CALIFORNIA PENAL CODE – PART 1

Table of Contents

Division - TITLE OF THE ACT

Section 1 - Short title; parts

This Act shall be known as The Penal Code of California, and is divided into four parts, as follows:

I.-OF CRIMES AND PUNISHMENTS.
II.-OF CRIMINAL PROCEDURE.
III.-OF THE STATE PRISON AND COUNTY JAILS.
IV.-OF PREVENTION OF CRIMES AND APPREHENSION OF CRIMINALS.

Amended by Stats. 1985, Ch. 367, Sec. 1.

Division - PRELIMINARY PROVISIONS

Section 2 - Effective date

This Code takes effect at twelve o'clock, noon, on the first day of January, eighteen hundred and seventy-three.

Enacted 1872.

Section 3 - Retroactivity

No part of it is retroactive, unless expressly so declared.

Enacted 1872.

Section 4 - Construction

The rule of the common law, that penal statutes are to be strictly construed, has no application to this Code. All its provisions are to be construed according to the fair import of their terms, with a view to effect its objects and to promote justice.

Enacted 1872.

Section 5 - Continuations

The provisions of this Code, so far as they are substantially the same as existing statutes, must be construed as continuations thereof, and not as new enactments.

Enacted 1872.

Section 6 - Criminality of act or omission

No act or omission, commenced after twelve o'clock noon of the day on which this Code takes effect as a law, is criminal or punishable, except as prescribed or authorized by this Code, or by some of the statutes which it specifies as continuing in force and as not affected by its provisions, or by some ordinance, municipal, county, or township regulation, passed or adopted, under such statutes and in force when this Code takes effect. Any act or omission commenced prior to that time may be inquired of, prosecuted, and punished in the same manner as if this Code had not been passed.

Enacted 1872.

Section 7 - Tense; gender; definitions

Words used in this code in the present tense include the future as well as the present; words used in the masculine gender include the feminine and neuter; the singular number includes the plural, and the plural the singular; the word "person" includes a corporation as well as a natural person; the word "county" includes "city and county"; writing includes printing and typewriting; oath includes affirmation or declaration; and every mode of oral statement, under oath or affirmation, is embraced by the term "testify," and every written one in the term "depose"; signature or subscription includes mark, when the person cannot write, his or her name being written near it, by a person who writes his or her own name as a witness; provided, that when a signature is made by mark it must, in order that the same may be acknowledged or serve as the signature to any sworn statement, be witnessed by two persons who must subscribe their own names as witnesses thereto.

The following words have in this code the signification attached to them in this section, unless otherwise apparent from the context:

(1) The word "willfully," when applied to the intent with which an act is done or omitted, implies simply a purpose or willingness to commit the act, or make the omission referred to. It does not require any intent to violate law, or to injure another, or to acquire any advantage.

(2) The words "neglect," "negligence," "negligent," and "negligently" import a want of such attention to the nature or probable consequences of the act or omission as a prudent man ordinarily bestows in acting in his own concerns.

(3) The word "corruptly" imports a wrongful design to acquire or cause some pecuniary or other advantage to the person guilty of the act or omission referred to, or to some other person.

(4) The words "malice" and "maliciously" import a wish to vex, annoy, or injure another person, or an intent to do a wrongful act, established either by proof or presumption of law.

(5) The word "knowingly" imports only a knowledge that the facts exist which bring the act or omission within the provisions of this code. It does not require any knowledge of the unlawfulness of such act or omission.

(6) The word "bribe" signifies anything of value or advantage, present or prospective, or any promise or undertaking to give any, asked, given, or accepted, with a corrupt intent to influence, unlawfully, the person to whom it is given, in his or her action, vote, or opinion, in any public or official capacity.

(7) The word "vessel," when used with reference to shipping, includes ships of all kinds, steamboats, canalboats, barges, and every structure adapted to be navigated from place to place for the transportation of merchandise or persons, except that, as used in Sections 192.5 and 193.5, the word "vessel" means a vessel as defined in subdivision (c) of Section 651 of the Harbors and Navigation Code.

(8) The words "peace officer" signify any one of the officers mentioned in Chapter 4.5 (commencing with Section 830) of Title 3 of Part 2.

(9) The word "magistrate" signifies any one of the officers mentioned in Section 808.

(10) The word "property" includes both real and personal property.

(11) The words "real property" are coextensive with lands, tenements, and hereditaments.

(12) The words "personal property" include money, goods, chattels, things in action, and evidences of debt.

(13) The word "month" means a calendar month, unless otherwise expressed; the word "daytime" means the period between sunrise and sunset, and the word "nighttime" means the period between sunset and sunrise.

(14) The word "will" includes codicil.

(15) The word "writ" signifies an order or precept in writing, issued in the name of the people, or of a court or judicial officer, and the word "process" a writ or summons issued in the course of judicial proceedings.

(16) Words and phrases must be construed according to the context and the approved usage of the language; but technical words and phrases, and such others as may have acquired a peculiar and appropriate meaning in law, must be construed according to such peculiar and appropriate meaning.

(17) Words giving a joint authority to three or more public officers or other persons, are construed as giving such authority to a majority of them, unless it is otherwise expressed in the act giving the authority.

(18) When the seal of a court or public officer is required by law to be affixed to any paper, the word "seal" includes an impression of such seal upon the paper alone, or upon any substance attached to the paper capable of receiving a visible impression. The seal of a private person may be made in like manner, or by the scroll of a pen, or by writing the word "seal" against his or her name.

(19) The word "state," when applied to the different parts of the United States, includes the District of Columbia and the territories, and the words "United States" may include the district and territories.

(20) The word "section," whenever hereinafter employed, refers to a section of this code, unless some other code or statute is expressly mentioned.

(21) To "book" signifies the recordation of an arrest in official police records, and the taking by the police of fingerprints and photographs of the person arrested, or any of these acts following an arrest.

(22) The word "spouse" includes "registered domestic partner," as required by Section 297.5 of the Family Code.

Amended by Stats 2016 ch 50 (SB 1005),s 65, eff. 1/1/2017.

Section 7.5 - Descriptive language

Whenever any offense is described in this code, the Uniform Controlled Substances Act (Division 10 (commencing with Section 11000) of the Health and Safety Code), or the Welfare and Institutions Code, as criminal conduct and as a violation of a specified code section or a particular provision of a code section, in the case of any ambiguity or conflict in interpretation, the code section or particular provision of the code section shall take precedence over the descriptive language. The descriptive language shall be deemed as being offered only for ease of reference unless it is otherwise clearly apparent from the context that the descriptive language is intended to narrow the application of the referenced code section or particular provision of the code section.

Added by Stats. 1998, Ch. 162, Sec. 1. Effective January 1, 1999.

Section 8 - Intent to defraud

Whenever, by any of the provisions of this Code, an intent to defraud is required in order to constitute any offense, it is sufficient if an intent appears to defraud any person, association, or body politic or corporate, whatever.

Enacted 1872.

Section 9 - Omission to specify liability to damages, penalty, forfeiture, or other remedy

The omission to specify or affirm in this Code any liability to damages, penalty, forfeiture, or other remedy imposed by law and allowed to be recovered or enforced in any civil action or proceeding, for any act or omission declared punishable herein, does not affect any right to recover or enforce the same.

Enacted 1872.

Section 10 - Omission to specify ground of forfeiture of public office

The omission to specify or affirm in this Code any ground of forfeiture of a public office, or other trust or special authority conferred by law, or any power conferred by law to impeach, remove, depose, or suspend any public officer or other person holding any trust, appointment, or other special authority conferred by law, does not affect such forfeiture or power, or any proceeding authorized by law to carry into effect such impeachment, removal, deposition, or suspension.

Enacted 1872.

Section 11 - Effect of court-martial or military authority

This code does not affect any power conferred by law upon any court-martial, or other military authority or officer, to impose or inflict punishment upon offenders; nor, except as provided in Section 19.2 of this code, any power conferred by law upon any public body, tribunal, or officer, to impose or inflict punishment for a contempt.

Amended by Stats. 1989, Ch. 897, Sec. 4.

Section 12 - Prescribed punishment

The several sections of this Code which declare certain crimes to be punishable as therein mentioned, devolve a duty upon the Court authorized to pass sentence, to determine and impose the punishment prescribed.

Enacted 1872.

Section 13 - Punishment determined by court

Whenever in this Code the punishment for a crime is left undetermined between certain limits, the punishment to be inflicted in a particular case must be determined by the Court authorized to pass sentence, within such limits as may be prescribed by this Code.

Enacted 1872.

Section 14 - Use of evidence obtained upon examination of person

The various sections of this Code which declare that evidence obtained upon the examination of a person as a witness cannot be received against him in any criminal proceeding, do not forbid such evidence being proved against such person upon any proceedings founded upon a charge of perjury committed in such examination.

Enacted 1872.

Section 15 - Crime or public offense defined

A crime or public offense is an act committed or omitted in violation of a law forbidding or commanding it, and to which is annexed, upon conviction, either of the following punishments:

1. Death;
2. Imprisonment;
3. Fine;
4. Removal from office; or,
5. Disqualification to hold and enjoy any office of honor, trust, or profit in this State.
Enacted 1872.

Section 16 - Crimes and public offenses

Crimes and public offenses include:
1. Felonies;
2. Misdemeanors; and
3. Infractions.
Amended by Stats. 1968, Ch. 1192.

Section 17 - Felony; misdemeanor; infraction

(a) A felony is a crime that is punishable with death, by imprisonment in the state prison, or, notwithstanding any other law, by imprisonment in a county jail under the provisions of subdivision (h) of Section 1170. Every other crime or public offense is a misdemeanor except those offenses that are classified as infractions.

(b) When a crime is punishable, in the discretion of the court, either by imprisonment in the state prison or imprisonment in a county jail under the provisions of subdivision (h) of Section 1170, or by fine or imprisonment in the county jail, it is a misdemeanor for all purposes under the following circumstances:

(1) After a judgment imposing a punishment other than imprisonment in the state prison or imprisonment in a county jail under the provisions of subdivision (h) of Section 1170.

(2) When the court, upon committing the defendant to the Division of Juvenile Justice, designates the offense to be a misdemeanor.

(3) When the court grants probation to a defendant and at the time of granting probation, or on application of the defendant or probation officer thereafter, the court declares the offense to be a misdemeanor.

(4) When the prosecuting attorney files in a court having jurisdiction over misdemeanor offenses a complaint specifying that the offense is a misdemeanor, unless the defendant at the time of arraignment or plea objects to the offense being made a misdemeanor, in which event the complaint shall be amended to charge the felony and the case shall proceed on the felony complaint.

(5) When, at or before the preliminary examination or prior to filing an order pursuant to Section 872, the magistrate determines that the offense is a misdemeanor, in which event the case shall proceed as if the defendant had been arraigned on a misdemeanor complaint.

(c) When a defendant is committed to the Division of Juvenile Justice for a crime punishable, in the discretion of the court, either by imprisonment in the state prison or imprisonment in a county jail under the provisions of subdivision (h) of Section 1170, or by fine or imprisonment in the county jail not exceeding one year, the offense shall, upon the discharge of the defendant from the Division of Juvenile Justice, thereafter be deemed a misdemeanor for all purposes.

(d) A violation of any code section listed in Section 19.8 is an infraction subject to the procedures described in Sections 19.6 and 19.7 in either of the following cases:

(1) The prosecutor files a complaint charging the offense as an infraction unless the defendant, at the time they are arraigned, after being informed of their rights, elects to have the case proceed as a misdemeanor.

(2) The court, with the consent of the defendant, determines that the offense is an infraction, in which event the case shall proceed as if the defendant had been arraigned on an infraction complaint.

(e) This section does not authorize a judge to relieve a defendant of the duty to register as a sex offender pursuant to Section 290 if the defendant is charged with an offense for which registration as a sex offender is required pursuant to Section 290, and for which the trier of fact has found the defendant guilty.

(f) When the court exercises its discretion under this section, an unfulfilled order of restitution or a restitution fine shall not be grounds for denial of a request or application for reduction.

Amended by Stats 2022 ch 734 (SB 1106),s 2, eff. 1/1/2023.
Amended by Stats 2018 ch 18 (AB 1941),s 1, eff. 1/1/2019.
Amended by Stats 2011 ch 12 (AB X1-17),s 6, eff. 9/20/2011, op. 10/1/2011.
Amended by Stats 2011 ch 39 (AB 117),s 68, eff. 6/30/2011.
Amended by Stats 2011 ch 15 (AB 109),s 228, eff. 4/4/2011, but operative no earlier than October 1, 2011, and only upon creation of a community corrections grant program to assist in implementing this act and upon an appropriation to fund the grant program.

Section 17.2 - Alternatives to incarceration

(a) It is the intent of the Legislature that the disposition of any criminal case use the least restrictive means available.

(b) The court presiding over a criminal matter shall consider alternatives to incarceration, including, without limitation, collaborative justice court programs, diversion, restorative justice, and probation.

(c) The court shall have the discretion to determine the appropriate sentence according to relevant statutes and the sentencing rules of the Judicial Council.

Added by Stats 2022 ch 775 (AB 2167),s 2, eff. 1/1/2023.

Section 17.5 - Legislative findings and declarations

(a) The Legislature finds and declares all of the following:

(1) The Legislature reaffirms its commitment to reducing recidivism among criminal offenders.

(2) Despite the dramatic increase in corrections spending over the past two decades, national reincarceration rates for people released from prison remain unchanged or have worsened. National data show that about 40 percent of released individuals are reincarcerated within three years. In California, the recidivism rate for persons who have served time in prison is even greater than the national average.

(3) Criminal justice policies that rely on building and operating more prisons to address community safety concerns are not sustainable, and will not result in improved public safety.

(4) California must reinvest its criminal justice resources to support community-based corrections programs and evidence-based practices that will achieve improved public safety returns on this state's substantial investment in its criminal justice system.

(5) Realigning low-level felony offenders who do not have prior convictions for serious, violent, or sex offenses to locally run community-based corrections programs, which are strengthened through community-based punishment, evidence-based practices, improved supervision strategies, and enhanced secured capacity, will improve public safety outcomes among adult felons and facilitate their reintegration back into society.

(6) Community-based corrections programs require a partnership between local public safety entities and the county to provide and expand the use of community-based punishment for low-level offender populations. Each county's Local Community Corrections Partnership, as established in paragraph (2) of subdivision (b) of Section 1230, should play a critical role in developing programs and ensuring appropriate outcomes for low-level offenders.

(7) Fiscal policy and correctional practices should align to promote a justice reinvestment strategy that fits each county. "Justice reinvestment" is a data-driven approach to reduce corrections and related criminal justice spending and reinvest savings in strategies designed to increase public safety. The purpose of justice reinvestment is to manage and allocate criminal justice populations more cost-effectively, generating savings that can be reinvested in evidence-based strategies that increase public safety while holding offenders accountable.

(8) "Community-based punishment" means correctional sanctions and programming encompassing a range of custodial and noncustodial responses to criminal or noncompliant offender activity. Community-based punishment may be provided by local public safety entities directly or through community-based public or private correctional service providers, and include, but are not limited to, the following:

(A) Short-term flash incarceration in jail for a period of not more than 10 days.

(B) Intensive community supervision.

(C) Home detention with electronic monitoring or GPS monitoring.

(D) Mandatory community service.

(E) Restorative justice programs such as mandatory victim restitution and victim-offender reconciliation.

(F) Work, training, or education in a furlough program pursuant to Section 1208.

(G) Work, in lieu of confinement, in a work release program pursuant to Section 4024.2.

(H) Day reporting.

(I) Mandatory residential or nonresidential substance abuse treatment programs.

(J) Mandatory random drug testing.

(K) Mother-infant care programs.

(L) Community-based residential programs offering structure, supervision, drug treatment, alcohol treatment, literacy programming, employment counseling, psychological counseling, mental health treatment, or any combination of these and other interventions.

(9) "Evidence-based practices" refers to supervision policies, procedures, programs, and practices demonstrated by scientific research to reduce recidivism among individuals under probation, parole, or post release supervision.

(b) The provisions of this act are not intended to alleviate state prison overcrowding.

Amended by Stats 2011 ch 39 (AB 117),s 68, eff. 6/30/2011.

Amended by Stats 2011 ch 39 (AB 117),s 5, eff. 6/30/2011.

Added by Stats 2011 ch 15 (AB 109),s 229, eff. 4/4/2011, but operative no earlier than October 1, 2011, and only upon creation of a community corrections grant program to assist in implementing this act and upon an appropriation to fund the grant program.

Section 17.7 - Legislative findings regarding California reentry program

The Legislature finds and declares the following:

(a) Strategies supporting reentering offenders through practices and programs, such as standardized risk and needs assessments, transitional community housing, treatment, medical and mental health services, and employment, have been demonstrated to significantly reduce recidivism among offenders in other states.

(b) Improving outcomes among offenders reentering the community after serving time in a correctional facility will promote public safety and will reduce California's prison and jail populations.

(c) Establishing a California reentry program that encompasses strategies known to reduce recidivism warrants a vigorous short-term startup in the 2014-15 fiscal year using readily available resources in the community, and a comprehensive long-term development plan for future budget years designed to expand the availability, impact, and sustainability of these strategies as further community partnerships are identified and developed.

Added by Stats 2014 ch 26 (AB 1468),s 11, eff. 6/20/2014.

Section 18 - Punishment for felony

(a) Except in cases where a different punishment is prescribed by any law of this state, every offense declared to be a felony is punishable by imprisonment for 16 months, or two or three years in the state prison unless the offense is punishable pursuant to subdivision (h) of Section 1170.

(b) Every offense which is prescribed by any law of the state to be a felony punishable by imprisonment or by a fine, but without an alternate sentence to the county jail for a period not exceeding one year, may be punishable by imprisonment in the county jail not exceeding one year or by a fine, or by both.

Amended by Stats 2011 ch 12 (AB X1-17),s 7, eff. 9/20/2011, op. 10/1/2011.

Amended by Stats 2011 ch 39 (AB 117),s 68, eff. 6/30/2011.

Amended by Stats 2011 ch 15 (AB 109),s 230, eff. 4/4/2011, but operative no earlier than October 1, 2011, and only upon creation of a community corrections grant program to assist in implementing this act and upon an appropriation to fund the grant program.

Section 18.5 - Imprisonment for misdemeanors

(a) Every offense which is prescribed by any law of the state to be punishable by imprisonment in a county jail up to or not exceeding one year shall be punishable by imprisonment in a county jail for a period not to exceed 364 days. This section shall apply retroactively, whether or not the case was final as of January 1, 2015.

(b) A person who was sentenced to a term of one year in county jail prior to January 1, 2015, may submit an application before the trial court that entered the judgment of conviction in the case to have the term of the sentence modified to the maximum term specified in subdivision (a).

Amended by Stats 2016 ch 789 (SB 1242),s 1, eff. 1/1/2017.

Added by Stats 2014 ch 174 (SB 1310),s 1, eff. 1/1/2015.

Section 19 - Punishment for misdemeanor

Except in cases where a different punishment is prescribed by any law of this state, every offense declared to be a misdemeanor is punishable by imprisonment in the county jail not exceeding six months, or by fine not exceeding one thousand dollars ($1,000), or by both.

Amended by Stats. 1983, Ch. 1092, Sec. 231. Effective September 27, 1983. Operative January 1, 1984, by Sec. 427 of Ch. 1092.

Section 19.2 - Sentence of confinement

In no case shall any person sentenced to confinement in a county or city jail, or in a county or joint county penal farm, road camp, work camp, or other county adult detention facility, or committed to the sheriff for placement in any county adult detention facility, on conviction of a misdemeanor, or as a condition of probation upon conviction of either a felony or a misdemeanor, or upon commitment for civil contempt, or upon default in the payment of a fine upon conviction of either a felony or a misdemeanor, or for any reason except upon conviction of a crime that specifies a felony punishment pursuant to subdivision (h) of Section 1170 or a conviction of more than one offense when consecutive sentences have been imposed, be committed for a period in excess of one year; provided, however, that the time allowed on parole shall not be considered as a part of the period of confinement.

Amended by Stats 2011 ch 39 (AB 117),s 68, eff. 6/30/2011.

Amended by Stats 2011 ch 15 (AB 109),s 231, eff. 4/4/2011, but operative no earlier than October 1, 2011, and only upon creation of a community corrections grant program to assist in implementing this act and upon an appropriation to fund the grant program.

Section 19.4 - Public offense punishable as misdemeanor

When an act or omission is declared by a statute to be a public offense and no penalty for the offense is prescribed in any statute, the act or omission is punishable as a misdemeanor.

Added by Stats. 1989, Ch. 897, Sec. 11.

Section 19.6 - Person charged with infraction

An infraction is not punishable by imprisonment. A person charged with an infraction shall not be entitled to a trial by jury. A person charged with an infraction shall not be entitled to have the public defender or other counsel appointed at public expense to represent him or her unless he or she is arrested and not released on his or her written promise to appear, his or her own recognizance, or a deposit of bail.

Added by renumbering Section 19c by Stats. 1989, Ch. 897, Sec. 8.

Section 19.7 - Application of law relating to misdemeanors to infractions

Except as otherwise provided by law, all provisions of law relating to misdemeanors shall apply to infractions including, but not limited to, powers of peace officers, jurisdiction of courts, periods for commencing action and for bringing a case to trial and burden of proof.

Added by renumbering Section 19d by Stats. 1989, Ch. 897, Sec. 9.

Section 19.8 - Certain offenses subject to law dealing with infractions

(a) The following offenses are subject to subdivision (d) of Section 17: Sections 193.8, 330, 415, 485, 490.7, 555, 602.13, and 853.7 of this code; subdivision (c) of Section 532b, and subdivision (o) of Section 602 of this code; subdivision (b) of Section 25658 and Sections 21672, 25661, and 25662 of the Business and Professions Code; Section 27204 of the Government Code; subdivision (c) of Section 23109 and Sections 5201.1, 12500, 14601.1, 27150.1, 40508, and 42005 of the Vehicle Code, and any other offense that the Legislature makes subject to subdivision (d) of Section 17. Except where a lesser maximum fine is expressly provided for a violation of those sections, a violation that is an infraction is punishable by a fine not exceeding two hundred fifty dollars ($250).

(b) Except in cases where a different punishment is prescribed, every offense declared to be an infraction is punishable by a fine not exceeding two hundred fifty dollars ($250).

(c) Except for the violations enumerated in subdivision (d) of Section 13202.5 of the Vehicle Code, and Section 14601.1 of the Vehicle Code based upon failure to appear, a conviction for an offense made an infraction under subdivision (d) of Section 17 is not grounds for the suspension, revocation, or denial of a license, or for the revocation of probation or parole of the person convicted.

Amended by Stats 2015 ch 303 (AB 731),s 383, eff. 1/1/2016.

Amended by Stats 2014 ch 54 (SB 1461),s 9, eff. 1/1/2015.

Amended by Stats 2012 ch 867 (SB 1144),s 14, eff. 1/1/2013.

Amended by Stats 2012 ch 702 (AB 2489),s 1, eff. 1/1/2013.

Amended by Stats 2010 ch 536 (AB 1675),s 1.5, eff. 1/1/2011.

Amended by Stats 2010 ch 366 (AB 1829),s 3, eff. 1/1/2011.

Amended by Stats 2006 ch 228 (AB 2612),s 1, eff. 1/1/2007.

Amended by Stats 2005 ch 307 (AB 646),s 1, eff. 1/1/2006.

Section 19.9 - "Mandatory supervision" defined

For purposes of this code, "mandatory supervision" shall mean the portion of a defendant's sentenced term during which time he or she is supervised by the county probation officer pursuant to subparagraph (B) of paragraph (5) of subdivision (h) of Section 1170.

Added by Stats 2012 ch 43 (SB 1023),s 14, eff. 6/27/2012.

Section 20 - Union of act or intent or criminal negligence

In every crime or public offense there must exist a union, or joint operation of act and intent, or criminal negligence.

Enacted 1872.

Section 21 - [Renumbered]
Renumbered as Ca. Pen. Code §29.2 by Stats 2012 ch 162 (SB 1171),s 118, eff. 1/1/2013.

Section 21a - Attempt
An attempt to commit a crime consists of two elements: a specific intent to commit the crime, and a direct but ineffectual act done toward its commission.

Added by Stats. 1986, Ch. 519, Sec. 1.

Section 22 - [Renumbered]
Renumbered as Ca. Pen. Code §29.4 by Stats 2012 ch 162 (SB 1171),s 119, eff. 1/1/2013.

Section 23 - Criminal proceeding against person issued license to engage in business or profession
In any criminal proceeding against a person who has been issued a license to engage in a business or profession by a state agency pursuant to provisions of the Business and Professions Code or the Education Code, or the Chiropractic Initiative Act, the state agency which issued the license may voluntarily appear to furnish pertinent information, make recommendations regarding specific conditions of probation, or provide any other assistance necessary to promote the interests of justice and protect the interests of the public, or may be ordered by the court to do so, if the crime charged is substantially related to the qualifications, functions, or duties of a licensee.

For purposes of this section, the term "license" shall include a permit or a certificate issued by a state agency.

For purposes of this section, the term "state agency" shall include any state board, commission, bureau, or division created pursuant to the provisions of the Business and Professions Code, the Education Code, or the Chiropractic Initiative Act to license and regulate individuals who engage in certain businesses and professions.

Amended by Stats 2002 ch 545 (SB 1852),s 3, eff. 1/1/2003.

Section 24 - Designation of act
This Act, whenever cited, enumerated, referred to, or amended, may be designated simply as The Penal Code, adding, when necessary, the number of the section.

Enacted 1872.

Part 1 - OF CRIMES AND PUNISHMENTS
Title 1 - OF PERSONS LIABLE TO PUNISHMENT FOR CRIME

Section 25 - Diminished capacity
(a) The defense of diminished capacity is hereby abolished. In a criminal action, as well as any juvenile court proceeding, evidence concerning an accused person's intoxication, trauma, mental illness, disease, or defect shall not be admissible to show or negate capacity to form the particular purpose, intent, motive, malice aforethought, knowledge, or other mental state required for the commission of the crime charged.

(b) In any criminal proceeding, including any juvenile court proceeding, in which a plea of not guilty by reason of insanity is entered, this defense shall be found by the trier of fact only when the accused person proves by a preponderance of the evidence that he or she was incapable of knowing or understanding the nature and quality of his or her act and of distinguishing right from wrong at the time of the commission of the offense.

(c) Notwithstanding the foregoing, evidence of diminished capacity or of a mental disorder may be considered by the court only at the time of sentencing or other disposition or commitment.

(d) The provisions of this section shall not be amended by the Legislature except by statute passed in each house by rollcall vote entered in the journal, two-thirds of the membership concurring, or by a statute that becomes effective only when approved by the electors.

Added June 8, 1982, by initiative Proposition 8, Sec. 4. Note: Prop. 8 is titled The Victims' Bill of Rights.

Section 25.5 - [Renumbered]
Renumbered as Ca. Pen. Code §29.8 by Stats 2012 ch 162 (SB 1171),s 120, eff. 1/1/2013.

Section 26 - Capability of committing crimes
All persons are capable of committing crimes except those belonging to the following classes:

One-Children under the age of 14, in the absence of clear proof that at the time of committing the act charged against them, they knew its wrongfulness.

Two-Persons who are mentally incapacitated.

Three-Persons who committed the act or made the omission charged under an ignorance or mistake of fact, which disproves any criminal intent.

Four-Persons who committed the act charged without being conscious thereof.

Five-Persons who committed the act or made the omission charged through misfortune or by accident, when it appears that there was no evil design, intention, or culpable negligence.

Six-Persons (unless the crime be punishable with death) who committed the act or made the omission charged under threats or menaces sufficient to show that they had reasonable cause to and did believe their lives would be endangered if they refused.

Amended by Stats 2007 ch 31 (AB 1640),s 3, eff. 1/1/2008.

Section 27 - Persons liable to punishment
(a) The following persons are liable to punishment under the laws of this state:

(1) All persons who commit, in whole or in part, any crime within this state.

(2) All who commit any offense without this state which, if committed within this state, would be larceny, carjacking, robbery, or embezzlement under the laws of this state, and bring the property stolen or embezzled, or any part of it, or are found with it, or any part of it, within this state.

(3) All who, being without this state, cause or aid, advise or encourage, another person to commit a crime within this state, and are afterwards found therein.

(b) Perjury, in violation of Section 118, is punishable also when committed outside of California to the extent provided in Section 118. Amended by Stats. 1993, Ch. 611, Sec. 2. Effective October 1, 1993.

Section 28 - Evidence of mental disease, mental defect, or mental disorder

(a) Evidence of mental disease, mental defect, or mental disorder shall not be admitted to show or negate the capacity to form any mental state, including, but not limited to, purpose, intent, knowledge, premeditation, deliberation, or malice aforethought, with which the accused committed the act. Evidence of mental disease, mental defect, or mental disorder is admissible solely on the issue of whether or not the accused actually formed a required specific intent, premeditated, deliberated, or harbored malice aforethought, when a specific intent crime is charged.

(b) As a matter of public policy there shall be no defense of diminished capacity, diminished responsibility, or irresistible impulse in a criminal action or juvenile adjudication hearing.

(c) This section shall not be applicable to an insanity hearing pursuant to Section 1026.

(d) Nothing in this section shall limit a court's discretion, pursuant to the Evidence Code, to exclude psychiatric or psychological evidence on whether the accused had a mental disease, mental defect, or mental disorder at the time of the alleged offense. Amended by Stats 2002 ch 784 (SB 1316), s 528, eff. 1/1/2003. Amended by Stats 2001 ch 854 (SB 205), s 18, eff. 1/1/2002.

Section 29 - Expert testimony about mental illness, mental disorder, or mental defect

In the guilt phase of a criminal action, any expert testifying about a defendant's mental illness, mental disorder, or mental defect shall not testify as to whether the defendant had or did not have the required mental states, which include, but are not limited to, purpose, intent, knowledge, or malice aforethought, for the crimes charged. The question as to whether the defendant had or did not have the required mental states shall be decided by the trier of fact. Repealed and added by Stats. 1984, Ch. 1433, Sec. 3.

Section 29.2 - Intent manifested by circumstances

(a) The intent or intention is manifested by the circumstances connected with the offense.

(b) In the guilt phase of a criminal action or a juvenile adjudication hearing, evidence that the accused lacked the capacity or ability to control his or her conduct for any reason shall not be admissible on the issue of whether the accused actually had any mental state with respect to the commission of any crime. This subdivision is not applicable to Section 26. Renumbered from Ca. Pen. Code §21 and amended by Stats 2012 ch 162 (SB 1171),s 118, eff. 1/1/2013.

Section 29.4 - Voluntary intoxication

(a) No act committed by a person while in a state of voluntary intoxication is less criminal by reason of his or her having been in that condition. Evidence of voluntary intoxication shall not be admitted to negate the capacity to form any mental states for the crimes charged, including, but not limited to, purpose, intent, knowledge, premeditation, deliberation, or malice aforethought, with which the accused committed the act.

(b) Evidence of voluntary intoxication is admissible solely on the issue of whether or not the defendant actually formed a required specific intent, or, when charged with murder, whether the defendant premeditated, deliberated, or harbored express malice aforethought.

(c) Voluntary intoxication includes the voluntary ingestion, injection, or taking by any other means of any intoxicating liquor, drug, or other substance. Renumbered from Ca. Pen. Code §22 and amended by Stats 2012 ch 162 (SB 1171),s 119, eff. 1/1/2013.

Section 29.8 - Defense of insanity

In any criminal proceeding in which a plea of not guilty by reason of insanity is entered, this defense shall not be found by the trier of fact solely on the basis of a personality or adjustment disorder, a seizure disorder, or an addiction to, or abuse of, intoxicating substances. This section shall apply only to persons who utilize this defense on or after the operative date of the section. Renumbered from Ca. Pen. Code §25.5 and amended by Stats 2012 ch 162 (SB 1171),s 120, eff. 1/1/2013.

Title 2 - OF PARTIES TO CRIME

Section 30 - Parties to crimes

The parties to crimes are classified as:
1. Principals; and,
2. Accessories.
Enacted 1872.

Section 31 - Principals

All persons concerned in the commission of a crime, whether it be felony or misdemeanor, and whether they directly commit the act constituting the offense, or aid and abet in its commission, or, not being present, have advised and encouraged its commission, and all persons counseling, advising, or encouraging children under the age of fourteen years, or persons who are mentally incapacitated, to commit any crime, or who, by fraud, contrivance, or force, occasion the drunkenness of another for the purpose of causing him to commit any crime, or who, by threats, menaces, command, or coercion, compel another to commit any crime, are principals in any crime so committed. Amended by Stats 2007 ch 31 (AB 1640),s 4, eff. 1/1/2008.

Section 32 - Accessory to felony by harboring, concealing, or aiding principal

Every person who, after a felony has been committed, harbors, conceals or aids a principal in such felony, with the intent that said principal may avoid or escape from arrest, trial, conviction or punishment, having knowledge that said principal has committed such felony or has been charged with such felony or convicted thereof, is an accessory to such felony. Amended by Stats. 1935, Ch. 436.

Section 33 - Punishment of accessory

Except in cases where a different punishment is prescribed, an accessory is punishable by a fine not exceeding five thousand dollars ($5,000), or by imprisonment pursuant to subdivision (h) of Section 1170, or in a county jail not exceeding one year, or by both such fine and imprisonment.

Amended by Stats 2011 ch 39 (AB 117),s 68, eff. 6/30/2011.

Amended by Stats 2011 ch 15 (AB 109),s 232, eff. 4/4/2011, but operative no earlier than October 1, 2011, and only upon creation of a community corrections grant program to assist in implementing this act and upon an appropriation to fund the grant program.

Title 3 - OF OFFENSES AGAINST THE SOVEREIGNTY OF THE STATE

Section 37 - Treason

(a) Treason against this state consists only in levying war against it, adhering to its enemies, or giving them aid and comfort, and can be committed only by persons owing allegiance to the state. The punishment of treason shall be death or life imprisonment without possibility of parole. The penalty shall be determined pursuant to Sections 190.3 and 190.4.

(b) Upon a trial for treason, the defendant cannot be convicted unless upon the testimony of two witnesses to the same overt act, or upon confession in open court; nor, except as provided in Sections 190.3 and 190.4, can evidence be admitted of an overt act not expressly charged in the indictment or information; nor can the defendant be convicted unless one or more overt acts be expressly alleged therein.

Amended by Stats. 1989, Ch. 897, Sec. 12.

Section 38 - Misprision of treason

Misprision of treason is the knowledge and concealment of treason, without otherwise assenting to or participating in the crime. It is punishable by imprisonment pursuant to subdivision (h) of Section 1170.

Amended by Stats 2011 ch 39 (AB 117),s 68, eff. 6/30/2011.

Amended by Stats 2011 ch 15 (AB 109),s 233, eff. 4/4/2011, but operative no earlier than October 1, 2011, and only upon creation of a community corrections grant program to assist in implementing this act and upon an appropriation to fund the grant program.

Title 5 - OF CRIMES BY AND AGAINST THE EXECUTIVE POWER OF THE STATE

Section 67 - Bribery of executive officer

Every person who gives or offers any bribe to any executive officer in this state, with intent to influence him in respect to any act, decision, vote, opinion, or other proceeding as such officer, is punishable by imprisonment in the state prison for two, three or four years, and is disqualified from holding any office in this state.

Amended by Stats. 1976, Ch. 1139.

Section 67.5 - Bribery of ministerial office, employee, or appointee

(a) Every person who gives or offers as a bribe to any ministerial officer, employee, or appointee of the State of California, county or city therein, or political subdivision thereof, any thing the theft of which would be petty theft is guilty of a misdemeanor.

(b) If the theft of the thing given or offered would be grand theft the offense is a felony punishable by imprisonment pursuant to subdivision (h) of Section 1170.

Amended by Stats 2011 ch 39 (AB 117),s 68, eff. 6/30/2011.

Amended by Stats 2011 ch 15 (AB 109),s 234, eff. 4/4/2011, but operative no earlier than October 1, 2011, and only upon creation of a community corrections grant program to assist in implementing this act and upon an appropriation to fund the grant program.

Section 68 - Receipt of bribe

(a) Every executive or ministerial officer, employee, or appointee of the State of California, a county or city therein, or a political subdivision thereof, who asks, receives, or agrees to receive, any bribe, upon any agreement or understanding that his or her vote, opinion, or action upon any matter then pending, or that may be brought before him or her in his or her official capacity, shall be influenced thereby, is punishable by imprisonment in the state prison for two, three, or four years and, in cases in which no bribe has been actually received, by a restitution fine of not less than two thousand dollars ($2,000) or not more than ten thousand dollars ($10,000) or, in cases in which a bribe was actually received, by a restitution fine of at least the actual amount of the bribe received or two thousand dollars ($2,000), whichever is greater, or any larger amount of not more than double the amount of any bribe received or ten thousand dollars ($10,000), whichever is greater, and, in addition thereto, forfeits his or her office, employment, or appointment, and is forever disqualified from holding any office, employment, or appointment, in this state.

(b) In imposing a restitution fine pursuant to this section, the court shall consider the defendant's ability to pay the fine.

Amended by Stats 2002 ch 664 (AB 3034), s 169, eff. 1/1/2003.

Amended by Stats 2001 ch 282 (SB 923), s 1, eff. 1/1/2002.

Section 69 - Threat or violence to deter or prevent executive officer

(a) Every person who attempts, by means of any threat or violence, to deter or prevent an executive officer from performing any duty imposed upon the officer by law, or who knowingly resists, by the use of force or violence, the officer, in the performance of his or her duty, is punishable by a fine not exceeding ten thousand dollars ($10,000), or by imprisonment pursuant to subdivision (h) of Section 1170, or in a county jail not exceeding one year, or by both such fine and imprisonment.

(b) The fact that a person takes a photograph or makes an audio or video recording of an executive officer, while the officer is in a public place or the person taking the photograph or making the recording is in a place he or she has the right to be, does not constitute, in and of itself, a violation of subdivision (a).

Amended by Stats 2015 ch 177 (SB 411),s 1, eff. 1/1/2016.

Amended by Stats 2011 ch 39 (AB 117),s 68, eff. 6/30/2011.

Amended by Stats 2011 ch 15 (AB 109),s 235, eff. 4/4/2011, but operative no earlier than October 1, 2011, and only upon creation of a community corrections grant program to assist in implementing this act and upon an appropriation to fund the grant program.

Section 70 - Receipt of emolument, gratuity, or reward

(a) Every executive or ministerial officer, employee, or appointee of the State of California, or any county or city therein, or any political subdivision thereof, who knowingly asks, receives, or agrees to receive any emolument, gratuity, or reward, or any promise thereof excepting such as may be authorized by law for doing an official act, is guilty of a misdemeanor.

(b) This section does not prohibit deputy registrars of voters from receiving compensation when authorized by local ordinance from any candidate, political committee, or statewide political organization for securing the registration of voters.

(c)

(1) Nothing in this section precludes a peace officer, as defined in Chapter 4.5 (commencing with Section 830) of Title 3 of Part 2, from engaging in, or being employed in, casual or part-time employment as a private security guard or patrolman for a public entity while off duty from his or her principal employment and outside his or her regular employment as a peace officer of a state or local agency, and exercising the powers of a peace officer concurrently with that employment, provided that the peace officer is in a police uniform and is subject to reasonable rules and regulations of the agency for which he or she is a peace officer. Notwithstanding the above provisions, any and all civil and criminal liability arising out of the secondary employment of any peace officer pursuant to this subdivision shall be borne by the officer's secondary employer.

(2) It is the intent of the Legislature by this subdivision to abrogate the holdings in People v. Corey, 21 Cal.3d 738, and Cervantez v. J.C. Penney Co., 24 Cal.3d 579, to reinstate prior judicial interpretations of this section as they relate to criminal sanctions for battery on peace officers who are employed, on a part-time or casual basis, by a public entity, while wearing a police uniform as private security guards or patrolmen, and to allow the exercise of peace officer powers concurrently with that employment.

(d)

(1) Nothing in this section precludes a peace officer, as defined in Chapter 4.5 (commencing with Section 830) of Title 3 of Part 2, from engaging in, or being employed in, casual or part-time employment as a private security guard or patrolman by a private employer while off duty from his or her principal employment and outside his or her regular employment as a peace officer, and exercising the powers of a peace officer concurrently with that employment, provided that all of the following are true:

(A) The peace officer is in his or her police uniform.

(B) The casual or part-time employment as a private security guard or patrolman is approved by the county board of supervisors with jurisdiction over the principal employer or by the board's designee or by the city council with jurisdiction over the principal employer or by the council's designee.

(C) The wearing of uniforms and equipment is approved by the principal employer.

(D) The peace officer is subject to reasonable rules and regulations of the agency for which he or she is a peace officer.

(2) Notwithstanding the above provisions, a peace officer while off duty from his or her principal employment and outside his or her regular employment as a peace officer of a state or local agency shall not exercise the powers of a police officer if employed by a private employer as a security guard during a strike, lockout, picketing, or other physical demonstration of a labor dispute at the site of the strike, lockout, picketing, or other physical demonstration of a labor dispute. The issue of whether or not casual or part-time employment as a private security guard or patrolman pursuant to this subdivision is to be approved shall not be a subject for collective bargaining. Any and all civil and criminal liability arising out of the secondary employment of any peace officer pursuant to this subdivision shall be borne by the officer's principal employer. The principal employer shall require the secondary employer to enter into an indemnity agreement as a condition of approving casual or part-time employment pursuant to this subdivision.

(3) It is the intent of the Legislature by this subdivision to abrogate the holdings in People v. Corey, 21 Cal. 3d 738, and Cervantez v. J. C. Penney Co., 24 Cal. 3d 579, to reinstate prior judicial interpretations of this section as they relate to criminal sanctions for battery on peace officers who are employed, on a part-time or casual basis, while wearing a police uniform approved by the principal employer, as private security guards or patrolmen, and to allow the exercise of peace officer powers concurrently with that employment.

(e)

(1) Nothing in this section precludes a peace officer, as defined in Chapter 4.5 (commencing with Section 830) of Title 3 of Part 2, from engaging in, or being employed in, other employment while off duty from his or her principal employment and outside his or her regular employment as a peace officer of a state or local agency.

(2) Subject to subdivisions (c) and (d), and except as provided by written regulations or policies adopted by the employing state or local agency, or pursuant to an agreement between the employing state or local agency and a recognized employee organization representing the peace officer, no peace officer shall be prohibited from engaging in, or being employed in, other employment while off duty from his or her principal employment and outside his or her regular employment as a peace officer of a state or local agency.

(3) If an employer withholds consent to allow a peace officer to engage in or be employed in other employment while off duty, the employer shall, at the time of denial, provide the reasons for denial in writing to the peace officer.

Amended by Stats 2003 ch 104 (AB 359), s 1, eff. 1/1/2004.

Section 70.5 - Acceptance of money by commissioner of civil marriages

Every commissioner of civil marriages or every deputy commissioner of civil marriages who accepts any money or other thing of value for performing any marriage pursuant to Section 401 of the Family Code, including any money or thing of value voluntarily tendered by the persons about to be married or who have been married by the commissioner of civil marriages or deputy commissioner of civil marriages, other than a fee expressly imposed by law for performance of a marriage, whether the acceptance occurs before or after performance of the marriage and whether or not performance of the marriage is conditioned on the giving of such money or the thing of value by the persons being married, is guilty of a misdemeanor.

It is not a necessary element of the offense described by this section that the acceptance of the money or other thing of value be committed with intent to commit extortion or with other criminal intent.

This section does not apply to the request or acceptance by any retired commissioner of civil marriages of a fee for the performance of a marriage.

This section is inapplicable to the acceptance of a fee for the performance of a marriage on Saturday, Sunday, or a legal holiday.

Amended by Stats. 1992, Ch. 163, Sec. 100. Effective January 1, 1993. Operative January 1, 1994, by Sec. 161 of Ch. 163.

Section 71 - Threatening officer or employee of public or private educational institution or public officer or employee

(a) Every person who, with intent to cause, attempts to cause, or causes, any officer or employee of any public or private educational institution or any public officer or employee to do, or refrain from doing, any act in the performance of his duties, by means of a threat, directly communicated to such person, to inflict an unlawful injury upon any person or property, and it reasonably appears to the recipient of the threat that such threat could be carried out, is guilty of a public offense punishable as follows:

(1) Upon a first conviction, such person is punishable by a fine not exceeding ten thousand dollars ($10,000), or by imprisonment pursuant to subdivision (h) of Section 1170, or in a county jail not exceeding one year, or by both that fine and imprisonment.

(2) If the person has been previously convicted of a violation of this section, such previous conviction shall be charged in the accusatory pleading, and if that previous conviction is found to be true by the jury, upon a jury trial, or by the court, upon a court trial, or is admitted by the defendant, he or she is punishable by imprisonment pursuant to subdivision (h) of Section 1170.

(b) As used in this section, "directly communicated" includes, but is not limited to, a communication to the recipient of the threat by telephone, telegraph, or letter.

Amended by Stats 2011 ch 39 (AB 117),s 68, eff. 6/30/2011.

Amended by Stats 2011 ch 15 (AB 109),s 236, eff. 4/4/2011, but operative no earlier than October 1, 2011, and only upon creation of a community corrections grant program to assist in implementing this act and upon an appropriation to fund the grant program.

Section 72 - Presentment of false or fraudulent claim, bill, account, voucher, or writing

Every person who, with intent to defraud, presents for allowance or for payment to any state board or officer, or to any county, city, or district board or officer, authorized to allow or pay the same if genuine, any false or fraudulent claim, bill, account, voucher, or writing, is punishable either by imprisonment in the county jail for a period of not more than one year, by a fine of not exceeding one thousand dollars ($1,000), or by both that imprisonment and fine, or by imprisonment pursuant to subdivision (h) of Section 1170, by a fine of not exceeding ten thousand dollars ($10,000), or by both such imprisonment and fine.

As used in this section "officer" includes a "carrier," as defined in subdivision (a) of Section 14124.70 of the Welfare and Institutions Code, authorized to act as an agent for a state board or officer or a county, city, or district board or officer, as the case may be.

Amended by Stats 2011 ch 39 (AB 117),s 68, eff. 6/30/2011.

Amended by Stats 2011 ch 15 (AB 109),s 237, eff. 4/4/2011, but operative no earlier than October 1, 2011, and only upon creation of a community corrections grant program to assist in implementing this act and upon an appropriation to fund the grant program.

Section 72.5 - Presenting claim for public funds for reimbursement of costs incurred in attending political function

(a) Every person who, knowing a claim seeks public funds for reimbursement of costs incurred in attending a political function organized to support or oppose any political party or political candidate, presents such a claim for allowance or for payment to any state board or officer, or to any county, city, or district board or officer authorized to allow or pay such claims, is punishable either by imprisonment in the county jail for a period of not more than one year, by a fine of not exceeding one thousand dollars ($1,000), or by both such imprisonment and fine, or by imprisonment pursuant to subdivision (h) of Section 1170, by a fine of not exceeding ten thousand dollars ($10,000), or by both such imprisonment and fine.

(b) Every person who, knowing a claim seeks public funds for reimbursement of costs incurred to gain admittance to a political function expressly organized to support or oppose any ballot measure, presents such a claim for allowance or for payment to any state board or officer, or to any county, city, or district board or officer authorized to allow or pay those claims is punishable either by imprisonment in the county jail for a period of not more than one year, by a fine of not exceeding one thousand dollars ($1,000), or by both that imprisonment and fine, or by imprisonment pursuant to subdivision (h) of Section 1170, by a fine of not exceeding ten thousand dollars ($10,000), or by both that imprisonment and fine.

Amended by Stats 2011 ch 39 (AB 117),s 68, eff. 6/30/2011.

Amended by Stats 2011 ch 15 (AB 109),s 238, eff. 4/4/2011, but operative no earlier than October 1, 2011, and only upon creation of a community corrections grant program to assist in implementing this act and upon an appropriation to fund the grant program.

Section 73 - Giving or offering gratuity or reward

Every person who gives or offers any gratuity or reward, in consideration that he or any other person shall be appointed to any public office, or shall be permitted to exercise or discharge the duties thereof, is guilty of a misdemeanor.

Enacted 1872.

Section 74 - Receipt of gratuity or reward

Every public officer who, for any gratuity or reward, appoints another person to a public office, or permits another person to exercise or discharge any of the duties of his office, is punishable by a fine not exceeding ten thousand dollars ($10,000), and, in addition thereto, forfeits his office and is forever disqualified from holding any office in this state.

Amended by Stats. 1983, Ch. 1092, Sec. 234. Effective September 27, 1983. Operative January 1, 1984, by Sec. 427 of Ch. 1092.

Section 76 - Threatening life or serious bodily harm

(a) Every person who knowingly and willingly threatens the life of, or threatens serious bodily harm to, any elected public official, county public defender, county clerk, exempt appointee of the Governor, judge, or Deputy Commissioner of the Board of Prison Terms, or the staff, immediate family, or immediate family of the staff of any elected public official, county public defender, county clerk, exempt appointee of the Governor, judge, or Deputy Commissioner of the Board of Prison Terms, with the specific intent that the statement is to be taken as a threat, and the apparent ability to carry out that threat by any means, is guilty of a public offense, punishable as follows:

(1) Upon a first conviction, the offense is punishable by a fine not exceeding five thousand dollars ($5,000), or by imprisonment pursuant to subdivision (h) of Section 1170, or in a county jail not exceeding one year, or by both that fine and imprisonment.

(2) If the person has been convicted previously of violating this section, the previous conviction shall be charged in the accusatory pleading, and if the previous conviction is found to be true by the jury upon a jury trial, or by the court upon a court trial, or is admitted by the defendant, the offense is punishable by imprisonment pursuant to subdivision (h) of Section 1170.

(b) Any law enforcement agency that has knowledge of a violation of this section involving a constitutional officer of the state, a Member of the Legislature, or a member of the judiciary shall immediately report that information to the Department of the California Highway Patrol.

(c) For purposes of this section, the following definitions shall apply:

(1) "Apparent ability to carry out that threat" includes the ability to fulfill the threat at some future date when the person making the threat is an incarcerated prisoner with a stated release date.

(2) "Serious bodily harm" includes serious physical injury or serious traumatic condition.

(3) "Immediate family" means a spouse, parent, or child, or anyone who has regularly resided in the household for the past six months.

(4) "Staff of a judge" means court officers and employees, including commissioners, referees, and retired judges sitting on assignment.

(5) "Threat" means a verbal or written threat or a threat implied by a pattern of conduct or a combination of verbal or written statements and conduct made with the intent and the apparent ability to carry out the threat so as to cause the person who is the target of the threat to reasonably fear for his or her safety or the safety of his or her immediate family.

(d) As for threats against staff or immediate family of staff, the threat must relate directly to the official duties of the staff of the elected public official, county public defender, county clerk, exempt appointee of the Governor, judge, or Deputy Commissioner of the Board of Prison Terms in order to constitute a public offense under this section.

(e) A threat must relate directly to the official duties of a Deputy Commissioner of the Board of Prison Terms in order to constitute a public offense under this section.

Amended by Stats 2011 ch 39 (AB 117),s 68, eff. 6/30/2011.

Amended by Stats 2011 ch 15 (AB 109),s 239, eff. 4/4/2011, but operative no earlier than October 1, 2011, and only upon creation of a community corrections grant program to assist in implementing this act and upon an appropriation to fund the grant program.

Amended by Stats 2004 ch 512 (AB 1433), s 1, eff. 1/1/2005.

Amended by Stats 2000 ch 233 (SB 1859), s 1, eff. 1/1/2001.

Section 77 - Application to administrative and ministerial officers

The various provisions of this title, except Section 76, apply to administrative and ministerial officers, in the same manner as if they were mentioned therein.

Amended by Stats. 1982, Ch. 1405, Sec. 2.

Title 6 - OF CRIMES AGAINST THE LEGISLATIVE POWER

Section 85 - Bribery

Every person who gives or offers to give a bribe to any Member of the Legislature, any member of the legislative body of a city, county, city and county, school district, or other special district, or to another person for the member, or attempts by menace, deceit, suppression of truth, or any corrupt means, to influence a member in giving or withholding his or her vote, or in not attending the house or any committee of which he or she is a member, is punishable by imprisonment in the state prison for two, three or four years.

Amended by Stats 2006 ch 435 (SB 1308),s 1, eff. 9/24/2006.

Section 86 - Receipt of bribe

Every Member of either house of the Legislature, or any member of the legislative body of a city, county, city and county, school district, or other special district, who asks, receives, or agrees to receive, any bribe, upon any understanding that his or her official vote, opinion, judgment, or action shall be influenced thereby, or shall give, in any particular manner, or upon any particular side of any question or matter upon which he or she may be required to act in his or her official capacity, or gives, or offers or promises to give, any official vote in consideration that another Member of the Legislature, or another member of the legislative body of a city, county, city and county, school district, or other special district shall give this vote either upon the same or another question, is punishable by imprisonment in the state prison for two, three, or four years and, in cases in which no bribe has been actually received, by a restitution fine of not less than four thousand dollars ($4,000) or not more than twenty thousand dollars ($20,000) or, in cases in which a bribe was actually received, by a restitution fine of at least the actual amount of the bribe received or four thousand dollars ($4,000), whichever is greater, or any larger amount of not more than double the amount of any bribe received or twenty thousand dollars ($20,000), whichever is greater.

In imposing a fine under this section, the court shall consider the defendant's ability to pay the fine.

Amended by Stats 2014 ch 881 (AB 1666),s 2, eff. 1/1/2015.

Amended by Stats 2006 ch 435 (SB 1308),s 2, eff. 9/24/2006.

Amended by Stats 2002 ch 664 (AB 3034), s 170, eff. 1/1/2003.

Amended by Stats 2001 ch 282 (SB 923), s 2, eff. 1/1/2002.

Section 88 - Forfeiture of office; disqualification from holding office

Every Member of the Legislature, and every member of a legislative body of a city, county, city and county, school district, or other special district convicted of any crime defined in this title, in addition to the punishment prescribed, forfeits his or her office and is forever disqualified from holding any office in this state or a political subdivision thereof.

Amended by Stats 2006 ch 435 (SB 1308),s 3, eff. 9/24/2006.

Amended by Stats 2002 ch 787 (SB 1798), s 7, eff. 1/1/2003.

Title 7 - OF CRIMES AGAINST PUBLIC JUSTICE

Chapter 1 - BRIBERY AND CORRUPTION

Section 92 - Bribery

Every person who gives or offers to give a bribe to any judicial officer, juror, referee, arbitrator, or umpire, or to any person who may be authorized by law to hear or determine any question or controversy, with intent to influence his vote, opinion, or decision upon any matter or question which is or may be brought before him for decision, is punishable by imprisonment in the state prison for two, three or four years.

Amended by Stats. 1976, Ch. 1139.

Section 93 - Receipt of bribe

(a) Every judicial officer, juror, referee, arbitrator, or umpire, and every person authorized by law to hear or determine any question or controversy, who asks, receives, or agrees to receive, any bribe, upon any agreement or understanding that his or her vote, opinion, or decision upon any matters or question which is or may be brought before him or her for decision, shall be influenced thereby, is punishable by imprisonment in the state prison for two, three, or four years and, in cases where no bribe has been actually received, by a restitution fine of not less than two thousand dollars ($2,000) or not more than ten thousand dollars ($10,000) or, in cases where a bribe was actually received, by a restitution fine of at least the actual amount of the bribe received or two thousand dollars ($2,000), whichever is greater, or any larger amount of not more than double the amount of any bribe received or ten thousand dollars ($10,000), whichever is greater.

(b) In imposing a restitution fine under this section, the court shall consider the defendant's ability to pay the fine.
Amended by Stats 2001 ch 282 (SB 923), s 3, eff. 1/1/2002.

Section 94 - Receipt of emolument, gratuity, or reward, or promise

Every judicial officer who asks or receives any emolument, gratuity, or reward, or any promise thereof, except such as may be authorized by law, for doing any official act, is guilty of a misdemeanor. The lawful compensation of a temporary judge shall be prescribed by Judicial Council rule. Every judicial officer who shall ask or receive the whole or any part of the fees allowed by law to any stenographer or reporter appointed by him or her, or any other person, to record the proceedings of any court or investigation held by him or her, shall be guilty of a misdemeanor, and upon conviction thereof shall forfeit his or her office. Any stenographer or reporter, appointed by any judicial officer in this state, who shall pay, or offer to pay, the whole or any part of the fees allowed him or her by law, for his or her appointment or retention in office, shall be guilty of a misdemeanor, and upon conviction thereof shall be forever disqualified from holding any similar office in the courts of this state.
Amended by Stats. 1993, Ch. 909, Sec. 13. Effective January 1, 1994.

Section 94.5 - Acceptance of money for performing marriage

Every judge, justice, commissioner, or assistant commissioner of a court of this state who accepts any money or other thing of value for performing any marriage, including any money or thing of value voluntarily tendered by the persons about to be married or who have been married by such judge, justice, commissioner, or assistant commissioner, whether the acceptance occurs before or after performance of the marriage and whether or not performance of the marriage is conditioned on the giving of such money or the thing of value by the persons being married, is guilty of a misdemeanor.

It is not a necessary element of the offense described by this section that the acceptance of the money or other thing of value be committed with intent to commit extortion or with other criminal intent.

This section does not apply to the request for or acceptance of a fee expressly imposed by law for performance of a marriage or to the request or acceptance by any retired judge, retired justice, or retired commissioner of a fee for the performance of a marriage. For the purposes of this section, a retired judge or retired justice sitting on assignment in court shall not be deemed to be a retired judge or retired justice.

This section does not apply to an acceptance of a fee for performing a marriage on Saturday, Sunday, or a legal holiday.
Amended by Stats. 1987, Ch. 753, Sec. 2.

Section 95 - Attempt to influence juror, arbitrator, umpire, or referee

Every person who corruptly attempts to influence a juror, or any person summoned or drawn as a juror, or chosen as an arbitrator or umpire, or appointed a referee, in respect to his or her verdict in, or decision of, any cause or proceeding, pending, or about to be brought before him or her, is punishable by a fine not exceeding ten thousand dollars ($10,000), or by imprisonment pursuant to subdivision (h) of Section 1170, if it is by means of any of the following:

(a) Any oral or written communication with him or her except in the regular course of proceedings.

(b) Any book, paper, or instrument exhibited, otherwise than in the regular course of proceedings.

(c) Any threat, intimidation, persuasion, or entreaty.

(d) Any promise, or assurance of any pecuniary or other advantage.
Amended by Stats 2011 ch 39 (AB 117),s 68, eff. 6/30/2011.
Amended by Stats 2011 ch 15 (AB 109),s 240, eff. 4/4/2011, but operative no earlier than October 1, 2011, and only upon creation of a community corrections grant program to assist in implementing this act and upon an appropriation to fund the grant program.

Section 95.1 - Threatening of juror with respect to criminal proceeding

Every person who threatens a juror with respect to a criminal proceeding in which a verdict has been rendered and who has the intent and apparent ability to carry out the threat so as to cause the target of the threat to reasonably fear for his or her safety or the safety of his or her immediate family, is guilty of a public offense and shall be punished by imprisonment in a county jail for not more than one year, or by imprisonment pursuant to subdivision (h) of Section 1170, or by a fine not exceeding ten thousand dollars ($10,000), or by both that imprisonment and fine.
Amended by Stats 2011 ch 39 (AB 117),s 68, eff. 6/30/2011.
Amended by Stats 2011 ch 15 (AB 109),s 241, eff. 4/4/2011, but operative no earlier than October 1, 2011, and only upon creation of a community corrections grant program to assist in implementing this act and upon an appropriation to fund the grant program.

Section 95.2 - Intentionally providing defendant with sealed records in order to locate or communicate with juror

Any person who, with knowledge of the relationship of the parties and without court authorization and juror consent, intentionally provides a defendant or former defendant to any criminal proceeding information from records sealed by the court pursuant to subdivision (b) of Section 237 of the Code of Civil Procedure, knowing that the records have been sealed, in order to locate or communicate with a juror to that proceeding and that information is used to violate Section 95 or 95.1, shall be guilty of a misdemeanor. Except as otherwise provided by any other law or court order limiting communication with a juror after a verdict has been reached, compliance with Section 206 of the Code of Civil Procedure shall constitute court authorization.
Added by Stats. 1992, Ch. 971, Sec. 5. Effective January 1, 1993.

Section 95.3 - Licensed individual intentionally providing defendant with sealed records in order to locate or communicate with juror

Any person licensed pursuant to Chapter 11.5 (commencing with Section 7512) of Division 3 of the Business and Professions Code who, with knowledge of the relationship of the parties and without court authorization and juror consent, knowingly provides a defendant or former defendant to any criminal proceeding information in order to locate or communicate with a juror to that proceeding is guilty of a misdemeanor. Conviction under this section shall be a basis for revocation or suspension of any license issued pursuant to Section 7561.1 of the Business and Professions Code. Except as otherwise provided by any law or court order limiting communication with a juror after a verdict has been reached, compliance with Section 206 of the Code of Civil Procedure shall constitute court authorization.

Added by Stats. 1992, Ch. 971, Sec. 6. Effective January 1, 1993.

Section 96 - Promise to give verdict or decision for or against party; communication

Every juror, or person drawn or summoned as a juror, or chosen arbitrator or umpire, or appointed referee, who either:

One-Makes any promise or agreement to give a verdict or decision for or against any party; or,

Two-Willfully and corruptly permits any communication to be made to him, or receives any book, paper, instrument, or information relating to any cause or matter pending before him, except according to the regular course of proceedings,

is punishable by fine not exceeding ten thousand dollars ($10,000), or by imprisonment pursuant to subdivision (h) of Section 1170.

Amended by Stats 2011 ch 39 (AB 117),s 68, eff. 6/30/2011.

Amended by Stats 2011 ch 15 (AB 109),s 242, eff. 4/4/2011, but operative no earlier than October 1, 2011, and only upon creation of a community corrections grant program to assist in implementing this act and upon an appropriation to fund the grant program.

Section 96.5 - Perversion or obstruction of justice by judicial officer, court commissioner, or referee

(a) Every judicial officer, court commissioner, or referee who commits any act that he or she knows perverts or obstructs justice, is guilty of a public offense punishable by imprisonment in a county jail for not more than one year.

(b) Nothing in this section prohibits prosecution under paragraph (5) of subdivision (a) of Section 182 of the Penal Code or any other law.

EFFECTIVE 1/1/2000. Amended October 10, 1999 (Bill Number: SB 832) (Chapter 853).

Section 98 - Forfeiture of office; disqualification from holding office

Every officer convicted of any crime defined in this Chapter, in addition to the punishment prescribed, forfeits his office and is forever disqualified from holding any office in this State.

Enacted 1872.

Section 99 - Restrictions on Superintendent of State Printing

The Superintendent of State Printing shall not, during his continuance in office, have any interest, either directly or indirectly, in any contract in any way connected with his office as Superintendent of State Printing; nor shall he, during said period, be interested, either directly or indirectly, in any state printing, binding, engraving. lithographing, or other state work of any kind connected with his said office; nor shall he, directly or indirectly, be interested in any contract for furnishing paper, or other printing stock or material, to or for use in his said office; and any violations of these provisions shall subject him, on conviction before a court of competent jurisdiction, to imprisonment pursuant to subdivision (h) of Section 1170 and to a fine of not less than one thousand dollars ($1,000) nor more than ten thousand dollars ($10,000), or by both that fine and imprisonment.

Amended by Stats 2011 ch 39 (AB 117),s 68, eff. 6/30/2011.

Amended by Stats 2011 ch 15 (AB 109),s 243, eff. 4/4/2011, but operative no earlier than October 1, 2011, and only upon creation of a community corrections grant program to assist in implementing this act and upon an appropriation to fund the grant program.

Section 100 - Collusion by Superintendent of State Printing

If the Superintendent of State Printing corruptly colludes with any person or persons furnishing paper or materials, or bidding therefor, or with any other person or persons, or has any secret understanding with him or them, by himself or through others, to defraud the state, or by which the state is defrauded or made to sustain a loss, contrary to the true intent and meaning of this chapter, he, upon conviction thereof, forfeits his office, and is subject to imprisonment in the state prison, and to a fine of not less than one thousand dollars ($1,000) nor more than ten thousand dollars ($10,000), or both such fine and imprisonment.

Amended by Stats. 1983, Ch. 1092, Sec. 238. Effective September 27, 1983. Operative January 1, 1984, by Sec. 427 of Ch. 1092.

Chapter 2 - RESCUES

Section 102 - Destruction or taking of personal property from custody of officer or person

Every person who willfully injures or destroys, or takes or attempts to take, or assists any person in taking or attempting to take, from the custody of any officer or person, any personal property which such officer or person has in charge under any process of law, is guilty of a misdemeanor.

Enacted 1872.

Chapter 3 - ESCAPES AND AIDING THEREIN

Section 107 - Escape from public training school or reformatory or county hospital

Every prisoner charged with or convicted of a felony who is an inmate of any public training school or reformatory or county hospital who escapes or attempts to escape from such public training school or reformatory or county hospital is guilty of a felony and is punishable by imprisonment pursuant to subdivision (h) of Section 1170, or by a fine not exceeding ten thousand dollars ($10,000), or by both that fine and imprisonment.

Amended by Stats 2011 ch 39 (AB 117),s 68, eff. 6/30/2011.

Amended by Stats 2011 ch 15 (AB 109),s 244, eff. 4/4/2011, but operative no earlier than October 1, 2011, and only upon creation of a community corrections grant program to assist in implementing this act and upon an appropriation to fund the grant program.

Section 109 - Assisting escape

Any person who willfully assists any inmate of any public training school or reformatory to escape, or in an attempt to escape from that public training school or reformatory is punishable by imprisonment pursuant to subdivision (h) of Section 1170, and fine not exceeding ten thousand dollars ($10,000).

Amended by Stats 2011 ch 39 (AB 117),s 68, eff. 6/30/2011.

Amended by Stats 2011 ch 15 (AB 109),s 245, eff. 4/4/2011, but operative no earlier than October 1, 2011, and only upon creation of a community corrections grant program to assist in implementing this act and upon an appropriation to fund the grant program.

Section 110 - Facilitation of escape

Every person who carries or sends into a public training school, or reformatory, anything useful to aid a prisoner or inmate in making his escape, with intent thereby to facilitate the escape of any prisoner or inmate confined therein, is guilty of a felony.

Amended by Stats. 1976, Ch. 1139.

Chapter 4 - FORGING, STEALING, MUTILATING, AND FALSIFYING JUDICIAL AND PUBLIC RECORDS AND DOCUMENTS

Section 112 - Manufacture or sale of false government document

(a) Any person who manufactures or sells any false government document with the intent to conceal the true citizenship or resident status for immigration purposes of another person is guilty of a misdemeanor and shall be punished by imprisonment in a county jail for one year. Every false government document that is manufactured or sold in violation of this section may be charged and prosecuted as a separate and distinct violation, and consecutive sentences may be imposed for each violation.

(b) A prosecuting attorney shall have discretion to charge a defendant with a violation of this section or any other law that applies.

(c) As used in this section, "government document" means any document issued by the United States government or any state or local government, including, but not limited to, any passport, immigration visa, employment authorization card, birth certificate, driver's license, identification card, or social security card.

Amended by Stats 2021 ch 296 (AB 1096),s 42, eff. 1/1/2022.

Renumbered from § 113 by Stats 2001 ch 854 (SB 205), s 19, eff. 1/1/2002.

Section 113 - Manufacture, distribution, or sale of false documents

Any person who manufactures, distributes, or sells false documents to conceal the true citizenship or resident status for immigration purposes of another person is guilty of a felony, and shall be punished by imprisonment pursuant to subdivision (h) of Section 1170 for five years or by a fine of seventy-five thousand dollars ($75,000).

Amended by Stats 2021 ch 296 (AB 1096),s 43, eff. 1/1/2022.

Amended by Stats 2011 ch 39 (AB 117),s 68, eff. 6/30/2011.

Amended by Stats 2011 ch 15 (AB 109),s 246, eff. 4/4/2011, but operative no earlier than October 1, 2011, and only upon creation of a community corrections grant program to assist in implementing this act and upon an appropriation to fund the grant program.

Former § 113, as added by Chapter 17 of the Statutes of 1994, 1st Extraordinary Session, was renumbered as § 112 by Stats 2001 ch 854 (SB 205), s 19, eff. 1/1/2002.

Section 114 - Use of false documents

Any person who uses false documents to conceal their true citizenship or resident status for immigration purposes is guilty of a felony, and shall be punished by imprisonment pursuant to subdivision (h) of Section 1170 for five years or by a fine of twenty-five thousand dollars ($25,000).

Amended by Stats 2021 ch 296 (AB 1096),s 44, eff. 1/1/2022.

Amended by Stats 2011 ch 39 (AB 117),s 68, eff. 6/30/2011.

Amended by Stats 2011 ch 15 (AB 109),s 247, eff. 4/4/2011, but operative no earlier than October 1, 2011, and only upon creation of a community corrections grant program to assist in implementing this act and upon an appropriation to fund the grant program.

Section 115 - Procurement or offering false or forged document

(a) Every person who knowingly procures or offers any false or forged instrument to be filed, registered, or recorded in any public office within this state, which instrument, if genuine, might be filed, registered, or recorded under any law of this state or of the United States, is guilty of a felony.

(b) Each instrument which is procured or offered to be filed, registered, or recorded in violation of subdivision (a) shall constitute a separate violation of this section.

(c) Except in unusual cases where the interests of justice would best be served if probation is granted, probation shall not be granted to, nor shall the execution or imposition of sentence be suspended for, any of the following persons:

(1) Any person with a prior conviction under this section who is again convicted of a violation of this section in a separate proceeding.

(2) Any person who is convicted of more than one violation of this section in a single proceeding, with intent to defraud another, and where the violations resulted in a cumulative financial loss exceeding one hundred thousand dollars ($100,000).

(d) For purposes of prosecution under this section, each act of procurement or of offering a false or forged instrument to be filed, registered, or recorded shall be considered a separately punishable offense.

(e)

(1) After a person is convicted of a violation of this section, or a plea is entered whereby a charge alleging a violation of this section is dismissed and waiver is obtained pursuant to People v. Harvey (1979) 25 Cal.3d 754, upon written motion of the prosecuting agency, the court, after a hearing described in subdivision (f), shall issue a written order that the false or forged instrument be adjudged void ab initio if the court determines that an order is appropriate under applicable law. The order shall state whether the instrument is false or forged, or both false and forged, and describe the nature of the falsity or forgery. A copy of the instrument shall be attached to the order at the time it is issued by the court and a certified copy of the order shall be filed, registered, or recorded at the appropriate public office by the prosecuting agency.

(2)

(A) If the order pertains to a false or forged instrument that has been recorded with a county recorder, an order made pursuant to this section shall be recorded in the county where the affected real property is located. The order shall also reference the county recorder's document recording number of any notice of pendency of action recorded pursuant to paragraph (2) of subdivision (f).

(B) As to any order, notice of pendency of action, or withdrawal of notice of pendency of action recorded pursuant to this section, recording fees shall be waived pursuant to Section 27383 of the Government Code.

(f) A prosecuting agency shall use the following procedures in filing a motion under subdivision (e):

(1) Within 10 calendar days of filing a criminal complaint or indictment alleging a violation of this section, the prosecuting agency shall provide written notice by certified mail to all parties who have an interest in the property affected by the false or forged instrument, or in the instrument itself, including those described in paragraph (5).

(2)

(A) Within 10 calendar days of filing a criminal complaint or indictment alleging a violation of this section, the prosecuting agency shall record a notice of pendency of action in the county in which the affected real property is located.

(B) Within 10 calendar days of the case being adjudicated or dismissed without obtaining an order pursuant to subdivision (e), the prosecuting agency shall record a withdrawal of the notice of pendency of action in the county where the affected real property is located.

(3) The written notice and notice of pendency of action described in paragraphs (1) and (2) shall inform the interested parties that a criminal action has commenced that may result in adjudications against the false or forged instrument or the property affected by the false or forged instrument, and shall notify the interested parties of their right to be heard if a motion is brought under subdivision (e) to void the false or forged instrument. The notice shall state the street address, if available, and the legal description of the affected real property.

(4) Failure of the prosecuting agency to provide written notice or record a pendency of action as required under paragraphs (1) and (2) within 10 calendar days shall not prevent the prosecuting agency from later making a motion under subdivision (e), but the court shall take the failure to provide notice or record a pendency of action as required under paragraphs (1) and (2) as reason to provide any interested parties additional time to respond to the motion. Failure of the prosecuting agency to so notify interested parties under this subdivision or record a pendency of action as required under paragraphs (1) and (2) within 10 calendar days shall create a presumption that a finding as described in paragraph (9) is necessary to protect the property rights of the interested party or parties.

(5) If the instrument sought to be declared void involves real property, "interested parties" include, but are not limited to, all parties who have recorded with the county recorder in the county where the affected property is located any of the following: a deed, lien, mortgage, deed of trust, security interest, lease, or other instrument declaring an interest in, or requesting notice relating to, the property affected by the false or forged instrument as of the date of the filing of the criminal complaint or indictment.

(6) Any party not required to be noticed under paragraph (1) or (5) who nonetheless notifies the prosecuting agency in writing of the party's desire to be notified if a motion is brought under subdivision (e) to void the false or forged instrument shall be treated as an interested party as defined in paragraph (1) or (5).

(7) The court shall set a hearing for the motion brought by the prosecuting agency under subdivision (e) no earlier than 90 calendar days from the date the motion is made. The prosecuting agency shall provide a copy by certified mail of the written motion and a notice of hearing to all interested parties described in paragraphs (1), (5), or (6), and all other persons who obtain an interest in the property prior to recordation of notice of pendency of action no later than 90 days before the hearing date set by the court. The notice shall state the street address, if available, and the legal description of the affected real property.

(8) At a hearing on a motion brought by the prosecuting agency under subdivision (e), the defendant, prosecuting agency, and interested parties described in paragraphs (1), (5), or (6), shall have a right to be heard and present information to the court. No party shall be denied a right to present information due to a lack of notice by the prosecuting agency or failure to contact the prosecuting agency or the court prior to the hearing.

(9)

(A) At a hearing on a motion brought by a prosecuting agency under subdivision (e), if the court determines that the interests of justice or the need to protect the property rights of any person or party so requires, including, but not limited to, a finding that the matter may be more appropriately determined in a civil proceeding, the court may decline to make a determination under subdivision (e).

(B) If, prior to the hearing on the motion, any person or party files a quiet title action that seeks a judicial determination of the validity of the same false or forged instrument that is the subject of the motion, or the status of an interested party as a bona fide purchaser of, or bona fide holder of an encumbrance on, the property affected by the false or forged instrument, the court may consider that as an additional but not dispositive factor in making its determination under subdivision (e); provided, however, that a final judgment previously entered in that quiet title action shall be followed to the extent otherwise required by law.

(g) As used in this section, "prosecuting agency" means a city attorney, a district attorney, the Attorney General, or other state or local agency actively prosecuting a case under this section.

(h) An order made pursuant to subdivision (e) shall be considered a judgment, and subject to appeal in accordance with, paragraph (1) of subdivision (a) of Section 904.1 of the Code of Civil Procedure.

Amended by Stats 2014 ch 455 (AB 1698),s 1, eff. 1/1/2015.

Section 115.1 - Campaign advertisement containing unauthorized signature

(a) The Legislature finds and declares that the voters of California are entitled to accurate representations in materials that are directed to them in efforts to influence how they vote.

(b) No person shall publish or cause to be published, with intent to deceive, any campaign advertisement containing a signature that the person knows to be unauthorized.

(c) For purposes of this section, "campaign advertisement" means any communication directed to voters by means of a mass mailing as defined in Section 82041.5 of the Government Code, a paid television, radio, or newspaper advertisement, an outdoor advertisement, or any other printed matter, if the expenditures for that communication are required to be reported by Chapter 4 (commencing with Section 84100) of Title 9 of the Government Code.

(d) For purposes of this section, an authorization to use a signature shall be oral or written.

(e) Nothing in this section shall be construed to prohibit a person from publishing or causing to be published a reproduction of all or part of a document containing an actual or authorized signature, provided that the signature so reproduced shall not, with the intent to deceive, be incorporated into another document in a manner that falsely suggests that the person whose signature is reproduced has signed the other document.

(f) Any knowing or willful violation of this section is a public offense punishable by imprisonment in a county jail not exceeding 6 months, or pursuant to subdivision (h) of Section 1170, or by a fine not to exceed fifty thousand dollars ($50,000), or by both that fine and imprisonment.

(g) As used in this section, "signature" means either of the following:

(1) A handwritten or mechanical signature, or a copy thereof.

(2) Any representation of a person's name, including, but not limited to, a printed or typewritten representation, that serves the same purpose as a handwritten or mechanical signature.

Amended by Stats 2011 ch 39 (AB 117),s 68, eff. 6/30/2011.

Amended by Stats 2011 ch 15 (AB 109),s 248, eff. 4/4/2011, but operative no earlier than October 1, 2011, and only upon creation of a community corrections grant program to assist in implementing this act and upon an appropriation to fund the grant program.

Section 115.2 - Campaign advertisement containing false or fraudulent depictions or misrepresentations of public documents

(a) No person shall publish or cause to be published, with actual knowledge, and intent to deceive, any campaign advertisement containing false or fraudulent depictions, or false or fraudulent representations, of official public documents or purported official public documents.

(b) For purposes of this section, "campaign advertisement" means any communication directed to voters by means of a mass mailing as defined in Section 82041.5 of the Government Code, a paid newspaper advertisement, an outdoor advertisement, or any other printed matter, if the expenditures for that communication are required to be reported by Chapter 4 (commencing with Section 84100) of Title 9 of the Government Code.

(c) Any violation of this section is a misdemeanor punishable by imprisonment in the county jail, or by a fine not to exceed fifty thousand dollars ($50,000), or both.

Added by Stats. 1991, Ch. 1051, Sec. 2.

Section 115.25 - Production or distribution of document containing inaccurate emergency service phone numbers

(a) No person or entity shall authorize the production or distribution, or participate in the authorization of the production or distribution, of any document, including, but not limited to, any campaign advertisement, as defined in subdivision (d), that the person or entity knows contains inaccurate emergency service phone numbers for various emergency services, including, but not limited to, police, fire, or ambulance services.

(b) A violation of subdivision (a) shall be an infraction, punishable by a fine not exceeding two hundred fifty dollars ($250).

(c) A violation of subdivision (a) resulting in the serious injury or death of persons who innocently rely on the erroneous phone numbers contained in the document is a misdemeanor, punishable by a fine not exceeding ten thousand dollars ($10,000), by imprisonment in a county jail not exceeding one year, or by both that fine and imprisonment.

(d) For purposes of this section, "campaign advertisement" means any communication directed to voters by means of a mass mailing, as defined in Section 82041.5 of the Government Code, a paid television, radio, or newspaper advertisement, an outdoor advertisement, or any other printed matter, if the expenditures for that communication are required to be reported by Chapter 4 (commencing with Section 84100) of Title 9 of the Government Code.

Added by Stats. 1992, Ch. 1010, Sec. 1. Effective January 1, 1993.

Section 115.3 - Alteration of certified copy of official record

Any person who alters a certified copy of an official record, or knowingly furnishes an altered certified copy of an official record, of this state, including the executive, legislative, and judicial branches thereof, or of any city, county, city and county, district, or political subdivision thereof, is guilty of a misdemeanor.

Added by Stats. 1984, Ch. 874, Sec. 1. Effective September 5, 1984.

Section 115.5 - Filing false or forged document with county recorder; false sworn statement to notary public

(a) Every person who files any false or forged document or instrument with the county recorder which affects title to, places an encumbrance on, or places an interest secured by a mortgage or deed of trust on, real property consisting of a single-family residence containing not more than four dwelling units, with knowledge that the document is false or forged, is punishable, in addition to any other punishment, by a fine not exceeding seventy-five thousand dollars ($75,000).

(b) Every person who makes a false sworn statement to a notary public, with knowledge that the statement is false, to induce the notary public to perform an improper notarial act on an instrument or document affecting title to, or placing an encumbrance on, real property consisting of a single-family residence containing not more than four dwelling units is guilty of a felony.

Added by Stats. 1984, Ch. 1397, Sec. 9.

Section 116 - Tampering with jury list

Every person who adds any names to the list of persons selected to serve as jurors for the county, either by placing the names in the jury box or otherwise, or extracts any name therefrom, or destroys the jury box or any of the pieces of paper containing the names of jurors, or mutilates or defaces the names so that they cannot be read, or changes the names on the pieces of paper, except in cases allowed by law, is guilty of a felony.

Amended by Stats. 1989, Ch. 1360, Sec. 104.

Section 116.5 - Tampering with jury

(a) A person is guilty of tampering with a jury when, prior to, or within 90 days of, discharge of the jury in a criminal proceeding, he or she does any of the following:

(1) Confers, or offers or agrees to confer, any payment or benefit upon a juror or upon a third person who is acting on behalf of a juror in consideration for the juror or third person supplying information in relation to an action or proceeding.

(2) Acting on behalf of a juror, accepts or agrees to accept any payment or benefit for himself or herself or for the juror in consideration for supplying any information in relation to an action or proceeding.

(3) Acting on behalf of himself or herself, agrees to accept, directly or indirectly, any payment or benefit in consideration for supplying any information in relation to an action or proceeding.

(b) Any person who violates this section is guilty of a misdemeanor.

(c) In the case of a juror who is within 90 days of having been discharged, otherwise lawful compensation not exceeding fifty dollars ($50) in value shall not constitute a criminal violation of this section.

(d) Upon conviction under this section, in addition to the penalty described in subdivision (b), any compensation received in violation of this section shall be forfeited by the defendant and deposited in the Victim Restitution Fund.

Added by Stats. 1994, Ch. 869, Sec. 2. Effective January 1, 1995.

Section 117 - Certification of false or incorrect list of persons selected as jurors

Every officer or person required by law to certify to the list of persons selected as jurors who maliciously, corruptly, or willfully certifies to a false or incorrect list, or a list containing other names than those selected, or who, being required by law to write down the names placed on the certified lists on separate pieces of paper, does not write down and place in the jury box the same names that are on the certified list, and no more and no less than are on such list, is guilty of a felony.

Enacted 1872.

Chapter 5 - PERJURY AND SUBORNATION OF PERJURY

Section 118 - Perjury

(a) Every person who, having taken an oath that he or she will testify, declare, depose, or certify truly before any competent tribunal, officer, or person, in any of the cases in which the oath may by law of the State of California be administered, willfully and contrary to the oath, states as true any material matter which he or she knows to be false, and every person who testifies, declares, deposes, or certifies under penalty of perjury in any of the cases in which the testimony, declarations, depositions, or certification is permitted by law of the State of California under penalty of perjury and willfully states as true any material matter which he or she knows to be false, is guilty of perjury. This subdivision is applicable whether the statement, or the testimony, declaration, deposition, or certification is made or subscribed within or without the State of California.

(b) No person shall be convicted of perjury where proof of falsity rests solely upon contradiction by testimony of a single person other than the defendant. Proof of falsity may be established by direct or indirect evidence.

Amended by Stats. 1990, Ch. 950, Sec. 2.

Section 118.1 - Filing false report by peace officer

(a) Every peace officer who, in their capacity as a peace officer, knowingly and intentionally makes, or causes to be made, any material statement in a peace officer report, or to another peace officer and the statement is included in a peace officer report, regarding the commission or investigation of any crime, knowing the statement to be false, is guilty of filing a false report, punishable by imprisonment in the county jail for up to one year, or in the state prison for one, two, or three years.

(b) This section does not apply to a peace officer writing or making a peace officer report, with regard to a false statement that the peace officer included in the report that is attributed to any other person, unless the peace officer writing or making the report knows the statement to be false and is including the statement to present the statement as being true.

Added by Stats 2021 ch 267 (AB 750),s 2, eff. 1/1/2022.

Repealed by Stats 2021 ch 267 (AB 750),s 1, eff. 1/1/2022.

Amended by Stats. 1992, Ch. 427, Sec. 124. Effective January 1, 1993.

Section 118a - Perjury related to false affidavit

Any person who, in any affidavit taken before any person authorized to administer oaths, swears, affirms, declares, deposes, or certifies that he will testify, declare, depose, or certify before any competent tribunal, officer, or person, in any case then pending or thereafter to be instituted, in any particular manner, or to any particular fact, and in such affidavit willfully and contrary to such oath states as true any material matter which he knows to be false, is guilty of perjury. In any prosecution under this section, the subsequent testimony of such person, in any action involving the matters in such affidavit contained, which is contrary to any of the matters in such affidavit contained, shall be prima facie evidence that the matters in such affidavit were false.

Added by Stats. 1905, Ch. 485.

Section 119 - "Oath" defined

The term "oath," as used in the last two sections, includes an affirmation and every other mode authorized by law of attesting the truth of that which is stated.

Amended by Stats. 1905, Ch. 485.

Section 120 - Oath of office

So much of an oath of office as relates to the future performance of official duties is not such an oath as is intended by the two preceding sections.

Enacted 1872.

Section 121 - Administration of oath in irregular manner

It is no defense to a prosecution for perjury that the oath was administered or taken in an irregular manner, or that the person accused of perjury did not go before, or was not in the presence of, the officer purporting to administer the oath, if such accused caused or procured such officer to certify that the oath had been taken or administered.

Amended by Stats. 1905, Ch. 485.

Section 122 - Competency of accused

It is no defense to a prosecution for perjury that the accused was not competent to give the testimony, deposition, or certificate of which falsehood is alleged. It is sufficient that he did give such testimony or make such deposition or certificate.

Enacted 1872.

Section 123 - Materiality of false statement

It is no defense to a prosecution for perjury that the accused did not know the materiality of the false statement made by him; or that it did not, in fact, affect the proceeding in or for which it was made. It is sufficient that it was material, and might have been used to affect such proceeding.

Enacted 1872.

Section 124 - Completion of deposition, affidavit, or certificate

The making of a deposition, affidavit or certificate is deemed to be complete, within the provisions of this chapter, from the time when it is delivered by the accused to any other person, with the intent that it be uttered or published as true.

Amended by Stats. 1905, Ch. 485.

Section 125 - Unqualified statement

An unqualified statement of that which one does not know to be true is equivalent to a statement of that which one knows to be false.

Enacted 1872.

Section 126 - Punishment for perjury

Perjury is punishable by imprisonment pursuant to subdivision (h) of Section 1170 for two, three or four years.

Amended by Stats 2011 ch 39 (AB 117),s 68, eff. 6/30/2011.

Amended by Stats 2011 ch 15 (AB 109),s 249, eff. 4/4/2011, but operative no earlier than October 1, 2011, and only upon creation of a community corrections grant program to assist in implementing this act and upon an appropriation to fund the grant program.

Section 127 - Procurement of perjury

Every person who willfully procures another person to commit perjury is guilty of subornation of perjury, and is punishable in the same manner as he would be if personally guilty of the perjury so procured.

Enacted 1872.

Section 128 - Procurement of conviction and execution of innocent person

Every person who, by willful perjury or subornation of perjury procures the conviction and execution of any innocent person, is punishable by death or life imprisonment without possibility of parole. The penalty shall be determined pursuant to Sections 190.3 and 190.4.

Amended by Stats. 1977, Ch. 316.

Section 129 - False return, statement, or report

Every person who, being required by law to make any return, statement, or report, under oath, willfully makes and delivers any such return, statement, or report, purporting to be under oath, knowing the same to be false in any particular, is guilty of perjury, whether such oath was in fact taken or not.

Added by Stats. 1905, Ch. 485.

Section 131 - False statement by person under investigation for violation of Corporate Securities Law

Every person in any matter under investigation for a violation of the Corporate Securities Law of 1968 (Part 1 (commencing with Section 25000) of Division 1 of Title 4 of the Corporations Code), the California Commodity Law of 1990 (Chapter 1 (commencing with Section 29500) of Division 4.5 of Title 4 of the Corporations Code), Section 16755 of the Business and Professions Code, or in connection with an investigation conducted by the head of a department of the State of California relating to the business activities and subjects under the jurisdiction of the department, who knowingly and willfully falsifies, misrepresents, or conceals a material fact or makes any materially false, fictitious, misleading, or fraudulent statement or representation, and any person who knowingly and willfully procures or causes another to violate this section, is guilty of a misdemeanor punishable by imprisonment in a county jail not exceeding one year, or by a fine not exceeding twenty-five thousand dollars ($25,000), or by both that imprisonment and fine for each violation of this section. This section does not apply to conduct charged as a violation of Section 118 of this code.

Added by Stats 2003 ch 876 (SB 434), s 14, eff. 1/1/2004.

Chapter 6 - FALSIFYING EVIDENCE, AND BRIBING, INFLUENCING, INTIMIDATING OR THREATENING WITNESSES

Section 132 - Offering forged or fraudulently altered or ante-dated evidence

Every person who upon any trial, proceeding, inquiry, or investigation whatever, authorized or permitted by law, offers in evidence, as genuine or true, any book, paper, document, record, or other instrument in writing, knowing the same to have been forged or fraudulently altered or ante-dated, is guilty of felony.

Enacted 1872.

Section 132.5 - [Multiple Versions] Witness of crime

(a) A person who is a witness to an event or occurrence that he or she knows, or reasonably should know, is a crime or who has personal knowledge of facts that he or she knows, or reasonably should know, may require that person to be called as a witness in a criminal prosecution shall not accept or receive, directly or indirectly, any payment or benefit in consideration for providing information obtained as a result of witnessing the event or occurrence or having personal knowledge of the facts.

(b) A violation of this section is a misdemeanor and shall be punished by imprisonment in a county jail for not exceeding six months, by a fine not exceeding one thousand dollars ($1,000), or by both that imprisonment and fine.

(c) Upon conviction under this section, in addition to the penalty described in subdivision (b), any compensation received in violation of this section shall be forfeited by the defendant and deposited in the Victim Restitution Fund.

(d) This section shall not apply if more than one year has elapsed from the date of any criminal act related to the information that is provided under subdivision (a) unless prosecution has commenced for that criminal act. If prosecution has commenced, this section shall remain applicable until the final judgment in the action.

(e) This section shall not apply to any of the following circumstances:

(1) Lawful compensation paid to expert witnesses, investigators, employees, or agents by a prosecutor, law enforcement agency, or an attorney employed to represent a person in a criminal matter.

(2) Lawful compensation provided to an informant by a prosecutor or law enforcement agency.

(3) Compensation paid to a publisher, editor, reporter, writer, or other person connected with or employed by a newspaper, magazine, or other publication or a television or radio news reporter or other person connected with a television or radio station, for disclosing information obtained in the ordinary course of business.

(4) Statutorily authorized rewards offered by governmental agencies for information leading to the arrest and conviction of specified offenders.

(5) Lawful compensation provided to a witness participating in the Witness Protection Program established pursuant to Title 7.5 (commencing with Section 14020) of Part 4.

(f) For purposes of this section, "information" does not include a photograph, videotape, audiotape, or any other direct recording of events or occurrences.

Amended by Stats 2003 ch 62 (SB 600), s 222, eff. 1/1/2004.

Amended by Stats 2002 ch 210 (SB 1739), s 1, eff. 1/1/2003.

Section 132.5 - [Multiple Versions] Legislative findings and declarations

(a) The Legislature supports and affirms the constitutional right of every person to communicate on any subject. This section is intended to preserve the right of every accused person to a fair trial, the right of the people to due process of law, and the integrity of judicial proceedings. This section is not intended to prevent any person from disseminating any information or opinion. The Legislature hereby finds and declares that the disclosure for valuable consideration of information relating to crimes by prospective witnesses can cause the loss of credible evidence in criminal trials and threatens to erode the reliability of verdicts.

The Legislature further finds and declares that the disclosure for valuable consideration of information relating to crimes by prospective witnesses creates an appearance of injustice that is destructive of public confidence.

(b) A person who is a witness to an event or occurrence that he or she knows is a crime or who has personal knowledge of facts that he or she knows or reasonably should know may require that person to be called as a witness in a criminal prosecution shall not accept or receive, directly or indirectly, any money or its equivalent in consideration for providing information obtained as a result of witnessing the event or occurrence or having personal knowledge of the facts.

(c) A person who is a witness to an event or occurrence that he or she reasonably should know is a crime shall not accept or receive, directly or indirectly, any money or its equivalent in consideration for providing information obtained as a result of his or her witnessing the event or occurrence.

(d) The Attorney General or the district attorney of the county in which an alleged violation of subdivision (c) occurs may institute a civil proceeding. Where a final judgment is rendered in the civil proceeding, the defendant shall be punished for the violation of subdivision (c) by a fine equal to 150 percent of the amount received or contracted for by the person.

(e) A violation of subdivision (b) is a misdemeanor punishable by imprisonment for a term not exceeding six months in a county jail, a fine not exceeding three times the amount of compensation requested, accepted, or received, or both the imprisonment and fine.

(f) This section does not apply if more than one year has elapsed from the date of any criminal act related to the information that is provided under subdivision (b) or (c) unless prosecution has commenced for that criminal act. If prosecution has commenced, this section shall remain applicable until the final judgment in the action.

(g) This section does not apply to any of the following circumstances:

(1) Lawful compensation paid to expert witnesses, investigators, employees, or agents by a prosecutor, law enforcement agency, or an attorney employed to represent a person in a criminal matter.

(2) Lawful compensation provided to an informant by a prosecutor or law enforcement agency.

(3) Compensation paid to a publisher, editor, reporter, writer, or other person connected with or employed by a newspaper, magazine, or other publication or a television or radio news reporter or other person connected with a television or radio station, for disclosing information obtained in the ordinary course of business.

(4) Statutorily authorized rewards offered by governmental agencies or private reward programs offered by victims of crimes for information leading to the arrest and conviction of specified offenders.

(5) Lawful compensation provided to a witness participating in the Witness Relocation and Assistance Program established pursuant to Title 7.5 (commencing with Section 14020) of Part 4.

(h) For purposes of this section, "information" does not include a photograph, videotape, audiotape, or any other direct recording of an event or occurrence.

(i) For purposes of this section, "victims of crimes" shall be construed in a manner consistent with Section 28 of Article I of the California Constitution, and shall include victims, as defined in subdivision (3) of Section 136.

Amended by Stats 2015 ch 303 (AB 731),s 384, eff. 1/1/2016.

Amended by Stats 2003 ch 62 (SB 600), s 223, eff. 1/1/2004.

Amended by Stats 2002 ch 210 (SB 1739), s 2, eff. 1/1/2003.

Section 133 - Fraud or deceit with intent to affect testimony

Every person who practices any fraud or deceit, or knowingly makes or exhibits any false statement, representation, token, or writing, to any witness or person about to be called as a witness upon any trial, proceeding, inquiry, or investigation whatever, authorized by law, with intent to affect the testimony of such witness, is guilty of a misdemeanor.

Enacted 1872.

Section 134 - Preparation of false or ante-dated evidence

Every person guilty of preparing any false or ante-dated book, paper, record, instrument in writing, or other matter or thing, with intent to produce it, or allow it to be produced for any fraudulent or deceitful purpose, as genuine or true, upon any trial, proceeding, or inquiry whatever, authorized by law, is guilty of felony.

Enacted 1872.

Section 135 - Willful destruction or concealment of evidence

A person who, knowing that any book, paper, record, instrument in writing, digital image, video recording owned by another, or other matter or thing, is about to be produced in evidence upon a trial, inquiry, or investigation, authorized by law, willfully destroys, erases, or conceals the same, with the intent to prevent it or its content from being produced, is guilty of a misdemeanor.

Amended by Stats 2015 ch 463 (AB 256),s 1, eff. 1/1/2016.

Section 135.5 - Alteration, concealment, or destruction of evidence in disciplinary proceeding against public safety officer

Any person who knowingly alters, tampers with, conceals, or destroys relevant evidence in any disciplinary proceeding against a public safety officer, for the purpose of harming that public safety officer, is guilty of a misdemeanor.

Added by Stats. 1998, Ch. 759, Sec. 1. Effective January 1, 1999.

Section 136 - Definitions

As used in this chapter:

(1) "Malice" means an intent to vex, annoy, harm, or injure in any way another person, or to thwart or interfere in any manner with the orderly administration of justice.

(2) "Witness" means any natural person, (i) having knowledge of the existence or nonexistence of facts relating to any crime, or (ii) whose declaration under oath is received or has been received as evidence for any purpose, or (iii) who has reported any crime to any peace officer, prosecutor, probation or parole officer, correctional officer or judicial officer, or (iv) who has been served with a subpoena issued under the authority of any court in the state, or of any other state or of the United States, or (v) who would be believed by any reasonable person to be an individual described in subparagraphs (i) to (iv), inclusive.

(3) "Victim" means any natural person with respect to whom there is reason to believe that any crime as defined under the laws of this state or any other state or of the United States is being or has been perpetrated or attempted to be perpetrated.

Repealed and added by Stats. 1980, Ch. 686, Sec. 2.

Section 136.1 - Preventing or dissuading witness or victim

(a) Except as provided in subdivision (c), any person who does any of the following is guilty of a public offense and shall be punished by imprisonment in a county jail for not more than one year or in the state prison:

(1) Knowingly and maliciously prevents or dissuades any witness or victim from attending or giving testimony at any trial, proceeding, or inquiry authorized by law.

(2) Knowingly and maliciously attempts to prevent or dissuade any witness or victim from attending or giving testimony at any trial, proceeding, or inquiry authorized by law.

(3) For purposes of this section, evidence that the defendant was a family member who interceded in an effort to protect the witness or victim shall create a presumption that the act was without malice.

(b) Except as provided in subdivision (c), every person who attempts to prevent or dissuade another person who has been the victim of a crime or who is witness to a crime from doing any of the following is guilty of a public offense and shall be punished by imprisonment in a county jail for not more than one year or in the state prison:

(1) Making any report of that victimization to any peace officer or state or local law enforcement officer or probation or parole or correctional officer or prosecuting agency or to any judge.

(2) Causing a complaint, indictment, information, probation or parole violation to be sought and prosecuted, and assisting in the prosecution thereof.

(3) Arresting or causing or seeking the arrest of any person in connection with that victimization.

(c) Every person doing any of the acts described in subdivision (a) or (b) knowingly and maliciously under any one or more of the following circumstances, is guilty of a felony punishable by imprisonment in the state prison for two, three, or four years under any of the following circumstances:

(1) Where the act is accompanied by force or by an express or implied threat of force or violence, upon a witness or victim or any third person or the property of any victim, witness, or any third person.

(2) Where the act is in furtherance of a conspiracy.

(3) Where the act is committed by any person who has been convicted of any violation of this section, any predecessor law hereto or any federal statute or statute of any other state which, if the act prosecuted was committed in this state, would be a violation of this section.

(4) Where the act is committed by any person for pecuniary gain or for any other consideration acting upon the request of any other person. All parties to such a transaction are guilty of a felony.

(d) Every person attempting the commission of any act described in subdivisions (a), (b), and (c) is guilty of the offense attempted without regard to success or failure of the attempt. The fact that no person was injured physically, or in fact intimidated, shall be no defense against any prosecution under this section.

(e) Nothing in this section precludes the imposition of an enhancement for great bodily injury where the injury inflicted is significant or substantial.

(f) The use of force during the commission of any offense described in subdivision (c) shall be considered a circumstance in aggravation of the crime in imposing a term of imprisonment under subdivision (b) of Section 1170.

Amended by Stats. 1997, Ch. 500, Sec. 1. Effective January 1, 1998.

Section 136.2 - Protective orders

(a)

(1) Upon a good cause belief that harm to, or intimidation or dissuasion of, a victim or witness has occurred or is reasonably likely to occur, a court with jurisdiction over a criminal matter may issue orders, including, but not limited to, the following:

(A) An order issued pursuant to Section 6320 of the Family Code.

(B) An order that a defendant shall not violate any provision of Section 136.1.

(C) An order that a person before the court other than a defendant, including, but not limited to, a subpoenaed witness or other person entering the courtroom of the court, shall not violate any provision of Section 136.1.

(D) An order that a person described in this section shall have no communication whatsoever with a specified witness or a victim except through an attorney under reasonable restrictions that the court may impose.

(E) An order calling for a hearing to determine if an order described in subparagraphs (A) to (D), inclusive, should be issued.

(F)

(i) An order that a particular law enforcement agency within the jurisdiction of the court provide protection for a victim, witness, or both, or for immediate family members of a victim or a witness who reside in the same household as the victim or witness or within reasonable proximity of the victim's or witness' household, as determined by the court. The order shall not be made without the consent of the law enforcement agency except for limited and specified periods of time and upon an express finding by the court of a clear and present danger of harm to the victim or witness or immediate family members of the victim or witness.

(ii) For purposes of this paragraph, "immediate family members" include the spouse, children, or parents of the victim or witness.

(G)

(i) An order protecting a victim or witness of violent crime from all contact by the defendant or contact with the intent to annoy, harass, threaten, or commit acts of violence by the defendant. The court or its designee shall transmit orders made under this paragraph to law enforcement personnel within one business day of the issuance, modification, extension, or termination of the order pursuant to subdivision (a) of Section 6380 of the Family Code. It is the responsibility of the court to transmit the modification, extension, or termination orders made under this paragraph to the same agency that entered the original protective order into the California Restraining and Protective Order System.

(ii)

(I) If a court does not issue an order pursuant to clause (i) when the defendant is charged with a crime involving domestic violence, as defined in Section 13700 of this code or in Section 6211 of the Family Code, the court, on its own motion, shall consider issuing a protective order upon a good cause belief that harm to, or intimidation or dissuasion of, a victim or witness has occurred or is reasonably likely to occur, that provides as follows:

(ia) The defendant shall not own, possess, purchase, receive, or attempt to purchase or receive a firearm while the protective order is in effect.

(ib) The defendant shall relinquish ownership or possession of any firearms pursuant to Section 527.9 of the Code of Civil Procedure.

(II) A person who owns, possesses, purchases, or receives, or attempts to purchase or receive a firearm while this protective order is in effect is punishable pursuant to Section 29825.

(iii) An order issued, modified, extended, or terminated by a court pursuant to this subparagraph shall be issued on forms adopted by the Judicial Council that have been approved by the Department of Justice pursuant to subdivision (i) of Section 6380 of the Family Code. However, the fact that an order issued by a court pursuant to this section was not issued on forms adopted by the Judicial Council and approved by the Department of Justice shall not make the order unenforceable.

(iv) A protective order issued under this subparagraph may require the defendant to be placed on electronic monitoring if the local government, with the concurrence of the county sheriff or the chief probation officer with jurisdiction, adopts a policy to authorize electronic monitoring of defendants and specifies the agency with jurisdiction for this purpose. If the court determines that the defendant has the ability to pay for the monitoring program, the court shall order the defendant to pay for the monitoring. If the court determines that the defendant does not have the ability to pay for the electronic monitoring, the court may order electronic monitoring to be paid for by the local government that adopted the policy to authorize electronic monitoring. The duration of electronic monitoring shall not exceed one year from the date the order is issued. The electronic monitoring shall not be in place if the protective order is not in place.

(2) For purposes of this subdivision, a minor who was not a victim of, but who was physically present at the time of, an act of domestic violence is a witness and is deemed to have suffered harm within the meaning of paragraph (1).

(b) A person violating an order made pursuant to subparagraphs (A) to (G), inclusive, of paragraph (1) of subdivision (a) may be punished for a substantive offense described in Section 136.1 or for a contempt of the court making the order. A finding of contempt shall not be a bar to prosecution for a violation of Section 136.1. However, a person held in contempt shall be entitled to credit for punishment imposed therein against a sentence imposed upon conviction of an offense described in Section 136.1. A conviction or acquittal for a substantive offense under Section 136.1 shall be a bar to a subsequent punishment for contempt arising out of the same act.

(c)

(1)

(A) Notwithstanding subdivision (e), an emergency protective order issued pursuant to Chapter 2 (commencing with Section 6250) of Part 3 of Division 10 of the Family Code or Section 646.91 shall have precedence in enforcement over any other restraining or protective order, provided the emergency protective order meets all of the following requirements:

(i) The emergency protective order is issued to protect one or more individuals who are already protected persons under another restraining or protective order.

(ii) The emergency protective order restrains the individual who is the restrained person in the other restraining or protective order specified in clause (i).

(iii) The provisions of the emergency protective order are more restrictive in relation to the restrained person than are the provisions of the other restraining or protective order specified in clause (i).

(B) An emergency protective order that meets the requirements of subparagraph (A) shall have precedence in enforcement over the provisions of any other restraining or protective order only with respect to those provisions of the emergency protective order that are more restrictive in relation to the restrained person.

(2) Except as described in paragraph (1), a no-contact order, as described in Section 6320 of the Family Code, shall have precedence in enforcement over any other restraining or protective order.

(d)

(1) A person subject to a protective order issued under this section shall not own, possess, purchase, or receive, or attempt to purchase or receive, a firearm while the protective order is in effect.

(2) The court shall order a person subject to a protective order issued under this section to relinquish ownership or possession of any firearms pursuant to Section 527.9 of the Code of Civil Procedure.

(3) A person who owns, possesses, purchases, or receives, or attempts to purchase or receive a firearm while the protective order is in effect is punishable pursuant to Section 29825.

(e)

(1) When the defendant is charged with a crime involving domestic violence, as defined in Section 13700 of this code or in Section 6211 of the Family Code, a violation of Section 261, 261.5, or former Section 262, or a crime that requires the defendant to register pursuant to subdivision (c) of Section 290, including, but not limited to, commercial sexual exploitation of a minor in violation of Section 236.1, the court shall consider issuing the above-described orders on its own motion. All interested parties shall receive a copy of those orders. To facilitate this, the court's records of all criminal cases involving domestic violence, a violation of Section 261, 261.5, or former Section 262, or a crime that requires the defendant to register pursuant to subdivision (c) of Section 290, including, but not limited to, commercial sexual exploitation of a minor in violation of Section 236.1, shall be marked to clearly alert the court to this issue.

(2) When a complaint, information, or indictment charging a crime involving domestic violence, as defined in Section 13700 or in Section 6211 of the Family Code, a violation of Section 261, 261.5, or former Section 262, or a crime that requires the defendant to register pursuant to subdivision (c) of Section 290, including, but not limited to, commercial sexual exploitation of a minor in violation of Section 236.1, has been issued, except as described in subdivision (c), a restraining order or protective order against the defendant issued by the criminal court in that case has precedence in enforcement over a civil court order against the defendant.

(3) Custody and visitation with respect to the defendant and the defendant's minor children may be ordered by a family or juvenile court consistent with the protocol established pursuant to subdivision (f), but if it is ordered after a criminal protective order has been issued pursuant to this section, the custody and visitation order shall make reference to and, if there is not an emergency protective order that has precedence in enforcement pursuant to paragraph (1) of subdivision (c) or a no-contact order, as described in Section 6320 of the Family Code, acknowledge the precedence of enforcement of an appropriate criminal protective order. On or before July 1, 2014, the Judicial Council shall modify the criminal and civil court forms consistent with this subdivision.

(f) On or before January 1, 2003, the Judicial Council shall promulgate a protocol, for adoption by each local court in substantially similar terms, to provide for the timely coordination of all orders against the same defendant and in favor of the same named victim or victims. The protocol shall include, but shall not be limited to, mechanisms for ensuring appropriate communication and information sharing between criminal, family, and juvenile courts concerning orders and cases that involve the same parties and shall permit a family or juvenile court order to coexist with a criminal court protective order subject to the following conditions:

(1) An order that permits contact between the restrained person and the person's children shall provide for the safe exchange of the children and shall not contain language, either printed or handwritten, that violates a "no-contact order" issued by a criminal court.

(2) The safety of all parties shall be the courts' paramount concern. The family or juvenile court shall specify the time, day, place, and manner of transfer of the child as provided in Section 3100 of the Family Code.

(g) On or before January 1, 2003, the Judicial Council shall modify the criminal and civil court protective order forms consistent with this section.

(h)

(1) When a complaint, information, or indictment charging a crime involving domestic violence, as defined in Section 13700 or in Section 6211 of the Family Code, has been filed, the court may consider, in determining whether good cause exists to issue an order under subparagraph (A) of paragraph (1) of subdivision (a), the underlying nature of the offense charged and the information provided to the court pursuant to Section 273.75.

(2) When a complaint, information, or indictment charging a violation of Section 261, 261.5, or former Section 262, or a crime that requires the defendant to register pursuant to subdivision (c) of Section 290, including, but not limited to, commercial sexual exploitation of a minor in violation of Section 236.1, has been filed, the court may consider, in determining whether good cause exists to issue an order under paragraph (1) of subdivision (a), the underlying nature of the offense charged, the defendant's relationship to the victim, the likelihood of continuing harm to the victim, any current restraining order or protective order issued by a civil or criminal court involving the defendant, and the defendant's criminal history, including, but not limited to, prior convictions for a violation of Section 261, 261.5, or former Section 262, a crime that requires the defendant to register pursuant to subdivision (c) of Section 290, including, but not limited to, commercial sexual exploitation of a minor in violation of Section 236.1, any other forms of violence, or a weapons offense.

(i)

(1) When a criminal defendant has been convicted of a crime involving domestic violence, as defined in Section 13700 or in Section 6211 of the Family Code, a violation of subdivision (a), (b), or (c) of Section 236.1 prohibiting human trafficking, Section 261, 261.5, former Section 262, subdivision (a) of Section 266h, or subdivision (a) of Section 266i, a violation of Section 186.22, or a crime that requires the defendant to register pursuant to subdivision (c) of Section 290, the court, at the time of sentencing, shall consider issuing an order restraining the defendant from any contact with a victim of the crime. The order may be valid for up to 10 years, as determined by the court. This protective order may be issued by the court regardless of whether the defendant is sentenced to the state prison or a county jail, whether the defendant is subject to mandatory supervision, or whether imposition of sentence is suspended and the defendant is placed on probation. The order may be modified by the sentencing court in the county in which it was issued throughout the duration of the order. It is the intent of the Legislature in enacting this subdivision that the duration of a restraining order issued by the court be based upon the seriousness of the facts before the court, the probability of future violations, and the safety of a victim and the victim's immediate family.

(2) When a criminal defendant has been convicted of a crime involving domestic violence, as defined in Section 13700 or in Section 6211 of the Family Code, a violation of Section 261, 261.5, or former Section 262, a violation of Section 186.22, or a crime that

requires the defendant to register pursuant to subdivision (c) of Section 290, the court, at the time of sentencing, shall consider issuing an order restraining the defendant from any contact with a percipient witness to the crime if it can be established by clear and convincing evidence that the witness has been harassed, as defined in paragraph (3) of subdivision (b) of Section 527.6 of the Code of Civil Procedure, by the defendant.

(3) An order under this subdivision may include provisions for electronic monitoring if the local government, upon receiving the concurrence of the county sheriff or the chief probation officer with jurisdiction, adopts a policy authorizing electronic monitoring of defendants and specifies the agency with jurisdiction for this purpose. If the court determines that the defendant has the ability to pay for the monitoring program, the court shall order the defendant to pay for the monitoring. If the court determines that the defendant does not have the ability to pay for the electronic monitoring, the court may order the electronic monitoring to be paid for by the local government that adopted the policy authorizing electronic monitoring. The duration of the electronic monitoring shall not exceed one year from the date the order is issued.

(j) For purposes of this section, "local government" means the county that has jurisdiction over the protective order.

Amended by Stats 2023 ch 14 (AB 467),s 1, eff. 1/1/2024.
Amended by Stats 2022 ch 87 (SB 382),s 1, eff. 1/1/2023.
Amended by Stats 2021 ch 626 (AB 1171),s 14, eff. 1/1/2022.
Amended by Stats 2019 ch 256 (SB 781),s 6, eff. 1/1/2020.
Amended by Stats 2018 ch 805 (AB 1735),s 1, eff. 1/1/2019.
Amended by Stats 2017 ch 270 (AB 264),s 1, eff. 1/1/2018.
Amended by Stats 2016 ch 86 (SB 1171),s 220, eff. 1/1/2017.
Amended by Stats 2015 ch 60 (SB 307),s 1, eff. 1/1/2016.
Amended by Stats 2014 ch 673 (AB 1850),s 1.3, eff. 1/1/2015.
Amended by Stats 2014 ch 665 (AB 1498),s 1, eff. 1/1/2015.
Amended by Stats 2014 ch 638 (SB 910),s 1, eff. 1/1/2015.
Amended by Stats 2014 ch 71 (SB 1304),s 115, eff. 1/1/2015.
Amended by Stats 2013 ch 291 (AB 307),s 1.5, eff. 1/1/2014, op 7/1/2014.
Amended by Stats 2013 ch 291 (AB 307),s 1, eff. 1/1/2014, op 7/1/2014.
Amended by Stats 2013 ch 263 (AB 176),s 4, eff. 1/1/2014, op. 7/1/2014.
Amended by Stats 2013 ch 76 (AB 383),s 145, eff. 1/1/2014.
Amended by Stats 2012 ch 513 (AB 2467),s 2, eff. 1/1/2013.
Amended by Stats 2012 ch 162 (SB 1171),s 121, eff. 1/1/2013.
Amended by Stats 2011 ch 155 (SB 723),s 1, eff. 1/1/2012.
Amended by Stats 2010 ch 178 (SB 1115),s 42, eff. 1/1/2011, op. 1/1/2012.
Amended by Stats 2008 ch 86 (AB 1771),s 1, eff. 1/1/2009.
Amended by Stats 2005 ch 702 (AB 1288),s 1.7, eff. 1/1/2006
Amended by Stats 2005 ch 631 (SB 720),s 3.4, eff. 1/1/2006
Amended by Stats 2005 ch 465 (AB 118),s 2.1, eff. 1/1/2006
Amended by Stats 2005 ch 132 (AB 112),s 1, eff. 1/1/2006
Amended by Stats 2003 ch 498 (SB 226), s 6, eff. 1/1/2004.
Amended by Stats 2001 ch 698 (AB 160), s 4, eff. 1/1/2002, op. 1/1/2003.
Previously Amended October 10, 1999 (Bill Number: AB 825) (Chapter 661).

Section 136.3 - Prohibition from obtaining address or location of protected party

(a) The court shall order that any party enjoined pursuant to Section 136.2 be prohibited from taking any action to obtain the address or location of a protected party or a protected party's family members, caretakers, or guardian, unless there is good cause not to make that order.

(b) The Judicial Council shall promulgate forms necessary to effectuate this section.

Added by Stats 2005 ch 472 (AB 978),s 4, eff. 1/1/2006.

Section 136.5 - Use of deadly weapon

Any person who has upon his person a deadly weapon with the intent to use such weapon to commit a violation of Section 136.1 is guilty of an offense punishable by imprisonment in the county jail for not more than one year, or in the state prison.

Added by Stats. 1982, Ch. 1101, Sec. 1.

Section 136.7 - Revealing name and address of witness or victim to sexual offense to other prisoner

(a) Every person imprisoned in a county jail or the state prison who has been convicted of a sexual offense, including, but not limited to, a violation of Section 243.4, 261, 261.5, 264.1, 266, 266a, 266b, 266c, 266f, 285, 286, 287, 288, or 289, or former Section 262 or 288a, who knowingly reveals the name and address of a witness or victim to that offense to any other prisoner with the intent that the other prisoner will intimidate or harass the witness or victim through the initiation of unauthorized correspondence with the witness or victim, is guilty of a public offense, punishable by imprisonment in the county jail not to exceed one year, or by imprisonment pursuant to subdivision (h) of Section 1170.

(b) This section shall not prevent the interviewing of witnesses.

Amended by Stats 2021 ch 626 (AB 1171),s 15, eff. 1/1/2022.
Amended by Stats 2018 ch 423 (SB 1494),s 41, eff. 1/1/2019.
Amended by Stats 2011 ch 39 (AB 117),s 68, eff. 6/30/2011.
Amended by Stats 2011 ch 15 (AB 109),s 250, eff. 4/4/2011, but operative no earlier than October 1, 2011, and only upon creation of a community corrections grant program to assist in implementing this act and upon an appropriation to fund the grant program.

Section 137 - Bribery of witness

(a) Every person who gives or offers, or promises to give, to any witness, person about to be called as a witness, or person about to give material information pertaining to a crime to a law enforcement official, any bribe, upon any understanding or agreement that the testimony of such witness or information given by such person shall be thereby influenced is guilty of a felony.

(b) Every person who attempts by force or threat of force or by the use of fraud to induce any person to give false testimony or withhold true testimony or to give false material information pertaining to a crime to, or withhold true material information pertaining to a crime from, a law enforcement official is guilty of a felony, punishable by imprisonment pursuant to subdivision (h) of Section 1170 for two, three, or four years. As used in this subdivision, "threat of force" means a credible threat of unlawful injury to any person or damage to the property of another which is communicated to a person for the purpose of inducing him to give false testimony or withhold true testimony or to give false material information pertaining to a crime to, or to withhold true material information pertaining to a crime from, a law enforcement official.

(c) Every person who knowingly induces another person to give false testimony or withhold true testimony not privileged by law or to give false material information pertaining to a crime to, or to withhold true material information pertaining to a crime from, a law enforcement official is guilty of a misdemeanor.

(d) At the arraignment, on a showing of cause to believe this section may be violated, the court, on motion of a party, shall admonish the person who there is cause to believe may violate this section and shall announce the penalties and other provisions of this section.

(e) As used in this section "law enforcement official" includes any district attorney, deputy district attorney, city attorney, deputy city attorney, the Attorney General or any deputy attorney general, or any peace officer included in Chapter 4.5 (commencing with Section 830) of Title 3 of Part 2.

(f) The provisions of subdivision (c) shall not apply to an attorney advising a client or to a person advising a member of his or her family.
Amended by Stats 2011 ch 39 (AB 117),s 68, eff. 6/30/2011.
Amended by Stats 2011 ch 15 (AB 109),s 251, eff. 4/4/2011, but operative no earlier than October 1, 2011, and only upon creation of a community corrections grant program to assist in implementing this act and upon an appropriation to fund the grant program.

Section 138 - Bribery of witness to dissuade attendance at trial

(a) Every person who gives or offers or promises to give to any witness or person about to be called as a witness, any bribe upon any understanding or agreement that the person shall not attend upon any trial or other judicial proceeding, or every person who attempts by means of any offer of a bribe to dissuade any person from attending upon any trial or other judicial proceeding, is guilty of a felony.

(b) Every person who is a witness, or is about to be called as such, who receives, or offers to receive, any bribe, upon any understanding that his or her testimony shall be influenced thereby, or that he or she will absent himself or herself from the trial or proceeding upon which his or her testimony is required, is guilty of a felony.
Amended by Stats. 1987, Ch. 828, Sec. 5.

Section 139 - Credible threat to use force or violence

(a) Except as provided in Sections 71 and 136.1, any person who has been convicted of any felony offense specified in Chapter 3 (commencing with Section 29900) of Division 9 of Title 4 of Part 6 who willfully and maliciously communicates to a witness to, or a victim of, the crime for which the person was convicted, a credible threat to use force or violence upon that person or that person's immediate family, shall be punished by imprisonment in the county jail not exceeding one year or by imprisonment pursuant to subdivision (h) of Section 1170 for two, three, or four years.

(b) Any person who is convicted of violating subdivision (a) who subsequently is convicted of making a credible threat, as defined in subdivision (c), which constitutes a threat against the life of, or a threat to cause great bodily injury to, a person described in subdivision (a), shall be sentenced to consecutive terms of imprisonment as prescribed in Section 1170.13.

(c) As used in this section, "a credible threat" is a threat made with the intent and the apparent ability to carry out the threat so as to cause the target of the threat to reasonably fear for his or her safety or the safety of his or her immediate family.

(d) The present incarceration of the person making the threat shall not be a bar to prosecution under this section.

(e) As used in this section, "malice," "witness," and "victim" have the meanings given in Section 136.
Amended by Stats 2011 ch 39 (AB 117),s 68, eff. 6/30/2011.
Amended by Stats 2011 ch 15 (AB 109),s 253, eff. 4/4/2011, but operative no earlier than October 1, 2011, and only upon creation of a community corrections grant program to assist in implementing this act and upon an appropriation to fund the grant program.
Amended by Stats 2010 ch 178 (SB 1115),s 43, eff. 1/1/2011, op. 1/1/2012.

Section 140 - Use of force or violence

(a) Except as provided in Section 139, every person who willfully uses force or threatens to use force or violence upon the person of a witness to, or a victim of, a crime or any other person, or to take, damage, or destroy any property of any witness, victim, or any other person, because the witness, victim, or other person has provided any assistance or information to a law enforcement officer, or to a public prosecutor in a criminal proceeding or juvenile court proceeding, shall be punished by imprisonment in the county jail not exceeding one year, or by imprisonment pursuant to subdivision (h) of Section 1170 for two, three, or four years.

(b) A person who is punished under another provision of law for an act described in subdivision (a) shall not receive an additional term of imprisonment under this section.
Amended by Stats 2011 ch 39 (AB 117),s 68, eff. 6/30/2011.
Amended by Stats 2011 ch 15 (AB 109),s 254, eff. 4/4/2011, but operative no earlier than October 1, 2011, and only upon creation of a community corrections grant program to assist in implementing this act and upon an appropriation to fund the grant program.

Section 141 - Alteration or planting of evidence

(a) Except as provided in subdivisions (b) and (c), a person who knowingly, willfully, intentionally, and wrongfully alters, modifies, plants, places, manufactures, conceals, or moves any physical matter, digital image, or video recording, with specific intent that the action will result in a person being charged with a crime or with the specific intent that the physical matter will be wrongfully produced as genuine or true upon a trial, proceeding, or inquiry, is guilty of a misdemeanor.

(b) A peace officer who knowingly, willfully, intentionally, and wrongfully alters, modifies, plants, places, manufactures, conceals, or moves any physical matter, digital image, or video recording, with specific intent that the action will result in a person being charged with a crime or with the specific intent that the physical matter, digital image, or video recording will be concealed or destroyed, or fraudulently represented as the original evidence upon a trial, proceeding, or inquiry, is guilty of a felony punishable by two, three, or five years in the state prison.

(c) A prosecuting attorney who intentionally and in bad faith alters, modifies, or withholds any physical matter, digital image, video recording, or relevant exculpatory material or information, knowing that it is relevant and material to the outcome of the case, with the specific intent that the physical matter, digital image, video recording, or relevant exculpatory material or information will be concealed or destroyed, or fraudulently represented as the original evidence upon a trial, proceeding, or inquiry, is guilty of a felony punishable by imprisonment pursuant to subdivision (h) of Section 1170 for 16 months, or two or three years.

(d) This section does not preclude prosecution under both this section and any other law.

Amended by Stats 2016 ch 879 (AB 1909),s 1, eff. 1/1/2017.

Amended by Stats 2015 ch 463 (AB 256),s 2, eff. 1/1/2016.

Added by Stats 2000 ch 620 (AB 1993), s 1, eff. 1/1/2001.

Chapter 7 - OTHER OFFENSES AGAINST PUBLIC JUSTICE

Section 142 - Willful refusal to arrest person

(a) Any peace officer who has the authority to receive or arrest a person charged with a criminal offense and willfully refuses to receive or arrest that person shall be punished by a fine not exceeding ten thousand dollars ($10,000), or by imprisonment in a county jail not exceeding one year, or pursuant to subdivision (h) of Section 1170, or by both that fine and imprisonment.

(b) Notwithstanding subdivision (a), the sheriff may determine whether any jail, institution, or facility under his or her direction shall be designated as a reception, holding, or confinement facility, or shall be used for several of those purposes, and may designate the class of prisoners for which any facility shall be used.

(c) This section shall not apply to arrests made pursuant to Section 837.

Amended by Stats 2011 ch 39 (AB 117),s 68, eff. 6/30/2011.

Amended by Stats 2011 ch 15 (AB 109),s 255, eff. 4/4/2011, but operative no earlier than October 1, 2011, and only upon creation of a community corrections grant program to assist in implementing this act and upon an appropriation to fund the grant program.

Amended by Stats 2002 ch 526 (AB 1835), s 1, eff. 1/1/2003.

Section 145 - Willful delay to take arrestee before magistrate

Every public officer or other person, having arrested any person upon a criminal charge, who willfully delays to take such person before a magistrate having jurisdiction, to take his examination, is guilty of a misdemeanor.

Enacted 1872.

Section 145.5 - Prohibition on aiding agency of armed forces; legislative intent

(a)

(1) Subject to paragraph (2), notwithstanding any law to the contrary, no agency of the State of California, no political subdivision of this state, no employee of an agency, or a political subdivision, of this state acting in his or her official capacity, and no member of the California National Guard on official state duty shall knowingly aid an agency of the armed forces of the United States in any investigation, prosecution, or detention of a person within California pursuant to (A) Sections 1021 and 1022 of the National Defense Authorization Act for Fiscal Year 2012 (NDAA), (B) the federal law known as the Authorization for Use of Military Force (Public Law 107-40), enacted in 2001, or (C) any other federal law, if the state agency, political subdivision, employee, or member of the California National Guard would violate the United States Constitution, the California Constitution, or any law of this state by providing that aid.

(2) Paragraph (1) does not apply to participation by state or local law enforcement or the California National Guard in a joint task force, partnership, or other similar cooperative agreement with federal law enforcement if that joint task force, partnership, or similar cooperative agreement is not for the purpose of investigating, prosecuting, or detaining any person pursuant to (A) Sections 1021 and 1022 of the NDAA, (B) the federal law known as the Authorization for Use of Military Force (Public Law 107-40), enacted in 2001, or (C) any other federal law, if the state agency, political subdivision, employee, or member of the California National Guard would violate the United States Constitution, the California Constitution, or any law of this state by providing that aid.

(b) It is the policy of this state to refuse to provide material support for or to participate in any way with the implementation within this state of any federal law that purports to authorize indefinite detention of a person within California. Notwithstanding any other law, no local law enforcement agency or local or municipal government, or the employee of that agency or government acting in his or her official capacity, shall knowingly use state funds or funds allocated by the state to local entities on or after January 1, 2013, in whole or in part, to engage in any activity that aids an agency of the armed forces of the United States in the detention of any person within California for purposes of implementing Sections 1021 and 1022 of the NDAA or the federal law known as the Authorization for Use of Military Force (Public Law 107-40), enacted in 2001, if that activity would violate the United States Constitution, the California Constitution, or any law of this state.

Amended by Stats 2014 ch 71 (SB 1304),s 116, eff. 1/1/2015.

Added by Stats 2013 ch 450 (AB 351),s 1, eff. 1/1/2014.

Section 146 - Acts done without regular process or other lawful authority

Every public officer, or person pretending to be a public officer, who, under the pretense or color of any process or other legal authority, does any of the following, without a regular process or other lawful authority, is guilty of a misdemeanor:

(a) Arrests any person or detains that person against his or her will.

(b) Seizes or levies upon any property.

(c) Dispossesses any one of any lands or tenements.

Amended by Stats. 1990, Ch. 350, Sec. 11.

Section 146a - False representation as deputy or clerk

(a) Any person who falsely represents himself or herself to be a deputy or clerk in any state department and who, in that assumed character, does any of the following is guilty of a misdemeanor punishable by imprisonment in a county jail not exceeding six months, by a fine not exceeding two thousand five hundred dollars ($2,500), or both the fine and imprisonment:

(1) Arrests, detains, or threatens to arrest or detain any person.

(2) Otherwise intimidates any person.

(3) Searches any person, building, or other property of any person.

(4) Obtains money, property, or other thing of value.

(b) Any person who falsely represents himself or herself to be a public officer, investigator, or inspector in any state department and who, in that assumed character, does any of the following shall be punished by imprisonment in a county jail not exceeding one year, by a fine not exceeding two thousand five hundred dollars ($2,500), or by both that fine and imprisonment, or by imprisonment pursuant to subdivision (h) of Section 1170:

(1) Arrests, detains, or threatens to arrest or detain any person.

(2) Otherwise intimidates any person.

(3) Searches any person, building, or other property of any person.

(4) Obtains money, property, or other thing of value.

Amended by Stats 2011 ch 39 (AB 117),s 68, eff. 6/30/2011.

Amended by Stats 2011 ch 15 (AB 109),s 256, eff. 4/4/2011, but operative no earlier than October 1, 2011, and only upon creation of a community corrections grant program to assist in implementing this act and upon an appropriation to fund the grant program.

Section 146b - False request or demand for information

Every person who, with intent to lead another to believe that a request or demand for information is being made by the State, a county, city, or other governmental entity, when such is not the case, sends to such other person a written or printed form or other communication which reasonably appears to be such request or demand by such governmental entity, is guilty of a misdemeanor.

Added by Stats. 1959, Ch. 2135.

Section 146c - False designation of nongovernmental organization

Every person who designates any nongovernmental organization by any name, including, but not limited to any name that incorporates the term "peace officer," "police," or "law enforcement," that would reasonably be understood to imply that the organization is composed of law enforcement personnel, when, in fact, less than 80 percent of the voting members of the organization are law enforcement personnel or firefighters, active or retired, is guilty of a misdemeanor.

Every person who solicits another to become a member of any organization so named, of which less than 80 percent of the voting members are law enforcement personnel or firefighters, or to make a contribution thereto or subscribe to or advertise in a publication of the organization, or who sells or gives to another any badge, pin, membership card, or other article indicating membership in the organization, knowing that less than 80 percent of the voting members are law enforcement personnel or firefighters, active or retired, is guilty of a misdemeanor.

As used in this section, "law enforcement personnel" includes those mentioned in Chapter 4.5 (commencing with Section 830) of Title 3 of Part 2, plus any other officers in any segment of law enforcement who are employed by the state or any of its political subdivisions.

Amended by Stats. 1994, Ch. 202, Sec. 1. Effective January 1, 1995.

Section 146d - Sale of membership card, badge, or other device

Every person who sells or gives to another a membership card, badge, or other device, where it can be reasonably inferred by the recipient that display of the device will have the result that the law will be enforced less rigorously as to such person than would otherwise be the case is guilty of a misdemeanor.

Added by Stats. 1963, Ch. 1180.

Section 146e - Disclosure of residence address or telephone number of peace officer and others

(a) Every person who maliciously, and with the intent to obstruct justice or the due administration of the laws, or with the intent to, or threat to, inflict bodily harm in retaliation for the due administration of the laws, publishes, disseminates, or otherwise discloses the residence address or telephone number of any peace officer, nonsworn police dispatcher, employee of a city police department or county sheriff's office, or public safety official, or that of the immediate family of these persons who reside with them, while designating the elected or appointed official, peace officer, nonsworn police dispatcher, employee of a city police department or county sheriff's office, or public safety official, or relative of these persons as such, without the authorization of the employing agency, is guilty of a misdemeanor.

(b) A violation of subdivision (a) with regard to any peace officer, nonsworn police dispatcher, employee of a city police department or county sheriff's office, or public safety official, or the immediate family of these persons, that results in bodily injury to the elected or appointed official, peace officer, nonsworn police dispatcher, employee of the city police department or county sheriff's office, or public safety official, or the immediate family of these persons, is a felony punishable by imprisonment pursuant to subdivision (h) of Section 1170.

(c) For the purposes of this section, the following terms have the following meanings:

(1) "Immediate family" means a spouse, parent, child, a person related by consanguinity or affinity within the second degree, or another person who regularly resides in the household, or who, within the prior six months, regularly resided in the household.

(2) "Public safety official" has the same meaning as defined in Section 7920.535 of the Government Code.

Amended by Stats 2023 ch 131 (AB 1754),s 147, eff. 1/1/2024.

Amended by Stats 2022 ch 697 (AB 2588),s 2, eff. 1/1/2023.

Amended by Stats 2021 ch 615 (AB 474),s 330, eff. 1/1/2022, op. 1/1/2023.

Amended by Stats 2011 ch 39 (AB 117),s 68, eff. 6/30/2011.

Amended by Stats 2011 ch 15 (AB 109),s 257, eff. 4/4/2011, but operative no earlier than October 1, 2011, and only upon creation of a community corrections grant program to assist in implementing this act and upon an appropriation to fund the grant program.

Amended by Stats 2002 ch 621 (AB 2238), s 4, eff. 1/1/2003.

Section 146f - No access to peace officer personnel information by inmates

No inmate under the control or supervision of the Department of Corrections or the Department of the Youth Authority shall be permitted to work with records or files containing peace officer personnel information or be allowed access to the immediate area where that information is normally stored, except for maintenance services and only after those records or files have been secured and locked. Added by Stats. 1983, Ch. 399, Sec. 2.

Section 146g - Unlawful disclosure or solicitation of information obtained in course of criminal investigation

(a) Any peace officer, as defined in Chapter 4.5 (commencing with Section 830) of Title 3 of Part 2, any employee of a law enforcement agency, any attorney as defined in Section 6125 of the Business and Professions Code employed by a governmental agency, or any trial court employee as defined in Section 71601 of the Government Code, who does either of the following is guilty of a misdemeanor punishable by a fine not to exceed one thousand dollars ($1,000):

(1) Discloses, for financial gain, information obtained in the course of a criminal investigation, the disclosure of which is prohibited by law.

(2) Solicits, for financial gain, the exchange of information obtained in the course of a criminal investigation, the disclosure of which is prohibited by law.

(b) Any person who solicits any other person described in subdivision (a) for the financial gain of the person described in subdivision (a) to disclose information obtained in the course of a criminal investigation, with the knowledge that the disclosure is prohibited by law, is guilty of a misdemeanor, punishable by a fine not to exceed one thousand dollars ($1,000).

(c)

(1) Any person described in subdivision (a) who, for financial gain, solicits or sells any photograph or video taken inside any secure area of a law enforcement or court facility, the taking of which was not authorized by the law enforcement or court facility administrator, is guilty of a misdemeanor punishable by a fine not to exceed one thousand dollars ($1,000).

(2) Any person who solicits any person described in subdivision (a) for financial gain to the person described in subdivision (a) to disclose any photograph or video taken inside any secure area of a law enforcement or court facility, the taking of which was not authorized by the law enforcement or court facility administrator, is guilty of a misdemeanor punishable by a fine not to exceed one thousand dollars ($1,000).

(d) Upon conviction of, and in addition to, any other penalty prescribed by this section, the defendant shall forfeit any monetary compensation received in the commission of a violation of this section and the money shall be deposited in the Victim Restitution Fund.

(e) Nothing in this section shall apply to officially sanctioned information, photographs, or video, or to information, photographs, or video obtained or distributed pursuant to the California Whistleblower Protection Act or the Local Government Disclosure of Information Act.

(f) This section shall not be construed to limit or prevent prosecution pursuant to any other applicable provision of law. Added by Stats 2007 ch 401 (AB 920),s 2, eff. 1/1/2008.

Section 147 - Willful inhumanity or oppression toward prisoner

Every officer who is guilty of willful inhumanity or oppression toward any prisoner under his care or in his custody, is punishable by fine not exceeding four thousand dollars ($4,000), and by removal from office. Amended by Stats. 1983, Ch. 1092, Sec. 240. Effective September 27, 1983. Operative January 1, 1984, by Sec. 427 of Ch. 1092.

Section 148 - Resistance, delay, or obstruction of public officer, peace officer, or emergency medical technician

(a)

(1) Every person who willfully resists, delays, or obstructs any public officer, peace officer, or an emergency medical technician, as defined in Division 2.5 (commencing with Section 1797) of the Health and Safety Code, in the discharge or attempt to discharge any duty of his or her office or employment, when no other punishment is prescribed, shall be punished by a fine not exceeding one thousand dollars ($1,000), or by imprisonment in a county jail not to exceed one year, or by both that fine and imprisonment.

(2) Except as provided by subdivision (d) of Section 653t, every person who knowingly and maliciously interrupts, disrupts, impedes, or otherwise interferes with the transmission of a communication over a public safety radio frequency shall be punished by a fine not exceeding one thousand dollars ($1,000), imprisonment in a county jail not exceeding one year, or by both that fine and imprisonment.

(b) Every person who, during the commission of any offense described in subdivision (a), removes or takes any weapon, other than a firearm, from the person of, or immediate presence of, a public officer or peace officer shall be punished by imprisonment in a county jail not to exceed one year or pursuant to subdivision (h) of Section 1170.

(c) Every person who, during the commission of any offense described in subdivision (a), removes or takes a firearm from the person of, or immediate presence of, a public officer or peace officer shall be punished by imprisonment pursuant to subdivision (h) of Section 1170.

(d) Except as provided in subdivision (c) and notwithstanding subdivision (a) of Section 489, every person who removes or takes without intent to permanently deprive, or who attempts to remove or take a firearm from the person of, or immediate presence of, a public officer or peace officer, while the officer is engaged in the performance of his or her lawful duties, shall be punished by imprisonment in a county jail not to exceed one year or pursuant to subdivision (h) of Section 1170. In order to prove a violation of this subdivision, the prosecution shall establish that the defendant had the specific intent to remove or take the firearm by demonstrating that any of the following direct, but ineffectual, acts occurred:

(1) The officer's holster strap was unfastened by the defendant.

(2) The firearm was partially removed from the officer's holster by the defendant.

(3) The firearm safety was released by the defendant.

(4) An independent witness corroborates that the defendant stated that he or she intended to remove the firearm and the defendant actually touched the firearm.

(5) An independent witness corroborates that the defendant actually had his or her hand on the firearm and tried to take the firearm away from the officer who was holding it.

(6) The defendant's fingerprint was found on the firearm or holster.

(7) Physical evidence authenticated by a scientifically verifiable procedure established that the defendant touched the firearm.

(8) In the course of any struggle, the officer's firearm fell and the defendant attempted to pick it up.

(e) A person shall not be convicted of a violation of subdivision (a) in addition to a conviction of a violation of subdivision (b), (c), or (d) when the resistance, delay, or obstruction, and the removal or taking of the weapon or firearm or attempt thereof, was committed against the same public officer, peace officer, or emergency medical technician. A person may be convicted of multiple violations of this section if more than one public officer, peace officer, or emergency medical technician are victims.

(f) This section shall not apply if the public officer, peace officer, or emergency medical technician is disarmed while engaged in a criminal act.

(g) The fact that a person takes a photograph or makes an audio or video recording of a public officer or peace officer, while the officer is in a public place or the person taking the photograph or making the recording is in a place he or she has the right to be, does not constitute, in and of itself, a violation of subdivision (a), nor does it constitute reasonable suspicion to detain the person or probable cause to arrest the person.

Amended by Stats 2015 ch 177 (SB 411),s 2, eff. 1/1/2016.

Amended by Stats 2011 ch 39 (AB 117),s 68, eff. 6/30/2011.

Amended by Stats 2011 ch 15 (AB 109),s 258, eff. 4/4/2011, but operative no earlier than October 1, 2011, and only upon creation of a community corrections grant program to assist in implementing this act and upon an appropriation to fund the grant program. EFFECTIVE 1/1/2000. Amended October 10, 1999 (Bill Number: SB 832) (Chapter 853).

Section 148.1 - False report of bomb

(a) Any person who reports to any peace officer listed in Section 830.1 or 830.2, or subdivision (a) of Section 830.33, employee of a fire department or fire service, district attorney, newspaper, radio station, television station, deputy district attorney, employees of the Department of Justice, employees of an airline, employees of an airport, employees of a railroad or busline, an employee of a telephone company, occupants of a building or a news reporter in the employ of a newspaper or radio or television station, that a bomb or other explosive has been or will be placed or secreted in any public or private place, knowing that the report is false, is guilty of a crime punishable by imprisonment in a county jail not to exceed one year, or pursuant to subdivision (h) of Section 1170.

(b) Any person who reports to any other peace officer defined in Chapter 4.5 (commencing with Section 830) of Title 3 of Part 2 that a bomb or other explosive has been or will be placed or secreted in any public or private place, knowing that the report is false, is guilty of a crime punishable by imprisonment in a county jail not to exceed one year or pursuant to subdivision (h) of Section 1170 if (1) the false information is given while the peace officer is engaged in the performance of his or her duties as a peace officer and (2) the person providing the false information knows or should have known that the person receiving the information is a peace officer.

(c) Any person who maliciously informs any other person that a bomb or other explosive has been or will be placed or secreted in any public or private place, knowing that the information is false, is guilty of a crime punishable by imprisonment in a county jail not to exceed one year, or pursuant to subdivision (h) of Section 1170.

(d) Any person who maliciously gives, mails, sends, or causes to be sent any false or facsimile bomb to another person, or places, causes to be placed, or maliciously possesses any false or facsimile bomb, with the intent to cause another to fear for his or her personal safety or the safety of others, is guilty of a crime punishable by imprisonment in a county jail not to exceed one year, or pursuant to subdivision (h) of Section 1170.

Amended by Stats 2011 ch 39 (AB 117),s 68, eff. 6/30/2011.

Amended by Stats 2011 ch 15 (AB 109),s 259, eff. 4/4/2011, but operative no earlier than October 1, 2011, and only upon creation of a community corrections grant program to assist in implementing this act and upon an appropriation to fund the grant program.

Section 148.2 - Unlawful acts at burning of building

Every person who willfully commits any of the following acts at the burning of a building or at any other time and place where any fireman or firemen or emergency rescue personnel are discharging or attempting to discharge an official duty, is guilty of a misdemeanor:

1.Resists or interferes with the lawful efforts of any fireman or firemen or emergency rescue personnel in the discharge or attempt to discharge an official duty.

2.Disobeys the lawful orders of any fireman or public officer.

3.Engages in any disorderly conduct which delays or prevents a fire from being timely extinguished.

4.Forbids or prevents others from assisting in extinguishing a fire or exhorts another person, as to whom he has no legal right or obligation to protect or control, from assisting in extinguishing a fire.

Amended by Stats. 1973, Ch. 471.

Section 148.3 - False report of emergency

(a) Any individual who reports, or causes any report to be made, to any city, county, city and county, or state department, district, agency, division, commission, or board, that an "emergency" exists, knowing that the report is false, is guilty of a misdemeanor and upon conviction thereof shall be punishable by imprisonment in a county jail for a period not exceeding one year, or by a fine not exceeding one thousand dollars ($1,000), or by both that imprisonment and fine.

(b) Any individual who reports, or causes any report to be made, to any city, county, city and county, or state department, district, agency, division, commission, or board, that an "emergency" exists, who knows that the report is false, and who knows or should know that the response to the report is likely to cause death or great bodily injury, and great bodily injury or death is sustained by any person as a result of the false report, is guilty of a felony and upon conviction thereof shall be punishable by imprisonment pursuant to subdivision (h) of Section 1170, or by a fine of not more than ten thousand dollars ($10,000), or by both that imprisonment and fine.

(c) "Emergency" as used in this section means any condition that results in, or could result in, the response of a public official in an authorized emergency vehicle, aircraft, or vessel, any condition that jeopardizes or could jeopardize public safety and results in, or could result in, the evacuation of any area, building, structure, vehicle, or of any other place that any individual may enter, or any situation that results in or could result in activation of the Emergency Alert System pursuant to Section 8594 of the Government Code. An activation or possible activation of the Emergency Alert System pursuant to Section 8594 of the Government Code shall not constitute an "emergency" for purposes of this section if it occurs as the result of a report made or caused to be made by a parent, guardian, or lawful custodian of a child that is based on a good faith belief that the child is missing.

(d) Nothing in this section precludes punishment for the conduct described in subdivision (a) or (b) under any other section of law providing for greater punishment for that conduct.

(e) Any individual convicted of violating this section, based upon a report that resulted in an emergency response, is liable to a public agency for the reasonable costs of the emergency response by that public agency.

Amended by Stats 2013 ch 284 (SB 333),s 1, eff. 1/1/2014.

Amended by Stats 2011 ch 39 (AB 117),s 68, eff. 6/30/2011.

Amended by Stats 2011 ch 15 (AB 109),s 260, eff. 4/4/2011, but operative no earlier than October 1, 2011, and only upon creation of a community corrections grant program to assist in implementing this act and upon an appropriation to fund the grant program.

Amended by Stats 2006 ch 227 (AB 2225),s 1, eff. 1/1/2007.

Amended by Stats 2002 ch 521 (SB 2057), s 1, eff. 1/1/2003.

Section 148.4 - Tampering with fire protection equipment; false alarm of fire

(a) Any person who does any of the following is guilty of a misdemeanor and upon conviction is punishable by imprisonment in a county jail, not exceeding one year, or by a fine, not exceeding one thousand dollars ($1,000), or by both that fine and imprisonment:

(1) Willfully and maliciously tampers with, molests, injures, or breaks any fire protection equipment, fire protection installation, fire alarm apparatus, wire, or signal.

(2) Willfully and maliciously sends, gives, transmits, or sounds any false alarm of fire, by means of any fire alarm system or signal or by any other means or methods.

(b) Any person who willfully and maliciously sends, gives, transmits, or sounds any false alarm of fire, by means of any fire alarm system or signal, or by any other means or methods, is guilty of a felony and upon conviction is punishable by imprisonment pursuant to subdivision (h) of Section 1170 or by a fine of not less than five hundred dollars ($500) nor more than ten thousand dollars ($10,000), or by both that fine and imprisonment, if any person sustains as a result thereof, any of the following:

(1) Great bodily injury.

(2) Death.

Amended by Stats 2011 ch 39 (AB 117),s 68, eff. 6/30/2011.

Amended by Stats 2011 ch 15 (AB 109),s 261, eff. 4/4/2011, but operative no earlier than October 1, 2011, and only upon creation of a community corrections grant program to assist in implementing this act and upon an appropriation to fund the grant program.

Section 148.5 - False report of felony or misdemeanor

(a) Every person who reports to any peace officer listed in Section 830.1 or 830.2, or subdivision (a) of Section 830.33, the Attorney General, or a deputy attorney general, or a district attorney, or a deputy district attorney that a felony or misdemeanor has been committed, knowing the report to be false, is guilty of a misdemeanor.

(b) Every person who reports to any other peace officer, as defined in Chapter 4.5 (commencing with Section 830) of Title 3 of Part 2, that a felony or misdemeanor has been committed, knowing the report to be false, is guilty of a misdemeanor if (1) the false information is given while the peace officer is engaged in the performance of his or her duties as a peace officer and (2) the person providing the false information knows or should have known that the person receiving the information is a peace officer.

(c) Except as provided in subdivisions (a) and (b), every person who reports to any employee who is assigned to accept reports from citizens, either directly or by telephone, and who is employed by a state or local agency which is designated in Section 830.1, 830.2, subdivision (e) of Section 830.3, Section 830.31, 830.32, 830.33, 830.34, 830.35, 830.36, 830.37, or 830.4, that a felony or misdemeanor has been committed, knowing the report to be false, is guilty of a misdemeanor if (1) the false information is given while the employee is engaged in the performance of his or her duties as an agency employee and (2) the person providing the false information knows or should have known that the person receiving the information is an agency employee engaged in the performance of the duties described in this subdivision.

(d) Every person who makes a report to a grand jury that a felony or misdemeanor has been committed, knowing the report to be false, is guilty of a misdemeanor. This subdivision shall not be construed as prohibiting or precluding a charge of perjury or contempt for any report made under oath in an investigation or proceeding before a grand jury.

(e) This section does not apply to reports made by persons who are required by statute to report known or suspected instances of child abuse, dependent adult abuse, or elder abuse.

(f) This section applies to a person who reports to a person described in subdivision (a), (b), or (c), that a firearm, as defined in subdivision (a) or (b) of Section 16520, has been lost or stolen, knowing the report to be false.

Amended by Stats 2016 ch 47 (AB 1695),s 1, eff. 1/1/2017.

Amended by Stats 2006 ch 901 (SB 1422),s 5, eff. 1/1/2007.

Section 148.6 - Allegation of misconduct against peace officer

(a)

(1) Every person who files any allegation of misconduct against any peace officer, as defined in Chapter 4.5 (commencing with Section 830) of Title 3 of Part 2, knowing the allegation to be false, is guilty of a misdemeanor.

(2) A law enforcement agency accepting an allegation of misconduct against a peace officer shall require the complainant to read and sign the following advisory, all in boldface type: YOU HAVE THE RIGHT TO MAKE A COMPLAINT AGAINST A POLICE OFFICER FOR ANY IMPROPER POLICE CONDUCT. CALIFORNIA LAW REQUIRES THIS AGENCY TO HAVE A PROCEDURE TO INVESTIGATE CIVILIANS' COMPLAINTS. YOU HAVE A RIGHT TO A WRITTEN DESCRIPTION OF THIS PROCEDURE. THIS AGENCY MAY FIND AFTER INVESTIGATION THAT THERE IS NOT ENOUGH EVIDENCE TO WARRANT ACTION ON YOUR COMPLAINT; EVEN IF THAT IS THE CASE, YOU HAVE THE RIGHT TO MAKE THE COMPLAINT AND HAVE IT INVESTIGATED IF YOU BELIEVE AN OFFICER BEHAVED IMPROPERLY. CIVILIAN COMPLAINTS AND ANY REPORTS OR FINDINGS RELATING TO COMPLAINTS MUST BE RETAINED BY THIS AGENCY FOR AT LEAST FIVE YEARS.

IT IS AGAINST THE LAW TO MAKE A COMPLAINT THAT YOU KNOW TO BE FALSE. IF YOU MAKE A COMPLAINT AGAINST AN OFFICER KNOWING THAT IT IS FALSE, YOU CAN BE PROSECUTED ON A MISDEMEANOR CHARGE.

I have read and understood the above statement.
Complainant _____

(3) The advisory shall be available in multiple languages.

(b) Every person who files a civil claim against a peace officer or a lien against his or her property, knowing the claim or lien to be false and with the intent to harass or dissuade the officer from carrying out his or her official duties, is guilty of a misdemeanor. This section applies only to claims pertaining to actions that arise in the course and scope of the peace officer's duties.

Amended by Stats 2016 ch 99 (AB 1953),s 2, eff. 1/1/2017.

Amended by Stats 2000 ch 289 (SB 2133), s 1, eff. 1/1/2001.

Section 148.7 - Misrepresentation that person required to serve term of confinement

Every person who, for the purpose of serving in any county or city jail, industrial farm or road camp, or other local correctional institution any part or all of the sentence of another person, or any part or all of a term of confinement that is required to be served by another person as a condition of probation, represents to any public officer or employee that he is such other person, is guilty of a misdemeanor.

Added by Stats. 1963, Ch. 577.

Section 148.9 - False representation or identification as another person or fictitious person

(a) Any person who falsely represents or identifies himself or herself as another person or as a fictitious person to any peace officer listed in Section 830.1 or 830.2, or subdivision (a) of Section 830.33, upon a lawful detention or arrest of the person, either to evade the process of the court, or to evade the proper identification of the person by the investigating officer is guilty of a misdemeanor.

(b) Any person who falsely represents or identifies himself or herself as another person or as a fictitious person to any other peace officer defined in Chapter 4.5 (commencing with Section 830) of Title 3 of Part 2, upon lawful detention or arrest of the person, either to evade the process of the court, or to evade the proper identification of the person by the arresting officer is guilty of a misdemeanor if (1) the false information is given while the peace officer is engaged in the performance of his or her duties as a peace officer and (2) the person providing the false information knows or should have known that the person receiving the information is a peace officer.

Amended by Stats. 1998, Ch. 760, Sec. 3. Effective January 1, 1999.

Section 148.10 - Resistance of peace officer

(a) Every person who willfully resists a peace officer in the discharge or attempt to discharge any duty of his or her office or employment and whose willful resistance proximately causes death or serious bodily injury to a peace officer shall be punished by imprisonment pursuant to subdivision (h) of Section 1170 for two, three, or four years, or by a fine of not less than one thousand dollars ($1,000) or more than ten thousand dollars ($10,000), or by both that fine and imprisonment, or by imprisonment in a county jail for not more than one year, or by a fine of not more than one thousand dollars ($1,000), or by both that fine and imprisonment.

(b) For purposes of subdivision (a), the following facts shall be found by the trier of fact:

(1) That the peace officer's action was reasonable based on the facts or circumstances confronting the officer at the time.

(2) That the detention and arrest was lawful and there existed probable cause or reasonable cause to detain.

(3) That the person who willfully resisted any peace officer knew or reasonably should have known that the other person was a peace officer engaged in the performance of his or her duties.

(c) This section does not apply to conduct that occurs during labor picketing, demonstrations, or disturbing the peace.

(d) For purposes of this section, "serious bodily injury" is defined in paragraph (4) of subdivision (f) of Section 243.

Amended by Stats 2011 ch 39 (AB 117),s 68, eff. 6/30/2011.

Amended by Stats 2011 ch 15 (AB 109),s 262, eff. 4/4/2011, but operative no earlier than October 1, 2011, and only upon creation of a community corrections grant program to assist in implementing this act and upon an appropriation to fund the grant program. EFFECTIVE 1/1/2000. Amended July 12, 1999 (Bill Number: SB 966) (Chapter 83).

Section 149 - Assault by public officer

Every public officer who, under color of authority, without lawful necessity, assaults or beats any person, is punishable by a fine not exceeding ten thousand dollars ($10,000), or by imprisonment in a county jail not exceeding one year, or pursuant to subdivision (h) of Section 1170, or by both that fine and imprisonment.

Amended by Stats 2011 ch 39 (AB 117),s 68, eff. 6/30/2011.

Amended by Stats 2011 ch 15 (AB 109),s 263, eff. 4/4/2011, but operative no earlier than October 1, 2011, and only upon creation of a community corrections grant program to assist in implementing this act and upon an appropriation to fund the grant program.

Section 150 - [Repealed]

Repealed by Stats 2019 ch 204 (SB 192),s 1, eff. 1/1/2020.

Section 151 - Advocating the killing or injuring of peace officer

(a) Any person who advocates the willful and unlawful killing or injuring of a peace officer, with the specific intent to cause the willful and unlawful killing or injuring of a peace officer, and such advocacy is done at a time, place, and under circumstances in which the advocacy is likely to cause the imminent willful and unlawful killing or injuring of a peace officer is guilty of (1) a misdemeanor if such advocacy does not cause the unlawful and willful killing or injuring of a peace officer, or (2) a felony if such advocacy causes the unlawful and willful killing or injuring of a peace officer.

(b) As used in this section, "advocacy" means the direct incitement of others to cause the imminent willful and unlawful killing or injuring of a peace officer, and not the mere abstract teaching of a doctrine.

Added by Stats. 1971, Ch. 1248.

Section 152 - Concealing accidental death

(a) Every person who, having knowledge of an accidental death, actively conceals or attempts to conceal that death, shall be guilty of a misdemeanor punishable by imprisonment in a county jail for not more than one year, or by a fine of not less than one thousand dollars ($1,000) nor more than ten thousand dollars ($10,000), or by both that fine and imprisonment.

(b) For purposes of this section, "to actively conceal an accidental death" means any of the following:

(1) To perform an overt act that conceals the body or directly impedes the ability of authorities or family members to discover the body.

(2) To directly destroy or suppress evidence of the actual physical body of the deceased, including, but not limited to, bodily fluids or tissues.

(3) To destroy or suppress the actual physical instrumentality of death.

EFFECTIVE 1/1/2000. Added9/15/1999 (Bill Number: SB 139) (Chapter 396).

Section 152.3 - Duty to notify peace officer of commission of offense where victim is child under age of 14 years

(a) Any person who reasonably believes that he or she has observed the commission of any of the following offenses where the victim is a child under 14 years of age shall notify a peace officer, as defined in Chapter 4.5 (commencing with Section 830) of Title 3 of Part 2:

(1) Murder.

(2) Rape.

(3) A violation of paragraph (1) of subdivision (b) of Section 288 of the Penal Code.

(b) This section shall not be construed to affect privileged relationships as provided by law.

(c) The duty to notify a peace officer imposed pursuant to subdivision (a) is satisfied if the notification or an attempt to provide notice is made by telephone or any other means.

(d) Failure to notify as required pursuant to subdivision (a) is a misdemeanor and is punishable by a fine of not more than one thousand five hundred dollars ($1,500), by imprisonment in a county jail for not more than six months, or by both that fine and imprisonment.

(e) The requirements of this section shall not apply to the following:

(1) A person who is related to either the victim or the offender, including a spouse, parent, child, brother, sister, grandparent, grandchild, or other person related by consanguinity or affinity.

(2) A person who fails to report based on a reasonable mistake of fact.

(3) A person who fails to report based on a reasonable fear for his or her own safety or for the safety of his or her family.

Amended by Stats 2016 ch 50 (SB 1005),s 66, eff. 1/1/2017.

Added by Stats 2000 ch 477 (AB 1422), s 1, eff. 1/1/2001.

Section 153 - Acceptance of reward or promise to conceal crime

Every person who, having knowledge of the actual commission of a crime, takes money or property of another, or any gratuity or reward, or any engagement, or promise thereof, upon any agreement or understanding to compound or conceal that crime, or to abstain from any prosecution thereof, or to withhold any evidence thereof, except in the cases provided for by law, in which crimes may be compromised by leave of court, is punishable as follows:

1. By imprisonment in a county jail not exceeding one year, or pursuant to subdivision (h) of Section 1170, where the crime was punishable by death or imprisonment in the state prison for life;

2. By imprisonment in a county jail not exceeding six months, or pursuant to subdivision (h) of Section 1170, where the crime was punishable by imprisonment in the state prison for any other term than for life;

3. By imprisonment in a county jail not exceeding six months, or by fine not exceeding one thousand dollars ($1,000), where the crime was a misdemeanor.

Amended by Stats 2011 ch 39 (AB 117),s 68, eff. 6/30/2011.

Amended by Stats 2011 ch 15 (AB 109),s 264, eff. 4/4/2011, but operative no earlier than October 1, 2011, and only upon creation of a community corrections grant program to assist in implementing this act and upon an appropriation to fund the grant program.

Section 154 - Fraudulent removal or sale of property to defraud creditors

(a) Every debtor who fraudulently removes his or her property or effects out of this state, or who fraudulently sells, conveys, assigns or conceals his or her property with intent to defraud, hinder or delay his or her creditors of their rights, claims, or demands, is punishable by imprisonment in the county jail not exceeding one year, or by fine not exceeding one thousand dollars ($1,000), or by both that fine and imprisonment.

(b) Where the property so removed, sold, conveyed, assigned, or concealed consists of a stock in trade, or a part thereof, of a value exceeding two hundred fifty dollars ($250), the offense shall be a felony and punishable as such.

Amended by Stats 2009 ch 28 (SB X3-18),s 6, eff. 1/1/2010.

Section 155 - Fraudulent concealment, sale, or disposition of property to hinder recovery of judgment

(a) Every person against whom an action is pending, or against whom a judgment has been rendered for the recovery of any personal property, who fraudulently conceals, sells, or disposes of that property, with intent to hinder, delay, or defraud the person bringing the action or recovering the judgment, or with such intent removes that property beyond the limits of the county in which it may be at the time of the commencement of the action or the rendering of the judgment, is punishable by imprisonment in a county jail not exceeding one year, or by fine not exceeding one thousand dollars ($1,000), or by both that fine and imprisonment.

(b) Where the property so concealed, sold, disposed of, or removed consists of a stock in trade, or a part thereof, of a value exceeding two hundred fifty dollars ($250), the offenses shall be a felony and punishable as such.

Amended by Stats 2009 ch 28 (SB X3-18),s 7, eff. 1/1/2010.

Section 155.5 - Sale, conveyance, or concealment of property to impair financial ability to pay fine or restitution

(a) Any defendant who is ordered to pay any fine or restitution in connection with the commission of a misdemeanor and who, after the plea or judgment and prior to sentencing, or during the period that a restitution fine or order remains unsatisfied and enforceable, sells, conveys, assigns, or conceals his or her property with the intent to lessen or impair his or her financial ability to pay in full any fine or restitution which he or she may lawfully be ordered to pay, or to avoid forfeiture of assets pursuant to the California Control of Profits of Organized Crime Act (Chapter 9 (commencing with Section 186) of this title), is guilty of a misdemeanor.

(b) Any defendant who is ordered to pay any fine or restitution in connection with the commission of a felony and who, after the plea or judgment and prior to sentencing for the same felony offense, or during the period that a restitution order remains unsatisfied and enforceable, sells, conveys, assigns, or conceals his or her property with the intent to lessen or impair his or her financial ability to pay in full any fine or restitution which he or she may lawfully be ordered to pay or to avoid forfeiture of assets derived from either criminal profiteering pursuant to Chapter 9 (commencing with Section 186) of this title or trafficking in controlled substances pursuant to Chapter 8 (commencing with Section 11470) of Division 10 of the Health and Safety Code, is guilty of a felony.
Amended by Stats. 1996, Ch. 629, Sec. 1. Effective January 1, 1997.

Section 156 - Fraudulent production of infant
Every person who fraudulently produces an infant, falsely pretending it to have been born of any parent whose child would be entitled to inherit any real estate or to receive a share of any personal estate, with intent to intercept the inheritance of any such real estate, or the distribution of any such personal estate from any person lawfully entitled thereto, is punishable by imprisonment pursuant to subdivision (h) of Section 1170 for two, three or four years.
Amended by Stats 2011 ch 39 (AB 117),s 68, eff. 6/30/2011.
Amended by Stats 2011 ch 15 (AB 109),s 265, eff. 4/4/2011, but operative no earlier than October 1, 2011, and only upon creation of a community corrections grant program to assist in implementing this act and upon an appropriation to fund the grant program.

Section 157 - Unlawful substitution of child
Every person to whom an infant has been confided for nursing, education, or any other purpose, who, with intent to deceive any parent or guardian of that child, substitutes or produces to that parent or guardian another child in the place of the one so confided, is punishable by imprisonment pursuant to subdivision (h) of Section 1170 for two, three or four years.
Amended by Stats 2011 ch 39 (AB 117),s 68, eff. 6/30/2011.
Amended by Stats 2011 ch 15 (AB 109),s 266, eff. 4/4/2011, but operative no earlier than October 1, 2011, and only upon creation of a community corrections grant program to assist in implementing this act and upon an appropriation to fund the grant program.

Section 158 - Common barratry
Common barratry is the practice of exciting groundless judicial proceedings, and is punishable by imprisonment in the county jail not exceeding six months and by fine not exceeding one thousand dollars ($1,000).
Amended by Stats. 1983, Ch. 1092, Sec. 246. Effective September 27, 1983. Operative January 1, 1984, by Sec. 427 of Ch. 1092.

Section 159 - Proof of common barratry
No person can be convicted of common barratry except upon proof that he has excited suits or proceedings at law in at least three instances, and with a corrupt or malicious intent to vex and annoy.
Enacted 1872.

Section 160 - Unlawful acts by bail licensee
(a) No bail licensee may employ, engage, solicit, pay, or promise any payment, compensation, consideration or thing of value to any person incarcerated in any prison, jail, or other place of detention for the purpose of that person soliciting bail on behalf of the licensee. A violation of this section is a misdemeanor.
(b) Nothing in this section shall prohibit prosecution under Section 1800 or 1814 of the Insurance Code, or any other applicable provision of law.
Added by Stats 2004 ch 165 (AB 1694), s 1, eff. 1/1/2005.

Section 165 - Bribery of member of common council, board of supervisors, or board of trustees
Every person who gives or offers a bribe to any member of any common council, board of supervisors, or board of trustees of any county, city and county, city, or public corporation, with intent to corruptly influence such member in his action on any matter or subject pending before, or which is afterward to be considered by, the body of which he is a member, and every member of any of the bodies mentioned in this section who receives, or offers or agrees to receive any bribe upon any understanding that his official vote, opinion, judgment, or action shall be influenced thereby, or shall be given in any particular manner or upon any particular side of any question or matter, upon which he may be required to act in his official capacity, is punishable by imprisonment in the state prison for two, three or four years, and upon conviction thereof shall, in addition to said punishment, forfeit his office, and forever be disfranchised and disqualified from holding any public office or trust.
Amended by Stats. 1976, Ch. 1139.

Section 166 - Contempt of court
(a) Except as provided in subdivisions (b), (c), and (d), a person guilty of any of the following contempts of court is guilty of a misdemeanor:
(1) Disorderly, contemptuous, or insolent behavior committed during the sitting of a court of justice, in the immediate view and presence of the court, and directly tending to interrupt its proceedings or to impair the respect due to its authority.
(2) Behavior specified in paragraph (1) that is committed in the presence of a referee, while actually engaged in a trial or hearing, pursuant to the order of a court, or in the presence of a jury while actually sitting for the trial of a cause, or upon an inquest or other proceeding authorized by law.
(3) A breach of the peace, noise, or other disturbance directly tending to interrupt the proceedings of the court.
(4) Willful disobedience of the terms, as written, of a process or court order or out-of-state court order, lawfully issued by a court, including orders pending trial.
(5) Resistance willfully offered by a person to the lawful order or process of a court.
(6) The contumacious and unlawful refusal of a person to be sworn as a witness or, when so sworn, the like refusal to answer a material question.
(7) The publication of a false or grossly inaccurate report of the proceedings of a court.
(8) Presenting to a court having power to pass sentence upon a prisoner under conviction, or to a member of the court, an affidavit, testimony, or representation of any kind, verbal or written, in aggravation or mitigation of the punishment to be imposed upon the prisoner, except as provided in this code.

(9) Willful disobedience of the terms of an injunction that restrains the activities of a criminal street gang or any of its members, lawfully issued by a court, including an order pending trial.

(b)

(1) A person who is guilty of contempt of court under paragraph (4) of subdivision (a) by willfully contacting a victim by telephone or mail, social media, electronic communication, or electronic communication device, or directly, and who has been previously convicted of a violation of Section 646.9 shall be punished by imprisonment in a county jail for not more than one year, by a fine of no more than five thousand dollars ($5,000), or by both that fine and imprisonment.

(2) For the purposes of sentencing under this subdivision, each contact shall constitute a separate violation of this subdivision.

(3) The present incarceration of a person who makes contact with a victim in violation of paragraph (1) is not a defense to a violation of this subdivision.

(4) For purposes of this subdivision, the following definitions shall apply:

(A) "Social media" has the same definition as in Section 632.01.

(B) "Electronic communication" has the same definition as in Section 646.9.

(C) "Electronic communication device" has the same definition as in Section 646.9.

(c)

(1) Notwithstanding paragraph (4) of subdivision (a), a willful and knowing violation of a protective order or stay-away court order described as follows shall constitute contempt of court, a misdemeanor, punishable by imprisonment in a county jail for not more than one year, by a fine of not more than one thousand dollars ($1,000), or by both that imprisonment and fine:

(A) An order issued pursuant to Section 136.2.

(B) An order issued pursuant to paragraph (2) of subdivision (a) of Section 1203.097.

(C) An order issued after a conviction in a criminal proceeding involving elder or dependent adult abuse, as defined in Section 368.

(D) An order issued pursuant to Section 1201.3.

(E) An order described in paragraph (3).

(F) An order issued pursuant to subdivision (j) of Section 273.5.

(2) If a violation of paragraph (1) results in a physical injury, the person shall be imprisoned in a county jail for at least 48 hours, whether a fine or imprisonment is imposed, or the sentence is suspended.

(3) Paragraphs (1) and (2) apply to the following court orders:

(A) An order issued pursuant to Section 6320 or 6389 of the Family Code.

(B) An order excluding one party from the family dwelling or from the dwelling of the other.

(C) An order enjoining a party from specified behavior that the court determined was necessary to effectuate the orders described in paragraph (1).

(4) A second or subsequent conviction for a violation of an order described in paragraph (1) occurring within seven years of a prior conviction for a violation of any of those orders and involving an act of violence or "a credible threat" of violence, as provided in subdivision (c) of Section 139, is punishable by imprisonment in a county jail not to exceed one year, or in the state prison for 16 months or two or three years.

(5) The prosecuting agency of each county shall have the primary responsibility for the enforcement of the orders described in paragraph (1).

(d)

(1) A person who owns, possesses, purchases, or receives a firearm knowing that person is prohibited from doing so by the provisions of a protective order as defined in Section 136.2 of this code, Section 6218 of the Family Code, or Section 527.6 or 527.8 of the Code of Civil Procedure, shall be punished under Section 29825.

(2) A person subject to a protective order described in paragraph (1) shall not be prosecuted under this section for owning, possessing, purchasing, or receiving a firearm to the extent that firearm is granted an exemption pursuant to subdivision (h) of Section 6389 of the Family Code.

(e)

(1) If probation is granted upon conviction of a violation of subdivision (c), the court shall impose probation consistent with Section 1203.097.

(2) If probation is granted upon conviction of a violation of subdivision (c), the conditions of probation may include, in lieu of a fine, one or both of the following requirements:

(A) That the defendant make payments to a domestic violence shelter-based program up to a maximum of one thousand dollars ($1,000).

(B) That the defendant provide restitution to reimburse the victim for reasonable costs of counseling and other reasonable expenses that the court finds are the direct result of the defendant's offense.

(3) For an order to pay a fine, make payments to a domestic violence shelter-based program, or pay restitution as a condition of probation under this subdivision or subdivision (c), the court shall make a determination of the defendant's ability to pay. An order to make payments to a domestic violence shelter-based program, shall not be made if it would impair the ability of the defendant to pay direct restitution to the victim or court-ordered child support.

(4) If the injury to a married person is caused, in whole or in part, by the criminal acts of the person's spouse in violation of subdivision (c), the community property shall not be used to discharge the liability of the offending spouse for restitution to the injured spouse required by Section 1203.04, as operative on or before August 2, 1995, or Section 1202.4, or to a shelter for costs with regard to the injured spouse and dependents required by this subdivision, until all separate property of the offending spouse is exhausted.

(5) A person violating an order described in subdivision (c) may be punished for any substantive offenses described under Section 136.1 or 646.9. A finding of contempt shall not be a bar to prosecution for a violation of Section 136.1 or 646.9. However, a person held in contempt for a violation of subdivision (c) shall be entitled to credit for any punishment imposed as a result of that violation against a sentence imposed upon conviction of an offense described in Section 136.1 or 646.9. A conviction or acquittal for a substantive offense under Section 136.1 or 646.9 shall be a bar to a subsequent punishment for contempt arising out of the same act.

Amended by Stats 2021 ch 704 (AB 764),s 1, eff. 1/1/2022.

Amended by Stats 2016 ch 342 (SB 883),s 1, eff. 1/1/2017.

Amended by Stats 2015 ch 279 (SB 352),s 1, eff. 1/1/2016.

Amended by Stats 2014 ch 99 (AB 2683),s 1, eff. 1/1/2015.

Amended by Stats 2013 ch 291 (AB 307),s 2, eff. 1/1/2014.

Amended by Stats 2013 ch 76 (AB 383),s 145.3, eff. 1/1/2014.

Amended by Stats 2011 ch 296 (AB 1023),s 199, eff. 1/1/2012.

Amended by Stats 2011 ch 285 (AB 1402),s 9, eff. 1/1/2012, op. 1/1/2012.

Amended by Stats 2010 ch 677 (AB 2632),s 1, eff. 1/1/2011.

Amended by Stats 2010 ch 178 (SB 1115),s 44, eff. 1/1/2011, op. 1/1/2012.

Amended by Stats 2009 ch 140 (AB 1164),s 139, eff. 1/1/2010.

Amended by Stats 2008 ch 152 (AB 1424),s 1, eff. 1/1/2009.

Amended by Stats 2002 ch 830 (AB 2695), s 1, eff. 1/1/2003.

Previously Amended October 10, 1999 (Bill Number: SB 218) (Chapter 662).

Section 166.5 - Suspension of proceedings or sentence

(a) After arrest and before plea or trial or after conviction or plea of guilty and before sentence under paragraph (4) of subdivision (a) of Section 166, for willful disobedience of any order for child, spousal, or family support issued pursuant to Division 9 (commencing with Section 3500) of the Family Code or Section 17400 of the Family Code, the court may suspend proceedings or sentence therein if:

    (1) The defendant appears before the court and affirms his or her obligation to pay to the person having custody of the child, or the spouse, that sum per month as shall have been previously fixed by the court in order to provide for the minor child or the spouse.

    (2) The defendant provides a bond or other undertaking with sufficient sureties to the people of the State of California in a sum as the court may fix to secure the defendant's performance of his or her support obligations and that bond or undertaking is valid and binding for two years, or any lesser time that the court shall fix.

(b) Upon the failure of the defendant to comply with the conditions imposed by the court in subdivision (a), the defendant may be ordered to appear before the court and show cause why further proceedings should not be had in the action or why sentence should not be imposed, whereupon the court may proceed with the action, or pass sentence, or for good cause shown may modify the order and take a new bond or undertaking and further suspend proceedings or sentence for a like period.

EFFECTIVE 1/1/2000. Added by Stats. 1999, Ch. 653, Sec. 20.

Section 167 - Unlawful recording of proceedings of trial jury

Every person who, by any means whatsoever, willfully and knowingly, and without knowledge and consent of the jury, records, or attempts to record, all or part of the proceedings of any trial jury while it is deliberating or voting, or listens to or observes, or attempts to listen to or observe, the proceedings of any trial jury of which he is not a member while such jury is deliberating or voting is guilty of a misdemeanor.

This section is not intended to prohibit the taking of notes by a trial juror in connection with and solely for the purpose of assisting him in the performance of his duties as such juror.

Amended by Stats. 1959, Ch. 501.

Section 168 - Disclosure of fact of warrant prior to execution

(a) Every district attorney, clerk, judge, or peace officer who, except by issuing or in executing a search warrant or warrant of arrest for a felony, willfully discloses the fact of the warrant prior to execution for the purpose of preventing the search or seizure of property or the arrest of any person shall be punished by imprisonment in a county jail not exceeding one year or pursuant to subdivision (h) of Section 1170.

(b) This section shall not prohibit the following:

    (1) A disclosure made by a district attorney or the Attorney General for the sole purpose of securing voluntary compliance with the warrant.

    (2) Upon the return of an indictment and the issuance of an arrest warrant, a disclosure of the existence of the indictment and arrest warrant by a district attorney or the Attorney General to assist in the apprehension of a defendant.

    (3) The disclosure of an arrest warrant pursuant to paragraph (1) of subdivision (a) of Section 14207.

Amended by Stats 2014 ch 437 (SB 1066),s 7, eff. 1/1/2015.

Amended by Stats 2011 ch 39 (AB 117),s 68, eff. 6/30/2011.

Amended by Stats 2011 ch 15 (AB 109),s 267, eff. 4/4/2011, but operative no earlier than October 1, 2011, and only upon creation of a community corrections grant program to assist in implementing this act and upon an appropriation to fund the grant program.

Section 169 - Unlawful picket or parade of court

Any person who pickets or parades in or near a building which houses a court of this state with the intent to interfere with, obstruct, or impede the administration of justice or with the intent to influence any judge, juror, witness, or officer of the court in the discharge of his duty is guilty of a misdemeanor.

Added by Stats. 1970, Ch. 1444.

Section 170 - Malicious procurement of warrant

Every person who maliciously and without probable cause procures a search warrant or warrant of arrest to be issued and executed, is guilty of a misdemeanor.

Enacted 1872.

Section 171 - Unlawful communication with person detained in reformatory

Every person, not authorized by law, who, without the permission of the officer in charge of any reformatory in this State, communicates with any person detained therein, or brings therein or takes therefrom any letter, writing, literature, or reading matter to or from any person confined therein, is guilty of a misdemeanor.

Amended by Stats. 1941, Ch. 106.

Section 171b - Bringing weapon in public building or meeting

(a) Any person who brings or possesses within any state or local public building or at any meeting required to be open to the public pursuant to Chapter 9 (commencing with Section 54950) of Part 1 of Division 2 of Title 5 of, or Article 9 (commencing with Section 11120) of Chapter 1 of Part 1 of Division 3 of Title 2 of, the Government Code, any of the following is guilty of a public offense punishable by imprisonment in a county jail for not more than one year, or in the state prison:

(1) Any firearm.

(2) Any deadly weapon described in Section 17235 or in any provision listed in Section 16590.

(3) Any knife with a blade length in excess of four inches, the blade of which is fixed or is capable of being fixed in an unguarded position by the use of one or two hands.

(4) Any unauthorized tear gas weapon.

(5) Any taser or stun gun as defined in Section 244.5.

(6) Any instrument that expels a metallic projectile, such as a BB or pellet, through the force of air pressure, CO2 pressure, or spring action, or any spot marker gun or paint gun.

(b) Subdivision (a) shall not apply to, or affect, any of the following:

(1) A person who possesses weapons in, or transports weapons into, a court of law to be used as evidence.

(2)

(A) A duly appointed peace officer as defined in Chapter 4.5 (commencing with Section 830) of Title 3 of Part 2, a retired peace officer with authorization to carry concealed weapons as described in Article 2 (commencing with Section 25450) of Chapter 2 of Division 5 of Title 4 of Part 6, a full-time paid peace officer of another state or the federal government who is carrying out official duties while in California, or any person summoned by any of these officers to assist in making arrests or preserving the peace while they are actually engaged in assisting the officer.

(B) Notwithstanding subparagraph (A), subdivision (a) shall apply to any person who brings or possesses any weapon specified therein within any courtroom if they are a party to an action pending before the court.

(3) A person holding a valid license to carry the firearm pursuant to Chapter 4 (commencing with Section 26150) of Division 5 of Title 4 of Part 6 who possesses the firearm within a building designated for a court proceeding, including matters before a superior court, district court of appeal, or the California Supreme Court, and is a justice, judge, or commissioner of the court.

(4) A person who has permission to possess that weapon granted in writing by a duly authorized official who is in charge of the security of the state or local government building.

(5) A person who lawfully resides in, lawfully owns, or is in lawful possession of, that building with respect to those portions of the building that are not owned or leased by the state or local government.

(6) A person licensed or registered in accordance with, and acting within the course and scope of, Chapter 11.5 (commencing with Section 7512) or Chapter 11.6 (commencing with Section 7590) of Division 3 of the Business and Professions Code who has been hired by the owner or manager of the building if the person has permission pursuant to paragraph (5).

(7)

(A) A person who, for the purpose of sale or trade, brings any weapon that may otherwise be lawfully transferred, into a gun show conducted pursuant to Article 1 (commencing with Section 27200) and Article 2 (commencing with Section 27300) of Chapter 3 of Division 6 of Title 4 of Part 6.

(B) A person who, for purposes of an authorized public exhibition, brings any weapon that may otherwise be lawfully possessed, into a gun show conducted pursuant to Article 1 (commencing with Section 27200) and Article 2 (commencing with Section 27300) of Chapter 3 of Division 6 of Title 4 of Part 6.

(c) As used in this section, "state or local public building" means a building that meets all of the following criteria:

(1) It is a building or part of a building owned or leased by the state or local government, if state or local public employees are regularly present for the purposes of performing their official duties. A state or local public building includes, but is not limited to, a building that contains a courtroom.

(2) It is not a building or facility, or a part thereof, that is referred to in Section 171c, 171d, 626.9, 626.95, or 626.10 of this code, or in Section 18544 of the Elections Code.

(3) It is a building not regularly used, and not intended to be used, by state or local employees as a place of residence.

Amended by Stats 2023 ch 249 (SB 2),s 2, eff. 1/1/2024.

Amended by Stats 2010 ch 178 (SB 1115),s 45, eff. 1/1/2011, op. 1/1/2012.

Amended August 30, 1999 (Bill Number: AB 295) (Chapter 247).

Section 171c - Bringing loaded firearm into State Capitol, legislative office, office of Governor or other constitutional officer, or hearing room

(a)

(1) Any person who brings a loaded firearm into, or possesses a loaded firearm within, the State Capitol, the state office building at 1021 O Street in the City of Sacramento, any legislative office, any office of the Governor or other constitutional officer, or any hearing room in which any committee of the Senate or Assembly is conducting a hearing, or upon the grounds of the State Capitol, which is bounded by 10th, L, 15th, and N Streets in the City of Sacramento, shall be punished by imprisonment in a county jail for a period of not more than one year, a fine of not more than one thousand dollars ($1,000), or both such imprisonment and fine, or by imprisonment pursuant to subdivision (h) of Section 1170.

(2) Any person who brings or possesses, within the State Capitol, any legislative office, any hearing room in which any committee of the Senate or Assembly is conducting a hearing, the Legislative Office Building at 1020 N Street in the City of Sacramento, the state

office building at 1021 O Street in the City of Sacramento, or upon the grounds of the State Capitol, which is bounded by 10th, L, 15th, and N Streets in the City of Sacramento, any of the following, is guilty of a misdemeanor punishable by imprisonment in a county jail for a period not to exceed one year, or by a fine not exceeding one thousand dollars ($1,000), or by both that fine and imprisonment, if the area is posted with a statement providing reasonable notice that prosecution may result from possession of any of these items:

(A) Any firearm.

(B) Any deadly weapon described in Section 21510 or in any provision listed in Section 16590.

(C) Any knife with a blade length in excess of four inches, the blade of which is fixed or is capable of being fixed in an unguarded position by the use of one or two hands.

(D) Any unauthorized tear gas weapon.

(E) Any stun gun, as defined in Section 244.5.

(F) Any instrument that expels a metallic projectile, such as a BB or pellet, through the force of air pressure, CO2 pressure, or spring action, or any spot marker gun or paint gun.

(G) Any ammunition as defined in Sections 16150 and 16650.

(H) Any explosive as defined in Section 12000 of the Health and Safety Code.

(b) Subdivision (a) shall not apply to, or affect, any of the following:

(1) A duly appointed peace officer as defined in Chapter 4.5 (commencing with Section 830) of Title 3 of Part 2, a retired peace officer with authorization to carry concealed weapons as described in Article 2 (commencing with Section 25450) of Chapter 2 of Division 5 of Title 4 of Part 6, a full-time paid peace officer of another state or the federal government who is carrying out official duties while in California, or any person summoned by any of these officers to assist in making arrests or preserving the peace while that person is actually engaged in assisting the officer.

(2) A person holding a valid license to carry the firearm pursuant to Chapter 4 (commencing with Section 26150) of Division 5 of Title 4 of Part 6, and who has permission granted by the Chief Sergeants at Arms of the State Assembly and the State Senate to possess a concealed weapon upon the premises described in subdivision (a).

(3) A person who has permission granted by the Chief Sergeants at Arms of the State Assembly and the State Senate to possess a weapon upon the premises described in subdivision (a).

(c)

(1) Nothing in this section shall preclude prosecution under Chapter 2 (commencing with Section 29800) or Chapter 3 (commencing with Section 29900) of Division 9 of Title 4 of Part 6 of this code, Section 8100 or 8103 of the Welfare and Institutions Code, or any other law with a penalty greater than is set forth in this section.

(2) The provisions of this section are cumulative, and shall not be construed as restricting the application of any other law. However, an act or omission punishable in different ways by different provisions of law shall not be punished under more than one provision.

Amended by Stats 2021 ch 253 (AB 173),s 1, eff. 9/23/2021.

Amended by Stats 2013 ch 76 (AB 383),s 145.5, eff. 1/1/2014.

Amended by Stats 2011 ch 285 (AB 1402),s 10, eff. 1/1/2012, op. 1/1/2012.

Amended by Stats 2011 ch 39 (AB 117),s 68, eff. 6/30/2011.

Amended by Stats 2011 ch 15 (AB 109),s 268, eff. 4/4/2011, but operative no earlier than October 1, 2011, and only upon creation of a community corrections grant program to assist in implementing this act and upon an appropriation to fund the grant program.

Added by Stats 2010 ch 689 (AB 2668),s 2, eff. 1/1/2011.

Repealed by Stats 2010 ch 689 (AB 2668),s 1, eff. 1/1/2011.

Section 171d - Bringing loaded firearm into Governor's Mansion, residence of constitutional officer, or residence of member of legislature

Any person, except a duly appointed peace officer as defined in Chapter 4.5 (commencing with Section 830) of Title 3 of Part 2, a full-time paid peace officer of another state or the federal government who is carrying out official duties while in California, any person summoned by that officer to assist in making arrests or preserving the peace while they are actually engaged in assisting the officer, a member of the military forces of this state or of the United States engaged in the performance of their duties, the Governor or a member of their immediate family or a person acting with their permission with respect to the Governor's Mansion or any other residence of the Governor, any other constitutional officer or a member of their immediate family or a person acting with their permission with respect to the officer's residence, or a Member of the Legislature or a member of their immediate family or a person acting with their permission with respect to the Member's residence, shall be punished by imprisonment in a county jail for not more than one year, by a fine of not more than one thousand dollars ($1,000), or by both the fine and imprisonment, or by imprisonment pursuant to subdivision (h) of Section 1170, if they do either of the following:

(a) Bring a firearm into, or possess a firearm within, the Governor's Mansion, or any other residence of the Governor, the residence of any other constitutional officer, or the residence of any Member of the Legislature.

(b) Bring a firearm upon, or possess a firearm upon, the grounds of the Governor's Mansion or any other residence of the Governor, the residence of any other constitutional officer, or the residence of any Member of the Legislature.

Amended by Stats 2023 ch 249 (SB 2),s 3, eff. 1/1/2024.

Amended by Stats 2011 ch 296 (AB 1023),s 200, eff. 1/1/2012.

Amended by Stats 2011 ch 39 (AB 117),s 68, eff. 6/30/2011.

Amended by Stats 2011 ch 15 (AB 109),s 270, eff. 4/4/2011, but operative no earlier than October 1, 2011, and only upon creation of a community corrections grant program to assist in implementing this act and upon an appropriation to fund the grant program.

Amended by Stats 2010 ch 178 (SB 1115),s 47, eff. 1/1/2011, op. 1/1/2012.

Section 171e - Loaded firearm

A firearm shall be deemed loaded for the purposes of Sections 171c and 171d whenever both the firearm and unexpended ammunition capable of being discharged from such firearm are in the immediate possession of the same person.

In order to determine whether or not a firearm is loaded for the purpose of enforcing Section 171c or 171d, peace officers are authorized to examine any firearm carried by anyone on his person or in a vehicle while in any place or on the grounds of any place in or on which the possession of a loaded firearm is prohibited by Section 171c or 171d. Refusal to allow a peace officer to inspect a firearm pursuant to the provisions of this section constitutes probable cause for arrest for violation of Section 171c or 171d. Added by Stats. 1967, Ch. 960.

Section 171f - Unlawful presence in chamber of Legislature

No person or group of persons shall willfully and knowingly:

1. Enter or remain within or upon any part of the chamber of either house of the Legislature unless authorized, pursuant to rules adopted or permission granted by either such house, to enter or remain within or upon a part of the chamber of either such house;
2. Engage in any conduct within the State Capitol which disrupts the orderly conduct of official business. A violation of this section is a misdemeanor.

As used in this section, "State Capitol" means the building which is intended primarily for use of the legislative department and situated in the area bounded by 10th, L, 15th, and N Streets in the City of Sacramento.

Nothing in this section shall forbid any act of any Member of the Legislature, or any employee of a Member of the Legislature, any officer or employee of the Legislature or any committee or subcommittee thereof, or any officer or employee of either house of the Legislature or any committee or subcommittee thereof, which is performed in the lawful discharge of his official duties. Amended by Stats. 1975, Ch. 548.

Section 171.5 - Unlawful possession of items in sterile area of airport or passenger vessel terminal

(a) For purposes of this section:

(1) "Airport" means an airport, with a secured area, that regularly serves an air carrier holding a certificate issued by the United States Secretary of Transportation.

(2) "Passenger vessel terminal" means only that portion of a harbor or port facility, as described in Section 105.105(a)(2) of Title 33 of the Code of Federal Regulations, with a secured area that regularly serves scheduled commuter or passenger operations.

(3) "Sterile area" means a portion of an airport defined in the airport security program to which access generally is controlled through the screening of persons and property, as specified in Section 1540.5 of Title 49 of the Code of Federal Regulations, or a portion of any passenger vessel terminal to which, pursuant to the requirements set forth in Sections 105.255 and 105.260(a) of Title 33 of the Code of Federal Regulations, access is generally controlled in a manner consistent with the passenger vessel terminal's security plan and the maritime security level in effect at the time.

(b) It is unlawful for any person to knowingly possess any firearm in any building, real property, or parking area under the control of an airport, except as provided for in subdivision (b), (c), or (e) of Section 26230.

(c) It is unlawful for any person to knowingly possess, within any sterile area of an airport or a passenger vessel terminal, any of the following items:

(1) Any knife with a blade length in excess of four inches, the blade of which is fixed, or is capable of being fixed, in an unguarded position by the use of one or two hands.

(2) Any box cutter or straight razor.

(3) Any metal military practice hand grenade.

(4) Any metal replica hand grenade.

(5) Any plastic replica hand grenade.

(6) Any imitation firearm as defined in Section 417.4.

(7) Any frame, receiver, barrel, or magazine of a firearm.

(8) Any unauthorized tear gas weapon.

(9) Any taser or stun gun as defined in Section 244.5.

(10) Any instrument that expels a metallic projectile, such as a BB or pellet, through the force of air pressure, CO2 pressure, or spring action, or any spot marker gun or paint gun.

(11) Any ammunition as defined in Section 16150.

(d) Subdivisions (b) and (c) shall not apply to, or affect, any of the following:

(1) A duly appointed peace officer as defined in Chapter 4.5 (commencing with Section 830) of Title 3 of Part 2, a retired peace officer with authorization to carry concealed weapons as described in Article 2 (commencing with Section 25450) of Chapter 2 of Division 5 of Title 4 of Part 6, a full-time paid peace officer of another state or the federal government who is carrying out official duties while in California, or any person summoned by any of these officers to assist in making arrests or preserving the peace while they are actually engaged in assisting the officer.

(2) A person who has authorization to possess a weapon specified in subdivision (c), granted in writing by an airport security coordinator who is designated as specified in Section 1542.3 of Title 49 of the Code of Federal Regulations, and who is responsible for the security of the airport.

(3) A person, including an employee of a licensed contract guard service, who has authorization to possess a weapon specified in subdivision (c) granted in writing by a person discharging the duties of Facility Security Officer or Company Security Officer pursuant to an approved United States Coast Guard facility security plan, and who is responsible for the security of the passenger vessel terminal.

(e) Subdivision (b) shall not apply to, or affect, any person possessing an unloaded firearm being transported in accordance with Sections 1540.111(c)(2)(iii) and 1540.111(c)(2)(iv) of Title 49 of the Code of Federal Regulations, which require a hard-sided, locked container, so long as the person is not within any sterile area of an airport or a passenger vessel terminal.

(f) A violation of this section is punishable by imprisonment in a county jail for a period not exceeding six months, or by a fine not exceeding one thousand dollars ($1,000), or by both that fine and imprisonment.

(g) The provisions of this section are cumulative, and shall not be construed as restricting the application of any other law. However, an act or omission that is punishable in different ways by this and any other provision of law shall not be punished under more than one provision.

(h) Nothing in this section is intended to affect existing state or federal law regarding the transportation of firearms on airplanes in checked luggage or the possession of the items listed in subdivision (c) in areas that are not "sterile areas."

Amended by Stats 2023 ch 249 (SB 2),s 4, eff. 1/1/2024.
Amended by Stats 2010 ch 178 (SB 1115),s 48, eff. 1/1/2011, op. 1/1/2012.
Amended by Stats 2005 ch 289 (AB 280),s 1, eff. 1/1/2006
Amended by Stats 2003 ch 62 (SB 600), s 224, eff. 1/1/2004.
Amended by Stats 2003 ch 468 (SB 851), s 7, eff. 1/1/2004.
Added by Stats 2002 ch 608 (SB 510), s 1, eff. 9/16/2002.

Section 171.7 - Unlawful possession of items in sterile area of public transit facility

(a) For purposes of this section:

(1) "Public transit facility" means any land, building, or equipment, or any interest therein, including any station on a public transportation route, to which access is controlled in a manner consistent with the public transit authority's security plan, whether or not the operation thereof produces revenue, that has as its primary purpose the operation of a public transit system or the providing of services to the passengers of a public transit system. A public transit system includes the vehicles used in the system, including, but not limited to, motor vehicles, streetcars, trackless trolleys, buses, light rail systems, rapid transit systems, subways, trains, or jitneys, that transport members of the public for hire.

(2) "Firearm" has the same meaning as specified in subdivisions (a) and (b) of Section 16520.

(b) It is unlawful for any person to knowingly possess any of the following in a public transit facility:

(1) Any firearm.
(2) Any imitation firearm as defined in Section 417.4.
(3) Any instrument that expels a metallic projectile, such as a BB or pellet, through the force of air pressure, CO_2 pressure, or spring action, or any spot marker gun or paint gun.
(4) Any metal military practice hand grenade.
(5) Any metal replica hand grenade.
(6) Any plastic replica hand grenade.
(7) Any unauthorized tear gas weapon.
(8) Any undetectable knife, as described in Section 17290.
(9) Any undetectable firearm, as described in Section 17280.

(c)

(1) Subdivision (b) shall not apply to, or affect, any of the following:

(A) A duly appointed peace officer as defined in Chapter 4.5 (commencing with Section 830) of Title 3 of Part 2.
(B) A retired peace officer with authorization to carry concealed weapons as described in Article 2 (commencing with Section 25450) of Chapter 2 of Division 5 of Title 4 of Part 6.
(C) A full-time paid peace officer of another state or the federal government who is carrying out official duties while in California.
(D) A qualified law enforcement officer of another state or the federal government, as permitted under the Law Enforcement Officers Safety Act pursuant to Section 926B or 926C of Title 18 of the United States Code.
(E) Any person summoned by any of the officers listed in subparagraphs (A) to (C), inclusive, to assist in making arrests or preserving the peace while they are actually engaged in assisting the officer.
(F) A person who is responsible for the security of the public transit system and who has been authorized by the public transit authority's security coordinator, in writing, to possess a weapon specified in subdivision (b).
(G) A person possessing an unloaded firearm while traveling on a public transit system that offers checked baggage services, so long as the firearm is stored in accordance with the public transit system's checked baggage policies.

(2) Paragraph (7) of subdivision (b) shall not apply to or affect the possession of a tear gas weapon when possession is permitted pursuant to Division 11 (commencing with Section 22810) of Title 3 of Part 6.

(d) A violation of this section is punishable by imprisonment in a county jail for a period not exceeding six months, or by a fine not exceeding one thousand dollars ($1,000), or by both that fine and imprisonment.

(e) The provisions of this section are cumulative, and shall not be construed as restricting the application of any other law. However, an act or omission that is punishable in different ways by this and any other provision of law shall not be punished under more than one provision.

(f) This section does not prevent prosecution under any other provision of law that may provide a greater punishment.

(g) This section shall be interpreted so as to be consistent with Section 926A of Title 18 of the United States Code.

Amended by Stats 2023 ch 249 (SB 2),s 5, eff. 1/1/2024.
Amended by Stats 2011 ch 285 (AB 1402),s 11, eff. 1/1/2012, op. 1/1/2012.
Added by Stats 2010 ch 675 (AB 2324),s 1, eff. 1/1/2011.

Section 172 - Unlawful sale of intoxicating liquors near certain lands

(a) Every person who, within one-half mile of the land belonging to this state upon which any state prison, or within 1,900 feet of the land belonging to this state upon which any Youth Authority institution is situated, or within one mile of the grounds belonging to the University of California, at Berkeley, or within one mile of the grounds belonging to the University of California at Santa Barbara, as such grounds existed as of January 1, 1961, or within one mile of the grounds belonging to Fresno State College, as such grounds existed as of January 1, 1959, or within three miles of the University Farm at Davis, or within $1^1/_2$ miles of any building actually occupied as a home, retreat, or asylum for ex-soldiers, sailors, and marines of the Army and Navy of the United States, established or to be established by this state, or by the United States within this state, or within the State Capitol, or within the limits of the grounds adjacent and belonging thereto, sells or exposes for sale, any alcoholic beverage, is guilty of a misdemeanor, and upon conviction thereof shall be punished by a fine of not less than one hundred dollars ($100), or by imprisonment for not less than 50 days or by both such fine and imprisonment, in the discretion of the court.

(b) The provision of subdivision (a) of this section prohibiting the sale or exposure for sale of any alcoholic beverage within 1,900 feet of the land belonging to this state upon which any Youth Authority institution is situated shall not apply with respect to the Fred C. Nelles School for Boys.

(c) Except within the State Capitol or the limits of the grounds adjacent and belonging thereto, as mentioned in subdivision (a) of this section, the provisions of this section shall not apply to the sale or exposing or offering for sale of ale, porter, wine, similar fermented malt or vinous liquor or fruit juice containing one-half of 1 percent or more of alcohol by volume and not more than 3.2 percent of alcohol by weight nor the sale or exposing or offering for sale of beer.

(d) Distances provided in this section shall be measured not by airline but by following the shortest highway or highways as defined in Section 360 of the Vehicle Code connecting the points in question. In measuring distances from the Folsom State Prison and the eastern facilities of the California Institution for Men at Chino and Youth Training School, the measurement shall start at the entrance gate.

(e) The provision of subdivision (a) prohibiting the sale or exposure for sale of any alcoholic beverage within $1^1/_2$ miles of any building actually occupied as a home, retreat, or asylum for ex-soldiers, sailors, and marines of the Army and Navy of the United States shall not apply to the Veterans' Home at Yountville, Napa County, California.

(f) The prohibition in subdivision (a) on the sale or exposure for sale of any alcoholic beverage within the State Capitol or within the limits of the grounds adjacent and belonging thereto does not apply with respect to an event that is held on those grounds if all of the following conditions are met:

   (1) The event is organized and operated by a nonprofit organization that is located in the City of Sacramento for purposes of increasing awareness of the Sacramento region and promoting education about the food and wine of the Sacramento region.

   (2) Tickets for the event are sold on a presale basis only and are not available for sale at the event.

   (3) Each attendee has purchased a ticket for the event, regardless of whether the attendee consumes any food or alcohol at the event.

   (4) Alcohol is not sold at the event, and any orders or any other activities that would constitute exposure for sale of alcoholic beverages do not occur at the event, except as authorized by this subdivision.

Amended by Stats 2017 ch 224 (AB 400),s 1, eff. 9/11/2017.

Section 172a - Unlawful sale of intoxicating liquor near university grounds or campus

Every person who, within one and one-half miles of the university grounds or campus, upon which are located the principal administrative offices of any university having an enrollment of more than 1,000 students, more than 500 of whom reside or lodge upon such university grounds or campus, sells or exposes for sale, any intoxicating liquor, is guilty of a misdemeanor; provided, however, that the provisions of this section shall not apply to nor prohibit the sale of any of said liquors by any regularly licensed pharmacist who shall maintain a fixed place of business in said territory, upon the written prescription of a physician regularly licensed to practice medicine under the laws of the State of California when such prescription is dated by the physician issuing it, contains the name of the person for whom the prescription is written, and is filled for such person only and within 48 hours of its date; provided further, that the provisions of this section shall not apply to nor prohibit the sale of any of said liquors for chemical or mechanical purposes; provided further, that the provisions of this section shall not apply to nor prohibit the sale or exposing or offering for sale of ale, porter, wine, similar fermented malt, or vinous liquor or fruit juice containing one-half of 1 percent or more of alcohol by volume and not more than 3.2 percent of alcohol by weight nor the sale or exposing or offering for sale of beer.

In measuring distances from the university grounds or campus of any such university, such distances shall not be measured by airline but by following the shortest road or roads connecting the points in question. With respect to Leland Stanford Junior University measurements from the university grounds or campus shall be by airline measurement.

Any license issued and in effect in the City and County of San Francisco on the effective date of the amendment of this section enacted at the 1961 Regular Session of the Legislature may be transferred to any location in the City and County of San Francisco.

Amended by Stats. 1965, Ch. 1588.

Section 172b - Unlawful sale of intoxicating liquor near grounds of University of California at Los Angeles

1.Every person who, within one and one-half miles of the boundaries of the grounds belonging to the University of California at Los Angeles on which the principal administrative offices of the university are located, as such boundaries were established as of July 1, 1959, sells or exposes for sale any intoxicating liquor, is guilty of a misdemeanor, and upon conviction thereof shall be punished by a fine of not less than one hundred dollars ($100), or by imprisonment for not less than 50 days, or by both such fine and imprisonment, in the discretion of the court.

2.The provisions of this section shall not apply to the sale or exposing or offering for sale of ale, porter, wine, similar fermented malt or vinous liquor or fruit juice containing one-half of 1 percent or more of alcohol by volume and not more than 3.2 percent of alcohol by weight nor the sale or exposing or offering for sale of beer.

3.Distances provided in this section shall be measured not by airline but by following the shortest road or roads connecting the points in question.

Amended by Stats. 1965, Ch. 1588.

Section 172c - Sale at auction of alcoholic beverages by nonprofit organization

Section 172a shall not apply to the sale at auction of alcoholic beverages by a nonprofit organization at the California Science Center premises located at Exposition Park, Los Angeles, California.

Amended by Stats. 1996, Ch. 841, Sec. 15. Effective January 1, 1997.

Section 172d - Unlawful sale of intoxicating liquor near grounds of Riverside

1.Every person who, within one mile of that portion of the grounds at Riverside (hereinafter described) belonging to the University of California, that will be used by the College of Letters and Sciences, sells, or exposes for sale, any intoxicating liquor, is guilty of a misdemeanor, and upon conviction thereof shall be punished by a fine of not less than one hundred dollars ($100), or by imprisonment for not less than 50 days or by both such fine and imprisonment in the discretion of the court.

2. The provisions of this section shall not apply to the sale or exposing or offering for sale of ale, porter, wine, similar fermented malt or vinous liquor or fruit juice containing one-half of 1 percent or more of alcohol by volume and not more than 3.2 percent of alcohol by weight nor the sale or exposing or offering for sale of beer.

3. Distances provided in this section shall be measured not by air line but by following the shortest vehicular road or roads connecting the points in question.

4. The portion of the grounds of the University of California referred to in paragraph 1 are situated in the County of Riverside and more particularly described as follows: beginning at the intersection of Canyon Crest Drive and U.S. Highway 60, thence southeasterly along said highway to a point opposite the intersection of said U.S. Highway 60 and Pennsylvania Avenue, thence northeasterly following centerline of present drive into University campus, thence continuing north along said centerline of drive on west side of Citrus Experiment Station buildings to a point intersecting the present east-west road running east from intersection of Canyon Crest Drive and U.S. Highway 60, thence east 500 feet more or less, thence north 1,300 feet more or less, thence east to intersection of east boundary of the Regents of the University of California property (Valencia Hill Drive), thence north along said east boundary to the north boundary of the Regents of the University of California property (Linden Street), thence west along said north boundary to the west boundary of the Regents of the University of California property (Canyon Crest Drive) thence south along said west boundary to the point of beginning.
Amended by Stats. 1972, Ch. 1241.

Section 172e - Inapplicability of statutes governing unlawful sale of intoxicating liquors to on-sale licensee

The provisions of Sections 172, 172a, 172b, 172d, and 172g of this code shall not apply to the sale or the exposing or offering for sale of alcoholic beverages by an on-sale licensee under the Alcoholic Beverage Control Act within premises licensed as a bona fide public eating place as provided in the Constitution and as defined in the Alcoholic Beverage Control Act (commencing at Section 23000, Business and Professions Code), or within premises licensed as a club as defined in Articles 4 and 5 of Chapter 3 of the Alcoholic Beverage Control Act, provided that such club shall have been in existence for not less than 5 years, have a membership of 300 or more, and serves meals daily to its members, or by the holder of a caterer's permit under the provisions of Section 23399 of the Business and Professions Code in connection with the serving of bona fide meals as defined in Section 23038 of the Business and Professions Code, and the provisions of such sections shall not be construed so as to preclude the Department of Alcoholic Beverage Control from issuing licenses for bona fide public eating places within the areas prescribed by the sections. The provisions of this section shall not permit the issuance of licenses to fraternities, sororities, or other student organizations.
Amended by Stats. 1973, Ch. 599.

Section 172f - Inapplicability of statutes governing unlawful sale of intoxicating liquor to licensee

The provisions of Sections 172, 172a, 172b, 172d, and 172g of this code shall not apply to the sale or the exposing or offering for sale of any intoxicating liquor in any premises within the areas prescribed by said sections for which a license was issued under the Alcoholic Beverage Control Act (Division 9 (commencing with Section 23000), Business and Professions Code) and is in effect on the effective date of this section or on the effective date of any amendment to Section 172g specifying an additional institution, or in any licensed premises which may become included in such a prescribed area because of the extension of the boundaries of any of the institutions mentioned in said sections or because of the increased enrollment or number of resident students at any of such institutions. Any such licenses may be transferred from person to person, and may be transferred from premises to premises if the premises to which the license is transferred are not located nearer to the boundaries of the institution, as they exist on the date of the transfer, than the premises from which the license is transferred, except that such license may be transferred once from premises to premises located nearer by not more than 300 feet to the boundaries of the institution as they exist on the date of transfer than the premises from which the license is transferred. If a license is transferred pursuant to this section from premises to premises located nearer by not more than 300 feet to the boundaries of the institution as they exist on the date of the transfer than the premises from which the license is transferred, such license shall not be thereafter transferred to any other premises located nearer to the boundaries of the institution as they exist on the date of the transfer than the premises from which the license is transferred.
Amended by Stats. 1976, Ch. 778.

Section 172g - Unlawful sale of intoxicating liquors near certain colleges

(a) Every person who, within one-half mile by air line from the intersection of Sierra Vista, Pierce, and Campus Drive streets at the entrance to La Sierra College in the City of Riverside, or within one mile of the grounds or campus of Loma Linda University in the County of San Bernardino, or within one mile of the grounds of the University of Santa Clara in the City of Santa Clara, sells, or exposes for sale, any intoxicating liquor, is guilty of a misdemeanor, and upon conviction thereof shall be punished by a fine of not less than one hundred dollars ($100), or by imprisonment in the county jail of not less than 50 days nor more than one year, or by both that fine and imprisonment in the discretion of the court.

(b) The provisions of this section shall not apply to the sale or exposing or offering for sale of ale, porter, wine, similar fermented malt or vinous liquor or fruit juice containing one-half of 1 percent or more of alcohol by volume and not more than 3.2 percent of alcohol by weight nor the sale or exposing or offering for sale of beer.

(c) Distances provided in this section shall be measured not by air line but by following the shortest road or roads connecting the points in question except those applying to La Sierra College.
Amended by Stats 2013 ch 43 (SB 120),s 1, eff. 6/28/2013.

Section 172h - Inapplicability of statutes governing unlawful sale of intoxicating liquor due to construction of dormitories

The provisions of Sections 172, 172a, 172b, 172d and 172g of this code shall not be applied to prohibit the sale or the exposing or offering for sale of any intoxicating liquor in, or the issuance of an alcoholic beverage license for, any premises because a university has constructed and occupied since January 1, 1960, or in the future constructs, dormitories for its students which has resulted or results in the premises being prohibited by the foregoing sections from selling, exposing or offering such liquor for sale because the premises are or become thereby within the area prescribed by these sections.
Added by Stats. 1965, Ch. 1309.

Section 172j - Inapplicability of statutes governing unlawful sale of intoxicating liquor to holder of retail package off-sale general license or retail package off-sale beer and wine license

The provisions of Sections 172, 172a, 172b, 172d, and 172g shall not apply to the sale or exposing for sale of any intoxicating liquor on the premises of, and by the holder or agent of, a holder of a retail package off-sale general license or retail package off-sale beer and wine license issued under the Alcoholic Beverage Control Act (Division 9 (commencing with Section 23000), Business and Professions Code).

Added by Stats. 1973, Ch. 210.

Section 172l - Inapplicability of statute governing unlawful sale of intoxicating liquor near Claremont Colleges

The provisions of Section 172a shall not apply to the sale or offering for sale of any intoxicating liquor on the premises of, and by the holder or agent of a holder of, a retail off-sale license, as defined in Section 23394 of the Business and Professions Code, outside one mile of the closest building of the Claremont Colleges to these premises; nor shall the provisions of Section 172a apply to the sale or offering for sale of any beer, or wine, or both, on the premises of, and by the holder or agent of a holder of, a retail package off-sale beer and wine license, as defined in Section 23393 of the Business and Professions Code, outside 2,000 feet of the closest building of the Claremont Colleges to these premises.

Distance provided in this section shall be measured not by air line but by following the shortest road or roads connecting the points in question.

Amended by Stats. 1973, Ch. 224.

Section 172m - Inapplicability of statute governing unlawful sale of intoxicating liquor near Leland Stanford Junior University

The provisions of Section 172a shall not apply to the sale or the exposing or offering for sale of alcoholic beverages at premises licensed under any type of on-sale license issued pursuant to Division 9 (commencing with Section 23000) of the Business and Professions Code, which premises are located off of the grounds or campus of Leland Stanford Junior University near the City of Palo Alto.

Added by Stats. 1970, Ch. 1442.

Section 172n - Inapplicability of statutes governing unlawful sale of intoxicating liquor near University of California at Los Angeles

The provisions of Sections 172a and 172b shall not apply to the sale or exposing or offering for sale of alcoholic beverages by any off-sale licensee under the Alcoholic Beverage Control Act situated more than 2,000 feet of the boundaries of the grounds belonging to the University of California at Los Angeles on which the principal administrative offices of the university are located, as such boundaries were established as of July 1, 1959, provided the licensee has conducted a retail grocery business and has held an off-sale beer and wine license at the same location for at least 15 years.

Distances provided in this section shall be measured not by airline but by following the shortest road or roads connecting the points in question.

Added by Stats. 1973, Ch. 210.

Section 172o - Inapplicability of statutes governing unlawful sale of intoxicating liquor to sale of wine for consumption off the premises

The provisions of Sections 172, 172a, 172b, 172d, and 172g shall not apply to the sale of wine for consumption off the premises where sold when the wine is sold at a bona fide public eating place by the holder of an on-sale general alcoholic beverage license or an on-sale beer and wine license issued under the Alcoholic Beverage Control Act (Division 9 (commencing with Section 23000) of the Business and Professions Code).

Added by Stats. 1985, Ch. 267, Sec. 1.

Section 172p - Inapplicability of statute governing unlawful sale of intoxicating liquor to licensees near Whittier College

The provisions of Section 172a shall not apply to the sale or exposing or offering for sale of beer or wine by any on-sale licensee under the Alcoholic Beverage Control Act whose licensed premises are situated more than 1,200 feet from the boundaries of Whittier College in the City of Whittier.

Added by Stats. 1997, Ch. 774, Sec. 6. Effective January 1, 1998.

Section 172.1 - Possession or use of wine for use in experimentation or instruction

No provision of law shall prevent the possession or use of wine on any state university, state college or community college premises solely for use in experimentation in or instruction of viticulture, enology, domestic science or home economics.

Amended by Stats. 1970, Ch. 102.

Section 172.3 - Inapplicability of statutes governing unlawful sale of intoxicating liquor near University of Redlands

The provisions of Section 172a shall not apply to the sale or exposing or offering for sale of any alcoholic beverages on the premises of, and by the holder or agent of a holder of, any off-sale license situated within 1 1/2 miles from the grounds of the University of Redlands.

Added by Stats. 1977, Ch. 760.

Section 172.5 - Inapplicability of statutes governing unlawful sale of intoxicating liquor to club near University of California at Berkeley

The provisions of Sections 172 and 172a of this code shall not apply to the sale or exposing or offering for sale of alcoholic beverages by a licensee under the Alcoholic Beverage Control Act within the premises occupied by any bona fide club which is situated within one mile of the grounds belonging to the University of California at Berkeley, if the club meets all of the following requirements:

(a) The membership in the club shall be limited to male American citizens over the age of 21 years.

(b) The club shall have been organized and have existed in the City of Berkeley for not less than 35 years continuously.

(c) The club shall have a bona fide membership of not less than 500 members.

(d) The premises occupied by the club are owned by the club, or by a corporation, at least 75 percent of whose capital stock is owned by the club, and have a value of not less than one hundred thousand dollars ($100,000).

Amended by Stats. 1967, Ch. 138.

Section 172.6 - Inapplicability of statute governing unlawful sale of intoxicating liquor to club near San Quentin Prison

The provisions of Section 172 of this code shall not apply to the sale, gift, or exposing or offering for sale of alcoholic beverages by a licensee under the Alcoholic Beverage Control Act within the premises occupied by any bona fide club which is situated within 2,000 feet of San Quentin Prison in Marin County, provided the club meets all the following requirements:

(a) The club shall have been organized and have existed in the County of Marin for not less than 25 years continuously.

(b) The club shall have a bona fide membership of not less than 1,000 persons.

(c) The premises occupied by the club are owned by the club or by club members.

Added by Stats. 1965, Ch. 1452.

Section 172.7 - Inapplicability of statute governing unlawful sale of intoxicating liquor to club near Leland Stanford Junior University

The provisions of Section 172a shall not apply to the sale, gift, or exposing or offering for sale of alcoholic beverages by a licensee under the Alcoholic Beverage Control Act within the premises occupied by any bona fide club which is situated within one mile of the campus of Whittier College in the City of Whittier, or one mile or more from the campus of Leland Stanford Junior University near the City of Palo Alto, provided the club meets all the following requirements:

(a) The club shall have been organized and have existed for not less than 10 years continuously.

(b) The club shall have a bona fide membership of not less than 350 persons.

(c) The club shall own the building which it occupies.

Amended by Stats. 1970, Ch. 1285.

Section 172.8 - Inapplicability of statute governing unlawful sale of intoxicating liquor to nonprofit organization at municipally owned conference near California Institute of Technology

The provisions of Section 172a shall not apply to the sale of alcoholic beverages for consumption on the premises, by a nonprofit organization at a municipally owned conference center located more than one but less than 1 1/2 miles from the California Institute of Technology in Pasadena.

Added by Stats. 1975, Ch. 88.

Section 172.9 - "University" defined

The word "university," when used in this chapter with reference to the sale, exposing or offering for sale, of alcoholic beverages, means an institution which has the authority to grant an academic graduate degree.

Amended by Stats. 1965, Ch. 1588.

Section 172.95 - Inapplicability of statutes to wholesalers or retailers

Sections 172 to 172.9, inclusive, do not apply to sales to wholesalers or retailers by licensed winegrowers, brandy manufacturers, beer manufacturers, distilled spirits manufacturers' agents, distilled spirits manufacturers, or wholesalers.

Added by Stats. 1965, Ch. 710.

Section 173 - Unlawful importation for foreign convict

Every Captain, Master of a vessel, or other person, who willfully imports, brings, or sends, or causes or procures to be brought or sent, into this State, any person who is a foreign convict of any crime which, if committed within this State, would be punishable therein (treason and misprision of treason excepted), or who is delivered or sent to him from any prison or place of confinement in any place without this State, is guilty of a misdemeanor.

Enacted 1872.

Section 175 - Separate prosecution and penalty

Every individual person of the classes referred to in Section 173, brought to or landed within this state contrary to the provisions of such section, renders the person bringing or landing liable to a separate prosecution and penalty.

Amended by Stats. 1972, Ch. 637.

Section 181 - Holding person in involuntary servitude

Every person who holds, or attempts to hold, any person in involuntary servitude, or assumes, or attempts to assume, rights of ownership over any person, or who sells, or attempts to sell, any person to another, or receives money or anything of value, in consideration of placing any person in the custody, or under the power or control of another, or who buys, or attempts to buy, any person, or pays money, or delivers anything of value, to another, in consideration of having any person placed in his or her custody, or under his or her power or control, or who knowingly aids or assists in any manner any one thus offending, is punishable by imprisonment pursuant to subdivision (h) of Section 1170 for two, three or four years.

Amended by Stats 2011 ch 39 (AB 117),s 68, eff. 6/30/2011.

Amended by Stats 2011 ch 15 (AB 109),s 271, eff. 4/4/2011, but operative no earlier than October 1, 2011, and only upon creation of a community corrections grant program to assist in implementing this act and upon an appropriation to fund the grant program.

Chapter 8 - CONSPIRACY

Section 182 - Conspiracy

(a) If two or more persons conspire:

    (1) To commit any crime.

    (2) Falsely and maliciously to indict another for any crime, or to procure another to be charged or arrested for any crime.

    (3) Falsely to move or maintain any suit, action, or proceeding.

    (4) To cheat and defraud any person of any property, by any means which are in themselves criminal, or to obtain money or property by false pretenses or by false promises with fraudulent intent not to perform those promises.

    (5) To commit any act injurious to the public health, to public morals, or to pervert or obstruct justice, or the due administration of the laws.

    (6) To commit any crime against the person of the President or Vice President of the United States, the Governor of any state or territory, any United States justice or judge, or the secretary of any of the executive departments of the United States. They are punishable as follows:

When they conspire to commit any crime against the person of any official specified in paragraph (6), they are guilty of a felony and are punishable by imprisonment pursuant to subdivision (h) of Section 1170 for five, seven, or nine years.

When they conspire to commit any other felony, they shall be punishable in the same manner and to the same extent as is provided for the punishment of that felony. If the felony is one for which different punishments are prescribed for different degrees, the jury or court which finds the defendant guilty thereof shall determine the degree of the felony the defendant conspired to commit. If the degree is not so determined, the punishment for conspiracy to commit the felony shall be that prescribed for the lesser degree, except in the case of conspiracy to commit murder, in which case the punishment shall be that prescribed for murder in the first degree.

If the felony is conspiracy to commit two or more felonies which have different punishments and the commission of those felonies constitute but one offense of conspiracy, the penalty shall be that prescribed for the felony which has the greater maximum term.

When they conspire to do an act described in paragraph (4), they shall be punishable by imprisonment in a county jail for not more than one year, or by imprisonment pursuant to subdivision (h) of Section 1170, or by a fine not exceeding ten thousand dollars ($10,000), or by both that imprisonment and fine.

When they conspire to do any of the other acts described in this section, they shall be punishable by imprisonment in a county jail for not more than one year, or pursuant to subdivision (h) of Section 1170, or by a fine not exceeding ten thousand dollars ($10,000), or by both that imprisonment and fine. When they receive a felony conviction for conspiring to commit identity theft, as defined in Section 530.5, the court may impose a fine of up to twenty-five thousand dollars ($25,000).

All cases of conspiracy may be prosecuted and tried in the superior court of any county in which any overt act tending to effect the conspiracy shall be done.

(b) Upon a trial for conspiracy, in a case where an overt act is necessary to constitute the offense, the defendant cannot be convicted unless one or more overt acts are expressly alleged in the indictment or information, nor unless one of the acts alleged is proved; but other overt acts not alleged may be given in evidence.

Amended by Stats 2011 ch 39 (AB 117),s 68, eff. 6/30/2011.

Amended by Stats 2011 ch 15 (AB 109),s 272, eff. 4/4/2011, but operative no earlier than October 1, 2011, and only upon creation of a community corrections grant program to assist in implementing this act and upon an appropriation to fund the grant program.

Amended by Stats 2002 ch 787 (SB 1798), s 8, eff. 1/1/2003.

Amended by Stats 2002 ch 907 (AB 1155), s 1, eff. 1/1/2003.

Amended by Stats 2001 ch 854 (SB 205), s 20, eff. 1/1/2002.

Section 182.5 - Active participation in criminal street gang

Notwithstanding subdivisions (a) or (b) of Section 182, any person who actively participates in any criminal street gang, as defined in subdivision (f) of Section 186.22, with knowledge that its members engage in or have engaged in a pattern of criminal gang activity, as defined in subdivision (e) of Section 186.22, and who willfully promotes, furthers, assists, or benefits from any felonious criminal conduct by members of that gang is guilty of conspiracy to commit that felony and may be punished as specified in subdivision (a) of Section 182.

Added March 7, 2000, by initiative Proposition 21, Sec. 3. Note: Prop. 21 is titled the Gang Violence and Juvenile Crime Prevention Act of 1998.

Section 183 - Conspiracies punishable criminally

No conspiracies, other than those enumerated in the preceding section, are punishable criminally.

Enacted 1872.

Section 184 - Agreement amounting to conspiracy

No agreement amounts to a conspiracy, unless some act, beside such agreement, be done within this state to effect the object thereof, by one or more of the parties to such agreement and the trial of cases of conspiracy may be had in any county in which any such act be done.

Amended by Stats. 1919, Ch. 125.

Section 185 - Unlawful wearing of mask, false whiskers, or personal disguise

Section One Hundred and Eighty-five. It shall be unlawful for any person to wear any mask, false whiskers, or any personal disguise (whether complete or partial) for the purpose of:

One-Evading or escaping discovery, recognition, or identification in the commission of any public offense.

Two-Concealment, flight, or escape, when charged with, arrested for, or convicted of, any public offense. Any person violating any of the provisions of this section shall be deemed guilty of a misdemeanor.

Amended by Code Amendments 1873-74, Ch. 614.

Chapter 9 - CRIMINAL PROFITEERING

Section 186 - Short title

This act may be cited as the "California Control of Profits of Organized Crime Act."

Added by Stats. 1982, Ch. 1281, Sec. 1.

Section 186.1 - Legislative findings and declarations

The Legislature hereby finds and declares that an effective means of punishing and deterring criminal activities of organized crime is through the forfeiture of profits acquired and accumulated as a result of such criminal activities. It is the intent of the Legislature that the "California Control of Profits of Organized Crime Act" be used by prosecutors to punish and deter only such activities.

Added by Stats. 1982, Ch. 1281, Sec. 1.

Section 186.2 - Definitions

For purposes of this chapter, the following definitions apply:

(a) "Criminal profiteering activity" means an act committed or attempted or a threat made for financial gain or advantage, which act or threat may be charged as a crime under any of the following sections:

    (1) Arson, as defined in Section 451.

    (2) Bribery, as defined in Sections 67, 67.5, and 68.

(3) Child pornography or exploitation, as defined in subdivision (b) of Section 311.2, or Section 311.3 or 311.4, which may be prosecuted as a felony.

(4) Felonious assault, as defined in Section 245.

(5) Embezzlement, as defined in Sections 424 and 503.

(6) Extortion, as defined in Section 518.

(7) Forgery, as defined in Section 470.

(8) Gambling, as defined in Sections 320, 321, 322, 323, 326, 330a, 330b, 330c, 330.1, 330.4, 337a to 337f, inclusive, and Section 337i, except the activities of a person who participates solely as an individual bettor.

(9) Kidnapping, as defined in Section 207.

(10) Mayhem, as defined in Section 203.

(11) Murder, as defined in Section 187.

(12) Pimping and pandering, as defined in Section 266.

(13) Receiving stolen property, as defined in Section 496.

(14) Robbery, as defined in Section 211.

(15) Solicitation of crimes, as defined in Section 653f.

(16) Grand theft, as defined in Section 487 or subdivision (a) of Section 487a.

(17) Trafficking in controlled substances, as defined in Sections 11351, 11352, and 11353 of the Health and Safety Code.

(18) Violation of the laws governing corporate securities, as defined in Section 25541 of the Corporations Code.

(19) Offenses contained in Chapter 7.5 (commencing with Section 311) of Title 9, relating to obscene matter, or in Chapter 7.6 (commencing with Section 313) of Title 9, relating to harmful matter that may be prosecuted as a felony.

(20) Presentation of a false or fraudulent claim, as defined in Section 550.

(21) False or fraudulent activities, schemes, or artifices, as described in Section 14107 of the Welfare and Institutions Code.

(22) Money laundering, as defined in Section 186.10.

(23) Offenses relating to the counterfeit of a registered mark, as specified in Section 350, or offenses relating to piracy, as specified in Section 653w.

(24) Offenses relating to the unauthorized access to computers, computer systems, and computer data, as specified in Section 502.

(25) Conspiracy to commit any of the crimes listed above, as defined in Section 182.

(26) Subdivision (a) of Section 186.22, or a felony subject to enhancement as specified in subdivision (b) of Section 186.22.

(27) Offenses related to fraud or theft against the state's beverage container recycling program, including, but not limited to, those offenses specified in this subdivision and those criminal offenses specified in the California Beverage Container Recycling and Litter Reduction Act (Division 12.1 (commencing with Section 14500) of the Public Resources Code).

(28) Human trafficking, as defined in Section 236.1.

(29) A crime in which the perpetrator induces, encourages, or persuades a person under 18 years of age to engage in a commercial sex act. For purposes of this paragraph, a commercial sex act means any sexual conduct on account of which anything of value is given or received by any person.

(30) A crime in which the perpetrator, through force, fear, coercion, deceit, violence, duress, menace, or threat of unlawful injury to the victim or to another person, causes a person under 18 years of age to engage in a commercial sex act. For purposes of this paragraph, a commercial sex act means any sexual conduct on account of which anything of value is given or received by any person.

(31) Theft of personal identifying information, as defined in Section 530.5.

(32) Offenses involving the theft of a motor vehicle, as specified in Section 10851 of the Vehicle Code.

(33) Abduction or procurement by fraudulent inducement for prostitution, as defined in Section 266a.

(34)

(A) Offenses relating to insurance fraud as specified in Sections 2106, 2108, 2109, 2110, 2110.3, 2110.5, 2110.7, and 2117 of the Unemployment Insurance Code.

(B) Fraud offenses relating to COVID-19 pandemic-related insurance programs administered by the Employment Development Department. For the purposes of this subparagraph, "fraud offenses" includes the offenses specified in subparagraph (A).

(b)

(1) "Pattern of criminal profiteering activity" means engaging in at least two incidents of criminal profiteering, as defined by this chapter, that meet the following requirements:

(A) Have the same or a similar purpose, result, principals, victims, or methods of commission, or are otherwise interrelated by distinguishing characteristics.

(B) Are not isolated events.

(C) Were committed as a criminal activity of organized crime.

(2) Acts that would constitute a "pattern of criminal profiteering activity" shall not be used by a prosecuting agency to seek the remedies provided by this chapter unless the underlying offense occurred after the effective date of this chapter and the prior act occurred within 10 years, excluding any period of imprisonment, of the commission of the underlying offense. A prior act shall not be used by a prosecuting agency to seek remedies provided by this chapter if a prosecution for that act resulted in an acquittal.

(c) "Prosecuting agency" means the Attorney General or the district attorney of any county.

(d) "Organized crime" means crime that is of a conspiratorial nature and that is either of an organized nature and seeks to supply illegal goods or services such as narcotics, prostitution, pimping and pandering, loan-sharking, counterfeiting of a registered mark in violation of Section 350, the piracy of a recording or audiovisual work in violation of Section 653w, gambling, and pornography, or that, through planning and coordination of individual efforts, seeks to conduct the illegal activities of arson for profit, hijacking, insurance fraud, smuggling, operating vehicle theft rings, fraud against the beverage container recycling program, embezzlement, securities fraud, insurance fraud in violation of the provisions listed in paragraph (34) of subdivision (a), grand theft, money laundering, forgery, or systematically encumbering the assets of a business for the purpose of defrauding creditors. "Organized crime" also means crime committed by a criminal street gang, as defined in subdivision (f) of Section 186.22. "Organized crime" also means false or fraudulent activities, schemes, or artifices, as described in Section 14107 of the Welfare and Institutions Code, and the theft of personal identifying information, as defined in Section 530.5.

(e) "Underlying offense" means an offense enumerated in subdivision (a) for which the defendant is being prosecuted.

Amended by Stats 2022 ch 950 (AB 1637),s 1, eff. 9/30/2022.
Amended by Stats 2019 ch 268 (AB 1294),s 1, eff. 1/1/2020.
Amended by Stats 2016 ch 86 (SB 1171),s 221, eff. 1/1/2017.
Amended by Stats 2015 ch 427 (AB 160),s 1, eff. 1/1/2016.
Amended by Stats 2013 ch 618 (AB 924),s 5, eff. 1/1/2014.
Amended by Stats 2011 ch 457 (AB 90),s 1, eff. 1/1/2012.
Amended by Stats 2009 ch 211 (AB 17),s 1, eff. 10/11/2009.
Amended by Stats 2007 ch 111 (AB 924),s 1, eff. 1/1/2008.
Amended by Stats 2006 ch 538 (SB 1852),s 498, eff. 1/1/2007.
Amended by Stats 2005 ch 240 (AB 22),s 6.5, eff. 1/1/2006
Amended by Stats 2005 ch 53 (AB 988),s 1, eff. 1/1/2006
Amended by Stats 2003 ch 125 (SB 968), s 1, eff. 1/1/2004.
Amended by Stats 2002 ch 991 (AB 1990), s 1, eff. 1/1/2003.
Amended by Stats 2000 ch 322 (AB 1098), s 11, eff. 1/1/2001.

Section 186.3 - Assets subject to forfeiture

(a) In any case in which a person is alleged to have been engaged in a pattern of criminal profiteering activity, upon a conviction of the underlying offense, the assets listed in subdivisions (b) and (c) shall be subject to forfeiture upon proof of the provisions of subdivision (d) of Section 186.5.

(b) Any property interest whether tangible or intangible, acquired through a pattern of criminal profiteering activity.

(c) All proceeds of a pattern of criminal profiteering activity, which property shall include all things of value that may have been received in exchange for the proceeds immediately derived from the pattern of criminal profiteering activity.

Added by Stats. 1982, Ch. 1281, Sec. 1.

Section 186.4 - Petition of forfeiture; service of process of notice

(a) The prosecuting agency shall, in conjunction with the criminal proceeding, file a petition of forfeiture with the superior court of the county in which the defendant has been charged with the underlying criminal offense, which shall allege that the defendant has engaged in a pattern of criminal profiteering activity, including the acts or threats chargeable as crimes and the property forfeitable pursuant to Section 186.3. The prosecuting agency shall make service of process of a notice regarding that petition upon every individual who may have a property interest in the alleged proceeds, which notice shall state that any interested party may file a verified claim with the superior court stating the amount of their claimed interest and an affirmation or denial of the prosecuting agency's allegation. If the notices cannot be given by registered mail or personal delivery, the notices shall be published for at least three successive weeks in a newspaper of general circulation in the county where the property is located. If the property alleged to be subject to forfeiture is real property, the prosecuting agency shall, at the time of filing the petition of forfeiture, record a lis pendens in each county in which the real property is situated which specifically identifies the real property alleged to be subject to forfeiture. The judgment of forfeiture shall not affect the interest in real property of any third party which was acquired prior to the recording of the lis pendens.

(b) All notices shall set forth the time within which a claim of interest in the property seized is required to be filed pursuant to Section 186.5.

Amended by Stats. 1983, Ch. 208, Sec. 1.

Section 186.5 - Verified claim

(a) Any person claiming an interest in the property or proceeds may, at any time within 30 days from the date of the first publication of the notice of seizure, or within 30 days after receipt of actual notice, file with the superior court of the county in which the action is pending a verified claim stating his or her interest in the property or proceeds. A verified copy of the claim shall be given by the claimant to the Attorney General or district attorney, as appropriate.

(b)

(1) If, at the end of the time set forth in subdivision (a), an interested person, other than the defendant, has not filed a claim, the court, upon motion, shall declare that the person has defaulted upon his or her alleged interest, and it shall be subject to forfeiture upon proof of the provisions of subdivision (d).

(2) The defendant may admit or deny that the property is subject to forfeiture pursuant to the provisions of this chapter. If the defendant fails to admit or deny or to file a claim of interest in the property or proceeds, the court shall enter a response of denial on behalf of the defendant.

(c)

(1) The forfeiture proceeding shall be set for hearing in the superior court in which the underlying criminal offense will be tried.

(2) If the defendant is found guilty of the underlying offense, the issue of forfeiture shall be promptly tried, either before the same jury or before a new jury in the discretion of the court, unless waived by the consent of all parties.

(d) At the forfeiture hearing, the prosecuting agency shall have the burden of establishing beyond a reasonable doubt that the defendant was engaged in a pattern of criminal profiteering activity and that the property alleged in the petition comes within the provisions of subdivision (b) or (c) of Section 186.3.

Added by Stats. 1982, Ch. 1281, Sec. 1.

Section 186.6 - Pendente lite orders to preserve status quo of property

(a) Concurrent with, or subsequent to, the filing of the petition, the prosecuting agency may move the superior court for the following pendente lite orders to preserve the status quo of the property alleged in the petition of forfeiture:

(1) An injunction to restrain all interested parties and enjoin them from transferring, encumbering, hypothecating or otherwise disposing of that property.

(2) Appointment of a receiver to take possession of, care for, manage, and operate the assets and properties so that such property may be maintained and preserved.

(b) No preliminary injunction may be granted or receiver appointed without notice to the interested parties and a hearing to determine that such an order is necessary to preserve the property, pending the outcome of the criminal proceedings, and that there is probable cause to believe that the property alleged in the forfeiture proceedings are proceeds or property interests forfeitable under Section 186.3. However, a temporary restraining order may issue pending that hearing pursuant to the provisions of Section 527 of the Code of Civil Procedure.

(c) Notwithstanding any other provision of law, the court in granting these motions may order a surety bond or undertaking to preserve the property interests of the interested parties.

(d) The court shall, in making its orders, seek to protect the interests of those who may be involved in the same enterprise as the defendant, but who were not involved in the commission of the criminal profiteering activity.

Added by Stats. 1982, Ch. 1281, Sec. 1.

Section 186.7 - Forfeiture

(a) If the trier of fact at the forfeiture hearing finds that the alleged property or proceeds is forfeitable pursuant to Section 186.3 and the defendant was engaged in a pattern of criminal profiteering activity, the court shall declare that property or proceeds forfeited to the state or local governmental entity, subject to distribution as provided in Section 186.8. No property solely owned by a bona fide purchaser for value shall be subject to forfeiture.

(b) If the trier of fact at the forfeiture hearing finds that the alleged property is forfeitable pursuant to Section 186.3 but does not find that a person holding a valid lien, mortgage, security interest, or interest under a conditional sales contract acquired that interest with actual knowledge that the property was to be used for a purpose for which forfeiture is permitted, and the amount due to that person is less than the appraised value of the property, that person may pay to the state or the local governmental entity which initiated the forfeiture proceeding, the amount of the registered owner's equity, which shall be deemed to be the difference between the appraised value and the amount of the lien, mortgage, security interest, or interest under a conditional sales contract. Upon that payment, the state or local governmental entity shall relinquish all claims to the property. If the holder of the interest elects not to make that payment to the state or local governmental entity, the property shall be deemed forfeited to the state or local governmental entity and the ownership certificate shall be forwarded. The appraised value shall be determined as of the date judgment is entered either by agreement between the legal owner and the governmental entity involved, or if they cannot agree, then by a court-appointed appraiser for the county in which the action is brought. A person holding a valid lien, mortgage, security interest, or interest under a conditional sales contract shall be paid the appraised value of his or her interest.

(c) If the amount due to a person holding a valid lien, mortgage, security interest, or interest under a conditional sales contract is less than the value of the property and the person elects not to make payment to the governmental entity, the property shall be sold at public auction by the Department of General Services or by the local governmental entity which shall provide notice of that sale by one publication in a newspaper published and circulated in the city, community, or locality where the sale is to take place.

(d) Notwithstanding subdivision (c), a county may dispose of any real property forfeited to the county pursuant to this chapter pursuant to Section 25538.5 of the Government Code.

Amended by Stats. 1992, Ch. 1020, Sec. 3.7. Effective January 1, 1993.

Section 186.8 - Distribution of money forfeited or proceeds of sale

Notwithstanding that no response or claim has been filed pursuant to Section 186.5, in all cases where property is forfeited pursuant to this chapter and, if necessary, sold by the Department of General Services or local governmental entity, the money forfeited or the proceeds of sale shall be distributed by the state or local governmental entity as follows:

(a) To the bona fide or innocent purchaser, conditional sales vendor, or holder of a valid lien, mortgage, or security interest, if any, up to the amount of their interest in the property or proceeds, when the court declaring the forfeiture orders a distribution to that person. The court shall endeavor to discover all those lienholders and protect their interests and may, at its discretion, order the proceeds placed in escrow for up to an additional 60 days to ensure that all valid claims are received and processed.

(b) To the Department of General Services or local governmental entity for all expenditures made or incurred by it in connection with the sale of the property, including expenditures for any necessary repairs, storage, or transportation of any property seized under this chapter.

(c) To the General Fund of the state or a general fund of a local governmental entity, whichever prosecutes.

(d) In any case involving a violation of subdivision (b) of Section 311.2, or Section 311.3 or 311.4, in lieu of the distribution of the proceeds provided for by subdivisions (b) and (c), the proceeds shall be deposited in the county children's trust fund, established pursuant to Section 18966 of the Welfare and Institutions Code, of the county that filed the petition of forfeiture. If the county does not have a children's trust fund, the funds shall be deposited in the State Children's Trust Fund, established pursuant to Section 18969 of the Welfare and Institutions Code.

(e) In any case involving crimes against the state beverage container recycling program, in lieu of the distribution of proceeds provided in subdivision (c), the proceeds shall be deposited in the penalty account established pursuant to subdivision (d) of Section 14580 of the Public Resources Code, except that a portion of the proceeds equivalent to the cost of prosecution in the case shall be distributed to the local prosecuting entity that filed the petition of forfeiture.

(f)

(1) In any case described in paragraph (29) or (30) of subdivision (a) of Section 186.2, or paragraph (33) of subdivision (a) of Section 186.2 where the victim is a minor, in lieu of the distribution provided for in subdivision (c), the proceeds shall be deposited in the Victim-Witness Assistance Fund to be available for appropriation to fund child sexual exploitation and child sexual abuse victim counseling centers and prevention programs under Section 13837. Fifty percent of the funds deposited in the Victim-Witness Assistance Fund pursuant to this subdivision shall be granted to community-based organizations that serve minor victims of human trafficking.

(2) Notwithstanding paragraph (1), any proceeds specified in paragraph (1) that would otherwise be distributed to the General Fund of the state under subdivision (c) pursuant to a paragraph in subdivision (a) of Section 186.2 other than paragraph (29) or (30) of subdivision (a) of Section 186.2, or paragraph (33) of subdivision (a) of Section 186.2 where the victim is a minor, shall, except as otherwise required by law, continue to be distributed to the General Fund of the state as specified in subdivision (c).

(g) In any case described in subparagraph (B) of paragraph (34) of subdivision (a) of Section 186.2, in lieu of the distribution provided for in subdivision (c), the proceeds shall be returned to the Employment Development Department.

Amended by Stats 2022 ch 950 (AB 1637),s 2, eff. 9/30/2022.

Amended by Stats 2012 ch 514 (SB 1133),s 1, eff. 1/1/2013.

Amended by Stats 2011 ch 457 (AB 90),s 2, eff. 1/1/2012.

Amended by Stats 2009 ch 211 (AB 17),s 2, eff. 10/11/2009.

Amended by Stats 2004 ch 183 (AB 3082), s 266, eff. 1/1/2005.

Amended by Stats 2003 ch 125 (SB 968), s 2, eff. 1/1/2004.

Chapter 10 - MONEY LAUNDERING

Section 186.9 - Definitions

As used in this chapter:

(a)"Conducts" includes, but is not limited to, initiating, concluding, or participating in conducting, initiating, or concluding a transaction.

(b)"Financial institution" means, when located or doing business in this state, any national bank or banking association, state bank or banking association, commercial bank or trust company organized under the laws of the United States or any state, any private bank, industrial savings bank, savings bank or thrift institution, savings and loan association, or building and loan association organized under the laws of the United States or any state, any insured institution as defined in Section 401 of the National Housing Act (12 U.S.C. Sec. 1724(a)), any credit union organized under the laws of the United States or any state, any national banking association or corporation acting under Chapter 6 (commencing with Section 601) of Title 12 of the United States Code, any agency, agent or branch of a foreign bank, any currency dealer or exchange, any person or business engaged primarily in the cashing of checks, any person or business who regularly engages in the issuing, selling, or redeeming of traveler's checks, money orders, or similar instruments, any broker or dealer in securities registered or required to be registered with the Securities and Exchange Commission under the Securities Exchange Act of 1934 or with the Commissioner of Financial Protection and Innovation under Part 3 (commencing with Section 25200) of Division 1 of Title 4 of the Corporations Code, any licensed transmitter of funds or other person or business regularly engaged in transmitting funds to a foreign nation for others, any investment banker or investment company, any insurer, any dealer in gold, silver, or platinum bullion or coins, diamonds, emeralds, rubies, or sapphires, any pawnbroker, any telegraph company, any person or business regularly engaged in the delivery, transmittal, or holding of mail or packages, any person or business that conducts a transaction involving the transfer of title to any real property, vehicle, vessel, or aircraft, any personal property broker, any person or business acting as a real property securities dealer within the meaning of Section 10237 of the Business and Professions Code, whether licensed to do so or not, any person or business acting within the meaning and scope of subdivisions (d) and (e) of Section 10131 and Section 10131.1 of the Business and Professions Code, whether licensed to do so or not, any person or business regularly engaged in gaming within the meaning and scope of Section 330, any person or business regularly engaged in pool selling or bookmaking within the meaning and scope of Section 337a, any person or business regularly engaged in horse racing whether licensed to do so or not under the Business and Professions Code, any person or business engaged in the operation of a gambling ship within the meaning and scope of Section 11317, any person or business engaged in controlled gambling within the meaning and scope of subdivision (e) of Section 19805 of the Business and Professions Code, whether registered to do so or not, and any person or business defined as a "bank," "financial agency," or "financial institution" by Section 5312 of Title 31 of the United States Code or Section 103.11 of Title 31 of the Code of Federal Regulations and any successor provisions thereto.

(c)"Transaction" includes the deposit, withdrawal, transfer, bailment, loan, pledge, payment, or exchange of currency, or a monetary instrument, as defined by subdivision (d), or the electronic, wire, magnetic, or manual transfer of funds between accounts by, through, or to, a financial institution as defined by subdivision (b).

(d)"Monetary instrument" means United States currency and coin; the currency, coin, and foreign bank drafts of any foreign country; payment warrants issued by the United States, this state, or any city, county, or city and county of this state or any other political subdivision thereof; any bank check, cashier's check, traveler's check, or money order; any personal check, stock, investment security, or negotiable instrument in bearer form or otherwise in a form in which title thereto passes upon delivery; gold, silver, or platinum bullion or coins; and diamonds, emeralds, rubies, or sapphires. Except for foreign bank drafts and federal, state, county, or city warrants, "monetary instrument" does not include personal checks made payable to the order of a named party which have not been endorsed or which bear restrictive endorsements, and also does not include personal checks which have been endorsed by the named party and deposited by the named party into the named party's account with a financial institution.

(e)"Criminal activity" means a criminal offense punishable under the laws of this state by death, imprisonment in the state prison, or imprisonment pursuant to subdivision (h) of Section 1170 or from a criminal offense committed in another jurisdiction punishable under the laws of that jurisdiction by death or imprisonment for a term exceeding one year.

(f)"Foreign bank draft" means a bank draft or check issued or made out by a foreign bank, savings and loan, casa de cambio, credit union, currency dealer or exchanger, check cashing business, money transmitter, insurance company, investment or private bank, or any other foreign financial institution that provides similar financial services, on an account in the name of the foreign bank or foreign financial institution held at a bank or other financial institution located in the United States or a territory of the United States.

Amended by Stats 2022 ch 452 (SB 1498),s 203, eff. 1/1/2023.

Amended by Stats 2019 ch 143 (SB 251),s 76, eff. 1/1/2020.

Amended by Stats 2012 ch 43 (SB 1023),s 15, eff. 6/27/2012.

Amended by Stats 2007 ch 130 (AB 299),s 185, eff. 1/1/2008.

Section 186.10 - Crime of money laundering

(a) Any person who conducts or attempts to conduct a transaction or more than one transaction within a seven-day period involving a monetary instrument or instruments of a total value exceeding five thousand dollars ($5,000), or a total value exceeding twenty-five thousand dollars ($25,000) within a 30-day period, through one or more financial institutions (1) with the specific intent to promote, manage, establish, carry on, or facilitate the promotion, management, establishment, or carrying on of any criminal activity, or (2) knowing that the monetary instrument represents the proceeds of, or is derived directly or indirectly from the proceeds of, criminal activity, is guilty of the crime of money laundering. The aggregation periods do not create an obligation for financial institutions to record, report, create, or implement tracking systems or otherwise monitor transactions involving monetary instruments in any time period. In consideration of the constitutional right to counsel afforded by the Sixth Amendment to the United States Constitution and Section 15 of Article I of the California Constitution, when a case involves an attorney who accepts a fee for representing a client in a criminal investigation or proceeding, the prosecution shall additionally be required to prove that the monetary instrument was accepted by the attorney with the intent to disguise or aid in disguising the source of the funds or the nature of the criminal activity. A violation of this section shall be punished by imprisonment in a county jail for not more than one year or pursuant to subdivision (h) of Section 1170, by a fine of not more than two hundred fifty thousand dollars ($250,000) or twice the value of the property transacted, whichever is greater, or by both that imprisonment and fine. However, for a second or subsequent conviction for a violation of this section, the maximum fine that may be imposed is five hundred thousand dollars ($500,000) or five times the value of the property transacted, whichever is greater.

(b) Notwithstanding any other law, for purposes of this section, each individual transaction conducted in excess of five thousand dollars ($5,000), each series of transactions conducted within a seven-day period that total in excess of five thousand dollars ($5,000), or each series of transactions conducted within a 30-day period that total in excess of twenty-five thousand dollars ($25,000), shall constitute a separate, punishable offense.

(c)

(1) Any person who is punished under subdivision (a) by imprisonment pursuant to subdivision (h) of Section 1170 shall also be subject to an additional term of imprisonment pursuant to subdivision (h) of Section 1170 as follows:

(A) If the value of the transaction or transactions exceeds fifty thousand dollars ($50,000) but is less than one hundred fifty thousand dollars ($150,000), the court, in addition to and consecutive to the felony punishment otherwise imposed pursuant to this section, shall impose an additional term of imprisonment of one year.

(B) If the value of the transaction or transactions exceeds one hundred fifty thousand dollars ($150,000) but is less than one million dollars ($1,000,000), the court, in addition to and consecutive to the felony punishment otherwise imposed pursuant to this section, shall impose an additional term of imprisonment of two years.

(C) If the value of the transaction or transactions exceeds one million dollars ($1,000,000), but is less than two million five hundred thousand dollars ($2,500,000), the court, in addition to and consecutive to the felony punishment otherwise imposed pursuant to this section, shall impose an additional term of imprisonment of three years.

(D) If the value of the transaction or transactions exceeds two million five hundred thousand dollars ($2,500,000), the court, in addition to and consecutive to the felony punishment otherwise prescribed by this section, shall impose an additional term of imprisonment of four years.

(2)

(A) An additional term of imprisonment as provided for in this subdivision shall not be imposed unless the facts of a transaction or transactions, or attempted transaction or transactions, of a value described in paragraph (1), are charged in the accusatory pleading, and are either admitted to by the defendant or are found to be true by the trier of fact.

(B) An additional term of imprisonment as provided for in this subdivision may be imposed with respect to an accusatory pleading charging multiple violations of this section, regardless of whether any single violation charged in that pleading involves a transaction or attempted transaction of a value covered by paragraph (1), if the violations charged in that pleading arise from a common scheme or plan and the aggregate value of the alleged transactions or attempted transactions is of a value covered by paragraph (1).

(d) All pleadings under this section shall remain subject to the rules of joinder and severance stated in Section 954.

Amended by Stats 2011 ch 39 (AB 117),s 68, eff. 6/30/2011.

Amended by Stats 2011 ch 15 (AB 109),s 273, eff. 4/4/2011, but operative no earlier than October 1, 2011, and only upon creation of a community corrections grant program to assist in implementing this act and upon an appropriation to fund the grant program.

Chapter 10.5 - FRAUD AND EMBEZZLEMENT: VICTIM RESTITUTION

Section 186.11 - Aggravated while collar crime enhancement

(a)

(1) Any person who commits two or more related felonies, a material element of which is fraud or embezzlement, which involve a pattern of related felony conduct, and the pattern of related felony conduct involves the taking of, or results in the loss by another person or entity of, more than one hundred thousand dollars ($100,000), shall be punished, upon conviction of two or more felonies in a single criminal proceeding, in addition and consecutive to the punishment prescribed for the felony offenses of which he or she has been convicted, by an additional term of imprisonment in the state prison as specified in paragraph (2) or (3). This enhancement shall be known as the aggravated white collar crime enhancement. The aggravated white collar crime enhancement shall only be imposed once in a single criminal proceeding. For purposes of this section, "pattern of related felony conduct" means engaging in at least two felonies that have the same or similar purpose, result, principals, victims, or methods of commission, or are otherwise interrelated by distinguishing characteristics, and that are not isolated events. For purposes of this section, "two or more related felonies" means felonies committed against two or more separate victims, or against the same victim on two or more separate occasions.

(2) If the pattern of related felony conduct involves the taking of, or results in the loss by another person or entity of, more than five hundred thousand dollars ($500,000), the additional term of punishment shall be two, three, or five years in the state prison.

(3) If the pattern of related felony conduct involves the taking of, or results in the loss by another person or entity of, more than one hundred thousand dollars ($100,000), but not more than five hundred thousand dollars ($500,000), the additional term of punishment shall be the term specified in paragraph (1) or (2) of subdivision (a) of Section 12022.6.

(b)

(1) The additional prison term and penalties provided for in subdivisions (a), (c), and (d) shall not be imposed unless the facts set forth in subdivision (a) are charged in the accusatory pleading and admitted or found to be true by the trier of fact.

(2) The additional prison term provided in paragraph (2) of subdivision (a) shall be in addition to any other punishment provided by law, including Section 12022.6, and shall not be limited by any other provision of law.

(c) Any person convicted of two or more felonies, as specified in subdivision (a), shall also be liable for a fine not to exceed five hundred thousand dollars ($500,000) or double the value of the taking, whichever is greater, if the existence of facts that would make the person subject to the aggravated white collar crime enhancement have been admitted or found to be true by the trier of fact. However, if the pattern of related felony conduct involves the taking of more than one hundred thousand dollars ($100,000), but not more than five hundred thousand dollars ($500,000), the fine shall not exceed one hundred thousand dollars ($100,000) or double the value of the taking, whichever is greater.

(d)

(1) If a person is alleged to have committed two or more felonies, as specified in subdivision (a), and the aggravated white collar crime enhancement is also charged, or a person is charged in an accusatory pleading with a felony, a material element of which is fraud or embezzlement, that involves the taking or loss of more than one hundred thousand dollars ($100,000), and an allegation as to the existence of those facts, any asset or property that is in the control of that person, and any asset or property that has been transferred by that person to a third party, subsequent to the commission of any criminal act alleged pursuant to subdivision (a), other than in a bona fide purchase, whether found within or outside the state, may be preserved by the superior court in order to pay restitution and fines. Upon conviction of two or more felonies, as specified in subdivision (a), or a felony, a material element of which is fraud or embezzlement, that involves the taking or loss of more than one hundred thousand dollars ($100,000), this property may be levied upon by the superior court to pay restitution and fines if the existence of facts that would make the person subject to the aggravated white collar crime enhancement or that demonstrate the taking or loss of more than one hundred thousand dollars ($100,000) in the commission of a felony, a material element of which is fraud or embezzlement, have been charged in the accusatory pleading and admitted or found to be true by the trier of fact.

(2) To prevent dissipation or secreting of assets or property, the prosecuting agency may, at the same time as or subsequent to the filing of a complaint or indictment charging two or more felonies, as specified in subdivision (a), and the enhancement specified in subdivision (a), or a felony, a material element of which is fraud or embezzlement, that involves the taking or loss of more than one hundred thousand dollars ($100,000), and an allegation as to the existence of those facts, file a petition with the criminal division of the superior court of the county in which the accusatory pleading was filed, seeking a temporary restraining order, preliminary injunction, the appointment of a receiver, or any other protective relief necessary to preserve the property or assets. This petition shall commence a proceeding that shall be pendent to the criminal proceeding and maintained solely to affect the criminal remedies provided for in this section. The proceeding shall not be subject to or governed by the provisions of the Civil Discovery Act as set forth in Title 4 (commencing with Section 2016.010) of Part 4 of the Code of Civil Procedure. The petition shall allege that the defendant has been charged with two or more felonies, as specified in subdivision (a), and is subject to the aggravated white collar crime enhancement specified in subdivision (a) or that the defendant has been charged with a felony, a material element of which is fraud or embezzlement, that involves the taking or loss of more than one hundred thousand dollars ($100,000), and an allegation as to the existence of those facts. The petition shall identify that criminal proceeding and the assets and property to be affected by an order issued pursuant to this section.

(3) A notice regarding the petition shall be provided, by personal service or registered mail, to every person who may have an interest in the property specified in the petition. Additionally, the notice shall be published for at least three successive weeks in a newspaper of general circulation in the county where the property affected by an order issued pursuant to this section is located. The notice shall state that any interested person may file a verified claim with the superior court stating the nature and amount of their claimed interest. The notice shall set forth the time within which a claim of interest in the protected property is required to be filed.

(4) If the property to be preserved is real property, the prosecuting agency shall record, at the time of filing the petition, a lis pendens in each county in which the real property is situated which specifically identifies the property by legal description, the name of the owner of record as shown on the latest equalized assessment roll, and the assessor's parcel number.

(5) If the property to be preserved are assets under the control of a banking or financial institution, the prosecuting agency, at the time of the filing of the petition, may obtain an order from the court directing the banking or financial institution to immediately disclose the account numbers and value of the assets of the accused held by the banking or financial institution. The prosecuting agency shall file a supplemental petition, specifically identifying which banking or financial institution accounts shall be subject to a temporary restraining order, preliminary injunction, or other protective remedy.

(6) Any person claiming an interest in the protected property may, at any time within 30 days from the date of the first publication of the notice of the petition, or within 30 days after receipt of actual notice, file with the superior court of the county in which the action is pending a verified claim stating the nature and amount of his or her interest in the property or assets. A verified copy of the claim shall be served by the claimant on the Attorney General or district attorney, as appropriate.

(7) The imposition of fines and restitution pursuant to this section shall be determined by the superior court in which the underlying criminal offense is sentenced. Any judge who is assigned to the criminal division of the superior court in the county where the petition is filed may issue a temporary restraining order in conjunction with, or subsequent to, the filing of an allegation pursuant to this section. Any subsequent hearing on the petition shall also be heard by a judge assigned to the criminal division of the superior court in the county in which the petition is filed. At the time of the filing of an information or indictment in the underlying criminal case, any subsequent hearing on the petition shall be heard by the superior court judge assigned to the underlying criminal case.

(e) Concurrent with or subsequent to the filing of the petition, the prosecuting agency may move the superior court for, and the superior court may issue, the following pendente lite orders to preserve the status quo of the property alleged in the petition:

(1) An injunction to restrain any person from transferring, encumbering, hypothecating, or otherwise disposing of that property.

(2) Appointment of a receiver to take possession of, care for, manage, and operate the assets and properties so that the property may be maintained and preserved. The court may order that a receiver appointed pursuant to this section shall be compensated for all reasonable expenditures made or incurred by him or her in connection with the possession, care, management, and operation of any property or assets that are subject to the provisions of this section.

(3) A bond or other undertaking, in lieu of other orders, of a value sufficient to ensure the satisfaction of restitution and fines imposed pursuant to this section.

(f)

(1) No preliminary injunction may be granted or receiver appointed by the court without notice that meets the requirements of paragraph (3) of subdivision (d) to all known and reasonably ascertainable interested parties and upon a hearing to determine that an order is necessary to preserve the property pending the outcome of the criminal proceedings. A temporary restraining order may be issued by the court, ex parte, pending that hearing in conjunction with or subsequent to the filing of the petition upon the application of the prosecuting attorney. The temporary restraining order may be based upon the sworn declaration of a peace officer with personal knowledge of the criminal investigation that establishes probable cause to believe that aggravated white collar crime or a felony, a material element of which is fraud or embezzlement, that involves the taking or loss of more than one hundred thousand dollars ($100,000) has taken place and that the amount of restitution and fines exceeds or equals the worth of the assets subject to the temporary restraining order. The declaration may include the hearsay statements of witnesses to establish the necessary facts. The temporary restraining order may be issued without notice upon a showing of good cause to the court.

(2) The defendant, or a person who has filed a verified claim as provided in paragraph (6) of subdivision (d), shall have the right to have the court conduct an order to show cause hearing within 10 days of the service of the request for hearing upon the prosecuting agency, in order to determine whether the temporary restraining order should remain in effect, whether relief should be granted from any lis pendens recorded pursuant to paragraph (4) of subdivision (d), or whether any existing order should be modified in the interests of justice. Upon a showing of good cause, the hearing shall be held within two days of the service of the request for hearing upon the prosecuting agency.

(3) In determining whether to issue a preliminary injunction or temporary restraining order in a proceeding brought by a prosecuting agency in conjunction with or subsequent to the filing of an allegation pursuant to this section, the court has the discretion to consider any matter that it deems reliable and appropriate, including hearsay statements, in order to reach a just and equitable decision. The court shall weigh the relative degree of certainty of the outcome on the merits and the consequences to each of the parties of granting the interim relief. If the prosecution is likely to prevail on the merits and the risk of the dissipation of assets outweighs the potential harm to the defendants and the interested parties, the court shall grant injunctive relief. The court shall give significant weight to the following factors:

(A) The public interest in preserving the property or assets pendente lite.

(B) The difficulty of preserving the property or assets pendente lite where the underlying alleged crimes involve issues of fraud and moral turpitude.

(C) The fact that the requested relief is being sought by a public prosecutor on behalf of alleged victims of white collar crimes.

(D) The likelihood that substantial public harm has occurred where aggravated white collar crime is alleged to have been committed.

(E) The significant public interest involved in compensating the victims of white collar crime and paying court-imposed restitution and fines.

(4) The court, in making its orders, may consider a defendant's request for the release of a portion of the property affected by this section in order to pay reasonable legal fees in connection with the criminal proceeding, any necessary and appropriate living expenses pending trial and sentencing, and for the purpose of posting bail. The court shall weigh the needs of the public to retain the property against the needs of the defendant to a portion of the property. The court shall consider the factors listed in paragraph (3) prior to making any order releasing property for these purposes.

(5) The court, in making its orders, shall seek to protect the interests of any innocent third persons, including an innocent spouse, who were not involved in the commission of any criminal activity.

(6) Any petition filed pursuant to this section is part of the criminal proceedings for purposes of appointment of counsel and shall be assigned to the criminal division of the superior court of the county in which the accusatory pleading was filed.

(7) Based upon a noticed motion brought by the receiver appointed pursuant to paragraph (2) of subdivision (e), the court may order an interlocutory sale of property named in the petition when the property is liable to perish, to waste, or to be significantly reduced in value, or when the expenses of maintaining the property are disproportionate to the value thereof. The proceeds of the interlocutory sale shall be deposited with the court or as directed by the court pending determination of the proceeding pursuant to this section.

(8) The court may make any orders that are necessary to preserve the continuing viability of any lawful business enterprise that is affected by the issuance of a temporary restraining order or preliminary injunction issued pursuant to this action.

(9) In making its orders, the court shall seek to prevent any asset subject to a temporary restraining order or preliminary injunction from perishing, spoiling, going to waste, or otherwise being significantly reduced in value. Where the potential for diminution in value exists, the court shall appoint a receiver to dispose of or otherwise protect the value of the property or asset.

(10) A preservation order shall not be issued against any assets of a business that are not likely to be dissipated and that may be subject to levy or attachment to meet the purposes of this section.

(g) If the allegation that the defendant is subject to the aggravated white collar crime enhancement or has committed a felony, a material element of which is fraud or embezzlement, that involves the taking or loss of more than one hundred thousand dollars ($100,000) is dismissed or found by the trier of fact to be untrue, any preliminary injunction or temporary restraining order issued pursuant to this section shall be dissolved. If a jury is the trier of fact, and the jury is unable to reach a unanimous verdict, the court shall have the discretion to continue or dissolve all or a portion of the preliminary injunction or temporary restraining order based upon the interests of justice. However, if the prosecuting agency elects not to retry the case, any preliminary injunction or temporary restraining order issued pursuant to this section shall be dissolved.

(h)

(1)

(A) If the defendant is convicted of two or more felonies, as specified in subdivision (a), and the existence of facts that would make the person subject to the aggravated white collar crime enhancement have been admitted or found to be true by the trier of fact, or the defendant is convicted of a felony, a material element of which is fraud or embezzlement, that involves the taking or loss of more than one hundred thousand dollars ($100,000), and an allegation as to the existence of those facts has been admitted or found to be true by the trier of fact, the trial judge shall continue the preliminary injunction or temporary restraining order until the date of the criminal sentencing and shall make a finding at that time as to what portion, if any, of the property or assets subject to the preliminary injunction or temporary restraining order shall be levied upon to pay fines and restitution to victims of the crime. The order imposing fines and restitution may exceed the total worth of the property or assets subjected to the preliminary injunction or temporary restraining order. The court may order the immediate transfer of the property or assets to satisfy any judgment and sentence made pursuant to this section. Additionally, upon motion of the prosecution, the court may enter an order as part of the judgment and sentence making the order imposing fines and restitution pursuant to this section enforceable pursuant to Title 9 (commencing with Section 680.010) of Part 2 of the Code of Civil Procedure.

(B) Additionally, the court shall order the defendant to make full restitution to the victim. The payment of the restitution ordered by the court pursuant to this section shall be made a condition of any probation granted by the court if the existence of facts that would make the defendant subject to the aggravated white collar crime enhancement or of facts demonstrating the person committed a felony, a material element of which is fraud or embezzlement, that involves the taking or loss of more than one hundred thousand dollars ($100,000) have been admitted or found to be true by the trier of fact. Notwithstanding any other provision of law, the court may order that the period of probation continue for up to 10 years or until full restitution is made to the victim, whichever is earlier.

(C) The sentencing court shall retain jurisdiction to enforce the order to pay additional fines and restitution and, in appropriate cases, may initiate probation violation proceedings or contempt of court proceedings against a defendant who is found to have willfully failed to comply with any lawful order of the court.

(D) If the execution of judgment is stayed pending an appeal of an order of the superior court pursuant to this section, the preliminary injunction or temporary restraining order shall be maintained in full force and effect during the pendency of the appellate period.

(2) The order imposing fines and restitution shall not affect the interest in real property of any third party that was acquired prior to the recording of the lis pendens, unless the property was obtained from the defendant other than as a bona fide purchaser for value. If any assets or property affected by this section are subject to a valid lien, mortgage, security interest, or interest under a conditional sales contract and the amount due to the holder of the lien, mortgage, interest, or contract is less than the appraised value of the property, that person may pay to the state or the local government that initiated the proceeding the amount of the difference between the appraised value of the property and the amount of the lien, mortgage, security interest, or interest under a conditional sales contract. Upon that payment, the state or local entity shall relinquish all claims to the property. If the holder of the interest elects not to make that payment to the state or local governmental entity, the interest in the property shall be deemed transferred to the state or local governmental entity and any indicia of ownership of the property shall be confirmed in the state or local governmental entity. The appraised value shall be determined as of the date judgment is entered either by agreement between the holder of the lien, mortgage, security interest, or interest under a conditional sales contract and the governmental entity involved, or, if they cannot agree, then by a court-appointed appraiser for the county in which the action is brought. A person holding a valid lien, mortgage, security interest, or interest under a conditional sales contract shall be paid the appraised value of his or her interest.

(3) In making its final order, the court shall seek to protect the legitimately acquired interests of any innocent third persons, including an innocent spouse, who were not involved in the commission of any criminal activity.

(i) In all cases where property is to be levied upon pursuant to this section, a receiver appointed by the court shall be empowered to liquidate all property or assets which shall be distributed in the following order of priority:

(1) To the receiver, or court-appointed appraiser, for all reasonable expenditures made or incurred by him or her in connection with the sale of the property or liquidation of assets, including all reasonable expenditures for any necessary repairs, storage, or transportation of any property levied upon under this section.

(2) To any holder of a valid lien, mortgage, or security interest up to the amount of his or her interest in the property or proceeds.

(3) To any victim as restitution for any fraudulent or unlawful acts alleged in the accusatory pleading that were proven by the prosecuting agency as part of the pattern of fraudulent or unlawful acts.

(4) For payment of any fine imposed pursuant to this section. The proceeds obtained in payment of a fine shall be paid to the treasurer of the county in which the judgment was entered, or if the action was undertaken by the Attorney General, to the Treasurer. If the payment of any fine imposed pursuant to this section involved losses resulting from violation of Section 550 of this code or Section 1871.4 of the Insurance Code, one-half of the fine collected shall be paid to the treasurer of the county in which the judgment was entered, and one-half of the fine collected shall be paid to the Department of Insurance for deposit in the appropriate account in the Insurance Fund. The proceeds from the fine first shall be used by a county to reimburse local prosecutors and enforcement agencies for the reasonable costs of investigation and prosecution of cases brought pursuant to this section.

(5) To the Restitution Fund, or in cases involving convictions relating to insurance fraud, to the Insurance Fund as restitution for crimes not specifically pleaded and proven in the accusatory pleading.

(j) If, after distribution pursuant to paragraphs (1) and (2) of subdivision (i), the value of the property to be levied upon pursuant to this section is insufficient to pay for restitution and fines, the court shall order an equitable sharing of the proceeds of the liquidation of the property, and any other recoveries, which shall specify the percentage of recoveries to be devoted to each purpose. At least 70 percent of the proceeds remaining after distribution pursuant to paragraphs (1) and (2) of subdivision (i) shall be devoted to restitution.

(k) Unless otherwise expressly provided, the remedies or penalties provided by this section are cumulative to each other and to the remedies or penalties available under all other laws of this state, except that two separate actions against the same defendant and pertaining to the same fraudulent or unlawful acts may not be brought by a district attorney or the Attorney General pursuant to this section and Chapter 5 (commencing with Section 17200) of Part 2 of Division 7 of the Business and Professions Code. If a fine is imposed under this section, it shall be in lieu of all other fines that may be imposed pursuant to any other provision of law for the crimes for which the defendant has been convicted in the action.

Amended by Stats 2016 ch 86 (SB 1171),s 222, eff. 1/1/2017.
Amended by Stats 2016 ch 37 (AB 2295),s 1, eff. 1/1/2017.
Amended by Stats 2011 ch 182 (AB 364),s 1, eff. 1/1/2012.
Amended by Stats 2007 ch 408 (AB 1199),s 1, eff. 1/1/2008.
Amended by Stats 2004 ch 182 (AB 3081), s 49, eff. 1/1/2005.
Amended by Stats 2001 ch 854 (SB 205), s 21, eff. 1/1/2002.

Section 186.12 - Felony; protective relief to preserve property

(a)

(1) A felony for purposes of this section means a felony violation of subdivision (d) or (e) of Section 368, or a felony violation of subdivision (c) of Section 15656 of the Welfare and Institutions Code, that involves the taking or loss of more than one hundred thousand dollars ($100,000).

(2) If a person is charged with a felony as described in paragraph (1) and an allegation as to the existence of those facts has been made, any property that is in the control of that person, and any property that has been transferred by that person to a third party, subsequent to the commission of any criminal act alleged pursuant to this subdivision, other than in a bona fide purchase, whether found within or outside the state, may be preserved by the superior court in order to pay restitution imposed pursuant to this section. Upon conviction of the felony, this property may be levied upon by the superior court to pay restitution imposed pursuant to this section.

(b)

(1) To prevent dissipation or secreting of property, the prosecuting agency may, at the same time as or subsequent to the filing of a complaint or indictment charging a felony subject to this section, file a petition with the criminal division of the superior court of the county in which the accusatory pleading was filed, seeking a temporary restraining order, preliminary injunction, the appointment of a receiver, or any other protective relief necessary to preserve the property. The filing of the petition shall commence a proceeding that shall be pendent to the criminal proceeding and maintained solely to affect the criminal remedies provided for in this section. The proceeding shall not be subject to or governed by the provisions of the Civil Discovery Act as set forth in Title 4 (commencing with Section 2016.010) of Part 4 of the Code of Civil Procedure. The petition shall allege that the defendant has been charged with a felony as described in paragraph (1) of subdivision (a) and shall identify that criminal proceeding and the property to be affected by an order issued pursuant to this section.

(2) A notice regarding the petition shall be provided, by personal service or registered mail, to every person who may have an interest in the property specified in the petition. Additionally, the notice shall be published for at least three successive weeks in a newspaper of general circulation in the county where the property affected by an order issued pursuant to this section is located. The notice shall state that any interested person may file a verified claim with the superior court stating the nature and amount of their claimed interest. The notice shall set forth the time within which a claim of interest in the protected property is required to be filed.

(3) If the property to be preserved is real property, the prosecuting agency shall record, at the time of filing the petition, a lis pendens in each county in which the real property is situated which specifically identifies the property by legal description, the name of the owner of record as shown on the latest equalized assessment roll, and the assessor's parcel number.

(4) If the property to be preserved are assets under the control of a banking or financial institution, the prosecuting agency, at the time of the filing of the petition, may obtain an order from the court directing the banking or financial institution to immediately disclose the account numbers and value of the assets of the accused held by the banking or financial institution. The prosecuting agency shall file a supplemental petition, specifically identifying which banking or financial institution accounts shall be subject to a temporary restraining order, preliminary injunction, or other protective remedy.

(5) Any person claiming an interest in the protected property may, at any time within 30 days from the date of the first publication of the notice of the petition, or within 30 days after receipt of actual notice, file with the superior court of the county in which the action is pending a verified claim stating the nature and amount of his or her interest in the property. A verified copy of the claim shall be served by the claimant on the Attorney General or district attorney, as appropriate.

(6) The imposition of restitution pursuant to this section shall be determined by the superior court in which the underlying criminal offense is sentenced. Any judge who is assigned to the criminal division of the superior court in the county where the petition is filed may issue a temporary restraining order in conjunction with, or subsequent to, the filing of an allegation pursuant to this section. Any subsequent hearing on the petition shall also be heard by a judge assigned to the criminal division of the superior court in the county in which the petition is filed. At the time of the filing of an information or indictment in the underlying criminal case, any subsequent hearing on the petition shall be heard by the superior court judge assigned to the underlying criminal case.

(c) Concurrent with or subsequent to the filing of the petition pursuant to this section, the prosecuting agency may move the superior court for, and the superior court may issue, the following pendente lite orders to preserve the status quo of the property identified in the petition:

(1) An injunction to restrain any person from transferring, encumbering, hypothecating, or otherwise disposing of that property.

(2) Appointment of a receiver to take possession of, care for, manage, and operate the properties so that the property may be maintained and preserved. The court may order that a receiver appointed pursuant to this section shall be compensated for all reasonable expenditures made or incurred by him or her in connection with the possession, care, management, and operation of any property that is subject to this section.

(3) A bond or other undertaking, in lieu of other orders, of a value sufficient to ensure the satisfaction of restitution imposed pursuant to this section.

(d)

(1) No preliminary injunction may be granted or receiver appointed by the court without notice that meets the requirements of paragraph (2) of subdivision (b) to all known and reasonably ascertainable interested parties and upon a hearing to determine that an order is necessary to preserve the property pending the outcome of the criminal proceedings. A temporary restraining order may be issued by the court, ex parte, pending that hearing in conjunction with or subsequent to the filing of the petition upon the application of the prosecuting attorney. The temporary restraining order may be based upon the sworn declaration of a peace officer with personal knowledge of the criminal investigation that establishes probable cause to believe that a felony has taken place and that the amount of restitution established by this section exceeds or equals the worth of the property subject to the temporary restraining order. The declaration may include the hearsay statements of witnesses to establish the necessary facts. The temporary restraining order may be issued without notice upon a showing of good cause to the court.

(2) The defendant, or a person who has filed a verified claim as provided in paragraph (5) of subdivision (b), shall have the right to have the court conduct an order to show cause hearing within 10 days of the service of the request for hearing upon the prosecuting agency, in order to determine whether the temporary restraining order should remain in effect, whether relief should be granted from any lis pendens recorded pursuant to paragraph (3) of subdivision (b), or whether any existing order should be modified in the interests of justice. Upon a showing of good cause, the hearing shall be held within two days of the service of the request for hearing upon the prosecuting agency.

(3) In determining whether to issue a preliminary injunction or temporary restraining order in a proceeding brought by a prosecuting agency in conjunction with or subsequent to the filing of an allegation pursuant to this section, the court has the discretion to consider any matter that it deems reliable and appropriate, including hearsay statements, in order to reach a just and equitable decision. The court shall weigh the relative degree of certainty of the outcome on the merits and the consequences to each of the parties of granting the interim relief. If the prosecution is likely to prevail on the merits and the risk of dissipation of the property outweighs the potential harm to the defendants and the interested parties, the court shall grant injunctive relief. The court shall give significant weight to the following factors:

(A) The public interest in preserving the property pendente lite.

(B) The difficulty of preserving the property pendente lite where the underlying alleged crimes involve issues of fraud and moral turpitude.

(C) The fact that the requested relief is being sought by a public prosecutor on behalf of alleged victims of elder or dependent adult financial abuse.

(D) The likelihood that substantial public harm has occurred where a felony is alleged to have been committed.

(E) The significant public interest involved in compensating the elder or dependent adult victim of financial abuse and paying court-imposed restitution.

(4) The court, in making its orders, may consider a defendant's request for the release of a portion of the property affected by this section in order to pay reasonable legal fees in connection with the criminal proceeding, any necessary and appropriate living expenses pending trial and sentencing, and for the purpose of posting bail. The court shall weigh the needs of the public to retain the property against the needs of the defendant to a portion of the property. The court shall consider the factors listed in paragraph (3) prior to making any order releasing property for these purposes.

(5) The court, in making its orders, shall seek to protect the interests of any innocent third persons, including an innocent spouse, who were not involved in the commission of any criminal activity.

(6) Any petition filed pursuant to this section shall be part of the criminal proceedings for purposes of appointment of counsel and shall be assigned to the criminal division of the superior court of the county in which the accusatory pleading was filed.

(7) Based upon a noticed motion brought by the receiver appointed pursuant to paragraph (2) of subdivision (c), the court may order an interlocutory sale of property identified in the petition when the property is liable to perish, to waste, or to be significantly reduced in value, or when the expenses of maintaining the property are disproportionate to the value thereof. The proceeds of the interlocutory sale shall be deposited with the court or as directed by the court pending determination of the proceeding pursuant to this section.

(8) The court may make any orders that are necessary to preserve the continuing viability of any lawful business enterprise that is affected by the issuance of a temporary restraining order or preliminary injunction issued pursuant to this action.

(9) In making its orders, the court shall seek to prevent any property subject to a temporary restraining order or preliminary injunction from perishing, spoiling, going to waste, or otherwise being significantly reduced in value. Where the potential for diminution in value exists, the court shall appoint a receiver to dispose of or otherwise protect the value of the property.

(10) A preservation order shall not be issued against any assets of a business that are not likely to be dissipated and that may be subject to levy or attachment to meet the purposes of this section.

(e) If the allegation that the defendant committed a felony subject to this section is dismissed or found by the trier of fact to be untrue, any preliminary injunction or temporary restraining order issued pursuant to this section shall be dissolved. If a jury is the trier of fact, and the jury is unable to reach a unanimous verdict, the court shall have the discretion to continue or dissolve all or a portion of the preliminary injunction or temporary restraining order based upon the interests of justice. However, if the prosecuting agency elects not to retry the case, any preliminary injunction or temporary restraining order issued pursuant to this section shall be dissolved.

(f)

(1)

(A) If the defendant is convicted of a felony subject to this section, the trial judge shall continue the preliminary injunction or temporary restraining order until the date of the criminal sentencing and shall make a finding at that time as to what portion, if any, of the property subject to the preliminary injunction or temporary restraining order shall be levied upon to pay restitution to victims of the crime. The order imposing restitution may exceed the total worth of the property subjected to the preliminary injunction or temporary restraining order. The court may order the immediate transfer of the property to satisfy any judgment and sentence made pursuant to this section. Additionally, upon motion of the prosecution, the court may enter an order as part of the judgment and sentence making the order imposing restitution pursuant to this section enforceable pursuant to Title 9 (commencing with Section 680.010) of Part 2 of the Code of Civil Procedure.

(B) Additionally, the court shall order the defendant to make full restitution to the victim. The payment of the restitution ordered by the court pursuant to this section shall be made a condition of any probation granted by the court. Notwithstanding any other provision of law, the court may order that the period of probation continue for up to 10 years or until full restitution is made to the victim, whichever is earlier.

(C) The sentencing court shall retain jurisdiction to enforce the order to pay additional restitution and, in appropriate cases, may initiate probation violation proceedings or contempt of court proceedings against a defendant who is found to have willfully failed to comply with any lawful order of the court.

(D) If the execution of judgment is stayed pending an appeal of an order of the superior court pursuant to this section, the preliminary injunction or temporary restraining order shall be maintained in full force and effect during the pendency of the appellate period.

(2) The order imposing restitution shall not affect the interest in real property of any third party that was acquired prior to the recording of the lis pendens, unless the property was obtained from the defendant other than as a bona fide purchaser for value. If any assets or property affected by this section are subject to a valid lien, mortgage, security interest, or interest under a conditional sales contract and the amount due to the holder of the lien, mortgage, interest, or contract is less than the appraised value of the property, that person may pay to the state or the local government that initiated the proceeding the amount of the difference between the appraised value of the property and the amount of the lien, mortgage, security interest, or interest under a conditional sales contract. Upon that payment, the state or local entity shall relinquish all claims to the property. If the holder of the interest elects not to make that payment to the state or local governmental entity, the interest in the property shall be deemed transferred to the state or local governmental entity and any indicia of ownership of the property shall be confirmed in the state or local governmental entity. The appraised value shall be determined as of the date judgment is entered either by agreement between the holder of the lien, mortgage, security interest, or interest under a conditional sales contract and the governmental entity involved, or if they cannot agree, then by a court-appointed appraiser for the county in which the action is brought. A person holding a valid lien, mortgage, security interest, or interest under a conditional sales contract shall be paid the appraised value of his or her interest.

(3) In making its final order, the court shall seek to protect the legitimately acquired interests of any innocent third persons, including an innocent spouse, who were not involved in the commission of any criminal activity.

(g) In all cases where property is to be levied upon pursuant to this section, a receiver appointed by the court shall be empowered to liquidate all property, the proceeds of which shall be distributed in the following order of priority:

(1) To the receiver, or court-appointed appraiser, for all reasonable expenditures made or incurred by him or her in connection with the sale or liquidation of the property, including all reasonable expenditures for any necessary repairs, storage, or transportation of any property levied upon under this section.

(2) To any holder of a valid lien, mortgage, or security interest up to the amount of his or her interest in the property or proceeds.

(3) To any victim as restitution for any fraudulent or unlawful acts alleged in the accusatory pleading that were proven by the prosecuting agency as part of the pattern of fraudulent or unlawful acts.

(h) Unless otherwise expressly provided, the remedies or penalties provided by this section are cumulative to each other and to the remedies or penalties available under all other laws of this state, except that two separate actions against the same defendant and pertaining to the same fraudulent or unlawful acts may not be brought by a district attorney or the Attorney General pursuant to this section and Chapter 5 (commencing with Section 17200) of Part 2 of Division 7 of the Business and Professions Code.

Amended by Stats 2016 ch 86 (SB 1171),s 223, eff. 1/1/2017.

Amended by Stats 2016 ch 37 (AB 2295),s 2, eff. 1/1/2017.

Added by Stats 2011 ch 371 (AB 1293),s 1, eff. 1/1/2012.

Chapter 11 - STREET TERRORISM ENFORCEMENT AND PREVENTION ACT

Section 186.20 - Short title

This chapter shall be known and may be cited as the "California Street Terrorism Enforcement and Prevention Act."

Added by Stats. 1988, Ch. 1256, Sec. 1. Effective September 26, 1988.

Section 186.21 - Legislative findings and declarations

The Legislature hereby finds and declares that it is the right of every person, regardless of race, color, creed, religion, national origin, gender, gender identity, gender expression, age, sexual orientation, or handicap, to be secure and protected from fear, intimidation, and physical harm caused by the activities of violent groups and individuals. It is not the intent of this chapter to interfere with the exercise of the constitutionally protected rights of freedom of expression and association. The Legislature hereby recognizes the constitutional right of every citizen to harbor and express beliefs on any lawful subject whatsoever, to lawfully associate with others who share similar beliefs, to petition lawfully constituted authority for a redress of perceived grievances, and to participate in the electoral process.

The Legislature, however, further finds that the State of California is in a state of crisis which has been caused by violent street gangs whose members threaten, terrorize, and commit a multitude of crimes against the peaceful citizens of their neighborhoods. These activities, both individually and collectively, present a clear and present danger to public order and safety and are not constitutionally protected. The Legislature finds that there are nearly 600 criminal street gangs operating in California, and that the number of gang-related murders is increasing. The Legislature also finds that in Los Angeles County alone there were 328 gang-related murders in 1986, and that gang homicides in 1987 have increased 80 percent over 1986. It is the intent of the Legislature in enacting this chapter to seek the eradication of criminal activity by street gangs by focusing upon patterns of criminal gang activity and upon the organized nature of street gangs, which together, are the chief source of terror created by street gangs. The Legislature further finds that an effective means of punishing and deterring the criminal activities of street gangs is through forfeiture of the profits, proceeds, and instrumentalities acquired, accumulated, or used by street gangs.

Section 186.22 - Active participation in criminal street gang

(a) A person who actively participates in a criminal street gang with knowledge that its members engage in, or have engaged in, a pattern of criminal gang activity, and who willfully promotes, furthers, or assists in felonious criminal conduct by members of that gang, shall be punished by imprisonment in a county jail for a period not to exceed one year, or by imprisonment in the state prison for 16 months, or two or three years.

(b)

(1) Except as provided in paragraphs (4) and (5), a person who is convicted of a felony committed for the benefit of, at the direction of, or in association with a criminal street gang, with the specific intent to promote, further, or assist in criminal conduct by gang members, shall, upon conviction of that felony, in addition and consecutive to the punishment prescribed for the felony or attempted felony of which the person has been convicted, be punished as follows:

(A) Except as provided in subparagraphs (B) and (C), the person shall be punished by an additional term of two, three, or four years at the court's discretion.

(B) If the felony is a serious felony, as defined in subdivision (c) of Section 1192.7, the person shall be punished by an additional term of five years.

(C) If the felony is a violent felony, as defined in subdivision (c) of Section 667.5, the person shall be punished by an additional term of 10 years.

(2) If the underlying felony described in paragraph (1) is committed on the grounds of, or within 1,000 feet of, a public or private elementary, vocational, junior high, or high school, during hours in which the facility is open for classes or school-related programs or when minors are using the facility, that fact shall be a circumstance in aggravation of the crime in imposing a term under paragraph (1).

(3) The court shall order the imposition of the middle term of the sentence enhancement, unless there are circumstances in aggravation or mitigation. The court shall state the reasons for its choice of sentencing enhancements on the record at the time of the sentencing.

(4) A person who is convicted of a felony enumerated in this paragraph committed for the benefit of, at the direction of, or in association with a criminal street gang, with the specific intent to promote, further, or assist in criminal conduct by gang members, shall, upon conviction of that felony, be sentenced to an indeterminate term of life imprisonment with a minimum term of the indeterminate sentence calculated as the greater of:

(A) The term determined by the court pursuant to Section 1170 for the underlying conviction, including any enhancement applicable under Chapter 4.5 (commencing with Section 1170) of Title 7 of Part 2, or any period prescribed by Section 3046, if the felony is any of the offenses enumerated in subparagraph (B) or (C) of this paragraph.

(B) Imprisonment in the state prison for 15 years, if the felony is a home invasion robbery, in violation of subparagraph (A) of paragraph (1) of subdivision (a) of Section 213; carjacking, as defined in Section 215; a felony violation of Section 246; or a violation of Section 12022.55.

(C) Imprisonment in the state prison for seven years, if the felony is extortion, as defined in Section 519; or threats to victims and witnesses, as defined in Section 136.1.

(5) Except as provided in paragraph (4), a person who violates this subdivision in the commission of a felony punishable by imprisonment in the state prison for life shall not be paroled until a minimum of 15 calendar years have been served.

(c) If the court grants probation or suspends the execution of sentence imposed upon the defendant for a violation of subdivision (a), or in cases involving a true finding of the enhancement enumerated in subdivision (b), the court shall require that the defendant serve a minimum of 180 days in a county jail as a condition thereof.

(d) A person who is convicted of a public offense, punishable as a felony or a misdemeanor, that is committed for the benefit of, at the direction of, or in association with, a criminal street gang, with the specific intent to promote, further, or assist in criminal conduct by gang members, shall be punished by imprisonment in a county jail not to exceed one year, or by imprisonment in a state prison for one, two, or three years, provided that a person sentenced to imprisonment in the county jail shall be imprisoned for a period not to exceed one year, but not less than 180 days, and shall not be eligible for release upon completion of sentence, parole, or any other basis, until the person has served 180 days. If the court grants probation or suspends the execution of sentence imposed upon the defendant, it shall require as a condition thereof that the defendant serve 180 days in a county jail.

(e)

(1) As used in this chapter, "pattern of criminal gang activity" means the commission of, attempted commission of, conspiracy to commit, or solicitation of, sustained juvenile petition for, or conviction of, two or more of the following offenses, provided at least one of these offenses occurred after the effective date of this chapter, and the last of those offenses occurred within three years of the prior offense and within three years of the date the current offense is alleged to have been committed, the offenses were committed on separate occasions or by two or more members, the offenses commonly benefited a criminal street gang, and the common benefit from the offenses is more than reputational.

(A) Assault with a deadly weapon or by means of force likely to produce great bodily injury, as defined in Section 245.

(B) Robbery, as defined in Chapter 4 (commencing with Section 211) of Title 8.

(C) Unlawful homicide or manslaughter, as defined in Chapter 1 (commencing with Section 187) of Title 8.

(D) The sale, possession for sale, transportation, manufacture, offer for sale, or offer to manufacture a controlled substance as defined in Section 11007 of the Health and Safety Code.

(E) Shooting at an inhabited dwelling or occupied motor vehicle, as defined in Section 246.

(F) Discharging or permitting the discharge of a firearm from a motor vehicle, as defined in subdivisions (a) and (b) of Section 12034 until January 1, 2012, and, on or after that date, subdivisions (a) and (b) of Section 26100.

(G) Arson, as defined in Chapter 1 (commencing with Section 450) of Title 13.

(H) The intimidation of witnesses and victims, as defined in Section 136.1.

(I) Grand theft, as defined in subdivision (a) or (c) of Section 487.

(J) Grand theft of any firearm, vehicle, trailer, or vessel.

(K) Burglary, as defined in Section 459.

(L) Rape, as defined in Section 261.

(M) Money laundering, as defined in Section 186.10.

(N) Kidnapping, as defined in Section 207.

(O) Mayhem, as defined in Section 203.

(P) Aggravated mayhem, as defined in Section 205.

(Q) Torture, as defined in Section 206.

(R) Felony extortion, as defined in Sections 518 and 520.

(S) Carjacking, as defined in Section 215.

(T) The sale, delivery, or transfer of a firearm, as defined in Section 12072 until January 1, 2012, and, on or after that date, Article 1 (commencing with Section 27500) of Chapter 4 of Division 6 of Title 4 of Part 6.

(U) Possession of a pistol, revolver, or other firearm capable of being concealed upon the person in violation of paragraph (1) of subdivision (a) of Section 12101 until January 1, 2012, and, on or after that date, Section 29610.

(V) Threats to commit crimes resulting in death or great bodily injury, as defined in Section 422.

(W) Theft and unlawful taking or driving of a vehicle, as defined in Section 10851 of the Vehicle Code.

(X) Prohibited possession of a firearm in violation of Section 12021 until January 1, 2012, and, on or after that date, Chapter 2 (commencing with Section 29800) of Division 9 of Title 4 of Part 6.

(Y) Carrying a concealed firearm in violation of Section 12025 until January 1, 2012, and, on or after that date, Section 25400.

(Z) Carrying a loaded firearm in violation of Section 12031 until January 1, 2012, and, on or after that date, Section 25850.

(2) The currently charged offense shall not be used to establish the pattern of criminal gang activity.

(f) As used in this chapter, "criminal street gang" means an ongoing, organized association or group of three or more persons, whether formal or informal, having as one of its primary activities the commission of one or more of the criminal acts enumerated in subdivision (e), having a common name or common identifying sign or symbol, and whose members collectively engage in, or have engaged in, a pattern of criminal gang activity.

(g) As used in this chapter, to benefit, promote, further, or assist means to provide a common benefit to members of a gang where the common benefit is more than reputational. Examples of a common benefit that are more than reputational may include, but are not limited to, financial gain or motivation, retaliation, targeting a perceived or actual gang rival, or intimidation or silencing of a potential current or previous witness or informant.

(h) Notwithstanding any other law, the court may strike the additional punishment for the enhancements provided in this section or refuse to impose the minimum jail sentence for misdemeanors in an unusual case where the interests of justice would best be served, if the court specifies on the record and enters into the minutes the circumstances indicating that the interests of justice would best be served by that disposition.

(i) Notwithstanding any other law, for each person committed to the Department of Corrections and Rehabilitation, Division of Juvenile Facilities for a conviction pursuant to subdivision (a) or (b) of this section, the offense shall be deemed one for which the state shall pay the rate of 100 percent of the per capita institutional cost of the Department of Corrections and Rehabilitation, Division of Juvenile Facilities, pursuant to former Section 912.5 of the Welfare and Institutions Code.

(j) In order to secure a conviction or sustain a juvenile petition, pursuant to subdivision (a) it is not necessary for the prosecution to prove that the person devotes all, or a substantial part, of their time or efforts to the criminal street gang, nor is it necessary to prove that the person is a member of the criminal street gang. Active participation in the criminal street gang is all that is required.

(k) This section shall become operative on January 1, 2023.

Amended by Stats 2021 ch 699 (AB 333),s 4, eff. 1/1/2022.

Amended by Stats 2017 ch 561 (AB 1516),s 179, eff. 1/1/2018.

Amended by Stats 2016 ch 887 (SB 1016),s 2, eff. 1/1/2017.

Amended by Stats 2013 ch 508 (SB 463),s 2, eff. 1/1/2014.

Amended by Stats 2011 ch 361 (SB 576),s 2, eff. 9/29/2011.

Amended by Stats 2011 ch 285 (AB 1402),s 12, eff. 1/1/2012, op. 1/1/2012.

Amended by Stats 2011 ch 39 (AB 117),s 68, eff. 6/30/2011.

Amended by Stats 2011 ch 39 (AB 117),s 7, eff. 6/30/2011.

Amended by Stats 2011 ch 15 (AB 109),s 276, eff. 4/4/2011, but operative no earlier than October 1, 2011, and only upon creation of a community corrections grant program to assist in implementing this act and upon an appropriation to fund the grant program.

Amended by Stats 2010 ch 256 (AB 2263),s 2, eff. 1/1/2011.

Amended by Stats 2010 ch 178 (SB 1115),s 49, eff. 1/1/2011, op. 1/1/2012.

Added by Stats 2009 ch 171 (SB 150),s 2, eff. 1/1/2010.

Stats 2021 ch 699 (AB 333) provides that this act shall be known, and may be cited, as the STEP Forward Act of 2021.

Section 186.22a - Nuisance

(a) Every building or place used by members of a criminal street gang for the purpose of the commission of the offenses listed in subdivision (e) of Section 186.22 or any offense involving dangerous or deadly weapons, burglary, or rape, and every building or place wherein or upon which that criminal conduct by gang members takes place, is a nuisance which shall be enjoined, abated, and prevented, and for which damages may be recovered, whether it is a public or private nuisance.

(b) Any action for injunction or abatement filed pursuant to subdivision (a), including an action filed by the Attorney General, shall proceed according to the provisions of Article 3 (commencing with Section 11570) of Chapter 10 of Division 10 of the Health and Safety Code, except that all of the following shall apply:

(1) The court shall not assess a civil penalty against any person unless that person knew or should have known of the unlawful acts.

(2) No order of eviction or closure may be entered.

(3) All injunctions issued shall be limited to those necessary to protect the health and safety of the residents or the public or those necessary to prevent further criminal activity.

(4) Suit may not be filed until 30-day notice of the unlawful use or criminal conduct has been provided to the owner by mail, return receipt requested, postage prepaid, to the last known address.

(c) Whenever an injunction is issued pursuant to subdivision (a), or Section 3479 of the Civil Code, to abate gang activity constituting a nuisance, the Attorney General or any district attorney or any prosecuting city attorney may maintain an action for money damages on behalf of the community or neighborhood injured by that nuisance. Any money damages awarded shall be paid by or collected from assets of the criminal street gang or its members. Only members of the criminal street gang who created, maintained, or contributed to the creation or maintenance of the nuisance shall be personally liable for the payment of the damages awarded. In a civil action for damages brought pursuant to this subdivision, the Attorney General, district attorney, or city attorney may use, but is not limited to the use of, the testimony of experts to establish damages suffered by the community or neighborhood injured by the nuisance. The damages recovered pursuant to this subdivision shall be deposited into a separate segregated fund for payment to the governing body of the city or county in whose political subdivision the community or neighborhood is located, and that governing body shall use those assets solely for the benefit of the community or neighborhood that has been injured by the nuisance.

(d) No nonprofit or charitable organization which is conducting its affairs with ordinary care or skill, and no governmental entity, shall be abated pursuant to subdivisions (a) and (b).

(e) Nothing in this chapter shall preclude any aggrieved person from seeking any other remedy provided by law.

(f)

(1) Any firearm, ammunition which may be used with the firearm, or any deadly or dangerous weapon which is owned or possessed by a member of a criminal street gang for the purpose of the commission of any of the offenses listed in subdivision (e) of Section 186.22, or the commission of any burglary or rape, may be confiscated by any law enforcement agency or peace officer.

(2) In those cases where a law enforcement agency believes that the return of the firearm, ammunition, or deadly weapon confiscated pursuant to this subdivision, is or will be used in criminal street gang activity or that the return of the item would be likely to result in endangering the safety of others, the law enforcement agency shall initiate a petition in the superior court to determine if the item confiscated should be returned or declared a nuisance.

(3) No firearm, ammunition, or deadly weapon shall be sold or destroyed unless reasonable notice is given to its lawful owner if his or her identity and address can be reasonably ascertained. The law enforcement agency shall inform the lawful owner, at that person's last known address by registered mail, that he or she has 30 days from the date of receipt of the notice to respond to the court clerk to confirm his or her desire for a hearing and that the failure to respond shall result in a default order forfeiting the confiscated firearm, ammunition, or deadly weapon as a nuisance.

(4) If the person requests a hearing, the court clerk shall set a hearing no later than 30 days from receipt of that request. The court clerk shall notify the person, the law enforcement agency involved, and the district attorney of the date, time, and place of the hearing.

(5) At the hearing, the burden of proof is upon the law enforcement agency or peace officer to show by a preponderance of the evidence that the seized item is or will be used in criminal street gang activity or that return of the item would be likely to result in endangering the safety of others. All returns of firearms shall be subject to Chapter 2 (commencing with Section 33850) of Division 11 of Title 4 of Part 6.

(6) If the person does not request a hearing within 30 days of the notice or the lawful owner cannot be ascertained, the law enforcement agency may file a petition that the confiscated firearm, ammunition, or deadly weapon be declared a nuisance. If the items are declared to be a nuisance, the law enforcement agency shall dispose of the items as provided in Sections 18000 and 18005.

Amended by Stats 2010 ch 178 (SB 1115),s 50, eff. 1/1/2011, op. 1/1/2012.

Amended by Stats 2008 ch 38 (SB 1126),s 1, eff. 6/25/2008.

Amended by Stats 2007 ch 34 (SB 271),s 1, eff. 1/1/2008.

Amended by Stats 2006 ch 901 (SB 1422),s 5.5, eff. 1/1/2007.

Section 186.23 - Inapplicability of chapter

This chapter does not apply to employees engaged in concerted activities for their mutual aid and protection, or the activities of labor organizations or their members or agents.

Added by Stats. 1988, Ch. 1256, Sec. 1. Effective September 26, 1988.

Section 186.24 - Severability

If any part or provision of this chapter, or the application thereof to any person or circumstance, is held invalid, the remainder of the chapter, including the application of that part or provision to other persons or circumstances, shall not be affected thereby and shall continue in full force and effect. To this end, the provisions of this chapter are severable.

Added by Stats. 1988, Ch. 1256, Sec. 1. Effective September 26, 1988.

Section 186.25 - Local regulation

Nothing in this chapter shall prevent a local governing body from adopting and enforcing laws consistent with this chapter relating to gangs and gang violence. Where local laws duplicate or supplement this chapter, this chapter shall be construed as providing alternative remedies and not as preempting the field.

Added by Stats. 1988, Ch. 1256, Sec. 1. Effective September 26, 1988.

Section 186.26 - Solicitation or recruitment

(a) Any person who solicits or recruits another to actively participate in a criminal street gang, as defined in subdivision (f) of Section 186.22, with the intent that the person solicited or recruited participate in a pattern of criminal street gang activity, as defined in subdivision (e) of Section 186.22, or with the intent that the person solicited or recruited promote, further, or assist in any felonious conduct by members of the criminal street gang, shall be punished by imprisonment in the state prison for 16 months, or two or three years.

(b) Any person who threatens another person with physical violence on two or more separate occasions within any 30-day period with the intent to coerce, induce, or solicit any person to actively participate in a criminal street gang, as defined in subdivision (f) of Section 186.22, shall be punished by imprisonment in the state prison for two, three, or four years.

(c) Any person who uses physical violence to coerce, induce, or solicit another person to actively participate in any criminal street gang, as defined in subdivision (f) of Section 186.22, or to prevent the person from leaving a criminal street gang, shall be punished by imprisonment in the state prison for three, four, or five years.

(d) If the person solicited, recruited, coerced, or threatened pursuant to subdivision (a), (b), or (c) is a minor, an additional term of three years shall be imposed in addition and consecutive to the penalty prescribed for a violation of any of these subdivisions.

(e) Nothing in this section shall be construed to limit prosecution under any other provision of law.

Amended by Stats 2011 ch 39 (AB 117),s 68, eff. 6/30/2011.

Amended by Stats 2011 ch 39 (AB 117),s 8, eff. 6/30/2011.

Amended by Stats 2011 ch 15 (AB 109),s 277, eff. 4/4/2011, but operative no earlier than October 1, 2011, and only upon creation of a community corrections grant program to assist in implementing this act and upon an appropriation to fund the grant program.

Amended by Stats 2001 ch 854 (SB 205), s 23, eff. 1/1/2002.

Section 186.28 - Knowingly supply sale or giving possession or control of firearm to another to commit felony

(a) Any person, corporation, or firm who shall knowingly supply, sell, or give possession or control of any firearm to another shall be punished by imprisonment pursuant to subdivision (h) of Section 1170, or in a county jail for a term not exceeding one year, or by a fine not exceeding one thousand dollars ($1,000), or by both that fine and imprisonment if all of the following apply:

    (1) The person, corporation, or firm has actual knowledge that the person will use the firearm to commit a felony described in subdivision (e) of Section 186.22, while actively participating in any criminal street gang, as defined in subdivision (f) of Section 186.22, the members of which engage in a pattern of criminal activity, as defined in subdivision (e) of Section 186.22.

    (2) The firearm is used to commit the felony.

    (3) A conviction for the felony violation under subdivision (e) of Section 186.22 has first been obtained of the person to whom the firearm was supplied, sold, or given possession or control pursuant to this section.

(b) This section shall only be applicable where the person is not convicted as a principal to the felony offense committed by the person to whom the firearm was supplied, sold, or given possession or control pursuant to this section.

Amended by Stats 2011 ch 39 (AB 117),s 68, eff. 6/30/2011.

Amended by Stats 2011 ch 15 (AB 109),s 278, eff. 4/4/2011, but operative no earlier than October 1, 2011, and only upon creation of a community corrections grant program to assist in implementing this act and upon an appropriation to fund the grant program.

Section 186.30 - Registration with chief of police

(a) Any person described in subdivision (b) shall register with the chief of police of the city in which he or she resides, or the sheriff of the county if he or she resides in an unincorporated area, within 10 days of release from custody or within 10 days of his or her arrival in any city, county, or city and county to reside there, whichever occurs first.

(b) Subdivision (a) shall apply to any person convicted in a criminal court or who has had a petition sustained in a juvenile court in this state for any of the following offenses:

    (1) Subdivision (a) of Section 186.22.

    (2) Any crime where the enhancement specified in subdivision (b) of Section 186.22 is found to be true.

    (3) Any crime that the court finds is gang related at the time of sentencing or disposition.

Added March 7, 2000, by initiative Proposition 21, Sec. 7.

Section 186.31 - Advisement of duty to register

At the time of sentencing in adult court, or at the time of the dispositional hearing in the juvenile court, the court shall inform any person subject to Section 186.30 of his or her duty to register pursuant to that section. This advisement shall be noted in the court minute order. The court clerk shall send a copy of the minute order to the law enforcement agency with jurisdiction for the last known address of the person subject to registration under Section 186.30. The parole officer or the probation officer assigned to that person shall verify that he or she has complied with the registration requirements of Section 186.30.

Added March 7, 2000, by initiative Proposition 21, Sec. 8.

Section 186.32 - Registration

(a) The registration required by Section 186.30 shall consist of the following:

    (1) Juvenile registration shall include the following:

        (A) The juvenile shall appear at the law enforcement agency with a parent or guardian.

        (B) The law enforcement agency shall serve the juvenile and the parent with a California Street Terrorism Enforcement and Prevention Act notification which shall include, where applicable, that the juvenile belongs to a gang whose members engage in or have engaged in a pattern of criminal gang activity as described in subdivision (e) of Section 186.22.

        (C) A written statement signed by the juvenile, giving any information that may be required by the law enforcement agency, shall be submitted to the law enforcement agency.

        (D) The fingerprints and current photograph of the juvenile shall be submitted to the law enforcement agency.

    (2) Adult registration shall include the following:

        (A) The adult shall appear at the law enforcement agency.

        (B) The law enforcement agency shall serve the adult with a California Street Terrorism Enforcement and Prevention Act notification which shall include, where applicable, that the adult belongs to a gang whose members engage in or have engaged in a pattern of criminal gang activity as described in subdivision (e) of Section 186.22.

        (C) A written statement, signed by the adult, giving any information that may be required by the law enforcement agency, shall be submitted to the law enforcement agency.

        (D) The fingerprints and current photograph of the adult shall be submitted to the law enforcement agency.

(b) Within 10 days of changing his or her residence address, any person subject to Section 186.30 shall inform, in writing, the law enforcement agency with whom he or she last registered of his or her new address. If his or her new residence address is located within the jurisdiction of a law enforcement agency other than the agency where he or she last registered, he or she shall register with the new law enforcement agency, in writing, within 10 days of the change of residence.

(c) All registration requirements set forth in this article shall terminate five years after the last imposition of a registration requirement pursuant to Section 186.30.

(d) The statements, photographs and fingerprints required under this section shall not be open to inspection by any person other than a regularly employed peace or other law enforcement officer.

(e) Nothing in this section or Section 186.30 or 186.31 shall preclude a court in its discretion from imposing the registration requirements as set forth in those sections in a gang-related crime.

Added March 7, 2000, by initiative Proposition 21, Sec. 9.

Section 186.33 - Failure to register

(a) Any person required to register pursuant to Section 186.30 who knowingly violates any of its provisions is guilty of a misdemeanor.

(b)

(1) Any person who knowingly fails to register pursuant to Section 186.30 and is subsequently convicted of, or any person for whom a petition is subsequently sustained for a violation of, any of the offenses specified in Section 186.30, shall be punished by an additional term of imprisonment in the state prison for 16 months, or two or three years. The court shall order imposition of the middle term unless there are circumstances in aggravation or mitigation. The court shall state its reasons for the enhancement choice on the record at the time of sentencing.

(2) The existence of any fact bringing a person under this subdivision shall be alleged in the information, indictment, or petition, and be either admitted by the defendant or minor in open court, or found to be true or not true by the trier of fact.

(c) This section shall become operative on January 1, 2022.

Amended by Stats 2016 ch 887 (SB 1016),s 4, eff. 1/1/2017.
Amended by Stats 2013 ch 508 (SB 463),s 4, eff. 1/1/2014.
Amended by Stats 2011 ch 361 (SB 576),s 4, eff. 9/29/2011.
Amended by Stats 2011 ch 39 (AB 117),s 68, eff. 6/30/2011.
Amended by Stats 2011 ch 39 (AB 117),s 10, eff. 6/30/2011.
Amended by Stats 2011 ch 15 (AB 109),s 280, eff. 4/4/2011, but operative no earlier than October 1, 2011, and only upon creation of a community corrections grant program to assist in implementing this act and upon an appropriation to fund the grant program.
Amended by Stats 2010 ch 256 (AB 2263),s 4, eff. 1/1/2011.
Added by Stats 2009 ch 171 (SB 150),s 4, eff. 1/1/2010.

Section 186.34 - Shared gang database; designation as gang member

(a) For purposes of this section and Sections 186.35 and 186.36, the following definitions apply:

(1) "Criminal street gang" means an ongoing organization, association, or group of three or more persons, whether formal or informal, having as one of its primary activities the commission of crimes enumerated in paragraphs (1) to (25), inclusive, and paragraphs (31) to (33), inclusive, of subdivision (e) of Section 186.22 who have a common identifying sign, symbol, or name, and whose members individually or collectively engage in or have engaged in a pattern of definable criminal activity.

(2) "Gang database" means any database accessed by a law enforcement agency that designates a person as a gang member or associate, or includes or points to information, including, but not limited to, fact-based or uncorroborated information, that reflects a designation of that person as a gang member or associate.

(3) "Law enforcement agency" means a governmental agency or a subunit of a governmental agency, and its authorized support staff and contractors, whose primary function is detection, investigation, or apprehension of criminal offenders, or whose primary duties include detention, pretrial release, posttrial release, correctional supervision, or the collection, storage, or dissemination of criminal history record information.

(4) "Shared gang database" means a gang database that is accessed by an agency or person outside of the agency that created the records that populate the database.

(b) Notwithstanding subdivision (a), the following are not subject to this section, or Sections 186.35 and 186.36:

(1) Databases that designate persons as gang members or associates using only criminal offender record information, as defined in Section 13102, or information collected pursuant to Section 186.30.

(2) Databases accessed solely by jail or custodial facility staff for classification or operational decisions in the administration of the facility.

(c)

(1) To the extent a local law enforcement agency elects to utilize a shared gang database prior to a local law enforcement agency designating a person as a suspected gang member, associate, or affiliate in a shared gang database, or submitting a document to the Attorney General's office for the purpose of designating a person in a shared gang database, or otherwise identifying the person in a shared gang database, the local law enforcement agency shall provide written notice to the person, and shall, if the person is under 18 years of age, provide written notice to the person and the person's parent or guardian, of the designation and the basis for the designation, unless providing that notification would compromise an active criminal investigation or compromise the health or safety of the minor.

(2) The notice described in paragraph (1) shall describe the process for the person, or, if the person is under 18 years of age, for the person's parent or guardian, or an attorney working on behalf of the person, to contest the designation of the person in the database. The notice shall also inform the person of the reason for the person's designation in the database.

(d)

(1)

(A) A person, or, if the person is under 18 years of age, the person's parent or guardian, or an attorney working on behalf of the person, may request information of any law enforcement agency as to whether the person is designated as a suspected gang member, associate, or affiliate in a shared gang database accessible by that law enforcement agency and the name of the law enforcement agency that made the designation. A request pursuant to this paragraph shall be in writing.

(B) If a person about whom information is requested pursuant to subparagraph (A) is designated as a suspected gang member, associate, or affiliate in a shared gang database by that law enforcement agency, the person making the request may also request information as to the basis for the designation for the purpose of contesting the designation as described in subdivision (e).

(2) The law enforcement agency shall provide information requested under paragraph (1), unless doing so would compromise an active criminal investigation or compromise the health or safety of the person if the person is under 18 years of age.

(3) The law enforcement agency shall respond to a valid request pursuant to paragraph (1) in writing to the person making the request within 30 calendar days of receipt of the request.

(e) Subsequent to the notice described in subdivision (c) or the law enforcement agency's response to an information request described in subdivision (d), the person designated or to be designated as a suspected gang member, associate, or affiliate, or the person's parent or guardian if the person is under 18 years of age, may submit written documentation to the local law enforcement agency contesting the designation. The local law enforcement agency shall review the documentation, and if the agency determines that the person is not a suspected gang member, associate, or affiliate, the agency shall remove the person from the shared gang database. The local law enforcement agency shall provide the person and, if the person is under 18 years of age, the person's parent or guardian, with written verification of the agency's decision within 30 days of submission of the written documentation contesting the designation. If the law enforcement agency denies the request for removal, the notice of its determination shall state the reason for the denial. If the law enforcement agency does not provide a verification of the agency's decision within the required 30-day period, the request to remove the person from the gang database shall be deemed denied. The person or, if the person is under 18 years of age, the person's parent or guardian may petition the court to review the law enforcement agency's denial of the request for removal and order the law enforcement agency to remove the person from the shared gang database pursuant to Section 186.35.

(f) Nothing in this section shall require a local law enforcement agency to disclose any information protected under Section 1040 or 1041 of the Evidence Code or any provision listed in Section 7920.505 of the Government Code.

Amended by Stats 2021 ch 615 (AB 474),s 331, eff. 1/1/2022, op. 1/1/2023.

Added by Stats 2017 ch 695 (AB 90),s 4, eff. 1/1/2018.

Section 186.35 - Contesting designation as gang member, suspected gang member, associate, or affiliate

(a) A person who is listed by a law enforcement agency in a shared gang database as a gang member, suspected gang member, associate, or affiliate and who has contested his or her designation pursuant to subdivision (e) of Section 186.34, may petition the court to review the law enforcement agency's denial of the request for removal and to order the law enforcement agency to remove the person from the shared gang database. The petition may be brought by the person or the person's attorney, or if the person is under 18 years of age, by his or her parent or guardian or an attorney on behalf of the parent or guardian.

(b) The petition shall be filed and served within 90 calendar days of the agency's mailing or personal service of the verification of the decision to deny the request for removal from the shared gang database or the date that the request is deemed denied under subdivision (e) of Section 186.34. A proceeding under this subdivision is not a criminal case. The petition shall be filed in either the superior court of the county in which the local law enforcement agency is located or, if the person resides in California, in the county in which the person resides. A copy of the petition shall be served on the agency in person or by first-class mail. Proof of service of the petition on the agency shall be filed in the superior court. For purposes of computing the 90-calendar-day period, Section 1013 of the Code of Civil Procedure shall be applicable.

(c) The evidentiary record for the court's determination of the petition shall be limited to the agency's statement of the basis of its designation made pursuant to subdivision (c) or (d) of Section 186.34, and the documentation provided to the agency by the person contesting the designation pursuant to subdivision (e) of Section 186.34.

(d) If, upon de novo review of the record and any arguments presented to the court, the court finds that the law enforcement agency has failed to establish the person's active gang membership, associate status, or affiliate status by clear and convincing evidence, the court shall order the law enforcement agency to remove the name of the person from the shared gang database.

(e) The fee for filing the petition is as provided in Section 70615 of the Government Code. The court shall notify the person of the appearance date by mail or personal delivery. The court shall retain the fee under Section 70615 of the Government Code regardless of the outcome of the petition. If the court finds in favor of the person, the amount of the fee shall be reimbursed to the person by the agency.

Added by Stats 2017 ch 695 (AB 90),s 6, eff. 1/1/2018.

Section 186.36 - Shared gang databases; CalGang database

(a) The Department of Justice is responsible for establishing regulations for shared gang databases. All shared gang databases shall comply with those regulations.

(b) The department shall administer and oversee the CalGang database. Commencing January 1, 2018, the CalGang Executive Board shall not administer or oversee the CalGang database.

(c) The department shall establish the Gang Database Technical Advisory Committee.

(d) Each appointee to the committee, regardless of the appointing authority, shall have the following characteristics:

(1) Substantial prior knowledge of issues related to gang intervention, suppression, or prevention efforts.

(2) Decisionmaking authority for, or direct access to those who have decisionmaking authority for, the agency or organization he or she represents.

(3) A willingness to serve on the committee and a commitment to contribute to the committee's work.

(e) The membership of the committee shall be as follows:

(1) The Attorney General, or his or her designee.

(2) The President of the California District Attorneys Association, or his or her designee.

(3) The President of the California Public Defenders Association, or his or her designee.

(4) A representative of organizations that specialize in gang violence intervention, appointed by the Senate Committee on Rules.

(5) A representative of organizations that provide immigration services, appointed by the Senate Committee on Rules.

(6) The President of the California Gang Investigators Association, or his or her designee.

(7) A representative of community organizations that specialize in civil or human rights, appointed by the Speaker of the Assembly.

(8) A person who has personal experience with a shared gang database as someone who is or was impacted by gang labeling, appointed by the Speaker of the Assembly.

(9) The chairperson of the California Gang Node Advisory Committee, or his or her designee.

(10) The President of the California Police Chiefs Association, or his or her designee.

(11) The President of the California State Sheriffs' Association, or his or her designee.

(f) The committee shall appoint a chairperson from among the members appointed pursuant to subdivision (e). The chairperson shall serve in that capacity at the pleasure of the committee.

(g) Each member of the committee who is appointed pursuant to this section shall serve without compensation.

(h) If a committee member is unable to adequately perform his or her duties, he or she is subject to removal from the board by a majority vote of the full committee.

(i) A vacancy on the committee as a result of the removal of a member shall be filled by the appointing authority of the removed member within 30 days of the vacancy.

(j) Committee meetings are subject to the Bagley-Keene Open Meeting Act (Article 9 (commencing with Section 11120) of Chapter 1 of Part 1 of Division 3 of Title 2 of the Government Code).

(k) The department, with the advice of the committee, shall promulgate regulations governing the use, operation, and oversight of shared gang databases. The regulations issued by the department shall, at minimum, ensure the following:

(1) The system integrity of a shared gang database.

(2) All law enforcement agency and criminal justice agency personnel who access a shared gang database undergo comprehensive and standardized training on the use of shared gang databases and related policies and procedures.

(3) Proper criteria are established for supervisory reviews of all database entries and regular reviews of records entered into a shared gang database.

(4) Reasonable measures are taken to locate equipment related to the operation of a shared gang database in a secure area in order to preclude access by unauthorized personnel.

(5) Law enforcement agencies and criminal justice agencies notify the department of any missing equipment that could potentially compromise a shared gang database.

(6) Personnel authorized to access a shared gang database are limited to sworn law enforcement personnel, nonsworn law enforcement support personnel, or noncriminal justice technical or maintenance personnel, including information technology and information security staff and contract employees, who have been subject to character or security clearance and who have received approved training.

(7) Any records contained in a shared gang database are not disclosed for employment or military screening purposes.

(8) Any records contained in a shared gang database are not disclosed for purposes of enforcing federal immigration law, unless required by state or federal statute or regulation.

(9) The committee does not discuss or access individual records contained in a shared gang database.

(l) The regulations issued by the department shall include, but not be limited to, establishing the following:

(1) Policies and procedures for entering, reviewing, and purging documentation.

(2) Criteria for designating a person as a gang member or associate that are unambiguous, not overbroad, and consistent with empirical research on gangs and gang membership.

(3) Retention periods for information about a person in a shared gang database that is consistent with empirical research on the duration of gang membership.

(4) Criteria for designating an organization as a criminal street gang and retention periods for information about criminal street gangs.

(5) Policies and procedures for notice to a person in a shared gang database. This includes policies and procedures for when notification would compromise an active criminal investigation or the health or safety of a minor.

(6) Policies and procedures for responding to an information request, a request for removal, or a petition for removal under Sections 186.34 and 186.35, respectively. This includes policies and procedures for a request or petition that could compromise an active criminal investigation or the health or safety of a minor.

(7) Policies and procedures for sharing information from a shared gang database with a federal agency, multistate agency, or agency of another state that is otherwise denied access. This includes sharing of information with a partner in a joint task force.

(8) Implementation of supervisory review procedures and periodic record reviews by law enforcement agencies and criminal justice agencies, and reporting of the results of those reviews to the department.

(m) Shared gang databases shall be used and operated in compliance with all applicable state and federal regulations, statutes, and guidelines. These include Part 23 of Title 28 of the Code of Federal Regulations and the department's Model Standards and Procedures for Maintaining Criminal Intelligence Files and Criminal Intelligence Operational Activities.

(n) The department, with the advice of the committee, no later than January 1, 2020, shall promulgate regulations to provide for periodic audits of each CalGang node and user agency to ensure the accuracy, reliability, and proper use of the CalGang database. The department shall mandate the purge of any information for which a user agency cannot establish adequate support.

(o) The department, with the advice of the committee, shall develop and implement standardized periodic training for everyone with access to the CalGang database.

(p) Commencing February 15, 2018, and annually on February 15 thereafter, the department shall publish an annual report on the CalGang database.

(1) The report shall include, in a format developed by the department, that contains, by ZIP Code, referring agency, race, gender, and age, the following information for each user agency:

    (A) The number of persons included in the CalGang database on the day of reporting.

    (B) The number of persons added to the CalGang database during the immediately preceding 12 months.

    (C) The number of requests for removal of information about a person from the CalGang database pursuant to Section 186.34 received during the immediately preceding 12 months.

    (D) The number of requests for removal of information about a person from the CalGang database pursuant to Section 186.34 that were granted during the immediately preceding 12 months.

    (E) The number of petitions for removal of information about a person from the CalGang database pursuant to Section 186.35 adjudicated in the immediately preceding 12 months, including their dispositions.

    (F) The number of persons whose information was removed from the CalGang database due to the expiration of a retention period during the immediately preceding 12 months.

    (G) The number of times an agency did not provide notice or documentation described in Section 186.34 because providing that notice or documentation would compromise an active criminal investigation, in the immediately preceding 12 months.

    (H) The number of times an agency did not provide notice or documentation described in Section 186.34 because providing that notice or documentation would compromise the health or safety of the designated minor, in the immediately preceding 12 months.

    (2) The report shall include the results from each user agency's periodic audit conducted pursuant to subdivision (n).

    (3) The department shall post the report on the department's Internet Web site.

    (4) The department shall invite and assess public comments following the report's release, and each report shall summarize public comments received on prior reports and the actions taken in response to comments.

(q) The department shall instruct all user agencies to review the records of criminal street gang members entered into a shared gang database to ensure the existence of proper support for each criterion for entry in the shared gang database.

(r)

    (1) The department shall instruct each CalGang node agency to purge from a shared gang database any record of a person entered into the database designated as a suspected gang member, associate, or affiliate that does not meet criteria for entry or whose entry was based upon the following criteria: jail classification, frequenting gang neighborhoods, or on the basis of an untested informant. Unsupported criteria shall be purged and the records of a person shall be purged if the remaining criteria are not sufficient to support the person's designation.

    (2) After the purge is completed, the shared gang database shall be examined using a statistically valid sample, pursuant to professional auditing standards to ensure that all fields in the database are accurate.

(s)

    (1) Commencing January 1, 2018, any shared gang database operated by law enforcement in California including, but not limited to, the CalGang database, shall be under a moratorium. During the moratorium, data shall not be added to the database. Data in the database shall not be accessed by participating agencies or shared with other entities. The moratorium on a shared gang database shall not be lifted until the Attorney General certifies that the purge required in subdivision (r) has been completed. After the purge has been completed and before the department adopts the regulations required by this section, new data may be entered, provided the new data meets the criteria established by the conditions of the purge.

    (2) The department shall not use regulations developed pursuant to this section to invalidate data entries entered prior to the adoption of those regulations.

(t) The department shall be responsible for overseeing shared gang database system discipline and conformity with all applicable state and federal regulations, statutes, and guidelines.

(u) The department may enforce a violation of a state or federal law or regulation with respect to a shared gang database, or a violation of regulation, policy, or procedure established by the department pursuant to this title by any of the following methods:

    (1) Letter of censure.

    (2) Temporary suspension of access privileges to the shared gang database system.

    (3) Revocation of access privileges to the shared gang database system.

(v) The department shall temporarily suspend access to a shared gang database system or revoke access to a shared gang database system for any individual who shares information from a shared gang database for employment or military screening purposes.

(w) The department shall temporarily suspend access to a shared gang database system or revoke access to a shared gang database system for an individual who shares information from a shared gang database for federal immigration law purposes, unless required by state or federal statute or regulation.

(x) The department shall ensure that the shared gang database user account of an individual is disabled if the individual no longer has a need or right to access a shared gang database because he or she has separated from his or her employment with a user agency or for another reason.

Added by Stats 2017 ch 695 (AB 90),s 7, eff. 1/1/2018.

Title 8 - OF CRIMES AGAINST THE PERSON

Chapter 1 - HOMICIDE

Section 187 - Murder

(a) Murder is the unlawful killing of a human being, or a fetus, with malice aforethought.

(b) This section shall not apply to any person who commits an act that results in the death of a fetus if any of the following apply:

    (1) The act complied with the former Therapeutic Abortion Act (Article 2 (commencing with Section 123400) of Chapter 2 of Part 2 of Division 106 of the Health and Safety Code) or the Reproductive Privacy Act (Article 2.5 (commencing with Section 123460) of Chapter 2 of Part 2 of Division 106 of the Health and Safety Code).

(2) The act was committed by a holder of a physician's and surgeon's certificate, as defined in the Business and Professions Code, in a case where, to a medical certainty, the result of childbirth would be death of the person pregnant with the fetus or where the pregnant person's death from childbirth, although not medically certain, would be substantially certain or more likely than not.

(3) It was an act or omission by the person pregnant with the fetus or was solicited, aided, abetted, or consented to by the person pregnant with the fetus.

(c) Subdivision (b) shall not be construed to prohibit the prosecution of any person under any other provision of law.

Amended by Stats 2023 ch 260 (SB 345),s 14, eff. 1/1/2024.

Amended by Stats. 1996, Ch. 1023, Sec. 385. Effective September 29, 1996.

Section 188 - Malice

(a) For purposes of Section 187, malice may be express or implied.

(1) Malice is express when there is manifested a deliberate intention to unlawfully take away the life of a fellow creature.

(2) Malice is implied when no considerable provocation appears, or when the circumstances attending the killing show an abandoned and malignant heart.

(3) Except as stated in subdivision (e) of Section 189, in order to be convicted of murder, a principal in a crime shall act with malice aforethought. Malice shall not be imputed to a person based solely on his or her participation in a crime.

(b) If it is shown that the killing resulted from an intentional act with express or implied malice, as defined in subdivision (a), no other mental state need be shown to establish the mental state of malice aforethought. Neither an awareness of the obligation to act within the general body of laws regulating society nor acting despite that awareness is included within the definition of malice.

Amended by Stats 2018 ch 1015 (SB 1437),s 2, eff. 1/1/2019.

Section 189 - Murder of the first degree

(a) All murder that is perpetrated by means of a destructive device or explosive, a weapon of mass destruction, knowing use of ammunition designed primarily to penetrate metal or armor, poison, lying in wait, torture, or by any other kind of willful, deliberate, and premeditated killing, or that is committed in the perpetration of, or attempt to perpetrate, arson, rape, carjacking, robbery, burglary, mayhem, kidnapping, train wrecking, or any act punishable under Section 206, 286, 287, 288, or 289, or former Section 288a, or murder that is perpetrated by means of discharging a firearm from a motor vehicle, intentionally at another person outside of the vehicle with the intent to inflict death, is murder of the first degree.

(b) All other kinds of murders are of the second degree.

(c) As used in this section, the following definitions apply:

(1) "Destructive device" has the same meaning as in Section 16460.

(2) "Explosive" has the same meaning as in Section 12000 of the Health and Safety Code.

(3) "Weapon of mass destruction" means any item defined in Section 11417.

(d) To prove the killing was "deliberate and premeditated," it is not necessary to prove the defendant maturely and meaningfully reflected upon the gravity of the defendant's act.

(e) A participant in the perpetration or attempted perpetration of a felony listed in subdivision (a) in which a death occurs is liable for murder only if one of the following is proven:

(1) The person was the actual killer.

(2) The person was not the actual killer, but, with the intent to kill, aided, abetted, counseled, commanded, induced, solicited, requested, or assisted the actual killer in the commission of murder in the first degree.

(3) The person was a major participant in the underlying felony and acted with reckless indifference to human life, as described in subdivision (d) of Section 190.2.

(f) Subdivision (e) does not apply to a defendant when the victim is a peace officer who was killed while in the course of the peace officer's duties, where the defendant knew or reasonably should have known that the victim was a peace officer engaged in the performance of the peace officer's duties.

Amended by Stats 2019 ch 497 (AB 991),s 192, eff. 1/1/2020.

Amended by Stats 2018 ch 1015 (SB 1437),s 3, eff. 1/1/2019.

Amended by Stats 2018 ch 423 (SB 1494),s 42, eff. 1/1/2019.

Amended by Stats 2010 ch 178 (SB 1115),s 51, eff. 1/1/2011, op. 1/1/2012.

Amended by Stats 2002 ch 606 (AB 1838), s 1, eff. 9/16/2002.

Previously Amended October 10, 1999 (Bill Number: AB 1547) (Chapter 694).

Note: This section was amended on June 5, 1990, by initiative Prop. 115.

Section 189.1 - Willful killing of peace officer

(a) The Legislature finds and declares that all unlawful killings that are willful, deliberate, and premeditated and in which the victim was a peace officer, as defined in Section 830, who was killed while engaged in the performance of his or her duties, where the defendant knew, or reasonably should have known, that the victim was a peace officer engaged in the performance of his or her duties, are considered murder of the first degree for all purposes, including the gravity of the offense and the support of the survivors.

(b) This section is declarative of existing law.

Added by Stats 2017 ch 214 (AB 1459),s 2, eff. 1/1/2018.

Section 189.5 - Burden of proof

(a) Upon a trial for murder, the commission of the homicide by the defendant being proved, the burden of proving circumstances of mitigation, or that justify or excuse it, devolves upon the defendant, unless the proof on the part of the prosecution tends to show that the crime committed only amounts to manslaughter, or that the defendant was justifiable or excusable.

(b) Nothing in this section shall apply to or affect any proceeding under Section 190.3 or 190.4.

Added by Stats. 1989, Ch. 897, Sec. 16.

Section 190 - Punishment

(a) Every person guilty of murder in the first degree shall be punished by death, imprisonment in the state prison for life without the possibility of parole, or imprisonment in the state prison for a term of 25 years to life. The penalty to be applied shall be determined as provided in Sections 190.1, 190.2, 190.3, 190.4, and 190.5. Except as provided in subdivision (b), (c), or (d), every person guilty of murder in the second degree shall be punished by imprisonment in the state prison for a term of 15 years to life.

(b) Except as provided in subdivision (c), every person guilty of murder in the second degree shall be punished by imprisonment in the state prison for a term of 25 years to life if the victim was a peace officer, as defined in subdivision (a) of Section 830.1, subdivision (a), (b), or (c) of Section 830.2, subdivision (a) of Section 830.33, or Section 830.5, who was killed while engaged in the performance of his or her duties, and the defendant knew, or reasonably should have known, that the victim was a peace officer engaged in the performance of his or her duties.

(c) Every person guilty of murder in the second degree shall be punished by imprisonment in the state prison for a term of life without the possibility of parole if the victim was a peace officer, as defined in subdivision (a) of Section 830.1, subdivision (a), (b), or (c) of Section 830.2, subdivision (a) of Section 830.33, or Section 830.5, who was killed while engaged in the performance of his or her duties, and the defendant knew, or reasonably should have known, that the victim was a peace officer engaged in the performance of his or her duties, and any of the following facts has been charged and found true:

(1) The defendant specifically intended to kill the peace officer.

(2) The defendant specifically intended to inflict great bodily injury, as defined in Section 12022.7, on a peace officer.

(3) The defendant personally used a dangerous or deadly weapon in the commission of the offense, in violation of subdivision (b) of Section 12022.

(4) The defendant personally used a firearm in the commission of the offense, in violation of Section 12022.5.

(d) Every person guilty of murder in the second degree shall be punished by imprisonment in the state prison for a term of 20 years to life if the killing was perpetrated by means of shooting a firearm from a motor vehicle, intentionally at another person outside of the vehicle with the intent to inflict great bodily injury.

(e) Article 2.5 (commencing with Section 2930) of Chapter 7 of Title 1 of Part 3 shall not apply to reduce any minimum term of a sentence imposed pursuant to this section. A person sentenced pursuant to this section shall not be released on parole prior to serving the minimum term of confinement prescribed by this section.

19 (2000).

Prior : Added Nov. 7, 1978, by initiative Prop. 7; amended June 7, 1988, by Prop. 67 (from Stats. 1987, Ch. 1006); amended June 7, 1994, by Prop. 179 (from Stats. 1993, Ch. 609); amended June 2, 1998, by Prop. 222 (from Stats. 1997, Ch. 413, Sec. 1, which incorporated Stats. 1996, Ch. 598).

Section 190.03 - Punishment for first-degree murder that is hate crime

(a) A person who commits first-degree murder that is a hate crime shall be punished by imprisonment in the state prison for life without the possibility of parole.

(b) The term authorized by subdivision (a) shall not apply unless the allegation is charged in the accusatory pleading and admitted by the defendant or found true by the trier of fact. The court shall not strike the allegation, except in the interest of justice, in which case the court shall state its reasons in writing for striking the allegation.

(c) For the purpose of this section, "hate crime" has the same meaning as in Section 422.55.

(d) Nothing in this section shall be construed to prevent punishment instead pursuant to any other provision of law that imposes a greater or more severe punishment.

Amended by Stats 2004 ch 700 (SB 1234), s 5, eff. 1/1/2005.

EFFECTIVE 1/1/2000. Amended September 29, 1999 (Bill Number: AB 208) (Chapter 566).

Section 190.05 - Penalty for defendant found guilty of second-degree murder who has served prior prison term for murder

(a) The penalty for a defendant found guilty of murder in the second degree, who has served a prior prison term for murder in the first or second degree, shall be confinement in the state prison for a term of life without the possibility of parole or confinement in the state prison for a term of 15 years to life. For purposes of this section, a prior prison term for murder of the first or second degree is that time period in which a defendant has spent actually incarcerated for his or her offense prior to release on parole.

(b) A prior prison term for murder for purposes of this section includes either of the following:

(1) A prison term served in any state prison or federal penal institution, including confinement in a hospital or other institution or facility credited as service of prison time in the jurisdiction of confinement, as punishment for the commission of an offense which includes all of the elements of murder in the first or second degree as defined under California law.

(2) Incarceration at a facility operated by the Youth Authority for murder of the first or second degree when the person was subject to the custody, control, and discipline of the Director of Corrections.

(c) The fact of a prior prison term for murder in the first or second degree shall be alleged in the accusatory pleading, and either admitted by the defendant in open court, or found to be true by the jury trying the issue of guilt or by the court where guilt is established by a plea of guilty or nolo contendere or by trial by the court sitting without a jury.

(d) In case of a reasonable doubt as to whether the defendant served a prior prison term for murder in the first or second degree, the defendant is entitled to a finding that the allegation is not true.

(e) If the trier of fact finds that the defendant has served a prior prison term for murder in the first or second degree, there shall be a separate penalty hearing before the same trier of fact, except as provided in subdivision (f).

(f) If the defendant was convicted by the court sitting without a jury, the trier of fact at the penalty hearing shall be a jury unless a jury is waived by the defendant and the people, in which case the trier of fact shall be the court. If the defendant was convicted by a plea of guilty or nolo contendere, the trier of fact shall be a jury unless a jury is waived by the defendant and the people. If the trier of fact is a jury and has been unable to reach a unanimous verdict as to what the penalty shall be, the court shall dismiss the jury and shall order a new jury impaneled to try the issue as to what the penalty shall be. If the new jury is unable to reach a unanimous verdict as to what the penalty shall be, the court in its discretion shall either order a new jury or impose a punishment of confinement in the state prison for a term of 15 years to life.

(g) Evidence presented at any prior phase of the trial, including any proceeding under a plea of not guilty by reason of insanity pursuant to Section 1026, shall be considered at any subsequent phase of the trial, if the trier of fact of the prior phase is the same trier of fact at the subsequent phase.

(h) In the proceeding on the question of penalty, evidence may be presented by both the people and the defendant as to any matter relevant to aggravation, mitigation, and sentence, including, but not limited to, the nature and circumstances of the present offense, any prior felony conviction or convictions whether or not such conviction or convictions involved a crime of violence, the presence or absence of other criminal activity by the defendant which involved the use or attempted use of force or violence or which involved the express or implied threat to use force or violence, and the defendant's character, background, history, mental condition, and physical condition. However, no evidence shall be admitted regarding other criminal activity by the defendant which did not involve the use or attempted use of force or violence or which did not involve the express or implied threat to use force or violence. As used in this section, criminal activity does not require a conviction.

However, in no event shall evidence of prior criminal activity be admitted for an offense for which the defendant was prosecuted and acquitted. The restriction on the use of this evidence is intended to apply only to proceedings pursuant to this section and is not intended to affect statutory or decisional law allowing such evidence to be used in any other proceedings.

Except for evidence in proof of the offense or the prior prison term for murder of the first or second degree which subjects a defendant to the punishment of life without the possibility of parole, no evidence may be presented by the prosecution in aggravation unless notice of the evidence to be introduced has been given to the defendant within a reasonable period of time as determined by the court, prior to trial. Evidence may be introduced without such notice in rebuttal to evidence introduced by the defendant in mitigation.

In determining the penalty, the trier of fact shall take into account any of the following factors if relevant:

(1) The circumstances of the crime of which the defendant was convicted in the present proceeding and the existence of the prior prison term for murder.

(2) The presence or absence of criminal activity by the defendant which involved the use or attempted use of force or violence or the express or implied threat to use force or violence.

(3) The presence or absence of any prior felony conviction.

(4) Whether or not the offense was committed while the defendant was under the influence of extreme mental or emotional disturbance.

(5) Whether or not the victim was a participant in the defendant's homicidal conduct or consented to the homicidal act.

(6) Whether or not the offense was committed under circumstances which the defendant reasonably believed to be a moral justification or extenuation for his or her conduct.

(7) Whether or not the defendant acted under extreme duress or under the substantial domination of another person.

(8) Whether or not at the time of the offense the ability of the defendant to appreciate the criminality of his or her conduct or to conform his or her conduct to the requirements of law was impaired as a result of mental disease or defect, or the effects of intoxication.

(9) The age of the defendant at the time of the crime.

(10) Whether or not the defendant was an accomplice to the offense and his or her participation in the commission of the offense was relatively minor.

(11) Any other circumstance which extenuates the gravity of the crime even though it is not a legal excuse for the crime. After having heard and received all of the evidence, and after having heard and considered the arguments of counsel, the trier of fact shall consider, take into account, and be guided by the aggravating and mitigating circumstances referred to in this section, and shall impose a sentence of life without the possibility of parole if the trier of fact concludes that the aggravating circumstances outweigh the mitigating circumstances. If the trier of fact determines that the mitigating circumstances outweigh the aggravating circumstances, the trier of fact shall impose a sentence of confinement in the state prison for 15 years to life.

(i) Nothing in this section shall be construed to prohibit the charging of finding of any special circumstance pursuant to Sections 190.1, 190.2, 190.3, 190.4, and 190.5.

Added by Stats. 1985, Ch. 1510, Sec. 1.

Section 190.1 - Separate phases for death penalty case

A case in which the death penalty may be imposed pursuant to this chapter shall be tried in separate phases as follows:

(a) The question of the defendant's guilt shall be first determined. If the trier of fact finds the defendant guilty of first degree murder, it shall at the same time determine the truth of all special circumstances charged as enumerated in Section 190.2 except for a special circumstance charged pursuant to paragraph (2) of subdivision (a) of Section 190.2 where it is alleged that the defendant had been convicted in a prior proceeding of the offense of murder in the first or second degree.

(b) If the defendant is found guilty of first degree murder and one of the special circumstances is charged pursuant to paragraph (2) of subdivision (a) of Section 190.2 which charges that the defendant had been convicted in a prior proceeding of the offense of murder of the first or second degree, there shall thereupon be further proceedings on the question of the truth of such special circumstance.

(c) If the defendant is found guilty of first degree murder and one or more special circumstances as enumerated in Section 190.2 has been charged and found to be true, his sanity on any plea of not guilty by reason of insanity under Section 1026 shall be determined as provided in Section 190.4. If he is found to be sane, there shall thereupon be further proceedings on the question of the penalty to be imposed. Such proceedings shall be conducted in accordance with the provisions of Section 190.3 and 190.4.

Repealed and added November 7, 1978, by initiative Proposition 7, Sec. 4.

Section 190.2 - Penalty for defendant found guilty of first-degree murder with special circumstance

(a) The penalty for a defendant who is found guilty of murder in the first degree is death or imprisonment in the state prison for life without the possibility of parole if one or more of the following special circumstances has been found under Section 190.4 to be true:

(1) The murder was intentional and carried out for financial gain.

(2) The defendant was convicted previously of murder in the first or second degree. For the purpose of this paragraph, an offense committed in another jurisdiction, which if committed in California would be punishable as first or second degree murder, shall be deemed murder in the first or second degree.

(3) The defendant, in this proceeding, has been convicted of more than one offense of murder in the first or second degree.

(4) The murder was committed by means of a destructive device, bomb, or explosive planted, hidden, or concealed in any place, area, dwelling, building, or structure, and the defendant knew, or reasonably should have known, that his or her act or acts would create a great risk of death to one or more human beings.

(5) The murder was committed for the purpose of avoiding or preventing a lawful arrest, or perfecting or attempting to perfect, an escape from lawful custody.

(6) The murder was committed by means of a destructive device, bomb, or explosive that the defendant mailed or delivered, attempted to mail or deliver, or caused to be mailed or delivered, and the defendant knew, or reasonably should have known, that his or her act or acts would create a great risk of death to one or more human beings.

(7) The victim was a peace officer, as defined in Section 830.1, 830.2, 830.3, 830.31, 830.32, 830.33, 830.34, 830.35, 830.36, 830.37, 830.4, 830.5, 830.6, 830.10, 830.11, or 830.12, who, while engaged in the course of the performance of his or her duties, was intentionally killed, and the defendant knew, or reasonably should have known, that the victim was a peace officer engaged in the performance of his or her duties; or the victim was a peace officer, as defined in the above-enumerated sections, or a former peace officer under any of those sections, and was intentionally killed in retaliation for the performance of his or her official duties.

(8) The victim was a federal law enforcement officer or agent who, while engaged in the course of the performance of his or her duties, was intentionally killed, and the defendant knew, or reasonably should have known, that the victim was a federal law enforcement officer or agent engaged in the performance of his or her duties; or the victim was a federal law enforcement officer or agent, and was intentionally killed in retaliation for the performance of his or her official duties.

(9) The victim was a firefighter, as defined in Section 245.1, who, while engaged in the course of the performance of his or her duties, was intentionally killed, and the defendant knew, or reasonably should have known, that the victim was a firefighter engaged in the performance of his or her duties.

(10) The victim was a witness to a crime who was intentionally killed for the purpose of preventing his or her testimony in any criminal or juvenile proceeding, and the killing was not committed during the commission or attempted commission, of the crime to which he or she was a witness; or the victim was a witness to a crime and was intentionally killed in retaliation for his or her testimony in any criminal or juvenile proceeding. As used in this paragraph, "juvenile proceeding" means a proceeding brought pursuant to Section 602 or 707 of the Welfare and Institutions Code.

(11) The victim was a prosecutor or assistant prosecutor or a former prosecutor or assistant prosecutor of any local or state prosecutor's office in this or any other state, or of a federal prosecutor's office, and the murder was intentionally carried out in retaliation for, or to prevent the performance of, the victim's official duties.

(12) The victim was a judge or former judge of any court of record in the local, state, or federal system in this or any other state, and the murder was intentionally carried out in retaliation for, or to prevent the performance of, the victim's official duties.

(13) The victim was an elected or appointed official or former official of the federal government, or of any local or state government of this or any other state, and the killing was intentionally carried out in retaliation for, or to prevent the performance of, the victim's official duties.

(14) The murder was especially heinous, atrocious, or cruel, manifesting exceptional depravity. As used in this section, the phrase "especially heinous, atrocious, or cruel, manifesting exceptional depravity" means a conscienceless or pitiless crime that is unnecessarily torturous to the victim.

(15) The defendant intentionally killed the victim by means of lying in wait.

(16) The victim was intentionally killed because of his or her race, color, religion, nationality, or country of origin.

(17) The murder was committed while the defendant was engaged in, or was an accomplice in, the commission of, attempted commission of, or the immediate flight after committing, or attempting to commit, the following felonies:

(A) Robbery in violation of Section 211 or 212.5.

(B) Kidnapping in violation of Section 207, 209, or 209.5.

(C) Rape in violation of Section 261.

(D) Sodomy in violation of Section 286.

(E) The performance of a lewd or lascivious act upon the person of a child under the age of 14 years in violation of Section 288.

(F) Oral copulation in violation of Section 287 or former Section 288a.

(G) Burglary in the first or second degree in violation of Section 460.

(H) Arson in violation of subdivision (b) of Section 451.

(I) Train wrecking in violation of Section 219.

(J) Mayhem in violation of Section 203.

(K) Rape by instrument in violation of Section 289.

(L) Carjacking, as defined in Section 215.

(M) To prove the special circumstances of kidnapping in subparagraph (B), or arson in subparagraph (H), if there is specific intent to kill, it is only required that there be proof of the elements of those felonies. If so established, those two special circumstances are proven even if the felony of kidnapping or arson is committed primarily or solely for the purpose of facilitating the murder.

(18) The murder was intentional and involved the infliction of torture.

(19) The defendant intentionally killed the victim by the administration of poison.

(20) The victim was a juror in any court of record in the local, state, or federal system in this or any other state, and the murder was intentionally carried out in retaliation for, or to prevent the performance of, the victim's official duties.

(21) The murder was intentional and perpetrated by means of discharging a firearm from a motor vehicle, intentionally at another person or persons outside the vehicle with the intent to inflict death. For purposes of this paragraph, "motor vehicle" means any vehicle as defined in Section 415 of the Vehicle Code.

(22) The defendant intentionally killed the victim while the defendant was an active participant in a criminal street gang, as defined in subdivision (f) of Section 186.22, and the murder was carried out to further the activities of the criminal street gang.

(b) Unless an intent to kill is specifically required under subdivision (a) for a special circumstance enumerated therein, an actual killer, as to whom the special circumstance has been found to be true under Section 190.4, need not have had any intent to kill at the time of the commission of the offense which is the basis of the special circumstance in order to suffer death or confinement in the state prison for life without the possibility of parole.

(c) Every person, not the actual killer, who, with the intent to kill, aids, abets, counsels, commands, induces, solicits, requests, or assists any actor in the commission of murder in the first degree shall be punished by death or imprisonment in the state prison for life without the possibility of parole if one or more of the special circumstances enumerated in subdivision (a) has been found to be true under Section 190.4.

(d) Notwithstanding subdivision (c), every person, not the actual killer, who, with reckless indifference to human life and as a major participant, aids, abets, counsels, commands, induces, solicits, requests, or assists in the commission of a felony enumerated in paragraph (17) of subdivision (a) which results in the death of some person or persons, and who is found guilty of murder in the first degree therefor, shall be punished by death or imprisonment in the state prison for life without the possibility of parole if a special circumstance enumerated in paragraph (17) of subdivision (a) has been found to be true under Section 190.4. The penalty shall be determined as provided in this section and Sections 190.1, 190.3, 190.4, and 190.5.

Amended by Stats 2018 ch 423 (SB 1494),s 43, eff. 1/1/2019.

18 (2000).

Prior : Added Nov. 7, 1978, by initiative Prop. 7; amended June 5, 1990, by Prop. 114 (from Stats. 1989, Ch. 1165) and by initiative Prop. 115; amended March 26, 1996, by Prop. 196 (from Stats. 1995, Ch. 478, Sec. 2).

Section 190.25 - Penalty for defendant found guilty of first-degree murder with special circumstance related to transportation

(a) The penalty for a defendant found guilty of murder in the first degree shall be confinement in state prison for a term of life without the possibility of parole in any case in which any of the following special circumstances has been charged and specially found under Section 190.4, to be true: the victim was the operator or driver of a bus, taxicab, streetcar, cable car, trackless trolley, or other motor vehicle operated on land, including a vehicle operated on stationary rails or on a track or rail suspended in the air, used for the transportation of persons for hire, or the victim was a station agent or ticket agent for the entity providing such transportation, who, while engaged in the course of the performance of his or her duties was intentionally killed, and such defendant knew or reasonably should have known that such victim was the operator or driver of a bus, taxicab, streetcar, cable car, trackless trolley, or other motor vehicle operated on land, including a vehicle operated on stationary rails or on a track or rail suspended in the air, used for the transportation of persons for hire, or was a station agent or ticket agent for the entity providing such transportation, engaged in the performance of his or her duties.

(b) Every person whether or not the actual killer found guilty of intentionally aiding, abetting, counseling, commanding, inducing, soliciting, requesting, or assisting any actor in the commission of murder in the first degree shall suffer confinement in state prison for a term of life without the possibility of parole, in any case in which one or more of the special circumstances enumerated in subdivision (a) of this section has been charged and specially found under Section 190.4 to be true.

(c) Nothing in this section shall be construed to prohibit the charging or finding of any special circumstance pursuant to Sections 190.1, 190.2, 190.3, 190.4, and 190.5.

Added by Stats. 1982, Ch. 172, Sec. 1. Effective April 27, 1982.

Section 190.3 - Death penalty for defendant found guilty of first degree murder with special circumstance

If the defendant has been found guilty of murder in the first degree, and a special circumstance has been charged and found to be true, or if the defendant may be subject to the death penalty after having been found guilty of violating subdivision (a) of Section 1672 of the Military and Veterans Code or Sections 37, 128, 219, or 4500 of this code, the trier of fact shall determine whether the penalty shall be death or confinement in state prison for a term of life without the possibility of parole. In the proceedings on the question of penalty, evidence may be presented by both the people and the defendant as to any matter relevant to aggravation, mitigation, and sentence including, but not limited to, the nature and circumstances of the present offense, any prior felony conviction or convictions whether or not such conviction or convictions involved a crime of violence, the presence or absence of other criminal activity by the defendant which involved the use or attempted use of force or violence or which involved the express or implied threat to use force or violence, and the defendant's character, background, history, mental condition and physical condition.

However, no evidence shall be admitted regarding other criminal activity by the defendant which did not involve the use or attempted use of force or violence or which did not involve the express or implied threat to use force or violence. As used in this section, criminal activity does not require a conviction.

However, in no event shall evidence of prior criminal activity be admitted for an offense for which the defendant was prosecuted and acquitted. The restriction on the use of this evidence is intended to apply only to proceedings pursuant to this section and is not intended to affect statutory or decisional law allowing such evidence to be used in any other proceedings.

Except for evidence in proof of the offense or special circumstances which subject a defendant to the death penalty, no evidence may be presented by the prosecution in aggravation unless notice of the evidence to be introduced has been given to the defendant within a reasonable period of time as determined by the court, prior to trial. Evidence may be introduced without such notice in rebuttal to evidence introduced by the defendant in mitigation.

The trier of fact shall be instructed that a sentence of confinement to state prison for a term of life without the possibility of parole may in future after sentence is imposed, be commuted or modified to a sentence that includes the possibility of parole by the Governor of the State of California.

In determining the penalty, the trier of fact shall take into account any of the following factors if relevant:

(a) The circumstances of the crime of which the defendant was convicted in the present proceeding and the existence of any special circumstances found to be true pursuant to Section 190.1.

(b) The presence or absence of criminal activity by the defendant which involved the use or attempted use of force or violence or the express or implied threat to use force or violence.

(c) The presence or absence of any prior felony conviction.

(d) Whether or not the offense was committed while the defendant was under the influence of extreme mental or emotional disturbance.

(e) Whether or not the victim was a participant in the defendant's homicidal conduct or consented to the homicidal act.

(f) Whether or not the offense was committed under circumstances which the defendant reasonably believed to be a moral justification or extenuation for his conduct.

(g) Whether or not defendant acted under extreme duress or under the substantial domination of another person.

(h) Whether or not at the time of the offense the capacity of the defendant to appreciate the criminality of his conduct or to conform his conduct to the requirements of law was impaired as a result of mental disease or defect, or the affects of intoxication.

(i) The age of the defendant at the time of the crime.

(j) Whether or not the defendant was an accomplice to the offense and his participation in the commission of the offense was relatively minor.

(k) Any other circumstance which extenuates the gravity of the crime even though it is not a legal excuse for the crime. After having heard and received all of the evidence, and after having heard and considered the arguments of counsel, the trier of fact shall consider, take into account and be guided by the aggravating and mitigating circumstances referred to in this section, and shall impose a sentence of death if the trier of fact concludes that the aggravating circumstances outweigh the mitigating circumstances. If the trier of fact determines that the mitigating circumstances outweigh the aggravating circumstances the trier of fact shall impose a sentence of confinement in state prison for a term of life without the possibility of parole.

Repealed and added November 7, 1978, by initiative Proposition 7, Sec. 8.

Section 190.4 - Special circumstances

(a) Whenever special circumstances as enumerated in Section 190.2 are alleged and the trier of fact finds the defendant guilty of first degree murder, the trier of fact shall also make a special finding on the truth of each alleged special circumstance. The determination of the truth of any or all of the special circumstances shall be made by the trier of fact on the evidence presented at the trial or at the hearing held pursuant to Subdivision (b) of Section 190.1. In case of a reasonable doubt as to whether a special circumstance is true, the defendant is entitled to a finding that is not true. The trier of fact shall make a special finding that each special circumstance charged is either true or not true. Whenever a special circumstance requires proof of the commission or attempted commission of a crime, such crime shall be charged and proved pursuant to the general law applying to the trial and conviction of the crime.

If the defendant was convicted by the court sitting without a jury, the trier of fact shall be a jury unless a jury is waived by the defendant and by the people, in which case the trier of fact shall be the court. If the defendant was convicted by a plea of guilty, the trier of fact shall be a jury unless a jury is waived by the defendant and by the people.

If the trier of fact finds that any one or more of the special circumstances enumerated in Section 190.2 as charged is true, there shall be a separate penalty hearing, and neither the finding that any of the remaining special circumstances charged is not true, nor if the trier of fact is a jury, the inability of the jury to agree on the issue of the truth or untruth of any of the remaining special circumstances charged, shall prevent the holding of a separate penalty hearing.

In any case in which the defendant has been found guilty by a jury, and the jury has been unable to reach an unanimous verdict that one or more of the special circumstances charged are true, and does not reach a unanimous verdict that all the special circumstances charged are not true, the court shall dismiss the jury and shall order a new jury impaneled to try the issues, but the issue of guilt shall not be tried by such jury, nor shall such jury retry the issue of the truth of any of the special circumstances which were found by an unanimous verdict of the previous jury to be untrue. If such new jury is unable to reach the unanimous verdict that one or more of the special circumstances it is trying are true, the court shall dismiss the jury and in the court's discretion shall either order a new jury impaneled to try the issues the previous jury was unable to reach the unanimous verdict on, or impose a punishment of confinement in state prison for a term of 25 years.

(b) If defendant was convicted by the court sitting without a jury the trier of fact at the penalty hearing shall be a jury unless a jury is waived by the defendant and the people, in which case the trier of fact shall be the court. If the defendant was convicted by a plea of guilty, the trier of fact shall be a jury unless a jury is waived by the defendant and the people. If the trier of fact is a jury and has been unable to reach a unanimous verdict as to what the penalty shall be, the court shall dismiss the jury and shall order a new jury impaneled to try the issue as to what the penalty shall be. If such new jury is unable to reach a unanimous verdict as to what the penalty shall be, the court in its discretion shall either order a new jury or impose a punishment of confinement in state prison for a term of life without the possibility of parole.

(c) If the trier of fact which convicted the defendant of a crime for which he may be subject to the death penalty was a jury, the same jury shall consider any plea of not guilty by reason of insanity pursuant to Section 1026, the truth of any special circumstances which may be alleged, and the penalty to be applied, unless for good cause shown the court discharges that jury in which case a new jury shall be drawn. The court shall state facts in support of the finding of good cause upon the record and cause them to be entered into the minutes.

(d) In any case in which the defendant may be subject to the death penalty, evidence presented at any prior phase of the trial, including any proceeding under a plea of not guilty by reason of insanity pursuant to Section 1026 shall be considered an any subsequent phase of the trial, if the trier of fact of the prior phase is the same trier of fact at the subsequent phase.

(e) In every case in which the trier of fact has returned a verdict or finding imposing the death penalty, the defendant shall be deemed to have made an application for modification of such verdict or finding pursuant to Subdivision 7 of Section 11. In ruling on the application, the judge shall review the evidence, consider, take into account, and be guided by the aggravating and mitigating circumstances referred to in Section 190.3, and shall make a determination as to whether the jury's findings and verdicts that the aggravating circumstances outweigh the mitigating circumstances are contrary to law or the evidence presented. The judge shall state on the record the reasons for his findings. The judge shall set forth the reasons for his ruling on the application and direct that they be entered on the Clerk's minutes. The denial of the modification of the death penalty verdict pursuant to subdivision (7) of Section 1181 shall be reviewed on the defendant's automatic appeal pursuant to subdivision (b) of Section 1239. The granting of the application shall be reviewed on the People's appeal pursuant to paragraph (6).

Repealed and added November 7, 1978, by initiative Proposition 7, Sec. 10.

Section 190.41 - Proof of corpus delicti of felony-based special circumstance

Notwithstanding Section 190.4 or any other provision of law, the corpus delicti of a felony-based special circumstance enumerated in paragraph (17) of subdivision (a) of Section 190.2 need not be proved independently of a defendant's extrajudicial statement.

Added June 5, 1990, by initiative Proposition 115, Sec. 11.

Section 190.5 - Death penalty prohibited for person under age of 18 at time of commission of crime

(a) Notwithstanding any other provision of law, the death penalty shall not be imposed upon any person who is under the age of 18 at the time of the commission of the crime. The burden of proof as to the age of such person shall be upon the defendant.

(b) The penalty for a defendant found guilty of murder in the first degree, in any case in which one or more special circumstances enumerated in Section 190.2 or 190.25 has been found to be true under Section 190.4, who was 16 years of age or older and under the age of 18 years at the time of the commission of the crime, shall be confinement in the state prison for life without the possibility of parole or, at the discretion of the court, 25 years to life.

(c) The trier of fact shall determine the existence of any special circumstance pursuant to the procedure set forth in Section 190.4.

Amended June 5, 1990, by initiative Proposition 115, Sec. 12.

Section 190.6 - Expeditious imposition of sentence in capital cases

(a) The Legislature finds that the sentence in all capital cases should be imposed expeditiously.

(b) Therefore, in all cases in which a sentence of death has been imposed on or after January 1, 1997, the opening appellate brief in the appeal to the State Supreme Court shall be filed no later than seven months after the certification of the record for completeness under subdivision (d) of Section 190.8 or receipt by the appellant's counsel of the completed record, whichever is later, except for good cause. However, in those cases where the trial transcript exceeds 10,000 pages, the briefing shall be completed within the time limits and pursuant to the procedures set by the rules of court adopted by the Judicial Council.

(c) In all cases in which a sentence of death has been imposed on or after January 1, 1997, it is the Legislature's goal that the appeal be decided and an opinion reaching the merits be filed within 210 days of the completion of the briefing. However, where the appeal and a petition for writ of habeas corpus is heard at the same time, the petition should be decided and an opinion reaching the merits should be filed within 210 days of the completion of the briefing for the petition.

(d) The right of victims of crime to a prompt and final conclusion, as provided in paragraph (9) of subdivision (b) of Section 28 of Article I of the California Constitution, includes the right to have judgments of death carried out within a reasonable time. Within 18 months of the effective date of this initiative, the Judicial Council shall adopt initial rules and standards of administration designed to expedite the processing of capital appeals and state habeas corpus review. Within five years of the adoption of the initial rules or the entry of judgment, whichever is later, the state courts shall complete the state appeal and the initial state habeas corpus review in capital cases. The Judicial Council shall continuously monitor the timeliness of review of capital cases and shall amend the rules and standards as necessary to complete the state appeal and initial state habeas corpus proceedings within the five-year period provided in this subdivision.

(e) The failure of the parties or of a court to comply with the time limit in subdivision (b) shall not affect the validity of the judgment or require dismissal of an appeal or habeas corpus petition. If a court fails to comply without extraordinary and compelling reasons justifying the delay, either party or any victim of the offense may seek relief by petition for writ of mandate. The court in which the petition is filed shall act on it within 60 days of filing. Paragraph (1) of subdivision (c) of Section 28 of Article I of the California Constitution, regarding standing to enforce victims' rights, applies to this subdivision and subdivision (d).

Amended by Proposition 66, approved by the voters at the November 8, 2016 election, effective immediately upon enactment.

Section 190.7 - Entire record

(a) The "entire record" referred to in Section 190.6 includes, but is not limited to, the following:

(1) The normal and additional record prescribed in the rules adopted by the Judicial Council pertaining to an appeal taken by the defendant from a judgment of conviction.

(2) A copy of any other paper or record on file or lodged with the superior or municipal court and a transcript of any other oral proceeding reported in the superior or municipal court pertaining to the trial of the cause.

(b) Notwithstanding this section, the Judicial Council may adopt rules, not inconsistent with the purpose of Section 190.6, specifically pertaining to the content, preparation and certification of the record on appeal when a judgment of death has been pronounced.

Amended by Stats. 1996, Ch. 1086, Sec. 2. Effective January 1, 1997.

Section 190.8 - Expeditious certification of record on appeal

(a) In any case in which a death sentence has been imposed, the record on appeal shall be expeditiously certified in two stages, the first for completeness and the second for accuracy, as provided by this section. The trial court may use all reasonable means to ensure compliance with all applicable statutes and rules of court pertaining to record certification in capital appeals, including, but not limited to, the imposition of sanctions.

(b) Within 30 days of the imposition of the death sentence, the clerk of the superior court shall provide to trial counsel copies of the clerk's transcript and shall deliver the transcript as provided by the court reporter. Trial counsel shall promptly notify the court if he or she has not received the transcript within 30 days.

(c) During the course of a trial in which the death penalty is being sought, trial counsel shall alert the court's attention to any errors in the transcripts incidentally discovered by counsel while reviewing them in the ordinary course of trial preparation. The court shall periodically request that trial counsel provide a list of errors in the trial transcript during the course of trial and may hold hearings in connection therewith. Corrections to the record shall not be required to include immaterial typographical errors that cannot conceivably cause confusion.

(d) The trial court shall certify the record for completeness and for incorporation of all corrections, as provided by subdivision (c), no later than 90 days after entry of the imposition of the death sentence unless good cause is shown. However, this time period may be extended for proceedings in which the trial transcript exceeds 10,000 pages in accordance with the timetable set forth in, or for good cause pursuant to the procedures set forth in, the rules of court adopted by the Judicial Council.

(e) Following the imposition of the death sentence and prior to the deadline set forth in subdivision (d), the trial court shall hold one or more hearings for trial counsel to address the completeness of the record and any outstanding errors that have come to their attention and to certify that they have reviewed all docket sheets to ensure that the record contains transcripts for any proceedings, hearings, or discussions that are required to be reported and that have occurred in the course of the case in any court, as well as all documents required by this code and the rules adopted by the Judicial Council.

(f) The clerk of the trial court shall deliver a copy of the record on appeal to appellate counsel when the clerk receives notice of counsel's appointment or retention, or when the record is certified for completeness under subdivision (d), whichever is later.

(g) The trial court shall certify the record for accuracy no later than 120 days after the record has been delivered to appellate counsel. However, this time may be extended pursuant to the timetable and procedures set forth in the rules of court adopted by the Judicial Council. The trial court may hold one or more status conferences for purposes of timely certification of the record for accuracy, as set forth in the rules of court adopted by the Judicial Council.

(h) The Supreme Court shall identify in writing to the Judicial Council any case that has not met the time limit for certification of the record for completeness under subdivision (d) or for accuracy under subdivision (g), and shall identify those cases, and its reasons, for which it has granted an extension of time. The Judicial Council shall include this information in its annual report to the Legislature.

(i) As used in this section, "trial counsel" means both the prosecution and the defense counsel in the trial in which the sentence of death has been imposed.

(j) This section shall be implemented pursuant to rules of court adopted by the Judicial Council.

(k) This section shall only apply to those proceedings in which a sentence of death has been imposed following a trial that was commenced on or after January 1, 1997.

Amended by Stats. 1996, Ch. 1086, Sec. 3. Effective January 1, 1997.

Section 190.9 - Proceedings conducted on record with court reporter

(a)

(1) In any case in which a death sentence may be imposed, all proceedings conducted in the superior court, including all conferences and proceedings, whether in open court, in conference in the courtroom, or in chambers, shall be conducted on the record with a court reporter present. The court reporter shall prepare and certify a daily transcript of all proceedings commencing with the preliminary hearing. Proceedings prior to the preliminary hearing shall be reported but need not be transcribed until the court receives notice as prescribed in paragraph (2).

(2) Upon receiving notification from the prosecution that the death penalty is being sought, the clerk shall order the transcription and preparation of the record of all proceedings prior to and including the preliminary hearing in the manner prescribed by the Judicial Council in the rules of court. The record of all proceedings prior to and including the preliminary hearing shall be certified by the court no later than 120 days following notification unless the time is extended pursuant to rules of court adopted by the Judicial Council. Upon certification, the record of all proceedings is incorporated into the superior court record.

(b)

(1) The court shall assign a court reporter who uses computer-aided transcription equipment to report all proceedings under this section.

(2) Failure to comply with the requirements of this section relating to the assignment of court reporters who use computer-aided transcription equipment is not a ground for reversal.

(c) Any computer-readable transcript produced by court reporters pursuant to this section shall conform to the requirements of Section 271 of the Code of Civil Procedure.

Amended by Stats 2002 ch 71 (SB 1371), s 6, eff. 1/1/2003.

Amended by Stats 2000 ch 287 (SB 1955), s 2, eff. 1/1/2001.

Section 191 - Abolishment of common law distinguishing killing of master by servant and husband by wife as petit treason

The rules of the common law, distinguishing the killing of a master by his servant, and of a husband by his wife, as petit treason, are abolished, and these offenses are homicides, punishable in the manner prescribed by this Chapter.

Enacted 1872.

Section 191.5 - Vehicular manslaughter while intoxicated

(a) Gross vehicular manslaughter while intoxicated is the unlawful killing of a human being without malice aforethought, in the driving of a vehicle, where the driving was in violation of Section 23140, 23152, or 23153 of the Vehicle Code, and the killing was either the proximate result of the commission of an unlawful act, not amounting to a felony, and with gross negligence, or the proximate result of the commission of a lawful act that might produce death, in an unlawful manner, and with gross negligence.

(b) Vehicular manslaughter while intoxicated is the unlawful killing of a human being without malice aforethought, in the driving of a vehicle, where the driving was in violation of Section 23140, 23152, or 23153 of the Vehicle Code, and the killing was either the proximate result of the commission of an unlawful act, not amounting to a felony, but without gross negligence, or the proximate result of the commission of a lawful act that might produce death, in an unlawful manner, but without gross negligence.

(c)

(1) Except as provided in subdivision (d), gross vehicular manslaughter while intoxicated in violation of subdivision (a) is punishable by imprisonment in the state prison for 4, 6, or 10 years.

(2) Vehicular manslaughter while intoxicated in violation of subdivision (b) is punishable by imprisonment in a county jail for not more than one year or by imprisonment pursuant to subdivision (h) of Section 1170 for 16 months or two or four years.

(d) A person convicted of violating subdivision (a) who has one or more prior convictions of this section or of paragraph (1) of subdivision (c) of Section 192, subdivision (a) or (b) of Section 192.5 of this code, or of violating Section 23152 punishable under Sections 23540, 23542, 23546, 23548, 23550, or 23552 of, or convicted of Section 23153 of, the Vehicle Code, shall be punished by imprisonment in the state prison for a term of 15 years to life. Article 2.5 (commencing with Section 2930) of Chapter 7 of Title 1 of Part 3 shall apply to reduce the term imposed pursuant to this subdivision.

(e) This section shall not be construed as prohibiting or precluding a charge of murder under Section 188 upon facts exhibiting wantonness and a conscious disregard for life to support a finding of implied malice, or upon facts showing malice consistent with the holding of the California Supreme Court in People v. Watson, 30 Cal. 3d 290.

(f) This section shall not be construed as making any homicide in the driving of a vehicle or the operation of a vessel punishable which is not a proximate result of the commission of an unlawful act, not amounting to felony, or of the commission of a lawful act which might produce death, in an unlawful manner.

(g) For the penalties in subdivision (d) to apply, the existence of any fact required under subdivision (d) shall be alleged in the information or indictment and either admitted by the defendant in open court or found to be true by the trier of fact.

Amended by Stats 2011 ch 39 (AB 117),s 68, eff. 6/30/2011.

Amended by Stats 2011 ch 15 (AB 109),s 281, eff. 4/4/2011, but operative no earlier than October 1, 2011, and only upon creation of a community corrections grant program to assist in implementing this act and upon an appropriation to fund the grant program.

Amended by Stats 2006 ch 91 (AB 2559),s 1, eff. 1/1/2007.

Amended by Stats 2002 ch 622 (AB 2471), s 1, eff. 1/1/2003.

Section 192 - Manslaughter

Manslaughter is the unlawful killing of a human being without malice. It is of three kinds:

(a) Voluntary-upon a sudden quarrel or heat of passion.

(b) Involuntary-in the commission of an unlawful act, not amounting to a felony; or in the commission of a lawful act which might produce death, in an unlawful manner, or without due caution and circumspection. This subdivision shall not apply to acts committed in the driving of a vehicle.

(c) Vehicular-

(1) Except as provided in subdivision (a) of Section 191.5, driving a vehicle in the commission of an unlawful act, not amounting to a felony, and with gross negligence; or driving a vehicle in the commission of a lawful act which might produce death, in an unlawful manner, and with gross negligence.

(2) Driving a vehicle in the commission of an unlawful act, not amounting to a felony, but without gross negligence; or driving a vehicle in the commission of a lawful act which might produce death, in an unlawful manner, but without gross negligence.

(3) Driving a vehicle in connection with a violation of paragraph (3) of subdivision (a) of Section 550, where the vehicular collision or vehicular accident was knowingly caused for financial gain and proximately resulted in the death of any person. This paragraph does not prevent prosecution of a defendant for the crime of murder.

(d) This section shall not be construed as making any homicide in the driving of a vehicle punishable that is not a proximate result of the commission of an unlawful act, not amounting to a felony, or of the commission of a lawful act which might produce death, in an unlawful manner.

(e)

(1) "Gross negligence," as used in this section, does not prohibit or preclude a charge of murder under Section 188 upon facts exhibiting wantonness and a conscious disregard for life to support a finding of implied malice, or upon facts showing malice, consistent with the holding of the California Supreme Court in People v. Watson (1981) 30 Cal.3d 290.

(2) "Gross negligence," as used in this section, may include, based on the totality of the circumstances, any of the following:

(A) Participating in a sideshow pursuant to subparagraph (A) of subparagraph (2) of subdivision (i) of Section 23109 of the Vehicle Code.

(B) Engaging in a motor vehicle speed contest pursuant to subdivision (a) of Section 23109 of the Vehicle Code.

(C) Speeding over 100 miles per hour.

(f)

(1) For purposes of determining sudden quarrel or heat of passion pursuant to subdivision (a), the provocation was not objectively reasonable if it resulted from the discovery of, knowledge about, or potential disclosure of the victim's actual or perceived gender, gender identity, gender expression, or sexual orientation, including under circumstances in which the victim made an unwanted nonforcible romantic or sexual advance towards the defendant, or if the defendant and victim dated or had a romantic or sexual relationship. Nothing in this section shall preclude the jury from considering all relevant facts to determine whether the defendant was in fact provoked for purposes of establishing subjective provocation.

(2) For purposes of this subdivision, "gender" includes a person's gender identity and gender-related appearance and behavior regardless of whether that appearance or behavior is associated with the person's gender as determined at birth.

Amended by Stats 2023 ch 311 (SB 883),s 3, eff. 1/1/2024.

Amended by Stats 2022 ch 626 (SB 1472),s 3, eff. 1/1/2023.

Amended by Stats 2014 ch 684 (AB 2501),s 1, eff. 1/1/2015.

Amended by Stats 2006 ch 91 (AB 2559),s 2, eff. 1/1/2007.

Stats 2022 ch 626 (SB 1472), which amended this section, shall be known, and may be cited, as Ryan's Law.

Section 192.5 - Vehicular manslaughter

Vehicular manslaughter pursuant to subdivision (b) of Section 191.5 and subdivision (c) of Section 192 is the unlawful killing of a human being without malice aforethought, and includes:

(a) Operating a vessel in violation of subdivision (b), (c), (d), (e), or (f) of Section 655 of the Harbors and Navigation Code, and in the commission of an unlawful act, not amounting to a felony, and with gross negligence; or operating a vessel in violation of subdivision (b), (c), (d), (e), or (f) of Section 655 of the Harbors and Navigation Code, and in the commission of a lawful act that might produce death, in an unlawful manner, and with gross negligence.

(b) Operating a vessel in violation of subdivision (b), (c), (d), (e), or (f) of Section 655 of the Harbors and Navigation Code, and in the commission of an unlawful act, not amounting to felony, but without gross negligence; or operating a vessel in violation of subdivision (b), (c), (d), (e), or (f) of Section 655 of the Harbors and Navigation Code, and in the commission of a lawful act that might produce death, in an unlawful manner, but without gross negligence.

(c) Operating a vessel in the commission of an unlawful act, not amounting to a felony, and with gross negligence; or operating a vessel in the commission of a lawful act that might produce death, in an unlawful manner, and with gross negligence.

(d) Operating a vessel in the commission of an unlawful act, not amounting to a felony, but without gross negligence; or operating a vessel in the commission of a lawful act that might produce death, in an unlawful manner, but without gross negligence.

(e) A person who flees the scene of the crime after committing a violation of subdivision (a), (b), or (c), upon conviction, in addition and consecutive to the punishment prescribed, shall be punished by an additional term of imprisonment of five years in the state prison. This additional term shall not be imposed unless the allegation is charged in the accusatory pleading and admitted by the defendant or found to be true by the trier of fact. The court shall not strike a finding that brings a person within the provisions of this subdivision or an allegation made pursuant to this subdivision.

Amended by Stats 2007 ch 747 (AB 678),s 5, eff. 1/1/2008.
Amended by Stats 2006 ch 91 (AB 2559),s 3, eff. 1/1/2007.

Section 193 - Voluntary manslaughter

(a) Voluntary manslaughter is punishable by imprisonment in the state prison for 3, 6, or 11 years.

(b) Involuntary manslaughter is punishable by imprisonment pursuant to subdivision (h) of Section 1170 for two, three, or four years.

(c) Vehicular manslaughter is punishable as follows:

(1) A violation of paragraph (1) of subdivision (c) of Section 192 is punishable either by imprisonment in the county jail for not more than one year or by imprisonment in the state prison for two, four, or six years.

(2) A violation of paragraph (2) of subdivision (c) of Section 192 is punishable by imprisonment in the county jail for not more than one year.

(3) A violation of paragraph (3) of subdivision (c) of Section 192 is punishable by imprisonment in the state prison for 4, 6, or 10 years.

Amended by Stats 2011 ch 39 (AB 117),s 68, eff. 6/30/2011.
Amended by Stats 2011 ch 15 (AB 109),s 282, eff. 4/4/2011, but operative no earlier than October 1, 2011, and only upon creation of a community corrections grant program to assist in implementing this act and upon an appropriation to fund the grant program.
Amended by Stats 2006 ch 91 (AB 2559),s 4, eff. 1/1/2007.

Section 193.5 - Manslaughter committed during operation of vessel

Manslaughter committed during the operation of a vessel is punishable as follows:

(a) A violation of subdivision (a) of Section 192.5 is punishable by imprisonment in the state prison for 4, 6, or 10 years.

(b) A violation of subdivision (b) of Section 192.5 is punishable by imprisonment in a county jail for not more than one year or by imprisonment pursuant to subdivision (h) of Section 1170 for 16 months or two or four years.

(c) A violation of subdivision (c) of Section 192.5 is punishable either by imprisonment in the county jail for not more than one year or by imprisonment in the state prison for two, four, or six years.

(d) A violation of subdivision (d) of Section 192.5 is punishable by imprisonment in the county jail for not more than one year.

Amended by Stats 2011 ch 39 (AB 117),s 68, eff. 6/30/2011.
Amended by Stats 2011 ch 15 (AB 109),s 283, eff. 4/4/2011, but operative no earlier than October 1, 2011, and only upon creation of a community corrections grant program to assist in implementing this act and upon an appropriation to fund the grant program.
Amended by Stats 2006 ch 91 (AB 2559),s 5, eff. 1/1/2007.

Section 193.7 - Habitual traffic offender

A person convicted of a violation of subdivision (b) of Section 191.5 that occurred within seven years of two or more separate violations of Section 23103, as specified in Section 23103.5, of, or Section 23152 or 23153 of, the Vehicle Code, or any combination thereof, that resulted in convictions, shall be designated as an habitual traffic offender subject to paragraph (3) of subdivision (e) of Section 14601.3 of the Vehicle Code, for a period of three years, subsequent to the conviction. The person shall be advised of this designation pursuant to subdivision (b) of Section 13350 of the Vehicle Code.

Amended by Stats 2007 ch 747 (AB 678),s 6, eff. 1/1/2008.

Section 193.8 - Unlawful relinquishment of possession of vehicle to minor for purpose of driving

(a) An adult, who is the registered owner of a motor vehicle or in possession of a motor vehicle, shall not relinquish possession of the vehicle to a minor for the purpose of driving if the following conditions exist:

(1) The adult owner or person in possession of the vehicle knew or reasonably should have known that the minor was intoxicated at the time possession was relinquished.

(2) A petition was sustained or the minor was convicted of a violation of Section 23103 as specified in Section 23103.5, 23140, 23152, or 23153 of the Vehicle Code or a violation of Section 191.5 or subdivision (a) of Section 192.5.

(3) The minor does not otherwise have a lawful right to possession of the vehicle.

(b) The offense described in subdivision (a) shall not apply to commercial bailments, motor vehicle leases, or parking arrangements, whether or not for compensation, provided by hotels, motels, or food facilities for customers, guests, or other invitees thereof. For purposes of this subdivision, hotel and motel shall have the same meaning as in subdivision (b) of Section 25503.16 of the Business and Professions Code and food facility shall have the same meaning as in Section 113785 of the Health and Safety Code.

(c) If an adult is convicted of the offense described in subdivision (a), that person shall be punished by a fine not exceeding one thousand dollars ($1,000), or by imprisonment in a county jail not exceeding six months, or by both the fine and imprisonment. An adult convicted of the offense described in subdivision (a) shall not be subject to driver's license suspension or revocation or attendance at a licensed alcohol or drug education and counseling program for persons who drive under the influence.

Amended by Stats 2007 ch 747 (AB 678),s 7, eff. 1/1/2008.

Section 194 - Rebuttable presumption that killing not criminal

To make the killing either murder or manslaughter, it is not requisite that the party die within three years and a day after the stroke received or the cause of death administered. If death occurs beyond the time of three years and a day, there shall be a rebuttable presumption that the killing was not criminal. The prosecution shall bear the burden of overcoming this presumption. In the computation of time, the whole of the day on which the act was done shall be reckoned the first.

Amended by Stats. 1996, Ch. 580, Sec. 1. Effective January 1, 1997.

Section 195 - Excusable homicide

Homicide is excusable in the following cases:

1. When committed by accident and misfortune, or in doing any other lawful act by lawful means, with usual and ordinary caution, and without any unlawful intent.

2. When committed by accident and misfortune, in the heat of passion, upon any sudden and sufficient provocation, or upon a sudden combat, when no undue advantage is taken, nor any dangerous weapon used, and when the killing is not done in a cruel or unusual manner.

Amended by Stats. 1984, Ch. 438, Sec. 1.

Section 196 - Justifiable homicide when committed by peace officers

Homicide is justifiable when committed by peace officers and those acting by their command in their aid and assistance, under either of the following circumstances:

(a) In obedience to any judgment of a competent court.

(b) When the homicide results from a peace officer's use of force that is in compliance with Section 835a.

Amended by Stats 2019 ch 170 (AB 392),s 1, eff. 1/1/2020.

Section 197 - Justifiable homicide

Homicide is also justifiable when committed by any person in any of the following cases:

(1) When resisting any attempt to murder any person, or to commit a felony, or to do some great bodily injury upon any person.

(2) When committed in defense of habitation, property, or person, against one who manifestly intends or endeavors, by violence or surprise, to commit a felony, or against one who manifestly intends and endeavors, in a violent, riotous, or tumultuous manner, to enter the habitation of another for the purpose of offering violence to any person therein.

(3) When committed in the lawful defense of such person, or of a spouse, parent, child, master, mistress, or servant of such person, when there is reasonable ground to apprehend a design to commit a felony or to do some great bodily injury, and imminent danger of such design being accomplished; but such person, or the person in whose behalf the defense was made, if he or she was the assailant or engaged in mutual combat, must really and in good faith have endeavored to decline any further struggle before the homicide was committed.

(4) When necessarily committed in attempting, by lawful ways and means, to apprehend any person for any felony committed, or in lawfully suppressing any riot, or in lawfully keeping and preserving the peace.

Amended by Stats 2016 ch 50 (SB 1005),s 67, eff. 1/1/2017.

Section 198 - Bare fear

A bare fear of the commission of any of the offenses mentioned in subdivisions 2 and 3 of Section 197, to prevent which homicide may be lawfully committed, is not sufficient to justify it. But the circumstances must be sufficient to excite the fears of a reasonable person, and the party killing must have acted under the influence of such fears alone.

Amended by Stats. 1987, Ch. 828, Sec. 8.

Section 198.5 - Use of force intended or likely to cause death or great bodily injury within residence

Any person using force intended or likely to cause death or great bodily injury within his or her residence shall be presumed to have held a reasonable fear of imminent peril of death or great bodily injury to self, family, or a member of the household when that force is used against another person, not a member of the family or household, who unlawfully and forcibly enters or has unlawfully and forcibly entered the residence and the person using the force knew or had reason to believe that an unlawful and forcible entry occurred.

As used in this section, great bodily injury means a significant or substantial physical injury.

Added by Stats. 1984, Ch. 1666, Sec. 1.

Section 199 - Effect of justifiable or excusable homicide

The homicide appearing to be justifiable or excusable, the person indicted must, upon his trial, be fully acquitted and discharged.

Enacted 1872.

Chapter 2 - MAYHEM

Section 203 - Mayhem

Every person who unlawfully and maliciously deprives a human being of a member of his body, or disables, disfigures, or renders it useless, or cuts or disables the tongue, or puts out an eye, or slits the nose, ear, or lip, is guilty of mayhem.

Amended by Stats. 1989, Ch. 1360, Sec. 106.

Section 204 - Punishment for mayhem

Mayhem is punishable by imprisonment in the state prison for two, four, or eight years.

Amended by Stats. 1986, Ch. 1424, Sec. 1.

Section 205 - Aggravated mayhem

A person is guilty of aggravated mayhem when he or she unlawfully, under circumstances manifesting extreme indifference to the physical or psychological well-being of another person, intentionally causes permanent disability or disfigurement of another human being or deprives a human being of a limb, organ, or member of his or her body. For purposes of this section, it is not necessary to prove an intent to kill. Aggravated mayhem is a felony punishable by imprisonment in the state prison for life with the possibility of parole.

Added by Stats. 1987, Ch. 785, Sec. 1.

Section 206 - Torture

Every person who, with the intent to cause cruel or extreme pain and suffering for the purpose of revenge, extortion, persuasion, or for any sadistic purpose, inflicts great bodily injury as defined in Section 12022.7 upon the person of another, is guilty of torture. The crime of torture does not require any proof that the victim suffered pain.

Added June 5, 1990, by initiative Proposition 115, Sec. 13.

Section 206.1 - Punishment for torture

Torture is punishable by imprisonment in the state prison for a term of life.

Added June 5, 1990, by initiative Proposition 115, Sec. 14.

Chapter 3 - KIDNAPPING

Section 207 - Kidnapping

(a) Every person who forcibly, or by any other means of instilling fear, steals or takes, or holds, detains, or arrests any person in this state, and carries the person into another country, state, or county, or into another part of the same county, is guilty of kidnapping.

(b) Every person, who for the purpose of committing any act defined in Section 288, hires, persuades, entices, decoys, or seduces by false promises, misrepresentations, or the like, any child under the age of 14 years to go out of this country, state, or county, or into another part of the same county, is guilty of kidnapping.

(c) Every person who forcibly, or by any other means of instilling fear, takes or holds, detains, or arrests any person, with a design to take the person out of this state, without having established a claim, according to the laws of the United States, or of this state, or who hires, persuades, entices, decoys, or seduces by false promises, misrepresentations, or the like, any person to go out of this state, or to be taken or removed therefrom, for the purpose and with the intent to sell that person into slavery or involuntary servitude, or otherwise to employ that person for his or her own use, or to the use of another, without the free will and consent of that persuaded person, is guilty of kidnapping.

(d) Every person who, being out of this state, abducts or takes by force or fraud any person contrary to the law of the place where that act is committed, and brings, sends, or conveys that person within the limits of this state, and is afterwards found within the limits thereof, is guilty of kidnapping.

(e) For purposes of those types of kidnapping requiring force, the amount of force required to kidnap an unresisting infant or child is the amount of physical force required to take and carry the child away a substantial distance for an illegal purpose or with an illegal intent.

(f) Subdivisions (a) to (d), inclusive, do not apply to any of the following:

    (1) To any person who steals, takes, entices away, detains, conceals, or harbors any child under the age of 14 years, if that act is taken to protect the child from danger of imminent harm.

    (2) To any person acting under Section 834 or 837.

Amended by Stats 2003 ch 23 (SB 450), eff. 7/1/2003.

Section 208 - Punishment

(a) Kidnapping is punishable by imprisonment in the state prison for three, five, or eight years.

(b) If the person kidnapped is under 14 years of age at the time of the commission of the crime, the kidnapping is punishable by imprisonment in the state prison for 5, 8, or 11 years. This subdivision is not applicable to the taking, detaining, or concealing, of a minor child by a biological parent, a natural father, as specified in Section 7611 of the Family Code, an adoptive parent, or a person who has been granted access to the minor child by a court order.

(c) In all cases in which probation is granted, the court shall, except in unusual cases where the interests of justice would best be served by a lesser penalty, require as a condition of the probation that the person be confined in the county jail for 12 months. If the court grants probation without requiring the defendant to be confined in the county jail for 12 months, it shall specify its reason or reasons for imposing a lesser penalty.

Amended by Stats. 1997, Ch. 817, Sec. 1. Effective January 1, 1998.

Section 209 - Kidnapping for ransom, reward or to commit extortion

(a) A person who seizes, confines, inveigles, entices, decoys, abducts, conceals, kidnaps, or carries away another person by any means whatsoever with intent to hold or detain, or who holds or detains, that person for ransom, reward, or to commit extortion or to exact from another person any money or valuable thing, or a person who aids or abets any such act, is guilty of a felony. When a person subjected to that act suffers death or bodily harm, or is intentionally confined in a manner that exposes that person to a substantial likelihood of death, the person, upon conviction, shall be punished by imprisonment in the state prison for life without possibility of parole. When no person subjected to that act suffers death or bodily harm, the person, upon conviction, shall be punished by imprisonment in the state prison for life with the possibility of parole.

(b)

    (1) A person who kidnaps or carries away an individual to commit robbery, rape, oral copulation, sodomy, or any violation of Section 264.1, 288, 289, or former Section 262, shall be punished by imprisonment in the state prison for life with the possibility of parole.

    (2) This subdivision shall only apply if the movement of the victim is beyond that merely incidental to the commission of, and increases the risk of harm to the victim over and above that necessarily present in, the intended underlying offense.

(c) When probation is granted, the court shall, except in unusual cases where the interests of justice would best be served by a lesser penalty, require as a condition of the probation that the person be confined in the county jail for 12 months. If the court grants probation without requiring the defendant to be confined in the county jail for 12 months, it shall specify its reason or reasons for imposing a lesser penalty.

(d) Subdivision (b) does not supersede or affect Section 667.61. A person may be charged with a violation of subdivision (b) and Section 667.61. However, a person may not be punished under subdivision (b) and Section 667.61 for the same act that constitutes a violation of both subdivision (b) and Section 667.61.

Amended by Stats 2021 ch 626 (AB 1171),s 16, eff. 1/1/2022.

Amended by Stats 2006 ch 337 (SB 1128),s 4, eff. 9/20/2006.

Amended by Stats 2000 ch 287 (SB 1955), s 3, eff. 1/1/2001.

Section 209.5 - Kidnapping during commission of carjacking

(a) Any person who, during the commission of a carjacking and in order to facilitate the commission of the carjacking, kidnaps another person who is not a principal in the commission of the carjacking shall be punished by imprisonment in the state prison for life with the possibility of parole.

(b) This section shall only apply if the movement of the victim is beyond that merely incidental to the commission of the carjacking, the victim is moved a substantial distance from the vicinity of the carjacking, and the movement of the victim increases the risk of harm to the victim over and above that necessarily present in the crime of carjacking itself.

(c) In all cases in which probation is granted, the court shall, except in unusual cases where the interests of justice would best be served by a lesser penalty, require as a condition of the probation that the person be confined in the county jail for 12 months. If the court grants probation without requiring the defendant to be confined in the county jail for 12 months, it shall specify its reason or reasons for imposing a lesser penalty.

Added by Stats. 1993, Ch. 611, Sec. 5. Effective October 1, 1993.

Section 210 - Representation as kidnapper

Every person who for the purpose of obtaining any ransom or reward, or to extort or exact from any person any money or thing of value, poses as, or in any manner represents himself to be a person who has seized, confined, inveigled, enticed, decoyed, abducted, concealed, kidnapped or carried away any person, or who poses as, or in any manner represents himself to be a person who holds or detains such person, or who poses as, or in any manner represents himself to be a person who has aided or abetted any such act, or who poses as or in any manner represents himself to be a person who has the influence, power, or ability, to obtain the release of such person so seized, confined, inveigled, enticed, decoyed, abducted, concealed, kidnapped or carried away, is guilty of a felony and upon conviction thereof shall be punished by imprisonment for two, three or four years.

Nothing in this section prohibits any person who, in good faith believes that he can rescue any person who has been seized, confined, inveigled, enticed, decoyed, abducted, concealed, kidnapped or carried away, and who has had no part in, or connection with, such confinement, inveigling, decoying, abducting, concealing, kidnapping, or carrying away, from offering to rescue or obtain the release of such person for a monetary consideration or other thing of value.

Amended by Stats. 1976, Ch. 1139.

Chapter 3.5 - HOSTAGES

Section 210.5 - False imprisonment for purposes of protection against arrest

Every person who commits the offense of false imprisonment, as defined in Section 236, against a person for purposes of protection from arrest, which substantially increases the risk of harm to the victim, or for purposes of using the person as a shield is punishable by imprisonment pursuant to subdivision (h) of Section 1170 for three, five, or eight years.

Amended by Stats 2011 ch 39 (AB 117),s 68, eff. 6/30/2011.

Amended by Stats 2011 ch 15 (AB 109),s 284, eff. 4/4/2011, but operative no earlier than October 1, 2011, and only upon creation of a community corrections grant program to assist in implementing this act and upon an appropriation to fund the grant program.

Chapter 4 - ROBBERY

Section 211 - Robbery

Robbery is the felonious taking of personal property in the possession of another, from his person or immediate presence, and against his will, accomplished by means of force or fear.

Enacted 1872.

Section 212 - Fear

The fear mentioned in Section 211 may be either:

1. The fear of an unlawful injury to the person or property of the person robbed, or of any relative of his or member of his family; or,

2. The fear of an immediate and unlawful injury to the person or property of anyone in the company of the person robbed at the time of the robbery.

Amended by Stats. 1963, Ch. 372.

Section 212.5 - Robbery in first degree

(a) Every robbery of any person who is performing his or her duties as an operator of any bus, taxicab, cable car, streetcar, trackless trolley, or other vehicle, including a vehicle operated on stationary rails or on a track or rail suspended in the air, and used for the transportation of persons for hire, every robbery of any passenger which is perpetrated on any of these vehicles, and every robbery which is perpetrated in an inhabited dwelling house, a vessel as defined in Section 21 of the Harbors and Navigation Code which is inhabited and designed for habitation, an inhabited floating home as defined in subdivision (d) of Section 18075.55 of the Health and Safety Code, a trailer coach as defined in the Vehicle Code which is inhabited, or the inhabited portion of any other building is robbery of the first degree.

(b) Every robbery of any person while using an automated teller machine or immediately after the person has used an automated teller machine and is in the vicinity of the automated teller machine is robbery of the first degree.

(c) All kinds of robbery other than those listed in subdivisions (a) and (b) are of the second degree.

Amended by Stats. 1994, Ch. 919, Sec. 1. Effective January 1, 1995.

Section 213 - Punishment

(a) Robbery is punishable as follows:

    (1) Robbery of the first degree is punishable as follows:

        (A) If the defendant, voluntarily acting in concert with two or more other persons, commits the robbery within an inhabited dwelling house, a vessel as defined in Section 21 of the Harbors and Navigation Code, which is inhabited and designed for habitation, an inhabited floating home as defined in subdivision (d) of Section 18075.55 of the Health and Safety Code, a trailer coach as defined in the Vehicle Code, which is inhabited, or the inhabited portion of any other building, by imprisonment in the state prison for three, six, or nine years.

(B) In all cases other than that specified in subparagraph (A), by imprisonment in the state prison for three, four, or six years.

(2) Robbery of the second degree is punishable by imprisonment in the state prison for two, three, or five years.

(b) Notwithstanding Section 664, attempted robbery in violation of paragraph (2) of subdivision (a) is punishable by imprisonment in the state prison.

Amended by Stats. 1994, Ch. 789, Sec. 1. Effective January 1, 1995.

Section 214 - Robbery of passenger on railroad

Every person who goes upon or boards any railroad train, car or engine, with the intention of robbing any passenger or other person on such train, car or engine, of any personal property thereon in the possession or care or under the control of any such passenger or other person, or who interferes in any manner with any switch, rail, sleeper, viaduct, culvert, embankment, structure or appliance pertaining to or connected with any railroad, or places any dynamite or other explosive substance or material upon or near the track of any railroad, or who sets fire to any railroad bridge or trestle, or who shows, masks, extinguishes or alters any light or other signal, or exhibits or compels any other person to exhibit any false light or signal, or who stops any such train, car or engine, or slackens the speed thereof, or who compels or attempts to compel any person in charge or control thereof to stop any such train, car or engine, or slacken the speed thereof, with the intention of robbing any passenger or other person on such train, car or engine, of any personal property thereon in the possession or charge or under the control of any such passenger or other person, is guilty of a felony.

Added by Stats. 1905, Ch. 494.

Section 215 - Carjacking

(a) "Carjacking" is the felonious taking of a motor vehicle in the possession of another, from his or her person or immediate presence, or from the person or immediate presence of a passenger of the motor vehicle, against his or her will and with the intent to either permanently or temporarily deprive the person in possession of the motor vehicle of his or her possession, accomplished by means of force or fear.

(b) Carjacking is punishable by imprisonment in the state prison for a term of three, five, or nine years.

(c) This section shall not be construed to supersede or affect Section 211. A person may be charged with a violation of this section and Section 211. However, no defendant may be punished under this section and Section 211 for the same act which constitutes a violation of both this section and Section 211.

Added by Stats. 1993, Ch. 611, Sec. 6. Effective October 1, 1993.

Chapter 5 - ATTEMPTS TO KILL

Section 217.1 - Assault of official in retaliation for or to prevent performance of victim's official duties

(a) Except as provided in subdivision (b), every person who commits any assault upon the President or Vice President of the United States, the Governor of any state or territory, any justice, judge, or former judge of any local, state, or federal court of record, any commissioner, referee, or other subordinate judicial officer of any court of record, the secretary or director of any executive agency or department of the United States or any state or territory, or any other official of the United States or any state or territory holding elective office, any mayor, city council member, county supervisor, sheriff, district attorney, prosecutor or assistant prosecutor of any local, state, or federal prosecutor's office, a former prosecutor or assistant prosecutor of any local, state, or federal prosecutor's office, public defender or assistant public defender of any local, state, or federal public defender's office, a former public defender or assistant public defender of any local, state, or federal public defender's office, the chief of police of any municipal police department, any peace officer, any juror in any local, state, or federal court of record, or the immediate family of any of these officials, in retaliation for or to prevent the performance of the victim's official duties, shall be punished by imprisonment in the county jail not exceeding one year or by imprisonment pursuant to subdivision (h) of Section 1170.

(b) Notwithstanding subdivision (a), every person who attempts to commit murder against any person listed in subdivision (a) in retaliation for or to prevent the performance of the victim's official duties, shall be confined in the state prison for a term of 15 years to life. The provisions of Article 2.5 (commencing with Section 2930) of Chapter 7 of Title 1 of Part 3 shall apply to reduce any minimum term of 15 years in a state prison imposed pursuant to this section, but that person shall not otherwise be released on parole prior to that time.

(c) For the purposes of this section, the following words have the following meanings:

(1) "Immediate family" means spouse, child, stepchild, brother, stepbrother, sister, stepsister, mother, stepmother, father, or stepfather.

(2) "Peace officer" means any person specified in subdivision (a) of Section 830.1 or Section 830.5.

Amended by Stats 2011 ch 39 (AB 117),s 68, eff. 6/30/2011.

Amended by Stats 2011 ch 15 (AB 109),s 285, eff. 4/4/2011, but operative no earlier than October 1, 2011, and only upon creation of a community corrections grant program to assist in implementing this act and upon an appropriation to fund the grant program.

EFFECTIVE 1/1/2000. Amended October 10, 1999 (Bill Number: SB 832) (Chapter 853).

Section 218 - Unlawful acts upon or near track of railroad with intent of wrecking train

Every person who unlawfully throws out a switch, removes a rail, or places any obstruction on any railroad with the intention of derailing any passenger, freight or other train, car or engine, or who unlawfully places any dynamite or other explosive material or any other obstruction upon or near the track of any railroad with the intention of blowing up or derailing any such train, car or engine, or who unlawfully sets fire to any railroad bridge or trestle, over which any such train, car or engine must pass with the intention of wrecking such train, car or engine, is guilty of a felony, and shall be punished by imprisonment in the state prison for life without possibility of parole.

Amended by Stats. 1976, Ch. 1139.

Section 218.1 - Placement of obstruction upon or near track of railroad

Any person who unlawfully and with gross negligence places or causes to be placed any obstruction upon or near the track of any railroad that proximately results in either the damaging or derailing of any passenger, freight, or other train, or injures a rail passenger or employee, shall be punished by imprisonment pursuant to subdivision (h) of Section 1170 for two, three, or four years, or by imprisonment in a county jail for not more than one year, or by a fine not to exceed two thousand five hundred dollars ($2,500), or by both that imprisonment and fine.

Amended by Stats 2011 ch 39 (AB 117),s 68, eff. 6/30/2011.

Amended by Stats 2011 ch 15 (AB 109),s 286, eff. 4/4/2011, but operative no earlier than October 1, 2011, and only upon creation of a community corrections grant program to assist in implementing this act and upon an appropriation to fund the grant program.

Added by Stats 2005 ch 716 (AB 1067),s 2, eff. 1/1/2006.

Section 219 - Unlawful acts with intention to derail train

Every person who unlawfully throws out a switch, removes a rail, or places any obstruction on any railroad with the intention of derailing any passenger, freight or other train, car or engine and thus derails the same, or who unlawfully places any dynamite or other explosive material or any other obstruction upon or near the track of any railroad with the intention of blowing up or derailing any such train, car or engine and thus blows up or derails the same, or who unlawfully sets fire to any railroad bridge or trestle over which any such train, car or engine must pass with the intention of wrecking such train, car or engine, and thus wrecks the same, is guilty of a felony and punishable with death or imprisonment in the state prison for life without possibility of parole in cases where any person suffers death as a proximate result thereof, or imprisonment in the state prison for life with the possibility of parole, in cases where no person suffers death as a proximate result thereof. The penalty shall be determined pursuant to Sections 190.3 and 190.4.

Amended by Stats. 1977, Ch. 316.

Section 219.1 - Unlawful acts related to wrecking of common carrier

Every person who unlawfully throws, hurls or projects at a vehicle operated by a common carrier, while such vehicle is either in motion or stationary, any rock, stone, brick, bottle, piece of wood or metal or any other missile of any kind or character, or does any unlawful act, with the intention of wrecking such vehicle and doing bodily harm, and thus wrecks the same and causes bodily harm, is guilty of a felony and punishable by imprisonment pursuant to subdivision (h) of Section 1170 for two, four, or six years.

Amended by Stats 2011 ch 39 (AB 117),s 68, eff. 6/30/2011.

Amended by Stats 2011 ch 15 (AB 109),s 287, eff. 4/4/2011, but operative no earlier than October 1, 2011, and only upon creation of a community corrections grant program to assist in implementing this act and upon an appropriation to fund the grant program.

Section 219.2 - Unlawful throwing of stone at train, etc.

Every person who willfully throws, hurls, or projects a stone or other hard substance, or shoots a missile, at a train, locomotive, railway car, caboose, cable railway car, street railway car, or bus or at a steam vessel or watercraft used for carrying passengers or freight on any of the waters within or bordering on this state, is punishable by imprisonment in the county jail not exceeding one year, or in a state prison, or by fine not exceeding two thousand dollars ($2,000), or by both such fine and imprisonment.

Amended by Stats. 1983, Ch. 1092, Sec. 248. Effective September 27, 1983. Operative January 1, 1984, by Sec. 427 of Ch. 1092.

Section 219.3 - Unlawful dropping or throwing object from toll bridge

Any person who wilfully drops or throws any object or missile from any toll bridge is guilty of a misdemeanor.

Added by Stats. 1957, Ch. 1053.

Chapter 6 - ASSAULTS WITH INTENT TO COMMIT FELONY, OTHER THAN ASSAULTS WITH INTENT TO MURDER

Section 220 - Assault with intent to commit mayhem, rape, sodomy, oral copulation, or other violations

(a)

(1) Except as provided in subdivision (b), any person who assaults another with intent to commit mayhem, rape, sodomy, oral copulation, or any violation of Section 264.1, 288, or 289 shall be punished by imprisonment in the state prison for two, four, or six years.

(2) Except as provided in subdivision (b), any person who assaults another person under 18 years of age with the intent to commit rape, sodomy, oral copulation, or any violation of Section 264.1, 288, or 289 shall be punished by imprisonment in the state prison for five, seven, or nine years.

(b) Any person who, in the commission of a burglary of the first degree, as defined in subdivision (a) of Section 460, assaults another with intent to commit rape, sodomy, oral copulation, or any violation of Section 264.1, 288, or 289 shall be punished by imprisonment in the state prison for life with the possibility of parole.

Amended by Stats 2010 ch 219 (AB 1844),s 2, eff. 9/9/2010.

Amended by Stats 2006 ch 337 (SB 1128),s 5, eff. 9/20/2006.

See Stats 2010 ch 219 (AB 1844), s 1.

Section 222 - Unlawful administering of intoxicating agent to commit felony

Every person guilty of administering to another any chloroform, ether, laudanum, or any controlled substance, anaesthetic, or intoxicating agent, with intent thereby to enable or assist himself or herself or any other person to commit a felony, is guilty of a felony punishable by imprisonment in the state prison for 16 months, or two or three years.

Amended by Stats 2011 ch 39 (AB 117),s 68, eff. 6/30/2011.

Amended by Stats 2011 ch 15 (AB 109),s 287.5, eff. 4/4/2011, but operative no earlier than October 1, 2011, and only upon creation of a community corrections grant program to assist in implementing this act and upon an appropriation to fund the grant program.

Chapter 8 - FALSE IMPRISONMENT AND HUMAN TRAFFICKING

Section 236 - False imprisonment

False imprisonment is the unlawful violation of the personal liberty of another.

Chapter heading amended by Proposition 35, approved by the people of the State of California 11/6/2012, eff. 11/7/2012.

Section 236.1 - Human trafficking

(a)A person who deprives or violates the personal liberty of another with the intent to obtain forced labor or services, is guilty of human trafficking and shall be punished by imprisonment in the state prison for 5, 8, or 12 years and a fine of not more than five hundred thousand dollars ($500,000).

(b)A person who deprives or violates the personal liberty of another with the intent to effect or maintain a violation of Section 266, 266h, 266i, 266j, 267, 311.1, 311.2, 311.3, 311.4, 311.5, 311.6, or 518 is guilty of human trafficking and shall be punished by imprisonment in the state prison for 8, 14, or 20 years and a fine of not more than five hundred thousand dollars ($500,000).

(c)A person who causes, induces, or persuades, or attempts to cause, induce, or persuade, a person who is a minor at the time of commission of the offense to engage in a commercial sex act, with the intent to effect or maintain a violation of Section 266, 266h, 266i, 266j, 267, 311.1, 311.2, 311.3, 311.4, 311.5, 311.6, or 518 is guilty of human trafficking. A violation of this subdivision is punishable by imprisonment in the state prison as follows:

(1)Five, 8, or 12 years and a fine of not more than five hundred thousand dollars ($500,000).

(2)Fifteen years to life and a fine of not more than five hundred thousand dollars ($500,000) when the offense involves force, fear, fraud, deceit, coercion, violence, duress, menace, or threat of unlawful injury to the victim or to another person.

(d)In determining whether a minor was caused, induced, or persuaded to engage in a commercial sex act, the totality of the circumstances, including the age of the victim, the victim's relationship to the trafficker or agents of the trafficker, and any handicap or disability of the victim, shall be considered.

(e)Consent by a victim of human trafficking who is a minor at the time of the commission of the offense is not a defense to a criminal prosecution under this section.

(f)Mistake of fact as to the age of a victim of human trafficking who is a minor at the time of the commission of the offense is not a defense to a criminal prosecution under this section.

(g)The Legislature finds that the definition of human trafficking in this section is equivalent to the federal definition of a severe form of trafficking found in Section 7102(11) of Title 22 of the United States Code.

(h)For purposes of this chapter, the following definitions apply:

(1)"Coercion" includes a scheme, plan, or pattern intended to cause a person to believe that failure to perform an act would result in serious harm to or physical restraint against any person; the abuse or threatened abuse of the legal process; debt bondage; or providing and facilitating the possession of a controlled substance to a person with the intent to impair the person's judgment.

(2)"Commercial sex act" means sexual conduct on account of which anything of value is given or received by a person.

(3)"Deprivation or violation of the personal liberty of another" includes substantial and sustained restriction of another's liberty accomplished through force, fear, fraud, deceit, coercion, violence, duress, menace, or threat of unlawful injury to the victim or to another person, under circumstances where the person receiving or apprehending the threat reasonably believes that it is likely that the person making the threat would carry it out.

(4)"Duress" includes a direct or implied threat of force, violence, danger, hardship, or retribution sufficient to cause a reasonable person to acquiesce in or perform an act which the person would otherwise not have submitted to or performed; a direct or implied threat to destroy, conceal, remove, confiscate, or possess an actual or purported passport or immigration document of the victim; or knowingly destroying, concealing, removing, confiscating, or possessing an actual or purported passport or immigration document of the victim.

(5)"Forced labor or services" means labor or services that are performed or provided by a person and are obtained or maintained through force, fraud, duress, or coercion, or equivalent conduct that would reasonably overbear the will of the person.

(6)"Great bodily injury" means a significant or substantial physical injury.

(7)"Minor" means a person less than 18 years of age.

(8)"Serious harm" includes any harm, whether physical or nonphysical, including psychological, financial, or reputational harm, that is sufficiently serious, under all the surrounding circumstances, to compel a reasonable person of the same background and in the same circumstances to perform or to continue performing labor, services, or commercial sexual acts in order to avoid incurring that harm.

(i)The total circumstances, including the age of the victim, the relationship between the victim and the trafficker or agents of the trafficker, and any handicap or disability of the victim, shall be factors to consider in determining the presence of "deprivation or violation of the personal liberty of another," "duress," and "coercion" as described in this section.

(j)In any case brought pursuant to this section, the prosecutor shall consider whether to seek protective orders pursuant to Section 136.2.

Amended by Stats 2022 ch 87 (SB 382),s 2, eff. 1/1/2023.

Amended by Stats 2021 ch 124 (AB 938),s 34, eff. 1/1/2022.

Amended by Stats 2016 ch 86 (SB 1171),s 223.5, eff. 1/1/2017.

Amended by Proposition 35, approved by the people of the State of California 11/6/2012, eff. 11/7/2012. .

Amended by Stats 2010 ch 219 (AB 1844),s 3, eff. 9/9/2010.

Added by Stats 2005 ch 240 (AB 22),s 7, eff. 1/1/2006.

Section 236.2 - Identification of victims of human trafficking

Law enforcement agencies shall use due diligence to identify all victims of human trafficking, regardless of the citizenship of the person. When a peace officer comes into contact with a person who has been deprived of his or her personal liberty, a minor who has engaged in a commercial sex act, a person suspected of violating subdivision (a) or (b) of Section 647, or a victim of a crime of domestic violence or sexual assault, the peace officer shall consider whether the following indicators of human trafficking are present:

(a) Signs of trauma, fatigue, injury, or other evidence of poor care.

(b) The person is withdrawn, afraid to talk, or his or her communication is censored by another person.

(c) The person does not have freedom of movement.

(d) The person lives and works in one place.

(e) The person owes a debt to his or her employer.

(f) Security measures are used to control who has contact with the person.

(g) The person does not have control over his or her own government-issued identification or over his or her worker immigration documents.

Amended by Proposition 35, approved by the people of the State of California 11/6/2012, eff. 11/7/2012.

Added by Stats 2008 ch 358 (AB 2810),s 4, eff. 1/1/2009.

Section 236.3 - Nuisance

Upon conviction of a violation of Section 236.1, if real property is used to facilitate the commission of the offense, the procedures for determining whether the property constitutes a nuisance and the remedies imposed therefor as provided in Article 2 (commencing with Section 11225) of Chapter 3 of Title 1 of Part 4 shall apply.

Added by Stats 2010 ch 625 (SB 677),s 1, eff. 1/1/2011.

Section 236.4 - Punishment for human trafficking

(a) Upon the conviction of a person of a violation of Section 236.1, the court may, in addition to any other penalty, fine, or restitution imposed, order the defendant to pay an additional fine not to exceed one million dollars ($1,000,000). In setting the amount of the fine, the court shall consider any relevant factors, including, but not limited to, the seriousness and gravity of the offense, the circumstances and duration of its commission, the amount of economic gain the defendant derived as a result of the crime, and the extent to which the victim suffered losses as a result of the crime.

(b) Any person who inflicts great bodily injury on a victim in the commission or attempted commission of a violation of Section 236.1 shall be punished by an additional and consecutive term of imprisonment in the state prison for 5, 7, or 10 years.

(c) Any person who has previously been convicted of a violation of any crime specified in Section 236.1 shall receive an additional and consecutive term of imprisonment in the state prison for 5 years for each additional conviction on charges separately brought and tried.

(d) Every fine imposed and collected pursuant to Section 236.1 and this section shall be deposited in the Victim-Witness Assistance Fund, to be administered by the California Emergency Management Agency (Cal EMA), to fund grants for services for victims of human trafficking. Seventy percent of the fines collected and deposited shall be granted to public agencies and nonprofit corporations that provide shelter, counseling, or other direct services for trafficked victims. Thirty percent of the fines collected and deposited shall be granted to law enforcement and prosecution agencies in the jurisdiction in which the charges were filed to fund human trafficking prevention, witness protection, and rescue operations.

Enacted by Proposition 35, approved by the people of the State of California 11/6/2012, eff. 11/7/2012.

Section 236.5 - [Renumbered]

(a) Within 15 business days of the first encounter with a victim of human trafficking, as defined by Section 236.1, law enforcement agencies shall provide brief letters that satisfy the following Law Enforcement Agency (LEA) endorsement regulations as found in paragraph (1) of subdivision (f) of Section 214.11 of Title 8 of the Code of Federal Regulations.

(b) The LEA must be submitted on Supplement B, Declaration of Law Enforcement Officer for Victim of Trafficking in Persons, of Form I-914. The LEA endorsement must be filled out completely in accordance with the instructions contained on the form and must attach the results of any name or database inquiry performed. In order to provide persuasive evidence, the LEA endorsement must contain a description of the victimization upon which the application is based, including the dates the trafficking in persons and victimization occurred, and be signed by a supervising official responsible for the investigation or prosecution of trafficking in persons. The LEA endorsement must address whether the victim had been recruited, harbored, transported, provided, or obtained specifically for either labor or services, or for the purposes of a commercial sex act.

(c) Where state law enforcement agencies find the grant of a LEA endorsement to be inappropriate for a victim of trafficking in persons, the agency shall within 15 days provide the victim with a letter explaining the grounds of the denial of the LEA. The victim may submit additional evidence to the law enforcement agency, which must reconsider the denial of the LEA within one week of the receipt of additional evidence.

Renumbered as Ca. Pen. Code §236.5 by Stats 2008 ch 358 (AB 2810),s 3, eff. 1/1/2009.

Added by Stats 2005 ch 240 (AB 22),s 8, eff. 1/1/2006.

Section 236.6 - Protective relief to preserve property or assets

(a) To prevent dissipation or secreting of assets or property, the prosecuting agency may, at the same time as or subsequent to the filing of a complaint or indictment charging human trafficking under Section 236.1, file a petition with the criminal division of the superior court of the county in which the accusatory pleading was filed, seeking a temporary restraining order, preliminary injunction, the appointment of a receiver, or any other protective relief necessary to preserve the property or assets. The filing of the petition shall start a proceeding that shall be pendent to the criminal proceeding and maintained solely to effect the remedies available for this crime, including, but not limited to, payment of restitution and payment of fines. The proceeding shall not be subject to or governed by the provisions of the Civil Discovery Act as set forth in Title 4 (commencing with Section 2016.010) of Part 4 of the Code of Civil Procedure. The petition shall allege that the defendant has been charged with human trafficking under Section 236.1 and shall identify that criminal proceeding and the assets and property to be affected by an order issued pursuant to this section.

(b) The prosecuting agency shall, by personal service or registered mail, provide notice of the petition to every person who may have an interest in the property specified in the petition. Additionally, the notice shall be published for at least three successive weeks in a newspaper of general circulation in the county where the property affected by the order is located. The notice shall state that any interested person may file a verified claim with the superior court stating the nature and amount of his or her claimed interest. The notice shall set forth the time within which a claim of interest in the protected property shall be filed.

(c) If the property to be preserved is real property, the prosecuting agency shall record, at the time of filing the petition, a lis pendens in each county in which the real property is situated that specifically identifies the property by legal description, the name of the owner of record, as shown on the latest equalized assessment roll, and the assessor's parcel number.

(d) If the property to be preserved consists of assets under the control of a banking or financial institution, the prosecuting agency, at the time of filing the petition, may obtain an order from the court directing the banking or financial institution to immediately disclose the account numbers and value of the assets of the accused held by the banking or financial institution. The prosecuting agency shall file a supplemental petition, specifically identifying which banking or financial institution accounts shall be subject to a temporary restraining order, preliminary injunction, or other protective remedy.

(e) A person claiming an interest in the protected property or assets may, at any time within 30 days from the date of the first publication of the notice of the petition, or within 30 days after receipt of actual notice, whichever is later, file with the superior court of the county in which the action is pending a verified claim stating the nature and amount of his or her interest in the property or assets. A verified copy of the claim shall be served by the claimant on the Attorney General or district attorney, as appropriate.

(f) Concurrent with or subsequent to the filing of the petition, the prosecuting agency may move the superior court for, and the superior court may issue, any of the following pendente lite orders to preserve the status quo of the property or assets alleged in the petition:

(1) An injunction to restrain any person from transferring, encumbering, hypothecating, or otherwise disposing of the property or assets.

(2) Appointment of a receiver to take possession of, care for, manage, and operate the assets and properties so that they may be maintained and preserved. The court may order that a receiver appointed pursuant to this section shall be compensated for all reasonable expenditures made or incurred by him or her in connection with the possession, care, management, and operation of property or assets that are subject to the provisions of this section.

(3) Requiring a bond or other undertaking, in lieu of other orders, of a value sufficient to ensure the satisfaction of restitution and fines imposed pursuant to Section 236.1.

(g) The following procedures shall be followed in processing the petition:

(1) No preliminary injunction shall be granted or receiver appointed without notice to the interested parties and a hearing to determine that the order is necessary to preserve the property or assets, pending the outcome of the criminal proceedings. However, a temporary restraining order may be issued pending that hearing pursuant to the provisions of Section 527 of the Code of Civil Procedure. The temporary restraining order may be based upon the sworn declaration of a peace officer with personal knowledge of the criminal investigation that establishes probable cause to believe that human trafficking has taken place and that the amount of restitution and fines established pursuant to subdivision (f) exceeds or equals the worth of the property or assets subject to the temporary restraining order. The declaration may include the hearsay statements of witnesses to establish the necessary facts. The temporary restraining order may be issued without notice upon a showing of good cause to the court.

(2) The defendant, or a person who has filed a verified claim, shall have the right to have the court conduct an order to show cause hearing within 10 days of the service of the request for a hearing upon the prosecuting agency, in order to determine whether the temporary restraining order should remain in effect, whether relief should be granted from a lis pendens recorded pursuant to subdivision (c), or whether an existing order should be modified in the interests of justice. Upon a showing of good cause, the hearing shall be held within two days of the service of the request for a hearing upon the prosecuting agency.

(3) In determining whether to issue a preliminary injunction or temporary restraining order in a proceeding brought by a prosecuting agency in conjunction with or subsequent to the filing of an allegation pursuant to this section, the court has the discretion to consider any matter that it deems reliable and appropriate, including hearsay statements, in order to reach a just and equitable decision. The court shall weigh the relative degree of certainty of the outcome on the merits and the consequences to each of the parties of granting the interim relief. If the prosecution is likely to prevail on the merits and the risk of the dissipation of assets outweighs the potential harm to the defendants and the interested parties, the court shall grant injunctive relief. The court shall give significant weight to the following factors:

(A) The public interest in preserving the property or assets pendente lite.

(B) The difficulty of preserving the property or assets pendente lite where the underlying alleged crimes involve human trafficking.

(C) The fact that the requested relief is being sought by a public prosecutor on behalf of alleged victims of human trafficking.

(D) The likelihood that substantial public harm has occurred where the human trafficking is alleged to have been committed.

(E) The significant public interest involved in compensating victims of human trafficking and paying court-imposed restitution and fines.

(4) The court, in making its orders, may consider a defendant's request for the release of a portion of the property affected by this section in order to pay reasonable legal fees in connection with the criminal proceeding, necessary and appropriate living expenses pending trial and sentencing, and for the purpose of posting bail. The court shall weigh the needs of the public to retain the property against the needs of the defendant to a portion of the property. The court shall consider the factors listed in paragraph (3) prior to making an order releasing property for these purposes.

(5) The court, in making its orders, shall seek to protect the interests of innocent third parties, including an innocent spouse, who were not involved in the commission of criminal activity.

(6) The orders shall be no more extensive than necessary to effect the remedies available for the crime. In determining the amount of property to be held, the court shall ascertain the amount of fines that are assessed for a violation of this chapter and the amount of possible restitution.

(7) A petition filed pursuant to this section is part of the criminal proceedings for purposes of appointment of counsel and shall be assigned to the criminal division of the superior court of the county in which the accusatory pleading was filed.

(8) Based upon a noticed motion brought by the receiver appointed pursuant to paragraph (2) of subdivision (f), the court may order an interlocutory sale of property named in the petition when the property is liable to perish, to waste, or to be significantly reduced in value, or when the expenses of maintaining the property are disproportionate to the value of the property. The proceeds of the interlocutory sale shall be deposited with the court or as directed by the court pending determination of the proceeding pursuant to this section.

(9) The court may make any orders that are necessary to preserve the continuing viability of a lawful business enterprise that is affected by the issuance of a temporary restraining order or preliminary injunction issued pursuant to this section.

(10) In making its orders, the court shall seek to prevent the property or asset subject to a temporary restraining order or preliminary injunction from perishing, spoiling, going to waste, or otherwise being significantly reduced in value. Where the potential for diminution in value exists, the court shall appoint a receiver to dispose of or otherwise protect the value of the property or asset.

(11) A preservation order shall not be issued against an asset of a business that is not likely to be dissipated and that may be subject to levy or attachment to meet the purposes of this section.

(h) If the allegation of human trafficking is dismissed or found by the trier of fact to be untrue, a preliminary injunction or temporary restraining order issued pursuant to this section shall be dissolved. If a jury is the trier of fact, and the jury is unable to reach a unanimous verdict, the court shall have the discretion to continue or dissolve all or a portion of the preliminary injunction or temporary restraining order based upon the interests of justice. However, if the prosecuting agency elects not to retry the case, a preliminary injunction or temporary restraining order issued pursuant to this section shall be dissolved.

(i)

    (1)

        (A) If the defendant is convicted of human trafficking, the trial judge shall continue the preliminary injunction or temporary restraining order until the date of the criminal sentencing and shall make a finding at that time as to what portion, if any, of the property or assets subject to the preliminary injunction or temporary restraining order shall be levied upon to pay fines and restitution to victims of the crime. The order imposing fines and restitution may exceed the total worth of the property or assets subjected to the preliminary injunction or temporary restraining order. The court may order the immediate transfer of the property or assets to satisfy a restitution order issued pursuant to Section 1202.4 and a fine imposed pursuant to this chapter.

        (B) If the execution of judgment is stayed pending an appeal of an order of the superior court pursuant to this section, the preliminary injunction or temporary restraining order shall be maintained in full force and effect during the pendency of the appellate period.

    (2) The order imposing fines and restitution shall not affect the interest in real property of a third party that was acquired prior to the recording of the lis pendens, unless the property was obtained from the defendant other than as a bona fide purchaser for value. If any assets or property affected by this section are subject to a valid lien, mortgage, security interest, or interest under a conditional sales contract and the amount due to the holder of the lien, mortgage, interest, or contract is less than the appraised value of the property, that person may pay to the state or the local government that initiated the proceeding the amount of the difference between the appraised value of the property and the amount of the lien, mortgage, security interest, or interest under a conditional sales contract. Upon that payment, the state or local entity shall relinquish all claims to the property. If the holder of the interest elects not to make that payment to the state or local governmental entity, the interest in the property shall be deemed transferred to the state or local governmental entity and any indicia of ownership of the property shall be confirmed in the state or local governmental entity. The appraised value shall be determined as of the date judgment is entered either by agreement between the holder of the lien, mortgage, security interest, or interest under a conditional sales contract and the governmental entity involved or, if they cannot agree, then by a court-appointed appraiser for the county in which the action is brought. A person holding a valid lien, mortgage, security interest, or interest under a conditional sales contract shall be paid the appraised value of his or her interest.

    (3) In making its final order, the court shall seek to protect the legitimately acquired interests of innocent third parties, including an innocent spouse, who were not involved in the commission of criminal activity.

(j) In all cases where property is to be levied upon pursuant to this section, a receiver appointed by the court shall be empowered to liquidate all property or assets, which shall be distributed in the following order of priority:

    (1) To the receiver, or court-appointed appraiser, for all reasonable expenditures made or incurred by him or her in connection with the sale of the property or liquidation of assets, including all reasonable expenditures for necessary repairs, storage, or transportation of property levied upon under this section.

    (2) To a holder of a valid lien, mortgage, or security interest, up to the amount of his or her interest in the property or proceeds.

    (3) To a victim as restitution for human trafficking that was alleged in the accusatory pleading and that was proven by the prosecution.

    (4) For payment of a fine imposed. The proceeds obtained in payment of a fine shall be paid in the manner set forth in subdivision (h) of Section 236.1.

Added by Stats 2012 ch 512 (AB 2466),s 1, eff. 1/1/2013.

Section 236.7 - Seizure and forfeiture of assets

(a) Any interest in a vehicle, boat, airplane, money, negotiable instruments, securities, real property, or other thing of value that was put to substantial use for the purpose of facilitating the crime of human trafficking that involves a commercial sex act, as defined in paragraph (2) of subdivision (g) of Section 236.1, where the victim was less than 18 years of age at the time of the commission of the crime, may be seized and ordered forfeited by the court upon the conviction of a person guilty of human trafficking that involves a commercial sex act where the victim is an individual under 18 years of age, pursuant to Section 236.1.

(b) In any case in which a defendant is convicted of human trafficking pursuant to Section 236.1 and an allegation is found to be true that the victim was a person under 18 years of age and the crime involved a commercial sex act, as defined in paragraph (2) of subdivision (g) of Section 236.1, the following assets shall be subject to forfeiture upon proof of the provisions of subdivision (d) of Section 236.9:

    (1) Any property interest, whether tangible or intangible, acquired through human trafficking that involves a commercial sex act where the victim was less than 18 years of age at the time of the commission of the crime.

    (2) All proceeds from human trafficking that involves a commercial sex act where the victim was less than 18 years of age at the time of the commission of the crime, which property shall include all things of value that may have been received in exchange for the proceeds immediately derived from the act.

(c) If a prosecuting agency petitions for forfeiture of an interest under subdivision (a) or (b), the process prescribed in Sections 236.8 to 236.12, inclusive, shall apply, but no local or state prosecuting agency shall be required to petition for forfeiture in any case.

(d) Real property that is used as a family residence or for other lawful purposes, or that is owned by two or more persons, one of whom had no knowledge of its unlawful use, shall not be subject to forfeiture.

(e) An interest in a vehicle that may be lawfully driven with a class C, class M1, or class M2 license, as prescribed in Section 12804.9 of the Vehicle Code, may not be forfeited under this section if there is a community property interest in the vehicle by a person other than the defendant and the vehicle is the sole vehicle of this type available to the defendant's immediate family.

(f) Real property subject to forfeiture may not be seized, absent exigent circumstances, without notice to the interested parties and a hearing to determine that seizure is necessary to preserve the property pending the outcome of the proceedings. At the hearing, the prosecution shall bear the burden of establishing that probable cause exists for the forfeiture of the property and that seizure is necessary to preserve the property pending the outcome of the forfeiture proceedings. The court may issue a seizure order pursuant to this section if it finds that seizure is warranted or a pendente lite order pursuant to Section 236.10 if it finds that the status quo or value of the property can be preserved without seizure.

(g) For purposes of this section, no allegation or proof of a pattern of criminal profiteering activity is required.

Added by Stats 2012 ch 514 (SB 1133),s 2, eff. 1/1/2013.

Section 236.8 - Service of process of notice

(a) If the prosecuting agency, in conjunction with the criminal proceeding, files a petition of forfeiture with the superior court of the county in which the defendant has been charged with human trafficking that involves a commercial sex act, as defined in paragraph (2) of subdivision (g) of Section 236.1, where the victim was less than 18 years of age at the time of the commission of the crime, the prosecuting agency shall make service of process of a notice regarding that petition upon every individual who may have a property interest in the alleged proceeds or instruments. The notice shall state that any interested party may file a verified claim with the superior court stating the amount of their claimed interest and an affirmation or denial of the prosecuting agency's allegation. If the notice cannot be given by registered mail or personal delivery, the notice shall be published for at least three successive weeks in a newspaper of general circulation in the county where the property is located. If the property alleged to be subject to forfeiture is real property, the prosecuting agency shall, at the time of filing the petition of forfeiture, record a lis pendens with the county recorder in each county in which the real property is situated that specifically identifies the real property alleged to be subject to forfeiture. The judgment of forfeiture shall not affect the interest in real property of a third party that was acquired prior to the recording of the lis pendens.

(b) All notices shall set forth the time within which a claim of interest in the property seized is required to be filed pursuant to Section 236.9.

Added by Stats 2012 ch 514 (SB 1133),s 3, eff. 1/1/2013.

Section 236.9 - Verified claim

(a) A person claiming an interest in the property, proceeds, or instruments may, at any time within 30 days from the date of the first publication of the notice of seizure or within 30 days after receipt of actual notice, file with the superior court of the county in which the action is pending a verified claim stating his or her interest in the property, proceeds, or instruments. A verified copy of the claim shall be given by the claimant to the Attorney General or district attorney, as appropriate.

(b)

(1) If, at the end of the time set forth in subdivision (a), an interested person, other than the defendant, has not filed a claim, the court, upon motion, shall declare that the person has defaulted upon his or her alleged interest and the interest shall be subject to forfeiture upon proof of the provisions of subdivision (d).

(2) The defendant may admit or deny that the property is subject to forfeiture pursuant to the provisions of this chapter. If the defendant fails to admit or deny or to file a claim of interest in the property, proceeds, or instruments, the court shall enter a response of denial on behalf of the defendant.

(c)

(1) The forfeiture proceeding shall be set for hearing in the superior court in which the underlying criminal offense will be tried.

(2) If the defendant is found guilty of the underlying offense, the issue of forfeiture shall be promptly tried, either before the same jury or before a new jury in the discretion of the court, unless waived by the consent of all parties.

(d) At the forfeiture hearing, the prosecuting agency shall have the burden of establishing beyond a reasonable doubt that the property alleged in the petition comes within the provisions of Section 236.7.

(e) Unless the trier of fact finds that the seized property was used for a purpose for which forfeiture is permitted, the court shall order the seized property released to the person that the court determines is entitled to possession of that property. If the trier of fact finds that the seized property was used for a purpose for which forfeiture is permitted, but does not find that a person who has a valid interest in the property had actual knowledge that the property would be or was used for a purpose for which forfeiture is permitted and consented to that use, the court shall order the property released to the claimant.

Added by Stats 2012 ch 514 (SB 1133),s 4, eff. 1/1/2013.

Section 236.10 - Pendente lite orders to preserve status quo of property

(a) Concurrent with or subsequent to the filing of the petition, the prosecuting agency may move the superior court for, and the superior court may issue, the following pendente lite orders to preserve the status quo of the property alleged in the petition:

(1) An injunction to restrain anyone from transferring, encumbering, hypothecating, or otherwise disposing of the property.

(2) Appointment of a receiver to take possession of, care for, manage, and operate the assets and properties so that the property may be maintained and preserved. The court may order that a receiver appointed pursuant to this section be compensated for all reasonable expenditures made or incurred by him or her in connection with the possession, care, management, and operation of property or assets that are subject to the provisions of this section.

(b) No preliminary injunction may be granted or receiver appointed without notice to the interested parties and a hearing to determine that an order is necessary to preserve the property, pending the outcome of the criminal proceedings, and that there is probable cause to believe that the property alleged in the forfeiture proceedings are proceeds, instruments, or property interests forfeitable under the provisions of Section 236.7. However, a temporary restraining order may issue pending that hearing pursuant to the provisions of Section 527 of the Code of Civil Procedure.

(c) Notwithstanding any other provision of law, the court in granting these motions may order a surety bond or undertaking to preserve the property interests of the interested parties.

(d) The court shall, in making its orders, seek to protect the interests of those who may be involved in the same enterprise as the defendant, but who were not involved in human trafficking that involves a commercial sex act, as defined in paragraph (2) of subdivision (g) of Section 236.1, where the victim was less than 18 years of age at the time of the commission of the crime.

Added by Stats 2012 ch 514 (SB 1133),s 5, eff. 1/1/2013.

Section 236.11 - Forfeiture

(a) If the trier of fact at the forfeiture hearing finds that the alleged property, instruments, or proceeds are forfeitable pursuant to Section 236.7 and the defendant was engaged in human trafficking that involves a commercial sex act, as defined in paragraph (2) of subdivision (g) of Section 236.1, where the victim was less than 18 years of age at the time of the commission of the crime, the court shall declare that property or proceeds forfeited to the state or local governmental entity, subject to distribution as provided in Section 236.12. No property solely owned by a bona fide purchaser for value shall be subject to forfeiture.

(b) If the trier of fact at the forfeiture hearing finds that the alleged property is forfeitable pursuant to Section 236.7 but does not find that a person holding a valid lien, mortgage, security interest, or interest under a conditional sales contract acquired that interest with actual knowledge that the property was to be used for a purpose for which forfeiture is permitted, and the amount due to that person is less than the appraised value of the property, that person may pay to the state or the local governmental entity that initiated the forfeiture proceeding the amount of the registered owner's equity, which shall be deemed to be the difference between the appraised value and the amount of the lien, mortgage, security interest, or interest under a conditional sales contract. Upon payment, the state or local governmental entity shall relinquish all claims to the property. If the holder of the interest elects not to pay the state or local governmental entity, the property shall be deemed forfeited to the state or local governmental entity and the ownership certificate shall be forwarded. The appraised value shall be determined as of the date judgment is entered either by agreement between the legal owner and the governmental entity involved, or, if they cannot agree, by a court-appointed appraiser for the county in which the action is brought. A person holding a valid lien, mortgage, security interest, or interest under a conditional sales contract shall be paid the appraised value of his or her interest.

(c) If the amount due to a person holding a valid lien, mortgage, security interest, or interest under a conditional sales contract is less than the value of the property and the person elects not to make payment to the governmental entity, the property shall be sold at public auction by the Department of General Services or by the local governmental entity. The seller shall provide notice of the sale by one publication in a newspaper published and circulated in the city, community, or locality where the sale is to take place.

(d) Notwithstanding subdivision (c), a county may dispose of real property forfeited to the county pursuant to this chapter by the process prescribed in Section 25538.5 of the Government Code.

Added by Stats 2012 ch 514 (SB 1133),s 6, eff. 1/1/2013.

Section 236.12 - Distribution of money forfeited or proceeds of sale

Notwithstanding that no response or claim has been filed pursuant to Section 236.9, in all cases where property is forfeited pursuant to this chapter and, if necessary, sold by the Department of General Services or local governmental entity, the money forfeited or the proceeds of sale shall be distributed by the state or local governmental entity as follows:

(a) To the bona fide or innocent purchaser, conditional sales vendor, or holder of a valid lien, mortgage, or security interest, if any, up to the amount of his or her interest in the property or proceeds, when the court declaring the forfeiture orders a distribution to that person. The court shall endeavor to discover all those lienholders and protect their interests and may, at its discretion, order the proceeds placed in escrow for up to an additional 60 days to ensure that all valid claims are received and processed.

(b) To the Department of General Services or local governmental entity for all expenditures made or incurred by it in connection with the sale of the property, including expenditures for necessary repairs, storage, or transportation of property seized under this chapter.

(c)

(1) Fifty percent to the General Fund of the state or local governmental entity, whichever prosecutes or handles the forfeiture hearing.

(2) Fifty percent to the Victim-Witness Assistance Fund to be used upon appropriation for grants to community-based organizations that serve victims of human trafficking.

Added by Stats 2012 ch 514 (SB 1133),s 7, eff. 1/1/2013.

Section 236.13 - Assistance for minor victims of human trafficking

(a) In a case involving a charge of human trafficking under Section 236.1, a minor who is a victim of the human trafficking shall be provided with assistance from the local county Victim Witness Assistance Center if the minor so desires.

(b) This section does not require a local agency to operate a Victim Witness Assistance Center.

Added by Stats 2016 ch 641 (AB 2221),s 1, eff. 1/1/2017.

Section 236.14 - Vacatur relief for victims of human trafficking

(a) If a person was arrested for or convicted of any nonviolent offense committed while they were a victim of human trafficking, including, but not limited to, prostitution as described in subdivision (b) of Section 647, the person may petition the court for vacatur relief of their convictions, arrests, and adjudications under this section. The petitioner shall establish, by clear and convincing evidence, that the arrest or conviction was the direct result of being a victim of human trafficking that demonstrates that the person lacked the requisite intent to commit the offense. Upon this showing, the court shall find that the person lacked the requisite intent to commit the offense and shall therefore vacate the conviction as invalid due to legal defect at the time of the arrest or conviction.

(b) The petition for relief shall be submitted under penalty of perjury and shall describe all of the available grounds and evidence that the petitioner was a victim of human trafficking and the arrest or conviction of a nonviolent offense was the direct result of being a victim of human trafficking.

(c) The petition for relief and supporting documentation shall be served on the state or local prosecutorial agency that obtained the conviction for which vacatur is sought or with jurisdiction over charging decisions with regard to the arrest. The state or local prosecutorial agency shall have 45 days from the date of receipt of service to respond to the petition for relief.

(d) If opposition to the petition is not filed by the applicable state or local prosecutorial agency, the court shall deem the petition unopposed and may grant the petition.

(e) The court may, with the agreement of the petitioner and all of the involved state or local prosecutorial agencies, consolidate into one hearing a petition with multiple convictions from different jurisdictions.

(f) If the petition is opposed or if the court otherwise deems it necessary, the court shall schedule a hearing on the petition. The hearing may consist of the following:

(1) Testimony by the petitioner, which may be required in support of the petition.

(2) Evidence and supporting documentation in support of the petition.

(3) Opposition evidence presented by any of the involved state or local prosecutorial agencies that obtained the conviction.

(g) After considering the totality of the evidence presented, the court may vacate the conviction and the arrests and issue an order if it finds all of the following:

(1) That the petitioner was a victim of human trafficking at the time of the alleged commission of the qualifying crime.

(2) The arrest for or conviction of the crime was a direct result of being a victim of human trafficking.

(3) It is in the best interest of justice.

(h) An order of vacatur shall do all of the following:

(1) Set forth a finding that the petitioner was a victim of human trafficking at the time of the alleged commission of the qualifying crime and therefore lacked the requisite intent to commit the offense.

(2) Set aside the arrest, finding of guilt, or the adjudication and dismiss the accusation or information against the petitioner as invalid due to a legal defect at the time of arrest or conviction.

(3) Notify the Department of Justice that the petitioner was a victim of human trafficking when they committed the crime and of the relief that has been ordered.

(i) Notwithstanding this section, a petitioner shall not be relieved of any financial restitution order that directly benefits the victim of a nonviolent crime unless it has already been paid. With the exception of restitution, the collection of fines imposed as a result of a nonviolent offense that is the subject of the petition shall be stayed while the petition is pending.

(j) A person who was arrested as, or found to be, a person described in Section 602 of the Welfare and Institutions Code because they committed a qualifying nonviolent offense while they were a victim of human trafficking, including, but not limited to, prostitution, as described in subdivision (b) of Section 647, may petition the court for relief under this section. If the petitioner establishes that the arrest or adjudication was the direct result of being a victim of human trafficking, the petitioner is entitled to a rebuttable presumption that the requirements for relief have been met.

(k)

(1) If the court issues an order as described in subdivision (a) or (j), the court shall also order all of the following agencies to seal and destroy their records:

(A) Any law enforcement agency having jurisdiction over the offense.

(B) The Department of Justice.

(C) Any law enforcement agency that arrested the petitioner.

(D) Any law enforcement agency that participated in the arrest of the petitioner.

(E) Any law enforcement agency that has taken action or maintains records because of the offense, including, but not limited to, departments of probation, rehabilitation, corrections, and parole.

(2) Any government agency described in paragraph (1) shall seal its records of arrest and the court order to seal and destroy the records within one year from the date of arrest or within 90 days after the court order is granted, whichever occurs later. The agency shall thereafter destroy their records of the arrest and court order to seal and destroy those records within one year of the date of the court order.

(3) The court shall provide the petitioner a certified copy of any court order concerning the sealing and destruction of the arrest records. The court shall provide the petitioner and petitioner's counsel a copy of any form that the court submits to any agency, including the Department of Justice, related to the sealing and destruction of the arrest records.

(4) The Department of Justice shall notify the petitioner and the petitioner's counsel that the department has complied with the order to seal the arrest records by the applicable deadline.

(l) A petition pursuant to this section shall be made and heard at any time after the person has ceased to be a victim of human trafficking or at any time after the petitioner has sought services for being a victim of human trafficking, whichever occurs later, subject to reasonable concerns for the safety of the petitioner, family members of the petitioner, or other victims of human trafficking who may be jeopardized by the bringing of the application or for other reasons consistent with the purposes of this section. The right to petition for relief pursuant to this section does not expire with the passage of time and may be made at any time after the time specified in this subdivision. A court shall not refuse to hear a petition that was properly made pursuant to this section on the basis of the petitioner's outstanding fines and fees or the petitioner's failure to meet the conditions of probation.

(m)

(1) For the purposes of this section, official documentation of a petitioner's status as a victim of human trafficking may be introduced as evidence that their participation in the offense was the result of their status as a victim of human trafficking.

(2) For the purposes of this subdivision, "official documentation" means any documentation issued by a federal, state, or local agency that tends to show the petitioner's status as a victim of human trafficking. Official documentation shall not be required for the issuance of an order described in subdivision (a).

(n) If the petition is unopposed, the petitioner may appear at all hearings on the petition, if any, by counsel. If the petition is opposed and the court orders a hearing for relief on the petition, the petitioner shall appear in person unless the court finds a compelling reason why the petitioner cannot attend the hearing, in which case the petitioner may appear by telephone, videoconference, or by other electronic means established by the court.

(o) Notwithstanding any other law, a petitioner who has obtained an order pursuant to this section may lawfully deny or refuse to acknowledge an arrest, conviction, or adjudication that is set aside pursuant to the order.

(p) Notwithstanding any other law, the records of the arrest, conviction, or adjudication shall not be distributed to any state licensing board.

(q) The record of a proceeding related to a petition pursuant to this section that is accessible by the public shall not disclose the petitioner's full name.

(r) A court that grants relief pursuant to this section may take additional action as appropriate under the circumstances to carry out the purposes of this section.

(s) If the court denies the application because the evidence is insufficient to establish grounds for vacatur, the denial may be without prejudice. The court may state the reasons for its denial in writing or on the record that is memorialized by transcription, audiotape, or videotape, and, if those reasons are based on curable deficiencies in the application, allow the applicant a reasonable time period to cure the deficiencies upon which the court based the denial.

(t) For the purposes of this section, the following terms apply:

  (1) "Nonviolent offense" means any offense not listed in subdivision (c) of Section 667.5.

  (2) "Vacate" means that the arrest and any adjudications or convictions suffered by the petitioner are deemed not to have occurred and that all records in the case are sealed and destroyed pursuant to this section. The court shall provide the petitioner with a copy of the orders described in subdivisions (a), (j), and (k), as applicable, and inform the petitioner that they may thereafter state that they were not arrested for the charge, or adjudicated or convicted of the charge, that was vacated.

  (3) "Victim of human trafficking" means the victim of a crime described in subdivisions (a), (b), and (c) of Section 236.1.

Amended by Stats 2023 ch 131 (AB 1754),s 148, eff. 1/1/2024.

Amended by Stats 2022 ch 776 (AB 2169),s 1, eff. 1/1/2023.

Amended by Stats 2021 ch 193 (AB 262),s 1, eff. 1/1/2022.

Added by Stats 2016 ch 650 (SB 823),s 1, eff. 1/1/2017.

Section 236.15 - Vacatur relief for convictions resulting from being a victim of intimate partner violence or sexual violence

(a) If a person was arrested for or convicted of any nonviolent offense committed while the person was a victim of intimate partner violence or sexual violence, the person may petition the court for vacatur relief of their convictions, arrests, and adjudications under this section. The petitioner shall establish, by clear and convincing evidence, that the arrest or conviction was the direct result of being a victim of intimate partner violence or sexual violence that demonstrates that the person lacked the requisite intent to commit the offense. Upon this showing, the court shall find that the person lacked the requisite intent to commit the offense and shall therefore vacate the conviction as invalid due to legal defect at the time of the arrest or conviction.

(b) The petition for relief shall be submitted under penalty of perjury and shall describe all of the available grounds and evidence that the petitioner was a victim of intimate partner violence or sexual violence and the arrest or conviction of a nonviolent offense was the direct result of being a victim of intimate partner violence or sexual violence.

(c) The petition for relief and supporting documentation shall be served on the state or local prosecutorial agency that obtained the conviction for which vacatur is sought or with jurisdiction over charging decisions with regard to the arrest. The state or local prosecutorial agency shall have 45 days from the date of receipt of service to respond to the petition for relief.

(d) If opposition to the petition is not filed by the applicable state or local prosecutorial agency, the court shall deem the petition unopposed and may grant the petition.

(e) The court may, with the agreement of the petitioner and all of the involved state or local prosecutorial agencies, consolidate into one hearing a petition with multiple convictions from different jurisdictions.

(f) If the petition is opposed or if the court otherwise deems it necessary, the court shall schedule a hearing on the petition. The hearing may consist of the following:

  (1) Testimony by the petitioner, which may be required in support of the petition.

  (2) Evidence and supporting documentation in support of the petition.

  (3) Opposition evidence presented by any of the involved state or local prosecutorial agencies that obtained the conviction.

(g) After considering the totality of the evidence presented, the court may vacate the conviction and expunge the arrests and issue an order if it finds all of the following:

  (1) That the petitioner was a victim of intimate partner violence or sexual violence at the time of the alleged commission of the qualifying crime.

  (2) The arrest or conviction of the crime was a direct result of being a victim of intimate partner violence or sexual violence.

  (3) It is in the best interest of justice.

(h) An order of vacatur shall do all of the following:

  (1) Set forth a finding that the petitioner was a victim of intimate partner violence or sexual violence at the time of the alleged commission of the qualifying crime and therefore lacked the requisite intent to commit the offense.

  (2) Set aside the arrest, finding of guilt, or the adjudication and dismiss the accusation or information against the petitioner as invalid due to a legal defect at the time of the arrest or conviction.

  (3) Notify the Department of Justice that the petitioner was a victim of intimate partner violence or sexual violence when they committed the crime and of the relief that has been ordered.

(i) Notwithstanding this section, a petitioner shall not be relieved of any financial restitution order that directly benefits the victim of a nonviolent offense unless it has already been paid.

(j) A person who was arrested as, or found to be, a person described in Section 602 of the Welfare and Institutions Code because they committed a qualifying nonviolent offense while they were a victim of intimate partner violence or sexual violence may petition the court for relief under this section. If the petitioner establishes that the arrest or adjudication was the direct result of being a victim of intimate partner violence or sexual violence, the petitioner is entitled to a rebuttable presumption that the requirements for relief have been met.

(k) If the court issues an order as described in subdivision (a) or (j), the court shall also order the law enforcement agency having jurisdiction over the offense, the Department of Justice, and any law enforcement agency that arrested the petitioner or participated in the arrest of the petitioner to seal their records of the arrest and the court order to seal and destroy the records within three years from the date of the arrest or within one year after the court order is granted, whichever occurs later and thereafter to destroy their records of the arrest and the court order to seal and destroy those records. The court shall provide the petitioner a copy of any court order concerning the destruction of the arrest records.

(l) A petition pursuant to this section shall be made and heard within a reasonable time after the person has ceased to be a victim of intimate partner violence or sexual violence or within a reasonable time after the petitioner has sought services for being a victim of intimate partner violence or sexual violence, whichever occurs later, subject to reasonable concerns for the safety of the petitioner, family members of the petitioner, or other victims of intimate partner violence or sexual violence who may be jeopardized by the bringing of the application or for other reasons consistent with the purposes of this section.

(m) For the purposes of this section, official documentation of a petitioner's status as a victim of intimate partner violence or sexual violence may be introduced as evidence that their participation in the offense was the result of their status as a victim of intimate partner violence or sexual violence. For the purposes of this subdivision, "official documentation" means any documentation issued by a federal, state, or local agency that tends to show the petitioner's status as a victim of intimate partner violence or sexual violence. Official documentation shall not be required for the issuance of an order described in subdivision (a).

(n) A petitioner, or their attorney, may be excused from appearing in person at a hearing for relief pursuant to this section only if the court finds a compelling reason why the petitioner cannot attend the hearing, in which case the petitioner may appear telephonically, via videoconference, or by other electronic means established by the court.

(o) Notwithstanding any other law, a petitioner who has obtained an order pursuant to this section may lawfully deny or refuse to acknowledge an arrest, conviction, or adjudication that is set aside pursuant to the order.

(p) Notwithstanding any other law, the records of the arrest, conviction, or adjudication shall not be distributed to any state licensing board.

(q) The record of a proceeding related to a petition pursuant to this section that is accessible by the public shall not disclose the petitioner's full name.

(r) A court that grants relief pursuant to this section may take additional action as appropriate under the circumstances to carry out the purposes of this section.

(s) If the court denies the application because the evidence is insufficient to establish grounds for vacatur, the denial may be without prejudice. The court may state the reasons for its denial in writing or on the record that is memorialized by transcription, audiotape, or videotape, and if those reasons are based on curable deficiencies in the application, allow the applicant a reasonable time period to cure the deficiencies upon which the court based the denial.

(t) For the purposes of this section, the following terms apply:

(1) "Nonviolent offense" means any offense not listed in subdivision (c) of Section 667.5.

(2) "Vacate" means that the arrest and any adjudications or convictions suffered by the petitioner are deemed not to have occurred and that all records in the case are sealed and destroyed pursuant to this section. The court shall provide the petitioner with a copy of the orders described in subdivisions (a), (j), and (k), as applicable, and inform the petitioner that they may thereafter state that they were not arrested for the charge, or adjudicated or convicted of the charge, that was vacated.

Amended by Stats 2023 ch 131 (AB 1754),s 149, eff. 1/1/2024.

Amended by Stats 2022 ch 776 (AB 2169),s 2, eff. 1/1/2023.

Added by Stats 2021 ch 695 (AB 124),s 1, eff. 1/1/2022.

Section 236.21 - Human trafficking; victim rights

(a)

(1) A victim of human trafficking or abuse, as defined in Section 236.1 of this code or Section 1038.2 of the Evidence Code, has the right to have a human trafficking advocate and a support person of the victim's choosing present at an interview by a law enforcement authority, prosecutor, or the suspect's defense attorney. The law enforcement officer or prosecutor may exclude the support person from the interview if the law enforcement officer or prosecutor believes that the support person's presence would be detrimental to the process.

(2) Prior to being present at an interview conducted by a law enforcement authority, prosecutor, or the suspect's defense attorney, a human trafficking advocate shall advise the victim of applicable limitations on the confidentiality of communications between the victim and the human trafficking advocate.

(3) For purposes of this section, the following definitions apply:

(A) "Human trafficking advocate" means a person employed by an organization specified in Section 1038.2 of the Evidence Code.

(B) "Support person" means a family member or friend of the survivor and does not include the human trafficking advocate.

(b)

(1) Prior to the commencement of the initial interview by a law enforcement authority or a prosecutor pertaining to a criminal action arising out of a human trafficking incident, a victim of human trafficking or abuse, as defined in Section 236.1 of this code or Section 1038.2 of the Evidence Code, shall be notified orally or in writing by the attending law enforcement authority or prosecutor that the victim has the right to have a human trafficking advocate and a support person of the victim's choosing present at the interview.

(2) At the time the victim is advised of their rights under paragraph (1), the attending law enforcement authority or prosecutor shall also advise the victim of the right to have a human trafficking advocate and a support person present at an interview by the suspect's defense attorney or investigators or agents employed by the suspect's defense attorney.

(3) This subdivision applies to investigators and agents employed or retained by law enforcement or the prosecutor.

(c) An initial investigation by law enforcement to determine whether a crime has been committed and the identity of the suspects does not constitute a law enforcement interview for purposes of this section.

Added by Stats 2023 ch 109 (SB 376),s 1, eff. 1/1/2024.

Section 236.23 - Being victim of human trafficking as affirmative defense

(a) In addition to any other affirmative defense, it is a defense to a charge of a crime that the person was coerced to commit the offense as a direct result of being a human trafficking victim at the time of the offense and had a reasonable fear of harm. This defense does not apply to a violent felony, as defined in subdivision (c) of Section 667.5.

(b) A defendant asserting the affirmative defense specified in subdivision (a) has the burden of establishing the affirmative defense by a preponderance of the evidence.

(c) Certified records of a federal, state, tribal, or local court or governmental agency documenting the person's status as a victim of human trafficking at the time of the offense, including identification of a victim of human trafficking by a peace officer pursuant to Section 236.2 and certified records of approval notices or enforcement certifications generated from federal immigration proceedings, may be presented to establish an affirmative defense pursuant to this section. Information contained in governmental agency reports, which is relevant to the identification of a victim of human trafficking by a peace officer pursuant to Section 236.2, may be presented pursuant to this subdivision even if a peace officer did not make an identification pursuant to Section 236.2.

(d) The affirmative defense may be asserted at any time before the entry of a plea of guilty or nolo contendere or admission to the truth of the charges and before the conclusion of any trial for the offense. If asserted before the preliminary hearing held in a case, the affirmative defense shall, upon request by the defendant, be determined at the preliminary hearing.

(e) If the defendant prevails on the affirmative defense provided under subdivision (a), the defendant is entitled to all of the following relief:

    (1)

        (A) The court shall order that all records in the case be sealed pursuant to Section 851.86.

        (B) Records that have been sealed pursuant to this paragraph may be accessed, inspected, or utilized by law enforcement for subsequent investigatory purposes involving persons other than the defendant.

    (2) The person shall be released from all penalties and disabilities resulting from the charge, and all actions and proceedings by law enforcement personnel, courts, or other government employees that led to the charge shall be deemed not to have occurred.

    (3)

        (A) The person may in all circumstances state that they have never been arrested for, or charged with, the crime that is the subject of the charge or conviction, including without limitation in response to questions on employment, housing, financial aid, or loan applications.

        (B) The person may not be denied rights or benefits, including, without limitation, employment, housing, financial aid, welfare, or a loan or other financial accommodation, based on the arrest or charge or their failure or refusal to disclose the existence of or information concerning those events.

        (C) The person may not be thereafter charged or convicted of perjury or otherwise of giving a false statement by reason of having failed to disclose or acknowledge the existence of the charge, or any arrest, indictment, trial, or other proceedings related thereto.

(f) If, in a proceeding pursuant to Section 602 of the Welfare and Institutions Code, the juvenile court finds that the offense on which the proceeding is based was committed as a direct result of the minor being a human trafficking victim, and the affirmative defense established in subdivision (a) is established by a preponderance of the evidence, the court shall dismiss the proceeding and order the relief prescribed in Section 786 of the Welfare and Institutions Code.

Amended by Stats 2021 ch 695 (AB 124),s 2, eff. 1/1/2022.

Added by Stats 2016 ch 636 (AB 1761),s 2, eff. 1/1/2017.

Section 236.24 - Coercion to commit offense due to being a victim of intimate partner violence or sexual violence is affirmative defense

(a) In addition to any other affirmative defense, it is a defense to a charge of a crime that the person was coerced to commit the offense as a direct result of being a victim of intimate partner violence or sexual violence at the time of the offense and had a reasonable fear of harm. This defense does not apply to a violent felony, as defined in subdivision (c) of Section 667.5.

(b) A defendant asserting the affirmative defense specified in subdivision (a) has the burden of establishing the affirmative defense by a preponderance of the evidence.

(c) Certified records of a federal, state, tribal, or local court or governmental agency documenting the person's status as a victim of intimate partner violence or sexual violence at the time of the offense, including identification of a victim of intimate partner violence or sexual violence by a peace officer and certified records of approval notices or enforcement certifications generated from federal immigration proceedings, may be presented to establish an affirmative defense pursuant to this section. Information contained in governmental agency reports, which is relevant to the identification of a victim of intimate partner violence or sexual violence, may be presented pursuant to this subdivision even if the defendant was not then identified as a victim of intimate partner violence or sexual violence.

(d) The affirmative defense may be asserted at any time before the entry of a plea of guilty or nolo contendere or admission to the truth of the charges and before the conclusion of any trial for the offense. If asserted before the preliminary hearing held in a case, the affirmative defense shall, upon request by the defendant, be determined at the preliminary hearing.

(e) If the defendant prevails on the affirmative defense provided under subdivision (a), the defendant is entitled to all of the following relief:

    (1)

        (A) The court shall order that all records in the case be sealed pursuant to Section 851.86.

        (B) Records that have been sealed pursuant to this paragraph may be accessed, inspected, or utilized by law enforcement for subsequent investigatory purposes involving persons other than the defendant.

    (2) The person shall be released from all penalties and disabilities resulting from the charge, and all actions and proceedings by law enforcement personnel, courts, or other government employees that led to the charge shall be deemed not to have occurred.

    (3)

(A) The person may in all circumstances state that they have never been arrested for, or charged with, the crime that is the subject of the charge or conviction, including without limitation in response to questions on employment, housing, financial aid, or loan applications.

(B) The person may not be denied rights or benefits, including, without limitation, employment, housing, financial aid, welfare, or a loan or other financial accommodation, based on the arrest or charge or their failure or refusal to disclose the existence of or information concerning those events.

(C) The person may not be thereafter charged or convicted of perjury or otherwise of giving a false statement by reason of having failed to disclose or acknowledge the existence of the charge, or any arrest, indictment, trial, or other proceedings related thereto.

(f) If, in a proceeding pursuant to Section 602 of the Welfare and Institutions Code, the juvenile court finds that the offense on which the proceeding is based was committed as a direct result of the minor being a victim of intimate partner violence or sexual violence, and the affirmative defense established in subdivision (a) is established by a preponderance of the evidence, the court shall dismiss the proceeding and order the relief prescribed in Section 786 of the Welfare and Institutions Code.

Added by Stats 2021 ch 695 (AB 124),s 3, eff. 1/1/2022.

Section 237 - Punishment for false imprisonment

(a) False imprisonment is punishable by a fine not exceeding one thousand dollars ($1,000), or by imprisonment in the county jail for not more than one year, or by both that fine and imprisonment. If the false imprisonment be effected by violence, menace, fraud, or deceit, it shall be punishable by imprisonment pursuant to subdivision (h) of Section 1170.

(b) False imprisonment of an elder or dependent adult by use of violence, menace, fraud, or deceit shall be punishable as described in subdivision (f) of Section 368.

Amended by Stats 2011 ch 39 (AB 117),s 68, eff. 6/30/2011.

Amended by Stats 2011 ch 15 (AB 109),s 288, eff. 4/4/2011, but operative no earlier than October 1, 2011, and only upon creation of a community corrections grant program to assist in implementing this act and upon an appropriation to fund the grant program.

Amended & effective October 10, 1999 (Bill Number: AB 1236) (Chapter 706).

Chapter 9 - ASSAULT AND BATTERY

Section 240 - Assault

An assault is an unlawful attempt, coupled with a present ability, to commit a violent injury on the person of another.

Enacted 1872.

Section 241 - Punishment

(a) An assault is punishable by a fine not exceeding one thousand dollars ($1,000), or by imprisonment in the county jail not exceeding six months, or by both the fine and imprisonment.

(b) When an assault is committed against the person of a parking control officer engaged in the performance of his or her duties, and the person committing the offense knows or reasonably should know that the victim is a parking control officer, the assault is punishable by a fine not exceeding two thousand dollars ($2,000), or by imprisonment in the county jail not exceeding six months, or by both the fine and imprisonment.

(c) When an assault is committed against the person of a peace officer, firefighter, emergency medical technician, mobile intensive care paramedic, lifeguard, process server, traffic officer, code enforcement officer, animal control officer, or search and rescue member engaged in the performance of his or her duties, or a physician or nurse engaged in rendering emergency medical care outside a hospital, clinic, or other health care facility, and the person committing the offense knows or reasonably should know that the victim is a peace officer, firefighter, emergency medical technician, mobile intensive care paramedic, lifeguard, process server, traffic officer, code enforcement officer, animal control officer, or search and rescue member engaged in the performance of his or her duties, or a physician or nurse engaged in rendering emergency medical care, the assault is punishable by a fine not exceeding two thousand dollars ($2,000), or by imprisonment in a county jail not exceeding one year, or by both the fine and imprisonment.

(d) As used in this section, the following definitions apply:

(1) Peace officer means any person defined in Chapter 4.5 (commencing with Section 830) of Title 3 of Part 2.

(2) "Emergency medical technician" means a person possessing a valid course completion certificate from a program approved by the State Department of Health Care Services for the medical training and education of ambulance personnel, and who meets the standards of Division 2.5 (commencing with Section 1797) of the Health and Safety Code.

(3) "Mobile intensive care paramedic" refers to a person who meets the standards set forth in Division 2.5 (commencing with Section 1797) of the Health and Safety Code.

(4) "Nurse" means a person who meets the standards of Division 2.5 (commencing with Section 1797) of the Health and Safety Code.

(5) "Lifeguard" means a person who is:

(A) Employed as a lifeguard by the state, a county, or a city, and is designated by local ordinance as a public officer who has a duty and responsibility to enforce local ordinances and misdemeanors through the issuance of citations.

(B) Wearing distinctive clothing which includes written identification of the person's status as a lifeguard and which clearly identifies the employing organization.

(6) "Process server" means any person who meets the standards or is expressly exempt from the standards set forth in Section 22350 of the Business and Professions Code.

(7) "Traffic officer" means any person employed by a county or city to monitor and enforce state laws and local ordinances relating to parking and the operation of vehicles.

(8) "Animal control officer" means any person employed by a county or city for purposes of enforcing animal control laws or regulations.

(9)

(A) "Code enforcement officer" means any person who is not described in Chapter 4.5 (commencing with Section 830) of Title 3 of Part 2 and who is employed by any governmental subdivision, public or quasi-public corporation, public agency, public service corporation, any town, city, county, or municipal corporation, whether incorporated or chartered, that has enforcement authority for health, safety, and welfare requirements, and whose duties include enforcement of any statute, rules, regulations, or standards, and who is authorized to issue citations, or file formal complaints.

(B) "Code enforcement officer" also includes any person who is employed by the Department of Housing and Community Development who has enforcement authority for health, safety, and welfare requirements pursuant to the Employee Housing Act (Part 1 (commencing with Section 17000) of Division 13 of the Health and Safety Code); the State Housing Law (Part 1.5 (commencing with Section 17910) of Division 13 of the Health and Safety Code); the Manufactured Housing Act of 1980 (Part 2 (commencing with Section 18000) of Division 13 of the Health and Safety Code); the Mobilehome Parks Act (Part 2.1 (commencing with Section 18200) of Division 13 of the Health and Safety Code); and the Special Occupancy Parks Act (Part 2.3 (commencing with Section 18860) of Division 13 of the Health and Safety Code).

(10) "Parking control officer" means any person employed by a city, county, or city and county, to monitor and enforce state laws and local ordinances relating to parking.

(11) "Search and rescue member" means any person who is part of an organized search and rescue team managed by a governmental agency.

Amended by Stats 2016 ch 86 (SB 1171),s 224, eff. 1/1/2017.
Amended by Stats 2011 ch 249 (SB 390),s 1, eff. 1/1/2012.
Amended by Stats 2007 ch 243 (AB 1686),s 1, eff. 1/1/2008.
Amended by Stats 2003 ch 274 (SB 919), s 1, eff. 1/1/2004.

Section 241.1 - Assault committed against person of custodial officer

When an assault is committed against the person of a custodial officer as defined in Section 831 or 831.5, and the person committing the offense knows or reasonably should know that the victim is a custodial officer engaged in the performance of his or her duties, the offense shall be punished by imprisonment in the county jail not exceeding one year or by imprisonment pursuant to subdivision (h) of Section 1170.

Amended by Stats 2011 ch 39 (AB 117),s 68, eff. 6/30/2011.
Amended by Stats 2011 ch 15 (AB 109),s 289, eff. 4/4/2011, but operative no earlier than October 1, 2011, and only upon creation of a community corrections grant program to assist in implementing this act and upon an appropriation to fund the grant program.

Section 241.2 - Assault committed on school or park property

(a)

(1) When an assault is committed on school or park property against any person, the assault is punishable by a fine not exceeding two thousand dollars ($2,000), or by imprisonment in the county jail not exceeding one year, or by both that fine and imprisonment.

(2) When a violation of this section is committed by a minor on school property, the court may, in addition to any other fine, sentence, or as a condition of probation, order the minor to attend counseling as deemed appropriate by the court at the expense of the minor's parents. The court shall take into consideration the ability of the minor's parents to pay, however, no minor shall be relieved of attending counseling because of the minor's parents' inability to pay for the counseling imposed by this section.

(b) "School," as used in this section, means any elementary school, junior high school, four-year high school, senior high school, adult school or any branch thereof, opportunity school, continuation high school, regional occupational center, evening high school, technical school, or community college.

(c) "Park," as used in this section, means any publicly maintained or operated park. It does not include any facility when used for professional sports or commercial events.

Amended by Stats 2001 ch 484 (AB 653), s 2, eff. 1/1/2002.

Section 241.3 - Assault committed on property or motor vehicle of public transportation provider

(a) When an assault is committed against any person on the property of, or on a motor vehicle of, a public transportation provider, the offense shall be punished by a fine not to exceed two thousand dollars ($2,000), or by imprisonment in a county jail not to exceed one year, or by both the fine and imprisonment.

(b) As used in this section, "public transportation provider" means a publicly or privately owned entity that operates, for the transportation of persons for hire, a bus, taxicab, streetcar, cable car, trackless trolley, or other motor vehicle, including a vehicle operated on stationary rails or on a track or rail suspended in air, or that operates a schoolbus.

(c) As used in this section, "on the property of" means the entire station where public transportation is available, including the parking lot reserved for the public who utilize the transportation system.

Repealed and added by Stats. 1996, Ch. 423, Sec. 2. Effective January 1, 1997.

Section 241.4 - Fine; assault committed against person of peace officer

An assault is punishable by fine not exceeding one thousand dollars ($1,000), or by imprisonment in the county jail not exceeding six months, or by both. When the assault is committed against the person of a peace officer engaged in the performance of his or her duties as a member of a police department of a school district pursuant to Section 38000 of the Education Code, and the person committing the offense knows or reasonably should know that the victim is a peace officer engaged in the performance of his or her duties, the offense shall be punished by imprisonment in the county jail not exceeding one year or by imprisonment pursuant to subdivision (h) of Section 1170.

Amended by Stats 2011 ch 39 (AB 117),s 68, eff. 6/30/2011.
Amended by Stats 2011 ch 15 (AB 109),s 290, eff. 4/4/2011, but operative no earlier than October 1, 2011, and only upon creation of a community corrections grant program to assist in implementing this act and upon an appropriation to fund the grant program.
Amended by Stats 2005 ch 279 (SB 1107),s 2, eff. 1/1/2006

Section 241.5 - Assault committed against highway worker

(a) When an assault is committed against a highway worker engaged in the performance of his or her duties and the person committing the offense knows or reasonably should know that the victim is a highway worker engaged in the performance of his or her duties, the offense shall be punishable by a fine not to exceed two thousand dollars ($2,000) or by imprisonment in a county jail up to one year or by both that fine and imprisonment.

(b) As used in this section, "highway worker" means an employee of the Department of Transportation, a contractor or employee of a contractor while working under contract with the Department of Transportation, an employee of a city, county, or city and county, a contractor or employee of a contractor while working under contract with a city, county, or city and county, or a volunteer as defined in Section 1720.4 of the Labor Code who does one or more of the following:

(1) Performs maintenance, repair, or construction of state highway or local street or road infrastructures and associated rights-of-way in highway or local street or road work zones.

(2) Operates equipment on state highway or local street or road infrastructures and associated rights-of-way in highway or local street or road work zones.

(3) Performs any related maintenance work, as required, on state highway or local street or road infrastructures in highway or local street or road work zones.

Amended by Stats 2009 ch 116 (AB 561),s 1, eff. 1/1/2010.

Added by Stats 2008 ch 410 (SB 1509),s 1, eff. 1/1/2009.

Section 241.6 - Assault committed against school employee

When an assault is committed against a school employee engaged in the performance of his or her duties, or in retaliation for an act performed in the course of his or her duties, whether on or off campus, during the schoolday or at any other time, and the person committing the offense knows or reasonably should know the victim is a school employee, the assault is punishable by imprisonment in a county jail not exceeding one year, or by a fine not exceeding two thousand dollars ($2,000), or by both the fine and imprisonment. For purposes of this section, "school employee" has the same meaning as defined in subdivision (d) of Section 245.5.

This section shall not apply to conduct arising during the course of an otherwise lawful labor dispute.

Amended by Stats. 1993, Ch. 1257, Sec. 5. Effective January 1, 1994.

Section 241.7 - Assault against juror

Any person who is a party to a civil or criminal action in which a jury has been selected to try the case and who, while the legal action is pending or after the conclusion of the trial, commits an assault against any juror or alternate juror who was selected and sworn in that legal action, shall be punished by a fine not to exceed two thousand dollars ($2,000), or by imprisonment in the county jail not exceeding one year, or by both such fine and imprisonment, or by imprisonment pursuant to subdivision (h) of Section 1170.

Amended by Stats 2011 ch 39 (AB 117),s 68, eff. 6/30/2011.

Amended by Stats 2011 ch 15 (AB 109),s 291, eff. 4/4/2011, but operative no earlier than October 1, 2011, and only upon creation of a community corrections grant program to assist in implementing this act and upon an appropriation to fund the grant program.

Section 241.8 - Assault against member of armed forces because of victim's service

(a) Any person who commits an assault against a member of the United States Armed Forces because of the victim's service in the United States Armed Forces shall be punished by a fine not exceeding two thousand dollars ($2,000), by imprisonment in a county jail for a period not exceeding one year, or by both that fine and imprisonment.

(b) "Because of" means that the bias motivation must be a cause in fact of the assault, whether or not other causes exist. When multiple concurrent motives exist, the prohibited bias must be a substantial factor in bringing about the assault.

Added by Stats 2003 ch 138 (AB 187), s 1, eff. 1/1/2004.

Section 242 - Battery

A battery is any willful and unlawful use of force or violence upon the person of another.

Enacted 1872.

Section 243 - Punishment

(a) A battery is punishable by a fine not exceeding two thousand dollars ($2,000), or by imprisonment in a county jail not exceeding six months, or by both that fine and imprisonment.

(b) When a battery is committed against the person of a peace officer, custodial officer, firefighter, emergency medical technician, lifeguard, security officer, custody assistant, process server, traffic officer, code enforcement officer, animal control officer, or search and rescue member engaged in the performance of their duties, whether on or off duty, including when the peace officer is in a police uniform and is concurrently performing the duties required of them as a peace officer while also employed in a private capacity as a part-time or casual private security guard or patrolman, or a nonsworn employee of a probation department engaged in the performance of their duties, whether on or off duty, or a physician or nurse engaged in rendering emergency medical care outside a hospital, clinic, or other health care facility, and the person committing the offense knows or reasonably should know that the victim is a peace officer, custodial officer, firefighter, emergency medical technician, lifeguard, security officer, custody assistant, process server, traffic officer, code enforcement officer, animal control officer, or search and rescue member engaged in the performance of their duties, nonsworn employee of a probation department, or a physician or nurse engaged in rendering emergency medical care, the battery is punishable by a fine not exceeding two thousand dollars ($2,000), or by imprisonment in a county jail not exceeding one year, or by both that fine and imprisonment.

(c)

(1) When a battery is committed against a custodial officer, firefighter, emergency medical technician, lifeguard, process server, traffic officer, or animal control officer engaged in the performance of their duties, whether on or off duty, or a nonsworn employee of a probation department engaged in the performance of their duties, whether on or off duty, or a physician or nurse engaged in rendering emergency medical care outside a hospital, clinic, or other health care facility, and the person committing the offense knows or reasonably should know that the victim is a nonsworn employee of a probation department, custodial officer, firefighter, emergency medical technician, lifeguard, process server, traffic officer, or animal control officer engaged in the performance of their duties, or a physician or nurse engaged in rendering emergency medical care, and an injury is inflicted on that victim, the battery is punishable by a

fine of not more than two thousand dollars ($2,000), by imprisonment in a county jail not exceeding one year, or by both that fine and imprisonment, or by imprisonment pursuant to subdivision (h) of Section 1170 for 16 months, or two or three years.

(2) When the battery specified in paragraph (1) is committed against a peace officer engaged in the performance of their duties, whether on or off duty, including when the peace officer is in a police uniform and is concurrently performing the duties required of them as a peace officer while also employed in a private capacity as a part-time or casual private security guard or patrolman and the person committing the offense knows or reasonably should know that the victim is a peace officer engaged in the performance of their duties, the battery is punishable by a fine of not more than ten thousand dollars ($10,000), or by imprisonment in a county jail not exceeding one year or pursuant to subdivision (h) of Section 1170 for 16 months, or two or three years, or by both that fine and imprisonment.

(d) When a battery is committed against any person and serious bodily injury is inflicted on the person, the battery is punishable by imprisonment in a county jail not exceeding one year or imprisonment pursuant to subdivision (h) of Section 1170 for two, three, or four years.

(e)

(1) When a battery is committed against a spouse, a person with whom the defendant is cohabiting, a person who is the parent of the defendant's child, former spouse, fiance, or fiancee, or a person with whom the defendant currently has, or has previously had, a dating or engagement relationship, the battery is punishable by a fine not exceeding two thousand dollars ($2,000), or by imprisonment in a county jail for a period of not more than one year, or by both that fine and imprisonment. If probation is granted, or the execution or imposition of the sentence is suspended, it shall be a condition thereof that the defendant participate in, for no less than one year, and successfully complete, a batterer's treatment program, as described in Section 1203.097, or if none is available, another appropriate counseling program designated by the court. However, this provision shall not be construed as requiring a city, a county, or a city and county to provide a new program or higher level of service as contemplated by Section 6 of Article XIII B of the California Constitution.

(2) Upon conviction of a violation of this subdivision, if probation is granted, the conditions of probation may include, in lieu of a fine, one or both of the following requirements:

(A) That the defendant make payments to a domestic violence shelter-based program, up to a maximum of five thousand dollars ($5,000).

(B) That the defendant reimburse the victim for reasonable costs of counseling and other reasonable expenses that the court finds are the direct result of the defendant's offense. For any order to pay a fine, make payments to a domestic violence shelter-based program, or pay restitution as a condition of probation under this subdivision, the court shall make a determination of the defendant's ability to pay. In no event shall any order to make payments to a domestic violence shelter-based program be made if it would impair the ability of the defendant to pay direct restitution to the victim or court-ordered child support. If the injury to a married person is caused in whole or in part by the criminal acts of their spouse in violation of this section, the community property shall not be used to discharge the liability of the offending spouse for restitution to the injured spouse, required by Section 1203.04, as operative on or before August 2, 1995, or Section 1202.4, or to a shelter for costs with regard to the injured spouse and dependents, required by this section, until all separate property of the offending spouse is exhausted.

(3) Upon conviction of a violation of this subdivision, if probation is granted or the execution or imposition of the sentence is suspended and the person has been previously convicted of a violation of this subdivision or Section 273.5, the person shall be imprisoned for not less than 48 hours in addition to the conditions in paragraph (1). However, the court, upon a showing of good cause, may elect not to impose the mandatory minimum imprisonment as required by this subdivision and may, under these circumstances, grant probation or order the suspension of the execution or imposition of the sentence.

(4) The Legislature finds and declares that these specified crimes merit special consideration when imposing a sentence so as to display society's condemnation for these crimes of violence upon victims with whom a close relationship has been formed.

(5) If a peace officer makes an arrest for a violation of paragraph (1) of subdivision (e) of this section, the peace officer is not required to inform the victim of their right to make a citizen's arrest pursuant to subdivision (b) of Section 836.

(f) As used in this section:

(1) "Peace officer" means any person defined in Chapter 4.5 (commencing with Section 830) of Title 3 of Part 2.

(2) "Emergency medical technician" means a person who is either an EMT-I, EMT-II, or EMT-P (paramedic), and possesses a valid certificate or license in accordance with the standards of Division 2.5 (commencing with Section 1797) of the Health and Safety Code.

(3) "Nurse" means a person who meets the standards of Division 2.5 (commencing with Section 1797) of the Health and Safety Code.

(4) "Serious bodily injury" means a serious impairment of physical condition, including, but not limited to, the following: loss of consciousness; concussion; bone fracture; protracted loss or impairment of function of any bodily member or organ; a wound requiring extensive suturing; and serious disfigurement.

(5) "Injury" means any physical injury which requires professional medical treatment.

(6) "Custodial officer" means any person who has the responsibilities and duties described in Section 831 and who is employed by a law enforcement agency of any city or county or who performs those duties as a volunteer.

(7) "Lifeguard" means a person defined in paragraph (5) of subdivision (d) of Section 241.

(8) "Traffic officer" means any person employed by a city, county, or city and county to monitor and enforce state laws and local ordinances relating to parking and the operation of vehicles.

(9) "Animal control officer" means any person employed by a city, county, or city and county for purposes of enforcing animal control laws or regulations.

(10) "Dating relationship" means frequent, intimate associations primarily characterized by the expectation of affectional or sexual involvement independent of financial considerations.

(11)

(A) "Code enforcement officer" means any person who is not described in Chapter 4.5 (commencing with Section 830) of Title 3 of Part 2 and who is employed by any governmental subdivision, public or quasi-public corporation, public agency, public service corporation, any town, city, county, or municipal corporation, whether incorporated or chartered, who has enforcement authority for health, safety, and welfare requirements, and whose duties include enforcement of any statute, rules, regulations, or standards, and who is authorized to issue citations, or file formal complaints.

(B) "Code enforcement officer" also includes any person who is employed by the Department of Housing and Community Development who has enforcement authority for health, safety, and welfare requirements pursuant to the Employee Housing Act (Part 1 (commencing with Section 17000) of Division 13 of the Health and Safety Code); the State Housing Law (Part 1.5 (commencing with Section 17910) of Division 13 of the Health and Safety Code); the Manufactured Housing Act of 1980 (Part 2 (commencing with Section 18000) of Division 13 of the Health and Safety Code); the Mobilehome Parks Act (Part 2.1 (commencing with Section 18200) of Division 13 of the Health and Safety Code); and the Special Occupancy Parks Act (Part 2.3 (commencing with Section 18860) of Division 13 of the Health and Safety Code).

(12) "Custody assistant" means any person who has the responsibilities and duties described in Section 831.7 and who is employed by a law enforcement agency of any city, county, or city and county.

(13) "Search and rescue member" means any person who is part of an organized search and rescue team managed by a government agency.

(14) "Security officer" means any person who has the responsibilities and duties described in Section 831.4 and who is employed by a law enforcement agency of any city, county, or city and county.

(g) It is the intent of the Legislature by amendments to this section at the 1981-82 and 1983-84 Regular Sessions to abrogate the holdings in cases such as People v. Corey, 21 Cal. 3d 738, and Cervantez v. J.C. Penney Co., 24 Cal. 3d 579, and to reinstate prior judicial interpretations of this section as they relate to criminal sanctions for battery on peace officers who are employed, on a part-time or casual basis, while wearing a police uniform as private security guards or patrolmen and to allow the exercise of peace officer powers concurrently with that employment.

Amended by Stats 2022 ch 197 (SB 1493),s 12, eff. 1/1/2023.
Amended by Stats 2015 ch 626 (AB 545),s 1, eff. 1/1/2016.
Amended by Stats 2012 ch 867 (SB 1144),s 15, eff. 1/1/2013.
Amended by Stats 2012 ch 162 (SB 1171),s 122, eff. 1/1/2013.
Amended by Stats 2011 ch 250 (SB 406),s 1.3, eff. 1/1/2012.
Amended by Stats 2011 ch 39 (AB 117),s 68, eff. 6/30/2011.
Amended by Stats 2011 ch 15 (AB 109),s 292, eff. 4/4/2011, but operative no earlier than October 1, 2011, and only upon creation of a community corrections grant program to assist in implementing this act and upon an appropriation to fund the grant program.
Amended by Stats 2011 ch 249 (SB 390),s 2, eff. 1/1/2012.
Amended by Stats 2003 ch 274 (SB 919), s 2, eff. 1/1/2004.
Amended by Stats 2000 ch 236 (AB 1899), s 1, eff. 1/1/2001.
Previously Amended October 10, 1999 (Bill Number: SB 563) (Chapter 660).

Section 243.1 - Batter committed against person of custodial officer
When a battery is committed against the person of a custodial officer as defined in Section 831 of the Penal Code, and the person committing the offense knows or reasonably should know that the victim is a custodial officer engaged in the performance of his or her duties, and the custodial officer is engaged in the performance of his or her duties, the offense shall be punished by imprisonment pursuant to subdivision (h) of Section 1170.
Amended by Stats 2011 ch 39 (AB 117),s 68, eff. 6/30/2011.
Amended by Stats 2011 ch 15 (AB 109),s 293, eff. 4/4/2011, but operative no earlier than October 1, 2011, and only upon creation of a community corrections grant program to assist in implementing this act and upon an appropriation to fund the grant program.
Amended by Stats 2001 ch 854 (SB 205), s 24, eff. 1/1/2002.

Section 243.2 - Battery committed on school property, park property, or grounds of hospital
(a)

(1) Except as otherwise provided in Section 243.6, when a battery is committed on school property, park property, or the grounds of a public or private hospital, against any person, the battery is punishable by a fine not exceeding two thousand dollars ($2,000), or by imprisonment in the county jail not exceeding one year, or by both the fine and imprisonment.

(2) When a violation of this section is committed by a minor on school property, the court may, in addition to any other fine, sentence, or as a condition of probation, order the minor to attend counseling as deemed appropriate by the court at the expense of the minor's parents. The court shall take into consideration the ability of the minor's parents to pay, however, no minor shall be relieved of attending counseling because of the minor's parents' inability to pay for the counseling imposed by this section.

(b) For the purposes of this section, the following terms have the following meanings:

(1) "Hospital" means a facility for the diagnosis, care, and treatment of human illness that is subject to, or specifically exempted from, the licensure requirements of Chapter 2 (commencing with Section 1250) of Division 2 of the Health and Safety Code.

(2) "Park" means any publicly maintained or operated park. It does not include any facility when used for professional sports or commercial events.

(3) "School" means any elementary school, junior high school, four-year high school, senior high school, adult school or any branch thereof, opportunity school, continuation high school, regional occupational center, evening high school, technical school, or community college.

(c) This section shall not apply to conduct arising during the course of an otherwise lawful labor dispute.
Amended by Stats 2001 ch 484 (AB 653), s 3, eff. 1/1/2002.

Section 243.25 - Battery committed against person of elder or dependent adult

When a battery is committed against the person of an elder or a dependent adult as defined in Section 368, with knowledge that he or she is an elder or a dependent adult, the offense shall be punishable by a fine not to exceed two thousand dollars ($2,000), or by imprisonment in a county jail not to exceed one year, or by both that fine and imprisonment.

Added by Stats 2002 ch 369 (AB 2140), s 1, eff. 1/1/2003.

Section 243.3 - Battery committed against transportation worker or passenger

When a battery is committed against the person of an operator, driver, or passenger on a bus, taxicab, streetcar, cable car, trackless trolley, or other motor vehicle, including a vehicle operated on stationary rails or on a track or rail suspended in the air, used for the transportation of persons for hire, or against a schoolbus driver, or against the person of a station agent or ticket agent for the entity providing the transportation, and the person who commits the offense knows or reasonably should know that the victim, in the case of an operator, driver, or agent, is engaged in the performance of his or her duties, or is a passenger the offense shall be punished by a fine not exceeding ten thousand dollars ($10,000), or by imprisonment in a county jail not exceeding one year, or by both that fine and imprisonment. If an injury is inflicted on that victim, the offense shall be punished by a fine not exceeding ten thousand dollars ($10,000), or by imprisonment in a county jail not exceeding one year or in the state prison for 16 months, or two or three years, or by both that fine and imprisonment.

Amended by Stats. 1997, Ch. 305, Sec. 1. Effective January 1, 1998.

Section 243.35 - Battery committed against person on property or in motor vehicle of public transportation provider

(a) Except as provided in Section 243.3, when a battery is committed against any person on the property of, or in a motor vehicle of, a public transportation provider, the offense shall be punished by a fine not to exceed two thousand dollars ($2,000), or by imprisonment in a county jail not to exceed one year, or by both the fine and imprisonment.

(b) As used in this section, "public transportation provider" means a publicly or privately owned entity that operates, for the transportation of persons for hire, a bus, taxicab, streetcar, cable car, trackless trolley, or other motor vehicle, including a vehicle operated on stationary rails or on a track or rail suspended in air, or that operates a schoolbus.

(c) As used in this section, "on the property of" means the entire station where public transportation is available, including the parking lot reserved for the public who utilize the transportation system.

Added by Stats. 1996, Ch. 423, Sec. 3. Effective January 1, 1997.

Section 243.4 - Sexual battery

(a)Any person who touches an intimate part of another person while that person is unlawfully restrained by the accused or an accomplice, and if the touching is against the will of the person touched and is for the purpose of sexual arousal, sexual gratification, or sexual abuse, is guilty of sexual battery. A violation of this subdivision is punishable by imprisonment in a county jail for not more than one year, and by a fine not exceeding two thousand dollars ($2,000); or by imprisonment in the state prison for two, three, or four years, and by a fine not exceeding ten thousand dollars ($10,000).

(b)Any person who touches an intimate part of another person who is institutionalized for medical treatment and who is seriously disabled or medically incapacitated, if the touching is against the will of the person touched, and if the touching is for the purpose of sexual arousal, sexual gratification, or sexual abuse, is guilty of sexual battery. A violation of this subdivision is punishable by imprisonment in a county jail for not more than one year, and by a fine not exceeding two thousand dollars ($2,000); or by imprisonment in the state prison for two, three, or four years, and by a fine not exceeding ten thousand dollars ($10,000).

(c)Any person who touches an intimate part of another person for the purpose of sexual arousal, sexual gratification, or sexual abuse, and the victim is at the time unconscious of the nature of the act because the perpetrator fraudulently represented that the touching served a professional purpose, is guilty of sexual battery. A violation of this subdivision is punishable by imprisonment in a county jail for not more than one year, and by a fine not exceeding two thousand dollars ($2,000); or by imprisonment in the state prison for two, three, or four years, and by a fine not exceeding ten thousand dollars ($10,000).

(d)Any person who, for the purpose of sexual arousal, sexual gratification, or sexual abuse, causes another, against that person's will while that person is unlawfully restrained either by the accused or an accomplice, or is institutionalized for medical treatment and is seriously disabled or medically incapacitated, to masturbate or touch an intimate part of either of those persons or a third person, is guilty of sexual battery. A violation of this subdivision is punishable by imprisonment in a county jail for not more than one year, and by a fine not exceeding two thousand dollars ($2,000); or by imprisonment in the state prison for two, three, or four years, and by a fine not exceeding ten thousand dollars ($10,000).

(e)

(1)Any person who touches an intimate part of another person, if the touching is against the will of the person touched, and is for the specific purpose of sexual arousal, sexual gratification, or sexual abuse, is guilty of misdemeanor sexual battery, punishable by a fine not exceeding two thousand dollars ($2,000), or by imprisonment in a county jail not exceeding six months, or by both that fine and imprisonment. However, if the defendant was an employer and the victim was an employee of the defendant, the misdemeanor sexual battery shall be punishable by a fine not exceeding three thousand dollars ($3,000), by imprisonment in a county jail not exceeding six months, or by both that fine and imprisonment. Notwithstanding any other provision of law, any amount of a fine above two thousand dollars ($2,000) which is collected from a defendant for a violation of this subdivision shall be transmitted to the State Treasury and, upon appropriation by the Legislature, distributed to the Civil Rights Department for the purpose of enforcement of the California Fair Employment and Housing Act (Part 2.8 (commencing with Section 12900) of Division 3 of Title 2 of the Government Code), including, but not limited to, laws that proscribe sexual harassment in places of employment. However, in no event shall an amount over two thousand dollars ($2,000) be transmitted to the State Treasury until all fines, including any restitution fines that may have been imposed upon the defendant, have been paid in full.

(2)As used in this subdivision, "touches" means physical contact with another person, whether accomplished directly, through the clothing of the person committing the offense, or through the clothing of the victim.

(f)As used in subdivisions (a), (b), (c), and (d), "touches" means physical contact with the skin of another person whether accomplished directly or through the clothing of the person committing the offense.

(g)As used in this section, the following terms have the following meanings:

(1)"Intimate part" means the sexual organ, anus, groin, or buttocks of any person, and the breast of a female.

(2)"Sexual battery" does not include the crimes defined in Section 261 or 289.

(3)"Seriously disabled" means a person with severe physical or sensory disabilities.

(4)"Medically incapacitated" means a person who is incapacitated as a result of prescribed sedatives, anesthesia, or other medication.

(5)"Institutionalized" means a person who is located voluntarily or involuntarily in a hospital, medical treatment facility, nursing home, acute care facility, or mental hospital.

(6)"Minor" means a person under 18 years of age.

(h)This section shall not be construed to limit or prevent prosecution under any other law which also proscribes a course of conduct that also is proscribed by this section.

(i)In the case of a felony conviction for a violation of this section, the fact that the defendant was an employer and the victim was an employee of the defendant shall be a factor in aggravation in sentencing.

(j)A person who commits a violation of subdivision (a), (b), (c), or (d) against a minor when the person has a prior felony conviction for a violation of this section shall be guilty of a felony, punishable by imprisonment in the state prison for two, three, or four years and a fine not exceeding ten thousand dollars ($10,000).

Amended by Stats 2022 ch 48 (SB 189),s 70, eff. 6/30/2022.

Amended by Stats 2002 ch 302 (SB 1421), s 1, eff. 1/1/2003.

Section 243.5 - Arrest of person who commits assault or battery on school property

(a) When a person commits an assault or battery on school property during hours when school activities are being conducted, a peace officer may, without a warrant, notwithstanding paragraph (2) or (3) of subdivision (a) of Section 836, arrest the person who commits the assault or battery:

(1) Whenever the person has committed the assault or battery, although not in the peace officer's presence.

(2) Whenever the peace officer has reasonable cause to believe that the person to be arrested has committed the assault or battery, whether or not it has in fact been committed.

(b) "School," as used in this section, means any elementary school, junior high school, four-year high school, senior high school, adult school or any branch thereof, opportunity school, continuation high school, regional occupational center, evening high school, technical school, or community college.

Amended by Stats. 1997, Ch. 324, Sec. 2. Effective January 1, 1998.

Section 243.6 - Battery committed against school employee

When a battery is committed against a school employee engaged in the performance of his or her duties, or in retaliation for an act performed in the course of his or her duties, whether on or off campus, during the schoolday or at any other time, and the person committing the offense knows or reasonably should know that the victim is a school employee, the battery is punishable by imprisonment in a county jail not exceeding one year, or by a fine not exceeding two thousand dollars ($2,000), or by both the fine and imprisonment. However, if an injury is inflicted on the victim, the battery shall be punishable by imprisonment in a county jail for not more than one year, or by a fine of not more than two thousand dollars ($2,000), or by imprisonment pursuant to subdivision (h) of Section 1170 for 16 months, or two or three years.

For purposes of this section, "school employee" has the same meaning as defined in subdivision (d) of Section 245.5.

This section shall not apply to conduct arising during the course of an otherwise lawful labor dispute.

Amended by Stats 2011 ch 39 (AB 117),s 68, eff. 6/30/2011.

Amended by Stats 2011 ch 15 (AB 109),s 294, eff. 4/4/2011, but operative no earlier than October 1, 2011, and only upon creation of a community corrections grant program to assist in implementing this act and upon an appropriation to fund the grant program.

Section 243.65 - Battery committed against highway worker

(a) When a battery is committed against the person of a highway worker engaged in the performance of his or her duties and the person committing the offense knows or reasonably should know that the victim is a highway worker engaged in the performance of his or her duties, the offense shall be punished by a fine not exceeding two thousand dollars ($2,000), or by imprisonment in a county jail not exceeding one year, or by both that fine and imprisonment.

(b) As used in this section, "highway worker" means an employee of the Department of Transportation, a contractor or employee of a contractor while working under contract with the Department of Transportation, an employee of a city, county, or city and county, a contractor or employee of a contractor while working under contract with a city, county, or city and county, or a volunteer as defined in Section 1720.4 of the Labor Code who does one or more of the following:

(1) Performs maintenance, repair, or construction of state highway or local street or road infrastructures and associated rights-of-way in highway or local street or road work zones.

(2) Operates equipment on state highway or local street or road infrastructures and associated rights-of-way in highway or local street or road work zones.

(3) Performs any related maintenance work, as required, on state highway or local street or road infrastructures in highway or local street or road work zones.

Amended by Stats 2009 ch 116 (AB 561),s 2, eff. 1/1/2010.

Added by Stats 2008 ch 410 (SB 1509),s 2, eff. 1/1/2009.

Section 243.7 - Battery against juror

Any person who is a party to a civil or criminal action in which a jury has been selected to try the case and who, while the legal action is pending or after the conclusion of the trial commits a battery against any juror or alternate juror who was selected and sworn in that legal action shall be punished by a fine not to exceed five thousand dollars ($5,000), or by imprisonment in the county jail not exceeding one year, or by both such fine and imprisonment, or by the imprisonment in the state prison for 16 months, or for two or three years.

Added by Stats. 1986, Ch. 616, Sec. 3.

Section 243.8 - Battery committed against sports official

(a) When a battery is committed against a sports official immediately prior to, during, or immediately following an interscholastic, intercollegiate, or any other organized amateur or professional athletic contest in which the sports official is participating, and the person who commits the offense knows or reasonably should know that the victim is engaged in the performance of his or her duties, the offense shall be punishable by a fine not exceeding two thousand dollars ($2,000), or by imprisonment in the county jail not exceeding one year, or by both that fine and imprisonment.

(b) For purposes of this section, "sports official" means any individual who serves as a referee, umpire, linesman, or who serves in a similar capacity but may be known by a different title or name and is duly registered by, or a member of, a local, state, regional, or national organization engaged in part in providing education and training to sports officials.

Added by Stats. 1991, Ch. 575, Sec. 1.

Section 243.83 - Unlawful acts while attending professional sporting event

(a) It is unlawful for any person attending a professional sporting event to do any of the following:

(1) Throw any object on or across the court or field of play with the intent to interfere with play or distract a player.

(2) Enter upon the court or field of play without permission from an authorized person any time after the authorized participants of play have entered the court or field to begin the sporting event and until the participants of play have completed the playing time of the sporting event.

(b)

(1) The owner of the facility in which a professional sporting event is to be held shall provide a notice specifying the unlawful activity prohibited by this section and the punishment for engaging in that prohibited activity.

(2) The notice shall be prominently displayed throughout the facility or may be provided by some other manner, such as on a big screen or by a general public announcement. In addition, notice shall be posted at all controlled entry areas of the sporting facility.

(3) Failure to provide the notice shall not be a defense to a violation of this section.

(c) For the purposes of this section, the following terms have the following meanings:

(1) "Player" includes any authorized participant of play, including, but not limited to, team members, referees however designated, and support staff, whether or not any of those persons receive compensation.

(2) "Professional sporting event" means a scheduled sporting event involving a professional sports team or organization or a professional athlete for which an admission fee is charged to the public.

(d) A violation of subdivision (a) is an infraction punishable by a fine not exceeding two hundred fifty dollars ($250). The fine shall not be subject to penalty assessments as provided in Section 1464 or 1465.7 of this code or Section 76000 of the Government Code.

(e) This section shall apply to attendees at professional sporting events; this section shall not apply to players or to sports officials, as defined in Section 243.8.

(f) Nothing in this section shall be construed to limit or prevent prosecution under any applicable provision of law.

Added by Stats 2003 ch 818 (AB 245), s 1, eff. 1/1/2004.

Section 243.85 - Posting of telephone number in order to report violent act at professional sports facility

The owner of any professional sports facility shall post, visible from a majority of the seating in the stands at all times, at controlled entry areas, and at parking facilities that are part of the professional sports facility, written notices displaying the text message number and telephone number to contact security in order to report a violent act.

Added by Stats 2012 ch 261 (AB 2464),s 1, eff. 1/1/2013.

Section 243.9 - Battery by gassing peace officer by person confined in local detention facility

(a) Every person confined in any local detention facility who commits a battery by gassing upon the person of any peace officer, as defined in Chapter 4.5 (commencing with Section 830) of Title 3 of Part 2, or employee of the local detention facility is guilty of aggravated battery and shall be punished by imprisonment in a county jail or by imprisonment in the state prison for two, three, or four years.

(b) For purposes of this section, "gassing" means intentionally placing or throwing, or causing to be placed or thrown, upon the person of another, any human excrement or other bodily fluids or bodily substances or any mixture containing human excrement or other bodily fluids or bodily substances that results in actual contact with the person's skin or membranes.

(c) The person in charge of the local detention facility shall use every available means to immediately investigate all reported or suspected violations of subdivision (a), including, but not limited to, the use of forensically acceptable means of preserving and testing the suspected gassing substance to confirm the presence of human excrement or other bodily fluids or bodily substances. If there is probable cause to believe that the inmate has violated subdivision (a), the chief medical officer of the local detention facility, or his or her designee, may, when he or she deems it medically necessary to protect the health of an officer or employee who may have been subject to a violation of this section, order the inmate to receive an examination or test for hepatitis or tuberculosis or both hepatitis and tuberculosis on either a voluntary or involuntary basis immediately after the event, and periodically thereafter as determined to be necessary by the medical officer in order to ensure that further hepatitis or tuberculosis transmission does not occur. These decisions shall be consistent with an occupational exposure as defined by the Center for Disease Control and Prevention. The results of any examination or test shall be provided to the officer or employee who has been subject to a reported or suspected violation of this section. Nothing in this subdivision shall be construed to otherwise supersede the operation of Title 8 (commencing with Section 7500). Any person performing tests, transmitting test results, or disclosing information pursuant to this section shall be immune from civil liability for any action taken in accordance with this section.

(d) The person in charge of the local detention facility shall refer all reports for which there is probable cause to believe that the inmate has violated subdivision (a) to the local district attorney for prosecution.

(e) Nothing in this section shall preclude prosecution under both this section and any other provision of law.

Added by Stats 2000 ch 627 (AB 1449), s 1, eff. 1/1/2001.

Section 243.10 - Battery against member of armed service because of victim's service

(a) Any person who commits a battery against a member of the United States Armed Forces because of the victim's service in the United States Armed Forces shall be punished by a fine not exceeding two thousand dollars ($2,000), by imprisonment in a county jail for a period not exceeding one year, or by both that fine and imprisonment.

(b) "Because of" means that the bias motivation must be a cause in fact of the battery, whether or not other causes exist. When multiple concurrent motives exist, the prohibited bias must be a substantial factor in bringing about the battery.

Added by Stats 2003 ch 138 (AB 187), s 2, eff. 1/1/2004.

Section 243.15 - Commission of battery

Every person confined in, sentenced to, or serving a sentence in, a city or county jail, industrial farm, or industrial road camp in this state, who commits a battery upon the person of any individual who is not himself or herself a person confined or sentenced therein, is guilty of a public offense and is subject to punishment by imprisonment pursuant to subdivision (h) of Section 1170, or in a county jail for not more than one year.

Renumbered from Ca. Pen. Code §4131.5 and amended by Stats 2015 ch 499 (SB 795),s 4, eff. 1/1/2016.

Amended by Stats 2011 ch 39 (AB 117),s 68, eff. 6/30/2011.

Amended by Stats 2011 ch 15 (AB 109),s 483, eff. 4/4/2011, but operative no earlier than October 1, 2011, and only upon creation of a community corrections grant program to assist in implementing this act and upon an appropriation to fund the grant program.

Section 244 - Unlawful throwing of flammable substance or caustic chemical on person

Any person who willfully and maliciously places or throws, or causes to be placed or thrown, upon the person of another, any vitriol, corrosive acid, flammable substance, or caustic chemical of any nature, with the intent to injure the flesh or disfigure the body of that person, is punishable by imprisonment in the state prison for two, three or four years.

As used in this section, "flammable substance" means gasoline, petroleum products, or flammable liquids with a flashpoint of 150 degrees Fahrenheit or less.

Amended by Stats. 1995, Ch. 468, Sec. 1. Effective January 1, 1996.

Section 244.5 - Punishment for assault with stun gun or less lethal weapon

(a) As used in this section, "stun gun" means any item, except a less lethal weapon, as defined in Section 16780, used or intended to be used as either an offensive or defensive weapon that is capable of temporarily immobilizing a person by the infliction of an electrical charge.

(b) Every person who commits an assault upon the person of another with a stun gun or less lethal weapon, as defined in Section 16780, shall be punished by imprisonment in a county jail for a term not exceeding one year, or by imprisonment pursuant to subdivision (h) of Section 1170 for 16 months, two, or three years.

(c) Every person who commits an assault upon the person of a peace officer or firefighter with a stun gun or less lethal weapon, as defined in Section 16780, who knows or reasonably should know that the person is a peace officer or firefighter engaged in the performance of his or her duties, when the peace officer or firefighter is engaged in the performance of his or her duties, shall be punished by imprisonment in the county jail for a term not exceeding one year, or by imprisonment pursuant to subdivision (h) of Section 1170 for two, three, or four years.

(d) This section shall not be construed to preclude or in any way limit the applicability of Section 245 in any criminal prosecution.

Amended by Stats 2011 ch 39 (AB 117),s 68, eff. 6/30/2011.

Amended by Stats 2011 ch 15 (AB 109),s 297, eff. 4/4/2011, but operative no earlier than October 1, 2011, and only upon creation of a community corrections grant program to assist in implementing this act and upon an appropriation to fund the grant program.

Amended by Stats 2010 ch 178 (SB 1115),s 52, eff. 1/1/2011, op. 1/1/2012.

Amended by Stats 2008 ch 556 (AB 2973),s 1, eff. 1/1/2009.

Section 245 - Assault with deadly weapon or instrument other than firearm; assault with firearm; assault with machinegun; assault by means of force likely to produce great bodily injury; assault with semiautomatic firearm

(a)

(1) Any person who commits an assault upon the person of another with a deadly weapon or instrument other than a firearm shall be punished by imprisonment in the state prison for two, three, or four years, or in a county jail for not exceeding one year, or by a fine not exceeding ten thousand dollars ($10,000), or by both the fine and imprisonment.

(2) Any person who commits an assault upon the person of another with a firearm shall be punished by imprisonment in the state prison for two, three, or four years, or in a county jail for not less than six months and not exceeding one year, or by both a fine not exceeding ten thousand dollars ($10,000) and imprisonment.

(3) Any person who commits an assault upon the person of another with a machinegun, as defined in Section 16880, or an assault weapon, as defined in Section 30510 or 30515, or a .50 BMG rifle, as defined in Section 30530, shall be punished by imprisonment in the state prison for 4, 8, or 12 years.

(4) Any person who commits an assault upon the person of another by any means of force likely to produce great bodily injury shall be punished by imprisonment in the state prison for two, three, or four years, or in a county jail for not exceeding one year, or by a fine not exceeding ten thousand dollars ($10,000), or by both the fine and imprisonment.

(b) Any person who commits an assault upon the person of another with a semiautomatic firearm shall be punished by imprisonment in the state prison for three, six, or nine years.

(c) Any person who commits an assault with a deadly weapon or instrument, other than a firearm, or by any means likely to produce great bodily injury upon the person of a peace officer or firefighter, and who knows or reasonably should know that the victim is a peace officer or firefighter engaged in the performance of his or her duties, when the peace officer or firefighter is engaged in the performance of his or her duties, shall be punished by imprisonment in the state prison for three, four, or five years.

(d)

(1) Any person who commits an assault with a firearm upon the person of a peace officer or firefighter, and who knows or reasonably should know that the victim is a peace officer or firefighter engaged in the performance of his or her duties, when the peace

officer or firefighter is engaged in the performance of his or her duties, shall be punished by imprisonment in the state prison for four, six, or eight years.

(2) Any person who commits an assault upon the person of a peace officer or firefighter with a semiautomatic firearm and who knows or reasonably should know that the victim is a peace officer or firefighter engaged in the performance of his or her duties, when the peace officer or firefighter is engaged in the performance of his or her duties, shall be punished by imprisonment in the state prison for five, seven, or nine years.

(3) Any person who commits an assault with a machinegun, as defined in Section 16880, or an assault weapon, as defined in Section 30510 or 30515, or a .50 BMG rifle, as defined in Section 30530, upon the person of a peace officer or firefighter, and who knows or reasonably should know that the victim is a peace officer or firefighter engaged in the performance of his or her duties, shall be punished by imprisonment in the state prison for 6, 9, or 12 years.

(e) When a person is convicted of a violation of this section in a case involving use of a deadly weapon or instrument or firearm, and the weapon or instrument or firearm is owned by that person, the court shall order that the weapon or instrument or firearm be deemed a nuisance, and it shall be confiscated and disposed of in the manner provided by Sections 18000 and 18005.

(f) As used in this section, "peace officer" refers to any person designated as a peace officer in Chapter 4.5 (commencing with Section 830) of Title 3 of Part 2.

Amended by Stats 2011 ch 183 (AB 1026),s 1, eff. 1/1/2012.
Amended by Stats 2011 ch 39 (AB 117),s 68, eff. 6/30/2011.
Amended by Stats 2011 ch 39 (AB 117),s 11, eff. 6/30/2011.
Amended by Stats 2011 ch 15 (AB 109),s 298, eff. 4/4/2011, but operative no earlier than October 1, 2011, and only upon creation of a community corrections grant program to assist in implementing this act and upon an appropriation to fund the grant program.
Amended by Stats 2010 ch 178 (SB 1115),s 53, eff. 1/1/2011, op. 1/1/2012.
Amended by Stats 2004 ch 494 (AB 50), s 1, eff. 1/1/2005.
Effective 1/1/2000. Amended July 19, 1999 (Bill Number: SB 23) (Chapter 129).

Section 245.1 - "Fireman" and "firefighter" defined; "emergency rescue personnel" defined

As used in Sections 148.2, 241, 243, 244.5, and 245, "fireman" or "firefighter" includes any person who is an officer, employee or member of a fire department or fire protection or firefighting agency of the federal government, the State of California, a city, county, city and county, district, or other public or municipal corporation or political subdivision of this state, whether this person is a volunteer or partly paid or fully paid.

As used in Section 148.2, "emergency rescue personnel" means any person who is an officer, employee or member of a fire department or fire protection or firefighting agency of the federal government, the State of California, a city, county, city and county, district, or other public or municipal corporation or political subdivision of this state, whether this person is a volunteer or partly paid or fully paid, while he or she is actually engaged in the on-the-site rescue of persons or property during an emergency as defined by subdivision (c) of Section 148.3.

Amended by Stats. 1998, Ch. 936, Sec. 3. Effective September 28, 1998.

Section 245.2 - Assault with deadly weapon or instrument or by means likely to produce great bodily injury upon person of operator, driver, or passenger

Every person who commits an assault with a deadly weapon or instrument or by any means of force likely to produce great bodily injury upon the person of an operator, driver, or passenger on a bus, taxicab, streetcar, cable car, trackless trolley, or other motor vehicle, including a vehicle operated on stationary rails or on a track or rail suspended in the air, used for the transportation of persons for hire, or upon the person of a station agent or ticket agent for the entity providing such transportation, when the driver, operator, or agent is engaged in the performance of his or her duties, and where the person who commits the assault knows or reasonably should know that the victim is engaged in the performance of his or her duties, or is a passenger, shall be punished by imprisonment in the state prison for three, four, or five years.

Amended by Stats. 1987, Ch. 801, Sec. 4.

Section 245.3 - Assault with deadly weapon or instrument or by means likely to produce great bodily injury upon person of custodial officer

Every person who commits an assault with a deadly weapon or instrument or by any means likely to produce great bodily injury upon the person of a custodial officer as defined in Section 831 or 831.5, and who knows or reasonably should know that the victim is a custodial officer engaged in the performance of that person's duties, shall be punished by imprisonment in the state prison for three, four, or five years.

When a person is convicted of a violation of this section in a case involving use of a deadly weapon or instrument, and such weapon or instrument is owned by that person, the court may, in its discretion, order that the weapon or instrument be deemed a nuisance and shall be confiscated and destroyed in the manner provided by Sections 18000 and 18005.

Amended by Stats 2010 ch 178 (SB 1115),s 54, eff. 1/1/2011, op. 1/1/2012.

Section 245.5 - Assault with deadly weapon or instrument, other than firearm, or by means likely to produce great bodily injury upon person of school employee

(a) Every person who commits an assault with a deadly weapon or instrument, other than a firearm, or by any means likely to produce great bodily injury upon the person of a school employee, and who knows or reasonably should know that the victim is a school employee engaged in the performance of his or her duties, when that school employee is engaged in the performance of his or her duties, shall be punished by imprisonment in the state prison for three, four, or five years, or in a county jail not exceeding one year.

(b) Every person who commits an assault with a firearm upon the person of a school employee, and who knows or reasonably should know that the victim is a school employee engaged in the performance of his or her duties, when the school employee is engaged in the performance of his or her duties, shall be punished by imprisonment in the state prison for four, six, or eight years, or in a county jail for not less than six months and not exceeding one year.

(c) Every person who commits an assault upon the person of a school employee with a stun gun or taser, and who knows or reasonably should know that the person is a school employee engaged in the performance of his or her duties, when the school employee is engaged in the performance of his or her duties, shall be punished by imprisonment in a county jail for a term not exceeding one year or by imprisonment in the state prison for two, three, or four years. This subdivision shall not be construed to preclude or in any way limit the applicability of Section 245 in any criminal prosecution.

(d) As used in the section, "school employee" means any person employed as a permanent or probationary certificated or classified employee of a school district on a part-time or full-time basis, including a substitute teacher. "School employee," as used in this section, also includes a student teacher, or a school board member. "School," as used in this section, has the same meaning as that term is defined in Section 626.

Amended by Stats. 1992, Ch. 334, Sec. 1. Effective January 1, 1993.

Section 245.6 - Hazing

(a) It shall be unlawful to engage in hazing, as defined in this section.

(b) "Hazing" means any method of initiation or preinitiation into a student organization or student body, whether or not the organization or body is officially recognized by an educational institution, which is likely to cause serious bodily injury to any former, current, or prospective student of any school, community college, college, university, or other educational institution in this state. The term "hazing" does not include customary athletic events or school-sanctioned events.

(c) A violation of this section that does not result in serious bodily injury is a misdemeanor, punishable by a fine of not less than one hundred dollars ($100), nor more than five thousand dollars ($5,000), or imprisonment in the county jail for not more than one year, or both.

(d) Any person who personally engages in hazing that results in death or serious bodily injury as defined in paragraph (4) of subdivision (f) of Section 243 of the Penal Code, is guilty of either a misdemeanor or a felony, and shall be punished by imprisonment in county jail not exceeding one year, or by imprisonment pursuant to subdivision (h) of Section 1170.

(e) The person against whom the hazing is directed may commence a civil action for injury or damages. The action may be brought against any participants in the hazing, or any organization to which the student is seeking membership whose agents, directors, trustees, managers, or officers authorized, requested, commanded, participated in, or ratified the hazing.

(f) Prosecution under this section shall not prohibit prosecution under any other provision of law.

Amended by Stats 2011 ch 39 (AB 117),s 68, eff. 6/30/2011.

Amended by Stats 2011 ch 15 (AB 109),s 299, eff. 4/4/2011, but operative no earlier than October 1, 2011, and only upon creation of a community corrections grant program to assist in implementing this act and upon an appropriation to fund the grant program. Added by Stats 2006 ch 601 (SB 1454),s 4, eff. 1/1/2007.

Section 246 - Unlawful discharge of firearm at inhabited dwelling house, occupied building, occupied motor vehicle, occupied aircraft, inhabited housecar, or inhabited camper

Any person who shall maliciously and willfully discharge a firearm at an inhabited dwelling house, occupied building, occupied motor vehicle, occupied aircraft, inhabited housecar, as defined in Section 362 of the Vehicle Code, or inhabited camper, as defined in Section 243 of the Vehicle Code, is guilty of a felony, and upon conviction shall be punished by imprisonment in the state prison for three, five, or seven years, or by imprisonment in the county jail for a term of not less than six months and not exceeding one year.

As used in this section, "inhabited" means currently being used for dwelling purposes, whether occupied or not.

Amended by Stats. 1988, Ch. 911, Sec. 1. Effective September 15, 1988.

Section 246.1 - Order that vehicle used in commission of offense be sold

(a) Except as provided in subdivision (f), upon the conviction of any person found guilty of murder in the first or second degree, manslaughter, attempted murder, assault with a deadly weapon, the unlawful discharge or brandishing of a firearm from or at an occupied vehicle where the victim was killed, attacked, or assaulted from or in a motor vehicle by the use of a firearm on a public street or highway, or the unlawful possession of a firearm by a member of a criminal street gang, as defined in subdivision (f) of Section 186.22, while present in a vehicle the court shall order a vehicle used in the commission of that offense sold. Any vehicle ordered to be sold pursuant to this subdivision shall be surrendered to the sheriff of the county or the chief of police of the city in which the violation occurred. The officer to whom the vehicle is surrendered shall promptly ascertain from the Department of Motor Vehicles the names and addresses of all legal and registered owners of the vehicle and within five days of receiving that information, shall send by certified mail a notice to all legal and registered owners of the vehicle other than the defendant, at the addresses obtained from the department, informing them that the vehicle has been declared a nuisance and will be sold or otherwise disposed of pursuant to this section, and of the approximate date and location of the sale or other disposition. The notice shall also inform any legal owner of its right to conduct the sale pursuant to subdivision (b).

(b) Any legal owner which in the regular course of its business conducts sales of repossessed or surrendered motor vehicles may take possession and conduct the sale of the vehicle if it notifies the officer to whom the vehicle is surrendered of its intent to conduct the sale within 15 days of the mailing of the notice pursuant to subdivision (a). Sale of the vehicle pursuant to this subdivision may be conducted at the time, in the manner, and on the notice usually given by the legal owner for the sale of repossessed or surrendered vehicles. The proceeds of any sale conducted by the legal owner shall be disposed of as provided in subdivision (d).

(c) If the legal owner does not notify the officer to whom the vehicle is surrendered of its intent to conduct the sale as provided in subdivision (b), the officer shall offer the vehicle for sale at public auction within 60 days of receiving the vehicle. At least 10 days but not more than 20 days prior to the sale, not counting the day of sale, the officer shall give notice of the sale by advertising once in a newspaper of general circulation published in the city or county, as the case may be, in which the vehicle is located, which notice shall contain a description of the make, year, model, identification number, and license number of the vehicle, and the date, time, and location of the sale. For motorcycles, the engine number shall also be included. If there is no newspaper of general circulation published in the county, notice shall be given by posting a notice of sale containing the information required by this subdivision in three of the most public places in the city or county in which the vehicle is located and at the place where the vehicle is to be sold for 10 consecutive days prior to and including the day of the sale.

(d) The proceeds of a sale conducted pursuant to this section shall be disposed of in the following priority:

(1) To satisfy the costs of the sale, including costs incurred with respect to the taking and keeping of the vehicle pending sale.

(2) To the legal owner in an amount to satisfy the indebtedness owed to the legal owner remaining as of the date of sale, including accrued interest or finance charges and delinquency charges.

(3) To the holder of any subordinate lien or encumbrance on the vehicle to satisfy any indebtedness so secured if written notification of demand is received before distribution of the proceeds is completed. The holder of a subordinate lien or encumbrance, if requested, shall reasonably furnish reasonable proof of its interest, and unless it does so on request is not entitled to distribution pursuant to this paragraph.

(4) To any other person who can establish an interest in the vehicle, including a community property interest, to the extent of his or her provable interest.

(5) The balance, if any, to the city or county in which the violation occurred, to be deposited in a special account in its general fund to be used exclusively to pay the costs or a part of the costs of providing services or education to prevent juvenile violence. The person conducting the sale shall disburse the proceeds of the sale as provided in this subdivision, and provide a written accounting regarding the disposition to all persons entitled to or claiming a share of the proceeds, within 15 days after the sale is conducted.

(e) If the vehicle to be sold under this section is not of the type that can readily be sold to the public generally, the vehicle shall be destroyed or donated to an eleemosynary institution.

(f) No vehicle may be sold pursuant to this section in either of the following circumstances:

(1) The vehicle is stolen, unless the identity of the legal and registered owners of the vehicle cannot be reasonably ascertained.

(2) The vehicle is owned by another, or there is a community property interest in the vehicle owned by a person other than the defendant and the vehicle is the only vehicle available to the defendant's immediate family which may be operated on the highway with a class 3 or class 4 driver's license.

(g) A vehicle is used in the commission of a violation of the offenses enumerated in subdivision (a) if a firearm is discharged either from the vehicle at another person or by an occupant of a vehicle other than the vehicle in which the victim is an occupant.

Amended by Stats. 1994, 1st Ex. Sess., Ch. 33, Sec. 1. Effective November 30, 1994.

Section 246.3 - Willful discharge of firearm in grossly negligent manner

(a) Except as otherwise authorized by law, any person who willfully discharges a firearm in a grossly negligent manner which could result in injury or death to a person is guilty of a public offense and shall be punished by imprisonment in a county jail not exceeding one year, or by imprisonment pursuant to subdivision (h) of Section 1170.

(b) Except as otherwise authorized by law, any person who willfully discharges a BB device in a grossly negligent manner which could result in injury or death to a person is guilty of a public offense and shall be punished by imprisonment in a county jail not exceeding one year.

(c) As used in this section, "BB device" means any instrument that expels a projectile, such as a BB or a pellet, through the force of air pressure, gas pressure, or spring action.

Amended by Stats 2011 ch 39 (AB 117),s 68, eff. 6/30/2011.

Amended by Stats 2011 ch 15 (AB 109),s 300, eff. 4/4/2011, but operative no earlier than October 1, 2011, and only upon creation of a community corrections grant program to assist in implementing this act and upon an appropriation to fund the grant program.

Amended by Stats 2006 ch 180 (SB 532),s 1, eff. 1/1/2007.

See Stats 2006 ch 180 (SB 532), s 2.

Section 247 - Unlawful discharge of firearm at unoccupied aircraft, motor vehicle, building, or dwelling house

(a) Any person who willfully and maliciously discharges a firearm at an unoccupied aircraft is guilty of a felony.

(b) Any person who discharges a firearm at an unoccupied motor vehicle or an uninhabited building or dwelling house is guilty of a public offense punishable by imprisonment in the county jail for not more than one year or in the state prison. This subdivision does not apply to shooting at an abandoned vehicle, unoccupied vehicle, uninhabited building, or dwelling house with the permission of the owner. As used in this section and Section 246"aircraft" means any contrivance intended for and capable of transporting persons through the airspace.

Amended by Stats. 1988, Ch. 911, Sec. 2. Effective September 15, 1988.

Section 247.5 - Unlawful discharge at aircraft while occupied

Any person who willfully and maliciously discharges a laser at an aircraft, whether in motion or in flight, while occupied, is guilty of a violation of this section, which shall be punishable as either a misdemeanor by imprisonment in the county jail for not more than one year or by a fine of one thousand dollars ($1,000), or a felony by imprisonment pursuant to subdivision (h) of Section 1170 for 16 months, two years, or three years, or by a fine of two thousand dollars ($2,000). This section does not apply to the conduct of laser development activity by or on behalf of the United States Armed Forces.

As used in this section, "aircraft" means any contrivance intended for and capable of transporting persons through the airspace.

As used in this section, "laser" means a device that utilizes the natural oscillations of atoms or molecules between energy levels for generating coherent electromagnetic radiation in the ultraviolet, visible, or infrared region of the spectrum, and when discharged exceeds one milliwatt continuous wave.

Amended by Stats 2011 ch 39 (AB 117),s 68, eff. 6/30/2011.

Amended by Stats 2011 ch 15 (AB 109),s 301, eff. 4/4/2011, but operative no earlier than October 1, 2011, and only upon creation of a community corrections grant program to assist in implementing this act and upon an appropriation to fund the grant program.

Section 248 - Unlawful shining of light at aircraft

Any person who, with the intent to interfere with the operation of an aircraft, willfully shines a light or other bright device, of an intensity capable of impairing the operation of an aircraft, at an aircraft, shall be punished by a fine not exceeding one thousand dollars ($1,000), or by imprisonment in a county jail not exceeding one year, or by both that fine and imprisonment.

Amended by Stats. 1998, Ch. 218, Sec. 1. Effective January 1, 1999.

Title 9 - OF CRIMES AGAINST THE PERSON INVOLVING SEXUAL ASSAULT, AND CRIMES AGAINST PUBLIC DECENCY AND GOOD MORALS

Chapter 1 - RAPE, ABDUCTION, CARNAL ABUSE OF CHILDREN, AND SEDUCTION

Section 261 - Rape

(a) Rape is an act of sexual intercourse accomplished under any of the following circumstances:

(1) If a person who is not the spouse of the person committing the act is incapable, because of a mental disorder or developmental or physical disability, of giving legal consent, and this is known or reasonably should be known to the person committing the act. Notwithstanding the existence of a conservatorship pursuant to the provisions of the Lanterman-Petris-Short Act (Part 1 (commencing with Section 5000) of Division 5 of the Welfare and Institutions Code), the prosecuting attorney shall prove, as an element of the crime, that a mental disorder or developmental or physical disability rendered the alleged victim incapable of giving consent. This paragraph does not preclude the prosecution of a spouse committing the act from being prosecuted under any other paragraph of this subdivision or any other law.

(2) If it is accomplished against a person's will by means of force, violence, duress, menace, or fear of immediate and unlawful bodily injury on the person or another.

(3) If a person is prevented from resisting by an intoxicating or anesthetic substance, or a controlled substance, and this condition was known, or reasonably should have been known by the accused.

(4) If a person is at the time unconscious of the nature of the act, and this is known to the accused. As used in this paragraph, "unconscious of the nature of the act" means incapable of resisting because the victim meets any one of the following conditions:

(A) Was unconscious or asleep.

(B) Was not aware, knowing, perceiving, or cognizant that the act occurred.

(C) Was not aware, knowing, perceiving, or cognizant of the essential characteristics of the act due to the perpetrator's fraud in fact.

(D) Was not aware, knowing, perceiving, or cognizant of the essential characteristics of the act due to the perpetrator's fraudulent representation that the sexual penetration served a professional purpose when it served no professional purpose.

(5) If a person submits under the belief that the person committing the act is someone known to the victim other than the accused, and this belief is induced by artifice, pretense, or concealment practiced by the accused, with intent to induce the belief.

(6) If the act is accomplished against the victim's will by threatening to retaliate in the future against the victim or any other person, and there is a reasonable possibility that the perpetrator will execute the threat. As used in this paragraph, "threatening to retaliate" means a threat to kidnap or falsely imprison, or to inflict extreme pain, serious bodily injury, or death.

(7) If the act is accomplished against the victim's will by threatening to use the authority of a public official to incarcerate, arrest, or deport the victim or another, and the victim has a reasonable belief that the perpetrator is a public official. As used in this paragraph, "public official" means a person employed by a governmental agency who has the authority, as part of that position, to incarcerate, arrest, or deport another. The perpetrator does not actually have to be a public official.

(b) For purposes of this section, the following definitions apply:

(1) "Duress" means a direct or implied threat of force, violence, danger, or retribution sufficient to coerce a reasonable person of ordinary susceptibilities to perform an act which otherwise would not have been performed, or acquiesce in an act to which one otherwise would not have submitted. The total circumstances, including the age of the victim, and the victim's relationship to the defendant, are factors to consider in appraising the existence of duress.

(2) "Menace" means any threat, declaration, or act that shows an intention to inflict an injury upon another.

Amended by Stats 2021 ch 626 (AB 1171),s 17, eff. 1/1/2022.

Amended by Stats 2013 ch 259 (AB 65),s 1, eff. 9/9/2013.

Amended by Stats 2002 ch 302 (SB 1421), s 2, eff. 1/1/2003.

Section 261.5 - Unlawful sexual intercourse

(a) Unlawful sexual intercourse is an act of sexual intercourse accomplished with a person who is not the spouse of the perpetrator, if the person is a minor. For the purposes of this section, a "minor" is a person under 18 years of age and an "adult" is a person who is 18 years of age or older.

(b) A person who engages in an act of unlawful sexual intercourse with a minor who is not more than three years older or three years younger than the perpetrator, is guilty of a misdemeanor.

(c) A person who engages in an act of unlawful sexual intercourse with a minor who is more than three years younger than the perpetrator is guilty of either a misdemeanor or a felony, and shall be punished by imprisonment in a county jail not exceeding one year, or by imprisonment pursuant to subdivision (h) of Section 1170.

(d) A person 21 years of age or older who engages in an act of unlawful sexual intercourse with a minor who is under 16 years of age is guilty of either a misdemeanor or a felony, and shall be punished by imprisonment in a county jail not exceeding one year, or by imprisonment pursuant to subdivision (h) of Section 1170 for two, three, or four years.

(e)

(1) Notwithstanding any other provision of this section, an adult who engages in an act of sexual intercourse with a minor in violation of this section may be liable for civil penalties in the following amounts:

(A) An adult who engages in an act of unlawful sexual intercourse with a minor less than two years younger than the adult is liable for a civil penalty not to exceed two thousand dollars ($2,000).

(B) An adult who engages in an act of unlawful sexual intercourse with a minor at least two years younger than the adult is liable for a civil penalty not to exceed five thousand dollars ($5,000).

(C) An adult who engages in an act of unlawful sexual intercourse with a minor at least three years younger than the adult is liable for a civil penalty not to exceed ten thousand dollars ($10,000).

(D) An adult over 21 years of age who engages in an act of unlawful sexual intercourse with a minor under 16 years of age is liable for a civil penalty not to exceed twenty-five thousand dollars ($25,000).

(2) The district attorney may bring actions to recover civil penalties pursuant to this subdivision. From the amounts collected for each case, an amount equal to the costs of pursuing the action shall be deposited with the treasurer of the county in which the judgment was entered, and the remainder shall be deposited in the Underage Pregnancy Prevention Fund, which is hereby created in the State Treasury. Amounts deposited in the Underage Pregnancy Prevention Fund may be used only for the purpose of preventing underage pregnancy upon appropriation by the Legislature.

(3) In addition to any punishment imposed under this section, the judge may assess a fine not to exceed seventy dollars ($70) against a person who violates this section with the proceeds of this fine to be used in accordance with Section 1463.23. The court shall, however, take into consideration the defendant's ability to pay, and a defendant shall not be denied probation because of their inability to pay the fine permitted under this subdivision.

(f) A person convicted of violating subdivision (d) who is granted probation shall not complete their community service at a school or location where children congregate.

Amended by Stats 2023 ch 838 (AB 1371),s 1, eff. 1/1/2024.

Amended by Stats 2011 ch 39 (AB 117),s 68, eff. 6/30/2011.

Amended by Stats 2011 ch 15 (AB 109),s 302, eff. 4/4/2011, but operative no earlier than October 1, 2011, and only upon creation of a community corrections grant program to assist in implementing this act and upon an appropriation to fund the grant program. EFFECTIVE 1/1/2000. Amended October 10, 1999 (Bill Number: SB 832) (Chapter 853).

Section 261.6 - Consent

(a) In prosecutions under Section 261, 286, 287, or 289, or former Section 262 or 288a, in which consent is at issue, "consent" means positive cooperation in act or attitude pursuant to an exercise of free will. The person must act freely and voluntarily and have knowledge of the nature of the act or transaction involved.

(b) A current or previous dating or marital relationship is not sufficient to constitute consent if consent is at issue in a prosecution under Section 261, 286, 287, or 289, or former Section 262 or 288a.

(c) This section shall not affect the admissibility of evidence or the burden of proof on the issue of consent.

Amended by Stats 2021 ch 626 (AB 1171),s 18, eff. 1/1/2022.

Amended by Stats 2018 ch 423 (SB 1494),s 44, eff. 1/1/2019.

Section 261.7 - Victim's communication to defendant that defendant use condom not sufficient to constitute consent

In prosecutions under Section 261, 286, 287, or 289, or former Section 262 or 288a, in which consent is at issue, evidence that the victim suggested, requested, or otherwise communicated to the defendant that the defendant use a condom or other birth control device, without additional evidence of consent, is not sufficient to constitute consent.

Amended by Stats 2021 ch 626 (AB 1171),s 19, eff. 1/1/2022.

Amended by Stats 2018 ch 423 (SB 1494),s 45, eff. 1/1/2019.

Section 261.9 - Fine for person convicted of seeking to procure or procuring sexual services of prostitute

(a) Any person convicted of seeking to procure or procuring the sexual services of a prostitute in violation of subdivision (b) of Section 647, if the prostitute is under 18 years of age, shall be ordered by the court, in addition to any other penalty or fine imposed, to pay an additional fine in an amount not to exceed twenty-five thousand dollars ($25,000).

(b) Every fine imposed and collected pursuant to this section shall, upon appropriation by the Legislature, be available to fund programs and services for commercially sexually exploited minors in the counties where the underlying offenses are committed.

Added by Stats 2011 ch 75 (AB 12),s 3, eff. 1/1/2012.

Section 262 - [Repealed]

Repealed by Stats 2021 ch 626 (AB 1171),s 20, eff. 1/1/2022.

Amended by Stats 2006 ch 45 (SB 1402),s 1, eff. 1/1/2007.

Section 263 - Essential guilt of rape; sexual penetration

The essential guilt of rape consists in the outrage to the person and feelings of the victim of the rape. Any sexual penetration, however slight, is sufficient to complete the crime.

Amended by Stats. 1979, Ch. 994.

Section 263.1 - All forms of nonconsensual sexual assault considered rape

(a) The Legislature finds and declares that all forms of nonconsensual sexual assault may be considered rape for purposes of the gravity of the offense and the support of survivors.

(b) This section is declarative of existing law.

Added by Stats 2016 ch 848 (AB 701),s 1, eff. 1/1/2017.

Section 264 - Punishment

(a) Except as provided in subdivision (c), rape, as defined in Section 261 or former Section 262, is punishable by imprisonment in the state prison for three, six, or eight years.

(b) In addition to any punishment imposed under this section the judge may assess a fine not to exceed seventy dollars ($70) against a person who violates Section 261 or former Section 262 with the proceeds of this fine to be used in accordance with Section 1463.23. The court shall, however, take into consideration the defendant's ability to pay, and no defendant shall be denied probation because of the defendant's inability to pay the fine permitted under this subdivision.

(c)

(1) A person who commits rape in violation of paragraph (2) of subdivision (a) of Section 261 upon a child who is under 14 years of age shall be punished by imprisonment in the state prison for 9, 11, or 13 years.

(2) A person who commits rape in violation of paragraph (2) of subdivision (a) of Section 261 upon a minor who is 14 years of age or older shall be punished by imprisonment in the state prison for 7, 9, or 11 years.

(3) This subdivision does not preclude prosecution under Section 269, Section 288.7, or any other law.

Amended by Stats 2021 ch 626 (AB 1171),s 21, eff. 1/1/2022.
Amended by Stats 2010 ch 219 (AB 1844),s 4, eff. 9/9/2010.
EFFECTIVE 1/1/2000. Amended October 10, 1999 (Bill Number: SB 832) (Chapter 853).

Section 264.1 - Punishment if victim is under 14 years of age

(a) The provisions of Section 264 notwithstanding, when the defendant, voluntarily acting in concert with another person, by force or violence and against the will of the victim, committed an act described in Section 261 or 289, either personally or by aiding and abetting the other person, that fact shall be charged in the indictment or information and if found to be true by the jury, upon a jury trial, or if found to be true by the court, upon a court trial, or if admitted by the defendant, the defendant shall suffer confinement in the state prison for five, seven, or nine years.

(b)

(1) If the victim of an offense described in subdivision (a) is a child who is under 14 years of age, the defendant shall be punished by imprisonment in the state prison for 10, 12, or 14 years.

(2) If the victim of an offense described in subdivision (a) is a minor who is 14 years of age or older, the defendant shall be punished by imprisonment in the state prison for 7, 9, or 11 years.

(3) This subdivision does not preclude prosecution under Section 269, Section 288.7, or any other law.

Amended by Stats 2021 ch 626 (AB 1171),s 22, eff. 1/1/2022.
Amended by Stats 2010 ch 219 (AB 1844),s 5, eff. 9/9/2010.

Section 264.2 - Victims of domestic violence card; notification to rape victim counseling center; right to have support person

(a) When there is an alleged violation or violations of subdivision (e) of Section 243, or Section 261, 261.5, 273.5, 286, 287, or 289, the law enforcement officer assigned to the case shall immediately provide the victim of the crime with the "Victims of Domestic Violence" card, as specified in subparagraph (H) of paragraph (9) of subdivision (c) of Section 13701, or with the card described in subdivision (a) of Section 680.2, whichever is more applicable.

(b)

(1) The law enforcement officer, or the law enforcement officer's agency, shall immediately notify the local rape victim counseling center, whenever a victim of an alleged violation of Section 261, 261.5, 286, 287, or 289 is transported to a hospital for a medical evidentiary or physical examination. The hospital shall notify the local rape victim counseling center, when the victim of the alleged violation of Section 261, 261.5, 286, 287, or 289 is presented to the hospital for the medical or evidentiary physical examination, upon approval of the victim. The victim has the right to have a sexual assault counselor, as defined in Section 1035.2 of the Evidence Code, and a support person of the victim's choosing present at any medical evidentiary or physical examination.

(2) Prior to the commencement of an initial medical evidentiary or physical examination arising out of a sexual assault, the medical provider shall give the victim the card described in subdivision (a) of Section 680.2. This requirement shall apply only if the law enforcement agency has provided the card to the medical provider in a language understood by the victim.

(3) The hospital may verify with the law enforcement officer, or the law enforcement officer's agency, whether the local rape victim counseling center has been notified, upon the approval of the victim.

(4) A support person may be excluded from a medical evidentiary or physical examination if the law enforcement officer or medical provider determines that the presence of that individual would be detrimental to the purpose of the examination.

(5) After conducting the medical evidentiary or physical examination, the medical provider shall give the victim the opportunity to shower or bathe at no cost to the victim, unless a showering or bathing facility is not available.

(6) A medical provider shall, within 24 hours of obtaining sexual assault forensic evidence from the victim, notify the law enforcement agency having jurisdiction over the alleged violation if the medical provider knows the appropriate jurisdiction. If the medical provider does not know the appropriate jurisdiction, the medical provider shall notify the local law enforcement agency.

Amended by Stats 2021 ch 626 (AB 1171),s 23, eff. 1/1/2022.
Amended by Stats 2018 ch 423 (SB 1494),s 46, eff. 1/1/2019.
Amended by Stats 2017 ch 692 (AB 1312),s 1, eff. 1/1/2018.
Amended by Stats 2015 ch 303 (AB 731),s 385, eff. 1/1/2016.
Amended by Stats 2014 ch 136 (SB 978),s 1, eff. 1/1/2015.
Amended by Stats 2006 ch 689 (SB 1743),s 11, eff. 1/1/2007.

Section 265 - Unlawful marriage

Every person who takes any woman unlawfully, against her will, and by force, menace or duress, compels her to marry him, or to marry any other person, or to be defiled, is punishable by imprisonment pursuant to subdivision (h) of Section 1170.

Amended by Stats 2011 ch 39 (AB 117),s 68, eff. 6/30/2011.
Amended by Stats 2011 ch 15 (AB 109),s 303, eff. 4/4/2011, but operative no earlier than October 1, 2011, and only upon creation of a community corrections grant program to assist in implementing this act and upon an appropriation to fund the grant program.

Section 266 - Unlawful inveiglement or enticement for purpose of prostitution

A person who inveigles or entices a person under 18 years of age into a house of ill fame, or of assignation, or elsewhere, for the purpose of prostitution, or to have illicit carnal connection with another person, and a person who aids or assists in that inveiglement or enticement, and a person who, by any false pretenses, false representation, or other fraudulent means, procures a person to have illicit carnal connection with another person, is punishable by imprisonment in the state prison, or by imprisonment in a county jail not exceeding one year, or by a fine not exceeding two thousand dollars ($2,000), or by both that fine and imprisonment.

Amended by Stats 2019 ch 615 (AB 662),s 1, eff. 1/1/2020.

Section 266a - Unlawful taking of person for purpose of prostitution

Each person who, within this state, takes any person against his or her will and without his or her consent, or with his or her consent procured by fraudulent inducement or misrepresentation, for the purpose of prostitution, as defined in subdivision (b) of Section 647, is punishable by imprisonment in the state prison, and a fine not exceeding ten thousand dollars ($10,000).

Amended by Stats 2014 ch 109 (AB 2424),s 1, eff. 1/1/2015.

Section 266b - Unlawful taking of person to live in illicit relation

Every person who takes any other person unlawfully, and against his or her will, and by force, menace, or duress, compels him or her to live with such person in an illicit relation, against his or her consent, or to so live with any other person, is punishable by imprisonment pursuant to subdivision (h) of Section 1170.

Amended by Stats 2011 ch 39 (AB 117),s 68, eff. 6/30/2011.

Amended by Stats 2011 ch 15 (AB 109),s 304, eff. 4/4/2011, but operative no earlier than October 1, 2011, and only upon creation of a community corrections grant program to assist in implementing this act and upon an appropriation to fund the grant program.

Section 266c - Unlawful inducement of person to engage in sexual intercourse by fear

Every person who induces any other person to engage in sexual intercourse, sexual penetration, oral copulation, or sodomy when his or her consent is procured by false or fraudulent representation or pretense that is made with the intent to create fear, and which does induce fear, and that would cause a reasonable person in like circumstances to act contrary to the person's free will, and does cause the victim to so act, is punishable by imprisonment in a county jail for not more than one year or in the state prison for two, three, or four years.

As used in this section, "fear" means the fear of physical injury or death to the person or to any relative of the person or member of the person's family.

Amended by Stats 2000 ch 287 (SB 1955), s 4, eff. 1/1/2001.

Section 266d - Receipt of money on account of placing in custody person for cohabitation

Any person who receives any money or other valuable thing for or on account of placing in custody any other person for the purpose of causing the other person to cohabit with any person to whom the other person is not married, is guilty of a felony.

Amended by Stats. 1975, Ch. 996.

Section 266e - Purchase of person for purpose of prostitution

Every person who purchases, or pays any money or other valuable thing for, any person for the purpose of prostitution as defined in subdivision (b) of Section 647, or for the purpose of placing such person, for immoral purposes, in any house or place against his or her will, is guilty of a felony punishable by imprisonment in the state prison for 16 months, or two or three years.

Amended by Stats 2011 ch 39 (AB 117),s 68, eff. 6/30/2011.

Amended by Stats 2011 ch 15 (AB 109),s 304.5, eff. 4/4/2011, but operative no earlier than October 1, 2011, and only upon creation of a community corrections grant program to assist in implementing this act and upon an appropriation to fund the grant program.

Section 266f - Sale of person for placing in custody for immoral purposes

Every person who sells any person or receives any money or other valuable thing for or on account of his or her placing in custody, for immoral purposes, any person, whether with or without his or her consent, is guilty of a felony punishable by imprisonment in the state prison for 16 months, or two or three years.

Amended by Stats 2011 ch 39 (AB 117),s 68, eff. 6/30/2011.

Amended by Stats 2011 ch 15 (AB 109),s 304.7, eff. 4/4/2011, but operative no earlier than October 1, 2011, and only upon creation of a community corrections grant program to assist in implementing this act and upon an appropriation to fund the grant program.

Section 266g - Placement, or procurement any other person to place, of wife in house of prostitution

Every man who, by force, intimidation, threats, persuasion, promises, or any other means, places or leaves, or procures any other person or persons to place or leave, his wife in a house of prostitution, or connives at or consents to, or permits, the placing or leaving of his wife in a house of prostitution, or allows or permits her to remain therein, is guilty of a felony and punishable by imprisonment pursuant to subdivision (h) of Section 1170 for two, three or four years; and in all prosecutions under this section a wife is a competent witness against her husband.

Amended by Stats 2011 ch 39 (AB 117),s 68, eff. 6/30/2011.

Amended by Stats 2011 ch 15 (AB 109),s 305, eff. 4/4/2011, but operative no earlier than October 1, 2011, and only upon creation of a community corrections grant program to assist in implementing this act and upon an appropriation to fund the grant program.

Section 266h - Pimping

(a) Except as provided in subdivision (b), any person who, knowing another person is a prostitute, lives or derives support or maintenance in whole or in part from the earnings or proceeds of the person's prostitution, or from money loaned or advanced to or charged against that person by any keeper or manager or inmate of a house or other place where prostitution is practiced or allowed, or who solicits or receives compensation for soliciting for the person, is guilty of pimping, a felony, and shall be punishable by imprisonment in the state prison for three, four, or six years.

(b) Any person who, knowing another person is a prostitute, lives or derives support or maintenance in whole or in part from the earnings or proceeds of the person's prostitution, or from money loaned or advanced to or charged against that person by any keeper or manager or inmate of a house or other place where prostitution is practiced or allowed, or who solicits or receives compensation for soliciting for the person, when the prostitute is a minor, is guilty of pimping a minor, a felony, and shall be punishable as follows:

(1) If the person engaged in prostitution is a minor 16 years of age or older, the offense is punishable by imprisonment in the state prison for three, four, or six years.

(2) If the person engaged in prostitution is under 16 years of age, the offense is punishable by imprisonment in the state prison for three, six, or eight years.

Amended by Stats 2010 ch 709 (SB 1062),s 8, eff. 1/1/2011.

Amended by Stats 2004 ch 405 (SB 1796), s 5, eff. 1/1/2005.

Section 266i - Pandering

(a) Except as provided in subdivision (b), any person who does any of the following is guilty of pandering, a felony, and shall be punishable by imprisonment in the state prison for three, four, or six years:

(1) Procures another person for the purpose of prostitution.

(2) By promises, threats, violence, or by any device or scheme, causes, induces, persuades, or encourages another person to become a prostitute.

(3) Procures for another person a place as an inmate in a house of prostitution or as an inmate of any place in which prostitution is encouraged or allowed within this state.

(4) By promises, threats, violence, or by any device or scheme, causes, induces, persuades, or encourages an inmate of a house of prostitution, or any other place in which prostitution is encouraged or allowed, to remain therein as an inmate.

(5) By fraud or artifice, or by duress of person or goods, or by abuse of any position of confidence or authority, procures another person for the purpose of prostitution, or to enter any place in which prostitution is encouraged or allowed within this state, or to come into this state or leave this state for the purpose of prostitution.

(6) Receives or gives, or agrees to receive or give, any money or thing of value for procuring, or attempting to procure, another person for the purpose of prostitution, or to come into this state or leave this state for the purpose of prostitution.

(b) Any person who does any of the acts described in subdivision (a) with another person who is a minor is guilty of pandering, a felony, and shall be punishable as follows:

(1) If the other person is a minor 16 years of age or older, the offense is punishable by imprisonment in the state prison for three, four, or six years.

(2) If the other person is under 16 years of age, the offense is punishable by imprisonment in the state prison for three, six, or eight years.

Amended by Stats 2010 ch 709 (SB 1062),s 9, eff. 1/1/2011.

Amended by Stats 2004 ch 405 (SB 1796), s 6, eff. 1/1/2005.

Section 266j - Making available child under age of 16 for purpose of lewd or lascivious act

Any person who intentionally gives, transports, provides, or makes available, or who offers to give, transport, provide, or make available to another person, a child under the age of 16 for the purpose of any lewd or lascivious act as defined in Section 288, or who causes, induces, or persuades a child under the age of 16 to engage in such an act with another person, is guilty of a felony and shall be imprisoned in the state prison for a term of three, six, or eight years, and by a fine not to exceed fifteen thousand dollars ($15,000).

Amended by Stats. 1987, Ch. 1068, Sec. 1.

Section 266k - Fines

(a) Upon the conviction of any person for a violation of Section 266h or 266i, the court may, in addition to any other penalty or fine imposed, order the defendant to pay an additional fine not to exceed five thousand dollars ($5,000). In setting the amount of the fine, the court shall consider any relevant factors including, but not limited to, the seriousness and gravity of the offense and the circumstances of its commission, whether the defendant derived any economic gain as the result of the crime, and the extent to which the victim suffered losses as a result of the crime. Every fine imposed and collected under this section shall be deposited in the Victim-Witness Assistance Fund to be available for appropriation to fund child sexual exploitation and child sexual abuse victim counseling centers and prevention programs under Section 13837.

(b) Upon the conviction of any person for a violation of Section 266j or 267, the court may, in addition to any other penalty or fine imposed, order the defendant to pay an additional fine not to exceed twenty-five thousand dollars ($25,000).

(c) Fifty percent of the fines collected pursuant to subdivision (b) and deposited in the Victim-Witness Assistance Fund pursuant to subdivision (a) shall be granted to community-based organizations that serve minor victims of human trafficking.

(d) If the court orders a fine to be imposed pursuant to this section, the actual administrative cost of collecting that fine, not to exceed 2 percent of the total amount paid, may be paid into the general fund of the county treasury for the use and benefit of the county.

Amended by Stats 2014 ch 714 (SB 1388),s 1, eff. 1/1/2015.

Amended by Stats 2009 ch 211 (AB 17),s 3, eff. 10/11/2009.

Section 267 - Taking of person under age of 18 for purpose of prostitution

Every person who takes away any other person under the age of 18 years from the father, mother, guardian, or other person having the legal charge of the other person, without their consent, for the purpose of prostitution, is punishable by imprisonment in the state prison, and a fine not exceeding two thousand dollars ($2,000).

Amended by Stats. 1983, Ch. 1092, Sec. 258. Effective September 27, 1983. Operative January 1, 1984, by Sec. 427 of Ch. 1092.

Section 269 - Aggravated sexual assault of child

(a) Any person who commits any of the following acts upon a child who is under 14 years of age and seven or more years younger than the person is guilty of aggravated sexual assault of a child:

(1) Rape, in violation of paragraph (2) or (6) of subdivision (a) of Section 261.

(2) Rape or sexual penetration, in concert, in violation of Section 264.1.

(3) Sodomy, in violation of paragraph (2) or (3) of subdivision (c), or subdivision (d), of Section 286.

(4) Oral copulation, in violation of paragraph (2) or (3) of subdivision (c), or subdivision (d), of Section 287 or former Section 288a.

(5) Sexual penetration, in violation of subdivision (a) of Section 289.

(b) Any person who violates this section is guilty of a felony and shall be punished by imprisonment in the state prison for 15 years to life.

(c) The court shall impose a consecutive sentence for each offense that results in a conviction under this section if the crimes involve separate victims or involve the same victim on separate occasions as defined in subdivision (d) of Section 667.6.

Amended by Stats 2018 ch 423 (SB 1494),s 47, eff. 1/1/2019.

Amended by Stats 2006 ch 337 (SB 1128),s 6, eff. 9/20/2006.

Chapter 2 - ABANDONMENT AND NEGLECT OF CHILDREN

Section 270 - Abandonment or desertion of child by parent

If a parent of a minor child willfully omits, without lawful excuse, to furnish necessary clothing, food, shelter or medical attendance, or other remedial care for his or her child, he or she is guilty of a misdemeanor punishable by a fine not exceeding two thousand dollars ($2,000), or by imprisonment in the county jail not exceeding one year, or by both such fine and imprisonment. If a court of competent jurisdiction has made a final adjudication in either a civil or a criminal action that a person is the parent of a minor child and the person has notice of such adjudication and he or she then willfully omits, without lawful excuse, to furnish necessary clothing, food, shelter, medical attendance or other remedial care for his or her child, this conduct is punishable by imprisonment in the county jail not exceeding one year or in a state prison for a determinate term of one year and one day, or by a fine not exceeding two thousand dollars ($2,000), or by both such fine and imprisonment. This statute shall not be construed so as to relieve such parent from the criminal liability defined herein for such omission merely because the other parent of such child is legally entitled to the custody of such child nor because the other parent of such child or any other person or organization voluntarily or involuntarily furnishes such necessary food, clothing, shelter or medical attendance or other remedial care for such child or undertakes to do so.

Proof of abandonment or desertion of a child by such parent, or the omission by such parent to furnish necessary food, clothing, shelter or medical attendance or other remedial care for his or her child is prima facie evidence that such abandonment or desertion or omission to furnish necessary food, clothing, shelter or medical attendance or other remedial care is willful and without lawful excuse. The court, in determining the ability of the parent to support his or her child, shall consider all income, including social insurance benefits and gifts.

The provisions of this section are applicable whether the parents of such child are or were ever married or divorced, and regardless of any decree made in any divorce action relative to alimony or to the support of the child. A child conceived but not yet born is to be deemed an existing person insofar as this section is concerned.

The husband of a woman who bears a child as a result of artificial insemination shall be considered the father of that child for the purpose of this section, if he consented in writing to the artificial insemination.

If a parent provides a minor with treatment by spiritual means through prayer alone in accordance with the tenets and practices of a recognized church or religious denomination, by a duly accredited practitioner thereof, such treatment shall constitute "other remedial care", as used in this section.

Amended by Stats. 1984, Ch. 1432, Sec. 1.

Section 270.1 - Parent or guardian of elementary school pupil who is chronic truant

(a) A parent or guardian of a pupil of six years of age or more who is in kindergarten or any of grades 1 to 8, inclusive, and who is subject to compulsory full-time education or compulsory continuation education, whose child is a chronic truant as defined in Section 48263.6 of the Education Code, who has failed to reasonably supervise and encourage the pupil's school attendance, and who has been offered language accessible support services to address the pupil's truancy, is guilty of a misdemeanor punishable by a fine not exceeding two thousand dollars ($2,000), or by imprisonment in a county jail not exceeding one year, or by both that fine and imprisonment. A parent or guardian guilty of a misdemeanor under this subdivision may participate in the deferred entry of judgment program defined in subdivision (b).

(b) A superior court may establish a deferred entry of judgment program that includes the components listed in paragraphs (1) to (7), inclusive, to adjudicate cases involving parents or guardians of elementary school pupils who are chronic truants as defined in Section 48263.6 of the Education Code:

    (1) A dedicated court calendar.

    (2) Leadership by a judge of the superior court in that county.

    (3) Meetings, scheduled and held periodically, with school district representatives designated by the chronic truant's school district of enrollment. Those representatives may include school psychologists, school counselors, teachers, school administrators, or other educational service providers deemed appropriate by the school district.

    (4) Service referrals for parents or guardians, as appropriate to each case that may include, but are not limited to, all of the following:

        (A) Case management.

        (B) Mental and physical health services.

        (C) Parenting classes and support.

        (D) Substance abuse treatment.

        (E) Child care and housing.

    (5) A clear statement that, in lieu of trial, the court may grant deferred entry of judgment with respect to the current crime or crimes charged if the defendant pleads guilty to each charge and waives time for the pronouncement of judgment and that, upon the defendant's compliance with the terms and conditions set forth by the court and agreed to by the defendant upon the entry of his or her plea, and upon the motion of the prosecuting attorney, the court will dismiss the charge or charges against the defendant and the same procedures specified for successful completion of a drug diversion program or a deferred entry of judgment program pursuant to Section 851.90 and the provisions of Section 1203.4 shall apply.

    (6) A clear statement that failure to comply with any condition under the program may result in the prosecuting attorney or the court making a motion for entry of judgment, whereupon the court will render a finding of guilty to the charge or charges pled, enter judgment, and schedule a sentencing hearing as otherwise provided in this code.

    (7) An explanation of criminal record retention and disposition resulting from participation in the deferred entry of judgment program and the defendant's rights relative to answering questions about his or her arrest and deferred entry of judgment following successful completion of the program.

(c) Funding for the deferred entry of judgment program pursuant to this section shall be derived solely from nonstate sources.

(d) A parent or guardian of an elementary school pupil who is a chronic truant, as defined in Section 48263.6 of the Education Code, may not be punished for a violation of both this section and the provisions of Section 272 that involve criminal liability for parents and guardians of truant children.

(e) If any district attorney chooses to charge a defendant with a violation of subdivision (a) and the defendant is found by the prosecuting attorney to be eligible or ineligible for deferred entry of judgment, the prosecuting attorney shall file with the court a declaration in writing, or state for the record, the grounds upon which that determination is based.

Added by Stats 2010 ch 647 (SB 1317),s 2, eff. 1/1/2011.

Section 270.5 - Failure to provide shelter

(a) Every parent who refuses, without lawful excuse, to accept his or her minor child into the parent's home, or, failing to do so, to provide alternative shelter, upon being requested to do so by a child protective agency and after being informed of the duty imposed by this statute to do so, is guilty of a misdemeanor and shall be punished by a fine of not more than five hundred dollars ($500).

(b) For purposes of this section, "child protective agency" means a police or sheriff's department, a county probation department, or a county welfare department.

(c) For purposes of this section, "lawful excuse" shall include, but not be limited to, a reasonable fear that the minor child's presence in the home will endanger the safety of the parent or other persons residing in the home.

Added by Stats. 1984, Ch. 1616, Sec. 1.

Section 270.6 - Failure to furnish spousal support

If a court of competent jurisdiction has made a temporary or permanent order awarding spousal support that a person must pay, the person has notice of that order, and he or she then leaves the state with the intent to willfully omit, without lawful excuse, to furnish the spousal support, he or she is punishable by imprisonment in a county jail for a period not exceeding one year, a fine not exceeding two thousand dollars ($2,000), or both that imprisonment and fine.

Added by Stats 2002 ch 410 (SB 1399), s 1, eff. 1/1/2003.

Section 270a - Abandonment of spouse

Every individual who has sufficient ability to provide for his or her spouse's support, or who is able to earn the means of such spouse's support, who willfully abandons and leaves his or her spouse in a destitute condition, or who refuses or neglects to provide such spouse with necessary food, clothing, shelter, or medical attendance, unless by such spouse's conduct the individual was justified in abandoning such spouse, is guilty of a misdemeanor.

Amended by Stats. 1976, Ch. 1170.

Section 270b - Suspension of proceeding

After arrest and before plea or trial, or after conviction or plea of guilty and before sentence under either Section 270 or 270a, if the defendant shall appear before the court and enter into an undertaking with sufficient sureties to the people of the State of California in such penal sum as the court may fix, to be approved by the court, and conditioned that the defendant will pay to the person having custody of such child or to such spouse, such sum per month as may be fixed by the court in order to thereby provide such minor child or such spouse as the case may be, with necessary food, shelter, clothing, medical attendance, or other remedial care, then the court may suspend proceedings or sentence therein; and such undertaking is valid and binding for two years, or such lesser time which the court shall fix; and upon the failure of defendant to comply with such undertaking, the defendant may be ordered to appear before the court and show cause why further proceedings should not be had in such action or why sentence should not be imposed, whereupon the court may proceed with such action, or pass sentence, or for good cause shown may modify the order and take a new undertaking and further suspend proceedings or sentence for a like period.

Amended by Stats. 1976, Ch. 1170.

Section 270c - Failure to provide for indigent parent

Except as provided in Chapter 2 (commencing with Section 4410) of Part 4 of Division 9 of the Family Code, every adult child who, having the ability so to do, fails to provide necessary food, clothing, shelter, or medical attendance for an indigent parent, is guilty of a misdemeanor.

Amended by Stats. 1992, Ch. 163, Sec. 102. Effective January 1, 1993. Operative January 1, 1994, by Sec. 161 of Ch. 163.

Section 270d - Payment of fine

In any case where there is a conviction and sentence under the provisions of either Section 270 or Section 270a, should a fine be imposed, such fine shall be directed by the court to be paid in whole or in part to the spouse of the defendant or guardian or custodian of the child or children of such defendant, except as follows:

If the children are receiving public assistance, all fines, penalties or forfeitures imposed and all funds collected from the defendant shall be paid to the county department. Money so paid shall be applied first to support for the calendar month following its receipt by the county department and any balance remaining shall be applied to future needs, or be treated as reimbursement for past support furnished from public assistance funds.

Amended by Stats. 1974, Ch. 893.

Section 270e - Proof of marriage or parentage; proof of abandonment and nonsupport

No other evidence shall be required to prove marriage or registered domestic partnership of spouses, or that a person is the lawful father or mother of a child or children, than is or shall be required to prove such facts in a civil action. In all prosecutions under either Section 270a or 270 of this code, Sections 970, 971, and 980 of the Evidence Code do not apply, and both spouses or domestic partners shall be competent to testify to any and all relevant matters, including the fact of marriage or registered domestic partnership and the parentage of a child or children. Proof of the abandonment and nonsupport of a spouse, or of the omission to furnish necessary food, clothing, shelter, or of medical attendance for a child or children is prima facie evidence that such abandonment and nonsupport or omission to furnish necessary food, clothing, shelter, or medical attendance is willful. In any prosecution under Section 270, it shall be competent for the people to prove nonaccess of husband to wife or any other fact establishing nonpaternity of a husband. In any prosecution pursuant to Section 270, the final establishment of paternity or nonpaternity in another proceeding shall be admissible as evidence of paternity or nonpaternity.

Amended by Stats 2016 ch 50 (SB 1005),s 68, eff. 1/1/2017.

Section 270f - Investigation of report of failure to provide support to child

Where, under the provisions of this chapter, a report is filed by a parent of a child with the district attorney averring:

(1) That the other parent has failed to provide necessary support and

(2) That neither the child in need of assistance nor another on his behalf is receiving public assistance, the district attorney shall immediately investigate the verity of such report and determine the defaulting parent's location and financial ability to provide the needed support, and upon a finding that the report is true shall immediately take all steps necessary to obtain support for the child in need of assistance.

Amended by Stats. 1974, Ch. 893.

Section 270g - Review of report

A review of each report filed with the district attorney under Section 270f shall be made at 90-day intervals unless the support payments have been legally terminated, the parties involved are permanently located beyond county jurisdiction, or the defaulting parent is complying with the provisions of this chapter.

Amended by Stats. 1974, Ch. 893.

Section 270h - Execution on order for support payments; earnings assignment order

In any case where there is a conviction under either Section 270 or 270a and there is an order granting probation which includes an order for support, the court may:

(a) Issue an execution on the order for the support payments that accrue during the time the probation order is in effect, in the same manner as on a judgment in a civil action for support payments. This remedy shall apply only when there is no existing civil order of this state or a foreign court order that has been reduced to a judgment of this state for support of the same person or persons included in the probation support order.

(b) Issue an earnings assignment order for support pursuant to Chapter 8 (commencing with Section 5200) of Part 5 of Division 9 of the Family Code as a condition of probation. This remedy shall apply only when there is no existing civil order for support of the same person or persons included in the probation support order upon which an assignment order has been entered pursuant to Chapter 8 (commencing with Section 5200) of Part 5 of Division 9 of the Family Code or pursuant to former Chapter 5 (commencing with Section 4390) of Title 1.5 of Part 5 of Division 4 of the Civil Code. These remedies are in addition to any other remedies available to the court.

Amended by Stats. 1992, Ch. 163, Sec. 103. Effective January 1, 1993. Operative January 1, 1994, by Sec. 161 of Ch. 163.

Section 271 - Desertion of child

Every parent of any child under the age of 14 years, and every person to whom any such child has been confided for nurture, or education, who deserts such child in any place whatever with intent to abandon it, is punishable by imprisonment pursuant to subdivision (h) of Section 1170 or in the county jail not exceeding one year or by fine not exceeding one thousand dollars ($1,000) or by both.

Amended by Stats 2011 ch 39 (AB 117),s 68, eff. 6/30/2011.

Amended by Stats 2011 ch 15 (AB 109),s 306, eff. 4/4/2011, but operative no earlier than October 1, 2011, and only upon creation of a community corrections grant program to assist in implementing this act and upon an appropriation to fund the grant program.

Section 271.5 - Voluntary surrender of child to personnel on duty at safe-surrender site

(a) No parent or other individual having lawful custody of a minor child 72 hours old or younger may be prosecuted for a violation of Section 270, 270.5, 271, or 271a if he or she voluntarily surrenders physical custody of the child to personnel on duty at a safe-surrender site.

(b) For purposes of this section, "safe-surrender site" has the same meaning as defined in paragraph (1) of subdivision (a) of Section 1255.7 of the Health and Safety Code.

(c)

(1) For purposes of this section, "lawful custody" has the same meaning as defined in subdivision (j) of Section 1255.7 of the Health and Safety Code.

(2) For purposes of this section, "personnel" has the same meaning as defined in paragraph (3) of subdivision (a) of Section 1255.7 of the Health and Safety Code.

Amended by Stats 2007 ch 130 (AB 299),s 186, eff. 1/1/2008.

Amended by Stats 2005 ch 625 (SB 116),s 2, eff. 1/1/2006

Amended by Stats 2005 ch 279 (SB 1107),s 3, eff. 1/1/2006

Amended by Stats 2004 ch 103 (SB 1413), s 2, eff. 1/1/2005.

Amended by Stats 2003 ch 150 (SB 139), s 2, eff. 1/1/2004.

Repealed by Stats 2003 ch 150 (SB 139), s 2, eff. 1/1/2006.

Added by Stats 2000 ch 824 (SB 1368), s 2, eff. 1/1/2001.

Amended by Stats 2004 ch 103 (SB 1413), s 2, eff. 1/1/2005.

Amended by Stats 2003 ch 150 (SB 139), s 2, eff. 1/1/2004.

Repealed by Stats 2003 ch 150 (SB 139), s 2, eff. 1/1/2006.

Added by Stats 2000 ch 824 (SB 1368), s 2, eff. 1/1/2001.

Section 271a - Abandonment of child; false representation that child is orphan

Every person who knowingly and willfully abandons, or who, having ability so to do, fails or refuses to maintain his or her minor child under the age of 14 years, or who falsely, knowing the same to be false, represents to any manager, officer or agent of any orphan asylum or charitable institution for the care of orphans, that any child for whose admission into that asylum or institution application has been made is an orphan, is punishable by imprisonment pursuant to subdivision (h) of Section 1170, or in the county jail not exceeding one year, or by fine not exceeding one thousand dollars ($1,000), or by both.

Amended by Stats 2011 ch 39 (AB 117),s 68, eff. 6/30/2011.

Amended by Stats 2011 ch 15 (AB 109),s 307, eff. 4/4/2011, but operative no earlier than October 1, 2011, and only upon creation of a community corrections grant program to assist in implementing this act and upon an appropriation to fund the grant program.

Section 272 - Inducing minor to fail to conform to lawful order of juvenile court; persuading or luring minor from home

(a)

(1) Every person who commits any act or omits the performance of any duty, which act or omission causes or tends to cause or encourage any person under the age of 18 years to come within the provisions of Section 300, 601, or 602 of the Welfare and Institutions Code or which act or omission contributes thereto, or any person who, by any act or omission, or by threats, commands, or persuasion, induces or endeavors to induce any person under the age of 18 years or any ward or dependent child of the juvenile court to fail or refuse to conform to a lawful order of the juvenile court, or to do or to perform any act or to follow any course of conduct or to

so live as would cause or manifestly tend to cause that person to become or to remain a person within the provisions of Section 300, 601, or 602 of the Welfare and Institutions Code, is guilty of a misdemeanor and upon conviction thereof shall be punished by a fine not exceeding two thousand five hundred dollars ($2,500), or by imprisonment in the county jail for not more than one year, or by both fine and imprisonment in a county jail, or may be released on probation for a period not exceeding five years.

(2) For purposes of this subdivision, a parent or legal guardian to any person under the age of 18 years shall have the duty to exercise reasonable care, supervision, protection, and control over their minor child.

(b)

(1) An adult stranger who is 21 years of age or older, who knowingly contacts or communicates with a minor who is under 14 years of age, who knew or reasonably should have known that the minor is under 14 years of age, for the purpose of persuading and luring, or transporting, or attempting to persuade and lure, or transport, that minor away from the minor's home or from any location known by the minor's parent, legal guardian, or custodian, to be a place where the minor is located, for any purpose, without the express consent of the minor's parent or legal guardian, and with the intent to avoid the consent of the minor's parent or legal guardian, is guilty of an infraction or a misdemeanor, subject to subdivision (d) of Section 17.

(2) This subdivision shall not apply in an emergency situation.

(3) As used in this subdivision, the following terms are defined to mean:

(A) "Emergency situation" means a situation where the minor is threatened with imminent bodily harm, emotional harm, or psychological harm.

(B) "Contact" or "communication" includes, but is not limited to, the use of a telephone or the Internet, as defined in Section 17538 of the Business and Professions Code.

(C) "Stranger" means a person of casual acquaintance with whom no substantial relationship exists, or an individual with whom a relationship has been established or promoted for the primary purpose of victimization, as defined in subdivision (e) of Section 6600 of the Welfare and Institutions Code.

(D) "Express consent" means oral or written permission that is positive, direct, and unequivocal, requiring no inference or implication to supply its meaning.

(4) This section shall not be interpreted to criminalize acts of persons contacting minors within the scope and course of their employment, or status as a volunteer of a recognized civic or charitable organization.

(5) This section is intended to protect minors and to help parents and legal guardians exercise reasonable care, supervision, protection, and control over minor children.

Amended by Stats 2005 ch 461 (AB 33),s 1, eff. 1/1/2006
Amended by Stats 2000 ch 621 (AB 2021), s 1, eff. 1/1/2001.
Amended by Stats 2001 ch 159 (SB 662), s 161, eff. 1/1/2002.

Section 273 - Unlawful payment for adoption or consent to adoption

(a) It is a misdemeanor for any person or agency to pay, offer to pay, or to receive money or anything of value for the placement for adoption or for the consent to an adoption of a child. This subdivision shall not apply to any fee paid for adoption services provided by the State Department of Social Services, a licensed adoption agency, adoption services providers, as defined in Section 8502 of the Family Code, or an attorney providing adoption legal services.

(b) This section shall not make it unlawful to pay or receive the maternity-connected medical or hospital and necessary living expenses of the mother preceding and during confinement as an act of charity, as long as the payment is not contingent upon placement of the child for adoption, consent to the adoption, or cooperation in the completion of the adoption.

(c) It is a misdemeanor punishable by imprisonment in a county jail not exceeding one year or by a fine not exceeding two thousand five hundred dollars ($2,500) for any parent to obtain the financial benefits set forth in subdivision (b) with the intent to receive those financial benefits where there is an intent to do either of the following:

(1) Not complete the adoption.

(2) Not consent to the adoption.

(d) It is a misdemeanor punishable by imprisonment in a county jail not exceeding one year or by a fine not exceeding two thousand five hundred dollars ($2,500) for any parent to obtain the financial benefits set forth in subdivision (b) from two or more prospective adopting families or persons, if either parent does both of the following:

(1) Knowingly fails to disclose to those families or persons that there are other prospective adopting families or persons interested in adopting the child, with knowledge that there is an obligation to disclose that information.

(2) Knowingly accepts the financial benefits set forth in subdivision (b) if the aggregate amount exceeds the reasonable maternity-connected medical or hospital and necessary living expenses of the mother preceding and during the pregnancy.

(e) Any person who has been convicted previously of an offense described in subdivision (c) or (d), who is separately tried and convicted of a subsequent violation of subdivision (c) or (d), is guilty of a public offense punishable by imprisonment in a county jail or in the state prison.

(f) Nothing in this section shall be construed to prohibit the prosecution of any person for a misdemeanor or felony pursuant to Section 487 or any other provision of law in lieu of prosecution pursuant to this section.

Amended by Stats. 1997, Ch. 185, Sec. 1. Effective January 1, 1998.

Section 273a - Endangerment of child

(a) Any person who, under circumstances or conditions likely to produce great bodily harm or death, willfully causes or permits any child to suffer, or inflicts thereon unjustifiable physical pain or mental suffering, or having the care or custody of any child, willfully causes or permits the person or health of that child to be injured, or willfully causes or permits that child to be placed in a situation where his or her person or health is endangered, shall be punished by imprisonment in a county jail not exceeding one year, or in the state prison for two, four, or six years.

(b) Any person who, under circumstances or conditions other than those likely to produce great bodily harm or death, willfully causes or permits any child to suffer, or inflicts thereon unjustifiable physical pain or mental suffering, or having the care or custody of any child, willfully causes or permits the person or health of that child to be injured, or willfully causes or permits that child to be placed in a situation where his or her person or health may be endangered, is guilty of a misdemeanor.

(c) If a person is convicted of violating this section and probation is granted, the court shall require the following minimum conditions of probation:

(1) A mandatory minimum period of probation of 48 months.

(2) A criminal court protective order protecting the victim from further acts of violence or threats, and, if appropriate, residence exclusion or stay-away conditions.

(3)

(A) Successful completion of no less than one year of a child abuser's treatment counseling program approved by the probation department. The defendant shall be ordered to begin participation in the program immediately upon the grant of probation. The counseling program shall meet the criteria specified in Section 273.1. The defendant shall produce documentation of program enrollment to the court within 30 days of enrollment, along with quarterly progress reports.

(B) The terms of probation for offenders shall not be lifted until all reasonable fees due to the counseling program have been paid in full, but in no case shall probation be extended beyond the term provided in subdivision (a) of Section 1203.1. If the court finds that the defendant does not have the ability to pay the fees based on the defendant's changed circumstances, the court may reduce or waive the fees.

(4) If the offense was committed while the defendant was under the influence of drugs or alcohol, the defendant shall abstain from the use of drugs or alcohol during the period of probation and shall be subject to random drug testing by his or her probation officer.

(5) The court may waive any of the above minimum conditions of probation upon a finding that the condition would not be in the best interests of justice. The court shall state on the record its reasons for any waiver.

Amended by Stats. 1997, Ch. 134, Sec. 1. Effective January 1, 1998.

Section 273ab - Assault of child under eight years of age

(a) Any person, having the care or custody of a child who is under eight years of age, who assaults the child by means of force that to a reasonable person would be likely to produce great bodily injury, resulting in the child's death, shall be punished by imprisonment in the state prison for 25 years to life. Nothing in this section shall be construed as affecting the applicability of subdivision (a) of Section 187 or Section 189.

(b) Any person, having the care or custody of a child who is under eight years of age, who assaults the child by means of force that to a reasonable person would be likely to produce great bodily injury, resulting in the child becoming comatose due to brain injury or suffering paralysis of a permanent nature, shall be punished by imprisonment in the state prison for life with the possibility of parole. As used in this subdivision, "paralysis" means a major or complete loss of motor function resulting from injury to the nervous system or to a muscular mechanism.

Amended by Stats 2010 ch 300 (AB 1280),s 1, eff. 1/1/2011.

Section 273b - Unlawful placement of child under age of 16 years with adults charged with or convicted of crime

No child under the age of 16 years shall be placed in any courtroom, or in any vehicle for transportation to any place, in company with adults charged with or convicted of crime, except in the presence of a proper official.

Amended by Stats. 1987, Ch. 828, Sec. 13.5.

Section 273c - Fines, payable to society for prevention of cruelty to children

All fines, penalties, and forfeitures imposed and collected under the provisions of Sections 270, 271, 271a, 273a, and 273b, or under the provisions of any law relating to, or affecting, children, in every case where the prosecution is instituted or conducted by a society incorporated under the laws of this state for the prevention of cruelty to children, inure to such society in aid of the purposes for which it is incorporated.

Amended by Stats. 1987, Ch. 828, Sec. 14.

Section 273d - Unlawful infliction of cruel or inhuman corporal punishment or injury resulting in traumatic condition

(a) Any person who willfully inflicts upon a child any cruel or inhuman corporal punishment or an injury resulting in a traumatic condition is guilty of a felony and shall be punished by imprisonment pursuant to subdivision (h) of Section 1170 for two, four, or six years, or in a county jail for not more than one year, by a fine of up to six thousand dollars ($6,000), or by both that imprisonment and fine.

(b) Any person who is found guilty of violating subdivision (a) shall receive a four-year enhancement for a prior conviction of that offense provided that no additional term shall be imposed under this subdivision for any prison term or term imposed under the provisions of subdivision (h) of Section 1170 served prior to a period of 10 years in which the defendant remained free of both the commission of an offense that results in a felony conviction and prison custody or custody in a county jail under the provisions of subdivision (h) of Section 1170.

(c) If a person is convicted of violating this section and probation is granted, the court shall require the following minimum conditions of probation:

(1) A mandatory minimum period of probation of 36 months.

(2) A criminal court protective order protecting the victim from further acts of violence or threats, and, if appropriate, residence exclusion or stay-away conditions.

(3)

(A) Successful completion of no less than one year of a child abuser's treatment counseling program. The defendant shall be ordered to begin participation in the program immediately upon the grant of probation. The counseling program shall meet the criteria specified in Section 273.1. The defendant shall produce documentation of program enrollment to the court within 30 days of enrollment, along with quarterly progress reports.

(B) The terms of probation for offenders shall not be lifted until all reasonable fees due to the counseling program have been paid in full, but in no case shall probation be extended beyond the term provided in subdivision (a) of Section 1203.1. If the court finds that the defendant does not have the ability to pay the fees based on the defendant's changed circumstances, the court may reduce or waive the fees.

(4) If the offense was committed while the defendant was under the influence of drugs or alcohol, the defendant shall abstain from the use of drugs or alcohol during the period of probation and shall be subject to random drug testing by his or her probation officer.

(5) The court may waive any of the above minimum conditions of probation upon a finding that the condition would not be in the best interests of justice. The court shall state on the record its reasons for any waiver.

Amended by Stats 2011 ch 12 (AB X1-17),s 8, eff. 9/20/2011, op. 10/1/2011.

Amended by Stats 2011 ch 39 (AB 117),s 68, eff. 6/30/2011.

Amended by Stats 2011 ch 15 (AB 109),s 312, eff. 4/4/2011, but operative no earlier than October 1, 2011, and only upon creation of a community corrections grant program to assist in implementing this act and upon an appropriation to fund the grant program.

Amended by Stats 2004 ch 229 (SB 1104), s 14, eff. 8/16/2004.

EFFECTIVE 1/1/2000. Amended October 10, 1999 (Bill Number: SB 218) (Chapter 662).

Section 273e - Unlawful use of minor to make delivery at house of prostitution

Every telephone, special delivery company or association, and every other corporation or person engaged in the delivery of packages, letters, notes, messages, or other matter, and every manager, superintendent, or other agent of such person, corporation, or association, who sends any minor in the employ or under the control of any such person, corporation, association, or agent, to the keeper of any house of prostitution, variety theater, or other place of questionable repute, or to any person connected with, or any inmate of, such house, theater, or other place, or who permits such minor to enter such house, theater, or other place, is guilty of a misdemeanor.

Added by Stats. 1905, Ch. 568.

Section 273f - Unlawful sending of minor to saloon, gambling house, house of prostitution, or other immoral place

Any person, whether as parent, guardian, employer, or otherwise, and any firm or corporation, who as employer or otherwise, shall send, direct, or cause to be sent or directed to any saloon, gambling house, house of prostitution, or other immoral place, any minor, is guilty of a misdemeanor.

Amended by Stats. 1972, Ch. 579.

Section 273g - Degrading, lewd, immoral or vicious habits or practices in presence of child; habitually drunk in presence of child

Any person who in the presence of any child indulges in any degrading, lewd, immoral or vicious habits or practices, or who is habitually drunk in the presence of any child in his care, custody or control, is guilty of a misdemeanor.

Added by Stats. 1907, Ch. 413.

Section 273h - Work upon public roads or highways

In all prosecutions under the provisions of either section 270, section 270a, section 270b, section 271 or section 271a, of this code, where a conviction is had and sentence of imprisonment in the county jail or in the city jail is imposed, the court may direct that the person so convicted shall be compelled to work upon the public roads or highways, or any other public work, in the county or in the city where such conviction is had, during the term of such sentence. And it shall be the duty of the board of supervisors of the county where such person is imprisoned in the county jail, and of the city council of the city where such person is imprisoned in the city jail, where such conviction and sentence are had and where such work is performed by a person under sentence to the county jail or to the city jail, to allow and order the payment out of any funds available, to the wife or to the guardian, or to the custodian of a child or children, or to an organization, or to an individual, appointed by the court as trustee, at the end of each calendar month, for the support of such wife or children, a sum not to exceed two dollars for each day's work of such person so imprisoned.

Amended by Stats. 1927, Ch. 243.

Section 273i - Unlawful publication of information relating to child

(a) Any person who publishes information describing or depicting a child, the physical appearance of a child, the location of a child, or locations where children may be found with the intent that another person imminently use the information to commit a crime against a child and the information is likely to aid in the imminent commission of a crime against a child, is guilty of a misdemeanor, punishable by imprisonment in a county jail for not more than one year, a fine of not more than one thousand dollars ($1,000), or by both a fine and imprisonment.

(b) For purposes of this section, "publishes" means making the information available to another person through any medium, including, but not limited to, the Internet, the World Wide Web, or e-mail.

(c) For purposes of this section, "child" means a person who is 14 years of age or younger.

(d) For purposes of this section, "information" includes, but is not limited to, an image, film, filmstrip, photograph, negative, slide, photocopy, videotape, video laser disc, or any other computer-generated image.

(e) Any parent or legal guardian of a child about whom information is published in violation of subdivision (a) may seek a preliminary injunction enjoining any further publication of that information.

Added by Stats 2008 ch 423 (AB 534),s 1, eff. 1/1/2009.

Section 273j - Notification of death of child; notification that child is missing person

(a)

(1) Any parent or guardian having the care, custody, or control of a child under 14 years of age who knows or should have known that the child has died shall notify a public safety agency, as defined in Section 53102 of the Government Code, within 24 hours of the time that the parent or guardian knew or should have known that the child has died.

(2) This subdivision shall not apply when a child is otherwise under the immediate care of a physician at the time of death, or if a public safety agency, a coroner, or a medical examiner is otherwise aware of the death.

(b)

(1) Any parent or guardian having the care, custody, or control of a child under 14 years of age shall notify law enforcement within 24 hours of the time that the parent or guardian knows or should have known that the child is a missing person and there is evidence that the child is a person at risk, as those terms are defined in Section 14215.

(2) This subdivision shall not apply if law enforcement is otherwise aware that the child is a missing person.

(c) A violation of this section is a misdemeanor punishable by imprisonment in a county jail for not more than one year, or by a fine not exceeding one thousand dollars ($1,000), or by both that fine and imprisonment.

(d) Nothing in this section shall preclude prosecution under any other provision of law.

Amended by Stats 2014 ch 437 (SB 1066),s 8, eff. 1/1/2015.

Added by Stats 2012 ch 805 (AB 1432),s 2, eff. 1/1/2013.

Section 273.1 - Criteria for treatment program for child abuser

(a) Any treatment program to which a child abuser convicted of a violation of Section 273a or 273d is referred as a condition of probation shall meet the following criteria:

(1) Substantial expertise and experience in the treatment of victims of child abuse and the families in which abuse and violence have occurred.

(2) Staff providing direct service are therapists licensed to practice in this state or are under the direct supervision of a therapist licensed to practice in this state.

(3) Utilization of a treatment regimen designed to specifically address the offense, including methods of preventing and breaking the cycle of family violence, anger management, and parenting education that focuses, among other things, on means of identifying the developmental and emotional needs of the child.

(4) Utilization of group and individual therapy and counseling, with groups no larger than 12 persons.

(5) Capability of identifying substance abuse and either treating the abuse or referring the offender to a substance abuse program, to the extent that the court has not already done so.

(6) Entry into a written agreement with the defendant that includes an outline of the components of the program, the attendance requirements, a requirement to attend group session free of chemical influence, and a statement that the defendant may be removed from the program if it is determined that the defendant is not benefiting from the program or is disruptive to the program.

(7) The program may include, on the recommendation of the treatment counselor, family counseling. However, no child victim shall be compelled or required to participate in the program, including family counseling, and no program may condition a defendant's enrollment on participation by the child victim. The treatment counselor shall privately advise the child victim that his or her participation is voluntary.

(b) If the program finds that the defendant is unsuitable, the program shall immediately contact the probation department or the court. The probation department or court shall either recalendar the case for hearing or refer the defendant to an appropriate alternative child abuser's treatment counseling program.

(c) Upon request by the child abuser's treatment counseling program, the court shall provide the defendant's arrest report, prior incidents of violence, and treatment history to the program.

(d) The child abuser's treatment counseling program shall provide the probation department and the court with periodic progress reports at least every three months that include attendance, fee payment history, and program compliance. The program shall submit a final evaluation that includes the program's evaluation of the defendant's progress, and recommendation for either successful or unsuccessful termination of the program.

(e) The defendant shall pay for the full costs of the treatment program, including any drug testing. However, the court may waive any portion or all of that financial responsibility upon a finding of an inability to pay. Upon the request of the defendant, the court shall hold a hearing to determine the defendant's ability to pay for the treatment program. At the hearing the court may consider all relevant information, but shall consider the impact of the costs of the treatment program on the defendant's ability to provide food, clothing, and shelter for the child injured by a violation of Section 273a or 273d. If the court finds that the defendant is unable to pay for any portion of the costs of the treatment program, its reasons for that finding shall be stated on the record. In the event of this finding, the program fees or a portion thereof shall be waived.

(f) All programs accepting referrals of child abusers pursuant to this section shall accept offenders for whom fees have been partially or fully waived. However, the court shall require each qualifying program to serve no more than its proportionate share of those offenders who have been granted fee waivers, and require all qualifying programs to share equally in the cost of serving those offenders with fee waivers.

Amended by Stats. 1997, Ch. 17, Sec. 95. Effective January 1, 1998.

Section 273.4 - Female genital mutilation

(a) If the act constituting a felony violation of subdivision (a) of Section 273a was female genital mutilation, as defined in subdivision (b), the defendant shall be punished by an additional term of imprisonment in the state prison for one year, in addition and consecutive to the punishment prescribed by Section 273a.

(b) "Female genital mutilation" means the excision or infibulation of the labia majora, labia minora, clitoris, or vulva, performed for nonmedical purposes.

(c) Nothing in this section shall preclude prosecution under Section 203, 205, or 206 or any other provision of law.

Amended by Stats 2011 ch 39 (AB 117),s 68, eff. 6/30/2011.

Amended by Stats 2011 ch 39 (AB 117),s 12, eff. 6/30/2011.

Amended by Stats 2011 ch 15 (AB 109),s 308, eff. 4/4/2011, but operative no earlier than October 1, 2011, and only upon creation of a community corrections grant program to assist in implementing this act and upon an appropriation to fund the grant program.

Section 273.5 - Infliction of corporal injury resulting in traumatic injury upon person who is spouse, former spouse, cohabitant, former cohabitant, or parent of child

(a) Any person who willfully inflicts corporal injury resulting in a traumatic condition upon a victim described in subdivision (b) is guilty of a felony, and upon conviction thereof shall be punished by imprisonment in the state prison for two, three, or four years, or in a county jail for not more than one year, or by a fine of up to six thousand dollars ($6,000), or by both that fine and imprisonment.

(b) Subdivision (a) shall apply if the victim is or was one or more of the following:

(1) The offender's spouse or former spouse.

(2) The offender's cohabitant or former cohabitant.

(3) The offender's fiance or fiancee, or someone with whom the offender has, or previously had, an engagement or dating relationship, as defined in paragraph (10) of subdivision (f) of Section 243.

(4) The mother or father of the offender's child.

(c) Holding oneself out to be the spouse of the person with whom one is cohabiting is not necessary to constitute cohabitation as the term is used in this section.

(d) As used in this section, "traumatic condition" means a condition of the body, such as a wound, or external or internal injury, including, but not limited to, injury as a result of strangulation or suffocation, whether of a minor or serious nature, caused by a physical force. For purposes of this section, "strangulation" and "suffocation" include impeding the normal breathing or circulation of the blood of a person by applying pressure on the throat or neck.

(e) For the purpose of this section, a person shall be considered the father or mother of another person's child if the alleged male parent is presumed the natural father under Sections 7611 and 7612 of the Family Code.

(f)

(1) Any person convicted of violating this section for acts occurring within seven years of a previous conviction under subdivision (a), or subdivision (d) of Section 243, or Section 243.4, 244, 244.5, or 245, shall be punished by imprisonment in a county jail for not more than one year, or by imprisonment in the state prison for two, four, or five years, or by both imprisonment and a fine of up to ten thousand dollars ($10,000).

(2) Any person convicted of a violation of this section for acts occurring within seven years of a previous conviction under subdivision (e) of Section 243 shall be punished by imprisonment in the state prison for two, three, or four years, or in a county jail for not more than one year, or by a fine of up to ten thousand dollars ($10,000), or by both that imprisonment and fine.

(g) If probation is granted to any person convicted under subdivision (a), the court shall impose probation consistent with the provisions of Section 1203.097.

(h) If probation is granted, or the execution or imposition of a sentence is suspended, for any defendant convicted under subdivision (a) who has been convicted of any prior offense specified in subdivision (f), the court shall impose one of the following conditions of probation:

(1) If the defendant has suffered one prior conviction within the previous seven years for a violation of any offense specified in subdivision (f), it shall be a condition of probation, in addition to the provisions contained in Section 1203.097, that the defendant be imprisoned in a county jail for not less than 15 days.

(2) If the defendant has suffered two or more prior convictions within the previous seven years for a violation of any offense specified in subdivision (f), it shall be a condition of probation, in addition to the provisions contained in Section 1203.097, that the defendant be imprisoned in a county jail for not less than 60 days.

(3) The court, upon a showing of good cause, may find that the mandatory imprisonment required by this subdivision shall not be imposed and shall state on the record its reasons for finding good cause.

(i) If probation is granted upon conviction of a violation of subdivision (a), the conditions of probation may include, consistent with the terms of probation imposed pursuant to Section 1203.097, in lieu of a fine, one or both of the following requirements:

(1) That the defendant make payments to a domestic violence shelter-based program, up to a maximum of five thousand dollars ($5,000), pursuant to Section 1203.097.

(2)

(A) That the defendant reimburse the victim for reasonable costs of counseling and other reasonable expenses that the court finds are the direct result of the defendant's offense.

(B) For any order to pay a fine, make payments to a domestic violence shelter-based program, or pay restitution as a condition of probation under this subdivision, the court shall make a determination of the defendant's ability to pay. An order to make payments to a domestic violence shelter-based program shall not be made if it would impair the ability of the defendant to pay direct restitution to the victim or court-ordered child support. If the injury to a person who is married or in a registered domestic partnership is caused in whole or in part by the criminal acts of their spouse or domestic partner in violation of this section, the community property may not be used to discharge the liability of the offending spouse or domestic partner for restitution to the injured spouse or domestic partner, required by Section 1203.04, as operative on or before August 2, 1995, or Section 1202.4, or to a shelter for costs with regard to the injured spouse or domestic partner and dependents, required by this section, until all separate property of the offending spouse or domestic partner is exhausted.

(j) Upon conviction under subdivision (a), the sentencing court shall also consider issuing an order restraining the defendant from any contact with the victim, which may be valid for up to 10 years, as determined by the court. It is the intent of the Legislature that the length of any restraining order be based upon the seriousness of the facts before the court, the probability of future violations, and the safety of the victim and their immediate family. This protective order may be issued by the court whether the defendant is sentenced to state prison or county jail, or if imposition of sentence is suspended and the defendant is placed on probation.

(k) If a peace officer makes an arrest for a violation of this section, the peace officer is not required to inform the victim of their right to make a citizen's arrest pursuant to subdivision (b) of Section 836.

Amended by Stats 2022 ch 197 (SB 1493),s 13, eff. 1/1/2023.
Amended by Stats 2016 ch 50 (SB 1005),s 69, eff. 1/1/2017.
Amended by Stats 2014 ch 71 (SB 1304),s 117, eff. 1/1/2015.
Amended by Stats 2013 ch 763 (AB 16),s 1, eff. 1/1/2014.
Amended by Stats 2012 ch 867 (SB 1144),s 16, eff. 1/1/2013.
Amended by Stats 2011 ch 129 (SB 430),s 2, eff. 1/1/2012.
Amended by Stats 2007 ch 582 (AB 289),s 1, eff. 1/1/2008.
Amended by Stats 2003 ch 262 (AB 134), s 1, eff. 1/1/2004.
Amended by Stats 2000 ch 287 (SB 1955), s 5, eff. 1/1/2001.
EFFECTIVE 1/1/2000. Amended October 10, 1999 (Bill Number: SB 218) (Chapter 662).

Section 273.55 - [Repealed]
Repealed 10/10/1999 (Bill Number: SB 218) (Chapter 662).

Section 273.56 - [Repealed]

Repealed 10/10/1999 (Bill Number: SB 218) (Chapter 662).

Section 273.6 - Violation of protective order

(a)Any intentional and knowing violation of a protective order, as defined in Section 6218 of the Family Code, or of an order issued pursuant to Section 527.6, 527.8, or 527.85 of the Code of Civil Procedure, or Section 15657.03 of the Welfare and Institutions Code, is a misdemeanor punishable by a fine of not more than one thousand dollars ($1,000), or by imprisonment in a county jail for not more than one year, or by both that fine and imprisonment.

(b)In the event of a violation of subdivision (a) that results in physical injury, the person shall be punished by a fine of not more than two thousand dollars ($2,000), or by imprisonment in a county jail for not less than 30 days nor more than one year, or by both that fine and imprisonment. However, if the person is imprisoned in a county jail for at least 48 hours, the court may, in the interest of justice and for reasons stated on the record, reduce or eliminate the 30-day minimum imprisonment required by this subdivision. In determining whether to reduce or eliminate the minimum imprisonment pursuant to this subdivision, the court shall consider the seriousness of the facts before the court, whether there are additional allegations of a violation of the order during the pendency of the case before the court, the probability of future violations, the safety of the victim, and whether the defendant has successfully completed or is making progress with counseling.

(c)Subdivisions (a) and (b) shall apply to the following court orders:

(1)Any order issued pursuant to Section 6320 or 6389 of the Family Code.

(2)An order excluding one party from the family dwelling or from the dwelling of the other.

(3)An order enjoining a party from specified behavior that the court determined was necessary to effectuate the order described in subdivision (a).

(4)Any order issued by another state that is recognized under Part 5 (commencing with Section 6400) of Division 10 of the Family Code.

(d)A subsequent conviction for a violation of an order described in subdivision (a), occurring within seven years of a prior conviction for a violation of an order described in subdivision (a) and involving an act of violence or "a credible threat" of violence, as defined in subdivision (c) of Section 139, is punishable by imprisonment in a county jail not to exceed one year, or pursuant to subdivision (h) of Section 1170.

(e)In the event of a subsequent conviction for a violation of an order described in subdivision (a) for an act occurring within one year of a prior conviction for a violation of an order described in subdivision (a) that results in physical injury to a victim, the person shall be punished by a fine of not more than two thousand dollars ($2,000), or by imprisonment in a county jail for not less than six months nor more than one year, by both that fine and imprisonment, or by imprisonment pursuant to subdivision (h) of Section 1170. However, if the person is imprisoned in a county jail for at least 30 days, the court may, in the interest of justice and for reasons stated in the record, reduce or eliminate the six-month minimum imprisonment required by this subdivision. In determining whether to reduce or eliminate the minimum imprisonment pursuant to this subdivision, the court shall consider the seriousness of the facts before the court, whether there are additional allegations of a violation of the order during the pendency of the case before the court, the probability of future violations, the safety of the victim, and whether the defendant has successfully completed or is making progress with counseling.

(f)The prosecuting agency of each county shall have the primary responsibility for the enforcement of orders described in subdivisions (a), (b), (d), and (e).

(g)

(1)Every person who owns, possesses, purchases, or receives a firearm knowing they are prohibited from doing so by the provisions of a protective order as defined in Section 136.2 of this code, Section 6218 of the Family Code, or Section 527.6, 527.8, or 527.85 of the Code of Civil Procedure, or Section 15657.03 of the Welfare and Institutions Code, shall be punished under Section 29825.

(2)Every person subject to a protective order described in paragraph (1) shall not be prosecuted under this section for owning, possessing, purchasing, or receiving a firearm to the extent that firearm is granted an exemption pursuant to subdivision (f) of Section 527.9 of the Code of Civil Procedure, or subdivision (h) of Section 6389 of the Family Code.

(h)If probation is granted upon conviction of a violation of subdivision (a), (b), (c), (d), or (e), the court shall impose probation consistent with Section 1203.097, and the conditions of probation may include, in lieu of a fine, one or both of the following requirements:

(1)That the defendant make payments to a domestic violence shelter-based program or to a shelter for abused elder persons or dependent adults, up to a maximum of five thousand dollars ($5,000), pursuant to Section 1203.097.

(2)That the defendant reimburse the victim for reasonable costs of counseling and other reasonable expenses that the court finds are the direct result of the defendant's offense.

(i)For any order to pay a fine, make payments to a domestic violence shelter-based program, or pay restitution as a condition of probation under subdivision (e), the court shall make a determination of the defendant's ability to pay. In no event shall any order to make payments to a domestic violence shelter-based program be made if it would impair the ability of the defendant to pay direct restitution to the victim or court-ordered child support. Where the injury to a married person is caused in whole or in part by the criminal acts of their spouse in violation of this section, the community property may not be used to discharge the liability of the offending spouse for restitution to the injured spouse, required by Section 1203.04, as operative on or before August 2, 1995, or Section 1202.4, or to a shelter for costs with regard to the injured spouse and dependents, required by this section, until all separate property of the offending spouse is exhausted.

Amended by Stats 2022 ch 197 (SB 1493),s 14, eff. 1/1/2023.

Amended by Stats 2013 ch 76 (AB 383),s 145.7, eff. 1/1/2014.

Amended by Stats 2011 ch 39 (AB 117),s 68, eff. 6/30/2011.

Amended by Stats 2011 ch 15 (AB 109),s 309, eff. 4/4/2011, but operative no earlier than October 1, 2011, and only upon creation of a community corrections grant program to assist in implementing this act and upon an appropriation to fund the grant program.

Amended by Stats 2010 ch 709 (SB 1062),s 10, eff. 1/1/2011.

Amended by Stats 2009 ch 566 (SB 188),s 2, eff. 1/1/2010.

Amended by Stats 2003 ch 498 (SB 226), s 7, eff. 1/1/2004.
Amended by Stats 2001 ch 816 (AB 731), s 4, eff. 1/1/2002.
Previously Amended October 10, 1999 (Bill Number: SB 218) (Chapter 662).

Section 273.65 - Violation of protective order

(a)Any intentional and knowing violation of a protective order issued pursuant to Section 213.5, 304, or 362.4 of the Welfare and Institutions Code is a misdemeanor punishable by a fine of not more than one thousand dollars ($1,000), or by imprisonment in a county jail for not more than one year, or by both the fine and imprisonment.

(b)In the event of a violation of subdivision (a) which results in physical injury, the person shall be punished by a fine of not more than two thousand dollars ($2,000), or by imprisonment in a county jail for not less than 30 days nor more than one year, or by both the fine and imprisonment. However, if the person is imprisoned in a county jail for at least 48 hours, the court may, in the interests of justice and for reasons stated on the record, reduce or eliminate the 30-day minimum imprisonment required by this subdivision. In determining whether to reduce or eliminate the minimum imprisonment pursuant to this subdivision, the court shall consider the seriousness of the facts before the court, whether there are additional allegations of a violation of the order during the pendency of the case before the court, the probability of future violations, the safety of the victim, and whether the defendant has successfully completed or is making progress with counseling.

(c)Subdivisions (a) and (b) shall apply to the following court orders:

(1)An order enjoining any party from molesting, attacking, striking, threatening, sexually assaulting, battering, harassing, contacting repeatedly by mail with the intent to harass, or disturbing the peace of the other party, or other named family and household members.

(2)An order excluding one party from the family dwelling or from the dwelling of the other.

(3)An order enjoining a party from specified behavior which the court determined was necessary to effectuate the order under subdivision (a).

(d)A subsequent conviction for a violation of an order described in subdivision (a), occurring within seven years of a prior conviction for a violation of an order described in subdivision (a) and involving an act of violence or "a credible threat" of violence, as defined in subdivision (c) of Section 139, is punishable by imprisonment in a county jail not to exceed one year, or pursuant to subdivision (h) of Section 1170.

(e)In the event of a subsequent conviction for a violation of an order described in subdivision (a) for an act occurring within one year of a prior conviction for a violation of an order described in subdivision (a) which results in physical injury to the same victim, the person shall be punished by a fine of not more than two thousand dollars ($2,000), or by imprisonment in a county jail for not less than six months nor more than one year, by both that fine and imprisonment, or by imprisonment pursuant to subdivision (h) of Section 1170. However, if the person is imprisoned in a county jail for at least 30 days, the court may, in the interests of justice and for reasons stated in the record, reduce or eliminate the six-month minimum imprisonment required by this subdivision. In determining whether to reduce or eliminate the minimum imprisonment pursuant to this subdivision, the court shall consider the seriousness of the facts before the court, whether there are additional allegations of a violation of the order during the pendency of the case before the court, the probability of future violations, the safety of the victim, and whether the defendant has successfully completed or is making progress with counseling.

(f)The prosecuting agency of each county shall have the primary responsibility for the enforcement of orders issued pursuant to subdivisions (a), (b), (d), and (e).

(g)The court may order a person convicted under this section to undergo counseling, and, if appropriate, to complete a batterer's treatment program.

(h)If probation is granted upon conviction of a violation of subdivision (a), (b), or (c), the conditions of probation may include, in lieu of a fine, one or both of the following requirements:

(1)That the defendant make payments to a domestic violence shelter-based program, up to a maximum of five thousand dollars ($5,000), pursuant to Section 1203.097.

(2)That the defendant reimburse the victim for reasonable costs of counseling and other reasonable expenses that the court finds are the direct result of the defendant's offense.

(i)For any order to pay a fine, make payments to a domestic violence shelter-based program, or pay restitution as a condition of probation under subdivision (e), the court shall make a determination of the defendant's ability to pay. In no event shall any order to make payments to a domestic violence shelter-based program be made if it would impair the ability of the defendant to pay direct restitution to the victim or court-ordered child support.

Amended by Stats 2022 ch 197 (SB 1493),s 15, eff. 1/1/2023.
Amended by Stats 2011 ch 39 (AB 117),s 68, eff. 6/30/2011.
Amended by Stats 2011 ch 15 (AB 109),s 311, eff. 4/4/2011, but operative no earlier than October 1, 2011, and only upon creation of a community corrections grant program to assist in implementing this act and upon an appropriation to fund the grant program.

Section 273.7 - Unlawful disclosure of location of shelter

(a) A person who maliciously publishes, disseminates, or otherwise discloses the location of a trafficking shelter or domestic violence shelter or a place designated as a trafficking shelter or domestic violence shelter, without the authorization of that trafficking shelter or domestic violence shelter, is guilty of a misdemeanor.

(b) For purposes of this section, the following definitions apply:

(1) "Domestic violence shelter" means a confidential location that provides emergency housing on a 24-hour basis for victims of sexual assault, spousal abuse, or both, and their families.

(2) "Trafficking shelter" means a confidential location that provides emergency housing on a 24-hour basis for victims of human trafficking, including any person who is a victim under Section 236.1.

(3) Sexual assault, spousal abuse, or both, include, but are not limited to, those crimes described in Sections 240, 242, 243.4, 261, 261.5, 264.1, 266, 266a, 266b, 266c, 266f, 273.5, 273.6, 285, 288, and 289.

(c) This section does not apply to confidential communications between an attorney and their client.

Amended by Stats 2021 ch 626 (AB 1171),s 24, eff. 1/1/2022.
Amended by Stats 2006 ch 538 (SB 1852),s 499, eff. 1/1/2007.
Amended by Stats 2005 ch 240 (AB 22),s 9, eff. 1/1/2006

Section 273.75 - Search of databases in prosecution of acts of domestic violence

(a) On any charge involving acts of domestic violence as defined in subdivisions (a) and (b) of Section 13700 of the Penal Code or Sections 6203 and 6211 of the Family Code, the district attorney or prosecuting city attorney shall perform or cause to be performed, by accessing the electronic databases enumerated in subdivision (b), a thorough investigation of the defendant's history, including, but not limited to, prior convictions for domestic violence, other forms of violence or weapons offenses and any current protective or restraining order issued by any civil or criminal court. This information shall be presented for consideration by the court (1) when setting bond or when releasing a defendant on his or her own recognizance at the arraignment, if the defendant is in custody, (2) upon consideration of any plea agreement, and (3) when issuing a protective order pursuant to Section 136.2 of the Penal Code, in accordance with subdivision (h) of that section. In determining bail or release upon a plea agreement, the court shall consider the safety of the victim, the victim's children, and any other person who may be in danger if the defendant is released.

(b) For purposes of this section, the district attorney or prosecuting city attorney shall search or cause to be searched the following databases, when readily available and reasonably accessible:

(1) The California Sex and Arson Registry (CSAR).

(2) The Supervised Release File.

(3) State summary criminal history information maintained by the Department of Justice pursuant to Section 11105 of the Penal Code.

(4) The Federal Bureau of Investigation's nationwide database.

(5) Locally maintained criminal history records or databases. However, a record or database need not be searched if the information available in that record or database can be obtained as a result of a search conducted in another record or database.

(c) If the investigation required by this section reveals a current civil protective or restraining order or a protective or restraining order issued by another criminal court and involving the same or related parties, and if a protective or restraining order is issued in the current criminal proceeding, the district attorney or prosecuting city attorney shall send relevant information regarding the contents of the order issued in the current criminal proceeding, and any information regarding a conviction of the defendant, to the other court immediately after the order has been issued. When requested, the information described in this subdivision may be sent to the appropriate family, juvenile, or civil court. When requested, and upon a showing of a compelling need, the information described in this section may be sent to a court in another state.

Amended by Stats 2014 ch 54 (SB 1461),s 10, eff. 1/1/2015.
Amended by Stats 2008 ch 86 (AB 1771),s 2, eff. 1/1/2009.
Added by Stats 2001 ch 572 (SB 66), s 4, eff. 1/1/2002.

Chapter 2.5 - SPOUSAL ABUSERS

Section 273.8 - Legislative finding

The Legislature hereby finds that spousal abusers present a clear and present danger to the mental and physical well-being of the citizens of the State of California. The Legislature further finds that the concept of vertical prosecution, in which a specially trained deputy district attorney, deputy city attorney, or prosecution unit is assigned to a case after arraignment and continuing to its completion, is a proven way of demonstrably increasing the likelihood of convicting spousal abusers and ensuring appropriate sentences for those offenders. In enacting this chapter, the Legislature intends to support increased efforts by district attorneys' and city attorneys' offices to prosecute spousal abusers through organizational and operational techniques that have already proven their effectiveness in selected cities and counties in this and other states.

Amended by Stats. 1994, Ch. 599, Sec. 2. Effective September 16, 1994.

Section 273.81 - Spousal Abuser Prosecution Program

(a) There is hereby established in the Department of Justice a program of financial and technical assistance for district attorneys' or city attorneys' offices, designated the Spousal Abuser Prosecution Program. All funds appropriated to the Department of Justice for the purposes of this chapter shall be administered and disbursed by the Attorney General, and shall to the greatest extent feasible, be coordinated or consolidated with any federal or local funds that may be made available for these purposes. The Department of Justice shall establish guidelines for the provision of grant awards to proposed and existing programs prior to the allocation of funds under this chapter. These guidelines shall contain the criteria for the selection of agencies to receive funding and the terms and conditions upon which the Department of Justice is prepared to offer grants pursuant to statutory authority. The guidelines shall not constitute rules, regulations, orders, or standards of general application.

(b) The Attorney General may allocate and award funds to cities or counties, or both, in which spousal abuser prosecution units are established or are proposed to be established in substantial compliance with the policies and criteria set forth in this chapter.

(c) The allocation and award of funds shall be made upon application executed by the county's district attorney or by the city's attorney and approved by the county board of supervisors or by the city council. Funds disbursed under this chapter shall not supplant local funds that would, in the absence of the California Spousal Abuser Prosecution Program, be made available to support the prosecution of spousal abuser cases. Local grant awards made under this program shall not be subject to review as specified in Section 10295 of the Public Contract Code.

(d) Local government recipients shall provide 20 percent matching funds for every grant awarded under this program.

Amended by Stats. 1994, Ch. 599, Sec. 3. Effective September 16, 1994.

Section 273.82 - Enhanced prosecution efforts and resources

Spousal abuser prosecution units receiving funds under this chapter shall concentrate enhanced prosecution efforts and resources upon individuals identified under selection criteria set forth in Section 273.83. Enhanced prosecution efforts and resources shall include, but not be limited to, all of the following:

(a)

(1) Vertical prosecutorial representation, whereby the prosecutor who, or prosecution unit that, makes all major court appearances on that particular case through its conclusion, including bail evaluation, preliminary hearing, significant law and motion litigation, trial, and sentencing.

(2) Vertical counselor representation, whereby a trained domestic violence counselor maintains liaison from initial court appearances through the case's conclusion, including the sentencing phase.

(b) The assignment of highly qualified investigators and prosecutors to spousal abuser cases. "Highly qualified" for the purposes of this chapter means any of the following:

(1) Individuals with one year of experience in the investigation and prosecution of felonies.

(2) Individuals with at least two years of experience in the investigation and prosecution of misdemeanors.

(3) Individuals who have attended a program providing domestic violence training as approved by the Office of Emergency Services or the Department of Justice.

(c) A significant reduction of caseloads for investigators and prosecutors assigned to spousal abuser cases.

(d) Coordination with local rape victim counseling centers, spousal abuse services programs, and victim-witness assistance programs. That coordination shall include, but not be limited to: referrals of individuals to receive client services; participation in local training programs; membership and participation in local task forces established to improve communication between criminal justice system agencies and community service agencies; and cooperating with individuals serving as liaison representatives of local rape victim counseling centers, spousal abuse victim programs, and victim-witness assistance programs.

Amended by Stats 2013 ch 352 (AB 1317),s 403, eff. 9/26/2013, op. 7/1/2013.

Amended by Stats 2010 ch 618 (AB 2791),s 191, eff. 1/1/2011.

Amended by Stats 2003 ch 229 (AB 1757), s 2.4, eff. 1/1/2004.

Section 273.83 - Spousal abuser selection criteria

(a) An individual shall be the subject of a spousal abuser prosecution effort who is under arrest for any act or omission described in subdivisions (a) and (b) of Section 13700.

(b) In applying the spousal abuser selection criteria set forth in subdivision (a), a district attorney or city attorney shall not reject cases for filing exclusively on the basis that there is a family or personal relationship between the victim and the alleged offender.

(c) In exercising the prosecutorial discretion granted by Section 273.85, the district attorney or city attorney shall consider the number and seriousness of the offenses currently charged against the defendant.

Amended by Stats. 1994, Ch. 599, Sec. 5. Effective September 16, 1994.

Section 273.84 - Policies for spousal abuser cases

Each district attorney's or city attorney's office establishing a spousal abuser prosecution unit and receiving state support under this chapter shall adopt and pursue the following policies for spousal abuser cases:

(a) All reasonable prosecutorial efforts shall be made to resist the pretrial release of a charged defendant meeting spousal abuser selection criteria.

(b) All reasonable prosecutorial efforts shall be made to persuade the court to impose the most severe authorized sentence upon a person convicted after prosecution as a spousal abuser. In the prosecution of an intrafamily sexual abuse case, discretion may be exercised as to the type and nature of sentence recommended to the court.

(c) All reasonable prosecutorial efforts shall be made to reduce the time between arrest and disposition of charge against an individual meeting spousal abuser criteria.

Amended by Stats 2000 ch 135 (AB 2539), s 131, eff. 1/1/2001.

Section 273.85 - Application of selection criteria

(a) The selection criteria set forth in Section 273.84 shall be adhered to for each spousal abuser case unless, in the reasonable exercise of prosecutor's discretion, extraordinary circumstances require departure from those policies in order to promote the general purposes and intent of this chapter.

(b) Each district attorney's and city attorney's office establishing a spousal abuser prosecution unit and receiving state support under this chapter shall submit the following information, on a quarterly basis, to the Department of Justice:

(1) The number of spousal abuser cases referred to the district attorney's or city attorney's office for possible filing.

(2) The number of spousal abuser cases filed for prosecution.

(3) The number of spousal abuser cases taken to trial.

(4) The number of spousal abuser cases tried that resulted in conviction.

Amended by Stats. 1994, Ch. 599, Sec. 7. Effective September 16, 1994.

Section 273.86 - No communication of characterization as spousal abuser to trier of fact

The characterization of a defendant as a "spousal abuser" as defined by this chapter shall not be communicated to the trier of fact.

Added by Stats. 1985, Ch. 1122, Sec. 1.

Section 273.87 - Use of federal funds

The Department of Justice is encouraged to utilize Federal Victims of Crimes Act (VOCA) funds or any other federal funds that may become available in order to implement this chapter.

Amended by Stats. 1994, Ch. 599, Sec. 8. Effective September 16, 1994.

Section 273.88 - Administrative costs

Administrative costs incurred by the Department of Justice pursuant to the Spousal Abuser Prosecution Program shall not exceed 5 percent of the total funds allocated for the program.

Added by Stats. 1994, Ch. 599, Sec. 9. Effective September 16, 1994.

Chapter 3 - [REPEALED] ABORTIONS

Section 274 through 276 - [Repealed]

Repealed by Stats 2000 ch 692 (SB 370), s 2, eff. 1/1/2001.

Chapter 4 - CHILD ABDUCTION

Section 277 - Definitions

The following definitions apply for the purposes of this chapter:

(a) "Child" means a person under the age of 18 years.

(b) "Court order" or "custody order" means a custody determination decree, judgment, or order issued by a court of competent jurisdiction, whether permanent or temporary, initial or modified, that affects the custody or visitation of a child, issued in the context of a custody proceeding. An order, once made, shall continue in effect until it expires, is modified, is rescinded, or terminates by operation of law.

(c) "Custody proceeding" means a proceeding in which a custody determination is an issue, including, but not limited to, an action for dissolution or separation, dependency, guardianship, termination of parental rights, adoption, paternity, except actions under Section 11350 or 11350.1 of the Welfare and Institutions Code, or protection from domestic violence proceedings, including an emergency protective order pursuant to Part 3 (commencing with Section 6240) of Division 10 of the Family Code.

(d) "Lawful custodian" means a person, guardian, or public agency having a right to custody of a child.

(e) A "right to custody" means the right to the physical care, custody, and control of a child pursuant to a custody order as defined in subdivision (b) or, in the absence of a court order, by operation of law, or pursuant to the Uniform Parentage Act contained in Part 3 (commencing with Section 7600) of Division 12 of the Family Code. Whenever a public agency takes protective custody or jurisdiction of the care, custody, control, or conduct of a child by statutory authority or court order, that agency is a lawful custodian of the child and has a right to physical custody of the child. In any subsequent placement of the child, the public agency continues to be a lawful custodian with a right to physical custody of the child until the public agency's right of custody is terminated by an order of a court of competent jurisdiction or by operation of law.

(f) In the absence of a court order to the contrary, a parent loses his or her right to custody of the child to the other parent if the parent having the right to custody is dead, is unable or refuses to take the custody, or has abandoned his or her family. A natural parent whose parental rights have been terminated by court order is no longer a lawful custodian and no longer has a right to physical custody.

(g) "Keeps" or "withholds" means retains physical possession of a child whether or not the child resists or objects.

(h) "Visitation" means the time for access to the child allotted to any person by court order.

(i) "Person" includes, but is not limited to, a parent or an agent of a parent.

(j) "Domestic violence" means domestic violence as defined in Section 6211 of the Family Code.

(k) "Abduct" means take, entice away, keep, withhold, or conceal.

Repealed and added by Stats. 1996, Ch. 988, Sec. 9. Effective January 1, 1997.

Section 278 - Unlawful taking, enticing, keeping, withholding, or concealment of child

Every person, not having a right to custody, who maliciously takes, entices away, keeps, withholds, or conceals any child with the intent to detain or conceal that child from a lawful custodian shall be punished by imprisonment in a county jail not exceeding one year, a fine not exceeding one thousand dollars ($1,000), or both that fine and imprisonment, or by imprisonment pursuant to subdivision (h) of Section 1170 for two, three, or four years, a fine not exceeding ten thousand dollars ($10,000), or both that fine and imprisonment.

Amended by Stats 2011 ch 39 (AB 117),s 68, eff. 6/30/2011.

Amended by Stats 2011 ch 15 (AB 109),s 313, eff. 4/4/2011, but operative no earlier than October 1, 2011, and only upon creation of a community corrections grant program to assist in implementing this act and upon an appropriation to fund the grant program.

Section 278.5 - Punishment

(a) Every person who takes, entices away, keeps, withholds, or conceals a child and maliciously deprives a lawful custodian of a right to custody, or a person of a right to visitation, shall be punished by imprisonment in a county jail not exceeding one year, a fine not exceeding one thousand dollars ($1,000), or both that fine and imprisonment, or by imprisonment pursuant to subdivision (h) of Section 1170 for 16 months, or two or three years, a fine not exceeding ten thousand dollars ($10,000), or both that fine and imprisonment.

(b) Nothing contained in this section limits the court's contempt power.

(c) A custody order obtained after the taking, enticing away, keeping, withholding, or concealing of a child does not constitute a defense to a crime charged under this section.

Amended by Stats 2011 ch 39 (AB 117),s 68, eff. 6/30/2011.

Amended by Stats 2011 ch 15 (AB 109),s 314, eff. 4/4/2011, but operative no earlier than October 1, 2011, and only upon creation of a community corrections grant program to assist in implementing this act and upon an appropriation to fund the grant program.

Section 278.6 - Aggravating circumstances

(a) At the sentencing hearing following a conviction for a violation of Section 278 or 278.5, or both, the court shall consider any relevant factors and circumstances in aggravation, including, but not limited to, all of the following:

    (1) The child was exposed to a substantial risk of physical injury or illness.

    (2) The defendant inflicted or threatened to inflict physical harm on a parent or lawful custodian of the child or on the child at the time of or during the abduction.

    (3) The defendant harmed or abandoned the child during the abduction.

    (4) The child was taken, enticed away, kept, withheld, or concealed outside the United States.

    (5) The child has not been returned to the lawful custodian.

    (6) The defendant previously abducted or threatened to abduct the child.

    (7) The defendant substantially altered the appearance or the name of the child.

    (8) The defendant denied the child appropriate education during the abduction.

    (9) The length of the abduction.

    (10) The age of the child.

(b) At the sentencing hearing following a conviction for a violation of Section 278 or 278.5, or both, the court shall consider any relevant factors and circumstances in mitigation, including, but not limited to, both of the following:

    (1) The defendant returned the child unharmed and prior to arrest or issuance of a warrant for arrest, whichever is first.

(2) The defendant provided information and assistance leading to the child's safe return.

(c) In addition to any other penalties provided for a violation of Section 278 or 278.5, a court shall order the defendant to pay restitution to the district attorney for any costs incurred in locating and returning the child as provided in Section 3134 of the Family Code, and to the victim for those expenses and costs reasonably incurred by, or on behalf of, the victim in locating and recovering the child. An award made pursuant to this section shall constitute a final judgment and shall be enforceable as such.

Added by Stats. 1996, Ch. 988, Sec. 9. Effective January 1, 1997.

Section 278.7 - Applicability of punishment

(a) Section 278.5 does not apply to a person with a right to custody of a child who, with a good faith and reasonable belief that the child, if left with the other person, will suffer immediate bodily injury or emotional harm, takes, entices away, keeps, withholds, or conceals that child.

(b) Section 278.5 does not apply to a person with a right to custody of a child who has been a victim of domestic violence who, with a good faith and reasonable belief that the child, if left with the other person, will suffer immediate bodily injury or emotional harm, takes, entices away, keeps, withholds, or conceals that child. "Emotional harm" includes having a parent who has committed domestic violence against the parent who is taking, enticing away, keeping, withholding, or concealing the child.

(c) The person who takes, entices away, keeps, withholds, or conceals a child shall do all of the following:

   (1) Within a reasonable time from the taking, enticing away, keeping, withholding, or concealing, make a report to the office of the district attorney of the county where the child resided before the action. The report shall include the name of the person, the current address and telephone number of the child and the person, and the reasons the child was taken, enticed away, kept, withheld, or concealed.

   (2) Within a reasonable time from the taking, enticing away, keeping, withholding, or concealing, commence a custody proceeding in a court of competent jurisdiction consistent with the federal Parental Kidnapping Prevention Act (Section 1738A, Title 28, United States Code) or the Uniform Child Custody Jurisdiction Act (Part 3 (commencing with Section 3400) of Division 8 of the Family Code).

   (3) Inform the district attorney's office of any change of address or telephone number of the person and the child.

(d) For the purposes of this article, a reasonable time within which to make a report to the district attorney's office is at least 10 days and a reasonable time to commence a custody proceeding is at least 30 days. This section shall not preclude a person from making a report to the district attorney's office or commencing a custody proceeding earlier than those specified times.

(e) The address and telephone number of the person and the child provided pursuant to this section shall remain confidential unless released pursuant to state law or by a court order that contains appropriate safeguards to ensure the safety of the person and the child.

Added by Stats. 1996, Ch. 988, Sec. 9. Effective January 1, 1997.

Section 279 - Punishment in California

A violation of Section 278 or 278.5 by a person who was not a resident of, or present in, this state at the time of the alleged offense is punishable in this state, whether the intent to commit the offense is formed within or outside of this state, if any of the following apply:

(a) The child was a resident of, or present in, this state at the time the child was taken, enticed away, kept, withheld, or concealed.

(b) The child thereafter is found in this state.

(c) A lawful custodian or a person with a right to visitation is a resident of this state at the time the child was taken, enticed away, kept, withheld, or concealed.

Repealed and added by Stats. 1996, Ch. 988, Sec. 9. Effective January 1, 1997.

Section 279.1 - Continuous nature of offenses

The offenses enumerated in Sections 278 and 278.5 are continuous in nature, and continue for as long as the minor child is concealed or detained.

Added by Stats. 1996, Ch. 988, Sec. 9. Effective January 1, 1997.

Section 279.5 - Bail

When a person is arrested for an alleged violation of Section 278 or 278.5, the court, in setting bail, shall take into consideration whether the child has been returned to the lawful custodian, and if not, shall consider whether there is an increased risk that the child may not be returned, or the defendant may flee the jurisdiction, or, by flight or concealment, evade the authority of the court.

Added by Stats. 1996, Ch. 988, Sec. 9. Effective January 1, 1997.

Section 279.6 - Protective custody

(a) A law enforcement officer may take a child into protective custody under any of the following circumstances:

   (1) It reasonably appears to the officer that a person is likely to conceal the child, flee the jurisdiction with the child, or, by flight or concealment, evade the authority of the court.

   (2) There is no lawful custodian available to take custody of the child.

   (3) There are conflicting custody orders or conflicting claims to custody and the parties cannot agree which party should take custody of the child.

   (4) The child is an abducted child.

(b) When a law enforcement officer takes a child into protective custody pursuant to this section, the officer shall do one of the following:

   (1) Release the child to the lawful custodian of the child, unless it reasonably appears that the release would cause the child to be endangered, abducted, or removed from the jurisdiction.

   (2) Obtain an emergency protective order pursuant to Part 3 (commencing with Section 6240) of Division 10 of the Family Code ordering placement of the child with an interim custodian who agrees in writing to accept interim custody.

   (3) Release the child to the social services agency responsible for arranging shelter or foster care.

   (4) Return the child as ordered by a court of competent jurisdiction.

(c) Upon the arrest of a person for a violation of Section 278 or 278.5, a law enforcement officer shall take possession of an abducted child who is found in the company of, or under the control of, the arrested person and deliver the child as directed in subdivision (b).

(d) Notwithstanding any other law, when a person is arrested for an alleged violation of Section 278 or 278.5, the court shall, at the time of the arraignment or thereafter, order that the child shall be returned to the lawful custodian by or on a specific date, or that the person show cause on that date why the child has not been returned as ordered. If conflicting custodial orders exist within this state, or between this state and a foreign state, the court shall set a hearing within five court days to determine which court has jurisdiction under the laws of this state and determine which state has subject matter jurisdiction to issue a custodial order under the laws of this state, the Uniform Child Custody Jurisdiction Act (Part 3 (commencing with Section 3400) of Division 8 of the Family Code), or federal law, if applicable. At the conclusion of the hearing, or if the child has not been returned as ordered by the court at the time of arraignment, the court shall enter an order as to which custody order is valid and is to be enforced. If the child has not been returned at the conclusion of the hearing, the court shall set a date within a reasonable time by which the child shall be returned to the lawful custodian, and order the defendant to comply by this date, or to show cause on that date why he or she has not returned the child as directed. The court shall only enforce its order, or any subsequent orders for the return of the child, under subdivision (a) of Section 1219 of the Code of Civil Procedure, to ensure that the child is promptly placed with the lawful custodian. An order adverse to either the prosecution or defense is reviewable by a writ of mandate or prohibition addressed to the appropriate court.
Added by Stats. 1996, Ch. 988, Sec. 9. Effective January 1, 1997.

Section 280 - Unlawful removal or concealment of child
Every person who willfully causes or permits the removal or concealment of any child in violation of Section 8713, 8803, or 8910 of the Family Code shall be punished as follows:
(a) By imprisonment in a county jail for not more than one year if the child is concealed within the county in which the adoption proceeding is pending or in which the child has been placed for adoption, or is removed from that county to a place within this state.
(b) By imprisonment pursuant to subdivision (h) of Section 1170, or by imprisonment in a county jail for not more than one year, if the child is removed from that county to a place outside of this state.
Amended by Stats 2011 ch 39 (AB 117),s 68, eff. 6/30/2011.
Amended by Stats 2011 ch 15 (AB 109),s 315, eff. 4/4/2011, but operative no earlier than October 1, 2011, and only upon creation of a community corrections grant program to assist in implementing this act and upon an appropriation to fund the grant program.

Chapter 5 - BIGAMY, INCEST, AND THE CRIME AGAINST NATURE

Section 281 - Bigamy
(a) Every person having a spouse living, who marries or enters into a registered domestic partnership with any other person, except in the cases specified in Section 282, is guilty of bigamy.
(b) Upon a trial for bigamy, it is not necessary to prove either of the marriages or registered domestic partnerships by the register, certificate, or other record evidence thereof, but the marriages or registered domestic partnerships may be proved by evidence which is admissible to prove a marriage or registered domestic partnership in other cases; and when the second marriage or registered domestic partnership took place out of this state, proof of that fact, accompanied with proof of cohabitation thereafter in this state, is sufficient to sustain the charge.
Amended by Stats 2016 ch 50 (SB 1005),s 70, eff. 1/1/2017.

Section 282 - Applicability of bigamy statute
Section 281 does not extend to any of the following:
(a) To any person by reason of any former marriage or former registered domestic partnership whose spouse by such marriage or registered domestic partnership has been absent for five successive years without being known to such person within that time to be living.
(b) To any person by reason of any former marriage, or any former registered domestic partnership, which has been pronounced void, annulled, or dissolved by the judgment of a competent court.
Amended by Stats 2016 ch 50 (SB 1005),s 71, eff. 1/1/2017.

Section 283 - Punishment
Bigamy is punishable by a fine not exceeding ten thousand dollars ($10,000) or by imprisonment in a county jail not exceeding one year or in the state prison.
Amended by Stats. 1983, Ch. 1092, Sec. 264. Effective September 27, 1983. Operative January 1, 1984, by Sec. 427 of Ch. 1092.

Section 284 - Unlawful marriage to or partnership with spouse of another
Every person who knowingly and willfully marries or enters into a registered domestic partnership with the spouse of another, in any case in which such spouse would be punishable under the provisions of this chapter, is punishable by a fine not less than five thousand dollars ($5,000), or by imprisonment pursuant to subdivision (h) of Section 1170.
Amended by Stats 2016 ch 50 (SB 1005),s 72, eff. 1/1/2017.
Amended by Stats 2011 ch 39 (AB 117),s 68, eff. 6/30/2011.
Amended by Stats 2011 ch 15 (AB 109),s 316, eff. 4/4/2011, but operative no earlier than October 1, 2011, and only upon creation of a community corrections grant program to assist in implementing this act and upon an appropriation to fund the grant program.

Section 285 - Incest
Persons being within the degrees of consanguinity within which marriages are declared by law to be incestuous and void, who intermarry with each other, or who being 14 years of age or older, commit fornication or adultery with each other, are punishable by imprisonment in the state prison.
Amended by Stats 2005 ch 477 (SB 33),s 1, eff. 1/1/2006

Section 286 - Sodomy
(a) Sodomy is sexual conduct consisting of contact between the penis of one person and the anus of another person. Any sexual penetration, however slight, is sufficient to complete the crime of sodomy.
(b)
(1) Except as provided in Section 288, any person who participates in an act of sodomy with another person who is under 18 years of age shall be punished by imprisonment in the state prison, or in a county jail for not more than one year.

(2) Except as provided in Section 288, any person over 21 years of age who participates in an act of sodomy with another person who is under 16 years of age shall be guilty of a felony.

(c)

(1) Any person who participates in an act of sodomy with another person who is under 14 years of age and more than 10 years younger than he or she shall be punished by imprisonment in the state prison for three, six, or eight years.

(2)

(A) Any person who commits an act of sodomy when the act is accomplished against the victim's will by means of force, violence, duress, menace, or fear of immediate and unlawful bodily injury on the victim or another person shall be punished by imprisonment in the state prison for three, six, or eight years.

(B) Any person who commits an act of sodomy with another person who is under 14 years of age when the act is accomplished against the victim's will by means of force, violence, duress, menace, or fear of immediate and unlawful bodily injury on the victim or another person shall be punished by imprisonment in the state prison for 9, 11, or 13 years.

(C) Any person who commits an act of sodomy with another person who is a minor 14 years of age or older when the act is accomplished against the victim's will by means of force, violence, duress, menace, or fear of immediate and unlawful bodily injury on the victim or another person shall be punished by imprisonment in the state prison for 7, 9, or 11 years.

(D) This paragraph does not preclude prosecution under Section 269, Section 288.7, or any other provision of law.

(3) Any person who commits an act of sodomy where the act is accomplished against the victim's will by threatening to retaliate in the future against the victim or any other person, and there is a reasonable possibility that the perpetrator will execute the threat, shall be punished by imprisonment in the state prison for three, six, or eight years.

(d)

(1) Any person who, while voluntarily acting in concert with another person, either personally or aiding and abetting that other person, commits an act of sodomy when the act is accomplished against the victim's will by means of force or fear of immediate and unlawful bodily injury on the victim or another person or where the act is accomplished against the victim's will by threatening to retaliate in the future against the victim or any other person, and there is a reasonable possibility that the perpetrator will execute the threat, shall be punished by imprisonment in the state prison for five, seven, or nine years.

(2) Any person who, while voluntarily acting in concert with another person, either personally or aiding and abetting that other person, commits an act of sodomy upon a victim who is under 14 years of age, when the act accomplished against the victim's will by means of force or fear of immediate and unlawful bodily injury on the victim or another person, shall be punished by imprisonment in the state prison for 10, 12, or 14 years.

(3) Any person who, while voluntarily acting in concert with another person, either personally or aiding and abetting that other person, commits an act of sodomy upon a victim who is a minor 14 years of age or older, when the act is accomplished against the victim's will by means of force or fear of immediate and unlawful bodily injury on the victim or another person, shall be punished by imprisonment in the state prison for 7, 9, or 11 years.

(4) This subdivision does not preclude prosecution under Section 269, Section 288.7, or any other provision of law.

(e) Any person who participates in an act of sodomy with any person of any age while confined in any state prison, as defined in Section 4504, or in any local detention facility, as defined in Section 6031.4, shall be punished by imprisonment in the state prison, or in a county jail for not more than one year.

(f) Any person who commits an act of sodomy, and the victim is at the time unconscious of the nature of the act and this is known to the person committing the act, shall be punished by imprisonment in the state prison for three, six, or eight years. As used in this subdivision, "unconscious of the nature of the act" means incapable of resisting because the victim meets one of the following conditions:

(1) Was unconscious or asleep.

(2) Was not aware, knowing, perceiving, or cognizant that the act occurred.

(3) Was not aware, knowing, perceiving, or cognizant of the essential characteristics of the act due to the perpetrator's fraud in fact.

(4) Was not aware, knowing, perceiving, or cognizant of the essential characteristics of the act due to the perpetrator's fraudulent representation that the sexual penetration served a professional purpose when it served no professional purpose.

(g) Except as provided in subdivision (h), a person who commits an act of sodomy, and the victim is at the time incapable, because of a mental disorder or developmental or physical disability, of giving legal consent, and this is known or reasonably should be known to the person committing the act, shall be punished by imprisonment in the state prison for three, six, or eight years. Notwithstanding the existence of a conservatorship pursuant to the Lanterman-Petris-Short Act (Part 1 (commencing with Section 5000) of Division 5 of the Welfare and Institutions Code), the prosecuting attorney shall prove, as an element of the crime, that a mental disorder or developmental or physical disability rendered the alleged victim incapable of giving consent.

(h) Any person who commits an act of sodomy, and the victim is at the time incapable, because of a mental disorder or developmental or physical disability, of giving legal consent, and this is known or reasonably should be known to the person committing the act, and both the defendant and the victim are at the time confined in a state hospital for the care and treatment of the mentally disordered or in any other public or private facility for the care and treatment of the mentally disordered approved by a county mental health director, shall be punished by imprisonment in the state prison, or in a county jail for not more than one year. Notwithstanding the existence of a conservatorship pursuant to the Lanterman-Petris-Short Act (Part 1 (commencing with Section 5000) of Division 5 of the Welfare and Institutions Code), the prosecuting attorney shall prove, as an element of the crime, that a mental disorder or developmental or physical disability rendered the alleged victim incapable of giving legal consent.

(i) Any person who commits an act of sodomy, where the victim is prevented from resisting by an intoxicating or anesthetic substance, or any controlled substance, and this condition was known, or reasonably should have been known by the accused, shall be punished by imprisonment in the state prison for three, six, or eight years.

(j) Any person who commits an act of sodomy, where the victim submits under the belief that the person committing the act is someone known to the victim other than the accused, and this belief is induced by any artifice, pretense, or concealment practiced by the accused, with intent to induce the belief, shall be punished by imprisonment in the state prison for three, six, or eight years.

(k) Any person who commits an act of sodomy, where the act is accomplished against the victim's will by threatening to use the authority of a public official to incarcerate, arrest, or deport the victim or another, and the victim has a reasonable belief that the perpetrator is a public official, shall be punished by imprisonment in the state prison for three, six, or eight years. As used in this subdivision, "public official" means a person employed by a governmental agency who has the authority, as part of that position, to incarcerate, arrest, or deport another. The perpetrator does not actually have to be a public official.

(l) As used in subdivisions (c) and (d), "threatening to retaliate" means a threat to kidnap or falsely imprison, or inflict extreme pain, serious bodily injury, or death.

(m) In addition to any punishment imposed under this section, the judge may assess a fine not to exceed seventy dollars ($70) against any person who violates this section, with the proceeds of this fine to be used in accordance with Section 1463.23. The court, however, shall take into consideration the defendant's ability to pay, and no defendant shall be denied probation because of his or her inability to pay the fine permitted under this subdivision.

Amended by Stats 2013 ch 259 (AB 65),s 2, eff. 9/9/2013.
Amended by Stats 2010 ch 219 (AB 1844),s 6, eff. 9/9/2010.
Amended by Stats 2002 ch 302 (SB 1421), s 3, eff. 1/1/2003.

Section 286.5 - Sexual contact with an animal

(a) Every person who has sexual contact with an animal is guilty of a misdemeanor.

(b) This section does not apply to any lawful and accepted practice related to veterinary medicine performed by a licensed veterinarian or a certified veterinary technician under the guidance of a licensed veterinarian, any artificial insemination of animals for reproductive purposes, any accepted animal husbandry practices such as raising, breeding, or assisting with the birthing process of animals or any other practice that provides care for an animal, or to any generally accepted practices related to the judging of breed conformation.

(c) As used in this section, the following terms have the following meanings:

(1) "Animal" means any nonhuman creature, whether alive or dead.

(2) "Sexual contact" means any act, committed for the purpose of sexual arousal or gratification, abuse, or financial gain, between a person and an animal involving contact between the sex organs or anus of one and the mouth, sex organs, or anus of the other, or, without a bona fide veterinary or animal husbandry purpose, the insertion, however slight, of any part of the body of a person or any object into the vaginal or anal opening of an animal, or the insertion of any part of the body of an animal into the vaginal or anal opening of a person.

(d)

(1) Any authorized officer investigating a violation of this section may seize an animal that has been used in the commission of an offense to protect the health or safety of the animal or the health or safety of others, and to obtain evidence of the offense.

(2) Any animal seized pursuant to this subdivision shall be promptly taken to a shelter facility or veterinary clinic to be examined by a veterinarian for evidence of sexual contact.

(3) Upon the conviction of a person charged with a violation of this section, all animals lawfully seized and impounded with respect to the violation shall be adjudged by the court to be forfeited and shall thereupon be transferred to the impounding officer or appropriate public entity for proper adoption or other disposition. A person convicted of a violation of this section shall be personally liable to the seizing agency for all costs of impoundment from the time of seizure to the time of proper disposition. Upon conviction, the court shall order the convicted person to make payment to the appropriate public entity for the costs incurred in the housing, care, feeding, and treatment of the seized or impounded animals. Each person convicted in connection with a particular animal may be held jointly and severally liable for restitution for that particular animal. The payment shall be in addition to any other fine or sentence ordered by the court.

(4) Except as otherwise specified in this section, if an animal is seized pursuant to paragraph (1), the disposition, care, or the responsibility for the financial cost of animals seized shall be in accordance with the provisions of Section 597.1.

Added by Stats 2019 ch 613 (AB 611),s 2, eff. 1/1/2020.

Section 287 - Oral copulation

(a) Oral copulation is the act of copulating the mouth of one person with the sexual organ or anus of another person.

(b)

(1) Except as provided in Section 288, any person who participates in an act of oral copulation with another person who is under 18 years of age shall be punished by imprisonment in the state prison, or in a county jail for a period of not more than one year.

(2) Except as provided in Section 288, any person over 21 years of age who participates in an act of oral copulation with another person who is under 16 years of age is guilty of a felony.

(c)

(1) Any person who participates in an act of oral copulation with another person who is under 14 years of age and more than 10 years younger than he or she shall be punished by imprisonment in the state prison for three, six, or eight years.

(2)

(A) Any person who commits an act of oral copulation when the act is accomplished against the victim's will by means of force, violence, duress, menace, or fear of immediate and unlawful bodily injury on the victim or another person shall be punished by imprisonment in the state prison for three, six, or eight years.

(B) Any person who commits an act of oral copulation upon a person who is under 14 years of age, when the act is accomplished against the victim's will by means of force, violence, duress, menace, or fear of immediate and unlawful bodily injury on the victim or another person, shall be punished by imprisonment in the state prison for 8, 10, or 12 years.

(C) Any person who commits an act of oral copulation upon a minor who is 14 years of age or older, when the act is accomplished against the victim's will by means of force, violence, duress, menace, or fear of immediate and unlawful bodily injury on the victim or another person, shall be punished by imprisonment in the state prison for 6, 8, or 10 years.

(D) This paragraph does not preclude prosecution under Section 269, Section 288.7, or any other provision of law.

(3) Any person who commits an act of oral copulation where the act is accomplished against the victim's will by threatening to retaliate in the future against the victim or any other person, and there is a reasonable possibility that the perpetrator will execute the threat, shall be punished by imprisonment in the state prison for three, six, or eight years.

(d)

(1) Any person who, while voluntarily acting in concert with another person, either personally or by aiding and abetting that other person, commits an act of oral copulation (A) when the act is accomplished against the victim's will by means of force or fear of immediate and unlawful bodily injury on the victim or another person, or (B) where the act is accomplished against the victim's will by threatening to retaliate in the future against the victim or any other person, and there is a reasonable possibility that the perpetrator will execute the threat, or (C) where the victim is at the time incapable, because of a mental disorder or developmental or physical disability, of giving legal consent, and this is known or reasonably should be known to the person committing the act, shall be punished by imprisonment in the state prison for five, seven, or nine years. Notwithstanding the appointment of a conservator with respect to the victim pursuant to the provisions of the Lanterman-Petris-Short Act (Part 1 (commencing with Section 5000) of Division 5 of the Welfare and Institutions Code), the prosecuting attorney shall prove, as an element of the crime described under paragraph (3), that a mental disorder or developmental or physical disability rendered the alleged victim incapable of giving legal consent.

(2) Any person who, while voluntarily acting in concert with another person, either personally or by aiding and abetting that other person, commits an act of oral copulation upon a victim who is under 14 years of age, when the act is accomplished against the victim's will by means of force or fear of immediate and unlawful bodily injury on the victim or another person, shall be punished by imprisonment in the state prison for 10, 12, or 14 years.

(3) Any person who, while voluntarily acting in concert with another person, either personally or by aiding and abetting that other person, commits an act of oral copulation upon a victim who is a minor 14 years of age or older, when the act is accomplished against the victim's will by means of force or fear of immediate and unlawful bodily injury on the victim or another person, shall be punished by imprisonment in the state prison for 8, 10, or 12 years.

(4) This paragraph does not preclude prosecution under Section 269, Section 288.7, or any other provision of law.

(e) Any person who participates in an act of oral copulation while confined in any state prison, as defined in Section 4504 or in any local detention facility as defined in Section 6031.4, shall be punished by imprisonment in the state prison, or in a county jail for a period of not more than one year.

(f) Any person who commits an act of oral copulation, and the victim is at the time unconscious of the nature of the act and this is known to the person committing the act, shall be punished by imprisonment in the state prison for a period of three, six, or eight years. As used in this subdivision, "unconscious of the nature of the act" means incapable of resisting because the victim meets one of the following conditions:

(1) Was unconscious or asleep.

(2) Was not aware, knowing, perceiving, or cognizant that the act occurred.

(3) Was not aware, knowing, perceiving, or cognizant of the essential characteristics of the act due to the perpetrator's fraud in fact.

(4) Was not aware, knowing, perceiving, or cognizant of the essential characteristics of the act due to the perpetrator's fraudulent representation that the oral copulation served a professional purpose when it served no professional purpose.

(g) Except as provided in subdivision (h), any person who commits an act of oral copulation, and the victim is at the time incapable, because of a mental disorder or developmental or physical disability, of giving legal consent, and this is known or reasonably should be known to the person committing the act, shall be punished by imprisonment in the state prison, for three, six, or eight years. Notwithstanding the existence of a conservatorship pursuant to the provisions of the Lanterman-Petris-Short Act (Part 1 (commencing with Section 5000) of Division 5 of the Welfare and Institutions Code), the prosecuting attorney shall prove, as an element of the crime, that a mental disorder or developmental or physical disability rendered the alleged victim incapable of giving consent.

(h) Any person who commits an act of oral copulation, and the victim is at the time incapable, because of a mental disorder or developmental or physical disability, of giving legal consent, and this is known or reasonably should be known to the person committing the act, and both the defendant and the victim are at the time confined in a state hospital for the care and treatment of the mentally disordered or in any other public or private facility for the care and treatment of the mentally disordered approved by a county mental health director, shall be punished by imprisonment in the state prison, or in a county jail for a period of not more than one year. Notwithstanding the existence of a conservatorship pursuant to the provisions of the Lanterman-Petris-Short Act (Part 1 (commencing with Section 5000) of Division 5 of the Welfare and Institutions Code), the prosecuting attorney shall prove, as an element of the crime, that a mental disorder or developmental or physical disability rendered the alleged victim incapable of giving legal consent.

(i) Any person who commits an act of oral copulation, where the victim is prevented from resisting by any intoxicating or anesthetic substance, or any controlled substance, and this condition was known, or reasonably should have been known by the accused, shall be punished by imprisonment in the state prison for a period of three, six, or eight years.

(j) Any person who commits an act of oral copulation, where the victim submits under the belief that the person committing the act is someone known to the victim other than the accused, and this belief is induced by any artifice, pretense, or concealment practiced by the accused, with intent to induce the belief, shall be punished by imprisonment in the state prison for a period of three, six, or eight years.

(k) Any person who commits an act of oral copulation, where the act is accomplished against the victim's will by threatening to use the authority of a public official to incarcerate, arrest, or deport the victim or another, and the victim has a reasonable belief that the perpetrator is a public official, shall be punished by imprisonment in the state prison for a period of three, six, or eight years. As used in this subdivision, "public official" means a person employed by a governmental agency who has the authority, as part of that position, to incarcerate, arrest, or deport another. The perpetrator does not actually have to be a public official.

(l) As used in subdivisions (c) and (d), "threatening to retaliate" means a threat to kidnap or falsely imprison, or to inflict extreme pain, serious bodily injury, or death.

(m) In addition to any punishment imposed under this section, the judge may assess a fine not to exceed seventy dollars ($70) against any person who violates this section, with the proceeds of this fine to be used in accordance with Section 1463.23. The court shall, however, take into consideration the defendant's ability to pay, and no defendant shall be denied probation because of his or her inability to pay the fine permitted under this subdivision.

Renumbered from Ca. Pen. Code §288a and amended by Stats 2018 ch 423 (SB 1494),s 49, eff. 1/1/2019.

Amended by Stats 2013 ch 282 (SB 59),s 1, eff. 9/9/2013.

Amended by Stats 2010 ch 219 (AB 1844),s 8, eff. 9/9/2010.

Amended by Stats 2002 ch 302 (SB 1421), s 4, eff. 1/1/2003.

Section 288 - Lewd or lascivious act upon child under age of 14 years

(a) Except as provided in subdivision (i), a person who willfully and lewdly commits any lewd or lascivious act, including any of the acts constituting other crimes provided for in Part 1, upon or with the body, or any part or member thereof, of a child who is under the age of 14 years, with the intent of arousing, appealing to, or gratifying the lust, passions, or sexual desires of that person or the child, is guilty of a felony and shall be punished by imprisonment in the state prison for three, six, or eight years.

(b)

(1) A person who commits an act described in subdivision (a) by use of force, violence, duress, menace, or fear of immediate and unlawful bodily injury on the victim or another person, is guilty of a felony and shall be punished by imprisonment in the state prison for 5, 8, or 10 years.

(2) A person who is a caretaker and commits an act described in subdivision (a) upon a dependent person by use of force, violence, duress, menace, or fear of immediate and unlawful bodily injury on the victim or another person, with the intent described in subdivision (a), is guilty of a felony and shall be punished by imprisonment in the state prison for 5, 8, or 10 years.

(c)

(1) A person who commits an act described in subdivision (a) with the intent described in that subdivision, and the victim is a child of 14 or 15 years, and that person is at least 10 years older than the child, is guilty of a public offense and shall be punished by imprisonment in the state prison for one, two, or three years, or by imprisonment in a county jail for not more than one year. In determining whether the person is at least 10 years older than the child, the difference in age shall be measured from the birth date of the person to the birth date of the child.

(2) A person who is a caretaker and commits an act described in subdivision (a) upon a dependent person, with the intent described in subdivision (a), is guilty of a public offense and shall be punished by imprisonment in the state prison for one, two, or three years, or by imprisonment in a county jail for not more than one year.

(d) In any arrest or prosecution under this section or Section 288.5, the peace officer, district attorney, and the court shall consider the needs of the child victim or dependent person and shall do whatever is necessary, within existing budgetary resources, and constitutionally permissible to prevent psychological harm to the child victim or to prevent psychological harm to the dependent person victim resulting from participation in the court process.

(e)

(1) Upon the conviction of a person for a violation of subdivision (a) or (b), the court may, in addition to any other penalty or fine imposed, order the defendant to pay an additional fine not to exceed ten thousand dollars ($10,000). In setting the amount of the fine, the court shall consider any relevant factors, including, but not limited to, the seriousness and gravity of the offense, the circumstances of its commission, whether the defendant derived any economic gain as a result of the crime, and the extent to which the victim suffered economic losses as a result of the crime. Every fine imposed and collected under this section shall be deposited in the Victim-Witness Assistance Fund to be available for appropriation to fund child sexual exploitation and child sexual abuse victim counseling centers and prevention programs pursuant to Section 13837.

(2) If the court orders a fine imposed pursuant to this subdivision, the actual administrative cost of collecting that fine, not to exceed 2 percent of the total amount paid, may be paid into the general fund of the county treasury for the use and benefit of the county.

(f) For purposes of paragraph (2) of subdivision (b) and paragraph (2) of subdivision (c), the following definitions apply:

(1) "Caretaker" means an owner, operator, administrator, employee, independent contractor, agent, or volunteer of any of the following public or private facilities when the facilities provide care for elder or dependent persons:

(A) Twenty-four hour health facilities, as defined in Sections 1250, 1250.2, and 1250.3 of the Health and Safety Code.

(B) Clinics.

(C) Home health agencies.

(D) Adult day health care centers.

(E) Secondary schools that serve dependent persons and postsecondary educational institutions that serve dependent persons or elders.

(F) Sheltered workshops.

(G) Camps.

(H) Community care facilities, as defined by Section 1402 of the Health and Safety Code, and residential care facilities for the elderly, as defined in Section 1569.2 of the Health and Safety Code.

(I) Respite care facilities.

(J) Foster homes.

(K) Regional centers for persons with developmental disabilities.

(L) A home health agency licensed in accordance with Chapter 8 (commencing with Section 1725) of Division 2 of the Health and Safety Code.

(M) An agency that supplies in-home supportive services.

(N) Board and care facilities.

(O) Any other protective or public assistance agency that provides health services or social services to elder or dependent persons, including, but not limited to, in-home supportive services, as defined in Section 14005.14 of the Welfare and Institutions Code.

(P) Private residences.

(2) "Board and care facilities" means licensed or unlicensed facilities that provide assistance with one or more of the following activities:

(A) Bathing.

(B) Dressing.

(C) Grooming.

(D) Medication storage.

(E) Medical dispensation.

(F) Money management.

(3) "Dependent person" means a person, regardless of whether the person lives independently, who has a physical or mental impairment that substantially restricts his or her ability to carry out normal activities or to protect his or her rights, including, but not limited to, persons who have physical or developmental disabilities or whose physical or mental abilities have significantly diminished because of age. "Dependent person" includes a person who is admitted as an inpatient to a 24-hour health facility, as defined in Sections 1250, 1250.2, and 1250.3 of the Health and Safety Code.

(g) Paragraph (2) of subdivision (b) and paragraph (2) of subdivision (c) apply to the owners, operators, administrators, employees, independent contractors, agents, or volunteers working at these public or private facilities and only to the extent that the individuals personally commit, conspire, aid, abet, or facilitate any act prohibited by paragraph (2) of subdivision (b) and paragraph (2) of subdivision (c).

(h) Paragraph (2) of subdivision (b) and paragraph (2) of subdivision (c) do not apply to a caretaker who is a spouse of, or who is in an equivalent domestic relationship with, the dependent person under care.

(i)

(1) A person convicted of a violation of subdivision (a) shall be imprisoned in the state prison for life with the possibility of parole if the defendant personally inflicted bodily harm upon the victim.

(2) The penalty provided in this subdivision shall only apply if the fact that the defendant personally inflicted bodily harm upon the victim is pled and proved.

(3) As used in this subdivision, "bodily harm" means any substantial physical injury resulting from the use of force that is more than the force necessary to commit the offense.

Amended by Stats 2018 ch 70 (AB 1934),s 2, eff. 1/1/2019.

Amended by Stats 2010 ch 219 (AB 1844),s 7, eff. 9/9/2010.

Amended by Stats 2004 ch 823 (AB 20), s 7, eff. 1/1/2005.

Section 288.1 - Suspension of sentence

Any person convicted of committing any lewd or lascivious act including any of the acts constituting other crimes provided for in Part 1 of this code upon or with the body, or any part or member thereof, of a child under the age of 14 years shall not have his or her sentence suspended until the court obtains a report from a reputable psychiatrist, from a reputable psychologist who meets the standards set forth in Section 1027, as to the mental condition of that person.

Amended by Stats 2005 ch 477 (SB 33),s 2, eff. 1/1/2006

Section 288.2 - Unlawful distribution of harmful matter to minor

(a)

(1) Every person who knows, should have known, or believes that another person is a minor, and who knowingly distributes, sends, causes to be sent, exhibits, or offers to distribute or exhibit by any means, including by physical delivery, telephone, electronic communication, or in person, any harmful matter that depicts a minor or minors engaging in sexual conduct, to the other person with the intent of arousing, appealing to, or gratifying the lust or passions or sexual desires of that person or of the minor, and with the intent or for the purposes of engaging in sexual intercourse, sodomy, or oral copulation with the other person, or with the intent that either person touch an intimate body part of the other, is guilty of a misdemeanor, punishable by imprisonment in a county jail not exceeding one year, or is guilty of a felony, punishable by imprisonment in the state prison for two, three, or five years.

(2) If the matter used by the person is harmful matter but does not include a depiction or depictions of a minor or minors engaged in sexual conduct, the offense is punishable by imprisonment in a county jail not exceeding one year, or by imprisonment in the state prison for 16 months, or two or three years.

(3) For purposes of this subdivision, the offense described in paragraph (2) shall include all of the elements described in paragraph (1), except as to the element modified in paragraph (2).

(b) For purposes of this section, "sexual conduct" has the same meaning as defined in subdivision (d) of Section 311.4.

(c) For purposes of this section, "harmful matter" has the same meaning as defined in Section 313.

(d) For purposes of this section, an intimate body part includes the sexual organ, anus, groin, or buttocks of any person, or the breasts of a female.

(e) Prosecution under this section shall not preclude prosecution under any other provision of law.

(f) It shall be a defense to any prosecution under this section that a parent or guardian committed the act charged in aid of legitimate sex education.

(g) It shall be a defense in any prosecution under this section that the act charged was committed in aid of legitimate scientific or educational purposes.

(h) It does not constitute a violation of this section for a telephone corporation, as defined in Section 234 of the Public Utilities Code, a cable television company franchised pursuant to Section 53066 of the Government Code, or any of its affiliates, an Internet service provider, or commercial online service provider, to carry, broadcast, or transmit messages described in this section or perform related activities in providing telephone, cable television, Internet, or commercial online services.

Added by Stats 2013 ch 777 (SB 145),s 2, eff. 1/1/2014.

Section 288.3 - Unlawful contact or communication with minor

(a) Every person who contacts or communicates with a minor, or attempts to contact or communicate with a minor, who knows or reasonably should know that the person is a minor, with intent to commit an offense specified in Section 207, 209, 261, 264.1, 273a, 286, 287, 288, 288.2, 289, 311.1, 311.2, 311.4 or 311.11, or former Section 288a, involving the minor shall be punished by imprisonment in the state prison for the term prescribed for an attempt to commit the intended offense.

(b) As used in this section, "contacts or communicates with" shall include direct and indirect contact or communication that may be achieved personally or by use of an agent or agency, any print medium, any postal service, a common carrier or communication common carrier, any electronic communications system, or any telecommunications, wire, computer, or radio communications device or system.

(c) A person convicted of a violation of subdivision (a) who has previously been convicted of a violation of subdivision (a) shall be punished by an additional and consecutive term of imprisonment in the state prison for five years.

Amended by Stats 2018 ch 423 (SB 1494),s 48, eff. 1/1/2019.

Approved by the voters at the General Election, Nov., 2006.

Section 288.4 - Unlawful arrangement of meeting with minor

(a)

(1) Every person who, motivated by an unnatural or abnormal sexual interest in children, arranges a meeting with a minor or a person he or she believes to be a minor for the purpose of exposing his or her genitals or pubic or rectal area, having the child expose his or her genitals or pubic or rectal area, or engaging in lewd or lascivious behavior, shall be punished by a fine not exceeding five thousand dollars ($5,000), by imprisonment in a county jail not exceeding one year, or by both the fine and imprisonment.

(2) Every person who violates this subdivision after a prior conviction for an offense listed in subdivision (c) of Section 290 shall be punished by imprisonment in the state prison.

(b) Every person described in paragraph (1) of subdivision (a) who goes to the arranged meeting place at or about the arranged time, shall be punished by imprisonment in the state prison for two, three, or four years.

(c) Nothing in this section shall preclude or prohibit prosecution under any other provision of law.

Renumbered from Ca. Pen. Code §288.3 by Stats 2007 ch 579 (SB 172),s 5, eff. 10/13/2007.

Added by Stats 2006 ch 337 (SB 1128),s 7, eff. 9/20/2006.

Section 288.5 - Continuous sexual abuse of child

(a) Any person who either resides in the same home with the minor child or has recurring access to the child, who over a period of time, not less than three months in duration, engages in three or more acts of substantial sexual conduct with a child under the age of 14 years at the time of the commission of the offense, as defined in subdivision (b) of Section 1203.066, or three or more acts of lewd or lascivious conduct, as defined in Section 288, with a child under the age of 14 years at the time of the commission of the offense is guilty of the offense of continuous sexual abuse of a child and shall be punished by imprisonment in the state prison for a term of 6, 12, or 16 years.

(b) To convict under this section the trier of fact, if a jury, need unanimously agree only that the requisite number of acts occurred not on which acts constitute the requisite number.

(c) No other act of substantial sexual conduct, as defined in subdivision (b) of Section 1203.066, with a child under 14 years of age at the time of the commission of the offenses, or lewd and lascivious acts, as defined in Section 288, involving the same victim may be charged in the same proceeding with a charge under this section unless the other charged offense occurred outside the time period charged under this section or the other offense is charged in the alternative. A defendant may be charged with only one count under this section unless more than one victim is involved in which case a separate count may be charged for each victim.

Amended by Stats 2006 ch 337 (SB 1128),s 8, eff. 9/20/2006.

Section 288.7 - Unlawful acts by person 18 years of age or older with child who is 10 years of age or younger

(a) Any person 18 years of age or older who engages in sexual intercourse or sodomy with a child who is 10 years of age or younger is guilty of a felony and shall be punished by imprisonment in the state prison for a term of 25 years to life.

(b) Any person 18 years of age or older who engages in oral copulation or sexual penetration, as defined in Section 289, with a child who is 10 years of age or younger is guilty of a felony and shall be punished by imprisonment in the state prison for a term of 15 years to life.

Added by Stats 2006 ch 337 (SB 1128),s 9, eff. 9/20/2006.

Section 288a - [Renumbered]

Renumbered as Ca. Pen. Code §287 by Stats 2018 ch 423 (SB 1494),s 49, eff. 1/1/2019.

Amended by Stats 2013 ch 282 (SB 59),s 1, eff. 9/9/2013.

Amended by Stats 2010 ch 219 (AB 1844),s 8, eff. 9/9/2010.

Amended by Stats 2002 ch 302 (SB 1421), s 4, eff. 1/1/2003.

Section 289 - Sexual penetration against victim's will

(a)

(1)

(A) Any person who commits an act of sexual penetration when the act is accomplished against the victim's will by means of force, violence, duress, menace, or fear of immediate and unlawful bodily injury on the victim or another person shall be punished by imprisonment in the state prison for three, six, or eight years.

(B) Any person who commits an act of sexual penetration upon a child who is under 14 years of age, when the act is accomplished against the victim's will by means of force, violence, duress, menace, or fear of immediate and unlawful bodily injury on the victim or another person, shall be punished by imprisonment in the state prison for 8, 10, or 12 years.

(C) Any person who commits an act of sexual penetration upon a minor who is 14 years of age or older, when the act is accomplished against the victim's will by means of force, violence, duress, menace, or fear of immediate and unlawful bodily injury on the victim or another person, shall be punished by imprisonment in the state prison for 6, 8, or 10 years.

(D) This paragraph does not preclude prosecution under Section 269, Section 288.7, or any other provision of law.

(2) Any person who commits an act of sexual penetration when the act is accomplished against the victim's will by threatening to retaliate in the future against the victim or any other person, and there is a reasonable possibility that the perpetrator will execute the threat, shall be punished by imprisonment in the state prison for three, six, or eight years.

(b) Except as provided in subdivision (c), any person who commits an act of sexual penetration, and the victim is at the time incapable, because of a mental disorder or developmental or physical disability, of giving legal consent, and this is known or reasonably should be known to the person committing the act or causing the act to be committed, shall be punished by imprisonment in the state prison for three, six, or eight years. Notwithstanding the appointment of a conservator with respect to the victim pursuant to the provisions of the Lanterman-Petris-Short Act (Part 1 (commencing with Section 5000) of Division 5 of the Welfare and Institutions Code), the prosecuting attorney shall prove, as an element of the crime, that a mental disorder or developmental or physical disability rendered the alleged victim incapable of giving legal consent.

(c) Any person who commits an act of sexual penetration, and the victim is at the time incapable, because of a mental disorder or developmental or physical disability, of giving legal consent, and this is known or reasonably should be known to the person committing the act or causing the act to be committed and both the defendant and the victim are at the time confined in a state hospital for the care and treatment of the mentally disordered or in any other public or private facility for the care and treatment of the mentally disordered approved by a county mental health director, shall be punished by imprisonment in the state prison, or in a county jail for a period of not more than one year. Notwithstanding the existence of a conservatorship pursuant to the provisions of the Lanterman-Petris-Short Act (Part 1 (commencing with Section 5000) of Division 5 of the Welfare and Institutions Code), the prosecuting attorney shall prove, as an element of the crime, that a mental disorder or developmental or physical disability rendered the alleged victim incapable of giving legal consent.

(d) Any person who commits an act of sexual penetration, and the victim is at the time unconscious of the nature of the act and this is known to the person committing the act or causing the act to be committed, shall be punished by imprisonment in the state prison for three, six, or eight years. As used in this subdivision, "unconscious of the nature of the act" means incapable of resisting because the victim meets one of the following conditions:

(1) Was unconscious or asleep.

(2) Was not aware, knowing, perceiving, or cognizant that the act occurred.

(3) Was not aware, knowing, perceiving, or cognizant of the essential characteristics of the act due to the perpetrator's fraud in fact.

(4) Was not aware, knowing, perceiving, or cognizant of the essential characteristics of the act due to the perpetrator's fraudulent representation that the sexual penetration served a professional purpose when it served no professional purpose.

(e) Any person who commits an act of sexual penetration when the victim is prevented from resisting by any intoxicating or anesthetic substance, or any controlled substance, and this condition was known, or reasonably should have been known by the accused, shall be punished by imprisonment in the state prison for a period of three, six, or eight years.

(f) Any person who commits an act of sexual penetration when the victim submits under the belief that the person committing the act or causing the act to be committed is someone known to the victim other than the accused, and this belief is induced by any artifice, pretense, or concealment practiced by the accused, with intent to induce the belief, shall be punished by imprisonment in the state prison for a period of three, six, or eight years.

(g) Any person who commits an act of sexual penetration when the act is accomplished against the victim's will by threatening to use the authority of a public official to incarcerate, arrest, or deport the victim or another, and the victim has a reasonable belief that the perpetrator is a public official, shall be punished by imprisonment in the state prison for a period of three, six, or eight years. As used in this subdivision, "public official" means a person employed by a governmental agency who has the authority, as part of that position, to incarcerate, arrest, or deport another. The perpetrator does not actually have to be a public official.

(h) Except as provided in Section 288, any person who participates in an act of sexual penetration with another person who is under 18 years of age shall be punished by imprisonment in the state prison or in a county jail for a period of not more than one year.

(i) Except as provided in Section 288, any person over 21 years of age who participates in an act of sexual penetration with another person who is under 16 years of age shall be guilty of a felony.

(j) Any person who participates in an act of sexual penetration with another person who is under 14 years of age and who is more than 10 years younger than he or she shall be punished by imprisonment in the state prison for three, six, or eight years.

(k) As used in this section:

(1) "Sexual penetration" is the act of causing the penetration, however slight, of the genital or anal opening of any person or causing another person to so penetrate the defendant's or another person's genital or anal opening for the purpose of sexual arousal, gratification, or abuse by any foreign object, substance, instrument, or device, or by any unknown object.

(2) "Foreign object, substance, instrument, or device" shall include any part of the body, except a sexual organ.

(3) "Unknown object" shall include any foreign object, substance, instrument, or device, or any part of the body, including a penis, when it is not known whether penetration was by a penis or by a foreign object, substance, instrument, or device, or by any other part of the body.

(l) As used in subdivision (a), "threatening to retaliate" means a threat to kidnap or falsely imprison, or inflict extreme pain, serious bodily injury or death.

(m) As used in this section, "victim" includes any person who the defendant causes to penetrate the genital or anal opening of the defendant or another person or whose genital or anal opening is caused to be penetrated by the defendant or another person and who otherwise qualifies as a victim under the requirements of this section.

Amended by Stats 2013 ch 282 (SB 59),s 2, eff. 9/9/2013.

Amended by Stats 2010 ch 219 (AB 1844),s 9, eff. 9/9/2010.

Amended by Stats 2002 ch 302 (SB 1421), s 5, eff. 1/1/2003.

Amended by Stats 2002 ch 787 (SB 1798), s 9, eff. 1/1/2003.

Previously Amended October 10, 1999 (Bill Number: AB 1236) (Chapter 706).

Section 289.5 - Fleeing to California with intent to avoid prosecution
(a) Every person who flees to this state with the intent to avoid prosecution for an offense which, if committed or attempted in this state, would have been punishable as one or more of the offenses described in subdivision (c) of Section 290, and who has been charged with that offense under the laws of the jurisdiction from which the person fled, is guilty of a misdemeanor.
(b) Every person who flees to this state with the intent to avoid custody or confinement imposed for conviction of an offense under the laws of the jurisdiction from which the person fled, which offense, if committed or attempted in this state, would have been punishable as one or more of the offenses described in subdivision (c) of Section 290, is guilty of a misdemeanor.
(c) No person shall be charged and prosecuted for an offense under this section unless the prosecutor has requested the other jurisdiction to extradite the person and the other jurisdiction has refused to do so.
(d) Any person who is convicted of any felony sex offense described in subdivision (c) of Section 290, that is committed after fleeing to this state under the circumstances described in subdivision (a) or (b) of this section, shall, in addition and consecutive to the punishment for that conviction, receive an additional term of two years' imprisonment.
Amended by Stats 2007 ch 579 (SB 172),s 6, eff. 10/13/2007.

Section 289.6 - Sexual activity with consenting adult confined in health facility, detention facility, or corrections facility
(a)
(1) An employee or officer of a public entity health facility, or an employee, officer, or agent of a private person or entity that provides a health facility or staff for a health facility under contract with a public entity, who engages in sexual activity with a consenting adult who is confined in a health facility is guilty of a public offense. As used in this paragraph, "health facility" means a health facility as defined in subdivisions (b), (e), (g), (h), and (j) of, and subparagraph (C) of paragraph (2) of subdivision (i) of, Section 1250 of the Health and Safety Code, in which the victim has been confined involuntarily.
(2) An employee or officer of a public entity detention facility, or an employee, officer, agent of a private person or entity that provides a detention facility or staff for a detention facility, a person or agent of a public or private entity under contract with a detention facility, a volunteer of a private or public entity detention facility, or a peace officer who engages in sexual activity with a consenting adult who is confined in a detention facility is guilty of a public offense.
(3) An employee with a department, board, or authority under the Department of Corrections and Rehabilitation or a facility under contract with a department, board, or authority under the Department of Corrections and Rehabilitation, who, during the course of his or her employment directly provides treatment, care, control, or supervision of inmates, wards, or parolees, and who engages in sexual activity with a consenting adult who is an inmate, ward, or parolee, is guilty of a public offense.
(b) As used in this section, the term "public entity" means the state, federal government, a city, a county, a city and county, a joint county jail district, or any entity created as a result of a joint powers agreement between two or more public entities.
(c) As used in this section, the term "detention facility" means:
(1) A prison, jail, camp, or other correctional facility used for the confinement of adults or both adults and minors.
(2) A building or facility used for the confinement of adults or adults and minors pursuant to a contract with a public entity.
(3) A room that is used for holding persons for interviews, interrogations, or investigations and that is separate from a jail or located in the administrative area of a law enforcement facility.
(4) A vehicle used to transport confined persons during their period of confinement, including transporting a person after he or she has been arrested but has not been booked.
(5) A court holding facility located within or adjacent to a court building that is used for the confinement of persons for the purpose of court appearances.
(d) As used in this section, "sexual activity" means:
(1) Sexual intercourse.
(2) Sodomy, as defined in subdivision (a) of Section 286.
(3) Oral copulation, as defined in subdivision (a) of Section 287 or former Section 288a.
(4) Sexual penetration, as defined in subdivision (k) of Section 289.
(5) The rubbing or touching of the breasts or sexual organs of another, or of oneself in the presence of and with knowledge of another, with the intent of arousing, appealing to, or gratifying the lust, passions, or sexual desires of oneself or another.
(e) Consent by a confined person or parolee to sexual activity proscribed by this section is not a defense to a criminal prosecution for violation of this section.
(f) This section does not apply to sexual activity between consenting adults that occurs during an overnight conjugal visit that takes place pursuant to a court order or with the written approval of an authorized representative of the public entity that operates or contracts for the operation of the detention facility where the conjugal visit takes place, to physical contact or penetration made pursuant to a lawful search, or bona fide medical examinations or treatments, including clinical treatments.
(g) Any violation of paragraph (1) of subdivision (a), or a violation of paragraph (2) or (3) of subdivision (a) as described in paragraph (5) of subdivision (d), is a misdemeanor.
(h) Any violation of paragraph (2) or (3) of subdivision (a), as described in paragraph (1), (2), (3), or (4) of subdivision (d), shall be punished by imprisonment in a county jail not exceeding one year, or in the state prison, or by a fine of not more than ten thousand dollars ($10,000) or by both that fine and imprisonment.
(i) Any person previously convicted of a violation of this section shall, upon a subsequent violation, be guilty of a felony.
(j) Anyone who is convicted of a felony violation of this section who is employed by a department, board, or authority within the Department of Corrections and Rehabilitation shall be terminated in accordance with the State Civil Service Act (Part 2 (commencing with Section 18500) of Division 5 of Title 2 of the Government Code). Anyone who has been convicted of a felony violation of this section shall not be eligible to be hired or reinstated by a department, board, or authority within the Department of Corrections and Rehabilitation.
Amended by Stats 2018 ch 423 (SB 1494),s 50, eff. 1/1/2019.
Amended by Stats 2014 ch 71 (SB 1304),s 118, eff. 1/1/2015.

Amended by Stats 2013 ch 76 (AB 383),s 146, eff. 1/1/2014.
Amended by Stats 2013 ch 59 (SB 514),s 1, eff. 1/1/2014.
Amended by Stats 2012 ch 123 (AB 2078),s 1, eff. 1/1/2013.
Amended by Stats 2000 ch 287 (SB 1955), s 6, eff. 1/1/2001.
Amended October 10, 1999 (Bill Number: SB 377) (Chapter 806).

Chapter 5.5 - SEX OFFENDERS

Section 290 - Short title; persons required to register

(a) Sections 290 to 290.024, inclusive, shall be known, and may be cited, as the Sex Offender Registration Act. All references to "the Act" in those sections are to the Sex Offender Registration Act.

(b) Every person described in subdivision (c), for the period specified in subdivision (d) while residing in California, or while attending school or working in California, as described in Sections 290.002 and 290.01, shall register with the chief of police of the city in which the person is residing, or the sheriff of the county if the person is residing in an unincorporated area or city that has no police department, and, additionally, with the chief of police of a campus of the University of California, the California State University, or community college if the person is residing upon the campus or in any of its facilities, within five working days of coming into, or changing the person's residence within, any city, county, or city and county, or campus in which the person temporarily resides, and shall register thereafter in accordance with the Act, unless the duty to register is terminated pursuant to Section 290.5 or as otherwise provided by law.

(c)

(1) The following persons shall register: Every person who, since July 1, 1944, has been or is hereafter convicted in any court in this state or in any federal or military court of a violation of Section 187 committed in the perpetration, or an attempt to perpetrate, rape, or any act punishable under Section 286, 287, 288, or 289 or former Section 288a, Section 207 or 209 committed with intent to violate Section 261, 286, 287, 288, or 289 or former Section 288a, Section 220, except assault to commit mayhem, subdivision (b) or (c) of Section 236.1, Section 243.4, Section 261, paragraph (1) of subdivision (a) of former Section 262 involving the use of force or violence for which the person is sentenced to the state prison, Section 264.1, 266, or 266c, subdivision (b) of Section 266h, subdivision (b) of Section 266i, Section 266j, 267, 269, 285, 286, 287, 288, 288.3, 288.4, 288.5, 288.7, 289, or 311.1, or former Section 288a, subdivision (b), (c), or (d) of Section 311.2, Section 311.3, 311.4, 311.10, 311.11, or 647.6, former Section 647a, subdivision (c) of Section 653f, subdivision 1 or 2 of Section 314, any offense involving lewd or lascivious conduct under Section 272, or any felony violation of Section 288.2; any statutory predecessor that includes all elements of one of the offenses described in this subdivision; or any person who since that date has been or is hereafter convicted of the attempt or conspiracy to commit any of the offenses described in this subdivision.

(2) Notwithstanding paragraph (1), a person convicted of a violation of subdivision (b) of Section 286, subdivision (b) of Section 287, or subdivision (h) or (i) of Section 289 shall not be required to register if, at the time of the offense, the person is not more than 10 years older than the minor, as measured from the minor's date of birth to the person's date of birth, and the conviction is the only one requiring the person to register. This paragraph does not preclude the court from requiring a person to register pursuant to Section 290.006.

(d) A person described in subdivision (c), or who is otherwise required to register pursuant to the Act shall register for 10 years, 20 years, or life, following a conviction and release from incarceration, placement, commitment, or release on probation or other supervision, as follows:

(1)

(A) A tier one offender is subject to registration for a minimum of 10 years. A person is a tier one offender if the person is required to register for conviction of a misdemeanor described in subdivision (c), or for conviction of a felony described in subdivision (c) that was not a serious or violent felony as described in subdivision (c) of Section 667.5 or subdivision (c) of Section 1192.7.

(B) This paragraph does not apply to a person who is subject to registration pursuant to paragraph (2) or (3).

(2)

(A) A tier two offender is subject to registration for a minimum of 20 years. A person is a tier two offender if the person was convicted of an offense described in subdivision (c) that is also described in subdivision (c) of Section 667.5 or subdivision (c) of Section 1192.7, Section 285, subdivision (g) or (h) of Section 286, subdivision (g) or (h) of Section 287 or former Section 288a, subdivision (b) of Section 289, or Section 647.6 if it is a second or subsequent conviction for that offense that was brought and tried separately.

(B) This paragraph does not apply if the person is subject to lifetime registration as required in paragraph (3).

(3) A tier three offender is subject to registration for life. A person is a tier three offender if any one of the following applies:

(A) Following conviction of a registerable offense, the person was subsequently convicted in a separate proceeding of committing an offense described in subdivision (c) and the conviction is for commission of a violent felony described in subdivision (c) of Section 667.5, or the person was subsequently convicted of committing an offense for which the person was ordered to register pursuant to Section 290.006, and the conviction is for the commission of a violent felony described in subdivision (c) of Section 667.5.

(B) The person was committed to a state mental hospital as a sexually violent predator pursuant to Article 4 (commencing with Section 6600) of Chapter 2 of Part 2 of Division 6 of the Welfare and Institutions Code.

(C) The person was convicted of violating any of the following:

(i) Section 187 while attempting to commit or committing an act punishable under Section 261, 286, 287, 288, or 289 or former Section 288a.

(ii) Section 207 or 209 with intent to violate Section 261, 286, 287, 288, or 289 or former Section 288a.

(iii) Section 220.

(iv) Subdivision (b) of Section 266h.

(v) Subdivision (b) of Section 266i.

(vi) Section 266j.

(vii) Section 267.

(viii) Section 269.

(ix) Subdivision (b) or (c) of Section 288.

(x) Section 288.2.

(xi) Section 288.3, unless committed with the intent to commit a violation of subdivision (b) of Section 286, subdivision (b) of Section 287 or former Section 288a, or subdivision (h) or (i) of Section 289.

(xii) Section 288.4.

(xiii) Section 288.5.

(xiv) Section 288.7.

(xv) Subdivision (c) of Section 653f.

(xvi) Any offense for which the person is sentenced to a life term pursuant to Section 667.61.

(D) The person's risk level on the static risk assessment instrument for sex offenders (SARATSO), pursuant to Section 290.04, is well above average risk at the time of release on the index sex offense into the community, as defined in the Coding Rules for that instrument.

(E) The person is a habitual sex offender pursuant to Section 667.71.

(F) The person was convicted of violating subdivision (a) of Section 288 in two proceedings brought and tried separately.

(G) The person was sentenced to 15 to 25 years to life for an offense listed in Section 667.61.

(H) The person is required to register pursuant to Section 290.004.

(I) The person was convicted of a felony offense described in subdivision (b) or (c) of Section 236.1.

(J) The person was convicted of a felony offense described in subdivision (a), (c), or (d) of Section 243.4.

(K) The person was convicted of violating paragraph (2), (3), or (4) of subdivision (a) of Section 261 or was convicted of violating Section 261 and punished pursuant to paragraph (1) or (2) of subdivision (c) of Section 264.

(L) The person was convicted of violating paragraph (1) of subdivision (a) of former Section 262.

(M) The person was convicted of violating Section 264.1.

(N) The person was convicted of any offense involving lewd or lascivious conduct under Section 272.

(O) The person was convicted of violating paragraph (2) of subdivision (c) or subdivision (d), (f), or (i) of Section 286.

(P) The person was convicted of violating paragraph (2) of subdivision (c) or subdivision (d), (f), or (i) of Section 287 or former Section 288a.

(Q) The person was convicted of violating paragraph (1) of subdivision (a) or subdivision (d), (e), or (j) of Section 289.

(R) The person was convicted of a felony violation of Section 311.1 or 311.11 or of violating subdivision (b), (c), or (d) of Section 311.2, Section 311.3, 311.4, or 311.10.

(4)

(A) A person who is required to register pursuant to Section 290.005 shall be placed in the appropriate tier if the offense is assessed as equivalent to a California registerable offense described in subdivision (c).

(B) If the person's duty to register pursuant to Section 290.005 is based solely on the requirement of registration in another jurisdiction, and there is no equivalent California registerable offense, the person shall be subject to registration as a tier two offender, except that the person is subject to registration as a tier three offender if one of the following applies:

(i) The person's risk level on the static risk assessment instrument (SARATSO), pursuant to Section 290.06, is well above average risk at the time of release on the index sex offense into the community, as defined in the Coding Rules for that instrument.

(ii) The person was subsequently convicted in a separate proceeding of an offense substantially similar to an offense listed in subdivision (c) which is also substantially similar to an offense described in subdivision (c) of Section 667.5, or is substantially similar to Section 269 or 288.7.

(iii) The person has ever been committed to a state mental hospital or mental health facility in a proceeding substantially similar to civil commitment as a sexually violent predator pursuant to Article 4 (commencing with Section 6600) of Chapter 2 of Part 2 of Division 6 of the Welfare and Institutions Code.

(5)

(A) The Department of Justice may place a person described in subdivision (c), or who is otherwise required to register pursuant to the Act, in a tier-to-be-determined category if the appropriate tier designation described in this subdivision cannot be immediately ascertained. An individual placed in this tier-to-be-determined category shall continue to register in accordance with the Act. The individual shall be given credit toward the mandated minimum registration period for any period for which the individual registers.

(B) The Department of Justice shall ascertain an individual's appropriate tier designation as described in this subdivision within 24 months of the individual's placement in the tier-to-be-determined category.

(e) The minimum time period for the completion of the required registration period in tier one or two commences on the date of release from incarceration, placement, or commitment, including any related civil commitment on the registerable offense. The minimum time for the completion of the required registration period for a designated tier is tolled during any period of subsequent incarceration, placement, or commitment, including any subsequent civil commitment, except that arrests not resulting in conviction, adjudication, or revocation of probation or parole shall not toll the required registration period. The minimum time period shall be extended by one year for each misdemeanor conviction of failing to register under this act, and by three years for each felony conviction of failing to register under this act, without regard to the actual time served in custody for the conviction. If a registrant is subsequently convicted of another offense requiring registration pursuant to the Act, a new minimum time period for the completion of the registration requirement for the applicable tier shall commence upon that person's release from incarceration, placement, or commitment, including any related civil commitment. If the subsequent conviction requiring registration pursuant to the Act occurs prior to an order to terminate the registrant from the registry after completion of a tier associated with the first conviction for a registerable offense, the applicable tier shall be the highest tier associated with the convictions.

(f) This section does not require a ward of the juvenile court to register under the Act, except as provided in Section 290.008.
Amended by Stats 2021 ch 626 (AB 1171),s 25, eff. 1/1/2022.

Amended by Stats 2020 ch 79 (SB 145),s 2, eff. 1/1/2021.
Amended by Stats 2018 ch 423 (SB 1494),s 52, eff. 1/1/2019.
Added by Stats 2017 ch 541 (SB 384),s 2.5, eff. 1/1/2018.

Section 290.001 - Registration

Every person who has ever been adjudicated a sexually violent predator, as defined in Section 6600 of the Welfare and Institutions Code, shall register in accordance with the Act.

Added by Stats 2007 ch 579 (SB 172),s 9, eff. 10/13/2007.

Section 290.002 - Registration of out-of-state residents

Persons required to register in their state of residence who are out-of-state residents employed, or carrying on a vocation in California on a full-time or part-time basis, with or without compensation, for more than 14 days, or for an aggregate period exceeding 30 days in a calendar year, shall register in accordance with the Act. Persons described in the Act who are out-of-state residents enrolled in any educational institution in California, as defined in Section 22129 of the Education Code, on a full-time or part-time basis, shall register in accordance with the Act. The place where the out-of-state resident is located, for purposes of registration, shall be the place where the person is employed, carrying on a vocation, or attending school. The out-of-state resident subject to this section shall, in addition to the information required pursuant to Section 290.015, provide the registering authority with the name of his or her place of employment or the name of the school attended in California, and his or her address or location in his or her state of residence. The registration requirement for persons subject to this section shall become operative on November 25, 2000. The terms "employed or carries on a vocation" include employment whether or not financially compensated, volunteered, or performed for government or educational benefit.

Added by Stats 2007 ch 579 (SB 172),s 10, eff. 10/13/2007.

Section 290.003 - Registration upon release, discharge, or parole from penal institution

Any person who, since July 1, 1944, has been or hereafter is released, discharged, or paroled from a penal institution where he or she was confined because of the commission or attempted commission of one of the offenses described in subdivision (c) of Section 290, shall register in accordance with the Act.

Added by Stats 2007 ch 579 (SB 172),s 11, eff. 10/13/2007.

Section 290.004 - Registration of mentally disordered sex offender of person found not guilty by reason of insanity

Any person who, since July 1, 1944, has been or hereafter is determined to be a mentally disordered sex offender under Article 1 (commencing with Section 6300) of Chapter 2 of Part 2 of Division 6 of the Welfare and Institutions Code, or any person who has been found guilty in the guilt phase of a trial for an offense for which registration is required by this act but who has been found not guilty by reason of insanity in the sanity phase of the trial shall register in accordance with the act.

Amended by Stats 2017 ch 269 (SB 811),s 8, eff. 1/1/2018.

Added by Stats 2007 ch 579 (SB 172),s 12, eff. 10/13/2007.

Section 290.005 - Persons required to register

The following persons shall register in accordance with the Act:

(a) Except as provided in subdivision (c) or (d), any person who, since July 1, 1944, has been, or is hereafter convicted in any other court, including any state, federal, or military court, of any offense that, if committed or attempted in this state, based on the elements of the convicted offense or facts admitted by the person or found true by the trier of fact or stipulated facts in the record of military proceedings, would have been punishable as one or more of the offenses described in subdivision (c) of Section 290, including offenses in which the person was a principal, as defined in Section 31.

(b) Any person ordered by any other court, including any state, federal, or military court, to register as a sex offender for any offense, if the court found at the time of conviction or sentencing that the person committed the offense as a result of sexual compulsion or for purposes of sexual gratification.

(c) Except as provided in subdivision (d), any person who would be required to register while residing in the state of conviction for a sex offense committed in that state.

(d) Notwithstanding any other law, a person convicted in another state of an offense similar to one of the following offenses who is required to register in the state of conviction shall not be required to register in California unless the out-of-state offense, based on the elements of the conviction offense or proven or stipulated facts in the record of conviction, contains all of the elements of a registerable California offense described in subdivision (c) of Section 290:

    (1) Indecent exposure, pursuant to Section 314.

    (2) Unlawful sexual intercourse, pursuant to Section 261.5.

    (3) Incest, pursuant to Section 285.

    (4) Sodomy, pursuant to Section 286, or oral copulation, pursuant to Section 287 or former Section 288a, provided that the offender notifies the Department of Justice that the sodomy or oral copulation conviction was for conduct between consenting adults, as described in Section 290.019, and the department is able, upon the exercise of reasonable diligence, to verify that fact.

    (5) Pimping, pursuant to Section 266h, or pandering, pursuant to Section 266i.

Amended by Stats 2018 ch 423 (SB 1494),s 53, eff. 1/1/2019.

Amended by Stats 2011 ch 362 (SB 622),s 1, eff. 1/1/2012.

Added by Stats 2007 ch 579 (SB 172),s 13, eff. 10/13/2007.

See Stats 2011 ch 362 (SB 622), s 2.

Section 290.006 - Registration if offense committed as result of sexual compulsion or for purposes of sexual gratification; tier registration

(a) Any person ordered by any court to register pursuant to the act, who is not required to register pursuant to Section 290, shall so register, if the court finds at the time of conviction or sentencing that the person committed the offense as a result of sexual compulsion or for purposes of sexual gratification. The court shall state on the record the reasons for its findings and the reasons for requiring registration.

(b) The person shall register as a tier one offender in accordance with paragraph (1) of subdivision (d) of Section 290, unless the court finds the person should register as a tier two or tier three offender and states on the record the reasons for its finding.

(c) In determining whether to require the person to register as a tier two or tier three offender, the court shall consider all of the following:

(1) The nature of the registerable offense.

(2) The age and number of victims, and whether any victim was personally unknown to the person at the time of the offense. A victim is personally unknown to the person for purposes of this paragraph if the victim was known to the offender for less than 24 hours.

(3) The criminal and relevant noncriminal behavior of the person before and after conviction for the registerable offense.

(4) Whether the person has previously been arrested for, or convicted of, a sexually motivated offense.

(5) The person's current risk of sexual or violent reoffense, including the person's risk level on the SARATSO static risk assessment instrument, and, if available from past supervision for a sexual offense, the person's risk level on the SARATSO dynamic and violence risk assessment instruments.

(d) This section shall become operative on January 1, 2021.

Amended by Stats 2020 ch 79 (SB 145),s 4, eff. 1/1/2021.

Added by Stats 2017 ch 541 (SB 384),s 4, eff. 1/1/2018.

Section 290.007 - Registration unless person obtains certificate of rehabilitation and is entitled to relief from registration

A person required to register pursuant to any provision of the Act shall register in accordance with the Act, regardless of whether the person's conviction has been dismissed pursuant to Section 1203.4, unless the person obtains a certificate of rehabilitation and is entitled to relief from registration pursuant to Section 290.5, or is exonerated pursuant to subdivision (e) of Section 3007.05 of the conviction requiring registration and the person is not otherwise required to register.

Amended by Stats 2018 ch 979 (SB 1050),s 1, eff. 1/1/2019.

Added by Stats 2007 ch 579 (SB 172),s 15, eff. 10/13/2007.

Section 290.008 - Registration of person adjudicated ward of juvenile court after discharge or parole

(a) Any person who, on or after January 1, 1986, is discharged or paroled from the Department of Corrections and Rehabilitation to the custody of which they were committed after having been adjudicated a ward of the juvenile court pursuant to Section 602 of the Welfare and Institutions Code because of the commission or attempted commission of any offense described in subdivision (c) shall register in accordance with the Act unless the duty to register is terminated pursuant to Section 290.5 or as otherwise provided by law.

(b) Any person who is discharged or paroled from a facility in another state that is equivalent to the Division of Juvenile Justice, to the custody of which they were committed because of an offense which, if committed or attempted in this state, would have been punishable as one or more of the offenses described in subdivision (c) shall register in accordance with the Act.

(c) Any person described in this section who committed an offense in violation of any of the following provisions shall be required to register pursuant to the Act:

(1) Assault with intent to commit rape, sodomy, oral copulation, or any violation of Section 264.1, 288, or 289 under Section 220.

(2) Any offense defined in paragraph (1), (2), (3), (4), or (6) of subdivision (a) of Section 261, Section 264.1, 266c, or 267, paragraph (1) of subdivision (b) of, or subdivision (c) or (d) of, Section 286, paragraph (1) of subdivision (b) of, or subdivision (c) or (d) of, Section 287, Section 288 or 288.5, paragraph (1) of subdivision (b) of, or subdivision (c) or (d) of, former Section 288a, subdivision (a) of Section 289, or Section 647.6.

(3) A violation of Section 207 or 209 committed with the intent to violate Section 261, 286, 287, 288, or 289, or former Section 288a.

(d)

(1) A tier one juvenile offender is subject to registration for a minimum of five years. A person is a tier one juvenile offender if the person is required to register after being adjudicated as a ward of the court and discharged or paroled from the Department of Corrections and Rehabilitation for an offense listed in subdivision (c) that is not a serious or violent felony as described in subdivision (c) of Section 667.5 or subdivision (c) of Section 1192.7.

(2) A tier two juvenile offender is subject to registration for a minimum of 10 years. A person is a tier two juvenile offender if the person is required to register after being adjudicated as a ward of the court and discharged or paroled from the Department of Corrections and Rehabilitation for an offense listed in subdivision (c) that is a serious or violent felony as described in subdivision (c) of Section 667.5 or subdivision (c) of Section 1192.7.

(3) A person who is required to register as a sex offender pursuant to this section may file a petition for termination from the sex offender registry in the juvenile court in the county in which they are registered at the expiration of their mandated minimum registration period, pursuant to Section 290.5.

(e) Prior to discharge or parole from the Department of Corrections and Rehabilitation, any person who is subject to registration under this section shall be informed of the duty to register under the procedures set forth in the Act. Department officials shall transmit the required forms and information to the Department of Justice.

(f) All records specifically relating to the registration in the custody of the Department of Justice, law enforcement agencies, and other agencies or public officials shall be destroyed when the person who is required to register has their records sealed under the procedures set forth in Section 781 of the Welfare and Institutions Code. This section shall not be construed as requiring the destruction of other criminal offender or juvenile records relating to the case that are maintained by the Department of Justice, law enforcement agencies, the juvenile court, or other agencies and public officials unless ordered by a court under Section 781 of the Welfare and Institutions Code.

(g) This section shall become operative on January 1, 2021.

(h) For purposes of this section, a discharged person shall include all of the following:

(1) A ward in the custody of the Department of Corrections and Rehabilitation, Division of Juvenile Justice on or after July 1, 2022, who, prior to discharge, is returned by the division or the chief probation officer of the county to the court of jurisdiction for alternative disposition, specifically due to the statutorily required closure of the division. The division shall inform the ward of the duty to register prior to the ward being returned to the court.

(2) A patient described in Section 1732.10 of the Welfare and Institutions Code. The division shall inform the patient of the duty to register immediately prior to closure of the division.

(3) A person described in Section 1732.9 of the Welfare and Institutions Code. The Department of Corrections and Rehabilitation shall inform the person of the duty to register immediately prior to the person being returned to the court of jurisdiction.

(i) The court of jurisdiction shall establish the point at which the ward described in subdivision (h) is required to register and notify the Department of Justice of its decision.

Amended by Stats 2022 ch 771 (AB 160),s 13, eff. 9/29/2022.

Amended by Stats 2018 ch 423 (SB 1494),s 55, eff. 1/1/2019.

Added by Stats 2017 ch 541 (SB 384),s 6, eff. 1/1/2018.

Section 290.009 - Registration of person enrolled as student or employee at institution of higher learning

Any person required to register under the Act who is enrolled as a student or is an employee or carries on a vocation, with or without compensation, at an institution of higher learning in this state, shall register pursuant to the provisions of the Act.

Added by Stats 2007 ch 579 (SB 172),s 17, eff. 10/13/2007.

Section 290.010 - Registration at addresses where person regularly resides

If the person who is registering has more than one residence address at which he or she regularly resides, he or she shall register in accordance with the Act in each of the jurisdictions in which he or she regularly resides, regardless of the number of days or nights spent there. If all of the addresses are within the same jurisdiction, the person shall provide the registering authority with all of the addresses where he or she regularly resides.

Added by Stats 2007 ch 579 (SB 172),s 18, eff. 10/13/2007.

Section 290.011 - Registration of transient

Every person who is required to register pursuant to the act who is living as a transient shall be required to register for the rest of his or her life as follows:

(a) He or she shall register, or reregister if the person has previously registered, within five working days from release from incarceration, placement or commitment, or release on probation, pursuant to subdivision (b) of Section 290, except that if the person previously registered as a transient less than 30 days from the date of his or her release from incarceration, he or she does not need to reregister as a transient until his or her next required 30-day update of registration. If a transient convicted in another jurisdiction enters the state, he or she shall register within five working days of coming into California with the chief of police of the city in which he or she is present or the sheriff of the county if he or she is present in an unincorporated area or city that has no police department. If a transient is not physically present in any one jurisdiction for five consecutive working days, he or she shall register in the jurisdiction in which he or she is physically present on the fifth working day following release, pursuant to subdivision (b) of Section 290. Beginning on or before the 30th day following initial registration upon release, a transient shall reregister no less than once every 30 days thereafter. A transient shall register with the chief of police of the city in which he or she is physically present within that 30-day period, or the sheriff of the county if he or she is physically present in an unincorporated area or city that has no police department, and additionally, with the chief of police of a campus of the University of California, the California State University, or community college if he or she is physically present upon the campus or in any of its facilities. A transient shall reregister no less than once every 30 days regardless of the length of time he or she has been physically present in the particular jurisdiction in which he or she reregisters. If a transient fails to reregister within any 30-day period, he or she may be prosecuted in any jurisdiction in which he or she is physically present.

(b) A transient who moves to a residence shall have five working days within which to register at that address, in accordance with subdivision (b) of Section 290. A person registered at a residence address in accordance with that provision who becomes transient shall have five working days within which to reregister as a transient in accordance with subdivision (a).

(c) Beginning on his or her first birthday following registration, a transient shall register annually, within five working days of his or her birthday, to update his or her registration with the entities described in subdivision (a). A transient shall register in whichever jurisdiction he or she is physically present on that date. At the 30-day updates and the annual update, a transient shall provide current information as required on the Department of Justice annual update form, including the information described in paragraphs (1) to (3), inclusive, of subdivision (a) of Section 290.015, and the information specified in subdivision (d).

(d) A transient shall, upon registration and reregistration, provide current information as required on the Department of Justice registration forms, and shall also list the places where he or she sleeps, eats, works, frequents, and engages in leisure activities. If a transient changes or adds to the places listed on the form during the 30-day period, he or she does not need to report the new place or places until the next required reregistration.

(e) Failure to comply with the requirement of reregistering every 30 days following initial registration pursuant to subdivision (a) shall be punished in accordance with subdivision (g) of Section 290.018. Failure to comply with any other requirement of this section shall be punished in accordance with either subdivision (a) or (b) of Section 290.018.

(f) A transient who moves out of state shall inform, in person, the chief of police in the city in which he or she is physically present, or the sheriff of the county if he or she is physically present in an unincorporated area or city that has no police department, within five working days, of his or her move out of state. The transient shall inform that registering agency of his or her planned destination, residence or transient location out of state, and any plans he or she has to return to California, if known. The law enforcement agency shall, within three days after receipt of this information, forward a copy of the change of location information to the Department of Justice. The department shall forward appropriate registration data to the law enforcement agency having local jurisdiction of the new place of residence or location.

(g) For purposes of the act, "transient" means a person who has no residence. "Residence" means one or more addresses at which a person regularly resides, regardless of the number of days or nights spent there, such as a shelter or structure that can be located by a street address, including, but not limited to, houses, apartment buildings, motels, hotels, homeless shelters, and recreational and other vehicles.

(h) The transient registrant's duty to update his or her registration no less than every 30 days shall begin with his or her second transient update following the date this section became effective.

Amended by Stats 2010 ch 328 (SB 1330),s 153, eff. 1/1/2011.

Amended by Stats 2009 ch 35 (SB 174),s 6, eff. 1/1/2010.

Added by Stats 2007 ch 579 (SB 172),s 19, eff. 10/13/2007.

Section 290.012 - Annual registration; verification of address and place of employment

(a) Beginning on his or her first birthday following registration or change of address, the person shall be required to register annually, within five working days of his or her birthday, to update his or her registration with the entities described in subdivision (b) of Section 290. At the annual update, the person shall provide current information as required on the Department of Justice annual update form, including the information described in paragraphs (1) to (4), inclusive, of subdivision (a) of Section 290.015. The registering agency shall give the registrant a copy of the registration requirements from the Department of Justice form.

(b) In addition, every person who has ever been adjudicated a sexually violent predator, as defined in Section 6600 of the Welfare and Institutions Code, shall, after his or her release from custody, verify his or her address no less than once every 90 days and place of employment, including the name and address of the employer, in a manner established by the Department of Justice. Every person who, as a sexually violent predator, is required to verify his or her registration every 90 days, shall be notified wherever he or she next registers of his or her increased registration obligations. This notice shall be provided in writing by the registering agency or agencies. Failure to receive this notice shall be a defense to the penalties prescribed in subdivision (f) of Section 290.018.

(c) In addition, every person subject to the Act, while living as a transient in California, shall update his or her registration at least every 30 days, in accordance with Section 290.011.

(d) No entity shall require a person to pay a fee to register or update his or her registration pursuant to this section. The registering agency shall submit registrations, including annual updates or changes of address, directly into the Department of Justice California Sex and Arson Registry (CSAR).

Amended by Stats 2016 ch 772 (SB 448),s 2, eff. 1/1/2017.

Amended by Stats 2014 ch 54 (SB 1461),s 11, eff. 1/1/2015.

Amended by Proposition 35, approved by the people of the State of California 11/6/2012, eff. 11/7/2012. .

Added by Stats 2007 ch 579 (SB 172),s 20, eff. 10/13/2007.

Section 290.013 - Change of address

(a) A person who was last registered at a residence address pursuant to the Act who changes his or her residence address, whether within the jurisdiction in which he or she is currently registered or to a new jurisdiction inside or outside the state, shall, in person, within five working days of the move, inform the law enforcement agency or agencies with which he or she last registered of the move, the new address or transient location, if known, and any plans he or she has to return to California.

(b) If the person does not know the new residence address or location at the time of the move, the registrant shall, in person, within five working days of the move, inform the last registering agency or agencies that he or she is moving. The person shall later notify the last registering agency or agencies, in writing, sent by certified or registered mail, of the new address or location within five working days of moving into the new residence address or location, whether temporary or permanent.

(c) The law enforcement agency or agencies shall, within three working days after receipt of this information, forward a copy of the change of address information to the Department of Justice. The Department of Justice shall forward appropriate registration data to the law enforcement agency or agencies having local jurisdiction of the new place of residence.

(d) If the person is being admitted to or released from a Department of Corrections and Rehabilitation facility, a county or local custodial facility, or state mental institution, an official of the place of incarceration, placement, or commitment shall, within 15 working days of both receipt and release of the person, forward the registrant's change of address information to the Department of Justice in a manner prescribed by the department. If the person is being admitted to the facility, the agency need not provide a physical address for the registrant but shall indicate that he or she is serving a period of incarceration or commitment in a facility under the agency's jurisdiction. This subdivision shall apply to persons received in a department facility, county or local custodial facility, or state mental institution on or after January 1, 1999. The Department of Justice shall forward the change of address information to the agency with which the person last registered.

Amended by Stats 2018 ch 811 (AB 1994),s 1, eff. 1/1/2019.

Added by Stats 2007 ch 579 (SB 172),s 21, eff. 10/13/2007.

Section 290.014 - Change of name; change of Internet account

(a) If any person who is required to register pursuant to the Act changes his or her name, the person shall inform, in person, the law enforcement agency or agencies with which he or she is currently registered within five working days. The law enforcement agency or agencies shall forward a copy of this information to the Department of Justice within three working days of its receipt.

(b) If any person who is required to register Internet identifiers pursuant to Section 290.024 adds or changes an Internet identifier, as defined in Section 290.024, the person shall send written notice by mail of the addition or change to the law enforcement agency or agencies with which he or she is currently registered within 30 working days of the addition or change. The law enforcement agency or agencies shall make the information available to the Department of Justice.

Amended by Stats 2016 ch 772 (SB 448),s 3, eff. 1/1/2017.

Amended by Proposition 35, approved by the people of the State of California 11/6/2012, eff. 11/7/2012. .

Added by Stats 2007 ch 579 (SB 172),s 22, eff. 10/13/2007.

Section 290.015 - Registration upon release from incarceration, placement, commitment, or release on probation

(a) A person who is subject to the Act shall register, or reregister if he or she has previously registered, upon release from incarceration, placement, commitment, or release on probation pursuant to subdivision (b) of Section 290. This section shall not apply to a person who is incarcerated for less than 30 days if he or she has registered as required by the Act, he or she returns after incarceration to the last registered address, and the annual update of registration that is required to occur within five working days of his or her birthday, pursuant to subdivision (a) of Section 290.012, did not fall within that incarceration period. The registration shall consist of all of the following:

(1) A statement in writing signed by the person, giving information as shall be required by the Department of Justice and giving the name and address of the person's employer, and the address of the person's place of employment if that is different from the employer's main address.

(2) The fingerprints and a current photograph of the person taken by the registering official.

(3) The license plate number of any vehicle owned by, regularly driven by, or registered in the name of the person.

(4) A list of all Internet identifiers actually used by the person, as required by Section 290.024.

(5) A statement in writing, signed by the person, acknowledging that the person is required to register and update the information in paragraph (4), as required by this chapter.

(6) Notice to the person that, in addition to the requirements of the Act, he or she may have a duty to register in any other state where he or she may relocate.

(7) Copies of adequate proof of residence, which shall be limited to a California driver's license, California identification card, recent rent or utility receipt, printed personalized checks or other recent banking documents showing that person's name and address, or any other information that the registering official believes is reliable. If the person has no residence and no reasonable expectation of obtaining a residence in the foreseeable future, the person shall so advise the registering official and shall sign a statement provided by the registering official stating that fact. Upon presentation of proof of residence to the registering official or a signed statement that the person has no residence, the person shall be allowed to register. If the person claims that he or she has a residence but does not have any proof of residence, he or she shall be allowed to register but shall furnish proof of residence within 30 days of the date he or she is allowed to register.

(b) Within three days thereafter, the registering law enforcement agency or agencies shall forward the statement, fingerprints, photograph, and vehicle license plate number, if any, to the Department of Justice.

(c)

(1) If a person fails to register in accordance with subdivision (a) after release, the district attorney in the jurisdiction where the person was to be paroled or to be on probation may request that a warrant be issued for the person's arrest and shall have the authority to prosecute that person pursuant to Section 290.018.

(2) If the person was not on parole or probation or on postrelease community supervision or mandatory supervision at the time of release, the district attorney in the following applicable jurisdiction shall have the authority to prosecute that person pursuant to Section 290.018:

(A) If the person was previously registered, in the jurisdiction in which the person last registered.

(B) If there is no prior registration, but the person indicated on the Department of Justice notice of sex offender registration requirement form where he or she expected to reside, in the jurisdiction where he or she expected to reside.

(C) If neither subparagraph (A) nor (B) applies, in the jurisdiction where the offense subjecting the person to registration pursuant to this Act was committed.

Amended by Stats 2016 ch 772 (SB 448),s 4, eff. 1/1/2017.

Amended by Proposition 35, approved by the people of the State of California 11/6/2012, eff. 11/7/2012. .

Amended by Stats 2011 ch 363 (SB 756),s 1, eff. 1/1/2012.

Added by Stats 2007 ch 579 (SB 172),s 23, eff. 10/13/2007.

Section 290.016 - Preregistration

(a) On or after January 1, 1998, upon incarceration, placement, or commitment, or prior to release on probation, any person who is required to register under the Act shall preregister. The preregistering official shall be the admitting officer at the place of incarceration, placement, or commitment, or the probation officer if the person is to be released on probation. The preregistration shall consist of all of the following:

(1) A preregistration statement in writing, signed by the person, giving information that shall be required by the Department of Justice.

(2) The fingerprints and a current photograph of the person.

(3) Any person who is preregistered pursuant to this subdivision is required to be preregistered only once.

(b) Within three days thereafter, the preregistering official shall forward the statement, fingerprints, photograph, and vehicle license plate number, if any, to the Department of Justice.

Added by Stats 2007 ch 579 (SB 172),s 24, eff. 10/13/2007.

Section 290.017 - Information as to duty to register

(a) Any person who is released, discharged, or paroled from a jail, state or federal prison, school, road camp, or other institution where he or she was confined, who is required to register pursuant to the Act, shall, prior to discharge, parole, or release, be informed of his or her duty to register under the Act by the official in charge of the place of confinement or hospital, and the official shall require the person to read and sign any form that may be required by the Department of Justice, stating that the duty of the person to register under the Act has been explained to the person. The official in charge of the place of confinement or hospital shall obtain the address where the person expects to reside upon his or her discharge, parole, or release and shall report the address to the Department of Justice. The official shall at the same time forward a current photograph of the person to the Department of Justice.

(b) The official in charge of the place of confinement or hospital shall give one copy of the form to the person and shall send one copy to the Department of Justice and one copy to the appropriate law enforcement agency or agencies having jurisdiction over the place the person expects to reside upon discharge, parole, or release. If the conviction that makes the person subject to the Act is a felony conviction, the official in charge shall, not later than 45 days prior to the scheduled release of the person, send one copy to the appropriate law enforcement agency or agencies having local jurisdiction where the person expects to reside upon discharge, parole, or release; one copy to the prosecuting agency that prosecuted the person; and one copy to the Department of Justice. The official in charge of the place of confinement or hospital shall retain one copy.

(c) Any person who is required to register pursuant to the Act and who is released on probation, shall, prior to release or discharge, be informed of the duty to register under the Act by the probation department, and a probation officer shall require the person to read and sign any form that may be required by the Department of Justice, stating that the duty of the person to register has been explained to him or her. The probation officer shall obtain the address where the person expects to reside upon release or discharge and shall report within three days the address to the Department of Justice. The probation officer shall give one copy of the form to the person, send one copy to the Department of Justice, and forward one copy to the appropriate law enforcement agency or agencies having local jurisdiction where the person expects to reside upon his or her discharge, parole, or release.

(d) Any person who is required to register pursuant to the Act and who is granted conditional release without supervised probation, or discharged upon payment of a fine, shall, prior to release or discharge, be informed of the duty to register under the Act in open court by the court in which the person has been convicted, and the court shall require the person to read and sign any form that may be required by the Department of Justice, stating that the duty of the person to register has been explained to him or her. If the court finds that it is in the interest of the efficiency of the court, the court may assign the bailiff to require the person to read and sign forms under the Act. The court shall obtain the address where the person expects to reside upon release or discharge and shall report within three days the address to the Department of Justice. The court shall give one copy of the form to the person, send one copy to the Department of Justice, and forward one copy to the appropriate law enforcement agency or agencies having local jurisdiction where the person expects to reside upon his or her discharge, parole, or release.

Added by Stats 2007 ch 579 (SB 172),s 25, eff. 10/13/2007.

Section 290.018 - Violation of duty to register

(a) A person who is required to register under the Act based on a misdemeanor conviction or juvenile adjudication who willfully violates any requirement of the act is guilty of a misdemeanor punishable by imprisonment in a county jail not exceeding one year.

(b) Except as provided in subdivisions (f), (h), (i), and (k), a person who is required to register under the act based on a felony conviction or juvenile adjudication who willfully violates any requirement of the act or who has a prior conviction or juvenile adjudication for the offense of failing to register under the act and who subsequently and willfully violates any requirement of the act is guilty of a felony and shall be punished by imprisonment in the state prison for 16 months, or two or three years.

(c) If probation is granted or if the imposition or execution of sentence is suspended, it shall be a condition of the probation or suspension that the person serve at least 90 days in a county jail. The penalty described in subdivision (b) or this subdivision shall apply whether or not the person has been released on parole or has been discharged from parole.

(d) A person determined to be a mentally disordered sex offender or who has been found guilty in the guilt phase of trial for an offense for which registration is required under the act, but who has been found not guilty by reason of insanity in the sanity phase of the trial, or who has had a petition sustained in a juvenile adjudication for an offense for which registration is required pursuant to Section 290.008, but who has been found not guilty by reason of insanity, who willfully violates any requirement of the act is guilty of a misdemeanor and shall be punished by imprisonment in a county jail not exceeding one year. For any second or subsequent willful violation of any requirement of the act, the person is guilty of a felony and shall be punished by imprisonment in the state prison for 16 months, or two or three years.

(e) If, after discharge from parole, the person is convicted of a felony or suffers a juvenile adjudication as specified in this act, he or she shall be required to complete parole of at least one year, in addition to any other punishment imposed under this section. A person convicted of a felony as specified in this section may be granted probation only in the unusual case where the interests of justice would best be served. When probation is granted under this act, the court shall specify on the record and shall enter into the minutes the circumstances indicating that the interests of justice would best be served by the disposition.

(f) A person who has ever been adjudicated a sexually violent predator, as defined in Section 6600 of the Welfare and Institutions Code, and who fails to verify his or her registration every 90 days as required pursuant to subdivision (b) of Section 290.012, shall be punished by imprisonment in the state prison or in a county jail not exceeding one year.

(g) Except as otherwise provided in subdivision (f), a person who is required to register or reregister pursuant to Section 290.011 and willfully fails to comply with the requirement that he or she reregister no less than every 30 days is guilty of a misdemeanor and shall be punished by imprisonment in a county jail for at least 30 days, but not exceeding six months. A person who willfully fails to comply with the requirement that he or she reregister no less than every 30 days shall not be charged with this violation more often than once for a failure to register in any period of 90 days. A person who willfully commits a third or subsequent violation of the requirements of Section 290.011 that he or she reregister no less than every 30 days shall be punished in accordance with either subdivision (a) or (b).

(h) A person who fails to provide proof of residence as required by paragraph (7) of subdivision (a) of Section 290.015, regardless of the offense upon which the duty to register is based, is guilty of a misdemeanor punishable by imprisonment in a county jail not exceeding six months.

(i) A person who fails to provide his or her Internet identifiers, as required by paragraph (4) of subdivision (a) of Section 290.015, regardless of the offense upon which the duty to register is based, is guilty of a misdemeanor punishable in a county jail not exceeding six months.

(j) A person who is required to register under the act who willfully violates any requirement of the act is guilty of a continuing offense as to each requirement he or she violated.

(k) In addition to any other penalty imposed under this section, the failure to provide information required on registration and reregistration forms of the Department of Justice, or the provision of false information, is a crime punishable by imprisonment in a county jail for a period not exceeding one year. This subdivision shall not be construed to limit or prevent prosecution under any applicable law.

(l) Whenever a person is released on parole or probation and is required to register under the act but fails to do so within the time prescribed, the parole authority or the court, as the case may be, shall order the parole or probation of the person revoked. For purposes of this subdivision, "parole authority" has the same meaning as described in Section 3000.

Amended by Stats 2016 ch 772 (SB 448),s 6, eff. 1/1/2017.
Amended by Stats 2011 ch 39 (AB 117),s 68, eff. 6/30/2011.
Amended by Stats 2011 ch 39 (AB 117),s 13, eff. 6/30/2011.
Amended by Stats 2011 ch 15 (AB 109),s 318, eff. 4/4/2011, but operative no earlier than October 1, 2011, and only upon creation of a community corrections grant program to assist in implementing this act and upon an appropriation to fund the grant program.
Amended by Stats 2009 ch 60 (SB 668),s 1, eff. 1/1/2010.
Added by Stats 2007 ch 579 (SB 172),s 26, eff. 10/13/2007.

Section 290.019 - Conviction for conduct between consenting adults

(a) Notwithstanding any other section in the Act, a person who was convicted before January 1, 1976, under subdivision (a) of Section 286, or former Section 288a, shall not be required to register pursuant to the Act for that conviction if the conviction was for conduct between consenting adults that was decriminalized by Chapter 71 of the Statutes of 1975 or Chapter 1139 of the Statutes of 1976. The Department of Justice shall remove that person from the California Sex Offender Registry, and the person is discharged from the person's duty to register pursuant to either of the following procedures:

(1) The person submits to the Department of Justice official documentary evidence, including court records or police reports, that demonstrate that the person's conviction pursuant to either of those sections was for conduct between consenting adults that was decriminalized.

(2) The person submits to the department a declaration stating that the person's conviction pursuant to either of those sections was for consensual conduct between adults that has been decriminalized. The declaration shall be confidential and not a public record, and shall include the person's name, address, telephone number, date of birth, and a summary of the circumstances leading to the conviction, including the date of the conviction and county of the occurrence.

(b) The department shall determine whether the person's conviction was for conduct between consensual adults that has been decriminalized. If the conviction was for consensual conduct between adults that has been decriminalized, and the person has no other offenses for which the person is required to register pursuant to the Act, the department shall, within 60 days of receipt of those documents, notify the person that the person is relieved of the duty to register, and shall notify the local law enforcement agency with which the person is registered that the person has been relieved of the duty to register. The local law enforcement agency shall remove the person's registration from its files within 30 days of receipt of notification. If the documentary or other evidence submitted is insufficient to establish the person's claim, the department shall, within 60 days of receipt of those documents, notify the person that the person's claim cannot be established, and that the person shall continue to register pursuant to the Act. The department shall provide, upon the person's request, any information relied upon by the department in making its determination that the person shall continue to register pursuant to the Act. Any person whose claim has been denied by the department pursuant to this subdivision may petition the court to appeal the department's denial of the person's claim.

Amended by Stats 2019 ch 497 (AB 991),s 193, eff. 1/1/2020.
Amended by Stats 2018 ch 423 (SB 1494),s 56, eff. 1/1/2019.
Added by Stats 2007 ch 579 (SB 172),s 27, eff. 10/13/2007.

Section 290.020 - Temporary assignment outside institution

In any case in which a person who would be required to register pursuant to the Act for a felony conviction is to be temporarily sent outside the institution where he or she is confined on any assignment within a city or county including firefighting, disaster control, or of whatever nature the assignment may be, the local law enforcement agency having jurisdiction over the place or places where the assignment shall occur shall be notified within a reasonable time prior to removal from the institution. This section shall not apply to any person who is temporarily released under guard from the institution where he or she is confined.

Added by Stats 2007 ch 579 (SB 172),s 28, eff. 10/13/2007.

Section 290.021 - Inspection of statements, photographs, and fingerprints

Except as otherwise provided by law, the statements, photographs, and fingerprints required by the Act shall not be open to inspection by the public or by any person other than a regularly employed peace officer or other law enforcement officer.

Added by Stats 2007 ch 579 (SB 172),s 29, eff. 10/13/2007.

Section 290.022 - Renovation of VCIN

On or before July 1, 2010, the Department of Justice shall renovate the VCIN to do the following:

(1) Correct all software deficiencies affecting data integrity and include designated data fields for all mandated sex offender data.

(2) Consolidate and simplify program logic, thereby increasing system performance and reducing system maintenance costs.

(3) Provide all necessary data storage, processing, and search capabilities.

(4) Provide law enforcement agencies with full Internet access to all sex offender data and photos.

(5) Incorporate a flexible design structure to readily meet future demands for enhanced system functionality, including public Internet access to sex offender information pursuant to Section 290.46.

Added by Stats 2007 ch 579 (SB 172),s 30, eff. 10/13/2007.

Section 290.023 - Applicability of registration provisions

The registration provisions of the Act are applicable to every person described in the Act, without regard to when his or her crime or crimes were committed or his or her duty to register pursuant to the Act arose, and to every offense described in the Act, regardless of when it was committed.

Added by Stats 2007 ch 579 (SB 172),s 31, eff. 10/13/2007.

Section 290.024 - Registration of Internet identifiers; "Internet identifier" and "private information" defined

For purposes of this chapter:

(a) A person who is convicted of a felony on or after January 1, 2017, requiring registration pursuant to the Act, shall register his or her Internet identifiers if a court determines at the time of sentencing that any of the following apply:

(1) The person used the Internet to collect any private information to identify the victim of the crime to further the commission of the crime.

(2) The person was convicted of a felony pursuant to subdivision (b) or (c) of Section 236.1 and used the Internet to traffic the victim of the crime.

(3) The person was convicted of a felony pursuant to Chapter 7.5 (commencing with Section 311) and used the Internet to prepare, publish, distribute, send, exchange, or download the obscene matter or matter depicting a minor engaging in sexual conduct, as defined in subdivision (d) of Section 311.4.

(b) For purposes of this chapter:

(1) "Internet identifier" means any electronic mail address or user name used for instant messaging or social networking that is actually used for direct communication between users on the Internet in a manner that makes the communication not accessible to the general public. "Internet identifier" does not include Internet passwords, date of birth, social security number, or PIN number.

(2) "Private information" means any information that identifies or describes an individual, including, but not limited to, his or her name; electronic mail, chat, instant messenger, social networking, or similar name used for Internet communication; social security number; account numbers; passwords; personal identification numbers; physical description; physical location; home address; home telephone number; education; financial matters; medical or employment history; and statements made by, or attributed to, the individual.
Amended by Stats 2016 ch 772 (SB 448),s 7, eff. 1/1/2017.
Enacted by Proposition 35, approved by the people of the State of California 11/6/2012, eff. 11/7/2012. .

Section 290.01 - Registration with campus police department

(a)

(1) Commencing October 28, 2002, every person required to register pursuant to Sections 290 to 290.009, inclusive, of the Sex Offender Registration Act who is enrolled as a student of any university, college, community college, or other institution of higher learning, or is, with or without compensation, a full-time or part-time employee of that university, college, community college, or other institution of higher learning, or is carrying on a vocation at the university, college, community college, or other institution of higher learning, for more than 14 days, or for an aggregate period exceeding 30 days in a calendar year, shall, in addition to the registration required by the Sex Offender Registration Act, register with the campus police department within five working days of commencing enrollment or employment at that university, college, community college, or other institution of higher learning, on a form as may be required by the Department of Justice. The terms "employed or carries on a vocation" include employment whether or not financially compensated, volunteered, or performed for government or educational benefit. The registrant shall also notify the campus police department within five working days of ceasing to be enrolled or employed, or ceasing to carry on a vocation, at the university, college, community college, or other institution of higher learning.

(2) For purposes of this section, a campus police department is a police department of the University of California, California State University, or California Community College, established pursuant to Section 72330, 89560, or 92600 of the Education Code, or is a police department staffed with deputized or appointed personnel with peace officer status as provided in Section 830.6 of the Penal Code and is the law enforcement agency with the primary responsibility for investigating crimes occurring on the college or university campus on which it is located.

(b) If the university, college, community college, or other institution of higher learning has no campus police department, the registrant shall instead register pursuant to subdivision (a) with the police of the city in which the campus is located or the sheriff of the county in which the campus is located if the campus is located in an unincorporated area or in a city that has no police department, on a form as may be required by the Department of Justice. The requirements of subdivisions (a) and (b) are in addition to the requirements of the Sex Offender Registration Act.

(c) A first violation of this section is a misdemeanor punishable by a fine not to exceed one thousand dollars ($1,000). A second violation of this section is a misdemeanor punishable by imprisonment in a county jail for not more than six months, by a fine not to exceed one thousand dollars ($1,000), or by both that imprisonment and fine. A third or subsequent violation of this section is a misdemeanor punishable by imprisonment in a county jail for not more than one year, by a fine not exceeding one thousand dollars ($1,000), or by both that imprisonment and fine.

(d)

(1)

(A) The following information regarding a registered sex offender on campus as to whom information shall not be made available to the public via the Internet Web site as provided in Section 290.46 may be released to members of the campus community by any campus police department or, if the university, college, community college, or other institution of higher learning has no police department, the police department or sheriff's department with jurisdiction over the campus, and any employees of those agencies, as required by Section 1092(f)(1)(I) of Title 20 of the United States Code:

(i) The offender's full name.
(ii) The offender's known aliases.
(iii) The offender's gender.
(iv) The offender's race.
(v) The offender's physical description.
(vi) The offender's photograph.
(vii) The offender's date of birth.
(viii) Crimes resulting in registration under Section 290.
(ix) The date of last registration or reregistration.

(B) The authority provided in this subdivision is in addition to the authority of a peace officer or law enforcement agency to provide information about a registered sex offender pursuant to Section 290.45, and exists notwithstanding Section 290.021 or any other provision of law.

(2) Any law enforcement entity and employees of any law enforcement entity listed in paragraph (1) shall be immune from civil or criminal liability for good faith conduct under this subdivision.

(3) Nothing in this subdivision shall be construed to authorize campus police departments or, if the university, college, community college, or other institution has no police department, the police department or sheriff's department with jurisdiction over the campus, to make disclosures about registrants intended to reach persons beyond the campus community.

(4)

(A) Before being provided any information by an agency pursuant to this subdivision, a member of the campus community who requests that information shall sign a statement, on a form provided by the Department of Justice, stating that he or she is not a registered sex offender, that he or she understands the purpose of the release of information is to allow members of the campus community to protect themselves and their children from sex offenders, and that he or she understands it is unlawful to use information obtained pursuant to this subdivision to commit a crime against any registrant or to engage in illegal discrimination or harassment of any registrant. The signed statement shall be maintained in a file in the agency's office for a minimum of five years.

(B) An agency disseminating printed information pursuant to this subdivision shall maintain records of the means and dates of dissemination for a minimum of five years.

(5) For purposes of this subdivision, "campus community" means those persons present at, and those persons regularly frequenting, any place associated with an institution of higher education, including campuses; administrative and educational offices; laboratories; satellite facilities owned or utilized by the institution for educational instruction, business, or institutional events; and public areas contiguous to any campus or facility that are regularly frequented by students, employees, or volunteers of the campus.

Amended by Stats 2007 ch 579 (SB 172),s 32, eff. 10/13/2007.

Amended by Stats 2005 ch 722 (AB 1323),s 4, eff. 10/7/2005.

Amended by Stats 2004 ch 405 (SB 1796), s 7, eff. 1/1/2005.

Amended by Stats 2003 ch 634 (AB 1313), eff. 9/30/2003.

Added by Stats 2001 ch 544 (AB 4), s 2, eff. 1/1/2002.

Section 290.02 - Identification of names of persons required to register

(a) Notwithstanding any other law, the Department of Justice shall identify the names of persons required to register pursuant to Section 290 from a list of persons provided by the requesting agency, and provide those names and other information necessary to verify proper identification, to any state governmental entity responsible for authorizing or providing publicly funded prescription drugs or other therapies to treat erectile dysfunction of those persons. State governmental entities shall use information received pursuant to this section to protect public safety by preventing the use of prescription drugs or other therapies to treat erectile dysfunction by convicted sex offenders.

(b) Use or disclosure of the information disclosed pursuant to this section is prohibited for any purpose other than that authorized by this section or Section 14133.225 of the Welfare and Institutions Code. The Department of Justice may establish a fee for requests, including all actual and reasonable costs associated with the service.

(c) Notwithstanding any other provision of law, any state governmental entity that is responsible for authorizing or providing publicly funded prescription drugs or other therapies to treat erectile dysfunction may use the sex offender database authorized by Section 290.46 to protect public safety by preventing the use of those drugs or therapies for convicted sex offenders.

Added by Stats 2005 ch 469 (AB 522),s 2, eff. 10/4/2005.

Section 290.03 - Legislative findings and declarations

(a) The Legislature finds and declares that a comprehensive system of risk assessment, supervision, monitoring and containment for registered sex offenders residing in California communities is necessary to enhance public safety and reduce the risk of recidivism posed by these offenders. The Legislature further affirms and incorporates the following findings and declarations, previously reflected in its enactment of "Megan's Law":

(1) Sex offenders pose a potentially high risk of committing further sex offenses after release from incarceration or commitment, and the protection of the public from reoffending by these offenders is a paramount public interest.

(2) It is a compelling and necessary public interest that the public have information concerning persons convicted of offenses involving unlawful sexual behavior collected pursuant to Sections 290 and 290.4 to allow members of the public to adequately protect themselves and their children from these persons.

(3) Persons convicted of these offenses involving unlawful sexual behavior have a reduced expectation of privacy because of the public's interest in public safety.

(4) In balancing the offenders' due process and other rights against the interests of public security, the Legislature finds that releasing information about sex offenders under the circumstances specified in the Sex Offender Punishment, Control, and Containment Act of 2006 will further the primary government interest of protecting vulnerable populations from potential harm.

(5) The registration of sex offenders, the public release of specified information about certain sex offenders pursuant to Sections 290 and 290.4, and public notice of the presence of certain high risk sex offenders in communities will further the governmental interests of public safety and public scrutiny of the criminal and mental health systems that deal with these offenders.

(6) To protect the safety and general welfare of the people of this state, it is necessary to provide for continued registration of sex offenders, for the public release of specified information regarding certain more serious sex offenders, and for community notification regarding high risk sex offenders who are about to be released from custody or who already reside in communities in this state. This policy of authorizing the release of necessary and relevant information about serious and high risk sex offenders to members of the general public is a means of assuring public protection and shall not be construed as punitive.

(7) The Legislature also declares, however, that in making information available about certain sex offenders to the public, it does not intend that the information be used to inflict retribution or additional punishment on any person convicted of a sex offense. While the Legislature is aware of the possibility of misuse, it finds that the dangers to the public of nondisclosure far outweigh the risk of possible misuse of the information. The Legislature is further aware of studies in Oregon and Washington indicating that community notification laws and public release of similar information in those states have resulted in little criminal misuse of the information and that the enhancement to public safety has been significant.

(b) In enacting the Sex Offender Punishment, Control, and Containment Act of 2006, the Legislature hereby creates a standardized, statewide system to identify, assess, monitor and contain known sex offenders for the purpose of reducing the risk of recidivism posed by these offenders, thereby protecting victims and potential victims from future harm.
Added by Stats 2006 ch 337 (SB 1128),s 12, eff. 9/20/2006.

Section 290.04 - State-Authorized Risk Assessment Tool for Sex Offenders (SARATSO)

(a)

(1) The sex offender risk assessment tools authorized by this section for use with selected populations shall be known, with respect to each population, as the State-Authorized Risk Assessment Tool for Sex Offenders (SARATSO). If a SARATSO has not been selected for a given population pursuant to this section, no duty to administer the SARATSO elsewhere in this code shall apply with respect to that population. Every person required to register as a sex offender shall be subject to assessment with the SARATSO as set forth in this section and elsewhere in this code.

(2) A representative of the Department of Corrections and Rehabilitation, in consultation with a representative of the State Department of State Hospitals and a representative of the Attorney General's office, shall comprise the SARATSO Review Committee. The purpose of the committee, which shall be staffed by the Department of Corrections and Rehabilitation, shall be to ensure that the SARATSO reflects the most reliable, objective, and well-established protocols for predicting sex offender risk of recidivism, has been scientifically validated and cross validated, and is, or is reasonably likely to be, widely accepted by the courts. The committee shall consult with experts in the fields of risk assessment and the use of actuarial instruments in predicting sex offender risk, sex offending, sex offender treatment, mental health, and law, as it deems appropriate.

(b)

(1) Commencing January 1, 2007, the SARATSO for adult males required to register as sex offenders shall be the STATIC-99 risk assessment scale, which shall be the SARATSO static tool for adult males.

(2) The SARATSO Review Committee shall determine whether the STATIC-99 should be supplemented with an empirically derived instrument that measures dynamic risk factors or whether the STATIC-99 should be replaced as the SARATSO with a different risk assessment tool. The SARATSO Review Committee shall select an empirically derived instrument that measures dynamic risk factors and an empirically derived instrument that measures risk of future violence. The selected instruments shall be the SARATSO dynamic tool for adult males and the SARATSO future violence tool for adult males. If the committee unanimously agrees on changes to be made to a designated SARATSO, it shall advise the Governor and the Legislature of the changes, and the Department of Corrections and Rehabilitation shall post the decision on its Internet Web site. Sixty days after the decision is posted, the selected tool shall become the SARATSO for adult males.

(c) On or before July 1, 2007, the SARATSO Review Committee shall research risk assessment tools for adult females required to register as sex offenders. If the committee unanimously agrees on an appropriate risk assessment tool to be used to assess this population, it shall advise the Governor and the Legislature of the selected tool, and the State Department of Mental Health shall post the decision on its Internet Web site. Sixty days after the decision is posted, the selected tool shall become the SARATSO for adult females.

(d) On or before July 1, 2007, the SARATSO Review Committee shall research risk assessment tools for male juveniles required to register as sex offenders. If the committee unanimously agrees on an appropriate risk assessment tool to be used to assess this population, it shall advise the Governor and the Legislature of the selected tool, and the State Department of Mental Health shall post the decision on its Internet Web site. Sixty days after the decision is posted, the selected tool shall become the SARATSO for male juveniles.

(e) On or before July 1, 2007, the SARATSO Review Committee shall research risk assessment tools for female juveniles required to register as sex offenders. If the committee unanimously agrees on an appropriate risk assessment tool to be used to assess this population, it shall advise the Governor and the Legislature of the selected tool, and the State Department of Mental Health shall post the decision on its Internet Web site. Sixty days after the decision is posted, the selected tool shall become the SARATSO for female juveniles.

(f) The committee shall periodically evaluate the SARATSO static, dynamic, and risk of future violence tools for each specified population. If the committee unanimously agrees on a change to the SARATSO for any population, it shall advise the Governor and the Legislature of the selected tool, and the Department of Corrections and Rehabilitation shall post the decision on its Internet Web site. Sixty days after the decision is posted, the selected tool shall become the SARATSO for that population.

(g) The committee shall perform other functions consistent with the provisions of this act or as may be otherwise required by law, including, but not limited to, defining tiers of risk based on the SARATSO. The committee shall be immune from liability for good faith conduct under this act.
Amended by Stats 2012 ch 24 (AB 1470),s 15, eff. 6/27/2012.
Amended by Stats 2011 ch 357 (AB 813),s 2, eff. 1/1/2012.
Amended by Stats 2010 ch 219 (AB 1844),s 10, eff. 9/9/2010.
Amended by Stats 2009 ch 582 (SB 325),s 1, eff. 1/1/2010.
Amended by Stats 2007 ch 579 (SB 172),s 33, eff. 10/13/2007.
Amended by Stats 2006 ch 886 (AB 1849),s 1, eff. 9/30/2006.
Added by Stats 2006 ch 337 (SB 1128),s 13, eff. 9/20/2006.
Added by Stats 2006 ch 336 (SB 1178),s 1, eff. 9/20/2006.

Section 290.05 - SARATSO Training Committee

(a) The SARATSO Training Committee shall be comprised of a representative of the State Department of State Hospitals, a representative of the Department of Corrections and Rehabilitation, a representative of the Attorney General's Office, and a representative of the Chief Probation Officers of California.

(b) On or before January 1, 2008, the SARATSO Training Committee, in consultation with the Corrections Standards Authority and the Commission on Peace Officer Standards and Training, shall develop a training program for persons authorized by this code to administer the static SARATSO, as set forth in Section 290.04.

(c)

(1) The Department of Corrections and Rehabilitation shall be responsible for overseeing the training of persons who will administer the static SARATSO pursuant to paragraph (1) or (2) of subdivision (a) of Section 290.06.

(2) The State Department of State Hospitals shall be responsible for overseeing the training of persons who will administer the static SARATSO pursuant to paragraph (3) of subdivision (a) of Section 290.06.

(3) The Correction Standards Authority shall be responsible for developing standards for the training of persons who will administer the static SARATSO pursuant to paragraph (5) or (6) of subdivision (a) of Section 290.06.

(4) The Commission on Peace Officer Standards and Training shall be responsible for developing standards for the training of persons who will administer the static SARATSO pursuant to subdivision (b) of Section 290.06.

(d) The training shall be conducted by experts in the field of risk assessment and the use of actuarial instruments in predicting sex offender risk. Subject to requirements established by the committee, the Department of Corrections and Rehabilitation, the State Department of State Hospitals, probation departments, and authorized local law enforcement agencies shall designate key persons within their organizations to attend training and, as authorized by the department, to train others within their organizations designated to perform risk assessments as required or authorized by law. Any person who administers the static SARATSO shall receive training no less frequently than every two years.

(e) If the agency responsible for scoring the static SARATSO believes an individual score does not represent the person's true risk level, based on factors in the offender's record, the agency may submit the case to the experts retained by the SARATSO Review Committee to monitor the scoring of the SARATSO. Those experts shall be guided by empirical research in determining whether to raise or lower the risk level. Agencies that score the static SARATSO shall develop a protocol for submission of risk level override requests to the experts retained in accordance with this subdivision.

(f) The static SARATSO may be performed for purposes authorized by statute only by persons trained pursuant to this section. Persons who administer the dynamic SARATSO and the future violence SARATSO shall be trained to administer the dynamic and future violence SARATSO tools as required in Section 290.09. Probation officers or parole agents may be trained by SARATSO experts on the dynamic SARATSO tool and perform assessments on that tool only if authorized by the SARATSO Training Committee to do so after successful completion of training.

Amended by Stats 2012 ch 24 (AB 1470),s 16, eff. 6/27/2012.
Amended by Stats 2010 ch 302 (SB 5),s 3.5, eff. 9/25/2010.
Amended by Stats 2010 ch 219 (AB 1844),s 11, eff. 9/9/2010.
Amended by Stats 2009 ch 582 (SB 325),s 2, eff. 1/1/2010.
Amended by Stats 2007 ch 579 (SB 172),s 34, eff. 10/13/2007.
Amended by Stats 2006 ch 886 (AB 1849),s 2, eff. 9/30/2006.
Added by Stats 2006 ch 337 (SB 1128),s 14, eff. 9/20/2006.
Added by Stats 2006 ch 336 (SB 1178),s 2, eff. 9/20/2006.

Section 290.06 - Administration of SARATSO

The static SARATSO, as set forth in Section 290.04, shall be administered as follows:

(a)

(1) The Department of Corrections and Rehabilitation shall assess every eligible person who is incarcerated in state prison. Whenever possible, the assessment shall take place at least four months, but no sooner than 10 months, prior to release from incarceration.

(2) The department shall assess every eligible person who is on parole if the person was not assessed prior to release from state prison. Whenever possible, the assessment shall take place at least four months, but no sooner than 10 months, prior to termination of parole. The department shall record in a database the risk assessment scores of persons assessed pursuant to this paragraph and paragraph (1), and any risk assessment score that was submitted to the department by a probation officer pursuant to Section 1203.

(3) The department shall assess every person on parole transferred from any other state or by the federal government to this state who has been, or is hereafter convicted in any other court, including any state, federal, or military court, of any offense that, if committed or attempted in this state, would have been punishable as one or more of the offenses described in subdivision (c) of Section 290. The assessment required by this paragraph shall occur no later than 60 days after a determination by the Department of Justice that the person is required to register as a sex offender in California pursuant to Section 290.005.

(4) The State Department of State Hospitals shall assess every eligible person who is committed to that department. Whenever possible, the assessment shall take place at least four months, but no sooner than 10 months, prior to release from commitment. The State Department of State Hospitals shall record in a database the risk assessment scores of persons assessed pursuant to this paragraph and any risk assessment score that was submitted to the department by a probation officer pursuant to Section 1203.

(5) Commencing January 1, 2010, the Department of Corrections and Rehabilitation and the State Department of State Hospitals shall send the scores obtained in accordance with paragraphs (2), (3), and (4) to the Department of Justice not later than 30 days after the date of the assessment. The risk assessment score of an offender shall be made part of his or her file maintained by the Department of Justice as soon as possible without financial impact, but no later than January 1, 2012.

(6) Each probation department shall, prior to sentencing, assess every eligible person as defined in subdivision (c), whether or not a report is prepared pursuant to Section 1203.

(7) Each probation department shall assess every eligible person under its supervision who was not assessed pursuant to paragraph (6). The assessment shall take place prior to the termination of probation, but no later than January 1, 2010.

(b) Eligible persons not assessed pursuant to subdivision (a) may be assessed as follows:

(1) Upon request of the law enforcement agency in the jurisdiction in which the person is registered pursuant to Sections 290 to 290.023, inclusive, the person shall be assessed. The law enforcement agency may enter into a memorandum of understanding with a probation department to perform the assessment. In the alternative, the law enforcement agency may arrange to have personnel trained to perform the risk assessment in accordance with subdivision (d) of Section 290.05.

(2) Eligible persons not assessed pursuant to subdivision (a) may request that a risk assessment be performed. A request form shall be available at registering law enforcement agencies. The person requesting the assessment shall pay a fee for the assessment that shall be sufficient to cover the cost of the assessment. The risk assessment so requested shall be performed either by the probation department, if a memorandum of understanding is established between the law enforcement agency and the probation department, or by personnel who have been trained to perform risk assessment in accordance with subdivision (d) of Section 290.05.

(c) For purposes of this section, "eligible person" means a person who was convicted of an offense that requires him or her to register as a sex offender pursuant to the Sex Offender Registration Act and who is eligible for assessment, pursuant to the official Coding Rules designated for use with the risk assessment instrument by the author of any risk assessment instrument (SARATSO) selected by the SARATSO Review Committee.

(d) Persons authorized to perform risk assessments pursuant to this section, Section 1203, and Section 706 of the Welfare and Institutions Code shall be immune from liability for good faith conduct under this act.

Amended by Stats 2016 ch 59 (SB 1474),s 1, eff. 1/1/2017.
Amended by Stats 2012 ch 24 (AB 1470),s 17, eff. 6/27/2012.
Amended by Stats 2010 ch 710 (SB 1201),s 1.7, eff. 1/1/2011.
Amended by Stats 2010 ch 709 (SB 1062),s 11, eff. 1/1/2011.
Amended by Stats 2010 ch 219 (AB 1844),s 12, eff. 9/9/2010.
Amended by Stats 2009 ch 582 (SB 325),s 3, eff. 1/1/2010.
Amended by Stats 2006 ch 886 (AB 1849),s 3, eff. 9/30/2006.
Added by Stats 2006 ch 337 (SB 1128),s 15, eff. 9/20/2006.
Added by Stats 2006 ch 336 (SB 1178),s 3, eff. 9/20/2006.

Section 290.07 - Access to relevant records

Notwithstanding any other provision of law, a person authorized by statute to administer the State Authorized Risk Assessment Tool for Sex Offenders (SARATSO) and trained pursuant to Section 290.06 or 290.09, and a person acting under authority from the SARATSO Review Committee as an expert to train, monitor, or review scoring by persons who administer the SARATSO pursuant to Section 290.05 or 1203 of this code or Section 706 of the Welfare and Institutions Code, shall be granted access to all relevant records pertaining to a registered sex offender, including, but not limited to, criminal histories, sex offender registration records, police reports, probation and presentencing reports, judicial records and case files, juvenile records, psychological evaluations and psychiatric hospital reports, sexually violent predator treatment program reports, and records that have been sealed by the courts or the Department of Justice. Records and information obtained under this section shall not be subject to the California Public Records Act, Division 10 (commencing with Section 7920.000) of Title 1 of the Government Code.

Amended by Stats 2021 ch 615 (AB 474),s 332, eff. 1/1/2022, op. 1/1/2023.
Amended by Stats 2012 ch 174 (AB 1835),s 1, eff. 1/1/2013.
Amended by Stats 2009 ch 582 (SB 325),s 4, eff. 1/1/2010.
Added by Stats 2006 ch 337 (SB 1128),s 16, eff. 9/20/2006.

Section 290.08 - Retention of records

Every district attorney's office and the Department of Justice shall retain records relating to a person convicted of an offense for which registration is required pursuant to Section 290 for a period of 75 years after disposition of the case.

Added by Stats 2006 ch 337 (SB 1128),s 17, eff. 9/20/2006.

Section 290.09 - Administration of SARATSO dynamic tool and SARATSO future violence tool

On or before July 2012, the SARATSO dynamic tool and the SARATSO future violence tool, as set forth in Section 290.04, shall be administered as follows:

(a)

(1) Every sex offender required to register pursuant to Sections 290 to 290.023, inclusive, shall, while on parole or formal probation, participate in an approved sex offender management program, pursuant to Sections 1203.067 and 3008.

(2) The sex offender management program shall meet the certification requirements developed by the California Sex Offender Management Board pursuant to Section 9003. Probation departments and the Department of Corrections and Rehabilitation shall not employ or contract with, and shall not allow a sex offender to employ or contract with, any individual or entity to provide sex offender evaluation or treatment services pursuant to this section unless the sex offender evaluation or treatment services to be provided by the individual or entity conforms with the standards developed pursuant to Section 9003.

(b)

(1) The sex offender management professionals certified by the California Sex Offender Management Board in accordance with Section 9003 who provide sex offender management programs for any probation department or the Department of Corrections and Rehabilitation shall assess each registered sex offender on formal probation or parole using the SARATSO dynamic tool, when a dynamic risk factor changes, and shall do a final dynamic assessment within six months of the offender's release from supervision. The management professional shall also assess the sex offenders in the program with the SARATSO future violence tool.

(2) The certified sex offender management professional shall, as soon as possible but not later than 30 days after the assessment, provide the person's score on the SARATSO dynamic tool and the future violence tool to the person's parole agent or probation officer. Within five working days of receipt of the score, the parole or probation officer shall send the score to the Department of Justice, and the score shall be accessible to law enforcement through the Department of Justice's Internet Web site for the California Sex and Arson Registry (CSAR).

(c) The certified sex offender management professional shall communicate with the offender's probation officer or parole agent on a regular basis, but at least once a month, about the offender's progress in the program and dynamic risk assessment issues, and shall share pertinent information with the certified polygraph examiner as required.

(d) The SARATSO Training Committee shall provide annual training on the SARATSO dynamic tool and the SARATSO future violence tool. Certified sex offender management professionals shall attend this training once to obtain authorization to perform the assessments, and thereafter attend training updates as required by the SARATSO Training Committee. If a sex offender management professional is certified pursuant to Section 9003 to conduct an approved sex offender management program prior to attending SARATSO training on the dynamic and violent risk assessment tools, he or she shall present to the SARATSO Training Committee proof of training on these tools from a risk assessment expert approved by the SARATSO Training Committee.

Amended by Stats 2011 ch 357 (AB 813),s 3, eff. 1/1/2012.
Amended by Stats 2010 ch 302 (SB 5),s 4, eff. 9/25/2010.
Added by Stats 2010 ch 219 (AB 1844),s 13, eff. 9/9/2010.

Section 290.3 - Fines

(a) Every person who is convicted of any offense specified in subdivision (c) of Section 290 shall, in addition to any imprisonment or fine, or both, imposed for commission of the underlying offense, be punished by a fine of three hundred dollars ($300) upon the first conviction or a fine of five hundred dollars ($500) upon the second and each subsequent conviction, unless the court determines that the defendant does not have the ability to pay the fine. An amount equal to all fines collected pursuant to this subdivision during the preceding month upon conviction of, or upon the forfeiture of bail by, any person arrested for, or convicted of, committing an offense specified in subdivision (c) of Section 290, shall be transferred once a month by the county treasurer to the Controller for deposit in the General Fund. Moneys deposited in the General Fund pursuant to this subdivision shall be transferred by the Controller as provided in subdivision (b).

(b) Except as provided in subdivision (d), out of the moneys deposited pursuant to subdivision (a) as a result of second and subsequent convictions of Section 290, one-third shall first be transferred to the Department of Justice Sexual Habitual Offender Fund, as provided in paragraph (1) of this subdivision. Out of the remainder of all moneys deposited pursuant to subdivision (a), 50 percent shall be transferred to the Department of Justice Sexual Habitual Offender Fund, as provided in paragraph (1), 25 percent shall be transferred to the DNA Identification Fund, as established by Section 76104.6 of the Government Code, and 25 percent shall be allocated equally to counties that maintain a local DNA testing laboratory, as provided in paragraph (2).

(1) Those moneys so designated shall be transferred to the Department of Justice Sexual Habitual Offender Fund created pursuant to paragraph (5) of subdivision (b) of Section 11170 and, when appropriated by the Legislature, shall be used for the purposes of Chapter 9.5 (commencing with Section 13885) and Chapter 10 (commencing with Section 13890) of Title 6 of Part 4 for the purpose of monitoring, apprehending, and prosecuting sexual habitual offenders.

(2) Those moneys so designated shall be allocated equally and distributed quarterly to counties that maintain a local DNA testing laboratory. Before making any allocations under this paragraph, the Controller shall deduct the estimated costs that will be incurred to set up and administer the payment of these funds to the counties. Any funds allocated to a county pursuant to this paragraph shall be used by that county for the exclusive purpose of testing DNA samples for law enforcement purposes.

(c) Notwithstanding any other provision of this section, the Department of Corrections and Rehabilitation may collect a fine imposed pursuant to this section from a person convicted of a violation of any offense listed in subdivision (c) of Section 290, that results in incarceration in a facility under the jurisdiction of the Department of Corrections and Rehabilitation. All moneys collected by the Department of Corrections and Rehabilitation under this subdivision shall be transferred, once a month, to the Controller for deposit in the General Fund, as provided in subdivision (a), for transfer by the Controller, as provided in subdivision (b).

(d) An amount equal to one-third of every first conviction fine collected and one-fifth of every second conviction fine collected pursuant to subdivision (a) shall be transferred to the Department of Corrections and Rehabilitation to help defray the cost of the global positioning system used to monitor sex offender parolees.

Amended by Stats 2008 ch 699 (SB 1241),s 9, eff. 1/1/2009.
Amended by Stats 2007 ch 579 (SB 172),s 35, eff. 10/13/2007.
Amended by Stats 2006 ch 337 (SB 1128),s 18, eff. 9/20/2006.
Amended by Stats 2006 ch 69 (AB 1806),s 27, eff. 7/12/2006.

Section 290.4 - Service to provide public information

(a) The department shall operate a service through which members of the public may provide a list of at least six persons on a form approved by the Department of Justice and inquire whether any of those persons is required to register as a sex offender and is subject to public notification. The Department of Justice shall respond with information on any person as to whom information may be available to the public via the Internet Web site as provided in Section 290.46, to the extent that information may be disclosed pursuant to Section 290.46. The Department of Justice may establish a fee for requests, including all actual and reasonable costs associated with the service.

(b) The income from the operation of the service specified in subdivision (a) shall be deposited in the Sexual Predator Public Information Account within the Department of Justice for the purpose of the implementation of this section by the Department of Justice. The moneys in the account shall consist of income from the operation of the service authorized by subdivision (a), and any other funds made available to the account by the Legislature. Moneys in the account shall be available to the Department of Justice upon appropriation by the Legislature for the purpose specified in subdivision (a).

(c)

(1) Any person who uses information disclosed pursuant to this section to commit a felony shall be punished, in addition and consecutive to, any other punishment, by a five-year term of imprisonment pursuant to subdivision (h) of Section 1170.

(2) Any person who, without authorization, uses information disclosed pursuant to this section to commit a misdemeanor shall be subject to, in addition to any other penalty or fine imposed, a fine of not less than five hundred dollars ($500) and not more than one thousand dollars ($1,000).

(d)

(1) A person is authorized to use information disclosed pursuant to this section only to protect a person at risk.

(2) Except as authorized under paragraph (1) or any other provision of law, use of any information that is disclosed pursuant to this section for purposes relating to any of the following is prohibited:

    (A) Health insurance.

    (B) Insurance.

    (C) Loans.

    (D) Credit.

    (E) Employment.

    (F) Education, scholarships, or fellowships.

    (G) Housing or accommodations.

    (H) Benefits, privileges, or services provided by any business establishment.

(3) This section shall not affect authorized access to, or use of, information pursuant to, among other provisions, Sections 11105 and 11105.3 of this code, Section 226.55 of the Civil Code, Sections 777.5 and 14409.2 of the Financial Code, Sections 1522.01 and 1596.871 of the Health and Safety Code, and Section 432.7 of the Labor Code.

(4)

    (A) Any use of information disclosed pursuant to this section for purposes other than those provided by paragraph (1) or in violation of paragraph (2) shall make the user liable for the actual damages, and any amount that may be determined by a jury or a court sitting without a jury, not exceeding three times the amount of actual damage, and not less than two hundred fifty dollars ($250), and attorney's fees, exemplary damages, or a civil penalty not exceeding twenty-five thousand dollars ($25,000).

    (B) Whenever there is reasonable cause to believe that any person or group of persons is engaged in a pattern or practice of misuse of the service specified in subdivision (a), in violation of paragraph (2), the Attorney General, any district attorney, or city attorney, or any person aggrieved by the misuse of the service is authorized to bring a civil action in the appropriate court requesting preventive relief, including an application for a permanent or temporary injunction, restraining order, or other order against the person or group of persons responsible for the pattern or practice of misuse. The foregoing remedies shall be independent of any other remedies or procedures that may be available to an aggrieved party under other provisions of law, including Part 2 (commencing with Section 43) of Division 1 of the Civil Code.

(e) The Department of Justice and its employees shall be immune from liability for good faith conduct under this section.

(f) The public notification provisions of this section are applicable to every person described in subdivision (a), without regard to when his or her crimes were committed or his or her duty to register pursuant to Section 290 arose, and to every offense subject to public notification pursuant to Section 290.46, regardless of when it was committed.

Amended by Stats 2011 ch 39 (AB 117),s 68, eff. 6/30/2011.

Amended by Stats 2011 ch 15 (AB 109),s 319, eff. 4/4/2011, but operative no earlier than October 1, 2011, and only upon creation of a community corrections grant program to assist in implementing this act and upon an appropriation to fund the grant program.

Amended by Stats 2009 ch 35 (SB 174),s 7, eff. 1/1/2010.

Amended by Stats 2005 ch 722 (AB 1323),s 5, eff. 10/7/2005.

Amended by Stats 2004 ch 731 (SB 1289), s 2, eff. 1/1/2005.

Amended by Stats 2003 ch 634 (AB 1313), eff. 9/30/2003.

Amended by Stats 2002 ch 118 (SB 1965), s 1, eff. 1/1/2003.

Amended by Stats 2000 ch 648 (AB 1340), s 2, eff. 1/1/2001.

Section 290.45 - Providing information to public; community notification

(a)

(1) Notwithstanding any other law, and except as provided in paragraph (2), any designated law enforcement entity may provide information to the public about a person required to register as a sex offender pursuant to Section 290, by whatever means the entity deems appropriate, when necessary to ensure the public safety based upon information available to the entity concerning that specific person's current risk of sexual or violent reoffense, including, but not limited to, the person's static, dynamic, and violence risk levels on the SARATSO risk tools described in subdivision (f) of Section 290.04.

(2) The law enforcement entity shall include, with the disclosure, a statement that the purpose of the release of information is to allow members of the public to protect themselves and their children from sex offenders.

(3) Community notification by way of an Internet Web site shall be governed by Section 290.46, and a designated law enforcement entity may not post on an Internet Web site any information identifying an individual as a person required to register as a sex offender except as provided in that section unless there is a warrant outstanding for that person's arrest.

(b) Information that may be provided pursuant to subdivision (a) may include, but is not limited to, the offender's name, known aliases, gender, race, physical description, photograph, date of birth, address, which shall be verified prior to publication, description and license plate number of the offender's vehicles or vehicles the offender is known to drive, type of victim targeted by the offender, relevant parole or probation conditions, crimes resulting in classification under this section, and date of release from confinement, but excluding information that would identify the victim. It shall not include any Internet identifier submitted pursuant to this chapter.

(c)

(1) The designated law enforcement entity may authorize persons and entities who receive the information pursuant to this section to disclose information to additional persons only if the entity determines that disclosure to the additional persons will enhance the public safety and identifies the appropriate scope of further disclosure. A law enforcement entity may not authorize any disclosure of this information by placing that information on an Internet Web site, and shall not authorize disclosure of Internet identifiers submitted pursuant to this chapter, except as provided in subdivision (h).

(2) A person who receives information from a law enforcement entity pursuant to paragraph (1) may disclose that information only in the manner and to the extent authorized by the law enforcement entity.

(d)

(1) A designated law enforcement entity and its employees shall be immune from liability for good faith conduct under this section.

(2) A public or private educational institution, a day care facility, or a child care custodian described in Section 11165.7, or an employee of a public or private educational institution or day care facility which in good faith disseminates information as authorized pursuant to subdivision (c) shall be immune from civil liability.

(e)

(1) A person who uses information disclosed pursuant to this section to commit a felony shall be punished, in addition and consecutive to any other punishment, by a five-year term of imprisonment pursuant to subdivision (h) of Section 1170.

(2) A person who uses information disclosed pursuant to this section to commit a misdemeanor shall be subject to, in addition to any other penalty or fine imposed, a fine of not less than five hundred dollars ($500) and not more than one thousand dollars ($1,000).

(f) For purposes of this section, "designated law enforcement entity" means the Department of Justice, a district attorney, the Department of Corrections and Rehabilitation, the Division of Juvenile Justice, and every state or local agency expressly authorized by statute to investigate or prosecute law violators.

(g) The public notification provisions of this section are applicable to every person required to register pursuant to Section 290, without regard to when his or her crimes were committed or his or her duty to register pursuant to Section 290 arose, and to each offense described in Section 290, regardless of when it was committed.

(h)

(1) Notwithstanding any other law, a designated law enforcement entity shall only use an Internet identifier submitted pursuant to this chapter, or release that Internet identifier to another law enforcement entity, for the purpose of investigating a sex-related crime, a kidnapping, or human trafficking.

(2) A designated law enforcement entity shall not disclose or authorize persons or entities to disclose an Internet identifier submitted pursuant to this chapter to the public or other persons, except as required by court order.

(i) This section shall become operative on January 1, 2021.

Added by Stats 2017 ch 541 (SB 384),s 8, eff. 1/1/2018.

Section 290.46 - Internet web site

(a)

(1) On or before the dates specified in this section, the Department of Justice shall make available information concerning persons who are required to register pursuant to Section 290 to the public via an internet website as specified in this section. The department shall update the internet website on an ongoing basis. All information identifying the victim by name, birth date, address, or relationship to the registrant shall be excluded from the internet website. The name or address of the person's employer and the listed person's criminal history other than the specific crimes for which the person is required to register shall not be included on the internet website. The internet website shall be translated into languages other than English as determined by the department.

(2)

(A) On or before July 1, 2010, the Department of Justice shall make available to the public, via an internet website as specified in this section, as to any person described in subdivision (b), the following information:

(i) The year of conviction of the person's most recent offense requiring registration pursuant to Section 290.

(ii) The year the person was released from incarceration for that offense. However, no year of conviction shall be made available to the public unless the department also is able to make available the corresponding year of release of incarceration for that offense, and the required notation regarding any subsequent felony.

(B)

(i) Any state facility that releases from incarceration a person who was incarcerated because of a crime for which the person is required to register as a sex offender pursuant to Section 290 shall, within 30 days of release, provide the year of release for the person's most recent offense requiring registration to the Department of Justice in a manner and format approved by the department.

(ii) Any state facility that releases a person who is required to register pursuant to Section 290 from incarceration whose incarceration was for a felony committed subsequently to the offense for which the person is required to register shall, within 30 days of release, advise the Department of Justice of that fact.

(iii) Any state facility that, prior to January 1, 2007, released from incarceration a person who was incarcerated because of a crime for which the person is required to register as a sex offender pursuant to Section 290 shall provide the year of release for the person's most recent offense requiring registration to the Department of Justice in a manner and format approved by the department. The information provided by the Department of Corrections and Rehabilitation shall be limited to information that is currently maintained in an electronic format.

(iv) Any state facility that, prior to January 1, 2007, released a person who is required to register pursuant to Section 290 from incarceration whose incarceration was for a felony committed subsequently to the offense for which the person is required to register shall advise the Department of Justice of that fact in a manner and format approved by the department. The information provided by the Department of Corrections and Rehabilitation shall be limited to information that is currently maintained in an electronic format.

(3) The State Department of State Hospitals shall provide to the Department of Justice the names of all persons committed to its custody pursuant to Article 4 (commencing with Section 6600) of Chapter 2 of Part 2 of Division 6 of the Welfare and Institutions Code, within 30 days of commitment, and shall provide the names of all of those persons released from its custody within five working days of release.

(b)

(1) With respect to a person who has been convicted of the commission or the attempted commission of any of the offenses listed in, or who is otherwise described in, paragraph (2), or who is a tier three offender as described in paragraph (3) of subdivision (d) of Section 290, the Department of Justice shall make available to the public via the internet website the person's name and known aliases, a photograph, a physical description, including gender and race, date of birth, criminal history, prior adjudication as a sexually violent

predator, the address at which the person resides, and any other information that the Department of Justice deems relevant, but not the information excluded pursuant to subdivision (a), except that information about persons required to register as a result of an adjudication as a ward of the juvenile court pursuant to Section 290.008 shall not be made available on the internet website. The department shall also make available to the public via the internet website the person's static SARATSO risk level, if any, and information on an elevated risk level based on the SARATSO future violence tool. Any registrant whose information is listed on the public internet website on January 1, 2022, by the Department of Justice pursuant to this subdivision, may continue to be included on the public internet website while the registrant is placed in the tier-to-be-determined category described in paragraph (5) of subdivision (d) of Section 290.

(2) This subdivision shall apply to the following offenses and offenders:

(A) Section 187 committed in the perpetration, or an attempt to perpetrate, rape or any act punishable under Section 286, 287, 288, or 289, or former Section 288a.

(B) Section 207 committed with intent to violate Section 261, 286, 287, 288, or 289, or former Section 288a.

(C) Section 209 committed with intent to violate Section 261, 286, 287, 288, or 289, or former Section 288a.

(D) Paragraph (2) or (6) of subdivision (a) of Section 261.

(E) Section 264.1.

(F) Section 269.

(G) Subdivision (c) or (d) of Section 286.

(H) Subdivision (a), (b), or (c) of Section 288, provided that the offense is a felony.

(I) Subdivision (c) or (d) of Section 287 or of former Section 288a.

(J) Section 288.3, provided that the offense is a felony.

(K) Section 288.4, provided that the offense is a felony.

(L) Section 288.5.

(M) Subdivision (a) or (j) of Section 289.

(N) Section 288.7.

(O) Any person who has ever been adjudicated a sexually violent predator, as defined in Section 6600 of the Welfare and Institutions Code.

(P) A felony violation of Section 311.1.

(Q) A felony violation of subdivision (b), (c), or (d) of Section 311.2.

(R) A felony violation of Section 311.3.

(S) A felony violation of subdivision (a), (b), or (c) of Section 311.4.

(T) Section 311.10.

(U) A felony violation of Section 311.11.

(V) A tier three offender, as described in paragraph (3) of subdivision (d) of Section 290.

(c)

(1) With respect to a person who has been convicted of the commission or the attempted commission of any of the offenses listed in, or who is otherwise described in, paragraph (2) of subdivision (d) of Section 290 and who is a tier two offender, and with respect to a person who has been convicted of the commission or the attempted commission of Section 647.6, the Department of Justice shall make available to the public via the internet website the person's name and known aliases, a photograph, a physical description, including gender and race, date of birth, criminal history, the community of residence and ZIP Code in which the person resides or the county in which the person is registered as a transient, and any other information that the Department of Justice deems relevant, but not the information excluded pursuant to subdivision (a) or the address at which the person resides, except that information about persons required to register as a result of an adjudication as a ward of the juvenile court pursuant to Section 290.008 shall not be made available on the internet website. Any registrant whose information is listed on the public internet website on January 1, 2022, by the Department of Justice pursuant to this subdivision may continue to be included on the public internet website while the registrant is placed in the tier-to-be-determined category described in paragraph (5) of subdivision (d) of Section 290.

(2) Any registrant whose information was not included on the public internet website on January 1, 2022, and who is placed in the tier-to-be-determined category described in paragraph (5) of subdivision (d) of Section 290 may have the information described in this subdivision made available to the public via the public internet website.

(d)

(1)

(A) An offender who is required to register pursuant to the Sex Offender Registration Act may apply for exclusion from the internet website if the offender demonstrates that the person's only registerable offense is either of the following:

(i) An offense for which the offender successfully completed probation, provided that the offender submits to the department a certified copy of a probation report, presentencing report, report prepared pursuant to Section 288.1, or other official court document that clearly demonstrates that the offender was the victim's parent, stepparent, sibling, or grandparent and that the crime did not involve either oral copulation or penetration of the vagina or rectum of either the victim or the offender by the penis of the other or by any foreign object.

(ii) An offense for which the offender is on probation at the time of the offender's application, provided that the offender submits to the department a certified copy of a probation report, presentencing report, report prepared pursuant to Section 288.1, or other official court document that clearly demonstrates that the offender was the victim's parent, stepparent, sibling, or grandparent and that the crime did not involve either oral copulation or penetration of the vagina or rectum of either the victim or the offender by the penis of the other or by any foreign object.

(B) If, subsequent to the offender's application, the offender commits a violation of probation resulting in the offender's incarceration in county jail or state prison, the offender's exclusion, or application for exclusion, from the internet website shall be terminated.

(C) For the purposes of this paragraph, "successfully completed probation" means that during the period of probation the offender neither received additional county jail or state prison time for a violation of probation nor was convicted of another offense resulting in a sentence to county jail or state prison.

(2) If the department determines that a person who was granted an exclusion under a former version of this subdivision would not qualify for an exclusion under the current version of this subdivision, the department shall rescind the exclusion, make a reasonable effort to provide notification to the person that the exclusion has been rescinded, and, no sooner than 30 days after notification is attempted, make information about the offender available to the public on the internet website as provided in this section.

(3) Effective January 1, 2012, no person shall be excluded pursuant to this subdivision unless the offender has submitted to the department documentation sufficient for the department to determine that the person has a SARATSO risk level of average, below average, or very low as determined by the Coding Rules for the SARATSO static risk assessment instrument.

(e)

(1) A designated law enforcement entity, as defined in subdivision (f) of Section 290.45, may make available information concerning persons who are required to register pursuant to Section 290 to the public via an internet website as specified in paragraph (2), provided that the information about that person is also displayed on the Department of Justice's Megan's Law internet website.

(2) The law enforcement entity may make available by way of an internet website the information described in subdivision (c) if it determines that the public disclosure of the information about a specific offender by way of the entity's internet website is necessary to ensure the public safety based upon information available to the entity concerning the current risk posed by a specific offender, including the offender's risk of sexual or violent reoffense, as indicated by the person's SARATSO static, dynamic, and violence risk levels, as described in Section 290.04, if available.

(3) The information that may be provided pursuant to this subdivision may include the information specified in subdivision (b) of Section 290.45. However, that offender's address may not be disclosed unless the offender is a person whose address is on the Department of Justice's internet website pursuant to subdivision (b).

(f) For purposes of this section, "offense" includes the statutory predecessors of that offense, or any offense committed in another jurisdiction that, if committed or attempted to be committed in this state, would have been punishable in this state as an offense listed in subdivision (c) of Section 290.

(g) Notwithstanding Section 7921.505 of the Government Code, disclosure of information pursuant to this section is not a waiver of exemptions under Division 10 (commencing with Section 7920.000) of Title 1 of the Government Code and does not affect other statutory restrictions on disclosure in other situations.

(h)

(1) Any person who uses information disclosed pursuant to this section to commit a misdemeanor shall be subject to, in addition to any other penalty or fine imposed, a fine of not less than ten thousand dollars ($10,000) and not more than fifty thousand dollars ($50,000).

(2) Any person who uses information disclosed pursuant to this section to commit a felony shall be punished, in addition and consecutive to any other punishment, by a five-year term of imprisonment pursuant to subdivision (h) of Section 1170.

(i) Any person who is required to register pursuant to Section 290 who enters an internet website established pursuant to this section shall be punished by a fine not exceeding one thousand dollars ($1,000), imprisonment in a county jail for a period not to exceed six months, or by both that fine and imprisonment.

(j)

(1) A person is authorized to use information disclosed pursuant to this section only to protect a person at risk.

(2) Except as authorized under paragraph (1) or any other provision of law, use of any information that is disclosed pursuant to this section for purposes relating to any of the following is prohibited:

    (A) Health insurance.

    (B) Insurance.

    (C) Loans.

    (D) Credit.

    (E) Employment.

    (F) Education, scholarships, or fellowships.

    (G) Housing or accommodations.

    (H) Benefits, privileges, or services provided by any business establishment.

(3) This section shall not affect authorized access to, or use of, information pursuant to, among other provisions, Sections 11105 and 11105.3 of this code, Section 8808 of the Family Code, Sections 777.5 and 14409.2 of the Financial Code, Sections 1522.01 and 1596.871 of the Health and Safety Code, and Section 432.7 of the Labor Code.

(4)

    (A) Any use of information disclosed pursuant to this section for purposes other than those provided by paragraph (1) or in violation of paragraph (2) shall make the user liable for the actual damages, and any amount that may be determined by a jury or a court sitting without a jury, not exceeding three times the amount of actual damage, and not less than two hundred fifty dollars ($250), and attorney's fees, exemplary damages, or a civil penalty not exceeding twenty-five thousand dollars ($25,000).

    (B) Whenever there is reasonable cause to believe that any person or group of persons is engaged in a pattern or practice of misuse of the information available via an internet website established pursuant to this section in violation of paragraph (2), the Attorney General, any district attorney, or city attorney, or any person aggrieved by the misuse is authorized to bring a civil action in the appropriate court requesting preventive relief, including an application for a permanent or temporary injunction, restraining order, or other order against the person or group of persons responsible for the pattern or practice of misuse. The foregoing remedies shall be independent of any other remedies or procedures that may be available to an aggrieved party under other provisions of law, including Part 2 (commencing with Section 43) of Division 1 of the Civil Code.

(k) The public notification provisions of this section are applicable to every person described in this section, without regard to when the person's crimes were committed or the person's duty to register pursuant to Section 290 arose, and to every offense described in this section, regardless of when it was committed.

(l) A designated law enforcement entity and its employees shall be immune from liability for good faith conduct under this section.

(m) The Attorney General, in collaboration with local law enforcement and others knowledgeable about sex offenders, shall develop strategies to assist members of the public in understanding and using publicly available information about registered sex offenders to further public safety. These strategies may include, but are not limited to, a hotline for community inquiries, neighborhood and business guidelines for how to respond to information posted on this internet website, and any other resource that promotes public education about these offenders.

(n) This section shall become operative on January 1, 2022.

Amended by Stats 2021 ch 615 (AB 474),s 333, eff. 1/1/2022, op. 1/1/2023.
Amended by Stats 2018 ch 423 (SB 1494),s 58, eff. 1/1/2019.
Added by Stats 2017 ch 541 (SB 384),s 10, eff. 1/1/2018.

Section 290.47 - Unique identifier for address of registered sex offender

The Department of Justice shall record the address at which a registered sex offender resides with a unique identifier for the address. The information for this identifier shall be captured pursuant to Section 290.015 and the identifier shall consist of a description of the nature of the dwelling, with the choices of a single family residence, an apartment/condominium, a motel/hotel, or a licensed facility. Each address and its association with any specific registered sex offender shall be stored by the department in the same database as the registration data recorded pursuant to Section 290.015. The department shall make that information available to the State Department of Social Services or any other state agency when the agency needs the information for law enforcement purposes relating to investigative responsibilities relative to sex offenders. This section shall become operative on January 1, 2012.

Added by Stats 2009 ch 55 (SB 583),s 1, eff. 1/1/2010.

Section 290.5 - Termination from registry

(a)

(1) A person who is required to register pursuant to Section 290 and who is a tier one or tier two offender may file a petition in the superior court in the county in which the person is registered for termination from the sex offender registry on or after their next birthday after July 1, 2021, following the expiration of the person's mandated minimum registration period, or if the person is required to register pursuant to Section 290.008, the person may file the petition in juvenile court on or after their next birthday after July 1, 2021, following the expiration of the mandated minimum registration period. The petition shall contain proof of the person's current registration as a sex offender.

(2) The petition shall be served on the registering law enforcement agency and the district attorney in the county where the petition is filed and on the law enforcement agency and the district attorney of the county of conviction of a registerable offense if different than the county where the petition is filed. The registering law enforcement agency shall report receipt of service of a filed petition to the Department of Justice in a manner prescribed by the department. The registering law enforcement agency and the law enforcement agency of the county of conviction of a registerable offense if different than the county where the petition is filed shall, within 60 days of receipt of the petition, report to the district attorney and the superior or juvenile court in which the petition is filed regarding whether the person has met the requirements for termination pursuant to subdivision (e) of Section 290. If an offense which may require registration pursuant to Section 290.005 is identified by the registering law enforcement agency which has not previously been assessed by the Department of Justice, the registering law enforcement agency shall refer that conviction to the department for assessment and determination of whether the conviction changes the tier designation assigned by the department to the offender. If the newly discovered offense changes the tier designation for that person, the department shall change the tier designation pursuant to subdivision (d) of Section 290 within three months of receipt of the request by the registering law enforcement agency and notify the registering law enforcement agency. If more time is required to obtain the documents needed to make the assessment, the department shall notify the registering law enforcement agency of the reason that an extension of time is necessary to complete the tier designation. The registering law enforcement agency shall report to the district attorney and the court that the department has requested an extension of time to determine the person's tier designation based on the newly discovered offense, the reason for the request, and the estimated time needed to complete the tier designation. The district attorney in the county where the petition is filed may, within 60 days of receipt of the report from either the registering law enforcement agency, the law enforcement agency of the county of conviction of a registerable offense if different than the county where the petition is filed, or the district attorney of the county of conviction of a registerable offense, request a hearing on the petition if the petitioner has not fulfilled the requirement described in subdivision (e) of Section 290, or if community safety would be significantly enhanced by the person's continued registration. If no hearing is requested, the petition for termination shall be granted if the court finds the required proof of current registration is presented in the petition, provided that the registering agency reported that the person met the requirement for termination pursuant to subdivision (e) of Section 290, there are no pending charges against the person which could extend the time to complete the registration requirements of the tier or change the person's tier status, and the person is not in custody or on parole, probation, or supervised release. The court may summarily deny a petition if the court determines the petitioner does not meet the statutory requirements for termination of sex offender registration or if the petitioner has not fulfilled the filing and service requirements of this section. In summarily denying a petition the court shall state the reason or reasons the petition is being denied.

(3) If the district attorney requests a hearing, the district attorney shall be entitled to present evidence regarding whether community safety would be significantly enhanced by requiring continued registration. In determining whether to order continued registration, the court shall consider: the nature and facts of the registerable offense; the age and number of victims; whether any victim was a stranger at the time of the offense (known to the offender for less than 24 hours); criminal and relevant noncriminal behavior before and after conviction for the registerable offense; the time period during which the person has not reoffended; successful completion, if any, of a Sex Offender Management Board-certified sex offender treatment program; and the person's current risk of sexual or violent reoffense, including the person's risk levels on SARATSO static, dynamic, and violence risk assessment instruments, if

available. Any judicial determination made pursuant to this section may be heard and determined upon declarations, affidavits, police reports, or any other evidence submitted by the parties which is reliable, material, and relevant.

(4) If termination from the registry is denied, the court shall set the time period after which the person can repetition for termination, which shall be at least one year from the date of the denial, but not to exceed five years, based on facts presented at the hearing. The court shall state on the record the reason for its determination setting the time period after which the person may repetition.

(5) The court shall notify the Department of Justice, California Sex Offender Registry, when a petition for termination from the registry is granted, denied, or summarily denied, in a manner prescribed by the department. If the petition is denied, the court shall also notify the Department of Justice, California Sex Offender Registry, of the time period after which the person can file a new petition for termination.

(b)

(1) A person required to register as a tier two offender, pursuant to paragraph (2) of subdivision (d) of Section 290, may petition the superior court for termination from the registry after 10 years from release from custody on the registerable offense if all of the following apply:

(A) the registerable offense involved no more than one victim 14 to 17 years of age, inclusive;

(B) the offender was under 21 years of age at the time of the offense;

(C) the registerable offense is not specified in subdivision (c) of Section 667.5, except subdivision (a) of Section 288; and

(D) the registerable offense is not specified in Section 236.1.

(2) A tier two offender described in paragraph (1) may file a petition with the superior court for termination from the registry only if the person has not been convicted of a new offense requiring sex offender registration or an offense described in subdivision (c) of Section 667.5 since the person was released from custody on the offense requiring registration pursuant to Section 290, and has registered for 10 years pursuant to subdivision (e) of Section 290. The court shall determine whether community safety would be significantly enhanced by requiring continued registration and may consider the following factors: whether the victim was a stranger (known less than 24 hours) at the time of the offense; the nature of the registerable offense, including whether the offender took advantage of a position of trust; criminal and relevant noncriminal behavior before and after the conviction for the registerable offense; whether the offender has successfully completed a Sex Offender Management Board-certified sex offender treatment program; whether the offender initiated a relationship for the purpose of facilitating the offense; and the person's current risk of sexual or violent reoffense, including the person's risk levels on SARATSO static, dynamic, and violence risk assessment instruments, if known. If the petition is denied, the person may not repetition for termination for at least one year.

(3) A person required to register as a tier three offender based solely on the person's risk level, pursuant to subparagraph (D) of paragraph (3) of subdivision (d) of Section 290, may petition the court for termination from the registry after 20 years from release from custody on the registerable offense, if the person (A) has not been convicted of a new offense requiring sex offender registration or an offense described in subdivision (c) of Section 667.5 since the person was released from custody on the offense requiring registration pursuant to Section 290, and (B) has registered for 20 years pursuant to subdivision (e) of Section 290; except that a person required to register for a conviction pursuant to Section 288 or an offense listed in subdivision (c) of Section 1192.7 who is a tier three offender based on the person's risk level, pursuant to subparagraph (D) of paragraph (3) of subdivision (d) of Section 290, shall not be permitted to petition for removal from the registry. The court shall determine whether community safety would be significantly enhanced by requiring continued registration and may consider the following factors: whether the victim was a stranger (known less than 24 hours) at the time of the offense; the nature of the registerable offense, including whether the offender took advantage of a position of trust; criminal and relevant noncriminal behavior before and after the conviction for the registerable offense; whether the offender has successfully completed a Sex Offender Management Board-certified sex offender treatment program; whether the offender initiated a relationship for the purpose of facilitating the offense; and the person's current risk of sexual or violent reoffense, including the person's risk levels on SARATSO static, dynamic, and violence risk assessment instruments, if known. If the petition is denied, the person may not re-petition for termination for at least three years.

(c) This section shall become operative on July 1, 2021.

Added by Stats 2017 ch 541 (SB 384),s 12, eff. 1/1/2018.

Section 290.6 - Provision of information before scheduled release of person required to register

(a) Fifteen days before the scheduled release date of a person described in subdivision (b), the Department of Corrections and Rehabilitation shall provide to local law enforcement all of the following information regarding the person:

(1) Name.

(2) Community residence and address, including ZIP Code.

(3) Physical description.

(4) Conviction information.

(b) This subdivision shall apply to any person sentenced to the state prison who is required to register pursuant to Section 290 for a conviction of an offense specified in subdivision (b), (c), or (d) of Section 290.46 and to any person described in those subdivisions.

(c) For the purpose of this section, "law enforcement" includes any agency with which the person will be required to register upon his or her release pursuant to Section 290 based upon the person's community of residence upon release.

(d) If it is not possible for the Department of Corrections and Rehabilitation to provide the information specified in subdivision (a) on a date that is 15 days before the scheduled release date, the information shall be provided on the next business day following that date.

(e) The Department of Corrections and Rehabilitation shall notify local law enforcement within 36 hours of learning of the change if the scheduled release date or any of the required information changes prior to the scheduled release date.

Amended by Stats 2006 ch 538 (SB 1852),s 501, eff. 1/1/2007.

Amended by Stats 2005 ch 722 (AB 1323),s 9, eff. 10/7/2005.

Section 290.7 - Provision of samples of blood and saliva taken from prison inmate

The Department of Corrections shall provide samples of blood and saliva taken from a prison inmate pursuant to the DNA and Forensic Identification Data Base and Data Bank Act of 1998 (Chapter 6 (commencing with Section 295) of Title 9 of Part 1 of the Penal Code) to the county in which the inmate is to be released if the county maintains a local DNA testing laboratory.

EFFECTIVE 1/1/2000. Amended September 23, 1999 (Bill Number: SB 654) (Chapter 475).

Section 290.8 - Notification of days, times, and locations available for registration

Effective January 1, 1999, any local law enforcement agency that does not register sex offenders during regular daytime business hours on a daily basis, excluding weekends and holidays, shall notify the regional parole office for the Department of Corrections and the regional parole office for the Department of the Youth Authority of the days, times, and locations the agency is available for registration of sex offenders pursuant to Section 290.

Added by Stats. 1998, Ch. 960, Sec. 4. Effective January 1, 1999.

Section 290.85 - Proof of registration to probation officer

(a) Every person released on probation or parole who is required to register as a sex offender, pursuant to Section 290, shall provide proof of registration to his or her probation officer or parole agent within six working days of release on probation or parole. The six-day period for providing proof of registration may be extended only upon determination by the probation officer or parole agent that unusual circumstances exist relating to the availability of local law enforcement registration capabilities that preclude the person's ability to meet the deadline.

(b) Every person released on probation or parole who is required to register as a sex offender pursuant to Section 290 shall provide proof of any change or update to his or her registration information to his or her probation officer or parole agent within five working days for so long as he or she is required to be under the supervision of a probation officer or parole agent.

(c) A probation officer or parole agent who supervises an individual who is required to register as a sex offender pursuant to Section 290 shall inform that individual of his or her duties under this section not fewer than six days prior to the date on which proof of registration or proof of any change or update to registration information is to be provided to the probation officer or parole agent.

(d) For purposes of this section, "proof of registration" means a photocopy of the actual registration form. A law enforcement agency that registers an individual as a sex offender pursuant to Section 290 who is released on probation or parole and is therefore subject to this section shall provide that individual with proof of his or her registration free of charge when requested by the registrant to fulfill the requirements of this section or any other provision of law.

Amended by Stats 2003 ch 245 (AB 1098), s 1, eff. 1/1/2004.

Section 290.9 - Provision of address of person who is in violation of duty to register [Second of two versions]

Notwithstanding any other provision of law, any state or local governmental agency shall, upon written request, provide to the Department of Justice the address of any person represented by the department to be a person who is in violation of his or her duty to register under Section 290.

Added by Stats 2004 ch 127 (AB 1937), s 1, eff. 1/1/2005.

Section 290.95 - Disclosure of status as registrant

(a) Every person required to register under Section 290, who applies for or accepts a position as an employee or volunteer with any person, group, or organization where the registrant would be working directly and in an unaccompanied setting with minor children on more than an incidental and occasional basis or have supervision or disciplinary power over minor children, shall disclose his or her status as a registrant, upon application or acceptance of a position, to that person, group, or organization.

(b) Every person required to register under Section 290 who applies for or accepts a position as an employee or volunteer with any person, group, or organization where the applicant would be working directly and in an accompanied setting with minor children, and the applicant's work would require him or her to touch the minor children on more than an incidental basis, shall disclose his or her status as a registrant, upon application or acceptance of the position, to that person, group, or organization.

(c) No person who is required to register under Section 290 because of a conviction for a crime where the victim was a minor under 16 years of age shall be an employer, employee, or independent contractor, or act as a volunteer with any person, group, or organization in a capacity in which the registrant would be working directly and in an unaccompanied setting with minor children on more than an incidental and occasional basis or have supervision or disciplinary power over minor children. This subdivision shall not apply to a business owner or an independent contractor who does not work directly in an unaccompanied setting with minors.

(d) For purposes of this section, "working directly and in an unaccompanied setting" includes, but is not limited to, providing goods or services to minors.

(e) A violation of this section is a misdemeanor punishable by imprisonment in a county jail for not exceeding six months, by a fine not exceeding one thousand dollars ($1,000), or by both that imprisonment and fine, and a violation of this section shall not constitute a continuing offense.

Amended by Stats 2009 ch 430 (AB 307),s 1, eff. 10/11/2009.

Amended by Stats 2006 ch 341 (AB 2263),s 1.5, eff. 1/1/2007.

Amended by Stats 2006 ch 340 (AB 1900),s 1, eff. 1/1/2007.

Amended by Stats 2001 ch 224 (SB 1192), s 1, eff. 1/1/2002.

Section 291 - Arrest of school employee

Every sheriff, chief of police, or the Commissioner of the California Highway Patrol, upon the arrest for any of the offenses enumerated in Section 290, subdivision (a) of Section 261, or Section 44010 of the Education Code, of any school employee, shall, provided that he or she knows that the arrestee is a school employee, do either of the following:

(a) If the school employee is a teacher in any of the public schools of this state, the sheriff, chief of police, or Commissioner of the California Highway Patrol shall immediately notify by telephone the superintendent of schools of the school district employing the teacher and shall immediately give written notice of the arrest to the Commission on Teacher Credentialing and to the superintendent of schools in the county where the person is employed. Upon receipt of the notice, the county superintendent of schools and the Commission on Teacher Credentialing shall immediately notify the governing board of the school district employing the person.

(b) If the school employee is a nonteacher in any of the public schools of this state, the sheriff, chief of police, or Commissioner of the California Highway Patrol shall immediately notify by telephone the superintendent of schools of the school district employing the nonteacher and shall immediately give written notice of the arrest to the governing board of the school district employing the person.
Amended by Stats 2003 ch 536 (AB 608), s 2, eff. 1/1/2004.

Section 291.1 - Arrest of teacher in private school
Every sheriff or chief of police, or Commissioner of the California Highway Patrol, upon the arrest for any of the offenses enumerated in Section 290 or Section 44010 of the Education Code, of any person who is employed as a teacher in any private school of this state, shall, provided that he or she knows that the arrestee is a school employee, immediately give written notice of the arrest to the private school authorities employing the teacher. The sheriff, chief of police, or Commissioner of the California Highway Patrol, provided that he or she knows that the arrestee is a school employee, shall immediately notify by telephone the private school authorities employing the teacher of the arrest.
Amended by Stats 2003 ch 536 (AB 608), s 3, eff. 1/1/2004.

Section 291.5 - Arrest of teacher or instructor employed in community college district
Every sheriff or chief of police, upon the arrest for any of the offenses enumerated in Section 290 or in subdivision (1) of Section 261 of any teacher or instructor employed in any community college district shall immediately notify by telephone the superintendent of the community college district employing the teacher or instructor and shall immediately give written notice of the arrest to the Office of the Chancellor of the California Community Colleges. Upon receipt of such notice, the district superintendent shall immediately notify the governing board of the community college district employing the person.
Added by Stats. 1983, Ch. 1032, Sec. 4.

Section 292 - Legislative intent
It is the intention of the Legislature in enacting this section to clarify that for the purposes of subdivisions (b) and (c) of Section 12 of Article I of the California Constitution, a violation of paragraph (2) or (6) of subdivision (a) of Section 261, paragraph (1) or (4) of subdivision (a) of former Section 262, Section 264.1, subdivision (c) or (d) of Section 286, subdivision (c) or (d) of Section 287 or former Section 288a, subdivision (b) of Section 288, or subdivision (a) of Section 289, shall be deemed to be a felony offense involving an act of violence and a felony offense involving great bodily harm.
Amended by Stats 2021 ch 626 (AB 1171),s 26, eff. 1/1/2022.
Amended by Stats 2018 ch 423 (SB 1494),s 60, eff. 1/1/2019.

Section 293 - Report that person is victim of sex offense or was forced to commit act of prostitution because person is victim of human trafficking
(a) An employee of a law enforcement agency who personally receives a report from a person, alleging that the person making the report has been the victim of a sex offense, shall inform that person that the person's name will become a matter of public record unless the person requests that it not become a matter of public record, pursuant to Section 7923.615 of the Government Code.
(b) A written report of an alleged sex offense shall indicate that the alleged victim has been properly informed pursuant to subdivision (a) and shall memorialize the victim's response.
(c) A law enforcement agency shall not disclose to a person, except the prosecutor, parole officers of the Department of Corrections and Rehabilitation, hearing officers of the parole authority, probation officers of county probation departments, or other persons or public agencies where authorized or required by law, the address of a person who alleges to be the victim of a sex offense.
(d) A law enforcement agency shall not disclose to a person, except the prosecutor, parole officers of the Department of Corrections and Rehabilitation, hearing officers of the parole authority, probation officers of county probation departments, or other persons or public agencies where authorized or required by law, the name of a person who alleges to be the victim of a sex offense if that person has elected to exercise the person's right pursuant to this section and Section 7923.615 of the Government Code.
(e) A law enforcement agency shall not disclose to a person, except the prosecutor, parole officers of the Department of Corrections and Rehabilitation, hearing officers of the parole authority, probation officers of county probation departments, or other persons or public agencies if authorized or required by law, names, addresses, or images of a person who alleges to be the victim of human trafficking, as defined in Section 236.1, or of that alleged victim's immediate family, other than a family member who is charged with a criminal offense arising from the same incident, and that information and those images shall be withheld and remain confidential. The law enforcement agency shall orally inform the person who alleges to be the victim of human trafficking of that person's right to have the person's name, addresses, and images, and the names, addresses, and images of the person's immediate family members withheld and kept confidential pursuant to this section and Section 7923.615 of the Government Code. For purposes of this subdivision, "immediate family" shall have the same meaning as that provided in paragraph (3) of subdivision (b) of Section 422.4 of the Penal Code.
(f) For purposes of this section, sex offense means any crime listed in subdivision (b) of Section 7923.615 of the Government Code.
(g) Parole officers of the Department of Corrections and Rehabilitation, hearing officers of the parole authority, and probation officers of county probation departments shall be entitled to receive information pursuant to subdivisions (c), (d), and (e) only if the person to whom the information pertains alleges that the person is the victim of a sex offense or is the victim of human trafficking, as defined in Section 236.1, the alleged perpetrator of which is a parolee who is alleged to have committed the offense while on parole, or in the case of a county probation officer, the person who is alleged to have committed the offense is a probationer or is under investigation by a county probation department.
Amended by Stats 2021 ch 615 (AB 474),s 334, eff. 1/1/2022, op. 1/1/2023.
Amended by Stats 2016 ch 644 (AB 2498),s 2, eff. 1/1/2017.
Amended by Stats 2010 ch 328 (SB 1330),s 154, eff. 1/1/2011.
Amended by Stats 2008 ch 596 (AB 3038),s 1.5, eff. 9/30/2008.
Amended by Stats 2008 ch 358 (AB 2810),s 5, eff. 1/1/2009.
Amended by Stats 2007 ch 578 (SB 449),s 2, eff. 1/1/2008.
Amended by Stats 2006 ch 92 (AB 2615),s 1, eff. 1/1/2007.

Section 293.5 - Identification of alleged victim in records and proceedings

(a) Except as provided in Chapter 10 (commencing with Section 1054) of Part 2 of Title 7, or for cases in which the alleged victim of a sex offense, as specified in subdivision (f) of Section 293, has not elected to exercise the alleged victim's right pursuant to Section 7923.615 of the Government Code, the court, at the request of the alleged victim, may order the identity of the alleged victim in all records and during all proceedings to be either Jane Doe or John Doe, if the court finds that type of order is reasonably necessary to protect the privacy of the person and will not unduly prejudice the prosecution or the defense.

(b) If the court orders the alleged victim to be identified as Jane Doe or John Doe pursuant to subdivision (a) and if there is a jury trial, the court shall instruct the jury, at the beginning and at the end of the trial, that the alleged victim is being so identified only for the purpose of protecting the alleged victim's privacy pursuant to this section.

Amended by Stats 2021 ch 615 (AB 474),s 335, eff. 1/1/2022, op. 1/1/2023.

Amended by Stats 2016 ch 644 (AB 2498),s 3, eff. 1/1/2017.

Section 294 - Restitution fine

(a) Upon conviction of any person for a violation of Section 273a, 273d, 288.5, 311.2, 311.3, or 647.6, the court may, in addition to any other penalty or restitution fine imposed, order the defendant to pay a restitution fine based on the defendant's ability to pay not to exceed five thousand dollars ($5,000), upon a felony conviction, or one thousand dollars ($1,000), upon a misdemeanor conviction, to be deposited in the Restitution Fund to be transferred to the county children's trust fund for the purposes of child abuse prevention.

(b) Upon conviction of any person for a violation of Section 261, 264.1, 285, 286, 287, or 289 or former Section 288a, where the violation is with a minor under the age of 14 years, the court may, in addition to any other penalty or restitution fine imposed, order the defendant to pay a restitution fine based on the defendant's ability to pay not to exceed five thousand dollars ($5,000), upon a felony conviction, or one thousand dollars ($1,000), upon a misdemeanor conviction, to be deposited in the Restitution Fund to be transferred to the county children's trust fund for the purpose of child abuse prevention.

(c) If the perpetrator is a member of the immediate family of the victim, the court shall consider in its decision to impose a fine under this section any hardship that may impact the victim from the imposition of the fine.

(d) If the court orders a fine to be imposed pursuant to this section, the actual administrative cost of collecting that fine, not to exceed 2 percent of the total amount paid, may be paid into the general fund of the county treasury for the use and benefit of the county.

Amended by Stats 2018 ch 423 (SB 1494),s 61, eff. 1/1/2019.

Chapter 6 - DNA AND FORENSIC IDENTIFICATION DATABASE AND DATA BANK ACT OF 1998
Article 1 - PURPOSE AND ADMINISTRATION

Section 295 - Short title; purpose; collection of DNA samples

(a) This chapter shall be known and may be cited as the DNA and Forensic Identification Database and Data Bank Act of 1998, as amended.

(b) The people of the State of California set forth all of the following:

(1) Deoxyribonucleic acid (DNA) and forensic identification analysis is a useful law enforcement tool for identifying and prosecuting criminal offenders and exonerating the innocent.

(2) It is the intent of the people of the State of California, in order to further the purposes of this chapter, to require DNA and forensic identification data bank samples from all persons, including juveniles, for the felony and misdemeanor offenses described in subdivision (a) of Section 296.

(3) It is necessary to enact this act defining and governing the state's DNA and forensic identification database and data bank in order to clarify existing law and to enable the state's DNA and Forensic Identification Database and Data Bank Program to become a more effective law enforcement tool.

(c) The purpose of the DNA and Forensic Identification Database and Data Bank Program is to assist federal, state, and local criminal justice and law enforcement agencies within and outside California in the expeditious and accurate detection and prosecution of individuals responsible for sex offenses and other crimes, the exclusion of suspects who are being investigated for these crimes, and the identification of missing and unidentified persons, particularly abducted children.

(d) Like the collection of fingerprints, the collection of DNA samples pursuant to this chapter is an administrative requirement to assist in the accurate identification of criminal offenders.

(e) Unless otherwise requested by the Department of Justice, collection of biological samples for DNA analysis from qualifying persons under this chapter is limited to collection of inner cheek cells of the mouth (buccal swab samples).

(f) The Department of Justice DNA Laboratory may obtain through federal, state, or local law enforcement agencies blood specimens from qualifying persons as defined in subdivision (a) of Section 296, and according to procedures set forth in Section 298, when it is determined in the discretion of the Department of Justice that such specimens are necessary in a particular case or would aid the department in obtaining an accurate forensic DNA profile for identification purposes.

(g) The Department of Justice, through its DNA Laboratory, shall be responsible for the management and administration of the state's DNA and Forensic Identification Database and Data Bank Program and for liaison with the Federal Bureau of Investigation (FBI) regarding the state's participation in a national or international DNA database and data bank program such as the FBI's Combined DNA Index System (CODIS) that allows the storage and exchange of DNA records submitted by state and local forensic DNA laboratories nationwide.

(h) The Department of Justice shall be responsible for implementing this chapter.

(1) The Department of Justice DNA Laboratory, and the Department of Corrections and Rehabilitation may adopt policies and enact regulations for the implementation of this chapter, as necessary, to give effect to the intent and purpose of this chapter, and to ensure that data bank blood specimens, buccal swab samples, and thumb and palm print impressions as required by this chapter are collected from qualifying persons in a timely manner, as soon as possible after arrest, conviction, or a plea or finding of guilty, no contest, or not guilty by reason of insanity, or upon any disposition rendered in the case of a juvenile who is adjudicated under Section 602 of the Welfare and Institutions Code for commission of any of this chapter's enumerated qualifying offenses, including attempts, or when it is determined that a qualifying person has not given the required specimens, samples, or print impressions. Before adopting any policy or

regulation implementing this chapter, the Department of Corrections and Rehabilitation shall seek advice from and consult with the Department of Justice DNA Laboratory Director.

(2) Given the specificity of this chapter, and except as provided in subdivision (c) of Section 298.1, any administrative bulletins, notices, regulations, policies, procedures, or guidelines adopted by the Department of Justice and its DNA Laboratory or the Department of Corrections and Rehabilitation for the purpose of implementing this chapter are exempt from the provisions of the Administrative Procedure Act, Chapter 3.5 (commencing with Section 11340), Chapter 4 (commencing with Section 11370), Chapter 4.5 (commencing with Section 11400), and Chapter 5 (commencing with Section 11500) of Part 1 of Division 3 of Title 2 of the Government Code.

(3) The Department of Corrections and Rehabilitation shall submit copies of any of its policies and regulations with respect to this chapter to the Department of Justice DNA Laboratory Director, and quarterly shall submit to the director written reports updating the director as to the status of its compliance with this chapter.

(4) On or before April 1 in the year following adoption of the act that added this paragraph, and quarterly thereafter, the Department of Justice DNA Laboratory shall submit a quarterly report to be published electronically on a Department of Justice internet website and made available for public review. The quarterly report shall state the total number of samples received, the number of samples received from the Department of Corrections and Rehabilitation, the number of samples fully analyzed for inclusion in the CODIS database, and the number of profiles uploaded into the CODIS database for the reporting period. Each quarterly report shall state the total, annual, and quarterly number of qualifying profiles in the Department of Justice DNA Laboratory data bank both from persons and case evidence, and the number of hits and investigations aided, as reported to the National DNA Index System. The quarterly report shall also confirm the laboratory's accreditation status and participation in CODIS and shall include an accounting of the funds collected, expended, and disbursed pursuant to subdivision (k).

(5) On or before April 1 in the year following adoption of the act that added this paragraph, and quarterly thereafter, the Department of Corrections and Rehabilitation shall submit a quarterly report to be published electronically on a Department of Corrections and Rehabilitation internet website and made available for public review. The quarterly report shall state the total number of inmates housed in state correctional facilities, including a breakdown of those housed in state prisons, camps, community correctional facilities, and other facilities such as prisoner mother facilities. Each quarterly report shall also state the total, annual, and quarterly number of inmates who have yet to provide specimens, samples, and print impressions pursuant to this chapter and the number of specimens, samples, and print impressions that have yet to be forwarded to the Department of Justice DNA Laboratory within 30 days of collection.

(i)

(1) When the specimens, samples, and print impressions required by this chapter are collected at a county jail or other county facility, including a private community correctional facility, the county sheriff or chief administrative officer of the county jail or other county facility shall be responsible for ensuring all of the following:

(A) The requisite specimens, samples, and print impressions are collected from qualifying persons immediately following arrest, conviction, or adjudication, or during the booking or intake or reception center process at that facility, or reasonably promptly thereafter.

(B) The requisite specimens, samples, and print impressions are collected as soon as administratively practicable after a qualifying person reports to the facility for the purpose of providing specimens, samples, and print impressions.

(C) The specimens, samples, and print impressions collected pursuant to this chapter are forwarded immediately to the Department of Justice, and in compliance with department policies.

(2) The specimens, samples, and print impressions required by this chapter shall be collected by a person using a collection kit approved by the Department of Justice and in accordance with the requirements and procedures set forth in subdivision (b) of Section 298.

(3) The counties shall be reimbursed for the costs of obtaining specimens, samples, and print impressions subject to the conditions and limitations set forth by the Department of Justice policies governing reimbursement for collecting specimens, samples, and print impressions pursuant to Section 76104.6 of the Government Code.

(j) The trial court may order that a portion of the costs assessed pursuant to Section 1203.1c or 1203.1m include a reasonable portion of the cost of obtaining specimens, samples, and print impressions in furtherance of this chapter and the funds collected pursuant to this subdivision shall be deposited in the DNA Identification Fund as created by Section 76104.6 of the Government Code.

(k) The Department of Justice DNA Laboratory shall be known as the Jan Bashinski DNA Laboratory.

(l) This section shall become operative on July 1, 2021.

Added by Stats 2020 ch 92 (AB 1869),s 30, eff. 9/18/2020.

Section 295.1 - DNA analysis; forensic identification analysis

(a) The Department of Justice shall perform DNA analysis and other forensic identification analysis pursuant to this chapter only for identification purposes.

(b) The Department of Justice Bureau of Criminal Identification and Information shall perform examinations of palm prints pursuant to this chapter only for identification purposes.

(c) The DNA Laboratory of the Department of Justice shall serve as a repository for blood specimens and buccal swab and other biological samples collected, and shall analyze specimens and samples, and store, compile, correlate, compare, maintain, and use DNA and forensic identification profiles and records related to the following:

(1) Forensic casework and forensic unknowns.

(2) Known and evidentiary specimens and samples from crime scenes or criminal investigations.

(3) Missing or unidentified persons.

(4) Persons required to provide specimens, samples, and print impressions under this chapter.

(5) Legally obtained samples.

(6) Anonymous DNA records used for training, research, statistical analysis of populations, quality assurance, or quality control.

(d) The computerized data bank and database of the DNA Laboratory of the Department of Justice shall include files as necessary to implement this chapter.

(e) Nothing in this section shall be construed as requiring the Department of Justice to provide specimens or samples for quality control or other purposes to those who request specimens or samples.

(f) Submission of samples, specimens, or profiles for the state DNA Database and Data Bank Program shall include information as required by the Department of Justice for ensuring search capabilities and compliance with National DNA Index System (NDIS) standards.

Amended by Proposition 69, enacted by the people of the State of California 11/2/2004, eff. 11/3/2004.

Section 295.2 - DNA and forensic identification database and databank

The DNA and forensic identification database and databank and the Department of Justice DNA Laboratory shall not be used as a source of genetic material for testing, research, or experiments, by any person, agency, or entity seeking to find a causal link between genetics and behavior or health.

Amended by Stats 2015 ch 303 (AB 731),s 386, eff. 1/1/2016.

Added by Stats 2014 ch 454 (AB 1697),s 1, eff. 1/1/2015.

Article 2 - OFFENDERS SUBJECT TO SAMPLE COLLECTION

Section 296 - Persons required to provide samples

(a) The following persons shall provide buccal swab samples, right thumbprints, and a full palm print impression of each hand, and any blood specimens or other biological samples required pursuant to this chapter for law enforcement identification analysis:

(1) Any person, including any juvenile, who is convicted of or pleads guilty or no contest to any felony offense, or is found not guilty by reason of insanity of any felony offense, or any juvenile who is adjudicated under Section 602 of the Welfare and Institutions Code for committing any felony offense.

(2) Any adult person who is arrested for or charged with any of the following felony offenses:

(A) Any felony offense specified in Section 290 or attempt to commit any felony offense described in Section 290, or any felony offense that imposes upon a person the duty to register in California as a sex offender under Section 290.

(B) Murder or voluntary manslaughter or any attempt to commit murder or voluntary manslaughter.

(C) Commencing on January 1 of the fifth year following enactment of the act that added this subparagraph, as amended, any adult person arrested or charged with any felony offense.

(3) Any person, including any juvenile, who is required to register under Section 290 or 457.1 because of the commission of, or the attempt to commit, a felony or misdemeanor offense, or any person, including any juvenile, who is housed in a mental health facility or sex offender treatment program after referral to such facility or program by a court after being charged with any felony offense.

(4) The term "felony" as used in this subdivision includes an attempt to commit the offense.

(5) Nothing in this chapter shall be construed as prohibiting collection and analysis of specimens, samples, or print impressions as a condition of a plea for a non-qualifying offense.

(b) The provisions of this chapter and its requirements for submission of specimens, samples and print impressions as soon as administratively practicable shall apply to all qualifying persons regardless of sentence imposed, including any sentence of death, life without the possibility of parole, or any life or indeterminate term, or any other disposition rendered in the case of an adult or juvenile tried as an adult, or whether the person is diverted, fined, or referred for evaluation, and regardless of disposition rendered or placement made in the case of juvenile who is found to have committed any felony offense or is adjudicated under Section 602 of the Welfare and Institutions Code.

(c) The provisions of this chapter and its requirements for submission of specimens, samples, and print impressions as soon as administratively practicable by qualified persons as described in subdivision (a) shall apply regardless of placement or confinement in any mental hospital or other public or private treatment facility, and shall include, but not be limited to, the following persons, including juveniles:

(1) Any person committed to a state hospital or other treatment facility as a mentally disordered sex offender under Article 1 (commencing with Section 6300) of Chapter 2 of Part 2 of Division 6 of the Welfare and Institutions Code.

(2) Any person who has a severe mental disorder as set forth within the provisions of Article 4 (commencing with Section 2960) of Chapter 7 of Title 1 of Part 3 of the Penal Code.

(3) Any person found to be a sexually violent predator pursuant to Article 4 (commencing with Section 6600) of Chapter 2 of Part 2 of Division 6 of the Welfare and Institutions Code.

(d) The provisions of this chapter are mandatory and apply whether or not the court advises a person, including any juvenile, that he or she must provide the data bank and database specimens, samples, and print impressions as a condition of probation, parole, or any plea of guilty, no contest, or not guilty by reason of insanity, or any admission to any of the offenses described in subdivision (a).

(e) If at any stage of court proceedings the prosecuting attorney determines that specimens, samples, and print impressions required by this chapter have not already been taken from any person, as defined under subdivision (a) of Section 296, the prosecuting attorney shall notify the court orally on the record, or in writing, and request that the court order collection of the specimens, samples, and print impressions required by law. However, a failure by the prosecuting attorney or any other law enforcement agency to notify the court shall not relieve a person of the obligation to provide specimens, samples, and print impressions pursuant to this chapter.

(f) Prior to final disposition or sentencing in the case the court shall inquire and verify that the specimens, samples, and print impressions required by this chapter have been obtained and that this fact is included in the abstract of judgment or dispositional order in the case of a juvenile. The abstract of judgment issued by the court shall indicate that the court has ordered the person to comply with the requirements of this chapter and that the person shall be included in the state's DNA and Forensic Identification Data Base and Data Bank program and be subject to this chapter. However, failure by the court to verify specimen, sample, and print impression collection or enter these facts in the abstract of judgment or dispositional order in the case of a juvenile shall not invalidate an arrest, plea, conviction, or disposition, or otherwise relieve a person from the requirements of this chapter.

Amended by Proposition 69, enacted by the people of the State of California 11/2/2004, eff. 11/3/2004.

Amended by Stats 2002 ch 160 (AB 2105), s 1, eff. 7/11/2002.

Amended by Stats 2001 ch 906 (AB 673), s 1, eff. 1/1/2002.

Amended by Stats 2000 ch 823 (AB 2814), s 1, eff. 1/1/2001.

Section 296.1 - Collection of samples

(a) The specimens, samples, and print impressions required by this chapter shall be collected from persons described in subdivision (a) of Section 296 for present and past qualifying offenses of record as follows:

(1) Collection from any adult person following arrest for a felony offense as specified in subparagraphs (A), (B), and (C) of paragraph (2) of subdivision (a) of Section 296:

(A) Each adult person arrested for a felony offense as specified in subparagraphs (A), (B), and (C) of paragraph (2) of subdivision (a) of Section 296 shall provide the buccal swab samples and thumb and palm print impressions and any blood or other specimens required pursuant to this chapter immediately following arrest, or during the booking or intake or prison reception center process or as soon as administratively practicable after arrest, but, in any case, prior to release on bail or pending trial or any physical release from confinement or custody.

(B) If the person subject to this chapter did not have specimens, samples, and print impressions taken immediately following arrest or during booking or intake procedures or is released on bail or pending trial or is not confined or incarcerated at the time of sentencing or otherwise bypasses a prison inmate reception center maintained by the Department of Corrections and Rehabilitation, the court shall order the person to report within five calendar days to a county jail facility or to a city, state, local, private, or other designated facility to provide the required specimens, samples, and print impressions in accordance with subdivision (i) of Section 295.

(2) Collection from persons confined or in custody after conviction or adjudication:

(A) Any person, including any juvenile who is imprisoned or confined or placed in a state correctional institution, a county jail, a facility within the jurisdiction of the Department of Corrections and Rehabilitation, the Corrections Standards Authority, a residential treatment program, or any state, local, city, private, or other facility after a conviction of any felony or misdemeanor offense, or any adjudication or disposition rendered in the case of a juvenile, whether or not that crime or offense is one set forth in subdivision (a) of Section 296, shall provide buccal swab samples and thumb and palm print impressions and any blood or other specimens required pursuant to this chapter, immediately at intake, or during the prison reception center process, or as soon as administratively practicable at the appropriate custodial or receiving institution or the program in which the person is placed, if:

(i) The person has a record of any past or present conviction or adjudication as a ward of the court in California of a qualifying offense described in subdivision (a) of Section 296 or has a record of any past or present conviction or adjudication in any other court, including any state, federal, or military court, of any offense that, if committed or attempted in this state, would have been punishable as an offense described in subdivision (a) of Section 296; and

(ii) The person's blood specimens, buccal swab samples, and thumb and palm print impressions authorized by this chapter are not in the possession of the Department of Justice DNA Laboratory or have not been recorded as part of the department's DNA databank program.

(3) Collection from persons on probation, parole, or other release:

(A) Any person, including any juvenile, who has a record of any past or present conviction or adjudication for an offense set forth in subdivision (a) of Section 296, and who is on probation, parole, postrelease community supervision, or mandatory supervision pursuant to paragraph (5) of subdivision (h) of Section 1170 for any felony or misdemeanor offense, whether or not that crime or offense is one set forth in subdivision (a) of Section 296, shall provide buccal swab samples and thumb and palm print impressions and any blood specimens required pursuant to this chapter, if:

(i) The person has a record of any past or present conviction or adjudication as a ward of the court in California of a qualifying offense described in subdivision (a) of Section 296 or has a record of any past or present conviction or adjudication in any other court, including any state, federal, or military court, of any offense that, if committed or attempted in this state, would have been punishable as an offense described in subdivision (a) of Section 296; and

(ii) The person's blood specimens, buccal swab samples, and thumb and palm print impressions authorized by this chapter are not in the possession of the Department of Justice DNA Laboratory or have not been recorded as part of the department's DNA databank program.

(B) The person shall have any required specimens, samples, and print impressions collected within five calendar days of being notified by the court, or a law enforcement agency or other agency authorized by the Department of Justice. The specimens, samples, and print impressions shall be collected in accordance with subdivision (i) of Section 295 at a county jail facility or a city, state, local, private, or other facility designated for this collection.

(4) Collection from parole violators and others returned to custody:

(A) If a person, including any juvenile, who has been released on parole, furlough, or other release for any offense or crime, whether or not set forth in subdivision (a) of Section 296, is returned to a state correctional or other institution for a violation of a condition of his or her parole, furlough, or other release, or for any other reason, that person shall provide buccal swab samples and thumb and palm print impressions and any blood or other specimens required pursuant to this chapter, at a state correctional or other receiving institution, if:

(i) The person has a record of any past or present conviction or adjudication as a ward of the court in California of a qualifying offense described in subdivision (a) of Section 296 or has a record of any past or present conviction or adjudication in any other court, including any state, federal, or military court, of any offense that, if committed or attempted in this state, would have been punishable as an offense described in subdivision (a) of Section 296; and

(ii) The person's blood specimens, buccal swab samples, and thumb and palm print impressions authorized by this chapter are not in the possession of the Department of Justice DNA Laboratory or have not been recorded as part of the department's DNA databank program.

(5) Collection from persons accepted into California from other jurisdictions:

(A) When an offender from another state is accepted into this state under any of the interstate compacts described in Article 3 (commencing with Section 11175) or Article 4 (commencing with Section 11189) of Chapter 2 of Title 1 of Part 4 of this code, or Chapter 4 (commencing with Section 1400) of Part 1 of Division 2 of the Welfare and Institutions Code, or under any other reciprocal agreement with any county, state, or federal agency, or any other provision of law, whether or not the offender is confined or released, the acceptance is conditional on the offender providing blood specimens, buccal swab samples, and palm and thumb print impressions pursuant to this chapter, if the offender has a record of any past or present conviction or adjudication in California of a qualifying offense described in subdivision (a) of Section 296 or has a record of any past or present conviction or adjudication or had a disposition rendered in any other court, including any state, federal, or military court, of any offense that, if committed or attempted in this state, would have been punishable as an offense described in subdivision (a) of Section 296.

(B) If the person is not confined, the specimens, samples, and print impressions required by this chapter must be provided within five calendar days after the person reports to the supervising agent or within five calendar days of notice to the person, whichever occurs first. The person shall report to a county jail facility in the county where he or she resides or temporarily is located to have the specimens, samples, and print impressions collected pursuant to this chapter. The specimens, samples, and print impressions shall be collected in accordance with subdivision (i) of Section 295.

(C) If the person is confined, he or she shall provide the blood specimens, buccal swab samples, and thumb and palm print impressions required by this chapter as soon as practicable after his or her receipt in a state, county, city, local, private, or other designated facility.

(6) Collection from persons in federal institutions:

(A) Subject to the approval of the Director of the FBI, persons confined or incarcerated in a federal prison or federal institution who have a record of any past or present conviction or juvenile adjudication for a qualifying offense described in subdivision (a) of Section 296, or of a similar crime under the laws of the United States or any other state that would constitute an offense described in subdivision (a) of Section 296, are subject to this chapter and shall provide blood specimens, buccal swab samples, and thumb and palm print impressions pursuant to this chapter if any of the following apply:

(i) The person committed a qualifying offense in California.

(ii) The person was a resident of California at the time of the qualifying offense.

(iii) The person has any record of a California conviction for an offense described in subdivision (a) of Section 296, regardless of when the crime was committed.

(iv) The person will be released in California.

(B) The Department of Justice DNA Laboratory shall, upon the request of the United States Department of Justice, forward portions of the specimens or samples, taken pursuant to this chapter, to the United States Department of Justice DNA databank laboratory. The specimens and samples required by this chapter shall be taken in accordance with the procedures set forth in subdivision (i) of Section 295. The Department of Justice DNA Laboratory is authorized to analyze and upload specimens and samples collected pursuant to this section upon approval of the Director of the FBI.

(b) Paragraphs (2), (3), (4), (5), and (6) of subdivision (a) shall have retroactive application. Collection shall occur pursuant to paragraphs (2), (3), (4), (5), and (6) of subdivision (a) regardless of when the crime charged or committed became a qualifying offense pursuant to this chapter, and regardless of when the person was convicted of the qualifying offense described in subdivision (a) of Section 296 or a similar crime under the laws of the United States or any other state, or pursuant to the United States Code of Military Justice, 10 U.S.C., Sections 801 and following, or when a juvenile petition is sustained for commission of a qualifying offense described in subdivision (a) of Section 296 or a similar crime under the laws of the United States or any other state.

Amended by Stats 2012 ch 43 (SB 1023),s 17, eff. 6/27/2012.

Amended by Stats 2006 ch 170 (AB 2850),s 1, eff. 1/1/2007.

Amended by Proposition 69, enacted by the people of the State of California 11/2/2004, eff. 11/3/2004. .

Amended by Stats 2000 ch 823 (AB 2814), s 2, eff. 1/1/2001.

This section does not contain subsection (a)(2)(B) nor (a)(4)(B).

Section 296.2 - Collection of additional samples

(a) Whenever the DNA Laboratory of the Department of Justice notifies the Department of Corrections and Rehabilitation or any law enforcement agency that a biological specimen or sample, or print impression is not usable for any reason, the person who provided the original specimen, sample, or print impression shall submit to collection of additional specimens, samples, or print impressions. The Department of Corrections and Rehabilitation or other responsible law enforcement agency shall collect additional specimens, samples, and print impressions from these persons as necessary to fulfill the requirements of this chapter, and transmit these specimens, samples, and print impressions to the appropriate agencies of the Department of Justice.

(b) If a person, including any juvenile, is convicted of, pleads guilty or no contest to, is found not guilty by reason of insanity of, or is adjudged a ward of the court under Section 602 of the Welfare and Institutions Code for committing, any of the offenses described in subdivision (a) of Section 296, and has given a blood specimen or other biological sample or samples to law enforcement for any purpose, the DNA Laboratory of the Department of Justice is authorized to analyze the blood specimen and other biological sample or samples for forensic identification markers, including DNA markers, and to include the DNA and forensic identification profiles from these specimens and samples in the state's DNA and forensic identification databank and databases. This subdivision applies whether or not the blood specimen or other biological sample originally was collected from the sexual or violent offender pursuant to the databank and database program, and whether or not the crime committed predated the enactment of the state's DNA and forensic identification databank program, or any amendments thereto. This subdivision does not relieve a person convicted of a crime described in subdivision (a) of Section 296, or otherwise subject to this chapter, from the requirement to give blood specimens, saliva samples, and thumb and palm print impressions for the DNA and forensic identification databank and database program as described in this chapter.

(c) Any person who is required to register under the Sex Offender Registration Act who has not provided the specimens, samples, and print impressions described in this chapter for any reason including the release of the person prior to the enactment of the state's DNA and forensic identification database and databank program, an oversight or error, or because of the transfer of the person from another state, the person, as an additional requirement of registration or of updating his or her annual registration pursuant to the Sex Offender Registration Act shall give specimens, samples, and print impressions as described in this chapter for inclusion in the state's DNA and forensic identification database and databank. At the time the person registers or updates his or her registration, he or she shall receive an appointment designating a time and place for the collection of the specimens, samples, and print impressions described in this chapter, if he or she has not already complied with the provisions of this chapter.

As specified in the appointment, the person shall report to a county jail facility in the county where he or she resides or is temporarily located to have specimens, samples, and print impressions collected pursuant to this chapter or other facility approved by the Department of Justice for this collection. The specimens, samples, and print impressions shall be collected in accordance with subdivision (f) of Section 295.

If, prior to the time of the annual registration update, a person is notified by the Department of Justice, a probation or parole officer, other law enforcement officer, or officer of the court, that he or she is subject to this chapter, then the person shall provide the specimens, samples, and print impressions required by this chapter within 10 calendar days of the notification at a county jail facility or other facility approved by the department for this collection.

Amended by Stats 2007 ch 579 (SB 172),s 37, eff. 10/13/2007.

Article 3 - DATA BASE APPLICATIONS

Section 297 - Authorized laboratories

(a) Subject to the limitations in paragraph (3) of this subdivision, only the following laboratories are authorized to analyze crime scene samples and other forensic identification samples of known and unknown origin and to upload and compare those profiles against available state and national DNA and forensic identification databanks and databases in order to establish identity and origin of samples for forensic identification purposes pursuant to this chapter:

(1) The DNA laboratories of the Department of Justice that meet state and federal requirements, including the Federal Bureau of Investigation (FBI) Quality Assurance Standards, and that are accredited by an organization approved by the National DNA Index System (NDIS) Procedures Board.

(2) Public law enforcement crime laboratories designated by the Department of Justice that meet state and federal requirements, including the FBI Quality Assurance Standards, and that are accredited by an organization approved by the NDIS Procedures Board.

(3) Only the laboratories of the Department of Justice that meet the requirements of paragraph (1) of subdivision (a) are authorized to upload DNA profiles from arrestees and other qualifying offender samples collected pursuant to this section, Section 296, and Section 296.2.

(b) The laboratories of the Department of Justice and public law enforcement crime laboratories that meet the requirements of subdivision (a) may, subject to the laboratory's discretion, and the limitations of paragraph (3) of subdivision (a), upload to available state and national DNA and forensic identification databanks and databases qualifying DNA profiles from forensic identification samples of known and unknown origin that are generated by private forensic laboratories that meet state and federal requirements, including the FBI Quality Assurance Standards, and that are accredited by an organization approved by the NDIS Procedures Board. Prior to uploading DNA profiles generated by a private laboratory, the public laboratory shall conduct the quality assessment and review required by the FBI Quality Assurance Standards.

(c)

(1) A biological sample obtained from a suspect in a criminal investigation for the commission of any crime may be analyzed for forensic identification profiles, including DNA profiles, by the DNA Laboratory of the Department of Justice or any law enforcement crime laboratory or private forensic laboratory that meets all of the FBI Quality Assurance Standards and accreditation requirements in paragraphs (1) and (2) of subdivision (a) and then compared by the Department of Justice in and between as many cases and investigations as necessary, and searched against the forensic identification profiles, including DNA profiles, stored in the files of the Department of Justice DNA databank or database or any available databanks or databases as part of the Department of Justice DNA Database and databank Program.

(2) The law enforcement investigating agency submitting a specimen, sample, or print impression to the DNA Laboratory of the Department of Justice or law enforcement crime laboratory pursuant to this section shall inform the Department of Justice DNA Laboratory within two years whether the person remains a suspect in a criminal investigation. Upon written notification from a law enforcement agency that a person is no longer a suspect in a criminal investigation, the Department of Justice DNA Laboratory shall remove the suspect sample from its databank files and databases. However, any identification, warrant, arrest, or prosecution based upon a databank or database match shall not be invalidated or dismissed due to a failure to purge or delay in purging records.

(d) All laboratories, including the Department of Justice DNA laboratories, contributing DNA profiles for inclusion in California's DNA databank shall meet state and federal requirements, including the FBI Quality Assurance Standards and accreditation requirements, and shall be accredited by an organization approved by the National DNA Index System (NDIS) Procedures Board. Additionally, each laboratory shall submit to the Department of Justice for review the annual report required by the submitting laboratory's accrediting organization that documents the laboratory's adherence to FBI Quality Assurance Standards and the standards of the accrediting organization. The requirements of this subdivision do not preclude DNA profiles developed in California from being searched in the NDIS.

(e) Nothing in this section precludes local law enforcement DNA laboratories from maintaining local forensic databases and databanks or performing forensic identification analyses, including DNA profiling, independently from the Department of Justice DNA laboratories and Forensic Identification Data Base and databank Program.

(f) The limitation on the types of offenses set forth in subdivision (a) of Section 296 as subject to the collection and testing procedures of this chapter is for the purpose of facilitating the administration of this chapter by the Department of Justice, and shall not be considered cause for dismissing an investigation or prosecution or reversing a verdict or disposition.

(g) The detention, arrest, wardship, adjudication, or conviction of a person based upon a databank match or database information is not invalidated if it is determined that the specimens, samples, or print impressions were obtained or placed or retained in a databank or database by mistake.

Amended by Stats 2006 ch 170 (AB 2850),s 2, eff. 1/1/2007.

Amended by Proposition 69, enacted by the people of the State of California 11/2/2004, eff. 11/3/2004. .

Amended by Stats 2000 ch 823 (AB 2814), s 3, eff. 1/1/2001.

Article 4 - COLLECTION AND FORWARDING OF SAMPLES
Section 298 - [For Operative Date See Text] Collection kit; forwarding of samples

Section 298 - [For Operative Date See Text] Collection kit; forwarding of samples

(a) The Secretary of the Department of Corrections and Rehabilitation, or the Chief Administrative Officer of the detention facility, jail, or other facility at which the blood specimens, buccal swab samples, and thumb and palm print impressions were collected shall cause these specimens, samples, and print impressions to be forwarded promptly to the Department of Justice. The specimens, samples, and print impressions shall be collected by a person using a Department of Justice approved collection kit and in accordance with the requirements and procedures set forth in subdivision (b).

(b)

   (1) The Department of Justice shall provide all blood specimen vials, buccal swab collectors, mailing tubes, labels, and instructions for the collection of the blood specimens, buccal swab samples, and thumbprints. The specimens, samples, and thumbprints shall thereafter be forwarded to the DNA Laboratory of the Department of Justice for analysis of DNA and other forensic identification markers. Additionally, the Department of Justice shall provide all full palm print cards, mailing envelopes, and instructions for the collection of full palm prints. The full palm prints, on a form prescribed by the Department of Justice, shall thereafter be forwarded to the Department of Justice for maintenance in a file for identification purposes.

   (2) The withdrawal of blood shall be performed in a medically approved manner. Only health care providers trained and certified to draw blood may withdraw the blood specimens for purposes of this section.

   (3) Buccal swab samples may be procured by law enforcement or corrections personnel or other individuals trained to assist in buccal swab collection.

   (4) Right thumbprints and a full palm print impression of each hand shall be taken on forms prescribed by the Department of Justice. The palm print forms shall be forwarded to and maintained by the Bureau of Criminal Identification and Information of the Department of Justice. Right thumbprints also shall be taken at the time of the collection of samples and specimens and shall be placed on the sample and specimen containers and forms as directed by the Department of Justice. The samples, specimens, and forms shall be forwarded to and maintained by the DNA Laboratory of the Department of Justice.

   (5) The law enforcement or custodial agency collecting specimens, samples, or print impressions is responsible for confirming that the person qualifies for entry into the Department of Justice DNA Database and Databank Program prior to collecting the specimens, samples, or print impressions pursuant to this chapter.

   (6) The DNA Laboratory of the Department of Justice is responsible for establishing procedures for entering databank and database information.

(c)

   (1) Persons authorized to draw blood or obtain samples or print impressions under this chapter for the databank or database shall not be civilly or criminally liable either for withdrawing blood when done in accordance with medically accepted procedures, or for obtaining buccal swab samples by scraping inner cheek cells of the mouth, or thumb or palm print impressions when performed in accordance with standard professional practices.

   (2) There is no civil or criminal cause of action against any law enforcement agency or the Department of Justice, or any employee thereof, for a mistake in confirming a person's or sample's qualifying status for inclusion within the database or databank or in placing an entry in a databank or a database.

   (3) The failure of the Department of Justice or local law enforcement to comply with Article 4 or any other provision of this chapter shall not invalidate an arrest, plea, conviction, or disposition.

(d) This section shall become inoperative if the California Supreme Court rules to uphold the California Court of Appeal decision in People v. Buza (2014) 231 Cal.App.4th 1446 in regard to the provisions of Section 298 of the Penal Code, as amended by Section 6 of the DNA Fingerprint, Unsolved Crime and Innocence Protection Act, Proposition 69, approved by the voters at the November 2, 2004, statewide general election, in which case this section shall become inoperative immediately upon that ruling becoming final.

Amended by Stats 2015 ch 487 (AB 1492),s 2, eff. 1/1/2016.

Amended by Stats 2000 ch 823 (AB 2814), s 4, eff. 1/1/2001.

Previously Amended July 12, 1999 (Bill Number: SB 966) (Chapter 83).

Section 298 - [For Operative Date See Text] Collection kit; forwarding of samples

(a)

   (1)

      (A) The Secretary of the Department of Corrections and Rehabilitation, or the Chief Administrative Officer of the detention facility, jail, or other facility at which the blood specimens, buccal swab samples, and thumb and palm print impressions were collected shall cause these specimens, samples, and print impressions to be forwarded promptly to the Department of Justice, except that a blood specimen or buccal swab sample taken from a person arrested for the commission of a felony as specified in paragraph (2) of subdivision (a) of Section 296 shall be forwarded to the Department of Justice only after one of the following has occurred, which shall be deemed a finding of probable cause, whichever occurs first:

         (i) A felony arrest warrant has been signed by a judicial officer pursuant to Section 813 or 817.

         (ii) A grand jury indictment has been found and issued pursuant to Section 939.8, 940, or 944.

         (iii) A judicial officer has determined that probable cause exists to believe the person has committed the offense for which he or she was arrested.

      (B) The specimens, samples, and print impressions shall be collected by a person using a Department of Justice approved collection kit and in accordance with the requirements and procedures set forth in subdivision (b).

   (2) A blood specimen or buccal swab sample taken from a person arrested for the commission of a felony as specified in paragraph (2) of subdivision (a) of Section 296 that has not been forwarded to the Department of Justice within six months following the arrest of that person because the agency that took the blood specimen or buccal swab sample has not received notice to forward the DNA specimen or sample to the Department of Justice for inclusion in the state's DNA and Forensic Identification Database and Databank Program pursuant to paragraph (1) following a determination of probable cause, shall be destroyed by the agency that collected the blood specimen or buccal swab sample.

(b)

(1) The Department of Justice shall provide all blood specimen vials, buccal swab collectors, mailing tubes, labels, and instructions for the collection of the blood specimens, buccal swab samples, and thumbprints. The specimens, samples, and thumbprints shall thereafter be forwarded to the DNA Laboratory of the Department of Justice for analysis of DNA and other forensic identification markers. Additionally, the Department of Justice shall provide all full palm print cards, mailing envelopes, and instructions for the collection of full palm prints. The full palm prints, on a form prescribed by the Department of Justice, shall thereafter be forwarded to the Department of Justice for maintenance in a file for identification purposes.

(2) The withdrawal of blood shall be performed in a medically approved manner. Only health care providers trained and certified to draw blood may withdraw the blood specimens for purposes of this section.

(3) Buccal swab samples may be procured by law enforcement or corrections personnel or other individuals trained to assist in buccal swab collection.

(4) Right thumbprints and a full palm print impression of each hand shall be taken on forms prescribed by the Department of Justice. The palm print forms shall be forwarded to and maintained by the Bureau of Criminal Identification and Information of the Department of Justice. Right thumbprints also shall be taken at the time of the collection of samples and specimens and shall be placed on the sample and specimen containers and forms as directed by the Department of Justice. The samples, specimens, and forms shall be forwarded to and maintained by the DNA Laboratory of the Department of Justice.

(5) The law enforcement or custodial agency collecting specimens, samples, or print impressions is responsible for confirming that the person qualifies for entry into the Department of Justice DNA and Forensic Identification Database and Databank Program prior to collecting the specimens, samples, or print impressions pursuant to this chapter.

(6) The DNA Laboratory of the Department of Justice is responsible for establishing procedures for entering databank and database information.

(c)

(1) Persons authorized to draw blood or obtain samples or print impressions under this chapter for the databank or database shall not be civilly or criminally liable either for withdrawing blood when done in accordance with medically accepted procedures, or for obtaining buccal swab samples by scraping inner cheek cells of the mouth, or thumb or palm print impressions when performed in accordance with standard professional practices.

(2) There is no civil or criminal cause of action against any law enforcement agency or the Department of Justice, or any employee thereof, for a mistake in confirming a person's or sample's qualifying status for inclusion within the database or databank or in placing an entry in a databank or a database.

(3) The failure of the Department of Justice or local law enforcement to comply with Article 4 or any other provision of this chapter shall not invalidate an arrest, plea, conviction, or disposition.

(d) This section shall only become operative if the California Supreme Court rules to uphold the California Court of Appeal decision in People v. Buza (2014) 231 Cal.App.4th 1446 in regard to the provisions of Section 298 of the Penal Code, as amended by Section 6 of the DNA Fingerprint, Unsolved Crime and Innocence Protection Act, Proposition 69, approved by the voters at the November 2, 2004, statewide general election, in which case this section shall become operative immediately upon that ruling becoming final.
Added by Stats 2015 ch 487 (AB 1492),s 3, eff. 1/1/2016.

Section 298.1 - Refusal or failure to give samples

(a) On and after January 1, 1999, any person who refuses to give any or all of the following, blood specimens, saliva samples, or thumb or palm print impressions as required by this chapter, once he or she has received written notice from the Department of Justice, the Department of Corrections and Rehabilitation, any law enforcement personnel, or officer of the court that he or she is required to provide specimens, samples, and print impressions pursuant to this chapter is guilty of a misdemeanor. The refusal or failure to give any or all of the following, a blood specimen, saliva sample, or thumb or palm print impression is punishable as a separate offense by both a fine of five hundred dollars ($500) and imprisonment of up to one year in a county jail, or if the person is already imprisoned in the state prison, by sanctions for misdemeanors according to a schedule determined by the Department of Corrections and Rehabilitation.

(b)

(1) Notwithstanding subdivision (a), authorized law enforcement, custodial, or corrections personnel, including peace officers as defined in Sections 830, 830.1, subdivision (d) of Section 830.2, Sections 830.38, 830.5, or 830.55, may employ reasonable force to collect blood specimens, saliva samples, or thumb or palm print impressions pursuant to this chapter from individuals who, after written or oral request, refuse to provide those specimens, samples, or thumb or palm print impressions.

(2) The withdrawal of blood shall be performed in a medically approved manner in accordance with the requirements of paragraph (2) of subdivision (b) of Section 298.

(3) The use of reasonable force as provided in this subdivision shall be carried out in a manner consistent with regulations and guidelines adopted pursuant to subdivision (c).

(c)

(1) The Department of Corrections and Rehabilitation and the Division of Juvenile Justice shall adopt regulations governing the use of reasonable force as provided in subdivision (b), which shall include the following:

(A) "Use of reasonable force" shall be defined as the force that an objective, trained, and competent correctional employee, faced with similar facts and circumstances, would consider necessary and reasonable to gain compliance with this chapter.

(B) The use of reasonable force shall not be authorized without the prior written authorization of the supervising officer on duty. The authorization shall include information that reflects the fact that the offender was asked to provide the requisite specimen, sample, or impression and refused.

(C) The use of reasonable force shall be preceded by efforts to secure voluntary compliance with this section.

(D) If the use of reasonable force includes a cell extraction, the regulations shall provide that the extraction be video recorded.

(2) The Corrections Standards Authority shall adopt guidelines governing the use of reasonable force as provided in subdivision (b) for local detention facilities, which shall include the following:

(A) "Use of reasonable force" shall be defined as the force that an objective, trained and competent correctional employee, faced with similar facts and circumstances, would consider necessary and reasonable to gain compliance with this chapter.

(B) The use of reasonable force shall not be authorized without the prior written authorization of the supervising officer on duty. The authorization shall include information that reflects the fact that the offender was asked to provide the requisite specimen, sample, or impression and refused.

(C) The use of reasonable force shall be preceded by efforts to secure voluntary compliance with this section.

(D) If the use of reasonable force includes a cell extraction, the extraction shall be video recorded.

(3) The Department of Corrections and Rehabilitation, the Division of Juvenile Justice, and the Corrections Standards Authority shall report to the Legislature not later than January 1, 2005, on the use of reasonable force pursuant to this section. The report shall include, but is not limited to, the number of refusals, the number of incidents of the use of reasonable force under this section, the type of force used, the efforts undertaken to obtain voluntary compliance, if any, and whether any medical attention was needed by the prisoner or personnel as a result of force being used.

Amended by Stats 2009 ch 88 (AB 176),s 71, eff. 1/1/2010.

Amended by Stats 2007 ch 130 (AB 299),s 189, eff. 1/1/2008.

Amended by Stats 2002 ch 632 (SB 1242), s 1, eff. 9/17/2002.

Section 298.2 - Unlawful acts by person required to submit sample

(a) Any person who is required to submit a specimen sample or print impression pursuant to this chapter who engages or attempts to engage in any of the following acts is guilty of a felony punishable by imprisonment in the state prison for two, three, or four years:

(1) Knowingly facilitates the collection of a wrongfully attributed blood specimen, buccal swab sample, or thumb or palm print impression, with the intent that a government agent or employee be deceived as to the origin of a DNA profile or as to any identification information associated with a specimen, sample, or print impression required for submission pursuant to this chapter.

(2) Knowingly tampers with any specimen, sample, print, or the collection container for any specimen or sample, with the intent that any government agent or employee be deceived as to the identity of the person to whom the specimen, sample, or print relates.

Amended by Stats 2011 ch 39 (AB 117),s 68, eff. 6/30/2011.

Amended by Stats 2011 ch 39 (AB 117),s 14, eff. 6/30/2011.

Amended by Stats 2011 ch 15 (AB 109),s 322, eff. 4/4/2011, but operative no earlier than October 1, 2011, and only upon creation of a community corrections grant program to assist in implementing this act and upon an appropriation to fund the grant program.

Added by Proposition 69, enacted by the people of the State of California 11/2/2004, eff. 11/3/2004.

Section 298.3 - Expeditious and economical processing of samples

(a) To ensure expeditious and economical processing of offender specimens and samples for inclusion in the FBI's CODIS System and the state's DNA Database and Data Bank Program, the Department of Justice DNA Laboratory is authorized to contract with other laboratories, whether public or private, including law enforcement laboratories, that have the capability of fully analyzing offender specimens or samples within 60 days of receipt, for the anonymous analysis of specimens and samples for forensic identification testing as provided in this chapter and in accordance with the quality assurance requirement established by CODIS and ASCLD/LAB.

(b) Contingent upon the availability of sufficient funds in the state's DNA Identification Fund established pursuant to Section 76104.6, the Department of Justice DNA Laboratory shall immediately contract with other laboratories, whether public or private, including law enforcement laboratories, for the anonymous analysis of offender reference specimens or samples and any arrestee reference specimens or samples collected pursuant to subdivision (a) of Section 296 for forensic identification testing as provided in subdivision (a) of this section and in accordance with the quality assurance requirements established by CODIS and ASCLD/LAB for any specimens or samples that are not fully analyzed and uploaded into the CODIS database within six months of the receipt of the reference specimens or samples by the Department of Justice DNA Laboratory.

Added by Proposition 69, enacted by the people of the State of California 11/2/2004, eff. 11/3/2004.

Article 5 - EXPUNGEMENT OF INFORMATION

Section 299 - Expungement

Section 299 - Expungement

(a) A person whose DNA profile has been included in the databank pursuant to this chapter shall have his or her DNA specimen and sample destroyed and searchable database profile expunged from the databank program pursuant to the procedures set forth in subdivision (b) if the person has no past or present offense or pending charge which qualifies that person for inclusion within the state's DNA and Forensic Identification Database and Databank Program and there otherwise is no legal basis for retaining the specimen or sample or searchable profile.

(b) Pursuant to subdivision (a), a person who has no past or present qualifying offense, and for whom there otherwise is no legal basis for retaining the specimen or sample or searchable profile, may make a written request to have his or her specimen and sample destroyed and searchable database profile expunged from the databank program if any of the following apply:

(1) Following arrest, no accusatory pleading has been filed within the applicable period allowed by law, charging the person with a qualifying offense as set forth in subdivision (a) of Section 296 or if the charges which served as the basis for including the DNA profile in the state's DNA and Forensic Identification Database and Databank Program have been dismissed prior to adjudication by a trier of fact;

(2) The underlying conviction or disposition serving as the basis for including the DNA profile has been reversed and the case dismissed;

(3) The person has been found factually innocent of the underlying offense pursuant to Section 851.8, or Section 781.5 of the Welfare and Institutions Code; or

(4) The defendant has been found not guilty or the defendant has been acquitted of the underlying offense.

(c)

(1) The person requesting the databank entry to be expunged must send a copy of his or her request to the trial court of the county where the arrest occurred, or that entered the conviction or rendered disposition in the case, to the DNA Laboratory of the Department of Justice, and to the prosecuting attorney of the county in which he or she was arrested or, convicted, or adjudicated, with proof of service on all parties. The court has the discretion to grant or deny the request for expungement. The denial of a request for expungement is a nonappealable order and shall not be reviewed by petition for writ.

(2) Except as provided in this section, the Department of Justice shall destroy a specimen and sample and expunge the searchable DNA database profile pertaining to the person who has no present or past qualifying offense of record upon receipt of a court order that verifies the applicant has made the necessary showing at a noticed hearing, and that includes all of the following:

(A) The written request for expungement pursuant to this section.

(B) A certified copy of the court order reversing and dismissing the conviction or case, or a letter from the district attorney certifying that no accusatory pleading has been filed or the charges which served as the basis for collecting a DNA specimen and sample have been dismissed prior to adjudication by a trier of fact, the defendant has been found factually innocent, the defendant has been found not guilty, the defendant has been acquitted of the underlying offense, or the underlying conviction has been reversed and the case dismissed.

(C) Proof of written notice to the prosecuting attorney and the Department of Justice that expungement has been requested.

(D) A court order verifying that no retrial or appeal of the case is pending, that it has been at least 180 days since the defendant or minor has notified the prosecuting attorney and the Department of Justice of the expungement request, and that the court has not received an objection from the Department of Justice or the prosecuting attorney.

(d) Upon order from the court, the Department of Justice shall destroy any specimen or sample collected from the person and any searchable DNA database profile pertaining to the person, unless the department determines that the person is subject to the provisions of this chapter because of a past qualifying offense of record or is or has otherwise become obligated to submit a blood specimen or buccal swab sample as a result of a separate arrest, conviction, juvenile adjudication, or finding of guilty or not guilty by reason of insanity for an offense described in subdivision (a) of Section 296, or as a condition of a plea. The Department of Justice is not required to destroy analytical data or other items obtained from a blood specimen or saliva, or buccal swab sample, if evidence relating to another person subject to the provisions of this chapter would thereby be destroyed or otherwise compromised.

Any identification, warrant, probable cause to arrest, or arrest based upon a databank or database match is not invalidated due to a failure to expunge or a delay in expunging records.

(e) Notwithstanding any other law, the Department of Justice DNA Laboratory is not required to expunge DNA profile or forensic identification information or destroy or return specimens, samples, or print impressions taken pursuant to this section if the duty to register under Section 290 or 457.1 is terminated.

(f) Notwithstanding any other law, including Sections 17, 1170.18, 1203.4, and 1203.4a, a judge is not authorized to relieve a person of the separate administrative duty to provide specimens, samples, or print impressions required by this chapter if a person has been found guilty or was adjudicated a ward of the court by a trier of fact of a qualifying offense as defined in subdivision (a) of Section 296, or was found not guilty by reason of insanity or pleads no contest to a qualifying offense as defined in subdivision (a) of Section 296.

(g) This section shall become inoperative if the California Supreme Court rules to uphold the California Court of Appeal decision in People v. Buza (2014) 231 Cal.App.4th 1446 in regard to the provisions of Section 299 of the Penal Code, as amended by Section 9 of the DNA Fingerprint, Unsolved Crime and Innocence Protection Act, Proposition 69, approved by the voters at the November 2, 2004, statewide general election, in which case this section shall become inoperative immediately upon that ruling becoming final.

Amended by Stats 2015 ch 487 (AB 1492),s 4, eff. 1/1/2016.

Amended by Proposition 69, enacted by the people of the State of California 11/2/2004, eff. 11/3/2004.

Amended by Stats 2000 ch 823 (AB 2814), s 5, eff. 1/1/2001.

Previously Amended July 12, 1999 (Bill Number: SB 966) (Chapter 83).

Section 299 - Expungement

(a) A person whose DNA profile has been included in the databank pursuant to this chapter shall have his or her DNA specimen and sample destroyed and searchable database profile expunged from the databank program if the person has no past or present offense or pending charge which qualifies that person for inclusion within the state's DNA and Forensic Identification Database and Databank Program and there otherwise is no legal basis for retaining the specimen or sample or searchable profile.

(b) Pursuant to subdivision (a), a person who has no past or present qualifying offense, and for whom there otherwise is no legal basis for retaining the specimen or sample or searchable profile shall have his or her specimen and sample destroyed and searchable database profile expunged from the databank program if any of the following apply:

(1) Following arrest, and after the applicable law enforcement agency has provided notice to the prosecuting attorney that the criminal case will not be presented to the prosecuting attorney for review, or after the applicable law enforcement agency has submitted a criminal case to the prosecuting attorney for review, no accusatory pleading has been filed within the applicable period allowed by law, charging the person with a qualifying offense as set forth in subdivision (a) of Section 296, in which case the prosecuting attorney shall immediately, or as soon as practically possible, submit a letter to the Department of Justice indicating that an accusatory pleading has not been filed.

(2) The charges which served as the basis for including the DNA profile in the state's DNA and Forensic Identification Database and Databank Program have been dismissed prior to adjudication by a trier of fact, in which case the court shall forward an order to the Department of Justice upon disposition of the case, indicating that the charges have been dismissed.

(3) The underlying conviction or disposition serving as the basis for including the DNA profile has been reversed and the case dismissed, in which case the court shall forward its order to the Department of Justice upon disposition of the case.

(4) The person has been found factually innocent of the underlying offense pursuant to Section 851.8, or Section 781.5 of the Welfare and Institutions Code, in which case the court shall forward its order to the Department of Justice upon disposition of the case.

(5) The defendant has been found not guilty or the defendant has been acquitted of the underlying offense, in which case the court shall forward its order to the Department of Justice upon disposition of the case.

(c) Except as provided in this section, the Department of Justice shall destroy a specimen and sample and expunge the searchable DNA database profile pertaining to the person who has no present or past qualifying offense of record upon receipt of the following:

(1) A certified copy of the court order reversing and dismissing the conviction or case, or a letter from the district attorney certifying that no accusatory pleading has been filed or the charges which served as the basis for collecting a DNA specimen and sample have been dismissed prior to adjudication by a trier of fact, the defendant has been found factually innocent, the defendant has been found not guilty, the defendant has been acquitted of the underlying offense, or the underlying conviction has been reversed and the case dismissed.

(2) A court order verifying that no retrial or appeal of the case is pending.

(d) Pursuant to this section, the Department of Justice shall destroy any specimen or sample collected from the person and any searchable DNA database profile pertaining to the person, unless the department determines that the person is subject to the provisions of this chapter because of a past qualifying offense of record or is or has otherwise become obligated to submit a blood specimen or buccal swab sample as a result of a separate arrest, conviction, juvenile adjudication, or finding of guilty or not guilty by reason of insanity for an offense described in subdivision (a) of Section 296, or as a condition of a plea. The Department of Justice is not required to destroy analytical data or other items obtained from a blood specimen or saliva, or buccal swab sample, if evidence relating to another person subject to the provisions of this chapter would thereby be destroyed or otherwise compromised.

Any identification, warrant, probable cause to arrest, or arrest based upon a databank or database match is not invalidated due to a failure to expunge or a delay in expunging records.

(e) Notwithstanding any other law, the Department of Justice DNA Laboratory is not required to expunge DNA profile or forensic identification information or destroy or return specimens, samples, or print impressions taken pursuant to this section if the duty to register under Section 290 or 457.1 is terminated.

(f) Notwithstanding any other law, including Sections 17, 1170.18, 1203.4, and 1203.4a, a judge is not authorized to relieve a person of the separate administrative duty to provide specimens, samples, or print impressions required by this chapter if a person has been found guilty or was adjudicated a ward of the court by a trier of fact of a qualifying offense as defined in subdivision (a) of Section 296, or was found not guilty by reason of insanity or pleads no contest to a qualifying offense as defined in subdivision (a) of Section 296.

(g) This section shall only become operative if the California Supreme Court rules to uphold the California Court of Appeal decision in People v. Buza (2014) 231 Cal.App.4th 1446 in regard to the provisions of Section 299 of the Penal Code, as amended by Section 9 of the DNA Fingerprint, Unsolved Crime and Innocence Protection Act, Proposition 69, approved by the voters at the November 2, 2004, statewide general election, in which case this section shall become operative immediately upon that ruling becoming final.

Added by Stats 2015 ch 487 (AB 1492),s 5, eff. 1/1/2016.

Article 6 - LIMITATIONS ON DISCLOSURE

Section 299.5 - Exemption from law requiring disclosure of information to public; confidentiality

(a) All DNA and forensic identification profiles and other identification information retained by the Department of Justice pursuant to this chapter are exempt from any law requiring disclosure of information to the public and shall be confidential except as otherwise provided in this chapter.

(b) All evidence and forensic samples containing biological material retained by the Department of Justice DNA Laboratory or other state law enforcement agency are exempt from any law requiring disclosure of information to the public or the return of biological specimens, samples, or print impressions.

(c) Non-DNA forensic identification information may be filed with the offender's file maintained by the Sex Registration Unit of the Department of Justice or in other computerized data bank or database systems maintained by the Department of Justice.

(d) The DNA and other forensic identification information retained by the Department of Justice pursuant to this chapter shall not be included in the state summary criminal history information. However, nothing in this chapter precludes law enforcement personnel from entering into a person's criminal history information or offender file maintained by the Department of Justice, the fact that the specimens, samples, and print impressions required by this chapter have or have not been collected from that person.

(e) The fact that the blood specimens, saliva or buccal swab samples, and print impressions required by this chapter have been received by the DNA Laboratory of the Department of Justice shall be included in the state summary criminal history information as soon as administratively practicable. The full palm prints of each hand shall be filed and maintained by the Automated Latent Print Section of the Bureau of Criminal Identification and Information of the Department of Justice, and may be included in the state summary criminal history information.

(f) DNA samples and DNA profiles and other forensic identification information shall be released only to law enforcement agencies, including, but not limited to, parole officers of the Department of Corrections, hearing officers of the parole authority, probation officers, the Attorney General's office, district attorneys' offices, and prosecuting city attorneys' offices, unless otherwise specifically authorized by this chapter. Dissemination of DNA specimens, samples, and DNA profiles and other forensic identification information to law enforcement agencies and district attorneys' offices outside this state shall be performed in conformity with the provisions of this chapter.

(g) A defendant's DNA and other forensic identification information developed pursuant to this chapter shall be available to his or her defense counsel upon court order made pursuant to Chapter 10 (commencing with Section 1054) of Title 6 of Part 2.

(h) Except as provided in subdivision (g) and in order to protect the confidentiality and privacy of database and data bank information, the Department of Justice and local public DNA laboratories shall not otherwise be compelled in a criminal or civil proceeding to provide any DNA profile or forensic identification database or data bank information or its computer database program software or structures to any person or party seeking such records or information whether by subpoena or discovery, or other procedural device or inquiry.

(i)

(1)

(A) Any person who knowingly uses an offender specimen, sample, or DNA profile collected pursuant to this chapter for other than criminal identification or exclusion purposes, or for other than the identification of missing persons, or who knowingly discloses DNA or other forensic identification information developed pursuant to this section to an unauthorized individual or agency, for other than criminal identification or exclusion purposes, or for the identification of missing persons, in violation of this chapter, shall be punished by imprisonment in a county jail not exceeding one year or by imprisonment in the state prison for 16 months, or two or three years.

(B) Any person who, for the purpose of financial gain, knowingly uses a specimen, sample, or DNA profile collected pursuant to this chapter for other than criminal identification or exclusion purposes or for the identification of missing persons or who, for the purpose of financial gain, knowingly discloses DNA or other forensic identification information developed pursuant to this section to an unauthorized individual or agency, for other than criminal identification or exclusion purposes or for other than the identification of missing persons, in violation of this chapter, shall, in addition to the penalty provided in subparagraph (A), be punished by a criminal fine in an amount three times that of any financial gain received or ten thousand dollars ($10,000), whichever is greater.

(2)

(A) If any employee of the Department of Justice knowingly uses a specimen, sample, or DNA profile collected pursuant to this chapter for other than criminal identification or exclusion purposes, or knowingly discloses DNA or other forensic identification information developed pursuant to this section to an unauthorized individual or agency, for other than criminal identification or exclusion purposes or for other than the identification of missing persons, in violation of this chapter, the department shall be liable in civil damages to the donor of the DNA identification information in the amount of five thousand dollars ($5,000) for each violation, plus attorney's fees and costs. In the event of multiple disclosures, the total damages available to the donor of the DNA is limited to fifty thousand dollars ($50,000) plus attorney's fees and costs.

(B)

(i) Notwithstanding any other law, this shall be the sole and exclusive remedy against the Department of Justice and its employees available to the donor of the DNA.

(ii) The Department of Justice employee disclosing DNA identification information in violation of this chapter shall be absolutely immune from civil liability under this or any other law.

(3) It is not a violation of this section for a law enforcement agency in its discretion to publicly disclose the fact of a DNA profile match, or the name of the person identified by the DNA match when this match is the basis of law enforcement's investigation, arrest, or prosecution of a particular person, or the identification of a missing or abducted person.

(j) It is not a violation of this chapter to furnish DNA or other forensic identification information of the defendant to his or her defense counsel for criminal defense purposes in compliance with discovery.

(k) It is not a violation of this section for law enforcement to release DNA and other forensic identification information developed pursuant to this chapter to a jury or grand jury, or in a document filed with a court or administrative agency, or as part of a judicial or administrative proceeding, or for this information to become part of the public transcript or record of proceedings when, in the discretion of law enforcement, disclosure is necessary because the DNA information pertains to the basis for law enforcement's identification, arrest, investigation, prosecution, or exclusion of a particular person related to the case.

(l) It is not a violation of this section to include information obtained from a file in a transcript or record of a judicial proceeding, or in any other public record when the inclusion of the information in the public record is authorized by a court, statute, or decisional law.

(m) It is not a violation of this section for the DNA Laboratory of the Department of Justice, or an organization retained as an agent of the Department of Justice, or a local public laboratory to use anonymous records or criminal history information obtained pursuant to this chapter for training, research, statistical analysis of populations, or quality assurance or quality control.

(n) The Department of Justice shall make public the methodology and procedures to be used in its DNA program prior to the commencement of DNA testing in its laboratories. The Department of Justice shall review and consider on an ongoing basis the findings and results of any peer review and validation studies submitted to the department by members of the relevant scientific community experienced in the use of DNA technology. This material shall be available to criminal defense counsel upon court order made pursuant to Chapter 10 (commencing with Section 1054) of Title 6 of Part 2.

(o) In order to maintain the computer system security of the Department of Justice DNA and Forensic Identification Database and Data Bank Program, the computer software and database structures used by the DNA Laboratory of the Department of Justice to implement this chapter are confidential.

Amended by Stats 2011 ch 39 (AB 117),s 68, eff. 6/30/2011.

Amended by Stats 2011 ch 39 (AB 117),s 15, eff. 6/30/2011.

Amended by Stats 2011 ch 15 (AB 109),s 323, eff. 4/4/2011, but operative no earlier than October 1, 2011, and only upon creation of a community corrections grant program to assist in implementing this act and upon an appropriation to fund the grant program.

Amended by Proposition 69, enacted by the people of the State of California 11/2/2004, eff. 11/3/2004.

Amended by Stats 2002 ch 664 (AB 3034), s 172, eff. 1/1/2003.

Amended by Stats 2001 ch 906 (AB 673), s 2, eff. 1/1/2002.

Amended by Stats 2000 ch 823 (AB 2814), s 6, eff. 1/1/2001.

Previously Amended September 23, 1999 (Bill Number: SB 654) (Chapter 475).

Section 299.6 - Sharing or dissemination of information

(a) Nothing in this chapter shall prohibit the Department of Justice, in its sole discretion, from the sharing or disseminating of population database or data bank information, DNA profile or forensic identification database or data bank information, analytical data and results generated for forensic identification database and data bank purposes, or protocol and forensic DNA analysis methods and quality assurance or quality control procedures with any of the following:

(1) Federal, state, or local law enforcement agencies.

(2) Crime laboratories, whether public or private, that serve federal, state, and local law enforcement agencies that have been approved by the Department of Justice.

(3) The attorney general's office of any state.

(4) Any state or federally authorized auditing agent or board that inspects or reviews the work of the Department of Justice DNA Laboratory for the purpose of ensuring that the laboratory meets ASCLD/LAB and FBI standards for accreditation and quality assurance standards necessary under this chapter and for the state's participation in CODIS and other national or international crime-solving networks.

(5) Any third party that the Department of Justice deems necessary to assist the department's crime laboratory with statistical analyses of population databases, or the analyses of forensic protocol, research methods, or quality control procedures, or to assist in the recovery or identification of human remains for humanitarian purposes, including identification of missing persons.

(b) The population databases and data banks of the DNA Laboratory of the Department of Justice may be made available to and searched by the FBI and any other agency participating in the FBI's CODIS System or any other national or international law enforcement database or data bank system.

(c) The Department of Justice may provide portions of biological samples including blood specimens, saliva samples, and buccal swab samples collected pursuant to this chapter to local public law enforcement DNA laboratories for identification purposes provided that the privacy provisions of this section are followed by the local public law enforcement laboratory and if each of the following conditions is met:

(1) The procedures used by the local public DNA laboratory for the handling of specimens and samples and the disclosure of results are the same as those established by the Department of Justice pursuant to Sections 297, 298, and 299.5.

(2) The methodologies and procedures used by the local public DNA laboratory for DNA or forensic identification analysis are compatible with those used by the Department of Justice, or otherwise are determined by the Department of Justice to be valid and appropriate for identification purposes.

(3) Only tests of value to law enforcement for identification purposes are performed and a copy of the results of the analysis are sent to the Department of Justice.

(4) All provisions of this section concerning privacy and security are followed.

(5) The local public law enforcement DNA laboratory assumes all costs of securing the specimens and samples and provides appropriate tubes, labels, and materials necessary to secure the specimens and samples.

(d) Any local DNA laboratory that produces DNA profiles of known reference samples for inclusion within the permanent files of the state's DNA Data Bank program shall follow the policies of the DNA Laboratory of the Department of Justice.

Amended by Proposition 69, enacted by the people of the State of California 11/2/2004, eff. 11/3/2004.

Amended by Stats 2001 ch 906 (AB 673), s 3, eff. 1/1/2002.

Previously Amended September 23, 1999 (Bill Number: SB 654) (Chapter 475).

See Stats 2001 ch 906 (AB 673), s 4.

Section 299.7 - Disposal of unused samples

The Department of Justice is authorized to dispose of unused specimens and samples, unused portions of specimens and samples, and expired specimens and samples in the normal course of business and in a reasonable manner as long as the disposal method is designed to protect the identity and origin of specimens and samples from disclosure to third persons who are not a part of law enforcement.

Added by Stats. 1998, Ch. 696, Sec. 2. Effective January 1, 1999.

Article 7 - CONSTRUCTION AND SEVERABILITY

Section 300 - No limitation or abrogation of existing authority of law enforcement officers

Nothing in this chapter shall limit or abrogate any existing authority of law enforcement officers to take, maintain, store, and utilize DNA or forensic identification markers, blood specimens, buccal swab samples, saliva samples, or thumb or palm print impressions for identification purposes.

Amended by Proposition 69, enacted by the people of the State of California 11/2/2004, eff. 11/3/2004.

Section 300.1 - No restriction on local authorities

(a) Nothing in this chapter shall be construed to restrict the authority of local law enforcement to maintain their own DNA-related databases or data banks, or to restrict the Department of Justice with respect to data banks and databases created by other statutory authority, including, but not limited to, databases related to fingerprints, firearms and other weapons, child abuse, domestic violence deaths, child deaths, driving offenses, missing persons, violent crime information as described in Title 12 (commencing with Section 14200) of Part 4, and criminal justice statistics permitted by Section 13305.

(b) Nothing in this chapter shall be construed to limit the authority of local or county coroners or their agents, in the course of their scientific investigation, to utilize genetic and DNA technology to inquire into and determine the circumstances, manner, and cause of death, or to employ or use outside laboratories, hospitals, or research institutions that utilize genetic and DNA technology.

Amended by Proposition 69, enacted by the people of the State of California 11/2/2004, eff. 11/3/2004.

Section 300.2 - Saliva samples

Any requirement to provide saliva samples pursuant to this chapter shall be construed as a requirement to provide buccal swab samples as of the effective date of the act that added this section. However, the Department of Justice may retain and use previously collected saliva and other biological samples as part of its database and databank program and for quality control purposes in conformity with the provisions of this chapter.

Added by Proposition 69, enacted by the people of the State of California 11/2/2004, eff. 11/2/2004.

Section 300.3 - Commencement of duties

The duties and requirements of the Department of Corrections and the Department of the Youth Authority pursuant to this chapter shall commence on July 1, 1999.

Added by Stats. 1998, Ch. 696, Sec. 2. Effective January 1, 1999.

Section 300.4 - Severability

The provisions of this chapter are severable. If any provision of this chapter or its application is held invalid, that invalidity shall not affect other provisions or applications that can be given effect without the invalid provision or application.

Renumbered from Ca. Pen. Code §300.2 by Stats 2015 ch 303 (AB 731),s 387, eff. 1/1/2016.

Chapter 7 - OF CRIMES AGAINST RELIGION AND CONSCIENCE, AND OTHER OFFENSES AGAINST GOOD MORALS

Section 302 - Unlawful disturbance of religious worship

(a) Every person who intentionally disturbs or disquiets any assemblage of people met for religious worship at a tax-exempt place of worship, by profane discourse, rude or indecent behavior, or by any unnecessary noise, either within the place where the meeting is held, or so near it as to disturb the order and solemnity of the meeting, is guilty of a misdemeanor punishable by a fine not exceeding one thousand dollars ($1,000), or by imprisonment in a county jail for a period not exceeding one year, or by both that fine and imprisonment.

(b) A court may require performance of community service of not less than 50 hours and not exceeding 80 hours as an alternative to imprisonment or a fine.

(c) In addition to the penalty set forth in subdivision (a), a person who has suffered a previous conviction of a violation of this section or Section 403, shall be required to perform community service of not less than 120 hours and not exceeding 160 hours.

(d) The existence of any fact which would bring a person under subdivision (c) or (d) shall be alleged in the complaint, information, or indictment and either:

    (1) Admitted by the defendant in open court.

    (2) Found to be true by a jury trying the issue of guilt.

    (3) Found to be true by the court where guilt is established by a plea of guilty or nolo contendere.

    (4) Found to be true by trial by the court sitting without a jury.

(e) Upon conviction of any person under this section for disturbances of religious worship, the court may, in accordance with the performance of community service imposed under this section, consistent with public safety interests and with the victim's consent, order the defendant to perform a portion of, or all of, the required community service at the place where the disturbance of religious worship occurred.

(f) The court may waive the mandatory minimum requirements for community service whenever it is in the interest of justice to do so. When a waiver is granted, the court shall state on the record all reasons supporting the waiver.

Amended by Stats. 1994, Ch. 401, Sec. 1. Effective January 1, 1995.

Section 303 - Unlawful procurement of encouragement of sale of alcoholic beverages

It shall be unlawful for any person engaged in the sale of alcoholic beverages, other than in the original package, to employ upon the premises where the alcoholic beverages are sold any person for the purpose of procuring or encouraging the purchase or sale of such beverages, or to pay any person a percentage or commission on the sale of such beverages for procuring or encouraging such purchase or sale. Violation of this section shall be a misdemeanor.

Added by Stats. 1935, Ch. 504.

Section 303a - Unlawful begging or solicitation of purchase of alcoholic beverage

It shall be unlawful, in any place of business where alcoholic beverages are sold to be consumed upon the premises, for any person to loiter in or about said premises for the purpose of begging or soliciting any patron or customer of, or visitor in, such premises to purchase any alcoholic beverage for the one begging or soliciting. Violation of this section shall be a misdemeanor.

Added by Stats. 1953, Ch. 1591.

Section 307 - Unlawful sale or gift of candy, cake, cookie, or chewing gum containing alcohol

Every person, firm, or corporation which sells or gives or in any way furnishes to another person, who is in fact under the age of 21 years, any candy, cake, cookie, or chewing gum which contains alcohol in excess of 1/2 of 1 percent by weight, is guilty of a misdemeanor.

Amended by Stats. 1985, Ch. 934, Sec. 4.

Section 308 - Unlawful sale or gift of tobacco, cigarettes, etc. of person under age of 21 years

(a)

    (1)

        (A)

            (i) Every person, firm, or corporation that knowingly or under circumstances in which it has knowledge, or should otherwise have grounds for knowledge, sells, gives, or in any way furnishes to another person who is under 21 years of age any tobacco, cigarette, or cigarette papers, or blunt wraps, or any other preparation of tobacco, or any other instrument or paraphernalia that is designed for the smoking or ingestion of tobacco, tobacco products, or any controlled substance, is subject to either a criminal action for a misdemeanor or a civil action brought by a city attorney, a county counsel, or a district attorney, punishable by a fine of two hundred dollars ($200) for the first offense, five hundred dollars ($500) for the second offense, and one thousand dollars ($1,000) for the third offense.

            (ii) This subparagraph does not apply to the sale, giving, or furnishing of any of the products specified in clause (i) to active duty military personnel who are 18 years of age or older. An identification card issued by the United States Armed Forces shall be used as proof of age for this purpose.

        (B) Notwithstanding Section 1464 or any other law, 25 percent of each civil and criminal penalty collected pursuant to this subdivision shall be paid to the office of the city attorney, county counsel, or district attorney, whoever is responsible for bringing the successful action.

        (C) Proof that a defendant, or his or her employee or agent, demanded, was shown, and reasonably relied upon evidence of majority shall be defense to any action brought pursuant to this subdivision. Evidence of majority of a person is a facsimile of, or a reasonable likeness of, a document issued by a federal, state, county, or municipal government, or subdivision or agency thereof, including, but not limited to, a motor vehicle operator's license, a registration certificate issued under the federal Military Selective Service Act (50 U.S.C. Sec. 3801 et seq.), or an identification card issued to a member of the Armed Forces.

(D) For purposes of this section, the person liable for selling or furnishing tobacco products to persons under 21 years of age by a tobacco vending machine shall be the person authorizing the installation or placement of the tobacco vending machine upon premises he or she manages or otherwise controls and under circumstances in which he or she has knowledge, or should otherwise have grounds for knowledge, that the tobacco vending machine will be utilized by persons under 21 years of age.

(2) For purposes of this section, "blunt wraps" means cigar papers or cigar wrappers of all types that are designed for smoking or ingestion of tobacco products and contain less than 50 percent tobacco.

(b) Every person, firm, or corporation that sells, or deals in tobacco or any preparation thereof, shall post conspicuously and keep so posted in his, her, or their place of business at each point of purchase the notice required pursuant to subdivision (b) of Section 22952 of the Business and Professions Code, and any person failing to do so shall, upon conviction, be punished by a fine of fifty dollars ($50) for the first offense, one hundred dollars ($100) for the second offense, two hundred fifty dollars ($250) for the third offense, and five hundred dollars ($500) for the fourth offense and each subsequent violation of this provision, or by imprisonment in a county jail not exceeding 30 days.

(c) For purposes of determining the liability of persons, firms, or corporations controlling franchises or business operations in multiple locations for the second and subsequent violations of this section, each individual franchise or business location shall be deemed a separate entity.

(d) It is the Legislature's intent to regulate the subject matter of this section. As a result, a city, county, or city and county shall not adopt any ordinance or regulation inconsistent with this section.

(e) For purposes of this section, "smoking" has the same meaning as in subdivision (c) of Section 22950.5 of the Business and Professions Code.

(f) For purposes of this section, "tobacco products" means a product or device as defined in subdivision (d) of Section 22950.5 of the Business and Professions Code.

Amended by Stats 2017 ch 561 (AB 1516),s 180, eff. 1/1/2018.
Amended by Stats 2016 ch 8 (SB X2-7),s 8.5, eff. 6/9/2016.
Amended by Stats 2016 ch 7 (SB X2-5),s 24, eff. 91 days after the adjournment of the 2015-16 Second Extraordinary Session Session.
Amended by Stats 2015 ch 303 (AB 731),s 388, eff. 1/1/2016.
Amended by Stats 2014 ch 442 (SB 1465),s 9, eff. 9/18/2014.
Amended by Stats 2012 ch 335 (AB 1301),s 5, eff. 1/1/2013.
Amended by Stats 2006 ch 501 (AB 1749),s 11, eff. 1/1/2007.
Amended by Stats 2004 ch 822 (AB 3092), s 5, eff. 9/27/2004.
Amended by Stats 2004 ch 798 (AB 384), s 2, eff. 1/1/2005, op. 7/1/2005.
Amended by Stats 2001 ch 376 (SB 757), s 4, eff. 1/1/2002.

Section 308.1 - Unlawful sale of "bidis" or "beedies"

(a) Notwithstanding any other law, no person shall sell, offer for sale, distribute, or import any tobacco product commonly referred to as "bidis" or "beedies," unless that tobacco product is sold, offered for sale, or intended to be sold in a business establishment that prohibits the presence of persons under 18 years of age on its premises.

(b) For purposes of this section, "bidis" or "beedies" means any of the following:

(1) A product containing tobacco that is wrapped in temburni leaf (diospyros melanoxylon) or tendu leaf (diospyros exculpra).

(2) A product that is marketed and sold as "bidis" or "beedies."

(c) Any person who violates this section is guilty of a misdemeanor and is also subject to a civil action brought by the Attorney General, a city attorney, county counsel, or district attorney for an injunction and a civil penalty of up to two thousand dollars ($2,000) per violation. This subdivision does not affect any other remedies available for a violation of this section.

Amended by Stats 2010 ch 265 (AB 2496),s 5, eff. 1/1/2011.
Added by Stats 2001 ch 375 (SB 322), s 1, eff. 1/1/2002.

Section 308.2 - Unlawful sale of cigarettes other than in sealed and labeled package

(a) Every person who sells one or more cigarettes, other than in a sealed and properly labeled package, is guilty of an infraction.

(b) "A sealed and properly labeled package," as used in this section, means the original packaging or sanitary wrapping of the manufacturer or importer which conforms to federal labeling requirements, including the federal warning label.

Added by Stats. 1991, Ch. 1231, Sec. 1.

Section 308.3 - Unlawful manufacture or sale of cigarettes

(a) A person, firm, corporation, or business may not manufacture for sale, distribute, sell, or offer to sell any cigarette, except in a package containing at least 20 cigarettes. A person, firm, corporation, or business may not manufacture for sale, distribute, sell, or offer to sell any roll-your-own tobacco, except in a package containing at least 0.60 ounces of tobacco.

(b) As used in subdivision (a), "cigarette" means any product that contains nicotine, is intended to be burned or heated under ordinary conditions of use, and consists of, or contains any of, the following:

(1) Any roll of tobacco wrapped in paper or in any substance not containing tobacco.

(2) Tobacco, in any form, that is functional in the product, that, because of its appearance, the type of tobacco used in the filler, or its packaging and labeling, is likely to be offered to, or purchased by, consumers as a cigarette.

(3) Any roll of tobacco wrapped in any substance containing tobacco which, because of its appearance, the type of tobacco used in the filler, or its packaging and labeling, is likely to be offered to, or purchased by, consumers as a cigarette described in this subdivision.

(c) Any person, firm, corporation, or business that violates this section is liable for an infraction, or in an action brought by the Attorney General, a district attorney, a county counsel, or a city attorney for a civil penalty of two hundred dollars ($200) for the first violation, five hundred dollars ($500) for the second violation, and one thousand dollars ($1,000) for each subsequent act constituting a violation.

Added by Stats 2001 ch 376 (SB 757), s 5, eff. 1/1/2002.

Section 308.5 - Unlawful sale, lease or provision of video game

(a) No person or business shall sell, lease, rent, or provide, or offer to sell, lease, rent, or otherwise offer to the public or to public establishments in this state, any video game intended for either private use or for use in a public establishment and intended primarily for use by any person under the age of 18 years, which contains, in its design and in the on-screen presentation of the video game, any paid commercial advertisement of alcoholic beverage or tobacco product containers or other forms of consumer packaging, particular brand names, trademarks, or copyrighted slogans of alcoholic beverages or tobacco products.

(b) As used in this section, "video game" means any electronic amusement device that utilizes a computer, microprocessor, or similar electronic circuitry and its own cathode ray tube, or is designed to be used with a television set or a monitor, that interacts with the user of the device.

(c) A violation of this section is a misdemeanor.

Added by Stats. 1990, Ch. 639, Sec. 2.

Section 308b - Unlawful delivery of tobacco products to residence

(a) Except as provided in subdivision (b), every person who knowingly delivers or causes to be delivered to any residence in this state any tobacco products unsolicited by any person residing therein is guilty of a misdemeanor.

(b) It is a defense to a violation of this section that the recipient of the tobacco products is personally known to the defendant at the time of the delivery.

(c) The distribution of unsolicited tobacco products to residences in violation of this section is a nuisance within the meaning of Section 3479 of the Civil Code.

(d) Nothing in this section shall be construed to impose any liability on any employee of the United States Postal Service for actions performed in the scope of his employment by the United States Postal Service.

Added by Stats. 1971, Ch. 1005.

Section 309 - Unlawful admission or keeping of minor in house of prostitution

Any proprietor, keeper, manager, conductor, or person having the control of any house of prostitution, or any house or room resorted to for the purpose of prostitution, who shall admit or keep any minor of either sex therein; or any parent or guardian of any such minor, who shall admit or keep such minor, or sanction, or connive at the admission or keeping thereof, into, or in any such house, or room, shall be guilty of a misdemeanor.

Added by Code Amendments 1880, Ch. 58.

Section 310 - Unlawful admission of minor to prizefight

(a) Any minor under 16 years of age who visits or attends any prizefight or place where any prizefight is advertised to take place, and any owner, lessee, or proprietor, or the agent of any owner, lessee, or proprietor of any place where any prizefight is advertised or represented to take place who admits any minor to a place where any prizefight is advertised or represented to take place or who admits, sells, or gives to any minor a ticket or other paper by which that minor may be admitted to a place where a prizefight is advertised to take place, is guilty of a misdemeanor, and is punishable by a fine not exceeding one hundred dollars ($100) or by imprisonment in the county jail for not more than 25 days.

(b) Any minor under 16 years of age who visits or attends any cockfight or place where any cockfight is advertised to take place, and any owner, lessee, or proprietor, or the agent of any owner, lessee, or proprietor of any place where any cockfight is advertised or represented to take place who admits any minor to a place where any cockfight is advertised or represented to take place or who admits, sells, or gives to any minor a ticket or other paper by which that minor may be admitted to a place where a cockfight is advertised to take place, is guilty of a misdemeanor, and is punishable by a fine not exceeding five hundred dollars ($500) or by imprisonment in the county jail for not more than 25 days.

Amended by Stats 2011 ch 562 (SB 425),s 1, eff. 1/1/2012.

Section 310.2 - Unlawful furnishing of diuretic, diet pill, or laxative to minor member of athletic team

(a) Any coach, trainer, or other person acting in an official or nonofficial capacity as an adult supervisor for an athletic team consisting of minors under the age of 18 who sells, gives, or otherwise furnishes to any member of that team a diuretic, diet pill, or laxative with the intent that it be consumed, injected, or administered for any nonmedical purpose such as loss of weight or altering the body in any way related to participation on the team or league, is guilty of a misdemeanor.

(b) Subdivision (a) does not apply to a minor's parent or guardian, or any person acting at the written direction of, or with the written consent of, the parent or guardian, if that person is in fact acting with that authority. Subdivision (a) does not apply to a physician.

Added by Stats. 1987, Ch. 999, Sec. 1.

Section 310.5 - Unlawful agreement relating to unlawful sex act upon child

(a) Any parent or guardian of a child who enters into an agreement on behalf of that child which is in violation of Section 1669.5 of the Civil Code, and any alleged perpetrator of an unlawful sex act upon that child who enters into such an agreement, is guilty of a misdemeanor.

(b) Every person convicted of a violation of subdivision (a) shall be punished by a fine of not less than one hundred dollars ($100) nor more than one thousand dollars ($1,000), by imprisonment in the county jail for not less than 30 days nor more than six months, or by both such a fine and imprisonment, at the discretion of the court.

(c) For purposes of this section, "unlawful sex act," means a felony sex offense committed against a minor.

Added by Stats. 1994, 1st Ex. Sess., Ch. 54, Sec. 2. Effective November 30, 1994.

Chapter 7.5 - OBSCENE MATTER

Section 311 - Definitions

As used in this chapter, the following definitions apply:

(a) "Obscene matter" means matter, taken as a whole, that to the average person, applying contemporary statewide standards, appeals to the prurient interest, that, taken as a whole, depicts or describes sexual conduct in a patently offensive way, and that, taken as a whole, lacks serious literary, artistic, political, or scientific value.

(1) If it appears from the nature of the matter or the circumstances of its dissemination, distribution, or exhibition that it is designed for clearly defined deviant sexual groups, the appeal of the matter shall be judged with reference to its intended recipient group.

(2) In prosecutions under this chapter, if circumstances of production, presentation, sale, dissemination, distribution, or publicity indicate that matter is being commercially exploited by the defendant for the sake of its prurient appeal, this evidence is probative with respect to the nature of the matter and may justify the conclusion that the matter lacks serious literary, artistic, political, or scientific value.

(3) In determining whether the matter taken as a whole lacks serious literary, artistic, political, or scientific value in description or representation of those matters, the fact that the defendant knew that the matter depicts persons under the age of 16 years engaged in sexual conduct, as defined in subdivision (c) of Section 311.4, is a factor that may be considered in making that determination.

(b) "Matter" means any book, magazine, newspaper, or other printed or written material, or any picture, drawing, photograph, motion picture, or other pictorial representation, or any statue or other figure, or any recording, transcription, or mechanical, chemical, or electrical reproduction, or any other article, equipment, machine, or material. "Matter" also means live or recorded telephone messages if transmitted, disseminated, or distributed as part of a commercial transaction.

(c) "Person" means any individual, partnership, firm, association, corporation, limited liability company, or other legal entity.

(d) "Distribute" means transfer possession of, whether with or without consideration.

(e) "Knowingly" means being aware of the character of the matter or live conduct.

(f) "Exhibit" means show.

(g) "Obscene live conduct" means any physical human body activity, whether performed or engaged in alone or with other persons, including but not limited to singing, speaking, dancing, acting, simulating, or pantomiming, taken as a whole, that to the average person, applying contemporary statewide standards, appeals to the prurient interest and is conduct that, taken as a whole, depicts or describes sexual conduct in a patently offensive way and that, taken as a whole, lacks serious literary, artistic, political, or scientific value.

(1) If it appears from the nature of the conduct or the circumstances of its production, presentation, or exhibition that it is designed for clearly defined deviant sexual groups, the appeal of the conduct shall be judged with reference to its intended recipient group.

(2) In prosecutions under this chapter, if circumstances of production, presentation, advertising, or exhibition indicate that live conduct is being commercially exploited by the defendant for the sake of its prurient appeal, that evidence is probative with respect to the nature of the conduct and may justify the conclusion that the conduct lacks serious literary, artistic, political, or scientific value.

(3) In determining whether the live conduct taken as a whole lacks serious literary, artistic, political, or scientific value in description or representation of those matters, the fact that the defendant knew that the live conduct depicts persons under the age of 16 years engaged in sexual conduct, as defined in subdivision (c) of Section 311.4, is a factor that may be considered in making that determination.

(h) The Legislature expresses its approval of the holding of People v. Cantrell, 7 Cal. App. 4th 523, that, for the purposes of this chapter, matter that "depicts a person under the age of 18 years personally engaging in or personally simulating sexual conduct" is limited to visual works that depict that conduct.

Amended by Stats. 1997, Ch. 17, Sec. 98. Effective January 1, 1998.

Section 311.1 - Distribution of obscene matter

(a) Every person who knowingly sends or causes to be sent, or brings or causes to be brought, into this state for sale or distribution, or in this state possesses, prepares, publishes, produces, develops, duplicates, or prints any representation of information, data, or image, including, but not limited to, any film, filmstrip, photograph, negative, slide, photocopy, videotape, video laser disc, computer hardware, computer software, computer floppy disc, data storage media, CD-ROM, or computer-generated equipment or any other computer-generated image that contains or incorporates in any manner, any film or filmstrip, with intent to distribute or to exhibit to, or to exchange with, others, or who offers to distribute, distributes, or exhibits to, or exchanges with, others, any obscene matter, knowing that the matter depicts a person under the age of 18 years personally engaging in or personally simulating sexual conduct, as defined in Section 311.4, shall be punished either by imprisonment in the county jail for up to one year, by a fine not to exceed one thousand dollars ($1,000), or by both the fine and imprisonment, or by imprisonment in the state prison, by a fine not to exceed ten thousand dollars ($10,000), or by the fine and imprisonment.

(b) This section does not apply to the activities of law enforcement and prosecuting agencies in the investigation and prosecution of criminal offenses or to legitimate medical, scientific, or educational activities, or to lawful conduct between spouses.

(c) This section does not apply to matter which depicts a child under the age of 18, which child is legally emancipated, including lawful conduct between spouses when one or both are under the age of 18.

(d) It does not constitute a violation of this section for a telephone corporation, as defined by Section 234 of the Public Utilities Code, to carry or transmit messages described in this chapter or perform related activities in providing telephone services.

Amended by Stats. 1996, Ch. 1080, Sec. 2. Effective January 1, 1997.

Section 311.2 - Punishment

(a) Every person who knowingly sends or causes to be sent, or brings or causes to be brought, into this state for sale or distribution, or in this state possesses, prepares, publishes, produces, or prints, with intent to distribute or to exhibit to others, or who offers to distribute, distributes, or exhibits to others, any obscene matter is for a first offense, guilty of a misdemeanor. If the person has previously been convicted of any violation of this section, the court may, in addition to the punishment authorized in Section 311.9, impose a fine not exceeding fifty thousand dollars ($50,000).

(b) Every person who knowingly sends or causes to be sent, or brings or causes to be brought, into this state for sale or distribution, or in this state possesses, prepares, publishes, produces, develops, duplicates, or prints any representation of information, data, or image, including, but not limited to, any film, filmstrip, photograph, negative, slide, photocopy, videotape, video laser disc, computer hardware, computer software, computer floppy disc, data storage media, CD-ROM, or computer-generated equipment or any other computer-generated image that contains or incorporates in any manner, any film or filmstrip, with intent to distribute or to exhibit to, or to exchange with, others for commercial consideration, or who offers to distribute, distributes, or exhibits to, or exchanges with, others for commercial consideration, any obscene matter, knowing that the matter depicts a person under the age of 18 years personally engaging in or personally simulating sexual conduct, as defined in Section 311.4, is guilty of a felony and shall be punished by imprisonment in the state prison for two, three, or six years, or by a fine not exceeding one hundred thousand dollars ($100,000), in the absence of a finding that the defendant would be incapable of paying that fine, or by both that fine and imprisonment.

(c) Every person who knowingly sends or causes to be sent, or brings or causes to be brought, into this state for sale or distribution, or in this state possesses, prepares, publishes, produces, develops, duplicates, or prints any representation of information, data, or image, including, but not limited to, any film, filmstrip, photograph, negative, slide, photocopy, videotape, video laser disc, computer hardware, computer software, computer floppy disc, data storage media, CD-ROM, or computer-generated equipment or any other computer-generated image that contains or incorporates in any manner, any film or filmstrip, with intent to distribute or exhibit to, or to exchange with, a person 18 years of age or older, or who offers to distribute, distributes, or exhibits to, or exchanges with, a person 18 years of age or older any matter, knowing that the matter depicts a person under the age of 18 years personally engaging in or personally simulating sexual conduct, as defined in Section 311.4, shall be punished by imprisonment in the county jail for up to one year, or by a fine not exceeding two thousand dollars ($2,000), or by both that fine and imprisonment, or by imprisonment in the state prison. It is not necessary to prove commercial consideration or that the matter is obscene in order to establish a violation of this subdivision. If a person has been previously convicted of a violation of this subdivision, he or she is guilty of a felony.

(d) Every person who knowingly sends or causes to be sent, or brings or causes to be brought, into this state for sale or distribution, or in this state possesses, prepares, publishes, produces, develops, duplicates, or prints any representation of information, data, or image, including, but not limited to, any film, filmstrip, photograph, negative, slide, photocopy, videotape, video laser disc, computer hardware, computer software, computer floppy disc, data storage media, CD-ROM, or computer-generated equipment or any other computer-generated image that contains or incorporates in any manner, any film or filmstrip, with intent to distribute or exhibit to, or to exchange with, a person under 18 years of age, or who offers to distribute, distributes, or exhibits to, or exchanges with, a person under 18 years of age any matter, knowing that the matter depicts a person under the age of 18 years personally engaging in or personally simulating sexual conduct, as defined in Section 311.4, is guilty of a felony. It is not necessary to prove commercial consideration or that the matter is obscene in order to establish a violation of this subdivision.

(e) Subdivisions (a) to (d), inclusive, do not apply to the activities of law enforcement and prosecuting agencies in the investigation and prosecution of criminal offenses, to legitimate medical, scientific, or educational activities, or to lawful conduct between spouses.

(f) This section does not apply to matter that depicts a legally emancipated child under the age of 18 years or to lawful conduct between spouses when one or both are under the age of 18 years.

(g) It does not constitute a violation of this section for a telephone corporation, as defined by Section 234 of the Public Utilities Code, to carry or transmit messages described in this chapter or to perform related activities in providing telephone services.

Amended by Stats 2006 ch 337 (SB 1128),s 20, eff. 9/20/2006.

Section 311.3 - Sexual exploitation of child

(a) A person is guilty of sexual exploitation of a child if he or she knowingly develops, duplicates, prints, or exchanges any representation of information, data, or image, including, but not limited to, any film, filmstrip, photograph, negative, slide, photocopy, videotape, video laser disc, computer hardware, computer software, computer floppy disc, data storage media, CD-ROM, or computer-generated equipment or any other computer-generated image that contains or incorporates in any manner, any film or filmstrip that depicts a person under the age of 18 years engaged in an act of sexual conduct.

(b) As used in this section, "sexual conduct" means any of the following:

(1) Sexual intercourse, including genital-genital, oral-genital, anal-genital, or oral-anal, whether between persons of the same or opposite sex or between humans and animals.

(2) Penetration of the vagina or rectum by any object.

(3) Masturbation for the purpose of sexual stimulation of the viewer.

(4) Sadomasochistic abuse for the purpose of sexual stimulation of the viewer.

(5) Exhibition of the genitals or the pubic or rectal area of any person for the purpose of sexual stimulation of the viewer.

(6) Defecation or urination for the purpose of sexual stimulation of the viewer.

(c) Subdivision (a) does not apply to the activities of law enforcement and prosecution agencies in the investigation and prosecution of criminal offenses or to legitimate medical, scientific, or educational activities, or to lawful conduct between spouses.

(d) Every person who violates subdivision (a) shall be punished by a fine of not more than two thousand dollars ($2,000) or by imprisonment in a county jail for not more than one year, or by both that fine and imprisonment. If the person has been previously convicted of a violation of subdivision (a) or any section of this chapter, he or she shall be punished by imprisonment in the state prison.

(e) The provisions of this section do not apply to an employee of a commercial film developer who is acting within the scope of his or her employment and in accordance with the instructions of his or her employer, provided that the employee has no financial interest in the commercial developer by which he or she is employed.

(f) Subdivision (a) does not apply to matter that is unsolicited and is received without knowledge or consent through a facility, system, or network over which the person or entity has no control.

Amended by Stats. 1996, Ch. 1080, Sec. 4.1. Effective January 1, 1997.

Section 311.4 - Unlawful use of minor

(a) Every person who, with knowledge that a person is a minor, or who, while in possession of any facts on the basis of which he or she should reasonably know that the person is a minor, hires, employs, or uses the minor to do or assist in doing any of the acts described in Section 311.2, shall be punished by imprisonment in the county jail for up to one year, or by a fine not exceeding two thousand dollars ($2,000), or by both that fine and imprisonment, or by imprisonment in the state prison. If the person has previously been convicted of any violation of this section, the court may, in addition to the punishment authorized in Section 311.9, impose a fine not exceeding fifty thousand dollars ($50,000).

(b) Every person who, with knowledge that a person is a minor under the age of 18 years, or who, while in possession of any facts on the basis of which he or she should reasonably know that the person is a minor under the age of 18 years, knowingly promotes, employs, uses, persuades, induces, or coerces a minor under the age of 18 years, or any parent or guardian of a minor under the age of

176

18 years under his or her control who knowingly permits the minor, to engage in or assist others to engage in either posing or modeling alone or with others for purposes of preparing any representation of information, data, or image, including, but not limited to, any film, filmstrip, photograph, negative, slide, photocopy, videotape, video laser disc, computer hardware, computer software, computer floppy disc, data storage media, CD-ROM, or computer-generated equipment or any other computer-generated image that contains or incorporates in any manner, any film, filmstrip, or a live performance involving, sexual conduct by a minor under the age of 18 years alone or with other persons or animals, for commercial purposes, is guilty of a felony and shall be punished by imprisonment in the state prison for three, six, or eight years.

(c) Every person who, with knowledge that a person is a minor under the age of 18 years, or who, while in possession of any facts on the basis of which he or she should reasonably know that the person is a minor under the age of 18 years, knowingly promotes, employs, uses, persuades, induces, or coerces a minor under the age of 18 years, or any parent or guardian of a minor under the age of 18 years under his or her control who knowingly permits the minor, to engage in or assist others to engage in either posing or modeling alone or with others for purposes of preparing any representation of information, data, or image, including, but not limited to, any film, filmstrip, photograph, negative, slide, photocopy, videotape, video laser disc, computer hardware, computer software, computer floppy disc, data storage media, CD-ROM, or computer-generated equipment or any other computer-generated image that contains or incorporates in any manner, any film, filmstrip, or a live performance involving, sexual conduct by a minor under the age of 18 years alone or with other persons or animals, is guilty of a felony. It is not necessary to prove commercial purposes in order to establish a violation of this subdivision.

(d)

(1) As used in subdivisions (b) and (c), "sexual conduct" means any of the following, whether actual or simulated: sexual intercourse, oral copulation, anal intercourse, anal oral copulation, masturbation, bestiality, sexual sadism, sexual masochism, penetration of the vagina or rectum by any object in a lewd or lascivious manner, exhibition of the genitals or pubic or rectal area for the purpose of sexual stimulation of the viewer, any lewd or lascivious sexual act as defined in Section 288, or excretory functions performed in a lewd or lascivious manner, whether or not any of the above conduct is performed alone or between members of the same or opposite sex or between humans and animals. An act is simulated when it gives the appearance of being sexual conduct.

(2) As used in subdivisions (b) and (c), "matter" means any film, filmstrip, photograph, negative, slide, photocopy, videotape, video laser disc, computer hardware, computer software, computer floppy disc, or any other computer-related equipment or computer-generated image that contains or incorporates in any manner, any film, filmstrip, photograph, negative, slide, photocopy, videotape, or video laser disc.

(e) This section does not apply to a legally emancipated minor or to lawful conduct between spouses if one or both are under the age of 18.

(f) In every prosecution under this section involving a minor under the age of 14 years at the time of the offense, the age of the victim shall be pled and proven for the purpose of the enhanced penalty provided in Section 647.6. Failure to plead and prove that the victim was under the age of 14 years at the time of the offense is not a bar to prosecution under this section if it is proven that the victim was under the age of 18 years at the time of the offense.

Amended by Stats 2006 ch 337 (SB 1128),s 21, eff. 9/20/2006.

Section 311.5 - Unlawful creation or promotion of obscene matter

Every person who writes, creates, or solicits the publication or distribution of advertising or other promotional material, or who in any manner promotes, the sale, distribution, or exhibition of matter represented or held out by him to be obscene, is guilty of a misdemeanor.

Amended by Stats. 1969, Ch. 249.

Section 311.6 - Unlawful presentation of obscene live conduct

Every person who knowingly engages or participates in, manages, produces, sponsors, presents or exhibits obscene live conduct to or before an assembly or audience consisting of at least one person or spectator in any public place or in any place exposed to public view, or in any place open to the public or to a segment thereof, whether or not an admission fee is charged, or whether or not attendance is conditioned upon the presentation of a membership card or other token, is guilty of a misdemeanor.

Amended by Stats. 1970, Ch. 1072.

Section 311.7 - Unlawful conditioning of purchase or consignment upon receipt of obscene matter

Every person who, knowingly, as a condition to a sale, allocation, consignment, or delivery for resale of any paper, magazine, book, periodical, publication or other merchandise, requires that the purchaser or consignee receive any obscene matter or who denies or threatens to deny a franchise, revokes or threatens to revoke, or imposes any penalty, financial or otherwise, by reason of the failure of any person to accept obscene matter, or by reason of the return of such obscene matter, is guilty of a misdemeanor.

Added by Stats. 1961, Ch. 2147.

Section 311.8 - Defenses

(a) It shall be a defense in any prosecution for a violation of this chapter that the act charged was committed in aid of legitimate scientific or educational purposes.

(b) It shall be a defense in any prosecution for a violation of this chapter by a person who knowingly distributed any obscene matter by the use of telephones or telephone facilities to any person under the age of 18 years that the defendant has taken either of the following measures to restrict access to the obscene matter by persons under 18 years of age:

(1) Required the person receiving the obscene matter to use an authorized access or identification code, as provided by the information provider, before transmission of the obscene matter begins, where the defendant has previously issued the code by mailing it to the applicant therefor after taking reasonable measures to ascertain that the applicant was 18 years of age or older and has established a procedure to immediately cancel the code of any person after receiving notice, in writing or by telephone, that the code has been lost, stolen, or used by persons under the age of 18 years or that the code is no longer desired.

(2) Required payment by credit card before transmission of the matter.

(c) Any list of applicants or recipients compiled or maintained by an information-access service provider for purposes of compliance with subdivision (b) is confidential and shall not be sold or otherwise disseminated except upon order of the court.
Amended by Stats. 1987, Ch. 1101, Sec. 1.

Section 311.9 - Fines

(a) Every person who violates subdivision (a) of Section 311.2 or Section 311.5 is punishable by fine of not more than one thousand dollars ($1,000) plus five dollars ($5) for each additional unit of material coming within the provisions of this chapter, which is involved in the offense, not to exceed ten thousand dollars ($10,000), or by imprisonment in the county jail for not more than six months plus one day for each additional unit of material coming within the provisions of this chapter, and which is involved in the offense, not to exceed a total of 360 days in the county jail, or by both that fine and imprisonment. If that person has previously been convicted of any offense in this chapter, or of a violation of Section 313.1, a violation of subdivision (a) of Section 311.2 or Section 311.5 is punishable as a felony by imprisonment pursuant to subdivision (h) of Section 1170.

(b) Every person who violates subdivision (a) of Section 311.4 is punishable by fine of not more than two thousand dollars ($2,000) or by imprisonment in the county jail for not more than one year, or by both that fine and imprisonment, or by imprisonment pursuant to subdivision (h) of Section 1170. If that person has been previously convicted of a violation of former Section 311.3 or Section 311.4 he or she is punishable by imprisonment pursuant to subdivision (h) of Section 1170.

(c) Every person who violates Section 311.7 is punishable by fine of not more than one thousand dollars ($1,000) or by imprisonment in the county jail for not more than six months, or by both that fine and imprisonment. For a second and subsequent offense he or she shall be punished by a fine of not more than two thousand dollars ($2,000), or by imprisonment in the county jail for not more than one year, or by both that fine and imprisonment. If the person has been twice convicted of a violation of this chapter, a violation of Section 311.7 is punishable as a felony by imprisonment pursuant to subdivision (h) of Section 1170.
Amended by Stats 2011 ch 39 (AB 117),s 68, eff. 6/30/2011.
Amended by Stats 2011 ch 15 (AB 109),s 324, eff. 4/4/2011, but operative no earlier than October 1, 2011, and only upon creation of a community corrections grant program to assist in implementing this act and upon an appropriation to fund the grant program.
Amended by Stats 2006 ch 337 (SB 1128),s 22, eff. 9/20/2006.

Section 311.10 - Unlawful advertisement for sale or distribution obscene matter knowing it depicts person under age of 18 years engaging in or simulating sexual conduct

(a) Any person who advertises for sale or distribution any obscene matter knowing that it depicts a person under the age of 18 years personally engaging in or personally simulating sexual conduct, as defined in Section 311.4, is guilty of a felony and is punishable by imprisonment in the state prison for two, three, or four years, or in a county jail not exceeding one year, or by a fine not exceeding fifty thousand dollars ($50,000), or by both such fine and imprisonment.

(b) Subdivision (a) shall not apply to the activities of law enforcement and prosecution agencies in the investigation and prosecution of criminal offenses.
Added by Stats. 1985, Ch. 1550, Sec. 1.

Section 311.11 - Unlawful possession of obscene matter knowing it depicts person under age of 18 years engaging in or simulating sexual conduct

(a) Every person who knowingly possesses or controls any matter, representation of information, data, or image, including, but not limited to, any film, filmstrip, photograph, negative, slide, photocopy, videotape, video laser disc, computer hardware, computer software, computer floppy disc, data storage media, CD-ROM, or computer-generated equipment or any other computer-generated image that contains or incorporates in any manner, any film or filmstrip, the production of which involves the use of a person under 18 years of age, knowing that the matter depicts a person under 18 years of age personally engaging in or simulating sexual conduct, as defined in subdivision (d) of Section 311.4, is guilty of a felony and shall be punished by imprisonment in the state prison, or a county jail for up to one year, or by a fine not exceeding two thousand five hundred dollars ($2,500), or by both the fine and imprisonment.

(b) Every person who commits a violation of subdivision (a), and who has been previously convicted of a violation of this section, an offense requiring registration under the Sex Offender Registration Act, or an attempt to commit any of the above-mentioned offenses, is guilty of a felony and shall be punished by imprisonment in the state prison for two, four, or six years.

(c) Each person who commits a violation of subdivision (a) shall be punished by imprisonment in the state prison for 16 months, or two or five years, or shall be punished by imprisonment in a county jail for up to one year, or by a fine not exceeding two thousand five hundred dollars ($2,500), or by both the fine and imprisonment, if one of the following factors exists:

    (1) The matter contains more than 600 images that violate subdivision (a), and the matter contains 10 or more images involving a prepubescent minor or a minor who has not attained 12 years of age.

    (2) The matter portrays sexual sadism or sexual masochism involving a person under 18 years of age. For purposes of this section, "sexual sadism" means the intentional infliction of pain for purposes of sexual gratification or stimulation. For purposes of this section, "sexual masochism" means intentionally experiencing pain for purposes of sexual gratification or stimulation.

(d) It is not necessary to prove that the matter is obscene in order to establish a violation of this section.

(e) This section does not apply to drawings, figurines, statues, or any film rated by the Motion Picture Association of America, nor does it apply to live or recorded telephone messages when transmitted, disseminated, or distributed as part of a commercial transaction.

(f) For purposes of determining the number of images under paragraph (1) of subdivision (c), the following shall apply:

    (1) Each photograph, picture, computer or computer-generated image, or any similar visual depiction shall be considered to be one image.

    (2) Each video, video-clip, movie, or similar visual depiction shall be considered to have 50 images.
Amended by Stats 2014 ch 71 (SB 1304),s 119, eff. 1/1/2015.
Amended by Stats 2014 ch 54 (SB 1461),s 12, eff. 1/1/2015.
Amended by Stats 2013 ch 777 (SB 145),s 3, eff. 1/1/2014.
Amended by Stats 2007 ch 579 (SB 172),s 38, eff. 10/13/2007.
Amended by Stats 2006 ch 337 (SB 1128),s 23, eff. 9/20/2006.

Amended by Stats 2001 ch 559 (AB 1012), s 1, eff. 1/1/2002.

Section 311.12 - Fines

(a)

(1) Every person who is convicted of a violation of Section 311.1, 311.2, 311.3, 311.10, or 311.11 in which the offense involves the production, use, possession, control, or advertising of matter or image that depicts a person under 18 years of age personally engaging in or simulating sexual conduct, as defined in subdivision (d) of Section 311.4, in which the violation is committed on, or via, a government-owned computer or via a government-owned computer network, shall, in addition to any imprisonment or fine imposed for the commission of the underlying offense, be punished by a fine not exceeding two thousand dollars ($2,000), unless the court determines that the defendant does not have the ability to pay.

(2) Every person who is convicted of a violation of Section 311.1, 311.2, 311.3, 311.10, or 311.11 in which the offense involves the production, use, possession, control, or advertising of matter or image that depicts a person under 18 years of age personally engaging in or simulating sexual conduct, as defined in subdivision (d) of Section 311.4, in which the production, transportation, or distribution of which involves the use, possession, or control of government-owned property shall, in addition to any imprisonment or fine imposed for the commission of the underlying offense, be punished by a fine not exceeding two thousand dollars ($2,000), unless the court determines that the defendant does not have the ability to pay.

(b) The fines in subdivision (a) shall not be subject to the provisions of Sections 70372, 76000, 76000.5, and 76104.6 of the Government Code, or Sections 1464 and 1465.7 of this code.

(c) Revenue from any fines collected pursuant to this section shall be deposited into a county fund established for that purpose and allocated as follows, and a county may transfer all or part of any of those allocations to another county for the allocated use:

(1) One-third for sexual assault investigator training.

(2) One-third for public agencies and nonprofit corporations that provide shelter, counseling, or other direct services for victims of human trafficking.

(3) One-third for multidisciplinary teams.

(d) As used in this section:

(1) "Computer" includes any computer hardware, computer software, computer floppy disk, data storage medium, or CD-ROM.

(2) "Government-owned" includes property and networks owned or operated by state government, city government, city and county government, county government, a public library, or a public college or university.

(3) "Multidisciplinary teams" means a child-focused, facility-based program in which representatives from many disciplines, including law enforcement, child protection, prosecution, medical and mental health, and victim and child advocacy work together to conduct interviews and make team decisions about the investigation, treatment, management, and prosecution of child abuse cases, including child sexual abuse cases. It is the intent of the Legislature that this multidisciplinary team approach will protect victims of child abuse from multiple interviews, result in a more complete understanding of case issues, and provide the most effective child- and family-focused system response possible.

(e) This section shall not be construed to require any government or government entity to retain data in violation of any provision of state or federal law.

Amended by Stats 2014 ch 71 (SB 1304),s 120, eff. 1/1/2015.

Added by Stats 2013 ch 143 (AB 20),s 1, eff. 1/1/2014.

Section 312 - Destruction of material

Upon the conviction of the accused, the court may, when the conviction becomes final, order any matter or advertisement, in respect whereof the accused stands convicted, and which remains in the possession or under the control of the district attorney or any law enforcement agency, to be destroyed, and the court may cause to be destroyed any such material in its possession or under its control.

Repealed and added by Stats. 1961, Ch. 2147.

Section 312.1 - Evidence of obscenity

In any prosecution for a violation of the provisions of this chapter or of Chapter 7.6 (commencing with Section 313), neither the prosecution nor the defense shall be required to introduce expert witness testimony concerning the obscene or harmful character of the matter or live conduct which is the subject of the prosecution. Any evidence which tends to establish contemporary community standards of appeal to prurient interest or of customary limits of candor in the description or representation of nudity, sex, or excretion, or which bears upon the question of significant literary, artistic, political, educational, or scientific value shall, subject to the provisions of the Evidence Code, be admissible when offered by either the prosecution or by the defense.

Amended by Stats 2001 ch 854 (SB 205), s 25, eff. 1/1/2002.

Section 312.3 - Forfeiture

(a) Matter that depicts a person under the age of 18 years personally engaging in or personally simulating sexual conduct as defined in Section 311.4 and that is in the possession of any city, county, city and county, or state official or agency is subject to forfeiture pursuant to this section.

(b) An action to forfeit matter described in subdivision (a) may be brought by the Attorney General, the district attorney, county counsel, or the city attorney. Proceedings shall be initiated by a petition of forfeiture filed in the superior court of the county in which the matter is located.

(c) The prosecuting agency shall make service of process of a notice regarding that petition upon every individual who may have a property interest in the alleged proceeds. The notice shall state that any interested party may file a verified claim with the superior court stating the amount of their claimed interest and an affirmation or denial of the prosecuting agency's allegation. If the notice cannot be given by registered mail or personal delivery, the notice shall be published for at least three successive weeks in a newspaper of general circulation in the county where the property is located. All notices shall set forth the time within which a claim of interest in the property seized is required to be filed.

(d)

(1) Any person claiming an interest in the property or proceeds may, at any time within 30 days from the date of the first publication of the notice of seizure, or within 30 days after receipt of actual notice, file with the superior court of the county in which the action is pending a verified claim stating his or her interest in the property or proceeds. A verified copy of the claim shall be given by the claimant to the Attorney General or district attorney, county counsel, or city attorney, as appropriate.

(2) If, at the end of the time set forth in paragraph (1), an interested person has not filed a claim, the court, upon motion, shall declare that the person has defaulted upon his or her alleged interest, and it shall be subject to forfeiture upon proof of compliance with subdivision (c).

(e) The burden is on the petitioner to prove beyond a reasonable doubt that matter is subject to forfeiture pursuant to this section.

(f) It is not necessary to seek or obtain a criminal conviction prior to the entry of an order for the destruction of matter pursuant to this section. Any matter described in subdivision (a) that is in the possession of any city, county, city and county, or state official or agency, including found property, or property obtained as the result of a case in which no trial was had or that has been disposed of by way of dismissal or otherwise than by way of conviction may be ordered destroyed.

(g) A court order for destruction of matter described in subdivision (a) may be carried out by a police or sheriff's department or by the Department of Justice. The court order shall specify the agency responsible for the destruction.

(h) As used in this section, "matter" means any book, magazine, newspaper, or other printed or written material or any picture, drawing, photograph, motion picture, or other pictorial representation, or any statue or other figure, or any recording, transcription or mechanical, chemical or electrical reproduction, or any other articles, equipment, machines, or materials. "Matter" also means any representation of information, data, or image, including, but not limited to, any film, filmstrip, photograph, negative, slide, photocopy, videotape, video laser disc, computer hardware, computer software, computer floppy disc, data storage media, CD-ROM, or computer-generated equipment or any other computer-generated image that contains or incorporates in any manner any film or filmstrip.

(i) This section does not apply to a depiction of a legally emancipated minor or to lawful conduct between spouses if one or both are under the age of 18.

(j) It is a defense in any forfeiture proceeding that the matter seized was lawfully possessed in aid of legitimate scientific or educational purposes.

Amended by Stats. 1996, Ch. 1080, Sec. 7. Effective January 1, 1997.

Section 312.5 - Severability

If any phrase, clause, sentence, section or provision of this chapter or application thereof to any person or circumstance is held invalid, such invalidity shall not affect any other phrase, clause, sentence, section, provision or application of this chapter, which can be given effect without the invalid phrase, clause, sentence, section, provision or application and to this end the provisions of this chapter are declared to be severable.

Added by Stats. 1969, Ch. 249.

Section 312.6 - Liability of person or entity providing access or connection; liability of employer; defense

(a) It does not constitute a violation of this chapter for a person or entity solely to provide access or connection to or from a facility, system, or network over which that person or entity has no control, including related capabilities that are incidental to providing access or connection. This subdivision does not apply to an individual or entity that is owned or controlled by, or a conspirator with, an entity actively involved in the creation, editing, or knowing distribution of communications that violate this chapter.

(b) An employer is not liable under this chapter for the actions of an employee or agent unless the employee's or agent's conduct is within the scope of his or her employment or agency and the employer has knowledge of, authorizes, or ratifies the employee's or agent's conduct.

(c) It is a defense to prosecution under this chapter and in any civil action that may be instituted based on a violation of this chapter that a person has taken reasonable, effective, and appropriate actions in good faith to restrict or prevent the transmission of, or access to, a communication specified in this chapter.

Added by Stats. 1996, Ch. 1080, Sec. 8. Effective January 1, 1997.

Section 312.7 - Inapplicability to interstate services

Nothing in this chapter shall be construed to apply to interstate services or to any other activities or actions for which states are prohibited from imposing liability pursuant to Paragraph (4) of subsection (g) of Section 223 of Title 47 of the United States Code.

Added by Stats. 1996, Ch. 1080, Sec. 9. Effective January 1, 1997.

Chapter 7.6 - HARMFUL MATTER

Section 313 - Definitions

As used in this chapter:

(a) "Harmful matter" means matter, taken as a whole, which to the average person, applying contemporary statewide standards, appeals to the prurient interest, and is matter which, taken as a whole, depicts or describes in a patently offensive way sexual conduct and which, taken as a whole, lacks serious literary, artistic, political, or scientific value for minors.

(1) When it appears from the nature of the matter or the circumstances of its dissemination, distribution or exhibition that it is designed for clearly defined deviant sexual groups, the appeal of the matter shall be judged with reference to its intended recipient group.

(2) In prosecutions under this chapter, where circumstances of production, presentation, sale, dissemination, distribution, or publicity indicate that matter is being commercially exploited by the defendant for the sake of its prurient appeal, that evidence is probative with respect to the nature of the matter and can justify the conclusion that the matter lacks serious literary, artistic, political, or scientific value for minors.

(b) "Matter" means any book, magazine, newspaper, video recording, or other printed or written material or any picture, drawing, photograph, motion picture, or other pictorial representation or any statue or other figure, or any recording, transcription, or mechanical, chemical, or electrical reproduction or any other articles, equipment, machines, or materials. "Matter" also includes live or recorded telephone messages when transmitted, disseminated, or distributed as part of a commercial transaction.

(c) "Person" means any individual, partnership, firm, association, corporation, limited liability company, or other legal entity.

(d) "Distribute" means to transfer possession of, whether with or without consideration.

(e) "Knowingly" means being aware of the character of the matter.

(f) "Exhibit" means to show.

(g) "Minor" means any natural person under 18 years of age.

Amended by Stats. 1994, Ch. 1010, Sec. 190. Effective January 1, 1995.

Section 313.1 - Unlawful distribution of harmful matter to minor

(a) Every person who, with knowledge that a person is a minor, or who fails to exercise reasonable care in ascertaining the true age of a minor, knowingly sells, rents, distributes, sends, causes to be sent, exhibits, or offers to distribute or exhibit by any means, including, but not limited to, live or recorded telephone messages, any harmful matter to the minor shall be punished as specified in Section 313.4. It does not constitute a violation of this section for a telephone corporation, as defined by Section 234 of the Public Utilities Code, to carry or transmit messages described in this chapter or to perform related activities in providing telephone services.

(b) Every person who misrepresents himself or herself to be the parent or guardian of a minor and thereby causes the minor to be admitted to an exhibition of any harmful matter shall be punished as specified in Section 313.4.

(c)

    (1) Any person who knowingly displays, sells, or offers to sell in any coin-operated or slug-operated vending machine or mechanically or electronically controlled vending machine that is located in a public place, other than a public place from which minors are excluded, any harmful matter displaying to the public view photographs or pictorial representations of the commission of any of the following acts shall be punished as specified in Section 313.4: sodomy, oral copulation, sexual intercourse, masturbation, bestiality, or a photograph of an exposed penis in an erect and turgid state.

    (2) Any person who knowingly displays, sells, or offers to sell in any coin-operated vending machine that is not supervised by an adult and that is located in a public place, other than a public place from which minors are excluded, any harmful matter, as defined in subdivision (a) of Section 313, shall be punished as specified in Section 313.4.

(d) Nothing in this section invalidates or prohibits the adoption of an ordinance by a city, county, or city and county that restricts the display of material that is harmful to minors, as defined in this chapter, in a public place, other than a public place from which minors are excluded, by requiring the placement of devices commonly known as blinder racks in front of the material, so that the lower two-thirds of the material is not exposed to view.

(e) Any person who sells or rents video recordings of harmful matter shall create an area within his or her business establishment for the placement of video recordings of harmful matter and for any material that advertises the sale or rental of these video recordings. This area shall be labeled "adults only." The failure to create and label the area is an infraction, punishable by a fine not to exceed one hundred dollars ($100). The failure to place a video recording or advertisement, regardless of its content, in this area shall not constitute an infraction. Any person who sells or distributes video recordings of harmful matter to others for resale purposes shall inform the purchaser of the requirements of this section. This subdivision shall not apply to public libraries as defined in Section 18710 of the Education Code.

(f) Any person who rents a video recording and alters the video recording by adding harmful material, and who then returns the video recording to a video rental store, shall be guilty of a misdemeanor. It shall be a defense in any prosecution for a violation of this subdivision that the video rental store failed to post a sign, reasonably visible to all customers, delineating the provisions of this subdivision.

(g) It shall be a defense in any prosecution for a violation of subdivision (a) by a person who knowingly distributed any harmful matter by the use of telephones or telephone facilities to any person under the age of 18 years that the defendant has taken either of the following measures to restrict access to the harmful matter by persons under 18 years of age:

    (1) Required the person receiving the harmful matter to use an authorized access or identification code, as provided by the information provider, before transmission of the harmful matter begins, where the defendant previously has issued the code by mailing it to the applicant after taking reasonable measures to ascertain that the applicant was 18 years of age or older and has established a procedure to immediately cancel the code of any person after receiving notice, in writing or by telephone, that the code has been lost, stolen, or used by persons under the age of 18 years or that the code is no longer desired.

    (2) Required payment by credit card before transmission of the matter.

(h) It shall be a defense in any prosecution for a violation of paragraph (2) of subdivision (c) that the defendant has taken either of the following measures to restrict access to the harmful matter by persons under 18 years of age:

    (1) Required the person receiving the harmful matter to use an authorized access or identification card to the vending machine after taking reasonable measures to ascertain that the applicant was 18 years of age or older and has established a procedure to immediately cancel the card of any person after receiving notice, in writing or by telephone, that the code has been lost, stolen, or used by persons under the age of 18 years or that the card is no longer desired.

    (2) Required the person receiving the harmful matter to use a token in order to utilize the vending machine after taking reasonable measures to ascertain that the person was 18 years of age or older.

(i) Any list of applicants or recipients compiled or maintained by an information-access service provider for purposes of compliance with paragraph (1) of subdivision (g) is confidential and shall not be sold or otherwise disseminated except upon order of the court.

Amended by Stats. 1994, Ch. 38, Sec. 1. Effective January 1, 1995.

Section 313.2 - Exceptions

(a) Nothing in this chapter shall prohibit any parent or guardian from distributing any harmful matter to his child or ward or permitting his child or ward to attend an exhibition of any harmful matter if the child or ward is accompanied by him.

(b) Nothing in this chapter shall prohibit any person from exhibiting any harmful matter to any of the following:

    (1) A minor who is accompanied by his parent or guardian.

    (2) A minor who is accompanied by an adult who represents himself to be the parent or guardian of the minor and whom the person, by the exercise of reasonable care, does not have reason to know is not the parent or guardian of the minor.

Amended by Stats. 1970, Ch. 257.

Section 313.3 - Defense

It shall be a defense in any prosecution for a violation of this chapter that the act charged was committed in aid of legitimate scientific or educational purposes.

Added by Stats. 1969, Ch. 248.

Section 313.4 - Punishment

Every person who violates Section 313.1, other than subdivision (e), is punishable by fine of not more than two thousand dollars ($2,000), by imprisonment in the county jail for not more than one year, or by both that fine and imprisonment. However, if the person has been previously convicted of a violation of Section 313.1, other than subdivision (e), or of any section of Chapter 7.5 (commencing with Section 311) of Title 9 of Part 1 of this code, the person shall be punished by imprisonment pursuant to subdivision (h) of Section 1170.

Amended by Stats 2011 ch 39 (AB 117),s 68, eff. 6/30/2011.

Amended by Stats 2011 ch 15 (AB 109),s 325, eff. 4/4/2011, but operative no earlier than October 1, 2011, and only upon creation of a community corrections grant program to assist in implementing this act and upon an appropriation to fund the grant program.

Section 313.5 - Severability

If any phrase, clause, sentence, section or provision of this chapter or application thereof to any person or circumstance is held invalid, such invalidity shall not affect any other phrase, clause, sentence, section, provision or application of this chapter, which can be given effect without the invalid phrase, clause, sentence, section, provision or application and to this end the provisions of this chapter are declared to be severable.

Added by Stats. 1969, Ch. 248.

Chapter 8 - INDECENT EXPOSURE, OBSCENE EXHIBITIONS, AND BAWDY AND OTHER DISORDERLY HOUSES

Section 314 - Indecent exposure

Every person who willfully and lewdly, either:

1. Exposes his person, or the private parts thereof, in any public place, or in any place where there are present other persons to be offended or annoyed thereby; or,

2. Procures, counsels, or assists any person so to expose himself or take part in any model artist exhibition, or to make any other exhibition of himself to public view, or the view of any number of persons, such as is offensive to decency, or is adapted to excite to vicious or lewd thoughts or acts, is guilty of a misdemeanor.

Every person who violates subdivision 1 of this section after having entered, without consent, an inhabited dwelling house, or trailer coach as defined in Section 635 of the Vehicle Code, or the inhabited portion of any other building, is punishable by imprisonment in the state prison, or in the county jail not exceeding one year.

Upon the second and each subsequent conviction under subdivision 1 of this section, or upon a first conviction under subdivision 1 of this section after a previous conviction under Section 288, every person so convicted is guilty of a felony, and is punishable by imprisonment in state prison.

Amended by Stats. 1982, Ch. 1113, Sec. 2.

Section 315 - House of ill-fame

Every person who keeps a house of ill-fame in this state, resorted to for the purposes of prostitution or lewdness, or who willfully resides in such house, is guilty of a misdemeanor; and in all prosecutions for keeping or resorting to such a house common repute may be received as competent evidence of the character of the house, the purpose for which it is kept or used, and the character of the women inhabiting or resorting to it.

Amended by Stats. 1905, Ch. 507.

Section 316 - Disorderly house, house for purpose of assignation or prostitution, or house of public resort

Every person who keeps any disorderly house, or any house for the purpose of assignation or prostitution, or any house of public resort, by which the peace, comfort, or decency of the immediate neighborhood is habitually disturbed, or who keeps any inn in a disorderly manner; and every person who lets any apartment or tenement, knowing that it is to be used for the purpose of assignation or prostitution, is guilty of a misdemeanor.

Amended by Stats. 1989, Ch. 1360, Sec. 108.

Section 318 - Unlawful prevailing upon person to visit place kept for illegal gambling or prostitution

Whoever, through invitation or device, prevails upon any person to visit any room, building, or other places kept for the purpose of illegal gambling or prostitution, is guilty of a misdemeanor, and, upon conviction thereof, shall be confined in the county jail not exceeding six months, or fined not exceeding five hundred dollars ($500), or be punished by both that fine and imprisonment.

Amended by Stats. 1991, Ch. 684, Sec. 2.

Section 318.5 - Ordinance regulating exposure in adult or sexually oriented business

(a) Nothing in this code shall invalidate an ordinance of, or be construed to prohibit the adoption of an ordinance by, a county or city, if that ordinance directly regulates the exposure of the genitals or buttocks of any person, or the breasts of any female person, who acts as a waiter, waitress, or entertainer, whether or not the owner of the establishment in which the activity is performed employs or pays any compensation to that person to perform the activity, in an adult or sexually oriented business. For purposes of this section, an "adult or sexually oriented business" includes any establishment that regularly features live performances which are distinguished or characterized by an emphasis on the exposure of the genitals or buttocks of any person, or the breasts of any female person, or specified sexual activities that involve the exposure of the genitals or buttocks of any person, or the breasts of any female person.

(b) The provisions of this section shall not be construed to apply to any adult or sexually oriented business, as defined herein, that has been adjudicated by a court of competent jurisdiction to be, or by action of a local body such as issuance of an adult entertainment establishment license or permit allowing the business to operate on or before July 1, 1998, as, a theater, concert hall, or similar establishment primarily devoted to theatrical performances for purposes of this section. This section shall be known and may be cited as the "Quimby-Walsh Act."

Amended by Stats. 1998, Ch. 294, Sec. 2. Effective January 1, 1999.

Section 318.6 - Ordinance regulating live acts in adult or sexually oriented businesses

(a) Nothing in this code shall invalidate an ordinance of, or be construed to prohibit the adoption of an ordinance by, a city or county, if that ordinance relates to any live acts, demonstrations, or exhibitions occurring within adult or sexually oriented businesses and involve the exposure of the genitals or buttocks of any participant or the breasts of any female participant, and if that ordinance prohibits an act or acts which are not expressly authorized or prohibited by this code.

(b) For purposes of this section, an "adult or sexually oriented business" includes any establishment that regularly features live performances which are distinguished or characterized by an emphasis on the exposure of the genitals or buttocks of any person, or the breasts of any female person or sexual activities that involve the exposure of the genitals or buttocks of any person, or the breasts of any female person.

(c) The provisions of this section shall not be construed to apply to any adult or sexually oriented business, as defined herein, that has been adjudicated by a court of competent jurisdiction to be, or by action of a local body such as issuance of an adult entertainment establishment license or permit allowing the business to operate on or before July 1, 1998, as, a theater, concert hall, or similar establishment primarily devoted to theatrical performances for purposes of this section.

(d) This section shall not be construed to preempt the legislative body of any city or county from regulating an adult or sexually oriented business, or similar establishment, in the manner and to the extent permitted by the United States Constitution and the California Constitution.

Amended by Stats. 1998, Ch. 294, Sec. 3. Effective January 1, 1999.

Chapter 9 - LOTTERIES

Section 319 - Lottery defined

A lottery is any scheme for the disposal or distribution of property by chance, among persons who have paid or promised to pay any valuable consideration for the chance of obtaining such property or a portion of it, or for any share or any interest in such property, upon any agreement, understanding, or expectation that it is to be distributed or disposed of by lot or chance, whether called a lottery, raffle, or gift enterprise, or by whatever name the same may be known.

Enacted 1872.

Section 319.3 - Grab bag game

(a) In addition to Section 319, a lottery also shall include a grab bag game which is a scheme whereby, for the disposal or distribution of sports trading cards by chance, a person pays valuable consideration to purchase a sports trading card grab bag with the understanding that the purchaser has a chance to win a designated prize or prizes listed by the seller as being contained in one or more, but not all, of the grab bags.

(b) For purposes of this section, the following definitions shall apply:

(1) "Sports trading card grab bag" means a sealed package which contains one or more sports trading cards that have been removed from the manufacturer's original packaging. A "sports trading card grab bag" does not include a sweepstakes, or procedure for the distribution of any sports trading card of value by lot or by chance, which is not unlawful under other provisions of law.

(2) "Sports trading card" means any card produced for use in commerce that contains a company name or logo, or both, and an image, representation, or facsimile of one or more players or other team member or members in any pose, and that is produced pursuant to an appropriate licensing agreement.

Added by Stats. 1994, Ch. 1074, Sec. 3. Effective January 1, 1995.

Section 319.5 - Inapplicability to possession or operation of reverse vending machine

Neither this chapter nor Chapter 10 (commencing with Section 330) applies to the possession or operation of a reverse vending machine. As used in this section a reverse vending machine is a machine in which empty beverage containers are deposited for recycling and which provides a payment of money, merchandise, vouchers, or other incentives at a frequency less than upon each deposit. The pay out of a reverse vending machine is made on a deposit selected at random within the designated number of required deposits. The deposit of an empty beverage container in a reverse vending machine does not constitute consideration within the definition of lottery in Section 319.

Added by Stats. 1982, Ch. 456, Sec. 1. Effective July 8, 1982.

Section 320 - Unlawful acts related to a lottery

Every person who contrives, prepares, sets up, proposes, or draws any lottery, is guilty of a misdemeanor.

Enacted 1872.

Section 320.5 - Inapplicability to raffle

(a) Nothing in this chapter applies to any raffle conducted by an eligible organization as defined in subdivision (c) for the purpose of directly supporting beneficial or charitable purposes or financially supporting another private, nonprofit, eligible organization that performs beneficial or charitable purposes if the raffle is conducted in accordance with this section.

(b) For purposes of this section, "raffle" means a scheme for the distribution of prizes by chance among persons who have paid money for paper tickets that provide the opportunity to win these prizes, where all of the following are true:

(1) Each ticket is sold with a detachable coupon or stub, and both the ticket and its associated coupon or stub are marked with a unique and matching identifier.

(2) Winners of the prizes are determined by draw from among the coupons or stubs described in paragraph (1) that have been detached from all tickets sold for entry in the draw.

(3) The draw is conducted in California under the supervision of a natural person who is 18 years of age or older.

(4)

(A) At least 90 percent of the gross receipts generated from the sale of raffle tickets for any given draw are used by the eligible organization conducting the raffle to benefit or provide support for beneficial or charitable purposes, or it may use those revenues to benefit another private, nonprofit organization, provided that an organization receiving these funds is itself an eligible organization as defined in subdivision (c). As used in this section, "beneficial purposes" excludes purposes that are intended to benefit officers, directors, or members, as defined by Section 5056 of the Corporations Code, of the eligible organization. In no event shall funds raised by raffles conducted pursuant to this section be used to fund any beneficial, charitable, or other purpose outside of California. This section does not preclude an eligible organization from using funds from sources other than the sale of raffle tickets to pay for the administration or other costs of conducting a raffle.

(B) An employee of an eligible organization who is a direct seller of raffle tickets shall not be treated as an employee for purposes of workers' compensation under Section 3351 of the Labor Code if the following conditions are satisfied:

(i) Substantially all of the remuneration (whether or not paid in cash) for the performance of the service of selling raffle tickets is directly related to sales rather than to the number of hours worked.

(ii) The services performed by the person are performed pursuant to a written contract between the seller and the eligible organization and the contract provides that the person will not be treated as an employee with respect to the selling of raffle tickets for workers' compensation purposes.

(C) For purposes of this section, employees selling raffle tickets shall be deemed to be direct sellers as described in Section 650 of the Unemployment Insurance Code as long as they meet the requirements of that section.

(c) For purposes of this section, "eligible organization" means a private, nonprofit organization that has been qualified to conduct business in California for at least one year prior to conducting a raffle and is exempt from taxation pursuant to Sections 23701a, 23701b, 23701d, 23701e, 23701f, 23701g, 23701k, 23701l, 23701t, or 23701w of the Revenue and Taxation Code.

(d) Any person who receives compensation in connection with the operation of the raffle shall be an employee of the eligible organization that is conducting the raffle, and in no event may compensation be paid from revenues required to be dedicated to beneficial or charitable purposes.

(e) No raffle otherwise permitted under this section may be conducted by means of, or otherwise utilize, any gaming machine, apparatus, or device, whether or not that machine, apparatus, or device meets the definition of slot machine contained in Section 330a, 330b, or 330.1.

(f)

(1) No raffle otherwise permitted under this section may be conducted, nor may tickets for a raffle be sold, within an operating satellite wagering facility or racetrack inclosure licensed pursuant to the Horse Racing Law (Chapter 4 (commencing with Section 19400) of Division 8 of the Business and Professions Code) or within a gambling establishment licensed pursuant to the Gambling Control Act (Chapter 5 (commencing with Section 19800) of Division 8 of the Business and Professions Code).

(2) A raffle may not be operated or conducted in any manner over the Internet, nor may raffle tickets be sold, traded, or redeemed over the Internet. For purposes of this paragraph, an eligible organization shall not be deemed to operate or conduct a raffle over the Internet, or sell raffle tickets over the Internet, if the eligible organization advertises its raffle on the Internet or permits others to do so. Information that may be conveyed on an Internet Web site pursuant to this paragraph includes, but is not limited to, all of the following:

(A) Lists, descriptions, photographs, or videos of the raffle prizes.

(B) Lists of the prize winners.

(C) The rules of the raffle.

(D) Frequently asked questions and their answers.

(E) Raffle entry forms, which may be downloaded from the Internet Web site for manual completion by raffle ticket purchasers, but shall not be submitted to the eligible organization through the Internet.

(F) Raffle contact information, including the eligible organization's name, address, telephone number, facsimile number, or e-mail address.

(g) No individual, corporation, partnership, or other legal entity shall hold a financial interest in the conduct of a raffle, except the eligible organization that is itself authorized to conduct that raffle, and any private, nonprofit, eligible organizations receiving financial support from that charitable organization pursuant to subdivisions (a) and (b).

(h)

(1) An eligible organization may not conduct a raffle authorized under this section, unless it registers annually with the Department of Justice. The department shall furnish a registration form via the Internet or upon request to eligible nonprofit organizations. The department shall, by regulation, collect only the information necessary to carry out the provisions of this section on this form. This information shall include, but is not limited to, the following:

(A) The name and address of the eligible organization.

(B) The federal tax identification number, the corporate number issued by the Secretary of State, the organization number issued by the Franchise Tax Board, or the California charitable trust identification number of the eligible organization.

(C) The name and title of a responsible fiduciary of the organization.

(2) The department may require an eligible organization to pay an annual registration fee of ten dollars ($10) to cover the actual costs of the department to administer and enforce this section. The department may, by regulation, adjust the annual registration fee as needed to ensure that revenues willfully offset, but do not exceed, the actual costs incurred by the department pursuant to this section. The fee shall be deposited by the department into the General Fund.

(3) The department shall receive General Fund moneys for the costs incurred pursuant to this section subject to an appropriation by the Legislature.

(4) The department shall adopt regulations necessary to effectuate this section, including emergency regulations, pursuant to the Administrative Procedure Act (Chapter 3.5 (commencing with Section 11340) of Part 1 of Division 3 of Title 2 of the Government Code).

(5) The department shall maintain an automated database of all registrants. Each local law enforcement agency shall notify the department of any arrests or investigation that may result in an administrative or criminal action against a registrant. The department may audit the records and other documents of a registrant to ensure compliance with this section.

(6) Once registered, an eligible organization must file annually thereafter with the department a report that includes the following:

(A) The aggregate gross receipts from the operation of raffles.

(B) The aggregate direct costs incurred by the eligible organization from the operation of raffles.

(C) The charitable or beneficial purposes for which proceeds of the raffles were used, or identify the eligible recipient organization to which proceeds were directed, and the amount of those proceeds.

(7) The department shall annually furnish to registrants a form to collect this information.

(8) The registration and reporting provisions of this section do not apply to any religious corporation sole or other religious corporation or organization that holds property for religious purposes, to a cemetery corporation regulated under Chapter 19 of Division 3 of the Business and Professions Code, or to any committee as defined in Section 82013 that is required to and does file any statement pursuant to the provisions of Article 2 (commencing with Section 84200) of Chapter 4 of Title 9, or to a charitable corporation organized and operated primarily as a religious organization, educational institution, hospital, or a health care service plan licensed pursuant to Section 1349 of the Health and Safety Code.

(i) The department may take legal action against a registrant if it determines that the registrant has violated this section or any regulation adopted pursuant to this section, or that the registrant has engaged in any conduct that is not in the best interests of the public's health, safety, or general welfare. Any action taken pursuant to this subdivision does not prohibit the commencement of an administrative or criminal action by the Attorney General, a district attorney, city attorney, or county counsel.

(j) Each action and hearing conducted to deny, revoke, or suspend a registry, or other administrative action taken against a registrant shall be conducted pursuant to the Administrative Procedure Act (Chapters 4.5 (commencing with Section 11400) and 5 (commencing with Section 11500) of Part 1 of Division 3 of Title 2 of the Government Code). The department may seek recovery of the costs incurred in investigating or prosecuting an action against a registrant or applicant in accordance with those procedures specified in Section 125.3 of the Business and Professions Code. A proceeding conducted under this subdivision is subject to judicial review pursuant to Section 1094.5 of the Code of Civil Procedure.

(k) The Department of Justice shall conduct a study and report to the Legislature by December 31, 2003, on the impact of this section on raffle practices in California. Specifically, the study shall include, but not be limited to, information on whether the number of raffles has increased, the amount of money raised through raffles and whether this amount has increased, whether there are consumer complaints, and whether there is increased fraud in the operation of raffles.

(l) This section shall become operative on July 1, 2001.

(m) A raffle shall be exempt from this section if it satisfies all of the following requirements:

(1) It involves a general and indiscriminate distribution of the tickets.

(2) The tickets are offered on the same terms and conditions as the tickets for which a donation is given.

(3) The scheme does not require any of the participants to pay for a chance to win.

Amended by Stats 2009 ch 38 (SB 200),s 1, eff. 1/1/2010.
Added by Stats 2000 ch 778 (SB 639), s 1, eff. 1/1/2001.
Amended by Stats 2001 ch 854 (SB 205), s 26, eff. 1/1/2002.

Section 320.6 - Raffles by eligible organizations

(a) Notwithstanding Section 320.5, this section applies to an eligible organization.

(b) A raffle that is conducted by an eligible organization for the purpose of directly supporting beneficial or charitable purposes or financially supporting another private, nonprofit eligible organization, as defined in subdivision (c) of Section 320.5, that performs beneficial or charitable purposes may be conducted in accordance with this section.

(c) For purposes of this section, "eligible organization" means a private, nonprofit organization established by, or affiliated with, a team from the Major League Baseball, National Hockey League, National Basketball Association, National Football League, Women's National Basketball Association, or Major League Soccer, or a private, nonprofit organization established by the Professional Golfers' Association of America, Ladies Professional Golf Association, or National Association for Stock Car Auto Racing that has been qualified to conduct business in California for at least one year before conducting a raffle, is qualified for an exemption under Section 501(c)(3) of the Internal Revenue Code, and is exempt from taxation pursuant to Section 23701a, 23701b, 23701d, 23701e, 23701f, 23701g, 23701k, 23701l, 23701t, or 23701w of the Revenue and Taxation Code.

(d) For purposes of this section, "raffle" means a scheme for the distribution of prizes by chance among persons who have paid money for paper tickets that provide the opportunity to win these prizes, in which all of the following are true:

(1) Each ticket sold contains a unique and matching identifier.

(2)

(A) Winners of the prizes are determined by a manual draw from tickets described in paragraph (1) that have been sold for entry in the manual draw.

(B) An electronic device may be used to sell tickets. The ticket receipt issued by the electronic device to the purchaser may include more than one unique and matching identifier, representative of and matched to the number of tickets purchased in a single transaction.

(C) A random number generator is not used for the manual draw or to sell tickets.

(D) The prize paid to the winner is comprised of one-half or 50 percent of the gross receipts generated from the sale of raffle tickets for a raffle.

(3) The manual draw is conducted in California under the supervision of a natural person who meets all of the following requirements:

(A) The person is 18 years of age or older.

(B) The person is affiliated with the eligible organization conducting the raffle.

(C) The person is registered with the Department of Justice pursuant to paragraph (4) of subdivision (o).

(4)

(A) Fifty percent of the gross receipts generated from the sale of raffle tickets for any given manual draw are used by the eligible organization conducting the raffle solely for charitable purposes, or used to benefit another private, nonprofit organization, provided that an organization receiving these funds is itself an eligible organization as defined in subdivision (c) of Section 320.5. As used in this section, "charitable purposes" excludes purposes that are intended to benefit officers, directors, or members, as defined by Section 5056 of the Corporations Code, of the eligible organization. Funds raised by raffles conducted pursuant to this section shall not be used to fund any beneficial, charitable, or other purpose outside of California. This section does not preclude an eligible organization from using funds from sources other than the sale of raffle tickets to pay for the administration or other costs of conducting a raffle if these expenses comply with legal standard of care requirements described in Sections 5231, 7231, and 9241 of the Corporations Code.

(B) An employee of an eligible organization who is a direct seller of raffle tickets shall not be treated as an employee for purposes of workers' compensation under Section 3351 of the Labor Code if both of the following conditions are satisfied:

(i) Substantially all of the remuneration, whether or not paid in cash, for the performance of the service of selling raffle tickets is directly related to sales rather than to the number of hours worked.

(ii) The services performed by the person are performed pursuant to a written contract between the seller and the eligible organization and the contract provides that the person will not be treated as an employee with respect to the selling of raffle tickets for workers' compensation purposes.

(C) For purposes of this section, an employee selling raffle tickets shall be deemed to be a direct seller, as described in Section 650 of the Unemployment Insurance Code, as long as the employee meets the requirements of that section.

(e) A person who receives compensation in connection with the operation of the raffle shall be an employee of the eligible organization that is conducting the raffle, and in no event may compensation be paid from revenues required to be dedicated to beneficial or charitable purposes.

(f) A raffle ticket shall not be sold in exchange for Bitcoin or any other cryptocurrency.

(g) A raffle that is otherwise permitted under this section shall not be conducted by means of, or otherwise utilize, any gaming machine that meets the definition of slot machine contained in Section 330a, 330b, or 330.1.

(h)

(1) A raffle otherwise permitted under this section shall not be conducted, nor may tickets for a raffle be sold, within an operating satellite wagering facility or racetrack inclosure licensed pursuant to the Horse Racing Law (Chapter 4 (commencing with Section 19400) of Division 8 of the Business and Professions Code) or within a gambling establishment licensed pursuant to the Gambling Control Act (Chapter 5 (commencing with Section 19800) of Division 8 of the Business and Professions Code).

(2) A raffle shall not be operated or conducted in any manner over the internet, nor may raffle tickets be sold, traded, or redeemed over the Internet. For purposes of this paragraph, an eligible organization shall not be deemed to operate or conduct a raffle over the internet, or sell raffle tickets over the internet, if the eligible organization advertises its raffle on the internet or permits others to do so. Information that may be conveyed on an internet website pursuant to this paragraph includes, but is not limited to, all of the following:

(A) Lists, descriptions, photographs, or videos of the raffle prizes.

(B) Lists of the prize winners.

(C) The rules of the raffle.

(D) Frequently asked questions and their answers.

(E) Raffle entry forms, which may be downloaded from the internet website for manual completion by raffle ticket purchasers, but shall not be submitted to the eligible organization through the Internet.

(F) Raffle contact information, including the eligible organization's name, address, telephone number, facsimile number, or email address.

(i) An individual, corporation, partnership, or other legal entity shall not hold a financial interest in the conduct of a raffle, except the eligible organization that is itself authorized to conduct that raffle, and any private, nonprofit, eligible organizations receiving financial support from that charitable organization pursuant to subdivisions (b) and (d).

(j)

(1) An eligible organization may conduct a major league sports raffle only at a home game.

(2) An eligible organization shall not conduct more than one major league sports raffle per home game.

(k) An employee shall not sell raffle tickets in any seating area designated as a family section.

(l) An eligible organization shall disclose to all ticket purchasers the designated private, nonprofit, eligible organization for which the raffle is being conducted.

(m) An eligible organization that conducts a raffle to financially support another private, nonprofit eligible organization, as defined in subdivision (c) of Section 320.5, shall distribute all proceeds not paid out to the winners of the prizes to the private, nonprofit organization within 15 days of conducting the raffle, in accordance with this section.

(n) Any raffle prize remaining unclaimed by a winner at the end of the season for a team with an affiliated eligible organization that conducted a raffle to financially support another private, nonprofit eligible organization, as defined in subdivision (c) of Section 320.5, shall be donated within 30 days from the end of the season by the eligible organization to the designated private, nonprofit organization for which the raffle was conducted.

(o)

(1)

(A) An eligible organization shall not conduct a raffle authorized under this section, unless it has a valid registration issued by the Department of Justice. The department shall furnish a registration form via the Internet or upon request to eligible nonprofit organizations. The department shall, by regulation, collect only the information necessary to carry out the provisions of this section on this form. This information shall include, but is not limited to, all of the following:

(i) The name and address of the eligible organization.

(ii) The federal tax identification number, the corporate number issued by the Secretary of State, the organization number issued by the Franchise Tax Board, or the California charitable trust identification number of the eligible organization.

(iii) The name and title of a responsible fiduciary of the organization.

(B)

(i) The department may require an eligible organization to pay a minimum annual registration fee of ten thousand dollars ($10,000) to cover the reasonable costs of the department to administer and enforce this section.

(ii) An eligible organization shall pay, in addition to the annual registration application fee, two hundred dollars ($200) for every individual raffle conducted at an eligible location to cover the reasonable costs of the department to administer and enforce this section. This fee shall be submitted in conjunction with the annual registration form.

(2)

(A) A manufacturer or distributor of raffle-related products or services shall not conduct business with an eligible organization for purposes of conducting a raffle pursuant to this section unless the manufacturer or distributor has a valid annual registration issued by the department.

(B) The department may require a manufacturer or distributor of raffle-related products or services to pay a minimum annual registration fee of ten thousand dollars ($10,000) to cover the reasonable costs of the department to administer and enforce this section.

(3) An eligible organization shall register the equipment used in the sale and distribution of raffle tickets, and shall have the equipment tested by an independent gaming testing lab.

(4)

(A) A person affiliated with an eligible organization who conducts the manual draw shall annually register with the department.

(B) The department may require a person affiliated with an eligible organization who conducts the manual draw to pay a minimum annual registration fee of twenty dollars ($20) to cover the reasonable costs of the department to administer and enforce this section.

(5)

(A) The department may, by regulation, adjust the annual registration fees described in this section as needed to ensure that revenues will fully offset, but not exceed, the reasonable costs incurred by the department pursuant to this section. The fees shall be deposited by the department into the Major League Sporting Event Raffle Fund, which is hereby created in the State Treasury.

(B) A loan is hereby authorized from the General Fund to the Major League Sporting Event Raffle Fund on or after July 1, 2016, in an amount of up to one million five thousand dollars ($1,005,000) to address department workload related to the initial implementation activities relating to this section by the department's Indian and Gaming Law Section. The terms and conditions of the loan shall first be approved by the Department of Finance pursuant to appropriate fiscal standards. The loan shall be subject to all of the following conditions:

(i) Of the total amount loaned, no more than three hundred thirty-five thousand dollars ($335,000) shall be provided annually to the department.

(ii) The loan shall be repaid to the General Fund as soon as there is sufficient money in the Major League Sporting Event Raffle Fund to repay the loan, but no later than December 31, 2023.

(iii) Interest on the loan shall be paid from the Major League Sporting Event Raffle Fund at the rate accruing to moneys in the Pooled Money Investment Account.

(6) The department shall receive moneys for the costs incurred pursuant to this section subject to an appropriation by the Legislature.

(7) The department shall adopt regulations necessary to effectuate this section, including emergency regulations, pursuant to the Administrative Procedure Act (Chapter 3.5 (commencing with Section 11340) of Part 1 of Division 3 of Title 2 of the Government Code).

(8) The department shall maintain an automated database of all registrants.

(9) A local law enforcement agency shall notify the department of any arrests or investigation that may result in an administrative or criminal action against a registrant.

(10) The department may, to the extent the Legislature appropriates funds for this purpose, investigate all suspected violations of this section or any regulation adopted pursuant to this section, or any activity that the registrant has engaged in that is not in the best interests of the public's health, safety, or general welfare as it pertains to charitable raffles.

(11) The department may, to the extent the Legislature appropriates funds for this purpose, audit the records and other documents of a registrant to ensure compliance with this section.

(12) Once registered, an eligible organization shall post all of the following information on either its internet website or the affiliated sport team's internet website for each raffle:

(A) The gross receipts generated from the sale of raffle tickets.

(B) Each eligible recipient organization and the amount each eligible recipient organization received.

(C) The prize total.

(D) The winning ticket number and whether the prize was claimed.

(13)

(A) Once registered, an eligible organization shall file with the department, each season or year thereafter, a report that includes all of the following information:

(i) For each raffle, all of the following information:

(I) The gross receipts generated from the sale of raffle tickets.

(II) Each eligible recipient organization and the amount each eligible recipient organization received.

(III) The prize total.

(IV) The winning ticket number and whether the prize was claimed.

(ii) The total number of raffles conducted for the season or year.

(iii) The gross receipts generated from the sale of raffle tickets for the season or year.

(iv) The average per raffle gross receipts generated from the sale of raffle tickets for the season or year.

(v) The prize total for the season or year, including any prize that was not claimed.

(vi) The average per raffle prize total for the season or year, including any prize that was not claimed.

(vii) The prize total that was not claimed, if any, during the season or year. For each raffle in which the prize was not claimed, the name of the eligible recipient organization who received the prize.

(viii) A schedule of all vendors used to operate the raffles and total payments made to each vendor.

(ix) An itemization of the direct costs of conducting the raffles, including labor, raffle equipment, software, marketing, and consulting costs.

(B) Failure to timely submit the seasonal or annual report to the department, as required in this paragraph, shall be grounds for denial of an annual registration and for the imposition of penalties under Section 12591.1 of the Government Code.

(C) Failure to submit a complete financial report shall be grounds for the denial of an annual registration and for the imposition of penalties under Section 12591.1 of the Government Code if the filer does not resubmit a complete form within 30 days of receiving a notice of incomplete filing.

(D)

(i) An eligible organization shall file with the department and post on either its internet website or the affiliated sport team's internet website the report required by this paragraph no later than 60 days after the end of the league season or year.

(ii) The department shall post the reports required by this paragraph on its internet website, but shall not post the report on the online search portal of the Attorney General's Registry of Charitable Trusts maintained pursuant to Section 12584 of the Government Code.

(14) The department shall annually furnish to registrants a form to collect this information.

(p) The department may take legal action against a registrant if it determines that the registrant has violated this section or a regulation adopted pursuant to this section, or that the registrant has engaged in any conduct that is not in the best interests of the public's health, safety, or general welfare. An action taken pursuant to this subdivision does not prohibit the commencement of an administrative or criminal action by the Attorney General, a district attorney, city attorney, or county counsel.

(q) An action and hearing conducted to deny, revoke, or suspend a registry, or other administrative action taken against a registrant, shall be conducted pursuant to the Administrative Procedure Act (Chapters 4.5 (commencing with Section 11400) and 5 (commencing with Section 11500) of Part 1 of Division 3 of Title 2 of the Government Code). The department may seek civil remedies, including imposing fines, for violations of this section, and may seek recovery of the costs incurred in investigating or prosecuting an action against a registrant or applicant in accordance with those procedures specified in Section 125.3 of the Business and Professions Code. A proceeding conducted under this subdivision is subject to judicial review pursuant to Section 1094.5 of the Code of Civil Procedure. A violation of this section shall not constitute a crime.

Amended by Stats 2023 ch 406 (SB 650),s 1, eff. 1/1/2024.

Amended by Stats 2019 ch 29 (SB 82),s 127, eff. 6/27/2019.

Amended by Stats 2018 ch 575 (AB 888),s 1, eff. 9/20/2018.

Amended by Stats 2016 ch 33 (SB 843),s 16, eff. 6/27/2016.

Added by Stats 2015 ch 509 (SB 549),s 1, eff. 1/1/2016.

Section 321 - Unlawful furnishing of ticket

Every person who sells, gives, or in any manner whatever, furnishes or transfers to or for any other person any ticket, chance, share, or interest, or any paper, certificate, or instrument purporting or understood to be or to represent any ticket, chance, share, or interest in, or depending upon the event of any lottery, is guilty of a misdemeanor.

Enacted 1872.

Section 322 - Unlawful setting up, managing, or drawing lottery

Every person who aids or assists, either by printing, writing, advertising, publishing, or otherwise in setting up, managing, or drawing any lottery, or in selling or disposing of any ticket, chance, or share therein, is guilty of a misdemeanor.

Enacted 1872.

Section 323 - Unlawful opening of office for sale of ticket in lottery

Every person who opens, sets up, or keeps, by himself or by any other person, any office or other place for the sale of, or for registering the number of any ticket in any lottery, or who, by printing, writing, or otherwise, advertises or publishes the setting up, opening, or using of any such office, is guilty of a misdemeanor.

Enacted 1872.

Section 324 - Unlawful insuring for or against drawing of ticket in lottery

Every person who insures or receives any consideration for insuring for or against the drawing of any ticket in any lottery whatever, whether drawn or to be drawn within this State or not, or who receives any valuable consideration upon any agreement to repay any sum, or deliver the same, or any other property, if any lottery ticket or number of any ticket in any lottery shall prove fortunate or unfortunate, or shall be drawn or not be drawn, at any particular time or in any particular order, or who promises or agrees to pay any sum of money, or to deliver any goods, things in action, or property, or to forbear to do anything for the benefit of any person, with or without consideration, upon any event or contingency dependent on the drawing of any ticket in any lottery, or who publishes any notice or proposal of any of the purposes aforesaid, is guilty of a misdemeanor.

Enacted 1872.

Section 325 - Forfeiture

All moneys and property offered for sale or distribution in violation of any of the provisions of this chapter are forfeited to the state, and may be recovered by information filed, or by an action brought by the Attorney General, or by any district attorney, in the name of the state. Upon the filing of the information or complaint, the clerk of the court must issue an attachment against the property mentioned in the complaint or information, which attachment has the same force and effect against such property, and is issued in the same manner as attachments issued from the superior courts in civil cases.

Amended by Stats. 1977, Ch. 1257.

Section 326 - Unlawful permission to use building or vessel for lottery

Every person who lets, or permits to be used, any building or vessel, or any portion thereof, knowing that it is to be used for setting up, managing, or drawing any lottery, or for the purpose of selling or disposing of lottery tickets, is guilty of a misdemeanor.
Enacted 1872.

Section 326.3 - [Repealed]
Amended by Stats 2014 ch 71 (SB 1304),s 121, eff. 1/1/2015.
Amended by Stats 2013 ch 353 (SB 820),s 120, eff. 9/26/2013, op. 7/1/2013.
Amended by Stats 2013 ch 32 (SB 76),s 5, eff. 6/27/2013.
Amended by Stats 2011 ch 296 (AB 1023),s 201, eff. 1/1/2012.
Amended by Stats 2010 ch 514 (SB 1090),s 1, eff. 1/1/2011.
Amended by Stats 2009 ch 562 (SB 126),s 2, eff. 10/11/2009.
Added by Stats 2008 ch 748 (SB 1369),s 4, eff. 1/1/2009.

Section 326.4 - Charity Bingo Mitigation Fund
(a) Consistent with the Legislature's finding that card-minding devices, as described in subdivision (p) of Section 326.5, are the only permissible electronic devices to be used by charity bingo players, and in an effort to ease the transition to remote caller bingo on the part of those nonprofit organizations that, as of July 1, 2008, used electronic devices other than card-minding devices to conduct games in reliance on an ordinance of a city, county, or city and county that, as of July 1, 2008, expressly recognized the operation of electronic devices other than card-minding devices by organizations purportedly authorized to conduct bingo in the city, county, or city and county, there is hereby created the Charity Bingo Mitigation Fund.
(b) The Charity Bingo Mitigation Fund shall be administered by the Department of Justice.
(c) Mitigation payments to be made by the Charity Bingo Mitigation Fund shall not exceed five million dollars ($5,000,000) in the aggregate.
(d)

(1) To allow the Charity Bingo Mitigation Fund to become immediately operable, five million dollars ($5,000,000) shall be loaned from the accrued interest in the Indian Gaming Special Distribution Fund to the Charity Bingo Mitigation Fund on or after January 1, 2009, to make mitigation payments to eligible nonprofit organizations. Five million dollars ($5,000,000) of this loan amount is hereby appropriated to the California Gambling Control Commission for the purposes of providing mitigation payments to certain charitable organizations, as described in subdivision (e). Pursuant to Section 16304 of the Government Code, after three years the unexpended balance shall revert back to the Charity Bingo Mitigation Fund.

(2) To reimburse the Special Distribution Fund, those nonprofit organizations that conduct a remote caller bingo game pursuant to Section 326.3 shall pay to the Department of Justice an amount equal to 5 percent of the gross revenues of each remote caller bingo game played until that time as the full advanced amount plus interest on the loan at the rate accruing to moneys in the Pooled Money Investment Account is reimbursed.

(e)

(1) An organization meeting the requirements in subdivision (a) shall be eligible to receive mitigation payments from the Charity Bingo Mitigation Fund only if the city, county, or city and county in which the organization is located maintained official records of the net revenues generated for the fiscal year ending June 30, 2008, by the organization from the use of electronic devices or the organization maintained audited financial records for the fiscal year ending June 30, 2008, which show the net revenues generated from the use of electronic devices.

(2) In addition, an organization applying for mitigation payments shall provide proof that its board of directors has adopted a resolution and its chief executive officer has signed a statement executed under penalty of perjury stating that, as of January 1, 2009, the organization has ceased using electronic devices other than card-minding devices, as described in subdivision (p) of Section 326.5, as a fundraising tool.

(3) Each eligible organization may apply to the California Gambling Control Commission no later than January 31, 2009, for the mitigation payments in the amount equal to net revenues from the fiscal year ending June 30, 2008, by filing an application, including therewith documents and other proof of eligibility, including any and all financial records documenting the organization's net revenues for the fiscal year ending June 30, 2008, as the California Gambling Control Commission may require. The California Gambling Control Commission is authorized to access and examine the financial records of charities requesting funding in order to confirm the legitimacy of the request for funding. In the event that the total of those requests exceeds five million dollars ($5,000,000), payments to all eligible applicants shall be reduced in proportion to each requesting organization's reported or audited net revenues from the operation of electronic devices.
Amended by Stats 2013 ch 353 (SB 820),s 121, eff. 9/26/2013, op. 7/1/2013.
Amended by Stats 2009 ch 140 (AB 1164),s 140, eff. 1/1/2010.
Added by Stats 2008 ch 748 (SB 1369),s 5, eff. 1/1/2009.

Section 326.45 - Appropriation from California Bingo Fund to California Gambling Control Commission
Up to five hundred thousand dollars ($500,000), as determined by order of the Director of Finance, is hereby appropriated from the California Bingo Fund to the California Gambling Control Commission for use in the 2008-09 fiscal year for the purposes described in subparagraph (C) of paragraph (3) of subdivision (q) of Section 326.3.
Amended by Stats 2009 ch 562 (SB 126),s 3, eff. 10/11/2009.
Added by Stats 2008 ch 734 (AB 334),s 1, eff. 1/1/2009.

Section 326.5 - Inapplicability of prohibition on gambling to bingo game
(a) Neither the prohibition on gambling in this chapter nor in Chapter 10 (commencing with Section 330) applies to any bingo game that is conducted in a city, county, or city and county pursuant to an ordinance enacted under Section 19 of Article IV of the State Constitution, if the ordinance allows games to be conducted only in accordance with this section and only by organizations exempted from the payment of the bank and corporation tax by Sections 23701a, 23701b, 23701d, 23701e, 23701f, 23701g, 23701k,

23701w, and 23701l of the Revenue and Taxation Code and by mobilehome park associations, senior citizens organizations, and charitable organizations affiliated with a school district; and if the receipts of those games are used only for charitable purposes.

(b) It is a misdemeanor for any person to receive or pay a profit, wage, or salary from any bingo game authorized by Section 19 of Article IV of the State Constitution. Security personnel employed by the organization conducting the bingo game may be paid from the revenues of bingo games, as provided in subdivisions (j) and (k).

(c) A violation of subdivision (b) shall be punishable by a fine not to exceed ten thousand dollars ($10,000), which fine is deposited in the general fund of the city, county, or city and county that enacted the ordinance authorizing the bingo game. A violation of any provision of this section, other than subdivision (b), is a misdemeanor.

(d) The city, county, or city and county that enacted the ordinance authorizing the bingo game may bring an action to enjoin a violation of this section.

(e) Minors shall not be allowed to participate in any bingo game.

(f) An organization authorized to conduct bingo games pursuant to subdivision (a) shall conduct a bingo game only on property owned or leased by it, or property whose use is donated to the organization, and which property is used by that organization for an office or for performance of the purposes for which the organization is organized. Nothing in this subdivision shall be construed to require that the property owned or leased by, or whose use is donated to, the organization be used or leased exclusively by, or donated exclusively to, that organization.

(g) All bingo games shall be open to the public, not just to the members of the authorized organization.

(h) A bingo game shall be operated and staffed only by members of the authorized organization that organized it. Those members shall not receive a profit, wage, or salary from any bingo game. Only the organization authorized to conduct a bingo game shall operate such a game, or participate in the promotion, supervision, or any other phase of a bingo game. This subdivision does not preclude the employment of security personnel who are not members of the authorized organization at a bingo game by the organization conducting the game.

(i) Any individual, corporation, partnership, or other legal entity, except the organization authorized to conduct a bingo game, shall not hold a financial interest in the conduct of a bingo game.

(j) With respect to organizations exempt from payment of the bank and corporation tax by Section 23701d of the Revenue and Taxation Code, all profits derived from a bingo game shall be kept in a special fund or account and shall not be commingled with any other fund or account. Those profits shall be used only for charitable purposes.

(k) With respect to other organizations authorized to conduct bingo games pursuant to this section, all proceeds derived from a bingo game shall be kept in a special fund or account and shall not be commingled with any other fund or account. Proceeds are the receipts of bingo games conducted by organizations not within subdivision (j). Those proceeds shall be used only for charitable purposes, except as follows:

    (1) The proceeds may be used for prizes.

    (2)

        (A) Except as provided in subparagraph (B), a portion of the proceeds, not to exceed 20 percent of the proceeds before the deduction for prizes, or two thousand dollars ($2,000) per month, whichever is less, may be used for the rental of property and for overhead, including the purchase of bingo equipment, administrative expenses, security equipment, and security personnel.

        (B) For the purposes of bingo games conducted by the Lake Elsinore Elks Lodge, a portion of the proceeds, not to exceed 20 percent of the proceeds before the deduction for prizes, or three thousand dollars ($3,000) per month, whichever is less, may be used for the rental of property and for overhead, including the purchase of bingo equipment, administrative expenses, security equipment, and security personnel. Any amount of the proceeds that is additional to that permitted under subparagraph (A), up to one thousand dollars ($1,000), shall be used for the purpose of financing the rebuilding of the facility and the replacement of equipment that was destroyed by fire in 2007. The exception to subparagraph (A) that is provided by this subparagraph shall remain in effect only until the cost of rebuilding the facility is repaid, or January 1, 2019, whichever occurs first.

    (3) The proceeds may be used to pay license fees.

    (4) A city, county, or city and county that enacts an ordinance permitting bingo games may specify in the ordinance that if the monthly gross receipts from bingo games of an organization within this subdivision exceed five thousand dollars ($5,000), a minimum percentage of the proceeds shall be used only for charitable purposes not relating to the conducting of bingo games and that the balance shall be used for prizes, rental of property, overhead, administrative expenses, and payment of license fees. The amount of proceeds used for rental of property, overhead, and administrative expenses is subject to the limitations specified in paragraph (2).

(l)

    (1) A city, county, or city and county may impose a license fee on each organization that it authorizes to conduct bingo games. The fee, whether for the initial license or renewal, shall not exceed fifty dollars ($50) annually, except as provided in paragraph (2). If an application for a license is denied, one-half of any license fee paid shall be refunded to the organization.

    (2) In lieu of the license fee permitted under paragraph (1), a city, county, or city and county may impose a license fee of fifty dollars ($50) paid upon application. If an application for a license is denied, one-half of the application fee shall be refunded to the organization. An additional fee for law enforcement and public safety costs incurred by the city, county, or city and county that are directly related to bingo activities may be imposed and shall be collected monthly by the city, county, or city and county issuing the license; however, the fee shall not exceed the actual costs incurred in providing the service.

(m) A person shall not be allowed to participate in a bingo game, unless the person is physically present at the time and place where the bingo game is being conducted.

(n) The total value of prizes available to be awarded during the conduct of any bingo games shall not exceed five hundred dollars ($500) in cash or kind, or both, for each separate game which is held.

(o) As used in this section, "bingo" means a game of chance in which prizes are awarded on the basis of designated numbers or symbols that are marked or covered by the player on a tangible card in the player's possession and that conform to numbers or symbols, selected at random and announced by a live caller. Notwithstanding Section 330c, as used in this section, the game of bingo includes tangible cards having numbers or symbols that are concealed and preprinted in a manner providing for distribution of prizes. Electronics or video displays shall not be used in connection with the game of bingo, except in connection with the caller's drawing of numbers or symbols and the public display of that drawing, and except as provided in subdivision (p). The winning cards shall not be known prior to the game by any person participating in the playing or operation of the bingo game. All preprinted cards shall bear the legend, "for sale or use only in a bingo game authorized under California law and pursuant to local ordinance." Only a covered or marked tangible card possessed by a player and presented to an attendant may be used to claim a prize. It is the intention of the Legislature that bingo as defined in this subdivision applies exclusively to this section and shall not be applied in the construction or enforcement of any other provision of law.

(p)

(1) Players who are physically present at a bingo game may use hand-held, portable card-minding devices, as described in this subdivision, to assist in monitoring the numbers or symbols announced by a live caller as those numbers or symbols are called in a live game. Card-minding devices may not be used in connection with any game where a bingo card may be sold or distributed after the start of the ball draw for that game. A card-minding device shall do all of the following:

(A) Be capable of storing in the memory of the device bingo faces of tangible cards purchased by a player.

(B) Provide a means for bingo players to input manually each individual number or symbol announced by a live caller.

(C) Compare the numbers or symbols entered by the player to the bingo faces previously stored in the memory of the device.

(D) Identify winning bingo patterns that exist on the stored bingo faces.

(2) A card-minding device shall perform no functions involving the play of the game other than those described in paragraph (1). Card-minding devices shall not do any of the following:

(A) Be capable of accepting or dispensing any coins, currency, or other representative of value or on which value has been encoded.

(B) Be capable of monitoring any bingo card face other than the faces of the tangible bingo card or cards purchased by the player for that game.

(C) Display or represent the game result through any means, including, but not limited to, video or mechanical reels or other slot machine or casino game themes, other than highlighting the winning numbers or symbols marked or covered on the tangible bingo cards or giving an audio alert that the player's card has a prize-winning pattern.

(D) Determine the outcome of any game or be physically or electronically connected to any component that determines the outcome of a game or to any other bingo equipment, including, but not limited to, the ball call station, or to any other card-minding device. No other player-operated or player-activated electronic or electromechanical device or equipment is permitted to be used in connection with a bingo game.

(3)

(A) A card-minding device shall be approved in advance by the department as meeting the requirements of this section and any additional requirements stated in regulations adopted by the department. Any proposed material change to the device, including any change to the software used by the device, shall be submitted to the department and approved by the department prior to implementation.

(B) In accordance with Chapter 5 (commencing with Section 19800) of Division 8 of the Business and Professions Code, the commission shall establish reasonable criteria for, and require the licensure of, any person that directly or indirectly manufactures, distributes, supplies, vends, leases, or otherwise provides card-minding devices or other supplies, equipment, or services related to card-minding devices designed for use in the playing of bingo games by any nonprofit organization.

(C) A person or entity that supplies or services any card-minding device shall meet all licensing requirements established by the commission in regulations.

(4) The costs of any testing, certification, license, or determination required by this subdivision shall be borne by the person or entity seeking it.

(5) On and after January 1, 2010, the Department of Justice may inspect all card-minding devices at any time without notice, and may immediately prohibit the use of any device that does not comply with the requirements established by the department in regulations. The Department of Justice may at any time, without notice, impound any device the use of which has been prohibited by the commission.

(6) The Department of Justice shall issue regulations to implement the requirements of this subdivision, and the California Gambling Control Commission may issue regulations regarding the means by which the operator of a bingo game, as required by applicable law, may offer assistance to a player with disabilities in order to enable that player to participate in a bingo game, provided that the means of providing that assistance shall not be through any electronic, electromechanical, or other device or equipment that accepts the insertion of any coin, currency, token, credit card, or other means of transmitting value, and does not constitute or is not a part of a system that constitutes a video lottery terminal, slot machine, or device prohibited by Chapter 10 (commencing with Section 330).

(7) The following definitions apply for purposes of this subdivision:

(A) "Commission" means the California Gambling Control Commission.

(B) "Department" means the Department of Justice.

(C) "Person" includes a natural person, corporation, limited liability company, partnership, trust, joint venture, association, or any other business organization.

Amended by Stats 2013 ch 353 (SB 820),s 122, eff. 9/26/2013, op. 7/1/2013.

Amended by Stats 2009 ch 562 (SB 126),s 4, eff. 10/11/2009.

Amended by Stats 2008 ch 748 (SB 1369),s 6, eff. 1/1/2009.

Amended by Stats 2008 ch 216 (AB 1924),s 1, eff. 1/1/2009.

See Stats 2008 ch 216 (AB 1924), s 2.

Section 327 - Endless chain

Every person who contrives, prepares, sets up, proposes, or operates any endless chain is guilty of a public offense, and is punishable by imprisonment in the county jail not exceeding one year or in state prison for 16 months, two, or three years.

As used in this section, an "endless chain" means any scheme for the disposal or distribution of property whereby a participant pays a valuable consideration for the chance to receive compensation for introducing one or more additional persons into participation in the scheme or for the chance to receive compensation when a person introduced by the participant introduces a new participant. Compensation, as used in this section, does not mean or include payment based upon sales made to persons who are not participants in the scheme and who are not purchasing in order to participate in the scheme.

Amended by Stats. 1989, Ch. 436, Sec. 2.

Section 328 - Advertisements for lottery conducted in other state or nation

Nothing in this chapter shall make unlawful the printing or other production of any advertisements for, or any ticket, chance, or share in a lottery conducted in any other state or nation where such lottery is not prohibited by the laws of such state or nation; or the sale of such materials by the manufacturer thereof to any person or entity conducting or participating in the conduct of such a lottery in any such state or nation. This section does not authorize any advertisement within California relating to lotteries, or the sale or resale within California of lottery tickets, chances, or shares to individuals, or acts otherwise in violation of any laws of the state.

Added by Stats. 1980, Ch. 216, Sec. 1. Effective June 23, 1980.

Section 329 - Evidence

Upon a trial for the violation of any of the provisions of this chapter, it is not necessary to prove the existence of any lottery in which any lottery ticket purports to have been issued, or to prove the actual signing of any such ticket or share, or pretended ticket or share, of any pretended lottery, nor that any lottery ticket, share, or interest was signed or issued by the authority of any manager, or of any person assuming to have authority as manager; but in all cases proof of the sale, furnishing, bartering, or procuring of any ticket, share, or interest therein, or of any instrument purporting to be a ticket, or part or share of any such ticket, is evidence that such share or interest was signed and issued according to the purport thereof.

Added by Stats. 1989, Ch. 897, Sec. 19.

Chapter 10 - GAMING

Section 330 - Unlawful gaming

Every person who deals, plays, or carries on, opens, or causes to be opened, or who conducts, either as owner or employee, whether for hire or not, any game of faro, monte, roulette, lansquenet, rouge et noire, rondo, tan, fan-tan, seven-and-a-half, twenty-one, hokey-pokey, or any banking or percentage game played with cards, dice, or any device, for money, checks, credit, or other representative of value, and every person who plays or bets at or against any of those prohibited games, is guilty of a misdemeanor, and shall be punishable by a fine not less than one hundred dollars ($100) nor more than one thousand dollars ($1,000), or by imprisonment in the county jail not exceeding six months, or by both the fine and imprisonment.

Amended by Stats. 1991, Ch. 71, Sec. 1.

Section 330a - Unlawful possession of gaming machine

(a) Every person, who has in his or her possession or under his or her control, either as owner, lessee, agent, employee, mortgagee, or otherwise, or who permits to be placed, maintained, or kept in any room, space, inclosure, or building owned, leased, or occupied by him or her, or under his or her management or control, any slot or card machine, contrivance, appliance or mechanical device, upon the result of action of which money or other valuable thing is staked or hazarded, and which is operated, or played, by placing or depositing therein any coins, checks, slugs, balls, or other articles or device, or in any other manner and by means whereof, or as a result of the operation of which any merchandise, money, representative or articles of value, checks, or tokens, redeemable in or exchangeable for money or any other thing of value, is won or lost, or taken from or obtained from the machine, when the result of action or operation of the machine, contrivance, appliance, or mechanical device is dependent upon hazard or chance, and every person, who has in his or her possession or under his or her control, either as owner, lessee, agent, employee, mortgagee, or otherwise, or who permits to be placed, maintained, or kept in any room, space, inclosure, or building owned, leased, or occupied by him or her, or under his or her management or control, any card dice, or any dice having more than six faces or bases each, upon the result of action of which any money or other valuable thing is staked or hazarded, or as a result of the operation of which any merchandise, money, representative or article of value, check or token, redeemable in or exchangeable for money or any other thing of value, is won or lost or taken, when the result of action or operation of the dice is dependent upon hazard or chance, is guilty of a misdemeanor.

(b) A first violation of this section shall be punishable by a fine of not less than five hundred dollars ($500) nor more than one thousand dollars ($1,000), or by imprisonment in a county jail not exceeding six months, or by both that fine and imprisonment.

(c) A second offense shall be punishable by a fine of not less than one thousand dollars ($1,000) nor more than ten thousand dollars ($10,000), or by imprisonment in a county jail not exceeding six months, or by both that fine and imprisonment.

(d) A third or subsequent offense shall be punishable by a fine of not less than ten thousand dollars ($10,000) nor more than twenty-five thousand dollars ($25,000), or by imprisonment in a county jail not exceeding one year, or by both that fine and imprisonment.

(e) If the offense involved more than one machine or more than one location, an additional fine of not less than one thousand dollars ($1,000) nor more than five thousand dollars ($5,000) shall be imposed per machine and per location.

Amended by Stats 2010 ch 577 (AB 1753),s 1, eff. 1/1/2011.

Section 330b - Unlawful manufacture or operation of slot machine or device

(a) It is unlawful for any person to manufacture, repair, own, store, possess, sell, rent, lease, let on shares, lend or give away, transport, or expose for sale or lease, or to offer to repair, sell, rent, lease, let on shares, lend or give away, or permit the operation, placement, maintenance, or keeping of, in any place, room, space, or building owned, leased, or occupied, managed, or controlled by that person, any slot machine or device, as defined in this section. It is unlawful for any person to make or to permit the making of an agreement with another person regarding any slot machine or device, by which the user of the slot machine or device, as a result of the element of hazard or chance or other unpredictable outcome, may become entitled to receive money, credit, allowance, or other thing of value or additional chance or right to use the slot machine or device, or to receive any check, slug, token, or memorandum entitling the holder to receive money, credit, allowance, or other thing of value.

(b) The limitations of subdivision (a), insofar as they relate to owning, storing, possessing, or transporting any slot machine or device, do not apply to any slot machine or device located upon or being transported by any vessel regularly operated and engaged in interstate or foreign commerce, so long as the slot machine or device is located in a locked compartment of the vessel, is not accessible for use, and is not used or operated within the territorial jurisdiction of this state.

(c) The limitations of subdivision (a) do not apply to a manufacturer's business activities that are conducted in accordance with the terms of a license issued by a tribal gaming agency pursuant to the tribal-state gaming compacts entered into in accordance with the Indian Gaming Regulatory Act (18 U.S.C. Sec. 1166 to 1168, inclusive, and 25 U.S.C. Sec. 2701 et seq.).

(d) For purposes of this section, "slot machine or device" means a machine, apparatus, or device that is adapted, or may readily be converted, for use in a way that, as a result of the insertion of any piece of money or coin or other object, or by any other means, the machine or device is caused to operate or may be operated, and by reason of any element of hazard or chance or of other outcome of operation unpredictable by him or her, the user may receive or become entitled to receive any piece of money, credit, allowance, or thing of value, or additional chance or right to use the slot machine or device, or any check, slug, token, or memorandum, whether of value or otherwise, which may be exchanged for any money, credit, allowance, or thing of value, or which may be given in trade, irrespective of whether it may, apart from any element of hazard or chance or unpredictable outcome of operation, also sell, deliver, or present some merchandise, indication of weight, entertainment, or other thing of value.

(e) Every person who violates this section is guilty of a misdemeanor.

(1) A first violation of this section shall be punishable by a fine of not less than five hundred dollars ($500) nor more than one thousand dollars ($1,000), or by imprisonment in a county jail not exceeding six months, or by both that fine and imprisonment.

(2) A second offense shall be punishable by a fine of not less than one thousand dollars ($1,000) nor more than ten thousand dollars ($10,000), or by imprisonment in a county jail not exceeding six months, or by both that fine and imprisonment.

(3) A third or subsequent offense shall be punishable by a fine of not less than ten thousand dollars ($10,000) nor more than twenty-five thousand dollars ($25,000), or by imprisonment in a county jail not exceeding one year, or by both that fine and imprisonment.

(4) If the offense involved more than one machine or more than one location, an additional fine of not less than one thousand dollars ($1,000) nor more than five thousand dollars ($5,000) shall be imposed per machine and per location.

(f) Pinball and other amusement machines or devices, which are predominantly games of skill, whether affording the opportunity of additional chances or free plays or not, are not included within the term slot machine or device, as defined in this section.

Amended by Stats 2010 ch 577 (AB 1753),s 2, eff. 1/1/2011.

Amended by Stats 2004 ch 183 (AB 3082), s 267, eff. 1/1/2005.

Amended by Stats 2003 ch 264 (AB 360), s 1, eff. 1/1/2004.

Section 330c - Punchboard

A punchboard as hereinafter defined is hereby declared to be a slot machine or device within the meaning of Section 330b of this code and shall be subject to the provisions thereof. For the purposes of this section, a punchboard is any card, board or other device which may be played or operated by pulling, pressing, punching out or otherwise removing any slip, tab, paper or other substance therefrom to disclose any concealed number, name or symbol.

Added by Stats. 1953, Ch. 379.

Section 330.1 - Unlawful manufacture or keeping of slot machine or device

(a) Every person who manufactures, owns, stores, keeps, possesses, sells, rents, leases, lets on shares, lends or gives away, transports, or exposes for sale or lease, or offers to sell, rent, lease, let on shares, lend or give away or who permits the operation of or permits to be placed, maintained, used, or kept in any room, space, or building owned, leased, or occupied by him or her or under his or her management or control, any slot machine or device as hereinafter defined, and every person who makes or permits to be made with any person any agreement with reference to any slot machine or device as hereinafter defined, pursuant to which agreement the user thereof, as a result of any element of hazard or chance, may become entitled to receive anything of value or additional chance or right to use that slot machine or device, or to receive any check, slug, token, or memorandum, whether of value or otherwise, entitling the holder to receive anything of value, is guilty of a misdemeanor.

(b) A first violation of this section shall be punishable by a fine of not more than one thousand dollars ($1,000), or by imprisonment in a county jail not exceeding six months, or by both that fine and imprisonment.

(c) A second offense shall be punishable by a fine of not less than one thousand dollars ($1,000) nor more than ten thousand dollars ($10,000), or by imprisonment in a county jail not exceeding six months, or by both that fine and imprisonment.

(d) A third or subsequent offense shall be punishable by a fine of not less than ten thousand dollars ($10,000) nor more than twenty-five thousand dollars ($25,000), or by imprisonment in a county jail not exceeding one year, or by both that fine and imprisonment.

(e) If the offense involved more than one machine or more than one location, an additional fine of not less than one thousand dollars ($1,000) nor more than five thousand dollars ($5,000) shall be imposed per machine and per location.

(f) A slot machine or device within the meaning of Sections 330.1 to 330.5, inclusive, of this code is one that is, or may be, used or operated in such a way that, as a result of the insertion of any piece of money or coin or other object the machine or device is caused to operate or may be operated or played, mechanically, electrically, automatically, or manually, and by reason of any element of hazard or chance, the user may receive or become entitled to receive anything of value or any check, slug, token, or memorandum, whether of value or otherwise, which may be given in trade, or the user may secure additional chances or rights to use such machine or device, irrespective of whether it may, apart from any element of hazard or chance, also sell, deliver, or present some merchandise, indication of weight, entertainment, or other thing of value.

Amended by Stats 2011 ch 296 (AB 1023),s 202, eff. 1/1/2012.

Amended by Stats 2010 ch 577 (AB 1753),s 3, eff. 1/1/2011.

Section 330.2 - "Thing of value" defined

As used in Sections 330.1 to 330.5, inclusive, of this code a "thing of value" is defined to be any money, coin, currency, check, chip, allowance, token, credit, merchandise, property, or any representative of value.

Added by Stats. 1950, 1st Ex. Sess., Ch. 18.

Section 330.3 - Seizure of slot machine or device

In addition to any other remedy provided by law any slot machine or device may be seized by any of the officers designated by Sections 335 and 335a of the Penal Code, and in such cases shall be disposed of, together with any and all money seized in or in connection with such machine or device, as provided in Section 335a of the Penal Code.

Added by Stats. 1950, 1st Ex. Sess., Ch. 18.

Section 330.4 - Mere possession or control of slot machine or device

It is specifically declared that the mere possession or control, either as owner, lessee, agent, employee, mortgagor, or otherwise of any slot machine or device, as defined in Section 330.1 of this code, is prohibited and penalized by the provisions of Sections 330.1 to 330.5, inclusive, of this code.

It is specifically declared that every person who permits to be placed, maintained or kept in any room, space, enclosure, or building owned, leased or occupied by him, or under his management or control, whether for use or operation or for storage, bailment, safekeeping or deposit only, any slot machine or device, as defined in Section 330.1 of this code, is guilty of a misdemeanor and punishable as provided in Section 330.1 of this code.

It is further declared that the provisions of this section specifically render any slot machine or device as defined in Section 330.1 of this code subject to confiscation as provided in Section 335a of this code.

Added by Stats. 1950, 1st Ex. Sess., Ch. 18.

Section 330.5 - Inapplicability to music machines, weighing machines, and vending machines

It is further expressly provided that Sections 330.1 to 330.4, inclusive, of this code shall not apply to music machines, weighing machines and machines which vend cigarettes, candy, ice cream, food, confections or other merchandise, in which there is deposited an exact consideration and from which in every case the customer obtains that which he purchases; and it is further expressly provided that with respect to the provisions of Sections 330.1 to 330.4, inclusive, only, of this code, pin ball, and other amusement machines or devices which are predominantly games of skill, whether affording the opportunity of additional chances or free plays or not, are not intended to be and are not included within the term slot machine or device as defined within Sections 330.1 to 330.4, inclusive, of this code.

Added by Stats. 1950, 1st Ex. Sess., Ch. 18.

Section 330.6 - Inapplicability to slot machine or device upon vessel

The provisions of Sections 330.1 to 330.5, inclusive, of this code, with respect to owning, storing, keeping, possessing, or transporting any slot machine or device as therein defined, shall not apply to any slot machine or device as therein defined, located upon or being transported by any vessel regularly operated and engaged in interstate or foreign commerce, so long as such slot machine or device is located in a locked compartment of the vessel, is not accessible for use and is not used or operated within the territorial jurisdiction of this State.

Added by Stats. 1950, 1st Ex. Sess., Ch. 18.

Section 330.7 - Defense of antique slot machine

(a) It shall be a defense to any prosecution under this chapter relating to slot machines, as defined in subdivision (d) of Section 330b, if the defendant shows that the slot machine is an antique slot machine and was not operated for gambling purposes while in the defendant's possession. For the purposes of this section, the term "antique slot machine" means a slot machine that is over 25 years of age.

(b) Notwithstanding Section 335a, whenever the defense provided by subdivision (a) is offered, no slot machine seized from a defendant shall be destroyed or otherwise altered until after a final court determination that the defense is not applicable. If the defense is applicable, the machine shall be returned pursuant to provisions of law providing for the return of property.

(c) It is the purpose of this section to protect the collection and restoration of antique slot machines not presently utilized for gambling purposes because of their aesthetic interest and importance in California history.

Amended by Stats 2004 ch 183 (AB 3082), s 268, eff. 1/1/2005.

Section 330.8 - Sale, transportation, storage, and manufacture of gambling devices

Notwithstanding Sections 330a, 330b, and 330.1 to 330.5, inclusive, the sale, transportation, storage, and manufacture of gambling devices, as defined in Section 330.1, including the acquisition of essential parts therefor and the assembly of such parts, is permitted, provided those devices are sold, transported, stored, and manufactured only for subsequent transportation in interstate or foreign commerce when that transportation is not prohibited by any applicable federal law. Those activities may be conducted only by persons who have registered with the United States government pursuant to Chapter 24 (commencing with Section 1171) of Title 15 of the United States Code, as amended. Those gambling devices shall not be displayed to the general public or sold for use in California regardless of where purchased, nor held nor manufactured in violation of any applicable federal law. A violation of this section is a misdemeanor.

Amended by Stats. 1987, Ch. 828, Sec. 18.5.

Section 330.9 - Transportation and possession of slot machine or device for display or as prop

(a) Notwithstanding Sections 330a, 330b, 330.1 to 330.5, inclusive, or any other provision of law, it shall be lawful for any person to transport and possess any slot machine or device for display at a trade show, conference, or convention being held within this state, or if used solely as a prop for a motion picture, television, or video production.

(b) Subdivision (a) shall apply only if the slot machine or device is adjusted to render the machine or device inoperable, or if the slot machine or device is set on demonstration mode.

(c) This section is intended to constitute a state exemption as provided in Section 1172 of Title 15 of the United States Code.

(d) For purposes of this section:

(1) "Demonstration mode" means that the programming or settings of a slot machine or device have been programmed, set, or selected to operate normally, but to not accept or pay out cash or any other consideration.

(2) "Slot machine or device" has the same meaning as "slot machine or device" as defined in Section 330.1, or "gambling device" as defined in paragraph (1) of subsection (a) of Section 1171 of Title 15 of the United States Code.
Amended by Stats 2005 ch 546 (AB 1753),s 2, eff. 1/1/2006
EFFECTIVE 1/1/2000. Added October 10, 1999 (Bill Number: SB 1207) (Chapter 642).

Section 330.11 - "Banking game" or "banked game" defined

"Banking game" or "banked game" does not include a controlled game if the published rules of the game feature a player-dealer position and provide that this position must be continuously and systematically rotated amongst each of the participants during the play of the game, ensure that the player-dealer is able to win or lose only a fixed and limited wager during the play of the game, and preclude the house, another entity, a player, or an observer from maintaining or operating as a bank during the course of the game. For purposes of this section it is not the intent of the Legislature to mandate acceptance of the deal by every player if the division finds that the rules of the game render the maintenance of or operation of a bank impossible by other means. The house shall not occupy the player-dealer position.
Added by Stats 2000 ch 1023 (AB 1416), s 17, eff. 1/1/2001.
Amended by Stats 2001 ch 941 (AB 54), s 2, eff. 1/1/2002.

Section 331 - Unlawful playing of games in house

Every person who knowingly permits any of the games mentioned in Sections 330 and 330a to be played, conducted, or dealt in any house owned or rented by such person, in whole or in part, is punishable as provided in Sections 330 and 330a.
Amended by Stats. 1987, Ch. 828, Sec. 19.

Section 332 - Fraudulently obtaining money or property by game, device, sleight of hand, or other means

(a) Every person who by the game of "three card monte," so-called, or any other game, device, sleight of hand, pretensions to fortune telling, trick, or other means whatever, by use of cards or other implements or instruments, or while betting on sides or hands of any play or game, fraudulently obtains from another person money or property of any description, shall be punished as in the case of larceny of property of like value for the first offense, except that the fine may not exceed more than five thousand dollars ($5,000). A second offense of this section is punishable, as in the case of larceny, except that the fine shall not exceed ten thousand dollars ($10,000), or both imprisonment and fine.
(b) For the purposes of this section, "fraudulently obtains" includes, but is not limited to, cheating, including, for example, gaining an unfair advantage for any player in any game through a technique or device not sanctioned by the rules of the game.
(c) For the purposes of establishing the value of property under this section, poker chips, tokens, or markers have the monetary value assigned to them by the players in any game.
Amended by Stats 2005 ch 546 (AB 1753),s 3, eff. 1/1/2006

Section 333 - Neglect or refusal to attend by witness

Every person duly summoned as a witness for the prosecution, on any proceedings had under this Chapter, who neglects or refuses to attend, as required, is guilty of a misdemeanor.
Enacted 1872.

Section 334 - Unlawful operation of concession

(a) Every person who owns or operates any concession, and who fraudulently obtains money from another by means of any hidden mechanical device or obstruction with intent to diminish the chance of any patron to win a prize, or by any other fraudulent means, shall be punished as in the case of theft of property of like value.
(b) Any person who manufactures or sells any mechanical device or obstruction for a concession which he knows or reasonably should know will be fraudulently used to diminish the chance of any patron to win a prize is guilty of a misdemeanor.
(c) Any person who owns or operates any game, at a fair or carnival of a type known as razzle-dazzle is guilty of a misdemeanor. As used in this subdivision, "razzle-dazzle" means a series of games of skill or chance in which the player pays money or other valuable consideration in return for each opportunity to make successive attempts to obtain points by the use of dice, darts, marbles or other implements, and where such points are accumulated in successive games by the player toward a total number of points, determined by the operator, which is required for the player to win a prize or other valuable consideration.
(d) As used in this section, "concession" means any game or concession open to the public and operated for profit in which the patron pays a fee for participating and may receive a prize upon a later happening.
(e) Nothing in this section shall be construed to prohibit or preempt more restrictive regulation of any concession at a fair or carnival by any local governmental entity.
Added by Stats. 1974, Ch. 626.

Section 335 - Diligent prosecution

Every district attorney, sheriff, or police officer must inform against and diligently prosecute persons whom they have reasonable cause to believe offenders against the provisions of this chapter, and every officer refusing or neglecting so to do, is guilty of a misdemeanor.
Amended by Stats. 1996, Ch. 872, Sec. 110. Effective January 1, 1997.

Section 335a - Seizure; destruction of machine or device

In addition to any other remedy provided by law any machine or other device the possession or control of which is penalized by the laws of this State prohibiting lotteries or gambling may be seized by any peace officer, and a notice of intention summarily to destroy such machine or device as provided in this section must be posted in a conspicuous place upon the premises in or upon which such machine or device was seized. Such machine or device shall be held by such officer for 30 days after such posting, and if no action is commenced to recover possession of such machine or device, within such time, the same shall be summarily destroyed by such officer, or if such machine or device shall be held by the court, in any such action, to be in violation of such laws, or any of them, the same shall be summarily destroyed by such officer immediately after the decision of the court has become final.
The superior court shall have jurisdiction of any such actions or proceedings commenced to recover the possession of such machine or device or any money seized in connection therewith.

Any and all money seized in or in connection with such machine or device shall, immediately after such machine or device has been so destroyed, be paid into the treasury of the city or county, as the case may be, where seized, said money to be deposited in the general fund.
Added by Stats. 1941, Ch. 192.

Section 336 - Unlawfully permitting person under 18 years of age to pay game of chance
Every owner, lessee, or keeper of any house used in whole, or in part, as a saloon or drinking place, who knowingly permits any person under 18 years of age to play at any game of chance therein, is guilty of a misdemeanor.
Amended by Stats. 1972, Ch. 579.

Section 336.5 - Gaming chips
Gaming chips may be used on the gaming floor by a patron of a gambling establishment, as defined in subdivision (o) of Section 19805 of the Business and Professions Code, to pay for food and beverage items that are served at the table.
Amended by Stats 2012 ch 162 (SB 1171),s 123, eff. 1/1/2013.
Added by Stats 2007 ch 438 (SB 730),s 9, eff. 1/1/2008.

Section 336.9 - Unlawful betting or betting pools
(a) Notwithstanding Section 337a, and except as provided in subdivision (b), any person who, not for gain, hire, or reward other than that at stake under conditions available to every participant, knowingly participates in any of the ways specified in paragraph (2), (3), (4), (5), or (6) of subdivision (a) of Section 337a in any bet, bets, wager, wagers, or betting pool or pools made between the person and any other person or group of persons who are not acting for gain, hire, or reward, other than that at stake under conditions available to every participant, upon the result of any lawful trial, or purported trial, or contest, or purported contest, of skill, speed, or power of endurance of person or animal, or between persons, animals, or mechanical apparatus, is guilty of an infraction, punishable by a fine not to exceed two hundred fifty dollars ($250).
(b) Subdivision (a) does not apply to either of the following situations:
(1) Any bet, bets, wager, wagers, or betting pool or pools made online.
(2) Betting pools with more than two thousand five hundred dollars ($2,500) at stake.
Amended by Stats 2010 ch 328 (SB 1330),s 155, eff. 1/1/2011.
Added by Stats 2009 ch 72 (AB 58),s 1, eff. 1/1/2010.

Section 337 - Unlawful acts by public officials
Every state, county, city, city and county, town, or judicial district officer, or other person who shall ask for, receive, or collect any money, or other valuable consideration, either for his own or the public use, for and with the understanding that he will aid, exempt, or otherwise assist any person from arrest or conviction for a violation of Section 330 of the Penal Code; or who shall issue, deliver, or cause to be given or delivered to any person or persons, any license, permit, or other privilege, giving, or pretending to give, any authority or right to any person or persons to carry on, conduct, open, or cause to be opened, any game or games which are forbidden or prohibited by Section 330 of said code; and any of such officer or officers who shall vote for the passage of any ordinance or by-law, giving, granting, or pretending to give or grant to any person or persons any authority or privilege to open, carry on, conduct, or cause to be opened, carried on, or conducted, any game or games prohibited by said Section 330 of the Penal Code, is guilty of a felony.
Amended by Stats. 1951, Ch. 1608.

Section 337a - Punishment
(a) Except as provided in Section 336.9, every person who engages in one of the following offenses, shall be punished for a first offense by imprisonment in a county jail for a period of not more than one year or in the state prison, or by a fine not to exceed five thousand dollars ($5,000), or by both imprisonment and fine:
(1) Pool selling or bookmaking, with or without writing, at any time or place.
(2) Whether for gain, hire, reward, or gratuitously, or otherwise, keeps or occupies, for any period of time whatsoever, any room, shed, tenement, tent, booth, building, float, vessel, place, stand or enclosure, of any kind, or any part thereof, with a book or books, paper or papers, apparatus, device or paraphernalia, for the purpose of recording or registering any bet or bets, any purported bet or bets, wager or wagers, any purported wager or wagers, selling pools, or purported pools, upon the result, or purported result, of any trial, purported trial, contest, or purported contest, of skill, speed or power of endurance of person or animal, or between persons, animals, or mechanical apparatus, or upon the result, or purported result, of any lot, chance, casualty, unknown or contingent event whatsoever.
(3) Whether for gain, hire, reward, or gratuitously, or otherwise, receives, holds, or forwards, or purports or pretends to receive, hold, or forward, in any manner whatsoever, any money, thing or consideration of value, or the equivalent or memorandum thereof, staked, pledged, bet or wagered, or to be staked, pledged, bet or wagered, or offered for the purpose of being staked, pledged, bet or wagered, upon the result, or purported result, of any trial, or purported trial, or contest, or purported contest, of skill, speed or power of endurance of person or animal, or between persons, animals, or mechanical apparatus, or upon the result, or purported result, of any lot, chance, casualty, unknown or contingent event whatsoever.
(4) Whether for gain, hire, reward, or gratuitously, or otherwise, at any time or place, records, or registers any bet or bets, wager or wagers, upon the result, or purported result, of any trial, or purported trial, or contest, or purported contest, of skill, speed or power of endurance of person or animal, or between persons, animals, or mechanical apparatus, or upon the result, or purported result, of any lot, chance, casualty, unknown or contingent event whatsoever.
(5) Being the owner, lessee or occupant of any room, shed, tenement, tent, booth, building, float, vessel, place, stand, enclosure or grounds, or any part thereof, whether for gain, hire, reward, or gratuitously, or otherwise, permits that space to be used or occupied for any purpose, or in any manner prohibited by paragraph (1), (2), (3), or (4).
(6) Lays, makes, offers or accepts any bet or bets, or wager or wagers, upon the result, or purported result, of any trial, or purported trial, or contest, or purported contest, of skill, speed or power of endurance of person or animal, or between persons, animals, or mechanical apparatus.

(b) In any accusatory pleading charging a violation of this section, if the defendant has been once previously convicted of a violation of any subdivision of this section, the previous conviction shall be charged in the accusatory pleading, and, if the previous conviction is found to be true by the jury, upon a jury trial, or by the court, upon a court trial, or is admitted by the defendant, the defendant shall, if he or she is not imprisoned in the state prison, be imprisoned in the county jail for a period of not more than one year and pay a fine of not less than one thousand dollars ($1,000) and not to exceed ten thousand dollars ($10,000). Nothing in this paragraph shall prohibit a court from placing a person subject to this subdivision on probation. However, that person shall be required to pay a fine of not less than one thousand dollars ($1,000) nor more than ten thousand dollars ($10,000) or be imprisoned in the county jail for a period of not more than one year, as a condition thereof. In no event does the court have the power to absolve a person convicted pursuant to this subdivision from either being imprisoned or from paying a fine of not less than one thousand dollars ($1,000) and not more than ten thousand dollars ($10,000).

(c) In any accusatory pleading charging a violation of this section, if the defendant has been previously convicted two or more times of a violation of any subdivision of this section, each previous conviction shall be charged in the accusatory pleadings. If two or more of the previous convictions are found to be true by the jury, upon a jury trial, or by the court, upon a court trial, or are admitted by the defendant, the defendant shall, if he or she is not imprisoned in the state prison, be imprisoned in the county jail for a period of not more than one year or pay a fine of not less than one thousand dollars ($1,000) nor more than fifteen thousand dollars ($15,000), or be punished by both imprisonment and fine. Nothing in this paragraph shall prohibit a court from placing a person subject to this subdivision on probation. However, that person shall be required to pay a fine of not less than one thousand dollars ($1,000) nor more than fifteen thousand dollars ($15,000), or be imprisoned in the county jail for a period of not more than one year as a condition thereof. In no event does the court have the power to absolve a person convicted and subject to this subdivision from either being imprisoned or from paying a fine of not more than fifteen thousand dollars ($15,000).

(d) Except where the existence of a previous conviction of any subdivision of this section was not admitted or not found to be true pursuant to this section, or the court finds that a prior conviction was invalid, the court shall not strike or dismiss any prior convictions alleged in the information or indictment.

(e) This section applies not only to persons who commit any of the acts designated in paragraphs (1) to (6), inclusive, of subdivision (a), as a business or occupation, but also applies to every person who in a single instance engages in any one of the acts specified in paragraphs (1) to (6), inclusive, of subdivision (a).

Amended by Stats 2009 ch 72 (AB 58),s 2, eff. 1/1/2010.

Amended by Stats 2005 ch 546 (AB 1753),s 4, eff. 1/1/2006

Section 337b - Unlawful bribery of participant or player in sporting event, contest, or exhibition

Any person who gives, or offers or promises to give, or attempts to give or offer, any money, bribe, or thing of value, to any participant or player, or to any prospective participant or player, in any sporting event, contest, or exhibition of any kind whatsoever, except a wrestling exhibition as defined in Section 18626 of the Business and Professions Code, and specifically including, but without being limited to, such sporting events, contests, and exhibitions as baseball, football, basketball, boxing, horse racing, and wrestling matches, with the intention or understanding or agreement that such participant or player or such prospective participant or player shall not use his or her best efforts to win such sporting event, contest, or exhibition, or shall so conduct himself or herself in such sporting event, contest, or exhibition that any other player, participant or team of players or participants shall thereby be assisted or enabled to win such sporting event, contest, or exhibition, or shall so conduct himself or herself in such sporting event, contest, or exhibition as to limit his or her or his or her team's margin of victory in such sporting event, contest, or exhibition, is guilty of a felony, and shall be punished by imprisonment pursuant to subdivision (h) of Section 1170, or by a fine not exceeding five thousand dollars ($5,000), or by both that fine and imprisonment.

Amended by Stats 2011 ch 39 (AB 117),s 68, eff. 6/30/2011.

Amended by Stats 2011 ch 15 (AB 109),s 328, eff. 4/4/2011, but operative no earlier than October 1, 2011, and only upon creation of a community corrections grant program to assist in implementing this act and upon an appropriation to fund the grant program.

Section 337c - Unlawful receipt of bribe by participant or player in sporting event, contest, or exhibition

Any person who accepts, or attempts to accept, or offers to accept, or agrees to accept, any money, bribe or thing of value, with the intention or understanding or agreement that he or she will not use his or her best efforts to win any sporting event, contest, or exhibition of any kind whatsoever, except a wrestling exhibition as defined in Section 18626 of the Business and Professions Code, and specifically including, but without being limited to, such sporting events, contests, or exhibitions as baseball, football, basketball, boxing, horse racing, and wrestling matches, in which he or she is playing or participating or is about to play or participate in, or will so conduct himself or herself in such sporting event, contest, or exhibition that any other player or participant or team of players or participants shall thereby be assisted or enabled to win such sporting event, contest, or exhibition, or will so conduct himself or herself in such sporting event, contest, or exhibition as to limit his or her or his or her team's margin of victory in such sporting event, contest, or exhibition, is guilty of a felony, and shall be punished by imprisonment pursuant to subdivision (h) of Section 1170, or by a fine not exceeding five thousand dollars ($5,000), or by both that fine and imprisonment.

Amended by Stats 2011 ch 39 (AB 117),s 68, eff. 6/30/2011.

Amended by Stats 2011 ch 15 (AB 109),s 329, eff. 4/4/2011, but operative no earlier than October 1, 2011, and only upon creation of a community corrections grant program to assist in implementing this act and upon an appropriation to fund the grant program.

Section 337d - Unlawful bribery of official in sporting event, contest, or exhibition

Any person who gives, offers to give, promises to give, or attempts to give, any money, bribe, or thing of value to any person who is umpiring, managing, directing, refereeing, supervising, judging, presiding, or officiating at, or who is about to umpire, manage, direct, referee, supervise, judge, preside, or officiate at any sporting event, contest, or exhibition of any kind whatsoever, including, but not limited to, sporting events, contests, and exhibitions such as baseball, football, boxing, horse racing, and wrestling matches, with the intention or agreement or understanding that the person shall corruptly or dishonestly umpire, manage, direct, referee, supervise, judge, preside, or officiate at, any sporting event, contest, or exhibition, or the players or participants thereof, with the intention or purpose that the result of the sporting event, contest, or exhibition will be affected or influenced thereby, is guilty of a felony and shall be

punished by imprisonment pursuant to subdivision (h) of Section 1170 or by a fine of not more than ten thousand dollars ($10,000), or by imprisonment and fine. A second offense of this section is a felony and shall be punished by imprisonment pursuant to subdivision (h) of Section 1170 or by a fine of not more than fifteen thousand dollars ($15,000), or by both that imprisonment and fine.
Amended by Stats 2011 ch 39 (AB 117),s 68, eff. 6/30/2011.
Amended by Stats 2011 ch 15 (AB 109),s 330, eff. 4/4/2011, but operative no earlier than October 1, 2011, and only upon creation of a community corrections grant program to assist in implementing this act and upon an appropriation to fund the grant program.
Amended by Stats 2005 ch 546 (AB 1753),s 5, eff. 1/1/2006

Section 337e - Unlawful receipt of bribe by official in sporting event, contest, or exhibition

Any person who as umpire, manager, director, referee, supervisor, judge, presiding officer or official receives or agrees to receive, or attempts to receive any money, bribe or thing of value, with the understanding or agreement that such umpire, manager, director, referee, supervisor, judge, presiding officer, or official shall corruptly conduct himself or shall corruptly umpire, manage, direct, referee, supervise, judge, preside, or officiate at, any sporting event, contest, or exhibition of any kind whatsoever, and specifically including, but without being limited to, such sporting events, contests, and exhibitions as baseball, football, boxing, horse racing, and wrestling matches, or any player or participant thereof, with the intention or purpose that the result of the sporting event, contest, or exhibition will be affected or influenced thereby, is guilty of a felony and shall be punished by imprisonment pursuant to subdivision (h) of Section 1170, or by a fine not exceeding five thousand dollars ($5,000), or by both that fine and imprisonment.
Amended by Stats 2011 ch 39 (AB 117),s 68, eff. 6/30/2011.
Amended by Stats 2011 ch 15 (AB 109),s 331, eff. 4/4/2011, but operative no earlier than October 1, 2011, and only upon creation of a community corrections grant program to assist in implementing this act and upon an appropriation to fund the grant program.

Section 337f - Unlawful acts related to horse racing

(a) Any person who does any of the following is punishable by a fine not exceeding five thousand dollars ($5,000), or by imprisonment in a county jail not exceeding one year, or by imprisonment pursuant to subdivision (h) of Section 1170, or by both that fine and imprisonment:

(1) Influences, or induces, or conspires with, any owner, trainer, jockey, groom, or other person associated with or interested in any stable, horse, or race in which a horse participates, to affect the result of that race by stimulating or depressing a horse through the administration of any drug to that horse, or by the use of any electrical device or any electrical equipment or by any mechanical or other device not generally accepted as regulation racing equipment, or so stimulates or depresses a horse.

(2) Knowingly enters any horse in any race within a period of 24 hours after any drug has been administered to that horse for the purpose of increasing or retarding the speed of that horse.

(3) Willfully or unjustifiably enters or races any horse in any running or trotting race under any name or designation other than the name or designation assigned to that horse by and registered with the Jockey Club or the United States Trotting Association or willfully sets on foot, instigates, engages in or in any way furthers any act by which any horse is entered or raced in any running or trotting race under any name or designation other than the name or designation duly assigned by and registered with the Jockey Club or the United States Trotting Association.

(b) For purposes of this section, the term "drug" includes all substances recognized as having the power of stimulating or depressing the central nervous system, respiration, or blood pressure of an animal, such as narcotics, hypnotics, benzedrine or its derivatives, but shall not include recognized vitamins or supplemental feeds approved by or in compliance with the rules and regulations or policies of the California Horse Racing Board.
Amended by Stats 2011 ch 39 (AB 117),s 68, eff. 6/30/2011.
Amended by Stats 2011 ch 15 (AB 109),s 332, eff. 4/4/2011, but operative no earlier than October 1, 2011, and only upon creation of a community corrections grant program to assist in implementing this act and upon an appropriation to fund the grant program.
Amended by Stats 2008 ch 509 (AB 3073),s 3, eff. 1/1/2009.

Section 337g - Unlawful possession, transport, or use of local anaesthetic within racing enclosure

The possession, transport or use of any local anaesthetic of the cocaine group, including but not limited to natural or synthetic drugs of this group, such as allocaine, apothesine, alypine, benzyl carbinol, butyn, procaine, nupercaine, beta-eucaine, novol or anestubes, within the racing inclosure is prohibited, except upon a bona fide veterinarian's prescription with complete statement of uses and purposes of same on the container. A copy of such prescription shall be filed with the stewards, and such substances may be used only with approval of the stewards and under the supervision of the veterinarian representing the board.
Added by Stats. 1943, Ch. 1001.

Section 337h - Unlawful administration of poison, drug, medicine or other noxious substance to animal in race or competition

Any person who, except for medicinal purposes, administers any poison, drug, medicine, or other noxious substance, to any horse, stud, mule, ass, mare, horned cattle, neat cattle, gelding, colt, filly, dog, animals, or other livestock, entered or about to be entered in any race or upon any race course, or entered or about to be entered at or with any agricultural park, or association, race course, or corporation, or other exhibition for competition for prize, reward, purse, premium, stake, sweepstakes, or other reward, or who exposes any poison, drug, medicine, or noxious substance, with intent that it shall be taken, inhaled, swallowed, or otherwise received by any of these animals or other livestock, with intent to impede or affect its speed, endurance, sense, health, physical condition, or other character or quality, or who causes to be taken by or placed upon or in the body of any of these animals or other livestock, entered or about to be entered in any race or competition described in this section any sponge, wood, or foreign substance of any kind, with intent to impede or affect its speed, endurance, sense, health, or physical condition, is guilty of a misdemeanor.
Added by Stats. 1953, Ch. 32.

Section 337i - Unlawful transmission of information regarding horserace

Every person who knowingly transmits information as to the progress or results of a horserace, or information as to wagers, betting odds, changes in betting odds, post or off times, jockey or player changes in any contest or trial, or purported contest or trial, involving humans, beasts, or mechanical apparatus by any means whatsoever including, but not limited to telephone, telegraph, radio, and semaphore when such information is transmitted to or by a person or persons engaged in illegal gambling operations, is punishable by imprisonment in the county jail for a period of not more than one year or in the state prison.

This section shall not be construed as prohibiting a newspaper from printing such results or information as news, or any television or radio station from telecasting or broadcasting such results or information as news. This section shall not be so construed as to place in jeopardy any common carrier or its agents performing operations within the scope of a public franchise, or any gambling operation authorized by law.

Amended by Stats. 1976, Ch. 1139.

Section 337j - Controlled games

(a) It is unlawful for any person, as owner, lessee, or employee, whether for hire or not, either solely or in conjunction with others, to do any of the following without having first procured and thereafter maintained in effect all federal, state, and local licenses required by law:

(1) To deal, operate, carry on, conduct, maintain, or expose for play in this state any controlled game.

(2) To receive, directly or indirectly, any compensation or reward or any percentage or share of the revenue, for keeping, running, or carrying on any controlled game.

(3) To manufacture, distribute, or repair any gambling equipment within the boundaries of this state, or to receive, directly or indirectly, any compensation or reward for the manufacture, distribution, or repair of any gambling equipment within the boundaries of this state.

(b) It is unlawful for any person to knowingly permit any controlled game to be conducted, operated, dealt, or carried on in any house or building or other premises that he or she owns or leases, in whole or in part, if that activity is undertaken by a person who is not licensed as required by state law, or by an employee of that person.

(c) It is unlawful for any person to knowingly permit any gambling equipment to be manufactured, stored, or repaired in any house or building or other premises that the person owns or leases, in whole or in part, if that activity is undertaken by a person who is not licensed as required by state law, or by an employee of that person.

(d) Any person who violates, attempts to violate, or conspires to violate this section shall be punished by imprisonment in a county jail for not more than one year or by a fine of not more than ten thousand dollars ($10,000), or by both imprisonment and fine. A second offense of this section is punishable by imprisonment in a county jail for a period of not more than one year or in the state prison or by a fine of not more than ten thousand dollars ($10,000), or by both imprisonment and fine.

(e)

(1) As used in this section, "controlled game" means any poker or Pai Gow game, and any other game played with cards or tiles, or both, and approved by the Department of Justice, and any game of chance, including any gambling device, played for currency, check, credit, or any other thing of value that is not prohibited and made unlawful by statute or local ordinance.

(2) As used in this section, "controlled game" does not include any of the following:

(A) The game of bingo conducted pursuant to Section 326.3 or 326.5.

(B) Parimutuel racing on horse races regulated by the California Horse Racing Board.

(C) Any lottery game conducted by the California State Lottery.

(D) Games played with cards in private homes or residences, in which no person makes money for operating the game, except as a player.

(f) This subdivision is intended to be dispositive of the law relating to the collection of player fees in gambling establishments. A fee may not be calculated as a fraction or percentage of wagers made or winnings earned. The amount of fees charged for all wagers shall be determined prior to the start of play of any hand or round. However, the gambling establishment may waive collection of the fee or portion of the fee in any hand or round of play after the hand or round has begun pursuant to the published rules of the game and the notice provided to the public. The actual collection of the fee may occur before or after the start of play. Ample notice shall be provided to the patrons of gambling establishments relating to the assessment of fees. Flat fees on each wager may be assessed at different collection rates, but no more than five collection rates may be established per table. However, if the gambling establishment waives its collection fee, this fee does not constitute one of the five collection rates.

Amended by Stats 2008 ch 748 (SB 1369),s 7, eff. 1/1/2009.
Amended by Stats 2007 ch 493 (AB 356),s 2, eff. 1/1/2008.
Amended by Stats 2007 ch 176 (SB 82),s 62, eff. 8/24/2007.
Amended by Stats 2005 ch 546 (AB 1753),s 6, eff. 1/1/2006
Amended by Stats 2004 ch 405 (SB 1796), s 8, eff. 1/1/2005.
Amended by Stats 2003 ch 756 (AB 278), s 1, eff. 1/1/2004.
Amended by Stats 2001 ch 941 (AB 54), s 3, eff. 1/1/2002.

Section 337k - Unlawful advertising of nonparimutuel wagering on horse races

(a) It is unlawful for any person to advertise, or to facilitate the advertisement of, nonparimutuel wagering on horse races.

(b) Violation of this section is an infraction punishable by a fine of five hundred dollars ($500). A second conviction for a violation of this section is a misdemeanor punishable by a fine of up to ten thousand dollars ($10,000).

Added by Stats 2006 ch 305 (SB 1229),s 1, eff. 1/1/2007.

Section 337s - Draw poker

(a) This section applies only in counties with a population exceeding 4,000,000.

(b) Every person who deals, plays, or carries on, opens, or causes to be opened, or who conducts, either as owner or employee, whether for hire or not, any game of draw poker, including lowball poker, is guilty of a misdemeanor.

(c) Subdivision (b) shall become operative in a county only if the board of supervisors thereof by resolution directs that there be placed on the ballot at a designated county election the question whether draw poker, including lowball poker, shall be prohibited in the county and a majority of electors voting thereon vote affirmatively. The question shall appear on the ballot in substantially the following form: "Shall draw poker, including lowball poker, be prohibited in _____ County? Yes _____ No _____"

If a majority of electors voting thereon vote affirmatively, draw poker shall be prohibited in the unincorporated territory in the county.

(d) Any county ordinance in any county prohibiting, restricting, or regulating the playing of draw poker and other acts relating to draw poker shall not be superseded until, pursuant to subdivision (c), the electorate of the county determines that subdivision (b) shall be operative in the county.

(e) The Legislature finds that in counties with a large, concentrated population, problems incident to the playing of draw poker are, in part, qualitatively, as well as quantitatively, different from the problems in smaller counties. The Legislature finds that counties with a population exceeding 4,000,000 constitute a special problem, and it is reasonable classification to adopt prohibitory legislation applicable only to such counties.

(f) If any provision of this section is held invalid, the entire section shall be invalid. The provisions of this section are not severable.
Amended by Stats. 1993, Ch. 98, Sec. 1. Effective January 1, 1994.

Section 337t - Definitions

The following definitions govern the construction of this section and Sections 337u, 337w, 337x, and 337y:

(a) "Associated equipment" means any equipment or mechanical, electromechanical, or electronic contrivance, component or machine used remotely or directly in connection with gaming or any game that would not otherwise be classified as a gaming device, including dice, playing cards, links which connect to progressive slot machines, equipment which affects the proper reporting of gross revenue, computerized systems for monitoring slot machines and devices for weighing or counting money.

(b) "Cashless wagering system" means a method of wagering and accounting in which the validity and value of a wagering instrument or wagering credits are determined, monitored, and retained by a computer that is operated and maintained by a licensee and that maintains a record of each transaction involving the wagering instrument or wagering credits, exclusive of the game or gaming device on which wagers are being made. The term includes computerized systems which facilitate electronic transfers of money directly to or from a game or gaming device.

(c) "Cheat" means to alter the normal elements of chance, method of selection, or criteria, excluding those alterations to the game generally done by the casino to provide variety to games and that are known, or should be known, by the wagering players, which determine any of the following:

    (1) The result of a gambling game.

    (2) The amount or frequency of payment in a gambling game.

    (3) The value of a wagering instrument.

    (4) The value of a wagering credit.

(d) "Drop box" means the box that serves as a repository for cash, chips, tokens, or other wagering instruments.

(e) "Gambling establishment" means any premises wherein or whereon any gaming is done.

(f) "Gambling game device" means any equipment or mechanical, electromechanical, or electronic contrivance, component or machine used remotely or directly in connection with gaming or any game which affects the result of a wager by determining win or loss. The term includes any of the following:

    (1) A slot machine.

    (2) A collection of two or more of the following components:

        (A) An assembled electronic circuit which cannot be reasonably demonstrated to have any use other than in a slot machine.

        (B) A cabinet with electrical wiring and provisions for mounting a coin, token, or currency acceptor and provisions for mounting a dispenser of coins, tokens, or anything of value.

        (C) A storage medium containing the source language or executable code of a computer program that cannot be reasonably demonstrated to have any use other than in a slot machine.

        (D) An assembled video display unit.

        (E) An assembled mechanical or electromechanical display unit intended for use in gambling.

        (F) An assembled mechanical or electromechanical unit which cannot be demonstrated to have any use other than in a slot machine.

    (3) Any mechanical, electrical, or other device that may be connected to or used with a slot machine to alter the normal criteria of random selection or affect the outcome of a game.

    (4) A system for the accounting or management of any game in which the result of the wager is determined electronically by using any combination of hardware or software for computers.

    (5) Any combination of one of the components set forth in subparagraphs (A) to (F), inclusive, of paragraph (2) and any other component that the commission determines, by regulation, to be a machine used directly or remotely in connection with gaming or any game which affects the results of a wager by determining a win or loss.

(g) "Past-posting" means the placing of a wager by an individual at a game after having knowledge of the result or outcome of that game.

(h) "Pinching wagers" means to reduce the amount wagered or to cancel the wager after acquiring knowledge of the outcome of the game or other event that is the subject of the wager.

(i) "Pressing wagers" means to increase a wager after acquiring knowledge of the outcome of the game or other event that is the subject of the wager.

(j) "Tribal Gaming Agency" means the person, agency, board, committee, commission, or council designated under tribal law, including, but not limited to, an intertribal gaming regulatory agency approved to fulfill those functions by the National Indian Gaming Commission, as primarily responsible for carrying out the regulatory responsibilities of the tribe under the Indian Gaming and Regulatory Act (25 U.S.C. Sec. 2701) and a tribal gaming ordinance.

(k) "Wagering credit" means a representative of value, other than a chip, token, or wagering instrument, that is used for wagering at a game or gaming device and is obtained by the payment of cash or a cash equivalent, the use of a wagering instrument or the electronic transfer of money.

(l) "Wagering instrument" means a representative of value, other than a chip or token, that is issued by a licensee and approved by the California Gambling Control Commission or a tribal gaming agency, for use in a cashless wagering system.

Added by Stats 2002 ch 624 (AB 2965), s 1, eff. 1/1/2003.

Section 337u - Unlawful acts related to gambling game or other event

It is unlawful for any person to commit any of the following acts:

(a) To alter or misrepresent the outcome of a gambling game or other event on which wagers lawfully have been made after the outcome is determined, but before it is revealed to the players.

(b) To place, increase, or decrease a wager or to determine the course of play after acquiring knowledge, not available to all players, of the outcome of the gambling game or any event that affects the outcome of the gambling game or which is the subject of the wager or to aid anyone in acquiring that knowledge for the purpose of placing, increasing, or decreasing a wager or determining the course of play contingent upon that event or outcome.

(c) To claim, collect, or take, or attempt to claim, collect, or take, money or anything of value in or from a gambling game, with intent to defraud, without having made a wager contingent on the game, or to claim, collect, or take an amount greater than the amount actually won.

(d) Knowingly to entice or induce another to go to any place where a gambling game is being conducted or operated in violation of this section, or Section 337v, 337w, 337x, or 337y, with the intent that the other person play or participate in that gambling game.

(e) To place or increase a wager after acquiring knowledge of the outcome of the gambling game or other event which is the subject of the wager, including past-posting and pressing wagers.

(f) To reduce the amount wagered or cancel the wager after acquiring knowledge of the outcome of the gambling game or other event which is the subject of the bet, including pinching wagers.

(g) To manipulate, with the intent to cheat, any component of a gambling game device in a manner contrary to the designed and normal operational purpose for the component, including, but not limited to, varying the pull of the handle of a slot machine, with knowledge that the manipulation affects the outcome of the gambling game or with knowledge of any event that affects the outcome of the gambling game.

Amended by Stats 2003 ch 62 (SB 600), s 225, eff. 1/1/2004.
Added by Stats 2002 ch 624 (AB 2965), s 2, eff. 1/1/2003.

Section 337v - Unlawful use of device by person at gambling establishment

It is unlawful for any person at a gambling establishment to use, or to possess with the intent to use, any device to assist in any of the following:

(a) In projecting the outcome of the gambling game.

(b) In keeping track of the cards played.

(c) In analyzing the probability of the occurrence of an event relating to the gambling game.

(d) In analyzing the strategy for playing or wagering to be used in the gambling game, except as permitted by the California Gambling Control Commission or a tribal gaming agency.

Added by Stats 2002 ch 624 (AB 2965), s 3, eff. 1/1/2003.

Section 337w - Unlawful use or possession of wagering instruments or devices

(a) It is unlawful for any person to use counterfeit chips, counterfeit debit instruments, or other counterfeit wagering instruments in a gambling game, the equipment associated with a gambling game, or a cashless wagering system.

(b) It is unlawful for any person, in playing or using any gambling game, the equipment associated with a gambling game, or a cashless wagering system designed to be played with, receive, or be operated by chips, tokens, wagering credits or other wagering instruments approved by the California Gambling Control Commission or a tribal gaming agency, or by lawful coin of the United States of America to either:

    (1) Knowingly use chips, tokens, wagering credits, or other wagering instruments not approved by the California Gambling Control Commission or a tribal gaming agency, or lawful coin, legal tender of the United States of America, or use coins or tokens not of the same denomination as the coins or tokens intended to be used in that gambling game, associated equipment, or cashless wagering system.

    (2) Use any device or means to violate this section or Section 337u, 337v, 337x, or 337y.

(c) It is unlawful for any person, not a duly authorized employee of a gambling establishment acting in furtherance of his or her employment within that establishment, to possess any device intended to be used to violate this section or Section 337u, 337v, 337x, or 337y.

(d) It is unlawful for any person, not a duly authorized employee of a gambling establishment acting in furtherance of his or her employment within that establishment, to possess any key or device known to have been designed for the purpose of, and suitable for, opening, entering, or affecting the operation of any gambling game, cashless wagering system, or dropbox, or for removing money or other contents from the game, system, or box.

(e) It is unlawful for any person to possess any paraphernalia for manufacturing slugs. As used in this subdivision, "paraphernalia for manufacturing slugs" means the equipment, products, and materials that are intended for use or designed for use in manufacturing, producing, fabricating, preparing, testing, analyzing, packaging, storing, or concealing a counterfeit facsimile of the chips, tokens, debit instruments, or other wagering instruments approved by the California Gambling Control Commission or a tribal gaming agency, or a lawful coin of the United States, the use of which is unlawful pursuant to subdivision (b). The term "paraphernalia for manufacturing slugs" includes, but is not limited to, any of the following:

    (1) Lead or lead alloys.

    (2) Molds, forms, or similar equipment capable of producing a likeness of a gaming token or lawful coin of the United States.

    (3) Melting pots or other receptacles.

    (4) Torches.

    (5) Tongs, trimming tools, or other similar equipment.

    (6) Equipment which can be reasonably demonstrated to manufacture facsimiles of debit instruments or wagering instruments approved by the California Gambling Control Commission or a tribal gaming agency.

Added by Stats 2002 ch 624 (AB 2965), s 4, eff. 1/1/2003.

Section 337x - Cheating at gambling game

It is unlawful to cheat at any gambling game in a gambling establishment.

Added by Stats 2002 ch 624 (AB 2965), s 5, eff. 1/1/2003.

Section 337y - Unlawful manufacture of device to cheat; unlawful modification of gambling equipment; unlawful instruction in cheating

It is unlawful to do either of the following:

(a) Manufacture, sell, or distribute any cards, chips, dice, game, or device which is intended to be used to violate Section 337u, 337v, 337w, or 337x.

(b) Mark, alter, or otherwise modify any gambling game device or associated equipment in a manner that either:

(1) Affects the result of a wager by determining win or loss.

(2) Alters the normal criteria of random selection, which affects the operation of a gambling game or which determines the outcome of a game.

(c) It is unlawful for any person to instruct another in cheating or in the use of any device for that purpose, with the knowledge or intent that the information or use conveyed may be employed to violate Section 337u, 337v, 337w, or 337x.

Added by Stats 2002 ch 624 (AB 2965), s 6, eff. 1/1/2003.

Section 337z - Punishment

(a) Any person who violates Section 337u, 337v, 337w, 337x, or 337y shall be punished as follows:

(1) For the first violation, by imprisonment in a county jail for a term not to exceed one year, or by a fine of not more than ten thousand dollars ($10,000), or by both imprisonment and fine.

(2) For a second or subsequent violation of any of those sections, by imprisonment in a county jail for a term not to exceed one year or by a fine of not more than fifteen thousand dollars ($15,000), or by both imprisonment and fine.

(b) A person who attempts to violate Section 337u, 337v, 337w, 337x, or 337y shall be punished in the same manner as the underlying crime.

(c) This section does not preclude prosecution under Section 332 or any other provision of law.

Amended by Stats 2005 ch 546 (AB 1753),s 7, eff. 1/1/2006

Added by Stats 2002 ch 624 (AB 2965), s 7, eff. 1/1/2003.

Chapter 10.5 - HORSE RACING

Section 337.1 - Touting

Any person, who knowingly and designedly by false representation attempts to, or does persuade, procure or cause another person to wager on a horse in a race to be run in this state or elsewhere, and upon which money is wagered in this state, and who asks or demands compensation as a reward for information or purported information given in such case is a tout, and is guilty of touting.

Amended by Stats. 1987, Ch. 828, Sec. 22.

Section 337.2 - Punishment

Any person who is a tout, or who attempts or conspires to commit touting, is guilty of a misdemeanor and is punishable by a fine of not more than five hundred dollars ($500) or by imprisonment in the county jail for not more than six months, or by both such fine and imprisonment. For a second offense in this State, he shall be imprisoned.

Added by Stats. 1945, Ch. 1524.

Section 337.3 - False use of official's name

Any person who in the commission of touting falsely uses the name of any official of the California Horse Racing Board, its inspectors or attaches, or of any official of any race track association, or the names of any owner, trainer, jockey or other person licensed by the California Horse Racing Board as the source of any information or purported information is guilty of a felony and is punishable by a fine of not more than five thousand dollars ($5,000) or by imprisonment pursuant to subdivision (h) of Section 1170, or by both that fine and imprisonment.

Amended by Stats 2011 ch 39 (AB 117),s 68, eff. 6/30/2011.

Amended by Stats 2011 ch 15 (AB 109),s 326, eff. 4/4/2011, but operative no earlier than October 1, 2011, and only upon creation of a community corrections grant program to assist in implementing this act and upon an appropriation to fund the grant program.

Section 337.4 - Obtaining money in excess of $950

Any person who in the commission of touting obtains money in excess of nine hundred fifty dollars ($950) may, in addition to being prosecuted for the violation of any provision of this chapter, be prosecuted for the violation of Section 487 of this code.

Amended by Stats 2009 ch 28 (SB X3-18),s 8, eff. 1/1/2010.

Section 337.5 - Exclusion from racetrack

Any person who has been convicted of touting, and the record of whose conviction on such charge is on file in the office of the California Horse Racing Board or in the State Bureau of Criminal Identification and Investigation or of the Federal Bureau of Investigation, or any person who has been ejected from any racetrack of this or any other state for touting or practices inimical to the public interest shall be excluded from all racetracks in this State. Any such person who refuses to leave such track when ordered to do so by inspectors of the California Horse Racing Board, or by any peace officer, or by an accredited attache of a racetrack or association is guilty of a misdemeanor.

Amended by Stats. 1963, Ch. 372.

Section 337.6 - Revocation of credential or license

Any credential or license issued by the California Horse Racing Board to licensees, if used by the holder thereof for a purpose other than identification and in the performance of legitimate duties on a race track, shall be automatically revoked whether so used on or off a race track.

Added by Stats. 1945, Ch. 1524.

Section 337.7 - Unlawful possession of credential or license

Any person other than the lawful holder thereof who has in his possession any credential or license issued by the California Horse Racing Board to licensees and any person who has a forged or simulated credential or license of said board in his possession, and who uses such credential or license for the purpose of misrepresentation, fraud or touting is guilty of a felony and shall be punished by a fine of five thousand dollars ($5,000) or by imprisonment pursuant to subdivision (h) of Section 1170, or by both that fine and imprisonment. If he or she has previously been convicted of any offense under this chapter, he or she shall be imprisoned pursuant to subdivision (h) of Section 1170.

Amended by Stats 2011 ch 39 (AB 117),s 68, eff. 6/30/2011.

Amended by Stats 2011 ch 15 (AB 109),s 327, eff. 4/4/2011, but operative no earlier than October 1, 2011, and only upon creation of a community corrections grant program to assist in implementing this act and upon an appropriation to fund the grant program.

Section 337.8 - Unlawful use of credential for purpose of touting

Any person who uses any credential, other than a credential or license issued by the California Horse Racing Board, for the purpose of touting is guilty of touting, and if the credential has been forged shall be imprisoned as provided in this chapter, whether the offense was committed on or off a race track.

Added by Stats. 1945, Ch. 1524.

Section 337.9 - Policy for enforcement

The secretary and chief investigator of the California Horse Racing Board shall coordinate a policy for the enforcement of this chapter with all other enforcement bureaus in the State in order to insure prosecution of all persons who commit any offense against the horse racing laws of this State. For such purposes the secretary and chief investigator are peace officers and have all the powers thereof.

Added by Stats. 1945, Ch. 1524.

Chapter 11 - PAWNBROKERS

Section 343 - Failure, refusal, or neglect to produce for inspection

Every person who purchases gold bullion, gold bars or gold quartz or mineral containing gold, who fails, refuses, or neglects to produce for inspection his register, or to exhibit all articles received by him in pledge, or his account of sales, to any officer holding a warrant authorizing him to search for personal property or to any person appointed by the sheriff or head of the police department of any city, city and county or town, or an order of a committing magistrate directing such officer to inspect such register, or examine such articles or account of sales, is guilty of a misdemeanor.

Amended by Stats. 1959, Ch. 638.

Chapter 12 - OTHER INJURIES TO PERSONS

Section 346 - Unlawful sale of ticket of admission

Any person who, without the written permission of the owner or operator of the property on which an entertainment event is to be held or is being held, sells a ticket of admission to the entertainment event, which was obtained for the purpose of resale, at any price which is in excess of the price that is printed or endorsed upon the ticket, while on the grounds of or in the stadium, arena, theater, or other place where an event for which admission tickets are sold is to be held or is being held, is guilty of a misdemeanor.

Added by Stats. 1972, Ch. 529.

Section 347 - Unlawful mingling of poison or harmful substance with food, drink, medicine, or water supply

(a)

(1) Every person who willfully mingles any poison or harmful substance with any food, drink, medicine, or pharmaceutical product or who willfully places any poison or harmful substance in any spring, well, reservoir, or public water supply, where the person knows or should have known that the same would be taken by any human being to his or her injury, is guilty of a felony punishable by imprisonment in the state prison for two, four, or five years.

(2) Any violation of paragraph (1) involving the use of a poison or harmful substance that may cause death if ingested or that causes the infliction of great bodily injury on any person shall be punished by an additional term of three years.

(b) Any person who maliciously informs any other person that a poison or other harmful substance has been or will be placed in any food, drink, medicine, pharmaceutical product, or public water supply, knowing that such report is false, is guilty of a crime punishable by imprisonment in the state prison, or by imprisonment in the county jail not to exceed one year.

(c) The court may impose the maximum fine for each item tampered with in violation of subdivision (a).

Amended by Stats 2000 ch 287 (SB 1955), s 8, eff. 1/1/2001.

Section 347b - Unlawful manufacture or furnishing of alcoholic solution of potable nature containing deleterious or poisonous substance

It shall be unlawful for any person, firm or corporation to manufacture, sell, furnish, or give away, or offer to manufacture, sell, furnish, or give away any alcoholic solution of a potable nature containing any deleterious or poisonous substance, and the burden of proof shall be upon the person, firm, or corporation manufacturing, selling, furnishing, or giving away, or offering to manufacture, sell, furnish, or give away, any such alcoholic solution of a potable nature containing any deleterious or poisonous substance, to show that such alcoholic solution of a potable nature did not contain any deleterious or poisonous substance. Every person who violates any of the provisions of this section is guilty of a misdemeanor, and shall be punished by a fine not exceeding two thousand five hundred dollars ($2,500), or by imprisonment in a county jail not exceeding one year, or by both such fine and imprisonment.

Amended by Stats. 1976, Ch. 1125.

Section 350 - Unlawful manufacture, sale, or possession for sale of counterfeit mark

(a) Any person who willfully manufactures, intentionally sells, or knowingly possesses for sale any counterfeit mark registered with the Secretary of State or registered on the Principal Register of the United States Patent and Trademark Office, shall, upon conviction, be punishable as follows:

(1) When the offense involves less than 1,000 of the articles described in this subdivision, with a total retail or fair market value less than that required for grand theft as defined in Section 487, and if the person is an individual, he or she shall be punished by a fine of

not more than ten thousand dollars ($10,000), or by imprisonment in a county jail for not more than one year, or by both that fine and imprisonment; or, if the person is a business entity, by a fine of not more than two hundred thousand dollars ($200,000).

(2) When the offense involves 1,000 or more of the articles described in this subdivision, or has a total retail or fair market value equal to or greater than that required for grand theft as defined in Section 487, and if the person is an individual, he or she shall be punished by imprisonment in a county jail not to exceed one year, or pursuant to subdivision (h) of Section 1170 for 16 months, or two or three years, or by a fine not to exceed five hundred thousand dollars ($500,000), or by both that imprisonment and fine; or, if the person is a business entity, by a fine not to exceed one million dollars ($1,000,000).

(b) Any person who has been convicted of a violation of either paragraph (1) or (2) of subdivision (a) shall, upon a subsequent conviction of paragraph (1) of subdivision (a), if the person is an individual, be punished by a fine of not more than one hundred thousand dollars ($100,000), or by imprisonment in a county jail for not more than one year, or pursuant to subdivision (h) of Section 1170 for 16 months, or two or three years, or by both that fine and imprisonment; or, if the person is a business entity, by a fine of not more than four hundred thousand dollars ($400,000).

(c) Any person who has been convicted of a violation of subdivision (a) and who, by virtue of the conduct that was the basis of the conviction, has directly and foreseeably caused death or great bodily injury to another through reliance on the counterfeited item for its intended purpose shall, if the person is an individual, be punished by a fine of not more than one hundred thousand dollars ($100,000), or by imprisonment pursuant to subdivision (h) of Section 1170 for two, three, or four years, or by both that fine and imprisonment; or, if the person is a business entity, by a fine of not more than four hundred thousand dollars ($400,000).

(d)

(1) Except as provided in paragraph (2), in any action brought under this section resulting in a conviction or a plea of nolo contendere, the court shall order the forfeiture and destruction of all of those marks and of all goods, articles, or other matter bearing the marks, and the forfeiture and destruction or other disposition of all means of making the marks, and any and all electrical, mechanical, or other devices for manufacturing, reproducing, transporting, or assembling these marks, that were used in connection with, or were part of, any violation of this section.

(2) Upon request of any law enforcement agency and consent from the specific registrants, the court may consider a motion to have the items described in paragraph (1), not including recordings or audiovisual works as defined in Section 653w, donated to a nonprofit organization for the purpose of distributing the goods to persons living in poverty at no charge to the persons served by the organization.

(3) Forfeiture of the proceeds of the crime shall be subject to Chapter 9 (commencing with Section 186) of Title 7 of Part 1. However, no vehicle shall be forfeited under this section that may be lawfully driven on the highway with a class C, M1, or M2 license, as prescribed in Section 12804.9 of the Vehicle Code, and that is any of the following:

(A) A community property asset of a person other than the defendant.

(B) The sole class C, M1, or M2 vehicle available to the immediate family of that person or of the defendant.

(C) Reasonably necessary to be retained by the defendant for the purpose of lawfully earning a living, or for any other reasonable and lawful purpose.

(e) For the purposes of this section, the following definitions shall apply:

(1) When counterfeited but unassembled components of computer software packages are recovered, including, but not limited to, counterfeited computer diskettes, instruction manuals, or licensing envelopes, the number of "articles" shall be equivalent to the number of completed computer software packages that could have been made from those components.

(2) "Business entity" includes, but is not limited to, a corporation, limited liability company, or partnership. "Business entity" does not include a sole proprietorship.

(3) "Counterfeit mark" means a spurious mark that is identical with, or confusingly similar to, a registered mark and is used, or intended to be used, on or in connection with the same type of goods or services for which the genuine mark is registered. It is not necessary for the mark to be displayed on the outside of an article for there to be a violation. For articles containing digitally stored information, it shall be sufficient to constitute a violation if the counterfeit mark appears on a video display when the information is retrieved from the article. The term "spurious mark" includes genuine marks used on or in connection with spurious articles and includes identical articles containing identical marks, where the goods or marks were reproduced without authorization of, or in excess of any authorization granted by, the registrant. When counterfeited but unassembled components of any articles described under subdivision (a) are recovered, including, but not limited to, labels, patches, fabric, stickers, wrappers, badges, emblems, medallions, charms, boxes, containers, cans, cases, hangtags, documentation, or packaging, or any other components of any type or nature that are designed, marketed, or otherwise intended to be used on or in connection with any articles described under subdivision (a), the number of "articles" shall be equivalent to the number of completed articles that could have been made from those components.

(4) "Knowingly possess" means that the person possessing an article knew or had reason to believe that it was spurious, or that it was used on or in connection with spurious articles, or that it was reproduced without authorization of, or in excess of any authorization granted by, the registrant.

(5) Notwithstanding Section 7, "person" includes, but is not limited to, a business entity.

(6) "Registrant" means any person to whom the registration of a mark is issued and that person's legal representatives, successors, or assigns.

(7) "Sale" includes resale.

(8) "Value" has the following meanings:

(A) When counterfeit items of computer software are manufactured or possessed for sale, the "value" of those items shall be equivalent to the retail price or fair market price of the true items that are counterfeited.

(B) When counterfeited but unassembled components of computer software packages or any other articles described under subdivision (a) are recovered, including, but not limited to, counterfeited digital disks, instruction manuals, licensing envelopes, labels, patches, fabric, stickers, wrappers, badges, emblems, medallions, charms, boxes, containers, cans, cases, hangtags, documentation, or packaging, or any other components of any type or nature that are designed, marketed, or otherwise intended to be used on or in connection with any articles described under subdivision (a), the "value" of those components shall be equivalent to the retail price or fair market value of the number of completed computer software packages or other completed articles described under subdivision (a) that could have been made from those components.

(C) "Retail or fair market value" of a counterfeit article means a value equivalent to the retail price or fair market value, as of the last day of the charged crime, of a completed similar genuine article containing a genuine mark.

(f) This section shall not be enforced against any party who has adopted and lawfully used the same or confusingly similar mark in the rendition of like services or the manufacture or sale of like goods in this state from a date prior to the earliest effective date of registration of the service mark or trademark either with the Secretary of State or on the Principle Register of the United States Patent and Trademark Office.

(g) An owner, officer, employee, or agent who provides, rents, leases, licenses, or sells real property upon which a violation of subdivision (a) occurs shall not be subject to a criminal penalty pursuant to this section, unless he or she sells, or possesses for sale, articles bearing a counterfeit mark in violation of this section. This subdivision shall not be construed to abrogate or limit any civil rights or remedies for a trademark violation.

(h) This section shall not be enforced against any party who engages in fair uses of a mark, as specified in Section 14247 of the Business and Professions Code.

(i) When a person is convicted of an offense under this section, the court shall order the person to pay restitution to the trademark owner and any other victim of the offense pursuant to Section 1202.4.

Amended by Stats 2012 ch 867 (SB 1144),s 19, eff. 1/1/2013.
Amended by Stats 2011 ch 39 (AB 117),s 68, eff. 6/30/2011.
Amended by Stats 2011 ch 15 (AB 109),s 333, eff. 4/4/2011, but operative no earlier than October 1, 2011, and only upon creation of a community corrections grant program to assist in implementing this act and upon an appropriation to fund the grant program.
Amended by Stats 2010 ch 351 (AB 819),s 2, eff. 9/25/2010.
Amended by Stats 2009 ch 581 (SB 324),s 1, eff. 1/1/2010.
Amended by Stats 2008 ch 431 (AB 1394),s 1, eff. 1/1/2009.
EFFECTIVE 1/1/2000. Amended July 12, 1999 (Bill Number: SB 966) (Chapter 83).

Section 351a - False representation of goods,, product, or output

Any person who sells, attempts to sell, offers for sale or assists in the sale of any goods, product or output, and who willfully and falsely represents such goods, product or output to be the goods, product or output of any dealer, manufacturer or producer, other than the true dealer, manufacturer or producer, or any member of a firm or any officer of a corporation, who knowingly permits any employee of such firm or corporation to sell, offer for sale or assist in the sale of any goods, product or output or to falsely represent such goods, product or output to be the goods, product or output of any dealer, manufacturer or producer, other than the true dealer, manufacturer or producer, is guilty of a misdemeanor and punishable by a fine of not less than one hundred dollars ($100) or more than six hundred dollars ($600), or by imprisonment in the county jail for not less than 20 or more than 90 days, or both. This section shall not apply to any person who sells or offers for sale under his own name or brand the product or output of another manufacturer or producer with the written consent of such manufacturer or producer.

Amended by Stats. 1983, Ch. 1092, Sec. 271. Effective September 27, 1983. Operative January 1, 1984, by Sec. 427 of Ch. 1092.

Section 355 - Defacement or obliteration of marks upon wrecked property

Every person who defaces or obliterates the marks upon wrecked property, or in any manner disguises the appearance thereof, with intent to prevent the owner from discovering its identity, or who destroys or suppresses any invoice, bill of lading, or other document tending to show the ownership, is guilty of a misdemeanor.

Enacted 1872.

Section 356 - Cutting out, altering, or defacing mark upon log, lumber, or wood

Every person who cuts out, alters, or defaces any mark made upon any log, lumber, or wood, or puts a false mark thereon with intent to prevent the owner from discovering its identity, is guilty of a misdemeanor.

Enacted 1872.

Section 359 - Solemnizing incestuous or other forbidden marriage

Every person authorized to solemnize marriage, who willfully and knowingly solemnizes any incestuous or other marriage forbidden by law, is punishable by fine of not less than one hundred nor more than one thousand dollars, or by imprisonment in the County Jail not less than three months nor more than one year, or by both.

Enacted 1872.

Section 360 - Unlawful solemnization of marriage

Every person authorized to solemnize any marriage, who solemnizes a marriage without first being presented with the marriage license, as required by Section 421 of the Family Code; or who solemnizes a marriage pursuant to Part 4 (commencing with Section 500) of Division 3 of the Family Code without the authorization required by that part; or who willfully makes a false return of any marriage or pretended marriage to the recorder or clerk and every person who willfully makes a false record of any marriage return, is guilty of a misdemeanor.

Amended by Stats 2001 ch 39 (AB 1323), s 11, eff. 1/1/2002.

Section 362 - Neglect or refusal to obey writ of habeas corpus

Every officer or person to whom a writ of habeas corpus may be directed, who, after service thereof, neglects or refuses to obey the command thereof, is guilty of a misdemeanor.

Enacted 1872.

Section 363 - Unlawful restraint of person who has been discharged upon writ of habeas corpus

Every person who, either solely or as member of a Court, knowingly and unlawfully recommits, imprisons, or restrains of his liberty, for the same cause, any person who has been discharged upon a writ of habeas corpus, is guilty of a misdemeanor.

Enacted 1872.

Section 364 - Unlawful concealment of person for whose relief writ of habeas corpus has been issued

Every person having in his custody, or under his restraint or power, any person for whose relief a writ of habeas corpus has been issued, who, with the intent to elude the service of such writ or to avoid the effect thereof, transfers such person to the custody of another, or places him under the power or control of another, or conceals or changes the place of his confinement or restraint, or removes him without the jurisdiction of the Court or Judge issuing the writ, is guilty of a misdemeanor.
Enacted 1872.

Section 365 - Unlawful refusal to receive guest or passenger

Every person, and every agent or officer of any corporation carrying on business as an innkeeper, or as a common carrier of passengers, who refuses, without just cause or excuse, to receive and entertain any guest, or to receive and carry any passenger, is guilty of a misdemeanor. However, an innkeeper who has proceeded as authorized by Section 1865 of the Civil Code shall be rebuttably presumed to have acted with just cause or excuse for purposes of this section.
EFFECTIVE 1/1/2000. Amended September 7, 1999 (Bill Number: SB 1171) (Chapter 354).

Section 365.5 - Unlawful acts related to guide, signal, or service dogs

(a) Any blind person, deaf person, or disabled person, who is a passenger on any common carrier, airplane, motor vehicle, railway train, motorbus, streetcar, boat, or any other public conveyance or mode of transportation operating within this state, shall be entitled to have with him or her a specially trained guide dog, signal dog, or service dog.

(b) No blind person, deaf person, or disabled person and his or her specially trained guide dog, signal dog, or service dog shall be denied admittance to accommodations, advantages, facilities, medical facilities, including hospitals, clinics, and physicians' offices, telephone facilities, adoption agencies, private schools, hotels, lodging places, places of public accommodation, amusement, or resort, and other places to which the general public is invited within this state because of that guide dog, signal dog, or service dog.

(c) Any person, firm, association, or corporation, or the agent of any person, firm, association, or corporation, who prevents a disabled person from exercising, or interferes with a disabled person in the exercise of, the rights specified in this section is guilty of a misdemeanor, punishable by a fine not exceeding two thousand five hundred dollars ($2,500).

(d) As used in this section, "guide dog" means any guide dog or Seeing Eye dog that was trained by a person licensed under Chapter 9.5 (commencing with Section 7200) of Division 3 of the Business and Professions Code or that meets the definitional criteria under federal regulations adopted to implement Title III of the Americans with Disabilities Act of 1990 (Public Law 101-336).

(e) As used in this section, "signal dog" means any dog trained to alert a deaf person, or a person whose hearing is impaired, to intruders or sounds.

(f) As used in this section, "service dog" means any dog individually trained to do work or perform tasks for the benefit of an individual with a disability, including, but not limited to, minimal protection work, rescue work, pulling a wheelchair, or fetching dropped items.

(g)

    (1) Nothing in this section is intended to affect any civil remedies available for a violation of this section.

    (2) This section is intended to provide equal accessibility for all owners or trainers of animals that are trained as guide dogs, signal dogs, or service dogs in a manner that is no less than that provided by the Americans with Disabilities Act of 1990 (Public Law 101-336) and the Air Carrier Access Act of 1986 (Public Law 99-435).

(h) The exercise of rights specified in subdivisions (a) and (b) by any person may not be conditioned upon payment of any extra charge, provided that the person shall be liable for any provable damage done to the premises or facilities by his or her dog.

(i) Any trainer or individual with a disability may take dogs in any of the places specified in subdivisions (a) and (b) for the purpose of training the dogs as guide dogs, signal dogs, or service dogs. The person shall ensure that the dog is on a leash and tagged as a guide dog, signal dog, or service dog by an identification tag issued by the county clerk or animal control department as authorized by Chapter 3.5 (commencing with Section 30850) of Division 14 of the Food and Agricultural Code. In addition, the person shall be liable for any provable damage done to the premises or facilities by his or her dog.
Amended by Stats. 1996, Ch. 498, Sec. 6. Effective January 1, 1997.

Section 365.6 - Intentional interference with use of guide, signal, or service dog or mobility aid

(a) Any person who, with no legal justification, intentionally interferes with the use of a guide, signal, or service dog or mobility aid by harassing or obstructing the guide, signal, or service dog or mobility aid user or his or her guide, signal, or service dog, is guilty of a misdemeanor, punishable by imprisonment in a county jail not exceeding six months, or by a fine of not less than one thousand five hundred dollars ($1,500) nor more than two thousand five hundred dollars ($2,500), or both that fine and imprisonment.

(b) As used in this section, the following definitions shall apply:

    (1) "Mobility aid" means any device enabling a person with a disability, as defined in subdivision (b) of Section 54 of the Civil Code, to travel independently, including, but not limited to, a guide, signal, or service dog, as defined in Section 54.1 of the Civil Code, a wheelchair, walker or white cane.

    (2) "Guide, signal, or service dog" means any dog trained to do work or perform tasks for the benefit of an individual with a disability, including, but not limited to, guiding individuals with impaired vision, alerting individuals with impaired hearing to intruders or sounds, pulling a wheelchair, or fetching dropped items.

(c) Nothing in this section is intended to affect any civil remedies available for a violation of this section.
Amended by Stats 2004 ch 322 (AB 1801), s 1, eff. 1/1/2005.

Section 365.7 - Unlawful representation to be owner or trainer of guide, signal, or service dog

(a) Any person who knowingly and fraudulently represents himself or herself, through verbal or written notice, to be the owner or trainer of any canine licensed as, to be qualified as, or identified as, a guide, signal, or service dog, as defined in subdivisions (d), (e), and (f) of Section 365.5 and paragraph (6) of subdivision (b) of Section 54.1 of the Civil Code, shall be guilty of a misdemeanor punishable by imprisonment in the county jail not exceeding six months, by a fine not exceeding one thousand dollars ($1,000), or by both that fine and imprisonment.

(b) As used in this section, "owner" means any person who owns a guide, signal, or service dog, or who is authorized by the owner to use the guide, signal, or service dog.

Added by Stats. 1994, Ch. 1257, Sec. 12. Effective January 1, 1995.

Section 367f - Unlawful transfer of human organ

(a) Except as provided in subdivisions (d) and (e), it shall be unlawful for any person to knowingly acquire, receive, sell, promote the transfer of, or otherwise transfer any human organ, for purposes of transplantation, for valuable consideration.

(b) Except as provided in subdivisions (d), (e), and (f), it shall be unlawful to remove or transplant any human organ with the knowledge that the organ has been acquired or will be transferred or sold for valuable consideration in violation of subdivision (a).

(c) For purposes of this section, the following definitions apply:

(1) "Human organ" includes, but is not limited to, a human kidney, liver, heart, lung, pancreas, or any other human organ or nonrenewable or nonregenerative tissue except plasma and sperm.

(2) "Valuable consideration" means financial gain or advantage, but does not include the reasonable costs associated with the removal, storage, transportation, and transplantation of a human organ, or reimbursement for those services, or the expenses of travel, housing, and lost wages incurred by the donor of a human organ in connection with the donation of the organ.

(d) No act respecting the nonsale donation of organs or other nonsale conduct pursuant to or in the furtherance of the purposes of the Uniform Anatomical Gift Act, Chapter 3.5 (commencing with Section 7150) Part 1 of Division 7 of the Health and Safety Code, including acts pursuant to anatomical gifts offered under Section 12811.3 of the Vehicle Code, shall be made unlawful by this section.

(e) This section shall not apply to the person from whom the organ is removed, nor to the person who receives the transplant, or those persons' next-of-kin who assisted in obtaining the organ for purposes of transplantations.

(f) A licensed physician and surgeon who transplants a human organ in violation of subdivision (b) shall not be criminally liable under that subdivision if the act is performed under emergency and life-threatening conditions.

(g) Any person who violates subdivision (a) or (b) shall be punished by a fine not to exceed fifty thousand dollars ($50,000), or by imprisonment pursuant to subdivision (h) of Section 1170 for three, four, or five years, or by both that fine and imprisonment.

Amended by Stats 2021 ch 211 (AB 1374),s 2, eff. 1/1/2022.

Amended by Stats 2011 ch 39 (AB 117),s 68, eff. 6/30/2011.

Amended by Stats 2011 ch 15 (AB 109),s 334, eff. 4/4/2011, but operative no earlier than October 1, 2011, and only upon creation of a community corrections grant program to assist in implementing this act and upon an appropriation to fund the grant program.

Section 367g - Unlawful use of sperm, ova, or embryos in assisted reproduction technology

(a) It shall be unlawful for anyone to knowingly use sperm, ova, or embryos in assisted reproduction technology, for any purpose other than that indicated by the sperm, ova, or embryo provider's signature on a written consent form.

(b) It shall be unlawful for anyone to knowingly implant sperm, ova, or embryos, through the use of assisted reproduction technology, into a recipient who is not the sperm, ova, or embryo provider, without the signed written consent of the sperm, ova, or embryo provider and recipient.

(c) Any person who violates this section shall be punished by imprisonment pursuant to subdivision (h) of Section 1170 for three, four, or five years, by a fine not to exceed fifty thousand dollars ($50,000), or by both that fine and imprisonment.

(d) Written consent, for the purposes of this section, shall not be required of men who donate sperm to a licensed tissue bank.

Amended by Stats 2011 ch 39 (AB 117),s 68, eff. 6/30/2011.

Amended by Stats 2011 ch 15 (AB 109),s 335, eff. 4/4/2011, but operative no earlier than October 1, 2011, and only upon creation of a community corrections grant program to assist in implementing this act and upon an appropriation to fund the grant program.

Chapter 13 - CRIMES AGAINST ELDERS, DEPENDENT ADULTS, AND PERSONS WITH DISABILITIES

Section 368 - Crimes against elders and dependent adults

(a) The Legislature finds and declares that elders, adults whose physical or mental disabilities or other limitations restrict their ability to carry out normal activities or to protect their rights, and adults admitted as inpatients to a 24-hour health facility deserve special consideration and protection.

(b)

(1) A person who knows or reasonably should know that a person is an elder or dependent adult and who, under circumstances or conditions likely to produce great bodily harm or death, willfully causes or permits any elder or dependent adult to suffer, or inflicts thereon unjustifiable physical pain or mental suffering, or having the care or custody of any elder or dependent adult, willfully causes or permits the person or health of the elder or dependent adult to be injured, or willfully causes or permits the elder or dependent adult to be placed in a situation in which his or her person or health is endangered, is punishable by imprisonment in a county jail not exceeding one year, or by a fine not to exceed six thousand dollars ($6,000), or by both that fine and imprisonment, or by imprisonment in the state prison for two, three, or four years.

(2) If, in the commission of an offense described in paragraph (1), the victim suffers great bodily injury, as defined in Section 12022.7, the defendant shall receive an additional term in the state prison as follows:

(A) Three years if the victim is under 70 years of age.

(B) Five years if the victim is 70 years of age or older.

(3) If, in the commission of an offense described in paragraph (1), the defendant proximately causes the death of the victim, the defendant shall receive an additional term in the state prison as follows:

(A) Five years if the victim is under 70 years of age.

(B) Seven years if the victim is 70 years of age or older.

(c) A person who knows or reasonably should know that a person is an elder or dependent adult and who, under circumstances or conditions other than those likely to produce great bodily harm or death, willfully causes or permits any elder or dependent adult to suffer, or inflicts thereon unjustifiable physical pain or mental suffering, or having the care or custody of any elder or dependent adult, willfully causes or permits the person or health of the elder or dependent adult to be injured or willfully causes or permits the elder or dependent adult to be placed in a situation in which his or her person or health may be endangered, is guilty of a misdemeanor. A second or subsequent violation of this subdivision is punishable by a fine not to exceed two thousand dollars ($2,000), or by imprisonment in a county jail not to exceed one year, or by both that fine and imprisonment.

(d) A person who is not a caretaker who violates any provision of law proscribing theft, embezzlement, forgery, or fraud, or who violates Section 530.5 proscribing identity theft, with respect to the property or personal identifying information of an elder or a dependent adult, and who knows or reasonably should know that the victim is an elder or a dependent adult, is punishable as follows:

(1) By a fine not exceeding two thousand five hundred dollars ($2,500), or by imprisonment in a county jail not exceeding one year, or by both that fine and imprisonment, or by a fine not exceeding ten thousand dollars ($10,000), or by imprisonment pursuant to subdivision (h) of Section 1170 for two, three, or four years, or by both that fine and imprisonment, when the moneys, labor, goods, services, or real or personal property taken or obtained is of a value exceeding nine hundred fifty dollars ($950).

(2) By a fine not exceeding one thousand dollars ($1,000), by imprisonment in a county jail not exceeding one year, or by both that fine and imprisonment, when the moneys, labor, goods, services, or real or personal property taken or obtained is of a value not exceeding nine hundred fifty dollars ($950).

(e) A caretaker of an elder or a dependent adult who violates any provision of law proscribing theft, embezzlement, forgery, or fraud, or who violates Section 530.5 proscribing identity theft, with respect to the property or personal identifying information of that elder or dependent adult, is punishable as follows:

(1) By a fine not exceeding two thousand five hundred dollars ($2,500), or by imprisonment in a county jail not exceeding one year, or by both that fine and imprisonment, or by a fine not exceeding ten thousand dollars ($10,000), or by imprisonment pursuant to subdivision (h) of Section 1170 for two, three, or four years, or by both that fine and imprisonment, when the moneys, labor, goods, services, or real or personal property taken or obtained is of a value exceeding nine hundred fifty dollars ($950).

(2) By a fine not exceeding one thousand dollars ($1,000), by imprisonment in a county jail not exceeding one year, or by both that fine and imprisonment, when the moneys, labor, goods, services, or real or personal property taken or obtained is of a value not exceeding nine hundred fifty dollars ($950).

(f) A person who commits the false imprisonment of an elder or a dependent adult by the use of violence, menace, fraud, or deceit is punishable by imprisonment pursuant to subdivision (h) of Section 1170 for two, three, or four years.

(g) As used in this section, "elder" means a person who is 65 years of age or older.

(h) As used in this section, "dependent adult" means a person, regardless of whether the person lives independently, who is between the ages of 18 and 64, who has physical or mental limitations which restrict his or her ability to carry out normal activities or to protect his or her rights, including, but not limited to, persons who have physical or developmental disabilities or whose physical or mental abilities have diminished because of age. "Dependent adult" includes a person between the ages of 18 and 64 who is admitted as an inpatient to a 24-hour health facility, as defined in Sections 1250, 1250.2, and 1250.3 of the Health and Safety Code.

(i) As used in this section, "caretaker" means a person who has the care, custody, or control of, or who stands in a position of trust with, an elder or a dependent adult.

(j) Nothing in this section shall preclude prosecution under both this section and Section 187 or 12022.7 or any other provision of law. However, a person shall not receive an additional term of imprisonment under both paragraphs (2) and (3) of subdivision (b) for a single offense, nor shall a person receive an additional term of imprisonment under both Section 12022.7 and paragraph (2) or (3) of subdivision (b) for a single offense.

(k) In any case in which a person is convicted of violating these provisions, the court may require him or her to receive appropriate counseling as a condition of probation. A defendant ordered to be placed in a counseling program shall be responsible for paying the expense of his or her participation in the counseling program as determined by the court. The court shall take into consideration the ability of the defendant to pay, and no defendant shall be denied probation because of his or her inability to pay.

(l) Upon conviction for a violation of subdivision (b), (c), (d), (e), or (f), the sentencing court shall also consider issuing an order restraining the defendant from any contact with the victim, which may be valid for up to 10 years, as determined by the court. It is the intent of the Legislature that the length of any restraining order be based upon the seriousness of the facts before the court, the probability of future violations, and the safety of the victim and his or her immediate family. This protective order may be issued by the court whether the defendant is sentenced to state prison or county jail, or if imposition of sentence is suspended and the defendant is placed on probation.

Amended by Stats 2018 ch 70 (AB 1934),s 3, eff. 1/1/2019.
Amended by Stats 2015 ch 279 (SB 352),s 2, eff. 1/1/2016.
Amended by Stats 2011 ch 366 (AB 332),s 1.5, eff. 1/1/2012.
Amended by Stats 2011 ch 39 (AB 117),s 68, eff. 6/30/2011.
Amended by Stats 2011 ch 15 (AB 109),s 336, eff. 4/4/2011, but operative no earlier than October 1, 2011, and only upon creation of a community corrections grant program to assist in implementing this act and upon an appropriation to fund the grant program.
Chapter 13 heading added by Stats 2010 ch 617 (SB 110),s 2, eff. 1/1/2011.
Amended by Stats 2009 ch 28 (SB X3-18),s 9, eff. 1/1/2010.
Amended by Stats 2009 ch 25 (SB 18),s 1, eff. 1/1/2010.
Amended by Stats 2004 ch 893 (AB 3095), s 1, eff. 1/1/2005.
Amended by Stats 2004 ch 886 (AB 2611), s 1, eff. 1/1/2005.
Amended by Stats 2003 ch 543 (AB 1131), s 1, eff. 1/1/2004.
Amended by Stats 2002 ch 369 (AB 2140), s 2, eff. 1/1/2003.
Amended by Stats 2001 ch 854 (SB 205), s 27, eff. 1/1/2002.
Amended by Stats 2000 ch 214 (AB 559), s 1, eff. 1/1/2001.

Section 368.5 - Jurisdiction; revision of policy manual

(a) Local law enforcement agencies and state law enforcement agencies with jurisdiction have concurrent jurisdiction to investigate elder and dependent adult abuse and all other crimes against elder victims and victims with disabilities.

(b) Adult protective services agencies and local long-term care ombudsman programs also have jurisdiction within their statutory authority to investigate elder and dependent adult abuse and criminal neglect, and may assist local law enforcement agencies in criminal investigations at the law enforcement agencies' request, if consistent with federal law; however, law enforcement agencies retain exclusive responsibility for criminal investigations, notwithstanding any law to the contrary.

(c)

    (1) Every local law enforcement agency shall, when the agency next undertakes the policy revision process, revise or include in the portion of its policy manual relating to elder and dependent adult abuse, if that policy manual exists, the following information:

        (A) The elements of the offense specified in subdivision (c) of Section 368.

        (B) The elements of the offense specified in subdivision (f) of Section 368.

        (C) The requirement, pursuant to subdivisions (a) and (b), that law enforcement agencies have the responsibility for criminal investigations of elder and dependent adult abuse and criminal neglect; however, adult protective services agencies and long-term care ombudsman programs have authority to investigate incidents of elder and dependent adult abuse and neglect and may, if requested and consistent with federal law, assist law enforcement agencies with criminal investigations.

        (D) As a guideline to investigators and first responders, the definition of elder and dependent adult abuse, as defined in subparagraph (A) of paragraph (2).

    (2) As used in this subdivision, the following terms have the following meanings:

        (A)

            (i) "Elder and dependent adult abuse" means any of the following:

                (I) Physical abuse, neglect, abandonment, isolation, abduction, or other treatment with resulting physical harm or pain or mental suffering.

                (II) The deprivation by a care custodian of goods or services that are necessary to avoid physical harm or mental suffering.

                (III) Financial abuse.

            (ii) For the purposes of this subparagraph, the terms "abandonment," "abduction," "financial abuse," "goods and services necessary to avoid physical harm or mental suffering," "isolation," "mental suffering," "neglect," and "physical abuse" have the same meanings as in Article 2 (commencing with Section 15610) of Chapter 11 of Part 3 of Division 9 of the Welfare and Institutions Code.

        (B) "Local law enforcement agency" means every municipal police department and county sheriffs' department.

        (C) "Policy manual" means any general orders, patrol manual, duty manual, or other written document or collection of documents that provides field or investigative personnel with policies, procedures, or guidelines for responding to or investigating crimes, complaints, or incidents.

Amended by Stats 2020 ch 247 (SB 1123),s 1, eff. 1/1/2021.

Amended by Stats 2019 ch 641 (SB 338),s 2, eff. 1/1/2020.

Amended by Stats 2019 ch 497 (AB 991),s 194, eff. 1/1/2020.

Amended by Stats 2018 ch 513 (SB 1191),s 1, eff. 1/1/2019.

Added by Stats 2010 ch 617 (SB 110),s 3, eff. 1/1/2011.

See Stats 2023 ch 18 (AB 751), s 1.

Section 368.6 - Senior and Disability Justice Act

(a) This section shall be known, and may be cited, as the Senior and Disability Justice Act.

(b) As used in this section, the following definitions apply:

    (1) "Agency protocol" means a procedure adopted by a local law enforcement agency consistent with the agency's organizational structure, and stated in a policy adopted pursuant to this section, to effectively and accountably carry out a particular agency responsibility.

    (2) "Caretaker" has the same meaning as defined in Section 368 and includes caretakers whether or not they are paid.

    (3) "Dependent adult" has the same meaning as defined in Section 368.

    (4) "Dependent person" has the same meaning as defined in Section 288.

    (5) "Disability" includes mental disability and physical disability as defined in Sections 12926 and 12926.1 of the Government Code, regardless of whether those disabilities are temporary, permanent, congenital, or acquired by heredity, accident, injury, illness, or advanced age.

    (6) "Domestic violence" has the same meaning as defined in Section 13700 and includes a violation of Section 273.5.

    (7) "Elder" has the same meaning as defined in Section 368.

    (8) "Elder and dependent adult abuse" means a violation of Section 368 and includes physical abuse, neglect, financial abuse, abandonment, isolation, abduction, or other treatment with resulting physical harm, pain, or mental suffering, or the deprivation by a care custodian of goods or services that are necessary to avoid physical harm or mental suffering.

    (9) "Hate crime" has the same meaning as set forth in Sections 422.55 and 422.56.

    (10) "Human trafficking" means a violation of Section 236.1.

    (11) "Local law enforcement agency" means every municipal police department and county sheriffs' department.

    (12) "Mandated reporting requirements" means any of the following:

        (A) The requirements of Article 2.5 (commencing with Section 11164) of Chapter 2 of Title 1 of Part 4.

        (B) The requirements of Sections 15630 and 15630.1 and subdivision (d) of Section 15640 of the Welfare and Institutions Code concerning reporting of elder and dependent adult abuse.

        (C) The prohibitions on inhibiting or impeding reporting pursuant to the requirements in subparagraph (A) or (B).

    (13) "Senior and disability victimization" means any of the following:

        (A) Elder and dependent adult abuse.

        (B) Unlawful interference with a mandated report.

        (C) Homicide of an elder, dependent adult, or other adult or child with a disability.

(D) Sex crimes against an elder, dependent adult, or other adult or child with a disability.

(E) Child abuse of children with disabilities.

(F) Violation of relevant protective orders.

(G) Hate crimes against persons with actual or perceived disabilities, including, but not limited to, disabilities caused by advanced age, or those associated with them.

(H) Domestic violence against an elder, dependent adult, or other adult or child with a disability, including any disability caused by advanced age.

(14) "Relevant protective order" means an order by a California or out-of-state court, including, but not limited to, a tribal, federal, United States territorial, or United States military court, protecting an elder, dependent adult, dependent person, or other adult or child with a disability.

(15) "Responsible agency" means a local, state, or federal agency with responsibilities concerning senior and disability victimization. This includes, but is not limited to, law enforcement agencies, adult protective services agencies, child protective services agencies, the Office of the State Long-Term Care Ombudsman and its designated local agencies, fire and emergency medical services, regional centers pursuant to the Lanterman Developmental Disabilities Services Act, elder and disability service agencies, sexual assault and domestic violence agencies, elder and dependent adult death review teams, local government human relations commissions, coroners, probate court investigators, public administrators, public guardians, public conservators, district attorney's offices, city attorney's offices or other prosecutors with jurisdiction, the Division of Medi-Cal Fraud and Elder Abuse, state licensing agencies, the United States Attorney's offices, and the Federal Bureau of Investigation.

(16) "Sex crime" means either of the following:

(A) An offense requiring registration pursuant to the Sex Offender Registration Act.

(B) A violation of Section 729 of the Business and Professions Code.

(17) "State protection and advocacy agency" means the agency designated pursuant to Division 4.7 (commencing with Section 4900) of the Welfare and Institutions Code.

(18) "Unlawful interference in a mandated report" includes, but is not limited to, inhibiting or impeding reporting in violation of the mandated reporting requirements or a violation of Section 136.1 that concerns the mandated reporting requirements.

(c) Each local law enforcement agency may adopt a policy regarding senior and disability victimization. A municipal police department or county sheriffs' department that adopts or revises a policy regarding elder and dependent adult abuse or senior and disability victimization on or after April 13, 2021, shall include, but not be limited to, all of the following items:

(1) Information on the wide prevalence of elder and dependent adult abuse, sexual assault, other sex crimes, hate crimes, domestic violence, human trafficking, and homicide against adults and children with disabilities, including disabilities caused by advanced age, and including those crimes often committed by caretakers.

(2) A statement of the agency's commitment to providing equal protection and demonstrating respect for all persons regardless of age or disabilities, and to conscientiously enforcing all criminal laws protecting elders, and adults and children with disabilities, regardless of whether these crimes also carry civil penalties.

(3) The definitions and elements of the offenses specified in paragraph (2) of subdivision (b) of Section 288 and in subdivisions (c) and (f) of Section 368, noting that they protect many persons with disabilities regardless of the fact they live independently.

(4)

(A) The fact that elder and dependent adult abuse, sex crimes, child abuse, domestic violence, and any other criminal act, when committed in whole or in part because of the victim's actual or perceived disability, including disability caused by advanced age, is also a hate crime.

(B) In recognizing suspected disability-bias hate crimes, the policy shall instruct officers to consider whether there is any indication that the perpetrator committed the criminal act because of bias, including, but not limited to, the bias motivations described in subparagraphs (B) and (C) of paragraph (3) of subdivision (a) of Section 422.87.

(5) An agency protocol and schedule for training officers with both of the following:

(A) The training materials made available by the Commission on Peace Officer Standards and Training pursuant to Sections 13515, 13515.25, 13515.27, 13515.28, 13515.29, 13515.295, 13515.30, 13515.35, and 13519.2. In the case of the training materials identified in each of these sections, the agency protocol shall require the training for, at a minimum, the category of officers for whom that section states that the training is intended or required or, if the section does not state for whom the training material is required or intended, those officers identified pursuant to paragraph (16).

(B) The agency's policy pursuant to this section.

(6) A requirement that when an officer intends to interview a victim or witness to an alleged crime and the victim or witness reports or demonstrates deafness or hearing loss, the officer first secure the services of an interpreter as defined in Section 754 of the Evidence Code. The agency shall have a protocol for securing the services of the interpreter to ensure accurate interpretation.

(7) An agency protocol for providing appropriate training concerning the agency's policy to dispatchers, community services officers, front desk personnel, and other civilian personnel who interact with the public.

(8)

(A) The fact that the agency requires officers to investigate every report of senior and disability victimization, and does not dismiss any reports as merely civil matters or for any other reason without an investigation.

(B) An appendix to the policy describing the requirements for these investigations, including, but not limited to, all of the following:

(i) An agency protocol or protocols for cooperating and collaborating whenever possible with the Division of Medi-Cal Fraud and Elder Abuse, other state law enforcement agencies with jurisdiction, adult and child protective services, local long-term care ombudsman programs, and, when appropriate, other responsible agencies.

(ii) Appropriate techniques for interviewing potential victims and witnesses with cognitive or communication disabilities, including, but not limited to, avoiding repeated interviews when possible.

(iii) The elements of the investigation, including, but not limited to, all of the following:

(I) Checking prior reports received by adult or child protective services agencies, local long-term care ombudsman programs, except as provided in Section 9725 of the Welfare and Institutions Code, and any other responsible agencies.

(II) Interviewing each alleged victim, each witness, and each suspect who is available.

(III) Viewing all body-worn camera videos and all other films.

(IV) Listening to all calls from mandated reports or other callers.

(V) Making reasonable efforts to determine whether any person committed unlawful interference in a mandated report.

(iv) An agency protocol for transmitting the crime report to the appropriate prosecution office if the law enforcement agency recommends prosecution.

(v) If the agency deems it appropriate, the Investigation Response section and Addendum B of the San Diego County Elder and Dependent Adult Abuse Blueprint or the Elder Abuse Guide for Law Enforcement of the National Center on Elder Abuse at the University of Southern California.

(9)

(A) A statement that it is the agency's policy to make arrests or to seek arrest warrants, in accordance with Section 836, and, in the case of domestic violence, as allowed by Section 13701. The policy shall also state the agency protocol for seeking those arrest warrants.

(B) The agency protocol for arrests for senior and disability victimization other than domestic violence, which shall include, but not be limited to, the following requirements:

(i) In the case of a senior and disability victimization committed in an officer's presence, including, but not limited to, a violation of a relevant protective order, the officer shall make a warrantless arrest based on probable cause when necessary or advisable to protect the safety of the victim or others.

(ii) In the case of a felony not committed in an officer's presence, the officer shall make a warrantless arrest based on probable cause when necessary or advisable to protect the safety of the victim or others.

(iii) In the case of a misdemeanor not committed in the officer's presence, including, but not limited to, misdemeanor unlawful interference with a mandated report or a misdemeanor violation of a relevant protective order, or when necessary or advisable to protect the safety of the victim or others, the agency shall seek an arrest warrant based on probable cause.

(iv) The policy shall state the agency protocol for seeking arrest warrants based on probable cause for crimes for which no arrest has been made.

(10) The fact that senior and disability victimization crimes are also domestic violence subject to the mandatory arrest requirements of Section 836 if they meet the elements described in Section 273.5, including, but not limited to, a violation by a caretaker or other person who is or was a cohabitant of the victim, regardless of whether the cohabitant is or was a relative of, or in an intimate personal relationship with, the victim.

(11)

(A) The fact that many victims of sexual assault and other sex crimes delay disclosing the crimes for reasons including, but not limited to, shame, embarrassment, self-doubt, fear of being disbelieved, and fear of retaliation by the perpetrator or others.

(B) An instruction pursuant to Sections 264.2 and 679.04 to notify potential victims of sex crimes that they have a right to have a support person of their choice present at all times.

(12) The agency's cross-reporting requirements, including, but not limited to, those pursuant to Section 15640 of the Welfare and Institutions Code, and an agency protocol for carrying out these cross-reporting requirements.

(13) Mandated reporting requirements, including, but not limited to, officers' mandated reporting responsibilities and an agency protocol for carrying out the officers' mandated reporting responsibilities.

(14) The fact that victims and witnesses with disabilities, including cognitive and communication disabilities, can be highly credible witnesses when interviewed appropriately by trained officers or other trained persons.

(15) A procedure for first-responding officers to follow when interviewing persons with cognitive and communication disabilities until officers, or staff of other responsible agencies, with more advanced training, are available. The procedure shall include an instruction to avoid repeated interviews whenever possible.

(16) The unit or office, or multiple units or offices of the agency, or the title or titles of an officer or officers, tasked with the following responsibilities:

(A) Receiving advanced officer training on senior and disability victimization, available from the Commission on Peace Officer Standards and Training, the United States Department of Justice, the Disability and Abuse Project of the Spectrum Institute, or other sources.

(B) Acting as a liaison to other responsible agencies to increase cooperation and collaboration among them while retaining the law enforcement agency's exclusive responsibility for criminal investigations.

(C) Reaching out to the senior and disability communities and to the public to encourage prevention and reporting of senior and disability victimization.

(17) An agency protocol for seeking emergency protective orders by phone from a court at any time of the day or night pursuant to subdivision (d) of Section 6250 of the Family Code, including the court system telephone number for an officer to call, and a requirement that an officer utilize the agency protocol whenever necessary or advisable to protect a victim's safety.

(18) A requirement that all officers treat an unexplained or suspicious death of an elder, dependent adult, or other adult or child with a disability as a potential homicide until a complete investigation, including an autopsy, is completed, and not to assume that the death of an elder or person with a disability is natural simply because of the age or disability of the deceased.

(19) A requirement that, whenever an officer verifies that a relevant protective order has been issued, the officer shall make reasonable efforts to determine if the order prohibits the possession of firearms or requires the relinquishment of firearms, and if the order does so, a requirement that the officer shall make reasonable efforts to do each of the following:

(A) Inquire whether the restrained person possesses firearms. The officer may make this effort by asking the restrained person and the protected person.

(B) Query through the California Law Enforcement Telecommunications System to determine if any firearms are registered to the restrained person.

(C) Receive or seize prohibited firearms located in plain view or pursuant to a consensual or other lawful search, in compliance with Division 4 (commencing with Section 18250) of Title 2 of Part 6.

(20) Civil remedies and resources available to victims, including, but not limited to, the program administered by the California Victim Compensation Board.

(21) The complete contents of any model policy on senior and disability victimization that the Commission on Peace Officer Standards and Training may develop based on this section, regardless of whether that model policy includes items in addition to those listed in this section.

(22) Use of the full term "elder and dependent adult abuse" in every reference to that crime, with no shorthand terms, including, but not limited to, "elder abuse" or "adult abuse."

(23) A detailed checklist of first-responding officers' responsibilities, including, but not limited to, all of the following:

(A) Taking responsibility for the safety and well-being of the potential victims and witnesses and treating all potential victims, witnesses, and suspects with dignity and respect.

(B) Complying with the provisions of the agency's policy requirements for arrests and mandatory seeking of arrest warrants pursuant to paragraph (9) and the requirements for seeking emergency protective orders pursuant to paragraph (17).

(C) Following the policy's guidelines for interviewing persons with cognitive or communication disabilities pursuant to paragraph (15).

(D) Recognizing that some elders and adults and children with cognitive or communication disabilities may have difficulty narrating events, appear to be poor historians, or lack short-term memory, which adds to their vulnerability and therefore requires officers to make special efforts to provide them with equal protection.

(E) Documenting the scene.

(F) Obtaining a signed medical release from potential victims.

(G) Interviewing caretakers separately, recognizing that in some cases, the caretaker is the perpetrator.

(H) Recognizing that victim cooperation is sometimes unnecessary for prosecution, and that in some cases allowing victims the option of preventing prosecution creates an opportunity for the perpetrators to obstruct justice by pressuring or threatening the victims. Each dispatch call or case should be investigated on its own evidential merits.

(I) Taking other actions necessary to comply with the provisions of the law enforcement agency's policy pursuant to this section.

(24) The relevant content of any memoranda of understanding or similar agreements or procedures for cooperating with other responsible agencies, consistent with Section 368.5.

(25) A statement of the agency chief executive's responsibilities, including, but not limited to, all of the following:

(A) Taking leadership within the agency and in the community, including by speaking out publicly in major cases of senior and disability victimization, to assure the community of the agency's support for the victims and their families and for others in the community who are terrorized and traumatized by the crimes, and to encourage victims and witnesses to the crimes or similar past or future crimes to report those crimes to help bring the perpetrators to justice and prevent further crimes.

(B) Carrying out specific responsibilities pursuant to this subdivision, including, but not limited to, developing and including agency protocols in this policy.

(C) Ensuring that all officers and staff carry out their responsibilities under the policy.

(26) An agency protocol for transmitting and periodically retransmitting the policy and any related orders to all officers, including a simple and immediate way for officers to access the policy in the field when needed.

(27)

(A) A requirement that all officers be familiar with the policy and carry out the policy at all times except in the case of unusual compelling circumstances as determined by the agency's chief executive or by another supervisory or command-level officer designated by the chief executive.

(B) A responsible officer who makes a determination allowing a deviation from the policy shall produce a report to the agency's chief executive stating the unusual compelling circumstances. The policy shall include an agency protocol for providing copies of those reports to the alleged victims and reporting parties. The chief executive shall retain the report for a minimum of five years and shall make it available to the state protection and advocacy agency upon request.

(28) For each agency protocol, either a specific title-by-title list of officers' responsibilities, or a specific office or unit in the law enforcement agency responsible for implementing the protocol.

(d) If a law enforcement agency adopts or revises a policy regarding senior and disability victimization on or after April 13, 2021, the chief executive shall make it available to the state protection and advocacy agency upon request.

(e) A law enforcement agency that adopts, revises, or has adopted or revised a policy regarding elder and dependent adult abuse in compliance with the requirements of Section 368.5 on or after April 13, 2021, shall also comply with the requirements of subdivision (c) and (d) of this section.

Amended by Stats 2023 ch 18 (AB 751),s 2, eff. 1/1/2024.

Amended by Stats 2021 ch 554 (SB 823),s 8, eff. 1/1/2022.

Added by Stats 2019 ch 641 (SB 338),s 3, eff. 1/1/2020.

Section 368.7 - Development and distribution of informational notice regarding about elder and dependent adult fraud

The Department of Justice shall develop and distribute an informational notice that warns the public about elder and dependent adult fraud and directs them to information and resources necessary to determine whether they are victims of fraud. The notice shall provide information regarding how and where to file complaints. The notice shall also be made available on the Internet Web site of the Attorney General.

Title 10 - OF CRIMES AGAINST THE PUBLIC HEALTH AND SAFETY
Section 369a - Rail transit safety
(a) The Legislature hereby finds and declares the following:

(1) Rail transit traffic safety programs are necessary to educate the public about the potential for harm and injury arising from an individual's disregard for, and violation of, rail-related traffic safety laws, and to increase the consequences for those persons violating rail-related traffic safety laws.

(2) Currently, there does not exist a unified statewide system to deal with the ever increasing problem of rail-related traffic safety violators, and to provide a method of educating the public.

(b) In each county with a population greater than 500,000 in which a transportation commission or authority has been established and it owns or operates rail transit facilities, the commission or authority may provide and disseminate appropriate educational materials to traffic schools to aid in reducing the number of rail-related traffic accidents, including, but not limited to, a film developed or caused to be developed by the transportation commission or authority on rail transit safety.

Added by Stats. 1993, Ch. 722, Sec. 2. Effective January 1, 1994.

Section 369b - Punishment of person convicted of rail transit related traffic violation
(a) This section shall only apply to counties with a population greater than 500,000.

(b) The court may order any person convicted of a rail transit related traffic violation, as listed in subdivision (c), to attend a traffic school that offers, as a part of its curriculum, a film developed or caused to be developed by a transportation commission or authority on rail transit safety.

(c) For a first offense, a court, at its discretion, may order any person cited for any of the following violations to attend a traffic school offering a rail safety presentation, Internet rail safety test, or rail transit safety film prepared by a county transportation commission or authority, pay an additional fine of one hundred dollars ($100), or both:

(1) Section 369g.

(2) Section 369i.

(3) Subdivision (c) of Section 21752, Section 22450, 22451, or 22452, or subdivision (c) of Section 22526, of the Vehicle Code, involving railroad grade crossings.

(d) For a second or subsequent violation as provided in subdivision (c), a court shall order a person to pay an additional fine of up to two hundred dollars ($200) and to attend a traffic school offering a rail safety presentation, Internet rail safety test, or rail safety film prepared by a county transportation commission or authority.

(e) All fines collected according to this section shall be distributed pursuant to Sections 1463 and 1463.12, as applicable.

Amended by Stats 2005 ch 716 (AB 1067),s 3, eff. 1/1/2006

EFFECTIVE 1/1/2000. Amended October 10, 1999 (Bill Number: AB 923) (Chapter 841).

Section 369d - Failure to close bars or gates
Any person who enters upon or crosses any railroad, at any private passway, which is inclosed by bars or gates, and neglects to leave the same securely closed after him, is guilty of a misdemeanor.

Added by Stats. 1905, Ch. 573.

Section 369g - Unlawful riding, driving, or propelling vehicle upon and along track
(a) Any person who rides, drives, or propels any vehicle upon and along the track of any railroad through or over its private right-of-way, without the authorization of its superintendent or other officer in charge thereof, is guilty of a misdemeanor.

(b) Any person who rides, drives, or propels any vehicle upon and along the track of any railline owned or operated by a county transportation commission or transportation authority without the authorization of the commission or authority is guilty of a misdemeanor.

Amended by Stats. 1993, Ch. 722, Sec. 4. Effective January 1, 1994.

Section 369h - Unlawful use of sign or light
Any person, partnership, firm or corporation installing, setting up, maintaining or operating upon public or private property, any sign or light in line of vision along any main line track of any railroad in this State of such type or in such form or manner that it may be mistaken for any fixed or standard railroad signal when viewed from an approaching locomotive cab, railway car, or train, by the operators or employees upon such locomotive cab, railway car or train, so as to hinder the safe and efficient operation of such locomotive, railway car or train, and endanger the safety of persons or property upon such locomotive, railway car, or train, shall be guilty of maintaining a public nuisance. No sign, signal, flare or light placed within the right of way of any street or highway by public authorities in charge thereof, considered necessary by them to direct or warn highway traffic, shall be deemed to violate this section.

Added by Stats. 1941, Ch. 153.

Section 369i - Unlawful entry on property of any railroad
(a)

(1) Any person who enters or remains upon the property of any railroad without the permission of the owner of the land, the owner's agent, or the person in lawful possession and whose entry, presence, or conduct upon the property interferes with, interrupts, or hinders, or which, if allowed to continue, would interfere with, interrupt, or hinder the safe and efficient operation of any locomotive, railway car, or train is guilty of a misdemeanor.

(2) As used in this subdivision, "property of any railroad" means any land owned, leased, or possessed by a railroad upon which is placed a railroad track and the land immediately adjacent thereto, to the distance of 20 feet on either side of the track, that is owned, leased, or possessed by a railroad.

(b)

(1) Any person who enters or remains upon any transit-related property without permission or whose entry, presence, or conduct upon the property interferes with, interrupts, or hinders the safe and efficient operation of the transit-related facility is guilty of a misdemeanor.

(2) As used in this subdivision, "transit-related property" means any land, facilities, or vehicles owned, leased, or possessed by a county transportation commission, transportation authority, or transit district, as defined in Section 99170 of the Public Utilities Code, that are used to provide public transportation by rail or passenger bus or are directly related to that use, or any property, facilities, or vehicles upon which the San Francisco Bay Area Rapid Transit District owes policing responsibilities to a local government pursuant to an operations and maintenance agreement or similar interagency agreement.

(c) This section does not prohibit picketing in the immediately adjacent area of the property of any railroad or transit-related property or any lawful activity by which the public is informed of the existence of an alleged labor dispute.

Amended by Stats 2021 ch 534 (AB 1337),s 1, eff. 1/1/2022.

Amended by Stats 2011 ch 534 (AB 716),s 1, eff. 1/1/2012.

Section 370 - Unlawful obstruction

Section Three Hundred and Seventy. Anything which is injurious to health, or is indecent, or offensive to the senses, or an obstruction to the free use of property, so as to interfere with the comfortable enjoyment of life or property by an entire community or neighborhood, or by any considerable number of persons, or unlawfully obstructs the free passage or use, in the customary manner, of any navigable lake, or river, bay, stream, canal, or basin, or any public park, square, street, or highway, is a public nuisance.

Amended by Code Amendments 1873-74, Ch. 614.

Section 371 - Act affecting entire community or neighborhood

An act which affects an entire community or neighborhood, or any considerable number of persons, as specified in the last section, is not less a nuisance because the extent of the annoyance or damage inflicted upon individuals is unequal.

Amended by Stats. 1989, Ch. 1360, Sec. 109.

Section 372 - Maintaining or committing public nuisance

Every person who maintains or commits any public nuisance, the punishment for which is not otherwise prescribed, or who willfully omits to perform any legal duty relating to the removal of a public nuisance, is guilty of a misdemeanor.

Enacted 1872.

Section 372.5 - Public nuisance sentencing

(a)Notwithstanding Section 372, if a defendant is sentenced for a violation of Section 370 based on a disposition negotiated between the defendant and the prosecution, or pursuant to an indicated sentence of the court, a term of which includes the dismissal of one or more infraction charges that allege unlawfully cultivating, manufacturing, transporting, giving away, or selling a drug, or offering to transport, give away, or sell a drug, unlawful use of a drug, or unlawful possession or use of a drug or drug paraphernalia, public nuisance is an infraction punishable by a fine not to exceed two hundred fifty dollars ($250).

(b)Notwithstanding Section 372, if a defendant is sentenced for a violation of Section 370 based on a disposition negotiated between the defendant and the prosecution, a term of which includes the dismissal of one or more misdemeanor charges that allege unlawfully cultivating, manufacturing, transporting, giving away, or selling a drug, or offering to transport, give away, or sell a drug, unlawful use of a drug, or unlawful possession or use of a drug or drug paraphernalia, public nuisance is punishable by a fine of not exceeding one thousand dollars ($1,000), or imprisonment in a county jail for not more than one year, or by both that fine and imprisonment, or as an infraction punishable by a fine not to exceed two hundred fifty dollars ($250).

(c)Notwithstanding Section 372, if a defendant is sentenced for a violation of Section 370 based on a disposition negotiated between the defendant and the prosecution, a term of which includes the dismissal of one or more felony charges that allege cultivating, manufacturing, transporting, giving away, or selling a drug, or offering to transport, give away, or to sell a drug, or unlawful possession of a drug, public nuisance is punishable pursuant to subdivision (h) of Section 1170 for a period of 16 months, or two or three years, or by imprisonment in a county jail for not more than one year.

(d)For purposes of this section, "drug" is defined as under Section 11014 of the Health and Safety Code.

Added by Stats 2022 ch 487 (AB 2195),s 1, eff. 1/1/2023.

Section 373a - Maintaining, permitting, or allowing public nuisance on property

Each person who maintains, permits, or allows a public nuisance to exist upon his or her property or premises, and each person occupying or leasing the property or premises of another who maintains, permits, or allows a public nuisance to exist on the property, after reasonable notice in writing from a health officer, district attorney, city attorney, or city prosecutor to remove, discontinue, or abate the public nuisance has been served upon the person, is guilty of a misdemeanor. The existence of the public nuisance for each and every day after the service of the notice is a separate and distinct offense, and it is the duty of the district attorney, or the city attorney or city prosecutor of any city the charter of which imposes the duty upon the city attorney or city prosecutor to prosecute state misdemeanors, to continuously prosecute all persons guilty of violating this section until the nuisance is abated and removed.

Amended by Stats 2017 ch 299 (AB 1418),s 1, eff. 1/1/2018.

Section 374 - Littering

(a) Littering means the willful or negligent throwing, dropping, placing, depositing, or sweeping, or causing any such acts, of any waste matter on land or water in other than appropriate storage containers or areas designated for such purposes.

(b) Waste matter means discarded, used, or leftover substance including, but not limited to, a lighted or nonlighted cigarette, cigar, match, or any flaming or glowing material, or any garbage, trash, refuse, paper, container, packaging or construction material, carcass of a dead animal, any nauseous or offensive matter of any kind, or any object likely to injure any person or create a traffic hazard.

Added by Stats. 1970, Ch. 1548.

Section 374.2 - Malicious discharge, dump, release, or deposit of substance into manhole, cleanout, or other sanitary sewer facility

(a) It is unlawful for any person to maliciously discharge, dump, release, place, drop, pour, or otherwise deposit, or to maliciously cause to be discharged, dumped, released, placed, dropped, poured, or otherwise deposited, any substance capable of causing substantial damage or harm to the operation of a public sewer sanitary facility, or to deposit in commercial quantities any other substance, into a manhole, cleanout, or other sanitary sewer facility, not intended for use as a point of deposit for sewage, which is connected to a public sanitary sewer system, without possessing a written authorization therefor granted by the public entity which is charged with the administration of the use of the affected public sanitary sewer system or the affected portion of the public sanitary sewer system. As used in this section, "maliciously" means an intent to do a wrongful act.

(b) For the purposes of this section "person" means an individual, trust, firm, partnership, joint stock company, limited liability company, or corporation, and "deposited in commercial quantities" refers to any substance deposited or otherwise discharged in any amount greater than for normal domestic sewer use.

(c) Lack of specific knowledge that the facility into which the prohibited discharge or release occurred is connected to a public sanitary sewer system shall not constitute a defense to a violation charged under this section.

(d) Any person who violates this section shall be punished by imprisonment in the county jail for not more than one year, or by a fine of up to twenty-five thousand dollars ($25,000), or by both a fine and imprisonment. If the conviction is for a second or subsequent violation, the person shall be punished by imprisonment in the county jail for not more than one year, or imprisonment pursuant to subdivision (h) of Section 1170 for 16, 20, or 24 months, and by a fine of not less than five thousand dollars ($5,000) or more than twenty-five thousand dollars ($25,000).

Amended by Stats 2011 ch 39 (AB 117),s 68, eff. 6/30/2011.

Amended by Stats 2011 ch 15 (AB 109),s 337, eff. 4/4/2011, but operative no earlier than October 1, 2011, and only upon creation of a community corrections grant program to assist in implementing this act and upon an appropriation to fund the grant program.

Section 374.3 - Unlawful dumping

(a) It is unlawful to dump or cause to be dumped waste matter in or upon a public or private highway or road, including any portion of the right-of-way thereof, or in or upon private property into or upon which the public is admitted by easement or license, or upon private property without the consent of the owner, or in or upon a public park or other public property other than property designated or set aside for that purpose by the governing board or body having charge of that property.

(b) It is unlawful to place, deposit, or dump, or cause to be placed, deposited, or dumped, rocks, concrete, asphalt, or dirt in or upon a private highway or road, including any portion of the right-of-way of the private highway or road, or private property, without the consent of the owner or a contractor under contract with the owner for the materials, or in or upon a public park or other public property, without the consent of the state or local agency having jurisdiction over the highway, road, or property.

(c) A person violating this section is guilty of an infraction. Each day that waste placed, deposited, or dumped in violation of subdivision (a) or (b) remains is a separate violation.

(d) This section does not restrict a private owner in the use of their own private property, unless the placing, depositing, or dumping of the waste matter on the property creates a public health and safety hazard, a public nuisance, or a fire hazard, as determined by a local health department, local fire department or district providing fire protection services, or the Department of Forestry and Fire Protection, in which case this section applies.

(e) A person convicted of a violation of this section shall be punished by a mandatory fine of not less than two hundred fifty dollars ($250) nor more than one thousand dollars ($1,000) upon a first conviction, by a mandatory fine of not less than five hundred dollars ($500) nor more than one thousand five hundred dollars ($1,500) upon a second conviction, and by a mandatory fine of not less than seven hundred fifty dollars ($750) nor more than three thousand dollars ($3,000) upon a third or subsequent conviction. If the court finds that the waste matter placed, deposited, or dumped was used tires, the fine prescribed in this subdivision shall be doubled.

(f) The court may require, in addition to any fine imposed upon a conviction, that a person convicted under this section remove, or pay the cost of removing, any waste matter which the convicted person dumped or caused to be dumped upon public or private property.

(g) The court may, in addition to the fine imposed upon a conviction, require that a person convicted of a violation of this section pick up waste matter at a time and place within the jurisdiction of the court for not less than 12 hours.

(h)

(1) Except as otherwise provided in paragraph (2), a person who places, deposits, or dumps, or causes to be placed, deposited, or dumped, waste matter in violation of this section in commercial quantities shall be guilty of a misdemeanor punishable by imprisonment in a county jail for not more than six months and by a fine. The fine is mandatory and shall amount to not less than one thousand dollars ($1,000) nor more than three thousand dollars ($3,000) upon a first conviction, not less than three thousand dollars ($3,000) nor more than six thousand dollars ($6,000) upon a second conviction, and not less than six thousand dollars ($6,000) nor more than ten thousand dollars ($10,000) upon a third or subsequent conviction.

(2) If a person convicted under paragraph (1) is the owner or operator of the business involved in the illegal dumping, and that business employs more than 10 full-time employees, the fine shall amount to not less than one thousand dollars ($1,000) nor more than five thousand dollars ($5,000) upon a first conviction, not less than three thousand dollars ($3,000) nor more than ten thousand dollars ($10,000) upon a second conviction, and not less than six thousand dollars ($6,000) nor more than twenty thousand dollars ($20,000) upon a third or subsequent conviction.

(3) The court shall require, in addition to the fine imposed upon a conviction, that a person convicted under this subdivision remove, or pay the cost of removing, any waste matter which the convicted person dumped or caused to be dumped upon public or private property.

(4)

(A) If a person convicted under this subdivision holds a license or permit to conduct business that is substantially related to the illegal dumping for which the person was convicted, the court shall notify the applicable licensing or permitting entity subject to the jurisdiction of the Department of Consumer Affairs as set forth in Section 101 of the Business and Professions Code, if any, of the conviction.

(B) The licensing or permitting entity shall record and post the offense on the public profile of the license or permitholder on the internet website of the entity.

(5) "Commercial quantities" means an amount of waste matter generated in the course of a trade, business, profession, or occupation, or an amount equal to or in excess of one cubic yard. This subdivision does not apply to the dumping of household waste at a person's own residence.

(i) For purposes of this section, "person" means an individual, trust, firm, partnership, joint stock company, joint venture, or corporation.

(j) When setting fines pursuant to this section, the court shall consider the defendant's ability to pay, including consideration of, without limitation, all of the following:

(1) The defendant's present financial position.

(2) The defendant's reasonably discernible future financial position, provided that the court shall not consider a period of more than one year from the date of the hearing for purposes of determining the reasonably discernible future financial position of the defendant.

(3) The likelihood that the defendant will be able to obtain employment within one year from the date of the hearing.

(4) Any other factor that may bear upon the defendant's financial capability to pay the fine.

Amended by Stats 2022 ch 784 (AB 2374),s 1, eff. 1/1/2023.

Amended by Stats 2006 ch 416 (AB 1992),s 7, eff. 1/1/2007.

Amended by Stats 2004 ch 137 (AB 1802), s 1, eff. 1/1/2005.

Section 374.4 - Unlawful littering upon public or private property

(a) It is unlawful to litter or cause to be littered in or upon public or private property. A person, firm, or corporation violating this section is guilty of an infraction.

(b) This section does not restrict a private owner in the use of his or her own property, unless the littering of waste matter on the property creates a public health and safety hazard, a public nuisance, or a fire hazard, as determined by a local health department, local fire department or district providing fire protection services, or the Department of Forestry and Fire Protection, in which case this section applies.

(c) As used in this section, "litter" means the discarding, dropping, or scattering of small quantities of waste matter ordinarily carried on or about the person, including, but not limited to, beverage containers and closures, packaging, wrappers, wastepaper, newspapers, and magazines, in a place other than a place or container for the proper disposal thereof, and including waste matter that escapes or is allowed to escape from a container, receptacle, or package.

(d) A person, firm, or corporation convicted of a violation of this section shall be punished by a mandatory fine of not less than two hundred fifty dollars ($250) nor more than one thousand dollars ($1,000) upon a first conviction, by a mandatory fine of not less than five hundred dollars ($500) nor more than one thousand five hundred dollars ($1,500) upon a second conviction, and by a mandatory fine of not less than seven hundred fifty dollars ($750) nor more than three thousand dollars ($3,000) upon a third or subsequent conviction.

(e) The court may, in addition to the fine imposed upon a conviction, require as a condition of probation, in addition to any other condition of probation, that any person convicted of a violation of this section pick up litter at a time and place within the jurisdiction of the court for not less than eight hours.

Amended by Stats 2006 ch 416 (AB 1992),s 8, eff. 1/1/2007.

Section 374.5 - Unlawful acts by grease waste hauler

(a) It is unlawful for any grease waste hauler to do either of the following:

(1) Reinsert, deposit, dump, place, release, or discharge into a grease trap, grease interceptor, manhole, cleanout, or other sanitary sewer appurtenance any materials that the hauler has removed from the grease trap or grease interceptor, or to cause those materials to be so handled.

(2) Cause or permit to be discharged in or on any waters of the state, or discharged in or deposited where it is, or probably will be, discharged in or on any waters of the state, any materials that the hauler has removed from the grease trap or grease interceptor, or to cause those materials to be so handled.

(b) The prohibition in subdivision (a), as it pertains to reinsertion of material removed from a grease trap or grease interceptor, shall not apply to a grease waste hauler if all of the following conditions are met:

(1) The local sewer authority having jurisdiction over the pumping and disposal of the material specifically allows a registered grease waste hauler to obtain written approval for the reinsertion of decanted liquid.

(2) The local sewer authority has determined that, if reinsertion is allowed, it is feasible to enforce local discharge limits for fats, oil, and grease, if any, and other local requirements for best management or operating practices, if any.

(3) The grease waste hauler is registered pursuant to Section 19310 of the Food and Agricultural Code.

(4) The registered grease waste hauler demonstrates to the satisfaction of the local sewer authority all of the following:

(A) It will use equipment that will adequately separate the water from the grease waste and solids in the material so as to comply with applicable regulations.

(B) Its employees are adequately trained in the use of that equipment.

(5) The registered grease waste hauler demonstrates both of the following:

(A) It has informed the managerial personnel of the owner or operator of the grease trap or interceptor, in writing, that the grease waste hauler may reinsert the decanted materials, unless the owner or operator objects to the reinsertion.

(B) The owner or operator has not objected to the reinsertion of the decanted materials. If the owner or operator of the grease trap or interceptor objects to the reinsertion, no decanted material may be inserted in that grease trap or interceptor.

(c) A grease waste hauler shall not transport grease removed from a grease trap or grease interceptor in the same vehicle used for transporting other waste, including, but not limited to, yellow grease, cooking grease, recyclable cooking oil, septic waste, or fluids collected at car washes.

(d) For purposes of this section, a "grease waste hauler" is a transporter of inedible kitchen grease subject to registration requirements pursuant to Section 19310 of the Food and Agricultural Code.

(e) Any person who violates this section shall be guilty of a misdemeanor punishable by imprisonment in a county jail for not more than six months or a fine of not more than ten thousand dollars ($10,000), or both a fine and imprisonment. A second and subsequent conviction, shall be punishable by imprisonment in a county jail for not more than one year, or a fine of not more than twenty-five thousand dollars ($25,000), or both a fine and imprisonment.

(f) Notwithstanding Section 1463, the fines paid pursuant to this section shall be apportioned as follows:

(1) Fifty percent shall be deposited in the Environmental Enforcement and Training Account established pursuant to Section 14303, and used for purposes of Title 13 (commencing with Section 14300) of Part 4.

(2) Twenty-five percent shall be distributed pursuant to Section 1463.001.

(3) Twenty-five percent to the local health officer or other local public officer or agency that investigated the matter which led to bringing the action.

(g) If the court finds that the violator has engaged in a practice or pattern of violation, consisting of two or more convictions, the court may bar the violating individual or business from engaging in the business of grease waste hauling for a period not to exceed five years.

(h) The court may require, in addition to any fine imposed upon conviction, that as a condition of probation and in addition to any other punishment or condition of probation, that a person convicted under this section remove, or pay the cost of removing, to the extent they are able, any materials which the convicted person dumped or caused to be dumped in violation of this section.

(i) This section does not prohibit the direct receipt of trucked grease by a publicly owned treatment works.

Amended by Stats 2007 ch 130 (AB 299),s 190, eff. 1/1/2008.

Added by Stats 2006 ch 186 (AB 1333),s 1, eff. 1/1/2007.

Section 374.7 - Unlawful littering into body of water

(a) A person who litters or causes to be littered, or dumps or causes to be dumped, waste matter into a bay, lagoon, channel, river, creek, slough, canal, lake, or reservoir, or other stream or body of water, or upon a bank, beach, or shore within 150 feet of the high water mark of a stream or body of water, is guilty of a misdemeanor.

(b) A person convicted of a violation of subdivision (a) shall be punished by a mandatory fine of not less than two hundred fifty dollars ($250) nor more than one thousand dollars ($1,000) upon a first conviction, by a mandatory fine of not less than five hundred dollars ($500) nor more than one thousand five hundred dollars ($1,500) upon a second conviction, and by a mandatory fine of not less than seven hundred fifty dollars ($750) nor more than three thousand dollars ($3,000) upon a third or subsequent conviction.

(c) The court may, in addition to the fine imposed upon a conviction, require as a condition of probation, in addition to any other condition of probation, that any person convicted of a violation of subdivision (a), pick up litter at a time and place within the jurisdiction of the court for not less than eight hours.

Amended by Stats 2006 ch 416 (AB 1992),s 9, eff. 1/1/2007.

Section 374.8 - Unlawful deposit of hazardous substance upon road or land of another

(a) In any prosecution under this section, proof of the elements of the offense shall not be dependent upon the requirements of Title 22 of the California Code of Regulations.

(b) Any person who knowingly causes any hazardous substance to be deposited into or upon any road, street, highway, alley, or railroad right-of-way, or upon the land of another, without the permission of the owner, or into the waters of this state is punishable by imprisonment in the county jail for not more than one year or by imprisonment pursuant to subdivision (h) of Section 1170 for a term of 16 months, two years, or three years, or by a fine of not less than fifty dollars ($50) nor more than ten thousand dollars ($10,000), or by both the fine and imprisonment, unless the deposit occurred as a result of an emergency that the person promptly reported to the appropriate regulatory authority.

(c) For purposes of this section, "hazardous substance" means either of the following:

(1) Any material that, because of its quantity, concentration, or physical or chemical characteristics, poses a significant present or potential hazard to human health and safety or to the environment if released into the environment, including, but not limited to, hazardous waste and any material that the administering agency or a handler, as defined in Chapter 6.91 (commencing with Section 25410) of Division 20 of the Health and Safety Code, has a reasonable basis for believing would be injurious to the health and safety of persons or harmful to the environment if released into the environment.

(2) Any substance or chemical product for which one of the following applies:

(A) The manufacturer or producer is required to prepare a MSDS, as defined in Section 6374 of the Labor Code, for the substance or product pursuant to the Hazardous Substances Information Training Act (Chapter 2.5 (commencing with Section 6360) of Part 1 of Division 5 of the Labor Code) or pursuant to any applicable federal law or regulation.

(B) The substance is described as a radioactive material in Chapter 1 of Title 10 of the Code of Federal Regulations maintained and updated by the Nuclear Regulatory Commission.

(C) The substance is designated by the Secretary of Transportation in Chapter 27 (commencing with Section 1801) of the appendix to Title 49 of the United States Code and taxed as a radioactive substance or material.

(D) The materials listed in subdivision (b) of Section 6382 of the Labor Code.

Amended by Stats 2011 ch 39 (AB 117),s 68, eff. 6/30/2011.

Amended by Stats 2011 ch 15 (AB 109),s 338, eff. 4/4/2011, but operative no earlier than October 1, 2011, and only upon creation of a community corrections grant program to assist in implementing this act and upon an appropriation to fund the grant program.

Section 374a - Reward for information leading to arrest and conviction

A person giving information leading to the arrest and conviction of a person for a violation of Section 374c, 374.2, 374.3, 374.4, or 374.7 is entitled to a reward for providing the information.

The amount of the reward for each arrest and conviction shall be 50 percent of the fine levied against and collected from the person who violated Section 374c, 374.2, 374.3, 374.4, or 374.7 and shall be paid by the court. If the reward is payable to two or more persons, it shall be divided equally. The amount of collected fine to be paid under this section shall be paid prior to any distribution of the fine that may be prescribed by any other section, including Section 1463.9, with respect to the same fine.

Amended by Stats 2006 ch 416 (AB 1992),s 6, eff. 1/1/2007.

Amended by Stats 2002 ch 787 (SB 1798), s 10, eff. 1/1/2003.

Section 374c - Unlawful shooting of firearm from or upon public road or highway

Every person who shoots any firearm from or upon a public road or highway is guilty of a misdemeanor.
Added by Stats. 1933, Ch. 203.

Section 374d - Unlawful acts related to carcass of dead animal

Every person who knowingly allows the carcass of any dead animal which belonged to him at the time of its death to be put, or to remain, within 100 feet of any street, alley, public highway, or road in common use, and every person who puts the carcass of any dead animal within 100 feet of any street, alley, highway, or road in common use is guilty of a misdemeanor.
Added by Stats. 1951, Ch. 657.

Section 375 - Unlawful discharge or exposure of substance about place of business or public assemblage

(a) It shall be unlawful to throw, drop, pour, deposit, release, discharge or expose, or to attempt to throw, drop, pour, deposit, release, discharge or expose in, upon or about any theater, restaurant, place of business, place of amusement or any place of public assemblage, any liquid, gaseous or solid substance or matter of any kind which is injurious to person or property, or is nauseous, sickening, irritating or offensive to any of the senses.

(b) It shall be unlawful to manufacture or prepare, or to possess any liquid, gaseous, or solid substance or matter of any kind which is injurious to person or property, or is nauseous, sickening, irritating or offensive, to any of the senses with intent to throw, drop, pour, deposit, release, discharge or expose the same in, upon or about any theater, restaurant, place of business, place of amusement, or any other place of public assemblage.

(c) Any person violating any of the provisions hereof shall be punished by imprisonment in the county jail for not less than three months and not more than one year, or by a fine of not less than five hundred dollars ($500) and not more than two thousand dollars ($2,000), or by both that fine and imprisonment.

(d) Any person who, in violating any of the provisions of subdivision (a), willfully employs or uses any liquid, gaseous or solid substance which may produce serious illness or permanent injury through being vaporized or otherwise dispersed in the air or who, in violating any of the provisions of subdivision (a), willfully employs or uses any tear gas, mustard gas or any of the combinations or compounds thereof, or willfully employs or uses acid or explosives, shall be guilty of a felony and shall be punished by imprisonment pursuant to subdivision (h) of Section 1170.
Amended by Stats 2011 ch 39 (AB 117),s 68, eff. 6/30/2011.
Amended by Stats 2011 ch 15 (AB 109),s 339, eff. 4/4/2011, but operative no earlier than October 1, 2011, and only upon creation of a community corrections grant program to assist in implementing this act and upon an appropriation to fund the grant program.

Section 377 - False representation that person is physician who can prescribe drug

Every person who, in order to obtain for himself or another any drug that can be lawfully dispensed by a pharmacist only on prescription, falsely represents himself to be a physician or other person who can lawfully prescribe such drug, or falsely represents that he is acting on behalf of a person who can lawfully prescribe such drug, in a telephone communication with a pharmacist, is guilty of a misdemeanor.
Added by Stats. 1963, Ch. 1272.

Section 379 - Unlawful sale or gift of Salvia divinorum or Salvinorin A to person less than 18 years of age

 Every person who sells, dispenses, distributes, furnishes, administers, gives, or offers to sell, dispense, distribute, furnish, administer, or give Salvia divinorum or Salvinorin A, or any substance or material containing Salvia divinorum or Salvinorin A, to any person who is less than 18 years of age, is guilty of a misdemeanor punishable by imprisonment in a county jail not exceeding six months, or by a fine not exceeding one thousand dollars ($1,000), or by both that fine and imprisonment.
Added by Stats 2008 ch 184 (AB 259),s 1, eff. 1/1/2009.

Section 380 - Unlawful sale or distribution of toluene

(a) Every person who sells, dispenses or distributes toluene, or any substance or material containing toluene, to any person who is less than 18 years of age shall be guilty of a misdemeanor, and upon conviction shall be fined in a sum of not less than one thousand dollars ($1,000), nor more than two thousand five hundred dollars ($2,500), or by imprisonment for not less than six months nor more than one year.

(b) The court shall order the suspension of the business license, for a period of one year, of a person who knowingly violates any of the provisions of this section after having been previously convicted of a violation of this section unless the owner of such business license can demonstrate a good faith attempt to prevent illegal sales or deliveries by employees. The provisions of this subdivision shall become operative on July 1, 1980.

(c) The provisions of this section shall apply to, but are not limited to, the sale or distribution of glue, cement, dope, paint thinners, paint, and any combination of hydrocarbons either alone or in combination with any substance or material including, but not limited to, paint, paint thinners, shellac thinners, and solvents which, when inhaled, ingested or breathed, can cause a person to be under the influence of, or intoxicated from, any such combination of hydrocarbons. This section shall not prohibit the sale of gasoline or other motor vehicle fuels to persons less than 18 years of age.

(d) This section shall not apply to any glue or cement which has been certified by the State Department of Health Services as containing a substance which makes such glue or cement malodorous or causes such glue or cement to induce sneezing, nor shall this section apply where the glue or cement is sold, delivered, or given away simultaneously with or as part of a kit used for the construction of model airplanes, model boats, model automobiles, model trains, or other similar models or used for the assembly or creation of hobby craft items using such components as beads, tiles, tiffany glass, ceramics, clay, or other craft-related components.
Amended by Stats. 1980, Ch. 1011, Sec. 1. Effective September 21, 1980.

Section 381 - Unlawful possession of toluene

(a) Any person who possesses toluene or any substance or material containing toluene, including, but not limited to, glue, cement, dope, paint thinner, paint and any combination of hydrocarbons, either alone or in combination with any substance or material including but not limited to paint, paint thinner, shellac thinner, and solvents, with the intent to breathe, inhale, or ingest for the purpose of causing a condition of intoxication, elation, euphoria, dizziness, stupefaction, or dulling of the senses or for the purpose of, in any manner, changing, distorting, or disturbing the audio, visual, or mental processes, or who knowingly and with the intent to do so is under the influence of toluene or any material containing toluene, or any combination of hydrocarbons is guilty of a misdemeanor.

(b) Any person who possesses any substance or material, which the State Department of Public Health has determined by regulations adopted pursuant to the Administrative Procedure Act (Chapter 3.5 (commencing with Section 11340) of Part 1 of Division 3 of Title 2 of the Government Code) has toxic qualities similar to toluene, with the intent to breathe, inhale, or ingest for the purpose of causing a condition of intoxication, elation, euphoria, dizziness, excitement, irrational behavior, exhilaration, satisfaction, stupefaction, or dulling of the senses or for the purpose of, in any manner, changing, distorting, or disturbing the audio, visual, or mental processes, or who is under the influence of such substance or material is guilty of a misdemeanor.

Amended by Stats 2011 ch 296 (AB 1023),s 203, eff. 1/1/2012.

Section 381a - Unlawful buying or selling of dairy product

Any person, or persons, whether as principals, agents, managers, or otherwise, who buy or sell dairy products, or deal in milk, cream or butter, and who buy or sell the same upon the basis of their richness or weight or the percentage of cream, or butter-fat contained therein, who use any apparatus, test bottle or other appliance, or who use the "Babcock test" or machine of like character for testing such dairy products, cream or butter, which is not accurate and correct, or which gives wrong or false percentages, or which is calculated in any way to defraud or injure the person with whom he deals, is guilty of a misdemeanor, and upon conviction shall be fined not more than one thousand dollars ($1,000) or imprisoned in the county jail not more than six (6) months.

Amended by Stats. 1983, Ch. 1092, Sec. 275. Effective September 27, 1983. Operative January 1, 1984, by Sec. 427 of Ch. 1092.

Section 381b - Unlawful possession of nitrous oxide

Any person who possesses nitrous oxide or any substance containing nitrous oxide, with the intent to breathe, inhale, or ingest for the purpose of causing a condition of intoxication, elation, euphoria, dizziness, stupefaction, or dulling of the senses or for the purpose of, in any manner, changing, distorting, or disturbing the audio, visual, or mental processes, or who knowingly and with the intent to do so is under the influence of nitrous oxide or any material containing nitrous oxide is guilty of a misdemeanor. This section shall not apply to any person who is under the influence of nitrous oxide or any material containing nitrous oxide pursuant to an administration for the purpose of medical, surgical, or dental care by a person duly licensed to administer such an agent.

Amended by Stats. 1984, Ch. 999, Sec. 1.

Section 381c - Unlawful sale of nitrous oxide

(a) As used in this section, "nitrous oxide" refers to any of the following substances: N2O, dinitrogen monoxide, dinitrogen oxide, nitrogen oxide, or laughing gas.

(b) Every person who sells, furnishes, administers, distributes, gives away, or offers to sell, furnish, administer, distribute, or give away a device, canister, tank, or receptacle either exclusively containing nitrous oxide or exclusively containing a chemical compound mixed with nitrous oxide, to a person under 18 years of age is guilty of a misdemeanor. The court shall consider ordering the person to perform community service as a condition of probation.

(c)

(1) It is a defense to this crime that the defendant honestly and reasonably believed that the minor involved in the offense was at least 18 years of age.

(2) The defendant shall bear the burden of establishing this defense by a preponderance of the evidence.

(d) For the purpose of preventing a violation of this section, any person may refuse to sell, furnish, administer, distribute, or give away a device, canister, tank, or receptacle either exclusively containing nitrous oxide or exclusively containing a chemical compound mixed with nitrous oxide to a person who is unable to produce adequate proof of age of majority.

(e) On and after July 1, 2010, the court shall order the suspension of the business license, for a period of up to one year, of a person who knowingly violates this section after having been previously convicted of a violation of this section, unless the owner of the business license can demonstrate a good faith attempt to prevent illegal sales or deliveries by the owner's employees.

(f) This section shall not apply to any person who administers nitrous oxide for the purpose of providing medical or dental care, if administered by a medical or dental practitioner licensed by this state or at the direction or under the supervision of a practitioner licensed by this state.

(g) This section does not apply to the sale of nitrous oxide contained in food products for use as a propellant.

Added by Stats 2009 ch 266 (AB 1015),s 1, eff. 1/1/2010.

Section 381d - Dispensing or distributing nitrous oxide; penalty

(a) A person who dispenses or distributes nitrous oxide to a person, and knows or should know that the person is going to use the nitrous oxide in violation of Section 381b, and that person proximately causes great bodily injury or death to himself, herself, or another person, is guilty of a misdemeanor, and shall be punished by imprisonment in a county jail, not to exceed six months, or by a fine not to exceed one thousand dollars ($1,000), or by both that fine and imprisonment.

(b) This section shall not preclude prosecution under any other law.

Added by Stats 2014 ch 458 (AB 1735),s 1, eff. 1/1/2015.

Section 381e - Dispensing or distributing nitrous oxide; records of transactions

(a) A person who dispenses or distributes nitrous oxide shall record each transaction involving the dispensing or distribution of nitrous oxide in a written or electronic document. The person dispensing or distributing the nitrous oxide shall require the purchaser to sign the document and provide a complete residential address and present a valid government-issued photo identification. The person dispensing or distributing the nitrous oxide shall sign and date the document and shall retain the document at the person's business address for one year from the date of the transaction. The person shall make the documents available during normal business hours for inspection and copying, upon presentation of a duly authorized search warrant, by officers or employees of the California State Board of Pharmacy or of other law enforcement agencies of this state or the United States.

(b) The document used to record each transaction shall inform the purchaser of all of the following:

(1) That inhalation of nitrous oxide outside of a clinical setting may have dangerous health effects.

(2) That it is a violation of state law to possess nitrous oxide or any substance containing nitrous oxide, with the intent to breathe, inhale, or ingest it for the purpose of intoxication.

(3) That it is a violation of state law to knowingly distribute or dispense nitrous oxide or any substance containing nitrous oxide, to a person who intends to breathe, inhale, or ingest it for the purpose of intoxication.

(c) This section shall not apply to any person who administers nitrous oxide for the purpose of providing medical or dental care, if administered by a medical or dental practitioner licensed by this state or at the direction or under the supervision of a practitioner licensed by this state.

(d) This section does not apply to the sale of nitrous oxide contained in food products for use as a propellant.

(e) This section shall not apply to the sale or distribution of nitrous oxide by a wholesaler licensed by the Board of Pharmacy or manufacturer classified under Code Number 325120 or 424690 of the North American Industry Classification System (NAICS).

(f)

(1) Information obtained from a person to whom nitrous oxide was distributed or dispensed pursuant to this section shall be confidential and shall be used solely for the purposes provided in this section.

(2) Except as provided in this section, a person who dispenses or distributes nitrous oxide shall not use, review, or disclose any information obtained pursuant to this section.

(3) A person who violates this subdivision shall be guilty of a misdemeanor, punishable by imprisonment in a county jail not to exceed six months, or by a fine not to exceed one thousand dollars ($1,000), or by both that fine and imprisonment.
Added by Stats 2014 ch 458 (AB 1735),s 2, eff. 1/1/2015.

Section 382 - Unlawful adulteration or dilution of food, drink or medicine

Every person who adulterates or dilutes any article of food, drink, drug, medicine, spirituous or malt liquor, or wine, or any article useful in compounding them, with the fraudulent intent to offer the same, or cause or permit it to be offered for sale as unadulterated or undiluted; and every person who fraudulently sells, or keeps or offers for sale the same, as unadulterated or undiluted, or who, in response to an inquiry for any article of food, drink, drug, medicine, spirituous or malt liquor, or wine, sells or offers for sale, a different article, or an article of a different character or manufacture, without first informing such purchaser of such difference, is guilty of a misdemeanor; provided, that no retail dealer shall be convicted under the provisions of this section if he shall prove a written guaranty of purity obtained from the person from whom he purchased such adulterated or diluted goods.
Amended by Stats. 1903, Ch. 254.

Section 382.4 - Unlawful administration of succinylcholine to dog or cat

No person, other than a licensed veterinarian, shall administer succinylcholine, also known as sucostrin, to any dog or cat. Violation of this section shall constitute a misdemeanor.
Added by Stats. 1976, Ch. 1083.

Section 382.5 - Unlawful sale or administration of dinitrophenol

Every person who sells, dispenses, administers or prescribes dinitrophenol for any purpose shall be guilty of a felony, punishable by a fine not less than one thousand dollars ($1,000) nor more than ten thousand dollars ($10,000), or by imprisonment pursuant to subdivision (h) of Section 1170, or by both that fine and imprisonment.

This section shall not apply to dinitrophenol manufactured or sold as an economic poison registered under the provision of Section 12811 of the Food and Agricultural Code nor to sales for use in manufacturing or for scientific purposes, and not for human consumption.
Amended by Stats 2011 ch 39 (AB 117),s 68, eff. 6/30/2011.
Amended by Stats 2011 ch 15 (AB 109),s 340, eff. 4/4/2011, but operative no earlier than October 1, 2011, and only upon creation of a community corrections grant program to assist in implementing this act and upon an appropriation to fund the grant program.

Section 382.6 - Unlawful sale or administration of preparations containing diphenylamine, paraphenylenediamine, or paratoluylenediamine

Every person who sells, dispenses, administers or prescribes preparations containing diphenylamine, paraphenylenediamine, or paratoluylenediamine, or a derivative of any such chemicals, to be used as eyebrow and eyelash dye, shall be guilty of a felony, punishable by a fine not less than one thousand dollars ($1,000) nor more than ten thousand dollars ($10,000), or by imprisonment pursuant to subdivision (h) of Section 1170, or by both that fine and imprisonment.
Amended by Stats 2011 ch 39 (AB 117),s 68, eff. 6/30/2011.
Amended by Stats 2011 ch 15 (AB 109),s 341, eff. 4/4/2011, but operative no earlier than October 1, 2011, and only upon creation of a community corrections grant program to assist in implementing this act and upon an appropriation to fund the grant program.

Section 382.7 - Unlawful furnishing of liquid silicone substance

Every person who knowingly prescribes, dispenses, administers, or furnishes any liquid silicone substance for the purpose of injection into a human breast or mammary is guilty of a misdemeanor.
Added by Stats. 1976, Ch. 949.

Section 383 - Unlawful sale or disposition of adulterated food, drink, drug or medicine

Every person who knowingly sells, or keeps or offers for sale, or otherwise disposes of any article of food, drink, drug, or medicine, knowing that the same is adulterated or has become tainted, decayed, spoiled, or otherwise unwholesome or unfit to be eaten or drunk, with intent to permit the same to be eaten or drunk, is guilty of a misdemeanor, and must be fined not exceeding one thousand dollars ($1,000), or imprisoned in the county jail not exceeding six months, or both, and may, in the discretion of the court, be adjudged to pay, in addition, all the necessary expenses, not exceeding one thousand dollars ($1,000), incurred in inspecting and analyzing such articles. The term "drug," as used herein, includes all medicines for internal or external use, antiseptics, disinfectants, and cosmetics. The term "food," as used herein, includes all articles used for food or drink by man, whether simple, mixed, or compound. Any article is deemed to be adulterated within the meaning of this section:

(a) In case of drugs:

(1) if, when sold under or by a name recognized in the United States Pharmacopoeia, it differs materially from the standard of strength, quality, or purity laid down therein;

(2) if, when sold under or by a name not recognized in the United States Pharmacopoeia, but which is found in some other pharmacopoeia or other standard work on materia medica, it differs materially from the standard of strength, quality, or purity laid down in such work;

(3) if its strength, quality, or purity falls below the professed standard under which it is sold.

(b) In the case of food:

(1) if any substance or substances have been mixed with it, so as to lower or depreciate, or injuriously affect its quality, strength, or purity;

(2) if any inferior or cheaper substance or substances have been substituted wholly or in part for it;

(3) if any valuable or necessary constituent or ingredient has been wholly or in part abstracted from it;

(4) if it is an imitation of, or is sold under the name of, another article;

(5) if it consists wholly, or in part, of a diseased, decomposed, putrid, infected, tainted, or rotten animal or vegetable substance or article, whether manufactured or not; or in the case of milk, if it is the produce of a diseased animal;

(6) if it is colored, coated, polished, or powdered, whereby damage or inferiority is concealed, or if by any means it is made to appear better or of greater value than it really is;

(7) if it contains any added substance or ingredient which is poisonous or injurious to health.

Amended by Stats. 1976, Ch. 1125.

Section 383a - Unlawful sale of stale, rancid, or decomposed butter

Any person, firm, or corporation, who sells or offers for sale, or has in his or its possession for sale, any butter manufactured by boiling, melting, deodorizing, or renovating, which is the product of stale, rancid, or decomposed butter, or by any other process whereby stale, rancid, or decomposed butter is manufactured to resemble or appear like creamery or dairy butter, unless the same is plainly stenciled or branded upon each and every package, barrel, firkin, tub, pail, square, or roll, in letters not less than one half inch in length, "process butter," or "renovated butter," in such a manner as to advise the purchaser of the real character of such "process" or "renovated" butter, is guilty of a misdemeanor.

Added by Stats. 1905, Ch. 573.

Section 383b - False representation that meat is kosher

Every person who with intent to defraud, sells or exposes for sale any meat or meat preparations, and falsely represents the same to be kosher, whether such meat or meat preparations be raw or prepared for human consumption, or as having been prepared under and from a product or products sanctioned by the orthodox Hebrew religious requirements; or falsely represents any food product, or the contents of any package or container, to be so constituted and prepared, by having or permitting to be inscribed thereon the words "kosher" in any language; or sells or exposes for sale in the same place of business both kosher and nonkosher meat or meat preparations, either raw or prepared for human consumption, who fails to indicate on his window signs in all display advertising in block letters at least four inches in height "kosher and nonkosher meats sold here"; or who exposes for sale in any show window or place of business as both kosher and nonkosher meat preparations, either raw or prepared for human consumption, who fails to display over each kind of meat or meat preparation so exposed a sign in block letters at least four inches in height, reading "kosher meat" or "nonkosher meat" as the case may be; or sells or exposes for sale in any restaurant or any other place where food products are sold for consumption on the premises, any article of food or food preparations and falsely represents the same to be kosher, or as having been prepared in accordance with the orthodox Hebrew religious requirements; or sells or exposes for sale in such restaurant, or such other place, both kosher and nonkosher food or food preparations for consumption on the premises, not prepared in accordance with the Jewish ritual, or not sanctioned by the Hebrew orthodox religious requirements, and who fails to display on his window signs in all display advertising, in block letters at least four inches in height "kosher and nonkosher food served here" is guilty of a misdemeanor and upon conviction thereof be punishable by a fine of not less than one hundred dollars ($100), nor more than six hundred dollars ($600), or imprisonment in the county jail of not less than 30 days, nor more than 90 days, or both such fine and imprisonment.

The word "kosher" is here defined to mean a strict compliance with every Jewish law and custom pertaining and relating to the killing of the animal or fowl from which the meat is taken or extracted, the dressing, treatment and preparation thereof for human consumption, and the manufacture, production, treatment and preparation of such other food or foods in connection wherewith Jewish laws and customs obtain and to the use of tools, implements, vessels, utensils, dishes and containers that are used in connection with the killing of such animals and fowls and the dressing, preparation, production, manufacture and treatment of such meats and other products, foods and food stuffs.

Amended by Stats. 1983, Ch. 1092, Sec. 278. Effective September 27, 1983. Operative January 1, 1984, by Sec. 427 of Ch. 1092.

Section 383c - False representation that meat is halal

Every person who with intent to defraud, sells or exposes for sale any meat or meat preparations, and falsely represents the same to be halal, whether the meat or meat preparations is raw or prepared for human consumption, or as having been prepared under and from a product or products sanctioned by the Islamic religious requirements; or falsely represents any food product, or the contents of any package or container, to be so constituted and prepared, by having or permitting to be inscribed thereon the word "halal" in any language; or sells or exposes for sale in the same place of business both halal and nonhalal meat or meat preparations, either raw or prepared for human consumption, who fails to indicate on his or her window signs in all display advertising in block letters at least four inches in height "halal and nonhalal meats sold here"; or who exposes for sale in any show window or place of business as both halal and nonhalal meat preparations, either raw or prepared for human consumption, who fails to display over each kind of meat or meat preparation so exposed a sign in block letters at least four inches in height, reading "halal meat" or "nonhalal meat" as the case may be; or sells or exposes for sale in any restaurant or any other place where food products are sold for consumption on the premises, any article of food or food preparations and falsely represents the same to be halal, or as having been prepared in accordance with the Islamic religious requirements; or sells or exposes for sale in a restaurant, or other place, both halal and nonhalal food or food preparations for consumption on the premises, not prepared in accordance with the Islamic ritual, or not sanctioned by Islamic religious requirements, and who fails to display on his or her window signs in all display advertising, in block letters at least four inches in height "halal and nonhalal food served here" is guilty of a misdemeanor and upon conviction thereof be punishable by a fine of not less than one hundred dollars ($100), nor more than six hundred dollars ($600), or imprisonment in a county jail of not less than 30 days, nor more than 90 days, or both that fine and imprisonment.

The word "halal" is here defined to mean a strict compliance with every Islamic law and custom pertaining and relating to the killing of the animal or fowl from which the meat is taken or extracted, the dressing, treatment, and preparation thereof for human consumption, and the manufacture, production, treatment, and preparation of other food or foods in connection wherewith Islamic laws and customs obtain and to the use of tools, implements, vessels, utensils, dishes, and containers that are used in connection with the killing of animals and fowls and the dressing, preparation, production, manufacture, and treatment of meats and other products, foods, and food stuffs.

Amended by Stats 2003 ch 62 (SB 600), s 226, eff. 1/1/2004.

Added by Stats 2002 ch 102 (AB 1828), s 1, eff. 1/1/2003.

Section 384 - Unlawful refusal to relinquish party line

(a) Any person who shall wilfully refuse to immediately relinquish a party line when informed that such line is needed for an emergency call, and in fact such line is needed for an emergency call, to a fire department or police department or for medical aid or ambulance service, or any person who shall secure the use of a party line by falsely stating that such line is needed for an emergency call, shall be guilty of a misdemeanor.

(b) "Party line" as used in this section means a subscribers' line telephone circuit, consisting of two or more main telephone stations connected therewith, each station with a distinctive ring or telephone number. "Emergency" as used in this section means a situation in which property or human life is in jeopardy and the prompt summoning of aid is essential.

(c) Every telephone directory hereafter published and distributed to the members of the general public in this State or in any portion thereof which lists the calling numbers of telephones of any telephone exchange located in this State shall contain a notice which explains the offense provided for in this section, such notice to be printed in type which is not smaller than any other type on the same page and to be preceded by the word "warning" printed in type at least as large as the largest type on the same page; provided, that the provisions of this subdivision shall not apply to those directories distributed solely for business advertising purposes, commonly known as classified directories, nor to any telephone directory heretofore distributed to the general public. Any person, firm or corporation providing telephone service which distributes or causes to be distributed in this State copies of a telephone directory which is subject to the provisions of this section and which do not contain the notice herein provided for shall be guilty of a misdemeanor. Added by Stats. 1957, Ch. 533.

Section 384.5 - Unlawful removal of minor forest products

(a)

(1) Any person who removes any minor forest products from the property where the products were cut and transports the products upon any public road or highway shall have in the person's possession a valid bill of sale for the products or a written permit issued by the owner of the property from which the products were removed authorizing the removal and transport.

(2) Any such permit or bill of sale shall include, but is not limited to, all of the following:

(A) The name, address, and signature of the landowner, and phone number, if available.

(B) The name, address, and signature of the permittee or purchaser.

(C) The amount, species, and type of minor forest products to be removed and transported.

(D) A description sufficient to identify the property from which the minor forest products are to be removed.

(E) The date of issuance of the permit or bill of sale and the duration of the period of time within which the minor forest products may be removed.

(F) Any conditions or additional information which the landowner may impose or include.

(3) Any permit for the removal of minor forest products from public lands that is issued by the United States Forest Service or the Bureau of Land Management is sufficient for the purposes of this subdivision, regardless of whether the permit conforms to the specific requirements as to content set forth in paragraph (2).

(4) For the purposes of this subdivision, "minor forest products" means firewood, posts, shakeboards, shake and shingle bolts, or split products, in quantities exceeding 20 cubic feet in volume, and burlwood or stumps, in quantities of two or more.

(b) This section shall not apply to the transport of any minor forest products carried in a passenger vehicle, as defined in Section 465 of the Vehicle Code.

(c) Violation of subdivision (a) is a misdemeanor punishable by a fine of not more than one thousand dollars ($1,000) or by imprisonment in a county jail for not more than six months or by both that fine and imprisonment.

Amended by Stats. 1988, Ch. 225, Sec. 1.

Section 384a - Unlawful cutting or removal of tree or shrub, fern, herb, bulb, cactus, flower etc. along highway rights of way

(a)

(1) A person shall not willfully or negligently cut, destroy, mutilate, or remove plant material that is growing upon state or county highway rights-of-way.

(2) A person shall not willfully or negligently cut, destroy, mutilate, or remove plant material that is growing upon public land or upon land that is not his or hers without a written permit from the owner of the land, signed by the owner of the land or the owner's authorized agent, as provided in subdivision (c).

(3) A person shall not knowingly sell, offer or expose for sale, or transport for sale plant material that is cut or removed in violation of this subdivision.

(b) For purposes of this section, "plant material" means a tree, shrub, fern, herb, bulb, cactus, flower, huckleberry, or redwood green, or a portion of any of those, or the leaf mold on those plants. "Plant material" does not include a tree, shrub, fern, herb, bulb, cactus, flower, or greens declared by law to be a public nuisance.

(c)

(1) The written permit required by paragraph (2) of subdivision (a) shall be signed by the landowner, or the landowner's authorized agent, and acknowledged before a notary public, or other person authorized by law to take acknowledgments. The permit shall contain the number and species of trees and amount of plant material, and shall contain the legal description of the real property as usually found in deeds and conveyances of the land on which cutting or removal shall take place. One copy of the permit shall be filed in the office of the sheriff of the county in which the land described in the permit is located. The permit shall be filed prior to the commencement of cutting or removal of plant material authorized by the permit.

(2) The permit required by this section need not be notarized or filed with the sheriff when five or less pounds of shrubs or boughs are to be cut or removed.

(d) A county or state fire warden; personnel of the Department of Forestry and Fire Protection, as designated by the Director of Forestry and Fire Protection; personnel of the United States Forest Service, as designated by the Regional Forester, Region 5, of the United States Forest Service; or a peace officer of the State of California, may enforce the provisions of this section and may confiscate any and all plant material unlawfully cut or removed or knowingly sold, offered, or exposed or transported for sale as provided in this section.

(e) This section does not apply to any of the following:

(1) An employee of the state or of a political subdivision of the state who is engaged in work upon a state, county, or public road or highway while performing work under the supervision of the state or a political subdivision of the state.

(2) A person engaged in the necessary cutting or trimming of plant material for the purpose of protecting or maintaining an electric powerline, telephone line, or other property of a public utility.

(3) A person engaged in logging operations or fire suppression.

(f) A violation of this section shall be a misdemeanor, punishable by a fine of not more than one thousand dollars ($1,000), by imprisonment in a county jail for not more than six months, or by both that fine and imprisonment.

Amended by Stats 2015 ch 499 (SB 795),s 2, eff. 1/1/2016.

Section 384b - Definitions

For the purposes of Sections 384c through 384f, inclusive, unless the context otherwise requires, the definitions contained in this section govern the construction of those sections.

(a) "Person" includes an employee with wages as his or her sole compensation.

(b) "Permit" means a permit as required by Section 384a.

(c) "Tree" means any evergreen tree or top thereof which is harvested without having the limbs and foliage removed.

(d) "Shrub" means any toyon or Christmas red-berry shrub or any of the following native desert plants: all species of the family Cactaceae (cactus family); and Agave deserti (desert agave), Agave utahensis (Utah agave), Nolina bigelovii, Nolina parryi (Parry nolina), Nolina wolfii, Yucca baccata, Yucca brevifolia (Joshua tree), Yucca schidigera (Mohave yucca), Yucca whipplei (Whipple yucca), Cercidium floridum (blue palo verde), Cercidium microphyllum (little leaf palo verde), Dalea spinosa (smoke tree), Olneya tesota (ironwood tree), and Fouquieria splendens (ocotillo), or any part thereof, except the fruit thereof, which is harvested without having the limbs and foliage removed.

(e) "Bough" means any limb or foliage removed from an evergreen tree.

(f) "Peace officer" means any county or state fire warden, personnel of the Department of Forestry and Fire Protection as designated by the Director of Forestry and Fire Protection, personnel of the United States Forest Service as designated by the Regional Forester, Region 5 of the United States Forest Service, personnel of the United States Department of the Interior as designated by them, or any peace officer of the State of California.

(g) "Harvest" means to remove or cut and remove from the place where grown.

(h) "Harvester" means a person who harvests a tree, shrub, or bough.

Amended by Stats. 1992, Ch. 427, Sec. 126. Effective January 1, 1993.

Section 384c - Unlawful transportation of trees, shrubs, or boughs

Persons purchasing trees, shrubs, or boughs from harvesters thereof shall not transport more than five trees or more than five pounds of shrubs or boughs on the public roads or highways without obtaining from the seller of the trees, shrubs, or boughs and having validated as provided in Section 384d a transportation tag for each load of the trees, shrubs, or boughs.

Unless a valid transportation tag issued in California for a tree, shrub, or bough has already been obtained, persons who harvest trees, shrubs, or boughs from their own land or the land of another or who are in possession of trees, shrubs, or boughs shall, before transporting on the public roads or highways or selling or consigning for removal and transportation over the public roads and highways more than five trees or more than five pounds of other shrubs or boughs, file with the sheriff of each county in which the trees, shrubs, or boughs are to be harvested an application for transportation tags and obtain a supply of these transportation tags sufficient to provide one tag for each load of trees, shrubs, or boughs to be so transported or sold.

No person shall knowingly make any false statement on any application for the transportation tags and the application shall contain, but is not limited to, the following information:

(a) The name and address of the applicant.

(b) The amount and species of trees, shrubs, or boughs to be transported.

(c) The name of the county from which the trees, shrubs, or boughs are to be removed.

(d) A legal description of the real property from which the trees, shrubs, or boughs are to be removed.

(e) The name or names of the owner of the real property from which the trees, shrubs, or boughs are to be removed.

(f) The applicant's timber operator permit number, if the harvesting of the trees, shrubs, or boughs is subject to the Z'berg-Nejedly Forest Practice Act of 1973 (Chapter 8 (commencing with Section 4511) of Part 2 of Division 4 of the Public Resources Code).

(g) The destination of the trees, shrubs, or boughs.

(h) The proposed date or dates of the transportation. Every applicant shall, at the time of application, show to the sheriff his or her permit or proof of ownership of the trees, shrubs, or boughs. The application forms and transportation tags shall be printed and distributed by the sheriff of each county.

Amended by Stats. 1982, Ch. 1318, Sec. 3.

Section 384d - Transportation tags

Upon the filing of an application containing the information required by Section 384c, and the presentation of a permit or proof of ownership as required by Section 384c, the county sheriff's office shall issue to persons who harvest or have in their possession, trees, shrubs or boughs within the county sufficient transportation tags stamped with the county seal and identified by the applicant's timber operator permit number, if any, to enable the person transporting any of the trees, shrubs or boughs harvested within the county by the applicant to have a tag accompany each and every load of such trees, shrubs or boughs. Harvesters of trees, shrubs or boughs, when selling from stockpile location, shall furnish to the purchaser of trees, shrubs or boughs a bill of sale and a transportation tag for each load or part thereof bearing the harvester's timber operator permit number, if any, and other information as hereinafter required.

The purchaser of harvested trees, shrubs or boughs or the harvester when transporting his own trees, shrubs or boughs shall have the transportation tag validated by a peace officer in the county of purchase or harvest or by the nearest peace officer in an adjacent county when the transportation route used does not pass an office of a peace officer in the county of purchase or harvest. The validated transportation tag or tags shall remain with the load to the marketing area.

The transportation tags shall be in two parts; one to be retained by the transporting party; one to be retained by the validating peace officer and forwarded to the county sheriff. The transportation tags shall be validated and in force only for the proposed date or dates of transportation as specified in the application for the transportation tags. The transportation tags will be validated without fee and each shall contain the following information: name and address of the person obtaining and using the tag; number or amount of each species of trees, shrubs and boughs in the load; make, model and license number of the transporting vehicle; the county of origin and county of destination; the specified period of time during which the transportation tag is in force; date and validating signature and title of a peace officer.

Amended by Stats. 1977, Ch. 32.

Section 384e - Presentation of transportation tag

(a) The transportation tag described in Section 384d shall be presented to any peace officer upon demand.

(b) Failure to produce a transportation tag properly filled out and validated upon demand of any peace officer shall constitute sufficient grounds to hold in protective custody the entire load of trees, shrubs or boughs, until proof of legal right to transport is furnished.

Added by Stats. 1963, Ch. 1830.

Section 384f - Punishment

Any person violating any of the provisions of Sections 384b through 384f shall be guilty of a misdemeanor and upon conviction thereof shall be punished by a fine of not more than one thousand dollars ($1,000) or by imprisonment in the county jail not exceeding six months or by both such fine and imprisonment.

Amended by Stats. 1983, Ch. 1092, Sec. 281. Effective September 27, 1983. Operative January 1, 1984, by Sec. 427 of Ch. 1092.

Section 384h - Unlawful killing or wounding of animal on property of another

Every person who willfully or negligently, while hunting upon the inclosed lands of another, kills, maims, or wounds an animal, the property of another, is guilty of a misdemeanor.

Added by renumbering Section 384c by Stats. 1963, Ch. 1830.

Section 384i - Applicability

(a) Sections 384a to 384f, inclusive, shall not apply to maintenance and construction activities of public agencies and their employees.

(b) Sections 384b to 384f, inclusive, shall not apply to native desert plants described in subdivision (b) of Section 384b, that have been propagated and cultivated by human beings and which are being transported under Section 6922 or 6923 of the Food and Agricultural Code, pursuant to a valid nursery stock certificate.

(c) Sections 384a to 384f, inclusive, shall not apply to any act regulated by the provisions of Division 23 (commencing with Section 80001) of the Food and Agricultural Code.

Amended by Stats. 1987, Ch. 828, Sec. 25.

Section 385 - Unlawful acts related to a high voltage overhead conductor

(a) The term "high voltage" as used in this section means a voltage in excess of 750 volts, measured between conductors or measured between the conductor and the ground. The term "overhead conductor" as used in this section means any electrical conductor (either bare or insulated) installed above the ground except such conductors as are enclosed in iron pipe or other metal covering of equal strength.

(b) Any person who either personally or through an employee or agent, or as an employee or agent of another, operates, places, erects or moves any tools, machinery, equipment, material, building or structure within six feet of a high voltage overhead conductor is guilty of a misdemeanor.

(c) It shall be a misdemeanor to own, operate or to employ any person to operate, any crane, derrick, power shovel, drilling rig, hay loader, hay stacker, pile driver, or similar apparatus, any part of which is capable of vertical, lateral or swinging motion, unless there is posted and maintained in plain view of the operator thereof, a durable warning sign legible at 12 feet, reading: "Unlawful to operate this equipment within six feet of high voltage lines." Each day's failure to post or maintain such sign shall constitute a separate violation.

(d) The provisions of this section shall not apply to (1) the construction, reconstruction, operation or maintenance of any high voltage overhead conductor, or its supporting structures or appurtenances by persons authorized by the owner, or (2) the operation of standard rail equipment which is normally used in the transportation of freight or passengers, or the operation of relief trains or other emergency railroad equipment by persons authorized by the owner, or (3) any construction, reconstruction, operation or maintenance of any overhead structures covered by the rules for overhead line construction prescribed by the Public Utilities Commission of the State of California.

Added by Stats. 1947, Ch. 1229.

Section 386 - Unlawful acts related to construction or maintenance of fire-protection system

(a) Any person who willfully or maliciously constructs or maintains a fire-protection system in any structure with the intent to install a fire protection system which is known to be inoperable or to impair the effective operation of a system, so as to threaten the safety of any occupant or user of the structure in the event of a fire, shall be subject to imprisonment pursuant to subdivision (h) of Section 1170 for two, three, or four years.

(b) A violation of subdivision (a) which proximately results in great bodily injury or death is a felony punishable by imprisonment pursuant to subdivision (h) of Section 1170 for five, six, or seven years.

(c) As used in this section, "fire-protection system" includes, but is not limited to, an automatic fire sprinkler system, standpipe system, automatic fixed fire extinguishing system, and fire alarm system.

(d) For purposes of this section, the following definitions shall control:

(1) "Automatic fire sprinkler system" means an integrated system of underground and overhead piping designed in accordance with fire protection engineering standards. The portion of the sprinkler system above ground is a network of specially sized or hydraulically designed piping installed in a building, structure, or area, generally overhead, and to which sprinklers are attached in a systematic pattern. The valve controlling each system riser is located in the system riser or its supply piping. Each sprinkler system riser includes a device for activating an alarm when the system is in operation. The system is normally activated by heat from a fire, and it discharges water over the fire area.

(2) "Standpipe system" means an arrangement of piping, valves, and hose connectors and allied equipment installed in a building or structure with the hose connectors located in a manner that water can be discharged in streams or spray patterns through attached hose and nozzles. The purpose of the system is to extinguish a fire, thereby protecting a building or structure and its contents and occupants. This system relies upon connections to water supply systems or pumps, tanks, and other equipment necessary to provide an adequate supply of water to the hose connectors.

(3) "Automatic fixed fire extinguishing system" means either of the following:

(A) An engineered fixed extinguishing system which is custom designed for a particular hazard, using components which are approved or listed only for their broad performance characteristics. Components may be arranged into a variety of configurations. These systems shall include, but not be limited to, dry chemical systems, carbon dioxide systems, halogenated agent systems, steam systems, high expansion foam systems, foam extinguishing systems, and liquid agent systems.

(B) A pre-engineered fixed extinguishing system is a system where the number of components and their configurations are included in the description of the system's approval and listing. These systems include, but are not limited to, dry chemical systems, carbon dioxide systems, halogenated agent systems, and liquid agent systems.

(4) "Fire alarm system" means a control unit and a combination of electrical interconnected devices designed and intended to cause an alarm or warning of fire in a building or structure by either manual or automatic activation, or by both, and includes the systems installed throughout any building or portion thereof.

(5) "Structure" means any building, whether private, commercial, or public, or any bridge, tunnel, or powerplant.

Amended by Stats 2011 ch 39 (AB 117),s 68, eff. 6/30/2011.

Amended by Stats 2011 ch 15 (AB 109),s 342, eff. 4/4/2011, but operative no earlier than October 1, 2011, and only upon creation of a community corrections grant program to assist in implementing this act and upon an appropriation to fund the grant program.

Section 387 - Knowledge of concealed danger

(a) Any corporation, limited liability company, or person who is a manager with respect to a product, facility, equipment, process, place of employment, or business practice, is guilty of a public offense punishable by imprisonment in the county jail for a term not exceeding one year, or by a fine not exceeding ten thousand dollars ($10,000), or by both that fine and imprisonment; or by imprisonment pursuant to subdivision (h) of Section 1170 for 16 months, two, or three years, or by a fine not exceeding twenty-five thousand dollars ($25,000); or by both that fine and imprisonment, but if the defendant is a corporation or a limited liability company the fine shall not exceed one million dollars ($1,000,000), if that corporation, limited liability company, or person does all of the following:

(1) Has actual knowledge of a serious concealed danger that is subject to the regulatory authority of an appropriate agency and is associated with that product or a component of that product or business practice.

(2) Knowingly fails during the period ending 15 days after the actual knowledge is acquired, or if there is imminent risk of great bodily harm or death, immediately, to do both of the following:

(A) Inform the Division of Occupational Safety and Health in the Department of Industrial Relations in writing, unless the corporation, limited liability company, or manager has actual knowledge that the division has been so informed. Where the concealed danger reported pursuant to this paragraph is subject to the regulatory authority of an agency other than the Division of Occupational Safety and Health in the Department of Industrial Relations, it shall be the responsibility of the Division of Occupational Safety and Health in the Department of Industrial Relations, within 24 hours of receipt of the information, to telephonically notify the appropriate government agency of the hazard, and promptly forward any written notification received.

(B) Warn its affected employees in writing, unless the corporation, limited liability company, or manager has actual knowledge that the employees have been so warned. The requirement for disclosure is not applicable if the hazard is abated within the time prescribed for reporting, unless the appropriate regulatory agency nonetheless requires disclosure by regulation.

Where the Division of Occupational Safety and Health in the Department of Industrial Relations was not notified, but the corporation, limited liability company, or manager reasonably and in good faith believed that they were complying with the notification requirements of this section by notifying another government agency, as listed in paragraph (8) of subdivision (d), no penalties shall apply.

(b) As used in this section:

(1) "Manager" means a person having both of the following:

(A) Management authority in or as a business entity.

(B) Significant responsibility for any aspect of a business that includes actual authority for the safety of a product or business practice or for the conduct of research or testing in connection with a product or business practice.

(2) "Product" means an article of trade or commerce or other item of merchandise that is a tangible or an intangible good, and includes services.

(3) "Actual knowledge," used with respect to a serious concealed danger, means has information that would convince a reasonable person in the circumstances in which the manager is situated that the serious concealed danger exists.

(4) "Serious concealed danger," used with respect to a product or business practice, means that the normal or reasonably foreseeable use of, or the exposure of an individual to, the product or business practice creates a substantial probability of death, great bodily harm, or serious exposure to an individual, and the danger is not readily apparent to an individual who is likely to be exposed.

(5) "Great bodily harm" means a significant or substantial physical injury.

(6) "Serious exposure" means any exposure to a hazardous substance, when the exposure occurs as a result of an incident or exposure over time and to a degree or in an amount sufficient to create a substantial probability that death or great bodily harm in the future would result from the exposure.

(7) "Warn its affected employees" means give sufficient description of the serious concealed danger to all individuals working for or in the business entity who are likely to be subject to the serious concealed danger in the course of that work to make those individuals aware of that danger.

(8) "Appropriate government agency" means an agency on the following list that has regulatory authority with respect to the product or business practice and serious concealed dangers of the sort discovered:

(A) The Division of Occupational Safety and Health in the Department of Industrial Relations.

(B) State Department of Health Services.

(C) Department of Agriculture.

(D) County departments of health.

(E) The United States Food and Drug Administration.

(F) The United States Environmental Protection Agency.

(G) The National Highway Traffic Safety Administration.

(H) The Federal Occupation Safety and Health Administration.

(I) The Nuclear Regulatory Commission.

(J) The Consumer Product Safety Commission.

(K) The Federal Aviation Administration.

(L) The Federal Mine Safety and Health Review Commission.

(c) Notification received pursuant to this section shall not be used against any manager in any criminal case, except a prosecution for perjury or for giving a false statement.

(d) No person who is a manager of a limited liability company shall be personally liable for acts or omissions for which the limited liability company is liable under subdivision (a) solely by reason of being a manager of the limited liability company. A person who is a manager of a limited liability company may be held liable under subdivision (a) if that person is also a "manager" within the meaning of paragraph (1) of subdivision (b).

Amended by Stats 2011 ch 39 (AB 117),s 68, eff. 6/30/2011.

Amended by Stats 2011 ch 15 (AB 109),s 343, eff. 4/4/2011, but operative no earlier than October 1, 2011, and only upon creation of a community corrections grant program to assist in implementing this act and upon an appropriation to fund the grant program.

Section 395 - False statement with intent to affect market price of property

Every person who willfully makes or publishes any false statement, spreads any false rumor, or employs any other false or fraudulent means or device, with intent to affect the market price of any kind of property, is guilty of a misdemeanor.

Enacted 1872.

Section 396 - Unlawful increase in price of consumer goods and services during emergencies

(a) The Legislature hereby finds that during a state of emergency or local emergency, including, but not limited to, an earthquake, flood, fire, riot, storm, drought, plant or animal infestation or disease, pandemic or epidemic disease outbreak, or other natural or manmade disaster, some merchants have taken unfair advantage of consumers by greatly increasing prices for essential consumer goods and services. While the pricing of consumer goods and services is generally best left to the marketplace under ordinary conditions, when a declared state of emergency or local emergency results in abnormal disruptions of the market, the public interest requires that excessive and unjustified increases in the prices of essential consumer goods and services be prohibited. It is the intent of the Legislature in enacting this act to protect citizens from excessive and unjustified increases in the prices charged during or shortly after a declared state of emergency or local emergency for goods and services that are vital and necessary for the health, safety, and welfare of consumers, whether those goods and services are offered or sold in person, in stores, or online. Further, it is the intent of the Legislature that this section be liberally construed so that its beneficial purposes may be served.

(b) Upon the proclamation of a state of emergency declared by the President of the United States or the Governor, or upon the declaration of a local emergency by an official, board, or other governing body vested with authority to make that declaration in any county, city, or city and county, and for a period of 30 days following that proclamation or declaration, it is unlawful for a person, contractor, business, or other entity to sell or offer to sell any consumer food items or goods, goods or services used for emergency cleanup, emergency supplies, medical supplies, home heating oil, building materials, housing, transportation, freight, and storage services, or gasoline or other motor fuels for a price of more than 10 percent greater than the price charged by that person for those goods or services immediately prior to the proclamation or declaration of emergency, or prior to a date set in the proclamation or declaration. However, a greater price increase is not unlawful if that person can prove that the increase in price was directly attributable to additional costs imposed on it by the supplier of the goods, or directly attributable to additional costs for labor or materials used to provide the services, during the state of emergency or local emergency, and the price is no more than 10 percent greater than the total of the cost to the seller plus the markup customarily applied by that seller for that good or service in the usual course of business immediately prior to the onset of the state of emergency or local emergency. If the person, contractor, business, or other entity did not charge a price for the goods or services immediately prior to the proclamation or declaration of emergency, it may not charge a price that is more than 50 percent greater than the cost thereof to the vendor as "cost" is defined in Section 17026 of the Business and Professions Code.

(c) Upon the proclamation of a state of emergency declared by the President of the United States or the Governor, or upon the declaration of a local emergency by an official, board, or other governing body vested with authority to make that declaration in any county, city, or city and county, and for a period of 180 days following that proclamation or declaration, it is unlawful for a contractor to sell or offer to sell any repair or reconstruction services or any services used in emergency cleanup for a price of more than 10 percent above the price charged by that person for those services immediately prior to the proclamation or declaration of emergency. However, a greater price increase is not unlawful if that person can prove that the increase in price was directly attributable to additional costs imposed on it by the supplier of the goods, or directly attributable to additional costs for labor or materials used to provide the services, during the state of emergency or local emergency, and the price represents no more than 10 percent greater than the total of the cost to the contractor plus the markup customarily applied by the contractor for that good or service in the usual course of business immediately prior to the onset of the state of emergency or local emergency.

(d) Upon the proclamation of a state of emergency declared by the President of the United States or the Governor, or upon the declaration of a local emergency by an official, board, or other governing body vested with authority to make that declaration in any county, city, or city and county, and for a period of 30 days following that proclamation or declaration, it is unlawful for an owner or operator of a hotel or motel to increase the hotel or motel's regular rates, as advertised immediately prior to the proclamation or declaration of emergency, by more than 10 percent. However, a greater price increase is not unlawful if the owner or operator can prove that the increase in price is directly attributable to additional costs imposed on it for goods or labor used in its business, to seasonal adjustments in rates that are regularly scheduled, or to previously contracted rates.

(e) Upon the proclamation of a state of emergency declared by the President of the United States or the Governor, or upon the declaration of a local emergency by an official, board, or other governing body vested with authority to make that declaration in any city, county, or city and county, and for a period of 30 days following that proclamation or declaration, or any period the proclamation or declaration is extended by the applicable authority, it is unlawful for any person, business, or other entity, to increase the rental price, as defined in paragraph (11) of subdivision (j), advertised, offered, or charged for housing, to an existing or prospective tenant, by more than 10 percent. However, a greater rental price increase is not unlawful if that person can prove that the increase is directly attributable to additional costs for repairs or additions beyond normal maintenance that were amortized over the rental term that caused the rent to be increased greater than 10 percent or that an increase was contractually agreed to by the tenant prior to the proclamation or declaration. It shall not be a defense to a prosecution under this subdivision that an increase in rental price was based on the length of the rental term, the inclusion of additional goods or services, except as provided in paragraph (11) of subdivision (j) with respect to furniture, or that the rent was offered by, or paid by, an insurance company, or other third party, on behalf of a tenant. This subdivision does not authorize a landlord to charge a price greater than the amount authorized by a local rent control ordinance.

(f) It is unlawful for a person, business, or other entity to evict any residential tenant of residential housing after the proclamation of a state of emergency declared by the President of the United States or the Governor, or upon the declaration of a local emergency by an official, board, or other governing body vested with authority to make that declaration in any city, county, or city and county, and for a period of 30 days following that proclamation or declaration, or any period that the proclamation or declaration is extended by the applicable authority and rent or offer to rent to another person at a rental price greater than the evicted tenant could be charged under this section. It shall not be a violation of this subdivision for a person, business, or other entity to continue an eviction process that was lawfully begun prior to the proclamation or declaration of emergency.

(g) The prohibitions of this section may be extended for additional periods, as needed, by a local legislative body, local official, the Governor, or the Legislature, if deemed necessary to protect the lives, property, or welfare of the citizens. Each extension by a local legislative body or local official shall not exceed 30 days. An extension may also authorize specified price increases that exceed the amount that would be permissible under this section during the initial 30 or 180 days after a proclamation or declaration of emergency.

(h) A violation of this section is a misdemeanor punishable by imprisonment in a county jail for a period not exceeding one year, by a fine of not more than ten thousand dollars ($10,000), or by both that fine and imprisonment.

(i) A violation of this section shall constitute an unlawful business practice and an act of unfair competition within the meaning of Section 17200 of the Business and Professions Code. The remedies and penalties provided by this section are cumulative to each other, the remedies under Section 17200 of the Business and Professions Code, and the remedies or penalties available under all other laws of this state.

(j) For the purposes of this section, the following terms have the following meanings:

(1) "State of emergency" means a natural or manmade emergency resulting from an earthquake, flood, fire, riot, storm, drought, plant or animal infestation or disease, pandemic or epidemic disease outbreak, or other natural or manmade disaster for which a state of emergency has been declared by the President of the United States or the Governor.

(2) "Local emergency" means a natural or manmade emergency resulting from an earthquake, flood, fire, riot, storm, drought, plant or animal infestation or disease, pandemic or epidemic disease outbreak, or other natural or manmade disaster for which a local emergency has been declared by an official, board, or other governing body vested with authority to make that declaration in any county, city, or city and county in California.

(3) "Consumer food item" means any article that is used or intended for use for food, drink, confection, or condiment by a person or animal.

(4) "Repair or reconstruction services" means services performed by any person who is required to be licensed under the Contractors' State License Law (Chapter 9 (commencing with Section 7000) of Division 3 of the Business and Professions Code), for repairs to residential or commercial property of any type that is damaged as a result of a disaster.

(5) "Emergency supplies" includes, but is not limited to, water, flashlights, radios, batteries, candles, blankets, soaps, diapers, temporary shelters, tape, toiletries, plywood, nails, and hammers.

(6) "Medical supplies" includes, but is not limited to, prescription and nonprescription medications, bandages, gauze, isopropyl alcohol, and antibacterial products.

(7) "Building materials" means lumber, construction tools, windows, and anything else used in the building or rebuilding of property.

(8) "Gasoline" means any fuel used to power any motor vehicle or power tool.

(9) "Transportation, freight, and storage services" means any service that is performed by any company that contracts to move, store, or transport personal or business property or that rents equipment for those purposes, including towing services.

(10) "Housing" means any rental housing with an initial lease term of no longer than one year, including, but not limited to, a space rented in a mobilehome park or campground.

(11) "Rental price" for housing means any of the following:

(A) For housing rented within one year prior to the time of the proclamation or declaration of emergency, the actual rental price paid by the tenant. For housing not rented at the time of the declaration or proclamation, but rented, or offered for rent, within one year prior to the proclamation or declaration of emergency, the most recent rental price offered before the proclamation or declaration of emergency. For housing rented at the time of the proclamation or declaration of emergency but which becomes vacant while the proclamation or declaration of emergency remains in effect and which is subject to any ordinance, rule, regulation, or initiative measure adopted by any local governmental entity that establishes a maximum amount that a landlord may charge a tenant for rent, the actual rental price paid by the previous tenant or the amount specified in subparagraph (B), whichever is greater. This amount may be increased by 5 percent if the housing was previously rented or offered for rent unfurnished, and it is now being offered for rent fully furnished. This amount shall not be adjusted for any other good or service, including, but not limited to, gardening or utilities currently or formerly provided in connection with the lease.

(B) For housing not rented and not offered for rent within one year prior to the proclamation or declaration of emergency, 160 percent of the fair market rent established by the United States Department of Housing and Urban Development. This amount may be increased by 5 percent if the housing is offered for rent fully furnished. This amount shall not be adjusted for any other good or service, including, but not limited to, gardening or utilities currently or formerly provided in connection with the lease.

(C) Housing advertised, offered, or charged, at a daily rate at the time of the declaration or proclamation of emergency, shall be subject to the rental price described in subparagraph (A), if the housing continues to be advertised, offered, or charged, at a daily rate. Housing advertised, offered, or charged, on a daily basis at the time of the declaration or proclamation of emergency, shall be subject to the rental price in subparagraph (B), if the housing is advertised, offered, or charged, on a periodic lease agreement after the declaration or proclamation of emergency.

(D) For mobilehome spaces rented to existing tenants at the time of the proclamation or declaration of emergency and subject to a local rent control ordinance, the amount authorized under the local rent control ordinance. For new tenants who enter into a rental agreement for a mobilehome space that is subject to rent control but not rented at the time of the proclamation or declaration of emergency, the amount of rent last charged for a space in the same mobilehome park. For mobilehome spaces not subject to a local rent control ordinance and not rented at the time of the proclamation or declaration of emergency, the amount of rent last charged for the space.

(12) "Goods" has the same meaning as defined in subdivision (c) of Section 1689.5 of the Civil Code.

(k) This section does not preempt any local ordinance prohibiting the same or similar conduct or imposing a more severe penalty for the same conduct prohibited by this section.

(l) A business offering an item for sale, or a service, at a reduced price immediately prior to the proclamation or declaration of the emergency may use the price it normally charges for the item or service to calculate the price pursuant to subdivision (b) or (c).

(m) This section does not prohibit an owner from evicting a tenant for any lawful reason, including pursuant to Section 1161 of the Code of Civil Procedure.

Amended by Stats 2020 ch 339 (SB 1196),s 1, eff. 1/1/2021.
Amended by Stats 2018 ch 631 (AB 1919),s 2, eff. 1/1/2019.
Amended by Stats 2016 ch 671 (AB 2820),s 1, eff. 1/1/2017.
Amended by Stats 2004 ch 492 (SB 1363),s 2, eff. 1/1/2005.

Section 396.5 - Unlawful sale of items not authorized by Food Stamp Act

It shall be unlawful for any retail food store or wholesale food concern, as defined in Section 3(k) of the federal Food and Nutrition Act of 2008 (Public Law 95-113) (7 U.S.C. Sec. 2012(k)), or any person, to sell, furnish or give away any goods or services, other than those items authorized by the Food Stamp Act of 1964, as amended (Public Law 88-525) (Chapter 51 (commencing with Section 2011) of Title 7 of the United States Code), in exchange for CalFresh benefits issued pursuant to Chapter 10 (commencing with Section 18900), Part 6, Division 9 of the Welfare and Institutions Code.

Any violator of this section is guilty of a misdemeanor and shall be punished by a fine of not more than five thousand dollars ($5,000) or by imprisonment in the county jail not exceeding 90 days, or by both that fine and imprisonment.

Amended by Stats 2011 ch 227 (AB 1400),s 15, eff. 1/1/2012.

Section 397 - Unlawful furnishing of intoxicating liquors to drunkard or incompetent or insane person

Every person who sells or furnishes, or causes to be sold or furnished, intoxicating liquors to any habitual or common drunkard, or to any person who has been adjudged legally incompetent or insane by any court of this State and has not been restored to legal capacity, knowing such person to have been so adjudged, is guilty of a misdemeanor.

Amended by Stats. 1953, Ch. 146.

Section 398 - Animal bites

(a) If a person owning or having custody or control of an animal knows, or has reason to know, that the animal bit another person, he or she shall, as soon as is practicable, but no later than 48 hours thereafter, provide the other person with his or her name, address, telephone number, and the name and license tag number of the animal who bit the other person. If the person with custody or control of the animal at the time the bite occurs is a minor, he or she shall instead provide identification or contact information of an adult owner or responsible party. If the animal is required by law to be vaccinated against rabies, the person owning or having custody or control of the animal shall, within 48 hours of the bite, provide the other person with information regarding the status of the animal's vaccinations. Violation of this section is an infraction punishable by a fine of not more than one hundred dollars ($100).

(b) For purposes of this section, it is necessary for the skin of the person to be broken or punctured by the animal for the contact to be classified as a bite.

Amended by Stats 2008 ch 179 (SB 1498),s 178, eff. 1/1/2009.
Added by Stats 2007 ch 136 (AB 670),s 1, eff. 1/1/2008.

Section 399 - Mischievous animal

(a) If any person owning or having custody or control of a mischievous animal, knowing its propensities, willfully suffers it to go at large, or keeps it without ordinary care, and the animal, while so at large, or while not kept with ordinary care, kills any human being who has taken all the precautions that the circumstances permitted, or which a reasonable person would ordinarily take in the same situation, is guilty of a felony.

(b) If any person owning or having custody or control of a mischievous animal, knowing its propensities, willfully suffers it to go at large, or keeps it without ordinary care, and the animal, while so at large, or while not kept with ordinary care, causes serious bodily injury to any human being who has taken all the precautions that the circumstances permitted, or which a reasonable person would ordinarily take in the same situation, is guilty of a misdemeanor or a felony.

Amended by Stats 2001 ch 257 (AB 1709), s 1, eff. 9/5/2001.

Section 399.5 - Custody or control of dog trained to fight, attack, or kill

(a) Any person owning or having custody or control of a dog trained to fight, attack, or kill is guilty of a felony or a misdemeanor, punishable by imprisonment in a county jail not to exceed one year, or imprisonment pursuant to subdivision (h) of Section 1170 for two, three, or four years, or by a fine not exceeding ten thousand dollars ($10,000), or by both the fine and imprisonment, if, as a result of that person's failure to exercise ordinary care, the dog bites a human being, on two separate occasions or on one occasion causing substantial physical injury. No person shall be criminally liable under this section, however, unless he or she knew or reasonably should have known of the vicious or dangerous nature of the dog, or if the victim failed to take all the precautions that a reasonable person would ordinarily take in the same situation.

(b) Following the conviction of an individual for a violation of this section, the court shall hold a hearing to determine whether conditions of the treatment or confinement of the dog or other circumstances existing at the time of the bite or bites have changed so as to remove the danger to other persons presented by the animal. The court, after hearing, may make any order it deems appropriate to prevent the recurrence of such an incident, including, but not limited to, the removal of the animal from the area or its destruction if necessary.

(c) Nothing in this section shall authorize the bringing of an action pursuant to subdivision (a) based on a bite or bites inflicted upon a trespasser, upon a person who has provoked the dog or contributed to his or her own injuries, or by a dog used in military or police work if the bite or bites occurred while the dog was actually performing in that capacity. As used in this subdivision, "provocation" includes, but is not limited to, situations where a dog held on a leash by its owner or custodian reacts in a protective manner to a person or persons who approach the owner or custodian in a threatening manner.

(d) Nothing in this section shall be construed to affect the liability of the owner of a dog under Section 399 or any other provision of law.

(e) This section shall not apply to a veterinarian or an on-duty animal control officer while in the performance of his or her duties, or to a peace officer, as defined in Chapter 4.5 (commencing with Section 830) of Title 3 of Part 2, if he or she is assigned to a canine unit.

Amended by Stats 2011 ch 39 (AB 117),s 68, eff. 6/30/2011.

Amended by Stats 2011 ch 15 (AB 109),s 344, eff. 4/4/2011, but operative no earlier than October 1, 2011, and only upon creation of a community corrections grant program to assist in implementing this act and upon an appropriation to fund the grant program.

EFFECTIVE 1/1/2000. Amended August 30, 1999 (Bill Number: SB 103) (Chapter 265).

Section 401 - Aiding suicide

(a) Any person who deliberately aids, advises, or encourages another to commit suicide is guilty of a felony.

(b) A person whose actions are compliant with the provisions of the End of Life Option Act (Part 1.85 (commencing with Section 443) of Division 1 of the Health and Safety Code) shall not be prosecuted under this section.

Amended by Stats 2018 ch 245 (AB 282),s 1, eff. 1/1/2019.

Section 402 - Impeding emergency personnel; resisting or interfering with efforts of lifeguard

(a)

(1) Every person who goes to the scene of an emergency, or stops at the scene of an emergency, for the purpose of viewing the scene or the activities of police officers, firefighters, emergency medical, or other emergency personnel, or military personnel coping with the emergency in the course of their duties during the time it is necessary for emergency vehicles or those personnel to be at the scene of the emergency or to be moving to or from the scene of the emergency for the purpose of protecting lives or property, unless it is part of the duties of that person's employment to view that scene or those activities, and thereby impedes police officers, firefighters, emergency medical, or other emergency personnel or military personnel, in the performance of their duties in coping with the emergency, is guilty of a misdemeanor.

(2) For purposes of this subdivision, a person shall include a person, regardless of his or her location, who operates or uses an unmanned aerial vehicle, remote piloted aircraft, or drone that is at the scene of an emergency.

(b) Every person who knowingly resists or interferes with the lawful efforts of a lifeguard in the discharge or attempted discharge of an official duty in an emergency situation, when the person knows or reasonably should know that the lifeguard is engaged in the performance of his or her official duty, is guilty of a misdemeanor.

(c) For the purposes of this section, an emergency includes a condition or situation involving injury to persons, damage to property, or peril to the safety of persons or property, which results from a fire, an explosion, an airplane crash, flooding, windstorm damage, a railroad accident, a traffic accident, a powerplant accident, a toxic chemical or biological spill, or any other natural or human-caused event.

Amended by Stats 2016 ch 817 (AB 1680),s 1, eff. 1/1/2017.

Section 402a - Adulterated candy

Every person who adulterates candy by using in its manufacture terra alba or other deleterious substances, or who sells or keeps for sale any candy or candies adulterated with terra alba, or any other deleterious substance, knowing the same to be adulterated, is guilty of a misdemeanor.

Added by renumbering Section 4021/4 by Stats. 1905, Ch. 573.

Section 402b - Unlawful discarding or abandonment of refrigerator or other appliance

Any person who discards or abandons or leaves in any place accessible to children any refrigerator, icebox, deep-freeze locker, clothes dryer, washing machine, or other appliance, having a capacity of one and one-half cubic feet or more, which is no longer in use, and which has not had the door removed or the hinges and such portion of the latch mechanism removed to prevent latching or locking of the door, is guilty of a misdemeanor. Any owner, lessee, or manager who knowingly permits such a refrigerator, icebox, deep-freeze locker, clothes dryer, washing machine, or other appliance to remain on premises under his control without having the door removed or the hinges and such portion of the latch mechanism removed to prevent latching or locking of the door, is guilty of a misdemeanor. Guilt of a violation of this section shall not, in itself, render one guilty of manslaughter, battery or other crime against a person who may suffer death or injury from entrapment in such a refrigerator, icebox, deep-freeze locker, clothes dryer, washing machine, or other appliance.

The provisions of this section shall not apply to any vendor or seller of refrigerators, iceboxes, deep-freeze lockers, clothes dryers, washing machines, or other appliances, who keeps or stores them for sale purposes, if the vendor or seller takes reasonable precautions to effectively secure the door of any such refrigerator, icebox, deep-freeze locker, clothes dryer, washing machine, or other appliance so as to prevent entrance by children small enough to fit therein.

Amended by Stats. 1976, Ch. 1122.

Section 402c - Unlawful sale of refrigerator, icebox, or deep-freeze locker not equipped with lock

On and after January 1, 1970, any person who sells a new refrigerator, icebox, or deep-freeze locker not equipped with an integral lock in this state, having a capacity of two cubic feet or more, which cannot be opened from the inside by the exertion of 15 pounds of force against the latch edge of the closed door is guilty of a misdemeanor.

Added by Stats. 1968, Ch. 232.

Title 11 - OF CRIMES AGAINST THE PUBLIC PEACE

Section 403 - Unlawful disturbance of assembly or meeting

Every person who, without authority of law, willfully disturbs or breaks up any assembly or meeting that is not unlawful in its character, other than an assembly or meeting referred to in Section 302 of the Penal Code or Section 18340 of the Elections Code, is guilty of a misdemeanor.

Amended by Stats. 1994, Ch. 923, Sec. 159. Effective January 1, 1995.

Section 404 - Riot

(a) Any use of force or violence, disturbing the public peace, or any threat to use force or violence, if accompanied by immediate power of execution, by two or more persons acting together, and without authority of law, is a riot.

(b) As used in this section, disturbing the public peace may occur in any place of confinement. Place of confinement means any state prison, county jail, industrial farm, or road camp, or any city jail, industrial farm, or road camp, or any juvenile hall, juvenile camp, juvenile ranch, or juvenile forestry camp.

Amended by Stats. 1995, Ch. 132, Sec. 1. Effective January 1, 1996.

Section 404.6 - Incitement to riot

(a) Every person who with the intent to cause a riot does an act or engages in conduct that urges a riot, or urges others to commit acts of force or violence, or the burning or destroying of property, and at a time and place and under circumstances that produce a clear and present and immediate danger of acts of force or violence or the burning or destroying of property, is guilty of incitement to riot.

(b) Incitement to riot is punishable by a fine not exceeding one thousand dollars ($1,000), or by imprisonment in a county jail not exceeding one year, or by both that fine and imprisonment.

(c) Every person who incites any riot in the state prison or a county jail that results in serious bodily injury, shall be punished by either imprisonment in a county jail for not more than one year, or imprisonment pursuant to subdivision (h) of Section 1170.

(d) The existence of any fact that would bring a person under subdivision (c) shall be alleged in the complaint, information, or indictment and either admitted by the defendant in open court, or found to be true by the jury trying the issue of guilt, by the court where guilt is established by a plea of guilty or nolo contendere, or by trial by the court sitting without a jury.

Amended by Stats 2011 ch 39 (AB 117),s 68, eff. 6/30/2011.

Amended by Stats 2011 ch 15 (AB 109),s 345, eff. 4/4/2011, but operative no earlier than October 1, 2011, and only upon creation of a community corrections grant program to assist in implementing this act and upon an appropriation to fund the grant program.

Section 405 - Participation in riot

Every person who participates in any riot is punishable by a fine not exceeding one thousand dollars, or by imprisonment in a county jail not exceeding one year, or by both such fine and imprisonment.

Amended by Stats. 1957, Ch. 139.

Section 405a - Taking by means of riot

A person who participates in the taking by means of a riot of another person from the lawful custody of a peace officer is guilty of a felony, punishable by imprisonment pursuant to subdivision (h) of Section 1170 for two, three, or four years.

Amended by Stats 2015 ch 47 (SB 629),s 1, eff. 1/1/2016.

Section 405b - [Repealed]

Repealed by Stats 2015 ch 47 (SB 629),s 2, eff. 1/1/2016.

Amended by Stats 2011 ch 39 (AB 117),s 68, eff. 6/30/2011.

Amended by Stats 2011 ch 15 (AB 109),s 346, eff. 4/4/2011, but operative no earlier than October 1, 2011, and only upon creation of a community corrections grant program to assist in implementing this act and upon an appropriation to fund the grant program.

Section 406 - Rout

Whenever two or more persons, assembled and acting together, make any attempt or advance toward the commission of an act which would be a riot if actually committed, such assembly is a rout.

Enacted 1872.

Section 407 - Unlawful assembly

Whenever two or more persons assemble together to do an unlawful act, or do a lawful act in a violent, boisterous, or tumultuous manner, such assembly is an unlawful assembly.

Amended by Stats. 1969, Ch. 365.

Section 408 - Participation in rout or unlawful assembly

Every person who participates in any rout or unlawful assembly is guilty of a misdemeanor.

Enacted 1872.

Section 409 - Remaining present at riot, rout, or unlawful assembly after warned to disperse

Every person remaining present at the place of any riot, rout, or unlawful assembly, after the same has been lawfully warned to disperse, except public officers and persons assisting them in attempting to disperse the same, is guilty of a misdemeanor.

Enacted 1872.

Section 409.3 - Management at scene of accident

Whenever law enforcement officers and emergency medical technicians are at the scene of an accident, management of the scene of the accident shall be vested in the appropriate law enforcement agency, whose representative shall consult with representatives of other response agencies at the scene to ensure that all appropriate resources are properly utilized. However, authority for patient care management at the scene of an accident shall be determined in accordance with Section 1798.6 of the Health and Safety Code. For purposes of this section, "management of the scene of an accident" means the coordination of operations which occur at the location of an accident.

Amended by Stats. 1987, Ch. 1058, Sec. 6.

Section 409.5 - Menace created by calamity

(a) When a menace to the public health or safety is created by a calamity including a flood, storm, fire, earthquake, explosion, accident, or other disaster, officers of the Department of the California Highway Patrol, police departments, marshal's office or sheriff's office, an officer or employee of the Department of Forestry and Fire Protection designated a peace officer by subdivision (g) of Section 830.2, an officer or employee of the Department of Parks and Recreation designated a peace officer by subdivision (f) of Section 830.2, an officer or employee of the Department of Fish and Wildlife designated a peace officer under subdivision (e) of Section 830.2, and a publicly employed full-time lifeguard or publicly employed full-time marine safety officer while acting in a supervisory position in the performance of their official duties, may close the area where the menace exists for the duration of the menace by means of ropes, markers, or guards to all persons not authorized by the lifeguard or officer to enter or remain within the enclosed area. If the calamity creates an immediate menace to the public health, the local health officer may close the area where the menace exists pursuant to the conditions set forth in this section.

(b) Officers of the Department of the California Highway Patrol, police departments, marshal's office or sheriff's office, officers of the Department of Fish and Wildlife designated as peace officers by subdivision (e) of Section 830.2, or officers of the Department of Forestry and Fire Protection designated as peace officers by subdivision (g) of Section 830.2 may close the immediate area surrounding any emergency field command post or any other command post activated for the purpose of abating a calamity enumerated in this section or a riot or other civil disturbance to all unauthorized persons pursuant to the conditions set forth in this section whether or not the field command post or other command post is located near the actual calamity or riot or other civil disturbance.

(c) An unauthorized person who willfully and knowingly enters an area closed pursuant to subdivision (a) or (b) and who willfully remains within the area after receiving notice to evacuate or leave shall be guilty of a misdemeanor.

(d)

(1) This section shall not prevent a duly authorized representative of a news service, newspaper, or radio or television station or network from entering the areas closed pursuant to this section.

(2) This subdivision does not authorize a duly authorized representative of a news service, newspaper, or radio or television station or network to facilitate the entry of a person into, or facilitate the transport of a person within, an area closed, unless for the safety of the person, pursuant to this section if that person is not a duly authorized representative of a news service, newspaper, or radio or television station or network.

(e) This section shall not prevent an individual who holds a valid livestock pass identification document, pursuant to Section 2350 of the Food and Agricultural Code, from entering the areas closed pursuant to this section, unless a peace officer identified in subdivision (a) finds that the disaster is of such a nature that it would be unsafe for the documentholder to enter or that the presence of the documentholder would interfere with disaster response.

Amended by Stats 2023 ch 17 (AB 750),s 1, eff. 1/1/2024.

Amended by Stats 2021 ch 609 (AB 1103),s 3, eff. 1/1/2022.

Amended by Stats. 1996, Ch. 305, Sec. 44. Effective January 1, 1997.

Section 409.6 - Menace created by avalanche

(a) Whenever a menace to the public health or safety is created by an avalanche, officers of the Department of the California Highway Patrol, police departments, or sheriff's offices, any officer or employee of the Department of Forestry and Fire Protection designated a peace officer by subdivision (g) of Section 830.2, and any officer or employee of the Department of Parks and Recreation designated a peace officer by subdivision (f) of Section 830.2, may close the area where the menace exists for the duration thereof by means of ropes, markers, or guards to any and all persons not authorized by that officer to enter or remain within the closed area. If an avalanche creates an immediate menace to the public health, the local health officer may close the area where the menace exists pursuant to the conditions which are set forth above in this section.

(b) Officers of the Department of the California Highway Patrol, police departments, or sheriff's offices, or officers of the Department of Forestry and Fire Protection designated as peace officers by subdivision (g) of Section 830.2, may close the immediate area surrounding any emergency field command post or any other command post activated for the purpose of abating hazardous conditions created by an avalanche to any and all unauthorized persons pursuant to the conditions which are set forth in this section whether or not that field command post or other command post is located near the avalanche.

(c) Any unauthorized person who willfully and knowingly enters an area closed pursuant to subdivision (a) or (b) and who willfully remains within that area, or any unauthorized person who willfully remains within an area closed pursuant to subdivision (a) or (b), after receiving notice to evacuate or leave from a peace officer named in subdivision (a) or (b), shall be guilty of a misdemeanor. If necessary, a peace officer named in subdivision (a) or (b) may use reasonable force to remove from the closed area any unauthorized person who willfully remains within that area after receiving notice to evacuate or leave.

(d) Nothing in this section shall prevent a duly authorized representative of any news service, newspaper, or radio or television station or network from entering the areas closed pursuant to this section.

Amended by Stats. 1996, Ch. 305, Sec. 45. Effective January 1, 1997.

Section 409.7 - Public peace; media access permitted

(a) If peace officers, as defined in Chapter 4.5 (commencing with Section 830) of Title 3 of Part 2, close the immediate area surrounding any emergency field command post or any other command post, or establish a police line, or rolling closure at a demonstration, march, protest, or rally where individuals are engaged in activity that is protected pursuant to the First Amendment to the United States Constitution or Article I of the California Constitution, the following requirements shall apply:

    (1) A duly authorized representative of any news service, online news service, newspaper, or radio or television station or network may enter the closed areas described in this section.

    (2) A peace officer or other law enforcement officer shall not intentionally assault, interfere with, or obstruct the duly authorized representative of any news service, online news service, newspaper, or radio or television station or network who is gathering, receiving, or processing information for communication to the public.

    (3) A duly authorized representative of any news service, online news service, newspaper, or radio or television station or network that is in a closed area described in this section shall not be cited for the failure to disperse, a violation of a curfew, or a violation of paragraph (1) of subdivision (a) of Section 148, for gathering, receiving, or processing information. If the duly authorized representative is detained by a peace officer or other law enforcement officer, that representative shall be permitted to contact a supervisory officer immediately for the purpose of challenging the detention, unless circumstances make it impossible to do so.

(b) This section does not prevent a law enforcement officer from enforcing other applicable laws if the person is engaged in activity that is unlawful.

(c) This section does not impose, and shall not be used as the basis for, criminal liability.

Added by Stats 2021 ch 759 (SB 98),s 2, eff. 1/1/2022.

Section 410 - Neglect to proceed to place of assembly

If a magistrate or officer, having notice of an unlawful or riotous assembly, mentioned in this Chapter, neglects to proceed to the place of assembly, or as near thereto as he can with safety, and to exercise the authority with which he is invested for suppressing the same and arresting the offenders, he is guilty of a misdemeanor.

Enacted 1872.

Section 412 - Unlawful acts related to pugilistic contest or fight

Any person, who, within this state, engages in, or instigates, aids, encourages, or does any act to further, a pugilistic contest, or fight, or ring or prize fight, or sparring or boxing exhibition, taking or to take place either within or without this state, between two or more persons, with or without gloves, for any price, reward or compensation, directly or indirectly, or who goes into training preparatory to such pugilistic contest, or fight, or ring or prize fight, or sparring or boxing exhibition, or acts as aider, abettor, backer, umpire, referee, trainer, second, surgeon, or assistant, at such pugilistic contest, or fight, or ring or prize fight, or sparring or boxing exhibition, or who sends or publishes a challenge or acceptance of a challenge, or who knowingly carries or delivers such challenge or acceptance, or who gives or takes or receives any tickets, tokens, prize, money, or thing of value, from any person or persons, for the purpose of seeing or witnessing any such pugilistic contest, or fight, or ring or prize fight, or sparring or boxing exhibition, or who, being the owner, lessee, agent, or occupant of any vessel, building, hotel, room, enclosure or ground, or any part thereof, whether for gain, hire, reward or gratuitously or otherwise, permits the same to be used or occupied for such a pugilistic contest, or fight, or ring or prize fight, or sparring or boxing exhibition, or who lays, makes, offers or accepts, a bet or bets, or wager or wagers, upon the result or any feature of any pugilistic contest, or fight, or ring or prize fight, or sparring or boxing exhibition, or acts as stakeholder of any such bet or bets, or wager or wagers, shall be guilty of a misdemeanor, and upon conviction thereof, shall be fined not less than one hundred dollars nor more than one thousand dollars and be imprisoned in the county jail not less than thirty days nor exceeding one year; provided, however, that amateur boxing exhibitions may be held within this state, of a limited number of rounds, not exceeding four of the duration of three minutes each; the interval between each round shall be one minute, and the contestants weighing one hundred and forty-five pounds or over shall wear gloves of not less than eight ounces each in weight, and contestants weighing under one hundred and forty-five pounds may wear gloves of not less than six ounces each in weight. All gloves used by contestants in such amateur boxing exhibitions shall be so constructed, as that the soft padding between the outside coverings shall be evenly distributed over the back of said gloves and cover the knuckles and back of the hands. And no bandages of any kind shall be used on the hands or arms of the contestants. For the purpose of this statute an amateur boxing exhibition shall be and is hereby defined as one in which no contestant has received or shall receive in any form, directly or indirectly, any money, prize, reward or compensation either for the expenses of training for such contest or for taking part therein, except as herein expressly provided. Nor shall any person appear as contestant in such amateur exhibition who prior thereto has received any compensation or reward in any form for displaying, exercising or giving any example of his skill in or knowledge of athletic exercises, or for rendering services of any kind to any athletic organization or to any person or persons as trainer, coach, instructor or otherwise, or who shall have been employed in any manner professionally by reason of his athletic skill or knowledge; provided, however, that a medal or trophy may be awarded to each contestant in such amateur boxing exhibitions, not to exceed in value the sum of $35.00 each, which such medal or trophy must have engraved thereon the name of the winner and the date of the event; but no portion of any admission fee or fees charged or received for any amateur boxing exhibition shall be paid or given to any contestant in such amateur boxing exhibition, either directly or indirectly, nor shall any gift be given to or received by such contestants for participating in such boxing exhibition, except said medal or trophy. At every amateur boxing exhibition held in this state and permitted by this section of the Penal Code, any sheriff, constable, marshal, policeman or other peace officer of the city, county or other political subdivision, where such exhibition is being held, shall have the right to, and it is hereby declared to be his duty to stop such exhibition, whenever it shall appear to him that the contestants are so unevenly matched or for any other reason, the said contestants have been, or either of them, has been seriously injured or there is danger that said contestants, or either of them, will be seriously injured if such contest continues, and he may call to his assistance in enforcing his order to stop said exhibition, as many peace officers or male citizens of the state as may be necessary for that purpose. Provided, further, that any contestant who shall continue to participate in such exhibition after an order to stop such exhibition shall have been given by such peace officer, or who shall violate any of the regulations herein prescribed, for governing amateur boxing exhibitions, shall be deemed guilty of violating this section of the Penal Code and subject to the punishment herein provided.

Nothing in this section contained shall be construed to prevent any county, city and county, or incorporated city or town from prohibiting, by ordinance, the holding or conducting of any boxing exhibition, or any person from engaging in any such boxing exhibition therein.

Amended November 3, 1914, by initiative Proposition 20.

Section 413 - Spectator at fight or contention

Every person wilfully present as spectator at any fight or contention prohibited in the preceding section, is guilty of a misdemeanor.

An information may be laid before any of the magistrates mentioned in section eight hundred and eight of this code, that a person has taken steps toward promoting or participating in a contemplated pugilistic contest, or fight, or ring or prize fight, or sparring or boxing exhibition, prohibited under the provision of section four hundred and twelve of this code, or is about to commit an offense under said section four hundred and twelve. When said information is laid before said magistrate, he must examine, on oath, the informer, and any witness or witnesses he may produce, and must take their depositions in writing and cause them to be subscribed by the parties making them. If it appears from the deposition that there is just reason to fear the commission of the offense contemplated by the person so informed against, the magistrate must issue a warrant directed generally to the sheriff of the county, or any constable, marshal, or policeman in the state, reciting the substance of the information and commanding the officer forthwith to arrest the person informed against and bring him before the magistrate. When the person informed against is brought before the magistrate, if the charge be controverted, the magistrate must take testimony in relation thereto. The evidence must be reduced to writing and subscribed by the witnesses. If it appears there is no just reason to fear the commission of the offense alleged to have been contemplated, the person complained against must be discharged. If, however, there is just reason to fear the commission of the offense, the person complained of must be required to enter into an undertaking in such sum, not less than three thousand dollars, as the magistrate may direct, with one or more sufficient sureties, conditioned that such person will not, for a period of one year thereafter, commit any such contemplated offense.

Amended November 3, 1914, by initiative Proposition 20.

Section 414 - Leaving state with intent to evade

Every person who leaves this state with intent to evade any of the provisions of Section 412 or 413, and to commit any act out of this state such as is prohibited by them, and who does any act which would be punishable under these provisions if committed within this state, is punishable in the same manner as he or she would have been in case such act had been committed within this state.

Amended by Stats. 1987, Ch. 828, Sec. 27.

Section 414a - Disqualification from testifying

No person, otherwise competent as a witness, is disqualified from testifying as such, concerning any offense under this act, on the ground that such testimony may incriminate himself, but no prosecution can afterwards be had against him for any offense concerning which he testified. The provisions of section 1111 of the Penal Code of this state are not applicable to any prosecutions brought under the provisions of this act.

Added November 3, 1914, by initiative Proposition 20.

Section 415 - Punishment for unlawful fighting; disturbance by noise, or use of offensive words

Any of the following persons shall be punished by imprisonment in the county jail for a period of not more than 90 days, a fine of not more than four hundred dollars ($400), or both such imprisonment and fine:

(1) Any person who unlawfully fights in a public place or challenges another person in a public place to fight.

(2) Any person who maliciously and willfully disturbs another person by loud and unreasonable noise.

(3) Any person who uses offensive words in a public place which are inherently likely to provoke an immediate violent reaction.

Amended by Stats. 1983, Ch. 1092, Sec. 283. Effective September 27, 1983. Operative January 1, 1984, by Sec. 427 of Ch. 1092.

Section 415.5 - Unlawful fighting, disturbance by noise, or use of offensive words on school property

(a) Any person who (1) unlawfully fights within any building or upon the grounds of any school, community college, university, or state university or challenges another person within any building or upon the grounds to fight, or (2) maliciously and willfully disturbs another person within any of these buildings or upon the grounds by loud and unreasonable noise, or (3) uses offensive words within any of these buildings or upon the grounds which are inherently likely to provoke an immediate violent reaction is guilty of a misdemeanor punishable by a fine not exceeding four hundred dollars ($400) or by imprisonment in the county jail for a period of not more than 90 days, or both.

(b) If the defendant has been previously convicted once of a violation of this section or of any offense defined in Chapter 1 (commencing with Section 626) of Title 15 of Part 1, the defendant shall be sentenced to imprisonment in the county jail for a period of not less than 10 days or more than six months, or by both that imprisonment and a fine of not exceeding one thousand dollars ($1,000), and shall not be released on probation, parole, or any other basis until not less than 10 days of imprisonment has been served.

(c) If the defendant has been previously convicted two or more times of a violation of this section or of any offense defined in Chapter 1 (commencing with Section 626) of Title 15 of Part 1, the defendant shall be sentenced to imprisonment in the county jail for a period of not less than 90 days or more than six months, or by both that imprisonment and a fine of not exceeding one thousand dollars ($1,000), and shall not be released on probation, parole, or any other basis until not less than 90 days of imprisonment has been served.

(d) For the purpose of determining the penalty to be imposed pursuant to this section, the court may consider a written report from the Department of Justice containing information from its records showing prior convictions; and the communication is prima facie evidence of such convictions, if the defendant admits them, regardless of whether or not the complaint commencing the proceedings has alleged prior convictions.

(e) As used in this section "state university," "university," "community college," and "school" have the same meaning as these terms are given in Section 626.

(f) This section shall not apply to any person who is a registered student of the school, or to any person who is engaged in any otherwise lawful employee concerted activity.

Amended by Stats. 1988, Ch. 1113, Sec. 3.

Section 416 - Unlawful assembly to disturb peace or commit unlawful act; failure to disperse

(a) If two or more persons assemble for the purpose of disturbing the public peace, or committing any unlawful act, and do not disperse on being desired or commanded so to do by a public officer, the persons so offending are severally guilty of a misdemeanor.

(b) Any person who, as a result of violating subdivision (a), personally causes damage to real or personal property, which is either publicly or privately owned, shall make restitution for the damage he or she caused, including, but not limited to, the costs of cleaning up, repairing, replacing, or restoring the property. Any restitution required to be paid pursuant to this subdivision shall be paid directly to the victim. If the court determines that the defendant is unable to pay restitution, the court shall order the defendant to perform community service, as the court deems appropriate, in lieu of the direct restitution payment.

(c) This section shall not preclude the court from imposing restitution in the form of a penalty assessment pursuant to Section 1464 if the court, in its discretion, deems that additional restitution appropriate.

(d) The burden of proof on the issue of whether any defendant or defendants personally caused any property damage shall rest with the prosecuting agency or claimant. In no event shall the burden of proof on this issue shift to the defendant or any of several defendants to prove that he or she was not responsible for the property damage.

Amended by Stats. 1989, Ch. 572, Sec. 1.

Section 417 - Unlawful exhibition of deadly weapon or firearm

(a)

   (1) Every person who, except in self-defense, in the presence of any other person, draws or exhibits any deadly weapon whatsoever, other than a firearm, in a rude, angry, or threatening manner, or who in any manner, unlawfully uses a deadly weapon other than a firearm in any fight or quarrel is guilty of a misdemeanor, punishable by imprisonment in a county jail for not less than 30 days.

   (2) Every person who, except in self-defense, in the presence of any other person, draws or exhibits any firearm, whether loaded or unloaded, in a rude, angry, or threatening manner, or who in any manner, unlawfully uses a firearm in any fight or quarrel is punishable as follows:

      (A) If the violation occurs in a public place and the firearm is a pistol, revolver, or other firearm capable of being concealed upon the person, by imprisonment in a county jail for not less than three months and not more than one year, by a fine not to exceed one thousand dollars ($1,000), or by both that fine and imprisonment.

      (B) In all cases other than that set forth in subparagraph (A), a misdemeanor, punishable by imprisonment in a county jail for not less than three months.

(b) Every person who, except in self-defense, in the presence of any other person, draws or exhibits any loaded firearm in a rude, angry, or threatening manner, or who, in any manner, unlawfully uses any loaded firearm in any fight or quarrel upon the grounds of any day care center, as defined in Section 1596.76 of the Health and Safety Code, or any facility where programs, including day care programs or recreational programs, are being conducted for persons under 18 years of age, including programs conducted by a nonprofit organization, during the hours in which the center or facility is open for use, shall be punished by imprisonment in the state prison for 16 months, or two or three years, or by imprisonment in a county jail for not less than three months, nor more than one year.

(c) Every person who, in the immediate presence of a peace officer, draws or exhibits any firearm, whether loaded or unloaded, in a rude, angry, or threatening manner, and who knows, or reasonably should know, by the officer's uniformed appearance or other action of identification by the officer, that he or she is a peace officer engaged in the performance of his or her duties, and that peace officer is engaged in the performance of his or her duties, shall be punished by imprisonment in a county jail for not less than nine months and not to exceed one year, or in the state prison for 16 months, or two or three years.

(d) Except where a different penalty applies, every person who violates this section when the other person is in the process of cleaning up graffiti or vandalism is guilty of a misdemeanor, punishable by imprisonment in a county jail for not less than three months nor more than one year.

(e) As used in this section, "peace officer" means any person designated as a peace officer pursuant to Chapter 4.5 (commencing with Section 830) of Title 3 of Part 2.

(f) As used in this section, "public place" means any of the following:

   (1) A public place in an incorporated city.

   (2) A public street in an incorporated city.

   (3) A public street in an unincorporated area.

Amended by Stats 2011 ch 39 (AB 117),s 68, eff. 6/30/2011.

Amended by Stats 2011 ch 15 (AB 109),s 347, eff. 4/4/2011, but operative no earlier than October 1, 2011, and only upon creation of a community corrections grant program to assist in implementing this act and upon an appropriation to fund the grant program.

Amended by Stats 2000 ch 478 (AB 2523), s 1, eff. 1/1/2001.

Section 417.2 - [Repealed]

Repealed by Stats 2004 ch 607 (SB 1858), s 2, eff. 9/20/2004.

Amended by Stats 2003 ch 246 (AB 1455), s 1, eff. 1/1/2004.

Amended by Stats 2001 ch 159 (SB 662), s 162, eff. 1/1/2002.

Amended by Stats 2000 ch 275 (AB 2053), s 1, eff. 1/1/2001.

Section 417.25 - Unlawful aiming or pointing of laser scope or pointer

(a) Every person who, except in self-defense, aims or points a laser scope, as defined in subdivision (b), or a laser pointer, as defined in subdivision (c), at another person in a threatening manner with the specific intent to cause a reasonable person fear of bodily harm is guilty of a misdemeanor, punishable by imprisonment in a county jail for up to 30 days. For purposes of this section, the laser scope need not be attached to a firearm.

(b) As used in this section, "laser scope" means a portable battery-powered device capable of being attached to a firearm and capable of projecting a laser light on objects at a distance.

(c) As used in this section, "laser pointer" means any hand held laser beam device or demonstration laser product that emits a single point of light amplified by the stimulated emission of radiation that is visible to the human eye.

EFFECTIVE 1/1/2000. Amended October 10, 1999 (Bill Number: AB 293) (Chapter 621).

Section 417.26 - Unlawful aiming or pointing of laser scope or pointer at peace officer

(a) Any person who aims or points a laser scope as defined in subdivision (b) of Section 417.25, or a laser pointer, as defined in subdivision (c) of that section, at a peace officer with the specific intent to cause the officer apprehension or fear of bodily harm and who knows or reasonably should know that the person at whom he or she is aiming or pointing is a peace officer, is guilty of a misdemeanor punishable by imprisonment in a county jail for a term not exceeding six months.

(b) Any person who commits a second or subsequent violation of subdivision (a) shall be punished by imprisonment in a county jail for not more than one year.

EFFECTIVE 1/1/2000. Added 9/21/1999 (Bill Number: AB 221) (Chapter 438).

Section 417.27 - Unlawful sale or possession of laser pointer to person 17 years or younger; unlawful directing of beam from laser

(a) No person, corporation, firm, or business entity of any kind shall knowingly sell a laser pointer to a person 17 years of age or younger, unless he or she is accompanied and supervised by a parent, legal guardian, or any other adult 18 years of age or older.

(b) No student shall possess a laser pointer on any elementary or secondary school premises unless possession of a laser pointer on the elementary or secondary school premises is for a valid instructional or other school-related purpose, including employment.

(c) No person shall direct the beam from a laser pointer directly or indirectly into the eye or eyes of another person or into a moving vehicle with the intent to harass or annoy the other person or the occupants of the moving vehicle.

(d) No person shall direct the beam from a laser pointer directly or indirectly into the eye or eyes of a guide dog, signal dog, service dog, or dog being used by a peace officer with the intent to harass or annoy the animal.

(e) A violation of subdivision (a), (b), (c), or (d) shall be an infraction that is punished by either a fine of fifty dollars ($50) or four hours of community service, and a second or subsequent violation of any of these subdivisions shall be an infraction that is punished by either a fine of one hundred dollars ($100) or eight hours of community service.

(f) As used in this section, "laser pointer" has the same meaning as set forth in subdivision (c) of Section 417.25.

(g) As used in this section, "guide dog," "signal dog," and "service dog," respectively, have the same meaning as set forth in subdivisions (d), (e), and (f) of Section 365.5.

Added 10/10/1999 (Bill Number: AB 293) (Chapter 621).

Section 417.3 - Unlawful drawing or exhibition of firearm in presence of person who is occupant in motor vehicle

Every person who, except in self-defense, in the presence of any other person who is an occupant of a motor vehicle proceeding on a public street or highway, draws or exhibits any firearm, whether loaded or unloaded, in a threatening manner against another person in such a way as to cause a reasonable person apprehension or fear of bodily harm is guilty of a felony punishable by imprisonment pursuant to subdivision (h) of Section 1170 for 16 months or two or three years or by imprisonment for 16 months or two or three years and a three thousand dollar ($3,000) fine.

Nothing in this section shall preclude or prohibit prosecution under any other statute.

Amended by Stats 2011 ch 39 (AB 117),s 68, eff. 6/30/2011.

Amended by Stats 2011 ch 15 (AB 109),s 348, eff. 4/4/2011, but operative no earlier than October 1, 2011, and only upon creation of a community corrections grant program to assist in implementing this act and upon an appropriation to fund the grant program.

Section 417.4 - Unlawful drawing or exhibition of imitation firearm

Every person who, except in self-defense, draws or exhibits an imitation firearm, as defined in subdivision (a) of Section 16700, in a threatening manner against another in such a way as to cause a reasonable person apprehension or fear of bodily harm is guilty of a misdemeanor punishable by imprisonment in a county jail for a term of not less than 30 days.

Amended by Stats 2010 ch 178 (SB 1115),s 56, eff. 1/1/2011, op. 1/1/2012.

Amended by Stats 2004 ch 607 (SB 1858), s 3, eff. 9/20/2004.

Section 417.6 - Serious bodily injury inflicted by person drawing or exhibiting firearm or deadly weapon

(a) If, in the commission of a violation of Section 417 or 417.8, serious bodily injury is intentionally inflicted by the person drawing or exhibiting the firearm or deadly weapon, the offense shall be punished by imprisonment in the county jail not exceeding one year or by imprisonment in state prison.

(b) As used in this section, "serious bodily injury" means a serious impairment of physical condition, including, but not limited to, the following: loss of consciousness; concussion; bone fracture; protracted loss or impairment of function of any bodily member or organ; a wound requiring extensive suturing; and serious disfigurement.

(c) When a person is convicted of a violation of Section 417 or 417.8 and the deadly weapon or firearm used by the person is owned by that person, the court shall order that the weapon or firearm be deemed a nuisance and disposed of in the manner provided by Sections 18000 and 18005.

Amended by Stats 2012 ch 43 (SB 1023),s 18, eff. 6/27/2012.

Amended by Stats 2011 ch 39 (AB 117),s 68, eff. 6/30/2011.

Amended by Stats 2011 ch 15 (AB 109),s 350, eff. 4/4/2011, but operative no earlier than October 1, 2011, and only upon creation of a community corrections grant program to assist in implementing this act and upon an appropriation to fund the grant program.

Amended by Stats 2011 ch 15 (AB 109),s 349, eff. 4/4/2011, but operative no earlier than October 1, 2011, and only upon creation of a community corrections grant program to assist in implementing this act and upon an appropriation to fund the grant program.

Amended by Stats 2010 ch 178 (SB 1115),s 57, eff. 1/1/2011, op. 1/1/2012.

Amended by Stats 2000 ch 478 (AB 2523), s 2, eff. 1/1/2001.

Section 417.8 - Unlawful drawing or exhibiting firearm to resist or prevent arrest

Every person who draws or exhibits any firearm, whether loaded or unloaded, or other deadly weapon, with the intent to resist or prevent the arrest or detention of himself or another by a peace officer shall be imprisoned in the state prison for two, three, or four years.

Added by Stats. 1982, Ch. 142, Sec. 2.5.

Section 418 - Using force or violence to enter upon lands of another

Every person using or procuring, encouraging or assisting another to use, any force or violence in entering upon or detaining any lands or other possessions of another, except in the cases and in the manner allowed by law, is guilty of a misdemeanor.

Enacted 1872.

Section 419 - Unlawful return to lands

Every person who has been removed from any lands by process of law, or who has removed from any lands pursuant to the lawful adjudication or direction of any Court, tribunal, or officer, and who afterwards unlawfully returns to settle, reside upon, or take possession of such lands, is guilty of a misdemeanor.

Enacted 1872.

Section 420 - Unlawful obstruction from entering public land

Every person who unlawfully prevents, hinders, or obstructs any person from peaceably entering upon or establishing a settlement or residence on any tract of public land of the United States within the State of California, subject to settlement or entry under any of the public land laws of the United States; or who unlawfully hinders, prevents, or obstructs free passage over or through the public lands of the United States within the State of California, for the purpose of entry, settlement, or residence, as aforesaid, is guilty of a misdemeanor.

Added by Stats. 1905, Ch. 516.

Section 420.1 - Unlawful obstruction from entering, passing over, or leaving land

Anyone who willfully and knowingly prevents, hinders, or obstructs any person from entering, passing over, or leaving land in which that person enjoys, either personally or as an agent, guest, licensee, successor-in-interest, or contractor, a right to enter, use, cross, or inspect the property pursuant to an easement, covenant, license, profit, or other interest in the land, is guilty of an infraction punishable by a fine not to exceed five hundred dollars ($500), provided that the interest to be exercised has been duly recorded with the county recorder's office. This section shall not apply to the following persons:

(1) any person engaged in lawful labor union activities that are permitted to be carried out by state or federal law; or

(2) any person who is engaging in activities protected by the California Constitution or the United States Constitution.

Added by Stats. 1998, Ch. 271, Sec. 1. Effective January 1, 1999.

Title 11.5 - CRIMINAL THREATS

Section 422 - Unlawful threat to commit crime

(a) Any person who willfully threatens to commit a crime which will result in death or great bodily injury to another person, with the specific intent that the statement, made verbally, in writing, or by means of an electronic communication device, is to be taken as a threat, even if there is no intent of actually carrying it out, which, on its face and under the circumstances in which it is made, is so unequivocal, unconditional, immediate, and specific as to convey to the person threatened, a gravity of purpose and an immediate prospect of execution of the threat, and thereby causes that person reasonably to be in sustained fear for his or her own safety or for his or her immediate family's safety, shall be punished by imprisonment in the county jail not to exceed one year, or by imprisonment in the state prison.

(b) For purposes of this section, "immediate family" means any spouse, whether by marriage or not, parent, child, any person related by consanguinity or affinity within the second degree, or any other person who regularly resides in the household, or who, within the prior six months, regularly resided in the household.

(c) "Electronic communication device" includes, but is not limited to, telephones, cellular telephones, computers, video recorders, fax machines, or pagers. "Electronic communication" has the same meaning as the term defined in Subsection 12 of Section 2510 of Title 18 of the United States Code.

Amended by Stats 2011 ch 39 (AB 117),s 68, eff. 6/30/2011.

Amended by Stats 2011 ch 39 (AB 117),s 16, eff. 6/30/2011.

Amended by Stats 2011 ch 15 (AB 109),s 351, eff. 4/4/2011, but operative no earlier than October 1, 2011, and only upon creation of a community corrections grant program to assist in implementing this act and upon an appropriation to fund the grant program.

Section 422.1 - Restitution

Every person who is convicted of a felony violation of Section 148.1 or 11418.1, under circumstances in which the defendant knew the underlying report was false, in addition to being ordered to comply with all other applicable restitution requirements and fine and fee provisions, shall also be ordered to pay full restitution to each of the following:

(a) Any person, corporation, business trust, estate, trust, partnership, association, joint venture, government, governmental subdivision, agency or instrumentality, or any other legal or commercial entity for any personnel, equipment, material, or clean up costs, and for any property damage, caused by the violation directly, or stemming from any emergency response to the violation or its aftermath.

(b) Any public or private entity incurring any costs for actual emergency response, for all costs of that response and for any clean up costs, including any overtime paid to uninvolved personnel made necessary by the allocation of resources to the emergency response and clean up.

(c) Restitution for the costs of response by a government entity under this section shall be determined in a hearing separate from the determination of guilt. The court shall order restitution in an amount no greater than the reasonable costs of the response. The burden shall be on the people to prove the reasonable costs of the response.

(d) In determining the restitution for the costs of response by a government entity, the court shall consider the amount of restitution to be paid to the direct victim, as defined in subdivision (k) of Section 1202.4.

Added by Stats 2002 ch 281 (SB 1267), s 1, eff. 1/1/2003.

Section 422.4 - Unlawful violence or threat of violence against academic researcher

(a) Any person who publishes information describing or depicting an academic researcher or his or her immediate family member, or the location or locations where an academic researcher or an immediate family member of an academic researcher may be found, with the intent that another person imminently use the information to commit a crime involving violence or a threat of violence against an academic researcher or his or her immediate family member, and the information is likely to produce the imminent commission of such a crime, is guilty of a misdemeanor, punishable by imprisonment in a county jail for not more than one year, a fine of not more than one thousand dollars ($1,000), or by both a fine and imprisonment.

(b) For the purposes of this section, all of the following apply:

(1) "Publishes" means making the information available to another person through any medium, including, but not limited to, the Internet, the World Wide Web, or e-mail.

(2) "Academic researcher" has the same meaning as in Section 602.12.

(3) "Immediate family" means any spouse, whether by marriage or not, domestic partner, parent, child, any person related by consanguinity or affinity within the second degree, or any other person who regularly resides in the household, or who, within the prior six months, regularly resided in the household.

(4) "Information" includes, but is not limited to, an image, film, filmstrip, photograph, negative, slide, photocopy, videotape, video laser disc, or any other computer-generated image.

(c) Any academic researcher about whom information is published in violation of subdivision (a) may seek a preliminary injunction enjoining any further publication of that information. This subdivision shall not apply to a person or entity protected pursuant to Section 1070 of the Evidence Code.

(d) This section shall not apply to any person who is lawfully engaged in labor union activities that are protected under state or federal law.

(e) This section shall not preclude prosecution under any other provision of law.

Added by Stats 2008 ch 492 (AB 2296),s 3, eff. 9/28/2008.

Title 11.6 - CIVIL RIGHTS

Chapter 1 - DEFINITIONS

Section 422.55 - "Hate crime" defined

For purposes of this title, and for purposes of all other state law unless an explicit provision of law or the context clearly requires a different meaning, the following shall apply:

(a) "Hate crime" means a criminal act committed, in whole or in part, because of one or more of the following actual or perceived characteristics of the victim:

(1) Disability.

(2) Gender.

(3) Nationality.

(4) Race or ethnicity.

(5) Religion.

(6) Sexual orientation.

(7) Association with a person or group with one or more of these actual or perceived characteristics.

(b) "Hate crime" includes, but is not limited to, a violation of Section 422.6.

Added by Stats 2004 ch 700 (SB 1234), s 6, eff. 1/1/2005.

Section 422.56 - Definitions

For purposes of this title, the following definitions shall apply:

(a) "Association with a person or group with one or more of these actual or perceived characteristics" includes advocacy for, identification with, or being on the premises owned or rented by, or adjacent to, any of the following: a community center, educational facility, family, individual, office, meeting hall, place of worship, private institution, public agency, library, or other entity, group, or person that has, or is identified with people who have, one or more of the characteristics listed in the definition of "hate crime" under paragraphs (1) to (6), inclusive, of subdivision (a) of Section 422.55.

(b) "Disability" includes mental disability and physical disability, as defined in Section 12926 of the Government Code, regardless of whether those disabilities are temporary, permanent, congenital, or acquired by heredity, accident, injury, advanced age, or illness. This definition is declaratory of existing law.

(c) "Gender" means sex, and includes a person's gender identity and gender expression. "Gender expression" means a person's gender-related appearance and behavior regardless of whether it is stereotypically associated with the person's assigned sex at birth.

(d) "In whole or in part because of" means that the bias motivation must be a cause in fact of the offense, whether or not other causes also exist. When multiple concurrent motives exist, the prohibited bias must be a substantial factor in bringing about the particular result. There is no requirement that the bias be a main factor, or that the crime would not have been committed but for the actual or perceived characteristic. This subdivision does not constitute a change in, but is declaratory of, existing law under In re M.S. (1995) 10 Cal.4th 698 and People v. Superior Court (Aishman) (1995) 10 Cal.4th 735.

(e) "Nationality" means country of origin, immigration status, including citizenship, and national origin. This definition is declaratory of existing law.

(f) "Race or ethnicity" includes ancestry, color, and ethnic background.

(g) "Religion" includes all aspects of religious belief, observance, and practice and includes agnosticism and atheism.

(h) "Sexual orientation" means heterosexuality, homosexuality, or bisexuality.

(i) "Victim" includes, but is not limited to, a community center, educational facility, entity, family, group, individual, office, meeting hall, person, place of worship, private institution, public agency, library, or other victim or intended victim of the offense.

Amended by Stats 2021 ch 295 (AB 600),s 1, eff. 1/1/2022.

Amended by Stats 2018 ch 26 (AB 1985),s 2, eff. 1/1/2019.

Amended by Stats 2011 ch 719 (AB 887),s 31, eff. 1/1/2012.

Added by Stats 2004 ch 700 (SB 1234), s 6, eff. 1/1/2005.

Section 422.57 - "Gender" defined

For purposes this code, unless an explicit provision of law or the context clearly requires a different meaning, "gender" has the same meaning as in Section 422.56.

Added by Stats 2004 ch 700 (SB 1234), s 6, eff. 1/1/2005.

Chapter 2 - CRIMES AND PENALTIES

Section 422.6 - Hate crime

(a) No person, whether or not acting under color of law, shall by force or threat of force, willfully injure, intimidate, interfere with, oppress, or threaten any other person in the free exercise or enjoyment of any right or privilege secured to him or her by the Constitution or laws of this state or by the Constitution or laws of the United States in whole or in part because of one or more of the actual or perceived characteristics of the victim listed in subdivision (a) of Section 422.55.

(b) No person, whether or not acting under color of law, shall knowingly deface, damage, or destroy the real or personal property of any other person for the purpose of intimidating or interfering with the free exercise or enjoyment of any right or privilege secured to the other person by the Constitution or laws of this state or by the Constitution or laws of the United States, in whole or in part because of one or more of the actual or perceived characteristics of the victim listed in subdivision (a) of Section 422.55.

(c) Any person convicted of violating subdivision (a) or (b) shall be punished by imprisonment in a county jail not to exceed one year, or by a fine not to exceed five thousand dollars ($5,000), or by both the above imprisonment and fine, and the court shall order the defendant to perform a minimum of community service, not to exceed 400 hours, to be performed over a period not to exceed 350 days, during a time other than his or her hours of employment or school attendance. However, no person may be convicted of violating subdivision (a) based upon speech alone, except upon a showing that the speech itself threatened violence against a specific person or group of persons and that the defendant had the apparent ability to carry out the threat.

(d) Conduct that violates this and any other provision of law, including, but not limited to, an offense described in Article 4.5 (commencing with Section 11410) of Chapter 3 of Title 1 of Part 4, may be charged under all applicable provisions. However, an act or omission punishable in different ways by this section and other provisions of law shall not be punished under more than one provision, and the penalty to be imposed shall be determined as set forth in Section 654.

Amended by Stats 2004 ch 700 (SB 1234), s 8, eff. 1/1/2005.

Amended by Stats 2004 ch 115 (AB 1920), s 1, eff. 1/1/2005.

Section 422.7 - Punishment of hate crime

Except in the case of a person punished under Section 422.6, any hate crime that is not made punishable by imprisonment in the state prison shall be punishable by imprisonment in a county jail not to exceed one year, or by imprisonment pursuant to subdivision (h) of Section 1170, or by a fine not to exceed ten thousand dollars ($10,000), or by both that imprisonment and fine, if the crime is committed against the person or property of another for the purpose of intimidating or interfering with that other person's free exercise or enjoyment of any right secured to him or her by the Constitution or laws of this state or by the Constitution or laws of the United States under any of the following circumstances, which shall be charged in the accusatory pleading:

(a) The crime against the person of another either includes the present ability to commit a violent injury or causes actual physical injury.

(b) The crime against property causes damage in excess of nine hundred fifty dollars ($950).

(c) The person charged with a crime under this section has been convicted previously of a violation of subdivision (a) or (b) of Section 422.6, or has been convicted previously of a conspiracy to commit a crime described in subdivision (a) or (b) of Section 422.6.

Amended by Stats 2011 ch 39 (AB 117),s 68, eff. 6/30/2011.

Amended by Stats 2011 ch 15 (AB 109),s 352, eff. 4/4/2011, but operative no earlier than October 1, 2011, and only upon creation of a community corrections grant program to assist in implementing this act and upon an appropriation to fund the grant program.

Amended by Stats 2009 ch 28 (SB X3-18),s 10, eff. 1/1/2010.

Amended by Stats 2004 ch 780 (AB 2288), s 1.1, eff. 1/1/2005.

Amended by Stats 2004 ch 700 (SB 1234), s 9, eff. 1/1/2005.

Section 422.75 - Punishment of felony that is hate crime

(a) Except in the case of a person punished under Section 422.7, a person who commits a felony that is a hate crime or attempts to commit a felony that is a hate crime, shall receive an additional term of one, two, or three years in the state prison, at the court's discretion.

(b) Except in the case of a person punished under Section 422.7 or subdivision (a) of this section, any person who commits a felony that is a hate crime, or attempts to commit a felony that is a hate crime, and who voluntarily acted in concert with another person, either personally or by aiding and abetting another person, shall receive an additional two, three, or four years in the state prison, at the court's discretion.

(c) For the purpose of imposing an additional term under subdivision (a) or (b), it shall be a factor in aggravation that the defendant personally used a firearm in the commission of the offense. Nothing in this subdivision shall preclude a court from also imposing a sentence enhancement pursuant to Section 12022.5, 12022.53, or 12022.55, or any other law.

(d) A person who is punished pursuant to this section also shall receive an additional term of one year in the state prison for each prior felony conviction on charges brought and tried separately in which it was found by the trier of fact or admitted by the defendant that the crime was a hate crime. This additional term shall only apply where a sentence enhancement is not imposed pursuant to Section 667 or 667.5.

(e) Any additional term authorized by this section shall not be imposed unless the allegation is charged in the accusatory pleading and admitted by the defendant or found to be true by the trier of fact.

(f) Any additional term imposed pursuant to this section shall be in addition to any other punishment provided by law.

(g) Notwithstanding any other provision of law, the court may strike any additional term imposed by this section if the court determines that there are mitigating circumstances and states on the record the reasons for striking the additional punishment.

Amended by Stats 2004 ch 700 (SB 1234), s 10, eff. 1/1/2005.

Section 422.76 - Aggravating circumstance [Renumbered from 1170.75]

Except where the court imposes additional punishment under Section 422.75 or in a case in which the person has been convicted of an offense subject to Section 1170.8, the fact that a person committed a felony or attempted to commit a felony that is a hate crime shall be considered a circumstance in aggravation of the crime in imposing a term under subdivision (b) of Section 1170.

Renumbered from Ca. Pen. Code §1170.75 and amended by Stats 2004 ch 700 (SB 1234), s 23, eff. 1/1/2005.

Section 422.77 - Willful and knowing violation of order

(a) Any willful and knowing violation of any order issued pursuant to subdivision (b) or (c) of Section 52.1 of the Civil Code shall be a misdemeanor punishable by a fine of not more than one thousand dollars ($1,000), or by imprisonment in the county jail for not more than six months, or by both the fine and imprisonment.

(b) A person who has previously been convicted one or more times of violating an order issued pursuant to subdivision (b) or (c) of Section 52.1 of the Civil Code upon charges separately brought and tried shall be imprisoned in the county jail for not more than one year. Subject to the discretion of the court, the prosecution shall have the opportunity to present witnesses and relevant evidence at the time of the sentencing of a defendant pursuant to this subdivision.

(c) The prosecuting agency of each county shall have the primary responsibility for the enforcement of orders issued pursuant to Section 52.1 of the Civil Code.

(d) The court may order a defendant who is convicted of a hate crime to perform a minimum of community service, not to exceed 400 hours, to be performed over a period not to exceed 350 days, during a time other than their hours of employment or school attendance.

Amended by Stats 2021 ch 434 (SB 827),s 3, eff. 1/1/2022.

Added by Stats 2004 ch 700 (SB 1234), s 12, eff. 1/1/2005.

Section 422.78 - Responsibility for enforcement of orders

The prosecuting agency of each county shall have the primary responsibility for the enforcement of orders issued pursuant to this title or Section 52.1 of the Civil Code.

Added by Stats 2004 ch 700 (SB 1234), s 13, eff. 1/1/2005.

Section 422.8 - Prosecution not prevented or limited

Except as otherwise required by law, nothing in this title shall be construed to prevent or limit the prosecution of any person pursuant to any provision of law.

Amended by Stats. 1991, Ch. 839, Sec. 4.

Section 422.85 - Protection order; conditions of probation

(a) In the case of any person who is convicted of any offense against the person or property of another individual, private institution, or public agency, committed because of the victim's actual or perceived race, color, ethnicity, religion, nationality, country of origin, ancestry, disability, gender, gender identity, gender expression, or sexual orientation, including, but not limited to, offenses defined in Section 302, 423.2, 594.3, 11411, 11412, or 11413, or for any hate crime, the court, absent compelling circumstances stated on the record, shall make an order protecting the victim, or known immediate family or domestic partner of the victim, from further acts of violence, threats, stalking, or harassment by the defendant, including any stay-away conditions the court deems appropriate, and shall make obedience of that order a condition of the defendant's probation. In these cases the court may also order that the defendant be required to do one or more of the following as a condition of probation:

(1) Complete a class or program on racial or ethnic sensitivity, or other similar training in the area of civil rights, or a one-year counseling program intended to reduce the tendency toward violent and antisocial behavior if that class, program, or training is available and was developed or authorized by the court or local agencies in cooperation with organizations serving the affected community.

(2) Make payments or other compensation to a community-based program or local agency that provides services to victims of hate violence.

(3) Reimburse the victim for reasonable costs of counseling and other reasonable expenses that the court finds are the direct result of the defendant's acts.

(b) Any payments or other compensation ordered under this section shall be in addition to restitution payments required under Section 1203.04, and shall be made only after that restitution is paid in full.

Amended by Stats 2011 ch 719 (AB 887),s 32, eff. 1/1/2012.

Renumbered from Ca. Pen. Code §422.95 and amended by Stats 2004 ch 809 (AB 2428), s 2.1, eff. 1/1/2005.

Renumbered from Ca. Pen. Code §422.95 and amended by Stats 2004 ch 700 (SB 1234), s 21, eff. 1/1/2005.

Section 422.86 - Goals of sentencing for hate crimes

(a) It is the public policy of this state that the principal goals of sentencing for hate crimes, are the following:

(1) Punishment for the hate crimes committed.

(2) Crime and violence prevention, including prevention of recidivism and prevention of crimes and violence in prisons and jails.

(3) Restorative justice for the immediate victims of the hate crimes and for the classes of persons terrorized by the hate crimes.

(b) The Judicial Council shall develop a rule of court guiding hate crime sentencing to implement the policy in subdivision (a). In developing the rule of court, the council shall consult experts including organizations representing hate crime victims.

Added by Stats 2004 ch 700 (SB 1234), s 14, eff. 1/1/2005.

Section 422.865 - Condition of outpatient status or conditional release

(a) In the case of any person who is committed to a state hospital or other treatment facility under the provisions of Section 1026 for any offense against the person or property of another individual, private institution, or public agency because of the victim's actual or perceived race, color, ethnicity, religion, nationality, country of origin, ancestry, disability, gender, or sexual orientation, including, but not limited to, offenses defined in Section 302, 423.2, 594.3, 11411, 11412, or for any hate crime, and then is either placed on outpatient status or conditional release from the state hospital or other treatment facility, the court or community program director may order that the defendant be required as a condition of outpatient status or conditional release to complete a class or program on racial or ethnic sensitivity, or other similar training in the area of civil rights, or a one-year counseling program intended to reduce the tendency toward violent and antisocial behavior if that class, program, or training is available and was developed or authorized by the court or local agencies in cooperation with organizations serving the affected community.

(b) In the case of any person who is committed to a state hospital or other treatment facility under the provisions of Section 1026 for any offense against the person or property of another individual, private institution, or public agency committed because of the victim's actual or perceived race, color, ethnicity, religion, nationality, country of origin, ancestry, disability, gender, or sexual orientation, including, but not limited to, offenses defined in Section 302, 423.2, 594.3, 11411, 11412, or 11413, or for any hate crime, and then is either placed on outpatient status or conditional release from the state hospital or other treatment facility, the court, absent compelling circumstances stated on the record, shall make an order protecting the victim, or known immediate family or domestic partner of the victim, from further acts of violence, threats, stalking, or harassment by the defendant, including any stay-away conditions as the court deems appropriate, and shall make obedience of that order a condition of the defendant's outpatient status or conditional release.

(c) It is the intent of the Legislature to encourage state agencies and treatment facilities to establish education and training programs to prevent violations of civil rights and hate crimes.

Added by Stats 2004 ch 809 (AB 2428), s 1, eff. 1/1/2005.

Chapter 2.5 - LAW ENFORCEMENT AGENCY POLICIES

Section 422.87 - General provisions

(a) Each state and local law enforcement agency shall, by July 1, 2024, adopt a hate crimes policy that shall include, but not be limited to, all of the following:

(1) The definitions in Sections 422.55 and 422.56.

(2) The content of the model policy framework that the Commission on Peace Officer Standards and Training developed pursuant to Section 13519.6, and any content that the commission may revise or add in the future, including any policy, definitions, response and reporting responsibilities, training resources, the supplemental hate crime report, and planning and prevention methods.

(3)

(A) Information regarding bias motivation.

(B) For the purposes of this paragraph, "bias motivation" is a preexisting negative attitude toward actual or perceived characteristics referenced in Section 422.55. Depending on the circumstances of each case, bias motivation may include, but is not limited to, hatred, animosity, discriminatory selection of victims, resentment, revulsion, contempt, unreasonable fear, paranoia, callousness, thrill-seeking, desire for social dominance, desire for social bonding with those of one's "own kind," or a perception of the vulnerability of the victim due to the victim being perceived as being weak, worthless, or fair game because of a protected characteristic, including, but not limited to, disability or gender.

(C)

(i) In recognizing suspected disability-bias hate crimes, the policy shall instruct officers to consider whether there is any indication that the perpetrator was motivated by hostility or other bias, occasioned by factors such as, but not limited to, dislike of persons who arouse fear or guilt, a perception that persons with disabilities are inferior and therefore "deserving victims," a fear of persons whose visible traits are perceived as being disturbing to others, or resentment of those who need, demand, or receive alternative educational, physical, or social accommodations.

(ii) In recognizing suspected disability-bias hate crimes, the policy also shall instruct officers to consider whether there is any indication that the perpetrator perceived the victim to be vulnerable and, if so, if this perception is grounded, in whole or in part, in antidisability bias. This includes, but is not limited to, if a perpetrator targets a person with a particular perceived disability while avoiding other vulnerable-appearing persons such as inebriated persons or persons with perceived disabilities different than those of the victim, those circumstances could be evidence that the perpetrator's motivations included bias against persons with the perceived disability of the victim and that the crime must be reported as a suspected hate crime and not a mere crime of opportunity.

(D) In recognizing suspected religion-bias hate crimes, the policy shall instruct officers to consider whether there were targeted attacks on, or biased references to, symbols of importance to a particular religion or articles considered of spiritual significance in a particular religion. Examples of religions and such symbols and articles include, but are not limited to:

(i) In Buddhism, statues of the Buddha.

(ii) In Christianity, crosses.

(iii) In Hinduism, forehead markings, known as bindis and tilaks, Aum/Om symbols, and images of deities known as murtis.

(iv) In Islam, hijabs.

(v) In Judaism, Stars of David, menorahs, and yarmulke.

(vi) In Sikhism, turbans, head coverings, and unshorn hair, including beards.

(4) Information regarding the general underreporting of hate crimes and the more extreme underreporting of antidisability and antigender hate crimes and a plan for the agency to remedy this underreporting.

(5) A protocol for reporting suspected hate crimes to the Department of Justice pursuant to Section 13023.

(6) A checklist of first responder responsibilities, including, but not limited to, being sensitive to effects of the crime on the victim, determining whether any additional resources are needed on the scene to assist the victim or whether to refer the victim to appropriate

community and legal services, and giving the victims and any interested persons the agency's hate crimes brochure, as required by Section 422.92.

(7) A specific procedure for transmitting and periodically retransmitting the policy and any related orders to all officers, including a simple and immediate way for officers to access the policy in the field when needed.

(8) The title or titles of the officer or officers responsible for ensuring that the department has a hate crime brochure as required by Section 422.92 and ensuring that all officers are trained to distribute the brochure to all suspected hate crime victims and all other interested persons.

(9) A requirement that all officers be familiar with the policy and carry out the policy at all times unless directed by the chief, sheriff, director, or other chief executive of the law enforcement agency or other command-level officer to whom the chief executive officer formally delegates this responsibility.

(10) A schedule of the hate crime training required by Section 13519.6 and any other hate crime or related training the agency may conduct.

(b) A law enforcement agency that updates an existing hate crimes policy or adopts a new hate crimes policy may include any of the provisions of a model hate crime policy and other relevant documents developed by the International Association of Chiefs of Police that are relevant to California and consistent with this chapter.

Amended by Stats 2023 ch 524 (AB 449),s 1, eff. 1/1/2024.
Amended by Stats 2021 ch 691 (AB 57),s 2, eff. 1/1/2022.
Added by Stats 2018 ch 26 (AB 1985),s 3, eff. 1/1/2019.

Chapter 3 - GENERAL PROVISIONS

Section 422.88 - Restraining orders

(a) The court in which a criminal proceeding stemming from a hate crime or alleged hate crime is filed shall take all actions reasonably required, including granting restraining orders, to safeguard the health, safety, or privacy of the alleged victim, or of a person who is a victim of, or at risk of becoming a victim of, a hate crime.

(b) Restraining orders issued pursuant to subdivision (a) may include provisions prohibiting or restricting the photographing of a person who is a victim of, or at risk of becoming a victim of, a hate crime when reasonably required to safeguard the health, safety, or privacy of that person.

Added by Stats 2004 ch 700 (SB 1234), s 15, eff. 1/1/2005.

Section 422.89 - Education and training programs

It is the intent of the Legislature to encourage counties, cities, law enforcement agencies, and school districts to establish education and training programs to prevent violations of civil rights and hate crimes and to assist victims.

Added by Stats 2004 ch 700 (SB 1234), s 16, eff. 1/1/2005.

Section 422.9 - Use of definition of "hate crime"

All state and local agencies shall use the definition of "hate crime" set forth in subdivision (a) of Section 422.55 exclusively, except as other explicit provisions of state or federal law may require otherwise.

Added by Stats 2004 ch 700 (SB 1234), s 18, eff. 1/1/2005.

Former § 422.9 was repealed by Stats 2004 ch 700 (SB 1234), s 17, eff. 1/1/2005.

Section 422.91 - Duties of Department of Corrections and California Youth Authority

The Department of Corrections and the California Youth Authority, subject to available funding, shall do each of the following:

(a) Cooperate fully and participate actively with federal, state, and local law enforcement agencies and community hate crime prevention and response networks and other anti-hate groups concerning hate crimes and gangs.

(b) Strive to provide inmates with safe environments in which they are not pressured to join gangs or hate groups and do not feel a need to join them in self-defense.

Added by Stats 2004 ch 700 (SB 1234), s 19, eff. 1/1/2005.

Section 422.92 - Brochure on hate crimes

(a)Every state and local law enforcement agency in this state shall make available a brochure on hate crimes to victims of these crimes and the public.

(b)The Civil Rights Department shall provide existing brochures, making revisions as needed, to local law enforcement agencies upon request for reproduction and distribution to victims of hate crimes and other interested parties. In carrying out these responsibilities, the department shall consult the Civil Rights Council, the Department of Justice, and the California Victim Compensation Board.

Amended by Stats 2022 ch 48 (SB 189),s 71, eff. 6/30/2022.
Amended by Stats 2016 ch 31 (SB 836),s 232, eff. 6/27/2016.
Amended by Stats 2012 ch 46 (SB 1038),s 115, eff. 6/27/2012, op. 1/1/2013.
Renumbered from Ca. Pen. Code §13873 and amended by Stats 2004 ch 700 (SB 1234), s 33, eff. 1/1/2005.

Section 422.93 - Public policy

(a) It is the public policy of this state to protect the public from crime and violence by encouraging all persons who are victims of or witnesses to crimes, or who otherwise can give evidence in a criminal investigation, to cooperate with the criminal justice system and not to penalize these persons for being victims or for cooperating with the criminal justice system.

(b) Whenever an individual who is a victim of or witness to a hate crime, or who otherwise can give evidence in a hate crime investigation, is not charged with or convicted of committing any crime under state law, a peace officer may not detain the individual exclusively for any actual or suspected immigration violation or report or turn the individual over to federal immigration authorities.

Added by Stats 2004 ch 700 (SB 1234), s 20, eff. 1/1/2005.

Section 422.94 - [Effective until 7/1/2029] Hate Crime Vertical Prosecution Pilot Grant Program (HCVP)

(a) The Hate Crime Vertical Prosecution Pilot Grant Program (HCVP) is hereby created to be administered by the Department of Justice.

(b) Beginning January 1, 2023, and subject to an appropriation of funds by the Legislature, the department shall award grants to prosecutorial agencies for the purpose of creating, supporting, or expanding vertical prosecution units for the prosecution of hate crimes. These units shall be primarily focused on better serving hate crime victims and achieving just, equitable, and appropriate resolutions to hate crime cases.

(c) One-time HCVP grants shall be made on a competitive basis to selected applicants in a manner and in an amount determined by the department.

(d) The department shall do all of the following to administer the grant program:

(1) Specify the form of the application and information required to be submitted by each applicant.

(2) Specify the criteria the department shall consider in selecting grant awardees.

(3) Select the number of awards to be granted.

(e) The department may use no more than 5 percent of the funds appropriated for HCVP for the costs of administering the program. Grant awardees shall not use grant funds to supplant existing spending for vertical prosecutions of hate crimes.

(f) By no later than July 1, 2028, each grant recipient shall prepare and submit a report to the department, in a form prescribed by the department, that includes any relevant data requested by the department.

(g) By no later than January 1, 2029, the department shall prepare and submit a report to the Legislature in compliance with Section 9795 of the Government Code summarizing the data provided by grant recipients and analyzing the effectiveness of vertical prosecution programs in better serving hate crime victims and achieving just, equitable, and appropriate resolutions to hate crime cases, and making policy recommendations to the Legislature.

(h) The department shall make evaluations of the grant program available to the public.

(i) As used in this section, the following terms have the following meanings:

(1) "Prosecutorial agency" means a district attorney, city attorney, or other governmental entity responsible for the prosecution of crimes within a local jurisdiction.

(2) "Vertical prosecution" refers to having the same individual prosecutor assigned to a case from the initial criminal investigation through the sentencing of the offender.

(j) This section shall remain in effect only until July 1, 2029, and as of that date is repealed.

Added by Stats 2022 ch 853 (AB 557),s 1, eff. 1/1/2023.

Section 422.95 - [Renumbered]

Renumbered as Ca. Pen. Code §422.85 by Stats 2004 ch 809 (AB 2428), s 2.1, eff. 1/1/2005.

Title 11.7 - CALIFORNIA FREEDOM OF ACCESS TO CLINIC AND CHURCH ENTRANCES ACT

Section 423 - Short title

This title shall be known and may be cited as the California Freedom of Access to Clinic and Church Entrances Act, or the California FACE Act.

Added by Stats 2001 ch 899 (SB 780), s 2, eff. 1/1/2002.

Section 423.1 - Definitions

The following definitions apply for the purposes of this title:

(a) "Crime of violence" means an offense that has as an element the use, attempted use, or threatened use of physical force against the person or property of another.

(b) "Interfere with" means to restrict a person's freedom of movement.

(c) "Intimidate" means to place a person in reasonable apprehension of bodily harm to themselves or to another.

(d) "Nonviolent" means conduct that would not constitute a crime of violence.

(e) "Physical obstruction" means rendering ingress to or egress from a reproductive health services facility or to or from a place of religious worship impassable to another person, or rendering passage to or from a reproductive health services facility or a place of religious worship unreasonably difficult or hazardous to another person.

(f) "Reproductive health services" means reproductive health services provided in a hospital, clinic, physician's office, or other facility and includes medical, surgical, counseling, or referral services relating to the human reproductive system, including services relating to pregnancy or the termination of a pregnancy.

(g) "Reproductive health services patient, provider, or assistant" means a person or entity, including, but not limited to, employees, staff, volunteers, and third-party vendors, that is or was involved in obtaining, seeking to obtain, providing, seeking to provide, or assisting or seeking to assist another person, at that other person's request, to obtain or provide services in a reproductive health services facility, or a person or entity that is or was involved in owning or operating or seeking to own or operate, a reproductive health services facility.

(h) "Reproductive health services facility" includes a hospital, clinic, physician's office, or other facility that provides or seeks to provide reproductive health services and includes the building or structure in which the facility is located.

Amended by Stats 2021 ch 191 (AB 1356),s 5, eff. 1/1/2022.

Added by Stats 2001 ch 899 (SB 780), s 2, eff. 1/1/2002.

Section 423.2 - Unlawful acts

Every person who, except a parent or guardian acting towards their minor child or ward, commits any of the following acts shall be subject to the punishment specified in Section 423.3.

(a) By force, threat of force, or physical obstruction that is a crime of violence, intentionally injures, intimidates, interferes with, or attempts to injure, intimidate, or interfere with, any person or entity because that person or entity is a reproductive health services patient, provider, or assistant, or in order to intimidate a person or entity, or a class of persons or entities, or from becoming or remaining a reproductive health services patient, provider, or assistant.

(b) By force, threat of force, or physical obstruction that is a crime of violence, intentionally injures, intimidates, interferes with, or attempts to injure, intimidate, or interfere with a person lawfully exercising or seeking to exercise the First Amendment right of religious freedom at a place of religious worship.

(c) By nonviolent physical obstruction, intentionally injures, intimidates, or interferes with, or attempts to injure, intimidate, or interfere with, any person or entity because that person or entity is a reproductive health services patient, provider, or assistant, or in order to intimidate any person or entity, or any class of persons or entities, from becoming or remaining a reproductive health services patient, provider, or assistant.

(d) By nonviolent physical obstruction, intentionally injures, intimidates, or interferes with, or attempts to injure, intimidate, or interfere with, a person lawfully exercising or seeking to exercise the First Amendment right of religious freedom at a place of religious worship.

(e) Intentionally damages or destroys the property of a person, entity, or facility, or attempts to do so, because the person, entity, or facility is a reproductive health services patient, provider, assistant, or facility.

(f) Intentionally damages or destroys the property of a place of religious worship.

(g) Within 100 feet of the entrance to, or within, a reproductive health services facility, intentionally videotapes, films, photographs, or records by electronic means, a reproductive health services patient, provider, or assistant without that person's consent with specific intent to intimidate the person from becoming or remaining a reproductive health services patient, provider, or assistant, and thereby causes the person to be intimidated.

(h) In any manner or forum, including, but not limited to, internet websites and social media, intentionally discloses or distributes a videotape, film, photograph, or recording knowing it was obtained in violation of subdivision (g) with the specific intent to intimidate the person from becoming or remaining a reproductive health services patient, provider, or assistant, and thereby causes the person to be intimidated. For purposes of this subdivision, "social media" means an electronic service or account, or electronic content, including, but not limited to, videos or still photographs, blogs, video blogs, podcasts, instant and text messages, email, online services or accounts, or internet website profiles or locations.

(i) Subdivisions (g) and (h) do not apply to a person described in subdivision (b) of Section 2 of Article I of the California Constitution.

Amended by Stats 2021 ch 191 (AB 1356),s 6, eff. 1/1/2022.

Added by Stats 2001 ch 899 (SB 780), s 2, eff. 1/1/2002.

Section 423.3 - Punishment

(a) A first violation of subdivision (c), (d), (g), or (h) of Section 423.2 is a misdemeanor, punishable by imprisonment in a county jail for a period of not more than one year, or a fine not to exceed ten thousand dollars ($10,000), or both that fine and imprisonment.

(b) A second or subsequent violation of subdivision (c), (d), (g), or (h) of Section 423.2 is a misdemeanor, punishable by imprisonment in a county jail for a period of not more than one year, or a fine not to exceed twenty-five thousand dollars ($25,000), or by both that fine and imprisonment.

(c) A first violation of subdivision (e) or (f) of Section 423.2 is a misdemeanor, punishable by imprisonment in a county jail for a period of not more than one year, or a fine not to exceed twenty-five thousand dollars ($25,000), or by both that fine and imprisonment.

(d) A first violation of subdivision (a) or (b) of Section 432.2 is a misdemeanor, punishable by imprisonment in a county jail for a period of not more than one year, or a fine not to exceed twenty-five thousand dollars ($25,000), or by both that fine and imprisonment.

(e) A second or subsequent violation of subdivision (a), (b), (e), or (f) of Section 423.2 is a misdemeanor, punishable by imprisonment in a county jail for a period of not more than one year, or a fine not to exceed fifty thousand dollars ($50,000), or by both that fine and imprisonment.

(f) In imposing fines pursuant to this section, the court shall consider applicable factors in aggravation and mitigation set out in Rules 4.421 and 4.423 of the California Rules of Court, and shall consider a prior violation of the federal Freedom of Access to Clinic Entrances Act of 1994 (18 U.S.C. Sec. 248), or a prior violation of a statute of another jurisdiction that would constitute a violation of Section 423.2 or of the federal Freedom of Access to Clinic Entrances Act of 1994, to be a prior violation of Section 423.2.

(g) This title establishes concurrent state jurisdiction over conduct that is also prohibited by the federal Freedom of Access to Clinic Entrances Act of 1994 (18 U.S.C. Sec. 248), which provides for misdemeanor penalties for first violations and felony-misdemeanor penalties for second and subsequent violations. State law enforcement agencies and prosecutors shall cooperate with federal authorities in the prevention, apprehension, and prosecution of these crimes, and shall seek federal prosecutions when appropriate.

(h) No person shall be convicted under this article for conduct in violation of Section 423.2 that was done on a particular occasion where the identical conduct on that occasion was the basis for a conviction of that person under the federal Freedom of Access to Clinic Entrances Act of 1994 (18 U.S.C. Sec. 248).

Amended by Stats 2021 ch 191 (AB 1356),s 7, eff. 1/1/2022.

Added by Stats 2001 ch 899 (SB 780), s 2, eff. 1/1/2002.

Section 423.4 - Civil action

(a) A person aggrieved by a violation of Section 423.2 may bring a civil action to enjoin the violation, for compensatory and punitive damages, and for the costs of suit and reasonable fees for attorneys and expert witnesses, except that only a reproductive health services client, provider, or assistant may bring an action under subdivision (a), (c), or (e) of Section 423.2, and only a person lawfully exercising or seeking to exercise the First Amendment right of religious freedom in a place of religious worship, or the entity that owns or operates a place of religious worship, may bring an action under subdivision (b), (d), or (f) of Section 423.2. With respect to compensatory damages, the plaintiff may elect, at any time prior to the rendering of a final judgment, to recover, in lieu of actual damages, an award of statutory damages in the amount of one thousand dollars ($1,000) per exclusively nonviolent violation, and five thousand dollars ($5,000) per any other violation, for each violation committed.

(b) The Attorney General, a district attorney, or a city attorney may bring a civil action to enjoin a violation of Section 423.2, for compensatory damages to persons aggrieved as described in subdivision (a) and for the assessment of a civil penalty against each respondent. The civil penalty shall not exceed two thousand dollars ($2,000) for an exclusively nonviolent first violation, and fifteen thousand dollars ($15,000) for any other first violation, and shall not exceed five thousand dollars ($5,000) for an exclusively nonviolent subsequent violation, and twenty-five thousand dollars ($25,000) for any other subsequent violation. In imposing civil penalties pursuant to this subdivision, the court shall consider a prior violation of the federal Freedom of Access to Clinic Entrances Act of 1994 (18 U.S.C. Sec. 248), or a prior violation of a statute of another jurisdiction that would constitute a violation of Section 423.2 or the federal Freedom of Access to Clinic Entrances Act of 1994, to be a prior violation of Section 423.2.

(c) No person shall be found liable under this section for conduct in violation of Section 423.2 done on a particular occasion where the identical conduct on that occasion was the basis for a finding of liability by that person under the federal Freedom of Access to Clinic Entrances Act of 1994 (18 U.S.C. Sec. 248).
Added by Stats 2001 ch 899 (SB 780), s 2, eff. 1/1/2002.

Section 423.5 - Restraining orders

(a)

 (1) The court in which a criminal or civil proceeding is filed for a violation of subdivision (a), (c), or (e) of Section 423.2 shall take all action reasonably required, including granting restraining orders, to safeguard the health, safety, or privacy of either of the following:

  (A) A reproductive health services client, provider, or assistant who is a party or witness in the proceeding.

  (B) A person who is a victim of, or at risk of becoming a victim of, conduct prohibited by subdivision (a), (c), or (e) of Section 423.2.

 (2) The court in which a criminal or civil proceeding is filed for a violation of subdivision (b), (d), or (f) of Section 423.2 shall take all action reasonably required, including granting restraining orders, to safeguard the health, safety, or privacy of either of the following:

  (A) A person lawfully exercising or seeking to exercise the First Amendment right of religious freedom at a place of religious worship.

  (B) An entity that owns or operates a place of religious worship.

(b) Restraining orders issued pursuant to paragraph (1) of subdivision (a) may include provisions prohibiting or restricting the photographing of persons described in subparagraphs (A) and (B) of paragraph (1) of subdivision (a) when reasonably required to safeguard the health, safety, or privacy of those persons. Restraining orders issued pursuant to paragraph (2) of subdivision (a) may include provisions prohibiting or restricting the photographing of persons described in subparagraphs (A) and (B) of paragraph (2) of subdivision (a) when reasonably required to safeguard the health, safety, or privacy of those persons.

(c) A court may, in its discretion, permit an individual described in subparagraph (A) or (B) of paragraph (1) of subdivision (a) to use a pseudonym in a civil proceeding described in paragraph (1) of subdivision (a) when reasonably required to safeguard the health, safety, or privacy of those persons. A court may, in its discretion, permit an individual described in subparagraph (A) or (B) of paragraph (2) of subdivision (a) to use a pseudonym in a civil proceeding described in paragraph (2) of subdivision (a) when reasonably required to safeguard the health, safety, or privacy of those persons.
Added by Stats 2001 ch 899 (SB 780), s 2, eff. 1/1/2002.

Section 423.6 - Construction of title

This title shall not be construed for any of the following purposes:

(a) To impair any constitutionally protected activity, or any activity protected by the laws of California or of the United States of America.

(b) To provide exclusive civil or criminal remedies or to preempt or to preclude any county, city, or city and county from passing any law to provide a remedy for the commission of any of the acts prohibited by this title or to make any of those acts a crime.

(c) To interfere with the enforcement of any federal, state, or local laws regulating the performance of abortions or the provision of other reproductive health services.

(d) To negate, supercede, or otherwise interfere with the operation of any provision of Chapter 10 (commencing with Section 1138) of Part 3 of Division 2 of the Labor Code.

(e) To create additional civil or criminal remedies or to limit any existing civil or criminal remedies to redress an activity that interferes with the exercise of any other rights protected by the First Amendment to the United States Constitution or of Article I of the California Constitution.

(f) To preclude prosecution under both this title and any other provision of law, except as provided in subdivision (g) of Section 423.3.
Added by Stats 2001 ch 899 (SB 780), s 2, eff. 1/1/2002.

Title 12 – OF CRIMES AGAINST THE REVENUE AND PROPERTY OF THIS STATE

Section 424 - Unlawful acts related to public moneys

(a) Each officer of this state, or of any county, city, town, or district of this state, and every other person charged with the receipt, safekeeping, transfer, or disbursement of public moneys, who either:

 1. Without authority of law, appropriates the same, or any portion thereof, to his or her own use, or to the use of another; or,

 2. Loans the same or any portion thereof; makes any profit out of, or uses the same for any purpose not authorized by law; or,

 3. Knowingly keeps any false account, or makes any false entry or erasure in any account of or relating to the same; or,

 4. Fraudulently alters, falsifies, conceals, destroys, or obliterates any account; or,

 5. Willfully refuses or omits to pay over, on demand, any public moneys in his or her hands, upon the presentation of a draft, order, or warrant drawn upon these moneys by competent authority; or,

 6. Willfully omits to transfer the same, when transfer is required by law; or,

 7. Willfully omits or refuses to pay over to any officer or person authorized by law to receive the same, any money received by him or her under any duty imposed by law so to pay over the same;- Is punishable by imprisonment in the state prison for two, three, or four years, and is disqualified from holding any office in this state.

(b) As used in this section, "public moneys" includes the proceeds derived from the sale of bonds or other evidence or indebtedness authorized by the legislative body of any city, county, district, or public agency.

(c) This section does not apply to the incidental and minimal use of public resources authorized by Section 8314 of the Government Code.
Amended by Stats 2003 ch 62 (SB 600), s 227, eff. 1/1/2004.
Amended by Stats 2002 ch 154 (AB 1714), s 2, eff. 1/1/2003.

Section 425 - Neglect or failure to keep and pay over public moneys

Every officer charged with the receipt, safe keeping, or disbursement of public moneys, who neglects or fails to keep and pay over the same in the manner prescribed by law, is guilty of felony.

Enacted 1872.
Section 426 - "Public moneys" defined
The phrase "public moneys," as used in Sections 424 and 425, includes all bonds and evidence of indebtedness, and all moneys belonging to the state, or any city, county, town, district, or public agency therein, and all moneys, bonds, and evidences of indebtedness received or held by state, county, district, city, town, or public agency officers in their official capacity.
Amended by Stats. 1987, Ch. 828, Sec. 29.
Section 428 - Obstruction or hindrance of public officer to collect money
Every person who willfully obstructs or hinders any public officer from collecting any revenue, taxes, or other sums of money in which the people of this State are interested, and which such officer is by law empowered to collect, is guilty of a misdemeanor.
Enacted 1872.
Section 429 - Unlawful failure to collect or remit fees or surcharges by provider of telecommunications services
Any provider of telecommunications services in this state that intentionally fails to collect or remit, as may be required, the annual fee imposed pursuant to Section 431 of the Public Utilities Code, the universal telephone service surcharge imposed pursuant to Section 879 or 879.5 of the Public Utilities Code, the fee for filing an application for a certificate of public convenience and necessity as provided in Section 1904 of the Public Utilities Code, or the surcharge imposed pursuant to subdivision (g) of Section 2881 of the Public Utilities Code, whether imposed on the provider or measured by the provider's service charges, is guilty of a misdemeanor.
Amended by Stats 2012 ch 162 (SB 1171),s 124, eff. 1/1/2013.
Section 431 - Unlawful acts related to receipt for poll tax, road tax, or license
Every person who uses or gives any receipt, except that prescribed by law, as evidence of the payment of any poll tax, road tax, or license of any kind, or who receives payment of such tax or license without delivering the receipt prescribed by law, or who inserts the name of more than one person therein, is guilty of a misdemeanor.
Enacted 1872.
Section 432 - Unlawful possession of blank licenses or poll tax receipts
Every person who has in his possession, with intent to circulate or sell, any blank licenses or poll tax receipts other than those furnished by the Controller of State or County Auditor, is guilty of felony.
Enacted 1872.
Section 436 - Unlawful acting as auctioneer
Every person who acts as an auctioneer in violation of the laws of this State relating to auctions and auctioneers, is guilty of a misdemeanor.
Enacted 1872.
Section 439 - Unlawful procurement of insurance
Every person who in this State procures, or agrees to procure, any insurance for a resident of this State, from any insurance company not incorporated under the laws of this State, unless such company or its agent has filed the bond required by the laws of this State relating to insurance, is guilty of a misdemeanor.
Enacted 1872.
Section 440 - Failure or refusal to permit Controller or Attorney General to inspect officer's records
Every officer charged with the collection, receipt, or disbursement of any portion of the revenue of this State, who, upon demand, fails or refuses to permit the Controller or Attorney General to inspect his books, papers, receipts, and records pertaining to his office, is guilty of a misdemeanor.
Enacted 1872.

Title 13 - OF CRIMES AGAINST PROPERTY

Chapter 1 - ARSON

Section 450 - Definitions
In this chapter, the following terms have the following meanings:
(a) "Structure" means any building, or commercial or public tent, bridge, tunnel, or powerplant.
(b) "Forest land" means any brush covered land, cut-over land, forest, grasslands, or woods.
(c) "Property" means real property or personal property, other than a structure or forest land.
(d) "Inhabited" means currently being used for dwelling purposes whether occupied or not. "Inhabited structure" and "inhabited property" do not include the real property on which an inhabited structure or an inhabited property is located.
(e) "Maliciously" imports a wish to vex, defraud, annoy, or injure another person, or an intent to do a wrongful act, established either by proof or presumption of law.
(f) "Recklessly" means a person is aware of and consciously disregards a substantial and unjustifiable risk that his or her act will set fire to, burn, or cause to burn a structure, forest land, or property. The risk shall be of such nature and degree that disregard thereof constitutes a gross deviation from the standard of conduct that a reasonable person would observe in the situation. A person who creates such a risk but is unaware thereof solely by reason of voluntary intoxication also acts recklessly with respect thereto.
Added by Stats. 1979, Ch. 145.
Section 451 - Arson
A person is guilty of arson when he or she willfully and maliciously sets fire to or burns or causes to be burned or who aids, counsels, or procures the burning of, any structure, forest land, or property.
(a) Arson that causes great bodily injury is a felony punishable by imprisonment in the state prison for five, seven, or nine years.
(b) Arson that causes an inhabited structure or inhabited property to burn is a felony punishable by imprisonment in the state prison for three, five, or eight years.
(c) Arson of a structure or forest land is a felony punishable by imprisonment in the state prison for two, four, or six years.

(d) Arson of property is a felony punishable by imprisonment in the state prison for 16 months, two, or three years. For purposes of this paragraph, arson of property does not include one burning or causing to be burned his or her own personal property unless there is an intent to defraud or there is injury to another person or another person's structure, forest land, or property.

(e) In the case of any person convicted of violating this section while confined in a state prison, prison road camp, prison forestry camp, or other prison camp or prison farm, or while confined in a county jail while serving a term of imprisonment for a felony or misdemeanor conviction, any sentence imposed shall be consecutive to the sentence for which the person was then confined.

Amended by Stats. 1994, Ch. 421, Sec. 1. Effective September 7, 1994.

Section 451.1 - Felony violation

(a) Notwithstanding any other law, any person who is convicted of a felony violation of Section 451 shall be punished by a three-, four-, or five-year enhancement if one or more of the following circumstances is found to be true:

　　(1) The defendant has been previously convicted of a felony violation of Section 451 or 452.

　　(2) A firefighter, peace officer, or other emergency personnel suffered great bodily injury as a result of the offense. The additional term provided by this subdivision shall be imposed whenever applicable, including any instance in which there is a violation of subdivision (a) of Section 451.

　　(3) The defendant proximately caused great bodily injury to more than one victim in any single violation of Section 451. The additional term provided by this subdivision shall be imposed whenever applicable, including any instance in which there is a violation of subdivision (a) of Section 451.

　　(4) The defendant proximately caused multiple structures to burn in any single violation of Section 451.

　　(5) The defendant committed arson as described in subdivision (a), (b), or (c) of Section 451 and the arson was caused by use of a device designed to accelerate the fire or delay ignition.

(b) The additional term specified in subdivision (a) shall not be imposed unless the existence of any fact required under this section shall be alleged in the accusatory pleading and either admitted by the defendant in open court or found to be true by the trier of fact.

Added by Stats. 1994, Ch. 421, Sec. 2. Effective September 7, 1994.

Section 451.5 - [Effective until 1/1/2029] Aggravated arson

(a) A person who willfully, maliciously, deliberately, with premeditation, and with intent to cause injury to one or more persons, or to cause damage to property under circumstances likely to produce injury to one or more persons, or to cause damage to one or more structures or inhabited dwellings, sets fire to, burns, or causes to be burned, or aids, counsels, or procures the burning of any residence, structure, forest land, or property, is guilty of aggravated arson if one or more of the following aggravating factors exists:

　　(1) The defendant has been previously convicted of arson on one or more occasions within the past 10 years.

　　(2)

　　　　(A) The fire caused property damage and other losses in excess of ten million one hundred thousand dollars ($10,100,000), exclusive of damage to, or destruction of, inhabited dwellings.

　　　　(B) In calculating the total amount of property damage and other losses under subparagraph (A), the court shall consider the cost of fire suppression. It is the intent of the Legislature that this paragraph be reviewed within five years to consider the effects of inflation on the dollar amount stated herein.

　　(3) The fire caused damage to, or the destruction of, five or more inhabited dwellings.

(b) A person who is convicted under subdivision (a) shall be punished by imprisonment in the state prison for 10 years to life.

(c) A person who is sentenced under subdivision (b) shall not be eligible for release on parole until 10 calendar years have elapsed.

(d) This section shall remain in effect only until January 1, 2029, and as of that date is repealed.

Amended by Stats 2023 ch 706 (SB 281),s 1, eff. 1/1/2024.

Amended by Stats 2018 ch 619 (SB 896),s 1, eff. 1/1/2019.

Amended by Stats 2014 ch 481 (SB 930),s 1, eff. 9/19/2014.

Amended by Stats 2009 ch 71 (AB 27),s 1, eff. 1/1/2010.

Amended by Stats 2004 ch 135 (AB 1907), s 1, eff. 1/1/2005.

EFFECTIVE 1/1/2000. Amended September 27, 1999 (Bill Number: SB 555) (Chapter 518).

This section is set out more than once due to postponed, multiple, or conflicting amendments.

Section 451.5 - [Operative 1/1/2029] Aggravated arson

(a) A person who willfully, maliciously, deliberately, with premeditation, and with intent to cause injury to one or more persons, or to cause damage to property under circumstances likely to produce injury to one or more persons, or to cause damage to one or more structures or inhabited dwellings, sets fire to, burns, or causes to be burned, or aids, counsels, or procures the burning of any residence, structure, forest land, or property, is guilty of aggravated arson if either of the following aggravating factors exists:

　　(1) The defendant has been previously convicted of arson on one or more occasions within the past 10 years.

　　(2) The fire caused damage to, or the destruction of, five or more inhabited dwellings.

(b) A person who is convicted under subdivision (a) shall be punished by imprisonment in the state prison for 10 years to life.

(c) A person who is sentenced under subdivision (b) shall not be eligible for release on parole until 10 calendar years have elapsed.

(d) This section shall become operative on January 1, 2029.

Amended by Stats 2023 ch 706 (SB 281),s 2, eff. 1/1/2024.

Amended by Stats 2018 ch 619 (SB 896),s 2, eff. 1/1/2019.

Added by Stats 2014 ch 481 (SB 930),s 2, eff. 9/19/2014.

This section is set out more than once due to postponed, multiple, or conflicting amendments.

Section 452 - Unlawfully causing fire

A person is guilty of unlawfully causing a fire when he recklessly sets fire to or burns or causes to be burned, any structure, forest land or property.

(a) Unlawfully causing a fire that causes great bodily injury is a felony punishable by imprisonment in the state prison for two, four or six years, or by imprisonment in the county jail for not more than one year, or by a fine, or by both such imprisonment and fine.

(b) Unlawfully causing a fire that causes an inhabited structure or inhabited property to burn is a felony punishable by imprisonment in the state prison for two, three or four years, or by imprisonment in the county jail for not more than one year, or by a fine, or by both such imprisonment and fine.

(c) Unlawfully causing a fire of a structure or forest land is a felony punishable by imprisonment in the state prison for 16 months, two or three years, or by imprisonment in the county jail for not more than six months, or by a fine, or by both such imprisonment and fine.

(d) Unlawfully causing a fire of property is a misdemeanor. For purposes of this paragraph, unlawfully causing a fire of property does not include one burning or causing to be burned his own personal property unless there is injury to another person or to another person's structure, forest land or property.

(e) In the case of any person convicted of violating this section while confined in a state prison, prison road camp, prison forestry camp, or other prison camp or prison farm, or while confined in a county jail while serving a term of imprisonment for a felony or misdemeanor conviction, any sentence imposed shall be consecutive to the sentence for which the person was then confined.

Amended by Stats. 1982, Ch. 1133, Sec. 2. Effective September 17, 1982.

Section 452.1 - Felony violation

(a) Notwithstanding any other law, any person who is convicted of a felony violation of Section 452 shall be punished by a one-, two-, or three-year enhancement for each of the following circumstances that is found to be true:

    (1) The defendant has been previously convicted of a felony violation of Section 451 or 452.

    (2) A firefighter, peace officer, or other emergency personnel suffered great bodily injury as a result of the offense. The additional term provided by this subdivision shall be imposed whenever applicable, including any instance in which there is a violation of subdivision (a) of Section 452.

    (3) The defendant proximately caused great bodily injury to more than one victim in any single violation of Section 452. The additional term provided by this subdivision shall be imposed whenever applicable, including any instance in which there is a violation of subdivision (a) of Section 452.

    (4) The defendant proximately caused multiple structures to burn in any single violation of Section 452.

(b) The additional term specified in subdivision (a) of Section 452.1 shall not be imposed unless the existence of any fact required under this section shall be alleged in the accusatory pleading and either admitted by the defendant in open court or found to be true by the trier of fact.

Added by Stats. 1994, Ch. 421, Sec. 4. Effective September 7, 1994.

Section 453 - Unlawful possession manufacture or disposal of flammable or combustible material or substance or incendiary device

(a) Every person who possesses, manufactures, or disposes of any flammable, or combustible material or substance, or any incendiary device in an arrangement or preparation, with intent to willfully and maliciously use this material, substance, or device to set fire to or burn any structure, forest land, or property, shall be punished by imprisonment pursuant to subdivision (h) of Section 1170, or in a county jail, not exceeding one year.

(b) For the purposes of this section:

    (1) "Disposes of" means to give, give away, loan, offer, offer for sale, sell, or transfer.

    (2) "Incendiary device" means a device that is constructed or designed to start an incendiary fire by remote, delayed, or instant means, but no device commercially manufactured primarily for the purpose of illumination shall be deemed to be an incendiary device for the purposes of this section.

    (3) "Incendiary fire" means a fire that is deliberately ignited under circumstances in which a person knows that the fire should not be ignited.

(c) Subdivision (a) does not prohibit the authorized use or possession of any material, substance or device described therein by a member of the armed forces of the United States or by firemen, police officers, peace officers, or law enforcement officers authorized by the properly constituted authorities; nor does that subdivision prohibit the use or possession of any material, substance or device described therein when used solely for scientific research or educational purposes, or for disposal of brush under permit as provided for in Section 4494 of the Public Resources Code, or for any other lawful burning. Subdivision (a) does not prohibit the manufacture or disposal of an incendiary device for the parties or purposes described in this subdivision.

Amended by Stats 2011 ch 39 (AB 117),s 68, eff. 6/30/2011.

Amended by Stats 2011 ch 15 (AB 109),s 353, eff. 4/4/2011, but operative no earlier than October 1, 2011, and only upon creation of a community corrections grant program to assist in implementing this act and upon an appropriation to fund the grant program.

Section 454 - Punishment

(a) Every person who violates Section 451 or 452 during and within an area of any of the following, when proclaimed by the Governor, shall be punished by imprisonment in the state prison, as specified in subdivision (b):

    (1) A state of insurrection pursuant to Section 143 of the Military and Veterans Code.

    (2) A state of emergency pursuant to Section 8625 of the Government Code.

(b) Any person who is described in subdivision (a) and who violates subdivision (a), (b), or (c) of Section 451 shall be punished by imprisonment in the state prison for five, seven, or nine years. All other persons who are described in subdivision (a) shall be punished by imprisonment in the state prison for three, five, or seven years.

(c) Probation shall not be granted to any person who is convicted of violating this section, except in unusual cases where the interest of justice would best be served.

Amended by Stats. 1997, Ch. 260, Sec. 3. Effective January 1, 1998.

Section 455 - Unlawful attempt to set fire

(a) Any person who willfully and maliciously attempts to set fire to or attempts to burn or to aid, counsel or procure the burning of any structure, forest land or property, or who commits any act preliminary thereto, or in furtherance thereof, is punishable by imprisonment in the state prison for 16 months, two or three years.

(b) The placing or distributing of any flammable, explosive or combustible material or substance, or any device in or about any structure, forest land or property in an arrangement or preparation with intent to eventually willfully and maliciously set fire to or burn same, or to procure the setting fire to or burning of the same shall, for the purposes of this act constitute an attempt to burn such structure, forest land or property.

Amended by Stats 2011 ch 39 (AB 117),s 68, eff. 6/30/2011.

Amended by Stats 2011 ch 39 (AB 117),s 17, eff. 6/30/2011.

Amended by Stats 2011 ch 15 (AB 109),s 354, eff. 4/4/2011, but operative no earlier than October 1, 2011, and only upon creation of a community corrections grant program to assist in implementing this act and upon an appropriation to fund the grant program.

Section 456 - Fines

(a) Upon conviction for any felony violation of this chapter, in addition to the penalty prescribed, the court may impose a fine not to exceed fifty thousand dollars ($50,000) unless a greater amount is provided by law.

(b) When any person is convicted of a violation of any provision of this chapter and the reason he committed the violation was for pecuniary gain, in addition to the penalty prescribed and instead of the fine provided in subdivision (a), the court may impose a fine of twice the anticipated or actual gross gain.

Amended by Stats. 1979, Ch. 145.

Section 457 - Psychiatric or psychological examination

Upon conviction of any person for a violation of any provision of this chapter, the court may order that such person, for the purpose of sentencing, submit to a psychiatric or psychological examination.

Added by renumbering Section 455 by Stats. 1979, Ch. 145.

Section 457.1 - Registration

(a) As used in this section, "arson" means a violation of Section 451, 451.5, or 453, and attempted arson, which includes, but is not limited to, a violation of Section 455.

(b)

(1) Every person described in paragraph (2), (3), and (4), for the periods specified therein, shall, while residing in, or if the person has no residence, while located in California, be required to, within 14 days of coming into, or changing the person's residence or location within any city, county, city and county, or campus wherein the person temporarily resides, or if the person has no residence, is located:

(A) Register with the chief of police of the city where the person is residing, or if the person has no residence, where the person is located.

(B) Register with the sheriff of the county where the person is residing, or if the person has no residence, where the person is located in an unincorporated area or city that has no police department.

(C) In addition to (A) or (B) above, register with the chief of police of a campus of the University of California, the California State University, or community college where the person is residing, or if the person has no residence, where the person is located upon the campus or any of its facilities.

(2) Any person who, on or after November 30, 1994, is convicted in any court in this state of arson or attempted arson shall be required to register, in accordance with the provisions of this section, for the rest of their life.

(3) Any person who, having committed the offense of arson or attempted arson, and after having been adjudicated a ward of the juvenile court on or after January 1, 1993, is discharged or paroled from the Division of Juvenile Justice shall be required to register, in accordance with the provisions of this section, until that person attains 25 years of age, or until the person has their records sealed pursuant to Section 781 of the Welfare and Institutions Code, whichever comes first.

(4) Any person convicted of the offense of arson or attempted arson on or after January 1, 1985, through November 29, 1994, inclusive, in any court of this state, shall be required to register, in accordance with the provisions of this section, for a period of five years commencing, in the case where the person was confined for the offense, from the date of their release from confinement, or in the case where the person was not confined for the offense, from the date of sentencing or discharge, if that person was ordered by the court at the time that person was sentenced to register as an arson offender. The law enforcement agencies shall make registration information available to the chief fire official of a legally organized fire department or fire protection district having local jurisdiction where the person resides.

(c) Any person required to register pursuant to this section who is discharged or paroled from a jail, prison, school, road camp, or other penal institution, or from the Division of Juvenile Justice where they were confined because of the commission or attempted commission of arson, shall, prior to the discharge, parole, or release, be informed of their duty to register under this section by the official in charge of the place of confinement. The official shall require the person to read and sign the form as may be required by the Department of Justice, stating that the duty of the person to register under this section has been explained to them. The official in charge of the place of confinement shall obtain the address where the person expects to reside upon their discharge, parole, or release and shall report the address to the Department of Justice. The official in charge of the place of confinement shall give one copy of the form to the person, and shall, not later than 45 days prior to the scheduled release of the person, send one copy to the appropriate law enforcement agency having local jurisdiction where the person expects to reside upon their discharge, parole, or release; one copy to the prosecuting agency that prosecuted the person; one copy to the chief fire official of a legally organized fire department or fire protection district having local jurisdiction where the person expects to reside upon their discharge, parole, or release; and one copy to the Department of Justice. The official in charge of the place of confinement shall retain one copy. All forms shall be transmitted in time so as to be received by the local law enforcement agency and prosecuting agency 30 days prior to the discharge, parole, or release of the person.

(d) All records relating specifically to the registration in the custody of the Department of Justice, law enforcement agencies, and other agencies or public officials shall be destroyed when the person required to register under this subdivision for offenses adjudicated by a juvenile court attains 25 years of age or has their records sealed under the procedures set forth in Section 781 of the Welfare and Institutions Code, whichever event occurs first. This subdivision shall not be construed to require the destruction of other criminal offender or juvenile records relating to the case that are maintained by the Department of Justice, law enforcement agencies, the juvenile court, or other agencies and public officials unless ordered by the court under Section 781 of the Welfare and Institutions Code.

(e) Any person who is required to register pursuant to this section who is released on probation or discharged upon payment of a fine shall, prior to the release or discharge, be informed of their duty to register under this section by the probation department of the county in which they have been convicted, and the probation officer shall require the person to read and sign the form as may be required by the Department of Justice, stating that the duty of the person to register under this section has been explained to them. The probation officer shall obtain the address where the person expects to reside upon their release or discharge and shall report within three days the address to the Department of Justice. The probation officer shall give one copy of the form to the person, and shall send one copy to the appropriate law enforcement agency having local jurisdiction where the person expects to reside upon their discharge or release, one copy to the prosecuting agency that prosecuted the person, one copy to the chief fire official of a legally organized fire department or fire protection district having local jurisdiction where the person expects to reside upon their discharge or release, and one copy to the Department of Justice. The probation officer shall also retain one copy.

(f) The registration shall consist of (1) a statement in writing signed by the person, giving the information as may be required by the Department of Justice, and (2) the fingerprints and photograph of the person. Within three days thereafter, the registering law enforcement agency shall electronically forward the statement, fingerprints, and photograph to the Department of Justice.

(g) If any person required to register by this section changes their residence address, they shall inform, in writing within 10 days, the law enforcement agency with whom they last registered of their new address. The law enforcement agency shall, within three days after receipt of the information, electronically forward it to the Department of Justice. The Department of Justice shall forward appropriate registration data to the law enforcement agency having local jurisdiction of the new place of residence.

(h) Any person required to register under this section who violates any of the provisions thereof is guilty of a misdemeanor. Any person who has been convicted of arson or attempted arson and who is required to register under this section who willfully violates any of the provisions thereof is guilty of a misdemeanor and shall be sentenced to serve a term of not less than 90 days nor more than one year in a county jail. In no event does the court have the power to absolve a person who willfully violates this section from the obligation of spending at least 90 days of confinement in a county jail and of completing probation of at least one year.

(i) Whenever any person is released on parole or probation and is required to register under this section but fails to do so within the time prescribed, the Division of Juvenile Justice, or the court, as the case may be, shall order the parole or probation of that person revoked.

(j) The statements, photographs, and fingerprints required by this section shall not be open to inspection by the public or by any person other than a regularly employed peace officer or other law enforcement officer.

(k) In any case in which a person who would be required to register pursuant to this section is to be temporarily sent outside the institution where they are confined on any assignment within a city or county, including, but not limited to, firefighting or disaster control, the local law enforcement agency having jurisdiction over the place or places where that assignment shall occur shall be notified within a reasonable time prior to removal from the institution. This subdivision shall not apply to any person temporarily released under guard from the institution where they are confined.

(l) Nothing in this section shall be construed to conflict with Section 1203.4 concerning termination of probation and release from penalties and disabilities of probation. A person required to register under this section may initiate a proceeding under Chapter 3.5 (commencing with Section 4852.01) of Title 6 of Part 3 and, upon obtaining a certificate of rehabilitation, shall be relieved of any further duty to register under this section. This certificate shall not relieve the petitioner of the duty to register under this section for any offense subject to this section of which they are convicted in the future.

Any person who is required to register under this section due to a misdemeanor conviction shall be relieved of the requirement to register if that person is granted relief pursuant to Section 1203.4.

(m) For purposes of this section, a discharged person shall include all of the following:

(1) A ward in the custody of the Department of Corrections and Rehabilitation, Division of Juvenile Justice on or after July 1, 2022, who, prior to discharge, is returned by the division or the chief probation officer of the county to the court of jurisdiction for alternative disposition, specifically due to the statutorily required closure of the division. The division shall inform the ward of the duty to register prior to the ward being returned to the court.

(2) A patient described in Section 1732.10 of the Welfare and Institutions Code. The division shall inform the patient of the duty to register immediately prior to closure of the division.

(3) A person described in Section 1732.9 of the Welfare and Institutions Code. The Department of Corrections and Rehabilitation shall inform the person of the duty to register immediately prior to the person being returned to the court of jurisdiction.

(n) The court of jurisdiction shall establish the point at which the ward described in subdivision (m) is required to register and notify the Department of Justice of its decision.

Amended by Stats 2023 ch 311 (SB 883),s 4, eff. 1/1/2024.
Amended by Stats 2022 ch 771 (AB 160),s 14, eff. 9/29/2022.
EFFECTIVE 1/1/2000. Amended September 27, 1999 (Bill Number: SB 555) (Chapter 518).

Chapter 2 - BURGLARY

Section 458 - "Cargo container" defined

As used in this chapter, the term "cargo container" means a receptacle with all of the following characteristics:

(a) Of a permanent character and accordingly strong enough to be suitable for repeated use.

(b) Specially designed to facilitate the carriage of goods, by one or more modes of transport, one of which shall be by vessels, without intermediate reloading.

(c) Fitted with devices permitting its ready handling, particularly its transfer from one mode of transport to another.

(d) So designed to be easy to fill and empty.

(e) Having a cubic displacement of 1,000 cubic feet or more.

Added by Stats. 1984, Ch. 854, Sec. 1.

Section 459 - Burglary

Every person who enters any house, room, apartment, tenement, shop, warehouse, store, mill, barn, stable, outhouse or other building, tent, vessel, as defined in Section 21 of the Harbors and Navigation Code, floating home, as defined in subdivision (d) of Section 18075.55 of the Health and Safety Code, railroad car, locked or sealed cargo container, whether or not mounted on a vehicle, trailer coach, as defined in Section 635 of the Vehicle Code, any house car, as defined in Section 362 of the Vehicle Code, inhabited camper, as defined in Section 243 of the Vehicle Code, vehicle as defined by the Vehicle Code, when the doors are locked, aircraft as defined by Section 21012 of the Public Utilities Code, or mine or any underground portion thereof, with intent to commit grand or petit larceny or any felony is guilty of burglary. As used in this chapter, "inhabited" means currently being used for dwelling purposes, whether occupied or not. A house, trailer, vessel designed for habitation, or portion of a building is currently being used for dwelling purposes if, at the time of the burglary, it was not occupied solely because a natural or other disaster caused the occupants to leave the premises. Amended by Stats. 1991, Ch. 942, Sec. 14.

Section 459.5 - Entry into commercial establishment

(a) Notwithstanding Section 459, shoplifting is defined as entering a commercial establishment with intent to commit larceny while that establishment is open during regular business hours, where the value of the property that is taken or intended to be taken does not exceed nine hundred fifty dollars ($950). Any other entry into a commercial establishment with intent to commit larceny is burglary. Shoplifting shall be punished as a misdemeanor, except that a person with one or more prior convictions for an offense specified in clause (iv) of subparagraph (C) of paragraph (2) of subdivision (e) of Section 667 or for an offense requiring registration pursuant to subdivision (c) of Section 290 may be punished pursuant to subdivision (h) of Section 1170.

(b) Any act of shoplifting as defined in subdivision (a) shall be charged as shoplifting. No person who is charged with shoplifting may also be charged with burglary or theft of the same property.
Added by Proposition 47, eff. 11/5/2014.

Section 460 - Burglary of first degree; burglary of second degree

(a) Every burglary of an inhabited dwelling house, vessel, as defined in the Harbors and Navigation Code, which is inhabited and designed for habitation, floating home, as defined in subdivision (d) of Section 18075.55 of the Health and Safety Code, or trailer coach, as defined by the Vehicle Code, or the inhabited portion of any other building, is burglary of the first degree.

(b) All other kinds of burglary are of the second degree.

(c) This section shall not be construed to supersede or affect Section 464 of the Penal Code.
Amended by Stats. 1991, Ch. 942, Sec. 15.

Section 461 - Punishment

Burglary is punishable as follows:

(a) Burglary in the first degree: by imprisonment in the state prison for two, four, or six years.

(b) Burglary in the second degree: by imprisonment in the county jail not exceeding one year or imprisonment pursuant to subdivision (h) of Section 1170.
Amended by Stats 2011 ch 39 (AB 117),s 68, eff. 6/30/2011.
Amended by Stats 2011 ch 15 (AB 109),s 355, eff. 4/4/2011, but operative no earlier than October 1, 2011, and only upon creation of a community corrections grant program to assist in implementing this act and upon an appropriation to fund the grant program.
Amended by Stats 2009 ch 28 (SB X3-18),s 11, eff. 1/1/2010.

Section 462 - Probation

(a) Except in unusual cases where the interests of justice would best be served if the person is granted probation, probation shall not be granted to any person who is convicted of a burglary of an inhabited dwelling house or trailer coach as defined in Section 635 of the Vehicle Code, an inhabited floating home as defined in subdivision (d) of Section 18075.55 of the Health and Safety Code, or the inhabited portion of any other building.

(b) If the court grants probation under subdivision (a), it shall specify the reason or reasons for that order on the court record.
Amended by Stats. 1993, Ch. 162, Sec. 2. Effective January 1, 1994.

Section 462.5 - Probation for conviction for custodial institution burglary

(a) Except in unusual cases where the interests of justice would best be served if the person is granted probation, probation shall not be granted to any person who is convicted of a felony custodial institution burglary. In any case in which a person is convicted of a misdemeanor custodial institution burglary, such person shall be confined in the county jail for not less than 90 days nor more than one year except in unusual cases where the interests of justice would best be served by the granting of probation.

(b) As used in this section, "custodial institution burglary" shall mean a violation of Section 459 on the grounds of any jail or correctional institution with the intent to steal items to use or convert for use as weapons, escape tools, or intoxicating drugs.

(c) If the court grants probation under subdivision (a), it shall specify the reason or reasons for such order on the court record.

(d) Any person convicted of custodial institution burglary shall serve his or her sentence, including enhancements, consecutive to any other sentence in effect or pending. The felony sentence shall be calculated under Section 1170.1.
Added by Stats. 1982, Ch. 1132, Sec. 1.

Section 463 - Burglary during state of emergency

(a) Every person who violates Section 459, punishable as a second-degree burglary pursuant to subdivision (b) of Section 461, during and within an affected county in a "state of emergency" or a "local emergency," or under an "evacuation order," resulting from an earthquake, fire, flood, riot, or other natural or manmade disaster shall be guilty of the crime of looting, punishable by imprisonment in a county jail for one year or pursuant to subdivision (h) of Section 1170. Any person convicted under this subdivision who is eligible for probation and who is granted probation shall, as a condition thereof, be confined in a county jail for at least 180 days, except that the court may, in the case where the interest of justice would best be served, reduce or eliminate that mandatory jail sentence, if the court specifies on the record and enters into the minutes the circumstances indicating that the interest of justice would best be served by that disposition. In addition to whatever custody is ordered, the court, in its discretion, may require any person granted probation following conviction under this subdivision to serve up to 240 hours of community service in any program deemed appropriate by the court, including any program created to rebuild the community. For purposes of this subdivision, the fact that the structure entered has been damaged by the earthquake, fire, flood, or other natural or manmade disaster shall not, in and of itself, preclude conviction.

(b) Every person who commits the crime of grand theft, as defined in Section 487 or subdivision (a) of Section 487a, except grand theft of a firearm, during and within an affected county in a "state of emergency" or a "local emergency," or under an "evacuation order," resulting from an earthquake, fire, flood, riot, or other natural or unnatural disaster shall be guilty of the crime of looting, punishable by imprisonment in a county jail for one year or pursuant to subdivision (h) of Section 1170. Every person who commits the crime of grand theft of a firearm, as defined in Section 487, during and within an affected county in a "state of emergency" or a "local emergency" resulting from an earthquake, fire, flood, riot, or other natural or unnatural disaster shall be guilty of the crime of looting, punishable by imprisonment in the state prison, as set forth in subdivision (a) of Section 489. Any person convicted under this subdivision who is eligible for probation and who is granted probation shall, as a condition thereof, be confined in a county jail for at least 180 days, except that the court may, in the case where the interest of justice would best be served, reduce or eliminate that mandatory jail sentence, if the court specifies on the record and enters into the minutes the circumstances indicating that the interest of justice would best be served by that disposition. In addition to whatever custody is ordered, the court, in its discretion, may require any person granted probation following conviction under this subdivision to serve up to 160 hours of community service in any program deemed appropriate by the court, including any program created to rebuild the community.

(c) Every person who commits the crime of petty theft, as defined in Section 488, during and within an affected county in a "state of emergency" or a "local emergency," or under an "evacuation order," resulting from an earthquake, fire, flood, riot, or other natural or manmade disaster shall be guilty of a misdemeanor, punishable by imprisonment in a county jail for six months. Any person convicted under this subdivision who is eligible for probation and who is granted probation shall, as a condition thereof, be confined in a county jail for at least 90 days, except that the court may, in the case where the interest of justice would best be served, reduce or eliminate that mandatory minimum jail sentence, if the court specifies on the record and enters into the minutes the circumstances indicating that the interest of justice would best be served by that disposition. In addition to whatever custody is ordered, the court, in its discretion, may require any person granted probation following conviction under this subdivision to serve up to 80 hours of community service in any program deemed appropriate by the court, including any program created to rebuild the community.

(d)

(1) For purposes of this section, "state of emergency" means conditions that, by reason of their magnitude, are, or are likely to be, beyond the control of the services, personnel, equipment, and facilities of any single county, city and county, or city and require the combined forces of a mutual aid region or regions to combat.

(2) For purposes of this section, "local emergency" means conditions that, by reason of their magnitude, are, or are likely to be, beyond the control of the services, personnel, equipment, and facilities of any single county, city and county, or city and require the combined forces of a mutual aid region or regions to combat.

(3) For purposes of this section, a "state of emergency" shall exist from the time of the proclamation of the condition of the emergency until terminated pursuant to Section 8629 of the Government Code. For purposes of this section only, a "local emergency" shall exist from the time of the proclamation of the condition of the emergency by the local governing body until terminated pursuant to Section 8630 of the Government Code.

(4) For purposes of this section, "evacuation order" means an order from the Governor, or a county sheriff, chief of police, or fire marshal, under which persons subject to the order are required to relocate outside of the geographic area covered by the order due to an imminent danger resulting from an earthquake, fire, flood, riot, or other natural or manmade disaster.

(5) Consensual entry into a commercial structure with the intent to commit a violation of Section 470, 476, 476a, 484f, or 484g shall not be charged as a violation under this section.

Amended by Stats 2018 ch 132 (AB 3078),s 1, eff. 1/1/2019.
Amended by Stats 2013 ch 618 (AB 924),s 6, eff. 1/1/2014.
Amended by Stats 2011 ch 39 (AB 117),s 68, eff. 6/30/2011.
Amended by Stats 2011 ch 15 (AB 109),s 356, eff. 4/4/2011, but operative no earlier than October 1, 2011, and only upon creation of a community corrections grant program to assist in implementing this act and upon an appropriation to fund the grant program.
Amended by Stats 2009 ch 28 (SB X3-18),s 12, eff. 1/1/2010.

Section 464 - Unlawful opening of vault, safe, or other secure place

Any person who, with intent to commit crime, enters, either by day or by night, any building, whether inhabited or not, and opens or attempts to open any vault, safe, or other secure place by use of acetylene torch or electric arc, burning bar, thermal lance, oxygen lance, or any other similar device capable of burning through steel, concrete, or any other solid substance, or by use of nitroglycerine, dynamite, gunpowder, or any other explosive, is guilty of a felony and, upon conviction, shall be punished by imprisonment pursuant to subdivision (h) of Section 1170 for a term of three, five, or seven years.

Amended by Stats 2011 ch 39 (AB 117),s 68, eff. 6/30/2011.
Amended by Stats 2011 ch 15 (AB 109),s 357, eff. 4/4/2011, but operative no earlier than October 1, 2011, and only upon creation of a community corrections grant program to assist in implementing this act and upon an appropriation to fund the grant program.

Chapter 3 - BURGLARIOUS AND LARCENOUS INSTRUMENTS AND DEADLY WEAPONS

Section 466 - Unlawful possession of burglarious and larcenous instruments

Every person having upon him or her in his or her possession a picklock, crow, keybit, crowbar, screwdriver, vise grip pliers, water-pump pliers, slidehammer, slim jim, tension bar, lock pick gun, tubular lock pick, bump key, floor-safe door puller, master key, ceramic or porcelain spark plug chips or pieces, or other instrument or tool with intent feloniously to break or enter into any building, railroad car, aircraft, or vessel, trailer coach, or vehicle as defined in the Vehicle Code, or who shall knowingly make or alter, or shall attempt to make or alter, any key or other instrument named above so that the same will fit or open the lock of a building, railroad car, aircraft, vessel, trailer coach, or vehicle as defined in the Vehicle Code, without being requested to do so by some person having the right to open the same, or who shall make, alter, or repair any instrument or thing, knowing or having reason to believe that it is intended to be used in committing a misdemeanor or felony, is guilty of a misdemeanor. Any of the structures mentioned in Section 459 shall be deemed to be a building within the meaning of this section.

Amended by Stats 2008 ch 119 (SB 1554),s 1, eff. 1/1/2009.

Amended by Stats 2002 ch 335 (AB 2015), s 1, eff. 1/1/2003.

Amended by Stats 2001 ch 854 (SB 205), s 28, eff. 1/1/2002.

Section 466.1 - Unlawful sale of burglarious and larcenous instruments

Any person who knowingly and willfully sells or provides a lock pick, a tension bar, a lock pick gun, a tubular lock pick, or a floor-safe door puller, to another, whether or not for compensation, shall obtain the name, address, telephone number, if any, date of birth, and driver's license number or identification number, if any, of the person to whom the device is sold or provided. This information, together with the date the device was sold or provided and the signature of the person to whom the device was sold or provided, shall be set forth on a bill of sale or receipt. A copy of each bill of sale or receipt shall be retained for one year and shall be open to inspection by any peace officer during business hours.

Any person who violates any provision of this section is guilty of a misdemeanor.

Added by Stats. 1984, Ch. 82, Sec. 2.

Section 466.3 - Unlawful possession of device to open or damage coin-operated machine

(a) Whoever possesses a key, tool, instrument, explosive, or device, or a drawing, print, or mold of a key, tool, instrument, explosive, or device, designed to open, break into, tamper with, or damage a coin-operated machine as defined in subdivision (b), with intent to commit a theft from such machine, is punishable by imprisonment in the county jail for not more than one year, or by fine of not more than one thousand dollars ($1,000), or by both.

(b) As used in this section, the term "coin-operated machine" shall include any automatic vending machine or any part thereof, parking meter, coin telephone, coin laundry machine, coin dry cleaning machine, amusement machine, music machine, vending machine dispensing goods or services, or moneychanger.

Added by Stats. 1972, Ch. 1088.

Section 466.5 - Unlawful possession, use, manufacture, or sale of motor vehicle master key

(a) Every person who, with the intent to use it in the commission of an unlawful act, possesses a motor vehicle master key or a motor vehicle wheel lock master key is guilty of a misdemeanor.

(b) Every person who, with the intent to use it in the commission of an unlawful act, uses a motor vehicle master key to open a lock or operate the ignition switch of any motor vehicle or uses a motor vehicle wheel lock master key to open a wheel lock on any motor vehicle is guilty of a misdemeanor.

(c) Every person who knowingly manufactures for sale, advertises for sale, offers for sale, or sells a motor vehicle master key or a motor vehicle wheel lock master key, except to persons who use such keys in their lawful occupations or businesses, is guilty of a misdemeanor.

(d) As used in this section:

(1) "Motor vehicle master key" means a key which will operate all the locks or ignition switches, or both the locks and ignition switches, in a given group of motor vehicle locks or motor vehicle ignition switches, or both motor vehicle locks and motor vehicle ignition switches, each of which can be operated by a key which will not operate one or more of the other locks or ignition switches in such group.

(2) "Motor vehicle wheel lock" means a device attached to a motor vehicle wheel for theft protection purposes which can be removed only by a key unit unique to the wheel lock attached to a particular motor vehicle.

(3) "Motor vehicle wheel lock master key" means a key unit which will operate all the wheel locks in a given group of motor vehicle wheel locks, each of which can be operated by a key unit which will not operate any of the other wheel locks in the group.

Amended by Stats. 1976, Ch. 138.

Section 466.6 - Making of key capable of operating ignition of motor vehicle

(a) Any person who makes a key capable of operating the ignition of a motor vehicle or personal property registered under the Vehicle Code for another by any method other than by the duplication of an existing key, whether or not for compensation, shall obtain the name, address, telephone number, if any, date of birth, and driver's license number or identification number of the person requesting or purchasing the key; and the registration or identification number, license number, year, make, model, color, and vehicle identification number of the vehicle or personal property registered under the Vehicle Code for which the key is to be made. Such information, together with the date the key was made and the signature of the person for whom the key was made, shall be set forth on a work order. A copy of each such work order shall be retained for two years, shall include the name and permit number of the locksmith performing the service, and shall be open to inspection by any peace officer or by the Bureau of Collection and Investigative Services during business hours or submitted to the bureau upon request. Any person who violates any provision of this subdivision is guilty of a misdemeanor.

(b) The provisions of this section shall include, but are not limited to, the making of a key from key codes or impressions.

(c) Nothing contained in this section shall be construed to prohibit the duplication of any key for a motor vehicle from another key.

Amended by Stats. 1992, Ch. 1135, Sec. 27. Effective January 1, 1993.

Section 466.65 - Unlawful possession, gift, or lending of device designed to bypass motorcycle ignition

(a) Every person who possesses, gives, or lends any device designed to bypass the factory-installed ignition of a motorcycle in order to start the engine of a motorcycle without a manufacturer's key, or who possesses, gives, or lends any motorcycle ignition, or part thereof, with the intent to unlawfully take or drive, or to facilitate the unlawful taking or driving of, a motorcycle without the consent of the owner, is guilty of a misdemeanor.

(b) Every person who possesses, gives, or lends any item of hardware, including, but not limited to, boltcutters, electrical tape, wirecutters, wire strippers, or allen wrenches, with the intent to unlawfully take or drive, or to facilitate the unlawful taking or driving of, a motorcycle without the consent of the owner, is guilty of a misdemeanor.

Added by Stats 2010 ch 120 (AB 1848),s 1, eff. 1/1/2011.

Section 466.7 - Unlawful possession of motor vehicle key

Every person who, with the intent to use it in the commission of an unlawful act, possesses a motor vehicle key with knowledge that such key was made without the consent of either the registered or legal owner of the motor vehicle or of a person who is in lawful possession of the motor vehicle, is guilty of a misdemeanor.

Added by Stats. 1977, Ch. 1147.

Section 466.8 - Unlawful making of key for residence or commercial establishment

(a) Any person who knowingly and willfully makes a key capable of opening any door or other means of entrance to any residence or commercial establishment for another by any method involving an onsite inspection of such door or entrance, whether or not for compensation, shall obtain, together with the date the key was made, the street address of the residence or commercial establishment, and the signature of the person for whom the key was made, on a work order form, the following information regarding the person requesting or purchasing the key:

   (1) Name.
   (2) Address.
   (3) Telephone number, if any.
   (4) Date of birth.
   (5) Driver's license number or identification number, if any. A copy of each such work order shall be retained for two years and shall be open to inspection by any peace officer or by the Bureau of Collection and Investigative Services during business hours or submitted to the bureau upon request.

Any person who violates any provision of this subdivision is guilty of a misdemeanor.

(b) Nothing contained in this section shall be construed to prohibit the duplication of any key for a residence or commercial establishment from another such key.

(c) Locksmiths licensed by the Bureau of Collection and Investigative Services are subject to the provisions set forth in Chapter 8.5 (commencing with Section 6980) of Division 3 of the Business and Professions Code.

(d) The provisions of this section shall include, but are not limited to, the making of a key from key codes or impressions.

Amended by Stats. 1992, Ch. 1135, Sec. 28. Effective January 1, 1993.

Section 466.9 - Unlawful possession or use of code grabbing device

(a) Every person who possesses a code grabbing device, with the intent to use it in the commission of an unlawful act, is guilty of a misdemeanor.

(b) Every person who uses a code grabbing device to disarm the security alarm system of a motor vehicle, with the intent to use the device in the commission of an unlawful act, is guilty of a misdemeanor.

(c) As used in this section, "code grabbing device" means a device that can receive and record the coded signal sent by the transmitter of a motor vehicle security alarm system and can play back the signal to disarm that system.

Added by renumbering Section 446.9 by Stats. 1995, Ch. 91, Sec. 124. Effective January 1, 1996.

Section 468 - Unlawful purchase, sale, receipt, disposal, concealment, or possession of sniperscope

Any person who knowingly buys, sells, receives, disposes of, conceals, or has in his possession a sniperscope shall be guilty of a misdemeanor, punishable by a fine not to exceed one thousand dollars ($1,000) or by imprisonment in the county jail for not more than one year, or by both such fine and imprisonment.

As used in this section, sniperscope means any attachment, device or similar contrivance designed for or adaptable to use on a firearm which, through the use of a projected infrared light source and electronic telescope, enables the operator thereof to visually determine and locate the presence of objects during the nighttime.

This section shall not prohibit the authorized use or possession of such sniperscope by a member of the armed forces of the United States or by police officers, peace officers, or law enforcement officers authorized by the properly constituted authorities for the enforcement of law or ordinances; nor shall this section prohibit the use or possession of such sniperscope when used solely for scientific research or educational purposes.

Added by Stats. 1958, 1st Ex. Sess., Ch. 76.

Section 469 - Unlawful making, duplicating, or use of key to public building

Any person who knowingly makes, duplicates, causes to be duplicated, or uses, or attempts to make, duplicate, cause to be duplicated, or use, or has in his possession any key to a building or other area owned, operated, or controlled by the State of California, any state agency, board, or commission, a county, city, or any public school or community college district without authorization from the person in charge of such building or area or his designated representative and with knowledge of the lack of such authorization is guilty of a misdemeanor.

Added by Stats. 1970, Ch. 1090.

Chapter 4 - FORGERY AND COUNTERFEITING

Section 470 - Forgery

(a) Every person who, with the intent to defraud, knowing that he or she has no authority to do so, signs the name of another person or of a fictitious person to any of the items listed in subdivision (d) is guilty of forgery.

(b) Every person who, with the intent to defraud, counterfeits or forges the seal or handwriting of another is guilty of forgery.

(c) Every person who, with the intent to defraud, alters, corrupts, or falsifies any record of any will, codicil, conveyance, or other instrument, the record of which is by law evidence, or any record of any judgment of a court or the return of any officer to any process of any court, is guilty of forgery.

(d) Every person who, with the intent to defraud, falsely makes, alters, forges, or counterfeits, utters, publishes, passes or attempts or offers to pass, as true and genuine, any of the following items, knowing the same to be false, altered, forged, or counterfeited, is guilty of forgery: any check, bond, bank bill, or note, cashier's check, traveler's check, money order, post note, draft, any controller's warrant for the payment of money at the treasury, county order or warrant, or request for the payment of money, receipt for money or goods, bill of exchange, promissory note, order, or any assignment of any bond, writing obligatory, or other contract for money or other property, contract, due bill for payment of money or property, receipt for money or property, passage ticket, lottery ticket or share purporting to be issued under the California State Lottery Act of 1984, trading stamp, power of attorney, certificate of ownership or other document evidencing ownership of a vehicle or undocumented vessel, or any certificate of any share, right, or interest in the stock of any corporation or association, or the delivery of goods or chattels of any kind, or for the delivery of any instrument of writing, or acquittance, release or discharge of any debt, account, suit, action, demand, or any other thing, real or personal, or any transfer or assurance of money, certificate of shares of stock, goods, chattels, or other property whatever, or any letter of attorney, or other power to receive money, or to receive or transfer certificates of shares of stock or annuities, or to let, lease, dispose of, alien, or convey any goods, chattels, lands, or tenements, or other estate, real or personal, or falsifies the acknowledgment of any notary public, or any notary public who issues an acknowledgment knowing it to be false; or any matter described in subdivision (b).

(e) Upon a trial for forging any bill or note purporting to be the bill or note of an incorporated company or bank, or for passing, or attempting to pass, or having in possession with intent to pass, any forged bill or note, it is not necessary to prove the incorporation of the bank or company by the charter or act of incorporation, but it may be proved by general reputation; and persons of skill are competent witnesses to prove that the bill or note is forged or counterfeited.

Amended by Stats 2005 ch 295 (AB 361),s 5, eff. 1/1/2006

Section 470a - Unlawful reproduction or counterfeiting of driver's license or identification card

Every person who alters, falsifies, forges, duplicates or in any manner reproduces or counterfeits any driver's license or identification card issued by a governmental agency with the intent that such driver's license or identification card be used to facilitate the commission of any forgery, is punishable by imprisonment in a county jail for not more than one year, or by imprisonment pursuant to subdivision (h) of Section 1170.

Amended by Stats 2011 ch 39 (AB 117),s 68, eff. 6/30/2011.

Amended by Stats 2011 ch 15 (AB 109),s 358, eff. 4/4/2011, but operative no earlier than October 1, 2011, and only upon creation of a community corrections grant program to assist in implementing this act and upon an appropriation to fund the grant program.

Section 470b - Unlawful display or possession of reproduced or counterfeit driver's license or identification card

Every person who displays or causes or permits to be displayed or has in his or her possession any driver's license or identification card of the type enumerated in Section 470a with the intent that the driver's license or identification card be used to facilitate the commission of any forgery, is punishable by imprisonment in a county jail for not more than one year, or by imprisonment pursuant to subdivision (h) of Section 1170.

Amended by Stats 2011 ch 39 (AB 117),s 68, eff. 6/30/2011.

Amended by Stats 2011 ch 15 (AB 109),s 359, eff. 4/4/2011, but operative no earlier than October 1, 2011, and only upon creation of a community corrections grant program to assist in implementing this act and upon an appropriation to fund the grant program.

Section 471 - Unlawful forgery or alteration of book of records

Every person who, with intent to defraud another, makes, forges, or alters any entry in any book of records, or any instrument purporting to be any record or return specified in Section 470, is guilty of forgery.

Amended by Stats 2002 ch 787 (SB 1798), s 11, eff. 1/1/2003.

Section 471.5 - Unlawful alteration or modification of medical record

Any person who alters or modifies the medical record of any person, with fraudulent intent, or who, with fraudulent intent, creates any false medical record, is guilty of a misdemeanor.

Amended by Stats. 1979, Ch. 644.

Section 472 - Forgery or counterfeit of seal

Every person who, with intent to defraud another, forges, or counterfeits the seal of this State, the seal of any public officer authorized by law, the seal of any Court of record, or the seal of any corporation, or any other public seal authorized or recognized by the laws of this State, or of any other State, Government, or country, or who falsely makes, forges, or counterfeits any impression purporting to be an impression of any such seal, or who has in his possession any such counterfeited seal or impression thereof, knowing it to be counterfeited, and willfully conceals the same, is guilty of forgery.

Enacted 1872.

Section 473 - Punishment of forgery

(a) Forgery is punishable by imprisonment in a county jail for not more than one year, or by imprisonment pursuant to subdivision (h) of Section 1170.

(b) Notwithstanding subdivision (a), any person who is guilty of forgery relating to a check, bond, bank bill, note, cashier's check, traveler's check, or money order, where the value of the check, bond, bank bill, note, cashier's check, traveler's check, or money order does not exceed nine hundred fifty dollars ($950), shall be punishable by imprisonment in a county jail for not more than one year, except that such person may instead be punished pursuant to subdivision (h) of Section 1170 if that person has one or more prior convictions for an offense specified in clause (iv) of subparagraph (C) of paragraph (2) of subdivision (e) of Section 667 or for an offense requiring registration pursuant to subdivision (c) of Section 290. This subdivision shall not be applicable to any person who is convicted both of forgery and of identity theft, as defined in Section 530.5.

Amended by Proposition 47, eff. 11/5/2014.

Amended by Stats 2011 ch 39 (AB 117),s 68, eff. 6/30/2011.

Amended by Stats 2011 ch 15 (AB 109),s 360, eff. 4/4/2011, but operative no earlier than October 1, 2011, and only upon creation of a community corrections grant program to assist in implementing this act and upon an appropriation to fund the grant program.

Section 474 - False or forged message

Every person who knowingly and willfully sends by telegraph or telephone to any person a false or forged message, purporting to be from a telegraph or telephone office, or from any other person, or who willfully delivers or causes to be delivered to any person any such message falsely purporting to have been received by telegraph or telephone, or who furnishes, or conspires to furnish, or causes to be furnished to any agent, operator, or employee, to be sent by telegraph or telephone, or to be delivered, any such message, knowing the same to be false or forged, with the intent to deceive, injure, or defraud another, is punishable by imprisonment in a county jail not exceeding one year, or by imprisonment pursuant to subdivision (h) of Section 1170, or by a fine not exceeding ten thousand dollars ($10,000), or by both that fine and imprisonment.

Amended by Stats 2011 ch 39 (AB 117),s 68, eff. 6/30/2011.

Amended by Stats 2011 ch 15 (AB 109),s 361, eff. 4/4/2011, but operative no earlier than October 1, 2011, and only upon creation of a community corrections grant program to assist in implementing this act and upon an appropriation to fund the grant program.

Section 475 - Unlawful possession or receipt of forged, altered, or counterfeit items; unlawful possession of check, note, bank bill, money order, or traveler's check

(a) Every person who possesses or receives, with the intent to pass or facilitate the passage or utterance of any forged, altered, or counterfeit items, or completed items contained in subdivision (d) of Section 470 with intent to defraud, knowing the same to be forged, altered, or counterfeit, is guilty of forgery.

(b) Every person who possesses any blank or unfinished check, note, bank bill, money order, or traveler's check, whether real or fictitious, with the intention of completing the same or the intention of facilitating the completion of the same, in order to defraud any person, is guilty of forgery.

(c) Every person who possesses any completed check, money order, traveler's check, warrant or county order, whether real or fictitious, with the intent to utter or pass or facilitate the utterance or passage of the same, in order to defraud any person, is guilty of forgery.

Repealed and added by Stats. 1998, Ch. 468, Sec. 4. Effective January 1, 1999.

Section 476 - Unlawful making, passing, uttering, or publishing fictitious or altered bill, note, or check

Every person who makes, passes, utters, or publishes, with intent to defraud any other person, or who, with the like intent, attempts to pass, utter, or publish, or who has in his or her possession, with like intent to utter, pass, or publish, any fictitious or altered bill, note, or check, purporting to be the bill, note, or check, or other instrument in writing for the payment of money or property of any real or fictitious financial institution as defined in Section 186.9 is guilty of forgery.

Repealed and added by Stats. 1998, Ch. 468, Sec. 7. Effective January 1, 1999.

Section 476a - Making or drawing or uttering or delivering check, draft, or order knowing funds are not sufficient

(a) Any person who, for himself or herself, as the agent or representative of another, or as an officer of a corporation, willfully, with intent to defraud, makes or draws or utters or delivers a check, draft, or order upon a bank or depositary, a person, a firm, or a corporation, for the payment of money, knowing at the time of that making, drawing, uttering, or delivering that the maker or drawer or the corporation has not sufficient funds in, or credit with the bank or depositary, person, firm, or corporation, for the payment of that check, draft, or order and all other checks, drafts, or orders upon funds then outstanding, in full upon its presentation, although no express representation is made with reference thereto, is punishable by imprisonment in a county jail for not more than one year, or pursuant to subdivision (h) of Section 1170.

(b) However, if the total amount of all checks, drafts, or orders that the defendant is charged with and convicted of making, drawing, or uttering does not exceed nine hundred fifty dollars ($950), the offense is punishable only by imprisonment in the county jail for not more than one year, except that such person may instead be punished pursuant to subdivision (h) of Section 1170 if that person has one or more prior convictions for an offense specified in clause (iv) of subparagraph (C) of paragraph (2) of subdivision (e) of Section 667 or for an offense requiring registration pursuant to subdivision (c) of Section 290. This subdivision shall not be applicable if the defendant has previously been convicted of three or more violations of Section 470, 475, or 476, or of this section, or of the crime of petty theft in a case in which defendant's offense was a violation also of Section 470, 475, or 476 or of this section or if the defendant has previously been convicted of any offense under the laws of any other state or of the United States which, if committed in this state, would have been punishable as a violation of Section 470, 475 or 476 or of this section or if he has been so convicted of the crime of petty theft in a case in which, if defendant's offense had been committed in this state, it would have been a violation also of Section 470, 475, or 476, or of this section.

(c) Where the check, draft, or order is protested on the ground of insufficiency of funds or credit, the notice of protest shall be admissible as proof of presentation, nonpayment, and protest and shall be presumptive evidence of knowledge of insufficiency of funds or credit with the bank or depositary, person, firm, or corporation.

(d) In any prosecution under this section involving two or more checks, drafts, or orders, it shall constitute prima facie evidence of the identity of the drawer of a check, draft, or order if both of the following occur:

(1) When the payee accepts the check, draft, or order from the drawer, he or she obtains from the drawer the following information: name and residence of the drawer, business or mailing address, either a valid driver's license number or Department of Motor Vehicles identification card number, and the drawer's home or work phone number or place of employment. That information may be recorded on the check, draft, or order itself or may be retained on file by the payee and referred to on the check, draft, or order by identifying number or other similar means.

(2) The person receiving the check, draft, or order witnesses the drawer's signature or endorsement, and, as evidence of that, initials the check, draft, or order at the time of receipt.

(e) The word "credit" as used herein shall be construed to mean an arrangement or understanding with the bank or depositary, person, firm, or corporation for the payment of a check, draft, or order.

(f) If any of the preceding paragraphs, or parts thereof, shall be found unconstitutional or invalid, the remainder of this section shall not thereby be invalidated, but shall remain in full force and effect.

(g) A sheriff's department, police department, or other law enforcement agency may collect a fee from the defendant for investigation, collection, and processing of checks referred to their agency for investigation of alleged violations of this section or Section 476.

(h) The amount of the fee shall not exceed twenty-five dollars ($25) for each bad check, in addition to the amount of any bank charges incurred by the victim as a result of the alleged offense. If the sheriff's department, police department, or other law enforcement agency collects a fee for bank charges incurred by the victim pursuant to this section, that fee shall be paid to the victim for any bank fees the victim may have been assessed. In no event shall reimbursement of the bank charge to the victim pursuant to this section exceed ten dollars ($10) per check.

Amended by Proposition 47, eff. 11/5/2014.

Amended by Stats 2012 ch 43 (SB 1023),s 19, eff. 6/27/2012.
Amended by Stats 2009 ch 28 (SB X3-18),s 13, eff. 1/1/2010.
Section 477 - Unlawful counterfeiting of gold or silver
Every person who counterfeits any of the species of gold or silver coin current in this State, or any kind or species of gold dust, gold or silver bullion, or bars, lumps, pieces, or nuggets, or who sells, passes, or gives in payment such counterfeit coin, dust, bullion, bars, lumps, pieces, or nuggets, or permits, causes, or procures the same to be sold, uttered, or passed, with intention to defraud any person, knowing the same to be counterfeited, is guilty of counterfeiting.

Enacted 1872.

Section 478 - Punishment for counterfeiting
Counterfeiting is punishable by imprisonment pursuant to subdivision (h) of Section 1170 for two, three or four years.

Amended by Stats 2011 ch 39 (AB 117),s 68, eff. 6/30/2011.
Amended by Stats 2011 ch 15 (AB 109),s 362, eff. 4/4/2011, but operative no earlier than October 1, 2011, and only upon creation of a community corrections grant program to assist in implementing this act and upon an appropriation to fund the grant program.

Section 479 - Unlawful possession or receipt of counterfeit gold or silver
Every person who has in his possession, or receives for any other person, any counterfeit gold or silver coin of the species current in this state, or any counterfeit gold dust, gold or silver bullion or bars, lumps, pieces or nuggets, with the intention to sell, utter, put off or pass the same, or permits, causes or procures the same to be sold, uttered or passed, with intention to defraud any person, knowing the same to be counterfeit, is punishable by imprisonment pursuant to subdivision (h) of Section 1170 for two, three or four years.

Amended by Stats 2011 ch 39 (AB 117),s 68, eff. 6/30/2011.
Amended by Stats 2011 ch 15 (AB 109),s 363, eff. 4/4/2011, but operative no earlier than October 1, 2011, and only upon creation of a community corrections grant program to assist in implementing this act and upon an appropriation to fund the grant program.

Section 480 - Unlawful making or possession of counterfeiting apparatus or machine
(a) Every person who makes, or knowingly has in his or her possession any die, plate, or any apparatus, paper, metal, machine, or other thing whatever, made use of in counterfeiting coin current in this state, or in counterfeiting gold dust, gold or silver bars, bullion, lumps, pieces, or nuggets, or in counterfeiting bank notes or bills, is punishable by imprisonment pursuant to subdivision (h) of Section 1170 for two, three, or four years; and all dies, plates, apparatus, papers, metals, or machines intended for the purpose aforesaid, must be destroyed.

(b)

(1) If the counterfeiting apparatus or machine used to violate this section is a computer, computer system, or computer network, the apparatus or machine shall be disposed of pursuant to Section 502.01.

(2) For the purposes of this section, "computer system" and "computer network" have the same meaning as that specified in Section 502. The terms "computer, computer system, or computer network" include any software or data residing on the computer, computer system, or computer network used in a violation of this section.

Amended by Stats 2011 ch 39 (AB 117),s 68, eff. 6/30/2011.
Amended by Stats 2011 ch 15 (AB 109),s 364, eff. 4/4/2011, but operative no earlier than October 1, 2011, and only upon creation of a community corrections grant program to assist in implementing this act and upon an appropriation to fund the grant program.
EFFECTIVE 1/1/2000. Amended August 30, 1999 (Bill Number: AB 451) (Chapter 254).

Section 481 - Unlawful counterfeiting of ticket issued by railroad or steamship company
Every person who counterfeits, forges, or alters any ticket, check, order, coupon, receipt for fare, or pass, issued by any railroad or steamship company, or by any lessee or manager thereof, designed to entitle the holder to ride in the cars or vessels of such company, or who utters, publishes, or puts into circulation, any such counterfeit or altered ticket, check, or order, coupon, receipt for fare, or pass, with intent to defraud any such railroad or steamship company, or any lessee thereof, or any other person, is punishable by imprisonment in a county jail, not exceeding one year, or by imprisonment pursuant to subdivision (h) of Section 1170, or by fine not exceeding one thousand dollars, or by both that imprisonment and fine.

Amended by Stats 2011 ch 39 (AB 117),s 68, eff. 6/30/2011.
Amended by Stats 2011 ch 15 (AB 109),s 365, eff. 4/4/2011, but operative no earlier than October 1, 2011, and only upon creation of a community corrections grant program to assist in implementing this act and upon an appropriation to fund the grant program.

Section 481.1 - Unlawful counterfeiting or possession of fare media
(a) Every person who counterfeits, forges, or alters any fare media designed to entitle the holder to a ride on vehicles of a public transportation system, as defined by Section 99211 of the Public Utilities Code, or on vehicles operated by entities subsidized by the Department of Transportation is punishable by imprisonment in a county jail, not exceeding one year, or in the state prison.

(b) Every person who knowingly possesses any counterfeit, forged, or altered fare media designed to entitle the holder to a ride on vehicles of a public transportation system, as defined by Section 99211 of the Public Utilities Code, or on vehicles operated by entities subsidized by the Department of Transportation, or who utters, publishes, or puts into circulation any fare media with intent to defraud is punishable by imprisonment in a county jail not exceeding one year, or by a fine not exceeding one thousand dollars ($1,000), or by both that imprisonment and fine.

Amended by Stats 2001 ch 854 (SB 205), s 29, eff. 1/1/2002.

Section 482 - Unlawful restoration of ticket of railroad or steamship company
Every person who, for the purpose of restoring to its original appearance and nominal value in whole or in part, removes, conceals, fills up, or obliterates, the cuts, marks, punch-holes, or other evidence of cancellation, from any ticket, check, order, coupon, receipt for fare, or pass, issued by any railroad or steamship company, or any lessee or manager thereof, canceled in whole or in part, with intent to dispose of by sale or gift, or to circulate the same, or with intent to defraud the railroad or steamship company, or lessee thereof, or any other person, or who, with like intent to defraud, offers for sale, or in payment of fare on the railroad or vessel of the company, such ticket, check, order, coupon, or pass, knowing the same to have been so restored, in whole or in part, is punishable by imprisonment in the county jail not exceeding six months, or by a fine not exceeding one thousand dollars, or by both such imprisonment and fine.

Amended by Stats. 1905, Ch. 515.

Section 483 - Unlawful sale of ticket for common carrier

Except as otherwise provided in Section 26002.5 of the Government Code and Sections 40180.5 and 99151 of the Public Utilities Code, any person, firm, corporation, partnership, or association that shall sell to another any ticket, pass, scrip, mileage or commutation book, coupon, or other instrument for passage on a common carrier, for the use of any person not entitled to use the same according to the terms thereof, or of the book or portion thereof from which it was detached, shall be guilty of a misdemeanor.

Amended by Stats. 1979, Ch. 161.

Section 483.5 - Unlawful manufacture, sale, or furnishing of deceptive identification document

(a) No deceptive identification document shall be manufactured, sold, offered for sale, furnished, offered to be furnished, transported, offered to be transported, or imported or offered to be imported into this state unless there is diagonally across the face of the document, in not less than 14-point type and printed conspicuously on the document in permanent ink, the following statement: NOT A GOVERNMENT DOCUMENT
and, also printed conspicuously on the document, the name of the manufacturer.

(b) No document-making device may be possessed with the intent that the device will be used to manufacture, alter, or authenticate a deceptive identification document.

(c) As used in this section, "deceptive identification document" means any document not issued by a governmental agency of this state, another state, the federal government, a foreign government, a political subdivision of a foreign government, an international government, or an international quasi-governmental organization, which purports to be, or which might deceive an ordinary reasonable person into believing that it is, a document issued by such an agency, including, but not limited to, a driver's license, identification card, birth certificate, passport, or social security card.

(d) As used in this section, "document-making device" includes, but is not limited to, an implement, tool, equipment, impression, laminate, card, template, computer file, computer disk, electronic device, hologram, laminate machine or computer hardware or software.

(e) Any person who violates or proposes to violate this section may be enjoined by any court of competent jurisdiction. Actions for injunction under this section may be prosecuted by the Attorney General, any district attorney, or any city attorney prosecuting on behalf of the people of the State of California under Section 41803.5 of the Government Code in this state in the name of the people of the State of California upon their own complaint or upon the complaint of any person.

(f) Any person who violates the provisions of subdivision (a) who knows or reasonably should know that the deceptive identification document will be used for fraudulent purposes is guilty of a crime, and upon conviction therefor, shall be punished by imprisonment in a county jail not to exceed one year, or by imprisonment pursuant to subdivision (h) of Section 1170. Any person who violates the provisions of subdivision (b) is guilty of a misdemeanor punishable by imprisonment in a county jail not exceeding one year, or by a fine not exceeding one thousand dollars ($1,000), or by both imprisonment and a fine. Any document-making device may be seized by law enforcement and shall be forfeited to law enforcement or destroyed by order of the court upon a finding that the device was intended to be used to manufacture, alter, or authenticate a deceptive identification document. The court may make such a finding in the absence of a defendant for whom a bench warrant has been issued by the court.

Amended by Stats 2011 ch 39 (AB 117),s 68, eff. 6/30/2011.

Amended by Stats 2011 ch 15 (AB 109),s 366, eff. 4/4/2011, but operative no earlier than October 1, 2011, and only upon creation of a community corrections grant program to assist in implementing this act and upon an appropriation to fund the grant program.

Amended by Stats 2005 ch 326 (AB 1069),s 1, eff. 1/1/2006

Chapter 5 - LARCENY

Section 484 - Theft

(a) Every person who shall feloniously steal, take, carry, lead, or drive away the personal property of another, or who shall fraudulently appropriate property which has been entrusted to him or her, or who shall knowingly and designedly, by any false or fraudulent representation or pretense, defraud any other person of money, labor or real or personal property, or who causes or procures others to report falsely of his or her wealth or mercantile character and by thus imposing upon any person, obtains credit and thereby fraudulently gets or obtains possession of money, or property or obtains the labor or service of another, is guilty of theft. In determining the value of the property obtained, for the purposes of this section, the reasonable and fair market value shall be the test, and in determining the value of services received the contract price shall be the test. If there be no contract price, the reasonable and going wage for the service rendered shall govern. For the purposes of this section, any false or fraudulent representation or pretense made shall be treated as continuing, so as to cover any money, property or service received as a result thereof, and the complaint, information or indictment may charge that the crime was committed on any date during the particular period in question. The hiring of any additional employee or employees without advising each of them of every labor claim due and unpaid and every judgment that the employer has been unable to meet shall be prima facie evidence of intent to defraud.

(b)

(1) Except as provided in Section 10855 of the Vehicle Code, where a person has leased or rented the personal property of another person pursuant to a written contract, and that property has a value greater than one thousand dollars ($1,000) and is not a commonly used household item, intent to commit theft by fraud shall be rebuttably presumed if the person fails to return the personal property to its owner within 10 days after the owner has made written demand by certified or registered mail following the expiration of the lease or rental agreement for return of the property so leased or rented.

(2) Except as provided in Section 10855 of the Vehicle Code, where a person has leased or rented the personal property of another person pursuant to a written contract, and where the property has a value no greater than one thousand dollars ($1,000), or where the property is a commonly used household item, intent to commit theft by fraud shall be rebuttably presumed if the person fails to return the personal property to its owner within 20 days after the owner has made written demand by certified or registered mail following the expiration of the lease or rental agreement for return of the property so leased or rented.

(c) Notwithstanding the provisions of subdivision (b), if one presents with criminal intent identification which bears a false or fictitious name or address for the purpose of obtaining the lease or rental of the personal property of another, the presumption created herein shall apply upon the failure of the lessee to return the rental property at the expiration of the lease or rental agreement, and no written demand for the return of the leased or rented property shall be required.

(d) The presumptions created by subdivisions (b) and (c) are presumptions affecting the burden of producing evidence.

(e) Within 30 days after the lease or rental agreement has expired, the owner shall make written demand for return of the property so leased or rented. Notice addressed and mailed to the lessee or renter at the address given at the time of the making of the lease or rental agreement and to any other known address shall constitute proper demand. Where the owner fails to make such written demand the presumption created by subdivision (b) shall not apply.

Amended by Stats 2000 ch 176 (SB 1867), s 1, eff. 1/1/2001.

Section 484.1 - Theft from pawnbroker or secondhand dealer

(a) Any person who knowingly gives false information or provides false verification as to the person's true identity or as to the person's ownership interest in property or the person's authority to sell property in order to receive money or other valuable consideration from a pawnbroker or secondhand dealer and who receives money or other valuable consideration from the pawnbroker or secondhand dealer is guilty of theft.

(b) Upon conviction of the offense described in subdivision (a), the court may require, in addition to any sentence or fine imposed, that the defendant make restitution to the pawnbroker or secondhand dealer in an amount not exceeding the actual losses sustained pursuant to the provisions of subdivision (c) of Section 13967 of the Government Code, as operative on or before September 28, 1994, if the defendant is denied probation, or Section 1203.04, as operative on or before August 2, 1995, if the defendant is granted probation or Section 1202.4.

(c) Upon the setting of a court hearing date for sentencing of any person convicted under this section, the probation officer, if one is assigned, shall notify the pawnbroker or secondhand dealer or coin dealer of the time and place of the hearing.

Amended by Stats. 1996, Ch. 1077, Sec. 18.5. Effective January 1, 1997.

Section 484b - Wrongful diversion of money received for obtaining or paying for services, labor, materials, and equipment

Any person who receives money for the purpose of obtaining or paying for services, labor, materials or equipment and willfully fails to apply such money for such purpose by either willfully failing to complete the improvements for which funds were provided or willfully failing to pay for services, labor, materials or equipment provided incident to such construction, and wrongfully diverts the funds to a use other than that for which the funds were received, shall be guilty of a public offense and shall be punishable by a fine not exceeding ten thousand dollars ($10,000), or by imprisonment in a county jail not exceeding one year, or by imprisonment pursuant to subdivision (h) of Section 1170, or by both that fine and that imprisonment if the amount diverted is in excess of two thousand three hundred fifty dollars ($2,350). If the amount diverted is less than or equal to two thousand three hundred fifty dollars ($2,350), the person shall be guilty of a misdemeanor.

Amended by Stats 2011 ch 39 (AB 117),s 68, eff. 6/30/2011.

Amended by Stats 2011 ch 15 (AB 109),s 367, eff. 4/4/2011, but operative no earlier than October 1, 2011, and only upon creation of a community corrections grant program to assist in implementing this act and upon an appropriation to fund the grant program.

Amended by Stats 2009 ch 28 (SB X3-18),s 14, eff. 1/1/2010.

Amended by Stats 2009 ch 35 (SB 174),s 9, eff. 1/1/2010.

Section 484c - Embezzlement by submission of false voucher to obtain construction loan funds

Any person who submits a false voucher to obtain construction loan funds and does not use the funds for the purpose for which the claim was submitted is guilty of embezzlement.

Added by Stats. 1965, Ch. 1145.

Section 484d - Definitions

As used in this section and Sections 484e to 484j, inclusive:

(1) "Cardholder" means any person to whom an access card is issued or any person who has agreed with the card issuer to pay obligations arising from the issuance of an access card to another person.

(2) "Access card" means any card, plate, code, account number, or other means of account access that can be used, alone or in conjunction with another access card, to obtain money, goods, services, or any other thing of value, or that can be used to initiate a transfer of funds, other than a transfer originated solely by a paper instrument.

(3) "Expired access card" means an access card which shows on its face it has elapsed.

(4) "Card issuer" means any person who issues an access card or the agent of that person with respect to that card.

(5) "Retailer" means every person who is authorized by an issuer to furnish money, goods, services, or anything else of value upon presentation of an access card by a cardholder.

(6) An access card is "incomplete" if part of the matter other than the signature of the cardholder which an issuer requires to appear on the access card before it can be used by a cardholder has not been stamped, embossed, imprinted, or written on it.

(7) "Revoked access card" means an access card which is no longer authorized for use by the issuer, that authorization having been suspended or terminated and written notice thereof having been given to the cardholder.

(8) "Counterfeit access card" means any access card that is counterfeit, fictitious, altered, or forged, or any false representation or depiction of an access card or a component thereof.

(9) "Traffic" means to transfer or otherwise dispose of property to another, or to obtain control of property with intent to transfer or dispose of it to another.

(10) "Card making equipment" means any equipment, machine, plate, mechanism, impression, or other device designed, used, or intended to be used to produce an access card.

Amended by Stats. 1986, Ch. 1436, Sec. 1.

Section 484e - Unlawful acts related to access cards

(a) Every person who, with intent to defraud, sells, transfers, or conveys, an access card, without the cardholder's or issuer's consent, is guilty of grand theft.

(b) Every person, other than the issuer, who within any consecutive 12-month period, acquires access cards issued in the names of four or more persons which he or she has reason to know were taken or retained under circumstances which constitute a violation of subdivision (a), (c), or (d) is guilty of grand theft.

(c) Every person who, with the intent to defraud, acquires or retains possession of an access card without the cardholder's or issuer's consent, with intent to use, sell, or transfer it to a person other than the cardholder or issuer is guilty of petty theft.

(d) Every person who acquires or retains possession of access card account information with respect to an access card validly issued to another person, without the cardholder's or issuer's consent, with the intent to use it fraudulently, is guilty of grand theft.

Repealed and added by Stats. 1998, Ch. 468, Sec. 9. Effective January 1, 1999.

Section 484f - Unlawful acts related to counterfeit access cards

(a) Every person who, with the intent to defraud, designs, makes, alters, or embosses a counterfeit access card or utters or otherwise attempts to use a counterfeit access card is guilty of forgery.

(b) A person other than the cardholder or a person authorized by him or her who, with the intent to defraud, signs the name of another or of a fictitious person to an access card, sales slip, sales draft, or instrument for the payment of money which evidences an access card transaction, is guilty of forgery.

Repealed and added by Stats. 1998, Ch. 468, Sec. 11. Effective January 1, 1999.

Section 484g - Unlawful use of access card

Every person who, with the intent to defraud, (a) uses, for the purpose of obtaining money, goods, services, or anything else of value, an access card or access card account information that has been altered, obtained, or retained in violation of Section 484e or 484f, or an access card which he or she knows is forged, expired, or revoked, or (b) obtains money, goods, services, or anything else of value by representing without the consent of the cardholder that he or she is the holder of an access card and the card has not in fact been issued, is guilty of theft. If the value of all money, goods, services, and other things of value obtained in violation of this section exceeds nine hundred fifty dollars ($950) in any consecutive six-month period, then the same shall constitute grand theft.

Amended by Stats 2009 ch 28 (SB X3-18),s 15, eff. 1/1/2010.

Section 484h - Unlawful acts by retailer

Every retailer or other person who, with intent to defraud:

(a) Furnishes money, goods, services or anything else of value upon presentation of an access card obtained or retained in violation of Section 484e or an access card which he or she knows is a counterfeit access card or is forged, expired, or revoked, and who receives any payment therefor, is guilty of theft. If the payment received by the retailer or other person for all money, goods, services, and other things of value furnished in violation of this section exceeds nine hundred fifty dollars ($950) in any consecutive six-month period, then the same shall constitute grand theft.

(b) Presents for payment a sales slip or other evidence of an access card transaction, and receives payment therefor, without furnishing in the transaction money, goods, services, or anything else of value that is equal in value to the amount of the sales slip or other evidence of an access card transaction, is guilty of theft. If the difference between the value of all money, goods, services, and anything else of value actually furnished and the payment or payments received by the retailer or other person therefor upon presentation of a sales slip or other evidence of an access card transaction exceeds nine hundred fifty dollars ($950) in any consecutive six-month period, then the same shall constitute grand theft.

Amended by Stats 2009 ch 28 (SB X3-18),s 16, eff. 1/1/2010.

Section 484i - Unlawful possession of incomplete access card; unlawful modification of access card account information

(a) Every person who possesses an incomplete access card, with intent to complete it without the consent of the issuer, is guilty of a misdemeanor.

(b) Every person who, with the intent to defraud, makes, alters, varies, changes, or modifies access card account information on any part of an access card, including information encoded in a magnetic stripe or other medium on the access card not directly readable by the human eye, or who authorizes or consents to alteration, variance, change, or modification of access card account information by another, in a manner that causes transactions initiated by that access card to be charged or billed to a person other than the cardholder to whom the access card was issued, is guilty of forgery.

(c) Every person who designs, makes, possesses, or traffics in card making equipment or incomplete access cards with the intent that the equipment or cards be used to make counterfeit access cards, is punishable by imprisonment in a county jail for not more than one year, or by imprisonment pursuant to subdivision (h) of Section 1170.

Amended by Stats 2011 ch 39 (AB 117),s 68, eff. 6/30/2011.

Amended by Stats 2011 ch 15 (AB 109),s 368, eff. 4/4/2011, but operative no earlier than October 1, 2011, and only upon creation of a community corrections grant program to assist in implementing this act and upon an appropriation to fund the grant program.

Section 484j - Unlawful publication

Any person who publishes the number or code of an existing, canceled, revoked, expired or nonexistent access card, personal identification number, computer password, access code, debit card number, bank account number, or the numbering or coding which is employed in the issuance of access cards, with the intent that it be used or with knowledge or reason to believe that it will be used to avoid the payment of any lawful charge, or with intent to defraud or aid another in defrauding, is guilty of a misdemeanor. As used in this section, "publishes" means the communication of information to any one or more persons, either orally, in person or by telephone, radio or television, or on a computer network or computer bulletin board, or in a writing of any kind, including without limitation a letter or memorandum, circular or handbill, newspaper or magazine article, or book.

Amended by Stats. 1986, Ch. 1437, Sec. 2.

Section 485 - Wrongful appropriation of lost property

One who finds lost property under circumstances which give him knowledge of or means of inquiry as to the true owner, and who appropriates such property to his own use, or to the use of another person not entitled thereto, without first making reasonable and just efforts to find the owner and to restore the property to him, is guilty of theft.

Amended by Stats. 1927, Ch. 619.

Section 486 - Degrees of theft
Theft is divided into two degrees, the first of which is termed grand theft; the second, petty theft.
Amended by Stats. 1927, Ch. 619.

Section 487 - Grand theft
Grand theft is theft committed in any of the following cases:

(a)When the money, labor, real property, or personal property taken is of a value exceeding nine hundred fifty dollars ($950), except as provided in subdivision (b).

(b)Notwithstanding subdivision (a), grand theft is committed in any of the following cases:

(1)

(A)When domestic fowls, avocados, olives, citrus or deciduous fruits, other fruits, vegetables, nuts, artichokes, or other farm crops are taken of a value exceeding two hundred fifty dollars ($250).

(B)For the purposes of establishing that the value of domestic fowls, avocados, olives, citrus or deciduous fruits, other fruits, vegetables, nuts, artichokes, or other farm crops under this paragraph exceeds two hundred fifty dollars ($250), that value may be shown by the presentation of credible evidence which establishes that on the day of the theft domestic fowls, avocados, olives, citrus or deciduous fruits, other fruits, vegetables, nuts, artichokes, or other farm crops of the same variety and weight exceeded two hundred fifty dollars ($250) in wholesale value.

(2)When fish, shellfish, mollusks, crustaceans, kelp, algae, or other aquacultural products are taken from a commercial or research operation which is producing that product, of a value exceeding two hundred fifty dollars ($250).

(3)Where the money, labor, real property, or personal property is taken by a servant, agent, or employee from their principal or employer and aggregates nine hundred fifty dollars ($950) or more in any 12 consecutive month period.

(c)When the property is taken from the person of another.

(d)When the property taken is any of the following:

(1)An automobile.

(2)A firearm.

(e)If the value of the money, labor, real property, or personal property taken exceeds nine hundred fifty dollars ($950) over the course of distinct but related acts, the value of the money, labor, real property, or personal property taken may properly be aggregated to charge a count of grand theft, if the acts are motivated by one intention, one general impulse, and one plan.

Amended by Stats 2022 ch 22 (AB 2356),s 1, eff. 1/1/2023.
Amended by Stats 2013 ch 618 (AB 924),s 7, eff. 1/1/2014.
Amended by Stats 2010 ch 694 (SB 1338),s 1.5, eff. 1/1/2011.
Amended by Stats 2010 ch 693 (AB 2372),s 1, eff. 1/1/2011.
Amended by Stats 2009 ch 28 (SB X3-18),s 17, eff. 1/1/2010.
Amended by Stats 2002 ch 787 (SB 1798), s 12, eff. 1/1/2003.

The amendment of Section 487 of the Penal Code made by Stats 2022 ch 22 (AB 2356) is declaratory of existing law in People v. Bailey (1961) 55 Cal.2d 514.

Section 487a - Felonious stealing or transporting carcass
(a) Every person who feloniously steals, takes, carries, leads, or drives away any horse, mare, gelding, any bovine animal, any caprine animal, mule, jack, jenny, sheep, lamb, hog, sow, boar, gilt, barrow, or pig, which is the personal property of another, or who fraudulently appropriates that same property which has been entrusted to him or her, or who knowingly and designedly, by any false or fraudulent representation or pretense, defrauds any other person of that same property, or who causes or procures others to report falsely of his or her wealth or mercantile character and by thus imposing upon any person, obtains credit and thereby fraudulently gets or obtains possession of that same property, is guilty of grand theft.

(b) Every person who shall feloniously steal, take, transport or carry the carcass of any bovine, caprine, equine, ovine, or suine animal or of any mule, jack or jenny, which is the personal property of another, or who shall fraudulently appropriate such property which has been entrusted to him or her, is guilty of grand theft.

(c) Every person who shall feloniously steal, take, transport, or carry any portion of the carcass of any bovine, caprine, equine, ovine, or suine animal or of any mule, jack, or jenny, which has been killed without the consent of the owner thereof, is guilty of grand theft.

Amended by Stats 2014 ch 71 (SB 1304),s 122, eff. 1/1/2015.
Amended by Stats 2013 ch 618 (AB 924),s 8, eff. 1/1/2014.

Section 487b - Conversion of real estate of value of $250 or more into personal property
Every person who converts real estate of the value of two hundred fifty dollars ($250) or more into personal property by severance from the realty of another, and with felonious intent to do so, steals, takes, and carries away that property is guilty of grand theft and is punishable by imprisonment pursuant to subdivision (h) of Section 1170.

Amended by Stats 2011 ch 39 (AB 117),s 68, eff. 6/30/2011.
Amended by Stats 2011 ch 15 (AB 109),s 369, eff. 4/4/2011, but operative no earlier than October 1, 2011, and only upon creation of a community corrections grant program to assist in implementing this act and upon an appropriation to fund the grant program.
Amended by Stats 2009 ch 28 (SB X3-18),s 18, eff. 1/1/2010.

Section 487c - Conversion of real estate of value of less than $250 into personal property
Every person who converts real estate of the value of less than two hundred fifty dollars ($250) into personal property by severance from the realty of another, and with felonious intent to do so steals, takes, and carries away that property is guilty of petty theft and is punishable by imprisonment in the county jail for not more than one year, or by a fine not exceeding one thousand dollars ($1,000), or by both that fine and imprisonment.

Amended by Stats 2009 ch 28 (SB X3-18),s 19, eff. 1/1/2010.
Amended by Stats 2000 ch 135 (AB 2539), s 133, eff. 1/1/2001.

Section 487d - Felonious stealing of gold dust, amalgam, or quick silver

Every person who feloniously steals, takes, and carries away, or attempts to take, steal, and carry from any mining claim, tunnel, sluice, undercurrent, riffle box, or sulfurate machine, another's gold dust, amalgam, or quicksilver is guilty of grand theft and is punishable by imprisonment pursuant to subdivision (h) of Section 1170.

Amended by Stats 2011 ch 39 (AB 117),s 68, eff. 6/30/2011.

Amended by Stats 2011 ch 15 (AB 109),s 370, eff. 4/4/2011, but operative no earlier than October 1, 2011, and only upon creation of a community corrections grant program to assist in implementing this act and upon an appropriation to fund the grant program.

Section 487e - Felonious stealing of companion animal of value exceeding $950

(a)Every person who feloniously steals, takes, or carries away a companion animal of another which is of a value exceeding nine hundred fifty dollars ($950) is guilty of grand theft.

(b)

(1)For purposes of this section, "companion animal" means an animal, including, but not limited to, a dog or a cat that a person keeps and provides care for as a household pet or otherwise for the purpose of companionship, emotional support, service, or protection.

(2)For purposes of this section, "companion animal" excludes feral animals, including, but not limited to, feral cats as defined in Section 31752.5 of the Food and Agricultural Code.

Amended by Stats 2022 ch 546 (AB 1290),s 1, eff. 1/1/2023.

Amended by Stats 2009 ch 28 (SB X3-18),s 20, eff. 1/1/2010.

Section 487f - Felonious stealing of companion animal of value not exceeding $950

(a)Every person who feloniously steals, takes, or carries away a companion animal of another which is of a value not exceeding nine hundred fifty dollars ($950) is guilty of petty theft.

(b)

(1)For purposes of this section, "companion animal" means an animal, including, but not limited to, a dog or a cat that a person keeps and provides care for as a household pet or otherwise for the purpose of companionship, emotional support, service, or protection.

(2)For purposes of this section, "companion animal" excludes feral animals, including, but not limited to, feral cats as defined in Section 31752.5 of the Food and Agricultural Code.

Amended by Stats 2022 ch 546 (AB 1290),s 2, eff. 1/1/2023.

Amended by Stats 2009 ch 28 (SB X3-18),s 21, eff. 1/1/2010.

Section 487g - Stealing or maliciously taking animal for purposes of sale, medical research, slaughter, or other commercial use

Every person who steals or maliciously takes or carries away any animal of another for purposes of sale, medical research, slaughter, or other commercial use, or who knowingly, by any false representation or pretense, defrauds another person of any animal for purposes of sale, medical research, slaughter, or other commercial use is guilty of a public offense punishable by imprisonment in a county jail not exceeding one year or in the state prison.

Amended by Stats. 1995, Ch. 151, Sec. 1. Effective January 1, 1996.

Section 487h - Stealing cargo of value exceeding $950

(a) Every person who steals, takes, or carries away cargo of another, if the cargo taken is of a value exceeding nine hundred fifty dollars ($950), except as provided in Sections 487, 487a, and 487d, is guilty of grand theft.

(b) For the purposes of this section, "cargo" means any goods, wares, products, or manufactured merchandise that has been loaded into a trailer, railcar, or cargo container, awaiting or in transit.

Amended by Stats 2009 ch 607 (SB 24),s 1, eff. 1/1/2010.

Amended by Stats 2009 ch 28 (SB X3-18),s 22, eff. 1/1/2010.

Added by Stats 2004 ch 515 (AB 1814), s 1, eff. 1/1/2005.

See Stats 2004 ch 515 (AB 1814), s 3.

Section 487i - Defrauding house program

Any person who defrauds a housing program of a public housing authority of more than four hundred dollars ($400) is guilty of grand theft.

Added by Stats 2008 ch 105 (AB 2827),s 1, eff. 1/1/2009.

Section 487j - Stealing copper materials

Every person who steals, takes, or carries away copper materials of another, including, but not limited to, copper wire, copper cable, copper tubing, and copper piping, which are of a value exceeding nine hundred fifty dollars ($950) is guilty of grand theft. Grand theft of copper shall be punishable by a fine not exceeding two thousand five hundred dollars ($2,500), by imprisonment in a county jail not exceeding one year, or by both that fine and imprisonment, or by imprisonment pursuant to subdivision (h) of Section 1170 and a fine not exceeding ten thousand dollars ($10,000).

Added by Stats 2011 ch 317 (AB 316),s 2, eff. 1/1/2012.

Section 487k - Theft of tractors, all-terrain vehicles, or other agricultural equipment

A person who steals, takes, or carries away tractors, all-terrain vehicles, or other agricultural equipment, or any portion thereof, used in the acquisition or production of food for public consumption, which are of a value exceeding nine hundred fifty dollars ($950), is guilty of grand theft.

Added by Stats 2019 ch 119 (SB 224),s 1, eff. 1/1/2020.

Section 487m - Wage theft; grand theft

(a) Notwithstanding Sections 215 and 216 of the Labor Code, the intentional theft of wages in an amount greater than nine hundred fifty dollars ($950) from any one employee, or two thousand three hundred fifty dollars ($2,350) in the aggregate from two or more employees, by an employer in any consecutive 12-month period may be punished as grand theft.

(b) For purposes of this section, "theft of wages" is the intentional deprivation of wages, as defined in Section 200 of the Labor Code, gratuities, as defined in Section 350 of the Labor Code, benefits, or other compensation, by unlawful means, with the knowledge that the wages, gratuities, benefits, or other compensation is due to the employee under the law.

(c) For purposes of this section, "employee" includes an independent contractor and "employer" includes the hiring entity of an independent contractor.

(d) Wages, gratuities, benefits, or other compensation that are the subject of a prosecution under this section may be recovered as restitution in accordance with Sections 1202.4 and 1203.1. This section does not prohibit the employee or the Labor Commissioner from commencing a civil action to seek remedies provided for under the Labor Code for acts prosecuted under this section.

(e) This section does not constitute a change in, and does not expand or limit the scope of conduct prohibited by, Section 487.
Added by Stats 2021 ch 325 (AB 1003),s 1, eff. 1/1/2022.

Section 488 - Petty theft
Theft in other cases is petty theft.
Amended by Stats. 1927, Ch. 619.

Section 489 - Punishment for grand theft
Grand theft is punishable as follows:

(a) If the grand theft involves the theft of a firearm, by imprisonment in the state prison for 16 months, or two or three years.

(b) If the grand theft involves a violation of Section 487a, by imprisonment in a county jail not exceeding one year or pursuant to subdivision (h) of Section 1170, or by a fine not exceeding five thousand dollars ($5,000), or by both that fine and imprisonment. The proceeds of this fine shall be allocated to the Bureau of Livestock Identification to be used, upon appropriation by the Legislature, for purposes relating to the investigation of cases involving grand theft of any animal or animals, or of the carcass or carcasses of, or any portion of the carcass or carcasses of, any animal specified in Section 487a.

(c)

(1) In all other convictions for grand theft not described in either subdivision (a) or (b), by imprisonment in a county jail not exceeding one year or pursuant to subdivision (h) of Section 1170.

(2) In a county participating in a rural crime prevention program pursuant to Title 11.5 (commencing with Section 14170) or Title 11.7 (commencing with Section 14180) of Part 4, the proceeds of a fine imposed pursuant to a conviction for a violation of Section 487k shall be allocated by the Controller, upon appropriation by the Legislature, to the Central Valley Rural Crime Prevention Program and the Central Coast Rural Crime Prevention Program, in accordance with the schedule specified in paragraph (12) of subdivision (c) of Section 13821.

Amended by Stats 2020 ch 232 (SB 903),s 1, eff. 9/28/2020.
Amended by Stats 2019 ch 119 (SB 224),s 2, eff. 1/1/2020.
Amended by Stats 2013 ch 618 (AB 924),s 9, eff. 1/1/2014.
Amended by Stats 2011 ch 39 (AB 117),s 68, eff. 6/30/2011.
Amended by Stats 2011 ch 15 (AB 109),s 371, eff. 4/4/2011, but operative no earlier than October 1, 2011, and only upon creation of a community corrections grant program to assist in implementing this act and upon an appropriation to fund the grant program.

Section 490 - Punishment of petty theft
Petty theft is punishable by fine not exceeding one thousand dollars ($1,000), or by imprisonment in the county jail not exceeding six months, or both.
Amended by Stats. 1976, Ch. 1125.

Section 490a - Statute mentioning larceny, embezzlement, or stealing
Wherever any law or statute of this state refers to or mentions larceny, embezzlement, or stealing, said law or statute shall hereafter be read and interpreted as if the word "theft" were substituted therefor.
Added by Stats. 1927, Ch. 619.

Section 490.1 - Petty theft charged as misdemeanor or infraction
(a) Petty theft, where the value of the money, labor, real or personal property taken is of a value which does not exceed fifty dollars ($50), may be charged as a misdemeanor or an infraction, at the discretion of the prosecutor, provided that the person charged with the offense has no other theft or theft-related conviction.

(b) Any offense charged as an infraction under this section shall be subject to the provisions of subdivision (d) of Section 17 and Sections 19.6 and 19.7. A violation which is an infraction under this section is punishable by a fine not exceeding two hundred fifty dollars ($250).
Added by Stats. 1991, Ch. 638, Sec. 2.

Section 490.2 - Theft of property under $950
(a) Notwithstanding Section 487 or any other provision of law defining grand theft, obtaining any property by theft where the value of the money, labor, real or personal property taken does not exceed nine hundred fifty dollars ($950) shall be considered petty theft and shall be punished as a misdemeanor, except that such person may instead be punished pursuant to subdivision (h) of Section 1170 if that person has one or more prior convictions for an offense specified in clause (iv) of subparagraph (C) of paragraph (2) of subdivision (e) of Section 667 or for an offense requiring registration pursuant to subdivision (c) of Section 290.

(b) This section shall not be applicable to any theft that may be charged as an infraction pursuant to any other provision of law.

(c) This section shall not apply to theft of a firearm.
Amended by Proposition 63, approved by the voters at the 11/8/2016 election.
Added by Proposition 47, eff. 11/5/2014.

Section 490.4 - [Effective until 1/1/2026] Organized retail theft
(a) A person who commits any of the following acts is guilty of organized retail theft, and shall be punished pursuant to subdivision (b):

(1) Acts in concert with one or more persons to steal merchandise from one or more merchant's premises or online marketplace with the intent to sell, exchange, or return the merchandise for value.

(2) Acts in concert with two or more persons to receive, purchase, or possess merchandise described in paragraph (1), knowing or believing it to have been stolen.

(3) Acts as an agent of another individual or group of individuals to steal merchandise from one or more merchant's premises or online marketplaces as part of an organized plan to commit theft.

(4) Recruits, coordinates, organizes, supervises, directs, manages, or finances another to undertake any of the acts described in paragraph (1) or (2) or any other statute defining theft of merchandise.

(b) Organized retail theft is punishable as follows:

(1) If violations of paragraph (1), (2), or (3) of subdivision (a) are committed on two or more separate occasions within a 12-month period, and if the aggregated value of the merchandise stolen, received, purchased, or possessed within that 12-month period exceeds nine hundred fifty dollars ($950), the offense is punishable by imprisonment in a county jail not exceeding one year or pursuant to subdivision (h) of Section 1170.

(2) Any other violation of paragraph (1), (2), or (3) of subdivision (a) that is not described in paragraph (1) of this subdivision is punishable by imprisonment in a county jail not exceeding one year.

(3) A violation of paragraph (4) of subdivision (a) is punishable by imprisonment in a county jail not exceeding one year or pursuant to subdivision (h) of Section 1170.

(c) For the purpose of determining whether the defendant acted in concert with another person or persons in any proceeding, the trier of fact may consider any competent evidence, including, but not limited to, all of the following:

(1) The defendant has previously acted in concert with another person or persons in committing acts constituting theft, or any related offense, including any conduct that occurred in counties other than the county of the current offense, if relevant to demonstrate a fact other than the defendant's disposition to commit the act.

(2) That the defendant used or possessed an artifice, instrument, container, device, or other article capable of facilitating the removal of merchandise from a retail establishment without paying the purchase price and use of the artifice, instrument, container, or device or other article is part of an organized plan to commit theft.

(3) The property involved in the offense is of a type or quantity that would not normally be purchased for personal use or consumption and the property is intended for resale.

(d) In a prosecution under this section, the prosecutor shall not be required to charge any other coparticipant of the organized retail theft.

(e) Upon conviction of an offense under this section, the court shall consider ordering, as a condition of probation, that the defendant stay away from retail establishments with a reasonable nexus to the crime committed.

(f) This section shall remain in effect only until January 1, 2026, and as of that date is repealed.

Added by Stats 2021 ch 113 (AB 331),s 1, eff. 7/21/2021.

Section 490.5 - Petty theft involving merchandise taken from merchant's premises or book or other library materials taken from library facility

(a) Upon a first conviction for petty theft involving merchandise taken from a merchant's premises or a book or other library materials taken from a library facility, a person shall be punished by a mandatory fine of not less than fifty dollars ($50) and not more than one thousand dollars ($1,000) for each such violation; and may also be punished by imprisonment in the county jail, not exceeding six months, or both such fine and imprisonment.

(b) When an unemancipated minor's willful conduct would constitute petty theft involving merchandise taken from a merchant's premises or a book or other library materials taken from a library facility, any merchant or library facility who has been injured by that conduct may bring a civil action against the parent or legal guardian having control and custody of the minor. For the purposes of those actions the misconduct of the unemancipated minor shall be imputed to the parent or legal guardian having control and custody of the minor. The parent or legal guardian having control or custody of an unemancipated minor whose conduct violates this subdivision shall be jointly and severally liable with the minor to a merchant or to a library facility for damages of not less than fifty dollars ($50) nor more than five hundred dollars ($500), plus costs. In addition to the foregoing damages, the parent or legal guardian shall be jointly and severally liable with the minor to the merchant for the retail value of the merchandise if it is not recovered in a merchantable condition, or to a library facility for the fair market value of its book or other library materials. Recovery of these damages may be had in addition to, and is not limited by, any other provision of law which limits the liability of a parent or legal guardian for the tortious conduct of a minor. An action for recovery of damages, pursuant to this subdivision, may be brought in small claims court if the total damages do not exceed the jurisdictional limit of that court, or in any other appropriate court; however, total damages, including the value of the merchandise or book or other library materials, shall not exceed five hundred dollars ($500) for each action brought under this section. The provisions of this subdivision are in addition to other civil remedies and do not limit merchants or other persons to elect to pursue other civil remedies, except that the provisions of Section 1714.1 of the Civil Code shall not apply herein.

(c) When an adult or emancipated minor has unlawfully taken merchandise from a merchant's premises, or a book or other library materials from a library facility, the adult or emancipated minor shall be liable to the merchant or library facility for damages of not less than fifty dollars ($50) nor more than five hundred dollars ($500), plus costs. In addition to the foregoing damages, the adult or emancipated minor shall be liable to the merchant for the retail value of the merchandise if it is not recovered in merchantable condition, or to a library facility for the fair market value of its book or other library materials. An action for recovery of damages, pursuant to this subdivision, may be brought in small claims court if the total damages do not exceed the jurisdictional limit of such court, or in any other appropriate court. The provisions of this subdivision are in addition to other civil remedies and do not limit merchants or other persons to elect to pursue other civil remedies.

(d) In lieu of the fines prescribed by subdivision (a), any person may be required to perform public services designated by the court, provided that in no event shall any such person be required to perform less than the number of hours of such public service necessary to satisfy the fine assessed by the court as provided by subdivision (a) at the minimum wage prevailing in the state at the time of sentencing.

(e) All fines collected under this section shall be collected and distributed in accordance with Sections 1463 and 1463.1 of the Penal Code; provided, however, that a county may, by a majority vote of the members of its board of supervisors, allocate any amount up to, but not exceeding 50 percent of such fines to the county superintendent of schools for allocation to local school districts. The fines allocated shall be administered by the county superintendent of schools to finance public school programs, which provide counseling or other educational services designed to discourage shoplifting, theft, and burglary. Subject to rules and regulations as may be adopted by the Superintendent of Public Instruction, each county superintendent of schools shall allocate such funds to school districts within the county which submit project applications designed to further the educational purposes of this section. The costs of administration of this section by each county superintendent of schools shall be paid from the funds allocated to the county superintendent of schools.

(f)

(1) A merchant may detain a person for a reasonable time for the purpose of conducting an investigation in a reasonable manner whenever the merchant has probable cause to believe the person to be detained is attempting to unlawfully take or has unlawfully taken merchandise from the merchant's premises. A theater owner may detain a person for a reasonable time for the purpose of conducting an investigation in a reasonable manner whenever the theater owner has probable cause to believe the person to be detained is attempting to operate a video recording device within the premises of a motion picture theater without the authority of the owner of the theater. A person employed by a library facility may detain a person for a reasonable time for the purpose of conducting an investigation in a reasonable manner whenever the person employed by a library facility has probable cause to believe the person to be detained is attempting to unlawfully remove or has unlawfully removed books or library materials from the premises of the library facility.

(2) In making the detention a merchant, theater owner, or a person employed by a library facility may use a reasonable amount of nondeadly force necessary to protect himself or herself and to prevent escape of the person detained or the loss of tangible or intangible property.

(3) During the period of detention any items which a merchant or theater owner, or any items which a person employed by a library facility has probable cause to believe are unlawfully taken from the premises of the merchant or library facility, or recorded on theater premises, and which are in plain view may be examined by the merchant, theater owner, or person employed by a library facility for the purposes of ascertaining the ownership thereof.

(4) A merchant, theater owner, a person employed by a library facility, or an agent thereof, having probable cause to believe the person detained was attempting to unlawfully take or has taken any item from the premises, or was attempting to operate a video recording device within the premises of a motion picture theater without the authority of the owner of the theater, may request the person detained to voluntarily surrender the item or recording. Should the person detained refuse to surrender the recording or item of which there is probable cause to believe has been recorded on or unlawfully taken from the premises, or attempted to be recorded or unlawfully taken from the premises, a limited and reasonable search may be conducted by those authorized to make the detention in order to recover the item. Only packages, shopping bags, handbags or other property in the immediate possession of the person detained, but not including any clothing worn by the person, may be searched pursuant to this subdivision. Upon surrender or discovery of the item, the person detained may also be requested, but may not be required, to provide adequate proof of his or her true identity.

(5) If any person admitted to a theater in which a motion picture is to be or is being exhibited, refuses or fails to give or surrender possession or to cease operation of any video recording device that the person has brought into or attempts to bring into that theater, then a theater owner shall have the right to refuse admission to that person or request that the person leave the premises and shall thereupon offer to refund and, unless that offer is refused, refund to that person the price paid by that person for admission to that theater. If the person thereafter refuses to leave the theater or cease operation of the video recording device, then the person shall be deemed to be intentionally interfering with and obstructing those attempting to carry on a lawful business within the meaning of Section 602.1.

(6) A peace officer who accepts custody of a person arrested for an offense contained in this section may, subsequent to the arrest, search the person arrested and his or her immediate possessions for any item or items alleged to have been taken.

(7) In any civil action brought by any person resulting from a detention or arrest by a merchant, it shall be a defense to such action that the merchant detaining or arresting such person had probable cause to believe that the person had stolen or attempted to steal merchandise and that the merchant acted reasonably under all the circumstances. In any civil action brought by any person resulting from a detention or arrest by a theater owner or person employed by a library facility, it shall be a defense to that action that the theater owner or person employed by a library facility detaining or arresting that person had probable cause to believe that the person was attempting to operate a video recording device within the premises of a motion picture theater without the authority of the owner of the theater or had stolen or attempted to steal books or library materials and that the person employed by a library facility acted reasonably under all the circumstances.

(g) As used in this section:

(1) "Merchandise" means any personal property, capable of manual delivery, displayed, held or offered for retail sale by a merchant.

(2) "Merchant" means an owner or operator, and the agent, consignee, employee, lessee, or officer of an owner or operator, of any premises used for the retail purchase or sale of any personal property capable of manual delivery.

(3) "Theater owner" means an owner or operator, and the agent, employee, consignee, lessee, or officer of an owner or operator, of any premises used for the exhibition or performance of motion pictures to the general public.

(4) The terms "book or other library materials" include any book, plate, picture, photograph, engraving, painting, drawing, map, newspaper, magazine, pamphlet, broadside, manuscript, document, letter, public record, microform, sound recording, audiovisual material in any format, magnetic or other tape, electronic data-processing record, artifact, or other documentary, written or printed material regardless of physical form or characteristics, or any part thereof, belonging to, on loan to, or otherwise in the custody of a library facility.

(5) The term "library facility" includes any public library; any library of an educational, historical or eleemosynary institution, organization or society; any museum; any repository of public records.

(h) Any library facility shall post at its entrance and exit a conspicuous sign to read as follows: "IN ORDER TO PREVENT THE THEFT OF BOOKS AND LIBRARY MATERIALS, STATE LAW AUTHORIZES THE DETENTION FOR A REASONABLE PERIOD OF ANY PERSON USING THESE FACILITIES SUSPECTED OF COMMITTING "LIBRARY THEFT" (PENAL CODE SECTION 490.5)."

Amended by Stats. 1994, 1st Ex. Sess., Ch. 34, Sec. 1. Effective November 30, 1994.

Section 490.6 - Detention for violating amusement park rules

(a) A person employed by an amusement park may detain a person for a reasonable time for the purpose of conducting an investigation in a reasonable manner whenever the person employed by the amusement park has probable cause to believe the person to be detained is violating lawful amusement park rules.

(b) If any person admitted to an amusement park refuses or fails to follow lawful amusement park rules, after being so informed, then an amusement park employee may request that the person either comply or leave the premises. If the person refuses to leave the premises or comply with lawful park rules, then the person shall be deemed to be intentionally interfering with and obstructing those attempting to carry on a lawful business within the meaning of Section 602.1.

(c) In any civil action brought by any person resulting from a detention or an arrest by a person employed by an amusement park, it shall be a defense to that action that the amusement park employee detaining or arresting the person had probable cause to believe that the person was not following lawful amusement park rules and that the amusement park employee acted reasonably under all the circumstances.

Added by Stats. 1996, Ch. 731, Sec. 1. Effective January 1, 1997.

Section 490.7 - Taking of more than 25 copies of free or complimentary newspaper

(a) The Legislature finds that free newspapers provide a key source of information to the public, in many cases providing an important alternative to the news and ideas expressed in other local media sources. The Legislature further finds that the unauthorized taking of multiple copies of free newspapers, whether done to sell them to recycling centers, to injure a business competitor, to deprive others of the opportunity to read them, or for any other reason, injures the rights of readers, writers, publishers, and advertisers, and impoverishes the marketplace of ideas in California.

(b) No person shall take more than twenty-five (25) copies of the current issue of a free or complimentary newspaper if done with the intent to do one or more of the following:

    (1) Recycle the newspapers for cash or other payment.

    (2) Sell or barter the newspaper.

    (3) Deprive others of the opportunity to read or enjoy the newspaper.

    (4) Harm a business competitor.

(c) This section does not apply to the owner or operator of the newsrack in which the copies are placed, the owner or operator of the property on which the newsrack is placed, the publisher, the printer, the distributor, the deliverer of the newspaper, or to any advertiser in that issue, or to any other person who has the express permission to do so from any of these entities.

(d) Any newspaper publisher may provide express permission to take more than twenty-five (25) copies of the current issue of a free or complimentary newspaper by indicating on the newsrack or in the newspaper itself, that people may take a greater number of copies if they wish.

(e) A first violation of subdivision (b) shall be an infraction punishable by a fine not exceeding two hundred fifty dollars ($250). A second or subsequent violation shall be punishable as an infraction or a misdemeanor. A misdemeanor conviction under this section is punishable by a fine not exceeding five hundred dollars ($500), imprisonment of up to 10 days in a county jail, or by both that fine and imprisonment. The court may order community service in lieu of the punishment otherwise provided for an infraction or misdemeanor in the amount of 20 hours for an infraction, and 40 hours for a misdemeanor. A misdemeanor conviction under this section shall not constitute a conviction for petty theft.

(f) This section shall not be construed to repeal, modify, or weaken any existing legal prohibitions against the taking of private property.

(g) For purposes of this section, an issue is current if no more than half of the period of time until the distribution of the next issue has passed.

Added by Stats 2006 ch 228 (AB 2612),s 2, eff. 1/1/2007.

Section 491 - Ascertainment of value of companion animal

(a) Companion animals are personal property, and their value is to be ascertained in the same manner as the value of other property.

(b)

    (1) For purposes of this section, "companion animal" means an animal, including, but not limited to, a dog or a cat that a person keeps and provides care for as a household pet or otherwise for the purpose of companionship, emotional support, service, or protection.

    (2) For purposes of this section, "companion animal" excludes feral animals, including, but not limited to, feral cats as defined in Section 31752.5 of the Food and Agricultural Code.

Amended by Stats 2022 ch 546 (AB 1290),s 3, eff. 1/1/2023.

Amended by Stats. 1887, Ch. 109.

Section 492 - Value of evidence of debt

If the thing stolen consists of any evidence of debt, or other written instrument, the amount of money due thereupon, or secured to be paid thereby, and remaining unsatisfied, or which in any contingency might be collected thereon, or the value of the property the title to which is shown thereby, or the sum which might be recovered in the absence thereof, is the value of the thing stolen.

Enacted 1872.

Section 493 - Value of passage ticket

If the thing stolen is any ticket or other paper or writing entitling or purporting to entitle the holder or proprietor thereof to a passage upon any railroad or vessel or other public conveyance, the price at which tickets entitling a person to a like passage are usually sold by the proprietors of such conveyance is the value of such ticket, paper, or writing.

Enacted 1872.

Section 494 - Value of unissued or undelivered instrument for payment of money, evidence of debt, public security or passage ticket

All the provisions of this Chapter apply where the property taken is an instrument for the payment of money, evidence of debt, public security, or passage ticket, completed and ready to be issued or delivered, although the same has never been issued or delivered by the makers thereof to any person as a purchaser or owner.

Enacted 1872.

Section 495 - Applicability to severed fixture of part of realty

The provisions of this Chapter apply where the thing taken is any fixture or part of the realty, and is severed at the time of the taking, in the same manner as if the thing had been severed by another person at some previous time.

Enacted 1872.

Section 496 - Buying or receipt of stolen property

(a) Every person who buys or receives any property that has been stolen or that has been obtained in any manner constituting theft or extortion, knowing the property to be so stolen or obtained, or who conceals, sells, withholds, or aids in concealing, selling, or withholding any property from the owner, knowing the property to be so stolen or obtained, shall be punished by imprisonment in a county jail for not more than one year, or imprisonment pursuant to subdivision (h) of Section 1170. However, if the value of the property does not exceed nine hundred fifty dollars ($950), the offense shall be a misdemeanor, punishable only by imprisonment in a county jail not exceeding one year, if such person has no prior convictions for an offense specified in clause (iv) of subparagraph (C) of paragraph (2) of subdivision (e) of Section 667 or for an offense requiring registration pursuant to subdivision (c) of Section 290. A principal in the actual theft of the property may be convicted pursuant to this section. However, no person may be convicted both pursuant to this section and of the theft of the same property.

(b) Every swap meet vendor, as defined in Section 21661 of the Business and Professions Code, and every person whose principal business is dealing in, or collecting, merchandise or personal property, and every agent, employee, or representative of that person, who buys or receives any property of a value in excess of nine hundred fifty dollars ($950) that has been stolen or obtained in any manner constituting theft or extortion, under circumstances that should cause the person, agent, employee, or representative to make reasonable inquiry to ascertain that the person from whom the property was bought or received had the legal right to sell or deliver it, without making a reasonable inquiry, shall be punished by imprisonment in a county jail for not more than one year, or imprisonment pursuant to subdivision (h) of Section 1170. Every swap meet vendor, as defined in Section 21661 of the Business and Professions Code, and every person whose principal business is dealing in, or collecting, merchandise or personal property, and every agent, employee, or representative of that person, who buys or receives any property of a value of nine hundred fifty dollars ($950) or less that has been stolen or obtained in any manner constituting theft or extortion, under circumstances that should cause the person, agent, employee, or representative to make reasonable inquiry to ascertain that the person from whom the property was bought or received had the legal right to sell or deliver it, without making a reasonable inquiry, shall be guilty of a misdemeanor.

(c) Any person who has been injured by a violation of subdivision (a) or (b) may bring an action for three times the amount of actual damages, if any, sustained by the plaintiff, costs of suit, and reasonable attorney's fees.

(d) Notwithstanding Section 664, any attempt to commit any act prohibited by this section, except an offense specified in the accusatory pleading as a misdemeanor, is punishable by imprisonment in a county jail for not more than one year, or by imprisonment pursuant to subdivision (h) of Section 1170.

Amended by Proposition 47, eff. 11/5/2014.

Amended by Stats 2011 ch 39 (AB 117),s 68, eff. 6/30/2011.

Amended by Stats 2011 ch 15 (AB 109),s 372, eff. 4/4/2011, but operative no earlier than October 1, 2011, and only upon creation of a community corrections grant program to assist in implementing this act and upon an appropriation to fund the grant program.

Amended by Stats 2009 ch 28 (SB X3-18),s 23, eff. 1/1/2010.

Section 496a - Buying of wire, cable, copper, etc. by dealer in or collector of junk, metals, or secondhand materials

(a) Every person who is a dealer in or collector of junk, metals, or secondhand materials, or the agent, employee, or representative of such dealer or collector, and who buys or receives any wire, cable, copper, lead, solder, mercury, iron, or brass which he or she knows or reasonably should know is ordinarily used by or ordinarily belongs to a railroad or other transportation, telephone, telegraph, gas, water, or electric light company, or a county, city, city and county, or other political subdivision of this state engaged in furnishing public utility service, without using due diligence to ascertain that the person selling or delivering the same has a legal right to do so, is guilty of criminally receiving that property, and shall be punished by imprisonment in a county jail for not more than one year, or by imprisonment pursuant to subdivision (h) of Section 1170, or by a fine of not more than one thousand dollars ($1,000), or by both that fine and imprisonment.

(b) Any person who buys or receives material pursuant to subdivision (a) shall obtain evidence of his or her identity from the seller, including, but not limited to, that person's full name, signature, address, driver's license number, and vehicle license number, and the license number of the vehicle delivering the material.

(c) The record of the transaction shall include an appropriate description of the material purchased and the record shall be maintained pursuant to Section 21607 of the Business and Professions Code.

Amended by Stats 2013 ch 76 (AB 383),s 147, eff. 1/1/2014.

Amended by Stats 2012 ch 82 (AB 1971),s 2, eff. 1/1/2013.

Amended by Stats 2011 ch 39 (AB 117),s 68, eff. 6/30/2011.

Amended by Stats 2011 ch 15 (AB 109),s 373, eff. 4/4/2011, but operative no earlier than October 1, 2011, and only upon creation of a community corrections grant program to assist in implementing this act and upon an appropriation to fund the grant program.

Section 496b - Buying of book, map, or other work of literature by dealer in or collector of secondhand books or other literary material

Every person who, being a dealer in or collector of second-hand books or other literary material, or the agent, employee or representative of such dealer, or collector, buys or receives any book, manuscript, map, chart, or other work of literature, belonging to, and bearing any mark or indicia of ownership by a public or incorporated library, college or university, without ascertaining by diligent inquiry that the person selling or delivering the same has a legal right to do so, is guilty of criminally receiving such property in the first degree if such property be of the value of more than fifty dollars, and is punishable by imprisonment in the county jail for not more than one year, or by a fine of not more than twice the value of the property received, or by both such fine and imprisonment; and is guilty of criminally receiving such property in the second degree if such property be of the value of fifty dollars or under, and is punishable by imprisonment in the county jail for not more than one month, or by a fine of not more than twice the value of the property received, or by both such fine and imprisonment.

Added by Stats. 1923, Ch. 192.

Section 496c - Copying or making record of information relating to title of real property

Any person who shall copy, transcribe, photograph or otherwise make a record or memorandum of the contents of any private and unpublished paper, book, record, map or file, containing information relating to the title to real property or containing information used in the business of examining, certifying or insuring titles to real property and belonging to any person, firm or corporation engaged in the business of examining, certifying, or insuring titles to real property, without the consent of the owner of such paper, book, record, map or file, and with the intent to use the same or the contents thereof, or to dispose of the same or the contents thereof to others for use, in the business of examining, certifying, or insuring titles to real property, shall be guilty of theft, and any person who shall induce another to violate the provisions of this section by giving, offering, or promising to such another any gift, gratuity, or thing of value or by doing or promising to do any act beneficial to such another, shall be guilty of theft; and any person who shall receive or acquire from another any copy, transcription, photograph or other record or memorandum of the contents of any private and unpublished paper, book, record, map or file containing information relating to the title to real property or containing information used in the business of examining, certifying or insuring titles to real property, with the knowledge that the same or the contents thereof has or have been acquired, prepared or compiled in violation of this section shall be guilty of theft. The contents of any such private and unpublished paper, book, record, map or file is hereby defined to be personal property, and in determining the value thereof for the purposes of this section the cost of acquiring and compiling the same shall be the test.

Added by Stats. 1931, Ch. 732.

Section 496d - Buying or receiving stolen motor vehicle, trailer, construction equipment, or vessel

(a) Every person who buys or receives any motor vehicle, as defined in Section 415 of the Vehicle Code, any trailer, as defined in Section 630 of the Vehicle Code, any special construction equipment, as defined in Section 565 of the Vehicle Code, or any vessel, as defined in Section 21 of the Harbors and Navigation Code, that has been stolen or that has been obtained in any manner constituting theft or extortion, knowing the property to be stolen or obtained, or who conceals, sells, withholds, or aids in concealing, selling, or withholding any motor vehicle, trailer, special construction equipment, or vessel from the owner, knowing the property to be so stolen or obtained, shall be punished by imprisonment pursuant to subdivision (h) of Section 1170 for 16 months or two or three years or a fine of not more than ten thousand dollars ($10,000), or both, or by imprisonment in a county jail not to exceed one year or a fine of not more than one thousand dollars ($1,000), or both.

(b) For the purposes of this section, the terms "special construction equipment" and "vessel" are limited to motorized vehicles and vessels.

Amended by Stats 2011 ch 39 (AB 117),s 68, eff. 6/30/2011.

Amended by Stats 2011 ch 15 (AB 109),s 374, eff. 4/4/2011, but operative no earlier than October 1, 2011, and only upon creation of a community corrections grant program to assist in implementing this act and upon an appropriation to fund the grant program.

Section 496e - Possession of stolen property belonging to local government or private utility by person engaged in salvage of scrap metal

(a) Any person who is engaged in the salvage, recycling, purchase, or sale of scrap metal and who possesses any of the following items that were owned or previously owned by any public agency, city, county, city and county, special district, or private utility that have been stolen or obtained in any manner constituting theft or extortion, knowing the property to be so stolen or obtained, or fails to report possession of the items pursuant to Section 21609.1 of the Business and Professions Code, is guilty of a crime:

(1) A fire hydrant or any reasonably recognizable part of that hydrant.

(2) Any fire department connection, including, but not limited to, reasonably recognizable bronze or brass fittings and parts.

(3) Manhole covers or lids, or any reasonably recognizable part of those manhole covers and lids.

(4) Backflow devices and connections to that device, or any part of that device.

(b) A person who violates subdivision (a) shall, in addition to any other penalty provided by law, be subject to a criminal fine of not more than three thousand dollars ($3,000).

Amended by Stats 2012 ch 656 (SB 1387),s 4, eff. 1/1/2013.

Added by Stats 2008 ch 659 (AB 1859),s 1, eff. 9/30/2008.

Section 497 - Stealing or embezzling property known to have stolen and embezzled

Every person who, in another state or country steals or embezzles the property of another, or receives such property knowing it to have been stolen or embezzled, and brings the same into this state, may be convicted and punished in the same manner as if such larceny, or embezzlement, or receiving, had been committed in this state.

Amended by Stats. 1905, Ch. 554.

Section 498 - Unlawful acts related to utility services

(a) The following definitions govern the construction of this section:

(1) "Person" means any individual, or any partnership, firm, association, corporation, limited liability company, or other legal entity.

(2) "Utility" means any electrical, gas, or water corporation as those terms are defined in the Public Utilities Code, and electrical, gas, or water systems operated by any political subdivision.

(3) "Customer" means the person in whose name utility service is provided.

(4) "Utility service" means the provision of electricity, gas, water, or any other service provided by the utility for compensation.

(5) "Divert" means to change the intended course or path of electricity, gas, or water without the authorization or consent of the utility.

(6) "Tamper" means to rearrange, injure, alter, interfere with, or otherwise prevent from performing a normal or customary function.

(7) "Reconnection" means the reconnection of utility service by a customer or other person after service has been lawfully disconnected by the utility.

(b) Any person who, with intent to obtain for himself or herself utility services without paying the full lawful charge therefor, or with intent to enable another person to do so, or with intent to deprive any utility of any part of the full lawful charge for utility services it provides, commits, authorizes, solicits, aids, or abets any of the following shall be guilty of a misdemeanor:

(1) Diverts or causes to be diverted utility services, by any means.

(2) Prevents any utility meter, or other device used in determining the charge for utility services, from accurately performing its measuring function by tampering or by any other means.

(3) Tampers with any property owned by or used by the utility to provide utility services.

(4) Makes or causes to be made any connection with or reconnection with property owned or used by the utility to provide utility services without the authorization or consent of the utility.

(5) Uses or receives the direct benefit of all or a portion of utility services with knowledge or reason to believe that the diversion, tampering, or unauthorized connection existed at the time of that use, or that the use or receipt was otherwise without the authorization or consent of the utility.

(c) In any prosecution under this section, the presence of any of the following objects, circumstances, or conditions on premises controlled by the customer or by the person using or receiving the direct benefit of all or a portion of utility services obtained in violation of this section shall permit an inference that the customer or person intended to and did violate this section:

(1) Any instrument, apparatus, or device primarily designed to be used to obtain utility services without paying the full lawful charge therefor.

(2) Any meter that has been altered, tampered with, or bypassed so as to cause no measurement or inaccurate measurement of utility services.

(d) If the value of all utility services obtained in violation of this section totals more than nine hundred fifty dollars ($950) or if the defendant has previously been convicted of an offense under this section or any former section which would be an offense under this section, or of an offense under the laws of another state or of the United States which would have been an offense under this section if committed in this state, then the violation is punishable by imprisonment in a county jail for not more than one year, or in the state prison.

(e) This section shall not be construed to preclude the applicability of any other provision of the criminal law of this state.
Amended by Stats 2009 ch 28 (SB X3-18),s 24, eff. 1/1/2010.

Section 499 - Subsequent convictions involving vehicle or vessel

(a) Any person who, having been convicted of a previous violation of Section 10851 of the Vehicle Code, or of subdivision (d) of Section 487, involving a vehicle or vessel, and having served a term therefor in any penal institution or having been imprisoned therein as a condition of probation for the offense, is subsequently convicted of a violation of Section 499b, involving a vehicle or vessel, is punishable for the subsequent offense by imprisonment in the county jail not exceeding one year or the state prison for 16 months, two, or three years.

(b) Any person convicted of a violation of Section 499b, who has been previously convicted under charges separately brought and tried two or more times of a violation of Section 499b, all such violations involving a vehicle or vessel, and who has been imprisoned therefore as a condition of probation or otherwise at least once, is punishable by imprisonment in the county jail for not more than one year or in the state prison for 16 months, two, or three years.

(c) This section shall become operative on January 1, 1997.
Repealed (in Sec. 7) and added by Stats. 1993, Ch. 1125, Sec. 8. Effective October 11, 1993. Section operative January 1, 1997, by its own provisions.

Section 499b - Unlawful taking of bicycle or vessel

(a) Any person who shall, without the permission of the owner thereof, take any bicycle for the purpose of temporarily using or operating the same, is guilty of a misdemeanor, and shall be punishable by a fine not exceeding four hundred dollars ($400), or by imprisonment in a county jail not exceeding three months, or by both that fine and imprisonment.

(b) Any person who shall, without the permission of the owner thereof, take any vessel for the purpose of temporarily using or operating the same, is guilty of a misdemeanor, and shall be punishable by a fine not exceeding one thousand dollars ($1,000), or by imprisonment in a county jail not exceeding one year, or by both that fine and imprisonment.
Amended by Stats 2003 ch 391 (AB 928), s 1, eff. 1/1/2004.

Section 499c - Unlawful acts related to trade secrets

(a) As used in this section:

(1) "Access" means to approach, a way or means of approaching, nearing, admittance to, including to instruct, communicate with, store information in, or retrieve information from a computer system or computer network.

(2) "Article" means any object, material, device, or substance or copy thereof, including any writing, record, recording, drawing, sample, specimen, prototype, model, photograph, micro-organism, blueprint, map, or tangible representation of a computer program or information, including both human and computer readable information and information while in transit.

(3) "Benefit" means gain or advantage, or anything regarded by the beneficiary as gain or advantage, including benefit to any other person or entity in whose welfare he or she is interested.

(4) "Computer system" means a machine or collection of machines, one or more of which contain computer programs and information, that performs functions, including, but not limited to, logic, arithmetic, information storage and retrieval, communications, and control.

(5) "Computer network" means an interconnection of two or more computer systems.

(6) "Computer program" means an ordered set of instructions or statements, and related information that, when automatically executed in actual or modified form in a computer system, causes it to perform specified functions.

(7) "Copy" means any facsimile, replica, photograph or other reproduction of an article, and any note, drawing or sketch made of or from an article.

(8) "Representing" means describing, depicting, containing, constituting, reflecting or recording.

(9) "Trade secret" means information, including a formula, pattern, compilation, program, device, method, technique, or process, that:

(A) Derives independent economic value, actual or potential, from not being generally known to the public or to other persons who can obtain economic value from its disclosure or use; and

(B) Is the subject of efforts that are reasonable under the circumstances to maintain its secrecy.

(b) Every person is guilty of theft who, with intent to deprive or withhold the control of a trade secret from its owner, or with an intent to appropriate a trade secret to his or her own use or to the use of another, does any of the following:

(1) Steals, takes, carries away, or uses without authorization, a trade secret.

(2) Fraudulently appropriates any article representing a trade secret entrusted to him or her.

(3) Having unlawfully obtained access to the article, without authority makes or causes to be made a copy of any article representing a trade secret.

(4) Having obtained access to the article through a relationship of trust and confidence, without authority and in breach of the obligations created by that relationship, makes or causes to be made, directly from and in the presence of the article, a copy of any article representing a trade secret.

(c) Every person who promises, offers or gives, or conspires to promise or offer to give, to any present or former agent, employee or servant of another, a benefit as an inducement, bribe or reward for conveying, delivering or otherwise making available an article representing a trade secret owned by his or her present or former principal, employer or master, to any person not authorized by the owner to receive or acquire the trade secret and every present or former agent, employee, or servant, who solicits, accepts, receives or takes a benefit as an inducement, bribe or reward for conveying, delivering or otherwise making available an article representing a trade secret owned by his or her present or former principal, employer or master, to any person not authorized by the owner to receive or acquire the trade secret, shall be punished by imprisonment in a county jail not exceeding one year, or by imprisonment pursuant to subdivision (h) of Section 1170, or by a fine not exceeding five thousand dollars ($5,000), or by both that fine and imprisonment.

(d) In a prosecution for a violation of this section, it shall be no defense that the person returned or intended to return the article.

Amended by Stats 2011 ch 39 (AB 117),s 68, eff. 6/30/2011.

Amended by Stats 2011 ch 15 (AB 109),s 375, eff. 4/4/2011, but operative no earlier than October 1, 2011, and only upon creation of a community corrections grant program to assist in implementing this act and upon an appropriation to fund the grant program.

Section 499d - Unlawful operating or taking aircraft

Any person who operates or takes an aircraft not his own, without the consent of the owner thereof, and with intent to either permanently or temporarily deprive the owner thereof of his title to or possession of such vehicle, whether with or without intent to steal the same, or any person who is a party or accessory to or an accomplice in any operation or unauthorized taking or stealing is guilty of a felony, and upon conviction thereof shall be punished by imprisonment in a county jail for not more than one year or by imprisonment pursuant to subdivision (h) of Section 1170, or by a fine of not more than ten thousand dollars ($10,000) or by both that fine and imprisonment.

Amended by Stats 2011 ch 39 (AB 117),s 68, eff. 6/30/2011.

Amended by Stats 2011 ch 15 (AB 109),s 376, eff. 4/4/2011, but operative no earlier than October 1, 2011, and only upon creation of a community corrections grant program to assist in implementing this act and upon an appropriation to fund the grant program.

Section 500 - Unlawful receipt of money for purpose of transmitting to foreign country

(a) Any person who receives money for the actual or purported purpose of transmitting the same or its equivalent to foreign countries as specified in Section 1800.5 of the Financial Code who fails to do at least one of the following acts unless otherwise instructed by the customer is guilty of a misdemeanor or felony as set forth in subdivision (b):

(1) Forward the money as represented to the customer within 10 days of receipt of the funds.

(2) Give instructions within 10 days of receipt of the customer's funds, committing equivalent funds to the person designated by the customer.

(3) Refund to the customer any money not forwarded as represented within 10 days of the customer's written request for a refund pursuant to subdivision (a) of Section 1810.5 of the Financial Code.

(b)

(1) If the total value of the funds received from the customer is less than nine hundred fifty dollars ($950), the offense set forth in subdivision (a) is punishable by imprisonment in a county jail not exceeding one year or by a fine not exceeding one thousand dollars ($1,000), or by both that imprisonment and fine.

(2) If the total value of the money received from the customer is nine hundred fifty dollars ($950) or more, or if the total value of all moneys received by the person from different customers is nine hundred fifty dollars ($950) or more, and the receipts were part of a common scheme or plan, the offense set forth in subdivision (a) is punishable by imprisonment pursuant to subdivision (h) of Section 1170 for 16 months, two, or three years, by a fine not exceeding ten thousand dollars ($10,000), or by both that imprisonment and fine.

Amended by Stats 2011 ch 39 (AB 117),s 68, eff. 6/30/2011.

Amended by Stats 2011 ch 15 (AB 109),s 377, eff. 4/4/2011, but operative no earlier than October 1, 2011, and only upon creation of a community corrections grant program to assist in implementing this act and upon an appropriation to fund the grant program.

Amended by Stats 2009 ch 28 (SB X3-18),s 25, eff. 1/1/2010.

Section 501 - Description of property in trial for larceny or embezzlement of money, bank notes, certificates of stock, or valuable securities

Upon a trial for larceny or embezzlement of money, bank notes, certificates of stock, or valuable securities, the allegation of the indictment or information, so far as regards the description of the property, is sustained, if the offender be proved to have embezzled or stolen any money, bank notes, certificates of stock, or valuable security, although the particular species of coin or other money, or the number, denomination, or kind of bank notes, certificates of stock, or valuable security, is not proved; and upon a trial for embezzlement, if the offender is proved to have embezzled any piece of coin or other money, any bank note, certificate of stock, or valuable security, although the piece of coin or other money, or bank note, certificate of stock, or valuable security, may have been delivered to him or her in order that some part of the value thereof should be returned to the party delivering the same, and such part shall have been returned accordingly.

Added by Stats. 1989, Ch. 897, Sec. 21.

Section 502 - Unauthorized access to computers, computer systems, and computer data

(a) It is the intent of the Legislature in enacting this section to expand the degree of protection afforded to individuals, businesses, and governmental agencies from tampering, interference, damage, and unauthorized access to lawfully created computer data and computer systems. The Legislature finds and declares that the proliferation of computer technology has resulted in a concomitant proliferation of computer crime and other forms of unauthorized access to computers, computer systems, and computer data. The Legislature further finds and declares that protection of the integrity of all types and forms of lawfully created computers, computer systems, and computer data is vital to the protection of the privacy of individuals as well as to the well-being of financial institutions, business concerns, governmental agencies, and others within this state that lawfully utilize those computers, computer systems, and data.

(b) For the purposes of this section, the following terms have the following meanings:

(1) "Access" means to gain entry to, instruct, cause input to, cause output from, cause data processing with, or communicate with, the logical, arithmetical, or memory function resources of a computer, computer system, or computer network.

(2) "Computer network" means any system that provides communications between one or more computer systems and input/output devices, including, but not limited to, display terminals, remote systems, mobile devices, and printers connected by telecommunication facilities.

(3) "Computer program or software" means a set of instructions or statements, and related data, that when executed in actual or modified form, cause a computer, computer system, or computer network to perform specified functions.

(4) "Computer services" includes, but is not limited to, computer time, data processing, or storage functions, internet services, electronic mail services, electronic message services, or other uses of a computer, computer system, or computer network.

(5) "Computer system" means a device or collection of devices, including support devices and excluding calculators that are not programmable and capable of being used in conjunction with external files, one or more of which contain computer programs, electronic instructions, input data, and output data, that performs functions, including, but not limited to, logic, arithmetic, data storage and retrieval, communication, and control. A "computer system" includes, without limitation, any such device or system that is located within, connected to, or otherwise integrated with, any motor vehicle as defined in Section 415 of the Vehicle Code.

(6) "Government computer system" means any computer system, or part thereof, that is owned, operated, or used by any federal, state, or local governmental entity.

(7) "Public safety infrastructure computer system" means any computer system, or part thereof, that is necessary for the health and safety of the public including computer systems owned, operated, or used by drinking water and wastewater treatment facilities, hospitals, emergency service providers, telecommunication companies, and gas and electric utility companies.

(8) "Data" means a representation of information, knowledge, facts, concepts, computer software, or computer programs or instructions. Data may be in any form, in storage media, or as stored in the memory of the computer or in transit or presented on a display device.

(9) "Supporting documentation" includes, but is not limited to, all information, in any form, pertaining to the design, construction, classification, implementation, use, or modification of a computer, computer system, computer network, computer program, or computer software, which information is not generally available to the public and is necessary for the operation of a computer, computer system, computer network, computer program, or computer software.

(10) "Injury" means any alteration, deletion, damage, or destruction of a computer system, computer network, computer program, or data caused by the access, or the denial of access to legitimate users of a computer system, network, or program.

(11) "Victim expenditure" means any expenditure reasonably and necessarily incurred by the owner or lessee to verify that a computer system, computer network, computer program, or data was or was not altered, deleted, damaged, or destroyed by the access.

(12) "Computer contaminant" means any set of computer instructions that are designed to modify, damage, destroy, record, or transmit information within a computer, computer system, or computer network without the intent or permission of the owner of the information. They include, but are not limited to, a group of computer instructions commonly called viruses or worms, that are self-replicating or self-propagating and are designed to contaminate other computer programs or computer data, consume computer resources, modify, destroy, record, or transmit data, or in some other fashion usurp the normal operation of the computer, computer system, or computer network.

(13) "Internet domain name" means a globally unique, hierarchical reference to an internet host or service, assigned through centralized internet naming authorities, comprising a series of character strings separated by periods, with the rightmost character string specifying the top of the hierarchy.

(14) "Electronic mail" means an electronic message or computer file that is transmitted between two or more telecommunications devices; computers; computer networks, regardless of whether the network is a local, regional, or global network; or electronic devices capable of receiving electronic messages, regardless of whether the message is converted to hard copy format after receipt, viewed upon transmission, or stored for later retrieval.

(15) "Profile" means either of the following:

(A) A configuration of user data required by a computer so that the user may access programs or services and have the desired functionality on that computer.

(B) An Internet website user's personal page or section of a page that is made up of data, in text or graphical form, that displays significant, unique, or identifying information, including, but not limited to, listing acquaintances, interests, associations, activities, or personal statements.

(c) Except as provided in subdivision (h), any person who commits any of the following acts is guilty of a public offense:

(1) Knowingly accesses and without permission alters, damages, deletes, destroys, or otherwise uses any data, computer, computer system, or computer network in order to either (A) devise or execute any scheme or artifice to defraud, deceive, or extort, or (B) wrongfully control or obtain money, property, or data.

(2) Knowingly accesses and without permission takes, copies, or makes use of any data from a computer, computer system, or computer network, or takes or copies any supporting documentation, whether existing or residing internal or external to a computer, computer system, or computer network.

(3) Knowingly and without permission uses or causes to be used computer services.

(4) Knowingly accesses and without permission adds, alters, damages, deletes, or destroys any data, computer software, or computer programs which reside or exist internal or external to a computer, computer system, or computer network.

(5) Knowingly and without permission disrupts or causes the disruption of computer services or denies or causes the denial of computer services to an authorized user of a computer, computer system, or computer network.

(6) Knowingly and without permission provides or assists in providing a means of accessing a computer, computer system, or computer network in violation of this section.

(7) Knowingly and without permission accesses or causes to be accessed any computer, computer system, or computer network.

(8) Knowingly introduces any computer contaminant into any computer, computer system, or computer network.

(9) Knowingly and without permission uses the internet domain name or profile of another individual, corporation, or entity in connection with the sending of one or more electronic mail messages or posts and thereby damages or causes damage to a computer, computer data, computer system, or computer network.

(10) Knowingly and without permission disrupts or causes the disruption of government computer services or denies or causes the denial of government computer services to an authorized user of a government computer, computer system, or computer network.

(11) Knowingly accesses and without permission adds, alters, damages, deletes, or destroys any data, computer software, or computer programs which reside or exist internal or external to a public safety infrastructure computer system computer, computer system, or computer network.

(12) Knowingly and without permission disrupts or causes the disruption of public safety infrastructure computer system computer services or denies or causes the denial of computer services to an authorized user of a public safety infrastructure computer system computer, computer system, or computer network.

(13) Knowingly and without permission provides or assists in providing a means of accessing a computer, computer system, or public safety infrastructure computer system computer, computer system, or computer network in violation of this section.

(14) Knowingly introduces any computer contaminant into any public safety infrastructure computer system computer, computer system, or computer network.

(d)

(1) Any person who violates any of the provisions of paragraph (1), (2), (4), (5), (10), (11), or (12) of subdivision (c) is guilty of a felony, punishable by imprisonment pursuant to subdivision (h) of Section 1170 for 16 months, or two or three years and a fine not exceeding ten thousand dollars ($10,000), or a misdemeanor, punishable by imprisonment in a county jail not exceeding one year, by a fine not exceeding five thousand dollars ($5,000), or by both that fine and imprisonment.

(2) Any person who violates paragraph (3) of subdivision (c) is punishable as follows:

(A) For the first violation that does not result in injury, and where the value of the computer services used does not exceed nine hundred fifty dollars ($950), by a fine not exceeding five thousand dollars ($5,000), or by imprisonment in a county jail not exceeding one year, or by both that fine and imprisonment.

(B) For any violation that results in a victim expenditure in an amount greater than five thousand dollars ($5,000) or in an injury, or if the value of the computer services used exceeds nine hundred fifty dollars ($950), or for any second or subsequent violation, by a fine not exceeding ten thousand dollars ($10,000), or by imprisonment pursuant to subdivision (h) of Section 1170 for 16 months, or two or three years, or by both that fine and imprisonment, or by a fine not exceeding five thousand dollars ($5,000), or by imprisonment in a county jail not exceeding one year, or by both that fine and imprisonment.

(3) Any person who violates paragraph (6), (7), or (13) of subdivision (c) is punishable as follows:

(A) For a first violation that does not result in injury, an infraction punishable by a fine not exceeding one thousand dollars ($1,000).

(B) For any violation that results in a victim expenditure in an amount not greater than five thousand dollars ($5,000), or for a second or subsequent violation, by a fine not exceeding five thousand dollars ($5,000), or by imprisonment in a county jail not exceeding one year, or by both that fine and imprisonment.

(C) For any violation that results in a victim expenditure in an amount greater than five thousand dollars ($5,000), by a fine not exceeding ten thousand dollars ($10,000), or by imprisonment pursuant to subdivision (h) of Section 1170 for 16 months, or two or three years, or by both that fine and imprisonment, or by a fine not exceeding five thousand dollars ($5,000), or by imprisonment in a county jail not exceeding one year, or by both that fine and imprisonment.

(4) Any person who violates paragraph (8) or (14) of subdivision (c) is punishable as follows:

(A) For a first violation that does not result in injury, a misdemeanor punishable by a fine not exceeding five thousand dollars ($5,000), or by imprisonment in a county jail not exceeding one year, or by both that fine and imprisonment.

(B) For any violation that results in injury, or for a second or subsequent violation, by a fine not exceeding ten thousand dollars ($10,000), or by imprisonment in a county jail not exceeding one year, or by imprisonment pursuant to subdivision (h) of Section 1170, or by both that fine and imprisonment.

(5) Any person who violates paragraph (9) of subdivision (c) is punishable as follows:

(A) For a first violation that does not result in injury, an infraction punishable by a fine not exceeding one thousand dollars ($1,000).

(B) For any violation that results in injury, or for a second or subsequent violation, by a fine not exceeding five thousand dollars ($5,000), or by imprisonment in a county jail not exceeding one year, or by both that fine and imprisonment.

(e)

(1) In addition to any other civil remedy available, the owner or lessee of the computer, computer system, computer network, computer program, or data who suffers damage or loss by reason of a violation of any of the provisions of subdivision (c) may bring a civil action against the violator for compensatory damages and injunctive relief or other equitable relief. Compensatory damages shall include any expenditure reasonably and necessarily incurred by the owner or lessee to verify that a computer system, computer network, computer program, or data was or was not altered, damaged, or deleted by the access. For the purposes of actions authorized by this subdivision, the conduct of an unemancipated minor shall be imputed to the parent or legal guardian having control or custody of the minor, pursuant to the provisions of Section 1714.1 of the Civil Code.

(2) In any action brought pursuant to this subdivision the court may award reasonable attorney's fees.

(3) A community college, state university, or academic institution accredited in this state is required to include computer-related crimes as a specific violation of college or university student conduct policies and regulations that may subject a student to disciplinary sanctions up to and including dismissal from the academic institution. This paragraph shall not apply to the University of California unless the Board of Regents adopts a resolution to that effect.

(4) In any action brought pursuant to this subdivision for a willful violation of the provisions of subdivision (c), where it is proved by clear and convincing evidence that a defendant has been guilty of oppression, fraud, or malice as defined in subdivision (c) of Section 3294 of the Civil Code, the court may additionally award punitive or exemplary damages.

(5) No action may be brought pursuant to this subdivision unless it is initiated within three years of the date of the act complained of, or the date of the discovery of the damage, whichever is later.

(f) This section shall not be construed to preclude the applicability of any other provision of the criminal law of this state which applies or may apply to any transaction, nor shall it make illegal any employee labor relations activities that are within the scope and protection of state or federal labor laws.

(g) Any computer, computer system, computer network, or any software or data, owned by the defendant, that is used during the commission of any public offense described in subdivision (c) or any computer, owned by the defendant, which is used as a repository for the storage of software or data illegally obtained in violation of subdivision (c) shall be subject to forfeiture, as specified in Section 502.01.

(h)

(1) Subdivision (c) does not apply to punish any acts which are committed by a person within the scope of lawful employment. For purposes of this section, a person acts within the scope of employment when the person performs acts which are reasonably necessary to the performance of their work assignment.

(2) Paragraph (3) of subdivision (c) does not apply to penalize any acts committed by a person acting outside of their lawful employment, provided that the employee's activities do not cause an injury, to the employer or another, or provided that the value of supplies or computer services which are used does not exceed an accumulated total of two hundred fifty dollars ($250).

(i) No activity exempted from prosecution under paragraph (2) of subdivision (h) which incidentally violates paragraph (2), (4), or (7) of subdivision (c) shall be prosecuted under those paragraphs.

(j) For purposes of bringing a civil or a criminal action under this section, a person who causes, by any means, the access of a computer, computer system, or computer network in one jurisdiction from another jurisdiction is deemed to have personally accessed the computer, computer system, or computer network in each jurisdiction.

(k) In determining the terms and conditions applicable to a person convicted of a violation of this section the court shall consider the following:

(1) The court shall consider prohibitions on access to and use of computers.

(2) Except as otherwise required by law, the court shall consider alternate sentencing, including community service, if the defendant shows remorse and recognition of the wrongdoing, and an inclination not to repeat the offense.

Amended by Stats 2019 ch 16 (AB 814),s 1, eff. 1/1/2020.

Amended by Stats 2015 ch 614 (AB 32),s 1, eff. 1/1/2016.

Amended by Stats 2014 ch 379 (AB 1649),s 1, eff. 1/1/2015.

Amended by Stats 2011 ch 39 (AB 117),s 68, eff. 6/30/2011.

Amended by Stats 2011 ch 15 (AB 109),s 378, eff. 4/4/2011, but operative no earlier than October 1, 2011, and only upon creation of a community corrections grant program to assist in implementing this act and upon an appropriation to fund the grant program.

Amended by Stats 2009 ch 28 (SB X3-18),s 26, eff. 1/1/2010.

Amended by Stats 2009 ch 70 (AB 22),s 1, eff. 1/1/2010.

Amended by Stats 2000 ch 634 (AB 2232), s 1.5, eff. 1/1/2001.

Previously Amended August 30, 1999 (Bill Number: AB 451) (Chapter 254).

Section 502.01 - Forfeiture

(a) As used in this section:

(1) "Property subject to forfeiture" means any property of the defendant that is illegal telecommunications equipment as defined in subdivision (g) of Section 502.8, or a computer, computer system, or computer network, and any software or data residing thereon, if the telecommunications device, computer, computer system, or computer network was used in committing a violation of, or conspiracy to commit a violation of, subdivision (b) of Section 272, Section 288, 288.2, 311.1, 311.2, 311.3, 311.4, 311.5, 311.10, 311.11, 422, 470, 470a, 472, 475, 476, 480, 483.5, 484g, or subdivision (a), (b), or (d) of Section 484e, subdivision (a) of Section 484f, subdivision (b) or (c) of Section 484i, subdivision (c) of Section 502, or Section 502.7, 502.8, 529, 529a, or 530.5, 537e, 593d, 593e, 646.9, or subdivision (j) of Section 647, or was used as a repository for the storage of software or data obtained in violation of those

provisions. Forfeiture shall not be available for any property used solely in the commission of an infraction. If the defendant is a minor, it also includes property of the parent or guardian of the defendant.

(2) "Sentencing court" means the court sentencing a person found guilty of violating or conspiring to commit a violation of subdivision (b) of Section 272, Section 288, 288.2, 311.1, 311.2, 311.3, 311.4, 311.5, 311.10, 311.11, 422, 470, 470a, 472, 475, 476, 480, 483.5, 484g, or subdivision (a), (b), or (d) of Section 484e, subdivision (d) of Section 484e, subdivision (a) of Section 484f, subdivision (b) or (c) of Section 484i, subdivision (c) of Section 502, or Section 502.7, 502.8, 529, 529a, 530.5, 537e, 593d, 593e, 646.9, or subdivision (j) of Section 647, or, in the case of a minor, found to be a person described in Section 602 of the Welfare and Institutions Code because of a violation of those provisions, the juvenile court.

(3) "Interest" means any property interest in the property subject to forfeiture.

(4) "Security interest" means an interest that is a lien, mortgage, security interest, or interest under a conditional sales contract.

(5) "Value" has the following meanings:

(A) When counterfeit items of computer software are manufactured or possessed for sale, the "value" of those items shall be equivalent to the retail price or fair market price of the true items that are counterfeited.

(B) When counterfeited but unassembled components of computer software packages are recovered, including, but not limited to, counterfeited computer diskettes, instruction manuals, or licensing envelopes, the "value" of those components of computer software packages shall be equivalent to the retail price or fair market price of the number of completed computer software packages that could have been made from those components.

(b) The sentencing court shall, upon petition by the prosecuting attorney, at any time following sentencing, or by agreement of all parties, at the time of sentencing, conduct a hearing to determine whether any property or property interest is subject to forfeiture under this section. At the forfeiture hearing, the prosecuting attorney shall have the burden of establishing, by a preponderance of the evidence, that the property or property interests are subject to forfeiture. The prosecuting attorney may retain seized property that may be subject to forfeiture until the sentencing hearing.

(c)

(1) Prior to the commencement of a forfeiture proceeding, the law enforcement agency seizing the property subject to forfeiture shall make an investigation as to any person other than the defendant who may have an interest in it. At least 30 days before the hearing to determine whether the property should be forfeited, the prosecuting agency shall send notice of the hearing to any person who may have an interest in the property that arose before the seizure.

(2) A person claiming an interest in the property shall file a motion for the redemption of that interest at least 10 days before the hearing on forfeiture, and shall send a copy of the motion to the prosecuting agency and to the probation department.

(3) If a motion to redeem an interest has been filed, the sentencing court shall hold a hearing to identify all persons who possess valid interests in the property. No person shall hold a valid interest in the property if, by a preponderance of the evidence, the prosecuting agency shows that the person knew or should have known that the property was being used in violation of, or conspiracy to commit a violation of, subdivision (b) of Section 272, Section 288, 288.2, 311.1, 311.2, 311.3, 311.4, 311.5, 311.10, 311.11, 470, 470a, 472, 475, 476, 480, 483.5, 484g, or subdivision (a), (b), or (d) of Section 484e, subdivision (a) of Section 484f, subdivision (b) or (c) of Section 484i, subdivision (c) of Section 502, or Section 502.7, 502.8, 529, 529a, 530.5, 537e, 593d, 593e, 646.9, or subdivision (j) of Section 647, and that the person did not take reasonable steps to prevent that use, or if the interest is a security interest, the person knew or should have known at the time that the security interest was created that the property would be used for a violation.

(d) If the sentencing court finds that a person holds a valid interest in the property, the following provisions shall apply:

(1) The court shall determine the value of the property.

(2) The court shall determine the value of each valid interest in the property.

(3) If the value of the property is greater than the value of the interest, the holder of the interest shall be entitled to ownership of the property upon paying the court the difference between the value of the property and the value of the valid interest. If the holder of the interest declines to pay the amount determined under paragraph (2), the court may order the property sold and designate the prosecutor or any other agency to sell the property. The designated agency shall be entitled to seize the property and the holder of the interest shall forward any documentation underlying the interest, including any ownership certificates for that property, to the designated agency. The designated agency shall sell the property and pay the owner of the interest the proceeds, up to the value of that interest.

(4) If the value of the property is less than the value of the interest, the designated agency shall sell the property and pay the owner of the interest the proceeds, up to the value of that interest.

(e) If the defendant was a minor at the time of the offense, this subdivision shall apply to property subject to forfeiture that is the property of the parent or guardian of the minor.

(1) The prosecuting agency shall notify the parent or guardian of the forfeiture hearing at least 30 days before the date set for the hearing.

(2) The computer or telecommunications device shall not be subject to forfeiture if the parent or guardian files a signed statement with the court at least 10 days before the date set for the hearing that the minor shall not have access to any computer or telecommunications device owned by the parent or guardian for two years after the date on which the minor is sentenced.

(3) If the minor is convicted of a violation of Section 288, 288.2, 311.1, 311.2, 311.3, 311.4, 311.5, 311.10, 311.11, 470, 470a, 472, 476, 480, or subdivision (b) of Section 484e, subdivision (d) of Section 484e, subdivision (a) of Section 484f, subdivision (b) of Section 484i, subdivision (c) of Section 502, or Section 502.7, 502.8, 529, 529a, 530.5, or subdivision (j) of Section 647, within two years after the date on which the minor is sentenced, and the violation involves a computer or telecommunications device owned by the parent or guardian, the original property subject to forfeiture, and the property involved in the new offense, shall be subject to forfeiture notwithstanding paragraph (2).

(4) Notwithstanding paragraph (1), (2), or (3), or any other provision of this chapter, if a minor's parent or guardian makes full restitution to the victim of a crime enumerated in this chapter in an amount or manner determined by the court, the forfeiture provisions

of this chapter do not apply to the property of that parent or guardian if the property was located in the family's primary residence during the commission of the crime.

(f) Notwithstanding any other provision of this chapter, the court may exercise its discretion to deny forfeiture where the court finds that the convicted defendant, or minor adjudicated to come within the jurisdiction of the juvenile court, is not likely to use the property otherwise subject to forfeiture for future illegal acts.

(g) If the defendant is found to have the only valid interest in the property subject to forfeiture, it shall be distributed as follows:

(1) First, to the victim, if the victim elects to take the property as full or partial restitution for injury, victim expenditures, or compensatory damages, as defined in paragraph (1) of subdivision (e) of Section 502. If the victim elects to receive the property under this paragraph, the value of the property shall be determined by the court and that amount shall be credited against the restitution owed by the defendant. The victim shall not be penalized for electing not to accept the forfeited property in lieu of full or partial restitution.

(2) Second, at the discretion of the court, to one or more of the following agencies or entities:

(A) The prosecuting agency.

(B) The public entity of which the prosecuting agency is a part.

(C) The public entity whose officers or employees conducted the investigation resulting in forfeiture.

(D) Other state and local public entities, including school districts.

(E) Nonprofit charitable organizations.

(h) If the property is to be sold, the court may designate the prosecuting agency or any other agency to sell the property at auction. The proceeds of the sale shall be distributed by the court as follows:

(1) To the bona fide or innocent purchaser or encumbrancer, conditional sales vendor, or mortgagee of the property up to the amount of his or her interest in the property, if the court orders a distribution to that person.

(2) The balance, if any, to be retained by the court, subject to the provisions for distribution under subdivision (g).

Amended by Stats 2015 ch 291 (SB 676),s 1, eff. 1/1/2016.
Amended by Stats 2005 ch 461 (AB 33),s 2, eff. 1/1/2006
Amended by Stats 2005 ch 22 (SB 1108),s 148, eff. 1/1/2006
Amended by Stats 2004 ch 751 (AB 1499), s 1, eff. 1/1/2005.
Amended by Stats 2000 ch 628 (AB 1767), s 1, eff. 1/1/2001.
Previously Amended August 30, 1999 (Bill Number: AB 451) (Chapter 254).

Section 502.5 - Unlawful taking of improvement after foreclosure or trustee's sale

Every person who, after mortgaging or encumbering by deed of trust any real property, and during the existence of such mortgage or deed of trust, or after such mortgaged or encumbered property shall have been sold under an order and decree of foreclosure or at trustee's sale, and with intent to defraud or injure the mortgagee or the beneficiary or trustee, under such deed of trust, his representatives, successors or assigns, or the purchaser of such mortgaged or encumbered premises at such foreclosure or trustee's sale, his representatives, successors or assigns, takes, removes or carries away from such mortgaged or encumbered premises, or otherwise disposes of or permits the taking, removal or carrying away or otherwise disposing of any house, barn, windmill, water tank, pump, engine or other part of the freehold that is attached or affixed to such premises as an improvement thereon, without the written consent of the mortgagee or beneficiary, under deed of trust, his representatives, successors or assigns, or the purchaser at such foreclosure or trustee's sale, his representatives, successors or assigns, is guilty of larceny and shall be punished accordingly.

Added by renumbering Section 5021/2 by Stats. 1979, Ch. 373.

Section 502.6 - Unlawful possession or use of scanning device or reencoder

(a) Any person who knowingly, willfully, and with the intent to defraud, possesses a scanning device, or who knowingly, willfully, and with intent to defraud, uses a scanning device to access, read, obtain, memorize or store, temporarily or permanently, information encoded on the magnetic strip or stripe of a payment card without the permission of the authorized user of the payment card is guilty of a misdemeanor, punishable by a term in a county jail not to exceed one year, or a fine of one thousand dollars ($1,000), or both the imprisonment and fine.

(b) Any person who knowingly, willfully, and with the intent to defraud, possesses a reencoder, or who knowingly, willfully, and with intent to defraud, uses a reencoder to place encoded information on the magnetic strip or stripe of a payment card or any electronic medium that allows an authorized transaction to occur, without the permission of the authorized user of the payment card from which the information is being reencoded is guilty of a misdemeanor, punishable by a term in a county jail not to exceed one year, or a fine of one thousand dollars ($1,000), or both the imprisonment and fine.

(c) Any scanning device or reencoder described in subdivision (e) owned by the defendant and possessed or used in violation of subdivision (a) or (b) may be seized and be destroyed as contraband by the sheriff of the county in which the scanning device or reencoder was seized.

(d) Any computer, computer system, computer network, or any software or data, owned by the defendant, which is used during the commission of any public offense described in this section or any computer, owned by the defendant, which is used as a repository for the storage of software or data illegally obtained in violation of this section shall be subject to forfeiture.

(e) As used in this section, the following definitions apply:

(1) "Scanning device" means a scanner, reader, or any other electronic device that is used to access, read, scan, obtain, memorize, or store, temporarily or permanently, information encoded on the magnetic strip or stripe of a payment card.

(2) "Reencoder" means an electronic device that places encoded information from the magnetic strip or stripe of a payment card on to the magnetic strip or stripe of a different payment card.

(3) "Payment card" means a credit card, debit card, or any other card that is issued to an authorized user and that allows the user to obtain, purchase, or receive goods, services, money, or anything else of value.

(f) Nothing in this section shall preclude prosecution under any other provision of law.

Added by Stats 2002 ch 861 (SB 1259), s 1, eff. 1/1/2003.

Section 502.7 - Unlawful avoiding of charge for telephone or telegraph service

(a) Any person who, knowingly, willfully, and with intent to defraud a person providing telephone or telegraph service, avoids or attempts to avoid, or aids, abets or causes another to avoid the lawful charge, in whole or in part, for telephone or telegraph service by any of the following means is guilty of a misdemeanor or a felony, except as provided in subdivision (g):

(1) By charging the service to an existing telephone number or credit card number without the authority of the subscriber thereto or the lawful holder thereof.

(2) By charging the service to a nonexistent telephone number or credit card number, or to a number associated with telephone service which is suspended or terminated, or to a revoked or canceled (as distinguished from expired) credit card number, notice of the suspension, termination, revocation, or cancellation of the telephone service or credit card having been given to the subscriber thereto or the holder thereof.

(3) By use of a code, prearranged scheme, or other similar stratagem or device whereby the person, in effect, sends or receives information.

(4) By rearranging, tampering with, or making connection with telephone or telegraph facilities or equipment, whether physically, electrically, acoustically, inductively, or otherwise, or by using telephone or telegraph service with knowledge or reason to believe that the rearrangement, tampering, or connection existed at the time of the use.

(5) By using any other deception, false pretense, trick, scheme, device, conspiracy, or means, including the fraudulent use of false, altered, or stolen identification.

(b) Any person who does either of the following is guilty of a misdemeanor or a felony, except as provided in subdivision (g):

(1) Makes, possesses, sells, gives, or otherwise transfers to another, or offers or advertises any instrument, apparatus, or device with intent to use it or with knowledge or reason to believe it is intended to be used to avoid any lawful telephone or telegraph toll charge or to conceal the existence or place of origin or destination of any telephone or telegraph message.

(2) Sells, gives, or otherwise transfers to another or offers, or advertises plans or instructions for making or assembling an instrument, apparatus, or device described in paragraph (1) of this subdivision with knowledge or reason to believe that they may be used to make or assemble the instrument, apparatus, or device.

(c) Any person who publishes the number or code of an existing, canceled, revoked, expired, or nonexistent credit card, or the numbering or coding which is employed in the issuance of credit cards, with the intent that it be used or with knowledge or reason to believe that it will be used to avoid the payment of any lawful telephone or telegraph toll charge is guilty of a misdemeanor. Subdivision (g) shall not apply to this subdivision. As used in this section, "publishes" means the communication of information to any one or more persons, either orally, in person or by telephone, radio, or television, or electronic means, including, but not limited to, a bulletin board system, or in a writing of any kind, including without limitation a letter or memorandum, circular or handbill, newspaper, or magazine article, or book.

(d) Any person who is the issuee of a calling card, credit card, calling code, or any other means or device for the legal use of telecommunications services and who receives anything of value for knowingly allowing another person to use the means or device in order to fraudulently obtain telecommunications services is guilty of a misdemeanor or a felony, except as provided in subdivision (g).

(e) Subdivision (a) applies when the telephone or telegraph communication involved either originates or terminates, or both originates and terminates, in this state, or when the charges for service would have been billable, in normal course, by a person providing telephone or telegraph service in this state, but for the fact that the charge for service was avoided, or attempted to be avoided, by one or more of the means set forth in subdivision (a).

(f) Jurisdiction of an offense under this section is in the jurisdictional territory where the telephone call or telegram involved in the offense originates or where it terminates, or the jurisdictional territory to which the bill for the service is sent or would have been sent but for the fact that the service was obtained or attempted to be obtained by one or more of the means set forth in subdivision (a).

(g) Theft of any telephone or telegraph services under this section by a person who has a prior misdemeanor or felony conviction for theft of services under this section within the past five years, is a felony.

(h) Any person or telephone company defrauded by any acts prohibited under this section shall be entitled to restitution for the entire amount of the charges avoided from any person or persons convicted under this section.

(i) Any instrument, apparatus, device, plans, instructions, or written publication described in subdivision (b) or (c) may be seized under warrant or incident to a lawful arrest, and, upon the conviction of a person for a violation of subdivision (a), (b), or (c), the instrument, apparatus, device, plans, instructions, or written publication may be destroyed as contraband by the sheriff of the county in which the person was convicted or turned over to the person providing telephone or telegraph service in the territory in which it was seized.

(j) Any computer, computer system, computer network, or any software or data, owned by the defendant, which is used during the commission of any public offense described in this section or any computer, owned by the defendant, which is used as a repository for the storage of software or data illegally obtained in violation of this section shall be subject to forfeiture.

Amended by Stats. 1993, Ch. 1014, Sec. 1. Effective January 1, 1994.

Section 502.8 - Unlawful advertising of illegal telecommunications equipment; unlawful possession or use

(a) Any person who knowingly advertises illegal telecommunications equipment is guilty of a misdemeanor.

(b) Any person who possesses or uses illegal telecommunications equipment intending to avoid the payment of any lawful charge for telecommunications service or to facilitate other criminal conduct is guilty of a misdemeanor.

(c) Any person found guilty of violating subdivision (b), who has previously been convicted of the same offense, shall be guilty of a felony, punishable by imprisonment in state prison, a fine of up to fifty thousand dollars ($50,000), or both.

(d) Any person who possesses illegal telecommunications equipment with intent to sell, transfer, or furnish or offer to sell, transfer, or furnish the equipment to another, intending to avoid the payment of any lawful charge for telecommunications service or to facilitate other criminal conduct is guilty of a misdemeanor punishable by one year in a county jail or imprisonment in state prison or a fine of up to ten thousand dollars ($10,000), or both.

(e) Any person who possesses 10 or more items of illegal telecommunications equipment with intent to sell or offer to sell the equipment to another, intending to avoid payment of any lawful charge for telecommunications service or to facilitate other criminal conduct, is guilty of a felony, punishable by imprisonment in state prison, a fine of up to fifty thousand dollars ($50,000), or both.

(f) Any person who manufactures 10 or more items of illegal telecommunications equipment with intent to sell or offer to sell the equipment to another, intending to avoid the payment of any lawful charge for telecommunications service or to facilitate other criminal conduct is guilty of a felony punishable by imprisonment in state prison or a fine of up to fifty thousand dollars ($50,000), or both.

(g) For purposes of this section, "illegal telecommunications equipment" means equipment that operates to evade the lawful charges for any telecommunications service; surreptitiously intercept electronic serial numbers or mobile identification numbers; alter electronic serial numbers; circumvent efforts to confirm legitimate access to a telecommunications account; conceal from any telecommunications service provider or lawful authority the existence, place of origin, or destination of any telecommunication; or otherwise facilitate any other criminal conduct. "Illegal telecommunications equipment" includes, but is not limited to, any unauthorized electronic serial number or mobile identification number, whether incorporated into a wireless telephone or other device or otherwise. Items specified in this subdivision shall be considered illegal telecommunications equipment notwithstanding any statement or disclaimer that the items are intended for educational, instructional, or similar purposes.

(h)

(1) In the event that a person violates the provisions of this section with the intent to avoid the payment of any lawful charge for telecommunications service to a telecommunications service provider, the court shall order the person to pay restitution to the telecommunications service provider in an amount that is the greater of the following:

(A) Five thousand dollars ($5,000).

(B) Three times the amount of actual damages, if any, sustained by the telecommunications service provider, plus reasonable attorney fees.

(2) It is not a necessary prerequisite to an order of restitution under this section that the telecommunications service provider has suffered, or be threatened with, actual damages.

Amended by Stats 2016 ch 86 (SB 1171),s 225, eff. 1/1/2017.

Section 502.9 - Aggravating circumstance that victim was elder or dependent person

Upon conviction of a felony violation under this chapter, the fact that the victim was an elder or dependent person, as defined in Section 288, shall be considered a circumstance in aggravation when imposing a term under subdivision (b) of Section 1170.

Amended by Stats 2004 ch 823 (AB 20), s 8, eff. 1/1/2005.

Chapter 6 - EMBEZZLEMENT

Section 503 - Embezzlement

Embezzlement is the fraudulent appropriation of property by a person to whom it has been intrusted.

Enacted 1872.

Section 504 - Fraudulent appropriation by public officer or agent of association, society, or corporation

Every officer of this state, or of any county, city, city and county, or other municipal corporation or subdivision thereof, and every deputy, clerk, or servant of that officer, and every officer, director, trustee, clerk, servant, or agent of any association, society, or corporation (public or private), who fraudulently appropriates to any use or purpose not in the due and lawful execution of that person's trust, any property in his or her possession or under his or her control by virtue of that trust, or secretes it with a fraudulent intent to appropriate it to that use or purpose, is guilty of embezzlement.

Amended by Stats 2002 ch 787 (SB 1798), s 13, eff. 1/1/2003.

Section 504a - Fraudulent removal, concealment, or disposal of goods, chattels, or effects

Every person who shall fraudulently remove, conceal or dispose of any goods, chattels or effects, leased or let to him by any instrument in writing, or any personal property or effects of another in his possession, under a contract of purchase not yet fulfilled, and any person in possession of such goods, chattels, or effects knowing them to be subject to such lease or contract of purchase who shall so remove, conceal or dispose of the same with intent to injure or defraud the lessor or owner thereof, is guilty of embezzlement.

Added by Stats. 1917, Ch. 180.

Section 504b - Unlawful appropriation of proceeds of sale of property covered by security agreement

Where under the terms of a security agreement, as defined in paragraph (74) of subdivision (a) of Section 9102 of the Commercial Code, the debtor has the right to sell the property covered thereby and is to account to the secured party for, and pay to the secured party the indebtedness secured by the security agreement from, the proceeds of the sale of any of the property, and where the debtor, having sold the property covered by the security agreement and having received the proceeds of the sale, willfully and wrongfully, and with the intent to defraud, fails to pay to the secured party the amounts due under the security agreement, or the proceeds of the sale, whichever is the lesser amount, and appropriates the money to his or her own use, the debtor shall be guilty of embezzlement and shall be punishable as provided in Section 514.

Amended by Stats 2013 ch 531 (AB 502),s 26, eff. 1/1/2014, op. 7/1/2014.

Section 505 - Fraudulent appropriation by carrier

Every carrier or other person having under his control personal property for the purpose of transportation for hire, who fraudulently appropriates it to any use or purpose inconsistent with the safe keeping of such property and its transportation according to his trust, is guilty of embezzlement, whether he has broken the package in which such property is contained, or has otherwise separated the items thereof, or not.

Enacted 1872.

Section 506 - Fraudulent appropriation by trustee, banker, merchant, broker, attorney, agent, assignee in trust, executor, administrator, or collector; fraudulent appropriation by contractor

Every trustee, banker, merchant, broker, attorney, agent, assignee in trust, executor, administrator, or collector, or person otherwise intrusted with or having in his control property for the use of any other person, who fraudulently appropriates it to any use or purpose not in the due and lawful execution of his trust, or secretes it with a fraudulent intent to appropriate it to such use or purpose, and any contractor who appropriates money paid to him for any use or purpose, other than for that which he received it, is guilty of embezzlement, and the payment of laborers and materialmen for work performed or material furnished in the performance of any contract is hereby declared to be the use and purpose to which the contract price of such contract, or any part thereof, received by the contractor shall be applied.

Amended by Stats. 1919, Ch. 518.

Section 506a - Prosecution of collector

Any person who, acting as collector, or acting in any capacity in or about a business conducted for the collection of accounts or debts owing by another person, and who violates Section 506 of the Penal Code, shall be deemed to be an agent or person as defined in Section 506, and subject for a violation of Section 506, to be prosecuted, tried, and punished in accordance therewith and with law; and "collector" means every such person who collects, or who has in his or her possession or under his or her control property or money for the use of any other person, whether in his or her own name and mixed with his or her own property or money, or otherwise, or whether he or she has any interest, direct or indirect, in or to such property or money, or any portion thereof, and who fraudulently appropriates to his or her own use, or the use of any person other than the true owner, or person entitled thereto, or secretes that property or money, or any portion thereof, or interest therein not his or her own, with a fraudulent intent to appropriate it to any use or purpose not in the due and lawful execution of his or her trust.

Amended by Stats. 1987, Ch. 828, Sec. 30.

Section 506b - Punishment for violation of statutory provisions relating to property sales contracts

Any person who violates Section 2985.3 or 2985.4 of the Civil Code, relating to real property sales contracts, is guilty of a public offense punishable by a fine not exceeding ten thousand dollars ($10,000), or by imprisonment in a the county jail not exceeding one year, or by imprisonment pursuant to subdivision (h) of Section 1170, or by both that fine and imprisonment.

Amended by Stats 2011 ch 39 (AB 117),s 68, eff. 6/30/2011.

Amended by Stats 2011 ch 15 (AB 109),s 379, eff. 4/4/2011, but operative no earlier than October 1, 2011, and only upon creation of a community corrections grant program to assist in implementing this act and upon an appropriation to fund the grant program.

Section 507 - Fraudulent conversion by person intrusted with property or with power of attorney for sale or transfer

Every person intrusted with any property as bailee, tenant, or lodger, or with any power of attorney for the sale or transfer thereof, who fraudulently converts the same or the proceeds thereof to his own use, or secretes it or them with a fraudulent intent to convert to his own use, is guilty of embezzlement.

Enacted 1872.

Section 508 - Fraudulent appropriation by clerk, agent, or servant

Every clerk, agent, or servant of any person who fraudulently appropriates to his own use, or secretes with a fraudulent intent to appropriate to his own use, any property of another which has come into his control or care by virtue of his employment as such clerk, agent, or servant, is guilty of embezzlement.

Enacted 1872.

Section 509 - Distinct act of taking

A distinct act of taking is not necessary to constitute embezzlement.

Enacted 1872.

Section 510 - Evidence of debt as subject of embezzlement

Any evidence of debt, negotiable by delivery only, and actually executed, is the subject of embezzlement, whether it has been delivered or issued as a valid instrument or not.

Enacted 1872.

Section 511 - Defense

Upon any indictment for embezzlement, it is a sufficient defense that the property was appropriated openly and avowedly, and under a claim of title preferred in good faith, even though such claim is untenable. But this provision does not excuse the unlawful retention of the property of another to offset or pay demands held against him.

Enacted 1872.

Section 512 - Intent to restore property embezzled

The fact that the accused intended to restore the property embezzled, is no ground of defense or mitigation of punishment, if it has not been restored before an information has been laid before a magistrate, or an indictment found by a grand jury, charging the commission of the offense.

Amended by Stats. 1905, Ch. 520.

Section 513 - Actual restoration or tender of restoration

Whenever, prior to an information laid before a magistrate, or an indictment found by a grand jury, charging the commission of embezzlement, the person accused voluntarily and actually restores or tenders restoration of the property alleged to have been embezzled, or any part thereof, such fact is not a ground of defense, but it authorizes the court to mitigate punishment, in its discretion.

Amended by Stats. 1905, Ch. 520.

Section 514 - Punishment

Every person guilty of embezzlement is punishable in the manner prescribed for theft of property of the value or kind embezzled; and where the property embezzled is an evidence of debt or right of action, the sum due upon it or secured to be paid by it must be taken as its value; if the embezzlement or defalcation is of the public funds of the United States, or of this state, or of any county or municipality within this state, the offense is a felony, and is punishable by imprisonment in the state prison; and the person so convicted is ineligible thereafter to any office of honor, trust, or profit in this state.

Amended by Stats. 1976, Ch. 1139.

Section 515 - Aggravating circumstance that victim was elder or dependent person

Upon conviction of a felony violation under this chapter, the fact that the victim was an elder or dependent person, as defined in Section 288, shall be considered a circumstance in aggravation when imposing a term under subdivision (b) of Section 1170.

Chapter 7 - EXTORTION

Section 518 - Extortion

(a) Extortion is the obtaining of property or other consideration from another, with his or her consent, or the obtaining of an official act of a public officer, induced by a wrongful use of force or fear, or under color of official right.

(b) For purposes of this chapter, "consideration" means anything of value, including sexual conduct as defined in subdivision (b) of Section 311.3, or an image of an intimate body part as defined in subparagraph (C) of paragraph (4) of subdivision (j) of Section 647.

(c) Notwithstanding subdivision (a), this section does not apply to a person under 18 years of age who has obtained consideration consisting of sexual conduct or an image of an intimate body part.

Amended by Stats 2017 ch 518 (SB 500),s 1, eff. 1/1/2018.

Section 519 - Fear

Fear, such as will constitute extortion, may be induced by a threat of any of the following:

1. To do an unlawful injury to the person or property of the individual threatened or of a third person.

2. To accuse the individual threatened, or a relative of his or her, or a member of his or her family, of a crime.

3. To expose, or to impute to him, her, or them a deformity, disgrace, or crime.

4. To expose a secret affecting him, her, or them.

5. To report his, her, or their immigration status or suspected immigration status.

Amended by Stats 2014 ch 71 (SB 1304),s 123, eff. 1/1/2015.

Amended by Stats 2013 ch 572 (AB 524),s 1, eff. 1/1/2014.

Section 520 - Punishment

Every person who extorts property or other consideration from another, under circumstances not amounting to robbery or carjacking, by means of force, or any threat, such as is mentioned in Section 519, shall be punished by imprisonment pursuant to subdivision (h) of Section 1170 for two, three or four years.

Amended by Stats 2017 ch 518 (SB 500),s 2, eff. 1/1/2018.

Amended by Stats 2011 ch 39 (AB 117),s 68, eff. 6/30/2011.

Amended by Stats 2011 ch 15 (AB 109),s 380, eff. 4/4/2011, but operative no earlier than October 1, 2011, and only upon creation of a community corrections grant program to assist in implementing this act and upon an appropriation to fund the grant program.

Section 521 - Extortion under color of official right

Every person who commits any extortion under color of official right, in cases for which a different punishment is not prescribed in this Code, is guilty of a misdemeanor.

Enacted 1872.

Section 522 - Obtaining signature to paper or instrument by extortionate means

Every person who, by any extortionate means, obtains from another his signature to any paper or instrument, whereby, if such signature were freely given, any property would be transferred, or any debt, demand, charge, or right of action created, is punishable in the same manner as if the actual delivery of such debt, demand, charge, or right of action were obtained.

Enacted 1872.

Section 523 - Sending letter or other writing expressing threat

(a) Every person who, with intent to extort property or other consideration from another, sends or delivers to any person any letter or other writing, whether subscribed or not, expressing or implying, or adapted to imply, any threat such as is specified in Section 519 is punishable in the same manner as if such property or other consideration were actually obtained by means of such threat.

(b)

(1) Every person who, with intent to extort property or other consideration from another, introduces ransomware into any computer, computer system, or computer network is punishable pursuant to Section 520 in the same manner as if such property or other consideration were actually obtained by means of the ransomware.

(2) Prosecution pursuant to this subdivision does not prohibit or limit prosecution under any other law.

(c)

(1) "Ransomware" means a computer contaminant, as defined in Section 502, or lock placed or introduced without authorization into a computer, computer system, or computer network that restricts access by an authorized person to the computer, computer system, computer network, or any data therein under circumstances in which the person responsible for the placement or introduction of the ransomware demands payment of money or other consideration to remove the computer contaminant, restore access to the computer, computer system, computer network, or data, or otherwise remediate the impact of the computer contaminant or lock.

(2) A person is responsible for placing or introducing ransomware into a computer, computer system, or computer network if the person directly places or introduces the ransomware or directs or induces another person to do so, with the intent of demanding payment or other consideration to remove the ransomware, restore access, or otherwise remediate the impact of the ransomware.

Amended by Stats 2017 ch 518 (SB 500),s 3, eff. 1/1/2018.

Amended by Stats 2016 ch 725 (SB 1137),s 1, eff. 1/1/2017.

Section 524 - Threat to extort money or property

Every person who attempts, by means of any threat, such as is specified in Section 519 of this code, to extort property or other consideration from another is punishable by imprisonment in the county jail not longer than one year or in the state prison or by fine not exceeding ten thousand dollars ($10,000), or by both such fine and imprisonment.

Amended by Stats 2017 ch 518 (SB 500),s 4, eff. 1/1/2018.

Section 525 - Aggravating circumstance that victim was elder or dependent person

Upon conviction of a felony violation under this chapter, the fact that the victim was an elder or dependent person, as defined in Section 288, shall be considered a circumstance in aggravation when imposing a term under subdivision (b) of Section 1170.

Amended by Stats 2004 ch 823 (AB 20), s 10, eff. 1/1/2005.

Section 526 - Delivery of paper purporting to be order or other process of court

Any person, who, with intent to obtain from another person any property or other consideration, delivers or causes to be delivered to the other person any paper, document or written, typed or printed form purporting to be an order or other process of a court, or designed or calculated by its writing, typing or printing, or the arrangement thereof, to cause or lead the other person to believe it to be an order or other process of a court, when in fact such paper, document or written, typed or printed form is not an order or process of a court, is guilty of a misdemeanor, and each separate delivery of any paper, document or written, typed or printed form shall constitute a separate offense.

Amended by Stats 2017 ch 518 (SB 500),s 5, eff. 1/1/2018.

Section 527 - Sale, offer to sell, printing, publishing, or distributing paper causing person to believe it is order or other process of court

Any person who shall sell or offer for sale, print, publish, or distribute any paper, document or written, typed or printed form, designed or calculated by its writing, typing or printing, or the arrangement thereof, to cause or lead any person to believe it to be, or that it will be used as an order or other process of a court when in fact such paper, document or written, typed or printed form is not to be used as the order or process of a court, is guilty of a misdemeanor, and each separate publication, printing, distribution, sale or offer to sell any such paper, document or written, typed or printed form shall constitute a separate offense, and upon conviction thereof in addition to any other sentence imposed the court may order that all such papers or documents or written, typed or printed forms in the possession or under the control of the person found guilty of such misdemeanor shall be delivered to such court or the clerk thereof for destruction.

Added by Stats. 1929, Ch. 593.

Chapter 8 - FALSE PERSONATION AND CHEATS

Section 528 - False personation

Every person who falsely personates another, and in such assumed character marries or pretends to marry, or to sustain the marriage relation towards another, with or without the connivance of such other, is guilty of a felony.

Enacted 1872.

Section 528.5 - False personation through or on Internet web site or by other electronic means

(a) Notwithstanding any other provision of law, any person who knowingly and without consent credibly impersonates another actual person through or on an Internet Web site or by other electronic means for purposes of harming, intimidating, threatening, or defrauding another person is guilty of a public offense punishable pursuant to subdivision (d).

(b) For purposes of this section, an impersonation is credible if another person would reasonably believe, or did reasonably believe, that the defendant was or is the person who was impersonated.

(c) For purposes of this section, "electronic means" shall include opening an e-mail account or an account or profile on a social networking Internet Web site in another person's name.

(d) A violation of subdivision (a) is punishable by a fine not exceeding one thousand dollars ($1,000), or by imprisonment in a county jail not exceeding one year, or by both that fine and imprisonment.

(e) In addition to any other civil remedy available, a person who suffers damage or loss by reason of a violation of subdivision (a) may bring a civil action against the violator for compensatory damages and injunctive relief or other equitable relief pursuant to paragraphs (1), (2), (4), and (5) of subdivision (e) and subdivision (g) of Section 502.

(f) This section shall not preclude prosecution under any other law.

Added by Stats 2010 ch 335 (SB 1411),s 1, eff. 1/1/2011.

Section 529 - False personation and in that assumed character doing prescribed acts

(a) Every person who falsely personates another in either his or her private or official capacity, and in that assumed character does any of the following, is punishable pursuant to subdivision (b):

(1) Becomes bail or surety for any party in any proceeding whatever, before any court or officer authorized to take that bail or surety.

(2) Verifies, publishes, acknowledges, or proves, in the name of another person, any written instrument, with intent that the same may be recorded, delivered, or used as true.

(3) Does any other act whereby, if done by the person falsely personated, he might, in any event, become liable to any suit or prosecution, or to pay any sum of money, or to incur any charge, forfeiture, or penalty, or whereby any benefit might accrue to the party personating, or to any other person.

(b) By a fine not exceeding ten thousand dollars ($10,000), or by imprisonment in a county jail not exceeding one year, or imprisonment pursuant to subdivision (h) of Section 1170, or by both that fine and imprisonment.

Amended by Stats 2011 ch 39 (AB 117),s 68, eff. 6/30/2011.

Amended by Stats 2011 ch 15 (AB 109),s 381, eff. 4/4/2011, but operative no earlier than October 1, 2011, and only upon creation of a community corrections grant program to assist in implementing this act and upon an appropriation to fund the grant program.

Section 529a - Unlawful manufacturing or sale of false or counterfeit certificate of birth

Every person who manufactures, produces, sells, offers, or transfers to another any document purporting to be either a certificate of birth or certificate of baptism, knowing such document to be false or counterfeit and with the intent to deceive, is guilty of a crime, and upon conviction therefor, shall be punished by imprisonment in a county jail not to exceed one year, or by imprisonment pursuant to subdivision (h) of Section 1170. Every person who offers, displays, or has in his or her possession any false or counterfeit certificate of birth or certificate of baptism, or any genuine certificate of birth which describes a person then living or deceased, with intent to represent himself or herself as another or to conceal his or her true identity, is guilty of a crime, and upon conviction therefor, shall be punished by imprisonment in the county jail not to exceed one year.

Amended by Stats 2011 ch 39 (AB 117),s 68, eff. 6/30/2011.

Amended by Stats 2011 ch 15 (AB 109),s 382, eff. 4/4/2011, but operative no earlier than October 1, 2011, and only upon creation of a community corrections grant program to assist in implementing this act and upon an appropriation to fund the grant program.

Section 529.5 - Unlawful manufacture or sale of purported government-issued identification card or driver's license
(a) Every person who manufactures, sells, offers for sale, or transfers any document, not amounting to counterfeit, purporting to be a government-issued identification card or driver's license, which by virtue of the wording or appearance thereon could reasonably deceive an ordinary person into believing that it is issued by a government agency, and who knows that the document is not a government-issued document, is guilty of a misdemeanor, punishable by imprisonment in a county jail not exceeding one year, or by a fine not exceeding one thousand dollars ($1,000), or by both the fine and imprisonment.
(b) Any person who, having been convicted of a violation of subdivision (a), is subsequently convicted of a violation of subdivision (a), is punishable for the subsequent conviction by imprisonment in a county jail not exceeding one year, or by a fine not exceeding five thousand dollars ($5,000), or by both the fine and imprisonment.
(c) Any person who possesses a document described in subdivision (a) and who knows that the document is not a government-issued document is guilty of a misdemeanor punishable by a fine of not less than one thousand dollars ($1,000) and not more than two thousand five hundred dollars ($2,500). The misdemeanor fine shall be imposed except in unusual cases where the interests of justice would be served. The court may allow an offender to work off the fine by doing community service. If community service work is not available, the misdemeanor shall be punishable by a fine of up to one thousand dollars ($1,000), based on the person's ability to pay.
Amended by Stats 2019 ch 505 (SB 485),s 6, eff. 1/1/2020.

Section 529.6 - Freedom to Count Act
(a)
  (1) This section shall be known, and may be cited, as the Freedom to Count Act.
  (2) It is the intent of the Legislature to ensure that all Californians have access to accurate, timely information about the census and that all Californians have the opportunity to participate in the census freely and without fear of fraud, intimidation, or harm.
(b) A person is guilty of a misdemeanor, punishable by imprisonment in a county jail not exceeding one year, or by a fine not exceeding one thousand dollars ($1,000), or by both that fine and imprisonment, who does either of the following:
  (1) Falsely represents that they are a census taker with the intent to interfere with the operation of the census or with the intent to obtain information or consent to an otherwise unlawful search or seizure.
  (2) Falsely assumes some or all of the activities of a census taker with the intent to interfere with the operation of the census or with the intent to obtain information or consent to an otherwise unlawful search or seizure.
Added by Stats 2019 ch 831 (AB 1563),s 2, eff. 1/1/2020.

Section 529.7 - Unlawful obtaining of official document issued by Department of Motor Vehicles
Any person who obtains, or assists another person in obtaining, a driver's license, identification card, vehicle registration certificate, or any other official document issued by the Department of Motor Vehicles, with knowledge that the person obtaining the document is not entitled to the document, is guilty of a misdemeanor, and is punishable by imprisonment in a county jail for up to one year, or a fine of up to one thousand dollars ($1,000), or both.
Added by Stats 2002 ch 907 (AB 1155), s 2, eff. 1/1/2003.

Section 530 - False personation and unlawful receipt of property and money
Every person who falsely personates another, in either his private or official capacity, and in such assumed character receives any money or property, knowing that it is intended to be delivered to the individual so personated, with intent to convert the same to his own use, or to that of another person, or to deprive the true owner thereof, is punishable in the same manner and to the same extent as for larceny of the money or property so received.
Amended by Stats. 1905, Ch. 523.

Section 530.5 - Unlawful obtaining or use or personal identifying information
(a) Every person who willfully obtains personal identifying information, as defined in subdivision (b) of Section 530.55, of another person, and uses that information for any unlawful purpose, including to obtain, or attempt to obtain, credit, goods, services, real property, or medical information without the consent of that person, is guilty of a public offense, and upon conviction therefor, shall be punished by a fine, by imprisonment in a county jail not to exceed one year, or by both a fine and imprisonment, or by imprisonment pursuant to subdivision (h) of Section 1170.
(b) In any case in which a person willfully obtains personal identifying information of another person, uses that information to commit a crime in addition to a violation of subdivision (a), and is convicted of that crime, the court records shall reflect that the person whose identity was falsely used to commit the crime did not commit the crime.
(c)
  (1) Every person who, with the intent to defraud, acquires or retains possession of the personal identifying information, as defined in subdivision (b) of Section 530.55, of another person is guilty of a public offense, and upon conviction therefor, shall be punished by a fine, by imprisonment in a county jail not to exceed one year, or by both a fine and imprisonment.
  (2) Every person who, with the intent to defraud, acquires or retains possession of the personal identifying information, as defined in subdivision (b) of Section 530.55, of another person, and who has previously been convicted of a violation of this section, upon conviction therefor shall be punished by a fine, by imprisonment in a county jail not to exceed one year, or by both a fine and imprisonment, or by imprisonment pursuant to subdivision (h) of Section 1170.
  (3) Every person who, with the intent to defraud, acquires or retains possession of the personal identifying information, as defined in subdivision (b) of Section 530.55, of 10 or more other persons is guilty of a public offense, and upon conviction therefor, shall be punished by a fine, by imprisonment in a county jail not to exceed one year, or by both a fine and imprisonment, or by imprisonment pursuant to subdivision (h) of Section 1170.
(d)
  (1) Every person who, with the intent to defraud, sells, transfers, or conveys the personal identifying information, as defined in subdivision (b) of Section 530.55, of another person is guilty of a public offense, and upon conviction therefor, shall be punished by a fine, by imprisonment in a county jail not to exceed one year, or by both a fine and imprisonment, or by imprisonment pursuant to subdivision (h) of Section 1170.

(2) Every person who, with actual knowledge that the personal identifying information, as defined in subdivision (b) of Section 530.55, of a specific person will be used to commit a violation of subdivision (a), sells, transfers, or conveys that same personal identifying information is guilty of a public offense, and upon conviction therefor, shall be punished by a fine, by imprisonment pursuant to subdivision (h) of Section 1170, or by both a fine and imprisonment.

(e) Every person who commits mail theft, as defined in Section 1708 of Title 18 of the United States Code, is guilty of a public offense, and upon conviction therefor shall be punished by a fine, by imprisonment in a county jail not to exceed one year, or by both a fine and imprisonment. Prosecution under this subdivision shall not limit or preclude prosecution under any other provision of law, including, but not limited to, subdivisions (a) to (c), inclusive, of this section.

(f) An interactive computer service or access software provider, as defined in subsection (f) of Section 230 of Title 47 of the United States Code, shall not be liable under this section unless the service or provider acquires, transfers, sells, conveys, or retains possession of personal information with the intent to defraud.

Amended by Stats 2011 ch 39 (AB 117),s 68, eff. 6/30/2011.

Amended by Stats 2011 ch 15 (AB 109),s 383, eff. 4/4/2011, but operative no earlier than October 1, 2011, and only upon creation of a community corrections grant program to assist in implementing this act and upon an appropriation to fund the grant program.

Amended by Stats 2007 ch 302 (SB 425),s 10, eff. 1/1/2008.

Amended by Stats 2006 ch 522 (AB 2886),s 2, eff. 1/1/2007.

Amended by Stats 2006 ch 10 (AB 424),s 1, eff. 2/24/2006.

Amended by Stats 2005 ch 432 (AB 1566),s 1, eff. 1/1/2006

Amended by Stats 2002 ch 254 (SB 1254), s 1, eff. 1/1/2003.

Amended by Stats 2001 ch 478 (AB 245), s 1, eff. 1/1/2002.

Amended by Stats 2000 ch 956 (AB 1897), s 1, eff. 1/1/2001.

Section 530.55 - "Person" and "personal identifying information" defined

(a) For purposes of this chapter, "person" means a natural person, living or deceased, firm, association, organization, partnership, business trust, company, corporation, limited liability company, or public entity, or any other legal entity.

(b) For purposes of this chapter, "personal identifying information" means any name, address, telephone number, health insurance number, taxpayer identification number, school identification number, state or federal driver's license, or identification number, social security number, place of employment, employee identification number, professional or occupational number, mother's maiden name, demand deposit account number, savings account number, checking account number, PIN (personal identification number) or password, United States Citizenship and Immigration Services-assigned number, government passport number, date of birth, unique biometric data including fingerprint, facial scan identifiers, voiceprint, retina or iris image, or other unique physical representation, unique electronic data including information identification number assigned to the person, address or routing code, telecommunication identifying information or access device, information contained in a birth or death certificate, or credit card number of an individual person, or an equivalent form of identification.

Amended by Stats 2021 ch 296 (AB 1096),s 45, eff. 1/1/2022.

Added by Stats 2006 ch 522 (AB 2886),s 3, eff. 1/1/2007.

Section 530.6 - Initiation of law enforcement investigation; petition for determination of factual innocence by victim of identity theft

(a) A person who has learned or reasonably suspects that his or her personal identifying information has been unlawfully used by another, as described in subdivision (a) of Section 530.5, may initiate a law enforcement investigation by contacting the local law enforcement agency that has jurisdiction over his or her actual residence or place of business, which shall take a police report of the matter, provide the complainant with a copy of that report, and begin an investigation of the facts. If the suspected crime was committed in a different jurisdiction, the local law enforcement agency may refer the matter to the law enforcement agency where the suspected crime was committed for further investigation of the facts.

(b) A person who reasonably believes that he or she is the victim of identity theft may petition a court, or the court, on its own motion or upon application of the prosecuting attorney, may move, for an expedited judicial determination of his or her factual innocence, where the perpetrator of the identity theft was arrested for, cited for, or convicted of a crime under the victim's identity, or where a criminal complaint has been filed against the perpetrator in the victim's name, or where the victim's identity has been mistakenly associated with a record of criminal conviction. Any judicial determination of factual innocence made pursuant to this section may be heard and determined upon declarations, affidavits, police reports, or other material, relevant, and reliable information submitted by the parties or ordered to be part of the record by the court. Where the court determines that the petition or motion is meritorious and that there is no reasonable cause to believe that the victim committed the offense for which the perpetrator of the identity theft was arrested, cited, convicted, or subject to a criminal complaint in the victim's name, or that the victim's identity has been mistakenly associated with a record of criminal conviction, the court shall find the victim factually innocent of that offense. If the victim is found factually innocent, the court shall issue an order certifying this determination.

(c) After a court has issued a determination of factual innocence pursuant to this section, the court may order the name and associated personal identifying information contained in court records, files, and indexes accessible by the public deleted, sealed, or labeled to show that the data is impersonated and does not reflect the defendant's identity.

(d) A court that has issued a determination of factual innocence pursuant to this section may at any time vacate that determination if the petition, or any information submitted in support of the petition, is found to contain any material misrepresentation or fraud.

(e) The Judicial Council of California shall develop a form for use in issuing an order pursuant to this section.

(f) For purposes of this section, "person" means a natural person, firm, association, organization, partnership, business trust, company, corporation, limited liability company, or public entity.

Amended by Stats 2006 ch 10 (AB 424),s 2, eff. 2/24/2006.

Amended by Stats 2003 ch 533 (SB 602), s 6, eff. 1/1/2004.

Amended by Stats 2002 ch 851 (AB 1219), s 1, eff. 1/1/2003.

Added by Stats 2000 ch 956 (AB 1897), s 2, eff. 1/1/2001.

Section 530.7 - Database of victims of identity theft

(a) In order for a victim of identity theft to be included in the data base established pursuant to subdivision (c), he or she shall submit to the Department of Justice a court order obtained pursuant to any provision of law, a full set of fingerprints, and any other information prescribed by the department.

(b) Upon receiving information pursuant to subdivision (a), the Department of Justice shall verify the identity of the victim against any driver's license or other identification record maintained by the Department of Motor Vehicles.

(c) The Department of Justice shall establish and maintain a data base of individuals who have been victims of identity theft. The department shall provide a victim of identity theft or his or her authorized representative access to the data base in order to establish that the individual has been a victim of identity theft. Access to the data base shall be limited to criminal justice agencies, victims of identity theft, and individuals and agencies authorized by the victims.

(d) The Department of Justice shall establish and maintain a toll-free telephone number to provide access to information under subdivision (c).

(e) This section shall be operative September 1, 2001.

Added by Stats 2000 ch 631 (AB 1862), s 1, eff. 1/1/2001.

Amended by Stats 2001 ch 854 (SB 205), s 30, eff. 1/1/2002, op. 9/1/2001.

Section 530.8 - Request for information related to application or account by unauthorized person

(a) If a person discovers that an application in their name for a loan, credit line or account, credit card, charge card, public utility service, mail receiving or forwarding service, office or desk space rental service, or commercial mobile radio service has been filed with any person or entity by an unauthorized person, or that an account in their name has been opened with a bank, trust company, savings association, credit union, public utility, mail receiving or forwarding service, office or desk space rental service, or commercial mobile radio service provider by an unauthorized person, then, upon presenting to the person or entity with which the application was filed or the account was opened a copy of a police report prepared pursuant to Section 530.6 or a copy of a signed and submitted Federal Trade Commission (FTC) identity theft report and identifying information in the categories of information that the unauthorized person used to complete the application or to open the account, the person, or a law enforcement officer specified by the person, shall be entitled to receive information related to the application or account, including a copy of the unauthorized person's application or application information and a record of transactions or charges associated with the application or account. Upon request by the person in whose name the application was filed or in whose name the account was opened, the person or entity with which the application was filed shall inform them of the categories of identifying information that the unauthorized person used to complete the application or to open the account. The person or entity with which the application was filed or the account was opened shall provide copies of all paper records, records of telephone applications or authorizations, or records of electronic applications or authorizations required by this section, without charge, within 10 business days of receipt of the person's request and submission of the required copy of the police report or Federal Trade Commission (FTC) identity theft report and identifying information.

(b) Any request made pursuant to subdivision (a) to a person or entity subject to the provisions of Section 2891 of the Public Utilities Code shall be in writing and the requesting person shall be deemed to be the subscriber for purposes of that section.

(c)

(1) Before a person or entity provides copies to a law enforcement officer pursuant to subdivision (a), the person or entity may require the requesting person to submit a signed and dated statement by which the requesting person does all of the following:

(A) Authorizes disclosure for a stated period.

(B) Specifies the name of the agency or department to which the disclosure is authorized.

(C) Identifies the types of records that the requesting person authorizes to be disclosed.

(2) The person or entity shall include in the statement to be signed by the requesting person a notice that the requesting person has the right at any time to revoke the authorization.

(d)

(1) A failure to produce records pursuant to subdivision (a) shall be addressed by the court in the jurisdiction in which the victim resides or in which the request for information was issued. At the victim's request, the Attorney General, the district attorney, or the prosecuting city attorney may file a petition to compel the attendance of the person or entity in possession of the records, as described in subdivision (a), and order the production of the requested records to the court. The petition shall contain a declaration from the victim stating when the request for information was made, that the information requested was not provided, and what response, if any, was made by the person or entity. The petition shall also contain copies of the police report prepared pursuant to Section 530.6 or the FTC identity theft report and the request for information made pursuant to this section upon the person or entity in possession of the records, as described in subdivision (a), and these two documents shall be kept confidential by the court. The petition and copies of the police report or the FTC identity theft report and the application shall be served upon the person or entity in possession of the records, as described in subdivision (a). The court shall hold a hearing on the petition no later than 10 court days after the petition is served and filed. The court shall order the release of records to the victim as required pursuant to this section.

(2) In addition to any other civil remedy available, the victim may bring a civil action against the entity for damages, injunctive relief, or other equitable relief, and a penalty of one hundred dollars ($100) per day of noncompliance, plus reasonable attorney's fees.

(e) For the purposes of this section, the following terms have the following meanings:

(1) "Application" means a new application for credit or service, the addition of authorized users to an existing account, the renewal of an existing account, or any other changes made to an existing account.

(2) "Commercial mobile radio service" means "commercial mobile radio service" as defined in Section 20.3 of Title 47 of the Code of Federal Regulations.

(3) "Law enforcement officer" means a peace officer as defined by Section 830.1.

(4) "Person" means a natural person, firm, association, organization, partnership, business trust, company, corporation, limited liability company, or public entity.

Amended by Stats 2021 ch 265 (AB 430),s 5, eff. 1/1/2022.
Amended by Stats 2006 ch 10 (AB 424),s 3, eff. 2/24/2006.
Amended by Stats 2003 ch 90 (AB 1772), s 1, eff. 1/1/2004.
Amended by Stats 2003 ch 533 (SB 602), s 7, eff. 1/1/2004.
Amended by Stats 2003 ch 534 (SB 684), s 2, eff. 1/1/2004.
Amended by Stats 2002 ch 254 (SB 1254), s 2, eff. 1/1/2003.
Added by Stats 2001 ch 493 (SB 125), s 5, eff. 1/1/2002.
See Stats 2003 ch 533 (SB 602), s 10.
See Stats 2003 ch 534 (SB 684), s 3.

Section 531 - Party to fraudulent conveyance of lands tenements or hereditaments goods or chattels etc.

Every person who is a party to any fraudulent conveyance of any lands, tenements, or hereditaments, goods or chattels, or any right or interest issuing out of the same, or to any bond, suit, judgment, or execution, contract or conveyance, had, made, or contrived with intent to deceive and defraud others, or to defeat, hinder, or delay creditors or others of their just debts, damages, or demands; or who, being a party as aforesaid, at any time wittingly and willingly puts in, uses, avows, maintains, justifies, or defends the same, or any of them, as true, and done, had, or made in good faith, or upon good consideration, or aliens, assigns, or sells any of the lands, tenements, hereditaments, goods, chattels, or other things before mentioned, to him or them conveyed as aforesaid, or any part thereof, is guilty of a misdemeanor.

Enacted 1872.

Section 531a - Unlawful execution or procurement of execution of instrument purporting to convey real property

Every person who, with intent to defraud, knowingly executes or procures another to execute any instrument purporting to convey any real property, or any right or interest therein, knowing that such person so executing has no right to or interest in such property, or who files or procures the filing of any such instrument, knowing that the person executing the same had no right, title or interest in the property so purported to be conveyed, is guilty of a misdemeanor and is punishable by imprisonment for not more than one year or by fine of five thousand dollars or both.

Added by Stats. 1929, Ch. 337.

Section 532 - Unlawful defrauding of person of money, labor, or property

(a) Every person who knowingly and designedly, by any false or fraudulent representation or pretense, defrauds any other person of money, labor, or property, whether real or personal, or who causes or procures others to report falsely of his or her wealth or mercantile character, and by thus imposing upon any person obtains credit, and thereby fraudulently gets possession of money or property, or obtains the labor or service of another, is punishable in the same manner and to the same extent as for larceny of the money or property so obtained.

(b) Upon a trial for having, with an intent to cheat or defraud another designedly, by any false pretense, obtained the signature of any person to a written instrument, or having obtained from any person any labor, money, or property, whether real or personal, or valuable thing, the defendant cannot be convicted if the false pretense was expressed in language unaccompanied by a false token or writing, unless the pretense, or some note or memorandum thereof is in writing, subscribed by or in the handwriting of the defendant, or unless the pretense is proven by the testimony of two witnesses, or that of one witness and corroborating circumstances. This section does not apply to a prosecution for falsely representing or personating another, and, in that assumed character, marrying, or receiving any money or property.

Amended by Stats. 1989, Ch. 897, Sec. 22.

Section 532a - False statement respecting financial condition

(1) Any person who shall knowingly make or cause to be made, either directly or indirectly or through any agency whatsoever, any false statement in writing, with intent that it shall be relied upon, respecting the financial condition, or means or ability to pay, of himself or herself, or any other person, firm or corporation, in whom he or she is interested, or for whom he or she is acting, for the purpose of procuring in any form whatsoever, either the delivery of personal property, the payment of cash, the making of a loan or credit, the extension of a credit, the execution of a contract of guaranty or suretyship, the discount of an account receivable, or the making, acceptance, discount, sale or endorsement of a bill of exchange, or promissory note, for the benefit of either himself or herself or of that person, firm or corporation shall be guilty of a public offense.

(2) Any person who knowing that a false statement in writing has been made, respecting the financial condition or means or ability to pay, of himself or herself, or a person, firm or corporation in which he or she is interested, or for whom he or she is acting, procures, upon the faith thereof, for the benefit either of himself or herself, or of that person, firm or corporation, either or any of the things of benefit mentioned in the first subdivision of this section shall be guilty of a public offense.

(3) Any person who knowing that a statement in writing has been made, respecting the financial condition or means or ability to pay of himself or herself or a person, firm or corporation, in which he or she is interested, or for whom he or she is acting, represents on a later day in writing that the statement theretofore made, if then again made on said day, would be then true, when in fact, said statement if then made would be false, and procures upon the faith thereof, for the benefit either of himself or herself or of that person, firm or corporation either or any of the things of benefit mentioned in the first subdivision of this section shall be guilty of a public offense.

(4) Any person committing a public offense under subdivision (1), (2), or (3) shall be guilty of a misdemeanor, punishable by a fine of not more than one thousand dollars ($1,000), or by imprisonment in the county jail for not more than six months, or by both that fine and imprisonment. Any person who violates the provisions of subdivision (1), (2), or (3), by using a fictitious name, social security number, business name, or business address, or by falsely representing himself or herself to be another person or another business, is guilty of a felony and is punishable by a fine not exceeding five thousand dollars ($5,000) or by imprisonment pursuant to subdivision (h) of Section 1170, or by both that fine and imprisonment, or by a fine not exceeding two thousand five hundred dollars ($2,500) or by imprisonment in the county jail not exceeding one year, or by both such fine and imprisonment.

(5) This section shall not be construed to preclude the applicability of any other provision of the criminal law of this state which applies or may apply to any transaction.

Amended by Stats 2011 ch 39 (AB 117),s 68, eff. 6/30/2011.

Amended by Stats 2011 ch 15 (AB 109),s 384, eff. 4/4/2011, but operative no earlier than October 1, 2011, and only upon creation of a community corrections grant program to assist in implementing this act and upon an appropriation to fund the grant program.

Section 532b - False representation as veteran

(a) A person who fraudulently represents themselves as a veteran or ex-serviceman of a war in which the United States was engaged, in connection with the soliciting of aid or the sale or attempted sale of any property, is guilty of a misdemeanor.

(b) A person who fraudulently claims, or presents themselves, to be a veteran or member of the Armed Forces of the United States, the California National Guard, the State Guard, the Naval Militia, the national guard of any other state, or any other reserve component of the Armed Forces of the United States, with the intent to obtain money, property, or other tangible benefit, is guilty of a misdemeanor.

(c)

(1) Except as provided in paragraph (2), a person who, orally, in writing, or by wearing any military decoration, fraudulently represents themselves to have been awarded a military decoration, with the intent to obtain money, property, or other tangible benefit, is guilty of a misdemeanor.

(2) This offense is an infraction or a misdemeanor, subject to Sections 19.6, 19.7, and 19.8, if the person committing the offense is a veteran of the Armed Forces of the United States.

(d) A person who forges documentation reflecting the awarding of a military decoration that the person has not received for the purposes of obtaining money, property, or receiving a tangible benefit is guilty of a misdemeanor.

(e) A person who knowingly, with the intent to impersonate and to deceive, for the purposes of obtaining money, property, or receiving a tangible benefit, misrepresents themselves as a member or veteran of the Armed Forces of the United States, the California National Guard, the State Guard, or the Naval Militia by wearing the uniform or military decoration authorized for use by the members or veterans of those forces, is guilty of a misdemeanor.

(f) A person who knowingly utilizes falsified military identification for the purposes of obtaining money, property, or receiving a tangible benefit, is guilty of a misdemeanor.

(g) A person who knowingly, with the intent to impersonate, for the purposes of promoting a business, charity, or endeavor, misrepresents themselves as a member or veteran of the Armed Forces of the United States, the California National Guard, the State Guard, or the Naval Militia by wearing the uniform or military decoration authorized for use by the members or veterans of those forces, is guilty of a misdemeanor.

(h) A person who knowingly, with the intent to gain an advantage for employment purposes, misrepresents themselves, as a member or veteran of the Armed Forces of the United States, the California National Guard, the State Guard, or the Naval Militia by wearing the uniform or military decoration authorized for use by the members or veterans of those forces, is guilty of a misdemeanor.

(i) This section does not apply to face-to-face solicitations involving less than ten dollars ($10).

(j) This section, Section 3003 of the Government Code, and Section 1821 of the Military and Veterans Code shall be known, and may be cited as, the California Stolen Valor Act.

(k) For purposes of this section, the following terms shall have the following meanings:

(1) "Military decoration" means any decoration or medal from the Armed Forces of the United States, the California National Guard, the State Guard, or the Naval Militia, or any service medals or badges awarded to the members of those forces, or the ribbon, button, or rosette of that badge, decoration, or medal, or any colorable imitation of that item.

(2) "Tangible benefit" means financial remuneration, an effect on the outcome of a criminal or civil court proceeding, or any benefit relating to service in the military that is provided by a federal, state, or local governmental entity.

Amended by Stats 2020 ch 97 (AB 2193),s 45, eff. 1/1/2021.

Amended by Stats 2017 ch 576 (AB 153),s 2, eff. 1/1/2018.

Amended by Stats 2011 ch 69 (AB 167),s 2, eff. 1/1/2012.

Section 532c - Unlawful offer or gift with winning numbers or tickets of admissions of real property and charge of fees in connection with transfer

Any person, firm, corporation or copartnership who knowingly and designedly offers or gives with winning numbers at any drawing of numbers or with tickets of admission to places of public assemblage, any lot or parcel of real property and charges or collects fees in connection with the transfer thereof, is guilty of a misdemeanor.

Added by renumbering Section 532a (as added by Stats. 1913, Ch. 70) by Stats. 1935, Ch. 338.

Section 532d - Unlawful solicitation or receipt of money or property for charitable, religious, or eleemosynary purpose

(a) Any person who solicits or attempts to solicit or receives money or property of any kind for a charitable, religious or eleemosynary purpose and who, directly or indirectly, makes, utters, or delivers, either orally or in writing, an unqualified statement of fact concerning the purpose or organization for which the money or property is solicited or received, or concerning the cost and expense of solicitation or the manner in which the money or property or any part thereof is to be used, which statement is in fact false and was made, uttered, or delivered by that person either willfully and with knowledge of its falsity or negligently without due consideration of those facts which by the use of ordinary care he or she should have known, is guilty of a misdemeanor, and is punishable by imprisonment in the county jail for not more than one year, by a fine not exceeding five thousand dollars ($5,000), or by both that imprisonment and fine.

(b) An offense charged in violation of this section shall be proven by the testimony of one witness and corroborating circumstances.

(c) Nothing contained in this section shall be construed to limit the right of any city, county, or city and county to adopt regulations for charitable solicitations which are not in conflict with this section.

Amended by Stats. 1998, Ch. 166, Sec. 1. Effective January 1, 1999.

Section 532e - Unlawful receipt of money incident to constructing improvements on real property

Any person who receives money for the purpose of obtaining or paying for services, labor, materials or equipment incident to constructing improvements on real property and willfully rebates any part of the money to or on behalf of anyone contracting with such person, for provision of the services, labor, materials or equipment for which the money was given, shall be guilty of a misdemeanor; provided, however, that normal trade discount for prompt payment shall not be considered a violation of this section.

Added by Stats. 1965, Ch. 1145.

Section 532f - Mortgage fraud

(a) A person commits mortgage fraud if, with the intent to defraud, the person does any of the following:

(1) Deliberately makes any misstatement, misrepresentation, or omission during the mortgage lending process with the intention that it be relied on by a mortgage lender, borrower, or any other party to the mortgage lending process.

(2) Deliberately uses or facilitates the use of any misstatement, misrepresentation, or omission, knowing the same to contain a misstatement, misrepresentation, or omission, during the mortgage lending process with the intention that it be relied on by a mortgage lender, borrower, or any other party to the mortgage lending process.

(3) Receives any proceeds or any other funds in connection with a mortgage loan closing that the person knew resulted from a violation of paragraph (1) or (2) of this subdivision.

(4) Files or causes to be filed with the recorder of any county in connection with a mortgage loan transaction any document the person knows to contain a deliberate misstatement, misrepresentation, or omission.

(b) An offense involving mortgage fraud shall not be based solely on information lawfully disclosed pursuant to federal disclosure laws, regulations, or interpretations related to the mortgage lending process.

(c)

(1) Notwithstanding any other provision of law, an order for the production of any or all relevant records possessed by a real estate recordholder in whatever form and however stored may be issued by a judge upon a written ex parte application made under penalty of perjury by a peace officer stating that there are reasonable grounds to believe that the records sought are relevant and material to an ongoing investigation of a felony fraud violation.

(2) The ex parte application shall specify with particularity the records to be produced, which shall relate to a party or parties in the criminal investigation.

(3) Relevant records may include, but are not limited to, purchase contracts, loan applications, settlement statements, closing statements, escrow instructions, payoff demands, disbursement reports, or checks.

(4) The ex parte application and any subsequent judicial order may be ordered sealed by the court upon a sufficient showing that it is necessary for the effective continuation of the investigation.

(5) The records ordered to be produced shall be provided to the peace officer applicant or his or her designee within a reasonable time period after service of the order upon the real estate recordholder.

(d)

(1) Nothing in this section shall preclude the real estate recordholder from notifying a customer of the receipt of the order for production of records, unless a court orders the real estate recordholder to withhold notification to the customer upon a finding that this notice would impede the investigation.

(2) If a court has made an order to withhold notification to the customer under this subdivision, the peace officer who or law enforcement agency that obtained the records shall notify the customer by delivering a copy of the ex parte order to the customer within 10 days of the termination of the investigation.

(e)

(1) Nothing in this section shall preclude the real estate recordholder from voluntarily disclosing information or providing records to law enforcement upon request.

(2) This section shall not preclude a real estate recordholder, in its discretion, from initiating contact with, and thereafter communicating with and disclosing records to, appropriate state or local agencies concerning a suspected violation of any law.

(f) No real estate recordholder, or any officer, employee, or agent of the real estate recordholder, shall be liable to any person for either of the following:

(1) Disclosing information in response to an order pursuant to this section.

(2) Complying with an order under this section not to disclose to the customer the order, or the dissemination of information pursuant to the order.

(g) Any records required to be produced pursuant to this section shall be accompanied by an affidavit of a custodian of records of the real estate recordholder or other qualified witness which states, or includes in substance, all of the following:

(1) The affiant is the duly authorized custodian of the records or other qualified witness and has authority to certify the records.

(2) The identity of the records.

(3) A description of the mode of preparation of the records.

(4) The records were prepared by the personnel of the business in the regular course of business at or near the time of an act, condition, or event.

(5) Any copies of records described in the order are true copies.

(h) A person who violates this section is guilty of a public offense punishable by imprisonment in a county jail for not more than one year or by imprisonment pursuant to subdivision (h) of Section 1170.

(i) For the purposes of this section, the following terms shall have the following meanings:

(1) "Person" means any individual, partnership, firm, association, corporation, limited liability company, or other legal entity.

(2) "Mortgage lending process" means the process through which a person seeks or obtains a mortgage loan, including, but not limited to, solicitation, application, origination, negotiation of terms, third-party provider services, underwriting, signing and closing, and funding of the loan.

(3) "Mortgage loan" means a loan or agreement to extend credit to a person that is secured by a deed of trust or other document representing a security interest or lien upon any interest in real property, including the renewal or refinancing of the loan.

(4) "Real estate recordholder" means any person, licensed or unlicensed, that meets any of the following conditions:

(A) Is a title insurer that engages in the "business of title insurance" as defined by Section 12340.3 of the Insurance Code, an underwritten title company, or an escrow company.

(B) Functions as a broker or salesperson by engaging in any of the type of acts set forth in Sections 10131, 10131.1, 10131.2, 10131.3, 10131.4, and 10131.6 of the Business and Professions Code.

(C) Engages in the making or servicing of loans secured by real property.

(j) Fraud involving a mortgage loan may only be prosecuted under this section when the value of the alleged fraud meets the threshold for grand theft as set out in subdivision (a) of Section 487.

Amended by Stats 2011 ch 39 (AB 117),s 68, eff. 6/30/2011.

Amended by Stats 2011 ch 15 (AB 109),s 385, eff. 4/4/2011, but operative no earlier than October 1, 2011, and only upon creation of a community corrections grant program to assist in implementing this act and upon an appropriation to fund the grant program.

Added by Stats 2009 ch 174 (SB 239),s 3, eff. 1/1/2010.

Section 533 - Unlawful sale or disposal of tract of land after selling or disposing of it

Every person who, after once selling, bartering, or disposing of any tract of land or town lot, or after executing any bond or agreement for the sale of any land or town lot, again willfully and with intent to defraud previous or subsequent purchasers, sells, barters, or disposes of the same tract of land or town lot, or any part thereof, or willfully and with intent to defraud previous or subsequent purchasers, executes any bond or agreement to sell, barter, or dispose of the same land or lot, or any part thereof, to any other person for a valuable consideration, is punishable by imprisonment pursuant to subdivision (h) of Section 1170.

Amended by Stats 2011 ch 39 (AB 117),s 68, eff. 6/30/2011.

Amended by Stats 2011 ch 15 (AB 109),s 386, eff. 4/4/2011, but operative no earlier than October 1, 2011, and only upon creation of a community corrections grant program to assist in implementing this act and upon an appropriation to fund the grant program.

Section 534 - Unlawful sale or mortgage of real estate by spouse

Every person who is married or in a registered domestic partnership, who falsely and fraudulently represents himself or herself as competent to sell or mortgage any real estate, to the validity of which sale or mortgage the assent or concurrence of his or her spouse is necessary, and under such representations willfully conveys or mortgages the same, is guilty of a felony.

Amended by Stats 2016 ch 50 (SB 1005),s 73, eff. 1/1/2017.

Section 535 - Unlawful obtaining of money or property by auction or mock auction

Every person who obtains any money or property from another, or obtains the signature of another to any written instrument, the false making of which would be forgery, by means of any false or fraudulent sale of property or pretended property, by auction, or by any of the practices known as mock auctions, is punishable by imprisonment in a county jail not exceeding one year, or by imprisonment pursuant to subdivision (h) of Section 1170, or by a fine not exceeding two thousand dollars ($2,000), or by both that fine and imprisonment, and, in addition, is disqualified for a period of three years from acting as an auctioneer in this state.

Amended by Stats 2011 ch 39 (AB 117),s 68, eff. 6/30/2011.

Amended by Stats 2011 ch 15 (AB 109),s 387, eff. 4/4/2011, but operative no earlier than October 1, 2011, and only upon creation of a community corrections grant program to assist in implementing this act and upon an appropriation to fund the grant program.

Section 536 - False statement as to price obtained for consigned property

Every commission merchant, broker, agent, factor, or consignee, who shall willfully and corruptly make, or cause to be made, to the principal or consignor of such commission merchant, agent, broker, factor, or consignee, a false statement as to the price obtained for any property consigned or entrusted for sale, or as to the quality or quantity of any property so consigned or entrusted, or as to any expenditures made in connection therewith, shall be deemed guilty of a misdemeanor, and on conviction thereof, shall be punished by fine not exceeding one thousand dollars ($1,000) and not less than two hundred dollars ($200), or by imprisonment in the county jail not exceeding six months and not less than 10 days, or by both such fine and imprisonment.

Amended by Stats. 1983, Ch. 1092, Sec. 299. Effective September 27, 1983. Operative January 1, 1984, by Sec. 427 of Ch. 1092.

Section 536a - Statement setting forth name and address of person to whom sale was made and price obtained

It is hereby made the duty of every commission merchant, broker, factor, or consignee, to whom any property is consigned or entrusted for sale, to make, when accounting therefor or subsequently, upon the written demand of his principal or consignor, a true written statement setting forth the name and address of the person or persons to whom a sale of the said property, or any portion thereof, was made, the quantity so sold to each purchaser, and the respective prices obtained therefor; provided, however, that unless separate written demand shall be made as to each consignment or shipment regarding which said statement is desired, prior to sale, it shall be sufficient to set forth in said statement only so many of said matters above enumerated as said commission merchant, broker, factor, or consignee may be able to obtain from the books of account kept by him; and that said statement shall not be required in case of cash sales where the amount of the transaction is less than fifty dollars. Any person violating the provisions of this section is guilty of a misdemeanor.

Added by Stats. 1909, Ch. 706.

Section 537 - Unlawfully obtaining credit, food, fuel, services or accommodations

(a) Any person who obtains any food, fuel, services, or accommodations at a hotel, inn, restaurant, boardinghouse, lodginghouse, apartment house, bungalow court, motel, marina, marine facility, autocamp, ski area, or public or private campground, without paying therefor, with intent to defraud the proprietor or manager thereof, or who obtains credit at an hotel, inn, restaurant, boardinghouse, lodginghouse, apartment house, bungalow court, motel, marina, marine facility, autocamp, or public or private campground by the use of any false pretense, or who, after obtaining credit, food, fuel, services, or accommodations, at an hotel, inn, restaurant, boardinghouse, lodginghouse, apartment house, bungalow court, motel, marina, marine facility, autocamp, or public or private campground, absconds, or surreptitiously, or by force, menace, or threats, removes any part of his or her baggage therefrom with the intent not to pay for his or her food or accommodations is guilty of a public offense punishable as follows:

(1) If the value of the credit, food, fuel, services, or accommodations is nine hundred fifty dollars ($950) or less, by a fine not exceeding one thousand dollars ($1,000) or by imprisonment in the county jail for a term not exceeding six months, or both.

(2) If the value of the credit, food, fuel, services, or accommodations is greater than nine hundred fifty dollars ($950), by imprisonment in a county jail for a term of not more than one year, or in the state prison.

(b) Any person who uses or attempts to use ski area facilities for which payment is required without paying as required, or who resells a ski lift ticket to another when the resale is not authorized by the proprietor, is guilty of an infraction.

(c) Evidence that a person left the premises of such an hotel, inn, restaurant, boardinghouse, lodginghouse, apartment house, bungalow court, motel, marina, marine facility, autocamp, ski area, or public or private campground, without paying or offering to pay for such food, fuel, services, use of facilities, or accommodation, or that the person, without authorization from the proprietor, resold his or her ski lift ticket to another person after making use of such facilities, shall be prima facie evidence of the following:

    (1) That the person obtained such food, fuel, services, use of facilities or accommodations with intent to defraud the proprietor or manager.

    (2) That, if, after obtaining the credit, food, fuel, services, or accommodations, the person absconded, or surreptitiously, or by force, menace, or threats, removed part of his or her baggage therefrom, the person did so with the intent not to pay for the credit, food, fuel, services, or accommodations.

Amended by Stats 2009 ch 28 (SB X3-18),s 27, eff. 1/1/2010.

Section 537b - Unlawfully obtaining livery hire or other accommodations

Any person who obtains any livery hire or other accommodation at any livery or feed stable, kept for profit, in this state, without paying therefor, with intent to defraud the proprietor or manager thereof; or who obtains credit at any such livery or feed stable by the use of any false pretense; or who after obtaining a horse, vehicle, or other property at such livery or feed stable, willfully or maliciously abuses the same by beating, goading, overdriving or other willful or malicious conduct, or who after obtaining such horse, vehicle, or other property, shall, with intent to defraud the owner, manager or proprietor of such livery or feed stable, keep the same for a longer period, or take the same to a greater distance than contracted for; or allow a feed bill or other charges to accumulate against such property, without paying therefor; or abandon or leave the same, is guilty of a misdemeanor.

Added by renumbering Section 5373/4 by Stats. 1905, Ch. 523.

Section 537c - Unlawfully permitting person to drive, ride, or otherwise use boarded horse, other animal, or vehicle

Every owner, manager, proprietor, or other person, having the management, charge or control of any livery stable, feed or boarding stable, and every person pasturing stock, who shall receive and take into his possession, charge, care or control, any horse, mare, or other animal, or any buggy, or other vehicle, belonging to any other person, to be by him kept, fed, or cared for, and who, while said horse, mare or other animal or buggy or other vehicle, is thus in his possession, charge, care or under his control, as aforesaid, shall drive, ride or use, or knowingly permit or allow any person other than the owner or other person entitled so to do, to drive, ride, or otherwise use the same, without the consent or permission of the owner thereof, or other person charged with the care, control or possession of such property, shall be guilty of a misdemeanor.

Added by Stats. 1909, Ch. 178.

Section 537e - Unlawful buying, selling, or possession of personal property from which distinguishing number or identification mark removed, defaced, or destroyed

(a) Any person who knowingly buys, sells, receives, disposes of, conceals, or has in his or her possession any personal property from which the manufacturer's serial number, identification number, electronic serial number, or any other distinguishing number or identification mark has been removed, defaced, covered, altered, or destroyed, is guilty of a public offense, punishable as follows:

    (1) If the value of the property does not exceed nine hundred fifty dollars ($950), by imprisonment in a county jail not exceeding six months.

    (2) If the value of the property exceeds nine hundred fifty dollars ($950), by imprisonment in a county jail not exceeding one year.

    (3) If the property is an integrated computer chip or panel of a value of nine hundred fifty dollars ($950) or more, by imprisonment pursuant to subdivision (h) of Section 1170 for 16 months, or two or three years or by imprisonment in a county jail not exceeding one year.

(b) For purposes of this subdivision, "personal property" includes, but is not limited to, the following:

    (1) Any television, radio, recorder, phonograph, telephone, piano, or any other musical instrument or sound equipment.

    (2) Any washing machine, sewing machine, vacuum cleaner, or other household appliance or furnishings.

    (3) Any typewriter, adding machine, dictaphone, or any other office equipment or furnishings.

    (4) Any computer, printed circuit, integrated chip or panel, or other part of a computer.

    (5) Any tool or similar device, including any technical or scientific equipment.

    (6) Any bicycle, exercise equipment, or any other entertainment or recreational equipment.

    (7) Any electrical or mechanical equipment, contrivance, material, or piece of apparatus or equipment.

    (8) Any clock, watch, watch case, or watch movement.

    (9) Any vehicle or vessel, or any component part thereof.

(c) When property described in subdivision (a) comes into the custody of a peace officer it shall become subject to the provision of Chapter 12 (commencing with Section 1407) of Title 10 of Part 2, relating to the disposal of stolen or embezzled property. Property subject to this section shall be considered stolen or embezzled property for the purposes of that chapter, and prior to being disposed of, shall have an identification mark imbedded or engraved in, or permanently affixed to it.

(d) This section does not apply to those cases or instances where any of the changes or alterations enumerated in subdivision (a) have been customarily made or done as an established practice in the ordinary and regular conduct of business, by the original manufacturer, or by his or her duly appointed direct representative, or under specific authorization from the original manufacturer.

Amended by Stats 2011 ch 39 (AB 117),s 68, eff. 6/30/2011.

Amended by Stats 2011 ch 15 (AB 109),s 388, eff. 4/4/2011, but operative no earlier than October 1, 2011, and only upon creation of a community corrections grant program to assist in implementing this act and upon an appropriation to fund the grant program.

Amended by Stats 2009 ch 28 (SB X3-18),s 28, eff. 1/1/2010.

Section 537f - Unlawful sale of rebuilt battery

No storage battery composed in whole or in part of a used container, or used plate or plates and intended for use in the starting, lighting or ignition of automobiles, shall be sold or offered for sale in this State unless: the word "Rebuilt" together with the rebuilder's name and address is labeled on one side of the battery in letters not less than one-half inch in height with a one-eighth inch stroke. Any person selling or offering for sale such a battery in violation of this section shall be guilty of a misdemeanor, punishable by a fine not exceeding two hundred fifty dollars, or by imprisonment in the county jail for not more than six months, or by both such fine and imprisonment.

Added by Stats. 1933, Ch. 925.

Section 537g - Unlawful removal of owner identification number from another's personal property

(a) Unless otherwise provided by law, any person who knowingly removes, defaces, covers, alters or destroys a National Crime Information Center owner identification number from the personal property of another without permission is guilty of a misdemeanor punishable by a fine not to exceed four hundred dollars ($400), imprisonment in the county jail not to exceed one year, or both.

(b) This section shall not apply to any action taken by an authorized person to dispose of property pursuant to Article 1 (commencing with Section 2080) of Chapter 4 of Title 6 of Part 4 of Division 3 of the Civil Code or pursuant to Chapter 12 (commencing with Section 1407) of Title 10 of Part 2 of this code.

Added by Stats. 1983, Ch. 878, Sec. 2.

Section 538 - Unlawful acts after mortgaging of property

Every person, who, after mortgaging any of the property permitted to be mortgaged by the provisions of Sections 9102 and 9109 of the Commercial Code, excepting locomotives, engines, rolling stock of a railroad, steamboat machinery in actual use, and vessels, during the existence of the mortgage, with intent to defraud the mortgagee, his or her representative or assigns, takes, drives, carries away, or otherwise removes or permits the taking, driving, or carrying away, or other removal of the mortgaged property, or any part thereof, from the county where it was situated when mortgaged, without the written consent of the mortgagee, or who sells, transfers, slaughters, destroys, or in any manner further encumbers the mortgaged property, or any part thereof, or causes it to be sold, transferred, slaughtered, destroyed, or further encumbered, is guilty of theft, and is punishable accordingly. In the case of a sale, transfer, or further encumbrance at or before the time of making the sale, transfer, or encumbrance, the mortgagor informs the person to whom the sale, transfer, or encumbrance is made, of the existence of the prior mortgage, and also informs the prior mortgagee of the intended sale, transfer, or encumbrance, in writing, by giving the name and place of residence of the party to whom the sale, transfer, or encumbrance is to be made.

EFFECTIVE 7/1/2001. Amended October 10, 1999 (Bill Number: SB 45) (Chapter 991).

Section 538a - Unlawful acts related to letter addressed to newspaper

Every person who signs any letter addressed to a newspaper with the name of a person other than himself and sends such letter to the newspaper, or causes it to be sent to such newspaper, with intent to lead the newspaper to believe that such letter was written by the person whose name is signed thereto, is guilty of a misdemeanor.

Added by renumbering Section 480 (as added by Stats. 1963, Ch. 1256) by Stats. 1972, Ch. 449.

Section 538b - Unlawful wearing of insignia or apparel of secret society or fraternal or religious organization to obtain aid or assistance

Any person who wilfully wears the badge, lapel button, rosette, or any part of the garb, robe, habit, or any other recognized and established insignia or apparel of any secret society, or fraternal or religious order or organization, or of any sect, church or religious denomination, or uses the same to obtain aid or assistance within this State, with intent to deceive, unless entitled to wear and use the same under the constitution, by-laws or rules and regulations, or other laws or enactments of such society, order, organization, sect, church or religious denomination is guilty of a misdemeanor.

Amended by Stats. 1937, Ch. 255.

Section 538c - Theft of advertising services

(a) Except as provided in subdivision (c), any person who attaches or inserts an unauthorized advertisement in a newspaper, whether alone or in concert with another, and who redistributes it to the public or who has the intent to redistribute it to the public, is guilty of the crime of theft of advertising services which shall be punishable as a misdemeanor.

(b) As used in this section:

(1) "Unauthorized advertisement" means any form of representation or communication, including any handbill, newsletter, pamphlet, or notice that contains any letters, words, or pictorial representation that is attached to or inserted in a newspaper without a contractual agreement between the publisher and an advertiser.

(2) "Newspaper" includes any newspaper, magazine, periodical, or other tangible publication, whether offered for retail sale or distributed without charge.

(c) This section does not apply if the publisher or authorized distributor of the newspaper consents to the attachment or insertion of the advertisement.

(d) This section does not apply to a newspaper distributor who is directed to insert an unauthorized advertisement by a person or company supplying the newspapers, and who is not aware that the advertisement is unauthorized.

(e) A conviction under this section shall not constitute a conviction for petty theft.

Amended by Stats 2002 ch 1134 (AB 2145), s 1, eff. 1/1/2003.

Section 538d - Fraudulent personation of peace officer

(a) Any person other than one who by law is given the authority of a peace officer, who willfully wears, exhibits, or uses the authorized uniform, insignia, emblem, device, label, certificate, card, or writing, of a peace officer, with the intent of fraudulently impersonating a peace officer, or of fraudulently inducing the belief that they are a peace officer, or who willfully and credibly impersonates a peace officer through or on an internet website, or by other electronic means, for purposes of defrauding another, is guilty of a misdemeanor.

(b)

(1) Any person, other than the one who by law is given the authority of a peace officer, who willfully wears, exhibits, or uses the badge of a peace officer with the intent of fraudulently impersonating a peace officer, or of fraudulently inducing the belief that they are

a peace officer, is guilty of a misdemeanor punishable by imprisonment in a county jail not to exceed one year, by a fine not to exceed two thousand dollars ($2,000), or by both that imprisonment and fine.

(2) Any person who willfully wears or uses any badge that falsely purports to be authorized for the use of one who by law is given the authority of a peace officer, or which so resembles the authorized badge of a peace officer as would deceive any ordinary reasonable person into believing that it is authorized for the use of one who by law is given the authority of a peace officer, for the purpose of fraudulently impersonating a peace officer, or of fraudulently inducing the belief that they are a peace officer, is guilty of a misdemeanor punishable by imprisonment in a county jail not to exceed one year, by a fine not to exceed two thousand dollars ($2,000), or by both that imprisonment and fine.

(c)

(1) Except as provided in subdivision (d), any person who willfully wears, exhibits, or uses, or who willfully makes, sells, loans, gives, or transfers to another, any badge, insignia, emblem, device, or any label, certificate, card, or writing, which falsely purports to be authorized for the use of one who by law is given the authority of a peace officer, or which so resembles the authorized badge, insignia, emblem, device, label, certificate, card, or writing of a peace officer as would deceive an ordinary reasonable person into believing that it is authorized for the use of one who by law is given the authority of a peace officer, is guilty of a misdemeanor punishable by imprisonment in a county jail not to exceed six months, by a fine not to exceed two thousand dollars ($2,000), or by both that imprisonment and fine, except that any person who makes or sells any badge under the circumstances described in this subdivision is subject to a fine not to exceed fifteen thousand dollars ($15,000).

(2) A local law enforcement agency in the jurisdiction that files charges against a person for a violation of paragraph (1) shall seize the badge, insignia, emblem, device, label, certificate, card, or writing described in paragraph (1).

(d)

(1) The head of an agency that employs peace officers, as defined in Sections 830.1 and 830.2, is authorized to issue identification in the form of a badge, insignia, emblem, device, label, certificate, card, or writing that clearly states that the person has honorably retired following service as a peace officer from that agency. The identification authorized pursuant to this subdivision is separate and distinct from the identification authorized by Article 2 (commencing with Section 25450) of Chapter 2 of Division 5 of Title 4 of Part 6.

(2) If the head of an agency issues a badge to an honorably retired peace officer that is not affixed to a plaque or other memento commemorating the retiree's service for the agency, the words "Honorably Retired" shall be clearly visible above, underneath, or on the badge itself.

(3) The head of an agency that employs peace officers as defined in Sections 830.1 and 830.2 is authorized to revoke identification granted pursuant to this subdivision in the event of misuse or abuse.

(4) For the purposes of this subdivision, the term "honorably retired" does not include an officer who has agreed to a service retirement in lieu of termination.

(e)

(1) Vendors of law enforcement uniforms shall verify that a person purchasing a uniform identifying a law enforcement agency is an employee of the agency identified on the uniform. Presentation and examination of a valid identification card with a picture of the person purchasing the uniform and identification, on the letterhead of the law enforcement agency, of the person buying the uniform as an employee of the agency identified on the uniform shall be sufficient verification.

(2) Any uniform vendor who sells a uniform identifying a law enforcement agency, without verifying that the purchaser is an employee of the agency, is guilty of a misdemeanor, punishable by a fine of not more than one thousand dollars ($1,000).

(3) This subdivision shall not apply if the uniform is to be used solely as a prop for a motion picture, television, video production, or a theatrical event, and prior written permission has been obtained from the identified law enforcement agency.

Amended by Stats 2022 ch 954 (AB 1899),s 1, eff. 1/1/2023.
Amended by Stats 2014 ch 514 (SB 702),s 1, eff. 1/1/2015.
Amended by Stats 2010 ch 178 (SB 1115),s 58, eff. 1/1/2011, op. 1/1/2012.
Amended by Stats 2009 ch 345 (SB 169),s 1, eff. 1/1/2010.
Amended by Stats 2008 ch 699 (SB 1241),s 10, eff. 1/1/2009.
Amended by Stats 2007 ch 241 (AB 1448),s 1, eff. 1/1/2008.
Amended by Stats 2000 ch 430 (SB 1942), s 1, eff. 1/1/2001.

Section 538e - Fraudulent personation of firefighter

(a) Any person, other than an officer or member of a fire department, who willfully wears, exhibits, or uses the authorized uniform, insignia, emblem, device, label, certificate, card, or writing of an officer or member of a fire department or a deputy state fire marshal, with the intent of fraudulently impersonating an officer or member of a fire department or the Office of the State Fire Marshal, or of fraudulently inducing the belief that they are an officer or member of a fire department or the Office of the State Fire Marshal, or who willfully and credibly impersonates such an officer or member on an internet website, or by other electronic means, for purposes of defrauding another, is guilty of a misdemeanor.

(b)

(1) Any person, other than the one who by law is given the authority of an officer or member of a fire department, or a deputy state fire marshal, who willfully wears, exhibits, or uses the badge of a fire department or the Office of the State Fire Marshal with the intent of fraudulently impersonating an officer, or member of a fire department, or a deputy state fire marshal, or of fraudulently inducing the belief that they are an officer or member of a fire department, or a deputy state fire marshal, is guilty of a misdemeanor punishable by imprisonment in a county jail not to exceed one year, by a fine not to exceed two thousand dollars ($2,000), or by both that imprisonment and fine.

(2) Any person who willfully wears or uses any badge that falsely purports to be authorized for the use of one who by law is given the authority of an officer or member of a fire department, or a deputy state fire marshal, or which so resembles the authorized badge of an officer or member of a fire department, or a deputy state fire marshal as would deceive any ordinary reasonable person into believing that it is authorized for the use of one who by law is given the authority of an officer or member of a fire department or a deputy state

fire marshal, for the purpose of fraudulently impersonating an officer or member of a fire department, or a deputy state fire marshal, or of fraudulently inducing the belief that they are an officer or member of a fire department, or a deputy state fire marshal, is guilty of a misdemeanor punishable by imprisonment in a county jail not to exceed one year, by a fine not to exceed two thousand dollars ($2,000), or by both that imprisonment and fine.

(c) Any person who willfully wears, exhibits, or uses, or who willfully makes, sells, loans, gives, or transfers to another, any badge, insignia, emblem, device, or any label, certificate, card, or writing, which falsely purports to be authorized for the use of one who by law is given the authority of an officer, or member of a fire department or a deputy state fire marshal, or which so resembles the authorized badge, insignia, emblem, device, label, certificate, card, or writing of an officer or member of a fire department or a deputy state fire marshal as would deceive an ordinary reasonable person into believing that it is authorized for use by an officer or member of a fire department or a deputy state fire marshal, is guilty of a misdemeanor, except that any person who makes or sells any badge under the circumstances described in this subdivision is guilty of a misdemeanor punishable by a fine not to exceed fifteen thousand dollars ($15,000).

(d) Any person who, for the purpose of selling, leasing or otherwise disposing of merchandise, supplies or equipment used in fire prevention or suppression, falsely represents, in any manner whatsoever, to any other person that they are a fire marshal, fire inspector or member of a fire department, or that they have the approval, endorsement or authorization of any fire marshal, fire inspector or fire department, or member thereof, is guilty of a misdemeanor.

(e)

(1) Vendors of uniforms shall verify that a person purchasing a uniform identifying a firefighting agency or department is an employee or authorized member of the agency or department identified on the uniform. Examination of a valid photo identification card issued by a firefighting agency or department that designates the person as an employee or authorized member of the agency or department identified on the uniform shall be sufficient verification.

(2) If a person purchasing a uniform does not have a valid photo identification card issued by a firefighting agency or department, the person shall present an official letter of authorization from the firefighting agency or department designating that person as an employee or authorized member of the agency or department. The person shall also present a government issued photo identification card bearing the same name as listed in the letter of authorization issued by the agency or department.

(3) Any uniform vendor who sells a uniform identifying a firefighting agency or department without verifying that the purchaser is an employee or authorized member of the agency or department is guilty of a misdemeanor, punishable by a fine of not more than one thousand dollars ($1,000).

(4) This subdivision shall not apply if the uniform is to be used solely as a prop for a motion picture, television, video production, or a theatrical event, and prior written permission has been obtained from the identified firefighting agency or department.

(f) This section shall not apply to either of the following:

(1) Use of a badge solely as a prop for a motion picture, television, or video production, or an entertainment or theatrical event.

(2) A badge supplied by a recognized employee organization as defined in Section 3501 of the Government Code representing firefighters or a state or international organization to which it is affiliated.

Amended by Stats 2022 ch 954 (AB 1899),s 2, eff. 1/1/2023.
Amended by Stats 2009 ch 100 (AB 388),s 1, eff. 1/1/2010.
Amended by Stats 2006 ch 901 (SB 1422),s 6, eff. 1/1/2007.
Amended by Stats 2004 ch 22 (AB 1153), s 1, eff. 3/5/2004.

Section 538f - Fraudulent personation of employee of public utility or district

Any person, other than an employee of a public utility or district as defined in Sections 216 and 11503 of the Public Utilities Code, respectively, who willfully presents themselves to a utility or district customer with the intent of fraudulently personating an employee of a public utility or district, or of fraudulently inducing the belief that they are an employee of a public utility or district, or who willfully and credibly impersonates an employee of a public utility or district on an internet website, or by other electronic means, for purposes of defrauding another, is guilty of a misdemeanor and shall be punished by imprisonment in a county jail not to exceed six months, or by a fine not to exceed one thousand dollars ($1,000), or by both that fine and imprisonment. Nothing in this section shall be construed to prohibit conduct that arguably constitutes protected activity under state labor law or the National Labor Relations Act (Title 29, United States Code, Section 151 and following).

Amended by Stats 2022 ch 954 (AB 1899),s 3, eff. 1/1/2023.
Added by Stats. 1995, Ch. 460, Sec. 1. Effective January 1, 1996.

Section 538g - Fraudulent personation of public officer or employee

(a) Any person, other than a state, county, city, special district, or city and county officer or employee, who willfully wears, exhibits, or uses the authorized badge, photographic identification card, or insignia of a state, county, city, special district, or city and county officer or employee, with the intent of fraudulently personating a state, county, city, special district, or city and county officer or employee, or of fraudulently inducing the belief that they are a state, county, city, special district, or city and county officer or employee, or who willfully and credibly impersonates such an officer or member on an internet website, or by other electronic means, for purposes of defrauding another, is guilty of a misdemeanor.

(b) Any person who willfully wears, exhibits, or uses, or willfully makes, sells, loans, gives, or transfers to another, any badge, photographic identification card, or insignia, which falsely purports to be for the use of a state, county, city, special district, or city and county officer or employee, or which so resembles the authorized badge, photographic identification card, or insignia of a state, county, city, special district, or city and county officer or employee as would deceive an ordinary reasonable person into believing that it is authorized for use by a state, county, city, special district, or city and county officer or employee, is guilty of a misdemeanor, except that any person who makes or sells any badge under the circumstances described in this subdivision is subject to a fine not to exceed fifteen thousand dollars ($15,000).

(c) This section shall not apply to either of the following:

(1) Use of a badge solely as a prop for a motion picture, television, or video production, or an entertainment or theatrical event.

(2) A badge supplied by a recognized employee organization as defined in Section 3501 of the Government Code or a state or international organization to which it is affiliated.

Amended by Stats 2022 ch 954 (AB 1899),s 4, eff. 1/1/2023.

Added by Stats 2004 ch 22 (AB 1153), s 2, eff. 3/5/2004.

Section 538h - Impersonating a search and rescue officer or member of unit or team

(a) Any person, other than an officer or member of a government agency managed or affiliated search and rescue unit or team, who willfully wears, exhibits, or uses the authorized uniform, insignia, emblem, device, label, certificate, card, or writing of an officer or member of a government agency managed or affiliated search and rescue unit or team, with the intent of fraudulently impersonating an officer or member of a government agency managed or affiliated search and rescue unit or team, or of fraudulently inducing the belief that they are an officer or member of a government agency managed or affiliated search and rescue unit or team, or uses the same to obtain aid, money, or assistance within this state, or who willfully and credibly impersonates such an officer or member on an internet website, or by other electronic means, for purposes of defrauding another, is guilty of a misdemeanor.

(b)

(1) Any person, other than the one who by law is given the authority of an officer or member of a government agency managed or affiliated search and rescue unit or team, who willfully wears, exhibits, or uses the badge of a government agency managed or affiliated search and rescue unit or team with the intent of fraudulently impersonating an officer or member of a government agency managed or affiliated search and rescue unit or team, or fraudulently inducing the belief that they are an officer or member of a government agency managed or affiliated search and rescue unit or team, is guilty of a misdemeanor punishable by imprisonment in a county jail not to exceed one year, by a fine not to exceed two thousand dollars ($2,000), or by both that imprisonment and fine.

(2) Any person who willfully wears or uses any badge that falsely purports to be authorized for the use of one who by law is given the authority of an officer or member of a government agency managed or affiliated search and rescue unit or team, or that resembles the authorized badge of an officer or member of a government agency managed or affiliated search and rescue unit or team as would deceive any ordinary reasonable person into believing that it is authorized for the use of one who by law is given the authority of an officer or member of a government agency managed or affiliated search and rescue unit or team, for the purpose of fraudulently impersonating an officer or member of a government agency managed or affiliated search and rescue unit or team, or of fraudulently inducing the belief that they are an officer or member of a government agency managed or affiliated search and rescue unit or team, is guilty of a misdemeanor punishable by imprisonment in a county jail not to exceed one year, by a fine not to exceed two thousand dollars ($2,000), or by both that fine and imprisonment.

(c) As used in this section, the following terms have the following meanings:

(1) "Member" means any natural person who is registered with an accredited disaster council for the purpose of engaging in disaster service without pay or other consideration. Food and lodging provided, or expenses reimbursed for these items, during a member's activation do not constitute other consideration.

(2) "Search and rescue unit or team" means an entity engaged in the acts of searching for, rescuing, or recovering by means of ground, marine, or air activity, any person that becomes lost, injured, or is killed while outdoors or as a result of a natural or manmade disaster, including instances involving searches for downed or missing aircraft.

Amended by Stats 2022 ch 954 (AB 1899),s 5, eff. 1/1/2023.

Added by Stats 2018 ch 252 (AB 1920),s 1, eff. 1/1/2019.

Section 538.5 - Unlawful acts to obtain confidential information from public utility

Every person who transmits or causes to be transmitted by means of wire, radio or television communication any words, sounds, writings, signs, signals, or pictures for the purpose of furthering or executing a scheme or artifice to obtain, from a public utility, confidential, privileged, or proprietary information, trade secrets, trade lists, customer records, billing records, customer credit data, or accounting data by means of false or fraudulent pretenses, representations, personations, or promises is guilty of an offense punishable by imprisonment pursuant to subdivision (h) of Section 1170, or by imprisonment in the county jail not exceeding one year.

Amended by Stats 2011 ch 39 (AB 117),s 68, eff. 6/30/2011.

Amended by Stats 2011 ch 15 (AB 109),s 389, eff. 4/4/2011, but operative no earlier than October 1, 2011, and only upon creation of a community corrections grant program to assist in implementing this act and upon an appropriation to fund the grant program.

Section 539 - Unlawful certification that person has completed community service

Every person who, with the intent to defraud, certifies that a person ordered by the court to participate in community service as a condition of probation has completed the number of hours of community service prescribed in the court order and the participant has not completed the prescribed number of hours, is guilty of a misdemeanor.

Added by Stats. 1993, Ch. 371, Sec. 1. Effective January 1, 1994.

Chapter 10 - CRIMES AGAINST INSURED PROPERTY AND INSURERS

Section 548 - Unlawful destruction or disposal of insured property

(a) Every person who willfully injures, destroys, secretes, abandons, or disposes of any property which at the time is insured against loss or damage by theft, or embezzlement, or any casualty with intent to defraud or prejudice the insurer, whether the property is the property or in the possession of that person or any other person, is punishable by imprisonment pursuant to subdivision (h) of Section 1170 for two, three, or five years and by a fine not exceeding fifty thousand dollars ($50,000). For purposes of this section, "casualty" does not include fire.

(b) Any person who violates subdivision (a) and who has a prior conviction of the offense set forth in that subdivision, in Section 550 of this code, or in former Section 556 or former Section 1871.1 of the Insurance Code, shall receive a two-year enhancement for each prior conviction in addition to the sentence provided under subdivision (a). The existence of any fact which would subject a person to a penalty enhancement shall be alleged in the information or indictment and either admitted by the defendant in open court, or found to be true by the jury trying the issue of guilt or by the court where guilt is established by plea of guilty or nolo contendere or by trial by the court sitting without a jury.

Amended by Stats 2011 ch 39 (AB 117),s 68, eff. 6/30/2011.

Amended by Stats 2011 ch 15 (AB 109),s 390, eff. 4/4/2011, but operative no earlier than October 1, 2011, and only upon creation of a community corrections grant program to assist in implementing this act and upon an appropriation to fund the grant program.

Section 549 - Unlawful solicitation, acceptance, or referral of business

Any firm, corporation, partnership, or association, or any person acting in his or her individual capacity, or in his or her capacity as a public or private employee, who solicits, accepts, or refers any business to or from any individual or entity with the knowledge that, or with reckless disregard for whether, the individual or entity for or from whom the solicitation or referral is made, or the individual or entity who is solicited or referred, intends to violate Section 550 of this code or Section 1871.4 of the Insurance Code is guilty of a crime, punishable upon a first conviction by imprisonment in the county jail for not more than one year or by imprisonment pursuant to subdivision (h) of Section 1170 for 16 months, two years, or three years, or by a fine not exceeding fifty thousand dollars ($50,000) or double the amount of the fraud, whichever is greater, or by both that imprisonment and fine. A second or subsequent conviction is punishable by imprisonment pursuant to subdivision (h) of Section 1170 or by that imprisonment and a fine of fifty thousand dollars ($50,000). Restitution shall be ordered, including restitution for any medical evaluation or treatment services obtained or provided. The court shall determine the amount of restitution and the person or persons to whom the restitution shall be paid.

Amended by Stats 2011 ch 39 (AB 117),s 68, eff. 6/30/2011.

Amended by Stats 2011 ch 15 (AB 109),s 391, eff. 4/4/2011, but operative no earlier than October 1, 2011, and only upon creation of a community corrections grant program to assist in implementing this act and upon an appropriation to fund the grant program.

Amended by Stats 2004 ch 2 (SB X4-2), s 5, eff. 1/1/2005.

Amended by Stats 2000 ch 843 (AB 2594), s 4, eff. 1/1/2001.

Section 550 - Unlawful acts

(a) It is unlawful to do any of the following, or to aid, abet, solicit, or conspire with any person to do any of the following:

(1) Knowingly present or cause to be presented any false or fraudulent claim for the payment of a loss or injury, including payment of a loss or injury under a contract of insurance.

(2) Knowingly present multiple claims for the same loss or injury, including presentation of multiple claims to more than one insurer, with an intent to defraud.

(3) Knowingly cause or participate in a vehicular collision, or any other vehicular accident, for the purpose of presenting any false or fraudulent claim.

(4) Knowingly present a false or fraudulent claim for the payments of a loss for theft, destruction, damage, or conversion of a motor vehicle, a motor vehicle part, or contents of a motor vehicle.

(5) Knowingly prepare, make, or subscribe any writing, with the intent to present or use it, or to allow it to be presented, in support of any false or fraudulent claim.

(6) Knowingly make or cause to be made any false or fraudulent claim for payment of a health care benefit.

(7) Knowingly submit a claim for a health care benefit that was not used by, or on behalf of, the claimant.

(8) Knowingly present multiple claims for payment of the same health care benefit with an intent to defraud.

(9) Knowingly present for payment any undercharges for health care benefits on behalf of a specific claimant unless any known overcharges for health care benefits for that claimant are presented for reconciliation at that same time.

(10) For purposes of paragraphs (6) to (9), inclusive, a claim or a claim for payment of a health care benefit also means a claim or claim for payment submitted by or on the behalf of a provider of any workers' compensation health benefits under the Labor Code.

(b) It is unlawful to do, or to knowingly assist or conspire with any person to do, any of the following:

(1) Present or cause to be presented any written or oral statement as part of, or in support of or opposition to, a claim for payment or other benefit pursuant to an insurance policy, knowing that the statement contains any false or misleading information concerning any material fact.

(2) Prepare or make any written or oral statement that is intended to be presented to any insurer or any insurance claimant in connection with, or in support of or opposition to, any claim or payment or other benefit pursuant to an insurance policy, knowing that the statement contains any false or misleading information concerning any material fact.

(3) Conceal, or knowingly fail to disclose the occurrence, of an event that affects any person's initial or continued right or entitlement to any insurance benefit or payment, or the amount of any benefit or payment to which the person is entitled.

(4) Prepare or make any written or oral statement, intended to be presented to any insurer or producer for the purpose of obtaining a motor vehicle insurance policy, that the person to be the insured resides or is domiciled in this state when, in fact, that person resides or is domiciled in a state other than this state.

(c)

(1) Every person who violates paragraph (1), (2), (3), (4), or (5) of subdivision (a) is guilty of a felony punishable by imprisonment pursuant to subdivision (h) of Section 1170 for two, three, or five years, and by a fine not exceeding fifty thousand dollars ($50,000), or double the amount of the fraud, whichever is greater.

(2) Every person who violates paragraph (6), (7), (8), or (9) of subdivision (a) is guilty of a public offense.

(A) When the claim or amount at issue exceeds nine hundred fifty dollars ($950), the offense is punishable by imprisonment pursuant to subdivision (h) of Section 1170 for two, three, or five years, or by a fine not exceeding fifty thousand dollars ($50,000) or double the amount of the fraud, whichever is greater, or by both that imprisonment and fine, or by imprisonment in a county jail not to exceed one year, by a fine of not more than ten thousand dollars ($10,000), or by both that imprisonment and fine.

(B) When the claim or amount at issue is nine hundred fifty dollars ($950) or less, the offense is punishable by imprisonment in a county jail not to exceed six months, or by a fine of not more than one thousand dollars ($1,000), or by both that imprisonment and fine, unless the aggregate amount of the claims or amount at issue exceeds nine hundred fifty dollars ($950) in any 12-consecutive-month period, in which case the claims or amounts may be charged as in subparagraph (A).

(3) Every person who violates paragraph (1), (2), (3), or (4) of subdivision (b) shall be punished by imprisonment pursuant to subdivision (h) of Section 1170 for two, three, or five years, or by a fine not exceeding fifty thousand dollars ($50,000) or double the

amount of the fraud, whichever is greater, or by both that imprisonment and fine, or by imprisonment in a county jail not to exceed one year, or by a fine of not more than ten thousand dollars ($10,000), or by both that imprisonment and fine.

(4) Restitution shall be ordered for a person convicted of violating this section, including restitution for any medical evaluation or treatment services obtained or provided. The court shall determine the amount of restitution and the person or persons to whom the restitution shall be paid.

(d) Notwithstanding any other provision of law, probation shall not be granted to, nor shall the execution or imposition of a sentence be suspended for, any adult person convicted of felony violations of this section who previously has been convicted of felony violations of this section or Section 548, or of Section 1871.4 of the Insurance Code, or former Section 556 of the Insurance Code, or former Section 1871.1 of the Insurance Code as an adult under charges separately brought and tried two or more times. The existence of any fact that would make a person ineligible for probation under this subdivision shall be alleged in the information or indictment, and either admitted by the defendant in an open court, or found to be true by the jury trying the issue of guilt or by the court where guilt is established by plea of guilty or nolo contendere or by trial by the court sitting without a jury. Except when the existence of the fact was not admitted or found to be true or the court finds that a prior felony conviction was invalid, the court shall not strike or dismiss any prior felony convictions alleged in the information or indictment.

This subdivision does not prohibit the adjournment of criminal proceedings pursuant to Division 3 (commencing with Section 3000) or Division 6 (commencing with Section 6000) of the Welfare and Institutions Code.

(e) Except as otherwise provided in subdivision (f), any person who violates subdivision (a) or (b) and who has a prior felony conviction of an offense set forth in either subdivision (a) or (b), in Section 548, in Section 1871.4 of the Insurance Code, in former Section 556 of the Insurance Code, or in former Section 1871.1 of the Insurance Code shall receive a two-year enhancement for each prior felony conviction in addition to the sentence provided in subdivision (c). The existence of any fact that would subject a person to a penalty enhancement shall be alleged in the information or indictment and either admitted by the defendant in open court, or found to be true by the jury trying the issue of guilt or by the court where guilt is established by plea of guilty or nolo contendere or by trial by the court sitting without a jury. Any person who violates this section shall be subject to appropriate orders of restitution pursuant to Section 13967 of the Government Code.

(f) Any person who violates paragraph (3) of subdivision (a) and who has two prior felony convictions for a violation of paragraph (3) of subdivision (a) shall receive a five-year enhancement in addition to the sentence provided in subdivision (c). The existence of any fact that would subject a person to a penalty enhancement shall be alleged in the information or indictment and either admitted by the defendant in open court, or found to be true by the jury trying the issue of guilt or by the court where guilt is established by plea of guilty or nolo contendere or by trial by the court sitting without a jury.

(g) Except as otherwise provided in Section 12022.7, any person who violates paragraph (3) of subdivision (a) shall receive a two-year enhancement for each person other than an accomplice who suffers serious bodily injury resulting from the vehicular collision or accident in a violation of paragraph (3) of subdivision (a).

(h) This section shall not be construed to preclude the applicability of any other provision of criminal law or equitable remedy that applies or may apply to any act committed or alleged to have been committed by a person.

(i) Any fine imposed pursuant to this section shall be doubled if the offense was committed in connection with any claim pursuant to any automobile insurance policy in an auto insurance fraud crisis area designated by the Insurance Commissioner pursuant to Article 4.6 (commencing with Section 1874.90) of Chapter 12 of Part 2 of Division 1 of the Insurance Code.

Amended by Stats 2011 ch 39 (AB 117),s 68, eff. 6/30/2011.
Amended by Stats 2011 ch 15 (AB 109),s 392, eff. 4/4/2011, but operative no earlier than October 1, 2011, and only upon creation of a community corrections grant program to assist in implementing this act and upon an appropriation to fund the grant program.
Amended by Stats 2009 ch 28 (SB X3-18),s 29, eff. 1/1/2010.
Amended by Stats 2004 ch 2 (SB X4-2), s 6, eff. 1/1/2005.
Amended by Stats 2000 ch 867 (SB 1988), s 21, eff. 1/1/2001.
Previously Amended July 12, 1999 (Bill Number: SB 966) (Chapter 83).

Section 551 - Unlawful referrals of insured

(a) It is unlawful for any automotive repair dealer, contractor, or employees or agents thereof to offer to any insurance agent, broker, or adjuster any fee, commission, profit sharing, or other form of direct or indirect consideration for referring an insured to an automotive repair dealer or its employees or agents for vehicle repairs covered under a policyholder's automobile physical damage or automobile collision coverage, or to a contractor or its employees or agents for repairs to or replacement of a structure covered by a residential or commercial insurance policy.

(b) Except in cases in which the amount of the repair or replacement claim has been determined by the insurer and the repair or replacement services are performed in accordance with that determination or in accordance with provided estimates that are accepted by the insurer, it is unlawful for any automotive repair dealer, contractor, or employees or agents thereof to knowingly offer or give any discount intended to offset a deductible required by a policy of insurance covering repairs to or replacement of a motor vehicle or residential or commercial structure. This subdivision does not prohibit an advertisement for repair or replacement services at a discount as long as the amount of the repair or replacement claim has been determined by the insurer and the repair or replacement services are performed in accordance with that determination or in accordance with provided estimates that are accepted by the insurer.

(c) A violation of this section is a public offense. Where the amount at issue exceeds nine hundred fifty dollars ($950), the offense is punishable by imprisonment pursuant to subdivision (h) of Section 1170 for 16 months, or two or three years, by a fine of not more than ten thousand dollars ($10,000), or by both that imprisonment and fine; or by imprisonment in a county jail not to exceed one year, by a fine of not more than one thousand dollars ($1,000), or by both that imprisonment and fine. In all other cases, the offense is punishable by imprisonment in a county jail not to exceed six months, by a fine of not more than one thousand dollars ($1,000), or by both that imprisonment and fine.

(d) Every person who, having been convicted of subdivision (a) or (b), or Section 7027.3 or former Section 9884.75 of the Business and Professions Code and having served a term therefor in any penal institution or having been imprisoned therein as a condition of probation for that offense, is subsequently convicted of subdivision (a) or (b), upon a subsequent conviction of one of those offenses, shall be punished by imprisonment pursuant to subdivision (h) of Section 1170 for 16 months, or two or three years, by a fine of not more than ten thousand dollars ($10,000), or by both that imprisonment and fine; or by imprisonment in a county jail not to exceed one year, by a fine of not more than one thousand dollars ($1,000), or by both that imprisonment and fine.

(e) For purposes of this section:

(1) "Automotive repair dealer" means a person who, for compensation, engages in the business of repairing or diagnosing malfunctions of motor vehicles.

(2) "Contractor" has the same meaning as set forth in Section 7026 of the Business and Professions Code.

Amended by Stats 2011 ch 39 (AB 117),s 68, eff. 6/30/2011.

Amended by Stats 2011 ch 15 (AB 109),s 393, eff. 4/4/2011, but operative no earlier than October 1, 2011, and only upon creation of a community corrections grant program to assist in implementing this act and upon an appropriation to fund the grant program.

Amended by Stats 2009 ch 28 (SB X3-18),s 30, eff. 1/1/2010.

Chapter 12 - UNLAWFUL INTERFERENCE WITH PROPERTY

Article 1 - TRESPASSING OR LOITERING NEAR POSTED INDUSTRIAL PROPERTY

Section 552 - Applicability of article

This article does not apply to any entry in the course of duty of any peace or police officer or other duly authorized public officer, nor does it apply to the lawful use of an established and existing right of way for public road purposes.

Added by Stats. 1953, Ch. 32.

Section 552.1 - Lawful acts not proscribed

This article does not prohibit:

(a) Any lawful activity for the purpose of engaging in any organizational effort on behalf of any labor union, agent, or member thereof, or of any employee group, or any member thereof, employed or formerly employed in any place of business or manufacturing establishment described in this article, or for the purpose of carrying on the lawful activities of labor unions, or members thereof.

(b) Any lawful activity for the purpose of investigation of the safety of working conditions on posted property by a representative of a labor union or other employee group who has upon his person written evidence of due authorization by his labor union or employee group to make such investigation.

Added by Stats. 1953, Ch. 32.

Section 553 - Definitions

The following definitions apply to this article only:

(a) "Sign" means a sign not less than one (1) square foot in area and upon which in letters not less than two inches in height appear the words "trespassing-loitering forbidden by law," or words describing the use of the property followed by the words "no trespassing."

(b) "Posted property" means any property specified in Section 554 which is posted in a manner provided in Section 554.1.

(c) "Posted boundary" means a line running from sign to sign and such line need not conform to the legal boundary or legal description of any lot, parcel, or acreage of land, but only the area within the posted boundary shall constitute posted property, except as otherwise provided in subdivision (e) of Section 554. 1.

Amended by Stats. 1988, Ch. 273, Sec. 1.

Section 554 - Posted property

Any property, except that portion of such property to which the general public is accorded access, may be posted against trespassing and loitering in the manner provided in Section 554.1, and thereby become posted property subject to the provisions of this article applicable to posted property, if such property consists of, or is used, or is designed to be used, for any one or more of the following:

(a) An oil well, oilfield, tank farm, refinery, compressor plant, absorption plant, bulk plant, marine terminal, pipeline, pipeline pumping station, or reservoir, or any other plant, structure, or works, used for the production, extraction, treatment, handling, storage, or transportation, of oil, gas, gasoline, petroleum, or any product or products thereof.

(b) A gas plant, gas storage station, gas meter, gas valve, or regulator station, gas odorant station, gas pipeline, or appurtenances, or any other property used in the transmission or distribution of gas.

(c) A reservoir, dam, generating plant, receiving station, distributing station, transformer, transmission line, or any appurtenances, used for the storage of water for the generation of hydroelectric power, or for the generation of electricity by water or steam or by any other apparatus or method suitable for the generation of electricity, or for the handling, transmission, reception, or distribution of electric energy.

(d) Plant, structures or facilities used for or in connection with the rendering of telephone or telegraph service or for radio or television broadcasting.

(e) A water well, dam, reservoir, pumping plant, aqueduct, canal, tunnel, siphon, conduit, or any other structure, facility, or conductor for producing, storing, diverting, conserving, treating, or conveying water.

(f) The production, storage, or manufacture of munitions, dynamite, black blasting powder, gunpowder, or other explosives.

(g) A railroad right-of-way, railroad bridge, railroad tunnel, railroad shop, railroad yard, or other railroad facility.

(h) A plant and facility for the collection, pumping, transmission, treatment, outfall, and disposal of sanitary sewerage or storm and waste water, including a water pollution or quality control facility.

(i) A quarry used for the purpose of extracting surface or subsurface material or where explosives are stored or used for that purpose.

Amended by Stats. 1982, Ch. 965, Sec. 1.

Section 554.1 - Manner of posting

Any property described in Section 554 may be posted against trespassing and loitering in the following manner:

(a) If it is not enclosed within a fence and if it is of an area not exceeding one (1) acre and has no lineal dimension exceeding one (1) mile, by posting signs at each corner of the area and at each entrance.

(b) If it is not enclosed within a fence, and if it is of an area exceeding one (1) acre, or contains any lineal dimension exceeding one (1) mile, by posting signs along or near the exterior boundaries of the area at intervals of not more than 600 feet, and also at each corner, and, if such property has a definite entrance or entrances, at each such entrance.

(c) If it is enclosed within a fence and if it is of an area not exceeding one (1) acre, and has no lineal dimension exceeding one (1) mile, by posting signs at each corner of such fence and at each entrance.

(d) If it is enclosed within a fence and if it is of an area exceeding one (1) acre, or has any lineal dimension exceeding one (1) mile, by posting signs on, or along the line of, such fence at intervals of not more than 600 feet, and also at each corner and at each entrance.

(e) If it consists of poles or towers or appurtenant structures for the suspension of wires or other conductors for conveying electricity or telegraphic or telephonic messages or of towers or derricks for the production of oil or gas, by affixing a sign upon one or more sides of such poles, towers, or derricks, but such posting shall render only the pole, tower, derrick, or appurtenant structure posted property.
Added by Stats. 1953, Ch. 32.

Section 555 - Unlawful entry or remaining upon posted property
It is unlawful to enter or remain upon any posted property without the written permission of the owner, tenant, or occupant in legal possession or control thereof. Every person who enters or remains upon posted property without such written permission is guilty of a separate offense for each day during any portion of which he enters or remains upon such posted property.
Added by Stats. 1953, Ch. 32.

Section 555.1 - Unlawful destruction of posted sign
It is unlawful, without authority, to tear down, deface or destroy any sign posted pursuant to this article.
Added by Stats. 1953, Ch. 32.

Section 555.2 - Unlawful loitering
It is unlawful to loiter in the immediate vicinity of any posted property. This section does not prohibit picketing in such immediate vicinity or any lawful activity by which the public is informed of the existence of an alleged labor dispute.
Added by Stats. 1953, Ch. 32.

Section 555.3 - Misdemeanor
Violation of any of the provisions of this article is a misdemeanor.
Added by Stats. 1953, Ch. 32.

Section 555.4 - Prohibition against ordinances
The provisions of this article are applicable throughout the State in all counties and municipalities and no local authority shall enact or enforce any ordinance in conflict with such provisions.
Added by Stats. 1953, Ch. 32.

Section 555.5 - Severability
If any provision of this article, or the application thereof to any person or circumstance, is held to be invalid, the remainder of the article, and the application of such provision to other persons or circumstances, shall not be affected thereby.

If any section, subsection, sentence, clause, or phrase of this article is for any reason held to be unconstitutional or invalid, such decision shall not affect the validity or constitutionality of the remaining portions of this article. The Legislature hereby declares that it would have passed this article and each section, subsection, sentence, clause, or phrase thereof, irrespective of the fact that one or more of the sections, subsections, sentences, clauses, or phrases thereof be declared unconstitutional or invalid.
Added by Stats. 1953, Ch. 32.

Article 2 - UNLAWFULLY PLACING SIGNS ON PUBLIC AND PRIVATE PROPERTY

Section 556 - Unlawful placing of advertising signs on public property
It is a misdemeanor for any person to place or maintain, or cause to be placed or maintained without lawful permission upon any property of the State, or of a city or of a county, any sign, picture, transparency, advertisement, or mechanical device which is used for the purpose of advertising or which advertises or brings to notice any person, article of merchandise, business or profession, or anything that is to be or has been sold, bartered, or given away.
Added by Stats. 1953, Ch. 32.

Section 556.1 - Unlawful placing of advertising signs on private property
It is a misdemeanor for any person to place or maintain or cause to be placed or maintained upon any property in which he has no estate or right of possession any sign, picture, transparency, advertisement, or mechanical device which is used for the purpose of advertising, or which advertises or brings to notice any person, article of merchandise, business or profession, or anything that is to be or has been sold, bartered, or given away, without the consent of the owner, lessee, or person in lawful possession of such property before such sign, picture, transparency, advertisement, or mechanical device is placed upon the property.
Added by Stats. 1953, Ch. 32.

Section 556.2 - Postings not prohibited
Sections 556 and 556.1 do not prevent the posting of any notice required by law or order of any court, to be posted, nor the posting or placing of any notice, particularly pertaining to the grounds or premises upon which the notice is so posted or placed, nor the posting or placing of any notice, sign, or device used exclusively for giving public notice of the name, direction or condition of any highway, street, lane, road or alley.
Added by Stats. 1953, Ch. 32.

Section 556.3 - Public nuisance
Any sign, picture, transparency, advertisement, or mechanical device placed on any property contrary to the provisions of Sections 556 and 556.1, is a public nuisance.
Added by Stats. 1953, Ch. 32.

Section 556.4 - Use of information on sign as evidence

For purposes of this article, information that appears on any sign, picture, transparency, advertisement, or mechanical device such as, but not limited to, the following, may be used as evidence to establish the fact, and may create an inference, that a person or entity is responsible for the posting of the sign, picture, transparency, advertisement, or mechanical device:

(a) The name, telephone number, address, or other identifying information regarding the real estate broker, real estate brokerage firm, real estate agent, or other person associated with the firm.

(b) The name, telephone number, address, or other identifying information of the owner or lessee of property used for a commercial activity or event.

(c) The name, telephone number, address, or other identifying information of the sponsor or promoter of a sporting event, concert, theatrical performance, or similar activity or event.

Added by Stats. 1998, Ch. 192, Sec. 1. Effective January 1, 1999.

Article 3 - TRESPASS ON PROPERTY BELONGING TO THE UNIVERSITY OF CALIFORNIA

Section 558 - Trespass

Every person other than an officer, employee or student of the University of California, or licensee of the Regents of the University of California, is forbidden to enter upon those lands bordering on the Pacific Ocean in San Diego County, which were granted by Section 1 of Chapter 514 of the Statutes of 1929 to the Regents of the University of California for the uses and purposes of the University of California in connection with scientific research and investigation at the Scripps Institution of Oceanography, or upon state waters adjacent thereto, or to trespass upon the same, or to interfere with the exclusive possession, occupation, and use thereof by the Regents of the University of California.

Nothing herein contained shall be deemed or construed to affect in any manner the rights of navigation and fishery reserved to the people by the Constitution.

Added by Stats. 1955, Ch. 41.

Section 558.1 - Violation; punishment

Every person who violates any of the provisions of Section 558 is guilty of a misdemeanor and upon conviction thereof shall be punished by a fine of not more than six hundred dollars ($600) or by imprisonment for not more than 30 days, or by both such fine and imprisonment.

Amended by Stats. 1983, Ch. 1092, Sec. 304. Effective September 27, 1983. Operative January 1, 1984, by Sec. 427 of Ch. 1092.

Chapter 12.5 - CRIMES INVOLVING BAILMENTS

Section 560 - Unlawful acts by bailee

Any bailee, as defined in Section 7102 of the Uniform Commercial Code, who issues or aids in issuing a document of title, or any person who secures the issue by a bailee of a document of title, or any person who negotiates or transfers for value a document of title knowing that the goods for which that document is issued have not been actually received by that bailee or are not under his or her control at the time of issuing that receipt shall be guilty of a crime and upon conviction shall be punished for each offense by imprisonment pursuant to subdivision (h) of Section 1170 or by a fine not exceeding ten thousand dollars ($10,000) or by both that fine and imprisonment.

Amended by Stats 2011 ch 39 (AB 117),s 68, eff. 6/30/2011.

Amended by Stats 2011 ch 15 (AB 109),s 394, eff. 4/4/2011, but operative no earlier than October 1, 2011, and only upon creation of a community corrections grant program to assist in implementing this act and upon an appropriation to fund the grant program.

Section 560.1 - Fraudulent issue of receipt for goods

Any bailee, as defined in Section 7102 of the Uniform Commercial Code, who fraudulently issues or aids in fraudulently issuing a receipt for goods knowing that it contains any false statement shall be guilty of a crime and upon conviction shall be punished for each offense by imprisonment not exceeding one year or by a fine not exceeding one thousand dollars ($1,000) or by both.

Added by Stats. 1963, Ch. 819.

Section 560.2 - Delivery of goods knowing that negotiable document of title is outstanding and uncanceled

Any bailee, as defined in Section 7102 of the Uniform Commercial Code, who delivers goods out of the possession of such bailee knowing that a negotiable document of title the negotiation of which would transfer the right to the possession of such goods is outstanding and uncanceled without obtaining possession of such document at or before the time for such delivery shall, except for the cases in Sections 7210, 7308, 7601 and 7602 of the Uniform Commercial Code, be guilty of a crime and upon conviction shall be punished for each offense by imprisonment not exceeding one year or by a fine not exceeding one thousand dollars ($1,000) or by both.

Added by Stats. 1963, Ch. 819.

Section 560.3 - Unlawful deposit of goods with bailee

Any person who deposits goods with a bailee, as defined in Section 7102 of the Uniform Commercial Code, to which he has not title or upon which there is a security interest and who takes for such goods a negotiable document of title which he afterwards negotiates for value with intent to deceive and without disclosing his want of title or the existence of the security interest shall be guilty of a crime, and upon conviction shall be punished for such offense by imprisonment not exceeding one year or by a fine not exceeding one thousand dollars ($1,000) or by both.

Added by Stats. 1963, Ch. 819.

Section 560.4 - Unlawful issuance of duplicate or additional negotiable document of title by bailee

Any bailee, as defined in Section 7102 of the Uniform Commercial Code, who issues or aids in issuing a duplicate or additional negotiable document of title for goods knowing that a former negotiable document of title for the same goods or any part of them is outstanding and uncanceled without plainly placing upon the face thereof the word "duplicate," except in cases of bills in a set and documents issued as substitutes for lost, stolen or destroyed documents, shall be guilty of a crime and upon conviction shall be punished for each offense by imprisonment pursuant to subdivision (h) of Section 1170 or by a fine not exceeding ten thousand dollars ($10,000) or by both that fine and imprisonment.

Amended by Stats 2011 ch 39 (AB 117),s 68, eff. 6/30/2011.

Amended by Stats 2011 ch 15 (AB 109),s 395, eff. 4/4/2011, but operative no earlier than October 1, 2011, and only upon creation of a community corrections grant program to assist in implementing this act and upon an appropriation to fund the grant program.

Section 560.5 - Unlawful issue of negotiable document of title by warehouseman

Where there are deposited with or held by a warehouseman goods of which he is owner either solely or jointly or in common with others such warehouseman or any of his officers, agents, or servants who knowing of this ownership issues or aids in issuing a negotiable document of title for such goods which does not state such ownership, shall be guilty of a crime and upon conviction shall be punished for each offense by imprisonment not exceeding one year or by a fine not exceeding one thousand dollars ($1,000) or by both.

Added by Stats. 1963, Ch. 819.

Section 560.6 - Unlawful issue, sale, or transfer of warehouse receipt

(1) A corporation, firm, or person, and its or his agents or employees shall not issue, sell, pledge, assign, or transfer in this State any receipt, certificate, or other written instrument purporting to be a warehouse receipt, or in the similitude of a warehouse receipt, or designed to be understood as a warehouse receipt, for goods, wares, or merchandise stored or deposited, or claimed to be stored or deposited, in any warehouse, public or private, in any other state, unless such receipt, certificate, or other written instrument has been issued by the warehouseman operating such warehouse.

(2) A corporation, firm, or person, and its or his agents or employees shall not issue, sell, pledge, assign, or transfer in this State any receipt, certificate, or other written instrument for goods, wares, or merchandise claimed to be stored or deposited, in any warehouse, public or private, in any other state, knowing that there is no such warehouse located at the place named in such receipt, certificate, or other written instrument, or if there is a warehouse at such place knowing that there are no goods, wares, or merchandise stored or deposited therein as specified in such receipt, certificate, or other written instrument.

(3) A corporation, firm, or person, and its or his agents or employees shall not issue, sign, sell, pledge, assign, or transfer in this State any receipt, certificate, or other written instrument evidencing, or purporting to evidence, the creation of a security interest in, or sale, or bailment, of any goods, wares, or merchandise stored or deposited, or claimed to be stored or deposited, in any warehouse, public or private, in any other state, unless such receipt, certificate, or other written instrument plainly designates the number and location of such warehouse and contains a full, true, and complete copy of the receipt issued by the warehouseman operating the warehouse in which such goods, wares, or merchandise is stored or deposited, or is claimed to be stored or deposited. This section shall not apply to the issue, signing, sale, pledge, assignment, or transfer of bona fide warehouse receipts issued by the warehouseman operating public or bonded warehouses in other states according to the laws of the state in which such warehouses are located.

(4) Every corporation, firm, person, agent, or employee, who knowingly violates any of the provisions of this section is guilty of a misdemeanor, and shall be fined not less than fifty dollars ($50) nor more than one thousand dollars ($1,000), and may in addition be imprisoned in the county jail for not exceeding six months.

Added by Stats. 1963, Ch. 819.

Chapter 12.6 - CRIMES INVOLVING BRANDED CONTAINERS, CABINETS, OR OTHER DAIRY EQUIPMENT

Section 565 - Misdemeanor

It is a misdemeanor, punishable by a fine not exceeding one thousand dollars ($1,000), or by imprisonment in the county jail not exceeding six months, or both, for an unauthorized person to possess or use, or to obliterate or destroy the brand registration upon, containers (including milk cases), cabinets, or other dairy equipment, which have a value of nine hundred fifty dollars ($950) or less, when the containers, cabinets, or other dairy equipment are marked with a brand that is registered pursuant to Chapter 10 (commencing with Section 34501) of Part 1 of Division 15 of the Food and Agricultural Code. "Unauthorized person" shall have the meaning of that term as defined in Section 34564 of the Food and Agricultural Code.

Amended by Stats 2009 ch 28 (SB X3-18),s 31, eff. 1/1/2010.

Section 566 - Felony

It is a felony, punishable by a fine not exceeding one thousand five hundred dollars ($1,500), or by imprisonment pursuant to subdivision (h) of Section 1170, or both, for an unauthorized person to possess or use, or to obliterate or destroy the brand registration upon, containers (including milk cases), cabinets, or other dairy equipment, which have a value in excess of nine hundred fifty dollars ($950), when the containers, cabinets, or other dairy equipment are marked with a brand that is registered pursuant to Chapter 10 (commencing with Section 34501) of Part 1 of Division 15 of the Food and Agricultural Code. "Unauthorized person" shall have the meaning of that term as defined in Section 34564 of the Food and Agricultural Code.

Amended by Stats 2011 ch 39 (AB 117),s 68, eff. 6/30/2011.

Amended by Stats 2011 ch 15 (AB 109),s 396, eff. 4/4/2011, but operative no earlier than October 1, 2011, and only upon creation of a community corrections grant program to assist in implementing this act and upon an appropriation to fund the grant program.

Amended by Stats 2009 ch 28 (SB X3-18),s 32, eff. 1/1/2010.

Chapter 12.7 - UNLAWFUL SUBLEASING OF MOTOR VEHICLES

Section 570 - Punishment

An act of unlawful subleasing of a motor vehicle, as defined in Section 571, shall be punishable by imprisonment in a county jail for not more than one year, or by imprisonment pursuant to subdivision (h) of Section 1170, or by a fine of not more than ten thousand dollars ($10,000), or by both that fine and imprisonment.

Amended by Stats 2011 ch 39 (AB 117),s 68, eff. 6/30/2011.

Amended by Stats 2011 ch 15 (AB 109),s 397, eff. 4/4/2011, but operative no earlier than October 1, 2011, and only upon creation of a community corrections grant program to assist in implementing this act and upon an appropriation to fund the grant program.

Section 571 - Unlawful subleasing of motor vehicle

(a) A person engages in an act of unlawful subleasing of a motor vehicle if all of the following conditions are met:

(1) The motor vehicle is subject to a lease contract, conditional sale contract, or security agreement the terms of which prohibit the transfer or assignment of any right or interest in the motor vehicle or under the lease contract, conditional sale contract, or security agreement.

(2) The person is not a party to the lease contract, conditional sale contract, or security agreement.

(3) The person transfers or assigns, or purports to transfer or assign, any right or interest in the motor vehicle or under the lease contract, conditional sale contract, or security agreement, to any person who is not a party to the lease contract, conditional sale contract, or security agreement.

(4) The person does not obtain, prior to the transfer or assignment described in paragraph (3), written consent to the transfer or assignment from the motor vehicle's lessor, seller, or secured party.

(5) The person receives compensation or some other consideration for the transfer or assignment described in paragraph (3).

(b) A person engages in an act of unlawful subleasing of a motor vehicle when the person is not a party to the lease contract, conditional sale contract, or security agreement, and assists, causes, or arranges an actual or purported transfer or assignment, as described in subdivision (a).

Added by Stats. 1987, Ch. 1072, Sec. 2.

Section 572 - Acts not constituting unlawful subleasing of motor vehicle

(a) The actual or purported transfer or assignment, or the assisting, causing, or arranging of an actual or purported transfer or assignment, of any right or interest in a motor vehicle or under a lease contract, conditional sale contract, or security agreement, by an individual who is a party to the lease contract, conditional sale contract, or security agreement is not an act of unlawful subleasing of a motor vehicle and is not subject to prosecution.

(b) This chapter shall not affect the enforceability of any provision of any lease contract, conditional sale contract, security agreement, or direct loan agreement by any party thereto.

Added by Stats. 1987, Ch. 1072, Sec. 2.

Section 573 - Penalties in addition to other remedies or penalties; severability

(a) The penalties under this chapter are in addition to any other remedies or penalties provided by law for the conduct proscribed by this chapter.

(b) If any provision of this chapter or the application thereof to any person or circumstance is held to be unconstitutional, the remainder of the chapter and the application of its provisions to other persons and circumstances shall not be affected thereby.

Added by Stats. 1987, Ch. 1072, Sec. 2.

Section 574 - Definitions

As used in this chapter, the following terms have the following meanings:

(a) "Buyer" has the meaning set forth in subdivision (c) of Section 2981 of the Civil Code.

(b) "Conditional sale contract" has the meaning set forth in subdivision (a) of Section 2981 of the Civil Code. Notwithstanding subdivision (k) of Section 2981 of the Civil Code, "conditional sale contract" includes any contract for the sale or bailment of a motor vehicle between a buyer and a seller primarily for business or commercial purposes.

(c) "Direct loan agreement" means an agreement between a lender and a purchaser whereby the lender has advanced funds pursuant to a loan secured by the motor vehicle which the purchaser has purchased.

(d) "Lease contract" means a lease contract between a lessor and lessee as this term and these parties are defined in Section 2985.7 of the Civil Code. Notwithstanding subdivision (d) of Section 2985.7 of the Civil Code, "lease contract" includes a lease for business or commercial purposes.

(e) "Motor vehicle" means any vehicle required to be registered under the Vehicle Code.

(f) "Person" means an individual, company, firm, association, partnership, trust, corporation, limited liability company, or other legal entity.

(g) "Purchaser" has the meaning set forth in paragraph (30) of subdivision (b) of Section 1201 of the Commercial Code.

(h) "Security agreement" and "secured party" have the meanings set forth, respectively, in paragraphs (74) and (73) of subdivision (a) of Section 9102 of the Commercial Code. "Security interest" has the meaning set forth in paragraph (35) of subdivision (b) of Section 1201 of the Commercial Code.

(i) "Seller" has the meaning set forth in subdivision (b) of Section 2981 of the Civil Code, and includes the present holder of the conditional sale contract.

Amended by Stats 2013 ch 531 (AB 502),s 27, eff. 1/1/2014, op. 7/1/2014.

Amended by Stats 2006 ch 254 (SB 1481),s 79, eff. 1/1/2007.

EFFECTIVE 7/01/2001. Amended October 10, 1999 (Bill Number: SB 45) (Chapter 991).

Chapter 14 - FRAUDULENT ISSUE OF DOCUMENTS OF TITLE TO MERCHANDISE

Section 577 - Fraudulent issue of bill of lading, receipt, other voucher by vessel, railroad, or transportation company

Every person, being the master, owner or agent of any vessel, or officer or agent of any railroad, express or transportation company, or otherwise being or representing any carrier, who delivers any bill of lading, receipt or other voucher, by which it appears that any merchandise of any description has been shipped on board any vessel, or delivered to any railroad, express or transportation company or other carrier, unless the same has been so shipped or delivered, and is at the time actually under the control of such carrier or the master, owner or agent of such vessel, or of some officer or agent of that company, to be forwarded as expressed in that bill of lading, receipt or voucher, is punishable by imprisonment pursuant to subdivision (h) of Section 1170, or by a fine not exceeding one thousand dollars ($1,000), or both.

Amended by Stats 2011 ch 39 (AB 117),s 68, eff. 6/30/2011.

Amended by Stats 2011 ch 15 (AB 109),s 398, eff. 4/4/2011, but operative no earlier than October 1, 2011, and only upon creation of a community corrections grant program to assist in implementing this act and upon an appropriation to fund the grant program.

Section 578 - Fraudulent issue of receipt, bill of lading, or other voucher by warehouseman, wharfinger, or other depositary of property

Every person carrying on the business of a warehouseman, wharfinger, or other depositary of property, who issues any receipt, bill of lading, or other voucher for any merchandise of any description, which has not been actually received upon the premises of that person, and is not under his or her actual control at the time of issuing such instrument, whether that instrument is issued to a person as being the owner of that merchandise or as security for any indebtedness, is punishable by imprisonment pursuant to subdivision (h) of Section 1170, or by a fine not exceeding one thousand dollars ($1,000), or both.

Amended by Stats 2011 ch 39 (AB 117),s 68, eff. 6/30/2011.

Amended by Stats 2011 ch 15 (AB 109),s 399, eff. 4/4/2011, but operative no earlier than October 1, 2011, and only upon creation of a community corrections grant program to assist in implementing this act and upon an appropriation to fund the grant program.

Section 579 - Substantial correspondence

No person shall be convicted of an offense under Section 577 or 578 by reason that the contents of any barrel, box, case, cask, or other vessel or package mentioned in the bill of lading, receipt, or other voucher did not correspond with the description given in the instrument of the merchandise received, if the description corresponded substantially with the marks, labels, or brands upon the outside of the vessel or package, unless it appears that the accused knew that the marks, labels, or brands were untrue.

Amended by Stats. 1987, Ch. 828, Sec. 33.

Section 580 - Unlawful issuance of second or duplicate receipt or voucher

Every person mentioned in this chapter, who issues any second or duplicate receipt or voucher, of a kind specified therein, at a time while any former receipt or voucher for the merchandise specified in that second receipt is outstanding and uncanceled, without writing across the face of the same the word "Duplicate," in a plain and legible manner, is punishable by imprisonment pursuant to subdivision (h) of Section 1170, or by a fine not exceeding one thousand dollars ($1,000), or both.

Amended by Stats 2011 ch 39 (AB 117),s 68, eff. 6/30/2011.

Amended by Stats 2011 ch 15 (AB 109),s 400, eff. 4/4/2011, but operative no earlier than October 1, 2011, and only upon creation of a community corrections grant program to assist in implementing this act and upon an appropriation to fund the grant program.

Section 581 - Unlawful sale without consent of person holding bill, receipt, or voucher

Every person mentioned in this chapter, who sells, hypothecates, or pledges any merchandise for which any bill of lading, receipt, or voucher has been issued by him or her, without the consent in writing thereto of the person holding that bill, receipt, or voucher, is punishable by imprisonment pursuant to subdivision (h) of Section 1170, or by a fine not exceeding one thousand dollars ($1,000), or both.

Amended by Stats 2011 ch 39 (AB 117),s 68, eff. 6/30/2011.

Amended by Stats 2011 ch 15 (AB 109),s 401, eff. 4/4/2011, but operative no earlier than October 1, 2011, and only upon creation of a community corrections grant program to assist in implementing this act and upon an appropriation to fund the grant program.

Section 583 - Sale by virtue of process of law

Section 581 does not apply where property is demanded or sold by virtue of process of law.

Amended by Stats. 1987, Ch. 828, Sec. 34.

Chapter 15 - MALICIOUS INJURIES TO RAILROAD BRIDGES, HIGHWAYS, BRIDGES, AND TELEGRAPHS

Section 587 - Malicious injury to railroad

Every person who maliciously does either of the following is punishable by imprisonment pursuant to subdivision (h) of Section 1170, or imprisonment in a county jail not exceeding one year:

(a) Removes, displaces, injures, or destroys any part of any railroad, whether for steam or horse cars, or any track of any railroad, or any branch or branchway, switch, turnout, bridge, viaduct, culvert, embankment, station house, or other structure or fixture, or any part thereof, attached to or connected with any railroad.

(b) Places any obstruction upon the rails or track of any railroad, or of any switch, branch, branchway, or turnout connected with any railroad.

Amended by Stats 2011 ch 39 (AB 117),s 68, eff. 6/30/2011.

Amended by Stats 2011 ch 15 (AB 109),s 402, eff. 4/4/2011, but operative no earlier than October 1, 2011, and only upon creation of a community corrections grant program to assist in implementing this act and upon an appropriation to fund the grant program.

Section 587.1 - Malicious moving of locomotive

(a) Every person who maliciously moves or causes to be moved, without authorization, any locomotive, is guilty of a misdemeanor punishable by imprisonment in the county jail not exceeding one year.

(b) Every person who maliciously moves or causes to be moved, without authorization, any locomotive, when the moving creates a substantial likelihood of causing personal injury or death to another, is guilty of a public offense punishable by imprisonment in a county jail not exceeding one year or by imprisonment pursuant to subdivision (h) of Section 1170.

Amended by Stats 2011 ch 39 (AB 117),s 68, eff. 6/30/2011.

Amended by Stats 2011 ch 15 (AB 109),s 403, eff. 4/4/2011, but operative no earlier than October 1, 2011, and only upon creation of a community corrections grant program to assist in implementing this act and upon an appropriation to fund the grant program.

Section 587a - Tampering with air brake or other device

Every person, who, without being thereunto duly authorized by the owner, lessee, or person or corporation engaged in the operation of any railroad, shall manipulate or in anywise tamper or interfere with any air brake or other device, appliance or apparatus in or upon any car or locomotive upon such railroad, and used or provided for use in the operation of such car or locomotive, or of any train upon such railroad, or with any switch, signal or other appliance or apparatus used or provided for use in the operation of such railroad, shall be deemed guilty of a misdemeanor.

Added by Stats. 1909, Ch. 372.

Section 587b - Unlawful entry or attachment to train

Every person, who shall, without being thereunto authorized by the owner, lessee, person or corporation operating any railroad, enter into, climb upon, hold to, or in any manner attach himself to any locomotive, locomotive-engine tender, freight or passenger car upon such railroad, or any portion of any train thereon, shall be deemed guilty of a misdemeanor, and, upon conviction thereof shall be punished by a fine not exceeding fifty dollars ($50), or by imprisonment not exceeding 30 days, or by both such fine and imprisonment. Amended by Stats. 1949, Ch. 137.

Section 587c - Evading payment of railroad fare

Every person who fraudulently evades, or attempts to evade the payment of his fare, while traveling upon any railroad, shall be deemed guilty of a misdemeanor, and upon conviction thereof, shall be punished by a fine of not more than five hundred dollars, or imprisonment not exceeding six months, or by both such fine and imprisonment.
Added by Stats. 1909, Ch. 345.

Section 588 - Unlawful destruction of public highway or bridge or private way

Every person who negligently, willfully or maliciously digs up, removes, displaces, breaks down or otherwise injures or destroys any state or other public highway or bridge, or any private way, laid out by authority of law, or bridge upon any such highway or private way, or who negligently, willfully or maliciously sprinkles, drains, diverts or in any manner permits water from any sprinkler, ditch, canal, flume, or reservoir to flow upon or saturate by seepage any public highway, which act tends to damage such highway or tends to be a hazard to traffic thereon, shall be guilty of a misdemeanor. This section shall not apply to the natural flow of surface or flood waters that are not diverted, accelerated or concentrated by such person.
Amended by Stats. 1963, Ch. 1625.

Section 588a - Unlawful throwing or depositing of substance upon public highway

Any person who throws or deposits any oil, glass bottle, glass, nails, tacks, hoops, wire, cans, or any other substance likely to injure any person, animal or vehicle upon any public highway in the State of California shall be guilty of a misdemeanor; provided, however, that any person who willfully deposits any such substance upon any public highway in the State of California with the intent to cause great bodily injury to other persons using the highway shall be guilty of a felony.
Amended by Stats. 1963, Ch. 250.

Section 588b - Unlawful removal or destruction of barrier or obstruction

Any person who wilfully breaks down, removes, injures, or destroys any barrier or obstruction erected or placed in or upon any road or highway by the authorities in charge thereof, or by any authorized contractor engaged in the construction or maintenance thereof, or who tears down, defaces, removes, or destroys any warnings, notices, or directional signs erected, placed or posted in, upon, or adjacent to any road or highway, or who extinguishes, removes, injures, or destroys any warning light or lantern, or reflectorized warning or directional sign, erected, placed or maintained by any such authority in, upon or adjacent to any such road or highway, shall be guilty of a misdemeanor.
Amended by Stats. 1933, Ch. 403.

Section 590 - Malicious removal, destruction, or defacement of mile post, board or stone, or guide post

Every person who maliciously removes, destroys, injures, breaks or defaces any mile post, board or stone, or guide post erected on or near any highway, or any inscription thereon, is guilty of a misdemeanor.
Amended by Stats. 1907, Ch. 489.

Section 590a - Fines

One-half of all fines imposed and collected under Section 590 shall be paid to the informer who first causes a complaint to be filed charging the defendant with the violation of Section 590.
Amended by Stats. 1987, Ch. 828, Sec. 35.

Section 591 - Unlawful and malicious removal or obstruction of line or wire

A person who unlawfully and maliciously takes down, removes, injures, disconnects, cuts, or obstructs a line of telegraph, telephone, or cable television, or any line used to conduct electricity, or any part thereof, or appurtenances or apparatus connected therewith, including, but not limited to, a backup deep cycle battery or other power supply, or severs any wire thereof, or makes an unauthorized connection with any line, other than a telegraph, telephone, or cable television line, used to conduct electricity, or any part thereof, or appurtenances or apparatus connected therewith, is subject to punishment by imprisonment in a county jail not exceeding one year, by a fine not exceeding one thousand dollars ($1,000), or by both that imprisonment and fine, or by imprisonment in a county jail for 16 months, two or three years pursuant to subdivision (h) of Section 1170 and a fine of up to ten thousand dollars ($10,000).
Amended by Stats 2014 ch 332 (AB 1782),s 1, eff. 1/1/2015.
Amended by Stats 2011 ch 39 (AB 117),s 68, eff. 6/30/2011.
Amended by Stats 2011 ch 15 (AB 109),s 404, eff. 4/4/2011, but operative no earlier than October 1, 2011, and only upon creation of a community corrections grant program to assist in implementing this act and upon an appropriation to fund the grant program.

Section 591.5 - Unlawful removal, destruction, or obstruction of wireless communication device

A person who unlawfully and maliciously removes, injures, destroys, damages, or obstructs the use of any wireless communication device with the intent to prevent the use of the device to summon assistance or notify law enforcement or any public safety agency of a crime is guilty of a misdemeanor.
Amended by Stats 2006 ch 695 (AB 44),s 1, eff. 1/1/2007.
Added by Stats 2003 ch 143 (AB 836), s 1, eff. 1/1/2004.

Section 592 - Unlawful taking of water

(a) Every person who shall, without authority of the owner or managing agent, and with intent to defraud, take water from any canal, ditch, flume, or reservoir used for the purpose of holding or conveying water for manufacturing, agricultural, mining, irrigating, generation of power, or domestic uses is guilty of a misdemeanor.

(b) If the total retail value of all the water taken is more than nine hundred fifty dollars ($950), or if the defendant has previously been convicted of an offense under this section or any former section that would be an offense under this section, or of an offense under the

laws of another state or of the United States that would have been an offense under this section if committed in this state, then the violation is punishable by imprisonment in a county jail for not more than one year, or in the state prison.
Amended by Stats 2009 ch 28 (SB X3-18),s 33, eff. 1/1/2010.

Section 593 - Unlawful removal, interference with, or obstruction of line transmitting electricity

Every person who unlawfully and maliciously takes down, removes, injures, interferes with, or obstructs any line erected or maintained by proper authority for the purpose of transmitting electricity for light, heat, or power, or any part thereof, or any insulator or crossarm, appurtenance or apparatus connected therewith, or severs or in any way interferes with any wire, cable, or current thereof, is punishable by imprisonment pursuant to subdivision (h) of Section 1170, or by fine not exceeding one thousand dollars ($1,000), or imprisonment in the county jail not exceeding one year.
Amended by Stats 2011 ch 39 (AB 117),s 68, eff. 6/30/2011.
Amended by Stats 2011 ch 15 (AB 109),s 405, eff. 4/4/2011, but operative no earlier than October 1, 2011, and only upon creation of a community corrections grant program to assist in implementing this act and upon an appropriation to fund the grant program.

Section 593a - Malicious placement in any tree of substance to injure saws

(a) Every person who maliciously drives or places, in any tree, saw-log, shingle-bolt, or other wood, any iron, steel, ceramic, or other substance sufficiently hard to injure saws, knowing that the tree is intended to be harvested or that the saw-log, shingle-bolt, or other wood is intended to be manufactured into any kind of lumber or other wood product, is guilty of a felony.
(b) Any person who violates subdivision (a) and causes bodily injury to another person other than an accomplice shall, in addition and consecutive to the punishment prescribed for that felony, be punished by an additional prison term of three years.
Amended by Stats. 1987, Ch. 1132, Sec. 1. Effective September 25, 1987. Operative September 30, 1987, by Sec. 4 of Ch. 1132.

Section 593b - Unlawful climbing upon pole, tower, or other structure designed to support wires or cables for transmission of electric energy

Every person who shall, without the written permission of the owner, lessee, or person or corporation operating any electrical transmission line, distributing line or system, climb upon any pole, tower or other structure which is a part of such line or system and is supporting or is designed to support a wire or wires, cable or cables, for the transmission or distribution of electric energy, shall be deemed guilty of a misdemeanor; provided, that nothing herein shall apply to employees of either privately or publicly owned public utilities engaged in the performance of their duties.
Added by Stats. 1935, Ch. 106.

Section 593c - Unlawful interference with or removal of pipe maintained for transporting gas

Every person who willfully and maliciously breaks, digs up, obstructs, interferes with, removes or injures any pipe or main or hazardous liquid pipeline erected, operated, or maintained for the purpose of transporting, conveying or distributing gas or other hazardous liquids for light, heat, power or any other purpose, or any part thereof, or any valve, meter, holder, compressor, machinery, appurtenance, equipment or apparatus connected with any such main or pipeline, or used in connection with or affecting the operation thereof or the conveying of gas or hazardous liquid therethrough, or shuts off, removes, obstructs, injures, or in any way interferes with any valve or fitting installed on, connected to, or operated in connection with any such main or pipeline, or controlling or affecting the flow of gas or hazardous liquid through any such main or pipeline, is guilty of a felony.
Amended by Stats. 1988, Ch. 844, Sec. 1.

Section 593d - Unlawful interception, receipt, or use of program or service carried by multichannel video or information services provider

(a) Except as provided in subdivision (e), any person who, for the purpose of intercepting, receiving, or using any program or other service carried by a multichannel video or information services provider that the person is not authorized by that provider to receive or use, commits any of the following acts is guilty of a public offense:
    (1) Knowingly and willfully makes or maintains an unauthorized connection or connections, whether physically, electrically, electronically, or inductively, to any cable, wire, or other component of a multichannel video or information services provider's system or to a cable, wire or other media, or receiver that is attached to a multichannel video or information services provider's system.
    (2) Knowingly and willfully purchases, possesses, attaches, causes to be attached, assists others in attaching, or maintains the attachment of any unauthorized device or devices to any cable, wire, or other component of a multichannel video or information services provider's system or to a cable, wire or other media, or receiver that is attached to a multichannel video or information services provider's system.
    (3) Knowingly and willfully makes or maintains any modification or alteration to any device installed with the authorization of a multichannel video or information services provider.
    (4) Knowingly and willfully makes or maintains any modifications or alterations to an access device that authorizes services or knowingly and willfully obtains an unauthorized access device and uses the modified, altered, or unauthorized access device to obtain services from a multichannel video or information services provider. For purposes of this section, each purchase, possession, connection, attachment, or modification shall constitute a separate violation of this section.
(b) Except as provided in subdivision (e), any person who knowingly and willfully manufactures, assembles, modifies, imports into this state, distributes, sells, offers to sell, advertises for sale, or possesses for any of these purposes, any device or kit for a device, designed, in whole or in part, to decrypt, decode, descramble, or otherwise make intelligible any encrypted, encoded, scrambled, or other nonstandard signal carried by a multichannel video or information services provider, unless the device has been granted an equipment authorization by the Federal Communications Commission (FCC), is guilty of a public offense. For purposes of this subdivision, "encrypted, encoded, scrambled, or other nonstandard signal" means any type of signal or transmission that is not intended to produce an intelligible program or service without the use of a special device, signal, or information provided by the multichannel video or information services provider or its agents to authorized subscribers.
(c) Every person who knowingly and willfully makes or maintains an unauthorized connection or connections with, whether physically, electrically, electronically, or inductively, or who attaches, causes to be attached, assists others in attaching, or maintains any attachment to, any cable, wire, or other component of a multichannel video or information services provider's system, for the purpose of interfering

with, altering, or degrading any multichannel video or information service being transmitted to others, or for the purpose of transmitting or broadcasting any program or other service not intended to be transmitted or broadcast by the multichannel video or information services provider, is guilty of a public offense. For purposes of this section, each transmission or broadcast shall constitute a separate violation of this section.

(d)

(1) Any person who violates subdivision (a) shall be punished by a fine not exceeding one thousand dollars ($1,000), by imprisonment in a county jail not exceeding 90 days, or by both that fine and imprisonment.

(2) Any person who violates subdivision (b) shall be punished as follows:

(A) If the violation involves the manufacture, assembly, modification, importation into this state, distribution, advertisement for sale, or possession for sale or for any of these purposes, of 10 or more of the items described in subdivision (b), or the sale or offering for sale of five or more items for financial gain, the person shall be punished by imprisonment in a county jail not exceeding one year, or in the state prison, by a fine not exceeding two hundred fifty thousand dollars ($250,000), or by both that imprisonment and fine.

(B) If the violation involves the manufacture, assembly, modification, importation into this state, distribution, advertisement for sale, or possession for sale or for any of these purposes, of nine or less of the items described in subdivision (b), or the sale or offering for sale of four or less items for financial gain, shall upon a conviction of a first offense, be punished by imprisonment in a county jail not exceeding one year, by a fine not exceeding twenty-five thousand dollars ($25,000), or by both that imprisonment and fine. A second or subsequent conviction shall be punished by imprisonment in a county jail not exceeding one year, or in the state prison, by a fine not exceeding one hundred thousand dollars ($100,000), or by both that imprisonment and fine.

(3) Any person who violates subdivision (c) shall be punished by a fine not exceeding ten thousand dollars ($10,000), by imprisonment in a county jail, or by both that fine and imprisonment.

(e) Any device or kit described in subdivision (a) or (b) seized under warrant or incident to a lawful arrest, upon the conviction of a person for a violation of subdivision (a) or (b), may be destroyed as contraband by the sheriff.

(f) Any person who violates this section shall be liable in a civil action to the multichannel video or information services provider for the greater of the following amounts:

(1) Five thousand dollars ($5,000).

(2) Three times the amount of actual damages, if any, sustained by the plaintiff plus reasonable attorney's fees. A defendant who prevails in the action shall be awarded his or her reasonable attorney's fees.

(g) Any multichannel video or information services provider may, in accordance with the provisions of Chapter 3 (commencing with Section 525) of Title 7 of Part 2 of the Code of Civil Procedure, bring an action to enjoin and restrain any violation of this section, and may in the same action seek damages as provided in subdivision (f).

(h) It is not a necessary prerequisite to an action pursuant to this section that the plaintiff has suffered, or be threatened with, actual damages.

(i) For the purposes of this section, a "multichannel video or information services provider" means a franchised or otherwise duly licensed cable television system, video dialtone system, Multichannel Multipoint Distribution Service system, Direct Broadcast Satellite system, or other system providing video or information services that are distributed via cable, wire, radio frequency, or other media. A video dialtone system is a platform operated by a public utility telephone corporation for the transport of video programming as authorized by the Federal Communications Commission pursuant to FCC Docket No. 87-266, and any subsequent decisions related to that docket, subject to any rules promulgated by the FCC pursuant to those decisions.

Amended by Stats 2001 ch 854 (SB 205), s 31, eff. 1/1/2002.

Section 593e - Unlawful interception, receipt, or use of program or service carried by subscription television system

(a) Every person who knowingly and willfully makes or maintains an unauthorized connection or connections, whether physically, electrically, or inductively, or purchases, possesses, attaches, causes to be attached, assists others in or maintains the attachment of any unauthorized device or devices to a television set or to other equipment designed to receive a television broadcast or transmission, or makes or maintains any modification or alteration to any device installed with the authorization of a subscription television system, for the purpose of intercepting, receiving, or using any program or other service carried by the subscription television system which the person is not authorized by that subscription television system to receive or use, is guilty of a misdemeanor punishable by a fine not exceeding one thousand dollars ($1,000), or by imprisonment in a county jail not exceeding 90 days, or by both that fine and imprisonment. For the purposes of this section, each purchase, possession, connection, attachment or modification shall constitute a separate violation of this section.

(b) Every person who, without the express authorization of a subscription television system, knowingly and willfully manufactures, imports into this state, assembles, distributes, sells, offers to sell, possesses, advertises for sale, or otherwise provides any device, any plan, or any kit for a device or for a printed circuit, designed in whole or in part to decode, descramble, intercept, or otherwise make intelligible any encoded, scrambled, or other nonstandard signal carried by that subscription television system, is guilty of a misdemeanor punishable by a fine not exceeding ten thousand dollars ($10,000), or by imprisonment in a county jail, or by both that fine and imprisonment. A second or subsequent conviction is punishable by a fine not exceeding twenty thousand dollars ($20,000), or by imprisonment in a county jail for up to one year, or by both that fine and imprisonment.

(c) Any person who violates the provisions of subdivision (a) shall be liable to the subscription television system for civil damages in the amount of the value of the connection and subscription fees service actually charged by the subscription television system for the period of unauthorized use according to proof. Any person who violates the provisions of subdivision (b) shall be liable to the subscription television system at the election of the subscription television system for either of the following amounts:

(1) An award of statutory damages in an aggregate amount of not less than five hundred dollars ($500) or more than ten thousand dollars ($10,000), as the court deems just, for each device, plan, or kit for a device, or for a printed circuit manufactured, imported, assembled, sold, offered for sale, possessed, advertised for sale, or otherwise provided in violation of subdivision (b), to be awarded instead of actual damages and profits.

(2) Three times the amount of actual damages sustained by the plaintiff as a result of the violation or violations of this section and any revenues which have been obtained by the defendant as a result of the violation or violations, or an amount equal to three times the value of the services unlawfully obtained, or the sum of five hundred dollars ($500) for each unauthorized device manufactured, sold, used, or distributed, whichever is greater, and, when appropriate, punitive damages. For the purposes of this subdivision, revenues which have been obtained by the defendant as a result of a violation or violations of this section shall not be included in computing actual damages. In a case where the court finds that any activity set forth in subdivision (b) was committed knowingly and willfully and for purposes of commercial advantage or private financial gain, the court in its discretion may increase the award of damages, whether actual or statutory, by an amount of not more than fifty thousand dollars ($50,000). It shall not constitute a use for "commercial advantage or private financial gain" for any person to receive a subscription television signal within a residential unit as defined herein.

(d) In any civil action filed pursuant to this section, the court shall allow the recovery of full costs plus an award of reasonable attorney's fees to the prevailing party.

(e) Any subscription television system may, in accordance with the provisions of Chapter 3 (commencing with Section 525) of Title 7 of Part 2 of the Code of Civil Procedure, bring an action to enjoin and restrain any violation of this section without having to make a showing of special or irreparable damage, and may in the same action seek damages as provided in subdivision (c). Upon the execution of a proper bond against damages for an injunction improvidently granted, a temporary restraining order or a preliminary injunction may be issued in any action before a final determination on the merits.

(f) It is not necessary that the plaintiff have incurred actual damages, or be threatened with incurring actual damages, as a prerequisite to bringing an action pursuant to this section.

(g) For the purposes of this section, an encoded, scrambled, or other nonstandard signal shall include, without limitation, any type of distorted signal or transmission that is not intended to produce an intelligible program or service without the use of special devices or information provided by the sender for the receipt of this type of signal or transmission.

(h)

(1) For the purposes of this section, a "subscription television system" means a television system which sends an encoded, scrambled, or other nonstandard signal over the air which is not intended to be received in an intelligible form without special equipment provided by or authorized by the sender.

(2) For purposes of this section, "residential unit" is defined as any single-family residence, mobilehome within a mobilehome park, condominium, unit or an apartment or multiple-housing unit leased or rented for residential purposes.

Amended by Stats 2001 ch 854 (SB 205), s 32, eff. 1/1/2002.

Section 593f - Unlawful manufacture, distribution, or sale of device to decode over-the-air transmission by Multi-point Distribution Service or Instructional Television Fixed Service

Every person who for profit knowingly and willfully manufactures, distributes, or sells any device or plan or kit for a device, or printed circuit containing circuitry for decoding or addressing with the purpose or intention of facilitating decoding or addressing of any over-the-air transmission by a Multi-point Distribution Service or Instructional Television Fixed Service made pursuant to authority granted by the Federal Communications Commission which is not authorized by the Multi-point Distribution Service or the Instructional Television Fixed Service is guilty of a misdemeanor punishable by a fine not exceeding two thousand five hundred dollars ($2,500) or by imprisonment in the county jail not exceeding 90 days, or both.

Added by Stats. 1984, Ch. 833, Sec. 1. Effective August 31, 1984.

Section 593g - Unlawful possession of substance sufficiently hard to injure saws or wood manufacturing or processing equipment

Every person who, with the intent to use it in a violation of Section 593a, possesses any iron, steel, ceramic, or other substance sufficiently hard to injure saws or wood manufacturing or processing equipment, shall be punished by imprisonment in the county jail not to exceed one year.

This section shall only become operative if Senate Bill 1176 of the 1987-88 Regular Session of the Legislature is enacted and becomes effective on or before January 1, 1988.

Added by Stats. 1987, Ch. 1414, Sec. 1. Note: SB 1176 was enacted as Stats. 1987, Ch. 1132.

Title 14 - MALICIOUS MISCHIEF

Section 594 - Vandalism

(a) Every person who maliciously commits any of the following acts with respect to any real or personal property not his or her own, in cases other than those specified by state law, is guilty of vandalism:

(1) Defaces with graffiti or other inscribed material.

(2) Damages.

(3) Destroys. Whenever a person violates this subdivision with respect to real property, vehicles, signs, fixtures, furnishings, or property belonging to any public entity, as defined by Section 811.2 of the Government Code, or the federal government, it shall be a permissive inference that the person neither owned the property nor had the permission of the owner to deface, damage, or destroy the property.

(b)

(1) If the amount of defacement, damage, or destruction is four hundred dollars ($400) or more, vandalism is punishable by imprisonment pursuant to subdivision (h) of Section 1170 or in a county jail not exceeding one year, or by a fine of not more than ten thousand dollars ($10,000), or if the amount of defacement, damage, or destruction is ten thousand dollars ($10,000) or more, by a fine of not more than fifty thousand dollars ($50,000), or by both that fine and imprisonment.

(2)

(A) If the amount of defacement, damage, or destruction is less than four hundred dollars ($400), vandalism is punishable by imprisonment in a county jail not exceeding one year, or by a fine of not more than one thousand dollars ($1,000), or by both that fine and imprisonment.

(B) If the amount of defacement, damage, or destruction is less than four hundred dollars ($400), and the defendant has been previously convicted of vandalism or affixing graffiti or other inscribed material under Section 594, 594.3, 594.4, 640.5, 640.6, or 640.7, vandalism is punishable by imprisonment in a county jail for not more than one year, or by a fine of not more than five thousand dollars ($5,000), or by both that fine and imprisonment.

(c) Upon conviction of any person under this section for acts of vandalism consisting of defacing property with graffiti or other inscribed materials, the court shall, when appropriate and feasible, in addition to any punishment imposed under subdivision (b), order the defendant to clean up, repair, or replace the damaged property himself or herself, or order the defendant, and his or her parents or guardians if the defendant is a minor, to keep the damaged property or another specified property in the community free of graffiti for up to one year. Participation of a parent or guardian is not required under this subdivision if the court deems this participation to be detrimental to the defendant, or if the parent or guardian is a single parent who must care for young children. If the court finds that graffiti cleanup is inappropriate, the court shall consider other types of community service, where feasible.

(d) If a minor is personally unable to pay a fine levied for acts prohibited by this section, the parent of that minor shall be liable for payment of the fine. A court may waive payment of the fine, or any part thereof, by the parent upon a finding of good cause.

(e) As used in this section, the term "graffiti or other inscribed material" includes any unauthorized inscription, word, figure, mark, or design, that is written, marked, etched, scratched, drawn, or painted on real or personal property.

(f) The court may order any person ordered to perform community service or graffiti removal pursuant to paragraph (1) of subdivision (c) to undergo counseling.

(g) This section shall become operative on January 1, 2002.
Amended by Stats 2011 ch 39 (AB 117),s 68, eff. 6/30/2011.
Amended by Stats 2011 ch 15 (AB 109),s 406, eff. 4/4/2011, but operative no earlier than October 1, 2011, and only upon creation of a community corrections grant program to assist in implementing this act and upon an appropriation to fund the grant program.
Amended by Stats 2008 ch 209 (AB 2609),s 1, eff. 1/1/2009.
Amended by Stats 2000 ch 50 (SB 1616), s 2, eff. 1/1/2001.
Previously Amended July 12, 1999 (Bill Number: SB 966) (Chapter 83).

Section 594.05 - "Damages" defined

(a) For purposes of Section 594, "damages" includes damage caused to public transit property and facilities, public parks property and facilities, and public utilities and water property and facilities, in the course of stealing or attempting to steal nonferrous material, as defined in Section 21608.5 of the Business and Professions Code.

(b) This section is declaratory of existing law.
Added by Stats 2012 ch 82 (AB 1971),s 3, eff. 1/1/2013.

Section 594.1 - Unlawful acts related to etching cream or aerosol container of paint

(a)

(1) It shall be unlawful for any person, firm, or corporation, except a parent or legal guardian, to sell or give or in any way furnish to another person, who is in fact under the age of 18 years, any etching cream or aerosol container of paint that is capable of defacing property without first obtaining bona fide evidence of majority and identity.

(2) For purposes of this section, "etching cream" means any caustic cream, gel, liquid, or solution capable, by means of a chemical action, of defacing, damaging, or destroying hard surfaces in a manner similar to acid.

(3) For purposes of this subdivision, "bona fide evidence of majority and identity" is any document evidencing the age and identity of an individual which has been issued by a federal, state, or local governmental entity, and includes, but is not limited to, a motor vehicle operator's license, a registration certificate issued under the federal Selective Service Act, or an identification card issued to a member of the armed forces.

(4) This subdivision shall not apply to the furnishing of six ounces or less of etching cream or an aerosol container of paint to a minor for the minor's use or possession under the supervision of the minor's parent, guardian, instructor, or employer.

(5) Etching cream, aerosol containers of paint, or related substances may be furnished for use in school-related activities that are part of the instructional program when used under controlled and supervised situations within the classroom or on the site of a supervised project. These containers may not leave the supervised site and shall be inventoried by the instructor. This use shall comply with Section 32060 of the Education Code regarding the safe use of toxic art supplies in schools.

(b) It shall be unlawful for any person under the age of 18 years to purchase etching cream or an aerosol container of paint that is capable of defacing property.

(c) Every retailer selling or offering for sale in this state etching cream or aerosol containers of paint capable of defacing property shall post in a conspicuous place a sign in letters at least three-eighths of an inch high stating: "Any person who maliciously defaces real or personal property with etching cream or paint is guilty of vandalism which is punishable by a fine, imprisonment, or both."

(d) It is unlawful for any person to carry on his or her person and in plain view to the public etching cream or an aerosol container of paint while in any posted public facility, park, playground, swimming pool, beach, or recreational area, other than a highway, street, alley, or way, unless he or she has first received valid authorization from the governmental entity which has jurisdiction over the public area. As used in this subdivision, "posted" means a sign placed in a reasonable location or locations stating it is a misdemeanor to possess etching cream or a spray can of paint in that public facility, park, playground, swimming pool, beach, or recreational area without valid authorization.

(e)

(1) It is unlawful for any person under the age of 18 years to possess etching cream or an aerosol container of paint for the purpose of defacing property while on any public highway, street, alley, or way, or other public place, regardless of whether that person is or is not in any automobile, vehicle, or other conveyance.

(2) As a condition of probation for any violation of this subdivision, the court may order a defendant convicted of a violation of this subdivision to perform community service as follows:

(A) For a first conviction under this subdivision, community service not to exceed 100 hours over a period not to exceed 90 days during a time other than his or her hours of school attendance or employment.

(B) If the person has a prior conviction under this subdivision, community service not to exceed 200 hours over a period of 180 days during a time other than his or her hours of school attendance or employment.

(C) If the person has two prior convictions under this subdivision, community service not to exceed 300 hours over a period not to exceed 240 days during a time other than his or her hours of school attendance or employment.

(f) Violation of any provision of this section is a misdemeanor. Upon conviction of any person under this section, the court may, in addition to any other punishment imposed, if the jurisdiction has adopted a graffiti abatement program as defined in subdivision (f) of Section 594, order the defendant, and his or her parents or guardians if the defendant is a minor, to keep the damaged property or another specified property in the community free of graffiti, as follows:

(1) For a first conviction under this section, for 90 days.

(2) If the defendant has a prior conviction under this section, for 180 days.

(3) If the defendant has two or more prior convictions under this section, for 240 days. Parti cipation of a parent or guardian is not required under this subdivision if the court deems this participation to be detrimental to the defendant, or if the parent or guardian is a single parent who must care for young children.

(g) The court may order any person ordered to perform community service or graffiti removal pursuant to subdivision (e) or (f) to undergo counseling.

Amended by Stats 2002 ch 523 (AB 1344), s 1, eff. 1/1/2003.

Section 594.2 - Unlawful possession of drill bit, glass cutter, marking substance, etc.

(a) Every person who possesses a masonry or glass drill bit, a carbide drill bit, a glass cutter, a grinding stone, an awl, a chisel, a carbide scribe, an aerosol paint container, a felt tip marker, or any other marking substance with the intent to commit vandalism or graffiti, is guilty of a misdemeanor.

(b) As a condition of probation for any violation of this section, the court may order the defendant to perform community service not to exceed 90 hours during a time other than his or her hours of school attendance or employment.

(c) For the purposes of this section:

(1) "Felt tip marker" means any broad-tipped marker pen with a tip exceeding three-eighths of one inch in width, or any similar implement containing an ink that is not water soluble.

(2) "Marking substance" means any substance or implement, other than aerosol paint containers and felt tip markers, that could be used to draw, spray, paint, etch, or mark.

Amended by Stats. 1994, Ch. 911, Sec. 1. Effective January 1, 1995.

Section 594.3 - Vandalism of place of worship or cemetery

(a) Any person who knowingly commits any act of vandalism to a church, synagogue, mosque, temple, building owned and occupied by a religious educational institution, or other place primarily used as a place of worship where religious services are regularly conducted or a cemetery is guilty of a crime punishable by imprisonment in a county jail for not exceeding one year or imprisonment pursuant to subdivision (h) of Section 1170.

(b) Any person who knowingly commits any act of vandalism to a church, synagogue, mosque, temple, building owned and occupied by a religious educational institution, or other place primarily used as a place of worship where religious services are regularly conducted or a cemetery, which is shown to have been a hate crime and to have been committed for the purpose of intimidating and deterring persons from freely exercising their religious beliefs, is guilty of a felony punishable by imprisonment pursuant to subdivision (h) of Section 1170.

(c) For purposes of this section, "hate crime" has the same meaning as Section 422.55.

Amended by Stats 2011 ch 39 (AB 117),s 68, eff. 6/30/2011.

Amended by Stats 2011 ch 15 (AB 109),s 407, eff. 4/4/2011, but operative no earlier than October 1, 2011, and only upon creation of a community corrections grant program to assist in implementing this act and upon an appropriation to fund the grant program.

Amended by Stats 2004 ch 700 (SB 1234), s 22, eff. 1/1/2005.

Amended by Stats 2000 ch 546 (AB 2580), s 2, eff. 1/1/2001.

Section 594.35 - Unlawful acts related to cemeteries or mortuaries

Every person is guilty of a crime and punishable by imprisonment pursuant to subdivision (h) of Section 1170 or by imprisonment in a county jail for not exceeding one year, who maliciously does any of the following:

(a) Destroys, cuts, mutilates, effaces, or otherwise injures, tears down, or removes any tomb, monument, memorial, or marker in a cemetery, or any gate, door, fence, wall, post or railing, or any enclosure for the protection of a cemetery or mortuary or any property in a cemetery or mortuary.

(b) Obliterates any grave, vault, niche, or crypt.

(c) Destroys, cuts, breaks or injures any mortuary building or any building, statuary, or ornamentation within the limits of a cemetery.

(d) Disturbs, obstructs, detains or interferes with any person carrying or accompanying human remains to a cemetery or funeral establishment, or engaged in a funeral service, or an interment.

Amended by Stats 2011 ch 39 (AB 117),s 68, eff. 6/30/2011.

Amended by Stats 2011 ch 15 (AB 109),s 408, eff. 4/4/2011, but operative no earlier than October 1, 2011, and only upon creation of a community corrections grant program to assist in implementing this act and upon an appropriation to fund the grant program.

Added by Stats 2000 ch 546 (AB 2580), s 3, eff. 1/1/2001.

Section 594.37 - Picketing targeted at funeral

(a) It is unlawful, except upon private property, for a person to engage in picketing targeted at a funeral during the time period beginning one hour prior to the funeral and ending one hour after the conclusion of the funeral.

(b) Any violation of subdivision (a) is punishable by a fine not exceeding one thousand dollars ($1,000), imprisonment in a county jail not exceeding six months, or by both that fine and imprisonment.

(c) For purposes of this section:

(1) "Funeral" means the ceremony or memorial service held in connection with the burial or cremation of a deceased person. "Funeral" does not mean any nonburial or noncremation activities, businesses, or services.

(2) "Picketing," for purposes of this section only, means protest activities engaged in by any person within 300 feet of a burial site, mortuary, or place of worship.

(3) "Protest activities" includes oration, speech, use of sound amplification equipment in a manner that is intended to make or makes speech, including, but not limited to, oration audible to participants in a funeral, or similar conduct that is not part of the funeral, before an assembled group of people.

(4) "Targeted at" means directed at or toward the deceased person or the attendees of a funeral.

(d) The provisions of this section are severable. If any provision of this section or its application is held invalid, that invalidity shall not affect other provisions or applications that can be given effect without the invalid provision or application.

Added by Stats 2012 ch 354 (SB 661),s 2, eff. 1/1/2013.

Section 594.39 - Vaccination sites; obstructing, intimidating, or harassing are unlawful activities

(a) It is unlawful to knowingly approach within 30 feet of any person while a person is within 100 feet of the entrance or exit of a vaccination site and is seeking to enter or exit a vaccination site, or any occupied motor vehicle seeking entry or exit to a vaccination site, for the purpose of obstructing, injuring, harassing, intimidating, or interfering with that person or vehicle occupant.

(b) A violation of subdivision (a) is punishable by a fine not exceeding one thousand dollars ($1,000), imprisonment in a county jail not exceeding six months, or by both that fine and imprisonment.

(c) For purposes of this section:

(1) "Harassing" means knowingly approaching, without consent, within 30 feet of another person or occupied vehicle for the purpose of passing a leaflet or handbill to, displaying a sign to, or engaging in oral protest, education, or counseling with, that other person in a public way or on a sidewalk area.

(2) "Interfering with" means restricting a person's freedom of movement.

(3) "Intimidating" means making a true threat directed to a person or group of persons with the intent of placing that person or group of persons in fear of bodily harm or death.

(4) "Obstructing" means rendering ingress to or egress from a vaccination site, or rendering passage to or from a vaccination site, unreasonably difficult or hazardous.

(5) "True threat" means a statement in which the speaker means to communicate a serious expression of an intent to commit an act of unlawful violence to a particular person or group of persons regardless of whether the person actually intends to act on the threat.

(6) "Vaccination site" means the physical location where vaccination services are provided, including, but not limited to, a hospital, physician's office, clinic, or any retail space or pop-up location made available for vaccination services.

(d) It is not a violation of this section to engage in lawful picketing arising out of a labor dispute, as provided in Section 527.3 of the Code of Civil Procedure.

(e) The provisions of this section are severable. If any provision of this section or its application is held invalid, that invalidity shall not affect other provisions or applications that can be given effect without the invalid provision or application.

Added by Stats 2021 ch 737 (SB 742),s 2, eff. 10/8/2021.

Section 594.4 - Unlawful defacement or contamination of structure with noxious or caustic chemical or substance

(a) Any person who willfully and maliciously injects into or throws upon, or otherwise defaces, damages, destroys, or contaminates, any structure with butyric acid, or any other similar noxious or caustic chemical or substance, is guilty of a public offense, punishable by imprisonment pursuant to subdivision (h) of Section 1170 or in a county jail not exceeding 6 months, by a fine as specified in subdivision (b), or by both that imprisonment and fine.

(b)

(1) If the amount of the defacement, damage, destruction, or contamination is fifty thousand dollars ($50,000) or more, by a fine of not more than fifty thousand dollars ($50,000).

(2) If the amount of the defacement, damage, destruction, or contamination is five thousand dollars ($5,000) or more, but less than fifty thousand dollars ($50,000), by a fine of not more than ten thousand dollars ($10,000).

(3) If the amount of defacement, damage, destruction, or contamination is nine hundred fifty dollars ($950) or more, but less than five thousand dollars ($5,000), by a fine of not more than five thousand dollars ($5,000).

(4) If the amount of the defacement, damage, destruction, or contamination is less than nine hundred fifty dollars ($950), by a fine of not more than one thousand dollars ($1,000).

(c) For purposes of this section, "structure" includes any house or other building being used at the time of the offense for a dwelling or for commercial purposes.

Amended by Stats 2011 ch 39 (AB 117),s 68, eff. 6/30/2011.

Amended by Stats 2011 ch 15 (AB 109),s 409, eff. 4/4/2011, but operative no earlier than October 1, 2011, and only upon creation of a community corrections grant program to assist in implementing this act and upon an appropriation to fund the grant program.

Amended by Stats 2009 ch 28 (SB X3-18),s 34, eff. 1/1/2010.

Section 594.5 - Ordinances regulating sale of aerosol containers of paint or other liquid substances capable of defacing property

Nothing in this code shall invalidate an ordinance of, nor be construed to prohibit the adoption of an ordinance by, a city, city and county, or county, if the ordinance regulates the sale of aerosol containers of paint or other liquid substances capable of defacing property or sets forth civil administrative regulations, procedures, or civil penalties governing the placement of graffiti or other inscribed material on public or private, real or personal property.

Amended by Stats. 1995, Ch. 42, Sec. 1. Effective January 1, 1996.

Section 594.6 - Community service for person convicted of vandalism or affixing graffiti

(a) Every person who, having been convicted of vandalism or affixing graffiti or other inscribed material under Section 594, 594.3, 594.4, or 640.7, or any combination of these offenses, may be ordered by the court as a condition of probation to perform community service not to exceed 300 hours over a period not to exceed one year during a time other than his or her hours of school attendance or employment. Nothing in this subdivision shall limit the court from ordering the defendant to perform a longer period of community service if a longer period of community service is authorized under other provisions of law.

(b) In lieu of the community service that may be ordered pursuant to subdivision (a), the court may, if a jurisdiction has adopted a graffiti abatement program as defined in subdivision (f) of Section 594, order the defendant, and his or her parents or guardians if the defendant is a minor, as a condition of probation, to keep a specified property in the community free of graffiti for up to one year. Participation of a parent or guardian is not required under this subdivision if the court deems this participation to be detrimental to the defendant, or if the parent or guardian is a single parent who must care for young children.

(c) The court may order any person ordered to perform community service or graffiti removal pursuant to subdivision (a) or (b) to undergo counseling.

Amended by Stats 2013 ch 791 (AB 1325),s 1, eff. 1/1/2014.

Section 594.7 - Subsequent convictions

Notwithstanding subdivision (b) of Section 594, every person who, having been convicted previously of vandalism under Section 594 for maliciously defacing with graffiti or other inscribed material any real or personal property not his or her own on two separate occasions and having been incarcerated pursuant to a sentence, a conditional sentence, or a grant of probation for at least one of the convictions, is subsequently convicted of vandalism under Section 594, shall be punished by imprisonment in a county jail not exceeding one year, or in the state prison.

Amended by Stats. 1994, Ch. 909, Sec. 6. Effective January 1, 1995.

Section 594.8 - Community service for person convicted of possession of destructive implement with intent to commit graffiti or willfully affixing graffiti

(a) Any person convicted of possession of a destructive implement with intent to commit graffiti or willfully affixing graffiti under Section 594.2, 640.5, 640.6, or 640.7, where the offense was committed when he or she was under the age of 18 years, shall perform not less than 24 hours of community service during a time other than his or her hours of school attendance or employment. One parent or guardian shall be present at the community service site for at least one-half of the hours of community service required under this section unless participation by the parent, guardian, or foster parent is deemed by the court to be inappropriate or potentially detrimental to the child.

(b) In lieu of the community service required pursuant to subdivision (a), the court may, if a jurisdiction has adopted a graffiti abatement program as defined in subdivision (f) of Section 594, order the defendant, and his or her parents or guardians if the defendant is a minor, to keep a specified property in the community free of graffiti for at least 60 days. Participation of a parent or guardian is not required under this subdivision if the court deems this participation to be detrimental to the defendant, or if the parent or guardian is a single parent who must care for young children.

(c) The court may order any person ordered to perform community service or graffiti removal pursuant to subdivision (a) or (b) to undergo counseling.

Amended by Stats. 1996, Ch. 600, Sec. 5. Effective January 1, 1997.

Section 595 - Effect of specification of acts

The specification of the Acts enumerated in the following sections of this Chapter is not intended to restrict or qualify the interpretation of the preceding section.

Enacted 1872.

Section 596 - Willfully administering poison to animal or property of another

Every person who, without the consent of the owner, wilfully administers poison to any animal, the property of another, or exposes any poisonous substance, with the intent that the same shall be taken or swallowed by any such animal, is guilty of a misdemeanor. However, the provisions of this section shall not apply in the case of a person who exposes poisonous substances upon premises or property owned or controlled by him for the purpose of controlling or destroying predatory animals or livestock-killing dogs and if, prior to or during the placing out of such poisonous substances, he shall have posted upon the property conspicuous signs located at intervals of distance not greater than one-third of a mile apart, and in any case not less than three such signs having words with letters at least one inch high reading "Warning-Poisoned bait placed out on these premises," which signs shall be kept in place until the poisonous substances have been removed. Whenever such signs have been conspicuously located upon the property or premises owned or controlled by him as hereinabove provided, such person shall not be charged with any civil liability to another party in the event that any domestic animal belonging to such party becomes injured or killed by trespassing or partaking of the poisonous substance or substances so placed.

Amended by Stats. 1941, Ch. 494.

Section 596.5 - Abusive behavior to elephant

It shall be a misdemeanor for any owner or manager of an elephant to engage in abusive behavior towards the elephant, which behavior shall include the discipline of the elephant by any of the following methods:

(a) Deprivation of food, water, or rest.

(b) Use of electricity.

(c) Physical punishment resulting in damage, scarring, or breakage of skin.

(d) Insertion of any instrument into any bodily orifice.

(e) Use of martingales.

(f) Use of block and tackle.

Added by Stats. 1989, Ch. 1423, Sec. 1.

Section 596.7 - Veterinarian at rodeo

(a)

(1) For purposes of this section, "rodeo" means a performance featuring competition between persons that includes three or more of the following events: bareback bronc riding, saddle bronc riding, bull riding, calf roping, steer wrestling, or team roping.

(2) A rodeo performed on private property for which admission is charged, or that sells or accepts sponsorships, or is open to the public constitutes a performance for the purpose of this subdivision.

(b) The management of any professionally sanctioned or amateur rodeo that intends to perform in any city, county, or city and county shall ensure that there is a veterinarian licensed to practice in this state present at all times during the performances of the rodeo, or a veterinarian licensed to practice in the state who is on-call and able to arrive at the rodeo within one hour after a determination has been made that there is an injury which requires treatment to be provided by a veterinarian.

(c)

    (1) The attending or on-call veterinarian shall have complete access to the site of any event in the rodeo that uses animals.

    (2) The attending or on-call veterinarian may, for good cause, declare any animal unfit for use in any rodeo event.

(d)

    (1) Any animal that is injured during the course of, or as a result of, any rodeo event shall receive immediate examination and appropriate treatment by the attending veterinarian or shall begin receiving examination and appropriate treatment by a veterinarian licensed to practice in this state within one hour of the determination of the injury requiring veterinary treatment.

    (2) The attending or on-call veterinarian shall submit a brief written listing of any animal injury requiring veterinary treatment to the Veterinary Medical Board within 48 hours of the conclusion of the rodeo.

    (3) The rodeo management shall ensure that there is a conveyance available at all times for the immediate and humane removal of any injured animal.

(e) The rodeo management shall ensure that no electric prod or similar device is used on any animal once the animal is in the holding chute, unless necessary to protect the participants and spectators of the rodeo.

(f) A violation of this section is an infraction and shall be punishable as follows:

    (1) A fine of not less than five hundred dollars ($500) and not more than two thousand dollars ($2,000) for a first violation.

    (2) A fine of not less than one thousand five hundred dollars ($1,500) and not more than five thousand dollars ($5,000) for a second or subsequent violation.

Amended by Stats 2007 ch 714 (AB 1614),s 1, eff. 1/1/2008.

Added by Stats 2000 ch 992 (SB 1462), s 1, eff. 1/1/2001.

Section 597 - Unlawful acts related to animals, mammals, birds, reptiles, amphibians, and fish

(a) Except as provided in subdivision (c) of this section or Section 599c, a person who maliciously and intentionally maims, mutilates, tortures, or wounds a living animal, or maliciously and intentionally kills an animal, is guilty of a crime punishable pursuant to subdivision (d).

(b) Except as otherwise provided in subdivision (a) or (c), a person who overdrives, overloads, drives when overloaded, overworks, tortures, torments, deprives of necessary sustenance, drink, or shelter, cruelly beats, mutilates, or cruelly kills an animal, or causes or procures an animal to be so overdriven, overloaded, driven when overloaded, overworked, tortured, tormented, deprived of necessary sustenance, drink, shelter, or to be cruelly beaten, mutilated, or cruelly killed; and whoever, having the charge or custody of an animal, either as owner or otherwise, subjects an animal to needless suffering, or inflicts unnecessary cruelty upon the animal, or in any manner abuses an animal, or fails to provide the animal with proper food, drink, or shelter, or protection from the weather, or who drives, rides, or otherwise uses the animal when unfit for labor, is, for each offense, guilty of a crime punishable pursuant to subdivision (d).

(c) A person who maliciously and intentionally maims, mutilates, or tortures a mammal, bird, reptile, amphibian, or fish, as described in subdivision (e), is guilty of a crime punishable pursuant to subdivision (d).

(d) A violation of subdivision (a), (b), or (c) is punishable as a felony by imprisonment pursuant to subdivision (h) of Section 1170, or by a fine of not more than twenty thousand dollars ($20,000), or by both that fine and imprisonment, or alternatively, as a misdemeanor by imprisonment in a county jail for not more than one year, or by a fine of not more than twenty thousand dollars ($20,000), or by both that fine and imprisonment.

(e)

    (1) Subdivision (c) applies to a mammal, bird, reptile, amphibian, or fish that is a creature described as follows:

        (A) Endangered species or threatened species as described in Chapter 1.5 (commencing with Section 2050) of Division 3 of the Fish and Game Code.

        (B) Fully protected birds described in Section 3511 of the Fish and Game Code.

        (C) Fully protected mammals described in Chapter 8 (commencing with Section 4700) of Part 3 of Division 4 of the Fish and Game Code.

        (D) Fully protected reptiles and amphibians described in Chapter 2 (commencing with Section 5050) of Division 5 of the Fish and Game Code.

        (E) Fully protected fish as described in Section 5515 of the Fish and Game Code.

    (2) This subdivision does not supersede or affect any law relating to taking of the described species, including, but not limited to, Section 12008 of the Fish and Game Code.

(f) For the purposes of subdivision (c), each act of malicious and intentional maiming, mutilating, or torturing a separate specimen of a creature described in subdivision (e) is a separate offense. If a person is charged with a violation of subdivision (c), the proceedings shall be subject to Section 12157 of the Fish and Game Code.

(g)

    (1) Upon the conviction of a person charged with a violation of this section by causing or permitting an act of cruelty, as defined in Section 599b, all animals lawfully seized and impounded with respect to the violation by a peace officer, officer of a humane society, or officer of an animal shelter or animal regulation department of a public agency shall be adjudged by the court to be forfeited and shall thereupon be awarded to the impounding officer for proper disposition. A person convicted of a violation of this section by causing or permitting an act of cruelty, as defined in Section 599b, shall be liable to the impounding officer for all costs of impoundment from the time of seizure to the time of proper disposition.

(2) Mandatory seizure or impoundment shall not apply to animals in properly conducted scientific experiments or investigations performed under the authority of the faculty of a regularly incorporated medical college or university of this state.

Amended by Stats 2023 ch 546 (AB 829),s 2, eff. 1/1/2024.

Amended by Stats 2019 ch 7 (AB 1553),s 18, eff. 1/1/2020.

Amended by Stats 2011 ch 131 (SB 917),s 1, eff. 1/1/2012.

Amended by Stats 2011 ch 39 (AB 117),s 68, eff. 6/30/2011.

Amended by Stats 2011 ch 15 (AB 109),s 410, eff. 4/4/2011, but operative no earlier than October 1, 2011, and only upon creation of a community corrections grant program to assist in implementing this act and upon an appropriation to fund the grant program.

Section 597.1 - Stray or abandoned animals; seizure or impoundment of animal

(a)

(1) Every owner, driver, or keeper of any animal who permits the animal to be in any building, enclosure, lane, street, square, or lot of any city, county, city and county, or judicial district without proper care and attention is guilty of a misdemeanor. Any peace officer, humane society officer, or animal control officer shall take possession of the stray or abandoned animal and shall provide care and treatment for the animal until the animal is deemed to be in suitable condition to be returned to the owner. When the officer has reasonable grounds to believe that very prompt action is required to protect the health or safety of the animal or the health or safety of others, the officer shall immediately seize the animal and comply with subdivision (f). In all other cases, the officer shall comply with the provisions of subdivision (g). The full cost of caring for and treating any animal properly seized under this subdivision or pursuant to a search warrant shall constitute a lien on the animal and the animal shall not be returned to its owner until the charges are paid, if the seizure is upheld pursuant to this section.

(2) Notwithstanding any other law, if an animal control officer or humane officer, when necessary to protect the health and safety of a wild, stray, or abandoned animal or the health and safety of others, seeks to administer a tranquilizer that contains a controlled substance, as defined in Division 10 (commencing with Section 11000) of the Health and Safety Code, to gain control of that animal, the officer may possess and administer that tranquilizer with direct or indirect supervision as determined by a licensed veterinarian, provided that the officer has met each of the following requirements:

(A) Has received training in the administration of tranquilizers from a licensed veterinarian. The training shall be approved by the California Veterinary Medical Board.

(B) Has successfully completed the firearms component of a course relating to the exercise of police powers, as set forth in Section 832.

(C) Is authorized by the officer's agency or organization to possess and administer the tranquilizer in accordance with a policy established by the agency or organization and approved by the veterinarian who obtained the controlled substance.

(D) Has successfully completed the euthanasia training set forth in Section 2039 of Title 16 of the California Code of Regulations.

(E) Has completed a state and federal fingerprinting background check and does not have any drug- or alcohol-related convictions.

(b) Every sick, disabled, infirm, or crippled animal, except a dog or cat, that is abandoned in any city, county, city and county, or judicial district may be humanely euthanized by the officer if, after a reasonable search, no owner of the animal can be found. It shall be the duty of all peace officers, humane society officers, and animal control officers to cause the animal to be humanely euthanized or rehabilitated and placed in a suitable home on information that the animal is stray or abandoned. The officer may likewise take charge of any animal, including a dog or cat, that by reason of lameness, sickness, feebleness, or neglect, is unfit for the labor it is performing, or that in any other manner is being cruelly treated, and provide care and treatment for the animal until it is deemed to be in a suitable condition to be returned to the owner. When the officer has reasonable grounds to believe that very prompt action is required to protect the health or safety of an animal or the health or safety of others, the officer shall immediately seize the animal and comply with subdivision (f). In all other cases, the officer shall comply with subdivision (g). The full cost of caring for and treating any animal properly seized under this subdivision or pursuant to a search warrant shall constitute a lien on the animal and the animal shall not be returned to its owner until the charges are paid.

(c)

(1) Any peace officer, humane society officer, or animal control officer shall convey all injured cats and dogs found without their owners in a public place directly to a veterinarian known by the officer to be a veterinarian who ordinarily treats dogs and cats for a determination of whether the animal shall be immediately and humanely euthanized or shall be hospitalized under proper care and given emergency treatment.

(2) If the owner does not redeem the animal within the locally prescribed waiting period, the veterinarian may personally perform euthanasia on the animal. If the animal is treated and recovers from its injuries, the veterinarian may keep the animal for purposes of adoption, provided the responsible animal control agency has first been contacted and has refused to take possession of the animal.

(3) Whenever any animal is transferred to a veterinarian in a clinic, such as an emergency clinic that is not in continuous operation, the veterinarian may, in turn, transfer the animal to an appropriate facility.

(4) If the veterinarian determines that the animal shall be hospitalized under proper care and given emergency treatment, the costs of any services that are provided pending the owner's inquiry to the responsible agency, department, or society shall be paid from the dog license fees, fines, and fees for impounding dogs in the city, county, or city and county in which the animal was licensed or, if the animal is unlicensed, shall be paid by the jurisdiction in which the animal was found, subject to the provision that this cost be repaid by the animal's owner. The full cost of caring for and treating any animal seized under this subdivision shall constitute a lien on the animal and the animal shall not be returned to the owner until the charges are paid. No veterinarian shall be criminally or civilly liable for any decision that the veterinarian makes or for services that the veterinarian provides pursuant to this subdivision.

(d) An animal control agency that takes possession of an animal pursuant to subdivision (c) shall keep records of the whereabouts of the animal from the time of possession to the end of the animal's impoundment, and those records shall be available for inspection by the public upon request for three years after the date the animal's impoundment ended.

(e) Notwithstanding any other provision of this section, any peace officer, humane society officer, or any animal control officer may, with the approval of the officer's immediate superior, humanely euthanize any stray or abandoned animal in the field in any case where the animal is too severely injured to move or where a veterinarian is not available and it would be more humane to euthanize the animal.

(f) Whenever an officer authorized under this section seizes or impounds an animal based on a reasonable belief that prompt action is required to protect the health or safety of the animal or the health or safety of others, the officer shall, before the commencement of any criminal proceedings authorized by this section, provide the owner or keeper of the animal, if known or ascertainable after reasonable investigation, with the opportunity for a postseizure hearing to determine the validity of the seizure or impoundment, or both.

(1) The agency shall cause a notice to be affixed to a conspicuous place where the animal was situated or personally deliver a notice of the seizure or impoundment, or both, to the owner or keeper within 48 hours, excluding weekends and holidays. The notice shall include all of the following:

(A) The name, business address, and telephone number of the officer providing the notice.

(B) A description of the animal seized, including any identification upon the animal.

(C) The authority and purpose for the seizure or impoundment, including the time, place, and circumstances under which the animal was seized.

(D) A statement that, in order to receive a postseizure hearing, the owner or person authorized to keep the animal, or their agent, shall request the hearing by signing and returning an enclosed declaration of ownership or right to keep the animal to the agency providing the notice within 10 days, including weekends and holidays, of the date of the notice. The declaration may be returned by personal delivery or mail.

(E) A statement that the full cost of caring for and treating any animal properly seized under this section is a lien on the animal and that the animal shall not be returned to the owner until the charges are paid, and that failure to request or to attend a scheduled hearing shall result in liability for this cost.

(2) The postseizure hearing shall be conducted within 48 hours of the request, excluding weekends and holidays. The seizing agency may authorize its own officer or employee to conduct the hearing if the hearing officer is not the same person who directed the seizure or impoundment of the animal and is not junior in rank to that person. The agency may use the services of a hearing officer from outside the agency for the purposes of complying with this section.

(3) Failure of the owner or keeper, or of their agent, to request or to attend a scheduled hearing shall result in a forfeiture of any right to a postseizure hearing or right to challenge their liability for costs incurred.

(4) The agency, department, or society employing the person who directed the seizure shall be responsible for the costs incurred for caring and treating the animal, if it is determined in the postseizure hearing that the seizing officer did not have reasonable grounds to believe very prompt action, including seizure of the animal, was required to protect the health or safety of the animal or the health or safety of others. If it is determined the seizure was justified, the owner or keeper shall be personally liable to the seizing agency for the full cost of the seizure and care of the animal. The charges for the seizure and care of the animal shall be a lien on the animal. The animal shall not be returned to its owner until the charges are paid and the owner demonstrates to the satisfaction of the seizing agency or the hearing officer that the owner can and will provide the necessary care for the animal.

(g) Where the need for immediate seizure is not present and before the commencement of any criminal proceedings authorized by this section, the agency shall provide the owner or keeper of the animal, if known or ascertainable after reasonable investigation, with the opportunity for a hearing before any seizure or impoundment of the animal. The owner shall produce the animal at the time of the hearing unless, before the hearing, the owner has made arrangements with the agency to view the animal upon request of the agency, or unless the owner can provide verification that the animal was humanely euthanized. Any person who willfully fails to produce the animal or provide the verification is guilty of an infraction, punishable by a fine of not less than two hundred fifty dollars ($250) nor more than one thousand dollars ($1,000).

(1) The agency shall cause a notice to be affixed to a conspicuous place where the animal was situated or personally deliver a notice stating the grounds for believing the animal should be seized under subdivision (a) or (b). The notice shall include all of the following:

(A) The name, business address, and telephone number of the officer providing the notice.

(B) A description of the animal to be seized, including any identification upon the animal.

(C) The authority and purpose for the possible seizure or impoundment.

(D) A statement that, in order to receive a hearing before any seizure, the owner or person authorized to keep the animal, or their agent, shall request the hearing by signing and returning the enclosed declaration of ownership or right to keep the animal to the officer providing the notice within two days, excluding weekends and holidays, of the date of the notice.

(E) A statement that the cost of caring for and treating any animal properly seized under this section is a lien on the animal, that any animal seized shall not be returned to the owner until the charges are paid, and that failure to request or to attend a scheduled hearing shall result in a conclusive determination that the animal may properly be seized and that the owner shall be liable for the charges.

(2) The preseizure hearing shall be conducted within 48 hours, excluding weekends and holidays, after receipt of the request. The seizing agency may authorize its own officer or employee to conduct the hearing if the hearing officer is not the same person who requests the seizure or impoundment of the animal and is not junior in rank to that person. The agency may use the services of a hearing officer from outside the agency for the purposes of complying with this section.

(3) Failure of the owner or keeper, or their agent, to request or to attend a scheduled hearing shall result in a forfeiture of any right to a preseizure hearing or right to challenge their liability for costs incurred pursuant to this section.

(4) The hearing officer, after the hearing, may affirm or deny the owner's or keeper's right to custody of the animal and, if reasonable grounds are established, may order the seizure or impoundment of the animal for care and treatment.

(h) If any animal is properly seized under this section or pursuant to a search warrant, the owner or keeper shall be personally liable to the seizing agency for the cost of the seizure and care of the animal. Further, if the charges for the seizure or impoundment and any other charges permitted under this section are not paid within 14 days of the seizure, or if the owner, within 14 days of notice of availability of the animal to be returned, fails to pay charges permitted under this section and take possession of the animal, the animal shall be deemed to have been abandoned and may be humanely euthanized or otherwise properly disposed of by the seizing agency.

(i) If the animal requires veterinary care and the humane society or public agency is not assured, within 14 days of the seizure of the animal, that the owner will provide the necessary care, the animal shall not be returned to its owner and shall be deemed to have been abandoned and may be humanely euthanized or otherwise properly disposed of by the seizing agency. A veterinarian may humanely euthanize an impounded animal without regard to the prescribed holding period when it has been determined that the animal has incurred severe injuries or is incurably crippled. A veterinarian also may immediately humanely euthanize an impounded animal afflicted with a serious contagious disease unless the owner or the owner's agent immediately authorizes treatment of the animal by a veterinarian at the expense of the owner or agent.

(j) No animal properly seized under this section or pursuant to a search warrant shall be returned to its owner until the owner can demonstrate to the satisfaction of the seizing agency or hearing officer that the owner can and will provide the necessary care for the animal.

(k)

(1) In the case of cats and dogs, before the final disposition of any criminal charges, the seizing agency or prosecuting attorney may file a petition in a criminal action requesting that, before that final disposition, the court issue an order forfeiting the animal to the city, county, or seizing agency. The petitioner shall serve a true copy of the petition upon the defendant and the prosecuting attorney.

(2) Upon receipt of the petition, the court shall set a hearing on the petition. The hearing shall be conducted within 14 days after the filing of the petition, or as soon as practicable.

(3) The petitioner shall have the burden of establishing beyond a reasonable doubt that, even in the event of an acquittal of the criminal charges, the owner will not legally be permitted to retain the animal in question. If the court finds that the petitioner has met its burden, the court shall order the immediate forfeiture of the animal as sought by the petition.

(4) Nothing in this subdivision is intended to authorize a seizing agency or prosecuting attorney to file a petition to determine an owner's ability to legally retain an animal pursuant to paragraph (3) of subdivision (l) if a petition has previously been filed pursuant to this subdivision.

(l)

(1) Upon the conviction of a person charged with a violation of this section, or Section 597 or 597a, all animals lawfully seized and impounded with respect to the violation shall be adjudged by the court to be forfeited and shall thereupon be transferred to the impounding officer or appropriate public entity for proper adoption or other disposition. A person convicted of a violation of this section shall be personally liable to the seizing agency for all costs of impoundment from the time of seizure to the time of proper disposition. Upon conviction, the court shall order the convicted person to make payment to the appropriate public entity for the costs incurred in the housing, care, feeding, and treatment of the seized or impounded animals. Each person convicted in connection with a particular animal may be held jointly and severally liable for restitution for that particular animal. The payment shall be in addition to any other fine or sentence ordered by the court.

(2) The court may also order, as a condition of probation, that the convicted person be prohibited from owning, possessing, caring for, or residing with, animals of any kind, and require the convicted person to immediately deliver all animals in the convicted person's possession to a designated public entity for adoption or other lawful disposition or provide proof to the court that the person no longer has possession, care, or control of any animals. In the event of the acquittal or final discharge without conviction of the person charged, if the animal is still impounded, the animal has not been previously deemed abandoned pursuant to subdivision (h), the court has not ordered that the animal be forfeited pursuant to subdivision (k), the court shall, on demand, direct the release of seized or impounded animals to the defendant upon a showing of proof of ownership.

(3) Any questions regarding ownership shall be determined in a separate hearing by the court where the criminal case was finally adjudicated and the court shall hear testimony from any persons who may assist the court in determining ownership of the animal. If the owner is determined to be unknown or the owner is prohibited or unable to retain possession of the animals for any reason, the court shall order the animals to be released to the appropriate public entity for adoption or other lawful disposition. This section is not intended to cause the release of any animal, bird, reptile, amphibian, or fish seized or impounded pursuant to any other statute, ordinance, or municipal regulation. This section shall not prohibit the seizure or impoundment of animals as evidence as provided for under any other provision of law.

(m) It shall be the duty of all peace officers, humane society officers, and animal control officers to use all currently acceptable methods of identification, both electronic and otherwise, to determine the lawful owner or caretaker of any seized or impounded animal. It shall also be their duty to make reasonable efforts to notify the owner or caretaker of the whereabouts of the animal and any procedures available for the lawful recovery of the animal and, upon the owner's and caretaker's initiation of recovery procedures, retain custody of the animal for a reasonable period of time to allow for completion of the recovery process. Efforts to locate or contact the owner or caretaker and communications with persons claiming to be the owner or caretaker shall be recorded and maintained and be made available for public inspection.

Amended by Stats 2019 ch 7 (AB 1553),s 19, eff. 1/1/2020.
Amended by Stats 2012 ch 598 (SB 1500),s 1.5, eff. 1/1/2013.
Amended by Stats 2012 ch 594 (SB 1162),s 1, eff. 9/26/2012.
Amended by Stats 2011 ch 553 (AB 1117),s 1, eff. 1/1/2012.

Section 597.2 - Abandonment or voluntary relinquishment of equine

(a) It shall be the duty of an officer of an animal shelter, a humane society, or an animal regulation department of a public agency to assist in a case involving the abandonment or voluntary relinquishment of an equine by the equine's owner. This section does not require an animal shelter, a humane society, or an animal regulation department of a public agency to take actual possession of the equine.

(b) If an animal shelter, a humane society, or an animal regulation department of a public agency sells an equine at a private or public auction or sale, it shall set the minimum bid for the sale of the equine at a price above the current slaughter price of the equine.

(c)

(1) This section does not prohibit an animal shelter, a humane society, or an animal regulation department of a public agency from placing an equine through an adoption program at an adoption fee that may be set below current slaughter price.

(2) A person adopting an equine under paragraph (1) shall submit a written statement declaring that the person is adopting the equine for personal use and not for purposes of resale, resale for slaughter, or holding or transporting the equine for slaughter.

Amended by Stats 2019 ch 7 (AB 1553),s 20, eff. 1/1/2020.

Repealed by Stats 2001 ch 854 (SB 205), s 33, eff. 1/1/2002.

Added by Stats 2000 ch 1061 (AB 2479), s 1, eff. 1/1/2001.

Section 597.3 - Live animal market

(a) Every person who operates a live animal market shall do all of the following:

(1) Provide that no animal will be dismembered, flayed, cut open, or have its skin, scales, feathers, or shell removed while the animal is still alive.

(2) Provide that no live animals will be confined, held, or displayed in a manner that results, or is likely to result, in injury, starvation, dehydration, or suffocation.

(b) As used in this section:

(1) "Animal" means frogs, turtles, and birds sold for the purpose of human consumption, with the exception of poultry.

(2) "Live animal market" means a retail food market where, in the regular course of business, animals are stored alive and sold to consumers for the purpose of human consumption.

(c) Any person who fails to comply with any requirement of subdivision (a) shall for the first violation, be given a written warning in a written language that is understood by the person receiving the warning. A second or subsequent violation of subdivision (a) shall be an infraction, punishable by a fine of not less than two hundred fifty dollars ($250), nor more than one thousand dollars ($1,000). However, a fine paid for a second violation of subdivision (a) shall be deferred for six months if a course is available that is administered by a state or local agency on state law and local ordinances relating to live animal markets. If the defendant successfully completes that course within six months of entry of judgment, the fine shall be waived. The state or local agency may charge the participant a fee to take the course, not to exceed one hundred dollars ($100).

Added by renumbering Section 597.2 (as added by Stats. 2000, Ch. 1061) by Stats. 2001, Ch. 854, Sec. 33. Effective January 1, 2002.

Section 597.4 - Unlawful acts related to sale of gift of live animals

(a) It shall be unlawful for any person to willfully do either of the following:

(1) Sell or give away as part of a commercial transaction a live animal on any street, highway, public right-of-way, parking lot, carnival, or boardwalk.

(2) Display or offer for sale, or display or offer to give away as part of a commercial transaction, a live animal, if the act of selling or giving away the live animal is to occur on any street, highway, public right-of-way, parking lot, carnival, or boardwalk.

(b)

(1) A person who violates this section for the first time shall be guilty of an infraction punishable by a fine not to exceed two hundred fifty dollars ($250).

(2) A person who violates this section for the first time and by that violation either causes or permits any animal to suffer or be injured, or causes or permits any animal to be placed in a situation in which its life or health may be endangered, shall be guilty of a misdemeanor.

(3) A person who violates this section for a second or subsequent time shall be guilty of a misdemeanor.

(c) A person who is guilty of a misdemeanor violation of this section shall be punishable by a fine not to exceed one thousand dollars ($1,000) per violation. The court shall weigh the gravity of the violation in setting the fine.

(d) A notice describing the charge and the penalty for a violation of this section may be issued by any peace officer, animal control officer, as defined in Section 830.9, or humane officer qualified pursuant to Section 14502 or 14503 of the Corporations Code.

(e) This section shall not apply to the following:

(1) Events held by 4-H Clubs, Junior Farmers Clubs, or Future Farmers Clubs.

(2) The California Exposition and State Fair, district agricultural association fairs, or county fairs.

(3) Stockyards with respect to which the Secretary of the United States Department of Agriculture has posted notice that the stockyards are regulated by the federal Packers and Stockyards Act, 1921 (7 U.S.C. Sec. 181 et seq.).

(4) The sale of cattle on consignment at any public cattle sales market, the sale of sheep on consignment at any public sheep sales market, the sale of swine on consignment at any public swine sales market, the sale of goats on consignment at any public goat sales market, and the sale of equines on consignment at any public equine sales market.

(5) Live animal markets regulated under Section 597.3.

(6) A public animal control agency or shelter, society for the prevention of cruelty to animals shelter, humane society shelter, or rescue group regulated under Division 14 (commencing with Section 30501) of the Food and Agricultural Code. For purposes of this section, "rescue group" is a not-for-profit entity whose primary purpose is the placement of dogs, cats, or other animals that have been removed from a public animal control agency or shelter, society for the prevention of cruelty to animals shelter, or humane society shelter, or that have been surrendered or relinquished to the entity by the previous owner.

(7) The sale of fish or shellfish, live or dead, from a fishing vessel or registered aquaculture facility, at a pier or wharf, or at a farmer's market by any licensed commercial fisherman or an owner or employee of a registered aquaculture facility to the public for human consumption.

(8) A cat show, dog show, or bird show, provided that all of the following circumstances exist:

(A) The show is validly permitted by the city or county in which the show is held.

(B) The show's sponsor or permittee ensures compliance with all federal, state, and local animal welfare and animal control laws.

(C) The participant has written documentation of the payment of a fee for the entry of his or her cat, dog, or bird in the show.

(D) The sale of a cat, dog, or bird occurs only on the premises and within the confines of the show.

(E) The show is a competitive event where the cats, dogs, or birds are exhibited and judged by an established standard or set of ideals established for each breed or species.

(9) A pet store as defined in subdivision (i) of Section 122350 of the Health and Safety Code.

(f) Nothing in this section shall be construed to in any way limit or affect the application or enforcement of any other law that protects animals or the rights of consumers, including, but not limited to, the Lockyer-Polanco-Farr Pet Protection Act contained in Article 2 (commencing with Section 122125) of Chapter 5 of Part 6 of Division 105 of the Health and Safety Code, or Sections 597 and 597l of this code.

(g) Nothing in this section limits or authorizes any act or omission that violates Section 597 or 597l, or any other local, state, or federal law. The procedures set forth in this section shall not apply to any civil violation of any other local, state, or federal law that protects animals or the rights of consumers, or to a violation of Section 597 or 597l, which is cited or prosecuted pursuant to one or both of those sections, or to a violation of any other local, state, or federal law that is cited or prosecuted pursuant to that law.

Amended by Stats 2012 ch 162 (SB 1171),s 125, eff. 1/1/2013.

Added by Stats 2011 ch 131 (SB 917),s 2, eff. 1/1/2012.

Section 597.5 - Unlawful acts related to fighting of dogs

(a) Any person who does any of the following is guilty of a felony and is punishable by imprisonment pursuant to subdivision (h) of Section 1170 for 16 months, or two or three years, or by a fine not to exceed fifty thousand dollars ($50,000), or by both that fine and imprisonment:

(1) Owns, possesses, keeps, or trains any dog, with the intent that the dog shall be engaged in an exhibition of fighting with another dog.

(2) For amusement or gain, causes any dog to fight with another dog, or causes any dogs to injure each other.

(3) Permits any act in violation of paragraph (1) or (2) to be done on any premises under his or her charge or control, or aids or abets that act.

(b) Any person who is knowingly present, as a spectator, at any place, building, or tenement where preparations are being made for an exhibition of the fighting of dogs, with the intent to be present at those preparations, or is knowingly present at that exhibition or at any other fighting or injuring as described in paragraph (2) of subdivision (a), with the intent to be present at that exhibition, fighting, or injuring, is guilty of an offense punishable by imprisonment in a county jail not to exceed one year, or by a fine not to exceed five thousand dollars ($5,000), or by both that imprisonment and fine.

(c) Nothing in this section shall prohibit any of the following:

(1) The use of dogs in the management of livestock, as defined by Section 14205 of the Food and Agricultural Code, by the owner of the livestock or his or her employees or agents or other persons in lawful custody thereof.

(2) The use of dogs in hunting as permitted by the Fish and Game Code, including, but not limited to, Sections 4002 and 4756, and by the rules and regulations of the Fish and Game Commission.

(3) The training of dogs or the use of equipment in the training of dogs for any purpose not prohibited by law.

Amended by Stats 2011 ch 39 (AB 117),s 68, eff. 6/30/2011.

Amended by Stats 2011 ch 15 (AB 109),s 411, eff. 4/4/2011, but operative no earlier than October 1, 2011, and only upon creation of a community corrections grant program to assist in implementing this act and upon an appropriation to fund the grant program.

Amended by Stats 2010 ch 328 (SB 1330),s 156, eff. 1/1/2011.

Amended by Stats 2009 ch 225 (AB 242),s 1, eff. 1/1/2010.

Section 597.6 - Declawing of cat

(a)

(1) No person may perform, or otherwise procure or arrange for the performance of, surgical claw removal, declawing, onychectomy, or tendonectomy on any cat that is a member of an exotic or native wild cat species, and shall not otherwise alter such a cat's toes, claws, or paws to prevent the normal function of the cat's toes, claws, or paws.

(2) This subdivision does not apply to a procedure performed solely for a therapeutic purpose.

(b) Any person who violates this section is guilty of a misdemeanor punishable by imprisonment in a county jail for a period not to exceed one year, by a fine of ten thousand dollars ($10,000), or by both that imprisonment and fine.

(c) For purposes of this section, the following terms have the following meanings:

(1) "Declawing" and "onychectomy" mean any surgical procedure in which a portion of the animal's paw is amputated in order to remove the animal's claws.

(2) "Tendonectomy" means a procedure in which the tendons to an animal's limbs, paws, or toes are cut or modified so that the claws cannot be extended.

(3) "Exotic or native wild cat species" include all members of the taxonomic family Felidae, except domestic cats (Felis catus or Felis domesticus) or hybrids of wild and domestic cats that are greater than three generations removed from an exotic or native cat. "Exotic or native wild cat species" include, but are not limited to, lions, tigers, cougars, leopards, lynxes, bobcats, caracals, ocelots, margays, servals, cheetahs, snow leopards, clouded leopards, jungle cats, leopard cats, and jaguars, or any hybrid thereof.

(4) "Therapeutic purpose" means for the purpose of addressing an existing or recurring infection, disease, injury, or abnormal condition in the claw that jeopardizes the cat's health, where addressing the infection, disease, injury, or abnormal condition is a medical necessity.

Added by Stats 2004 ch 876 (AB 1857), s 1, eff. 1/1/2005.

Section 597.7 - Unlawful leaving of animal in unattended motor vehicle

(a) A person shall not leave or confine an animal in any unattended motor vehicle under conditions that endanger the health or well-being of an animal due to heat, cold, lack of adequate ventilation, or lack of food or water, or other circumstances that could reasonably be expected to cause suffering, disability, or death to the animal.

(b)

(1) This section does not prevent a person from taking reasonable steps that are necessary to remove an animal from a motor vehicle if the person holds a reasonable belief that the animal's safety is in immediate danger from heat, cold, lack of adequate ventilation, lack of food or water, or other circumstances that could reasonably be expected to cause suffering, disability, or death to the animal.

(2) A person who removes an animal from a vehicle in accordance with paragraph (1) is not criminally liable for actions taken reasonably and in good faith if the person does all of the following:

(A) Determines the vehicle is locked or there is otherwise no reasonable manner for the animal to be removed from the vehicle.

(B) Has a good faith belief that forcible entry into the vehicle is necessary because the animal is in imminent danger of suffering harm if it is not immediately removed from the vehicle, and, based upon the circumstances known to the person at the time, the belief is a reasonable one.

(C) Has contacted a local law enforcement agency, the fire department, animal control, or the "911" emergency service prior to forcibly entering the vehicle.

(D) Remains with the animal in a safe location, out of the elements but reasonably close to the vehicle, until a peace officer, humane officer, animal control officer, or another emergency responder arrives.

(E) Used no more force to enter the vehicle and remove the animal from the vehicle than was necessary under the circumstances.

(F) Immediately turns the animal over to a representative from law enforcement, animal control, or another emergency responder who responds to the scene.

(c) Unless the animal suffers great bodily injury, a first conviction for violation of this section is punishable by a fine not exceeding one hundred dollars ($100) per animal. If the animal suffers great bodily injury, a violation of this section is punishable by a fine not exceeding five hundred dollars ($500), imprisonment in a county jail not exceeding six months, or by both a fine and imprisonment. Any subsequent violation of this section, regardless of injury to the animal, is also punishable by a fine not exceeding five hundred dollars ($500), imprisonment in a county jail not exceeding six months, or by both a fine and imprisonment.

(d)

(1) This section does not prevent a peace officer, firefighter, humane officer, animal control officer, or other emergency responder from removing an animal from a motor vehicle if the animal's safety appears to be in immediate danger from heat, cold, lack of adequate ventilation, lack of food or water, or other circumstances that could reasonably be expected to cause suffering, disability, or death to the animal.

(2) A peace officer, firefighter, humane officer, animal control officer, or other emergency responder who removes an animal from a motor vehicle, or who takes possession of an animal that has been removed from a motor vehicle, shall take it to an animal shelter or other place of safekeeping or, if the officer deems necessary, to a veterinary hospital for treatment. The owner of the animal removed from the vehicle may be required to pay for charges that have accrued for the maintenance, care, medical treatment, or impoundment of the animal.

(3) A peace officer, firefighter, humane officer, animal control officer, or other emergency responder is authorized to take all steps that are reasonably necessary for the removal of an animal from a motor vehicle, including, but not limited to, breaking into the motor vehicle, after a reasonable effort to locate the owner or other person responsible.

(4) A peace officer, firefighter, humane officer, animal control officer, or other emergency responder who removes an animal from a motor vehicle or who receives an animal rescued from a vehicle from another person shall, in a secure and conspicuous location on or within the motor vehicle, leave written notice bearing his or her name and office, and the address of the location where the animal can be claimed. The animal may be claimed by the owner only after payment of all charges that have accrued for the maintenance, care, medical treatment, or impoundment of the animal.

(5) Except as provided in subdivision (b), this section does not affect in any way existing liabilities or immunities in current law, or create any new immunities or liabilities.

(e) Nothing in this section shall preclude prosecution under both this section and Section 597 or any other provision of law, including city or county ordinances.

(f) Nothing in this section shall be deemed to prohibit the transportation of horses, cattle, pigs, sheep, poultry, or other agricultural animals in motor vehicles designed to transport such animals for agricultural purposes.

Amended by Stats 2016 ch 554 (AB 797),s 2, eff. 1/1/2017.

Added by Stats 2006 ch 431 (SB 1806),s 2, eff. 1/1/2007.

Section 597.9 - Unlawful ownership, possession, or custody of animal after conviction

(a) Except as provided in subdivision (c) or (d), a person who has been convicted of a misdemeanor violation of Section 286.5, subdivision (a) or (b) of Section 597, or Section 597a, 597b, 597h, 597j, 597s, or 597.1, and who, within five years after the conviction, owns, possesses, maintains, has custody of, resides with, or cares for any animal is guilty of a public offense, punishable by a fine of one thousand dollars ($1,000).

(b) Except as provided in subdivision (c) or (d), a person who has been convicted of a felony violation of subdivision (a) or (b) of Section 597, or Section 597b or 597.5, and who, within 10 years after the conviction, owns, possesses, maintains, has custody of, resides with, or cares for any animal is guilty of a public offense, punishable by a fine of one thousand dollars ($1,000).

(c)

(1) In cases of owners of livestock, as defined in Section 14205 of the Food and Agricultural Code, a court may, in the interest of justice, exempt a defendant from the injunction required under subdivision (a) or (b), as it would apply to livestock, if the defendant files a petition with the court to establish, and does establish by a preponderance of the evidence, that the imposition of the provisions of this section would result in substantial or undue economic hardship to the defendant's livelihood and that the defendant has the ability to properly care for all livestock in their possession.

(2) Upon receipt of a petition from the defendant, the court shall set a hearing to be conducted within 30 days after the filing of the petition. The petitioner shall serve a copy of the petition upon the prosecuting attorney 10 calendar days prior to the requested hearing.

The court shall grant the petition for exemption from subdivision (a) or (b) unless the prosecuting attorney shows by a preponderance of the evidence that either or both of the criteria for exemption under this subdivision are untrue.

(d)

(1) A defendant may petition the court to reduce the duration of the mandatory ownership prohibition. Upon receipt of a petition from the defendant, the court shall set a hearing to be conducted within 30 days after the filing of the petition. The petitioner shall serve a copy of the petition upon the prosecuting attorney 10 calendar days prior to the requested hearing. At the hearing, the petitioner shall have the burden of establishing by a preponderance of the evidence all of the following:

(A) The petitioner does not present a danger to animals.

(B) The petitioner has the ability to properly care for all animals in their possession.

(C) The petitioner has successfully completed all classes or counseling ordered by the court.

(2) If the petitioner has met their burden, the court may reduce the mandatory ownership prohibition and may order that the defendant comply with reasonable and unannounced inspections by animal control agencies or law enforcement.

(e) An animal shelter administered by a public animal control agency, a humane society, or any society for the prevention of cruelty to animals, and an animal rescue or animal adoption organization may ask a person who is attempting to adopt an animal from that entity whether the person is prohibited from owning, possessing, maintaining, having custody of, or residing with an animal pursuant to this section.

Amended by Stats 2019 ch 613 (AB 611),s 3, eff. 1/1/2020.

Amended by Stats 2018 ch 877 (AB 2774),s 1, eff. 1/1/2019.

Amended by Stats 2012 ch 598 (SB 1500),s 2, eff. 1/1/2013.

Added by Stats 2011 ch 553 (AB 1117),s 2, eff. 1/1/2012.

Section 597a - Cruelty to domestic animal

Whoever carries or causes to be carried in or upon any vehicle or otherwise any domestic animal in a cruel or inhuman manner, or knowingly and willfully authorizes or permits it to be subjected to unnecessary torture, suffering, or cruelty of any kind, is guilty of a misdemeanor; and whenever any such person is taken into custody therefor by any officer, such officer must take charge of such vehicle and its contents, together with the horse or team attached to such vehicle, and deposit the same in some place of custody; and any necessary expense incurred for taking care of and keeping the same, is a lien thereon, to be paid before the same can be lawfully recovered; and if such expense, or any part thereof, remains unpaid, it may be recovered, by the person incurring the same, of the owner of such domestic animal, in an action therefor.

Added by Stats. 1905, Ch. 519.

Section 597b - Unlawful fighting of animals

(a) Except as provided in subdivisions (b) and (c), any person who, for amusement or gain, causes any bull, bear, or other animal, not including any dog, to fight with like kind of animal or creature, or causes any animal, including any dog, to fight with a different kind of animal or creature, or with any human being, or who, for amusement or gain, worries or injures any bull, bear, dog, or other animal, or causes any bull, bear, or other animal, not including any dog, to worry or injure each other, or any person who permits the same to be done on any premises under his or her charge or control, or any person who aids or abets the fighting or worrying of an animal or creature, is guilty of a misdemeanor punishable by imprisonment in a county jail for a period not to exceed one year, by a fine not to exceed ten thousand dollars ($10,000), or by both that imprisonment and fine.

(b) Any person who, for amusement or gain, causes any cock to fight with another cock or with a different kind of animal or creature or with any human being; or who, for amusement or gain, worries or injures any cock, or causes any cock to worry or injure another animal; and any person who permits the same to be done on any premises under his or her charge or control, and any person who aids or abets the fighting or worrying of any cock is guilty of a misdemeanor punishable by imprisonment in a county jail for a period not to exceed one year, or by a fine not to exceed ten thousand dollars ($10,000), or by both that imprisonment and fine.

(c) A second or subsequent conviction of this section is a misdemeanor or a felony punishable by imprisonment in a county jail for a period not to exceed one year or the state prison for 16 months, two, or three years, by a fine not to exceed twenty-five thousand dollars ($25,000), or by both that imprisonment and fine, except in unusual circumstances in which the interests of justice would be better served by the imposition of a lesser sentence.

(d) For the purposes of this section, aiding and abetting a violation of this section shall consist of something more than merely being present or a spectator at a place where a violation is occurring.

Amended by Stats 2012 ch 133 (SB 1145),s 1, eff. 1/1/2013.

Amended by Stats 2006 ch 430 (SB 1349),s 2, eff. 1/1/2007.

Amended by Stats 2004 ch 183 (AB 3082), s 269, eff. 1/1/2005.

Amended by Stats 2003 ch 256 (SB 732), s 1, eff. 1/1/2004.

Section 597c - Spectator at exhibition of animal fighting

Any person who is knowingly present as a spectator at any place, building, or tenement for an exhibition of animal fighting, or who is knowingly present at that exhibition or is knowingly present where preparations are being made for the acts described in subdivision (a) or (b) of Section 597b, is guilty of a misdemeanor punishable by imprisonment in a county jail for a period not to exceed six months, or by a fine of five thousand dollars ($5,000), or by both that imprisonment and fine.

Amended by Stats 2012 ch 133 (SB 1145),s 2, eff. 1/1/2013.

Added by Stats 2006 ch 430 (SB 1349),s 4, eff. 1/1/2007.

Amended by Stats 2004 ch 183 (AB 3082), s 270, eff. 1/1/2005.

Amended by Stats 2003 ch 256 (SB 732), s 2, eff. 1/1/2004.

Section 597d - Entry of place where there is exhibition of fighting of birds or animals by peace officer

Any sheriff, police, or peace officer, or officer qualified as provided in Section 14502 of the Corporations Code, may enter any place, building, or tenement, where there is an exhibition of the fighting of birds or animals, or where preparations are being made for such an exhibition, and, without a warrant, arrest all persons present.

Amended by Stats. 1997, Ch. 598, Sec. 11. Effective January 1, 1998.

Section 597e - Supply of food and water to impounded domestic animal

Any person who impounds, or causes to be impounded in any animal shelter, any domestic animal, shall supply it during confinement with a sufficient quantity of good and wholesome food and water, and in default thereof, is guilty of a misdemeanor. In case any domestic animal is at any time so impounded and continues to be without necessary food and water for more than 12 consecutive hours, it is lawful for any person, from time to time, as may be deemed necessary, to enter into and upon any animal shelter in which the animal is confined, and supply it with necessary food and water so long as it remains so confined. That person is not liable for the entry and may collect the reasonable cost of the food and water from the owner of the animal, and the animal is subject to enforcement of a money judgment for the reasonable cost of food and water.

Amended by Stats 2019 ch 7 (AB 1553),s 21, eff. 1/1/2020.

Section 597f - [Repealed]

Repealed by Stats 2021 ch 434 (SB 827),s 4, eff. 1/1/2022.

Amended by Stats 2019 ch 7 (AB 1553),s 22, eff. 1/1/2020.

Repealed by Stats 2019 ch 256 (SB 781),s 8, eff. 1/1/2020.

Section 597g - Poling of horse

(a) Poling a horse is a method of training horses to jump which consists of (1) forcing, persuading, or enticing a horse to jump in such manner that one or more of its legs will come in contact with an obstruction consisting of any kind of wire, or a pole, stick, rope or other object with brads, nails, tacks or other sharp points imbedded therein or attached thereto or (2) raising, throwing or moving a pole, stick, wire, rope or other object, against one or more of the legs of a horse while it is jumping an obstruction so that the horse, in either case, is induced to raise such leg or legs higher in order to clear the obstruction. Tripping a horse is an act that consists of the use of any wire, pole, stick, rope, or other object or apparatus whatsoever to cause a horse to fall or lose its balance. The poling or tripping of any horse is unlawful and any person violating the provisions of this section is guilty of a misdemeanor.

(b) It is a misdemeanor for any person to intentionally trip or fell an equine by the legs by any means whatsoever for the purposes of entertainment or sport.

(c) This section does not apply to the lawful laying down of a horse for medical or identification purposes, nor shall the section be construed as condemning or limiting any cultural or historical activities, except those prohibited herein.

Amended by Stats. 1994, 1st Ex. Sess., Ch. 8, Sec. 1. Effective November 30, 1994.

Section 597h - Unlawful attachment of animal to machine or device for purpose of being pursued by dogs

(a) It shall be unlawful for any person to tie or attach or fasten any live animal to any machine or device propelled by any power for the purpose of causing that animal to be pursued by a dog or dogs.

(b) Any person violating any of the provisions of this section shall be guilty of a misdemeanor punishable by a fine of two thousand five hundred dollars ($2,500) or by imprisonment in a county jail not exceeding six months, or by both that imprisonment and fine.

Amended by Stats 2011 ch 562 (SB 425),s 2, eff. 1/1/2012.

Section 597i - Unlawful manufacture, buying, selling, or possession of gaffs or slashers

(a) It shall be unlawful for anyone to manufacture, buy, sell, barter, exchange, or have in his or her possession any of the implements commonly known as gaffs or slashers, or any other sharp implement designed to be attached in place of the natural spur of a gamecock or other fighting bird.

(b) Any person who violates any of the provisions of this section is guilty of a misdemeanor punishable by imprisonment in a county jail for a period not to exceed one year, by a fine not to exceed ten thousand dollars ($10,000), or by both that imprisonment and fine and upon conviction thereof shall, in addition to any judgment or sentence imposed by the court, forfeit possession or ownership of those implements.

Amended by Stats 2012 ch 133 (SB 1145),s 3, eff. 1/1/2013.

Amended by Stats 2003 ch 256 (SB 732), s 3, eff. 1/1/2004.

Section 597j - Unlawful possession, keeping, or training of bird or other animal for fighting

(a) Any person who owns, possesses, keeps, or trains any bird or other animal with the intent that it be used or engaged by himself or herself, by his or her vendee, or by any other person in an exhibition of fighting as described in Section 597b is guilty of a misdemeanor punishable by imprisonment in a county jail for a period not to exceed one year, by a fine not to exceed ten thousand dollars ($10,000), or by both that imprisonment and fine.

(b) This section shall not apply to an exhibition of fighting of a dog with another dog.

(c) A second or subsequent conviction of this section is a misdemeanor punishable by imprisonment in a county jail for a period not to exceed one year or by a fine not to exceed twenty-five thousand dollars ($25,000), or by both that imprisonment and fine, except in unusual circumstances in which the interests of justice would be better served by the imposition of a lesser sentence.

Amended by Stats 2012 ch 133 (SB 1145),s 4, eff. 1/1/2013.

Amended by Stats 2006 ch 430 (SB 1349),s 5, eff. 1/1/2007.

Amended by Stats 2003 ch 256 (SB 732), s 4, eff. 1/1/2004.

Section 597k - Use of bristle bur, tack bur, or other like device on horse or other animal

Anyone who, having care, custody or control of any horse or other animal, uses what is known as the bristle bur, tack bur, or other like device, by whatsoever name known or designated, on such horse or other animal for any purpose whatsoever, is guilty of a misdemeanor and is punishable by a fine of not less than fifty dollars ($50) nor more than five hundred dollars ($500), or by imprisonment in the county jail for not less than 10 days nor more than 175 days, or by both such fine and imprisonment.

Amended by Stats. 1983, Ch. 1092, Sec. 308. Effective September 27, 1983. Operative January 1, 1984, by Sec. 427 of Ch. 1092.

Section 597l - Unlawful acts of pet shop operator

(a) It shall be unlawful for any person who operates a pet shop to fail to do all of the following:

(1) Maintain the facilities used for the keeping of pet animals in a sanitary condition.

(2) Provide proper heating and ventilation for the facilities used for the keeping of pet animals.

(3) Provide adequate nutrition for, and humane care and treatment of, all pet animals under his or her care and control.

(4) Take reasonable care to release for sale, trade, or adoption only those pet animals that are free of disease or injuries.

(5) Provide adequate space appropriate to the size, weight, and specie of pet animals.

(b)

(1) Sellers of pet animals shall provide buyers of a pet animal with general written recommendations for the generally accepted care of the class of pet animal sold, including recommendations as to the housing, equipment, cleaning, environment, and feeding of the animal. This written information shall be in a form determined by the sellers of pet animals and may include references to Web sites, books, pamphlets, videos, and compact discs.

(2) If a seller of pet animals distributes material prepared by a third party, the seller shall not be liable for damages caused by any erroneous information in that material unless a reasonable person exercising ordinary care should have known of the error causing the damage.

(3) This subdivision shall apply to any private or public retail business that sells pet animals to the public and is required to possess a permit pursuant to Section 6066 of the Revenue and Taxation Code.

(4) Charges brought against a seller of pet animals for a first violation of the provisions of this subdivision shall be dismissed if the person charged produces in court satisfactory proof of compliance. A second or subsequent violation is an infraction punishable by a fine not to exceed two hundred fifty dollars ($250).

(c) As used in this section, the following terms have the following meanings:

(1) "Pet animals" means dogs, cats, monkeys and other primates, rabbits, birds, guinea pigs, hamsters, mice, snakes, iguanas, turtles, and any other species of animal sold or retained for the purpose of being kept as a household pet.

(2) "Pet shop" means every place or premises where pet animals are kept for the purpose of either wholesale or retail sale. "Pet shop" does not include any place or premises where pet animals are occasionally sold.

(d) Any person who violates any provision of subdivision (a) is guilty of a misdemeanor and is punishable by a fine not exceeding one thousand dollars ($1,000), or by imprisonment in the county jail not exceeding 90 days, or by both that fine and imprisonment.

Amended by Stats 2003 ch 62 (SB 600), s 228, eff. 1/1/2004.

Amended by Stats 2002 ch 710 (SB 1357), s 1, eff. 1/1/2003.

Section 597m - Bullfight exhibitions

It shall be unlawful for any person to promote, advertise, stage, hold, manage, conduct, participate in, engage in, or carry on any bullfight exhibition, any bloodless bullfight contest or exhibition, or any similar contest or exhibition, whether for amusement or gain or otherwise; provided, that nothing herein shall be construed to prohibit rodeos or to prohibit measures necessary to the safety of participants at rodeos.

This section shall not, however, be construed as prohibiting bloodless bullfights, contests, or exhibitions held in connection with religious celebrations or religious festivals.

Any person violating the provisions of this section is guilty of a misdemeanor.

Added by Stats. 1957, Ch. 2243.

Section 597n - Unlawful docking of horse or cattle

(a) Any person who cuts the solid part of the tail of any horse or cattle in the operation known as "docking," or in any other operation performed for the purpose of shortening the tail of any horse or cattle, within the State of California, or procures the same to be done, or imports or brings into this state any docked horse, or horses, or drives, works, uses, races, or deals in any unregistered docked horse, or horses, within the State of California except as provided in Section 597r, is guilty of a misdemeanor.

(b) Subdivision (a) shall not apply to "docking" when the solid part of any cattle's tail must be removed in an emergency for the purpose of saving the cattle's life or relieving the cattle's pain, provided that the emergency treatment is performed consistent with the Veterinary Medicine Practice Act (commencing with Section 4811) of Article 1 of Chapter 11 of Division 2 of the Business and Professions Code.

(c) For the purposes of this section, "cattle" means any animal of the bovine species.

Amended by Stats 2009 ch 344 (SB 135),s 1, eff. 1/1/2010.

Section 597o - Transport of equine in vehicle to slaughter

(a) Any person who transports an equine in a vehicle to slaughter shall meet the following requirements:

(1) The vehicle shall have sufficient clearance to allow the equine to be transported in a standing position with its head in a normal upright position above its withers.

(2) Any ramps and floors in the vehicle shall be covered with a nonskid surface to prevent the equine from slipping.

(3) The vehicle shall provide adequate ventilation to the equine while the equine is being transported.

(4) The sides and overhead of the vehicle shall be constructed to withstand the weight of any equine which may put pressure against the sides or overhead.

(5) Any compartments in the interior of the vehicle shall be constructed of smooth materials and shall contain no protrusions or sharp objects.

(6) The size of the vehicle shall be appropriate for the number of equine being transported and the welfare of the equine shall not be jeopardized by overcrowding.

(7) Stallions shall be segregated during transportation to slaughter.

(8) Diseased, sick, blind, dying, or otherwise disabled equine shall not be transported out of this state.

(9) Any equine being transported shall be able to bear weight on all four feet.

(10) Unweaned foals shall not be transported.

(11) Mares in their last trimester of pregnancy shall not be transported.

(12) The person shall notify a humane officer having jurisdiction 72 hours before loading the equine in order that the humane officer may perform a thorough inspection of the vehicle to determine if all requirements of this section have been satisfied.

(b)

(1) Any person who violates this section is guilty of a misdemeanor and is subject to a fine of one hundred dollars ($100) per equine being transported.

(2) Any person who violates this section for a second or subsequent time is guilty of a misdemeanor and shall be fined five hundred dollars ($500) per equine being transported.

(c) Whenever a person is taken into custody by an officer for a violation of this section, the officer shall take charge of the vehicle and its contents and deposit the property in some place of custody.

(d)

(1) Any necessary expense incurred for taking care of and keeping the property described in subdivision (c) is a lien thereon, to be paid before the property can be lawfully recovered.

(2) If the expense, or any part thereof, remains unpaid, it may be recovered by the person incurring the expense from the owner of the equine in an action therefor.

(e) For the purposes of this section, "equine" means any horse, pony, burro, or mule.

Added by Stats. 1993, Ch. 1183, Sec. 1. Effective January 1, 1994.

Section 597p - Registration of docked horse

Within 30 days after the passage of this act, every owner, or user of any docked horse, within the State of California, shall register his or her docked horse, or horses by filing in the office of the county clerk of the county in which such docked horse, or horses, may then be kept, a certificate, which certificate shall contain the name, or names of the owner, together with his or her post office address, a full description of the color, age, size and the use made of such docked horse, or horses; which certificate shall be signed by the owner, or his, or her agent. The county clerk shall number such certificate consecutively and record the name in a book, or register to be kept for that purpose only; and shall receive as a fee for recording of such certificate, the sum of fifty cents ($0.50), and the clerk shall thereupon issue to such person so registering such horse or horses a certificate containing the facts recited in this section which upon demand shall be exhibited to any peace officer, and the same shall be conclusive evidence of a compliance with the provisions of Section 597n of this code.

Added by renumbering Section 597b (as added by Stats. 1907, Ch. 220) by Stats. 1963, Ch. 372.

Section 597q - Unlawful keeping or use of unregistered docked horse

The driving, working, keeping, racing or using of any unregistered docked horse, or horses, after 60 days after the passage of this act, shall be deemed prima facie evidence of the fact that the party driving, working, keeping, racing or using such unregistered docked horse, or horses, docked the tail of such horse or horses.

Added by renumbering Section 597c (as added by Stats. 1907, Ch. 220) by Stats. 1963, Ch. 372.

Section 597r - Misdemeanor

Any person or persons violating any of the provisions of this act, shall be deemed guilty of a misdemeanor; provided, however, that the provisions of Sections 597n, 597p, and 597q, shall not be applied to persons owning or possessing any docked purebred stallions and mares imported from foreign countries for breeding or exhibition purposes only, as provided by an act of Congress entitled "An act regulating the importation of breeding animals" and approved March 3, 1903, and to docked native-bred stallions and mares brought into this State and used for breeding or exhibition purposes only; and provided further, that a description of each such animal so brought into the State, together with the date of importation and name and address of importer, be filed with the county clerk of the county where such animal is kept, within 30 days after the importation of such animal.

Added by renumbering Section 597d (as added by Stats. 1907, Ch. 220) by Stats. 1963, Ch. 372.

Section 597s - Willful abandonment of animal

(a) Every person who willfully abandons any animal is guilty of a misdemeanor.

(b) This section shall not apply to the release or rehabilitation and release of native California wildlife pursuant to statute or regulations of the California Department of Fish and Game.

EFFECTIVE 1/1/2000. Amended September 2, 1999 (Bill Number: AB 1540) (Chapter 303).

Section 597t - Provision of adequate exercise area for confined animal; access to adequate shelter, food, and water for restricted animal

Every person who keeps an animal confined in an enclosed area shall provide it with an adequate exercise area. If the animal is restricted by a leash, rope, or chain, the leash, rope, or chain shall be affixed in such a manner that it will prevent the animal from becoming entangled or injured and permit the animal's access to adequate shelter, food, and water. Violation of this section constitutes a misdemeanor.

This section shall not apply to an animal which is in transit, in a vehicle, or in the immediate control of a person.

Amended by Stats. 1971, Ch. 243.

Section 597u - Unlawful methods of killing animal

(a) A person, peace officer, officer of a humane society, or officer of an animal shelter or animal regulation department of a public agency shall not kill an animal by using either of the following methods:

(1) Carbon monoxide gas.

(2) Intracardiac injection of a euthanasia agent on a conscious animal, unless the animal is heavily sedated or anesthetized in a humane manner, or comatose, or unless, in light of all the relevant circumstances, the procedure is justifiable.

(b) With respect to the killing of a dog or cat, a person, peace officer, officer of a humane society, or officer of an animal shelter or animal regulation department of a public agency shall not use any of the methods specified in subdivision (a) or any of the following methods:

(1) High-altitude decompression chamber.

(2) Nitrogen gas.

(3) Carbon dioxide gas.

Amended by Stats 2019 ch 7 (AB 1553),s 23, eff. 1/1/2020.

Amended by Stats 2016 ch 105 (AB 2505),s 1, eff. 1/1/2017.

Amended by Stats 2005 ch 652 (AB 1426),s 1, eff. 1/1/2006

Section 597v - Unlawful method of killing newborn dog or cat

No person, peace officer, officer of a humane society, or officer of an animal shelter or animal regulation department of a public agency shall kill any newborn dog or cat whose eyes have not yet opened by any other method than by the use of chloroform vapor or by inoculation of barbiturates.

Amended by Stats 2019 ch 7 (AB 1553),s 24, eff. 1/1/2020.

Section 597x - Unlawful transport of disabled horse, mule, burro, or pony

(a) Notwithstanding Section 18734 of the Food and Agricultural Code or any other provision of law, it is unlawful for any person to sell, attempt to sell, load, cause to be loaded, transport, or attempt to transport any live horse, mule, burro, or pony that is disabled, if the animal is intended to be sold, loaded, or transported for commercial slaughter out of the state.

(b) For the purposes of this section, "disabled animal" includes, but is not limited to, any animal that has broken limbs, is unable to stand and balance itself without assistance, cannot walk, or is severely injured.

(c) A person who violates this section is guilty of a misdemeanor and subject to the same penalties imposed upon a person convicted of a misdemeanor under Section 597a.

Added by Stats. 1993, Ch. 1213, Sec. 1. Effective January 1, 1994.

Section 597y - Misdemeanor

A violation of Section 597u or 597v is a misdemeanor.

Amended by Stats 2011 ch 296 (AB 1023),s 206, eff. 1/1/2012.

Section 597z - Unlawful sale of dog under eight weeks of age

(a)

(1) Except as otherwise authorized under any other provision of law, it shall be a crime, punishable as specified in subdivision (b), for any person to sell one or more dogs under eight weeks of age, unless, prior to any physical transfer of the dog or dogs from the seller to the purchaser, the dog or dogs are approved for sale, as evidenced by written documentation from a veterinarian licensed to practice in California.

(2) For the purposes of this section, the sale of a dog or dogs shall not be considered complete, and thereby subject to the requirements and penalties of this section, unless and until the seller physically transfers the dog or dogs to the purchaser.

(b)

(1) Any person who violates this section shall be guilty of an infraction or a misdemeanor.

(2) An infraction under this section shall be punishable by a fine not to exceed two hundred fifty dollars ($250).

(3) With respect to the sale of two or more dogs in violation of this section, each dog unlawfully sold shall represent a separate offense under this section.

(c) This section shall not apply to any of the following:

(1) An organization, as defined in Section 501(c)(3) of the Internal Revenue Code, or any other organization that provides, or contracts to provide, services as a public animal sheltering agency.

(2) A pet dealer as defined under Article 2 (commencing with Section 122125) of Chapter 5 of Part 6 of Division 105 of the Health and Safety Code.

(3) A public animal control agency or shelter, society for the prevention of cruelty to animals shelter, humane society shelter, or rescue group regulated under Division 14 (commencing with Section 30501) of the Food and Agricultural Code.

Added by Stats 2005 ch 669 (SB 914),s 1, eff. 1/1/2006.

Section 598 - Unlawful acts related to birds within public cemetery

Every person who, within any public cemetery or burying ground, kills, wounds, or traps any bird, or destroys any bird's nest other than swallows' nests, or removes any eggs or young birds from any nest, is guilty of a misdemeanor.

Enacted 1872.

Section 598.1 - Forfeiture

(a) The prosecuting agency in a criminal proceeding in which the defendant has been charged with the commission of any of the crimes listed in subdivision (a) of Section 597.5 or subdivision (b) of Section 597b may, in conjunction with the criminal proceeding, file a petition for forfeiture as provided in subdivision (c). If the prosecuting agency has filed a petition for forfeiture pursuant to subdivision (c) and the defendant is convicted of any of the crimes described in subdivision (a) of Section 597.5 or subdivision (b) of Section 597b, the assets listed in subdivision (b) shall be subject to forfeiture upon proof of the elements of subdivision (b) and in accordance with this section.

(b)

(1) Any property interest, whether tangible or intangible, that was acquired through the commission of any of the crimes listed in subdivision (a) of Section 597.5 or subdivision (b) of Section 597b shall be subject to forfeiture, including both personal and real property, profits, proceeds, and the instrumentalities acquired, accumulated, or used by cockfighting or dogfighting participants, organizers, transporters of animals and equipment, breeders and trainers of fighting birds or fighting dogs, and persons who steal or illegally obtain dogs or other animals for fighting, including bait and sparring animals.

(2) Notwithstanding paragraph (1), the following property shall not be subject to forfeiture under this section:

(A) Property solely owned by a bona fide purchaser for value, who was without knowledge that the property was intended to be used for a purpose which would subject it to forfeiture under this section, or is subject to forfeiture under this section.

(B) Property used as a family residence and owned by two or more inhabitants, one of whom had no knowledge of its unlawful use.

(c)

(1) If the prosecuting agency proceeds under subdivision (a), that agency shall, in conjunction with the criminal proceeding, file a petition for forfeiture with the superior court of the county in which the defendant has been charged with the commission of any of the

crimes listed in subdivision (a) of Section 597.5 or subdivision (b) of Section 597b, that shall allege that the defendant has committed those crimes and the property is forfeitable pursuant to subdivision (a).

(2) The prosecuting agency shall make service of process of a notice regarding that petition upon every individual who may have a property interest in the alleged proceeds, and that notice shall state that any interested party may file a verified claim with the superior court stating the amount of the party's claimed interest and an affirmation or denial of the prosecuting agency's allegation.

(3) If the notices cannot be served by registered mail or personal delivery, the notices shall be published for at least three consecutive weeks in a newspaper of general circulation in the county where the property is located.

(4) If the property alleged to be subject to forfeiture is real property, the prosecuting agency shall, at the time of filing the petition for forfeiture, record a lis pendens in each county in which real property alleged to be subject to forfeiture is located.

(5) The judgment of forfeiture shall not affect the interest of any third party in real property that was acquired prior to the recording of the lis pendens.

(6) All notices shall set forth the time within which a claim of interest in the property seized is required to be filed pursuant to this section.

(d) Any person claiming an interest in the property or proceeds seized may, at any time within 30 days from the date of the first publication of the notice of seizure, or within 30 days after receipt of the actual notice, file with the superior court of the county in which the action is pending a verified claim stating his or her interest in the property or proceeds. A verified copy of the claim shall be given by the claimant to the Attorney General, or the district or city attorney, whichever is the prosecuting agency of the underlying crime.

(e)

(1) If, at the end of the time set forth in subdivision (d), an interested person, other than the defendant, has not filed a claim, the court, upon a motion, shall declare that the person has defaulted upon his or her alleged interest, and that interest shall be subject to forfeiture upon proof of the elements of subdivision (b).

(2) The defendant may admit or deny that the property is subject to forfeiture pursuant to this section. If the defendant fails to admit or deny, or fails to file a claim of interest in the property or proceeds, the court shall enter a response of denial on behalf of the defendant.

(f)

(1) The forfeiture proceeding shall be set for hearing in the superior court in which the underlying criminal offense will be tried.

(2) If the defendant is found guilty of the underlying offense, the issue of forfeiture shall be promptly tried, either before the same jury or before a new jury in the discretion of the court, unless waived by the consent of all parties.

(g) At the forfeiture hearing, the prosecuting agency shall have the burden of establishing beyond a reasonable doubt that the defendant was engaged in any of the crimes described in subdivision (a) of Section 597.5 or subdivision (b) of Section 597b and that the property comes within the provisions of subdivision (b).

(h) Concurrent with, or subsequent to, the filing of the petition, the prosecuting agency may move the superior court for the following pendente lite orders to preserve the status quo of the property alleged in the petition of forfeiture:

(1) An injunction to restrain all interested parties and enjoin them from transferring, encumbering, hypothecating, or otherwise disposing of that property.

(2) Appointment of a receiver to take possession of, care for, manage, and operate the assets and properties so that the property may be maintained and preserved.

(i)

(1) No preliminary injunction may be granted or receiver appointed without notice to the interested parties and a hearing to determine that the order is necessary to preserve the property, pending the outcome of the criminal proceedings, and that there is probable cause to believe that the property alleged in the forfeiture proceedings are proceeds or property interests forfeitable under subdivision (a). However, a temporary restraining order may issue pending that hearing pursuant to the provisions of Section 527 of the Code of Civil Procedure.

(2) Notwithstanding any other provision of law, the court, when granting or issuing these orders may order a surety bond or undertaking to preserve the property interests of the interested parties. The court shall, in making its orders, seek to protect the interest of those who may be involved in the same enterprise as the defendant, but who are not involved in any of the crimes described in subdivision (a) of Section 597.5 or subdivision (b) of Section 597b.

(j) If the trier of fact at the forfeiture hearing finds that the alleged property or proceeds are forfeitable pursuant to subdivision (a), and that the defendant was convicted of a crime listed in subdivision (a) of Section 597.5 or subdivision (b) of Section 597b, the court shall declare that property or proceeds forfeited to the state or local governmental entity, subject to distribution as provided in subdivision (l).

(k)

(1) If the trier of fact at the forfeiture hearing finds that the alleged property is forfeitable pursuant to subdivision (a) but does not find that a person holding a valid lien, mortgage, security interest, or interest under a conditional sales contract acquired that interest with actual knowledge that the property was to be used for a purpose for which forfeiture is permitted, and the amount due to that person is less than the appraised value of the property, that person may pay to the state or the local governmental entity that initiated the forfeiture proceeding the amount of the registered owner's equity, which shall be deemed to be the difference between the appraised value and the amount of the lien, mortgage, security interest, or interest under a conditional sales contract. Upon that payment, the state or local governmental entity shall relinquish all claims to the property.

(2) If the holder of the interest elects not to make that payment to the state or local governmental entity, the property shall be deemed forfeited to the state or local governmental entity.

(3) The appraised value shall be determined as of the date judgment is entered either by agreement between the legal owner and the governmental entity involved, or if they cannot agree, then by a court-appointed appraiser for the county in which the action is brought.

(4) If the amount due to a person holding a valid lien, mortgage, security interest, or interest under a conditional sales contract is less than the value of the property and the person elects not to make payment to the governmental entity, the property shall be sold at

public auction by the Department of General Services or by the local governmental entity which shall provide notice of that sale by one publication in a newspaper published and circulated in the city, community, or locality where the sale is to take place. Proceeds of the sale shall be distributed pursuant to subdivision (l).

(l) Notwithstanding that no response or claim has been filed pursuant to subdivision (d), in all cases where property is forfeited pursuant to this section and is sold by the Department of General Services or a local governmental entity, the property forfeited or the proceeds of the sale shall be distributed by the state or local governmental entity, as follows:

(1) To the bona fide or innocent purchaser, conditional sales vendor, or holder of a valid lien, mortgage, or security interest, if any, up to the amount of his or her interest in the property or proceeds, when the court declaring the forfeiture orders a distribution to that person. The court shall endeavor to discover all those lienholders and protect their interests and may, at its discretion, order the proceeds placed in escrow for a period not to exceed 60 additional days to ensure that all valid claims are received and processed.

(2) To the Department of General Services or local governmental entity for all expenditures made or incurred by it in connection with the sale of the property, including expenditures for any necessary repairs, storage, or transportation of any property seized under this section.

(3) To local nonprofit organizations exempt under Section 501(c)(3) of the Internal Revenue Code, the primary activities of which include ongoing rescue, foster, or other care of animals that are the victims of cockfighting or dogfighting, and to law enforcement entities, including multiagency task forces, that actively investigate and prosecute animal fighting crimes.

(4) Any remaining funds not fully distributed to organizations or entities pursuant to paragraph (3) shall be deposited in an escrow account or restricted fund to be distributed as soon as possible in accordance with paragraph (3).

Amended by Stats 2011 ch 562 (SB 425),s 3, eff. 1/1/2012.

Added by Stats 2009 ch 302 (SB 318),s 2, eff. 1/1/2010.

Section 598a - Unlawful killing of dog or cate for pelt; unlawful import, sale, or buying of pelt

(a) Every person is guilty of a misdemeanor who kills any dog or cat with the sole intent of selling or giving away the pelt of such animal.

(b) Every person is guilty of a misdemeanor who possesses, imports into this state, sells, buys, gives away or accepts any pelt of a dog or cat with the sole intent of selling or giving away the pelt of the dog or cat, or who possesses, imports into this state, sells, buys, gives away, or accepts any dog or cat, with the sole intent of killing or having killed such dog or cat for the purpose of selling or giving away the pelt of such animal.

Added by Stats. 1973, Ch. 778.

Section 598b - Unlawful possession, importation, exportation, sale, buy, gift, or acceptance of carcass

(a) Every person is guilty of a misdemeanor who possesses, imports into, or exports from, this state, sells, buys, gives away, or accepts any carcass or part of any carcass of any animal traditionally or commonly kept as a pet or companion with the intent of using or having another person use any part of that carcass for food.

(b) Every person is guilty of a misdemeanor who possesses, imports into, or exports from, this state, sells, buys, gives away, or accepts any animal traditionally or commonly kept as a pet or companion with the intent of killing or having another person kill that animal for the purpose of using or having another person use any part of the animal for food.

(c) This section shall not be construed to interfere with the production, marketing, or disposal of any livestock, poultry, fish, shellfish, or any other agricultural commodity produced in this state. Nor shall this section be construed to interfere with the lawful killing of wildlife, or the lawful killing of any other animal under the laws of this state pertaining to game animals.

Amended by Stats. 1996, Ch. 381, Sec. 1. Effective January 1, 1997.

Section 598c - Unlawful possession, importation, exportation, sale, purchase, or holding of horse with intent of killing for human consumption

(a) Notwithstanding any other provision of law, it is unlawful for any person to possess, to import into or export from the state, or to sell, buy, give away, hold, or accept any horse with the intent of killing, or having another kill, that horse, if that person knows or should have known that any part of that horse will be used for human consumption.

(b) For purposes of this section, "horse" means any equine, including any horse, pony, burro, or mule.

(c) Violation of this section is a felony punishable by imprisonment in the state prison for 16 months, or two or three years.

(d) It is not the intent of this section to affect any commonly accepted commercial, noncommercial, recreational, or sporting activity that relates to horses.

(e) It is not the intent of this section to affect any existing law that relates to horse taxation or zoning.

Amended by Stats 2011 ch 39 (AB 117),s 68, eff. 6/30/2011.

Amended by Stats 2011 ch 39 (AB 117),s 18, eff. 6/30/2011.

Amended by Stats 2011 ch 15 (AB 109),s 412, eff. 4/4/2011, but operative no earlier than October 1, 2011, and only upon creation of a community corrections grant program to assist in implementing this act and upon an appropriation to fund the grant program.

Section 598d - Unlawful offer for sale of horsemeat for human consumption

(a) Notwithstanding any other provision of law, horsemeat may not be offered for sale for human consumption. No restaurant, cafe, or other public eating place may offer horsemeat for human consumption.

(b) Violation of this section is a misdemeanor punishable by a fine of not more than one thousand dollars ($1,000), or by confinement in jail for not less than 30 days nor more than two years, or by both that fine and confinement.

(c) A second or subsequent offense under this section is punishable by imprisonment in the state prison for not less than two years nor more than five years.

Amended by Stats 2011 ch 39 (AB 117),s 68, eff. 6/30/2011.

Amended by Stats 2011 ch 39 (AB 117),s 19, eff. 6/30/2011.

Amended by Stats 2011 ch 15 (AB 109),s 413, eff. 4/4/2011, but operative no earlier than October 1, 2011, and only upon creation of a community corrections grant program to assist in implementing this act and upon an appropriation to fund the grant program.

Section 599 - Unlawful acts related to live chicks, rabbits, ducklings, or other fowl

Every person is guilty of a misdemeanor who:

(a) Sells or gives away, any live chicks, rabbits, ducklings, or other fowl as a prize for, or as an inducement to enter, any contest, game or other competition or as an inducement to enter a place of amusement or place of business; or

(b) Dyes or otherwise artificially colors any live chicks, rabbits, ducklings or other fowl, or sells, offers for sale, or gives away any live chicks, rabbits, ducklings, or other fowl which has been dyed or artificially colored; or

(c) Maintains or possesses any live chicks, rabbits, ducklings, or other fowl for the purpose of sale or display without adequate facilities for supplying food, water and temperature control needed to maintain the health of such fowl or rabbit; or

(d) Sells, offers for sale, barters, or for commercial purposes gives away, any live chicks, rabbits, ducklings, or other fowl on any street or highway. This section shall not be construed to prohibit established hatchery management procedures or the display, or sale of natural chicks, rabbits, ducklings, or other fowl in proper facilities by dealers, hatcheries, poultrymen, or stores regularly engaged in the business of selling the same.

Amended by Stats. 1967, Ch. 708.

Section 599a - Complaint that dumb animals or birds are being violated in particular building or place

When complaint is made, on oath, to any magistrate authorized to issue warrants in criminal cases, that the complainant believes that any provision of law relating to, or in any way affecting, dumb animals or birds, is being, or is about to be violated in any particular building or place, the magistrate must issue and deliver immediately a warrant directed to any sheriff, police or peace officer or officer of any incorporated association qualified as provided by law, authorizing him to enter and search that building or place, and to arrest any person there present violating, or attempting to violate, any law relating to, or in any way affecting, dumb animals or birds, and to bring that person before some court or magistrate of competent jurisdiction, within the city, city and county, or judicial district within which the offense has been committed or attempted, to be dealt with according to law, and the attempt must be held to be a violation of Section 597.

Amended by Stats. 1996, Ch. 872, Sec. 112. Effective January 1, 1997.

Section 599aa - Arrest; seizure of birds and animals and paraphernalia

(a) Any authorized officer making an arrest under Section 597.5 shall, and any authorized officer making an arrest under Section 597b, 597c, 597j, or 599a may, lawfully take possession of all birds or animals and all paraphernalia, implements, or other property or things used or employed, or about to be employed, in the violation of any of the provisions of this code relating to the fighting of birds or animals that can be used in animal or bird fighting, in training animals or birds to fight, or to inflict pain or cruelty upon animals or birds with respect to animal or bird fighting.

(b)

(1) Upon taking possession, the officer shall inventory the items seized and question the persons present as to the identity of the owner or owners of the items. The inventory list shall identify the location where the items were seized, the names of the persons from whom the property was seized, and the names of any known owners of the property.

(2) Any person claiming ownership or possession of any item shall be provided with a signed copy of the inventory list, which shall identify the seizing officer and the officer's employing agency. If no person claims ownership or possession of the items, a copy of the inventory list shall be left at the location from which the items were seized.

(c) The officer shall file with the magistrate before whom the complaint against the arrested person is made, a copy of the inventory list and an affidavit stating the affiant's basis for the officer's belief that the property and items taken were in violation of this code. On receipt of the affidavit, the magistrate shall order the items seized to be held until the final disposition of any charges filed in the case subject to subdivision (e).

(d) All animals and birds seized shall, at the discretion of the seizing officer, be taken promptly to an appropriate animal storage facility. For purposes of this subdivision, an appropriate animal storage facility is one in which the animals or birds may be stored humanely. However, if an appropriate animal storage facility is not available, the officer may cause the animals or birds used in committing or possessed for the purpose of the alleged offenses to remain at the location at which they were found. In determining whether it is more humane to leave the animals or birds at the location at which they were found than to take the animals or birds to an animal storage facility, the officer shall, at a minimum, consider the difficulty of transporting the animals or birds and the adequacy of the available animal storage facility. When the officer does not seize and transport all animals or birds to a storage facility, the officer shall do both of the following:

(1) Seize a representative sample of animals or birds for evidentiary purposes from the animals or birds found at the site of the alleged offenses. The animals or birds seized as a representative sample shall be transported to an appropriate animal storage facility.

(2) Cause all animals or birds used in committing or possessed for the purpose of the alleged offenses to be banded, tagged, or marked by microchip, and photographed or video recorded for evidentiary purposes.

(e)

(1) If ownership of the seized animals or birds cannot be determined after reasonable efforts, the officer or other person named and designated in the order as custodian of the animals or birds may, after holding the animals and birds for a period of not less than 10 days, petition the magistrate for permission to humanely euthanize or otherwise dispose of the animals or birds. The petition shall be published for three successive days in a newspaper of general circulation. The magistrate shall hold a hearing on the petition not less than 10 days after seizure of the animals or birds, after which the magistrate may order the animals or birds to be humanely euthanized or otherwise disposed of, or to be retained by the officer or person with custody until the conviction or final discharge of the arrested person. No animal or bird may be euthanized or otherwise disposed of until four days after the order.

(2) Paragraph (1) shall apply only to those animals and birds seized under any of the following circumstances:

(A) After having been used in violation of any of the provisions of this code relating to the fighting of birds or animals.

(B) At the scene or site of a violation of any of the provisions of this code relating to the fighting of birds or animals.

(f) Upon the conviction of the arrested person, all property seized shall be adjudged by the court to be forfeited and shall then be, in the case of animals or birds, humanely euthanized or otherwise disposed of, and, in the case of other property, destroyed or otherwise disposed of, as the court may order. Upon the conviction of the arrested person, the court may order the person to make payment to the appropriate public entity for the costs incurred in the housing, care, feeding, and treatment of the animals or birds. Each person convicted in connection with a particular animal or bird, excluding any person convicted as a spectator pursuant to Section 597b or 597c, or subdivision (b) of Section 597.5, may be held jointly and severally liable for restitution pursuant to this subdivision. This payment shall be in addition to any other fine or other sentence ordered by the court. The court shall specify in the order that the public entity shall not enforce the order until the defendant satisfies all other outstanding fines, penalties, assessments, restitution fines, and restitution orders. The court may relieve any convicted person of the obligation to make payment pursuant to this subdivision for good cause but shall state the reasons for that decision in the record. In the event of the acquittal or final discharge without conviction of the arrested person, the court shall, on demand, direct the delivery of the property held in custody to the owner. If the owner is unknown, the court shall order the animals or birds to be humanely euthanized or otherwise disposed of.

Amended by Stats 2019 ch 7 (AB 1553),s 25, eff. 1/1/2020.

Amended by Stats 2009 ch 88 (AB 176),s 72, eff. 1/1/2010.

Section 599b - Definitions

In this title, the word "animal" includes every dumb creature; the words "torment," "torture," and "cruelty" include every act, omission, or neglect whereby unnecessary or unjustifiable physical pain or suffering is caused or permitted; and the words "owner" and "person" include corporations as well as individuals; and the knowledge and acts of any agent of, or person employed by, a corporation in regard to animals transported, owned, or employed by, or in the custody of, the corporation, must be held to be the act and knowledge of the corporation as well as the agent or employee.

Amended by Stats 2002 ch 787 (SB 1798), s 14, eff. 1/1/2003.

Section 599c - Scope of part

No part of this title shall be construed as interfering with any of the laws of this state known as the "game laws," or any laws for or against the destruction of certain birds, nor must this title be construed as interfering with the right to destroy any venomous reptile, or any animal known as dangerous to life, limb, or property, or to interfere with the right to kill all animals used for food, or with properly conducted scientific experiments or investigations performed under the authority of the faculty of a regularly incorporated medical college or university of this state.

Added by Stats. 1905, Ch. 519.

Section 599d - No adoptable or treatable animal should be euthanized

(a) It is the policy of the state that no adoptable animal should be euthanized if it can be adopted into a suitable home. Adoptable animals include only those animals eight weeks of age or older that, at or subsequent to the time the animal is impounded or otherwise taken into possession, have manifested no sign of a behavioral or temperamental defect that could pose a health or safety risk or otherwise make the animal unsuitable for placement as a pet, and have manifested no sign of disease, injury, or congenital or hereditary condition that adversely affects the health of the animal or that is likely to adversely affect the animal's health in the future.

(b) It is the policy of the state that no treatable animal should be euthanized. A treatable animal shall include any animal that is not adoptable but that could become adoptable with reasonable efforts. This subdivision, by itself, shall not be the basis of liability for damages regarding euthanasia.

Added by Stats. 1998, Ch. 752, Sec. 20. Effective January 1, 1999.

Section 599e - Unfit animals

Every animal which is unfit, by reason of its physical condition, for the purpose for which those animals are usually employed, and when there is no reasonable probability of that animal ever becoming fit for the purpose for which it is usually employed, shall be by the owner or lawful possessor of the same, deprived of life within 12 hours after being notified by any peace officer, officer of said society, or employee of an animal shelter or animal regulation department of a public agency who is a veterinarian, to kill the animal, and the owner, possessor, or person omitting or refusing to comply with the provisions of this section shall, upon conviction, be deemed guilty of a misdemeanor, and after that conviction the court or magistrate having jurisdiction of that offense shall order any peace officer, officer of said society, or officer of an animal shelter or animal regulation department of a public agency, to immediately kill that animal; provided, that this shall not apply to the owner of any old or diseased animal keeping the animal on the owner's premises with proper care.

Amended by Stats 2019 ch 7 (AB 1553),s 26, eff. 1/1/2020.

Section 599f - Restrictions on slaughterhouses regarding nonambulatory animals

(a) No slaughterhouse, stockyard, auction, market agency, or dealer shall buy, sell, or receive a nonambulatory animal.

(b) No slaughterhouse shall process, butcher, or sell meat or products of nonambulatory animals for human consumption.

(c) No slaughterhouse shall hold a nonambulatory animal without taking immediate action to humanely euthanize the animal.

(d) No stockyard, auction, market agency, or dealer shall hold a nonambulatory animal without taking immediate action to humanely euthanize the animal or to provide immediate veterinary treatment.

(e) While in transit or on the premises of a stockyard, auction, market agency, dealer, or slaughterhouse, a nonambulatory animal may not be dragged at any time, or pushed with equipment at any time, but shall be moved with a sling or on a stoneboat or other sled-like or wheeled conveyance.

(f) No person shall sell, consign, or ship any nonambulatory animal for the purpose of delivering a nonambulatory animal to a slaughterhouse, stockyard, auction, market agency, or dealer.

(g) No person shall accept a nonambulatory animal for transport or delivery to a slaughterhouse, stockyard, auction, market agency, or dealer.

(h) A violation of this section is subject to imprisonment in a county jail for a period not to exceed one year, or by a fine of not more than twenty thousand dollars ($20,000), or by both that fine and imprisonment.

(i) As used in this section, "nonambulatory" means unable to stand and walk without assistance.

(j) As used in this section, "animal" means live cattle, swine, sheep, or goats.

(k) As used in this section, "humanely euthanize" means to kill by a mechanical, chemical, or electrical method that rapidly and effectively renders the animal insensitive to pain.

Amended by Stats 2009 ch 140 (AB 1164),s 141, eff. 1/1/2010.
Amended by Stats 2008 ch 194 (AB 2098),s 1, eff. 1/1/2009.

Section 600 - Unlawful acts related to horse or dog being used by peace officer

(a) Any person who willfully and maliciously and with no legal justification strikes, beats, kicks, cuts, stabs, shoots with a firearm, administers any poison or other harmful or stupefying substance to, or throws, hurls, or projects at, or places any rock, object, or other substance which is used in such a manner as to be capable of producing injury and likely to produce injury, on or in the path of, a horse being used by, or a dog under the supervision of, a peace officer in the discharge or attempted discharge of his or her duties, or a volunteer who is acting under the direct supervision of a peace officer in the discharge or attempted discharge of his or her assigned volunteer duties, is guilty of a public offense. If the injury inflicted is a serious injury, as described in subdivision (c), the person shall be punished by imprisonment pursuant to subdivision (h) of Section 1170 for 16 months, two or three years, or in a county jail for not exceeding one year, or by a fine not exceeding two thousand dollars ($2,000), or by both a fine and imprisonment. If the injury inflicted is not a serious injury, the person shall be punished by imprisonment in the county jail for not exceeding one year, or by a fine not exceeding one thousand dollars ($1,000), or by both a fine and imprisonment.

(b) Any person who willfully and maliciously and with no legal justification interferes with or obstructs a horse or dog being used by a peace officer in the discharge or attempted discharge of his or her duties, or a volunteer who is acting under the direct supervision of a peace officer in the discharge or attempted discharge of his or her assigned volunteer duties, by frightening, teasing, agitating, harassing, or hindering the horse or dog shall be punished by imprisonment in a county jail for not exceeding one year, or by a fine not exceeding one thousand dollars ($1,000), or by both a fine and imprisonment.

(c) Any person who, in violation of this section, and with intent to inflict that injury or death, personally causes the death, destruction, or serious physical injury including bone fracture, loss or impairment of function of any bodily member, wounds requiring extensive suturing, or serious crippling, of a horse or dog, shall, upon conviction of a felony under this section, in addition and consecutive to the punishment prescribed for the felony, be punished by an additional term of imprisonment pursuant to subdivision (h) of Section 1170 for one year.

(d) Any person who, in violation of this section, and with the intent to inflict that injury, personally causes great bodily injury, as defined in Section 12022.7, to any person not an accomplice, shall, upon conviction of a felony under this section, in addition and consecutive to the punishment prescribed for the felony, be punished by an additional term of imprisonment in the state prison for two years unless the conduct described in this subdivision is an element of any other offense of which the person is convicted or receives an enhancement under Section 12022.7.

(e) A defendant convicted of a violation of this section shall be ordered to make restitution to the agency owning the animal and employing the peace officer, to a volunteer who is acting under the direct supervision of a peace officer who is using his or her horse or supervising his or her dog in the performance of his or her assigned duties, or to the agency that provides, or the individual who provides, veterinary health care coverage or veterinary care for a horse or dog being used by, or under the supervision of, a volunteer who is acting under the direct supervision of a peace officer for any veterinary bills, replacement costs of the animal if it is disabled or killed, and, if applicable, the salary of the peace officer for the period of time his or her services are lost to the agency.

Amended by Stats 2015 ch 201 (AB 794),s 1, eff. 1/1/2016.
Amended by Stats 2011 ch 39 (AB 117),s 68, eff. 6/30/2011.
Amended by Stats 2011 ch 39 (AB 117),s 20, eff. 6/30/2011.
Amended by Stats 2011 ch 15 (AB 109),s 414, eff. 4/4/2011, but operative no earlier than October 1, 2011, and only upon creation of a community corrections grant program to assist in implementing this act and upon an appropriation to fund the grant program.
Amended by Stats 2000 ch 287 (SB 1955), s 9, eff. 1/1/2001.

Section 600.2 - Unlawful acts related to guide, signal, or service dog

(a) It is a crime for a person to permit a dog that is owned, harbored, or controlled by the person to cause injury to, or the death of, a guide, signal, or service dog.

(b) A violation of this section is an infraction punishable by a fine not to exceed two hundred fifty dollars ($250) if the injury or death to a guide, signal, or service dog is caused by the person's failure to exercise ordinary care in the control of the person's dog.

(c) A violation of this section is a misdemeanor if the injury or death to a guide, signal, or service dog is caused by the person's reckless disregard in the exercise of control over the person's dog, under circumstances that constitute such a departure from the conduct of a reasonable person as to be incompatible with a proper regard for the safety and life of a guide, signal, or service dog. A violation of this subdivision is punishable by imprisonment in a county jail not exceeding one year, or by a fine of not less than two thousand five hundred dollars ($2,500) nor more than five thousand dollars ($5,000), or both that fine and imprisonment. The court shall consider the costs ordered pursuant to subdivision (d) when determining the amount of any fines.

(d) A defendant who is convicted of a violation of this section shall be ordered to make restitution to the person with a disability who has custody or ownership of the guide, signal, or service dog for any veterinary bills, replacement costs of the dog if it is disabled or killed, medical or medical-related expenses of the person with a disability, loss of wages or income of the person with a disability, or other reasonable costs deemed appropriate by the court. The costs ordered pursuant to this subdivision shall be paid prior to any fines. The person with the disability may apply for compensation by the California Victim Compensation Board pursuant to Chapter 5 (commencing with Section 13950) of Part 4 of Division 3 of Title 2 of the Government Code, in an amount not to exceed ten thousand dollars ($10,000).

(e) For the purposes of this section, the following definitions apply:

(1) "Guide, signal, or service dog" means a guide dog, signal dog, or service dog, as defined in Section 54.1 of the Civil Code. "Guide, signal, or service dog" also includes a dog enrolled in a training school or program, located in this state, for guide, signal, or service dogs.

(2) "Located in this state" includes the training of a guide, signal, or service dog that occurs in this state, even if the training school or program is located in another state.

(3) "Loss of wages or income" means wages or income that are lost by the person with a disability as a direct result of a violation of this section.

(4) "Replacement costs" means all costs that are incurred in the replacement of the guide, signal, or service dog, including, but not limited to, the training costs for a new dog, if needed, the cost of keeping the now-disabled dog in a kennel while the handler travels to receive the new dog, and, if needed, the cost of the travel required for the handler to receive the new dog.

Amended by Stats 2019 ch 604 (AB 169),s 1, eff. 1/1/2020.
Amended by Stats 2016 ch 31 (SB 836),s 233, eff. 6/27/2016.
Amended by Stats 2014 ch 502 (AB 2264),s 3, eff. 1/1/2015.
Amended by Stats 2004 ch 322 (AB 1801), s 2, eff. 1/1/2005.

Section 600.5 - Causing injury or death to guide, signal, or service dog

(a) A person who intentionally causes injury to, or the death of, a guide, signal, or service dog is guilty of a misdemeanor, punishable by imprisonment in a county jail not exceeding one year, or by a fine not exceeding ten thousand dollars ($10,000), or by both that fine and imprisonment. The court shall consider the costs ordered pursuant to subdivision (b) when determining the amount of any fines.

(b) A defendant who is convicted of a violation of this section shall be ordered to make restitution to the person with a disability who has custody or ownership of the dog for any veterinary bills, replacement costs of the dog if it is disabled or killed, medical or medical-related expenses of the person with a disability, loss of wages or income of the person with a disability, or other reasonable costs deemed appropriate by the court. The costs ordered pursuant to this subdivision shall be paid prior to any fines. The person with the disability may apply for compensation by the California Victim Compensation Board pursuant to Chapter 5 (commencing with Section 13950) of Part 4 of Division 3 of Title 2 of the Government Code, in an amount not to exceed ten thousand dollars ($10,000).

(c) For the purposes of this section, the following definitions apply:

(1) "Guide, signal, or service dog" means a guide dog, signal dog, or service dog, as defined in Section 54.1 of the Civil Code. "Guide, signal, or service dog" also includes a dog enrolled in a training school or program, located in this state, for guide, signal, or service dogs.

(2) "Located in this state" includes the training of a guide, signal, or service dog that occurs in this state, even if the training school or program is located in another state.

(3) "Loss of wages or income" means wages or income that are lost by the person with a disability as a direct result of a violation of this section.

(4) "Replacement costs" means all costs that are incurred in the replacement of the guide, signal, or service dog, including, but not limited to, the training costs for a new dog, if needed, the cost of keeping the now-disabled dog in a kennel while the handler travels to receive the new dog, and, if needed, the cost of the travel required for the handler to receive the new dog.

Amended by Stats 2019 ch 604 (AB 169),s 2, eff. 1/1/2020.
Amended by Stats 2016 ch 31 (SB 836),s 234, eff. 6/27/2016.
Amended by Stats 2014 ch 502 (AB 2264),s 4, eff. 1/1/2015.
Amended by Stats 2004 ch 322 (AB 1801), s 3, eff. 1/1/2005.

Section 600.8 - Court-ordered counseling for certain offenses involving animal cruelty

(a) For a defendant who is granted probation for an offense specified in subdivision (d), the court shall order the defendant to successfully complete counseling, as determined by the court, designed to evaluate and treat behavior or conduct disorders, unless the defendant is ordered to complete treatment as specified in subdivision (b).

(b) The court shall consider whether to order the convicted person to undergo a mental health evaluation by an evaluator chosen by the court. Upon evaluation, if the evaluating mental health professional deems a higher level of treatment than described in subdivision (a) is necessary, the defendant shall complete such treatment as directed by the court.

(c) Counseling or mental health evaluations and any subsequent treatment described in subdivisions (a) and (b) shall be paid for by the defendant. The court shall determine the defendant's ability to pay. If the court finds that the defendant is financially unable to pay, the court may develop a sliding fee schedule based on the defendant's ability to pay. A person who meets the criteria set forth in Section 68632 of the Government Code shall not be responsible for any costs. The counseling specified in this section shall be in addition to any other terms and conditions of probation, including any term of imprisonment and fine.

(d) This section applies to a conviction for any of the following offenses:

(1) Section 286.5.
(2) Section 596.
(3) Section 597.
(4) Section 597.1.
(5) Section 600.5.

(e) A finding that the defendant suffers from a mental disorder, and any progress reports concerning the defendant's treatment, or any other records created pursuant to this section, shall be confidential and shall not be released or used in connection with any civil or criminal proceeding without the defendant's consent.

Added by Stats 2023 ch 546 (AB 829),s 3, eff. 1/1/2024.

Section 601 - Trespass

(a) Any person is guilty of trespass who makes a credible threat to cause serious bodily injury, as defined in subdivision (a) of Section 417.6, to another person with the intent to place that other person in reasonable fear for his or her safety, or the safety of his or her immediate family, as defined in subdivision (l) of Section 646.9, and who does any of the following:

(1) Within 30 days of the threat, unlawfully enters into the residence or real property contiguous to the residence of the person threatened without lawful purpose, and with the intent to execute the threat against the target of the threat.

(2) Within 30 days of the threat, knowing that the place is the threatened person's workplace, unlawfully enters into the workplace of the person threatened and carries out an act or acts to locate the threatened person within the workplace premises without lawful purpose, and with the intent to execute the threat against the target of the threat.

(b) Subdivision (a) shall not apply if the residence, real property, or workplace described in paragraph (1) or (2) that is entered is the residence, real property, or workplace of the person making the threat.

(c) This section shall not apply to any person who is engaged in labor union activities which are permitted to be carried out on the property by the California Agricultural Labor Relations Act, Part 3.5 (commencing with Section 1140) of Division 2 of the Labor Code, or by the National Labor Relations Act.

(d) A violation of this section shall be punishable by imprisonment pursuant to subdivision (h) of Section 1170, or by imprisonment in a county jail not exceeding one year, or by a fine not exceeding two thousand dollars ($2,000), or by both that fine and imprisonment.

Amended by Stats 2011 ch 39 (AB 117),s 68, eff. 6/30/2011.

Amended by Stats 2011 ch 15 (AB 109),s 415, eff. 4/4/2011, but operative no earlier than October 1, 2011, and only upon creation of a community corrections grant program to assist in implementing this act and upon an appropriation to fund the grant program.

Amended by Stats 2005 ch 279 (SB 1107),s 5, eff. 1/1/2006

Section 602 - Misdemeanor

Except as provided in subdivisions (u), (v), and (x), and Section 602.8, a person who willfully commits a trespass by any of the following acts is guilty of a misdemeanor:

(a) Cutting down, destroying, or injuring any kind of wood or timber standing or growing upon the lands of another.

(b) Carrying away any kind of wood or timber lying on those lands.

(c) Maliciously injuring or severing from the freehold of another anything attached to it, or its produce.

(d) Digging, taking, or carrying away from a lot situated within the limits of an incorporated city, without the license of the owner or legal occupant, any earth, soil, or stone.

(e) Digging, taking, or carrying away from land in a city or town laid down on the map or plan of the city, or otherwise recognized or established as a street, alley, avenue, or park, without the license of the proper authorities, any earth, soil, or stone.

(f) Maliciously tearing down, damaging, mutilating, or destroying a sign, signboard, or notice placed upon, or affixed to, a property belonging to the state, or to a city, county, city and county, town, or village, or upon the property of a person, by the state or by an automobile association, which sign, signboard, or notice is intended to indicate or designate a road or a highway, or is intended to direct travelers from one point to another, or relates to fires, fire control, or any other matter involving the protection of the property, or putting up, affixing, fastening, printing, or painting upon any property belonging to the state, or to any city, county, town, or village, or dedicated to the public, or upon the property of a person, without license from the owner, a notice, advertisement, or designation of, or a name for a commodity, whether for sale or otherwise, or a picture, sign, or device intended to call attention to it.

(g) Entering upon lands owned by another person whereon oysters or other shellfish are planted or growing; or injuring, gathering, or carrying away oysters or other shellfish planted, growing, or on any of those lands, whether covered by water or not, without the license of the owner or legal occupant; or damaging, destroying, or removing, or causing to be removed, damaged, or destroyed, any stakes, marks, fences, or signs intended to designate the boundaries and limits of those lands.

(h)

(1) Entering upon lands or buildings owned by another person without the license of the owner or legal occupant, where signs forbidding trespass are displayed, and whereon cattle, goats, pigs, sheep, fowl, or any other animal is being raised, bred, fed, or held for the purpose of food for human consumption; or injuring, gathering, or carrying away any animal being housed on any of those lands, without the license of the owner or legal occupant; or damaging, destroying, or removing, or causing to be removed, damaged, or destroyed, any stakes, marks, fences, or signs intended to designate the boundaries and limits of those lands.

(2) In order for there to be a violation of this subdivision, the trespass signs under paragraph (1) shall be displayed at intervals not less than three per mile along all exterior boundaries and at all roads and trails entering the land.

(3) This subdivision does not preclude prosecution or punishment under any other law, including, but not limited to, grand theft or any provision that provides for a greater penalty or longer term of imprisonment.

(i) Willfully opening, tearing down, or otherwise destroying a fence on the enclosed land of another, or opening a gate, bar, or fence of another and willfully leaving it open without the written permission of the owner, or maliciously tearing down, mutilating, or destroying a sign, signboard, or other notice forbidding shooting on private property.

(j) Building fires upon lands owned by another where signs forbidding trespass are displayed at intervals not greater than one mile along the exterior boundaries and at all roads and trails entering the lands, without first having obtained written permission from the owner of the lands or the owner's agent, or the person in lawful possession.

(k) Entering lands, whether unenclosed or enclosed by fence, for the purpose of injuring property or property rights or with the intention of interfering with, obstructing, or injuring a lawful business or occupation carried on by the owner of the land, the owner's agent, or the person in lawful possession.

(l) Entering lands under cultivation or enclosed by fence, belonging to, or occupied by, another, or entering upon uncultivated or unenclosed lands where signs forbidding trespass are displayed at intervals not less than three to the mile along all exterior boundaries and at all roads and trails entering the lands without the written permission of the owner of the land, the owner's agent, or the person in lawful possession, and any of the following:

(1) Refusing or failing to leave the lands immediately upon being requested by the owner of the land, the owner's agent, or by the person in lawful possession to leave the lands.

(2) Tearing down, mutilating, or destroying a sign, signboard, or notice forbidding trespass or hunting on the lands.

(3) Removing, injuring, unlocking, or tampering with a lock on a gate on or leading into the lands.

(4) Discharging a firearm.

(m) Entering and occupying real property or structures of any kind without the consent of the owner, the owner's agent, or the person in lawful possession.

(n) Driving a vehicle, as defined in Section 670 of the Vehicle Code, upon real property belonging to, or lawfully occupied by, another and known not to be open to the general public, without the consent of the owner, the owner's agent, or the person in lawful possession. This subdivision does not apply to a person described in Section 22350 of the Business and Professions Code who is making a lawful service of process, provided that upon exiting the vehicle, the person proceeds immediately to attempt the service of process, and leaves immediately upon completing the service of process or upon the request of the owner, the owner's agent, or the person in lawful possession.

(o)

(1) Refusing or failing to leave land, real property, or structures belonging to, or lawfully occupied by, another and not open to the general public, upon being requested to leave by (1) a peace officer at the request of the owner, the owner's agent, or the person in lawful possession, and upon being informed by the peace officer that they are acting at the request of the owner, the owner's agent, or the person in lawful possession, or (2) the owner, the owner's agent, or the person in lawful possession. The owner, the owner's agent, or the person in lawful possession shall make a separate request to the peace officer on each occasion when the peace officer's assistance in dealing with a trespass is requested. However, a single request for a peace officer's assistance, made in a notarized writing on a form provided by the law enforcement agency, may be made to cover a limited period of time not to exceed a time period determined by local ordinance or 12 months, whichever is shorter, and identified by specific dates, during which there is a fire hazard or the owner, owner's agent, or person in lawful possession is absent from the premises or property. In addition, a single request for a peace officer's assistance, made in a notarized writing on a form provided by the law enforcement agency, may be made for a period not to exceed 12 months when the premises or property is closed to the public and posted as being closed. The requestor shall inform the law enforcement agency to which the request was made, in writing, when the assistance is no longer desired, before the period not exceeding 12 months expires. However, this subdivision does not apply to persons engaged in lawful labor union activities that are permitted to be carried out on the property by the Alatorre-Zenovich-Dunlap-Berman Agricultural Labor Relations Act of 1975 (Part 3.5 (commencing with Section 1140) of Division 2 of the Labor Code) or by the federal National Labor Relations Act. For purposes of this section, land, real property, or structures owned or operated by a housing authority for tenants, as defined in Section 34213.5 of the Health and Safety Code, constitutes property not open to the general public; however, this subdivision does not apply to persons on the premises who are engaging in activities protected by the California or United States Constitution, or to persons who are on the premises at the request of a resident or management and who are not loitering or otherwise suspected of violating or actually violating a law or ordinance.

(2) A request for a peace officer's assistance shall expire upon transfer of ownership of the property or upon a change in the person in lawful possession.

(3) A request for a peace officer's assistance in dealing with a trespass may be submitted electronically. A local government may accept electronic submissions of requests pursuant to this subdivision.

(p) Entering upon lands declared closed to entry, as provided in Section 4256 of the Public Resources Code, if the closed areas have been posted with notices declaring the closure, at intervals not greater than one mile along the exterior boundaries or along roads and trails passing through the lands.

(q) Refusing or failing to leave a public building of a public agency during those hours of the day or night when the building is regularly closed to the public upon being requested to do so by a regularly employed guard, watchperson, or custodian of the public agency owning or maintaining the building or property, if the surrounding circumstances would indicate to a reasonable person that the person has no apparent lawful business to pursue.

(r) Knowingly skiing in an area or on a ski trail that is closed to the public and that has signs posted indicating the closure.

(s) Refusing or failing to leave a hotel or motel, where the person has obtained accommodations and has refused to pay for those accommodations, upon request of the proprietor or manager and the occupancy is exempt, pursuant to subdivision (b) of Section 1940 of the Civil Code, from Chapter 2 (commencing with Section 1940) of Title 5 of Part 4 of Division 3 of the Civil Code. For purposes of this subdivision, occupancy at a hotel or motel for a continuous period of 30 days or less shall, in the absence of a written agreement to the contrary, or other written evidence of a periodic tenancy of indefinite duration, be exempt from Chapter 2 (commencing with Section 1940) of Title 5 of Part 4 of Division 3 of the Civil Code.

(t)

(1) Entering upon private property, including contiguous land, real property, or structures thereon belonging to the same owner, whether or not generally open to the public, after having been informed by a peace officer at the request of the owner, the owner's agent, or the person in lawful possession, and upon being informed by the peace officer that the peace officer is acting at the request of the owner, the owner's agent, or the person in lawful possession, that the property is not open to the particular person; or refusing or failing to leave the property upon being asked to leave the property in the manner provided in this subdivision.

(2) This subdivision applies only to a person who has been convicted of a crime committed upon the particular private property.

(3) A single notification or request to the person as set forth above shall be valid and enforceable under this subdivision unless and until rescinded by the owner, the owner's agent, or the person in lawful possession of the property.

(4) Where the person has been convicted of a violent felony, as described in subdivision (c) of Section 667.5, this subdivision applies without time limitation. Where the person has been convicted of any other felony, this subdivision applies for no more than five years from the date of conviction. Where the person has been convicted of a misdemeanor, this subdivision applies for no more than two years from the date of conviction. Where the person was convicted for an infraction pursuant to Section 490.1, this subdivision applies for no more than one year from the date of conviction. This subdivision does not apply to convictions for any other infraction.

(u)

(1) Knowingly entering, by an unauthorized person, upon an airport operations area, passenger vessel terminal, or public transit facility if the area has been posted with notices restricting access to authorized personnel only and the postings occur not greater than every 150 feet along the exterior boundary, to the extent, in the case of a passenger vessel terminal, as defined in subparagraph (B) of paragraph (3), that the exterior boundary extends shoreside. To the extent that the exterior boundary of a passenger vessel terminal operations area extends waterside, this prohibition applies if notices have been posted in a manner consistent with the requirements for the shoreside exterior boundary, or in any other manner approved by the captain of the port.

(2) A person convicted of a violation of paragraph (1) shall be punished as follows:

(A) By a fine not exceeding one hundred dollars ($100).

(B) By imprisonment in a county jail not exceeding six months, or by a fine not exceeding one thousand dollars ($1,000), or by both that fine and imprisonment, if the person refuses to leave the airport or passenger vessel terminal after being requested to leave by a peace officer or authorized personnel.

(C) By imprisonment in a county jail not exceeding six months, or by a fine not exceeding one thousand dollars ($1,000), or by both that fine and imprisonment, for a second or subsequent offense.

(3) As used in this subdivision, the following definitions shall control:

(A) "Airport operations area" means that part of the airport used by aircraft for landing, taking off, surface maneuvering, loading and unloading, refueling, parking, or maintenance, where aircraft support vehicles and facilities exist, and which is not for public use or public vehicular traffic.

(B) "Passenger vessel terminal" means only that portion of a harbor or port facility, as described in Section 105.105(a)(2) of Title 33 of the Code of Federal Regulations, with a secured area that regularly serves scheduled commuter or passenger operations. For the purposes of this section, "passenger vessel terminal" does not include any area designated a public access area pursuant to Section 105.106 of Title 33 of the Code of Federal Regulations.

(C) "Public transit facility" has the same meaning as specified in Section 171.7.

(D)

(i) "Authorized personnel" means a person who has a valid airport identification card issued by the airport operator or has a valid airline identification card recognized by the airport operator, or any person not in possession of an airport or airline identification card who is being escorted for legitimate purposes by a person with an airport or airline identification card.

(ii) "Authorized personnel" also means a person who has a valid port identification card issued by the harbor operator, or who has a valid company identification card issued by a commercial maritime enterprise recognized by the harbor operator, or any other person who is being escorted for legitimate purposes by a person with a valid port or qualifying company identification card.

(iii) "Authorized personnel" also means a person who has a valid public transit employee identification card.

(E) "Airport" means a facility whose function is to support commercial aviation.

(v)

(1) Except as permitted by federal law, intentionally avoiding submission to the screening and inspection of one's person and accessible property in accordance with the procedures being applied to control access when entering or reentering a sterile area of an airport, passenger vessel terminal, as defined in subdivision (u), or public transit facility, as defined in Section 171.7, if the sterile area is posted with a statement providing reasonable notice that prosecution may result from a trespass described in this subdivision, is a violation of this subdivision, punishable by a fine of not more than five hundred dollars ($500) for the first offense. A second and subsequent violation is a misdemeanor, punishable by imprisonment in a county jail for a period of not more than one year, or by a fine not to exceed one thousand dollars ($1,000), or by both that fine and imprisonment.

(2) Notwithstanding paragraph (1), if a first violation of this subdivision is responsible for the evacuation of an airport terminal, passenger vessel terminal, or public transit facility and is responsible in any part for delays or cancellations of scheduled flights or departures, it is punishable by imprisonment of not more than one year in a county jail.

(w) Refusing or failing to leave the location of a domestic violence shelter-based program at any time after being requested to leave by a managing authority of the shelter.

(1) A person who is convicted of violating this subdivision shall be punished by imprisonment in a county jail for not more than one year.

(2) The court may order a defendant who is convicted of violating this subdivision to make restitution to a victim of domestic violence in an amount equal to the relocation expenses of the victim of domestic violence and the victim's children if those expenses are incurred as a result of trespass by the defendant at the location of a domestic violence shelter-based program.

(x)

(1) Knowingly entering or remaining in a neonatal unit, maternity ward, or birthing center located in a hospital or clinic without lawful business to pursue therein, if the area has been posted so as to give reasonable notice restricting access to those with lawful business to pursue therein and the surrounding circumstances would indicate to a reasonable person that the person has no lawful business to pursue therein. Reasonable notice is that which would give actual notice to a reasonable person, and is posted, at a minimum, at each entrance into the area.

(2) A person convicted of a violation of paragraph (1) shall be punished as follows:

(A) As an infraction, by a fine not exceeding one hundred dollars ($100).

(B) By imprisonment in a county jail not exceeding one year, or by a fine not exceeding one thousand dollars ($1,000), or by both that fine and imprisonment, if the person refuses to leave the posted area after being requested to leave by a peace officer or other authorized person.

(C) By imprisonment in a county jail not exceeding one year, or by a fine not exceeding two thousand dollars ($2,000), or by both that fine and imprisonment, for a second or subsequent offense.

(D) If probation is granted or the execution or imposition of sentencing is suspended for a person convicted under this subdivision, it shall be a condition of probation that the person participate in counseling, as designated by the court, unless the court finds good cause not to impose this requirement. The court shall require the person to pay for this counseling, if ordered, unless good cause not to pay is shown.

(y) Except as permitted by federal law, intentionally avoiding submission to the screening and inspection of one's person and accessible property in accordance with the procedures being applied to control access when entering or reentering a courthouse or a city, county, city and county, or state building if entrances to the courthouse or the city, county, city and county, or state building have been posted with a statement providing reasonable notice that prosecution may result from a trespass described in this subdivision.

Amended by Stats 2023 ch 404 (SB 602),s 1, eff. 1/1/2024.

Amended by Stats 2022 ch 197 (SB 1493),s 16, eff. 1/1/2023.

Amended by Stats 2015 ch 303 (AB 731),s 389, eff. 1/1/2016.

Amended by Stats 2014 ch 453 (AB 1686),s 1.5, eff. 1/1/2015.
Amended by Stats 2014 ch 373 (SB 1295),s 1, eff. 1/1/2015.
Amended by Stats 2011 ch 296 (AB 1023),s 207, eff. 1/1/2012.
Amended by Stats 2010 ch 675 (AB 2324),s 2.5, eff. 1/1/2011.
Amended by Stats 2010 ch 531 (AB 668),s 1, eff. 1/1/2011.
Amended by Stats 2005 ch 378 (SB 584),s 3, eff. 1/1/2006
Amended by Stats 2005 ch 289 (AB 280),s 2, eff. 1/1/2006
Amended by Stats 2003 ch 355 (AB 936), s 1, eff. 1/1/2004.
Amended by Stats 2003 ch 805 (SB 993), s 1.3, eff.
Amended by Stats 2002 ch 608 (SB 510), s 2, eff. 9/16/2002.
Amended by Stats 2000 ch 149 (AB 1787), s 1, eff. 1/1/2001.
 See Stats 2003 ch 361 (AB 1263), s 2.
 See Stats 2003 ch 805 (SB 993), s 2.

Section 602.1 - Intentional interference with lawful business or occupation open to public by obstruction or intimidation or refusal to leave premises

(a) Any person who intentionally interferes with any lawful business or occupation carried on by the owner or agent of a business establishment open to the public, by obstructing or intimidating those attempting to carry on business, or their customers, and who refuses to leave the premises of the business establishment after being requested to leave by the owner or the owner's agent, or by a peace officer acting at the request of the owner or owner's agent, is guilty of a misdemeanor, punishable by imprisonment in a county jail for up to 90 days, or by a fine of up to four hundred dollars ($400), or by both that imprisonment and fine.

(b) Any person who intentionally interferes with any lawful business carried on by the employees of a public agency open to the public, by obstructing or intimidating those attempting to carry on business, or those persons there to transact business with the public agency, and who refuses to leave the premises of the public agency after being requested to leave by the office manager or a supervisor of the public agency, or by a peace officer acting at the request of the office manager or a supervisor of the public agency, is guilty of a misdemeanor, punishable by imprisonment in a county jail for up to 90 days, or by a fine of up to four hundred dollars ($400), or by both that imprisonment and fine.

(c) Any person who intentionally interferes with any lawful business carried on by the employees of a public agency open to the public, by knowingly making a material misrepresentation of the law to those persons there to transact business with the public agency, and who refuses to leave the premises of the public agency after being requested to leave by the office manager or a supervisor of the public agency, or by a peace officer acting at the request of the office manager or a supervisor of the public agency, is guilty of an infraction, punishable by a fine of up to four hundred dollars ($400).

(d) This section shall not apply to any of the following persons:

   (1) Any person engaged in lawful labor union activities that are permitted to be carried out on the property by state or federal law.

   (2) Any person on the premises who is engaging in activities protected by the California Constitution or the United States Constitution.

(e) Nothing in this section shall be deemed to supersede the application of any other law.

Amended by Stats 2017 ch 381 (AB 660),s 1, eff. 1/1/2018.

Section 602.2 - Applicability of ordinance requiring written permission to enter vacant or unimproved land

Any ordinance or resolution adopted by a county which requires written permission to enter vacant or unimproved private land from either the owner, the owner's agent, or the person in lawful possession of private land, shall not apply unless the land is immediately adjacent and contiguous to residential property, or enclosed by fence, or under cultivation, or posted with signs forbidding trespass, displayed at intervals of not less than three to a mile, along all exterior boundaries and at all roads and trails entering the private land.

Added by Stats. 1986, Ch. 34, Sec. 1.

Section 602.3 - Unlawfully remaining on premises of owner-occupied dwelling unit by lodger

(a) A lodger who is subject to Section 1946.5 of the Civil Code and who remains on the premises of an owner-occupied dwelling unit after receipt of a notice terminating the hiring, and expiration of the notice period, provided in Section 1946.5 of the Civil Code is guilty of an infraction and may, pursuant to Section 837, be arrested for the offense by the owner, or in the event the owner is represented by a court-appointed conservator, executor, or administrator, by the owner's representative. Notwithstanding Section 853.5, the requirement of that section for release upon a written promise to appear shall not preclude an assisting peace officer from removing the person from the owner-occupied dwelling unit.

(b) The removal of a lodger from a dwelling unit by the owner pursuant to subdivision (a) is not a forcible entry under the provisions of Section 1159 of the Code of Civil Procedure and shall not be a basis for civil liability under that section.

(c) Chapter 5 (commencing with Section 1980) of Title 5 of Part 4 of Division 3 of the Civil Code applies to any personal property of the lodger which remains on the premises following the lodger's removal from the premises pursuant to this section.

(d) Nothing in this section shall be construed to limit the owner's right to have a lodger removed under other provisions of law.

(e) Except as provided in subdivision (b), nothing in this section shall be construed to limit or affect in any way any cause of action an owner or lodger may have for damages for any breach of the contract of the parties respecting the lodging.

(f) This section applies only to owner-occupied dwellings where a single lodger resides. Nothing in this section shall be construed to determine or affect in any way the rights of persons residing as lodgers in an owner-occupied dwelling where more than one lodger resides.

Amended by Stats. 1991, Ch. 930, Sec. 1.

Section 602.4 - Unlawful sale, peddling, or offering for sale of goods, merchandise, property, or services on airport property

(a) A person who enters or remains on airport property owned by a city, county, or city and county, but located in another county, and sells, peddles, or offers for sale any goods, merchandise, property, or services of any kind whatsoever, including transportation services to, on, or from the airport property, to members of the public without the express written consent of the governing board of the airport property, or its duly authorized representative, is guilty of a misdemeanor.

(b) Nothing in this section affects the power of a county, city, or city and county to regulate the sale, peddling, or offering for sale of goods, merchandise, property, or services.

(c) For purposes of this section, when a charter-party carrier licensed by the Public Utilities Commission operates at an airport on a prearranged basis, as defined in Section 5360.5 of the Public Utilities Code, that operation shall not constitute the sale, peddling, or offering of goods, merchandise, property, or services.

Amended by Stats 2014 ch 323 (SB 1430),s 1, eff. 9/15/2014.

Amended by Stats 2010 ch 584 (AB 1885),s 1, eff. 1/1/2011.

Section 602.5 - Unlawful entry in noncommercial dwelling house, apartment, or other residential place

(a) Every person other than a public officer or employee acting within the course and scope of his or her employment in performance of a duty imposed by law, who enters or remains in any noncommercial dwelling house, apartment, or other residential place without consent of the owner, his or her agent, or the person in lawful possession thereof, is guilty of a misdemeanor.

(b) Every person other than a public officer or an employee acting within the course and scope of his employment in performance of a duty imposed by law, who, without the consent of the owner, his or her agent, or the person in lawful possession thereof, enters or remains in any noncommercial dwelling house, apartment, or other residential place while a resident, or another person authorized to be in the dwelling, is present at any time during the course of the incident is guilty of aggravated trespass punishable by imprisonment in a county jail for not more than one year or by a fine of not more than one thousand dollars ($1,000), or by both that fine and imprisonment.

(c) If the court grants probation, it may order a person convicted of a misdemeanor under subdivision (b) to up to three years of supervised probation. It shall be a condition of probation that the person participate in counseling, as designated by the court.

(d) If a person is convicted of a misdemeanor under subdivision (b), the sentencing court shall also consider issuing an order restraining the defendant from any contact with the victim, that may be valid for up to three years, as determined by the court. In determining the length of the restraining order, the court shall consider, among other factors, the seriousness of the facts before the court, the probability of future violations, and the safety of the victim and his or her immediate family.

(e) Nothing in this section shall preclude prosecution under Section 459 or any other provision of law.

Amended by Stats 2000 ch 563 (SB 1486), s 1, eff. 1/1/2001.

Section 602.6 - Unlawful entry of public fair buildings or grounds

Every person who enters or remains in, or upon, any state, county, district, or citrus fruit fair buildings or grounds, when the buildings or grounds are not open to the general public, after having been ordered or directed by a peace officer or a fair manager to leave the building or grounds and when the order or direction to leave is issued after determination that the person has no apparent lawful business or other legitimate reason for remaining on the property, and fails to identify himself or herself and account for his or her presence, is guilty of a misdemeanor.

Added by Stats. 1990, Ch. 631, Sec. 1.

Section 602.7 - Unlawful entry of property, facility, or vehicle owned San Francisco Bay Area Rapid Transit District or the Southern California Rapid Transit District; unlawful peddling

Every person who enters or remains on any property, facility, or vehicle owned by the San Francisco Bay Area Rapid Transit District or the Southern California Rapid Transit District, and sells or peddles any goods, merchandise, property, or services of any kind whatsoever on the property, facilities, or vehicles, without the express written consent of the governing board of the San Francisco Bay Area Rapid Transit District or the governing board of the Southern California Rapid Transit District, or its duly authorized representatives, is guilty of an infraction.

Nothing in this section affects the power of a county, city, transit district, or city and county to regulate the sale or peddling of goods, merchandise, property, or services.

Added by Stats. 1986, Ch. 1232, Sec. 1.

Section 602.8 - Unlawful entry of lands under cultivation or enclosed by fence, or uncultivated lands or unenclosed lands posted with no trespass signs

(a) Any person who without the written permission of the landowner, the owner's agent, or the person in lawful possession of the land, willfully enters any lands under cultivation or enclosed by fence, belonging to, or occupied by, another, or who willfully enters upon uncultivated or unenclosed lands where signs forbidding trespass are displayed at intervals not less than three to the mile along all exterior boundaries and at all roads and trails entering the lands, is guilty of a public offense.

(b) Any person convicted of a violation of subdivision (a) shall be punished as follows:

(1) A first offense is an infraction punishable by a fine of seventy-five dollars ($75).

(2) A second offense on the same land or any contiguous land of the same landowner, without the permission of the landowner, the landowner's agent, or the person in lawful possession of the land, is an infraction punishable by a fine of two hundred fifty dollars ($250).

(3) A third or subsequent offense on the same land or any contiguous land of the same landowner, without the permission of the landowner, the landowner's agent, or the person in lawful possession of the land, is a misdemeanor.

(c) Subdivision (a) shall not apply to any of the following:

(1) Any person engaged in lawful labor union activities which are permitted to be carried out on property by the California Agricultural Labor Relations Act, Part 3.5 (commencing with Section 1140) of Division 2 of the Labor Code, or by the National Labor Relations Act.

(2) Any person on the premises who is engaging in activities protected by the California or United States Constitution.

(3) Any person described in Section 22350 of the Business and Professions Code who is making a lawful service of process.

(4) Any person licensed pursuant to Chapter 15 (commencing with Section 8700) of Division 3 of the Business and Professions Code who is engaged in the lawful practice of land surveying as authorized by Section 846.5 of the Civil Code.

(d) For any infraction charged pursuant to this section, the defendant shall have the option to forfeit bail in lieu of making a court appearance. Notwithstanding subdivision (e) of Section 853.6, if the offender elects to forfeit bail pursuant to this subdivision, no further proceedings shall be had in the case.

Amended by Stats 2003 ch 101 (AB 924), s 1, eff. 1/1/2004.

Section 602.9 - Unlawful claims of ownership or taking possession of residential dwelling for purpose of renting that dwelling

(a) Except as provided in subdivision (c), any person who, without the owner's or owner's agent's consent, claims ownership or claims or takes possession of a residential dwelling for the purpose of renting that dwelling to another is guilty of a misdemeanor punishable by imprisonment in a county jail not exceeding one year, or by a fine not exceeding two thousand five hundred dollars ($2,500), or by both that imprisonment and fine. Each violation is a separate offense.

(b) Except as provided in subdivision (c), any person who, without the owner's or owner's agent's consent, causes another person to enter or remain in any residential dwelling for the purpose of renting that dwelling to another, is guilty of a misdemeanor punishable by imprisonment in a county jail not exceeding one year, or by a fine not exceeding two thousand five hundred dollars ($2,500), or by both that imprisonment and fine. Each violation is a separate offense.

(c) This section does not apply to any tenant, subtenant, lessee, sublessee, or assignee, nor to any other hirer having a lawful occupancy interest in the residential dwelling.

(d) Nothing in this section shall preclude the prosecution of a person under any other applicable provision of law.

(e) It is the intent of the Legislature that this section shall not preclude the prosecution of a person on grand theft or fraud charges. The Legislature finds that this section has never precluded prosecution of a person on grand theft or fraud charges.

Amended by Stats 2010 ch 580 (AB 1800),s 1, eff. 1/1/2011.

Section 602.10 - Unlawful obstruction of student or teacher

Every person who, by physical force and with the intent to prevent attendance or instruction, willfully obstructs or attempts to obstruct any student or teacher seeking to attend or instruct classes at any of the campuses or facilities owned, controlled, or administered by the Regents of the University of California, the Trustees of the California State University, or the governing board of a community college district shall be punished by a fine not exceeding five hundred dollars ($500), by imprisonment in a county jail for a period of not exceeding one year, or by both such fine and imprisonment.

As used in this section, "physical force" includes, but is not limited to, use of one's person, individually or in concert with others, to impede access to, or movement within, or otherwise to obstruct the students and teachers of the classes to which the premises are devoted.

Amended by Stats. 1983, Ch. 143, Sec. 202.

Section 602.11 - Intentionally preventing individual from entering or exiting health care facility, place of worship, or school

(a) Any person, alone or in concert with others, who intentionally prevents an individual from entering or exiting a health care facility, place of worship, or school by physically detaining the individual or physically obstructing the individual's passage shall be guilty of a misdemeanor punishable by imprisonment in the county jail, or a fine of not more than two hundred fifty dollars ($250), or both, for the first offense; imprisonment in the county jail for not less than five days and a fine of not more than five hundred dollars ($500) for the second offense; and imprisonment in the county jail for not less than 30 days and a fine of not more than two thousand dollars ($2,000) for a third or subsequent offense. However, the court may order the defendant to perform community service, in lieu of any fine or any imprisonment imposed under this section, if it determines that paying the fine would result in undue hardship to the defendant or his or her dependents.

(b) As used in subdivision (a), the following terms have the following meanings:

(1) "Physically" does not include speech.

(2) "Health care facility" means a facility licensed pursuant to Chapter 1 (commencing with Section 1200) of Division 2 of the Health and Safety Code, a health facility licensed pursuant to Chapter 2 (commencing with Section 1250) of Division 2 of the Health and Safety Code, or any facility where medical care is regularly provided to individuals by persons licensed under Division 2 (commencing with Section 500) of the Business and Professions Code, the Osteopathic Initiative Act, or the Chiropractic Initiative Act.

(3) "Person" does not include an officer, employee, or agent of the health care facility, or a law enforcement officer, acting in the course of his or her employment.

(c) This section shall not be interpreted to prohibit any lawful activities permitted under the laws of the State of California or by the National Labor Relations Act in connection with a labor dispute.

Added by Stats. 1992, Ch. 935, Sec. 2. Effective January 1, 1993.

Section 602.12 - Unlawfully entering residential real property of academic researcher

(a) Any person who enters the residential real property of an academic researcher for the purpose of chilling, preventing the exercise of, or interfering with the researcher's academic freedom is guilty of trespass, a misdemeanor.

(b) For the purposes of this section, the following definitions apply:

(1) "Academic researcher" means any person lawfully engaged in academic research who is a student, trainee, employee, or affiliated physician of an accredited California community college, a campus of the California State University or the University of California, or a Western Association of Schools and Colleges accredited, degree granting, nonprofit institution. Academic research does not include routine, nonlaboratory coursework or assignments.

(2) "Academic freedom" means the lawful performance, dissemination, or publication of academic research or instruction.

(c) This section shall not apply to any person who is lawfully engaged in labor union activities that are protected under state or federal law.

(d) This section shall not preclude prosecution under any other provision of law.

Added by Stats 2008 ch 492 (AB 2296),s 4, eff. 9/28/2008.

Section 602.13 - Unlawful entry of animal enclosure at zoo, circus, or traveling animal exhibit

(a) Every person who enters into an animal enclosure at a zoo, circus, or traveling animal exhibit, if the zoo, circus, or exhibit is licensed or permitted to display living animals to the public, and if signs prohibiting entrance into the animal enclosures have been posted either at the entrance to the zoo, circus, or traveling animal exhibit, or on the animal enclosure itself, without the consent of the governing authority of the zoo, circus, or traveling animal exhibit, or a representative authorized by the governing authority, is guilty of an infraction or a misdemeanor, subject to Section 19.8. This subdivision shall not apply to an employee of the zoo, circus, or traveling animal exhibit, or to a public officer acting within the course and scope of his or her employment.

(b) For purposes of this section, "zoo" means a permanent or semipermanent collection of living animals kept in enclosures for the purpose of displaying the animals to the public. The term "zoo" includes a public aquarium displaying aquatic animals.

(c) For purposes of this section, an "animal enclosure" means the interior of any cage, stall, container, pen, aquarium or tank, or other discrete containment area that is used to house or display an animal and that is not generally accessible to the public.

(d) Prosecution under this section does not preclude prosecution under any other provision of law.

Added by Stats 2010 ch 536 (AB 1675),s 2, eff. 1/1/2011.

Section 603 - Forcible entry of dwelling house without consent

Every person other than a peace officer engaged in the performance of his duties as such who forcibly and without the consent of the owner, representative of the owner, lessee or representative of the lessee thereof, enters a dwelling house, cabin, or other building occupied or constructed for occupation by humans, and who damages, injures or destroys any property of value in, around or appertaining to such dwelling house, cabin or other building, is guilty of a misdemeanor.

Added by Stats. 1941, Ch. 635.

Section 604 - Malicious destruction of standing crops, grains, cultivated fruits or vegetables

Every person who maliciously injures or destroys any standing crops, grain, cultivated fruits or vegetables, the property of another, in any case for which a punishment is not otherwise prescribed by this Code, is guilty of a misdemeanor.

Enacted 1872.

Section 605 - Unlawful acts related to monuments

Every person who either:

1. Maliciously removes any monument erected for the purpose of designating any point in the boundary of any lot or tract of land, or a place where a subaqueous telegraph cable lies; or,

2. Maliciously defaces or alters the marks upon any such monument; or,

3. Maliciously cuts down or removes any tree upon which any such marks have been made for such purpose, with intent to destroy such marks; -Is guilty of a misdemeanor.

Enacted 1872.

Section 607 - Unlawful destruction of structure erected to create hydraulic power, to drain or reclaim marsh land, or to store or conduct water

Every person who willfully and maliciously cuts, breaks, injures, or destroys, or who, without the authority of the owner or managing agent, operates any gate or control of, any bridge, dam, canal, flume, aqueduct, levee, embankment, reservoir, or other structure erected to create hydraulic power, or to drain or reclaim any swamp, overflow, tide, or marsh land, or to store or conduct water for mining, manufacturing, reclamation, or agricultural purposes, or for the supply of the inhabitants of any city or town, or any embankment necessary to the same, or either of them, or willfully or maliciously makes, or causes to be made, any aperture or plows up the bottom or sides in the dam, canal, flume, aqueduct, reservoir, embankment, levee, or structure, with intent to injure or destroy the same; or draws up, cuts, or injures any piles fixed in the ground for the purpose of securing any sea bank, sea wall, dock, quay, jetty, or lock; or who, between the first day of October and the fifteenth day of April of each year, plows up or loosens the soil in the bed on the side of any natural water course, reclamation ditch, or drainage ditch, with an intent to destroy the same without removing the soil within 24 hours from the water course, reclamation ditch, or drainage ditch, or who, between the fifteenth day of April and the first day of October of each year, plows up or loosens the soil in the bed or on the sides of the natural water course, reclamation ditch, or drainage ditch, with an intent to destroy the same and does not remove therefrom the soil so plowed up or loosened before the first day of October next thereafter, is guilty of vandalism under Section 594. Nothing in this section shall be construed so as to in any manner prohibit any person from digging or removing soil from any water course, reclamation ditch, or drainage ditch for the purpose of mining.

Amended by Stats. 1992, Ch. 402, Sec. 2. Effective January 1, 1993.

Section 610 - Unlawful masking, altering, or removing light or signal to bring vessel into danger

Every person who unlawfully masks, alters, or removes any light or signal, or willfully exhibits any light or signal, with intent to bring any vessel into danger, is punishable by imprisonment pursuant to subdivision (h) of Section 1170.

Amended by Stats 2011 ch 39 (AB 117),s 68, eff. 6/30/2011.

Amended by Stats 2011 ch 15 (AB 109),s 416, eff. 4/4/2011, but operative no earlier than October 1, 2011, and only upon creation of a community corrections grant program to assist in implementing this act and upon an appropriation to fund the grant program.

Section 615 - Unlawful defacement or removal of signal, monument, building, or appurtenance used by persons engaged in United States Coast Survey

Every person who willfully injures, defaces, or removes any signal, monument, building, or appurtenance thereto, placed, erected, or used by persons engaged in the United States Coast Survey, is guilty of a misdemeanor.

Enacted 1872.

Section 616 - Unlawful defacement or destruction of proclamation, advertisement, or notification set up by United States, California, or any court

Every person who intentionally defaces, obliterates, tears down, or destroys any copy or transcript, or extract from or of any law of the United States or of this State, or any proclamation, advertisement, or notification set up at any place in this State, by authority of any law of the United States or of this State, or by order of any Court, before the expiration of the time for which the same was to remain set up, is punishable by fine not less than twenty nor more than one hundred dollars, or by imprisonment in the County Jail not more than one month.

Enacted 1872.

Section 617 - Unlawful defacement or destruction of written property, the property of another, the false making of which would be forgery

Every person who maliciously mutilates, tears, defaces, obliterates, or destroys any written instrument, the property of another, the false making of which would be forgery, is punishable by imprisonment pursuant to subdivision (h) of Section 1170.

Amended by Stats 2011 ch 39 (AB 117),s 68, eff. 6/30/2011.

Amended by Stats 2011 ch 15 (AB 109),s 417, eff. 4/4/2011, but operative no earlier than October 1, 2011, and only upon creation of a community corrections grant program to assist in implementing this act and upon an appropriation to fund the grant program.

Section 618 - Unlawful opening, or reading sealed letter; unlawful publication of contents

Every person who willfully opens or reads, or causes to be read, any sealed letter not addressed to himself, without being authorized so to do, either by the writer of such letter or by the person to whom it is addressed, and every person who, without the like authority, publishes any of the contents of such letter, knowing the same to have been unlawfully opened, is guilty of a misdemeanor.

Enacted 1872.

Section 620 - Unlawful alteration of meaning of telegraphic or telephonic message

Every person who willfully alters the purport, effect, or meaning of a telegraphic or telephonic message to the injury of another, is punishable by imprisonment pursuant to subdivision (h) of Section 1170, or in a county jail not exceeding one year, or by fine not exceeding ten thousand dollars ($10,000), or by both that fine and imprisonment.

Amended by Stats 2011 ch 39 (AB 117),s 68, eff. 6/30/2011.

Amended by Stats 2011 ch 15 (AB 109),s 418, eff. 4/4/2011, but operative no earlier than October 1, 2011, and only upon creation of a community corrections grant program to assist in implementing this act and upon an appropriation to fund the grant program.

Section 621 - Unlawful destruction or removal of law enforcement or firefighter's memorial

(a) Every person who maliciously destroys, cuts, breaks, mutilates, effaces, or otherwise injures, tears down, or removes any law enforcement memorial or firefighter's memorial is guilty of a crime punishable by imprisonment pursuant to subdivision (h) of Section 1170 or by imprisonment in a county jail for less than one year.

(b) This section does not preclude prosecution under any other provision of law, including Section 1318 of the Military and Veterans Code.

Amended by Stats 2018 ch 549 (AB 2801),s 1, eff. 1/1/2019.

Amended by Stats 2011 ch 39 (AB 117),s 68, eff. 6/30/2011.

Amended by Stats 2011 ch 15 (AB 109),s 419, eff. 4/4/2011, but operative no earlier than October 1, 2011, and only upon creation of a community corrections grant program to assist in implementing this act and upon an appropriation to fund the grant program.

Section 622 - Unlawful disfigurement or destruction of monument, work of art, or useful or ornamental improvement

Every person, not the owner thereof, who willfully injures, disfigures, or destroys any monument, work of art, or useful or ornamental improvement within the limits of any village, town, or city, or any shade tree or ornamental plant growing therein, whether situated upon private ground or on any street, sidewalk, or public park or place, is guilty of a misdemeanor.

Enacted 1872.

Section 622 1/2 - Unlawful disfigurement of archeological or historical object

Every person, not the owner thereof, who wilfully injures, disfigures, defaces, or destroys any object or thing of archeological or historical interest or value, whether situated on private lands or within any public park or place, is guilty of a misdemeanor.

Section 623 - Unlawful acts related to caves

(a) Except as otherwise provided in Section 599c, any person who, without the prior written permission of the owner of a cave, intentionally and knowingly does any of the following acts is guilty of a misdemeanor punishable by imprisonment in the county jail not exceeding one year, or by a fine not exceeding one thousand dollars ($1,000), or by both such fine and imprisonment:

(1) Breaks, breaks off, cracks, carves upon, paints, writes or otherwise marks upon or in any manner destroys, mutilates, injures, defaces, mars, or harms any natural material found in any cave.

(2) Disturbs or alters any archaeological evidence of prior occupation in any cave.

(3) Kills, harms, or removes any animal or plant life found in any cave.

(4) Burns any material which produces any smoke or gas which is harmful to any plant or animal found in any cave.

(5) Removes any material found in any cave.

(6) Breaks, forces, tampers with, removes or otherwise disturbs any lock, gate, door, or any other structure or obstruction designed to prevent entrance to any cave, whether or not entrance is gained.

(b) For purposes of this section:

(1) "Cave" means any natural geologically formed void or cavity beneath the surface of the earth, not including any mine, tunnel, aqueduct, or other manmade excavation, which is large enough to permit a person to enter.

(2) "Owner" means the person or private or public agency which has the right of possession to the cave.

(3) "Natural material" means any stalactite, stalagmite, helictite, anthodite, gypsum flower or needle, flowstone, drapery, column, tufa dam, clay or mud formation or concretion, crystalline mineral formation, and any wall, ceiling, or mineral protuberance therefrom, whether attached or broken, found in any cave.

(4) "Material" means all or any part of any archaeological, paleontological, biological, or historical item including, but not limited to, any petroglyph, pictograph, basketry, human remains, tool, beads, pottery, projectile point, remains of historical mining activity or any other occupation found in any cave.

(c) The entering or remaining in a cave by itself shall not constitute a violation of this section.

Amended by Stats. 1983, Ch. 1092, Sec. 312. Effective September 27, 1983. Operative January 1, 1984, by Sec. 427 of Ch. 1092.

Section 624 - Unlawful breaking, digging up, or obstruction of pipe or main for conducting water

Every person who wilfully breaks, digs up, obstructs, or injures any pipe or main for conducting water, or any works erected for supplying buildings with water, or any appurtenances or appendages connected thereto, is guilty of a misdemeanor.

Amended by Stats. 1939, Ch. 369.

Section 625 - Unlawful opening of stopcock or faucet

Every person who, with intent to defraud or injure, opens or causes to be opened, or draws water from any stopcock or faucet by which the flow of water is controlled, after having been notified that the same has been closed or shut for specific cause, by order of competent authority, is guilty of a misdemeanor.

Enacted 1872.

Section 625b - Unlawful injuring or tampering with aircraft

(a) Every person who willfully injures or tampers with any aircraft or the contents or parts thereof, or removes any part of or from an aircraft without the consent of the owner, and every person who, with intent to commit any malicious mischief, injury or other crime, climbs into or upon an aircraft or attempts to manipulate any of the controls, starting mechanism, brakes or other mechanism or device of an aircraft while it is at rest and unattended or who sets in motion any aircraft while it is at rest and unattended, is guilty of a misdemeanor and upon conviction shall be punished by imprisonment for not more than six months or by a fine of not more than one thousand dollars ($1,000), or by both that fine and imprisonment.

(b) Every person who willfully and maliciously damages, injures, or destroys any aircraft, or the contents or any part thereof, in such a manner as to render the aircraft unsafe for those flight operations for which it is designed and equipped is punishable by imprisonment pursuant to subdivision (h) of Section 1170, or by imprisonment in a county jail not exceeding one year, or by a fine not exceeding ten thousand dollars ($10,000), or by both such fine and imprisonment.

Amended by Stats 2011 ch 39 (AB 117),s 68, eff. 6/30/2011.

Amended by Stats 2011 ch 15 (AB 109),s 420, eff. 4/4/2011, but operative no earlier than October 1, 2011, and only upon creation of a community corrections grant program to assist in implementing this act and upon an appropriation to fund the grant program.

Section 625c - Unlawful removing, tampering with, or destruction of passenger transit vehicle or contents or parts thereof

Any person who, with the intent to cause great bodily injury to another person, willfully removes, tampers with, injures or destroys any passenger transit vehicle or the contents or parts thereof, or who willfully removes, tampers with or destroys, or places an obstruction upon any part of the transit system, including its right-of-way, structures, fixtures, tracks, switches or controls, or who willfully sets a vehicle in motion while it is at rest and unattended is guilty of a felony.

Added by Stats. 1980, Ch. 993, Sec. 1.

Title 15 - MISCELLANEOUS CRIMES

Chapter 1 - SCHOOLS

Section 626 - Definitions

(a)As used in this chapter, the following definitions apply:

(1)"University" means the University of California, and includes any affiliated institution thereof and any campus or facility owned, operated, or controlled by the Regents of the University of California.

(2)"State university" means any California state university, and includes any campus or facility owned, operated, or controlled by the Trustees of the California State University.

(3)"Community college" means any public community college established pursuant to the Education Code.

(4)"Independent institutions of higher education" means nonpublic higher education institutions that grant undergraduate degrees, graduate degrees, or both, and that are formed as nonprofit corporations in this state and are accredited by an agency recognized by the United States Department of Education.

(5)"School" means any public or private elementary school, junior high school, four-year high school, senior high school, adult school or any branch thereof, opportunity school, continuation high school, regional occupational center, evening high school, or technical school or any public right-of-way situated immediately adjacent to school property or any other place if a teacher and one or more pupils are required to be at that place in connection with assigned school activities.

(6)"Chief administrative officer" means either of the following:

(A)The president of the university, a state university, or an independent institution of higher education, or an officer designated by the president, the Chancellor of the California State University, or the officer designated by the Regents of the University of California or pursuant to authority granted by the Regents of the University of California to administer and be the officer in charge of a campus or other facility owned, operated, or controlled by the Regents of the University of California, or the superintendent of a community college district.

(B)For a school, the principal of the school, a person who possesses a standard supervision credential or a standard administrative credential and who is designated by the principal, or a person who carries out the same functions as a person who possesses a credential and who is designated by the principal.

(b)For the purpose of determining the penalty to be imposed pursuant to this chapter, the court may consider a written report from the Department of Justice containing information from its records showing prior convictions; and that communication is prima facie evidence of the convictions, if the defendant admits them, regardless of whether or not the complaint commencing the proceedings has alleged prior convictions.

(c)As used in this code, the following definitions apply:

(1)"Pupil currently attending school" means a pupil enrolled in a public or private school who has been in attendance or has had an excused absence, for purposes of attendance accounting, for a majority of the days for which the pupil has been enrolled in that school during the school year.

(2)"Safe school zone" means an area that encompasses any of the following places during regular school hours or within 60 minutes before or after the schoolday or 60 minutes before or after a school-sponsored activity at the schoolsite:

(A)Within 100 feet of a bus stop, whether or not a public transit bus stop, that has been publicly designated by the school district as a schoolbus stop. This definition applies only if the school district has chosen to mark the bus stop as a schoolbus stop.

(B)Within 1,500 feet of a school, as designated by the school district.

Amended by Stats 2022 ch 134 (SB 748),s 1, eff. 7/19/2022.

Amended by Stats 2008 ch 726 (SB 1666),s 1, eff. 1/1/2009.

Section 626.1 - [Repealed]

Repealed 10/10/1999 (Bill Number: SB 832) (Chapter 853).

Section 626.2 - Unlawful entry of campus or facility to which person has been denied access

Every student or employee who, after a hearing or institutional process, has been suspended or dismissed from a community college, a state university, the university, an independent institution of higher education, or a public or private school for disrupting the orderly operation of the campus or facility of the institution, and as a condition of the suspension or dismissal has been denied access to the campus or facility, or both, of the institution for the period of the suspension or in the case of dismissal for a period not to exceed one year; who has been served by registered or certified mail, at the last address given by that person, with a written notice of the suspension or dismissal and condition; and who willfully and knowingly enters upon the campus or facility of the institution to which that person has been denied access, without the express written permission of the chief administrative officer of the campus or facility, is guilty of a misdemeanor and shall be punished by a fine not exceeding five hundred dollars ($500), by imprisonment in a county jail for a period of not more than six months, or by both that fine and imprisonment.

Knowledge shall be presumed if notice has been given as prescribed in this section. The presumption established by this section is a presumption affecting the burden of proof.

Amended by Stats 2022 ch 134 (SB 748),s 2, eff. 7/19/2022.

Amended by Stats 2009 ch 140 (AB 1164),s 142, eff. 1/1/2010.

Amended by Stats 2008 ch 726 (SB 1666),s 2, eff. 1/1/2009.

Section 626.4 - Withdrawal of consent to remain on campus

(a)The chief administrative officer of a campus or other facility of a community college, a state university, the university, an independent institution of higher education, or a school, or an officer or employee designated by the chief administrative officer to maintain order on such campus or facility, may notify a person that consent to remain on the campus or other facility under the control of the chief administrative officer has been withdrawn whenever there is reasonable cause to believe that such person has willfully disrupted the orderly operation of such campus or facility.

(b)Whenever consent is withdrawn by any authorized officer or employee, other than the chief administrative officer, the officer or employee shall as soon as is reasonably possible submit a written report to the chief administrative officer or designee. The report shall contain all of the following:

(1)The description of the person from whom consent was withdrawn, including, if available, the person's name, address, and phone number.

(2)A statement of the facts giving rise to the withdrawal of consent. If the chief administrative officer or, in the chief administrative officer's absence, a person designated by the chief administrative officer for this purpose, upon reviewing the report, finds that there was reasonable cause to believe that such person has willfully disrupted the orderly operation of the campus or facility, the chief administrative officer may enter written confirmation upon the report of the action taken by the officer or employee. If the chief administrative officer or, in the chief administrative officer's absence, the person designated by the chief administrative officer, does not confirm the action of the officer or employee within 24 hours after the time that consent was withdrawn, the action of the officer or employee shall be deemed void and of no force or effect, except that any arrest made during such period shall not for this reason be deemed not to have been made for probable cause.

(c)Consent shall be reinstated by the chief administrative officer whenever they have reason to believe that the presence of the person from whom consent was withdrawn will not constitute a substantial and material threat to the orderly operation of the campus or facility. In no case shall consent be withdrawn for longer than 14 days from the date upon which consent was initially withdrawn. The person from whom consent has been withdrawn may submit a written request for a hearing on the withdrawal within the two-week period. The written request shall state the address to which notice of hearing is to be sent. The chief administrative officer shall grant such a hearing not later than seven days from the date of receipt of the request and shall immediately mail a written notice of the time, place, and date of such hearing to such person.

(d)Any person who has been notified by the chief administrative officer of a campus or other facility of a community college, a state university, the university, an independent institution of higher education, or a school, or by an officer or employee designated by the chief administrative officer to maintain order on such campus or facility, that consent to remain on the campus or facility has been withdrawn pursuant to subdivision (a); who has not had such consent reinstated; and who willfully and knowingly enters or remains upon such campus or facility during the period for which consent has been withdrawn is guilty of a misdemeanor. This subdivision does not apply to any person who enters or remains on such campus or facility for the sole purpose of applying to the chief administrative officer for the reinstatement of consent or for the sole purpose of attending a hearing on the withdrawal.

(e)This section shall not affect the power of the duly constituted authorities of a community college, a state university, an independent institution of higher education, the university, or a school, to suspend, dismiss, or expel any student or employee at the college, state university, university, an independent institution of higher education, or school.

(f)Any person convicted under this section shall be punished by a fine not exceeding five hundred dollars ($500), by imprisonment in a county jail for a period of not more than six months, or by both that fine and imprisonment.

(g)This section shall not affect the rights of representatives of employee organizations to enter, or remain upon, school grounds while actually engaged in activities related to representation, as provided for in Chapter 10.7 (commencing with Section 3540) of Division 4 of Title 1 of the Government Code.

Amended by Stats 2022 ch 134 (SB 748),s 3, eff. 7/19/2022.

Amended by Stats. 1983, Ch. 143, Sec. 205.

Section 626.6 - Direction to leave campus or facility due to interference with peaceful conduct; failure to leave or reentry

(a)If a person who is not a student, officer, or employee of a college, or university, or an independent institution of higher education, and who is not required by their employment to be on the campus or any other facility owned, operated, or controlled by the governing board of that college, university, or an independent institution of higher education enters a campus or facility, and it reasonably appears to the chief administrative officer of the campus or facility, or to an officer or employee designated by the chief administrative officer to maintain order on the campus or facility, that the person is committing any act likely to interfere with the peaceful conduct of the activities of the campus or facility, or has entered the campus or facility for the purpose of committing any such act, the chief administrative officer or their designee may direct the person to leave the campus or facility. If that person fails to do so or if the person willfully and knowingly reenters upon the campus or facility within seven days after being directed to leave, the person is guilty of a misdemeanor and shall be punished by a fine not exceeding five hundred dollars ($500), by imprisonment in a county jail for a period of not more than six months, or by both that fine and imprisonment.

(b) The provisions of this section shall not be utilized to impinge upon the lawful exercise of constitutionally protected rights of freedom of speech or assembly.

(c) When a person is directed to leave pursuant to subdivision (a), the individual directing the person to leave shall inform the person that if the person reenters the campus or facility within seven days the person will be guilty of a crime.

Amended by Stats 2022 ch 134 (SB 748),s 4, eff. 7/19/2022.

Amended by Stats. 1995, Ch. 163, Sec. 1. Effective January 1, 1996.

Section 626.7 - Direction to leave campus or facility for committing act likely to interfere with peaceful conduct; failure to do so or return

(a) If a person who is not a student, officer, or employee of a public school, and who is not required by his or her employment to be on the campus or any other facility owned, operated, or controlled by the governing board of that school, enters a campus or facility outside of the common areas where public business is conducted, and it reasonably appears to the chief administrative officer of the campus or facility, or to an officer or employee designated by the chief administrative officer to maintain order on the campus or facility, that the person is committing any act likely to interfere with the peaceful conduct of the activities of the campus or facility, or has entered the campus or facility for the purpose of committing any such act, the chief administrative officer or his or her designee may direct the person to leave the campus or facility. If that person fails to do so or if the person returns without following the posted requirements to contact the administrative offices of the campus, he or she is guilty of a misdemeanor and shall be punished as follows:

(1) Upon a first conviction, by a fine of not more than five hundred dollars ($500), by imprisonment in a county jail for a period of not more than six months, or by both that fine and imprisonment.

(2) If the defendant has been previously convicted once of a violation of any offense defined in this chapter or Section 415.5, by imprisonment in a county jail for a period of not less than 10 days or more than six months, or by both that imprisonment and a fine of not more than five hundred dollars ($500), and the defendant shall not be released on probation, parole, or any other basis until he or she has served not less than 10 days.

(3) If the defendant has been previously convicted two or more times of a violation of any offense defined in this chapter or Section 415.5, by imprisonment in a county jail for a period of not less than 90 days or more than six months, or by both that imprisonment and a fine of not more than five hundred dollars ($500), and the defendant shall not be released on probation, parole, or any other basis until he or she has served not less than 90 days. For purposes of this section, a representative of a school employee organization engaged in activities related to representation, as provided for in Chapter 10.7 (commencing with Section 3540) of Division 4 of Title 1 of the Government Code, shall be deemed a person required by his or her employment to be in a school building or on the grounds of a school.

(b) The provisions of this section shall not be utilized to impinge upon the lawful exercise of constitutionally protected rights of freedom of speech or assembly.

(c) When a person is directed to leave pursuant to subdivision (a), the person directing him or her to leave shall inform the person that if he or she reenters the campus or facility without following the posted requirements to contact the administrative offices of the campus, he or she will be guilty of a crime.

(d) Notwithstanding any other subdivision of this section, the chief administrative officer, or his or her designee, shall allow a person previously directed to leave the campus or facility pursuant to this section to reenter the campus if the person is a parent or guardian of a pupil enrolled at the campus or facility who has to retrieve the pupil for disciplinary reasons, for medical attention, or for a family emergency.

Amended by Stats 2002 ch 343 (AB 2593), s 1, eff. 1/1/2003.

Section 626.8 - Unlawful interference with peaceful conduct of activities of school or disruption of school, pupils, or school activities

(a) Any person who comes into any school building or upon any school ground, or street, sidewalk, or public way adjacent thereto, without lawful business thereon, and whose presence or acts interfere with the peaceful conduct of the activities of the school or disrupt the school or its pupils or school activities, is guilty of a misdemeanor if he or she does any of the following:

(1) Remains there after being asked to leave by the chief administrative official of that school or his or her designated representative, or by a person employed as a member of a security or police department of a school district pursuant to Chapter 1 (commencing with Section 38000) of Part 23 of Division 3 of Title 2 of the Education Code, or a city police officer, or sheriff or deputy sheriff, or a Department of the California Highway Patrol peace officer.

(2) Reenters or comes upon that place within seven days of being asked to leave by a person specified in paragraph (1).

(3) Has otherwise established a continued pattern of unauthorized entry.

(4) Willfully or knowingly creates a disruption with the intent to threaten the immediate physical safety of any pupil in preschool, kindergarten, or any of grades 1 to 8, inclusive, arriving at, attending, or leaving from school.

(b) Punishment for violation of this section shall be as follows:

(1) Upon a first conviction by a fine not exceeding five hundred dollars ($500), by imprisonment in a county jail for a period of not more than six months, or by both that fine and imprisonment.

(2) If the defendant has been previously convicted once of a violation of any offense defined in this chapter or Section 415.5, by imprisonment in a county jail for a period of not less than 10 days or more than six months, or by both imprisonment and a fine not

exceeding five hundred dollars ($500), and shall not be released on probation, parole, or any other basis until he or she has served not less than 10 days.

(3) If the defendant has been previously convicted two or more times of a violation of any offense defined in this chapter or Section 415.5, by imprisonment in a county jail for a period of not less than 90 days or more than six months, or by both imprisonment and a fine not exceeding five hundred dollars ($500), and shall not be released on probation, parole, or any other basis until he or she has served not less than 90 days.

(c) As used in this section, the following definitions apply:

(1) "Lawful business" means a reason for being present upon school property which is not otherwise prohibited by statute, by ordinance, or by any regulation adopted pursuant to statute or ordinance.

(2) "Continued pattern of unauthorized entry" means that on at least two prior occasions in the same school year the defendant came into any school building or upon any school ground, or street, sidewalk, or public way adjacent thereto, without lawful business thereon, and his or her presence or acts interfered with the peaceful conduct of the activities of the school or disrupted the school or its pupils or school activities, and the defendant was asked to leave by a person specified in paragraph (1) of subdivision (a).

(3) "School" means any preschool or public or private school having kindergarten or any of grades 1 to 12, inclusive.

(d) When a person is directed to leave pursuant to paragraph (1) of subdivision (a), the person directing him or her to leave shall inform the person that if he or she reenters the place within seven days he or she will be guilty of a crime.

(e) This section shall not be utilized to impinge upon the lawful exercise of constitutionally protected rights of speech or assembly.

Amended by Stats 2011 ch 161 (AB 123),s 1A, eff. 1/1/2012.

Amended by Stats 2009 ch 140 (AB 1164),s 143, eff. 1/1/2010.

Amended by Stats 2008 ch 726 (SB 1666),s 3, eff. 1/1/2009.

Amended by Stats 2006 ch 337 (SB 1128),s 24, eff. 9/20/2006.

Section 626.81 - Unlawful entry into school building or upon school grounds by registered sex offender

(a) A person who is required to register as a sex offender pursuant to Section 290, who comes into any school building or upon any school ground without lawful business thereon and written permission indicating the date or dates and times for which permission has been granted from the chief administrative official of that school, is guilty of a misdemeanor.

(b)

(1) The chief administrative official of a school may grant a person who is subject to this section and not a family member of a pupil who attends that school, permission to come into a school building or upon the school grounds to volunteer at the school, provided that, notwithstanding subdivisions (a) and (c) of Section 290.45, at least 14 days prior to the first date for which permission has been granted, the chief administrative official notifies or causes to be notified the parent or guardian of each child attending the school that a person who is required to register as a sex offender pursuant to Section 290 has been granted permission to come into a school building or upon school grounds, the date or dates and times for which permission has been granted, and his or her right to obtain information regarding the person from a designated law enforcement entity pursuant to Section 290.45. The notice required by this paragraph shall be provided by one of the methods identified in Section 48981 of the Education Code.

(2) Any chief administrative official or school employee who in good faith disseminates the notification and information as required by paragraph (1) shall be immune from civil liability for action taken in accordance with that paragraph.

(c) Punishment for a violation of this section shall be as follows:

(1) Upon a first conviction by a fine of not exceeding five hundred dollars ($500), by imprisonment in a county jail for a period of not more than six months, or by both the fine and imprisonment.

(2) If the defendant has been previously convicted once of a violation of this section, by imprisonment in a county jail for a period of not less than 10 days or more than six months, or by both imprisonment and a fine of not exceeding five hundred dollars ($500), and shall not be released on probation, parole, or any other basis until he or she has served not less than 10 days.

(3) If the defendant has been previously convicted two or more times of a violation of this section, by imprisonment in a county jail for a period of not less than 90 days or more than six months, or by both imprisonment and a fine of not exceeding five hundred dollars ($500), and shall not be released on probation, parole, or any other basis until he or she has served not less than 90 days.

(d) Nothing in this section shall preclude or prohibit prosecution under any other provision of law.

Amended by Stats 2013 ch 279 (SB 326),s 1, eff. 1/1/2014.

Added by Stats 2006 ch 337 (SB 1128),s 25, eff. 9/20/2006.

Section 626.85 - Unlawful entry into school building or upon school ground by drug offender

(a) Any specified drug offender who, at any time, comes into any school building or upon any school ground, or adjacent street, sidewalk, or public way, unless the person is a parent or guardian of a child attending that school and his or her presence is during any school activity, or is a student at the school and his or her presence is during any school activity, or has prior written permission for the entry from the chief administrative officer of that school, is guilty of a misdemeanor if he or she does any of the following:

(1) Remains there after being asked to leave by the chief administrative officer of that school or his or her designated representative, or by a person employed as a member of a security or police department of a school district pursuant to Section 39670 of the Education Code, or a city police officer, sheriff, or a Department of the California Highway Patrol peace officer.

(2) Reenters or comes upon that place within seven days of being asked to leave by a person specified in paragraph (1) of subdivision (a).

(3) Has otherwise established a continued pattern of unauthorized entry. This section shall not be utilized to impinge upon the lawful exercise of constitutionally protected rights of freedom of speech or assembly, or to prohibit any lawful act, including picketing, strikes, or collective bargaining.

(b) Punishment for violation of this section shall be as follows:

(1) Upon a first conviction, by a fine not exceeding one thousand dollars ($1,000), by imprisonment in the county jail for a period of not more than six months, or by both that fine and imprisonment.

(2) If the defendant has been previously convicted once of a violation of any offense defined in this chapter or Section 415.5, by imprisonment in the county jail for a period of not less than 10 days or more than six months, or by both imprisonment and a fine not exceeding one thousand dollars ($1,000), and the defendant shall not be released on probation, parole, or any other basis until he or she has served not less than 10 days.

(3) If the defendant has been previously convicted two or more times of a violation of any offense defined in this chapter or Section 415.5, by imprisonment in the county jail for a period of not less than 90 days or more than six months, or by both imprisonment and a fine not exceeding one thousand dollars ($1,000), and the defendant shall not be released on probation, parole, or any other basis until he or she has served not less than 90 days.

(c) As used in this section:

(1) "Specified drug offender" means any person who, within the immediately preceding three years, has a felony or misdemeanor conviction of either:

(A) Unlawful sale, or possession for sale, of any controlled substance, as defined in Section 11007 of the Health and Safety Code.

(B) Unlawful use, possession, or being under the influence of any controlled substance, as defined in Section 11007 of the Health and Safety Code, where that conviction was based on conduct which occurred, wholly or partly, in any school building or upon any school ground, or adjacent street, sidewalk, or public way.

(2) "Continued pattern of unauthorized entry" means that on at least two prior occasions in the same calendar year the defendant came into any school building or upon any school ground, or adjacent street, sidewalk, or public way, and the defendant was asked to leave by a person specified in paragraph (1) of subdivision (a).

(3) "School" means any preschool or public or private school having any of grades kindergarten to 12, inclusive.

(4) "School activity" means and includes any school session, any extracurricular activity or event sponsored by or participated in by the school, and the 30-minute periods immediately preceding and following any session, activity, or event.

(d) When a person is directed to leave pursuant to paragraph (1) of subdivision (a), the person directing him or her to leave shall inform the person that if he or she reenters the place he or she will be guilty of a crime.

Amended by Stats 2008 ch 726 (SB 1666),s 4, eff. 1/1/2009.

Section 626.9 - Gun-Free School Zone Act of 1995

(a) This section shall be known, and may be cited, as the Gun-Free School Zone Act of 1995.

(b) Any person who possesses a firearm in a place that the person knows, or reasonably should know, is a school zone as defined in paragraph (4) of subdivision (e), shall be punished as specified in subdivision (f).

(c) Subdivision (b) does not apply to the possession of a firearm under any of the following circumstances:

(1) Within a place of residence or place of business or on private property, if the place of residence, place of business, or private property is not part of the school grounds and the possession of the firearm is otherwise lawful.

(2)

(A) When the firearm is an unloaded pistol, revolver, or other firearm capable of being concealed on the person is within a locked container in a motor vehicle or is within the locked trunk of a motor vehicle at all times.

(B) This section does not prohibit or limit the otherwise lawful transportation of any other firearm, other than a pistol, revolver, or other firearm capable of being concealed on the person, in accordance with state law.

(3) When the person possessing the firearm reasonably believes that they are in grave danger because of circumstances forming the basis of a current restraining order issued by a court against another person or persons who has or have been found to pose a threat to their life or safety. This subdivision does not apply when the circumstances involve a mutual restraining order issued pursuant to Division 10 (commencing with Section 6200) of the Family Code absent a factual finding of a specific threat to the person's life or safety. Upon a trial for violating subdivision (b), the trier of a fact shall determine whether the defendant was acting out of a reasonable belief that they were in grave danger.

(4) When the person is exempt from the prohibition against carrying a concealed firearm pursuant to Section 25615, 25625, 25630, or 25645.

(5) When the person holds a valid license to carry the firearm pursuant to Chapter 4 (commencing with Section 26150) of Division 5 of Title 4 of Part 6, who is carrying that firearm in an area that is within a distance of 1,000 feet from the grounds of the public or private school, but is not within any building, real property, or parking area under the control of a public or private school providing instruction in kindergarten or grades 1 to 12, inclusive, or on a street or sidewalk immediately adjacent to a building, real property, or parking area under the control of that public or private school. Nothing in this paragraph shall prohibit a person holding a valid license to carry the firearm pursuant to Chapter 4 (commencing with Section 26150) of Division 5 of Title 4 of Part 6 from carrying a firearm in accordance with that license as provided in subdivisions (b), (c), or (e) of Section 26230.

(d) Except as provided in subdivision (b), it shall be unlawful for any person, with reckless disregard for the safety of another, to discharge, or attempt to discharge, a firearm in a school zone as defined in paragraph (4) of subdivision (e). The prohibition contained in this subdivision does not apply to the discharge of a firearm to the extent that the conditions of paragraph (1) of subdivision (c) are satisfied.

(e) As used in this section, the following definitions shall apply:

(1) "Concealed firearm" has the same meaning as that term is given in Sections 25400 and 25610.

(2) "Firearm" has the same meaning as that term is given in subdivisions (a) to (d), inclusive, of Section 16520.

(3) "Locked container" has the same meaning as that term is given in Section 16850.

(4) "School zone" means an area in, or on the grounds of, a public or private school providing instruction in kindergarten or grades 1 to 12, inclusive, or within a distance of 1,000 feet from the grounds of the public or private school.

(f)

(1) A person who violates subdivision (b) by possessing a firearm in, or on the grounds of, a public or private school providing instruction in kindergarten or grades 1 to 12, inclusive, shall be punished by imprisonment pursuant to subdivision (h) of Section 1170 for two, three, or five years.

(2) A person who violates subdivision (b) by possessing a firearm within a distance of 1,000 feet from the grounds of a public or private school providing instruction in kindergarten or grades 1 to 12, inclusive, shall be punished as follows:

(A) By imprisonment pursuant to subdivision (h) of Section 1170 for two, three, or five years, if any of the following circumstances apply:

(i) If the person previously has been convicted of any felony, or of any crime made punishable by any provision listed in Section 16580.

(ii) If the person is within a class of persons prohibited from possessing or acquiring a firearm pursuant to Chapter 2 (commencing with Section 29800) or Chapter 3 (commencing with Section 29900) of Division 9 of Title 4 of Part 6 of this code or Section 8100 or 8103 of the Welfare and Institutions Code.

(iii) If the firearm is any pistol, revolver, or other firearm capable of being concealed upon the person and the offense is punished as a felony pursuant to Section 25400.

(B) By imprisonment in a county jail for not more than one year or by imprisonment pursuant to subdivision (h) of Section 1170 for two, three, or five years, in all cases other than those specified in subparagraph (A).

(3) A person who violates subdivision (d) shall be punished by imprisonment pursuant to subdivision (h) of Section 1170 for three, five, or seven years.

(g)

(1) A person convicted under this section for a misdemeanor violation of subdivision (b) who has been convicted previously of a misdemeanor offense enumerated in Section 23515 shall be punished by imprisonment in a county jail for not less than three months, or if probation is granted or if the execution or imposition of sentence is suspended, it shall be a condition thereof that they be imprisoned in a county jail for not less than three months.

(2) A person convicted under this section of a felony violation of subdivision (b) or (d) who has been convicted previously of a misdemeanor offense enumerated in Section 23515, if probation is granted or if the execution of sentence is suspended, it shall be a condition thereof that they be imprisoned in a county jail for not less than three months.

(3) A person convicted under this section for a felony violation of subdivision (b) or (d) who has been convicted previously of any felony, or of any crime made punishable by any provision listed in Section 16580, if probation is granted or if the execution or imposition of sentence is suspended, it shall be a condition thereof that they be imprisoned in a county jail for not less than three months.

(4) The court shall apply the three-month minimum sentence specified in this subdivision, except in unusual cases where the interests of justice would best be served by granting probation or suspending the execution or imposition of sentence without the minimum imprisonment required in this subdivision or by granting probation or suspending the execution or imposition of sentence with conditions other than those set forth in this subdivision, in which case the court shall specify on the record and shall enter on the minutes the circumstances indicating that the interests of justice would best be served by this disposition.

(h) Notwithstanding Section 25605, any person who brings or possesses a loaded firearm upon the grounds of a campus of, or buildings owned or operated for student housing, teaching, research, or administration by, a public or private university or college, that are contiguous or are clearly marked university property, unless it is with the written permission of the university or college president, their designee, or equivalent university or college authority, shall be punished by imprisonment pursuant to subdivision (h) of Section 1170 for two, three, or four years. Notwithstanding subdivision (k), a university or college shall post a prominent notice at primary entrances on noncontiguous property stating that firearms are prohibited on that property pursuant to this subdivision.

(i) Notwithstanding Section 25605, any person who brings or possesses a firearm upon the grounds of a campus of, or buildings owned or operated for student housing, teaching, research, or administration by, a public or private university or college, that are contiguous or are clearly marked university property, unless it is with the written permission of the university or college president, their designee, or equivalent university or college authority, shall be punished by imprisonment pursuant to subdivision (h) of Section 1170 for one, two, or three years. Notwithstanding subdivision (k), a university or college shall post a prominent notice at primary entrances on noncontiguous property stating that firearms are prohibited on that property pursuant to this subdivision.

(j) For purposes of this section, a firearm shall be deemed to be loaded when there is an unexpended cartridge or shell, consisting of a case that holds a charge of powder and a bullet or shot, in, or attached in any manner to, the firearm, including, but not limited to, in the firing chamber, magazine, or clip thereof attached to the firearm. A muzzle-loader firearm shall be deemed to be loaded when it is capped or primed and has a powder charge and ball or shot in the barrel or cylinder.

(k) This section does not require that notice be posted regarding the proscribed conduct.

(l) This section does not apply to a duly appointed peace officer as defined in Chapter 4.5 (commencing with Section 830) of Title 3 of Part 2, a full-time paid peace officer of another state or the federal government who is carrying out official duties while in California, any person summoned by any of these officers to assist in making arrests or preserving the peace while they are actually engaged in assisting the officer, a member of the military forces of this state or of the United States who is engaged in the performance of their duties, or an armored vehicle guard, engaged in the performance of their duties as defined in subdivision (d) of Section 7582.1 of the Business and Professions Code.

(m) This section does not apply to a security guard authorized to carry a loaded firearm pursuant to Article 4 (commencing with Section 26000) of Chapter 3 of Division 5 of Title 4 of Part 6.

(n) This section does not apply to an existing shooting range at a public or private school or university or college campus.

(o) This section does not apply to an honorably retired peace officer authorized to carry a concealed or loaded firearm pursuant to any of the following:

(1) Article 2 (commencing with Section 25450) of Chapter 2 of Division 5 of Title 4 of Part 6.

(2) Section 25650.

(3) Sections 25900 to 25910, inclusive.

(4) Section 26020.

(5) Paragraph (2) of subdivision (c) of Section 26300.

(p) This section does not apply to a peace officer appointed pursuant to Section 830.6 who is authorized to carry a firearm by the appointing agency.

(q)

(1) This section does not apply to the activities of a program involving shooting sports or activities, including, but not limited to, trap shooting, skeet shooting, sporting clays, and pistol shooting, that are sanctioned by a school, school district, college, university, or other governing body of the institution, that occur on the grounds of a public or private school or university or college campus.

(2) This section does not apply to the activities of a state-certified hunter education program pursuant to Section 3051 of the Fish and Game Code if all firearms are unloaded and participants do not possess live ammunition in a school building.

Amended by Stats 2023 ch 249 (SB 2),s 6, eff. 1/1/2024.

Amended by Stats 2017 ch 779 (AB 424),s 1, eff. 1/1/2018.

Amended by Stats 2015 ch 766 (SB 707),s 1, eff. 1/1/2016.

Amended by Stats 2015 ch 303 (AB 731),s 390, eff. 1/1/2016.

Amended by Stats 2011 ch 39 (AB 117),s 68, eff. 6/30/2011.

Amended by Stats 2011 ch 15 (AB 109),s 422, eff. 4/4/2011, but operative no earlier than October 1, 2011, and only upon creation of a community corrections grant program to assist in implementing this act and upon an appropriation to fund the grant program.

Amended by Stats 2011 ch 15 (AB 109),s 421, eff. 4/4/2011, but operative no earlier than October 1, 2011, and only upon creation of a community corrections grant program to assist in implementing this act and upon an appropriation to fund the grant program.

Amended by Stats 2010 ch 178 (SB 1115),s 59, eff. 1/1/2011, op. 1/1/2012.

EFFECTIVE 1/1/2000. Amended July 12, 1999 (Bill Number: SB 966) (Chapter 83).

Section 626.91 - Possession of ammunition on school grounds

Possession of ammunition on school grounds is governed by Section 30310.

Added by Stats 2010 ch 711 (SB 1080),s 1, eff. 1/1/2011, op. 1/1/2012.

Section 626.92 - Applicability of Gun-Free School Zone Act of 1995

Section 626.9 does not apply to or affect any of the following:

(a) A security guard authorized to openly carry an unloaded handgun pursuant to Chapter 6 (commencing with Section 26350) of Division 5 of Title 4 of Part 6.

(b) An honorably retired peace officer authorized to openly carry an unloaded handgun pursuant to Section 26361.

(c) A security guard authorized to openly carry an unloaded firearm that is not a handgun pursuant to Chapter 7 (commencing with Section 26400) of Division 5 of Title 4 of Part 6.

(d) An honorably retired peace officer authorized to openly carry an unloaded firearm that is not a handgun pursuant to Section 26405.

Amended by Stats 2012 ch 700 (AB 1527),s 3, eff. 1/1/2013.

Added by Stats 2011 ch 725 (AB 144),s 3, eff. 1/1/2012.

Section 626.95 - Unlawful presence at playground or youth center

(a) Any person who is in violation of paragraph (2) of subdivision (a), or subdivision (b), of Section 417, or Section 25400 or 25850, upon the grounds of or within a playground, or a public or private youth center during hours in which the facility is open for business, classes, or school-related programs, or at any time when minors are using the facility, knowing that he or she is on or within those grounds, shall be punished by imprisonment pursuant to subdivision (h) of Section 1170 for one, two, or three years, or in a county jail not exceeding one year.

(b) State and local authorities are encouraged to cause signs to be posted around playgrounds and youth centers giving warning of prohibition of the possession of firearms upon the grounds of or within playgrounds or youth centers.

(c) For purposes of this section, the following definitions shall apply:

(1) "Playground" means any park or recreational area specifically designed to be used by children that has play equipment installed, including public grounds designed for athletic activities such as baseball, football, soccer, or basketball, or any similar facility located on public or private school grounds, or on city or county parks.

(2) "Youth center" means any public or private facility that is used to host recreational or social activities for minors while minors are present.

(d) It is the Legislature's intent that only an actual conviction of a felony of one of the offenses specified in this section would subject the person to firearms disabilities under the federal Gun Control Act of 1968 (P.L. 90-618; 18 U.S.C. Sec. 921 et seq.).

Amended by Stats 2013 ch 76 (AB 383),s 147.3, eff. 1/1/2014.

Amended by Stats 2011 ch 296 (AB 1023),s 208, eff. 1/1/2012.

Amended by Stats 2011 ch 39 (AB 117),s 68, eff. 6/30/2011.

Amended by Stats 2011 ch 15 (AB 109),s 424, eff. 4/4/2011, but operative no earlier than October 1, 2011, and only upon creation of a community corrections grant program to assist in implementing this act and upon an appropriation to fund the grant program.

Amended by Stats 2010 ch 178 (SB 1115),s 60, eff. 1/1/2011, op. 1/1/2012.

Section 626.10 - Unlawful possession of dirk, dagger, ice pick, knife, razor, taser, stun gun, BB or pellet gun, or spot marker gun on school or university grounds

(a)

(1) Any person, except a duly appointed peace officer as defined in Chapter 4.5 (commencing with Section 830) of Title 3 of Part 2, a full-time paid peace officer of another state or the federal government who is carrying out official duties while in this state, a person summoned by any officer to assist in making arrests or preserving the peace while the person is actually engaged in assisting any officer, or a member of the military forces of this state or the United States who is engaged in the performance of his or her duties, who brings or possesses any dirk, dagger, ice pick, knife having a blade longer than 2^1/$_2$ inches, folding knife with a blade that locks into place, razor with an unguarded blade, taser, or stun gun, as defined in subdivision (a) of Section 244.5, any instrument that expels a metallic projectile, such as a BB or a pellet, through the force of air pressure, CO_2 pressure, or spring action, or any spot marker gun, upon the grounds of, or within, any public or private school providing instruction in kindergarten or any of grades 1 to 12, inclusive, is guilty of a public offense, punishable by imprisonment in a county jail not exceeding one year, or by imprisonment pursuant to subdivision (h) of Section 1170.

(2) Any person, except a duly appointed peace officer as defined in Chapter 4.5 (commencing with Section 830) of Title 3 of Part 2, a full-time paid peace officer of another state or the federal government who is carrying out official duties while in this state, a person summoned by any officer to assist in making arrests or preserving the peace while the person is actually engaged in assisting any officer, or a member of the military forces of this state or the United States who is engaged in the performance of his or her duties, who brings or possesses a razor blade or a box cutter upon the grounds of, or within, any public or private school providing instruction in kindergarten or any of grades 1 to 12, inclusive, is guilty of a public offense, punishable by imprisonment in a county jail not exceeding one year.

(b) Any person, except a duly appointed peace officer as defined in Chapter 4.5 (commencing with Section 830) of Title 3 of Part 2, a full-time paid peace officer of another state or the federal government who is carrying out official duties while in this state, a person summoned by any officer to assist in making arrests or preserving the peace while the person is actually engaged in assisting any officer, or a member of the military forces of this state or the United States who is engaged in the performance of his or her duties, who brings or possesses any dirk, dagger, ice pick, or knife having a fixed blade longer than $2^1/_2$ inches upon the grounds of, or within, any private university, the University of California, the California State University, or the California Community Colleges is guilty of a public offense, punishable by imprisonment in a county jail not exceeding one year, or by imprisonment pursuant to subdivision (h) of Section 1170.

(c) Subdivisions (a) and (b) do not apply to any person who brings or possesses a knife having a blade longer than $2^1/_2$ inches, a razor with an unguarded blade, a razor blade, or a box cutter upon the grounds of, or within, a public or private school providing instruction in kindergarten or any of grades 1 to 12, inclusive, or any private university, state university, or community college at the direction of a faculty member of the private university, state university, or community college, or a certificated or classified employee of the school for use in a private university, state university, community college, or school-sponsored activity or class.

(d) Subdivisions (a) and (b) do not apply to any person who brings or possesses an ice pick, a knife having a blade longer than $2^1/_2$ inches, a razor with an unguarded blade, a razor blade, or a box cutter upon the grounds of, or within, a public or private school providing instruction in kindergarten or any of grades 1 to 12, inclusive, or any private university, state university, or community college for a lawful purpose within the scope of the person's employment.

(e) Subdivision (b) does not apply to any person who brings or possesses an ice pick or a knife having a fixed blade longer than $2^1/_2$ inches upon the grounds of, or within, any private university, state university, or community college for lawful use in or around a residence or residential facility located upon those grounds or for lawful use in food preparation or consumption.

(f) Subdivision (a) does not apply to any person who brings an instrument that expels a metallic projectile, such as a BB or a pellet, through the force of air pressure, CO_2 pressure, or spring action, or any spot marker gun, or any razor blade or box cutter upon the grounds of, or within, a public or private school providing instruction in kindergarten or any of grades 1 to 12, inclusive, if the person has the written permission of the school principal or his or her designee.

(g) Any certificated or classified employee or school peace officer of a public or private school providing instruction in kindergarten or any of grades 1 to 12, inclusive, may seize any of the weapons described in subdivision (a), and any certificated or classified employee or school peace officer of any private university, state university, or community college may seize any of the weapons described in subdivision (b), from the possession of any person upon the grounds of, or within, the school if he or she knows, or has reasonable cause to know, the person is prohibited from bringing or possessing the weapon upon the grounds of, or within, the school.

(h) As used in this section, "dirk" or "dagger" means a knife or other instrument with or without a handguard that is capable of ready use as a stabbing weapon that may inflict great bodily injury or death.

(i) Any person who, without the written permission of the college or university president or chancellor or his or her designee, brings or possesses a less lethal weapon, as defined in Section 16780, or a stun gun, as defined in Section 17230, upon the grounds of, or within, a public or private college or university campus is guilty of a misdemeanor.

Amended by Stats 2013 ch 76 (AB 383),s 147.5, eff. 1/1/2014.

Amended by Stats 2011 ch 39 (AB 117),s 68, eff. 6/30/2011.

Amended by Stats 2011 ch 15 (AB 109),s 426, eff. 4/4/2011, but operative no earlier than October 1, 2011, and only upon creation of a community corrections grant program to assist in implementing this act and upon an appropriation to fund the grant program.

Amended by Stats 2011 ch 15 (AB 109),s 425, eff. 4/4/2011, but operative no earlier than October 1, 2011, and only upon creation of a community corrections grant program to assist in implementing this act and upon an appropriation to fund the grant program.

Amended by Stats 2010 ch 328 (SB 1330),s 157, eff. 1/1/2011.

Amended by Stats 2009 ch 258 (AB 870),s 1, eff. 1/1/2010.

Amended by Stats 2008 ch 676 (AB 2470),s 1, eff. 1/1/2009.

Section 626.11 - Seizure of evidence

(a) Any evidence seized by a teacher, official, employee, or governing board member of any university, state university, or community college, or by any person acting under his or her direction or with his or her consent in violation of standards relating to rights under the Fourth Amendment to the United States Constitution or under Section 13 of Article I of the State Constitution to be free from unreasonable searches and seizures, or in violation of state or federal constitutional rights to privacy, or any of them, is inadmissible in administrative disciplinary proceedings.

(b) Any provision in an agreement between a student and an educational institution specified in subdivision (a) relating to the leasing, renting, or use of a room of any student dormitory owned or operated by the institution by which the student waives a constitutional right under the Fourth Amendment to the United States Constitution or under Section 13 of Article I of the State Constitution, or under state or federal constitutional provision guaranteeing a right to privacy, or any of them, is contrary to public policy and void.

(c) Any evidence seized by a person specified in subdivision (a) after a nonconsensual entry not in violation of subdivision (a) into a dormitory room, which evidence is not directly related to the purpose for which the entry was initially made, is not admissible in administrative disciplinary proceedings.

Amended by Stats. 1983, Ch. 143, Sec. 208.

Chapter 1.1 - ACCESS TO SCHOOL PREMISES

Section 627 - Legislative findings and declarations

(a) The Legislature finds the following:

(1) Violent crimes perpetrated on public school grounds interfere with the education of students and threaten the health and safety of teachers, other employees, and students.

(2) Many serious crimes of violence are committed on school grounds by persons who are neither students nor school employees and who are not otherwise authorized to be present on school grounds.

(3) School officials and law enforcement officers, in seeking to control these persons, have been hindered by the lack of effective legislation restricting the access of unauthorized persons to school grounds and providing appropriate criminal sanctions for unauthorized entry.

(b) The Legislature declares that the purpose of this chapter is to safeguard the teachers, other employees, students, and property of public schools. The Legislature recognizes the right to visit school grounds for legitimate nonviolent purposes and does not intend by this enactment to interfere with the exercise of that right.

(c) The Legislature finds and declares that a disproportionate share of crimes committed on school campuses are committed by persons who are neither students, school officials, or staff, and who have no lawful business on the school grounds. It is the intent of the Legislature in enacting this chapter to promote the safety and security of the public schools by restricting and conditioning the access of unauthorized persons to school campuses and to thereby implement the provisions of Section 28 of Article 1 of the California Constitution which guarantee all students and staff the inalienable constitutional right to attend safe, secure, and peaceful public schools. It is also the intent of the Legislature that the provisions of this chapter shall not be construed to infringe upon the legitimate exercise of constitutionally protected rights of freedom of speech and expression which may be expressed through rallies, demonstrations, and other forms of expression which may be appropriately engaged in by students and nonstudents in a campus setting.

Amended by Stats. 1984, Ch. 395, Sec. 1.

Section 627.1 - Definitions

As used in this chapter, with regard to a public school:

(a) An "outsider" is any person other than:

(1) A student of the school; except that a student who is currently suspended from the school shall be deemed an outsider for purposes of this chapter.

(2) A parent or guardian of a student of the school.

(3) An officer or employee of the school district that maintains the school.

(4) A public employee whose employment requires him or her to be on school grounds, or any person who is on school grounds at the request of the school.

(5) A representative of a school employee organization who is engaged in activities related to the representation of school employees.

(6) An elected public official.

(7) A person who comes within the provisions of Section 1070 of the Evidence Code by virtue of his or her current employment or occupation.

(b) "School grounds" are the buildings and grounds of the public school.

(c) "School hours" extend from one hour before classes begin until one hour after classes end.

(d) "Principal" is the chief administrative officer of the public school.

(e) "Designee" is a person whom the principal has authorized to register outsiders pursuant to this chapter.

(f) "Superintendent" is the superintendent of the school district that maintains the school or a person (other than the principal or someone employed under the principal's supervision) who the superintendent has authorized to conduct hearings pursuant to Section 627.5.

Added by Stats. 1982, Ch. 76, Sec. 1. Effective March 1, 1982.

Section 627.2 - Presence of outsider on school grounds

No outsider shall enter or remain on school grounds during school hours without having registered with the principal or designee, except to proceed expeditiously to the office of the principal or designee for the purpose of registering. If signs posted in accordance with Section 627.6 restrict the entrance or route that outsiders may use to reach the office of the principal or designee, an outsider shall comply with such signs.

Added by Stats. 1982, Ch. 76, Sec. 1. Effective March 1, 1982.

Section 627.3 - Registration of outsider

In order to register, an outsider shall upon request furnish the principal or designee with the following:

(1) His or her name, address, and occupation.

(2) His or her age, if less than 21.

(3) His or her purpose in entering school grounds.

(4) Proof of identity.

(5) Other information consistent with the purposes of this chapter and with other provisions of law. No person who furnishes the information and the proof of identity required by this section shall be refused registration except as provided by Section 627.4.

Added by Stats. 1982, Ch. 76, Sec. 1. Effective March 1, 1982.

Section 627.4 - Refusal to register; revocation of outsider's registration

(a) The principal or his or her designee may refuse to register an outsider if he or she has a reasonable basis for concluding that the outsider's presence or acts would disrupt the school, its students, its teachers, or its other employees; would result in damage to property; or would result in the distribution or use of unlawful or controlled substances.

(b) The principal, his or her designee, or school security officer may revoke an outsider's registration if he or she has a reasonable basis for concluding that the outsider's presence on school grounds would interfere or is interfering with the peaceful conduct of the activities of the school, or would disrupt or is disrupting the school, its students, its teachers, or its other employees.

Repealed and added by Stats. 1984, Ch. 395, Sec. 3.

Section 627.5 - Hearing

Any person who is denied registration or whose registration is revoked may request a hearing before the principal or superintendent on the propriety of the denial or revocation. The request shall be in writing, shall state why the denial or revocation was improper, shall give the address to which notice of hearing is to be sent, and shall be delivered to either the principal or the superintendent within five days after the denial or revocation. The principal or superintendent shall promptly mail a written notice of the date, time, and place of the hearing to the person who requested the hearing. A hearing before the principal shall be held within seven days after the principal receives the request. A hearing before the superintendent shall be held within seven days after the superintendent receives the request.

Added by Stats. 1982, Ch. 76, Sec. 1. Effective March 1, 1982.

Section 627.6 - Posting of signs

At each entrance to the school grounds of every public school at which this chapter is in force, signs shall be posted specifying the hours during which registration is required pursuant to Section 627.2, stating where the office of the principal or designee is located and what route to take to that office, and setting forth the applicable requirements of Section 627.2 and the penalties for violation of this chapter.

Added by Stats. 1982, Ch. 76, Sec. 1. Effective March 1, 1982.

Section 627.7 - Unlawful failure or refusal to leave school grounds

(a) It is a misdemeanor punishable by imprisonment in the county jail not to exceed six months, or by a fine not to exceed five hundred dollars ($500), or by both, for an outsider to fail or refuse to leave the school grounds promptly after the principal, designee, or school security officer has requested the outsider to leave or to fail to remain off the school grounds for 7 days after being requested to leave, if the outsider does any of the following:

(1) Enters or remains on school grounds without having registered as required by Section 627.2.

(2) Enters or remains on school grounds after having been denied registration pursuant to subdivision (a) of Section 627.4.

(3) Enters or remains on school grounds after having registration revoked pursuant to subdivision (b) of Section 627.4.

(b) The provisions of this section shall not be utilized to impinge upon the lawful exercise of constitutionally protected rights of freedom of speech or assembly.

(c) When a person is directed to leave pursuant to subdivision (a), the person directing him or her to leave shall inform the person that if he or she reenters the place within 7 days he or she will be guilty of a crime.

Amended by Stats. 1989, Ch. 1054, Sec. 3.

Section 627.8 - Subsequent conviction

Every outsider who willfully and knowingly violates this chapter after having been previously convicted of a violation of this chapter committed within seven years of the date of two or more prior violations that resulted in conviction, shall be punished by imprisonment in the county jail for not less than 10 days nor more than six months, or by both such imprisonment and a fine not exceeding five hundred dollars ($500).

Amended by Stats. 1984, Ch. 395, Sec. 6.

Section 627.8a - Penalties

The penalties imposed by the provisions of this chapter shall be utilized to prevent, deter, and punish those committing crimes on school campuses. The penalties imposed by the provisions of this chapter shall not be utilized to infringe upon the legitimate exercise of constitutionally protected rights of free speech or assembly.

Added by Stats. 1984, Ch. 395, Sec. 7.

Section 627.9 - Authority of governing board of school district

The governing board of any school district may:

(a) Exempt the district or any school or class of schools in the district from the operation of this chapter.

(b) Make exceptions to Section 627.2 for particular classes of outsiders.

(c) Authorize principals to exempt individual outsiders from the operation of Section 627.2; but any such exemption shall be in a writing which is signed and dated by the principal and which specifies the person or persons exempted and the date on which the exemption will expire.

(d) Exempt, or authorize principals to exempt, designated portions of school grounds from the operation of this chapter during some or all school hours.

Added by Stats. 1982, Ch. 76, Sec. 1. Effective March 1, 1982.

Section 627.10 - Other punishment

A person whose presence or conduct on school grounds violates another provision of law may be punished for that violation, regardless of whether he or she was registered pursuant to this chapter at the time of the violation; but no punishment shall be imposed contrary to Section 654.

Added by Stats. 1982, Ch. 76, Sec. 1. Effective March 1, 1982.

Chapter 1.3 - MASSAGE THERAPY

Section 628 - Unlawful representation that person has received instruction in massage therapy

A person who provides a certificate, transcript, diploma, or other document, or otherwise affirms that a person has received instruction in massage therapy knowing that the person has not received instruction in massage therapy or knowing that the person has not received massage therapy instruction consistent with that document or affirmation is guilty of a misdemeanor and is punishable by a fine of not more than two thousand five hundred dollars ($2,500) per violation, or imprisonment in a county jail for not more than one year, or by both that fine and imprisonment.

Added by Stats 2011 ch 149 (SB 285),s 1, eff. 1/1/2012.

Section 628.5 - Provision of information to California Massage Therapy Council

For any person that is criminally prosecuted for a violation of law in connection with massage therapy, including for crimes relating to prostitution, the arresting law enforcement agency may provide to the California Massage Therapy Council, created pursuant to Section 4600.5 of the Business and Professions Code, information concerning the massage therapy instruction received by the person prosecuted, including the name of the school attended, if any.

Added by Stats 2011 ch 149 (SB 285),s 1, eff. 1/1/2012.

Chapter 1.2 - [REPEALED] REPORTING OF SCHOOL CRIME

Section 628 through 628.6 - [Repealed]

Repealed by Stats 2005 ch 677 (SB 512),s 49, eff. 10/7/2005.

Chapter 1.4 - INTERCEPTION OF WIRE, ELECTRONIC DIGITAL PAGER, OR ELECTRONIC CELLULAR TELEPHONE COMMUNICATIONS

Section 629.50 - [Effective until 1/1/2030] Application for order authorizing interception of wire or electronic communication

(a) Each application for an order authorizing the interception of a wire or electronic communication shall be made in writing upon the personal oath or affirmation of the Attorney General, Chief Deputy Attorney General, or Chief Assistant Attorney General, Criminal Law Division, or of a district attorney, or the person designated to act as district attorney in the district attorney's absence, to the presiding judge of the superior court or one other judge designated by the presiding judge. An ordered list of additional judges may be authorized by the presiding judge to sign an order authorizing an interception. One of these judges may hear an application and sign an order only if that judge makes a determination that the presiding judge, the first designated judge, and those judges higher on the list are unavailable. Each application shall include all of the following information:

(1) The identity of the investigative or law enforcement officer making the application, and the officer authorizing the application.

(2) The identity of the law enforcement agency that is to execute the order.

(3) A statement attesting to a review of the application and the circumstances in support thereof by the chief executive officer, or his or her designee, of the law enforcement agency making the application. This statement shall name the chief executive officer or the designee who effected this review.

(4) A full and complete statement of the facts and circumstances relied upon by the applicant to justify his or her belief that an order should be issued, including (A) details as to the particular offense that has been, is being, or is about to be committed, (B) the fact that conventional investigative techniques had been tried and were unsuccessful, or why they reasonably appear to be unlikely to succeed or to be too dangerous, (C) a particular description of the nature and location of the facilities from which or the place where the communication is to be intercepted, (D) a particular description of the type of communication sought to be intercepted, and (E) the identity, if known, of the person committing the offense and whose communications are to be intercepted, or if that person's identity is not known, then the information relating to the person's identity that is known to the applicant.

(5) A statement of the period of time for which the interception is required to be maintained, and if the nature of the investigation is such that the authorization for interception should not automatically terminate when the described type of communication has been first obtained, a particular description of the facts establishing probable cause to believe that additional communications of the same type will occur thereafter.

(6) A full and complete statement of the facts concerning all previous applications known, to the individual authorizing and to the individual making the application, to have been made to any judge of a state or federal court for authorization to intercept wire or electronic communications involving any of the same persons, facilities, or places specified in the application, and the action taken by the judge on each of those applications. This requirement may be satisfied by making inquiry of the California Attorney General and the United States Department of Justice and reporting the results of these inquiries in the application.

(7) If the application is for the extension of an order, a statement setting forth the number of communications intercepted pursuant to the original order, and the results thus far obtained from the interception, or a reasonable explanation of the failure to obtain results.

(8) An application for modification of an order may be made when there is probable cause to believe that the person or persons identified in the original order have commenced to use a facility or device that is not subject to the original order. Any modification under this subdivision shall only be valid for the period authorized under the order being modified. The application for modification shall meet all of the requirements in paragraphs (1) to (6), inclusive, and shall include a statement of the results thus far obtained from the interception, or a reasonable explanation for the failure to obtain results.

(b) The judge may require the applicant to furnish additional testimony or documentary evidence in support of an application for an order under this section.

(c) The judge shall accept a facsimile copy of the signature of any person required to give a personal oath or affirmation pursuant to subdivision (a) as an original signature to the application. The original signed document shall be sealed and kept with the application pursuant to the provisions of Section 629.66 and custody of the original signed document shall be in the same manner as the judge orders for the application.

Amended by Stats 2010 ch 707 (SB 1428),s 1, eff. 1/1/2011.

Amended by Stats 2006 ch 146 (SB 1714),s 1, eff. 1/1/2007.

Amended by Stats 2002 ch 605 (AB 74), s 1, eff. 1/1/2003.

Section 629.51 - [Effective until 1/1/2030] Definitions; applicability of chapter

(a)For the purposes of this chapter, the following terms have the following meanings:

(1)"Wire communication" means any aural transfer made in whole or in part through the use of facilities for the transmission of communications by the aid of wire, cable, or other like connection between the point of origin and the point of reception (including the use of a like connection in a switching station), furnished or operated by any person engaged in providing or operating these facilities for the transmission of communications.

(2)"Electronic communication" means any transfer of signs, signals, writings, images, sounds, data, or intelligence of any nature in whole or in part by a wire, radio, electromagnetic, photoelectric, or photo-optical system, but does not include any of the following:

(A)Any wire communication defined in paragraph (1).

(B)Any communication made through a tone-only paging device.

(C)Any communication from a tracking device.

(D)Electronic funds transfer information stored by a financial institution in a communications system used for the electronic storage and transfer of funds.

(3)"Tracking device" means an electronic or mechanical device that permits the tracking of the movement of a person or object.

(4)"Aural transfer" means a transfer containing the human voice at any point between and including the point of origin and the point of reception.

(5)

(A)"Prohibited violation" means any violation of law that creates liability for, or arising out of, either of the following:

(i)Providing, facilitating, or obtaining an abortion that is lawful under California law.

(ii)Intending or attempting to provide, facilitate, or obtain an abortion that is lawful under California law.

(B)As used in this paragraph, "facilitating" or "facilitate" means assisting, directly or indirectly in any way, with the obtaining of an abortion that is lawful under California law.

(b)This chapter applies to the interceptions of wire and electronic communications. It does not apply to stored communications or stored content.

(c)The act that added this subdivision is not intended to change the law as to stored communications or stored content.

Amended by Stats 2022 ch 627 (AB 1242),s 2, eff. 9/27/2022.

Amended by Stats 2010 ch 707 (SB 1428),s 2, eff. 1/1/2011.

Amended by Stats 2005 ch 17 (AB 1305),s 1, eff. 1/1/2006

Amended by Stats 2002 ch 605 (AB 74), s 2, eff. 1/1/2003.

Section 629.52 - [Effective until 1/1/2030] Ex parte order

Upon application made under Section 629.50, the judge may enter an ex parte order, as requested or modified, authorizing interception of wire or electronic communications initially intercepted within the territorial jurisdiction of the court in which the judge is sitting, if the judge determines, on the basis of the facts submitted by the applicant, all of the following:

(a)There is probable cause to believe that an individual is committing, has committed, or is about to commit, one of the following offenses:

(1)Importation, possession for sale, transportation, manufacture, or sale of controlled substances in violation of Section 11351, 11351.5, 11352, 11370.6, 11378, 11378.5, 11379, 11379.5, or 11379.6 of the Health and Safety Code with respect to a substance containing heroin, cocaine, PCP, methamphetamine, fentanyl, or their precursors or analogs where the substance exceeds 10 gallons by liquid volume or three pounds of solid substance by weight.

(2)Murder, solicitation to commit murder, a violation of Section 209, or the commission of a felony involving a destructive device in violation of Section 18710, 18715, 18720, 18725, 18730, 18740, 18745, 18750, or 18755.

(3)A felony violation of Section 186.22.

(4)A felony violation of Section 11418, relating to weapons of mass destruction, Section 11418.5, relating to threats to use weapons of mass destruction, or Section 11419, relating to restricted biological agents.

(5)A violation of Section 236.1.

(6)An attempt or conspiracy to commit any of the above-mentioned crimes.

(b)There is probable cause to believe that particular communications concerning the illegal activities will be obtained through that interception, including, but not limited to, communications that may be utilized for locating or rescuing a kidnap victim.

(c)There is probable cause to believe that the facilities from which, or the place where, the wire or electronic communications are to be intercepted are being used, or are about to be used, in connection with the commission of the offense, or are leased to, listed in the name of, or commonly used by the person whose communications are to be intercepted.

(d)Normal investigative procedures have been tried and have failed or reasonably appear either unlikely to succeed if tried or too dangerous.

(e)Notwithstanding any other provision in this section, no magistrate shall enter an ex parte order authorizing interception of wire or electronic communications for the purpose of investigating or recovering evidence of a prohibited violation, as defined in Section 629.51.

Amended by Stats 2022 ch 627 (AB 1242),s 3, eff. 9/27/2022.

Amended by Stats 2018 ch 294 (AB 1948),s 1, eff. 1/1/2019.

Amended by Stats 2014 ch 712 (SB 955),s 1, eff. 1/1/2015.

Amended by Stats 2011 ch 285 (AB 1402),s 16, eff. 1/1/2012, op. 1/1/2012.

Amended by Stats 2010 ch 707 (SB 1428),s 3, eff. 1/1/2011.

Amended by Stats 2010 ch 178 (SB 1115),s 62, eff. 1/1/2011, op. 1/1/2012.

Amended by Stats 2002 ch 605 (AB 74), s 3, eff. 1/1/2003.

Section 629.53 - [Effective until 1/1/2030] Guidelines

The Judicial Council may establish guidelines for judges to follow in granting an order authorizing the interception of any wire or electronic communications.

Amended by Stats 2010 ch 707 (SB 1428),s 4, eff. 1/1/2011.

Added by Stats 2002 ch 605 (AB 74), s 4, eff. 1/1/2003.

Section 629.54 - [Effective until 1/1/2030] Order authorizing interception

Each order authorizing the interception of any wire or electronic communication shall specify all of the following:

(a) The identity, if known, of the person whose communications are to be intercepted, or if the identity is not known, then that information relating to the person's identity known to the applicant.

(b) The nature and location of the communication facilities as to which, or the place where, authority to intercept is granted.

(c) A particular description of the type of communication sought to be intercepted, and a statement of the illegal activities to which it relates.

(d) The identity of the agency authorized to intercept the communications and of the person making the application.

(e) The period of time during which the interception is authorized including a statement as to whether or not the interception shall automatically terminate when the described communication has been first obtained.

Amended by Stats 2010 ch 707 (SB 1428),s 5, eff. 1/1/2011.

Amended by Stats 2002 ch 605 (AB 74), s 5, eff. 1/1/2003.

Section 629.56 - [Effective until 1/1/2030] Oral approval for interception

(a) Upon informal application by the Attorney General, Chief Deputy Attorney General, or Chief Assistant Attorney General, Criminal Law Division, or a district attorney, or the person designated to act as district attorney in the district attorney's absence, the presiding judge of the superior court or the first available judge designated as provided in Section 629.50 may grant oral approval for an interception, without an order, if he or she determines all of the following:

(1) There are grounds upon which an order could be issued under this chapter.

(2) There is probable cause to believe that an emergency situation exists with respect to the investigation of an offense enumerated in this chapter.

(3) There is probable cause to believe that a substantial danger to life or limb exists justifying the authorization for immediate interception of a private wire or electronic communication before an application for an order could with due diligence be submitted and acted upon.

(b) Approval for an interception under this section shall be conditioned upon filing with the judge, by midnight of the second full court day after the oral approval, a written application for an order which, if granted consistent with this chapter, shall also recite the oral approval under this subdivision and be retroactive to the time of the oral approval.

Amended by Stats 2010 ch 707 (SB 1428),s 6, eff. 1/1/2011.

Amended by Stats 2002 ch 605 (AB 74), s 6, eff. 1/1/2003.

Section 629.58 - [Effective until 1/1/2030] Term of order

No order entered under this chapter shall authorize the interception of any wire or electronic communication for any period longer than is necessary to achieve the objective of the authorization, nor in any event longer than 30 days, commencing on the day of the initial interception, or 10 days after the issuance of the order, whichever comes first. Extensions of an order may be granted, but only upon application for an extension made in accordance with Section 629.50 and upon the court making findings required by Section 629.52. The period of extension shall be no longer than the authorizing judge deems necessary to achieve the purposes for which it was granted and in no event any longer than 30 days. Every order and extension thereof shall contain a provision that the authorization to intercept shall be executed as soon as practicable, shall be conducted so as to minimize the interception of communications not otherwise subject to interception under this chapter, and shall terminate upon attainment of the authorized objective, or in any event at the time expiration of the term designated in the order or any extensions. In the event the intercepted communication is in a foreign language, an interpreter of that foreign language may assist peace officers in executing the authorization provided in this chapter, provided that the interpreter has the same training as any other interceptor authorized under this chapter and provided that the interception shall be conducted so as to minimize the interception of communications not otherwise subject to interception under this chapter.

Amended by Stats 2010 ch 707 (SB 1428),s 7, eff. 1/1/2011.

Amended by Stats 2002 ch 605 (AB 74), s 7, eff. 1/1/2003.

Section 629.60 - [Effective until 1/1/2030] Report to judge

Whenever an order authorizing an interception is entered, the order shall require reports in writing or otherwise to be made to the judge who issued the order showing the number of communications intercepted pursuant to the original order, and a statement setting forth what progress has been made toward achievement of the authorized objective, or a satisfactory explanation for its lack, and the need for continued interception. If the judge finds that progress has not been made, that the explanation for its lack is not satisfactory, or that no need exists for continued interception, he or she shall order that the interception immediately terminate. The reports shall be filed with the court at the intervals that the judge may require, but not less than one for each period of 10 days, commencing with the date of the signing of the order, and shall be made by any reasonable and reliable means, as determined by the judge.

Amended by Stats 2010 ch 707 (SB 1428),s 8, eff. 1/1/2011.

Amended by Stats 2002 ch 605 (AB 74), s 8, eff. 1/1/2003.

Section 629.61 - [Effective until 1/1/2030] Report to attorney general

(a) Whenever an order authorizing an interception is entered, the order shall require a report in writing or otherwise to be made to the Attorney General showing what persons, facilities, places, or any combination of these are to be intercepted pursuant to the application, and the action taken by the judge on each of those applications. The report shall be made at the interval that the order may require, but not more than 10 days after the order was issued, and shall be made by any reasonable and reliable means, as determined by the Attorney General.

(b) The Attorney General may issue regulations prescribing the collection and dissemination of information collected pursuant to this chapter.

(c) The Attorney General shall, upon the request of an individual making an application for an interception order pursuant to this chapter, provide any information known as a result of these reporting requirements and in compliance with paragraph (6) of subdivision (a) of Section 629.50.

Amended by Stats 2004 ch 405 (SB 1796), s 9, eff. 1/1/2005.

Added by Stats 2002 ch 605 (AB 74), s 9, eff. 1/1/2003.

Section 629.62 - [Effective until 1/1/2030] Annual report

(a) The Attorney General shall prepare and submit an annual report to the Legislature, the Judicial Council, and the Director of the Administrative Office of the United States Courts on interceptions conducted under the authority of this chapter during the preceding year. Information for this report shall be provided to the Attorney General by any prosecutorial agency seeking an order pursuant to this chapter.

(b) The report shall include all of the following data:

(1) The number of orders or extensions applied for.

(2) The kinds of orders or extensions applied for.

(3) The fact that the order or extension was granted as applied for, was modified, or was denied.

(4) The number of wire or electronic communication devices that are the subject of each order granted.

(5) The period of interceptions authorized by the order, and the number and duration of any extensions of the order.

(6) The offense specified in the order or application, or extension of an order.

(7) The identity of the applying law enforcement officer and agency making the application and the person authorizing the application.

(8) The nature of the facilities from which or the place where communications were to be intercepted.

(9) A general description of the interceptions made under the order or extension, including (A) the number of persons whose communications were intercepted, (B) the number of communications intercepted, (C) the percentage of incriminating communications intercepted and the percentage of other communications intercepted, and (D) the approximate nature, amount, and cost of the manpower and other resources used in the interceptions.

(10) The number of arrests resulting from interceptions made under the order or extension, and the offenses for which arrests were made.

(11) The number of trials resulting from the interceptions.

(12) The number of motions to suppress made with respect to the interceptions, and the number granted or denied.

(13) The number of convictions resulting from the interceptions and the offenses for which the convictions were obtained and a general assessment of the importance of the interceptions.

(14) Except with regard to the initial report required by this section, the information required by paragraphs (9) to (13), inclusive, with respect to orders or extensions obtained in a preceding calendar year.

(15) The date of the order for service of inventory made pursuant to Section 629.68, confirmation of compliance with the order, and the number of notices sent.

(16) Other data that the Legislature, the Judicial Council, or the Director of the Administrative Office of the United States Courts shall require.

(c) The annual report shall be filed no later than April of each year, and shall also include a summary analysis of the data reported pursuant to subdivision (b). The Attorney General may issue regulations prescribing the content and form of the reports required to be filed pursuant to this section by any prosecutorial agency seeking an order to intercept wire or electronic communications.

(d) The Attorney General shall, upon the request of an individual making an application, provide any information known to him or her as a result of these reporting requirements that would enable the individual making an application to comply with paragraph (6) of subdivision (a) of Section 629.50.

Amended by Stats 2012 ch 162 (SB 1171),s 126, eff. 1/1/2013.

Amended by Stats 2011 ch 663 (SB 61),s 1, eff. 1/1/2012.

Amended by Stats 2010 ch 707 (SB 1428),s 9, eff. 1/1/2011.

Amended by Stats 2003 ch 468 (SB 851), s 8, eff. 1/1/2004.

Amended by Stats 2002 ch 605 (AB 74), s 10, eff. 1/1/2003.

Section 629.64 - [Effective until 1/1/2030] Recording

The contents of any wire or electronic communication intercepted by any means authorized by this chapter shall, if possible, be recorded on any recording media. The recording of the contents of any wire or electronic communication pursuant to this chapter shall be done in a way that will protect the recording from editing or other alterations and ensure that the recording can be immediately verified as to its authenticity and originality and that any alteration can be immediately detected. In addition, the monitoring or recording device shall be of a type and shall be installed to preclude any interruption or monitoring of the interception by any unauthorized means. Immediately upon the expiration of the period of the order, or extensions thereof, the recordings shall be made available to the judge issuing the order and sealed under his or her directions. Custody of the recordings shall be where the judge orders. They shall not be destroyed except upon an order of the issuing or denying judge and in any event shall be kept for 10 years. Duplicate recordings may be made for use or disclosure pursuant to the provisions of Sections 629.74 and 629.76 for investigations. The presence of the seal provided for by this section, or a satisfactory explanation for the absence thereof, shall be a prerequisite for the use or disclosure of the contents of any wire or electronic communication or evidence derived therefrom under Section 629.78.

Amended by Stats 2010 ch 707 (SB 1428),s 10, eff. 1/1/2011.

Amended by Stats 2002 ch 605 (AB 74), s 11, eff. 1/1/2003.

Section 629.66 - [Effective until 1/1/2030] Sealing of applications and orders

Applications made and orders granted pursuant to this chapter shall be sealed by the judge. Custody of the applications and orders shall be where the judge orders. The applications and orders shall be disclosed only upon a showing of good cause before a judge or for compliance with the provisions of subdivisions (b) and (c) of Section 629.70 and shall not be destroyed except on order of the issuing or denying judge, and in any event shall be kept for 10 years.

Amended by Stats 2010 ch 707 (SB 1428),s 11, eff. 1/1/2011.

Section 629.68 - [Effective until 1/1/2030] Order to serve inventory

Within a reasonable time, but no later than 90 days, after the termination of the period of an order or extensions thereof, or after the filing of an application for an order of approval under Section 629.56 which has been denied, the issuing judge shall issue an order that shall require the requesting agency to serve upon persons named in the order or the application, and other known parties to intercepted communications, an inventory which shall include notice of all of the following:

(a) The fact of the entry of the order.

(b) The date of the entry and the period of authorized interception.

(c) The fact that during the period wire or electronic communications were or were not intercepted. The judge, upon filing of a motion, may, in his or her discretion, make available to the person or his or her counsel for inspection the portions of the intercepted communications, applications, and orders that the judge determines to be in the interest of justice. On an ex parte showing of good cause to a judge, the serving of the inventory required by this section may be postponed. The period of postponement shall be no longer than the authorizing judge deems necessary to achieve the purposes for which it was granted.

Amended by Stats 2010 ch 707 (SB 1428),s 12, eff. 1/1/2011.

Amended by Stats 2002 ch 605 (AB 74), s 12, eff. 1/1/2003.

Section 629.70 - [Effective until 1/1/2030] Notice; copy of recorded interceptions

(a) A defendant shall be notified that he or she was identified as the result of an interception that was obtained pursuant to this chapter. The notice shall be provided prior to the entry of a plea of guilty or nolo contendere, or at least 10 days prior to any trial, hearing, or proceeding in the case other than an arraignment or grand jury proceeding.

(b) Within the time period specified in subdivision (c), the prosecution shall provide to the defendant a copy of all recorded interceptions from which evidence against the defendant was derived, including a copy of the court order, accompanying application, and monitoring logs.

(c) Neither the contents of any intercepted wire or electronic communication nor evidence derived from those contents shall be received in evidence or otherwise disclosed in any trial, hearing, or other proceeding, except a grand jury proceeding, unless each party, not less than 10 days before the trial, hearing, or proceeding, has been furnished with a transcript of the contents of the interception and with the materials specified in subdivision (b). This 10-day period may be waived by the judge with regard to the transcript if he or she finds that it was not possible to furnish the party with the transcript 10 days before the trial, hearing, or proceeding, and that the party will not be prejudiced by the delay in receiving that transcript.

(d) A court may issue an order limiting disclosures pursuant to subdivisions (a) and (b) upon a showing of good cause.

Amended by Stats 2010 ch 707 (SB 1428),s 13, eff. 1/1/2011.

Amended by Stats 2002 ch 605 (AB 74), s 13, eff. 1/1/2003.

Section 629.72 - [Effective until 1/1/2030] Motion to suppress

Any person in any trial, hearing, or proceeding, may move to suppress some or all of the contents of any intercepted wire or electronic communications, or evidence derived therefrom, only on the basis that the contents or evidence were obtained in violation of the Fourth Amendment of the United States Constitution or of this chapter. The motion shall be made, determined, and be subject to review in accordance with the procedures set forth in Section 1538.5.

Amended by Stats 2010 ch 707 (SB 1428),s 14, eff. 1/1/2011.

Amended by Stats 2002 ch 605 (AB 74), s 14, eff. 1/1/2003.

Section 629.74 - [Effective until 1/1/2030] Disclosure of contents of wire or electronic communication

The Attorney General, any deputy attorney general, district attorney, or deputy district attorney, or any peace officer who, by any means authorized by this chapter, has obtained knowledge of the contents of any wire or electronic communication, or evidence derived therefrom, may disclose the contents to one of the individuals referred to in this section, to any judge or magistrate in the state, and to any investigative or law enforcement officer as defined in subdivision (7) of Section 2510 of Title 18 of the United States Code to the extent that the disclosure is permitted pursuant to Section 629.82 and is appropriate to the proper performance of the official duties of the individual making or receiving the disclosure. No other disclosure, except to a grand jury, of intercepted information is permitted prior to a public court hearing by any person regardless of how the person may have come into possession thereof.

Amended by Stats 2010 ch 707 (SB 1428),s 15, eff. 1/1/2011.

Amended by Stats 2002 ch 605 (AB 74), s 15, eff. 1/1/2003.

Section 629.76 - [Effective until 1/1/2030] Use of contents of wire or electronic communication

The Attorney General, any deputy attorney general, district attorney, or deputy district attorney, or any peace officer or federal law enforcement officer who, by any means authorized by this chapter, has obtained knowledge of the contents of any wire or electronic communication, or evidence derived therefrom, may use the contents or evidence to the extent the use is appropriate to the proper performance of his or her official duties and is permitted pursuant to Section 629.82.

Amended by Stats 2010 ch 707 (SB 1428),s 16, eff. 1/1/2011.

Amended by Stats 2002 ch 605 (AB 74), s 16, eff. 1/1/2003.

Section 629.78 - [Effective until 1/1/2030] Disclosure while giving testimony

Any person who has received, by any means authorized by this chapter, any information concerning a wire or electronic communication, or evidence derived therefrom, intercepted in accordance with the provisions of this chapter, may, pursuant to Section 629.82, disclose the contents of that communication or derivative evidence while giving testimony under oath or affirmation in any criminal court proceeding or in any grand jury proceeding, or in an administrative or disciplinary hearing involving the employment of a peace officer.

Amended by Stats 2019 ch 645 (SB 439),s 1, eff. 1/1/2020.

Amended by Stats 2010 ch 707 (SB 1428),s 17, eff. 1/1/2011.

Amended by Stats 2002 ch 605 (AB 74), s 17, eff. 1/1/2003.

Section 629.80 - [Effective until 1/1/2030] Intercepted privileged communication

No otherwise privileged communication intercepted in accordance with, or in violation of, the provisions of this chapter shall lose its privileged character. When a peace officer or federal law enforcement officer, while engaged in intercepting wire or electronic communications in the manner authorized by this chapter, intercepts wire or electronic communications that are of a privileged nature he or she shall immediately cease the interception for at least two minutes. After a period of at least two minutes, interception may be resumed for up to 30 seconds during which time the officer shall determine if the nature of the communication is still privileged. If still of a privileged nature, the officer shall again cease interception for at least two minutes, after which the officer may again resume interception for up to 30 seconds to redetermine the nature of the communication. The officer shall continue to go online and offline in this manner until the time that the communication is no longer privileged or the communication ends. The recording device shall be metered so as to authenticate upon review that interruptions occurred as set forth in this chapter.

Amended by Stats 2010 ch 707 (SB 1428),s 18, eff. 1/1/2011.

Amended by Stats 2002 ch 605 (AB 74), s 18, eff. 1/1/2003.

Section 629.82 - [Effective until 1/1/2030] Interception of wire or electronic communications relating to crimes other than those specified in order of authorization

(a) If a peace officer or federal law enforcement officer, while engaged in intercepting wire or electronic communications in the manner authorized by this chapter, intercepts wire or electronic communications relating to crimes other than those specified in the order of authorization, but that are enumerated in subdivision (a) of Section 629.52, grand theft involving a firearm, a violation of Section 18750 or 18755, or a violent felony as defined in subdivision (c) of Section 667.5, (1) the contents thereof, and evidence derived therefrom, may be disclosed or used as provided in Sections 629.74 and 629.76 and (2) the contents and any evidence derived therefrom may be used under Section 629.78 when authorized by a judge if the judge finds, upon subsequent application, that the contents were otherwise intercepted in accordance with the provisions of this chapter. The application shall be made as soon as practicable.

(b) If a peace officer or federal law enforcement officer, while engaged in intercepting wire or electronic communications in the manner authorized by this chapter, intercepts wire or electronic communications relating to crimes other than those specified in subdivision (a), the contents thereof, and evidence derived therefrom, may not be disclosed or used as provided in Sections 629.74 and 629.76, except to prevent the commission of a public offense. The contents and any evidence derived therefrom may not be used under Section 629.78, except where the evidence was obtained through an independent source or inevitably would have been discovered, and the use is authorized by a judge who finds that the contents were intercepted in accordance with this chapter.

(c) The use of the contents of an intercepted wire or electronic communication relating to crimes other than those specified in the order of authorization to obtain a search or arrest warrant entitles the person named in the warrant to notice of the intercepted wire or electronic communication and a copy of the contents thereof that were used to obtain the warrant.

(d)

(1) If a peace officer or federal law enforcement officer, while engaged in intercepting wire or electronic communications in the manner authorized by this chapter, intercepts wire or electronic communications relating to crimes, other than those specified in subdivision (a), and involving the employment of a peace officer, the contents thereof, and evidence derived therefrom, may not be disclosed or used as provided in Sections 629.74 and 629.76, except to prevent the commission of a public offense or in an administrative or disciplinary hearing involving the employment of a peace officer. The contents and any evidence derived therefrom may not be used under Section 629.78, except if the evidence was obtained through an independent source or inevitably would have been discovered, and the use is authorized by a judge who finds that the contents were intercepted in accordance with this chapter.

(2) This section does not authorize the use of an intercepted wire or electronic communication involving acts that only involve a violation of a departmental rule or guideline that is not a public offense under California law.

(3) If an agency employing peace officers utilizes evidence obtained pursuant to this subdivision in an administrative or disciplinary proceeding, the agency shall, on an annual basis, report both of the following to the Attorney General:

(A) The number of administrative or disciplinary proceedings involving the employment of a peace officer in which the agency utilized evidence obtained pursuant to this subdivision.

(B) The specific offenses for which evidence obtained pursuant to this subdivision was used in those administrative or disciplinary proceedings.

(4)

(A) The Attorney General may issue regulations prescribing the form of the reports required to be filed pursuant to paragraph (3) by an agency utilizing intercepted wire or electronic communications in an administrative or disciplinary proceeding against a peace officer.

(B) The Attorney General shall include information received pursuant to paragraph (3) in its annual report made pursuant to Section 629.62.

Amended by Stats 2019 ch 645 (SB 439),s 2, eff. 1/1/2020.

Amended by Stats 2010 ch 707 (SB 1428),s 19, eff. 1/1/2011.

Amended by Stats 2002 ch 605 (AB 74), s 19, eff. 1/1/2003.

Section 629.84 - [Effective until 1/1/2030] Punishment for violation of chapter

Any violation of this chapter is punishable by a fine not exceeding two thousand five hundred dollars ($2,500), or by imprisonment in the county jail not exceeding one year, or by imprisonment pursuant to subdivision (h) of Section 1170, or by both that fine and imprisonment.

Amended by Stats 2011 ch 39 (AB 117),s 68, eff. 6/30/2011.

Amended by Stats 2011 ch 15 (AB 109),s 427, eff. 4/4/2011, but operative no earlier than October 1, 2011, and only upon creation of a community corrections grant program to assist in implementing this act and upon an appropriation to fund the grant program.

Section 629.86 - [Effective until 1/1/2030] Remedies

Any person whose wire or electronic communication is intercepted, disclosed, or used in violation of this chapter shall have the following remedies:

(a) Have a civil cause of action against any person who intercepts, discloses, or uses, or procures any other person to intercept, disclose, or use, the communications.

(b) Be entitled to recover, in that action, all of the following:

(1) Actual damages but not less than liquidated damages computed at the rate of one hundred dollars ($100) a day for each day of violation or one thousand dollars ($1,000), whichever is greater.

(2) Punitive damages.

(3) Reasonable attorney's fees and other litigation costs reasonably incurred. A good faith reliance on a court order is a complete defense to any civil or criminal action brought under this chapter, or under Chapter 1.5 (commencing with Section 630) or any other law.

Amended by Stats 2010 ch 707 (SB 1428),s 20, eff. 1/1/2011.

Amended by Stats 2002 ch 605 (AB 74), s 20, eff. 1/1/2003.

Section 629.88 - [Effective until 1/1/2030] Acts not prohibited

Nothing in Section 631, 632.5, 632.6, or 632.7 shall be construed as prohibiting any peace officer or federal law enforcement officer from intercepting any wire or electronic communication pursuant to an order issued in accordance with the provisions of this chapter. Nothing in Section 631, 632.5, 632.6, or 632.7 shall be construed as rendering inadmissible in any criminal proceeding in any court or before any grand jury any evidence obtained by means of an order issued in accordance with the provisions of this chapter. Nothing in Section 637 shall be construed as prohibiting the disclosure of the contents of any wire or electronic communication obtained by any means authorized by this chapter, if the disclosure is authorized by this chapter. Nothing in this chapter shall apply to any conduct authorized by Section 633.

Amended by Stats 2010 ch 707 (SB 1428),s 21, eff. 1/1/2011.

Amended by Stats 2002 ch 605 (AB 74), s 21, eff. 1/1/2003.

Section 629.89 - [Effective until 1/1/2030] Covert entry prohibited

No order issued pursuant to this chapter shall either directly or indirectly authorize covert entry into or upon the premises of a residential dwelling, hotel room, or motel room for installation or removal of any interception device or for any other purpose. Notwithstanding that this entry is otherwise prohibited by any other section or code, this chapter expressly prohibits covert entry of a residential dwelling, hotel room, or motel room to facilitate an order to intercept wire or electronic communications.

Amended by Stats 2010 ch 707 (SB 1428),s 22, eff. 1/1/2011.

Amended by Stats 2002 ch 605 (AB 74), s 22, eff. 1/1/2003.

Section 629.90 - [Effective until 1/1/2030] Assistance of public utility, landlord, custodian, or other person

An order authorizing the interception of a wire or electronic communication shall direct, upon request of the applicant, that a public utility engaged in the business of providing communications services and facilities, a landlord, custodian, or any other person furnish the applicant forthwith all information, facilities, and technical assistance necessary to accomplish the interception unobtrusively and with a minimum of interference with the services which the public utility, landlord, custodian, or other person is providing the person whose communications are to be intercepted. Any such public utility, landlord, custodian, or other person furnishing facilities or technical assistance shall be fully compensated by the applicant for the reasonable costs of furnishing the facilities and technical assistance.

Amended by Stats 2010 ch 707 (SB 1428),s 23, eff. 1/1/2011.

Amended by Stats 2002 ch 605 (AB 74), s 23, eff. 1/1/2003.

Section 629.91 - [Effective until 1/1/2030] Good faith reliance on court order

A good faith reliance on a court order issued in accordance with this chapter by any public utility, landlord, custodian, or any other person furnishing information, facilities, and technical assistance as directed by the order is a complete defense to any civil or criminal action brought under this chapter, Chapter 1.5 (commencing with Section 630), or any other law.

Added by Stats. 1995, Ch. 971, Sec. 10. Effective January 1, 1996. Repealed as of January 1, 2025, pursuant to Section 629.98.

Section 629.92 - [Effective until 1/1/2030] Taking evidence, making findings, or issuing order

Notwithstanding any other provision of law, any court to which an application is made in accordance with this chapter may take any evidence, make any finding, or issue any order required to conform the proceedings or the issuance of any order of authorization or approval to the provisions of the Constitution of the United States, any law of the United States, or this chapter.

Added by Stats. 1995, Ch. 971, Sec. 10. Effective January 1, 1996. Repealed as of January 1, 2025, pursuant to Section 629.98.

Section 629.94 - [Effective until 1/1/2030] Course of training, certification

(a) The Commission on Peace Officer Standards and Training, in consultation with the Attorney General, shall establish a course of training in the legal, practical, and technical aspects of the interception of private wire or electronic communications and related investigative techniques.

(b) The Attorney General shall set minimum standards for certification and periodic recertification of the following persons as eligible to apply for orders authorizing the interception of private wire or electronic communications, to conduct the interceptions, and to use the communications or evidence derived from them in official proceedings:

   (1) Investigative or law enforcement officers.

   (2) Other persons, when necessary, to provide linguistic interpretation who are designated by the Attorney General, Chief Deputy Attorney General, or Chief Assistant Attorney General, Criminal Law Division, or the district attorney, or the district attorney's designee and are supervised by an investigative or law enforcement officer.

(c) The Commission on Peace Officer Standards and Training may charge a reasonable enrollment fee for those students who are employed by an agency not eligible for reimbursement by the commission to offset the costs of the training. The Attorney General may charge a reasonable fee to offset the cost of certification.

Amended by Stats 2010 ch 707 (SB 1428),s 24, eff. 1/1/2011.

Amended by Stats 2002 ch 605 (AB 74), s 24, eff. 1/1/2003.

Section 629.96 - [Effective until 1/1/2030] Severability

If any provision of this chapter, or the application thereof to any person or circumstances, is held invalid, the remainder of the chapter, and the application of its provisions to other persons or circumstances, shall not be affected thereby.

Added by Stats. 1995, Ch. 971, Sec. 10. Effective January 1, 1996. Repealed as of January 1, 2025, pursuant to Section 629.98.

Section 629.98 - [Effective until 1/1/2030] Repealer

This chapter shall remain in effect only until January 1, 2030, and as of that date is repealed.

Amended by Stats 2023 ch 488 (SB 514),s 1, eff. 1/1/2024.

Amended by Stats 2019 ch 607 (AB 304),s 1, eff. 1/1/2020.

Amended by Stats 2014 ch 745 (SB 35),s 1, eff. 1/1/2015.

Amended by Stats 2011 ch 663 (SB 61),s 2, eff. 1/1/2012.

Amended by Stats 2007 ch 391 (AB 569),s 1, eff. 1/1/2008.

Amended by Stats 2002 ch 605 (AB 74), s 25, eff. 1/1/2003.

Chapter 1.5 - INVASION OF PRIVACY

Section 630 - Legislative declarations

The Legislature hereby declares that advances in science and technology have led to the development of new devices and techniques for the purpose of eavesdropping upon private communications and that the invasion of privacy resulting from the continual and increasing use of such devices and techniques has created a serious threat to the free exercise of personal liberties and cannot be tolerated in a free and civilized society.

The Legislature by this chapter intends to protect the right of privacy of the people of this state.

The Legislature recognizes that law enforcement agencies have a legitimate need to employ modern listening devices and techniques in the investigation of criminal conduct and the apprehension of lawbreakers. Therefore, it is not the intent of the Legislature to place greater restraints on the use of listening devices and techniques by law enforcement agencies than existed prior to the effective date of this chapter.

Added by Stats. 1967, Ch. 1509.

Section 631 - Unlawful tapping

(a)Any person who, by means of any machine, instrument, or contrivance, or in any other manner, intentionally taps, or makes any unauthorized connection, whether physically, electrically, acoustically, inductively, or otherwise, with any telegraph or telephone wire, line, cable, or instrument, including the wire, line, cable, or instrument of any internal telephonic communication system, or who willfully and without the consent of all parties to the communication, or in any unauthorized manner, reads, or attempts to read, or to learn the contents or meaning of any message, report, or communication while the same is in transit or passing over any wire, line, or cable, or is being sent from, or received at any place within this state; or who uses, or attempts to use, in any manner, or for any purpose, or to communicate in any way, any information so obtained, or who aids, agrees with, employs, or conspires with any person or persons to unlawfully do, or permit, or cause to be done any of the acts or things mentioned above in this section, is punishable by a fine not exceeding two thousand five hundred dollars ($2,500), or by imprisonment in the county jail not exceeding one year, or by imprisonment pursuant to subdivision (h) of Section 1170, or by both a fine and imprisonment in the county jail or pursuant to subdivision (h) of Section 1170. If the person has previously been convicted of a violation of this section or Section 632, 632.5, 632.6, 632.7, or 636, the offense is punishable by a fine not exceeding ten thousand dollars ($10,000), or by imprisonment in the county jail not exceeding one year, or by imprisonment pursuant to subdivision (h) of Section 1170, or by both that fine and imprisonment.

(b)This section shall not apply to any of the following:

(1)Any public utility, or telephone company, engaged in the business of providing communications services and facilities, or to the officers, employees or agents thereof, where the acts otherwise prohibited herein are for the purpose of construction, maintenance, conduct or operation of the services and facilities of the public utility or telephone company.

(2)The use of any instrument, equipment, facility, or service furnished and used pursuant to the tariffs of a public utility.

(3)Any telephonic communication system used for communication exclusively within a state, county, city and county, or city correctional facility.

(c)For purposes of this section, "telephone company" is defined in paragraph (3) of subdivision (c) of Section 638.

(d)Except as proof in an action or prosecution for violation of this section, no evidence obtained in violation of this section shall be admissible in any judicial, administrative, legislative, or other proceeding.

Amended by Stats 2022 ch 27 (SB 1272),s 1, eff. 1/1/2023.

Amended by Stats 2011 ch 39 (AB 117),s 68, eff. 6/30/2011.

Amended by Stats 2011 ch 15 (AB 109),s 428, eff. 4/4/2011, but operative no earlier than October 1, 2011, and only upon creation of a community corrections grant program to assist in implementing this act and upon an appropriation to fund the grant program.

Section 632 - Unlawful eavesdropping or recording

(a) A person who, intentionally and without the consent of all parties to a confidential communication, uses an electronic amplifying or recording device to eavesdrop upon or record the confidential communication, whether the communication is carried on among the parties in the presence of one another or by means of a telegraph, telephone, or other device, except a radio, shall be punished by a fine not exceeding two thousand five hundred dollars ($2,500) per violation, or imprisonment in a county jail not exceeding one year, or in the state prison, or by both that fine and imprisonment. If the person has previously been convicted of a violation of this section or Section 631, 632.5, 632.6, 632.7, or 636, the person shall be punished by a fine not exceeding ten thousand dollars ($10,000) per violation, by imprisonment in a county jail not exceeding one year, or in the state prison, or by both that fine and imprisonment.

(b) For the purposes of this section, "person" means an individual, business association, partnership, corporation, limited liability company, or other legal entity, and an individual acting or purporting to act for or on behalf of any government or subdivision thereof, whether federal, state, or local, but excludes an individual known by all parties to a confidential communication to be overhearing or recording the communication.

(c) For the purposes of this section, "confidential communication" means any communication carried on in circumstances as may reasonably indicate that any party to the communication desires it to be confined to the parties thereto, but excludes a communication made in a public gathering or in any legislative, judicial, executive, or administrative proceeding open to the public, or in any other circumstance in which the parties to the communication may reasonably expect that the communication may be overheard or recorded.

(d) Except as proof in an action or prosecution for violation of this section, evidence obtained as a result of eavesdropping upon or recording a confidential communication in violation of this section is not admissible in any judicial, administrative, legislative, or other proceeding.

(e) This section does not apply (1) to any public utility engaged in the business of providing communications services and facilities, or to the officers, employees, or agents thereof, if the acts otherwise prohibited by this section are for the purpose of construction, maintenance, conduct, or operation of the services and facilities of the public utility, (2) to the use of any instrument, equipment, facility, or service furnished and used pursuant to the tariffs of a public utility, or (3) to any telephonic communication system used for communication exclusively within a state, county, city and county, or city correctional facility.

(f) This section does not apply to the use of hearing aids and similar devices, by persons afflicted with impaired hearing, for the purpose of overcoming the impairment to permit the hearing of sounds ordinarily audible to the human ear.

Amended by Stats 2016 ch 855 (AB 1671),s 1, eff. 1/1/2017.

Section 632.01 - Penalty for intentional distribution of information unlawfully collected via web site or social media

(a)

(1) A person who violates subdivision (a) of Section 632 shall be punished pursuant to subdivision (b) if the person intentionally discloses or distributes, in any manner, in any forum, including, but not limited to, Internet Web sites and social media, or for any purpose, the contents of a confidential communication with a health care provider that is obtained by that person in violation of subdivision (a) of Section 632. For purposes of this subdivision, "social media" means an electronic service or account, or electronic content, including, but not limited to, videos or still photographs, blogs, video blogs, podcasts, instant and text messages, email, online services or accounts, or Internet Web site profiles or locations.

(2) Notwithstanding any other provision of law, to aid and abet a violation of paragraph (1), for the purposes of Section 31, the person shall either violate, or aid and abet in a violation of, both Section 632 and paragraph (1).

(b) A violation of subdivision (a) shall be punished by a fine not exceeding two thousand five hundred dollars ($2,500) per violation, or imprisonment in a county jail not exceeding one year, or in the state prison, or by both that fine and imprisonment. If the person has previously been convicted of a violation of this section, the person shall be punished by a fine not exceeding ten thousand dollars ($10,000) per violation, by imprisonment in a county jail not exceeding one year, or in the state prison, or by both that fine and imprisonment.

(c) For purposes of this section, "health care provider" means any of the following:

(1) A person licensed or certified pursuant to Division 2 (commencing with Section 500) of the Business and Professions Code.

(2) A person licensed pursuant to the Osteopathic Initiative Act or the Chiropractic Initiative Act.

(3) A person certified pursuant to Division 2.5 (commencing with Section 1797) of the Health and Safety Code.

(4) A clinic, health dispensary, or health facility licensed or exempt from licensure pursuant to Division 2 (commencing with Section 1200) of the Health and Safety Code.

(5) An employee, volunteer, or contracted agent of any group practice prepayment health care service plan regulated pursuant to the Knox-Keene Health Care Service Plan Act of 1975 (Chapter 2.2 (commencing with Section 1340) of Division 2 of the Health and Safety Code).

(6) An employee, volunteer, independent contractor, or professional student of a clinic, health dispensary, or health care facility or health care provider described in this subdivision.

(7) A professional organization that represents any of the other health care providers described in this subdivision.

(d)

(1) Subdivision (a) does not apply to the disclosure or distribution of a confidential communication pursuant to any of the following:

(A) Any party as described in Section 633 acting within the scope of his or her authority overhearing or recording a confidential communication that he or she may lawfully overhear or record pursuant to that section.

(B) Any party as described in Section 633.02 overhearing or recording a confidential communication related to sexual assault or other sexual offense that he or she may lawfully overhear or record pursuant to that section, or using or operating a body-worn camera as authorized pursuant to that section.

(C) A city attorney as described in Section 633.05 overhearing or recording any communication that he or she may lawfully overhear or record pursuant to that section.

(D) An airport law enforcement officer recording a communication received on an incoming telephone line pursuant to Section 633.1.

(E) A party to a confidential communication recording the communication for the purpose of obtaining evidence reasonably believed to relate to the commission by another party to the communication of a crime as specified in Section 633.5.

(F) A victim of domestic violence recording a prohibited communication made to him or her by the perpetrator pursuant to Section 633.6.

(G) A peace officer using electronic amplifying or recording devices to eavesdrop on and record the otherwise confidential oral communications of individuals within a location when responding to an emergency situation that involves the taking of a hostage or the barricading of a location pursuant to Section 633.8.

(2) This section does not affect the admissibility of any evidence that would otherwise be admissible pursuant to the authority of any section specified in paragraph (1).

Added by Stats 2016 ch 855 (AB 1671),s 2, eff. 1/1/2017.

Section 632.5 - Malicious interception or receipt of communication transmitted between cellular radio telephones or between cellular radio telephone and landline telephone

(a) Every person who, maliciously and without the consent of all parties to the communication, intercepts, receives, or assists in intercepting or receiving a communication transmitted between cellular radio telephones or between any cellular radio telephone and a landline telephone shall be punished by a fine not exceeding two thousand five hundred dollars ($2,500), by imprisonment in the county jail not exceeding one year or in the state prison, or by both that fine and imprisonment. If the person has been previously convicted of a violation of this section or Section 631, 632, 632.6, 632.7, or 636, the person shall be punished by a fine not exceeding ten thousand dollars ($10,000), by imprisonment in the county jail not exceeding one year or in the state prison, or by both that fine and imprisonment.

(b) In the following instances, this section shall not apply:

(1) To any public utility engaged in the business of providing communications services and facilities, or to the officers, employees, or agents thereof, where the acts otherwise prohibited are for the purpose of construction, maintenance, conduct, or operation of the services and facilities of the public utility.

(2) To the use of any instrument, equipment, facility, or service furnished and used pursuant to the tariffs of the public utility.

(3) To any telephonic communication system used for communication exclusively within a state, county, city and county, or city correctional facility.

(c) As used in this section and Section 635, "cellular radio telephone" means a wireless telephone authorized by the Federal Communications Commission to operate in the frequency bandwidth reserved for cellular radio telephones.

Amended by Stats. 1992, Ch. 298, Sec. 4. Effective January 1, 1993.

Section 632.6 - Unlawful interception or receipt of communication transmitted involving cordless telephone

(a) Every person who, maliciously and without the consent of all parties to the communication, intercepts, receives, or assists in intercepting or receiving a communication transmitted between cordless telephones as defined in subdivision (c), between any cordless telephone and a landline telephone, or between a cordless telephone and a cellular telephone shall be punished by a fine not exceeding two thousand five hundred dollars ($2,500), by imprisonment in the county jail not exceeding one year, or in the state prison, or by both that fine and imprisonment. If the person has been convicted previously of a violation of Section 631, 632, 632.5, 632.7, or 636, the person shall be punished by a fine not exceeding ten thousand dollars ($10,000), or by imprisonment in the county jail not exceeding one year, or in the state prison, or by both that fine and imprisonment.

(b) This section shall not apply in any of the following instances:

(1) To any public utility engaged in the business of providing communications services and facilities, or to the officers, employees, or agents thereof, where the acts otherwise prohibited are for the purpose of construction, maintenance, conduct, or operation of the services and facilities of the public utility.

(2) To the use of any instrument, equipment, facility, or service furnished and used pursuant to the tariffs of the public utility.

(3) To any telephonic communications system used for communication exclusively within a state, county, city and county, or city correctional facility.

(c) As used in this section and in Section 635, "cordless telephone" means a two-way low power communication system consisting of two parts-a "base" unit which connects to the public switched telephone network and a handset or "remote" unit-which are connected by a radio link and authorized by the Federal Communications Commission to operate in the frequency bandwidths reserved for cordless telephones.

Amended by Stats. 1992, Ch. 298, Sec. 5. Effective January 1, 1993.

Section 632.7 - Unlawful interception or reception and intention recordation of communications transmitted between certain telephones

(a) Every person who, without the consent of all of the parties to a communication, intercepts or receives and intentionally records, or assists in the interception or reception and intentional recordation of, a communication transmitted between two cellular radio telephones, a cellular radio telephone and a landline telephone, two cordless telephones, a cordless telephone and a landline telephone, or a cordless telephone and a cellular radio telephone, shall be punished by a fine not exceeding two thousand five hundred dollars ($2,500), or by imprisonment in a county jail not exceeding one year, or in the state prison, or by both that fine and imprisonment. If the person has been convicted previously of a violation of this section or of Section 631, 632, 632.5, 632.6, or 636, the person shall be punished by a fine not exceeding ten thousand dollars ($10,000), by imprisonment in a county jail not exceeding one year, or in the state prison, or by both that fine and imprisonment.

(b) This section shall not apply to any of the following:

(1) Any public utility, or telephone company, engaged in the business of providing communications services and facilities, or to the officers, employees, or agents thereof, where the acts otherwise prohibited are for the purpose of construction, maintenance, conduct, or operation of the services and facilities of the public utility or telephone company.

(2) The use of any instrument, equipment, facility, or service furnished and used pursuant to the tariffs of the public utility.

(3) Any telephonic communication system used for communication exclusively within a state, county, city and county, or city correctional facility.

(c) For purposes of this section, "telephone company" is defined in paragraph (3) of subdivision (c) of Section 638.

(d) As used in this section, each of the following terms have the following meaning:

(1) "Cellular radio telephone" means a wireless telephone authorized by the Federal Communications Commission to operate in the frequency bandwidth reserved for cellular radio telephones.

(2) "Cordless telephone" means a two-way, low power communication system consisting of two parts, a "base" unit which connects to the public switched telephone network and a handset or "remote" unit, that are connected by a radio link and authorized by the Federal Communications Commission to operate in the frequency bandwidths reserved for cordless telephones.

(3) "Communication" includes, but is not limited to, communications transmitted by voice, data, or image, including facsimile.

Amended by Stats 2022 ch 27 (SB 1272),s 2, eff. 1/1/2023.

Amended by Stats. 1993, Ch. 536, Sec. 1. Effective September 27, 1993.

Section 633 - No prohibition of attorney general or other law enforcement officer from overhearing or recording communication that they could prior to effective date

(a) Nothing in Section 631, 632, 632.5, 632.6, or 632.7 prohibits the Attorney General, any district attorney, or any assistant, deputy, or investigator of the Attorney General or any district attorney, any officer of the California Highway Patrol, any peace officer of the Office of Internal Affairs of the Department of Corrections and Rehabilitation, any chief of police, assistant chief of police, or police officer of a city or city and county, any sheriff, undersheriff, or deputy sheriff regularly employed and paid in that capacity by a county, police officer of the County of Los Angeles, or any person acting pursuant to the direction of one of these law enforcement officers acting within the scope of his or her authority, from overhearing or recording any communication that they could lawfully overhear or record prior to January 1, 1968.

(b) Nothing in Section 631, 632, 632.5, 632.6, or 632.7 renders inadmissible any evidence obtained by the above-named persons by means of overhearing or recording any communication that they could lawfully overhear or record prior to January 1, 1968.

Amended by Stats 2018 ch 175 (AB 2669),s 1, eff. 1/1/2019.

Amended by Stats 2003 ch 468 (SB 851), s 9, eff. 1/1/2004.

Section 633.02 - Use of overheard or recorded communications in sexual offense cases

(a) Nothing in Section 631, 632, 632.5, 632.6, or 632.7 prohibits any POST-certified chief of police, assistant chief of police, or police officer of a university or college campus acting within the scope of his or her authority, from overhearing or recording any communication that he or she could lawfully overhear or record prior to January 1, 1968, in any criminal investigation related to sexual assault or other sexual offense.

(b) Nothing in Section 631, 632, 632.5, 632.6, or 632.7 shall prohibit any POST-certified chief of police, assistant chief of police, or police officer of a university or college campus from using or operating body-worn cameras.

(c) This section shall not be construed to affect Section 633.

(d) This section shall not be used to impinge upon the lawful exercise of constitutionally protected rights of freedom of speech or assembly, or the constitutionally protected right of personal privacy.

Added by Stats 2015 ch 159 (SB 424),s 1, eff. 1/1/2016.

Section 633.05 - No prohibition of city attorneys from overhearing or recording that they could lawfully overhear or record prior to effective date

(a) Nothing in Section 632, 632.5, 632.6, or 632.7 prohibits a city attorney acting under authority of Section 41803.5 of the Government Code, provided that authority is granted prior to January 1, 2012, or any person acting pursuant to the direction of one of those city attorneys acting within the scope of his or her authority, from overhearing or recording any communication that they could lawfully overhear or record.

(b) Nothing in Section 632, 632.5, 632.6, or 632.7 renders inadmissible any evidence obtained by the above-named persons by means of overhearing or recording any communication that they could lawfully overhear or record.

Added by Stats 2011 ch 659 (AB 1010),s 1, eff. 1/1/2012.

Section 633.1 - No prohibition of airport law enforcement officer from recording incoming telephone line

(a) Nothing in Section 631, 632, 632.5, 632.6, or 632.7 prohibits any person regularly employed as an airport law enforcement officer, as described in subdivision (d) of Section 830.33, acting within the scope of his or her authority, from recording any communication which is received on an incoming telephone line, for which the person initiating the call utilized a telephone number known to the public to be a means of contacting airport law enforcement officers. In order for a telephone call to be recorded under this subdivision, a series of electronic tones shall be used, placing the caller on notice that his or her telephone call is being recorded.

(b) Nothing in Section 631, 632, 632.5, 632.6, or 632.7 renders inadmissible any evidence obtained by an officer described in subdivision (a) if the evidence was received by means of recording any communication which is received on an incoming public telephone line, for which the person initiating the call utilized a telephone number known to the public to be a means of contacting airport law enforcement officers.

(c) This section shall only apply to airport law enforcement officers who are employed at an airport which maintains regularly scheduled international airport service and which maintains permanent facilities of the United States Customs Service.

Amended by Stats. 1995, Ch. 62, Sec. 1. Effective January 1, 1996.

Section 633.5 - No prohibition of one party recording confidential communication relating to commission of certain crimes

Sections 631, 632, 632.5, 632.6, and 632.7 do not prohibit one party to a confidential communication from recording the communication for the purpose of obtaining evidence reasonably believed to relate to the commission by another party to the communication of the crime of extortion, kidnapping, bribery, any felony involving violence against the person, including, but not limited to, human trafficking, as defined in Section 236.1, or a violation of Section 653m, or domestic violence as defined in Section 13700. Sections 631, 632, 632.5, 632.6, and 632.7 do not render any evidence so obtained inadmissible in a prosecution for extortion, kidnapping, bribery, any felony involving violence against the person, including, but not limited to, human trafficking, as defined in Section 236.1, a violation of Section 653m, or domestic violence as defined in Section 13700, or any crime in connection therewith.

Amended by Stats 2017 ch 191 (AB 413),s 1, eff. 1/1/2018.

Amended by Stats 2016 ch 855 (AB 1671),s 3, eff. 1/1/2017.

Section 633.6 - Recording of prohibited communication to victim of domestic violence

(a) Notwithstanding the provisions of this chapter, and in accordance with federal law, upon the request of a victim of domestic violence who is seeking a domestic violence restraining order, a judge issuing the order may include a provision in the order that permits the victim to record any prohibited communication made to him or her by the perpetrator.

(b) Notwithstanding the provisions of this chapter, and in accordance with federal law, a victim of domestic violence who is seeking a domestic violence restraining order from a court, and who reasonably believes that a confidential communication made to him or her by the perpetrator may contain evidence germane to that restraining order, may record that communication for the exclusive purpose and use of providing that evidence to the court.

(c) The Judicial Council shall amend its domestic violence prevention application and order forms to incorporate the provisions of this section.

Amended by Stats 2017 ch 191 (AB 413),s 2, eff. 1/1/2018.

EFFECTIVE 1/1/2000. Amended September 13, 1999 (Bill Number: AB 207) (Chapter 367).

Section 633.8 - Use of electronic amplifying or recording devices by law enforcement to eavesdrop and record

(a) It is the intent of the Legislature in enacting this section to provide law enforcement with the ability to use electronic amplifying or recording devices to eavesdrop on and record the otherwise confidential oral communications of individuals within a location when responding to an emergency situation that involves the taking of a hostage or the barricading of a location. It is the intent of the Legislature that eavesdropping on oral communications pursuant to this section comply with paragraph (7) of Section 2518 of Title 18 of the United States Code.

(b) Notwithstanding the provisions of this chapter, and in accordance with federal law, a designated peace officer described in subdivision (c) may use, or authorize the use of, an electronic amplifying or recording device to eavesdrop on or record, or both, any oral communication within a particular location in response to an emergency situation involving the taking of a hostage or hostages or the barricading of a location if all of the following conditions are satisfied:

(1) The officer reasonably determines that an emergency situation exists involving the immediate danger of death or serious physical injury to any person, within the meaning of Section 2518(7)(a)(i) of Title 18 of the United States Code.

(2) The officer reasonably determines that the emergency situation requires that the eavesdropping on oral communication occur immediately.

(3) There are grounds upon which an order could be obtained pursuant to Section 2516(2) of Title 18 of the United States Code in regard to the offenses enumerated therein.

(c) Only a peace officer who has been designated by either a district attorney in the county where the emergency exists, or by the Attorney General to make the necessary determinations pursuant to paragraphs (1), (2), and (3) of subdivision (b) may make those determinations for purposes of this section.

(d) If the determination is made by a designated peace officer described in subdivision (c) that an emergency situation exists, a peace officer shall not be required to knock and announce his or her presence before entering, installing, and using any electronic amplifying or recording devices.

(e) If the determination is made by a designated peace officer described in subdivision (c) that an emergency situation exists and an eavesdropping device has been deployed, an application for an order approving the eavesdropping shall be made within 48 hours of the beginning of the eavesdropping and shall comply with the requirements of Section 629.50. A court may grant an application authorizing the use of electronic amplifying or recording devices to eavesdrop on and record otherwise confidential oral communications in barricade or hostage situations where there is probable cause to believe that an individual is committing, has committed, or is about to commit an offense listed in Section 2516(2) of Title 18 of the United States Code.

(f) The contents of any oral communications overheard pursuant to this section shall be recorded on tape or other comparable device. The recording of the contents shall be done so as to protect the recording from editing or other alterations.

(g) For purposes of this section, a "barricading" occurs when a person refuses to come out from a covered or enclosed position. Barricading also occurs when a person is held against his or her will and the captor has not made a demand.

(h) For purposes of this section, a "hostage situation" occurs when a person is held against his or her will and the captor has made a demand.

(i) A judge shall not grant an application made pursuant to this section in anticipation that an emergency situation will arise. A judge shall grant an application authorizing the use of electronic amplifying or recording devices to eavesdrop on and record otherwise confidential oral communications in barricade or hostage situations where there is probable cause to believe that an individual is committing, has committed, or is about to commit an offense listed in Section 2516(2) of Title 18 of the United States Code, and only if the peace officer has fully complied with the requirements of this section. If an application is granted pursuant to this section, an inventory shall be served pursuant to Section 629.68.

(j) This section does not require that a peace officer designated pursuant to subdivision (c) undergo training pursuant to Section 629.94.

(k) A peace officer who has been designated pursuant to subdivision (c) to use an eavesdropping device shall cease use of the device upon the termination of the barricade or hostage situation, or upon the denial by a judge of an application for an order to approve the eavesdropping, whichever is earlier.

(l) Nothing in this section shall be deemed to affect the admissibility or inadmissibility of evidence.

Amended by Stats 2011 ch 304 (SB 428),s 6, eff. 1/1/2012.

Added by Stats 2010 ch 380 (AB 2210),s 1, eff. 1/1/2011.

Section 634 - Trespass

Any person who trespasses on property for the purpose of committing any act, or attempting to commit any act, in violation of Section 631, 632, 632.5, 632.6, 632.7, or 636 shall be punished by a fine not exceeding two thousand five hundred dollars ($2,500), by imprisonment in the county jail not exceeding one year or in the state prison, or by both that fine and imprisonment. If the person has previously been convicted of a violation of this section or Section 631, 632, 632.5, 632.6, 632.7, or 636, the person shall be punished by a fine not exceeding ten thousand dollars ($10,000), by imprisonment in the county jail not exceeding one year or in the state prison, or by both that fine and imprisonment.

Amended by Stats. 1992, Ch. 298, Sec. 10. Effective January 1, 1993.

Section 635 - Unlawful manufacture, sale, possession, transport, import, or furnishing of eavesdropping device

(a) Every person who manufactures, assembles, sells, offers for sale, advertises for sale, possesses, transports, imports, or furnishes to another any device which is primarily or exclusively designed or intended for eavesdropping upon the communication of another, or any device which is primarily or exclusively designed or intended for the unauthorized interception or reception of communications between cellular radio telephones or between a cellular radio telephone and a landline telephone in violation of Section 632.5, or communications between cordless telephones or between a cordless telephone and a landline telephone in violation of Section 632.6, shall be punished by a fine not exceeding two thousand five hundred dollars ($2,500), by imprisonment in the county jail not exceeding one year, or in the state prison, or by both that fine and imprisonment. If the person has previously been convicted of a violation of this section, the person shall be punished by a fine not exceeding ten thousand dollars ($10,000), by imprisonment in the county jail not exceeding one year, or in the state prison, or by both that fine and imprisonment.

(b) This section does not apply to either of the following:

(1) An act otherwise prohibited by this section when performed by any of the following:

(A) A communication utility or an officer, employee or agent thereof for the purpose of construction, maintenance, conduct, or operation of, or otherwise incident to the use of, the services or facilities of the utility.

(B) A state, county, or municipal law enforcement agency or an agency of the federal government.

(C) A person engaged in selling devices specified in subdivision (a) for use by, or resale to, agencies of a foreign government under terms approved by the federal government, communication utilities, state, county, or municipal law enforcement agencies, or agencies of the federal government.

(2) Possession by a subscriber to communication utility service of a device specified in subdivision (a) furnished by the utility pursuant to its tariffs.

Amended by Stats. 1990, Ch. 696, Sec. 8.

Section 636 - Unlawful eavesdropping on person who is custody of law enforcement officer

(a) Every person who, without permission from all parties to the conversation, eavesdrops on or records, by means of an electronic device, a conversation, or any portion thereof, between a person who is in the physical custody of a law enforcement officer or other public officer, or who is on the property of a law enforcement agency or other public agency, and that person's attorney, religious adviser, or licensed physician, is guilty of a felony punishable by imprisonment pursuant to subdivision (h) of Section 1170.

(b) Every person who, intentionally and without permission from all parties to the conversation, nonelectronically eavesdrops upon a conversation, or any portion thereof, that occurs between a person who is in the physical custody of a law enforcement officer or other public officer and that person's attorney, religious adviser, or licensed physician, is guilty of a public offense. This subdivision applies to conversations that occur in a place, and under circumstances, where there exists a reasonable expectation of privacy, including a custody holding area, holding area, or anteroom. This subdivision does not apply to conversations that are inadvertently overheard or that take place in a courtroom or other room used for adjudicatory proceedings. A person who is convicted of violating this subdivision shall be punished by imprisonment pursuant to subdivision (h) of Section 1170, or in a county jail for a term not to exceed one year, or by a fine not to exceed two thousand five hundred dollars ($2,500), or by both that fine and imprisonment.

(c) This section shall not apply to any employee of a public utility engaged in the business of providing service and facilities for telephone or telegraph communications while engaged in the construction, maintenance, conduct, or operation of the service or facilities of that public utility who listens in to conversations for the limited purpose of testing or servicing equipment.

Amended by Stats 2011 ch 39 (AB 117),s 68, eff. 6/30/2011.

Amended by Stats 2011 ch 15 (AB 109),s 429, eff. 4/4/2011, but operative no earlier than October 1, 2011, and only upon creation of a community corrections grant program to assist in implementing this act and upon an appropriation to fund the grant program.

Section 636.5 - Unlawful interception of public safety radio service communication

Any person not authorized by the sender, who intercepts any public safety radio service communication, by use of a scanner or any other means, for the purpose of using that communication to assist in the commission of a criminal offense or to avoid or escape arrest, trial, conviction, or punishment or who divulges to any person he or she knows to be a suspect in the commission of any criminal offense, the existence, contents, substance, purport, effect or meaning of that communication concerning the offense with the intent that the suspect may avoid or escape from arrest, trial, conviction, or punishment is guilty of a misdemeanor.

Nothing in this section shall preclude prosecution of any person under Section 31 or 32.

As used in this section, "public safety radio service communication" means a communication authorized by the Federal Communications Commission to be transmitted by a station in the public safety radio service.

EFFECTIVE 1/1/2000. Amended October 10, 1999 (Bill Number: SB 832) (Chapter 853).

Section 637 - Unlawful disclosure of contents of telegraphic or telephonic message

Every person not a party to a telegraphic or telephonic communication who willfully discloses the contents of a telegraphic or telephonic message, or any part thereof, addressed to another person, without the permission of that person, unless directed so to do by the lawful order of a court, is punishable by imprisonment pursuant to subdivision (h) of Section 1170, or in a county jail not exceeding one year, or by fine not exceeding five thousand dollars ($5,000), or by both that fine and imprisonment.

Amended by Stats 2011 ch 39 (AB 117),s 68, eff. 6/30/2011.

Amended by Stats 2011 ch 15 (AB 109),s 430, eff. 4/4/2011, but operative no earlier than October 1, 2011, and only upon creation of a community corrections grant program to assist in implementing this act and upon an appropriation to fund the grant program.

Section 637.1 - Unlawful opening of sealed envelope enclosing telegraphic or telephonic message

Every person not connected with any telegraph or telephone office who, without the authority or consent of the person to whom the same may be directed, willfully opens any sealed envelope enclosing a telegraphic or telephonic message, addressed to another person, with the purpose of learning the contents of such message, or who fraudulently represents another person and thereby procures to be delivered to himself any telegraphic or telephonic message addressed to such other person, with the intent to use, destroy, or detain the same from the person entitled to receive such message, is punishable as provided in Section 637.

Added by Stats. 1967, Ch. 1509.

Section 637.2 - Action against person who committed violation; injunctive relief

(a) Any person who has been injured by a violation of this chapter may bring an action against the person who committed the violation for the greater of the following amounts:

(1) Five thousand dollars ($5,000) per violation.

(2) Three times the amount of actual damages, if any, sustained by the plaintiff.

(b) Any person may, in accordance with Chapter 3 (commencing with Section 525) of Title 7 of Part 2 of the Code of Civil Procedure, bring an action to enjoin and restrain any violation of this chapter, and may in the same action seek damages as provided by subdivision (a).

(c) It is not a necessary prerequisite to an action pursuant to this section that the plaintiff has suffered, or be threatened with, actual damages.

(d) This section shall not be construed to affect Title 4 (commencing with Section 3425.1) of Part 1 of Division 4 of the Civil Code.

Amended by Stats 2016 ch 855 (AB 1671),s 4, eff. 1/1/2017.

Section 637.3 - Unlawful use of voice prints or other voice stress patterns

(a) No person or entity in this state shall use any system which examines or records in any manner voice prints or other voice stress patterns of another person to determine the truth or falsity of statements made by such other person without his or her express written consent given in advance of the examination or recordation.

(b) This section shall not apply to any peace officer, as defined in Section 830, while he is carrying out his official duties.

(c) Any person who has been injured by a violator of this section may bring an action against the violator for his actual damages or one thousand dollars ($1,000), whichever is greater.

Added by Stats. 1978, Ch. 1251.

Section 637.4 - Submission to polygraph examination as prerequisite to filing accusatory pleading prohibited

(a) No state or local governmental agency involved in the investigation or prosecution of crimes, or any employee thereof, shall require or request any complaining witness, in a case involving the use of force, violence, duress, menace, or threat of great bodily harm in the commission of any sex offense, to submit to a polygraph examination as a prerequisite to filing an accusatory pleading.

(b) Any person who has been injured by a violator of this section may bring an action against the violator for his actual damages or one thousand dollars ($1,000), whichever is greater.

Added by Stats. 1980, Ch. 880, Sec. 1.

Section 637.5 - Unlawful acts by owner or manager of satellite or cable television corporation

(a) No person who owns, controls, operates, or manages a satellite or cable television corporation, or who leases channels on a satellite or cable system shall:

(1) Use any electronic device to record, transmit, or observe any events or listen to, record, or monitor any conversations that take place inside a subscriber's residence, workplace, or place of business, without obtaining the express written consent of the subscriber. A satellite or cable television corporation may conduct electronic sweeps of subscriber households to monitor for signal quality.

(2) Provide any person with any individually identifiable information regarding any of its subscribers, including, but not limited to, the subscriber's television viewing habits, shopping choices, interests, opinions, energy uses, medical information, banking data or information, or any other personal or private information, without the subscriber's express written consent.

(b) Individual subscriber viewing responses or other individually identifiable information derived from subscribers may be retained and used by a satellite or cable television corporation only to the extent reasonably necessary for billing purposes and internal business practices, and to monitor for unauthorized reception of services. A satellite or cable television corporation may compile, maintain, and distribute a list containing the names and addresses of its subscribers if the list contains no other individually identifiable information and if subscribers are afforded the right to elect not to be included on the list. However, a satellite or cable television corporation shall maintain adequate safeguards to ensure the physical security and confidentiality of the subscriber information.

(c)

(1) A satellite or cable television corporation shall not make individual subscriber information available to government agencies in the absence of legal compulsion, including, but not limited to, a court order or subpoena. If requests for information are made, a satellite or cable television corporation shall promptly notify the subscriber of the nature of the request and what government agency has requested the information prior to responding unless otherwise prohibited from doing so by law.

(2) Nothing in this section shall be construed to prevent local franchising authorities from obtaining information necessary to monitor franchise compliance pursuant to franchise or license agreements. This information shall be provided so as to omit individually identifiable subscriber information whenever possible. Information obtained by local franchising authorities shall be used solely for monitoring franchise compliance and shall not be subject to the California Public Records Act (Division 10 (commencing with Section 7920.000) of Title 1 of the Government Code).

(d) Any individually identifiable subscriber information gathered by a satellite or cable television corporation shall be made available for subscriber examination within 30 days of receiving a request by a subscriber to examine the information on the premises of the corporation. Upon a reasonable showing by the subscriber that the information is inaccurate, a satellite or cable television corporation shall correct the information.

(e) Upon a subscriber's application for satellite or cable television service, including, but not limited to, interactive service, a satellite or cable television corporation shall provide the applicant with a separate notice in an appropriate form explaining the subscriber's right to privacy protection afforded by this section.

(f) As used in this section:

(1) "Cable television corporation" shall have the same meaning as that term is given by Section 216.4 of the Public Utilities Code.

(2) "Individually identifiable information" means any information identifying an individual or the individual's use of any service provided by a satellite or cable system other than the mere fact that the individual is a satellite or cable television subscriber. "Individually identifiable information" shall not include anonymous, aggregate, or any other information that does not identify an individual subscriber of a video provider service.

(3) "Person" includes an individual, business association, partnership, corporation, limited liability company, or other legal entity, and an individual acting or purporting to act for or on behalf of any government, or subdivision thereof, whether federal, state, or local.

(4) "Interactive service" means any service offered by a satellite or cable television corporation involving the collection, reception, aggregation, storage, or use of electronic information transmitted from a subscriber to any other receiving point under the control of the satellite or cable television corporation, or vice versa.

(g) Nothing in this section shall be construed to limit the ability of a satellite or cable television corporation to market satellite or cable television or ancillary services to its subscribers.

(h) Any person receiving subscriber information from a satellite or cable television corporation shall be subject to the provisions of this section.

(i) Any aggrieved person may commence a civil action for damages for invasion of privacy against any satellite or cable television corporation, service provider, or person that leases a channel or channels on a satellite or cable television system that violates the provisions of this section.

(j) Any person who violates the provisions of this section is guilty of a misdemeanor punishable by a fine not exceeding three thousand dollars ($3,000), or by imprisonment in the county jail not exceeding one year, or by both that fine and imprisonment.

(k) The penalties and remedies provided by subdivisions (i) and (j) are cumulative, and shall not be construed as restricting any penalty or remedy, provisional or otherwise, provided by law for the benefit of any person, and no judgment under this section shall preclude any person from obtaining additional relief based upon the same facts.

(l) The provisions of this section are intended to set forth minimum state standards for protecting the privacy of subscribers to cable television services and are not intended to preempt more restrictive local standards.

Amended by Stats 2021 ch 615 (AB 474),s 336, eff. 1/1/2022, op. 1/1/2023.

Amended by Stats 2006 ch 198 (AB 3073),s 5, eff. 1/1/2007.

Amended by Stats 2002 ch 664 (AB 3034), s 173, eff. 1/1/2003.

Amended by Stats 2001 ch 731 (SB 1090), s 1, eff. 1/1/2002.

Section 637.6 - Unlawful disclosure of personal information acquired for carpooling or ridesharing program

(a) No person who, in the course of business, acquires or has access to personal information concerning an individual, including, but not limited to, the individual's residence address, employment address, or hours of employment, for the purpose of assisting private entities in the establishment or implementation of carpooling or ridesharing programs, shall disclose that information to any other person or use that information for any other purpose without the prior written consent of the individual.

(b) As used in this section, "carpooling or ridesharing programs" include, but shall not be limited to, the formation of carpools, vanpools, buspools, the provision of transit routes, rideshare research, and the development of other demand management strategies such as variable working hours and telecommuting.

(c) Any person who violates this section is guilty of a misdemeanor, punishable by imprisonment in the county jail for not exceeding one year, or by a fine of not exceeding one thousand dollars ($1,000), or by both that imprisonment and fine.

Added by Stats. 1990, Ch. 304, Sec. 1.

Section 637.7 - Unlawful use of electronic tracking device

(a) No person or entity in this state shall use an electronic tracking device to determine the location or movement of a person.

(b) This section shall not apply when the registered owner, lessor, or lessee of a vehicle has consented to the use of the electronic tracking device with respect to that vehicle.

(c) This section shall not apply to the lawful use of an electronic tracking device by a law enforcement agency.

(d) As used in this section, "electronic tracking device" means any device attached to a vehicle or other movable thing that reveals its location or movement by the transmission of electronic signals.

(e) A violation of this section is a misdemeanor.

(f) A violation of this section by a person, business, firm, company, association, partnership, or corporation licensed under Division 3 (commencing with Section 5000) of the Business and Professions Code shall constitute grounds for revocation of the license issued to that person, business, firm, company, association, partnership, or corporation, pursuant to the provisions that provide for the revocation of the license as set forth in Division 3 (commencing with Section 5000) of the Business and Professions Code.

Added by Stats. 1998, Ch. 449, Sec. 2. Effective January 1, 1999.

Section 637.9 - Unlawful acts by person who provides mailing lists, computerized or telephone-based reference services, or similar products or services utilizing lists

(a) Any person who, in the course of business, provides mailing lists, computerized or telephone-based reference services, or similar products or services utilizing lists, as defined, knowingly does any of the following is guilty of a misdemeanor:

(1) Fails, prior to selling or distributing a list to a first-time buyer, to obtain the buyer's name, address, telephone number, tax identification number if the buyer is a forprofit entity, a sample of the type of material to be distributed using the list, or to make a good-faith effort to verify the nature and legitimacy of the business or organization to which the list is being sold or distributed.

(2) Knowingly provides access to personal information about children to any person who he or she knows is registered or required to register as a sex offender.

(b) Any person who uses personal information about a child that was obtained for commercial purposes to directly contact the child or the child's parent to offer a commercial product or service to the child and who knowingly fails to comply with the parent's request to take steps to limit access to personal information about a child only to authorized persons is guilty of a misdemeanor.

(c) Any person who knowingly distributes or receives any personal information about a child with knowledge that the information will be used to abuse or physically harm the child is guilty of a misdemeanor.

(d)

(1) List brokers shall, upon a written request from a parent that specifically identifies the child, provide the parent with procedures that the parent must follow in order to withdraw consent to use personal information relating to his or her child. Any list broker who fails to discontinue disclosing personal information about a child within 20 days after being so requested in writing by the child's parent, is guilty of a misdemeanor.

(2) Any person who, through the mail, markets or sells products or services directed to children, shall maintain a list of all individuals, and their addresses, who have requested in writing that the person discontinue sending any marketing or sales materials to the individual or the individual's child or children. No person who is obligated to maintain that list shall cause any marketing or sales materials, other than those that are already in the process of dissemination, to be sent to any individual's child or children, after that individual has made that written request. Any person who is subject to the provisions of this paragraph, who fails to comply with the requirements of this paragraph or who violates the provisions of this paragraph is guilty of a misdemeanor.

(e) The following shall be exempt from subdivisions (a) and (b):

(1) Any federal, state, or local government agency or law enforcement agency.

(2) The National Center for Missing and Exploited Children.

(3) Any educational institution, consortia, organization, or professional association, which shall include, but not be limited to, the California community colleges; the California State University, and each campus, branch, and function thereof; each campus, branch, and

function of the University of California; the California Maritime Academy; or any independent institution of higher education accredited by an agency recognized by the federal Department of Education. For the purposes of this paragraph, "independent institution of higher education" means any nonpublic higher education institution that grants undergraduate degrees, graduate degrees, or both undergraduate and graduate degrees, is formed as a nonprofit corporation in this state, and is accredited by an agency recognized by the federal Department of Education; or any private postsecondary vocational institution registered, approved, or exempted by the Bureau of Private Postsecondary Vocational Education.

(4) Any nonprofit organization that is exempt from taxation under Section 23701d of the Revenue and Taxation Code.

(f) As used in this section:

(1) "Child" means a person who is under 16 years of age.

(2) "Parent" shall include a legal guardian.

(3) "Personal information" means any information that identifies a child and that would suffice to locate and contact the child, including, but not limited to, the name, postal or electronic mail address, telephone number, social security number, date of birth, physical description of the child, or family income.

(4) "List" may include, but is not limited to, a collection of name and address records of individuals sharing a common interest, purchase history, demographic profile, membership, or affiliation.

Added by Stats. 1998, Ch. 763, Sec. 1. Effective January 1, 1999.

Section 638 - Unlawful purchase or sale of telephone calling pattern record or list

(a) Any person who purchases, sells, offers to purchase or sell, or conspires to purchase or sell any telephone calling pattern record or list, without the written consent of the subscriber, or any person who procures or obtains through fraud or deceit, or attempts to procure or obtain through fraud or deceit any telephone calling pattern record or list shall be punished by a fine not exceeding two thousand five hundred dollars ($2,500), or by imprisonment in a county jail not exceeding one year, or by both a fine and imprisonment. If the person has previously been convicted of a violation of this section, he or she is punishable by a fine not exceeding ten thousand dollars ($10,000), or by imprisonment in a county jail not exceeding one year, or by both a fine and imprisonment.

(b) Any personal information contained in a telephone calling pattern record or list that is obtained in violation of this section shall be inadmissible as evidence in any judicial, administrative, legislative, or other proceeding except when that information is offered as proof in an action or prosecution for a violation of this section, or when otherwise authorized by law, in any criminal prosecution.

(c) For purposes of this section:

(1) "Person" includes an individual, business association, partnership, limited partnership, corporation, limited liability company, or other legal entity.

(2) "Telephone calling pattern record or list" means information retained by a telephone company that relates to the telephone number dialed by the subscriber, or other person using the subscriber's telephone with permission, or the incoming number of a call directed to the subscriber, or other data related to such calls typically contained on a subscriber telephone bill such as the time the call started and ended, the duration of the call, any charges applied, and any information described in subdivision (a) of Section 2891 of the Public Utilities Code whether the call was made from or to a telephone connected to the public switched telephone network, a cordless telephone, as defined in Section 632.6, a telephony device operating over the Internet utilizing voice over Internet protocol, a satellite telephone, or commercially available interconnected mobile phone service that provides access to the public switched telephone network via a mobile communication device employing radiowave technology to transmit calls, including cellular radiotelephone, broadband Personal Communications Services, and digital Specialized Mobile Radio.

(3) "Telephone company" means a telephone corporation as defined in Section 234 of the Public Utilities Code or any other person that provides residential or commercial telephone service to a subscriber utilizing any of the technologies or methods enumerated in paragraph (2).

(4) For purposes of this section, "purchase" and "sell" shall not include information provided to a collection agency or assignee of the debt by the telephone corporation, and used exclusively for the collection of the unpaid debt assigned by the telephone corporation, provided that the collection agency or assignee of the debt shall be liable for any disclosure of the information that is in violation of this section.

(d) An employer of, or entity contracting with, a person who violates subdivision (a) shall only be subject to prosecution pursuant to that provision if the employer or contracting entity knowingly allowed the employee or contractor to engage in conduct that violated subdivision (a).

(e) It is the intent of the Legislature to ensure that telephone companies maintain telephone calling pattern records or lists in the strictest confidence, and protect the privacy of their subscribers with all due care. While it is not the intent of the Legislature in this act to preclude the sharing of information that is currently allowed by both state and federal laws and rules governing those records, it is the Legislature's intent in this act to preclude any unauthorized purchase or sale of that information.

(f) This section shall not be construed to prevent a law enforcement or prosecutorial agency, or any officer, employee, or agent thereof from obtaining telephone records in connection with the performance of the official duties of the agency consistent with any other applicable state and federal law.

(g) Nothing in this section shall preclude prosecution under any other provision of law.

(h) The Legislature hereby finds and declares that, notwithstanding the prohibition on specific means of making available or obtaining personal calling records pursuant to this section, the disclosure of personal calling records through any other means is no less harmful to the privacy and security interests of Californians. This section is not intended to limit the scope or force of Section 2891 of the Public Utilities Code in any way.

Added by Stats 2006 ch 626 (SB 202),s 1, eff. 1/1/2007.

Section 638.50 - Definitions

For purposes of this chapter, the following terms have the following meanings:

(a)"Wire communication" and "electronic communication" have the meanings set forth in subdivision (a) of Section 629.51.

(b)"Pen register" means a device or process that records or decodes dialing, routing, addressing, or signaling information transmitted by an instrument or facility from which a wire or electronic communication is transmitted, but not the contents of a communication. "Pen register" does not include a device or process used by a provider or customer of a wire or electronic communication service for billing, or recording as an incident to billing, for communications services provided by such provider, or a device or process used by a provider or customer of a wire communication service for cost accounting or other similar purposes in the ordinary course of its business.

(c)"Trap and trace device" means a device or process that captures the incoming electronic or other impulses that identify the originating number or other dialing, routing, addressing, or signaling information reasonably likely to identify the source of a wire or electronic communication, but not the contents of a communication.

(d)"Prohibited violation" has the same meaning as that term is defined in Section 629.51.

Amended by Stats 2022 ch 627 (AB 1242),s 4, eff. 9/27/2022.

Added by Stats 2015 ch 204 (AB 929),s 1, eff. 1/1/2016.

Section 638.51 - Installation or use of pen register or trap and trace device

(a) Except as provided in subdivision (b), a person may not install or use a pen register or a trap and trace device without first obtaining a court order pursuant to Section 638.52 or 638.53.

(b) A provider of electronic or wire communication service may use a pen register or a trap and trace device for any of the following purposes:

(1) To operate, maintain, and test a wire or electronic communication service.

(2) To protect the rights or property of the provider.

(3) To protect users of the service from abuse of service or unlawful use of service.

(4) To record the fact that a wire or electronic communication was initiated or completed to protect the provider, another provider furnishing service toward the completion of the wire communication, or a user of that service, from fraudulent, unlawful, or abusive use of service.

(5) If the consent of the user of that service has been obtained.

(c) A violation of this section is punishable by a fine not exceeding two thousand five hundred dollars ($2,500), or by imprisonment in the county jail not exceeding one year, or by imprisonment pursuant to subdivision (h) of Section 1170, or by both that fine and imprisonment.

(d) A good faith reliance on an order issued pursuant to Section 638.52, or an authorization made pursuant to Section 638.53, is a complete defense to a civil or criminal action brought under this section or under this chapter.

Added by Stats 2015 ch 204 (AB 929),s 2, eff. 1/1/2016.

Section 638.52 - Application for order or extension of authorization for installation or use of pen register or trap and trace device

(a)A peace officer may make an application to a magistrate for an order or an extension of an order authorizing or approving the installation and use of a pen register or a trap and trace device. The application shall be in writing under oath or equivalent affirmation, and shall include the identity of the peace officer making the application and the identity of the law enforcement agency conducting the investigation. The applicant shall certify that the information likely to be obtained is relevant to an ongoing criminal investigation and shall include a statement of the offense to which the information likely to be obtained by the pen register or trap and trace device relates.

(b) The magistrate shall enter an ex parte order authorizing the installation and use of a pen register or a trap and trace device if the magistrate finds that the information likely to be obtained by the installation and use of a pen register or a trap and trace device is relevant to an ongoing investigation and that there is probable cause to believe that the pen register or trap and trace device will lead to any of the following:

(1) Recovery of stolen or embezzled property.

(2) Property or things used as the means of committing a felony.

(3) Property or things in the possession of a person with the intent to use them as a means of committing a public offense, or in the possession of another to whom they may have delivered them for the purpose of concealing them or preventing them from being discovered.

(4) Evidence that tends to show a felony has been committed, or tends to show that a particular person has committed or is committing a felony.

(5) Evidence that tends to show that sexual exploitation of a child, in violation of Section 311.3, or possession of matter depicting sexual conduct of a person under 18 years of age, in violation of Section 311.11, has occurred or is occurring.

(6) The location of a person who is unlawfully restrained or reasonably believed to be a witness in a criminal investigation or for whose arrest there is probable cause.

(7) Evidence that tends to show a violation of Section 3700.5 of the Labor Code, or tends to show that a particular person has violated Section 3700.5 of the Labor Code.

(8) Evidence that does any of the following:

(A) Tends to show that a felony, a misdemeanor violation of the Fish and Game Code, or a misdemeanor violation of the Public Resources Code, has been committed or is being committed.

(B) Tends to show that a particular person has committed or is committing a felony, a misdemeanor violation of the Fish and Game Code, or a misdemeanor violation of the Public Resources Code.

(C) Will assist in locating an individual who has committed or is committing a felony, a misdemeanor violation of the Fish and Game Code, or a misdemeanor violation of the Public Resources Code.

(c) Information acquired solely pursuant to the authority for a pen register or a trap and trace device shall not include any information that may disclose the physical location of the subscriber, except to the extent that the location may be determined from the telephone number. Upon the request of the person seeking the pen register or trap and trace device, the magistrate may seal portions of the application pursuant to People v. Hobbs (1994) 7 Cal.4th 948, and Sections 1040, 1041, and 1042 of the Evidence Code.

(d) An order issued pursuant to subdivision (b) shall specify all of the following:

(1) The identity, if known, of the person to whom is leased or in whose name is listed the telephone line to which the pen register or trap and trace device is to be attached.

(2) The identity, if known, of the person who is the subject of the criminal investigation.

(3) The number and, if known, physical location of the telephone line to which the pen register or trap and trace device is to be attached and, in the case of a trap and trace device, the geographic limits of the trap and trace order.

(4) A statement of the offense to which the information likely to be obtained by the pen register or trap and trace device relates.

(5) The order shall direct, if the applicant has requested, the furnishing of information, facilities, and technical assistance necessary to accomplish the installation of the pen register or trap and trace device.

(e) An order issued under this section shall authorize the installation and use of a pen register or a trap and trace device for a period not to exceed 60 days.

(f) Extensions of the original order may be granted upon a new application for an order under subdivisions (a) and (b) if the officer shows that there is a continued probable cause that the information or items sought under this subdivision are likely to be obtained under the extension. The period of an extension shall not exceed 60 days.

(g) An order or extension order authorizing or approving the installation and use of a pen register or a trap and trace device shall direct that the order be sealed until the order, including any extensions, expires, and that the person owning or leasing the line to which the pen register or trap and trace device is attached not disclose the existence of the pen register or trap and trace device or the existence of the investigation to the listed subscriber or to any other person.

(h) Upon the presentation of an order, entered under subdivisions (b) or (f), by a peace officer authorized to install and use a pen register, a provider of wire or electronic communication service, landlord, custodian, or other person shall immediately provide the peace officer all information, facilities, and technical assistance necessary to accomplish the installation of the pen register unobtrusively and with a minimum of interference with the services provided to the party with respect to whom the installation and use is to take place, if the assistance is directed by the order.

(i) Upon the request of a peace officer authorized to receive the results of a trap and trace device, a provider of a wire or electronic communication service, landlord, custodian, or other person shall immediately install the device on the appropriate line and provide the peace officer all information, facilities, and technical assistance, including installation and operation of the device unobtrusively and with a minimum of interference with the services provided to the party with respect to whom the installation and use is to take place, if the installation and assistance is directed by the order.

(j) A provider of a wire or electronic communication service, landlord, custodian, or other person who provides facilities or technical assistance pursuant to this section shall be reasonably compensated by the requesting peace officer's law enforcement agency for the reasonable expenses incurred in providing the facilities and assistance.

(k) Unless otherwise ordered by the magistrate, the results of the pen register or trap and trace device shall be provided to the peace officer at reasonable intervals during regular business hours for the duration of the order.

(l) The magistrate, before issuing the order pursuant to subdivision (b), may examine on oath the person seeking the pen register or the trap and trace device, and any witnesses the person may produce, and shall take their affidavit or their affidavits in writing, and cause the affidavit or affidavits to be subscribed by the parties making them.

(m) Notwithstanding any other provision in this section, no magistrate shall enter an ex parte order authorizing the installation and use of a pen register or a trap and trace device for the purpose of investigating or recovering evidence of a prohibited violation, as defined in Section 629.51.

Amended by Stats 2022 ch 627 (AB 1242),s 5, eff. 9/27/2022.
Amended by Stats 2016 ch 511 (AB 1924),s 1, eff. 9/23/2016.
Added by Stats 2015 ch 204 (AB 929),s 3, eff. 1/1/2016.

Section 638.53 - Oral approval

(a) Except as otherwise provided in this chapter, upon an oral application by a peace officer, a magistrate may grant oral approval for the installation and use of a pen register or a trap and trace device, without an order, if he or she determines all of the following:

(1) There are grounds upon which an order could be issued under Section 638.52.

(2) There is probable cause to believe that an emergency situation exists with respect to the investigation of a crime.

(3) There is probable cause to believe that a substantial danger to life or limb exists justifying the authorization for immediate installation and use of a pen register or a trap and trace device before an order authorizing the installation and use can, with due diligence, be submitted and acted upon.

(b)

(1) By midnight of the second full court day after the pen register or trap and trace device is installed, a written application pursuant to Section 638.52 shall be submitted by the peace officer who made the oral application to the magistrate who orally approved the installation and use of a pen register or trap and trace device. If an order is issued pursuant to Section 638.52, the order shall also recite the time of the oral approval under subdivision (a) and shall be retroactive to the time of the original oral approval.

(2) In the absence of an authorizing order pursuant to paragraph (1), the use shall immediately terminate when the information sought is obtained, when the application for the order is denied, or by midnight of the second full court day after the pen register or trap and trace device is installed, whichever is earlier.

(c) A provider of a wire or electronic communication service, landlord, custodian, or other person who provides facilities or technical assistance pursuant to this section shall be reasonably compensated by the requesting peace officer's law enforcement agency for the reasonable expenses incurred in providing the facilities and assistance.

Added by Stats 2015 ch 204 (AB 929),s 4, eff. 1/1/2016.

Section 638.54 - Notice to targets

(a) Except as otherwise provided in this section, a government entity that obtains information pursuant to Section 638.52, or obtains information pursuant to oral authorization pursuant to Section 638.53, shall serve upon, or deliver to by registered or first-class mail, electronic mail, or other means reasonably calculated to be effective, the identified targets of the order a notice that informs the recipient that information about the recipient has been compelled or requested and states with reasonable specificity the nature of the government investigation under which the information is sought. The notice shall include a copy of the order or a written statement setting forth facts giving rise to the emergency. The notice shall be provided no later than 30 days after the termination of the period of the order, any extensions, or an emergency request.

(b)

(1) Prior to the expiration of the 30-day period specified in subdivision (a), the government entity may submit a request, supported by a sworn affidavit, for an order delaying unsealing of the order and notification and prohibiting the person owning or leasing the line to which the pen register or trap and trace device is attached from disclosing the existence of the pen register or trap and trace device or the existence of the investigation to the listed subscriber or any other person. The court shall issue the order if the court determines that there is reason to believe that notification may have an adverse result, but only for the period of time that the court finds there is reason to believe that the notification may have that adverse result, and not to exceed 90 days.

(2) The court may grant extensions of the delay of up to 90 days each on the same grounds as provided in paragraph (1).

(3) Upon expiration of the period of delay of the notification, the government entity shall serve upon, or deliver to by registered or first-class mail, electronic mail, or other means reasonably calculated to be effective as specified by the court issuing the order authorizing delayed notification, the identified targets of the order or emergency authorization a document that includes the information described in subdivision (a) and a copy of all electronic information obtained or a summary of that information, including, at a minimum, the number and types of records disclosed, the date and time when the earliest and latest records were created, and a statement of the grounds for the court's determination to grant a delay in notifying the individual. The notice shall be provided no later than three days after the expiration of the period of delay of the notification.

(c) If there is no identified target of an order or emergency request at the time of its issuance, the government entity shall submit to the Department of Justice, no later than three days after the termination of the period of the order, any extensions, or an emergency request, all of the information required in subdivision (a). If an order delaying notice is obtained pursuant to subdivision (b), the government entity shall submit to the department, no later than three days after the expiration of the period of delay of the notification, all of the information required in paragraph (3) of subdivision (b). The department shall publish all those reports on its Internet Web site within 90 days of receipt. The department may redact names or other personal identifying information from the reports.

(d) For the purposes of this section, "adverse result" has the meaning set forth in subdivision (a) of Section 1546.

Added by Stats 2016 ch 511 (AB 1924),s 2, eff. 9/23/2016.

Section 638.55 - Motion to suppress

(a) Any person in a trial, hearing, or proceeding may move to suppress wire or electronic information obtained or retained in violation of the Fourth Amendment to the United States Constitution or of this chapter. The motion shall be made, determined, and be subject to review in accordance with the procedures set forth in subdivisions (b) to (q), inclusive, of Section 1538.5.

(b) The Attorney General may commence a civil action to compel any government entity to comply with the provisions of this chapter.

(c) An individual whose information is targeted by a warrant, order, or other legal process that is not in compliance with this chapter, the California Constitution, or the United States Constitution, or a service provider or any other recipient of the warrant, order, or other legal process may petition the issuing court to void or modify the warrant, order, or process, or to order the destruction of any information obtained in violation of this chapter, the California Constitution, or the United States Constitution.

Added by Stats 2016 ch 511 (AB 1924),s 3, eff. 9/23/2016.

Chapter 2 - OF OTHER AND MISCELLANEOUS OFFENSES

Section 639 - Unlawful gift to financial institution employee for procuring loan or extension of credit

Every person who gives, offers, or agrees to give to any director, officer, or employee of a financial institution any emolument, gratuity, or reward, or any money, property, or thing of value for his own personal benefit or of personal advantage, for procuring or endeavoring to procure for any person a loan or extension of credit from such financial institution is guilty of a felony.

As used in this section and Section 639a, "financial institution" means any person or persons engaged in the business of making loans or extending credit or procuring the making of loans or extension of credit, including, but not limited to, state and federal banks, savings and loan associations, trust companies, industrial loan companies, personal property brokers, consumer finance lenders, commercial finance lenders, credit unions, escrow companies, title insurance companies, insurance companies, small business investment companies, pawnbrokers, and retirement funds.

As used in this section and Section 639a the word "person" includes any person, firm, partnership, association, corporation, limited liability company, company, syndicate, estate, trust, business trust, or organization of any kind.

Amended by Stats. 1994, Ch. 1010, Sec. 196. Effective January 1, 1995.

Section 639a - Unlawful solicitation or receipt of reward by financial institution employee for procuring loan or extension of credit

Any officer, director or employee of a financial institution who asks, receives, consents, or agrees to receive any commission, emolument, gratuity, or reward or any money, property, or thing of value for his own personal benefit or of personal advantage for procuring or endeavoring to procure for any person a loan from such financial institution is guilty of a felony.

Added by Stats. 1967, Ch. 1023.

Section 640 - Unlawful acts committed on or in facility or vehicle of public transportation system

(a)

(1) Any of the acts described in paragraphs (1) to (6), inclusive, of subdivision (b) is an infraction punishable by a fine not to exceed two hundred fifty dollars ($250) and by community service for a total time not to exceed 48 hours over a period not to exceed 30 days, during a time other than during the violator's hours of school attendance or employment. Except as provided in subdivision (g), any of the acts described in paragraphs (1) to (3), inclusive, of subdivision (c), upon a first or second violation, is an infraction punishable by a fine not to exceed two hundred fifty dollars ($250) and by community service for a total time not to exceed 48 hours over a period not to exceed 30 days, during a time other than during the violator's hours of school attendance or employment. Except as provided in subdivision (g), a third or subsequent violation of any of the acts described in paragraphs (1) to (3), inclusive, of subdivision (c) is a misdemeanor punishable by a fine of not more than four hundred dollars ($400) or by imprisonment in a county jail for a period of not

more than 90 days, or by both that fine and imprisonment. Any of the acts described in subdivision (d) shall be punishable by a fine of not more than four hundred dollars ($400), by imprisonment in a county jail for a period of not more than 90 days, or by both that fine and imprisonment.

(2) This section shall apply only to acts committed on or in a facility or vehicle of a public transportation system.

(b)

(1) Eating or drinking in or on a system facility or vehicle in areas where those activities are prohibited by that system.

(2) Playing unreasonably loud sound equipment on or in a system facility or vehicle, or failing to comply with the warning of a transit official related to disturbing another person by loud or unreasonable noise.

(3) Smoking in or on a system facility or vehicle in areas where those activities are prohibited by that system.

(4) Expectorating upon a system facility or vehicle.

(5) Skateboarding, roller skating, bicycle riding, roller blading, or operating a motorized scooter or similar device, as defined in Section 407.5 of the Vehicle Code, in a system facility, vehicle, or parking structure. This paragraph does not apply to an activity that is necessary for utilization of the transit facility by a bicyclist, including, but not limited to, an activity that is necessary for parking a bicycle or transporting a bicycle aboard a transit vehicle, if that activity is conducted with the permission of the transit agency in a manner that does not interfere with the safety of the bicyclist or other patrons of the transit facility.

(6) Selling or peddling any goods, merchandise, property, or services of any kind whatsoever on the facilities, vehicles, or property of the public transportation system if the public transportation system has prohibited those acts and neither the public transportation system nor its duly authorized representatives have granted written consent to engage in those acts.

(c)

(1) Evasion of the payment of a fare of the system. For purposes of this section, fare evasion includes entering an enclosed area of a public transit facility beyond posted signs prohibiting entrance without obtaining valid fare, in addition to entering a transit vehicle without valid fare.

(2) Misuse of a transfer, pass, ticket, or token with the intent to evade the payment of a fare.

(3)

(A) Unauthorized use of a discount ticket or failure to present, upon request from a transit system representative, acceptable proof of eligibility to use a discount ticket, in accordance with Section 99155 of the Public Utilities Code and posted system identification policies when entering or exiting a transit station or vehicle. Acceptable proof of eligibility must be clearly defined in the posting.

(B) If an eligible discount ticket user is not in possession of acceptable proof at the time of request, a citation issued shall be held for a period of 72 hours to allow the user to produce acceptable proof. If the proof is provided, the citation shall be voided. If the proof is not produced within that time period, the citation shall be processed.

(d)

(1) Willfully disturbing others on or in a system facility or vehicle by engaging in boisterous or unruly behavior.

(2) Carrying an explosive, acid, or flammable liquid in a public transit facility or vehicle.

(3) Urinating or defecating in a system facility or vehicle, except in a lavatory. However, this paragraph shall not apply to a person who cannot comply with this paragraph as a result of a disability, age, or a medical condition.

(4) Willfully blocking the free movement of another person in a system facility or vehicle. This paragraph shall not be interpreted to affect any lawful activities permitted or First Amendment rights protected under the laws of this state or applicable federal law, including, but not limited to, laws related to collective bargaining, labor relations, or labor disputes.

(5) Willfully tampering with, removing, displacing, injuring, or destroying any part of a facility or vehicle of a public transportation system.

(e) Notwithstanding subdivision (a) or (g), a public transportation agency, as defined in paragraph (4) of subdivision (c) of Section 99580 of the Public Utilities Code, may do either of the following:

(1) Enact and enforce an ordinance providing that a person who is the subject of a citation for any of the acts described in subdivision (b) of Section 99580 of the Public Utilities Code on or in a facility or vehicle described in subdivision (a) for which the public transportation agency has jurisdiction shall, under the circumstances set forth by the ordinance, be afforded an opportunity to complete an administrative process that imposes only an administrative penalty enforced in a civil proceeding. The ordinance for imposing and enforcing the administrative penalty shall be governed by Chapter 8 (commencing with Section 99580) of Part 11 of Division 10 of the Public Utilities Code.

(2) Enforce as an infraction pursuant to subdivision (b) the act of failing to yield seating reserved for an elderly or disabled person in a facility or vehicle for which the public transportation agency has jurisdiction, provided that the governing board of the public transportation agency enacts an ordinance to that effect after a public hearing on the issue.

(f) For purposes of this section, "facility or vehicle of a public transportation system" means any of the following:

(1) A facility or vehicle of a public transportation system as defined by Section 99211 of the Public Utilities Code.

(2) A facility of, or vehicle operated by, an entity subsidized by, the Department of Transportation.

(3) A facility or vehicle of a rail authority, whether owned or leased, including, but not limited to, any part of a railroad, or track of a railroad, or any branch or branchway, switch, turnout, bridge, viaduct, culvert, embankment, station house, or other structure or fixture, or any part thereof, attached or connected to a railroad.

(4) A leased or rented facility or vehicle for which any of the entities described in paragraph (1), (2), or (3) incurs costs of cleanup, repair, or replacement as a result of any of those acts.

(g) A minor shall not be charged with an infraction or a misdemeanor for violation of paragraphs (1) to (3), inclusive, of subdivision (c). Nothing in this subdivision shall limit the ability of a public transportation agency to assess an administrative penalty as established in paragraph (1) of subdivision (e) and in Section 99580 of the Public Utilities Code, not to exceed one hundred twenty-five dollars ($125) upon a first or second violation and not to exceed two hundred dollars ($200) upon a third or subsequent violation, to permit the performance of community service in lieu of payment of the fare evasion or passenger conduct penalty pursuant to Section 99580 of the Public Utilities Code, or to allow payment of the fare evasion or passenger conduct penalty in installments or deferred payment pursuant to Section 99580 of the Public Utilities Code.

Amended by Stats 2017 ch 219 (SB 614),s 1, eff. 1/1/2018.
Amended by Stats 2016 ch 167 (SB 882),s 1, eff. 1/1/2017.
Amended by Stats 2015 ch 765 (SB 413),s 1, eff. 1/1/2016.
Amended by Stats 2012 ch 750 (AB 2247),s 1.5, eff. 1/1/2013.
Amended by Stats 2012 ch 366 (AB 492),s 1, eff. 1/1/2013.
Amended by Stats 2011 ch 100 (AB 426),s 1, eff. 1/1/2012.
Amended by Stats 2010 ch 675 (AB 2324),s 3.5, eff. 1/1/2011.
Amended by Stats 2010 ch 493 (SB 1320),s 1, eff. 1/1/2011.
Amended by Stats 2006 ch 258 (SB 1749),s 1, eff. 1/1/2007.
Amended by Stats 2000 ch 860 (AB 2908), s 1, eff. 1/1/2001.

Section 640.2 - Unlawful placement of writing on consumer product offered for sale

(a) Any person who stamps, prints, places, or inserts any writing in or on any product or box, package, or other container containing a consumer product offered for sale is guilty of a misdemeanor.

(b) This section does not apply if the owner or manager of the premises where the product is stored or sold, or his or her designee, or the product manufacturer or authorized distributor or retailer of the product consents to the placing or inserting of the writing.

(c) As used in this section, "writing" means any form of representation or communication, including handbills, notices, or advertising, that contains letters, words, or pictorial representations.

Added by Stats. 1996, Ch. 140, Sec. 1. Effective July 12, 1996.

Section 640.5 - Defacement of facilities or vehicles of governmental entity

(a)

(1) Any person who defaces with graffiti or other inscribed material the interior or exterior of the facilities or vehicles of a governmental entity, as defined by Section 811.2 of the Government Code, or the interior or exterior of the facilities or vehicles of a public transportation system as defined by Section 99211 of the Public Utilities Code, or the interior or exterior of the facilities of or vehicles operated by entities subsidized by the Department of Transportation or the interior or exterior of any leased or rented facilities or vehicles for which any of the above entities incur costs of less than two hundred fifty dollars ($250) for cleanup, repair, or replacement is guilty of an infraction, punishable by a fine not to exceed one thousand dollars ($1,000) and by a minimum of 48 hours of community service for a total time not to exceed 200 hours over a period not to exceed 180 days, during a time other than his or her hours of school attendance or employment. This subdivision does not preclude application of Section 594.

(2) In lieu of the community service required pursuant to paragraph (1), the court may, if a jurisdiction has adopted a graffiti abatement program as defined in subdivision (f) of Section 594, order the defendant, and his or her parents or guardians if the defendant is a minor, to keep a specified property in the community free of graffiti for 90 days. Participation of a parent or guardian is not required under this paragraph if the court deems this participation to be detrimental to the defendant, or if the parent or guardian is a single parent who must care for young children.

(b)

(1) If the person has been convicted previously of an infraction under subdivision (a) or has a prior conviction of Section 594, 594.3, 594.4, 640.6, or 640.7, the offense is a misdemeanor, punishable by imprisonment in a county jail not to exceed six months, by a fine not to exceed two thousand dollars ($2,000), or by both that imprisonment and fine. As a condition of probation, the court shall order the defendant to perform a minimum of 96 hours of community service not to exceed 400 hours over a period not to exceed 350 days during a time other than his or her hours of school attendance or employment.

(2) In lieu of the community service required pursuant to paragraph (1), the court may, if a jurisdiction has adopted a graffiti abatement program as defined in subdivision (f) of Section 594, order the defendant, and his or her parents or guardians if the defendant is a minor, as a condition of probation, to keep a specified property in the community free of graffiti for 180 days. Participation of a parent or guardian is not required under this paragraph if the court deems this participation to be detrimental to the defendant, or if the parent or guardian is a single parent who must care for young children.

(c)

(1) Every person who, having been convicted previously under this section or Section 594, 594.3, 594.4, 640.6, or 640.7, or any combination of these offenses, on two separate occasions, and having been incarcerated pursuant to a sentence, a conditional sentence, or a grant of probation for at least one of the convictions, is subsequently convicted under this section, shall be punished by imprisonment in a county jail not to exceed one year, by a fine not to exceed three thousand dollars ($3,000), or by both that imprisonment and fine. As a condition of probation, the court may order the defendant to perform community service not to exceed 600 hours over a period not to exceed 480 days during a time other than his or her hours of school attendance or employment.

(2) In lieu of the community service that may be ordered pursuant to paragraph (1), the court may, if a jurisdiction has adopted a graffiti abatement program as defined in subdivision (f) of Section 594, order the defendant, and his or her parents or guardians if the defendant is a minor, as a condition of probation, to keep a specified property in the community free of graffiti for 240 days. Participation of a parent or guardian is not required under this paragraph if the court deems this participation to be detrimental to the defendant, or if the parent or guardian is a single parent who must care for young children.

(d)

(1) Upon conviction of any person under subdivision (a), the court, in addition to any punishment imposed pursuant to subdivision (a), (b), or (c), at the victim's option, may order the defendant to perform the necessary labor to clean up, repair, or replace the property damaged by that person.

(2) If a minor is personally unable to pay any fine levied for violating subdivision (a), (b), or (c), the parent or legal guardian of the minor shall be liable for payment of the fine. A court may waive payment of the fine or any part thereof by the parent or legal guardian upon a finding of good cause.

(e) Any fine levied for a violation of subdivision (a), (b), or (c) shall be credited by the county treasurer pursuant to Section 1463.29 to the governmental entity having jurisdiction over, or responsibility for, the facility or vehicle involved, to be used for removal of the graffiti or other inscribed material or replacement or repair of the property defaced by the graffiti or other inscribed material. Before crediting these fines to the appropriate governmental entity, the county may determine the administrative costs it has incurred pursuant to this section, and retain an amount equal to those costs. Any community service which is required pursuant to subdivision (a), (b), or (c) of a person under the age of 18 years may be performed in the presence, and under the direct supervision, of the person's parent or legal guardian.

(f) As used in this section, the term "graffiti or other inscribed material" includes any unauthorized inscription, word, figure, mark, or design that is written, marked, etched, scratched, drawn, or painted on real or personal property.

(g) The court may order any person ordered to perform community service or graffiti removal pursuant to subdivision (a), (b), (c), or (d) to undergo counseling.

Amended by Stats. 1996, Ch. 847, Sec. 1.5. Effective January 1, 1997.

Section 640.6 - Defacement of real or personal property

(a)

(1) Except as provided in Section 640.5, any person who defaces with graffiti or other inscribed material any real or personal property not his or her own, when the amount of the defacement, damage, or destruction is less than two hundred fifty dollars ($250), is guilty of an infraction, punishable by a fine not to exceed one thousand dollars ($1,000). This subdivision does not preclude application of Section 594. In addition to the penalty set forth in this section, the court shall order the defendant to perform a minimum of 48 hours of community service not to exceed 200 hours over a period not to exceed 180 days during a time other than his or her hours of school attendance or employment.

(2) In lieu of the community service required pursuant to paragraph (1), the court may, if a jurisdiction has adopted a graffiti abatement program as defined in subdivision (f) of Section 594, order the defendant, and his or her parents or guardians if the defendant is a minor, to keep a specified property in the community free of graffiti for 90 days. Participation of a parent or guardian is not required under this paragraph if the court deems this participation to be detrimental to the defendant, or if the parent or guardian is a single parent who must care for young children.

(b)

(1) If the person has been convicted previously of an infraction under subdivision (a) or has a prior conviction of Section 594, 594.3, 594.4, 640.5, or 640.7, the offense is a misdemeanor, punishable by not to exceed six months in a county jail, by a fine not to exceed two thousand dollars ($2,000), or by both that imprisonment and fine. As a condition of probation, the court shall order the defendant to perform a minimum of 96 hours of community service not to exceed 400 hours over a period not to exceed 350 days during a time other than his or her hours of school attendance or employment.

(2) In lieu of the community service required pursuant to paragraph (1), the court may, if a jurisdiction has adopted a graffiti abatement program as defined in subdivision (f) of Section 594, order the defendant, and his or her parents or guardians if the defendant is a minor, as a condition of probation, to keep a specified property in the community free of graffiti for 180 days. Participation of a parent or guardian is not required under this paragraph if the court deems this participation to be detrimental to the defendant, or if the parent or guardian is a single parent who must care for young children.

(c)

(1) Every person who, having been convicted previously under this section or Section 594, 594.3, 594.4, 640.5, or 640.7, or any combination of these offenses, on two separate occasions, and having been incarcerated pursuant to a sentence, a conditional sentence, or a grant of probation for at least one of the convictions, is subsequently convicted under this section, shall be punished by imprisonment in a county jail not to exceed one year, by a fine not to exceed three thousand dollars ($3,000), or by both that imprisonment and fine. As a condition of probation, the court may order the defendant to perform community service not to exceed 600 hours over a period not to exceed 480 days during a time other than his or her hours of school attendance or employment.

(2) In lieu of the community service that may be ordered pursuant to paragraph (1), the court may, if a jurisdiction has adopted a graffiti abatement program as defined in subdivision (f) of Section 594, order the defendant, and his or her parents or guardians if the defendant is a minor, as a condition of probation, to keep a specified property in the community free of graffiti for 240 days. Participation of a parent or guardian is not required under this paragraph if the court deems this participation to be detrimental to the defendant, or if the parent or guardian is a single parent who must care for young children.

(d) Upon conviction of any person under subdivision (a), the court, in addition to any punishment imposed pursuant to subdivision (a), (b), or (c), at the victim's option, may order the defendant to perform the necessary labor to clean up, repair, or replace the property damaged by that person.

(e) If a minor is personally unable to pay any fine levied for violating subdivision (a), (b), or (c), the parent or legal guardian of the minor shall be liable for payment of the fine. A court may waive payment of the fine or any part thereof by the parent or legal guardian upon a finding of good cause. Any community service which is required pursuant to subdivision (a), (b), or (c) of a person under the age of 18 years may be performed in the presence, and under the direct supervision, of the person's parent or legal guardian.

(f) As used in this section, the term "graffiti or other inscribed material" includes any unauthorized inscription, word, figure, mark, or design that is written, marked, etched, scratched, drawn, or painted on real or personal property.

(g) The court may order any person ordered to perform community service or graffiti removal pursuant to subdivision (a), (b), (c), or (d) to undergo counseling.

Amended by Stats. 1996, Ch. 847, Sec. 2.5. Effective January 1, 1997.

Section 640.7 - Defacement on or within 100 feet of highway

Any person who violates Section 594, 640.5, or 640.6 on or within 100 feet of a highway, or its appurtenances, including, but not limited to, guardrails, signs, traffic signals, snow poles, and similar facilities, excluding signs naming streets, is guilty of a misdemeanor, punishable by imprisonment in a county jail not exceeding six months, or by a fine not exceeding one thousand dollars ($1,000), or by both that imprisonment and fine. A second conviction is punishable by imprisonment in a county jail not exceeding one year, or by a fine not exceeding one thousand dollars ($1,000), or by both that imprisonment and fine.

Amended by Stats. 1998, Ch. 853, Sec. 3. Effective January 1, 1999.

Section 640.8 - Defacement on freeway

Any person who violates Section 594, 640.5, or 640.6, on a freeway, or its appurtenances, including sound walls, overpasses, overpass supports, guardrails, signs, signals, and other traffic control devices, is guilty of a misdemeanor, punishable by imprisonment in a county jail not to exceed one year, by a fine not to exceed five thousand dollars ($5,000), or by both that imprisonment and fine. As a condition of probation, the court may order the defendant to perform community service not to exceed 480 hours over a period not to exceed 420 days during a time other than his or her hours of school attendance or employment.

Added by Stats. 1996, Ch. 847, Sec. 3. Effective January 1, 1997.

Section 640a - Unlawful operation of automatic vending machines

1.Any person who shall knowingly and wilfully operate, or cause to be operated, or who shall attempt to operate, or attempt to cause to be operated, any automatic vending machine, slot machine or other receptacle designed to receive lawful coin of the United States of America in connection with the sale, use or enjoyment of property or service, by means of a slug or any false, counterfeited, mutilated, sweated or foreign coin, or by any means, method, trick or device whatsoever not lawfully authorized by the owner, lessee or licensee of such machine or receptacle, or who shall take, obtain or receive from or in connection with any automatic vending machine, slot machine or other receptacle designed to receive lawful coin of the United States of America in connection with the sale, use or enjoyment of property or service, any goods, wares, merchandise, gas, electric current, article of value, or the use or enjoyment of any musical instrument, phonograph or other property, without depositing in and surrendering to such machine or receptacle lawful coin of the United States of America to the amount required therefor by the owner, lessee or licensee of such machine or receptacle shall be guilty of a misdemeanor.

2.Any person who, with intent to cheat or defraud the owner, lessee, licensee or other person entitled to the contents of any automatic vending machine, slot machine or other receptacle, depository or contrivance designed to receive lawful coin of the United States of America in connection with the sale, use or enjoyment of property or service, or who, knowing or having cause to believe that the same is intended for unlawful use, shall manufacture for sale, or sell or give away any slug, device or substance whatsoever intended or calculated to be placed or deposited in any such automatic vending machine, slot machine or other such receptacle, depository or contrivance, shall be guilty of a misdemeanor.

Amended by Stats. 1957, Ch. 2096.

Section 640b - Unlawful operation of coin-box telephone

1.Any person who knowingly, wilfully and with intent to defraud the owner, lessee or licensee of any coin-box telephone, shall operate or cause to be operated, attempt to operate, or attempt to cause to be operated, any coin-box telephone by means of any slug or any false, counterfeited, mutilated, sweated or foreign coin, or by any means, method, trick or device whatsoever not lawfully authorized by such owner, lessee or licensee, or any person who, knowingly, wilfully and with intent to defraud the owner, lessee or licensee of any coin-box telephone, shall take, obtain or receive from or in connection with any such coin-box telephone, the use or enjoyment of any telephone or telegraph facilities or service, without depositing in or surrendering to such coin-box telephone lawful coin of the United States of America to the amount required therefor by such owner, lessee or licensee, shall be guilty of a misdemeanor.

2.Any person who, with the intent to cheat or defraud the owner, lessee or licensee or other person entitled to the contents of any coin-box telephone, or who, knowing or having cause to believe that the same is intended for unlawful use, shall manufacture for sale, or sell or give away any slug, device or substance whatsoever intended or calculated to be placed or deposited in any such coin-box telephone, shall be guilty of a misdemeanor.

Added by Stats. 1957, Ch. 2096.

Section 641 - Unlawful procurement of telegraph or telephone employee to disclose private message

Every person who, by the payment or promise of any bribe, inducement, or reward, procures or attempts to procure any telegraph or telephone agent, operator, or employee to disclose any private message, or the contents, purport, substance, or meaning thereof, or offers to any agent, operator, or employee any bribe, compensation, or reward for the disclosure of any private information received by him or her by reason of his or her trust as agent, operator, or employee, or uses or attempts to use any information so obtained, is punishable as provided in Section 639.

Amended by Stats. 1987, Ch. 828, Sec. 40.

Section 641.3 - Commercial bribery

(a) Any employee who solicits, accepts, or agrees to accept money or any thing of value from a person other than his or her employer, other than in trust for the employer, corruptly and without the knowledge or consent of the employer, in return for using or agreeing to use his or her position for the benefit of that other person, and any person who offers or gives an employee money or any thing of value under those circumstances, is guilty of commercial bribery.

(b) This section does not apply where the amount of money or monetary worth of the thing of value is two hundred fifty dollars ($250) or less.

(c) Commercial bribery is punishable by imprisonment in the county jail for not more than one year if the amount of the bribe is one thousand dollars ($1,000) or less, or by imprisonment in the county jail, or in the state prison for 16 months, or two or three years if the amount of the bribe exceeds one thousand dollars ($1,000).

(d) For purposes of this section:

(1) "Employee" means an officer, director, agent, trustee, partner, or employee.

(2) "Employer" means a corporation, association, organization, trust, partnership, or sole proprietorship.

(3) "Corruptly" means that the person specifically intends to injure or defraud (A) his or her employer, (B) the employer of the person to whom he or she offers, gives, or agrees to give the money or a thing of value, (C) the employer of the person from whom he or she requests, receives, or agrees to receive the money or a thing of value, or (D) a competitor of any such employer.

Amended by Stats 2009 ch 28 (SB X3-18),s 35, eff. 1/1/2010.

Section 641.4 - Commercial bribery involving title insurer, underwritten title company, or controlled escrow company

(a) An employee of a title insurer, underwritten title company, or controlled escrow company who corruptly violates Section 12404 of the Insurance Code by paying, directly or indirectly, a commission, compensation, or other consideration to a licensee, as defined in Section 10011 of the Business and Professions Code, or a licensee who corruptly violates Section 10177.4 of the Business and Professions Code by receiving from an employee of a title insurer, underwritten title company, or controlled escrow company a commission, compensation, or other consideration, as an inducement for the placement or referral of title business, is guilty of commercial bribery.

(b) For purposes of this section, commercial bribery is punishable by imprisonment in a county jail for not more than one year, or by a fine of ten thousand dollars ($10,000) for each unlawful transaction, or by both a fine and imprisonment.

(c) For purposes of this section, "title business" has the same meaning as that used in Section 12404 of the Insurance Code.

(d) This section shall not preclude prosecution under any other law.

(e) This section shall not be construed to supersede or affect Section 641.3. A person may be charged with a violation of this section and Section 641.3. However, a defendant may not be punished under this section and Section 641.3 for the same act that constitutes a violation of both this section and Section 641.3.

Added by Stats. 1997, Ch. 718, Sec. 3. Effective January 1, 1998.

Section 641.5 - Unlawful use of volatile, commercially moisture-free solvent by clothes cleaning establishment

(a) In any clothes cleaning establishment in which more than one gallon of a volatile, commercially moisture-free solvent of the chlorinated hydrocarbon type is used for dry cleaning, the performance of all the dry cleaning, drying, and deodorizing processes shall be completed entirely within fluid-tight machines or apparatus vented to the open air at a point not less than eight feet from any window or other opening and so used and operated as to prevent the escape of fumes, gases, or vapors into workrooms or workplaces.

(b) Except when operations are performed as provided in subdivision (a), no person shall operate a clothes cleaning establishment in which more than one gallon of a volatile, commercially moisture-free solvent of the chlorinated hydrocarbon type is used for dry cleaning except under either of the following conditions:

(1) All of the dry cleaning, drying, and deodorizing processes are performed in a single room or compartment designed and ventilated in such a manner that dangerous toxic concentrations of vapors will not accumulate in working areas.

(2) The dry cleaning processes are performed in fluid-tight machines or apparatus designed, installed, and operated in a manner that will prevent the escape of dangerous toxic concentrations of vapors to the working areas.

(c) "Volatile, commercially moisture-free solvent" means either of the following:

(1) Any commercially moisture-free liquid, volatile product or substance having the capacity to evaporate and, during evaporation, to generate and emit a gas or vapor.

(2) Any solvent commonly known to the clothes cleaning industry as a "chlorinated hydrocarbon solvent."

(d) Any violation of this section is a misdemeanor.

Added by Stats. 1986, Ch. 478, Sec. 2.

Section 641.6 - Unlawful use of cleaning agent by dry cleaners

Notwithstanding any other provision of law, no person engaged in the business of dry cleaning shall use carbon tetrachloride or trichlorethylene as a cleaning agent when engaged in onsite dry cleaning. For purposes of this section, "onsite dry cleaning" means dry cleaning which is performed in a residence or any commercial or public building other than a clothes cleaning establishment or plant. A violation of this section is a misdemeanor.

Added by Stats. 1986, Ch. 478, Sec. 3.

Section 642 - Theft from dead human body

Every person who wilfully and maliciously removes and keeps possession of and appropriates for his own use articles of value from a dead human body, the theft of which articles would be petty theft is guilty of a misdemeanor, or if the theft of the articles would be grand theft, a felony. This section shall not apply to articles removed at the request or direction of one of the persons enumerated in section 7111 of the Health and Safety Code.

Added by Stats. 1939, Ch. 691.

Section 643 - Unlawful disposal of fetal remains

No person knowingly shall dispose of fetal remains in a public or private dump, refuse, or disposal site or place open to public view. For the purposes of this section, "fetal remains" means the lifeless product of conception regardless of the duration of the pregnancy. Any violation of this section is a misdemeanor.

Added by Stats. 1971, Ch. 377.

Section 645 - Medroxyprogesterone acetate treatment

(a) Any person guilty of a first conviction of any offense specified in subdivision (c), where the victim has not attained 13 years of age, may, upon parole, undergo medroxyprogesterone acetate treatment or its chemical equivalent, in addition to any other punishment prescribed for that offense or any other provision of law, at the discretion of the court.

(b) Any person guilty of a second conviction of any offense specified in subdivision (c), where the victim has not attained 13 years of age, shall, upon parole, undergo medroxyprogesterone acetate treatment or its chemical equivalent, in addition to any other punishment prescribed for that offense or any other provision of law.

(c) This section shall apply to the following offenses:

(1) Subdivision (c) or (d) of Section 286.

(2) Paragraph (1) of subdivision (b) of Section 288.

(3) Subdivision (c) or (d) of Section 287 or of former Section 288a.

(4) Subdivision (a) or (j) of Section 289.

(d) The parolee shall begin medroxyprogesterone acetate treatment one week prior to his or her release from confinement in the state prison or other institution and shall continue treatments until the Department of Corrections demonstrates to the Board of Prison Terms that this treatment is no longer necessary.

(e) If a person voluntarily undergoes a permanent, surgical alternative to hormonal chemical treatment for sex offenders, he or she shall not be subject to this section.

(f) The Department of Corrections shall administer this section and implement the protocols required by this section. Nothing in the protocols shall require an employee of the Department of Corrections who is a physician and surgeon licensed pursuant to Chapter 5 (commencing with Section 2000) of Division 2 of the Business and Professions Code or the Osteopathic Initiative Act to participate against his or her will in the administration of the provisions of this section. These protocols shall include, but not be limited to, a requirement to inform the person about the effect of hormonal chemical treatment and any side effects that may result from it. A person subject to this section shall acknowledge the receipt of this information.

Amended by Stats 2018 ch 423 (SB 1494),s 62, eff. 1/1/2019.

Amended by Stats 2001 ch 854 (SB 205), s 34, eff. 1/1/2002.

Section 646 - Unlawful institution of suit outside of California

It is unlawful for any person with the intent, or for the purpose of instituting a suit thereon outside of this state, to seek or solicit the business of collecting any claim for damages for personal injury sustained within this state, or for death resulting therefrom, with the intention of instituting suit thereon outside of this state, in cases where such right of action rests in a resident of this state, or his legal representative, and is against a person, copartnership, or corporation subject to personal service within this state.

Any person violating any of the provisions of this section is guilty of a misdemeanor, and is punishable by a fine of not less than one hundred dollars ($100) nor more than one thousand dollars ($1,000), by imprisonment in the county jail not less than 30 days nor more than six months, or by both fine and imprisonment at the discretion of the court but within said limits.

Amended by Stats. 1983, Ch. 1092, Sec. 314. Effective September 27, 1983. Operative January 1, 1984, by Sec. 427 of Ch. 1092.

Section 646.5 - Unlawful solicitation of employment from injured person as investigator

No person shall knowingly and directly solicit employment from any injured person or from any other person to obtain authorization on behalf of the injured person, as an investigator to investigate the accident or act which resulted in injury or death to such person or damage to the property of such person. Nothing in this section shall prohibit the soliciting of employment as an investigator from such injured person's attorney.

Any person violating any provision of this section is guilty of a misdemeanor.

This section shall not apply to any business agent or attorney employed by a labor organization.

Added by Stats. 1971, Ch. 694.

Section 646.6 - Unlawful solicitation of injured person for sale or use of photographs relating to accident

No person shall knowingly and directly solicit any injured person, or anyone acting on behalf of any injured person, for the sale or use of photographs relating to the accident which resulted in the injury or death of such injured person.

Any person violating any provision of this section is guilty of a misdemeanor. Nothing in this section shall prohibit a person, other than a public employee acting within the scope of his or her employment, from soliciting the injured person's attorney for the sale or use of such photographs.

Amended by Stats. 1976, Ch. 495.

Section 646.9 - Stalking

(a) Any person who willfully, maliciously, and repeatedly follows or willfully and maliciously harasses another person and who makes a credible threat with the intent to place that person in reasonable fear for his or her safety, or the safety of his or her immediate family is guilty of the crime of stalking, punishable by imprisonment in a county jail for not more than one year, or by a fine of not more than one thousand dollars ($1,000), or by both that fine and imprisonment, or by imprisonment in the state prison.

(b) Any person who violates subdivision (a) when there is a temporary restraining order, injunction, or any other court order in effect prohibiting the behavior described in subdivision (a) against the same party, shall be punished by imprisonment in the state prison for two, three, or four years.

(c)

(1) Every person who, after having been convicted of a felony under Section 273.5, 273.6, or 422, commits a violation of subdivision (a) shall be punished by imprisonment in a county jail for not more than one year, or by a fine of not more than one thousand dollars ($1,000), or by both that fine and imprisonment, or by imprisonment in the state prison for two, three, or five years.

(2) Every person who, after having been convicted of a felony under subdivision (a), commits a violation of this section shall be punished by imprisonment in the state prison for two, three, or five years.

(d) In addition to the penalties provided in this section, the sentencing court may order a person convicted of a felony under this section to register as a sex offender pursuant to Section 290.006.

(e) For the purposes of this section, "harasses" means engages in a knowing and willful course of conduct directed at a specific person that seriously alarms, annoys, torments, or terrorizes the person, and that serves no legitimate purpose.

(f) For the purposes of this section, "course of conduct" means two or more acts occurring over a period of time, however short, evidencing a continuity of purpose. Constitutionally protected activity is not included within the meaning of "course of conduct."

(g) For the purposes of this section, "credible threat" means a verbal or written threat, including that performed through the use of an electronic communication device, or a threat implied by a pattern of conduct or a combination of verbal, written, or electronically communicated statements and conduct, made with the intent to place the person that is the target of the threat in reasonable fear for his or her safety or the safety of his or her family, and made with the apparent ability to carry out the threat so as to cause the person who is the target of the threat to reasonably fear for his or her safety or the safety of his or her family. It is not necessary to prove that the defendant had the intent to actually carry out the threat. The present incarceration of a person making the threat shall not be a bar to prosecution under this section. Constitutionally protected activity is not included within the meaning of "credible threat."

(h) For purposes of this section, the term "electronic communication device" includes, but is not limited to, telephones, cellular phones, computers, video recorders, fax machines, or pagers. "Electronic communication" has the same meaning as the term defined in Subsection 12 of Section 2510 of Title 18 of the United States Code.

(i) This section shall not apply to conduct that occurs during labor picketing.

(j) If probation is granted, or the execution or imposition of a sentence is suspended, for any person convicted under this section, it shall be a condition of probation that the person participate in counseling, as designated by the court. However, the court, upon a showing of good cause, may find that the counseling requirement shall not be imposed.

(k)

(1) The sentencing court also shall consider issuing an order restraining the defendant from any contact with the victim, that may be valid for up to 10 years, as determined by the court. It is the intent of the Legislature that the length of any restraining order be based upon the seriousness of the facts before the court, the probability of future violations, and the safety of the victim and his or her immediate family.

(2) This protective order may be issued by the court whether the defendant is sentenced to state prison, county jail, or if imposition of sentence is suspended and the defendant is placed on probation.

(l) For purposes of this section, "immediate family" means any spouse, parent, child, any person related by consanguinity or affinity within the second degree, or any other person who regularly resides in the household, or who, within the prior six months, regularly resided in the household.

(m) The court shall consider whether the defendant would benefit from treatment pursuant to Section 2684. If it is determined to be appropriate, the court shall recommend that the Department of Corrections and Rehabilitation make a certification as provided in Section 2684. Upon the certification, the defendant shall be evaluated and transferred to the appropriate hospital for treatment pursuant to Section 2684.

Amended by Stats 2007 ch 582 (AB 289),s 2.5, eff. 1/1/2008.
Amended by Stats 2007 ch 579 (SB 172),s 39, eff. 10/13/2007.
Amended by Stats 2002 ch 832 (SB 1320), s 1, eff. 1/1/2003.
Amended by Stats 2000 ch 669 (AB 2425), s 1, eff. 1/1/2001.

Section 646.91 - Emergency protective order

(a) Notwithstanding any other law, a judicial officer may issue an ex parte emergency protective order if a peace officer, as defined in Section 830.1, 830.2, 830.32, or subdivision (a) of Section 830.33, asserts reasonable grounds to believe that a person is in immediate and present danger of stalking based upon the person's allegation that he or she has been willfully, maliciously, and repeatedly followed or harassed by another person who has made a credible threat with the intent of placing the person who is the target of the threat in reasonable fear for his or her safety, or the safety of his or her immediate family, within the meaning of Section 646.9.

(b) A peace officer who requests an emergency protective order shall reduce the order to writing and sign it.

(c) An emergency protective order shall include all of the following:

(1) A statement of the grounds asserted for the order.

(2) The date and time the order expires.

(3) The address of the superior court for the district or county in which the protected party resides.

(4) The following statements, which shall be printed in English and Spanish:

(A) "To the protected person: This order will last until the date and time noted above. If you wish to seek continuing protection, you will have to apply for an order from the court at the address noted above. You may seek the advice of an attorney as to any matter connected with your application for any future court orders. The attorney should be consulted promptly so that the attorney may assist you in making your application."

(B) "To the restrained person: This order will last until the date and time noted above. The protected party may, however, obtain a more permanent restraining order from the court. You may seek the advice of an attorney as to any matter connected with the application. The attorney should be consulted promptly so that the attorney may assist you in responding to the application. You may not own, possess, purchase, or receive, or attempt to purchase or receive, a firearm while this order is in effect."

(d) An emergency protective order may be issued under this section only if the judicial officer finds both of the following:

(1) That reasonable grounds have been asserted to believe that an immediate and present danger of stalking, as defined in Section 646.9, exists.

(2) That an emergency protective order is necessary to prevent the occurrence or reoccurrence of the stalking activity.

(e) An emergency protective order may include either of the following specific orders as appropriate:

(1) A harassment protective order as described in Section 527.6 of the Code of Civil Procedure.

(2) A workplace violence protective order as described in Section 527.8 of the Code of Civil Procedure.

(f) An emergency protective order shall be issued without prejudice to any person.

(g) An emergency protective order expires at the earlier of the following times:

(1) The close of judicial business on the fifth court day following the day of its issuance.

(2) The seventh calendar day following the day of its issuance.

(h) A peace officer who requests an emergency protective order shall do all of the following:

(1) Serve the order on the restrained person, if the restrained person can reasonably be located.

(2) Give a copy of the order to the protected person, or, if the protected person is a minor child, to a parent or guardian of the protected child if the parent or guardian can reasonably be located, or to a person having temporary custody of the child.

(3) File a copy of the order with the court as soon as practicable after issuance.

(4) Have the order entered into the computer database system for protective and restraining orders maintained by the Department of Justice.

(i) A peace officer shall use every reasonable means to enforce an emergency protective order.

(j) A peace officer who acts in good faith to enforce an emergency protective order is not civilly or criminally liable.

(k) A peace officer described in subdivision (a) or (b) of Section 830.32 who requests an emergency protective order pursuant to this section shall also notify the sheriff or police chief of the city in whose jurisdiction the peace officer's college or school is located after issuance of the order.

(l) "Judicial officer," as used in this section, means a judge, commissioner, or referee.

(m) A person subject to an emergency protective order under this section shall not own, possess, purchase, or receive a firearm while the order is in effect.

(n) Nothing in this section shall be construed to permit a court to issue an emergency protective order prohibiting speech or other activities that are constitutionally protected or protected by the laws of this state or by the United States or activities occurring during a labor dispute, as defined by Section 527.3 of the Code of Civil Procedure, including, but not limited to, picketing and hand billing.

(o) The Judicial Council shall develop forms, instructions, and rules for the scheduling of hearings and other procedures established pursuant to this section.

(p) Any intentional disobedience of any emergency protective order granted under this section is punishable pursuant to Section 166. Nothing in this subdivision shall be construed to prevent punishment under Section 646.9, in lieu of punishment under this section, if a violation of Section 646.9 is also pled and proven.

Amended by Stats 2014 ch 559 (SB 1154),s 1, eff. 1/1/2015.

Amended by Stats 2014 ch 71 (SB 1304),s 124, eff. 1/1/2015.

Amended by Stats 2013 ch 145 (AB 238),s 3, eff. 1/1/2014.

Amended by Stats 2003 ch 495 (AB 1290), s 1, eff. 1/1/2004.

EFFECTIVE 1/1/2000. Amended October 10, 1999 (Bill Number: SB 355) (Chapter 659).

Section 646.91a - Prohibition from taking action to obtain address or location of protected person

(a) The court shall order that any party enjoined pursuant to Section 646.91 be prohibited from taking any action to obtain the address or location of a protected party or a protected party's family members, caretakers, or guardian, unless there is good cause not to make that order.

(b) The Judicial Council shall promulgate forms necessary to effectuate this section.

Amended by Stats 2006 ch 901 (SB 1422),s 6.1, eff. 1/1/2007.

Added by Stats 2005 ch 472 (AB 978),s 5, eff. 1/1/2006.

Section 646.92 - Notification of release or change in in parole status

(a)

(1) The Department of Corrections and Rehabilitation, county sheriff, or director of the local department of corrections shall give notice not less than 15 days prior to the release from the state prison or a county jail of any person who is convicted of violating Section 646.9 or convicted of a felony offense involving domestic violence, as defined in Section 6211 of the Family Code, or any change in the parole status or relevant change in the parole location of the convicted person, or if the convicted person absconds from supervision while on parole, to any person the court identifies as a victim of the offense, a family member of the victim, or a witness to the offense by telephone, electronic mail, or certified mail at his or her last known address, upon request and using the method of communication selected by the requesting party, if that method is available. A victim, family member, or witness shall keep the department or county sheriff informed of his or her current contact information to be entitled to receive notice. A victim may designate another person for the purpose of receiving notification. The department, county sheriff, or director of the local department of corrections, shall make reasonable attempts to locate a person who has requested notification but whose contact information is incorrect or not current. However, the duty to keep the department or county sheriff informed of current contact information shall remain with the victim.

(2) Following notification by the department pursuant to Section 3058.61, in the event the victim had not originally requested notification under this section, the sheriff or the chief of police, as appropriate, shall make an attempt to advise the victim or, if the victim is a minor, the parent or guardian of the victim, of the victim's right to notification under this section.

(b) All information relating to any person who receives notice under this section shall remain confidential and shall not be made available to the person convicted of violating this section.

(c) For purposes of this section, "release" includes a release from the state prison or a county jail because time has been served, a release from the state prison or a county jail to parole or probation supervision, or an escape from an institution or reentry facility.

(d) The department or county sheriff shall give notice of an escape from an institution or reentry facility of any person convicted of violating Section 646.9 or convicted of a felony offense involving domestic violence, as defined in Section 6211 of the Family Code, to the notice recipients described in subdivision (a).

(e) Substantial compliance satisfies the notification requirements of subdivision (a).

Amended by Stats 2011 ch 364 (SB 852),s 1, eff. 9/29/2011.

Amended by Stats 2000 ch 561 (SB 580), s 1, eff. 1/1/2001.

Section 646.93 - Telephone number to inquire about bail status or release; request for lower bail; conditions of release on bail

(a)

(1) In those counties where the arrestee is initially incarcerated in a jail operated by the county sheriff, the sheriff shall designate a telephone number that shall be available to the public to inquire about bail status or to determine if the person arrested has been released and if not yet released, the scheduled release date, if known. This subdivision does not require a county sheriff or jail administrator to establish a new telephone number but shall require that the information contained on the victim resource card, as defined in Section 264.2, specify the phone number that a victim should call to obtain this information. This subdivision shall not require the county sheriff or municipal police departments to produce new victim resource cards containing a designated phone number for the public to inquire about the bail or custody status of a person who has been arrested until their existing supply of victim resource cards has been exhausted.

(2) In those counties where the arrestee is initially incarcerated in an incarceration facility other than a jail operated by the county sheriff and in those counties that do not operate a Victim Notification (VNE) system, a telephone number shall be available to the public to inquire about bail status or to determine if the person arrested has been released and if not yet released, the scheduled release date, if known. This subdivision does not require a municipal police agency or jail administrator to establish a new telephone number but shall require that the information contained on the victim resource card, as defined in Section 264.2, specify the phone number that a victim

should call to obtain this information. This subdivision shall not require the county sheriff or municipal police departments to produce new victim resource cards containing a designated phone number for the public to inquire about the bail or custody status of a person who has been arrested until their existing supply of victim resource cards has been exhausted.

(3) If an arrestee is transferred to another incarceration facility and is no longer in the custody of the initial arresting agency, the transfer date and new incarceration location shall be made available through the telephone number designated by the arresting agency.

(4) The resource card provided to victims pursuant to Section 264.2 shall list the designated telephone numbers to which this section refers.

(b) Any request to lower bail shall be heard in open court in accordance with Section 1270.1. In addition, the prosecutor shall make all reasonable efforts to notify the victim or victims of the bail hearing. The victims may be present at the hearing and shall be permitted to address the court on the issue of bail.

(c) Unless good cause is shown not to impose the following conditions, the judge shall impose as additional conditions of release on bail that:

(1) The defendant shall not initiate contact in person, by telephone, or any other means with the alleged victims.

(2) The defendant shall not knowingly go within 100 yards of the alleged victims, their residence, or place of employment.

(3) The defendant shall not possess any firearms or other deadly or dangerous weapons.

(4) The defendant shall obey all laws.

(5) The defendant, upon request at the time of his or her appearance in court, shall provide the court with an address where he or she is residing or will reside, a business address and telephone number if employed, and a residence telephone number if the defendant's residence has a telephone. A showing by declaration that any of these conditions are violated shall, unless good cause is shown, result in the issuance of a no-bail warrant.

Amended by Stats 2001 ch 854 (SB 205), s 35, eff. 1/1/2002.

Amended by Stats 2000 ch 669 (AB 2425), s 2, eff. 1/1/2001.

Added October 10, 1999 (Bill Number: AB 1284) (Chapter 703).

Section 646.94 - Intensive and specialized parole supervision program for parolees deemed to pose high risk of committing repeat stalking offense

(a) Contingent upon a Budget Act appropriation, the Department of Corrections shall ensure that any parolee convicted of violating Section 646.9 on or after January 1, 2002, who is deemed to pose a high risk of committing a repeat stalking offense be placed on an intensive and specialized parole supervision program for a period not to exceed the period of parole.

(b)

(1) The program shall include referral to specialized services, for example substance abuse treatment, for offenders needing those specialized services.

(2) Parolees participating in this program shall be required to participate in relapse prevention classes as a condition of parole.

(3) Parole agents may conduct group counseling sessions as part of the program.

(4) The department may include other appropriate offenders in the treatment program if doing so facilitates the effectiveness of the treatment program.

(c) The program shall be established with the assistance and supervision of the staff of the department primarily by obtaining the services of mental health providers specializing in the treatment of stalking patients. Each parolee placed into this program shall be required to participate in clinical counseling programs aimed at reducing the likelihood that the parolee will commit or attempt to commit acts of violence or stalk their victim.

(d) The department may require persons subject to this section to pay some or all of the costs associated with this treatment, subject to the person's ability to pay. "Ability to pay" means the overall capability of the person to reimburse the costs, or a portion of the costs, of providing mental health treatment, and shall include, but shall not be limited to, consideration of all of the following factors:

(1) Present financial position.

(2) Reasonably discernible future financial position.

(3) Likelihood that the person shall be able to obtain employment after the date of parole.

(4) Any other factor or factors that may bear upon the person's financial capability to reimburse the department for the costs.

(e) For purposes of this section, a mental health provider specializing in the treatment of stalking patients shall meet all of the following requirements:

(1) Be a licensed clinical social worker, as defined in Article 4 (commencing with Section 4996) of Chapter 14 of Division 2 of the Business and Professions Code, a clinical psychologist, as defined in Section 1316.5 of the Health and Safety Code, or a physician and surgeon engaged in the practice of psychiatry.

(2) Have clinical experience in the area of assessment and treatment of stalking patients.

(3) Have two letters of reference from professionals who can attest to the applicant's experience in counseling stalking patients.

(f) The program shall target parolees convicted of violating Section 646.9 who meet the following conditions:

(1) The offender has been subject to a clinical assessment.

(2) A review of the offender's criminal history indicates that the offender poses a high risk of committing further acts of stalking or acts of violence against his or her victim or other persons upon his or her release on parole.

(3) The parolee, based on his or her clinical assessment, may be amenable to treatment.

(g) On or before January 1, 2006, the Department of Corrections shall evaluate the intensive and specialized parole supervision program and make a report to the Legislature regarding the results of the program, including, but not limited to, the recidivism rate for repeat stalking related offenses committed by persons placed into the program and a cost-benefit analysis of the program.

(h) This section shall become operative upon the appropriation of sufficient funds in the Budget Act to implement this section.

Added by Stats 2000 ch 669 (AB 2425), s 3, eff. 1/1/2001.

Amended by Stats 2001 ch 159 (SB 662), s 163, eff. 1/1/2002.

Section 647 - Disorderly conduct

Except as provided in paragraph (5) of subdivision (b) and subdivision (k), every person who commits any of the following acts is guilty of disorderly conduct, a misdemeanor:

(a) An individual who solicits anyone to engage in or who engages in lewd or dissolute conduct in any public place or in any place open to the public or exposed to public view.

(b)

(1) An individual who solicits, or who agrees to engage in, or who engages in, any act of prostitution with the intent to receive compensation, money, or anything of value from another person. An individual agrees to engage in an act of prostitution when, with specific intent to so engage, the individual manifests an acceptance of an offer or solicitation by another person to so engage, regardless of whether the offer or solicitation was made by a person who also possessed the specific intent to engage in an act of prostitution.

(2) An individual who solicits, or who agrees to engage in, or who engages in, any act of prostitution with another person who is 18 years of age or older in exchange for the individual providing compensation, money, or anything of value to the other person. An individual agrees to engage in an act of prostitution when, with specific intent to so engage, the individual manifests an acceptance of an offer or solicitation by another person who is 18 years of age or older to so engage, regardless of whether the offer or solicitation was made by a person who also possessed the specific intent to engage in an act of prostitution.

(3) An individual who solicits, or who agrees to engage in, or who engages in, any act of prostitution with another person who is a minor in exchange for the individual providing compensation, money, or anything of value to the minor. An individual agrees to engage in an act of prostitution when, with specific intent to so engage, the individual manifests an acceptance of an offer or solicitation by someone who is a minor to so engage, regardless of whether the offer or solicitation was made by a minor who also possessed the specific intent to engage in an act of prostitution.

(4) A manifestation of acceptance of an offer or solicitation to engage in an act of prostitution does not constitute a violation of this subdivision unless some act, in addition to the manifestation of acceptance, is done within this state in furtherance of the commission of the act of prostitution by the person manifesting an acceptance of an offer or solicitation to engage in that act. As used in this subdivision, "prostitution" includes any lewd act between persons for money or other consideration.

(5) Notwithstanding paragraphs (1) to (3), inclusive, this subdivision does not apply to a child under 18 years of age who is alleged to have engaged in conduct to receive money or other consideration that would, if committed by an adult, violate this subdivision. A commercially exploited child under this paragraph may be adjudged a dependent child of the court pursuant to paragraph (2) of subdivision (b) of Section 300 of the Welfare and Institutions Code and may be taken into temporary custody pursuant to subdivision (a) of Section 305 of the Welfare and Institutions Code, if the conditions allowing temporary custody without warrant are met.

(c) Who accosts other persons in any public place or in any place open to the public for the purpose of begging or soliciting alms.

(d) Who loiters in or about any toilet open to the public for the purpose of engaging in or soliciting any lewd or lascivious or any unlawful act.

(e) Who lodges in any building, structure, vehicle, or place, whether public or private, without the permission of the owner or person entitled to the possession or in control of it.

(f) Who is found in any public place under the influence of intoxicating liquor, any drug, controlled substance, toluene, or any combination of any intoxicating liquor, drug, controlled substance, or toluene, in a condition that they are unable to exercise care for their own safety or the safety of others, or by reason of being under the influence of intoxicating liquor, any drug, controlled substance, toluene, or any combination of any intoxicating liquor, drug, or toluene, interferes with or obstructs or prevents the free use of any street, sidewalk, or other public way.

(g) If a person has violated subdivision (f), a peace officer, if reasonably able to do so, shall place the person, or cause the person to be placed, in civil protective custody. The person shall be taken to a facility, designated pursuant to Section 5170 of the Welfare and Institutions Code, for the 72-hour treatment and evaluation of inebriates. A peace officer may place a person in civil protective custody with that kind and degree of force authorized to effect an arrest for a misdemeanor without a warrant. A person who has been placed in civil protective custody shall not thereafter be subject to any criminal prosecution or juvenile court proceeding based on the facts giving rise to this placement. This subdivision does not apply to the following persons:

(1) A person who is under the influence of any drug, or under the combined influence of intoxicating liquor and any drug.

(2) A person who a peace officer has probable cause to believe has committed any felony, or who has committed any misdemeanor in addition to subdivision (f).

(3) A person who a peace officer in good faith believes will attempt escape or will be unreasonably difficult for medical personnel to control.

(h) Who loiters, prowls, or wanders upon the private property of another, at any time, without visible or lawful business with the owner or occupant. As used in this subdivision, "loiter" means to delay or linger without a lawful purpose for being on the property and for the purpose of committing a crime as opportunity may be discovered.

(i) Who, while loitering, prowling, or wandering upon the private property of another, at any time, peeks in the door or window of any inhabited building or structure, without visible or lawful business with the owner or occupant.

(j)

(1) A person who looks through a hole or opening, into, or otherwise views, by means of any instrumentality, including, but not limited to, a periscope, telescope, binoculars, camera, motion picture camera, camcorder, mobile phone, electronic device, or unmanned aircraft system, the interior of a bedroom, bathroom, changing room, fitting room, dressing room, or tanning booth, or the interior of any other area in which the occupant has a reasonable expectation of privacy, with the intent to invade the privacy of a person or persons inside. This subdivision does not apply to those areas of a private business used to count currency or other negotiable instruments.

(2) A person who uses a concealed camcorder, motion picture camera, or photographic camera of any type, to secretly videotape, film, photograph, or record by electronic means, another identifiable person under or through the clothing being worn by that other person, for the purpose of viewing the body of, or the undergarments worn by, that other person, without the consent or knowledge of

that other person, with the intent to arouse, appeal to, or gratify the lust, passions, or sexual desires of that person and invade the privacy of that other person, under circumstances in which the other person has a reasonable expectation of privacy. For the purposes of this paragraph, "identifiable" means capable of identification, or capable of being recognized, meaning that someone, including the victim, could identify or recognize the victim. It does not require the victim's identity to actually be established.

(3)

(A) A person who uses a concealed camcorder, motion picture camera, or photographic camera of any type, to secretly videotape, film, photograph, or record by electronic means, another identifiable person who may be in a state of full or partial undress, for the purpose of viewing the body of, or the undergarments worn by, that other person, without the consent or knowledge of that other person, in the interior of a bedroom, bathroom, changing room, fitting room, dressing room, or tanning booth, or the interior of any other area in which that other person has a reasonable expectation of privacy, with the intent to invade the privacy of that other person. For the purposes of this paragraph, "identifiable" means capable of identification, or capable of being recognized, meaning that someone, including the victim, could identify or recognize the victim. It does not require the victim's identity to actually be established.

(B) Neither of the following is a defense to the crime specified in this paragraph:

(i) The defendant was a cohabitant, landlord, tenant, cotenant, employer, employee, or business partner or associate of the victim, or an agent of any of these.

(ii) The victim was not in a state of full or partial undress.

(4)

(A) A person who intentionally distributes or causes to be distributed the image of the intimate body part or parts of another identifiable person, or an image of the person depicted engaged in an act of sexual intercourse, sodomy, oral copulation, sexual penetration, or an image of masturbation by the person depicted or in which the person depicted participates, under circumstances in which the persons agree or understand that the image shall remain private, the person distributing the image knows or should know that distribution of the image will cause serious emotional distress, and the person depicted suffers that distress.

(B)

(i) A person intentionally distributes an image described in subparagraph (A) when that person personally distributes the image.

(ii) A person intentionally causes an image described in subparagraph (A) to be distributed when that person arranges, specifically requests, or intentionally causes another person to distribute the image.

(C) As used in this paragraph, the following terms have the following meanings:

(i) "Distribute" includes exhibiting in public or giving possession.

(ii) "Identifiable" has the same meaning as in paragraphs (2) and (3).

(iii) "Intimate body part" means any portion of the genitals, the anus and, in the case of a female, also includes any portion of the breasts below the top of the areola, that is either uncovered or clearly visible through clothing.

(D) It shall not be a violation of this paragraph to distribute an image described in subparagraph (A) if any of the following applies:

(i) The distribution is made in the course of reporting an unlawful activity.

(ii) The distribution is made in compliance with a subpoena or other court order for use in a legal proceeding.

(iii) The distribution is made in the course of a lawful public proceeding.

(iv) The distribution is related to a matter of public concern or public interest. Distribution is not a matter of public concern or public interest solely because the depicted individual is a public figure.

(5) This subdivision does not preclude punishment under any section of law providing for greater punishment.

(k)

(1) A second or subsequent violation of subdivision (j) is punishable by imprisonment in a county jail not exceeding one year, or by a fine not exceeding two thousand dollars ($2,000), or by both that fine and imprisonment.

(2) If the victim of a violation of subdivision (j) was a minor at the time of the offense, the violation is punishable by imprisonment in a county jail not exceeding one year, or by a fine not exceeding two thousand dollars ($2,000), or by both that fine and imprisonment.

(l)

(1) If a crime is committed in violation of subdivision (b) and the person who was solicited was a minor at the time of the offense, and if the defendant knew or should have known that the person who was solicited was a minor at the time of the offense, the violation is punishable by imprisonment in a county jail for not less than two days and not more than one year, or by a fine not exceeding ten thousand dollars ($10,000), or by both that fine and imprisonment.

(2) The court may, in unusual cases, when the interests of justice are best served, reduce or eliminate the mandatory two days of imprisonment in a county jail required by this subdivision. If the court reduces or eliminates the mandatory two days' imprisonment, the court shall specify the reason on the record.

Amended by Stats 2022 ch 882 (SB 1081),s 1, eff. 1/1/2023.
Amended by Stats 2020 ch 370 (SB 1371),s 229, eff. 1/1/2021.
Amended by Stats 2019 ch 749 (AB 1129),s 1.5, eff. 1/1/2020.
Amended by Stats 2019 ch 505 (SB 485),s 7, eff. 1/1/2020.
Amended by Stats 2018 ch 246 (AB 324),s 2, eff. 1/1/2019.
Amended by Stats 2016 ch 734 (SB 420),s 1.4, eff. 1/1/2017.
Amended by Stats 2016 ch 724 (SB 1129),s 1, eff. 1/1/2017.
Amended by Stats 2016 ch 654 (SB 1322),s 1, eff. 1/1/2017.
Amended by Stats 2014 ch 863 (SB 1255),s 1.7, eff. 1/1/2015.
Amended by Stats 2014 ch 714 (SB 1388),s 2, eff. 1/1/2015.
Amended by Stats 2014 ch 710 (AB 1791),s 1, eff. 1/1/2015.
Amended by Stats 2014 ch 71 (SB 1304),s 125, eff. 1/1/2015.

Amended by Stats 2013 ch 466 (SB 255),s 1, eff. 10/1/2013.
Amended by Stats 2011 ch 658 (AB 665),s 1, eff. 1/1/2012.
Amended by Stats 2007 ch 302 (SB 425),s 11, eff. 1/1/2008.
Amended by Stats 2004 ch 666 (SB 1484), s 1, eff. 1/1/2005.
 See Stats 2018 ch 246 (AB 324), s 1.

Section 647.1 - Fine

In addition to any fine assessed under Section 647, the judge may assess a fine not to exceed seventy dollars ($70) against any person who violates subdivision (a) or (b) of Section 647, or, if the offense involves intravenous use of a controlled substance, subdivision (f) of Section 647, with the proceeds of this fine to be used in accordance with Section 1463.23.

The court shall, however, take into consideration the defendant's ability to pay and no defendant shall be denied probation because of his or her inability to pay the fine permitted under this section.

Added by Stats. 1988, Ch. 1243, Sec. 8.

Section 647.2 - Condition of probation

If a person is convicted of a violation of subdivision (f) of Section 647 and is granted probation, the court may order, with the consent of the defendant, as a term and condition of probation, in addition to any other term and condition required or authorized by law, that the defendant participate in the program prescribed in Section 23509 of the Vehicle Code.

Amended by Stats. 1998, Ch. 118, Sec. 1.21. Effective January 1, 1999. Operative July 1, 1999, by Sec. 85 of Ch. 118.

Section 647.3 - Arrest for violation of CUCSA or sex work crimes prohibited if person is victim or witness to crime

(a)A person who reports being a victim of, or a witness to, a serious felony as defined in subdivision (c) of Section 1192.7, an assault in violation of subdivision (a) of Section 245, domestic violence in violation of Section 273.5, extortion in violation of Section 518, human trafficking in violation of Section 236.1, sexual battery in violation of subdivision (a) of Section 243.4, or stalking in violation of Section 646.9 shall not be arrested for any of the following offenses if that offense is related to the crime that the person is reporting or if the person was engaged in that offense at or around the time that the person was the victim of or witness to the crime they are reporting:

   (1)A misdemeanor violation of the California Uniform Controlled Substances Act (Division 10 (commencing with Section 11000) of the Health and Safety Code).

   (2)A violation of Section 372 or subdivision (a) or (b) of Section 647, or former Section 653.22, if the offense is related to an act of prostitution.

(b)Possession of condoms in any amount shall not provide a basis for probable cause for arrest for a violation of Section 372 or subdivision (a) or (b) of Section 647, or former Section 653.22 if the offense is related to an act of prostitution.

Amended by Stats 2022 ch 86 (SB 357),s 2, eff. 1/1/2023.
Added by Stats 2019 ch 141 (SB 233),s 4, eff. 1/1/2020.

Section 647.6 - Annoying or molesting child under 18 years of age

(a)

   (1) Every person who annoys or molests any child under 18 years of age shall be punished by a fine not exceeding five thousand dollars ($5,000), by imprisonment in a county jail not exceeding one year, or by both the fine and imprisonment.

   (2) Every person who, motivated by an unnatural or abnormal sexual interest in children, engages in conduct with an adult whom he or she believes to be a child under 18 years of age, which conduct, if directed toward a child under 18 years of age, would be a violation of this section, shall be punished by a fine not exceeding five thousand dollars ($5,000), by imprisonment in a county jail for up to one year, or by both that fine and imprisonment.

(b) Every person who violates this section after having entered, without consent, an inhabited dwelling house, or trailer coach as defined in Section 635 of the Vehicle Code, or the inhabited portion of any other building, shall be punished by imprisonment in the state prison, or in a county jail not exceeding one year, and by a fine not exceeding five thousand dollars ($5,000).

(c)

   (1) Every person who violates this section shall be punished upon the second and each subsequent conviction by imprisonment in the state prison.

   (2) Every person who violates this section after a previous felony conviction under Section 261, 264.1, 269, 285, 286, 287, 288.5, or 289, or former Section 288a, any of which involved a minor under 16 years of age, or a previous felony conviction under this section, a conviction under Section 288, or a felony conviction under Section 311.4 involving a minor under 14 years of age shall be punished by imprisonment in the state prison for two, four, or six years.

(d)

   (1) In any case in which a person is convicted of violating this section and probation is granted, the court shall require counseling as a condition of probation, unless the court makes a written statement in the court record, that counseling would be inappropriate or ineffective.

   (2) In any case in which a person is convicted of violating this section, and as a condition of probation, the court prohibits the defendant from having contact with the victim, the court order prohibiting contact shall not be modified except upon the request of the victim and a finding by the court that the modification is in the best interest of the victim. As used in this paragraph, "contact with the victim" includes all physical contact, being in the presence of the victim, communication by any means, any communication by a third party acting on behalf of the defendant, and any gifts.

(e) Nothing in this section prohibits prosecution under any other provision of law.

Amended by Stats 2018 ch 423 (SB 1494),s 63, eff. 1/1/2019.
Amended by Stats 2012 ch 43 (SB 1023),s 20, eff. 6/27/2012.
Amended by Stats 2011 ch 39 (AB 117),s 68, eff. 6/30/2011.
Amended by Stats 2011 ch 15 (AB 109),s 431, eff. 4/4/2011, but operative no earlier than October 1, 2011, and only upon creation of a community corrections grant program to assist in implementing this act and upon an appropriation to fund the grant program.
Amended by Stats 2006 ch 337 (SB 1128),s 26, eff. 9/20/2006.

Amended by Stats 2000 ch 657 (SB 1784), s 1, eff. 1/1/2001.

Section 647.7 - Counseling program as condition of probation for peeking toms

(a) In any case in which a person is convicted of violating subdivision (i) or (j) of Section 647, the court may require counseling as a condition of probation. Any defendant so ordered to be placed in a counseling program shall be responsible for paying the expense of his or her participation in the counseling program as determined by the court. The court shall take into consideration the ability of the defendant to pay, and no defendant shall be denied probation because of his or her inability to pay.

(b) Every person who, having been convicted of violating subdivision (i) or (j) of Section 647, commits a second or subsequent violation of subdivision (i) or (j) of Section 647, shall be punished by imprisonment in a county jail not exceeding one year, by a fine not exceeding one thousand dollars ($1,000), or by both that fine and imprisonment, except as provided in subdivision (c).

(c) Every person who, having been previously convicted of violating subdivision (i) or (j) of Section 647, commits a violation of paragraph (3) of subdivision (j) of Section 647 regardless of whether it is a first, second, or subsequent violation of that paragraph, shall be punished by imprisonment in a county jail not exceeding one year, by a fine not exceeding five thousand dollars ($5,000), or by both that fine and imprisonment.

Amended by Stats 2011 ch 296 (AB 1023),s 209, eff. 1/1/2012.

Amended by Stats 2004 ch 666 (SB 1484), s 2, eff. 1/1/2005.

See Stats 2004 ch 666 (SB 1484), s 4.

Section 647.8 - Matter obtained in violation of person's privacy; forfeiture

(a) Matter that is obtained or distributed in violation of subdivision (j) of Section 647 and that is in the possession of any city, county, city and county, or state official or agency is subject to forfeiture pursuant to this section.

(b) An action to forfeit matter described in subdivision (a) may be brought by the Attorney General, the district attorney, county counsel, or the city attorney. Proceedings shall be initiated by a petition of forfeiture filed in the superior court of the county in which the matter is located.

(c) The prosecuting agency shall make service of process of a notice regarding that petition upon every individual who may have a property interest in the alleged proceeds. The notice shall state that any interested party may file a verified claim with the superior court stating the amount of his or her claimed interest and an affirmation or denial of the prosecuting agency's allegation. If the notice cannot be given by registered mail or personal delivery, the notice shall be published for at least three successive weeks in a newspaper of general circulation in the county where the property is located. All notices shall set forth the time within which a claim of interest in the property seized is required to be filed.

(d)

(1) Any person claiming an interest in the property or proceeds may, at any time within 30 days from the date of the first publication of the notice of seizure, or within 30 days after receipt of actual notice, file with the superior court of the county in which the action is pending a verified claim stating his or her interest in the property or proceeds. A verified copy of the claim shall be given by the claimant to the Attorney General or district attorney, county counsel, or city attorney, as appropriate.

(2) If, at the end of the time set forth in paragraph (1), an interested person has not filed a claim, the court, upon motion, shall declare that the person has defaulted upon his or her alleged interest, and it shall be subject to forfeiture upon proof of compliance with subdivision (c).

(e) The burden is on the petitioner to prove beyond a reasonable doubt that matter is subject to forfeiture pursuant to this section.

(f) It is not necessary to seek or obtain a criminal conviction prior to the entry of an order for the destruction of matter pursuant to this section. Any matter described in subdivision (a) that is in the possession of any city, county, city and county, or state official or agency, including found property, or property obtained as the result of a case in which no trial was had or that has been disposed of by way of dismissal or otherwise than by way of conviction may be ordered destroyed.

(g) A court order for destruction of matter described in subdivision (a) may be carried out by a police or sheriff's department or by the Department of Justice. The court order shall specify the agency responsible for the destruction.

(h) As used in this section, "matter" means any picture, photograph, image, motion picture, video tape, film, filmstrip, negative, slide, photocopy, or other pictorial representation, recording, or electrical reproduction. "Matter" also means any data storage media that contains the image at issue, but does not include the computer, camera, telecommunication or electronic device, unless the matter consists solely of electronic information stored on a device that cannot be altered or erased.

(i) Prior for granting an order for destruction of matter pursuant to this section, the court may require the petitioner to demonstrate that the petition covers no more property than necessary to remove possession of the offending matter.

(j) It is a defense in any forfeiture proceeding that the matter seized was lawfully possessed in aid of legitimate scientific or educational purposes.

Added by Stats 2015 ch 291 (SB 676),s 2, eff. 1/1/2016.

Section 647.9 - Capturing image of deceased person by first responder

(a) A first responder, operating under color of authority, who responds to the scene of an accident or crime and captures the photographic image of a deceased person by any means, including, but not limited to, by use of a personal electronic device or a device belonging to their employing agency, for any purpose other than an official law enforcement purpose or a genuine public interest is guilty of a misdemeanor punishable by a fine not exceeding one thousand dollars ($1,000) per violation.

(b) An agency that employs first responders shall, on January 1, 2021, notify its employees who are first responders of the prohibition imposed by this section.

(c) For purposes of this section, "first responder" means a state or local peace officer, paramedic, emergency medical technician, rescue service personnel, emergency manager, firefighter, coroner, or employee of a coroner.

Added by Stats 2020 ch 219 (AB 2655),s 1, eff. 1/1/2021.

Section 647a - Transportation to homeless shelter or runaway shelter

(a) Any peace officer, as defined in subdivision (a) of Section 830.1 or Section 830.31, 830.32, or 830.33, may transport any person, as quickly as is feasible, to the nearest homeless shelter, or any runaway youth or youth in crisis to the nearest runaway shelter, if the officer inquires whether the person desires the transportation, and the person does not object to the transportation. Any officer exercising due care and precaution shall not be liable for any damages or injury incurred during transportation.

(b) Notwithstanding any other provision of law, this section shall become operative in a county only if the board of supervisors adopts the provisions of this section by ordinance. The ordinance shall include a provision requiring peace officers to determine the availability of space at the nearest homeless or runaway shelter prior to transporting any person.

Amended by Stats. 1998, Ch. 1065, Sec. 1. Effective January 1, 1999.

Section 647b - Loitering about school in which adults are in attendance; annoying or molesting person in attendance

Every person who loiters about any school in which adults are in attendance at courses established pursuant to Chapter 10 (commencing with Section 52500) of Part 28 of the Education Code, and who annoys or molests any person in attendance therein shall be punished by a fine of not exceeding one thousand dollars ($1,000) or by imprisonment in the county jail for not exceeding six months, or by both such fine and imprisonment.

Amended by Stats. 1987, Ch. 828, Sec. 42.

Section 647c - Unlawful obstruction of free movement of person on street, sidewalk, or other public place

Every person who willfully and maliciously obstructs the free movement of any person on any street, sidewalk, or other public place or on or in any place open to the public is guilty of a misdemeanor.

Nothing in this section affects the power of a county or a city to regulate conduct upon a street, sidewalk, or other public place or on or in a place open to the public.

Amended by Stats. 1968, Ch. 122.

Section 647d - Conditional attendance of alcohol treatment and recovery program

(a) Notwithstanding any other provision of law, subdivision (b) shall become operative in a county only if the board of supervisors adopts the provisions of subdivision (b) by ordinance after a finding that sufficient alcohol treatment and recovery facilities exist or will exist to accommodate the persons described in that subdivision.

(b) In any accusatory pleading charging a violation of subdivision (f) of Section 647, if the defendant has been previously convicted two or more times of a violation of subdivision (f) of Section 647 within the previous 12 months, each such previous conviction shall be charged in the accusatory pleading. If two or more of the previous convictions are found to be true by the jury, upon a jury trial, or by the court, upon a court trial, or are admitted by the defendant, the defendant shall be imprisoned in the county jail for a period of not less than 90 days. The trial court may grant probation or suspend the execution of sentence imposed upon the defendant if the court, as a condition of the probation or suspension, orders the defendant to spend 60 days in an alcohol treatment and recovery program in a facility which, as a minimum, meets the standards described in the guidelines for alcoholic recovery home programs issued by the Division of Alcohol Programs of the Department of Alcohol and Drug Abuse.

(c) The provisions of Section 4019 shall apply to the conditional attendance of an alcohol treatment and recovery program described in subdivision (b).

Added by Stats. 1981, Ch. 1009, Sec. 1.

Section 647e - Open container on licensed and posted premises

(a) A city, county, or city and county may by local ordinance provide that no person who has in his or her possession any bottle, can or other receptacle containing any alcoholic beverage which has been opened, or a seal broken, or the contents of which have been partially removed, shall enter, be, or remain on the posted premises of, including the posted parking lot immediately adjacent to, any retail package off-sale alcoholic beverage licensee licensed pursuant to Division 9 (commencing with Section 23000) of the Business and Professions Code, or on any public sidewalk immediately adjacent to the licensed and posted premises. Any person violating any provision of such an ordinance shall be guilty of an infraction.

(b) As used in subdivision (a), "posted premises" means those premises which are subject to licensure under any retail package off-sale alcoholic beverage license, the parking lot immediately adjacent to the licensed premises and any public sidewalk immediately adjacent to the licensed premises on which clearly visible notices indicate to the patrons of the licensee and parking lot and to persons on the public sidewalk, that the provisions of subdivision (a) are applicable. Any local ordinance adopted pursuant to this section shall require posting of the premises.

(c) The provisions of this section shall not apply to a private residential parking lot which is immediately adjacent to the posted premises. Nothing in this section shall affect the power of a county or a city, or city and county, to regulate the possession of an opened alcoholic beverage in any public place or in a place open to the public.

Added by Stats. 1983, Ch. 514, Sec. 1. Effective July 28, 1983.

Section 647f - [Repealed]

Repealed by Stats 2017 ch 537 (SB 239),s 8, eff. 1/1/2018.

Section 648 - Unlawful making, issuing, or putting into circulation money, except as authorized by law

Every person who makes, issues, or puts in circulation any bill, check, ticket, certificate, promissory note, or the paper of any bank, to circulate as money, except as authorized by the laws of the United States, for the first offense, is guilty of a misdemeanor, and for each and every subsequent offense, is guilty of felony.

Enacted 1872.

Section 648a - Unlawful possession or making, selling, issuing or putting into circulation slug or token

(a) Every person who has in his or her possession for any illegal purpose or who makes, sells, issues, or puts in circulation any slug or token that does not conform to the limitations on size, shape, weight, construction, and use specified in subdivision (b) is guilty of a misdemeanor. The term "slug" and the term "token," as used in this section, mean any piece of metal or other material not a coin of the United States or a foreign country. However, tokens sold by and accepted as fares by electric railways and lettered checks having a returnable trade value shall not be subject to the provisions of this section.

(b)

(1) The slug or token shall either be clearly identified with the name and location of the establishment from which it originates on at least one side or shall contain an identifying mark or logo that clearly indicates the identity of the manufacturer.

(2) The slug or token shall not be within any of the following diameter ranges in inches:

    (A) 0.680-0.775.
    (B) 0.810-0.860.
    (C) 0.910-0.980.
    (D) 1.018-1.068.
    (E) 1.180-1.230.
    (F) 1.475-1.525.

(3) The slug or token shall not be manufactured from a three-layered material consisting of a copper-nickel alloy clad on both sides of a pure core, nor from a copper-based material except if the total of zinc, nickel, aluminum, magnesium, and other alloying materials is at least 20 percent of the token's weight.

(4) The slug or token shall not possess sufficient magnetic properties so as to be accepted by a coin mechanism.

(5) The design on the slug or token shall not resemble any current or past foreign or United States coinage.

(6) Establishments using these slugs or tokens shall prominently and conspicuously post signs on their premises notifying patrons that federal law prohibits the use of the slugs or tokens outside the premises for any monetary purpose.

(7) The issuing establishment shall not accept slugs or tokens as payment for any goods or services offered by the establishment with the exception of the specific use for which the slugs or tokens were designed.

Amended by Stats. 1997, Ch. 354, Sec. 1. Effective January 1, 1998.

Section 649 - Unlawful misdirection of prospective guest by person engaged in transportation of persons

Any person engaged in the transportation of persons by taxicab or other means of conveyance who knowingly misdirects a prospective guest of any hotel, inn, boardinghouse or lodginghouse or knowingly takes such a prospective guest to a hotel, inn, boardinghouse or lodginghouse different from that of his instructions from such prospective guest is guilty of a misdemeanor.

Added by Stats. 1953, Ch. 32.

Section 649a - Unlawful payment of compensation for inducement of prospective guests

Any person engaged in the operation of any hotel, inn, boardinghouse or lodginghouse who pays another any compensation for inducing or attempting to induce, by false statement or misrepresentation, prospective guests of a given hotel, inn, boardinghouse or lodginghouse to enter, lodge at or become a guest of any other hotel, inn, boardinghouse or lodginghouse is guilty of a misdemeanor.

Added by Stats. 1953, Ch. 32.

Section 651 - Unlawful use of Federal order stamps

It is a misdemeanor for any person to buy, receive, sell, give away, dispose of, exchange or barter any Federal order stamps except for the foods or cotton goods for which they are issued.

This section does not apply to any person buying, receiving, selling, giving away, disposing of, exchanging or bartering any Federal order stamps subsequent to the redemption of such stamps in the manner provided by State or Federal law for the foods or cotton goods for which they are issued.

As used in this section, Federal order stamps refers to stamps issued by the United States Department of Agriculture or its duly authorized agent for food and surplus food or cotton and surplus cotton.

Added by Stats. 1941, Ch. 682.

Section 652 - Unlawful performance of body piercing upon person under age of 18 years

(a) It shall be an infraction for any person to perform or offer to perform body piercing upon a person under the age of 18 years, unless the body piercing is performed in the presence of, or as directed by a notarized writing by, the person's parent or guardian.

(b) This section does not apply to the body piercing of an emancipated minor.

(c) As used in this section, "body piercing" means the creation of an opening in the body of a human being for the purpose of inserting jewelry or other decoration, including, but not limited to, the piercing of a lip, tongue, nose, or eyebrow. "Body piercing" does not include the piercing of an ear.

(d) Neither the minor upon whom the body piercing was performed, nor the parent or guardian of that minor, nor any other minor is liable for punishment under this section.

Amended by Stats 2006 ch 538 (SB 1852),s 502, eff. 1/1/2007.

Added by Stats 2005 ch 307 (AB 646),s 2, eff. 1/1/2006.

Section 653 - Unlawful tattooing of person under age of 18 years

Every person who tattoos or offers to tattoo a person under the age of 18 years is guilty of a misdemeanor.

As used in this section, to "tattoo" means to insert pigment under the surface of the skin of a human being, by pricking with a needle or otherwise, so as to produce an indelible mark or figure visible through the skin.

This section is not intended to apply to any act of a licensed practitioner of the healing arts performed in the course of his practice.

Added by Stats. 1955, Ch. 1422.

Section 653b - Unlawful loitering about school or public place at or near which children attend or congregate

(a) Except as provided in subdivision (b) or (c), every person who loiters about any school or public place at or near which children attend or normally congregate and who remains at any school or public place at or near which children attend or normally congregate, or who reenters or comes upon a school or place within 72 hours, after being asked to leave by the chief administrative official of that school or, in the absence of the chief administrative official, the person acting as the chief administrative official, or by a member of the security patrol of the school district who has been given authorization, in writing, by the chief administrative official of that school to act as his or her agent in performing this duty, or a city police officer, or sheriff or deputy sheriff, or Department of the California Highway Patrol peace officer is a vagrant, and is punishable by a fine of not exceeding one thousand dollars ($1,000) or by imprisonment in a county jail for a period not exceeding six months, or by both that fine and imprisonment.

(b) Every person required to register as a sex offender who violates subdivision (a) shall be punished as follows:

    (1) Upon a first conviction, by a fine not exceeding two thousand dollars ($2,000), by imprisonment in a county jail for a period of not more than six months, or by both that fine and imprisonment.

(2) If the defendant has been previously convicted once of a violation of this section or former Section 653g, by imprisonment in a county jail for a period of not less than 10 days or more than six months, or by both imprisonment and a fine of not exceeding two thousand dollars ($2,000), and shall not be released on probation, parole, or any other basis until he or she has served at least 10 days.

(3) If the defendant has been previously convicted two or more times of a violation of this section or former Section 653g, by imprisonment in a county jail for a period of not less than 90 days or more than six months, or by both imprisonment and a fine of not exceeding two thousand dollars ($2,000), and shall not be released on probation, parole, or any other basis until he or she has served at least 90 days.

(c) Any person required to register with the chief of police or sheriff pursuant to Section 186.30 who violates subdivision (a) shall be punished as follows:

(1) Upon first conviction, by a fine not exceeding one thousand dollars ($1,000), by imprisonment in a county jail for a period of not more than one year, or by both that fine and imprisonment.

(2) Upon a second conviction, by a fine not exceeding two thousand dollars ($2,000), by imprisonment in a county jail for a period of not more than one year, or by both that fine and imprisonment. The court shall consider a period of imprisonment of at least 10 days.

(3) If the defendant has been previously convicted two or more times, by a fine not exceeding two thousand dollars ($2,000), by imprisonment in a county jail for a period of not more than one year, or by both that fine and imprisonment. The court shall consider a period of imprisonment of at least 90 days.

(d) As used in this section, "loiter" means to delay, to linger, or to idle about a school or public place without lawful business for being present.

(e) Nothing in this section shall preclude or prohibit prosecution under any other provision of law.

Amended by Stats 2009 ch 592 (SB 492),s 1, eff. 1/1/2010.

Renumbered from Ca. Pen. Code §653g by Stats 2006 ch 337 (SB 1128),s 27, eff. 9/20/2006.

Section 653c - Unlawful entry or remaining on grounds of day care or residential facility for elders or dependent adults

(a) No person required to register as a sex offender pursuant to Section 290 for an offense committed against an elder or dependent adult, as defined in Section 368, other than a resident of the facility, shall enter or remain on the grounds of a day care or residential facility where elders or dependent adults are regularly present or living, without having registered with the facility administrator or his or her designees, except to proceed expeditiously to the office of the facility administrator or designee for the purpose of registering.

(b) In order to register pursuant to subdivision (a), a sex offender shall advise the facility administrator or designee that he or she is a sex offender; provide his or her name, address, and purpose for entering the facility; and provide proof of identity.

(c) The facility administrator may refuse to register, impose restrictions on registration, or revoke the registration of a sex offender if he or she has a reasonable basis for concluding that the offender's presence or acts would disrupt, or have disrupted, the facility, any resident, employee, volunteer, or visitor; would result, or has resulted, in damage to property; the offender's presence at the facility would interfere, or has interfered, with the peaceful conduct of the activities of the facility; or would otherwise place at risk the facility, or any employee, volunteer or visitor.

(d) Punishment for any violation of this section shall be as follows:

(1) Upon a first conviction by a fine of not exceeding two thousand dollars ($2,000), by imprisonment in a county jail for a period of not more than six months, or by both that fine and imprisonment.

(2) If the defendant has been previously convicted once of a violation of this section, by imprisonment in a county jail for a period of not less than 10 days or more than six months, or by both imprisonment and a fine of not exceeding two thousand dollars ($2,000), and shall not be released on probation, parole, or any other basis until he or she has served at least 10 days.

(3) If the defendant has been previously convicted two or more times of a violation of this section, by imprisonment in a county jail for a period of not less than 90 days or more than six months, or by both imprisonment and a fine of not exceeding two thousand dollars ($2,000), and shall not be released on probation, parole, or any other basis until he or she has served at least 90 days.

(e) Nothing in this section shall preclude or prohibit prosecution under any other provision of law.

Added by Stats 2006 ch 337 (SB 1128),s 28, eff. 9/20/2006.

Section 653d - Records required for sale of mining machinery

Every person who sells machinery used or to be used for mining purposes who fails to give to the buyer, at the time of sale, a bill of sale for the machinery, or who fails to keep a written record of the sale, giving the date thereof, describing the machinery, and showing the name and address of the buyer, and every buyer of such machinery, if in this State, who fails to keep a record of his purchase of such machinery, giving the name and address of the seller, describing the machinery, and showing the date of the purchase, is guilty of a misdemeanor.

Added by Stats. 1959, Ch. 222.

Section 653f - Solicitation to commit crime

(a) Every person who, with the intent that the crime be committed, solicits another to offer, accept, or join in the offer or acceptance of a bribe, or to commit or join in the commission of carjacking, robbery, burglary, grand theft, receiving stolen property, extortion, perjury, subornation of perjury, forgery, kidnapping, arson or assault with a deadly weapon or instrument or by means of force likely to produce great bodily injury, or, by the use of force or a threat of force, to prevent or dissuade any person who is or may become a witness from attending upon, or testifying at, any trial, proceeding, or inquiry authorized by law, shall be punished by imprisonment in a county jail for not more than one year or pursuant to subdivision (h) of Section 1170, or by a fine of not more than ten thousand dollars ($10,000), or the amount which could have been assessed for commission of the offense itself, whichever is greater, or by both the fine and imprisonment.

(b) Every person who, with the intent that the crime be committed, solicits another to commit or join in the commission of murder shall be punished by imprisonment in the state prison for three, six, or nine years.

(c) Every person who, with the intent that the crime be committed, solicits another to commit rape by force or violence, sodomy by force or violence, oral copulation by force or violence, or any violation of Section 264.1, 288, or 289, shall be punished by imprisonment in the state prison for two, three, or four years.

(d)

(1) Every person who, with the intent that the crime be committed, solicits another to commit an offense specified in Section 11352, 11379, 11379.5, 11379.6, or 11391 of the Health and Safety Code shall be punished by imprisonment in a county jail not exceeding six months. Every person who, having been convicted of soliciting another to commit an offense specified in this subdivision, is subsequently convicted of the proscribed solicitation, shall be punished by imprisonment in a county jail not exceeding one year, or pursuant to subdivision (h) of Section 1170.

(2) This subdivision does not apply where the term of imprisonment imposed under other provisions of law would result in a longer term of imprisonment.

(e) Every person who, with the intent that the crime be committed, solicits another to commit an offense specified in Section 14014 of the Welfare and Institutions Code shall be punished by imprisonment in a county jail for not exceeding six months. Every person who, having been convicted of soliciting another to commit an offense specified in this subdivision, is subsequently convicted of the proscribed solicitation, shall be punished by imprisonment in a county jail not exceeding one year, or pursuant to subdivision (h) of Section 1170.

(f)

(1) Every person who, with the intent that the crime be committed, solicits another to commit an offense set forth in Section 502 shall be punished as set forth in paragraph (3).

(2) Every person who, with the intent that the crime be committed, offers to solicit assistance for another to conduct activities in violation of Section 502 shall be punished as set forth in paragraph (3). This includes persons operating Internet Web sites that offer to assist others in locating hacking services. For the purposes of this section "hacking services" means assistance in the unauthorized access to computers, computer systems, or data in violation of Section 502.

(3) Every person who violates this subdivision shall be punished by imprisonment in a county jail for a period not to exceed six months. Every subsequent violation of this subdivision by that same person shall be punished by imprisonment in a county jail not exceeding one year.

(g) An offense charged in violation of subdivision (a), (b), or (c) shall be proven by the testimony of two witnesses, or of one witness and corroborating circumstances. An offense charged in violation of subdivision (d), (e), or (f) shall be proven by the testimony of one witness and corroborating circumstances.

(h) Nothing in this section precludes prosecution under any other law that provides for a greater punishment.

Amended by Stats 2015 ch 552 (AB 195),s 1, eff. 1/1/2016.
Amended by Stats 2012 ch 43 (SB 1023),s 21, eff. 6/27/2012.
Amended by Stats 2011 ch 39 (AB 117),s 68, eff. 6/30/2011.
Amended by Stats 2011 ch 15 (AB 109),s 432, eff. 4/4/2011, but operative no earlier than October 1, 2011, and only upon creation of a community corrections grant program to assist in implementing this act and upon an appropriation to fund the grant program.

Section 653g - [Renumbered as 653b]
Renumbered as Ca. Pen. Code §653b by Stats 2006 ch 337 (SB 1128),s 27, eff. 9/20/2006.

Section 653h - Unlawful transfer of recorded sounds
(a) Every person is guilty of a public offense punishable as provided in subdivisions (b) and (c), who:

(1) Knowingly and willfully transfers or causes to be transferred any sounds that have been recorded on a phonograph record, disc, wire, tape, film or other article on which sounds are recorded, with intent to sell or cause to be sold, or to use or cause to be used for commercial advantage or private financial gain through public performance, the article on which the sounds are so transferred, without the consent of the owner.

(2) Transports for monetary or like consideration within this state or causes to be transported within this state any such article with the knowledge that the sounds thereon have been so transferred without the consent of the owner.

(b) Any person who has been convicted of a violation of subdivision (a), shall be punished by imprisonment in the county jail not to exceed one year, by imprisonment pursuant to subdivision (h) of Section 1170 for two, three, or five years, or by a fine not to exceed five hundred thousand dollars ($500,000), or by both that fine and imprisonment, if the offense involves the transfer or transportation, or conduct causing that transfer or transportation, of not less than 1,000 of the articles described in subdivision (a).

(c) Any person who has been convicted of any other violation of subdivision (a) not described in subdivision (b), shall be punished by imprisonment in the county jail not to exceed one year, or by a fine of not more than fifty thousand dollars ($50,000), or by both that fine and imprisonment. A second or subsequent conviction under subdivision (a) not described in subdivision (b) shall be punished by imprisonment pursuant to subdivision (h) of Section 1170 or by a fine not to exceed two hundred thousand dollars ($200,000), or by both that fine and imprisonment.

(d) Every person who offers for sale or resale, or sells or resells, or causes the sale or resale, or rents, or possesses for these purposes, any article described in subdivision (a) with knowledge that the sounds thereon have been so transferred without the consent of the owner is guilty of a public offense.

(1) A violation of subdivision (d) involving not less than 100 of those articles shall be punishable by imprisonment in a county jail not to exceed one year or by a fine not to exceed twenty thousand dollars ($20,000), or by both that fine and imprisonment. A second or subsequent conviction for the conduct described in this paragraph shall be punishable by imprisonment in the county jail not to exceed one year or pursuant to subdivision (h) of Section 1170, or by a fine not to exceed fifty thousand dollars ($50,000), or by both that fine and imprisonment.

(2) A person who has been convicted of any violation of this subdivision not described in paragraph (1) shall be punished by imprisonment in the county jail not to exceed six months or by a fine not to exceed ten thousand dollars ($10,000), or by both that fine and imprisonment. A second conviction for the conduct described in this paragraph shall be punishable by imprisonment in the county

jail not to exceed one year or by a fine not to exceed twenty thousand dollars ($20,000), or by both that fine and imprisonment. A third or subsequent conviction for the conduct described in this paragraph shall be punishable by imprisonment in the county jail not to exceed one year or pursuant to subdivision (h) of Section 1170, or by a fine not to exceed fifty thousand dollars ($50,000), or by both that fine and imprisonment.

(e) As used in this section, "person" means any individual, partnership, partnership's member or employee, corporation, limited liability company, association or corporation or association employee, officer or director; "owner" means the person who owns the original master recording embodied in the master phonograph record, master disc, master tape, master film or other article used for reproducing recorded sounds on phonograph records, discs, tapes, films or other articles on which sound is or can be recorded, and from which the transferred recorded sounds are directly or indirectly derived; and "master recording" means the original fixation of sounds upon a recording from which copies can be made.

(f) This section shall neither enlarge nor diminish the right of parties in private litigation.

(g) This section does not apply to any person engaged in radio or television broadcasting who transfers, or causes to be transferred, any such sounds (other than from the sound track of a motion picture) intended for, or in connection with, broadcast transmission or related uses, or for archival purposes.

(h) This section does not apply to any not-for-profit educational institution or any federal or state governmental entity, if the institution or entity has as a primary purpose the advancement of the public's knowledge and the dissemination of information regarding America's musical cultural heritage, provided that this purpose is clearly set forth in the institution's or entity's charter, bylaws, certificate of incorporation, or similar document, and the institution or entity has, prior to the transfer, made a good faith effort to identify and locate the owner or owners of the sound recordings to be transferred and, provided that the owner or owners could not be and have not been located. Nothing in this section shall be construed to relieve an institution or entity of its contractual or other obligation to compensate the owners of sound recordings to be transferred. In order to continue the exemption permitted by this subdivision, the institution or entity shall make continuing efforts to locate such owners and shall make an annual public notice of the fact of the transfers in newspapers of general circulation serving the jurisdictions where the owners were incorporated or doing business at the time of initial affixations. The institution or entity shall keep on file a record of the efforts made to locate such owners for inspection by appropriate governmental agencies.

(i) This section applies only to those articles that were initially mastered prior to February 15, 1972.

Amended by Stats 2011 ch 39 (AB 117),s 68, eff. 6/30/2011.

Amended by Stats 2011 ch 15 (AB 109),s 433, eff. 4/4/2011, but operative no earlier than October 1, 2011, and only upon creation of a community corrections grant program to assist in implementing this act and upon an appropriation to fund the grant program.

Amended by Stats 2010 ch 351 (AB 819),s 3, eff. 9/25/2010.

Section 653i - Leaving scene of skiing accident

Any person who is involved in a skiing accident and who leaves the scene of the accident knowing or having reason to believe that any other person involved in the accident is in need of medical and other assistance, except to notify the proper authorities or to obtain assistance, shall be guilty of an infraction punishable by fine not exceeding one thousand dollars ($1,000).

Added by Stats. 1977, Ch. 870.

Section 653j - Unlawful solicitation or intimidation of minor with intent that minor commit felony

(a) Every person 18 years of age or older who, in any voluntary manner, solicits, induces, encourages, or intimidates any minor with the intent that the minor shall commit a felony in violation of paragraph (1) of subdivision (c) of Section 136.1 or Section 187, 211, 215, 245, 246, 451, 459, or 520 of the Penal Code, or Section 10851 of the Vehicle Code, shall be punished by imprisonment pursuant to subdivision (h) of Section 1170 for a period of three, five, or seven years. If the minor is 16 years of age or older at the time of the offense, this section shall only apply when the adult is at least five years older than the minor at the time the offense is committed.

(b) In no case shall the court impose a sentence pursuant to subdivision (a) which exceeds the maximum penalty prescribed for the felony offense for which the minor was solicited, induced, encouraged, or intimidated to commit.

(c) Whenever a sentence is imposed under subdivision (a), the court shall consider the severity of the underlying crime as one of the circumstances in aggravation.

Amended by Stats 2011 ch 39 (AB 117),s 68, eff. 6/30/2011.

Amended by Stats 2011 ch 15 (AB 109),s 434, eff. 4/4/2011, but operative no earlier than October 1, 2011, and only upon creation of a community corrections grant program to assist in implementing this act and upon an appropriation to fund the grant program.

Section 653k - [Repealed]

Repealed by Stats 2010 ch 711 (SB 1080),s 2, eff. 1/1/2011, op. 1/1/2012.

Amended by Stats 2001 ch 128 (SB 274), s 1, eff. 1/1/2002.

Section 653m - Unlawful annoyance or harassment by telephone or electronic communications device

(a) Every person who, with intent to annoy, telephones or makes contact by means of an electronic communication device with another and addresses to or about the other person any obscene language or addresses to the other person any threat to inflict injury to the person or property of the person addressed or any member of his or her family, is guilty of a misdemeanor. Nothing in this subdivision shall apply to telephone calls or electronic contacts made in good faith.

(b) Every person who, with intent to annoy or harass, makes repeated telephone calls or makes repeated contact by means of an electronic communication device, or makes any combination of calls or contact, to another person is, whether or not conversation ensues from making the telephone call or contact by means of an electronic communication device, guilty of a misdemeanor. Nothing in this subdivision shall apply to telephone calls or electronic contacts made in good faith or during the ordinary course and scope of business.

(c) Any offense committed by use of a telephone may be deemed to have been committed when and where the telephone call or calls were made or received. Any offense committed by use of an electronic communication device or medium, including the Internet, may be deemed to have been committed when and where the electronic communication or communications were originally sent or first viewed by the recipient.

(d) Subdivision (a) or (b) is violated when the person acting with intent to annoy makes a telephone call or contact by means of an electronic communication device requesting a return call and performs the acts prohibited under subdivision (a) or (b) upon receiving the return call.

(e) Subdivision (a) or (b) is violated when a person knowingly permits any telephone or electronic communication under the person's control to be used for the purposes prohibited by those subdivisions.

(f) If probation is granted, or the execution or imposition of sentence is suspended, for any person convicted under this section, the court may order as a condition of probation that the person participate in counseling.

(g) For purposes of this section, the term "electronic communication device" includes, but is not limited to, telephones, cellular phones, computers, video recorders, facsimile machines, pagers, personal digital assistants, smartphones, and any other device that transfers signs, signals, writing, images, sounds, or data. "Electronic communication device" also includes, but is not limited to, videophones, TTY/TDD devices, and all other devices used to aid or assist communication to or from deaf or disabled persons. "Electronic communication" has the same meaning as the term defined in Subsection 12 of Section 2510 of Title 18 of the United States Code. Amended by Stats 2008 ch 109 (SB 129),s 1, eff. 1/1/2009.

EFFECTIVE 1/1/2000. Amended July 12, 1999 (Bill Number: SB 966) (Chapter 83).

Section 653n - Unlawful installation of two-way mirror

Any person who installs or who maintains after April 1, 1970, any two-way mirror permitting observation of any restroom, toilet, bathroom, washroom, shower, locker room, fitting room, motel room, or hotel room, is guilty of a misdemeanor.

This section does not apply to such areas (a) in state or local public penal, correctional, custodial, or medical institutions which are used by, or for the treatment of, persons who are committed or voluntarily confined to such institutions or voluntarily receive treatment therein; (b) in private custodial or medical institutions, which are used by, or for the treatment of, persons who are committed or voluntarily confined to such institutions or voluntarily receive treatment therein; (c) in public or private treatment facilities which are used by, or for the treatment of, persons who are committed or voluntarily confined to such facilities or voluntarily receive treatment therein; (d) in buildings operated by state or local law enforcement agencies; or (e) in public or private educational institutions.

"Two-way mirror" as used in this section means a mirror or other surface which permits any person on one side thereof to see through it under certain conditions of lighting, while any person on the other side thereof or other surface at that time can see only the usual mirror or other surface reflection.

Added by Stats. 1969, Ch. 428.

Section 653o - Unlawful importation, possession with intent to sell, or sale of dead body of certain animals

(a) It is unlawful to import into this state for commercial purposes, to possess with intent to sell, or to sell within the state, the dead body, or a part or product thereof, of a polar bear, leopard, ocelot, tiger, cheetah, jaguar, sable antelope, wolf (Canis lupus), zebra, whale, cobra, python, sea turtle, colobus monkey, kangaroo, vicuna, sea otter, free-roaming feral horse, dolphin or porpoise (Delphinidae), Spanish lynx, or elephant.

(b)

(1) Commencing January 1, 2020, it is unlawful to import into this state for commercial purposes, to possess with intent to sell, or to sell within the state, the dead body, or a part or product thereof, of a crocodile or alligator.

(2) This subdivision does not authorize the importation or sale of any alligator or crocodilian species, or products thereof, that are listed as endangered under the federal Endangered Species Act, or to allow the importation or sale of any alligator or crocodilian species, or products thereof, in violation of federal law or international treaty to which the United States is a party.

(c) Commencing January 1, 2022, it is unlawful to import into this state for commercial purposes, to possess with intent to sell, or to sell within the state, the dead body, or any part or product thereof, of an iguana, skink, caiman, hippopotamus, or a Teju, Ring, or Nile lizard.

(d) A person who violates this section is guilty of a misdemeanor and shall be subject to a fine of not less than one thousand dollars ($1,000) and not to exceed five thousand dollars ($5,000) or imprisonment in the county jail not to exceed six months, or both that fine and imprisonment, for each violation.

(e) The prohibitions against importation for commercial purposes, possession with intent to sell, and sale of the species listed in this section are severable. A finding of the invalidity of any one or more prohibitions shall not affect the validity of any remaining prohibitions.

Amended by Stats 2019 ch 767 (AB 1260),s 1, eff. 1/1/2020.

Amended by Stats 2014 ch 464 (AB 2075),s 1, eff. 1/1/2015.

Amended by Stats 2010 ch 412 (SB 1345),s 1, eff. 1/1/2011.

Amended by Stats 2009 ch 15 (SB 609),s 1, eff. 1/1/2010.

Amended by Stats 2007 ch 576 (SB 880),s 1, eff. 10/13/2007.

Amended by Stats 2006 ch 660 (SB 1485),s 1, eff. 1/1/2007.

Section 653p - Unlawful possession with intent to sell or sale of dead body of protected species or subspecies

It is unlawful to possess with the intent to sell, or to sell, within the state, the dead body, or any part or product thereof, of any species or subspecies of any fish, bird, mammal, amphibian, reptile, mollusk, invertebrate, or plant, the importation of which is illegal under the Federal Endangered Species Act of 1973 (Title 16, United States Code Sec. 1531 et seq.) and subsequent amendments, or under the Marine Mammal Protection Act of 1972 (Title 16, United States Code Sec. 1361 et seq.), or which is listed in the Federal Register by the Secretary of the Interior pursuant to the above acts. The violation of any federal regulations adopted pursuant to the above acts shall also be deemed a violation of this section and shall be prosecuted by the appropriate state or local officials.

Amended by Stats. 1976, Ch. 692.

Section 653q - Unlawful importation, possession with intent to sell, or sale of dead body of seal

It is unlawful to import into this state for commercial purposes, to possess with intent to sell, or to sell within the state, the dead body, or any part or product thereof, of any seal.

Any person who violates any provision of this section is guilty of a misdemeanor and shall be subject to a fine of not less than one thousand dollars ($1,000) and not to exceed five thousand dollars ($5,000) or imprisonment in the county jail for not to exceed six months, or both such fine and imprisonment, for each violation.

Added by Stats. 1971, Ch. 1200.

Section 653r - Unlawful possession with intent to sell or sale of dead body of specified fish, bird, amphibian, reptile, or mammal

Notwithstanding the provisions of Section 3 of Chapter 1557 of the Statutes of 1970, it shall be unlawful to possess with intent to sell, or to sell, within this state, after June 1, 1972, the dead body, or any part or product thereof, of any fish, bird, amphibian, reptile, or mammal specified in Section 653o or 653p.

Violation of this section constitutes a misdemeanor.

Added by Stats. 1971, Ch. 1283.

Section 653s - Unlawful transport of article containing sounds of live performance recorded without consent

(a) Any person who transports or causes to be transported for monetary or other consideration within this state, any article containing sounds of a live performance with the knowledge that the sounds thereon have been recorded or mastered without the consent of the owner of the sounds of the live performance is guilty of a public offense punishable as provided in subdivision (g) or (h).

(b) As used in this section and Section 653u:

(1) "Live performance" means the recitation, rendering, or playing of a series of musical, spoken, or other sounds in any audible sequence thereof.

(2) "Article" means the original disc, wire, tape, film, phonograph record, or other recording device used to record or master the sounds of the live performance and any copy or reproduction thereof which duplicates, in whole or in part, the original.

(3) "Person" means any individual, partnership, partnership member or employee, corporation, association, or corporation or association employee, officer, or director, limited liability company, or limited liability company manager or officer.

(c) In the absence of a written agreement or operation of law to the contrary, the performer or performers of the sounds of a live performance shall be presumed to own the right to record or master those sounds.

(d) For purposes of this section, a person who is authorized to maintain custody and control over business records reflecting the consent of the owner to the recordation or master recording of a live performance shall be a proper witness in any proceeding regarding the issue of consent. Any witness called pursuant to this section shall be subject to all rules of evidence relating to the competency of a witness to testify and the relevance and admissibility of the testimony offered.

(e) This section shall neither enlarge nor diminish the rights and remedies of parties to a recording or master recording which they might otherwise possess by law.

(f) This section shall not apply to persons engaged in radio or television broadcasting or cablecasting who record or fix the sounds of a live performance for, or in connection with, broadcast or cable transmission and related uses in educational television or radio programs, for archival purposes, or for news programs or purposes if the recordation or master recording is not commercially distributed independent of the broadcast or cablecast by or through the broadcasting or cablecasting entity to subscribers or the general public.

(g) Any person who has been convicted of a violation of subdivision (a), shall be punished by imprisonment in the county jail not to exceed one year, or by imprisonment pursuant to subdivision (h) of Section 1170 for two, three, or five years, or by a fine not to exceed five hundred thousand dollars ($500,000), or by both, if the offense involves the transportation or causing to be transported of not less than 1,000 articles described in subdivision (a).

(h) Any person who has been convicted of any other violation of subdivision (a) not described in subdivision (g) shall be punished by imprisonment in the county jail not to exceed one year, or by a fine not to exceed fifty thousand dollars ($50,000), or by both that fine and imprisonment. A second or subsequent conviction under subdivision (a) not described in subdivision (g) shall be punished by imprisonment in the county jail not to exceed one year or pursuant to subdivision (h) of Section 1170, or by a fine not to exceed two hundred thousand dollars ($200,000), or by both that fine and imprisonment.

(i) Every person who offers for sale or resale, or sells or resells, or causes the sale or resale, or rents, or possesses for these purposes, any article described in subdivision (a) with knowledge that the sounds thereon have been so recorded or mastered without the consent of the owner of the sounds of a live performance is guilty of a public offense.

(1) A violation of subdivision (i) involving not less than 100 of those articles shall be punishable by imprisonment in a county jail not to exceed one year or by a fine not to exceed twenty thousand dollars ($20,000), or by both that fine and imprisonment. A second or subsequent conviction for the conduct described in this paragraph shall be punishable by imprisonment in the county jail not to exceed one year or pursuant to subdivision (h) of Section 1170, or by a fine not to exceed fifty thousand dollars ($50,000), or by both.

(2) A person who has been convicted of any violation of this subdivision not described in paragraph (1) shall be punished by imprisonment in the county jail not to exceed six months or by a fine not to exceed ten thousand dollars ($10,000), or by both that fine and imprisonment. A second conviction for the conduct described in this paragraph shall be punishable by imprisonment in the county jail not to exceed one year or by a fine not to exceed twenty thousand dollars ($20,000), or by both that fine and imprisonment. A third or subsequent conviction for the conduct described in this paragraph shall be punishable by imprisonment in the county jail not to exceed one year or pursuant to subdivision (h) of Section 1170, or by a fine not to exceed fifty thousand dollars ($50,000), or by both that fine and imprisonment.

Amended by Stats 2011 ch 39 (AB 117),s 68, eff. 6/30/2011.

Amended by Stats 2011 ch 15 (AB 109),s 435, eff. 4/4/2011, but operative no earlier than October 1, 2011, and only upon creation of a community corrections grant program to assist in implementing this act and upon an appropriation to fund the grant program.

Amended by Stats 2010 ch 351 (AB 819),s 4, eff. 9/25/2010.

Section 653t - Unlawful interference with transmission of emergency communication over amateur or citizen's band radio frequency

(a) A person commits a public offense if the person knowingly and maliciously interrupts, disrupts, impedes, or otherwise interferes with the transmission of a communication over an amateur or a citizen's band radio frequency, the purpose of which communication is to inform or inquire about an emergency.

(b) For purposes of this section, "emergency" means a condition or circumstance in which an individual is or is reasonably believed by the person transmitting the communication to be in imminent danger of serious bodily injury, in which property is or is reasonably believed by the person transmitting the communication to be in imminent danger of extensive damage or destruction, or in which that injury or destruction has occurred and the person transmitting is attempting to summon assistance.

(c) A violation of subdivision (a) is a misdemeanor punishable by a fine not to exceed one thousand dollars ($1,000), by imprisonment in a county jail not to exceed six months, or by both, unless, as a result of the commission of the offense, serious bodily injury or property loss in excess of ten thousand dollars ($10,000) occurs, in which event the offense is a felony punishable by imprisonment pursuant to subdivision (h) of Section 1170.

(d) Any person who knowingly and maliciously interrupts, disrupts, impedes, or otherwise interferes with the transmission of an emergency communication over a public safety radio frequency, when the offense results in serious bodily injury or property loss in excess of ten thousand dollars ($10,000), is guilty of a felony punishable by imprisonment pursuant to subdivision (h) of Section 1170.

Amended by Stats 2011 ch 39 (AB 117),s 68, eff. 6/30/2011.

Amended by Stats 2011 ch 15 (AB 109),s 436, eff. 4/4/2011, but operative no earlier than October 1, 2011, and only upon creation of a community corrections grant program to assist in implementing this act and upon an appropriation to fund the grant program.

Amended by Stats 2002 ch 787 (SB 1798), s 15, eff. 1/1/2003.

Previously Amended October 10, 1999 (Bill Number: SB 832) (Chapter 853).

Section 653u - Unlawful recording of sounds of live performance without consent

(a) Any person who records or masters or causes to be recorded or mastered on any article with the intent to sell for commercial advantage or private financial gain, the sounds of a live performance with the knowledge that the sounds thereon have been recorded or mastered without the consent of the owner of the sounds of the live performance is guilty of a public offense punishable as provided in subdivisions (d) and (e).

(b) In the absence of a written agreement or operation of law to the contrary, the performer or performers of the sounds of a live performance shall be presumed to own the right to record or master those sounds.

(c)

(1) For purposes of this section, a person who is authorized to maintain custody and control over business records reflecting the consent of the owner to the recordation or master recording of a live performance shall be a proper witness in any proceeding regarding the issue of consent.

(2) Any witness called pursuant to this section shall be subject to all rules of evidence relating to the competency of a witness to testify and the relevance and admissibility of the testimony offered.

(d) Any person who has been convicted of a violation of subdivision (a) shall be punished by imprisonment in the county jail not to exceed one year, or by imprisonment pursuant to subdivision (h) of Section 1170 for two, three, or five years, or by a fine not to exceed five hundred thousand dollars ($500,000), or by both that fine and imprisonment, if the offense involves the recording, mastering, or causing to be recorded or mastered at least 1,000 articles described in subdivision (a).

(e) Any person who has been convicted of any other violation of subdivision (a) not described in subdivision (d), shall be punished by imprisonment in the county jail not to exceed one year, or by a fine not to exceed fifty thousand dollars ($50,000), or by both that fine and imprisonment. A second or subsequent conviction under subdivision (a) not described in subdivision (d) shall be punished by imprisonment in the county jail not to exceed one year or pursuant to subdivision (h) of Section 1170 or by a fine not to exceed two hundred thousand dollars ($200,000), or by both that fine and imprisonment.

Amended by Stats 2011 ch 39 (AB 117),s 68, eff. 6/30/2011.

Amended by Stats 2011 ch 15 (AB 109),s 437, eff. 4/4/2011, but operative no earlier than October 1, 2011, and only upon creation of a community corrections grant program to assist in implementing this act and upon an appropriation to fund the grant program.

Amended by Stats 2010 ch 351 (AB 819),s 5, eff. 9/25/2010.

Section 653v - Forfeiture and destruction of article upon which sounds or images recorded

Whenever any person is convicted of any violation of Section 653h, 653s, 653u, or 653w the court, in its judgment of conviction, shall, in addition to the penalty therein prescribed, order the forfeiture and destruction or other disposition of all articles, including, but not limited to, phonograph records, discs, wires, tapes, films, or any other article upon which sounds or images can be recorded or stored, and any and all electronic, mechanical, or other devices for manufacturing, reproducing or assembling these articles, which were used in connection with, or which were part of, any violation of Section 653h, 653s, 653u, or 653w.

Amended by Stats. 1985, Ch. 364, Sec. 2.

Section 653w - Failure to disclose origin of recording or audiovisual work

(a)

(1) A person is guilty of failure to disclose the origin of a recording or audiovisual work if, for commercial advantage or private financial gain, he or she knowingly advertises or offers for sale or resale, or sells or resells, or causes the rental, sale, or resale of, or rents, or manufactures, or possesses for these purposes, any recording or audiovisual work, the outside cover, box, jacket, or label of which does not clearly and conspicuously disclose the actual true name and address of the manufacturer thereof and the name of the actual author, artist, performer, producer, programmer, or group thereon. This section does not require the original manufacturer or authorized licensees of software producers to disclose the contributing authors or programmers.

(2) As used in this section, "recording" means any tangible medium upon which information or sounds are recorded or otherwise stored, including, but not limited to, any phonograph record, disc, tape, audio cassette, wire, film, memory card, flash drive, hard drive, data storage device, or other medium on which information or sounds are recorded or otherwise stored, but does not include sounds accompanying a motion picture or other audiovisual work.

(3) As used in this section, "audiovisual works" are the physical embodiment of works that consist of related images that are intrinsically intended to be shown using machines or devices, such as projectors, viewers, or electronic equipment, together with accompanying sounds, if any, regardless of the nature of the material objects, such as films, tapes, discs, memory cards, flash drives, hard drives, data storage devices, or other devices, on which the works are embodied.

(b) A person who has been convicted of a violation of subdivision (a) shall be punished as follows:

(1) If the offense involves the advertisement, offer for sale or resale, sale, rental, manufacture, or possession for these purposes, of at least 100 articles of audio recordings or 100 articles of audiovisual works described in subdivision (a), or the commercial equivalent thereof, the person shall be punished by imprisonment in a county jail not to exceed one year, or by imprisonment pursuant to subdivision (h) of Section 1170 for two, three, or five years, or by a fine not to exceed five hundred thousand dollars ($500,000), or by both that fine and imprisonment.

(2) Any other violation of subdivision (a) not described in paragraph (1) shall, upon a first offense, be punished by imprisonment in a county jail not to exceed one year, or by a fine not to exceed fifty thousand dollars ($50,000), or by both that fine and imprisonment.

(3) A second or subsequent conviction under subdivision (a) not described in paragraph (1) shall be punished by imprisonment in a county jail not to exceed one year or pursuant to subdivision (h) of Section 1170, or by a fine of not less than one thousand dollars ($1,000), but not to exceed two hundred thousand dollars ($200,000), or by both that fine and imprisonment.

Amended by Stats 2017 ch 561 (AB 1516),s 181, eff. 1/1/2018.
Amended by Stats 2016 ch 657 (AB 1241),s 1, eff. 1/1/2017.
Amended by Stats 2014 ch 857 (AB 2122),s 1, eff. 1/1/2015.
Amended by Stats 2011 ch 39 (AB 117),s 68, eff. 6/30/2011.
Amended by Stats 2011 ch 15 (AB 109),s 438, eff. 4/4/2011, but operative no earlier than October 1, 2011, and only upon creation of a community corrections grant program to assist in implementing this act and upon an appropriation to fund the grant program.
Amended by Stats 2010 ch 480 (SB 830),s 1.5, eff. 1/1/2011.
Amended by Stats 2010 ch 351 (AB 819),s 6, eff. 9/25/2010.
Amended by Stats 2006 ch 9 (AB 64),s 1, eff. 1/1/2007

Section 653x - Unlawful telephoning 911 emergency line

(a) A person who telephones or uses an electronic communication device to initiate communication with the 911 emergency system with the intent to annoy or harass another person is guilty of a misdemeanor punishable by a fine of not more than one thousand dollars ($1,000), by imprisonment in a county jail for not more than six months, or by both the fine and imprisonment. Nothing in this section shall apply to telephone calls or communications using electronic devices made in good faith.

(b) An intent to annoy or harass is established by proof of repeated calls or communications over a period of time, however short, that are unreasonable under the circumstances.

(c) Upon conviction of a violation of this section, a person also shall be liable for all reasonable costs incurred by any unnecessary emergency response.

Amended by Stats 2016 ch 96 (AB 1769),s 1, eff. 1/1/2017.

Section 653y - Unlawful use of 911 telephone system

(a) A person who knowingly allows the use of or who uses the 911 emergency system for any reason other than because of an emergency is guilty of an infraction, punishable as follows:

(1) For a first violation, a written warning shall be issued to the violator by the public safety entity originally receiving the telephone call or the communication from an electronic device describing the punishment for subsequent violations. The written warning shall inform the recipient to notify the issuing agency that the warning was issued inappropriately if the recipient did not make, or knowingly allow the use of the 911 emergency system for, the nonemergency 911 telephone call or the communication from an electronic device. The law enforcement agency may provide educational materials regarding the appropriate use of the 911 emergency system.

(2) For a second or subsequent violation, a citation may be issued by the public safety entity originally receiving the telephone call or the communication from an electronic device pursuant to which the violator shall be subject to the following penalties that may be reduced by a court upon consideration of the violator's ability to pay:

(A) For a second violation, a fine of fifty dollars ($50).

(B) For a third violation, a fine of one hundred dollars ($100).

(C) For a fourth or subsequent violation, a fine of two hundred and fifty dollars ($250).

(3) The parent or legal guardian having custody and control of an unemancipated minor who violates this section is jointly and severally liable with the minor for the fine imposed pursuant to this subdivision.

(b) Knowingly allowing the use of or using the 911 emergency system for the purpose of harassing another is a crime that is punishable as follows:

(1) For a first violation, as an infraction punishable by a two-hundred-fifty dollar ($250) fine or as a misdemeanor punishable by up to six months in a county jail, a fine of up to one thousand dollars ($1,000), or both that imprisonment and fine.

(2) For a second or subsequent violation, as a misdemeanor punishable by up to six months in a county jail, a fine of up to one thousand dollars ($1,000), or both that imprisonment and fine.

(c) If a person knowingly allows the use of or uses the 911 emergency system for the purpose of harassing another person and that act is an act described in Section 422.55 or 422.85, the person who commits the act is guilty of a misdemeanor punishable by up to one year in a county jail, a fine of not less than five hundred dollars ($500) nor more than two thousand dollars ($2,000), or both that imprisonment and fine.

(d) For purposes of this section, "emergency" means any condition in which emergency services will result in the saving of a life, a reduction in the destruction of property, quicker apprehension of criminals, or assistance with potentially life-threatening medical problems, a fire, a need for rescue, an imminent potential crime, or a similar situation in which immediate assistance is required.

(e)

(1) Notwithstanding subdivision (a), this section does not apply to a telephone corporation or any other entity for acts or omissions relating to the routine maintenance, repair, or operation of the 911 emergency system or the 311 telephone system.

(2) This section does not apply to uses of the 911 emergency system by a person with an intellectual disability or other mental disability that makes it difficult or impossible for the person to understand the potential consequences of their actions.

Amended by Stats 2020 ch 327 (AB 1775),s 4, eff. 1/1/2021.

Amended by Stats 2016 ch 96 (AB 1769),s 2, eff. 1/1/2017.

Amended by Stats 2008 ch 89 (AB 1976),s 1, eff. 1/1/2009.

Added by Stats 2004 ch 295 (AB 911), s 2, eff. 1/1/2005.

Section 653z - Unlawful operation of recording device in motion picture theater

(a) Every person who operates a recording device in a motion picture theater while a motion picture is being exhibited, for the purpose of recording a theatrical motion picture and without the express written authority of the owner of the motion picture theater, is guilty of a public offense and shall be punished by imprisonment in a county jail not exceeding one year, by a fine not exceeding five thousand dollars ($5,000), or by both that fine and imprisonment.

(b) For the purposes of this section, the following terms have the following meanings:

(1) "Recording device" means a photographic, digital or video camera, or other audio or video recording device capable of recording the sounds and images of a motion picture or any portion of a motion picture.

(2) "Motion picture theater" means a theater or other premises in which a motion picture is exhibited.

(c) Nothing in this section shall preclude prosecution under any other provision of law.

Amended by Stats 2010 ch 351 (AB 819),s 7, eff. 9/25/2010.

Added by Stats 2003 ch 670 (SB 1032), s 1, eff. 1/1/2004.

Section 653aa - Unlawful electronic transmission of commercial recording or audiovisual work

(a) Any person, except a minor, who is located in California, who, knowing that a particular recording or audiovisual work is commercial, knowingly electronically disseminates all or substantially all of that commercial recording or audiovisual work to more than 10 other people without disclosing his or her e-mail address, and the title of the recording or audiovisual work is punishable by a fine not exceeding five thousand dollars ($5,000), imprisonment in a county jail for a period not exceeding one year, or by both that fine and imprisonment.

(b) Any minor who violates subdivision (a) is punishable by a fine not exceeding five hundred dollars ($500). Any minor who commits a third or subsequent violation of subdivision (a) is punishable by a fine not exceeding two thousand dollars ($2,000), imprisonment in a county jail for a period not to exceed one year, or by both that imprisonment and fine.

(c) Subdivisions (a) and (b) do not apply:

(1) To a person who electronically disseminates a commercial recording or audiovisual work to his or her immediate family, or within his or her personal network, defined as a restricted access network controlled by and accessible to only that person or people in his or her immediate household.

(2) If the copyright owner, or a person acting under the authority of the copyright owner, of a commercial recording or audiovisual work has explicitly given permission for all or substantially all of that recording or audiovisual work to be freely disseminated electronically by or to anyone without limitation.

(3) To a person who has been licensed either by the copyright owner or a person acting under the authority of the copyright owner to disseminate electronically all or substantially all of a commercial audiovisual work or recording.

(4) To the licensed electronic dissemination of a commercial audiovisual work or recording by means of a cable television service offered over a cable system or direct to home satellite service as defined in Title 47 of the United States Code.

(d) Nothing in this section shall restrict the copyright owner from disseminating his or her own copyrighted material.

(e) Upon conviction for a violation of this section, in addition to the penalty prescribed, the court shall order the permanent deletion or destruction of any electronic file containing a commercial recording or audiovisual work, the dissemination of which was the basis of the violation. This subdivision shall not apply to the copyright owner or to a person acting under the authority of the copyright owner.

(f) An Internet service provider does not violate, and does not aid and abet a violation of subdivision (a), and subdivision (a) shall not be enforced against an Internet service provider, to the extent that the Internet service provider enables a user of its service to electronically disseminate an audiovisual work or sound recording, if the Internet service provider maintains its valid e-mail address or other means of electronic notification on its Internet Web site in a location that is accessible to the public. For the purposes of this section, "Internet service provider" means an entity, to the extent that the entity is transmitting, routing, or providing connections for Internet communications initiated by or at the direction of another person, between or among points specified by a user, of material placed online by a user, storing or hosting that material at the direction of a user, or referring or linking users to that material.

(g) For purposes of this section:

(1) "Recording" means the electronic or physical embodiment of any recorded images, sounds, or images and sounds, but does not include audiovisual works or sounds accompanying audiovisual works.

(2) "Audiovisual work" means the electronic or physical embodiment of motion pictures, television programs, video or computer games, or other audiovisual presentations that consist of related images that are intrinsically intended to be shown by the use of machines or devices such as projectors, viewers, or electronic equipment, or a computer program, software, or system, as defined in Section 502, together with accompanying sounds, if any.

(3) "Commercial recording or audiovisual work" means a recording or audiovisual work whose copyright owner, or assignee, authorized agent, or licensee, has made or intends to make available for sale, rental, or for performance or exhibition to the public under license, but does not include an excerpt consisting of less than substantially all of a recording or audiovisual work. A recording or audiovisual work may be commercial regardless of whether the person who electronically disseminates it seeks commercial advantage or private financial gain from that dissemination.

(4) "Electronic dissemination" means initiating a transmission of, making available, or otherwise offering, a commercial recording or audiovisual work for distribution on the Internet or other digital network, regardless of whether someone else had previously electronically disseminated the same commercial recording or audiovisual work.

(5) "E-mail address" means a valid e-mail address, or the valid e-mail address of the holder of the account from which the dissemination took place.

(6) "Disclosing" means providing information in, attached to, or discernable or available in or through the process of disseminating or obtaining a commercial recording or audiovisual work in a manner that is accessible by any person engaged in disseminating or receiving the commercial recording or audiovisual work.

(h) Nothing in this section shall preclude prosecution under any other provision of law.

Amended by Stats 2010 ch 351 (AB 819),s 8, eff. 9/25/2010.

Added by Stats 2004 ch 617 (SB 1506), s 1, eff. 1/1/2005.

Section 653.1 - Release of balloons made of electrically conductive material

(a) No person or group shall release, outdoors, balloons made of electrically conductive material and filled with a gas lighter than air, as part of a public or civic event, promotional activity, or product advertisement.

(b) Any person who violates this section shall be guilty of an infraction punishable by a fine not exceeding one hundred dollars ($100). Any person who violates this section who has been previously convicted twice of violating this section shall be guilty of a misdemeanor.

(c) This section shall not apply to manned hot air balloons, or to balloons used in governmental or scientific research projects.

Amended by Stats 2018 ch 262 (AB 2450),s 2, eff. 1/1/2019.

Amended by Stats 2004 ch 193 (SB 111), s 141, eff. 1/1/2005.

Section 653.2 - Unlawful electronic distribution of personal identifying information

(a) Every person who, with intent to place another person in reasonable fear for his or her safety, or the safety of the other person's immediate family, by means of an electronic communication device, and without consent of the other person, and for the purpose of imminently causing that other person unwanted physical contact, injury, or harassment, by a third party, electronically distributes, publishes, e-mails, hyperlinks, or makes available for downloading, personal identifying information, including, but not limited to, a digital image of another person, or an electronic message of a harassing nature about another person, which would be likely to incite or produce that unlawful action, is guilty of a misdemeanor punishable by up to one year in a county jail, by a fine of not more than one thousand dollars ($1,000), or by both that fine and imprisonment.

(b) For purposes of this section, "electronic communication device" includes, but is not limited to, telephones, cell phones, computers, Internet Web pages or sites, Internet phones, hybrid cellular/Internet/wireless devices, personal digital assistants (PDAs), video recorders, fax machines, or pagers. "Electronic communication" has the same meaning as the term is defined in Section 2510(12) of Title 18 of the United States Code.

(c) For purposes of this section, the following terms apply:

(1) "Harassment" means a knowing and willful course of conduct directed at a specific person that a reasonable person would consider as seriously alarming, seriously annoying, seriously tormenting, or seriously terrorizing the person and that serves no legitimate purpose.

(2) "Of a harassing nature" means of a nature that a reasonable person would consider as seriously alarming, seriously annoying, seriously tormenting, or seriously terrorizing of the person and that serves no legitimate purpose.

Amended by Stats 2009 ch 140 (AB 1164),s 144, eff. 1/1/2010.

Added by Stats 2008 ch 583 (AB 919),s 1, eff. 1/1/2009.

Chapter 2.5 - LOITERING FOR THE PURPOSE OF ENGAGING IN A PROSTITUTION OFFENSE

Section 653.20 - [Repealed]

Repealed by Stats 2022 ch 86 (SB 357),s 3, eff. 1/1/2023.

Added by Stats. 1995, Ch. 981, Sec. 4. Effective January 1, 1996.

Section 653.22 - [Repealed]

Repealed by Stats 2022 ch 86 (SB 357),s 4, eff. 1/1/2023.

Amended by Stats 2016 ch 654 (SB 1322),s 2, eff. 1/1/2017.

Section 653.23 - Unlawful recruiting or aiding of person; unlawful collection of proceeds earned from act of prostitution committed by another person

(a) It is unlawful for a person to do either of the following:

(1) Direct, supervise, recruit, or otherwise aid another person in the commission of a violation of subdivision (b) of Section 647.

(2) Collect or receive all or part of the proceeds earned from an act or acts of prostitution committed by another person in violation of subdivision (b) of Section 647.

(b) Nothing in this section shall preclude the prosecution of a suspect for a violation of Section 266h or 266i or for any other offense, or for a violation of this section in conjunction with a violation of Section 266h or 266i or any other offense.

Amended by Stats 2022 ch 86 (SB 357),s 5, eff. 1/1/2023.

Added by Stats. 1998, Ch. 460, Sec. 1. Effective January 1, 1999.

Section 653.24 - Severability

If any section, subdivision, sentence, clause, phrase, or portion of this chapter is for any reason held invalid or unconstitutional by any court of competent jurisdiction, that portion shall be deemed a separate, distinct, and independent provision, and that holding shall not affect the validity of the remaining portion of the chapter.

Added by Stats. 1995, Ch. 981, Sec. 4. Effective January 1, 1996.

Section 653.26 - Misdemeanor

A violation of any provision of this chapter is a misdemeanor.

Added by Stats. 1995, Ch. 981, Sec. 4. Effective January 1, 1996.

Section 653.28 - Local laws

Nothing in this chapter or Chapter 2 (commencing with Section 639) shall prevent a local governing body from adopting and enforcing laws consistent with these chapters relating to prostitution or prostitution-related activity. Where local laws duplicate or supplement this chapter or Chapter 2 (commencing with Section 639), these chapters shall be construed as providing alternative remedies and not to preempt the field.

Added by Stats. 1995, Ch. 981, Sec. 4. Effective January 1, 1996.

Section 653.29 - Petition for a recall or dismissal of sentence for conviction of violating former Section 653.22

(a)

(1) A person currently serving a sentence for a conviction of violating former Section 653.22, whether by trial or by open or negotiated plea, may petition for a recall or dismissal of sentence before the trial court that entered the judgment of conviction in the case to request resentencing or dismissal, and sealing, as applicable.

(2) Upon receiving a petition under paragraph (1), the court shall presume the petitioner satisfies the criteria in paragraph (1) unless the party opposing the petition proves by clear and convincing evidence that the petitioner does not satisfy the criteria. If the petitioner satisfies the criteria in paragraph (1), the court shall grant the petition to recall the sentence or dismiss the sentence because it is legally invalid and shall seal the conviction as legally invalid.

(b)

(1) A person who has completed their sentence for a conviction of violating former Section 653.22, whether by trial or open or negotiated plea, may file an application before the trial court that entered the judgment of conviction in their case to have the conviction dismissed and sealed because the prior conviction is now legally invalid.

(2) The court shall presume the petitioner satisfies the criteria in paragraph (1) unless the party opposing the application proves by clear and convincing evidence that the petitioner does not satisfy the criteria in paragraph (1). Once the applicant satisfies the criteria in paragraph (1), the court shall seal the conviction as legally invalid.

(c) Unless requested by the applicant, no hearing is necessary to grant or deny an application filed under subdivision (b).

(d) If the court that originally sentenced the petitioner is not available, the presiding judge shall designate another judge to rule on the petition or application.

(e) Nothing in this section is intended to diminish or abrogate any rights or remedies otherwise available to the petitioner or applicant.

(f) The Judicial Council shall promulgate and make available all necessary forms to enable the filing of the petitions and applications provided in this section.

Amended by Stats 2023 ch 131 (AB 1754),s 150, eff. 1/1/2024.

Added by Stats 2022 ch 86 (SB 357),s 6, eff. 1/1/2023.

Chapter 3 - IMMIGRATION MATTERS

Section 653.55 - False or misleading material statement in preparation of immigration matter

It is a misdemeanor for any person for compensation to knowingly make a false or misleading material statement or assertion of fact in the preparation of an immigration matter which statement or assertion is detrimentally relied upon by another. Such a misdemeanor is punishable by imprisonment in the county jail not exceeding six months, or by a fine not exceeding two thousand five hundred dollars ($2,500), or by both.

Amended by Stats. 1976, Ch. 1125.

Section 653.56 - Definitions

For purposes of this chapter:

(a) "Compensation" means money, property, or anything else of value.

(b) "Immigration matter" means any proceeding, filing, or action affecting the immigration or citizenship status of any person which arises under immigration and naturalization law, executive order or presidential proclamation, or action of the United States Immigration and Customs Enforcement, the United States Department of State, or the United States Department of Labor.

(c) "Person" means any individual, firm, partnership, corporation, limited liability company, association, other organization, or any employee or agent thereof.

(d) "Preparation" means giving advice on an immigration matter and includes drafting an application, brief, document, petition, or other paper, or completing a form provided by a federal or state agency in an immigration matter.

Amended by Stats 2011 ch 296 (AB 1023),s 210, eff. 1/1/2012.

Section 653.57 - Injunctive relief

Any person violating the provisions of this chapter may be enjoined by any superior court of competent jurisdiction upon an action for injunction, brought by the Attorney General, or any district attorney, county counsel, city attorney, or city prosecutor in this state, and the superior court shall, after proof of violation, issue an injunction or other appropriate order restraining such conduct.

Added by Stats. 1974, Ch. 999.

Section 653.58 - Intentional violation of injunction

Any person who intentionally violates any injunction issued pursuant to Section 653.57 shall be liable for a civil penalty not to exceed two thousand five hundred dollars ($2,500) for each violation. Where the conduct constituting a violation is of a continuing nature, each day of such conduct is a separate and distinct violation.

Amended by Stats. 1976, Ch. 1125.

Section 653.59 - Civil penalty

Any person who violates any provision of this chapter shall be liable for a civil penalty not to exceed two thousand five hundred dollars ($2,500) for each violation, which shall be assessed and recovered in a civil action brought in the name of the people of the State of California by the Attorney General, or any district attorney, county counsel, city attorney, or city prosecutor in this state in any court of competent jurisdiction. If the civil action was brought by the Attorney General, one-half of the penalty collected shall be paid to the treasurer of the county in which the judgment was entered, and one-half to the State General Fund. If the civil action was brought by a district attorney or county counsel, the entire amount of the penalty collected shall be paid to the treasurer of the county in which the judgment was entered. If the civil action was brought by a city attorney or city prosecutor, one-half of the penalty shall be paid to the treasurer of the county in which the judgment was entered and one-half to the city.

The action may be brought upon the complaint of any person acting for the interests of itself, or members, or the general public.

Added by Stats. 1974, Ch. 999.

Section 653.60 - Recovery of damages and costs of suit

Any person injured by violation of this chapter may recover:

(a) his actual damages or five hundred dollars ($500), whichever is greater; and

(b) the costs of the suit, including reasonable attorney's fees.

Added by Stats. 1974, Ch. 999.

Section 653.61 - Cumulative remedies or penalties

The remedies or penalties provided by this chapter are cumulative to each other and to the remedies or penalties available under all other laws of this state.

Added by Stats. 1974, Ch. 999.

Chapter 4 - CRIMES COMMITTED WHILE IN CUSTODY IN CORRECTIONAL FACILITIES

Section 653.75 - Commission of public offense while in custody of local detention facility or state prison

Any person who commits any public offense while in custody in any local detention facility, as defined in Section 6031.4, or any state prison, as defined in Section 4504, is guilty of a crime. That crime shall be punished as provided in the section prescribing the punishment for that public offense.

Added by Stats. 1987, Ch. 1005, Sec. 1.

Title 16 - GENERAL PROVISIONS

Section 654 - Single punishment

(a) An act or omission that is punishable in different ways by different provisions of law may be punished under either of such provisions, but in no case shall the act or omission be punished under more than one provision. An acquittal or conviction and sentence under any one bars a prosecution for the same act or omission under any other.

(b) Notwithstanding subdivision (a), a defendant sentenced pursuant to subdivision (a) shall not be granted probation if any of the provisions that would otherwise apply to the defendant prohibits the granting of probation.

Amended by Stats 2021 ch 441 (AB 518),s 1, eff. 1/1/2022.

Amended by Stats. 1997, Ch. 410, Sec. 1. Effective January 1, 1998.

Section 654.1 - Unlawful sale of transportation of person unless transportation provided by carrier holding certificate or permit

It shall be unlawful for any person, acting individually or as an officer or employee of a corporation, or as a member of a copartnership or as a commission agent or employee of another person, firm or corporation, to sell or offer for sale or, to negotiate, provide or arrange for, or to advertise or hold himself out as one who sells or offers for sale or negotiates, provides or arranges for transportation of a person or persons on an individual fare basis over the public highways of the State of California unless such transportation is to be furnished or provided solely by, and such sale is authorized by, a carrier having a valid and existing certificate of convenience and necessity, or other valid and existing permit from the Public Utilities Commission of the State of California, or from the Interstate Commerce Commission of the United States, authorizing the holder of such certificate or permit to provide such transportation.

Added by Stats. 1947, Ch. 1215.

Section 654.2 - Applicability

The provisions of Section 654.1 of the Penal Code shall not apply to the selling, furnishing, or providing of transportation of any person or persons in any of the following circumstances:

(a) When no compensation is paid or to be paid, either directly or indirectly, for the transportation.

(b) For the furnishing or providing of transportation to or from work of employees engaged in farmwork on any farm of the State of California.

(c) For the furnishing or providing of transportation to and from work of employees of any nonprofit cooperative association, organized pursuant to any law of the State of California.

(d) For the transportation of persons wholly or substantially within the limits of a single municipality or of contiguous municipalities.

(e) For transportation of persons over a route wholly or partly within a national park or state park where the transportation is sold in conjunction with, or as part of, a rail trip or trip over a regularly operated motorbus transportation system or line.

(f) For the transportation of persons between home and work locations or of persons having a common work-related trip purpose in a vehicle having a seating capacity of 15 passengers or less, including the driver, which is used for the purpose of ridesharing, as defined in Section 522 of the Vehicle Code, when the ridesharing is incidental to another purpose of the driver. This exemption does not apply if the primary purpose for the transportation of those persons is to make a profit. "Profit," as used in this subdivision, does not include the recovery of the actual costs incurred in owning and operating a vanpool vehicle, as defined in Section 668 of the Vehicle Code.

Amended by Stats. 1982, Ch. 185, Sec. 2.

Section 654.3 - Punishment

Violation of Section 654.1 shall be a misdemeanor, and upon first conviction the punishment shall be a fine of not over five hundred dollars ($500), or imprisonment in jail for not over 90 days, or both such fine and imprisonment. Upon second conviction the punishment shall be imprisonment in jail for not less than 30 days and not more than 180 days. Upon a third or subsequent conviction the punishment shall be confinement in jail for not less than 90 days and not more than one year, and a person suffering three or more convictions shall not be eligible to probation, the provisions of any law to the contrary notwithstanding.

Amended by Stats. 1983, Ch. 1092, Sec. 319. Effective September 27, 1983. Operative January 1, 1984, by Sec. 427 of Ch. 1092.

Section 655 - Act punishable under laws of another state, government, or county

An act or omission declared punishable by this Code is not less so because it is also punishable under the laws of another State, Government, or country, unless the contrary is expressly declared.

Enacted 1872.

Section 656 - Defense

Whenever on the trial of an accused person it appears that upon a criminal prosecution under the laws of the United States, or of another state or territory of the United States based upon the act or omission in respect to which he or she is on trial, he or she has been acquitted or convicted, it is a sufficient defense.

Amended by Stats 2004 ch 511 (AB 1432), s 1, eff. 1/1/2005.

Section 656.5 - Credit for time served

Any person convicted of a crime based upon an act or omission for which he or she has been acquitted or convicted in another country shall be entitled to credit for any actual time served in custody in a penal institution in that country for the crime, and for any additional time credits that would have actually been awarded had the person been incarcerated in California.

Added by Stats 2004 ch 511 (AB 1432), s 2, eff. 1/1/2005.

Section 656.6 - Violation of international treaties or laws prohibited

No international treaties or laws shall be violated to secure the return of a person who has been convicted in another country of a crime committed in California in order to prosecute the person in California.

Added by Stats 2004 ch 511 (AB 1432), s 3, eff. 1/1/2005.

Section 657 - Crime punishable as contempt

A criminal act is not the less punishable as a crime because it is also declared to be punishable as a contempt.

Enacted 1872.

Section 658 - Mitigation of punishment if person already paid fine or suffered imprisonment for act

When it appears, at the time of passing sentence upon a person convicted upon indictment, that such person has already paid a fine or suffered an imprisonment for the act of which he stands convicted, under an order adjudging it a contempt, the Court authorized to pass sentence may mitigate the punishment to be imposed, in its discretion.

Enacted 1872.

Section 659 - Unlawful counseling or aiding another

Whenever an act is declared a misdemeanor, and no punishment for counseling or aiding in the commission of such act is expressly prescribed by law, every person who counsels or aids another in the commission of such act is guilty of a misdemeanor.

Enacted 1872.

Section 660 - Offense deemed complete from time letter deposited or delivered

In the various cases in which the sending of a letter is made criminal by this Code, the offense is deemed complete from the time when such letter is deposited in any Post Office or any other place, or delivered to any person, with intent that it shall be forwarded.

Enacted 1872.

Section 661 - Removal from office

In addition to the penalty affixed by express terms, to every neglect or violation of official duty on the part of public officers, State, county, city, or township, where it is not so expressly provided, they may, in the discretion of the Court, be removed from office.

Enacted 1872.

Section 662 - Omission to perform act, where act performed by another

No person is punishable for an omission to perform an act, where such act has been performed by another person acting in his behalf and competent by law to perform it.

Enacted 1872.

Section 663 - Attempt to commit crime

Any person may be convicted of an attempt to commit a crime, although it appears on the trial that the crime intended or attempted was perpetrated by such person in pursuance of such attempt, unless the Court, in its discretion, discharges the jury and directs such person to be tried for such crime.

Enacted 1872.

Section 664 - Punishment for attempt to commit crime

Every person who attempts to commit any crime, but fails, or is prevented or intercepted in its perpetration, shall be punished where no provision is made by law for the punishment of those attempts, as follows:

(a) If the crime attempted is punishable by imprisonment in the state prison, or by imprisonment pursuant to subdivision (h) of Section 1170, the person guilty of the attempt shall be punished by imprisonment in the state prison or in a county jail, respectively, for one-half the term of imprisonment prescribed upon a conviction of the offense attempted. However, if the crime attempted is willful, deliberate, and premeditated murder, as defined in Section 189, the person guilty of that attempt shall be punished by imprisonment in the state prison for life with the possibility of parole. If the crime attempted is any other one in which the maximum sentence is life imprisonment or death, the person guilty of the attempt shall be punished by imprisonment in the state prison for five, seven, or nine years. The additional term provided in this section for attempted willful, deliberate, and premeditated murder shall not be imposed unless the fact that the attempted murder was willful, deliberate, and premeditated is charged in the accusatory pleading and admitted or found to be true by the trier of fact.

(b) If the crime attempted is punishable by imprisonment in a county jail, the person guilty of the attempt shall be punished by imprisonment in a county jail for a term not exceeding one-half the term of imprisonment prescribed upon a conviction of the offense attempted.

(c) If the offense so attempted is punishable by a fine, the offender convicted of that attempt shall be punished by a fine not exceeding one-half the largest fine which may be imposed upon a conviction of the offense attempted.

(d) If a crime is divided into degrees, an attempt to commit the crime may be of any of those degrees, and the punishment for the attempt shall be determined as provided by this section.

(e) Notwithstanding subdivision (a), if attempted murder is committed upon a peace officer or firefighter, as those terms are defined in paragraphs (7) and (9) of subdivision (a) of Section 190.2, a custodial officer, as that term is defined in subdivision (a) of Section 831 or subdivision (a) of Section 831.5, a custody assistant, as that term is defined in subdivision (a) of Section 831.7, or a nonsworn uniformed employee of a sheriff's department whose job entails the care or control of inmates in a detention facility, as defined in subdivision (c) of Section 289.6, and the person who commits the offense knows or reasonably should know that the victim is a peace officer, firefighter, custodial officer, custody assistant, or nonsworn uniformed employee of a sheriff's department engaged in the performance of his or her duties, the person guilty of the attempt shall be punished by imprisonment in the state prison for life with the possibility of parole. This subdivision shall apply if it is proven that a direct but ineffectual act was committed by one person toward killing another human being and the person committing the act harbored express malice aforethought, namely, a specific intent to unlawfully kill another human being. The Legislature finds and declares that this paragraph is declaratory of existing law.

(f) Notwithstanding subdivision (a), if the elements of subdivision (e) are proven in an attempted murder and it is also charged and admitted or found to be true by the trier of fact that the attempted murder was willful, deliberate, and premeditated, the person guilty of the attempt shall be punished by imprisonment in the state prison for 15 years to life. Article 2.5 (commencing with Section 2930) of Chapter 7 of Title 1 of Part 3 shall not apply to reduce this minimum term of 15 years in state prison, and the person shall not be released prior to serving 15 years' confinement.

Amended by Stats 2011 ch 39 (AB 117),s 68, eff. 6/30/2011.

Amended by Stats 2011 ch 15 (AB 109),s 439, eff. 4/4/2011, but operative no earlier than October 1, 2011, and only upon creation of a community corrections grant program to assist in implementing this act and upon an appropriation to fund the grant program.

Amended by Stats 2006 ch 468 (SB 1184),s 1, eff. 1/1/2007.

Amended by Stats 2005 ch 52 (AB 999),s 1, eff. 1/1/2006

Section 665 - Accomplishing commission of another and different crime

Sections 663 and 664 do not protect a person who, in attempting unsuccessfully to commit a crime, accomplishes the commission of another and different crime, whether greater or less in guilt, from suffering the punishment prescribed by law for the crime committed.

Amended by Stats. 1987, Ch. 828, Sec. 45.

Section 666 - Subsequent conviction of petty theft

(a) Notwithstanding Section 490, any person described in subdivision (b) who, having been convicted of petty theft, grand theft, a conviction pursuant to subdivision (d) or (e) of Section 368, auto theft under Section 10851 of the Vehicle Code, burglary, carjacking, robbery, or a felony violation of Section 496, and having served a term of imprisonment therefor in any penal institution or having been imprisoned therein as a condition of probation for that offense, and who is subsequently convicted of petty theft, is punishable by imprisonment in the county jail not exceeding one year, or in the state prison.

(b) Subdivision (a) shall apply to any person who is required to register pursuant to the Sex Offender Registration Act, or who has a prior violent or serious felony conviction, as specified in clause (iv) of subparagraph (C) of paragraph (2) of subdivision (e) of Section 667, or has a conviction pursuant to subdivision (d) or (e) of Section 368.

(c) This section shall not be construed to preclude prosecution or punishment pursuant to subdivisions (b) to (i), inclusive, of Section 667, or Section 1170.12.

Amended by Proposition 47, eff. 11/5/2014.

Amended by Stats 2013 ch 782 (SB 543),s 1, eff. 1/1/2014.

Amended by Stats 2011 ch 39 (AB 117),s 68, eff. 6/30/2011.

Amended by Stats 2011 ch 39 (AB 117),s 21, eff. 6/30/2011.

Amended by Stats 2011 ch 15 (AB 109),s 440, eff. 4/4/2011, but operative no earlier than October 1, 2011, and only upon creation of a community corrections grant program to assist in implementing this act and upon an appropriation to fund the grant program.

Amended by Stats 2010 ch 219 (AB 1844),s 15, eff. 9/9/2010.

Amended by Stats 2000 ch 135 (AB 2539), s 134, eff. 1/1/2001.

Section 666.5 - Subsequent conviction involving felony violations involving motor vehicles, trailers, special construction equipment, or vessels

(a) Every person who, having been previously convicted of a felony violation of Section 10851 of the Vehicle Code, or felony grand theft involving an automobile in violation of subdivision (d) of Section 487 or former subdivision (3) of Section 487, as that section read prior to being amended by Section 4 of Chapter 1125 of the Statutes of 1993, or felony grand theft involving a motor vehicle, as defined in Section 415 of the Vehicle Code, any trailer, as defined in Section 630 of the Vehicle Code, any special construction equipment, as defined in Section 565 of the Vehicle Code, or any vessel, as defined in Section 21 of the Harbors and Navigation Code in violation of former Section 487h, or a felony violation of Section 496d regardless of whether or not the person actually served a prior prison term for those offenses, is subsequently convicted of any of these offenses shall be punished by imprisonment pursuant to subdivision (h) of Section 1170 for two, three, or four years, or a fine of ten thousand dollars ($10,000), or both the fine and the imprisonment.

(b) For the purposes of this section, the terms "special construction equipment" and "vessel" are limited to motorized vehicles and vessels.

(c) The existence of any fact which would bring a person under subdivision (a) shall be alleged in the information or indictment and either admitted by the defendant in open court, or found to be true by the jury trying the issue of guilt or by the court where guilt is established by plea of guilty or nolo contendere or by trial by the court sitting without a jury.

Amended by Stats 2011 ch 39 (AB 117),s 68, eff. 6/30/2011.

Amended by Stats 2011 ch 15 (AB 109),s 441, eff. 4/4/2011, but operative no earlier than October 1, 2011, and only upon creation of a community corrections grant program to assist in implementing this act and upon an appropriation to fund the grant program.

Amended & effective October 10, 1999 (Bill Number: AB 1236) (Chapter 706).

Section 666.7 - [Repealed]

Repealed by Stats 2006 ch 901 (SB 1422),s 7, eff. 1/1/2007.

Amended by Stats 2005 ch 722 (AB 1323),s 10, eff. 10/7/2005.

Amended by Stats 2004 ch 405 (SB 1796), s 10, eff. 1/1/2005.

Amended by Stats 2003 ch 499 (SB 238), s 2, eff. 1/1/2004.

Amended by Stats 2001 ch 854 (SB 205), s 36, eff. 1/1/2002.

Previously Amended October 10, 1999 (Bill Number: AB 1236) (Chapter 706).

Section 667 - Subsequent conviction of serious felony

(a)

(1) A person convicted of a serious felony who previously has been convicted of a serious felony in this state or of any offense committed in another jurisdiction that includes all of the elements of any serious felony, shall receive, in addition to the sentence

imposed by the court for the present offense, a five-year enhancement for each such prior conviction on charges brought and tried separately. The terms of the present offense and each enhancement shall run consecutively.

(2) This subdivision shall not be applied when the punishment imposed under other provisions of law would result in a longer term of imprisonment. There is no requirement of prior incarceration or commitment for this subdivision to apply.

(3) The Legislature may increase the length of the enhancement of sentence provided in this subdivision by a statute passed by majority vote of each house thereof.

(4) As used in this subdivision, "serious felony" means a serious felony listed in subdivision (c) of Section 1192.7.

(5) This subdivision does not apply to a person convicted of selling, furnishing, administering, or giving, or offering to sell, furnish, administer, or give to a minor any methamphetamine-related drug or any precursors of methamphetamine unless the prior conviction was for a serious felony described in subparagraph (24) of subdivision (c) of Section 1192.7.

(b) It is the intent of the Legislature in enacting subdivisions (b) to (i), inclusive, to ensure longer prison sentences and greater punishment for those who commit a felony and have been previously convicted of one or more serious or violent felony offenses.

(c) Notwithstanding any other law, if a defendant has been convicted of a felony and it has been pled and proved that the defendant has one or more prior serious or violent felony convictions as defined in subdivision (d), the court shall adhere to each of the following:

(1) There shall not be an aggregate term limitation for purposes of consecutive sentencing for any subsequent felony conviction.

(2) Probation for the current offense shall not be granted, nor shall execution or imposition of the sentence be suspended for any prior offense.

(3) The length of time between the prior serious or violent felony conviction and the current felony conviction shall not affect the imposition of sentence.

(4) There shall not be a commitment to any other facility other than the state prison. Diversion shall not be granted, nor shall the defendant be eligible for commitment to the California Rehabilitation Center as provided in Article 2 (commencing with Section 3050) of Chapter 1 of Division 3 of the Welfare and Institutions Code.

(5) The total amount of credits awarded pursuant to Article 2.5 (commencing with Section 2930) of Chapter 7 of Title 1 of Part 3 shall not exceed one-fifth of the total term of imprisonment imposed and shall not accrue until the defendant is physically placed in the state prison.

(6) If there is a current conviction for more than one felony count not committed on the same occasion, and not arising from the same set of operative facts, the court shall sentence the defendant consecutively on each count pursuant to subdivision (e).

(7) If there is a current conviction for more than one serious or violent felony as described in paragraph (6), the court shall impose the sentence for each conviction consecutive to the sentence for any other conviction for which the defendant may be consecutively sentenced in the manner prescribed by law.

(8) A sentence imposed pursuant to subdivision (e) shall be imposed consecutive to any other sentence that the defendant is already serving, unless otherwise provided by law.

(d) Notwithstanding any other law and for the purposes of subdivisions (b) to (i), inclusive, a prior conviction of a serious or violent felony shall be defined as:

(1) An offense defined in subdivision (c) of Section 667.5 as a violent felony or an offense defined in subdivision (c) of Section 1192.7 as a serious felony in this state. The determination of whether a prior conviction is a prior felony conviction for purposes of subdivisions (b) to (i), inclusive, shall be made upon the date of that prior conviction and is not affected by the sentence imposed unless the sentence automatically, upon the initial sentencing, converts the felony to a misdemeanor. The following dispositions shall not affect the determination that a prior conviction is a prior felony for purposes of subdivisions (b) to (i), inclusive:

(A) The suspension of imposition of judgment or sentence.

(B) The stay of execution of sentence.

(C) The commitment to the State Department of State Hospitals as a mentally disordered sex offender following a conviction of a felony.

(D) The commitment to the California Rehabilitation Center or any other facility whose function is rehabilitative diversion from the state prison.

(2) A prior conviction in another jurisdiction for an offense that, if committed in California, is punishable by imprisonment in the state prison constitutes a prior conviction of a particular serious or violent felony if the prior conviction in the other jurisdiction is for an offense that includes all of the elements of a particular violent felony as defined in subdivision (c) of Section 667.5 or serious felony as defined in subdivision (c) of Section 1192.7.

(3) A prior juvenile adjudication constitutes a prior serious or violent felony conviction for purposes of sentence enhancement if it meets all of the following:

(A) The juvenile was 16 years of age or older at the time the juvenile committed the prior offense.

(B) The prior offense is listed in subdivision (b) of Section 707 of the Welfare and Institutions Code or described in paragraph (1) or (2) as a serious or violent felony.

(C) The juvenile was found to be a fit and proper subject to be dealt with under the juvenile court law.

(D) The juvenile was adjudged a ward of the juvenile court within the meaning of Section 602 of the Welfare and Institutions Code because the person committed an offense listed in subdivision (b) of Section 707 of the Welfare and Institutions Code.

(e) For purposes of subdivisions (b) to (i), inclusive, and in addition to any other enhancement or punishment provisions that apply, the following apply if a defendant has one or more prior serious or violent felony convictions:

(1) If a defendant has one prior serious or violent felony conviction as defined in subdivision (d) that has been pled and proved, the determinate term or minimum term for an indeterminate term shall be twice the term otherwise provided as punishment for the current felony conviction.

(2)

(A) Except as provided in subparagraph (C), if a defendant has two or more prior serious or violent felony convictions as defined in subdivision (d) that have been pled and proved, the term for the current felony conviction shall be an indeterminate term of life imprisonment with a minimum term of the indeterminate sentence calculated as the greatest of:

(i) Three times the term otherwise provided as punishment for each current felony conviction subsequent to the two or more prior serious or violent felony convictions.

(ii) Imprisonment in the state prison for 25 years.

(iii) The term determined by the court pursuant to Section 1170 for the underlying conviction, including any enhancement applicable under Chapter 4.5 (commencing with Section 1170) of Title 7 of Part 2, or any period prescribed by Section 190 or 3046.

(B) The indeterminate term described in subparagraph (A) shall be served consecutive to any other term of imprisonment for which a consecutive term may be imposed by law. Any other term imposed subsequent to an indeterminate term described in subparagraph (A) shall not be merged therein but shall commence at the time the person would otherwise have been released from prison.

(C) If a defendant has two or more prior serious or violent felony convictions as defined in subdivision (c) of Section 667.5 or subdivision (c) of Section 1192.7 that have been pled and proved, and the current offense is not a serious or violent felony as defined in subdivision (d), the defendant shall be sentenced pursuant to paragraph (1) of subdivision (e) unless the prosecution pleads and proves any of the following:

(i) The current offense is a controlled substance charge, in which an allegation under Section 11370.4 or 11379.8 of the Health and Safety Code was admitted or found true.

(ii) The current offense is a felony sex offense, defined in subdivision (d) of Section 261.5 or former Section 262, or a felony offense that results in mandatory registration as a sex offender pursuant to subdivision (c) of Section 290 except for violations of Sections 266 and 285, paragraph (1) of subdivision (b) and subdivision (e) of Section 286, paragraph (1) of subdivision (b) and subdivision (e) of Section 288a, Section 311.11, and Section 314.

(iii) During the commission of the current offense, the defendant used a firearm, was armed with a firearm or deadly weapon, or intended to cause great bodily injury to another person.

(iv) The defendant suffered a prior serious or violent felony conviction, as defined in subdivision (d) of this section, for any of the following felonies:

(I) A "sexually violent offense" as defined in subdivision (b) of Section 6600 of the Welfare and Institutions Code.

(II) Oral copulation with a child who is under 14 years of age and more than 10 years younger than the defendant as defined by Section 288a, sodomy with another person who is under 14 years of age and more than 10 years younger than the defendant as defined by Section 286, or sexual penetration with another person who is under 14 years of age and more than 10 years younger than the defendant, as defined by Section 289.

(III) A lewd or lascivious act involving a child under 14 years of age, in violation of Section 288.

(IV) Any homicide offense, including any attempted homicide offense, defined in Sections 187 to 191.5, inclusive.

(V) Solicitation to commit murder as defined in Section 653f.

(VI) Assault with a machinegun on a peace officer or firefighter, as defined in paragraph (3) of subdivision (d) of Section 245.

(VII) Possession of a weapon of mass destruction, as defined in paragraph (1) of subdivision (a) of Section 11418.

(VIII) Any serious or violent felony offense punishable in California by life imprisonment or death.

(f)

(1) Notwithstanding any other law, subdivisions (b) to (i), inclusive, shall be applied in every case in which a defendant has one or more prior serious or violent felony convictions as defined in subdivision (d). The prosecuting attorney shall plead and prove each prior serious or violent felony conviction except as provided in paragraph (2).

(2) The prosecuting attorney may move to dismiss or strike a prior serious or violent felony conviction allegation in the furtherance of justice pursuant to Section 1385, or if there is insufficient evidence to prove the prior serious or violent felony conviction. If upon the satisfaction of the court that there is insufficient evidence to prove the prior serious or violent felony conviction, the court may dismiss or strike the allegation. This section shall not be read to alter a court's authority under Section 1385.

(g) Prior serious or violent felony convictions shall not be used in plea bargaining as defined in subdivision (b) of Section 1192.7. The prosecution shall plead and prove all known prior serious or violent felony convictions and shall not enter into any agreement to strike or seek the dismissal of any prior serious or violent felony conviction allegation except as provided in paragraph (2) of subdivision (f).

(h) All references to existing statutes in subdivisions (c) to (g), inclusive, are to statutes as they existed on November 7, 2012.

(i) If any provision of subdivisions (b) to (h), inclusive, or the application thereof to any person or circumstance is held invalid, that invalidity shall not affect other provisions or applications of those subdivisions that can be given effect without the invalid provision or application, and to this end the provisions of those subdivisions are severable.

(j) The provisions of this section shall not be amended by the Legislature except by statute passed in each house by rollcall vote entered in the journal, two-thirds of the membership concurring, or by a statute that becomes effective only when approved by the electors.

Amended by Stats 2021 ch 626 (AB 1171),s 27, eff. 1/1/2022.

Amended by Stats 2019 ch 497 (AB 991),s 195, eff. 1/1/2020.

Amended by Stats 2018 ch 1013 (SB 1393),s 1, eff. 1/1/2019.

Amended by Stats 2018 ch 423 (SB 1494),s 64, eff. 1/1/2019.

Amended by Proposition 36, approved by the people of the State of California 11/6/2012, eff. 11/7/2012.

Note: This section was added on June 8, 1982, by initiative Prop. 8.

Section 667.1 - References to existing statutes

(a) Notwithstanding subdivision (h) of Section 667, for all offenses committed on or after November 7, 2012, but before January 1, 2024, all references to existing statutes in subdivisions (c) to (g), inclusive, of Section 667, are to those statutes as they read on November 7, 2012.

(b) Notwithstanding subdivision (h) of Section 667, for all offenses committed on or after January 1, 2024, all references to existing statutes in subdivisions (c) to (g), inclusive, of Section 667, are to those statutes as they read on January 1, 2024.

Amended by Stats 2023 ch 230 (SB 14),s 2, eff. 1/1/2024.

Amended by Proposition 36, approved by the people of the State of California 11/6/2012, eff. 11/7/2012.

Amended by Stats 2006 ch 337 (SB 1128),s 29, eff. 9/20/2006.

Section 667.2 - Reentry programs

(a) The Legislature finds and declares that assisting offenders released pursuant to Proposition 36, adopted at the November 6, 2012, statewide general election, with their transition back into communities will increase the offenders' likelihood of successful reintegration.

(b) Subject to the availability of funding for and space in the programs and services, the Department of Corrections and Rehabilitation may provide programs and services, including, but not limited to, transitional housing, mental health, and substance abuse treatment to an offender who is released from the department's custody and satisfies both of the following conditions:

    (1) The offender is released pursuant to any of the following provisions, as they were amended or added by Sections 2 to 6, inclusive, of Proposition 36, as adopted at the November 6, 2012, statewide general election:

        (A) Section 667.

        (B) Section 667.1.

        (C) Section 1170.12.

        (D) Section 1170.125.

        (E) Section 1170.126.

    (2) The offender is not subject to either of the following:

        (A) Parole pursuant to Article 3 (commencing with Section 3040) of Chapter 8 of Title 1 of Part 3.

        (B) Postrelease community supervision pursuant to Title 2.05 (commencing with Section 3450) of Part 3.

(c)

    (1) The Department of Corrections and Rehabilitation, in consultation with the Administrative Office of the Courts, shall establish a referral process for offenders described in subdivision (b) to participate in programs and receive services that the department has existing contracts to provide.

    (2) The Administrative Office of the Courts shall inform courts of the availability of the programs and services described in this section.

Added by Stats 2014 ch 26 (AB 1468),s 12, eff. 6/20/2014.

Section 667.5 - Enhancement of prison terms for new offenses because of prior prison terms

Enhancement of prison terms for new offenses because of prior prison terms shall be imposed as follows:

(a) If one of the new offenses is one of the violent felonies specified in subdivision (c), in addition to and consecutive to any other prison terms therefor, the court shall impose a three-year term for each prior separate prison term served by the defendant when the prior offense was one of the violent felonies specified in subdivision (c). However, an additional term shall not be imposed under this subdivision for any prison term served prior to a period of 10 years in which the defendant remained free of both prison custody and the commission of an offense that results in a felony conviction.

(b) Except when subdivision (a) applies, if the new offense is any felony for which a prison sentence or a sentence of imprisonment in a county jail under subdivision (h) of Section 1170 is imposed or is not suspended, in addition and consecutive to any other sentence therefor, the court shall impose a one-year term for each prior separate prison term for a sexually violent offense as defined in subdivision (b) of Section 6600 of the Welfare and Institutions Code, provided that an additional term shall not be imposed under this subdivision for any prison term served prior to a period of five years in which the defendant remained free of both the commission of an offense that results in a felony conviction, and prison custody or the imposition of a term of jail custody imposed under subdivision (h) of Section 1170 or any felony sentence that is not suspended.

(c) The Legislature finds and declares that the following specified crimes merit special consideration when imposing a sentence to display society's condemnation for these extraordinary crimes of violence against the person. For the purpose of this section, "violent felony" means any of the following:

    (1) Murder or voluntary manslaughter.

    (2) Mayhem.

    (3) Rape as defined in paragraph (2) or (6) of subdivision (a) of Section 261 or paragraph (1) or (4) of subdivision (a) of former Section 262.

    (4) Sodomy as defined in subdivision (c) or (d) of Section 286.

    (5) Oral copulation as defined in subdivision (c) or (d) of Section 287 or of former Section 288a.

    (6) Lewd or lascivious act as defined in subdivision (a) or (b) of Section 288.

    (7) Any felony punishable by death or imprisonment in the state prison for life.

    (8) Any felony in which the defendant inflicts great bodily injury on a person other than an accomplice, which has been charged and proved as provided for in Section 12022.7, 12022.8, or 12022.9 on or after July 1, 1977, or as specified prior to July 1, 1977, in Sections 213, 264, and 461, or any felony in which the defendant uses a firearm which use has been charged and proved as provided in subdivision (a) of Section 12022.3, or Section 12022.5 or 12022.55.

    (9) Any robbery.

    (10) Arson, in violation of subdivision (a) or (b) of Section 451.

    (11) Sexual penetration as defined in subdivision (a) or (j) of Section 289.

    (12) Attempted murder.

    (13) A violation of Section 18745, 18750, or 18755.

    (14) Kidnapping.

    (15) Assault with the intent to commit a specified felony, in violation of Section 220.

    (16) Continuous sexual abuse of a child, in violation of Section 288.5.

(17) Carjacking, as defined in subdivision (a) of Section 215.

(18) Rape or sexual penetration, in concert, in violation of Section 264.1.

(19) Extortion, as defined in Section 518, which would constitute a felony violation of Section 186.22.

(20) Threats to victims or witnesses, as defined in Section 136.1, which would constitute a felony violation of Section 186.22.

(21) Any burglary of the first degree, as defined in subdivision (a) of Section 460, wherein it is charged and proved that another person, other than an accomplice, was present in the residence during the commission of the burglary.

(22) Any violation of Section 12022.53.

(23) A violation of subdivision (b) or (c) of Section 11418.

(d) For the purposes of this section, the defendant shall be deemed to remain in prison custody for an offense until the official discharge from custody, including any period of mandatory supervision, or until release on parole or postrelease community supervision, whichever first occurs, including any time during which the defendant remains subject to reimprisonment or custody in county jail for escape from custody or is reimprisoned on revocation of parole or postrelease community supervision. The additional penalties provided for prior prison terms shall not be imposed unless they are charged and admitted or found true in the action for the new offense.

(e) The additional penalties provided for prior prison terms shall not be imposed for any felony for which the defendant did not serve a prior separate term in state prison or in county jail under subdivision (h) of Section 1170.

(f) A prior conviction of a felony shall include a conviction in another jurisdiction for an offense which, if committed in California, is punishable by imprisonment in the state prison or in county jail under subdivision (h) of Section 1170 if the defendant served one year or more in prison for the offense in the other jurisdiction. A prior conviction of a particular felony shall include a conviction in another jurisdiction for an offense that includes all of the elements of the particular felony as defined under California law if the defendant served one year or more in prison for the offense in the other jurisdiction.

(g) A prior separate prison term for the purposes of this section shall mean a continuous completed period of prison incarceration imposed for the particular offense alone or in combination with concurrent or consecutive sentences for other crimes, including any reimprisonment on revocation of parole that is not accompanied by a new commitment to prison, and including any reimprisonment after an escape from incarceration.

(h) Serving a prison term includes any confinement time in any state prison or federal penal institution as punishment for commission of an offense, including confinement in a hospital or other institution or facility credited as service of prison time in the jurisdiction of the confinement.

(i) For the purposes of this section, a commitment to the State Department of Mental Health, or its successor the State Department of State Hospitals, as a mentally disordered sex offender following a conviction of a felony, which commitment exceeds one year in duration, shall be deemed a prior prison term.

(j) For the purposes of this section, when a person subject to the custody, control, and discipline of the Secretary of the Department of Corrections and Rehabilitation is incarcerated at a facility operated by the Division of Juvenile Justice, that incarceration shall be deemed to be a term served in state prison.

(k)

(1) Notwithstanding subdivisions (d) and (g) or any other law, when one of the new offenses is committed while the defendant is temporarily removed from prison pursuant to Section 2690 or while the defendant is transferred to a community facility pursuant to Section 3416, 6253, or 6263, or while the defendant is on furlough pursuant to Section 6254, the defendant shall be subject to the full enhancements provided for in this section.

(2) This subdivision does not apply when a full, separate, and consecutive term is imposed pursuant to any other law.

Amended by Stats 2021 ch 626 (AB 1171),s 28, eff. 1/1/2022.
Amended by Stats 2019 ch 590 (SB 136),s 1, eff. 1/1/2020.
Amended by Stats 2018 ch 423 (SB 1494),s 65, eff. 1/1/2019.
Amended by Stats 2014 ch 442 (SB 1465),s 10, eff. 9/18/2014.
Amended by Stats 2012 ch 43 (SB 1023),s 22, eff. 6/27/2012.
Amended by Stats 2012 ch 24 (AB 1470),s 19, eff. 6/27/2012.
Amended by Stats 2011 ch 12 (AB X1-17),s 10, eff. 9/20/2011, op. 10/1/2011.
Amended by Stats 2011 ch 12 (AB X1-17),s 9, eff. 9/20/2011, op. 10/1/2011.
Amended by Stats 2011 ch 39 (AB 117),s 68, eff. 6/30/2011.
Amended by Stats 2011 ch 39 (AB 117),s 23, eff. 6/30/2011.
Amended by Stats 2011 ch 39 (AB 117),s 22, eff. 6/30/2011.
Amended by Stats 2011 ch 15 (AB 109),s 443, eff. 4/4/2011.
Amended by Stats 2011 ch 15 (AB 109),s 442, eff. .
Amended by Stats 2010 ch 178 (SB 1115),s 63, eff. 1/1/2011, op. 1/1/2012.
Amended by Proposition 83, § 9, eff. 11/7/2006.
Amended by Stats 2006 ch 337 (SB 1128),s 30, eff. 9/20/2006.
Amended by Stats 2002 ch 606 (AB 1838), s 2, eff. 9/16/2002.

Section 667.51 - Five-year enhancement for prior conviction of enumerated offenses

(a) A person who is convicted of violating Section 288 or 288.5 shall receive a five-year enhancement for a prior conviction of an offense specified in subdivision (b).

(b) Section 261, 264.1, 269, 285, 286, 287, 288, 288.5, or 289, former Section 262 or 288a, or any offense committed in another jurisdiction that includes all of the elements of any of the offenses specified in this subdivision.

(c) A violation of Section 288 or 288.5 by a person who has been previously convicted two or more times of an offense specified in subdivision (b) shall be punished by imprisonment in the state prison for 15 years to life.

Amended by Stats 2021 ch 626 (AB 1171),s 29, eff. 1/1/2022.
Amended by Stats 2018 ch 423 (SB 1494),s 66, eff. 1/1/2019.

Amended by Stats 2006 ch 337 (SB 1128),s 31, eff. 9/20/2006.

Section 667.6 - Five-year enhancement for subsequent conviction of sexual crime

(a) A person who is convicted of an offense specified in subdivision (e) and who has been convicted previously of any of those offenses shall receive a five-year enhancement for each of those prior convictions.

(b) A person who is convicted of an offense specified in subdivision (e) and who has served two or more prior prison terms as defined in Section 667.5 for any of those offenses shall receive a 10-year enhancement for each of those prior terms.

(c) In lieu of the term provided in Section 1170.1, a full, separate, and consecutive term may be imposed for each violation of an offense specified in subdivision (e) if the crimes involve the same victim on the same occasion. A term may be imposed consecutively pursuant to this subdivision if a person is convicted of at least one offense specified in subdivision (e). If the term is imposed consecutively pursuant to this subdivision, it shall be served consecutively to any other term of imprisonment, and shall commence from the time the person otherwise would have been released from imprisonment. The term shall not be included in any determination pursuant to Section 1170.1. Any other term imposed subsequent to that term shall not be merged therein but shall commence at the time the person otherwise would have been released from prison.

(d)

(1) A full, separate, and consecutive term shall be imposed for each violation of an offense specified in subdivision (e) if the crimes involve separate victims or involve the same victim on separate occasions.

(2) In determining whether crimes against a single victim were committed on separate occasions under this subdivision, the court shall consider whether, between the commission of one sex crime and another, the defendant had a reasonable opportunity to reflect upon the defendant's actions and nevertheless resumed sexually assaultive behavior. Neither the duration of time between crimes, nor whether or not the defendant lost or abandoned the opportunity to attack, shall be, in and of itself, determinative on the issue of whether the crimes in question occurred on separate occasions.

(3) The term shall be served consecutively to any other term of imprisonment and shall commence from the time the person otherwise would have been released from imprisonment. The term shall not be included in any determination pursuant to Section 1170.1. Any other term imposed subsequent to that term shall not be merged therein but shall commence at the time the person otherwise would have been released from prison.

(e) This section shall apply to the following offenses:

(1) Rape, in violation of paragraph (2), (3), (6), or (7) of subdivision (a) of Section 261.

(2) Rape, in violation of paragraph (1), (4), or (5) of subdivision (a) of former Section 262.

(3) Rape or sexual penetration, in concert, in violation of Section 264.1.

(4) Sodomy, in violation of paragraph (2) or (3) of subdivision (c), or subdivision (d) or (k), of Section 286.

(5) Lewd or lascivious act, in violation of subdivision (b) of Section 288.

(6) Continuous sexual abuse of a child, in violation of Section 288.5.

(7) Oral copulation, in violation of paragraph (2) or (3) of subdivision (c), or subdivision (d) or (k), of Section 287 or of former Section 288a.

(8) Sexual penetration, in violation of subdivision (a) or (g) of Section 289.

(9) As a present offense under subdivision (c) or (d), assault with intent to commit a specified sexual offense, in violation of Section 220.

(10) As a prior conviction under subdivision (a) or (b), an offense committed in another jurisdiction that includes all of the elements of an offense specified in this subdivision.

(f) In addition to any enhancement imposed pursuant to subdivision (a) or (b), the court may also impose a fine not to exceed twenty thousand dollars ($20,000) for anyone sentenced under those provisions. The fine imposed and collected pursuant to this subdivision shall be deposited in the Victim-Witness Assistance Fund to be available for appropriation to fund child sexual exploitation and child sexual abuse victim counseling centers and prevention programs established pursuant to Section 13837. If the court orders a fine to be imposed pursuant to this subdivision, the actual administrative cost of collecting that fine, not to exceed 2 percent of the total amount paid, may be paid into the general fund of the county treasury for the use and benefit of the county.

Amended by Stats 2021 ch 626 (AB 1171),s 30, eff. 1/1/2022.
Amended by Stats 2018 ch 423 (SB 1494),s 67, eff. 1/1/2019.
Amended by Stats 2006 ch 337 (SB 1128),s 32, eff. 9/20/2006.
Amended by Stats 2002 ch 787 (SB 1798), s 16, eff. 1/1/2003.

Section 667.61 - Punishment for sexual crime under specified circumstances

(a) Except as provided in subdivision (j), (l), or (m), a person who is convicted of an offense specified in subdivision (c) under one or more of the circumstances specified in subdivision (d) or under two or more of the circumstances specified in subdivision (e) shall be punished by imprisonment in the state prison for 25 years to life.

(b) Except as provided in subdivision (a), (j), (l), or (m), a person who is convicted of an offense specified in subdivision (c) under one of the circumstances specified in subdivision (e) shall be punished by imprisonment in the state prison for 15 years to life.

(c) This section shall apply to any of the following offenses:

(1) Rape, in violation of paragraph (2) or (6) of subdivision (a) of Section 261.

(2) Rape, in violation of paragraph (1) or (4) of subdivision (a) of former Section 262.

(3) Rape or sexual penetration, in concert, in violation of Section 264.1.

(4) Lewd or lascivious act, in violation of subdivision (b) of Section 288.

(5) Sexual penetration, in violation of subdivision (a) of Section 289.

(6) Sodomy, in violation of paragraph (2) or (3) of subdivision (c), or subdivision (d), of Section 286.

(7) Oral copulation, in violation of paragraph (2) or (3) of subdivision (c), or subdivision (d), of Section 287 or former Section 288a.

(8) Lewd or lascivious act, in violation of subdivision (a) of Section 288.

(9) Continuous sexual abuse of a child, in violation of Section 288.5.

(d) The following circumstances shall apply to the offenses specified in subdivision (c):

(1) The defendant has been previously convicted of an offense specified in subdivision (c), including an offense committed in another jurisdiction that includes all of the elements of an offense specified in subdivision (c).

(2) The defendant kidnapped the victim of the present offense and the movement of the victim substantially increased the risk of harm to the victim over and above that level of risk necessarily inherent in the underlying offense in subdivision (c).

(3) The defendant inflicted aggravated mayhem or torture on the victim or another person in the commission of the present offense in violation of Section 205 or 206.

(4) The defendant committed the present offense during the commission of a burglary of the first degree, as defined in subdivision (a) of Section 460, with intent to commit an offense specified in subdivision (c).

(5) The defendant committed the present offense in violation of Section 264.1, subdivision (d) of Section 286, or subdivision (d) of Section 287 or former Section 288a, and, in the commission of that offense, any person committed any act described in paragraph (2), (3), or (4) of this subdivision.

(6) The defendant personally inflicted great bodily injury on the victim or another person in the commission of the present offense in violation of Section 12022.53, 12022.7, or 12022.8.

(7) The defendant personally inflicted bodily harm on the victim who was under 14 years of age.

(e) The following circumstances shall apply to the offenses specified in subdivision (c):

(1) Except as provided in paragraph (2) of subdivision (d), the defendant kidnapped the victim of the present offense in violation of Section 207, 209, or 209.5.

(2) Except as provided in paragraph (4) of subdivision (d), the defendant committed the present offense during the commission of a burglary in violation of Section 459.

(3) The defendant personally used a dangerous or deadly weapon or a firearm in the commission of the present offense in violation of Section 12022, 12022.3, 12022.5, or 12022.53.

(4) The defendant has been convicted in the present case or cases of committing an offense specified in subdivision (c) against more than one victim.

(5) The defendant engaged in the tying or binding of the victim or another person in the commission of the present offense.

(6) The defendant administered a controlled substance to the victim in the commission of the present offense in violation of Section 12022.75.

(7) The defendant committed the present offense in violation of Section 264.1, subdivision (d) of Section 286, or subdivision (d) of Section 287 or former Section 288a, and, in the commission of that offense, any person committed an act described in paragraph (1), (2), (3), (5), or (6) of this subdivision or paragraph (6) of subdivision (d).

(f) If only the minimum number of circumstances specified in subdivision (d) or (e) that are required for the punishment provided in subdivision (a), (b), (j), (l), or (m) to apply have been pled and proved, that circumstance or those circumstances shall be used as the basis for imposing the term provided in subdivision (a), (b), (j), (l), or (m) whichever is greater, rather than being used to impose the punishment authorized under any other law, unless another law provides for a greater penalty or the punishment under another law can be imposed in addition to the punishment provided by this section. However, if any additional circumstance or circumstances specified in subdivision (d) or (e) have been pled and proved, the minimum number of circumstances shall be used as the basis for imposing the term provided in subdivision (a), (j), or (l) and any other additional circumstance or circumstances shall be used to impose any punishment or enhancement authorized under any other law.

(g) Notwithstanding Section 1385 or any other law, the court shall not strike any allegation, admission, or finding of any of the circumstances specified in subdivision (d) or (e) for any person who is subject to punishment under this section.

(h) Notwithstanding any other law, probation shall not be granted to, nor shall the execution or imposition of sentence be suspended for, a person who is subject to punishment under this section.

(i) For any offense specified in paragraphs (1) to (7), inclusive, of subdivision (c), or in paragraphs (1) to (6), inclusive, of subdivision (n), the court shall impose a consecutive sentence for each offense that results in a conviction under this section if the crimes involve separate victims or involve the same victim on separate occasions as defined in subdivision (d) of Section 667.6.

(j)

(1) A person who is convicted of an offense specified in subdivision (c), with the exception of a violation of subdivision (a) of Section 288, upon a victim who is a child under 14 years of age under one or more of the circumstances specified in subdivision (d) or under two or more of the circumstances specified in subdivision (e), shall be punished by imprisonment in the state prison for life without the possibility of parole. Where the person was under 18 years of age at the time of the offense, the person shall be punished by imprisonment in the state prison for 25 years to life.

(2) A person who is convicted of an offense specified in subdivision (c) under one of the circumstances specified in subdivision (e), upon a victim who is a child under 14 years of age, shall be punished by imprisonment in the state prison for 25 years to life.

(k) As used in this section, "bodily harm" means any substantial physical injury resulting from the use of force that is more than the force necessary to commit an offense specified in subdivision (c).

(l) A person who is convicted of an offense specified in subdivision (n) under one or more of the circumstances specified in subdivision (d) or under two or more of the circumstances specified in subdivision (e), upon a victim who is a minor 14 years of age or older shall be punished by imprisonment in the state prison for life without the possibility of parole. If the person who was convicted was under 18 years of age at the time of the offense, the person shall be punished by imprisonment in the state prison for 25 years to life.

(m) A person who is convicted of an offense specified in subdivision (n) under one of the circumstances specified in subdivision (e) against a minor 14 years of age or older shall be punished by imprisonment in the state prison for 25 years to life.

(n) Subdivisions (l) and (m) shall apply to any of the following offenses:

(1) Rape, in violation of paragraph (2) of subdivision (a) of Section 261.

(2) Rape, in violation of paragraph (1) of subdivision (a) of former Section 262.

(3) Rape or sexual penetration, in concert, in violation of Section 264.1.

(4) Sexual penetration, in violation of paragraph (1) of subdivision (a) of Section 289.

(5) Sodomy, in violation of paragraph (2) of subdivision (c) of Section 286, or in violation of subdivision (d) of Section 286.

(6) Oral copulation, in violation of paragraph (2) of subdivision (c) of Section 287 or former Section 288a, or in violation of subdivision (d) of Section 287 or former Section 288a.

(o) The penalties provided in this section shall apply only if the existence of any circumstance specified in subdivision (d) or (e) is alleged in the accusatory pleading pursuant to this section, and is either admitted by the defendant in open court or found to be true by the trier of fact.

Amended by Stats 2021 ch 626 (AB 1171),s 31, eff. 1/1/2022.

Amended by Stats 2018 ch 423 (SB 1494),s 68, eff. 1/1/2019.

Amended by Stats 2011 ch 361 (SB 576),s 5, eff. 9/29/2011.

Amended by Stats 2010 ch 219 (AB 1844),s 16, eff. 9/9/2010.

Amended by Stats 2006 ch 337 (SB 1128),s 33, eff. 9/20/2006.

Section 667.7 - Punishment for person convicted of felony in which person inflicted great bodily injury and who has served two or more separate prison terms

(a) Any person convicted of a felony in which the person inflicted great bodily injury as provided in Section 12022.53 or 12022.7, or personally used force which was likely to produce great bodily injury, who has served two or more prior separate prison terms as defined in Section 667.5 for the crime of murder; attempted murder; voluntary manslaughter; mayhem; rape by force, violence, or fear of immediate and unlawful bodily injury on the victim or another person; oral copulation by force, violence, duress, menace, or fear of immediate and unlawful bodily injury on the victim or another person; sodomy by force, violence, duress, menace, or fear of immediate and unlawful bodily injury on the victim or another person; lewd acts on a child under the age of 14 years by use of force, violence, duress, menace, or fear of immediate and unlawful bodily injury on the victim or another person; a violation of subdivision (a) of Section 289 where the act is accomplished against the victim's will by means of force, violence, duress, menace, or fear of immediate and unlawful bodily injury on the victim or another person; kidnapping as punished in former subdivision (d) of Section 208, or for ransom, extortion, or robbery; robbery involving the use of force or a deadly weapon; carjacking involving the use of a deadly weapon; assault with intent to commit murder; assault with a deadly weapon; assault with a force likely to produce great bodily injury; assault with intent to commit rape, sodomy, oral copulation, sexual penetration in violation of Section 289, or lewd and lascivious acts on a child; arson of a structure; escape or attempted escape by an inmate with force or violence in violation of subdivision (a) of Section 4530, or of Section 4532; exploding a destructive device with intent to murder in violation of Section 18745; exploding a destructive device which causes bodily injury in violation of Section 18750, or mayhem or great bodily injury in violation of Section 18755; exploding a destructive device with intent to injure, intimidate, or terrify, in violation of Section 18740; any felony in which the person inflicted great bodily injury as provided in Section 12022.53 or 12022.7; or any felony punishable by death or life imprisonment with or without the possibility of parole is a habitual offender and shall be punished as follows:

(1) A person who served two prior separate prison terms shall be punished by imprisonment in the state prison for life and shall not be eligible for release on parole for 20 years, or the term determined by the court pursuant to Section 1170 for the underlying conviction, including any enhancement applicable under Chapter 4.5 (commencing with Section 1170) of Title 7 of Part 2, or any period prescribed by Section 190 or 3046, whichever is greatest. Article 2.5 (commencing with Section 2930) of Chapter 7 of Title 1 of Part 3 shall apply to reduce any minimum term in a state prison imposed pursuant to this section, but the person shall not otherwise be released on parole prior to that time.

(2) Any person convicted of a felony specified in this subdivision who has served three or more prior separate prison terms, as defined in Section 667.5, for the crimes specified in subdivision (a) of this section shall be punished by imprisonment in the state prison for life without the possibility of parole.

(b) This section shall not prevent the imposition of the punishment of death or imprisonment for life without the possibility of parole. No prior prison term shall be used for this determination which was served prior to a period of 10 years in which the person remained free of both prison custody and the commission of an offense which results in a felony conviction. As used in this section, a commitment to the Department of the Youth Authority after conviction for a felony shall constitute a prior prison term. The term imposed under this section shall be imposed only if the prior prison terms are alleged under this section in the accusatory pleading, and either admitted by the defendant in open court, or found to be true by the jury trying the issue of guilt or by the court where guilt is established by a plea of guilty or nolo contendere or by a trial by the court sitting without a jury.

Amended by Stats 2010 ch 178 (SB 1115),s 64, eff. 1/1/2011, op. 1/1/2012.

Amended by Stats 2006 ch 901 (SB 1422),s 8, eff. 1/1/2007.

Amended by Stats 2001 ch 854 (SB 205), s 37, eff. 1/1/2002.

Section 667.70 - Eligibility for credit for person convicted of murder committed prior to June 3, 1998, and sentenced

Any person who is convicted of murder, which was committed prior to June 3, 1998, and sentenced pursuant to paragraph (1) of subdivision (a) of Section 667.7, shall be eligible only for credit pursuant to subdivisions (a), (b), and (c) of Section 2931.

Amended & effective 10/10/1999 (Bill Number: AB 1236) (Chapter 706).

Section 667.71 - Punishment of habitual sexual offender

(a) For the purpose of this section, a habitual sexual offender is a person who has been previously convicted of one or more of the offenses specified in subdivision (c) and who is convicted in the present proceeding of one of those offenses.

(b) A habitual sexual offender shall be punished by imprisonment in the state prison for 25 years to life.

(c) This section shall apply to any of the following offenses:

(1) Rape, in violation of paragraph (2) or (6) of subdivision (a) of Section 261.

(2) Rape, in violation of paragraph (1) or (4) of subdivision (a) of former Section 262.

(3) Rape or sexual penetration, in concert, in violation of Section 264.1.

(4) Lewd or lascivious act, in violation of subdivision (a) or (b) of Section 288.

(5) Sexual penetration, in violation of subdivision (a) or (j) of Section 289.

(6) Continuous sexual abuse of a child, in violation of Section 288.5.

(7) Sodomy, in violation of subdivision (c) or (d) of Section 286.

(8) Oral copulation, in violation of subdivision (c) or (d) of Section 287 or of former Section 288a.

(9) Kidnapping, in violation of subdivision (b) of Section 207.

(10) Kidnapping, in violation of former subdivision (d) of Section 208 (kidnapping to commit specified sex offenses).

(11) Kidnapping, in violation of subdivision (b) of Section 209 with the intent to commit a specified sexual offense.

(12) Aggravated sexual assault of a child, in violation of Section 269.

(13) An offense committed in another jurisdiction that includes all of the elements of an offense specified in this subdivision.

(d) Notwithstanding Section 1385 or any other law, the court shall not strike any allegation, admission, or finding of any prior conviction specified in subdivision (c) for a person who is subject to punishment under this section.

(e) Notwithstanding any other law, probation shall not be granted to, nor shall the execution or imposition of sentence be suspended for, a person who is subject to punishment under this section.

(f) This section shall apply only if the defendant's status as a habitual sexual offender is alleged in the accusatory pleading, and either admitted by the defendant in open court, or found to be true by the trier of fact.

Amended by Stats 2021 ch 626 (AB 1171),s 32, eff. 1/1/2022.

Amended by Stats 2018 ch 423 (SB 1494),s 69, eff. 1/1/2019.

Amended by Stats 2006 ch 337 (SB 1128),s 34, eff. 9/20/2006.

Amended by Stats 2000 ch 287 (SB 1955), s 10, eff. 1/1/2001.

Section 667.72 - [Repealed]

Repealed effective 10/10/1999 (Bill Number: AB 1236) (Chapter 706).

Section 667.75 - Punishment for person convicted of violation of Health and Safety Code and who has previously served two or more prior separate prison terms

Any person convicted of a violation of Section 11353, 11353.5, 11361, 11380, or 11380.5 of the Health and Safety Code who has previously served two or more prior separate prison terms, as defined in Section 667.5, for a violation of Section 11353, 11353.5, 11361, 11380, or 11380.5 of the Health and Safety Code, may be punished by imprisonment in the state prison for life and shall not be eligible for release on parole for 17 years, or the term determined by the court pursuant to Section 1170 for the underlying conviction, including any enhancement applicable under Chapter 4.5 (commencing with Section 1170) of Title 7 of Part 2, whichever is greatest. The provisions of Article 2.5 (commencing with Section 2930) of Chapter 7 of Title 1 of Part 3 shall apply to reduce any minimum term in a state prison imposed pursuant to this section, but the person shall not otherwise be released on parole prior to that time. No prior prison term shall be used for this determination which was served prior to a period of 10 years in which the person remained free of both prison custody and the commission of an offense which results in a felony conviction. As used in this section, a commitment to the Department of the Youth Authority after conviction for a felony shall constitute a prior prison term. The term imposed under this section shall be imposed only if the prior prison terms are alleged under this section in the accusatory pleading, and either admitted by the defendant in open court, or found to be true by the jury trying the issue of guilt or by the court where guilt is established by a plea of guilty or nolo contendere or by a trial by the court sitting without a jury.

Added by Stats. 1987, Ch. 729, Sec. 1.

Section 667.8 - Punishment for person convicted of felony violation, who, for purpose of committing sexual offense, kidnapped victim

(a) Except as provided in subdivision (b), a person convicted of a felony violation of Section 261, 264.1, 286, 287, or 289 or former Section 262 or 288a who, for the purpose of committing that sexual offense, kidnapped the victim in violation of Section 207 or 209, shall be punished by an additional term of nine years.

(b) A person convicted of a felony violation of subdivision (c) of Section 286, subdivision (c) of Section 287 or former Section 288a, or Section 288 who, for the purpose of committing that sexual offense, kidnapped the victim, who was under 14 years of age at the time of the offense, in violation of Section 207 or 209, shall be punished by an additional term of 15 years. This subdivision does not apply to conduct proscribed by Section 277, 278, or 278.5.

(c) The following shall govern the imposition of an enhancement pursuant to this section:

(1) Only one enhancement shall be imposed for a victim per incident.

(2) If there are two or more victims, one enhancement can be imposed for each victim per incident.

(3) The enhancement may be in addition to the punishment for either, but not both, of the following:

(A) A violation of Section 207 or 209.

(B) A violation of the sexual offenses enumerated in this section.

Amended by Stats 2021 ch 626 (AB 1171),s 33, eff. 1/1/2022.

Amended by Stats 2018 ch 423 (SB 1494),s 70, eff. 1/1/2019.

Section 667.85 - Punishment for person convicted of specified crime who kidnapped or carried away child under age of 14 years with intent to permanently deprive parent or legal guardian custody of child

Any person convicted of a violation of Section 207 or 209, who kidnapped or carried away any child under the age of 14 years with the intent to permanently deprive the parent or legal guardian custody of that child, shall be punished by imprisonment in the state prison for an additional five years.

Amended by Stats. 1997, Ch. 817, Sec. 11. Effective January 1, 1998.

Section 667.9 - Punishment for person who committed specified crimes against elderly or disabled person

(a) A person who commits one or more of the crimes specified in subdivision (c) against a person who is 65 years of age or older, or against a person who is blind, deaf, developmentally disabled, a paraplegic, or a quadriplegic, or against a person who is under 14 years of age, and that disability or condition is known or reasonably should be known to the person committing the crime, shall receive a one-year enhancement for each violation.

(b) A person who commits a violation of subdivision (a) and who has a prior conviction for any of the offenses specified in subdivision (c), shall receive a two-year enhancement for each violation in addition to the sentence provided under Section 667.

(c) Subdivisions (a) and (b) apply to the following crimes:

(1) Mayhem, in violation of Section 203 or 205.

(2) Kidnapping, in violation of Section 207, 209, or 209.5.

(3) Robbery, in violation of Section 211.

(4) Carjacking, in violation of Section 215.

(5) Rape, in violation of paragraph (2) or (6) of subdivision (a) of Section 261.

(6) Rape, in violation of paragraph (1) or (4) of subdivision (a) of former Section 262.

(7) Rape or sexual penetration in concert, in violation of Section 264.1.

(8) Sodomy, in violation of paragraph (2) or (3) of subdivision (c), or subdivision (d), of Section 286.

(9) Oral copulation, in violation of paragraph (2) or (3) of subdivision (c), or subdivision (d), of Section 287 or of former Section 288a.

(10) Sexual penetration, in violation of subdivision (a) of Section 289.

(11) Burglary of the first degree, as defined in Section 460, in violation of Section 459.

(d) As used in this section, "developmentally disabled" means a severe, chronic disability of a person, which is all of the following:

(1) Attributable to a mental or physical impairment or a combination of mental and physical impairments.

(2) Likely to continue indefinitely.

(3) Results in substantial functional limitation in three or more of the following areas of life activity:

(A) Self-care.

(B) Receptive and expressive language.

(C) Learning.

(D) Mobility.

(E) Self-direction.

(F) Capacity for independent living.

(G) Economic self-sufficiency.

Amended by Stats 2021 ch 626 (AB 1171),s 34, eff. 1/1/2022.

Amended by Stats 2018 ch 423 (SB 1494),s 71, eff. 1/1/2019.

EFFECTIVE 1/1/2000. Amended September 29, 1999 (Bill Number: AB 313) (Chapter 569).

Section 667.95 - Recording video as aggravating factor

In sentencing a person convicted of a violent felony listed in subdivision (c) of Section 667.5, the court may consider, as a factor in aggravation, that the defendant willfully recorded a video of the commission of the violent felony with the intent to encourage or facilitate the offense.

Added by Stats 2017 ch 668 (AB 1542),s 1, eff. 1/1/2018.

Section 667.10 - Punishment for person who committed crime of sexual penetration against person's will against elderly or disabled person

(a) Any person who has a prior conviction of the offense set forth in Section 289 and who commits that crime against a person who is 65 years of age or older, or against a person who is blind, deaf, developmentally disabled, as defined in subdivision (d) of Section 667.9, a paraplegic, or a quadriplegic, or against a person who is under the age of 14 years, and that disability or condition is known or reasonably should be known to the person committing the crime, shall receive a two-year enhancement for each violation in addition to the sentence provided under Section 289.

(b) The existence of any fact which would bring a person under subdivision (a) shall be alleged in the information or indictment and either admitted by the defendant in open court, or found to be true by the jury trying the issue of guilt or by the court where guilt is established by plea of guilty or nolo contendere or by trial by the court sitting without a jury.

Amended by Stats. 1992, Ch. 265, Sec. 3. Effective January 1, 1993.

Section 667.15 - Punishment for person who committed specified crimes and exhibits to minor any matter depicting person under age of 14 years engaging in or simulating sexual conduct

Any adult who, prior to or during the commission or attempted commission of a violation of Section 288 or 288.5, exhibits to the minor any matter, as defined in subdivision (d) of Section 311.11, the production of which involves the use of a person under the age of 14 years, knowing that the matter depicts a person under the age of 14 years personally engaging in or simulating sexual conduct, as defined in subdivision (d) of Section 311.4, with the intent of arousing, appealing to, or gratifying the lust, passions, or sexual desires of that person or of the minor, or with the intent, or for the purpose, of seducing the minor, shall be punished for a violation of this section as follows:

(a) If convicted of the commission or attempted commission of a violation of Section 288, the adult shall receive an additional term of one year, which punishment shall be imposed in addition and consecutive to the punishment imposed for the commission or attempted commission of a violation of Section 288.

(b) If convicted of the commission or attempted commission of a violation of Section 288.5, the adult shall receive an additional term of two years, which punishment shall be imposed in addition and consecutive to the punishment imposed for the commission or attempted commission of a violation of Section 288.5.

Added by Stats. 1993, Ch. 591, Sec. 1. Effective January 1, 1994.

Section 667.16 - Enhancement for person convicted of felony violation as part of plan or scheme to defraud owner of structure in connection with offer or performance of repairs for damage caused by natural disaster

(a) Any person convicted of a felony violation of Section 470, 487, or 532 as part of a plan or scheme to defraud an owner of a residential or nonresidential structure, including a mobilehome or manufactured home, in connection with the offer or performance of repairs or improvements to the structure or property, or by adding to, or subtracting from, grounds in connection therewith, for damage caused by a natural disaster, shall receive a one-year enhancement in addition and consecutive to the penalty prescribed. The additional term shall not be imposed unless the allegation is charged in the accusatory pleading and admitted by the defendant or found to be true by the trier of fact.

(b) This enhancement applies to natural disasters for which a state of emergency is proclaimed by the Governor pursuant to Section 8625 of the Government Code or for which an emergency or major disaster is declared by the President of the United States.

(c) Notwithstanding any other law, the court may strike the additional term provided in subdivision (a) if the court determines that there are mitigating circumstances and states on the record the reasons for striking the additional punishment.

Amended by Stats 2020 ch 364 (SB 1189),s 5, eff. 1/1/2021.

Section 667.17 - Punishment for violation of Section 538d during commission of felony

Any person who violates the provisions of Section 538d during the commission of a felony shall receive an additional one-year term of imprisonment to be imposed consecutive to the term imposed for the felony, in lieu of the penalty that would have been imposed under Section 538d.

Added by Stats. 1998, Ch. 279, Sec. 2. Effective January 1, 1999.

Section 668 - Prior conviction in other state, government, country, or jurisdiction

Every person who has been convicted in any other state, government, country, or jurisdiction of an offense for which, if committed within this state, that person could have been punished under the laws of this state by imprisonment in the state prison, is punishable for any subsequent crime committed within this state in the manner prescribed by law and to the same extent as if that prior conviction had taken place in a court of this state. The application of this section includes, but is not limited to, all statutes that provide for an enhancement or a term of imprisonment based on a prior conviction or a prior prison term or a term pursuant to subdivision (h) of Section 1170.

Amended by Stats 2011 ch 39 (AB 117),s 68, eff. 6/30/2011.

Amended by Stats 2011 ch 15 (AB 109),s 444, eff. 4/4/2011, but operative no earlier than October 1, 2011, and only upon creation of a community corrections grant program to assist in implementing this act and upon an appropriation to fund the grant program. Amended and effective September 7, 1999 (Bill Number: SB 786) (Chapter 350).

Section 668.5 - Prior felony conviction under predecessor statute

An offense specified as a prior felony conviction by reference to a specific code section shall include any prior felony conviction under any predecessor statute of that specified offense that includes all of the elements of that specified offense. The application of this section includes, but is not limited to, all statutes that provide for an enhancement or a term of imprisonment based on a prior conviction or a prior prison term.

Amended and effective 9/7/1999 (Bill Number: SB 786) (Chapter 350).

Section 669 - Conviction of two or more crimes

(a) When a person is convicted of two or more crimes, whether in the same proceeding or court or in different proceedings or courts, and whether by judgment rendered by the same judge or by different judges, the second or other subsequent judgment upon which sentence is ordered to be executed shall direct whether the terms of imprisonment or any of them to which he or she is sentenced shall run concurrently or consecutively. Life sentences, whether with or without the possibility of parole, may be imposed to run consecutively with one another, with any term imposed for applicable enhancements, or with any other term of imprisonment for a felony conviction. Whenever a person is committed to prison on a life sentence which is ordered to run consecutive to any determinate term of imprisonment, the determinate term of imprisonment shall be served first and no part thereof shall be credited toward the person's eligibility for parole as calculated pursuant to Section 3046 or pursuant to any other section of law that establishes a minimum period of confinement under the life sentence before eligibility for parole.

(b) In the event that the court at the time of pronouncing the second or other judgment upon that person had no knowledge of a prior existing judgment or judgments, or having knowledge, fails to determine how the terms of imprisonment shall run in relation to each other, then, upon that failure to determine, or upon that prior judgment or judgments being brought to the attention of the court at any time prior to the expiration of 60 days from and after the actual commencement of imprisonment upon the second or other subsequent judgments, the court shall, in the absence of the defendant and within 60 days of the notice, determine how the term of imprisonment upon the second or other subsequent judgment shall run with reference to the prior incompleted term or terms of imprisonment. Upon the failure of the court to determine how the terms of imprisonment on the second or subsequent judgment shall run, the term of imprisonment on the second or subsequent judgment shall run concurrently.

(c) The Department of Corrections and Rehabilitation shall advise the court pronouncing the second or other subsequent judgment of the existence of all prior judgments against the defendant, the terms of imprisonment of which have not been completely served.

(d) When a court imposes a concurrent term of imprisonment and imprisonment for one of the crimes is required to be served in the state prison, the term for all crimes shall be served in the state prison, even if the term for any other offense specifies imprisonment in a county jail pursuant to subdivision (h) of Section 1170.

Amended by Stats 2012 ch 43 (SB 1023),s 23, eff. 6/27/2012.

Section 670 - Punishment for violation of Business and Professions Code or Penal Code as part of plan to defraud owner or lessee in connection with repairs for damage caused by natural disaster

(a) Any person who violates Section 7158 or 7159 of, or subdivision (b), (c), (d), or (e) of Section 7161 of, the Business and Professions Code or Section 470, 484, 487, or 532 of this code as part of a plan or scheme to defraud an owner or lessee of a residential or nonresidential structure in connection with the offer or performance of repairs or improvements to the structure or property, or the adding to, or subtracting from, grounds in connection therewith, for damage or destruction caused by a natural disaster specified in subdivision (b), shall be subject to the penalties and enhancements specified in subdivisions (c) and (d). The existence of any fact which would bring a person under this section shall be alleged in the information or indictment and either admitted by the defendant in open court, or found to be true by the jury trying the issue of guilt or by the court where guilt is established by a plea of guilty or nolo contendere or by trial by the court sitting without a jury.

(b) This section applies to natural disasters for which a state of emergency is proclaimed by the Governor pursuant to Section 8625 of the Government Code or for which an emergency or major disaster is declared by the President of the United States.

(c) The maximum or prescribed amounts of fines for offenses subject to this section shall be doubled. If the person has been previously convicted of a felony offense specified in subdivision (a), the person shall receive a one-year enhancement in addition to, and to run consecutively to, the term of imprisonment for any felony otherwise prescribed by this subdivision.

(d) Additionally, the court shall order any person sentenced pursuant to this section to make full restitution to the victim or to make restitution to the victim based on the person's ability to pay, as defined in subdivision (e) of Section 1203.1b. The payment of the restitution ordered by the court pursuant to this subdivision shall be made a condition of any probation granted by the court for an offense punishable under this section. Notwithstanding any other provision of law, the period of probation shall be at least five years or until full restitution is made to the victim, whichever first occurs.

(e) Notwithstanding any other provision of law, the prosecuting agency shall be entitled to recover its costs of investigation and prosecution from any fines imposed for a conviction under this section.

Amended by Stats 2020 ch 364 (SB 1189),s 6, eff. 1/1/2021.

Amended by Stats 2016 ch 86 (SB 1171),s 226, eff. 1/1/2017.

Amended by Stats 2001 ch 854 (SB 205), s 38, eff. 1/1/2002.

Section 672 - Fine

Upon a conviction for any crime punishable by imprisonment in any jail or prison, in relation to which no fine is herein prescribed, the court may impose a fine on the offender not exceeding one thousand dollars ($1,000) in cases of misdemeanors or ten thousand dollars ($10,000) in cases of felonies, in addition to the imprisonment prescribed.

Amended by Stats. 1983, Ch. 1092, Sec. 320. Effective September 27, 1983. Operative January 1, 1984, by Sec. 427 of Ch. 1092.

Section 673 - Unlawful punishment or injury of prisoner, inmate, or person confined

It shall be unlawful to use in the reformatories, institutions, jails, state hospitals or any other state, county, or city institution any cruel, corporal or unusual punishment or to inflict any treatment or allow any lack of care whatever which would injure or impair the health of the prisoner, inmate, or person confined; and punishment by the use of the strait jacket, gag, thumbscrew, shower bath or the tricing up of a prisoner, inmate or person confined is hereby prohibited. Any person who violates the provisions of this section or who aids, abets, or attempts in any way to contribute to the violation of this section shall be guilty of a misdemeanor.

Added by renumbering Section 681 (as added by Stats. 1913, Ch. 583) by Stats. 1953, Ch. 615.

Section 674 - Punishment of primary care provider in day care facility who is convicted of specified crime where victim was minor entrusted to care

(a) Any person who is a primary care provider in a day care facility and who is convicted of a felony violation of Section 261, 285, 286, 287, 288, or 289 or former Section 288a, where the victim of the crime was a minor entrusted to his or her care by the minor's parent or guardian, a court, any public agency charged with the provision of social services, or a probation department, may be punished by an additional term of two years.

(b) If the crime described in subdivision (a) was committed while voluntarily acting in concert with another, the person so convicted may be punished by an additional term of three years.

(c) The enhancements authorized by this section may be imposed in addition to any other required or authorized enhancement.

Amended by Stats 2018 ch 423 (SB 1494),s 72, eff. 1/1/2019.

Section 675 - Punishment for felony conviction where offense was committed with minor for money or other consideration

(a) Any person suffering a felony conviction for a violation of subdivision (c) or (d) of Section 261.5, paragraph (1) or (2) of subdivision (b) or paragraph (1) of subdivision (c) of Section 286, paragraph (1) or (2) of subdivision (b) or paragraph (1) of subdivision (c) of Section 287 or former Section 288a, or subdivision (a) or paragraph (1) of subdivision (c) of Section 288, where the offense was committed with a minor for money or other consideration, is punishable by an additional term of imprisonment in the state prison of one year.

(b) The enhancements authorized by this section may be imposed in addition to any other required or authorized enhancement.

Amended by Stats 2018 ch 423 (SB 1494),s 73, eff. 1/1/2019.

Added by Stats 2004 ch 769 (AB 3042), s 1, eff. 1/1/2005.

Section 678 - Estimate of value of property

Whenever in this code the character or grade of an offense, or its punishment, is made to depend upon the value of property, such value shall be estimated exclusively in lawful money of the United States.

Amended by Stats. 1953, Ch. 616.

Title 17 - RIGHTS OF VICTIMS AND WITNESSES OF CRIME

Section 679 - Legislative intent

In recognition of the civil and moral duty of victims and witnesses of crime to fully and voluntarily cooperate with law enforcement and prosecutorial agencies, and in further recognition of the continuing importance of this citizen cooperation to state and local law enforcement efforts and the general effectiveness and well-being of the criminal justice system of this state, the Legislature declares its intent, in the enactment of this title, to ensure that all victims and witnesses of crime are treated with dignity, respect, courtesy, and sensitivity. It is the further intent that the rights enumerated in Section 679.02 relating to victims and witnesses of crime are honored and protected by law enforcement agencies, prosecutors, and judges in a manner no less vigorous than the protections afforded criminal defendants. It is the intent of the Legislature to add to Section 679.02 references to new rights as or as soon after they are created. The failure to enumerate in that section a right which is enumerated elsewhere in the law shall not be deemed to diminish the importance or enforceability of that right.

Added by Stats. 1986, Ch. 1427, Sec. 1.

Section 679.01 - Definitions

As used in this title, the following definitions shall control:

(a) "Crime" means an act committed in this state which, if committed by a competent adult, would constitute a misdemeanor or felony.

(b) "Victim" means a person against whom a crime has been committed.

(c) "Witness" means any person who has been or is expected to testify for the prosecution, or who, by reason of having relevant information, is subject to call or likely to be called as a witness for the prosecution, whether or not any action or proceeding has yet been commenced.

Added by Stats. 1986, Ch. 1427, Sec. 1.

Section 679.015 - Detention of victim of or witness to crime exclusively for actual or suspected immigration violation prohibited

(a) It is the public policy of this state to protect the public from crime and violence by encouraging all persons who are victims of or witnesses to crimes, or who otherwise can give evidence in a criminal investigation, to cooperate with the criminal justice system and not to penalize these persons for being victims or for cooperating with the criminal justice system.

(b) Whenever an individual who is a victim or witness to a crime, or who otherwise can give evidence in a criminal investigation, is not charged with or convicted of committing any crime under state law, a peace officer may not detain the individual exclusively for any actual or suspected immigration violation or turn the individual over to federal immigration authorities absent a judicial warrant.

Added by Stats 2017 ch 194 (AB 493),s 1, eff. 1/1/2018.

Section 679.02 - Statutory rights of victims and witnesses of crimes

(a) The following rights are hereby established as the statutory rights of victims and witnesses of crimes:

(1) To be notified as soon as feasible that a court proceeding to which the victim or witness has been subpoenaed as a witness will not proceed as scheduled, provided the prosecuting attorney determines that the witness' attendance is not required.

(2) Upon request of the victim or a witness, to be informed by the prosecuting attorney of the final disposition of the case, as provided by Section 11116.10.

(3) For the victim, the victim's parents or guardian if the victim is a minor, or the next of kin of the victim if the victim has died, to be notified of all sentencing proceedings, and of the right to appear, to reasonably express their views, have those views preserved by audio or video means as provided in Section 1191.16, and to have the court consider their statements, as provided by Sections 1191.1 and 1191.15.

(4) For the victim, the victim's parents or guardian if the victim is a minor, or the next of kin of the victim if the victim has died, to be notified of all juvenile disposition hearings in which the alleged act would have been a felony if committed by an adult, and of the right to attend and to express their views, as provided by Section 656.2 of the Welfare and Institutions Code.

(5) Upon request by the victim or the next of kin of the victim if the victim has died, to be notified of any parole eligibility hearing and of the right to appear, either personally as provided by Section 3043, or by other means as provided by Sections 3043.2 and 3043.25, to reasonably express their views, and to have their statements considered, as provided by Section 3043 of this code and by Section 1767 of the Welfare and Institutions Code.

(6) Upon request by the victim or the next of kin of the victim if the crime was a homicide, to be notified of an inmate's placement in a reentry or work furlough program, or notified of the inmate's escape as provided by Section 11155.

(7) To be notified that a witness may be entitled to witness fees and mileage, as provided by Section 1329.1.

(8) For the victim, to be provided with information concerning the victim's right to civil recovery and the opportunity to be compensated from the Restitution Fund pursuant to Chapter 5 (commencing with Section 13959) of Part 4 of Division 3 of Title 2 of the Government Code and Section 1191.2 of this code.

(9) To the expeditious return of property that has allegedly been stolen or embezzled, when it is no longer needed as evidence, as provided by Chapter 12 (commencing with Section 1407) and Chapter 13 (commencing with Section 1417) of Title 10 of Part 2.

(10) To an expeditious disposition of the criminal action.

(11) To be notified, if applicable, in accordance with Sections 679.03 and 3058.8 if the defendant is to be placed on parole.

(12) For the victim, upon request, to be notified of any pretrial disposition of the case, to the extent required by Section 28 of Article I of the California Constitution.

　　(A) A victim may request to be notified of a pretrial disposition.

　　(B) The victim may be notified by any reasonable means available.

　　(C) This paragraph is not intended to affect the right of the people and the defendant to an expeditious disposition as provided in Section 1050.

(13) For the victim, to be notified by the district attorney's office of the right to request, upon a form provided by the district attorney's office, and receive a notice pursuant to paragraph (14), if the defendant is convicted of any of the following offenses:

　　(A) Assault with intent to commit rape, sodomy, oral copulation, or any violation of Section 264.1, 288, or 289, in violation of Section 220.

　　(B) A violation of Section 207 or 209 committed with the intent to commit a violation of Section 261, 286, 287, 288, or 289, or former Section 262 or 288a.

　　(C) Rape, in violation of Section 261.

　　(D) Oral copulation, in violation of Section 287 or former Section 288a.

　　(E) Sodomy, in violation of Section 286.

　　(F) A violation of Section 288.

　　(G) A violation of Section 289.

(14) When a victim has requested notification pursuant to paragraph (13), the sheriff shall inform the victim that the person who was convicted of the offense has been ordered to be placed on probation, and give the victim notice of the proposed date upon which the person will be released from the custody of the sheriff.

(15) For the victim, to be notified of the availability of community-based restorative justice programs and processes available to them, including, but not limited to, programs serving their community, county, county jails, juvenile detention facilities, and the Department of Corrections and Rehabilitation. The victim has a right to be notified as early and often as possible, including during the initial contact, during followup investigation, at the point of diversion, throughout the process of the case, and in postconviction proceedings.

(b) The rights set forth in subdivision (a) shall be set forth in the information and educational materials prepared pursuant to Section 13897.1. The information and educational materials shall be distributed to local law enforcement agencies and local victims' programs by the Victims' Legal Resource Center established pursuant to Chapter 11 (commencing with Section 13897) of Title 6 of Part 4.

(c) Local law enforcement agencies shall make available copies of the materials described in subdivision (b) to victims and witnesses.

(d) This section is not intended to affect the rights and services provided to victims and witnesses by the local assistance centers for victims and witnesses.

(e) The court shall not release statements made pursuant to paragraph (3) or (4) of subdivision (a) to the public prior to the statement being heard in court.

Amended by Stats 2023 ch 513 (AB 60),s 2, eff. 1/1/2024.

Amended by Stats 2021 ch 626 (AB 1171),s 35, eff. 1/1/2022.

Amended by Stats 2018 ch 423 (SB 1494),s 74, eff. 1/1/2019.

Amended by Stats 2011 ch 77 (AB 886),s 1, eff. 1/1/2012.

Amended by Stats 2009 ch 12 (AB X4-12),s 28, eff. 7/28/2009.

Section 679.026 - "Marsy Rights" card; Victims' Survival and Resource Guide

(a) It is the intent of the people of the State of California in enacting this section to implement the rights of victims of crime established in Section 28 of Article I of the California Constitution to be informed of the rights of crime victims enumerated in the Constitution and in the statutes of this state.

(b) Every victim of crime has the right to receive without cost or charge a list of the rights of victims of crime recognized in Section 28 of Article I of the California Constitution. These rights shall be known as "Marsy Rights."

(c)

(1) Every law enforcement agency investigating a criminal act and every agency prosecuting a criminal act shall, as provided herein, at the time of initial contact with a crime victim, during follow-up investigation, or as soon thereafter as deemed appropriate by investigating officers or prosecuting attorneys, provide or make available to each victim of the criminal act without charge or cost a "Marsy Rights" card described in paragraphs (3) and (4).

(2) The victim disclosures required under this section shall be available to the public at a state funded and maintained Web site authorized pursuant to Section 14260 of the Penal Code to be known as "Marsy's Page."

(3) The Attorney General shall design and make available in ".pdf" or other imaging format to every agency listed in paragraph (1) a "Marsy Rights" card, which shall contain the rights of crime victims described in subdivision (b) of Section 28 of Article I of the California Constitution, information on the means by which a crime victim can access the web page described in paragraph (2), and a toll-free telephone number to enable a crime victim to contact a local victim's assistance office.

(4) Every law enforcement agency which investigates criminal activity shall, if provided without cost to the agency by any organization classified as a nonprofit organization under paragraph (3) of subdivision (c) of Section 501 of the Internal Revenue Code, make available and provide to every crime victim a "Victims' Survival and Resource Guide" pamphlet and/or video that has been approved by the Attorney General. The "Victims' Survival and Resource Guide" and video shall include an approved "Marsy Rights" card, a list of government agencies, nonprofit victims' rights groups, support groups, and local resources that assist crime victims, and any other information which the Attorney General determines might be helpful to victims of crime.

(5) Any agency described in paragraph (1) may in its discretion design and distribute to each victim of a criminal act its own Victims' Survival and Resource Guide and video, the contents of which have been approved by the Attorney General, in addition to or in lieu of the materials described in paragraph (4).

Added November 4, 2008, by initiative Proposition 9, Sec. 6.1. Note: Prop. 9 is titled the Victims' Bill of Rights Act of 2008: Marsy's Law.

Added by Proposition 9, approved by the voters 11/4/2008, effective 11/5/2008.

Section 679.027 - [For Operative Date See Text] Informing victims of rights; "Victim Protections and Resources" card ; contents

(a) Every law enforcement agency investigating a criminal act and every agency prosecuting a criminal act shall, as provided herein, at the time of initial contact with a crime victim, during followup investigation, or as soon thereafter as deemed appropriate by investigating officers or prosecuting attorneys, inform each victim, or the victim's next of kin if the victim is deceased, of the rights they may have under applicable law relating to the victimization, including rights relating to housing, employment, compensation, and immigration relief.

(b)

(1) Every law enforcement agency investigating a criminal act and every agency prosecuting a criminal act shall, as provided herein, at the time of initial contact with a crime victim, during followup investigation, or as soon thereafter as deemed appropriate by investigating officers or prosecuting attorneys, provide or make available to each victim of the criminal act without charge or cost a "Victim Protections and Resources" card described in paragraph (3).

(2) The Victim Protections and Resources card may be designed as part of and included with the "Marsy Rights" card described by Section 679.026.

(3) By June 1, 2025, the Attorney General shall design and make available in PDF or other imaging format to every agency listed in paragraph (1) a "Victim Protections and Resources" card, which shall contain information in lay terms about victim rights and resources, including, but not limited to, the following:

(A) Information about the rights provided by Sections 230 and 230.1 of the Labor Code.

(B) Information about the rights provided by Section 1946.7 of the Civil Code.

(C) Information about the rights provided by Section 1161.3 of the Civil Code, including information in lay terms about which crimes and tenants are eligible and under what circumstances.

(D) Information about federal immigration relief available to certain victims of crime.

(E) Information about the program established by Chapter 5 (commencing with Section 13950) of Part 4 of Division 3 of Title 2 of the Government Code, including information about the types of expenses the program may reimburse, eligibility, and how to apply.

(F) Information about the program established by Chapter 3.1 (commencing with Section 6205) of Division 7 of Title 1 of the Government Code.

(G) Information about eligibility for filing a restraining or protective order.

(H) Contact information for the Victims' Legal Resource Center established by Chapter 11 (commencing with Section 13897) of Title 6 of Part 4.

(I) A list of trauma recovery centers funded by the state pursuant to Section 13963.1 of the Government Code, with their contact information, which shall be updated annually.

(J) The availability of community-based restorative justice programs and processes available to them, including programs serving their community, county, county jails, juvenile detention facilities, and the Department of Corrections and Rehabilitation.

(c) This section shall become operative on July 1, 2024, only if General Fund moneys over the multiyear forecasts beginning in the 2024-25 fiscal year are available to support ongoing augmentations and actions, and if an appropriation is made to backfill the Restitution Fund to support the actions in this section.

Amended by Stats 2023 ch 513 (AB 60),s 3, eff. 1/1/2024.

Amended by Stats 2023 ch 311 (SB 883),s 5, eff. 1/1/2024.

Added by Stats 2022 ch 771 (AB 160),s 15, eff. 9/29/2022.

Section 679.03 - Right to request and receive notice of release, escape, scheduled execution, or death of violent offender

(a) With respect to the conviction of a defendant involving a violent offense, as defined in Section 29905, the county district attorney, probation department, and victim-witness coordinator shall confer and establish an annual policy within existing resources to decide which one of their agencies shall inform each witness involved in the conviction who was threatened by the defendant following the defendant's arrest and each victim or next of kin of the victim of that offense of the right to request and receive a notice pursuant to Section 3058.8 or 3605. If no agreement is reached, the presiding judge shall designate the appropriate county agency or department to provide this notification.

(b) The Department of Corrections and Rehabilitation shall supply a form to the agency designated pursuant to subdivision (a) in order to enable persons specified in subdivision (a) to request and receive notification from the department of the release, escape, scheduled execution, or death of the violent offender. That agency shall give the form to the victim, witness, or next of kin of the victim for completion, explain to that person or persons the right to be so notified, and forward the completed form to the department. The department or the Board of Parole Hearings is responsible for notifying all victims, witnesses, or next of kin of victims who request to be notified of a violent offender's release or scheduled execution, as provided by Sections 3058.8 and 3605.

(c) All information relating to any person receiving notice pursuant to subdivision (b) shall remain confidential and is not subject to disclosure pursuant to the California Public Records Act (Division 10 (commencing with Section 7920.000) of Title 1 of the Government Code).

(d) Nothing in this section precludes a victim, witness, or next of kin of the victim from requesting notification using an automated electronic notification process, if available.

Amended by Stats 2021 ch 615 (AB 474),s 337, eff. 1/1/2022, op. 1/1/2023.

Amended by Stats 2011 ch 364 (SB 852),s 2, eff. 9/29/2011.

Amended by Stats 2010 ch 178 (SB 1115),s 65, eff. 1/1/2011, op. 1/1/2012.

Section 679.04 - Right of victim of sexual assault to have victim advocates and support person

(a) A victim of sexual assault as the result of any offense specified in paragraph (1) of subdivision (b) of Section 264.2 has the right to have victim advocates and a support person of the victim's choosing present at any interview by law enforcement authorities, district attorneys, or defense attorneys. A victim retains this right regardless of whether he or she has waived the right in a previous medical evidentiary or physical examination or in a previous interview by law enforcement authorities, district attorneys, or defense attorneys. However, the support person may be excluded from an interview by law enforcement or the district attorney if the law enforcement authority or the district attorney determines that the presence of that individual would be detrimental to the purpose of the interview. As used in this section, "victim advocate" means a sexual assault counselor, as defined in Section 1035.2 of the Evidence Code, or a victim advocate working in a center established under Article 2 (commencing with Section 13835) of Chapter 4 of Title 6 of Part 4.

(b)

(1) Prior to the commencement of the initial interview by law enforcement authorities or the district attorney pertaining to any criminal action arising out of a sexual assault, a victim of sexual assault as the result of any offense specified in Section 264.2 shall be notified in writing by the attending law enforcement authority or district attorney that he or she has the right to have victim advocates and a support person of the victim's choosing present at the interview or contact, about any other rights of the victim pursuant to law in the card described in subdivision (a) of Section 680.2, and that the victim has the right to request to have a person of the same gender or opposite gender as the victim present in the room during any interview with a law enforcement official or district attorney, unless no such person is reasonably available. This subdivision applies to investigators and agents employed or retained by law enforcement or the district attorney.

(2) At the time the victim is advised of his or her rights pursuant to paragraph (1), the attending law enforcement authority or district attorney shall also advise the victim of the right to have victim advocates and a support person present at any interview by the defense attorney or investigators or agents employed by the defense attorney.

(3) The presence of a victim advocate shall not defeat any existing right otherwise guaranteed by law. A victim's waiver of the right to a victim advocate is inadmissible in court, unless a court determines the waiver is at issue in the pending litigation.

(4) The victim has the right to request to have a person of the same gender or opposite gender as the victim present in the room during any interview with a law enforcement official or district attorney, unless no such person is reasonably available. It is the intent of the Legislature to encourage every interviewer in this context to have trauma-based training.

(c) An initial investigation by law enforcement to determine whether a crime has been committed and the identity of the suspects shall not constitute a law enforcement interview for purposes of this section.

(d) A law enforcement official shall not, for any reason, discourage a victim of an alleged sexual assault from receiving a medical evidentiary or physical examination.

Amended by Stats 2017 ch 692 (AB 1312),s 2, eff. 1/1/2018.

Amended by Stats 2006 ch 689 (SB 1743),s 12, eff. 1/1/2007.

Section 679.05 - Right of victim of domestic violence or abuse to have domestic violence advocate and support person

(a) A victim of domestic violence or abuse, as defined in Sections 6203 or 6211 of the Family Code, or Section 13700 of the Penal Code, has the right to have a domestic violence advocate and a support person of the victim's choosing present at any interview by law enforcement authorities, prosecutors, or defense attorneys. However, the support person may be excluded from an interview by law enforcement or the prosecutor if the law enforcement authority or the prosecutor determines that the presence of that individual would be detrimental to the purpose of the interview. As used in this section, "domestic violence advocate" means either a person employed by a program specified in Section 13835.2 for the purpose of rendering advice or assistance to victims of domestic violence, or a domestic violence counselor, as defined in Section 1037.1 of the Evidence Code. Prior to being present at any interview conducted by law enforcement authorities, prosecutors, or defense attorneys, a domestic violence advocate shall advise the victim of any applicable limitations on the confidentiality of communications between the victim and the domestic violence advocate.

(b)

(1) Prior to the commencement of the initial interview by law enforcement authorities or the prosecutor pertaining to any criminal action arising out of a domestic violence incident, a victim of domestic violence or abuse, as defined in Section 6203 or 6211 of the Family Code, or Section 13700 of this code, shall be notified orally or in writing by the attending law enforcement authority or prosecutor that the victim has the right to have a domestic violence advocate and a support person of the victim's choosing present at the interview or contact. This subdivision applies to investigators and agents employed or retained by law enforcement or the prosecutor.

(2) At the time the victim is advised of his or her rights pursuant to paragraph (1), the attending law enforcement authority or prosecutor shall also advise the victim of the right to have a domestic violence advocate and a support person present at any interview by the defense attorney or investigators or agents employed by the defense attorney.

(c) An initial investigation by law enforcement to determine whether a crime has been committed and the identity of the suspects shall not constitute a law enforcement interview for purposes of this section.

Amended by Stats 2007 ch 206 (SB 407),s 6, eff. 1/1/2008.

Amended by Stats 2005 ch 279 (SB 1107),s 6, eff. 1/1/2006

Amended by Stats 2005 ch 22 (SB 1108),s 149, eff. 1/1/2006

Added by Stats 2004 ch 159 (SB 1441), s 1, eff. 1/1/2005.

Section 679.06 - Notification of release to victims of domestic violence and stalking

(a) The county probation department shall notify a victim of domestic violence or abuse, as defined in Section 13700 or in Section 6203 or 6211 of the Family Code, or a victim of stalking, as defined in Section 646.9, of the perpetrator's current community of residence or proposed community of residence upon release, when the perpetrator, after conviction, is placed on or being released on probation pursuant to subdivision (a) of Section 1203 and under the supervision of the county probation department.

(b) Subdivision (a) shall only apply if the victim has requested notification and has provided the probation department with a current address at which they may be notified.

(c) The district attorney shall advise every victim described in subdivision (a) of their right to request and receive notification pursuant to this section.

Added by Stats 2022 ch 941 (AB 547),s 1, eff. 1/1/2023.

Section 679.08 - Victim's rights card

(a)

(1) Whenever there has been a crime committed against a victim, the law enforcement officer assigned to the case may provide the victim of the crime with a "Victim's Rights Card," as specified in subdivision (b).

(2) This section shall be operative in a city or county only upon the adoption of a resolution by the city council or board of supervisors to that effect.

(3) This section shall not be interpreted as replacing or prohibiting any services currently offered to victims of crime by any agency or person affected by this section.

(b) A "Victim's Rights Card" means a card or paper that provides a printed notice with a disclaimer, in at least 10-point type, to a victim of a crime regarding potential services that may be available under existing state law to assist the victim. The printed notice shall include the following language or language substantially similar to the following: "California law provides crime victims with important rights. If you are a victim of crime, you may be entitled to the assistance of a victim advocate who can answer many of the questions you might have about the criminal justice system."

"Victim advocates can assist you with the following:

(1) Explaining what information you are entitled to receive while criminal proceedings are pending.

(2) Assisting you in applying for restitution to compensate you for crime-related losses.

(3) Communicating with the prosecution.

(4) Assisting you in receiving victim support services.

(5) Helping you prepare a victim impact statement before an offender is sentenced." "To speak with a victim advocate, please call any of the following numbers:"

[Set forth the name and phone number, including area code, of all victim advocate agencies in the local jurisdiction]

"PLEASE NOTE THAT THIS INFORMATION IS PROVIDED IN AN ATTEMPT TO ASSIST THE VICTIM, BY NOTIFYING THE VICTIM ABOUT SOME, BUT NOT NECESSARILY ALL, SERVICES AVAILABLE TO THE VICTIM; THE PROVISION OF THIS INFORMATION AND THE

INFORMATION CONTAINED THEREIN IS NOT LEGAL ADVICE AND IS NOT INTENDED TO CONSTITUTE A GUARANTEE OF ANY VICTIM'S RIGHTS OR OF A VICTIM'S ELIGIBILITY OR ENTITLEMENT TO ANY SPECIFIC BENEFITS OR SERVICES."

(c) Any act or omission covered by this section is a discretionary act pursuant to Section 820.2 of the Government Code.

Added by Stats 2006 ch 94 (AB 2705),s 1, eff. 1/1/2007.

Section 679.09 - Victims of crime; family access to information

(a)In the event of a death of a minor being investigated by law enforcement, the law enforcement agency that bears the primary responsibility for the investigation shall provide the victim's parent or guardian, with the following information, if and when the parent or guardian are located:

(1)Contact information for each law enforcement agency involved in the investigation and the identification of the primary contact, if known, for the particular investigation at the involved law enforcement agency.

(2)The case number referencing the investigation, if applicable.

(3)A list of the personal effects found with the minor and contact information necessary to permit an immediate family member to collect the victim's personal effects collected pursuant to Section 27491.3 of the Government Code. The list of the victim's personal effects may be withheld from the immediate family if providing information about the personal effects would interfere with the investigation being conducted by law enforcement.

(4)Information regarding the status of the investigation, at the discretion of the law enforcement agency.

(b)In the event that a parent or guardian is not located, the law enforcement agency that bears the primary responsibility for the investigation shall provide the victim's immediate family, at their request, with the following information:

(1)Contact information for each law enforcement agency involved in the investigation and the identification of the primary contact, if known, for the particular investigation at the involved law enforcement agency.

(2)The case number referencing the investigation, if applicable.

(3)A list of the personal effects found with the minor and contact information necessary to permit an immediate family member to collect the victim's personal effects collected pursuant to Section 27491.3 of the Government Code. The list of victim's personal effects may be withheld from the immediate family if providing information about the personal effects would interfere with the investigation being conducted by law enforcement.

(4)Information regarding the status of the investigation, at the discretion of the law enforcement agency.

(c)Law enforcement shall not be required to provide any information that would jeopardize or otherwise allow an individual to interfere with the ongoing investigation. This section shall not be interpreted to require law enforcement to provide investigative records generated pursuant to their investigation for inspection by a victim's immediate family.

(d)This section does not require law enforcement agencies to provide more than one copy of the information provided pursuant to this section to immediate family.

(e)Law enforcement agencies providing information pursuant to this section may require any family member receiving the information to confirm their identity through a certified declaration. Any person knowingly or willingly making a false certification for a declaration pursuant to this subdivision shall be punishable by an infraction.

(f)For the purposes of this section, "immediate family" means the victim's spouse, parent, guardian, grandparent, aunt, uncle, brother, sister, and children or grandchildren who are related by blood, marriage, or adoption.

Added by Stats 2022 ch 227 (SB 1268),s 1, eff. 1/1/2023.

Section 679.10 - Certification of victim helpfulness

(a) For purposes of this section, a "certifying entity" is any of the following:

(1) A state or local law enforcement agency, including, without limitation, the police department of the University of California, a California State University campus, or the police department of a school district, established pursuant to Section 38000 of the Education Code.

(2) A prosecutor.

(3) A judge.

(4) Any other authority that has responsibility for the detection or investigation or prosecution of a qualifying crime or criminal activity.

(5) Agencies that have criminal detection or investigative jurisdiction in their respective areas of expertise, including, but not limited to, child protective services, the Civil Rights Department, and the Department of Industrial Relations.

(b) For purposes of this section, a "certifying official" is any of the following:

(1) The head of the certifying entity.

(2) A person in a supervisory role who has been specifically designated by the head of the certifying entity to issue Form I-918 Supplement B certifications on behalf of that agency.

(3) A judge.

(4) Any other certifying official defined under Section 214.14 (a)(2) of Title 8 of the Code of Federal Regulations.

(c) "Qualifying criminal activity" has the same meaning as qualifying criminal activity pursuant to Section 101(a)(15)(U)(iii) of the federal Immigration and Nationality Act which includes, but is not limited to, the following crimes:

(1) Rape.

(2) Torture.

(3) Human trafficking.

(4) Incest.

(5) Domestic violence.

(6) Sexual assault.

(7) Abusive sexual conduct.

(8) Prostitution.

(9) Sexual exploitation.

(10) Female genital mutilation.

(11) Being held hostage.

(12) Peonage.

(13) Perjury.

(14) Involuntary servitude.

(15) Slavery.

(16) Kidnapping.

(17) Abduction.

(18) Unlawful criminal restraint.

(19) False imprisonment.

(20) Blackmail.

(21) Extortion.

(22) Manslaughter.

(23) Murder.

(24) Felonious assault.

(25) Witness tampering.

(26) Obstruction of justice.

(27) Fraud in foreign labor contracting.

(28) Stalking.

(d) A "qualifying crime" includes criminal offenses for which the nature and elements of the offenses are substantially similar to the criminal activity described in subdivision (c), and the attempt, conspiracy, or solicitation to commit any of those offenses.

(e) A "representative fully accredited by the United States Department of Justice" is a person who is approved by the United States Department of Justice to represent individuals before the Board of Immigration Appeals, the immigration courts, or the Department of Homeland Security. The representative shall be a person who works for a specific nonprofit, religious, charitable, social service, or similar organization that has been recognized by the United States Department of Justice to represent those individuals and whose accreditation is in good standing.

(f) Upon the request of a victim, licensed attorney representing the victim, or representative fully accredited by the United States Department of Justice authorized to represent the victim in immigration proceedings, a state or local law enforcement agency with whom the victim had filed a police report shall provide a copy of the police report within seven days of the request.

(g)

(1) Upon the request of the victim, victim's family member, licensed attorney representing the victim, or representative fully accredited by the United States Department of Justice authorized to represent the victim in immigration proceedings, a certifying official from a certifying entity shall certify victim helpfulness on the Form I-918 Supplement B certification, when the victim was a victim of a qualifying criminal activity and has been helpful, is being helpful, or is likely to be helpful to the detection or investigation or prosecution of that qualifying criminal activity. The certifying entity shall forward completed Form I-918 Supplemental B certification to the victim, victim's family member, licensed attorney representing the victim, or representative fully accredited by the United States Department of Justice authorized to represent the victim in immigration proceedings without requiring the victim to provide government-issued identification.

(2) A victim who submits a Form I-918 Supplement B certification to a certifying entity does not have to be present in the United States at time of submitting the certification request or filing the petition with the government and may apply for certification while outside of the United States.

(h) For purposes of determining helpfulness pursuant to subdivision (g), there is a rebuttable presumption that a victim is helpful, has been helpful, or is likely to be helpful to the detection or investigation or prosecution of that qualifying criminal activity, if the victim has not refused or failed to provide information and assistance reasonably requested by law enforcement. If the victim reasonably asserts they were unaware of a request for cooperation, their failure to cooperate does not rebut the presumption of helpfulness.

(i)

(1) The certifying official shall fully complete and sign the Form I-918 Supplement B certification and, regarding victim helpfulness, include specific details about the nature of the crime investigated or prosecuted and a detailed description of the victim's helpfulness or likely helpfulness to the detection or investigation or prosecution of the criminal activity.

(2) If a certifying entity does not certify a Form I-918 Supplement B certification, they shall provide a written explanation for the denial of the Form I-918 Supplement B certification. The written denial shall include specific details of any reasonable requests for cooperation and a detailed description of how the victim refused to cooperate.

(j)

(1) A certifying entity shall process a Form I-918 Supplement B certification within 30 days of request, unless the noncitizen is in removal proceedings, in which case the certification shall be processed within 7 days of the first business day following the day the request was received.

(2) A certifying agency shall process a Form I-918 Supplement B certification within 7 days of the first business day following the day the request was received if the victim asserts a qualifying family member of the victim will lose eligibility for U nonimmigrant status in 60 days or fewer because the victim's noncitizen sibling will turn 18 years of age, the victim's noncitizen child will turn 21 years of age, or the victim will turn 21 years of age.

(k)

(1) A current investigation, the filing of charges, an apprehension of the suspect who committed the qualifying crime, closing of a case, and a prosecution or conviction are not required for the victim to request and obtain the Form I-918 Supplement B certification from a certifying official.

(2) A certifying official shall not refuse to complete the Form I-918 Supplement B certification or to otherwise certify that a victim has been helpful, solely because a case has already been prosecuted or otherwise closed, or because the time for commencing a criminal action has expired.

(3) A certifying entity shall not refuse to complete the Form I-918 Supplement B certification and provide it to the victim, the victim's family member, licensed attorney representing the victim, or representative fully accredited by the United States Department of Justice authorized to represent the victim in immigration proceedings for any of the following reasons:

(A) The victim's criminal history information.

(B) The victim's immigration history.

(C) The victim's gang membership or gang affiliation.

(D) The certifying entity's belief that the Form I-918 Supplement B petition will not be approved by United States Citizenship and Immigration Services.

(E) The victim has an open case with another certifying entity.

(F) The extent of the harm the victim suffered.

(G) The victim's inability to produce a crime report from a law enforcement agency.

(H) The victim's cooperation or refusal to cooperate in a separate case.

(l) A certifying official may only withdraw the certification if the victim refuses to provide information and assistance when reasonably requested.

(m) A certifying entity is prohibited from disclosing the immigration status of a victim or person requesting the Form I-918 Supplement B certification, except to comply with federal law or legal process, or if authorized by the victim or person requesting the Form I-918 Supplement B certification.

(n) A certifying entity that receives a request for a Form I-918 Supplement B certification shall report to the Legislature, on or before January 1, 2017, and annually thereafter, the number of victims that requested Form I-918 Supplement B certifications from the entity, the number of those certification forms that were signed, and the number that were denied. A report pursuant to this subdivision shall comply with Section 9795 of the Government Code.

(o)

(1) A certifying entity may certify a Form I-918 Supplement B certification for direct victims, indirect victims, and bystander or witness victims.

(2) A direct victim is any person who has suffered direct harm or who is directly and proximately harmed as a result of the criminal activity.

(3)

(A) An indirect victim is a qualifying family member of a direct victim if the direct victim is incompetent, incapacitated, or deceased, including spouses, unmarried children under the age of 21, parents if the direct victim was under the age of 21, and siblings under the age of 18 if the direct victim was under 21 years of age. Indirect victims shall cooperate in the investigation or prosecution but are not required to possess information about the crime itself.

(B) Indirect victim cooperation includes parents who make their children available to communicate with the certifying entity.

(4) A bystander or witness victim is any individual who was not the direct target of a crime, but who nevertheless suffered unusually direct injury as a result of the qualifying crime.

Amended by Stats 2023 ch 679 (AB 1261),s 1, eff. 1/1/2024.
Amended by Stats 2022 ch 48 (SB 189),s 72, eff. 6/30/2022.
Amended by Stats 2020 ch 187 (AB 2426),s 1, eff. 1/1/2021.
Amended by Stats 2019 ch 576 (AB 917),s 1, eff. 1/1/2020.
Amended by Stats 2016 ch 86 (SB 1171),s 227, eff. 1/1/2017.
Added by Stats 2015 ch 721 (SB 674),s 1, eff. 1/1/2016.

Section 679.11 - Certification of victim cooperation for federal Form I-914

(a) For purposes of this section, a "certifying entity" is any of the following:

(1) A state or local law enforcement agency, including, without limitation, the police department of the University of California, a California State University campus, or the police department of a school district, established pursuant to Section 38000 of the Education Code.

(2) A prosecutor.

(3) A judge.

(4) The Department of Industrial Relations.

(5) Any other state or local government agencies that have criminal, civil, or administrative investigative or prosecutorial authority relating to human trafficking.

(b) For purposes of this section, a "certifying official" is any of the following:

(1) The head of the certifying entity.

(2) A person in a supervisory role who has been specifically designated by the head of the certifying entity to issue Form I-914 Supplement B declarations on behalf of that agency.

(3) A judge.

(4) Any other certifying official defined under Section 214.14(a)(2) of Title 8 of the Code of Federal Regulations.

(c) "Human trafficking" has the same meaning as "severe forms of trafficking in persons" pursuant to Section 7102 of Title 22 of the United States Code and includes either of the following:

(1) Sex trafficking in which a commercial sex act is induced by force, fraud, or coercion, or in which the person induced to perform such act has not attained 18 years of age.

(2) The recruitment, harboring, transportation, provision, or obtaining of a person for labor or services, through the use of force, fraud, or coercion for the purpose of subjection to involuntary servitude, peonage, debt bondage, or slavery.

(d) "Human trafficking" also includes criminal offenses for which the nature and elements of the offenses are substantially similar to the criminal activity described in subdivision (c), and the attempt, conspiracy, or solicitation to commit any of those offenses.

(e) A "representative fully accredited by the United States Department of Justice" is a person who is approved by the United States Department of Justice to represent individuals before the Board of Immigration Appeals, the immigration courts, or the Department of Homeland Security. The representative shall be a person who works for a specific nonprofit, religious, charitable, social service, or similar organization that has been recognized by the United States Department of Justice to represent those individuals and whose accreditation is in good standing.

(f)

   (1) Upon the request of the victim, victim's family member, licensed attorney representing the victim, or representative fully accredited by the United States Department of Justice authorized to represent the victim in immigration proceedings, a certifying official from a certifying entity shall certify victim cooperation on the Form I-914 Supplement B declaration, when the victim was a victim of human trafficking and has been cooperative, is being cooperative, or is likely to be cooperative to the investigation or prosecution of human trafficking. The certifying entity shall forward completed Form I-914 Supplemental B certification to the victim, victim's family member, licensed attorney representing the victim, or representative fully accredited by the United States Department of Justice authorized to represent the victim in immigration proceedings without requiring the victim to provide government-issued identification.

   (2) A victim who submits a Form I-914 Supplement B declaration to a certifying entity does not have to be present in the United States at time of submitting the certification request or filing the petition with the government and may apply for certification while outside of the United States.

(g) For purposes of determining cooperation pursuant to subdivision (f), there is a rebuttable presumption that a victim is cooperative, has been cooperative, or is likely to be cooperative to the investigation or prosecution of human trafficking, if the victim has not refused or failed to provide information and assistance reasonably requested by law enforcement. If the victim reasonably asserts they were unaware of a request for cooperation, their failure to cooperate does not rebut the presumption of helpfulness.

(h) The certifying official shall fully complete and sign the Form I-914 Supplement B declaration and, regarding victim cooperation, include specific details about the nature of the crime investigated or prosecuted and a detailed description of the victim's cooperation or likely cooperation to the detection, investigation, or prosecution of the criminal activity.

(i)

   (1) A certifying entity shall process a Form I-914 Supplement B declaration within 30 days of request, unless the noncitizen is in removal proceedings, in which case the declaration shall be processed within 7 days of the first business day following the day the request was received.

   (2) A certifying agency shall process a Form I-918 Supplement B certification within 7 days of the first business day following the day the request was received if the victim asserts a qualifying family member of the victim will lose eligibility for T nonimmigrant status in 60 days or fewer because the victim's noncitizen sibling will turn 18 years of age, the victim's noncitizen child will turn 21 years of age, or the victim will turn 21 years of age.

(j)

   (1) A current investigation, an apprehension of the suspect who committed the qualifying crime, the filing of charges, closing of a case, or a prosecution or conviction is not required for the victim to request and obtain the Form I-914 Supplement B declaration from a certifying official.

   (2) A certifying official shall not refuse to complete the Form I-914 Supplement B declaration and provide it to the victim, the victim's family member, licensed attorney representing the victim, or representative fully accredited by the United States Department of Justice authorized to represent the victim in immigration proceedings or to otherwise certify that a victim has been helpful, solely because a case has already been prosecuted or otherwise closed, or because the time for commencing a criminal action has expired.

   (3) A certifying entity shall not refuse to complete the Form I-914 Supplement B declaration for any of the following reasons:

   (A) The victim's criminal history information.

   (B) The victim's immigration history.

   (C) The victim's gang membership or gang affiliation.

   (D) The certifying entity's belief that the Form I-914 Supplement B petition will not be approved by United States Citizenship and Immigration Services.

   (E) The victim has an open case with another certifying entity.

   (F) The certifying entity's belief that the victim is eligible for relief or protection under Section 679.10 or any other provision of law.

   (G) The victim's inability to produce a crime report from a law enforcement agency.

   (H) The victim's cooperation or refusal to cooperate in a separate case.

(k) A certifying official may only withdraw the certification if the victim refuses to provide information and assistance when reasonably requested.

(l) A certifying entity is prohibited from disclosing the immigration status of a victim or person requesting the Form I-914 Supplement B declaration, except to comply with federal law or legal process, or if authorized by the victim or person requesting the Form I-914 Supplement B declaration.

(m) A certifying entity that receives a request for a Form I-914 Supplement B declaration shall report to the Legislature, on or before January 1, 2018, and annually thereafter, the number of victims who requested Form I-914 Supplement B declarations from the entity, the number of those declaration forms that were signed, and the number that were denied. A report pursuant to this subdivision shall comply with Section 9795 of the Government Code.

Amended by Stats 2023 ch 679 (AB 1261),s 2, eff. 1/1/2024.
Amended by Stats 2020 ch 187 (AB 2426),s 2, eff. 1/1/2021.
Amended by Stats 2019 ch 576 (AB 917),s 2, eff. 1/1/2020.
Added by Stats 2016 ch 749 (AB 2027),s 1, eff. 1/1/2017.

Section 679.12 - Procedures for reference samples of DNA from victims; applicability

(a) The following procedures apply to known reference samples of DNA from a victim of a crime or alleged crime, and to known reference samples of DNA from any individual that were voluntarily provided for the purpose of exclusion, as well as to any profiles developed from those samples:

(1) Law enforcement agencies and their agents shall use these DNA samples or profiles only for purposes directly related to the incident being investigated.

(2) No law enforcement agency or agent thereof may compare any of these samples or profiles with DNA samples or profiles that do not relate to the incident being investigated.

(3) No law enforcement agency or agent thereof may include any of these DNA profiles in any database that allows these samples to be compared to or matched with profiles derived from DNA evidence obtained from crime scenes.

(4) No law enforcement agency or agent thereof may provide any other person or entity with access to any of these DNA samples or profiles, unless that person or entity agrees to abide by the statutory restrictions on the use and disclosure of that sample or profile.

(5) Any part of a DNA sample that remains after the requested testing or analysis has been performed shall be securely stored and may only be used in accordance with the restrictions on use and disclosure of the sample provided in this section.

(6) No agent of a law enforcement agency may provide any part of these DNA samples or profiles to any person or entity other than the law enforcement agency that provided them, except portions of these remaining DNA samples may be provided to the defendant when authorized by court order.

(7) A person whose DNA profile has been voluntarily provided for purposes of exclusion shall have their searchable database profile expunged from all public and private databases if the person has no past or present offense or pending charge that qualifies that person for inclusion within the state's DNA and Forensic Identification Database and Databank Program.

(8) This section does not prohibit crime laboratories from collecting, retaining, and using for comparison purposes in multiple cases the following DNA profiles:

(i) The DNA profiles from persons whose proximity or access to DNA case evidence during the collection, handling, or processing of that evidence might result in DNA contamination, including first responders, crime scene investigators, laboratory staff, or others at the laboratory, if these kinds of elimination samples are voluntarily provided with written consent for their use as quality assurance or control samples, or if the elimination samples are obtained as a condition of employment with written consent, so that the crime laboratory can assure reliable results.

(ii) The DNA profiles from persons associated with the manufacturing or production of consumable supplies or reagents or positive control samples used in laboratory testing, if these kinds of elimination samples are voluntarily provided with written consent.

(iii) The DNA profiles that may be incidentally encountered on consumable supplies or reagents such as plastic tubes, plastic plates, swabs, and buffers.

(9) The requirement for written consent for voluntary elimination samples does not preclude a DNA testing laboratory from retaining, for use consistent with this section, the voluntary quality assurance or control samples described in paragraph (8) that were provided without written consent by persons prior to the enactment of this section, or if the laboratory is otherwise required to retain such case samples by another provision of law.

(10) This section does not preclude a DNA testing laboratory from conducting a limited comparison of samples that were analyzed concurrently in order to evaluate the DNA typing results for potential contamination, determine the source of contamination when detected, and to ensure that the contaminating profiles were not misidentified as DNA profiles from putative perpetrators.

(11) This section does not affect the inclusion of samples in state DNA databases as described in Section 295, the use of state DNA databases for identifying missing persons, the compliance with other provisions of law that allow the release of samples for postconviction testing, or the use of reference samples from a suspect lawfully collected in a manner that does not violate this section.

(b) For the purposes of this section, the following definitions apply:

(1) The "incident being investigated" means the crime or alleged crime that caused a law enforcement agency or agent to analyze or request a DNA sample from a victim of or witness to that crime or alleged crime.

(2) An "agent" of a law enforcement agency includes any person or entity that the agency provides with access to a DNA sample collected directly from the person of a victim of or witness to a crime or alleged crime, or to any profile developed from those samples. This includes, but is not limited to, public or private DNA testing facilities.

(3) A "victim" or "witness" does not include any person who is a target of the investigation of the incident being investigated, if law enforcement agents have probable cause to believe that person has committed a public offense relating to the incident under investigation.

(4) A sample is "voluntarily provided for the purpose of exclusion" if law enforcement agents do not consider the individual to be a suspect and have requested a voluntary DNA sample in order to exclude that person's DNA profile from consideration in the current investigation.

(c) This section does not apply to evidence arising from the victim that is biological material that is not the victim's own and is not from an individual who voluntarily provided a reference sample for exclusion, such as DNA transferred from an assailant.

Amended by Stats 2023 ch 131 (AB 1754),s 151, eff. 1/1/2024.

Added by Stats 2022 ch 994 (SB 1228),s 1, eff. 1/1/2023.

Section 679.13 - Form I-854A certification for qualified criminal informants

(a) For purposes of this section, a "certifying entity" is any of the following:

(1) A state or local law enforcement agency, including, without limitation, the police department of the University of California, a California State University campus, or the police department of a school district, established pursuant to Section 38000 of the Education Code.

(2) A prosecutor.

(3) A judge.

(4) Any other authority that has responsibility for the detection or investigation or prosecution of a qualifying crime or criminal activity.

(5) Agencies that have criminal detection or investigative jurisdiction in their respective areas of expertise, including, but not limited to, child protective services, the Civil Rights Department, and the Department of Industrial Relations.

(b) For purposes of this section, a "certifying official" is any of the following:

(1) The head of the certifying entity.

(2) A person in a supervisory role who has been specifically designated by the head of the certifying entity to issue Form I-854A certifications on behalf of that agency.

(3) A judge.

(4) Any other certifying official defined under Section 214.14 (a)(2) of Title 8 of the Code of Federal Regulations.

(c) "Qualified criminal informant" is an individual who meets the following requirements:

(1) The informant must have reliable information about an important aspect of a crime or pending commission of a crime.

(2) The informant must be willing to share that information with United States law enforcement officials or become a witness in court.

(3) The informant's presence in the United States is important and leads to the successful investigation or prosecution of that crime.

(d) A certifying entity may apply for and may certify a Form I-854A certification for a qualified criminal informant. A qualified informant does not have to be present in the United States for certification pursuant to this section.

(e) The certifying official shall fully complete and sign the Form I-854A certification and, regarding the qualified criminal informant's helpfulness, include specific details about the nature of the crime investigated or prosecuted and a detailed description of the qualified criminal informant's helpfulness or likely helpfulness to the detection or investigation or prosecution of the criminal activity.

(f) A certifying official may only withdraw the certification if the qualified criminal informant refuses to provide information and assistance when reasonably requested.

(g) A certifying entity is prohibited from disclosing the immigration status of the qualified criminal informant for whom Form I-854A certification has been completed, except to comply with federal law or legal process, or if authorized by the qualified criminal informant.
Added by Stats 2023 ch 679 (AB 1261),s 3, eff. 1/1/2024.

Section 680 - Sexual Assault Victims' DNA Bill of Rights

(a) This section shall be known as and may be cited as the "Sexual Assault Victims' DNA Bill of Rights."

(b) The Legislature finds and declares all of the following:

(1) Deoxyribonucleic acid (DNA) and forensic identification analysis is a powerful law enforcement tool for identifying and prosecuting sexual assault offenders.

(2) Existing law requires an adult arrested for or charged with a felony and a juvenile adjudicated for a felony to submit DNA samples as a result of that arrest, charge, or adjudication.

(3) Victims of sexual assaults have a strong interest in the investigation and prosecution of their cases.

(4) Law enforcement agencies have an obligation to victims of sexual assaults in the proper handling, retention, and timely DNA testing of rape kit evidence or other crime scene evidence and to be responsive to victims concerning the developments of forensic testing and the investigation of their cases.

(5) The growth of the Department of Justice's Cal-DNA databank and the national databank through the Combined DNA Index System (CODIS) makes it possible for many sexual assault perpetrators to be identified after their first offense, provided that rape kit evidence is analyzed in a timely manner.

(6) Timely DNA analysis of rape kit evidence is a core public safety issue affecting men, women, and children in the State of California. It is the intent of the Legislature, in order to further public safety, to encourage DNA analysis of rape kit evidence within the time limit imposed by paragraph (1) of subdivision (g) of Section 803.

(7) DNA reference samples collected directly from a victim of sexual assault, and reference samples of DNA collected from any individual that were voluntarily provided for the purpose of exclusion, shall be protected as provided in Section 679.12.

(c) In order to ensure that sexual assault forensic evidence is analyzed within the timeframe required by paragraph (1) of subdivision (g) of Section 803 and to ensure the longest possible statute of limitations for sex offenses, including sex offenses designated pursuant to those subparagraphs, the following shall occur:

(1) A law enforcement agency in whose jurisdiction a sex offense specified in Section 261, 261.5, 286, 287, or 289 or former Section 262 or 288a occurred shall do one of the following for any sexual assault forensic evidence received by the law enforcement agency on or after January 1, 2016:

(A) Submit sexual assault forensic evidence to the crime lab within 20 days after it is booked into evidence.

(B) Ensure that a rapid turnaround DNA program is in place to submit forensic evidence collected from the victim of a sexual assault directly from the medical facility where the victim is examined to the crime lab within five days after the evidence is obtained from the victim.

(2) The crime lab shall do one of the following for any sexual assault forensic evidence received by the crime lab on or after January 1, 2016:

(A) Process sexual assault forensic evidence, create DNA profiles when able, and upload qualifying DNA profiles into CODIS as soon as practically possible, but no later than 120 days after initially receiving the evidence.

(B) Transmit the sexual assault forensic evidence to another crime lab as soon as practically possible, but no later than 30 days after initially receiving the evidence, for processing of the evidence for the presence of DNA. If a DNA profile is created, the transmitting crime lab shall upload the profile into CODIS as soon as practically possible, but no longer than 30 days after being notified about the presence of DNA.

(3) This subdivision does not require a lab to test all items of forensic evidence obtained in a sexual assault forensic evidence examination. A lab is considered to be in compliance with the guidelines of this section when representative samples of the evidence are processed by the lab in an effort to detect the foreign DNA of the perpetrator.

(4) This section does not require a DNA profile to be uploaded into CODIS if the DNA profile does not meet federal guidelines regarding the uploading of DNA profiles into CODIS.

(5) For purposes of this section, a "rapid turnaround DNA program" is a program for the training of sexual assault team personnel in the selection of representative samples of forensic evidence from the victim to be the best evidence, based on the medical evaluation and patient history, the collection and preservation of that evidence, and the transfer of the evidence directly from the medical facility to the crime lab, which is adopted pursuant to a written agreement between the law enforcement agency, the crime lab, and the medical facility where the sexual assault team is based.

(6) For the purpose of this section, "law enforcement" means the law enforcement agency with the primary responsibility for investigating an alleged sexual assault.

(d)

(1) Upon the request of a sexual assault victim, the law enforcement agency investigating a violation of Section 261, 261.5, 286, 287, or 289 or of former Section 262 or 288a shall inform the victim of the status of the DNA testing of the rape kit evidence or other crime scene evidence from the victim's case. The law enforcement agency may, at its discretion, require that the victim's request be in writing. The law enforcement agency shall respond to the victim's request with either an oral or written communication, or by email, if an email address is available. This subdivision does not require that the law enforcement agency communicate with the victim or the victim's designee regarding the status of DNA testing absent a specific request from the victim or the victim's designee.

(2) Sexual assault victims have the right to access the Department of Justice's SAFE-T database portal consistent with subdivision (e) of Section 680.3 for information involving their own forensic kit and the status of the kit.

(3) Sexual assault victims have the right to be informed of the following:

(A) Whether or not a DNA profile of the assailant was obtained from the testing of the rape kit evidence or other crime scene evidence from their case.

(B) Whether or not the DNA profile of the assailant developed from the rape kit evidence or other crime scene evidence has been entered into the Department of Justice Data Bank or the federal Department of Justice or Federal Bureau of Investigation CODIS database of case evidence.

(C) Whether or not there is a confirmed match between the DNA profile of the assailant developed from the rape kit evidence or other crime scene evidence and a DNA profile contained in the Department of Justice Convicted Offender DNA Database, provided that disclosure would not impede or compromise an ongoing investigation.

(4) This subdivision is intended to encourage law enforcement agencies to notify victims of information that is in their possession. It is not intended to affect the manner of or frequency with which the Department of Justice provides this information to law enforcement agencies.

(e) If the law enforcement agency does not analyze DNA evidence within six months prior to the time limit established by paragraph (1) of subdivision (g) of Section 803, a victim of a sexual assault offense specified in Section 261, 261.5, 286, 287, or 289 or of former Section 262 or 288a shall be informed, either orally or in writing, of that fact by the law enforcement agency.

(f)

(1) If the law enforcement agency intends to destroy or dispose of rape kit evidence or other crime scene evidence from an unsolved sexual assault case, a victim of a violation of Section 261, 261.5, 286, 287, or 289 or former Section 262 or 288a shall be given written notification by the law enforcement agency of that intention.

(2) A law enforcement agency shall not destroy or dispose of rape kit evidence or other crime scene evidence from an unsolved sexual assault case before at least 20 years, or if the victim was under 18 years of age at the time of the alleged offense, before the victim's 40th birthday.

(g) Written notification under subdivision (e) or (f) shall be made at least 60 days prior to the destruction or disposal of the rape kit evidence or other crime scene evidence from an unsolved sexual assault case.

(h)

(1) A sexual assault victim may designate a sexual assault victim advocate, or other support person of the victim's choosing, to act as a recipient of the above information required to be provided by this section.

(2) A sexual assault victim may request that a kit collected from them not be tested. A kit for which this request has been made shall not be tested and shall not be subject to the requirements of this section, Section 680.3, or Section 680.4.

(i) It is the intent of the Legislature that a law enforcement agency responsible for providing information under subdivision (d) do so in a timely manner and, upon request of the victim or the victim's designee, advise the victim or the victim's designee of any significant changes in the information of which the law enforcement agency is aware. In order to be entitled to receive notice under this section, the victim or the victim's designee shall keep appropriate authorities informed of the name, address, telephone number, and email address of the person to whom the information should be provided, and any changes of the name, address, telephone number, and email address, if an email address is available.

(j) A defendant or person accused or convicted of a crime against the victim shall have no standing to object to any failure to comply with this section. The failure to provide a right or notice to a sexual assault victim under this section may not be used by a defendant to seek to have the conviction or sentence set aside.

(k) The sole civil or criminal remedy available to a sexual assault victim for a law enforcement agency's failure to fulfill its responsibilities under this section is standing to file a writ of mandamus to require compliance with subdivision (e) or (f).

Amended by Stats 2023 ch 715 (SB 464),s 1, eff. 1/1/2024.
Amended by Stats 2023 ch 131 (AB 1754),s 152, eff. 1/1/2024.
Amended by Stats 2022 ch 994 (SB 1228),s 2.5, eff. 1/1/2023.
Amended by Stats 2022 ch 709 (SB 916),s 1, eff. 1/1/2023.
Amended by Stats 2021 ch 626 (AB 1171),s 36, eff. 1/1/2022.
Amended by Stats 2019 ch 588 (SB 22),s 1, eff. 1/1/2020.
Amended by Stats 2018 ch 423 (SB 1494),s 75, eff. 1/1/2019.

Amended by Stats 2017 ch 692 (AB 1312),s 3, eff. 1/1/2018.

Amended by Stats 2014 ch 874 (AB 1517),s 1, eff. 1/1/2015.

Added by Stats 2003 ch 537 (AB 898), s 1, eff. 1/1/2004.

Section 680.1 - Process to track and receive updates privately, securely, and electronically regarding the status, location, and information regarding sexual assault evidence kit in the department's SAFE-T database

The Department of Justice, on or before July 1, 2022, and in consultation with law enforcement agencies and crime victims groups, shall establish a process that allows a survivor of sexual assault to track and receive updates privately, securely, and electronically regarding the status, location, and information regarding their sexual assault evidence kit in the department's SAFE-T database.

Amended by Stats 2021 ch 634 (SB 215),s 1, eff. 1/1/2022.

Added by Stats 2016 ch 884 (AB 2499),s 2, eff. 1/1/2017.

Section 680.2 - Notification of rights to sexual assault victim

(a) Upon the initial interaction with a sexual assault victim, a law enforcement officer or medical provider shall provide the victim with a card to be developed by every local law enforcement agency, in consultation with sexual assault experts, that explains all of the rights of sexual assault victims in clear language that is comprehensible to a person proficient in English at the fifth grade level, in at least 12-point font, and available in all major languages of the state. This card shall include, but is not limited to, all of the following:

(1) A clear statement that a sexual assault victim is not required to participate in the criminal justice system or to receive a medical evidentiary or physical examination in order to retain their rights under law.

(2) A clear statement that, under Section 1219 of the Code of Civil Procedure, a court may not imprison or otherwise confine or place in custody a victim of sexual assault or domestic violence for contempt if the contempt consists of refusing to testify concerning the crime.

(3) Telephone or internet website contact information for a nearby rape crisis center and sexual assault counselor.

(4) Information about the types of law enforcement protection available to the sexual assault victim, including a temporary protection order, and the process to obtain that protection.

(5) Instructions for requesting the results of the analysis of the victim's sexual assault forensic evidence.

(6) Information about state and federal compensation funds for medical and other costs associated with the sexual assault and information on any municipal, state, or federal right to restitution for sexual assault victims if a criminal trial occurs.

(7) A clear statement that the victim has the right to have a sexual assault counselor and at least one other support person of the victim's choosing present at any initial medical evidentiary examination, physical examination, or investigative interview arising out of a sexual assault, and that a sexual assault counselor can be contacted 24 hours a day.

(8) Information about the rate of potential evidence degradation.

(9) A clear statement that if sexual assault forensic evidence will be tested, it should be transported to the crime laboratory and analyzed within the time limits imposed by subparagraphs (A) and (B) of paragraph (1) of subdivision (g) of Section 803.

(10) A clear statement that the law enforcement agency or crime laboratory will retain the sexual assault forensic evidence for at least 20 years, or if the victim was under 18 years of age at the time of the alleged offense, at least until the victim's 40th birthday.

(b) A law enforcement official shall, upon written request by a sexual assault victim, furnish a free copy of the initial crime report related to the sexual assault, regardless of whether the report has been closed by the law enforcement agency, to the victim. A law enforcement agency may redact personal, identifying information in the copy furnished to the victim.

(c) A prosecutor shall, pursuant to Section 290.46, upon written request by a sexual assault victim, provide the convicted defendant's information on a sex offender registry to the victim, if the defendant is required to register as a sex offender.

(d) The law enforcement agency shall provide sufficient copies of the card described in subdivision (a) to each provider in its jurisdiction of medical evidentiary examinations or physical examinations arising out of sexual assault.

Amended by Stats 2022 ch 709 (SB 916),s 2, eff. 1/1/2023.

Added by Stats 2017 ch 692 (AB 1312),s 4, eff. 1/1/2018.

Section 680.3 - Information profiles for sexual assault kits on federal database

(a) Each law enforcement agency that has investigated a case involving the collection of sexual assault kit evidence from a victim shall, within 120 days of collection, create an information record for the kit on the Department of Justice's SAFE-T database and report the following:

(1) If biological evidence samples from the kit were submitted to a DNA laboratory for analysis.

(2) If the kit generated a probative DNA profile.

(3) If evidence was not submitted to a DNA laboratory for processing, the reason or reasons for not submitting evidence from the kit to a DNA laboratory for processing.

(b) After 120 days following submission of sexual assault kit biological evidence for processing, if a public DNA laboratory has not conducted DNA testing, that laboratory shall provide the reasons for the status in the appropriate SAFE-T data field. If the investigating law enforcement agency has contracted with a private vendor laboratory to conduct DNA testing on kit evidence, the submitting law enforcement agency shall provide the 120-day update in SAFE-T. The process described in this subdivision shall take place every 120 days until DNA testing is complete, except as provided in subdivision (c).

(c)

(1) Upon expiration of a sexual assault case's statute of limitations, or if a law enforcement agency elects not to analyze the DNA or intends to destroy or dispose of the crime scene evidence pursuant to subdivision (g) of Section 680, the investigating law enforcement agency shall state in writing the reason the kit collected as part of that case's investigation was not analyzed. This written statement relieves the investigating law enforcement agency or public laboratory of any further duty to report information related to that kit pursuant to this section.

(2) A record of a kit collected prior to January 1, 2016, that is created in SAFE-T pursuant to subdivision (b) of Section 680.4 is excluded from the 120-day update requirement.

(d) The SAFE-T database shall not contain any identifying information about a victim or a suspect, shall not contain any DNA profiles, and shall not contain any information that would impair a pending criminal investigation.

(e) The SAFE-T database shall, on or before July 1, 2022, allow a survivor of sexual assault to track and receive updates privately, securely, and electronically regarding the status and location of the survivor's sexual assault evidence kit, as provided in Section 680.1.

(f) On an annual basis, the Department of Justice shall file a report to the Legislature in compliance with Section 9795 of the Government Code summarizing data entered into the SAFE-T database during that year. The report shall not reference individual victims, suspects, investigations, or prosecutions. The report shall be made public by the department.

(g) Except as provided in subdivision (e), in order to protect the confidentiality of the SAFE-T database information, SAFE-T database contents shall be confidential, and a participating law enforcement agency or laboratory shall not be compelled in a criminal or civil proceeding, except as required by Brady v. Maryland (1963) 373 U.S. 83, to provide any SAFE-T database contents to a person or party seeking those records or information.

(h) The requirements of this section shall only apply to sexual assault kit evidence from a victim collected on or after January 1, 2018, and to sexual assault kit evidence from a victim required to be entered into the SAFE-T database pursuant to subdivision (b) of Section 680.4.

Amended by Stats 2023 ch 715 (SB 464),s 2, eff. 1/1/2024.
Amended by Stats 2021 ch 634 (SB 215),s 2, eff. 1/1/2022.
Amended by Stats 2019 ch 588 (SB 22),s 2, eff. 1/1/2020.
Amended by Stats 2018 ch 36 (AB 1812),s 15, eff. 6/27/2018.
Added by Stats 2017 ch 694 (AB 41),s 2, eff. 1/1/2018.

Section 680.4 - Audit of sexual assault kits

(a) Each law enforcement agency, medical facility, public crime laboratory, and any other entity that receives, maintains, stores, or preserves sexual assault evidence kits shall participate in an audit of all untested sexual assault kits in their possession pursuant to this section.

(b) No later than July 1, 2026, each law enforcement agency and public crime laboratory subject to subdivision (a) shall create a record in the SAFE-T database, pursuant to Section 680.3, for every victim sexual assault kit in their possession that has not had DNA testing completed as of July 1, 2026.

    (1) If a medical facility submitted selected evidence samples directly to a crime laboratory under a rapid turnaround DNA program, and those samples have been taken through the DNA testing process, the entire sexual assault kit shall be considered tested for the purposes of this section.

    (2) A kit that has only undergone biological screening shall not be considered tested for the purposes of this section. A tested kit is one that has been taken, at minimum, through the DNA quantitation process, and either of the following:

        (A) If the DNA quantitation results indicate that there is no DNA foreign to the victim, or the foreign DNA is of insufficient quality and quantity for DNA typing to provide genetic information about an alleged perpetrator, analysis can stop at DNA quantitation, and the kit shall be considered tested for the purposes of this section.

        (B) If the DNA quantitation results indicate that DNA typing may provide genetic information about an alleged perpetrator, and the DNA is of sufficient quantity and quality to be successfully typed, the analysis shall continue through DNA typing for the kit to be considered tested for the purposes of this section.

    (3) The SAFE-T database shall only contain records for sexual assault evidence kits collected from victims. Sexual assault evidence kits collected from suspects shall also be subject to the audit pursuant to this section, but they shall not be entered into the SAFE-T database. The following information shall be reported separately by each entity in a format prescribed by the Department of Justice:

        (A) The total number of untested suspect sexual assault kits in their possession.

        (B) For each suspect kit, the following information:

            (i) The date the suspect kit was collected.

            (ii) The date the suspect kit was picked up by a law enforcement agency, for each law enforcement agency that has taken custody of the kit.

            (iii) The date the suspect kit was delivered to a crime laboratory.

            (iv) The reason the suspect kit has not been tested, if applicable.

    (4) Sexual assault evidence other than evidence collected in kits, including clothing and bedding, DNA reference samples collected from suspects and consensual partners, and kits collected under circumstances where no sexual assault is alleged or suspected to have occurred, are not subject to this audit and shall not be entered into the SAFE-T database or reported for this audit.

(c) No later than July 1, 2026, each medical facility and other non-law enforcement entity subject to subdivision (a) shall report to the Department of Justice, in the format prescribed by the department, all of the following:

    (1) The total number of untested sexual assault kits in their possession that were not submitted to a law enforcement agency or public crime laboratory because the victim chose not to report the assault to law enforcement at the time of collection, and had not chosen to report the assault to law enforcement by the time of the audit.

    (2) For untested sexual assault evidence kits in their possession where the victim chose to report the assault to law enforcement:

        (A) The total number of untested sexual assault kits in their possession.

        (B) For each kit, the following information:

            (i) The date the kit was collected.

            (ii) The name of the medical facility, law enforcement agency, public crime laboratory, or other entity from which the kit was received.

            (iii) The date the kit was received by the entity.

            (iv) The reason the kit has not been submitted to a law enforcement agency or public crime laboratory.

        (C) This reporting requirement does not apply to untested kits that have been recently collected and are temporarily being stored pending release to a law enforcement agency or public crime laboratory.

(d) The Department of Justice shall, by no later than July 1, 2027, prepare and submit a report to the Legislature summarizing the information received pursuant to subdivisions (b) and (c).

(e) The report required by subdivision (d) shall be submitted in compliance with Section 9795 of the Government Code.

Added by Stats 2023 ch 715 (SB 464),s 4, eff. 1/1/2024.
Repealed by Stats 2023 ch 715 (SB 464),s 3, eff. 1/1/2024.
Added by Stats 2018 ch 950 (AB 3118),s 1, eff. 1/1/2019.

Part 2 - OF CRIMINAL PROCEDURE

Title - PRELIMINARY PROVISIONS

Section 681 - Legal conviction required for punishment for public offense

No person can be punished for a public offense, except upon a legal conviction in a Court having jurisdiction thereof.

Section 682 - Prosecution by indictment of information

Every public offense must be prosecuted by indictment or information, except:

1. Where proceedings are had for the removal of civil officers of the state;
2. Offenses arising in the militia when in actual service, and in the land and naval forces in the time of war, or which the state may keep, with the consent of Congress, in time of peace;
3. Misdemeanors and infractions;
4. A felony to which the defendant has pleaded guilty to the complaint before a magistrate, where permitted by law.

Section 683 - Criminal action

The proceeding by which a party charged with a public offense is accused and brought to trial and punishment, is known as a criminal action.

Section 684 - Prosecution of criminal action in name of people of State of California

A criminal action is prosecuted in the name of the people of the State of California, as a party, against the person charged with the offense.

Section 685 - Defendant

The party prosecuted in a criminal action is designated in this Code as the defendant.

Section 686 - Rights of defendant

In a criminal action the defendant is entitled:

1. To a speedy and public trial.
2. To be allowed counsel as in civil actions, or to appear and defend in person and with counsel, except that in a capital case he shall be represented in court by counsel at all stages of the preliminary and trial proceedings.
3. To produce witnesses on his behalf and to be confronted with the witnesses against him, in the presence of the court, except that:
    (a) Hearsay evidence may be admitted to the extent that it is otherwise admissible in a criminal action under the law of this state.
    (b) The deposition of a witness taken in the action may be read to the extent that it is otherwise admissible under the law of this state.

Section 686.1 - Representation of defendant in capital case

Notwithstanding any other provision of law, the defendant in a capital case shall be represented in court by counsel at all stages of the preliminary and trial proceedings.

Section 686.2 - Removal of spectator

(a) The court may, after holding a hearing and making the findings set forth in subdivision (b), order the removal of any spectator who is intimidating a witness.

(b) The court may order the removal of a spectator only if it finds all of the following by clear and convincing evidence:
    (1) The spectator to be removed is actually engaging in intimidation of the witness.
    (2) The witness will not be able to give full, free, and complete testimony unless the spectator is removed.
    (3) Removal of the spectator is the only reasonable means of ensuring that the witness may give full, free, and complete testimony.

(c) Subdivision (a) shall not be used as a means of excluding the press or a defendant from attendance at any portion of a criminal proceeding.

Section 686.5 - Return of person to place of arrest if released without trial or acquitted

In any case in which a person is arrested and released without trial or in which a person is arrested, tried, and acquitted, if such person is indigent and is released or acquitted at a place to which he has been transported by the arresting agency and which is more than 25 airline miles from the place of his arrest, the arresting agency shall, at his request, return or provide for return of such person to the place of his arrest.

Section 687 - Double jeopardy

No person can be subjected to a second prosecution for a public offense for which he has once been prosecuted and convicted or acquitted.

Section 688 - Limitations on restraint before conviction

No person charged with a public offense may be subjected, before conviction, to any more restraint than is necessary for his detention to answer the charge.

Section 688.5 - Charging criminal defendants for costs prohibited

(a) A city, county, or city and county, including an attorney acting on behalf of a city, county, or city and county, shall not charge a defendant for the costs of investigation, prosecution, or appeal in a criminal case, including, but not limited to, a criminal violation of a local ordinance. This prohibition shall not apply in any civil action or civil proceeding.

(b) This section shall not apply to any of the following:
    (1) A violation of Section 186.8, 186.11, or 670.
    (2) Costs ordered by a court pursuant to paragraph (1) of subdivision (d) of Section 17062 of the Health and Safety Code.

(3) A violation of Section 1871.4 of the Insurance Code.

(4) A violation of Section 3700.5 of the Labor Code.

(5) A violation of Section 19542.3, 19701, 19701.5, 19705, 19706, 19720, 19721, 30165.1, 30482, 38800, 46701, 46702, 46704, or 46705 of the Revenue and Taxation Code.

(6) A violation of Section 2126 of the Unemployment Insurance Code.

(7) A violation of any other provision of state law where recovery of the costs of investigation, prosecution, or appeal in a criminal case is specifically authorized by statute or ordered by a court. This paragraph does not apply to a local ordinance.

(c) Nothing in this section shall be interpreted to affect the authority of a probation department to assess and collect fees or other charges authorized by statute.

(d) For the purposes of this section, the term "costs" means the salary, fees, and hourly rate paid to attorneys, law enforcement, and inspectors for hours spent either investigating or enforcing the charged crime. Costs shall not include the cost, including oversight, to remediate, abate, restore, or otherwise clean-up harms caused by criminal conduct.

Added by Stats 2018 ch 264 (AB 2495),s 1, eff. 1/1/2019.

Section 689 - Conviction by verdict of jury or plea of guilty

No person can be convicted of a public offense unless by verdict of a jury, accepted and recorded by the court, by a finding of the court in a case where a jury has been waived, or by a plea of guilty.

Section 690 - Applicability to criminal actions and proceedings

The provisions of Part 2 (commencing with Section 681) shall apply to all criminal actions and proceedings in all courts, except where jurisdictional limitations or the nature of specific provisions prevent, or special provision is made for particular courts or proceedings.

Section 690.5 - Permissive filing and service of documents

(a) Subdivisions (a) and (e) of Section 1010.6 of the Code of Civil Procedure, pertaining to the permissive filing and service of documents, are applicable to criminal actions, except as otherwise provided in Section 959.1 or any other provision of this code.

(b) The Judicial Council shall adopt uniform rules for the electronic filing and service of documents in criminal cases in the trial courts of this state.

Amended by Stats 2022 ch 215 (AB 2961),s 5, eff. 1/1/2023.

Added by Stats 2017 ch 319 (AB 976),s 5, eff. 1/1/2018.

Section 691 - Definitions

The following words have in Part 2 (commencing with Section 681) the signification attached to them in this section, unless it is otherwise apparent from the context:

(a) The words "competent court" when used with reference to the jurisdiction over any public offense, mean any court the subject matter jurisdiction of which includes the offense so mentioned.

(b) The words "jurisdictional territory" when used with reference to a court, mean the city and county, county, city, township, or other limited territory over which the criminal jurisdiction of the court extends, as provided by law, and in case of a superior court mean the county in which the court sits.

(c) The words "accusatory pleading" include an indictment, an information, an accusation, and a complaint.

(d) The words "prosecuting attorney" include any attorney, whether designated as district attorney, city attorney, city prosecutor, prosecuting attorney, or by any other title, having by law the right or duty to prosecute, on behalf of the people, any charge of a public offense.

(e) The word "county" includes county, city and county, and city.

(f) "Felony case" means a criminal action in which a felony is charged and includes a criminal action in which a misdemeanor or infraction is charged in conjunction with a felony.

(g) "Misdemeanor or infraction case" means a criminal action in which a misdemeanor or infraction is charged and does not include a criminal action in which a felony is charged in conjunction with a misdemeanor or infraction.

Title 1 - OF THE PREVENTION OF PUBLIC OFFENSES

Chapter 1 - OF LAWFUL RESISTANCE

Section 692 - Lawful resistance to commission of public offense

Lawful resistance to the commission of a public offense may be made:

1. By the party about to be injured;

2. By other parties.

Enacted 1872.

Section 693 - Resistance to prevent offense by person about to be injured

Resistance sufficient to prevent the offense may be made by the party about to be injured:

1.To prevent an offense against his person, or his family, or some member thereof.

2.To prevent an illegal attempt by force to take or injure property in his lawful possession.

Enacted 1872.

Section 694 - Resistance to prevent offense by person in aid or defense of person about to be injured

Any other person, in aid or defense of the person about to be injured, may make resistance sufficient to prevent the offense.

Enacted 1872.

Chapter 2 - OF THE INTERVENTION OF THE OFFICERS OF JUSTICE

Section 697 - Intervention by officers of justice

Public offenses may be prevented by the intervention of the officers of justice:

1. By requiring security to keep the peace;

2. By forming a police in cities and towns, and by requiring their attendance in exposed places;

3. By suppressing riots.

Enacted 1872.
Section 698 - Justification
When the officers of justice are authorized to act in the prevention of public offenses, other persons, who, by their command, act in their aid, are justified in so doing.
Enacted 1872.

Chapter 3 - SECURITY TO KEEP THE PEACE
Section 701 - Information that person had threatened to commit offense
An information may be laid before any of the magistrates mentioned in Section 808, that a person has threatened to commit an offense against the person or property of another.
Enacted 1872.
Section 701.5 - Minor informants
(a) Notwithstanding subdivision (b), no peace officer or agent of a peace officer shall use a person who is 12 years of age or younger as a minor informant.
(b) No peace officer or agent of a peace officer shall use a person under the age of 18 years as a minor informant, except as authorized pursuant to the Stop Tobacco Access to Kids Enforcement Act (Division 8.5 (commencing with Section 22950) of the Business and Professions Code) for the purposes of that act, unless the peace officer or agent of a peace officer has obtained an order from the court authorizing the minor's cooperation.
(c) Prior to issuing any order pursuant to subdivision (b), the court shall find, after consideration of (1) the age and maturity of the minor, (2) the gravity of the minor's alleged offense, (3) the safety of the public, and (4) the interests of justice, that the agreement to act as a minor informant is voluntary and is being entered into knowingly and intelligently.
(d) Prior to the court making the finding required in subdivision (c), all of the following conditions shall be satisfied:
    (1) The court has found probable cause that the minor committed the alleged offense. The finding of probable cause shall only be for the purpose of issuing the order pursuant to subdivision (b), and shall not prejudice the minor in any future proceedings.
    (2) The court has advised the minor of the mandatory minimum and maximum sentence for the alleged offense.
    (3) The court has disclosed the benefit the minor may obtain by cooperating with the peace officer or agent of a peace officer.
    (4) The minor's parent or guardian has consented to the agreement by the minor unless the parent or guardian is a suspect in the criminal investigation.
(e) For purposes of this section, "minor informant" means a minor who participates, on behalf of a law enforcement agency, in a prearranged transaction or series of prearranged transactions with direct face-to-face contact with any party, when the minor's participation in the transaction is for the purpose of obtaining or attempting to obtain evidence of illegal activity by a third party and where the minor is participating in the transaction for the purpose of reducing or dismissing a pending juvenile petition against the minor.
Added by Stats. 1998, Ch. 833, Sec. 1. Effective September 25, 1998.
Section 702 - Examination of informer and witnesses
When the information is laid before such magistrate he must examine on oath the informer, and any witness he may produce, and must take their depositions in writing, and cause them to be subscribed by the parties making them.
Enacted 1872.
Section 703 - Issuance of warrant
If it appears from the depositions that there is just reason to fear the commission of the offense threatened, by the person so informed against, the magistrate must issue a warrant, directed generally to the sheriff of the county, or any marshal, or policeman in the state, reciting the substance of the information, and commanding the officer forthwith to arrest the person informed of and bring him or her before the magistrate.
Amended by Stats. 1996, Ch. 872, Sec. 113. Effective January 1, 1997.
Section 704 - Taking of testimony
When the person informed against is brought before the magistrate, if the charge be controverted, the magistrate shall take testimony in relation thereto. The evidence shall be reduced to writing and subscribed by the witnesses. The magistrate may, in his or her discretion, order the testimony and proceedings to be taken down in shorthand, and for that purpose he or she may appoint a shorthand reporter. The deposition or testimony of the witnesses shall be authenticated in the form prescribed in Section 869.
Amended by Stats. 1987, Ch. 828, Sec. 48.
Section 705 - Discharge of person complained of
If it appears that there is no just reason to fear the commission of the offense alleged to have been threatened, the person complained of must be discharged.
Enacted 1872.
Section 706 - Undertaking
If, however, there is just reason to fear the commission of the offense, the person complained of may be required to enter into an undertaking in such sum, not exceeding five thousand dollars, as the magistrate may direct, to keep the peace towards the people of this state, and particularly towards the informer. The undertaking is valid and binding for six months, and may, upon the renewal of the information, be extended for a longer period, or a new undertaking may be required.
Amended by Stats. 1982, Ch. 517, Sec. 315.
Section 707 - Discharge after undertaking is given
If the undertaking required by the last section is given, the party informed of must be discharged. If he does not give it, the magistrate must commit him to prison, specifying in the warrant the requirement to give security, the amount thereof, and the omission to give the same.
Enacted 1872.
Section 708 - Discharge after commitment for not giving undertaking

If the person complained of is committed for not giving the undertaking required, he may be discharged by any magistrate, upon giving the same.
Enacted 1872.

Section 709 - Filing of undertaking
The undertaking must be filed by the magistrate in the office of the Clerk of the county.
Enacted 1872.

Section 710 - Assault or threaten to assault in presence of court or magistrate
A person who, in the presence of a Court or magistrate, assaults or threatens to assault another, or to commit an offense against his person or property, or who contends with another with angry words, may be ordered by the Court or magistrate to give security, as in this Chapter provided, and if he refuse to do so, may be committed as provided in Section 707.
Enacted 1872.

Section 711 - Broken undertaking
Upon the conviction of the person informed against of a breach of the peace, the undertaking is broken.
Enacted 1872.

Section 712 - Prosecution of undertaking
Upon the District Attorney's producing evidence of such conviction to the Superior Court of the county, the Court must order the undertaking to be prosecuted, and the District Attorney must thereupon commence an action upon it in the name of the people of this State.
Amended by Code Amendments 1880, Ch. 56.

Section 713 - Breach of undertaking
In the action the offense stated in the record of conviction must be alleged as a breach of the undertaking, and such record is conclusive evidence of the breach.
Enacted 1872.

Section 714 - Security
Security to keep the peace, or be of good behavior, cannot be required except as prescribed in this Chapter.
Enacted 1872.

Chapter 5 - SUPPRESSION OF RIOTS

Section 723 - Commanding inhabitants to assist in overcoming resistance
When a sheriff or other public officer authorized to execute process finds, or has reason to apprehend, that resistance will be made to the execution of the process, the officer may command as many able-bodied inhabitants of the officer's county as he or she may think proper to assist in overcoming the resistance and, if necessary, in seizing, arresting, and confining the persons resisting, and their aiders and abettors.
Amended by Stats. 1988, Ch. 160, Sec. 128.

Section 724 - Certification of names of persons resisting and their aiders and abettors
The officer must certify to the Court from which the process issued the names of the persons resisting, and their aiders and abettors, to the end that they may be proceeded against for their contempt of Court.
Enacted 1872.

Section 726 - Command to disperse immediately
Where any number of persons, whether armed or not, are unlawfully or riotously assembled, the sheriff of the county and his or her deputies, the officials governing the town or city, or any of them, must go among the persons assembled, or as near to them as possible, and command them, in the name of the people of the state, immediately to disperse.
Amended by Stats. 1998, Ch. 931, Sec. 355. Effective September 28, 1998.

Section 727 - Arrest
If the persons assembled do not immediately disperse, such magistrates and officers must arrest them, and to that end may command the aid of all persons present or within the county.
Enacted 1872.

Title 2 - MODE OF PROSECUTION

Section 737 - Prosecution of felonies
All felonies shall be prosecuted by indictment or information, except as provided in Section 859a. A proceeding pursuant to Section 3060 of the Government Code shall be prosecuted by accusation.
Amended by Stats. 1998, Ch. 931, Sec. 356. Effective September 28, 1998.

Section 738 - Preliminary examination
Before an information is filed there must be a preliminary examination of the case against the defendant and an order holding him to answer made under Section 872. The proceeding for a preliminary examination must be commenced by written complaint, as provided elsewhere in this code.
Added by Stats. 1951, Ch. 1674.

Section 739 - Information
When a defendant has been examined and committed, as provided in Section 872, it shall be the duty of the district attorney of the county in which the offense is triable to file in the superior court of that county within 15 days after the commitment, an information against the defendant which may charge the defendant with either the offense or offenses named in the order of commitment or any offense or offenses shown by the evidence taken before the magistrate to have been committed. The information shall be in the name of the people of the State of California and subscribed by the district attorney.
Added by Stats. 1951, Ch. 1674.

Section 740 - Prosecution of misdemeanors and infractions by written complaint under oath

Except as otherwise provided by law, all misdemeanors and infractions must be prosecuted by written complaint under oath subscribed by the complainant. Such complaint may be verified on information and belief.

Amended by Stats. 1998, Ch. 931, Sec. 357. Effective September 28, 1998.

Section 741 - "Race-Blind Charging" guidelines

(a) Beginning January 1, 2024, the Department of Justice shall develop, issue, and publish "Race-Blind Charging" guidelines for a process whereby all prosecution agencies, for purposes of this section defined as agencies, or branches of agencies, that prosecute criminal violations of the law as felonies or misdemeanors, shall implement a process by which an initial review of a case for potential charging is performed based on information, including police reports and criminal histories from the Department of Justice, from which direct means of identifying the race of the suspect, victim, or witness have been removed or redacted.

(b) Following the department's guidelines, prosecution agencies shall independently develop and execute versions of this redaction and review process with the following general criteria:

(1) Beginning January 1, 2025, cases received from law enforcement agencies and suspect criminal history documentation shall be redacted, by the receiving prosecution agency, in order to be used for a race-blind initial charging evaluation, which shall precede the ordinary charging evaluation. This redaction may occur in a separate version of the documents and may be done mechanically, by hand performed by personnel not associated with the charging of the case, or by automation with the use of computer programming, so long as the method used reasonably ensures correct redaction. The redaction may be applied to the entire report or to only the "narrative" portion of the report so long as the portion submitted for initial review is sufficient to perform that review and the unredacted portions are not part of the initial charging evaluation.

(2) The initial charging evaluation based on redacted information, including redacted reports, criminal histories, and narratives, shall determine whether the case should be charged or not be charged. Individual charges shall not be determined at this initial charging evaluation stage. Other evidence may be considered as part of this initial charging evaluation so long as the other evidence does not reveal redacted facts. The initial charging evaluation shall be performed by a prosecutor who does not have knowledge of the redacted facts for that case.

(3) After completion of a race-blind initial charging evaluation, the case shall proceed to a second, complete review for charging using unredacted reports and all available evidence in which the most applicable individual charges and enhancements may be considered and charged in a criminal complaint, or the case may be submitted to a grand jury.

(4)

(A) Each of the following circumstances shall be documented as part of the case record:

(i) The initial charging evaluation determined that the case not be charged and the second review determined that a charge shall be filed.

(ii) The initial charging evaluation determined that the case shall be charged and the second review determined that no charge be filed.

(B) The explanation for the charging decision change shall be documented as part of the case record.

(C) The documented change between the result of the initial charging evaluation and the second review, as well as the explanation for the change, shall be disclosed, upon request, after sentencing in the case or dismissal of all charges comprising the case, subject to Section 1054.6 or any other applicable law.

(5) If a prosecution agency was unable to put a case through a race-blind initial charging evaluation, the reason for that inability shall be documented and retained by the agency. This documentation shall be made available by the agency upon request.

(6) The county shall collect the data resulting from the race-blind initial charging evaluation process and make the data available for research purposes.

(c) Each prosecution agency may remove or exclude certain classes of crimes or factual circumstances from a race-blind initial charging evaluation. This list of exclusions and the reasons for exclusion shall be available upon request to the Department of Justice and members of the public. Due to the increased reliance on victim or witness credibility, the availability of additional defenses, the increased reliance on forensics for the charging decision, or the relevance of racial animus to the charging decision, each of the following crimes may be excluded from a race-blind initial charging evaluation process:

(1) Homicides.

(2) Hate crimes.

(3) Charges arising from a physical confrontation where that confrontation is captured in video as evidence.

(4) Domestic violence and sex crimes.

(5) Gang crimes.

(6) Cases alleging either sexual assault or physical abuse or neglect where the charging decision relies upon either a forensic interview of a child or interviews of multiple victims or multiple defendants.

(7) Cases involving financial crimes where the redaction of documentation is not practicable or is cost prohibitive due to the volume of redactions, including, but not limited to, violations of Sections 368 and 503 and other crimes sounding in fraud consisting of voluminous documentation.

(8) Cases involving public integrity, including, but not limited to, conflict of interest crimes under Section 1090 of the Government Code.

(9) Cases in which the prosecution agency itself investigated the alleged crime or participated in the precharging investigation of the crime by law enforcement, including, but not limited to, the review of search warrants or advising law enforcement in the course of the investigation.

(10) Cases in which the prosecution agency initiated the charging and filing of the case by way of a grand jury indictment or where the charges arose from a grand jury investigation.

Added by Stats 2022 ch 806 (AB 2778),s 2, eff. 1/1/2023.

Section 745 - Conviction based on race, ethnicity, or national origin; remedy

(a) The state shall not seek or obtain a criminal conviction or seek, obtain, or impose a sentence on the basis of race, ethnicity, or national origin. A violation is established if the defendant proves, by a preponderance of the evidence, any of the following:

(1) The judge, an attorney in the case, a law enforcement officer involved in the case, an expert witness, or juror exhibited bias or animus towards the defendant because of the defendant's race, ethnicity, or national origin.

(2) During the defendant's trial, in court and during the proceedings, the judge, an attorney in the case, a law enforcement officer involved in the case, an expert witness, or juror, used racially discriminatory language about the defendant's race, ethnicity, or national origin, or otherwise exhibited bias or animus towards the defendant because of the defendant's race, ethnicity, or national origin, whether or not purposeful. This paragraph does not apply if the person speaking is relating language used by another that is relevant to the case or if the person speaking is giving a racially neutral and unbiased physical description of the suspect.

(3) The defendant was charged or convicted of a more serious offense than defendants of other races, ethnicities, or national origins who have engaged in similar conduct and are similarly situated, and the evidence establishes that the prosecution more frequently sought or obtained convictions for more serious offenses against people who share the defendant's race, ethnicity, or national origin in the county where the convictions were sought or obtained.

(4)

(A) A longer or more severe sentence was imposed on the defendant than was imposed on other similarly situated individuals convicted of the same offense, and longer or more severe sentences were more frequently imposed for that offense on people that share the defendant's race, ethnicity, or national origin than on defendants of other races, ethnicities, or national origins in the county where the sentence was imposed.

(B) A longer or more severe sentence was imposed on the defendant than was imposed on other similarly situated individuals convicted of the same offense, and longer or more severe sentences were more frequently imposed for the same offense on defendants in cases with victims of one race, ethnicity, or national origin than in cases with victims of other races, ethnicities, or national origins, in the county where the sentence was imposed.

(b) A defendant may file a motion pursuant to this section, or a petition for writ of habeas corpus or a motion under Section 1473.7, in a court of competent jurisdiction, alleging a violation of subdivision (a). For claims based on the trial record, a defendant may raise a claim alleging a violation of subdivision (a) on direct appeal from the conviction or sentence. The defendant may also move to stay the appeal and request remand to the superior court to file a motion pursuant to this section. If the motion is based in whole or in part on conduct or statements by the judge, the judge shall disqualify themselves from any further proceedings under this section.

(c) If a motion is filed in the trial court and the defendant makes a prima facie showing of a violation of subdivision (a), the trial court shall hold a hearing. A motion made at trial shall be made as soon as practicable upon the defendant learning of the alleged violation. A motion that is not timely may be deemed waived, in the discretion of the court.

(1) At the hearing, evidence may be presented by either party, including, but not limited to, statistical evidence, aggregate data, expert testimony, and the sworn testimony of witnesses. The court may also appoint an independent expert. For the purpose of a motion and hearing under this section, out-of-court statements that the court finds trustworthy and reliable, statistical evidence, and aggregated data are admissible for the limited purpose of determining whether a violation of subdivision (a) has occurred.

(2) The defendant shall have the burden of proving a violation of subdivision (a) by a preponderance of the evidence. The defendant does not need to prove intentional discrimination.

(3) At the conclusion of the hearing, the court shall make findings on the record.

(d) A defendant may file a motion requesting disclosure to the defense of all evidence relevant to a potential violation of subdivision (a) in the possession or control of the state. A motion filed under this section shall describe the type of records or information the defendant seeks. Upon a showing of good cause, the court shall order the records to be released. Upon a showing of good cause, and in order to protect a privacy right or privilege, the court may permit the prosecution to redact information prior to disclosure or may subject disclosure to a protective order. If a statutory privilege or constitutional privacy right cannot be adequately protected by redaction or a protective order, the court shall not order the release of the records.

(e) Notwithstanding any other law, except as provided in subdivision (k), or for an initiative approved by the voters, if the court finds, by a preponderance of evidence, a violation of subdivision (a), the court shall impose a remedy specific to the violation found from the following list:

(1) Before a judgment has been entered, the court may impose any of the following remedies:

(A) Declare a mistrial, if requested by the defendant.

(B) Discharge the jury panel and empanel a new jury.

(C) If the court determines that it would be in the interest of justice, dismiss enhancements, special circumstances, or special allegations, or reduce one or more charges.

(2)

(A) After a judgment has been entered, if the court finds that a conviction was sought or obtained in violation of subdivision (a), the court shall vacate the conviction and sentence, find that it is legally invalid, and order new proceedings consistent with subdivision (a). If the court finds that the only violation of subdivision (a) that occurred is based on paragraph (3) of subdivision (a), the court may modify the judgment to a lesser included or lesser related offense. On resentencing, the court shall not impose a new sentence greater than that previously imposed.

(B) After a judgment has been entered, if the court finds that only the sentence was sought, obtained, or imposed in violation of subdivision (a), the court shall vacate the sentence, find that it is legally invalid, and impose a new sentence. On resentencing, the court shall not impose a new sentence greater than that previously imposed.

(3) When the court finds there has been a violation of subdivision (a), the defendant shall not be eligible for the death penalty.

(4) The remedies available under this section do not foreclose any other remedies available under the United States Constitution, the California Constitution, or any other law.

(f) This section also applies to adjudications and dispositions in the juvenile delinquency system and adjudications to transfer a juvenile case to adult court.

(g) This section shall not prevent the prosecution of hate crimes pursuant to Sections 422.6 to 422.865, inclusive.

(h) As used in this section, the following definitions apply:

(1) "More frequently sought or obtained" or "more frequently imposed" means that the totality of the evidence demonstrates a significant difference in seeking or obtaining convictions or in imposing sentences comparing individuals who have engaged in similar conduct and are similarly situated, and the prosecution cannot establish race-neutral reasons for the disparity. The evidence may include statistical evidence, aggregate data, or nonstatistical evidence. Statistical significance is a factor the court may consider, but is not necessary to establish a significant difference. In evaluating the totality of the evidence, the court shall consider whether systemic and institutional racial bias, racial profiling, and historical patterns of racially biased policing and prosecution may have contributed to, or caused differences observed in, the data or impacted the availability of data overall. Race-neutral reasons shall be relevant factors to charges, convictions, and sentences that are not influenced by implicit, systemic, or institutional bias based on race, ethnicity, or national origin.

(2) "Prima facie showing" means that the defendant produces facts that, if true, establish that there is a substantial likelihood that a violation of subdivision (a) occurred. For purposes of this section, a "substantial likelihood" requires more than a mere possibility, but less than a standard of more likely than not.

(3) "Relevant factors," as that phrase applies to sentencing, means the factors in the California Rules of Court that pertain to sentencing decisions and any additional factors required to or permitted to be considered in sentencing under state law and under the state and federal constitutions.

(4) "Racially discriminatory language" means language that, to an objective observer, explicitly or implicitly appeals to racial bias, including, but not limited to, racially charged or racially coded language, language that compares the defendant to an animal, or language that references the defendant's physical appearance, culture, ethnicity, or national origin. Evidence that particular words or images are used exclusively or disproportionately in cases where the defendant is of a specific race, ethnicity, or national origin is relevant to determining whether language is discriminatory.

(5) "State" includes the Attorney General, a district attorney, or a city prosecutor.

(6) "Similarly situated" means that factors that are relevant in charging and sentencing are similar and do not require that all individuals in the comparison group are identical. A defendant's conviction history may be a relevant factor to the severity of the charges, convictions, or sentences. If it is a relevant factor and the defense produces evidence that the conviction history may have been impacted by racial profiling or historical patterns of racially biased policing, the court shall consider the evidence.

(i) A defendant may share a race, ethnicity, or national origin with more than one group. A defendant may aggregate data among groups to demonstrate a violation of subdivision (a).

(j) This section applies as follows:

(1) To all cases in which judgment is not final.

(2) Commencing January 1, 2023, to all cases in which, at the time of the filing of a petition pursuant to subdivision (f) of Section 1473 raising a claim under this section, the petitioner is sentenced to death or to cases in which the motion is filed pursuant to Section 1473.7 because of actual or potential immigration consequences related to the conviction or sentence, regardless of when the judgment or disposition became final.

(3) Commencing January 1, 2024, to all cases in which, at the time of the filing of a petition pursuant to subdivision (f) of Section 1473 raising a claim under this section, the petitioner is currently serving a sentence in the state prison or in a county jail pursuant to subdivision (h) of Section 1170, or committed to the Division of Juvenile Justice for a juvenile disposition, regardless of when the judgment or disposition became final.

(4) Commencing January 1, 2025, to all cases filed pursuant to Section 1473.7 or subdivision (f) of Section 1473 in which judgment became final for a felony conviction or juvenile disposition that resulted in a commitment to the Division of Juvenile Justice on or after January 1, 2015.

(5) Commencing January 1, 2026, to all cases filed pursuant to Section 1473.7 or subdivision (f) of Section 1473 in which judgment was for a felony conviction or juvenile disposition that resulted in a commitment to the Division of Juvenile Justice, regardless of when the judgment or disposition became final.

(k) For petitions that are filed in cases for which judgment was entered before January 1, 2021, and only in those cases, if the petition is based on a violation of paragraph (1) or (2) of subdivision (a), the petitioner shall be entitled to relief as provided in subdivision (e), unless the state proves beyond a reasonable doubt that the violation did not contribute to the judgment.

Amended by Stats 2023 ch 464 (AB 1118),s 1, eff. 1/1/2024.

Amended by Stats 2023 ch 311 (SB 883),s 6, eff. 1/1/2024.

Amended by Stats 2022 ch 739 (AB 256),s 2, eff. 1/1/2023.

Added by Stats 2020 ch 317 (AB 2542),s 3.5, eff. 1/1/2021.

See Stats 2022 ch 739 (AB 256), s 1.

Title 2.5 - NIGHTCOURT

Section 750 - Nightcourt policy or program

Notwithstanding any other provision of law, in the event that the superior court of a county having a population in excess of six million has discontinued, on or after December 1, 1991, a nightcourt policy or program with respect to criminal cases, the policy or program shall, upon approval of the board of supervisors, be substantially reinstated, with at least the average level of staffing and session scheduling which occurred during the period of six months immediately prior to December 1, 1991.

Added by Stats. 1992, Ch. 284, Sec. 1. Effective July 21, 1992.

Title 3 - ADDITIONAL PROVISIONS REGARDING CRIMINAL PROCEDURE

Chapter 1 - OF THE LOCAL JURISDICTION OF PUBLIC OFFENSES

Section 777 - Liability; jurisdiction of public offense

Every person is liable to punishment by the laws of this State, for a public offense committed by him therein, except where it is by law cognizable exclusively in the courts of the United States; and except as otherwise provided by law the jurisdiction of every public offense is in any competent court within the jurisdictional territory of which it is committed.

Amended by Stats. 1951, Ch. 1674.

Section 777a - Jurisdiction in which minor child is cared for or parent is apprehended

If a parent violates the provisions of Section 270 of this code, the jurisdiction of such offense is in any competent court of either the jurisdictional territory in which the minor child is cared for or in which such parent is apprehended.

Added by Stats. 1951, Ch. 1674.

Section 777b - Perjury committed outside of state

Perjury, in violation of Section 118, committed outside of the State of California is punishable in a competent court in the jurisdictional territory in this state in which occurs the act, transaction, matter, action, or proceeding, in relation to which the testimony, declaration, deposition, or certification was given or made.

Added by Stats. 1980, Ch. 889, Sec. 4.

Section 778 - Commission of public offense commenced without state consummated within its boundaries

When the commission of a public offense, commenced without the State, is consummated within its boundaries by a defendant, himself outside the State, through the intervention of an innocent or guilty agent or any other means proceeding directly from said defendant, he is liable to punishment therefor in this State in any competent court within the jurisdictional territory of which the offense is consummated.

Amended by Stats. 1951, Ch. 1674.

Section 778a - Act culminating in commission of crime within or without state; kidnapping

(a) Whenever a person, with intent to commit a crime, does any act within this state in execution or part execution of that intent, which culminates in the commission of a crime, either within or without this state, the person is punishable for that crime in this state in the same manner as if the crime had been committed entirely within this state.

(b) Whenever a person who, within this state, kidnaps another person within the meaning of Sections 207 and 209, and thereafter carries the person into another state or country and commits any crime of violence or theft against that person in the other state or country, the person is punishable for that crime of violence or theft in this state in the same manner as if the crime had been committed within this state.

Amended by Stats 2001 ch 854 (SB 205), s 39, eff. 1/1/2002.

Section 778b - Causing, aiding, advising or encouraging person to commit crime within state by person out of state

Every person who, being out of this state, causes, aids, advises, or encourages any person to commit a crime within this state, and is afterwards found within this state, is punishable in the same manner as if he had been within this state when he caused, aided, advised, or encouraged the commission of such crime.

Added by Stats. 1905, Ch. 529.

Section 781 - Acts occurring in two or more jurisdictional territories

Except as provided in Section 923, when a public offense is committed in part in one jurisdictional territory and in part in another jurisdictional territory, or the acts or effects thereof constituting or requisite to the consummation of the offense occur in two or more jurisdictional territories, the jurisdiction for the offense is in any competent court within either jurisdictional territory.

Amended by Stats 2013 ch 76 (AB 383),s 148, eff. 1/1/2014.

Amended by Stats 2013 ch 59 (SB 514),s 2, eff. 1/1/2014.

Amended by Stats 2012 ch 568 (SB 1474),s 1, eff. 1/1/2013.

Section 782 - Public offense committed on boundary of two or more jurisdictional territories

When a public offense is committed on the boundary of two or more jurisdictional territories, or within 500 yards thereof, the jurisdiction of such offense is in any competent court within either jurisdictional territory.

Amended by Stats. 1951, Ch. 1674.

Section 783 - Public offense committed on board a vessel, train, car, motor vehicle, common carrier, or aircraft

When a public offense is committed in this State, on board a vessel navigating a river, bay, slough, lake, or canal, or lying therein, in the prosecution of its voyage, or on a railroad train or car, motor vehicle, common carrier transporting passengers or on an aircraft prosecuting its trip, the jurisdiction is in any competent court, through, on, or over the jurisdictional territory of which the vessel, train, car, motor vehicle, common carrier or aircraft passes in the course of its voyage or trip, or in the jurisdictional territory of which the voyage or trip terminates.

Amended by Stats. 1951, Ch. 1674.

Section 783.5 - Public offense committed in park situated in more than one county

When a public offense is committed in a park situated in more than one county, the jurisdiction over such an offense is in any competent court in any county in which any part of the park is situated. "Park," as used in this section means any area of land, or water, or both, which has been designated as a park or recreation area by any public agency or political subdivision of this state.

Added by Stats. 1965, Ch. 582.

Section 784 - Jurisdiction of criminal action for seizing and confining person or taking person for purpose of concubinage or prostitution

The jurisdiction of a criminal action:

(a) For forcibly and without lawful authority seizing and confining another, or inveigling or kidnapping another, with intent, against his or her will, to cause him or her to be secretly confined or imprisoned in this state, or to be sent out of the state, or from one county to another, or to be sold as a slave, or in any way held to service;

(b) For inveigling, enticing, or taking away any person for the purpose of concubinage or prostitution, as defined in subdivision (b) of Section 647; Is in any competent court within the jurisdictional territory in which the offense was committed, or in the jurisdictional territory out of which the person upon whom the offense was committed was taken or within the jurisdictional territory in which an act was done by the defendant in instigating, procuring, promoting, or aiding in the commission of the offense, or in abetting the parties concerned therein.

Amended by Stats. 1983, Ch. 990, Sec. 6.

Section 784.5 - Jurisdiction for criminal action for violation of Section 277 278 or 278.5

The jurisdiction of a criminal action for a violation of Section 277, 278, or 278.5 shall be in any one of the following jurisdictional territories:

(a) Any jurisdictional territory in which the victimized person resides, or where the agency deprived of custody is located, at the time of the taking or deprivation.

(b) The jurisdictional territory in which the minor child was taken, detained, or concealed.

(c) The jurisdictional territory in which the minor child is found. When the jurisdiction lies in more than one jurisdictional territory, the district attorneys concerned may agree which of them will prosecute the case.

Amended by Stats. 1984, Ch. 1207, Sec. 5.

Section 784.7 - Jurisdiction when more than one violation of specified crimes occurs in more than one jurisdictional territory

(a) If more than one violation of Section 220, except assault with intent to commit mayhem, 261, 264.1, 269, 286, 287, 288, 288.5, 288.7, or 289 or former Section 262 or 288a occurs in more than one jurisdictional territory, the jurisdiction of any of those offenses, and for any offenses properly joinable with that offense, is in any jurisdiction where at least one of the offenses occurred, subject to a hearing pursuant to Section 954 in the jurisdiction of the proposed trial. At the hearing pursuant to Section 954, the prosecution shall present written evidence that all district attorneys in counties with jurisdiction over the offenses agree to the venue. Charged offenses from jurisdictions where there is not a written agreement from the district attorney shall be returned to that jurisdiction.

(b) If more than one violation of Section 243.4, 261.5, 273a, 273.5, 646.9, or any crime of domestic violence as defined in subdivision (b) of Section 13700 occurs in more than one jurisdictional territory, and the defendant and the victim are the same for all of the offenses, the jurisdiction of any of those offenses and for any offenses properly joinable with that offense is in any jurisdiction where at least one of the offenses occurred, subject to a hearing pursuant to Section 954 in the jurisdiction of the proposed trial. At the hearing pursuant to Section 954, the prosecution shall present written evidence that all district attorneys in counties with jurisdiction over the offenses agree to the venue. Charged offenses from jurisdictions where there is not a written agreement from the district attorney shall be returned to that jurisdiction.

(c) If more than one violation of Section 236.1, 266h, or 266i occurs in more than one jurisdictional territory, the jurisdiction of any of those offenses, and for any offenses properly joinable with that offense, is in any jurisdiction where at least one of the offenses occurred, subject to a hearing pursuant to Section 954 in the jurisdiction of the proposed trial. At the hearing pursuant to Section 954, the prosecution shall present written evidence that all district attorneys in counties with jurisdiction over the offenses agree to the venue. Charged offenses from jurisdictions where there is not a written agreement from the district attorney shall be returned to that jurisdiction. In determining whether all counts in the complaint should be joined in one county for prosecution, the court shall consider the location and complexity of the likely evidence, where the majority of the offenses occurred, the rights of the defendant and the people, and the convenience of, or hardship to, the victim or victims and witnesses.

Amended by Stats 2023 ch 666 (AB 806),s 1, eff. 1/1/2024.

Amended by Stats 2021 ch 626 (AB 1171),s 37, eff. 1/1/2022.

Amended by Stats 2018 ch 962 (AB 1746),s 1.5, eff. 1/1/2019.

Amended by Stats 2018 ch 423 (SB 1494),s 76, eff. 1/1/2019.

Amended by Stats 2017 ch 379 (AB 368),s 1, eff. 1/1/2018.

Amended by Stats 2014 ch 246 (SB 939),s 1, eff. 1/1/2015.

Amended by Stats 2002 ch 194 (AB 2252), s 2, eff. 1/1/2003.

Section 784.8 - Jurisdiction in multi-jurisdictional elder abuse cases

If more than one felony violation of subdivision (d) or (e) of Section 368 occurs in more than one jurisdictional territory, the jurisdiction of any of those offenses, and for any offenses properly joinable with that offense, is in any jurisdiction where at least one of the offenses occurred, subject to a hearing, pursuant to Section 954, within the jurisdiction of the proposed trial. At the hearing held pursuant to Section 954, the prosecution shall present written evidence that all district attorneys in counties with jurisdiction of the offenses agree to the venue. Charged offenses from any jurisdiction where there is not a written agreement from the district attorney shall be returned to that jurisdiction. In determining whether all counts in the complaint should be joined in one county for prosecution, the court shall consider the location and complexity of the likely evidence, where the majority of the offenses occurred, the rights of the defendant and the people, and the convenience of, or hardship to, the victim or victims and witnesses.

Added by Stats 2019 ch 206 (SB 304),s 1, eff. 1/1/2020.

Section 785 - Jurisdiction for incest or bigamy

When the offense of incest is committed in the jurisdictional territory of one competent court and the defendant is apprehended in the jurisdictional territory of another competent court the jurisdiction is in either court.

When the offense of bigamy is committed, the jurisdiction is in any competent court within the jurisdictional territory of which the marriage took place, or cohabitation occurred or the defendant was apprehended.

Amended by Stats. 1951, Ch. 1674.

Section 786 - Jurisdiction for burglary, carjacking robbery, theft, embezzlement, or unauthorized use, retention, or transfer of personal identifying information

(a) If property taken in one jurisdictional territory by burglary, carjacking, robbery, theft, or embezzlement has been brought into another, or when property is received in one jurisdictional territory with the knowledge that it has been stolen or embezzled and the property was stolen or embezzled in another jurisdictional territory, the jurisdiction of the offense is in any competent court within either jurisdictional territory, or any contiguous jurisdictional territory if the arrest is made within the contiguous territory, the prosecution secures on the record the defendant's knowing, voluntary, and intelligent waiver of the right of vicinage, and the defendant is charged with one or more property crimes in the arresting territory.

(b)

(1) The jurisdiction of a criminal action for unauthorized use, retention, or transfer of personal identifying information, as defined in subdivision (b) of Section 530.55, shall also include the county where the theft of the personal identifying information occurred, the county in which the victim resided at the time the offense was committed, or the county where the information was used for an illegal purpose. If multiple offenses of unauthorized use of personal identifying information, either all involving the same defendant or defendants and the same personal identifying information belonging to the one person, or all involving the same defendant or defendants and the same scheme or substantially similar activity, occur in multiple jurisdictions, then any of those jurisdictions is a proper jurisdiction for all of the offenses. Jurisdiction also extends to all associated offenses connected together in their commission to the underlying identity theft offense or identity theft offenses.

(2) When charges alleging multiple offenses of unauthorized use of personal identifying information occurring in multiple territorial jurisdictions are filed in one county pursuant to this section, the court shall hold a hearing to consider whether the matter should proceed in the county of filing, or whether one or more counts should be severed. The district attorney filing the complaint shall present evidence to the court that the district attorney in each county where any of the charges could have been filed has agreed that the matter should proceed in the county of filing. In determining whether all counts in the complaint should be joined in one county for prosecution, the court shall consider the location and complexity of the likely evidence, where the majority of the offenses occurred, whether or not the offenses involved substantially similar activity or the same scheme, the rights of the defendant and the people, and the convenience of, or hardship to, the victim and witnesses.

(3) When an action for unauthorized use, retention, or transfer of personal identifying information is filed in the county in which the victim resided at the time the offense was committed, and no other basis for the jurisdiction applies, the court, upon its own motion or the motion of the defendant, shall hold a hearing to determine whether the county of the victim's residence is the proper venue for trial of the case. In ruling on the matter, the court shall consider the rights of the parties, the access of the parties to evidence, the convenience to witnesses, and the interests of justice.

(c)

(1) The jurisdiction of a criminal action for conduct specified in paragraph (4) of subdivision (j) of Section 647 shall also include the county in which the offense occurred, the county in which the victim resided at the time the offense was committed, or the county in which the intimate image was used for an illegal purpose. If multiple offenses of unauthorized distribution of an intimate image, either all involving the same defendant or defendants and the same intimate image belonging to the one person, or all involving the same defendant or defendants and the same scheme or substantially similar activity, occur in multiple jurisdictions, then any of those jurisdictions is a proper jurisdiction for all of the offenses. Jurisdiction also extends to all associated offenses connected together in their commission to the underlying unauthorized distribution of an intimate image.

(2) When charges alleging multiple offenses of unauthorized distribution of an intimate image occurring in multiple territorial jurisdictions are filed in one county pursuant to this section, the court shall hold a hearing to consider whether the matter should proceed in the county of filing, or whether one or more counts should be severed. The district attorney filing the complaint shall present evidence to the court that the district attorney in each county where any of the charges could have been filed has agreed that the matter should proceed in the county of filing. In determining whether all counts in the complaint should be joined in one county for prosecution, the court shall consider the location and complexity of the likely evidence, where the majority of the offenses occurred, whether the offenses involved substantially similar activity or the same scheme, the rights of the defendant and the people, and the convenience of, or hardship to, the victim and witnesses.

(3) When an action for unauthorized distribution of an intimate image is filed in the county in which the victim resided at the time the offense was committed, and no other basis for the jurisdiction applies, the court, upon its own motion or the motion of the defendant, shall hold a hearing to determine whether the county of the victim's residence is the proper venue for trial of the case. In ruling on the matter, the court shall consider the rights of the parties, the access of the parties to evidence, the convenience to witnesses, and the interests of justice.

(d) This section does not alter victims' rights under Section 530.6.

Amended by Stats 2015 ch 643 (AB 1310),s 1, eff. 1/1/2016.

Amended by Stats 2010 ch 709 (SB 1062),s 12, eff. 1/1/2011.

Amended by Stats 2009 ch 40 (SB 226),s 1, eff. 1/1/2010.

Amended by Stats 2008 ch 47 (SB 612),s 1, eff. 1/1/2009.

Amended by Stats 2002 ch 908 (AB 1773), s 1, eff. 1/1/2003.

Section 786.5 - Jurisdiction for theft extended

The jurisdiction of a criminal action brought by the Attorney General for theft, as defined in subdivision (a) of Section 484, or a violation of Section 490.4 or 496, shall also include the county where an offense involving the theft or receipt of the stolen merchandise occurred, the county in which the merchandise was recovered, or the county where any act was done by the defendant in instigating, procuring, promoting, or aiding in the commission of a theft offense or a violation of Section 490.4 or 496 or in abetting the parties concerned therein. If multiple offenses of theft or violations of Section 490.4 or 496, either all involving the same defendant or defendants and the same merchandise, or all involving the same defendant or defendants and the same scheme or substantially similar activity, occur in multiple jurisdictions, then any of those jurisdictions are a proper jurisdiction for all of the offenses. Jurisdiction also extends to all associated offenses connected together in their commission to the underlying theft offenses or violations of Section 490.4 or 496.

Added by Stats 2022 ch 949 (AB 1613),s 1, eff. 1/1/2023.

Amended by Stats 2019 ch 25 (SB 94),s 29, eff. 6/27/2019.

Added by Stats 2018 ch 803 (AB 1065),s 2, eff. 1/1/2019.

Section 787 - Jurisdiction for terrorist attack

When multiple offenses punishable under one or more of Sections 11418, 11418.5, and 11419 occur in more than one jurisdictional territory, and the offenses are part of a single scheme or terrorist attack, the jurisdiction of any of those offenses is in any jurisdiction where at least one of those offenses occurred.

Added by Stats 2002 ch 64 (AB 2106), s 1, eff. 6/20/2002.

Section 788 - Jurisdiction of criminal action for treason

The jurisdiction of a criminal action for treason, when the overt act is committed out of the State, is in any county of the State.

Amended by Code Amendments 1880, Ch. 47.

Section 789 - Jurisdiction of criminal action for stealing or embezzling, in any other state, the property of another

The jurisdiction of a criminal action for stealing or embezzling, in any other state, the property of another, or receiving it knowing it to have been stolen or embezzled, and bringing the same into this State, is in any competent court into or through the jurisdictional territory of which such stolen or embezzled property has been brought.

Amended by Stats. 1951, Ch. 1674.

Section 790 - Jurisdiction of criminal action for murder or manslaughter

(a) The jurisdiction of a criminal action for murder or manslaughter is in the county where the fatal injury was inflicted or in the county in which the injured party died or in the county in which his or her body was found. However, if the defendant is indicted in the county in which the fatal injury was inflicted, at any time before his or her trial in another county, the sheriff of the other county shall, if the defendant is in custody, deliver the defendant upon demand to the sheriff of the county in which the fatal injury was inflicted. When the fatal injury was inflicted and the injured person died or his or her body was found within five hundred yards of the boundary of two or more counties, jurisdiction is in either county.

(b) If a defendant is charged with a special circumstance pursuant to paragraph (3) of subdivision (a) of Section 190.2, the jurisdiction for any charged murder, and for any crimes properly joinable with that murder, shall be in any county that has jurisdiction pursuant to subdivision (a) for one or more of the murders charged in a single complaint or indictment as long as the charged murders are "connected together in their commission," as that phrase is used in Section 954, and subject to a hearing in the jurisdiction where the prosecution is attempting to consolidate the charged murders. If the charged murders are not joined or consolidated, the murder that was charged outside of the county that has jurisdiction pursuant to subdivision (a) shall be returned to that county.

EFFECTIVE 1/1/2000. Amended July 12, 1999 (Bill Number: SB 966) (Chapter 83).

Section 791 - Jurisdiction in case of accessory

In the case of an accessory, as defined in Section 32, in the commission of a public offense, the jurisdiction is in any competent court within the jurisdictional territory of which the offense of the accessory was committed, notwithstanding the principal offense was committed in another jurisdictional territory.

Amended by Stats. 1951, Ch. 1674.

Section 792 - Jurisdiction of criminal action against principal

The jurisdiction of a criminal action against a principal in the commission of a public offense, when such principal is not present at the commission of the offense is in the same court it would be under this code if he were so present and aiding and abetting therein.

Amended by Stats. 1951, Ch. 1674.

Section 793 - Conviction or acquittal in other jurisdiction as bar to prosecution or indictment in California

When an act charged as a public offense is within the jurisdiction of the United States, or of another state or territory of the United States, as well as of this state, a conviction or acquittal thereof in that other jurisdiction is a bar to the prosecution or indictment in this state.

Amended by Stats 2004 ch 511 (AB 1432), s 4, eff. 1/1/2005.

Section 793.5 - No credit for actual time served in another country

Any person convicted of a crime based upon an act or omission for which he or she has been acquitted or convicted in another country shall be entitled to credit for any actual time served in custody in a penal institution in that country for the crime.

Added by Stats 2004 ch 511 (AB 1432), s 5, eff. 1/1/2005.

Section 794 - Conviction or acquittal in one court as bar to prosecution in another

Where an offense is within the jurisdiction of two or more courts, a conviction or acquittal thereof in one court is a bar to a prosecution therefor in another.

Amended by Stats. 1951, Ch. 1674.

Section 795 - Jurisdiction of violation of Sections 412, 413, or 414, or conspiracy to violate

The jurisdiction of a violation of Sections 412, 413, or 414, or a conspiracy to violate any of said sections, is in any competent court within the jurisdictional territory of which:

First. Any act is done towards the commission of the offense; or,

Second. The offender passed, whether into, out of, or through it, to commit the offense; or,

Third. The offender is arrested.

Amended by Stats. 1951, Ch. 1674.

Chapter 2 - TIME OF COMMENCING CRIMINAL ACTIONS

Section 799 - Prosecution for offense punishable by death or by imprisonment for life or for life without possibility of parole, or for embezzlement of public money

(a) Prosecution for an offense punishable by death or by imprisonment in the state prison for life or for life without the possibility of parole, or for the embezzlement of public money, may be commenced at any time.

(b)

(1) Prosecution for a felony offense described in paragraph (1), (2), (3), (4), (6), or (7) of subdivision (a) of Section 261, paragraph (1), (2), (3), (4), or (5) of subdivision (a) of former Section 262, Section 264.1, paragraph (2) or (3) of subdivision (c) of, or subdivision (d), (f), (g), (i), or (k) of, Section 286, paragraph (2) or (3) of subdivision (c) of, or subdivision (d), (f), (g), (i), or (k) of, Section 287 or former Section 288a, subdivision (a) of Section 288 involving substantial sexual conduct as defined in subdivision (b) of Section

1203.066, subdivision (b) of Section 288, Section 288.5, or subdivision (a), (b), (d), (e), or (g) of Section 289 may be commenced at any time.

(2) This subdivision applies to crimes that were committed on or after January 1, 2017, and to crimes for which the statute of limitations that was in effect prior to January 1, 2017, has not run as of January 1, 2017.

(c) This section applies when the defendant was a minor at the time of the commission of the offense and the prosecuting attorney could have petitioned the court for a fitness hearing pursuant to Section 707 of the Welfare and Institutions Code.

Amended by Stats 2021 ch 626 (AB 1171),s 38, eff. 1/1/2022.

Amended by Stats 2019 ch 497 (AB 991),s 196, eff. 1/1/2020.

Amended by Stats 2018 ch 423 (SB 1494),s 77, eff. 1/1/2019.

Amended by Stats 2016 ch 777 (SB 813),s 1, eff. 1/1/2017.

Section 800 - Prosecution for offense punishable by imprisonment for eight years or more

Except as provided in Section 799, prosecution for an offense punishable by imprisonment in the state prison for eight years or more or by imprisonment pursuant to subdivision (h) of Section 1170 for eight years or more shall be commenced within six years after commission of the offense.

Amended by Stats 2011 ch 12 (AB X1-17),s 11, eff. 9/20/2011, op. 10/1/2011.

Amended by Stats 2011 ch 39 (AB 117),s 68, eff. 6/30/2011.

Amended by Stats 2011 ch 39 (AB 117),s 24, eff. 6/30/2011.

Amended by Stats 2011 ch 15 (AB 109),s 445, eff. 4/4/2011, but operative no earlier than October 1, 2011, and only upon creation of a community corrections grant program to assist in implementing this act and upon an appropriation to fund the grant program.

Section 801 - Prosecution for offense punishable by imprisonment

Except as provided in Sections 799 and 800, prosecution for an offense punishable by imprisonment in the state prison or pursuant to subdivision (h) of Section 1170 shall be commenced within three years after commission of the offense.

Amended by Stats 2011 ch 39 (AB 117),s 68, eff. 6/30/2011.

Amended by Stats 2011 ch 15 (AB 109),s 446, eff. 4/4/2011, but operative no earlier than October 1, 2011, and only upon creation of a community corrections grant program to assist in implementing this act and upon an appropriation to fund the grant program.

Section 801.1 - Prosecution for felony offense relating to penetration by unknown object that is alleged to have been committed when victim was under age of 18 years

(a)

(1) Notwithstanding any other limitation of time described in this chapter, prosecution for a felony offense described in Section 261, 286, 287, 288, 288.5, or 289, or former Section 288a, or Section 289.5, as enacted by Chapter 293 of the Statutes of 1991 relating to penetration by an unknown object, that is alleged to have been committed when the victim was under 18 years of age, may be commenced any time prior to the victim's 40th birthday.

(2) Paragraph (1) shall only apply to crimes that were committed on or after January 1, 2015, or for which the statute of limitations that was in effect prior to January 1, 2015, has not run as of January 1, 2015.

(b) Notwithstanding any other limitation of time described in this chapter, if either subdivision (a) of this section or subdivision (b) of Section 799 does not apply, prosecution for a felony offense described in subdivision (c) of Section 290 shall be commenced within 10 years after commission of the offense.

Amended by Stats 2018 ch 423 (SB 1494),s 78, eff. 1/1/2019.

Amended by Stats 2016 ch 777 (SB 813),s 2, eff. 1/1/2017.

Amended by Stats 2014 ch 921 (SB 926),s 1, eff. 1/1/2015.

Amended by Stats 2007 ch 579 (SB 172),s 40, eff. 10/13/2007.

Amended by Stats 2005 ch 479 (SB 111),s 2, eff. 1/1/2006

Added by Stats 2004 ch 368 (AB 1667), s 1, eff. 1/1/2005.

Section 801.2 - Prosecution for violation of Section 311.4(b)

Notwithstanding any other limitation of time prescribed in this chapter, prosecution for a violation of subdivision (b) of Section 311.4 shall commence within 10 years of the date of production of the pornographic material.

Added by Stats 2006 ch 337 (SB 1128),s 35, eff. 9/20/2006.

Section 801.5 - Prosecution for any offense described in Section 803(c)

Notwithstanding Section 801 or any other provision of law, prosecution for any offense described in subdivision (c) of Section 803 shall be commenced within four years after discovery of the commission of the offense, or within four years after the completion of the offense, whichever is later.

Amended by Stats. 1995, Ch. 704, Sec. 1. Effective January 1, 1996.

Section 801.6 - Prosecution for any offense proscribed by Section 368

Notwithstanding any other limitation of time described in this chapter, prosecution for any offense proscribed by Section 368, except for a violation of any provision of law proscribing theft or embezzlement, may be filed at any time within five years from the date of occurrence of such offense.

Amended by Stats 2022 ch 587 (AB 2274),s 1, eff. 1/1/2023.

Amended by Stats 2018 ch 943 (AB 2302),s 1, eff. 1/1/2019.

Section 801.7 - Limitations of actions for felony offense in Section 502

(a) Notwithstanding Section 801 or any other law, prosecution for a felony offense described in Section 502 shall be commenced within three years after discovery of the commission of the offense, or within three years after the offense could have reasonably been discovered, provided, however, that in any case a complaint shall not be filed more than six years after the commission of the offense.

(b) This section applies to crimes that are committed on or after January 1, 2022, and to crimes for which the statute of limitations that was in effect prior to January 1, 2022, has not elapsed as of January 1, 2022.

Added by Stats 2021 ch 206 (AB 1247),s 1, eff. 1/1/2022.

Section 801.8 - Mandated reporters; statute of limitations

(a)Notwithstanding any other limitation of time described in this chapter, prosecution for the failure of a mandated reporter to report an incident under Section 11166 known or reasonably suspected by the mandated reporter to be sexual assault as defined in Section 11165.1, may be filed at any time within five years from the date of occurrence of such offense.

(b)Notwithstanding any other limitation of time described in this chapter, prosecution for the failure of a mandated reporter to report an incident under Section 11166 known or reasonably suspected by the mandated reporter to be child abuse or severe neglect that is not described in subdivision (a), may be filed within one year of the discovery of the offense, but in no case later than four years after the commission of the offense.

Added by Stats 2022 ch 587 (AB 2274),s 2, eff. 1/1/2023.

Section 802 - Prosecution for offense not punishable by death or imprisonment; prosecution for misdemeanor violations

(a) Except as provided in subdivision (b), (c), (d), or (e), prosecution for an offense not punishable by death or imprisonment in the state prison or pursuant to subdivision (h) of Section 1170 shall be commenced within one year after commission of the offense.

(b) Prosecution for a misdemeanor violation of Section 647.6 or former Section 647a committed with or upon a minor under 14 years of age shall be commenced within three years after commission of the offense.

(c) Prosecution of a misdemeanor violation of Section 729 of the Business and Professions Code shall be commenced within two years after commission of the offense.

(d) Prosecution of a misdemeanor violation of Chapter 9 (commencing with Section 7000) of Division 3 of the Business and Professions Code shall be commenced as follows:

(1) With respect to Sections 7028.17, 7068.5, and 7068.7 of the Business and Professions Code, within one year of the commission of the offense.

(2) With respect to Sections 7027.1, 7028.1, 7028.15, 7118.4, 7118.5, 7118.6, 7126, 7153, 7156, 7157, 7158, 7159.5 (licensee only), 7159.14 (licensee only), 7161, and 7189 of the Business and Professions Code, within two years of the commission of the offense.

(3) With respect to Sections 7027.3 and 7028.16 of the Business and Professions Code, within three years of the commission of the offense.

(4) With respect to Sections 7028, 7159.5(nonlicensee only), and 7159.14(nonlicensee only) of the Business and Professions Code, within four years of the commission of the offense.

(e)

(1) Prosecution for a misdemeanor violation of Section 6126, 10085.6, 10139, or 10147.6 of the Business and Professions Code or Section 2944.6 or 2944.7 of the Civil Code shall be commenced within three years after discovery of the commission of the offense, or within three years after completion of the offense, whichever is later.

(2) Prosecution for a misdemeanor violation of subdivisions (b) and (e) of Section 119 of the Business and Professions Code, by parties licensed or subject to licensure pursuant to Chapter 9 (commencing with Section 7000) of Division 3 of that code, within three years after discovery of the commission of the offense, or within three years after completion of the offense, whichever is later.

Amended by Stats 2023 ch 403 (SB 601),s 2, eff. 1/1/2024.

Amended by Stats 2012 ch 569 (AB 1950),s 4, eff. 1/1/2013.

Amended by Stats 2012 ch 43 (SB 1023),s 24, eff. 6/27/2012.

Added by Stats 2004 ch 586 (AB 2216), s 4, eff. 1/1/2005.

Repealed by Stats 2004 ch 586 (AB 2216), s 3, eff. 1/1/2006, op. 7/1/2005.

Amended by Stats 2004 ch 586 (AB 2216), s 3, eff. 1/1/2005.

Amended by Stats 2002 ch 828 (AB 2499), s 2, eff. 1/1/2003.

Section 802.5 - Prosecution for offense described in Business and Professions Code Section 18897.93

Notwithstanding Section 802 or any other provision of law, prosecution for the offense described in Section 18897.93 of the Business and Professions Code shall be commenced within three years after discovery of the commission of the offense.

Added by Stats 2011 ch 146 (SB 238),s 2, eff. 1/1/2012.

Section 803 - Tolling or extension of limitation of time

(a)Except as provided in this section, a limitation of time prescribed in this chapter is not tolled or extended for any reason.

(b)The time during which prosecution of the same person for the same conduct is pending in a court of this state is not a part of a limitation of time prescribed in this chapter.

(c)A limitation of time prescribed in this chapter does not commence to run until the discovery of an offense described in this subdivision. This subdivision applies to an offense punishable by imprisonment in the state prison or imprisonment pursuant to subdivision (h) of Section 1170, a material element of which is fraud or breach of a fiduciary obligation, the commission of the crimes of theft or embezzlement upon an elder or dependent adult, or the basis of which is misconduct in office by a public officer, employee, or appointee, including, but not limited to, the following offenses:

(1)Grand theft of any type, forgery, falsification of public records, or acceptance of, or asking, receiving, or agreeing to receive, a bribe, by a public official or a public employee, including, but not limited to, a violation of Section 68, 86, or 93.

(2)A violation of Section 72, 118, 118a, 132, 134, or 186.10.

(3)A violation of Section 25540, of any type, or Section 25541 of the Corporations Code.

(4)A violation of Section 1090 or 27443 of the Government Code.

(5)Felony welfare fraud or Medi-Cal fraud in violation of Section 11483 or 14107 of the Welfare and Institutions Code.

(6)Felony insurance fraud in violation of Section 548 or 550 of this code or former Section 1871.1, or Section 1871.4, of the Insurance Code.

(7)A violation of Section 580, 581, 582, 583, or 584 of the Business and Professions Code.

(8)A violation of Section 22430 of the Business and Professions Code.

(9)A violation of Section 103800 of the Health and Safety Code.

(10)A violation of Section 529a.

(11)A violation of subdivision (d) or (e) of Section 368.

(d)If the defendant is out of the state when or after the offense is committed, the prosecution may be commenced as provided in Section 804 within the limitations of time prescribed by this chapter, and no time up to a maximum of three years during which the defendant is not within the state shall be a part of those limitations.

(e)A limitation of time prescribed in this chapter does not commence to run until the offense has been discovered, or could have reasonably been discovered, with regard to offenses under Division 7 (commencing with Section 13000) of the Water Code, under Chapter 6.5 (commencing with Section 25100) or Chapter 6.7 (commencing with Section 25280) of Division 20 of, or Part 4 (commencing with Section 41500) of Division 26 of, or Part 2 (commencing with Section 78000) of Division 45 of, the Health and Safety Code, or under Section 386, or offenses under Chapter 5 (commencing with Section 2000) of Division 2 of, Chapter 9 (commencing with Section 4000) of Division 2 of, Section 6126 of, Chapter 10 (commencing with Section 7301) of Division 3 of, or Chapter 19.5 (commencing with Section 22440) of Division 8 of, the Business and Professions Code.

(f)

(1)Notwithstanding any other limitation of time described in this chapter, if subdivision (b) of Section 799 does not apply, a criminal complaint may be filed within one year of the date of a report to a California law enforcement agency by a person of any age alleging that the person, while under 18 years of age, was the victim of a crime described in Section 261, 286, 287, 288, 288.5, or 289, former Section 288a, or Section 289.5, as enacted by Chapter 293 of the Statutes of 1991 relating to penetration by an unknown object.

(2)This subdivision applies only if all of the following occur:

(A)The limitation period specified in Section 800, 801, or 801.1, whichever is later, has expired.

(B)The crime involved substantial sexual conduct, as described in subdivision (b) of Section 1203.066, excluding masturbation that is not mutual.

(C)There is independent evidence that corroborates the victim's allegation. If the victim was 21 years of age or older at the time of the report, the independent evidence shall clearly and convincingly corroborate the victim's allegation.

(3)Evidence shall not be used to corroborate the victim's allegation if that evidence would otherwise be inadmissible during trial. Independent evidence excludes the opinions of mental health professionals.

(4)

(A)In a criminal investigation involving any of the crimes listed in paragraph (1) committed against a child, if the applicable limitations period has not expired, that period shall be tolled from the time a party initiates litigation challenging a grand jury subpoena until the end of the litigation, including any associated writ or appellate proceeding, or until the final disclosure of evidence to the investigating or prosecuting agency, if that disclosure is ordered pursuant to the subpoena after the litigation.

(B)This subdivision does not affect the definition or applicability of any evidentiary privilege.

(C)This subdivision shall not apply if a court finds that the grand jury subpoena was issued or caused to be issued in bad faith.

(g)

(1)Notwithstanding any other limitation of time described in this chapter, a criminal complaint may be filed within one year of the date on which the identity of the suspect is conclusively established by DNA testing, if both of the following conditions are met:

(A)The crime is one that is described in subdivision (c) of Section 290.

(B)The offense was committed before January 1, 2001, and biological evidence collected in connection with the offense is analyzed for DNA type no later than January 1, 2004, or the offense was committed on or after January 1, 2001, and biological evidence collected in connection with the offense is analyzed for DNA type no later than two years from the date of the offense.

(2)For purposes of this section, "DNA" means deoxyribonucleic acid.

(h)For any crime, the proof of which depends substantially upon evidence that was seized under a warrant, but which is unavailable to the prosecuting authority under the procedures described in People v. Superior Court (Laff) (2001) 25 Cal.4th 703, People v. Superior Court (Bauman & Rose) (1995) 37 Cal.App.4th 1757, or subdivision (c) of Section 1524, relating to claims of evidentiary privilege or attorney work product, the limitation of time prescribed in this chapter shall be tolled from the time of the seizure until final disclosure of the evidence to the prosecuting authority. This section does not otherwise affect the definition or applicability of any evidentiary privilege or attorney work product.

(i)

(1)Notwithstanding any other limitation of time described in this chapter, a criminal complaint may be filed within one year of the date on which a hidden recording is discovered related to a violation of paragraph (2) or (3) of subdivision (j) of Section 647.

(2)Notwithstanding any other limitation of time described in this chapter, a criminal complaint may be filed within one year of the date on which it is discovered that, but not more than four years after, an image was intentionally distributed in violation of paragraph (4) of subdivision (j) of Section 647.

(j)Notwithstanding any other limitation of time described in this chapter, if a person flees the scene of an accident that caused death or permanent, serious injury, as defined in subdivision (d) of Section 20001 of the Vehicle Code, a criminal complaint brought pursuant to paragraph (2) of subdivision (b) of Section 20001 of the Vehicle Code may be filed within the applicable time period described in Section 801 or 802 or one year after the person is initially identified by law enforcement as a suspect in the commission of the offense, whichever is later, but in no case later than six years after the commission of the offense.

(k)Notwithstanding any other limitation of time described in this chapter, if a person flees the scene of an accident, a criminal complaint brought pursuant to paragraph (1) or (2) of subdivision (c) of Section 192 may be filed within the applicable time period described in Section 801 or 802, or one year after the person is initially identified by law enforcement as a suspect in the commission of that offense, whichever is later, but in no case later than six years after the commission of the offense.

(l)A limitation of time prescribed in this chapter does not commence to run until the discovery of an offense involving the offering or giving of a bribe to a public official or public employee, including, but not limited to, a violation of Section 67, 67.5, 85, 92, or 165, or Section 35230 or 72530 of the Education Code.

(m) Notwithstanding any other limitation of time prescribed in this chapter, if a person actively conceals or attempts to conceal an accidental death in violation of Section 152, a criminal complaint may be filed within one year after the person is initially identified by law enforcement as a suspect in the commission of that offense, provided, however, that in any case a complaint may not be filed more than four years after the commission of the offense.

(n)

(1) Notwithstanding any other limitation of time described in this chapter, a criminal complaint brought pursuant to a violation of Section 367g may be filed within one year of the discovery of the offense or within one year after the offense could have reasonably been discovered.

(2) This subdivision applies to crimes that were committed on or after January 1, 2021, and to crimes for which the statute of limitations that was in effect before January 1, 2021, has not run as of January 1, 2021.

Amended by Stats 2022 ch 258 (AB 2327),s 115, eff. 1/1/2023, op. 1/1/2024.
Amended by Stats 2021 ch 483 (SB 23),s 1, eff. 1/1/2022.
Amended by Stats 2020 ch 244 (AB 2014),s 1, eff. 1/1/2021.
Amended by Stats 2018 ch 423 (SB 1494),s 79, eff. 1/1/2019.
Amended by Stats 2017 ch 74 (SB 610),s 2, eff. 1/1/2018.
Amended by Stats 2016 ch 777 (SB 813),s 3, eff. 1/1/2017.
Amended by Stats 2015 ch 338 (AB 835),s 1, eff. 1/1/2016.
Amended by Stats 2014 ch 191 (SB 950),s 1, eff. 1/1/2015.
Amended by Stats 2013 ch 765 (AB 184),s 1, eff. 1/1/2014.
Amended by Stats 2012 ch 162 (SB 1171),s 238, eff. 1/1/2013.
Amended by Stats 2011 ch 211 (AB 708),s 1.5, eff. 1/1/2012.
Amended by Stats 2011 ch 39 (AB 117),s 68, eff. 6/30/2011.
Amended by Stats 2011 ch 15 (AB 109),s 447, eff. 4/4/2011, but operative no earlier than October 1, 2011, and only upon creation of a community corrections grant program to assist in implementing this act and upon an appropriation to fund the grant program.
Amended by Stats 2007 ch 579 (SB 172),s 41, eff. 10/13/2007.
Amended by Stats 2005 ch 479 (SB 111),s 3, eff. 1/1/2006
Added by Stats 2005 ch 2 (SB 16),s 3, eff. 2/28/2005.
Previously amended by Stats 2004 ch 368 (AB 1667), s 2, eff. 1/1/2005.
Previously amended by Stats 2004 ch 2 (SB X4-2), s 7, eff. 1/1/2005.
Previously amended by Stats 2003 ch 73 (AB 1105), s 1, eff. 1/1/2004.
Previously amended by Stats 2003 ch 152 (SB 337), s 1, eff. 1/1/2004.
Previously amended by Stats 2003 ch 468 (SB 851), s 10, eff. 1/1/2004.
Previously amended by Stats 2002 ch 787 (SB 1798), s 17, eff. 1/1/2003.
Previously amended by Stats 2002 ch 1059 (AB 2055), s 2, eff. 9/29/2002.
Previously amended by Stats 2001 ch 235 (AB 78), s 1, eff. 1/1/2002.
Previously amended by Stats 2000 ch 235 (AB 1742), s 1, eff. 1/1/2001.
Previously amended October 10, 1999 (Bill Number: SB 1307) (Chapter 983).

Section 803.5 - Limitation of time commencing with discovery of violation of Section 115 or 530.5
With respect to a violation of Section 115 or 530.5, a limitation of time prescribed in this chapter does not commence to run until the discovery of the offense.
Added by Stats 2003 ch 468 (SB 851), s 10.5, eff. 1/1/2004.

Section 803.6 - More than one time period applicable; change of time period
(a) If more than one time period described in this chapter applies, the time for commencing an action shall be governed by that period that expires the latest in time.
(b) Any change in the time period for the commencement of prosecution described in this chapter applies to any crime if prosecution for the crime was not barred on the effective date of the change by the statute of limitations in effect immediately prior to the effective date of the change.
(c) This section is declaratory of existing law.
Added by Stats 2004 ch 368 (AB 1667), s 3, eff. 1/1/2005.

Section 803.7 - Prosecution for Infliction of corporal injury resulting in traumatic injury upon person who is spouse, former spouse, cohabitant, former cohabitant, or parent of child; applicability of section
(a) Notwithstanding any other law, prosecution for a violation of Section 273.5 may be commenced within 5 years of the crime.
(b) This section applies to crimes that are committed on or after January 1, 2020, and to crimes for which the statute of limitations that was in effect prior to January 1, 2020, has not elapsed as of January 1, 2020.
Added by Stats 2019 ch 546 (SB 273),s 3, eff. 1/1/2020.

Section 804 - Commencement of prosecution for offense
 Except as otherwise provided in this chapter, for the purpose of this chapter, prosecution for an offense is commenced when any of the following occurs:
(a) An indictment or information is filed.
(b) A complaint is filed charging a misdemeanor or infraction.
(c) The defendant is arraigned on a complaint that charges the defendant with a felony.
(d) An arrest warrant or bench warrant is issued, provided the warrant names or describes the defendant with the same degree of particularity required for an indictment, information, or complaint.
Amended by Stats 2008 ch 110 (SB 610),s 1, eff. 1/1/2009.
Amended by Stats 2006 ch 901 (SB 1422),s 8.1, eff. 1/1/2007.

Section 805 - Applicable limitation of time

For the purpose of determining the applicable limitation of time pursuant to this chapter:

(a) An offense is deemed punishable by the maximum punishment prescribed by statute for the offense, regardless of the punishment actually sought or imposed. Any enhancement of punishment prescribed by statute shall be disregarded in determining the maximum punishment prescribed by statute for an offense.

(b) The limitation of time applicable to an offense that is necessarily included within a greater offense is the limitation of time applicable to the lesser included offense, regardless of the limitation of time applicable to the greater offense.

Added by Stats. 1984, Ch. 1270, Sec. 2.

Chapter 3 - COMPLAINTS BEFORE MAGISTRATES

Section 806 - Complaint

A proceeding for the examination before a magistrate of a person on a charge of a felony must be commenced by written complaint under oath subscribed by the complainant and filed with the magistrate. Such complaint may be verified on information and belief. When the complaint is used as a pleading to which the defendant pleads guilty under Section 859a of this code, the complaint shall contain the same allegations, including the charge of prior conviction or convictions of crime, as are required for indictments and informations and, wherever applicable, shall be construed and shall have substantially the same effect as provided in this code for indictments and informations.

Amended by Stats. 1998, Ch. 931, Sec. 359. Effective September 28, 1998.

Section 807 - Magistrate

A magistrate is an officer having power to issue a warrant for the arrest of a person charged with a public offense.

Enacted 1872.

Section 808 - Persons who are magistrates

The following persons are magistrates:

(a) The judges of the Supreme Court.

(b) The judges of the courts of appeal.

(c) The judges of the superior courts.

Amended by Stats 2003 ch 62 (SB 600), s 229, eff. 1/1/2004.

Amended by Stats 2002 ch 784 (SB 1316), s 529, eff. 1/1/2003.

Section 809 - Night-time commissioner of Santa Clara County Superior Court

The night-time commissioner of the Santa Clara County Superior Court shall be considered a magistrate for the purpose of conducting prompt probable cause hearings for persons arrested without an arrest warrant as mandated by law.

Added by Stats. 1993, Ch. 909, Sec. 14. Effective January 1, 1994.

Section 810 - Schedule; contacting magistrate

(a) The presiding judge of the superior court in a county shall, as often as is necessary, designate on a schedule not less than one judge of the court to be reasonably available on call as a magistrate for the setting of orders for discharge from actual custody upon bail, the issuance of search warrants, and for such other matters as may by the magistrate be deemed appropriate, at all times when a court is not in session in the county.

(b) The officer in charge of a jail, or a person the officer designates, in which an arrested person is held in custody shall assist the arrested person or the arrested person's attorney in contacting the magistrate on call as soon as possible for the purpose of obtaining release on bail.

(c) Any telephone call made pursuant to this section by an arrested person while in custody or by such person's attorney shall not count or be considered as a telephone call for purposes of Section 851.5 of the Penal Code.

Amended by Stats 2002 ch 784 (SB 1316), s 530, eff. 1/1/2003.

Chapter 4 - THE WARRANT OF ARREST

Section 813 - Arrest warrant; summons

(a) When a complaint is filed with a magistrate charging a felony originally triable in the superior court of the county in which he or she sits, if, and only if, the magistrate is satisfied from the complaint that the offense complained of has been committed and that there is reasonable ground to believe that the defendant has committed it, the magistrate shall issue a warrant for the arrest of the defendant, except that, upon the request of the prosecutor, a summons instead of an arrest warrant shall be issued.

(b) A summons issued pursuant to this section shall be in substantially the same form as an arrest warrant and shall contain all of the following:

(1) The name of the defendant.

(2) The date and time the summons was issued.

(3) The city or county where the summons was issued.

(4) The signature of the magistrate, judge, justice, or other issuing authority who is issuing the summons with the title of his or her office and the name of the court or other issuing agency.

(5) The offense or offenses with which the defendant is charged.

(6) The time and place at which the defendant is to appear.

(7) Notification that the defendant is to complete the booking process on or before his or her first court appearance, as well as instructions for the defendant on completing the booking process.

(8) A provision for certification by the booking agency that the defendant has completed the booking process which shall be presented to the court by the defendant as proof of booking.

(c) If a defendant has been properly served with a summons and thereafter fails to appear at the designated time and place, a bench warrant for arrest shall issue. In the absence of proof of actual receipt of the summons by the defendant, a failure to appear shall not be used in any future proceeding.

(d) A defendant who responds to a summons issued pursuant to this section and who has not been booked as provided in subdivision (b) shall be ordered by the court to complete the booking process.

(e) The prosecutor shall not request the issuance of a summons in lieu of an arrest warrant as provided in this section under any of the following circumstances:

(1) The offense charged involves violence.

(2) The offense charged involves a firearm.

(3) The offense charged involves resisting arrest.

(4) There are one or more outstanding arrest warrants for the person.

(5) The prosecution of the offense or offenses with which the person is charged, or the prosecution of any other offense or offenses would be jeopardized.

(6) There is a reasonable likelihood that the offense or offenses would continue or resume, or that the safety of persons or property would be imminently endangered.

(7) There is reason to believe that the person would not appear at the time and place specified in the summons.

Amended by Stats. 1998, Ch. 931, Sec. 362. Effective September 28, 1998.

Section 814 - Warrant of arrest

A warrant of arrest issued under Section 813 may be in substantially the following form:

County of _____

The people of the State of California to any peace officer of said State:

Complaint on oath having this day been laid before me that the crime of _____ (designating it generally) has been committed and accusing _____ (naming defendant) thereof, you are therefore commanded forthwith to arrest the above named defendant and bring him or her before me at _____ (naming the place), or in case of my absence or inability to act, before the nearest or most accessible magistrate in this county.

Dated at (place) this day of , 20__.

(Signature and full official title of magistrate.)

Amended by Stats 2015 ch 303 (AB 731),s 391, eff. 1/1/2016.

Amended by Stats 2014 ch 54 (SB 1461),s 13, eff. 1/1/2015.

Section 815 - Name of defendant

A warrant of arrest shall specify the name of the defendant or, if it is unknown to the magistrate, judge, justice, or other issuing authority, the defendant may be designated therein by any name. It shall also state the time of issuing it, and the city or county where it is issued, and shall be signed by the magistrate, judge, justice, or other issuing authority issuing it with the title of his office and the name of the court or other issuing agency.

Amended by Stats. 1970, Ch. 1490.

Section 815a - Bail

At the time of issuing a warrant of arrest, the magistrate shall fix the amount of bail which in his judgment in accordance with the provisions of section 1275 will be reasonable and sufficient for the appearance of the defendant following his arrest, if the offense is bailable, and said magistrate shall endorse upon said warrant a statement signed by him, with the name of his office, dated at the county, city or town where it is made to the following effect "The defendant is to be admitted to bail in the sum of _____ dollars" (stating the amount).

Added by Stats. 1933, Ch. 242.

Section 816 - Execution of warrant of arrest

A warrant of arrest shall be directed generally to any peace officer, or to any public officer or employee authorized to serve process where the warrant is for a violation of a statute or ordinance which such person has the duty to enforce, in the state, and may be executed by any of those officers to whom it may be delivered.

When a warrant of arrest has been delivered to a peace officer and the person named in the warrant is otherwise lawfully in the custody of the peace officer, the warrant may be executed by the peace officer or by any clerk of a city or county jail authorized to act and acting under the peace officer's direction.

Amended by Stats. 1969, Ch. 1205, Sec. 2.

Section 816a - Service of summons

A summons issued pursuant to Section 813 shall be served by any peace officer, or any public officer or employee authorized to serve process when the summons is for a violation of a statute or ordinance which that person has the duty to enforce, within the state. Upon service of the summons, the officer or employee shall deliver one copy of the summons to the defendant and shall file a duplicate copy with the magistrate before whom the defendant is to appear.

Added by Stats. 1988, Ch. 664, Sec. 2.

Section 817 - Declaration of probable cause; warrant of probable cause for arrest

(a)

(1) Before issuing an arrest warrant, the magistrate shall examine a declaration of probable cause made by a peace officer or, when the defendant is a peace officer, an employee of a public prosecutor's office of this state, in accordance with subdivisions (b), (c), and (d), as applicable. The magistrate shall issue a warrant of probable cause for the arrest of the defendant only if the magistrate is satisfied after reviewing the declaration that there exists probable cause that the offense described in the declaration has been committed and that the defendant described therein has committed the offense.

(2) The warrant of probable cause for arrest shall not begin a complaint process pursuant to Section 740 or 813. The warrant of probable cause for arrest shall have the same authority for service as set forth in Section 840 and the same time limitations as that of an arrest warrant issued pursuant to Section 813.

(b) The declaration in support of the warrant of probable cause for arrest shall be a sworn statement made in writing. If the declarant transmits the proposed warrant and all affidavits and supporting documents to the magistrate using facsimile transmission equipment, email, or computer server, the conditions in subdivision (d) shall apply.

(c) In lieu of the written declaration required in subdivision (b), the magistrate may accept an oral statement made under penalty of perjury and recorded and transcribed. The transcribed statement shall be deemed to be the declaration for the purposes of this section. The recording of the sworn oral statement and the transcribed statement shall be certified by the magistrate receiving it and shall be filed with the clerk of the court. In the alternative, the sworn oral statement may be recorded by a certified court reporter who shall certify the transcript of the statement, after which the magistrate receiving it shall certify the transcript, which shall be filed with the clerk of the court.

(d)

   (1) The declarant shall sign under penalty of perjury their declaration in support of the warrant of probable cause for arrest. The declarant's signature shall be in the form of a digital signature or electronic signature if email or computer server is used for transmission to the magistrate. The proposed warrant and all supporting declarations and attachments shall be transmitted to the magistrate utilizing facsimile transmission equipment, email, or computer server.

   (2) The magistrate shall verify that all the pages sent have been received, that all the pages are legible, and that the declarant's signature, digital signature, or electronic signature is genuine.

(e) A warrant of probable cause for arrest shall contain the information required pursuant to Sections 815 and 815a.

(f) A warrant of probable cause for arrest may be in substantially the following form:

County of _____, State of California.

The people of the State of California to any peace officer of the STATE:

Proof by declaration under penalty of perjury having been made this day to me by _____ (name of declarant) _____ ,
I find that there is probable cause to believe that the crime(s)of _____ (designate the crime/s) _____ has (have) been committed by the defendant named and described below.

Therefore, you are commanded to arrest _____ (name of defendant) _____ and to bring the defendantbefore any magistrate in _____ County pursuant to Sections 821, 825, 826, and 848 of the Penal Code.

Defendant is admitted to bail in the amount of_____dollars ($_____).

Time Issued: _____ (Signature of the Judge) _____
Dated: Judge of the Court

(g) Before issuing a warrant, the magistrate may examine under oath the person seeking the warrant and any witness the person may produce, take the written declaration of the person or witness, and cause the person or witness to subscribe the declaration. If the magistrate decides to issue the warrant, the magistrate shall do all of the following:

   (1) Sign the warrant. The magistrate's signature may be in the form of a digital signature or electronic signature if email or computer server was used for transmission to the magistrate.

   (2) Note on the warrant the date and time of the issuance of the warrant.

   (3) Transmit via facsimile transmission equipment, email, or computer server the signed warrant to the declarant. The warrant, signed by the magistrate and received by the declarant, shall be deemed to be the original warrant.

(h) An original warrant of probable cause for arrest or the duplicate original warrant of probable cause for arrest is sufficient for booking a defendant into custody.

(i) After the defendant named in the warrant of probable cause for arrest has been taken into custody, the agency that obtained the warrant shall file a "certificate of service" with the clerk of the issuing court. The certificate of service shall contain all of the following:

   (1) The date and time of service.

   (2) The name of the defendant arrested.

   (3) The location of the arrest.

   (4) The location where the defendant was incarcerated.

Amended by Stats 2021 ch 20 (AB 127),s 1, eff. 1/1/2022.
Amended by Stats 2018 ch 176 (AB 2710),s 1, eff. 1/1/2019.
Amended by Stats 2013 ch 460 (AB 1004),s 1, eff. 1/1/2014.

Section 817.5 - Entry of warrant information into Wanted Persons System

(a) On or after June 30, 2001, upon the issuance of any arrest warrant, the issuing law enforcement agency may enter the warrant information into the Department of Justice's Wanted Persons System.

(b) Notwithstanding any other provision of law, any state or local governmental agency shall, upon request, provide to the Department of Justice, a court, or any California law enforcement agency, the address of any person represented by the department, the court, or the law enforcement agency to be a person for whom there is an outstanding arrest warrant.

Added by Stats 2000 ch 940 (SB 1310), s 2, eff. 1/1/2001.

Section 818 - Notice to appear and promise to appear

In any case in which a peace officer serves upon a person a warrant of arrest for a misdemeanor offense under the Vehicle Code or under any local ordinance relating to stopping, standing, parking, or operation of a motor vehicle and where no written promise to appear has been filed and the warrant states on its face that a citation may be used in lieu of physical arrest, the peace officer may, instead of taking the person before a magistrate, prepare a notice to appear and release the person on his promise to appear, as prescribed by Sections 853. 6 through 853.8 of the Penal Code. Issuance of a notice to appear and securing of a promise to appear shall be deemed a compliance with the directions of the warrant, and the peace officer issuing such notice to appear and obtaining such promise to appear shall endorse on the warrant "Section 818, Penal Code, complied with" and return the warrant to the magistrate who issued it.

Amended by Stats. 1980, Ch. 336, Sec. 1.

Section 819 - Cooperation and participation of persecution regarding gender-affirming health care or gender-affirming mental health care of a child prohibited

(a) It is the public policy of the state that an out-of-state arrest warrant for an individual based on violating another state's law against providing, receiving, or allowing their child to receive gender-affirming health care or gender-affirming mental health care is the lowest law enforcement priority.

(b) California law enforcement agencies shall not knowingly make or participate in the arrest or participate in any extradition of an individual pursuant to an out-of-state arrest warrant for violation of another state's law against providing, receiving, or allowing a child to receive gender-affirming health care and gender-affirming mental health care in this state, if that care is lawful under the laws of this state, to the fullest extent permitted by federal law.

(c) No state or local law enforcement agency shall cooperate with or provide information to any individual or out-of-state agency or department regarding the provision of lawful gender-affirming health care or gender-affirming mental health care performed in this state.

(d) Nothing in this section shall prohibit the investigation of any criminal activity in this state which may involve the performance of gender-affirming health care or gender-affirming mental health care provided that no information relating to any medical procedure performed on a specific individual may be shared with an out-of-state agency or any other individual.

(e) For the purpose of this subdivision, "gender-affirming health care" and "gender-affirming mental health care" shall have the same meaning as provided in Section 16010.2 of the Welfare and Institutions Code.

Added by Stats 2022 ch 810 (SB 107),s 9, eff. 1/1/2023.

Section 821 - Taking defendant charged with felony before magistrate

If the offense charged is a felony, and the arrest occurs in the county in which the warrant was issued, the officer making the arrest must take the defendant before the magistrate who issued the warrant or some other magistrate of the same county.

If the defendant is arrested in another county, the officer must, without unnecessary delay, inform the defendant in writing of his right to be taken before a magistrate in that county, note on the warrant that he has so informed defendant, and, upon being required by defendant, take him before a magistrate in that county, who must admit him to bail in the amount specified in the endorsement referred to in Section 815a, and direct the defendant to appear before the court or magistrate by whom the warrant was issued on or before a day certain which shall in no case be more than 25 days after such admittance to bail. If bail be forthwith given, the magistrate shall take the same and endorse thereon a memorandum of the aforesaid order for the appearance of the defendant, or, if the defendant so requires, he may be released on bail set on the warrant by the issuing court, as provided in Section 1269b of this code, without an appearance before a magistrate.

If the warrant on which the defendant is arrested in another county does not have bail set thereon, or if the defendant arrested in another county does not require the arresting officer to take him before a magistrate in that county for the purpose of being admitted to bail, or if such defendant, after being admitted to bail, does not forthwith give bail, the arresting officer shall immediately notify the law enforcement agency requesting the arrest in the county in which the warrant was issued that such defendant is in custody, and thereafter such law enforcement agency shall take custody of the defendant within five days, or five court days if the law enforcement agency requesting the arrest is more than 400 miles from the county in which the defendant is held in custody, in the county in which he was arrested and shall take such defendant before the magistrate who issued the warrant, or before some other magistrate of the same county.

Amended by Stats. 1983, Ch. 1083, Sec. 1.

Section 822 - Taking defendant charged with misdemeanor before magistrate

If the offense charged is a misdemeanor, and the defendant is arrested in another county, the officer must, without unnecessary delay, inform the defendant in writing of his right to be taken before a magistrate in that county, note on the warrant that he has so informed defendant, and, upon being required by defendant, take him before a magistrate in that county, who must admit him to bail in the amount specified in the indorsement referred to in Section 815a, or if no bail is specified, the magistrate may set bail; if the defendant is admitted to bail the magistrate shall direct the defendant to appear before the court or magistrate by whom the warrant was issued on or before a day certain which shall in no case be more than 25 days after such admittance to bail. If bail be forthwith given, the magistrate shall take the same and indorse thereon a memorandum of the aforesaid order for the appearance of the defendant.

If the defendant arrested in another county on a misdemeanor charge does not require the arresting officer to take him before a magistrate in that county for the purpose of being admitted to bail, or if such defendant, after being admitted to bail, does not forthwith give bail, the arresting officer shall immediately notify the law enforcement agency requesting the arrest in the county in which the warrant was issued that such defendant is in custody, and thereafter such law enforcement agency shall take custody of such defendant within five days in the county in which he was arrested and shall take such defendant before the magistrate who issued the warrant, or before some other magistrate of the same county.

If a defendant is arrested in another county on a warrant charging the commission of a misdemeanor, upon which warrant the amount of bail is indorsed as provided in Section 815a, and defendant is held in jail in the county of arrest pending appearance before a magistrate, the officer in charge of the jail shall, to the same extent as provided by Section 1269b, have authority to approve and accept bail from defendant in the amount indorsed on the warrant, to issue and sign an order for the release of the defendant, and, on posting of such bail, shall discharge defendant from custody.

Amended by Stats. 1983, Ch. 236, Sec. 2.

Section 823 - Taking bail

On taking the bail, the magistrate must certify that fact on the warrant, and deliver the warrant to the officer having charge of the defendant. The magistrate shall issue to defendant a receipt for the undertaking of bail. The officer must then discharge the defendant from arrest, and must, without delay, deliver the warrant to the clerk of the court at which the defendant is required to appear. If the undertaking of bail is in the form of a bond, the magistrate shall forward the bond to the court at which defendant is required to appear. If the undertaking is in the form of cash, the magistrate shall deposit the cash in the county treasury, notifying the county auditor thereof, and the county auditor shall, by warrant, transmit the amount of the undertaking to the court at which the defendant is required to appear. If authorized by the county auditor, the magistrate may deposit the money in a bank account pursuant to Section 68084 of the Government Code, and by check drawn on such bank account transmit the amount of the undertaking to the court at which the defendant is required to appear.

Amended by Stats. 1959, Ch. 133.

Section 824 - Misrepresentation of age

When an adult willfully misrepresents himself or herself to be a minor under 18 years of age when taken into custody and this misrepresentation effects a material delay in investigation which prevents the filing of a criminal complaint against him or her in a court of competent jurisdiction within 48 hours, the complaint shall be filed within 48 hours from the time the true age is determined, excluding nonjudicial days.

Added by Stats. 1981, Ch. 205, Sec. 1.

Section 825 - 48-hour period; visit by attorney

(a)

(1) Except as provided in paragraph (2), the defendant shall in all cases be taken before the magistrate without unnecessary delay, and, in any event, within 48 hours after his or her arrest, excluding Sundays and holidays.

(2) When the 48 hours prescribed by paragraph (1) expire at a time when the court in which the magistrate is sitting is not in session, that time shall be extended to include the duration of the next court session on the judicial day immediately following. If the 48-hour period expires at a time when the court in which the magistrate is sitting is in session, the arraignment may take place at any time during that session. However, when the defendant's arrest occurs on a Wednesday after the conclusion of the day's court session, and if the Wednesday is not a court holiday, the defendant shall be taken before the magistrate not later than the following Friday, if the Friday is not a court holiday.

(b) After the arrest, any attorney at law entitled to practice in the courts of record of California, may, at the request of the prisoner or any relative of the prisoner, visit the prisoner. Any officer having charge of the prisoner who willfully refuses or neglects to allow that attorney to visit a prisoner is guilty of a misdemeanor. Any officer having a prisoner in charge, who refuses to allow the attorney to visit the prisoner when proper application is made, shall forfeit and pay to the party aggrieved the sum of five hundred dollars ($500), to be recovered by action in any court of competent jurisdiction.

Amended by Stats 2003 ch 149 (SB 79), s 66, eff. 1/1/2004.

Section 825.5 - Visit by physician

Any physician and surgeon, including a psychiatrist, licensed to practice in this state, or any psychologist licensed to practice in this state who holds a doctoral degree and has at least two years of experience in the diagnosis and treatment of emotional and mental disorders, who is employed by the prisoner or his or her attorney to assist in the preparation of the defense, shall be permitted to visit the prisoner while he or she is in custody.

Amended by Stats. 1984, Ch. 1123, Sec. 1.

Section 826 - Filing of new complaint

If on a warrant issued under Section 813 or 817 the defendant is brought before a magistrate other than the one who issued the warrant, the complaint on which the warrant was issued must be sent to that magistrate, or if it cannot be procured, a new complaint may be filed before that magistrate.

Amended by Stats. 1995, Ch. 563, Sec. 3. Effective January 1, 1996.

Section 827 - Complaint filed with magistrate of commission of felony originally triable in superior court of another county

When a complaint is filed with a magistrate of the commission of a felony originally triable in the superior court of another county of the state than that in which the magistrate sits, but showing that the defendant is in the county where the complaint is filed, the same proceedings must be had as prescribed in this chapter, except that the warrant must require the defendant to be taken before the nearest or most accessible magistrate of the county in which the offense is triable, and the complaint must be delivered by the magistrate to the officer to whom the warrant is delivered.

Amended by Stats. 1998, Ch. 931, Sec. 363. Effective September 28, 1998.

Section 827.1 - Release upon issuance of citation

A person who is specified or designated in a warrant of arrest for a misdemeanor offense may be released upon the issuance of a citation, in lieu of physical arrest, unless one of the following conditions exists:

(a) The misdemeanor cited in the warrant involves violence.

(b) The misdemeanor cited in the warrant involves a firearm.

(c) The misdemeanor cited in the warrant involves resisting arrest.

(d) The misdemeanor cited in the warrant involves giving false information to a peace officer.

(e) The person arrested is a danger to himself or herself or others due to intoxication or being under the influence of drugs or narcotics.

(f) The person requires medical examination or medical care or was otherwise unable to care for his or her own safety.

(g) The person has other ineligible charges pending against him or her.

(h) There is reasonable likelihood that the offense or offenses would continue or resume, or that the safety of persons or property would be immediately endangered by the release of the person.

(i) The person refuses to sign the notice to appear.

(j) The person cannot provide satisfactory evidence of personal identification.

(k) The warrant of arrest indicates that the person is not eligible to be released on a citation. The issuance of a citation under this section shall be undertaken in the manner set forth in Sections 853.6 to 853.8, inclusive.

Amended by Stats. 1988, Ch. 403, Sec. 1.

Section 828 - Taking defendant before magistrate and delivery of complaint and warrant

The officer who executes the warrant must take the defendant before the nearest or most accessible magistrate of the county in which the offense is triable, and must deliver to him the complaint and the warrant, with his return endorsed thereon, and the magistrate must then proceed in the same manner as upon a warrant issued by himself.

Amended by Stats. 1951, Ch. 1674.

Section 829 - Complaint filed with magistrate of commission of misdemeanor or infraction triable in another county

When a complaint is filed with a magistrate of the commission of a misdemeanor or infraction triable in another county of the state than that in which the magistrate sits, but showing that the defendant is in the county where the complaint is filed, the officer must, upon being required by the defendant, take the defendant before a magistrate of the county in which the warrant was issued, who must admit the defendant to bail in the amount specified in the endorsement referred to in Section 815a, and immediately transmit the warrant, complaint, and undertaking to the clerk of the court in which the defendant is required to appear.

Amended by Stats. 1998, Ch. 931, Sec. 364. Effective September 28, 1998.

Chapter 4.2 - CODE ENFORCEMENT OFFICERS

Section 829.5 - "Code enforcement officer" defined

(a) "Code enforcement officer" means any person who is not described in Chapter 4.5 (commencing with Section 830) and who is employed by any governmental subdivision, public or quasi-public corporation, public agency, public service corporation, any town, city, county, or municipal corporation, whether incorporated or chartered, who has enforcement authority for health, safety, and welfare requirements, whose duties include enforcement of any statute, rule, regulation, or standard, and who is authorized to issue citations, or file formal complaints.

(b) "Code enforcement officer" also includes any person who is employed by the Department of Housing and Community Development who has enforcement authority for health, safety, and welfare requirements pursuant to the Employee Housing Act (Part 1 (commencing with Section 17000) of Division 13 of the Health and Safety Code); the State Housing Law (Part 1.5 (commencing with Section 17910) of Division 13 of the Health and Safety Code); the Manufactured Housing Act of 1980 (Part 2 (commencing with Section 18000) of Division 13 of the Health and Safety Code); the Mobilehome Parks Act (Part 2.1 (commencing with Section 18200) of Division 13 of the Health and Safety Code); and the Special Occupancy Parks Act (Part 2.3 (commencing with Section 18860) of Division 13 of the Health and Safety Code).

Amended by Stats 2011 ch 296 (AB 1023),s 211, eff. 1/1/2012.

Added by Stats 2010 ch 117 (AB 1532),s 1, eff. 7/19/2010.

Section 829.7 - Code enforcement officer safety standards

Each local jurisdiction that employs code enforcement officers shall develop code enforcement officer safety standards appropriate for the code enforcement officers employed in their jurisdiction.

Added by Stats 2021 ch 637 (SB 296),s 2, eff. 1/1/2022.

Chapter 4.5 - PEACE OFFICERS

Section 830 - Peace officer

Any person who comes within the provisions of this chapter and who otherwise meets all standards imposed by law on a peace officer is a peace officer, and notwithstanding any other provision of law, no person other than those designated in this chapter is a peace officer. The restriction of peace officer functions of any public officer or employee shall not affect his or her status for purposes of retirement.

Amended by Stats. 1989, Ch. 1165, Sec. 19.

Section 830.1 - Persons who are peace officers; authority of peace officers

(a)A sheriff, undersheriff, or deputy sheriff, employed in that capacity, of a county, a chief of police of a city or chief, director, or chief executive officer of a consolidated municipal public safety agency that performs police functions, a police officer, employed in that capacity and appointed by the chief of police or chief, director, or chief executive of a public safety agency, of a city, a chief of police, or police officer of a district, including police officers of the San Diego Unified Port District Harbor Police, authorized by statute to maintain a police department, a marshal or deputy marshal of a superior court or county, a port warden or port police officer of the Harbor Department of the City of Los Angeles, or an inspector or investigator employed in that capacity in the office of a district attorney, is a peace officer. The authority of these peace officers extends to any place in the state, as follows:

(1) As to a public offense committed or for which there is probable cause to believe has been committed within the political subdivision that employs the peace officer or in which the peace officer serves.

(2) If the peace officer has the prior consent of the chief of police or chief, director, or chief executive officer of a consolidated municipal public safety agency, or person authorized by that chief, director, or officer to give consent, if the place is within a city, or of the sheriff, or person authorized by the sheriff to give consent, if the place is within a county.

(3) As to a public offense committed or for which there is probable cause to believe has been committed in the peace officer's presence, and with respect to which there is immediate danger to person or property, or of the escape of the perpetrator of the offense.

(b) The Attorney General and special agents and investigators of the Department of Justice are peace officers, and those assistant chiefs, deputy chiefs, chiefs, deputy directors, and division directors designated as peace officers by the Attorney General are peace officers. The authority of these peace officers extends to any place in the state where a public offense has been committed or where there is probable cause to believe one has been committed.

(c)A deputy sheriff of the County of Los Angeles, and a deputy sheriff of the Counties of Butte, Calaveras, Colusa, Del Norte, Glenn, Humboldt, Imperial, Inyo, Kern, Kings, Lake, Lassen, Madera, Mariposa, Mendocino, Merced, Mono, Plumas, Riverside, San Benito, San Diego, San Luis Obispo, San Mateo, Santa Barbara, Santa Clara, Shasta, Siskiyou, Solano, Sonoma, Stanislaus, Sutter, Tehama, Trinity, Tulare, Tuolumne, and Yuba who is employed to perform duties exclusively or initially relating to custodial assignments with responsibilities for maintaining the operations of county custodial facilities, including the custody, care, supervision, security, movement, and transportation of inmates, is a peace officer whose authority extends to any place in the state only while engaged in the performance of the duties of the officer's respective employment and for the purpose of carrying out the primary function of employment relating to the officer's custodial assignments, or when performing other law enforcement duties directed by the officer's employing agency during a local state of emergency.

Amended by Stats 2022 ch 416 (AB 2735),s 1, eff. 1/1/2023.
Amended by Stats 2021 ch 588 (AB 779),s 1, eff. 1/1/2022.
Amended by Stats 2012 ch 66 (SB 1254),s 1, eff. 1/1/2013.
Amended by Stats 2010 ch 575 (AB 1695),s 1, eff. 1/1/2011.
Amended by Stats 2009 ch 52 (SB 490),s 1, eff. 1/1/2010.
Amended by Stats 2008 ch 15 (AB 2215),s 1, eff. 5/16/2008.
Amended by Stats 2007 ch 84 (AB 151),s 1, eff. 7/17/2007.
Amended by Stats 2006 ch 127 (AB 272),s 1, eff. 8/21/2006.
Amended by Stats 2004 ch 516 (AB 1931), s 1, eff. 1/1/2005.
Amended by Stats 2003 ch 47 (AB 354), s 1, eff. 1/1/2004.
Amended by Stats 2003 ch 149 (SB 79), s 67, eff. 1/1/2004.
Amended by Stats 2003 ch 710 (SB 570), s 3, eff. 1/1/2004.
Amended by Stats 2002 ch 56 (SB 183), s 7, eff. 1/1/2003.
Amended by Stats 2002 ch 185 (AB 2346), s 2, eff. 1/1/2003.
Amended by Stats 2002 ch 784 (SB 1316), s 531, eff. 1/1/2003.
Amended by Stats 2001 ch 68 (SB 926), s 1, eff. 1/1/2002.
Amended by Stats 2000 ch 61 (SB 1762), s 1, eff. 1/1/2001.
See Stats 2003 ch 47 (AB 354), s 2.
See Stats 2003 ch 70 (AB 1254), s 3.

Section 830.2 - Peace officers whose authority extends to any place in state

The following persons are peace officers whose authority extends to any place in the state:

(a) Any member of the Department of the California Highway Patrol including those members designated under subdivision (a) of Section 2250.1 of the Vehicle Code, provided that the primary duty of the peace officer is the enforcement of any law relating to the use or operation of vehicles upon the highways, or laws pertaining to the provision of police services for the protection of state officers, state properties, and the occupants of state properties, or both, as set forth in the Vehicle Code and Government Code.

(b) A member of the University of California Police Department appointed pursuant to Section 92600 of the Education Code, provided that the primary duty of the peace officer shall be the enforcement of the law within the area specified in Section 92600 of the Education Code.

(c) A member of the California State University Police Departments appointed pursuant to Section 89560 of the Education Code, provided that the primary duty of the peace officer shall be the enforcement of the law within the area specified in Section 89560 of the Education Code.

(d)

(1) Any member of the Office of Correctional Safety of the Department of Corrections and Rehabilitation, provided that the primary duties of the peace officer shall be the investigation or apprehension of inmates, wards, parolees, parole violators, or escapees from state institutions, the transportation of those persons, the investigation of any violation of criminal law discovered while performing the usual and authorized duties of employment, and the coordination of those activities with other criminal justice agencies.

(2) Any member of the Office of Internal Affairs of the Department of Corrections and Rehabilitation, provided that the primary duties shall be criminal investigations of Department of Corrections and Rehabilitation personnel and the coordination of those activities with other criminal justice agencies. For purposes of this subdivision, the member of the Office of Internal Affairs shall possess certification from the Commission on Peace Officer Standards and Training for investigators, or have completed training pursuant to Section 6126.1.

(e) Employees of the Department of Fish and Game designated by the director, provided that the primary duty of those peace officers shall be the enforcement of the law as set forth in Section 856 of the Fish and Game Code.

(f) Employees of the Department of Parks and Recreation designated by the director pursuant to Section 5008 of the Public Resources Code, provided that the primary duty of the peace officer shall be the enforcement of the law as set forth in Section 5008 of the Public Resources Code.

(g) The Director of Forestry and Fire Protection and employees or classes of employees of the Department of Forestry and Fire Protection designated by the director pursuant to Section 4156 of the Public Resources Code, provided that the primary duty of the peace officer shall be the enforcement of the law as that duty is set forth in Section 4156 of the Public Resources Code.

(h) Persons employed by the Department of Alcoholic Beverage Control for the enforcement of Division 9 (commencing with Section 23000) of the Business and Professions Code and designated by the Director of Alcoholic Beverage Control, provided that the primary duty of any of these peace officers shall be the enforcement of the laws relating to alcoholic beverages, as that duty is set forth in Section 25755 of the Business and Professions Code.

(i) Marshals and police appointed by the Board of Directors of the California Exposition and State Fair pursuant to Section 3332 of the Food and Agricultural Code, provided that the primary duty of the peace officers shall be the enforcement of the law as prescribed in that section.

(j) Persons employed by the Department of Cannabis Control for the enforcement of Division 10 (commencing with Section 26000) of the Business and Professions Code and designated by the Director of the Department of Cannabis Control, provided that the primary duty of any of these peace officers shall be the enforcement of the laws as that duty is set forth in Section 26015 of the Business and Professions Code.

Amended by Stats 2021 ch 70 (AB 141),s 106, eff. 7/12/2021.
Amended by Stats 2020 ch 14 (AB 82),s 7, eff. 6/29/2020.
Amended by Stats 2011 ch 36 (SB 92),s 19, eff. 6/30/2011.
Amended by Stats 2011 ch 10 (SB 78),s 5, eff. 3/24/2011.
Amended by Stats 2009 ch 35 (SB 174),s 10, eff. 1/1/2010.
Amended by Stats 2008 ch 699 (SB 1241),s 11, eff. 1/1/2009.
EFFECTIVE 1/1/2000. Amended October 10, 1999 (Bill Number: SB 868) (Chapter 918).
Amended October 10, 1999 (Bill Number: AB 1502) (Chapter 917).

Section 830.29 - [Repealed]

Amended and repealed effective 1/1/2004 by Stats 2001 ch 859 (SB 826), s 2, eff. 1/1/2002.
Previously Amended and effective October 10, 1999 (Bill Number: AB 900) (Chapter 840).

Section 830.3 - Peace officers whose authority extends to any place in state for purpose of performing their primary duty or when making certain arrests

The following persons are peace officers whose authority extends to any place in the state for the purpose of performing their primary duty or when making an arrest pursuant to Section 836 as to any public offense with respect to which there is immediate danger to person or property, or of the escape of the perpetrator of that offense, or pursuant to Section 8597 or 8598 of the Government Code. These peace officers may carry firearms only if authorized and under those terms and conditions as specified by their employing agencies:

(a)Persons employed by the Division of Investigation of the Department of Consumer Affairs and investigators of the Dental Board of California, who are designated by the Director of Consumer Affairs, provided that the primary duty of these peace officers shall be the enforcement of the law as that duty is set forth in Section 160 of the Business and Professions Code.

(b)Voluntary fire wardens designated by the Director of Forestry and Fire Protection pursuant to Section 4156 of the Public Resources Code, provided that the primary duty of these peace officers shall be the enforcement of the law as that duty is set forth in Section 4156 of that code.

(c)Employees of the Department of Motor Vehicles designated in Section 1655 of the Vehicle Code, provided that the primary duty of these peace officers shall be the enforcement of the law as that duty is set forth in Section 1655 of that code.

(d)Investigators of the California Horse Racing Board designated by the board, provided that the primary duty of these peace officers shall be the enforcement of Chapter 4 (commencing with Section 19400) of Division 8 of the Business and Professions Code and Chapter 10 (commencing with Section 330) of Title 9 of Part 1.

(e)The State Fire Marshal and assistant or deputy state fire marshals appointed pursuant to Section 13103 of the Health and Safety Code, provided that the primary duty of these peace officers shall be the enforcement of the law as that duty is set forth in Section 13104 of that code.

(f)Inspectors of the food and drug section designated by the chief pursuant to subdivision (a) of Section 106500 of the Health and Safety Code, provided that the primary duty of these peace officers shall be the enforcement of the law as that duty is set forth in Section 106500 of that code.

(g)All investigators of the Division of Labor Standards Enforcement designated by the Labor Commissioner, provided that the primary duty of these peace officers shall be the enforcement of the law as prescribed in Section 95 of the Labor Code.

(h)All investigators of the State Departments of Health Care Services, Public Health, and Social Services, the Department of Toxic Substances Control, the Office of Statewide Health Planning and Development, and the Public Employees' Retirement System, provided that the primary duty of these peace officers shall be the enforcement of the law relating to the duties of their department or office. Notwithstanding any other law, investigators of the Public Employees' Retirement System shall not carry firearms.

(i)Either the Deputy Commissioner, Enforcement Branch of, or the Fraud Division Chief of, the Department of Insurance and those investigators designated by the deputy or the chief, provided that the primary duty of those investigators shall be the enforcement of Section 550.

(j)Employees of the Department of Housing and Community Development designated under Section 18023 of the Health and Safety Code, provided that the primary duty of these peace officers shall be the enforcement of the law as that duty is set forth in Section 18023 of that code.

(k)Investigators of the office of the Controller, provided that the primary duty of these investigators shall be the enforcement of the law relating to the duties of that office. Notwithstanding any other law, except as authorized by the Controller, the peace officers designated pursuant to this subdivision shall not carry firearms.

(l)Investigators of the Department of Financial Protection and Innovation designated by the Commissioner of Financial Protection and Innovation, provided that the primary duty of these investigators shall be the enforcement of the provisions of law administered by the Department of Financial Protection and Innovation. Notwithstanding any other law, the peace officers designated pursuant to this subdivision shall not carry firearms.

(m)Persons employed by the Contractors' State License Board designated by the Director of Consumer Affairs pursuant to Section 7011.5 of the Business and Professions Code, provided that the primary duty of these persons shall be the enforcement of the law as that duty is set forth in Section 7011.5, and in Chapter 9 (commencing with Section 7000) of Division 3, of that code. The Director of Consumer Affairs may designate as peace officers not more than 12 persons who shall at the time of their designation be assigned to the special investigations unit of the board. Notwithstanding any other law, the persons designated pursuant to this subdivision shall not carry firearms.

(n)The Chief and coordinators of the Law Enforcement Branch of the Office of Emergency Services.

(o)Investigators of the office of the Secretary of State designated by the Secretary of State, provided that the primary duty of these peace officers shall be the enforcement of the law as prescribed in Chapter 3 (commencing with Section 8200) of Division 1 of Title 2 of, and Section 12172.5 of, the Government Code. Notwithstanding any other law, the peace officers designated pursuant to this subdivision shall not carry firearms.

(p)The Deputy Director for Security designated by Section 8880.38 of the Government Code, and all lottery security personnel assigned to the California State Lottery and designated by the director, provided that the primary duty of any of those peace officers shall be the enforcement of the laws related to ensuring the integrity, honesty, and fairness of the operation and administration of the California State Lottery.

(q)Investigators employed by the Investigation Division of the Employment Development Department designated by the director of the department, provided that the primary duty of those peace officers shall be the enforcement of the law as that duty is set forth in Section 317 of the Unemployment Insurance Code. Notwithstanding any other law, the peace officers designated pursuant to this subdivision shall not carry firearms.

(r)The chief, assistant chief, and all security and safety officers of museum security and safety of Exposition Park, as designated by the Exposition Park Manager pursuant to Section 4108 of the Food and Agricultural Code, provided that the primary duty of those peace officers shall be the enforcement of the law as that duty is set forth in Section 4108 of the Food and Agricultural Code.

(s)Employees of the Franchise Tax Board designated by the board, provided that the primary duty of these peace officers shall be the enforcement of the law as set forth in Chapter 9 (commencing with Section 19701) of Part 10.2 of Division 2 of the Revenue and Taxation Code.

(t)

(1)Notwithstanding any other provision of this section, a peace officer authorized by this section shall not be authorized to carry firearms by their employing agency until that agency has adopted a policy on the use of deadly force by those peace officers, and until those peace officers have been instructed in the employing agency's policy on the use of deadly force.

(2)Every peace officer authorized pursuant to this section to carry firearms by their employing agency shall qualify in the use of the firearms at least every six months.

(u)Investigators of the Department of Managed Health Care designated by the Director of the Department of Managed Health Care, provided that the primary duty of these investigators shall be the enforcement of the provisions of laws administered by the Director of the Department of Managed Health Care. Notwithstanding any other law, the peace officers designated pursuant to this subdivision shall not carry firearms.

(v)The Chief, Deputy Chief, supervising investigators, and investigators of the Office of Protective Services of the State Department of Developmental Services, the Office of Protective Services of the State Department of State Hospitals, and the Office of Law Enforcement Support of the California Health and Human Services Agency, provided that the primary duty of each of those persons shall be the enforcement of the law relating to the duties of their department or office.

Amended by Stats 2022 ch 452 (SB 1498),s 204, eff. 1/1/2023.
Amended by Stats 2021 ch 411 (AB 483),s 3, eff. 1/1/2022.
Amended by Stats 2017 ch 561 (AB 1516),s 182, eff. 1/1/2018.
Amended by Stats 2016 ch 59 (SB 1474),s 3, eff. 1/1/2017.
Amended by Stats 2014 ch 71 (SB 1304),s 126, eff. 1/1/2015.
Amended by Stats 2014 ch 26 (AB 1468),s 13, eff. 6/20/2014.
Added by Stats 2013 ch 515 (SB 304),s 38, eff. 1/1/2014.

Section 830.31 - Certain police officer of County or City of Los Angeles; park ranger; housing authority patrol officer

The following persons are peace officers whose authority extends to any place in the state for the purpose of performing their primary duty or when making an arrest pursuant to Section 836 as to any public offense with respect to which there is immediate danger to person or property, or of the escape of the perpetrator of that offense, or pursuant to Section 8597 or 8598 of the Government Code. These peace officers may carry firearms only if authorized, and under the terms and conditions specified, by their employing agency.

(a) A police officer of the County of Los Angeles, if the primary duty of the officer is the enforcement of the law in or about properties owned, operated, or administered by his or her employing agency or when performing necessary duties with respect to patrons, employees, and properties of his or her employing agency.

(b) A person designated by a local agency as a park ranger and regularly employed and paid in that capacity, if the primary duty of the officer is the protection of park and other property of the agency and the preservation of the peace therein.

(c)

(1) A peace officer of the Department of General Services of the City of Los Angeles who was transferred to the Los Angeles Police Department and designated by the Chief of Police of the Los Angeles Police Department, or his or her designee, if the primary duty of the officer is the enforcement of the law in or about properties owned, operated, or administered by the City of Los Angeles or when performing necessary duties with respect to patrons, employees, and properties of the City of Los Angeles. For purposes of this section, "properties" means city offices, city buildings, facilities, parks, yards, and warehouses.

(2) A peace officer designated pursuant to this subdivision, and authorized to carry firearms by the Los Angeles Police Department, shall satisfactorily complete the introductory course of firearm training required by Section 832 and shall requalify in the use of firearms every six months.

(3) Notwithstanding any other provision of law, a peace officer designated pursuant to this subdivision who is authorized to carry a firearm by his or her employing agency while on duty shall not be authorized to carry a firearm when he or she is not on duty.

(d) A housing authority patrol officer employed by the housing authority of a city, district, county, or city and county or employed by the police department of a city and county, if the primary duty of the officer is the enforcement of the law in or about properties owned, operated, or administered by his or her employing agency or when performing necessary duties with respect to patrons, employees, and properties of his or her employing agency.

Amended by Stats 2012 ch 795 (SB 1466),s 1, eff. 1/1/2013.
Amended by Stats 2003 ch 468 (SB 851), s 11, eff. 1/1/2004.

Section 830.32 - Police officer at community college; members of police department of school district

The following persons are peace officers whose authority extends to any place in the state for the purpose of performing their primary duty or when making an arrest pursuant to Section 836 as to any public offense with respect to which there is immediate danger to person or property, or of the escape of the perpetrator of that offense, or pursuant to Section 8597 or 8598 of the Government Code. Those peace officers may carry firearms only if authorized and under terms and conditions specified by their employing agency.

(a) Members of a California Community College police department appointed pursuant to Section 72330 of the Education Code, if the primary duty of the police officer is the enforcement of the law as prescribed in Section 72330 of the Education Code.

(b) Persons employed as members of a police department of a school district pursuant to Section 38000 of the Education Code, if the primary duty of the police officer is the enforcement of the law as prescribed in Section 38000 of the Education Code.

(c) Any peace officer employed by a K-12 public school district or California Community College district who has completed training as prescribed by subdivision (f) of Section 832.3 shall be designated a school police officer.

Amended by Stats 2000 ch 135 (AB 2539), s 135, eff. 1/1/2001.

Section 830.33 - Harbor or port police; transit police officers; airport law enforcement officers

The following persons are peace officers whose authority extends to any place in the state for the purpose of performing their primary duty or when making an arrest pursuant to Section 836 as to any public offense with respect to which there is immediate danger to person or property, or of the escape of the perpetrator of that offense, or pursuant to Section 8597 or 8598 of the Government Code. Those peace officers may carry firearms only if authorized and under terms and conditions specified by their employing agency.

(a) A member of the San Francisco Bay Area Rapid Transit District Police Department appointed pursuant to Section 28767.5 of the Public Utilities Code, if the primary duty of the peace officer is the enforcement of the law in or about properties owned, operated, or administered by the district or when performing necessary duties with respect to patrons, employees, and properties of the district.

(b) Harbor or port police regularly employed and paid in that capacity by a county, city, or district other than peace officers authorized under Section 830.1, if the primary duty of the peace officer is the enforcement of the law in or about the properties owned, operated, or administered by the harbor or port or when performing necessary duties with respect to patrons, employees, and properties of the harbor or port.

(c) Transit police officers or peace officers of a county, city, transit development board, or district, if the primary duty of the peace officer is the enforcement of the law in or about properties owned, operated, or administered by the employing agency or when performing necessary duties with respect to patrons, employees, and properties of the employing agency.

(d) Any person regularly employed as an airport law enforcement officer by a city, county, or district operating the airport or by a joint powers agency, created pursuant to Article 1 (commencing with Section 6500) of Chapter 5 of Division 7 of Title 1 of the Government Code, operating the airport, if the primary duty of the peace officer is the enforcement of the law in or about properties owned, operated, and administered by the employing agency or when performing necessary duties with respect to patrons, employees, and properties of the employing agency.

(e)

(1) Any railroad police officer commissioned by the Governor pursuant to Section 8226 of the Public Utilities Code, if the primary duty of the peace officer is the enforcement of the law in or about properties owned, operated, or administered by the employing agency or when performing necessary duties with respect to patrons, employees, and properties of the employing agency.

(2) Notwithstanding any other provision of law, a railroad police officer who has met the current requirements of the Commission on Peace Officer Standards and Training necessary for exercising the powers of a peace officer, and who has been commissioned by the Governor as described herein, and the officer's employing agency, may apply for access to information from the California Law Enforcement Telecommunications System (CLETS) through a local law enforcement agency that has been granted direct access to CLETS, provided that, in addition to other review standards and conditions of eligibility applied by the Department of Justice, the CLETS Advisory Committee and the Attorney General, before access is granted the following are satisfied:

(A) The employing agency shall enter into a Release of CLETS Information agreement as provided for in the CLETS policies, practices, and procedures, and the required background check on the peace officer and other pertinent personnel has been completed, together with all required training.

(B) The Release of CLETS Information agreement shall be in substantially the same form as prescribed by the CLETS policies, practices, and procedures for public agencies of law enforcement who subscribe to CLETS services, and shall be subject to the provisions of Chapter 2.5 (commencing with Section 15150) of Title 2 of Division 3 of the Government Code and the CLETS policies, practices, and procedures.

(C)

(i) The employing agency shall expressly waive any objections to jurisdiction in the courts of the State of California for any liability arising from use, abuse, or misuse of CLETS access or services or the information derived therefrom, or with respect to any legal actions to enforce provisions of California law relating to CLETS access, services, or information under this subdivision, and provided that this liability shall be in addition to that imposed by Public Utilities Code Section 8226.

(ii) The employing agency shall further agree to utilize CLETS access, services, or information only for law enforcement activities by peace officers who have met the current requirements of the Commission on Peace Officer Standards and Training necessary for exercising the powers of a peace officer, and who have been commissioned as described herein who are operating within the State of California, where the activities are directly related to investigations or arrests arising from conduct occurring within the State of California.

(iii) The employing agency shall further agree to pay to the Department of Justice and the providing local law enforcement agency all costs related to the provision of access or services, including, but not limited to, any and all hardware, interface modules, and costs for telephonic communications, as well as administrative costs.

Amended by Stats 2004 ch 510 (SB 1768), s 1, eff. 1/1/2005.

Section 830.34 - Security officers; park ranger

The following persons are peace officers whose authority extends to any place in the state for the purpose of performing their primary duty or when making an arrest pursuant to Section 836 as to any public offense with respect to which there is immediate danger to person or property, or of the escape of the perpetrator of that offense, or pursuant to Section 8597 or 8598 of the Government Code. Those peace officers may carry firearms only if authorized and under terms and conditions specified by their employing agency.

(a) Persons designated as a security officer by a municipal utility district pursuant to Section 12820 of the Public Utilities Code, if the primary duty of the officer is the protection of the properties of the utility district and the protection of the persons thereon.

(b) Persons designated as a security officer by a county water district pursuant to Section 30547 of the Water Code, if the primary duty of the officer is the protection of the properties of the county water district and the protection of the persons thereon.

(c) The security director of the public utilities commission of a city and county, if the primary duty of the security director is the protection of the properties of the commission and the protection of the persons thereon.

(d) Persons employed as a park ranger by a municipal water district pursuant to Section 71341.5 of the Water Code, if the primary duty of the park ranger is the protection of the properties of the municipal water district and the protection of the persons thereon.

Amended by Stats 2004 ch 799 (AB 1119), s 1, eff. 9/27/2004.

Section 830.35 - Welfare fraud investigators or inspectors; child support investigators or inspectors, and coroner

The following persons are peace officers whose authority extends to any place in the state for the purpose of performing their primary duty or when making an arrest pursuant to Section 836 as to any public offense with respect to which there is immediate danger to person or property, or of the escape of the perpetrator of that offense, or pursuant to Section 8597 or 8598 of the Government Code. Those peace officers may carry firearms only if authorized and under terms and conditions specified by their employing agency.

(a) A welfare fraud investigator or inspector, regularly employed and paid in that capacity by a county, if the primary duty of the peace officer is the enforcement of the provisions of the Welfare and Institutions Code.

(b) A child support investigator or inspector, regularly employed and paid in that capacity by a district attorney's office, if the primary duty of the peace officer is the enforcement of the provisions of the Family Code and Section 270.

(c) The coroner and deputy coroners, regularly employed and paid in that capacity, of a county, if the primary duty of the peace officer are those duties set forth in Sections 27469 and 27491 to 27491.4, inclusive, of the Government Code.

Amended by Stats 2000 ch 808 (AB 1358), s 110.3, eff. 9/28/2000.

Section 830.36 - Sergeant-at- Arms; marshals and bailiffs; court service officer

The following persons are peace officers whose authority extends to any place in the state for the purpose of performing their primary duty or when making an arrest pursuant to Section 836 as to any public offense with respect to which there is immediate danger to person or property, or of the escape of the perpetrator of that offense, or pursuant to Section 8597 or 8598 of the Government Code. Those peace officers may carry firearms only if authorized and under terms and conditions specified by their employing agency.

(a) The Sergeant-at-Arms of each house of the Legislature, if the primary duty of the peace officer is the enforcement of the law in or about properties owned, operated, or administered by the employing agency or when performing necessary duties with respect to patrons, employees, and properties of the employing agency.

(b) Marshals of the Supreme Court and bailiffs of the courts of appeal, and coordinators of security for the judicial branch, if the primary duty of the peace officer is the enforcement of the law in or about properties owned, operated, or administered by the employing agency or when performing necessary duties with respect to patrons, employees, and properties of the employing agency.

(c) Court service officer in a county of the second class and third class, if the primary duty of the peace officer is the enforcement of the law in or about properties owned, operated, or administered by the employing agency or when performing necessary duties with respect to patrons, employees, and properties of the employing agency.

EFFECTIVE 1/1/2000. Amended October 10, 1999 (Bill Number: AB 1673) (Chapter 891).

Section 830.37 - Members of arson-investigating unit; members of fire department; voluntary fire wardens

The following persons are peace officers whose authority extends to any place in the state for the purpose of performing their primary duty or when making an arrest pursuant to Section 836 as to any public offense with respect to which there is immediate danger to person or property, or of the escape of the perpetrator of that offense, or pursuant to Section 8597 or 8598 of the Government Code. These peace officers may carry firearms only if authorized and under terms and conditions specified by their employing agency:

(a) Members of an arson-investigating unit, regularly paid and employed in that capacity, of a fire department or fire protection agency of a county, city, city and county, district, or the state, if the primary duty of these peace officers is the detection and apprehension of persons who have violated any fire law or committed insurance fraud.

(b) Members other than members of an arson-investigating unit, regularly paid and employed in that capacity, of a fire department or fire protection agency of a county, city, city and county, district, or the state, if the primary duty of these peace officers, when acting in that capacity, is the enforcement of laws relating to fire prevention or fire suppression.

(c) Voluntary fire wardens as are designated by the Director of Forestry and Fire Protection pursuant to Section 4156 of the Public Resources Code, provided that the primary duty of these peace officers shall be the enforcement of the law as that duty is set forth in Section 4156 of the Public Resources Code.

(d) Firefighter/security guards by the Military Department, if the primary duty of the peace officer is the enforcement of the law in or about properties owned, operated, or administered by the employing agency or when performing necessary duties with respect to patrons, employees, and properties of the employing agency.

Amended by Stats. 1992, Ch. 427, Sec. 129. Effective January 1, 1993.

Section 830.38 - Officers of state hospital

(a) The officers of a state hospital under the jurisdiction of the State Department of State Hospitals or the State Department of Developmental Services appointed pursuant to Section 4313 or 4493 of the Welfare and Institutions Code, are peace officers whose authority extends to any place in the state for the purpose of performing their primary duty or when making an arrest pursuant to Section 836 as to any public offense with respect to which there is immediate danger to person or property, or of the escape of the perpetrator of that offense, or pursuant to Section 8597 or 8598 of the Government Code provided that the primary duty of the peace officers shall be the enforcement of the law as set forth in Sections 4311, 4313, 4491, and 4493 of the Welfare and Institutions Code. Those peace officers may carry firearms only if authorized and under terms and conditions specified by their employing agency.

(b) By July 1, 2015, the California Health and Human Services Agency shall develop training protocols and policies and procedures for peace officers specified in subdivision (a). When appropriate, training protocols and policies and procedures shall be uniformly implemented in both state hospitals and developmental centers. Additional training protocols and policies and procedures shall be developed to address the unique characteristics of the residents in each type of facility.

(c) In consultation with system stakeholders, the agency shall develop recommendations to further improve the quality and stability of law enforcement and investigative functions at both developmental centers and state hospitals in a meaningful and sustainable manner. These recommendations shall be submitted to the budget committees and relevant policy committees of both houses of the Legislature no later than January 10, 2015.

Amended by Stats 2014 ch 26 (AB 1468),s 14, eff. 6/20/2014.

Amended by Stats 2012 ch 24 (AB 1470),s 20, eff. 6/27/2012.

Section 830.39 - Law enforcement officer of Oregon State Police, Nevada Department of Motor Vehicles and Public Safety, or Arizona Department of Public Safety

(a) Any regularly employed law enforcement officer of the Oregon State Police, the Nevada Department of Motor Vehicles and Public Safety, or the Arizona Department of Public Safety is a peace officer in this state if all of the following conditions are met:

(1) The officer is providing, or attempting to provide, law enforcement services within this state on the state or county highways and areas immediately adjacent thereto, within a distance of up to 50 statute miles of the contiguous border of this state and the state employing the officer.

(2) The officer is providing, or attempting to provide, law enforcement services pursuant to either of the following:

(A) In response to a request for services initiated by a member of the California Highway Patrol.

(B) In response to a reasonable belief that emergency law enforcement services are necessary for the preservation of life, and a request for services by a member of the Department of the California Highway Patrol is impractical to obtain under the circumstances. In those situations, the officer shall obtain authorization as soon as practical.

(3) The officer is providing, or attempting to provide, law enforcement services for the purpose of assisting a member of the California Highway Patrol to provide emergency service in response to misdemeanor or felony criminal activity, pursuant to the authority of a peace officer as provided in subdivision (a) of Section 830.2, or, in the event of highway-related traffic accidents, emergency incidents or other similar public safety problems, whether or not a member of the California Highway Patrol is present at the scene of the event. Nothing in this section shall be construed to confer upon the officer the authority to enforce traffic or motor vehicle infractions.

(4) An agreement pursuant to Section 2403.5 of the Vehicle Code is in effect between the Department of the California Highway Patrol and the agency of the adjoining state employing the officer, the officer acts in accordance with that agreement, and the agreement specifies that the officer and employing agency of the adjoining state shall be subject to the same civil immunities and liabilities as a peace officer and his or her employing agency in this state.

(5) The officer receives no separate compensation from this state for providing law enforcement services within this state.

(6) The adjoining state employing the officer confers similar rights and authority upon a member of the California Highway Patrol who renders assistance within that state.

(b) Whenever, pursuant to Nevada law, a Nevada correctional officer is working or supervising Nevada inmates who are performing conservation-related projects or fire suppression duties within California, the correctional officer may maintain custody of the inmates in California, and retake any inmate who should escape in California, to the same extent as if the correctional officer were a peace officer in this state and the inmate had been committed to his or her custody in proceedings under California law.

(c) Notwithstanding any other provision of law, any person who is acting as a peace officer in this state in the manner described in this section shall be deemed to have met the requirements of Section 1031 of the Government Code and the selection and training standards of the Commission on Peace Officer Standards and Training if the officer has completed the basic training required for peace officers in his or her state.

(d) In no case shall a peace officer of an adjoining state be authorized to provide services within a California jurisdiction during any period in which the regular law enforcement agency of the jurisdiction is involved in a labor dispute.

Amended by Stats. 1992, Ch. 131, Sec. 1. Effective January 1, 1993.

Section 830.4 - Members of California National Guard; security officers of Department of Justice; security officers of the college named in Section 92200 of the Education Code

The following persons are peace officers whose authority extends to any place in the state for the purpose of performing their duties under the conditions as specified by statute. Those peace officers may carry firearms only if authorized and under terms and conditions specified by their employing agency.

(a) Members of the California National Guard have the powers of peace officers when they are involved in any or all of the following:

(1) Called or ordered into active state service by the Governor pursuant to the provisions of Section 143 or 146 of the Military and Veterans Code.

(2) Serving within the area wherein military assistance is required.

(3) Directly assisting civil authorities in any of the situations specified in Section 143 or 146 of the Military and Veterans Code. The authority of the peace officer under this subdivision extends to the area wherein military assistance is required as to a public offense committed or which there is reasonable cause to believe has been committed within that area. The requirements of Section 1031 of the Government Code are not applicable under those circumstances.

(b) Security officers of the Department of Justice when performing assigned duties as security officers.

(c) Security officers of the college named in Section 92200 of the Education Code. These officers shall have authority of peace officers only within the City and County of San Francisco. Notwithstanding any other law, the peace officers designated by this subdivision shall not be authorized by this subdivision to carry firearms either on or off duty. Notwithstanding any other law, the act which designated the persons described in this subdivision as peace officers shall serve only to define those persons as peace officers, the extent of their jurisdiction, and the nature and scope of their authority, powers, and duties, and their status shall not change for purposes of retirement, workers' compensation or similar injury or death benefits, or other employee benefits.

Amended by Stats 2022 ch 478 (AB 1936),s 63, eff. 1/1/2023.

Amended by Stats 2012 ch 227 (SB 1578),s 4, eff. 1/1/2013.

Section 830.41 - Mutual aid agreement between City of Tulelake, California and City of Malin, Oregon

Notwithstanding any other provision of law, the City of Tulelake, California, is authorized to enter into a mutual aid agreement with the City of Malin, Oregon, for the purpose of permitting their police departments to provide mutual aid to each other when necessary. Before the effective date of the agreement, the agreement shall be reviewed and approved by the Commissioner of the California Highway Patrol.

Amended by Stats 2013 ch 76 (AB 383),s 149, eff. 1/1/2014.

Added by Stats 2012 ch 269 (SB 1067),s 1, eff. 1/1/2013.

Section 830.5 - Parole or probation officers; correctional officers

The following persons are peace officers whose authority extends to any place in the state while engaged in the performance of the duties of their respective employment and for the purpose of carrying out the primary function of their employment or as required under Sections 8597, 8598, and 8617 of the Government Code. Except as specified in this section, these peace officers may carry firearms only if authorized and under those terms and conditions specified by their employing agency:

(a) A parole officer of the Department of Corrections and Rehabilitation, or the Department of Corrections and Rehabilitation, Division of Juvenile Parole Operations, probation officer, deputy probation officer, or a board coordinating parole agent employed by the Juvenile Parole Board. Except as otherwise provided in this subdivision, the authority of these parole or probation officers shall extend only as follows:

(1) To conditions of parole, probation, mandatory supervision, or postrelease community supervision by any person in this state on parole, probation, mandatory supervision, or postrelease community supervision.

(2) To the escape of any inmate or ward from a state or local institution.

(3) To the transportation of persons on parole, probation, mandatory supervision, or postrelease community supervision.

(4) To violations of any penal provisions of law which are discovered while performing the usual or authorized duties of the officer's employment.

(5)

(A) To the rendering of mutual aid to any other law enforcement agency.

(B) For the purposes of this subdivision, "parole agent" shall have the same meaning as parole officer of the Department of Corrections and Rehabilitation or of the Department of Corrections and Rehabilitation, Division of Juvenile Justice.

(C) Any parole officer of the Department of Corrections and Rehabilitation, or the Department of Corrections and Rehabilitation, Division of Juvenile Parole Operations, is authorized to carry firearms, but only as determined by the director on a case-by-case or unit-by-unit basis and only under those terms and conditions specified by the director or chairperson. The Department of Corrections and Rehabilitation, Division of Juvenile Justice, shall develop a policy for arming peace officers of the Department of Corrections and Rehabilitation, Division of Juvenile Justice, who comprise "high-risk transportation details" or "high-risk escape details" no later than June 30, 1995. This policy shall be implemented no later than December 31, 1995.

(D) The Department of Corrections and Rehabilitation, Division of Juvenile Justice, shall train and arm those peace officers who comprise tactical teams at each facility for use during "high-risk escape details."

(b) A correctional officer employed by the Department of Corrections and Rehabilitation, or of the Department of Corrections and Rehabilitation, Division of Juvenile Justice, having custody of wards or any employee of the Department of Corrections and Rehabilitation designated by the secretary or any correctional counselor series employee of the Department of Corrections and Rehabilitation or any medical technical assistant series employee designated by the secretary or designated by the secretary and employed by the State Department of State Hospitals or any employee of the Board of Parole Hearings designated by the secretary or employee of the Department of Corrections and Rehabilitation, Division of Juvenile Justice, designated by the secretary or any superintendent, supervisor, or employee having custodial responsibilities in an institution operated by a probation department, or any transportation officer of a probation department.

(c) The following persons may carry a firearm while not on duty: a parole officer of the Department of Corrections and Rehabilitation, or the Department of Corrections and Rehabilitation, Division of Juvenile Justice, a correctional officer or correctional counselor employed by the Department of Corrections and Rehabilitation, or an employee of the Department of Corrections and Rehabilitation, Division of Juvenile Justice, having custody of wards or any employee of the Department of Corrections and Rehabilitation designated by the secretary or any medical technical assistant series employee designated by the secretary or designated by the secretary and employed by the State Department of State Hospitals. A parole officer of the Juvenile Parole Board may carry a firearm while not on duty only when so authorized by the chairperson of the board and only under the terms and conditions specified by the chairperson. Nothing in this section shall be interpreted to require licensure pursuant to Section 25400. The director or chairperson may deny, suspend, or revoke for good cause a person's right to carry a firearm under this subdivision. That person shall, upon request, receive a hearing, as provided for in the negotiated grievance procedure between the exclusive employee representative and the Department of Corrections and Rehabilitation, Division of Juvenile Justice, or the Juvenile Parole Board, to review the director's or the chairperson's decision.

(d) Persons permitted to carry firearms pursuant to this section, either on or off duty, shall meet the training requirements of Section 832 and shall qualify with the firearm at least quarterly. It is the responsibility of the individual officer or designee to maintain their eligibility to carry concealable firearms off duty. Failure to maintain quarterly qualifications by an officer or designee with any concealable firearms carried off duty shall constitute good cause to suspend or revoke that person's right to carry firearms off duty.

(e) The Department of Corrections and Rehabilitation shall allow reasonable access to its ranges for officers and designees of either department to qualify to carry concealable firearms off duty. The time spent on the range for purposes of meeting the qualification requirements shall be the person's own time during the person's off-duty hours.

(f) The secretary shall promulgate regulations consistent with this section.

(g) "High-risk transportation details" and "high-risk escape details" as used in this section shall be determined by the secretary, or the secretary's designee. The secretary, or the secretary's designee, shall consider at least the following in determining "high-risk transportation details" and "high-risk escape details": protection of the public, protection of officers, flight risk, and violence potential of the wards.

(h) "Transportation detail" as used in this section shall include transportation of wards outside the facility, including, but not limited to, court appearances, medical trips, and interfacility transfers.

Added by Stats 2020 ch 337 (SB 823),s 11, eff. 9/30/2020.

Repealed by Stats 2020 ch 337 (SB 823),s 10, eff. 9/30/2020.

Added by Stats 2019 ch 25 (SB 94),s 31, eff. 6/27/2019.

Section 830.53 - [Repealed]

Repealed by Stats 2020 ch 337 (SB 823),s 12, eff. 9/30/2020.

Added by Stats 2019 ch 25 (SB 94),s 32, eff. 6/27/2019.

Section 830.55 - Correctional officer

(a)

(1) As used in this section, a correctional officer is a peace officer, employed by a city, county, or city and county that operates a facility described in Section 2910.5 of this code or Section 1753.3 of the Welfare and Institutions Code or facilities operated by counties pursuant to Section 6241 or 6242 of this code under contract with the Department of Corrections and Rehabilitation or the Division of Juvenile Justice within the department, who has the authority and responsibility for maintaining custody of specified state prison inmates or wards, and who performs tasks related to the operation of a detention facility used for the detention of persons who have violated parole or are awaiting parole back into the community or, upon court order, either for their own safekeeping or for the specific purpose of serving a sentence therein.

(2) As used in this section, a correctional officer is also a peace officer, employed by a city, county, or city and county that operates a facility described in Section 4115.55, who has the authority and responsibility for maintaining custody of inmates sentenced to or housed in that facility, and who performs tasks related to the operation of that facility.

(b) A correctional officer shall have no right to carry or possess firearms in the performance of his or her prescribed duties, except, under the direction of the superintendent of the facility, while engaged in transporting prisoners, guarding hospitalized prisoners, or suppressing riots, lynchings, escapes, or rescues in or about a detention facility established pursuant to Section 2910.5 or 4115.55 of this code or Section 1753.3 of the Welfare and Institutions Code.

(c) Each person described in this section as a correctional officer, within 90 days following the date of the initial assignment to that position, shall satisfactorily complete the training course specified in Section 832. In addition, each person designated as a correctional officer, within one year following the date of the initial assignment as an officer, shall have satisfactorily met the minimum selection and training standards prescribed by the Board of State and Community Corrections pursuant to Section 6035. Persons designated as correctional officers, before the expiration of the 90-day and one-year periods described in this subdivision, who have not yet completed the required training, may perform the duties of a correctional officer only while under the direct supervision of a correctional officer who has completed the training required in this section, and shall not carry or possess firearms in the performance of their prescribed duties.

(d) This section shall not be construed to confer any authority upon a correctional officer except while on duty.

(e) A correctional officer may use reasonable force in establishing and maintaining custody of persons delivered to him or her by a law enforcement officer, may make arrests for misdemeanors and felonies within the local detention facility pursuant to a duly issued warrant, and may make warrantless arrests pursuant to Section 836.5 only during the duration of his or her job.

Amended by Stats 2013 ch 76 (AB 383),s 150, eff. 1/1/2014.

Amended by Stats 2012 ch 68 (SB 1351),s 1, eff. 7/9/2012.

Section 830.6 - Reserve or auxiliary sheriff, police officer, marshal, or park ranger

(a)

(1) Whenever any qualified person is deputized or appointed by the proper authority as a reserve or auxiliary sheriff or city police officer, a reserve deputy sheriff, a reserve deputy marshal, a reserve police officer of a regional park district or of a transit district, a reserve park ranger, a reserve harbor or port police officer of a county, city, or district as specified in Section 663.5 of the Harbors and Navigation Code, a reserve deputy of the Department of Fish and Game, a reserve special agent of the Department of Justice, a reserve officer of a community service district which is authorized under subdivision (h) of Section 61600 of the Government Code to maintain a police department or other police protection, a reserve officer of a school district police department under Section 35021.5 of the Education Code, a reserve officer of a community college police department under Section 72330, a reserve officer of a police protection district formed under Part 1 (commencing with Section 20000) of Division 14 of the Health and Safety Code, or a reserve housing authority patrol officer employed by a housing authority defined in subdivision (d) of Section 830.31, and is assigned specific police functions by that authority, the person is a peace officer, if the person qualifies as set forth in Section 832.6. The authority of a person designated as a peace officer pursuant to this paragraph extends only for the duration of the person's specific assignment. A reserve park ranger or a transit, harbor, or port district reserve officer may carry firearms only if authorized by, and under those terms and conditions as are specified by, his or her employing agency.

(2) Whenever any qualified person is deputized or appointed by the proper authority as a reserve or auxiliary sheriff or city police officer, a reserve deputy sheriff, a reserve deputy marshal, a reserve park ranger, a reserve police officer of a regional park district, transit district, community college district, or school district, a reserve harbor or port police officer of a county, city, or district as specified in Section 663.5 of the Harbors and Navigation Code, a reserve officer of a community service district that is authorized under subdivision (h) of Section 61600 of the Government Code to maintain a police department or other police protection, or a reserve officer of a police protection district formed under Part 1 (commencing with Section 20000) of Division 14 of the Health and Safety Code, and is so designated by local ordinance or, if the local agency is not authorized to act by ordinance, by resolution, either individually or by class, and is assigned to the prevention and detection of crime and the general enforcement of the laws of this state by that authority, the person is a peace officer, if the person qualifies as set forth in paragraph (1) of subdivision (a) of Section 832.6. The authority of a person designated as a peace officer pursuant to this paragraph includes the full powers and duties of a peace officer

as provided by Section 830.1. A transit, harbor, or port district reserve police officer, or a city or county reserve peace officer who is not provided with the powers and duties authorized by Section 830.1, has the powers and duties authorized in Section 830.33, or in the case of a reserve park ranger, the powers and duties that are authorized in Section 830.31, or in the case of a reserve housing authority patrol officer, the powers and duties that are authorized in subdivision (d) of Section 830.31, and a school district reserve police officer or a community college district reserve police officer has the powers and duties authorized in Section 830.32.

(b) Whenever any person designated by a Native American tribe recognized by the United States Secretary of the Interior is deputized or appointed by the county sheriff as a reserve or auxiliary sheriff or a reserve deputy sheriff, and is assigned to the prevention and detection of crime and the general enforcement of the laws of this state by the county sheriff, the person is a peace officer, if the person qualifies as set forth in paragraph (1) of subdivision (a) of Section 832.6. The authority of a peace officer pursuant to this subdivision includes the full powers and duties of a peace officer as provided by Section 830.1.

(c) Whenever any person is summoned to the aid of any uniformed peace officer, the summoned person is vested with the powers of a peace officer that are expressly delegated to him or her by the summoning officer or that are otherwise reasonably necessary to properly assist the officer.

Amended by Stats 2007 ch 118 (AB 1374),s 1, eff. 1/1/2008.

Amended by Stats 2003 ch 292 (AB 1436), s 4, eff. 1/1/2004.

Section 830.61 - [Repealed]

This section was repealed 1/1/2001 pursuant to its own terms.

Section 830.65 - Campaign Against Marijuana Planting emergency appointee

(a) Any person who is a regularly employed police officer of a city or a regularly employed deputy sheriff of a county, or a reserve peace officer of a city or county and is appointed in the manner described in paragraph (1) or (2) of subdivision (a) of Section 832.6, may be appointed as a Campaign Against Marijuana Planting emergency appointee by the Attorney General pursuant to Section 5 of Chapter 1563 of the Statutes of 1985 to assist with a specific investigation, tactical operation, or search and rescue operation. When so appointed, the person shall be a peace officer of the Department of Justice, provided that the person's authority shall extend only for the duration of the specific assignment.

(b) Notwithstanding any other provision of law, any person who is appointed as a peace officer in the manner described in this section shall be deemed to have met the requirements of Section 1031 of the Government Code and the selection and training standards of the Commission on Peace Officer Standards and Training.

Added by Stats. 1988, Ch. 1482, Sec. 4.

Section 830.7 - Persons who are not peace officers but may exercise the powers of arrest of a peace officer

The following persons are not peace officers but may exercise the powers of arrest of a peace officer as specified in Section 836 during the course and within the scope of their employment, if they successfully complete a course in the exercise of those powers pursuant to Section 832:

(a)Persons designated by a cemetery authority pursuant to Section 8325 of the Health and Safety Code.

(b)Persons regularly employed as security officers for independent institutions of higher education, recognized under subdivision (b) of Section 66010 of the Education Code, if the institution has concluded a memorandum of understanding, permitting the exercise of that authority, with the sheriff or the chief of police within whose jurisdiction the institution lies.

(c)Persons regularly employed as security officers for health facilities, as defined in Section 1250 of the Health and Safety Code, that are owned and operated by cities, counties, and cities and counties, if the facility has concluded a memorandum of understanding, permitting the exercise of that authority, with the sheriff or the chief of police within whose jurisdiction the facility lies.

(d)Employees or classes of employees of the California Department of Forestry and Fire Protection designated by the Director of Forestry and Fire Protection, provided that the primary duty of the employee shall be the enforcement of the law as that duty is set forth in Section 4156 of the Public Resources Code.

(e)Persons regularly employed as inspectors, supervisors, or security officers for transit districts, as defined in Section 99213 of the Public Utilities Code, if the district has concluded a memorandum of understanding permitting the exercise of that authority, with, as applicable, the sheriff, the chief of police, or the Department of the California Highway Patrol within whose jurisdiction the district lies. For the purposes of this subdivision, the exercise of peace officer authority may include the authority to remove a vehicle from a railroad right-of-way as set forth in Section 22656 of the Vehicle Code.

(f)Nonpeace officers regularly employed as county parole officers pursuant to Section 3089.

(g)Persons regularly employed as investigators by the Department of Transportation for the City of Los Angeles and designated by local ordinance as public officers, to the extent necessary to enforce laws related to public transportation, and authorized by a memorandum of understanding with the chief of police, permitting the exercise of that authority. For the purposes of this subdivision, "investigator" means an employee defined in Section 53075.61 of the Government Code authorized by local ordinance to enforce laws related to public transportation. Transportation investigators authorized by this section shall not be deemed "peace officers" for purposes of Sections 241 and 243.

(h)Persons regularly employed by any department of the City of Los Angeles who are designated as security officers and authorized by local ordinance to enforce laws related to the preservation of peace in or about the properties owned, controlled, operated, or administered by any department of the City of Los Angeles and authorized by a memorandum of understanding with the Chief of Police of the City of Los Angeles permitting the exercise of that authority. Security officers authorized pursuant to this subdivision shall not be deemed peace officers for purposes of Sections 241 and 243.

(i)Illegal dumping enforcement officers or code enforcement officers, to the extent necessary to enforce laws related to illegal waste dumping or littering, and authorized by a memorandum of understanding with, as applicable, the sheriff or chief of police within whose jurisdiction the person is employed, permitting the exercise of that authority. An "illegal dumping enforcement officer or code enforcement officer" is defined, for purposes of this section, as a person employed full time, part time, or as a volunteer after completing training prescribed by law, by a city, county, or city and county, whose duties include illegal dumping enforcement and who is designated by local ordinance as a public officer. An illegal dumping enforcement officer or code enforcement officer may also be a person who is not regularly employed by a city, county, or city and county, but who has met all training requirements and is directly supervised by a regularly employed illegal dumping enforcement officer or code enforcement officer conducting illegal dumping enforcement. This person shall not have the power of arrest or access to summary criminal history information pursuant to this section. No person may be appointed as an illegal dumping enforcement officer or code enforcement officer if that person is disqualified pursuant to the criteria set forth in Section 1029 of the Government Code. Persons regularly employed by a city, county, or city and county designated pursuant to this subdivision may be furnished state summary criminal history information upon a showing of compelling need pursuant to subdivision (c) of Section 11105.

(j)Until January 1, 2025, persons who, pursuant to Section 4108 of the Food and Agricultural Code, were appointed as Museum Security Officers and Supervising Museum Security Officers by the Exposition Park General Manager before March 1, 2022, and have not yet completed the regular basic training course prescribed by the Commission on Peace Officer Standards and Training.

Amended by Stats 2022 ch 58 (AB 200),s 4, eff. 6/30/2022.
Amended by Stats 2021 ch 411 (AB 483),s 4, eff. 1/1/2022.
Amended by Stats 2012 ch 298 (AB 801),s 1, eff. 1/1/2013.
Amended by Stats 2008 ch 217 (AB 1931),s 1, eff. 1/1/2009.
Amended by Stats 2007 ch 201 (AB 1048),s 2, eff. 1/1/2008.
Amended by Stats 2006 ch 271 (AB 1980),s 2, eff. 1/1/2007.
Amended by Stats 2006 ch 267 (AB 1688),s 1, eff. 1/1/2007.
EFFECTIVE 1/1/2000. Amended September 7, 1999 (Bill Number: AB 89) (Chapter 331).

Section 830.75 - Deputizing security officers regularly employed by institution of higher education

(a) Notwithstanding subdivision (b) of Section 830.7, a person regularly employed as a security officer for an independent institution of higher education recognized under subdivision (b) of Section 66010 of the Education Code may be deputized or appointed by the sheriff or the chief of police of the jurisdiction in which the institution is located as a reserve deputy or officer pursuant to Section 830.6, notwithstanding that he or she is compensated by the institution of higher education or that the assigned specific law enforcement functions and duties may be of a recurring or continuous nature, if both of the following requirements are met:

(1) The person meets the requirements specified in paragraph (1) of subdivision (a) of Section 832.6.

(2) The institution of higher education and the appropriate local law enforcement agency have entered into a memorandum of understanding.

(b) The authority of a person designated as a peace officer pursuant to this section extends to any place in the state and applies only while he or she is engaged in the performance of his or her assigned duties for his or her institution of higher education pursuant to the memorandum entered into pursuant to paragraph (2) of subdivision (a). The primary duty of a person designated as a peace officer pursuant to this section shall be the enforcement of the law upon the campuses of his or her institution of higher education and within one mile of the exterior of those campuses, and in or about other grounds and properties owned, operated, controlled, or administered by that institution of higher education.

(c) Vehicles owned by an independent institution of higher education that are specifically designated for use by persons designated as peace officers pursuant to this section shall be deemed authorized emergency vehicles for all purposes of the law within the institution's jurisdiction.

Added by Stats 2016 ch 356 (AB 2361),s 1, eff. 1/1/2017.

Section 830.8 - Federal criminal investigators and law enforcement officers; national park rangers

(a) Federal criminal investigators and law enforcement officers are not California peace officers, but may exercise the powers of arrest of a peace officer in any of the following circumstances:

(1) Any circumstances specified in Section 836 of this code or Section 5150 of the Welfare and Institutions Code for violations of state or local laws.

(2) When these investigators and law enforcement officers are engaged in the enforcement of federal criminal laws and exercise the arrest powers only incidental to the performance of these duties.

(3) When requested by a California law enforcement agency to be involved in a joint task force or criminal investigation.

(4) When probable cause exists to believe that a public offense that involves immediate danger to persons or property has just occurred or is being committed. In all of these instances, the provisions of Section 847 shall apply. These investigators and law enforcement officers, prior to the exercise of these arrest powers, shall have been certified by their agency heads as having satisfied the training requirements of Section 832, or the equivalent thereof.

This subdivision does not apply to federal officers of the Bureau of Land Management or the United States Forest Service. These officers have no authority to enforce California statutes without the written consent of the sheriff or the chief of police in whose jurisdiction they are assigned.

(b) Duly authorized federal employees who comply with the training requirements set forth in Section 832 are peace officers when they are engaged in enforcing applicable state or local laws on property owned or possessed by the United States government, or on any street, sidewalk, or property adjacent thereto, and with the written consent of the sheriff or the chief of police, respectively, in whose jurisdiction the property is situated.

(c) National park rangers are not California peace officers but may exercise the powers of arrest of a peace officer as specified in Section 836 and the powers of a peace officer specified in Section 5150 of the Welfare and Institutions Code for violations of state or local laws provided these rangers are exercising the arrest powers incidental to the performance of their federal duties or providing or attempting to provide law enforcement services in response to a request initiated by California state park rangers to assist in preserving the peace and protecting state parks and other property for which California state park rangers are responsible. National park rangers, prior to the exercise of these arrest powers, shall have been certified by their agency heads as having satisfactorily completed the training requirements of Section 832.3, or the equivalent thereof.

(d) Notwithstanding any other provision of law, during a state of war emergency or a state of emergency, as defined in Section 8558 of the Government Code, federal criminal investigators and law enforcement officers who are assisting California law enforcement officers in carrying out emergency operations are not deemed California peace officers, but may exercise the powers of arrest of a peace officer as specified in Section 836 and the powers of a peace officer specified in Section 5150 of the Welfare and Institutions Code for violations of state or local laws. In these instances, the provisions of Section 847 of this code and of Section 8655 of the Government Code shall apply.

(e)

(1) Any qualified person who is appointed as a Washoe tribal law enforcement officer is not a California peace officer, but may exercise the powers of a Washoe tribal peace officer when engaged in the enforcement of Washoe tribal criminal laws against any person who is an Indian, as defined in subsection (d) of Section 450b of Title 25 of the United States Code, on Washoe tribal land. The respective prosecuting authorities, in consultation with law enforcement agencies, may agree on who shall have initial responsibility for prosecution of specified infractions. This subdivision is not meant to confer cross-deputized status as California peace officers, nor to confer California peace officer status upon Washoe tribal law enforcement officers when enforcing state or local laws in the State of California. Nothing in this section shall be construed to impose liability upon or to require indemnification by the County of Alpine or the State of California for any act performed by an officer of the Washoe Tribe. Washoe tribal law enforcement officers shall have the right to travel to and from Washoe tribal lands within California in order to carry out tribal duties.

(2) Washoe tribal law enforcement officers are exempted from the provisions of subdivision (a) of Section 25400 and subdivision (a) and subdivisions (c) to (h), inclusive, of Section 25850 while performing their official duties on their tribal lands or while proceeding by a direct route to or from the tribal lands. Tribal law enforcement vehicles are deemed to be emergency vehicles within the meaning of Section 30 of the Vehicle Code while performing official police services.

(3) As used in this subdivision, the term "Washoe tribal lands" includes the following:

(A) All lands located in the County of Alpine within the limits of the reservation created for the Washoe Tribe of Nevada and California, notwithstanding the issuance of any patent and including rights-of-way running through the reservation and all tribal trust lands.

(B) All Indian allotments, the Indian titles to which have not been extinguished, including rights-of-way running through the same.

(4) As used in this subdivision, the term "Washoe tribal law" refers to the laws codified in the Law and Order Code of the Washoe Tribe of Nevada and California, as adopted by the Tribal Council of the Washoe Tribe of Nevada and California.

Amended by Stats 2011 ch 296 (AB 1023),s 212, eff. 1/1/2012.

Amended by Stats 2010 ch 178 (SB 1115),s 67, eff. 1/1/2011, op. 1/1/2012.

Amended by Stats 2002 ch 545 (SB 1852), s 4, eff. 1/1/2003.

Section 830.85 - ICE and CBP officers not state peace officers

Notwithstanding any other law, United States Immigration and Customs Enforcement officers and United States Customs and Border Protection officers are not California peace officers.

Added by Stats 2017 ch 116 (AB 1440),s 2, eff. 1/1/2018.

Section 830.9 - Animal control officers

Animal control officers are not peace officers but may exercise the powers of arrest of a peace officer as specified in Section 836 and the power to serve warrants as specified in Sections 1523 and 1530 during the course and within the scope of their employment, if those officers successfully complete a course in the exercise of those powers pursuant to Section 832. That part of the training course specified in Section 832 pertaining to the carrying and use of firearms shall not be required for any animal control officer whose employing agency prohibits the use of firearms.

For the purposes of this section, "firearms" includes capture guns, blowguns, carbon dioxide operated rifles and pistols, air guns, handguns, rifles, and shotguns.

Amended by Stats. 1990, Ch. 82, Sec. 13. Effective May 3, 1990.

Section 830.95 - Unlawful wearing of uniform of peace officer while engaged in picketing

(a) Any person who wears the uniform of a peace officer while engaged in picketing, or other informational activities in a public place relating to a concerted refusal to work, is guilty of a misdemeanor, whether or not the person is a peace officer.

(b) This section shall not be construed to authorize or ratify any picketing or other informational activities not otherwise authorized by law.

Added by Stats 2010 ch 711 (SB 1080),s 3, eff. 1/1/2011, op. 1/1/2012.

Section 830.10 - Badge, nameplate, or other identifying device

Any uniformed peace officer shall wear a badge, nameplate, or other device which bears clearly on its face the identification number or name of the officer.

Amended by Stats. 1989, Ch. 1165, Sec. 38.

Section 830.11 - Enforcement officers and investigators

(a) The following persons are not peace officers but may exercise the powers of arrest of a peace officer as specified in Section 836 and the power to serve warrants as specified in Sections 1523 and 1530 during the course and within the scope of their employment, if they receive a course in the exercise of those powers pursuant to Section 832. The authority and powers of the persons designated under this section extend to any place in the state:

(1) A person employed by the Department of Financial Protection and Innovation designated by the Commissioner of Financial Protection and Innovation, provided that the person's primary duty is the enforcement of, and investigations relating to, the provisions of law administered by the Commissioner of Financial Protection and Innovation.

(2) A person employed by the Bureau of Real Estate designated by the Real Estate Commissioner, provided that the person's primary duty is the enforcement of the laws set forth in Part 1 (commencing with Section 10000) and Part 2 (commencing with Section 11000) of Division 4 of the Business and Professions Code. The Real Estate Commissioner may designate a person under this section who, at the time of their designation, is assigned to the Special Investigations Unit, internally known as the Crisis Response Team.

(3)A person employed by the State Lands Commission designated by the executive officer, provided that the person's primary duty is the enforcement of the law relating to the duties of the State Lands Commission.

(4)A person employed as an investigator of the Investigations Bureau of the Department of Insurance, who is designated by the Chief of the Investigations Bureau, provided that the person's primary duty is the enforcement of the Insurance Code and other laws relating to persons and businesses, licensed and unlicensed by the Department of Insurance, who are engaged in the business of insurance.

(5)A person employed as an investigator or investigator supervisor by the Public Utilities Commission, who is designated by the commission's executive director and approved by the commission, provided that the person's primary duty is the enforcement of the law as that duty is set forth in Section 308.5 of the Public Utilities Code.

(6)

(A)A person employed by the California Department of Tax and Fee Administration, who is designated by the department's director, provided that the person's primary duty is the enforcement of laws administered by the California Department of Tax and Fee Administration.

(B)A person designated pursuant to this paragraph is not entitled to peace officer retirement benefits.

(7)A person employed by the Department of Food and Agriculture and designated by the Secretary of Food and Agriculture as an investigator, investigator supervisor, or investigator manager, provided that the person's primary duty is enforcement of, and investigations relating to, the Food and Agricultural Code or Division 5 (commencing with Section 12001) of the Business and Professions Code.

(8)The Inspector General and those employees of the Office of the Inspector General designated by the Inspector General, provided that the person's primary duty is the enforcement of the law relating to the duties of the Office of the Inspector General.

(9)A person employed by the Department of Cannabis Control and designated by the director of the department as an investigator, investigator supervisor, or investigator manager, provided that the person's primary duty is enforcement of, and investigations relating to, Division 10 (commencing with Section 26000) of the Business and Professions Code. This section shall apply to only those investigator positions occupied by persons previously designated by the Secretary of the Department of Food and Agriculture as an investigator, investigator supervisor, or investigative manager whose primary duty was to enforce Division 10 (commencing with Section 26000) of the Business and Professions Code.

(b)Notwithstanding any other law, a person designated pursuant to this section may not carry a firearm.

(c)A person designated pursuant to this section shall be included as a "peace officer of the state" under paragraph (2) of subdivision (c) of Section 11105 for the purpose of receiving state summary criminal history information and shall be furnished that information on the same basis as other peace officers designated in paragraph (2) of subdivision (c) of Section 11105.

Amended by Stats 2022 ch 474 (SB 1496),s 1.5, eff. 1/1/2023.
Amended by Stats 2022 ch 452 (SB 1498),s 205, eff. 1/1/2023. Not implemented per s 211
Amended by Stats 2021 ch 70 (AB 141),s 107, eff. 7/12/2021.
Amended by Stats 2018 ch 138 (AB 873),s 1, eff. 1/1/2019.
Amended by Stats 2016 ch 842 (SB 1222),s 3, eff. 1/1/2017.
Amended by Stats 2013 ch 352 (AB 1317),s 405, eff. 9/26/2013, op. 7/1/2013.
Amended by Stats 2011 ch 36 (SB 92),s 21, eff. 6/30/2011.
Amended by Stats 2006 ch 501 (AB 1749),s 12, eff. 1/1/2007.
Amended by Stats 2006 ch 501 (AB 1749),s 13, eff. 1/1/2007.
Amended by Stats 2003 ch 890 (AB 71), s 4, eff. 1/1/2004.
EFFECTIVE 1/1/2000. Amended October 10, 1999 (Bill Number: AB 1658) (Chapter 1005).

Section 830.12 - Litter control officers, vehicle abatement officers, registered sanitarians, and solid waste specialists

Notwithstanding any other provision of law, persons designated by a local agency as litter control officers, vehicle abatement officers, registered sanitarians, and solid waste specialists, are not peace officers, may not exercise the powers of arrest of a peace officer, as specified in Section 836, and shall not be authorized to carry or use firearms within the scope and course of their employment. These persons may, however, be authorized by the governing board of the particular local agency to issue citations involving violations of laws relating to abandoned vehicles and littering.

Added by Stats. 1988, Ch. 726, Sec. 1.

Section 830.13 - Investigators of auditor-controller or director of finance; investigative auditors

(a) The following persons are not peace officers but may exercise the power to serve warrants as specified in Sections 1523 and 1530 during the course and within the scope of their employment, if they receive a course in the exercise of that power pursuant to Section 832. The authority and power of the persons designated under this section shall extend to any place in the state:

(1) Persons employed as investigators of an auditor-controller or director of finance of any county or persons employed by a city and county who conduct investigations under the supervision of the controller of the city and county, who are regularly employed and paid in that capacity, provided that the primary duty of these persons shall be to engage in investigations related to the theft of funds or the misappropriation of funds or resources, or investigations related to the duties of the auditor-controller or finance director as set forth in Chapter 3.5 (commencing with Section 26880), Chapter 4 (commencing with Section 26900), Chapter 4.5 (commencing with Section 26970), and Chapter 4.6 (commencing with Section 26980) of Part 3 of Division 2 of Title 3 of the Government Code.

(2) Persons employed by the Department of Justice as investigative auditors, provided that the primary duty of these persons shall be to investigate financial crimes. Investigative auditors shall only serve warrants for the production of documentary evidence held by financial institutions, Internet service providers, telecommunications companies, and third parties who are not reasonably suspected of engaging or having engaged in criminal activity related to the documentary evidence for which the warrant is requested.

(b) Notwithstanding any other provision of law, persons designated pursuant to this section shall not carry firearms.

(c) Persons designated pursuant to this section shall be included as "peace officers of the state" under paragraph (2) of subdivision (c) of Section 11105 for the purpose of receiving state summary criminal history information and shall be furnished that information on the same basis as peace officers of the state designated in paragraph (2) of subdivision (c) of Section 11105.

(d) Unless otherwise specifically provided, this section confers to persons designated in this section the same authority and power to serve warrants as conferred by Section 830.11.

Amended by Stats 2008 ch 81 (SB 1164),s 1, eff. 1/1/2009.

Section 830.14 - Designation of enforcement agents by local or regional transit agency or joint powers agency

(a) A local or regional transit agency or a joint powers agency operating rail service identified in an implementation program adopted pursuant to Article 10 (commencing with Section 130450) of Chapter 4 of Division 12 of the Public Utilities Code may authorize by contract designated persons as conductors performing fare inspection duties who are employed by a railroad corporation that operates public rail commuter transit services for that agency to act as its agent in the enforcement of subdivisions (a) to (d), inclusive, of Section 640 relating to the operation of the rail service if they complete the training requirement specified in this section.

(b) The governing board of the Altamont Commuter Express Authority, a joint powers agency duly formed pursuant to Article 1 (commencing with Section 6500) of Chapter 5 of Division 7 of Title 1 of the Government Code, by and between the Alameda County Congestion Management Agency, the Santa Clara Valley Transportation Authority, and the San Joaquin Regional Rail Commission, may contract with designated persons to act as its agents in the enforcement of subdivisions (a) to (d), inclusive, of Section 640 relating to the operation of a public transportation system if these persons complete the training requirement specified in this section.

(c) The governing board of the Peninsula Corridor Joint Powers Board, a joint powers agency duly formed pursuant to Article 1 (commencing with Section 6500) of Chapter 5 of Division 7 of Title 1 of the Government Code, by and between the San Mateo County Transit District, the Santa Clara Valley Transportation Authority, and the City and County of San Francisco, may appoint designated persons to act as its agents in the enforcement of subdivisions (a) to (d), inclusive, of Section 640 relating to the operation of a public transportation system if these persons complete the training requirement specified in this section.

(d) The governing board of Foothill Transit, a joint powers agency duly formed pursuant to Article 1 (commencing with Section 6500) of Chapter 5 of Division 7 of Title 1 of the Government Code, by and between the Cities of Arcadia, Azusa, Baldwin Park, Bradbury, Claremont, Covina, Diamond Bar, Duarte, El Monte, Glendora, Industry, Irwindale, La Habra Heights, La Puente, La Verne, Monrovia, Pomona, San Dimas, South El Monte, Temple City, Walnut, West Covina, and the County of Los Angeles, may resolve to contract with designated persons to act as its agents in the enforcement of subdivisions (a) to (d), inclusive, of Section 640 relating to the operation of a public transportation system if these persons complete the training requirement specified in this section.

(e) The governing board of the Sacramento Regional Transit District, a transit district duly formed pursuant to Part 14 (commencing with Section 102000) of Division 10 of the Public Utilities Code, may designate persons regularly employed by the district as inspectors or supervisors to enforce subdivisions (a) to (d), inclusive, of Section 640, relating to the operation of a public transportation system, and any ordinance adopted by the district pursuant to subdivision (a) of Section 102122 of the Public Utilities Code, if these persons complete the training requirement specified in this section.

(f) The governing board of a transit district, as defined in subdivision (b) of Section 99170 of the Public Utilities Code, may designate employees, except for union-represented employees employed to drive revenue-generating transit vehicles, or security officers contracted by the transit district, to enforce subdivisions (a) to (d), inclusive, of Section 640, and Section 640.5, and violations of Section 99170 of the Public Utilities Code.

(g) Persons authorized pursuant to this section to enforce subdivisions (a) to (d), inclusive, of Section 640, or Section 640.5, or Section 99170 of the Public Utilities Code, shall complete a specialized fare compliance course that shall be provided by the authorizing agency. This training course shall include, but not be limited to, the following topics:

(1) An overview of barrier-free fare inspection concepts.

(2) The scope and limitations of inspector authority.

(3) Familiarization with the elements of the infractions enumerated in subdivisions (a) to (d), inclusive, of Section 640, and, as applicable, the crimes enumerated in Section 640.5, and Section 99170 of the Public Utilities Code.

(4) Techniques for conducting fare checks, including inspection procedures, demeanor, and contacting violators.

(5) Citation issuance and court appearances.

(6) Fare media recognition.

(7) Handling argumentative violators and diffusing conflict.

(8) The mechanics of law enforcement support and interacting with law enforcement for effective incident resolution.

(h) Persons described in this section are public officers, not peace officers, have no authority to carry firearms or any other weapon while performing the duties authorized in this section, and may not exercise the powers of arrest of a peace officer while performing the duties authorized in this section. These persons may be authorized by the agencies specified in this section to issue citations involving infractions relating to the operation of the rail service specified in this section.

(i) This section does not affect the retirement or disability benefits provided to employees described in this section or be in violation of any collective bargaining agreement between a labor organization and a railroad corporation.

(j) Notwithstanding any other provision of this section, the primary responsibility of a conductor of a commuter passenger train shall be functions related to safe train operation.

Amended by Stats 2015 ch 303 (AB 731),s 392, eff. 1/1/2016.

Amended by Stats 2014 ch 253 (SB 1236),s 1, eff. 1/1/2015.

Amended by Stats 2011 ch 534 (AB 716),s 2, eff. 1/1/2012.

Amended by Stats 2006 ch 260 (AB 343),s 1, eff. 9/14/2006.

EFFECTIVE 1/1/2000. Amended October 10, 1999 (Bill Number: SB 532) (Chapter 1007).

Section 830.15 - Persons employed as law enforcement officer by Los Angeles World Airports

(a) Notwithstanding subdivision (d) of Section 830.33, a person regularly employed as an airport law enforcement officer by Los Angeles World Airports is a peace officer for purposes of Section 830.1 if and when the Los Angeles Police Commission and the Los

Angeles Board of Airport Commissioners enter into an agreement to enable the Inspector General of the Los Angeles Police Commission to conduct audits and investigations of the Los Angeles Airport Police Division.

(b) For purposes of this section, "Los Angeles World Airports" means the department of the City of Los Angeles that owns and operates the Los Angeles International Airport, the Ontario International Airport, the Palmdale Regional Airport, and the Van Nuys Airport.

(c) If the Los Angeles Police Commission and the Los Angeles Board of Airport Commissioners do not take the necessary actions provided in subdivision (a) and do not make a record of that action publicly available on or before April 1, 2014, this section shall become inoperative on that date and, as of January 1, 2015, is repealed, unless a later enacted statute that is enacted before January 1, 2015, deletes or extends the dates on which this section becomes inoperative and is repealed.

Added by Stats 2013 ch 783 (AB 128),s 1, eff. 1/1/2014.

Section 831 - Custodial officer

(a) A custodial officer is a public officer, not a peace officer, employed by a law enforcement agency of a city or county who has the authority and responsibility for maintaining custody of prisoners and performs tasks related to the operation of a local detention facility used for the detention of persons usually pending arraignment or upon court order either for their own safekeeping or for the specific purpose of serving a sentence in that facility.

(b) A custodial officer shall not carry or possess firearms in the performance of his or her official duties. A custodial officer may use a firearm that is a less lethal weapon, as defined in Section 16780, in the performance of his or her official duties, at the discretion of the employing sheriff or chief of police, as applicable, or his or her designee. A custodial officer who uses a less lethal weapon shall be trained in its use and shall comply with the policy on the use of less lethal weapons as set forth by the sheriff or chief of police.

(c) Each person described in this section as a custodial officer shall, within 90 days following the date of the initial assignment to the position, satisfactorily complete the training course specified in Section 832. In addition, each person designated as a custodial officer shall, within one year following the date of the initial assignment as a custodial officer, have satisfactorily met the minimum selection and training standards prescribed by the Board of State and Community Corrections pursuant to Section 6035. Persons designated as custodial officers, before the expiration of the 90-day and one-year periods described in this subdivision, who have not yet completed the required training, may perform the duties of a custodial officer only while under the direct supervision of a peace officer as described in Section 830.1, who has completed the training prescribed by the Commission on Peace Officer Standards and Training, or a custodial officer who has completed the training required by this section.

(d) At any time 20 or more custodial officers are on duty, there shall be at least one peace officer, as described in Section 830.1, on duty at the same time to supervise the performance of the custodial officers.

(e) This section does not confer any authority upon any custodial officer, except while he or she is on duty.

(f) A custodial officer may do all of the following:

(1) Use reasonable force in establishing and maintaining custody of persons delivered to him or her by a law enforcement officer.

(2) Make arrests for misdemeanors and felonies within the local detention facility pursuant to a duly issued warrant.

(3) Release without further criminal process persons arrested for intoxication.

(4) Release misdemeanants on citation to appear in lieu of or after booking.

Amended by Stats 2017 ch 73 (SB 324),s 1, eff. 1/1/2018.

Section 831.4 - Sheriff or police security officer

(a)

(1) A sheriff's or police security officer is a public officer, employed by the sheriff of a county, a police chief of a city police department, or a police chief of a police division that is within a city department and that operates independently of the city police department commanded by the police chief of a city, whose primary duty is the security of locations or facilities as directed by the sheriff or police chief. The duties of a sheriff's or police security officer shall be limited to the physical security and protection of properties owned, operated, controlled, or administered by the county or city, or any municipality or special district contracting for police services from the county or city pursuant to Section 54981 of the Government Code, or necessary duties with respect to the patrons, employees, and properties of the employing county, city, or contracting entities.

(2) In addition to the duties in paragraph (1), the duties of a security officer employed by the Chief of Police of the City of Sacramento or the Sheriff of the County of Sacramento may also include the physical security and protection of any properties owned, operated, or administered by a public agency, privately owned company, or nonprofit entity contracting for security services from the City or County of Sacramento, whose primary business supports national defense, or whose facility is qualified as a national critical infrastructure under federal law or by a federal agency, or that stores or manufactures material that, if stolen, vandalized, or otherwise compromised, may compromise national security or pose a danger to residents within the County of Sacramento. A contract entered into pursuant to this paragraph shall provide for full reimbursement to the City or County of Sacramento of the actual costs of providing those services, as determined by the county auditor or auditor-controller, or by the city. Before contracting for services pursuant to this paragraph, the Sacramento County Board of Supervisors or the governing board of the City of Sacramento shall discuss the contract and the requirements of this paragraph at a duly noticed public hearing.

(b) A sheriff's or police security officer is neither a peace officer nor a public safety officer as defined in Section 3301 of the Government Code. A sheriff's or police security officer may carry or possess a firearm, baton, and other safety equipment and weapons authorized by the sheriff or police chief while performing the duties authorized in this section, and under the terms and conditions specified by the sheriff or police chief. These persons may not exercise the powers of arrest of a peace officer, but may issue citations for infractions if authorized by the sheriff or police chief.

(c) Each sheriff's or police security officer shall satisfactorily complete a course of training as specified in Section 832 before being assigned to perform his or her duties. This section does not preclude the sheriff or police chief from requiring additional training requirements.

(d) Notwithstanding any other law, this section does not confer any authority upon a sheriff's or police security officer except while on duty, or confer any additional retirement benefits to persons employed within this classification.

Amended by Stats 2018 ch 92 (SB 1289),s 164, eff. 1/1/2019.

Amended by Stats 2017 ch 107 (AB 585),s 1, eff. 1/1/2018.
Amended by Stats 2012 ch 48 (AB 1643),s 1, eff. 1/1/2013.
EFFECTIVE 1/1/2000. Amended July 13, 1999 (Bill Number: SB 1163) (Chapter 112).

Section 831.5 - Custodial officer

(a) As used in this section, a custodial officer is a public officer, not a peace officer, who is employed by a law enforcement agency of San Diego County, Fresno County, Kern County, Stanislaus County, Riverside County, Santa Clara County, Napa County, or a county having a population of 425,000 or less who has the authority and responsibility for maintaining custody of prisoners and performs tasks related to the operation of a local detention facility used for the detention of persons usually pending arraignment or upon court order either for their own safekeeping or for the specific purpose of serving a sentence in the local detention facility. Custodial officers of a county shall be employees of, and under the authority of, the sheriff, except in counties in which the sheriff, as of July 1, 1993, is not in charge of and the sole and exclusive authority to keep the county jail and the prisoners in it. A custodial officer includes a person designated as a correctional officer, jailer, or other similar title. The duties of a custodial officer may include the serving of warrants, court orders, writs, and subpoenas in the detention facility or under circumstances arising directly out of maintaining custody of prisoners and related tasks.

(b) A custodial officer has no right to carry or possess firearms in the performance of the officer's prescribed duties, except, under the direction of the sheriff or chief of police, while engaged in transporting prisoners; guarding hospitalized prisoners; or suppressing jail riots, lynchings, escapes, or rescues in or about a detention facility falling under the care and custody of the sheriff or chief of police.

(c) A person described in this section as a custodial officer shall, within 90 days following the date of the initial assignment to that position, satisfactorily complete the training course specified in Section 832. In addition, a person designated as a custodial officer shall, within one year following the date of the initial assignment as a custodial officer, have satisfactorily met the minimum selection and training standards prescribed by the Board of State and Community Corrections pursuant to Section 6035. Persons designated as custodial officers, before the expiration of the 90-day and one-year periods described in this subdivision, who have not yet completed the required training, shall not carry or possess firearms in the performance of their prescribed duties, but may perform the duties of a custodial officer only while under the direct supervision of a peace officer, as described in Section 830.1, who has completed the training prescribed by the Commission on Peace Officer Standards and Training, or a custodial officer who has completed the training required in this section.

(d) At any time 20 or more custodial officers are on duty, there shall be at least one peace officer, as described in Section 830.1, on duty at the same time to supervise the performance of the custodial officers.

(e) This section does not confer any authority upon any custodial officer except while on duty.

(f) A custodial officer may use reasonable force in establishing and maintaining custody of persons delivered to the custodial officer by a law enforcement officer; may make arrests for misdemeanors and felonies within the local detention facility pursuant to a duly issued warrant; may make warrantless arrests pursuant to Section 836.5 only during the duration of the custodial officer's job; may release without further criminal process persons arrested for intoxication; and may release misdemeanants on citation to appear in lieu of or after booking.

(g) Custodial officers employed by the Santa Clara County Department of Correction are authorized to perform the following additional duties in the facility:

(1) Arrest a person without a warrant whenever the custodial officer has reasonable cause to believe that the person to be arrested has committed a misdemeanor or felony in the presence of the officer that is a violation of a statute or ordinance that the officer has the duty to enforce.

(2) Search property, cells, prisoners, or visitors.

(3) Conduct strip or body cavity searches of prisoners pursuant to Section 4030.

(4) Conduct searches and seizures pursuant to a duly issued warrant.

(5) Segregate prisoners.

(6) Classify prisoners for the purpose of housing or participation in supervised activities. These duties may be performed at the Santa Clara Valley Medical Center, or at other health care facilities in the County of Santa Clara, as needed and only as they directly relate to guarding in-custody inmates. This subdivision does not authorize the performance of any law enforcement activity involving any person other than the inmate or the inmate's visitors.

(h)

(1) Upon resolution by the Napa County Board of Supervisors, custodial officers employed by the Napa County Department of Corrections are authorized to perform all of the following duties in a facility located in that county:

(A) Arrest a person without a warrant whenever the custodial officer has reasonable cause to believe that the person to be arrested has committed a misdemeanor or felony in the presence of the officer that is a violation of a statute or ordinance that the officer has the duty to enforce.

(B) Search property, cells, prisoners, or visitors.

(C) Conduct strip or body cavity searches of prisoners pursuant to Section 4030.

(D) Conduct searches and seizures pursuant to a duly issued warrant.

(E) Segregate prisoners.

(F) Classify prisoners for the purpose of housing or participation in supervised activities.

(2) This subdivision does not authorize the performance of any law enforcement activity involving any person other than an inmate or the inmate's visitors.

(i)

(1) Upon resolution by the County of Madera Board of Supervisors, custodial officers employed by the Madera County Department of Corrections are authorized to perform all of the following duties in a facility located in that county:

(A) Arrest a person without a warrant whenever the custodial officer has reasonable cause to believe that the person to be arrested has committed a misdemeanor or felony in the presence of the officer that is a violation of a statute or ordinance that the officer has the duty to enforce.

(B) Search property, cells, prisoners, or visitors.

(C) Conduct strip or body cavity searches of prisoners pursuant to Section 4030.

(D) Conduct searches and seizures pursuant to a duly issued warrant.

(E) Segregate prisoners.

(F) Classify prisoners for the purpose of housing or participation in supervised activities.

(2) This subdivision does not authorize the performance of any law enforcement activity involving any person other than an inmate or the inmate's visitors.

(j) This section does not authorize a custodial officer to carry or possess a firearm when the officer is not on duty.

(k) It is the intent of the Legislature that this section, as it relates to Santa Clara, Madera, and Napa Counties, enumerate specific duties of custodial officers known as "correctional officers" in Santa Clara, Madera, and Napa Counties and to clarify the relationships of the correctional officers and deputy sheriffs in those counties. These duties are the same duties of the custodial officers prior to the date of enactment of Chapter 635 of the Statutes of 1999 pursuant to local rules and judicial decisions. It is further the intent of the Legislature that all issues regarding compensation for custodial officers remain subject to the collective bargaining process between the counties and the authorized bargaining representative for the custodial officers. However, this section does not assert that the duties of custodial officers are equivalent to the duties of deputy sheriffs and does not affect the ability of the county to negotiate pay that reflects the different duties of custodial officers and deputy sheriffs.

Amended by Stats 2019 ch 497 (AB 991),s 197, eff. 1/1/2020.

Amended by Stats 2018 ch 19 (AB 2197),s 1, eff. 1/1/2019.

Amended by Stats 2014 ch 53 (SB 1406),s 1, eff. 1/1/2015.

Amended by Stats 2010 ch 575 (AB 1695),s 2, eff. 1/1/2011.

Amended by Stats 2009 ch 140 (AB 1164),s 145, eff. 1/1/2010.

Amended and effective October 20, 1999 (Bill Number: SB 1019) (Chapter 635).

Section 831.6 - Transportation officer

(a) A transportation officer is a public officer, not a peace officer, appointed on a contract basis by a peace officer to transport a prisoner or prisoners.

(b) A transportation officer shall have the authority of a public officer, and shall have the right to carry or possess firearms, only while engaged in the transportation of a prisoner or prisoners for the duration of the contract.

(c) Each person described in this section as a transportation officer shall, prior to the transportation of any prisoner, have satisfactorily completed the training course specified in Section 832.

(d) A transportation officer may use reasonable force in establishing and maintaining custody of persons delivered to him or her by a peace officer.

Added by Stats. 1982, Ch. 416, Sec. 1. Effective July 8, 1982.

Section 831.7 - Custody assistant

(a) As used in this section, a custody assistant is a person who is a full-time employee, not a peace officer, employed by the county sheriff's department who assists peace officer personnel in maintaining order and security in a custody detention, court detention, or station jail facility of the sheriff's department. A custody assistant is responsible for maintaining custody of prisoners and performs tasks related to the operation of a local detention facility used for the detention of persons usually pending arraignment or upon court order either for their own safekeeping or for the specific purpose of serving a sentence therein. Custody assistants of the sheriff's department shall be employees of, and under the authority of, the sheriff.

(b) A custody assistant has no right to carry or possess firearms in the performance of his or her prescribed duties.

(c) Each person described in this section as a custody assistant shall satisfactorily complete a training course specified by the sheriff's department. In addition, each person designated as a custody assistant shall satisfactorily meet the minimum selection and training standards prescribed by the Department of Corrections and Rehabilitation pursuant to Section 6035.

(d) A custody assistant may use reasonable force in establishing and maintaining custody of persons housed at a local detention facility, court detention facility, or station jail facility.

(e) Custody assistants employed by the county sheriff's department are authorized to perform the following additional duties in a custody facility, court detention facility, or station jail facility:

(1) Assist in supervising the conduct of inmates in sleeping quarters, during meals and bathing, at recreation, and on work assignments.

(2) Assist in overseeing the work of, and instructing, a group of inmates assigned to various operational, maintenance, or other rehabilitative activities.

(3) Assist in the operation of main or dormitory control booths.

(4) Assist in processing inmates for court appearances.

(5) Control, or assist in the monitoring and control of, access to attorney rooms and visiting areas.

(6) Fingerprint, photograph, or operate livescan machines with respect to inmates, or assist in the fingerprinting or photographing of inmates.

(7) Obtain criminal history information relating to an inmate including any warrant or other hold, and update classification or housing information relating to an inmate, as necessary.

(8) Interview inmates and review records related to the classification process to determine the appropriate security level for an inmate or the eligibility of an inmate for transfer to another facility.

(9) Ensure compliance of a custody facility, court detention facility, or station jail facility with the provisions of Title 15 of the California Code of Regulations, or with any other applicable legislative or judicial mandate.

(10) Assist in receiving and processing inmates in a sheriff's station, court detention area, or type I jail facility.

(11) Secure inmates and their personal property and moneys as necessary in compliance with the rules and regulations of the sheriff's department.

(12) Order, inspect, or serve meals to inmates.

(13) Maintain sanitary conditions within a custody facility, court detention facility, or station jail facility.

(14) Respond to public inquiries regarding any inmate.

(f) Notwithstanding any other law, nothing in this section shall be construed to confer any authority upon a custody assistant except while on duty, or to grant any additional retirement benefits to persons employed within this classification.

(g) This section shall apply only in a county of the first class, as established by Sections 28020 and 28022 of the Government Code, but shall not be operative in a county until adopted by resolution of the board of supervisors.

Added by Stats 2006 ch 468 (SB 1184),s 2, eff. 1/1/2007.

Section 832 - Course of training

(a) Every person described in this chapter as a peace officer shall satisfactorily complete an introductory training course prescribed by the Commission on Peace Officer Standards and Training. On or after July 1, 1989, satisfactory completion of the course shall be demonstrated by passage of an appropriate examination developed or approved by the commission. Training in the carrying and use of firearms shall not be required of a peace officer whose employing agency prohibits the use of firearms.

(b)

(1) Every peace officer described in this chapter, prior to the exercise of the powers of a peace officer, shall have satisfactorily completed the training course described in subdivision (a).

(2) Every peace officer described in Section 13510 or in subdivision (a) of Section 830.2 may satisfactorily complete the training required by this section as part of the training prescribed pursuant to Section 13510.

(c) Persons described in this chapter as peace officers who have not satisfactorily completed the course described in subdivision (a), as specified in subdivision (b), shall not have the powers of a peace officer until they satisfactorily complete the course.

(d) A peace officer who, on March 4, 1972, possesses or is qualified to possess the basic certificate as awarded by the Commission on Peace Officer Standards and Training is exempted from this section.

(e)

(1) A person completing the training described in subdivision (a) who does not become employed as a peace officer within three years from the date of passing the examination described in subdivision (a), or who has a three-year or longer break in service as a peace officer, shall pass the examination described in subdivision (a) prior to the exercise of the powers of a peace officer, except for a person described in paragraph (2).

(2) The requirement in paragraph (1) does not apply to a person who meets any of the following requirements:

(A) Is returning to a management position that is at the second level of supervision or higher.

(B) Has successfully requalified for a basic course through the Commission on Peace Officer Standards and Training.

(C) Has maintained proficiency through teaching the course described in subdivision (a).

(D) During the break in California service, was continuously employed as a peace officer in another state or at the federal level.

(E) Has previously met the requirements of subdivision (a), has been appointed as a peace officer under subdivision (c) of Section 830.1, and has been continuously employed as a custodial officer as defined in Section 831 or 831.5 by the agency making the peace officer appointment since completing the training prescribed in subdivision (a).

(f) The commission may charge appropriate fees for the examination required by subdivision (e), not to exceed actual costs.

(g) Notwithstanding any other law, the commission may charge appropriate fees for the examination required by subdivision (a) to each applicant who is not sponsored by a local or other law enforcement agency, or is not a peace officer employed by, or under consideration for employment by, a state or local agency, department, or district, or is not a custodial officer as defined in Sections 831 and 831.5. The fees shall not exceed actual costs.

(h)

(1) When evaluating a certification request from a probation department for a training course described in this section, the commission shall deem there to be an identifiable and unmet need for the training course.

(2) A probation department that is a certified provider of the training course described in this section shall not be required to offer the course to the general public.

Amended by Stats 2015 ch 200 (AB 546),s 1, eff. 1/1/2016.
Amended by Stats 2014 ch 87 (AB 1860),s 1, eff. 1/1/2015.
Amended by Stats 2003 ch 70 (AB 1254), s 2, eff. 1/1/2004.

Section 832.05 - Emotional and mental evaluation

(a) Each state or local department or agency that employs peace officers shall utilize a person meeting the requirements set forth in subdivision (f) of Section 1031 of the Government Code, applicable to emotional and mental examinations, for any emotional and mental evaluation done in the course of the department or agency's screening of peace officer recruits or the evaluation of peace officers to determine their fitness for duty.

(b) This section shall become operative on January 1, 2005.

Added by Stats 2003 ch 777 (AB 1669), s 5, eff. 1/1/2004.

Section 832.1 - Course of training relative to airport security

Any airport security officer, airport policeman, or airport special officer, regularly employed and paid by a city, county, city and county, or district who is a peace officer shall have completed a course of training relative to airport security approved by the Commission on Peace Officers Standards and Training. Any such airport officer so employed on the effective date of this section shall have completed the course of instruction required by this section by September 1, 1973. Any airport officer so employed after such effective date shall have completed the course of instruction within 90 days after such employment.

Any officer who has not satisfactorily completed such course within such prescribed time shall not continue to have the powers of a peace officer until they have satisfactorily completed such course.

Amended by Stats. 1975, Ch. 168.

Section 832.2 - School police reserve officer training course

Every school police reserve officer, as described in Section 38000 of the Education Code, shall complete a course of training approved by the Commission on Peace Officer Standards and Training relating directly to the role of school police reserve officers.

The school police reserve officer training course shall address guidelines and procedures for reporting offenses to other law enforcement agencies that deal with violence on campus and other school related matters, as determined by the Commission on Peace Officer Standards and Training.

Amended by Stats. 1998, Ch. 745, Sec. 5. Effective January 1, 1999.

Section 832.25 - Specialized investigators basic course for welfare fraud investigators or inspectors

(a) Notwithstanding any other provision of law, all welfare fraud investigators or inspectors who are appointed as peace officers pursuant to subdivision (a) of Section 830.35 on or after January 1, 2001, shall attend and complete a specialized investigators basic course approved by the Commission on Peace Officer Standards and Training within one year of being hired as a welfare investigator or inspector. Any welfare fraud investigator or inspector appointed prior to January 1, 2001, shall not be required to attend and complete the training required by this section, provided that he or she has been continuously employed in that capacity prior to January 1, 2001, by the county that made the appointment.

(b) Any investigator or inspector who possesses a valid basic peace officer certificate as awarded by the Commission on Peace Officer Standards and Training or who has successfully completed the regular basic course certified by the Commission on Peace Officer Standards and Training basic course within three years prior to appointment shall be exempt from the training requirements of subdivision (a).

Added by Stats 2000 ch 633 (AB 2059), s 1, eff. 1/1/2001.

Section 832.3 - Course of training for sheriffs and police officers

(a) Except as provided in subdivision (e), any sheriff, undersheriff, or deputy sheriff of a county, any police officer of a city, and any police officer of a district authorized by statute to maintain a police department, who is first employed after January 1, 1975, shall successfully complete a course of training prescribed by the Commission on Peace Officer Standards and Training before exercising the powers of a peace officer, except while participating as a trainee in a supervised field training program approved by the Commission on Peace Officer Standards and Training. Each police chief, or any other person in charge of a local law enforcement agency, appointed on or after January 1, 1999, as a condition of continued employment, shall complete the course of training pursuant to this subdivision within two years of appointment. The training course for a sheriff, an undersheriff, and a deputy sheriff of a county, and a police chief and a police officer of a city or any other local law enforcement agency, shall be the same.

(b) For the purpose of ensuring competent peace officers and standardizing the training required in subdivision (a), the commission shall develop a testing program, including standardized tests that enable (1) comparisons between presenters of the training and (2) assessments of trainee achievement. The trainees' test scores shall be used only for the purposes enumerated in this subdivision and those research purposes as shall be approved in advance by the commission. The commission shall take all steps necessary to maintain the confidentiality of the test scores, test items, scoring keys, and other examination data used in the testing program required by this subdivision. The commission shall determine the minimum passing score for each test and the conditions for retesting students who fail. Passing these tests shall be required for successful completion of the training required in subdivision (a). Presenters approved by the commission to provide the training required in subdivision (a) shall administer the standardized tests or, at the commission's option, shall facilitate the commission's administration of the standardized tests to all trainees.

(c) Community colleges may give preference in enrollment to employed law enforcement trainees who shall complete training as prescribed by this section. At least 15 percent of each presentation shall consist of non-law-enforcement trainees if they are available. Preference should only be given when the trainee could not complete the course within the time required by statute, and only when no other training program is reasonably available. Average daily attendance for these courses shall be reported for state aid.

(d) Prior to July 1, 1987, the commission shall make a report to the Legislature on academy proficiency testing scores. This report shall include an evaluation of the correlation between academy proficiency test scores and performance as a peace officer.

(e)

(1) Any deputy sheriff described in subdivision (c) of Section 830.1 shall be exempt from the training requirements specified in subdivisions (a) and (b) as long as his or her assignments remain custodial related.

(2) Deputy sheriffs described in subdivision (c) of Section 830.1 shall complete the training for peace officers pursuant to subdivision (a) of Section 832, and within 120 days after the date of employment, shall complete the training required by the Board of State and Community Corrections for custodial personnel pursuant to Section 6035, and the training required for custodial personnel of local detention facilities pursuant to Subchapter 1 (commencing with Section 100) of Chapter 1 of Division 1 of Title 15 of the California Code of Regulations.

(3) Deputy sheriffs described in subdivision (c) of Section 830.1 shall complete the course of training pursuant to subdivision (a) prior to being reassigned from custodial assignments to duties with responsibility for the prevention and detection of crime and the general enforcement of the criminal laws of this state. A deputy sheriff who has completed the course of training pursuant to subdivision (a) and has been hired as a deputy sheriff described in subdivision (c) of Section 830.1 shall be eligible to be reassigned from custodial assignments to duties with the responsibility for the prevention and detection of crime and the general enforcement of the criminal laws of this state within three years of completing the training pursuant to subdivision (a). A deputy sheriff shall be eligible for reassignment within five years of having completed the training pursuant to subdivision (a) without having to complete a requalification for the regular basic course provided that all of the following are satisfied:

(A) The deputy sheriff remains continuously employed by the same department in which the deputy sheriff is being reassigned from custodial assignments to duties with the responsibility for the prevention and detection of crime and the general enforcement of the criminal laws of this state.

(B) The deputy sheriff maintains the perishable skills training required by the commission for peace officers assigned to duties with the responsibility for the prevention and detection of crime and the general enforcement of the criminal laws of this state.

(f) Any school police officer first employed by a K-12 public school district or California Community College district after July 1, 1999, shall successfully complete a basic course of training as prescribed by subdivision (a) before exercising the powers of a peace officer. A school police officer shall not be subject to this subdivision while participating as a trainee in a supervised field training program approved by the Commission on Peace Officer Standards and Training.

(g) The commission shall prepare a specialized course of instruction for the training of school peace officers, as defined in Section 830.32, to meet the unique safety needs of a school environment. This course is intended to supplement any other training requirements.

(h) Any school peace officer first employed by a K-12 public school district or California Community College district before July 1, 1999, shall successfully complete the specialized course of training prescribed in subdivision (g) no later than July 1, 2002. Any school police officer first employed by a K-12 public school district or California Community College district after July 1, 1999, shall successfully complete the specialized course of training prescribed in subdivision (g) within two years of the date of first employment.

Amended by Stats 2018 ch 17 (AB 1888),s 1, eff. 1/1/2019.

Amended by Stats 2016 ch 86 (SB 1171),s 228, eff. 1/1/2017.

Amended by Stats 2015 ch 207 (AB 1168),s 1, eff. 1/1/2016.

EFFECTIVE 1/1/2000. Amended October 10, 1999 (Bill Number: SB 747) (Chapter 852).

Section 832.4 - Basic certificate for undersheriffs, deputy sheriffs, and police officers

(a) Any undersheriff or deputy sheriff of a county, any police officer of a city, and any police officer of a district authorized by statute to maintain a police department, who is first employed after January 1, 1974, and is responsible for the prevention and detection of crime and the general enforcement of the criminal laws of this state, shall obtain the basic certificate issued by the Commission on Peace Officer Standards and Training within 18 months of his or her employment in order to continue to exercise the powers of a peace officer after the expiration of the 18-month period.

(b) Every peace officer listed in subdivision (a) of Section 830.1, except a sheriff, or elected marshal, or a deputy sheriff described in subdivision (c) of Section 830.1, who is employed after January 1, 1988, shall obtain the basic certificate issued by the Commission on Peace Officer Standards and Training upon completion of probation, but in no case later than 24 months after his or her employment, in order to continue to exercise the powers of a peace officer after the expiration of the 24-month period. Deputy sheriffs described in subdivision (c) of Section 830.1 shall obtain the basic certificate issued by the Commission on Peace Officer Standards and Training within 24 months after being reassigned from custodial duties to general law enforcement duties.

In those cases where the probationary period established by the employing agency is 24 months, the peace officers described in this subdivision may continue to exercise the powers of a peace officer for an additional three-month period to allow for the processing of the certification application.

(c) Each police chief, or any other person in charge of a local law enforcement agency, appointed on or after January 1, 1999, as a condition of continued employment, shall obtain the basic certificate issued by the Commission on Peace Officer Standards and Training within two years of appointment.

Amended by Stats. 1998, Ch. 931, Sec. 366.5. Effective September 28, 1998. Operative January 1, 1999, by Sec. 496 of Ch. 931.

Section 832.5 - Complaints by members of public

(a)

　(1)Each department or agency in this state that employs peace officers shall establish a procedure to investigate complaints by members of the public against the personnel of these departments or agencies, and shall make a written description of the procedure available to the public.

　(2)Each department or agency that employs custodial officers, as defined in Section 831.5, may establish a procedure to investigate complaints by members of the public against those custodial officers employed by these departments or agencies, provided, however, that any procedure so established shall comply with the provisions of this section and with the provisions of Section 832.7.

(b) Complaints and any reports or findings relating to these complaints, including all complaints and any reports currently in the possession of the department or agency, shall be retained for a period of no less than 5 years for records where there was not a sustained finding of misconduct and for not less than 15 years where there was a sustained finding of misconduct. A record shall not be destroyed while a request related to that record is being processed or any process or litigation to determine whether the record is subject to release is ongoing. All complaints retained pursuant to this subdivision may be maintained either in the peace or custodial officer's general personnel file or in a separate file designated by the department or agency as provided by department or agency policy, in accordance with all applicable requirements of law. However, prior to any official determination regarding promotion, transfer, or disciplinary action by an officer's employing department or agency, the complaints described by subdivision (c) shall be removed from the officer's general personnel file and placed in a separate file designated by the department or agency, in accordance with all applicable requirements of law.

(c) Complaints by members of the public that are determined by the peace or custodial officer's employing agency to be frivolous, as defined in Section 128.5 of the Code of Civil Procedure, or unfounded or exonerated, or any portion of a complaint that is determined to be frivolous, unfounded, or exonerated, shall not be maintained in that officer's general personnel file. However, these complaints shall be retained in other, separate files that shall be deemed personnel records for purposes of the California Public Records Act (Division 10 (commencing with Section 7920.000) of Title 1 of the Government Code) and Section 1043 of the Evidence Code.

　(1)Management of the peace or custodial officer's employing agency shall have access to the files described in this subdivision.

　(2)Management of the peace or custodial officer's employing agency shall not use the complaints contained in these separate files for punitive or promotional purposes except as permitted by subdivision (f) of Section 3304 of the Government Code.

　(3)Management of the peace or custodial officer's employing agency may identify any officer who is subject to the complaints maintained in these files which require counseling or additional training. However, if a complaint is removed from the officer's personnel file, any reference in the personnel file to the complaint or to a separate file shall be deleted.

(d) As used in this section, the following definitions apply:

(1) "General personnel file" means the file maintained by the agency containing the primary records specific to each peace or custodial officer's employment, including evaluations, assignments, status changes, and imposed discipline.

(2) "Unfounded" means that the investigation clearly established that the allegation is not true.

(3) "Exonerated" means that the investigation clearly established that the actions of the peace or custodial officer that formed the basis for the complaint are not violations of law or department policy.

Amended by Stats 2022 ch 28 (SB 1380),s 125, eff. 1/1/2023.
Amended by Stats 2021 ch 615 (AB 474),s 338, eff. 1/1/2022, op. 1/1/2023.
Amended by Stats 2021 ch 402 (SB 16),s 2, eff. 1/1/2022.
Amended by Stats 2002 ch 391 (AB 2040), s 5, eff. 1/1/2003.

Section 832.6 - Deputized or appointed person

(a) Every person deputized or appointed, as described in subdivision (a) of Section 830.6, shall have the powers of a peace officer only when the person is any of the following:

(1) A level I reserve officer deputized or appointed pursuant to paragraph (1) or (2) of subdivision (a) or subdivision (b) of Section 830.6 and assigned to the prevention and detection of crime and the general enforcement of the laws of this state, whether or not working alone, and the person has completed the basic training course for deputy sheriffs and police officers prescribed by the Commission on Peace Officer Standards and Training. For level I reserve officers appointed prior to January 1, 1997, the basic training requirement shall be the course that was prescribed at the time of their appointment. Reserve officers appointed pursuant to this paragraph shall satisfy the continuing professional training requirement prescribed by the commission.

(2)

(A) A level II reserve officer assigned to the prevention and detection of crime and the general enforcement of the laws of this state while under the immediate supervision of a peace officer who has completed the basic training course for deputy sheriffs and police officers prescribed by the Commission on Peace Officer Standards and Training, and the level II reserve officer has completed the course required by Section 832 and any other training prescribed by the commission.

(B) Level II reserve officers appointed pursuant to this paragraph may be assigned, without immediate supervision, to those limited duties that are authorized for level III reserve officers pursuant to paragraph (3). Reserve officers appointed pursuant to this paragraph shall satisfy the continuing professional training requirement prescribed by the commission.

(3) Level III reserve officers may be deployed and are authorized only to carry out limited support duties not requiring general law enforcement powers in their routine performance. Those limited duties shall include traffic control, security at parades and sporting events, report taking, evidence transportation, parking enforcement, and other duties that are not likely to result in physical arrests. Level III reserve officers, while assigned these duties, shall be supervised in the accessible vicinity by a level I reserve officer or a full-time, regular peace officer employed by a law enforcement agency authorized to have reserve officers. Level III reserve officers may transport prisoners without immediate supervision. Those persons shall have completed the training required under Section 832 and any other training prescribed by the commission for those persons.

(4) A person assigned to the prevention and detection of a particular crime or crimes or to the detection or apprehension of a particular individual or individuals while working under the supervision of a California peace officer in a county adjacent to the state border who possesses a basic certificate issued by the Commission on Peace Officer Standards and Training, and the person is a law enforcement officer who is regularly employed by a local or state law enforcement agency in an adjoining state and has completed the basic training required for peace officers in his or her state.

(5)

(A) For purposes of this section, a reserve officer who has previously satisfied the training requirements pursuant to this section and has served as a level I or II reserve officer within the three-year period prior to the date of a new appointment shall be deemed to remain qualified as to the Commission on Peace Officer Standards and Training requirements if that reserve officer accepts a new appointment at the same or lower level with another law enforcement agency. If the reserve officer has more than a three-year break in service, he or she shall satisfy current training requirements.

(B) This training shall fully satisfy any other training requirements required by law, including those specified in Section 832.

(C) In no case shall a peace officer of an adjoining state provide services within a California jurisdiction during any period in which the regular law enforcement agency of the jurisdiction is involved in a labor dispute.

(b) Notwithstanding subdivision (a), a person who is issued a level I reserve officer certificate before January 1, 1981, shall have the full powers and duties of a peace officer, as provided by Section 830.1, if so designated by local ordinance or, if the local agency is not authorized to act by ordinance, by resolution, either individually or by class, if the appointing authority determines the person is qualified to perform general law enforcement duties by reason of the person's training and experience. Persons who were qualified to be issued the level I reserve officer certificate before January 1, 1981, and who state in writing under penalty of perjury that they applied for, but were not issued, the certificate before January 1, 1981, may be issued the certificate before July 1, 1984. For purposes of this section, certificates that are issued shall be deemed to have the full force and effect of any level I reserve officer certificate issued prior to January 1, 1981.

(c) In carrying out this section, the commission:

(1) May use proficiency testing to satisfy reserve training standards.

(2) Shall provide for convenient training to remote areas in the state.

(3) Shall establish a professional certificate for reserve officers, as defined in paragraph (1) of subdivision (a), and may establish a professional certificate for reserve officers, as defined in paragraphs (2) and (3) of subdivision (a).

(4) Shall facilitate the voluntary transition of reserve officers to regular officers with no unnecessary redundancy between the training required for level I and level II reserve officers.

(d) In carrying out paragraphs (1) and (3) of subdivision (c), the commission may establish and levy appropriate fees, provided the fees do not exceed the cost for administering the respective services. These fees shall be deposited in the State Penalty Fund established by Section 1464.

(e) The commission shall include an amount in its annual budget request to carry out this section.

Amended by Stats 2018 ch 36 (AB 1812),s 16, eff. 6/27/2018.

Amended by Stats 2001 ch 473 (SB 485), s 6, eff. 1/1/2002.

Amended by Stats 2000 ch 287 (SB 1955), s 11, eff. 1/1/2001.

Previously Amended July 13, 1999 (Bill Number: SB 359) (Chapter 111).

Section 832.7 - Peace officer or custodial officer personnel records

(a) Except as provided in subdivision (b), the personnel records of peace officers and custodial officers and records maintained by a state or local agency pursuant to Section 832.5, or information obtained from these records, are confidential and shall not be disclosed in any criminal or civil proceeding except by discovery pursuant to Sections 1043 and 1046 of the Evidence Code. This section does not apply to investigations or proceedings concerning the conduct of peace officers or custodial officers, or an agency or department that employs those officers, conducted by a grand jury, a district attorney's office, the Attorney General's office, or the Commission on Peace Officer Standards and Training.

(b)

(1) Notwithstanding subdivision (a), Section 7923.600 of the Government Code, or any other law, the following peace officer or custodial officer personnel records and records maintained by a state or local agency shall not be confidential and shall be made available for public inspection pursuant to the California Public Records Act (Division 10 (commencing with Section 7920.000) of Title 1 of the Government Code):

(A) A record relating to the report, investigation, or findings of any of the following:

(i) An incident involving the discharge of a firearm at a person by a peace officer or custodial officer.

(ii) An incident involving the use of force against a person by a peace officer or custodial officer that resulted in death or in great bodily injury.

(iii) A sustained finding involving a complaint that alleges unreasonable or excessive force.

(iv) A sustained finding that an officer failed to intervene against another officer using force that is clearly unreasonable or excessive.

(B)

(i) Any record relating to an incident in which a sustained finding was made by any law enforcement agency or oversight agency that a peace officer or custodial officer engaged in sexual assault involving a member of the public.

(ii) As used in this subparagraph, "sexual assault" means the commission or attempted initiation of a sexual act with a member of the public by means of force, threat, coercion, extortion, offer of leniency or other official favor, or under the color of authority. For purposes of this definition, the propositioning for or commission of any sexual act while on duty is considered a sexual assault.

(iii) As used in this subparagraph, "member of the public" means any person not employed by the officer's employing agency and includes any participant in a cadet, explorer, or other youth program affiliated with the agency.

(C) Any record relating to an incident in which a sustained finding was made by any law enforcement agency or oversight agency involving dishonesty by a peace officer or custodial officer directly relating to the reporting, investigation, or prosecution of a crime, or directly relating to the reporting of, or investigation of misconduct by, another peace officer or custodial officer, including, but not limited to, any false statements, filing false reports, destruction, falsifying, or concealing of evidence, or perjury.

(D) Any record relating to an incident in which a sustained finding was made by any law enforcement agency or oversight agency that a peace officer or custodial officer engaged in conduct including, but not limited to, verbal statements, writings, online posts, recordings, and gestures, involving prejudice or discrimination against a person on the basis of race, religious creed, color, national origin, ancestry, physical disability, mental disability, medical condition, genetic information, marital status, sex, gender, gender identity, gender expression, age, sexual orientation, or military and veteran status.

(E) Any record relating to an incident in which a sustained finding was made by any law enforcement agency or oversight agency that the peace officer made an unlawful arrest or conducted an unlawful search.

(2) Records that are subject to disclosure under clause (iii) or (iv) of subparagraph (A) of paragraph (1), or under subparagraph (D) or (E) of paragraph (1), relating to an incident that occurs before January 1, 2022, shall not be subject to the time limitations in paragraph (11) until January 1, 2023.

(3) Records that shall be released pursuant to this subdivision include all investigative reports; photographic, audio, and video evidence; transcripts or recordings of interviews; autopsy reports; all materials compiled and presented for review to the district attorney or to any person or body charged with determining whether to file criminal charges against an officer in connection with an incident, whether the officer's action was consistent with law and agency policy for purposes of discipline or administrative action, or what discipline to impose or corrective action to take; documents setting forth findings or recommended findings; and copies of disciplinary records relating to the incident, including any letters of intent to impose discipline, any documents reflecting modifications of discipline due to the Skelly or grievance process, and letters indicating final imposition of discipline or other documentation reflecting implementation of corrective action. Records that shall be released pursuant to this subdivision also include records relating to an incident specified in paragraph (1) in which the peace officer or custodial officer resigned before the law enforcement agency or oversight agency concluded its investigation into the alleged incident.

(4) A record from a separate and prior investigation or assessment of a separate incident shall not be released unless it is independently subject to disclosure pursuant to this subdivision.

(5) If an investigation or incident involves multiple officers, information about allegations of misconduct by, or the analysis or disposition of an investigation of, an officer shall not be released pursuant to subparagraph (B), (C), (D), or (E) of paragraph (1), unless it relates to a sustained finding regarding that officer that is itself subject to disclosure pursuant to this section. However, factual information about that action of an officer during an incident, or the statements of an officer about an incident, shall be released if they are relevant to a finding against another officer that is subject to release pursuant to subparagraph (B), (C), (D), or (E) of paragraph (1).

(6) An agency shall redact a record disclosed pursuant to this section only for any of the following purposes:

(A) To remove personal data or information, such as a home address, telephone number, or identities of family members, other than the names and work-related information of peace and custodial officers.

(B) To preserve the anonymity of whistleblowers, complainants, victims, and witnesses.

(C) To protect confidential medical, financial, or other information of which disclosure is specifically prohibited by federal law or would cause an unwarranted invasion of personal privacy that clearly outweighs the strong public interest in records about possible misconduct and use of force by peace officers and custodial officers.

(D) Where there is a specific, articulable, and particularized reason to believe that disclosure of the record would pose a significant danger to the physical safety of the peace officer, custodial officer, or another person.

(7) Notwithstanding paragraph (6), an agency may redact a record disclosed pursuant to this section, including personal identifying information, where, on the facts of the particular case, the public interest served by not disclosing the information clearly outweighs the public interest served by disclosure of the information.

(8) An agency may withhold a record of an incident described in paragraph (1) that is the subject of an active criminal or administrative investigation, in accordance with any of the following:

(A)

(i) During an active criminal investigation, disclosure may be delayed for up to 60 days from the date the misconduct or use of force occurred or until the district attorney determines whether to file criminal charges related to the misconduct or use of force, whichever occurs sooner. If an agency delays disclosure pursuant to this clause, the agency shall provide, in writing, the specific basis for the agency's determination that the interest in delaying disclosure clearly outweighs the public interest in disclosure. This writing shall include the estimated date for disclosure of the withheld information.

(ii) After 60 days from the misconduct or use of force, the agency may continue to delay the disclosure of records or information if the disclosure could reasonably be expected to interfere with a criminal enforcement proceeding against an officer who engaged in misconduct or used the force. If an agency delays disclosure pursuant to this clause, the agency shall, at 180-day intervals as necessary, provide, in writing, the specific basis for the agency's determination that disclosure could reasonably be expected to interfere with a criminal enforcement proceeding. The writing shall include the estimated date for the disclosure of the withheld information. Information withheld by the agency shall be disclosed when the specific basis for withholding is resolved, when the investigation or proceeding is no longer active, or by no later than 18 months after the date of the incident, whichever occurs sooner.

(iii) After 60 days from the misconduct or use of force, the agency may continue to delay the disclosure of records or information if the disclosure could reasonably be expected to interfere with a criminal enforcement proceeding against someone other than the officer who engaged in the misconduct or used the force. If an agency delays disclosure under this clause, the agency shall, at 180-day intervals, provide, in writing, the specific basis why disclosure could reasonably be expected to interfere with a criminal enforcement proceeding, and shall provide an estimated date for the disclosure of the withheld information. Information withheld by the agency shall be disclosed when the specific basis for withholding is resolved, when the investigation or proceeding is no longer active, or by no later than 18 months after the date of the incident, whichever occurs sooner, unless extraordinary circumstances warrant continued delay due to the ongoing criminal investigation or proceeding. In that case, the agency must show by clear and convincing evidence that the interest in preventing prejudice to the active and ongoing criminal investigation or proceeding outweighs the public interest in prompt disclosure of records about misconduct or use of force by peace officers and custodial officers. The agency shall release all information subject to disclosure that does not cause substantial prejudice, including any documents that have otherwise become available.

(iv) In an action to compel disclosure brought pursuant to Section 7923.000 of the Government Code, an agency may justify delay by filing an application to seal the basis for withholding, in accordance with Rule 2.550 of the California Rules of Court, or any successor rule, if disclosure of the written basis itself would impact a privilege or compromise a pending investigation.

(B) If criminal charges are filed related to the incident in which misconduct occurred or force was used, the agency may delay the disclosure of records or information until a verdict on those charges is returned at trial or, if a plea of guilty or no contest is entered, the time to withdraw the plea pursuant to Section 1018.

(C) During an administrative investigation into an incident described in paragraph (1), the agency may delay the disclosure of records or information until the investigating agency determines whether the misconduct or use of force violated a law or agency policy, but no longer than 180 days after the date of the employing agency's discovery of the misconduct or use of force, or allegation of misconduct or use of force, by a person authorized to initiate an investigation.

(9) A record of a complaint, or the investigations, findings, or dispositions of that complaint, shall not be released pursuant to this section if the complaint is frivolous, as defined in Section 128.5 of the Code of Civil Procedure, or if the complaint is unfounded.

(10) The cost of copies of records subject to disclosure pursuant to this subdivision that are made available upon the payment of fees covering direct costs of duplication pursuant to subdivision (a) of Section 7922.530 of the Government Code shall not include the costs of searching for, editing, or redacting the records.

(11) Except to the extent temporary withholding for a longer period is permitted pursuant to paragraph (8), records subject to disclosure under this subdivision shall be provided at the earliest possible time and no later than 45 days from the date of a request for their disclosure.

(12)

(A) For purposes of releasing records pursuant to this subdivision, the lawyer-client privilege does not prohibit the disclosure of either of the following:

(i) Factual information provided by the public entity to its attorney or factual information discovered in any investigation conducted by, or on behalf of, the public entity's attorney.

(ii) Billing records related to the work done by the attorney so long as the records do not relate to active and ongoing litigation and do not disclose information for the purpose of legal consultation between the public entity and its attorney.

(B) This paragraph does not prohibit the public entity from asserting that a record or information within the record is exempted or prohibited from disclosure pursuant to any other federal or state law.

(c) Notwithstanding subdivisions (a) and (b), a department or agency shall release to the complaining party a copy of the complaining party's own statements at the time the complaint is filed.

(d) Notwithstanding subdivisions (a) and (b), a department or agency that employs peace or custodial officers may disseminate data regarding the number, type, or disposition of complaints (sustained, not sustained, exonerated, or unfounded) made against its officers if that information is in a form which does not identify the individuals involved.

(e) Notwithstanding subdivisions (a) and (b), a department or agency that employs peace or custodial officers may release factual information concerning a disciplinary investigation if the officer who is the subject of the disciplinary investigation, or the officer's agent or representative, publicly makes a statement they know to be false concerning the investigation or the imposition of disciplinary action. Information may not be disclosed by the peace or custodial officer's employer unless the false statement was published by an established medium of communication, such as television, radio, or a newspaper. Disclosure of factual information by the employing agency pursuant to this subdivision is limited to facts contained in the officer's personnel file concerning the disciplinary investigation or imposition of disciplinary action that specifically refute the false statements made public by the peace or custodial officer or their agent or representative.

(f)

(1) The department or agency shall provide written notification to the complaining party of the disposition of the complaint within 30 days of the disposition.

(2) The notification described in this subdivision is not conclusive or binding or admissible as evidence in any separate or subsequent action or proceeding brought before an arbitrator, court, or judge of this state or the United States.

(g) This section does not affect the discovery or disclosure of information contained in a peace or custodial officer's personnel file pursuant to Section 1043 of the Evidence Code.

(h) This section does not supersede or affect the criminal discovery process outlined in Chapter 10 (commencing with Section 1054) of Title 6 of Part 2, or the admissibility of personnel records pursuant to subdivision (a), which codifies the court decision in Pitchess v. Superior Court (1974) 11 Cal.3d 531.

(i) Nothing in this chapter is intended to limit the public's right of access as provided for in Long Beach Police Officers Association v. City of Long Beach (2014) 59 Cal.4th 59.

Amended by Stats 2023 ch 47 (AB 134),s 3, eff. 7/10/2023.
Amended by Stats 2023 ch 131 (AB 1754),s 153, eff. 1/1/2024.
Amended by Stats 2022 ch 58 (AB 200),s 5, eff. 6/30/2022.
Amended by Stats 2022 ch 28 (SB 1380),s 126, eff. 1/1/2023. Not implemented per s 168.
Amended by Stats 2021 ch 615 (AB 474),s 339, eff. 1/1/2022, op. 1/1/2023.
Amended by Stats 2021 ch 409 (SB 2),s 5.5, eff. 1/1/2022.
Amended by Stats 2021 ch 402 (SB 16),s 3, eff. 1/1/2022.
Amended by Stats 2018 ch 988 (SB 1421),s 2, eff. 1/1/2019.
Amended by Stats 2003 ch 102 (AB 1106), s 1, eff. 1/1/2004.
Amended by Stats 2002 ch 63 (AB 1873), s 1, eff. 1/1/2003.
Amended by Stats 2002 ch 391 (AB 2040), s 6, eff. 1/1/2003.
Amended by Stats 2000 ch 971 (AB 2559), s 1, eff. 1/1/2001.
See Stats 2023 ch 47 (AB 134), s 33.

Section 832.8 - "Personnel records," "Sustained," and "Unfounded" defined

As used in Section 832.7, the following words or phrases have the following meanings:

(a) "Personnel records" means any file maintained under that individual's name by his or her employing agency and containing records relating to any of the following:

(1) Personal data, including marital status, family members, educational and employment history, home addresses, or similar information.

(2) Medical history.

(3) Election of employee benefits.

(4) Employee advancement, appraisal, or discipline.

(5) Complaints, or investigations of complaints, concerning an event or transaction in which he or she participated, or which he or she perceived, and pertaining to the manner in which he or she performed his or her duties.

(6) Any other information the disclosure of which would constitute an unwarranted invasion of personal privacy.

(b) "Sustained" means a final determination by an investigating agency, commission, board, hearing officer, or arbitrator, as applicable, following an investigation and opportunity for an administrative appeal pursuant to Sections 3304 and 3304.5 of the Government Code, that the actions of the peace officer or custodial officer were found to violate law or department policy.

(c) "Unfounded" means that an investigation clearly establishes that the allegation is not true.

Amended by Stats 2018 ch 988 (SB 1421),s 3, eff. 1/1/2019.

Section 832.9 - Reimbursement of moving and relocation expenses due to credible threat

(a) A governmental entity employing a peace officer, as defined in Section 830, judge, court commissioner, or an attorney employed by the Department of Justice, the State Public Defender, or a county office of a district attorney or public defender shall reimburse the moving and relocation expenses of those employees, or any member of his or her immediate family residing with the officer in the same household or on the same property when it is necessary to move because the officer has received a credible threat that a life threatening action may be taken against the officer, judge, court commissioner, or an attorney employed by the Department of Justice, the State Public Defender, or a county office of the district attorney or public defender or his or her immediate family as a result of his or her employment.

(b) The person relocated shall receive actual and necessary moving and relocation expenses incurred both before and after the change of residence, including reimbursement for the costs of moving household effects either by a commercial household goods carrier or by the employee.

(1) Actual and necessary moving costs shall be those costs that are set forth in the Department of Human Resources rules governing promotional relocations while in the state service. The department shall not be required to administer this section.

(2) The public entity shall not be liable for any loss in value to a residence or for the decrease in value due to a forced sale.

(3) Except as provided in subdivision (c), peace officers, judges, court commissioners, and attorneys employed by the Department of Justice, the State Public Defender, or a county office of a district attorney or public defender shall receive approval of the appointing authority prior to incurring any cost covered by this section.

(4) Peace officers, judges, court commissioners, and attorneys employed by the Department of Justice, the State Public Defender, or a county office of a district attorney or public defender shall not be considered to be on duty while moving unless approved by the appointing authority.

(5) For a relocation to be covered by this section, the appointing authority shall be notified as soon as a credible threat has been received.

(6) Temporary relocation housing shall not exceed 60 days.

(7) The public entity ceases to be liable for relocation costs after 120 days of the original notification of a viable threat if the peace officer, judge, court commissioner, or attorney employed by the Department of Justice, the State Public Defender, or a county office of a district attorney or public defender has failed to relocate.

(c)

(1) For purposes of the right to reimbursement of moving and relocation expenses pursuant to this section, judges shall be deemed to be employees of the State of California and a court commissioner is an employee of the court by which he or she is employed.

(2) For purposes of paragraph (3) of subdivision (b), a court commissioner shall receive approval by the presiding judge of the superior court in the county in which he or she is located.

(3) For purposes of paragraph (3) of subdivision (b), judges, including justices of the Supreme Court and the Courts of Appeal, shall receive approval from the Chief Justice, or his or her designee.

(d) As used in this section, "credible threat" means a verbal or written statement or a threat implied by a pattern of conduct or a combination of verbal or written statements and conduct made with the intent and the apparent ability to carry out the threat so as to cause the person who is the target of the threat to reasonably fear for his or her safety or the safety of his or her immediate family.

(e) As used in this section, "immediate family" means the spouse, parents, siblings, and children residing with the peace officer, judge, court commissioner, or attorney employed by the Department of Justice, the State Public Defender, or a county office of a district attorney or public defender.

Amended by Stats 2012 ch 665 (SB 1308),s 182, eff. 1/1/2013.

Amended by Stats 2008 ch 218 (AB 1949),s 6, eff. 1/1/2009.

Amended by Stats 2004 ch 248 (AB 2905), s 1, eff. 1/1/2005.

Section 832.10 - [Operative 7/1/2024] Records regarding death investigation available for public inspection

(a) For purposes of this section, the following definitions shall apply:

(1) "Death incident" means an event where a person has died in the custody or supervision of the local detention facility.

(2) "Local detention facility" means any city, county, city and county, or regional jail, camp, court holding facility, private detention facility, or other facility in which persons are incarcerated.

(3) "Private detention facility" has the same meaning as in Section 7320 of the Government Code.

(4) "Person" includes, but is not limited to, a custodial officer or health care staff.

(5) "Custodial officer" means those officers with the rank of deputy, correctional officer, patrol person, or another equivalent sworn or civilian rank whose duties include the supervision of incarcerated or detained persons at a local detention facility.

(6) "Health care staff" means the health authority, individual, or agency that is designated with responsibility for providing health care in the local detention facility.

(b) Notwithstanding subdivision (a) of Section 832.7, or any other law, any record relating to an investigation conducted by the local detention facility involving a death incident maintained by a local detention facility shall not be confidential and shall be made available for public inspection pursuant to the California Public Records Act (Division 10 (commencing with Section 7920.000) of Title 1 of the Government Code).

(c) Records disclosed under subdivision (b) shall be subject to all of the following:

(1) The record shall include all investigative reports; photographic, audio, and video evidence; transcripts or recordings of interviews; autopsy reports; all materials compiled and presented for review to the district attorney or to any person or body charged with determining whether to file criminal charges against a person, whether the person's action was consistent with law and agency policy for purposes of discipline or administrative action, or what discipline to impose or corrective action to take; documents setting forth findings or recommended findings; and copies of disciplinary records relating to the death incident, including any letters of intent to impose discipline, any documents reflecting modifications of discipline due to the Skelly or grievance process, and letters indicating final imposition of discipline or other documentation reflecting implementation of corrective action.

(2) An agency shall redact a record disclosed pursuant to this section only for any of the following purposes:

(A) To remove personal data or information, such as a home address, telephone number, or identities of family members, other than the people's names and work-related information.

(B) To preserve the anonymity of whistleblowers, complainants, victims, and witnesses.

(C) To protect confidential medical, financial, or other information of which disclosure is specifically prohibited by federal law or would cause an unwarranted invasion of personal privacy that clearly outweighs the strong public interest in records about possible misconduct.

(D) Where there is a specific, articulable, and particularized reason to believe that disclosure of the record would pose a significant danger to the physical safety of any person.

(3) Notwithstanding paragraph (2), an agency may redact a record disclosed pursuant to this section, including personal identifying information, where, on the facts of the particular case, the public interest served by not disclosing the information clearly outweighs the public interest served by disclosure of the information.

(4) A local detention facility may withhold a record of a death incident described in subdivision (b) that is the subject of an active criminal or administrative investigation, in accordance with any of the following:

(A)

(i) During an active criminal investigation, disclosure may be delayed for up to 60 days from the date the death incident occurred or until the district attorney determines whether to file criminal charges related to the death incident, whichever occurs sooner. If a local detention facility delays disclosure pursuant to this clause, the local detention facility shall provide, in writing, the specific basis for the facility's determination that the interest in delaying disclosure clearly outweighs the public interest in disclosure. This writing shall include the estimated date for disclosure of the withheld information.

(ii) After 60 days from the death incident, the local detention facility may continue to delay the disclosure of records or information if the disclosure could reasonably be expected to interfere with a criminal enforcement proceeding against any person. If an agency delays disclosure pursuant to this clause, the agency shall, at 180-day intervals as necessary, provide, in writing, the specific basis for the agency's determination that disclosure could reasonably be expected to interfere with a criminal enforcement proceeding. The writing shall include the estimated date for the disclosure of the withheld information. Information withheld by the agency shall be disclosed when the specific basis for withholding is resolved, when the investigation or proceeding is no longer active, or by no later than 18 months after the date of the death incident, whichever occurs sooner.

(iii) In an action to compel disclosure brought pursuant to Section 7923.000 of the Government Code, a local detention facility may justify delay by filing an application to seal the basis for withholding, in accordance with Rule 2.550 of the California Rules of Court, or any successor rule, if disclosure of the written basis itself would impact a privilege or compromise a pending investigation. This clause does not prohibit a court from conducting in camera review to determine whether privilege exists.

(B) If criminal charges are filed related to the death incident, the local detention facility may delay the disclosure of records or information until a verdict on those charges is returned at trial or, if a plea of guilty or no contest is entered, the time to withdraw the plea pursuant to Section 1018.

(C) During an administrative investigation into an incident described in subdivision (b), the local detention facility may delay the disclosure of records or information until the facility determines whether the death incident violated a law or agency policy.

(5) The cost of copies of records subject to disclosure pursuant to this subdivision that are made available upon the payment of fees covering direct costs of duplication pursuant to subdivision (a) of Section 7922.530 of the Government Code shall not include the costs of searching for, editing, or redacting the records.

(6) Except to the extent temporary withholding for a longer period is permitted pursuant to paragraph (4), records subject to disclosure under this section shall be provided at the earliest possible time and no later than 45 days from the date of a request for their disclosure.

(7)

(A) For purposes of releasing records pursuant to this subdivision, the attorney-client privilege does not prohibit the disclosure of either of the following:

(i) Factual information provided by the local detention facility to its attorney or factual information discovered in any investigation conducted by, or on behalf of, the local detention facility's attorney.

(ii) Billing records related to the work done by the attorney so long as the records do not relate to active and ongoing litigation and do not disclose information for the purpose of legal consultation between the local detention facility and its attorney.

(B) This paragraph does not prohibit the local detention facility from asserting that a record or information within the record is exempted or prohibited from disclosure pursuant to any other federal or state law. However, to the extent that the local detention facility asserts attorney-client privilege or any other prohibitive disclosure provided by federal or state law, the court may conduct in camera review unless prohibited by law.

(d) This section does not affect the discovery or disclosure of information contained in a subject officer's personnel file pursuant to Section 1043 of the Evidence Code.

(e) This section does not affect the disclosure of other records provided under this chapter or any other law.

(f) This section does not supersede or affect the criminal discovery process outlined in Chapter 10 (commencing with Section 1054) of Title 6 of Part 2, or the admissibility of personnel records pursuant to Section 832.7, which codifies the court decision in Pitchess v. Superior Court (1974) 11 Cal.3d 531.

(g) Nothing in this chapter is intended to limit the public's right of access as provided for in Long Beach Police Officers Association v. City of Long Beach (2014) 59 Cal.4th 59.

(h) This section shall become operative on July 1, 2024.

Added by Stats 2023 ch 306 (SB 519),s 1, eff. 1/1/2024.

Section 832.12 - Records of any investigations of misconduct involving a peace officer

(a) Each department or agency in this state that employs peace officers shall make a record of any investigations of misconduct involving a peace officer in the officer's general personnel file or a separate file designated by the department or agency. A peace officer seeking employment with a department or agency in this state that employs peace officers shall give written permission for the hiring department or agency to view the officer's general personnel file and any separate file designated by a department or agency.

(b) Prior to employing any peace officer, each department or agency in this state that employs peace officers shall request, and the hiring department or agency shall review, any records made available pursuant to subdivision (a).

Amended by Stats 2021 ch 402 (SB 16),s 4, eff. 1/1/2022.

Added by Stats 2018 ch 966 (AB 2327),s 1, eff. 1/1/2019.

Section 832.13 - All uses of force to be reported

Every person employed as a peace officer shall immediately report all uses of force by the officer to the officer's department or agency.

Added by Stats 2021 ch 402 (SB 16),s 5, eff. 1/1/2022.

Section 832.15 - Notice that individual applying for position of peace officer or custodial officer is prohibited from possessing, receiving, owning, or purchasing firearm

(a) On and after October 1, 1993, the Department of Justice shall notify a state or local agency as to whether an individual applying for a position as a peace officer, as defined by this chapter, a custodial officer authorized by the employing agency to carry a firearm pursuant to Section 831.5, or a transportation officer pursuant to Section 831.6 authorized by the employing agency to carry a firearm, is prohibited from possessing, receiving, owning, or purchasing a firearm pursuant to state or federal law. If the prohibition is temporary, the notice shall indicate the date that the prohibition expires. However, the notice shall not provide any other information with respect to the basis for the prohibition.

(b) Before providing the information specified in subdivision (a), the applicant shall provide the Department of Justice with fingerprints and other identifying information deemed necessary by the department.

(c) The Department of Justice may charge the applicant a fee sufficient to reimburse its costs for furnishing the information specified in subdivision (a).

(d) The notice required by this section shall not apply to persons receiving treatment under subdivision (a) of Section 8100 of the Welfare and Institutions Code.

Amended by Stats 2008 ch 698 (AB 837),s 9, eff. 1/1/2009.

Amended by Stats 2004 ch 593 (SB 1797), s 1, eff. 1/1/2005.

See Stats 2004 ch 593 (SB 1797), s 9. Section 9 provides, "Any section of any act enacted by the Legislature during the 2004 calendar year that takes effect on or before January 1, 2005, and that amends ... any one or more of the sections affected by this act, with the exception of Assembly Bill 3082, shall prevail over this act, whether that act is enacted prior to, or subsequent to, the enactment of this act."

Section 832.16 - Notice that peace officer is prohibited from possessing, receiving, owning, or purchasing firearm

(a) On and after October 1, 1993, the Department of Justice shall notify a state or local agency employing a peace officer, as defined by this chapter, who is authorized by the employing agency to carry a firearm, as to whether a peace officer is prohibited from possessing, receiving, owning, or purchasing a firearm pursuant to state or federal law. If the prohibition is temporary, the notice shall indicate the date that the prohibition expires. However, the notice shall not provide any other information with respect to the basis for the prohibition.

(b) Before providing the information specified in subdivision (a), the agency employing the peace officer shall provide the Department of Justice with the officer's fingerprints and other identifying information deemed necessary by the department.

(c) The information specified in this section shall only be provided by the Department of Justice subject to the availability of funding.

(d) The notice required by this section shall not apply to persons receiving treatment under subdivision (a) of Section 8100 of the Welfare and Institutions Code.

Amended by Stats 2008 ch 698 (AB 837),s 10, eff. 1/1/2009.

Section 832.17 - Notice that custodial or transportation officer is prohibited from possessing, receiving, owning, or purchasing firearm

(a) Upon request by a state or local agency, the Department of Justice shall notify the state or local agency as to whether an individual employed as a custodial or transportation officer and authorized by the employing agency to carry a firearm, is prohibited or subsequently becomes prohibited from possessing, receiving, owning, or purchasing a firearm pursuant to state or federal law. If the prohibition is temporary, the notice shall indicate the date on which the prohibition expires. However, the notice shall not provide any other information with respect to the basis for the prohibition.

(b) Before the department provides the information specified in subdivision (a), the officer shall provide the department with his or her fingerprints and other identifying information deemed necessary by the department.

(c) The department may charge the officer a fee sufficient to reimburse its costs for furnishing the information specified in subdivision (a). A local law enforcement agency may pay this fee for the officer.

(d) The notice required by this section shall not apply to persons receiving treatment under subdivision (a) of Section 8100 of the Welfare and Institutions Code.

Amended by Stats 2008 ch 698 (AB 837),s 11, eff. 1/1/2009.

Added by Stats 2004 ch 593 (SB 1797), s 2, eff. 1/1/2005.

See Stats 2004 ch 593 (SB 1797), s 9. Section 9 provides, "Any section of any act enacted by the Legislature during the 2004 calendar year that takes effect on or before January 1, 2005, and that ... adds ... any one or more of the sections affected by this act, with the exception of Assembly Bill 3082, shall prevail over this act, whether that act is enacted prior to, or subsequent to, the enactment of this act."

Section 832.18 - Policies and procedures for downloading and storing data recorded by body-worn cameras

(a) It is the intent of the Legislature to establish policies and procedures to address issues related to the downloading and storage data recorded by a body-worn camera worn by a peace officer. These policies and procedures shall be based on best practices.

(b) When establishing policies and procedures for the implementation and operation of a body-worn camera system, law enforcement agencies, departments, or entities shall consider the following best practices regarding the downloading and storage of body-worn camera data:

(1) Designate the person responsible for downloading the recorded data from the body-worn camera. If the storage system does not have automatic downloading capability, the officer's supervisor should take immediate physical custody of the camera and should be responsible for downloading the data in the case of an incident involving the use of force by an officer, an officer-involved shooting, or other serious incident.

(2) Establish when data should be downloaded to ensure the data is entered into the system in a timely manner, the cameras are properly maintained and ready for the next use, and for purposes of tagging and categorizing the data.

(3) Establish specific measures to prevent data tampering, deleting, and copying, including prohibiting the unauthorized use, duplication, or distribution of body-worn camera data.

(4) Categorize and tag body-worn camera video at the time the data is downloaded and classified according to the type of event or incident captured in the data.

(5) Specifically state the length of time that recorded data is to be stored.

(A) Unless subparagraph (B) or (C) applies, nonevidentiary data including video and audio recorded by a body-worn camera should be retained for a minimum of 60 days, after which it may be erased, destroyed, or recycled. An agency may keep data for more than 60 days to have it available in case of a civilian complaint and to preserve transparency.

(B) Evidentiary data including video and audio recorded by a body-worn camera under this section should be retained for a minimum of two years under any of the following circumstances:

(i) The recording is of an incident involving the use of force by a peace officer or an officer-involved shooting.

(ii) The recording is of an incident that leads to the detention or arrest of an individual.

(iii) The recording is relevant to a formal or informal complaint against a law enforcement officer or a law enforcement agency.

(C) If evidence that may be relevant to a criminal prosecution is obtained from a recording made by a body-worn camera under this section, the law enforcement agency should retain the recording for any time in addition to that specified in subparagraphs (A) and (B), and in the same manner as is required by law for other evidence that may be relevant to a criminal prosecution.

(D) In determining a retention schedule, the agency should work with its legal counsel to determine a retention schedule to ensure that storage policies and practices are in compliance with all relevant laws and adequately preserve evidentiary chains of custody.

(E) Records or logs of access and deletion of data from body-worn cameras should be retained permanently.

(6) State where the body-worn camera data will be stored, including, for example, an in-house server that is managed internally, or an online cloud database that is managed by a third-party vendor.

(7) If using a third-party vendor to manage the data storage system, the following factors should be considered to protect the security and integrity of the data:

(A) Using an experienced and reputable third-party vendor.

(B) Entering into contracts that govern the vendor relationship and protect the agency's data.

(C) Using a system that has a built-in audit trail to prevent data tampering and unauthorized access.

(D) Using a system that has a reliable method for automatically backing up data for storage.

(E) Consulting with internal legal counsel to ensure the method of data storage meets legal requirements for chain-of-custody concerns.

(F) Using a system that includes technical assistance capabilities.

(8) Require that all recorded data from body-worn cameras are property of their respective law enforcement agency and shall not be accessed or released for any unauthorized purpose, explicitly prohibit agency personnel from accessing recorded data for personal use and from uploading recorded data onto public and social media internet websites, and include sanctions for violations of this prohibition.

(c)

(1) For purposes of this section, "evidentiary data" refers to data of an incident or encounter that could prove useful for investigative purposes, including, but not limited to, a crime, an arrest or citation, a search, a use of force incident, or a confrontational encounter with a member of the public. The retention period for evidentiary data are subject to state evidentiary laws.

(2) For purposes of this section, "nonevidentiary data" refers to data that does not necessarily have value to aid in an investigation or prosecution, such as data of an incident or encounter that does not lead to an arrest or citation, or data of general activities the officer might perform while on duty.

(d) This section shall not be interpreted to limit the public's right to access recorded data under the California Public Records Act (Division 10 (commencing with Section 7920.000) of Title 1 of the Government Code).

Amended by Stats 2021 ch 615 (AB 474),s 340, eff. 1/1/2022, op. 1/1/2023.

Amended by Stats 2017 ch 561 (AB 1516),s 183, eff. 1/1/2018.

Amended by Stats 2016 ch 99 (AB 1953),s 3, eff. 1/1/2017.

Added by Stats 2015 ch 461 (AB 69),s 1, eff. 1/1/2016.

Section 832.19 - Prohibition against use of facial recognition and other biometric surveillance in connection with officer cameras

(a) For the purposes of this section, the following terms have the following meanings:

(1) "Biometric data" means a physiological, biological, or behavioral characteristic that can be used, singly or in combination with each other or with other information, to establish individual identity.

(2) "Biometric surveillance system" means any computer software or application that performs facial recognition or other biometric surveillance.

(3) "Facial recognition or other biometric surveillance" means either of the following, alone or in combination:

(A) An automated or semiautomated process that captures or analyzes biometric data of an individual to identify or assist in identifying an individual.

(B) An automated or semiautomated process that generates, or assists in generating, surveillance information about an individual based on biometric data.

(4) "Facial recognition or other biometric surveillance" does not include the use of an automated or semiautomated process for the purpose of redacting a recording for release or disclosure outside the law enforcement agency to protect the privacy of a subject depicted in the recording, if the process does not generate or result in the retention of any biometric data or surveillance information.

(5) "Law enforcement agency" means any police department, sheriff's department, district attorney, county probation department, transit agency police department, school district police department, highway patrol, the police department of any campus of the University of California, the California State University, or a community college, the Department of the California Highway Patrol, and the Department of Justice.

(6) "Law enforcement officer" means an officer, deputy, employee, or agent of a law enforcement agency.

(7) "Officer camera" means a body-worn camera or similar device that records or transmits images or sound and is attached to the body or clothing of, or carried by, a law enforcement officer.

(8) "Surveillance information" means either of the following, alone or in combination:

(A) Any information about a known or unknown individual, including, but not limited to, a person's name, date of birth, gender, or criminal background.

(B) Any information derived from biometric data, including, but not limited to, assessments about an individual's sentiment, state of mind, or level of dangerousness.

(9) "Use" means either of the following, alone or in combination:

(A) The direct use of a biometric surveillance system by a law enforcement officer or law enforcement agency.

(B) A request or agreement by a law enforcement officer or law enforcement agency that another law enforcement agency or other third party use a biometric surveillance system on behalf of the requesting officer or agency.

(b) A law enforcement agency or law enforcement officer shall not install, activate, or use any biometric surveillance system in connection with an officer camera or data collected by an officer camera.

(c) In addition to any other sanctions, penalties, or remedies provided by law, a person may bring an action for equitable or declaratory relief in a court of competent jurisdiction against a law enforcement agency or law enforcement officer that violates this section.

(d) This section does not preclude a law enforcement agency or law enforcement officer from using a mobile fingerprint scanning device during a lawful detention to identify a person who does not have proof of identification if this use is lawful and does not generate or result in the retention of any biometric data or surveillance information.

(e) This section shall remain in effect only until January 1, 2023, and as of that date is repealed.

Added by Stats 2019 ch 579 (AB 1215),s 2, eff. 1/1/2020.

Chapter 5 - ARREST, BY WHOM AND HOW MADE

Section 833 - Search for dangerous weapons

A peace officer may search for dangerous weapons any person whom he has legal cause to arrest, whenever he has reasonable cause to believe that the person possesses a dangerous weapon. If the officer finds a dangerous weapon, he may take and keep it until the completion of the questioning, when he shall either return it or arrest the person. The arrest may be for the illegal possession of the weapon.

Added by Stats. 1957, Ch. 2147.

Section 833.2 - Protocols addressing issues related to child safety when caretaker parent or guardian is arrested

(a) It is the intent of the Legislature to encourage law enforcement and county child welfare agencies to develop protocols in collaboration with other local entities, which may include local educational, judicial, correctional, and community-based organizations, when appropriate, regarding how to best cooperate in their response to the arrest of a caretaker parent or guardian of a minor child, to ensure the child's safety and well-being.

(b) The Legislature encourages the Department of Justice to apply to the federal government for a statewide training grant on behalf of California law enforcement agencies, with the purpose of enabling local jurisdictions to provide training for their law enforcement officers to assist them in developing protocols and adequately addressing issues related to child safety when a caretaker parent or guardian is arrested.

Added by Stats 2006 ch 729 (AB 1942),s 1, eff. 1/1/2007.

Section 833.5 - Detention to determine whether crime relating to firearms or deadly weapons has been committed

(a) In addition to any other detention permitted by law, if a peace officer has reasonable cause to believe that a person has a firearm or other deadly weapon with him or her in violation of any provision of law relating to firearms or deadly weapons the peace officer may detain that person to determine whether a crime relating to firearms or deadly weapons has been committed. For purposes of this section, "reasonable cause to detain" requires that the circumstances known or apparent to the officer must include specific and articulable facts causing him or her to suspect that some offense relating to firearms or deadly weapons has taken place or is occurring or is about to occur and that the person he or she intends to detain is involved in that offense. The circumstances must be such as would cause any reasonable peace officer in like position, drawing when appropriate on his or her training and experience, to suspect the same offense and the same involvement by the person in question.

(b) Incident to any detention permitted pursuant to subdivision (a), a peace officer may conduct a limited search of the person for firearms or weapons if the peace officer reasonably concludes that the person detained may be armed and presently dangerous to the peace officer or others. Any firearm or weapon seized pursuant to a valid detention or search pursuant to this section shall be admissible in evidence in any proceeding for any purpose permitted by law.

(c) This section shall not be construed to otherwise limit the authority of a peace officer to detain any person or to make an arrest based on reasonable cause.

(d) This section shall not be construed to permit a peace officer to conduct a detention or search of any person at the person's residence or place of business absent a search warrant or other reasonable cause to detain or search.

(e) If a firearm or weapon is seized pursuant to this section and the person from whom it was seized owned the firearm or weapon and is convicted of a violation of any offense relating to the possession of such firearm or weapon, the court shall order the firearm or weapon to be deemed a nuisance and disposed of in the manner provided by Sections 18000 and 18005.

Amended by Stats 2011 ch 296 (AB 1023),s 213, eff. 1/1/2012.

Amended by Stats 2010 ch 178 (SB 1115),s 68, eff. 1/1/2011, op. 1/1/2012.

Section 834 - Arrest

An arrest is taking a person into custody, in a case and in the manner authorized by law. An arrest may be made by a peace officer or by a private person.

Enacted 1872.

Section 834a - Duty to refrain from using force or weapon to resist arrest

If a person has knowledge, or by the exercise of reasonable care, should have knowledge, that he is being arrested by a peace officer, it is the duty of such person to refrain from using force or any weapon to resist such arrest.

Added by Stats. 1957, Ch. 2147.

Section 834b - [Repealed]

Repealed by Stats 2014 ch 318 (SB 396),s 5, eff. 1/1/2015.

Section 834c - Arrest of foreign national

(a)

(1) In accordance with federal law and the provisions of this section, every peace officer, upon arrest and booking or detention for more than two hours of a known or suspected foreign national, shall advise the foreign national that he or she has a right to communicate with an official from the consulate of his or her country, except as provided in subdivision (d). If the foreign national chooses to exercise that right, the peace officer shall notify the pertinent official in his or her agency or department of the arrest or detention and that the foreign national wants his or her consulate notified.

(2) The law enforcement official who receives the notification request pursuant to paragraph (1) shall be guided by his or her agency's procedures in conjunction with the Department of State Guidelines Regarding Foreign Nationals Arrested or Detained in the United States, and make the appropriate notifications to the consular officers at the consulate of the arrestee.

(3) The law enforcement official in charge of the custodial facility where an arrestee subject to this subdivision is located shall ensure that the arrestee is allowed to communicate with, correspond with, and be visited by, a consular officer of his or her country.

(b) The 1963 Vienna Convention on Consular Relations Treaty was signed by 140 nations, including the United States, which ratified the agreement in 1969. This treaty guarantees that individuals arrested or detained in a foreign country must be told by police "without delay" that they have a right to speak to an official from their country's consulate and if an individual chooses to exercise that right a law enforcement official is required to notify the consulate.

(c) California law enforcement agencies shall ensure that policy or procedure and training manuals incorporate language based upon provisions of the treaty that set forth requirements for handling the arrest and booking or detention for more than two hours of a foreign national pursuant to this section prior to December 31, 2000.

(d) Countries requiring mandatory notification under Article 36 of the Vienna Convention shall be notified as set forth in this section without regard to an arrested or detained foreign national's request to the contrary. Those countries, as identified by the United States Department of State on July 1, 1999, are as follows:

(1) Antigua and Barbuda.
(2) Armenia.
(3) Azerbaijan.
(4) The Bahamas.
(5) Barbados.
(6) Belarus.
(7) Belize.
(8) Brunei.
(9) Bulgaria.
(10) China.
(11) Costa Rica.
(12) Cyprus.
(13) Czech Republic.
(14) Dominica.
(15) Fiji.
(16) The Gambia.
(17) Georgia.
(18) Ghana.
(19) Grenada.
(20) Guyana.
(21) Hong Kong.
(22) Hungary.
(23) Jamaica.
(24) Kazakhstan.
(25) Kiribati.
(26) Kuwait.
(27) Kyrgyzstan.
(28) Malaysia.

(29) Malta.

(30) Mauritius.

(31) Moldova.

(32) Mongolia.

(33) Nigeria.

(34) Philippines.

(35) Poland (nonpermanent residents only).

(36) Romania.

(37) Russia.

(38) Saint Kitts and Nevis.

(39) Saint Lucia.

(40) Saint Vincent and the Grenadines.

(41) Seychelles.

(42) Sierra Leone.

(43) Singapore.

(44) Slovakia.

(45) Tajikistan.

(46) Tanzania.

(47) Tonga.

(48) Trinidad and Tobago.

(49) Turkmenistan.

(50) Tuvalu.

(51) Ukraine.

(52) United Kingdom.

(53) U.S.S.R.

(54) Uzbekistan.

(55) Zambia.

(56) Zimbabwe. However, any countries requiring notification that the above list does not identify because the notification requirement became effective after July 1, 1999, shall also be required to be notified.

EFFECTIVE 1/1/2000. Added8/30/1999 (Bill Number: SB 287) (Chapter 268).

Section 835 - Restraint of person arrested

An arrest is made by an actual restraint of the person, or by submission to the custody of an officer. The person arrested may be subjected to such restraint as is reasonable for his arrest and detention.

Amended by Stats. 1957, Ch. 2147.

Section 835a - Objectively reasonable force to effect arrest; use of deadly force

(a) The Legislature finds and declares all of the following:

(1) That the authority to use physical force, conferred on peace officers by this section, is a serious responsibility that shall be exercised judiciously and with respect for human rights and dignity and for the sanctity of every human life. The Legislature further finds and declares that every person has a right to be free from excessive use of force by officers acting under color of law.

(2) As set forth below, it is the intent of the Legislature that peace officers use deadly force only when necessary in defense of human life. In determining whether deadly force is necessary, officers shall evaluate each situation in light of the particular circumstances of each case, and shall use other available resources and techniques if reasonably safe and feasible to an objectively reasonable officer.

(3) That the decision by a peace officer to use force shall be evaluated carefully and thoroughly, in a manner that reflects the gravity of that authority and the serious consequences of the use of force by peace officers, in order to ensure that officers use force consistent with law and agency policies.

(4) That the decision by a peace officer to use force shall be evaluated from the perspective of a reasonable officer in the same situation, based on the totality of the circumstances known to or perceived by the officer at the time, rather than with the benefit of hindsight, and that the totality of the circumstances shall account for occasions when officers may be forced to make quick judgments about using force.

(5) That individuals with physical, mental health, developmental, or intellectual disabilities are significantly more likely to experience greater levels of physical force during police interactions, as their disability may affect their ability to understand or comply with commands from peace officers. It is estimated that individuals with disabilities are involved in between one-third and one-half of all fatal encounters with law enforcement.

(b) Any peace officer who has reasonable cause to believe that the person to be arrested has committed a public offense may use objectively reasonable force to effect the arrest, to prevent escape, or to overcome resistance.

(c)

(1) Notwithstanding subdivision (b), a peace officer is justified in using deadly force upon another person only when the officer reasonably believes, based on the totality of the circumstances, that such force is necessary for either of the following reasons:

(A) To defend against an imminent threat of death or serious bodily injury to the officer or to another person.

(B) To apprehend a fleeing person for any felony that threatened or resulted in death or serious bodily injury, if the officer reasonably believes that the person will cause death or serious bodily injury to another unless immediately apprehended. Where feasible, a peace officer shall, prior to the use of force, make reasonable efforts to identify themselves as a peace officer and to warn that deadly force may be used, unless the officer has objectively reasonable grounds to believe the person is aware of those facts.

465

(2) A peace officer shall not use deadly force against a person based on the danger that person poses to themselves, if an objectively reasonable officer would believe the person does not pose an imminent threat of death or serious bodily injury to the peace officer or to another person.

(d) A peace officer who makes or attempts to make an arrest need not retreat or desist from their efforts by reason of the resistance or threatened resistance of the person being arrested. A peace officer shall not be deemed an aggressor or lose the right to self-defense by the use of objectively reasonable force in compliance with subdivisions (b) and (c) to effect the arrest or to prevent escape or to overcome resistance. For the purposes of this subdivision, "retreat" does not mean tactical repositioning or other deescalation tactics.

(e) For purposes of this section, the following definitions shall apply:

(1) "Deadly force" means any use of force that creates a substantial risk of causing death or serious bodily injury, including, but not limited to, the discharge of a firearm.

(2) A threat of death or serious bodily injury is "imminent" when, based on the totality of the circumstances, a reasonable officer in the same situation would believe that a person has the present ability, opportunity, and apparent intent to immediately cause death or serious bodily injury to the peace officer or another person. An imminent harm is not merely a fear of future harm, no matter how great the fear and no matter how great the likelihood of the harm, but is one that, from appearances, must be instantly confronted and addressed.

(3) "Totality of the circumstances" means all facts known to the peace officer at the time, including the conduct of the officer and the subject leading up to the use of deadly force.

Amended by Stats 2019 ch 170 (AB 392),s 2, eff. 1/1/2020.

Section 836 - Arrest with warrant and without warrant; domestic violence call

(a) A peace officer may arrest a person in obedience to a warrant, or, pursuant to the authority granted to him or her by Chapter 4.5 (commencing with Section 830) of Title 3 of Part 2, without a warrant, may arrest a person whenever any of the following circumstances occur:

(1) The officer has probable cause to believe that the person to be arrested has committed a public offense in the officer's presence.

(2) The person arrested has committed a felony, although not in the officer's presence.

(3) The officer has probable cause to believe that the person to be arrested has committed a felony, whether or not a felony, in fact, has been committed.

(b) Any time a peace officer is called out on a domestic violence call, it shall be mandatory that the officer make a good faith effort to inform the victim of his or her right to make a citizen's arrest, unless the peace officer makes an arrest for a violation of paragraph (1) of subdivision (e) of Section 243 or 273.5. This information shall include advising the victim how to safely execute the arrest.

(c)

(1) When a peace officer is responding to a call alleging a violation of a domestic violence protective or restraining order issued under Section 527.6 of the Code of Civil Procedure, the Family Code, Section 136.2, 646.91, or paragraph (2) of subdivision (a) of Section 1203.097 of this code, Section 213.5 or 15657.03 of the Welfare and Institutions Code, or of a domestic violence protective or restraining order issued by the court of another state, tribe, or territory and the peace officer has probable cause to believe that the person against whom the order is issued has notice of the order and has committed an act in violation of the order, the officer shall, consistent with subdivision (b) of Section 13701, make a lawful arrest of the person without a warrant and take that person into custody whether or not the violation occurred in the presence of the arresting officer. The officer shall, as soon as possible after the arrest, confirm with the appropriate authorities or the Domestic Violence Protection Order Registry maintained pursuant to Section 6380 of the Family Code that a true copy of the protective order has been registered, unless the victim provides the officer with a copy of the protective order.

(2) The person against whom a protective order has been issued shall be deemed to have notice of the order if the victim presents to the officer proof of service of the order, the officer confirms with the appropriate authorities that a true copy of the proof of service is on file, or the person against whom the protective order was issued was present at the protective order hearing or was informed by a peace officer of the contents of the protective order.

(3) In situations where mutual protective orders have been issued under Division 10 (commencing with Section 6200) of the Family Code, liability for arrest under this subdivision applies only to those persons who are reasonably believed to have been the dominant aggressor. In those situations, prior to making an arrest under this subdivision, the peace officer shall make reasonable efforts to identify, and may arrest, the dominant aggressor involved in the incident. The dominant aggressor is the person determined to be the most significant, rather than the first, aggressor. In identifying the dominant aggressor, an officer shall consider (A) the intent of the law to protect victims of domestic violence from continuing abuse, (B) the threats creating fear of physical injury, (C) the history of domestic violence between the persons involved, and (D) whether either person involved acted in self-defense.

(d) Notwithstanding paragraph (1) of subdivision (a), if a suspect commits an assault or battery upon a current or former spouse, fiance, fiancee, a current or former cohabitant as defined in Section 6209 of the Family Code, a person with whom the suspect currently is having or has previously had an engagement or dating relationship, as defined in paragraph (10) of subdivision (f) of Section 243, a person with whom the suspect has parented a child, or is presumed to have parented a child pursuant to the Uniform Parentage Act (Part 3 (commencing with Section 7600) of Division 12 of the Family Code), a child of the suspect, a child whose parentage by the suspect is the subject of an action under the Uniform Parentage Act, a child of a person in one of the above categories, any other person related to the suspect by consanguinity or affinity within the second degree, or any person who is 65 years of age or older and who is related to the suspect by blood or legal guardianship, a peace officer may arrest the suspect without a warrant where both of the following circumstances apply:

(1) The peace officer has probable cause to believe that the person to be arrested has committed the assault or battery, whether or not it has in fact been committed.

(2) The peace officer makes the arrest as soon as probable cause arises to believe that the person to be arrested has committed the assault or battery, whether or not it has in fact been committed.

(e) In addition to the authority to make an arrest without a warrant pursuant to paragraphs (1) and (3) of subdivision (a), a peace officer may, without a warrant, arrest a person for a violation of Section 25400 when all of the following apply:

    (1) The officer has reasonable cause to believe that the person to be arrested has committed the violation of Section 25400.

    (2) The violation of Section 25400 occurred within an airport, as defined in Section 21013 of the Public Utilities Code, in an area to which access is controlled by the inspection of persons and property.

    (3) The peace officer makes the arrest as soon as reasonable cause arises to believe that the person to be arrested has committed the violation of Section 25400.

Amended by Stats 2012 ch 867 (SB 1144),s 20, eff. 1/1/2013.

Amended by Stats 2010 ch 178 (SB 1115),s 69, eff. 1/1/2011, op. 1/1/2012.

Amended by Stats 2009 ch 92 (AB 258),s 1, eff. 1/1/2010.

Amended by Stats 2004 ch 405 (SB 1796), s 11, eff. 1/1/2005.

Amended by Stats 2003 ch 468 (SB 851), s 12, eff. 1/1/2004.

Amended by Stats 2003 ch 495 (AB 1290), s 2, eff. 1/1/2004.

Amended by Stats 2002 ch 534 (AB 2826), s 1, eff. 1/1/2003.

Amended by Stats 2000 ch 47 (AB 2003), s 1, eff. 1/1/2001.

Section 836.1 - Arrest, without warrant, of person who commits assault or battery against firefighter, emergency medical technician, or mobile intensive care paramedic

When a person commits an assault or battery against the person of a firefighter, emergency medical technician, or mobile intensive care paramedic while that person is on duty engaged in the performance of his or her duties in violation of subdivision (b) of Section 241 or subdivision (b) of Section 243, a peace officer may, without a warrant, arrest the person who commits the assault or battery:

(a) Whenever the peace officer has reasonable cause to believe that the person to be arrested has committed the assault or battery, although the assault or battery was not committed in the peace officer's presence.

(b) Whenever the peace officer has reasonable cause to believe that the person to be arrested has committed the assault or battery, whether or not the assault or battery has in fact been committed.

Added by Stats. 1995, Ch. 52, Sec. 1. Effective January 1, 1996.

Section 836.3 - Arrest of person who, while charged with or convicted of misdemeanor, escaped

A peace officer may make an arrest in obedience to a warrant delivered to him, or may, without a warrant, arrest a person who, while charged with or convicted of a misdemeanor, has escaped from any county or city jail, prison, industrial farm or industrial road camp or from the custody of the officer or person in charge of him while engaged on any county road or other county work or going to or returning from such county road or other county work or from the custody of any officer or person in whose lawful custody he is when such escape is not by force or violence.

Added by Stats. 1955, Ch. 609.

Section 836.5 - Arrest by public officer or employee

(a) A public officer or employee, when authorized by ordinance, may arrest a person without a warrant whenever the officer or employee has reasonable cause to believe that the person to be arrested has committed a misdemeanor in the presence of the officer or employee that is a violation of a statute or ordinance that the officer or employee has the duty to enforce.

(b) There shall be no civil liability on the part of, and no cause of action shall arise against, any public officer or employee acting pursuant to subdivision (a) and within the scope of his or her authority for false arrest or false imprisonment arising out of any arrest that is lawful or that the public officer or employee, at the time of the arrest, had reasonable cause to believe was lawful. No officer or employee shall be deemed an aggressor or lose his or her right to self-defense by the use of reasonable force to effect the arrest, prevent escape, or overcome resistance.

(c) In any case in which a person is arrested pursuant to subdivision (a) and the person arrested does not demand to be taken before a magistrate, the public officer or employee making the arrest shall prepare a written notice to appear and release the person on his or her promise to appear, as prescribed by Chapter 5C (commencing with Section 853.5). The provisions of that chapter shall thereafter apply with reference to any proceeding based upon the issuance of a written notice to appear pursuant to this authority.

(d) The governing body of a local agency, by ordinance, may authorize its officers and employees who have the duty to enforce a statute or ordinance to arrest persons for violations of the statute or ordinance as provided in subdivision (a).

(e) For purposes of this section, "ordinance" includes an order, rule, or regulation of any air pollution control district.

(f) For purposes of this section, a "public officer or employee" includes an officer or employee of a nonprofit transit corporation wholly owned by a local agency and formed to carry out the purposes of the local agency.

Amended by Stats. 1997, Ch. 324, Sec. 3. Effective January 1, 1998.

Section 836.6 - Escape

(a) It is unlawful for any person who is remanded by a magistrate or judge of any court in this state to the custody of a sheriff, marshal, or other police agency, to thereafter escape or attempt to escape from that custody.

(b) It is unlawful for any person who has been lawfully arrested by any peace officer and who knows, or by the exercise of reasonable care should have known, that he or she has been so arrested, to thereafter escape or attempt to escape from that peace officer.

(c) Any person who violates subdivision (a) or (b) is guilty of a misdemeanor, punishable by imprisonment in a county jail not to exceed one year. However, if the escape or attempted escape is by force or violence, and the person proximately causes a peace officer serious bodily injury, the person shall be punished by imprisonment in the state prison for two, three, or four years, or by imprisonment in a county jail not to exceed one year.

Amended by Stats 2012 ch 43 (SB 1023),s 26, eff. 6/27/2012.

Amended by Stats 2011 ch 39 (AB 117),s 68, eff. 6/30/2011.

Amended by Stats 2011 ch 15 (AB 109),s 448, eff. 4/4/2011, but operative no earlier than October 1, 2011, and only upon creation of a community corrections grant program to assist in implementing this act and upon an appropriation to fund the grant program.

Section 837 - Arrest by private person

A private person may arrest another:

1. For a public offense committed or attempted in his presence.

2. When the person arrested has committed a felony, although not in his presence.

3. When a felony has been in fact committed, and he has reasonable cause for believing the person arrested to have committed it.

Enacted 1872.

Section 838 - Oral order to arrest one committing public offense in presence of magistrate

A magistrate may orally order a peace officer or private person to arrest any one committing or attempting to commit a public offense in the presence of such magistrate.

Enacted 1872.

Section 839 - Oral summon of persons to aid person making arrest

Any person making an arrest may orally summon as many persons as he deems necessary to aid him therein.

Enacted 1872.

Section 840 - Time for arrest

An arrest for the commission of a felony may be made on any day and at any time of the day or night. An arrest for the commission of a misdemeanor or an infraction cannot be made between the hours of 10 o'clock p.m. of any day and 6 o'clock a.m. of the succeeding day, unless:

(1) The arrest is made without a warrant pursuant to Section 836 or 837.

(2) The arrest is made in a public place.

(3) The arrest is made when the person is in custody pursuant to another lawful arrest.

(4) The arrest is made pursuant to a warrant which, for good cause shown, directs that it may be served at any time of the day or night.

Amended by Stats. 1976, Ch. 436.

Section 841 - Informing person of intention to arrest, cause of arrest, and authority to make it

The person making the arrest must inform the person to be arrested of the intention to arrest him, of the cause of the arrest, and the authority to make it, except when the person making the arrest has reasonable cause to believe that the person to be arrested is actually engaged in the commission of or an attempt to commit an offense, or the person to be arrested is pursued immediately after its commission, or after an escape.

The person making the arrest must, on request of the person he is arresting, inform the latter of the offense for which he is being arrested.

Amended by Stats. 1961, Ch. 1863.

Section 841.5 - Address or telephone number of victim or witness

(a) Except as otherwise required by Chapter 10 (commencing with Section 1054) of Title 7, or by the United States Constitution or the California Constitution, no law enforcement officer or employee of a law enforcement agency shall disclose to any arrested person, or to any person who may be a defendant in a criminal action, the address or telephone number of any person who is a victim or witness in the alleged offense.

(b) Nothing in this section shall impair or interfere with the right of a defendant to obtain information necessary for the preparation of his or her defense through the discovery process.

(c) Nothing in this section shall impair or interfere with the right of an attorney to obtain the address or telephone number of any person who is a victim of, or a witness to, an alleged offense where a client of that attorney has been arrested for, or may be a defendant in, a criminal action related to the alleged offense.

(d) Nothing in this section shall preclude a law enforcement agency from releasing the entire contents of an accident report as required by Section 20012 of the Vehicle Code.

Added by Stats. 1992, Ch. 3, Sec. 2. Effective February 10, 1992.

Section 842 - Arrest without warrant in possession of peace officer at time of arrest

An arrest by a peace officer acting under a warrant is lawful even though the officer does not have the warrant in his possession at the time of the arrest, but if the person arrested so requests it, the warrant shall be shown to him as soon as practicable.

Amended by Stats. 1957, Ch. 2147.

Section 843 - Fleeing or forcibly resisting arrest

When the arrest is being made by an officer under the authority of a warrant, after information of the intention to make the arrest, if the person to be arrested either flees or forcibly resists, the officer may use all necessary means to effect the arrest.

Enacted 1872.

Section 844 - Breaking open door or window of house in which person to be arrested is

To make an arrest, a private person, if the offense is a felony, and in all cases a peace officer, may break open the door or window of the house in which the person to be arrested is, or in which they have reasonable grounds for believing the person to be, after having demanded admittance and explained the purpose for which admittance is desired.

Amended by Stats. 1989, Ch. 1360, Sec. 112.

Section 845 - Breaking door or window to liberate person making arrest

Any person who has lawfully entered a house for the purpose of making an arrest, may break open the door or window thereof if detained therein, when necessary for the purpose of liberating himself, and an officer may do the same, when necessary for the purpose of liberating a person who, acting in his aid, lawfully entered for the purpose of making an arrest, and is detained therein.

Enacted 1872.

Section 846 - Taking offensive weapons from person arrested

Any person making an arrest may take from the person arrested all offensive weapons which he may have about his person, and must deliver them to the magistrate before whom he is taken.

Enacted 1872.

Section 847 - Taking person arrested by private person before magistrate or delivering person to peace officer

(a) A private person who has arrested another for the commission of a public offense must, without unnecessary delay, take the person arrested before a magistrate, or deliver him or her to a peace officer.

(b) There shall be no civil liability on the part of, and no cause of action shall arise against, any peace officer or federal criminal investigator or law enforcement officer described in subdivision (a) or (d) of Section 830.8, acting within the scope of his or her authority, for false arrest or false imprisonment arising out of any arrest under any of the following circumstances:

(1) The arrest was lawful, or the peace officer, at the time of the arrest, had reasonable cause to believe the arrest was lawful.

(2) The arrest was made pursuant to a charge made, upon reasonable cause, of the commission of a felony by the person to be arrested.

(3) The arrest was made pursuant to the requirements of Section 142, 837, 838, or 839.

Amended by Stats 2003 ch 468 (SB 851), s 13, eff. 1/1/2004.

Amended by Stats 2002 ch 526 (AB 1835), s 2, eff. 1/1/2003.

Section 847.5 - Warrant for arrest for fugitive admitted to bail in another state

(a) Except as provided in subdivision (b), if a person has been admitted to bail in another state, escapes bail, and is present in this state, the bail bondsman or other person who is bail for such fugitive, may file with a magistrate in the county where the fugitive is present an affidavit stating the name and whereabouts of the fugitive, the offense with which the alleged fugitive was charged or of which they were convicted, the time and place of same, and the particulars in which the fugitive has violated the terms of their bail, and may request the issuance of a warrant for arrest of the fugitive, and the issuance, after hearing, of an order authorizing the affiant to return the fugitive to the jurisdiction from which they escaped bail. The magistrate may require such additional evidence under oath as they deem necessary to decide the issue. If the magistrate concludes that there is probable cause for believing that the person alleged to be a fugitive is such, the magistrate may issue a warrant for the person's arrest. The magistrate shall notify the district attorney of the action and shall direct the district attorney to investigate the case and determine the facts of the matter. When the fugitive is brought before the magistrate pursuant to the warrant, the magistrate shall set a time and place for hearing, and shall advise the fugitive of their right to counsel and to produce evidence at the hearing. The magistrate may admit the fugitive to bail pending the hearing. The district attorney shall appear at the hearing. If, after hearing, the magistrate is satisfied from the evidence that the person is a fugitive, the magistrate may issue an order authorizing affiant to return the fugitive to the jurisdiction from which they escaped bail.

(b) A magistrate shall not issue a warrant for the arrest of an individual whose alleged offense or conviction is for the violation of the laws of another state that authorize a criminal penalty to an individual performing, receiving, supporting, or aiding in the performance or receipt of sexual or reproductive health care, including, but not limited to, an abortion, contraception, or gender-affirming care if the sexual or reproductive health care is lawful under the laws of this state, regardless of the recipient's location.

(c) A bondsman or person authorized, pursuant to subdivision (a) of Section 1299.02, to apprehend, detain, or arrest a fugitive admitted to bail in another state who takes into custody a fugitive admitted to bail in another state whose alleged offense or conviction is for the violation of the laws of another state that authorize a criminal penalty to an individual performing, receiving, supporting, or aiding in the performance or receipt of an abortion, contraception, reproductive care, or gender-affirming care if the abortion, contraception, reproductive care, or gender-affirming care is lawful under the laws of this state, regardless of the recipient's location, without a magistrate's order, is ineligible for a license issued pursuant to Chapter 11.3 (commencing with Section 7512) of Division 3 of the Business and Professions Code or Section 1800 of the Insurance Code, and shall forfeit any license already obtained pursuant to those laws.

(d) A person who is taken into custody by a bail agent in violation of subdivision (b) may institute and prosecute a civil action for injunctive, monetary, or other appropriate relief against the bondsman and bond company within three years after the cause of action accrues.

(e) A bondsman or other person who is bail for a fugitive admitted to bail in another state who takes the fugitive into custody, except pursuant to an order issued under this section, is guilty of an infraction punishable by a fine of five thousand dollars ($5,000).

Amended by Stats 2023 ch 260 (SB 345),s 15, eff. 1/1/2024.

Added by Stats. 1961, Ch. 2185.

Section 848 - Proceed with person arrested as commanded by warrant or as provided by law

An officer making an arrest, in obedience to a warrant, must proceed with the person arrested as commanded by the warrant, or as provided by law.

Enacted 1872.

Section 849 - Taking person arrested without warrant before magistrate or releasing from custody

(a) When an arrest is made without a warrant by a peace officer or private person, the person arrested, if not otherwise released, shall, without unnecessary delay, be taken before the nearest or most accessible magistrate in the county in which the offense is triable, and a complaint stating the charge against the arrested person shall be laid before the magistrate.

(b) A peace officer may release from custody, instead of taking the person before a magistrate, a person arrested without a warrant in the following circumstances:

(1) The officer is satisfied that there are insufficient grounds for making a criminal complaint against the person arrested.

(2) The person arrested was arrested for intoxication only, and no further proceedings are desirable.

(3) The person was arrested only for being under the influence of a controlled substance or drug and the person is delivered to a facility or hospital for treatment and no further proceedings are desirable.

(4) The person was arrested for driving under the influence of alcohol or drugs and the person is delivered to a hospital for medical treatment that prohibits immediate delivery before a magistrate.

(5) The person was arrested and subsequently delivered to a hospital or other urgent care facility, including, but not limited to, a facility for the treatment of co-occurring substance use disorders, for mental health evaluation and treatment, and no further proceedings are desirable.

(c) The record of arrest of a person released pursuant to paragraph (1), (3), or (5) of subdivision (b) shall include a record of release. Thereafter, the arrest shall not be deemed an arrest, but a detention only.

Amended by Stats 2017 ch 566 (SB 238),s 1, eff. 10/7/2017.

Amended by Stats 2015 ch 499 (SB 795),s 3, eff. 1/1/2016.

Section 849.5 - Record of release

In any case in which a person is arrested and released and no accusatory pleading is filed charging him with an offense, any record of arrest of the person shall include a record of release. Thereafter, the arrest shall not be deemed an arrest, but a detention only.

Added by Stats. 1975, Ch. 1117.

Section 850 - Copy or abstract or warrant

(a) A telegraphic copy of a warrant or an abstract of a warrant may be sent by telegraph, teletype, or any other electronic devices, to one or more peace officers, and such copy or abstract is as effectual in the hands of any officer, and he shall proceed in the same manner under it, as though he held the original warrant issued by a magistrate or the issuing authority or agency.

(b) Except as otherwise provided in Section 1549.2 relating to Governor's warrants of extradition, an abstract of the warrant as herein referred to shall contain the following information: the warrant number, the charge, the court or agency of issuance, the subject's name, address and description, the bail, the name of the issuing magistrate or authority, and if the offense charged is a misdemeanor, whether the warrant has been certified for night service.

(c) When the subject of a written or telegraphic warrant or abstract of warrant is in custody on another charge, the custodial officer shall, immediately upon receipt of information as to the existence of any such warrant or abstract, obtain and deliver a written copy of the warrant or abstract to the subject and shall inform him of his rights under Section 1381, where applicable, to request a speedy trial and under Section 858.7 relating to Vehicle Code violations.

Amended by Stats. 1983, Ch. 793, Sec. 1.

Section 851 - Certification of telegraphic copies or abstracts of warrants

Every officer causing telegraphic copies or abstracts of warrants to be sent, must certify as correct, and file in the telegraphic office from which such copies are sent, a copy of the warrant, and must return the original with a statement of his action thereunder.

Amended by Stats. 1965, Ch. 1990.

Section 851.5 - Right to telephone calls

(a)

(1) Immediately upon being booked and, except where physically impossible, no later than three hours after arrest, an arrested person has the right to make at least three completed telephone calls, as described in subdivision (b).

(2) The arrested person shall be entitled to make at least three calls at no expense if the calls are completed to telephone numbers within the local calling area or at his or her own expense if outside the local calling area.

(b) At any police facility or place where an arrestee is detained, a sign containing the following information in bold block type shall be posted in a conspicuous place: The arrestee has the right to free telephone calls within the local calling area, or at his or her own expense if outside the local calling area, to three of the following:

(1) An attorney of his or her choice or, if he or she has no funds, the public defender or other attorney assigned by the court to assist indigents, whose telephone number shall be posted. This telephone call shall not be monitored, eavesdropped upon, or recorded.

(2) A bail bondsman.

(3) A relative or other person.

(c) As soon as practicable upon being arrested but, except where physically impossible, no later than three hours after arrest, the arresting or booking officer shall inquire as to whether the arrested person is a custodial parent with responsibility for a minor child. The arresting or booking officer shall notify the arrested person who is a custodial parent with responsibility for a minor child that he or she is entitled to, and may request to, make two additional telephone calls at no expense if the telephone calls are completed to telephone numbers within the local calling area, or at his or her own expense if outside the local calling area, to a relative or other person for the purpose of arranging for the care of the minor child or children in the parent's absence.

(d) At any police facility or place where an arrestee is detained, a sign containing the following information in bold block type shall be posted in a conspicuous place: The arrestee, if he or she is a custodial parent with responsibility for a minor child, has the right to two additional telephone calls within the local dialing area, or at his or her own expense if outside the local area, for the purpose of arranging for the care of the minor child or children in the parent's absence.

(e) These telephone calls shall be given immediately upon request, or as soon as practicable.

(f) The signs posted pursuant to subdivisions (b) and (d) shall make the specified notifications in English and any non-English language spoken by a substantial number of the public, as specified in Section 7296.2 of the Government Code, who are served by the police facility or place of detainment.

(g) The rights and duties set forth in this section shall be enforced regardless of the arrestee's immigration status.

(h) This provision shall not abrogate a law enforcement officer's duty to advise a suspect of his or her right to counsel or of any other right.

(i) Any public officer or employee who willfully deprives an arrested person of any right granted by this section is guilty of a misdemeanor.

Amended by Stats 2012 ch 816 (AB 2015),s 1, eff. 1/1/2013.

Amended by Stats 2005 ch 635 (AB 760),s 1, eff. 1/1/2006

Section 851.6 - Certificate describing action as detention

(a) In any case in which a person is arrested and released pursuant to paragraph (1), (3), or (5) of subdivision (b) of Section 849, the person shall be issued a certificate, signed by the releasing officer or his superior officer, describing the action as a detention.

(b) In any case in which a person is arrested and released and an accusatory pleading is not filed charging him or her with an offense, the person shall be issued a certificate by the law enforcement agency which arrested him or her describing the action as a detention.

(c) The Attorney General shall prescribe the form and content of the certificate.

(d) Any reference to the action as an arrest shall be deleted from the arrest records of the arresting agency and of the Department of Justice. Thereafter, any record of the action shall refer to it as a detention.

Section 851.7 - Petition by minor arrested for misdemeanor for order sealing records

(a) Any person who has been arrested for a misdemeanor, with or without a warrant, while a minor, may, during or after minority, petition the court in which the proceedings occurred or, if there were no court proceedings, the court in whose jurisdiction the arrest occurred, for an order sealing the records in the case, including any records of arrest and detention, if any of the following occurred:

(1) The person was released pursuant to paragraph (1) of subdivision (b) of Section 849.

(2) Proceedings against the person were dismissed, or the person was discharged, without a conviction.

(3) The person was acquitted.

(b) If the court finds that the petitioner is eligible for relief under subdivision (a), it shall issue its order granting the relief prayed for. Thereafter, the arrest, detention, and any further proceedings in the case shall be deemed not to have occurred, and the petitioner may answer accordingly any question relating to their occurrence.

(c) This section applies to arrests and any further proceedings that occurred before, as well as those that occur after, the effective date of this section.

(d) This section does not apply to any person taken into custody pursuant to Section 625 of the Welfare and Institutions Code, or to any case within the scope of Section 781 of the Welfare and Institutions Code, unless, after a finding of unfitness for the juvenile court or otherwise, there were criminal proceedings in the case, not culminating in conviction. If there were criminal proceedings not culminating in conviction, this section shall be applicable to the criminal proceedings if the proceedings are otherwise within the scope of this section.

(e) This section does not apply to arrests for, and any further proceedings relating to, any of the following:

(1) Offenses for which registration is required under Section 290.

(2) Offenses under Division 10 (commencing with Section 11000) of the Health and Safety Code.

(3) Offenses under the Vehicle Code or any local ordinance relating to the operation, stopping, standing, or parking of a vehicle.

(f) In any action or proceeding based upon defamation, a court, upon a showing of good cause, may order any records sealed under this section to be opened and admitted in evidence. The records shall be confidential and shall be available for inspection only by the court, jury, parties, counsel for the parties, and any other person who is authorized by the court to inspect them. Upon the judgment in the action or proceeding becoming final, the court shall order the records sealed.

(g)

(1) A record that has been sealed pursuant to this section may be accessed, inspected, or utilized by the prosecuting attorney in order to meet a statutory or constitutional obligation to disclose favorable or exculpatory evidence to a defendant in a criminal case in which the prosecuting attorney has reason to believe that access to the record is necessary to meet the disclosure obligation. A request to access information in the sealed record for this purpose, including the prosecutor's rationale for believing that access to the information in the record may be necessary to meet the disclosure obligation and the date by which the records are needed, shall be submitted by the prosecuting attorney to the juvenile court. The juvenile court shall review the case file and records that have been referenced by the prosecutor as necessary to meet the disclosure obligation and any response submitted by the person having the sealed record. The court shall approve the prosecutor's request to the extent that the court has, upon review of the relevant records, determined that access to a specific sealed record or portion of a sealed record is necessary to enable the prosecuting attorney to comply with the disclosure obligation. If the juvenile court approves the prosecuting attorney's request, the court shall state on the record appropriate limits on the access, inspection, and utilization of the sealed record information in order to protect the confidentiality of the person whose sealed record is accessed pursuant to this subdivision. A ruling allowing disclosure of information pursuant to this subdivision does not affect whether the information is admissible in a criminal or juvenile proceeding. This subdivision does not impose any discovery obligations on a prosecuting attorney that do not already exist.

(2) This subdivision does not apply to juvenile case files pertaining to matters within the jurisdiction of the juvenile court pursuant to Section 300 of the Welfare and Institutions Code.

(h) This section applies in any case in which a person was under 21 years of age at the time of the commission of an offense to which this section applies if that offense was committed prior to March 7, 1973.

Amended by Stats 2021 ch 124 (AB 938),s 35, eff. 1/1/2022.

Amended by Stats 2019 ch 50 (AB 1537),s 1, eff. 1/1/2020.

Section 851.8 - Petition for destruction of records of arrest

(a) In any case where a person has been arrested and no accusatory pleading has been filed, the person arrested may petition the law enforcement agency having jurisdiction over the offense to destroy its records of the arrest. A copy of the petition shall be served upon the prosecuting attorney of the county or city having jurisdiction over the offense. The law enforcement agency having jurisdiction over the offense, upon a determination that the person arrested is factually innocent, shall, with the concurrence of the prosecuting attorney, seal its arrest records, and the petition for relief under this section for three years from the date of the arrest and thereafter destroy its arrest records and the petition. The law enforcement agency having jurisdiction over the offense shall notify the Department of Justice, and any law enforcement agency that arrested the petitioner or participated in the arrest of the petitioner for an offense for which the petitioner has been found factually innocent under this subdivision, of the sealing of the arrest records and the reason therefor. The Department of Justice and any law enforcement agency so notified shall forthwith seal their records of the arrest and the notice of sealing for three years from the date of the arrest, and thereafter destroy their records of the arrest and the notice of sealing. The law enforcement agency having jurisdiction over the offense and the Department of Justice shall request the destruction of any records of the arrest which they have given to any local, state, or federal agency or to any other person or entity. Each agency, person, or entity within the State of California receiving the request shall destroy its records of the arrest and the request, unless otherwise provided in this section.

(b) If, after receipt by both the law enforcement agency and the prosecuting attorney of a petition for relief under subdivision (a), the law enforcement agency and prosecuting attorney do not respond to the petition by accepting or denying the petition within 60 days after the running of the relevant statute of limitations or within 60 days after receipt of the petition in cases where the statute of limitations has previously lapsed, then the petition shall be deemed to be denied. In any case where the petition of an arrestee to the law enforcement agency to have an arrest record destroyed is denied, petition may be made to the superior court that would have had territorial jurisdiction over the matter. A copy of the petition shall be served on the law enforcement agency and the prosecuting attorney of the county or city having jurisdiction over the offense at least 10 days prior to the hearing thereon. The prosecuting attorney and the law enforcement agency through the district attorney may present evidence to the court at the hearing. Notwithstanding Section 1538.5 or 1539, any judicial determination of factual innocence made pursuant to this section may be heard and determined upon declarations, affidavits, police reports, or any other evidence submitted by the parties which is material, relevant, and reliable. A finding of factual innocence and an order for the sealing and destruction of records pursuant to this section shall not be made unless the court finds that no reasonable cause exists to believe that the arrestee committed the offense for which the arrest was made. In any court hearing to determine the factual innocence of a party, the initial burden of proof shall rest with the petitioner to show that no reasonable cause exists to believe that the arrestee committed the offense for which the arrest was made. If the court finds that this showing of no reasonable cause has been made by the petitioner, then the burden of proof shall shift to the respondent to show that a reasonable cause exists to believe that the petitioner committed the offense for which the arrest was made. If the court finds the arrestee to be factually innocent of the charges for which the arrest was made, then the court shall order the law enforcement agency having jurisdiction over the offense, the Department of Justice, and any law enforcement agency which arrested the petitioner or participated in the arrest of the petitioner for an offense for which the petitioner has been found factually innocent under this section to seal their records of the arrest and the court order to seal and destroy the records, for three years from the date of the arrest and thereafter to destroy their records of the arrest and the court order to seal and destroy those records. The court shall also order the law enforcement agency having jurisdiction over the offense and the Department of Justice to request the destruction of any records of the arrest which they have given to any local, state, or federal agency, person or entity. Each state or local agency, person or entity within the State of California receiving such a request shall destroy its records of the arrest and the request to destroy the records, unless otherwise provided in this section. The court shall give to the petitioner a copy of any court order concerning the destruction of the arrest records.

(c) In any case where a person has been arrested, and an accusatory pleading has been filed, but where no conviction has occurred, the defendant may, at any time after dismissal of the action, petition the court that dismissed the action for a finding that the defendant is factually innocent of the charges for which the arrest was made. A copy of the petition shall be served on the prosecuting attorney of the county or city in which the accusatory pleading was filed at least 10 days prior to the hearing on the petitioner's factual innocence. The prosecuting attorney may present evidence to the court at the hearing. The hearing shall be conducted as provided in subdivision (b). If the court finds the petitioner to be factually innocent of the charges for which the arrest was made, then the court shall grant the relief as provided in subdivision (b).

(d) In any case where a person has been arrested and an accusatory pleading has been filed, but where no conviction has occurred, the court may, with the concurrence of the prosecuting attorney, grant the relief provided in subdivision (b) at the time of the dismissal of the accusatory pleading.

(e) Whenever any person is acquitted of a charge and it appears to the judge presiding at the trial at which the acquittal occurred that the defendant was factually innocent of the charge, the judge may grant the relief provided in subdivision (b).

(f) In any case where a person who has been arrested is granted relief pursuant to subdivision (a) or (b), the law enforcement agency having jurisdiction over the offense or court shall issue a written declaration to the arrestee stating that it is the determination of the law enforcement agency having jurisdiction over the offense or court that the arrestee is factually innocent of the charges for which the person was arrested and that the arrestee is thereby exonerated. Thereafter, the arrest shall be deemed not to have occurred and the person may answer accordingly any question relating to its occurrence.

(g) The Department of Justice shall furnish forms to be utilized by persons applying for the destruction of their arrest records and for the written declaration that one person was found factually innocent under subdivisions (a) and (b).

(h) Documentation of arrest records destroyed pursuant to subdivision (a), (b), (c), (d), or (e) that are contained in investigative police reports shall bear the notation "Exonerated" whenever reference is made to the arrestee. The arrestee shall be notified in writing by the law enforcement agency having jurisdiction over the offense of the sealing and destruction of the arrest records pursuant to this section.

(i)

(1) Any finding that an arrestee is factually innocent pursuant to subdivision (a), (b), (c), (d), or (e) shall not be admissible as evidence in any action.

(2) Notwithstanding paragraph (1), a finding that an arrestee is factually innocent pursuant to subdivisions (a) to (e), inclusive, shall be admissible as evidence at a hearing before the California Victim Compensation Board.

(j) Destruction of records of arrest pursuant to subdivision (a), (b), (c), (d), or (e) shall be accomplished by permanent obliteration of all entries or notations upon the records pertaining to the arrest, and the record shall be prepared again so that it appears that the arrest never occurred. However, where (1) the only entries on the record pertain to the arrest and (2) the record can be destroyed without necessarily affecting the destruction of other records, then the document constituting the record shall be physically destroyed.

(k) No records shall be destroyed pursuant to subdivision (a), (b), (c), (d), or (e) if the arrestee or a codefendant has filed a civil action against the peace officers or law enforcement jurisdiction which made the arrest or instituted the prosecution and if the agency which is the custodian of the records has received a certified copy of the complaint in the civil action, until the civil action has been resolved. Any records sealed pursuant to this section by the court in the civil actions, upon a showing of good cause, may be opened and submitted into evidence. The records shall be confidential and shall be available for inspection only by the court, jury, parties, counsel for the parties, and any other person authorized by the court. Immediately following the final resolution of the civil action, records subject to subdivision (a), (b), (c), (d), or (e) shall be sealed and destroyed pursuant to subdivision (a), (b), (c), (d), or (e).

(l) For arrests occurring on or after January 1, 1981, and for accusatory pleadings filed on or after January 1, 1981, petitions for relief under this section may be filed up to two years from the date of the arrest or filing of the accusatory pleading, whichever is later. Until January 1, 1983, petitioners can file for relief under this section for arrests which occurred or accusatory pleadings which were filed up to five years prior to the effective date of the statute. Any time restrictions on filing for relief under this section may be waived upon a showing of good cause by the petitioner and in the absence of prejudice.

(m) Any relief which is available to a petitioner under this section for an arrest shall also be available for an arrest which has been deemed to be or described as a detention under Section 849.5 or 851.6.

(n) This section shall not apply to any offense which is classified as an infraction.

(o)

(1) This section shall be repealed on the effective date of a final judgment based on a claim under the California or United States Constitution holding that evidence that is relevant, reliable, and material may not be considered for purposes of a judicial determination of factual innocence under this section. For purposes of this subdivision, a judgment by the appellate division of a superior court is a final judgment if it is published and if it is not reviewed on appeal by a court of appeal. A judgment of a court of appeal is a final judgment if it is published and if it is not reviewed by the California Supreme Court.

(2) Any decision referred to in this subdivision shall be stayed pending appeal.

(3) If not otherwise appealed by a party to the action, any decision referred to in this subdivision which is a judgment by the appellate division of the superior court shall be appealed by the Attorney General.

(p) A judgment of the court under subdivision (b), (c), (d), or (e) is subject to the following appeal path:

(1) In a felony case, appeal is to the court of appeal.

(2) In a misdemeanor case, or in a case in which no accusatory pleading was filed, appeal is to the appellate division of the superior court.

Amended by Stats 2016 ch 31 (SB 836),s 235, eff. 6/27/2016.
Amended by Stats 2010 ch 328 (SB 1330),s 159, eff. 1/1/2011.
Amended by Stats 2009 ch 432 (AB 316),s 3, eff. 1/1/2010.
Amended by Stats 2007 ch 390 (AB 475),s 1, eff. 1/1/2008.
Amended by Stats 2006 ch 901 (SB 1422),s 8.2, eff. 1/1/2007.
Amended by Stats 2002 ch 784 (SB 1316), s 532, eff. 1/1/2003.

Section 851.85 - Sealing of records if person acquitted

Whenever a person is acquitted of a charge and it appears to the judge presiding at the trial wherein such acquittal occurred that the defendant was factually innocent of the charge, the judge may order that the records in the case be sealed, including any record of arrest or detention, upon the written or oral motion of any party in the case or the court, and with notice to all parties to the case. If such an order is made, the court shall give to the defendant a copy of such order and inform the defendant that he may thereafter state that he was not arrested for such charge and that he was found innocent of such charge by the court.

Added by Stats. 1980, Ch. 1172, Sec. 3. Effective September 29, 1980. Conditionally operative, upon repeal of Section 851.8, by Sec. 4 of Ch. 1172.

Section 851.86 - Sealing of records if conviction is set aside based upon determination that person was factually innocent of charge

Whenever a person is convicted of a charge, and the conviction is set aside based upon a determination that the person was factually innocent of the charge, the judge shall order that the records in the case be sealed, including any record of arrest or detention, upon written or oral motion of any party in the case or the court, and with notice to all parties to the case. If such an order is made, the court shall give the defendant a copy of that order and inform the defendant that he or she may thereafter state he or she was not arrested for that charge and that he or she was not convicted of that charge, and that he or she was found innocent of that charge by the court. The court shall also inform the defendant of the availability of indemnity for persons erroneously convicted pursuant to Chapter 5 (commencing with Section 4900) of Title 6 of Part 3, and the time limitations for presenting those claims.

Added by Stats 2009 ch 432 (AB 316),s 4, eff. 1/1/2010.

Section 851.865 - Effect of declaration of factual innocence for claim

(a) If a person has secured a declaration of factual innocence from the court pursuant to Section 851.8 or 851.86, the finding shall be binding on the California Victim Compensation Board for a claim presented to the board pursuant to Section 4900. Upon application by the person, the California Victim Compensation Board shall, without a hearing, approve payment to the claimant pursuant to Section 4904, if sufficient funds are available, upon appropriation by the Legislature.

(b) If the declaration of factual innocence is granted pursuant to a stipulation of the prosecutor, upon application by the person, the board shall, without a hearing, approve payment pursuant to Section 4904, if sufficient funds are available, upon appropriation by the Legislature.

Amended by Stats 2023 ch 702 (SB 78),s 1, eff. 1/1/2024.
Amended by Stats 2016 ch 31 (SB 836),s 236, eff. 6/27/2016.
Added by Stats 2013 ch 800 (SB 618),s 1, eff. 1/1/2014.

Section 851.87 - Completion of prefiling diversion program; order to seal records

(a)

(1) In any case where a person is arrested and successfully completes a prefiling diversion program administered by a prosecuting attorney in lieu of filing an accusatory pleading, the person may petition the superior court that would have had jurisdiction over the matter to issue an order to seal the records pertaining to an arrest and the court may order those records sealed as described in Section 851.92. A copy of the petition shall be served on the law enforcement agency and the prosecuting attorney of the county or city having jurisdiction over the offense, who may request a hearing within 60 days of receipt of the petition. The court may hear the matter no less than 60 days from the date the law enforcement agency and prosecuting attorney receive a copy of the petition. The prosecuting attorney and the law enforcement agency, through the prosecuting attorney, may present evidence to the court at the hearing.

(2) If the order is made, the court shall give a copy of the order to the person and inform the person that he or she may thereafter state that he or she was not arrested for the charge.

(3) The person may, except as specified in subdivisions (b) and (c), indicate in response to any question concerning the person's prior criminal record that the person was not arrested.

(4) Subject to subdivisions (b) and (c), a record pertaining to the arrest shall not, without the person's permission, be used in any way that could result in the denial of any employment, benefit, or certificate.

(b) The person shall be advised that, regardless of the person's successful completion of the program, the arrest shall be disclosed by the Department of Justice in response to any peace officer application request, and that, notwithstanding subdivision (a), this section does not relieve the person of the obligation to disclose the arrest in response to any direct question contained in any questionnaire or application for a position as a peace officer, as defined in Section 830.

(c) The person shall be advised that an order to seal records pertaining to an arrest made pursuant to this section has no effect on a criminal justice agency's ability to access and use those sealed records and information regarding sealed arrests, as described in Section 851.92.

(d) As used in this section, "prefiling diversion" is a diversion from prosecution that is offered to a person by the prosecuting attorney in lieu of, or prior to, the filing of an accusatory pleading in court as set forth in Section 950.

Amended by Stats 2017 ch 680 (SB 393),s 1, eff. 1/1/2018.

Added by Stats 2013 ch 798 (SB 513),s 2, eff. 1/1/2014.

Section 851.90 - Sealing of records if diverted person successfully completes program

(a)

(1) Whenever a person is diverted pursuant to a drug diversion program administered by a superior court pursuant to Section 1000.5 or is admitted to a deferred entry of judgment program pursuant to Section 1000 or 1000.8, and the person successfully completes the program, the judge may order those records pertaining to the arrest to be sealed as described in Section 851.92, upon the written or oral motion of any party in the case, or upon the court's own motion, and with notice to all parties in the case.

(2) If the order is made, the court shall give a copy of the order to the defendant and inform the defendant that he or she may thereafter state that he or she was not arrested for the charge.

(3) The defendant may, except as specified in subdivisions (b) and (c), indicate in response to any question concerning the defendant's prior criminal record that the defendant was not arrested or granted statutorily authorized drug diversion or deferred entry of judgment for the offense.

(4) Subject to subdivisions (b) and (c), a record pertaining to an arrest resulting in the successful completion of a statutorily authorized drug diversion or deferred entry of judgment program shall not, without the defendant's permission, be used in any way that could result in the denial of any employment, benefit, or certificate.

(b) The defendant shall be advised that, regardless of the defendant's successful completion of a statutorily authorized drug diversion or deferred entry of judgment program, the arrest upon which the case was based shall be disclosed by the Department of Justice in response to any peace officer application request, and that, notwithstanding subdivision (a), this section does not relieve the defendant of the obligation to disclose the arrest in response to any direct question contained in any questionnaire or application for a position as a peace officer, as defined in Section 830.

(c) The defendant shall be advised that, regardless of the defendant's successful completion of a statutorily authorized drug diversion or deferred entry of judgment program, an order to seal records pertaining to an arrest made pursuant to this section has no effect on a criminal justice agency's ability to access and use those sealed records and information regarding sealed arrests, as described in Section 851.92.

Amended by Stats 2017 ch 680 (SB 393),s 2, eff. 1/1/2018.

Amended by Stats 2009 ch 372 (AB 750),s 2, eff. 1/1/2010.

Added by Stats 2003 ch 792 (SB 599), s 1, eff. 1/1/2004.

Section 851.91 - Arrest not resulting in conviction

(a) A person who has suffered an arrest that did not result in a conviction may petition the court to have his or her arrest and related records sealed, as described in Section 851.92.

(1) For purposes of this section, an arrest did not result in a conviction if any of the following are true:

(A) The statute of limitations has run on every offense upon which the arrest was based and the prosecuting attorney of the city or county that would have had jurisdiction over the offense or offenses upon which the arrest was based has not filed an accusatory pleading based on the arrest.

(B) The prosecuting attorney filed an accusatory pleading based on the arrest, but, with respect to all charges, one or more of the following has occurred:

(i) No conviction occurred, the charge has been dismissed, and the charge may not be refiled.

(ii) No conviction occurred and the arrestee has been acquitted of the charges.

(iii) A conviction occurred, but has been vacated or reversed on appeal, all appellate remedies have been exhausted, and the charge may not be refiled.

(2) A person is not eligible for relief under this section in any of the following circumstances:

(A) He or she may still be charged with any of the offenses upon which the arrest was based.

(B) Any of the arrest charges, as specified by the law enforcement agency that conducted the arrest, or any of the charges in the accusatory pleading based on the arrest, if filed, is a charge of murder or any other offense for which there is no statute of limitations, except when the person has been acquitted or found factually innocent of the charge.

(C) The petitioner intentionally evaded law enforcement efforts to prosecute the arrest, including by absconding from the jurisdiction in which the arrest occurred. The existence of bench warrants or failures to appear that were adjudicated before the case closed with no conviction does not establish intentional evasion.

(D) The petitioner intentionally evaded law enforcement efforts to prosecute the arrest by engaging in identity fraud and was subsequently charged with a crime for that act of identity fraud.

(b)

(1) A petition to seal an arrest shall:

(A) Be verified.

(B) Be filed in the court in which the accusatory pleading based on the arrest was filed or, if no accusatory pleading was filed, in a court with criminal jurisdiction in the city or county in which the arrest occurred.

(C) Be filed at least 15 days prior to the hearing on the petition.

(D) Be served, by copy, upon the prosecuting attorney of the city or county in which the arrest occurred and upon the law enforcement agency that made the arrest at least 15 days prior to the hearing on the petition.

(E) Include all of the following information:

(i) The petitioner's name and date of birth.

(ii) The date of the arrest for which sealing is sought.

(iii) The city and county where the arrest took place.

(iv) The law enforcement agency that made the arrest.

(v) Any other information identifying the arrest that is available from the law enforcement agency that conducted the arrest or from the court in which the accusatory pleading, if any, based on the arrest was filed, including, but not limited to, the case number for the police investigative report documenting the arrest, and the court number under which the arrest was reviewed by the prosecuting attorney or under which the prosecuting attorney filed an accusatory pleading.

(vi) The offenses upon which the arrest was based or, if an accusatory pleading was filed based on the arrest, the charges in the accusatory pleading.

(vii) A statement that the petitioner is entitled to have his or her arrest sealed as a matter of right or, if the petitioner is requesting to have his or her arrest sealed in the interests of justice, how the interests of justice would be served by granting the petition, accompanied by declarations made directly and verified by the petitioner, his or her supporting declarants, or both.

(2) The court may deny a petition for failing to meet any of the requirements described in paragraph (1).

(3)

(A) The Judicial Council shall furnish forms to be utilized by a person applying to have his or her arrest sealed pursuant to this section. The petition form shall include all of the information required to be included in the petition by paragraph (1) of subdivision (b), shall be available in English, Spanish, Chinese, Vietnamese, and Korean, and shall include a statement that the petition form is available in additional languages and the Internet Web site where the form is available in alternative languages. The forms shall include notice of other means to address arrest records, including a determination of factual innocence under Section 851.8 and deeming an arrest a detention under Section 849.5.

(B)

(i) A facility at which an arrestee is detained shall, at the request of an arrestee upon release, provide the forms furnished by Judicial Council pursuant to subparagraph (A) to the arrestee.

(ii) A facility at which an arrestee is detained shall post a sign containing the following information: "A person who has been arrested but not convicted may petition the court to have his or her arrest and related records sealed. The petition form is available on the Internet or upon request in this facility."

(c) A petition to seal an arrest record pursuant to this section may be granted as a matter of right or in the interests of justice.

(1) A petitioner who is eligible for relief under subdivision (a) is entitled to have his or her arrest sealed as a matter of right unless he or she is subject to paragraph (2).

(2)

(A)

(i) A petitioner may have his or her arrest sealed only upon a showing that the sealing would serve the interests of justice if any of the offenses upon which the arrest was based, as specified by the law enforcement agency that made the arrest, or, if an accusatory pleading was filed, any of the charges in the accusatory pleading, was one of the following:

(I) Domestic violence, if the petitioner's record demonstrates a pattern of domestic violence arrests, convictions, or both.

(II) Child abuse, if the petitioner's record demonstrates a pattern of child abuse arrests, convictions, or both.

(III) Elder abuse, if the petitioner's record demonstrates a pattern of elder abuse arrests, convictions, or both.

(ii) For purposes of this subparagraph, "pattern" means two or more convictions, or five or more arrests, for separate offenses occurring on separate occasions within three years from at least one of the other convictions or arrests.

(B) In determining whether the interests of justice would be served by sealing an arrest record pursuant to this section, the court may consider any relevant factors, including, but not limited to, any of the following:

(i) Hardship to the petitioner caused by the arrest that is the subject of the petition.

(ii) Declarations or evidence regarding the petitioner's good character.

(iii) Declarations or evidence regarding the arrest.

(iv) The petitioner's record of convictions.

(d)

(1) At a hearing on a petition under this section, the petitioner, the prosecuting attorney, and, through the prosecuting attorney, the arresting agency may present evidence to the court. Notwithstanding Section 1538.5 or 1539, the hearing may be heard and determined upon declarations, affidavits, police investigative reports, copies of state summary criminal history information and local summary criminal history information, or any other evidence submitted by the parties that is material, relevant, and reliable.

(2) The petitioner has the initial burden of proof to show that he or she is entitled to have his or her arrest sealed as a matter of right or that sealing would serve the interests of justice. If the court finds that petitioner has satisfied his or her burden of proof, then the burden of proof shall shift to the respondent prosecuting attorney.

(e) If the court grants a petition pursuant to this section, the court shall do all of the following:

(1) Furnish a disposition report to the Department of Justice, pursuant to Section 13151, stating that relief was granted under this section.

(2)

(A) Issue a written ruling and order to the petitioner, the prosecuting attorney, and to the law enforcement agency that made the arrest that states all of the following:

(B) The record of arrest has been sealed as to petitioner, the arrest is deemed not to have occurred, the petitioner may answer any question relating to the sealed arrest accordingly, and the petitioner is released from all penalties and disabilities resulting from the arrest, except as provided in Section 851.92 and as follows:

(i) The sealed arrest may be pleaded and proved in any subsequent prosecution of the petitioner for any other offense, and shall have the same effect as if it had not been sealed.

(ii) The sealing of an arrest pursuant to this section does not relieve the petitioner of the obligation to disclose the arrest, if otherwise required by law, in response to any direct question contained in a questionnaire or application for public office, for employment as a peace officer, for licensure by any state or local agency, or for contracting with the California State Lottery Commission.

(iii) The sealing of an arrest pursuant to this section does not affect petitioner's authorization to own, possess, or have in his or her custody or control any firearm, or his or her susceptibility to conviction under Chapter 2 (commencing with Section 29800) of Division 9 of Title 4 of Part 6, if the arrest would otherwise affect this authorization or susceptibility.

(iv) The sealing of an arrest pursuant to this section does not affect any prohibition from holding public office that would otherwise apply under law as a result of the arrest.

Amended by Stats 2018 ch 653 (AB 2599),s 1, eff. 1/1/2019.

Added by Stats 2017 ch 680 (SB 393),s 3, eff. 1/1/2018.

Section 851.92 - Sealing of records

(a) This section applies when an arrest record is sealed pursuant to Sections 851.87, 851.90, 851.91, 1000.4, and 1001.9.

(b) When the court issues an order to seal an arrest, the sealing shall be accomplished as follows:

(1) The court shall provide copies of the order and a report on the disposition of the arrest, as follows:

(A) Upon issuing the order, the court shall provide a copy to the person whose arrest was sealed and to the prosecuting attorney.

(B) Within 30 days of issuing the order, the court shall forward a copy of the order to the law enforcement agency that made the arrest, to any other law enforcement agency that participated in the arrest, and to the law enforcement agency that administers the master local summary criminal history information that contains the arrest record for the sealed arrest.

(C) Within 30 days of issuing the order, the court shall furnish a disposition report to the Department of Justice indicating that relief has been ordered and providing the section of the Penal Code under which that relief was granted and the date that relief was granted.

(D) A sealing order made pursuant to this subdivision shall not be forwarded to the Department of Justice to be included or notated in the department's manual or electronic fingerprint image or criminal history record systems. Any sealing order made pursuant to this subdivision and received by the Department of Justice shall not be processed by the department.

(2) The arrest record shall be updated, as follows:

(A) The local summary criminal history information shall include, directly next to or below the entry or entries regarding the sealed arrest, a note stating "arrest sealed" and providing the date that the court issued the order, and the section pursuant to which the arrest was sealed. This note shall be included in all master copies of the arrest record, digital or otherwise.

(B) The state summary criminal history information shall include, directly next to or below the entry or entries regarding the sealed arrest, a note stating "arrest relief granted," providing the date that the court issued the order and the section of the Penal Code pursuant to which the relief was granted. This note shall be included in all master copies of the arrest record, digital or otherwise.

(3) A police investigative report related to the sealed arrest shall, only as to the person whose arrest was sealed, be stamped "ARREST SEALED: DO NOT RELEASE OUTSIDE THE CRIMINAL JUSTICE SECTOR," and shall note next to the stamp the date the arrest was sealed and the section pursuant to which the arrest was sealed. The responsible local law enforcement agency shall ensure that this note is included in all master copies, digital or otherwise, of the police investigative report related to the arrest that was sealed.

(4) Court records related to the sealed arrest shall, only as to the person whose arrest was sealed, be stamped "ARREST SEALED: DO NOT RELEASE OUTSIDE OF THE CRIMINAL JUSTICE SECTOR," and shall note next to the stamp the date of the sealing and the section pursuant to which the arrest was sealed. This stamp and note shall be included on all master court dockets, digital or otherwise, relating to the arrest.

(5) Arrest records, police investigative reports, and court records that are sealed under this section shall not be disclosed to any person or entity except the person whose arrest was sealed or a criminal justice agency. Nothing shall prohibit disclosure of information between criminal history providers.

(6) Notwithstanding the sealing of an arrest, a criminal justice agency may continue, in the regular course of its duties, to access, furnish to other criminal justice agencies, and use, including, but not limited to, by discussing in open court and in unsealed court filings, sealed arrests, sealed arrest records, sealed police investigative reports, sealed court records, and information relating to sealed arrests, to the same extent that would have been permitted for a criminal justice agency if the arrest had not been sealed.

(c) Unless specifically authorized by this section, a person or entity, other than a criminal justice agency or the person whose arrest was sealed, who disseminates information relating to a sealed arrest is subject to a civil penalty of not less than five hundred dollars ($500) and not more than two thousand five hundred dollars ($2,500) per violation. The civil penalty may be enforced by a city attorney, district attorney, or the Attorney General. This subdivision does not limit any existing private right of action. A civil penalty imposed under this section shall be cumulative to civil remedies or penalties imposed under any other law.

(d) As used in this section and Sections 851.87, 851.90, 851.91, 1000.4, and 1001.9, all of the following terms have the following meanings:

(1) "Arrest record" and "record pertaining to an arrest" mean information about the arrest or detention that is contained in either of the following:

   (A) The master, or a copy of the master, local summary criminal history information, as defined in subdivision (a) of Section 13300.

   (B) The master, or a copy of the master, state summary criminal history information as defined in subparagraph (A) of paragraph (2) of subdivision (a) of Section 11105.

(2) "Court records" means records, files, and materials created, compiled, or maintained by or for the court in relation to court proceedings, and includes, but is not limited to, indexes, registers of actions, court minutes, court orders, court filings, court exhibits, court progress and status reports, court history summaries, copies of state summary criminal history information and local summary criminal history information, and any other criminal history information contained in any of those materials.

(3) "Criminal history provider" means a person or entity that is not a criminal justice agency and that provides background screening services or criminal history information on identified individuals to the public or to those outside the criminal justice sector upon request, charge, or pursuant to a contractual agreement or that aggregates into databases that are open to the public or to those outside the criminal justice sector upon request or charge, or pursuant to a contractual agreement, that are not created or maintained by a criminal justice agency, criminal history information on identified individuals. For the purposes of this paragraph, a criminal history provider includes an investigative consumer reporting agency, as defined in Section 1786.2 of the Civil Code, a consumer credit reporting agency, as defined in Section 1785.3 of the Civil Code, and a consumer reporting agency, as defined in Section 603(f) of the Fair Credit Reporting Act (15 U.S.C. 1681a(f)).

(4) "Criminal justice agency" means an agency at any level of government that performs, as its principal function, activities relating to the apprehension, prosecution, defense, adjudication, incarceration, or correction of criminal suspects and criminal offenders. A criminal justice agency includes, but is not limited to, any of the following:

   (A) A court of this state.

   (B) A peace officer, as defined in Section 830.1, subdivisions (a) and (e) of Section 830.2, subdivision (a) of Section 830.3, subdivision (a) of Section 830.31, and subdivisions (a) and (b) of Section 830.5.

   (C) A district attorney.

   (D) A prosecuting city attorney.

   (E) A city attorney pursuing civil gang injunctions pursuant to Section 186.22a or drug abatement actions pursuant to Section 3479 or 3480 of the Civil Code or Section 11571 of the Health and Safety Code.

   (F) A probation officer.

   (G) A parole officer.

   (H) A public defender or an attorney representing a person, or a person representing himself or herself, in a criminal proceeding, a proceeding to revoke parole, mandatory supervision, or postrelease community supervision, or in proceeding described in Chapter 3.5 (commencing with Section 4852.01) of Title 6 of Part 3.

   (I) An expert, investigator, or other specialist contracted by a prosecuting attorney or defense attorney to accomplish the purpose of the prosecution, defense, or representation in the criminal proceeding.

   (J) A correctional officer.

(5) "Police investigative report" means intelligence, analytical, and investigative reports and files created, compiled, and maintained by a law enforcement criminal justice agency and relating to a potential crime, violation of the law, arrest, detention, prosecution, or law enforcement investigation.

Added by Stats 2017 ch 680 (SB 393),s 4, eff. 1/1/2018.

Section 851.93 - [Effective Until 7/1/2024] Monthly review of criminal justice databases; arrest record relief

(a)

   (1) On a monthly basis, the Department of Justice shall review the records in the statewide criminal justice databases, and based on information in the state summary criminal history repository, shall identify persons with records of arrest that meet the criteria set forth in paragraph (2) and are eligible for arrest record relief.

   (2) A person is eligible for relief pursuant to this section, if the arrest occurred on or after January 1, 1973, and meets any of the following conditions:

      (A) The arrest was for a misdemeanor offense and the charge was dismissed.

      (B) The arrest was for a misdemeanor offense, there is no indication that criminal proceedings have been initiated, at least one calendar year has elapsed since the date of the arrest, and no conviction occurred, or the arrestee was acquitted of any charges that arose, from that arrest.

      (C) The arrest was for an offense that is punishable by imprisonment pursuant to paragraph (1) or (2) of subdivision (h) of Section 1170, there is no indication that criminal proceedings have been initiated, at least three calendar years have elapsed since the date of the arrest, and no conviction occurred, or the arrestee was acquitted of any charges arising, from that arrest.

      (D) The person successfully completed any of the following, relating to that arrest:

         (i) A prefiling diversion program, as defined in Section 851.87, administered by a prosecuting attorney in lieu of filing an accusatory pleading.

         (ii) A drug diversion program administered by a superior court pursuant to Section 1000.5, or a deferred entry of judgment program pursuant to Section 1000 or 1000.8.

         (iii) A pretrial diversion program, pursuant to Section 1000.4.

         (iv) A diversion program, pursuant to Section 1001.9.

         (v) A diversion program described in Chapter 2.8 (commencing with Section 1001.20), Chapter 2.8A (commencing with Section 1001.35), Chapter 2.81 (commencing with Section 1001.40), Chapter 2.9 (commencing with Section 1001.50), Chapter 2.9A (commencing with Section 1001.60), Chapter 2.9B (commencing with Section 1001.70), Chapter 2.9C (commencing with Section 1001.80), Chapter 2.9D (commencing with Section 1001.81), or Chapter 2.92 (commencing with Section 1001.85), of Title 6.

(b)

(1) The department shall grant relief to a person identified pursuant to subdivision (a), without requiring a petition or motion by a party for that relief if the relevant information is present in the department's electronic records.

(2) The state summary criminal history information shall include, directly next to or below the entry or entries regarding the person's arrest record, a note stating "arrest relief granted," listing the date that the department granted relief, and this section. This note shall be included in all statewide criminal databases with a record of the arrest.

(3) Except as otherwise provided in subdivision (d), an arrest for which arrest relief has been granted is deemed not to have occurred, and a person who has been granted arrest relief is released from any penalties and disabilities resulting from the arrest, and may answer any question relating to that arrest accordingly.

(c) On a monthly basis, the department shall electronically submit a notice to the superior court having jurisdiction over the criminal case, informing the court of all cases for which a complaint was filed in that jurisdiction and for which relief was granted pursuant to this section. Commencing on August 1, 2022, for any record retained by the court pursuant to Section 68152 of the Government Code, except as provided in subdivision (d), the court shall not disclose information concerning an arrest that is granted relief pursuant to this section to any person or entity, in any format, except to the person whose arrest was granted relief or a criminal justice agency, as defined in Section 851.92.

(d) Relief granted pursuant to this section is subject to the following conditions:

(1) Arrest relief does not relieve a person of the obligation to disclose an arrest in response to a direct question contained in a questionnaire or application for employment as a peace officer, as defined in Section 830.

(2) Relief granted pursuant to this section has no effect on the ability of a criminal justice agency, as defined in Section 851.92, to access and use records that are granted relief to the same extent that would have been permitted for a criminal justice agency had relief not been granted.

(3) This section does not limit the ability of a district attorney to prosecute, within the applicable statute of limitations, an offense for which arrest relief has been granted pursuant to this section.

(4) Relief granted pursuant to this section does not affect a person's authorization to own, possess, or have in the person's custody or control a firearm, or the person's susceptibility to conviction under Chapter 2 (commencing with Section 29800) of Division 9 of Title 4 of Part 6, if the arrest would otherwise affect this authorization or susceptibility.

(5) Relief granted pursuant to this section does not affect any prohibition from holding public office that would otherwise apply under law as a result of the arrest.

(6) Relief granted pursuant to this section does not affect the authority to receive, or take adverse action based on, criminal history information, including the authority to receive certified court records received or evaluated pursuant to Section 1522, 1568.09, 1569.17, or 1596.871 of the Health and Safety Code, or pursuant to any statutory or regulatory provisions that incorporate the criteria of those sections.

(e) This section does not limit petitions, motions, or orders for arrest record relief, as required or authorized by any other law, including, but not limited to, Sections 851.87, 851.90, 851.91, 1000.4, and 1001.9.

(f) The department shall annually publish statistics for each county regarding the total number of arrests granted relief pursuant to this section and the percentage of arrests for which the state summary criminal history information does not include a disposition, on the OpenJustice Web portal, as defined in Section 13010.

(g) This section shall be operative commencing July 1, 2022, subject to an appropriation in the annual Budget Act.

(h) This section shall remain in effect only until July 1, 2024, and as of that date is repealed.

Amended by Stats 2023 ch 47 (AB 134),s 4, eff. 7/10/2023.

Amended by Stats 2022 ch 814 (SB 731),s 3, eff. 1/1/2023.

Amended by Stats 2021 ch 80 (AB 145),s 2, eff. 7/16/2021.

Amended by Stats 2020 ch 29 (SB 118),s 12, eff. 8/6/2020.

Added by Stats 2019 ch 578 (AB 1076),s 7, eff. 1/1/2020.

Section 851.93 - [Effective 7/1/2024] Monthly review of criminal justice databases; arrest record relief

(a)

(1) On a monthly basis, the Department of Justice shall review the records in the statewide criminal justice databases, and based on information in the state summary criminal history repository, shall identify persons with records of arrest that meet the criteria set forth in paragraph (2) and are eligible for arrest record relief.

(2) A person is eligible for relief pursuant to this section, if the arrest occurred on or after January 1, 1973, and meets any of the following conditions:

(A) The arrest was for a misdemeanor offense and the charge was dismissed.

(B) The arrest was for a misdemeanor offense, there is no indication that criminal proceedings have been initiated, at least one calendar year has elapsed since the date of the arrest, and no conviction occurred, or the arrestee was acquitted of any charges that arose, from that arrest.

(C)

(i) The arrest was for a felony offense not described in clause (ii), there is no indication that criminal proceedings have been initiated, at least three calendar years have elapsed since the date of the arrest, and no conviction occurred, or the arrestee was acquitted of any charges arising, from that arrest.

(ii) If the arrest was for an offense punishable by imprisonment in the state prison for eight years or more or by imprisonment pursuant to subdivision (h) of Section 1170 for eight years or more, there is no indication that criminal proceedings have been initiated, at least six years have elapsed since the date of the arrest, and no conviction occurred, or the arrestee was acquitted of any charges arising, from that arrest.

(D) The person successfully completed any of the following, relating to that arrest:

(i) A prefiling diversion program, as defined in subdivision (d) of Section 851.87, administered by a prosecuting attorney in lieu of filing an accusatory pleading.

(ii) A drug diversion program administered by a superior court pursuant to Section 1000.5, or a deferred entry of judgment program pursuant to Section 1000 or 1000.8.

(iii) A pretrial diversion program, pursuant to Section 1000.4.

(iv) A diversion program, pursuant to Section 1001.9.

(v) A diversion program described in Chapter 2.8 (commencing with Section 1001.20), Chapter 2.8A (commencing with Section 1001.35), Chapter 2.81 (commencing with Section 1001.40), Chapter 2.9 (commencing with Section 1001.50), Chapter 2.9A (commencing with Section 1001.60), Chapter 2.9B (commencing with Section 1001.70), Chapter 2.9C (commencing with Section 1001.80), Chapter 2.9D (commencing with Section 1001.81), or Chapter 2.92 (commencing with Section 1001.85), of Title 6.

(b)

(1) The department shall grant relief to a person identified pursuant to subdivision (a), without requiring a petition or motion by a party for that relief if the relevant information is present in the department's electronic records.

(2) The state summary criminal history information shall include, directly next to or below the entry or entries regarding the person's arrest record, a note stating "arrest relief granted," listing the date that the department granted relief, and this section. This note shall be included in all statewide criminal databases with a record of the arrest.

(3) Except as otherwise provided in subdivision (d), an arrest for which arrest relief has been granted is deemed not to have occurred, and a person who has been granted arrest relief is released from any penalties and disabilities resulting from the arrest, and may answer any question relating to that arrest accordingly.

(c) On a monthly basis, the department shall electronically submit a notice to the superior court having jurisdiction over the criminal case, informing the court of all cases for which a complaint was filed in that jurisdiction and for which relief was granted pursuant to this section. Commencing on August 1, 2022, for any record retained by the court pursuant to Section 68152 of the Government Code, except as provided in subdivision (d), the court shall not disclose information concerning an arrest that is granted relief pursuant to this section to any person or entity, in any format, except to the person whose arrest was granted relief or a criminal justice agency, as defined in Section 851.92.

(d) Relief granted pursuant to this section is subject to all of the following conditions:

(1) Arrest relief does not relieve a person of the obligation to disclose an arrest in response to a direct question contained in a questionnaire or application for employment as a peace officer, as defined in Section 830.

(2) Relief granted pursuant to this section has no effect on the ability of a criminal justice agency, as defined in Section 851.92, to access and use records that are granted relief to the same extent that would have been permitted for a criminal justice agency had relief not been granted.

(3) This section does not limit the ability of a district attorney to prosecute, within the applicable statute of limitations, an offense for which arrest relief has been granted pursuant to this section.

(4) Relief granted pursuant to this section does not affect a person's authorization to own, possess, or have in the person's custody or control a firearm, or the person's susceptibility to conviction under Chapter 2 (commencing with Section 29800) of Division 9 of Title 4 of Part 6, if the arrest would otherwise affect this authorization or susceptibility.

(5) Relief granted pursuant to this section does not affect any prohibition from holding public office that would otherwise apply under law as a result of the arrest.

(6) Relief granted pursuant to this section does not affect the authority to receive, or take adverse action based on, criminal history information, including the authority to receive certified court records received or evaluated pursuant to Section 1522, 1568.09, 1569.17, or 1596.871 of the Health and Safety Code, or pursuant to any statutory or regulatory provisions that incorporate the criteria of those sections.

(e) This section does not limit petitions, motions, or orders for arrest record relief, as required or authorized by any other law, including, but not limited to, Sections 851.87, 851.90, 851.91, 1000.4, and 1001.9.

(f) The department shall annually publish on the OpenJustice Web portal, as described under Section 13010, statistics for each county regarding the total number of arrests granted relief pursuant to this section and the percentage of arrests for which the state summary criminal history information does not include a disposition.

(g) This section shall be operative commencing July 1, 2024, subject to an appropriation in the annual Budget Act.

Amended by Stats 2023 ch 47 (AB 134),s 5, eff. 7/10/2023.

Added by Stats 2022 ch 814 (SB 731),s 4, eff. 1/1/2023.

Chapter 5A - UNIFORM ACT ON FRESH PURSUIT

Section 852 - Short title

This chapter may be cited as the Uniform Act on Fresh Pursuit.

Chapter heading amended by Stats 2015 ch 303 (AB 731),s 393, eff. 1/1/2016.

Added by Stats. 1937, Ch. 301.

Section 852.1 - Definitions

As used in this chapter:

(a) "State" means any State of the United States and the District of Columbia.

(b) "Peace officer" means any peace officer or member of any duly organized State, county, or municipal peace unit or police force of another State.

(c) "Fresh Pursuit" includes close pursuit and hot pursuit.

Added by Stats. 1937, Ch. 301.

Section 852.2 - Authority to arrest and hold person in custody

Any peace officer of another State, who enters this State in fresh pursuit, and continues within this State in fresh pursuit, of a person in order to arrest him on the ground that he has committed a felony in the other State, has the same authority to arrest and hold the

person in custody, as peace officers of this State have to arrest and hold a person in custody on the ground that he has committed a felony in this State.
Added by Stats. 1937, Ch. 301.

Section 852.3 - Hearing
If an arrest is made in this State by a peace officer of another State in accordance with the provisions of section 852.2 of this code, he shall without unnecessary delay take the person arrested before a magistrate of the county in which the arrest was made, who shall conduct a hearing for the purpose of determining the lawfulness of the arrest. If the magistrate determines that the arrest was lawful, he shall commit the person arrested to await a reasonable time for the issuance of an extradition warrant by the Governor of this State or admit him to bail for such purpose. If the magistrate determines that the arrest was unlawful he shall discharge the person arrested.
Added by Stats. 1937, Ch. 301.

Section 852.4 - Construction
Section 852.2 of this code shall not be construed so as to make unlawful any arrest in this State which would otherwise be lawful.
Added by Stats. 1937, Ch. 301.

Chapter 5B - INTERSTATE JURISDICTION
Article 1 - COLORADO RIVER CRIME ENFORCEMENT COMPACT
Section 853.1 - Ratification; purpose; operative date
(a) Pursuant to the authority vested in this state by Section 112 of Title 4 of the United States Code, the Legislature of the State of California hereby ratifies the Colorado River Crime Enforcement Compact as set forth in Section 853.2.
(b) The purpose of this compact is to promote the interests of justice with regard to crimes committed on the Colorado River by avoiding jurisdictional issues as to whether a criminal act sought to be prosecuted was committed on one side or the other of the exact boundary of the channel, and thus avoiding the risk that an offender may go free on technical grounds because neither state is able to establish that the offense was committed within its boundaries.
(c) This compact shall become operative when ratified by law in the State of Arizona; and shall remain in full force and effect so long as the provisions of this compact, as ratified by the State of Arizona, remain substantively the same as the provisions of this compact, as ratified by this section. This compact may be amended in the same manner as is required for it to be ratified to become operative.
Added by Stats. 1985, Ch. 754, Sec. 1.

Section 853.2 - Concurrent jurisdiction
(a) All courts and officers now or hereafter having and exercising jurisdiction in any county which is now or may hereafter be formed in any part of this state bordering upon the Colorado River, or any lake formed by, or which is a part of, the Colorado River, shall have and exercise jurisdiction in all criminal cases upon those waters concurrently with the courts of and officers of the State of Arizona, so far and to the extent that any of these bodies of water form a common boundary between this state and the State of Arizona. In addition, the officers shall have concurrent jurisdiction with the officers of the State of Arizona on any land mass within 25 air miles of the Colorado River, or within 25 air miles of any lake formed by, or that is a part of, the Colorado River.
(b) This section applies only to those crimes which are established in common between the States of Arizona and California; and an acquittal or conviction and sentence by one state shall bar a prosecution for the same act or omission by the other.
(c) This compact shall not be construed to bar the enforcement of the penal laws of either state not established in common with the other, provided that the act or omission proscribed occurs on that state's side of the river channel boundary.
(d) This compact does not apply to Division 3.5 (commencing with Section 9840) of the Vehicle Code, relating to registration of vessels, or to Section 658.7 of the Harbors and Navigation Code, relating to the display of a ski flag.
Amended by Stats. 1994, Ch. 348, Sec. 1. Effective January 1, 1995. Note: This section constitutes the primary text of the Colorado River Crime Enforcement Compact. Section 853.1 provides for ratification, operation, and amendment of the compact.

Article 2 - CALIFORNIA-NEVADA COMPACT FOR JURISDICTION ON INTERSTATE WATERS
Section 853.3 - Ratification; legislative findings and intent
(a) Pursuant to the authority vested in this state by Section 112 of Title 4 of the United States Code, the Legislature of the State of California hereby ratifies the California-Nevada Compact for Jurisdiction on Interstate Waters as set forth in Section 853.4.
(b) The Legislature finds that law enforcement has been impaired in sections of Lake Tahoe and Topaz Lake forming an interstate boundary between California and Nevada because of difficulty in determining precisely where a criminal act was committed.
(c) The Legislature intends that a person arrested for an act that is illegal in both states should not be freed merely because neither state could establish that a crime was committed within its boundaries.
(d) The California-Nevada Compact for Jurisdiction on Interstate Waters is enacted to provide for the enforcement of the laws of this state with regard to certain acts committed on Lake Tahoe or Topaz Lake, on either side of the boundary line between California and Nevada.
Added by Stats. 1995, Ch. 526, Sec. 5. Effective January 1, 1996.

Section 853.4 - Concurrent jurisdiction
(a) As used in this compact, unless the context otherwise requires, "party state" means a state that has enacted this compact.
(b) If conduct is prohibited by the party states, courts and law enforcement officers in either state who have jurisdiction over criminal offenses committed in a county where Lake Tahoe or Topaz Lake forms a common interstate boundary have concurrent jurisdiction to arrest, prosecute, and try offenders for the prohibited conduct committed anywhere on the body of water forming a boundary between the two states.
(c) This section applies only to those crimes that are established in common between the States of Nevada and California, and an acquittal or conviction and sentence by one state shall bar a prosecution for the same act or omission by the other.
(d) This compact does not authorize any conduct prohibited by a party state.

(e) This compact shall become operative when ratified by law by the party states and shall remain in full force and effect so long as the provisions of this compact, as ratified by the State of Nevada, remain substantively the same as the provisions of this compact, as ratified by this section. This compact may be amended in the same manner as is required for it to become operative.

Added by Stats. 1995, Ch. 526, Sec. 5. Effective January 1, 1996. [Note: This section constitutes the primary text of the California-Nevada Compact for Jurisdiction on Interstate Waters, with subd. (e) providing for its operation and amendment. Section 853.3 provides for ratification of the compact.]

Chapter 5C - CITATIONS FOR MISDEMEANORS

Section 853.5 - Release of person arrested for infraction; submission of thumbprint; factual innocence

(a) Except as otherwise provided by law, in any case in which a person is arrested for an offense declared to be an infraction, the person may be released according to the procedures set forth by this chapter for the release of persons arrested for an offense declared to be a misdemeanor. In all cases, except as specified in Sections 40302, 40303, 40305, and 40305.5 of the Vehicle Code, in which a person is arrested for an infraction, a peace officer shall only require the arrestee to present his or her driver's license or other satisfactory evidence of his or her identity for examination and to sign a written promise to appear contained in a notice to appear. If the arrestee does not have a driver's license or other satisfactory evidence of identity in his or her possession, the officer may require the arrestee to place a right thumbprint, or a left thumbprint or fingerprint if the person has a missing or disfigured right thumb, on the notice to appear. Except for law enforcement purposes relating to the identity of the arrestee, no person or entity may sell, give away, allow the distribution of, include in a database, or create a database with, this print. Only if the arrestee refuses to sign a written promise, has no satisfactory identification, or refuses to provide a thumbprint or fingerprint may the arrestee be taken into custody.

(b) A person contesting a charge by claiming under penalty of perjury not to be the person issued the notice to appear may choose to submit a right thumbprint, or a left thumbprint if the person has a missing or disfigured right thumb, to the issuing court through his or her local law enforcement agency for comparison with the one placed on the notice to appear. A local law enforcement agency providing this service may charge the requester no more than the actual costs. The issuing court may refer the thumbprint submitted and the notice to appear to the prosecuting attorney for comparison of the thumbprints. When there is no thumbprint or fingerprint on the notice to appear, or when the comparison of thumbprints is inconclusive, the court shall refer the notice to appear or copy thereof back to the issuing agency for further investigation, unless the court finds that referral is not in the interest of justice.

(c) Upon initiation of the investigation or comparison process by referral of the court, the court shall continue the case and the speedy trial period shall be tolled for 45 days.

(d) Upon receipt of the issuing agency's or prosecuting attorney's response, the court may make a finding of factual innocence pursuant to Section 530.6 if the court determines that there is insufficient evidence that the person cited is the person charged and shall immediately notify the Department of Motor Vehicles of its determination. If the Department of Motor Vehicles determines the citation or citations in question formed the basis of a suspension or revocation of the person's driving privilege, the department shall immediately set aside the action.

(e) If the prosecuting attorney or issuing agency fails to respond to a court referral within 45 days, the court shall make a finding of factual innocence pursuant to Section 530.6, unless the court finds that a finding of factual innocence is not in the interest of justice.

Amended by Stats 2003 ch 467 (SB 752), s 2, eff. 1/1/2004.

Section 853.6 - [Effective until 1/1/2026] Release of person arrested for misdemeanor; notice to appear

(a)

(1) When a person is arrested for an offense declared to be a misdemeanor, including a violation of a city or county ordinance, and does not demand to be taken before a magistrate, that person shall, instead of being taken before a magistrate, be released according to the procedures set forth by this chapter, although nothing prevents an officer from first booking an arrestee pursuant to subdivision (g). If the person is released, the officer or the officer's superior shall prepare in duplicate a written notice to appear in court, containing the name and address of the person, the offense charged, and the time when, and place where, the person shall appear in court. If, pursuant to subdivision (i), the person is not released prior to being booked and the officer in charge of the booking or the officer's superior determines that the person should be released, the officer or the officer's superior shall prepare a written notice to appear in a court.

(2) When a person is arrested for a misdemeanor violation of a protective court order involving domestic violence, as defined in Section 13700, or arrested pursuant to a policy, as described in Section 13701, the person shall be taken before a magistrate instead of being released according to the procedures set forth in this chapter, unless the arresting officer determines that there is not a reasonable likelihood that the offense will continue or resume or that the safety of persons or property would be imminently endangered by release of the person arrested. Prior to adopting these provisions, each city, county, or city and county shall develop a protocol to assist officers to determine when arrest and release is appropriate, rather than taking the arrested person before a magistrate. The county shall establish a committee to develop the protocol, consisting of, at a minimum, the police chief or county sheriff within the jurisdiction, the district attorney, county counsel, city attorney, representatives from domestic violence shelters, domestic violence councils, and other relevant community agencies.

(3) This subdivision does not apply to the crimes specified in Section 1270.1, including crimes defined in each of the following:

(A) Paragraph (1) of subdivision (e) of Section 243.

(B) Section 273.5.

(C) Section 273.6, if the detained person made threats to kill or harm, has engaged in violence against, or has gone to the residence or workplace of, the protected party.

(D) Section 646.9.

(4) This subdivision shall not affect a defendant's ability to be released on bail or on their own recognizance, except as specified in Section 1270.1.

(b) Unless waived by the person, the time specified in the notice to appear shall be at least 10 days after arrest if the duplicate notice is to be filed by the officer with the magistrate.

(c) The place specified in the notice shall be the court of the magistrate before whom the person would be taken if the requirement of taking an arrested person before a magistrate were complied with, or shall be an officer authorized by that court to receive a deposit of bail.

(d) The officer shall deliver one copy of the notice to appear to the arrested person, and the arrested person, in order to secure release, shall give their written promise to appear in court as specified in the notice by signing the duplicate notice, which shall be retained by the officer, and the officer may require the arrested person, if the arrested person has no satisfactory identification, to place a right thumbprint, or a left thumbprint or fingerprint if the person has a missing or disfigured right thumb, on the notice to appear. Except for law enforcement purposes relating to the identity of the arrestee, a person or entity shall not sell, give away, allow the distribution of, include in a database, or create a database with, this print. Upon the signing of the duplicate notice, the arresting officer shall immediately release the person arrested from custody.

(e) The officer shall, as soon as practicable, file the duplicate notice, as follows:

(1) It shall be filed with the magistrate if the offense charged is an infraction.

(2) It shall be filed with the magistrate if the prosecuting attorney has previously directed the officer to do so.

(3)

(A) The duplicate notice and underlying police reports in support of the charge or charges shall be filed with the prosecuting attorney in cases other than those specified in paragraphs (1) and (2).

(B) If the duplicate notice is filed with the prosecuting attorney, the prosecuting attorney, within their discretion, may initiate prosecution by filing the notice or a formal complaint with the magistrate specified in the duplicate notice within 25 days from the time of arrest. If the prosecution is not to be initiated, the prosecutor shall send notice to the person arrested at the address on the notice to appear. The failure by the prosecutor to file the notice or formal complaint within 25 days of the time of the arrest shall not bar further prosecution of the misdemeanor charged in the notice to appear. However, any further prosecution shall be preceded by a new and separate citation or an arrest warrant.

(C) Upon the filing of the notice with the magistrate by the officer, or the filing of the notice or formal complaint by the prosecutor, the magistrate may fix the amount of bail that in the magistrate's judgment, in accordance with Section 1275, is reasonable and sufficient for the appearance of the defendant and shall endorse upon the notice a statement signed by the magistrate in the form set forth in Section 815a. The defendant may, prior to the date upon which the defendant promised to appear in court, deposit with the magistrate the amount of bail set by the magistrate. At the time the case is called for arraignment before the magistrate, if the defendant does not appear, either in person or by counsel, the magistrate may declare the bail forfeited, and may, in the magistrate's discretion, order that further proceedings shall not be had in the case, unless the defendant has been charged with a violation of Section 374.3 or 374.7 of this code or of Section 11357, 11360, or 13002 of the Health and Safety Code, or a violation punishable under Section 5008.7 of the Public Resources Code, and the defendant has previously been convicted of a violation of that section or a violation that is punishable under that section, except when the magistrate finds that undue hardship will be imposed upon the defendant by requiring the defendant to appear, the magistrate may declare the bail forfeited and order that further proceedings not be had in the case.

(D) Upon the making of the order that further proceedings not be had, all sums deposited as bail shall immediately be paid into the county treasury for distribution pursuant to Section 1463.

(f) A warrant shall not be issued for the arrest of a person who has given a written promise to appear in court, unless and until the person has violated that promise or has failed to deposit bail, to appear for arraignment, trial, or judgment, or to comply with the terms and provisions of the judgment, as required by law.

(g) The officer may book the arrested person at the scene or at the arresting agency prior to release or indicate on the citation that the arrested person shall appear at the arresting agency to be booked or indicate on the citation that the arrested person shall appear at the arresting agency to be fingerprinted prior to the date the arrested person appears in court. If it is indicated on the citation that the arrested person shall be booked or fingerprinted prior to the date of the person's court appearance, the arresting agency, at the time of booking or fingerprinting, shall provide the arrested person with verification of the booking or fingerprinting by making an entry on the citation. If it is indicated on the citation that the arrested person is to be booked or fingerprinted, the magistrate, judge, or court shall, before the proceedings begin, order the defendant to provide verification that the defendant was booked or fingerprinted by the arresting agency. If the defendant cannot produce the verification, the magistrate, judge, or court shall require that the defendant be booked or fingerprinted by the arresting agency before the next court appearance, and that the defendant provide the verification at the next court appearance unless both parties stipulate that booking or fingerprinting is not necessary.

(h) A peace officer shall use the written notice to appear procedure set forth in this section for any misdemeanor offense in which the officer has arrested a person without a warrant pursuant to Section 836 or in which the officer has taken custody of a person pursuant to Section 847.

(i) When a person is arrested by a peace officer for a misdemeanor, that person shall be released according to the procedures set forth in this chapter unless one of the following is a reason for nonrelease, in which case the arresting officer may release the person, except as provided in subdivision (a), or the arresting officer shall indicate, on a form to be established by the officer's employing law enforcement agency, which of the following was a reason for the nonrelease:

(1) The person arrested was so intoxicated that they could have been a danger to themselves or to others.

(2) The person arrested required medical examination or medical care or was otherwise unable to care for their own safety.

(3) The person was arrested under one or more of the circumstances listed in Sections 40302 and 40303 of the Vehicle Code.

(4) There were one or more outstanding arrest warrants for the person.

(5) The person could not provide satisfactory evidence of personal identification.

(6) The prosecution of the offense or offenses for which the person was arrested, or the prosecution of any other offense or offenses, would be jeopardized by immediate release of the person arrested.

(7) There was a reasonable likelihood that the offense or offenses would continue or resume, or that the safety of persons or property would be imminently endangered by release of the person arrested.

(8) The person arrested demanded to be taken before a magistrate or refused to sign the notice to appear.

(9) There is reason to believe that the person would not appear at the time and place specified in the notice. The basis for this determination shall be specifically stated.

(10)

    (A) The person was subject to Section 1270.1.

    (B) The form shall be filed with the arresting agency as soon as practicable and shall be made available to any party having custody of the arrested person, subsequent to the arresting officer, and to any person authorized by law to release the arrested person from custody before trial.

(11) The person has been cited, arrested, or convicted for misdemeanor or felony theft from a store in the previous six months.

(12) There is probable cause to believe that the person arrested is guilty of committing organized retail theft, as defined in subdivision (a) of Section 490.4.

(j)

    (1) Once the arresting officer has prepared the written notice to appear and has delivered a copy to the person arrested, the officer shall deliver the remaining original and all copies as provided by subdivision (e).

    (2) Any person, including the arresting officer and any member of the officer's department or agency, or any peace officer, who alters, conceals, modifies, nullifies, or destroys, or causes to be altered, concealed, modified, nullified, or destroyed, the face side of the remaining original or a copy of a citation that was retained by the officer, for any reason, before it is filed with the magistrate or with a person authorized by the magistrate to receive deposit of bail, is guilty of a misdemeanor.

    (3) If, after an arrested person has signed and received a copy of a notice to appear, the arresting officer determines that, in the interest of justice, the citation or notice should be dismissed, the arresting agency may recommend, in writing, to the magistrate that the charges be dismissed. The recommendation shall cite the reasons for the recommendation and shall be filed with the court.

    (4) If the magistrate makes a finding that there are grounds for dismissal, the finding shall be entered in the record and the charges dismissed.

    (5) A personal relationship with any officer, public official, or law enforcement agency shall not be grounds for dismissal.

(k)

    (1) A person contesting a charge by claiming under penalty of perjury not to be the person issued the notice to appear may choose to submit a right thumbprint, or a left thumbprint if the person has a missing or disfigured right thumb, to the issuing court through the person's local law enforcement agency for comparison with the one placed on the notice to appear. A local law enforcement agency providing this service may charge the requester no more than the actual costs. The issuing court may refer the thumbprint submitted and the notice to appear to the prosecuting attorney for comparison of the thumbprints. When there is no thumbprint or fingerprint on the notice to appear, or when the comparison of thumbprints is inconclusive, the court shall refer the notice to appear or copy thereof back to the issuing agency for further investigation, unless the court finds that referral is not in the interest of justice.

    (2) Upon initiation of the investigation or comparison process by referral of the court, the court shall continue the case and the speedy trial period shall be tolled for 45 days.

    (3) Upon receipt of the issuing agency's or prosecuting attorney's response, the court may make a finding of factual innocence pursuant to Section 530.6 if the court determines that there is insufficient evidence that the person cited is the person charged and shall immediately notify the Department of Motor Vehicles of its determination. If the Department of Motor Vehicles determines the citation or citations in question formed the basis of a suspension or revocation of the person's driving privilege, the department shall immediately set aside the action.

    (4) If the prosecuting attorney or issuing agency fails to respond to a court referral within 45 days, the court shall make a finding of factual innocence pursuant to Section 530.6, unless the court finds that a finding of factual innocence is not in the interest of justice.

    (5) The citation or notice to appear may be held by the prosecuting attorney or issuing agency for future adjudication should the arrestee who received the citation or notice to appear be found.

(l) For purposes of this section, the term "arresting agency" includes any other agency designated by the arresting agency to provide booking or fingerprinting services.

(m) This section shall remain in effect only until January 1, 2026, and as of that date is repealed.

Amended by Stats 2022 ch 856 (AB 2294),s 1, eff. 9/30/2022.

Amended by Stats 2019 ch 497 (AB 991),s 199, eff. 1/1/2020.

Amended by Stats 2019 ch 25 (SB 94),s 34, eff. 6/27/2019.

Added by Stats 2018 ch 803 (AB 1065),s 4, eff. 1/1/2019.

Section 853.6 - [Operative 1/1/2026] Release of person arrested for misdemeanor; notice to appear

(a)

    (1) When a person is arrested for an offense declared to be a misdemeanor, including a violation of a city or county ordinance, and does not demand to be taken before a magistrate, that person shall, instead of being taken before a magistrate, be released according to the procedures set forth by this chapter, however an officer may first book an arrestee pursuant to subdivision (g). If the person is released, the officer or the officer's superior shall prepare, in duplicate, a written notice to appear in court, containing the name and address of the person, the offense charged, and the time when, and place where, the person shall appear in court. If, pursuant to subdivision (i), the person is not released prior to being booked and the officer in charge of the booking or the officer's superior determines that the person should be released, the officer or the officer's superior shall prepare a written notice to appear in a court.

    (2) When a person is arrested for a misdemeanor violation of a protective court order involving domestic violence, as defined in subdivision (b) of Section 13700, or arrested pursuant to a policy described in Section 13701, the person shall be taken before a magistrate instead of being released according to the procedures set forth in this chapter, unless the arresting officer determines that there is not a reasonable likelihood that the offense will continue or resume or that the safety of persons or property would be imminently endangered by release of the person arrested. Prior to adopting these provisions, each city, county, or city and county shall develop a protocol to assist officers to determine when arrest and release is appropriate, rather than taking the arrested person before a magistrate. The county shall establish a committee to develop the protocol, consisting of, at a minimum, the police chief or county sheriff within the jurisdiction, the district attorney, county counsel, city attorney, representatives from domestic violence shelters, domestic violence councils, and other relevant community agencies.

(3) This subdivision shall not apply to the crimes specified in Section 1270.1, including crimes defined in each of the following:

(A) Paragraph (1) of subdivision (e) of Section 243.

(B) Section 273.5.

(C) Section 273.6, if the detained person made threats to kill or harm, has engaged in violence against, or has gone to the residence or workplace of, the protected party.

(D) Section 646.9.

(4) This subdivision does not affect a defendant's ability to be released on bail or on their own recognizance, except as specified in Section 1270.1.

(b) Unless waived by the person, the time specified in the notice to appear shall be at least 10 days after arrest if the duplicate notice is to be filed by the officer with the magistrate.

(c) The place specified in the notice shall be the court of the magistrate before whom the person would be taken if the requirement of taking an arrested person before a magistrate were complied with, or shall be an officer authorized by that court to receive a deposit of bail.

(d) The officer shall deliver one copy of the notice to appear to the arrested person, and the arrested person, in order to secure release, shall give their written promise to appear in court as specified in the notice by signing the duplicate notice, which shall be retained by the officer. The officer may require the arrested person, if the arrested person has no satisfactory identification, to place a right thumbprint, or a left thumbprint or fingerprint if the person has a missing or disfigured right thumb, on the notice to appear. Except for law enforcement purposes relating to the identity of the arrestee, a person or entity may not sell, give away, allow the distribution of, include in a database, or create a database with, this print. Upon the person signing the duplicate notice, the arresting officer shall immediately release the person arrested from custody.

(e) The officer shall, as soon as practicable, file the duplicate notice, as follows:

(1) It shall be filed with the magistrate if the offense charged is an infraction.

(2) It shall be filed with the magistrate if the prosecuting attorney has previously directed the officer to do so.

(3)

(A) The duplicate notice and underlying police reports in support of the charge or charges shall be filed with the prosecuting attorney in cases other than those specified in paragraphs (1) and (2).

(B) If the duplicate notice is filed with the prosecuting attorney, the prosecuting attorney, within their discretion, may initiate prosecution by filing the notice or a formal complaint with the magistrate specified in the duplicate notice within 25 days from the time of arrest. If the prosecution is not to be initiated, the prosecutor shall send notice to the person arrested at the address on the notice to appear. The failure by the prosecutor to file the notice or formal complaint within 25 days of the time of the arrest shall not bar further prosecution of the misdemeanor charged in the notice to appear. However, any further prosecution shall be preceded by a new and separate citation or an arrest warrant.

(C) Upon the filing of the notice with the magistrate by the officer, or the filing of the notice or formal complaint by the prosecutor, the magistrate may fix the amount of bail that in the magistrate's judgment, in accordance with Section 1275, is reasonable and sufficient for the appearance of the defendant and shall endorse upon the notice a statement signed by the magistrate in the form set forth in Section 815a. The defendant may, prior to the date upon which the defendant promised to appear in court, deposit with the magistrate the amount of bail set by the magistrate. When the case is called for arraignment before the magistrate, if the defendant does not appear, either in person or by counsel, the magistrate may declare the bail forfeited, and may, in the magistrate's discretion, order that no further proceedings shall be had in the case, unless the defendant has been charged with a violation of Section 374.3 or 374.7 of this code or of Section 11357, 11360, or 13002 of the Health and Safety Code, or a violation punishable under Section 5008.7 of the Public Resources Code, and the defendant has previously been convicted of a violation of that section or a violation that is punishable under that section, except in cases where the magistrate finds that undue hardship will be imposed upon the defendant by requiring the defendant to appear, the magistrate may declare the bail forfeited and order that no further proceedings be had in the case.

(D) Upon the making of the order that no further proceedings be had, all sums deposited as bail shall immediately be paid into the county treasury for distribution pursuant to Section 1463.

(f) A warrant shall not be issued for the arrest of a person who has given a written promise to appear in court, unless and until the person has violated that promise or has failed to deposit bail, to appear for arraignment, trial, or judgment or to comply with the terms and provisions of the judgment, as required by law.

(g) The officer may book the arrested person at the scene or at the arresting agency prior to release or indicate on the citation that the arrested person shall appear at the arresting agency to be booked or indicate on the citation that the arrested person shall appear at the arresting agency to be fingerprinted prior to the date the arrested person appears in court. If it is indicated on the citation that the arrested person shall be booked or fingerprinted prior to the date of the person's court appearance, the arresting agency, at the time of booking or fingerprinting, shall provide the arrested person with verification of the booking or fingerprinting by making an entry on the citation. If it is indicated on the citation that the arrested person is to be booked or fingerprinted, the magistrate, judge, or court shall, before the proceedings begin, order the defendant to provide verification that the defendant was booked or fingerprinted by the arresting agency. If the defendant cannot produce the verification, the magistrate, judge, or court shall require that the defendant be booked or fingerprinted by the arresting agency before the next court appearance, and that the defendant provide the verification at the next court appearance unless both parties stipulate that booking or fingerprinting is not necessary.

(h) A peace officer shall use the written notice to appear procedure set forth in this section for any misdemeanor offense in which the officer has arrested a person without a warrant pursuant to Section 836 or in which the officer has taken custody of a person pursuant to Section 847.

(i) When a person is arrested by a peace officer for a misdemeanor, that person shall be released according to the procedures set forth by this chapter unless one of the following is a reason for nonrelease, in which case the arresting officer may release the person, except as provided in subdivision (a), or the arresting officer shall indicate, on a form to be established by the officer's employing law enforcement agency, which of the following was a reason for the nonrelease:

(1) The person arrested was so intoxicated that they could have been a danger to themselves or to others.

(2) The person arrested required medical examination or medical care or was otherwise unable to care for their own safety.

(3) The person was arrested under one or more of the circumstances listed in Sections 40302 and 40303 of the Vehicle Code.

(4) There were one or more outstanding arrest warrants for the person.

(5) The person could not provide satisfactory evidence of personal identification.

(6) The prosecution of the offense or offenses for which the person was arrested, or the prosecution of any other offense or offenses, would be jeopardized by immediate release of the person arrested.

(7) There was a reasonable likelihood that the offense or offenses would continue or resume, or that the safety of persons or property would be imminently endangered by release of the person arrested.

(8) The person arrested demanded to be taken before a magistrate or refused to sign the notice to appear.

(9) There is reason to believe that the person would not appear at the time and place specified in the notice. The basis for this determination shall be specifically stated.

(10)

    (A) The person was subject to Section 1270.1.

    (B) The form shall be filed with the arresting agency as soon as practicable and shall be made available to any party having custody of the arrested person, subsequent to the arresting officer, and to any person authorized by law to release the arrested person from custody before trial.

(j)

(1) Once the arresting officer has prepared the written notice to appear and has delivered a copy to the person arrested, the officer shall deliver the remaining original and all copies as provided by subdivision (e).

(2) A person, including the arresting officer and any member of the officer's department or agency, or any peace officer, who alters, conceals, modifies, nullifies, or destroys, or causes to be altered, concealed, modified, nullified, or destroyed, the face side of the remaining original or any copy of a citation that was retained by the officer, for any reason, before it is filed with the magistrate or with a person authorized by the magistrate to receive deposit of bail, is guilty of a misdemeanor.

(3) If, after an arrested person has signed and received a copy of a notice to appear, the arresting officer determines that, in the interest of justice, the citation or notice should be dismissed, the arresting agency may recommend, in writing, to the magistrate that the charges be dismissed. The recommendation shall cite the reasons for the recommendation and shall be filed with the court.

(4) If the magistrate makes a finding that there are grounds for dismissal, the finding shall be entered in the record and the charges dismissed.

(5) A personal relationship with any officer, public official, or law enforcement agency shall not be grounds for dismissal.

(k)

(1) A person contesting a charge by claiming under penalty of perjury not to be the person issued the notice to appear may choose to submit a right thumbprint, or a left thumbprint if the person has a missing or disfigured right thumb, to the issuing court through the person's local law enforcement agency for comparison with the one placed on the notice to appear. A local law enforcement agency providing this service may charge the requester no more than the actual costs. The issuing court may refer the thumbprint submitted and the notice to appear to the prosecuting attorney for comparison of the thumbprints. When there is no thumbprint or fingerprint on the notice to appear, or when the comparison of thumbprints is inconclusive, the court shall refer the notice to appear, or a copy thereof, back to the issuing agency for further investigation, unless the court finds that referral is not in the interest of justice.

(2) Upon initiation of the investigation or comparison process by referral of the court, the court shall continue the case and the speedy trial period shall be tolled for 45 days.

(3) Upon receipt of the issuing agency's or prosecuting attorney's response, the court may make a finding of factual innocence pursuant to Section 530.6 if the court determines that there is insufficient evidence that the person cited is the person charged and shall immediately notify the Department of Motor Vehicles of its determination. If the Department of Motor Vehicles determines the citation or citations in question formed the basis of a suspension or revocation of the person's driving privilege, the department shall immediately set aside the action.

(4) If the prosecuting attorney or issuing agency fails to respond to a court referral within 45 days, the court shall make a finding of factual innocence pursuant to Section 530.6, unless the court finds that a finding of factual innocence is not in the interest of justice.

(5) The citation or notice to appear may be held by the prosecuting attorney or issuing agency for future adjudication should the arrestee who received the citation or notice to appear be found.

(l) For purposes of this section, the term "arresting agency" includes any other agency designated by the arresting agency to provide booking or fingerprinting services.

(m) This section shall become operative January 1, 2026.

Added by Stats 2022 ch 856 (AB 2294),s 2, eff. 9/30/2022.

Section 853.6a - Arrest of juvenile

(a) Except as provided in subdivision (b), if the person arrested appears to be under the age of 18 years, and the arrest is for a violation listed in Section 256 of the Welfare and Institutions Code, other than an offense involving a firearm, the notice under Section 853.6 shall instead provide that the person shall appear before the juvenile court, a juvenile court referee, or a juvenile hearing officer within the county in which the offense charged is alleged to have been committed, and the officer shall instead, as soon as practicable, file the duplicate notice with the prosecuting attorney unless the prosecuting attorney directs the officer to file the duplicate notice with the clerk of the juvenile court, the juvenile court referee, or the juvenile hearing officer. If the notice is filed with the prosecuting attorney, within 48 hours before the date specified on the notice to appear, the prosecutor, within his or her discretion, may initiate proceedings by filing the notice or a formal petition with the clerk of the juvenile court, or the juvenile court referee or juvenile hearing officer, before whom the person is required to appear by the notice.

(b) A juvenile court may exercise the option of not requiring a mandatory appearance of the juvenile before the court for infractions contained in the Vehicle Code, except those related to drivers' licenses as specified in Division 6 (commencing with Section 12500), those related to financial responsibility as specified in Division 7 (commencing with Section 16000), those related to speeding violations as specified in Division 11 (commencing with Section 21000) in which the speed limit was violated by 15 or more miles per hour, and those involving the use or possession of alcoholic beverages as specified in Division 11.5 (commencing with Section 23500).

(c) In counties where an Expedited Youth Accountability Program is operative, as established under Section 660.5 of the Welfare and Institutions Code, a peace officer may issue a citation and written promise to appear in juvenile court or record the minor's refusal to sign the promise to appear and serve notice to appear in juvenile court, according to the requirements and procedures provided in that section.

(d) This section may not be construed to limit the discretion of a peace officer or other person with the authority to enforce laws pertaining to juveniles to take the minor into custody pursuant to Article 15 (commencing with Section 625) of the Welfare and Institutions Code.

Amended by Stats 2003 ch 149 (SB 79), s 68, eff. 1/1/2004.

Section 853.7 - Willful violation of promise to appear

Any person who willfully violates his or her written promise to appear or a lawfully granted continuance of his or her promise to appear in court is guilty of a misdemeanor, regardless of the disposition of the charge upon which he or she was originally arrested.

Amended by Stats. 1988, Ch. 403, Sec. 2.

Section 853.7a - Assessment

(a) In addition to the fees authorized or required by any other provision of law, a county may, by resolution of the board of supervisors, require the courts of that county to impose an assessment of fifteen dollars ($15) upon every person who violates his or her written promise to appear or a lawfully granted continuance of his or her promise to appear in court or before a person authorized to receive a deposit of bail, or who otherwise fails to comply with any valid court order for a violation of any provision of this code or local ordinance adopted pursuant to this code. This assessment shall apply whether or not a violation of Section 853.7 is concurrently charged or a warrant of arrest is issued pursuant to Section 853.8.

(b) The clerk of the court shall deposit the amounts collected under this section in the county treasury. All money so deposited shall be used first for the development and operation of an automated county warrant system. If sufficient funds are available after appropriate expenditures to develop, modernize, and maintain the automated warrant system, a county may use the balance to fund a warrant service task force for the purpose of serving all bench warrants within the county.

Amended by Stats 2002 ch 148 (SB 1754), s 1, eff. 1/1/2003.

Section 853.8 - Warrant for arrest after failure to appear

When a person signs a written promise to appear at the time and place specified in the written promise to appear and has not posted bail as provided in Section 853.6, the magistrate shall issue and have delivered for execution a warrant for his or her arrest within 20 days after his or her failure to appear as promised or within 20 days after his or her failure to appear after a lawfully granted continuance of his or her promise to appear.

Amended by Stats. 1988, Ch. 403, Sec. 3.

Section 853.85 - Applicability of chapter

This chapter shall not apply in any case where a person is arrested for an offense declared to be a felony.

Added by Stats. 1992, Ch. 1009, Sec. 1. Effective January 1, 1993.

Chapter 5D - FILING COMPLAINT AFTER CITATION

Section 853.9 - Complaint

(a)

(1) If written notice to appear has been prepared, delivered, and filed by an officer or the prosecuting attorney with the court pursuant to Section 853.6, an exact and legible duplicate copy of the notice when filed with the magistrate, in lieu of a verified complaint, shall constitute a complaint to which the defendant may plead "guilty" or "nolo contendere."

(2) If the defendant violates his or her promise to appear in court, or does not deposit lawful bail, or pleads other than "guilty" or "nolo contendere" to the offense charged, a complaint shall be filed which shall conform to the provisions of this code and which shall be deemed to be an original complaint; and thereafter proceedings shall be had as provided by law, except that a defendant may, by an agreement in writing, subscribed by him or her and filed with the court, waive the filing of a verified complaint and elect that the prosecution may proceed upon a written notice to appear.

(b) Notwithstanding subdivision (a), if the written notice to appear has been prepared on a form approved by the Judicial Council, an exact and legible duplicate copy of the notice when filed with the magistrate shall constitute a complaint to which the defendant may enter a plea and, if the notice to appear is verified, upon which a warrant may be issued. If the notice to appear is not verified, the defendant may, at the time of arraignment, request that a verified complaint be filed.

(c) If the notice to appear issued to and signed by the arrested person is being transmitted in electronic form, the copy of the notice to appear issued to the arrested person need not include the signature of the arrested person, unless specifically requested by the arrested person.

Amended by Stats 2016 ch 19 (AB 1927),s 1, eff. 1/1/2017.

Chapter 6 - RETAKING AFTER AN ESCAPE OR RESCUE

Section 854 - Pursuing and retaking

If a person arrested escape or is rescued, the person from whose custody he escaped or was rescued, may immediately pursue and retake him at any time and in any place within the State.

Enacted 1872.

Section 855 - Breaking open door or window of dwelling house

To retake the person escaping or rescued, the person pursuing may break open an outer or inner door or window of a dwelling house, if, after notice of his intention, he is refused admittance.

Enacted 1872.

Chapter 7 - EXAMINATION OF THE CASE, AND DISCHARGE OF THE DEFENDANT, OR HOLDING HIM TO ANSWER

Section 858 - Duties of magistrate

(a) When the defendant first appears for arraignment on a charge of having committed a public offense, the magistrate shall immediately inform the defendant of the charge against him or her, and of his or her right to the aid of counsel in every stage of the proceedings.

(b) If it appears that the defendant may be a minor, the magistrate shall ascertain whether that is the case, and if the magistrate concludes that it is probable that the defendant is a minor, and unless the defendant is a member of the Armed Forces of the United States and the offense charged is a misdemeanor, he or she shall immediately either notify the parent or guardian of the minor of the arrest or appoint counsel to represent the minor.

(c) For the purposes of this section, the Judicial Council shall revise its military service form to include information explaining the rights under Section 1170.9 and related statutes of individuals who have active duty or veteran status and shall include a space for the local court to provide the contact information for the county veterans service office. For purposes of this section, "active duty or veteran status" includes active military duty service, reserve duty status, national guard service, and veteran status.

(d) The court shall inform the defendant that there are certain provisions of law specifically designed for individuals who have active duty or veteran status and who have been charged with a crime. The court shall inform the defendant that if the defendant is on active duty in the United States military, or is a veteran of the United States military, the defendant may request a copy of the Judicial Council military form that explains those rights and may file that form with the court so that the defendant's active duty or veteran status is on file with the court. The court shall advise the defendant that the defendant should consult with counsel prior to submitting the form and that the defendant may, without penalty, decline to provide this information to the court.

(e) If the defendant acknowledges active duty or veteran status and submits the Judicial Council military service form to the court, the defendant shall file the form with the court and serve the form on the prosecuting attorney and defense counsel. The form may be used to assist in determining eligibility for services pursuant to Section 1170.9. The court shall transmit a copy of the form to the county veterans service officer for confirmation of the defendant's military service. The court shall also transmit a copy of the form to the Department of Veterans Affairs.

Amended by Stats 2014 ch 655 (SB 1110),s 1, eff. 1/1/2015.

Section 858.5 - Duties of magistrate in case in which defendant has been arrested for misdemeanor Vehicle Code violation

(a) In any case in which a defendant is, on his demand, brought before a magistrate pursuant to Section 822 after arrest for a misdemeanor Vehicle Code violation, the magistrate shall give such instructions to the defendant as required by law and inform the defendant of his rights under this section, and, if the defendant desires to plead guilty or nolo contendere to the charge in the complaint, he may so advise the magistrate. If the magistrate determines that such plea would be in the interest of justice, he shall direct the defendant to appear before a specified appropriate court in the county in which defendant has been arrested at a designated certain time, which in no case shall be more than 10 calendar days from the date of arrest, for plea and sentencing. The magistrate shall request the court in which the complaint has been filed to transmit a certified copy of the complaint and any citation and any factual report which may have been prepared by the law enforcement agency that investigated the case to the court in which defendant is to appear for plea and sentencing. If the court of which the request is made deems such action to be in the interest of justice, and the district attorney of the county in which that court sits, after notice from the court of the request it has received, does not object to such action, the court shall immediately transmit a certified copy of the complaint and the report of the law enforcement agency that investigated the case, and, if not, shall advise the requesting magistrate of its decision not to take such action. When defendant appears for plea and sentencing, and if a copy of the complaint has been transmitted, the court shall read the copy of the complaint to him, and the defendant may plead guilty or nolo contendere. Such court shall have jurisdiction to accept the plea and impose a sentence. Such court shall notify the court in which the complaint was originally filed of the disposition of the case. If defendant does not plead guilty or nolo contendere, or if transmittal of a copy of the complaint has been refused or if a copy of the complaint has not been received, the court shall terminate the proceedings under this section and shall direct the defendant to appear before the court or magistrate by whom the warrant was issued on or before a certain day which in no case shall be more than five days after the date such direction is made.

(b) Any fines imposed by a court which is given authority to sentence pursuant to this section shall be remitted to the court in which the complaint was originally filed for disposition as required by law. The county of the sentencing court shall bear all costs incurred incident to acceptance of the plea and sentencing, and no part of such costs shall be deducted from the fine remitted to the court in which the complaint was filed.

Added by Stats. 1965, Ch. 947.

Section 858.7 - Duties of magistrate in case in which defendant convicted of misdemeanor and serving sentence is charged with misdemeanor Vehicle Code violation

(a) In any case in which the defendant has been convicted of a misdemeanor and is serving a sentence as a result of such conviction and there has been filed and is pending in another county a complaint charging him with a misdemeanor Vehicle Code violation, the defendant may appear before the court that sentenced him, and a magistrate of that court shall give such instructions to the defendant as required by law and inform the defendant of his rights under this section, and, if the defendant desires to plead guilty or nolo contendere to the charge in the complaint, he may so advise the magistrate. If the magistrate determines that such plea would be in the interest of justice, he shall direct the defendant to appear before a specified appropriate court in the county in which defendant is serving his sentence at a designated certain time for plea and sentencing. The magistrate shall request the court in which the complaint has been filed to transmit a certified copy of the complaint and any citation and any factual report which may have been prepared by the law enforcement agency that investigated the case to the court in which defendant is to appear for plea and sentencing. If the court of which the request is made deems such action to be in the interest of justice, and the district attorney of the county in which that court sits, after notice from the court of the request it has received, does not object to such action, the court shall immediately transmit a certified copy of the complaint and any report of the law enforcement agency that investigated the case, and, if not, shall advise the requesting magistrate of its decision not to take such action. When defendant appears for plea and sentencing, and if a copy of the complaint has been transmitted, the court shall read the copy of the complaint to him, and the defendant may plead guilty or nolo contendere. Such court shall have jurisdiction to accept the plea and impose a sentence. Such court shall notify the court in which the complaint was originally filed of the disposition of the case. If defendant does not plead guilty or nolo contendere, or if transmittal of a copy of the complaint has been refused or if a copy of the complaint has not been received, the court shall terminate the proceedings under this section and shall direct the defendant to appear before the court in which the complaint was filed and is pending on or before a certain day.

(b)

(1) Any fines imposed by a court which is given authority to sentence pursuant to this section shall be remitted to the court in which the complaint was originally filed for disposition as required by law. Except as otherwise provided in paragraph (2) of this subdivision, the county of the sentencing court shall bear all costs incurred incident to acceptance of the plea and sentencing, and no part of such costs shall be deducted from the fine remitted to the court in which the complaint was filed.

(2) In any case in which a defendant is sentenced to imprisonment pursuant to this section, and as a result of such sentence he is required to be imprisoned for a time in addition to, and not concurrent with, the time he is imprisoned as a result of the sentence he is otherwise serving, the county in which the complaint was originally filed shall bear the cost of such additional time of imprisonment that the defendant is required to serve. Such cost may be deducted from any fine required to be remitted pursuant to paragraph (1) of this subdivision to the court in which the complaint was originally filed.

(c) As used in this section, "complaint" includes, but is not limited to, a notice to appear which is within the provisions of Section 40513 of the Vehicle Code.

Added by Stats. 1968, Ch. 973.

Section 859 - Duties of magistrate when defendant charged with felony

When the defendant is charged with the commission of a felony by a written complaint subscribed under oath and on file in a court within the county in which the felony is triable, he or she shall, without unnecessary delay, be taken before a magistrate of the court in which the complaint is on file. The magistrate shall immediately deliver to the defendant a copy of the complaint, inform the defendant that he or she has the right to have the assistance of counsel, ask the defendant if he or she desires the assistance of counsel, and allow the defendant reasonable time to send for counsel. However, in a capital case, the court shall inform the defendant that the defendant must be represented in court by counsel at all stages of the preliminary and trial proceedings and that the representation will be at the defendant's expense if the defendant is able to employ counsel or at public expense if he or she is unable to employ counsel, inquire of him or her whether he or she is able to employ counsel and, if so, whether the defendant desires to employ counsel of the defendant's choice or to have counsel assigned for him or her, and allow the defendant a reasonable time to send for his or her chosen or assigned counsel. If the defendant desires and is unable to employ counsel, the court shall assign counsel to defend him or her; in a capital case, if the defendant is able to employ counsel and either refuses to employ counsel or appears without counsel after having had a reasonable time to employ counsel, the court shall assign counsel to defend him or her. If it appears that the defendant may be a minor, the magistrate shall ascertain whether that is the case, and if the magistrate concludes that it is probable that the defendant is a minor, he or she shall immediately either notify the parent or guardian of the minor, by telephone or messenger, of the arrest, or appoint counsel to represent the minor.

Amended by Stats. 1998, Ch. 931, Sec. 368. Effective September 28, 1998. Note: This section was added on June 5, 1990, by initiative Prop. 115.

Section 859.1 - Hearing to determine whether testimony of minor or dependent person shall be closed to public

(a) In any criminal proceeding in which the defendant is charged with any offense specified in Section 868.8 on a minor under the age of 16 years, or a dependent person with a substantial cognitive impairment, as defined in paragraph (3) of subdivision (f) of Section 288, the court shall, upon motion of the prosecuting attorney, conduct a hearing to determine whether the testimony of, and testimony relating to, a minor or dependent person shall be closed to the public in order to protect the minor's or the dependent person's reputation.

(b) In making this determination, the court shall consider all of the following:

(1) The nature and seriousness of the offense.

(2) The age of the minor, or the level of cognitive development of the dependent person.

(3) The extent to which the size of the community would preclude the anonymity of the victim.

(4) The likelihood of public opprobrium due to the status of the victim.

(5) Whether there is an overriding public interest in having an open hearing.

(6) Whether the prosecution has demonstrated a substantial probability that the identity of the witness would otherwise be disclosed to the public during that proceeding, and demonstrated a substantial probability that the disclosure of his or her identity would cause serious harm to the witness.

(7) Whether the witness has disclosed information concerning the case to the public through press conferences, public meetings, or other means.

(8) Other factors the court may deem necessary to protect the interests of justice.

Amended by Stats 2004 ch 823 (AB 20), s 11, eff. 1/1/2005.

Section 859.5 - Custodial interrogation of murder suspect; electronic recording

(a) Except as otherwise provided in this section, a custodial interrogation of any person, including an adult or a minor, who is in a fixed place of detention, and suspected of committing murder, as listed in Section 187 or 189 of this code, or paragraph (1) of subdivision (b) of Section 707 of the Welfare and Institutions Code, shall be electronically recorded in its entirety. A statement that is electronically recorded as required pursuant to this section creates a rebuttable presumption that the electronically recorded statement was, in fact, given and was accurately recorded by the prosecution's witnesses, provided that the electronic recording was made of the custodial interrogation in its entirety and the statement is otherwise admissible.

(b) The requirement for the electronic recordation of a custodial interrogation pursuant to this section shall not apply under any of the following circumstances:

(1) Electronic recording is not feasible because of exigent circumstances. An explanation of the exigent circumstances shall be documented in the police report.

(2) The person to be interrogated states that he or she will speak to a law enforcement officer only if the interrogation is not electronically recorded. If feasible, that statement shall be electronically recorded. The requirement also does not apply if the person being interrogated indicates during interrogation that he or she will not participate in further interrogation unless electronic recording ceases. If the person being interrogated refuses to record any statement, the officer shall document that refusal in writing.

(3) The custodial interrogation occurred in another jurisdiction and was conducted by law enforcement officers of that jurisdiction in compliance with the law of that jurisdiction, unless the interrogation was conducted with intent to avoid the requirements of this section.

(4) The interrogation occurs when no law enforcement officer conducting the interrogation has knowledge of facts and circumstances that would lead an officer to reasonably believe that the individual being interrogated may have committed murder for which this section requires that a custodial interrogation be recorded. If during a custodial interrogation, the individual reveals facts and circumstances giving a law enforcement officer conducting the interrogation reason to believe that murder has been committed, continued custodial interrogation concerning that offense shall be electronically recorded pursuant to this section.

(5) A law enforcement officer conducting the interrogation or the officer's superior reasonably believes that electronic recording would disclose the identity of a confidential informant or jeopardize the safety of an officer, the individual being interrogated, or another individual. An explanation of the circumstances shall be documented in the police report.

(6) The failure to create an electronic recording of the entire custodial interrogation was the result of a malfunction of the recording device, despite reasonable maintenance of the equipment, and timely repair or replacement was not feasible.

(7) The questions presented to a person by law enforcement personnel and the person's responsive statements were part of a routine processing or booking of that person. Electronic recording is not required for spontaneous statements made in response to questions asked during the routine processing of the arrest of the person.

(8) The interrogation of a person who is in custody on a charge of a violation of Section 187 or 189 of this code or paragraph (1) of subdivision (b) of Section 707 of the Welfare and Institutions Code if the interrogation is not related to any of these offenses. If, during the interrogation, any information concerning one of these offenses is raised or mentioned, continued custodial interrogation concerning that offense shall be electronically recorded pursuant to this section.

(c) If the prosecution relies on an exception in subdivision (b) to justify a failure to make an electronic recording of a custodial interrogation, the prosecution shall show by clear and convincing evidence that the exception applies.

(d) A person's statements that were not electronically recorded pursuant to this section may be admitted into evidence in a criminal proceeding or in a juvenile court proceeding, as applicable, if the court finds that all of the following apply:

(1) The statements are admissible under applicable rules of evidence.

(2) The prosecution has proven by clear and convincing evidence that the statements were made voluntarily.

(3) Law enforcement personnel made a contemporaneous audio or audio and visual recording of the reason for not making an electronic recording of the statements. This provision does not apply if it was not feasible for law enforcement personnel to make that recording.

(4) The prosecution has proven by clear and convincing evidence that one or more of the circumstances described in subdivision (b) existed at the time of the custodial interrogation.

(e) Unless the court finds that an exception in subdivision (b) applies, all of the following remedies shall be granted as relief for noncompliance:

(1) Failure to comply with any of the requirements of this section shall be considered by the court in adjudicating motions to suppress a statement of a defendant made during or after a custodial interrogation.

(2) Failure to comply with any of the requirements of this section shall be admissible in support of claims that a defendant's statement was involuntary or is unreliable, provided the evidence is otherwise admissible.

(3) If the court finds that a defendant was subject to a custodial interrogation in violation of subdivision (a), the court shall provide the jury with an instruction, to be developed by the Judicial Council, that advises the jury to view with caution the statements made in that custodial interrogation.

(f) The interrogating entity shall maintain the original or an exact copy of an electronic recording made of a custodial interrogation until a conviction for any offense relating to the interrogation is final and all direct and habeas corpus appeals are exhausted or the prosecution for that offense is barred by law or, in a juvenile court proceeding, as otherwise provided in subdivision (b) of Section 626.8 of the Welfare and Institutions Code. The interrogating entity may make one or more true, accurate, and complete copies of the electronic recording in a different format.

(g) For the purposes of this section, the following terms have the following meanings:

(1) "Custodial interrogation" means any interrogation in a fixed place of detention involving a law enforcement officer's questioning that is reasonably likely to elicit incriminating responses, and in which a reasonable person in the subject's position would consider himself or herself to be in custody, beginning when a person should have been advised of his or her constitutional rights, including the right to remain silent, the right to have counsel present during any interrogation, and the right to have counsel appointed if the person is unable to afford counsel, and ending when the questioning has completely finished.

(2)

(A) For the purposes of the custodial interrogation of a minor, pursuant to subdivision (a) or (b), "electronically recorded," "electronic recordation," and "electronic recording" refer to a video recording that accurately records a custodial interrogation.

(B) For the purposes of the custodial interrogation of an adult, pursuant to subdivision (a) or (b), "electronically recorded," "electronic recordation," and "electronic recording" refer to a video or audio recording that accurately records a custodial interrogation. The Legislature encourages law enforcement agencies to use video recording when available.

(3) "Fixed place of detention" means a fixed location under the control of a law enforcement agency where an individual is held in detention in connection with a criminal offense that has been, or may be, filed against that person, including a jail, police or sheriff's station, holding cell, correctional or detention facility, juvenile hall, or a facility of the Division of Juvenile Facilities.

(4) "Law enforcement officer" means a person employed by a law enforcement agency whose duties include enforcing criminal laws or investigating criminal activity, or any other person who is acting at the request or direction of that person.

Amended by Stats 2016 ch 791 (SB 1389),s 2, eff. 1/1/2017.

Added by Stats 2013 ch 799 (SB 569),s 2, eff. 1/1/2014.

Section 859.7 - Regulations for conducting photo lineups and live lineups with eyewitnesses

(a) All law enforcement agencies and prosecutorial entities shall adopt regulations for conducting photo lineups and live lineups with eyewitnesses. The regulations shall be developed to ensure reliable and accurate suspect identifications. In order to ensure reliability and accuracy, the regulations shall comply with, at a minimum, the following requirements:

(1) Prior to conducting the identification procedure, and as close in time to the incident as possible, the eyewitness shall provide the description of the perpetrator of the offense.

(2) The investigator conducting the identification procedure shall use blind administration or blinded administration during the identification procedure.

(3) The investigator shall state in writing the reason that the presentation of the lineup was not conducted using blind administration, if applicable.

(4) An eyewitness shall be instructed of the following, prior to any identification procedure:

(A) The perpetrator may or may not be among the persons in the identification procedure.

(B) The eyewitness should not feel compelled to make an identification.

(C) An identification or failure to make an identification will not end the investigation.

(5) An identification procedure shall be composed so that the fillers generally fit the eyewitness' description of the perpetrator. In the case of a photo lineup, the photograph of the person suspected as the perpetrator should, if practicable, resemble his or her appearance at the time of the offense and not unduly stand out.

(6) In a photo lineup, writings or information concerning any previous arrest of the person suspected as the perpetrator shall not be visible to the eyewitness.

(7) Only one suspected perpetrator shall be included in any identification procedure.

(8) All eyewitnesses shall be separated when viewing an identification procedure.

(9) Nothing shall be said to the eyewitness that might influence the eyewitness' identification of the person suspected as the perpetrator.

(10) If the eyewitness identifies a person he or she believes to be the perpetrator, all of the following shall apply:

(A) The investigator shall immediately inquire as to the eyewitness' confidence level in the accuracy of the identification and record in writing, verbatim, what the eyewitness says.

(B) Information concerning the identified person shall not be given to the eyewitness prior to obtaining the eyewitness' statement of confidence level and documenting the exact words of the eyewitness.

(C) The officer shall not validate or invalidate the eyewitness' identification.

(11) An electronic recording shall be made that includes both audio and visual representations of the identification procedures. Whether it is feasible to make a recording with both audio and visual representations shall be determined on a case-by-case basis. When it is not feasible to make a recording with both audio and visual representations, audio recording may be used. When audio recording without video recording is used, the investigator shall state in writing the reason that video recording was not feasible.

(b) Nothing in this section is intended to affect policies for field show up procedures.

(c) For purposes of this section, the following terms have the following meanings:

(1) "Blind administration" means the administrator of an eyewitness identification procedure does not know the identity of the suspect.

(2) "Blinded administration" means the administrator of an eyewitness identification procedure may know who the suspect is, but does not know where the suspect, or his or her photo, as applicable, has been placed or positioned in the identification procedure through the use of any of the following:

(A) An automated computer program that prevents the administrator from seeing which photos the eyewitness is viewing until after the identification procedure is completed.

(B) The folder shuffle method, which refers to a system for conducting a photo lineup by placing photographs in folders, randomly numbering the folders, shuffling the folders, and then presenting the folders sequentially so that the administrator cannot see or track which photograph is being presented to the eyewitness until after the procedure is completed.

(C) Any other procedure that achieves neutral administration and prevents the lineup administrator from knowing where the suspect or his or her photo, as applicable, has been placed or positioned in the identification procedure.

(3) "Eyewitness" means a person whose identification of another person may be relevant in a criminal investigation.

(4) "Field show up" means a procedure in which a suspect is detained shortly after the commission of a crime and who, based on his or her appearance, his or her distance from the crime scene, or other circumstantial evidence, is suspected of having just committed a crime. In these situations, the victim or an eyewitness is brought to the scene of the detention and is asked if the detainee was the perpetrator.

(5) "Filler" means either a person or a photograph of a person who is not suspected of an offense and is included in an identification procedure.

(6) "Identification procedure" means either a photo lineup or a live lineup.

(7) "Investigator" means the person conducting the identification procedure.

(8) "Live lineup" means a procedure in which a group of persons, including the person suspected as the perpetrator of an offense and other persons not suspected of the offense, are displayed to an eyewitness for the purpose of determining whether the eyewitness is able to identify the suspect as the perpetrator.

(9) "Photo lineup" means a procedure in which an array of photographs, including a photograph of the person suspected as the perpetrator of an offense and additional photographs of other persons not suspected of the offense, are displayed to an eyewitness for the purpose of determining whether the eyewitness is able to identify the suspect as the perpetrator.

(d) Nothing in this section is intended to preclude the admissibility of any relevant evidence or to affect the standards governing the admissibility of evidence under the United States Constitution.

(e) This section shall become operative on January 1, 2020.

Added by Stats 2018 ch 977 (SB 923),s 2, eff. 1/1/2019.

Section 859a - Duties of magistrate if public offense charged is felony and punishable with death

(a) If the public offense charged is a felony not punishable with death, the magistrate shall immediately upon the appearance of counsel for the defendant read the complaint to the defendant and ask him or her whether he or she pleads guilty or not guilty to the offense charged therein and to a previous conviction or convictions of crime if charged. While the charge remains pending before the magistrate and when the defendant's counsel is present, the defendant may plead guilty to the offense charged, or, with the consent of the magistrate and the district attorney or other counsel for the people, plead nolo contendere to the offense charged or plead guilty or nolo contendere to any other offense the commission of which is necessarily included in that with which he or she is charged, or to an attempt to commit the offense charged and to the previous conviction or convictions of crime if charged upon a plea of guilty or nolo contendere. The magistrate may then fix a reasonable bail as provided by this code, and upon failure to deposit the bail or surety, shall immediately commit the defendant to the sheriff. Upon accepting the plea of guilty or nolo contendere the magistrate shall certify the case, including a copy of all proceedings therein and any testimony that in his or her discretion he or she may require to be taken, to the court in which judgment is to be pronounced at the time specified under subdivision (b), and thereupon the proceedings shall be had as if the defendant had pleaded guilty in that court. This subdivision shall not be construed to authorize the receiving of a plea of guilty or nolo contendere from any defendant not represented by counsel. If the defendant subsequently files a written motion to withdraw the plea under Section 1018, the motion shall be heard and determined by the court before which the plea was entered.

(b) Notwithstanding Section 1191 or 1203, the magistrate shall, upon the receipt of a plea of guilty or nolo contendere and upon the performance of the other duties of the magistrate under this section, immediately appoint a time for pronouncing judgment in the superior court and refer the case to the probation officer if eligible for probation, as prescribed in Section 1191.

Amended by Stats 2002 ch 784 (SB 1316), s 533, eff. 1/1/2003.

Section 859b - Duties of magistrate if public offense is felony to which defendant has not pleaded guilty

At the time the defendant appears before the magistrate for arraignment, if the public offense is a felony to which the defendant has not pleaded guilty in accordance with Section 859a, the magistrate, immediately upon the appearance of counsel, or if none appears, after waiting a reasonable time therefor as provided in Section 859, shall set a time for the examination of the case and shall allow not less than two days, excluding Sundays and holidays, for the district attorney and the defendant to prepare for the examination. The magistrate shall also issue subpoenas, duly subscribed, for witnesses within the state, required either by the prosecution or the defense. Both the defendant and the people have the right to a preliminary examination at the earliest possible time, and unless both waive that right or good cause for a continuance is found as provided for in Section 1050, the preliminary examination shall be held within 10 court days of the date the defendant is arraigned or pleads, whichever occurs later, or within 10 court days of the date criminal proceedings are reinstated pursuant to Chapter 6 (commencing with Section 1367) of Title 10 of Part 2.

Whenever the defendant is in custody, the magistrate shall dismiss the complaint if the preliminary examination is set or continued beyond 10 court days from the time of the arraignment, plea, or reinstatement of criminal proceedings pursuant to Chapter 6 (commencing with Section 1367) of Title 10 of Part 2, and the defendant has remained in custody for 10 or more court days solely on that complaint, unless either of the following occur:

(a) The defendant personally waives his or her right to preliminary examination within the 10 court days.

(b) The prosecution establishes good cause for a continuance beyond the 10-court-day period. For purposes of this subdivision, "good cause" includes, but is not limited to, those cases involving allegations that a violation of one or more of the sections specified in subdivision (a) of Section 11165.1 or in Section 11165.6 has occurred and the prosecuting attorney assigned to the case has another trial, preliminary hearing, or motion to suppress in progress in that court or another court. Any continuance under this paragraph shall be limited to a maximum of three additional court days.

If the preliminary examination is set or continued beyond the 10-court-day period, the defendant shall be released pursuant to Section 1318 unless:

(1) The defendant requests the setting of continuance of the preliminary examination beyond the 10-court-day period.

(2) The defendant is charged with a capital offense in a cause where the proof is evident and the presumption great.

(3) A witness necessary for the preliminary examination is unavailable due to the actions of the defendant.

(4) The illness of counsel.

(5) The unexpected engagement of counsel in a jury trial.

(6) Unforeseen conflicts of interest which require appointment of new counsel. The magistrate shall dismiss the complaint if the preliminary examination is set or continued more than 60 days from the date of the arraignment, plea, or reinstatement of criminal proceedings pursuant to Chapter 6 (commencing with Section 1367) of Title 10 of Part 2, unless the defendant personally waives his or her right to a preliminary examination within the 60 days.

Amended by Stats. 1996, Ch. 122, Sec. 1. Effective January 1, 1997.

Section 859c - Review of challenged ruling or order

Procedures under this code that provide for superior court review of a challenged ruling or order made by a superior court judge or a magistrate shall be performed by a superior court judge other than the judge or magistrate who originally made the ruling or order, unless agreed to by the parties.

Added by Stats. 1998, Ch. 931, Sec. 370. Effective September 28, 1998.

Section 860 - Aid of counsel if public offense is felony punishable by death or felony to which defendant has not pleaded guilty

At the time set for the examination of the case, if the public offense is a felony punishable with death, or is a felony to which the defendant has not pleaded guilty in accordance with Section 859a of this code, then, if the defendant requires the aid of counsel, the magistrate must allow the defendant a reasonable time to send for counsel, and may postpone the examination for not less than two nor more than five days for that purpose. The magistrate must, immediately after the appearance of counsel, or if, after waiting a reasonable time therefor, none appears, proceed to examine the case; provided, however, that a defendant represented by counsel may when brought before the magistrate as provided in Section 858 or at any time subsequent thereto, waive the right to an examination before such magistrate, and thereupon it shall be the duty of the magistrate to make an order holding the defendant to answer, and it shall be the duty of the district attorney within 15 days thereafter, to file in the superior court of the county in which the offense is triable the information; provided, further, however, that nothing contained herein shall prevent the district attorney nor the magistrate from requiring that an examination be held as provided in this chapter.

Amended by Stats. 1998, Ch. 931, Sec. 371. Effective September 28, 1998.

Section 861 - Preliminary examination

(a) The preliminary examination shall be completed at one session or the complaint shall be dismissed, unless the magistrate, for good cause shown by affidavit, postpones it. The postponement shall not be for more than 10 court days, unless either of the following occur:

(1) The defendant personally waives his or her right to a continuous preliminary examination.

(2) The prosecution establishes good cause for a postponement beyond the 10-court-day period. If the magistrate postpones the preliminary examination beyond the 10-court-day period, and the defendant is in custody, the defendant shall be released pursuant to subdivision (b) of Section 859b.

(b) The preliminary examination shall not be postponed beyond 60 days from the date the motion to postpone the examination is granted, unless by consent or on motion of the defendant.

(c) Nothing in this section shall preclude the magistrate from interrupting the preliminary examination to conduct brief court matters so long as a substantial majority of the court's time is devoted to the preliminary examination.

(d) A request for a continuance of the preliminary examination that is made by the defendant or his or her attorney of record for the purpose of filing a motion pursuant to paragraph (2) of subdivision (f) of Section 1538.5 shall be deemed a personal waiver of the defendant's right to a continuous preliminary examination.

Amended by Stats. 1997, Ch. 279, Sec. 2. Effective January 1, 1998.

Section 861.5 - Postponement of preliminary examination

Notwithstanding subdivision (a) of Section 861, the magistrate may postpone the preliminary examination for one court day in order to accommodate the special physical, mental, or emotional needs of a child witness who is 10 years of age or younger or a dependent person, as defined in paragraph (3) of subdivision (f) of Section 288.

The magistrate shall admonish both the prosecution and defense against coaching the witness prior to the witness' next appearance in the preliminary examination.

Amended by Stats 2005 ch 279 (SB 1107),s 7, eff. 1/1/2006

Amended by Stats 2004 ch 823 (AB 20), s 12, eff. 1/1/2005.

Section 862 - Duties of magistrate if postponement is had

If a postponement is had, the magistrate must commit the defendant for examination, admit him to bail or discharge him from custody upon the deposit of money as provided in this Code, as security for his appearance at the time to which the examination is postponed.

Enacted 1872.

Section 863 - Commitment for examination

The commitment for examination is made by an indorsement, signed by the magistrate on the warrant of arrest, to the following effect: "The within named A. B. having been brought before me under this warrant, is committed for examination to the Sheriff of _____." If the Sheriff is not present, the defendant may be committed to the custody of a peace officer.

Enacted 1872.

Section 864 - Reading of depositions of witnesses

At the examination, the magistrate must first read to the defendant the depositions of the witnesses examined on taking the information.

Amended by Stats. 1963, Ch. 1174.

Section 865 - Examination of witnesses

The witnesses must be examined in the presence of the defendant, and may be cross-examined in his behalf.

Enacted 1872.

Section 866 - Defense witnesses

(a) When the examination of witnesses on the part of the people is closed, any witness the defendant may produce shall be sworn and examined. Upon the request of the prosecuting attorney, the magistrate shall require an offer of proof from the defense as to the testimony expected from the witness. The magistrate shall not permit the testimony of any defense witness unless the offer of proof discloses to the satisfaction of the magistrate, in his or her sound discretion, that the testimony of that witness, if believed, would be reasonably likely to establish an affirmative defense, negate an element of a crime charged, or impeach the testimony of a prosecution witness or the statement of a declarant testified to by a prosecution witness.

(b) It is the purpose of a preliminary examination to establish whether there exists probable cause to believe that the defendant has committed a felony. The examination shall not be used for purposes of discovery.

(c) This section shall not be construed to compel or authorize the taking of depositions of witnesses.

Amended June 5, 1990, by initiative Proposition 115, Sec. 16.

Section 866.5 - Examination of defendant

The defendant may not be examined at the examination, unless he is represented by counsel, or unless he waives his right to counsel after being advised at such examination of his right to aid of counsel.
Added by Stats. 1953, Ch. 1482.

Section 867 - Exclusion of witnesses

While a witness is under examination, the magistrate shall, upon motion of either party, exclude all potential and actual witness who have not been examined.

The magistrate shall also order the witnesses not to converse with each other until they are all examined. The magistrate may also order, where feasible, that the witnesses be kept separated from each other until they are all examined.

This section does not apply to the investigating officer or the investigator for the defendant, nor does it apply to officers having custody of persons brought before the magistrate.

Either party may challenge the exclusion of any person under this section. Upon motion of either party, the magistrate shall hold a hearing, on the record, to determine if the person sought to be excluded is, in fact, a person excludable under this section.
Amended by Stats. 1986, Ch. 868, Sec. 1.

Section 868 - Open and public examination; exclusion

The examination shall be open and public. However, upon the request of the defendant and a finding by the magistrate that exclusion of the public is necessary in order to protect the defendant's right to a fair and impartial trial, the magistrate shall exclude from the examination every person except the clerk, court reporter and bailiff, the prosecutor and his or her counsel, the Attorney General, the district attorney of the county, the investigating officer, the officer having custody of a prisoner witness while the prisoner is testifying, the defendant and his or her counsel, the officer having the defendant in custody, and a person chosen by the prosecuting witness who is not himself or herself a witness but who is present to provide the prosecuting witness moral support, provided that the person so chosen shall not discuss prior to or during the preliminary examination the testimony of the prosecuting witness with any person, other than the prosecuting witness, who is a witness in the examination. Upon motion of the prosecution, members of the alleged victim's family shall be entitled to be present and seated during the examination. The court shall grant the motion unless the magistrate finds that the exclusion is necessary to protect the defendant's right to a fair and impartial trial, or unless information provided by the defendant or noticed by the court establishes that there is a reasonable likelihood that the attendance of members of the alleged victim's family poses a risk of affecting the content of the testimony of the victim or any other witness. The court shall admonish members of the alleged victim's family who are present and seated during the examination not to discuss any testimony with family members, witnesses, or the public. Nothing in this section shall affect the exclusion of witnesses as provided in Section 867 of the Penal Code.

For purposes of this section, members of the alleged victim's family shall include the alleged victim's spouse, parents, legal guardian, children, or siblings.
Amended by Stats. 1988, Ch. 277, Sec. 2.

Section 868.4 - Use of therapy or facility dog while testifying

(a) If requested by either party in a criminal or juvenile hearing, and if a therapy or facility dog is available to the party within the jurisdiction of the judicial district in which the case is being adjudicated, the following individuals shall be afforded the opportunity to have a therapy or facility dog accompany him or her while testifying in court, subject to the approval of the court:

(1) A child witness in a court proceeding involving any serious felony, as defined in subdivision (c) of Section 1192.7, or any violent felony, as defined in subdivision (c) of Section 667.5.

(2) A victim who is entitled to support persons pursuant to Section 868.5, in addition to any support persons selected pursuant to that section.

(b) Before a therapy or facility dog may be used pursuant to subdivision (a), the party seeking to utilize the therapy or facility dog shall file a motion with the court, which shall include the following:

(1) The training or credentials of the therapy or facility dog.

(2) The training of the therapy or facility dog handler.

(3) Facts justifying that the presence of the therapy or facility dog may reduce anxiety or otherwise be helpful to the witness while testifying.

(c) If a party, pursuant to subdivision (b), makes a showing that the therapy or facility dog and handler are suitably qualified and will reasonably assist the testifying witness, the court may grant the motion, unless the court finds the use of a therapy or facility dog would cause undue prejudice to the defendant or would be unduly disruptive to the court proceeding.

(d) The court shall take appropriate measures to make the presence of the therapy or facility dog as unobtrusive and nondisruptive as possible, including requiring the dog to be accompanied by a handler in the courtroom at all times.

(e) If a therapy or facility dog is used during a criminal jury trial, the court shall, upon request, issue an appropriate jury instruction designed to prevent prejudice for or against any party.

(f) This section does not prevent the court from removing or excluding a therapy or facility dog from the courtroom to maintain order or to ensure the fair presentation of evidence, as stated on the record.

(g)

(1) It is the intent of the Legislature in adding this section to codify the holding in People v. Chenault (2014) 227 Cal.App.4th 1503 with respect to allowing an individual witness to have a support dog accompany him or her when testifying in proceedings as provided in subdivision (a).

(2) Nothing in this section abrogates the holding in People v. Chenault regarding the need to present appropriate jury instructions.

(3) Nothing in this section limits the use of a service dog, as defined in Section 54.1 of the Civil Code, by a person with a disability.

(h) As used in this section, the following definitions shall apply:

(1) "Child witness" means any witness who is under the age of 18 at the time he or she testifies.

(2) "Facility dog" means a dog that has successfully completed a training program in providing emotional comfort in a high-stress environment for the purpose of enhancing the ability of a witness to speak in a judicial proceeding and reducing his or her stress level, provided by an assistance dog organization accredited by Assistance Dogs International or a similar nonprofit organization that sets standards of training for dogs, and that has passed a public access test for service animals.

(3) "Handler" means a person who has successfully completed training on offering an animal for assistance purposes from an organization accredited by Assistance Dogs International, Therapy Dogs Incorporated, or a similar nonprofit organization, and has received additional training on policies and protocols of the court and the responsibilities of a courtroom dog handler.

(4) "Therapy dog" means a dog that has successfully completed training, certification, or evaluation in providing emotional support therapy in settings including, but not limited to, hospitals, nursing homes, and schools, provided by the American Kennel Club, Therapy Dogs Incorporated, or a similar nonprofit organization, and has been performing the duties of a therapy dog for not less than one year.
Added by Stats 2017 ch 290 (AB 411),s 1, eff. 1/1/2018.

Section 868.5 - Support persons for prosecuting witness

(a) Notwithstanding any other law, a prosecuting witness in a case involving a violation or attempted violation of Section 187, 203, 205, or 207, subdivision (b) of Section 209, Section 211, 215, 220, 236.1, 240, 242, 243.4, 245, 261, 266, 266a, 266b, 266c, 266d, 266e, 266f, 266g, 266h, 266i, 266j, 266k, 267, 269, 273a, 273d, 273.5, 273.6, 278, 278.5, 285, 286, 287, 288, 288.5, 288.7, 289, 311.1, 311.2, 311.3, 311.4, 311.5, 311.6, 311.10, 311.11, 422, 646.9, or 647.6, former Section 262, 277, 288a, or 647a, subdivision (1) of Section 314, or subdivision (b), (d), or (e) of Section 368 when the prosecuting witness is the elder or dependent adult, shall be entitled, for support, to the attendance of up to two persons of the prosecuting witness' own choosing, one of whom may be a witness, at the preliminary hearing and at the trial, or at a juvenile court proceeding, during the testimony of the prosecuting witness. Only one of those support persons may accompany the witness to the witness stand, although the other may remain in the courtroom during the witness' testimony. The person or persons so chosen shall not be a person described in Section 1070 of the Evidence Code unless the person or persons are related to the prosecuting witness as a parent, guardian, or sibling and do not make notes during the hearing or proceeding.

(b) If the person or persons so chosen are also witnesses, the prosecution shall present evidence that the person's attendance is both desired by the prosecuting witness for support and will be helpful to the prosecuting witness. Upon that showing, the court shall grant the request unless information presented by the defendant or noticed by the court establishes that the support person's attendance during the testimony of the prosecuting witness would pose a substantial risk of influencing or affecting the content of that testimony. In the case of a juvenile court proceeding, the judge shall inform the support person or persons that juvenile court proceedings are confidential and may not be discussed with anyone not in attendance at the proceedings. In all cases, the judge shall admonish the support person or persons to not prompt, sway, or influence the witness in any way. This section does not preclude a court from exercising its discretion to remove a person from the courtroom whom it believes is prompting, swaying, or influencing the witness.

(c) The testimony of the person or persons so chosen who are also witnesses shall be presented before the testimony of the prosecuting witness. The prosecuting witness shall be excluded from the courtroom during that testimony. Whenever the evidence given by that person or those persons would be subject to exclusion because it has been given before the corpus delicti has been established, the evidence shall be admitted subject to the court's or the defendant's motion to strike that evidence from the record if the corpus delicti is not later established by the testimony of the prosecuting witness.
Amended by Stats 2021 ch 626 (AB 1171),s 39, eff. 1/1/2022.
Amended by Stats 2018 ch 423 (SB 1494),s 80, eff. 1/1/2019.
Amended by Stats 2013 ch 44 (SB 130),s 1, eff. 1/1/2014.
Amended by Stats 2012 ch 148 (SB 1091),s 1, eff. 7/17/2012.
Amended by Stats 2008 ch 48 (SB 1343),s 1, eff. 1/1/2009.

Section 868.6 - Minors under age of 16

(a) It is the purpose of this section to provide a nonthreatening environment for minors involved in the judicial system in order to better enable them to speak freely and accurately of the experiences that are the subject of judicial inquiry.

(b) Each county is encouraged to provide a room, located within, or within a reasonable distance from, the courthouse, for the use of minors under the age of 16. Should any such room reach full occupancy, preference shall be given to minors under the age of 16 whose appearance has been subpoenaed by the court. The room may be multipurpose in character. The county may seek the assistance of civic groups in the furnishing of the room and the provision of volunteers to aid in its operation and maintenance. If a county newly constructs, substantially remodels or refurbishes any courthouse or facility used as a courthouse on or after January 1, 1988, that courthouse or facility shall contain the room described in this subdivision.
Added by Stats. 1986, Ch. 976, Sec. 1.

Section 868.7 - Closing of examination

(a) Notwithstanding any other provision of law, the magistrate may, upon motion of the prosecutor, close the examination in the manner described in Section 868 during the testimony of a witness:

(1) Who is a minor or a dependent person, as defined in paragraph (3) of subdivision (f) of Section 288, with a substantial cognitive impairment and is the complaining victim of a sex offense, where testimony before the general public would be likely to cause serious psychological harm to the witness and where no alternative procedures, including, but not limited to, video recorded deposition or contemporaneous examination in another place communicated to the courtroom by means of closed-circuit television, are available to avoid the perceived harm.

(2) Whose life would be subject to a substantial risk in appearing before the general public, and where no alternative security measures, including, but not limited to, efforts to conceal his or her features or physical description, searches of members of the public attending the examination, or the temporary exclusion of other actual or potential witnesses, would be adequate to minimize the perceived threat.

(b) In any case where public access to the courtroom is restricted during the examination of a witness pursuant to this section, a transcript of the testimony of the witness shall be made available to the public as soon as is practicable.

Amended by Stats 2009 ch 88 (AB 176),s 73, eff. 1/1/2010.

Amended by Stats 2004 ch 823 (AB 20), s 13, eff. 1/1/2005.

Section 868.8 - Special precautions for persons with disability or minor

Notwithstanding any other provision of law, in any criminal proceeding in which the defendant is charged with a violation or attempted violation of subdivision (b) of Section 209, Section 220, 236.1, 243.4, 261, 269, 273a, 273d, 285, 286, 287, 288, 288.5, 288.7, or 289, subdivision (1) of Section 314, Section 422, 646.9, 647.6, or former Section 288a or 647a, or any crime that constitutes domestic violence defined in Section 13700, committed with or upon a person with a disability or a minor under 11 years of age, the court shall take special precautions to provide for the comfort and support of the person with a disability or minor and to protect him or her from coercion, intimidation, or undue influence as a witness, including, but not limited to, any of the following:

(a) In the court's discretion, the witness may be allowed reasonable periods of relief from examination and cross-examination during which he or she may retire from the courtroom. The judge may also allow other witnesses in the proceeding to be examined when the person with a disability or child witness retires from the courtroom.

(b) Notwithstanding Section 68110 of the Government Code, in his or her discretion, the judge may remove his or her robe if the judge believes that this formal attire intimidates the person with a disability or the minor.

(c) In the court's discretion the judge, parties, witnesses, support persons, and court personnel may be relocated within the courtroom to facilitate a more comfortable and personal environment for the person with a disability or the child witness.

(d) In the court's discretion, the taking of the testimony of the person with a disability or the minor may be limited to normal school hours if there is no good cause to take the testimony of the person with a disability or the minor during other hours.

(e) For the purposes of this section, the term "disability" is defined in subdivision (j) of Section 12926 of the Government Code.

Amended by Stats 2018 ch 423 (SB 1494),s 81, eff. 1/1/2019.

Amended by Stats 2013 ch 44 (SB 130),s 2, eff. 1/1/2014.

Amended by Stats 2011 ch 261 (SB 559),s 21, eff. 1/1/2012.

Amended by Stats 2001 ch 62 (AB 77), s 1, eff. 1/1/2002.

Section 869 - Testimony reduced to writing; authentication

The testimony of each witness in cases of homicide shall be reduced to writing, as a deposition, by the magistrate, or under his or her direction, and in other cases upon the demand of the prosecuting attorney, or the defendant, or his or her counsel. The magistrate before whom the examination is had may, in his or her discretion, order the testimony and proceedings to be taken down in shorthand in all examinations herein mentioned, and for that purpose he or she may appoint a shorthand reporter. The deposition or testimony of the witness shall be authenticated in the following form:

(a) It shall state the name of the witness, his or her place of residence, and his or her business or profession; except that if the witness is a peace officer, it shall state his or her name, and the address given in his or her testimony at the hearing.

(b) It shall contain the questions put to the witness and his or her answers thereto, each answer being distinctly read to him or her as it is taken down, and being corrected or added to until it conforms to what he or she declares is the truth, except in cases where the testimony is taken down in shorthand, the answer or answers of the witness need not be read to him or her.

(c) If a question put be objected to on either side and overruled, or the witness declines answering it, that fact, with the ground on which the question was overruled or the answer declined, shall be stated.

(d) The deposition shall be signed by the witness, or if he or she refuses to sign it, his or her reason for refusing shall be stated in writing, as he or she gives it, except in cases where the deposition is taken down in shorthand, it need not be signed by the witness.

(e) The reporter shall, within 10 days after the close of the examination, if the defendant be held to answer the charge of a felony, or in any other case if either the defendant or the prosecution orders the transcript, transcribe his or her shorthand notes, making an original and one copy and as many additional copies thereof as there are defendants (other than fictitious defendants), regardless of the number of charges or fictitious defendants included in the same examination, and certify and deliver the original and all copies to the clerk of the superior court in the county in which the defendant was examined. The reporter shall, before receiving any compensation as a reporter, file his or her affidavit setting forth that the transcript has been delivered within the time herein provided for. The compensation of the reporter for any services rendered by him or her as the reporter in any court of this state shall be reduced one-half if the provisions of this section as to the time of filing said transcript have not been complied with by him or her.

(f) In every case in which a transcript is delivered as provided in this section, the clerk of the court shall file the original of the transcript with the papers in the case, and shall deliver a copy of the transcript to the district attorney immediately upon his or her receipt thereof and shall deliver a copy of said transcript to each defendant (other than a fictitious defendant) at least five days before trial or upon earlier demand by him or her without cost to him or her; provided, that if any defendant be held to answer to two or more charges upon the same examination and thereafter the district attorney shall file separate informations upon said several charges, the delivery to each such defendant of one copy of the transcript of the examination shall be a compliance with this section as to all of those informations.

(g) If the transcript is delivered by the reporter within the time hereinbefore provided for, the reporter shall be entitled to receive the compensation fixed and allowed by law to reporters in the superior courts of this state.

Amended by Stats 2002 ch 784 (SB 1316), s 534, eff. 1/1/2003.

Section 870 - Depositions

The magistrate or his or her clerk shall keep the depositions taken on the information or the examination, until they are returned to the proper court; and shall not permit them to be examined or copied by any person except a judge of a court having jurisdiction of the offense, or authorized to issue writs of habeas corpus, the Attorney General, district attorney, or other prosecuting attorney, and the defendant and his or her counsel; provided however, upon demand by the defendant or his or her attorney the magistrate shall order a transcript of the depositions taken on the information, or on the examination, to be immediately furnished the defendant or his or her attorney, after the commitment of the defendant as provided by Sections 876 and 877, and the reporter furnishing the depositions, shall receive compensation in accordance with Section 869.

Amended by Stats 2002 ch 784 (SB 1316), s 535, eff. 1/1/2003.

Section 871 - Dismissal of complaint and discharge of defendant

If, after hearing the proofs, it appears either that no public offense has been committed or that there is not sufficient cause to believe the defendant guilty of a public offense, the magistrate shall order the complaint dismissed and the defendant to be discharged, by an indorsement on the depositions and statement, signed by the magistrate, to the following effect: "There being no sufficient cause to believe the within named A. B. guilty of the offense within mentioned, I order that the complaint be dismissed and that he or she shall be discharged."

Amended by Stats. 1980, Ch. 938, Sec. 3.

Section 871.5 - Motion to compel reinstatement of complaint and custodial status of defendant

(a) When an action is dismissed by a magistrate pursuant to Section 859b, 861, 871, 1008, 1381, 1381.5, 1385, 1387, or 1389 of this code or Section 41403 of the Vehicle Code, or a portion thereof is dismissed pursuant to those same sections which may not be charged by information under Section 739, the prosecutor may make a motion in the superior court within 15 days to compel the magistrate to reinstate the complaint or a portion thereof and to reinstate the custodial status of the defendant under the same terms and conditions as when the defendant last appeared before the magistrate.

(b) Notice of the motion shall be made to the defendant and the magistrate. The only ground for the motion shall be that, as a matter of law, the magistrate erroneously dismissed the action or a portion thereof.

(c) The superior court shall hear and determine the motion on the basis of the record of the proceedings before the magistrate. If the motion is litigated to decision by the prosecutor, the prosecution is prohibited from refiling the dismissed action, or portion thereof.

(d) Within 10 days after the magistrate has dismissed the action or a portion thereof, the prosecuting attorney may file a written request for a transcript of the proceedings with the clerk of the magistrate. The reporter shall immediately transcribe his or her shorthand notes pursuant to Section 869 and file with the clerk of the superior court an original plus one copy, and as many copies as there are defendants (other than a fictitious defendant). The reporter shall be entitled to compensation in accordance with Section 869. The clerk of the superior court shall deliver a copy of the transcript to the prosecuting attorney immediately upon its receipt and shall deliver a copy of the transcript to each defendant (other than a fictitious defendant) upon his or her demand without cost.

(e) When a court has ordered the resumption of proceedings before the magistrate, the magistrate shall resume the proceedings and when so ordered, issue an order of commitment for the reinstated offense or offenses within 10 days after the superior court has entered an order to that effect or within 10 days after the remittitur is filed in the superior court. Upon receipt of the remittitur, the superior court shall forward a copy to the magistrate.

(f) Pursuant to paragraph (9) of subdivision (a) of Section 1238 the people may take an appeal from the denial of the motion by the superior court to reinstate the complaint or a portion thereof. If the motion to reinstate the complaint is granted, the defendant may seek review thereof only pursuant to Sections 995 and 999a. That review may only be sought in the event the defendant is held to answer pursuant to Section 872.

(g) Nothing contained herein shall preclude a magistrate, upon the resumption of proceedings, from considering a motion made pursuant to Section 1318. If the superior court grants the motion for reinstatement and orders the magistrate to issue an order of commitment, the defendant, in lieu of resumed proceedings before the magistrate, may elect to waive his or her right to be committed by a magistrate, and consent to the filing of an amended or initial information containing the reinstated charge or charges. After arraignment thereon, he or she may adopt as a motion pursuant to Section 995, the record and proceedings of the motion taken pursuant to this section and the order issued pursuant thereto, and may seek review of the order in the manner prescribed in Section 999a.

Amended by Stats. 1993, Ch. 542, Sec. 1. Effective January 1, 1994.

Section 871.6 - Immediate appellate review of ruling setting hearing or granting continuance in felony case

If in a felony case the magistrate sets the preliminary examination beyond the time specified in Section 859b, in violation of Section 859b, or continues the preliminary hearing without good cause and good cause is required by law for such a continuance, the people or the defendant may file a petition for writ of mandate or prohibition in the superior court seeking immediate appellate review of the ruling setting the hearing or granting the continuance. Such a petition shall have precedence over all other cases in the court to which the petition is assigned. If the superior court grants a peremptory writ, it shall issue the writ and a remittitur three court days after its decision becomes final as to the court if this action is necessary to prevent mootness or to prevent frustration of the relief granted, notwithstanding the rights of the parties to seek review in a court of appeal. When the superior court issues the writ and remittitur as provided in this section, the writ shall command the magistrate to proceed with the preliminary hearing without further delay, other than that reasonably necessary for the parties to obtain the attendance of their witnesses.

The court of appeal may stay or recall the issuance of the writ and remittitur. The failure of the court of appeal to stay or recall the issuance of the writ and remittitur shall not deprive the parties of any right they would otherwise have to appellate review or extraordinary relief.

Added June 5, 1990, by initiative Proposition 115, Sec. 17.

Section 872 - Finding of probable cause

(a) If, however, it appears from the examination that a public offense has been committed, and there is sufficient cause to believe that the defendant is guilty, the magistrate shall make or indorse on the complaint an order, signed by him or her, to the following effect: "It appearing to me that the offense in the within complaint mentioned (or any offense, according to the fact, stating generally the nature thereof), has been committed, and that there is sufficient cause to believe that the within named A. B. is guilty, I order that he or she be held to answer to the same."

(b) Notwithstanding Section 1200 of the Evidence Code, the finding of probable cause may be based in whole or in part upon the sworn testimony of a law enforcement officer or honorably retired law enforcement officer relating the statements of declarants made out of court offered for the truth of the matter asserted. An honorably retired law enforcement officer may only relate statements of declarants made out of court and offered for the truth of the matter asserted that were made when the honorably retired officer was an active law enforcement officer. Any law enforcement officer or honorably retired law enforcement officer testifying as to hearsay statements shall either have five years of law enforcement experience or have completed a training course certified by the Commission on Peace Officer Standards and Training that includes training in the investigation and reporting of cases and testifying at preliminary hearings.

(c) For purposes of subdivision (b), a law enforcement officer is any officer or agent employed by a federal, state, or local government agency to whom all of the following apply:

   (1) Has either five years of law enforcement experience or who has completed a training course certified by the Commission on Peace Officer Standards and Training that includes training in the investigation and reporting of cases and testifying at preliminary hearings.

   (2) Whose primary responsibility is the enforcement of any law, the detection and apprehension of persons who have violated any law, or the investigation and preparation for prosecution of cases involving violation of laws.

Amended by Stats 2013 ch 125 (AB 568),s 1, eff. 1/1/2014.

Amended by Stats 2005 ch 18 (AB 557),s 1, eff. 1/1/2006

Note: This section was amended on June 5, 1990, by initiative Prop. 115.

Section 872.5 - Proof of content of writing in preliminary examination

Notwithstanding Article 1 (commencing with Section 1520) of Chapter 2 of Division 11 of the Evidence Code, in a preliminary examination the content of a writing may be proved by an otherwise admissible original or otherwise admissible secondary evidence.

Repealed and added by Stats. 1998, Ch. 100, Sec. 7. Effective January 1, 1999.

Section 873 - Offense not bailable

If the offense is not bailable, the following words must be added to the indorsement: "And he is hereby committed to the Sheriff of the County of ____. "

Enacted 1872.

Section 875 - Bailable offense

If the offense is bailable, and the defendant is admitted to bail, the following words must be added to the order, "and that he be admitted to bail in the sum of ____ dollars, and is committed to the Sheriff of the County of ____ until he gives such bail."

Amended by Code Amendments 1880, Ch. 60.

Section 876 - Commitment

If the magistrate order the defendant to be committed, he must make out a commitment, signed by him, with his name of office, and deliver it, with the defendant, to the officer to whom he is committed, or, if that officer is not present, to a peace officer, who must deliver the defendant into the proper custody, together with the commitment.

Enacted 1872.

Section 877 - Form of commitment

The commitment must be to the following effect except when it is made under the provisions of section 859a of this code.

County of ____ (as the case may be).

The people of the State of California to the sheriff of the county of ____:

An order having been this day made by me, that A. B. be held to answer upon a charge of (stating briefly the nature of the offense, and giving as near as may be the time when and the place where the same was committed), you are commanded to receive him into your custody and detain him until he is legally discharged.

Dated this ____ day of ____ nineteen ____.

Amended by Stats. 1935, Ch. 217.

Section 877a - Form of commitment made under Section 859a

When the commitment is made under the provisions of section 859a of this code, it must be made to the following effect:

County of ____ (as the case may be).

The people of the State of California to the sheriff of the county of ____.

A. B. having pleaded guilty to the offense of (stating briefly the nature of the offense, and giving as near as may be the time when and the place where the same was committed), you are commanded to receive him into your custody and detain him until he is legally discharged.

Dated this ____ day of ____ nineteen ____.

Added by Stats. 1935, Ch. 217.

Section 878 - Written undertaking from material witnesses

On holding the defendant to answer or on a plea of guilty where permitted by law, the magistrate may take from each of the material witnesses examined before him on the part of the people a written undertaking, to the effect that he will appear and testify at the court to which the depositions and statements or case are to be sent, or that he will forfeit the sum of five hundred dollars.

Amended by Stats. 1935, Ch. 217.

Section 879 - Written undertaking if there is reason to believe witness will not appear and testify

When the magistrate or a Judge of the Court in which the action is pending is satisfied, by proof on oath, that there is reason to believe that any such witness will not appear and testify unless security is required, he may order the witness to enter into a written undertaking, with sureties, in such sum as he may deem proper, for his appearance as specified in the preceding section.

Enacted 1872.

Section 880 - Infants who are material witnesses

Infants who are material witnesses against the defendant may be required to procure sureties for their appearance, as provided in the last section.

Amended by Stats. 1977, Ch. 579.

Section 881 - Refusal to comply with order to enter into undertaking; failure to appear; material witness

(a) If a witness, required to enter into an undertaking to appear and testify, either with or without sureties, refuses compliance with the order for that purpose, the magistrate shall commit him or her to prison until he or she complies or is legally discharged.

(b) If a witness fails to appear at the preliminary hearing in response to a subpoena, the court may hear evidence, including testimony or an affidavit from the arresting or interviewing officer, and if the court determines on the basis of the evidence that the witness is a material witness, the court shall issue a bench warrant for the arrest of the witness, and upon the appearance of the witness, may commit him or her into custody until the conclusion of the preliminary hearing, or until the defendant enters a plea of nolo contendere, or the witness is otherwise legally discharged. The court may order the witness to enter into a written undertaking to the effect that he or she will appear and testify at the time and place ordered by the court or that he or she will forfeit an amount that the court deems proper.

(c) Once the material witness has been taken into custody on the bench warrant he or she shall be brought before the magistrate issuing the warrant, if available, within two court days for a hearing to determine if the witness should be released on security of appearance or maintained in custody.

(d) A material witness shall remain in custody under this section for no longer than 10 days.

(e) If a material witness is being held in custody under this section the prosecution is entitled to have the preliminary hearing proceed, as to this witness only, within 10 days of the arraignment of the defendant. Once this material witness has completed his or her testimony the defendant shall be entitled to a reasonable continuance.

Amended by Stats. 1987, Ch. 828, Sec. 53.

Section 882 - Conditional examination

When, however, it satisfactorily appears by examination, on oath of the witness, or any other person, that the witness is unable to procure sureties, he or she may be forthwith conditionally examined on behalf of the people. The examination shall be by question and answer, in the presence of the defendant, or after notice to him or her, if on bail, and conducted in the same manner as the examination before a committing magistrate is required by this code to be conducted, and the witness thereupon discharged; and the deposition may be used upon the trial of the defendant, except in cases of homicide, under the same conditions as mentioned in Section 1345; but this section does not apply to an accomplice in the commission of the offense charged.

Amended by Stats. 1987, Ch. 828, Sec. 54.

Section 883 - Duties of defendant when discharged or held to answer

When a magistrate has discharged a defendant, or has held him to answer, he must return, without delay, to the Clerk of the Court at which the defendant is required to appear, the warrant, if any, the depositions, and all undertakings of bail, or for the appearance of witnesses taken by him.

Enacted 1872.

Title 4 - GRAND JURY PROCEEDINGS
Chapter 1 - GENERAL PROVISIONS

Section 888 - Grand jury

A grand jury is a body of the required number of persons returned from the citizens of the county before a court of competent jurisdiction, and sworn to inquire of public offenses committed or triable within the county.

Each grand jury or, if more than one has been duly impaneled pursuant to Sections 904.5 to 904.9, inclusive, one grand jury in each county, shall be charged and sworn to investigate or inquire into county matters of civil concern, such as the needs of county officers, including the abolition or creation of offices for, the purchase, lease, or sale of equipment for, or changes in the method or system of, performing the duties of the agencies subject to investigation pursuant to Section 914.1.

Amended by Stats. 1988, Ch. 1297, Sec. 1.

Section 888.2 - "Required number" defined

As used in this title as applied to a grand jury, "required number" means:

(a) Twenty-three in a county having a population exceeding 4,000,000.

(b) Eleven in a county having a population of 20,000 or less, upon the approval of the board of supervisors.

(c) Nineteen in all other counties.

Amended by Stats. 1994, Ch. 295, Sec. 1. Effective January 1, 1995.

Section 889 - Indictment

An indictment is an accusation in writing, presented by the grand jury to a competent court, charging a person with a public offense.

Added by Stats. 1959, Ch. 501.

Section 890 - Fees for grand jurors

Unless a higher fee or rate of mileage is otherwise provided by statute or county or city and county ordinance, the fees for grand jurors are fifteen dollars ($15) a day for each day's attendance as a grand juror, and the mileage reimbursement applicable to county employees for each mile actually traveled in attending court as a grand juror.

Amended by Stats 2001 ch 218 (AB 1161), s 1, eff. 1/1/2002, op. 7/1/2002.

Section 890.1 - Payment of per diem and mileage of grand jurors

The per diem and mileage of grand jurors where allowed by law shall be paid by the treasurer of the county out of the general fund of the county upon warrants drawn by the county auditor upon the written order of the judge of the superior court of the county.

Added by Stats. 1959, Ch. 501.

Section 891 - Unlawful recording of proceedings of grand jury

Every person who, by any means whatsoever, willfully and knowingly, and without knowledge and consent of the grand jury, records, or attempts to record, all or part of the proceedings of any grand jury while it is deliberating or voting, or listens to or observes, or attempts to listen to or observe, the proceedings of any grand jury of which he is not a member while such jury is deliberating or voting is guilty of a misdemeanor.

This section is not intended to prohibit the taking of notes by a grand juror in connection with and solely for the purpose of assisting him in the performance of his duties as such juror.

Added by Stats. 1959, Ch. 501.

Section 892 - Proceeding against corporation

The grand jury may proceed against a corporation.

Amended by Stats. 1973, Ch. 249.

Chapter 2 - FORMATION OF GRAND JURY
Article 1 - QUALIFICATIONS OF GRAND JURORS
Section 893 - Competency
(a) A person is competent to act as a grand juror only if he possesses each of the following qualifications:

(1) He is a citizen of the United States of the age of 18 years or older who shall have been a resident of the state and of the county or city and county for one year immediately before being selected and returned.

(2) He is in possession of his natural faculties, of ordinary intelligence, of sound judgment, and of fair character.

(3) He is possessed of sufficient knowledge of the English language.

(b) A person is not competent to act as a grand juror if any of the following apply:

(1) The person is serving as a trial juror in any court of this state.

(2) The person has been discharged as a grand juror in any court of this state within one year.

(3) The person has been convicted of malfeasance in office or any felony or other high crime.

(4) The person is serving as an elected public officer.

Amended by Stats. 1973, Ch. 416.

Section 894 - Exemptions and excuses
Sections 204, 218, and 219 of the Code of Civil Procedure specify the exemptions and the excuses which relieve a person from liability to serve as a grand juror.

Amended by Stats. 1989, Ch. 1416, Sec. 37.

Article 2 - LISTING AND SELECTION OF GRAND JURORS
Section 895 - Order designating estimated number of grand jurors required
During the month preceding the beginning of the fiscal year of the county, the superior court of each county shall make an order designating the estimated number of grand jurors that will, in the opinion of the court, be required for the transaction of the business of the court during the ensuing fiscal year as provided in Section 905.5.

Amended by Stats. 1974, Ch. 393.

Section 896 - Selection of grand jurors
(a) Immediately after an order is made pursuant to Section 895, the court shall select the grand jurors required by personal interview for the purpose of ascertaining whether they possess the qualifications prescribed by subdivision (a) of Section 893. If a person so interviewed, in the opinion of the court, possesses the necessary qualifications, in order to be listed the person shall sign a statement declaring that the person will be available for jury service for the number of hours usually required of a member of the grand jury in that county.

(b) The selections shall be made of men and women who are not exempt from serving and who are suitable and competent to serve as grand jurors pursuant to Sections 893, 898, and 899. The court shall list the persons so selected and required by the order to serve as grand jurors during the ensuing fiscal year of the county, or until a new list of grand jurors is provided, and shall at once place this list in the possession of the jury commissioner.

Amended by Stats 2003 ch 149 (SB 79), s 69, eff. 1/1/2004.

Section 898 - List of grand jurors
The list of grand jurors made in a county having a population in excess of four million shall contain the number of persons which has been designated by the court in its order.

Amended by Stats. 1963, Ch. 259.

Section 899 - Selection of names for grand jury list
The names for the grand jury list shall be selected from the different wards, judicial districts, or supervisorial districts of the respective counties in proportion to the number of inhabitants therein, as nearly as the same can be estimated by the persons making the lists. The grand jury list shall be kept separate and distinct from the trial jury list. In a county of the first class, the names for such list may be selected from the county at large.

Amended by Stats. 1969, Ch. 64.

Section 900 - Publication of list
On receiving the list of persons selected by the court, the jury commissioner shall file it in the jury commissioner's office and have the list, which shall include the name of the judge who selected each person on the list, published one time in a newspaper of general circulation, as defined in Section 6000 of the Government Code, in the county. The jury commissioner shall then do either of the following:

(a) Write down the names on the list onto separate pieces of paper of the same size and appearance, fold each piece so as to conceal the name, and deposit the pieces in a box to be called the "grand jury box."

(b) Assign a number to each name on the list and place, in a box to be called the "grand jury box," markers of the same size, shape, and color, each containing a number which corresponds with a number on the list.

Amended by Stats 2003 ch 149 (SB 79), s 70, eff. 1/1/2004.

Section 901 - Regular jurors
(a) The persons whose names are so returned shall be known as regular jurors, and shall serve for one year and until other persons are selected and returned.

(b) If the superior court so decides, the presiding judge may name up to 10 regular jurors not previously so named, who served on the previous grand jury and who so consent, to serve for a second year.

(c) The court may also decide to select grand jurors pursuant to Section 908.2.

Amended by Stats. 1988, Ch. 886, Sec. 1.

Section 902 - Drawing of names

The names of persons drawn for grand jurors shall be drawn from the grand jury box by withdrawing either the pieces of paper placed therein pursuant to subdivision (a) of Section 900 or the markers placed therein pursuant to subdivision (b) of Section 900. If, at the end of the fiscal year of the county, there are the names of persons in the grand jury box who have not been drawn during the fiscal year to serve and have not served as grand jurors, the names of such persons may be placed on the list of grand jurors drawn for the succeeding fiscal year.
Amended by Stats. 1974, Ch. 393.

Article 3 - JURY COMMISSIONERS

Section 903 - [Repealed]
Repealed by Stats 2003 ch 149 (SB 79), s 71, eff. 1/1/2004.

Section 903.1 - Furnishing of list of persons qualified to serve as grand jurors
Pursuant to written rules or instructions adopted by a majority of the judges of the superior court of the county, the jury commissioner shall furnish the judges of the court annually a list of persons qualified to serve as grand jurors during the ensuing fiscal year of the county, or until a new list of jurors is required. From time to time, a majority of the judges of the superior court may adopt such rules or instructions as may be necessary for the guidance of the jury commissioner, who shall at all times be under the supervision and control of the judges of the court. Any list of jurors prepared pursuant to this article must, however, meet the requirements of Section 899.
Amended by Stats. 1974, Ch. 393.

Section 903.2 - Qualifications of persons who may be summoned for grand jury duty; administration of oaths
The jury commissioner shall diligently inquire and inform himself or herself in respect to the qualifications of persons resident in his or her county who may be liable to be summoned for grand jury duty. He or she may require a person to answer, under oath to be administered by him or her, all questions as he or she may address to that person, touching his or her name, age, residence, occupation, and qualifications as a grand juror, and also all questions as to similar matters concerning other persons of whose qualifications for grand jury duty he or she has knowledge.
The commissioner and his or her assistants, referred to in Sections 69895 and 69896 of the Government Code, shall have the power to administer oaths and shall be allowed actual traveling expenses incurred in the performance of their duties. Those traveling expenses shall be audited, allowed, and paid out of the general fund of the county.
Amended by Stats 2008 ch 179 (SB 1498),s 179, eff. 1/1/2009.

Section 903.3 - List of persons recommended for grand jury duty
Pursuant to the rules or instructions adopted by a majority of the judges of the superior court, the jury commissioner shall return to the judges the list of persons recommended by him for grand jury duty. The judges of the superior court shall examine the jury list so returned and from such list a majority of the judges may select, to serve as grand jurors in the superior court of the county during the ensuing year or until a new list of jurors is required, such persons as, in their opinion, should be selected for grand jury duty. The persons so selected shall, in the opinion of the judges selecting them, be persons suitable and competent to serve as jurors, as required by law.
Added by Stats. 1959, Ch. 501.

Section 903.4 - Selection
The judges are not required to select any name from the list returned by the jury commissioner, but may, if in their judgment the due administration of justice requires, make every or any selection from among the body of persons in the county suitable and competent to serve as grand jurors regardless of the list returned by the jury commissioner.
Amended by Stats 2011 ch 296 (AB 1023),s 214, eff. 1/1/2012.

Article 4 - IMPANELING OF GRAND JURY

Section 904 - Order directing grand jury to be drawn
Every superior court, whenever in its opinion the public interest so requires, shall make and file with the jury commissioner an order directing a grand jury to be drawn. The order shall designate the number of grand jurors to be drawn, which may not be less than 29 nor more than 40 in counties having a population exceeding four million and not less than 25 nor more than 30 in other counties.
Amended by Stats 2003 ch 149 (SB 79), s 72, eff. 1/1/2004.

Section 904.4 - Additional grand jury in county having population of more than 370,000 but less than 400,000
(a) In any county having a population of more than 370,000 but less than 400,000 as established by Section 28020 of the Government Code, the presiding judge of the superior court, upon application by the district attorney, may order and direct the drawing and impanelment at any time of one additional grand jury.
(b) The presiding judge may select persons, at random, from the list of trial jurors in civil and criminal cases and shall examine them to determine if they are competent to serve as grand jurors. When a sufficient number of competent persons have been selected, they shall constitute the additional grand jury.
(c) Any additional grand jury which is impaneled pursuant to this section may serve for a period of one year from the date of impanelment, but may be discharged at any time within the one-year period by order of the presiding judge. In no event shall more than one additional grand jury be impaneled pursuant to this section at the same time.
(d) Whenever an additional grand jury is impaneled pursuant to this section, it may inquire into any matters that are subject to grand jury inquiry and shall have the sole and exclusive jurisdiction to return indictments, except for any matters that the regular grand jury is inquiring into at the time of its impanelment.
(e) If an additional grand jury is also authorized by another section, the county may impanel the additional grand jury authorized by this section, or by the other section, but not both.
Added by Stats. 1991, Ch. 1109, Sec. 1.

Section 904.6 - Additional grand jury in any county or city and county

(a) In any county or city and county, the presiding judge of the superior court, or the judge appointed by the presiding judge to supervise the grand jury, may, upon the request of the Attorney General or the district attorney or upon his or her own motion, order and direct the impanelment, of one additional grand jury pursuant to this section.

(b) The presiding judge or the judge appointed by the presiding judge to supervise the grand jury shall select persons, at random, from the list of trial jurors in civil and criminal cases and shall examine them to determine if they are competent to serve as grand jurors. When a sufficient number of competent persons have been selected, they shall constitute the additional grand jury.

(c) Any additional grand jury which is impaneled pursuant to this section may serve for a period of one year from the date of impanelment, but may be discharged at any time within the one-year period by order of the presiding judge or the judge appointed by the presiding judge to supervise the grand jury. In no event shall more than one additional grand jury be impaneled pursuant to this section at the same time.

(d) Whenever an additional grand jury is impaneled pursuant to this section, it may inquire into any matters which are subject to grand jury inquiry and shall have the sole and exclusive jurisdiction to return indictments, except for any matters which the regular grand jury is inquiring into at the time of its impanelment.

(e) It is the intent of the Legislature that all persons qualified for jury service shall have an equal opportunity to be considered for service as criminal grand jurors in the county in which they reside, and that they have an obligation to serve, when summoned for that purpose. All persons selected for the additional criminal grand jury shall be selected at random from a source or sources reasonably representative of a cross section of the population which is eligible for jury service in the county.

Amended by Stats 2005 ch 25 (SB 416),s 1, eff. 1/1/2006

Section 904.7 - Additional civil grand jury in County of San Bernardino

(a) Notwithstanding subdivision (a) of Section 904.6 or any other provision, in the County of San Bernardino, the presiding judge of the superior court, or the judge appointed by the presiding judge to supervise the grand jury, may, upon the request of the Attorney General or the district attorney or upon his or her own motion, order and direct the impanelment of an additional civil grand jury pursuant to this section.

(b) The presiding judge or the judge appointed by the presiding judge to supervise the grand jury shall select persons, at random, from the list of trial jurors in civil and criminal cases and shall examine them to determine if they are competent to serve as grand jurors. When a sufficient number of competent persons have been selected, they shall constitute an additional grand jury.

(c) Any additional civil grand jury that is impaneled pursuant to this section may serve for a term as determined by the presiding judge or the judge appointed by the presiding judge to supervise the civil grand jury, but may be discharged at any time within the set term by order of the presiding judge or the judge appointed by the presiding judge to supervise the civil grand jury. In no event shall more than one additional civil grand jury be impaneled pursuant to this section at the same time.

(d) Whenever an additional civil grand jury is impaneled pursuant to this section, it may inquire into matters of oversight, conduct investigations, issue reports, and make recommendations, except for any matters that the regular grand jury is inquiring into at the time of its impanelment. Any additional civil grand jury impaneled pursuant to this section shall not have jurisdiction to issue indictments.

(e) It is the intent of the Legislature that, in the County of San Bernardino, all persons qualified for jury service shall have an equal opportunity to be considered for service as grand jurors within the county, and that they have an obligation to serve, when summoned for that purpose. All persons selected for an additional grand jury shall be selected at random from a source or sources reasonably representative of a cross section of the population that is eligible for jury service in the county.

Amended by Stats 2011 ch 304 (SB 428),s 7, eff. 1/1/2012.
Added by Stats 2010 ch 87 (AB 1906),s 1, eff. 1/1/2011.

Section 904.8 - Additional grand juries in County of Los Angeles

(a) Notwithstanding subdivision (a) of Section 904.6 or any other provision, in the County of Los Angeles, the presiding judge of the superior court, or the judge appointed by the presiding judge to supervise the grand jury, may, upon the request of the Attorney General or the district attorney or upon his or her own motion, order and direct the impanelment of up to two additional grand juries pursuant to this section.

(b) The presiding judge or the judge appointed by the presiding judge to supervise the grand jury shall select persons, at random, from the list of trial jurors in civil and criminal cases and shall examine them to determine if they are competent to serve as grand jurors. When a sufficient number of competent persons have been selected, they shall constitute an additional grand jury.

(c) Any additional grand juries that are impaneled pursuant to this section may serve for a period of one year from the date of impanelment, but may be discharged at any time within the one-year period by order of the presiding judge or the judge appointed by the presiding judge to supervise the grand jury. In no event shall more than two additional grand juries be impaneled pursuant to this section at the same time.

(d) Whenever additional grand juries are impaneled pursuant to this section, they may inquire into any matters that are subject to grand jury inquiry and shall have the sole and exclusive jurisdiction to return indictments, except for any matters that the regular grand jury is inquiring into at the time of its impanelment.

(e) It is the intent of the Legislature that, in the County of Los Angeles, all persons qualified for jury service shall have an equal opportunity to be considered for service as criminal grand jurors within the county, and that they have an obligation to serve, when summoned for that purpose. All persons selected for an additional criminal grand jury shall be selected at random from a source or sources reasonably representative of a cross section of the population that is eligible for jury service in the county.

Added by Stats 2007 ch 82 (SB 796),s 1, eff. 1/1/2008.

Section 905 - Minimum of one grand jury in all counties

In all counties there shall be at least one grand jury drawn and impaneled in each year.

Amended by Stats. 1982, Ch. 1408, Sec. 3.

Section 905.5 - Impanelment and service during fiscal year or calendar year

(a) Except as otherwise provided in subdivision (b), the grand jury shall be impaneled and serve during the fiscal year of the county in the manner provided in this chapter.

(b) The board of supervisors of a county may provide that the grand jury shall be impaneled and serve during the calendar year. The board of supervisors shall provide for an appropriate transition from fiscal year term to calendar year term or from calendar year term to fiscal year term for the grand jury. The provisions of subdivisions (a) and (b) of Section 901 shall not be deemed a limitation on any appropriate transition provisions as determined by resolution or ordinance; and, except as otherwise provided in this chapter, no transition grand jury shall serve more than 18 months.
Amended by Stats. 1984, Ch. 344, Sec. 1. Effective July 10, 1984.

Section 906 - Drawing and summoning of grand jurors
The order shall designate the time at which the drawing will take place. The names of the grand jurors shall be drawn, and the list of names certified and summoned, as is provided for drawing and summoning trial jurors. The names of any persons drawn, who are not impaneled upon the grand jury, may be again placed in the grand jury box.
Added by Stats. 1959, Ch. 501.

Section 907 - Fine imposed for failure to attend
Any grand juror summoned, who willfully and without reasonable excuse fails to attend, may be attached and compelled to attend and the court may also impose a fine not exceeding fifty dollars ($50), upon which execution may issue. If the grand juror was not personally served, the fine shall not be imposed until upon an order to show cause an opportunity has been offered the grand juror to be heard.
Repealed and added by Stats. 1959, Ch. 501.

Section 908 - Required number of persons
If the required number of the persons summoned as grand jurors are present and not excused, the required number shall constitute the grand jury. If more than the required number of persons are present, the jury commissioner shall write their names on separate ballots, which the jury commissioner shall fold so that the names cannot be seen, place them in a box, and draw out the required number of them. The persons whose names are on the ballots so drawn shall constitute the grand jury. If less than the required number of persons are present, the panel may be filled as provided in Section 211 of the Code of Civil Procedure. If more of the persons summoned to complete a grand jury attend than are required, the requisite number shall be obtained by writing the names of those summoned and not excused on ballots, depositing them in a box, and drawing as provided above.
Amended by Stats 2003 ch 149 (SB 79), s 73, eff. 1/1/2004.

Section 908.1 - Vacancies
When, after the grand jury consisting of the required number of persons has been impaneled pursuant to law, the membership is reduced for any reason, vacancies within an existing grand jury may be filled, so as to maintain the full membership at the required number of persons, by the jury commissioner, in the presence of the court, drawing out sufficient names to fill the vacancies from the grand jury box, pursuant to law, or from a special venire as provided in Section 211 of the Code of Civil Procedure. A person selected as a grand juror to fill a vacancy pursuant to this section may not vote as a grand juror on any matter upon which evidence has been taken by the grand jury prior to the time of the person's selection.
Amended by Stats 2003 ch 149 (SB 79), s 74, eff. 1/1/2004.

Section 908.2 - Ballots
(a) Upon the decision of the superior court pursuant to Section 901 to adopt this method of selecting grand jurors, when the required number of persons have been impaneled as the grand jury pursuant to law, the jury commissioner shall write the names of each person on separate ballots. The jury commissioner shall fold the ballots so that the names cannot be seen, place them in a box, and draw out half of the ballots, or in a county where the number of grand jurors is uneven, one more than half. The persons whose names are on the ballots so drawn shall serve for 12 months until July 1 of the following year. The persons whose names are not on the ballots so drawn shall serve for six months until January 1 of the following year.
(b) Each subsequent year, on January 2 and July 2, a sufficient number of grand jurors shall be impaneled to replace those whose service concluded the previous day. Those persons impaneled on January 2 shall serve until January 1 of the following year. Those persons impaneled on July 2 shall serve until July 1 of the following year. A person may not serve on the grand jury for more than one year.
(c) The provisions of subdivisions (a) and (b) do not apply to the selection of grand jurors for an additional grand jury authorized pursuant to Section 904.6.
Amended by Stats 2003 ch 149 (SB 79), s 75, eff. 1/1/2004.

Section 909 - Qualification to act as grand juror
Before accepting a person drawn as a grand juror, the court shall be satisfied that such person is duly qualified to act as such juror. When a person is drawn and found qualified he shall be accepted unless the court, on the application of the juror and before he is sworn, excuses him from such service for any of the reasons prescribed in this title or in Chapter 1 (commencing with Section 190), Title 3, Part 1 of the Code of Civil Procedure.
Added by Stats. 1959, Ch. 501.

Section 910 - Challenge
No challenge shall be made or allowed to the panel from which the grand jury is drawn, nor to an individual grand juror, except when made by the court for want of qualification, as prescribed in Section 909.
Added by Stats. 1959, Ch. 501.

Section 911 - Oath
The following oath shall be taken by each member of the grand jury: "I do solemnly swear (affirm) that I will support the Constitution of the United States and of the State of California, and all laws made pursuant to and in conformity therewith, will diligently inquire into, and true presentment make, of all public offenses against the people of this state, committed or triable within this county, of which the grand jury shall have or can obtain legal evidence. Further, I will not disclose any evidence brought before the grand jury, nor anything which I or any other grand juror may say, nor the manner in which I or any other grand juror may have voted on any matter before the grand jury. I will keep the charge that will be given to me by the court."
Amended by Stats. 1983, Ch. 111, Sec. 4.

Section 912 - Foreman

From the persons summoned to serve as grand jurors and appearing, the court shall appoint a foreman. The court shall also appoint a foreman when the person already appointed is excused or discharged before the grand jury is dismissed.
Added by Stats. 1959, Ch. 501.

Section 913 - Demand for impaneling of grand jury by Attorney General

If a grand jury is not in existence, the Attorney General may demand the impaneling of a grand jury by those charged with the duty to do so, and upon such demand by him, it shall be their duty to do so.
Added by Stats. 1959, Ch. 501.

Chapter 3 - POWERS AND DUTIES OF GRAND JURY

Article 1 - GENERAL PROVISIONS

Section 914 - Information; training

(a) When the grand jury is impaneled and sworn, it shall be charged by the court. In doing so, the court shall give the grand jurors such information as it deems proper, or as is required by law, as to their duties, and as to any charges for public offenses returned to the court or likely to come before the grand jury.

(b) To assist a grand jury in the performance of its statutory duties regarding civil matters, the court, in consultation with the district attorney, the county counsel, and at least one former grand juror, shall ensure that a grand jury that considers or takes action on civil matters receives training that addresses, at a minimum, report writing, interviews, and the scope of the grand jury's responsibility and statutory authority.

(c) Any costs incurred by the court as a result of this section shall be absorbed by the court or the county from existing resources.
Amended by Stats. 1997, Ch. 443, Sec. 3. Effective January 1, 1998.

Section 914.1 - Providing information when investigation of, or inquiry into, county matters of civil concern

When a grand jury is impaneled, for purposes which include the investigation of, or inquiry into, county matters of civil concern, the judge of the superior court of the county, in addition to other matters requiring action, shall call its attention to the provisions of Chapter 1 (commencing with Section 23000) of Division 1 of Title 3, and Sections 24054 and 26525 of the Government Code, and instruct it to ascertain by a careful and diligent investigation whether such provisions have been complied with, and to note the result of such investigation in its report. At such time the judge shall also inform and charge the grand jury especially as to its powers, duties, and responsibilities under Article 1 (commencing with Section 888) of Chapter 2, and Article 2 (commencing with Section 925), Article 3 (commencing with Section 934) of this chapter, Article 3 (commencing with Section 3060) of Chapter 7 of Division 4 of Title 1 of the Government Code, and Section 17006 of the Welfare and Institutions Code.
Amended by Stats. 1988, Ch. 1297, Sec. 2.

Section 914.5 - Expenditures

The grand jury shall not spend money or incur obligations in excess of the amount budgeted for its investigative activities pursuant to this chapter by the county board of supervisors unless the proposed expenditure is approved in advance by the presiding judge of the superior court after the board of supervisors has been advised of the request.
Added by Stats. 1970, Ch. 740.

Section 915 - Retiring to private room

When the grand jury has been impaneled, sworn, and charged, it shall retire to a private room, except when operating under a finding pursuant to Section 939.1, and inquire into the offenses and matters of civil concern cognizable by it. On the completion of the business before the grand jury or expiration of the term of prescribed service of one or more grand jurors, the court shall discharge it or the affected individual jurors.
Amended by Stats. 1988, Ch. 1297, Sec. 3.

Section 916 - Officers; adoption of rules of procedure and public actions

Each grand jury shall choose its officers, except the foreman, and shall determine its rules of proceeding. Adoption of its rules of procedure and all public actions of the grand jury, whether concerning criminal or civil matters unless otherwise prescribed in law, including adoption of final reports, shall be only with the concurrence of that number of grand jurors necessary to find an indictment pursuant to Section 940. Rules of procedure shall include guidelines for that grand jury to ensure that all findings included in its final reports are supported by documented evidence, including reports of contract auditors or consultants, official records, or interviews attended by no fewer than two grand jurors and that all problems identified in a final report are accompanied by suggested means for their resolution, including financial, when applicable.
Amended by Stats. 1988, Ch. 1297, Sec. 4.

Section 916.1 - Foreman pro tempore

If the foreman of a grand jury is absent from any meeting or if he is disqualified to act, the grand jury may select a member of that body to act as foreman pro tempore, who shall perform the duties, and have all the powers, of the regularly appointed foreman in his absence or disqualification.
Added by Stats. 1959, Ch. 501.

Section 916.2 - Recusal

(a) Notwithstanding any other provision of law, a grand juror who is a current employee of, or a former or retired employee last employed within the prior three years by, an agency within the investigative jurisdiction of the civil grand jury shall inform the foreperson and court of that fact and shall recuse himself or herself from participating in any grand jury civil investigation of that agency, including any discussion or vote concerning a civil investigation of that agency.

(b) This section shall be in addition to any local policies or rules regarding conflict of interest for grand jurors.

(c) For purposes of this section, "agency" means a department or operational part of a government entity, such as a city, county, city and county, school district, or other local government body.
Amended by Stats 2012 ch 867 (SB 1144),s 21, eff. 1/1/2013.

Added by Stats 2011 ch 184 (AB 1133),s 1, eff. 1/1/2012.

Section 917 - Inquiry into public offenses

(a) The grand jury may inquire into all public offenses committed or triable within the county and present them to the court by indictment.

(b) Except as provided in Section 918, the grand jury shall not inquire into an offense that involves a shooting or use of excessive force by a peace officer described in Section 830.1, subdivision (a) of Section 830.2, or Section 830.39, that led to the death of a person being detained or arrested by the peace officer pursuant to Section 836.

Amended by Stats 2015 ch 175 (SB 227),s 1, eff. 1/1/2016.

Section 918 - Declaration that public offense has been committed and investigation

If a member of a grand jury knows, or has reason to believe, that a public offense, triable within the county, has been committed, he may declare it to his fellow jurors, who may thereupon investigate it.

Amended by Stats. 1976, Ch. 895.

Section 919 - Inquiry into case of person imprisoned but not indicted, condition and management of prisons, and misconduct in office of public officers

(a) The grand jury may inquire into the case of every person imprisoned in the jail of the county on a criminal charge and not indicted.

(b) The grand jury shall inquire into the condition and management of the public prisons within the county.

(c) The grand jury shall inquire into the willful or corrupt misconduct in office of public officers of every description within the county. Except as provided in Section 918, this subdivision does not apply to misconduct that involves a shooting or use of excessive force by a peace officer described in Section 830.1, subdivision (a) of Section 830.2, or Section 830.39, that led to the death of a person being detained or arrested by the peace officer pursuant to Section 836.

Amended by Stats 2015 ch 175 (SB 227),s 2, eff. 1/1/2016.

Section 920 - Inquiry into sales and transfers of land which might escheat to state

The grand jury may investigate and inquire into all sales and transfers of land, and into the ownership of land, which, under the state laws, might or should escheat to the State of California. For this purpose, the grand jury may summon witnesses before it and examine them and the records. The grand jury shall direct that proper escheat proceedings be commenced when, in the opinion of the grand jury, the evidence justifies such proceedings.

Amended by Stats. 1976, Ch. 895.

Section 921 - Access to prisons and public records

The grand jury is entitled to free access, at all reasonable times, to the public prisons, and to the examination, without charge, of all public records within the county.

Added by Stats. 1959, Ch. 501.

Section 922 - Removal of district, county, or city officers

The powers and duties of the grand jury in connection with proceedings for the removal of district, county, or city officers are prescribed in Article 3 (commencing with Section 3060), Chapter 7, Division 4, Title 1, of the Government Code.

Added by Stats. 1959, Ch. 501.

Section 923 - Powers of Attorney General

(a) Whenever the Attorney General considers that the public interest requires, he or she may, with or without the concurrence of the district attorney, direct the grand jury to convene for the investigation and consideration of those matters of a criminal nature that he or she desires to submit to it. He or she may take full charge of the presentation of the matters to the grand jury, issue subpoenas, prepare indictments, and do all other things incident thereto to the same extent as the district attorney may do.

(b) Whenever the Attorney General considers that the public interest requires, he or she may, with or without the concurrence of the district attorney, petition the court to impanel a special grand jury to investigate, consider, or issue indictments for any of the activities subject to fine, imprisonment, or asset forfeiture under Section 14107 of the Welfare and Institutions Code. He or she may take full charge of the presentation of the matters to the grand jury, issue subpoenas, prepare indictments, and do all other things incident thereto to the same extent as the district attorney may do. If the evidence presented to the grand jury shows the commission of an offense or offenses for which venue would be in a county other than the county where the grand jury is impaneled, the Attorney General, with or without the concurrence of the district attorney in the county with jurisdiction over the offense or offenses, may petition the court to impanel a special grand jury in that county. Notwithstanding any other law, upon request of the Attorney General, a grand jury convened by the Attorney General pursuant to this subdivision may submit confidential information obtained by that grand jury, including, but not limited to, documents and testimony, to a second grand jury that has been impaneled at the request of the Attorney General pursuant to this subdivision in any other county where venue for an offense or offenses shown by evidence presented to the first grand jury is proper. All confidentiality provisions governing information, testimony, and evidence presented to a grand jury shall be applicable, except as expressly permitted by this subdivision. The Attorney General shall inform the grand jury that transmits confidential information and the grand jury that receives confidential information of any exculpatory evidence, as required by Section 939.71. The grand jury that transmits information to another grand jury shall include the exculpatory evidence disclosed by the Attorney General in the transmission of the confidential information. The Attorney General shall inform both the grand jury transmitting the confidential information and the grand jury receiving that information of their duties under Section 939.7. A special grand jury convened pursuant to this subdivision shall be in addition to the other grand juries authorized by this section, this chapter, or Chapter 2 (commencing with Section 893).

(c) Whenever the Attorney General considers that the public interest requires, he or she may, with or without the concurrence of the district attorney, impanel a special statewide grand jury to investigate, consider, or issue indictments in any matters in which there are two or more activities, in which fraud or theft is a material element, that have occurred in more than one county and were conducted either by a single defendant or multiple defendants acting in concert.

(1) This special statewide grand jury may be impaneled in the Counties of Fresno, Los Angeles, Sacramento, San Diego, or San Francisco, at the Attorney General's discretion. When impaneling a special statewide grand jury pursuant to this subdivision, the

Attorney General shall use an existing regularly impaneled criminal grand jury within the period of its regular impanelment to serve as the special statewide grand jury and make arrangements with the grand jury coordinator in the applicable county, or with the presiding judge or whoever is charged with scheduling the grand jury hearings, in order to ensure orderly coordination and use of the grand jurors' time for both regular grand jury duties and special statewide grand jury duties. Whenever the Attorney General impanels a special statewide grand jury, the prosecuting attorney representing the Attorney General shall inform the special statewide grand jury at the outset of the case that the special statewide grand jury is acting as a special statewide grand jury with statewide jurisdiction.

(2) For special statewide grand juries impaneled pursuant to this subdivision, the Attorney General may issue subpoenas for documents and witnesses located anywhere in the state in order to obtain evidence to present to the special statewide grand jury. The special statewide grand jury may hear all evidence in the form of testimony or physical evidence presented to the special statewide grand jury, irrespective of the location of the witness or physical evidence prior to subpoena. The special statewide grand jury impaneled pursuant to this subdivision may indict a person or persons with charges for crimes that occurred in counties other than where the special statewide grand jury is impaneled. The indictment shall then be submitted to the court in any county in which any of the charges could otherwise have been properly brought. The court where the indictment is filed under this subdivision shall have proper jurisdiction over all counts in the indictment.

(3) Notwithstanding Section 944, an indictment found by a special statewide grand jury convened pursuant to this subdivision and endorsed as a true bill by the special statewide grand jury foreperson, may be presented to the court, as set forth in paragraph (2), solely by the Attorney General and within five court days of the endorsement of the indictment. For indictments presented to the court in this manner, the Attorney General shall also file with the court or court clerk, at the time of presenting the indictment, an affidavit signed by the special statewide grand jury foreperson attesting that all the jurors who voted on the indictment heard all of the evidence presented by the Attorney General, and that a proper number of jurors voted for the indictment pursuant to Section 940. The Attorney General's office shall be responsible for prosecuting an indictment produced by the special statewide grand jury.

(4) If a defendant makes a timely and successful challenge to the Attorney General's right to convene a special statewide grand jury by clearly demonstrating that the charges brought are not encompassed by this subdivision, the court shall dismiss the indictment without prejudice to the Attorney General, who may bring the same or other charges against the defendant at a later date by way of another special statewide grand jury, properly convened, or a regular grand jury, or by any other procedure available.

(5) The provisions of Section 939.71 shall apply to the special statewide grand jury.

(6) Unless otherwise set forth in this section, a law applying to a regular grand jury impaneled pursuant to Section 23 of Article I of the California Constitution shall apply to a special statewide grand jury unless the application of the law to a special statewide grand jury would substantially interfere with the execution of one or more of the provisions of this section. If there is substantial interference, the provision governing the special statewide grand jury will govern.

(d) Upon certification by the Attorney General, a statement of the costs directly related to the impanelment and activities of the grand jury pursuant to subdivisions (b) and (c) from the presiding judge of the superior court where the grand jury was impaneled shall be submitted for state reimbursement of the costs to the county or courts.

Amended by Stats 2012 ch 568 (SB 1474),s 2, eff. 1/1/2013.

Amended by Stats 2000 ch 322 (AB 1098), s 12, eff. 1/1/2001.

Section 924 - Unlawful disclosure of information or indictment

Every grand juror who willfully discloses the fact of an information or indictment having been made for a felony, until the defendant has been arrested, is guilty of a misdemeanor.

Added by Stats. 1959, Ch. 501.

Section 924.1 - Unlawful disclosure of evidence

(a) Every grand juror who, except when required by a court, willfully discloses any evidence adduced before the grand jury, or anything which he himself or any other member of the grand jury has said, or in what manner he or she or any other grand juror has voted on a matter before them, is guilty of a misdemeanor.

(b) Every interpreter for the disabled appointed to assist a member of the grand jury pursuant to Section 939.11 who, except when required by a court, willfully discloses any evidence adduced before the grand jury, or anything which he or she or any member of the grand jury has said, or in what manner any grand juror has voted on a matter before them, is guilty of a misdemeanor.

Amended by Stats. 1986, Ch. 357, Sec. 1.

Section 924.2 - Secrecy

Each grand juror shall keep secret whatever he himself or any other grand juror has said, or in what manner he or any other grand juror has voted on a matter before them. Any court may require a grand juror to disclose the testimony of a witness examined before the grand jury, for the purpose of ascertaining whether it is consistent with that given by the witness before the court, or to disclose the testimony given before the grand jury by any person, upon a charge against such person for perjury in giving his testimony or upon trial therefor.

Added by Stats. 1959, Ch. 501.

Section 924.3 - Questioning grand juror

A grand juror cannot be questioned for anything he may say or any vote he may give in the grand jury relative to a matter legally pending before the jury, except for a perjury of which he may have been guilty in making an accusation or giving testimony to his fellow jurors.

Added by Stats. 1959, Ch. 501.

Section 924.4 - Passing on records, information, or evidence to succeeding grand jury

Notwithstanding the provisions of Sections 924.1 and 924.2, any grand jury or, if the grand jury is no longer impaneled, the presiding judge of the superior court, may pass on and provide the succeeding grand jury with any records, information, or evidence acquired by the grand jury during the course of any investigation conducted by it during its term of service, except any information or evidence that relates to a criminal investigation or that could form part or all of the basis for issuance of an indictment. Transcripts of testimony reported during any session of the grand jury shall be made available to the succeeding grand jury upon its request.

Amended by Stats 2002 ch 784 (SB 1316), s 536, eff. 1/1/2003.

Section 924.6 - Disclosure of testimony of grand jury witness in connection with criminal proceeding; inquiries involving shooting or excessive force by peace officer

(a) If no indictment is returned, the court that impaneled the grand jury shall, upon application of either party, order disclosure of all or part of the testimony of a witness before the grand jury to a defendant and the prosecutor in connection with any pending or subsequent criminal proceeding before any court if the court finds following an in camera hearing, which shall include the court's review of the grand jury's testimony, that the testimony is relevant, and appears to be admissible.

(b) If a grand jury decides not to return an indictment in a grand jury inquiry into an offense that involves a shooting or use of excessive force by a peace officer described in Section 830.1, subdivision (a) of Section 830.2, or Section 830.39, that led to the death of a person being detained or arrested by the peace officer pursuant to Section 836, the court that impaneled the grand jury shall, upon application of the district attorney, a legal representative of the decedent, or a legal representative of the news media or public, and with notice to the district attorney and the affected witness involved, and an opportunity to be heard, order disclosure of all or part of the indictment proceeding transcript, excluding the grand jury's private deliberations and voting, to the movant, unless the court expressly finds, following an in camera hearing, that there exists an overriding interest that outweighs the right of public access to the record, the overriding interest supports sealing the record, a substantial probability exists that the overriding interest will be prejudiced if the record is not sealed, the proposed sealing is narrowly tailored, and no less restrictive means exist to achieve the overriding interest.

Amended by Stats 2017 ch 204 (AB 1024),s 1, eff. 1/1/2018.

Article 2 - INVESTIGATION OF COUNTY, CITY, AND DISTRICT AFFAIRS

Section 925 - Investigation of officers, departments, or functions of county

The grand jury shall investigate and report on the operations, accounts, and records of the officers, departments, or functions of the county including those operations, accounts, and records of any special legislative district or other district in the county created pursuant to state law for which the officers of the county are serving in their ex officio capacity as officers of the districts. The investigations may be conducted on some selective basis each year, but the grand jury shall not duplicate any examination of financial statements which has been performed by or for the board of supervisors pursuant to Section 25250 of the Government Code; this provision shall not be construed to limit the power of the grand jury to investigate and report on the operations, accounts, and records of the officers, departments, or functions of the county. The grand jury may enter into a joint contract with the board of supervisors to employ the services of an expert as provided for in Section 926.

Repealed and added by Stats. 1977, Ch. 107.

Section 925a - Investigation of incorporated city or joint powers agency in county

The grand jury may at any time examine the books and records of any incorporated city or joint powers agency located in the county. In addition to any other investigatory powers granted by this chapter, the grand jury may investigate and report upon the operations, accounts, and records of the officers, departments, functions, and the method or system of performing the duties of any such city or joint powers agency and make such recommendations as it may deem proper and fit.

The grand jury may investigate and report upon the needs of all joint powers agencies in the county, including the abolition or creation of agencies and the equipment for, or the method or system of performing the duties of, the several agencies. It shall cause a copy of any such report to be transmitted to the governing body of any affected agency.

As used in this section, "joint powers agency" means an agency described in Section 6506 of the Government Code whose jurisdiction encompasses all or part of a county.

Amended by Stats. 1983, Ch. 590, Sec. 1.

Section 926 - Employment of experts

(a) If, in the judgment of the grand jury, the services of one or more experts are necessary for the purposes of Sections 925, 925a, 928, 933.1, and 933.5 or any of them, the grand jury may employ one or more experts, at an agreed compensation, to be first approved by the court. If, in the judgment of the grand jury, the services of assistants to such experts are required, the grand jury may employ such assistants, at a compensation to be agreed upon and approved by the court. Expenditures for the services of experts and assistants for the purposes of Section 933.5 shall not exceed the sum of thirty thousand dollars ($30,000) annually, unless such expenditures shall also be approved by the board of supervisors.

(b) When making an examination of the books, records, accounts, and documents maintained and processed by the county assessor, the grand jury, with the consent of the board of supervisors, may employ expert auditors or appraisers to assist in the examination. Auditors and appraisers, while performing pursuant to the directive of the grand jury, shall have access to all records and documents that may be inspected by the grand jury subject to the same limitations on public disclosure as apply to the grand jury.

(c) Any contract entered into by a grand jury pursuant to this section may include services to be performed after the discharge of the jury, but in no event may a jury contract for services to be performed later than six months after the end of the fiscal year during which the jury was impaneled.

(d) Any contract entered into by a grand jury pursuant to this section shall stipulate that the product of that contract shall be delivered on or before a time certain to the then-current grand jury of that county for such use as that jury finds appropriate to its adopted objectives.

Amended by Stats. 1988, Ch. 1297, Sec. 4.5.

Section 927 - Investigation of needs for increase or decrease in salaries of county-elected officials

A grand jury may, and when requested by the board of supervisors shall, investigate and report upon the needs for increase or decrease in salaries of the county-elected officials. A copy of such report shall be transmitted to the board of supervisors.

Amended by Stats. 1976, Ch. 481.

Section 928 - Investigation of needs of county officers

Every grand jury may investigate and report upon the needs of all county officers in the county, including the abolition or creation of offices and the equipment for, or the method or system of performing the duties of, the several offices. Such investigation and report shall be conducted selectively each year. The grand jury shall cause a copy of such report to be transmitted to each member of the board of supervisors of the county.

Amended by Stats. 1981, Ch. 800, Sec. 5.

Section 929 - Making evidentiary material available to public

As to any matter not subject to privilege, with the approval of the presiding judge of the superior court or the judge appointed by the presiding judge to supervise the grand jury, a grand jury may make available to the public part or all of the evidentiary material, findings, and other information relied upon by, or presented to, a grand jury for its final report in any civil grand jury investigation provided that the name of any person, or facts that lead to the identity of any person who provided information to the grand jury, shall not be released. Prior to granting approval pursuant to this section, a judge may require the redaction or masking of any part of the evidentiary material, findings, or other information to be released to the public including, but not limited to, the identity of witnesses and any testimony or materials of a defamatory or libelous nature.

Added by Stats. 1998, Ch. 79, Sec. 1. Effective January 1, 1999.

Section 930 - Comment on person or official who has not been indicted

If any grand jury shall, in the report above mentioned, comment upon any person or official who has not been indicted by such grand jury such comments shall not be deemed to be privileged.

Added by Stats. 1959, Ch. 501.

Section 931 - Payment of expenses of grand jurors

All expenses of the grand jurors incurred under this article shall be paid by the treasurer of the county out of the general fund of the county upon warrants drawn by the county auditor upon the written order of the judge of the superior court of the county.

Added by Stats. 1959, Ch. 501.

Section 932 - Order to institute suit to recover money due county

After investigating the books and accounts of the various officials of the county, as provided in the foregoing sections of this article, the grand jury may order the district attorney of the county to institute suit to recover any money that, in the judgment of the grand jury, may from any cause be due the county. The order of the grand jury, certified by the foreman of the grand jury and filed with the clerk of the superior court of the county, shall be full authority for the district attorney to institute and maintain any such suit.

Amended by Stats 2002 ch 784 (SB 1316), s 537, eff. 1/1/2003.

Section 933 - Final report

(a) Each grand jury shall submit to the presiding judge of the superior court a final report of its findings and recommendations that pertain to county government matters during the fiscal or calendar year. Final reports on any appropriate subject may be submitted to the presiding judge of the superior court at any time during the term of service of a grand jury. A final report may be submitted for comment to responsible officers, agencies, or departments, including the county board of supervisors, when applicable, upon finding of the presiding judge that the report is in compliance with this title. For 45 days after the end of the term, the foreperson and his or her designees shall, upon reasonable notice, be available to clarify the recommendations of the report.

(b) One copy of each final report, together with the responses thereto, found to be in compliance with this title shall be placed on file with the clerk of the court and remain on file in the office of the clerk. The clerk shall immediately forward a true copy of the report and the responses to the State Archivist who shall retain that report and all responses in perpetuity.

(c) No later than 90 days after the grand jury submits a final report on the operations of any public agency subject to its reviewing authority, the governing body of the public agency shall comment to the presiding judge of the superior court on the findings and recommendations pertaining to matters under the control of the governing body, and every elected county officer or agency head for which the grand jury has responsibility pursuant to Section 914.1 shall comment within 60 days to the presiding judge of the superior court, with an information copy sent to the board of supervisors, on the findings and recommendations pertaining to matters under the control of that county officer or agency head and any agency or agencies which that officer or agency head supervises or controls. In any city and county, the mayor shall also comment on the findings and recommendations. All of these comments and reports shall forthwith be submitted to the presiding judge of the superior court who impaneled the grand jury. A copy of all responses to grand jury reports shall be placed on file with the clerk of the public agency and the office of the county clerk, or the mayor when applicable, and shall remain on file in those offices. One copy shall be placed on file with the applicable grand jury final report by, and in the control of the currently impaneled grand jury, where it shall be maintained for a minimum of five years.

(d) As used in this section "agency" includes a department.

Amended by Stats 2002 ch 784 (SB 1316), s 538, eff. 1/1/2003.

Section 933.05 - Duties of responding person or entity

(a) For purposes of subdivision (b) of Section 933, as to each grand jury finding, the responding person or entity shall indicate one of the following:

(1) The respondent agrees with the finding.

(2) The respondent disagrees wholly or partially with the finding, in which case the response shall specify the portion of the finding that is disputed and shall include an explanation of the reasons therefor.

(b) For purposes of subdivision (b) of Section 933, as to each grand jury recommendation, the responding person or entity shall report one of the following actions:

(1) The recommendation has been implemented, with a summary regarding the implemented action.

(2) The recommendation has not yet been implemented, but will be implemented in the future, with a timeframe for implementation.

(3) The recommendation requires further analysis, with an explanation and the scope and parameters of an analysis or study, and a timeframe for the matter to be prepared for discussion by the officer or head of the agency or department being investigated or reviewed, including the governing body of the public agency when applicable. This timeframe shall not exceed six months from the date of publication of the grand jury report.

(4) The recommendation will not be implemented because it is not warranted or is not reasonable, with an explanation therefor.

(c) However, if a finding or recommendation of the grand jury addresses budgetary or personnel matters of a county agency or department headed by an elected officer, both the agency or department head and the board of supervisors shall respond if requested by the grand jury, but the response of the board of supervisors shall address only those budgetary or personnel matters over which it has some decisionmaking authority. The response of the elected agency or department head shall address all aspects of the findings or recommendations affecting his or her agency or department.

(d) A grand jury may request a subject person or entity to come before the grand jury for the purpose of reading and discussing the findings of the grand jury report that relates to that person or entity in order to verify the accuracy of the findings prior to their release.

(e) During an investigation, the grand jury shall meet with the subject of that investigation regarding the investigation, unless the court, either on its own determination or upon request of the foreperson of the grand jury, determines that such a meeting would be detrimental.

(f) A grand jury shall provide to the affected agency a copy of the portion of the grand jury report relating to that person or entity two working days prior to its public release and after the approval of the presiding judge. No officer, agency, department, or governing body of a public agency shall disclose any contents of the report prior to the public release of the final report.

Amended by Stats. 1997, Ch. 443, Sec. 5. Effective January 1, 1998.

Section 933.06 - Final report in county having population of 20,000 or less

(a) Notwithstanding Sections 916 and 940, in a county having a population of 20,000 or less, a final report may be adopted and submitted pursuant to Section 933 with the concurrence of at least 10 grand jurors if all of the following conditions are met:

(1) The grand jury consisting of 19 persons has been impaneled pursuant to law, and the membership is reduced from 19 to fewer than 12.

(2) The vacancies have not been filled pursuant to Section 908.1 within 30 days from the time that the clerk of the superior court is given written notice that the vacancy has occurred.

(3) A final report has not been submitted by the grand jury pursuant to Section 933.

(b) Notwithstanding Section 933, no responsible officers, agencies, or departments shall be required to comment on a final report submitted pursuant to this section.

Amended by Stats 2001 ch 854 (SB 205), s 40, eff. 1/1/2002.

Section 933.1 - Examination of books and records of redevelopment agency, housing authority, or joint powers agency

A grand jury may at any time examine the books and records of a redevelopment agency, a housing authority, created pursuant to Division 24 (commencing with Section 33000) of the Health and Safety Code, or a joint powers agency created pursuant to Chapter 5 (commencing with Section 6500) of Division 7 of Title 1 of the Government Code, and, in addition to any other investigatory powers granted by this chapter, may investigate and report upon the method or system of performing the duties of such agency or authority.

Amended by Stats. 1986, Ch. 279, Sec. 1.

Section 933.5 - Examination of books and records of special-purpose assessing or taxing district or local agency formation commission

A grand jury may at any time examine the books and records of any special-purpose assessing or taxing district located wholly or partly in the county or the local agency formation commission in the county, and, in addition to any other investigatory powers granted by this chapter, may investigate and report upon the method or system of performing the duties of such district or commission.

Amended by Stats. 1979, Ch. 306.

Section 933.6 - Examination of books and records of nonprofit corporation

A grand jury may at any time examine the books and records of any nonprofit corporation established by or operated on behalf of a public entity the books and records of which it is authorized by law to examine, and, in addition to any other investigatory powers granted by this chapter, may investigate and report upon the method or system of performing the duties of such nonprofit corporation.

Added by Stats. 1986, Ch. 279, Sec. 2.

Article 3 - LEGAL AND OTHER ASSISTANTS FOR GRAND JURIES

Section 934 - Request for advice

(a) The grand jury may, at all times, request the advice of the court, or the judge thereof, the district attorney, the county counsel, or the Attorney General. Unless advice is requested, the judge of the court, or county counsel as to civil matters, shall not be present during the sessions of the grand jury.

(b) The Attorney General may grant or deny a request for advice from the grand jury. If the Attorney General grants a request for advice from the grand jury, the Attorney General shall fulfill that request within existing financial and staffing resources.

Amended by Stats. 1998, Ch. 230, Sec. 3. Effective January 1, 1999.

Section 935 - Appearance of district attorney before grand jury

The district attorney of the county may at all times appear before the grand jury for the purpose of giving information or advice relative to any matter cognizable by the grand jury, and may interrogate witnesses before the grand jury whenever he thinks it necessary. When a charge against or involving the district attorney, or assistant district attorney, or deputy district attorney, or anyone employed by or connected with the office of the district attorney, is being investigated by the grand jury, such district attorney, or assistant district attorney, or deputy district attorney, or all or anyone or more of them, shall not be allowed to be present before such grand jury when such charge is being investigated, in an official capacity but only as a witness, and he shall only be present while a witness and after his appearance as such witness shall leave the place where the grand jury is holding its session.

Added by Stats. 1959, Ch. 501.

Section 936 - Employment of special counsel and special investigators by attorney general

When requested so to do by the grand jury of any county, the Attorney General may employ special counsel and special investigators, whose duty it shall be to investigate and present the evidence in such investigation to such grand jury.

The services of such special counsel and special investigators shall be a county charge of such county.

Added by Stats. 1959, Ch. 501.

Section 936.5 - Employment of special counsel and special investigators by presiding judge of superior court

(a) When requested to do so by the grand jury of any county, the presiding judge of the superior court may employ special counsel and special investigators, whose duty it shall be to investigate and present the evidence of the investigation to the grand jury.

(b) Prior to the appointment, the presiding judge shall conduct an evidentiary hearing and find that a conflict exists that would prevent the local district attorney, the county counsel, and the Attorney General from performing such investigation. Notice of the hearing shall be given to each of them unless he or she is a subject of the investigation. The finding of the presiding judge may be appealed by the district attorney, the county counsel, or the Attorney General. The order shall be stayed pending the appeal made under this section.

(c) The authority to appoint is contingent upon the certification by the auditor-comptroller of the county, that the grand jury has funds appropriated to it sufficient to compensate the special counsel and investigator for services rendered pursuant to the court order. In the absence of a certification the court has no authority to appoint. In the event the county board of supervisors or a member thereof is under investigation, the county has an obligation to appropriate the necessary funds.

Added by Stats. 1980, Ch. 290, Sec. 2.

Section 936.7 - Special counsel to grand jury in county of eighth class

(a) In a county of the eighth class, as defined by Sections 28020 and 28029 of the Government Code, upon a request by the grand jury, the presiding judge of the superior court may retain, in the name of the county, a special counsel to the grand jury. The request shall be presented to the presiding judge in camera, by an affidavit, executed by the foreperson of the grand jury, which specifies the reason for the request and the nature of the services sought, and which certifies that the appointment of the special counsel is reasonably necessary to aid the work of the grand jury. The affidavit shall be confidential and its contents may not be made public except by order of the presiding judge upon a showing of good cause. The special counsel shall be selected by the presiding judge following submission of the name of the nominee to the board of supervisors for comment. The special counsel shall be retained under a contract executed by the presiding judge in the name of the county. The contract shall contain the following terms:

(1) The types of legal services to be rendered to the grand jury; provided, (i) that the special counsel's duties shall not include any legal advisory, investigative, or prosecutorial service that by statute is vested within the powers of the district attorney, and (ii) that the special counsel may not perform any investigative or prosecutorial service whatsoever except upon advance written approval by the presiding judge, which specifies the number of hours of these services, the hourly rate therefor, and the subject matter of the inquiry.

(2) The hourly rate of compensation of the special counsel for legal advisory services delivered, together with a maximum contract amount payable for all services rendered under the contract during the term thereof, and all service authorizations issued pursuant thereto.

(3) That the contract may be canceled in advance of the expiration of its term by the presiding judge pursuant to service upon the special counsel of 10 days' advance written notice.

(b) The maximum contract amount shall be determined by the board of supervisors and included in the grand jury's annual operational budget. The maximum amount shall be subject to increase by the presiding judge through contract amendment during the term thereof, subject to and in compliance with the procedure prescribed by Section 914.5.

(c) The contract shall constitute a public record and shall be subject to public inspection and copying pursuant to the provisions of the California Public Records Act (Division 10 (commencing with Section 7920.000) of Title 1 of the Government Code). However, at the sole discretion of the board of supervisors, any or all of the following steps may be taken:

(1) The nomination by the presiding judge, and any or all actions by the board of supervisors in commenting upon the nominee and the comments, may be made confidential.

(2) The deliberations and actions may be undertaken in meetings from which the public is excluded, and the communication containing comments may constitute a confidential record that is not subject to public inspection or copying except at the sole discretion of the board of supervisors. Moreover, any written authorization by the presiding judge pursuant to paragraph (1) of subdivision (a) shall constitute a confidential record that is not subject to public inspection or copying except in connection with a dispute concerning compensation for services rendered.

Amended by Stats 2021 ch 615 (AB 474),s 341, eff. 1/1/2022, op. 1/1/2023.

Added by Stats. 1988, Ch. 886, Sec. 2.

Section 937 - Interpreter

The grand jury or district attorney may require by subpoena the attendance of any person before the grand jury as interpreter. While his services are necessary, such interpreter may be present at the examination of witnesses before the grand jury. The compensation for services of such interpreter constitutes a charge against the county, and shall be fixed by the grand jury.

Amended by Stats. 1976, Ch. 1264.

Section 938 - Stenographic reporter

(a) Whenever criminal causes are being investigated before the grand jury, it shall appoint a competent stenographic reporter. He shall be sworn and shall report in shorthand the testimony given in such causes and shall transcribe the shorthand in all cases where an indictment is returned or accusation presented.

(b) At the request of the grand jury, the reporter shall also prepare transcripts of any testimony reported during any session of the immediately preceding grand jury.

Amended by Stats. 1975, Ch. 298.

Section 938.1 - Certification and delivery of transcript

(a) If an indictment has been found or accusation presented against a defendant, such stenographic reporter shall certify and deliver to the clerk of the superior court in the county an original transcription of the reporter's shorthand notes and a copy thereof and as many additional copies as there are defendants, other than fictitious defendants, regardless of the number of charges or fictitious defendants included in the same investigation. The reporter shall complete the certification and delivery within 10 days after the indictment has been found or the accusation presented unless the court for good cause makes an order extending the time. The time shall not be extended more than 20 days. The clerk shall file the original of the transcript, deliver a copy of the transcript to the district attorney immediately upon receipt thereof and deliver a copy of such transcript to each such defendant or the defendant's attorney. If the copy of the testimony is not served as provided in this section, the court shall on motion of the defendant continue the trial to such time as may be necessary to secure to the defendant receipt of a copy of such testimony 10 days before such trial. If several criminal charges are investigated against a defendant on one investigation and thereafter separate indictments are returned or accusations presented upon said several charges, the delivery to such defendant or the defendant's attorney of one copy of the transcript of such investigation shall be a compliance with this section as to all of such indictments or accusations.

(b) The transcript shall not be open to the public until 10 days after its delivery to the defendant or the defendant's attorney. Thereafter the transcript shall be open to the public unless the court orders otherwise on its own motion or on motion of a party pending a determination as to whether all or part of the transcript should be sealed. If the court determines that there is a reasonable likelihood that making all or any part of the transcript public may prejudice a defendant's right to a fair and impartial trial, that part of the transcript shall be sealed until the defendant's trial has been completed.

Amended by Stats 2002 ch 784 (SB 1316), s 539, eff. 1/1/2003.

Section 938.2 - Payment for preparing transcript

(a) For preparing any transcript in any case pursuant to subdivision (a) of Section 938.1, the stenographic reporter shall draw no salary or fees from the county for preparing such transcript in any case until all such transcripts of testimony in such case so taken by him are written up and delivered. Before making the order for payment to the reporter, the judge of the superior court shall require the reporter to show by affidavit or otherwise that he has written up and delivered all testimony taken by him, in accordance with subdivision (a) of Section 938 and Section 938.1.

(b) Before making the order for payment to a reporter who has prepared transcripts pursuant to subdivision (b) of Section 938, the judge of the superior court shall require the reporter to show by affidavit or otherwise that he has written up and delivered all testimony requested of him in accordance with that sudivision.

Amended by Stats. 1975, Ch. 298.

Section 938.3 - Payment for services of stenographic reporter

The services of the stenographic reporter shall constitute a charge against the county, and the stenographic reporter shall be compensated for reporting and transcribing at the same rates as prescribed in Sections 69947 to 69954, inclusive, of the Government Code, to be paid out of the county treasury on a warrant of the county auditor when ordered by the judge of the superior court.

Amended by Stats. 1987, Ch. 828, Sec. 56.

Section 938.4 - Suitable meeting room and other support

The superior court shall arrange for a suitable meeting room and other support as the court determines is necessary for the grand jury. Any costs incurred by the court as a result of this section shall be absorbed by the court or the county from existing resources.

Added by Stats. 1997, Ch. 443, Sec. 6. Effective January 1, 1998.

Article 4 - CONDUCT OF INVESTIGATIONS

Section 939 - Presence during criminal sessions

No person other than those specified in Article 3 (commencing with Section 934), and in Sections 939.1, 939.11, and 939.21, and the officer having custody of a prisoner witness while the prisoner is testifying, is permitted to be present during the criminal sessions of the grand jury except the members and witnesses actually under examination. Members of the grand jury who have been excused pursuant to Section 939.5 shall not be present during any part of these proceedings. No persons other than grand jurors shall be permitted to be present during the expression of the opinions of the grand jurors, or the giving of their votes, on any criminal or civil matter before them.

Amended by Stats. 1998, Ch. 755, Sec. 1. Effective January 1, 1999.

Section 939.1 - Request for public sessions

The grand jury acting through its foreman and the attorney general or the district attorney may make a joint written request for public sessions of the grand jury. The request shall be filed with the superior court. If the court, or the judge thereof, finds that the subject matter of the investigation affects the general public welfare, involving the alleged corruption, misfeasance, or malfeasance in office or dereliction of duty of public officials or employees or of any person allegedly acting in conjunction or conspiracy with such officials or employees in such alleged acts, the court or judge may make an order directing the grand jury to conduct its investigation in a session or sessions open to the public. The order shall state the finding of the court. The grand jury shall comply with the order.

The conduct of such investigation and the examination of witnesses shall be by the members of the grand jury and the district attorney. The deliberation of the grand jury and its voting upon such investigation shall be in private session. The grand jury may find indictments based wholly or partially upon the evidence introduced at such public session.

Added by Stats. 1959, Ch. 501.

Section 939.11 - Interpreter to assist grand juror

Any member of the grand jury who has a hearing, sight, or speech disability may request an interpreter when his or her services are necessary to assist the juror to carry out his or her duties. The request shall be filed with the superior court. If the court, or the judge thereof, finds that an interpreter is necessary, the court shall make an order to that effect and may require by subpoena the attendance of any person before the grand jury as interpreter. If the services of an interpreter are necessary, the court shall instruct the grand jury and the interpreter that the interpreter is not to participate in the jury's deliberations in any manner except to facilitate communication between the disabled juror and the other jurors. The court shall place the interpreter under oath not to disclose any grand jury matters, including the testimony of any witness, statements of any grand juror, or the vote of any grand juror, except in the due course of judicial proceedings.

Added by Stats. 1986, Ch. 357, Sec. 3.

Section 939.2 - Subpoena requiring attendance of witness

A subpoena requiring the attendance of a witness before the grand jury may be signed and issued by the district attorney, his investigator or, upon request of the grand jury, by any judge of the superior court, for witnesses in the state, in support of the prosecution, for those witnesses whose testimony, in his opinion is material in an investigation before the grand jury, and for such other witnesses as the grand jury, upon an investigation pending before them, may direct.

Amended by Stats. 1971, Ch. 1196.

Section 939.21 - Support person for prosecuting witness who is minor or dependent person; confidentiality; prompting, swaying, or influencing witness

(a) Any prosecution witness before the grand jury in a proceeding involving a violation of Section 243.4, 261, 273a, 273d, 285, 286, 287, 288, 288.5, or 289, subdivision (1) of Section 314, Section 368, 647.6, or former Section 288a or 647a, who is a minor or a dependent person, may, at the discretion of the prosecution, select a person of his or her own choice to attend the testimony of the prosecution witness for the purpose of providing support. The person chosen shall not be a witness in the same proceeding, or a person described in Section 1070 of the Evidence Code.

(b) The grand jury foreperson shall inform any person permitted to attend the grand jury proceedings pursuant to this section that grand jury proceedings are confidential and may not be discussed with anyone not in attendance at the proceedings. The foreperson also shall admonish that person not to prompt, sway, or influence the witness in any way. Nothing in this section shall preclude the presiding judge from exercising his or her discretion to remove a person from the grand jury proceeding whom the judge believes is prompting, swaying, or influencing the witness.

Amended by Stats 2018 ch 423 (SB 1494),s 82, eff. 1/1/2019.
Amended by Stats 2004 ch 823 (AB 20), s 14, eff. 1/1/2005.

Section 939.22 - [Repealed]

Added by Stats 2011 ch 679 (AB 622),s 1, eff. 1/1/2012.

Section 939.3 - Refusal to answer question or produce evidence on ground that person may be incriminated

In any investigation or proceeding before a grand jury for any felony offense when a person refuses to answer a question or produce evidence of any other kind on the ground that he may be incriminated thereby, proceedings may be had under Section 1324.

Added by Stats. 1959, Ch. 501.

Section 939.4 - Administration of oath by foreman

The foreman may administer an oath to any witness appearing before the grand jury.

Added by Stats. 1959, Ch. 501.

Section 939.5 - Duties of foreman

Before considering a charge against any person, the foreman of the grand jury shall state to those present the matter to be considered and the person to be charged with an offense in connection therewith. He shall direct any member of the grand jury who has a state of mind in reference to the case or to either party which will prevent him from acting impartially and without prejudice to the substantial rights of the party to retire. Any violation of this section by the foreman or any member of the grand jury is punishable by the court as a contempt.

Added by Stats. 1959, Ch. 501.

Section 939.6 - Receipt of evidence

(a) Subject to subdivision (b), in the investigation of a charge, the grand jury shall receive no other evidence than what is:

(1) Given by witnesses produced and sworn before the grand jury;

(2) Furnished by writings, material objects, or other things presented to the senses; or

(3) Contained in a deposition that is admissible under subdivision 3 of Section 686.

(b) Except as provided in subdivision (c), the grand jury shall not receive any evidence except that which would be admissible over objection at the trial of a criminal action, but the fact that evidence that would have been excluded at trial was received by the grand jury does not render the indictment void where sufficient competent evidence to support the indictment was received by the grand jury.

(c) Notwithstanding Section 1200 of the Evidence Code, as to the evidence relating to the foundation for admissibility into evidence of documents, exhibits, records, and other items of physical evidence, the evidence to support the indictment may be based in whole or in part upon the sworn testimony of a law enforcement officer relating the statement of a declarant made out of court and offered for the truth of the matter asserted. Any law enforcement officer testifying as to a hearsay statement pursuant to this subdivision shall have either five years of law enforcement experience or have completed a training course certified by the Commission on Peace Officer Standards and Training that includes training in the investigation and reporting of cases and testifying at preliminary hearings.

Amended by Stats. 1998, Ch. 757, Sec. 4. Effective January 1, 1999.

Section 939.7 - Hearing of evidence; order to produce evidence

The grand jury is not required to hear evidence for the defendant, but it shall weigh all the evidence submitted to it, and when it has reason to believe that other evidence within its reach will explain away the charge, it shall order the evidence to be produced, and for that purpose may require the district attorney to issue process for the witnesses.

Added by Stats. 1959, Ch. 501.

Section 939.71 - Exculpatory evidence

(a) If the prosecutor is aware of exculpatory evidence, the prosecutor shall inform the grand jury of its nature and existence. Once the prosecutor has informed the grand jury of exculpatory evidence pursuant to this section, the prosecutor shall inform the grand jury of its duties under Section 939.7. If a failure to comply with the provisions of this section results in substantial prejudice, it shall be grounds for dismissal of the portion of the indictment related to that evidence.

(b) It is the intent of the Legislature by enacting this section to codify the holding in Johnson v. Superior Court, 15 Cal. 3d 248, and to affirm the duties of the grand jury pursuant to Section 939.7.

Added by Stats. 1997, Ch. 22, Sec. 1. Effective January 1, 1998.

Section 939.8 - Indictment

The grand jury shall find an indictment when all the evidence before it, taken together, if unexplained or uncontradicted, would, in its judgment, warrant a conviction by a trial jury.

Added by Stats. 1959, Ch. 501.

Section 939.9 - Report, declaration, or recommendation

A grand jury shall make no report, declaration, or recommendation on any matter except on the basis of its own investigation of the matter made by such grand jury. A grand jury shall not adopt as its own the recommendation of another grand jury unless the grand jury adopting such recommendation does so after its own investigation of the matter as to which the recommendation is made, as required by this section.

Added by Stats. 1959, Ch. 501.

Section 939.91 - Request of report or declaration that grand jury could not find indictment

(a) A grand jury which investigates a charge against a person, and as a result thereof cannot find an indictment against such person, shall, at the request of such person and upon the approval of the court which impaneled the grand jury, report or declare that a charge against such person was investigated and that the grand jury could not as a result of the evidence presented find an indictment. The report or declaration shall be issued upon completion of the investigation of the suspected criminal conduct, or series of related suspected criminal conduct, and in no event beyond the end of the grand jury's term.

(b) A grand jury shall, at the request of the person called and upon the approval of the court which impaneled the grand jury, report or declare that any person called before the grand jury for a purpose, other than to investigate a charge against such person, was called only as a witness to an investigation which did not involve a charge against such person. The report or declaration shall be issued upon completion of the investigation of the suspected criminal conduct, or series of related suspected criminal conduct, and in no event beyond the end of the grand jury's term.

Added by Stats. 1975, Ch. 467.

Title 5 - THE PLEADINGS

Chapter 1 - FINDING AND PRESENTMENT OF THE INDICTMENT

Section 940 - Concurrence of grand jurors

An indictment cannot be found without concurrence of at least 14 grand jurors in a county in which the required number of members of the grand jury prescribed by Section 888.2 is 23, at least eight grand jurors in a county in which the required number of members is 11, and at least 12 grand jurors in all other counties. When so found it shall be endorsed, "A true bill," and the endorsement shall be signed by the foreman of the grand jury.

Amended by Stats. 1994, Ch. 295, Sec. 2. Effective January 1, 1995.

Section 943 - Names of witnesses

When an indictment is found, the names of the witnesses examined before the Grand Jury, or whose depositions may have been read before them, must be inserted at the foot of the indictment, or indorsed thereon, before it is presented to the Court.

Enacted 1872.

Section 944 - Presentment and filing of indictment

An indictment, when found by the grand jury, must be presented by their foreman, in their presence, to the court, and must be filed with the clerk. No recommendation as to the dollar amount of bail to be fixed shall be made to any court by any grand jury.

Amended by Stats. 1974, Ch. 695.

Section 945 - Indictment found against defendant not in custody

When an indictment is found against a defendant not in custody, the same proceedings must be had as are prescribed in Sections 979 to 984, inclusive, against a defendant who fails to appear for arraignment.

Enacted 1872.

Chapter 2 - RULES OF PLEADING

Section 948 - Forms of pleading in criminal actions

All the forms of pleading in criminal actions, and the rules by which the sufficiency of pleadings is to be determined, are those prescribed by this Code.

Enacted 1872.

Section 949 - First pleading

The first pleading on the part of the people in the superior court in a felony case is the indictment, information, or the complaint in any case certified to the superior court under Section 859a. The first pleading on the part of the people in a misdemeanor or infraction case is the complaint except as otherwise provided by law. The first pleading on the part of the people in a proceeding pursuant to Section 3060 of the Government Code is an accusation.

Amended by Stats. 1998, Ch. 931, Sec. 373. Effective September 28, 1998.

Section 950 - Accusatory pleading

The accusatory pleading must contain:

1. The title of the action, specifying the name of the court to which the same is presented, and the names of the parties;
2. A statement of the public offense or offenses charged therein.

Amended by Stats. 1951, Ch. 1674.

Section 951 - Form of indictment or information

An indictment or information may be in substantially the following form: The people of the State of California against A. B. In the superior court of the State of California, in and for the county of ____. The grand jury (or the district attorney) of the county of ____ hereby accuses A. B. of a felony (or misdemeanor), to wit: (giving the name of the crime, as murder, burglary, etc.), in that on or about the ____ day of ____, 19__, in the county of ____, State of California, he (here insert statement of act or omission, as for example, "murdered C. D.").

Amended by Stats. 1927, Ch. 613.

Section 952 - Charging offense

In charging an offense, each count shall contain, and shall be sufficient if it contains in substance, a statement that the accused has committed some public offense therein specified. Such statement may be made in ordinary and concise language without any technical averments or any allegations of matter not essential to be proved. It may be in the words of the enactment describing the offense or declaring the matter to be a public offense, or in any words sufficient to give the accused notice of the offense of which he is accused. In charging theft it shall be sufficient to allege that the defendant unlawfully took the labor or property of another.

Amended by Stats. 1929, Ch. 159.

Section 953 - Defendant charged by fictitious or erroneous name and true name discovered

When a defendant is charged by a fictitious or erroneous name, and in any stage of the proceedings his true name is discovered, it must be inserted in the subsequent proceedings, referring to the fact of his being charged by the name mentioned in the accusatory pleading.
Amended by Stats. 1951, Ch. 1674.

Section 954 - Charge of two or more different offenses in accusatory pleading; consolidation

An accusatory pleading may charge two or more different offenses connected together in their commission, or different statements of the same offense or two or more different offenses of the same class of crimes or offenses, under separate counts, and if two or more accusatory pleadings are filed in such cases in the same court, the court may order them to be consolidated. The prosecution is not required to elect between the different offenses or counts set forth in the accusatory pleading, but the defendant may be convicted of any number of the offenses charged, and each offense of which the defendant is convicted must be stated in the verdict or the finding of the court; provided, that the court in which a case is triable, in the interests of justice and for good cause shown, may in its discretion order that the different offenses or counts set forth in the accusatory pleading be tried separately or divided into two or more groups and each of said groups tried separately. An acquittal of one or more counts shall not be deemed an acquittal of any other count.
Amended by Stats. 1951, Ch. 1674.

Section 954.1 - Admissibility of evidence in trial of jointly charged offenses

In cases in which two or more different offenses of the same class of crimes or offenses have been charged together in the same accusatory pleading, or where two or more accusatory pleadings charging offenses of the same class of crimes or offenses have been consolidated, evidence concerning one offense or offenses need not be admissible as to the other offense or offenses before the jointly charged offenses may be tried together before the same trier of fact.
Added June 5, 1990, by initiative Proposition 115, Sec. 19.

Section 955 - Time at which offense was committed

The precise time at which the offense was committed need not be stated in the accusatory pleading, but it may be alleged to have been committed at any time before the finding or filing thereof, except where the time is a material ingredient in the offense.
Amended by Stats. 1951, Ch. 1674.

Section 956 - Erroneous allegation as to person injured, place where offense committed, or property involved

When an offense involves the commission of, or an attempt to commit a private injury, and is described with sufficient certainty in other respects to identify the act, an erroneous allegation as to the person injured, or intended to be injured, or of the place where the offense was committed, or of the property involved in its commission, is not material.
Amended by Stats. 1927, Ch. 611.

Section 957 - Constructions of words used in accusatory pleading

The words used in an accusatory pleading are construed in their usual acceptance in common language, except such words and phrases as are defined by law, which are construed according to their legal meaning.
Amended by Stats. 1951, Ch. 1674.

Section 958 - Words used in statute

Words used in a statute to define a public offense need not be strictly pursued in the accusatory pleading, but other words conveying the same meaning may be used.
Amended by Stats. 1951, Ch. 1674.

Section 959 - Sufficiency of accusatory pleading

The accusatory pleading is sufficient if it can be understood therefrom:

1. That it is filed in a court having authority to receive it, though the name of the court be not stated.
2. If an indictment, that it was found by a grand jury of the county in which the court was held, or if an information, that it was subscribed and presented to the court by the district attorney of the county in which the court was held.
3. If a complaint, that it is made and subscribed by some natural person and sworn to before some officer entitled to administer oaths.
4. That the defendant is named, or if his name is unknown, that he is described by a fictitious name, with a statement that his true name is to the grand jury, district attorney, or complainant, as the case may be, unknown.
5. That the offense charged therein is triable in the court in which it is filed, except in case of a complaint filed with a magistrate for the purposes of a preliminary examination.
6. That the offense was committed at some time prior to the filing of the accusatory pleading.

Amended by Stats. 1951, Ch. 1674.

Section 959.1 - Filing of accusatory pleading in electronic form

(a) Notwithstanding Sections 740, 806, 949, and 959 or any other law to the contrary, a criminal prosecution may be commenced by filing an accusatory pleading in electronic form with the magistrate or in a court having authority to receive it.

(b) As used in this section, accusatory pleadings include, but are not limited to, the complaint, the information, and the indictment.

(c) A magistrate or court is authorized to receive and file an accusatory pleading in electronic form if all of the following conditions are met:

(1) The accusatory pleading is issued in the name of, and transmitted by, a public prosecutor or law enforcement agency filing pursuant to Chapter 5c (commencing with Section 853.5) or Chapter 5d (commencing with Section 853.9), or by a clerk of the court with respect to complaints issued for the offenses of failure to appear, pay a fine, or comply with an order of the court.

(2) The magistrate or court has the facility to electronically store the accusatory pleading for the statutory period of record retention.

(3) The magistrate or court has the ability to reproduce the accusatory pleading in physical form upon demand and payment of any costs involved. An accusatory pleading shall be deemed to have been filed when it has been received by the magistrate or court.

When transmitted in electronic form, the accusatory pleading shall be exempt from any requirement that it be subscribed by a natural person. It is sufficient to satisfy any requirement that an accusatory pleading, or any part of it, be sworn to before an officer entitled to administer oaths, if the pleading, or any part of it, was in fact sworn to and the electronic form indicates which parts of the pleading were sworn to and the name of the officer who administered the oath.

(d) Notwithstanding any other law, a notice to appear issued on a form approved by the Judicial Council may be received and filed by a court in electronic form, if the following conditions are met:

(1) The notice to appear is issued and transmitted by a law enforcement agency prosecuting pursuant to Chapter 5c (commencing with Section 853.5) or Chapter 5d (commencing with Section 853.9) of Title 3 of Part 2 of this code, or Chapter 2 (commencing with Section 40300) of Division 17 of the Vehicle Code.

(2) The court has all of the following:

(A) The ability to receive the notice to appear in electronic format.

(B) The facility to electronically store an electronic copy and the data elements of the notice to appear for the statutory period of record retention.

(C) The ability to reproduce the electronic copy of the notice to appear and those data elements in printed form upon demand and payment of any costs involved.

(3) The issuing agency has the ability to reproduce the notice to appear in physical form upon demand and payment of any costs involved.

(e) A notice to appear that is received under subdivision (d) is deemed to have been filed when it has been accepted by the court and is in the form approved by the Judicial Council.

(f) If transmitted in electronic form, the notice to appear is deemed to have been signed by the defendant if it includes a digitized facsimile of the defendant's signature on the notice to appear. A notice to appear filed electronically under subdivision (d) need not be subscribed by the citing officer. An electronically submitted notice to appear need not be verified by the citing officer with a declaration under penalty of perjury if the electronic form indicates which parts of the notice are verified by that declaration and the name of the officer making the declaration.

Amended by Stats 2006 ch 567 (AB 2303),s 23, eff. 1/1/2007.

Section 960 - Defect in form not prejudicing substantial right of defendant

No accusatory pleading is insufficient, nor can the trial, judgment, or other proceeding thereon be affected by reason of any defect or imperfection in matter of form which does not prejudice a substantial right of the defendant upon the merits.

Amended by Stats. 1951, Ch. 1674.

Section 961 - Presumptions of law or judicial notice

Neither presumptions of law, nor matters of which judicial notice is authorized or required to be taken, need be stated in an accusatory pleading.

Amended by Stats. 1965, Ch. 299.

Section 962 - Jurisdiction

In pleading a judgment or other determination of, or proceeding before, a Court or officer of special jurisdiction, it is not necessary to state the facts constituting jurisdiction; but the judgment or determination may be stated as given or made, or the proceedings had. The facts constituting jurisdiction, however, must be established on the trial.

Enacted 1872.

Section 963 - Pleading private statute or ordinance

In pleading a private statute, or an ordinance of a county or a municipal corporation, or a right derived therefrom, it is sufficient to refer to the statute or ordinance by its title and the day of its passage, and the court must thereupon take judicial notice thereof in the same manner that it takes judicial notice of matters listed in Section 452 of the Evidence Code.

Amended by Stats. 1965, Ch. 299.

Section 964 - Procedure to protect confidential personal information regarding witness or victim

(a) In each county, the district attorney and the courts, in consultation with any local law enforcement agencies that may desire to provide information or other assistance, shall establish a mutually agreeable procedure to protect confidential personal information regarding any witness or victim contained in a police report, arrest report, or investigative report if one of these reports is submitted to a court by a prosecutor in support of a criminal complaint, indictment, or information, or by a prosecutor or law enforcement officer in support of a search warrant or an arrest warrant.

(b) For purposes of this section, "confidential personal information" includes, but is not limited to, an address, telephone number, driver's license or California Identification Card number, social security number, date of birth, place of employment, employee identification number, mother's maiden name, demand deposit account number, savings or checking account number, or credit card number.

(c)

(1) This section may not be construed to impair or affect the provisions of Chapter 10 (commencing with Section 1054) of Title 6 of Part 2.

(2) This section may not be construed to impair or affect procedures regarding informant disclosure provided by Sections 1040 to 1042, inclusive, of the Evidence Code, or as altering procedures regarding sealed search warrant affidavits as provided by People v. Hobbs (1994) 7 Cal.4th 948.

(3) This section shall not be construed to impair or affect a criminal defense counsel's access to unredacted reports otherwise authorized by law, or the submission of documents in support of a civil complaint.

(4) This section applies as an exception to California Rule of Court 2.550, as provided by paragraph (2) of subdivision (a) of that rule.

Amended by Stats 2012 ch 867 (SB 1144),s 22, eff. 1/1/2013.

Added by Stats 2004 ch 507 (SB 58), s 1, eff. 9/14/2004.

Section 965 - Misdescription of instrument when it has been destroyed or withheld by defendant

When an instrument which is the subject of an indictment or information for forgery has been destroyed or withheld by the act or the procurement of the defendant, and the fact of such destruction or withholding is alleged in the indictment, or information, and established on the trial, the misdescription of the instrument is immaterial.

Amended by Code Amendments 1880, Ch. 47.

Section 966 - Accusatory pleading for perjury

In an accusatory pleading for perjury, or subornation of perjury, it is sufficient to set forth the substance of the controversy or matter in respect to which the offense was committed, and in what court and before whom the oath alleged to be false was taken, and that the court, or the person before whom it was taken, had authority to administer it, with proper allegations of the falsity of the matter on which the perjury is assigned; but the accusatory pleading need not set forth the pleadings, records, or proceedings with which the oath is connected, nor the commission or authority of the court or person before whom the perjury was committed.

Amended by Stats. 1951, Ch. 1674.

Section 967 - Accusatory pleading charging theft of money, bank notes, certificates of stock or valuable securities, or conspiracy to cheat or defraud person of such property

In an accusatory pleading charging the theft of money, bank notes, certificates of stock or valuable securities, or a conspiracy to cheat or defraud a person of any such property, it is sufficient to allege the theft, or the conspiracy to cheat or defraud, to be of money, bank notes, certificates of stock or valuable securities without specifying the coin, number, denomination, or kind thereof.

Amended by Stats. 1951, Ch. 1674.

Section 968 - Accusatory pleading charging exhibiting, publishing, passing, selling, or offering to sell, or having in possession, with such intent, any lewd or obscene book, pamphlet, picture, print, card, paper, or writing

An accusatory pleading charging exhibiting, publishing, passing, selling, or offering to sell, or having in possession, with such intent, any lewd or obscene book, pamphlet, picture, print, card, paper, or writing, need not set forth any portion of the language used or figures shown upon such book, pamphlet, picture, print, card, paper, or writing; but it is sufficient to state generally the fact of the lewdness or obscenity thereof.

Amended by Stats. 1951, Ch. 1674.

Section 969 - Charging fact of previous conviction of felony, attempt to commit felony, or theft

In charging the fact of a previous conviction of felony, or of an attempt to commit an offense which, if perpetrated, would have been a felony, or of theft, it is sufficient to state, "That the defendant, before the commission of the offense charged herein, was in (giving the title of the court in which the conviction was had) convicted of a felony (or attempt, etc., or of theft)." If more than one previous conviction is charged, the date of the judgment upon each conviction may be stated, and all known previous convictions, whether in this State or elsewhere, must be charged.

Amended by Stats. 1951, Ch. 1674.

Section 969a - Amendment of indictment or information to charge prior conviction or convictions

Whenever it shall be discovered that a pending indictment or information does not charge all prior felonies of which the defendant has been convicted either in this State or elsewhere, said indictment or information may be forthwith amended to charge such prior conviction or convictions, and if such amendment is made it shall be made upon order of the court, and no action of the grand jury (in the case of an indictment) shall be necessary. Defendant shall promptly be rearraigned on such information or indictment as amended and be required to plead thereto.

Amended by Stats. 1957, Ch. 1617.

Section 969b - Prima facie evidence of prior conviction

For the purpose of establishing prima facie evidence of the fact that a person being tried for a crime or public offense under the laws of this State has been convicted of an act punishable by imprisonment in a state prison, county jail or city jail of this State, and has served a term therefor in any penal institution, or has been convicted of an act in any other state, which would be punishable as a crime in this State, and has served a term therefor in any state penitentiary, reformatory, county jail or city jail, or has been convicted of an act declared to be a crime by any act or law of the United States, and has served a term therefor in any penal institution, the records or copies of records of any state penitentiary, reformatory, county jail, city jail, or federal penitentiary in which such person has been imprisoned, when such records or copies thereof have been certified by the official custodian of such records, may be introduced as such evidence.

Amended by Stats. 1949, Ch. 701.

Section 969c - [Repealed]

Repealed by Stats 2002 ch 787 (SB 1798), s 18, eff. 1/1/2003.

Section 969d - [Repealed]

Repealed by Stats 2002 ch 787 (SB 1798), s 19, eff. 1/1/2003.

Section 969e - Charging fact of previous conviction of enumerated statutes

In charging the fact of a previous conviction for a violation of Section 5652 of the Fish and Game Code, or of Section 13001 or 13002 of the Health and Safety Code or of Section 374b or 374d of the Penal Code or of Section 23111, 23112, or 23113 of the Vehicle Code, it is sufficient to state, "That the defendant, before the commission of the offense charged herein, was in (giving the title of the court in which the conviction was had) convicted of a violation of (specifying the section violated)."

Added by Stats. 1977, Ch. 1161. Note: Former termination clause was deleted by Stats. 1980, Ch. 364, Sec. 34.

Section 969f - Charging of serious felony

(a) Whenever a defendant has committed a serious felony as defined in subdivision (c) of Section 1192.7, the facts that make the crime constitute a serious felony may be charged in the accusatory pleading. However, the crime shall not be referred to as a serious felony nor shall the jury be informed that the crime is defined as a serious felony. This charge, if made, shall be added to and be a part of the count or each of the counts of the accusatory pleading which charged the offense. If the defendant pleads not guilty to the offense charged in any count which alleges that the defendant committed a serious felony, the question whether or not the defendant committed a serious felony as alleged shall be tried by the court or jury which tries the issue upon the plea of not guilty. If the defendant pleads guilty of the offense charged, the question whether or not the defendant committed a serious felony as alleged shall be separately admitted or denied by the defendant.

(b) In charging an act or acts that bring the defendant within the operation of paragraph (8) or (23) of subdivision (c) of Section 1192.7, it is sufficient for purposes of subdivision (a) if the pleading states the following: "It is further alleged that in the commission and attempted commission of the foregoing offense, the defendant ____, personally [inflicted great bodily injury on another person, other than an accomplice] [used a firearm, to wit: ____,] [used a dangerous and deadly weapon, to wit: ____,] within the meaning of Sections 667 and 1192.7 of the Penal Code."

Added by Stats. 1991, Ch. 249, Sec. 1.

Section 969.5 - Amendment to charge prior conviction or convictions where plea of guilty has been made

(a) Whenever it shall be discovered that a pending complaint to which a plea of guilty has been made under Section 859a does not charge all prior felonies of which the defendant has been convicted either in this state or elsewhere, the complaint may be forthwith amended to charge the prior conviction or convictions and the amendments may and shall be made upon order of the court. The defendant shall thereupon be arraigned before the court to which the complaint has been certified and shall be asked whether he or she has suffered the prior conviction. If the defendant enters a denial, his or her answer shall be entered in the minutes of the court. The refusal of the defendant to answer is equivalent to a denial that he or she has suffered the prior conviction.

(b) Except as provided in subdivision (c), the question of whether or not the defendant has suffered the prior conviction shall be tried by a jury impaneled for that purpose unless a jury is waived, in which case it may be tried by the court.

(c) Notwithstanding the provisions of subdivision (b), the question of whether the defendant is the person who has suffered the prior conviction shall be tried by the court without a jury.

Added by renumbering Section 9691/2 by Stats. 1998, Ch. 235, Sec. 1. Effective January 1, 1999.

Section 970 - Conviction or acquittal where several defendants named in one accusatory pleading

When several defendants are named in one accusatory pleading, any one or more may be convicted or acquitted.

Amended by Stats. 1951, Ch. 1674.

Section 971 - Distinction between accessory before fact and principal and betweEn principals in first and second degree abrogated

The distinction between an accessory before the fact and a principal, and between principals in the first and second degree is abrogated; and all persons concerned in the commission of a crime, who by the operation of other provisions of this code are principals therein, shall hereafter be prosecuted, tried and punished as principals and no other facts need be alleged in any accusatory pleading against any such person than are required in an accusatory pleading against a principal.

Amended by Stats. 1951, Ch. 1674.

Section 972 - Prosecution, trying, and punishment of accessory to commission of felony

An accessory to the commission of a felony may be prosecuted, tried, and punished, though the principal may be neither prosecuted nor tried, and though the principal may have been acquitted.

Amended by Code Amendments 1880, Ch. 47.

Section 973 - Accusatory pleading lost or destroyed

If the accusatory pleading in any criminal action has heretofore been lost or destroyed or shall hereafter be lost or destroyed, the court must, upon the application of the prosecuting attorney or of the defendant, order a copy of such pleading to be filed and substituted for the original, and when filed and substituted, as provided in this section, the copy shall have the same force and effect as if it were the original pleading.

Added by Stats. 1951, Ch. 1674.

Title 6 - PLEADINGS AND PROCEEDINGS BEFORE TRIAL

Chapter 1 - OF THE ARRAIGNMENT OF THE DEFENDANT

Section 976 - Arraignment

(a) When the accusatory pleading is filed, the defendant shall be arraigned thereon before the court in which it is filed, unless the action is transferred to some other court for trial. However, within any county, if the defendant is in custody, upon the approval of both the presiding judge of the court in which the accusatory pleading is filed and the presiding judge of the court nearest to the place in which he or she is held in custody the arraignment may be before the court nearest to that place of custody.

(b) A defendant arrested in another county shall have the right to be taken before a magistrate in the arresting county for the purpose of being admitted to bail, as provided in Section 821 or 822. The defendant shall be informed of this right.

(c) Prior to being taken from the place where he or she is in custody to the place where he or she is to be arraigned, the defendant shall be allowed to make three completed telephone calls, at no expense to the defendant, in addition to any other telephone calls which the defendant is entitled to make pursuant to law.

Amended by Stats. 1982, Ch. 395, Sec. 1.

Section 976.5 - [Repealed]

Amended by Stats 2000 ch 287 (SB 1955), s 12, eff. 1/1/2001.

Section 977 - [Effective until 1/1/2025] Accused charged with misdemeanor; accused charged with felony

(a)

(1) In all cases in which the accused is charged with a misdemeanor only, they may appear by counsel only, except as provided in paragraphs (2) and (3). If the accused agrees, the initial court appearance, arraignment, plea, and all other proceedings, except jury and court trials, may be conducted remotely through the use of technology, as provided by subdivision (c).

(2) If the accused is charged with a misdemeanor offense involving domestic violence, as defined in Section 6211 of the Family Code, or a misdemeanor violation of Section 273.6, the accused shall be present for arraignment and sentencing, and at any time during the proceedings when ordered by the court for the purpose of being informed of the conditions of a protective order issued pursuant to Section 136.2.

(3) If the accused is charged with a misdemeanor offense involving driving under the influence, in an appropriate case, the court may order a defendant to be present for arraignment, at the time of plea, or at sentencing. For purposes of this paragraph, a misdemeanor offense involving driving under the influence shall include a misdemeanor violation of any of the following:

   (A) Subdivision (b) of Section 191.5.

   (B) Section 23103 as specified in Section 23103.5 of the Vehicle Code.

   (C) Section 23152 of the Vehicle Code.

   (D) Section 23153 of the Vehicle Code.

(b)

   (1) Except as provided in subdivision (c), in all cases in which a felony is charged, the accused shall be physically present at the arraignment, at the time of plea, during the preliminary hearing, during those portions of the trial when evidence is taken before the trier of fact, and at the time of the imposition of sentence. The accused shall be physically or remotely present at all other proceedings unless they waive their right to be physically or remotely present, with leave of court and with approval by defendant's counsel.

   (2) The waiver of a defendant's right to be physically or remotely present may be in writing and filed with the court or, with the court's consent, may be entered personally by the defendant or by the defendant's counsel of record.

   (A) A defendant's personal waiver of the right to be physically or remotely present shall be on the record and state that the defendant has been advised of the right to be physically or remotely present for the hearing at issue and agrees that notice to the attorney that the defendant's physical or remote presence in court at a future date and time is required is notice to the defendant of that requirement.

   (B) A waiver of the defendant's physical or remote presence may be entered by counsel, after counsel has stated on the record that the defendant has been advised of the right to be physically or remotely present for the hearing at issue, has waived that right, and agrees that notice to the attorney that the defendant's physical or remote presence in court at a future date and time is required is notice to the defendant of that requirement.

   (3) The court may specifically direct the defendant, either personally or through counsel, to be physically or remotely present at any particular proceeding or portion thereof, including upon request of a victim, to the extent required by Section 28 of Article I of the California Constitution.

   (4) A written waiver of the defendant's physical or remote presence shall be substantially in the following form: "Waiver of Defendant's Physical or Remote Presence"

"The undersigned defendant, having been advised of their right to be present at all stages of the proceedings, including, but not limited to, presentation of and arguments on questions of fact and law, and to be confronted by and cross-examine all witnesses, hereby knowingly, intelligently, and voluntarily waives the right to be physically or remotely present at the hearing of any motion or other proceeding in this cause. The undersigned defendant hereby requests the court to proceed during every absence of the defendant that the court may permit pursuant to this waiver, and hereby agrees that their interest is represented at all times by the presence of their attorney the same as if the defendant were physically or remotely present in court, and further agrees that notice to their attorney that their physical or remote presence in court on a particular day at a particular time is required is notice to the defendant of the requirement of their physical or remote appearance at that time and place."

(c)

   (1)

   (A) Upon waiver of the right to be physically present by the defendant, criminal proceedings may be conducted through the use of remote technology, except as provided in subparagraphs (D) and (E). The defendant may withdraw the waiver at any time.

   (B) The court may specifically direct the defendant, either personally or through counsel, to be physically present at any particular felony proceeding or portion thereof, including as provided in subdivision (f).

   (C) If the defendant is represented by counsel, the attorney shall not be required to be physically present with the defendant if remote technology allows for private communication between the defendant and the attorney prior to and during the proceeding, unless, upon request of defense counsel, the court allows the appearance without private communication. Any private communication shall be confidential and privileged pursuant to Section 952 of the Evidence Code.

   (D) A defendant charged with a felony or misdemeanor shall not appear remotely for a jury trial or court trial, except as provided in subparagraph (A) of paragraph (2).

   (E) A defendant charged with a felony shall not appear remotely at sentencing, except for postconviction relief proceedings and as otherwise provided by law.

   (F) A witness may appear at any misdemeanor or felony criminal proceeding, except for felony trial, remotely pursuant to section 977.3.

   (2)

   (A) A felony defendant who does not wish to be physically or remotely present for noncritical portions of the trial when no testimonial evidence is taken may make an oral waiver in open court prior to the proceeding, or may submit a written request to the court, which the court may grant in its discretion.

   (B) This paragraph does not expand or limit the right of a defendant to be personally present with their counsel at a particular proceeding as required by Section 15 of Article 1 of the California Constitution.

(d)

   (1) Notwithstanding any other provision in this section, the court may allow a defendant to appear by counsel on that day, at a trial, hearing, or other proceeding, with or without a written waiver, if the court finds, by clear and convincing evidence, all of the following to be true:

   (A) The defendant is in custody and is refusing, without good cause, to appear in court on that day for that trial, hearing, or other proceeding.

   (B) The defendant has been informed of their right and obligation to be personally present in court.

(C) The defendant has been informed that the trial, hearing, or other proceeding will proceed without the defendant being present.

(D) The defendant has been informed that they have the right to remain silent during the trial, hearing, or other proceeding.

(E) The defendant has been informed that their absence without good cause will constitute a voluntary waiver of any constitutional or statutory right to confront any witnesses against them or to testify on their own behalf.

(F) The defendant has been informed whether or not defense counsel will be present.

(2) The court shall state on the record the reasons for the court's findings and shall cause those findings and reasons to be entered into the minutes.

(3) If the trial, hearing, or other proceeding lasts for more than one day, the court is required to make the findings required by this subdivision anew for each day that the defendant is absent.

(4) This subdivision does not apply to any trial, hearing, or other proceeding in which the defendant was personally present in court at the commencement of the trial, hearing, or other proceeding.

(e) A court may, as appropriate and practicable, allow a prosecuting attorney or defense counsel to participate in a criminal proceeding through the use of remote technology without being physically present in the courtroom and in accordance with subdivision (f).

(f) Except as otherwise provided by law, the court shall require a prosecuting attorney, defense counsel, defendant, or witness to appear in person at a proceeding, if any of the following conditions are present and cannot be resolved in a reasonable amount of time:

(1) The court does not have the technology necessary to conduct the proceeding remotely.

(2) Although the court has the requisite technology, the quality of the technology or audibility at a proceeding prevents the effective management or resolution of the proceeding.

(3) The quality of the technology or audibility at a proceeding inhibits the court reporter's ability to accurately prepare a transcript of the proceeding.

(4) The quality of the technology or audibility at a proceeding prevents defense counsel from being able to provide effective representation to the defendant.

(5) The quality of the technology or audibility at a proceeding inhibits a court interpreter's ability to provide language access, including the ability to communicate and translate directly with the defendant and the court during the proceeding.

(g)

(1) Before the court may proceed with a remote proceeding, the court shall have a process for a defendant, defense counsel, prosecuting attorney, witness, official reporter, official reporter pro tempore, court interpreter, or other court personnel to alert the judicial officer of technological or audibility issues that arise during the proceeding.

(2) When the court conducts a remote proceeding that will be reported by an official reporter or official reporter pro tempore, the reporter shall be physically present in a courtroom.

(h) The court shall make findings on the record that any waiver entered into pursuant to this section is knowingly, voluntarily, and intelligently made by the defendant.

(i) The Judicial Council shall adopt rules and standards that are necessary to implement the policies and provisions of this section and the intent of the Legislature.

(j) This section shall remain in effect only until January 1, 2025, and as of that date is repealed.

Amended by Stats 2023 ch 190 (SB 135),s 3, eff. 9/13/2023.
Amended by Stats 2022 ch 57 (AB 199),s 12, eff. 6/30/2022.
Amended by Stats 2021 ch 196 (AB 700),s 1, eff. 1/1/2022.
Amended by Stats 2014 ch 167 (AB 2397),s 1, eff. 1/1/2015.
Amended by Stats 2007 ch 747 (AB 678),s 8.5, eff. 1/1/2008.
Amended by Stats 2007 ch 302 (SB 425),s 12, eff. 1/1/2008.
Amended by Stats 2007 ch 130 (AB 299),s 191, eff. 1/1/2008.
Amended by Stats 2007 ch 43 (SB 649),s 18, eff. 1/1/2008.
Amended by Stats 2006 ch 744 (AB 2174),s 1, eff. 1/1/2007.
Amended by Stats 2003 ch 29 (AB 383), s 1, eff. 1/1/2004.
Amended by Stats 2001 ch 82 (AB 477), s 1, eff. 1/1/2002.

Section 977 - [Operative 1/1/2025] Accused charged with misdemeanor; accused charged with felony

(a)

(1) In all cases in which the accused is charged with a misdemeanor only, they may appear by counsel only, except as provided in paragraphs (2) and (3). If the accused agrees, the initial court appearance, arraignment, and plea may be by video, as provided by subdivision (c).

(2) If the accused is charged with a misdemeanor offense involving domestic violence, as defined in Section 6211 of the Family Code, or a misdemeanor violation of Section 273.6, the accused shall be present for arraignment and sentencing, and at any time during the proceedings when ordered by the court for the purpose of being informed of the conditions of a protective order issued pursuant to Section 136.2.

(3) If the accused is charged with a misdemeanor offense involving driving under the influence, in an appropriate case, the court may order a defendant to be present for arraignment, at the time of plea, or at sentencing. For purposes of this paragraph, a misdemeanor offense involving driving under the influence shall include a misdemeanor violation of any of the following:

(A) Subdivision (b) of Section 191.5.

(B) Section 23103 as specified in Section 23103.5 of the Vehicle Code.

(C) Section 23152 of the Vehicle Code.

(D) Section 23153 of the Vehicle Code.

(b)

(1) Except as provided in subdivision (c), in all cases in which a felony is charged, the accused shall be personally present at the arraignment, at the time of plea, during the preliminary hearing, during those portions of the trial when evidence is taken before the trier of fact, and at the time of the imposition of sentence. The accused shall be personally present at all other proceedings unless they shall, with leave of court, execute in open court, a written waiver of their right to be personally present, as provided by paragraph (2). If the accused agrees, the initial court appearance, arraignment, and plea may be by video, as provided by subdivision (c).

(2) The accused may execute a written waiver of their right to be personally present, approved by their counsel, and the waiver shall be filed with the court. However, the court may specifically direct the defendant to be personally present at any particular proceeding or portion thereof. The waiver shall be substantially in the following form: "Waiver of Defendant's Personal Presence"
"The undersigned defendant, having been advised of their right to be present at all stages of the proceedings, including, but not limited to, presentation of and arguments on questions of fact and law, and to be confronted by and cross-examine all witnesses, hereby waives the right to be present at the hearing of any motion or other proceeding in this cause. The undersigned defendant hereby requests the court to proceed during every absence of the defendant that the court may permit pursuant to this waiver, and hereby agrees that their interest is represented at all times by the presence of their attorney the same as if the defendant were personally present in court, and further agrees that notice to their attorney that their presence in court on a particular day at a particular time is required is notice to the defendant of the requirement of their appearance at that time and place."

(c)

(1) The court may permit the initial court appearance and arraignment of defendants held in any state, county, or local facility within the county on felony or misdemeanor charges, except for those defendants who were indicted by a grand jury, to be conducted by two-way electronic audiovideo communication between the defendant and the courtroom in lieu of the physical presence of the defendant in the courtroom. If the defendant is represented by counsel, the attorney shall be present with the defendant at the initial court appearance and arraignment, and may enter a plea during the arraignment. However, if the defendant is represented by counsel at an arraignment on an information in a felony case, and if the defendant does not plead guilty or nolo contendere to any charge, the attorney shall be present with the defendant or if the attorney is not present with the defendant, the attorney shall be present in court during the hearing. The defendant shall have the right to make their plea while physically present in the courtroom if they request to do so. If the defendant decides not to exercise the right to be physically present in the courtroom they shall execute a written waiver of that right. A judge may order a defendant's personal appearance in court for the initial court appearance and arraignment. In a misdemeanor case, a judge may, pursuant to this subdivision, accept a plea of guilty or no contest from a defendant who is not physically in the courtroom. In a felony case, a judge may, pursuant to this subdivision, accept a plea of guilty or no contest from a defendant who is not physically in the courtroom if the parties stipulate thereto.

(2)

(A) A defendant who does not wish to be personally present for noncritical portions of the trial when no testimonial evidence is taken may make an oral waiver in open court prior to the proceeding or may submit a written request to the court, which the court may grant in its discretion. The court may, when a defendant has waived the right to be personally present, require a defendant held in any state, county, or local facility within the county on felony or misdemeanor charges to be present for noncritical portions of the trial when no testimonial evidence is taken, including, but not limited to, confirmation of the preliminary hearing, status conferences, trial readiness conferences, discovery motions, receipt of records, the setting of the trial date, a motion to vacate the trial date, and motions in limine, by two-way electronic audiovideo communication between the defendant and the courtroom in lieu of the physical presence of the defendant in the courtroom. If the defendant is represented by counsel, the attorney shall not be required to be personally present with the defendant for noncritical portions of the trial, if the audiovideo conferencing system or other technology allows for private communication between the defendant and the attorney prior to and during the noncritical portion of trial. Any private communication shall be confidential and privileged pursuant to Section 952 of the Evidence Code.

(B) This paragraph does not expand or limit the right of a defendant to be personally present with their counsel at a particular proceeding as required by Section 15 of Article 1 of the California Constitution.

(d)

(1) Notwithstanding any other provision in this section, the court may allow a defendant to appear by counsel on that day, at a trial, hearing, or other proceeding, with or without a written waiver, if the court finds, by clear and convincing evidence, all of the following to be true:

(A) The defendant is in custody and is refusing, without good cause, to appear in court on that day for that trial, hearing, or other proceeding.

(B) The defendant has been informed of their right and obligation to be personally present in court.

(C) The defendant has been informed that the trial, hearing, or other proceeding will proceed without the defendant being present.

(D) The defendant has been informed that they have the right to remain silent during the trial, hearing, or other proceeding.

(E) The defendant has been informed that their absence without good cause will constitute a voluntary waiver of any constitutional or statutory right to confront any witnesses against them or to testify on their own behalf.

(F) The defendant has been informed whether or not defense counsel will be present.

(2) The court shall state on the record the reasons for the court's findings and shall cause those findings and reasons to be entered into the minutes.

(3) If the trial, hearing, or other proceeding lasts for more than one day, the court is required to make the findings required by this subdivision anew for each day that the defendant is absent.

(4) This subdivision does not apply to any trial, hearing, or other proceeding in which the defendant was personally present in court at the commencement of the trial, hearing, or other proceeding.

(e) This section shall become operative on January 1, 2025.

Amended by Stats 2023 ch 190 (SB 135),s 4, eff. 9/13/2023.

Added by Stats 2022 ch 57 (AB 199),s 13, eff. 6/30/2022.

Section 977.1 - Effect of pending proceedings to determine whether defendant is mentally incompetent or gravely disabled

The resolution of questions of fact or issues of law by trial or hearing which can be made without the assistance or participation of the defendant is not prohibited by the existence of any pending proceeding to determine whether the defendant is or remains mentally incompetent or gravely disabled pursuant to the provisions of either this code or the Welfare and Institutions Code.

Added by Stats. 1974, Ch. 1511.

Section 977.2 - Court appearances of incarcerated defendant conducted by two-way electronic audiovideo communication

(a) Notwithstanding Section 977 or any other law, in any case in which the defendant is charged with a misdemeanor or a felony and is currently incarcerated in the state prison, the Department of Corrections and Rehabilitation may arrange for all court appearances in superior court, except for the preliminary hearing and trial, to be conducted by two-way electronic audiovideo communication between the defendant and the courtroom in lieu of the physical presence of the defendant in the courtroom. If the defendant agrees, the preliminary hearing and trial may be held by two-way electronic audiovideo communication. This section shall not be interpreted to eliminate the authority of the court to issue an order requiring the defendant to be physically present in the courtroom in those cases where the court finds circumstances that require the physical presence of the defendant in the courtroom. For those court appearances that are conducted by two-way electronic audiovideo communication, the department shall arrange for two-way electronic audiovideo communication between the superior court and any state prison facility. The department shall provide properly maintained equipment, adequately trained staff at the prison, and appropriate training for court staff to ensure that consistently effective two-way electronic audiovideo communication is provided between the prison facility and the courtroom for all appearances conducted by two-way electronic audiovideo communication.

(b) If the defendant is represented by counsel, the attorney shall be present with the defendant at the initial court appearance and arraignment, and may enter a plea during the arraignment. However, if the defendant is represented by counsel at an arraignment on an information or indictment in a felony case, and if the defendant does not plead guilty or nolo contendere to any charge, the attorney shall be present with the defendant or if the attorney is not present with the defendant, the attorney shall be present in court during the hearing.

(c) In lieu of the physical presence of the defendant's counsel at the institution with the defendant, the court and the department shall establish a confidential telephone line between the court and the institution for communication between the defendant's counsel in court and the defendant at the institution. In this case, counsel for the defendant shall not be required to be physically present at the institution during any court appearance that is conducted via electronic audiovideo communication. This section shall not be construed to prohibit the physical presence of the defense counsel with the defendant at the state prison.

Amended by Stats 2020 ch 29 (SB 118),s 13, eff. 8/6/2020.

Amended by Stats 2007 ch 43 (SB 649),s 19, eff. 1/1/2008.

Amended by Stats 2004 ch 293 (AB 99), s 1, eff. 1/1/2005.

EFFECTIVE 1/1/2000. Amended October 10, 1999 (Bill Number: SB 1126) (Chapter 888).

Section 977.3 - [Effective until 1/1/2025] Witness may testify in misdemeanor or felony criminal proceeding through remote technology; felony trials excepted

(a) A witness may testify in any misdemeanor or felony criminal proceeding, except for felony trials, through the use of remote technology with the written or oral consent of the parties on the record and with the consent of the court. The defendant shall waive the right to have a witness testify in person on the record.

(b) Notwithstanding subdivision (a), the court may allow a witness to testify through the use of remote technology as otherwise provided by statutes regarding the examination of victims of sexual crimes and conditional examinations of witnesses.

(c) The court shall make findings on the record that any waiver entered into pursuant to this section is knowingly, voluntarily, and intelligently made by the defendant.

(d) The Judicial Council shall adopt rules and standards that are necessary to implement the policies and provisions of this section and the intent of the Legislature.

(e) This section shall remain in effect only until January 1, 2025, and as of that date is repealed.

Amended by Stats 2023 ch 190 (SB 135),s 5, eff. 9/13/2023.

Added by Stats 2022 ch 57 (AB 199),s 14, eff. 6/30/2022.

Section 978 - Personal appearance required

When his personal appearance is necessary, if he is in custody, the Court may direct and the officer in whose custody he is must bring him before it to be arraigned.

Enacted 1872.

Section 978.5 - [Effective until 1/1/2026] Bench warrant of arrest

(a) A bench warrant of arrest may be issued when a defendant fails to appear in court as required by law, including, but not limited to, the following situations:

(1) If the defendant is ordered by a judge or magistrate to personally appear in court at a specific time and place.

(2) If the defendant is released from custody on bail and is ordered by a judge or magistrate, or other person authorized to accept bail, to personally appear in court at a specific time and place.

(3) If the defendant is released from custody on their own recognizance and promises to personally appear in court at a specific time and place.

(4) If the defendant is released from custody or arrest upon citation by a peace officer or other person authorized to issue citations and the defendant has signed a promise to personally appear in court at a specific time and place.

(5) If a defendant is authorized to appear by counsel and the court or magistrate orders that the defendant personally appear in court at a specific time and place.

(6) If an information or indictment has been filed in the superior court and the court has fixed the date and place for the defendant personally to appear for arraignment.

(7) If a defendant has been cited or arrested for misdemeanor or felony theft from a store and has failed to appear in court in connection with that charge or those charges in the previous six months.

(b) The bench warrant may be served in any county in the same manner as a warrant of arrest.

(c) This section shall remain in effect only until January 1, 2026, and as of that date is repealed.

Amended by Stats 2022 ch 856 (AB 2294),s 3, eff. 9/30/2022.

Amended by Stats 2019 ch 497 (AB 991),s 201, eff. 1/1/2020.

Amended by Stats 2019 ch 25 (SB 94),s 36, eff. 6/27/2019.

Added by Stats 2018 ch 803 (AB 1065),s 6, eff. 1/1/2019.

Section 978.5 - [Operative 1/1/2026] Bench warrant of arrest

(a) A bench warrant of arrest may be issued when a defendant fails to appear in court as required by law, including, but not limited to, the following situations:

(1) If the defendant is ordered by a judge or magistrate to personally appear in court at a specific time and place.

(2) If the defendant is released from custody on bail and is ordered by a judge or magistrate, or other person authorized to accept bail, to personally appear in court at a specific time and place.

(3) If the defendant is released from custody on their own recognizance and promises to personally appear in court at a specific time and place.

(4) If the defendant is released from custody or arrest upon citation by a peace officer or other person authorized to issue citations and the defendant has signed a promise to personally appear in court at a specific time and place.

(5) If a defendant is authorized to appear by counsel and the court or magistrate orders that the defendant personally appear in court at a specific time and place.

(6) If an information or indictment has been filed in the superior court and the court has fixed the date and place for the defendant personally to appear for arraignment.

(b) The bench warrant may be served in any county in the same manner as a warrant of arrest.

(c) This section shall become operative January 1, 2026.

Added by Stats 2022 ch 856 (AB 2294),s 4, eff. 9/30/2022.

Section 979 - Forfeiture and issuance of bench warrant for arrest

If the defendant has been discharged on bail or has deposited money or other property instead thereof, and does not appear to be arraigned when his personal presence is necessary, the court, in addition to the forfeiture of the undertaking of bail or of the money or other property deposited, may order the issuance of a bench warrant for his arrest.

Amended by Stats. 1951, Ch. 1674.

Section 980 - Issuance of bench warrant to one or more counties; entry into national warrant system

(a) At any time after the order for a bench warrant is made, whether the court is sitting or not, the clerk may issue a bench warrant to one or more counties.

(b) The clerk shall require the appropriate agency to enter each bench warrant issued on a private surety-bonded felony case into the national warrant system (National Crime Information Center (NCIC)). If the appropriate agency fails to enter the bench warrant into the national warrant system (NCIC), and the court finds that this failure prevented the surety or bond agent from surrendering the fugitive into custody, prevented the fugitive from being arrested or taken into custody, or resulted in the fugitive's subsequent release from custody, the court having jurisdiction over the bail shall, upon petition, set aside the forfeiture of the bond and declare all liability on the bail bond to be exonerated.

Amended by Stats. 1998, Ch. 520, Sec. 2. Effective January 1, 1999.

Section 981 - Form of bench warrant

The bench warrant must be substantially in the following form:

County of ____. The People of the State of California to any Sheriff, Marshal, or Policeman in this State: An accusatory pleading having been filed on the ____ day of ____, A.D. ____, in the Superior Court of the County of ____, charging C. D. with the crime of ____ (designating it generally); you are, therefore, commanded forthwith to arrest the above named C. D., and bring him or her before that Court (or if the accusatory pleading has been sent to another Court, then before that Court, naming it), to answer said accusatory pleading, or if the Court is not in session, that you deliver him or her into the custody of the Sheriff of the County of ____.

Given under my hand, with the seal of said Court affixed, this ____ day of ____, A.D. ____.

By order of said Court.

[seal.]   E. F., Clerk.

Amended by Stats 2003 ch 468 (SB 851), s 14, eff. 1/1/2004.

Section 982 - Arrest under warrant for offense not bailable

The defendant, when arrested under a warrant for an offense not bailable, must be held in custody by the Sheriff of the county in which the indictment is found or information filed, unless admitted to bail after an examination upon a writ of habeas corpus; but if the offense is bailable, there must be added to the body of the bench warrant a direction to the following effect: "Or, if he requires it, that you take him before any magistrate in that county, or in the county in which you arrest him, that he may give bail to answer to the indictment (or information);" and the Court, upon directing it to issue, must fix the amount of bail, and an indorsement must be made thereon and signed by the Clerk, to the following effect: "The defendant is to be admitted to bail in the sum of ____ dollars."

Amended by Code Amendments 1880, Ch. 47.

Section 983 - Service of bench warrant

The bench warrant may be served in any county in the same manner as a warrant of arrest.

Amended by Stats. 1951, Ch. 1674.

Section 984 - Proceedings when defendant brought before magistrate for purpose of giving bail

If the defendant is brought before a magistrate of another county for the purpose of giving bail, the magistrate must proceed in respect thereto in the same manner as if the defendant had been brought before him upon a warrant of arrest, and the same proceedings must be had thereon.

Enacted 1872.

Section 985 - Order that defendant be committed to actual custody unless defendant gives bail in increased amount

When the information or indictment is for a felony, and the defendant, before the filing thereof, has given bail for his appearance to answer the charge, the Court to which the indictment or information is presented, or in which it is pending, may order the defendant to be committed to actual custody, unless he gives bail in an increased amount, to be specified in the order.

Amended by Code Amendments 1880, Ch. 47.

Section 986 - Commitment or issuance of bench warrant

If the defendant is present when the order is made, he must be forthwith committed. If he is not present, a bench warrant must be issued and proceeded upon in the manner provided in this chapter.

Enacted 1872.

Section 987 - Right to counsel

(a) In a noncapital case, if the defendant appears for arraignment without counsel, the defendant shall be informed by the court that it is their right to have counsel before being arraigned, and shall be asked if they desire the assistance of counsel. If the defendant desires and is unable to employ counsel the court shall assign counsel to defend them.

(b) In a capital case, if the defendant appears for arraignment without counsel, the court shall inform the defendant that they shall be represented by counsel at all stages of the preliminary and trial proceedings and that the representation is at their expense if they are able to employ counsel or at public expense if they are unable to employ counsel, inquire of them whether they are able to employ counsel and, if so, whether they desire to employ counsel of their choice or to have counsel assigned, and allow them a reasonab e time to send for their chosen or assigned counsel. If the defendant is unable to employ counsel, the court shall assign counsel to defend them. If the defendant is able to employ counsel and either refuses to employ counsel or appears without counsel after having had a reasonable time to employ counsel, the court shall assign counsel. The court shall at the first opportunity inform the defendant's trial counsel, whether retained by the defendant or court-appointed, of the additional duties imposed upon trial counsel in any capital case as set forth in paragraph (1) of subdivision (b) of Section 1240.1.

(c) In order to assist the court in determining whether a defendant is able to employ counsel in any case, the court may require a defendant to file a financial statement or other financial information under penalty of perjury with the court or, in its discretion, order a defendant to appear before a county officer designated by the court to make an inquiry into the ability of the defendant to employ their own counsel. If a county officer is designated, the county officer shall provide to the court a written recommendation and the reason or reasons in support of the recommendation. The determination by the court shall be made on the record. Except as provided in Section 1214, the financial statement or other financial information obtained from the defendant shall be confidential and privileged and shall not be admissible in evidence in any criminal proceeding except the prosecution of an alleged offense of perjury based upon false material contained in the financial statement. The financial statement shall be made available to the prosecution only for purposes of investigation of an alleged offense of perjury based upon false material contained in the financial statement at the conclusion of the proceedings for which the financial statement was required to be submitted.

(d) In a capital case, the court may appoint an additional attorney as a cocounsel upon a written request of the first attorney appointed. The request shall be supported by an affidavit of the first attorney setting forth in detail the reasons why a second attorney should be appointed. Any affidavit filed with the court shall be confidential and privileged. The court shall appoint a second attorney when it is convinced by the reasons stated in the affidavit that the appointment is necessary to provide the defendant with effective representation. If the request is denied, the court shall state on the record its reasons for denial of the request.

(e) This section shall become operative on July 1, 2021.

Added by Stats 2020 ch 92 (AB 1869),s 32, eff. 9/18/2020.

Section 987.05 - Assignment of defense counsel in felony cases

In assigning defense counsel in felony cases, whether it is the public defender or private counsel, the court shall only assign counsel who represents, on the record, that he or she will be ready to proceed with the preliminary hearing or trial, as the case may be, within the time provisions prescribed in this code for preliminary hearings and trials, except in those unusual cases where the court finds that, due to the nature of the case, counsel cannot reasonably be expected to be ready within the presribed period if he or she were to begin preparing the case forthwith and continue to make diligent and constant efforts to be ready. In the case where the time of preparation for preliminary hearing or trial is deemed greater than the statutory time, the court shall set a reasonable time period for preparation. In making this determination, the court shall not consider counsel's convenience, counsel's calendar conflicts, or counsel's other business. The court may allow counsel a reasonable time to become familiar with the case in order to determine whether he or she can be ready. In cases where counsel, after making representations that he or she will be ready for preliminary examination or trial, and without good cause is not ready on the date set, the court may relieve counsel from the case and may impose sanctions upon counsel, including, but not limited to, finding the assigned counsel in contempt of court, imposing a fine, or denying any public funds as compensation for counsel's services. Both the prosecuting attorney and defense counsel shall have a right to present evidence and argument as to a reasonable length of time for preparation and on any reasons why counsel could not be prepared in the set time.

Added June 5, 1990, by initiative Proposition 115, Sec. 20.

Section 987.1 - Continued representation unless relieved by court

Counsel at the preliminary examination shall continue to represent a defendant who has been ordered to stand trial for a felony until the date set for arraignment on the information unless relieved by the court upon the substitution of other counsel or for cause.

Amended by Stats. 1998, Ch. 931, Sec. 377. Effective September 28, 1998.

Section 987.2 - Compensation of assigned counsel

(a) In any case in which a person, including a person who is a minor, desires but is unable to employ counsel, and in which counsel is assigned in the superior court to represent the person in a criminal trial, proceeding, or appeal, the following assigned counsel shall receive a reasonable sum for compensation and for necessary expenses, the amount of which shall be determined by the court, to be paid out of the general fund of the county:

(1) In a county or city and county in which there is no public defender.

(2) In a county of the first, second, or third class where there is no contract for criminal defense services between the county and one or more responsible attorneys.

(3) In a case in which the court finds that, because of a conflict of interest or other reasons, the public defender has properly refused.

(4) In a county of the first, second, or third class where attorneys contracted by the county are unable to represent the person accused.

(b) The sum provided for in subdivision (a) may be determined by contract between the court and one or more responsible attorneys after consultation with the board of supervisors as to the total amount of compensation and expenses to be paid, which shall be within the amount of funds allocated by the board of supervisors for the cost of assigned counsel in those cases.

(c) In counties that utilize an assigned private counsel system as either the primary method of public defense or as the method of appointing counsel in cases where the public defender is unavailable, the county, the courts, or the local county bar association working with the courts are encouraged to do all of the following:

(1) Establish panels that shall be open to members of the State Bar of California.

(2) Categorize attorneys for panel placement on the basis of experience.

(3) Refer cases to panel members on a rotational basis within the level of experience of each panel, except that a judge may exclude an individual attorney from appointment to an individual case for good cause.

(4) Seek to educate those panel members through an approved training program.

(d) In a county of the first, second, or third class, the court shall first utilize the services of the public defender to provide criminal defense services for indigent defendants. In the event that the public defender is unavailable and the county and the courts have contracted with one or more responsible attorneys or with a panel of attorneys to provide criminal defense services for indigent defendants, the court shall utilize the services of the county-contracted attorneys prior to assigning any other private counsel. Nothing in this subdivision shall be construed to require the appointment of counsel in any case in which the counsel has a conflict of interest. In the interest of justice, a court may depart from that portion of the procedure requiring appointment of a county-contracted attorney after making a finding of good cause and stating the reasons therefor on the record.

(e) In a county of the first, second, or third class, the court shall first utilize the services of the public defender to provide criminal defense services for indigent defendants. In the event that the public defender is unavailable and the county has created a second public defender and contracted with one or more responsible attorneys or with a panel of attorneys to provide criminal defense services for indigent defendants, and if the quality of representation provided by the second public defender is comparable to the quality of representation provided by the public defender, the court shall next utilize the services of the second public defender and then the services of the county-contracted attorneys prior to assigning any other private counsel. Nothing in this subdivision shall be construed to require the appointment of counsel in any case in which the counsel has a conflict of interest. In the interest of justice, a court may depart from that portion of the procedure requiring appointment of the second public defender or a county-contracted attorney after making a finding of good cause and stating the reasons therefor on the record.

(f) In any case in which counsel is assigned as provided in subdivision (a), that counsel appointed by the court and any court-appointed licensed private investigator shall have the same rights and privileges to information as the public defender and the public defender investigator. It is the intent of the Legislature in enacting this subdivision to equalize any disparity that exists between the ability of private, court-appointed counsel and investigators, and public defenders and public defender investigators, to represent their clients. This subdivision is not intended to grant to private investigators access to any confidential Department of Motor Vehicles' information not otherwise available to them. This subdivision is not intended to extend to private investigators the right to issue subpoenas.

(g) Notwithstanding any other provision of this section, where an indigent defendant is first charged in one county and establishes an attorney-client relationship with the public defender, defense services contract attorney, or private attorney, and where the defendant is then charged with an offense in a second or subsequent county, the court in the second or subsequent county may appoint the same counsel as was appointed in the first county to represent the defendant when all of the following conditions are met:

(1) The offense charged in the second or subsequent county would be joinable for trial with the offense charged in the first if it took place in the same county, or involves evidence which would be cross-admissible.

(2) The court finds that the interests of justice and economy will be best served by unitary representation.

(3) Counsel appointed in the first county consents to the appointment.

(h) The county may recover costs of public defender services under Chapter 6 (commencing with Section 4750) of Title 5 of Part 3 for any case subject to Section 4750.

(i) Counsel shall be appointed to represent, in a misdemeanor case, a person who desires but is unable to employ counsel, when it appears that the appointment is necessary to provide an adequate and effective defense for the defendant. Appointment of counsel in an infraction case is governed by Section 19.6.

(j) As used in this section, "county of the first, second, or third class" means the county of the first class, county of the second class, and county of the third class as provided by Sections 28020, 28022, 28023, and 28024 of the Government Code.

(k) This section shall become operative on July 1, 2021.

Added by Stats 2020 ch 92 (AB 1869),s 34, eff. 9/18/2020.

Section 987.3 - Factors to consider

Whenever in this code a court-appointed attorney is entitled to reasonable compensation and necessary expenses, the judge of the court shall consider the following factors, no one of which alone shall be controlling:

(a) Customary fee in the community for similar services rendered by privately retained counsel to a nonindigent client.

(b) The time and labor required to be spent by the attorney.

(c) The difficulty of the defense.

(d) The novelty or uncertainty of the law upon which the decision depended.

(e) The degree of professional ability, skill, and experience called for and exercised in the performance of the services.

(f) The professional character, qualification, and standing of the attorney.

Added by Stats. 1973, Ch. 101.

Section 987.4 - [Repealed]

Amended by Stats 2020 ch 92 (AB 1869),s 35, eff. 9/18/2020.

Section 987.5 - [Repealed]

Amended by Stats 2020 ch 92 (AB 1869),s 36, eff. 9/18/2020.

Amended by Stats 2009 ch 606 (SB 676),s 4, eff. 1/1/2010.

Section 987.6 - Payment to counties by Department of Finance

(a) From any state moneys made available to it for such purpose, the Department of Finance shall, pursuant to this section, pay to the counties an amount not to exceed 10 percent of the amounts actually expended by the counties in providing counsel in accordance with the law whether by public defender, assigned counsel, or both, for persons charged with violations of state criminal law or involuntarily detained under the Lanterman-Petris-Short Act, Division 5 (commencing with Section 5000) of the Welfare and Institutions Code, who desire, but are unable to afford, counsel.

(b) Application for payment shall be made in such manner and at such times as prescribed by the Department of Finance and the department may adopt rules necessary or appropriate to carry out the purposes of this section.

Added by renumbering Section 987b by Stats. 1970, Ch. 723.

Section 987.8 - [Repealed]

Amended by Stats 2020 ch 92 (AB 1869),s 37, eff. 9/18/2020.

Amended by Stats 2017 ch 62 (SB 355),s 1, eff. 1/1/2018.

Amended by Stats 2017 ch 561 (AB 1516),s 184, eff. 1/1/2018.

Amended by Stats 2016 ch 534 (SB 614),s 1, eff. 1/1/2017.

Section 987.81 - [Repealed]

Amended by Stats 2020 ch 92 (AB 1869),s 38, eff. 9/18/2020.

Amended by Stats 2017 ch 62 (SB 355),s 2, eff. 1/1/2018.

Section 987.9 - Application for funds in capital case

(a) In the trial of a capital case or a case under subdivision (a) of Section 190.05, the indigent defendant, through the defendant's counsel, may request the court for funds for the specific payment of investigators, experts, and others for the preparation or presentation of the defense. The application for funds shall be by affidavit and shall specify that the funds are reasonably necessary for the preparation or presentation of the defense. The fact that an application has been made shall be confidential and the contents of the application shall be confidential. Upon receipt of an application, a judge of the court, other than the trial judge presiding over the case in question, shall rule on the reasonableness of the request and shall disburse an appropriate amount of money to the defendant's attorney. The ruling on the reasonableness of the request shall be made at an in camera hearing. In making the ruling, the court shall be guided by the need to provide a complete and full defense for the defendant.

(b)

(1) The Controller shall not reimburse any county for costs that exceed Department of General Services' standards for travel and per diem expenses. The Controller may reimburse extraordinary costs in unusual cases if the county provides sufficient documentation of the need for those expenditures.

(2) At the termination of the proceedings, the attorney shall furnish to the court a complete accounting of all moneys received and disbursed pursuant to this section.

(c) The Controller shall adopt regulations pursuant to Chapter 3.5 (commencing with Section 11340) of Part 1 of Division 3 of Title 2 of the Government Code, controlling reimbursements under this section. The regulations shall consider compensation for investigators, expert witnesses, and other expenses that may or may not be reimbursable pursuant to this section. Notwithstanding the provisions of Chapter 3.5 (commencing with Section 11340) of Part 1 of Division 3 of Title 2 of the Government Code, the Controller shall follow any regulations adopted until final approval by the Office of Administrative Law.

(d) The confidentiality provided in this section shall not preclude any court from providing the Attorney General with access to documents protected by this section when the defendant raises an issue on appeal or collateral review where the recorded portion of the record, created pursuant to this section, relates to the issue raised. When the defendant raises that issue, the funding records, or relevant portions thereof, shall be provided to the Attorney General at the Attorney General's request. In this case, the documents shall remain under seal and their use shall be limited solely to the pending proceeding.

Amended by Stats 2016 ch 31 (SB 836),s 237, eff. 6/27/2016.

Amended by Stats 2006 ch 538 (SB 1852),s 503, eff. 1/1/2007.

Section 988 - Arraignment

The arraignment must be made by the court, or by the clerk or prosecuting attorney under its direction, and consists in reading the accusatory pleading to the defendant and delivering to the defendant a true copy thereof, and of the endorsements thereon, if any, including the list of witnesses, and asking the defendant whether the defendant pleads guilty or not guilty to the accusatory pleading; provided, that where the accusatory pleading is a complaint charging a misdemeanor, a copy of the same need not be delivered to any defendant unless requested by the defendant.

Amended by Stats. 1998, Ch. 931, Sec. 379. Effective September 28, 1998.

Section 989 - True name

When the defendant is arraigned, he must be informed that if the name by which he is prosecuted is not his true name, he must then declare his true name, or be proceeded against by the name in the accusatory pleading. If he gives no other name, the court may proceed accordingly; but if he alleges that another name is his true name, the court must direct an entry thereof in the minutes of the arraignment, and the subsequent proceedings on the accusatory pleading may be had against him by that name, referring also to the name by which he was first charged therein.

Amended by Stats. 1951, Ch. 1674.

Section 990 - Time to answer

If on the arraignment, the defendant requires it, the defendant must be allowed a reasonable time to answer, which shall be not less than one day in a felony case and not more than seven days in a misdemeanor or infraction case.

Amended by Stats. 1998, Ch. 931, Sec. 380. Effective September 28, 1998.

Section 991 - Determination of probable cause

(a) If the defendant is in custody at the time he appears before the magistrate for arraignment and, if the public offense is a misdemeanor to which the defendant has pleaded not guilty, the magistrate, on motion of counsel for the defendant or the defendant, shall determine whether there is probable cause to believe that a public offense has been committed and that the defendant is guilty thereof.

(b) The determination of probable cause shall be made immediately unless the court grants a continuance for good cause not to exceed three court days.

(c) In determining the existence of probable cause, the magistrate shall consider any warrant of arrest with supporting affidavits, and the sworn complaint together with any documents or reports incorporated by reference thereto, which, if based on information and belief, state the basis for such information, or any other documents of similar reliability.

(d) If, after examining these documents, the court determines that there exists probable cause to believe that the defendant has committed the offense charged in the complaint, it shall set the matter for trial. If the court determines that no such probable cause exists, it shall dismiss the complaint and discharge the defendant.

(e) Within 15 days of the dismissal of a complaint pursuant to this section the prosecution may refile the complaint. A second dismissal pursuant to this section is a bar to any other prosecution for the same offense.

Added by Stats. 1980, Ch. 1379, Sec. 1.

Section 991.5 - [Repealed]

Amended by Stats 2017 ch 561 (AB 1516),s 185, eff. 1/1/2018.

Added by Stats 2016 ch 689 (AB 2013),s 1, eff. 1/1/2017.

Section 992 - Thumbprint

(a)

(1) In any case in which the defendant is charged with a felony, the court shall require the defendant to provide a right thumbprint on a form developed for this purpose. Unless the court has obtained the thumbprint at an earlier proceeding, it shall do so at the arraignment on the information or indictment, or upon entry of a guilty or no contest plea under Section 859a. The fingerprint form shall include the name and superior court case number of the defendant, the date, and the printed name, position, and badge or serial number of the court bailiff who imprints the defendant's thumbprint. In the event the defendant is physically unable to provide a right thumbprint, the defendant shall provide a left thumbprint. In the event the defendant is physically unable to provide a left thumbprint, the court shall make a determination as to how the defendant might otherwise provide a suitable identifying characteristic to be imprinted on the judgment of conviction. The clerk shall note on the fingerprint form which digit, if any, of the defendant's was imprinted thereon. In the event that the defendant is convicted, this fingerprint form shall be attached to the minute order reflecting the defendant's sentence. The fingerprint form shall be permanently maintained in the superior court file.

(2) This thumbprint or fingerprint shall not be used to create a database. The Judicial Council shall develop a form to implement this section.

(b) In the event that a county implements a countywide policy in which every felony defendant's photograph and fingerprints are permanently maintained in the superior court file, the presiding judge of that county may elect, after consultation with the district attorney, to continue compliance with this section.

Amended by Stats 2011 ch 304 (SB 428),s 8, eff. 1/1/2012.

Section 993 - Information regarding guardianship for defendant who is sole custodial parent

(a) At the arraignment of a defendant who is charged with a felony and who is, or whom the court reasonably deems to be, the sole custodial parent of one or more minor children, the court shall provide the following to the defendant:

(1) Judicial Council Form GC-205, the "Guardianship Pamphlet."

(2) Information regarding a power of attorney for a minor child.

(3) Information regarding trustline background examinations pertaining to child care providers as provided in Chapter 3.35 (commencing with Section 1596.60) of Division 2 of the Health and Safety Code.

(b) If the defendant states, orally or in writing, at the arraignment that the defendant is a sole custodial parent of one or more minor children, the court may reasonably deem the defendant to be a sole custodial parent of one or more minor children without further investigation. The court may, but is not required to, make that determination on the basis of information other than the defendant's statement.

Amended by Stats 2019 ch 497 (AB 991),s 202, eff. 1/1/2020.

Amended by Stats 2019 ch 256 (SB 781),s 9, eff. 1/1/2020.

Added by Stats 2016 ch 882 (AB 2380),s 1, eff. 1/1/2017.

Chapter 2 - SETTING ASIDE THE INDICTMENT OR INFORMATION

Section 995 - Setting aside indictment or information

(a) Subject to subdivision (b) of Section 995a, the indictment or information shall be set aside by the court in which the defendant is arraigned, upon his or her motion, in either of the following cases:

(1) If it is an indictment:

(A) Where it is not found, endorsed, and presented as prescribed in this code.

(B) That the defendant has been indicted without reasonable or probable cause.

(2) If it is an information:

   (A) That before the filing thereof the defendant had not been legally committed by a magistrate.

   (B) That the defendant had been committed without reasonable or probable cause.

(b) In cases in which the procedure set out in subdivision (b) of Section 995a is utilized, the court shall reserve a final ruling on the motion until those procedures have been completed.

Amended by Stats. 1982, Ch. 1505, Sec. 3.

Section 995a - Names of witnesses; correction of errors

(a) If the names of the witnesses examined before the grand jury are not inserted at the foot of the indictment or indorsed thereon, the court shall order them to be so inserted or indorsed; and if the information be not subscribed by the district attorney, the court may order it to be so subscribed.

(b)

   (1) Without setting aside the information, the court may, upon motion of the prosecuting attorney, order further proceedings to correct errors alleged by the defendant if the court finds that such errors are minor errors of omission, ambiguity, or technical defect which can be expeditiously cured or corrected without a rehearing of a substantial portion of the evidence. The court may remand the cause to the committing magistrate for further proceedings, or if the parties and the court agree, the court may itself sit as a magistrate and conduct further proceedings. When remanding the cause to the committing magistrate, the court shall state in its remand order which minor errors it finds could be expeditiously cured or corrected.

   (2) Any further proceedings conducted pursuant to this subdivision may include the taking of testimony and shall be deemed to be a part of the preliminary examination.

   (3) The procedure specified in this subdivision may be utilized only once for each information filed. Any further proceedings conducted pursuant to this subdivision shall not be deemed to extend the time within which a defendant must be brought to trial under Section 1382.

Amended by Stats. 1982, Ch. 1505, Sec. 4.

Section 996 - Failure to make motion to set aside indictment or information

If the motion to set aside the indictment or information is not made, the defendant is precluded from afterwards taking the objections mentioned in Section 995.

Amended by Stats. 1967, Ch. 138.

Section 997 - Hearing of motion

The motion must be heard at the time it is made, unless for cause the court postpones the hearing to another time. The court may entertain such motion prior to trial whether or not a plea has been entered and such plea need not be set aside in order to consider the motion. If the motion is denied, and the accused has not previously answered the indictment or information, either by demurring or pleading thereto, he shall immediately do so. If the motion is granted, the court must order that the defendant, if in custody, be discharged therefrom; or, if admitted to bail, that his bail be exonerated; or, if he has deposited money, or if money has been deposited by another or others instead of bail for his appearance, that the same be refunded to him or to the person or persons found by the court to have deposited said money on behalf of said defendant, unless it directs that the case be resubmitted to the same or another grand jury, or that an information be filed by the district attorney; provided, that after such order of resubmission the defendant may be examined before a magistrate, and discharged or committed by him, as in other cases, if before indictment or information filed he has not been examined and committed by a magistrate.

Amended by Stats. 1968, Ch. 1064.

Section 998 - Resubmission of case or filing of indictment

If the court directs the case to be resubmitted, or an information to be filed, the defendant, if already in custody, shall remain, unless he or she is admitted to bail; or, if already admitted to bail, or money has been deposited instead thereof, the bail or money is answerable for the appearance of the defendant to answer a new indictment or information; and, unless a new indictment is found or information filed before the next grand jury of the county is discharged, the court shall, on the discharge of such grand jury, make the order prescribed by Section 997.

Amended by Stats. 1987, Ch. 828, Sec. 58.

Section 999 - Order to set aside not bar to future prosecution

An order to set aside an indictment or information, as provided in this chapter, is no bar to a future prosecution for the same offense.

Amended by Code Amendments 1880, Ch. 47.

Section 999a - Petition for writ of prohibition

A petition for a writ of prohibition, predicated upon the ground that the indictment was found without reasonable or probable cause or that the defendant had been committed on an information without reasonable or probable cause, or that the court abused its discretion in utilizing the procedure set out in subdivision (b) of Section 995a, must be filed in the appellate court within 15 days after a motion made under Section 995 to set aside the indictment on the ground that the defendant has been indicted without reasonable or probable cause or that the defendant had been committed on an information without reasonable or probable cause, has been denied by the trial court. A copy of such petition shall be served upon the district attorney of the county in which the indictment is returned or the information is filed. The alternative writ shall not issue until five days after the service of notice upon the district attorney and until he has had an opportunity to appear before the appellate court and to indicate to the court the particulars in which the evidence is sufficient to sustain the indictment or commitment.

Amended by Stats. 1982, Ch. 1505, Sec. 5.

Chapter 2.2 - CAREER CRIMINALS

Section 999b - Legislative findings and intent

The Legislature hereby finds a substantial and disproportionate amount of serious crime is committed against the people of California by a relatively small number of multiple and repeat felony offenders, commonly known as career criminals. In enacting this chapter, the

Legislature intends to support increased efforts by district attorneys' offices to prosecute career criminals through organizational and operational techniques that have been proven effective in selected counties in this and other states.
Added by Stats. 1982, Ch. 42, Sec. 1. Effective February 17, 1982.

Section 999c - California Career Criminal Prosecution Program

(a) There is hereby established in the Office of Emergency Services a program of financial and technical assistance for district attorneys' offices, designated the California Career Criminal Prosecution Program. All funds appropriated to the office for the purposes of this chapter shall be administered and disbursed by the Director of Emergency Services, and shall to the greatest extent feasible be coordinated or consolidated with federal funds that may be made available for these purposes.

(b) The Director of Emergency Services is authorized to allocate and award funds to counties in which career criminal prosecution units are established in substantial compliance with the policies and criteria set forth below in Sections 999d, 999e, 999f, and 999g.

(c) The allocation and award of funds shall be made upon application executed by the county's district attorney and approved by its board of supervisors. Funds disbursed under this chapter shall not supplant local funds that would, in the absence of the California Career Criminal Prosecution Program, be made available to support the prosecution of felony cases. Funds available under this program shall not be subject to review as specified in Section 14780 of the Government Code.
Amended by Stats 2013 ch 352 (AB 1317),s 406, eff. 9/26/2013, op. 7/1/2013.
Amended by Stats 2011 ch 36 (SB 92),s 22, eff. 6/30/2011, op. 1/1/2012.
Amended by Stats 2010 ch 618 (AB 2791),s 193, eff. 1/1/2011.
Amended by Stats 2003 ch 229 (AB 1757), s 2.5, eff. 1/1/2004.

Section 999d - Enhanced prosecution efforts and resources

Career criminal prosecution units receiving funds under this chapter shall concentrate enhanced prosecution efforts and resources upon individuals identified under selection criteria set forth in Section 999e. Enhanced prosecution efforts and resources shall include, but not be limited to:

(a) "Vertical" prosecutorial representation, whereby the prosecutor who makes the initial filing or appearance in a career criminal case will perform all subsequent court appearances on that particular case through its conclusion, including the sentencing phase;

(b) Assignment of highly qualified investigators and prosecutors to career criminal cases; and

(c) Significant reduction of caseloads for investigators and prosecutors assigned to career criminal cases.
Added by Stats. 1982, Ch. 42, Sec. 1. Effective February 17, 1982.

Section 999e - Subject of career criminal prosecution efforts

(a) An individual who is under arrest for the commission or attempted commission of one or more of the felonies listed in paragraph (1) and who is either being prosecuted for three or more separate offenses not arising out of the same transaction involving one or more of those felonies, or has been convicted during the preceding 10 years for any felony listed in paragraph (2) of this subdivision, or at least two convictions during the preceding 10 years for any felony listed in paragraph (3) of this subdivision shall be the subject of career criminal prosecution efforts.

(1) Murder, manslaughter, rape, sexual assault, child molestation, robbery, carjacking, burglary, arson, receiving stolen property, grand theft, grand theft auto, lewd and lascivious conduct upon a child, assault with a firearm, discharging a firearm into an inhabited structure or vehicle, owning, possessing, or having custody or control of a firearm, as specified in subdivision (a) or (b) of Section 29800, or any unlawful act relating to controlled substances in violation of Section 11351, 11351.5, 11352, or 11378 of the Health and Safety Code.

(2) Robbery of the first degree, carjacking, burglary of the first degree, arson as defined in Section 451, unlawfully causing a fire as defined in Section 452, forcible rape, sodomy or oral copulation committed with force, lewd or lascivious conduct committed upon a child, kidnapping as defined in Section 209 or 209.5, murder, or manslaughter.

(3) Grand theft, grand theft auto, receiving stolen property, robbery of the second degree, burglary of the second degree, kidnapping as defined in Section 207, assault with a deadly weapon or instrument, or any unlawful act relating to controlled substances in violation of Section 11351 or 11352 of the Health and Safety Code. For purposes of this chapter, the 10-year periods specified in this section shall be exclusive of any time which the arrested person has served in state prison.

(b) In applying the career criminal selection criteria set forth above, a district attorney may elect to limit career criminal prosecution efforts to persons arrested for any one or more of the felonies listed in subdivision (a) of this section if crime statistics demonstrate that the incidence of one or more of these felonies presents a particularly serious problem in the county.

(c) In exercising the prosecutorial discretion granted by Section 999g, the district attorney shall consider the character, background, and prior criminal background of the defendant, and the number and the seriousness of the offenses currently charged against the defendant.
Amended by Stats 2010 ch 178 (SB 1115),s 70, eff. 1/1/2011, op. 1/1/2012.

Section 999f - Policies for career criminal cases

(a) Each district attorney's office establishing a career criminal prosecution unit and receiving state support under this chapter shall adopt and pursue the following policies for career criminal cases:

(1) A plea of guilty or a trial conviction will be sought on all the offenses charged in the accusatory pleading against an individual meeting career criminal selection criteria.

(2) All reasonable prosecutorial efforts will be made to resist the pretrial release of a charged defendant meeting career criminal selection criteria.

(3) All reasonable prosecutorial efforts will be made to persuade the court to impose the most severe authorized sentence upon a person convicted after prosecution as a career criminal.

(4) All reasonable prosecutorial efforts will be made to reduce the time between arrest and disposition of charge against an individual meeting career criminal selection criteria.

(b) The prosecution shall not negotiate a plea agreement with a defendant in a career criminal prosecution; and Sections 1192.1 to 1192.5, inclusive, shall not apply, nor shall any plea of guilty or nolo contendere authorized by any such section, or any plea of guilty or nolo contendere as a result of any plea agreement be approved by the court in a career criminal prosecution.

(c) For purposes of this section a "plea agreement" means an agreement by the defendant to plead guilty or nolo contendere in exchange for any or all of the following: a dismissal of charges, a reduction in the degree of a charge, a change of a charge to a lesser or different crime, a specific manner or extent of punishment.

(d) This section does not prohibit the reduction of the offense charged or dismissal of counts in the interest of justice when a written declaration by the prosecuting attorney stating the specific factual and legal basis for such reduction or dismissal is presented to the court and the court, in writing, acknowledges acceptance of such declaration. A copy of such declaration and acceptance shall be retained in the case file. The only basis upon which charges may be reduced or counts dismissed by the court shall be in cases where the prosecuting attorney decides that there is insufficient evidence to prove the people's case, the testimony of a material witness cannot be obtained, or a reduction or dismissal would not result in a substantial change in sentence. In any case in which the court or magistrate grants the prosecuting attorney's motion for a reduction of charges or dismissal of counts because there would be no substantial change in sentence, the court or magistrate shall require the prosecuting attorney to put on the record in open court the following:

   (1) The charges filed in the complaint or information and the maximum statutory penalty that could be given if the defendant were convicted of all such charges.

   (2) The charges which would be filed against the defendant if the court or magistrate grants the prosecuting attorney's motion and the maximum statutory penalty which can be given for these charges.

(e) This section does not prohibit a plea agreement when there are codefendants, and the prosecuting attorney determines that the information or testimony of the defendant making the agreement is necessary for the conviction of one or more of the other codefendants. The court shall condition its acceptance of the plea agreement on the defendant giving the information or testimony. Before the court can accept the plea agreement, the prosecuting attorney shall present a written declaration to the court, specifying the legal and factual reasons for the agreement, and the court shall acknowledge in writing its acceptance of that declaration. A copy of the declaration and acceptance shall be retained in the case file.

Added by Stats. 1982, Ch. 42, Sec. 1. Effective February 17, 1982.

Section 999g - Adherence to selection criteria

The selection criteria set forth in Section 999e shall be adhered to for each career criminal case unless, in the reasonable exercise of prosecutor's discretion, extraordinary circumstances require the departure from such policies in order to promote the general purposes and intent of this chapter.

Added by Stats. 1982, Ch. 42, Sec. 1. Effective February 17, 1982.

Section 999h - Communication of characterization of defendant as career criminal

The characterization of a defendant as a "career criminal" as defined by this chapter may not be communicated to the trier of fact.

Added by Stats. 1982, Ch. 42, Sec. 1. Effective February 17, 1982.

Chapter 2.3 - REPEAT SEXUAL OFFENDERS

Section 999i - Legislative findings and intent

The Legislature hereby finds that repeat sexual offenders present a clear and present danger to the mental and physical well-being of the citizens of the State of California, especially of its children. The Legislature further finds that the concept of vertical prosecution, in which one deputy district attorney is assigned to a case from its filing to its completion, is a proven way of demonstrably increasing the likelihood of convicting repeat sex offenders and ensuring appropriate sentences for such offenders. In enacting this chapter, the Legislature intends to support increased efforts by district attorneys' offices to prosecute repeat sexual offenders through organizational and operational techniques that have already proven their effectiveness in selected counties in this and other states, as demonstrated by the California Career Criminal Prosecution Program and the California Gang Violence Suppression Program, as well as sexual assault prosecution units in several counties.

Added by Stats. 1983, Ch. 1078, Sec. 1.

Section 999j - Repeat Sexual Offender Prosecution Program

(a) There is hereby established in the Office of Emergency Services a program of financial and technical assistance for district attorneys' offices, designated the Repeat Sexual Offender Prosecution Program. All funds appropriated to the office for the purposes of this chapter shall be administered and disbursed by the Director of Emergency Services, and shall to the greatest extent feasible, be coordinated or consolidated with any federal or local funds that may be made available for these purposes. The Office of Emergency Services shall establish guidelines for the provision of grant awards to proposed and existing programs prior to the allocation of funds under this chapter. These guidelines shall contain the criteria for the selection of agencies to receive funding, as developed in consultation with an advisory group to be known as the Repeat Sexual Offender Prosecution Program Steering Committee. The membership of the steering committee shall be designated by the secretary of the office.

A draft of the guidelines shall be developed and submitted to the Chairpersons of the Assembly Criminal Law and Public Safety Committee and the Senate Judiciary Committee within 60 days of the effective date of this chapter and issued within 90 days of the same effective date. These guidelines shall set forth the terms and conditions upon which the Office of Emergency Services is prepared to offer grants pursuant to statutory authority. The guidelines shall not constitute rules, regulations, orders, or standards of general application.

(b) The Director of Emergency Services is authorized to allocate and award funds to counties in which repeat sexual offender prosecution units are established or are proposed to be established in substantial compliance with the policies and criteria set forth below in Sections 999k, 999l, and 999m.

(c) The allocation and award of funds shall be made upon application executed by the county's district attorney and approved by its board of supervisors. Funds disbursed under this chapter shall not supplant local funds that would, in the absence of the California

Repeat Sexual Offender Prosecution Program, be made available to support the prosecution of repeat sexual offender felony cases. Local grant awards made under this program shall not be subject to review as specified in Section 14780 of the Government Code.

Amended by Stats 2013 ch 352 (AB 1317),s 407, eff. 9/26/2013, op. 7/1/2013.

Amended by Stats 2010 ch 618 (AB 2791),s 194, eff. 1/1/2011.

Amended by Stats 2003 ch 229 (AB 1757), s 3, eff. 1/1/2004.

Section 999k - Enhanced prosecution efforts and resources

Repeat sexual offender prosecution units receiving funds under this chapter shall concentrate enhanced prosecution efforts and resources upon individuals identified under selection criteria set forth in Section 999l. Enhanced prosecution efforts and resources shall include, but not be limited to:

(a) Vertical prosecutorial representation, whereby the prosecutor who makes the initial filing or appearance in a repeat sexual offender case will perform all subsequent court appearances on that particular case through its conclusion, including the sentencing phase.

(b) The assignment of highly qualified investigators and prosecutors to repeat sexual offender cases. "Highly qualified" for the purposes of this chapter shall be defined as:

(1) individuals with one year of experience in the investigation and prosecution of felonies or specifically the felonies listed in subdivision (a) of Section 999l; or

(2) individuals whom the district attorney has selected to receive training as set forth in Section 13836; or

(3) individuals who have attended a program providing equivalent training as approved by the Office of Emergency Services.

(c) A significant reduction of caseloads for investigators and prosecutors assigned to repeat sexual offender cases.

(d) Coordination with local rape victim counseling centers, child abuse services programs, and victim witness assistance programs. Coordination shall include, but not be limited to: referrals of individuals to receive client services; participation in local training programs; membership and participation in local task forces established to improve communication between criminal justice system agencies and community service agencies; and cooperating with individuals serving as liaison representatives of local rape victim counseling centers and victim witness assistance programs.

Amended by Stats 2013 ch 352 (AB 1317),s 408, eff. 9/26/2013, op. 7/1/2013.

Amended by Stats 2010 ch 618 (AB 2791),s 195, eff. 1/1/2011.

Amended by Stats 2003 ch 229 (AB 1757), s 4, eff. 1/1/2004.

Section 999l - Subject of repeat sexual offender prosecution effort

(a) An individual shall be the subject of a repeat sexual offender prosecution effort who is under arrest for the commission or attempted commission of one or more of the following offenses: assault with intent to commit rape, sodomy, oral copulation or any violation of Section 264.1, Section 288, or Section 289; rape, in violation of Section 261; sexual battery, in violation of Section 243.4; sodomy, in violation of Section 286; lewd acts on a child under 14, in violation of Section 288; oral copulation, in violation of Section 287 or former Section 288a; sexual penetration, in violation of Section 289; and (1) who is being prosecuted for offenses involving two or more separate victims, or (2) who is being prosecuted for the commission or attempted commission of three or more separate offenses not arising out of the same transaction involving one or more of the above-listed offenses, or (3) who has suffered at least one conviction during the preceding 10 years for any of the above-listed offenses. For purposes of this chapter, the 10-year periods specified in this section shall be exclusive of any time which the arrested person has served in state prison or in a state hospital pursuant to a commitment as a mentally disordered sex offender.

(b) In applying the repeat sexual offender selection criteria set forth above:

(1) a district attorney may elect to limit repeat sexual offender prosecution efforts to persons arrested for any one or more of the offenses listed in subdivision (a) if crime statistics demonstrate that the incidence of such one or more offenses presents a particularly serious problem in the county;

(2) a district attorney shall not reject cases for filing exclusively on the basis that there is a family or personal relationship between the victim and the alleged offender.

(c) In exercising the prosecutorial discretion granted by Section 999n, the district attorney shall consider the following:

(1) the character, the background, and prior criminal background of the defendant, and

(2) the number and seriousness of the offenses currently charged against the defendant.

Amended by Stats 2018 ch 423 (SB 1494),s 83, eff. 1/1/2019.

Amended by Stats 2000 ch 287 (SB 1955), s 13, eff. 1/1/2001.

Section 999m - Policies for repeat sexual offender cases

Each district attorney's office establishing a repeat sexual offender prosecution unit and receiving state support under this chapter shall adopt and pursue the following policies for repeat sexual offender cases:

(a) All reasonable prosecutorial efforts will be made to resist the pretrial release of a charged defendant meeting repeat sexual offender selection criteria.

(b) All reasonable prosecutorial efforts will be made to persuade the court to impose the most severe authorized sentence upon a person convicted after prosecution as a repeat sexual offender. In the prosecution of an intrafamily sexual abuse case, discretion may be exercised as to the type and nature of sentence recommended to the court.

(c) All reasonable prosecutorial efforts will be made to reduce the time between arrest and disposition of charge against an individual meeting repeat sexual offender criteria.

Added by Stats. 1983, Ch. 1078, Sec. 1.

Section 999n - Adherence to selection criteria

(a) The selection criteria set forth in Section 999l shall be adhered to for each repeat sexual offender case unless, in the reasonable exercise of prosecutor's discretion, extraordinary circumstances require departure from those policies in order to promote the general purposes and intent of this chapter.

(b) Each district attorney's office establishing a repeat sexual offender prosecution unit and receiving state support under this chapter shall submit the following information, on a quarterly basis, to the Office of Emergency Services:

(1) The number of sexual assault cases referred to the district attorney's office for possible filing.

(2) The number of sexual assault cases filed for felony prosecution.

(3) The number of sexual assault cases taken to trial.

(4) The percentage of sexual assault cases tried which resulted in conviction.

Amended by Stats 2013 ch 352 (AB 1317),s 409, eff. 9/26/2013, op. 7/1/2013.

Amended by Stats 2010 ch 618 (AB 2791),s 196, eff. 1/1/2011.

Amended by Stats 2003 ch 229 (AB 1757), s 5, eff. 1/1/2004.

Section 999o - Communication of characterization of defendant as repeat sexual offender

The characterization of a defendant as a "repeat sexual offender" as defined by this chapter shall not be communicated to the trier of fact.

Added by Stats. 1983, Ch. 1078, Sec. 1.

Section 999p - Utilization of federal funds

The Office of Emergency Services is encouraged to utilize any federal funds which may become available in order to implement the provisions of this chapter.

Amended by Stats 2013 ch 352 (AB 1317),s 410, eff. 9/26/2013, op. 7/1/2013.

Amended by Stats 2010 ch 618 (AB 2791),s 197, eff. 1/1/2011.

Amended by Stats 2003 ch 229 (AB 1757), s 6, eff. 1/1/2004.

Chapter 2.4 - CHILD ABUSERS

Section 999q - Legislative findings and intent

The Legislature hereby finds that child abusers present a clear and present danger to the mental health and physical well-being of the citizens of the State of California, especially of its children. The Legislature further finds that the concept of vertical prosecution, in which a specially trained deputy district attorney or prosecution unit is assigned to a case from its filing to its completion, is a proven way of demonstrably increasing the likelihood of convicting child abusers and ensuring appropriate sentences for such offenders. In enacting this chapter, the Legislature intends to support increased efforts by district attorneys' offices to prosecute child abusers through organizational and operational techniques that have already proven their effectiveness in selected counties in this and other states, as demonstrated by the California Career Criminal Prosecution Program, the California Gang Violence Suppression Program, and the Repeat Sexual Offender Prosecution Program.

Added by Stats. 1985, Ch. 1097, Sec. 1.

Section 999r - Child Abuser Prosecution Program

(a) There is hereby established in the Office of Emergency Services a program of financial and technical assistance for district attorneys' offices, designated the Child Abuser Prosecution Program. All funds appropriated to the agency for the purposes of this chapter shall be administered and disbursed by the executive director of that agency or agencies, and shall to the greatest extent feasible, be coordinated or consolidated with any federal or local funds that may be made available for these purposes. The Office of Emergency Services shall establish guidelines for the provision of grant awards to proposed and existing programs prior to the allocation of funds under this chapter. These guidelines shall contain the criteria for the selection of agencies to receive funding and the terms and conditions upon which the agency is prepared to offer grants pursuant to statutory authority. The guidelines shall not constitute rules, regulations, orders, or standards of general application. The guidelines shall be submitted to the appropriate policy committees of the Legislature prior to their adoption.

(b) The Director of Emergency Services is authorized to allocate and award funds to counties in which child abuser offender prosecution units are established or are proposed to be established in substantial compliance with the policies and criteria set forth below in Sections 999s, 999t, and 999u.

(c) The allocation and award of funds shall be made upon application executed by the county's district attorney and approved by its board of supervisors. Funds disbursed under this chapter shall not supplant local funds that would, in the absence of the California Child Abuser Prosecution Program, be made available to support the prosecution of child abuser felony cases. Local grant awards made under this program shall not be subject to review as specified in Section 14780 of the Government Code.

Amended by Stats 2013 ch 352 (AB 1317),s 411, eff. 9/26/2013, op. 7/1/2013.

Amended by Stats 2010 ch 618 (AB 2791),s 198, eff. 1/1/2011.

Amended by Stats 2003 ch 229 (AB 1757), s 7, eff. 1/1/2004.

Section 999s - Enhanced prosecution efforts and resources

Child abuser prosecution units receiving funds under this chapter shall concentrate enhanced prosecution efforts and resources upon individuals identified under selection criteria set forth in Section 999t. Enhanced prosecution efforts and resources shall include, but not be limited to:

(a) Vertical prosecutorial representation, whereby the prosecutor who, or prosecution unit which, makes the initial filing or appearance in a case performs all subsequent court appearances on that particular case through its conclusion, including the sentencing phase.

(b) The assignment of highly qualified investigators and prosecutors to child abuser cases. "Highly qualified" for the purposes of this chapter means:

(1) individuals with one year of experience in the investigation and prosecution of felonies or specifically the felonies listed in subdivision (a) of Section 999l or 999t; or

(2) individuals whom the district attorney has selected to receive training as set forth in Section 13836; or

(3) individuals who have attended a program providing equivalent training as approved by the Office of Emergency Services.

(c) A significant reduction of caseloads for investigators and prosecutors assigned to child abuser cases.

(d) Coordination with local rape victim counseling centers, child abuse services programs, and victim witness assistance programs. That coordination shall include, but not be limited to: referrals of individuals to receive client services; participation in local training programs; membership and participation in local task forces established to improve communication between criminal justice system agencies and community service agencies; and cooperating with individuals serving as liaison representatives of child abuse and child sexual abuse programs, local rape victim counseling centers and victim witness assistance programs.

Amended by Stats 2013 ch 352 (AB 1317),s 412, eff. 9/26/2013, op. 7/1/2013.

Amended by Stats 2010 ch 618 (AB 2791),s 199, eff. 1/1/2011.

Amended by Stats 2003 ch 229 (AB 1757), s 8, eff. 1/1/2004.

Section 999t - Subject of child abuser prosecution effort

(a) An individual may be the subject of a child abuser prosecution effort who is under arrest for the sexual assault of a child, as defined in Section 11165, or a violation of subdivision (a) or (b) of Section 273a, or a violation of Section 273ab, or 273d, or a violation of Section 288.2 when committed in conjunction with any other violation listed in this subdivision.

(b) In applying the child abuser selection criteria set forth above:

(1) a district attorney may elect to limit child abuser prosecution efforts to persons arrested for any one or more of the offenses described in subdivision (a) if crime statistics demonstrate that the incidence of such one or more offenses presents a particularly serious problem in the county;

(2) a district attorney shall not reject cases for filing exclusively on the basis that there is a family or personal relationship between the victim and the alleged offender.

(c) In exercising the prosecutorial discretion granted by Section 999v, the district attorney shall consider the character, the background, and the prior criminal background of the defendant.

Amended by Stats 2001 ch 210 (AB 929), s 1, eff. 1/1/2002.

Section 999u - Policies for child abuser cases

Each district attorney's office establishing a child abuser prosecution unit and receiving state support under this chapter shall adopt and pursue the following policies for child abuser cases:

(a) Except as provided in subdivision (b), all reasonable prosecutorial efforts will be made to resist the pretrial release of a charged defendant meeting child abuser selection criteria.

(b) Nothing in this chapter shall be construed to limit the application of diversion programs authorized by law. All reasonable efforts shall be made to utilize diversion alternatives in appropriate cases.

(c) All reasonable prosecutorial efforts will be made to reduce the time between arrest and disposition of charge against an individual meeting child abuser criteria.

Added by Stats. 1985, Ch. 1097, Sec. 1.

Section 999v - Adherence to selection criteria

(a) The selection criteria set forth in Section 999t shall be adhered to for each child abuser case unless, in the reasonable exercise of prosecutor's discretion, extraordinary circumstances require departure from those policies in order to promote the general purposes and intent of this chapter.

(b) Each district attorney's office establishing a child abuser prosecution unit and receiving state support under this chapter shall submit the following information, on a quarterly basis, to the Office of Emergency Services:

(1) The number of child abuser cases referred to the district attorney's office for possible filing.

(2) The number of child abuser cases filed for felony prosecution.

(3) The number of sexual assault cases taken to trial.

(4) The number of child abuser cases tried which resulted in conviction.

Amended by Stats 2013 ch 352 (AB 1317),s 413, eff. 9/26/2013, op. 7/1/2013.

Amended by Stats 2010 ch 618 (AB 2791),s 200, eff. 1/1/2011.

Amended by Stats 2003 ch 229 (AB 1757), s 9, eff. 1/1/2004.

Section 999w - Characterization of defendant as child abuser

The characterization of a defendant as a "child abuser" as defined by this chapter shall not be communicated to the trier of fact.

Added by Stats. 1985, Ch. 1097, Sec. 1.

Section 999x - Utilization of federal funds

The Office of Emergency Services is encouraged to utilize any federal funds which may become available in order to implement the provisions of this chapter.

Amended by Stats 2013 ch 352 (AB 1317),s 414, eff. 9/26/2013, op. 7/1/2013.

Amended by Stats 2010 ch 618 (AB 2791),s 201, eff. 1/1/2011.

Amended by Stats 2003 ch 229 (AB 1757), s 10, eff. 1/1/2004.

Section 999y - Annual report; evaluation

The Office of Emergency Services shall report annually to the Legislature concerning the program established by this chapter. The office shall prepare and submit to the Legislature on or before December 15, 2002, and within six months of the completion of subsequent funding cycles for this program, an evaluation of the Child Abuser Prosecution Program. This evaluation shall identify outcome measures to determine the effectiveness of the programs established under this chapter, which shall include, but not be limited to, both of the following, to the extent that data is available:

(a) Child abuse conviction rates of Child Abuser Prosecution Program units compared to those of nonfunded counties.

(b) Quantification of the annual per capita costs of the Child Abuser Prosecution Program compared to the costs of prosecuting child abuse crimes in nonfunded counties.

Amended by Stats 2013 ch 352 (AB 1317),s 415, eff. 9/26/2013, op. 7/1/2013.

Amended by Stats 2010 ch 618 (AB 2791),s 202, eff. 1/1/2011.

Amended by Stats 2003 ch 229 (AB 1757), s 11, eff. 1/1/2004.

Amended by Stats 2001 ch 210 (AB 929), s 2, eff. 1/1/2002.

Chapter 2.5 - SPECIAL PROCEEDINGS IN NARCOTICS AND DRUG ABUSE CASES

Section 1000 - Applicability of chapter

(a) This chapter shall apply whenever a case is before any court upon an accusatory pleading for a violation of Section 11350, 11357, 11364, or 11365, paragraph (2) of subdivision (b) of Section 11375, Section 11377, or Section 11550 of the Health and Safety Code, or subdivision (b) of Section 23222 of the Vehicle Code, or Section 11358 of the Health and Safety Code if the marijuana planted, cultivated, harvested, dried, or processed is for personal use, or Section 11368 of the Health and Safety Code if the narcotic drug was secured by a fictitious prescription and is for the personal use of the defendant and was not sold or furnished to another, or subdivision (d) of Section 653f if the solicitation was for acts directed to personal use only, or Section 381 or subdivision (f) of Section 647 of the Penal Code, if for being under the influence of a controlled substance, or Section 4060 of the Business and Professions Code, and it appears to the prosecuting attorney that, except as provided in subdivision (b) of Section 11357 of the Health and Safety Code, all of the following apply to the defendant:

(1) Within five years prior to the alleged commission of the charged offense, the defendant has not suffered a conviction for any offense involving controlled substances other than the offenses listed in this subdivision.

(2) The offense charged did not involve a crime of violence or threatened violence.

(3) There is no evidence of a contemporaneous violation relating to narcotics or restricted dangerous drugs other than a violation of the offenses listed in this subdivision.

(4) The defendant has no prior felony conviction within five years prior to the alleged commission of the charged offense.

(b) The prosecuting attorney shall review his or her file to determine whether or not paragraphs (1) to (4), inclusive, of subdivision (a) apply to the defendant. If the defendant is found eligible, the prosecuting attorney shall file with the court a declaration in writing or state for the record the grounds upon which the determination is based, and shall make this information available to the defendant and his or her attorney. This procedure is intended to allow the court to set the hearing for pretrial diversion at the arraignment. If the defendant is found ineligible for pretrial diversion, the prosecuting attorney shall file with the court a declaration in writing or state for the record the grounds upon which the determination is based, and shall make this information available to the defendant and his or her attorney. The sole remedy of a defendant who is found ineligible for pretrial diversion is a postconviction appeal.

(c) All referrals for pretrial diversion granted by the court pursuant to this chapter shall be made only to programs that have been certified by the county drug program administrator pursuant to Chapter 1.5 (commencing with Section 1211) of Title 8, or to programs that provide services at no cost to the participant and have been deemed by the court and the county drug program administrator to be credible and effective. The defendant may request to be referred to a program in any county, as long as that program meets the criteria set forth in this subdivision.

(d) Pretrial diversion for an alleged violation of Section 11368 of the Health and Safety Code shall not prohibit any administrative agency from taking disciplinary action against a licensee or from denying a license. This subdivision does not expand or restrict the provisions of Section 1000.4.

(e) Any defendant who is participating in a program authorized in this section may be required to undergo analysis of his or her urine for the purpose of testing for the presence of any drug as part of the program. However, urinalysis results shall not be admissible as a basis for any new criminal prosecution or proceeding.

Amended by Stats 2017 ch 778 (AB 208),s 1, eff. 1/1/2018.
Amended by Stats 2014 ch 471 (AB 2309),s 1, eff. 1/1/2015.
Amended by Stats 2002 ch 545 (SB 1852), s 5, eff. 1/1/2003.
Amended by Stats 2002 ch 784 (SB 1316), s 541, eff. 1/1/2003.
Amended by Stats 2001 ch 473 (SB 485) s 7, eff. 1/1/2002.

Section 1000.1 - Notification of defendant and attorney

(a) If the prosecuting attorney determines that this chapter may be applicable to the defendant, he or she shall advise the defendant and his or her attorney in writing of that determination. This notification shall include all of the following:

(1) A full description of the procedures for pretrial diversion.

(2) A general explanation of the roles and authorities of the probation department, the prosecuting attorney, the program, and the court in the process.

(3) A clear statement that the court may grant pretrial diversion with respect to any offense specified in subdivision (a) of Section 1000 that is charged, provided that the defendant pleads not guilty to the charge or charges, waives the right to a speedy trial, to a speedy preliminary hearing, and to a trial by jury, if applicable, and that upon the defendant's successful completion of a program, as specified in subdivision (c) of Section 1000, the positive recommendation of the program authority and the motion of the defendant, prosecuting attorney, the court, or the probation department, but no sooner than 12 months and no later than 18 months from the date of the defendant's referral to the program, the court shall dismiss the charge or charges against the defendant.

(4) A clear statement that upon any failure of treatment or condition under the program, or any circumstance specified in Section 1000.3, the prosecuting attorney or the probation department or the court on its own may make a motion to the court to terminate pretrial diversion and schedule further proceedings as otherwise provided in this code.

(5) An explanation of criminal record retention and disposition resulting from participation in the pretrial diversion program and the defendant's rights relative to answering questions about his or her arrest and pretrial diversion following successful completion of the program.

(b) If the defendant consents and waives his or her right to a speedy trial, a speedy preliminary hearing, and to a trial by jury, if applicable, the court may refer the case to the probation department or the court may summarily grant pretrial diversion. When directed by the court, the probation department shall make an investigation and take into consideration the defendant's age, employment and service records, educational background, community and family ties, prior controlled substance use, treatment history, if any, demonstrable motivation, and other mitigating factors in determining whether the defendant is a person who would be benefited by education, treatment, or rehabilitation. The probation department shall also determine which programs the defendant would benefit from and which programs would accept the defendant. The probation department shall report its findings and recommendations to the court. The court shall make the final determination regarding education, treatment, or rehabilitation for the defendant. If the court determines that it is appropriate, the court shall grant pretrial diversion if the defendant pleads not guilty to the charge or charges and waives the right to a speedy trial, to a speedy preliminary hearing, and to a trial by jury, if applicable.

(c)

(1) No statement, or any information procured therefrom, made by the defendant to any probation officer or drug treatment worker, that is made during the course of any investigation conducted by the probation department or treatment program pursuant to subdivision (b), and prior to the reporting of the probation department's findings and recommendations to the court, shall be admissible in any action or proceeding brought subsequent to the investigation.

(2) No statement, or any information procured therefrom, with respect to the specific offense with which the defendant is charged, that is made to any probation officer or drug program worker subsequent to the granting of pretrial diversion shall be admissible in any action or proceeding.

(d) A defendant's participation in pretrial diversion pursuant to this chapter shall not constitute a conviction or an admission of guilt for any purpose.

Amended by Stats 2017 ch 778 (AB 208),s 2, eff. 1/1/2018.

Amended by Stats 2010 ch 328 (SB 1330),s 160, eff. 1/1/2011.

Section 1000.2 - Hearing

(a) The court shall hold a hearing and, after consideration of any information relevant to its decision, shall determine if the defendant consents to further proceedings under this chapter and if the defendant should be granted pretrial diversion. If the defendant does not consent to participate in pretrial diversion, the proceedings shall continue as in any other case.

(b) At the time that pretrial diversion is granted, any bail bond or undertaking, or deposit in lieu thereof, on file by or on behalf of the defendant shall be exonerated, and the court shall enter an order so directing.

(c) The period during which pretrial diversion is granted shall be for no less than 12 months nor longer than 18 months. However, the defendant may request, and the court shall grant, for good cause shown, an extension of time to complete a program specified in subdivision (c) of Section 1000. Progress reports shall be filed by the probation department with the court as directed by the court.

Amended by Stats 2017 ch 778 (AB 208),s 3, eff. 1/1/2018.

Section 1000.3 - Defendant not performing satisfactorily; hearing

(a) If it appears to the prosecuting attorney, the court, or the probation department that the defendant is performing unsatisfactorily in the assigned program, that the defendant is convicted of an offense that reflects the defendant's propensity for violence, or that the defendant is convicted of a felony, the prosecuting attorney, the court on its own, or the probation department may make a motion for termination from pretrial diversion.

(b) After notice to the defendant, the court shall hold a hearing to determine whether pretrial diversion shall be terminated.

(c) If the court finds that the defendant is not performing satisfactorily in the assigned program, or the court finds that the defendant has been convicted of a crime as indicated in subdivision (a), the court shall schedule the matter for further proceedings as otherwise provided in this code.

(d) If the defendant has completed pretrial diversion, at the end of that period, the criminal charge or charges shall be dismissed.

(e) Prior to dismissing the charge or charges or terminating pretrial diversion, the court shall consider the defendant's ability to pay and whether the defendant has paid a diversion restitution fee pursuant to Section 1001.90, if ordered, and has met their financial obligation to the program, if any.

(f) This section shall become operative on July 1, 2021.

Added by Stats 2020 ch 92 (AB 1869),s 40, eff. 9/18/2020.

Section 1000.4 - Successful completion of pretrial diversion program

(a) Any record filed with the Department of Justice shall indicate the disposition in those cases referred to pretrial diversion pursuant to this chapter. Upon successful completion of a pretrial diversion program, the arrest upon which the defendant was diverted shall be deemed to have never occurred and the court may issue an order to seal the records pertaining to the arrest as described in Section 851.92. The defendant may indicate in response to any question concerning his or her prior criminal record that he or she was not arrested or granted pretrial diversion for the offense, except as specified in subdivision (c). A record pertaining to an arrest resulting in successful completion of a pretrial diversion program shall not, without the defendant's consent, be used in any way that could result in the denial of any employment, benefit, license, or certificate, except that, as specified in Section 492 of the Business and Professions Code, successful completion of a pretrial diversion program shall not prohibit any agency established under Division 2 (commencing with Section 500) of the Business and Professions Code, or under any initiative act referred to in that division, from taking disciplinary action against a licensee or from denying a license for professional misconduct, notwithstanding that evidence of that misconduct may be recorded in a record pertaining to an arrest leading to successful completion of a pretrial diversion program.

(b) Notwithstanding any other law, any licensing agency listed in Section 144 of the Business and Professions Code may request, and is authorized to receive, from a local or state agency certified records regarding referral to, participation in, successful completion of, and termination from, diversion programs described in this section.

(c) The defendant shall be advised that, regardless of his or her successful completion of the pretrial diversion program, the arrest upon which the pretrial diversion was based may be disclosed by the Department of Justice in response to any peace officer application request and that, notwithstanding subdivision (a), this section does not relieve him or her of the obligation to disclose the arrest in response to any direct question contained in any questionnaire or application for a position as a peace officer, as defined in Section 830.

(d) The defendant shall be advised that, regardless of the defendant's successful completion of a pretrial diversion program, an order to seal records pertaining to an arrest made pursuant to this section has no effect on a criminal justice agency's ability to access and use those sealed records and information regarding sealed arrests, as described in Section 851.92.

Amended by Stats 2017 ch 778 (AB 208),s 5.5, eff. 1/1/2018.

Amended by Stats 2017 ch 680 (SB 393),s 5, eff. 1/1/2018.

Section 1000.5 - Preguilty plea drug court program

(a)

(1) The presiding judge of the superior court, or a judge designated by the presiding judge, together with the district attorney and the public defender, may agree in writing to establish and conduct a preguilty plea drug court program pursuant to the provisions of this chapter, wherein criminal proceedings are suspended without a plea of guilty for designated defendants. The drug court program shall include a regimen of graduated sanctions and rewards, individual and group therapy, urinalysis testing commensurate with treatment needs, close court monitoring and supervision of progress, educational or vocational counseling as appropriate, and other requirements as agreed to by the presiding judge or his or her designee, the district attorney, and the public defender. If there is no agreement in writing for a preguilty plea program by the presiding judge or his or her designee, the district attorney, and the public defender, the program shall be operated as a pretrial diversion program as provided in this chapter.

(2) A person charged with a misdemeanor under paragraph (3) of subdivision (b) of Section 11357.5 or paragraph (3) of subdivision (b) of Section 11375.5 of the Health and Safety Code shall be eligible to participate in a preguilty plea drug court program established pursuant to this chapter, as set forth in Section 11375.7 of the Health and Safety Code.

(b) The provisions of Section 1000.3 and Section 1000.4 regarding satisfactory and unsatisfactory performance in a program shall apply to preguilty plea programs, except as provided in Section 11375.7 of the Health and Safety Code. If the court finds that (1) the defendant is not performing satisfactorily in the assigned program, (2) the defendant is not benefiting from education, treatment, or rehabilitation, (3) the defendant has been convicted of a crime specified in Section 1000.3, or (4) the defendant has engaged in criminal conduct rendering him or her unsuitable for the preguilty plea program, the court shall reinstate the criminal charge or charges. If the defendant has performed satisfactorily during the period of the preguilty plea program, at the end of that period, the criminal charge or charges shall be dismissed and the provisions of Section 1000.4 shall apply.

Amended by Stats 2017 ch 778 (AB 208),s 6, eff. 1/1/2018.

Amended by Stats 2016 ch 624 (SB 139),s 5, eff. 9/25/2016.

Amended by Stats 2002 ch 784 (SB 1316), s 542, eff. 1/1/2003.

Section 1000.6 - Participation in program; authorized medications

(a) A person who is participating in a pretrial diversion program or a preguilty plea program pursuant to this chapter is authorized under the direction of a licensed health care practitioner, to use medications including, but not limited to, methadone, buprenorphine, or levoalphacetylmethadol (LAAM) to treat substance use disorders if the participant allows release of his or her medical records to the court presiding over the participant's preguilty plea or pretrial diversion program for the limited purpose of determining whether or not the participant is using such medications under the direction of a licensed health care practitioner and is in compliance with the pretrial diversion or preguilty plea program rules.

(b) If the conditions specified in subdivision (a) are met, the use by a participant of medications to treat substance use disorders shall not be the sole reason for exclusion from a pretrial diversion or preguilty plea program. A patient who uses medications to treat substance use disorders and participates in a preguilty plea or pretrial diversion program shall comply with all court program rules.

(c) A person who is participating in a pretrial diversion program or preguilty plea program pursuant to this chapter who uses medications to treat substance use disorders shall present to the court a declaration from his or her health care practitioner, or his or her health care practitioner's authorized representative, that the person is currently under their care.

(d) Urinalysis results that only establish that a person described in this section has ingested medication duly prescribed to that person by his or her physician or psychiatrist, or medications used to treat substance use disorders, shall not be considered a violation of the terms of the pretrial diversion or preguilty plea program under this chapter.

(e) Except as provided in subdivisions (a) to (d), inclusive, this section does not affect any other law governing diversion programs.

Amended by Stats 2017 ch 778 (AB 208),s 7, eff. 1/1/2018.

Renumbered from Ca. Pen. Code §1000.8 by Stats 2009 ch 372 (AB 750),s 3, eff. 1/1/2010.

Added by Stats 2000 ch 815 (SB 1807) s 3, eff. 1/1/2001.

Section 1000.65 - Pretrial diversion program

This chapter does not affect a pretrial diversion program provided pursuant to Chapter 2.7 (commencing with Section 1001).

Added by Stats 2017 ch 778 (AB 208),s 8, eff. 1/1/2018.

Chapter 2.55 - DEFERRED ENTRY OF JUDGMENT PILOT PROGRAM

Section 1000.7 - [Effective until 1/1/2026] Participating counties

(a) The following counties may establish a pilot program pursuant to this section to operate a deferred entry of judgment pilot program for eligible defendants described in subdivision (b):

(1) County of Alameda.

(2) County of Butte.

(3) County of Nevada.

(4) County of Santa Clara.

(b) A defendant may participate in a deferred entry of judgment pilot program within the county's juvenile hall if that person is charged with committing a felony offense, other than the offenses listed under subdivision (d), pleads guilty to the charge or charges, and the probation department determines that the person meets all of the following requirements:

(1) Is 18 years of age or older, but under 21 years of age on the date the offense was committed. A defendant who is 21 years of age or older, but under 25 years of age on the date the offense was committed, may participate in the program with the approval of the multidisciplinary team established pursuant to paragraph (2) of subdivision (m).

(2) Is suitable for the program after evaluation using a risk assessment tool, as described in subdivision (c).

(3) Shows the ability to benefit from services generally reserved for delinquents, including, but not limited to, cognitive behavioral therapy, other mental health services, and age-appropriate educational, vocational, and supervision services, that are currently deployed under the jurisdiction of the juvenile court.

(4) Meets the rules of the juvenile hall developed in accordance with the applicable regulations set forth in Title 15 of the California Code of Regulations.

(5) Does not have a prior or current conviction for committing an offense listed under subdivision (c) of Section 1192.7 or subdivision (c) of Section 667.5, or subdivision (b) of Section 707 of the Welfare and Institutions Code.

(6) Is not required to register as a sex offender pursuant to Chapter 5.5 (commencing with Section 290) of Title 9 of Part 1.

(c) The probation department, in consultation with the superior court, district attorney, and sheriff of the county or the governmental body charged with operating the county jail, shall develop an evaluation process using a risk assessment tool to determine eligibility for the program.

(d) A defendant is ineligible for the program if the defendant is required to register as a sex offender pursuant to Chapter 5.5 (commencing with Section 290) of Title 9 of Part 1 or has been convicted of one or more of the following offenses:

(1) An offense listed under subdivision (c) of Section 1192.7.

(2) An offense listed under subdivision (c) of Section 667.5.

(3) An offense listed under subdivision (b) of Section 707 of the Welfare and Institutions Code.

(e) The court shall grant deferred entry of judgment if an eligible defendant consents to participate in the program, waives the right to a speedy trial or a speedy preliminary hearing, pleads guilty to the charge or charges, and waives time for the pronouncement of judgment.

(f)

(1) If the probation department determines that the defendant is ineligible for the deferred entry of judgment pilot program or the defendant does not consent to participate in the program, the proceedings shall continue as in any other case.

(2) If it appears to the probation department that the defendant is performing unsatisfactorily in the program as a result of the commission of a new crime or the violation of any of the rules of the juvenile hall, or that the defendant is not benefiting from the services in the program, the probation department may make a motion for entry of judgment. After notice to the defendant, the court shall hold a hearing to determine whether judgment should be entered. If the court finds that the defendant is performing unsatisfactorily in the program or that the defendant is not benefiting from the services in the program, the court shall render a finding of guilt to the charge or charges pleaded, enter judgment, and schedule a sentencing hearing as otherwise provided in this code, and the probation department, in consultation with the county sheriff, shall remove the defendant from the program and return the defendant to custody in county jail. The mechanism of when and how the defendant is moved from custody in juvenile hall to custody in a county jail shall be determined by the local multidisciplinary team specified in paragraph (2) of subdivision (m).

(3) If the defendant has performed satisfactorily during the period in which deferred entry of judgment was granted, at the end of that period, the court shall dismiss the criminal charge or charges.

(g) A defendant shall serve no longer than one year in custody within a county's juvenile hall pursuant to the program.

(h) The probation department shall develop a plan for reentry services, including, but not limited to, housing, employment, and education services, as a component of the program.

(i) The probation department shall submit data relating to the effectiveness of the program to the Division of Recidivism Reduction and Re-Entry, within the Department of Justice, including recidivism rates for program participants as compared to recidivism rates for similar populations in the adult system within the county.

(j) A defendant participating in this program shall not come into contact with minors within the juvenile hall for any purpose, including, but not limited to, housing, recreation, or education.

(k) Before establishing a pilot program pursuant to this section, the county shall apply to the Board of State and Community Corrections for approval of a county institution as a suitable place for confinement for the purpose of the pilot program. The board shall review and approve or deny the application of the county within 30 days of receiving notice of this proposed use. In its review, the board shall take into account the available programming, capacity, and safety of the institution as a place for the confinement and rehabilitation of individuals within the jurisdiction of the criminal court, and those within the jurisdiction of the juvenile court.

(l) The Board of State and Community Corrections shall review a county's pilot program to ensure compliance with requirements of the federal Juvenile Justice and Delinquency Prevention Act of 1974 (34 U.S.C. Sec. 11101 et seq.), as amended, relating to "sight and sound" separation between juveniles and adult inmates.

(m)

(1) This section applies to a defendant who would otherwise serve time in custody in a county jail. Participation in a program pursuant to this section shall not be authorized as an alternative to a sentence involving community supervision.

(2) Each county shall establish a multidisciplinary team that shall meet periodically to review and discuss the implementation, practices, and impact of the program. The team shall include representatives from all of the following:

(A) Probation department.

(B) The district attorney's office.

(C) The public defender's office.

(D) The sheriff's department.

(E) Courts located in the county.

(F) The county board of supervisors.

(G) The county health and human services department.

(H) A youth advocacy group.

(n)

(1) A county that establishes a pilot program pursuant to this section shall conduct an evaluation of the pilot program's impact and effectiveness in their county. The evaluation shall include, but not be limited to, evaluating the pilot program's impact on sentencing and impact on opportunities for community supervision, monitoring the program's effect on minors in the juvenile facility, if any, and its effectiveness with respect to program participants, including outcome-related data for program participants compared to young adult offenders sentenced for comparable crimes.

(2) Each county shall prepare a report based on the evaluation conducted pursuant to paragraph (1) and shall submit the report to the Assembly and Senate Committees on Public Safety, no later than December 31, 2024.

(3) Counties may contract with an independent entity, including, but not limited to, the Regents of the University of California, for the purposes of conducting the evaluation and preparing the report pursuant to this subdivision.

(4) To continue to participate in the pilot program, authorized counties shall comply with the reporting requirement in paragraph (2).

(o) This chapter shall remain in effect only until January 1, 2026, and as of that date is repealed, unless a later enacted statute, that is enacted before January 1, 2026, deletes or extends that date.

Amended by Stats 2023 ch 418 (AB 58),s 1, eff. 1/1/2024.

Amended by Stats 2021 ch 210 (AB 1318),s 1, eff. 1/1/2022.

Amended by Stats 2019 ch 129 (AB 1390),s 1, eff. 1/1/2020.

Amended by Stats 2019 ch 256 (SB 781),s 10, eff. 1/1/2020.

Amended by Stats 2018 ch 1007 (SB 1106),s 1, eff. 1/1/2019.

Added by Stats 2016 ch 865 (SB 1004),s 1, eff. 1/1/2017.

Chapter 2.6 - DEFERRED ENTRY OF JUDGMENT REENTRY PROGRAM

Section 1000.8 - "Back on Track" deferred entry of judgment reentry program

A superior court, with the concurrence of the prosecuting attorney of the county, may create a "Back on Track" deferred entry of judgment reentry program aimed at preventing recidivism among first-time nonviolent felony drug offenders. No defendant who has been convicted of a violation of an offense enumerated in subdivision (c) of Section 290 or in Section 1192.7 shall be eligible for the program established in this chapter. When creating this program, the prosecuting attorney, together with the presiding judge and a representative of the criminal defense bar selected by the presiding judge of the superior court may agree to establish a "Back on Track" deferred entry of judgment program pursuant to the provisions of this chapter. The agreement shall specify which low-level nonviolent felony drug offenses under the Health and Safety Code will be eligible for the program and a process for selecting participants. The program shall have the following characteristics:

(a) A dedicated calendar.

(b) Leadership by a superior court judicial officer who is assigned by the presiding judge.

(c) Clearly defined eligibility criteria to enter the program and clearly defined criteria for completion of the program.

(d) Legal incentives for defendants to successfully complete the program, including dismissal or reduction of criminal charges upon successful completion of the program.

(e) Close supervision to hold participants accountable to program compliance, including the use of graduated sanctions and frequent, ongoing appearances before the court regarding participants' program progress and compliance with all program terms and conditions. The court may use available legal mechanisms, including return to custody if necessary, for failure to comply with the supervised plan.

(f) Appropriate transitional programming for participants, based on available resources from county and community service providers and other agencies. The transitional programming may include, but is not limited to, any of the following:

(1) Vocational training, readiness, and placement.

(2) Educational training, including assistance with acquiring a G.E.D. or high school diploma and assistance with admission to college.

(3) Substance abuse treatment.

(4) Assistance with obtaining identification cards and driver's licenses.

(5) Parenting skills training and assistance in becoming compliant with child support obligations.

(g) The program may develop a local, public-private partnership between law enforcement, government agencies, private employers, and community-based organizations for the purpose of creating meaningful employment opportunities for participants and to take advantage of incentives for hiring program participants.

Added by Stats 2009 ch 372 (AB 750),s 4, eff. 1/1/2010.

Renumbered as Ca. Pen. Code §1000.6 by Stats 2009 ch 372 (AB 750),s 3, eff. 1/1/2010.

Added by Stats 2000 ch 815 (SB 1807) s 3, eff. 1/1/2001.

Section 1000.9 - Eligibility for program; notification of defendant and attorney

The prosecuting attorney shall determine whether a defendant is eligible for participation in the deferred entry of judgment reentry program.

(a) If the prosecuting attorney determines that this section may be applicable to the defendant, he or she shall advise the defendant and his or her attorney in writing of that determination. This notification shall include the following:

(1) A full description of the procedures for deferred entry of judgment.

(2) A general explanation of the role and authority of the prosecuting attorney, the program, and the court in the process.

(3) A clear statement that in lieu of trial, the court may grant deferred entry of judgment with respect to the current crime or crimes charged if the defendant pleads guilty to each charge and waives time for the pronouncement of judgment, and that, upon the defendant's successful completion of the program and the motion of the prosecuting attorney, the court will dismiss the charge or charges against the defendant and the provisions of Sections 851.90 and 1203.4 will apply.

(4) A clear statement that failure to comply with any condition under the program may result in the prosecuting attorney or the court making a motion for entry of judgment, whereupon the court will render a finding of guilty to the charge or charges pled, enter judgment, and schedule a sentencing hearing as otherwise provided in this code.

(5) An explanation of criminal record retention and disposition resulting from participation in the deferred entry of judgment program and the defendant's rights relative to answering questions about his or her arrest and deferred entry of judgment following successful completion of the program.

(b) If the prosecuting attorney determines that the defendant is eligible for the program, the prosecuting attorney shall state for the record the grounds upon which the determination is based and shall make this information available to the defendant and his or her attorney. This procedure is intended to allow the court to set the hearing for deferred entry of judgment at the arraignment.

(c) If the prosecuting attorney determines that the defendant is ineligible for the program, the prosecuting attorney shall state for the record the grounds upon which the determination is based and shall make this information available to the defendant and his or her attorney. The sole remedy of a defendant who is found ineligible for deferred entry of judgment is a postconviction appeal. If the prosecuting attorney does not deem the defendant eligible, or the defendant does not consent to participate, the proceedings shall continue as in any other case.

(d) Upon a motion by the prosecuting attorney for an entry of judgment, before entering a judgment of guilty, the court may hold a hearing to determine whether the defendant has failed to comply with the program and should be terminated from the program.
Added by Stats 2009 ch 372 (AB 750),s 4, eff. 1/1/2010.

Section 1000.10 - Provisions applicable to chapter
The following provisions apply to this chapter:

(a) A defendant's plea of guilty shall not constitute a conviction for any purpose unless a judgment of guilty is entered pursuant to Section 1000.3.

(b) Counties that opt to create a deferred entry of judgment reentry program pursuant to Section 1000.8 of the Penal Code shall not seek state reimbursement for costs associated with the implementation, development, or operation of that program.

(c) To the extent county resources beyond those of the superior court and the district attorney are needed to implement the program, those agencies shall consult with the county board of supervisors and other impacted county agencies to assess resources before program implementation.

(d) Local law enforcement agencies and counties administering the programs may seek federal or private funding for the purpose of implementing the provisions of this chapter.
Added by Stats 2009 ch 372 (AB 750),s 4, eff. 1/1/2010.

Chapter 2.65 - CHILD ABUSE AND NEGLECT COUNSELING
Section 1000.12 - Referral for counseling or psychological treatment in lieu of prosecution
(a) It is the intent of the Legislature that nothing in this chapter deprive a prosecuting attorney of the ability to prosecute any person who is suspected of committing any crime in which a minor is a victim of an act of physical abuse or neglect to the fullest extent of the law, if the prosecuting attorney so chooses.

(b) In lieu of prosecuting a person suspected of committing any crime, involving a minor victim, of an act of physical abuse or neglect, the prosecuting attorney may refer that person to the county department in charge of public social services or the probation department for counseling or psychological treatment and such other services as the department deems necessary. The prosecuting attorney shall seek the advice of the county department in charge of public social services or the probation department in determining whether or not to make the referral.

(c) This section shall not apply to any person who is charged with sexual abuse or molestation of a minor victim, or any sexual offense involving force, violence, duress, menace, or fear of immediate and unlawful bodily injury on the minor victim or another person.
Amended by Stats 2005 ch 477 (SB 33),s 3, eff. 1/1/2006

Section 1000.17 - Administrative cost of referral and expense of counseling
If the person is referred pursuant to this chapter he or she shall be responsible for paying the administrative cost of the referral and the expense of such counseling as determined by the county department responsible for public social services or the probation department. The administrative cost of the referral shall not exceed one hundred dollars ($100) for any person referred pursuant to this chapter for an offense punishable as a felony and shall not exceed fifty dollars ($50) for any person referred pursuant to the chapter for an offense punishable as a misdemeanor. The department shall take into consideration the ability of the referred party to pay and no such person shall be denied counseling services because of his or her inability to pay.
Added by Stats. 1983, Ch. 804, Sec. 2.

Chapter 2.67 - [REPEALED] COUNSELING FOR CHILD ABUSE OR SEXUAL MOLESTATION
Section 1000.30 through 1000.36 - [Repealed]
Repealed by Stats 2001 ch 115 (SB 153), s 25, eff. 1/1/2002.

Chapter 2.7 - MISDEMEANOR DIVERSION
Section 1001 - Legislative intent
It is the intent of the Legislature that this chapter, Chapter 2.5 (commencing with Section 1000) of this title, or any other provision of law not be construed to preempt other current or future pretrial or precomplaint diversion programs. It is also the intent of the Legislature that current or future posttrial diversion programs not be preempted, except as provided in Section 13201 or 13352.5 of the Vehicle Code. Sections 1001.2 to 1001.9, inclusive, of this chapter apply only to pretrial diversion programs as defined in Section 1001.1.
Amended by Stats 2017 ch 537 (SB 239),s 9, eff. 1/1/2018.

Section 1001.1 - Pretrial diversion
As used in Sections 1001.2 to 1001.9, inclusive, of this chapter, pretrial diversion refers to the procedure of postponing prosecution of an offense filed as a misdemeanor either temporarily or permanently at any point in the judicial process from the point at which the accused is charged until adjudication.
Amended by Stats 2017 ch 537 (SB 239),s 10, eff. 1/1/2018.

Section 1001.2 - Applicability of chapter
(a) This chapter shall not apply to any pretrial diversion or posttrial programs for the treatment of problem drinking or alcoholism utilized for persons convicted of one or more offenses under Section 23152 or 23153 or former Section 23102 of the Vehicle Code or to pretrial diversion programs established pursuant to Chapter 2.5 (commencing with Section 1000) of this title nor shall this chapter be deemed to authorize any pretrial diversion or posttrial programs for persons alleged to have committed violation of Section 23152 or 23153 of the Vehicle Code.

(b) The district attorney of each county shall review annually any diversion program established pursuant to this chapter, and no program shall continue without the approval of the district attorney. No person shall be diverted under a program unless it has been approved by the district attorney. Nothing in this subdivision shall authorize the prosecutor to determine whether a particular defendant shall be diverted.

Added by Stats. 1982, Ch. 42, Sec. 2. Effective February 17, 1982.

Section 1001.3 - Admission of guilt not required

At no time shall a defendant be required to make an admission of guilt as a prerequisite for placement in a pretrial diversion program.

Added by Stats. 1982, Ch. 42, Sec. 2. Effective February 17, 1982.

Section 1001.4 - Hearing before pretrial diversion terminated for cause

A divertee is entitled to a hearing, as set forth by law, before his or her pretrial diversion can be terminated for cause.

Added by Stats. 1982, Ch. 42, Sec. 2. Effective February 17, 1982.

Section 1001.5 - Use of information regarding diversion

No statement, or information procured therefrom, made by the defendant in connection with the determination of his or her eligibility for diversion, and no statement, or information procured therefrom, made by the defendant, subsequent to the granting of diversion or while participating in such program, and no information contained in any report made with respect thereto, and no statement or other information concerning the defendant's participation in such program shall be admissible in any action or proceeding. However, if a divertee is recommended for termination for cause, information regarding his or her participation in such program may be used for purposes of the termination proceedings.

Added by Stats. 1982, Ch. 42, Sec. 2. Effective February 17, 1982.

Section 1001.6 - Exoneration of bail bond or undertaking, or deposit in lieu thereof

At such time that a defendant's case is diverted, any bail bond or undertaking, or deposit in lieu thereof, on file by or on behalf of the defendant shall be exonerated, and the court shall enter an order so directing.

Added by Stats. 1982, Ch. 42, Sec. 2. Effective February 17, 1982.

Section 1001.7 - Dismissal of criminal charges

If the divertee has performed satisfactorily during the period of diversion, the criminal charges shall be dismissed at the end of the period of diversion.

Added by Stats. 1982, Ch. 42, Sec. 2. Effective February 17, 1982.

Section 1001.8 - Indication of disposition of diverted cases

Any record filed with the Department of Justice shall indicate the disposition of those cases diverted pursuant to this chapter.

Added by Stats. 1982, Ch. 42, Sec. 2. Effective February 17, 1982.

Section 1001.9 - Effect of successful completion of diversion program

(a) Any record filed with the Department of Justice shall indicate the disposition in those cases diverted pursuant to this chapter. Upon successful completion of a diversion program, the arrest upon which the diversion was based shall be deemed to have never occurred and the court may issue an order to seal the records pertaining to the arrest as described in Section 851.92. The divertee may indicate in response to any question concerning his or her prior criminal record that he or she was not arrested or diverted for the offense, except as specified in subdivision (b). A record pertaining to an arrest resulting in successful completion of a diversion program shall not, without the divertee's consent, be used in any way that could result in the denial of any employment, benefit, license, or certificate.

(b) The divertee shall be advised that, regardless of his or her successful completion of diversion, the arrest upon which the diversion was based may be disclosed by the Department of Justice in response to any peace officer application request and that, notwithstanding subdivision (a), this section does not relieve him or her of the obligation to disclose the arrest in response to any direct question contained in any questionnaire or application for a position as a peace officer, as defined in Section 830.

(c) The divertee shall be advised that, regardless of the defendant's successful completion of a deferred entry of judgment program, an order to seal records pertaining to an arrest made pursuant to this section has no effect on a criminal justice agency's ability to access and use those sealed records and information regarding sealed arrests, as described in Section 851.92.

Amended by Stats 2017 ch 680 (SB 393),s 6, eff. 1/1/2018.

Chapter 2.71 - AIDS PREVENTION PROGRAM IN DRUG ABUSE AND PROSTITUTION CASES

Section 1001.10 - [Repealed]

Repealed by Stats 2017 ch 537 (SB 239),s 11, eff. 1/1/2018.

Section 1001.11 - [Repealed]

Repealed by Stats 2017 ch 537 (SB 239),s 12, eff. 1/1/2018.

Chapter 2.8 - DIVERSION OF DEFENDANTS WITH COGNITIVE DEVELOPMENTAL DISABILITIES

Section 1001.20 - Definitions

(a) "Developmental disability" means a disability as defined in subdivision (a) of Section 4512 of the Welfare and Institutions Code and for which a regional center finds eligibility for services under the Lanterman Developmental Disabilities Services Act.

(b) "Diversion-related treatment and habilitation" means, but is not limited to, specialized services or special adaptations of generic services, directed toward the alleviation of developmental disability or toward social, personal, physical, or economic habilitation or rehabilitation of an individual with a developmental disability, and includes, but is not limited to, diagnosis, evaluation, treatment, personal care, day care, domiciliary care, special living arrangements, physical, occupational, and speech therapy, training, education, sheltered employment, mental health services, recreation, counseling of the individual with this disability and of the individual's family, protective and other social and sociolegal services, information and referral services, follow-along services, and transportation services necessary to ensure delivery of services to persons with developmental disabilities.

(c) "Regional center" means a regional center for the developmentally disabled established under the Lanterman Developmental Disabilities Services Act that is organized as a private nonprofit community agency to plan, purchase, and coordinate the delivery of services that cannot be provided by state agencies to developmentally disabled persons residing in a particular geographic catchment area, and that is licensed and funded by the State Department of Developmental Services.

(d) "Director of a regional center" means the executive director of a regional center for the developmentally disabled individual or their designee.

(e) "Agency" means the prosecutor, the probation department, and the regional center involved in a particular defendant's case.

(f) "Dual agency diversion" means a treatment and habilitation program developed with court approval by the regional center, administered jointly by the regional center and by the probation department, that is individually tailored to the needs of the defendant as derived from the defendant's individual program plan pursuant to Section 4646 of the Welfare and Institutions Code, and that includes, but is not limited to, treatment specifically addressed to the criminal offense charged, for a specified period of time as prescribed in Section 1001.28.

(g) "Single agency diversion" means a treatment and habilitation program developed with court approval by the regional center, administered solely by the regional center without involvement by the probation department, that is individually tailored to the needs of the defendant as derived from the defendant's individual program plan pursuant to Section 4646 of the Welfare and Institutions Code, and that includes, but is not limited to, treatment specifically addressed to the criminal offense charged, for a specified period of time as prescribed in Section 1001.28.

(h) This section is operative January 1, 2021.

Added by Stats 2020 ch 11 (AB 79),s 15, eff. 6/29/2020.

Section 1001.21 - Applicability of chapter

(a) This chapter shall apply whenever a case is before any court upon an accusatory pleading at any stage of the criminal proceedings, for any person who has been evaluated by a regional center and who is determined to be a person with a developmental disability by the regional center, and who therefore is eligible for its services.

(b) This chapter applies to any offense that is charged as a misdemeanor or felony offense, except that a defendant may not be placed into a diversion program, pursuant to this section, for any of the following current charged offenses:

    (1) Murder or voluntary manslaughter.

    (2) An offense for which a person, if convicted, would be required to register pursuant to Section 290, except for a violation of Section 314.

    (3) Rape.

    (4) Lewd or lascivious act on a child under 14 years of age.

    (5) Assault with intent to commit rape, sodomy, or oral copulation, in violation of Section 220.

    (6) Commission of rape or sexual penetration in concert with another person, in violation of Section 264.1.

    (7) Continuous sexual abuse of a child, in violation of Section 288.5.

    (8) A violation of subdivision (b) or (c) of Section 11418.

(c) Diversion shall not be ordered when the defendant previously has been diverted under this chapter within two years prior to the present criminal proceedings.

(d) This section is operative January 1, 2021.

Added by Stats 2020 ch 11 (AB 79),s 17, eff. 6/29/2020.

Section 1001.22 - Determination of whether defendant may be diverted; report

The court shall consult with the prosecutor, the defense counsel, the probation department, and the appropriate regional center in order to determine whether a defendant may be diverted pursuant to this chapter. If the defendant is not represented by counsel, the court shall appoint counsel to represent the defendant. When the court suspects that a defendant may have a developmental disability, as defined in subdivision (a) of Section 1001.20, and the defendant consents to the diversion process and to the case being evaluated for eligibility for regional center services, and waives their right to a speedy trial, the court shall order the prosecutor, the probation department, and the regional center to prepare reports on specified aspects of the defendant's case. Each report shall be prepared concurrently.

(a) The regional center shall submit a report to the probation department within 25 judicial days of the court's order. The regional center's report shall include a determination as to whether the defendant has a developmental disability and is eligible for regional center diversion-related treatment and habilitation services, and the regional center shall also submit to the court a proposed diversion program, individually tailored to the needs of the defendant as derived from the defendant's individual program plan pursuant to Section 4646 of the Welfare and Institutions Code, which shall include, but not be limited to, treatment addressed to the criminal offense charged for a period of time as prescribed in Section 1001.28. The regional center's report shall also contain a statement whether the proposed program is available for the defendant through the treatment and habilitation services of the regional centers pursuant to Section 4648 of the Welfare and Institutions Code.

(b) The prosecutor shall submit a report on specified aspects of the defendant's case, within 30 judicial days of the court's order, to the court, to each of the other agencies involved in the case, and to the defendant. The prosecutor's report shall include all of the following:

    (1) A statement of whether the defendant's record indicates the defendant's diversion pursuant to this chapter within two years prior to the alleged commission of the charged divertible offense.

    (2) If the prosecutor recommends that this chapter may be applicable to the defendant, the prosecutor shall recommend either a dual or single agency diversion program and shall advise the court, the probation department, the regional center, and the defendant, in writing, of that determination within 20 judicial days of the court's order to prepare the report.

    (3) If the prosecutor recommends against diversion, the prosecutor's report shall include a declaration in writing to state for the record the grounds upon which the recommendation was made, and the court shall determine, pursuant to Section 1001.23, whether the defendant shall be diverted.

    (4) If dual agency diversion is recommended by the prosecutor, a copy of the prosecutor's report shall also be provided by the prosecutor to the probation department, the regional center, and the defendant within the above prescribed time period. This notification shall include all of the following:

(A) A full description of the proceedings for diversion and the prosecutor's investigation procedures.

(B) A general explanation of the role and authority of the probation department, the prosecutor, the regional center, and the court in the diversion program process.

(C) A clear statement that the court may decide in a hearing not to divert the defendant and that the defendant may have to stand trial for the alleged offense.

(D) A clear statement that should the defendant fail in meeting the terms of the diversion, or if, during the period of diversion, the defendant is subsequently charged with a felony, the defendant may be required, after a hearing, to stand trial for the original diverted offense.

(c) The probation department shall submit a report on specified aspects of the defendant's case within 30 judicial days of the court's order, to the court, to each of the other agencies involved in the case, and to the defendant. The probation department's report to the court shall be based upon an investigation by the probation department and consideration of the defendant's age, developmental disability, employment record, educational background, ties to community agencies and family, treatment history, criminal record if any, and demonstrable motivation and other mitigating factors in determining whether the defendant is a person who would benefit from a diversion-related treatment and habilitation program. The regional center's report in full shall be appended to the probation department's report to the court.

(d) This section is operative January 1, 2021.

Added by Stats 2020 ch 11 (AB 79),s 19, eff. 6/29/2020.

Section 1001.23 - Criminal proceedings or diversion

(a) Upon the court's receipt of the reports from the prosecutor, the probation department, and the regional center, and a determination by the regional center that the defendant does not have a developmental disability, the criminal proceedings for the offense charged shall proceed. If the defendant is found to have a developmental disability and to be eligible for regional center services, and the court determines from the various reports submitted to it that the proposed diversion program is acceptable to the court, the prosecutor, the probation department, and the regional center, and if the defendant consents to diversion and waives their right to a speedy trial, the court may order, without a hearing, that the diversion program be implemented for a period of time as prescribed in Section 1001.28.

(b) After consideration of the probation department's report, the report of the regional center, the report of the prosecutor relating to the prosecutor's recommendation for or against diversion, the defendant's violence and criminal history, the relationship of the developmental disability to the charged offense, and the current charged offense, and any other relevant information, and the court is satisfied that the defendant will not pose an unreasonable risk of danger to public safety, as defined in Section 1170.18, if treated in the community, the court shall determine if the defendant shall be diverted under either dual or single agency supervision, and referred for habilitation or rehabilitation diversion pursuant to this chapter. If the court does not deem the defendant a person who would benefit by diversion at the time of the hearing, the suspended criminal proceedings may be reinstituted, or any other disposition as authorized by law may be made, and diversion may be ordered at a later date.

(c) If a dual agency diversion program is ordered by the court, the regional center shall submit a report to the probation department on the defendant's progress in the diversion program not less than every six months. Within five judicial days after receiving the regional center's report, the probation department shall submit its report on the defendant's progress in the diversion program, with the full report of the regional center appended, to the court and to the prosecutor. If single agency diversion is ordered by the court, the regional center alone shall report the defendant's progress to the court and to the prosecutor not less than every six months.

(d) This section is operative January 1, 2021.

Added by Stats 2020 ch 11 (AB 79),s 21, eff. 6/29/2020.

Section 1001.24 - Use of information procured from defendant during course of information

No statement, or information procured therefrom, made by the defendant to any probation officer, the prosecutor, or any regional center designee during the course of the investigation conducted by either the regional center or the probation department pursuant to this chapter, and prior to the reporting to the probation department of the regional center's findings of eligibility and recommendations to the court, shall be admissible in any action or proceeding brought subsequent to this investigation.

Added by Stats. 1980, Ch. 1253, Sec. 1.

Section 1001.25 - Use of information procured subsequent to granting of diversion

No statement, or information procured therefrom, with respect to the specific offense with which the defendant is charged, which is made to a probation officer, a prosecutor, or a regional center designee subsequent to the granting of diversion shall be admissible in any action or proceeding brought subsequent to the investigation.

Added by Stats. 1980, Ch. 1253, Sec. 1.

Section 1001.26 - Use of information in event diversion denied or subsequently revoked

In the event that diversion is either denied or is subsequently revoked once it has been granted, neither the probation investigation nor the statements or other information divulged by the defendant during the investigation by the probation department or the regional center shall be used in any sentencing procedures.

Added by Stats. 1980, Ch. 1253, Sec. 1.

Section 1001.27 - Exoneration of bail, bond, or undertaking, or deposit in lieu thereof

At such time as the defendant's case is diverted, any bail, bond, or undertaking, or deposit in lieu thereof, on file or on behalf of the defendant shall be exonerated, and the court shall enter an order so directing.

Added by Stats. 1980, Ch. 1253, Sec. 1.

Section 1001.28 - Length of diversion; progress reports

The period during which criminal proceedings against the defendant may be diverted shall be no longer than two years. The responsible agency or agencies shall file reports on the defendant's progress in the diversion program with the court and with the prosecutor not less than every six months.

(a) Where dual agency diversion has been ordered, the probation department shall be responsible for the progress reports. The probation department shall append to its own report a copy of the regional center's assessment of the defendant's progress.

(b) Where single agency diversion has been ordered, the regional center alone shall be responsible for the progress reports.
Added by Stats. 1980, Ch. 1253, Sec. 1.

Section 1001.29 - Modification of diversion order; hearing to determine whether diverted criminal proceedings should re reinstituted

(a) If it appears that the divertee is not meeting the terms and conditions of the diversion program, the court may hold a hearing and amend the program to provide for greater supervision by the responsible regional center alone, by the probation department alone, or by both the regional center and the probation department. However, notwithstanding the modification of a diversion order, the court may hold a hearing to determine whether the diverted criminal proceedings should be reinstituted if any of the following circumstances exists:

(1) The defendant is charged with an additional misdemeanor allegedly committed during the pretrial diversion and that reflects the defendant's propensity for violence.

(2) The defendant is charged with an additional felony allegedly committed during the pretrial diversion.

(3) The defendant is engaged in criminal conduct rendering the defendant unsuitable for diversion.

(4) The defendant's performance in the diversion program is unsatisfactory.

(b) In cases of dual agency diversion, a hearing to reinstitute the diverted criminal proceedings may be initiated by either the court, the prosecutor, the regional center, or the probation department.

(c) In cases of single agency diversion, a hearing to reinstitute the diverted criminal proceedings may be initiated only by the court, the prosecutor, or the regional center.

(d) No hearing for either of these purposes shall be held unless the moving agency or the court has given the divertee prior notice of the hearing.

(e) Where the cause of the hearing is a subsequent charge of a felony against the divertee subsequent to the diversion order, any hearing to reinstitute the diverted criminal proceedings shall be delayed until such time as probable cause has been established in court to bind the defendant over for trial on the subsequently charged felony.

(f) This section is operative January 1, 2021.
Added by Stats 2020 ch 11 (AB 79),s 23, eff. 6/29/2020.

Section 1001.30 - Withdrawal of consent to participate in diversion program

At any time during which the defendant is participating in a diversion program, he or she may withdraw consent to further participate in the diversion program, and at such time as such consent is withdrawn, the suspended criminal proceedings may resume or such other disposition may be made as is authorized by law.
Added by Stats. 1980, Ch. 1253, Sec. 1.

Section 1001.31 - Dismissal of criminal charges

If the divertee has performed satisfactorily during the period of diversion, the criminal charges shall be dismissed at the end of the diversion period.
Added by Stats. 1980, Ch. 1253, Sec. 1.

Section 1001.32 - Indication of disposition of diverted cases

Any record filed with the State Department of Justice shall indicate the disposition of those cases diverted pursuant to this chapter.
Added by Stats. 1980, Ch. 1253, Sec. 1.

Section 1001.33 - Effect of successful completion of diversion program

(a) Any record filed with the Department of Justice shall indicate the disposition in those cases diverted pursuant to this chapter. Upon successful completion of a diversion program, the arrest upon which the diversion was based shall be deemed to have never occurred. The divertee may indicate in response to any question concerning his or her prior criminal record that he or she was not arrested or diverted for the offense, except as specified in subdivision (b). A record pertaining to an arrest resulting in successful completion of a diversion program shall not, without the divertee's consent, be used in any way that could result in the denial of any employment, benefit, license, or certificate.

(b) The divertee shall be advised that, regardless of his or her successful completion of diversion, the arrest upon which the diversion was based may be disclosed by the Department of Justice in response to any peace officer application request and that, notwithstanding subdivision (a), this section does not relieve him or her of the obligation to disclose the arrest in response to any direct question contained in any questionnaire or application for a position as a peace officer, as defined in Section 830.
Amended by Stats. 1996, Ch. 743, Sec. 3. Effective January 1, 1997.

Section 1001.34 - Implementation of diversion-related individual program plan

Notwithstanding any other provision of law, the diversion-related individual program plan shall be fully implemented by the regional centers upon court order and approval of the diversion-related treatment and habilitation plan.
Added by Stats. 1980, Ch. 1253, Sec. 1.

Chapter 2.8A - DIVERSION OF INDIVIDUALS WITH MENTAL DISORDERS

Section 1001.35 - Purpose

The purpose of this chapter is to promote all of the following:

(a) Increased diversion of individuals with mental disorders to mitigate the individuals' entry and reentry into the criminal justice system while protecting public safety.

(b) Allowing local discretion and flexibility for counties in the development and implementation of diversion for individuals with mental disorders across a continuum of care settings.

(c) Providing diversion that meets the unique mental health treatment and support needs of individuals with mental disorders.
Added by Stats 2018 ch 34 (AB 1810),s 24, eff. 6/27/2018.

Section 1001.36 - [Operative until 7/1/2024] Pretrial diversion for persons with mental disorders

(a) On an accusatory pleading alleging the commission of a misdemeanor or felony offense not set forth in subdivision (d), the court may, in its discretion, and after considering the positions of the defense and prosecution, grant pretrial diversion to a defendant pursuant to this section if the defendant satisfies the eligibility requirements for pretrial diversion set forth in subdivision (b) and the court determines that the defendant is suitable for that diversion under the factors set forth in subdivision (c).

(b) A defendant is eligible for pretrial diversion pursuant to this section if both of the following criteria are met:

(1) The defendant has been diagnosed with a mental disorder as identified in the most recent edition of the Diagnostic and Statistical Manual of Mental Disorders, including, but not limited to, bipolar disorder, schizophrenia, schizoaffective disorder, or post-traumatic stress disorder, but excluding antisocial personality disorder and pedophilia. Evidence of the defendant's mental disorder shall be provided by the defense and shall include a diagnosis or treatment for a diagnosed mental disorder within the last five years by a qualified mental health expert. In opining that a defendant suffers from a qualifying disorder, the qualified mental health expert may rely on an examination of the defendant, the defendant's medical records, arrest reports, or any other relevant evidence.

(2) The defendant's mental disorder was a significant factor in the commission of the charged offense. If the defendant has been diagnosed with a mental disorder, the court shall find that the defendant's mental disorder was a significant factor in the commission of the offense unless there is clear and convincing evidence that it was not a motivating factor, causal factor, or contributing factor to the defendant's involvement in the alleged offense. A court may consider any relevant and credible evidence, including, but not limited to, police reports, preliminary hearing transcripts, witness statements, statements by the defendant's mental health treatment provider, medical records, records or reports by qualified medical experts, or evidence that the defendant displayed symptoms consistent with the relevant mental disorder at or near the time of the offense.

(c) For any defendant who satisfies the eligibility requirements in subdivision (b), the court must consider whether the defendant is suitable for pretrial diversion. A defendant is suitable for pretrial diversion if all of the following criteria are met:

(1) In the opinion of a qualified mental health expert, the defendant's symptoms of the mental disorder causing, contributing to, or motivating the criminal behavior would respond to mental health treatment.

(2) The defendant consents to diversion and waives the defendant's right to a speedy trial, unless a defendant has been found to be an appropriate candidate for diversion in lieu of commitment pursuant to clause (iv) of subparagraph (B) of paragraph (1) of subdivision (a) of Section 1370 and, as a result of the defendant's mental incompetence, cannot consent to diversion or give a knowing and intelligent waiver of the defendant's right to a speedy trial.

(3) The defendant agrees to comply with treatment as a condition of diversion, unless the defendant has been found to be an appropriate candidate for diversion in lieu of commitment for restoration of competency treatment pursuant to clause (iv) of subparagraph (B) of paragraph (1) of subdivision (a) of Section 1370 and, as a result of the defendant's mental incompetence, cannot agree to comply with treatment.

(4) The defendant will not pose an unreasonable risk of danger to public safety, as defined in Section 1170.18, if treated in the community. The court may consider the opinions of the district attorney, the defense, or a qualified mental health expert, and may consider the defendant's treatment plan, the defendant's violence and criminal history, the current charged offense, and any other factors that the court deems appropriate.

(d) A defendant may not be placed into a diversion program, pursuant to this section, for the following current charged offenses:

(1) Murder or voluntary manslaughter.

(2) An offense for which a person, if convicted, would be required to register pursuant to Section 290, except for a violation of Section 314.

(3) Rape.

(4) Lewd or lascivious act on a child under 14 years of age.

(5) Assault with intent to commit rape, sodomy, or oral copulation, in violation of Section 220.

(6) Commission of rape or sexual penetration in concert with another person, in violation of Section 264.1.

(7) Continuous sexual abuse of a child, in violation of Section 288.5.

(8) A violation of subdivision (b) or (c) of Section 11418.

(e) At any stage of the proceedings, the court may require the defendant to make a prima facie showing that the defendant will meet the minimum requirements of eligibility for diversion and that the defendant and the offense are suitable for diversion. The hearing on the prima facie showing shall be informal and may proceed on offers of proof, reliable hearsay, and argument of counsel. If a prima facie showing is not made, the court may summarily deny the request for diversion or grant any other relief as may be deemed appropriate.

(f) As used in this chapter, the following terms have the following meanings:

(1) "Pretrial diversion" means the postponement of prosecution, either temporarily or permanently, at any point in the judicial process from the point at which the accused is charged until adjudication, to allow the defendant to undergo mental health treatment, subject to all of the following:

(A)

(i) The court is satisfied that the recommended inpatient or outpatient program of mental health treatment will meet the specialized mental health treatment needs of the defendant.

(ii) The defendant may be referred to a program of mental health treatment utilizing existing inpatient or outpatient mental health resources. Before approving a proposed treatment program, the court shall consider the request of the defense, the request of the prosecution, the needs of the defendant, and the interests of the community. The treatment may be procured using private or public funds, and a referral may be made to a county mental health agency, existing collaborative courts, or assisted outpatient treatment only if that entity has agreed to accept responsibility for the treatment of the defendant, and mental health services are provided only to the extent that resources are available and the defendant is eligible for those services.

(iii) If the court refers the defendant to a county mental health agency pursuant to this section and the agency determines that it is unable to provide services to the defendant, the court shall accept a written declaration to that effect from the agency in lieu of requiring live testimony. That declaration shall serve only to establish that the program is unable to provide services to the defendant at that time and does not constitute evidence that the defendant is unqualified or unsuitable for diversion under this section.

(B) The provider of the mental health treatment program in which the defendant has been placed shall provide regular reports to the court, the defense, and the prosecutor on the defendant's progress in treatment.

(C) The period during which criminal proceedings against the defendant may be diverted is limited as follows:

    (i) If the defendant is charged with a felony, the period shall be no longer than two years.

    (ii) If the defendant is charged with a misdemeanor, the period shall be no longer than one year.

    (D) Upon request, the court shall conduct a hearing to determine whether restitution, as defined in subdivision (f) of Section 1202.4, is owed to any victim as a result of the diverted offense and, if owed, order its payment during the period of diversion. However, a defendant's inability to pay restitution due to indigence or mental disorder shall not be grounds for denial of diversion or a finding that the defendant has failed to comply with the terms of diversion.

(2) "Qualified mental health expert" includes, but is not limited to, a psychiatrist, psychologist, a person described in Section 5751.2 of the Welfare and Institutions Code, or a person whose knowledge, skill, experience, training, or education qualifies them as an expert.

(g) If any of the following circumstances exists, the court shall, after notice to the defendant, defense counsel, and the prosecution, hold a hearing to determine whether the criminal proceedings should be reinstated, whether the treatment should be modified, or whether the defendant should be conserved and referred to the conservatorship investigator of the county of commitment to initiate conservatorship proceedings for the defendant pursuant to Chapter 3 (commencing with Section 5350) of Part 1 of Division 5 of the Welfare and Institutions Code:

(1) The defendant is charged with an additional misdemeanor allegedly committed during the pretrial diversion and that reflects the defendant's propensity for violence.

(2) The defendant is charged with an additional felony allegedly committed during the pretrial diversion.

(3) The defendant is engaged in criminal conduct rendering the defendant unsuitable for diversion.

(4) Based on the opinion of a qualified mental health expert whom the court may deem appropriate, either of the following circumstances exists:

    (A) The defendant is performing unsatisfactorily in the assigned program.

    (B) The defendant is gravely disabled, as defined in subparagraph (B) of paragraph (1) of subdivision (h) of Section 5008 of the Welfare and Institutions Code. A defendant shall only be conserved and referred to the conservatorship investigator pursuant to this finding.

(h) If the defendant has performed satisfactorily in diversion, at the end of the period of diversion, the court shall dismiss the defendant's criminal charges that were the subject of the criminal proceedings at the time of the initial diversion. A court may conclude that the defendant has performed satisfactorily if the defendant has substantially complied with the requirements of diversion, has avoided significant new violations of law unrelated to the defendant's mental health condition, and has a plan in place for long-term mental health care. If the court dismisses the charges, the clerk of the court shall file a record with the Department of Justice indicating the disposition of the case diverted pursuant to this section. Upon successful completion of diversion, if the court dismisses the charges, the arrest upon which the diversion was based shall be deemed never to have occurred, and the court shall order access to the record of the arrest restricted in accordance with Section 1001.9, except as specified in subdivisions (j) and (k). The defendant who successfully completes diversion may indicate in response to any question concerning the defendant's prior criminal record that the defendant was not arrested or diverted for the offense, except as specified in subdivision (j).

(i) A record pertaining to an arrest resulting in successful completion of diversion, or any record generated as a result of the defendant's application for or participation in diversion, shall not, without the defendant's consent, be used in any way that could result in the denial of any employment, benefit, license, or certificate.

(j) The defendant shall be advised that, regardless of the defendant's completion of diversion, both of the following apply:

(1) The arrest upon which the diversion was based may be disclosed by the Department of Justice to any peace officer application request and that, notwithstanding subdivision (i), this section does not relieve the defendant of the obligation to disclose the arrest in response to any direct question contained in any questionnaire or application for a position as a peace officer, as defined in Section 830.

(2) An order to seal records pertaining to an arrest made pursuant to this section has no effect on a criminal justice agency's ability to access and use those sealed records and information regarding sealed arrests, as described in Section 851.92.

(k) A finding that the defendant suffers from a mental disorder, any progress reports concerning the defendant's treatment, or any other records related to a mental disorder that were created as a result of participation in, or completion of, diversion pursuant to this section or for use at a hearing on the defendant's eligibility for diversion under this section may not be used in any other proceeding without the defendant's consent, unless that information is relevant evidence that is admissible under the standards described in paragraph (2) of subdivision (f) of Section 28 of Article I of the California Constitution. However, when determining whether to exercise its discretion to grant diversion under this section, a court may consider previous records of participation in diversion under this section.

(l) The county agency administering the diversion, the defendant's mental health treatment providers, the public guardian or conservator, and the court shall, to the extent not prohibited by federal law, have access to the defendant's medical and psychological records, including progress reports, during the defendant's time in diversion, as needed, for the purpose of providing care and treatment and monitoring treatment for diversion or conservatorship.

(m) This section shall remain in effect until July 1, 2024, and as of that date is repealed.

Amended by Stats 2023 ch 687 (AB 1412),s 1.1, eff. 1/1/2024.

Amended by Stats 2023 ch 236 (AB 455),s 1, eff. 1/1/2024.

Amended by Stats 2022 ch 735 (SB 1223),s 1, eff. 1/1/2023.

Amended by Stats 2022 ch 47 (SB 184),s 38, eff. 6/30/2022.

Amended by Stats 2019 ch 497 (AB 991),s 203, eff. 1/1/2020.

Amended by Stats 2018 ch 1005 (SB 215),s 1, eff. 1/1/2019.

Added by Stats 2018 ch 34 (AB 1810),s 24, eff. 6/27/2018.

This section is set out more than once due to postponed, multiple, or conflicting amendments.

Section 1001.36 - [Operative 7/1/2024] Pretrial diversion for persons with mental disorders

(a) On an accusatory pleading alleging the commission of a misdemeanor or felony offense not set forth in subdivision (d), the court may, in its discretion, and after considering the positions of the defense and prosecution, grant pretrial diversion to a defendant pursuant to this section if the defendant satisfies the eligibility requirements for pretrial diversion set forth in subdivision (b) and the court determines that the defendant is suitable for that diversion under the factors set forth in subdivision (c).

(b) A defendant is eligible for pretrial diversion pursuant to this section if both of the following criteria are met:

    (1) The defendant has been diagnosed with a mental disorder as identified in the most recent edition of the Diagnostic and Statistical Manual of Mental Disorders, including, but not limited to, bipolar disorder, schizophrenia, schizoaffective disorder, or post-traumatic stress disorder, but excluding antisocial personality disorder and pedophilia. Evidence of the defendant's mental disorder shall be provided by the defense and shall include a diagnosis or treatment for a diagnosed mental disorder within the last five years by a qualified mental health expert. In opining that a defendant suffers from a qualifying disorder, the qualified mental health expert may rely on an examination of the defendant, the defendant's medical records, arrest reports, or any other relevant evidence.

    (2) The defendant's mental disorder was a significant factor in the commission of the charged offense. If the defendant has been diagnosed with a mental disorder, the court shall find that the defendant's mental disorder was a significant factor in the commission of the offense unless there is clear and convincing evidence that it was not a motivating factor, causal factor, or contributing factor to the defendant's involvement in the alleged offense. A court may consider any relevant and credible evidence, including, but not limited to, police reports, preliminary hearing transcripts, witness statements, statements by the defendant's mental health treatment provider, medical records, records or reports by qualified medical experts, or evidence that the defendant displayed symptoms consistent with the relevant mental disorder at or near the time of the offense.

(c) For any defendant who satisfies the eligibility requirements in subdivision (b), the court must consider whether the defendant is suitable for pretrial diversion. A defendant is suitable for pretrial diversion if all of the following criteria are met:

    (1) In the opinion of a qualified mental health expert, the defendant's symptoms of the mental disorder causing, contributing to, or motivating the criminal behavior would respond to mental health treatment.

    (2) The defendant consents to diversion and waives the defendant's right to a speedy trial, unless a defendant has been found to be an appropriate candidate for diversion in lieu of commitment pursuant to clause (iv) of subparagraph (B) of paragraph (1) of subdivision (a) of Section 1370 and, as a result of the defendant's mental incompetence, cannot consent to diversion or give a knowing and intelligent waiver of the defendant's right to a speedy trial.

    (3) The defendant agrees to comply with treatment as a condition of diversion, unless the defendant has been found to be an appropriate candidate for diversion in lieu of commitment for restoration of competency treatment pursuant to clause (iv) of subparagraph (B) of paragraph (1) of subdivision (a) of Section 1370 and, as a result of the defendant's mental incompetence, cannot agree to comply with treatment.

    (4) The defendant will not pose an unreasonable risk of danger to public safety, as defined in Section 1170.18, if treated in the community. The court may consider the opinions of the district attorney, the defense, or a qualified mental health expert, and may consider the defendant's treatment plan, the defendant's violence and criminal history, the current charged offense, and any other factors that the court deems appropriate.

(d) A defendant may not be placed into a diversion program, pursuant to this section, for the following current charged offenses:

    (1) Murder or voluntary manslaughter.

    (2) An offense for which a person, if convicted, would be required to register pursuant to Section 290, except for a violation of Section 314.

    (3) Rape.

    (4) Lewd or lascivious act on a child under 14 years of age.

    (5) Assault with intent to commit rape, sodomy, or oral copulation, in violation of Section 220.

    (6) Commission of rape or sexual penetration in concert with another person, in violation of Section 264.1.

    (7) Continuous sexual abuse of a child, in violation of Section 288.5.

    (8) A violation of subdivision (b) or (c) of Section 11418.

(e) At any stage of the proceedings, the court may require the defendant to make a prima facie showing that the defendant will meet the minimum requirements of eligibility for diversion and that the defendant and the offense are suitable for diversion. The hearing on the prima facie showing shall be informal and may proceed on offers of proof, reliable hearsay, and argument of counsel. If a prima facie showing is not made, the court may summarily deny the request for diversion or grant any other relief as may be deemed appropriate.

(f) As used in this chapter, the following terms have the following meanings:

    (1) "Pretrial diversion" means the postponement of prosecution, either temporarily or permanently, at any point in the judicial process from the point at which the accused is charged until adjudication, to allow the defendant to undergo mental health treatment, subject to all of the following:

        (A)

            (i) The court is satisfied that the recommended inpatient or outpatient program of mental health treatment will meet the specialized mental health treatment needs of the defendant.

            (ii) The defendant may be referred to a program of mental health treatment utilizing existing inpatient or outpatient mental health resources. Before approving a proposed treatment program, the court shall consider the request of the defense, the request of the prosecution, the needs of the defendant, and the interests of the community. The treatment may be procured using private or public funds, and a referral may be made to a county mental health agency, existing collaborative courts, or assisted outpatient treatment only if that entity has agreed to accept responsibility for the treatment of the defendant, and mental health services are provided only to the extent that resources are available and the defendant is eligible for those services.

            (iii) If the court refers the defendant to a county mental health agency pursuant to this section and the agency determines that it is unable to provide services to the defendant, the court shall accept a written declaration to that effect from the agency in lieu of requiring live testimony. That declaration shall serve only to establish that the program is unable to provide services to the defendant at that time and does not constitute evidence that the defendant is unqualified or unsuitable for diversion under this section.

(B) The provider of the mental health treatment program in which the defendant has been placed shall provide regular reports to the court, the defense, and the prosecutor on the defendant's progress in treatment.

(C) The period during which criminal proceedings against the defendant may be diverted is limited as follows:

    (i) If the defendant is charged with a felony, the period shall be no longer than two years.

    (ii) If the defendant is charged with a misdemeanor, the period shall be no longer than one year.

(D) Upon request, the court shall conduct a hearing to determine whether restitution, as defined in subdivision (f) of Section 1202.4, is owed to any victim as a result of the diverted offense and, if owed, order its payment during the period of diversion. However, a defendant's inability to pay restitution due to indigence or mental disorder shall not be grounds for denial of diversion or a finding that the defendant has failed to comply with the terms of diversion.

(2) "Qualified mental health expert" includes, but is not limited to, a psychiatrist, psychologist, a person described in Section 5751.2 of the Welfare and Institutions Code, or a person whose knowledge, skill, experience, training, or education qualifies them as an expert.

(g) If any of the following circumstances exists, the court shall, after notice to the defendant, defense counsel, and the prosecution, hold a hearing to determine whether the criminal proceedings should be reinstated, whether the treatment should be modified, or whether the defendant should be conserved and referred to the conservatorship investigator of the county of commitment to initiate conservatorship proceedings for the defendant pursuant to Chapter 3 (commencing with Section 5350) of Part 1 of Division 5 of the Welfare and Institutions Code:

(1) The defendant is charged with an additional misdemeanor allegedly committed during the pretrial diversion and that reflects the defendant's propensity for violence.

(2) The defendant is charged with an additional felony allegedly committed during the pretrial diversion.

(3) The defendant is engaged in criminal conduct rendering the defendant unsuitable for diversion.

(4) Based on the opinion of a qualified mental health expert whom the court may deem appropriate, either of the following circumstances exists:

    (A) The defendant is performing unsatisfactorily in the assigned program.

    (B) The defendant is gravely disabled, as defined in subparagraph (B) of paragraph (1) of subdivision (h) of Section 5008 of the Welfare and Institutions Code. A defendant shall only be conserved and referred to the conservatorship investigator pursuant to this finding.

(h) If the defendant has performed satisfactorily in diversion, at the end of the period of diversion, the court shall dismiss the defendant's criminal charges that were the subject of the criminal proceedings at the time of the initial diversion. A court may conclude that the defendant has performed satisfactorily if the defendant has substantially complied with the requirements of diversion, has avoided significant new violations of law unrelated to the defendant's mental health condition, and has a plan in place for long-term mental health care. If the court dismisses the charges, the clerk of the court shall file a record with the Department of Justice indicating the disposition of the case diverted pursuant to this section. Upon successful completion of diversion, if the court dismisses the charges, the arrest upon which the diversion was based shall be deemed never to have occurred, and the court shall order access to the record of the arrest restricted in accordance with Section 1001.9, except as specified in subdivisions (j) and (k). The defendant who successfully completes diversion may indicate in response to any question concerning the defendant's prior criminal record that the defendant was not arrested or diverted for the offense, except as specified in subdivision (j).

(i) A record pertaining to an arrest resulting in successful completion of diversion, or any record generated as a result of the defendant's application for or participation in diversion, shall not, without the defendant's consent, be used in any way that could result in the denial of any employment, benefit, license, or certificate.

(j) The defendant shall be advised that, regardless of the defendant's completion of diversion, both of the following apply:

(1) The arrest upon which the diversion was based may be disclosed by the Department of Justice to any peace officer application request and that, notwithstanding subdivision (i), this section does not relieve the defendant of the obligation to disclose the arrest in response to any direct question contained in any questionnaire or application for a position as a peace officer, as defined in Section 830.

(2) An order to seal records pertaining to an arrest made pursuant to this section has no effect on a criminal justice agency's ability to access and use those sealed records and information regarding sealed arrests, as described in Section 851.92.

(k) A finding that the defendant suffers from a mental disorder, any progress reports concerning the defendant's treatment, including, but not limited to, any finding that the defendant be prohibited from owning or controlling a firearm because they are a danger to themselves or others pursuant to subdivision (m), or any other records related to a mental disorder that were created as a result of participation in, or completion of, diversion pursuant to this section or for use at a hearing on the defendant's eligibility for diversion under this section may not be used in any other proceeding without the defendant's consent, unless that information is relevant evidence that is admissible under the standards described in paragraph (2) of subdivision (f) of Section 28 of Article I of the California Constitution. However, when determining whether to exercise its discretion to grant diversion under this section, a court may consider previous records of participation in diversion under this section.

(l) The county agency administering the diversion, the defendant's mental health treatment providers, the public guardian or conservator, and the court shall, to the extent not prohibited by federal law, have access to the defendant's medical and psychological records, including progress reports, during the defendant's time in diversion, as needed, for the purpose of providing care and treatment and monitoring treatment for diversion or conservatorship.

(m)

(1) The prosecution may request an order from the court that the defendant be prohibited from owning or possessing a firearm until they successfully complete diversion because they are a danger to themselves or others pursuant to subdivision (i) of Section 8103 of the Welfare and Institutions Code.

(2) The prosecution shall bear the burden of proving, by clear and convincing evidence, both of the following are true:

    (A) The defendant poses a significant danger of causing personal injury to themselves or another by having in their custody or control, owning, purchasing, possessing, or receiving a firearm.

(B) The prohibition is necessary to prevent personal injury to the defendant or any other person because less restrictive alternatives either have been tried and found to be ineffective or are inadequate or inappropriate for the circumstances of the defendant.

(3)

(A) If the court finds that the prosecution has not met that burden, the court shall not order that the person is prohibited from having, owning, purchasing, possessing, or receiving a firearm.

(B) If the court finds that the prosecution has met the burden, the court shall order that the person is prohibited, and shall inform the person that they are prohibited, from owning or controlling a firearm until they successfully complete diversion because they are a danger to themselves or others.

(4) An order imposed pursuant to this subdivision shall be in effect until the defendant has successfully completed diversion or until their firearm rights are restored pursuant to paragraph (4) of subdivision (g) of Section 8103 of the Welfare and Institutions Code.

(n) This section shall become operative on July 1, 2024.

Added by Stats 2023 ch 687 (AB 1412),s 1.2, eff. 1/1/2024.

Added by Stats 2023 ch 236 (AB 455),s 2, eff. 1/1/2024.

Amended by Stats 2022 ch 735 (SB 1223),s 1, eff. 1/1/2023.

Amended by Stats 2022 ch 47 (SB 184),s 38, eff. 6/30/2022.

Amended by Stats 2019 ch 497 (AB 991),s 203, eff. 1/1/2020.

Amended by Stats 2018 ch 1005 (SB 215),s 1, eff. 1/1/2019.

Added by Stats 2018 ch 34 (AB 1810),s 24, eff. 6/27/2018.

Chapter 2.81 - PRETRIAL DIVERSION OF TRAFFIC VIOLATORS

Section 1001.40 - Establishment of pretrial diversion program for traffic violators

Notwithstanding any other provision of law, a county acting on behalf of one or more individual courts may by ordinance establish a program that provides for pretrial diversion by the court of any person issued a notice to appear for a traffic violation to attend any traffic violator school licensed pursuant to Chapter 1.5 (commencing with Section 11200) of Division 5 of the Vehicle Code.

Added by Stats. 1990, Ch. 1303, Sec. 1.

Chapter 2.9 - DIVERSION OF MISDEMEANOR OFFENDERS

Section 1001.50 - Adoption of chapter by ordinance; approval of district attorney

(a) Notwithstanding any other provision of law, this chapter shall become operative in a county only if the board of supervisors adopts the provisions of this chapter by ordinance.

(b) The district attorney of each county shall review annually any diversion program established pursuant to this chapter, and no program shall continue without the approval of the district attorney. No person shall be diverted under a program unless it has been approved by the district attorney. Nothing in this subdivision shall authorize the prosecutor to determine whether a particular defendant shall be diverted.

(c) As used in this chapter, "pretrial diversion" means the procedure of postponing prosecution either temporarily or permanently at any point in the judicial process from the point at which the accused is charged until adjudication.

Added by Stats. 1982, Ch. 1251, Sec. 2.

Section 1001.51 - Applicability of chapter

(a) This chapter shall apply whenever a case is before any court upon an accusatory pleading concerning the commission of a misdemeanor, except a misdemeanor specified in subdivision (b), and it appears to the court that all of the following apply to the defendant:

(1) The defendant's record does not indicate that probation or parole has ever been revoked without thereafter being completed.

(2) The defendant's record does not indicate that he has been diverted pursuant to this chapter within five years prior to the filing of the accusatory pleading which charges the divertible offense.

(3) The defendant has never been convicted of a felony, and has not been convicted of a misdemeanor within five years prior to the filing of the accusatory pleading which charges the divertible offense.

(b) This chapter shall not apply to any pretrial diversion or posttrial program otherwise established by this code, nor shall this chapter be deemed to authorize any pretrial diversion or posttrial program for any person alleged to have committed a violation of Section 23152 or 23153 of the Vehicle Code.

(c) This chapter shall not apply whenever the accusatory pleading charges the commission of a misdemeanor:

(1) For which incarceration would be mandatory upon conviction of the defendant.

(2) For which registration would be required pursuant to Section 290 upon conviction of the defendant.

(3) Which the magistrate determines shall be prosecuted as a misdemeanor pursuant to paragraph (5) of subdivision (b) of Section 17.

(4) Which involves the use of force or violence against a person, unless the charge is of a violation of Section 241 or 243.

(5) For which the granting of probation is prohibited.

(6) Which is a driving offense punishable as a misdemeanor pursuant to the Vehicle Code.

Added by Stats. 1982, Ch. 1251, Sec. 2.

Section 1001.52 - Referral to probation department; investigation; use of information

(a) If the defendant consents and waives his right to a speedy trial, the case shall be referred to the probation department. The probation department shall conduct such investigation as is necessary to determine whether the defendant qualifies for diversion under subdivision (a) of Section 1001.51, and whether he or she is a person who would be benefited by education, treatment or rehabilitation. The probation department shall also determine which educational, treatment or rehabilitative plan would benefit the defendant. The probation department shall report its findings and recommendation to the court. If the recommendation includes referral to a community program, the report shall contain a statement regarding the program's willingness to accept the defendant and the manner in which the services they offer can assist the defendant in completing the diversion program successfully.

(b) No statement, or any information procured therefrom, made by the defendant to any probation officer, which is made during the course of any investigation conducted by the probation department pursuant to subdivision (b), and prior to the reporting of the probation department's findings and recommendations to the court, shall be admissible in any action or proceeding brought subsequent to the investigation. No statement, or any information procured therefrom, with respect to the specific offense with which the defendant is charged, which is made to any probation officer subsequent to the granting of diversion, shall be admissible in any action or proceeding.

In the event that diversion is either denied, or is subsequently revoked once it has been granted, neither the probation investigation nor statements or information divulged during that investigation shall be used in any pretrial sentencing procedures.

Added by Stats. 1982, Ch. 1251, Sec. 2.

Section 1001.53 - Hearing

The court shall hold a hearing and, after consideration of the probation department's report, and any other relevant information, shall determine if the defendant consents to further proceedings under this chapter and waives his or her right to a speedy trial. If the court orders a defendant to be diverted, the court may make inquiry into the financial condition of the defendant, and upon a finding that the defendant is able in whole or in part, to pay the reasonable cost of diversion, the court may order him or her to pay all or part of such expense. The reasonable cost of diversion shall not exceed the amount determined to be the actual average cost of diversion services. If the court does not deem the defendant to be a person who would be benefited by diversion, or if the defendant does not consent to participate, the proceedings shall continue as in any other case.

At such time that a defendant's case is diverted, any bail bond or undertaking, or deposit in lieu thereof, on file by or on behalf of the defendant shall be exonerated, and the court shall enter an order so directing.

The period during which the further criminal proceedings against the defendant may be diverted shall be for the length of time required to complete and verify the diversion program but in no case shall it exceed two years.

Added by Stats. 1982, Ch. 1251, Sec. 2.

Section 1001.54 - Hearing to determine whether criminal proceedings should be reinstituted

If it appears to the probation department that the divertee is performing unsatisfactorily in the assigned program, or that the divertee is not benefiting from education, treatment or rehabilitation, or that the divertee is convicted of a misdemeanor in which force or violence is used, or if the divertee is convicted of a felony, after notice to the divertee, the court shall hold a hearing to determine whether the criminal proceedings should be reinstituted. If the court finds that the divertee is not performing satisfactorily in the assigned program, or that the divertee is not benefiting from diversion, or the court finds that the divertee has been convicted of a crime as indicated above, the criminal case shall be referred back to the court for resumption of the criminal proceedings. If the divertee has performed satisfactorily during the period of diversion, at the end of the period of diversion, the criminal charges shall be dismissed.

Added by Stats. 1982, Ch. 1251, Sec. 2.

Section 1001.55 - Effect of successful completion of diversion program

(a) Any record filed with the Department of Justice shall indicate the disposition in those cases diverted pursuant to this chapter. Upon successful completion of a diversion program, the arrest upon which the diversion was based shall be deemed to have never occurred. The divertee may indicate in response to any question concerning his or her prior criminal record that he or she was not arrested or diverted for the offense, except as specified in subdivision (b). A record pertaining to an arrest resulting in successful completion of a diversion program shall not, without the divertee's consent, be used in any way that could result in the denial of any employment, benefit, license, or certificate.

(b) The divertee shall be advised that, regardless of his or her successful completion of diversion, the arrest upon which the diversion was based may be disclosed by the Department of Justice in response to any peace officer application request and that, notwithstanding subdivision (a), this section does not relieve him or her of the obligation to disclose the arrest in response to any direct question contained in any questionnaire or application for a position as a peace officer, as defined in Section 830.

Amended by Stats. 1996, Ch. 743, Sec. 4. Effective January 1, 1997.

Chapter 2.9A - BAD CHECK DIVERSION

Section 1001.60 - Diversion program for persons who write bad checks

Upon the adoption of a resolution by the board of supervisors declaring that there are sufficient funds available to fund the program, the district attorney may create within his or her office a diversion program pursuant to this chapter for persons who write bad checks. For purposes of this chapter, "writing a bad check" means making, drawing, uttering, or delivering any check or draft upon any bank or depository for the payment of money where there is probable cause to believe there has been a violation of Section 476a. The program may be conducted by the district attorney or by a private entity under contract with the district attorney.

Amended by Stats 2008 ch 264 (AB 2606),s 1, eff. 1/1/2009.

Section 1001.61 - Referral by district attorney

The district attorney may refer a bad check case to the diversion program. Except as provided in Section 1001.64, this chapter does not limit the power of the district attorney to prosecute bad check complaints.

Added by Stats. 1985, Ch. 1059, Sec. 1.

Section 1001.62 - Determination of whether to refer case

On receipt of a bad check case, the district attorney shall determine if the case is one which is appropriate to be referred to the bad check diversion program. In determining whether to refer a case to the bad check diversion program, the district attorney shall consider, but is not limited to, all of the following:

(a) The amount of the bad check.

(b) If the person has a prior criminal record or has previously been diverted.

(c) The number of bad check grievances against the person previously received by the district attorney.

(d) Whether there are other bad check grievances currently pending against the person.

(e) The strength of the evidence, if any, of intent to defraud the victim.

Added by Stats. 1985, Ch. 1059, Sec. 1.

Section 1001.63 - Notice upon referral

On referral of a bad check case to the diversion program, a notice shall be forwarded by mail to the person alleged to have written the bad check which contains all of the following:

(a) The date and amount of the bad check.

(b) The name of the payee.

(c) The date before which the person must contact the person designated by the district attorney concerning the bad check.

(d) A statement of the penalty for issuance of a bad check.

Added by Stats. 1985, Ch. 1059, Sec. 1.

Section 1001.64 - Agreement to forego prosecution

The district attorney may enter into a written agreement with the person to forego prosecution on the bad check for a period to be determined by the district attorney, not to exceed six months, pending all of the following:

(a) Completion of a class or classes conducted by the district attorney or private entity under contract with the district attorney.

(b) Full restitution being made to the victim of the bad check to hold offenders accountable for victims' losses as a result of criminal conduct. For the purpose of this subdivision, "restitution" means the face value of the bad check or bad checks and any bank charges, as described in Section 1001.65.

(c) Full payment of the diversion fees, if any, specified in Section 1001.65.

Amended by Stats 2008 ch 264 (AB 2606),s 2, eff. 1/1/2009.

Section 1001.65 - Processing fee

(a) A district attorney may collect a processing fee if his or her office collects and processes a bad check. The amount of the fee shall not exceed fifty dollars ($50) for each bad check in addition to the actual amount of any bank charges, including the returned check fee, if any, incurred by the victim as a result of the offense.

(b) Notwithstanding subdivision (a), when a criminal complaint is filed in a bad check case after the maker of the check fails to comply with the terms of the bad check diversion program, the court, after conviction, may impose a bad check processing fee for the recovery and processing efforts by the district attorney of not more than fifty dollars ($50) for each bad check in addition to the actual amount of any bank charges incurred by the victim as a result of the offense, including the returned check fee, if any, not to exceed one thousand two hundred dollars ($1,200) in the aggregate. The court also may, as a condition of probation, require a defendant to participate in and successfully complete a check writing education class. If so required, the court shall make inquiry into the financial condition of the defendant and, upon a finding that the defendant is able in whole or part to pay the expense of the education class, the court may order him or her to pay for all or part of that expense.

(c) If the district attorney elects to collect any fee for bank charges incurred by the victim pursuant to this section, including any fee charged for a returned check, that fee shall be paid to the victim for any bank fees that the victim may have been assessed. In no event shall reimbursement of a bank charge to the victim pursuant to subdivision (a) or (b) exceed fifteen dollars ($15) per check.

Amended by Stats 2008 ch 264 (AB 2606),s 3, eff. 1/1/2009.

Amended by Stats 2001 ch 745 (SB 1191) s 160, eff. 10/11/2001.

Section 1001.66 - Admission of guilt not required

At no time shall a defendant be required to make an admission of guilt as a prerequisite for placement in a precomplaint diversion program.

Added by Stats. 1985, Ch. 1059, Sec. 1.

Section 1001.67 - Use of information

No statement, or information procured therefrom, made by the defendant in connection with the determination of his or her eligibility for diversion, and no statement, or information procured therefrom, made by the defendant, subsequent to the granting of diversion or while participating in the program, and no information contained in any report made with respect thereto, and no statement or other information concerning the defendant's participation in the program shall be admissible in any action or proceeding.

Added by Stats. 1985, Ch. 1059, Sec. 1.

Chapter 2.9B - PARENTAL DIVERSION

Section 1001.70 - Approval of local prosecutor

(a) Every local prosecutor with jurisdiction to prosecute violations of Section 272 shall review annually any diversion program established pursuant to this chapter, and no program shall commence or continue without the approval of the local prosecutor. No person shall be diverted under a program unless it has been approved by the local prosecutor. Nothing in this subdivision shall authorize the prosecutor to determine whether a particular defendant shall be diverted.

(b) As used in this chapter, "pretrial diversion" means the procedure of postponing prosecution either temporarily or permanently at any point in the judicial process from the point at which the accused is charged until adjudication.

Added by Stats. 1988, Ch. 1256, Sec. 3. Effective September 26, 1988.

Section 1001.71 - Applicability of chapter

This chapter shall apply whenever a case is before any court upon an accusatory pleading alleging a parent or legal guardian to have violated Section 272 with respect to his or her minor child, and all of the following apply to the defendant:

(a) The defendant's record does not indicate that probation or parole has ever been revoked without thereafter being completed.

(b) The defendant's record does not indicate that he or she has previously been diverted pursuant to this chapter.

Amended by Stats. 1989, Ch. 144, Sec. 2.

Section 1001.72 - Referral to probation department; investigation

(a) If the defendant consents and waives his or her right to a speedy trial, the case shall be referred to the probation department. The probation department shall conduct an investigation as is necessary to determine whether the defendant qualifies for diversion under this chapter, and whether he or she is a person who would be benefited by education, treatment, or rehabilitation. The probation department shall also determine which education, treatment, or rehabilitative plan would benefit the defendant. The probation department shall report its findings and recommendations to the court. If the recommendation includes referral to a community program, the report shall contain a statement regarding the program's willingness to accept the defendant and the manner in which the services they offer can assist the defendant in completing the diversion program successfully.

(b) No statement, or any information procured therefrom, made by the defendant to any probation officer, which is made during the course of any investigation conducted by the probation department pursuant to subdivision (a), and prior to the reporting of the probation department's findings and recommendations to the court, shall be admissible in any action or proceeding brought subsequent to the investigation. No statement, or any information procured therefrom, with respect to the specific offense with which the defendant is charged which is made to any probation officer subsequent to the granting of diversion, shall be admissible in any action or proceeding.

In the event that diversion is either denied or is subsequently revoked once it has been granted, neither the probation investigation nor statements or information divulged during that investigation shall be used in any pretrial sentencing procedures.

Added by Stats. 1988, Ch. 1256, Sec. 3. Effective September 26, 1988.

Section 1001.73 - Hearing

The court shall hold a hearing and, after consideration of the probation department's report, and any other relevant information, shall determine if the defendant consents to further proceedings under this chapter and waives his or her right to a speedy trial. If the court orders a defendant to be diverted, the court may make inquiry into the financial condition of the defendant, and upon a finding that the defendant is able, in whole or in part, to pay the reasonable cost of diversion, the court may order him or her to pay all or part of the expense. The reasonable cost of diversion shall not exceed the amount determined to be the actual average cost of diversion services.

If the court does not deem the defendant to be a person who would be benefited by diversion or if the defendant does not consent to participate, the proceedings shall continue as in any other case.

At the time that a defendant's case is diverted, any bail bond or undertaking, or deposit in lieu thereof, on file by or on behalf of the defendant shall be exonerated, and the court shall enter an order so directing.

The period during which the further criminal proceedings against the defendant may be diverted shall be for the length of time required to complete and verify the diversion program but in no case shall it exceed two years.

Added by Stats. 1988, Ch. 1256, Sec. 3. Effective September 26, 1988.

Section 1001.74 - Hearing to determine whether criminal proceedings should be reinstituted

If it appears to the probation department that the divertee is performing unsatisfactorily in the assigned program, or that the divertee is not benefiting from education, treatment, or rehabilitation, or that the divertee is convicted of a misdemeanor in which force or violence was used, or if the divertee is convicted of a felony, after notice to the divertee, the court shall hold a hearing to determine whether the criminal proceedings should be reinstituted. If the court finds that the divertee is not performing satisfactorily in the assigned program, or that the divertee has been convicted of a crime as indicated above, the criminal case shall be referred back to the court for resumption of the criminal proceedings. If the divertee has performed satisfactorily during the period of diversion, the criminal charges shall be dismissed.

Added by Stats. 1988, Ch. 1256, Sec. 3. Effective September 26, 1988.

Section 1001.75 - Effect of successful completion of diversion program

(a) Any record filed with the Department of Justice shall indicate the disposition in those cases diverted pursuant to this chapter. Upon successful completion of a diversion program, the arrest upon which the diversion was based shall be deemed to have never occurred. The divertee may indicate in response to any question concerning his or her prior criminal record that he or she was not arrested or diverted for that offense, except as specified in subdivision (b). A record pertaining to an arrest resulting in successful completion of a diversion program shall not, without the divertee's consent, be used in any way that would result in the denial of any employment, benefit, license, or certificate.

(b) The divertee shall be advised that, regardless of his or her successful completion of diversion, the arrest upon which the diversion was based may be disclosed by the Department of Justice in response to any peace officer application request and that, notwithstanding subdivision (a), this section does not relieve him or her of the obligation to disclose the arrest in response to any direct question contained in any questionnaire or application for a position as a peace officer, as defined in Section 830.

Amended by Stats. 1996, Ch. 743, Sec. 5. Effective January 1, 1997.

Chapter 2.9C - MILITARY DIVERSION PROGRAM

Section 1001.80 - Military diversion program

(a) This chapter shall apply to a case before a court on an accusatory pleading alleging the commission of a misdemeanor offense if both of the following apply to the defendant:

    (1) The defendant was, or currently is, a member of the United States military.

    (2) The defendant may be suffering from sexual trauma, traumatic brain injury, post-traumatic stress disorder, substance abuse, or mental health problems as a result of his or her military service. The court may request, using existing resources, an assessment to aid in the determination that this paragraph applies to a defendant.

(b) If the court determines that a defendant charged with an applicable offense under this chapter is a person described in subdivision (a), the court, with the consent of the defendant and a waiver of the defendant's speedy trial right, may place the defendant in a pretrial diversion program, as defined in subdivision (k).

(c) If it appears to the court that the defendant is performing unsatisfactorily in the assigned program, or that the defendant is not benefiting from the treatment and services provided under the diversion program, after notice to the defendant, the court shall hold a hearing to determine whether the criminal proceedings should be reinstituted. If the court finds that the defendant is not performing satisfactorily in the assigned program, or that the defendant is not benefiting from diversion, the court may end the diversion and order resumption of the criminal proceedings. If the defendant has performed satisfactorily during the period of diversion, at the end of the period of diversion, the criminal charges shall be dismissed.

(d) If a referral is made to the county mental health authority as part of the pretrial diversion program, the county shall provide mental health treatment services only to the extent that resources are available for that purpose, as described in paragraph (5) of subdivision (b) of Section 5600.3 of the Welfare and Institutions Code. If mental health treatment services are ordered by the court, the county mental health agency shall coordinate appropriate referral of the defendant to the county veterans service officer, as described in paragraph (5) of subdivision (b) of Section 5600.3 of the Welfare and Institutions Code. The county mental health agency is not responsible for providing services outside its traditional scope of services. An order shall be made referring a defendant to a county mental health agency only if that agency has agreed to accept responsibility for all of the following:

    (1) The treatment of the defendant.

    (2) The coordination of appropriate referral to a county veterans service officer.

    (3) The filing of reports pursuant to subdivision (h).

(e) When determining the requirements of a pretrial diversion program pursuant to this chapter, the court shall assess whether the defendant should be ordered to participate in a federal or community-based treatment service program with a demonstrated history of specializing in the treatment of mental health problems, including substance abuse, post-traumatic stress disorder, traumatic brain injury, military sexual trauma, and other related mental health problems.

(f) The court, in making an order pursuant to this section to commit a defendant to an established treatment program, shall give preference to a treatment program that has a history of successfully treating veterans who suffer from sexual trauma, traumatic brain injury, post-traumatic stress disorder, substance abuse, or mental health problems as a result of military service, including, but not limited to, programs operated by the United States Department of Defense or the United States Department of Veterans Affairs.

(g) The court and the assigned treatment program may collaborate with the Department of Veterans Affairs and the United States Department of Veterans Affairs to maximize benefits and services provided to a veteran.

(h) The period during which criminal proceedings against the defendant may be diverted shall be no longer than two years. The responsible agency or agencies shall file reports on the defendant's progress in the diversion program with the court and with the prosecutor not less than every six months.

(i) A record filed with the Department of Justice shall indicate the disposition of those cases diverted pursuant to this chapter. Upon successful completion of a diversion program, the arrest upon which the diversion was based shall be deemed to have never occurred. The defendant may indicate in response to a question concerning his or her prior criminal record that he or she was not arrested or diverted for the offense, except as specified in subdivision (j). A record pertaining to an arrest resulting in successful completion of a diversion program shall not, without the defendant's consent, be used in any way that could result in the denial of any employment, benefit, license, or certificate.

(j) The defendant shall be advised that, regardless of his or her successful completion of diversion, the arrest upon which the diversion was based may be disclosed by the Department of Justice in response to a peace officer application request and that, notwithstanding subdivision (i), this section does not relieve him or her of the obligation to disclose the arrest in response to a direct question contained in a questionnaire or application for a position as a peace officer, as defined in Section 830.

(k)

    (1) As used in this chapter, "pretrial diversion" means the procedure of postponing prosecution, either temporarily or permanently, at any point in the judicial process from the point at which the accused is charged until adjudication.

    (2) A pretrial diversion program shall utilize existing resources available to current or former members of the United States military to address and treat those suffering from sexual trauma, traumatic brain injury, post-traumatic stress disorder, substance abuse, or mental health problems as a result of military service.

(l) Notwithstanding any other law, including Section 23640 of the Vehicle Code, a misdemeanor offense for which a defendant may be placed in a pretrial diversion program in accordance with this section includes a misdemeanor violation of Section 23152 or 23153 of the Vehicle Code. However, this section does not limit the authority of the Department of Motor Vehicles to take administrative action concerning the driving privileges of a person arrested for a violation of Section 23152 or 23153 of the Vehicle Code.

Amended by Stats 2017 ch 179 (SB 725),s 1, eff. 8/7/2017.

Added by Stats 2014 ch 658 (SB 1227),s 1, eff. 1/1/2015.

Chapter 29D - THEFT AND REPEAT THEFT CRIMES DIVERSION OR DEFERRED ENTRY OF JUDGMENT PROGRAM

Section 1001.81 - [Effective until 1/1/2026] Diversion or deferred entry of judgment program; theft

(a) The city or county prosecuting attorney or county probation department may create a diversion or deferred entry of judgment program pursuant to this section for persons who commit a theft offense or repeat theft offenses. The program may be conducted by the prosecuting attorney's office or the county probation department.

(b) Except as provided in subdivision (e), this chapter does not limit the power of the prosecuting attorney to prosecute theft or repeat theft.

(c) If a county creates a diversion or deferred entry of judgment program for individuals committing a theft offense or repeat theft offenses, on receipt of a case or at arraignment, the prosecuting attorney shall either refer the case to the county probation department to conduct a prefiling investigation report to assess the appropriateness of program placement or, if the prosecuting attorney's office operates the program, determine if the case is one that is appropriate to be referred to the program. In determining whether to refer a case to the program, the probation department or prosecuting attorney shall consider, but is not limited to, all of the following factors:

    (1) Any prefiling investigation report conducted by the county probation department or nonprofit contract agency operating the program that evaluates the individual's risk and needs and the appropriateness of program placement.

    (2) If the person demonstrates a willingness to engage in community service, restitution, or other mechanisms to repair the harm caused by the criminal activity and address the underlying drivers of the criminal activity.

    (3) If a risk and needs assessment identifies underlying substance abuse or mental health needs or other drivers of criminal activity that can be addressed through the diversion or deferred entry of judgment program.

    (4) If the person has a violent or serious prior criminal record or has previously been referred to a diversion program and failed that program.

(5) Any relevant information concerning the efficacy of the program in reducing the likelihood of participants committing future offenses.

(d) On referral of a case to the program, a notice shall be provided, or forwarded by mail, to the person alleged to have committed the offense with both of the following:

(1) The date by which the person must contact the diversion program or deferred entry of judgment program in the manner designated by the supervising agency.

(2) A statement of the penalty for the offense or offenses with which that person has been charged.

(e) The prosecuting attorney may enter into a written agreement with the person to refrain from, or defer, prosecution on the offense or offenses on the following conditions:

(1) Completion of the program requirements such as community service or courses reasonably required by the prosecuting attorney.

(2) Making adequate restitution or an appropriate substitute for restitution to the establishment or person from which property was stolen at the face value of the stolen property, if required by the program.

(f) For the purposes of this section, "repeat theft offenses" means being cited or convicted for misdemeanor or felony theft from a store or from a vehicle two or more times in the previous 12 months and failing to appear in court when cited for these crimes or continuing to engage in these crimes after release or after conviction.

Amended by Stats 2023 ch 131 (AB 1754),s 154, eff. 1/1/2024.

Added by Stats 2022 ch 856 (AB 2294),s 5, eff. 9/30/2022.

Added by Stats 2018 ch 803 (AB 1065),s 7, eff. 1/1/2019.

Section 1001.82 - [Effective until 1/1/2026] Repealer

This chapter shall remain in effect only until January 1, 2026, and as of that date is repealed.

Added by Stats 2022 ch 856 (AB 2294),s 5, eff. 9/30/2022.

Chapter 2.9E - PRIMARY CAREGIVER DIVERSION

Section 1001.83 - Establishment of pretrial diversion program for primary caregivers

(a) The presiding judge of the superior court, or a judge designated by the presiding judge, in consultation with the presiding juvenile court judge and criminal court judges, and together with the prosecuting entity and the public defender or the contracted criminal defense office that provides the services of a public defender, may agree in writing to establish and conduct a pretrial diversion program for primary caregivers, pursuant to the provisions of this chapter, wherein criminal proceedings are suspended without a plea of guilty for a period of not less than 6 months and not more than 24 months. If the defendant is also participating in juvenile court proceedings, the juvenile and criminal courts shall not duplicate efforts.

(b) The program described in this section may include, but not be limited to, all of the following components:

(1) Parenting classes.

(2) Family and individual counseling.

(3) Mental health screening, education, and treatment.

(4) Family case management services.

(5) Drug and alcohol treatment.

(6) Domestic violence education and prevention.

(7) Physical and sexual abuse counseling.

(8) Anger management.

(9) Vocational and educational services.

(10) Job training and placement.

(11) Affordable and safe housing assistance.

(12) Financial literacy courses.

(c) The defendant may be referred to supportive services and classes in already existing diversion programs and county outpatient services. Before approving a proposed treatment program, the court shall consider the request of the defense, the request of the prosecution, the needs of the defendant and the dependent child or children, and the interests of the community. The programming may be procured using public or private funds. A referral may be made to a county agency, existing collaborative court, or assisted outpatient treatment or services, if the entity agrees to provide the required programming.

(d) On an accusatory pleading alleging the commission of a misdemeanor or felony offense, the court may, after considering the positions of the defense and prosecution, grant pretrial diversion to a defendant pursuant to this section if the defendant meets all of the following requirements:

(1) The defendant is a custodial parent or legal guardian of a minor child under 18 years of age, presently resides in the same household as that child, presently provides care or financial support for that minor child either alone or with the assistance of other household members, and the defendant's absence in the child's life would be detrimental to the child.

(2) The defendant has been advised of and waived the right to a speedy trial and a speedy preliminary hearing.

(3) The defendant has been informed of and agrees to comply with the requirements of the program.

(4) The court is satisfied that the defendant will not pose an unreasonable risk of danger to public safety, as defined in Section 1170.18, or to the minor child in their custody, if allowed to remain in the community. The court may consider the positions of the prosecuting entity and defense counsel, the defendant's violence and criminal history, the recency of the defendant's criminal history, the defendant's history of behavior towards minors, the risk of the dependent minor's exposure to or involvement in criminal activity, the current charged offense, child welfare history involving the defendant, and any other factors that the court deems appropriate.

(5) The defendant is not being placed into a diversion program, pursuant to this section, for any serious felony as described in Section 1192.7 or 1192.8 or violent felony as described in subdivision (c) of Section 667.5.

(6) The defendant is not being placed into a diversion program pursuant to this section for a crime alleged to have been committed against a person for whom the defendant is the primary caregiver.

(e) The provider of the pretrial diversion services in which the defendant has been placed shall provide regular reports to the court, the defense, and the prosecutor on the defendant's progress in the programming.

(f)

(1) If it appears to the prosecuting attorney, the court, pretrial services, or the probation department that the defendant is performing unsatisfactorily in the assigned program, or if the defendant is, subsequent to entering the program, convicted of a felony or any offense that reflects a propensity for violence, the prosecuting attorney or the probation department may make a motion to reinstate criminal proceedings. The court may also reinstate criminal proceedings on its own motion.

(2) After notice to the defendant, the court shall hold a hearing to determine whether to reinstate criminal proceedings.

(3) If the court finds that the defendant is not performing satisfactorily in the assigned program, or the court finds that the defendant has been convicted of a crime as indicated in paragraph (1), the court may end the diversion program and order the resumption of criminal proceedings.

(g) If the defendant has performed satisfactorily in diversion, at the end of the period of diversion, the court shall dismiss the defendant's criminal charges that were the subject of the criminal proceedings at the time of the initial diversion. A court may conclude that the defendant has performed satisfactorily if the defendant has substantially complied with the requirements of diversion, and has avoided significant new violations of law. If the court dismisses the charges, the clerk of the court shall file a record with the Department of Justice indicating the disposition of the case diverted pursuant to this section. Upon successful completion of diversion, if the court dismisses the charges, the arrest upon which the diversion was based shall be deemed never to have occurred, and the court shall order access to the record of the arrest restricted in accordance with Section 1001.9, except as specified in subdivision (i). The defendant who successfully completes diversion may indicate in response to any question concerning the defendant's prior criminal record that they were not arrested or diverted for the offense, except as specified in subdivision (i).

(h) A record pertaining to an arrest resulting in successful completion of diversion, or any record generated as a result of the defendant's application for or participation in diversion, shall not, without the defendant's consent, be used in any way that could result in the denial of any employment, benefit, license, or certificate.

(i) The defendant shall be advised that, regardless of the defendant's completion of diversion, both of the following apply:

(1) The arrest upon which the diversion was based may be disclosed by the Department of Justice to any peace officer application request and that, notwithstanding subdivision (h), this section does not relieve the defendant of the obligation to disclose the arrest in response to any direct question contained in any questionnaire or application for a position as a peace officer, as defined in Section 830.

(2) An order to seal records pertaining to an arrest made pursuant to this section has no effect on a criminal justice agency's ability to access and use those sealed records and information regarding sealed arrests, as described in Section 851.92.

Added by Stats 2019 ch 593 (SB 394),s 1, eff. 1/1/2020.

Chapter 2.92 - LAW ENFORCEMENT ASSISTED DIVERSION (LEAD) PILOT PROGRAM

Section 1001.85 - Law Enforcement Assisted Diversion (LEAD) pilot program

(a) The Law Enforcement Assisted Diversion (LEAD) pilot program is hereby established. The purpose of the LEAD program is to improve public safety and reduce recidivism by increasing the availability and use of social service resources while reducing costs to law enforcement agencies and courts stemming from repeated incarceration.

(b) LEAD pilot programs shall be consistent with the following principles, implemented to address and reflect the priorities of the community in which the program exists:

(1) Providing intensive case management services and an individually tailored intervention plan that acts as a blueprint for assisting LEAD participants.

(2) Prioritizing temporary and permanent housing that includes individualized supportive services, without preconditions of drug or alcohol treatment or abstinence from drugs or alcohol.

(3) Employing human and social service resources in coordination with law enforcement in a manner that improves individual outcomes and community safety, and promotes community wellness.

(4) Participation in LEAD services shall be voluntary throughout the duration of the program and shall not require abstinence from drug or alcohol use as a condition of continued participation.

Added by Stats 2016 ch 33 (SB 843),s 17, eff. 6/27/2016.

Section 1001.86 - Administration

(a) The LEAD program shall be administered by the Board of State and Community Corrections.

(b) The board shall award grants, on a competitive basis, to up to three jurisdictions as authorized by this chapter. The board shall establish minimum standards, funding schedules, and procedures for awarding grants, which shall take into consideration, but not be limited to, all of the following:

(1) Information from the applicant demonstrating a clear understanding of the program's purpose and the applicant's willingness and ability to implement the LEAD program as described in this chapter.

(2) Key local partners who would be committed to, and involved in, the development and successful implementation of a LEAD program, including, but not limited to, balanced representation from law enforcement agencies, prosecutorial agencies, public defenders and defense counsel, public health and social services agencies, case management service providers, and any other entities identified by the applicant as integral to the successful implementation of a LEAD program in the jurisdiction.

(3) The jurisdiction's capacity and commitment to coordinate social services, law enforcement efforts, and justice system decisionmaking processes, and to work to ensure that the discretionary decisions made by each participant in the administration of the program operates in a manner consistent with the purposes of this chapter.

(c) Successful grant applicants shall collect and maintain data pertaining to the effectiveness of the program as indicated by the board in the request for proposals.

Added by Stats 2016 ch 33 (SB 843),s 17, eff. 6/27/2016.

Section 1001.87 - Programs funded

(a) LEAD programs funded pursuant to this chapter shall consist of a strategy of effective intervention for eligible participants consistent with the following gateways to services:

    (1) Prebooking referral. As an alternative to arrest, a law enforcement officer may take or refer a person for whom the officer has probable cause for arrest for any of the offenses in subdivision (b) to a case manager to be screened for immediate crisis services and to schedule a complete assessment intake interview. Participation in LEAD shall be voluntary, and the person may decline to participate in the program at any time. Criminal charges based on the conduct for which a person is diverted to LEAD shall not be filed, provided that the person finishes the complete assessment intake interview within a period set by the local jurisdictional partners, but not to exceed 30 days after the referral.

    (2) Social contact referral. A law enforcement officer may refer an individual to LEAD whom he or she believes is at high risk of arrest in the future for any of the crimes specified in subdivision (b), provided that the individual meets the criteria specified in this paragraph and expresses interest in voluntarily participating in the program. LEAD may accept these referrals if the program has capacity after responding to prebooking diversion referrals described in paragraph (1). All social contact referrals to LEAD shall meet the following criteria:

        (A) Verification by law enforcement that the individual has had prior involvement with low-level drug activity or prostitution. Verification shall consist of any of the following:

            (i) Criminal history records, including, but not limited to, prior police reports, arrests, jail bookings, criminal charges, or convictions indicating that he or she was engaged in low-level drug or prostitution activity.

            (ii) Law enforcement has directly observed the individual's low-level drug or prostitution activity on prior occasions.

            (iii) Law enforcement has a reliable basis of information to believe that the individual is engaged in low-level drug or prostitution activity, including, but not limited to, information provided by another first responder, a professional, or a credible community member.

        (B) The individual's prior involvement with low-level drug or prostitution activity occurred within the LEAD pilot program area.

        (C) The individual's prior involvement with low-level drug or prostitution activity occurred within 24 months of the date of referral.

        (D) The individual does not have a pending case in drug court or mental health court.

        (E) The individual is not prohibited, by means of an existing no-contact order, temporary restraining order, or antiharassment order, from making contact with a current LEAD participant.

(b) The following offenses are eligible for either prebooking diversion, social contact referral, or both:

    (1) Possession for sale or transfer of a controlled substance or other prohibited substance where the circumstances indicate that the sale or transfer is intended to provide a subsistence living or to allow the person to obtain or afford drugs for his or her own consumption.

    (2) Sale or transfer of a controlled substance or other prohibited substance where the circumstances indicate that the sale or transfer is intended to provide a subsistence living or to allow the person to obtain or afford drugs for his or her own consumption.

    (3) Possession of a controlled substance or other prohibited substance.

    (4) Being under the influence of a controlled substance or other prohibited substance.

    (5) Being under the influence of alcohol and a controlled substance or other prohibited substance.

    (6) Prostitution pursuant to subdivision (b) of Section 647.

Amended by Stats 2017 ch 561 (AB 1516),s 186, eff. 1/1/2018.
Added by Stats 2016 ch 33 (SB 843),s 17, eff. 6/27/2016.

Section 1001.88 - Services provided

(a) Services provided pursuant to this chapter may include, but are not limited to, case management, housing, medical care, mental health care, treatment for alcohol or substance use disorders, nutritional counseling and treatment, psychological counseling, employment, employment training and education, civil legal services, and system navigation. Grant funding may be used to support any of the following:

    (1) Project management and community engagement.

    (2) Temporary services and treatment necessary to stabilize a participant's condition, including necessary housing.

    (3) Outreach and direct service costs for services described in this section.

    (4) Civil legal services for LEAD participants.

    (5) Dedicated prosecutorial resources, including for coordinating any nondiverted criminal cases of LEAD participants.

    (6) Dedicated law enforcement resources, including for overtime required for participation in operational meetings and training.

    (7) Training and technical assistance from experts in the implementation of LEAD in other jurisdictions.

    (8) Collecting and maintaining the data necessary for program evaluation.

(b)

    (1) The board shall contract with a nonprofit research entity, university, or college to evaluate the effectiveness of the LEAD program. The evaluation design shall include measures to assess the cost-benefit outcomes of LEAD programs compared to booking and prosecution, and may include evaluation elements such as comparing outcomes for LEAD participants to similarly situated offenders who are arrested and booked, the number of jail bookings, total number of jail days, the prison incarceration rate, subsequent felony and misdemeanor arrests or convictions, and costs to the criminal justice and court systems. Savings will be compared to costs of LEAD participation. By January 1, 2020, a report of the findings shall be submitted to the Governor and the Legislature pursuant to Section 9795 of the Government Code.

    (2) The requirement for submitting a report pursuant to this subdivision is inoperative on January 1, 2024, pursuant to Section 10231.5 of the Government Code.

(c) The board may contract with experts in the implementation of LEAD in other jurisdictions for the purpose of providing technical assistance to participating jurisdictions.

(d) The sum of fifteen million dollars ($15,000,000) is hereby appropriated from the General Fund for the LEAD pilot program authorized in this chapter. The board may spend up to five hundred fifty thousand dollars ($550,000) of the amount appropriated in this subdivision for the contracts authorized in subdivisions (b) and (c).
Added by Stats 2016 ch 33 (SB 843),s 17, eff. 6/27/2016.

Chapter 2.95 - DIVERSION RESTITUTION FEE

Section 1001.90 - Diversion restitution fee

(a) For all persons charged with a felony or misdemeanor whose case is diverted by the court pursuant to this title, the court shall impose on the defendant a diversion restitution fee in addition to any other administrative fee provided or imposed under the law. This fee shall not be imposed upon persons whose case is diverted by the court pursuant to Chapter 2.8 (commencing with Section 1001.20).

(b) The diversion restitution fee imposed pursuant to this section shall be set at the discretion of the court and shall be commensurate with the seriousness of the offense, but shall not be less than one hundred dollars ($100), and not more than one thousand dollars ($1,000).

(c) The diversion restitution fee shall be ordered regardless of the defendant's present ability to pay. However, if the court finds that there are compelling and extraordinary reasons, the court may waive imposition of the fee. When the waiver is granted, the court shall state on the record all reasons supporting the waiver. Except as provided in this subdivision, the court shall impose the separate and additional diversion restitution fee required by this section.

(d) In setting the amount of the diversion restitution fee in excess of the one hundred dollar ($100) minimum, the court shall consider any relevant factors, including, but not limited to, the defendant's ability to pay, the seriousness and gravity of the offense and the circumstances of its commission, any economic gain derived by the defendant as a result of the crime, and the extent to which any other person suffered any losses as a result of the crime. Those losses may include pecuniary losses to the victim or the victim's dependents as well as intangible losses, such as psychological harm caused by the crime. Consideration of a defendant's ability to pay may include the defendant's future earning capacity. A defendant shall bear the burden of demonstrating the lack of the defendant's ability to pay. Express findings by the court as to the factors bearing on the amount of the fee shall not be required. A separate hearing for the diversion restitution fee shall not be required.

(e) The court shall not limit the ability of the state to enforce the fee imposed by this section in the manner of a judgment in a civil action. The court shall not modify the amount of this fee except to correct an error in the setting of the amount of the fee imposed.

(f) The fee imposed pursuant to this section shall be immediately deposited in the Restitution Fund for use pursuant to Section 13967 of the Government Code.

(g) As used in this section, "diversion" also means deferred entry of judgment pursuant to Chapter 2.5 (commencing with Section 1000).

(h) This section shall become operative on January 1, 2022.
Added by Stats 2021 ch 257 (AB 177),s 18, eff. 9/23/2021.

Chapter 2.96 - COURT INITIATED MISDEMEANOR DIVERSION

Section 1001.95 - Procedure; offenses for which diversion may not be offered

(a) A judge in the superior court in which a misdemeanor is being prosecuted may, at the judge's discretion, and over the objection of a prosecuting attorney, offer diversion to a defendant pursuant to these provisions.

(b) A judge may continue a diverted case for a period not to exceed 24 months and order the defendant to comply with terms, conditions, or programs that the judge deems appropriate based on the defendant's specific situation.

(c) If the defendant has complied with the imposed terms and conditions, at the end of the period of diversion, the judge shall dismiss the action against the defendant.

(d) If it appears to the court that the defendant is not complying with the terms and conditions of diversion, after notice to the defendant, the court shall hold a hearing to determine whether the criminal proceedings should be reinstituted. If the court finds that the defendant has not complied with the terms and conditions of diversion, the court may end the diversion and order resumption of the criminal proceedings.

(e) A defendant may not be offered diversion pursuant to this section for any of the following current charged offenses:

    (1) Any offense for which a person, if convicted, would be required to register pursuant to Section 290.

    (2) Any offense involving domestic violence, as defined in Section 6211 of the Family Code or subdivision (b) of Section 13700 of this code.

    (3) A violation of Section 646.9.
Amended by Stats 2022 ch 58 (AB 200),s 6, eff. 6/30/2022.
Added by Stats 2020 ch 334 (AB 3234),s 1, eff. 1/1/2021.

Section 1001.96 - Duties of defendant

A defendant who is diverted pursuant to this chapter shall be required to complete all of the following in order to have their action dismissed:

(a) Complete all conditions ordered by the court.

(b) Make full restitution. However, a defendant's inability to pay restitution due to indigence shall not be grounds for denial of diversion or a finding that the defendant has failed to comply with the terms of diversion.

(c) Comply with a court-ordered protective order, stay-away order, or order prohibiting firearm possession, if applicable.
Added by Stats 2020 ch 334 (AB 3234),s 1, eff. 1/1/2021.

Section 1001.97 - Effect of diversion

(a) Upon successful completion of the terms, conditions, or programs ordered by the court pursuant to Section 1001.95, the arrest upon which diversion was imposed shall be deemed to have never occurred. The defendant may indicate in response to any question concerning their prior criminal record that they were not arrested. A record pertaining to an arrest resulting in successful completion of the terms, conditions, or programs ordered by the court shall not, without the defendant's consent, be used in any way that could result in the denial of any employment, benefit, license, or certificate.

(b) The defendant shall be advised that, regardless of their successful completion of diversion, the arrest upon which the diversion was based may be disclosed by the Department of Justice in response to a peace officer application request and that, notwithstanding subdivision (a), this section does not relieve them of the obligation to disclose the arrest in response to a direct question contained in a questionnaire or application for a position as a peace officer, as defined in Section 830.

Added by Stats 2020 ch 334 (AB 3234),s 1, eff. 1/1/2021.

Chapter 2.96 - DEFERRAL OF SENTENCING PILOT PROGRAM

Section 1001.94 et seq - [Repealed]
Added by Stats 2014 ch 732 (AB 2124),s 1, eff. 1/1/2015.

Chapter 3 - DEMURRER AND AMENDMENT

Section 1002 - Pleading on part of defendant
The only pleading on the part of the defendant is either a demurrer or a plea.

Enacted 1872.

Section 1003 - Time to put in demurrer and plea
Both the demurrer and plea must be put in, in open Court, either at the time of the arraignment or at such other time as may be allowed to the defendant for that purpose.

Enacted 1872.

Section 1004 - Demurrer to accusatory pleading
 The defendant may demur to the accusatory pleading at any time prior to the entry of a plea, when it appears upon the face thereof either:

(a) If an indictment, that the grand jury by which it was found had no legal authority to inquire into the offense charged, or, if any information or complaint that the court has no jurisdiction of the offense charged therein.

(b) That it does not substantially conform to the provisions of Sections 950 and 952, and also Section 951 in case of an indictment or information.

(c) That more than one offense is charged, except as provided in Section 954.

(d) That the facts stated do not constitute a public offense.

(e) That it contains matter which, if true, would constitute a legal justification or excuse of the offense charged, or other legal bar to the prosecution.

(f) That the statutory provision alleged in the accusatory pleading is constitutionally invalid.

Amended by Stats 2023 ch 311 (SB 883),s 7, eff. 1/1/2024.

Amended by Stats. 1951, Ch. 1674.

Section 1005 - Writing, signature, and grounds of objection
The demurrer must be in writing, signed either by the defendant or his counsel, and filed. It must distinctly specify the grounds of objection to the accusatory pleading or it must be disregarded.

Amended by Stats. 1951, Ch. 1674.

Section 1006 - Argument upon objections; continuance
Upon the demurrer being filed, the argument upon the objections presented thereby must be heard immediately, unless for exceptional cause shown, the court shall grant a continuance. Such continuance shall be for no longer time than the ends of justice require, and the court shall enter in its minutes the facts requiring it.

Amended by Stats. 1927, Ch. 609.

Section 1007 - Order either overruling or sustaining demurrer
Upon considering the demurrer, the court must make an order either overruling or sustaining it. If the demurrer to an indictment or information is overruled, the court must permit the defendant, at the defendant's election, to plead, which the defendant must do forthwith, unless the court extends the time. If the demurrer is sustained, the court must, if the defect can be remedied by amendment, permit the indictment or information to be amended, either forthwith or within such time, not exceeding 10 days, as it may fix, or, if the defect or insufficiency therein cannot be remedied by amendment, the court may direct the filing of a new information or the submission of the case to the same or another grand jury. If the demurrer to a complaint is sustained, the court must, if the defect can be remedied, permit the filing of an amended complaint within such time not exceeding 10 days as it may fix. The orders made under this section shall be entered in the docket or minutes of the court.

Amended by Stats. 1998, Ch. 931, Sec. 382. Effective September 28, 1998.

Section 1008 - Dismissal of action
If the demurrer is sustained, and no amendment of the accusatory pleading is permitted, or, in case an amendment is permitted, no amendment is made or amended pleading is filed within the time fixed therefor, the action shall be dismissed, and, except as provided in Section 1010, the court must order, if the defendant is in custody, that he be discharged or if he has been admitted to bail, that his bail be exonerated, or, if money or other property has been deposited instead of bail for his appearance, that such money or other property be refunded to him or to the person or persons found by the court to have deposited such money or other property on his behalf.

Amended by Stats. 1951, Ch. 1674.

Section 1009 - Amendment
An indictment, accusation or information may be amended by the district attorney, and an amended complaint may be filed by the prosecuting attorney, without leave of court at any time before the defendant pleads or a demurrer to the original pleading is sustained. The court in which an action is pending may order or permit an amendment of an indictment, accusation or information, or the filing of an amended complaint, for any defect or insufficiency, at any stage of the proceedings, or if the defect in an indictment or information

be one that cannot be remedied by amendment, may order the case submitted to the same or another grand jury, or a new information to be filed. The defendant shall be required to plead to such amendment or amended pleading forthwith, or, at the time fixed for pleading, if the defendant has not yet pleaded and the trial or other proceeding shall continue as if the pleading had been originally filed as amended, unless the substantial rights of the defendant would be prejudiced thereby, in which event a reasonable postponement, not longer than the ends of justice require, may be granted. An indictment or accusation cannot be amended so as to change the offense charged, nor an information so as to charge an offense not shown by the evidence taken at the preliminary examination. A complaint cannot be amended to charge an offense not attempted to be charged by the original complaint, except that separate counts may be added which might properly have been joined in the original complaint. The amended complaint must be verified but may be verified by some person other than the one who made oath to the original complaint.

Amended by Stats. 1998, Ch. 931, Sec. 383. Effective September 28, 1998.

Section 1010 - Resubmission of case to grand jury or filing of new information

When an indictment or information is dismissed after the sustaining of a demurrer, or at any other stage of the proceedings because of any defect or insufficiency of the indictment or information, if the court directs that the case be resubmitted to the same or another grand jury or that a new information be filed, the defendant shall not be discharged from custody, nor the defendant's bail exonerated nor money or other property deposited instead of bail on the defendant's behalf refunded, but the same proceedings must be had on such direction as are prescribed in Sections 997 and 998.

Amended by Stats. 1998, Ch. 931, Sec. 384. Effective September 28, 1998.

Section 1012 - Failure to object by demurrer

When any of the objections mentioned in Section 1004 appears on the face of the accusatory pleading, it can be taken only by demurrer, and failure so to take it shall be deemed a waiver thereof, except that the objection to the jurisdiction of the court and the objection that the facts stated do not constitute a public offense may be taken by motion in arrest of judgment.

Amended by Stats. 1951, Ch. 1674.

Chapter 4 - PLEA

Section 1016 - Kinds of pleas

There are six kinds of pleas to an indictment or an information, or to a complaint charging a misdemeanor or infraction:

1. Guilty.
2. Not guilty.
3. Nolo contendere, subject to the approval of the court. The court shall ascertain whether the defendant completely understands that a plea of nolo contendere shall be considered the same as a plea of guilty and that, upon a plea of nolo contendere, the court shall find the defendant guilty. The legal effect of such a plea, to a crime punishable as a felony, shall be the same as that of a plea of guilty for all purposes. In cases other than those punishable as felonies, the plea and any admissions required by the court during any inquiry it makes as to the voluntariness of, and factual basis for, the plea may not be used against the defendant as an admission in any civil suit based upon or growing out of the act upon which the criminal prosecution is based.
4. A former judgment of conviction or acquittal of the offense charged.
5. Once in jeopardy.
6. Not guilty by reason of insanity. A defendant who does not plead guilty may enter one or more of the other pleas. A defendant who does not plead not guilty by reason of insanity shall be conclusively presumed to have been sane at the time of the commission of the offense charged; provided, that the court may for good cause shown allow a change of plea at any time before the commencement of the trial. A defendant who pleads not guilty by reason of insanity, without also pleading not guilty, thereby admits the commission of the offense charged.

Amended by Stats. 1998, Ch. 931, Sec. 385. Effective September 28, 1998.

Section 1016.2 - Legislative findings; codification of Padilla v. Kentucky

The Legislature finds and declares all of the following:

(a) In Padilla v. Kentucky, 559 U.S. 356 (2010), the United States Supreme Court held that the Sixth Amendment requires defense counsel to provide affirmative and competent advice to noncitizen defendants regarding the potential immigration consequences of their criminal cases. California courts also have held that defense counsel must investigate and advise regarding the immigration consequences of the available dispositions, and should, when consistent with the goals of and informed consent of the defendant, and as consistent with professional standards, defend against adverse immigration consequences (People v. Soriano, 194 Cal.App.3d 1470 (1987), People v. Barocio, 216 Cal.App.3d 99 (1989), People v. Bautista, 115 Cal.App.4th 229 (2004)).

(b) In Padilla v. Kentucky, the United States Supreme Court sanctioned the consideration of immigration consequences by both parties in the plea negotiating process. The court stated that "informed consideration of possible deportation can only benefit both the State and noncitizen defendants during the plea-bargaining process. By bringing deportation consequences into this process, the defense and prosecution may well be able to reach agreements that better satisfy the interests of both parties."

(c) In Padilla v. Kentucky, the United States Supreme Court found that for noncitizens, deportation is an integral part of the penalty imposed for criminal convictions. Deportation may result from serious offenses or a single minor offense. It may be by far the most serious penalty flowing from the conviction.

(d) With an accurate understanding of immigration consequences, many noncitizen defendants are able to plead to a conviction and sentence that satisfy the prosecution and court, but that have no, or fewer, adverse immigration consequences than the original charge.

(e) Defendants who are misadvised or not advised at all of the immigration consequences of criminal charges often suffer irreparable damage to their current or potential lawful immigration status, resulting in penalties such as mandatory detention, deportation, and permanent separation from close family. In some cases, these consequences could have been avoided had counsel provided informed advice and attempted to defend against such consequences.

(f) Once in removal proceedings, a noncitizen may be transferred to any of over 200 immigration detention facilities across the country. Many criminal offenses trigger mandatory detention, so that the person may not request bond. In immigration proceedings, there is no court-appointed right to counsel and as a result, the majority of detained immigrants go unrepresented. Immigration judges often lack the power to consider whether the person should remain in the United States in light of equitable factors such as serious hardship to United States citizen family members, length of time living in the United States, or rehabilitation.

(g) The immigration consequences of criminal convictions have a particularly strong impact in California. One out of every four persons living in the state is foreign-born. One out of every two children lives in a household headed by at least one foreign-born person. The majority of these children are United States citizens. It is estimated that 50,000 parents of California United States citizen children were deported in a little over two years. Once a person is deported, especially after a criminal conviction, it is extremely unlikely that he or she ever is permitted to return.

(h) It is the intent of the Legislature to codify Padilla v. Kentucky and related California case law and to encourage the growth of such case law in furtherance of justice and the findings and declarations of this section.

Added by Stats 2015 ch 705 (AB 1343),s 1, eff. 1/1/2016.

Section 1016.3 - Advice to noncitizen defendants regarding the potential immigration consequences of their criminal cases

(a) Defense counsel shall provide accurate and affirmative advice about the immigration consequences of a proposed disposition, and when consistent with the goals of and with the informed consent of the defendant, and consistent with professional standards, defend against those consequences.

(b) The prosecution, in the interests of justice, and in furtherance of the findings and declarations of Section 1016.2, shall consider the avoidance of adverse immigration consequences in the plea negotiation process as one factor in an effort to reach a just resolution.

(c) This code section shall not be interpreted to change the requirements of Section 1016.5, including the requirement that no defendant shall be required to disclose his or her immigration status to the court.

Added by Stats 2015 ch 705 (AB 1343),s 2, eff. 1/1/2016.

Section 1016.5 - Advisement

(a) Prior to acceptance of a plea of guilty or nolo contendere to any offense punishable as a crime under state law, except offenses designated as infractions under state law, the court shall administer the following advisement on the record to the defendant: If you are not a citizen, you are hereby advised that conviction of the offense for which you have been charged may have the consequences of deportation, exclusion from admission to the United States, or denial of naturalization pursuant to the laws of the United States.

(b) Upon request, the court shall allow the defendant additional time to consider the appropriateness of the plea in light of the advisement as described in this section. If, after January 1, 1978, the court fails to advise the defendant as required by this section and the defendant shows that conviction of the offense to which defendant pleaded guilty or nolo contendere may have the consequences for the defendant of deportation, exclusion from admission to the United States, or denial of naturalization pursuant to the laws of the United States, the court, on defendant's motion, shall vacate the judgment and permit the defendant to withdraw the plea of guilty or nolo contendere, and enter a plea of not guilty. Absent a record that the court provided the advisement required by this section, the defendant shall be presumed not to have received the required advisement.

(c) With respect to pleas accepted prior to January 1, 1978, it is not the intent of the Legislature that a court's failure to provide the advisement required by subdivision (a) of Section 1016.5 should require the vacation of judgment and withdrawal of the plea or constitute grounds for finding a prior conviction invalid. Nothing in this section, however, shall be deemed to inhibit a court, in the sound exercise of its discretion, from vacating a judgment and permitting a defendant to withdraw a plea.

(d) The Legislature finds and declares that in many instances involving an individual who is not a citizen of the United States charged with an offense punishable as a crime under state law, a plea of guilty or nolo contendere is entered without the defendant knowing that a conviction of such offense is grounds for deportation, exclusion from admission to the United States, or denial of naturalization pursuant to the laws of the United States. Therefore, it is the intent of the Legislature in enacting this section to promote fairness to such accused individuals by requiring in such cases that acceptance of a guilty plea or plea of nolo contendere be preceded by an appropriate warning of the special consequences for such a defendant which may result from the plea. It is also the intent of the Legislature that the court in such cases shall grant the defendant a reasonable amount of time to negotiate with the prosecuting agency in the event the defendant or the defendant's counsel was unaware of the possibility of deportation, exclusion from admission to the United States, or denial of naturalization as a result of conviction. It is further the intent of the Legislature that at the time of the plea no defendant shall be required to disclose his or her legal status to the court.

Added by Stats. 1977, Ch. 1088.

Section 1016.7 - Considerations during plea negotiations

(a) In the interest of justice, and in order to reach a just resolution during plea negotiations, the prosecutor shall consider during plea negotiations, among other factors, the following circumstances as factors in support of a mitigated sentence if any of the following were a contributing factor in the commission of the alleged offense:

(1) The person has experienced psychological, physical, or childhood trauma, including, but not limited to, abuse, neglect, exploitation, or sexual violence.

(2) The person is a youth, or was a youth at the time of the commission of the offense.

(3) Prior to the instant offense, or during the commission of the offense, the person is or was a victim of intimate partner violence or human trafficking.

(b)A "youth" for purposes of this section includes any person under 26 years of age on the date the offense was committed.

Added by Stats 2021 ch 695 (AB 124),s 4, eff. 1/1/2022.

Section 1016.8 - Plea bargain that requires defendant to waive unknown future benefits of legislative enactments, initiatives, appellate decisions, or other changes in law

(a) The Legislature finds and declares all of the following:

(1) The California Supreme Court held in Doe v. Harris (2013) 57 Cal.4th 64 that, as a general rule, plea agreements are deemed to incorporate the reserve power of the state to amend the law or enact additional laws for the public good and in pursuance of public policy. That the parties enter into a plea agreement does not have the effect of insulating them from changes in the law that the Legislature has intended to apply to them.

(2) In Boykin v. Alabama (1969) 395 U.S. 238, the United States Supreme Court held that because of the significant constitutional rights at stake in entering a guilty plea, due process requires that a defendant's guilty plea be knowing, intelligent, and voluntary.

(3) Waiver is the voluntary, intelligent, and intentional relinquishment of a known right or privilege (Estelle v. Smith (1981) 451 U.S. 454, 471, fn. 16, quoting Johnson v. Zerbst (1938) 304 U.S. 458, 464) . Waiver requires knowledge that the right exists (Taylor v. U.S. (1973) 414 U.S. 17, 19).

(4) A plea bargain that requires a defendant to generally waive unknown future benefits of legislative enactments, initiatives, appellate decisions, or other changes in the law that may occur after the date of the plea is not knowing and intelligent.
(b) A provision of a plea bargain that requires a defendant to generally waive future benefits of legislative enactments, initiatives, appellate decisions, or other changes in the law that may retroactively apply after the date of the plea is void as against public policy.
(c) For purposes of this section, "plea bargain" has the same meaning as defined in subdivision (b) of Section 1192.7.
Added by Stats 2019 ch 586 (AB 1618),s 1, eff. 1/1/2020.

Section 1017 - Making of plea

Every plea must be made in open court and, may be oral or in writing, shall be entered upon the minutes of the court, and shall be taken down in shorthand by the official reporter if one is present. All pleas of guilty or nolo contendere to misdemeanors or felonies shall be oral or in writing. The plea, whether oral or in writing, shall be in substantially the following form:
1. If the defendant plead guilty: "The defendant pleads that he or she is guilty of the offense charged."
2. If he or she plead not guilty: "The defendant pleads that he or she is not guilty of the offense charged."
3. If he or she plead a former conviction or acquittal: "The defendant pleads that he or she has already been convicted (or acquitted) of the offense charged, by the judgment of the court of ____ (naming it), rendered at ____ (naming the place), on the ____ day of ____."
4. If he or she plead once in jeopardy: "The defendant pleads that he or she has been once in jeopardy for the offense charged (specifying the time, place, and court)."
5. If he or she plead not guilty by reason of insanity: "The defendant pleads that he or she is not guilty of the offense charged because he or she was insane at the time that he or she is alleged to have committed the unlawful act."
Amended by Stats. 1990, Ch. 632, Sec. 2.

Section 1018 - Entry or withdrawal of plea

Unless otherwise provided by law, every plea shall be entered or withdrawn by the defendant himself or herself in open court. No plea of guilty of a felony for which the maximum punishment is death, or life imprisonment without the possibility of parole, shall be received from a defendant who does not appear with counsel, nor shall that plea be received without the consent of the defendant's counsel. No plea of guilty of a felony for which the maximum punishment is not death or life imprisonment without the possibility of parole shall be accepted from any defendant who does not appear with counsel unless the court shall first fully inform him or her of the right to counsel and unless the court shall find that the defendant understands the right to counsel and freely waives it, and then only if the defendant has expressly stated in open court, to the court, that he or she does not wish to be represented by counsel. On application of the defendant at any time before judgment or within six months after an order granting probation is made if entry of judgment is suspended, the court may, and in case of a defendant who appeared without counsel at the time of the plea the court shall, for a good cause shown, permit the plea of guilty to be withdrawn and a plea of not guilty substituted. Upon indictment or information against a corporation a plea of guilty may be put in by counsel. This section shall be liberally construed to effect these objects and to promote justice.
Amended by Stats. 1991, Ch. 421, Sec. 1.

Section 1019 - Effect of plea of not guilty

The plea of not guilty puts in issue every material allegation of the accusatory pleading, except those allegations regarding previous convictions of the defendant to which an answer is required by Section 1025.
Amended by Stats. 1951, Ch. 1674.

Section 1020 - Defenses under plea of not guilty

All matters of fact tending to establish a defense other than one specified in the fourth, fifth, and sixth subdivisions of Section 1016, may be given in evidence under the plea of not guilty.
Amended by Stats. 1968, Ch. 122.

Section 1021 - Former acquittal

If the defendant was formerly acquitted on the ground of variance between the accusatory pleading and the proof or the accusatory pleading was dismissed upon an objection to its form or substance, or in order to hold the defendant for a higher offense, without a judgment of acquittal, it is not an acquittal of the same offense.
Amended by Stats. 1951, Ch. 1674.

Section 1022 - Acquittal on merits

Whenever the defendant is acquitted on the merits, he is acquitted of the same offense, notwithstanding any defect in form or substance in the accusatory pleading on which the trial was had.
Amended by Stats. 1951, Ch. 1674.

Section 1023 - Bar to another prosecution

When the defendant is convicted or acquitted or has been once placed in jeopardy upon an accusatory pleading, the conviction, acquittal, or jeopardy is a bar to another prosecution for the offense charged in such accusatory pleading, or for an attempt to commit the same, or for an offense necessarily included therein, of which he might have been convicted under that accusatory pleading.
Amended by Stats. 1951, Ch. 1674.

Section 1024 - Entry of plea of not guilty if defendant refuses to answer

If the defendant refuses to answer the accusatory pleading, by demurrer or plea, a plea of not guilty must be entered.
Amended by Stats. 1951, Ch. 1674.

Section 1025 - Prior conviction

(a) When a defendant who is charged in the accusatory pleading with having suffered a prior conviction pleads either guilty or not guilty of the offense charged against him or her, he or she shall be asked whether he or she has suffered the prior conviction. If the defendant enters an admission, his or her answer shall be entered in the minutes of the court, and shall, unless withdrawn by consent of the court, be conclusive of the fact of his or her having suffered the prior conviction in all subsequent proceedings. If the defendant enters a denial, his or her answer shall be entered in the minutes of the court. The refusal of the defendant to answer is equivalent to a denial that he or she has suffered the prior conviction.

(b) Except as provided in subdivision (c), the question of whether or not the defendant has suffered the prior conviction shall be tried by the jury that tries the issue upon the plea of not guilty, or in the case of a plea of guilty or nolo contendere, by a jury impaneled for that purpose, or by the court if a jury is waived.

(c) Notwithstanding the provisions of subdivision (b), the question of whether the defendant is the person who has suffered the prior conviction shall be tried by the court without a jury.

(d) Subdivision (c) shall not apply to prior convictions alleged pursuant to Section 190.2 or to prior convictions alleged as an element of a charged offense.

(e) If the defendant pleads not guilty, and answers that he or she has suffered the prior conviction, the charge of the prior conviction shall neither be read to the jury nor alluded to during trial, except as otherwise provided by law.

(f) Nothing in this section alters existing law regarding the use of prior convictions at trial.

Amended by Stats. 1997, Ch. 95, Sec. 1. Effective January 1, 1998.

Section 1026 - Plea of not guilty by reason of insanity joined with another plea

(a) If a defendant pleads not guilty by reason of insanity, and also joins with it another plea or pleas, the defendant shall first be tried as if only the other plea or pleas had been entered, and in that trial the defendant shall be conclusively presumed to have been sane at the time the offense is alleged to have been committed. If the jury finds the defendant guilty, or if the defendant pleads only not guilty by reason of insanity, the question whether the defendant was sane or insane at the time the offense was committed shall be promptly tried, either before the same jury or before a new jury in the discretion of the court. In that trial, the jury shall return a verdict either that the defendant was sane at the time the offense was committed or was insane at the time the offense was committed. If the verdict or finding is that the defendant was sane at the time the offense was committed, the court shall sentence the defendant as provided by law. If the verdict or finding is that the defendant was insane at the time the offense was committed, the court, unless it appears to the court that the sanity of the defendant has been recovered fully, shall direct that the defendant be committed to the State Department of State Hospitals for the care and treatment of persons with mental health disorders or any other appropriate public or private treatment facility approved by the community program director, or the court may order the defendant placed on outpatient status pursuant to Title 15 (commencing with Section 1600) of Part 2.

(b) Prior to making the order directing that the defendant be committed to the State Department of State Hospitals or other treatment facility or placed on outpatient status, the court shall order the community program director or a designee to evaluate the defendant and to submit to the court within 15 judicial days of the order a written recommendation as to whether the defendant should be placed on outpatient status or committed to the State Department of State Hospitals or other treatment facility. A person shall not be admitted to a state hospital or other treatment facility or placed on outpatient status under this section without having been evaluated by the community program director or a designee. If, however, it appears to the court that the sanity of the defendant has been recovered fully, the defendant shall be remanded to the custody of the sheriff until the issue of sanity has been finally determined in the manner prescribed by law. A defendant committed to a state hospital or other treatment facility or placed on outpatient status pursuant to Title 15 (commencing with Section 1600) of Part 2 shall not be released from confinement, parole, or outpatient status unless and until the court that committed the person, after notice and hearing, finds and determines that the person's sanity has been restored, or meets the criteria for release pursuant to Section 4146 of the Welfare and Institutions Code. This section does not prohibit the transfer of the patient from one state hospital to any other state hospital by proper authority. This section does not prohibit the transfer of the patient to a hospital in another state in the manner provided in Section 4119 of the Welfare and Institutions Code.

(c) If the defendant is committed or transferred to the State Department of State Hospitals pursuant to this section, the court may, upon receiving the written recommendation of the medical director of the state hospital and the community program director, or their designee, or, pursuant to Section 4360.5 of the Welfare and Institutions Code, the recommendation of the independent evaluation panel, that the defendant be transferred to a public or private treatment facility approved by the community program director or their designee, or, pursuant to Section 4360.5 of the Welfare and Institutions Code, the independent evaluation panel, order the defendant transferred to that facility. If the defendant is committed or transferred to a public or private treatment facility approved by the community program director, the court may, upon receiving the written recommendation of the community program director, order the defendant transferred to the State Department of State Hospitals or to another public or private treatment facility approved by the community program director. If either the defendant or the prosecuting attorney chooses to contest either kind of order of transfer, a petition may be filed in the court requesting a hearing, which shall be held if the court determines that sufficient grounds exist. At that hearing, the prosecuting attorney or the defendant may present evidence bearing on the order of transfer. The court shall use the same procedures and standards of proof as used in conducting probation revocation hearings pursuant to Section 1203.2.

(d) Prior to making an order for transfer under this section, the court shall notify the defendant, the attorney of record for the defendant, the prosecuting attorney, and the community program director or a designee.

(e) If the court, after considering the placement recommendation of the community program director or independent evaluation panel required in subdivision (b), orders that the defendant be committed to the State Department of State Hospitals or other public or private treatment facility, the court shall provide copies of the following documents prior to the admission of the defendant to the State Department of State Hospitals or other treatment facility where the defendant is to be committed:

    (1) The commitment order, including a specification of the charges.

    (2) A computation or statement setting forth the maximum term of commitment in accordance with Section 1026.5.

    (3) A computation or statement setting forth the amount of credit for time served, if any, to be deducted from the maximum term of commitment.

(4)State summary criminal history information.

(5)Any arrest reports prepared by the police department or other law enforcement agency.

(6)Any court-ordered psychiatric examination or evaluation reports.

(7)The community program director's placement recommendation report.

(8)Any medical records.

(f)If the defendant is confined in a state hospital or other treatment facility as an inpatient, the medical director of the facility shall, at six-month intervals, submit a report in writing to the court and the community program director of the county of commitment, or a designee, setting forth the status and progress of the defendant. The court shall transmit copies of these reports to the prosecutor and defense counsel.

(g)For purposes of this section and Sections 1026.1 to 1026.6, inclusive, "community program director" means the person, agency, or entity designated by the State Department of State Hospitals pursuant to Section 1605 of this code and Section 4360 of the Welfare and Institutions Code.

Amended by Stats 2022 ch 47 (SB 184),s 39, eff. 6/30/2022.

Amended by Stats 2019 ch 9 (AB 46),s 3, eff. 1/1/2020.

Amended by Stats 2016 ch 715 (SB 955),s 1, eff. 1/1/2017.

Amended by Stats 2014 ch 26 (AB 1468),s 15, eff. 6/20/2014.

Amended by Stats 2012 ch 24 (AB 1470),s 22, eff. 6/27/2012.

Section 1026.1 - Release from state hospital or other treatment facility

A person committed to a state hospital or other treatment facility under the provisions of Section 1026 shall be released from the state hospital or other treatment facility only under one or more of the following circumstances:

(a) Pursuant to the provisions of Section 1026.2.

(b) Upon expiration of the maximum term of commitment as provided in subdivision (a) of Section 1026.5, except as such term may be extended under the provisions of subdivision (b) of Section 1026.5.

(c) As otherwise expressly provided in Title 15 (commencing with Section 1600) of Part 2.

Amended by Stats. 1984, Ch. 1488, Sec. 2.

Section 1026.2 - Application for release; hearing

(a)An application for the release of a person who has been committed to a state hospital or other treatment facility, as provided in Section 1026, upon the ground that sanity has been restored, may be made to the superior court of the county from which the commitment was made, either by the person, or by the medical director of the state hospital or other treatment facility to which the person is committed or by the community program director where the person is on outpatient status under Title 15 (commencing with Section 1600). The court shall give notice of the hearing date to the prosecuting attorney, the community program director or a designee, and the medical director or person in charge of the facility providing treatment to the committed person at least 15 judicial days in advance of the hearing date.

(b)Pending the hearing, the medical director or person in charge of the facility in which the person is confined shall prepare a summary of the person's programs of treatment and shall forward the summary to the community program director or a designee and to the court. The community program director or a designee shall review the summary and shall designate a facility within a reasonable distance from the court in which the person may be detained pending the hearing on the application for release. The facility so designated shall continue the program of treatment, shall provide adequate security, and shall, to the greatest extent possible, minimize interference with the person's program of treatment.

(c)A designated facility need not be approved for 72-hour treatment and evaluation pursuant to the Lanterman-Petris-Short Act (Part 1 (commencing with Section 5000) of Division 5 of the Welfare and Institutions Code). However, a county jail may not be designated unless the services specified in subdivision (b) are provided and accommodations are provided which ensure both the safety of the person and the safety of the general population of the jail. If there is evidence that the treatment program is not being complied with or accommodations have not been provided which ensure both the safety of the committed person and the safety of the general population of the jail, the court shall order the person transferred to an appropriate facility or make any other appropriate order, including continuance of the proceedings.

(d)No hearing upon the application shall be allowed until the person committed has been confined or placed on outpatient status for a period of not less than 180 days from the date of the order of commitment.

(e)The court shall hold a hearing to determine whether the person applying for restoration of sanity would be a danger to the health and safety of others, due to mental defect, disease, or disorder, if under supervision and treatment in the community. If the court at the hearing determines the applicant will not be a danger to the health and safety of others, due to mental defect, disease, or disorder, while under supervision and treatment in the community, the court shall order the applicant placed with an appropriate forensic conditional release program for one year. All or a substantial portion of the program shall include outpatient supervision and treatment. The court shall retain jurisdiction. The court at the end of the one year, shall have a trial to determine if sanity has been restored, which means the applicant is no longer a danger to the health and safety of others, due to mental defect, disease, or disorder. The court shall not determine whether the applicant has been restored to sanity until the applicant has completed the one year in the appropriate forensic conditional release program, unless the community program director sooner makes a recommendation for restoration of sanity and unconditional release as described in subdivision (h). The court shall notify the persons required to be notified in subdivision (a) of the hearing date.

(f)If the applicant is on parole or outpatient status and has been on it for one year or longer, then it is deemed that the applicant has completed the required one year in an appropriate forensic conditional release program and the court shall, if all other applicable provisions of law have been met, hold the trial on restoration of sanity as provided for in this section.

(g)Before placing an applicant in an appropriate forensic conditional release program, the community program director or their designee, or, pursuant to Section 4360.5 of the Welfare and Institutions Code, the independent evaluation panel, shall submit to the court a written recommendation as to what forensic conditional release program is the most appropriate for supervising and treating the applicant. If the court does not accept the recommendation of the community program director or panel, the court shall specify the reason or reasons for its order on the court record. Sections 1605 to 1610, inclusive, shall be applicable to the person placed in the forensic conditional release program unless otherwise ordered by the court.

(h)

(1) If the court determines that the person should be transferred to an appropriate forensic conditional release program, the community program director or a designee shall make the necessary placement arrangements, and, within 21 days after receiving notice of the court finding, the person shall be placed in the community in accordance with the treatment and supervision plan, unless good cause for not doing so is made known to the court.

(2) During the one year of supervision and treatment, if the community program director is of the opinion that the person is no longer a danger to the health and safety of others due to a mental defect, disease, or disorder, the community program director shall submit a report of their opinion and recommendations to the committing court, the prosecuting attorney, and the attorney for the person. The court shall then set and hold a trial to determine whether restoration of sanity and unconditional release should be granted. The trial shall be conducted in the same manner as is required at the end of one full year of supervision and treatment.

(i)If at the trial for restoration of sanity the court rules adversely to the applicant, the court may place the applicant on outpatient status, pursuant to Title 15 (commencing with Section 1600) of Part 2, unless the applicant does not meet all of the requirements of Section 1603.

(j)If the court denies the application to place the person in an appropriate forensic conditional release program or if restoration of sanity is denied, no new application may be filed by the person until one year has elapsed from the date of the denial.

(k)In any hearing authorized by this section, the applicant shall have the burden of proof by a preponderance of the evidence.

(l)If the application for the release is not made by the medical director of the state hospital or other treatment facility to which the person is committed or by the community program director where the person is on outpatient status under Title 15 (commencing with Section 1600), no action on the application shall be taken by the court without first obtaining the written recommendation of the medical director of the state hospital or other treatment facility or of the community program director where the person is on outpatient status under Title 15 (commencing with Section 1600).

(m)This subdivision shall apply only to persons who, at the time of the petition or recommendation for restoration of sanity, are subject to a term of imprisonment with prison time remaining to serve or are subject to the imposition of a previously stayed sentence to a term of imprisonment. Any person to whom this subdivision applies who petitions or is recommended for restoration of sanity may not be placed in a forensic conditional release program for one year, and a finding of restoration of sanity may be made without the person being in a forensic conditional release program for one year. If a finding of restoration of sanity is made, the person shall be transferred to the custody of the California Department of Corrections to serve the term of imprisonment remaining or shall be transferred to the appropriate court for imposition of the sentence that is pending, whichever is applicable.

Amended by Stats 2022 ch 47 (SB 184),s 40, eff. 6/30/2022.

Amended by Stats 2003 ch 230 (AB 1762), eff. 8/11/2003.

Section 1026.3 - Placement on outpatient status

A person committed to a state hospital or other treatment facility under Section 1026, and a person placed pursuant to subdivision (e) of Section 1026.2 as amended by Section 3.5 of Chapter 1488 of the Statutes of 1984, may be placed on outpatient status from the commitment as provided in Title 15 (commencing with Section 1600) of Part 2.

Amended by Stats. 1985, Ch. 260, Sec. 2.

Section 1026.4 - Escape

(a) Every person committed to a state hospital or other public or private mental health facility pursuant to the provisions of Section 1026, who escapes from or who escapes while being conveyed to or from the state hospital or facility, is punishable by imprisonment in the county jail not to exceed one year or in a state prison for a determinate term of one year and one day. The term of imprisonment imposed pursuant to this section shall be served consecutively to any other sentence or commitment.

(b) The medical director or person in charge of a state hospital or other public or private mental health facility to which a person has been committed pursuant to the provisions of Section 1026 shall promptly notify the chief of police of the city in which the hospital or facility is located, or the sheriff of the county if the hospital or facility is located in an unincorporated area, of the escape of the person, and shall request the assistance of the chief of police or sheriff in apprehending the person, and shall within 48 hours of the escape of the person orally notify the court that made the commitment, the prosecutor in the case, and the Department of Justice of the escape.

Amended by Stats. 1989, Ch. 568, Sec. 1.

Section 1026.5 - Maximum term of commitment

(a)

(1) In the case of any person committed to a state hospital or other treatment facility pursuant to Section 1026 or placed on outpatient status pursuant to Section 1604, who committed a felony on or after July 1, 1977, the court shall state in the commitment order the maximum term of commitment, and the person may not be kept in actual custody longer than the maximum term of commitment, except as provided in this section. For the purposes of this section, "maximum term of commitment" shall mean the longest term of imprisonment which could have been imposed for the offense or offenses of which the person was convicted, including the upper term of the base offense and any additional terms for enhancements and consecutive sentences which could have been imposed less any applicable credits as defined by Section 2900.5, and disregarding any credits which could have been earned pursuant to Article 2.5 (commencing with Section 2930) of Chapter 7 of Title 1 of Part 3.

(2) In the case of a person confined in a state hospital or other treatment facility pursuant to Section 1026 or placed on outpatient status pursuant to Section 1604, who committed a felony prior to July 1, 1977, and who could have been sentenced under Section 1168 or 1170 if the offense was committed after July 1, 1977, the Board of Prison Terms shall determine the maximum term of commitment which could have been imposed under paragraph (1), and the person may not be kept in actual custody longer than the maximum term of commitment, except as provided in subdivision (b). The time limits of this section are not jurisdictional. In fixing a term under this section, the board shall utilize the upper term of imprisonment which could have been imposed for the offense or offenses of

which the person was convicted, increased by any additional terms which could have been imposed based on matters which were found to be true in the committing court. However, if at least two of the members of the board after reviewing the person's file determine that a longer term should be imposed for the reasons specified in Section 1170.2, a longer term may be imposed following the procedures and guidelines set forth in Section 1170.2, except that any hearings deemed necessary by the board shall be held within 90 days of September 28, 1979. Within 90 days of the date the person is received by the state hospital or other treatment facility, or of September 28, 1979, whichever is later, the Board of Prison Terms shall provide each person with the determination of the person's maximum term of commitment or shall notify the person that a hearing will be scheduled to determine the term.

Within 20 days following the determination of the maximum term of commitment the board shall provide the person, the prosecuting attorney, the committing court, and the state hospital or other treatment facility with a written statement setting forth the maximum term of commitment, the calculations, and any materials considered in determining the maximum term.

(3) In the case of a person committed to a state hospital or other treatment facility pursuant to Section 1026 or placed on outpatient status pursuant to Section 1604 who committed a misdemeanor, the maximum term of commitment shall be the longest term of county jail confinement which could have been imposed for the offense or offenses which the person was found to have committed, and the person may not be kept in actual custody longer than this maximum term.

(4) Nothing in this subdivision limits the power of any state hospital or other treatment facility or of the committing court to release the person, conditionally or otherwise, for any period of time allowed by any other provision of law.

(b)

(1) A person may be committed beyond the term prescribed by subdivision (a) only under the procedure set forth in this subdivision and only if the person has been committed under Section 1026 for a felony and by reason of a mental disease, defect, or disorder represents a substantial danger of physical harm to others.

(2) Not later than 180 days prior to the termination of the maximum term of commitment prescribed in subdivision (a), the medical director of a state hospital in which the person is being treated, or the medical director of the person's treatment facility or the local program director, if the person is being treated outside a state hospital setting, shall submit to the prosecuting attorney his or her opinion as to whether or not the patient is a person described in paragraph (1). If requested by the prosecuting attorney, the opinion shall be accompanied by supporting evaluations and relevant hospital records. The prosecuting attorney may then file a petition for extended commitment in the superior court which issued the original commitment. The petition shall be filed no later than 90 days before the expiration of the original commitment unless good cause is shown. The petition shall state the reasons for the extended commitment, with accompanying affidavits specifying the factual basis for believing that the person meets each of the requirements set forth in paragraph (1).

(3) When the petition is filed, the court shall advise the person named in the petition of the right to be represented by an attorney and of the right to a jury trial. The rules of discovery in criminal cases shall apply. If the person is being treated in a state hospital when the petition is filed, the court shall notify the community program director of the petition and the hearing date.

(4) The court shall conduct a hearing on the petition for extended commitment. The trial shall be by jury unless waived by both the person and the prosecuting attorney. The trial shall commence no later than 30 calendar days prior to the time the person would otherwise have been released, unless that time is waived by the person or unless good cause is shown.

(5) Pending the hearing, the medical director or person in charge of the facility in which the person is confined shall prepare a summary of the person's programs of treatment and shall forward the summary to the community program director or a designee, and to the court. The community program director or a designee shall review the summary and shall designate a facility within a reasonable distance from the court in which the person may be detained pending the hearing on the petition for extended commitment. The facility so designated shall continue the program of treatment, shall provide adequate security, and shall, to the greatest extent possible, minimize interference with the person's program of treatment.

(6) A designated facility need not be approved for 72-hour treatment and evaluation pursuant to the provisions of the Lanterman-Petris-Short Act (Part 1 (commencing with Section 5000) of Division 5 of the Welfare and Institutions Code). However, a county jail may not be designated unless the services specified in paragraph (5) are provided and accommodations are provided which ensure both the safety of the person and the safety of the general population of the jail. If there is evidence that the treatment program is not being complied with or accommodations have not been provided which ensure both the safety of the committed person and the safety of the general population of the jail, the court shall order the person transferred to an appropriate facility or make any other appropriate order, including continuance of the proceedings.

(7) The person shall be entitled to the rights guaranteed under the federal and State Constitutions for criminal proceedings. All proceedings shall be in accordance with applicable constitutional guarantees. The state shall be represented by the district attorney who shall notify the Attorney General in writing that a case has been referred under this section. If the person is indigent, the county public defender or State Public Defender shall be appointed. The State Public Defender may provide for representation of the person in any manner authorized by Section 15402 of the Government Code. Appointment of necessary psychologists or psychiatrists shall be made in accordance with this article and Penal Code and Evidence Code provisions applicable to criminal defendants who have entered pleas of not guilty by reason of insanity.

(8) If the court or jury finds that the patient is a person described in paragraph (1), the court shall order the patient recommitted to the facility in which the patient was confined at the time the petition was filed. This commitment shall be for an additional period of two years from the date of termination of the previous commitment, and the person may not be kept in actual custody longer than two years unless another extension of commitment is obtained in accordance with the provisions of this subdivision. Time spent on outpatient status, except when placed in a locked facility at the direction of the outpatient supervisor, shall not count as actual custody and shall not be credited toward the person's maximum term of commitment or toward the person's term of extended commitment.

(9) A person committed under this subdivision shall be eligible for release to outpatient status pursuant to the provisions of Title 15 (commencing with Section 1600) of Part 2.

(10) Prior to termination of a commitment under this subdivision, a petition for recommitment may be filed to determine whether the patient remains a person described in paragraph (1). The recommitment proceeding shall be conducted in accordance with the provisions of this subdivision.

(11) Any commitment under this subdivision places an affirmative obligation on the treatment facility to provide treatment for the underlying causes of the person's mental disorder.

Amended by Stats. 1994, 1st Ex. Sess., Ch. 9, Sec. 1. Effective November 30, 1994.

Section 1026.6 - Notification of release

Whenever any person who has been committed to a state hospital pursuant to Section 1026 is released for any reason, including placement on outpatient status, the director of the hospital shall notify the community program director of the county, and the chief law enforcement officer of the jurisdiction, in which the person will reside upon release, if that information is available.

Amended by Stats. 1985, Ch. 1232, Sec. 4. Effective September 30, 1985. Note: This text was suspended from Jan. 1, 1987, until Jan. 1, 1989, during operation of the temporary amendment by Stats. 1986, Ch. 64.

Section 1027 - Examination and investigation of defendant who pleads not guilty by reason of insanity

(a) When a defendant pleads not guilty by reason of insanity the court shall select and appoint two, and may select and appoint three, psychiatrists, or licensed psychologists who have a doctoral degree in psychology and at least five years of postgraduate experience in the diagnosis and treatment of emotional and mental disorders, to examine the defendant and investigate his or her mental status. It is the duty of the psychiatrists or psychologists selected and appointed to make the examination and investigation, and to testify, whenever summoned, in any proceeding in which the sanity of the defendant is in question. The psychiatrists or psychologists appointed by the court shall be allowed, in addition to their actual traveling expenses, those fees that in the discretion of the court seem just and reasonable, having regard to the services rendered by the witnesses. The fees allowed shall be paid by the county where the indictment was found or in which the defendant was held for trial.

(b) Any report on the examination and investigation made pursuant to subdivision (a) shall include, but not be limited to, the psychological history of the defendant, the facts surrounding the commission of the acts forming the basis for the present charge used by the psychiatrist or psychologist in making his or her examination of the defendant, the present psychological or psychiatric symptoms of the defendant, if any, the substance abuse history of the defendant, the substance use history of the defendant on the day of the offense, a review of the police report for the offense, and any other credible and relevant material reasonably necessary to describe the facts of the offense.

(c) This section does not presume that a psychiatrist or psychologist can determine whether a defendant was sane or insane at the time of the alleged offense. This section does not limit a court's discretion to admit or exclude, pursuant to the Evidence Code, psychiatric or psychological evidence about the defendant's state of mind or mental or emotional condition at the time of the alleged offense.

(d) Nothing contained in this section shall be deemed or construed to prevent any party to any criminal action from producing any other expert evidence with respect to the mental status of the defendant. If expert witnesses are called by the district attorney in the action, they shall only be entitled to those witness fees as may be allowed by the court.

(e) Any psychiatrist or psychologist appointed by the court may be called by either party to the action or by the court, and shall be subject to all legal objections as to competency and bias and as to qualifications as an expert. When called by the court or by either party to the action, the court may examine the psychiatrist or psychologist, as deemed necessary, but either party shall have the same right to object to the questions asked by the court and the evidence adduced as though the psychiatrist or psychologist were a witness for the adverse party. When the psychiatrist or psychologist is called and examined by the court, the parties may cross-examine him or her in the order directed by the court. When called by either party to the action, the adverse party may examine him or her the same as in the case of any other witness called by the party.

Amended by Stats 2012 ch 150 (SB 1281),s 1, eff. 7/17/2012.

Chapter 5 - TRANSMISSION OF CERTAIN INDICTMENTS AND INFORMATION

Section 1029 - Indictment found or information filed against superior court judge

When an indictment is found or an information filed in the superior court against a judge thereof, a certificate of that fact must be transmitted by the clerk to the chairman of the Judicial Council, who shall thereupon designate and assign a judge of the superior court of another county to preside at the trial of such indictment or information, and hear and determine all pleas and motions affecting the defendant thereunder before and after judgment.

Amended by Stats. 1935, Ch. 573.

Chapter 6 - CHANGE OF VENUE

Section 1033 - Order of change of venue

In a criminal action pending in the superior court, the court shall order a change of venue:

(a) On motion of the defendant, to another county when it appears that there is a reasonable likelihood that a fair and impartial trial cannot be had in the county. When a change of venue is ordered by the superior court, it shall be for the trial itself. All proceedings before trial shall occur in the county of original venue, except when it is evident that a particular proceeding must be heard by the judge who is to preside over the trial.

(b) On its own motion or on motion of any party, to an adjoining county when it appears as a result of the exhaustion of all of the jury panels called that it will be impossible to secure a jury to try the cause in the county.

Amended by Stats. 1983, Ch. 562, Sec. 1.

Section 1033.1 - Return to original place of trial

In any criminal action or proceeding in which the place of trial has been changed for any of the reasons set forth in Section 1033, the court, upon its own motion or upon the motion of any party, may return the action or proceeding to the original place of trial if both of the following conditions apply:

(a) The action or proceeding is pending before the court after reversal of the original judgment by the appellate court.

(b) The court finds that the conditions which originally required the order to change venue, as set forth in Section 1033, no longer apply. Prior to making such a finding, the court shall conduct a hearing, upon notice to all parties. At the hearing, the burden shall be on the prosecution to establish that the conditions which originally required the order to change venue no longer apply, unless the defendant and his or her attorney consent to the return of the action or proceeding to the original place of trial.

Added by Stats. 1993, Ch. 837, Sec. 1. Effective October 6, 1993.

Section 1034 - [Repealed]

Repealed by Stats 2003 ch 449 (AB 1712), s 31, eff. 1/1/2004.

Section 1035 - Transfer to county in which defendant was arrested, held, or present

A defendant arrested, held, or present in a county other than that in which an indictment, information, felony complaint, or felony probation violation is pending against the defendant, may state in writing his or her agreement to plead guilty or nolo contendere to some or all of the pending charges, to waive trial or hearing in the county in which the pleading is pending, and to consent to disposition of the case in the county in which that defendant was arrested, held, or present, subject to the approval of the district attorney for each county. Upon receipt of the defendant's statement and of the written approval of the district attorneys, the clerk of the court in which the pleading is pending shall transmit the papers in the proceeding or certified copies thereof to the clerk of the court for the county in which the defendant is arrested, held, or present, and the prosecution shall continue in that county. However, the proceedings shall be limited solely to the purposes of plea and sentencing and not for trial. If, after the proceeding has been transferred pursuant to this section, the defendant pleads not guilty, the clerk shall return the papers to the court in which the prosecution was commenced and the proceeding shall be restored to the docket of that court. The defendant's statement that the defendant wishes to plead guilty or nolo contendere may not be used against the defendant.

Amended by Stats 2003 ch 449 (AB 1712), s 32, eff. 1/1/2004.

Section 1036 - Delivery of defendant to custody of sheriff

(a) Unless the court reserves jurisdiction to hear other pretrial motions, if a defendant is incarcerated and the court orders a change of venue to another county, the court shall direct the sheriff to deliver the defendant to the custody of the sheriff of the other county for the purpose of trial.

(b) If the defendant is incarcerated and the court orders that the jury be selected from the county to which the venue would otherwise have been transferred pursuant to Section 1036.7, the court shall direct the sheriff to deliver the defendant to the custody of the sheriff of that county for the purpose of jury selection.

Amended by Stats. 1987, Ch. 780, Sec. 1.

Section 1036.5 - Setting aside order to change venue

Following the resolution of pre-trial motions, and prior to the issuance of an order under Section 1036 or the transmittal of the case file for the purpose of trial to the court to which venue has been ordered transferred, the court may, upon its own motion or the motion of any party and on appropriate notice to the court to which venue has been transferred, set aside its order to change venue on the ground that the conditions which originally required the order to change venue, as set forth in Section 1033 or 1034, no longer apply.

Added by Stats. 1983, Ch. 947, Sec. 7.

Section 1036.7 - Moving of jury rather than pending action

When a change of venue is ordered and the court, upon motion to transfer a jury or on its own motion and upon unanimous consent of all defendants, determines that it would be in the interests of the administration of justice to move the jury rather than to move the pending action, a change of venue may be accomplished by the selection of a jury in the county or judicial district to which the venue would otherwise have been transferred, and the selected jury shall be moved to the court in which the criminal action is pending.

Added by Stats. 1987, Ch. 780, Sec. 2.

Section 1037 - Payment of costs

(a) When a court orders a change of venue to a court in another county, all costs incurred by the receiving court or county, that are not payable pursuant to Section 4750, shall be paid by the transferring court or county as provided in Sections 1037.1 and 1037.2. Those costs may include, but are not limited to, the expenses for the following:

(1) The transfer, preparation, and trial of the action.

(2) The guarding, keeping, and transportation of the prisoner.

(3) Any appeal or other proceeding relating to the action.

(4) Execution of the sentence.

(b) The term "all costs" means all reasonable and necessary costs incurred by the receiving court or county as a result of the change of venue that would not have been incurred but for the change of venue. "All costs" does not include normal salaries, overhead, and other expenses that would have been incurred by the receiving court or county if it did not receive the trial.

Amended by Stats 2005 ch 282 (AB 27),s 1, eff. 1/1/2006

Amended by Stats 2000 ch 447 (SB 1533) s 11, eff. 1/1/2001.

Section 1037.1 - Change of venue costs

(a) Change of venue costs, as defined in Section 1037, that are court operations, as defined in Section 77003 of the Government Code and Rule 10.810 of the California Rules of Court, shall be considered court costs to be charged against and paid by the transferring court to the receiving court.

(b) The Judicial Council shall adopt financial policies and procedures to ensure the timely payment of court costs pursuant to this section. The policies and procedures shall include, but are not limited to, both of the following:

(1) The requirement that courts approve a budget and a timeline for reimbursement before the beginning of the trial.

(2) A process for the Administrative Office of the Courts to mediate any disputes regarding costs between transferring and receiving courts.

(c)

(1) The presiding judge of the transferring court, or his or her designee, shall authorize the payment for the reimbursement of court costs out of the court operations fund of the transferring court.

(2) Payments for the reimbursement of court costs shall be deposited into the court operations fund of the receiving court.

Amended by Stats 2007 ch 130 (AB 299),s 192, eff. 1/1/2008.

Amended by Stats 2006 ch 538 (SB 1852),s 504, eff. 1/1/2007.

Added by Stats 2005 ch 282 (AB 27),s 2, eff. 1/1/2006.

Section 1037.2 - County costs

(a) Change of venue costs, as defined in Section 1037, that are incurred by the receiving county and not defined as court operations under Section 77003 of the Government Code or Rule 10.810 of the California Rules of Court shall be considered to be county costs to be paid by the transferring county to the receiving county. County costs include, but are not limited to, alterations, including all construction-related costs, to a courthouse made that only resulted from the transfer of the trial, rental of furniture or equipment that only resulted from the transfer of the trial, inmate transportation provided by the county sheriff from the jail to the courthouse, security of the inmate or other participants in the trial, unique or extraordinary costs for the extended storage and safekeeping of evidence related to the trial, rental of jury parking lot, jury parking lot security and related costs, security expenses incurred by the county sheriff or a contracted agency that resulted only from the transfer of the trial, and information services for the court, jury, public, or media.

(b) Transferring counties shall approve a budget and a timeline for the payment of county costs before the beginning of trial.

(c) Claims for the costs described in subdivision (a) shall be forwarded to the treasurer and auditor of the transferring county on a monthly basis. The treasurer shall pay the amount of county costs out of the general funds of the transferring county within 30 days of receiving the claim for costs from the receiving county.

(d)

(1) The transferring court may, in its sound discretion, determine the reasonable and necessary costs under this section.

(2) The transferring court's approval of costs shall become effective 10 days after the court has given written notice of the costs to the auditor of the transferring county.

(3) During the 10-day period specified in paragraph (2), the auditor of the transferring county may contest the costs approved by the transferring court.

(4) If the auditor of the transferring county fails to contest the costs within the 10-day period specified in paragraph (2), the transferring county shall be deemed to have waived the right to contest the imposition of these costs.

Amended by Stats 2007 ch 130 (AB 299),s 193, eff. 1/1/2008.

Amended by Stats 2006 ch 287 (AB 3017),s 1, eff. 1/1/2007.

Added by Stats 2005 ch 282 (AB 27),s 3, eff. 1/1/2006.

Section 1038 - Adoption of rules of practice and procedure

The Judicial Council shall adopt rules of practice and procedure for the change of venue in criminal actions.

Amended by Stats 2003 ch 449 (AB 1712), s 33, eff. 1/1/2004.

Section 1039 - [Repealed]

Repealed by Stats 2003 ch 449 (AB 1712), s 34, eff. 1/1/2004.

Chapter 7 - THE MODE OF TRIAL

Section 1041 - Issue of fact

An issue of fact arises:

1.Upon a plea of not guilty.

2.Upon a plea of a former conviction or acquittal of the same offense.

3.Upon a plea of once in jeopardy.

4.Upon a plea of not guilty by reason of insanity.

Amended by Stats. 1949, Ch. 1314.

Section 1042 - Trial of issues of fact

Issues of fact shall be tried in the manner provided in Article I, Section 16 of the Constitution of this state.

Amended by Stats 2002 ch 787 (SB 1798), s 20, eff. 1/1/2003.

Section 1042.5 - Trial of infraction; trial of infraction and public offense

Trial of an infraction shall be by the court, but when a defendant has been charged with an infraction and with a public offense for which there is a right to jury trial and a jury trial is not waived, the court may order that the offenses be tried together by jury or that they be tried separately with the infraction being tried by the court either in the same proceeding or a separate proceeding as may be appropriate.

Added by Stats. 1968, Ch. 1192.

Section 1043 - Presence of defendant

(a) Except as otherwise provided in this section, the defendant in a felony case shall be personally present at the trial.

(b) The absence of the defendant in a felony case after the trial has commenced in their physical presence shall not prevent continuing the trial to, and including, the return of the verdict in any of the following cases:

(1) Any case in which the defendant, after being warned by the judge that they will be removed if they continue their disruptive behavior, nevertheless insists on acting in a manner so disorderly, disruptive, and disrespectful of the court that the trial cannot be carried on with the defendant present in the courtroom.

(2) Any prosecution for an offense which is not punishable by death in which the defendant is voluntarily absent.

(c) Any defendant who is absent from a trial pursuant to paragraph (1) of subdivision (b) may reclaim the right to be present at the trial as soon as they are willing to act consistently with the decorum and respect inherent in the concept of courts and judicial proceedings.

(d) Subdivisions (a) and (b) shall not limit the right of a defendant to waive the right to be present in accordance with Section 977.

(e) If the defendant in a misdemeanor case fails to appear in person at the time set for trial or during the course of trial, the court shall proceed with the trial, unless good cause for a continuance exists, if the defendant has authorized their counsel to proceed in their absence pursuant to subdivision (a) of Section 977. If there is no authorization pursuant to subdivision (a) of Section 977 and if the defendant fails to appear in person at the time set for trial or during the course of trial, the court, in its discretion, may do one or more of the following, as it deems appropriate:

(1)Continue the matter.

(2)Order bail forfeited or revoke release on the defendant's own recognizance.

(3)Issue a bench warrant.

(4)

(A)If the defendant is in custody, proceed with the trial in the defendant's absence as authorized in subdivision (f).

(B)If the defendant is out of custody, proceed with the trial if the court finds the defendant has absented themselves voluntarily with full knowledge that the trial is to be held or is being held.

(f)

(1)A trial shall be deemed to have commenced in the presence of the defendant for purposes of subdivision (b), or may proceed pursuant to paragraph (4) of subdivision (e), if the court finds, by clear and convincing evidence, all of the following to be true:

(A)The defendant is in custody and is refusing, without good cause, to appear in court on that day for that trial.

(B)The defendant has been informed of their right and obligation to be personally present in court.

(C)The defendant has been informed that the trial will proceed without the defendant being present.

(D)The defendant has been informed that they have the right to remain silent during the trial.

(E)The defendant has been informed that their absence without good cause will constitute a voluntary waiver of any constitutional or statutory right to confront any witnesses against them or to testify on their own behalf.

(F)The defendant has been informed whether or not defense counsel will be present.

(2)The court shall state on the record the reasons for the court's findings and shall cause those findings and reasons to be entered into the minutes.

(3)If the trial lasts for more than one day, the court is required to make the findings required by this subdivision anew for each day that the defendant is absent.

(4)This subdivision does not apply to any trial in which the defendant was personally present in court at the commencement of trial.

(g)Nothing herein shall limit the right of the court to order the defendant to be personally present at the trial for purposes of identification unless counsel stipulate to the issue of identity.

Amended by Stats 2022 ch 197 (SB 1493),s 17, eff. 1/1/2023.

Amended by Stats 2021 ch 196 (AB 700),s 2, eff. 1/1/2022.

Amended by Stats. 1977, Ch. 1152.

Section 1043.5 - [Effective until 1/1/2025] Presence of defendant in preliminary hearing

(a) Except as otherwise provided in this section, the defendant in a preliminary hearing shall be personally present.

(b) The absence of the defendant in a preliminary hearing after the hearing has commenced in their physical presence shall not prevent continuing the hearing to, and including, holding to answer, filing an information, or discharging the defendant in any of the following cases:

(1) Any case in which the defendant, after being warned by the judge that they will be removed if they continued their disruptive behavior, nevertheless insists on acting in a manner so disorderly, disruptive, and disrespectful of the court that the hearing cannot be carried on with the defendant present in the courtroom.

(2) Any prosecution for an offense which is not punishable by death in which the defendant is voluntarily absent.

(c) Any defendant who is absent from a preliminary hearing pursuant to paragraph (1) of subdivision (b) may reclaim their right to be present at the hearing as soon as they are willing to act consistently with the decorum and respect inherent in the concept of courts and judicial proceedings.

(d) Subdivisions (a) and (b) shall not limit the right of a defendant to waive the right to be physically present or to appear through the use of remote technology in accordance with Section 977.

(e)

(1) For purposes of subdivision (b), a preliminary hearing shall be deemed to have commenced in the presence of the defendant if the court finds, by clear and convincing evidence, all of the following to be true:

(A) The defendant is in custody and is refusing, without good cause, to appear in court on that day for that preliminary hearing.

(B) The defendant has been informed of their right and obligation to be personally present in court.

(C) The defendant has been informed that the preliminary hearing will proceed without the defendant being present.

(D) The defendant has been informed that they have the right to remain silent during the preliminary hearing.

(E) The defendant has been informed that their absence without good cause will constitute a voluntary waiver of any constitutional or statutory right to confront any witnesses against them or to testify on their own behalf.

(F) The defendant has been informed whether or not defense counsel will be present.

(2) The court shall state on the record the reasons for the court's findings and shall cause those findings and reasons to be entered into the minutes.

(3) If the preliminary hearing lasts for more than one day, the court is required to make the findings required by this subdivision anew for each day that the defendant is absent.

(4) This subdivision does not apply to any preliminary hearing in which the defendant was personally present in court at the commencement of the preliminary hearing.

(f) This section shall remain in effect only until January 1, 2025, and as of that date is repealed.

Amended by Stats 2023 ch 190 (SB 135),s 6, eff. 9/13/2023.

Amended by Stats 2022 ch 57 (AB 199),s 15, eff. 6/30/2022.

Amended by Stats 2021 ch 196 (AB 700),s 3, eff. 1/1/2022.

Added by Stats. 1980, Ch. 1379, Sec. 2.

Section 1043.5 - [Operative 1/1/2025] Presence of defendant in preliminary hearing

(a) Except as otherwise provided in this section, the defendant in a preliminary hearing shall be personally present.

(b) The absence of the defendant in a preliminary hearing after the hearing has commenced in their physical presence shall not prevent continuing the hearing to, and including, holding to answer, filing an information, or discharging the defendant in any of the following cases:

    (1) Any case in which the defendant, after being warned by the judge that they will be removed if they continued their disruptive behavior, nevertheless insists on acting in a manner so disorderly, disruptive, and disrespectful of the court that the hearing cannot be carried on with the defendant present in the courtroom.

    (2) Any prosecution for an offense which is not punishable by death in which the defendant is voluntarily absent.

(c) Any defendant who is absent from a preliminary hearing pursuant to paragraph (1) of subdivision (b) may reclaim their right to be present at the hearing as soon as they are willing to act consistently with the decorum and respect inherent in the concept of courts and judicial proceedings.

(d) Subdivisions (a) and (b) shall not limit the right of a defendant to waive the right to be present in accordance with Section 977.

(e)

    (1) For purposes of subdivision (b), a preliminary hearing shall be deemed to have commenced in the presence of the defendant if the court finds, by clear and convincing evidence, all of the following to be true:

        (A) The defendant is in custody and is refusing, without good cause, to appear in court on that day for that preliminary hearing.

        (B) The defendant has been informed of their right and obligation to be personally present in court.

        (C) The defendant has been informed that the preliminary hearing will proceed without the defendant being present.

        (D) The defendant has been informed that they have the right to remain silent during the preliminary hearing.

        (E) The defendant has been informed that their absence without good cause will constitute a voluntary waiver of any constitutional or statutory right to confront any witnesses against them or to testify on their own behalf.

        (F) The defendant has been informed whether or not defense counsel will be present.

    (2) The court shall state on the record the reasons for the court's findings and shall cause those findings and reasons to be entered into the minutes.

    (3) If the preliminary hearing lasts for more than one day, the court is required to make the findings required by this subdivision anew for each day that the defendant is absent.

    (4) This subdivision does not apply to any preliminary hearing in which the defendant was personally present in court at the commencement of the preliminary hearing.

(f) This section shall become operative on January 1, 2025.

Amended by Stats 2023 ch 190 (SB 135),s 7, eff. 9/13/2023.

Added by Stats 2022 ch 57 (AB 199),s 16, eff. 6/30/2022.

Section 1044 - Control of proceedings by judge

It shall be the duty of the judge to control all proceedings during the trial, and to limit the introduction of evidence and the argument of counsel to relevant and material matters, with a view to the expeditious and effective ascertainment of the truth regarding the matters involved.

Added by Stats. 1927, Ch. 607.

Section 1045 - Verbatim record

In any misdemeanor or infraction matter, where a verbatim record of the proceedings is not required to be made and where the right of a party to request a verbatim record is not provided for pursuant to any other provision of law or rule of court, if any party makes a request at least five days in advance and deposits the required fees, the court shall order that a verbatim record be made of all proceedings. Except as otherwise provided by law or rule the party requesting any reporting, recording, or transcript pursuant to this section shall pay the cost of such reporting, recording, or transcript.

This section shall cease to be operative upon a final decision of an appellate court holding that there is a constitutional right or other requirement that a verbatim record or transcript be provided at public expense for indigent or any other defendants in cases subject to the provisions of this section.

Added by Stats. 1980, Ch. 1200, Sec. 1.

Chapter 8 - FORMATION OF THE TRIAL JURY AND THE CALENDAR OF ISSUES FOR TRIAL

Section 1046 - Formation of trial juries

Trial juries for criminal actions are formed in the same manner as trial juries in civil actions.

Enacted 1872.

Section 1048 - Order of disposal of issues on calendar

(a) The issues on the calendar shall be disposed of in the following order, unless for good cause the court directs an action to be tried out of its order:

    (1) Prosecutions for felony, when the defendant is in custody.

    (2) Prosecutions for misdemeanor, when the defendant is in custody.

    (3) Prosecutions for felony, when the defendant is on bail.

    (4) Prosecutions for misdemeanor, when the defendant is on bail.

(b) Notwithstanding subdivision (a), all criminal actions in which (1) a minor is detained as a material witness or is the victim of the alleged offense, (2) a person who was 70 years of age or older at the time of the alleged offense or is a dependent adult, as defined in subdivision (h) of Section 368, was a witness to, or is the victim of, the alleged offense or (3) any person is a victim of an alleged violation of Section 261, 264.1, 273a, 273d, 285, 286, 287, 288, or 289 or former Section 262 or 288a, committed by the use of force, violence, or the threat thereof, shall be given precedence over all other criminal actions in the order of trial. In those actions, continuations shall be granted by the court only after a hearing and determination of the necessity thereof, and in any event, the trial shall be commenced within 30 days after arraignment, unless for good cause the court shall direct the action to be continued, after a hearing and determination of the necessity of the continuance, and states the findings for a determination of good cause on the record.

(c) This section does not provide a statutory right to a trial within 30 days.

Amended by Stats 2021 ch 626 (AB 1171),s 40, eff. 1/1/2022.

Amended by Stats 2018 ch 423 (SB 1494),s 84, eff. 1/1/2019.

Amended by Stats 2012 ch 867 (SB 1144),s 23, eff. 1/1/2013.

Section 1048.1 - Avoidance of setting trial dates on same day when assigned to same prosecuting attorney

(a) In scheduling a trial date at an arraignment in superior court involving any of the following offenses, reasonable efforts shall be made to avoid setting that trial, when that case is assigned to a particular prosecuting attorney, on the same day that another case is set for trial involving the same prosecuting attorney:

(1) Murder, as defined in subdivision (a) of Section 187.

(2) An alleged sexual assault offense, as described in subdivisions (a) and (b) of Section 11165.1.

(3) An alleged child abuse offense, as described in Section 11165.6.

(4) A case being handled in the Career Criminal Prosecution Program pursuant to Chapter 2.2 (commencing with Section 999b).

(5) An alleged offense against a person with a developmental disability.

(b) For purposes of this section, "developmental disability" has the same meaning as found in Section 4512 of the Welfare and Institutions Code.

Amended by Stats 2016 ch 91 (AB 1272),s 1, eff. 1/1/2017.

EFFECTIVE 1/1/2000. Amended September 15, 1999 (Bill Number: AB 501) (Chapter 382).

Section 1048.2 - Priority for actions alleging human trafficking

Notwithstanding subdivision (b) of Section 1048, for good cause shown, the court may grant priority to an action for an alleged violation of Section 236.1 as the court, in its discretion, may determine to be appropriate.

Added by Stats 2016 ch 644 (AB 2498),s 4, eff. 1/1/2017.

Section 1049 - Time for preparation for trial

After his plea, the defendant is entitled to at least five days to prepare for trial.

Amended by Stats. 1927, Ch. 606.

Section 1049.5 - Setting of trial date in felony cases

In felony cases, the court shall set a date for trial which is within 60 days of the defendant's arraignment in the superior court unless, upon a showing of good cause as prescribed in Section 1050, the court lengthens the time. If the court, after a hearing as prescribed in Section 1050, finds that there is good cause to set the date for trial beyond the 60 days, it shall state on the record the facts proved that justify its finding. A statement of facts proved shall be entered in the minutes.

Added June 5, 1990, by initiative Proposition 115, Sec. 21.

Section 1050 - Continuances

(a) The welfare of the people of the State of California requires that all proceedings in criminal cases shall be set for trial and heard and determined at the earliest possible time. To this end, the Legislature finds that the criminal courts are becoming increasingly congested with resulting adverse consequences to the welfare of the people and the defendant. Excessive continuances contribute substantially to this congestion and cause substantial hardship to victims and other witnesses. Continuances also lead to longer periods of presentence confinement for those defendants in custody and the concomitant overcrowding and increased expenses of local jails. It is therefore recognized that the people, the defendant, and the victims and other witnesses have the right to an expeditious disposition, and to that end it shall be the duty of all courts and judicial officers and of all counsel, both for the prosecution and the defense, to expedite these proceedings to the greatest degree that is consistent with the ends of justice. In accordance with this policy, criminal cases shall be given precedence over, and set for trial and heard without regard to the pendency of, any civil matters or proceedings. In further accordance with this policy, death penalty cases in which both the prosecution and the defense have informed the court that they are prepared to proceed to trial shall be given precedence over, and set for trial and heard without regard to the pendency of, other criminal cases and any civil matters or proceedings, unless the court finds in the interest of justice that it is not appropriate.

(b) To continue any hearing in a criminal proceeding, including the trial, (1) a written notice shall be filed and served on all parties to the proceeding at least two court days before the hearing sought to be continued, together with affidavits or declarations detailing specific facts showing that a continuance is necessary and (2) within two court days of learning that he or she has a conflict in the scheduling of any court hearing, including a trial, an attorney shall notify the calendar clerk of each court involved, in writing, indicating which hearing was set first. A party shall not be deemed to have been served within the meaning of this section until that party actually has received a copy of the documents to be served, unless the party, after receiving actual notice of the request for continuance, waives the right to have the documents served in a timely manner. Regardless of the proponent of the motion, the prosecuting attorney shall notify the people's witnesses and the defense attorney shall notify the defense's witnesses of the notice of motion, the date of the hearing, and the witnesses' right to be heard by the court.

(c) Notwithstanding subdivision (b), a party may make a motion for a continuance without complying with the requirements of that subdivision. However, unless the moving party shows good cause for the failure to comply with those requirements, the court may impose sanctions as provided in Section 1050.5.

(d) When a party makes a motion for a continuance without complying with the requirements of subdivision (b), the court shall hold a hearing on whether there is good cause for the failure to comply with those requirements. At the conclusion of the hearing, the court shall make a finding whether good cause has been shown and, if it finds that there is good cause, shall state on the record the facts proved that justify its finding. A statement of the finding and a statement of facts proved shall be entered in the minutes. If the moving party is unable to show good cause for the failure to give notice, the motion for continuance shall not be granted.

(e) Continuances shall be granted only upon a showing of good cause. Neither the convenience of the parties nor a stipulation of the parties is in and of itself good cause.

(f) At the conclusion of the motion for continuance, the court shall make a finding whether good cause has been shown and, if it finds that there is good cause, shall state on the record the facts proved that justify its finding. A statement of facts proved shall be entered in the minutes.

(g)

(1) When deciding whether or not good cause for a continuance has been shown, the court shall consider the general convenience and prior commitments of all witnesses, including peace officers. Both the general convenience and prior commitments of each witness also shall be considered in selecting a continuance date if the motion is granted. The facts as to inconvenience or prior commitments may be offered by the witness or by a party to the case.

(2) For purposes of this section, "good cause" includes, but is not limited to, those cases involving murder, as defined in subdivision (a) of Section 187, allegations that stalking, as defined in Section 646.9, a violation of one or more of the sections specified in subdivision (a) of Section 11165.1 or Section 11165.6, or domestic violence as defined in Section 13700, or a case being handled in the Career Criminal Prosecution Program pursuant to Sections 999b through 999h, or a hate crime, as defined in Title 11.6 (commencing with Section 422.6) of Part 1, has occurred and the prosecuting attorney assigned to the case has another trial, preliminary hearing, or motion to suppress in progress in that court or another court. A continuance under this paragraph shall be limited to a maximum of 10 additional court days.

(3) Only one continuance per case may be granted to the people under this subdivision for cases involving stalking, hate crimes, or cases handled under the Career Criminal Prosecution Program. Any continuance granted to the people in a case involving stalking or handled under the Career Criminal Prosecution Program shall be for the shortest time possible, not to exceed 10 court days.

(h) Upon a showing that the attorney of record at the time of the defendant's first appearance in the superior court on an indictment or information is a Member of the Legislature of this state and that the Legislature is in session or that a legislative interim committee of which the attorney is a duly appointed member is meeting or is to meet within the next seven days, the defendant shall be entitled to a reasonable continuance not to exceed 30 days.

(i) A continuance shall be granted only for that period of time shown to be necessary by the evidence considered at the hearing on the motion. Whenever any continuance is granted, the court shall state on the record the facts proved that justify the length of the continuance, and those facts shall be entered in the minutes.

(j) Whenever it shall appear that any court may be required, because of the condition of its calendar, to dismiss an action pursuant to Section 1382, the court must immediately notify the Chair of the Judicial Council.

(k) This section shall not apply when the preliminary examination is set on a date less than 10 court days from the date of the defendant's arraignment on the complaint, and the prosecution or the defendant moves to continue the preliminary examination to a date not more than 10 court days from the date of the defendant's arraignment on the complaint.

(l) This section is directory only and does not mandate dismissal of an action by its terms.

Amended by Stats 2003 ch 133 (AB 1273), s 1, eff. 1/1/2004.
Amended by Stats 2002 ch 784 (SB 1316), s 544, eff. 1/1/2003.
Amended by Stats 2002 ch 788 (AB 2653), s 1, eff. 1/1/2003.
Amended by Stats 2000 ch 268 (AB 2125) s 1, eff. 1/1/2001.
Amended September 29, 1999 (Bill Number: SB 69) (Chapter 580).
Previously Amended September 15, 1999 (Bill Number: AB 501) (Chapter 382).

Section 1050.1 - Continuances in case in which two or more defendants are jointly charged

In any case in which two or more defendants are jointly charged in the same complaint, indictment, or information, and the court or magistrate, for good cause shown, continues the arraignment, preliminary hearing, or trial of one or more defendants, the continuance shall, upon motion of the prosecuting attorney, constitute good cause to continue the remaining defendants' cases so as to maintain joinder. The court or magistrate shall not cause jointly charged cases to be severed due to the unavailability or unpreparedness of one or more defendants unless it appears to the court or magistrate that it will be impossible for all defendants to be available and prepared within a reasonable period of time.

Added June 5, 1990, by initiative Proposition 115, Sec. 22.

Section 1050.5 - Sanctions

(a) When, pursuant to subdivision (c) of Section 1050, the court imposes sanctions for failure to comply with the provisions of subdivision (b) of Section 1050, the court may impose one or both of the following sanctions when the moving party is the prosecuting or defense attorney:

(1) A fine not exceeding one thousand dollars ($1,000) upon counsel for the moving party.

(2) The filing of a report with an appropriate disciplinary committee.

(b) The authority to impose sanctions provided for by this section shall be in addition to any other authority or power available to the court, except that the court or magistrate shall not dismiss the case.

Amended by Stats 2003 ch 133 (AB 1273), s 2, eff. 1/1/2004.

Section 1051 - Continuance after testimony of defense witness

Upon a trial for any offense, if a defense witness testifies, there shall be good cause for a reasonable continuance unless the court finds that the prosecutor was or should, with due diligence, have been aware of such evidence. If the continuance is granted because of the defendant's testimony, it shall not exceed one day.

Amended by Stats. 1983, Ch. 782, Sec. 1.

Chapter 9 - POSTPONEMENT OF THE TRIAL

Section 1053 - Death or illness of judge or justice

If after the commencement of the trial of a criminal action or proceeding in any court the judge or justice presiding at the trial shall die, become ill, or for any other reason be unable to proceed with the trial, any other judge or justice of the court in which the trial is proceeding may proceed with and finish the trial; or if there be no other judge or justice of that court available, then the clerk, sheriff, or marshal shall adjourn the court and notify the Chairman of the Judicial Council of the facts, and shall continue the case from day to day until the time that the chairman shall designate and assign a judge or justice of some other court, and the judge or justice shall arrive, to proceed with and complete the trial, or until such time as by stipulation in writing between the prosecuting attorney and the attorney for the defendant, filed with the court, a judge or justice shall be agreed upon by them, and the judge or justice shall arrive to complete the trial. The judge or justice authorized by this section to proceed with and complete the trial shall have the same power, authority, and jurisdiction as if the trial had been commenced before that judge or justice.

Amended by Stats. 1996, Ch. 872, Sec. 118. Effective January 1, 1997.

Chapter 10 - DISCOVERY

Section 1054 - Purposes

This chapter shall be interpreted to give effect to all of the following purposes:

(a) To promote the ascertainment of truth in trials by requiring timely pretrial discovery.

(b) To save court time by requiring that discovery be conducted informally between and among the parties before judicial enforcement is requested.

(c) To save court time in trial and avoid the necessity for frequent interruptions and postponements.

(d) To protect victims and witnesses from danger, harassment, and undue delay of the proceedings.

(e) To provide that no discovery shall occur in criminal cases except as provided by this chapter, other express statutory provisions, or as mandated by the Constitution of the United States.

Added June 5, 1990, by initiative Proposition 115.

Section 1054.1 - Disclosure to defendant

The prosecuting attorney shall disclose to the defendant or his or her attorney all of the following materials and information, if it is in the possession of the prosecuting attorney or if the prosecuting attorney knows it to be in the possession of the investigating agencies:

(a) The names and addresses of persons the prosecutor intends to call as witnesses at trial.

(b) Statements of all defendants.

(c) All relevant real evidence seized or obtained as a part of the investigation of the offenses charged.

(d) The existence of a felony conviction of any material witness whose credibility is likely to be critical to the outcome of the trial.

(e) Any exculpatory evidence.

(f) Relevant written or recorded statements of witnesses or reports of the statements of witnesses whom the prosecutor intends to call at the trial, including any reports or statements of experts made in conjunction with the case, including the results of physical or mental examinations, scientific tests, experiments, or comparisons which the prosecutor intends to offer in evidence at the trial.

Added June 5, 1990, by initiative Proposition 115.

Section 1054.2 - Disclosure of address or telephone number of victim or witness

(a)

(1) Except as provided in paragraph (2), no attorney shall disclose or permit to be disclosed to a defendant, members of the defendant's family, or anyone else, the personal identifying information of a victim or witness whose name is disclosed to the attorney pursuant to subdivision (a) of Section 1054.1, other than the name of the victim or witness, unless specifically permitted to do so by the court after a hearing and a showing of good cause.

(2) Notwithstanding paragraph (1), an attorney may disclose or permit to be disclosed the personal identifying information of a victim or witness to persons employed by the attorney or to persons appointed by the court to assist in the preparation of a defendant's case if that disclosure is required for that preparation. Persons provided this information by an attorney shall be informed by the attorney that further dissemination of the information, except as provided by this section, is prohibited.

(b) If the defendant is acting as their own attorney, the court shall endeavor to protect the personal identifying information of a victim or witness by providing for contact only through a private investigator licensed by the Department of Consumer Affairs and appointed by the court or by imposing other reasonable restrictions, absent a showing of good cause as determined by the court.

(c) For the purposes of this section, personal identifying information has the same definition as in Section 530.55, except that it does not include name, place of employment, or an equivalent form of identification.

Amended by Stats 2021 ch 91 (AB 419),s 1, eff. 1/1/2022.

Amended by Stats. 1998, Ch. 485, Sec. 133. Effective January 1, 1999. Note: This section was added June 5, 1990, by initiative Prop. 115. Prop. 115 allows the Legislature to directly amend its provisions by 2/3 vote.

Section 1054.3 - Disclosure to prosecuting attorney

(a) The defendant and his or her attorney shall disclose to the prosecuting attorney:

(1) The names and addresses of persons, other than the defendant, he or she intends to call as witnesses at trial, together with any relevant written or recorded statements of those persons, or reports of the statements of those persons, including any reports or statements of experts made in connection with the case, and including the results of physical or mental examinations, scientific tests, experiments, or comparisons which the defendant intends to offer in evidence at the trial.

(2) Any real evidence which the defendant intends to offer in evidence at the trial.

(b)

(1) Unless otherwise specifically addressed by an existing provision of law, whenever a defendant in a criminal action or a minor in a juvenile proceeding brought pursuant to a petition alleging the juvenile to be within Section 602 of the Welfare and Institutions Code places in issue his or her mental state at any phase of the criminal action or juvenile proceeding through the proposed testimony of any mental health expert, upon timely request by the prosecution, the court may order that the defendant or juvenile submit to examination by a prosecution-retained mental health expert.

(A) The prosecution shall bear the cost of any such mental health expert's fees for examination and testimony at a criminal trial or juvenile court proceeding.

(B) The prosecuting attorney shall submit a list of tests proposed to be administered by the prosecution expert to the defendant in a criminal action or a minor in a juvenile proceeding. At the request of the defendant in a criminal action or a minor in a juvenile proceeding, a hearing shall be held to consider any objections raised to the proposed tests before any test is administered. Before ordering that the defendant submit to the examination, the trial court must make a threshold determination that the proposed tests bear some reasonable relation to the mental state placed in issue by the defendant in a criminal action or a minor in a juvenile proceeding.

For the purposes of this subdivision, the term "tests" shall include any and all assessment techniques such as a clinical interview or a mental status examination.

(2) The purpose of this subdivision is to respond to Verdin v. Superior Court 43 Cal.4th 1096, which held that only the Legislature may authorize a court to order the appointment of a prosecution mental health expert when a defendant has placed his or her mental state at issue in a criminal case or juvenile proceeding pursuant to Section 602 of the Welfare and Institutions Code. Other than authorizing the court to order testing by prosecution-retained mental health experts in response to Verdin v. Superior Court, supra, it is not the intent of the Legislature to disturb, in any way, the remaining body of case law governing the procedural or substantive law that controls the administration of these tests or the admission of the results of these tests into evidence.

Amended by Stats 2009 ch 297 (AB 1516),s 1, eff. 1/1/2010.

Note: This section was added on June 5, 1990, by initiative Prop. 115.

Section 1054.4 - No limitation on law enforcement or prosecuting agency from obtaining nontestimonial evidence

Nothing in this chapter shall be construed as limiting any law enforcement or prosecuting agency from obtaining nontestimonial evidence to the extent permitted by law on the effective date of this section.

Added June 5, 1990, by initiative Proposition 115.

Section 1054.5 - Order requiring discovery

(a) No order requiring discovery shall be made in criminal cases except as provided in this chapter. This chapter shall be the only means by which the defendant may compel the disclosure or production of information from prosecuting attorneys, law enforcement agencies which investigated or prepared the case against the defendant, or any other persons or agencies which the prosecuting attorney or investigating agency may have employed to assist them in performing their duties.

(b) Before a party may seek court enforcement of any of the disclosures required by this chapter, the party shall make an informal request of opposing counsel for the desired materials and information. If within 15 days the opposing counsel fails to provide the materials and information requested, the party may seek a court order. Upon a showing that a party has not complied with Section 1054.1 or 1054.3 and upon a showing that the moving party complied with the informal discovery procedure provided in this subdivision, a court may make any order necessary to enforce the provisions of this chapter, including, but not limited to, immediate disclosure, contempt proceedings, delaying or prohibiting the testimony of a witness or the presentation of real evidence, continuance of the matter, or any other lawful order. Further, the court may advise the jury of any failure or refusal to disclose and of any untimely disclosure.

(c) The court may prohibit the testimony of a witness pursuant to subdivision (b) only if all other sanctions have been exhausted. The court shall not dismiss a charge pursuant to subdivision (b) unless required to do so by the Constitution of the United States.

Added June 5, 1990, by initiative Proposition 115.

Section 1054.6 - Work product or privileged information

Neither the defendant nor the prosecuting attorney is required to disclose any materials or information which are work product as defined in subdivision (a) of Section 2018.030 of the Code of Civil Procedure, or which are privileged pursuant to an express statutory provision, or are privileged as provided by the Constitution of the United States.

Amended by Stats 2004 ch 182 (AB 3081), s 50, eff. 1/1/2005.

Note: This section was added on June 5, 1990, by initiative Prop. 115.

Section 1054.7 - Time of disclosure; in camera showing of good cause for denial or regulation of disclosures

The disclosures required under this chapter shall be made at least 30 days prior to the trial, unless good cause is shown why a disclosure should be denied, restricted, or deferred. If the material and information becomes known to, or comes into the possession of, a party within 30 days of trial, disclosure shall be made immediately, unless good cause is shown why a disclosure should be denied, restricted, or deferred. "Good cause" is limited to threats or possible danger to the safety of a victim or witness, possible loss or destruction of evidence, or possible compromise of other investigations by law enforcement.

Upon the request of any party, the court may permit a showing of good cause for the denial or regulation of disclosures, or any portion of that showing, to be made in camera. A verbatim record shall be made of any such proceeding. If the court enters an order granting relief following a showing in camera, the entire record of the showing shall be sealed and preserved in the records of the court, and shall be made available to an appellate court in the event of an appeal or writ. In its discretion, the trial court may after trial and conviction, unseal any previously sealed matter.

Added June 5, 1990, by initiative Proposition 115.

Section 1054.8 - Interview of victim or witness

(a) No prosecuting attorney, attorney for the defendant, or investigator for either the prosecution or the defendant shall interview, question, or speak to a victim or witness whose name has been disclosed by the opposing party pursuant to Section 1054.1 or 1054.3 without first clearly identifying himself or herself, identifying the full name of the agency by whom he or she is employed, and identifying whether he or she represents, or has been retained by, the prosecution or the defendant. If the interview takes place in person, the party shall also show the victim or witness a business card, official badge, or other form of official identification before commencing the interview or questioning.

(b) Upon a showing that a person has failed to comply with this section, a court may issue any order authorized by Section 1054.5.

Added by Stats. 1998, Ch. 630, Sec. 1. Effective January 1, 1999.

Section 1054.9 - Reasonable access to discovery materials upon prosecution of postconviction writ of habeas corpus or motion to vacate judgment

(a) In a case in which a defendant is or has ever been convicted of a serious felony or a violent felony resulting in a sentence of 15 years or more, upon the prosecution of a postconviction writ of habeas corpus or a motion to vacate a judgment, or in preparation to file that writ or motion, and on a showing that good faith efforts to obtain discovery materials from trial counsel were made and were unsuccessful, the court shall, except as provided in subdivision (b) or (d), order that the defendant be provided reasonable access to any of the materials described in subdivision (c).

(b) Notwithstanding subdivision (a), in a case in which a sentence other than death or life in prison without the possibility of parole is or has ever been imposed, if a court has entered a previous order granting discovery pursuant to this section, a subsequent order granting discovery pursuant to subdivision (a) may be made in the court's discretion. A request for discovery subject to this subdivision shall include a statement by the person requesting discovery as to whether that person has previously been granted an order for discovery pursuant to this section.

(c) For purposes of this section, "discovery materials" means materials in the possession of the prosecution and law enforcement authorities to which the same defendant would have been entitled at time of trial.

(d) In response to a writ or motion satisfying the conditions in subdivision (a), the court may order that the defendant be provided access to physical evidence for the purpose of examination, including, but not limited to, any physical evidence relating to the investigation, arrest, and prosecution of the defendant only upon a showing that there is good cause to believe that access to physical evidence is reasonably necessary to the defendant's effort to obtain relief. The procedures for obtaining access to physical evidence for purposes of postconviction DNA testing are provided in Section 1405, and this section does not provide an alternative means of access to physical evidence for those purposes.

(e) The actual costs of examination or copying pursuant to this section shall be borne or reimbursed by the defendant.

(f) This section does not require the retention of any discovery materials not otherwise required by law or court order.

(g) In criminal matters involving a conviction for a serious or a violent felony resulting in a sentence of 15 years or more, trial counsel shall retain a copy of a former client's files for the term of that client's imprisonment. An electronic copy is sufficient only if every item in the file is digitally copied and preserved.

(h) As used in this section, a "serious felony" is a conviction of a felony enumerated in subdivision (c) of Section 1192.7.

(i) As used in this section, a "violent felony" is a conviction of a felony enumerated in subdivision (c) of Section 667.5.

(j) Subdivision (g) only applies prospectively, commencing January 1, 2019.

Amended by Stats 2019 ch 483 (SB 651),s 1, eff. 1/1/2020.
Amended by Stats 2018 ch 482 (AB 1987),s 2, eff. 1/1/2019.
Added by Stats 2002 ch 1105 (SB 1391), s 1, eff. 1/1/2003.

Section 1054.10 - Disclosure of copies of child pornography evidence

(a) Except as provided in subdivision (b), no attorney may disclose or permit to be disclosed to a defendant, members of the defendant's family, or anyone else copies of child pornography evidence, unless specifically permitted to do so by the court after a hearing and a showing of good cause.

(b) Notwithstanding subdivision (a), an attorney may disclose or permit to be disclosed copies of child pornography evidence to persons employed by the attorney or to persons appointed by the court to assist in the preparation of a defendant's case if that disclosure is required for that preparation. Persons provided this material by an attorney shall be informed by the attorney that further dissemination of the material, except as provided by this section, is prohibited.

Added by Stats 2003 ch 238 (SB 877), eff. 8/11/2003.

Title 7 - OF PROCEEDINGS AFTER THE COMMENCEMENT OF THE TRIAL AND BEFORE JUDGMENT

Chapter 1 - CHALLENGING THE JURY

Section 1065 - Allowance or disallowance of challenge

If, either upon an exception to the challenge or a denial of the facts, the challenge is allowed, the Court must discharge the jury so far as the trial in question is concerned. If it is disallowed, the Court must direct the jury to be impaneled.

Amended by Code Amendments 1880, Ch. 47.

Section 1083 - Decision

Section Ten Hundred and Eighty-three. The Court must allow or disallow the challenge, and its decision must be entered in the minutes of the Court.

Amended by Code Amendments 1873-74, Ch. 614.

Section 1089 - Alternate jurors

Whenever, in the opinion of a judge of a superior court about to try a defendant against whom has been filed any indictment or information or complaint, the trial is likely to be a protracted one, the court may cause an entry to that effect to be made in the minutes of the court, and thereupon, immediately after the jury is impaneled and sworn, the court may direct the calling of one or more additional jurors, in its discretion, to be known as "alternate jurors."

The alternate jurors must be drawn from the same source, and in the same manner, and have the same qualifications as the jurors already sworn, and be subject to the same examination and challenges, provided that the prosecution and the defendant shall each be entitled to as many peremptory challenges to the alternate jurors as there are alternate jurors called. When two or more defendants are tried jointly each defendant shall be entitled to as many peremptory challenges to the alternate jurors as there are alternate jurors called. The prosecution shall be entitled to additional peremptory challenges equal to the number of all the additional separate challenges allowed the defendant or defendants to the alternate jurors.

The alternate jurors shall be seated so as to have equal power and facilities for seeing and hearing the proceedings in the case, and shall take the same oath as the jurors already selected, and must attend at all times upon the trial of the cause in company with the other jurors, and for a failure so to do are liable to be punished for contempt.

They shall obey the orders of and be bound by the admonition of the court, upon each adjournment of the court; but if the regular jurors are ordered to be kept in the custody of the sheriff or marshal during the trial of the cause, the alternate jurors shall also be kept in confinement with the other jurors; and upon final submission of the case to the jury the alternate jurors shall be kept in the custody of the sheriff or marshal and shall not be discharged until the original jurors are discharged, except as hereinafter provided.

If at any time, whether before or after the final submission of the case to the jury, a juror dies or becomes ill, or upon other good cause shown to the court is found to be unable to perform his or her duty, or if a juror requests a discharge and good cause appears therefor, the court may order the juror to be discharged and draw the name of an alternate, who shall then take a place in the jury box, and be subject to the same rules and regulations as though the alternate juror had been selected as one of the original jurors.

Amended by Stats 2003 ch 62 (SB 600), s 230, eff. 1/1/2004.

Amended by Stats 2002 ch 784 (SB 1316), s 545, eff. 1/1/2003.

Chapter 2 - THE TRIAL

Section 1093 - Order of trial

The jury having been impaneled and sworn, unless waived, the trial shall proceed in the following order, unless otherwise directed by the court:

(a) If the accusatory pleading be for a felony, the clerk shall read it, and state the plea of the defendant to the jury, and in cases where it charges a previous conviction, and the defendant has confessed the same, the clerk in reading it shall omit therefrom all that relates to such previous conviction. In all other cases this formality may be dispensed with.

(b) The district attorney, or other counsel for the people, may make an opening statement in support of the charge. Whether or not the district attorney, or other counsel for the people, makes an opening statement, the defendant or his or her counsel may then make an opening statement, or may reserve the making of an opening statement until after introduction of the evidence in support of the charge.

(c) The district attorney, or other counsel for the people shall then offer the evidence in support of the charge. The defendant or his or her counsel may then offer his or her evidence in support of the defense.

(d) The parties may then respectively offer rebutting testimony only, unless the court, for good reason, in furtherance of justice, permit them to offer evidence upon their original case.

(e) When the evidence is concluded, unless the case is submitted on either side, or on both sides, without argument, the district attorney, or other counsel for the people, and counsel for the defendant, may argue the case to the court and jury; the district attorney, or other counsel for the people, opening the argument and having the right to close.

(f) The judge may then charge the jury, and shall do so on any points of law pertinent to the issue, if requested by either party; and the judge may state the testimony, and he or she may make such comment on the evidence and the testimony and credibility of any witness as in his or her opinion is necessary for the proper determination of the case and he or she may declare the law. At the beginning of the trial or from time to time during the trial, and without any request from either party, the trial judge may give the jury such instructions on the law applicable to the case as the judge may deem necessary for their guidance on hearing the case. Upon the jury retiring for deliberation, the court shall advise the jury of the availability of a written copy of the jury instructions. The court may, at its discretion, provide the jury with a copy of the written instructions given. However, if the jury requests the court to supply a copy of the written instructions, the court shall supply the jury with a copy.

Amended by Stats. 1986, Ch. 1045, Sec. 2.

Section 1093.5 - Instructions in criminal case tried before court with jury

In any criminal case which is being tried before the court with a jury, all requests for instructions on points of law must be made to the court and all proposed instructions must be delivered to the court before commencement of argument. Before the commencement of the argument, the court, on request of counsel, must:

(1) decide whether to give, refuse, or modify the proposed instructions;

(2) decide which instructions shall be given in addition to those proposed, if any; and

(3) advise counsel of all instructions to be given. However, if, during the argument, issues are raised which have not been covered by instructions given or refused, the court may, on request of counsel, give additional instructions on the subject matter thereof.

Added by Stats. 1957, Ch. 1698.

Section 1094 - Departure from order regarding instructions

When the state of the pleadings requires it, or in any other case, for good reasons, and in the sound discretion of the court, the order prescribed in Section 1093 may be departed from.

Amended by Stats 2009 ch 35 (SB 174),s 11, eff. 1/1/2010.

Section 1095 - Number of counsel

If the offense charged is punishable with death, two counsel on each side may argue the cause. In any other case the court may, in its discretion, restrict the argument to one counsel on each side.

Amended by Stats. 1951, Ch. 1674.

Section 1096 - Presumption of innocence; reasonable doubt

A defendant in a criminal action is presumed to be innocent until the contrary is proved, and in case of a reasonable doubt whether his or her guilt is satisfactorily shown, he or she is entitled to an acquittal, but the effect of this presumption is only to place upon the state the burden of proving him or her guilty beyond a reasonable doubt. Reasonable doubt is defined as follows: "It is not a mere possible doubt; because everything relating to human affairs is open to some possible or imaginary doubt. It is that state of the case, which, after the entire comparison and consideration of all the evidence, leaves the minds of jurors in that condition that they cannot say they feel an abiding conviction of the truth of the charge."

Amended by Stats. 1995, Ch. 46, Sec. 1. Effective July 3, 1995.

Section 1096a - Charging jury on subject of presumption of innocence or definition of reasonable doubt

In charging a jury, the court may read to the jury Section 1096, and no further instruction on the subject of the presumption of innocence or defining reasonable doubt need be given.

Amended by Stats. 1995, Ch. 46, Sec. 2. Effective July 3, 1995.

Section 1097 - Conviction of lowest degree if reasonable ground of doubt

When it appears that the defendant has committed a public offense, or attempted to commit a public offense, and there is reasonable ground of doubt in which of two or more degrees of the crime or attempted crime he is guilty, he can be convicted of the lowest of such degrees only.

Amended by Stats. 1978, Ch. 1166.

Section 1098 - Joint trials; separate trials

When two or more defendants are jointly charged with any public offense, whether felony or misdemeanor, they must be tried jointly, unless the court order separate trials. In ordering separate trials, the court in its discretion may order a separate trial as to one or more defendants, and a joint trial as to the others, or may order any number of the defendants to be tried at one trial, and any number of the others at different trials, or may order a separate trial for each defendant; provided, that where two or more persons can be jointly tried, the fact that separate accusatory pleadings were filed shall not prevent their joint trial.
Amended by Stats. 1955, Ch. 103.

Section 1099 - Discharge of defendant to be witness for people

When two or more defendants are included in the same accusatory pleading, the court may, at any time before the defendants have gone into their defense, on the application of the prosecuting attorney, direct any defendant to be discharged, that he may be a witness for the people.
Amended by Stats. 1951, Ch. 1674.

Section 1100 - Discharge of defendant to be witness for codefendant

When two or more defendants are included in the same accusatory pleading, and the court is of opinion that in regard to a particular defendant there is not sufficient evidence to put him on his defense, it must order him to be discharged before the evidence is closed, that he may be a witness for his codefendant.
Amended by Stats. 1951, Ch. 1674.

Section 1101 - Discharge of defendant to witness as acquittal

The order mentioned in Sections 1099 and 1100 is an acquittal of the defendant discharged, and is a bar to another prosecution for the same offense.
Amended by Stats. 1987, Ch. 828, Sec. 64.

Section 1102 - Rules of evidence

The rules of evidence in civil actions are applicable also to criminal actions, except as otherwise provided in this Code.
Enacted 1872.

Section 1102.6 - Right of victim of crime to be present

The right of a victim of crime to be present during any criminal proceeding shall be secured as follows:
(a) Notwithstanding any other law, and except as specified in subdivision (d), a victim shall be entitled to be present and seated at all criminal proceedings where the defendant, the prosecuting attorney, and the general public are entitled to be present.
(b) A victim may be excluded from a criminal proceeding only if each of the following criteria are met:
(1) Any movant, including the defendant, who seeks to exclude the victim from any criminal proceeding demonstrates that there is a substantial probability that overriding interests will be prejudiced by the presence of the victim. "Overriding interests" may include, but are not limited to, the following:
(A) The defendant's right to a fair trial.
(B) The government's interest in inhibiting the disclosure of sensitive information.
(C) The protection of witnesses from harassment and physical harm.
(D) The court's interest in maintaining order.
(E) The protection of sexual offense victims from the trauma and embarrassment of testifying.
(F) Safeguarding the physical and psychological well-being of a minor.
(G) The preservation of trade secrets.
(2) The court considers reasonable alternatives to exclusion of the victim from the criminal proceeding.
(3) The exclusion of the victim from any criminal proceeding, or any limitation on his or her presence at any criminal proceeding, is narrowly tailored to serve the overriding interests identified by the movant.
(4) Following a hearing at which any victim who is to be excluded from a criminal proceeding is afforded an opportunity to be heard, the court makes specific factual findings that support the exclusion of the victim from, or any limitation on his or her presence at, the criminal proceeding.
(c) As used in this section, "victim" means
(1) the alleged victim of the offense and one person of his or her choosing or however many more the court may allow under the particular circumstances surrounding the proceeding,
(2) in the event that the victim is unable to attend the proceeding, two persons designated by the victim or however many more the court may allow under the particular circumstances surrounding the proceeding, or
(3) if the victim is no longer living, two members of the victim's immediate family or however many more the court may allow under the particular circumstances surrounding the proceeding.
(d) Nothing in this section shall prevent a court from excluding a victim from a criminal proceeding, pursuant to Section 777 of the Evidence Code, when the victim is subpoenaed as a witness. An order of exclusion shall be consistent with the objectives of paragraphs (1) to (4), inclusive, of subdivision (b) to allow the victim to be present, whenever possible, at all proceedings.
Repealed and added by Stats. 1995, Ch. 332, Sec. 3. Effective January 1, 1996.

Section 1108 - Corroboration of testimony of woman upon or with whom offense was committed

Upon a trial for procuring or attempting to procure an abortion, or aiding or assisting therein, or for inveigling, enticing, or taking away an unmarried female of previous chaste character, under the age of eighteen years, for the purpose of prostitution, or aiding or assisting therein, the defendant cannot be convicted upon the testimony of the woman upon or with whom the offense was committed, unless she is corroborated by other evidence.
Amended by Stats. 1905, Ch. 533.

Section 1109 - Gang enhancement may be tried in separate phases

(a) If requested by the defense, a case in which a gang enhancement is charged under subdivision (b) or (d) of Section 186.22 shall be tried in separate phases as follows:
(1) The question of the defendant's guilt of the underlying offense shall be first determined.

(2) If the defendant is found guilty of the underlying offense and there is an allegation of an enhancement under subdivision (b) or (d) of Section 186.22, there shall be further proceedings to the trier of fact on the question of the truth of the enhancement. Allegations that the underlying offense was committed for the benefit of, at the direction of, or in association with, a criminal street gang and that the underlying offense was committed with the specific intent to promote, further, or assist in criminal conduct by gang members shall be proved by direct or circumstantial evidence.

(b) If a defendant is charged with a violation of subdivision (a) of Section 186.22, this count shall be tried separately from all other counts that do not otherwise require gang evidence as an element of the crime. This charge may be tried in the same proceeding with an allegation of an enhancement under subdivision (b) or (d) of Section 186.22.

Added by Stats 2021 ch 699 (AB 333),s 5, eff. 1/1/2022.

Section 1111 - Corroboration of testimony of accomplice

A conviction can not be had upon the testimony of an accomplice unless it be corroborated by such other evidence as shall tend to connect the defendant with the commission of the offense; and the corroboration is not sufficient if it merely shows the commission of the offense or the circumstances thereof.

An accomplice is hereby defined as one who is liable to prosecution for the identical offense charged against the defendant on trial in the cause in which the testimony of the accomplice is given.

Amended by Stats. 1915, Ch. 457.

Section 1111.5 - Corroboration of in-custody informant

(a) A jury or judge may not convict a defendant, find a special circumstance true, or use a fact in aggravation based on the uncorroborated testimony of an in-custody informant. The testimony of an in-custody informant shall be corroborated by other evidence that connects the defendant with the commission of the offense, the special circumstance, or the evidence offered in aggravation to which the in-custody informant testifies. Corroboration is not sufficient if it merely shows the commission of the offense or the special circumstance or the circumstance in aggravation. Corroboration of an in-custody informant shall not be provided by the testimony of another in-custody informant unless the party calling the in-custody informant as a witness establishes by a preponderance of the evidence that the in-custody informant has not communicated with another in-custody informant on the subject of the testimony.

(b) As used in this section, "in-custody informant" means a person, other than a codefendant, percipient witness, accomplice, or coconspirator, whose testimony is based on statements allegedly made by the defendant while both the defendant and the informant were held within a city or county jail, state penal institution, or correctional institution. Nothing in this section limits or changes the requirements for corroboration of accomplice testimony pursuant to Section 1111.

Added by Stats 2011 ch 153 (SB 687),s 1, eff. 1/1/2012.

Section 1112 - Order requiring submission to psychiatric or psychological examination for purposes of assessing credibility of any prosecuting witness, complaining witness, or any other witness, or victim in any sexual assault prosecution prohibited

Notwithstanding the provisions of subdivision (d) of Section 28 of Article I of the California Constitution, the trial court shall not order any prosecuting witness, complaining witness, or any other witness, or victim in any sexual assault prosecution to submit to a psychiatric or psychological examination for the purpose of assessing his or her credibility.

Amended by Stats. 1984, Ch. 1101, Sec. 1. Effective September 13, 1984.

Section 1113 - Discharge of jury

The Court may direct the jury to be discharged where it appears that it has not jurisdiction of the offense, or that the facts charged do not constitute an offense punishable by law.

Amended by Code Amendments 1880, Ch. 47.

Section 1114 - Discharge of defendant if jury discharged because court does not have jurisdiction of offense

If the jury be discharged because the Court has not jurisdiction of the offense charged, and it appear that it was committed out of the jurisdiction of this State, the defendant must be discharged.

Amended by Code Amendments 1880, Ch. 47.

Section 1115 - Commitment of defendant

If the offense was committed within the exclusive jurisdiction of another county of this State, the Court must direct the defendant to be committed for such time as it deems reasonable, to await a warrant from the proper county for his arrest; or if the offense is a misdemeanor only, it may admit him to bail in an undertaking, with sufficient sureties, that he will, within such time as the Court may appoint, render himself amenable to a warrant for his arrest from the proper county; and, if not sooner arrested thereon, will attend at the office of the Sheriff of the county where the trial was had, at a certain time particularly specified in the undertaking, to surrender himself upon the warrant, if issued, or that his bail will forfeit such sum as the Court may fix, to be mentioned in the undertaking; and the Clerk must forthwith transmit a certified copy of the indictment or information, and of all the papers filed in the action, to the District Attorney of the proper county, the expense of which transmission is chargeable to that county.

Amended by Code Amendments 1880, Ch. 47.

Section 1116 - Discharge from custody

If the defendant is not arrested on a warrant from the proper county, as provided in section 1115, he must be discharged from custody, or his bail in the action is exonerated, or money deposited instead of bail must be refunded to him or to the person or persons found by the court to have deposited said money on behalf of said defendant, as the case may be, and the sureties in the undertaking, as mentioned in that section, must be discharged. If he is arrested, the same proceedings must be had thereon as upon the arrest of a defendant in another county on a warrant of arrest issued by a magistrate.

Amended by Stats. 1935, Ch. 657.

Section 1117 - Discharge of defendant if jury discharged because facts as charged do not constitute defense

If the jury is discharged because the facts as charged do not constitute an offense punishable by law, the court must order that the defendant, if in custody, be discharged; or if admitted to bail, that his bail be exonerated; or, if he has deposited money or if money has been deposited by another or others instead of bail for his appearance, that the money be refunded to him or to the person or persons found by the court to have deposited said money on behalf of said defendant, unless in its opinion a new indictment or information can

be framed upon which the defendant can be legally convicted, in which case it may direct the district attorney to file a new information, or (if the defendant has not been committed by a magistrate) direct that the case be submitted to the same or another grand jury; and the same proceedings must be had thereon as are prescribed in section 998; provided, that after such order or submission the defendant may be examined before a magistrate, and discharged or committed by him as in other cases.
Amended by Stats. 1935, Ch. 657.

Section 1118 - Acquittal at close of prosecution evidence in case tried by court without jury

In a case tried by the court without a jury, a jury having been waived, the court on motion of the defendant or on its own motion shall order the entry of a judgment of acquittal of one or more of the offenses charged in the accusatory pleading after the evidence of the prosecution has been closed if the court, upon weighing the evidence then before it, finds the defendant not guilty of such offense or offenses. If such a motion for judgment of acquittal at the close of the evidence offered by the prosecution is not granted, the defendant may offer evidence without first having reserved that right.
Repealed and added by Stats. 1967, Ch. 256.

Section 1118.1 - Acquittal at close of prosecution evidence in case tried before jury

In a case tried before a jury, the court on motion of the defendant or on its own motion, at the close of the evidence on either side and before the case is submitted to the jury for decision, shall order the entry of a judgment of acquittal of one or more of the offenses charged in the accusatory pleading if the evidence then before the court is insufficient to sustain a conviction of such offense or offenses on appeal. If such a motion for judgment of acquittal at the close of the evidence offered by the prosecution is not granted, the defendant may offer evidence without first having reserved that right.
Added by Stats. 1967, Ch. 256.

Section 1118.2 - Judgment of acquittal at close of prosecution evidence not appealable

A judgment of acquittal entered pursuant to the provisions of Section 1118 or 1118.1 shall not be appealable and is a bar to any other prosecution for the same offense.
Added by Stats. 1967, Ch. 256.

Section 1119 - Jury's view of place or property

When, in the opinion of the court, it is proper that the jury should view the place in which the offense is charged to have been committed, or in which any other material fact occurred, or any personal property which has been referred to in the evidence and cannot conveniently be brought into the courtroom, it may order the jury to be conducted in a body, in the custody of the sheriff or marshal, as the case may be, to the place, or to the property, which must be shown to them by a person appointed by the court for that purpose; and the officer must be sworn to suffer no person to speak or communicate with the jury, nor to do so himself or herself, on any subject connected with the trial, and to return them into court without unnecessary delay, or at a specified time.
Amended by Stats. 1996, Ch. 872, Sec. 119. Effective January 1, 1997.

Section 1120 - Juror's personal knowledge respecting fact in controversy

If a juror has any personal knowledge respecting a fact in controversy in a cause, he or she must declare the same in open court during the trial. If, during the retirement of the jury, a juror declares a fact that could be evidence in the cause, as of his or her own knowledge, the jury must return into court. In either of these cases, the juror making the statement must be sworn as a witness and examined in the presence of the parties in order that the court may determine whether good cause exists for his or her discharge as a juror.
Amended by Stats 2010 ch 328 (SB 1330),s 161, eff. 1/1/2011.

Section 1121 - Separation of jurors; admonishment

The jurors sworn to try an action may, in the discretion of the court, be permitted to separate or be kept in charge of a proper officer. Where the jurors are permitted to separate, the court shall properly admonish them. Where the jurors are kept in charge of a proper officer, the officer must be sworn to keep the jurors together until the next meeting of the court, to suffer no person to speak to them or communicate with them, nor to do so himself, on any subject connected with the trial, and to return them into court at the next meeting thereof.
Amended by Stats. 1969, Ch. 520.

Section 1122 - General instructions concerning functions, duties, and conduct of jury

(a) After the jury has been sworn and before the people's opening address, the court shall instruct the jury generally concerning its basic functions, duties, and conduct. The instructions shall include, among other matters, all of the following admonitions:

(1) That the jurors shall not converse among themselves, or with anyone else, conduct research, or disseminate information on any subject connected with the trial. The court shall clearly explain, as part of the admonishment, that the prohibition on conversation, research, and dissemination of information applies to all forms of electronic and wireless communication.

(2) That they shall not read or listen to any accounts or discussions of the case reported by newspapers or other news media.

(3) That they shall not visit or view the premises or place where the offense or offenses charged were allegedly committed or any other premises or place involved in the case.

(4) That prior to, and within 90 days of, discharge, they shall not request, accept, agree to accept, or discuss with any person receiving or accepting, any payment or benefit in consideration for supplying any information concerning the trial.

(5) That they shall promptly report to the court any incident within their knowledge involving an attempt by any person to improperly influence any member of the jury.

(b) The jury shall also, at each adjournment of the court before the submission of the cause to the jury, whether permitted to separate or kept in charge of officers, be admonished by the court that it is their duty not to conduct research, disseminate information, or converse among themselves, or with anyone else, on any subject connected with the trial, or to form or express any opinion about the case until the cause is finally submitted to them. The court shall clearly explain, as part of the admonishment, that the prohibition on research, dissemination of information, and conversation applies to all forms of electronic and wireless communication.
Amended by Stats 2011 ch 181 (AB 141),s 5, eff. 1/1/2012.

Section 1122.5 - Admonishment at adjournment of court

(a) The court, in its discretion, may, at each adjournment of the court before the submission of the cause to the jury, admonish the jury, whether permitted to be separate or kept in charge of officers, that, on pain of contempt of court, no juror shall, prior to discharge, accept, agree to accept, or benefit, directly or indirectly, from any payment or other consideration for supplying any information concerning the trial.

(b) In enacting this section, the Legislature recognizes that the appearance of justice, and justice itself, may be undermined by any juror who, prior to discharge, accepts, agrees to accept, or benefits from valuable consideration for providing information concerning a criminal trial.

Amended by Stats. 1995, Ch. 91, Sec. 128. Effective January 1, 1996.

Section 1124 - Questions of law
The Court must decide all questions of law which arise in the course of a trial.

Enacted 1872.

Section 1126 - Questions of fact
In a trial for any offense, questions of law are to be decided by the court, and questions of fact by the jury. Although the jury has the power to find a general verdict, which includes questions of law as well as of fact, they are bound, nevertheless, to receive as law what is laid down as such by the court.

Amended by Stats 2008 ch 699 (SB 1241),s 12, eff. 1/1/2009.

Section 1127 - Giving of instructions
All instructions given shall be in writing, unless there is a phonographic reporter present and he takes them down, in which case they may be given orally; provided however, that in all misdemeanor cases oral instructions may be given pursuant to stipulation of the prosecuting attorney and counsel for the defendant. In charging the jury the court may instruct the jury regarding the law applicable to the facts of the case, and may make such comment on the evidence and the testimony and credibility of any witness as in its opinion is necessary for the proper determination of the case and in any criminal case, whether the defendant testifies or not, his failure to explain or to deny by his testimony any evidence or facts in the case against him may be commented upon by the court. The court shall inform the jury in all cases that the jurors are the exclusive judges of all questions of fact submitted to them and of the credibility of the witnesses. Either party may present to the court any written charge on the law, but not with respect to matters of fact, and request that it be given. If the court thinks it correct and pertinent, it must be given; if not, it must be refused. Upon each charge presented and given or refused, the court must endorse and sign its decision and a statement showing which party requested it. If part be given and part refused, the court must distinguish, showing by the endorsement what part of the charge was given and what part refused.

Amended by Stats. 1951, Ch. 1674.

Section 1127a - Instruction on testimony of in-custody informant
(a) As used in this section, an "in-custody informant" means a person, other than a codefendant, percipient witness, accomplice, or coconspirator whose testimony is based upon statements made by the defendant while both the defendant and the informant are held within a correctional institution.

(b) In any criminal trial or proceeding in which an in-custody informant testifies as a witness, upon the request of a party, the court shall instruct the jury as follows: "The testimony of an in-custody informant should be viewed with caution and close scrutiny. In evaluating such testimony, you should consider the extent to which it may have been influenced by the receipt of, or expectation of, any benefits from the party calling that witness. This does not mean that you may arbitrarily disregard such testimony, but you should give it the weight to which you find it to be entitled in the light of all the evidence in the case."

(c) When the prosecution calls an in-custody informant as a witness in any criminal trial, contemporaneous with the calling of that witness, the prosecution shall file with the court a written statement setting out any and all consideration promised to, or received by, the in-custody informant. The statement filed with the court shall not expand or limit the defendant's right to discover information that is otherwise provided by law. The statement shall be provided to the defendant or the defendant's attorney prior to trial and the information contained in the statement shall be subject to rules of evidence.

(d) For purposes of subdivision (c), "consideration" means any plea bargain, bail consideration, reduction or modification of sentence, or any other leniency, benefit, immunity, financial assistance, reward, or amelioration of current or future conditions of incarceration in return for, or in connection with, the informant's testimony in the criminal proceeding in which the prosecutor intends to call him or her as a witness.

Added by Stats. 1989, Ch. 901, Sec. 1.

Section 1127b - Instruction on expert witness
When, in any criminal trial or proceeding, the opinion of any expert witness is received in evidence, the court shall instruct the jury substantially as follows:

Duly qualified experts may give their opinions on questions in controversy at a trial. To assist the jury in deciding such questions, the jury may consider the opinion with the reasons stated therefor, if any, by the expert who gives the opinion. The jury is not bound to accept the opinion of any expert as conclusive, but should give to it the weight to which they shall find it to be entitled. The jury may, however, disregard any such opinion, if it shall be found by them to be unreasonable.

No further instruction on the subject of opinion evidence need be given.

Added by Stats. 1929, Ch. 876.

Section 1127c - Instruction on flight of defendant
In any criminal trial or proceeding where evidence of flight of a defendant is relied upon as tending to show guilt, the court shall instruct the jury substantially as follows:

The flight of a person immediately after the commission of a crime, or after he is accused of a crime that has been committed, is not sufficient in itself to establish his guilt, but is a fact which, if proved, the jury may consider in deciding his guilt or innocence. The weight to which such circumstance is entitled is a matter for the jury to determine.

No further instruction on the subject of flight need be given.

Added by Stats. 1929, Ch. 875.

Section 1127d - Instruction on prior sexual conduct of complaining witness

(a) In any criminal prosecution for the crime of rape, or for violation of Section 261.5, or for an attempt to commit, or assault with intent to commit, any such crime, the jury shall not be instructed that it may be inferred that a person who has previously consented to sexual intercourse with persons other than the defendant or with the defendant would be therefore more likely to consent to sexual intercourse again. However, if evidence was received that the victim consented to and did engage in sexual intercourse with the defendant on one or more occasions prior to that charged against the defendant in this case, the jury shall be instructed that this evidence may be considered only as it relates to the question of whether the victim consented to the act of intercourse charged against the defendant in the case, or whether the defendant had a good faith reasonable belief that the victim consented to the act of sexual intercourse. The jury shall be instructed that it shall not consider this evidence for any other purpose.

(b) A jury shall not be instructed that the prior sexual conduct in and of itself of the complaining witness may be considered in determining the credibility of the witness pursuant to Chapter 6 (commencing with Section 780) of Division 6 of the Evidence Code.
Amended by Stats. 1990, Ch. 269, Sec. 1.

Section 1127e - Use of term "unchaste character"

The term "unchaste character" shall not be used by any court in any criminal case in which the defendant is charged with a violation of Section 261 or 261.5, or former Section 262, or attempt to commit or assault with intent to commit any crime defined in any of these sections, in any instruction to the jury.
Amended by Stats 2022 ch 197 (SB 1493),s 18, eff. 1/1/2023.
Amended by Stats 2021 ch 626 (AB 1171),s 41, eff. 1/1/2022.
Amended by Stats. 1994, Ch. 1188, Sec. 11. Effective January 1, 1995.

Section 1127f - Instruction on testimony of child 10 years of age or younger

In any criminal trial or proceeding in which a child 10 years of age or younger testifies as a witness, upon the request of a party, the court shall instruct the jury, as follows:
In evaluating the testimony of a child you should consider all of the factors surrounding the child's testimony, including the age of the child and any evidence regarding the child's level of cognitive development. Although, because of age and level of cognitive development, a child may perform differently as a witness from an adult, that does not mean that a child is any more or less credible a witness than an adult. You should not discount or distrust the testimony of a child solely because he or she is a child.
Added by Stats. 1986, Ch. 1051, Sec. 3.

Section 1127g - Instruction on testimony of person with developmental disability or cognitive, mental, or communication impairment

In any criminal trial or proceeding in which a person with a developmental disability, or cognitive, mental, or communication impairment testifies as a witness, upon the request of a party, the court shall instruct the jury, as follows:
In evaluating the testimony of a person with a developmental disability, or cognitive, mental, or communication impairment, you should consider all of the factors surrounding the person's testimony, including their level of cognitive development. Although, because of his or her level of cognitive development, a person with a developmental disability, or cognitive, mental, or communication impairment may perform differently as a witness, that does not mean that a person with a developmental disability, or cognitive, mental, or communication impairment is any more or less credible a witness than another witness. You should not discount or distrust the testimony of a person with a developmental disability, or cognitive, mental, or communication impairment solely because he or she is a person with a developmental disability, or cognitive, mental, or communication impairment.
Added by Stats 2004 ch 823 (AB 20), s 15, eff. 1/1/2005.

Section 1127h - Instruction on bias sympathy prejudice or public opinion

In any criminal trial or proceeding, upon the request of a party, the court shall instruct the jury substantially as follows:
"Do not let bias, sympathy, prejudice, or public opinion influence your decision. Bias includes bias against the victim or victims, witnesses, or defendant based upon his or her disability, gender, nationality, race or ethnicity, religion, gender identity, or sexual orientation."
Added by Stats 2006 ch 550 (AB 1160),s 3, eff. 1/1/2007.

Section 1128 - Deliberation

After hearing the charge, the jury may either decide in court or may retire for deliberation. If they do not agree without retiring for deliberation, an officer shall be sworn to keep them together for deliberation in some private and convenient place, and, during the deliberation, not to permit any person to speak to or communicate with them, including any form of electronic or wireless communication, nor to do so himself or herself, unless by order of the court, or to ask them whether they have agreed upon a verdict, and to return them into court when they have so agreed, or when ordered by the court. The court shall fix the time and place for deliberation. The jurors shall not deliberate on the case except under those circumstances. If the jurors are permitted by the court to separate, the court shall properly admonish them as provided in subdivision (b) of Section 1122. If the jury is composed of both men and women, and the jurors are not permitted by the court to separate, in the event that it becomes necessary to retire for the night, the women shall be kept in a room or rooms separate and apart from the men.
Amended by Stats 2011 ch 181 (AB 141),s 6, eff. 1/1/2012.

Section 1129 - Commitment of defendant who has given bail

When a defendant who has given bail appears for trial, the Court may, in its discretion, at any time after his appearance for trial, order him to be committed to the custody of the proper officer of the county, to abide the judgment or further order of the court, and he must be committed and held in custody accordingly.
Enacted 1872.

Section 1130 - Failure of prosecuting attorney to attend felony trial

If the prosecuting attorney fails to attend at the trial of a felony, the court must appoint an attorney at law to perform the duties of the prosecuting attorney on such trial.
Amended by Stats. 1998, Ch. 931, Sec. 389. Effective September 28, 1998.

Chapter 3 - CONDUCT OF THE JURY AFTER THE CAUSE IS SUBMITTED TO THEM

Section 1137 - Papers, copies of records or documents, and written instructions

Upon retiring for deliberation, the jury may take with them all papers (except depositions) which have been received as evidence in the cause, or copies of such public records or private documents given in evidence as ought not, in the opinion of the court, to be taken from the person having them in possession. They may also take with them the written instructions given, and notes of the testimony or other proceedings on the trial, taken by themselves or any of them, but none taken by any other person. The court shall provide for the custody and safekeeping of such items.

Amended by Stats. 1969, Ch. 520.

Section 1138 - Disagreement as to testimony or desire for information on point of law

After the jury have retired for deliberation, if there be any disagreement between them as to the testimony, or if they desire to be informed on any point of law arising in the case, they must require the officer to conduct them into court. Upon being brought into court, the information required must be given in the presence of, or after notice to, the prosecuting attorney, and the defendant or his counsel, or after they have been called.

Amended by Stats. 1951, Ch. 1674.

Section 1138.5 - Presence of judge not required while testimony read to jury

Except for good cause shown, the judge in his of her discretion need not be present in the court while testimony previously received in evidence is read to the jury.

Added by Stats. 1987, Ch. 88, Sec. 2. Effective July 2, 1987.

Section 1140 - Discharge of jury

Except as provided by law, the jury cannot be discharged after the cause is submitted to them until they have agreed upon their verdict and rendered it in open court, unless by consent of both parties, entered upon the minutes, or unless, at the expiration of such time as the court may deem proper, it satisfactorily appears that there is no reasonable probability that the jury can agree.

Amended by Stats. 1949, Ch. 1313.

Section 1141 - Retrying case where jury is discharged or prevented from giving verdict

In all cases where a jury is discharged or prevented from giving a verdict by reason of an accident or other cause, except where the defendant is discharged during the progress of the trial, or after the cause is submitted to them, the cause may be again tried.

Amended by Code Amendments 1880, Ch. 47.

Section 1142 - Adjournment of court

While the jury are absent the Court may adjourn from time to time, as to other business, but it must nevertheless be open for every purpose connected with the cause submitted to the jury until a verdict is rendered or the jury discharged.

Enacted 1872.

Chapter 4 - THE VERDICT OR FINDING

Section 1147 - Appearance of jury after agreement upon verdict

When the jury have agreed upon their verdict, they must be conducted into court by the officer having them in charge. Their names must then be called, and if all do not appear, the rest must be discharged without giving a verdict. In that case the action may be again tried.

Amended by Stats. 1905, Ch. 534.

Section 1148 - Presence of defendant charged with felony

If charged with a felony the defendant must, before the verdict is received, appear in person, unless, after the exercise of reasonable diligence to procure the presence of the defendant, the court shall find that it will be in the interest of justice that the verdict be received in his absence. If for a misdemeanor, the verdict may be rendered in his absence.

Amended by Stats. 1931, Ch. 124.

Section 1149 - Questioning jury about agreement upon verdict

When the jury appear they must be asked by the Court, or Clerk, whether they have agreed upon their verdict, and if the foreman answers in the affirmative, they must, on being required, declare the same.

Enacted 1872.

Section 1150 - General verdict or special verdict

The jury must render a general verdict, except that in a felony case, when they are in doubt as to the legal effect of the facts proved, they may, except upon a trial for libel, find a special verdict.

Amended by Stats. 1998, Ch. 931, Sec. 390. Effective September 28, 1998.

Section 1151 - General verdict

A general verdict upon a plea of not guilty is either "guilty" or "not guilty," which imports a conviction or acquittal of the offense charged in the accusatory pleading. Upon a plea of a former conviction or acquittal of the offense charged, or upon a plea of once in jeopardy, the general verdict is either "for the people" or "for the defendant." When the defendant is acquitted on the ground of a variance between the accusatory pleading and the proof, the verdict is "not guilty by reason of variance between charge and proof."

Amended by Stats. 1951, Ch. 1674.

Section 1152 - Special verdict

A special verdict is that by which the jury find the facts only, leaving the judgment to the Court. It must present the conclusions of fact as established by the evidence, and not the evidence to prove them, and these conclusions of fact must be so presented as that nothing remains to the Court but to draw conclusions of law upon them.

Enacted 1872.

Section 1153 - Requirements as to special verdict

The special verdict must be reduced to writing by the jury, or in their presence entered upon the minutes of the Court, read to the jury and agreed to by them, before they are discharged.

Enacted 1872.

Section 1154 - Sufficiency of special verdict

The special verdict need not be in any particular form, but is sufficient if it presents intelligibly the facts found by the jury.
Amended by Stats. 1987, Ch. 828, Sec. 65.

Section 1155 - Judgment upon special verdict

The court must give judgment upon the special verdict as follows:

1.If the plea is not guilty, and the facts prove the defendant guilty of the offense charged in the indictment or information, or of any other offense of which he could be convicted under that indictment or information, judgment must be given accordingly. But if otherwise, judgment of acquittal must be given.

2.If the plea is a former conviction or acquittal or once in jeopardy of the same offense, the court must give judgment of acquittal or conviction, as the facts prove or fail to prove the former conviction or acquittal or jeopardy.
Amended by Stats. 1951, Ch. 1674.

Section 1156 - Defect or insufficiency in special verdict returned

If the jury do not, in a special verdict, pronounce affirmatively or negatively on the facts necessary to enable the court to give judgment, or if they find the evidence of facts merely, and not the conclusions of fact, from the evidence, as established to their satisfaction, the court shall direct the jury to retire and return another special verdict. The court may explain to the jury the defect or insufficiency in the special verdict returned, and the form which the special verdict to be returned must take.
Amended by Stats. 1927, Ch. 602.

Section 1157 - Finding of degree of crime

Whenever a defendant is convicted of a crime or attempt to commit a crime which is distinguished into degrees, the jury, or the court if a jury trial is waived, must find the degree of the crime or attempted crime of which he is guilty. Upon the failure of the jury or the court to so determine, the degree of the crime or attempted crime of which the defendant is guilty, shall be deemed to be of the lesser degree.
Amended by Stats. 1978, Ch. 1166.

Section 1158 - Verdict or finding upon charge of previous conviction

Whenever the fact of a previous conviction of another offense is charged in an accusatory pleading, and the defendant is found guilty of the offense with which he is charged, the jury, or the judge if a jury trial is waived, must unless the answer of the defendant admits such previous conviction, find whether or not he has suffered such previous conviction. The verdict or finding upon the charge of previous conviction may be: "We (or I) find the charge of previous conviction true" or "We (or I) find the charge of previous conviction not true," according as the jury or the judge find that the defendant has or has not suffered such conviction. If more than one previous conviction is charged a separate finding must be made as to each.
Amended by Stats. 1951, Ch. 1674.

Section 1158a - Verdict of jury upon charge of being armed or using firearm

(a) Whenever the fact that a defendant was armed with a weapon either at the time of his commission of the offense or at the time of his arrest, or both, is charged in accordance with section 969c of this code, in any count of the indictment or information to which the defendant has entered a plea of not guilty, the jury, if they find a verdict of guilty of the offense with which the defendant is charged, or of any offense included therein, must also find whether or not the defendant was armed as charged in the count to which the plea of not guilty was entered. The verdict of the jury upon a charge of being armed may be: "We find the charge of being armed contained in the _____ count true," or "We find the charge of being armed contained in the _____ count not true," as they find that the defendant was or was not armed as charged in any particular count of the indictment or information. A separate verdict upon the charge of being armed must be returned for each count which alleges that the defendant was armed.

(b) Whenever the fact that a defendant used a firearm is charged in accordance with Section 969d in any count of the indictment or information to which the defendant has entered a plea of not guilty, the jury if they find a verdict of guilty of the offense with which the defendant is charged must also find whether or not the defendant used a firearm as charged in the count to which the plea of not guilty was entered. A verdict of the jury upon a charge of using a firearm may be: "We find the charge of using a firearm contained in the _____ count true," or "We find the charge of using a firearm contained in the _____ count not true," as they find that the defendant used or did not use a firearm as charged in any particular count of the indictment or information. A separate verdict upon the charge of using a firearm shall be returned for each count which alleges that defendant used a firearm.
Amended by Stats. 1972, Ch. 1131, Sec. 2.

Section 1159 - Finding of guilt of any offense, commission of which is necessarily included in that with which defendant is charged

The jury, or the judge if a jury trial is waived, may find the defendant guilty of any offense, the commission of which is necessarily included in that with which he is charged, or of an attempt to commit the offense.
Amended by Stats. 1951, Ch. 1674.

Section 1160 - Verdict as to charge against two or more defendants jointly or where two or more offenses are charged

On a charge against two or more defendants jointly, if the jury cannot agree upon a verdict as to all, they may render a verdict as to the defendant or defendants in regard to whom they do agree, on which a judgment must be entered accordingly, and the case as to the other may be tried again.

Where two or more offenses are charged in any accusatory pleading, if the jury cannot agree upon a verdict as to all of them, they may render a verdict as to the charge or charges upon which they do agree, and the charges on which they do not agree may be tried again.
Amended by Stats. 1951, Ch. 1674.

Section 1161 - Reconsideration of verdict

When there is a verdict of conviction, in which it appears to the Court that the jury have mistaken the law, the Court may explain the reason for that opinion and direct the jury to reconsider their verdict, and if, after the reconsideration, they return the same verdict, it must be entered; but when there is a verdict of acquittal, the Court cannot require the jury to reconsider it. If the jury render a verdict which is neither general nor special, the Court may direct them to reconsider it, and it cannot be recorded until it is rendered in some form from which it can be clearly understood that the intent of the jury is either to render a general verdict or to find the facts specially and to leave the judgment to the Court.

Enacted 1872.

Section 1162 - Informal verdict

If the jury persist in finding an informal verdict, from which, however, it can be clearly understood that their intention is to find in favor of the defendant upon the issue, it must be entered in the terms in which it is found, and the Court must give judgment of acquittal. But no judgment of conviction can be given unless the jury expressly find against the defendant upon the issue, or judgment is given against him on a special verdict.

Enacted 1872.

Section 1163 - Polling of jury

When a verdict is rendered, and before it is recorded, the jury may be polled, at the request of either party, in which case they must be severally asked whether it is their verdict, and if any one answer in the negative, the jury must be sent out for further deliberation.

Enacted 1872.

Section 1164 - Completion of verdict; discharge of jury

(a) When the verdict given is receivable by the court, the clerk shall record it in full upon the minutes, and if requested by any party shall read it to the jury, and inquire of them whether it is their verdict. If any juror disagrees, the fact shall be entered upon the minutes and the jury again sent out; but if no disagreement is expressed, the verdict is complete, and the jury shall, subject to subdivision (b), be discharged from the case.

(b) No jury shall be discharged until the court has verified on the record that the jury has either reached a verdict or has formally declared its inability to reach a verdict on all issues before it, including, but not limited to, the degree of the crime or crimes charged, and the truth of any alleged prior conviction whether in the same proceeding or in a bifurcated proceeding.

Amended by Stats. 1990, Ch. 800, Sec. 1.

Section 1165 - Judgment of acquittal

Where a general verdict is rendered or a finding by the court is made in favor of the defendant, except on a plea of not guilty by reason of insanity, a judgment of acquittal must be forthwith given. If such judgment is given, or a judgment imposing a fine only, without imprisonment for nonpayment is given, and the defendant is not detained for any other legal cause, he must be discharged, if in custody, as soon as the judgment is given, except that where the acquittal is because of a variance between the pleading and the proof which may be obviated by a new accusatory pleading, the court may order his detention, to the end that a new accusatory pleading may be preferred, in the same manner and with like effect as provided in Section 1117.

Amended by Stats. 1951, Ch. 1674.

Section 1166 - General verdict rendered against defendant or special verdict given

(a) Except as provided in subdivision (b), if a general verdict is rendered against the defendant, or a special verdict is given, they shall be remanded, if in custody, or if on bail they shall be committed to the proper officer of the county to await the judgment of the court upon the verdict, unless, upon considering the protection of the public, the seriousness of the offense charged and proven, the previous criminal record of the defendant, the probability of the defendant failing to appear for the judgment of the court upon the verdict, and public safety, the court concludes the evidence supports its decision to allow the defendant to remain out on bail.

(b) The judicial officer shall order that a person who has been found guilty of an offense punishable by life in prison without the possibility of parole or death, and is awaiting imposition or execution of sentence, be remanded.

(c) When a defendant is committed or remanded pursuant to this section, their bail is exonerated, or if money is deposited instead of bail, it shall be refunded to the defendant or to the person who deposited money on behalf of the defendant.

Amended by Stats 2023 ch 545 (AB 791),s 1, eff. 1/1/2024.

EFFECTIVE 1/1/2000. Amended September 29, 1999 (Bill Number: AB 476) (Chapter 570).

Section 1167 - Announcement of findings by judge when jury trial is waived

When a jury trial is waived, the judge or justice before whom the trial is had shall, at the conclusion thereof, announce his findings upon the issues of fact, which shall be in substantially the form prescribed for the general verdict of a jury and shall be entered upon the minutes.

Added by Stats. 1951, Ch. 1674.

Section 1168 - Sentencing

(a) Every person who commits a public offense, for which any specification of three time periods of imprisonment in any state prison or imprisonment pursuant to subdivision (h) of Section 1170 is now prescribed by law or for which only a single term of imprisonment in state prison or imprisonment pursuant to subdivision (h) of Section 1170 is specified shall, unless such convicted person be placed on probation, a new trial granted, or the imposing of sentence suspended, be sentenced pursuant to Chapter 4.5 (commencing with Section 1170) of Title 7 of Part 2.

(b) For any person not sentenced under such provision, but who is sentenced to be imprisoned in the state prison or imprisonment pursuant to subdivision (h) of Section 1170, including imprisonment not exceeding one year and one day, the court imposing the sentence shall not fix the term or duration of the period of imprisonment.

Amended by Stats 2011 ch 39 (AB 117),s 68, eff. 6/30/2011.

Amended by Stats 2011 ch 15 (AB 109),s 449, eff. 4/4/2011, but operative no earlier than October 1, 2011, and only upon creation of a community corrections grant program to assist in implementing this act and upon an appropriation to fund the grant program.

Chapter 4.5 - TRIAL COURT SENTENCING

Article 1 - INITIAL SENTENCING

Section 1170 - Legislative findings and declarations; sentence choice; recall

(a)

(1) The Legislature finds and declares that the purpose of sentencing is public safety achieved through punishment, rehabilitation, and restorative justice. When a sentence includes incarceration, the deprivation of liberty satisfies the punishment purpose of sentencing. The purpose of incarceration is rehabilitation and successful community reintegration achieved through education, treatment, and active participation in rehabilitative and restorative justice programs. This purpose is best served by terms that are proportionate to the seriousness of the offense with provision for uniformity in the sentences of people incarcerated for committing the same offense under similar circumstances.

(2) The Legislature further finds and declares that programs should be available for incarcerated persons, including, but not limited to, educational, rehabilitative, and restorative justice programs that are designed to promote behavioral change and to prepare all incarcerated persons for successful reentry into the community. The Legislature encourages the development of policies and programs designed to educate and rehabilitate all incarcerated persons. In implementing this section, the Department of Corrections and Rehabilitation is encouraged to allow all incarcerated persons the opportunity to enroll in programs that promote successful return to the community. The Legislature finds and declares that community-based organizations are an integral part of achieving the state's objective of ensuring that all people incarcerated in a state prison have access to rehabilitative programs. The Department of Corrections and Rehabilitation is directed to maintain a mission statement consistent with these principles and shall facilitate access for community-based programs in order to meaningfully effectuate the principles set forth in this section.

(3) In any case in which the sentence prescribed by statute for a person convicted of a public offense is a term of imprisonment in the state prison, or a term pursuant to subdivision (h), of any specification of three time periods, the court shall sentence the defendant to one of the terms of imprisonment specified unless the convicted person is given any other disposition provided by law, including a fine, jail, probation, or the suspension of imposition or execution of sentence or is sentenced pursuant to subdivision (b) of Section 1168 because they had committed their crime prior to July 1, 1977. In sentencing the convicted person, the court shall apply the sentencing rules of the Judicial Council. The court, unless it determines that there are circumstances in mitigation of the sentence prescribed, shall also impose any other term that it is required by law to impose as an additional term. Nothing in this article shall affect any provision of law that imposes the death penalty, that authorizes or restricts the granting of probation or suspending the execution or imposition of sentence, or expressly provides for imprisonment in the state prison for life, except as provided in subdivision (d). In any case in which the amount of preimprisonment credit under Section 2900.5 or any other provision of law is equal to or exceeds any sentence imposed pursuant to this chapter, except for a remaining portion of mandatory supervision imposed pursuant to subparagraph (B) of paragraph (5) of subdivision (h), the entire sentence shall be deemed to have been served, except for the remaining period of mandatory supervision, and the defendant shall not be actually delivered to the custody of the secretary or the county correctional administrator. The court shall advise the defendant that they shall serve an applicable period of parole, postrelease community supervision, or mandatory supervision and order the defendant to report to the parole or probation office closest to the defendant's last legal residence, unless the in-custody credits equal the total sentence, including both confinement time and the period of parole, postrelease community supervision, or mandatory supervision. The sentence shall be deemed a separate prior prison term or a sentence of imprisonment in a county jail under subdivision (h) for purposes of Section 667.5, and a copy of the judgment and other necessary documentation shall be forwarded to the secretary.

(b)

(1) When a judgment of imprisonment is to be imposed and the statute specifies three possible terms, the court shall, in its sound discretion, order imposition of a sentence not to exceed the middle term, except as otherwise provided in paragraph (2).

(2) The court may impose a sentence exceeding the middle term only when there are circumstances in aggravation of the crime that justify the imposition of a term of imprisonment exceeding the middle term and the facts underlying those circumstances have been stipulated to by the defendant or have been found true beyond a reasonable doubt at trial by the jury or by the judge in a court trial. Except where evidence supporting an aggravating circumstance is admissible to prove or defend against the charged offense or enhancement at trial, or it is otherwise authorized by law, upon request of a defendant, trial on the circumstances in aggravation alleged in the indictment or information shall be bifurcated from the trial of charges and enhancements. The jury shall not be informed of the bifurcated allegations until there has been a conviction of a felony offense.

(3) Notwithstanding paragraphs (1) and (2), the court may consider the defendant's prior convictions in determining sentencing based on a certified record of conviction without submitting the prior convictions to a jury. This paragraph does not apply to enhancements imposed on prior convictions.

(4) At least four days prior to the time set for imposition of judgment, either party or the victim, or the family of the victim if the victim is deceased, may submit a statement in aggravation or mitigation to dispute facts in the record or the probation officer's report or to present additional facts. The court may consider the record in the case, the probation officer's report, other reports, including reports received pursuant to Section 1203.03, and statements in aggravation or mitigation submitted by the prosecution, the defendant, or the victim, or the family of the victim if the victim is deceased, and any further evidence introduced at the sentencing hearing.

(5) The court shall set forth on the record the facts and reasons for choosing the sentence imposed. The court may not impose an upper term by using the fact of any enhancement upon which sentence is imposed under any provision of law. A term of imprisonment shall not be specified if imposition of sentence is suspended.

(6) Notwithstanding paragraph (1), and unless the court finds that the aggravating circumstances outweigh the mitigating circumstances that imposition of the lower term would be contrary to the interests of justice, the court shall order imposition of the lower term if any of the following was a contributing factor in the commission of the offense:

(A) The person has experienced psychological, physical, or childhood trauma, including, but not limited to, abuse, neglect, exploitation, or sexual violence.

(B) The person is a youth or was a youth as defined under subdivision (b) of Section 1016.7 at the time of the commission of the offense.

(C) Prior to the instant offense, or at the time of the commission of the offense, the person is or was a victim of intimate partner violence or human trafficking.

(7) Paragraph (6) does not preclude the court from imposing the lower term even if there is no evidence of those circumstances listed in paragraph (6) present.

(c) The court shall state the reasons for its sentence choice on the record at the time of sentencing. The court shall also inform the defendant that as part of the sentence after expiration of the term they may be on parole for a period as provided in Section 3000 or 3000.08 or postrelease community supervision for a period as provided in Section 3451.

(d)

   (1)

      (A) When a defendant who was under 18 years of age at the time of the commission of the offense for which the defendant was sentenced to imprisonment for life without the possibility of parole has been incarcerated for at least 15 years, the defendant may submit to the sentencing court a petition for recall and resentencing.

      (B) Notwithstanding subparagraph (A), this paragraph shall not apply to defendants sentenced to life without parole for an offense where it was pled and proved that the defendant tortured, as described in Section 206, their victim or the victim was a public safety official, including any law enforcement personnel mentioned in Chapter 4.5 (commencing with Section 830) of Title 3, or any firefighter as described in Section 245.1, as well as any other officer in any segment of law enforcement who is employed by the federal government, the state, or any of its political subdivisions.

   (2) The defendant shall file the original petition with the sentencing court. A copy of the petition shall be served on the agency that prosecuted the case. The petition shall include the defendant's statement that the defendant was under 18 years of age at the time of the crime and was sentenced to life in prison without the possibility of parole, the defendant's statement describing their remorse and work towards rehabilitation, and the defendant's statement that one of the following is true:

      (A) The defendant was convicted pursuant to felony murder or aiding and abetting murder provisions of law.

      (B) The defendant does not have juvenile felony adjudications for assault or other felony crimes with a significant potential for personal harm to victims prior to the offense for which the sentence is being considered for recall.

      (C) The defendant committed the offense with at least one adult codefendant.

      (D) The defendant has performed acts that tend to indicate rehabilitation or the potential for rehabilitation, including, but not limited to, availing themselves of rehabilitative, educational, or vocational programs, if those programs have been available at their classification level and facility, using self-study for self-improvement, or showing evidence of remorse.

   (3) If any of the information required in paragraph (2) is missing from the petition, or if proof of service on the prosecuting agency is not provided, the court shall return the petition to the defendant and advise the defendant that the matter cannot be considered without the missing information.

   (4) A reply to the petition, if any, shall be filed with the court within 60 days of the date on which the prosecuting agency was served with the petition unless a continuance is granted for good cause.

   (5) If the court finds by a preponderance of the evidence that one or more of the statements specified in subparagraphs (A) to (D), inclusive, of paragraph (2) is true, the court shall recall the sentence and commitment previously ordered and hold a hearing to resentence the defendant in the same manner as if the defendant had not previously been sentenced, provided that the new sentence, if any, is not greater than the initial sentence. Victims, or victim family members if the victim is deceased, shall retain the rights to participate in the hearing.

   (6) The factors that the court may consider when determining whether to resentence the defendant to a term of imprisonment with the possibility of parole include, but are not limited to, the following:

      (A) The defendant was convicted pursuant to felony murder or aiding and abetting murder provisions of law.

      (B) The defendant does not have juvenile felony adjudications for assault or other felony crimes with a significant potential for personal harm to victims prior to the offense for which the defendant was sentenced to life without the possibility of parole.

      (C) The defendant committed the offense with at least one adult codefendant.

      (D) Prior to the offense for which the defendant was sentenced to life without the possibility of parole, the defendant had insufficient adult support or supervision and had suffered from psychological or physical trauma or significant stress.

      (E) The defendant suffers from cognitive limitations due to mental illness, developmental disabilities, or other factors that did not constitute a defense but influenced the defendant's involvement in the offense.

      (F) The defendant has performed acts that tend to indicate rehabilitation or the potential for rehabilitation, including, but not limited to, availing themselves of rehabilitative, educational, or vocational programs, if those programs have been available at their classification level and facility, using self-study for self-improvement, or showing evidence of remorse.

      (G) The defendant has maintained family ties or connections with others through letter writing, calls, or visits or has eliminated contact with individuals outside of prison who are currently involved with crime.

      (H) The defendant has had no disciplinary actions for violent activities in the last five years in which the defendant was determined to be the aggressor.

   (7) The court shall have the discretion to resentence the defendant in the same manner as if the defendant had not previously been sentenced, provided that the new sentence, if any, is not greater than the initial sentence. The discretion of the court shall be exercised in consideration of the criteria in paragraph (6). Victims, or victim family members if the victim is deceased, shall be notified of the resentencing hearing and shall retain their rights to participate in the hearing.

   (8) Notwithstanding paragraph (7), the court may also resentence the defendant to a term that is less than the initial sentence if any of the following were a contributing factor in the commission of the alleged offense:

      (A) The person has experienced psychological, physical, or childhood trauma, including, but not limited to, abuse, neglect, exploitation, or sexual violence.

      (B) The person is a youth or was a youth as defined under subdivision (b) of Section 1016.7 at the time of the commission of the offense.

      (C) Prior to the instant offense, or at the time of the commission of the offense, the person is or was a victim of intimate partner violence or human trafficking.

(9) Paragraph (8) does not prohibit the court from resentencing the defendant to a term that is less than the initial sentence, even if none of the circumstances listed in paragraph (8) are present.

(10) If the sentence is not recalled or the defendant is resentenced to imprisonment for life without the possibility of parole, the defendant may submit another petition for recall and resentencing to the sentencing court when the defendant has been committed to the custody of the department for at least 20 years. If the sentence is not recalled or the defendant is resentenced to imprisonment for life without the possibility of parole under that petition, the defendant may file another petition after having served 24 years. The final petition may be submitted, and the response to that petition shall be determined, during the 25th year of the defendant's sentence.

(11) In addition to the criteria in paragraph (6), the court may consider any other criteria that the court deems relevant to its decision, so long as the court identifies them on the record, provides a statement of reasons for adopting them, and states why the defendant does or does not satisfy the criteria.

(12) This subdivision shall have retroactive application.

(13) Nothing in this paragraph is intended to diminish or abrogate any rights or remedies otherwise available to the defendant.

(e) Notwithstanding subdivision (a), the court may recall and resentence an incarcerated person pursuant to the compassionate release program set forth in Section 1172.2.

(f) Notwithstanding any other provision of this section, for purposes of paragraph (3) of subdivision (h), an allegation that a defendant is eligible for state prison due to a prior or current conviction, sentence enhancement, or because the defendant is required to register as a sex offender shall not be subject to dismissal pursuant to Section 1385.

(g) A sentence to the state prison for a determinate term for which only one term is specified is a sentence to state prison under this section.

(h)

(1) Except as provided in paragraph (3), a felony punishable pursuant to this subdivision where the term is not specified in the underlying offense shall be punishable by a term of imprisonment in a county jail for 16 months, or two or three years.

(2) Except as provided in paragraph (3), a felony punishable pursuant to this subdivision shall be punishable by imprisonment in a county jail for the term described in the underlying offense.

(3) Notwithstanding paragraphs (1) and (2), where the defendant (A) has a prior or current felony conviction for a serious felony described in subdivision (c) of Section 1192.7 or a prior or current conviction for a violent felony described in subdivision (c) of Section 667.5, (B) has a prior felony conviction in another jurisdiction for an offense that has all the elements of a serious felony described in subdivision (c) of Section 1192.7 or a violent felony described in subdivision (c) of Section 667.5, (C) is required to register as a sex offender pursuant to Chapter 5.5 (commencing with Section 290) of Title 9 of Part 1, or (D) is convicted of a crime and as part of the sentence an enhancement pursuant to Section 186.11 is imposed, an executed sentence for a felony punishable pursuant to this subdivision shall be served in the state prison.

(4) Nothing in this subdivision shall be construed to prevent other dispositions authorized by law, including pretrial diversion, deferred entry of judgment, or an order granting probation pursuant to Section 1203.1.

(5)

(A) Unless the court finds, in the interest of justice, that it is not appropriate in a particular case, the court, when imposing a sentence pursuant to paragraph (1) or (2), shall suspend execution of a concluding portion of the term for a period selected at the court's discretion.

(B) The portion of a defendant's sentenced term that is suspended pursuant to this paragraph shall be known as mandatory supervision, and, unless otherwise ordered by the court, shall commence upon release from physical custody or an alternative custody program, whichever is later. During the period of mandatory supervision, the defendant shall be supervised by the county probation officer in accordance with the terms, conditions, and procedures generally applicable to persons placed on probation for the remaining unserved portion of the sentence imposed by the court. The period of supervision shall be mandatory and may not be earlier terminated, except by court order. Any proceeding to revoke or modify mandatory supervision under this subparagraph shall be conducted pursuant to either subdivisions (a) and (b) of Section 1203.2 or Section 1203.3. During the period when the defendant is under that supervision, unless in actual custody related to the sentence imposed by the court, the defendant shall be entitled to only actual time credit against the term of imprisonment imposed by the court. Any time period that is suspended because a person has absconded shall not be credited toward the period of supervision. A defendant who is subject to search or seizure as part of the terms and conditions of mandatory supervision, is subject to search or seizure only by a probation officer or other peace officer.

(6) When the court is imposing a judgment pursuant to this subdivision concurrent or consecutive to a judgment or judgments previously imposed pursuant to this subdivision in another county or counties, the court rendering the second or other subsequent judgment shall determine the county or counties of incarceration and supervision of the defendant.

(7) The sentencing changes made by the act that added this subdivision shall be applied prospectively to any person sentenced on or after October 1, 2011.

(8) The sentencing changes made to paragraph (5) by the act that added this paragraph shall become effective and operative on January 1, 2015, and shall be applied prospectively to any person sentenced on or after January 1, 2015.

(9) Notwithstanding the separate punishment for any enhancement, any enhancement shall be punishable in a county jail or state prison as required by the underlying offense and not as would be required by the enhancement. The intent of the Legislature in enacting this paragraph is to abrogate the holding in People v. Vega (2014) 222 Cal.App.4th 1374, that if an enhancement specifies service of sentence in state prison, the entire sentence is served in state prison, even if the punishment for the underlying offense is a term of imprisonment in the county jail.

Amended by Stats 2023 ch 560 (AB 1104),s 2.5, eff. 1/1/2024.
Amended by Stats 2023 ch 218 (SB 852),s 3, eff. 1/1/2024.
Amended by Stats 2023 ch 131 (AB 1754),s 155, eff. 1/1/2024.
Amended by Stats 2022 ch 744 (AB 960),s 1, eff. 1/1/2023.
Amended by Stats 2021 ch 731 (SB 567),s 1.3, eff. 1/1/2022.

Amended by Stats 2021 ch 719 (AB 1540),s 2, eff. 1/1/2022.
Amended by Stats 2021 ch 695 (AB 124),s 5, eff. 1/1/2022.
Amended by Stats 2020 ch 29 (SB 118),s 15, eff. 8/6/2020.
Amended by Stats 2018 ch 1001 (AB 2942),s 2, eff. 1/1/2019.
Amended by Stats 2018 ch 36 (AB 1812),s 18, eff. 6/27/2018.
Amended by Stats 2017 ch 287 (SB 670),s 2, eff. 1/1/2018.
Amended by Stats 2017 ch 561 (AB 1516),s 188, eff. 1/1/2018.
Amended by Stats 2016 ch 887 (SB 1016),s 6.3, eff. 1/1/2017.
Amended by Stats 2016 ch 867 (SB 1084),s 2.1, eff. 1/1/2017.
Amended by Stats 2016 ch 696 (AB 2590),s 1, eff. 1/1/2017.
Amended by Stats 2015 ch 378 (AB 1156),s 2, eff. 1/1/2016.
Amended by Stats 2014 ch 612 (AB 2499),s 2, eff. 1/1/2015.
Amended by Stats 2014 ch 26 (AB 1468),s 17, eff. 6/20/2014.
Amended by Stats 2013 ch 508 (SB 463),s 6, eff. 1/1/2014.
Amended by Stats 2013 ch 76 (AB 383),s 152, eff. 1/1/2014.
Amended by Stats 2013 ch 32 (SB 76),s 6, eff. 6/27/2013.
Amended by Stats 2012 ch 828 (SB 9),s 2, eff. 1/1/2013.
Amended by Stats 2012 ch 43 (SB 1023),s 28, eff. 6/27/2012.
Amended by Stats 2011 ch 361 (SB 576),s 7.7, eff. 9/29/2011.
Amended by Stats 2011 ch 12 (AB X1-17),s 12.4, eff. 9/20/2011, op. 10/1/2011.
Amended by Stats 2011 ch 136 (AB 116),s 4, eff. 7/27/2011.
Amended by Stats 2011 ch 39 (AB 117),s 68, eff. 6/30/2011.
Amended by Stats 2011 ch 39 (AB 117),s 28, eff. 6/30/2011.
Amended by Stats 2011 ch 15 (AB 109),s 451, eff. 4/4/2011, but operative no earlier than October 1, 2011, and only upon creation of a community corrections grant program to assist in implementing this act and upon an appropriation to fund the grant program.
Amended by Stats 2010 ch 256 (AB 2263),s 6, eff. 1/1/2011.
Amended by Stats 2010 ch 328 (SB 1330),s 162, eff. 1/1/2011.
Amended by Stats 2008 ch 416 (SB 1701),s 2, eff. 1/1/2009.
Amended by Stats 2007 ch 740 (AB 1539),s 2, eff. 1/1/2008.
Amended by Stats 2007 ch 3 (SB 40),s 3, eff. 3/30/2007.
Amended by Stats 2007 ch 3 (SB 40),s 2, eff. 3/30/2007.
Amended by Stats 2004 ch 747 (AB 854), s 1, eff. 1/1/2005.
This act (Stats 2023 ch 218 (SB 852)) shall be known, and may be cited, as the Prohibiting Rogue Officer Tricks and Ensuring Community Trust (PROTECT) Act.

Section 1170.01 - [Renumbered as 1172]

Renumbered as Ca. Pen. Code §1172 by Stats 2022 ch 58 (AB 200),s 8, eff. 6/30/2022.
Added by Stats 2021 ch 80 (AB 145),s 3, eff. 7/16/2021.

Section 1170.02 - Exemption from medical parole and compassionate release eligibility

A prisoner is not eligible for resentence or recall pursuant to Section 1172.2 if they were convicted of first-degree murder, if the victim was a peace officer, as defined in Section 830.1, 830.2, 830.3, 830.31, 830.32, 830.33, 830.34, 830.35, 830.36, 830.37, 830.4, 830.5, 830.6, 830.10, 830.11, or 830.12, who was killed while engaged in the performance of their duties, and the individual knew, or reasonably should have known, that the victim was a peace officer engaged in the performance of their duties, or the victim was a peace officer or a former peace officer under any of the above-enumerated sections and was intentionally killed in retaliation for the performance of their official duties.
Amended by Stats 2023 ch 131 (AB 1754),s 156, eff. 1/1/2024.
Amended by Stats 2022 ch 744 (AB 960),s 2, eff. 1/1/2023.
Added by Stats 2016 ch 886 (SB 6),s 1, eff. 1/1/2017.

Section 1170.03 - [Renumbered as 1172.1]

Renumbered as Ca. Pen. Code §1172.1 by Stats 2022 ch 58 (AB 200),s 9, eff. 6/30/2022.
Added by Stats 2021 ch 719 (AB 1540),s 3.1, eff. 1/1/2022.

Section 1170.05 - Alternative custody program for inmates

(a) Notwithstanding any other law, the Secretary of the Department of Corrections and Rehabilitation may offer a program under which inmates, as specified in subdivision (c), who are not precluded by subdivision (d), and who have been committed to state prison may be allowed to participate in a voluntary alternative custody program as defined in subdivision (b) in lieu of their confinement in state prison. In order to qualify for the program an offender need not be confined in an institution under the jurisdiction of the Department of Corrections and Rehabilitation. Under this program, one day of participation in an alternative custody program shall be in lieu of one day of incarceration in the state prison. Participants in the program shall receive any sentence reduction credits that they would have received had they served their sentence in the state prison, and shall be subject to denial and loss of credit pursuant to subdivision (a) of Section 2932. The department may enter into contracts with county agencies, not-for-profit organizations, for-profit organizations, and others in order to promote alternative custody placements.

(b) As used in this section, an alternative custody program shall include, but not be limited to, the following:

    (1) Confinement to a residential home during the hours designated by the department.

    (2) Confinement to a residential drug or treatment program during the hours designated by the department.

    (3) Confinement to a transitional care facility that offers appropriate services.

(c) Except as provided by subdivision (d), only inmates sentenced to state prison for a determinate term of imprisonment pursuant to Section 1170 are eligible to participate in the alternative custody program authorized by this section.

(d) An inmate committed to the state prison who meets any of the following criteria is not eligible to participate in the alternative custody program:

(1) The person has a current conviction for a violent felony as defined in Section 667.5.

(2) The person has a current conviction for a serious felony as defined in Sections 1192.7 and 1192.8.

(3) The person has a current or prior conviction for an offense that requires the person to register as a sex offender as provided in Chapter 5.5 (commencing with Section 290) of Title 9 of Part 1.

(4) The person was screened by the department using a validated risk assessment tool and determined to pose a high risk to commit a violent offense.

(5) The person has a history, within the last 10 years, of escape from a facility while under juvenile or adult custody, including, but not limited to, any detention facility, camp, jail, or state prison facility.

(e) An alternative custody program shall include the use of electronic monitoring, global positioning system devices, or other supervising devices for the purpose of helping to verify a participant's compliance with the rules and regulations of the program. The devices shall not be used to eavesdrop or record any conversation, except a conversation between the participant and the person supervising the participant, in which case the recording of such a conversation is to be used solely for the purposes of voice identification.

(f)

(1) In order to implement alternative custody for the population specified in subdivision (c), the department shall create, and the participant shall agree to and fully participate in, an individualized treatment and rehabilitation plan. When available and appropriate for the individualized treatment and rehabilitation plan, the department shall prioritize the use of evidence-based programs and services that will aid in the successful reentry into society while the participant takes part in alternative custody. Case management services shall be provided to support rehabilitation and to track the progress and individualized treatment plan compliance of the inmate.

(2) For purposes of this section, "evidence-based practices" means supervision policies, procedures, programs, and practices demonstrated by scientific research to reduce recidivism among individuals under probation, parole, or postrelease community supervision.

(g) The secretary shall prescribe reasonable rules and regulations under which the alternative custody program shall operate. The department shall adopt regulations necessary to effectuate this section, including emergency regulations as provided under Section 5058.3 and adopted pursuant to the Administrative Procedure Act (Chapter 3.5 (commencing with Section 11340) of Part 1 of Division 3 of Title 2 of the Government Code). The participant shall be informed in writing that compliance with the rules and regulations of the program is required, including, but not limited to, the following rules:

(1) The participant shall remain within the interior premises of the participant's residence during the hours designated by the secretary or the secretary's designee.

(2) The participant shall be subject to search and seizure by a peace officer at any time of the day or night, with or without cause. In addition, the participant shall admit any peace officer designated by the secretary or the secretary's designee into the participant's residence at any time for purposes of verifying the participant's compliance with the conditions of detention. Prior to participation in the alternative custody program, all participants shall agree, in writing, to these terms and conditions.

(3) The secretary or the secretary's designee may immediately retake the participant into custody to serve the balance of the participant's sentence if the electronic monitoring or supervising devices are unable for any reason to properly perform their function at the designated place of detention, if the participant fails to remain within the place of detention as stipulated in the agreement, or if the participant for any other reason no longer meets the established criteria under this section.

(h) Whenever a peace officer supervising a participant has reasonable suspicion to believe that the participant is not complying with the rules or conditions of the program, or that the electronic monitoring devices are unable to function properly in the designated place of confinement, the peace officer may, under general or specific authorization of the secretary or the secretary's designee, and without a warrant of arrest, retake the participant into custody to complete the remainder of the original sentence.

(i) This section does not require the secretary or the secretary's designee to allow an inmate to participate in this program if it appears from the record that the inmate has not satisfactorily complied with reasonable rules and regulations while in custody. An inmate is eligible for participation in an alternative custody program only if the secretary or the secretary's designee concludes that the inmate meets the criteria for program participation established under this section and that the inmate's participation is consistent with any reasonable rules and regulations prescribed by the secretary.

(1) The rules and regulations and administrative policies of the program shall be written and shall be given or made available to the participant upon assignment to the alternative custody program.

(2) The secretary or the secretary's designee shall have the sole discretion concerning whether to permit program participation as an alternative to custody in state prison. A risk and needs assessment shall be completed on each inmate to assist in the determination of eligibility for participation and the type of alternative custody.

(3) An inmate's existing psychiatric or medical condition that requires ongoing care is not a basis for excluding the inmate from eligibility to participate in an alternative custody program authorized by this section.

(j) The secretary or the secretary's designee shall establish a timeline for the application process. The secretary or the secretary's designee shall respond to an applicant within two weeks of receiving the application to inform the inmate that the application was received, and to notify the inmate of the eligibility criteria of the program. The secretary or the secretary's designee shall provide a written notice to the inmate of acceptance or denial into the program. The individualized treatment and rehabilitation plan described in subdivision (f) shall be developed, in consultation with the inmate, after the applicant has been found potentially eligible for participation in the program and no later than 30 calendar days after the potential eligibility determination. Except as necessary to comply with any release notification requirements, the inmate shall be released to the program no later than seven business days following notice of acceptance into the program or, if this is not possible in the case of an inmate to be placed in a residential drug or treatment program or in a transitional care facility, the first day a contracted bed becomes available at the requested location. If the inmate is denied participation in the program, the notice of denial shall specify the reason the inmate was denied. The secretary or the secretary's designee shall maintain a record of the application and notice of denials for participation. The inmate may appeal the decision through normal grievance procedures or reapply for participation in the program 30 days after the notice of the denial.

(k) The secretary or the secretary's designee shall permit program participants to seek and retain employment in the community, attend psychological counseling sessions or educational or vocational training classes, participate in life skills or parenting training, utilize substance abuse treatment services, or seek medical and dental assistance based upon the participant's individualized treatment and release plan. Participation in other rehabilitative services and programs may be approved by the case manager if it is specified as a requirement of the inmate's individualized treatment and rehabilitative case plan. Willful failure of the program participant to return to the place of detention not later than the expiration of any period of time during which the participant is authorized to be away from the place of detention pursuant to this section, unauthorized departures from the place of detention, or tampering with or disabling, or attempting to tamper with or disable, an electronic monitoring device shall subject the participant to a return to custody pursuant to subdivisions (g) and (h). In addition, participants may be subject to forfeiture of credits pursuant to the provisions of Section 2932, or to discipline for violation of rules established by the secretary.

(l)

(1) Notwithstanding any other law, the secretary or the secretary's designee shall provide the information specified in paragraph (2) regarding participants in an alternative custody program to the law enforcement agencies of the jurisdiction in which persons participating in an alternative custody program reside.

(2) The information required by paragraph (1) shall consist of the following:

(A) The participant's name, address, and date of birth.

(B) The offense committed by the participant.

(C) The period of time the participant will be subject to an alternative custody program.

(3) The information received by a law enforcement agency pursuant to this subdivision may be used for the purpose of monitoring the impact of an alternative custody program on the community.

(m) It is the intent of the Legislature that the alternative custody program established under this section maintain the highest public confidence, credibility, and public safety. In the furtherance of these standards, the secretary may administer an alternative custody program pursuant to written contracts with appropriate public agencies or entities to provide specified program services. A public agency or entity entering into a contract may not itself employ a person who is in an alternative custody program. The department shall determine the recidivism rate of each participant in an alternative custody program.

(n) An inmate participating in this program shall voluntarily agree to all of the provisions of the program in writing, including that the inmate may be returned to confinement at any time with or without cause, and shall not be charged fees or costs for the program.

(o)

(1) The secretary or the secretary's designee shall assist an individual participating in the alternative custody program in obtaining health care coverage, including, but not limited to, assistance with having suspended Medi-Cal benefits reinstated, applying for Medi-Cal benefits, or obtaining health care coverage under a private health plan or policy.

(2) To the extent not covered by a participant's health care coverage, the state shall retain responsibility for the medical, dental, and mental health needs of individuals participating in the alternative custody program.

(p) The secretary shall adopt emergency regulations specifically governing participants in this program.

(q) If a phrase, clause, sentence, or provision of this section or application thereof to a person or circumstance is held invalid, that invalidity shall not affect any other phrase, clause, sentence, or provision or application of this section that can be given effect without the invalid phrase, clause, sentence, or provision or application and to this end the provisions of this section are declared to be severable.

Amended by Stats 2019 ch 256 (SB 781),s 11, eff. 1/1/2020.

Amended by Stats 2015 ch 762 (SB 219),s 1, eff. 1/1/2016.

Amended by Stats 2012 ch 41 (SB 1021),s 62, eff. 6/27/2012.

Added by Stats 2010 ch 644 (SB 1266),s 2, eff. 1/1/2011.

Section 1170.06 - Voluntary alternative custody programs

(a) Notwithstanding any other law, a sheriff or a county director of corrections is authorized to offer a program under which inmates as specified in subdivision (c), who are not precluded by subdivision (d), and who have been committed to a county jail may be allowed to participate in a voluntary alternative custody program as defined in subdivision (b) in lieu of their confinement in a county jail. Under this program, one day of participation is in lieu of one day of incarceration in a county jail. Participants in the program shall receive any sentence reduction credits that they would have received had they served their sentence in a county jail, and are subject to denial and loss of credit pursuant to subdivision (d) of Section 4019. The sheriff or the county director of corrections may enter into contracts with county agencies, not-for-profit organizations, for-profit organizations, and others in order to promote alternative custody placements.

(b) As used in this section, an alternative custody program shall include, but is not limited to, the following:

(1) Confinement to a residential home during the hours designated by the sheriff or the county director of corrections.

(2) Confinement to a residential drug or treatment program during the hours designated by the county sheriff or the county director of corrections.

(3) Confinement to a transitional care facility that offers appropriate services.

(4) Confinement to a mental health clinic or hospital that offers appropriate mental health services.

(c) Except as provided by subdivision (d), inmates sentenced to a county jail for a determinate term of imprisonment pursuant to a misdemeanor or a felony pursuant to subdivision (h) of Section 1170, and only those persons, are eligible to participate in the alternative custody program authorized by this section.

(d) An inmate committed to a county jail who meets any of the following criteria is not eligible to participate in the alternative custody program:

587

(1) The person was screened by the sheriff or the county director of corrections using a validated risk assessment tool and determined to pose a high risk to commit a violent offense.

(2) The person has a history, within the last 10 years, of escape from a facility while under juvenile or adult custody, including, but not limited to, any detention facility, camp, jail, or state prison facility.

(3) The person has a current or prior conviction for an offense that requires the person to register as a sex offender as provided in Chapter 5.5. (commencing with Section 290) of Title 9 of Part 1.

(e) An alternative custody program may include the use of electronic monitoring, global positioning system devices, or other supervising devices for the purpose of helping to verify a participant's compliance with the rules and regulations of the program. The devices shall not be used to eavesdrop or record any conversation, except a conversation between the participant and the person supervising the participant, in which case the recording of the conversation is to be used solely for the purposes of voice identification.

(f)

(1) In order to implement alternative custody for the population specified in subdivision (c), the sheriff or the county director of corrections shall create, and the participant shall agree to and fully participate in, an individualized treatment and rehabilitation plan. When available and appropriate for the individualized treatment and rehabilitation plan, the sheriff or the county director of corrections shall prioritize the use of evidence-based programs and services that will aid in the participant's successful reentry into society while he or she takes part in alternative custody. Case management services shall be provided to support rehabilitation and to track the progress and individualized treatment plan compliance of the inmate.

(2) For purposes of this section, "evidence-based practices" means supervision policies, procedures, programs, and practices demonstrated by scientific research to reduce recidivism among individuals under probation, parole, or postrelease community supervision.

(g) The sheriff or the county director of corrections shall prescribe reasonable rules to govern the operation of the alternative custody program. Each participant shall be informed in writing that he or she is required to comply with the rules of the program, including, but not limited to, the following rules:

(1) The participant shall remain within the interior premises of his or her residence during the hours designated by the sheriff or his or her designee or the county director of corrections or his or her designee.

(2) The participant shall be subject to search and seizure by a peace officer at any time of the day or night, with or without cause. In addition, the participant shall admit any peace officer designated by the sheriff or his or her designee or the county director of corrections or his or her designee into the participant's residence at any time for purposes of verifying the participant's compliance with the conditions of his or her detention. Prior to participation in the alternative custody program, each participant shall agree in writing to these terms and conditions.

(3) The sheriff or his or her designee, or the county director of corrections or his or her designee, may immediately retake the participant into custody to serve the balance of his or her sentence if an electronic monitoring or supervising device is unable for any reason to properly perform its function at the designated place of detention, if the participant fails to remain within the place of detention as stipulated in the agreement, or if the participant for any other reason no longer meets the criteria under this section.

(h) Whenever a peace officer supervising a participant has reasonable suspicion to believe that the participant is not complying with the rules or conditions of the program, or that a required electronic monitoring device is unable to function properly in the designated place of confinement, the peace officer may, under general or specific authorization of the sheriff or his or her designee, or the county director of corrections or his or her designee, and without a warrant of arrest, retake the participant into custody to complete the remainder of the original sentence.

(i) This section shall not be construed to require a sheriff or his or her designee, or a county director of corrections or his or her designee, to allow an inmate to participate in this program if it appears from the record that the inmate has not satisfactorily complied with reasonable rules and regulations while in custody. An inmate shall be eligible for participation in an alternative custody program only if the sheriff or his or her designee or the county director of corrections or his or her designee concludes that the inmate meets the criteria for program participation established under this section and that the inmate's participation is consistent with any reasonable rules prescribed by the sheriff or the county director of corrections.

(1) The rules and administrative policies of the program shall be written and shall be given or made available to each participant upon assignment to the alternative custody program.

(2) The sheriff or his or her designee or the county director of corrections or his or her designee shall have the sole discretion concerning whether to permit program participation as an alternative to custody in a county jail. A risk and needs assessment shall be completed on each inmate to assist in the determination of eligibility for participation and the type of alternative custody.

(j)

(1) The sheriff or his or her designee or the county director of corrections or his or her designee shall permit program participants to seek and retain employment in the community, attend psychological counseling sessions or educational or vocational training classes, participate in life skills or parenting training, utilize substance abuse treatment services, or seek medical, mental health, and dental assistance based upon the participant's individualized treatment and release plan. Participation in other rehabilitative services and programs may be approved by the case manager if it is specified as a requirement of the inmate's individualized treatment and rehabilitative case plan.

(2) Willful failure of the program participant to return to the place of detention prior to the expiration of any period of time during which he or she is authorized to be away from the place of detention, unauthorized departures from the place of detention, or tampering with or disabling, or attempting to tamper with or disable, an electronic monitoring device is punishable pursuant to Section 4532 and shall additionally subject the participant to a return to custody pursuant to subdivisions (g) and (h). In addition, participants may be subject to forfeiture of credits pursuant to the provisions of Section 4019, or to discipline for violation of rules established by the sheriff or the county director of corrections.

(k)

(1) Notwithstanding any other law, the sheriff or his or her designee or the county director of corrections or his or her designee shall provide the information specified in paragraph (2) regarding participants in an alternative custody program to the law enforcement agencies of the jurisdiction in which persons participating in an alternative custody program reside.

(2) The information required by paragraph (1) shall consist of the following:

(A) The participant's name, address, and date of birth.

(B) The offense committed by the participant.

(C) The period of time the participant will be subject to an alternative custody program.

(3) The information received by a law enforcement agency pursuant to this subdivision may be used for the purpose of monitoring the impact of an alternative custody program on the community.

(l) It is the intent of the Legislature that the alternative custody programs established under this section maintain the highest public confidence, credibility, and public safety. In the furtherance of these standards, the sheriff or the county director of corrections may administer an alternative custody program pursuant to written contracts with appropriate public agencies or entities to provide specified program services. No public agency or entity entering into a contract may itself employ any person who is in an alternative custody program. The sheriff or the county director of corrections shall determine the recidivism rate of each participant in an alternative custody program.

(m) An inmate participating in this program shall voluntarily agree to all of the provisions of the program in writing, including that he or she may be returned to confinement at any time with or without cause, and shall not be charged fees or costs for the program.

(n) If a phrase, clause, sentence, or provision of this section or application thereof to a person or circumstance is held invalid, that invalidity shall not affect any other phrase, clause, sentence, or provision or application of this section, which can be given effect without the invalid phrase, clause, sentence, or provision or application and to this end the provisions of this section are declared to be severable.

Added by Stats 2014 ch 26 (AB 1468),s 18, eff. 6/20/2014.

Section 1170.1 - Aggregate term of imprisonment when person convicted of two or more felonies; enhancements

(a) Except as otherwise provided by law, and subject to Section 654, when any person is convicted of two or more felonies, whether in the same proceeding or court or in different proceedings or courts, and whether by judgment rendered by the same or by a different court, and a consecutive term of imprisonment is imposed under Sections 669 and 1170, the aggregate term of imprisonment for all these convictions shall be the sum of the principal term, the subordinate term, and any additional term imposed for applicable enhancements for prior convictions, prior prison terms, and Section 12022.1. The principal term shall consist of the greatest term of imprisonment imposed by the court for any of the crimes, including any term imposed for applicable specific enhancements. The subordinate term for each consecutive offense shall consist of one-third of the middle term of imprisonment prescribed for each other felony conviction for which a consecutive term of imprisonment is imposed, and shall include one-third of the term imposed for any specific enhancements applicable to those subordinate offenses. Whenever a court imposes a term of imprisonment in the state prison, whether the term is a principal or subordinate term, the aggregate term shall be served in the state prison, regardless as to whether or not one of the terms specifies imprisonment in a county jail pursuant to subdivision (h) of Section 1170.

(b) If a person is convicted of two or more violations of kidnapping, as defined in Section 207, involving separate victims, the subordinate term for each consecutive offense of kidnapping shall consist of the full middle term and shall include the full term imposed for specific enhancements applicable to those subordinate offenses.

(c) In the case of any person convicted of one or more felonies committed while the person is confined in the state prison or is subject to reimprisonment for escape from custody and the law either requires the terms to be served consecutively or the court imposes consecutive terms, the term of imprisonment for all the convictions that the person is required to serve consecutively shall commence from the time the person would otherwise have been released from prison. If the new offenses are consecutive with each other, the principal and subordinate terms shall be calculated as provided in subdivision (a). This subdivision shall be applicable in cases of convictions of more than one offense in the same or different proceedings.

(d)

(1) When the court imposes a sentence for a felony pursuant to Section 1170 or subdivision (b) of Section 1168, the court shall also impose, in addition and consecutive to the offense of which the person has been convicted, the additional terms provided for any applicable enhancements. If an enhancement is punishable by one of three terms, the court shall, in its sound discretion, order imposition of a sentence not to exceed the middle term, except as otherwise provided in paragraph (2).

(2) The court may impose a sentence exceeding the middle term only when there are circumstances in aggravation that justify the imposition of a term of imprisonment exceeding the middle term, and the facts underlying those circumstances have been stipulated to by the defendant, or have been found true beyond a reasonable doubt at trial by the jury or by the judge in a court trial.

(3) The court shall also impose any other additional term that the court determines in its discretion or as required by law shall run consecutive to the term imposed under Section 1170 or subdivision (b) of Section 1168. In considering the imposition of the additional term, the court shall apply the sentencing rules of the Judicial Council.

(e) All enhancements shall be alleged in the accusatory pleading and either admitted by the defendant in open court or found to be true by the trier of fact.

(f) When two or more enhancements may be imposed for being armed with or using a dangerous or deadly weapon or a firearm in the commission of a single offense, only the greatest of those enhancements shall be imposed for that offense. This subdivision shall not limit the imposition of any other enhancements applicable to that offense, including an enhancement for the infliction of great bodily injury.

(g) When two or more enhancements may be imposed for the infliction of great bodily injury on the same victim in the commission of a single offense, only the greatest of those enhancements shall be imposed for that offense. This subdivision shall not limit the imposition of any other enhancements applicable to that offense, including an enhancement for being armed with or using a dangerous or deadly weapon or a firearm.

(h) For any violation of an offense specified in Section 667.6, the number of enhancements that may be imposed shall not be limited, regardless of whether the enhancements are pursuant to this section, Section 667.6, or some other provision of law. Each of the enhancements shall be a full and separately served term.

Amended by Stats 2021 ch 731 (SB 567),s 2, eff. 1/1/2022.

Amended by Stats 2016 ch 887 (SB 1016),s 8, eff. 1/1/2017.

Amended by Stats 2013 ch 508 (SB 463),s 8, eff. 1/1/2014.

Amended by Stats 2011 ch 361 (SB 576),s 9.7, eff. 9/29/2011.

Amended by Stats 2011 ch 12 (AB X1-17),s 13.2, eff. 9/20/2011, op. 10/1/2011.

Amended by Stats 2011 ch 39 (AB 117),s 30, eff. 6/30/2011.

Amended by Stats 2010 ch 256 (AB 2263),s 8, eff. 1/1/2011.

Added by Stats 2009 ch 171 (SB 150),s 6, eff. 1/1/2010.

Section 1170.11 - "Specific enhancement" defined

As used in Section 1170.1, the term "specific enhancement" means an enhancement that relates to the circumstances of the crime. It includes, but is not limited to, the enhancements provided in Sections 186.10, 186.11, 186.22, 186.26, 186.33, 192.5, 273.4, 289.5, 290.4, 290.45, 290.46, 347, and 368, subdivisions (a) and (b) of Section 422.75, paragraphs (2), (3), (4), and (5) of subdivision (a) of Section 451.1, paragraphs (2), (3), and (4) of subdivision (a) of Section 452.1, subdivision (g) of Section 550, Sections 593a, 600, 667.8, 667.85, 667.9, 667.10, 667.15, 667.16, 667.17, 674, 675, 12021.5, 12022, 12022.2, 12022.3, 12022.4, 12022.5, 12022.53, 12022.55, 12022.6, 12022.7, 12022.75, 12022.8, 12022.85, 12022.9, 12022.95, 27590, 30600, and 30615 of this code, and in Sections 1522.01 and 11353.1, subdivision (b) of Section 11353.4, Sections 11356.5, 11370.4, 11379.7, 11379.8, 11379.9, 11380.1, 11380.7, 25189.5, and 25189.7 of the Health and Safety Code, and in Sections 20001 and 23558 of the Vehicle Code, and in Sections 10980 and 14107 of the Welfare and Institutions Code.

Amended by Stats 2010 ch 178 (SB 1115),s 71, eff. 1/1/2011, op. 1/1/2012.

Amended by Stats 2008 ch 699 (SB 1241),s 13, eff. 1/1/2009.

Amended by Stats 2007 ch 302 (SB 425),s 13, eff. 1/1/2008.

Amended by Stats 2005 ch 279 (SB 1107),s 8, eff. 1/1/2006

Amended by Stats 2004 ch 405 (SB 1796), s 12, eff. 1/1/2005.

Amended by Stats 2003 ch 468 (SB 851), s 15, eff. 1/1/2004.

Amended by Stats 2001 ch 854 (SB 205) s 41, eff. 1/1/2002.

Amended by Stats 2000 ch 287 (SB 1955) s 14, eff. 1/1/2001.

Section 1170.12 - Aggregate and consecutive terms for multiple convictions; prior conviction as prior felony; commitment and other enhancements or punishment

(a) Notwithstanding any other law, if a defendant has been convicted of a felony and it has been pled and proved that the defendant has one or more prior serious or violent felony convictions, as defined in subdivision (b), the court shall adhere to each of the following:

(1) There shall not be an aggregate term limitation for purposes of consecutive sentencing for any subsequent felony conviction.

(2) Probation for the current offense shall not be granted, nor shall execution or imposition of the sentence be suspended for any prior offense.

(3) The length of time between the prior serious or violent felony conviction and the current felony conviction shall not affect the imposition of sentence.

(4) There shall not be a commitment to any other facility other than the state prison. Diversion shall not be granted nor shall the defendant be eligible for commitment to the California Rehabilitation Center as provided in Article 2 (commencing with Section 3050) of Chapter 1 of Division 3 of the Welfare and Institutions Code.

(5) The total amount of credits awarded pursuant to Article 2.5 (commencing with Section 2930) of Chapter 7 of Title 1 of Part 3 shall not exceed one-fifth of the total term of imprisonment imposed and shall not accrue until the defendant is physically placed in the state prison.

(6) If there is a current conviction for more than one felony count not committed on the same occasion, and not arising from the same set of operative facts, the court shall sentence the defendant consecutively on each count pursuant to this section.

(7) If there is a current conviction for more than one serious or violent felony as described in subdivision (b), the court shall impose the sentence for each conviction consecutive to the sentence for any other conviction for which the defendant may be consecutively sentenced in the manner prescribed by law.

(b) Notwithstanding any other law and for the purposes of this section, a prior serious or violent conviction of a felony is defined as:

(1) Any offense defined in subdivision (c) of Section 667.5 as a violent felony or any offense defined in subdivision (c) of Section 1192.7 as a serious felony in this state. The determination of whether a prior conviction is a prior serious or violent felony conviction for purposes of this section shall be made upon the date of that prior conviction and is not affected by the sentence imposed unless the sentence automatically, upon the initial sentencing, converts the felony to a misdemeanor. The following dispositions shall not affect the determination that a prior serious or violent conviction is a serious or violent felony for purposes of this section:

(A) The suspension of imposition of judgment or sentence.

(B) The stay of execution of sentence.

(C) The commitment to the State Department of State Hospitals as a mentally disordered sex offender following a conviction of a felony.

(D) The commitment to the California Rehabilitation Center or any other facility whose function is rehabilitative diversion from the state prison.

(2) A prior conviction in another jurisdiction for an offense that, if committed in California, is punishable by imprisonment in the state prison constitutes a prior conviction of a particular serious or violent felony if the prior conviction in the other jurisdiction is for an offense that includes all of the elements of the particular violent felony as defined in subdivision (c) of Section 667.5 or serious felony as defined in subdivision (c) of Section 1192.7.

(3) A prior juvenile adjudication constitutes a prior serious or violent felony conviction for the purposes of sentence enhancement if it meets all of the following criteria:

    (A) The juvenile was 16 years of age or older at the time the juvenile committed the prior offense.

    (B) The prior offense is either of the following:

        (i) Listed in subdivision (b) of Section 707 of the Welfare and Institutions Code.

        (ii) Listed in this subdivision as a serious or violent felony.

    (C) The juvenile was found to be a fit and proper subject to be dealt with under the juvenile court law.

    (D) The juvenile was adjudged a ward of the juvenile court within the meaning of Section 602 of the Welfare and Institutions Code because the person committed an offense listed in subdivision (b) of Section 707 of the Welfare and Institutions Code.

(c) For purposes of this section, and in addition to any other enhancements or punishment provisions that may apply, the following apply if a defendant has one or more prior serious or violent felony convictions:

    (1) If a defendant has one prior serious or violent felony conviction as defined in subdivision (b) that has been pled and proved, the determinate term or minimum term for an indeterminate term shall be twice the term otherwise provided as punishment for the current felony conviction.

    (2)

        (A) Except as provided in subparagraph (C), if a defendant has two or more prior serious or violent felony convictions, as defined in subdivision (b), that have been pled and proved, the term for the current felony conviction shall be an indeterminate term of life imprisonment with a minimum term of the indeterminate sentence calculated as the greatest of any of the following:

            (i) Three times the term otherwise provided as punishment for each current felony conviction subsequent to the two or more prior serious or violent felony convictions.

            (ii) Twenty-five years.

            (iii) The term determined by the court pursuant to Section 1170 for the underlying conviction, including any enhancement applicable under Chapter 4.5 (commencing with Section 1170) of Title 7 of Part 2, or any period prescribed by Section 190 or 3046.

        (B) The indeterminate term described in subparagraph (A) shall be served consecutive to any other term of imprisonment for which a consecutive term may be imposed by law. Any other term imposed subsequent to an indeterminate term described in subparagraph (A) shall not be merged therein but shall commence at the time the person would otherwise have been released from prison.

        (C) If a defendant has two or more prior serious or violent felony convictions as defined in subdivision (c) of Section 667.5 or subdivision (c) of Section 1192.7 that have been pled and proved, and the current offense is not a felony described in paragraph (1) of subdivision (b), the defendant shall be sentenced pursuant to paragraph (1) of subdivision (c), unless the prosecution pleads and proves any of the following:

            (i) The current offense is a controlled substance charge, in which an allegation under Section 11370.4 or 11379.8 of the Health and Safety Code was admitted or found true.

            (ii) The current offense is a felony sex offense, defined in subdivision (d) of Section 261.5, or any felony offense that results in mandatory registration as a sex offender pursuant to subdivision (c) of Section 290 except for violations of Sections 266 and 285, paragraph (1) of subdivision (b) and subdivision (e) of Section 286, paragraph (1) of subdivision (b) and subdivision (e) of Section 287, Section 314, and Section 311.11.

            (iii) During the commission of the current offense, the defendant used a firearm, was armed with a firearm or deadly weapon, or intended to cause great bodily injury to another person.

            (iv) The defendant suffered a prior conviction, as defined in subdivision (b), for any of the following serious or violent felonies:

                (I) A "sexually violent offense" as defined by subdivision (b) of Section 6600 of the Welfare and Institutions Code.

                (II) Oral copulation with a child who is under 14 years of age, and more than 10 years younger than the defendant as defined by Section 287 or former Section 288a, sodomy with another person who is under 14 years of age and more than 10 years younger than the defendant as defined by Section 286, or sexual penetration with another person who is under 14 years of age and more than 10 years younger than the defendant as defined by Section 289.

                (III) A lewd or lascivious act involving a child under 14 years of age, in violation of Section 288.

                (IV) Any homicide offense, including any attempted homicide offense, defined in Sections 187 to 191.5, inclusive.

                (V) Solicitation to commit murder as defined in Section 653f.

                (VI) Assault with a machinegun on a peace officer or firefighter, as defined in paragraph (3) of subdivision (d) of Section 245.

                (VII) Possession of a weapon of mass destruction, as defined in paragraph (1) of subdivision (a) of Section 11418.

                (VIII) Any serious or violent felony offense punishable in California by life imprisonment or death.

(d)

    (1) Notwithstanding any other law, this section shall be applied in every case in which a defendant has one or more prior serious or violent felony convictions as defined in this section. The prosecuting attorney shall plead and prove each prior serious or violent felony conviction except as provided in paragraph (2).

    (2) The prosecuting attorney may move to dismiss or strike a prior serious or violent felony conviction allegation in the furtherance of justice pursuant to Section 1385, or if there is insufficient evidence to prove the prior serious or violent conviction. If upon the satisfaction of the court that there is insufficient evidence to prove the prior serious or violent felony conviction, the court may dismiss or strike the allegation. This section does not alter a court's authority under Section 1385.

(e) Prior serious or violent felony convictions shall not be used in plea bargaining, as defined in subdivision (b) of Section 1192.7. The prosecution shall plead and prove all known prior serious or violent felony convictions and shall not enter into any agreement to strike or seek the dismissal of any prior serious or violent felony conviction allegation except as provided in paragraph (2) of subdivision (d).

(f) If any provision of subdivisions (a) to (e), inclusive, or of Section 1170.126, or the application thereof to any person or circumstance is held invalid, that invalidity does not affect other provisions or applications of those subdivisions that can be given effect without the invalid provision or application, and to this end the provisions of those subdivisions are severable.

(g) The provisions of this section shall not be amended by the Legislature except by statute passed in each house by rollcall vote entered in the journal, two-thirds of the membership concurring, or by a statute that becomes effective only when approved by the electors.

Amended by Stats 2021 ch 626 (AB 1171),s 42, eff. 1/1/2022.

Amended by Stats 2019 ch 497 (AB 991),s 204, eff. 1/1/2020.

Amended by Stats 2018 ch 423 (SB 1494),s 85, eff. 1/1/2019.

Amended by Proposition 36, approved by the people of the State of California 11/6/2012, eff. 11/7/2012.

Section 1170.125 - References to existing statutes

(a) Notwithstanding Section 2 of Proposition 184, as adopted at the November 8, 1994, statewide general election, for all offenses committed on or after November 7, 2012, but before January 1, 2024, all references to existing statutes in Sections 1170.12 and 1170.126 are to those sections as they read on November 7, 2012.

(b) Notwithstanding Section 2 of Proposition 184, as adopted at the November 8, 1994, statewide general election, for all offenses committed on or after January 1, 2024, all references to existing statutes in Sections 1170.12 and 1170.126 are to those sections as they read on January 1, 2024.

Amended by Stats 2023 ch 230 (SB 14),s 3, eff. 1/1/2024.

Amended by Proposition 36, approved by the people of the State of California 11/6/2012, eff. 11/7/2012.

Amended by Stats 2006 ch 337 (SB 1128),s 36, eff. 9/20/2006.

Section 1170.126 - Resentencing provisions for persons serving indeterminate term of life imprisonment

(a) The resentencing provisions under this section and related statutes are intended to apply exclusively to persons presently serving an indeterminate term of imprisonment pursuant to paragraph (2) of subdivision (e) of Section 667 or paragraph (2) of subdivision (c) of Section 1170.12, whose sentence under this act would not have been an indeterminate life sentence.

(b) Any person serving an indeterminate term of life imprisonment imposed pursuant to paragraph (2) of subdivision (e) of Section 667 or paragraph (2) of subdivision (c) of Section 1170.12 upon conviction, whether by trial or plea, of a felony or felonies that are not defined as serious and/or violent felonies by subdivision (c) of Section 667.5 or subdivision (c) of Section 1192.7, may file a petition for a recall of sentence, within two years after the effective date of the act that added this section or at a later date upon a showing of good cause, before the trial court that entered the judgment of conviction in his or her case, to request resentencing in accordance with the provisions of subdivision (e) of Section 667, and subdivision (c) of Section 1170.12, as those statutes have been amended by the act that added this section.

(c) No person who is presently serving a term of imprisonment for a "second strike" conviction imposed pursuant to paragraph (1) of subdivision (e) of Section 667 or paragraph (1) of subdivision (c) of Section 1170.12, shall be eligible for resentencing under the provisions of this section.

(d) The petition for a recall of sentence described in subdivision (b) shall specify all of the currently charged felonies, which resulted in the sentence under paragraph (2) of subdivision (e) of Section 667 or paragraph (2) of subdivision (c) of Section 1170.12, or both, and shall also specify all of the prior convictions alleged and proved under subdivision (d) of Section 667 and subdivision (b) of Section 1170.12.

(e) An inmate is eligible for resentencing if:

(1) The inmate is serving an indeterminate term of life imprisonment imposed pursuant to paragraph (2) of subdivision (e) of Section 667 or subdivision (c) of Section 1170.12 for a conviction of a felony or felonies that are not defined as serious and/or violent felonies by subdivision (c) of Section 667.5 or subdivision (c) of Section 1192.7.

(2) The inmate's current sentence was not imposed for any of the offenses appearing in clauses (i) to (iii), inclusive, of subparagraph (C) of paragraph (2) of subdivision (e) of Section 667 or clauses (i) to (iii), inclusive, of subparagraph (C) of paragraph (2) of subdivision (c) of Section 1170.12.

(3) The inmate has no prior convictions for any of the offenses appearing in clause (iv) of subparagraph (C) of paragraph (2) of subdivision (e) of Section 667 or clause (iv) of subparagraph (C) of paragraph (2) of subdivision (c) of Section 1170.12.

(f) Upon receiving a petition for recall of sentence under this section, the court shall determine whether the petitioner satisfies the criteria in subdivision (e). If the petitioner satisfies the criteria in subdivision (e), the petitioner shall be resentenced pursuant to paragraph (1) of subdivision (e) of Section 667 and paragraph (1) of subdivision (c) of Section 1170.12 unless the court, in its discretion, determines that resentencing the petitioner would pose an unreasonable risk of danger to public safety.

(g) In exercising its discretion in subdivision (f), the court may consider:

(1) The petitioner's criminal conviction history, including the type of crimes committed, the extent of injury to victims, the length of prior prison commitments, and the remoteness of the crimes;

(2) The petitioner's disciplinary record and record of rehabilitation while incarcerated; and

(3) Any other evidence the court, within its discretion, determines to be relevant in deciding whether a new sentence would result in an unreasonable risk of danger to public safety.

(h) Under no circumstances may resentencing under this act result in the imposition of a term longer than the original sentence.

(i) Notwithstanding subdivision (b) of Section 977, a defendant petitioning for resentencing may waive his or her appearance in court for the resentencing, provided that the accusatory pleading is not amended at the resentencing, and that no new trial or retrial of the individual will occur. The waiver shall be in writing and signed by the defendant.

(j) If the court that originally sentenced the defendant is not available to resentence the defendant, the presiding judge shall designate another judge to rule on the defendant's petition.

(k) Nothing in this section is intended to diminish or abrogate any rights or remedies otherwise available to the defendant.

(l) Nothing in this and related sections is intended to diminish or abrogate the finality of judgments in any case not falling within the purview of this act.

(m) A resentencing hearing ordered under this act shall constitute a "post-conviction release proceeding" under paragraph (7) of subdivision (b) of Section 28 of Article I of the California Constitution (Marsy's Law).

Enacted by Proposition 36, approved by the people of the State of California 11/6/2012, eff. 11/7/2012.

Section 1170.127 - Petition to reduce maximum term of commitment

(a) A person who is committed to a state hospital after being found not guilty by reason of insanity pursuant to Section 1026 may petition the court to have his or her maximum term of commitment, as established by Section 1026.5, reduced to the length it would have been had Section 1170.126 been in effect at the time of the original determination. Both of the following conditions are required for the maximum term of commitment to be reduced:

(1) The person would have met all of the criteria for a reduction in sentence pursuant to Section 1170.126 had he or she been found guilty.

(2) The person files the petition for a reduction of the maximum term of commitment before January 1, 2021, or on a later date upon a showing of good cause.

(b) If a petitioner's maximum term of confinement is ordered reduced under this section, the new term of confinement must provide opportunity to meet requirements provided in subdivision (b) of Section 1026.5. If a petitioner's new maximum term of confinement ordered under this section does not provide sufficient time to meet requirements provided in subdivision (b) of Section 1026.5, the new maximum term of confinement may be extended, not more than 240 days from the date the petition is granted, in order to meet requirements provided in subdivision (b) of Section 1026.5.

Added by Stats 2017 ch 17 (AB 103),s 25, eff. 6/27/2017.

Section 1170.13 - Subordinate terms for each consecutive offense

Notwithstanding subdivision (a) of Section 1170.1 which provides for the imposition of a subordinate term for a consecutive offense of one-third of the middle term of imprisonment, if a person is convicted pursuant to subdivision (b) of Section 139, the subordinate term for each consecutive offense shall consist of the full middle term.

Amended by Stats. 1998, Ch. 926, Sec. 3. Effective January 1, 1999.

Section 1170.15 - Subordinate term for consecutive offense if committed against victim or witness

Notwithstanding subdivision (a) of Section 1170.1 which provides for the imposition of a subordinate term for a consecutive offense of one-third of the middle term of imprisonment, if a person is convicted of a felony, and of an additional felony that is a violation of Section 136.1 or 137 and that was committed against the victim of, or a witness or potential witness with respect to, or a person who was about to give material information pertaining to, the first felony, or of a felony violation of Section 653f that was committed to dissuade a witness or potential witness to the first felony, the subordinate term for each consecutive offense that is a felony described in this section shall consist of the full middle term of imprisonment for the felony for which a consecutive term of imprisonment is imposed, and shall include the full term prescribed for any enhancements imposed for being armed with or using a dangerous or deadly weapon or a firearm, or for inflicting great bodily injury.

Amended by Stats. 1998, Ch. 926, Sec. 4. Effective January 1, 1999.

Section 1170.16 - Full, separate, and consecutive term

In lieu of the term provided in Section 1170.1, a full, separate, and consecutive term may be imposed for each violation of subdivision (a) of Section 192, whether or not the offenses were committed during a single transaction.

Added by Stats. 1996, Ch. 421, Sec. 1. Effective January 1, 1997.

Section 1170.17 - [Repealed]

Repealed by Stats 2021 ch 434 (SB 827),s 5, eff. 1/1/2022.

Amended by Stats 2015 ch 234 (SB 382),s 1, eff. 1/1/2016.

Amended by Stats 2000 ch 287 (SB 1955) s 15, eff. 1/1/2001.

Section 1170.18 - Petition for resentencing for conviction of nonserious or nonviolent crimes

(a) A person who, on November 5, 2014, was serving a sentence for a conviction, whether by trial or plea, of a felony or felonies who would have been guilty of a misdemeanor under the act that added this section ("this act") had this act been in effect at the time of the offense may petition for a recall of sentence before the trial court that entered the judgment of conviction in their case to request resentencing in accordance with Sections 11350, 11357, or 11377 of the Health and Safety Code, or Section 459.5, 473, 476a, 490.2, 496, or 666 of the Penal Code, as those sections have been amended or added by this act.

(b) Upon receiving a petition under subdivision (a), the court shall determine whether the petitioner satisfies the criteria in subdivision (a). If the petitioner satisfies the criteria in subdivision (a), the petitioner's felony sentence shall be recalled and the petitioner resentenced to a misdemeanor pursuant to Sections 11350, 11357, or 11377 of the Health and Safety Code, or Section 459.5, 473, 476a, 490.2, 496, or 666 of the Penal Code, as those sections have been amended or added by this act, unless the court, in its discretion, determines that resentencing the petitioner would pose an unreasonable risk of danger to public safety. In exercising its discretion, the court may consider all of the following:

(1) The petitioner's criminal conviction history, including the type of crimes committed, the extent of injury to victims, the length of prior prison commitments, and the remoteness of the crimes.

(2) The petitioner's disciplinary record and record of rehabilitation while incarcerated.

(3) Any other evidence the court, within its discretion, determines to be relevant in deciding whether a new sentence would result in an unreasonable risk of danger to public safety.

(c) As used throughout this code, "unreasonable risk of danger to public safety" means an unreasonable risk that the petitioner will commit a new violent felony within the meaning of clause (iv) of subparagraph (C) of paragraph (2) of subdivision (e) of Section 667.

(d) A person who is resentenced pursuant to subdivision (b) shall be given credit for time served and shall be subject to parole for one year following completion of their sentence, unless the court, in its discretion, as part of its resentencing order, releases the person from parole. The person is subject to parole supervision by the Department of Corrections and Rehabilitation pursuant to Section 3000.08

and the jurisdiction of the court in the county in which the parolee is released or resides, or in which an alleged violation of supervision has occurred, for the purpose of hearing petitions to revoke parole and impose a term of custody.

(e) Resentencing pursuant to this section shall not result in the imposition of a term longer than the original sentence.

(f) A person who has completed their sentence for a conviction, whether by trial or plea, of a felony or felonies who would have been guilty of a misdemeanor under this act had this act been in effect at the time of the offense, may file an application before the trial court that entered the judgment of conviction in their case to have the felony conviction or convictions designated as misdemeanors.

(g) If the application satisfies the criteria in subdivision (f), the court shall designate the felony offense or offenses as a misdemeanor.

(h) Unless the applicant requests a hearing, a hearing is not necessary to grant or deny an application filed under subdivision (f).

(i) This section does not apply to a person who has one or more prior convictions for an offense specified in clause (iv) of subparagraph (C) of paragraph (2) of subdivision (e) of Section 667 or for an offense requiring registration pursuant to subdivision (c) of Section 290.

(j) A felony conviction that is recalled and resentenced under subdivision (b) or designated as a misdemeanor under subdivision (g) shall be considered a misdemeanor for all purposes, except that resentencing shall not permit that person to own, possess, or have in their custody or control a firearm or prevent their conviction under Chapter 2 (commencing with Section 29800) of Division 9 of Title 4 of Part 6.

(k) If the court that originally sentenced the petitioner is not available, the presiding judge shall designate another judge to rule on the petition or application.

(l) This section does not diminish or abrogate any rights or remedies otherwise available to the petitioner or applicant.

(m) Resentencing pursuant to this section does not diminish or abrogate the finality of judgments in any case that does not come within the purview of this section.

(n) A resentencing hearing ordered under this section shall constitute a "post'"conviction release proceeding" under paragraph (7) of subdivision (b) of Section 28 of Article I of the California Constitution (Marsy's Law).

(o)

(1) A person who is committed to a state hospital after being found not guilty by reason of insanity pursuant to Section 1026 may petition the court to have their maximum term of commitment, as established by Section 1026.5, reduced to the length it would have been had the act that added this section been in effect at the time of the original determination. Both of the following conditions are required for the maximum term of commitment to be reduced:

(A) The person would have met all of the criteria for a reduction in sentence pursuant to this section had they been found guilty.

(B) The person files the petition for a reduction of the maximum term of commitment before January 1, 2021, or on a later date upon a showing of good cause.

(2) If a petitioner's maximum term of confinement is ordered reduced under this subdivision, the new term of confinement must provide opportunity to meet requirements provided in subdivision (b) of Section 1026.5. If a petitioner's new maximum term of confinement ordered under this section does not provide sufficient time to meet requirements provided in subdivision (b) of Section 1026.5, the new maximum term of confinement may be extended, not more than 240 days from the date the petition is granted, in order to meet requirements provided in subdivision (b) of Section 1026.5.

Amended by Stats 2023 ch 633 (SB 749),s 1, eff. 10/8/2023.
Amended by Stats 2017 ch 561 (AB 1516),s 189, eff. 1/1/2018.
Amended by Stats 2017 ch 17 (AB 103),s 26, eff. 6/27/2017.
Amended by Stats 2016 ch 767 (AB 2765),s 1, eff. 1/1/2017.
Added by Proposition 47, eff. 11/5/2014.

Section 1170.19 - [Repealed]

Repealed by Stats 2021 ch 434 (SB 827),s 6, eff. 1/1/2022.
Added by Stats. 1999, Ch. 996, Sec. 12.1. Effective January 1, 2000.

Section 1170.2 - Determination of length of time of imprisonment without consideration of good-time credit and using middle term

(a) In the case of any inmate who committed a felony prior to July 1, 1977, who would have been sentenced under Section 1170 if he or she had committed it after July 1, 1977, the Board of Prison Terms shall determine what the length of time of imprisonment would have been under Section 1170 without consideration of good-time credit and utilizing the middle term of the offense bearing the longest term of imprisonment of which the prisoner was convicted increased by any enhancements justified by matters found to be true and which were imposed by the court at the time of sentencing for such felony. These matters include: being armed with a deadly or dangerous weapon as specified in Section 211a, 460, 3024, or 12022 prior to July 1, 1977, which may result in a one-year enhancement pursuant to the provisions of Section 12022; using a firearm as specified in Section 12022.5 prior to July 1, 1977, which may result in a two-year enhancement pursuant to the provisions of Section 12022.5; infliction of great bodily injury as specified in Section 213, 264, or 461 prior to July 1, 1977, which may result in a three-year enhancement pursuant to the provisions of Section 12022.7; any prior felony conviction as specified in any statute prior to July 1, 1977, which prior felony conviction is the equivalent of a prior prison term as defined in Section 667.5, which may result in the appropriate enhancement pursuant to the provisions of Section 667.5; and any consecutive sentence.

(b) If the calculation required under subdivision (a) is less than the time to be served prior to a release date set prior to July 1, 1977, or if a release date had not been set, the Board of Prison Terms shall establish the prisoner's parole date, subject to subdivision (d), on the date calculated under subdivision (a) unless at least two of the commissioners of the Board of Prison Terms after reviewing the prisoner's file, determine that due to the number of crimes of which the prisoner was convicted, or due to the number of prior convictions suffered by the prisoner, or due to the fact that the prisoner was armed with a deadly weapon when the crime was committed, or used a deadly weapon during the commission of the crime, or inflicted or attempted to inflict great bodily injury on the victim of the crime, the prisoner should serve a term longer than that calculated in subdivision (a), in which event the prisoner shall be entitled to a hearing before a panel consisting of at least two commissioners of the Board of Prison Terms as provided for in Section 3041.5. The Board of Prison Terms shall notify each prisoner who is scheduled for such a hearing within 90 days of July 1, 1977, or within 90 days of the date the prisoner is received by or returned to the custody of the Department of Corrections, whichever is later. The hearing shall be held before October 1, 1978, or within 120 days of receipt of the prisoner, whichever is later. It is the intent of the Legislature that the hearings provided for in this subdivision shall be accomplished in the most expeditious manner possible. At the hearing the prisoner shall be entitled to be represented by legal counsel, a release date shall be set, and the prisoner shall be informed in writing of the extraordinary factors specifically considered determinative and on what basis the release date has been calculated. In fixing a term under this section the board shall be guided by, but not limited to, the term which reasonably could be imposed on a person who committed a similar offense under similar circumstances on or after July 1, 1977, and further, the board shall be guided by the following finding and declaration hereby made by the Legislature: that the necessity to protect the public from repetition of extraordinary crimes of violence against the person is the paramount consideration.

(c) Nothing in this section shall be deemed to keep an inmate in the custody of the Department of Corrections for a period of time longer than he would have been kept in its custody under the provisions of law applicable to him prior to July 1, 1977. Nothing in this section shall be deemed to require the release of an inmate sentenced to consecutive sentences under the provisions of law applicable to him prior to July 1, 1977, earlier than if he had been sentenced to concurrent sentences.

(d) In the case of any prisoner who committed a felony prior to July 1, 1977, who would have been sentenced under Section 1170 if the felony was committed on or after July 1, 1977, the good behavior and participation provisions of Article 2.5 (commencing with Section 2930) of Chapter 7 of Title 1 of Part 3 shall apply from July 1, 1977, and thereafter.

(e) In the case of any inmate who committed a felony prior to July 1, 1977, who would have been sentenced under Section 1168 if the felony was committed on or after July 1, 1977, the Board of Prison Terms shall provide for release from prison as provided for by this code.

(f) In the case of any inmate who committed a felony prior to July 1, 1977, the length, conditions, revocation, and other incidents of parole shall be the same as if the prisoner had been sentenced for an offense committed on or after July 1, 1977.

(g) Nothing in this chapter shall affect the eligibility for parole under Article 3 (commencing with Section 3040) of Chapter 8 of Title 1 of Part 3 of an inmate sentenced pursuant to Section 1168 as operative prior to July 1, 1977, for a period of parole as specified in subdivision (b) of Section 3000.

(h) In fixing a term under this section, the Board of Prison Terms shall utilize the terms of imprisonment as provided in Chapter 1139 of the Statutes of 1976 and Chapter 165 of the Statutes of 1977.

Amended by Stats. 1989, Ch. 568, Sec. 1.5.

Section 1170.21 - Effect of repeal of former section 647f on convictions, charges and arrests

A conviction for a violation of Section 647f as it read on December 31, 2017, is invalid and vacated. All charges alleging violation of Section 647f are dismissed and all arrests for violation of Section 647f are deemed to have never occurred. An individual who was arrested, charged, or convicted for a violation of Section 647f may indicate in response to any question concerning his or her prior arrest, charge, or conviction under Section 647f that he or she was not arrested, charged, or convicted for a violation of Section 647f. Notwithstanding any other law, information pertaining to an individual's arrest, charge, or conviction for violation of Section 647f shall not, without the individual's consent, be used in any way adverse to his or her interests, including, but not limited to, denial of any employment, benefit, license, or certificate.

Added by Stats 2017 ch 537 (SB 239),s 13, eff. 1/1/2018.

Section 1170.22 - Recall or dismissal of sentence under former section 647f

(a) A person who is serving a sentence as a result of a violation of Section 647f as it read on December 31, 2017, whether by trial or by open or negotiated plea, may petition for a recall or dismissal of sentence before the trial court that entered the judgment of conviction in his or her case.

(b) If the court's records show that the petitioner was convicted for a violation of Section 647f as it read on December 31, 2017, the court shall vacate the conviction and resentence the person for any remaining counts.

(c) A person who is serving a sentence and resentenced pursuant to subdivision (b) shall be given credit for any time already served and shall be subject to whatever supervision time he or she would have otherwise been subject to after release, whichever is shorter, unless the court, in its discretion, as part of its resentencing order, releases the person from supervision.

(d) Under no circumstances may resentencing under this section result in the imposition of a term longer than the original sentence, or the reinstatement of charges dismissed pursuant to a negotiated plea agreement.

(e) Upon completion of sentence for a conviction under Section 647f as it read on December 31, 2017, the provisions of Section 1170.21 shall apply.

(f) Nothing in this and related sections is intended to diminish or abrogate the finality of judgments in any case not falling within the purview of this section.

(g) A resentencing hearing ordered under this section shall constitute a "post-conviction release proceeding" under paragraph (7) of subdivision (b) of Section 28 of Article I of the California Constitution.

(h) The provisions of this section apply to juvenile delinquency adjudications and dispositions under Section 602 of the Welfare and Institutions Code if the juvenile would not have been guilty of an offense or would not have been guilty of an offense governed by this section.

(i) The Judicial Council shall promulgate and make available all necessary forms to enable the filing of petitions and applications provided in this section.

Added by Stats 2017 ch 537 (SB 239),s 14, eff. 1/1/2018.

Section 1170.3 - Promotion of uniformity in sentencing

The Judicial Council shall seek to promote uniformity in sentencing under Section 1170 by:

(a) The adoption of rules providing criteria for the consideration of the trial judge at the time of sentencing regarding the court's decision to:

(1) Grant or deny probation.

(2) Impose the lower or upper prison term.

(3) Impose the lower or upper term pursuant to paragraph (1) or (2) of subdivision (h) of Section 1170.

(4) Impose concurrent or consecutive sentences.

(5) Determine whether or not to impose an enhancement where that determination is permitted by law.

(6) Deny a period of mandatory supervision in the interests of justice under paragraph (5) of subdivision (h) of Section 1170 or determine the appropriate period and conditions of mandatory supervision. The rules implementing this paragraph shall be adopted no later than January 1, 2015.

(7) Determine the county or counties of incarceration and supervision when the court is imposing a judgment pursuant to subdivision (h) of Section 1170 concurrent or consecutive to a judgment or judgments previously imposed pursuant to subdivision (h) of Section 1170 in a county or counties.

(b) The adoption of rules standardizing the minimum content and the sequential presentation of material in probation officer reports submitted to the court regarding probation and mandatory supervision under paragraph (5) of subdivision (h) of Section 1170.

(c) This section shall become operative on January 1, 2022.

Amended by Stats 2017 ch 287 (SB 670),s 4, eff. 1/1/2018.
Amended by Stats 2016 ch 887 (SB 1016),s 10, eff. 1/1/2017.
Amended by Stats 2015 ch 378 (AB 1156),s 4, eff. 1/1/2016.
Amended by Stats 2014 ch 26 (AB 1468),s 20, eff. 6/20/2014.
Amended by Stats 2013 ch 508 (SB 463),s 10, eff. 1/1/2014.
Amended by Stats 2011 ch 361 (SB 576),s 11, eff. 9/29/2011.
Amended by Stats 2010 ch 256 (AB 2263),s 10, eff. 1/1/2011.
Amended by Stats 2009 ch 140 (AB 1164),s 147, eff. 1/1/2010.
Amended by Stats 2009 ch 140 (AB 1164),s 146, eff. 1/1/2010.
Amended by Stats 2008 ch 416 (SB 1701),s 3, eff. 1/1/2009.
Amended by Stats 2007 ch 3 (SB 40),s 5, eff. 3/30/2007.
Amended by Stats 2007 ch 3 (SB 40),s 4, eff. 3/30/2007.

Section 1170.4 - Collection and analysis of information relating to sentencing practices

The Judicial Council shall collect and analyze relevant information relating to sentencing practices in this state and other jurisdictions. Such information shall be taken into consideration by the Judicial Council in the adoption of rules pursuant to Section 1170.3.
Amended by Stats. 1993, Ch. 909, Sec. 15. Effective January 1, 1994.

Section 1170.45 - Collection of data on criminal cases relating to disposition according to race and ethnicity of defendant

The Judicial Council shall collect data on criminal cases statewide relating to the disposition of those cases according to the race and ethnicity of the defendant, and report annually thereon to the Legislature beginning no later than January 1, 1999. It is the intent of the Legislature to appropriate funds to the Judicial Council for this purpose.
Added by Stats. 1997, Ch. 850, Sec. 48.5. Effective January 1, 1998.

Section 1170.5 - Annual sentencing institutes for trial court judges

The Judicial Council shall conduct annual sentencing institutes for trial court judges pursuant to Section 68551 of the Government Code, toward the end of assisting the judge in the imposition of appropriate sentences.
Added by Stats. 1976, Ch. 1139.

Section 1170.6 - [Repealed]

Repealed by Stats 2001 ch 745 (SB 1191), s 158.2, eff. 10/11/2001.

Section 1170.7 - Robbery or attempted robbery for purpose of obtaining controlled substance when committed against pharmacist or other person lawfully possessing controlled substances

Robbery or attempted robbery for the purpose of obtaining any controlled substance, as defined in Division 10 (commencing with Section 11000) of the Health and Safety Code, when committed against a pharmacist, pharmacy employee, or other person lawfully possessing controlled substances, shall be considered a circumstance in aggravation of the crime in imposing a term under subdivision (b) of Section 1170.
Amended by Stats. 1987, Ch. 828, Sec. 67.

Section 1170.71 - Use of obscene or harmful matter to induce minor to engage in lewd or lascivious act

The fact that a person who commits a violation of Section 288 has used obscene or harmful matter to induce, persuade, or encourage the minor to engage in a lewd or lascivious act shall be considered a circumstance in aggravation of the crime in imposing a term under subdivision (b) of Section 1170.
Added by Stats. 1985, Ch. 165, Sec. 1.

Section 1170.72 - Minor 11 years of age or younger

Upon conviction of a violation of Section 11353, 11353.5, 11353.7, 11354, 11361, or 11380 of the Health and Safety Code, or a finding of truth of an enhancing allegation pursuant to paragraph (3) of subdivision (a) of Section 11353.1, Section 11353.6, or paragraph (3) of subdivision (a) of Section 11380.1, the fact that the minor was 11 years of age or younger shall be considered a circumstance in aggravation when imposing a term under subdivision (b) of Section 1170.
Added by Stats. 1993, Ch. 131, Sec. 1. Effective January 1, 1994.

Section 1170.73 - Quantity of controlled substance

Upon conviction of a felony violation of Section 11377, 11378, or 11378.5 of the Health and Safety Code, the court shall consider the quantity of controlled substance involved in determining whether to impose an aggravated term under subdivision (b) of Section 1170.
Added by Stats. 1990, Ch. 777, Sec. 1.

Section 1170.74 - Crystalline form of methamphetamine

Upon conviction of a felony violation of Section 11377, 11378, 11379, or 11379.6 of the Health and Safety Code, for an offense involving methamphetamine, the fact that the controlled substance is the crystalline form of methamphetamine shall be considered a circumstance in aggravation of the crime in imposing a term under subdivision (b) of Section 1170.

Added by Stats. 1990, Ch. 952, Sec. 1.

Section 1170.75 - [Renumbered as 422.76]

Renumbered as Ca. Pen. Code §422.76 by Stats 2004 ch 700 (SB 1234), s 23, eff. 1/1/2005.

Section 1170.76 - Member of household of minor or victim; relative of minor or victim

The fact that a defendant who commits or attempts to commit a violation of Section 243.4, 245, or 273.5 is or has been a member of the household of a minor or of the victim of the offense, or the defendant is a marital or blood relative of the minor or the victim, or the defendant or the victim is the natural parent, adoptive parent, stepparent, or foster parent of the minor, and the offense contemporaneously occurred in the presence of, or was witnessed by, the minor shall be considered a circumstance in aggravation of the crime in imposing a term under subdivision (b) of Section 1170.

Amended by Stats 2005 ch 279 (SB 1107),s 9, eff. 1/1/2006

Section 1170.78 - Retaliation for eviction or other legal action taken by owner or occupant

Upon a conviction of a violation of Section 451, the fact that the person committed the offense in retaliation against the owner or occupant of the property or structure burned, or against one believed by the person to be the owner or occupant of the property or structure burned, for any eviction or other legal action taken by the owner or occupant, or believed owner or occupant, shall be a circumstance in aggravation of the crime in imposing a term under subdivision (b) of Section 1170.

Added by Stats. 1991, Ch. 602, Sec. 7.

Section 1170.8 - Robbery or assault against person in place of worship

(a) The fact that a robbery or an assault with a deadly weapon or instrument or by means of any force likely to produce great bodily injury was committed against a person while that person was in a church, synagogue, or building owned and occupied by a religious educational institution, or any other place primarily used as a place of worship where religious services are regularly conducted, shall be considered a circumstance in aggravation of the crime in imposing a term under subdivision (b) of Section 1170.

(b) Upon conviction of any person for a violation of Section 451 or 453, the fact that the person intentionally burned, or intended to burn, a church, synagogue, or building owned and occupied by a religious educational institution, or any other place primarily used as a place of worship where religious services are regularly conducted, shall be considered a circumstance in aggravation of the crime in imposing a term under subdivision (b) of Section 1170.

Added by Stats. 1982, Ch. 929, Sec. 1.

Section 1170.81 - Peace officer as victim

The fact that the intended victim of an attempted life term crime was a peace officer, as described in subdivisions (a) and (b) of Section 830.1, or Section 830.2, 830.5 or 830.6, while the peace officer was engaged in the performance of his or her duties, and the defendant knew or reasonably should have known that the victim was a peace officer engaged in the performance of his or her duties, shall be considered a circumstance in aggravation of the crime in imposing a term under subdivision (b) of Section 1170.

Added by Stats. 1990, Ch. 1031, Sec. 1.

Section 1170.82 - Sale, furnishing, administering, or giving away controlled substance to pregnant woman, person convicted of violent felony, or person in psychological treatment for mental disorder or substance abuse

Upon a conviction of a violation of Section 11352, 11360, 11379, or 11379.5 of the Health and Safety Code, the fact that the person who committed the offense knew, or reasonably should have known, that any of the following circumstances existed with regard to the person to whom he or she unlawfully sold, furnished, administered, or gave away a controlled substance, shall be a circumstance in aggravation of the crime in imposing a term pursuant to subdivision (b) of Section 1170:

(a) The person was pregnant at the time of the selling, furnishing, administering, or giving away of the controlled substance.

(b) The person had been previously convicted of a violent felony, as defined in subdivision (c) of Section 667.5.

(c) The person was in psychological treatment for a mental disorder or for substance abuse at the time of the selling, furnishing, administering, or giving away of the controlled substance.

Added by Stats. 1994, Ch. 352, Sec. 1. Effective January 1, 1995.

Section 1170.84 - Tying, binding, or confining victim

Upon conviction of any serious felony, listed in subdivision (c) of Section 1192.7, it shall be considered a circumstance in aggravation of the crime in imposing a term under subdivision (b) of Section 1170 if, during the course of the serious felony, the person engaged in the tying, binding, or confining of any victim.

Added by Stats. 1990, Ch. 1216, Sec. 1.

Section 1170.85 - Prevention or dissuading of witness from testifying

(a) Upon conviction of any felony assault or battery offense, it shall be considered a circumstance in aggravation of the crime in imposing a term under subdivision (b) of Section 1170 if the offense was committed to prevent or dissuade a person who is or may become a witness from attending upon or testifying at any trial, proceeding, or inquiry authorized by law, or if the offense was committed because the person provided assistance or information to a law enforcement officer, or to a public prosecutor in a criminal or juvenile court proceeding.

(b) Upon conviction of any felony it shall be considered a circumstance in aggravation in imposing a term under subdivision (b) of Section 1170 if the victim of an offense is particularly vulnerable, or unable to defend himself or herself, due to age or significant disability.

Amended by Stats. 1985, Ch. 1108, Sec. 3.

Section 1170.86 - Commission of felony in safe school zone

Upon conviction of a felony violation of Section 220, 261, 261.5, 264.1, or 266j the fact that the felony was committed within a safe school zone, as defined in subdivision (c) of Section 626, against a victim who was a pupil currently attending school, shall be considered a circumstance in aggravation in imposing a term under subdivision (b) of Section 1170.

Amended by Stats 2005 ch 279 (SB 1107),s 10, eff. 1/1/2006

Section 1170.89 - Stolen firearm

Where there is an applicable triad for an enhancement related to the possession of, being armed with, use of, or furnishing or supplying a firearm, set forth in Section 12021.5, 12022, 12022.2, 12022.3, 12022.4, 12022.5, or 12022.55 the fact that a person knew or had reason to believe that a firearm was stolen shall constitute a circumstance in aggravation of the enhancement justifying imposition of the upper term on that enhancement.

Amended by Stats 2005 ch 279 (SB 1107),s 11, eff. 1/1/2006

Section 1170.9 - Commission of offense as result of sexual trauma, traumatic brain injury, PTSD, substance abuse, or mental health problems stemming from military service

(a) In the case of any person convicted of a criminal offense who could otherwise be sentenced to county jail or state prison and who alleges that the person committed the offense as a result of sexual trauma, traumatic brain injury, post-traumatic stress disorder, substance abuse, or mental health problems stemming from service in the United States military, the court shall, prior to sentencing, make a determination as to whether the defendant was, or currently is, a member of the United States military and whether the defendant may be suffering from sexual trauma, traumatic brain injury, post-traumatic stress disorder, substance abuse, or mental health problems as a result of the person's service. The court may request, through existing resources, an assessment to aid in that determination.

(b)

(1) If the court concludes that a defendant convicted of a criminal offense is a person described in subdivision (a), and if the defendant is otherwise eligible for probation, the court shall consider the circumstances described in subdivision (a) as a factor in favor of granting probation.

(2) If the court places the defendant on probation, the court may order the defendant into a local, state, federal, or private nonprofit treatment program for a period not to exceed that period which the defendant would have served in state prison or county jail, provided the defendant agrees to participate in the program and the court determines that an appropriate treatment program exists.

(c) If a referral is made to the county mental health authority, the county shall be obligated to provide mental health treatment services only to the extent that resources are available for that purpose, as described in paragraph (5) of subdivision (b) of Section 5600.3 of the Welfare and Institutions Code. If mental health treatment services are ordered by the court, the county mental health agency shall coordinate appropriate referral of the defendant to the county veterans service officer, as described in paragraph (5) of subdivision (b) of Section 5600.3 of the Welfare and Institutions Code. The county mental health agency shall not be responsible for providing services outside its traditional scope of services. An order shall be made referring a defendant to a county mental health agency only if that agency has agreed to accept responsibility for the treatment of the defendant.

(d) When determining the "needs of the defendant," for purposes of Section 1202.7, the court shall consider the fact that the defendant is a person described in subdivision (a) in assessing whether the defendant should be placed on probation and ordered into a federal or community-based treatment service program with a demonstrated history of specializing in the treatment of mental health problems, including substance abuse, post-traumatic stress disorder, traumatic brain injury, military sexual trauma, and other related mental health problems.

(e) A defendant granted probation under this section and committed to a residential treatment program shall earn sentence credits for the actual time the defendant serves in residential treatment.

(f) The court, in making an order under this section to commit a defendant to an established treatment program, shall give preference to a treatment program that has a history of successfully treating veterans who suffer from sexual trauma, traumatic brain injury, post-traumatic stress disorder, substance abuse, or mental health problems as a result of that service, including, but not limited to, programs operated by the United States Department of Defense or the United States Department of Veterans Affairs.

(g) The court and the assigned treatment program may collaborate with the Department of Veterans Affairs and the United States Department of Veterans Affairs to maximize benefits and services provided to the veteran.

(h)

(1) It is in the interests of justice to restore a defendant who acquired a criminal record due to a mental health disorder stemming from service in the United States military to the community of law abiding citizens. The restorative provisions of this subdivision apply to cases in which a trial court or a court monitoring the defendant's performance of probation pursuant to this section finds at a public hearing, held after not less than 15 days' notice to the prosecution, the defense, and any victim of the offense, that all of the following describe the defendant:

(A) The defendant was granted probation and was at the time that probation was granted a person described in subdivision (a).

(B) The defendant is in substantial compliance with the conditions of that probation.

(C) The defendant has successfully participated in court-ordered treatment and services to address the sexual trauma, traumatic brain injury, post-traumatic stress disorder, substance abuse, or mental health problems stemming from military service.

(D) The defendant does not represent a danger to the health and safety of others.

(E) The defendant has demonstrated significant benefit from court-ordered education, treatment, or rehabilitation to clearly show that granting restorative relief pursuant to this subdivision would be in the interests of justice.

(2) When determining whether granting restorative relief pursuant to this subdivision is in the interests of justice, the court may consider, among other factors, all of the following:

(A) The defendant's completion and degree of participation in education, treatment, and rehabilitation as ordered by the court.

(B) The defendant's progress in formal education.

(C) The defendant's development of career potential.

(D) The defendant's leadership and personal responsibility efforts.

(E) The defendant's contribution of service in support of the community.

(3) If the court finds that a case satisfies each of the requirements described in paragraph (1), then the court may take any of the following actions by a written order setting forth the reasons for so doing:

(A) Deem all conditions of probation to be satisfied, including fines, fees, assessments, and programs, and terminate probation prior to the expiration of the term of probation. This subparagraph does not apply to any court-ordered victim restitution.

(B) Reduce an eligible felony to a misdemeanor pursuant to subdivision (b) of Section 17.

(C) Grant relief in accordance with Section 1203.4.

(4) Notwithstanding anything to the contrary in Section 1203.4, a dismissal of the action pursuant to this subdivision has the following effect:

(A) Except as otherwise provided in this paragraph, a dismissal of the action pursuant to this subdivision releases the defendant from all penalties and disabilities resulting from the offense of which the defendant has been convicted in the dismissed action.

(B) A dismissal pursuant to this subdivision does not apply to any of the following:

(i) A conviction pursuant to subdivision (c) of Section 42002.1 of the Vehicle Code.

(ii) A felony conviction pursuant to subdivision (d) of Section 261.5.

(iii) A conviction pursuant to subdivision (c) of Section 286.

(iv) A conviction pursuant to Section 288.

(v) A conviction pursuant to subdivision (c) of Section 287 or former Section 288a.

(vi) A conviction pursuant to Section 288.5.

(vii) A conviction pursuant to subdivision (j) of Section 289.

(viii) The requirement to register pursuant to Section 290.

(C) The defendant is not obligated to disclose the arrest on the dismissed action, the dismissed action, or the conviction that was set aside when information concerning prior arrests or convictions is requested to be given under oath, affirmation, or otherwise. The defendant may indicate that the defendant has not been arrested when the defendant's only arrest concerns the dismissed action, except when the defendant is required to disclose the arrest, the conviction that was set aside, and the dismissed action in response to any direct question contained in any questionnaire or application for any law enforcement position.

(D) A dismissal pursuant to this subdivision may, in the discretion of the court, order the sealing of police records of the arrest and court records of the dismissed action, thereafter viewable by the public only in accordance with a court order.

(E) The dismissal of the action pursuant to this subdivision is a bar to any future action based on the conduct charged in the dismissed action.

(F) In any subsequent prosecution for any other offense, a conviction that was set aside in the dismissed action may be pleaded and proved as a prior conviction and has the same effect as if the dismissal pursuant to this subdivision had not been granted.

(G) A conviction that was set aside in the dismissed action may be considered a conviction for the purpose of administratively revoking or suspending or otherwise limiting the defendant's driving privilege on the ground of two or more convictions.

(H) The defendant's DNA sample and profile in the DNA data bank shall not be removed by a dismissal pursuant to this subdivision.

(I) Dismissal of an accusation, information, or conviction pursuant to this section does not authorize a defendant to own, possess, or have in the defendant's custody or control any firearm or prevent the defendant's conviction pursuant to Chapter 2 (commencing with Section 29800) of Division 9 of Title 4 of Part 6.

Amended by Stats 2019 ch 497 (AB 991),s 205, eff. 1/1/2020.

Amended by Stats 2018 ch 423 (SB 1494),s 86, eff. 1/1/2019.

Amended by Stats 2014 ch 163 (AB 2098),s 1, eff. 1/1/2015.

Amended by Stats 2013 ch 46 (SB 769),s 1, eff. 1/1/2014.

Amended by Stats 2012 ch 403 (AB 2371),s 1, eff. 1/1/2013.

Amended by Stats 2010 ch 347 (AB 674),s 1, eff. 1/1/2011.

Amended by Stats 2006 ch 788 (AB 2586),s 2, eff. 1/1/2007.

Section 1170.91 - Mitigation if defendant member of military suffering from sexual trauma, traumatic brain injury, post-traumatic stress disorder, substance abuse, or mental health problems

(a) If the court concludes that a defendant convicted of a felony offense is, or was, a member of the United States military who may be suffering from sexual trauma, traumatic brain injury, post-traumatic stress disorder, substance abuse, or mental health problems as a result of the defendant's military service, the court shall consider the circumstance as a factor in mitigation when imposing a sentence. This consideration does not preclude the court from considering similar trauma, injury, substance abuse, or mental health problems due to other causes, as evidence or factors in mitigation.

(b)

(1) A person currently serving a sentence for a felony conviction, whether by trial or plea, who is, or was, a member of the United States military and who may be suffering from sexual trauma, traumatic brain injury, post-traumatic stress disorder, substance abuse, or mental health problems as a result of the person's military service may petition for a recall of sentence, before the trial court that entered the judgment of conviction in the case, to request resentencing if the circumstance of suffering from sexual trauma, traumatic brain injury, post-traumatic stress disorder, substance abuse, or mental health problems as a result of the person's military service was not considered as a factor in mitigation at the time of sentencing.

(2) If the court that originally sentenced the person is not available, the presiding judge shall designate another judge to rule on the petition.

(3) Upon receiving a petition under this subdivision, the court shall determine, at a public hearing held after not less than 15 days' notice to the prosecution, the defense, and any victim of the offense, whether the person satisfies the criteria in this subdivision. At that hearing, the prosecution shall have an opportunity to be heard on the petitioner's eligibility and suitability for resentencing. If the person satisfies the criteria, the court may, in the interest of justice, and regardless of whether the original sentence was imposed after a trial or plea, do either of the following:

(A) Reduce the defendant's term of imprisonment by modifying the sentence.

(B) Vacate the conviction and impose judgment on any necessarily included lesser offense or lesser related offense, whether or not that offense was charged in the original pleading, and then resentence the defendant to a reduced term of imprisonment with the concurrence of both the defendant and the district attorney of the county in which the defendant was sentenced or by the Attorney General if the case was originally prosecuted by the Department of Justice.

(4) A person who is resentenced pursuant to this subdivision shall be given credit for time served.

(5) Resentencing under this subdivision shall not result in the imposition of a term longer than the original sentence.

(6) This subdivision does not alter or diminish any rights conferred under Section 28 of Article I of the California Constitution (Marsy's Law).

(7) This subdivision does not diminish or abrogate any rights or remedies otherwise available to the person.

(8) This subdivision does not diminish or abrogate the finality of judgments in any case not falling within the purview of this subdivision.

(9) This subdivision does not impose an obligation on the Department of Corrections and Rehabilitation to provide medical or mental health assessments in order to identify potential service-related injuries.

(10) This subdivision shall apply retroactively.

(c) This section does not apply to a person convicted of, or having one or more prior convictions for, an offense specified in clause (iv) of subparagraph (C) of paragraph (2) of subdivision (e) of Section 667 or an offense requiring registration pursuant to subdivision (c) of Section 290.

Amended by Stats 2022 ch 721 (SB 1209),s 1, eff. 1/1/2023.

Amended by Stats 2018 ch 523 (AB 865),s 1, eff. 1/1/2019.

Added by Stats 2014 ch 163 (AB 2098),s 2, eff. 1/1/2015.

Section 1170.95 - [Renumbered as 1172.6]

Renumbered as Ca. Pen. Code §1172.6 by Stats 2022 ch 58 (AB 200),s 10, eff. 6/30/2022.

Amended by Stats 2021 ch 551 (SB 775),s 2, eff. 1/1/2022.

Added by Stats 2018 ch 1015 (SB 1437),s 4, eff. 1/1/2019.

 See Stats 2021 ch 551 (SB 775), s 1.

Section 1171 - [Renumbered as 1172.7]

Renumbered as Ca. Pen. Code §1172.7 by Stats 2022 ch 58 (AB 200),s 11, eff. 6/30/2022.

Added by Stats 2021 ch 728 (SB 483),s 2, eff. 1/1/2022.

Section 1171.1 - [Renumbered as 1172.75]

Renumbered as Ca. Pen. Code §1172.75 by Stats 2022 ch 58 (AB 200),s 12, eff. 6/30/2022.

Added by Stats 2021 ch 728 (SB 483),s 3, eff. 1/1/2022.

Article 1.5 - RECALL AND RESENTENCING

Section 1172 - County Resentencing Pilot Program

(a)The County Resentencing Pilot Program (pilot) is hereby established to support and evaluate a collaborative approach to exercising prosecutorial resentencing discretion pursuant to Section 1172.1. Participants in the pilot shall include a county district attorney's office, a county public defender's office, and may include a community-based organization in each county pilot site.

(b)Each participating district attorney's office shall do all of the following:

(1)Develop and implement a written policy which, at minimum, outlines the factors, criteria, and processes that shall be used to identify, investigate, and recommend individuals for recall and resentencing. The district attorney's office may take into account any input provided by the participating public defender's office or a qualified contracted community-based organization in developing this policy.

(2)Identify, investigate, and recommend the recall and resentencing of incarcerated persons consistent with its written policy.

(3)Direct all funding provided for the pilot be used for the purposes of resentencing individuals pursuant to the pilot, including, but not limited to, ensuring adequate staffing of deputy district attorneys, paralegals, and data analysts who will coordinate obtaining records and case files, support data entry, assist in the preparation and filing of pleadings, coordinate with victim services, and any other tasks required to complete the processing and facilitation of resentencing recommendations and to comply with the requirements of the pilot.

(c)A participating district attorney's office may contract with a qualifying community-based organization for the duration of the pilot. The community-based organization shall have experience working with currently or formerly incarcerated individuals and their support networks, and shall have expertise in at least two of the following areas:

(1)Supporting and developing prerelease and reentry plans.

(2)Family reunification services.

(3)Referrals to postrelease wraparound programs, including, but not limited to, employment, education, housing, substance use disorder, and mental health service programs.

(4)Restorative justice programs.

(d)Nothing in this section shall be construed to limit the discretion or authority granted to prosecutors under Section 1172.1.

(e)All funding provided to a participating public defender's office shall be used for the purposes of supporting the resentencing of individuals pursuant to the pilot, including, but not limited to, ensuring adequate staffing of deputy public defenders and other support staff to represent incarcerated persons under consideration for resentencing, identifying and recommending incarcerated persons to the district attorney's office for resentencing consideration, and developing reentry and release plans. A participating public defender's office may provide input to the county district attorney's office regarding the factors, criteria, and processes to be used by the district attorney in their exercise of discretion under Section 1172.1.

(f)Each participating district attorney's office shall utilize the same template developed by the evaluator to identify and trac specific measures consistent with the goals of this section. The template shall be finalized no later than October 1, 2021. The measures shall include, but not be limited to, the following:

(1)A summary of expenditures by each entity receiving funds.

(2)A summary of any implementation delays or challenges, as well as steps being taken to address them.

(3)The total number of people incarcerated in state prison on the first day of each reporting year for convictions obtained in the reporting county.

(4)The factors and criteria used to identify cases to be considered for prosecutor-initiated resentencing.

(5)The total number of cases considered by a pilot participant for prosecutor-initiated resentencing. For each case, information collected shall include the date the case was considered, along with the defendant's race, ethnicity, gender, age at commitment, categories of controlling offenses, date of prison admission, earliest possible release date or minimum eligible parole date, and date of birth.

(6)The total number of prosecutor-initiated resentencing recommendations by the pilot participant to the court for recall of sentence, date of referral, and information on the defendant's race, ethnicity, gender, age at commitment, groups of controlling offenses, age at time of recall consideration, time served, and time remaining.

(7)The total number of prosecutor-initiated resentencing recommendations by the pilot participant in which the court responded, the date the court considered each case referred, how many cases the court considered, and information on the defendant's race, ethnicity, gender, age at commitment, groups of controlling offenses, age at time of recall consideration, time served, and time remaining.

(8)The total number of prosecutor-initiated resentencing recommendations denied by the court, and for each case the date of the denial and the reasons for the denial, and information on the defendant's race, ethnicity, gender, age at commitment, groups of controlling offenses, age at time of recall consideration, time served, and time remaining.

(9)The total number of people who were resentenced, the date of resentencing, and information on the defendant's race, ethnicity, gender, age at commitment, groups of controlling offenses, age at time of recall consideration, time served, and time remaining.

(10)The total number of people released from state prison due to prosecutor-initiated resentencing by the pilot participant, how many were released from state prison and the date of release, and information on the defendant's race, ethnicity, gender, age at commitment, groups of controlling offenses, age at time of recall consideration, time served, and time remaining.

(g)The participating district attorneys' offices shall provide the data listed in subdivision (f) to the evaluator on a quarterly basis.

(h)To the extent possible, the evaluation of data reported by the participating district attorneys' offices shall be conducted in a manner that allows for comparison between the pilot participant sites. This includes, but is not limited to, collection and reporting of data at the individual case level using the same definitions. Each pilot participant shall provide any information necessary to the evaluator's completion of its analysis.

(i)Notwithstanding any other law, state entities, including, but not limited to, the Department of Corrections and Rehabilitation, the State Department of Social Services, and the Department of Child Support Services, shall provide any information needed for the completion of the evaluator's analysis.

(j)The evaluator shall do all of the following:

(1)For each case considered by a pilot participant, calculate the time served by an individual and the time remaining on their sentence.

(2)Analyze the data and prepare two preliminary reports and a final report to the Legislature. The first preliminary report shall be submitted to the Legislature on or before October 1, 2022. The second preliminary report shall be submitted to the Legislature on or before October 1, 2023. The final report shall be submitted to the Legislature on or before January 31, 2025.

(3)As part of the evaluation, the evaluator shall conduct, at minimum, four assessments, as follows:

(A)An implementation assessment shall be conducted to determine if pilot activities were implemented as intended. This assessment shall include semi-structured in-depth interviews with all relevant stakeholders, including, but not limited to, representatives from the district attorney agencies, public defender agencies and community-based organizations participating in the pilot jurisdictions. The assessment shall document the different strategies the pilot sites used, the development and implementation of the written resentencing policies and procedures, which cases were prioritized for resentencing and the referral process, and factors that facilitated or hindered implementation.

(B)A cost study that shall estimate the resources required to implement the pilot activities, to include both new expenditures on personnel and other goods and services, and the reallocation of resources from prior activities to the pilot activities. The assessment shall include total cost and cost per case.

(C)An assessment of the estimated amount of time by which an individual's earliest possible release date or minimum eligible parole date was advanced due to prosecutor-initiated resentencing, including a descriptive analysis of the process of cases from initial recommendation to final resentencing outcomes to document points of attrition in the process and allow for comparison between individuals based on age, gender, race, offense, and county. This assessment shall include a description of recidivism outcomes for individuals released from prison, based on definitions created in collaboration with pilot participants. This assessment shall include a calculation of the total number of days of incarceration avoided, and amount of time by which the person's earliest possible release date or minimum eligible parole date was advanced due to prosecutor-initiated resentencing for those individuals released from prison using data maintained by the Department of Corrections and Rehabilitation data systems.

(D)An assessment which compares, to the extent feasible, records at the individual case level with county or state administrative data files that capture utilization of government benefit and social service programs, such as Temporary Assistance for Needy Families, Supplemental Nutrition Assistance Program, and other government cash or in-kind social services, and court-ordered child support and visitation. The evaluator shall document changes in these indicators at the individual case level during the evaluation period, in order to determine whether any observed changes can be attributed to the pilot. The evaluator shall combine the descriptive information on outcomes from the third and fourth evaluation components with the cost analysis findings from the second component to estimate the potential for cost savings to state and local governments from the pilot activities. The evaluator shall, using the data collected from the pilot, estimate the potential for cost savings to state and local governments from the pilot activities.

(k)The pilot term shall begin on September 1, 2021, and end on September 1, 2024. The evaluation term shall begin on September 1, 2021, and end on January 31, 2025.

Renumbered from Ca. Pen. Code §1170.01 and amended by Stats 2022 ch 58 (AB 200),s 8, eff. 6/30/2022.

Added by Stats 2021 ch 80 (AB 145),s 3, eff. 7/16/2021.

Section 1172.1 - Resentencing requests

(a)

(1) When a defendant, upon conviction for a felony offense, has been committed to the custody of the Secretary of the Department of Corrections and Rehabilitation or to the custody of the county correctional administrator pursuant to subdivision (h) of Section 1170, the court may, on its own motion, within 120 days of the date of commitment or at any time if the applicable sentencing laws at the time of original sentencing are subsequently changed by new statutory authority or case law, at any time upon the recommendation of the secretary or the Board of Parole Hearings in the case of a defendant incarcerated in state prison, the county correctional administrator in the case of a defendant incarcerated in county jail, the district attorney of the county in which the defendant was sentenced, or the Attorney General if the Department of Justice originally prosecuted the case, recall the sentence and commitment previously ordered and resentence the defendant in the same manner as if they had not previously been sentenced, whether or not the defendant is still in custody, and provided the new sentence, if any, is no greater than the initial sentence. Recall and resentencing under this section may be initiated by the original sentencing judge, a judge designated by the presiding judge, or any judge with jurisdiction in the case.

(2) The court, in recalling and resentencing under this subdivision, shall apply the sentencing rules of the Judicial Council and apply any changes in law that reduce sentences or provide for judicial discretion so as to eliminate disparity of sentences and to promote uniformity of sentencing.

(3) The resentencing court may, in the interest of justice and regardless of whether the original sentence was imposed after a trial or plea agreement, do the following:

(A) Reduce a defendant's term of imprisonment by modifying the sentence.

(B) Vacate the defendant's conviction and impose judgment on any necessarily included lesser offense or lesser related offense, whether or not that offense was charged in the original pleading, with the concurrence of the defendant, and then resentence the defendant to a reduced term of imprisonment.

(4) If the court has recalled the sentence on its own motion, the court shall not impose a judgment on any necessarily included lesser offense or lesser related offense if the conviction was a result of a plea bargain without the concurrence of both the defendant and the district attorney of the county in which the defendant was sentenced, or the Attorney General if the Department of Justice originally prosecuted the case.

(5) In recalling and resentencing pursuant to this provision, the court shall consider postconviction factors, including, but not limited to, the disciplinary record and record of rehabilitation of the defendant while incarcerated, evidence that reflects whether age, time served, and diminished physical condition, if any, have reduced the defendant's risk for future violence, and evidence that reflects that circumstances have changed since the original sentencing so that continued incarceration is no longer in the interest of justice. Evidence that the defendant's incarceration is no longer in the interest of justice includes, but is not limited to, evidence that the defendant's constitutional rights were violated in the proceedings related to the conviction or sentence at issue, and any other evidence that undermines the integrity of the underlying conviction or sentence. The court shall consider if the defendant has experienced psychological, physical, or childhood trauma, including, but not limited to, abuse, neglect, exploitation, or sexual violence, if the defendant was a victim of intimate partner violence or human trafficking prior to or at the time of the commission of the offense, or if the defendant is a youth or was a youth as defined under subdivision (b) of Section 1016.7 at the time of the commission of the offense, and whether those circumstances were a contributing factor in the commission of the offense.

(6) Credit shall be given for time served.

(7) The court shall state on the record the reasons for its decision to grant or deny recall and resentencing.

(8)

(A) Resentencing may be granted without a hearing upon stipulation by the parties.

(B) Notwithstanding subparagraph (A), if a victim of a crime wishes to be heard pursuant to the provisions of Section 28 of Article I of the California Constitution, or pursuant to any other provision of law applicable to the hearing, the victim shall notify the prosecution of their request to be heard within 15 days of being notified that resentencing is being sought and the court shall provide an opportunity for the victim to be heard.

(9) Resentencing shall not be denied, nor a stipulation rejected, without a hearing where the parties have an opportunity to address the basis for the intended denial or rejection. If a hearing is held, the defendant may appear remotely and the court may conduct the hearing through the use of remote technology, unless counsel requests their physical presence in court.

(b) If a resentencing request pursuant to subdivision (a) is from the Secretary of the Department of Corrections and Rehabilitation, the Board of Parole Hearings, a county correctional administrator, a district attorney, or the Attorney General, all of the following shall apply:

(1) The court shall provide notice to the defendant and set a status conference within 30 days after the date that the court received the request. The court's order setting the conference shall also appoint counsel to represent the defendant.

(2) There shall be a presumption favoring recall and resentencing of the defendant, which may only be overcome if a court finds the defendant currently poses an unreasonable risk of danger to public safety, as defined in subdivision (c) of Section 1170.18.

(c) A defendant is not entitled to file a petition seeking relief from the court under this section. If a defendant requests consideration for relief under this section, the court is not required to respond.

(d) After ruling on a referral authorized by this section, the court shall advise the defendant of their right to appeal and the necessary steps and time for taking an appeal.

Amended by Stats 2023 ch 795 (AB 88),s 1.5, eff. 1/1/2024.

Amended by Stats 2023 ch 446 (AB 600),s 2, eff. 1/1/2024.

Amended by Stats 2023 ch 131 (AB 1754),s 157, eff. 1/1/2024.

Renumbered from Ca. Pen. Code §1170.03 and amended by Stats 2022 ch 58 (AB 200),s 9, eff. 6/30/2022.

Added by Stats 2021 ch 719 (AB 1540),s 3.1, eff. 1/1/2022.

Section 1172.2 - Compassionate release

(a) Notwithstanding any other law and consistent with paragraph (1) of subdivision (a) of Section 1170, if the statewide chief medical executive, in consultation with other clinical executives, as needed, determines that an incarcerated person satisfies the medical criteria set forth in subdivision (b), the department shall recommend to the court that the incarcerated person's sentence be recalled.

(b) There shall be a presumption favoring recall and resentencing under this section if the court finds that the facts described in paragraph (1) or (2) exist, which may only be overcome if a court finds the defendant is an unreasonable risk of danger to public safety, as defined in subdivision (c) of Section 1170.18, based on the incarcerated person's current physical and mental condition.

    (1) The incarcerated person has a serious and advanced illness with an end-of-life trajectory. Examples include, but are not limited to, metastatic solid-tumor cancer, amyotrophic lateral sclerosis (ALS), end-stage organ disease, and advanced end-stage dementia.

    (2) The incarcerated person is permanently medically incapacitated with a medical condition or functional impairment that renders them permanently unable to complete basic activities of daily living, including, but not limited to, bathing, eating, dressing, toileting, transferring, and ambulation, or has progressive end-stage dementia and that incapacitation did not exist at the time of the original sentencing.

(c) Within 10 days of receipt of a positive recommendation by the department, the court shall hold a hearing to consider whether the incarcerated person's sentence should be recalled.

(d) Any physician employed by the department, or their designee, who determines that an incarcerated person has a serious and advanced illness with an end-of-life trajectory or has a medical condition or functional impairment that renders them permanently medically incapacitated shall notify the chief medical executive of the prognosis. If the chief medical executive concurs with the prognosis, they shall notify the warden. Within 48 hours of receiving notification, the warden or the warden's representative shall notify the incarcerated person of the recall and resentencing procedures and shall arrange for the incarcerated person to designate a family member or other outside agent to be notified as to the incarcerated person's medical condition and prognosis and as to the recall and resentencing procedures. If the incarcerated person is deemed mentally unfit, the warden or the warden's representative shall contact the incarcerated person's emergency contact and provide the information described in subdivision (b).

(e) The department shall refer the matter to the court for recall and resentencing within 45 days of the primary physician's, or their designee's, diagnosis and referral to the chief medical executive.

(f) The warden or the warden's representative shall provide the incarcerated person and their family member, agent, or emergency contact, as described in subdivision (d), updated information throughout the recall and resentencing process with regard to the incarcerated person's medical condition and the status of the incarcerated person's recall and resentencing proceedings.

(g) Notwithstanding any other provisions of this section, the incarcerated person or their family member or designee may independently request consideration for recall and resentencing by contacting the chief medical executive at the prison. Upon receipt of the request, the chief medical executive and the warden or the warden's representative shall follow the procedures described in subdivision (d). If the department determines that the incarcerated person satisfies the criteria set forth in subdivision (b), the department shall recommend to the court that the incarcerated person's sentence be recalled. The department shall submit a recommendation for release within 45 days.

(h) Any recommendation for recall submitted to the court by the department shall include one or more medical evaluations, a postrelease plan, and findings pursuant to subdivision (b).

(i) If possible, the matter shall be heard before the same judge of the court who sentenced the incarcerated person.

(j) The referring physician or their designees from the department shall be available to the court or defense counsel as necessary throughout the recall and resentencing proceedings.

(k) Upon recommendation to the court for recall of sentence, the incarcerated person shall have the right to counsel and, if indigent, the right to court-appointed counsel.

(l) If the court grants the recall and resentencing application, the incarcerated person shall be released by the department within 48 hours of receipt of the court's order, unless a longer time period is agreed to by the incarcerated person. At the time of release, the warden or the warden's representative shall ensure that the incarcerated person has each of the following in their possession: a discharge medical summary, full medical records, state identification, parole or postrelease community supervision medications, and all property belonging to the incarcerated person. After discharge, any additional records shall be sent to the incarcerated person's forwarding address.

(m) The secretary shall issue a directive to medical and correctional staff employed by the department that details the guidelines and procedures for initiating a recall and resentencing procedure. The directive shall clearly state that any incarcerated person who has a serious and advanced illness with an end-of-life trajectory or who is found to be permanently medically incapacitated is eligible for recall and resentencing consideration and that recall and resentencing procedures shall be initiated upon that prognosis.

(n) The provisions of this section shall be available to an incarcerated person who is sentenced to a county jail pursuant to subdivision (h) of Section 1170. For purposes of those incarcerated persons, "secretary" or "warden" shall mean the county correctional administrator and "chief medical executive" shall mean a physician designated by the county correctional administrator, for this purpose.

(o) This section does not apply to an incarcerated person sentenced to death or a term of life without the possibility of parole.

(p) Beginning January 1, 2024, the California Judicial Council shall publicly release an annual report on the compassionate release program based on records provided by the department pursuant to this section and subsequent court records. The report shall include, but is not limited to, all of the following:

    (1) The number of people who were referred to the court for recall and resentencing disaggregated by race, ethnicity, age, and gender identity and further disaggregated by the type of criteria on which the referral was based. The report shall identify the following categories of criteria for recall and resentencing referrals:

        (A) A serious and advanced illness with an end-of-life trajectory.

        (B) Functional impairment.

        (C) Cognitive impairment.

    (2) The number of people released by the court pursuant to this section, disaggregated by race, ethnicity, age, and gender identity.

    (3) The number of people denied resentencing sought pursuant to this section disaggregated by race, ethnicity, age, and gender identity.

(4) Number of people who pass away before completing the recall and resentencing process disaggregated by race, ethnicity, age, and gender identity.

(5) Number of people denied resentencing sought pursuant to this section for lack of release plans with data disaggregated by race, ethnicity, age, and gender identity.

(6) Number of cases pending decision with data disaggregated by race, ethnicity, age, and gender identity.

Amended by Stats 2023 ch 131 (AB 1754),s 158, eff. 1/1/2024.

Added by Stats 2022 ch 744 (AB 960),s 3, eff. 1/1/2023.

Section 1172.6 - Persons convicted of felony murder or murder under a natural and probable consequences theory; petition for resentencing

(a)A person convicted of felony murder or murder under the natural and probable consequences doctrine or other theory under which malice is imputed to a person based solely on that person's participation in a crime, attempted murder under the natural and probable consequences doctrine, or manslaughter may file a petition with the court that sentenced the petitioner to have the petitioner's murder, attempted murder, or manslaughter conviction vacated and to be resentenced on any remaining counts when all of the following conditions apply:

(1)A complaint, information, or indictment was filed against the petitioner that allowed the prosecution to proceed under a theory of felony murder, murder under the natural and probable consequences doctrine or other theory under which malice is imputed to a person based solely on that person's participation in a crime, or attempted murder under the natural and probable consequences doctrine.

(2) The petitioner was convicted of murder, attempted murder, or manslaughter following a trial or accepted a plea offer in lieu of a trial at which the petitioner could have been convicted of murder or attempted murder.

(3) The petitioner could not presently be convicted of murder or attempted murder because of changes to Section 188 or 189 made effective January 1, 2019.

(b)

(1) The petition shall be filed with the court that sentenced the petitioner and served by the petitioner on the district attorney, or on the agency that prosecuted the petitioner, and on the attorney who represented the petitioner in the trial court or on the public defender of the county where the petitioner was convicted. If the judge that originally sentenced the petitioner is not available to resentence the petitioner, the presiding judge shall designate another judge to rule on the petition. The petition shall include all of the following:

(A)A declaration by the petitioner that the petitioner is eligible for relief under this section, based on all the requirements of subdivision (a).

(B) The superior court case number and year of the petitioner's conviction.

(C) Whether the petitioner requests the appointment of counsel.

(2) If any of the information required by this subdivision is missing from the petition and cannot be readily ascertained by the court, the court may deny the petition without prejudice to the filing of another petition and advise the petitioner that the matter cannot be considered without the missing information.

(3) Upon receiving a petition in which the information required by this subdivision is set forth or a petition where any missing information can readily be ascertained by the court, if the petitioner has requested counsel, the court shall appoint counsel to represent the petitioner.

(c) Within 60 days after service of a petition that meets the requirements set forth in subdivision (b), the prosecutor shall file and serve a response. The petitioner may file and serve a reply within 30 days after the prosecutor's response is served. These deadlines shall be extended for good cause. After the parties have had an opportunity to submit briefings, the court shall hold a hearing to determine whether the petitioner has made a prima facie case for relief. If the petitioner makes a prima facie showing that the petitioner is entitled to relief, the court shall issue an order to show cause. If the court declines to make an order to show cause, it shall provide a statement fully setting forth its reasons for doing so.

(d)

(1) Within 60 days after the order to show cause has issued, the court shall hold a hearing to determine whether to vacate the murder, attempted murder, or manslaughter conviction and to recall the sentence and resentence the petitioner on any remaining counts in the same manner as if the petitioner had not previously been sentenced, provided that the new sentence, if any, is not greater than the initial sentence. This deadline may be extended for good cause.

(2) The parties may waive a resentencing hearing and stipulate that the petitioner is eligible to have the murder, attempted murder, or manslaughter conviction vacated and to be resentenced. If there was a prior finding by a court or jury that the petitioner did not act with reckless indifference to human life or was not a major participant in the felony, the court shall vacate the petitioner's conviction and resentence the petitioner.

(3) At the hearing to determine whether the petitioner is entitled to relief, the burden of proof shall be on the prosecution to prove, beyond a reasonable doubt, that the petitioner is guilty of murder or attempted murder under California law as amended by the changes to Section 188 or 189 made effective January 1, 2019. The admission of evidence in the hearing shall be governed by the Evidence Code, except that the court may consider evidence previously admitted at any prior hearing or trial that is admissible under current law, including witness testimony, stipulated evidence, and matters judicially noticed. The court may also consider the procedural history of the case recited in any prior appellate opinion. However, hearsay evidence that was admitted in a preliminary hearing pursuant to subdivision (b) of Section 872 shall be excluded from the hearing as hearsay, unless the evidence is admissible pursuant to another exception to the hearsay rule. The prosecutor and the petitioner may also offer new or additional evidence to meet their respective burdens. A finding that there is substantial evidence to support a conviction for murder, attempted murder, or manslaughter is insufficient to prove, beyond a reasonable doubt, that the petitioner is ineligible for resentencing. If the prosecution fails to sustain its burden of proof, the prior conviction, and any allegations and enhancements attached to the conviction, shall be vacated and the petitioner shall be resentenced on the remaining charges.

(e)The petitioner's conviction shall be redesignated as the target offense or underlying felony for resentencing purposes if the petitioner is entitled to relief pursuant to this section, murder or attempted murder was charged generically, and the target offense was not charged. Any applicable statute of limitations shall not be a bar to the court's redesignation of the offense for this purpose.

(f)This section does not diminish or abrogate any rights or remedies otherwise available to the petitioner.

(g)A person convicted of murder, attempted murder, or manslaughter whose conviction is not final may challenge on direct appeal the validity of that conviction based on the changes made to Sections 188 and 189 by Senate Bill 1437 (Chapter 1015 of the Statutes of 2018).

(h)A person who is resentenced pursuant to this section shall be given credit for time served. The judge may order the petitioner to be subject to parole supervision for up to two years following the completion of the sentence.

Renumbered from Ca. Pen. Code §1170.95 and amended by Stats 2022 ch 58 (AB 200),s 10, eff. 6/30/2022.

Amended by Stats 2021 ch 551 (SB 775),s 2, eff. 1/1/2022.

Added by Stats 2018 ch 1015 (SB 1437),s 4, eff. 1/1/2019.

See Stats 2021 ch 551 (SB 775), s 1.

Section 1172.7 - Sentence enhancements imposed prior to January 1, 2018, pursuant to Section 11370.2 invalid; exception

(a)Any sentence enhancement that was imposed prior to January 1, 2018, pursuant to Section 11370.2 of the Health and Safety Code, except for any enhancement imposed for a prior conviction of violating or conspiring to violate Section 11380 of the Health and Safety Code, is legally invalid.

(b)The Secretary of the Department of Corrections and Rehabilitation and the county correctional administrator of each county shall identify those persons in their custody currently serving a term for a judgment that includes an enhancement described in subdivision (a) and shall provide the name of each person, along with the person's date of birth and the relevant case number or docket number, to the sentencing court that imposed the enhancement. This information shall be provided as follows:

(1)By March 1, 2022, for individuals who have served their base term and any other enhancements and are currently serving a sentence based on the enhancement. For purposes of this paragraph, all other enhancements shall be considered to have been served first.

(2)By July 1, 2022, for all other individuals.

(c)Upon receiving the information described in subdivision (b), the court shall review the judgment and verify that the current judgment includes a sentence enhancement described in subdivision (a). If the court determines that the current judgment includes an enhancement described in subdivision (a), the court shall recall the sentence and resentence the defendant. The review and resentencing shall be completed as follows:

(1)By October 1, 2022, for individuals who have served their base term and any other enhancement and are currently serving a sentence based on the enhancement.

(2)By December 31, 2023, for all other individuals.

(d)

(1)Resentencing pursuant to this section shall result in a lesser sentence than the one originally imposed as a result of the elimination of the repealed enhancement, unless the court finds by clear and convincing evidence that imposing a lesser sentence would endanger public safety. Resentencing pursuant to this section shall not result in a longer sentence than the one originally imposed.

(2)The court shall apply the sentencing rules of the Judicial Council and apply any other changes in law that reduce sentences or provide for judicial discretion so as to eliminate disparity of sentences and to promote uniformity of sentencing.

(3)The court may consider postconviction factors, including, but not limited to, the disciplinary record and record of rehabilitation of the defendant while incarcerated, evidence that reflects whether age, time served, and diminished physical condition, if any, have reduced the defendant's risk for future violence, and evidence that reflects that circumstances have changed since the original sentencing so that continued incarceration is no longer in the interest of justice.

(4)Unless the court originally imposed the upper term, the court may not impose a sentence exceeding the middle term unless there are circumstances in aggravation that justify the imposition of a term of imprisonment exceeding the middle term, and those facts have been stipulated to by the defendant, or have been found true beyond a reasonable doubt at trial by the jury or by the judge in a court trial.

(5)The court shall appoint counsel.

(e)The parties may waive a resentencing hearing. If the hearing is not waived, the resentencing hearing may be conducted remotely through the use of remote technology, if the defendant agrees.

Renumbered from Ca. Pen. Code §1171 and amended by Stats 2022 ch 58 (AB 200),s 11, eff. 6/30/2022.

Added by Stats 2021 ch 728 (SB 483),s 2, eff. 1/1/2022.

Section 1172.75 - Sentence enhancements imposed prior to January 1, 2020, pursuant to subdivision (b) of Section 667.5 invalid; exception

(a)Any sentence enhancement that was imposed prior to January 1, 2020, pursuant to subdivision (b) of Section 667.5, except for any enhancement imposed for a prior conviction for a sexually violent offense as defined in subdivision (b) of Section 6600 of the Welfare and Institutions Code is legally invalid.

(b)The Secretary of the Department of Corrections and Rehabilitation and the county correctional administrator of each county shall identify those persons in their custody currently serving a term for a judgment that includes an enhancement described in subdivision (a) and shall provide the name of each person, along with the person's date of birth and the relevant case number or docket number, to the sentencing court that imposed the enhancement. This information shall be provided as follows:

(1)By March 1, 2022, for individuals who have served their base term and any other enhancements and are currently serving a sentence based on the enhancement. For purposes of this paragraph, all other enhancements shall be considered to have been served first.

(2)By July 1, 2022, for all other individuals.

(c)Upon receiving the information described in subdivision (b), the court shall review the judgment and verify that the current judgment includes a sentencing enhancement described in subdivision (a). If the court determines that the current judgment includes an enhancement described in subdivision (a), the court shall recall the sentence and resentence the defendant. The review and resentencing shall be completed as follows:

(1)By October 1, 2022, for individuals who have served their base term and any other enhancement and are currently serving a sentence based on the enhancement.

(2)By December 31, 2023, for all other individuals.

(d)

(1)Resentencing pursuant to this section shall result in a lesser sentence than the one originally imposed as a result of the elimination of the repealed enhancement, unless the court finds by clear and convincing evidence that imposing a lesser sentence would endanger public safety. Resentencing pursuant to this section shall not result in a longer sentence than the one originally imposed.

(2)The court shall apply the sentencing rules of the Judicial Council and apply any other changes in law that reduce sentences or provide for judicial discretion so as to eliminate disparity of sentences and to promote uniformity of sentencing.

(3)The court may consider postconviction factors, including, but not limited to, the disciplinary record and record of rehabilitation of the defendant while incarcerated, evidence that reflects whether age, time served, and diminished physical condition, if any, have reduced the defendant's risk for future violence, and evidence that reflects that circumstances have changed since the original sentencing so that continued incarceration is no longer in the interest of justice.

(4)Unless the court originally imposed the upper term, the court may not impose a sentence exceeding the middle term unless there are circumstances in aggravation that justify the imposition of a term of imprisonment exceeding the middle term, and those facts have been stipulated to by the defendant, or have been found true beyond a reasonable doubt at trial by the jury or by the judge in a court trial.

(5)The court shall appoint counsel.

(e)The parties may waive a resentencing hearing. If the hearing is not waived, the resentencing hearing may be conducted remotely through the use of remote technology, if the defendant agrees.

Renumbered from Ca. Pen. Code §1171.1 and amended by Stats 2022 ch 58 (AB 200),s 12, eff. 6/30/2022.

Added by Stats 2021 ch 728 (SB 483),s 3, eff. 1/1/2022.

Chapter 4.8 - PREGNANT AND PARENTING WOMEN'S ALTERNATIVE SENTENCING PROGRAM ACT

Section 1174 - Short title

This chapter shall be known as the Pregnant and Parenting Women's Alternative Sentencing Program Act.

Added by Stats. 1994, Ch. 63, Sec. 2. Effective May 9, 1994.

Section 1174.1 - Definitions

For purposes of this chapter, the following definitions shall apply:

(a) "Agency" means the private agency selected by the department to operate this program.

(b) "Construction" means the purchase, new construction, reconstruction, remodeling, renovation, or replacement of facilities, or a combination thereof.

(c) "County" means each individual county as represented by the county board of supervisors.

(d) "Court" means the superior court sentencing the offender to the custody of the department.

(e) "Department" means the Department of Corrections.

(f) "Facility" means the nonsecure physical buildings, rooms, areas, and equipment.

(g) "Program" means an intensive substance abusing pregnant and parenting women's alternative sentencing program.

Added by Stats. 1994, Ch. 63, Sec. 2. Effective May 9, 1994.

Section 1174.2 - Appropriation; use of funds

(a) Notwithstanding any other law, the unencumbered balance of Item 5240-311-751 of Section 2 of the Budget Act of 1990 shall revert to the unappropriated surplus of the 1990 Prison Construction Fund. The sum of fifteen million dollars ($15,000,000) is hereby appropriated to the Department of Corrections from the 1990 Prison Construction Fund for site acquisition, site studies, environmental studies, master planning, architectural programming, schematics, preliminary plans, working drawings, construction, and long lead and equipment items for the purpose of constructing facilities for pregnant and parenting women's alternative sentencing programs. These funds shall not be expended for any operating costs, including those costs reimbursed by the department pursuant to subdivision (c) of Section 1174.3. Funds not expended pursuant to this chapter shall be used for planning, construction, renovation, or remodeling by, or under the supervision of, the Department of Corrections and Rehabilitation, of community-based facilities for programs designed to reduce drug use and recidivism, including, but not limited to, restitution centers, facilities for the incarceration and rehabilitation of drug offenders, multipurpose correctional centers, and centers for intensive programs for parolees. These funds shall not be expended until legislation authorizing the establishment of these programs is enacted. If the Legislature finds that the Department of Corrections and Rehabilitation has made a good faith effort to site community-based facilities, but funds designated for these community-based facilities are unexpended as of January 1, 1998, the Legislature may appropriate these funds for other Level I housing.

(b) The Department of Corrections and Rehabilitation shall purchase, design, construct, and renovate facilities in counties or multicounty areas with a population of more than 450,000 people pursuant to this chapter. The department shall target for selection, among other counties, Los Angeles County, San Diego County, and a bay area, central valley, and an inland empire county as determined by the Secretary of the Department of Corrections and Rehabilitation. The department, in consultation with the State Department of Health Care Services, shall design core alcohol and drug treatment programs, with specific requirements and standards. Residential facilities shall be licensed by the State Department of Health Care Services in accordance with provisions of the Health and Safety Code governing licensure of alcoholism or drug abuse recovery or treatment facilities. Residential and nonresidential programs shall be certified by the

State Department of Health Care Services as meeting its standards for perinatal services. Funds shall be awarded to selected agency service providers based upon all of the following criteria and procedures:

(1) A demonstrated ability to provide comprehensive services to pregnant women or women with children who are substance abusers consistent with this chapter. Criteria shall include, but not be limited to, each of the following:

(A) The success records of the types of programs proposed based upon standards for successful programs.

(B) Expertise and actual experience of persons who will be in charge of the proposed program.

(C) Cost-effectiveness, including the costs per client served.

(D) A demonstrated ability to implement a program as expeditiously as possible.

(E) An ability to accept referrals and participate in a process with the probation department determining eligible candidates for the program.

(F) A demonstrated ability to seek and obtain supplemental funding as required in support of the overall administration of this facility from any county, state, or federal source that may serve to support this program, including the State Department of Health Care Services, the Office of Emergency Services, the State Department of Social Services, the State Department of State Hospitals, or any county public health department. In addition, the agency shall also attempt to secure other available funding from all county, state, or federal sources for program implementation.

(G) An ability to provide intensive supervision of the program participants to ensure complete daily programming.

(2) Staff from the department shall be available to selected agencies for consultation and technical services in preparation and implementation of the selected proposals.

(3) The department shall consult with existing program operators that are then currently delivering similar program services, the State Department of Health Care Services, and others it may identify in the development of the program.

(4) Funds shall be made available by the department to the agencies selected to administer the operation of this program.

(5) Agencies shall demonstrate an ability to provide offenders a continuing supportive network of outpatient drug treatment and other services upon the women's completion of the program and reintegration into the community.

(6) The department may propose any variation of types and sizes of facilities to carry out the purposes of this chapter.

(7) The department shall secure all other available funding for its eligible population from all county, state, or federal sources.

(8) Each program proposal shall include a plan for the required 12-month residential program, plus a 12-month outpatient transitional services program to be completed by participating women and children.

Amended by Stats 2013 ch 22 (AB 75),s 77, eff. 6/27/2013, op. 7/1/2013.

Amended by Stats 2012 ch 24 (AB 1470),s 23, eff. 6/27/2012.

Amended by Stats 2010 ch 618 (AB 2791),s 203, eff. 1/1/2011.

Amended by Stats 2003 ch 229 (AB 1757), s 12, eff. 1/1/2004.

Section 1174.3 - Facility designs; operation of center and program

(a) The department shall ensure that the facility designs provide adequate space to carry out this chapter, including the capability for nonsecure housing, programming, child care, food services, treatment services, educational or vocational services, intensive day treatment, and transitional living skills services.

(b) The agency selected to operate the program shall administer and operate the center and program consistent with the criteria set forth in this chapter and any criteria established by the department. These responsibilities shall include maintenance and compliance with all laws, regulations, and health standards. The department shall contract to reimburse the agency selected to operate this program for women who would otherwise be sentenced to state prison based upon actual costs not provided by other funding sources.

(c) Notwithstanding any other law, Division 13 (commencing with Section 21000) of the Public Resources Code shall not apply to any facility used for multiperson residential use in the last five years, including, but not limited to, motels, hotels, long-term care facilities, apartment buildings, and rooming houses, or to any project for which facilities intended to house no more than 75 women and children are constructed or leased pursuant to this chapter.

(d) Proposals submitted pursuant to this chapter are exempt from approval and submittal of plans and specifications to the Joint Legislative Committee on Prison Construction Operations and other legislative fiscal committees.

Added by Stats. 1994, Ch. 63, Sec. 2. Effective May 9, 1994.

Section 1174.4 - Criteria for eligibility for participation

(a) Persons eligible for participation in this alternative sentencing program shall meet all of the following criteria:

(1) Pregnant women with an established history of substance abuse, or pregnant or parenting women with an established history of substance abuse who have one or more children under six years old at the time of entry into the program. For women with children, at least one eligible child shall reside with the mother in the facility.

(2) Never served a prior prison term for, nor been convicted in the present proceeding of, committing or attempting to commit, any of the following offenses:

(A) Murder or voluntary manslaughter.

(B) Mayhem.

(C) Rape.

(D) Kidnapping.

(E) Sodomy by force, violence, duress, menace, or fear of immediate and unlawful bodily injury on the victim or another person.

(F) Oral copulation by force, violence, duress, menace, or fear of immediate and unlawful bodily injury on the victim or another person.

(G) Lewd acts on a child under 14 years of age, as defined in Section 288.

(H) Any felony punishable by death or imprisonment in the state prison for life.

(I) Any felony in which the defendant inflicts great bodily injury on any person, other than an accomplice, that has been charged and proved as provided for in Section 12022.53, 12022.7, or 12022.9, or any felony in which the defendant uses a firearm, as provided in Section 12022.5, 12022.53, or 12022.55, in which the use has been charged and proved.

(J) Robbery.

(K) Any robbery perpetrated in an inhabited dwelling house or trailer coach as defined in the Vehicle Code, or in the inhabited portion of any other building, wherein it is charged and proved that the defendant personally used a deadly or dangerous weapon, as provided in subdivision (b) of Section 12022, in the commission of that robbery.

(L) Arson in violation of subdivision (a) of Section 451.

(M) Sexual penetration in violation of subdivision (a) of Section 289 if the act is accomplished against the victim's will by force, violence, duress, menace, or fear of immediate and unlawful bodily injury on the victim or another person.

(N) Rape or sexual penetration in concert, in violation of Section 264.1.

(O) Continual sexual abuse of a child in violation of Section 288.5.

(P) Assault with intent to commit mayhem, rape, sodomy, oral copulation, rape in concert with another, lascivious acts upon a child, or sexual penetration.

(Q) Assault with a deadly weapon or with force likely to produce great bodily injury in violation of subdivision (a) of Section 245.

(R) Any violent felony defined in Section 667.5.

(S) A violation of Section 12022.

(T) A violation of Section 18745.

(U) Burglary of the first degree.

(V) A violation of Section 11351, 11351.5, 11352, 11353, 11358, 11359, 11360, 11370.1, 11370.6, 11378, 11378.5, 11379, 11379.5, 11379.6, 11380, or 11383 of the Health and Safety Code.

(3) Has not been sentenced to state prison for a term exceeding 36 months.

(b) Prior to sentencing, if the court proposes to give consideration to a placement, the court shall consider a written evaluation by the probation department, which shall include the following:

(1) Whether the defendant is eligible for participation pursuant to this section.

(2) Whether participation by the defendant and her eligible children is deemed to be in the best interests of the children.

(3) Whether the defendant is amenable to treatment for substance abuse and would benefit from participation in the program.

(4) Whether the program is deemed to be in the best interests of an eligible child of the defendant, as determined by a representative of the appropriate child welfare services agency of the county if the child is a dependent child of the juvenile court pursuant to Section 300 of the Welfare and Institutions Code.

(c) The district attorney shall make a recommendation to the court as to whether or not the defendant would benefit from the program, which the court shall consider in making its decision. If the court's decision is without the concurrence of the district attorney, the court shall specify its reasons in writing and enter them into the record.

(d) If the court determines that the defendant may benefit from participation in this program, the court may impose a sentence of imprisonment pursuant to subdivision (h) of Section 1170 with the recommendation that the defendant participate in the program pursuant to this chapter. The court shall notify the department within 48 hours of imposition of this sentence.

(e) The Director of Corrections shall consider the court's recommendation in making a determination on the inmate's placement in the program.

(f) Women accepted for the program by the Director of Corrections shall be delivered by the county, pursuant to Section 1202a, to the facility selected by the department. Before the director accepts a woman for the program, the county shall provide to the director the necessary information to determine her eligibility and appropriate placement status. Priority for services and aftercare shall be given to inmates who are incarcerated in a county, or adjacent to a county, in which a program facility is located.

(g) Prior to being admitted to the program, each participant shall voluntarily sign an agreement specifying the terms and conditions of participation in the program.

(h) The department may refer inmates back to the sentencing court if the department determines that an eligible inmate has not been recommended for the program. The department shall refer the inmate to the court by an evaluative report so stating the department's assessment of eligibility, and requesting a recommendation by the court.

(i) Women who successfully complete the program, including the minimum of one year of transition services under intensive parole supervision, shall be discharged from parole. Women who do not successfully complete the program shall be returned to imprisonment pursuant to subdivision (h) of Section 1170 where they shall serve their original sentences. These persons shall receive full credit against their original sentences for the time served in the program, pursuant to Section 2933.

Amended by Stats 2011 ch 39 (AB 117),s 68, eff. 6/30/2011.

Amended by Stats 2011 ch 15 (AB 109),s 453, eff. 4/4/2011, but operative no earlier than October 1, 2011, and only upon creation of a community corrections grant program to assist in implementing this act and upon an appropriation to fund the grant program.

Amended by Stats 2011 ch 15 (AB 109),s 452, eff. 4/4/2011, but operative no earlier than October 1, 2011, and only upon creation of a community corrections grant program to assist in implementing this act and upon an appropriation to fund the grant program.

Amended by Stats 2010 ch 178 (SB 1115),s 72, eff. 1/1/2011, op. 1/1/2012.

Amended by Stats 2000 ch 287 (SB 1955) s 16, eff. 1/1/2001.

Amended by Stats 2001 ch 854 (SB 205) s 42, eff. 1/1/2002.

Section 1174.5 - Responsibility for program

The department shall be responsible for the funding and monitoring of the progress, activities, and performance of each program.

Added by Stats. 1994, Ch. 63, Sec. 2. Effective May 9, 1994.

Section 1174.7 - [Repealed]

Repealed by Stats 2012 ch 728 (SB 71),s 124, eff. 1/1/2013.

Section 1174.8 - Adoption of regulations

(a) The department shall adopt regulations pursuant to the Administrative Procedure Act (Chapter 3.5 (commencing with Section 11340) of Part 1 of Division 3 of Title 2 of the Government Code) to implement this chapter.

(b) Notwithstanding subdivision (a) and any other law, and except as otherwise specifically provided in this chapter, until July 1, 1996, the Director of Corrections shall have the power to implement, interpret, and make specific the changes made in this chapter by issuing director's criteria. These criteria shall be exempt from the requirements of Articles 5 (commencing with Section 11346) and 6 (commencing with Section 11349) of the Administrative Procedure Act (Chapter 3.5 (commencing with Section 11340) of Part 1 of Division 3 of Title 2 of the Government Code) and shall remain in effect until July 1, 1996, unless terminated or replaced by, or readopted as, emergency regulations pursuant to subdivision (c).

(c) On or before July 1, 1995, the department shall file emergency regulations to implement this chapter with the Office of Administrative Law. These emergency regulations shall be considered by the office as necessary for the immediate preservation of the public peace, health and safety, or general welfare and shall remain in effect until July 1, 1996, unless terminated or replaced by, or readopted as, permanent regulations in compliance with Articles 5 (commencing with Section 11346) and 6 (commencing with Section 11349) of the Administrative Procedure Act (Chapter 3.5 (commencing with Section 11340) of Part 1 of Division 3 of Title 2 of the Government Code) pursuant to subdivision (d).

(d) The department shall file a certificate of compliance with the Office of Administrative Law to adopt permanent regulations on or before May 15, 1996.

Added by Stats. 1994, Ch. 63, Sec. 2. Effective May 9, 1994.

Section 1174.9 - Exemption for program facility

A program facility administered by the Department of Corrections pursuant to this chapter is exempt from the requirements and provisions of Chapter 3.4 (commencing with Section 1596.70), Chapter 3.5 (commencing with Section 1596.90), and Chapter 3.6 (commencing with Section 1597.30) of Division 2 of the Health and Safety Code.

Added by Stats. 1995, Ch. 372, Sec. 4. Effective January 1, 1996.

Chapter 5 - BILLS OF EXCEPTION

Section 1176 - Instructions or charge

When written instructions have been presented, and given, modified, or refused, or when the charge of the court has been taken down by the reporter, the questions presented in such instructions or charge need not be excepted to; but the judge must make and sign an indorsement upon such instructions, showing the action of the court thereon.

Amended by Stats. 1945, Ch. 40.

Chapter 6 - NEW TRIALS

Section 1179 - New trial

A new trial is a reëxamination of the issue in the same Court, before another jury, after a verdict has been given.

Enacted 1872.

Section 1180 - Effect of granting of new trial

The granting of a new trial places the parties in the same position as if no trial had been had. All the testimony must be produced anew, and the former verdict or finding cannot be used or referred to, either in evidence or in argument, or be pleaded in bar of any conviction which might have been had under the accusatory pleading.

Amended by Stats. 1951, Ch. 1674.

Section 1181 - Grant of new trial

When a verdict has been rendered or a finding made against the defendant, the court may, upon his application, grant a new trial, in the following cases only:

1. When the trial has been had in his absence except in cases where the trial may lawfully proceed in his absence;

2. When the jury has received any evidence out of court, other than that resulting from a view of the premises, or of personal property;

3. When the jury has separated without leave of the court after retiring to deliberate upon their verdict, or been guilty of any misconduct by which a fair and due consideration of the case has been prevented;

4. When the verdict has been decided by lot, or by any means other than a fair expression of opinion on the part of all the jurors;

5. When the court has misdirected the jury in a matter of law, or has erred in the decision of any question of law arising during the course of the trial, and when the district attorney or other counsel prosecuting the case has been guilty of prejudicial misconduct during the trial thereof before a jury;

6. When the verdict or finding is contrary to law or evidence, but if the evidence shows the defendant to be not guilty of the degree of the crime of which he was convicted, but guilty of a lesser degree thereof, or of a lesser crime included therein, the court may modify the verdict, finding or judgment accordingly without granting or ordering a new trial, and this power shall extend to any court to which the cause may be appealed;

7. When the verdict or finding is contrary to law or evidence, but in any case wherein authority is vested by statute in the trial court or jury to recommend or determine as a part of its verdict or finding the punishment to be imposed, the court may modify such verdict or finding by imposing the lesser punishment without granting or ordering a new trial, and this power shall extend to any court to which the case may be appealed;

8. When new evidence is discovered material to the defendant, and which he could not, with reasonable diligence, have discovered and produced at the trial. When a motion for a new trial is made upon the ground of newly discovered evidence, the defendant must produce at the hearing, in support thereof, the affidavits of the witnesses by whom such evidence is expected to be given, and if time is required by the defendant to procure such affidavits, the court may postpone the hearing of the motion for such length of time as, under all circumstances of the case, may seem reasonable.

9. When the right to a phonographic report has not been waived, and when it is not possible to have a phonographic report of the trial transcribed by a stenographic reporter as provided by law or by rule because of the death or disability of a reporter who participated as a stenographic reporter at the trial or because of the loss or destruction, in whole or in substantial part, of the notes of such reporter, the trial court or a judge, thereof, or the reviewing court shall have power to set aside and vacate the judgment, order or decree from which an appeal has been taken or is to be taken and to order a new trial of the action or proceeding.

Amended by Stats. 1973, Ch. 167.

Section 1182 - Application for new trial

The application for a new trial must be made and determined before judgment, the making of an order granting probation, the commitment of a defendant for observation as a mentally disordered sex offender, or the commitment of a defendant for narcotics addiction or insanity, whichever first occurs, and the order granting or denying the application shall be immediately entered by the clerk in the minutes.

Amended by Stats. 1980, Ch. 676, Sec. 252.

Chapter 7 - ARREST OF JUDGMENT

Section 1185 - Motion in arrest of judgment

A motion in arrest of judgment is an application on the part of the defendant that no judgment be rendered on a plea, finding, or verdict of guilty, or on a finding or verdict against the defendant, on a plea of a former conviction, former acquittal or once in jeopardy. It may be founded on any of the defects in the accusatory pleading mentioned in Section 1004, unless the objection has been waived by a failure to demur, and must be made and determined before the judgment is pronounced. When determined, the order must be immediately entered in the minutes.

Amended by Stats. 1951, Ch. 1674.

Section 1186 - Arrest of judgment

The court may, on its own motion, at any time before judgment is pronounced, arrest the judgment for any of the defects in the accusatory pleading upon which a motion in arrest of judgment may be founded as provided in Section 1185, by order for that purpose entered upon its minutes.

Amended by Stats. 1951, Ch. 1674.

Section 1187 - Effect of order arresting judgment

The effect of an order arresting judgment, in a felony case, is to place the defendant in the same situation in which the defendant was immediately before the indictment was found or information filed. In a misdemeanor or infraction case, the effect is to place the defendant in the situation in which the defendant was before the trial was had.

Amended by Stats. 1998, Ch. 931, Sec. 391. Effective September 28, 1998.

Section 1188 - Recommitment or discharge

If, from the evidence on the trial, there is reason to believe the defendant guilty, and a new indictment or information can be framed upon which he may be convicted, the court may order him to be recommitted to the officer of the proper county, or admitted to bail anew, to answer the new indictment or information. If the evidence shows him guilty of another offense, he must be committed or held thereon, and in neither case shall the verdict be a bar to another prosecution. But if no evidence appears sufficient to charge him with any offense, he must, if in custody, be discharged; or if admitted to bail, his bail is exonerated; or if money has been deposited instead of bail, it must be refunded to the defendant or to the person or persons found by the court to have deposited said money on behalf of said defendant; and the arrest of judgment shall operate as an acquittal of the charge upon which the indictment or information was founded.

Amended by Stats. 1935, Ch. 657.

Title 8 - OF JUDGMENT AND EXECUTION

Chapter 1 - THE JUDGMENT

Section 1191 - Time for pronouncing judgment

In a felony case, after a plea, finding, or verdict of guilty, or after a finding or verdict against the defendant on a plea of a former conviction or acquittal, or once in jeopardy, the court shall appoint a time for pronouncing judgment, which shall be within 20 judicial days after the verdict, finding, or plea of guilty, during which time the court shall refer the case to the probation officer for a report if eligible for probation and pursuant to Section 1203. However, the court may extend the time not more than 10 days for the purpose of hearing or determining any motion for a new trial, or in arrest of judgment, and may further extend the time until the probation officer's report is received and until any proceedings for granting or denying probation have been disposed of. If, in the opinion of the court, there is a reasonable ground for believing a defendant insane, the court may extend the time for pronouncing sentence until the question of insanity has been heard and determined, as provided in this code. If the court orders the defendant placed in a diagnostic facility pursuant to Section 1203.03, the time otherwise allowed by this section for pronouncing judgment is extended by a period equal to (1) the number of days which elapse between the date of the order and the date on which notice is received from the Director of Corrections advising whether or not the Department of Corrections will receive the defendant in the facility, and (2) if the director notifies the court that it will receive the defendant, the time which elapses until his or her return to the court from the facility.

Amended by Stats. 1998, Ch. 931, Sec. 392. Effective September 28, 1998.

Section 1191.1 - Right to attend sentencing proceedings

The victim of any crime, or the parents or guardians of the victim if the victim is a minor, or the next of kin of the victim if the victim has died, have the right to attend all sentencing proceedings under this chapter and shall be given adequate notice by the probation officer of all sentencing proceedings concerning the person who committed the crime.

The victim, or up to two of the victim's parents or guardians if the victim is a minor, or the next of kin of the victim if the victim has died, have the right to appear, personally or by counsel, at the sentencing proceeding and to reasonably express his, her, or their views concerning the crime, the person responsible, and the need for restitution. The court in imposing sentence shall consider the statements of victims, parents or guardians, and next of kin made pursuant to this section and shall state on the record its conclusion concerning whether the person would pose a threat to public safety if granted probation.

The provisions of this section shall not be amended by the Legislature except by statute passed in each house by rollcall vote entered in the journal, two-thirds of the membership concurring, or by a statute that becomes effective only when approved by the electors.

Amended by Stats. 1993, Ch. 338, Sec. 1. Effective January 1, 1994. Note: This section was added on June 8, 1982, by initiative Prop. 8.

Section 1191.10 - "Victim" defined

The definition of the term "victim" as used in Section 1191.1 includes any insurer or employer who was the victim of workers' compensation fraud for the crimes specified in Section 549 of this code, Sections 2314 and 6152 of the Business and Professions Code, Sections 1871.4, 11760, and 11880 of the Insurance Code, and Section 3215 of the Labor Code.

Added by Stats. 1993, Ch. 120, Sec. 9. Effective July 16, 1993.

Section 1191.15 - Written, audio, or video statement by victim or next of kin

(a) The court may permit the victim of any crime, his or her parent or guardian if the victim is a minor, or the next of kin of the victim if the victim has died, to file with the court a written, audiotaped, or videotaped statement, or statement stored on a CD-ROM, DVD, or any other recording medium acceptable to the court, expressing his or her views concerning the crime, the person responsible, and the need for restitution, in lieu of or in addition to the person personally appearing at the time of judgment and sentence. The court shall consider the statement filed with the court prior to imposing judgment and sentence. Whenever an audio or video statement or statement stored on a CD-ROM, DVD, or other medium is filed with the court, a written transcript of the statement shall also be provided by the person filing the statement, and shall be made available as a public record of the court after the judgment and sentence have been imposed.

(b) Whenever a written, audio, or video statement or statement stored on a CD-ROM, DVD, or other medium is filed with the court, it shall remain sealed until the time set for imposition of judgment and sentence except that the court, the probation officer, and counsel for the parties may view and listen to the statement not more than two court days prior to the date set for imposition of judgment and sentence.

(c) A person or a court shall not permit any person to duplicate, copy, or reproduce by audio or visual means a statement submitted to the court under the provisions of this section.

(d) Nothing in this section shall be construed to prohibit the prosecutor from representing to the court the views of the victim, his or her parent or guardian, the next of kin, or the California Victim Compensation Board.

(e) In the event the court permits an audio or video statement or statement stored on a CD-ROM, DVD, or other medium to be filed, the court shall not be responsible for providing any equipment or resources needed to assist the victim in preparing the statement.

Amended by Stats 2016 ch 31 (SB 836),s 238, eff. 6/27/2016.

Amended by Stats 2015 ch 303 (AB 731),s 394, eff. 1/1/2016.

Amended by Stats 2014 ch 508 (AB 2685),s 2, eff. 1/1/2015.

Amended by Stats 2004 ch 1 (AB 2), s 1, eff. 1/21/2004.

Section 1191.16 - Recording and preservation of victim's statement

The victim of any crime, or the parents or guardians of the victim if the victim is a minor, or the next of kin of the victim if the victim has died, who choose to exercise their rights with respect to sentencing proceedings as described in Section 1191.1 may, in any case where the defendant is subject to an indeterminate term of imprisonment, have their statements simultaneously recorded and preserved by means of videotape, videodisc, or any other means of preserving audio and video, if they notify the prosecutor in advance of the sentencing hearing and the prosecutor reasonably is able to provide the means to record and preserve the statement. If a video and audio record is developed, that record shall be maintained and preserved by the prosecution and used in accordance with the regulations of the Board of Prison Terms at any hearing to review parole suitability or the setting of a parole date.

Added by Stats. 1997, Ch. 902, Sec. 2. Effective January 1, 1998.

Section 1191.2 - Notice of victim's right to civil recovery against defendant and restitution

In providing notice to the victim pursuant to Section 1191.1, the probation officer shall also provide the victim with information concerning the victim's right to civil recovery against the defendant, the requirement that the court order restitution for the victim, the victim's right to receive a copy of the restitution order from the court and to enforce the restitution order as a civil judgment, the victim's responsibility to furnish the probation department, district attorney, and court with information relevant to his or her losses, and the victim's opportunity to be compensated from the Restitution Fund if eligible under Article 1 (commencing with Section 13959) of Chapter 5 of Part 4 of Division 3 of Title 2 of the Government Code. This information shall be in the form of written material prepared by the Judicial Council in consultation with the California Victim Compensation Board, shall include the relevant sections of the Penal Code, and shall be provided to each victim for whom the probation officer has a current mailing address.

Amended by Stats 2016 ch 31 (SB 836),s 239, eff. 6/27/2016.

Amended by Stats 2006 ch 538 (SB 1852),s 505, eff. 1/1/2007.

Section 1191.21 - Notification of eligibility card for victims

(a)

(1) The Office of Emergency Services shall develop and make available a "notification of eligibility" card for victims and derivative victims of crimes as defined in subdivision (c) of Section 13960 of the Government Code that includes, but is not limited to, the following information:"If you have been the victim of a crime that meets the required definition, you or others may be eligible to receive payment from the California State Restitution Fund for losses directly resulting from the crime. To learn about eligibility and receive an application to receive payments, call the Victims of Crime Program at (800) 777-9229 or call your local county Victim Witness Assistance Center."

(2) At a minimum, the Office of Emergency Services shall develop a template available for downloading on its Internet Web site the information requested in subdivision (b).

(b) In a case involving a crime as defined in subdivision (c) of Section 13960 of the Government Code, the law enforcement officer with primary responsibility for investigating the crime committed against the victim and the district attorney may provide the "notification of eligibility" card to the victim and derivative victim of a crime.

(c) The terms "victim" and "derivative victim" shall be given the same meaning given those terms in Section 13960 of the Government Code.

Amended by Stats 2013 ch 352 (AB 1317),s 416, eff. 9/26/2013, op. 7/1/2013.

Amended by Stats 2010 ch 618 (AB 2791),s 204, eff. 1/1/2011.

Amended by Stats 2003 ch 229 (AB 1757), s 13, eff. 1/1/2004.
Added by Stats 2000 ch 444 (AB 2685) s 1, eff. 1/1/2001.

Section 1191.25 - Notification of victim of crime committed by in-custody informant before testimony

The prosecution shall make a good faith attempt to notify any victim of a crime which was committed by, or is alleged to have been committed by, an in-custody informant, as defined in subdivision (a) of Section 1127a, within a reasonable time before the in-custody informant is called to testify. The notice shall include information concerning the prosecution's intention to offer the in-custody informant a modification or reduction in sentence or dismissal of the case or early parole in exchange for the in-custody informant's testimony in another case. The notification or attempt to notify the victim shall be made prior to the commencement of the trial in which the in-custody informant is to testify where the intention to call him or her is known at that time, but in no case shall the notice be made later than the time the in-custody informant is called to the stand.

Nothing contained in this section is intended to affect the right of the people and the defendant to an expeditious disposition of a criminal proceeding, as provided in Section 1050. The victim of any case alleged to have been committed by the in-custody informant may exercise his or her right to appear at the sentencing of the in-custody informant pursuant to Section 1191.1, but the victim shall not have a right to intervene in the trial in which the in-custody informant is called to testify.

Added by Stats. 1989, Ch. 901, Sec. 2.

Section 1191.3 - Oral statement regarding credits

(a) At the time of sentencing or pronouncement of judgment in which sentencing is imposed, the court shall make an oral statement that statutory law permits the award of conduct and worktime credits up to one-third or one-half of the sentence that is imposed by the court, that the award and calculation of credits is determined by the sheriff in cases involving imprisonment in county jails and by the Department of Corrections in cases involving imprisonment in the state prison, and that credit for presentence incarceration served by the defendant is calculated by the probation department under current state law. As used in this section, "victim" means the victim of the offense, the victim's parent or guardian if the victim is a minor, or the victim's next of kin.

(b) The probation officer shall provide a general estimate of the credits to which the defendant may be entitled for previous time served, and conduct or worktime credits authorized under Sections 2931, 2933, or 4019, and shall inform the victim pursuant to Section 1191.1. The probation officer shall file this estimate with the court and it shall become a part of the court record.

(c) This section applies to all felony convictions.

Added by Stats. 1987, Ch. 1247, Sec. 3.

Section 1192 - Degree of crime

Upon a plea of guilty, or upon conviction by the court without a jury, of a crime or attempted crime distinguished or divided into degrees, the court must, before passing sentence, determine the degree. Upon the failure of the court to so determine, the degree of the crime or attempted crime of which the defendant is guilty, shall be deemed to be of the lesser degree.

Amended by Stats. 1978, Ch. 1166.

Section 1192.1 - Plea of guilty to information or indictment specifying degree of crime

Upon a plea of guilty to an information or indictment accusing the defendant of a crime or attempted crime divided into degrees when consented to by the prosecuting attorney in open court and approved by the court, such plea may specify the degree thereof and in such event the defendant cannot be punished for a higher degree of the crime or attempted crime than the degree specified.

Amended by Stats. 1978, Ch. 1166.

Section 1192.2 - Pleas of guilty before committing magistrate specifying degree of crime

Upon a plea of guilty before a committing magistrate as provided in Section 859a, to a crime or attempted crime divided into degrees, when consented to by the prosecuting attorney in open court and approved by such magistrate, such plea may specify the degree thereof and in such event, the defendant cannot be punished for a higher degree of the crime or attempted crime than the degree specified.

Amended by Stats. 1978, Ch. 1166.

Section 1192.3 - Plea of guilty or nolo contendere specifying payment of restitution

(a) A plea of guilty or nolo contendere to an accusatory pleading charging a public offense, other than a felony specified in Section 1192.5 or 1192.7, which public offense did not result in damage for which restitution may be ordered, made on the condition that charges be dismissed for one or more public offenses arising from the same or related course of conduct by the defendant which did result in damage for which restitution may be ordered, may specify the payment of restitution by the defendant as a condition of the plea or any probation granted pursuant thereto, so long as the plea is freely and voluntarily made, there is factual basis for the plea, and the plea and all conditions are approved by the court.

(b) If restitution is imposed which is attributable to a count dismissed pursuant to a plea bargain, as described in this section, the court shall obtain a waiver pursuant to People v. Harvey (1979) 25 Cal. 3d 754 from the defendant as to the dismissed count.

Added by Stats. 1988, Ch. 287, Sec. 1.

Section 1192.4 - Plea of guilty not accepted by prosecuting attorney and approved by court

If the defendant's plea of guilty pursuant to Section 1192.1 or 1192.2 is not accepted by the prosecuting attorney and approved by the court, the plea shall be deemed withdrawn and the defendant may then enter such plea or pleas as would otherwise have been available. The plea so withdrawn may not be received in evidence in any criminal, civil, or special action or proceeding of any nature, including proceedings before agencies, commissions, boards, and tribunals.

Amended by Stats. 1970, Ch. 1123.

Section 1192.5 - Pleas of guilty or nolo contendere specifying punishment

(a) Upon a plea of guilty or nolo contendere to an accusatory pleading charging a felony, other than a violation of paragraph (2), (3), or (6) of subdivision (a) of Section 261, paragraph (1) or (4) of subdivision (a) of former Section 262, Section 264.1, Section 286 or 287 or former Section 288a by force, violence, duress, menace, or threat of great bodily harm, subdivision (b) of Section 288, or subdivision (a) of Section 289, the plea may specify the punishment to the same extent as it may be specified by the jury on a plea of not guilty or fixed by the court on a plea of guilty, nolo contendere, or not guilty, and may specify the exercise by the court thereafter of other powers legally available to it.

(b)When the plea is accepted by the prosecuting attorney in open court and is approved by the court, the defendant, except as otherwise provided in this section, cannot be sentenced on the plea to a punishment more severe than that specified in the plea and the court may not proceed as to the plea other than as specified in the plea.

(c) If the court approves of the plea, it shall inform the defendant prior to the making of the plea that (1) its approval is not binding, (2) it may, at the time set for the hearing on the application for probation or pronouncement of judgment, withdraw its approval in the light of further consideration of the matter, and (3) in that case, the defendant shall be permitted to withdraw the plea if the defendant desires to do so. The court shall also cause an inquiry to be made of the defendant to satisfy itself that the plea is freely and voluntarily made, and that there is a factual basis for the plea.

(d) If the plea is not accepted by the prosecuting attorney and approved by the court, the plea shall be deemed withdrawn and the defendant may then enter the plea or pleas as would otherwise have been available.

(e) If the plea is withdrawn or deemed withdrawn, it may not be received in evidence in any criminal, civil, or special action or proceeding of any nature, including proceedings before agencies, commissions, boards, and tribunals.

Amended by Stats 2022 ch 197 (SB 1493),s 19, eff. 1/1/2023.
Amended by Stats 2021 ch 626 (AB 1171),s 43, eff. 1/1/2022.
Amended by Stats 2018 ch 423 (SB 1494),s 87, eff. 1/1/2019.

Section 1192.6 - Amendment or dismissal of charges

(a) In each felony case in which the charges contained in the original accusatory pleading are amended or dismissed, the record shall contain a statement explaining the reason for the amendment or dismissal.

(b) In each felony case in which the prosecuting attorney seeks a dismissal of a charge in the complaint, indictment, or information, he or she shall state the specific reasons for the dismissal in open court, on the record.

(c) When, upon a plea of guilty or nolo contendere to an accusatory pleading charging a felony, whether or not that plea is entered pursuant to Section 1192.5, the prosecuting attorney recommends what punishment the court should impose or how it should exercise any of the powers legally available to it, the prosecuting attorney shall state the specific reasons for the recommendation in open court, on the record. The reasons for the recommendation shall be transcribed and made part of the court file.

Added by Stats. 1981, Ch. 759, Sec. 1.

Section 1192.7 - Prohibited plea bargaining

(a)

(1) It is the intent of the Legislature that district attorneys prosecute violent sex crimes under statutes that provide sentencing under a "one strike," "three strikes" or habitual sex offender statute instead of engaging in plea bargaining over those offenses.

(2) Plea bargaining in any case in which the indictment or information charges any serious felony, any felony in which it is alleged that a firearm was personally used by the defendant, or any offense of driving while under the influence of alcohol, drugs, narcotics, or any other intoxicating substance, or any combination thereof, is prohibited, unless there is insufficient evidence to prove the people's case, or testimony of a material witness cannot be obtained, or a reduction or dismissal would not result in a substantial change in sentence.

(3) If the indictment or information charges the defendant with a violent sex crime, as listed in subdivision (c) of Section 667.61, that could be prosecuted under Sections 269, 288.7, subdivisions (b) through (i) of Section 667, Section 667.61, or 667.71, plea bargaining is prohibited unless there is insufficient evidence to prove the people's case, or testimony of a material witness cannot be obtained, or a reduction or dismissal would not result in a substantial change in sentence. At the time of presenting the agreement to the court, the district attorney shall state on the record why a sentence under one of those sections was not sought.

(b) As used in this section, "plea bargaining" means any bargaining, negotiation, or discussion between a criminal defendant, or their counsel, and a prosecuting attorney or judge, whereby the defendant agrees to plead guilty or nolo contendere, in exchange for any promises, commitments, concessions, assurances, or consideration by the prosecuting attorney or judge relating to any charge against the defendant or to the sentencing of the defendant.

(c) As used in this section, "serious felony" means any of the following:

(1) Murder or voluntary manslaughter;

(2) mayhem;

(3) rape;

(4) sodomy by force, violence, duress, menace, threat of great bodily injury, or fear of immediate and unlawful bodily injury on the victim or another person;

(5) oral copulation by force, violence, duress, menace, threat of great bodily injury, or fear of immediate and unlawful bodily injury on the victim or another person;

(6) lewd or lascivious act on a child under 14 years of age;

(7) any felony punishable by death or imprisonment in the state prison for life;

(8) any felony in which the defendant personally inflicts great bodily injury on any person, other than an accomplice, or any felony in which the defendant personally uses a firearm;

(9) attempted murder;

(10) assault with intent to commit rape or robbery;

(11) assault with a deadly weapon or instrument on a peace officer;

(12) assault by a life prisoner on a noninmate;

(13) assault with a deadly weapon by an inmate;

(14) arson;

(15) exploding a destructive device or any explosive with intent to injure;

(16) exploding a destructive device or any explosive causing bodily injury, great bodily injury, or mayhem;

(17) exploding a destructive device or any explosive with intent to murder;

(18) any burglary of the first degree;

(19) robbery or bank robbery;

(20) kidnapping;

(21) holding of a hostage by a person confined in a state prison;

(22) attempt to commit a felony punishable by death or imprisonment in the state prison for life;

(23) any felony in which the defendant personally used a dangerous or deadly weapon;

(24) selling, furnishing, administering, giving, or offering to sell, furnish, administer, or give to a minor any heroin, cocaine, phencyclidine (PCP), or any methamphetamine-related drug, as described in paragraph (2) of subdivision (d) of Section 11055 of the Health and Safety Code, or any of the precursors of methamphetamines, as described in subparagraph (A) of paragraph (1) of subdivision (f) of Section 11055 or subdivision (a) of Section 11100 of the Health and Safety Code;

(25) any violation of subdivision (a) of Section 289 where the act is accomplished against the victim's will by force, violence, duress, menace, or fear of immediate and unlawful bodily injury on the victim or another person;

(26) grand theft involving a firearm;

(27) carjacking;

(28) any felony offense, which would also constitute a felony violation of Section 186.22;

(29) assault with the intent to commit mayhem, rape, sodomy, or oral copulation, in violation of Section 220;

(30) throwing acid or flammable substances, in violation of Section 244;

(31) assault with a deadly weapon, firearm, machinegun, assault weapon, or semiautomatic firearm or assault on a peace officer or firefighter, in violation of Section 245;

(32) assault with a deadly weapon against a public transit employee, custodial officer, or school employee, in violation of Section 245.2, 245.3, or 245.5;

(33) discharge of a firearm at an inhabited dwelling, vehicle, or aircraft, in violation of Section 246;

(34) commission of rape or sexual penetration in concert with another person, in violation of Section 264.1;

(35) continuous sexual abuse of a child, in violation of Section 288.5;

(36) shooting from a vehicle, in violation of subdivision (c) or (d) of Section 26100;

(37) intimidation of victims or witnesses, in violation of Section 136.1;

(38) criminal threats, in violation of Section 422;

(39) any attempt to commit a crime listed in this subdivision other than an assault;

(40) any violation of Section 12022.53;

(41) a violation of subdivision (b) or (c) of Section 11418;

(42) human trafficking of a minor, in violation of subdivision (c) of Section 236.1, except, with respect to a violation of paragraph (1) of subdivision (c) of Section 236.1, where the person who committed the offense was a victim of human trafficking, as described in subdivision (b) or (c) of Section 236.1, at the time of the offense; and

(43) any conspiracy to commit an offense described in this subdivision.

(d) As used in this section, "bank robbery" means to take or attempt to take, by force or violence, or by intimidation from the person or presence of another any property or money or any other thing of value belonging to, or in the care, custody, control, management, or possession of, any bank, credit union, or any savings and loan association. As used in this subdivision, the following terms have the following meanings:

(1) "Bank" means any member of the Federal Reserve System, and any bank, banking association, trust company, savings bank, or other banking institution organized or operating under the laws of the United States, and any bank the deposits of which are insured by the Federal Deposit Insurance Corporation.

(2) "Savings and loan association" means any federal savings and loan association and any "insured institution" as defined in Section 401 of the National Housing Act, as amended, and any federal credit union as defined in Section 2 of the Federal Credit Union Act.

(3) "Credit union" means any federal credit union and any state-chartered credit union the accounts of which are insured by the Administrator of the National Credit Union administration.

(e) The provisions of this section shall not be amended by the Legislature except by statute passed in each house by rollcall vote entered in the journal, two-thirds of the membership concurring, or by a statute that becomes effective only when approved by the electors.

Amended by Stats 2023 ch 230 (SB 14),s 4, eff. 1/1/2024.

Amended by Stats 2010 ch 178 (SB 1115),s 73, eff. 1/1/2011, op. 1/1/2012.

Amended by Stats 2006 ch 337 (SB 1128),s 37, eff. 9/20/2006.

Amended by Stats 2002 ch 606 (AB 1838), s 3, eff. 9/16/2002.

21 (2000).

Previously Amended September 2, 1999 (Bill Number: AB 381) (Chapter 298).

Note: This section was added on June 8, 1982, by initiative Prop. 8, and amended on March 7, 2000, by initiative Prop. 21.

Section 1192.8 - "Serious felony" defined

(a) For purposes of subdivision (c) of Section 1192.7, "serious felony" also means any violation of Section 191.5, paragraph (1) of subdivision (c) of Section 192, subdivision (a), (b), or (c) of Section 192.5 of this code, or Section 2800.3, subdivision (b) of Section 23104, or Section 23153 of the Vehicle Code, when any of these offenses involve the personal infliction of great bodily injury on any person other than an accomplice, or the personal use of a dangerous or deadly weapon, within the meaning of paragraph (8) or (23) of subdivision (c) of Section 1192.7.

(b) It is the intent of the Legislature, in enacting subdivision (a), to codify the court decisions of People v. Gonzales, 29 Cal. App. 4th 1684, and People v. Bow, 13 Cal. App. 4th 1551, and to clarify that the crimes specified in subdivision (a) have always been, and continue to be, serious felonies within the meaning of subdivision (c) of Section 1192.7.

Amended by Stats 2007 ch 747 (AB 678),s 9, eff. 1/1/2008.
Amended October 10, 1999 (Bill Number: AB 1236) (Chapter 706).

Section 1193 - Pronouncement of judgment

Judgment upon persons convicted of commission of crime shall be pronounced as follows:

(a) If the conviction is for a felony, the defendant shall be personally present when judgment is pronounced against him or her, unless the defendant, in open court and on the record, or in a notarized writing, requests that judgment be pronounced against him or her in his or her absence, and that he or she be represented by an attorney when judgment is pronounced, and the court approves his or her absence during the pronouncement of judgment, or unless, after the exercise of reasonable diligence to procure the presence of the defendant, the court shall find that it will be in the interest of justice that judgment be pronounced in his or her absence; provided, that when any judgment imposing the death penalty has been affirmed by the appellate court, sentence may be reimposed upon the defendant in his or her absence by the court from which the appeal was taken, and in the following manner: upon receipt by the superior court from which the appeal is taken of the certificate of the appellate court affirming the judgment, the judge of the superior court shall forthwith make and cause to be entered an order pronouncing sentence against the defendant, and a warrant signed by the judge, and attested by the clerk under the seal of the court, shall be drawn, and it shall state the conviction and judgment and appoint a day upon which the judgment shall be executed, which shall not be less than 60 days nor more than 90 days from the time of making the order; and that, within five days thereafter, a certified copy of the order, attested by the clerk under the seal of the court, and attached to the warrant, shall, for the purpose of execution, be transmitted by registered mail to the warden of the state prison having the custody of the defendant and certified copies thereof shall be transmitted by registered mail to the Governor; and provided further, that when any judgment imposing the death penalty has been affirmed and sentence has been reimposed as above provided there shall be no appeal from the order fixing the time for and directing the execution of the judgment as herein provided. If a pro se defendant requests that judgment in a noncapital case be pronounced against him or her in his or her absence, the court shall appoint an attorney to represent the defendant in the in absentia sentencing.

(b) If the conviction be of a misdemeanor, judgment may be pronounced against the defendant in his absence.

Amended by Stats. 1986, Ch. 1222, Sec. 1.

Section 1194 - Defendant in custody

When the defendant is in custody, the Court may direct the officer in whose custody he is to bring him before it for judgment, and the officer must do so.

Enacted 1872.

Section 1195 - Defendant's failure to appear; treatment of bail

If the defendant has been released on bail, or has deposited money or property instead thereof, and does not appear for judgment when his personal appearance is necessary, the court, in addition to the forfeiture of the undertaking of bail, or of the money or property deposited, must, on application of the prosecuting attorney, direct the issuance of a bench warrant for the arrest of the defendant.

If the defendant, who is on bail, does appear for judgment and judgment is pronounced upon him or probation is granted to him, then the bail shall be exonerated or, if money or property has been deposited instead of bail, it must be returned to the defendant or to the person or persons found by the court to have deposited said money or property on behalf of said defendant.

Amended by Stats. 1959, Ch. 1187.

Section 1196 - Issuance of bench warrant

(a) The clerk must, at any time after the order, issue a bench warrant into one or more counties.

(b) The clerk shall require the appropriate agency to enter each bench warrant issued on a private surety-bonded felony case into the national warrant system (National Crime Information Center (NCIC)). If the appropriate agency fails to enter the bench warrant into the national warrant system (NCIC), and the court finds that this failure prevented the surety or bond agent from surrendering the fugitive into custody, prevented the fugitive from being arrested or taken into custody, or resulted in the fugitive's subsequent release from custody, the court having jurisdiction over the bail shall, upon petition, set aside the forfeiture of the bond and declare all liability on the bail bond to be exonerated.

Amended by Stats 2007 ch 263 (AB 310),s 27, eff. 1/1/2008.

Section 1197 - Form of bench warrant

The bench warrant must be substantially in the following form:

County of ____

The people of the State of California to any peace officer in this State: _____ (name of defendant) having been on the ____ day of ____, 19_, duly convicted in the ____ court of ____ (naming the court) of the crime of ____ (designating it generally), you are therefore commanded forthwith to arrest the above named defendant and bring him before that court for judgment.

Given under my hand with the seal of said court affixed, this ____ day of ____, 19_.

By order of said court.

_____

(seal)Clerk (or Judge, or Justice)

Amended by Stats. 1951, Ch. 1674.

Section 1198 - Service of bench warrant

The bench warrant may be served in any county in the same manner as a warrant of arrest.

Amended by Stats. 1951, Ch. 1674.

Section 1199 - Arrest of defendant

Whether the bench warrant is served in the county in which it was issued or in another county, the officer must arrest the defendant and bring him before the court, or deliver him to any peace officer of the county from which the warrant issued, who must bring him before said court according to the command thereof.

Amended by Stats. 1951, Ch. 1674.

Section 1200 - Appearance for judgment

When the defendant appears for judgment he must be informed by the Court, or by the Clerk, under its direction, of the nature of the charge against him and of his plea, and the verdict, if any thereon, and must be asked whether he has any legal cause to show why judgment should not be pronounced against him.

Amended by Code Amendments 1880, Ch. 47.

Section 1201 - Showing for cause against judgment

He or she may show, for cause against the judgment:

(a) That he or she is insane; and if, in the opinion of the court, there is reasonable ground for believing him or her insane, the question of insanity shall be tried as provided in Chapter 6 (commencing with Section 1367) of Title 10 of Part 2. If, upon the trial of that question, the jury finds that he or she is sane, judgment shall be pronounced, but if they find him or her insane, he or she shall be committed to the state hospital for the care and treatment of the insane, until he or she becomes sane; and when notice is given of that fact, as provided in Section 1372, he or she shall be brought before the court for judgment.

(b) That he or she has good cause to offer, either in arrest of judgment or for a new trial; in which case the court may, in its discretion, order the judgment to be deferred, and proceed to decide upon the motion in arrest of judgment or for a new trial.

Amended by Stats. 1987, Ch. 828, Sec. 68.

Section 1201.3 - Order prohibiting harassing, intimidating, or threatening victim or victim's family

(a) Upon the conviction of a defendant for a sexual offense involving a minor victim or, in the case of a minor appearing in juvenile court, if a petition is admitted or sustained for a sexual offense involving a minor victim, the court is authorized to issue orders that would prohibit the defendant or juvenile, for a period up to 10 years, from harassing, intimidating, or threatening the victim or the victim's family members or spouse.

(b) No order issued pursuant to this section shall be interpreted to apply to counsel acting on behalf of the defendant or juvenile, or to investigators working on behalf of counsel, in an action relating to a conviction, petition in juvenile court, or any civil action arising therefrom, provided, however, that no counsel or investigator shall harass or threaten any person protected by an order issued pursuant to subdivision (a).

(c) Notice of the intent to request an order pursuant to this section shall be given to counsel for the defendant or juvenile by the prosecutor or the court at the time of conviction, or disposition of the petition in juvenile court, and counsel shall have adequate time in which to respond to the request before the order is made.

(d) A violation of an order issued pursuant to subdivision (a) is punishable as provided in Section 166.

Amended by Stats 2011 ch 296 (AB 1023),s 215, eff. 1/1/2012.

Added by Stats 2010 ch 627 (SB 834),s 1, eff. 1/1/2011.

Section 1201.5 - Motions subsequent to judgment

Any motions made subsequent to judgment must be made only upon written notice served upon the prosecution at least three days prior to the date of hearing thereon. No affidavit or other writing shall be presented or considered in support thereof unless a copy of the same has been duly served upon the prosecution at least three days prior to a hearing thereon. Any appeal from an order entered upon a motion made other than as herein provided, must be dismissed by the court.

Added by Stats. 1937, Ch. 31.

Section 1202 - New trial

If no sufficient cause is alleged or appears to the court at the time fixed for pronouncing judgment, as provided in Section 1191, why judgment should not be pronounced, it shall thereupon be rendered; and if not rendered or pronounced within the time so fixed or to which it is continued under the provisions of Section 1191, then the defendant shall be entitled to a new trial. If the court shall refuse to hear a defendant's motion for a new trial or when made shall neglect to determine such motion before pronouncing judgment or the making of an order granting probation, then the defendant shall be entitled to a new trial.

Amended by Stats. 1987, Ch. 828, Sec. 69.

Section 1202a - Judgment for imprisonment or death

If the judgment is for imprisonment in the state prison the judgment shall direct that the defendant be delivered into the custody of the Director of Corrections at the state prison or institution designated by the Director of Corrections as the place for the reception of persons convicted of felonies, except where the judgment is for death in which case the defendant shall be taken to the warden of the California State Prison at San Quentin.

Unless a different place or places are so designated by the Director of Corrections, the judgment shall direct that the defendant be delivered into the custody of the Director of Corrections at the California State Prison at San Quentin. The Director of Corrections shall designate a place or places for the reception of persons convicted of felonies by order, which order or orders shall be served by registered mail, return receipt requested, upon each judge of each superior court in the state. The Director of Corrections may change the place or places of commitment by the issuance of a new order. Nothing contained in this section affects any provision of Section 3400.

Amended by Stats. 1987, Ch. 828, Sec. 70.

Section 1202.05 - Prohibition of visitation between defendant and child victim

(a) Whenever a person is sentenced to the state prison on or after January 1, 1993, for violating Section 261, 264.1, 266c, 285, 286, 287, 288, 288.5, or 289, or former Section 288a, and the victim of one or more of those offenses is a child under the age of 18 years, the court shall prohibit all visitation between the defendant and the child victim. The court's order shall be transmitted to the Department of Corrections, to the parents, adoptive parents, or guardians, or a combination thereof, of the child victim, and to the child victim. If any parent, adoptive parent, or legal guardian of the child victim, or the child victim objects to the court's order, he or she may request a hearing on the matter. Any request for a hearing on the matter filed with the sentencing court shall be referred to the appropriate juvenile court pursuant to Section 362.6 of the Welfare and Institutions Code.

(b) The Department of Corrections is authorized to notify the sentencing court of persons who were sentenced to the state prison prior to January 1, 1993, for violating Section 261, 264.1, 266c, 285, 286, 288, 288.5, or 289, or former Section 288a, when the victim of one or more of those offenses was a child under the age of 18 years. Upon notification by the department pursuant to this subdivision, the sentencing court shall prohibit all visitation between the defendant and the child victim, according to the procedures specified in subdivision (a).

Amended by Stats 2018 ch 423 (SB 1494),s 88, eff. 1/1/2019.

Section 1202.1 - Submission to blood or oral mucosal transudate saliva test

(a) Notwithstanding Sections 120975 and 120990 of the Health and Safety Code, the court shall order every person who is convicted of, or adjudged by the court to be a person described by Section 601 or 602 of the Welfare and Institutions Code as provided in Section 725 of the Welfare and Institutions Code by reason of a violation of, a sexual offense listed in subdivision (e), whether or not a sentence or fine is imposed or probation is granted, to submit to a blood or oral mucosal transudate saliva test for evidence of antibodies to the probable causative agent of acquired immunodeficiency syndrome (AIDS) within 180 days of the date of conviction. Each person tested under this section shall be informed of the results of the blood or oral mucosal transudate saliva test.

(b) Notwithstanding Section 120980 of the Health and Safety Code, the results of the blood or oral mucosal transudate saliva test to detect antibodies to the probable causative agent of AIDS shall be transmitted by the clerk of the court to the Department of Justice and the local health officer.

(c) Notwithstanding Section 120980 of the Health and Safety Code, the Department of Justice shall provide the results of a test or tests as to persons under investigation or being prosecuted under Section 12022.85, if the results are on file with the department, to the defense attorney upon request and the results also shall be available to the prosecuting attorney upon request for the purpose of either preparing counts for a sentence enhancement under Section 12022.85 or complying with subdivision (d).

(d)

(1) When a person is convicted of a sexual offense listed in subdivision (e) or adjudged by the court to be a person described by Section 601 or 602 of the Welfare and Institutions Code as provided in Section 725 of the Welfare and Institutions Code by reason of the commission of a sexual offense listed in subdivision (e), the prosecutor or the prosecutor's victim-witness assistance bureau shall advise the victim of the right to receive the results of the blood or oral mucosal transudate saliva test performed pursuant to subdivision (a). The prosecutor or the prosecutor's victim-witness assistance bureau shall refer the victim to the local health officer for counseling to assist the victim in understanding the extent to which the particular circumstances of the crime may or may not have placed the victim at risk of transmission of the human immunodeficiency virus (HIV) from the accused, to ensure that the victim understands the limitations and benefits of current tests for HIV, and to assist the victim in determining whether the victim should make the request.

(2) Notwithstanding any other law, upon the victim's request, the local health officer shall be responsible for disclosing test results to the victim who requested the test and the person who was tested. However, as specified in subdivision (g), positive test results shall not be disclosed to the victim or the person who was tested without offering or providing professional counseling appropriate to the circumstances as follows:

(A) To help the victim understand the extent to which the particular circumstances of the crime may or may not have put the victim at risk of transmission of HIV from the perpetrator.

(B) To ensure that the victim understands both the benefits and limitations of the current tests for HIV.

(C) To obtain referrals to appropriate health care and support services.

(e) For purposes of this section, "sexual offense" includes any of the following:

(1) Rape in violation of Section 261, 261.4, or former Section 262.

(2) Unlawful intercourse with a person under 18 years of age in violation of Section 261.5 or 266c.

(3) Sodomy in violation of Section 266c or 286.

(4) Oral copulation in violation of Section 266c or 287, or former Section 288a.

(5)

(A) Any of the following offenses if the court finds that there is probable cause to believe that blood, semen, or any other bodily fluid capable of transmitting HIV has been transferred from the defendant to the victim:

(i) Sexual penetration in violation of Section 264.1, 266c, or 289.

(ii) Aggravated sexual assault of a child in violation of Section 269.

(iii) Lewd or lascivious conduct with a child in violation of Section 288.

(iv) Continuous sexual abuse of a child in violation of Section 288.5.

(v) The attempt to commit any offense described in clauses (i) to (iv), inclusive.

(B) For purposes of this paragraph, the court shall note its finding on the court docket and minute order if one is prepared.

(f) Any blood or oral mucosal transudate saliva tested pursuant to subdivision (a) shall be subjected to appropriate confirmatory tests to ensure accuracy of the first test results, and under no circumstances shall test results be transmitted to the victim or the person who is tested unless any initially reactive test result has been confirmed by appropriate confirmatory tests for positive reactors.

(g) The local health officer shall be responsible for disclosing test results to the victim who requested the test and the person who was tested. However, positive test results shall not be disclosed to the victim or the person who was tested without offering or providing professional counseling appropriate to the circumstances.

(h) The local health officer and the victim shall comply with all laws and policies relating to medical confidentiality, subject to the disclosure authorized by subdivisions (g) and (i).

(i) A victim who receives information from the local health officer pursuant to subdivision (g) may disclose the information as the victim deems necessary to protect the victim's health and safety or the health and safety of the victim's family or sexual partner.

(j) A person who transmits test results or discloses information pursuant to this section shall be immune from civil liability for any action taken in compliance with this section.

Amended by Stats 2021 ch 626 (AB 1171),s 44, eff. 1/1/2022.

Amended by Stats 2018 ch 423 (SB 1494),s 89, eff. 1/1/2019.

Amended by Stats 2017 ch 537 (SB 239),s 15, eff. 1/1/2018.

Amended by Stats 2003 ch 468 (SB 851), s 16, eff. 1/1/2004.

Section 1202.4 - Restitution

(a)

(1) It is the intent of the Legislature that a victim of crime who incurs an economic loss as a result of the commission of a crime shall receive restitution directly from a defendant convicted of that crime.

(2) Upon a person being convicted of a crime in the State of California, the court shall order the defendant to pay a fine in the form of a penalty assessment in accordance with Section 1464.

(3) The court, in addition to any other penalty provided or imposed under the law, shall order the defendant to pay both of the following:

(A) A restitution fine in accordance with subdivision (b).

(B) Restitution to the victim or victims, if any, in accordance with subdivision (f), which shall be enforceable as if the order were a civil judgment.

(b) In every case where a person is convicted of a crime, the court shall impose a separate and additional restitution fine, unless it finds compelling and extraordinary reasons for not doing so and states those reasons on the record.

(1) The restitution fine shall be set at the discretion of the court and commensurate with the seriousness of the offense. If the person is convicted of a felony, the fine shall not be less than three hundred dollars ($300) and not more than ten thousand dollars ($10,000). If the person is convicted of a misdemeanor, the fine shall not be less than one hundred fifty dollars ($150) and not more than one thousand dollars ($1,000).

(2) In setting a felony restitution fine, the court may determine the amount of the fine as the product of the minimum fine pursuant to paragraph (1) multiplied by the number of years of imprisonment the defendant is ordered to serve, multiplied by the number of felony counts of which the defendant is convicted.

(c) The court shall impose the restitution fine unless it finds compelling and extraordinary reasons for not doing so and states those reasons on the record. A defendant's inability to pay shall not be considered a compelling and extraordinary reason not to impose a restitution fine. Inability to pay may be considered only in increasing the amount of the restitution fine in excess of the minimum fine pursuant to paragraph (1) of subdivision (b). The court may specify that funds confiscated at the time of the defendant's arrest, except for funds confiscated pursuant to Chapter 8 (commencing with Section 11469) of Division 10 of the Health and Safety Code, be applied to the restitution fine if the funds are not exempt for spousal or child support or subject to any other legal exemption.

(d) In setting the amount of the fine pursuant to subdivision (b) in excess of the minimum fine pursuant to paragraph (1) of subdivision (b), the court shall consider any relevant factors, including, but not limited to, the defendant's inability to pay, the seriousness and gravity of the offense and the circumstances of its commission, any economic gain derived by the defendant as a result of the crime, the extent to which any other person suffered losses as a result of the crime, and the number of victims involved in the crime. Those losses may include pecuniary losses to the victim or the victim's dependents as well as intangible losses, such as psychological harm caused by the crime. Consideration of a defendant's inability to pay may include the defendant's future earning capacity. A defendant shall bear the burden of demonstrating the defendant's inability to pay. Express findings by the court as to the factors bearing on the amount of the fine shall not be required. A separate hearing for the fine shall not be required.

(e) The restitution fine shall not be subject to penalty assessments authorized in Section 1464 or Chapter 12 (commencing with Section 76000) of Title 8 of the Government Code, or the state surcharge authorized in Section 1465.7, and shall be deposited in the Restitution Fund in the State Treasury.

(f) Except as provided in subdivisions (p) and (q), in every case in which a victim has suffered economic loss as a result of the defendant's conduct, the court shall require that the defendant make restitution to the victim or victims in an amount established by court order, based on the amount of loss claimed by the victim or victims or any other showing to the court. If the amount of loss cannot be ascertained at the time of sentencing, the restitution order shall include a provision that the amount shall be determined at the direction of the court. The court shall order full restitution. The court may specify that funds confiscated at the time of the defendant's arrest, except for funds confiscated pursuant to Chapter 8 (commencing with Section 11469) of Division 10 of the Health and Safety Code, be applied to the restitution order if the funds are not exempt for spousal or child support or subject to any other legal exemption.

(1) The defendant has the right to a hearing before a judge to dispute the determination of the amount of restitution. The court may modify the amount, on its own motion or on the motion of the district attorney, the victim or victims, or the defendant. If a motion is made for modification of a restitution order, the victim shall be notified of that motion at least 10 days prior to the proceeding held to decide the motion. A victim at a restitution hearing or modification hearing described in this paragraph may testify by live, two-way audio and video transmission, if testimony by live, two-way audio and video transmission is available at the court.

(2) Determination of the amount of restitution ordered pursuant to this subdivision shall not be affected by the indemnification or subrogation rights of a third party. Restitution ordered pursuant to this subdivision shall be ordered to be deposited in the Restitution Fund to the extent that the victim, as defined in subdivision (k), has received assistance from the California Victim Compensation Board pursuant to Chapter 5 (commencing with Section 13950) of Part 4 of Division 3 of Title 2 of the Government Code.

(3) To the extent possible, the restitution order shall be prepared by the sentencing court, shall identify each victim and each loss to which it pertains, and shall be of a dollar amount that is sufficient to fully reimburse the victim or victims for every determined economic loss incurred as the result of the defendant's criminal conduct, including, but not limited to, all of the following:

(A) Full or partial payment for the value of stolen or damaged property. The value of stolen or damaged property shall be the replacement cost of like property, or the actual cost of repairing the property when repair is possible.

(B) Medical expenses.

(C) Mental health counseling expenses.

(D) Wages or profits lost due to injury incurred by the victim, and if the victim is a minor, wages or profits lost by the minor's parent, parents, guardian, or guardians, while caring for the injured minor. Lost wages shall include commission income as well as base wages. Commission income shall be established by evidence of commission income during the 12-month period prior to the date of the crime for which restitution is being ordered, unless good cause for a shorter time period is shown.

(E) Wages or profits lost by the victim, and if the victim is a minor, wages or profits lost by the minor's parent, parents, guardian, or guardians, due to time spent as a witness or in assisting the police or prosecution. Lost wages shall include commission income as well as base wages. Commission income shall be established by evidence of commission income during the 12-month period prior to the date of the crime for which restitution is being ordered, unless good cause for a shorter time period is shown.

(F) Noneconomic losses, including, but not limited to, psychological harm, for felony violations of Section 288, 288.5, or 288.7.

(G) Interest, at the rate of 10 percent per annum, that accrues as of the date of sentencing or loss, as determined by the court.

(H) Actual and reasonable attorney's fees and other costs of collection accrued by a private entity on behalf of the victim.

(I) Expenses incurred by an adult victim in relocating away from the defendant, including, but not limited to, deposits for utilities and telephone service, deposits for rental housing, temporary lodging and food expenses, clothing, and personal items. Expenses incurred pursuant to this section shall be verified by law enforcement to be necessary for the personal safety of the victim or by a mental health treatment provider to be necessary for the emotional well-being of the victim.

(J) Expenses to install or increase residential security incurred related to a violation of Section 273.5, or a violent felony as defined in subdivision (c) of Section 667.5, including, but not limited to, a home security device or system, or replacing or increasing the number of locks.

(K) Expenses to retrofit a residence or vehicle, or both, to make the residence accessible to or the vehicle operational by the victim, if the victim is permanently disabled, whether the disability is partial or total, as a direct result of the crime.

(L) Expenses for a period of time reasonably necessary to make the victim whole, for the costs to monitor the credit report of, and for the costs to repair the credit of, a victim of identity theft, as defined in Section 530.5.

(4)

(A) If, as a result of the defendant's conduct, the Restitution Fund has provided assistance to or on behalf of a victim or derivative victim pursuant to Chapter 5 (commencing with Section 13950) of Part 4 of Division 3 of Title 2 of the Government Code, the amount of assistance provided shall be presumed to be a direct result of the defendant's criminal conduct and shall be included in the amount of the restitution ordered.

(B) The amount of assistance provided by the Restitution Fund shall be established by copies of bills submitted to the California Victim Compensation Board reflecting the amount paid by the board and whether the services for which payment was made were for medical or dental expenses, funeral or burial expenses, mental health counseling, wage or support losses, or rehabilitation. Certified copies of these bills provided by the board and redacted to protect the privacy and safety of the victim or any legal privilege, together with a statement made under penalty of perjury by the custodian of records that those bills were submitted to and were paid by the board, shall be sufficient to meet this requirement.

(C) If the defendant offers evidence to rebut the presumption established by this paragraph, the court may release additional information contained in the records of the board to the defendant only after reviewing that information in camera and finding that the information is necessary for the defendant to dispute the amount of the restitution order.

(5) Except as provided in paragraph (6), in any case in which an order may be entered pursuant to this subdivision, the defendant shall prepare and file a disclosure identifying all assets, income, and liabilities in which the defendant held or controlled a present or future interest as of the date of the defendant's arrest for the crime for which restitution may be ordered. The financial disclosure statements shall be made available to the victim and the board pursuant to Section 1214. The disclosure shall be signed by the defendant upon a form approved or adopted by the Judicial Council for the purpose of facilitating the disclosure. A defendant who willfully states as true a material matter that the defendant knows to be false on the disclosure required by this subdivision is guilty of a misdemeanor, unless this conduct is punishable as perjury or another provision of law provides for a greater penalty.

(6) A defendant who fails to file the financial disclosure required in paragraph (5), but who has filed a financial affidavit or financial information pursuant to subdivision (c) of Section 987, shall be deemed to have waived the confidentiality of that affidavit or financial information as to a victim in whose favor the order of restitution is entered pursuant to subdivision (f). The affidavit or information shall serve in lieu of the financial disclosure required in paragraph (5), and paragraphs (7) to (10), inclusive, shall not apply.

(7) Except as provided in paragraph (6), the defendant shall file the disclosure with the clerk of the court no later than the date set for the defendant's sentencing, unless otherwise directed by the court. The disclosure may be inspected or copied as provided by subdivision (b), (c), or (d) of Section 1203.05.

(8) In its discretion, the court may relieve the defendant of the duty under paragraph (7) of filing with the clerk by requiring that the defendant's disclosure be submitted as an attachment to, and be available to, those authorized to receive the following:

(A) A report submitted pursuant to subparagraph (D) of paragraph (2) of subdivision (b) of Section 1203 or subdivision (g) of Section 1203.

(B) A stipulation submitted pursuant to paragraph (4) of subdivision (b) of Section 1203.

(C) A report by the probation officer, or information submitted by the defendant applying for a conditional sentence pursuant to subdivision (d) of Section 1203.

(9) The court may consider a defendant's unreasonable failure to make a complete disclosure pursuant to paragraph (5) as any of the following:

(A) A circumstance in aggravation of the crime in imposing a term under subdivision (b) of Section 1170.

(B) A factor indicating that the interests of justice would not be served by admitting the defendant to probation under Section 1203.

(C) A factor indicating that the interests of justice would not be served by conditionally sentencing the defendant under Section 1203.

(D) A factor indicating that the interests of justice would not be served by imposing less than the maximum fine and sentence fixed by law for the case.

(10) A defendant's failure or refusal to make the required disclosure pursuant to paragraph (5) shall not delay entry of an order of restitution or pronouncement of sentence. In appropriate cases, the court may do any of the following:

(A) Require the defendant to be examined by the district attorney pursuant to subdivision (h).

(B) If sentencing the defendant under Section 1170, provide that the victim shall receive a copy of the portion of the probation report filed pursuant to Section 1203.10 concerning the defendant's employment, occupation, finances, and liabilities.

(C) If sentencing the defendant under Section 1203, set a date and place for submission of the disclosure required by paragraph (5) as a condition of probation or suspended sentence.

(11) If a defendant has any remaining unpaid balance on a restitution order or fine 120 days prior to the defendant's scheduled release from probation or 120 days prior to the defendant's completion of a conditional sentence, the defendant shall prepare and file a new and updated financial disclosure identifying all assets, income, and liabilities in which the defendant holds or controls or has held or controlled a present or future interest during the defendant's period of probation or conditional sentence. The financial disclosure shall be made available to the victim and the board pursuant to Section 1214. The disclosure shall be signed and prepared by the defendant on the same form as described in paragraph (5). A defendant who willfully states as true a material matter that the defendant knows to be false on the disclosure required by this subdivision is guilty of a misdemeanor, unless this conduct is punishable as perjury or another provision of law provides for a greater penalty. The financial disclosure required by this paragraph shall be filed with the clerk of the court no later than 90 days prior to the defendant's scheduled release from probation or completion of the defendant's conditional sentence.

(12) In cases where an employer is convicted of a crime against an employee, a payment to the employee or the employee's dependent that is made by the employer's workers' compensation insurance carrier shall not be used to offset the amount of the restitution order unless the court finds that the defendant substantially met the obligation to pay premiums for that insurance coverage.

(g) A defendant's inability to pay shall not be a consideration in determining the amount of a restitution order.

(h) The district attorney may request an order of examination pursuant to the procedures specified in Article 2 (commencing with Section 708.110) of Chapter 6 of Division 2 of Title 9 of Part 2 of the Code of Civil Procedure, in order to determine the defendant's financial assets for purposes of collecting on the restitution order.

(i) A restitution order imposed pursuant to subdivision (f) shall be enforceable as if the order were a civil judgment.

(j) The making of a restitution order pursuant to subdivision (f) shall not affect the right of a victim to recovery from the Restitution Fund as otherwise provided by law, except to the extent that restitution is actually collected pursuant to the order. Restitution collected pursuant to this subdivision shall be credited to any other judgments for the same losses obtained against the defendant arising out of the crime for which the defendant was convicted.

(k) For purposes of this section, "victim" shall include all of the following:

(1) The immediate surviving family of the actual victim.

(2) A corporation, business trust, estate, trust, partnership, association, joint venture, government, governmental subdivision, agency, or instrumentality, or any other legal or commercial entity when that entity is a direct victim of a crime.

(3) A person who has sustained economic loss as the result of a crime and who satisfies any of the following conditions:

(A) At the time of the crime was the parent, grandparent, sibling, spouse, child, or grandchild of the victim.

(B) At the time of the crime was living in the household of the victim.

(C) At the time of the crime was a person who had previously lived in the household of the victim for a period of not less than two years in a relationship substantially similar to a relationship listed in subparagraph (A).

(D) Is another family member of the victim, including, but not limited to, the victim's fiance or fiancee, and who witnessed the crime.

(E) Is the primary caretaker of a minor victim.

(4) A person who is eligible to receive assistance from the Restitution Fund pursuant to Chapter 5 (commencing with Section 13950) of Part 4 of Division 3 of Title 2 of the Government Code.

(5) A governmental entity that is responsible for repairing, replacing, or restoring public or privately owned property that has been defaced with graffiti or other inscribed material, as defined in subdivision (e) of Section 594, and that has sustained an economic loss as the result of a violation of Section 594, 594.3, 594.4, 640.5, 640.6, or 640.7.

(l) In every case in which the defendant is granted probation, the court shall make the payment of restitution fines and orders imposed pursuant to this section a condition of probation. Any portion of a restitution order that remains unsatisfied after a defendant is no longer on probation shall continue to be enforceable by a victim pursuant to Section 1214 until the obligation is satisfied.

(m) If the court finds and states on the record compelling and extraordinary reasons why a restitution fine should not be required, the court shall order, as a condition of probation, that the defendant perform specified community service, unless it finds and states on the record compelling and extraordinary reasons not to require community service in addition to the finding that a restitution fine should not be required. Upon revocation of probation, the court shall impose the restitution fine pursuant to this section.

(n) The provisions of Section 13963 of the Government Code shall apply to restitution imposed pursuant to this section.

(o) The court clerk shall notify the California Victim Compensation and Government Claims Board within 90 days of an order of restitution being imposed if the defendant is ordered to pay restitution to the board due to the victim receiving compensation from the Restitution Fund. Notification shall be accomplished by mailing a copy of the court order to the board, which may be done periodically by bulk mail or email.

(p) Upon conviction for a violation of Section 236.1, the court shall, in addition to any other penalty or restitution, order the defendant to pay restitution to the victim in a case in which a victim has suffered economic loss as a result of the defendant's conduct. The court shall require that the defendant make restitution to the victim or victims in an amount established by court order, based on the amount of loss claimed by the victim or victims or another showing to the court. In determining restitution pursuant to this section, the court shall base its order upon the greater of the following: the gross value of the victim's labor or services based upon the comparable value of similar services in the labor market in which the offense occurred, or the value of the victim's labor as guaranteed under California law, or the actual income derived by the defendant from the victim's labor or services or any other appropriate means to provide reparations to the victim.

(q)

(1) In addition to any other penalty or fine, the court shall order a person who has been convicted of a violation of Section 350, 653h, 653s, 653u, 653w, or 653aa that involves a recording or audiovisual work to make restitution to an owner or lawful producer, or trade association acting on behalf of the owner or lawful producer, of a phonograph record, disc, wire, tape, film, or other device or article from which sounds or visual images are derived that suffered economic loss resulting from the violation. The order of restitution shall be based on the aggregate wholesale value of lawfully manufactured and authorized devices or articles from which sounds or visual images are devised corresponding to the number of nonconforming devices or articles involved in the offense, unless a higher value can be proved in the case of (A) an unreleased audio work, or (B) an audiovisual work that, at the time of unauthorized distribution, has not been made available in copies for sale to the general public in the United States on a digital versatile disc. For purposes of this subdivision, possession of nonconforming devices or articles intended for sale constitutes actual economic loss to an owner or lawful producer in the form of displaced legitimate wholesale purchases. The order of restitution shall also include reasonable costs incurred as a result of an investigation of the violation undertaken by the owner, lawful producer, or trade association acting on behalf of the owner or lawful producer. "Aggregate wholesale value" means the average wholesale value of lawfully manufactured and authorized sound or audiovisual recordings. Proof of the specific wholesale value of each nonconforming device or article is not required.

(2) As used in this subdivision, "audiovisual work" and "recording" shall have the same meaning as in Section 653w.

(r) This section shall become operative on January 1, 2022.

Added by Stats 2021 ch 257 (AB 177),s 20, eff. 9/23/2021.

Section 1202.41 - Hearing to impose or amend restitution order

(a)

(1) Notwithstanding Section 977 or any other law, if a defendant is currently incarcerated in a state prison with two-way audiovideo communication capability, the Department of Corrections, at the request of the California Victim Compensation Board, may collaborate with a court in any county to arrange for a hearing to impose or amend a restitution order, if the victim has received assistance pursuant to Article 5 (commencing with Section 13959) of Chapter 5 of Part 4 of Division 3 of Title 2 of the Government Code, to be conducted by two-way electronic audiovideo communication between the defendant and the courtroom in lieu of the defendant's physical presence in the courtroom, provided the county has agreed to make the necessary equipment available.

(2) Nothing in this subdivision shall be interpreted to eliminate the authority of the court to issue an order requiring the defendant to be physically present in the courtroom in those cases where the court finds circumstances that require the physical presence of the defendant in the courtroom.

(3) In lieu of the physical presence of the defendant's counsel at the institution with the defendant, the court and the Department of Corrections shall establish a confidential telephone and facsimile transmission line between the court and the institution for communication between the defendant's counsel in court and the defendant at the institution. In this case, counsel for the defendant shall not be required to be physically present at the institution during the hearing via electronic audiovideo communication. Nothing in this subdivision shall be construed to prohibit the physical presence of the defense counsel with the defendant at the state prison.

(b) If an inmate who is not incarcerated in a state prison with two-way audiovideo communication capability or ward does not waive his or her right to attend a restitution hearing for the amendment of a restitution order, the California Victim Compensation Board shall determine if the cost of holding the hearing is justified. If the board determines that the cost of holding the hearing is not justified, the amendment of the restitution order affecting that inmate or ward shall not be pursued at that time.

(c) Nothing in this section shall be construed to prohibit an individual or district attorney's office from independently pursuing the imposition or amendment of a restitution order that may result in a hearing, regardless of whether the victim has received assistance pursuant to Article 1 (commencing with Section 13959) of Chapter 5 of Part 4 of Division 3 of Title 2 of the Government Code.

Amended by Stats 2016 ch 31 (SB 836),s 241, eff. 6/27/2016.

Amended by Stats 2005 ch 238 (SB 972),s 2, eff. 1/1/2006

EFFECTIVE 1/1/2000. Amended October 10, 1999 (Bill Number: SB 1126) (Chapter 888).

Section 1202.42 - Income deduction order

Upon entry of a restitution order under subdivision (c) of Section 13967 of the Government Code, as operative on or before September 28, 1994, paragraph (3) of subdivision (a) of Section 1202.4 of this code, or Section 1203.04 as operative on or before August 2, 1995, the following shall apply:

(a) The court shall enter a separate order for income deduction upon determination of the defendant's ability to pay, regardless of the probation status, in accordance with Section 1203. Determination of a defendant's ability to pay may include his or her future earning capacity. A defendant shall bear the burden of demonstrating lack of his or her ability to pay. Express findings by the court as to the factors bearing on the amount of the fine shall not be required.

(b)

(1) In any case in which the court enters a separate order for income deduction under this section, the order shall be stayed until the agency in the county responsible for collection of restitution determines that the defendant has failed to meet his or her obligation under the restitution order and the defendant has not provided the agency with good cause for the failure in accordance with paragraph (2).

(2) If the agency responsible for collection of restitution receives information that the defendant has failed to meet his or her obligation under the restitution order, the agency shall request the defendant to provide evidence indicating that timely payments have been made or provide information establishing good cause for the failure. If the defendant fails to either provide the agency with the evidence or fails to establish good cause within five days of the request, the agency shall immediately inform the defendant of that fact, and shall inform the clerk of the court in order that an income deduction order will be served pursuant to subdivision (f) following a 15-day appeal period. The defendant may apply for a hearing to contest the lifting of the stay pursuant to subdivision (f).

(c) The income deduction order shall direct a payer to deduct from all income due and payable to the defendant the amount required by the court to meet the defendant's obligation.

(d) The income deduction order shall be effective so long as the order for restitution upon which it is based is effective or until further order of the court.

(e) When the court orders the income deduction, the court shall furnish to the defendant a statement of his or her rights, remedies, and duties in regard to the income deduction order. The statement shall state all of the following:

(1) All fees or interest that will be imposed.

(2) The total amount of income to be deducted for each pay period.

(3) That the income deduction order applies to current and subsequent payers and periods of employment.

(4) That a copy of the income deduction order will be served on the defendant's payer or payers.

(5) That enforcement of the income deduction order may only be contested on the ground of mistake of fact regarding the amount of restitution owed.

(6) That the defendant is required to notify the clerk of the court within seven days after changes in the defendant's address, payers, and the addresses of his or her payers.

(7) That the court order will be stayed in accordance with subdivision (b) and that a hearing is available in accordance with subdivision (f).

(f)

(1) Upon receiving the notice described in paragraph (2) of subdivision (b), the clerk of the court or officer of the agency responsible for collection of restitution shall serve an income deduction order and the notice to payer on the defendant's payer unless the defendant has applied for a hearing to contest the enforcement of the income deduction order.

(2)

(A) Service by or upon any person who is a party to a proceeding under this section shall be made in the manner prescribed for service upon parties in a civil action.

(B) Service upon the defendant's payer or successor payer under this section shall be made by prepaid certified mail, return receipt requested.

(3) The defendant, within 15 days after being informed that the order staying the income deduction order will be lifted, may apply for a hearing to contest the enforcement of the income deduction order on the ground of mistake of fact regarding the amount of restitution owed or on the ground that the defendant has established good cause for the nonpayment. The timely request for a hearing shall stay the service of an income deduction order on all payers of the defendant until a hearing is held and a determination is made as to whether the enforcement of the income deduction order is proper.

(4) The notice to any payer required by this subdivision shall contain only information necessary for the payer to comply with the income deduction order. The notice shall do all of the following:

(A) Require the payer to deduct from the defendant's income the amount specified in the income deduction order, and to pay that amount to the clerk of the court.

(B) Instruct the payer to implement the income deduction order no later than the first payment date that occurs more than 14 days after the date the income deduction order was served on the payer.

(C) Instruct the payer to forward, within two days after each payment date, to the clerk of the court the amount deducted from the defendant's income and a statement as to whether the amount totally or partially satisfies the periodic amount specified in the income deduction order.

(D) Specify that if a payer fails to deduct the proper amount from the defendant's income, the payer is liable for the amount the payer should have deducted, plus costs, interest, and reasonable attorney's fees.

(E) Provide that the payer may collect up to five dollars ($5) against the defendant's income to reimburse the payer for administrative costs for the first income deduction and up to one dollar ($1) for each deduction thereafter.

(F) State that the income deduction order and the notice to payer are binding on the payer until further notice by the court or until the payer no longer provides income to the defendant.

(G) Instruct the payer that, when he or she no longer provides income to the defendant, he or she shall notify the clerk of the court and shall also provide the defendant's last known address and the name and address of the defendant's new payer, if known, and that, if the payer violates this provision, the payer is subject to a civil penalty not to exceed two hundred fifty dollars ($250) for the first violation or five hundred dollars ($500) for any subsequent violation.

(H) State that the payer shall not discharge, refuse to employ, or take disciplinary action against the defendant because of an income deduction order and shall state that a violation of this provision subjects the payer to a civil penalty not to exceed two hundred fifty dollars ($250) for the first violation or five hundred dollars ($500) for any subsequent violation.

(I) Inform the payer that when he or she receives income deduction orders requiring that the income of two or more defendants be deducted and sent to the same clerk of a court, he or she may combine the amounts that are to be paid to the depository in a single payment as long as he or she identifies that portion of the payment attributable to each defendant.

(J) Inform the payer that if the payer receives more than one income deduction order against the same defendant, he or she shall contact the court for further instructions.

(5) The clerk of the court shall enforce income deduction orders against the defendant's successor payer who is located in this state in the same manner prescribed in this subdivision for the enforcement of an income deduction order against a payer.

(6) A person may not discharge, refuse to employ, or take disciplinary action against an employee because of the enforcement of an income deduction order. An employer who violates this provision is subject to a civil penalty not to exceed two hundred fifty dollars ($250) for the first violation or five hundred dollars ($500) for any subsequent violation.

(7) When a payer no longer provides income to a defendant, he or she shall notify the clerk of the court and shall provide the defendant's last known address and the name and address of the defendant's new payer, if known. A payer who violates this provision is

subject to a civil penalty not to exceed two hundred fifty dollars ($250) for the first violation or five hundred dollars ($500) for a subsequent violation.

(g) If the defendant has failed to meet his or her obligation under the restitution order and the defendant has not provided good cause for the failure in accordance with the process set forth in paragraph (2) of subdivision (b), the court may, upon the request of the prosecuting attorney, order that the prosecuting attorney be given authority to use lien procedures applicable to the defendant, including, but not limited to, a writ of attachment of property. This authority is in addition to any authority granted to the prosecuting attorney in subdivision (h).

(1) If the court authorizes a lien or other similar encumbrance on real property pursuant to this subdivision, the court shall, within 15 days, furnish to the defendant a statement of his or her rights, remedies, and duties in regard to the order. The statement shall state all of the following:

(A) That the lien is enforceable and collectible by execution issued by order of the court, except that a lien shall not be enforced by writ of execution on a defendant's principal place of residence.

(B) A legal description of the property to be encumbered.

(C) The total amount of restitution still owed by the defendant.

(D) That enforcement of the lien order may only be contested on the ground of mistake of fact regarding the amount of restitution owed or on the ground of mistake of fact regarding the defendant's ownership interest of the property to be encumbered.

(E) That a hearing is available in accordance with paragraph (2).

(F) That, upon paying the restitution order in full, the defendant may petition the court for a full release of any related encumbrance in accordance with paragraph (3).

(2) The defendant, within 15 days after being informed that a lien or other similar encumbrance on real property has been ordered, may apply for a hearing to contest the enforcement order on the ground of mistake of fact regarding the amount of restitution owed, on the ground of mistake of fact regarding the defendant's ownership interest of the property to be encumbered, or on the ground that the defendant has established good cause for the nonpayment. The timely request for a hearing shall stay any execution on the lien until a hearing is held and a determination is made as to whether the enforcement order is proper.

(3) Upon payment of the restitution order in full, the defendant may petition the court to issue an order directing the clerk of the court to execute a full reconveyance of title, a certificate of discharge, or a full release of any lien against real property created to secure performance of the restitution order.

(4) Neither a prosecutorial agency nor a prosecuting attorney shall be liable for an injury caused by an act or omission in exercising the authority granted by this subdivision.

(h) If there is no agency in the county responsible for the collection of restitution, the county probation office or the prosecuting attorney may carry out the functions and duties of such an agency as specified in subdivisions (b) and (f).

(i) A prosecuting attorney shall not make any collection against, or take any percentage of, the defendant's income or assets to reimburse the prosecuting attorney for administrative costs in carrying out any action authorized by this section.

(j) As used in this section, "good cause" for failure to meet an obligation or "good cause" for nonpayment means, but shall not be limited to, any of the following:

(1) That there has been a substantial change in the defendant's economic circumstances, such as involuntary unemployment, involuntary cost-of-living increases, or costs incurred as the result of medical circumstances or a natural disaster.

(2) That the defendant reasonably believes there has been an administrative error with regard to his or her obligation for payment.

(3) Any other similar and justifiable reasons.

Amended by Stats 2010 ch 582 (AB 1847),s 1, eff. 1/1/2011.

Added by Stats 2002 ch 1141 (SB 1423), s 14, eff. 1/1/2003.

Section 1202.43 - Payment of restitution fine

(a) The restitution fine imposed pursuant to subdivision (a) of Section 13967 of the Government Code, as operative on or before September 28, 1994, subparagraph (B) of paragraph (2) of subdivision (a) of Section 1203.04, as operative on or before August 2, 1995, or Section 1202.4 shall be payable to the clerk of the court, the probation officer, or any other person responsible for the collection of criminal fines. If the defendant is unable or otherwise fails to pay that fine in a felony case and there is an amount unpaid of one thousand dollars ($1,000) or more within 60 days after the imposition of sentence, or in a case in which probation is granted, within the period of probation, the clerk of the court, probation officer, or other person to whom the fine is to be paid shall forward to the Controller the abstract of judgment along with any information which may be relevant to the present and future location of the defendant and his or her assets, if any, and any verifiable amount which the defendant may have paid to the victim as a result of the crime.

(b) A restitution fine shall be deemed a debt of the defendant owing to the state for the purposes of Sections 12418 and 12419.5 of the Government Code, excepting any amounts the defendant has paid to the victim as a result of the crime. Upon request by the Controller, the district attorney of a county or the Attorney General may take any necessary action to recover amounts owing on a restitution fine. The amount of the recovery shall be increased by a sum sufficient to cover any costs incurred by any state or local agency in the administration of this section. The remedies provided by this subdivision are in addition to any other remedies provided by law for the enforcement of a judgment.

Added by Stats 2002 ch 1141 (SB 1423), s 15, eff. 1/1/2003.

Section 1202.44 - Probation revocation restitution fine

In every case in which a person is convicted of a crime and a conditional sentence or a sentence that includes a period of probation is imposed, the court shall, at the time of imposing the restitution fine pursuant to subdivision (b) of Section 1202.4, assess an additional probation revocation restitution fine in the same amount as that imposed pursuant to subdivision (b) of Section 1202.4. This additional probation revocation restitution fine shall become effective upon the revocation of probation or of a conditional sentence, and shall not be waived or reduced by the court, absent compelling and extraordinary reasons stated on record. Probation revocation restitution fines shall be deposited in the Restitution Fund in the State Treasury.

Added by Stats 2004 ch 223 (SB 631), s 3, eff. 8/16/2004.

Section 1202.45 - Parole revocation restitution fine

(a) In every case where a person is convicted of a crime and his or her sentence includes a period of parole, the court shall, at the time of imposing the restitution fine pursuant to subdivision (b) of Section 1202.4, assess an additional parole revocation restitution fine in the same amount as that imposed pursuant to subdivision (b) of Section 1202.4.

(b) In every case where a person is convicted of a crime and is subject to either postrelease community supervision under Section 3451 or mandatory supervision under subparagraph (B) of paragraph (5) of subdivision (h) of Section 1170, the court shall, at the time of imposing the restitution fine pursuant to subdivision (b) of Section 1202.4, assess an additional postrelease community supervision revocation restitution fine or mandatory supervision revocation restitution fine in the same amount as that imposed pursuant to subdivision (b) of Section 1202.4, that may be collected by the agency designated pursuant to subdivision (b) of Section 2085.5 by the board of supervisors of the county in which the prisoner is incarcerated.

(c) The fines imposed pursuant to subdivisions (a) and (b) shall not be subject to penalty assessments authorized by Section 1464 or Chapter 12 (commencing with Section 76000) of Title 8 of the Government Code, or the state surcharge authorized by Section 1465.7, and shall be suspended unless the person's parole, postrelease community supervision, or mandatory supervision is revoked. Fine moneys shall be deposited in the Restitution Fund in the State Treasury.

Amended by Stats 2012 ch 762 (SB 1210),s 1, eff. 1/1/2013.
Amended by Stats 2007 ch 302 (SB 425),s 15, eff. 1/1/2008.
Amended by Stats 2004 ch 223 (SB 631), s 4, eff. 8/16/2004.

Section 1202.46 - Retention of jurisdiction to impose or modify restitution

Notwithstanding Section 1170, when the economic losses of a victim cannot be ascertained at the time of sentencing pursuant to subdivision (f) of Section 1202.4, the court shall retain jurisdiction over a person subject to a restitution order for purposes of imposing or modifying restitution until such time as the losses may be determined. This section does not prohibit a victim, the district attorney, or a court on its own motion from requesting correction, at any time, of a sentence when the sentence is invalid due to the omission of a restitution order or fine pursuant to Section 1202.4.

Amended by Stats 2016 ch 37 (AB 2295),s 4, eff. 1/1/2017.
EFFECTIVE 1/1/2000. Amended October 10, 1999 (Bill Number: SB 1126) (Chapter 888).

Section 1202.5 - Additional $10 fine for specified offenses

(a) In any case in which a defendant is convicted of any of the offenses enumerated in Section 211, 215, 459, 470, 484, 487, subdivision (a) of Section 487a, or Section 488, or 594, the court shall order the defendant to pay a fine of ten dollars ($10) in addition to any other penalty or fine imposed. If the court determines that the defendant has the ability to pay all or part of the fine, the court shall set the amount to be reimbursed and order the defendant to pay that sum to the county in the manner in which the court believes reasonable and compatible with the defendant's financial ability. In making a determination of whether a defendant has the ability to pay, the court shall take into account the amount of any other fine imposed upon the defendant and any amount the defendant has been ordered to pay in restitution.

(b)

(1) All fines collected pursuant to this section shall be held in trust by the county collecting them, until transferred to the local law enforcement agency to be used exclusively for the jurisdiction where the offense took place. All moneys collected shall implement, support, and continue local crime prevention programs.

(2) All amounts collected pursuant to this section shall be in addition to, and shall not supplant funds received for crime prevention purposes from other sources.

(c) As used in this section, "law enforcement agency" includes, but is not limited to, police departments, sheriffs departments, and probation departments.

Amended by Stats 2013 ch 618 (AB 924),s 10, eff. 1/1/2014.
Amended by Stats 2000 ch 399 (AB 1840) s 1, eff. 1/1/2001.

Section 1202.51 - Additional $100 or $200 fine for specified offenses

In any case in which a defendant is convicted of any of the offenses enumerated in Section 372, 373a, 374.3, 374.4, 374.7, or 374.8, the court shall order the defendant to pay a fine of one hundred dollars ($100) if the conviction is for an infraction or two hundred dollars ($200) if the conviction is for a misdemeanor, in addition to any other penalty or fine imposed. If the court determines that the defendant has the ability to pay all or part of the fine, the court shall set the amount to be paid and order the defendant to pay that sum to the city or, if not within a city, the county, where the violation occurred, to be used for the city's or county's illegal dumping enforcement program. Notwithstanding any other provision of law, no state or county penalty, assessment, fee, or surcharge shall be imposed on the fine ordered under this section.

Added by Stats 2007 ch 394 (AB 679),s 1, eff. 1/1/2008.

Section 1202.6 - First conviction for prostitution; referral to drug diversion or Welfare-to-Work program or both

Notwithstanding Sections 120975, 120980, and 120990 of the Health and Safety Code, upon the first conviction of a person for a violation of subdivision (b) of Section 647, the court shall refer the defendant, where appropriate, to a program under Article 3.2 (commencing with Section 11320) of Chapter 2 of Part 3 of Division 9 of the Welfare and Institutions Code or to a drug diversion program, or to both.

Added by Stats 2017 ch 537 (SB 239),s 17, eff. 1/1/2018.

Section 1202.7 - Probation services

The Legislature finds and declares that the provision of probation services is an essential element in the administration of criminal justice. The safety of the public, which shall be a primary goal through the enforcement of court-ordered conditions of probation; the nature of the offense; the interests of justice, including punishment, reintegration of the offender into the community, and enforcement of conditions of probation; the loss to the victim; and the needs of the defendant shall be the primary considerations in the granting of probation. It is the intent of the Legislature that efforts be made with respect to persons who are subject to Section 290.011 who are on probation to engage them in treatment.

Amended by Stats 2007 ch 579 (SB 172),s 42, eff. 10/13/2007.

Amended by Stats 2001 ch 485 (AB 1004), s 2, eff. 1/1/2002.

Section 1202.8 - Supervision of persons placed on probation

(a) Persons placed on probation by a court shall be under the supervision of the county probation officer who shall determine both the level and type of supervision consistent with the court-ordered conditions of probation.

(b) Commencing January 1, 2009, every person who has been assessed with the State Authorized Risk Assessment Tool for Sex Offenders (SARATSO) pursuant to Sections 290.04 to 290.06, inclusive, and who has a SARATSO risk level of high shall be continuously electronically monitored while on probation, unless the court determines that such monitoring is unnecessary for a particular person. The monitoring device used for these purposes shall be identified as one that employs the latest available proven effective monitoring technology. Nothing in this section prohibits probation authorities from using electronic monitoring technology pursuant to any other provision of law.

(c) Within 30 days of a court making an order to provide restitution to a victim or to the Restitution Fund, the probation officer shall establish an account into which any restitution payments that are not deposited into the Restitution Fund shall be deposited.

(d) Beginning January 1, 2009, and every two years thereafter, each probation department shall report to the Corrections Standards Authority all relevant statistics and relevant information regarding the effectiveness of continuous electronic monitoring of offenders pursuant to subdivision (b). The report shall include the costs of monitoring and the recidivism rates of those persons who have been monitored. The Corrections Standards Authority shall compile the reports and submit a single report to the Legislature and the Governor every two years through 2017.

Amended by Stats 2010 ch 328 (SB 1330),s 164, eff. 1/1/2011.

Amended by Stats 2006 ch 886 (AB 1849),s 5, eff. 9/30/2006.

Amended by Stats 2006 ch 336 (SB 1178),s 4, eff. 9/20/2006.

Section 1203 - Referral to probation officer; investigation; report

(a) As used in this code, "probation" means the suspension of the imposition or execution of a sentence and the order of conditional and revocable release in the community under the supervision of a probation officer. As used in this code, "conditional sentence" means the suspension of the imposition or execution of a sentence and the order of revocable release in the community subject to conditions established by the court without the supervision of a probation officer. It is the intent of the Legislature that both conditional sentence and probation are authorized whenever probation is authorized in any code as a sentencing option for infractions or misdemeanors.

(b)

(1) Except as provided in subdivision (j), if a person is convicted of a felony and is eligible for probation, before judgment is pronounced, the court shall immediately refer the matter to a probation officer to investigate and report to the court, at a specified time, upon the circumstances surrounding the crime and the prior history and record of the person, which may be considered either in aggravation or mitigation of the punishment.

(2)

(A) The probation officer shall immediately investigate and make a written report to the court containing findings and recommendations, including recommendations as to the granting or denying of probation and the conditions of probation, if granted.

(B) Pursuant to Section 828 of the Welfare and Institutions Code, the probation officer shall include in the report any information gathered by a law enforcement agency relating to the taking of the defendant into custody as a minor, which shall be considered for purposes of determining whether adjudications of commissions of crimes as a juvenile warrant a finding that there are circumstances in aggravation pursuant to Section 1170 or to deny probation.

(C) If the person was convicted of an offense that requires that person to register as a sex offender pursuant to Sections 290 to 290.023, inclusive, or if the probation report recommends that registration be ordered at sentencing pursuant to Section 290.006, the probation officer's report shall include the results of the State-Authorized Risk Assessment Tool for Sex Offenders (SARATSO) administered pursuant to Sections 290.04 to 290.06, inclusive, if applicable.

(D) The probation officer may also include in the report recommendations for both of the following:

(i) The amount the defendant should be required to pay as a restitution fine pursuant to subdivision (b) of Section 1202.4.

(ii) Whether the court shall require, as a condition of probation, restitution to the victim or to the Restitution Fund and the amount thereof.

(E) The report shall be made available to the court and the prosecuting and defense attorneys at least five days, or upon request of the defendant or prosecuting attorney nine days, prior to the time fixed by the court for the hearing and determination of the report, and shall be filed with the clerk of the court as a record in the case at the time of the hearing. The time within which the report shall be made available and filed may be waived by written stipulation of the prosecuting and defense attorneys that is filed with the court or an oral stipulation in open court that is made and entered upon the minutes of the court.

(3) At a time fixed by the court, the court shall hear and determine the application, if one has been made, or, in any case, the suitability of probation in the particular case. At the hearing, the court shall consider any report of the probation officer, including the results of the SARATSO, if applicable, and shall make a statement that it has considered the report, which shall be filed with the clerk of the court as a record in the case. If the court determines that there are circumstances in mitigation of the punishment prescribed by law or that the ends of justice would be served by granting probation to the person, it may place the person on probation. If probation is denied, the clerk of the court shall immediately send a copy of the report to the Department of Corrections and Rehabilitation at the prison or other institution to which the person is delivered.

(4) The preparation of the report or the consideration of the report by the court may be waived only by a written stipulation of the prosecuting and defense attorneys that is filed with the court or an oral stipulation in open court that is made and entered upon the minutes of the court, except that a waiver shall not be allowed unless the court consents thereto. However, if the defendant is ultimately sentenced and committed to the state prison, a probation report shall be completed pursuant to Section 1203c.

(c) If a defendant is not represented by an attorney, the court shall order the probation officer who makes the probation report to discuss its contents with the defendant.

(d) If a person is convicted of a misdemeanor, the court may either refer the matter to the probation officer for an investigation and a report or summarily pronounce a conditional sentence. If the person was convicted of an offense that requires that person to register as a sex offender pursuant to Sections 290 to 290.023, inclusive, or if the probation officer recommends that the court, at sentencing, order the offender to register as a sex offender pursuant to Section 290.006, the court shall refer the matter to the probation officer for the purpose of obtaining a report on the results of the State-Authorized Risk Assessment Tool for Sex Offenders administered pursuant to Sections 290.04 to 290.06, inclusive, if applicable, which the court shall consider. If the case is not referred to the probation officer, in sentencing the person, the court may consider any information concerning the person that could have been included in a probation report. The court shall inform the person of the information to be considered and permit the person to answer or controvert the information. For this purpose, upon the request of the person, the court shall grant a continuance before the judgment is pronounced.

(e) Except in unusual cases in which the interests of justice would best be served if the person is granted probation, probation shall not be granted to any of the following persons:

(1) Unless the person had a lawful right to carry a deadly weapon, other than a firearm, at the time of the perpetration of the crime or the person's arrest, any person who has been convicted of arson, robbery, carjacking, burglary, burglary with explosives, rape with force or violence, torture, aggravated mayhem, murder, attempt to commit murder, trainwrecking, kidnapping, escape from the state prison, or a conspiracy to commit one or more of those crimes and who was armed with the weapon at either of those times.

(2) Any person who used, or attempted to use, a deadly weapon upon a human being in connection with the perpetration of the crime of which that person has been convicted.

(3) Any person who willfully inflicted great bodily injury or torture in the perpetration of the crime of which that person has been convicted.

(4) Any person who has been previously convicted twice in this state of a felony or in any other place of a public offense which, if committed in this state, would have been punishable as a felony.

(5) Unless the person has never been previously convicted once in this state of a felony or in any other place of a public offense which, if committed in this state, would have been punishable as a felony, any person who has been convicted of burglary with explosives, rape with force or violence, torture, aggravated mayhem, murder, attempt to commit murder, trainwrecking, extortion, kidnapping, escape from the state prison, a violation of Section 286, 287, 288, or 288.5, or of former Section 288a, or a conspiracy to commit one or more of those crimes.

(6) Any person who has been previously convicted once in this state of a felony or in any other place of a public offense which, if committed in this state, would have been punishable as a felony, if that person committed any of the following acts:

(A) Unless the person had a lawful right to carry a deadly weapon at the time of the perpetration of the previous crime or the person's arrest for the previous crime, the person was armed with a weapon at either of those times.

(B) The person used, or attempted to use, a deadly weapon upon a human being in connection with the perpetration of the previous crime.

(C) The person willfully inflicted great bodily injury or torture in the perpetration of the previous crime.

(7) Any public official or peace officer of this state or any city, county, or other political subdivision who, in the discharge of the duties of public office or employment, accepted or gave or offered to accept or give any bribe, embezzled public money, or was guilty of extortion.

(8) Any person who knowingly furnishes or gives away phencyclidine.

(9) Any person who intentionally inflicted great bodily injury in the commission of arson under subdivision (a) of Section 451 or who intentionally set fire to, burned, or caused the burning of, an inhabited structure or inhabited property in violation of subdivision (b) of Section 451.

(10) Any person who, in the commission of a felony, inflicts great bodily injury or causes the death of a human being by the discharge of a firearm from or at an occupied motor vehicle proceeding on a public street or highway.

(11) Any person who possesses a short-barreled rifle or a short-barreled shotgun under Section 33215, a machinegun under Section 32625, or a silencer under Section 33410.

(12) Any person who is convicted of violating Section 8101 of the Welfare and Institutions Code.

(13) Any person who is described in subdivision (b) or (c) of Section 27590.

(f) When probation is granted in a case which comes within subdivision (e), the court shall specify on the record and shall enter on the minutes the circumstances indicating that the interests of justice would best be served by that disposition.

(g) If a person is not eligible for probation, the judge shall refer the matter to the probation officer for an investigation of the facts relevant to determination of the amount of a restitution fine pursuant to subdivision (b) of Section 1202.4 in all cases in which the determination is applicable. The judge, in their discretion, may direct the probation officer to investigate all facts relevant to the sentencing of the person. Upon that referral, the probation officer shall immediately investigate the circumstances surrounding the crime and the prior record and history of the person and make a written report to the court containing findings. The findings shall include a recommendation of the amount of the restitution fine as provided in subdivision (b) of Section 1202.4.

(h) If a defendant is convicted of a felony and a probation report is prepared pursuant to subdivision (b) or (g), the probation officer may obtain and include in the report a statement of the comments of the victim concerning the offense. The court may direct the probation officer not to obtain a statement if the victim has in fact testified at any of the court proceedings concerning the offense.

(i) A probationer shall not be released to enter another state unless the case has been referred to the Administrator of the Interstate Probation and Parole Compacts, pursuant to the Uniform Act for Out-of-State Probationer or Parolee Supervision (Article 3 (commencing with Section 11175) of Chapter 2 of Title 1 of Part 4).

(j) In any court in which a county financial evaluation officer is available, in addition to referring the matter to the probation officer, the court may order the defendant to appear before the county financial evaluation officer for a financial evaluation of the defendant's ability to pay restitution, in which case the county financial evaluation officer shall report the findings regarding restitution and other court-related costs to the probation officer on the question of the defendant's ability to pay those costs. Any order made pursuant to this subdivision may be enforced as a violation of the terms and conditions of probation upon willful failure to pay and at the discretion of the court, may be enforced in the same manner as a judgment in a civil action, if any balance remains unpaid at the end of the defendant's probationary period.

(k) Probation shall not be granted to, nor shall the execution of, or imposition of sentence be suspended for, any person who is convicted of a violent felony, as defined in subdivision (c) of Section 667.5, or a serious felony, as defined in subdivision (c) of Section 1192.7, and who was on probation for a felony offense at the time of the commission of the new felony offense.

(l) For any person granted probation prior to January 1, 2028, at the time the court imposes probation, the court may take a waiver from the defendant permitting flash incarceration by the probation officer, pursuant to Section 1203.35.

(m) A person who is granted probation is subject to search or seizure as part of their terms and conditions only by a probation officer or other peace officer.

Amended by Stats 2023 ch 218 (SB 852),s 4, eff. 1/1/2024.

Amended by Stats 2022 ch 756 (AB 1744),s 1, eff. 1/1/2023.

Added by Stats 2020 ch 92 (AB 1869),s 42, eff. 9/18/2020.

This act (Stats 2023 ch 218 (SB 852)) shall be known, and may be cited, as the Prohibiting Rogue Officer Tricks and Ensuring Community Trust (PROTECT) Act.

Section 1203.01 - Statements of views respecting person convicted or sentenced

(a) Immediately after judgment has been pronounced, the judge and the district attorney, respectively, may cause to be filed with the clerk of the court a brief statement of their views respecting the person convicted or sentenced and the crime committed, together with any reports the probation officer may have filed relative to the prisoner. The judge and district attorney shall cause those statements to be filed if no probation officer's report has been filed. The attorney for the defendant and the law enforcement agency that investigated the case may likewise file with the clerk of the court statements of their views respecting the defendant and the crime of which they were convicted. Immediately after the filing of those statements and reports, the clerk of the court shall mail a copy thereof, certified by that clerk, with postage prepaid, addressed to the Department of Corrections and Rehabilitation at the prison or other institution to which the person convicted is delivered. The clerk shall also mail a copy of any statement submitted by the court, district attorney, or law enforcement agency, pursuant to this section, with postage prepaid, addressed to the attorney for the defendant, if any, and to the defendant, in care of the Department of Corrections and Rehabilitation, and a copy of any statement submitted by the attorney for the defendant, with postage prepaid, shall be mailed to the district attorney.

(b)

(1) In all cases in which the judgment imposed includes a sentence of death or an indeterminate term with or without the possibility of parole, the clerk shall, within 60 days after judgment has been pronounced, mail with postage prepaid, to the prison or other institution to which the person convicted is delivered, a copy of the charging documents, a copy of waiver and plea forms, if any, the transcript of the proceedings at the time of the defendant's guilty or nolo contendere plea, if the defendant pleaded guilty or nolo contendere, and the transcript of the proceedings at the time of sentencing.

(2) In all other cases not described in paragraph (1), the clerk shall mail with postage prepaid, to the prison or other institution to which the person convicted is delivered, a copy of the charging documents, a copy of the waiver and plea forms, if any, and upon written request by the Department of Corrections and Rehabilitation or by an inmate, or by their counsel, for, among other purposes on a particular case, appeals, review of custody credits and release dates, and restitution orders, the transcript of the proceedings at the time of the defendant's guilty or nolo contendere plea, if the defendant pleaded guilty or nolo contendere, and the transcript of the proceedings at the time of sentencing.

(c) With the consent of the recipient expressed in writing, or orally on the record, the clerk of the court may deliver the documents, or the data contained in the documents, described in subdivisions (a) and (b) by electronic means rather than by mail if the recipient is not the person convicted.

Amended by Stats 2021 ch 434 (SB 827),s 7, eff. 1/1/2022.

Amended by Stats 2011 ch 193 (AB 110),s 7, eff. 8/30/2011.

Section 1203.016 - Home detention program

(a) Notwithstanding any other law, the board of supervisors of any county may authorize the correctional administrator, as defined in subdivision (g), to offer a program under which inmates committed to a county jail or other county correctional facility or granted probation, or inmates participating in a work furlough program, may voluntarily participate or involuntarily be placed in a home detention program during their sentence in lieu of confinement in a county jail or other county correctional facility or program under the auspices of the probation officer.

(b) The board of supervisors, in consultation with the correctional administrator, may prescribe reasonable rules and regulations under which a home detention program may operate. As a condition of participation in the home detention program, the inmate shall give consent in writing to participate in the home detention program and shall in writing agree to comply or, for involuntary participation, the inmate shall be informed in writing that the inmate shall comply, with the rules and regulations of the program, including, but not limited to, the following rules:

(1) The participant shall remain within the interior premises of the participant's residence during the hours designated by the correctional administrator.

(2) The participant shall admit any probation officer or other peace officer designated by the correctional administrator into the participant's residence at any time for purposes of verifying the participant's compliance with the conditions of the detention.

(3) The participant shall agree to the use of electronic monitoring, which may include Global Positioning System devices or other supervising devices for the purpose of helping to verify compliance with the rules and regulations of the home detention program. The devices shall not be used to eavesdrop or record any conversation, except a conversation between the participant and the person supervising the participant which is to be used solely for the purposes of voice identification.

(4) The participant shall agree that the correctional administrator in charge of the county correctional facility from which the participant was released may, without further order of the court, immediately retake the person into custody to serve the balance of the person's sentence if the electronic monitoring or supervising devices are unable for any reason to properly perform their function at the designated place of home detention, if the person fails to remain within the place of home detention as stipulated in the agreement, or if the person for any other reason no longer meets the established criteria under this section. A copy of the agreement shall be delivered to the participant and a copy retained by the correctional administrator.

(c) If the peace officer supervising a participant has reasonable cause to believe that the participant is not complying with the rules or conditions of the program, or that the electronic monitoring devices are unable to function properly in the designated place of confinement, the peace officer may, under general or specific authorization of the correctional administrator, and without a warrant of arrest, retake the person into custody to complete the remainder of the original sentence.

(d) Nothing in this section shall be construed to require the correctional administrator to allow a person to participate in this program if it appears from the record that the person has not satisfactorily complied with reasonable rules and regulations while in custody. A person shall be eligible for participation in a home detention program only if the correctional administrator concludes that the person meets the criteria for release established under this section and that the person's participation is consistent with any reasonable rules and regulations prescribed by the board of supervisors or the administrative policy of the correctional administrator.

(1) The rules and regulations and administrative policy of the program shall be written and reviewed on an annual basis by the county board of supervisors and the correctional administrator. The rules and regulations shall be given to or made available to any participant upon request.

(2) The correctional administrator, or the administrator's designee, shall have the sole discretionary authority to permit program participation as an alternative to physical custody. All persons referred or recommended by the court to participate in the home detention program pursuant to subdivision (e) who are denied participation or all persons removed from program participation shall be notified in writing of the specific reasons for the denial or removal. The notice of denial or removal shall include the participant's appeal rights, as established by program administrative policy.

(e) The court may recommend or refer a person to the correctional administrator for consideration for placement in the home detention program. The recommendation or referral of the court shall be given great weight in the determination of acceptance or denial. At the time of sentencing or at any time that the court deems it necessary, the court may restrict or deny the defendant's participation in a home detention program.

(f) The correctional administrator may permit home detention program participants to seek and retain employment in the community, attend psychological counseling sessions or educational or vocational training classes, or seek medical and dental assistance. Willful failure of the program participant to return to the place of home detention not later than the expiration of any period of time during which the participant is authorized to be away from the place of home detention pursuant to this section and unauthorized departures from the place of home detention are punishable as provided in Section 4532.

(g) As used in this section, "correctional administrator" means the sheriff, probation officer, or director of the county department of corrections.

(h) Notwithstanding any other law, the police department of a city where an office is located to which persons on an electronic monitoring program report may request the county correctional administrator to provide information concerning those persons. This information shall be limited to the name, address, date of birth, offense committed by the home detainee, and if available, at the discretion of the supervising agency and solely for investigatory purposes, current and historical GPS coordinates of the home detainee. A law enforcement department that does not have the primary responsibility to supervise participants in the electronic monitoring program that receives information pursuant to this subdivision shall not use the information to conduct enforcement actions based on administrative violations of the home detention program. A law enforcement department that has knowledge that the subject in a criminal investigation is a participant in an electronic monitoring program shall make reasonable efforts to notify the supervising agency prior to serving a warrant or taking any law enforcement action against a participant in an electronic monitoring program.

(i) It is the intent of the Legislature that home detention programs established under this section maintain the highest public confidence, credibility, and public safety. In the furtherance of these standards, the following shall apply:

(1) The correctional administrator, with the approval of the board of supervisors, may administer a home detention program pursuant to written contracts with appropriate public or private agencies or entities to provide specified program services. No public or private agency or entity may operate a home detention program in any county without a written contract with that county's correctional administrator. However, this does not apply to the use of electronic monitoring by the Department of Corrections and Rehabilitation. No public or private agency or entity entering into a contract may itself employ any person who is in the home detention program.

(2) Program acceptance shall not circumvent the normal booking process for sentenced offenders. All home detention program participants shall be supervised.

(3)

(A) All privately operated home detention programs shall be under the jurisdiction of, and subject to the terms and conditions of the contract entered into with, the correctional administrator.

(B) Each contract shall include, but not be limited to, all of the following:

(i) A provision whereby the private agency or entity agrees to operate in compliance with any available standards promulgated by state correctional agencies and bodies, including the Corrections Standards Authority, and all statutory provisions and mandates, state and county, as appropriate and applicable to the operation of home detention programs and the supervision of sentenced offenders in a home detention program.

(ii) A provision that clearly defines areas of respective responsibility and liability of the county and the private agency or entity.

(iii) A provision that requires the private agency or entity to demonstrate evidence of financial responsibility, submitted and approved by the board of supervisors, in amounts and under conditions sufficient to fully indemnify the county for reasonably foreseeable public liability, including legal defense costs, that may arise from, or be proximately caused by, acts or omissions of the contractor. The contract shall provide for annual review by the correctional administrator to ensure compliance with requirements set by the board of supervisors and for adjustment of the financial responsibility requirements if warranted by caseload changes or other factors.

(iv) A provision that requires the private agency or entity to provide evidence of financial responsibility, such as certificates of insurance or copies of insurance policies, prior to commencing any operations pursuant to the contract or at any time requested by the board of supervisors or correctional administrator.

(v) A provision that permits the correctional administrator to immediately terminate the contract with a private agency or entity at any time that the contractor fails to demonstrate evidence of financial responsibility.

(C) All privately operated home detention programs shall comply with all appropriate, applicable ordinances and regulations specified in subdivision (a) of Section 1208.

(D) The board of supervisors, the correctional administrator, and the designee of the correctional administrator shall comply with Section 1090 of the Government Code in the consideration, making, and execution of contracts pursuant to this section.

(E) The failure of the private agency or entity to comply with statutory provisions and requirements or with the standards established by the contract and with the correctional administrator may be sufficient cause to terminate the contract.

(F) Upon the discovery that a private agency or entity with whom there is a contract is not in compliance pursuant to this paragraph, the correctional administrator shall give 60 days' notice to the director of the private agency or entity that the contract may be canceled if the specified deficiencies are not corrected.

(G) Shorter notice may be given or the contract may be canceled without notice whenever a serious threat to public safety is present because the private agency or entity has failed to comply with this section.

(j) For purposes of this section, "evidence of financial responsibility" may include, but is not limited to, certified copies of any of the following:

(1) A current liability insurance policy.

(2) A current errors and omissions insurance policy.

(3) A surety bond.

(k) This section shall become operative on July 1, 2021.
Amended by Stats 2023 ch 218 (SB 852),s 5, eff. 1/1/2024.
Added by Stats 2020 ch 92 (AB 1869),s 44, eff. 9/18/2020.

Section 1203.017 - Involuntary home detention program

(a) Notwithstanding any other provision of law, upon determination by the correctional administrator that conditions in a jail facility warrant the necessity of releasing sentenced misdemeanor inmates prior to them serving the full amount of a given sentence due to lack of jail space, the board of supervisors of any county may authorize the correctional administrator to offer a program under which inmates committed to a county jail or other county correctional facility or granted probation, or inmates participating in a work furlough program, may be required to participate in an involuntary home detention program, which shall include electronic monitoring, during their sentence in lieu of confinement in the county jail or other county correctional facility or program under the auspices of the probation officer. Under this program, one day of participation shall be in lieu of one day of incarceration. Participants in the program shall receive any sentence reduction credits that they would have received had they served their sentences in a county correctional facility.

(b) The board of supervisors may prescribe reasonable rules and regulations under which an involuntary home detention program may operate. The inmate shall be informed in writing that they shall comply with the rules and regulations of the program, including, but not limited to, the following rules:

(1) The participant shall remain within the interior premises of their residence during the hours designated by the correctional administrator.

(2) The participant shall admit any probation officer or other peace officer designated by the correctional administrator into their residence at any time for purposes of verifying the participant's compliance with the conditions of their detention.

(3) The use of electronic monitoring may include global positioning system devices or other supervising devices for the purpose of helping to verify their compliance with the rules and regulations of the home detention program. The devices shall not be used to eavesdrop or record any conversation, except a conversation between the participant and the person supervising the participant which is to be used solely for the purposes of voice identification.

(4) The correctional administrator in charge of the county correctional facility from which the participant was released may, without further order of the court, immediately retake the person into custody to serve the balance of their sentence if the electronic monitoring or supervising devices are unable for any reason to properly perform their function at the designated place of home detention, if the person fails to remain within the place of home detention as stipulated in the agreement, or if the person for any other reason no longer meets the established criteria under this section.

(c) Whenever the peace officer supervising a participant has reasonable cause to believe that the participant is not complying with the rules or conditions of the program, or that the electronic monitoring devices are unable to function properly in the designated place of confinement, the peace officer may, under general or specific authorization of the correctional administrator, and without a warrant of arrest, retake the person into custody to complete the remainder of the original sentence.

(d) Nothing in this section shall be construed to require the correctional administrator to allow a person to participate in this program if it appears from the record that the person has not satisfactorily complied with reasonable rules and regulations while in custody. A person shall be eligible for participation in a home detention program only if the correctional administrator concludes that the person meets the criteria for release established under this section and that the person's participation is consistent with any reasonable rules and regulations prescribed by the board of supervisors or the administrative policy of the correctional administrator.

(1) The rules and regulations and administrative policy of the program shall be written and reviewed on an annual basis by the county board of supervisors and the correctional administrator. The rules and regulations shall be given to or made available to any participant upon request.

(2) The correctional administrator, or their designee, shall have the sole discretionary authority to permit program participation as an alternative to physical custody. All persons referred or recommended by the court to participate in the home detention program pursuant to subdivision (e) who are denied participation or all persons removed from program participation shall be notified in writing of the specific reasons for the denial or removal. The notice of denial or removal shall include the participant's appeal rights, as established by program administrative policy.

(e) The court may recommend or refer a person to the correctional administrator for consideration for placement in the home detention program. The recommendation or referral of the court shall be given great weight in the determination of acceptance or denial. At the time of sentencing or at any time that the court deems it necessary, the court may restrict or deny the defendant's participation in a home detention program.

(f) The correctional administrator may permit home detention program participants to seek and retain employment in the community, attend psychological counseling sessions or educational or vocational training classes, or seek medical and dental assistance. Willful failure of the program participant to return to the place of home detention not later than the expiration of any period of time during which they are authorized to be away from the place of home detention pursuant to this section and unauthorized departures from the place of home detention are punishable as provided in Section 4532.

(g) As used in this section, "correctional administrator" means the sheriff, probation officer, or director of the county department of corrections.

(h)

   (1) Notwithstanding any other law, the correctional administrator shall provide the information specified in paragraph (2) regarding persons on involuntary home detention to the Corrections Standards Authority, and upon request, shall provide that information to the law enforcement agency of a city or unincorporated area where an office is located to which persons on involuntary home detention report.

   (2) The information required by paragraph (1) shall consist of the following:

      (A) The participant's name, address, and date of birth.

      (B) The offense committed by the participant.

      (C) The period of time the participant will be placed on home detention.

      (D) Whether the participant successfully completed the prescribed period of home detention or was returned to a county correctional facility, and if the person was returned to a county correctional facility, the reason for that return.

      (E) The gender and ethnicity of the participant.

   (3) Any information received by a police department pursuant to this subdivision shall be used only for the purpose of monitoring the impact of home detention programs on the community.

(i) It is the intent of the Legislature that home detention programs established under this section maintain the highest public confidence, credibility, and public safety. In the furtherance of these standards, the following shall apply:

   (1) The correctional administrator, with the approval of the board of supervisors, may administer a home detention program pursuant to written contracts with appropriate public or private agencies or entities to provide specified program services. No public or private agency or entity may operate a home detention program in any county without a written contract with that county's correctional administrator. However, this does not apply to the use of electronic monitoring by the Department of Corrections and Rehabilitation as established in Section 3004. No public or private agency or entity entering into a contract may itself employ any person who is in the home detention program.

   (2) Program acceptance shall not circumvent the normal booking process for sentenced offenders. All home detention program participants shall be supervised.

   (3)

      (A) All privately operated home detention programs shall be under the jurisdiction of, and subject to the terms and conditions of the contract entered into with, the correctional administrator.

      (B) Each contract shall include, but not be limited to, all of the following:

         (i) A provision whereby the private agency or entity agrees to operate in compliance with any available standards promulgated by state correctional agencies and bodies, including the Corrections Standards Authority, and all statutory provisions and mandates, state and county, as appropriate and applicable to the operation of home detention programs and the supervision of sentenced offenders in a home detention program.

         (ii) A provision that clearly defines areas of respective responsibility and liability of the county and the private agency or entity.

         (iii) A provision that requires the private agency or entity to demonstrate evidence of financial responsibility, submitted and approved by the board of supervisors, in amounts and under conditions sufficient to fully indemnify the county for reasonably foreseeable public liability, including legal defense costs, that may arise from, or be proximately caused by, acts or omissions of the contractor. The contract shall provide for annual review by the correctional administrator to ensure compliance with requirements set by the board of supervisors and for adjustment of the financial responsibility requirements if warranted by caseload changes or other factors.

         (iv) A provision that requires the private agency or entity to provide evidence of financial responsibility, such as certificates of insurance or copies of insurance policies, prior to commencing any operations pursuant to the contract or at any time requested by the board of supervisors or correctional administrator.

         (v) A provision that permits the correctional administrator to immediately terminate the contract with a private agency or entity at any time that the contractor fails to demonstrate evidence of financial responsibility.

      (C) All privately operated home detention programs shall comply with all appropriate, applicable ordinances and regulations specified in subdivision (a) of Section 1208.

      (D) The board of supervisors, the correctional administrator, and the designee of the correctional administrator shall comply with Section 1090 of the Government Code in the consideration, making, and execution of contracts pursuant to this section.

(E) The failure of the private agency or entity to comply with statutory provisions and requirements or with the standards established by the contract and with the correctional administrator may be sufficient cause to terminate the contract.

(F) Upon the discovery that a private agency or entity with whom there is a contract is not in compliance pursuant to this paragraph, the correctional administrator shall give 60 days' notice to the director of the private agency or entity that the contract may be canceled if the specified deficiencies are not corrected.

(G) Shorter notice may be given or the contract may be canceled without notice whenever a serious threat to public safety is present because the private agency or entity has failed to comply with this section.

(j) Inmates participating in this program shall not be charged fees or costs for the program.

(k) For purposes of this section, "evidence of financial responsibility" may include, but is not limited to, certified copies of any of the following:

(1) A current liability insurance policy.

(2) A current errors and omissions insurance policy.

(3) A surety bond.

Amended by Stats 2023 ch 218 (SB 852),s 6, eff. 1/1/2024.

Added by Stats 2007 ch 252 (SB 959),s 1, eff. 9/26/2007.

Section 1203.018 - Electronic monitoring program

(a) Notwithstanding any other law, this section shall only apply to inmates being held in lieu of bail and on no other basis.

(b) Notwithstanding any other law, the board of supervisors of any county may authorize the correctional administrator, as defined in paragraph (1) of subdivision (j), to offer a program under which inmates being held in lieu of bail in a county jail or other county correctional facility may participate in an electronic monitoring program if the conditions specified in subdivision (c) are met.

(c)

(1) In order to qualify for participation in an electronic monitoring program pursuant to this section, the inmate shall be an inmate with no holds or outstanding warrants to whom one of the following circumstances applies:

(A) The inmate has been held in custody for at least 30 calendar days from the date of arraignment pending disposition of only misdemeanor charges.

(B) The inmate has been held in custody pending disposition of charges for at least 60 calendar days from the date of arraignment.

(C) The inmate is appropriate for the program based on a determination by the correctional administrator that the inmate's participation would be consistent with the public safety interests of the community.

(2) All participants shall be subject to discretionary review for eligibility and compliance by the correctional administrator consistent with this section.

(d) The board of supervisors, after consulting with the sheriff and district attorney, may prescribe reasonable rules and regulations under which an electronic monitoring program pursuant to this section may operate. As a condition of participation in the electronic monitoring program, the participant shall give consent in writing to participate and shall agree in writing to comply with the rules and regulations of the program, including, but not limited to, all of the following:

(1) The participant shall remain within the interior premises of the participant's residence during the hours designated by the correctional administrator.

(2) The participant shall admit any probation officer or other peace officer designated by the correctional administrator into the participant's residence at any time for purposes of verifying the participant's compliance with the conditions of the detention.

(3) The electronic monitoring may include global positioning system devices or other supervising devices for the purpose of helping to verify the participant's compliance with the rules and regulations of the electronic monitoring program. The electronic devices shall not be used to eavesdrop or record any conversation, except a conversation between the participant and the person supervising the participant to be used solely for the purposes of voice identification.

(4) The correctional administrator in charge of the county correctional facility from which the participant was released may, without further order of the court, immediately retake the person into custody if the electronic monitoring or supervising devices are unable for any reason to properly perform their function at the designated place of home detention, if the person fails to remain within the place of home detention as stipulated in the agreement, or if the person for any other reason no longer meets the established criteria under this section.

(5) A copy of the signed consent to participate and a copy of the agreement to comply with the rules and regulations shall be provided to the participant and a copy shall be retained by the correctional administrator.

(e) The rules and regulations and administrative policy of the program shall be reviewed on an annual basis by the county board of supervisors and the correctional administrator. The rules and regulations shall be given to every participant.

(f) Whenever the peace officer supervising a participant has reasonable cause to believe that the participant is not complying with the rules or conditions of the program, or that the electronic monitoring devices are unable to function properly in the designated place of confinement, the peace officer may, under general or specific authorization of the correctional administrator, and without a warrant of arrest, retake the person into custody.

(g)

(1) Nothing in this section shall be construed to require the correctional administrator to allow a person to participate in this program if it appears from the record that the person has not satisfactorily complied with reasonable rules and regulations while in custody. A person shall be eligible for participation in an electronic monitoring program only if the correctional administrator concludes that the person meets the criteria for release established under this section and that the person's participation is consistent with any reasonable rules and regulations prescribed by the board of supervisors or the administrative policy of the correctional administrator.

(2) The correctional administrator, or the administrator's designee, shall have discretionary authority consistent with this section to permit program participation as an alternative to physical custody. All persons approved by the correctional administrator to participate in the electronic monitoring program pursuant to subdivision (c) who are denied participation and all persons removed from program participation shall be notified in writing of the specific reasons for the denial or removal. The notice of denial or removal shall include the participant's appeal rights, as established by program administrative policy.

(h) The correctional administrator may permit electronic monitoring program participants to seek and retain employment in the community, attend psychological counseling sessions or educational or vocational training classes, or seek medical and dental assistance.

(i) Willful failure of the program participant to return to the place of home detention prior to the expiration of any period of time during which the participant is authorized to be away from the place of home detention pursuant to this section and unauthorized departures from the place of home detention is punishable pursuant to Section 4532.

(j) For purposes of this section, the following terms have the following meanings:

(1) "Correctional administrator" means the sheriff, probation officer, or director of the county department of corrections.

(2) "Electronic monitoring program" includes, but is not limited to, home detention programs, work furlough programs, and work release programs.

(k) Notwithstanding any other law, upon request of a local law enforcement agency with jurisdiction over the location where a participant in an electronic monitoring program is placed, the correctional administrator shall provide the following information regarding participants in the electronic monitoring program:

(1) The participant's name, address, and date of birth.

(2) The offense or offenses alleged to have been committed by the participant.

(3) The period of time the participant will be placed on home detention.

(4) Whether the participant successfully completed the prescribed period of home detention or was returned to a county correctional facility, and if the person was returned to a county correctional facility, the reason for the return.

(5) The gender and ethnicity of the participant.

(l) Notwithstanding any other law, upon request of a local law enforcement agency with jurisdiction over the location where a participant in an electronic monitoring program is placed, the correctional administrator may, in the administrator's discretion and solely for investigatory purposes, provide current and historical GPS coordinates, if available.

(m) A law enforcement agency that does not have the primary responsibility to supervise participants in the electronic monitoring program that receives information pursuant to subdivision (k) shall not use the information to conduct enforcement actions based on administrative violations of the home detention program. An agency that has knowledge that the subject in a criminal investigation is a participant in an electronic monitoring program shall make reasonable efforts to notify the supervising agency prior to serving a warrant or taking any law enforcement action against a participant in an electronic monitoring program.

(n) It is the intent of the Legislature that electronic monitoring programs established under this section maintain the highest public confidence, credibility, and public safety. In the furtherance of these standards, the following shall apply:

(1) The correctional administrator, with the approval of the board of supervisors, may administer an electronic monitoring program as provided in this section pursuant to written contracts with appropriate public or private agencies or entities to provide specified program services. A public or private agency or entity shall not operate a home detention program pursuant to this section in any county without a written contract with that county's correctional administrator. A public or private agency or entity entering into a contract pursuant to this subdivision shall not itself employ any person who is in the electronic monitoring program.

(2) Program participants shall undergo the normal booking process for arrestees entering the jail. All electronic monitoring program participants shall be supervised.

(3)

(A) All privately operated electronic monitoring programs shall be under the jurisdiction of, and subject to the terms and conditions of the contract entered into with, the correctional administrator.

(B) Each contract specified in subparagraph (A) shall include, but not be limited to, all of the following:

(i) A provision whereby the private agency or entity agrees to operate in compliance with any available standards and all state and county laws applicable to the operation of electronic monitoring programs and the supervision of offenders in an electronic monitoring program.

(ii) A provision that clearly defines areas of respective responsibility and liability of the county and the private agency or entity.

(iii) A provision that requires the private agency or entity to demonstrate evidence of financial responsibility, submitted to and approved by the board of supervisors, in amounts and under conditions sufficient to fully indemnify the county for reasonably foreseeable public liability, including legal defense costs that may arise from, or be proximately caused by, acts or omissions of the contractor.

(iv) A provision that requires the private agency or entity to provide evidence of financial responsibility, such as certificates of insurance or copies of insurance policies, prior to commencing any operations pursuant to the contract or at any time requested by the board of supervisors or correctional administrator.

(v) A provision that requires an annual review by the correctional administrator to ensure compliance with requirements set by the board of supervisors and for adjustment of the financial responsibility requirements if warranted by caseload changes or other factors.

(vi) A provision that permits the correctional administrator to immediately terminate the contract with a private agency or entity at any time that the contractor fails to demonstrate evidence of financial responsibility.

(C) All privately operated electronic monitoring programs shall comply with all applicable ordinances and regulations specified in subdivision (a) of Section 1208.

(D) The board of supervisors, the correctional administrator, and the designee of the correctional administrator shall comply with Section 1090 of the Government Code in the consideration, making, and execution of contracts pursuant to this section.

(E) The failure of the private agency or entity to comply with state or county laws or with the standards established by the contract with the correctional administrator shall constitute cause to terminate the contract.

(F) Upon the discovery that a private agency or entity with which there is a contract is not in compliance with this paragraph, the correctional administrator shall give 60 days' notice to the director of the private agency or entity that the contract may be canceled if the specified deficiencies are not corrected.

(G) Shorter notice may be given or the contract may be canceled without notice whenever a serious threat to public safety is present because the private agency or entity has failed to comply with this section.

(H) For purposes of this section, "evidence of financial responsibility" may include, but is not limited to, certified copies of any of the following:

    (i) A current liability insurance policy.

    (ii) A current errors and omissions insurance policy.

    (iii) A surety bond.

(o) This section shall become operative on July 1, 2021.

Amended by Stats 2023 ch 218 (SB 852),s 7, eff. 1/1/2024.

Added by Stats 2020 ch 92 (AB 1869),s 46, eff. 9/18/2020.

Section 1203.02 - Abstention from use of alcoholic liquor or beverages as condition of probation

The court, or judge thereof, in granting probation to a defendant convicted of any of the offenses enumerated in Section 290 of this code shall inquire into the question whether the defendant at the time the offense was committed was intoxicated or addicted to the excessive use of alcoholic liquor or beverages at that time or immediately prior thereto, and if the court, or judge thereof, believes that the defendant was so intoxicated, or so addicted, such court, or judge thereof, shall require as a condition of such probation that the defendant totally abstain from the use of alcoholic liquor or beverages.

Amended by Stats. 1951, Ch. 1608.

Section 1203.03 - Diagnosis and treatment services

(a) In any case in which a defendant is convicted of an offense punishable by imprisonment in the state prison, the court, if it concludes that a just disposition of the case requires such diagnosis and treatment services as can be provided at a diagnostic facility of the Department of Corrections, may order that defendant be placed temporarily in such facility for a period not to exceed 90 days, with the further provision in such order that the Director of the Department of Corrections report to the court his diagnosis and recommendations concerning the defendant within the 90-day period.

(b) The Director of the Department of Corrections shall, within the 90 days, cause defendant to be observed and examined and shall forward to the court his diagnosis and recommendation concerning the disposition of defendant's case. Such diagnosis and recommendation shall be embodied in a written report and copies of the report shall be served only upon the defendant or his counsel, the probation officer, and the prosecuting attorney by the court receiving such report. After delivery of the copies of the report, the information contained therein shall not be disclosed to anyone else without the consent of the defendant. After disposition of the case, all copies of the report, except the one delivered to the defendant or his counsel, shall be filed in a sealed file and shall be available thereafter only to the defendant or his counsel, the prosecuting attorney, the court, the probation officer, or the Department of Corrections.

(c) Notwithstanding subdivision (b), the probation officer may retain a copy of the report for the purpose of supervision of the defendant if the defendant is placed on probation by the court. The report and information contained therein shall be confidential and shall not be disclosed to anyone else without the written consent of the defendant. Upon the completion or termination of probation, the copy of the report shall be returned by the probation officer to the sealed file prescribed in subdivision (b).

(d) The Department of Corrections shall designate the place to which a person referred to it under the provisions of this section shall be transported. After the receipt of any such person, the department may return the person to the referring court if the director of the department, in his discretion, determines that the staff and facilities of the department are inadequate to provide such services.

(e) The sheriff of the county in which an order is made placing a defendant in a diagnostic facility pursuant to this section, or any other peace officer designated by the court, shall execute the order placing such defendant in the center or returning him therefrom to the court. The expense of such sheriff or other peace officer incurred in executing such order is a charge upon the county in which the court is situated.

(f) It is the intention of the Legislature that the diagnostic facilities made available to the counties by this section shall only be used for the purposes designated and not in lieu of sentences to local facilities.

(g) Time spent by a defendant in confinement in a diagnostic facility of the Department of Corrections pursuant to this section or as an inpatient of the California Rehabilitation Center shall be credited on the term of imprisonment in state prison, if any, to which defendant is sentenced in the case.

(h) In any case in which a defendant has been placed in a diagnostic facility pursuant to this section and, in the course of his confinement, he is determined to be suffering from a remediable condition relevant to his criminal conduct, the department may, with the permission of defendant, administer treatment for such condition. If such treatment will require a longer period of confinement than the period for which defendant was placed in the diagnostic facility, the Director of Corrections may file with the court which placed defendant in the facility a petition for extension of the period of confinement, to which shall be attached a writing signed by defendant giving his consent to the extension. If the court finds the petition and consent in order, it may order the extension, and transmit a copy of the order to the Director of Corrections.

Amended by Stats. 1977, Ch. 165.

Section 1203.044 - [Repealed]

Amended by Stats 2001 ch 854 (SB 205) s 43, eff. 1/1/2002.

Section 1203.045 - Probation prohibited for defendant convicted of theft of amount exceeding $100,000

(a) Except in unusual cases where the interests of justice would best be served if the person is granted probation, probation shall not be granted to any person convicted of a crime of theft of an amount exceeding one hundred thousand dollars ($100,000).

(b) The fact that the theft was of an amount exceeding one hundred thousand dollars ($100,000) shall be alleged in the accusatory pleading, and either admitted by the defendant in open court, or found to be true by the jury trying the issue of guilt or by the court where guilt is established by plea of guilty or nolo contendere or by trial by the court sitting without a jury.

(c) When probation is granted, the court shall specify on the record and shall enter on the minutes the circumstances indicating that the interests of justice would best be served by such a disposition.

Added by Stats. 1983, Ch. 327, Sec. 1.

Section 1203.046 - Restrictions on probation for person convicted of violating Section 653j

(a) Except in unusual cases where the interests of justice would best be served if the person is granted probation, probation shall not be granted to any person who is convicted of violating Section 653j by using, soliciting, inducing, encouraging, or intimidating a minor to commit a felony in violation of that section.

(b) When probation is granted pursuant to subdivision (a), the court shall specify on the record and shall enter into the minutes the circumstances indicating that the interests of justice would best be served by that disposition.

Amended by Stats. 1989, Ch. 897, Sec. 37.5.

Section 1203.047 - Probation for person convicted of Section 502 or Section 502.7

A person convicted of a violation of paragraph (1), (2), (4), or (5) of subdivision (c) of Section 502, or of a felony violation of paragraph (3), (6), (7), or (8) of subdivision (c) of Section 502, or a violation of subdivision (b) of Section 502.7 may be granted probation, but, except in unusual cases where the ends of justice would be better served by a shorter period, the period of probation shall not be less than three years and the following terms shall be imposed. During the period of probation, that person shall not accept employment where that person would use a computer connected by any means to any other computer, except upon approval of the court and notice to and opportunity to be heard by the prosecuting attorney, probation department, prospective employer, and the convicted person. Court approval shall not be given unless the court finds that the proposed employment would not pose a risk to the public.

Added by Stats. 1989, Ch. 1357, Sec. 3.

Section 1203.048 - Probation prohibited for certain convictions of Section 502 or Section 502.7(b)

(a) Except in unusual cases where the interests of justice would best be served if the person is granted probation, probation shall not be granted to any person convicted of a violation of Section 502 or subdivision (b) of Section 502.7 involving the taking of or damage to property with a value exceeding one hundred thousand dollars ($100,000).

(b) The fact that the value of the property taken or damaged was an amount exceeding one hundred thousand dollars ($100,000) shall be alleged in the accusatory pleading, and either admitted by the defendant in open court, or found to be true by the jury trying the issue of guilt or by the court where guilt is established by plea of guilt or nolo contendere or by trial by the court sitting without a jury.

(c) When probation is granted, the court shall specify on the record and shall enter on the minutes the circumstances indicating that the interests of justice would best be served by such a disposition.

Added by Stats. 1989, Ch. 1357, Sec. 4.

Section 1203.049 - Probation prohibited for violation of Welfare and Institutions Code Section 10980(f) or (g)

(a) Except in unusual cases where the interest of justice would best be served if the person is granted probation, probation shall not be granted to any person who violates subdivision (f) or (g) of Section 10980 of the Welfare and Institutions Code, when the violation has been committed by means of the electronic transfer of CalFresh benefits, and the amount of the electronically transferred CalFresh benefits exceeds one hundred thousand dollars ($100,000).

(b) The fact that the violation was committed by means of an electronic transfer of CalFresh benefits and the amount of the electronically transferred CalFresh benefits exceeds one hundred thousand dollars ($100,000) shall be alleged in the accusatory pleading, and either admitted by the defendant in open court, or found to be true by the jury trying the issue of guilt or by the court where guilt is established by a plea of guilty or nolo contendere or by trial by the court sitting without a jury.

(c) If probation is granted, the court shall specify on the record and shall enter on the minutes the circumstances indicating that the interests of justice would best be served by that disposition of the case.

Amended by Stats 2011 ch 227 (AB 1400),s 16, eff. 1/1/2012.

Amended October 10, 1999 (Bill Number: AB 1236) (Chapter 706).

Section 1203.05 - Inspection and copying of report of probation officer

Any report of the probation officer filed with the court, including any report arising out of a previous arrest of the person who is the subject of the report, may be inspected or copied only as follows:

(a) By any person, from the date judgment is pronounced or probation granted or, in the case of a report arising out of a previous arrest, from the date the subsequent accusatory pleading is filed, to and including 60 days from the date judgment is pronounced or probation is granted, whichever is earlier.

(b) By any person, at any time, by order of the court, upon filing a petition therefor by the person.

(c) By the general public, if the court upon its own motion orders that a report or reports shall be open or that the contents of the report or reports shall be disclosed.

(d) By any person authorized or required by law to inspect or receive copies of the report.

(e) By the district attorney of the county at any time.

(f) By the subject of the report at any time.

Amended by Stats. 1997, Ch. 128, Sec. 1. Effective January 1, 1998.

Section 1203.055 - Mandatory period of confinement for certain crimes committed person in public transit vehicle

(a)

(1) Notwithstanding any other law, in sentencing a person convicted of committing or of attempting to commit one or more of the offenses listed in subdivision (b) against a person who is a passenger, operator, driver, or other occupant of any public transit vehicle whether the offense or attempt is committed within the vehicle or directed at the vehicle, the court shall require that the person serve some period of confinement. If probation is granted, it shall be a condition of probation that the person shall be confined in the county

jail for some period of time. If the time spent in jail prior to arraignment is less than 24 hours, it shall not be considered to satisfy the requirement that some period of confinement be imposed.

(2)As used in this subdivision, "public transit vehicle" means a motor vehicle, streetcar, trackless trolley, bus, shuttle, light rail system, rapid transit system, subway, train, taxicab, or jitney that transports members of the public for hire.

(b)Subdivision (a) applies to the following crimes:

(1)Murder.

(2)A violation of Section 241, 241.3, 241.4, 244, 245, 245.2, or 246.

(3)Robbery, in violation of Section 211.

(4)Kidnapping, in violation of Section 207.

(5)Kidnapping, in violation of Section 209.

(6)Battery, in violation of Section 243, 243.1, or 243.3.

(7)Rape, in violation of Section 261, 264, or 264.1, or former Section 262.

(8)Assault with intent to commit rape or sodomy, in violation of Section 220.

(9)Any other offense in which the defendant inflicts great bodily injury on a person other than an accomplice. As used in this paragraph, "great bodily injury" has the same meaning as defined in Section 12022.7.

(10)Grand theft, in violation of subdivision (1) of Section 487.

(11)Throwing of a hard substance or shooting a missile at a transit vehicle, in violation of Section 219.2.

(12)Unlawfully causing a fire, in violation of Section 452.

(13)Drawing, exhibiting, or using a firearm or deadly weapon, in violation of Section 417.

(14)A violation of Section 214.

(15)A violation of Section 215.

(16)Kidnapping, in violation of Section 209.5.

(c)Probation shall not be granted to, nor shall the execution or imposition of sentence be suspended for, a person convicted of a felony offense falling within this section if the person has been previously convicted and sentenced pursuant to this section.

(d)

(1)The existence of any fact that would make a person ineligible for probation under subdivisions (a) and (c) shall be alleged in the accusatory pleading, and either admitted by the defendant in open court, or found to be true by the jury trying the issue of guilt or by the court where guilt is established by a plea of guilty or nolo contendere or by a trial by the court sitting without a jury. A finding bringing the defendant within this section shall not be stricken pursuant to Section 1385 or any law.

(2)This subdivision does not prohibit the adjournment of criminal proceedings pursuant to Division 3 (commencing with Section 3000) or Division 6 (commencing with Section 6000) of the Welfare and Institutions Code.

(e)The court shall require, as a condition of probation for a person convicted of committing a crime that took place on a public transit vehicle, except when the court makes a finding and states on the record clear and compelling reasons why the condition would be inappropriate, that the person make restitution to the victim. If restitution is found to be inappropriate, the court shall require as a condition of probation, except when the court makes a finding and states on the record its reasons that the condition would be inappropriate, that the defendant perform specified community service. This subdivision does not limit the authority of a court to provide additional conditions of probation.

(f)When a person is convicted of committing a crime that took place on a public transit vehicle, the probation officer shall immediately investigate and report to the court at a specified time whether, as a result of the crime, property damage or loss or personal injury was caused by the defendant, the amount of the damage, loss, or injury, and the feasibility of requiring restitution to be made by the defendant. When a probation report is required pursuant to Section 1203 the information required by this subdivision shall be added to that probation report.

Amended by Stats 2022 ch 197 (SB 1493),s 20, eff. 1/1/2023.

Amended by Stats 2021 ch 626 (AB 1171),s 45, eff. 1/1/2022.

Amended by Stats. 1994, Ch. 224, Sec. 3. Effective January 1, 1995.

Section 1203.06 - Probation prohibited for persons who used firearm during commission of enumerated crimes

(a) Notwithstanding any other law, probation shall not be granted to, nor shall the execution or imposition of sentence be suspended for, nor shall a finding bringing the defendant within this section be stricken pursuant to Section 1385 for, any of the following persons:

(1) A person who personally used a firearm during the commission or attempted commission of any of the following crimes:

(A) Murder.

(B) Robbery, in violation of Section 211.

(C) Kidnapping, in violation of Section 207, 209, or 209.5.

(D) Lewd or lascivious act, in violation of Section 288.

(E) Burglary of the first degree, as defined in Section 460.

(F) Rape, in violation of Section 261, 264.1, or former Section 262.

(G) Assault with intent to commit a specified sexual offense, in violation of Section 220.

(H) Escape, in violation of Section 4530 or 4532.

(I) Carjacking, in violation of Section 215.

(J) Aggravated mayhem, in violation of Section 205.

(K) Torture, in violation of Section 206.

(L) Continuous sexual abuse of a child, in violation of Section 288.5.

(M) A felony violation of Section 136.1 or 137.

(N) Sodomy, in violation of Section 286.

(O) Oral copulation, in violation of Section 287 or former Section 288a.

(P) Sexual penetration, in violation of Section 289 or 264.1.

(Q) Aggravated sexual assault of a child, in violation of Section 269.

(2) A person previously convicted of a felony specified in paragraph (1), or assault with intent to commit murder under former Section 217, who is convicted of a subsequent felony and who was personally armed with a firearm at any time during its commission or attempted commission or was unlawfully armed with a firearm at the time of arrest for the subsequent felony.

(3) Aggravated arson, in violation of Section 451.5.

(b) The existence of any fact that would make a person ineligible for probation under subdivision (a) shall be alleged in the accusatory pleading, and either admitted by the defendant in open court or found to be true by the trier of fact.

(c) For purposes of this section, the following definitions apply:

(1) "Armed with a firearm" means to knowingly carry or have available for use a firearm as a means of offense or defense.

(2) "Used a firearm" means to display a firearm in a menacing manner, to intentionally fire it, to intentionally strike or hit a human being with it, or to use it in any manner that qualifies under Section 12022.5.

Amended by Stats 2021 ch 626 (AB 1171),s 46, eff. 1/1/2022.

Amended by Stats 2018 ch 423 (SB 1494),s 91, eff. 1/1/2019.

Amended by Stats 2006 ch 337 (SB 1128),s 42, eff. 9/20/2006.

Section 1203.065 - Grant of probation prohibited

(a) Notwithstanding any other law, probation shall not be granted to, nor shall the execution or imposition of sentence be suspended for, a person who is convicted of violating paragraph (2), (3), (4), or (6) of subdivision (a) of Section 261, Section 264.1, 266h, 266i, 266j, or 269, paragraph (2) or (3) of subdivision (c), or subdivision (d), (f), or (i) of Section 286, paragraph (2) or (3) of subdivision (c), or subdivision (d), (f), or (i) of Section 287 or former Section 288a, Section 288.7, subdivision (a), (d), or (e) of Section 289, or subdivision (b) of Section 311.4.

(b)

(1) Except in unusual cases where the interests of justice would best be served if the person is granted probation, probation shall not be granted to a person who is convicted of violating paragraph (7) of subdivision (a) of Section 261, subdivision (k) of Section 286, subdivision (k) of Section 287 or former Section 288a, subdivision (g) of Section 289, or Section 220 for assault with intent to commit a specified sexual offense.

(2) If probation is granted, the court shall specify on the record and shall enter on the minutes the circumstances indicating that the interests of justice would best be served by the disposition.

Amended by Stats 2018 ch 423 (SB 1494),s 92, eff. 1/1/2019.

Amended by Stats 2016 ch 863 (AB 2888),s 1, eff. 1/1/2017.

Amended by Stats 2008 ch 599 (SB 1302),s 2, eff. 1/1/2009.

Amended by Stats 2006 ch 337 (SB 1128),s 43, eff. 9/20/2006.

Section 1203.066 - Grant of probation prohibited for enumerated crimes

(a) Notwithstanding Section 1203 or any other law, probation shall not be granted to, nor shall the execution or imposition of sentence be suspended for, nor shall a finding bringing the defendant within the provisions of this section be stricken pursuant to Section 1385 for, any of the following persons:

(1) A person who is convicted of violating Section 288 or 288.5 when the act is committed by the use of force, violence, duress, menace, or fear of immediate and unlawful bodily injury on the victim or another person.

(2) A person who caused bodily injury on the child victim in committing a violation of Section 288 or 288.5.

(3) A person who is convicted of a violation of Section 288 or 288.5 and who was a stranger to the child victim or befriended the child victim for the purpose of committing an act in violation of Section 288 or 288.5, unless the defendant honestly and reasonably believed the victim was 14 years of age or older.

(4) A person who used a weapon during the commission of a violation of Section 288 or 288.5.

(5) A person who is convicted of committing a violation of Section 288 or 288.5 and who has been previously convicted of a violation of Section 261, 264.1, 266, 266c, 267, 285, 286, 287, 288, 288.5, or 289, or former Section 262 or 288a, or of assaulting another person with intent to commit a crime specified in this paragraph in violation of Section 220, or who has been previously convicted in another state of an offense which, if committed or attempted in this state, would constitute an offense enumerated in this paragraph.

(6) A person who violated Section 288 or 288.5 while kidnapping the child victim in violation of Section 207, 209, or 209.5.

(7) A person who is convicted of committing a violation of Section 288 or 288.5 against more than one victim.

(8) A person who, in violating Section 288 or 288.5, has substantial sexual conduct with a victim who is under 14 years of age.

(9) A person who, in violating Section 288 or 288.5, used obscene matter, as defined in Section 311, or matter, as defined in Section 311, depicting sexual conduct, as defined in Section 311.3.

(b) "Substantial sexual conduct" means penetration of the vagina or rectum of either the victim or the offender by the penis of the other or by any foreign object, oral copulation, or masturbation of either the victim or the offender.

(c)

(1) Except for a violation of subdivision (b) of Section 288, this section shall only apply if the existence of any fact required in subdivision (a) is alleged in the accusatory pleading and is either admitted by the defendant in open court, or found to be true by the trier of fact.

(2) For the existence of any fact under paragraph (7) of subdivision (a), the allegation must be made pursuant to this section.

(d)

(1) If a person is convicted of a violation of Section 288 or 288.5, and the factors listed in subdivision (a) are not pled or proven, probation may be granted only if the following terms and conditions are met:

(A) If the defendant is a member of the victim's household, the court finds that probation is in the best interest of the child victim.

(B) The court finds that rehabilitation of the defendant is feasible and that the defendant is amenable to undergoing treatment, and the defendant is placed in a recognized treatment program designed to deal with child molestation immediately after the grant of probation or the suspension of execution or imposition of sentence.

(C) If the defendant is a member of the victim's household, probation shall not be granted unless the defendant is removed from the household of the victim until the court determines that the best interests of the victim would be served by the defendant's return. While removed from the household, the court shall prohibit contact by the defendant with the victim, with the exception that the court may permit supervised contact, upon the request of the director of the court-ordered supervised treatment program, and with the agreement of the victim and the victim's parent or legal guardian, other than the defendant.

(D) If the defendant is not a member of the victim's household, the court shall prohibit the defendant from being placed or residing within one-half mile of the child victim's residence for the duration of the probation term unless the court, on the record, states its reasons for finding that this residency restriction would not serve the best interests of the victim.

(E) The court finds that there is no threat of physical harm to the victim if probation is granted.

(2) The court shall state its reasons on the record for whatever sentence it imposes on the defendant.

(3) The court shall order the psychiatrist or psychologist who is appointed pursuant to Section 288.1 to include a consideration of the factors specified in subparagraphs (A), (B), and (C) of paragraph (1) in making the report to the court.

(4) The court shall order the defendant to comply with all probation requirements, including the requirements to attend counseling, keep all program appointments, and pay program fees based upon ability to pay.

(5) A victim shall not be compelled to participate in a program or counseling, and a program may not condition a defendant's enrollment on participation by the victim.

(e) As used in subdivision (d), the following definitions apply:

(1) "Contact with the victim" includes all physical contact, being in the presence of the victim, communicating by any means, including by a third party acting on behalf of the defendant, or sending any gifts.

(2) "Recognized treatment program" means a program that consists of the following components:

(A) Substantial expertise in the treatment of child sexual abuse.

(B) A treatment regimen designed to specifically address the offense.

(C) The ability to serve indigent clients.

(D) Adequate reporting requirements to ensure that all persons who, after being ordered to attend and complete a program, may be identified for either failure to enroll in, or failure to successfully complete, the program, or for the successful completion of the program as ordered. The program shall notify the court and the probation department, in writing, within the period of time and in the manner specified by the court of any person who fails to complete the program. Notification shall be given if the program determines that the defendant is performing unsatisfactorily or if the defendant is not benefiting from the education, treatment, or counseling.

Amended by Stats 2021 ch 626 (AB 1171),s 47, eff. 1/1/2022.
Amended by Stats 2018 ch 423 (SB 1494),s 93, eff. 1/1/2019.
Amended by Stats 2011 ch 296 (AB 1023),s 216, eff. 1/1/2012.
Amended by Stats 2010 ch 49 (SB 1253),s 1, eff. 1/1/2011.
Amended by Stats 2006 ch 538 (SB 1852),s 506, eff. 1/1/2007.
Amended by Stats 2005 ch 477 (SB 33),s 5, eff. 1/1/2006

Section 1203.067 - Evaluation before grant of probation

(a) Notwithstanding any other law, before probation may be granted to any person convicted of a felony specified in Section 261, 264.1, 286, 287, 288, 288.5, or 289, or former Section 262 or 288a, who is eligible for probation, the court shall do all of the following:

(1) Order the defendant evaluated pursuant to Section 1203.03, or similar evaluation by the county probation department.

(2) Conduct a hearing at the time of sentencing to determine if probation of the defendant would pose a threat to the victim. The victim shall be notified of the hearing by the prosecuting attorney and given an opportunity to address the court.

(3) Order any psychiatrist or psychologist appointed pursuant to Section 288.1 to include a consideration of the threat to the victim and the defendant's potential for positive response to treatment in making the report to the court. This section does not require the court to order an examination of the victim.

(b) The terms of probation for persons placed on formal probation for an offense that requires registration pursuant to Sections 290 to 290.023, inclusive, shall include all of the following:

(1) A person placed on formal probation prior to July 1, 2012, shall participate in an approved sex offender management program, following the standards developed pursuant to Section 9003, for a period of not less than one year or the remaining term of probation if it is less than one year. The length of the period in the program is to be determined by the certified sex offender management professional in consultation with the probation officer and as approved by the court. Participation in this program applies to every person described without regard to when the person's crime or crimes were committed.

(2) A person placed on formal probation on or after July 1, 2012, shall successfully complete a sex offender management program, following the standards developed pursuant to Section 9003, as a condition of release from probation. The length of the period in the program shall be not less than one year, up to the entire period of probation, as determined by the certified sex offender management professional in consultation with the probation officer and as approved by the court. Participation in this program applies to each person without regard to when the person's crime or crimes were committed.

(3) Waiver of any privilege against self-incrimination and participation in polygraph examinations, which shall be part of the sex offender management program.

(4) Waiver of any psychotherapist-patient privilege to enable communication between the sex offender management professional and supervising probation officer, pursuant to Section 290.09.

(c) A defendant ordered to be placed in an approved sex offender management program pursuant to subdivision (b) shall be responsible for paying the expense of participation in the program as determined by the court. The court shall take into consideration the ability of the defendant to pay, and a defendant shall not be denied probation because of their inability to pay.

Amended by Stats 2021 ch 626 (AB 1171),s 48, eff. 1/1/2022.
Amended by Stats 2018 ch 423 (SB 1494),s 94, eff. 1/1/2019.
Amended by Stats 2014 ch 611 (AB 2411),s 1, eff. 9/26/2014.
Amended by Stats 2011 ch 357 (AB 813),s 4, eff. 1/1/2012.
Amended by Stats 2010 ch 219 (AB 1844),s 17, eff. 9/9/2010.
Amended by Stats 2008 ch 599 (SB 1302),s 3, eff. 1/1/2009.

Section 1203.07 - Probation prohibited for enumerated crimes involving controlled substances

(a) Notwithstanding Section 1203 and except as provided in subdivision (c), probation shall not be granted to, nor shall the execution or imposition of sentence be suspended for, either of the following:

(1) A person who is convicted of violating Section 11380 of the Health and Safety Code by using, soliciting, inducing, encouraging, or intimidating a minor to act as an agent to manufacture, compound, or sell a controlled substance specified in subdivision (d) of Section 11054 of the Health and Safety Code, except paragraphs (13), (14), (15), (20), (21), (22), and (23) of subdivision (d), or specified in subdivision (d), (e), or (f) of Section 11055 of the Health and Safety Code, except paragraph (3) of subdivision (e) and subparagraphs (A) and (B) of paragraph (2) of subdivision (f) of Section 11055 of the Health and Safety Code.

(2) A person who is convicted of violating Section 11380 of the Health and Safety Code by using a minor as an agent or who solicits, induces, encourages, or intimidates a minor with the intent that the minor shall violate the provisions of Section 11378.5, 11379.5, or 11379.6 of the Health and Safety Code insofar as the violation relates to phencyclidine or any of its analogs or precursors.

(b) The existence of a fact that would make a person ineligible for probation under subdivision (a) shall be alleged in the information or indictment, and either admitted by the defendant in open court, or found to be true by the jury trying the issue of guilt or by the court where guilt is established by plea of guilty or nolo contendere or by trial by the court sitting without a jury.

(c) A person who is made ineligible for probation pursuant to this section may be granted probation only in an unusual case where the interests of justice would best be served. When probation is granted pursuant to this subdivision, the court shall specify on the record and shall enter into the minutes the circumstances supporting the finding.

Added by Stats 2021 ch 537 (SB 73),s 3, eff. 1/1/2022.
Repealed by Stats 2021 ch 537 (SB 73),s 2, eff. 1/1/2022.
Amended by Stats. 1989, Ch. 1135, Sec. 2.

Section 1203.073 - [Repealed]

Repealed by Stats 2021 ch 537 (SB 73),s 4, eff. 1/1/2022.
Amended by Stats 2014 ch 749 (SB 1010),s 5, eff. 1/1/2015.
EFFECTIVE 1/1/2000. Amended October 10, 1999 (Bill Number: SB 832) (Chapter 853).

Section 1203.074 - Probation prohibited for person convicted of violating Health and Safety Code Section 11366.6

(a) A person convicted of a felony specified in subdivision (b) may be granted probation only in an unusual case where the interests of justice would best be served; when probation is granted in such a case, the court shall specify on the record and shall enter in the minutes the circumstances indicating that the interests of justice would best be served by such a disposition.

(b) Except as provided in subdivision (a), probation shall not be granted to, nor shall the execution or imposition of sentence be suspended for, any person who is convicted of violating Section 11366.6 of the Health and Safety Code.

Added by Stats. 1985, Ch. 1533, Sec. 3.

Section 1203.075 - Probation prohibited for person who inflicts great bodily injury in commission of enumerated crimes

(a) Notwithstanding any other law, probation shall not be granted to, nor shall the execution or imposition of sentence be suspended for, nor shall a finding bringing the defendant within this section be stricken pursuant to Section 1385 for, any person who personally inflicts great bodily injury, as defined in Section 12022.7, on the person of another in the commission or attempted commission of any of the following crimes:

(1) Murder.
(2) Robbery, in violation of Section 211.
(3) Kidnapping, in violation of Section 207, 209, or 209.5.
(4) Lewd or lascivious act, in violation of Section 288.
(5) Burglary of the first degree, as defined in Section 460.
(6) Rape, in violation of Section 261, 264.1, or former Section 262.
(7) Assault with intent to commit a specified sexual offense, in violation of Section 220.
(8) Escape, in violation of Section 4530 or 4532.
(9) Sexual penetration, in violation of Section 289 or 264.1.
(10) Sodomy, in violation of Section 286.
(11) Oral copulation, in violation of Section 287 or former Section 288a.
(12) Carjacking, in violation of Section 215.
(13) Continuous sexual abuse of a child, in violation of Section 288.5.
(14) Aggravated sexual assault of a child, in violation of Section 269.

(b) The existence of any fact that would make a person ineligible for probation under subdivision (a) shall be alleged in the accusatory pleading, and either admitted by the defendant in open court, or found to be true by the trier of fact.

Amended by Stats 2021 ch 626 (AB 1171),s 49, eff. 1/1/2022.
Amended by Stats 2018 ch 423 (SB 1494),s 95, eff. 1/1/2019.
Amended by Stats 2006 ch 337 (SB 1128),s 44, eff. 9/20/2006.

Section 1203.076 - Imposition of minimum 180-day sentence for person convicted of Health and Safety Code Section 11352 of Section 11379.5

A person convicted of violating Section 11352 of the Health and Safety Code relating to the sale of cocaine, cocaine hydrochloride, or heroin, or Section 11379.5 of the Health and Safety Code, who is eligible for probation and who is granted probation may, as a condition thereof, be confined in the county jail for at least 180 days. The imposition of the minimum 180-day sentence may be imposed in every case in which probation has been granted.
Amended by Stats 2019 ch 574 (AB 484),s 1, eff. 1/1/2020.

Section 1203.08 - Probation prohibited for person convicted designated felony who has previously been convicted of designated felony

(a) Notwithstanding any other law, probation shall not be granted to, nor shall the execution or imposition of sentence be suspended for, an adult person convicted of a designated felony who has been previously convicted as an adult under charges separately brought and tried two or more times of any designated felony or in any other place of a public offense which, if committed in this state, would have been punishable as a designated felony, if all the convictions occurred within a 10-year period. The 10-year period shall be calculated exclusive of any period of time during which the person has been confined in a state or federal prison.
(b)

(1) The existence of any fact that would make a person ineligible for probation under subdivision (a) shall be alleged in the information or indictment, and either admitted by the defendant in open court, or found to be true by the jury trying the issue of guilt or by the court where guilt is established by plea of guilty or nolo contendere or by trial by the court sitting without a jury.

(2) Except where the existence of the fact was not admitted or found to be true pursuant to paragraph (1), or the court finds that a prior conviction was invalid, the court shall not strike or dismiss any prior convictions alleged in the information or indictment.

(3) This subdivision does not prohibit the adjournment of criminal proceedings pursuant to Division 3 (commencing with Section 3000) or Division 6 (commencing with Section 6000) of the Welfare and Institutions Code.

(c) As used in this section, "designated felony" means any felony specified in Section 187, 192, 207, 209, 209.5, 211, 215, 217, 245, 288, or paragraph (2), (6), or (7) of subdivision (a) of Section 261, paragraph (1), (4), or (5) of subdivision (a) of former Section 262, subdivision (a) of Section 460, or when great bodily injury occurs in perpetration of an assault to commit robbery, mayhem, or rape, as defined in Section 220.
Amended by Stats 2021 ch 626 (AB 1171),s 50, eff. 1/1/2022.
Amended by Stats. 1994, Ch. 1188, Sec. 15. Effective January 1, 1995.

Section 1203.085 - Probation prohibited for person convicted of offense punishable by imprisonment in state prison but without alternate sentence to county jail; probation prohibited for violent felony

(a) Any person convicted of an offense punishable by imprisonment in the state prison but without an alternate sentence to a county jail shall not be granted probation or have the execution or imposition of sentence suspended, if the offense was committed while the person was on parole from state prison pursuant to Section 3000, following a term of imprisonment imposed for a violent felony, as defined in subdivision (c) of Section 667.5, or a serious felony, as defined in subdivision (c) of Section 1192.7.
(b) Any person convicted of a violent felony, as defined in subdivision (c) of Section 667.5, or a serious felony, as defined in subdivision (c) of Section 1192.7, shall not be granted probation or have the execution or imposition of sentence suspended, if the offense was committed while the person was on parole from state prison pursuant to Section 3000.
(c) The existence of any fact that would make a person ineligible for probation under subdivision (a) or (b) shall be alleged in the information or indictment, and either admitted by the defendant in open court, or found to be true by the jury trying the issue of guilt or by the court where guilt is established by plea of guilty or nolo contendere or by trial by the court sitting without a jury.
Amended by Stats. 1997, Ch. 160, Sec. 1. Effective January 1, 1998.

Section 1203.09 - Probation prohibited for designated crimes against older or disabled person

(a) Notwithstanding any other law, probation shall not be granted to, nor shall the execution or imposition of sentence be suspended for, a person who commits or attempts to commit one or more of the crimes listed in subdivision (b) against a person who is 60 years of age or older; or against a person who is blind, a paraplegic, a quadriplegic, or a person confined to a wheelchair and that disability is known or reasonably should be known to the person committing the crime; and who during the course of the offense inflicts great bodily injury upon the person.
(b) Subdivision (a) applies to the following crimes:

(1) Murder.

(2) Robbery, in violation of Section 211.

(3) Kidnapping, in violation of Section 207.

(4) Kidnapping, in violation of Section 209.

(5) Burglary of the first degree, as defined in Section 460.

(6) Rape by force or violence, in violation of paragraph (2) or (6) of subdivision (a) of Section 261 or paragraph (1) or (4) of subdivision (a) of former Section 262.

(7) Assault with intent to commit rape or sodomy, in violation of Section 220.

(8) Carjacking, in violation of Section 215.

(9) Kidnapping, in violation of Section 209.5.

(c) The existence of any fact that would make a person ineligible for probation under either subdivision (a) or (f) shall be alleged in the information or indictment, and either admitted by the defendant in open court, or found to be true by the jury trying the issue of guilt or by the court where guilt is established by plea of guilty or nolo contendere or by trial by the court sitting without a jury.
(d) As used in this section, "great bodily injury" has the same meaning as defined in Section 12022.7.
(e) This section shall apply in all cases, including those cases where the infliction of great bodily injury is an element of the offense.
(f) Except in unusual cases where the interests of justice would best be served if the person is granted probation, probation shall not be granted to, nor shall the execution or imposition of sentence be suspended for, a person convicted of having committed one or more of

the following crimes against a person who is 60 years of age or older: assault with a deadly weapon or instrument, battery that results in physical injury that requires professional medical treatment, carjacking, robbery, or mayhem.

Amended by Stats 2021 ch 626 (AB 1171),s 51, eff. 1/1/2022.

Amended by Stats. 1994, Ch. 1188, Sec. 16. Effective January 1, 1995.

Section 1203.095 - Prohibited probation for persons convicted of certain violations of Sections 245, 246, or 417

(a) Except as provided in subdivision (b), but notwithstanding any other provision of law, if any person convicted of a violation of paragraph (2) of subdivision (a) of Section 245, of a violation of paragraph (1) of subdivision (d) of Section 245, of a violation of Section 246, or a violation of subdivision (c) of Section 417, is granted probation or the execution or imposition of sentence is suspended, it shall be a condition thereof that he or she be imprisoned for at least six months, and if any person convicted of a violation of paragraph (2) of subdivision (a) of Section 417 is granted probation or the execution or imposition of sentence is suspended, it shall be a condition thereof that he or she be imprisoned for at least three months.

(b) The provisions of subdivision (a) shall apply except in unusual cases where the interests of justice would best be served by granting probation or suspending the imposition or execution of sentence without the imprisonment required by subdivision (a), or by granting probation or suspending the imposition or execution of sentence with conditions other than those set forth in subdivision (a), in which case the court shall specify on the record and shall enter on the minutes the circumstances indicating that the interests of justice would best be served by such a disposition.

(c) This section does not prohibit the adjournment of criminal proceedings pursuant to Division 3 (commencing with Section 3000) or Division 6 (commencing with Section 6000) of the Welfare and Institutions Code.

Amended by Stats. 1995, Ch. 377, Sec. 4. Effective January 1, 1996.

Section 1203.096 - Counseling or education program having substance abuse component

(a) Upon conviction of any felony in which the defendant is sentenced to state prison and in which the court makes the findings set forth in subdivision (b), a court shall, in addition to any other terms of imprisonment, fine, and conditions, recommend in writing that the defendant participate in a counseling or education program having a substance abuse component while imprisoned.

(b) The court shall make the recommendation specified in subdivision (a) if it finds that any of the following are true:

(1) That the defendant at the time of the commission of the offense was under the influence of any alcoholic beverages.

(2) That the defendant at the time of the commission of the offense was under the influence of any controlled substance.

(3) That the defendant has a demonstrated history of substance abuse.

(4) That the offense or offenses for which the defendant was convicted are drug related.

Added by Stats. 1991, Ch. 552, Sec. 1.

Section 1203.097 - Additional terms of probation for crime involving domestic violence

(a)If a person is granted probation for a crime in which the victim is a person defined in Section 6211 of the Family Code, the terms of probation shall include all of the following:

(1)A minimum period of probation of 36 months, which may include a period of summary probation as appropriate.

(2)A criminal court protective order protecting the victim from further acts of violence, threats, stalking, sexual abuse, and harassment, and, if appropriate, containing residence exclusion or stay-away conditions.

(3)Notice to the victim of the disposition of the case.

(4)Booking the defendant within one week of sentencing if the defendant has not already been booked.

(5)

(A)A minimum payment by the defendant of a fee of five hundred dollars ($500) to be disbursed as specified in this paragraph. If, after a hearing in open court, the court finds that the defendant does not have the ability to pay, the court may reduce or waive this fee. If the court exercises its discretion to reduce or waive the fee, it shall state the reason on the record.

(B)Two-thirds of the moneys deposited with the county treasurer pursuant to this section shall be retained by counties and deposited in the domestic violence programs special fund created pursuant to Section 18305 of the Welfare and Institutions Code, to be expended for the purposes of Chapter 5 (commencing with Section 18290) of Part 6 of Division 9 of the Welfare and Institutions Code. Of the moneys deposited in the domestic violence programs special fund, no more than 8 percent may be used for administrative costs, as specified in Section 18305 of the Welfare and Institutions Code.

(C)The remaining one-third of the moneys shall be transferred, once a month, to the Controller for deposit in equal amounts in the Domestic Violence Restraining Order Reimbursement Fund and in the Domestic Violence Training and Education Fund, which are hereby created, in an amount equal to one-third of funds collected during the preceding month. Moneys deposited into these funds pursuant to this section shall be available upon appropriation by the Legislature and shall be distributed each fiscal year as follows:

(i)Funds from the Domestic Violence Restraining Order Reimbursement Fund shall be distributed to local law enforcement or other criminal justice agencies for state-mandated local costs resulting from the notification requirements set forth in subdivision (b) of Section 6380 of the Family Code, based on the annual notification from the Department of Justice of the number of restraining orders issued and registered in the state domestic violence restraining order registry maintained by the Department of Justice, for the development and maintenance of the domestic violence restraining order databank system.

(ii)Funds from the Domestic Violence Training and Education Fund shall support a statewide training and education program to increase public awareness of domestic violence and to improve the scope and quality of services provided to the victims of domestic violence. Grants to support this program shall be awarded on a competitive basis and be administered by the State Department of Public Health, in consultation with the statewide domestic violence coalition, which is eligible to receive funding under this section.

(D)The fee imposed by this paragraph shall be treated as a fee, not as a fine, and shall not be subject to reduction for time served as provided pursuant to Section 1205 or 2900.5.

(E)The fee imposed by this paragraph may be collected by the collecting agency, or the agency's designee, after the termination of the period of probation, whether probation is terminated by revocation or by completion of the term.

(6) Successful completion of a batterer's program, as defined in subdivision (c), or if none is available, another appropriate counseling program designated by the court, for a period not less than one year with periodic progress reports by the program to the court every three months or less and weekly sessions of a minimum of two hours class time duration. The defendant shall attend consecutive weekly sessions, unless granted an excused absence for good cause by the program for no more than three individual sessions during the entire program, and shall complete the program within 18 months, unless, after a hearing, the court finds good cause to modify the requirements of consecutive attendance or completion within 18 months.

(7)

(A)

(i) The court shall order the defendant to comply with all probation requirements, including the requirements to attend counseling, keep all program appointments, and pay program fees based upon the ability to pay.

(ii) The terms of probation for offenders shall not be lifted until all reasonable fees due to the counseling program have been paid in full, but in no case shall probation be extended beyond the term provided in subdivision (a) of Section 1203.1. If the court finds that the defendant does not have the ability to pay the fees based on the defendant's changed circumstances, the court may reduce or waive the fees.

(B) Upon request by the batterer's program, the court shall provide the defendant's arrest report, prior incidents of violence, and treatment history to the program.

(8) The court also shall order the defendant to perform a specified amount of appropriate community service, as designated by the court. The defendant shall present the court with proof of completion of community service and the court shall determine if the community service has been satisfactorily completed. If sufficient staff and resources are available, the community service shall be performed under the jurisdiction of the local agency overseeing a community service program.

(9) If the program finds that the defendant is unsuitable, the program shall immediately contact the probation department or the court. The probation department or court shall either recalendar the case for hearing or refer the defendant to an appropriate alternative batterer's program.

(10)

(A) Upon recommendation of the program, a court shall require a defendant to participate in additional sessions throughout the probationary period, unless it finds that it is not in the interests of justice to do so, states its reasons on the record, and enters them into the minutes. In deciding whether the defendant would benefit from more sessions, the court shall consider whether any of the following conditions exists:

(i) The defendant has been violence free for a minimum of six months.

(ii) The defendant has cooperated and participated in the batterer's program.

(iii) The defendant demonstrates an understanding of and practices positive conflict resolution skills.

(iv) The defendant blames, degrades, or has committed acts that dehumanize the victim or puts at risk the victim's safety, including, but not limited to, molesting, stalking, striking, attacking, threatening, sexually assaulting, or battering the victim.

(v) The defendant demonstrates an understanding that the use of coercion or violent behavior to maintain dominance is unacceptable in an intimate relationship.

(vi) The defendant has made threats to harm anyone in any manner.

(vii) The defendant has complied with applicable requirements under paragraph (6) of subdivision (c) or subparagraph (C) to receive alcohol counseling, drug counseling, or both.

(viii) The defendant demonstrates acceptance of responsibility for the abusive behavior perpetrated against the victim.

(B) The program shall immediately report any violation of the terms of the protective order, including any new acts of violence or failure to comply with the program requirements, to the court, the prosecutor, and, if formal probation has been ordered, to the probation department. The probationer shall file proof of enrollment in a batterer's program with the court within 30 days of conviction.

(C) Concurrent with other requirements under this section, in addition to, and not in lieu of, the batterer's program, and unless prohibited by the referring court, the probation department or the court may make provisions for a defendant to use their resources to enroll in a chemical dependency program or to enter voluntarily a licensed chemical dependency recovery hospital or residential treatment program that has a valid license issued by the state to provide alcohol or drug services to receive program participation credit, as determined by the court. The probation department shall document evidence of this hospital or residential treatment participation in the defendant's program file.

(11) The conditions of probation may include, in lieu of a fine, but not in lieu of the fund payment required under paragraph (5), one or more of the following requirements:

(A) That the defendant make payments to a domestic violence shelter-based program, up to a maximum of five thousand dollars ($5,000).

(B) That the defendant reimburse the victim for reasonable expenses that the court finds are the direct result of the defendant's offense. For any order to pay a fine, to make payments to a domestic violence shelter-based program, or to pay restitution as a condition of probation under this subdivision, the court shall make a determination of the defendant's ability to pay. Determination of a defendant's ability to pay may include their future earning capacity. A defendant shall bear the burden of demonstrating lack of their ability to pay. Express findings by the court as to the factors bearing on the amount of the fine shall not be required. In no event shall any order to make payments to a domestic violence shelter-based program be made if it would impair the ability of the defendant to pay direct restitution to the victim or court-ordered child support. When the injury to a married person is caused, in whole or in part, by the criminal acts of their spouse in violation of this section, the community property shall not be used to discharge the liability of the offending spouse for restitution to the injured spouse, as required by Section 1203.04, as operative on or before August 2, 1995, or Section 1202.4, or to a shelter for costs with regard to the injured spouse, until all separate property of the offending spouse is exhausted.

(12) If it appears to the prosecuting attorney, the court, or the probation department that the defendant is performing unsatisfactorily in the assigned program, is not benefiting from counseling, or has engaged in criminal conduct, upon request of the probation officer, the prosecuting attorney, or on its own motion, the court, as a priority calendar item, shall hold a hearing to determine whether further sentencing should proceed. The court may consider factors, including, but not limited to, any violence by the defendant against the former or a new victim while on probation and noncompliance with any other specific condition of probation. If the court finds that the defendant is not performing satisfactorily in the assigned program, is not benefiting from the program, has not complied with a condition of probation, or has engaged in criminal conduct, the court shall terminate the defendant's participation in the program and shall proceed with further sentencing.

(b)If a person is granted formal probation for a crime in which the victim is a person defined in Section 6211 of the Family Code, in addition to the terms specified in subdivision (a), all of the following shall apply:

(1)The probation department shall make an investigation and take into consideration the defendant's age, medical history, employment and service records, educational background, community and family ties, prior incidents of violence, police report, treatment history, if any, demonstrable motivation, and other mitigating factors in determining which batterer's program would be appropriate for the defendant. This information shall be provided to the batterer's program if it is requested. The probation department shall also determine which community programs the defendant would benefit from and which of those programs would accept the defendant. The probation department shall report its findings and recommendations to the court.

(2)The court shall advise the defendant that the failure to report to the probation department for the initial investigation, as directed by the court, or the failure to enroll in a specified program, as directed by the court or the probation department, shall result in possible further incarceration. The court, in the interests of justice, may relieve the defendant from the prohibition set forth in this subdivision based upon the defendant's mistake or excusable neglect. Application for this relief shall be filed within 20 court days of the missed deadline. This time limitation may not be extended. A copy of any application for relief shall be served on the office of the prosecuting attorney.

(3)After the court orders the defendant to a batterer's program, the probation department shall conduct an initial assessment of the defendant, including, but not limited to, all of the following:

(A)Social, economic, and family background.

(B)Education.

(C)Vocational achievements.

(D)Criminal history.

(E)Medical history.

(F)Substance abuse history.

(G)Consultation with the probation officer.

(H)Verbal consultation with the victim, only if the victim desires to participate.

(I)Assessment of the future probability of the defendant committing murder.

(4)The probation department shall attempt to notify the victim regarding the requirements for the defendant's participation in the batterer's program, as well as regarding available victim resources. The victim also shall be informed that attendance in any program does not guarantee that an abuser will not be violent.

(c)The court or the probation department shall refer defendants only to batterer's programs that follow standards outlined in paragraph (1), which may include, but are not limited to, lectures, classes, group discussions, and counseling. The probation department shall design and implement an approval and renewal process for batterer's programs and shall solicit input from criminal justice agencies and domestic violence victim advocacy programs.

(1)The goal of a batterer's program under this section shall be to stop domestic violence. A batterer's program shall consist of the following components:

(A)Strategies to hold the defendant accountable for the violence in a relationship, including, but not limited to, providing the defendant with a written statement that the defendant shall be held accountable for acts or threats of domestic violence.

(B)A requirement that the defendant participate in ongoing same-gender group sessions.

(C)An initial intake that provides written definitions to the defendant of physical, emotional, sexual, economic, and verbal abuse, and the techniques for stopping these types of abuse.

(D)Procedures to inform the victim regarding the requirements for the defendant's participation in the intervention program as well as regarding available victim resources. The victim also shall be informed that attendance in any program does not guarantee that an abuser will not be violent.

(E)A requirement that the defendant attend group sessions free of chemical influence.

(F)Educational programming that examines, at a minimum, gender roles, socialization, the nature of violence, the dynamics of power and control, and the effects of abuse on children and others.

(G)A requirement that excludes any couple counseling or family counseling, or both.

(H)Procedures that give the program the right to assess whether or not the defendant would benefit from the program and to refuse to enroll the defendant if it is determined that the defendant would not benefit from the program, so long as the refusal is not because of the defendant's inability to pay. If possible, the program shall suggest an appropriate alternative program.

(I)Program staff who, to the extent possible, have specific knowledge regarding, but not limited to, spousal abuse, child abuse, sexual abuse, substance abuse, the dynamics of violence and abuse, the law, and procedures of the legal system.

(J)Program staff who are encouraged to utilize the expertise, training, and assistance of local domestic violence centers.

(K)A requirement that the defendant enter into a written agreement with the program, which shall include an outline of the contents of the program, the attendance requirements, the requirement to attend group sessions free of chemical influence, and a statement that the defendant may be removed from the program if it is determined that the defendant is not benefiting from the program or is disruptive to the program.

(L)A requirement that the defendant sign a confidentiality statement prohibiting disclosure of any information obtained through participating in the program or during group sessions regarding other participants in the program.

(M)Program content that provides cultural and ethnic sensitivity.

(N)A requirement of a written referral from the court or probation department prior to permitting the defendant to enroll in the program. The written referral shall state the number of minimum sessions required by the court.

(O)Procedures for submitting to the probation department all of the following uniform written responses:

(i)Proof of enrollment, to be submitted to the court and the probation department and to include the fee determined to be charged to the defendant, based upon the ability to pay, for each session.

(ii)Periodic progress reports that include attendance, fee payment history, and program compliance.

(iii)Final evaluation that includes the program's evaluation of the defendant's progress, using the criteria set forth in subparagraph (A) of paragraph (10) of subdivision (a), and recommendation for either successful or unsuccessful termination or continuation in the program.

(P)A sliding fee schedule based on the defendant's ability to pay. The batterer's program shall develop and utilize a sliding fee scale that recognizes both the defendant's ability to pay and the necessity of programs to meet overhead expenses. An indigent defendant may negotiate a deferred payment schedule, but shall pay a nominal fee, if the defendant has the ability to pay the nominal fee. Upon a hearing and a finding by the court that the defendant does not have the financial ability to pay the nominal fee, the court shall waive this fee. The payment of the fee shall be made a condition of probation if the court determines the defendant has the present ability to pay the fee. The fee shall be paid during the term of probation unless the program sets other conditions. The acceptance policies shall be in accordance with the scaled fee system.

(2)The court shall refer persons only to batterer's programs that have been approved by the probation department pursuant to paragraph (5). The probation department shall do both of the following:

(A)Provide for the issuance of a provisional approval, provided that the applicant is in substantial compliance with applicable laws and regulations and an urgent need for approval exists. A provisional approval shall be considered an authorization to provide services and shall not be considered a vested right.

(B)If the probation department determines that a program is not in compliance with standards set by the department, the department shall provide written notice of the noncompliant areas to the program. The program shall submit a written plan of corrections within 14 days from the date of the written notice on noncompliance. A plan of correction shall include, but not be limited to, a description of each corrective action and timeframe for implementation. The department shall review and approve all or any part of the plan of correction and notify the program of approval or disapproval in writing. If the program fails to submit a plan of correction or fails to implement the approved plan of correction, the department shall consider whether to revoke or suspend approval and, upon revoking or suspending approval, shall have the option to cease referrals of defendants under this section.

(3)No program, regardless of its source of funding, shall be approved unless it meets all of the following standards:

(A)The establishment of guidelines and criteria for education services, including standards of services that may include lectures, classes, and group discussions.

(B)Supervision of the defendant for the purpose of evaluating the person's progress in the program.

(C)Adequate reporting requirements to ensure that all persons who, after being ordered to attend and complete a program, may be identified for either failure to enroll in, or failure to successfully complete, the program or for the successful completion of the program as ordered. The program shall notify the court and the probation department, in writing, within the period of time and in the manner specified by the court of any person who fails to complete the program. Notification shall be given if the program determines that the defendant is performing unsatisfactorily or if the defendant is not benefiting from the education, treatment, or counseling.

(D)No victim shall be compelled to participate in a program or counseling, and no program may condition a defendant's enrollment on participation by the victim.

(4)In making referrals of indigent defendants to approved batterer's programs, the probation department shall apportion these referrals evenly among the approved programs.

(5)The probation department shall have the sole authority to approve a batterer's program for probation. The program shall be required to obtain only one approval but shall renew that approval annually.

(A)The procedure for the approval of a new or existing program shall include all of the following:

(i)The completion of a written application containing necessary and pertinent information describing the applicant program.

(ii)The demonstration by the program that it possesses adequate administrative and operational capability to operate a batterer's treatment program. The program shall provide documentation to prove that the program has conducted batterer's programs for at least one year prior to application. This requirement may be waived under subparagraph (A) of paragraph (2) if there is no existing batterer's program in the city, county, or city and county.

(iii)The onsite review of the program, including monitoring of a session to determine that the program adheres to applicable statutes and regulations.

(iv)The payment of the approval fee.

(B)The probation department shall fix a fee for approval not to exceed two hundred fifty dollars ($250) and for approval renewal not to exceed two hundred fifty dollars ($250) every year in an amount sufficient to cover its costs in administering the approval process under this section. No fee shall be charged for the approval of local governmental entities.

(C)The probation department has the sole authority to approve the issuance, denial, suspension, or revocation of approval and to cease new enrollments or referrals to a batterer's program under this section. The probation department shall review information relative to a program's performance or failure to adhere to standards, or both. The probation department may suspend or revoke an approval issued under this subdivision or deny an application to renew an approval or to modify the terms and conditions of approval, based on grounds established by probation, including, but not limited to, either of the following:

(i)Violation of this section by any person holding approval or by a program employee in a program under this section.

(ii)Misrepresentation of any material fact in obtaining the approval.

(6)For defendants who are chronic users or serious abusers of drugs or alcohol, standard components in the program shall include concurrent counseling for substance abuse and violent behavior, and in appropriate cases, detoxification and abstinence from the abused substance.

(7) The program shall conduct an exit conference that assesses the defendant's progress during the defendant's participation in the batterer's program.

(d) An act or omission relating to the approval of a batterer's treatment programs under paragraph (5) of subdivision (c) is a discretionary act pursuant to Section 820.2 of the Government Code.

Amended by Stats 2022 ch 197 (SB 1493),s 21, eff. 1/1/2023.
Amended by Stats 2013 ch 144 (AB 139),s 2, eff. 1/1/2014.
Amended by Stats 2013 ch 76 (AB 383),s 153, eff. 1/1/2014.
Amended by Stats 2013 ch 59 (SB 514),s 3, eff. 1/1/2014.
Amended by Stats 2012 ch 628 (AB 1165),s 1.5, eff. 1/1/2013.
Amended by Stats 2012 ch 511 (AB 2094),s 1, eff. 1/1/2013.
Amended by Stats 2010 ch 132 (AB 2011),s 1, eff. 8/13/2010.
Amended by Stats 2007 ch 483 (SB 1039),s 42, eff. 1/1/2008.
Amended by Stats 2006 ch 476 (AB 2695),s 5, eff. 1/1/2007.
Amended by Stats 2003 ch 431 (AB 352), s 1, eff. 1/1/2004.
Repealed by Stats 2003 ch 431 (AB 352), s 1, eff. 1/1/2007.
Amended by Stats 2002 ch 2 (AB 217), s 1, eff. 1/23/2002.
Amended by Stats 2002 ch 265 (SB 1627), s 3, eff. 1/1/2003.
Amended by Stats 2001 ch 854 (SB 205) s 44, eff. 1/1/2002.
Previously Amended July 12, 1999 (Bill Number: SB 966) (Chapter 83).

Section 1203.098 - Facilitator in batterers' intervention program

(a) Unless otherwise provided, a person who works as a facilitator in a batterers' intervention program that provides programs for batterers pursuant to subdivision (c) of Section 1203.097 shall complete the following requirements before being eligible to work as a facilitator in a batterers' intervention program:

(1) Forty hours of basic core training. A minimum of eight hours of this instruction shall be provided by a shelter-based or shelter-approved trainer. The core curriculum shall include the following components:

(A) A minimum of eight hours in basic domestic violence knowledge focusing on victim safety and the role of domestic violence shelters in a community-coordinated response.

(B) A minimum of eight hours in multicultural, cross-cultural, and multiethnic diversity and domestic violence.

(C) A minimum of four hours in substance abuse and domestic violence.

(D) A minimum of four hours in intake and assessment, including the history of violence and the nature of threats and substance abuse.

(E) A minimum of eight hours in group content areas focusing on gender roles and socialization, the nature of violence, the dynamics of power and control, and the effects of abuse on children and others as required by Section 1203.097.

(F) A minimum of four hours in group facilitation.

(G) A minimum of four hours in domestic violence and the law, ethics, all requirements specified by the probation department pursuant to Section 1203.097, and the role of batterers' intervention programs in a coordinated-community response.

(H) Any person that provides documentation of coursework, or equivalent training, that he or she has satisfactorily completed, shall be exempt from that part of the training that was covered by the satisfactorily completed coursework.

(I) The coursework that this person performs shall count toward the continuing education requirement.

(2) Fifty-two weeks or no less than 104 hours in six months, as a trainee in an approved batterers' intervention program with a minimum of a two-hour group each week. A training program shall include at least one of the following:

(A) Cofacilitation internship in which an experienced facilitator is present in the room during the group session.

(B) Observation by a trainer of the trainee conducting a group session via a one-way mirror.

(C) Observation by a trainer of the trainee conducting a group session via a video or audio recording.

(D) Consultation or supervision twice a week in a six-month program or once a week in a 52-week program.

(3) An experienced facilitator is one who has the following qualifications:

(A) Documentation on file, approved by the agency, evidencing that the experienced facilitator has the skills needed to provide quality supervision and training.

(B) Documented experience working with batterers for three years, and a minimum of two years working with batterers' groups.

(C) Documentation by January 1, 2003, of coursework or equivalent training that demonstrates satisfactory completion of the 40-hour basic core training.

(b) A facilitator of a batterers' intervention program shall complete, as a minimum continuing education requirement, 16 hours annually of continuing education in either domestic violence or a related field with a minimum of eight hours in domestic violence.

(c) A person or agency with a specific hardship may request the probation department, in writing, for an extension of time to complete the training or to complete alternative training options.

(d)

(1) An experienced facilitator, as defined in paragraph (3) of subdivision (a), is not subject to the supervision requirements of this section, if he or she meets the requirements of subparagraph (C) of paragraph (3) of subdivision (a).

(2) This section does not apply to a person who provides batterers' treatment through a jail education program if the person in charge of that program determines that the person providing treatment has adequate education or training in domestic violence or a related field.

(e) A person who satisfactorily completes the training requirements of a county probation department whose training program is equivalent to or exceeds the training requirements of this act shall be exempt from the training requirements of this act.

Amended by Stats 2010 ch 328 (SB 1330),s 165, eff. 1/1/2011.
Amended by Stats 2009 ch 88 (AB 176),s 74, eff. 1/1/2010.

Added by Stats 2000 ch 544 (AB 1886) s 1, eff. 1/1/2001.

Section 1203.099 - [Effective until 7/1/2026] Authority for certain counties to offer alternative program for domestic violence offenders

(a) The Counties of Napa, San Luis Obispo, Santa Barbara, Santa Clara, Santa Cruz, and Yolo may offer a program for individuals convicted of domestic violence that does not comply with the requirement of the batterer's program in Sections 1203.097 and 1203.098 if the program meets all of the following conditions:

(1) The county develops the program in consultation with the domestic violence service providers and other relevant community partners.

(2) The county performs a risk and needs assessment utilizing an assessment demonstrated to be appropriate for domestic violence offenders for each offender entering the program.

(3) The offender's treatment within the program is based on the findings of the risk and needs assessment.

(4) The program includes components which are evidence-based or promising practices.

(5) The program has a comprehensive written curriculum that informs the operations of the program and outlines the treatment and intervention modalities.

(6) The offender's treatment within the program is for not less than one year in length, unless an alternative length is established by a validated risk and needs assessment completed by the probation department or an organization approved by the probation department.

(7) The county collects all of the following data for participants in the program:

(A) The offender's demographic information, including age, gender, race, ethnicity, marital status, familial status, and employment status.

(B) The offender's criminal history.

(C) The offender's risk level as determined by the risk and needs assessment.

(D) The treatment provided to the offender during the program and if the offender completed that treatment.

(E) The offender's outcome at the time of program completion, and six months after completion, including subsequent restraining order violations, arrests and convictions, and feedback provided by the victim if the victim desires to participate.

(8) The county reports all of the following information annually to the Legislature:

(A) The risk and needs assessment tool used for the program.

(B) The curriculum used by each program.

(C) The number of participants with a program length other than one year, and the alternative program lengths used.

(D) Individual data on the number of offenders participating in the program.

(E) Individual data for the items described in paragraph (7).

(b) Offenders who complete a program described in subdivision (a) shall be deemed to have met the batterer's program requirements set forth in Section 1203.097.

(c) As used in this section, the following definitions shall apply:

(1) "Evidence-based program or practice" means a program or practice that has a high level of research indicating its effectiveness, determined as a result of multiple rigorous evaluations including randomized controlled trials and evaluations that incorporate strong comparison group designs, or a single large multisite randomized study, and, typically, has specified procedures that allow for successful replication.

(2) "Promising program or practice" means a program or practice that has some research demonstrating its effectiveness but does not meet the full criteria for an evidence-based designation.

(d) A report to be submitted pursuant to paragraph (8) of subdivision (a) shall be submitted in compliance with Section 9795 of the Government Code.

(e) This section shall become operative on July 1, 2019.

(f) This section shall remain in effect only until July 1, 2026, and as of that date is repealed.

Amended by Stats 2023 ch 86 (AB 479),s 1, eff. 7/21/2023.

Amended by Stats 2021 ch 434 (SB 827),s 8, eff. 1/1/2022.

Added by Stats 2018 ch 290 (AB 372),s 1, eff. 1/1/2019.

Section 1203.1 - Order granting probation

(a) The court, or judge thereof, in the order granting probation, may suspend the imposing or the execution of the sentence and may direct that the suspension may continue for a period of time not exceeding two years, and upon those terms and conditions as it shall determine. The court, or judge thereof, in the order granting probation and as a condition thereof, may imprison the defendant in a county jail for a period not exceeding the maximum time fixed by law in the case. The following shall apply to this subdivision:

(1) The court may fine the defendant in a sum not to exceed the maximum fine provided by law in the case.

(2) The court may, in connection with granting probation, impose either imprisonment in a county jail or a fine, both, or neither.

(3) The court shall provide for restitution in proper cases. The restitution order shall be fully enforceable as a civil judgment forthwith and in accordance with Section 1202.4 of the Penal Code.

(4) The court may require bonds for the faithful observance and performance of any or all of the conditions of probation.

(b) The court shall consider whether the defendant as a condition of probation shall make restitution to the victim or the Restitution Fund. Any restitution payment received by a court or probation department in the form of cash or money order shall be forwarded to the victim within 30 days from the date the payment is received by the department. Any restitution payment received by a court or probation department in the form of a check or draft shall be forwarded to the victim within 45 days from the date the payment is received, provided, that payment need not be forwarded to a victim until 180 days from the date the first payment is received, if the restitution payments for that victim received by the court or probation department total less than fifty dollars ($50). In cases where the court has ordered the defendant to pay restitution to multiple victims and where the administrative cost of disbursing restitution payments to multiple victims involves a significant cost, any restitution payment received by a probation department shall be forwarded to multiple victims when it is cost effective to do so, but in no event shall restitution disbursements be delayed beyond 180 days from the date the payment is received by the probation department.

(c) In counties or cities and counties where road camps, farms, or other public work is available the court may place the probationer in the road camp, farm, or other public work instead of in jail. In this case, Section 25359 of the Government Code shall apply to probation and the court shall have the same power to require adult probationers to work, as prisoners confined in the county jail are required to work, at public work. Each county board of supervisors may fix the scale of compensation of the adult probationers in that county.

(d) In all cases of probation the court may require as a condition of probation that the probationer go to work and earn money for the support of the probationer's dependents or to pay any fine imposed or reparation condition, to keep an account of the probationer's earnings, to report them to the probation officer and apply those earnings as directed by the court.

(e) The court shall also consider whether the defendant as a condition of probation shall make restitution to a public agency for the costs of an emergency response pursuant to Article 8 (commencing with Section 53150) of Chapter 1 of Part 1 of Division 2 of the Government Code.

(f) In all felony cases in which, as a condition of probation, a judge of the superior court sitting by authority of law elsewhere than at the county seat requires a convicted person to serve their sentence at intermittent periods the sentence may be served on the order of the judge at the city jail nearest to the place at which the court is sitting, and the cost of the convicted person's maintenance shall be a county charge.

(g)

(1) The court and prosecuting attorney shall consider whether any defendant who has been convicted of a nonviolent or nonserious offense and ordered to participate in community service as a condition of probation shall be required to engage in the removal of graffiti in the performance of the community service. For the purpose of this subdivision, a nonserious offense shall not include the following:

(A) Offenses in violation of the Dangerous Weapons Control Law, as defined in Section 23500.

(B) Offenses involving the use of a dangerous or deadly weapon, including all violations of Section 417.

(C) Offenses involving the use or attempted use of violence against the person of another or involving injury to a victim.

(D) Offenses involving annoying or molesting children.

(2) Notwithstanding subparagraph (A) of paragraph (1), any person who violates Chapter 1 (commencing with Section 29610) of Division 9 of Title 4 of Part 6 shall be ordered to perform not less than 100 hours and not more than 500 hours of community service as a condition of probation.

(3) The court and the prosecuting attorney need not consider a defendant pursuant to paragraph (1) if the following circumstances exist:

(A) The defendant was convicted of any offense set forth in subdivision (c) of Section 667.5 or subdivision (c) of Section 1192.7.

(B) The judge believes that the public safety may be endangered if the person is ordered to do community service or the judge believes that the facts or circumstances or facts and circumstances call for imposition of a more substantial penalty.

(h) The probation officer or their designated representative shall consider whether any defendant who has been convicted of a nonviolent and nonserious offense and ordered to participate in community service as a condition of probation shall be required to engage in the performance of house repairs or yard services for senior citizens and the performance of repairs to senior centers through contact with local senior service organizations in the performance of the community service.

(i)

(1) Upon conviction of any offense involving child abuse or neglect, the court may require, in addition to any or all of the terms of imprisonment, fine, and other reasonable conditions specified in this section, that the defendant participate in counseling or education programs, or both, including, but not limited to, parent education or parenting programs operated by community colleges, school districts, other public agencies, or private agencies.

(2) Upon conviction of any sex offense subjecting the defendant to the registration requirements of Section 290, the court may order as a condition of probation, at the request of the victim or in the court's discretion, that the defendant stay away from the victim and the victim's residence or place of employment, and that the defendant have no contact with the victim in person, by telephone or electronic means, or by mail.

(j) The court may impose and require any or all of the terms of imprisonment, fine, and conditions specified in this section, and other reasonable conditions, as it may determine are fitting and proper to the end that justice may be done, that amends may be made to society for the breach of the law, for any injury done to any person resulting from that breach, and generally and specifically for the reformation and rehabilitation of the probationer, and that should the probationer violate any of the terms or conditions imposed by the court in the matter, it shall have authority to modify and change any and all the terms and conditions and to reimprison the probationer in the county jail within the limitations of the penalty of the public offense involved. Upon the defendant being released from the county jail under the terms of probation as originally granted or any modification subsequently made, and in all cases where confinement in a county jail has not been a condition of the grant of probation, the court shall place the defendant or probationer in and under the charge of the probation officer of the court, for the period or term fixed for probation. However, upon the payment of any fine imposed and the fulfillment of all conditions of probation, probation shall cease at the end of the term of probation, or sooner, in the event of modification. In counties and cities and counties in which there are facilities for taking fingerprints, those of each probationer shall be taken and a record of them kept and preserved.

(k) Notwithstanding any other provisions of law to the contrary, except as provided in Section 13967, as operative on or before September 28, 1994, of the Government Code and Section 13967.5 of the Government Code and Sections 1202.4, 1463.16, paragraph (1) of subdivision (a) of Section 1463.18, and Section 1464, and Section 1203.04, as operative on or before August 2, 1995, all fines collected by a county probation officer in any of the courts of this state, as a condition of the granting of probation or as a part of the terms of probation, shall be paid into the county treasury and placed in the general fund for the use and benefit of the county.

(l) The two-year probation limit in subdivision (a) shall not apply to:

(1) An offense listed in subdivision (c) of Section 667.5 and an offense that includes specific probation lengths within its provisions. For these offenses, the court, or judge thereof, in the order granting probation, may suspend the imposing or the execution of the sentence and may direct that the suspension may continue for a period of time not exceeding the maximum possible term of the sentence and under conditions as it shall determine. All other provisions of subdivision (a) shall apply.

(2) A felony conviction for paragraph (3) of subdivision (b) of Section 487, Section 503, and Section 532a, if the total value of the property taken exceeds twenty-five thousand dollars ($25,000). For these offenses, the court, or judge thereof, in the order granting probation, may suspend the imposing or the execution of the sentence and may direct that the suspension may continue for a period of time not exceeding three years, and upon those terms and conditions as it shall determine. All other provisions of subdivision (a) shall apply.

(m) This section shall become operative on January 1, 2022.

Added by Stats 2021 ch 257 (AB 177),s 22, eff. 9/23/2021.

Section 1203.1a - Temporary removal

The probation officer of the county may authorize the temporary removal under custody or temporary release without custody of any inmate of the county jail, honor farm, or other detention facility, who is confined or committed as a condition of probation, after suspension of imposition of sentence or suspension of execution of sentence, for purposes preparatory to his return to the community, within 30 days prior to his release date, if he concludes that such an inmate is a fit subject therefor. Any such temporary removal shall not be for a period of more than three days. When an inmate is released for purposes preparatory to his return to the community, the probation officer may require the inmate to reimburse the county, in whole or in part, for expenses incurred by the county in connection therewith.

Added by Stats. 1971, Ch. 1357.

Section 1203.1ab - Drug and substance abuse testing as condition of probation

(a) Upon conviction of any offense involving the unlawful possession, use, sale, or other furnishing of any controlled substance, as defined in Chapter 2 (commencing with Section 11053) of Division 10 of the Health and Safety Code, in addition to any or all of the terms of imprisonment, fine, and other reasonable conditions specified in or permitted by Section 1203.1, unless it makes a finding that this condition would not serve the interests of justice, the court, when recommended by the probation officer, shall require as a condition of probation that the defendant shall not use or be under the influence of any controlled substance and shall submit to drug and substance abuse testing as directed by the probation officer.

(b) This section shall become operative on January 1, 2022.

Added by Stats 2021 ch 257 (AB 177),s 24, eff. 9/23/2021.

Section 1203.1abc - [Repealed]

Amended by Stats 2004 ch 74 (AB 1901), s 2, eff. 1/1/2005.

Amended by Stats 2003 ch 468 (SB 851), s 17, eff. 1/1/2004.

Section 1203.1b - [Repealed]

Amended by Stats 2020 ch 92 (AB 1869),s 47, eff. 9/18/2020.

Amended by Stats 2014 ch 468 (AB 2199),s 1, eff. 1/1/2015.

Amended by Stats 2009 ch 606 (SB 676),s 6, eff. 1/1/2010.

Amended by Stats 2002 ch 784 (SB 1316), s 546, eff. 1/1/2003.

Amended by Stats 2001 ch 473 (SB 485) s 8, eff. 1/1/2002.

Section 1203.1bb - Cost of ignition interlock device

(a) If a defendant is granted probation and ordered to install an ignition interlock device, the defendant shall be required to pay the cost of purchasing and installing an ignition interlock device pursuant to Section 13386 of the Vehicle Code. The cost shall be determined pursuant to subdivision (k) of Section 23575.3 of the Vehicle Code. Any defendant subject to this section shall pay the manufacturer of the ignition interlock device directly for the cost of its purchase and installation, in accordance with the payment schedule ordered by the court. If practicable, the court shall order payment to be made to the manufacturer of the ignition interlock device within a six-month period.

(b) This section does not require any county to pay the costs of purchasing and installing any ignition interlock devices ordered pursuant to Section 13386 of the Vehicle Code. The Office of Traffic Safety shall consult with the presiding judge or the presiding judge's designee in each county to determine an appropriate means, if any, to provide for installation of ignition interlock devices in cases in which the defendant has no ability to pay.

(c) This section shall become operative on July 1, 2021.

Added by Stats 2020 ch 92 (AB 1869),s 49, eff. 9/18/2020.

Section 1203.1bc - [Repealed]

Added by Stats 2002 ch 919 (AB 2075), s 1, eff. 1/1/2003.

Section 1203.1d - Amount and manner of disbursement

(a) In determining the amount and manner of disbursement under an order made pursuant to this code requiring a defendant to make reparation or restitution to a victim of a crime, to pay any cost of jail or other confinement, or to pay any other reimbursable costs, the court, after determining the amount of any fine and penalty assessments, and a county financial evaluation officer when making a financial evaluation, shall first determine the amount of restitution to be ordered paid to any victim, and shall determine the amount of the other reimbursable costs. If payment is made in full, the payment shall be apportioned and disbursed in the amounts ordered by the court.

If reasonable and compatible with the defendant's financial ability, the court may order payments to be made in installments.

(b) With respect to installment payments and amounts collected by the Franchise Tax Board pursuant to Section 19280 of the Revenue and Taxation Code and subsequently transferred by the Controller pursuant to Section 19282 of the Revenue and Taxation Code, the board of supervisors shall provide that disbursements be made in the following order of priority:

(1) Restitution ordered to, or on behalf of, the victim pursuant to subdivision (f) of Section 1202.4.

(2) The state surcharge ordered pursuant to Section 1465.7.

(3) Any fines, penalty assessments, and restitution fines ordered pursuant to subdivision (b) of Section 1202.4. Payment of each of these items shall be made on a proportional basis to the total amount levied for all of these items.

(4) Any other reimbursable costs.

(c) The board of supervisors shall apply these priorities of disbursement to orders or parts of orders in cases where defendants have been ordered to pay more than one court order.

(d) Documentary evidence, such as bills, receipts, repair estimates, insurance payment statements, payroll stubs, business records, and similar documents relevant to the value of the stolen or damaged property, medical expenses, and wages and profits lost shall not be excluded as hearsay evidence.

(e) This section shall become operative on July 1, 2021.

Added by Stats 2020 ch 92 (AB 1869),s 51, eff. 9/18/2020.

Section 1203.1e - [Repealed]

Amended by Stats 2020 ch 92 (AB 1869),s 52, eff. 9/18/2020.

Section 1203.1f - Consolidation of ability to pay determination hearings

If practicable, the court shall consolidate the ability to pay determination hearings authorized by this code into one proceeding, and the determination of ability to pay made at the consolidated hearing may be used for all purposes.

Amended by Stats 2002 ch 198 (AB 2526), s 1, eff. 1/1/2003.

Section 1203.1g - Restitution for costs of medical or psychological treatment incurred by minor victim of sexual assault

In any case in which a defendant is convicted of sexual assault on a minor, and the defendant is eligible for probation, the court, as a condition of probation, shall order him or her to make restitution for the costs of medical or psychological treatment incurred by the victim as a result of the assault and that he or she seek and maintain employment and apply that portion of his or her earnings specified by the court toward those costs.

As used in this section, "sexual assault" has the meaning specified in subdivisions (a) and (b) of Section 11165.1. The defendant is entitled to a hearing concerning any modification of the amount of restitution based on the costs of medical and psychological treatment incurred by the victim subsequent to the issuance of the order of probation.

Amended by Stats. 1994, Ch. 146, Sec. 168. Effective January 1, 1995.

Section 1203.1h - Cost of medical examinations conducted on victim

(a) In addition to any other costs which a court is authorized to require a defendant to pay, upon conviction of any offense involving child abuse or neglect, the court may require that the defendant pay to a law enforcement agency incurring the cost, the cost of any medical examinations conducted on the victim in order to determine the nature or extent of the abuse or neglect. If the court determines that the defendant has the ability to pay all or part of the medical examination costs, the court may set the amount to be reimbursed and order the defendant to pay that sum to the law enforcement agency in the manner in which the court believes reasonable and compatible with the defendant's financial ability. In making a determination of whether a defendant has the ability to pay, the court shall take into account the amount of any fine imposed upon the defendant and any amount the defendant has been ordered to pay in restitution.

(b) In addition to any other costs that a court is authorized to require a defendant to pay, upon conviction of any offense involving sexual assault or attempted sexual assault, including child sexual abuse, the court may require that the defendant pay, to the law enforcement agency, county, or local governmental agency incurring the cost, the cost of any medical examinations conducted on the victim for the collection and preservation of evidence. If the court determines that the defendant has the ability to pay all or part of the cost of the medical examination, the court may set the amount to be reimbursed and order the defendant to pay that sum to the law enforcement agency, county, or local governmental agency, in the manner in which the court believes reasonable and compatible with the defendant's financial ability. In making the determination of whether a defendant has the ability to pay, the court shall take into account the amount of any fine imposed upon the defendant and any amount the defendant has been ordered to pay in restitution. In no event shall a court penalize an indigent defendant by imposing an additional period of imprisonment in lieu of payment.

Amended by Stats 2019 ch 714 (AB 538),s 2, eff. 1/1/2020.

Section 1203.1i - House confinement for defendant convicted of violation of building standards

(a) In any case in which a defendant is convicted of a violation of any building standards adopted by a local entity by ordinance or resolution, including, but not limited to, local health, fire, building, or safety ordinances or resolutions, or any other ordinance or resolution relating to the health and safety of occupants of buildings, by maintaining a substandard building, as specified in Section 17920.3 of the Health and Safety Code, the court, or judge thereof, in making an order granting probation, in addition to any other orders, may order the defendant placed under house confinement, or may order the defendant to serve both a term of imprisonment in the county jail and to be placed under house confinement. This section only applies to violations involving a dwelling unit occupied by persons specified in subdivision (a) of Section 1940 of the Civil Code who are not excluded by subdivision (b) of that section.

(b) If the court orders a defendant to serve all or part of his or her sentence under house confinement, pursuant to subdivision (a), he or she may also be ordered to pay the cost of having a police officer or guard stand guard outside the area in which the defendant has been confined under house confinement if it has been determined that the defendant is able to pay these costs.

(c) As used in this section, "house confinement" means confinement to a residence or location designated by the court and specified in the probation order.

Added by Stats. 1987, Ch. 1063, Sec. 1.

Section 1203.1j - Restitution for costs of medical or psychological treatment incurred by victim 65 years of age or older

In any case in which the defendant is convicted of assault, battery, or assault with a deadly weapon on a victim 65 years of age or older, and the defendant knew or reasonably should have known the elderly status of the victim, the court, as a condition of probation, shall order the defendant to make restitution for the costs of medical or psychological treatment incurred by the victim as a result of the crime, and that the defendant seek and maintain legitimate employment and apply that portion of his or her earnings specified by the court toward those costs.

The defendant shall be entitled to a hearing, concerning any modification of the amount of restitution, based on the costs of medical and psychological treatment incurred by the victim subsequent to the issuance of the order of probation.
Amended by Stats. 1990, Ch. 45, Sec. 8.

Section 1203.1k - Specific amount of restitution and manner of payment

For any order of restitution made under Section 1203.1, the court may order the specific amount of restitution and the manner in which restitution shall be made to a victim or the Restitution Fund, to the extent that the victim has received payment from the Victims of Crime Program, based on the probation officer's report or it may, with the consent of the defendant, order the probation officer to set the amount of restitution and the manner in which restitution shall be made to a victim or the Restitution Fund, to the extent that the victim has received payment from the Victims of Crime Program. The defendant shall have the right to a hearing before the judge to dispute the determinations made by the probation officer in regard to the amount or manner in which restitution is to be made to the victim or the Restitution Fund, to the extent that the victim has received payment from the Victims of Crime Program. If the court orders restitution to be made to the Restitution Fund, the court, and not the probation officer, shall determine the amount and the manner in which restitution is to be made to the Restitution Fund.
Amended by Stats 2000 ch 1016 (AB 2491) s 10, eff. 9/29/2000.

Section 1203.1l - Restitution to public agency for costs of emergency response

In any case in which, pursuant to Section 1203.1, the court orders the defendant, as a condition of probation, to make restitution to a public agency for the costs of an emergency response, all of the following shall apply:

(a) The probation department shall obtain the actual costs for an emergency response from a public agency, and shall include the public agency's documents supporting the actual costs for the emergency response in the probation department's sentencing report to the court.

(b) At the sentencing hearing, the defendant has the right to confront witnesses and present evidence in opposition to the amount claimed to be due to the public agency for its actual costs for the emergency response.

(c) The collection of the emergency response costs is the responsibility of the public agency seeking the reimbursement. If a defendant fails to make restitution payment when a payment is due, the public agency shall by verified declaration notify the probation department of the delinquency. The probation department shall make an investigation of the delinquency and shall make a report to the court of the delinquency. The report shall contain any recommendation that the probation officer finds to be relevant regarding the delinquency and future payments. The court, after a hearing on the delinquency, may make modifications to the existing order in the furtherance of justice.

(d) The defendant has the right to petition the court for a modification of the emergency response reimbursement order whenever he or she has sustained a substantial change in economic circumstances. The defendant has a right to a hearing on the proposed modification, and the court may make any modification to the existing order in the furtherance of justice.
Added by renumbering Section 1203.1i (as added by Stats. 1987, Ch. 713) by Stats. 1989, Ch. 1360, Sec. 114.

Section 1203.2 - Rearrest of supervised person

(a) At any time during the period of supervision of a person (1) released on probation under the care of a probation officer pursuant to this chapter, (2) released on conditional sentence or summary probation not under the care of a probation officer, (3) placed on mandatory supervision pursuant to subparagraph (B) of paragraph (5) of subdivision (h) of Section 1170, (4) subject to revocation of postrelease community supervision pursuant to Section 3455, or (5) subject to revocation of parole supervision pursuant to Section 3000.08, if any probation officer, parole officer, or peace officer has probable cause to believe that the supervised person is violating any term or condition of the person's supervision, the officer may, without warrant or other process and at any time until the final disposition of the case, rearrest the supervised person and bring them before the court or the court may, in its discretion, issue a warrant for their rearrest. Unless the person on probation is otherwise serving a period of flash incarceration, whenever a person on probation who is subject to this section is arrested, with or without a warrant or the filing of a petition for revocation as described in subdivision (b), the court shall consider the release of a person on probation from custody in accordance with Section 1203.25. Notwithstanding Section 3056, and unless the supervised person is otherwise serving a period of flash incarceration, whenever any supervised person who is subject to this section and who is not on probation is arrested, with or without a warrant or the filing of a petition for revocation as described in subdivision (b), the court may order the release of the supervised person from custody under any terms and conditions the court deems appropriate. Upon rearrest, or upon the issuance of a warrant for rearrest, the court may revoke and terminate the supervision of the person if the interests of justice so require and the court, in its judgment, has reason to believe from the report of the probation or parole officer or otherwise that the person has violated any of the conditions of their supervision, or has subsequently committed other offenses, regardless of whether the person has been prosecuted for those offenses. However, the court shall not terminate parole pursuant to this section. Supervision shall not be revoked solely for failure of a person to make restitution, or to pay fines, fees, or assessments, imposed as a condition of supervision unless the court determines that the defendant has willfully failed to pay and has the ability to pay. Restitution shall be consistent with a person's ability to pay. The revocation, summary or otherwise, shall serve to toll the running of the period of supervision.

(b)

(1) Upon its own motion or upon the petition of the supervised person, the probation or parole officer, or the district attorney, the court may modify, revoke, or terminate supervision of the person pursuant to this subdivision, except that the court shall not terminate parole pursuant to this section. The court in the county in which the person is supervised has jurisdiction to hear the motion or petition, or for those on parole, either the court in the county of supervision or the court in the county in which the alleged violation of supervision occurred. A person supervised on parole or postrelease community supervision pursuant to Section 3455 may not petition the court pursuant to this section for early release from supervision, and a petition under this section shall not be filed solely for the purpose of modifying parole. This section does not prohibit the court in the county in which the person is supervised or in which the alleged violation of supervision occurred from modifying a person's parole when acting on the court's own motion or a petition to revoke parole. The court shall give notice of its motion, and the probation or parole officer or the district attorney shall give notice of their petition to the supervised person, the supervised person's attorney of record, and the district attorney or the probation or parole

officer, as the case may be. The supervised person shall give notice of their petition to the probation or parole officer and notice of any motion or petition shall be given to the district attorney in all cases. The court shall refer its motion or the petition to the probation or parole officer. After the receipt of a written report from the probation or parole officer, the court shall read and consider the report and either its motion or the petition and may modify, revoke, or terminate the supervision of the supervised person upon the grounds set forth in subdivision (a) if the interests of justice so require.

(2) The notice required by this subdivision may be given to the supervised person upon their first court appearance in the proceeding. Upon the agreement by the supervised person in writing to the specific terms of a modification or termination of a specific term of supervision, any requirement that the supervised person make a personal appearance in court for the purpose of a modification or termination shall be waived. Prior to the modification or termination and waiver of appearance, the supervised person shall be informed of their right to consult with counsel, and if indigent the right to secure court-appointed counsel. If the supervised person waives their right to counsel a written waiver shall be required. If the supervised person consults with counsel and thereafter agrees to a modification, revocation, or termination of the term of supervision and waiver of personal appearance, the agreement shall be signed by counsel showing approval for the modification or termination and waiver.

(c) Upon any revocation and termination of probation the court may, if the sentence has been suspended, pronounce judgment for any time within the longest period for which the person might have been sentenced. However, if the judgment has been pronounced and the execution thereof has been suspended, the court may revoke the suspension and order that the judgment shall be in full force and effect. In either case, the person shall be delivered over to the proper officer to serve their sentence, less any credits herein provided for.

(d) In any case of revocation and termination of probation, including, but not limited to, cases in which the judgment has been pronounced and the execution thereof has been suspended, upon the revocation and termination, the court may, in lieu of any other sentence, commit the person to the Department of Corrections and Rehabilitation, Division of Juvenile Facilities if the person is otherwise eligible for that commitment.

(e) If probation has been revoked before the judgment has been pronounced, the order revoking probation may be set aside for good cause upon motion made before pronouncement of judgment. If probation has been revoked after the judgment has been pronounced, the judgment and the order which revoked the probation may be set aside for good cause within 30 days after the court has notice that the execution of the sentence has commenced. If an order setting aside the judgment, the revocation of probation, or both is made after the expiration of the probationary period, the court may again place the person on probation for that period and with those terms and conditions as it could have done immediately following conviction.

(f) As used in this section, the following definitions shall apply:

(1) "Court" means a judge, magistrate, or revocation hearing officer described in Section 71622.5 of the Government Code.

(2) "Probation officer" means a probation officer as described in Section 1203 or an officer of the agency designated by the board of supervisors of a county to implement postrelease community supervision pursuant to Section 3451.

(3) "Supervised person" means a person who satisfies any of the following:

(A) The person is released on probation subject to the supervision of a probation officer.

(B) The person is released on conditional sentence or summary probation not under the care of a probation officer.

(C) The person is subject to mandatory supervision pursuant to subparagraph (B) of paragraph (5) of subdivision (h) of Section 1170.

(D) The person is subject to revocation of postrelease community supervision pursuant to Section 3455.

(E) The person is subject to revocation of parole pursuant to Section 3000.08.

(g) This section does not affect the authority of the supervising agency to impose intermediate sanctions, including flash incarceration, to persons supervised on parole pursuant to Section 3000.8 or postrelease community supervision pursuant to Title 2.05 (commencing with Section 3450) of Part 3.

Amended by Stats 2021 ch 533 (AB 1228),s 1, eff. 1/1/2022.
Amended by Stats 2019 ch 111 (AB 1421),s 1, eff. 1/1/2020.
Amended by Stats 2015 ch 61 (SB 517),s 1, eff. 1/1/2016.
Amended by Stats 2013 ch 32 (SB 76),s 7, eff. 6/27/2013.
Amended by Stats 2013 ch 31 (SB 75),s 9, eff. 6/27/2013.
Amended by Stats 2012 ch 43 (SB 1023),s 30, eff. 6/27/2012.

Section 1203.2a - Imposition of sentence after person released on probation is committed to prison for another offense

If any defendant who has been released on probation is committed to a prison in this state or another state for another offense, the court which released him or her on probation shall have jurisdiction to impose sentence, if no sentence has previously been imposed for the offense for which he or she was granted probation, in the absence of the defendant, on the request of the defendant made through his or her counsel, or by himself or herself in writing, if such writing is signed in the presence of the warden of the prison in which he or she is confined or the duly authorized representative of the warden, and the warden or his or her representative attests both that the defendant has made and signed such request and that he or she states that he or she wishes the court to impose sentence in the case in which he or she was released on probation, in his or her absence and without him or her being represented by counsel.

The probation officer may, upon learning of the defendant's imprisonment, and must within 30 days after being notified in writing by the defendant or his or her counsel, or the warden or duly authorized representative of the prison in which the defendant is confined, report such commitment to the court which released him or her on probation.

Upon being informed by the probation officer of the defendant's confinement, or upon receipt from the warden or duly authorized representative of any prison in this state or another state of a certificate showing that the defendant is confined in prison, the court shall issue its commitment if sentence has previously been imposed. If sentence has not been previously imposed and if the defendant has requested the court through counsel or in writing in the manner herein provided to impose sentence in the case in which he or she was released on probation in his or her absence and without the presence of counsel to represent him or her, the court shall impose sentence and issue its commitment, or shall make other final order terminating its jurisdiction over the defendant in the case in which the order of probation was made. If the case is one in which sentence has previously been imposed, the court shall be deprived of jurisdiction over defendant if it does not issue its commitment or make other final order terminating its jurisdiction over defendant in the case within 60 days after being notified of the confinement. If the case is one in which sentence has not previously been imposed, the court is deprived of jurisdiction over defendant if it does not impose sentence and issue its commitment or make other final order terminating its jurisdiction over defendant in the case within 30 days after defendant has, in the manner prescribed by this section, requested imposition of sentence.

Upon imposition of sentence hereunder the commitment shall be dated as of the date upon which probation was granted. If the defendant is then in a state prison for an offense committed subsequent to the one upon which he or she has been on probation, the term of imprisonment of such defendant under a commitment issued hereunder shall commence upon the date upon which defendant was delivered to prison under commitment for his or her subsequent offense. Any terms ordered to be served consecutively shall be served as otherwise provided by law.

In the event the probation officer fails to report such commitment to the court or the court fails to impose sentence as herein provided, the court shall be deprived thereafter of all jurisdiction it may have retained in the granting of probation in said case.

Amended by Stats. 1989, Ch. 1420, Sec. 2.

Section 1203.25 - Release of persons on their own recognizance

(a) All persons released by a court at or after the initial hearing and prior to a formal probation violation hearing pursuant to subdivision (a) of Section 1203.2 shall be released on their own recognizance unless the court finds, by clear and convincing evidence, that the particular circumstances of the case require the imposition of an order to provide reasonable protection to the public and reasonable assurance of the person's future appearance in court.

(1) The court shall make an individualized determination of the factors that do or do not indicate that the person would be a danger to the public if released pending a formal revocation hearing. Any finding of danger to the public must be based on clear and convincing evidence.

(2) The court shall not require the use of any algorithm-based risk assessment tool in setting conditions of release.

(3) The court shall impose the least restrictive conditions of release necessary to provide reasonable protection of the public and reasonable assurance of the person's future appearance in court.

(b) Reasonable conditions of release may include, but are not limited to, reporting telephonically to a probation officer, protective orders, a global positioning system (GPS) monitoring device or other electronic monitoring, an alcohol use detection device, or search and seizure by a probation officer or other peace officer. The person shall not be required to bear the expense of any conditions of release ordered by the court.

(c)

(1) Bail shall not be imposed unless the court finds by clear and convincing evidence that other reasonable conditions of release are not adequate to provide reasonable protection of the public and reasonable assurance of the person's future appearance in court.

(2) "Bail" as used in this section is defined as cash bail. A bail bond or property bond is not bail. In determining the amount of bail, the court shall make an individualized determination based on the particular circumstances of the case, and it shall consider the person's ability to pay cash bail, not a bail bond or property bond. Bail shall be set at a level the person can reasonably afford.

(d) The court shall not deny release for a person on probation for misdemeanor conduct before the court holds a formal probation revocation hearing, unless the person fails to comply with an order of the court, including an order to appear in court in the underlying case, in which case subdivision (a) shall apply.

(e) The court shall not deny release for a person on probation for felony conduct before the court holds a formal probation revocation hearing unless the court finds by clear and convincing evidence that there are no means reasonably available to provide reasonable protection of the public and reasonable assurance of the person's future appearance in court.

(f) All findings required to be made by clear and convincing evidence under this section shall, based on all evidence presented, including, but not limited to, any probation report, be made orally on the record by the court. The court also shall set forth the reason in an order entered upon the minutes if requested by either party in any case in which the proceedings are not being reported by a court reporter.

(g) If a new charge is the basis for a probation violation, nothing in this section shall be construed to limit the court's authority to hold, release, limit release, or impose conditions of release for that charge as permitted by applicable law.

Amended by Stats 2023 ch 218 (SB 852),s 8, eff. 1/1/2024.

Added by Stats 2021 ch 533 (AB 1228),s 2, eff. 1/1/2022.

Section 1203.3 - Authority to revoke, modify, or change order of suspension of imposition or execution of sentence

(a) The court has the authority at any time during the term of probation to revoke, modify, or change its order of suspension of imposition or execution of sentence. The court may at any time when the ends of justice will be subserved thereby, and when the good conduct and reform of the person so held on probation shall warrant it, terminate the period of probation, and discharge the person held. The court also has the authority at any time during the term of mandatory supervision pursuant to subparagraph (B) of paragraph (5) of subdivision (h) of Section 1170 to revoke, modify, or change the conditions of the court's order suspending the execution of the concluding portion of the supervised person's term.

(b) The exercise of the court's authority in subdivision (a) to revoke, modify, or change probation or mandatory supervision, or to terminate probation, is subject to the following:

(1) Before any sentence or term or condition of probation or condition of mandatory supervision is modified, a hearing shall be held in open court before the judge. The prosecuting attorney shall be given a two-day written notice and an opportunity to be heard on the matter, except that, as to modifying or terminating a protective order in a case involving domestic violence, as defined in Section 6211 of the Family Code, the prosecuting attorney shall be given a five-day written notice and an opportunity to be heard.

(A) If the sentence or term or condition of probation or the term or any condition of mandatory supervision is modified pursuant to this section, the judge shall state the reasons for that modification on the record.

(B) As used in this section, modification of sentence shall include reducing a felony to a misdemeanor.

(2)

(A) An order shall not be made without written notice first given by the court or the clerk thereof to the proper probation officer of the intention to revoke, modify, or change its order.

(B) Before an order terminating probation early may be made, a hearing shall be held in open court before the judge. The prosecuting attorney shall be given a two-day written notice and an opportunity to be heard on the matter. The prosecuting attorney shall provide notice to the victim if the victim has requested to be notified about the progress of the case. If the victim advises the prosecuting attorney that there is an outstanding restitution order or restitution fine, as specified in Section 1202.4, the prosecuting attorney shall request a continuance of the hearing.

(3) In all probation cases, if the court has not seen fit to revoke the order of probation and impose sentence or pronounce judgment, the defendant shall at the end of the term of probation or any extension thereof, be discharged by the court subject to the provisions of these sections.

(4) The court may modify the time and manner of the term of probation for purposes of measuring the timely payment of restitution obligations or the good conduct and reform of the defendant while on probation. The court shall not modify the dollar amount of the restitution obligations due to the good conduct and reform of the defendant, absent compelling and extraordinary reasons, nor shall the court limit the ability of payees to enforce the obligations in the manner of judgments in civil actions.

(5) This section does not prohibit the court from modifying the dollar amount of a restitution order pursuant to subdivision (f) of Section 1202.4 at any time during the term of the probation.

(6) The court may limit or terminate a protective order that is a condition of probation or mandatory supervision in a case involving domestic violence, as defined in Section 6211 of the Family Code. In determining whether to limit or terminate the protective order, the court shall consider if there has been any material change in circumstances since the crime for which the order was issued, and any issue that relates to whether there exists good cause for the change, including, but not limited to, consideration of all of the following:

(A) Whether the probationer or supervised person has accepted responsibility for the abusive behavior perpetrated against the victim.

(B) Whether the probationer or supervised person is currently attending and actively participating in counseling sessions.

(C) Whether the probationer or supervised person has completed parenting counseling, or attended alcoholics or narcotics counseling.

(D) Whether the probationer or supervised person has moved from the state, or is incarcerated.

(E) Whether the probationer or supervised person is still cohabiting, or intends to cohabit, with any subject of the order.

(F) Whether the defendant has performed well on probation or mandatory supervision, including consideration of any progress reports.

(G) Whether the victim desires the change, and if so, the victim's reasons, whether the victim has consulted a victim advocate, and whether the victim has prepared a safety plan and has access to local resources.

(H) Whether the change will impact any children involved, including consideration of any child protective services information.

(I) Whether the ends of justice would be served by limiting or terminating the order.

(c) If a probationer is ordered to serve time in jail, and the probationer escapes while serving that time, the probation is revoked as a matter of law on the day of the escape.

(d) If probation is revoked pursuant to subdivision (c), upon taking the probationer into custody, the probationer shall be accorded a hearing or hearings consistent with the holding in the case of People v. Vickers (1972) 8 Cal.3d 451. The purpose of that hearing or hearings is not to revoke probation, as the revocation has occurred as a matter of law in accordance with subdivision (c), but rather to afford the defendant an opportunity to require the prosecution to establish that the alleged violation did in fact occur and to justify the revocation.

(e) This section does not apply to cases covered by Section 1203.2.

Amended by Stats 2019 ch 573 (AB 433),s 1, eff. 1/1/2020.
Amended by Stats 2012 ch 43 (SB 1023),s 31, eff. 6/27/2012.
Amended by Stats 2003 ch 62 (SB 600), s 231, eff. 1/1/2004.
Amended by Stats 2003 ch 468 (SB 851), s 18, eff. 1/1/2004.
Amended by Stats 2002 ch 66 (AB 2563), s 1, eff. 1/1/2003.
Amended by Stats 2000 ch 1016 (AB 2491) s 11, eff. 9/29/2000.

Section 1203.35 - [Effective until 1/1/2028] Flash incarceration for violation of probation or mandatory supervision

(a)

(1) In any case in which the court grants probation or imposes a sentence that includes mandatory supervision, the county probation department is authorized to use flash incarceration for any violation of the conditions of probation or mandatory supervision if, at the time of granting probation or ordering mandatory supervision, the court obtains from the defendant a waiver to a court hearing prior to the imposition of a period of flash incarceration. Probation shall not be denied for refusal to sign the waiver.

(2) Each county probation department shall develop a response matrix that establishes protocols for the imposition of graduated sanctions for violations of the conditions of probation to determine appropriate interventions to include the use of flash incarceration.

(3) A supervisor shall approve the term of flash incarceration prior to the imposition of flash incarceration.

(4) Upon a decision to impose a period of flash incarceration, the probation department shall notify the court, public defender, district attorney, and sheriff of each imposition of flash incarceration.

(5) If the person on probation or mandatory supervision does not agree to accept a recommended period of flash incarceration, upon a determination that there has been a violation, the probation officer is authorized to address the alleged violation by filing a declaration or revocation request with the court.

(b) For purposes of this section, "flash incarceration" is a period of detention in a county jail due to a violation of an offender's conditions of probation or mandatory supervision. The length of the detention period may range between 1 and 10 consecutive days. Shorter, but if necessary more frequent, periods of detention for violations of an offender's conditions of probation or mandatory supervision shall appropriately punish an offender while preventing the disruption in a work or home establishment that typically arises from longer periods of detention. In cases in which there are multiple violations in a single incident, only one flash incarceration booking is authorized and may range between 1 and 10 consecutive days.

(c) This section shall not apply to any defendant sentenced pursuant to Section 1210.1.

(d) This section shall remain in effect only until January 1, 2028, and as of that date is repealed, unless a later enacted statute, that is enacted before January 1, 2028, deletes or extends that date.

Amended by Stats 2022 ch 756 (AB 1744),s 2, eff. 1/1/2023.
Amended by Stats 2019 ch 44 (AB 597),s 2, eff. 1/1/2020.
Added by Stats 2016 ch 706 (SB 266),s 2, eff. 1/1/2017.

Section 1203.4 - Fulfillment of conditions of probation; change; dismissal of accusations or information

(a)

(1) When a defendant has fulfilled the conditions of probation for the entire period of probation, or has been discharged prior to the termination of the period of probation, or in any other case in which a court, in its discretion and the interest of justice, determines that a defendant should be granted the relief available under this section, the defendant shall, at any time after the termination of the period of probation, if they are not then serving a sentence for an offense, on probation for an offense, or charged with the commission of an offense, be permitted by the court to withdraw their plea of guilty or plea of nolo contendere and enter a plea of not guilty; or, if they have been convicted after a plea of not guilty, the court shall set aside the verdict of guilty; and, in either case, the court shall thereupon dismiss the accusations or information against the defendant and except as noted below, the defendant shall thereafter be released from all penalties and disabilities resulting from the offense of which they have been convicted, except as provided in Section 13555 of the Vehicle Code. The probationer shall be informed, in their probation papers, of this right and privilege and the right, if any, to petition for a certificate of rehabilitation and pardon. The probationer may make the application and change of plea in person or by attorney, or by the probation officer authorized in writing. However, in any subsequent prosecution of the defendant for any other offense, the prior conviction may be pleaded and proved and shall have the same effect as if probation had not been granted or the accusation or information dismissed. The order shall state, and the probationer shall be informed, that the order does not relieve them of the obligation to disclose the conviction in response to any direct question contained in any questionnaire or application for public office, for licensure by any state or local agency, or for contracting with the California State Lottery Commission.

(2) Dismissal of an accusation or information pursuant to this section does not permit a person to own, possess, or have custody or control of a firearm or to prevent conviction under Chapter 2 (commencing with Section 29800) of Division 9 of Title 4 of Part 6.

(3) Dismissal of an accusation or information underlying a conviction pursuant to this section does not permit a person prohibited from holding public office as a result of that conviction to hold public office.

(4) Dismissal of an accusation or information pursuant to this section does not release the defendant from the terms and conditions of an unexpired criminal protective order that has been issued by the court pursuant to paragraph (1) of subdivision (i) of Section 136.2, subdivision (j) of Section 273.5, subdivision (l) of Section 368, or subdivision (k) of Section 646.9. These protective orders shall remain in full effect until expiration or until any further order by the court modifying or terminating the order, despite the dismissal of the underlying accusation or information.

(5) This subdivision shall apply to all applications for relief under this section which are filed on or after November 23, 1970.

(b) Subdivision (a) of this section does not apply to a misdemeanor that is within the provisions of Section 42002.1 of the Vehicle Code, to a violation of subdivision (c) of Section 286, Section 288, subdivision (c) of Section 287 or of former Section 288a, Section 288.5, subdivision (j) of Section 289, Section 311.1, 311.2, 311.3, or 311.11, or a felony conviction pursuant to subdivision (d) of Section 261.5, or to an infraction.

(c)

(1) Except as provided in paragraph (2), subdivision (a) does not apply to a person who receives a notice to appear or is otherwise charged with a violation of an offense described in subdivisions (a) to (e), inclusive, of Section 12810 of the Vehicle Code.

(2) If a defendant who was convicted of a violation listed in paragraph (1) petitions the court, the court in its discretion and in the interest of justice, may order the relief provided pursuant to subdivision (a) to that defendant.

(3)

(A) A petition for relief under this section shall not be denied due to an unfulfilled order of restitution or restitution fine.

(B) An unfulfilled order of restitution or a restitution fine shall not be grounds for finding that a defendant did not fulfil the condition of probation for the entire period of probation.

(C) When the court considers a petition for relief under this section, in its discretion and in the interest of justice, an unpaid order of restitution or restitution fine shall not be grounds for denial of the petition for relief.

(d)

(1) Relief shall not be granted under this section unless the prosecuting attorney has been given 15 days' notice of the petition for relief. The probation officer shall notify the prosecuting attorney when a petition is filed, pursuant to this section.

(2) It shall be presumed that the prosecuting attorney has received notice if proof of service is filed with the court.

(e) If, after receiving notice pursuant to subdivision (d), the prosecuting attorney fails to appear and object to a petition for dismissal, the prosecuting attorney may not move to set aside or otherwise appeal the grant of that petition.

(f) Notwithstanding the above provisions or any other law, the Governor shall have the right to pardon a person convicted of a violation of subdivision (c) of Section 286, Section 288, subdivision (c) of Section 287 or of former Section 288a, Section 288.5, or subdivision (j) of Section 289, if there are extraordinary circumstances.

Amended by Stats 2023 ch 47 (AB 134),s 6, eff. 7/10/2023.
Amended by Stats 2022 ch 734 (SB 1106),s 3, eff. 1/1/2023.
Amended by Stats 2021 ch 209 (AB 1281),s 1, eff. 1/1/2022.
Amended by Stats 2018 ch 423 (SB 1494),s 96, eff. 1/1/2019.
Amended by Stats 2013 ch 143 (AB 20),s 2, eff. 1/1/2014.
Amended by Stats 2011 ch 304 (SB 428),s 9, eff. 1/1/2012.

Amended by Stats 2011 ch 285 (AB 1402),s 17, eff. 1/1/2012, op. 1/1/2012.
Amended by Stats 2009 ch 606 (SB 676),s 7, eff. 1/1/2010.
Amended by Stats 2008 ch 94 (AB 2092),s 1, eff. 1/1/2009.
Amended by Stats 2007 ch 161 (AB 645),s 1, eff. 1/1/2008.
Amended by Stats 2005 ch 704 (AB 439),s 3, eff. 1/1/2006
Amended by Stats 2003 ch 49 (AB 580), s 1, eff. 1/1/2004.
Amended by Stats 2000 ch 226 (AB 2320) s 1, eff. 1/1/2001.

Section 1203.4a - Withdrawal of plea and setting aside verdict of guilty by defendant convicted of misdemeanor and not granted probation or convicted of infraction; dismissal of accusatory pleading

(a) Every defendant convicted of a misdemeanor and not granted probation, and every defendant convicted of an infraction shall, at any time after the lapse of one year from the date of pronouncement of judgment, if they have fully complied with and performed the sentence of the court, are not then serving a sentence for an offense and are not under charge of commission of a crime, and have, since the pronouncement of judgment, lived an honest and upright life and have conformed to and obeyed the laws of the land, be permitted by the court to withdraw their plea of guilty or nolo contendere and enter a plea of not guilty; or if they have been convicted after a plea of not guilty, the court shall set aside the verdict of guilty; and in either case the court shall dismiss the accusatory pleading against the defendant, who shall be released from all penalties and disabilities resulting from the offense of which they have been convicted, except as provided in Chapter 3 (commencing with Section 29900) of Division 9 of Title 4 of Part 6 of this code or Section 13555 of the Vehicle Code.

(b) If a defendant does not satisfy all the requirements of subdivision (a), after a lapse of one year from the date of pronouncement of judgment, a court, in its discretion and in the interest of justice, may grant the relief available pursuant to subdivision (a) to a defendant convicted of an infraction, or of a misdemeanor and not granted probation, or both, if the defendant has fully complied with and performed the sentence of the court, is not then serving a sentence for any offense, and is not under charge of commission of a crime.

(c)

(1) The defendant shall be informed of the provisions of this section, either orally or in writing, at the time they are sentenced. The defendant may make an application and change of plea in person or by attorney, or by the probation officer authorized in writing, provided that, in any subsequent prosecution of the defendant for any other offense, the prior conviction may be pleaded and proved and shall have the same effect as if relief had not been granted pursuant to this section.

(2) Dismissal of an accusatory pleading pursuant to this section does not permit a person to own, possess, or have in their custody or control a firearm or prevent their conviction under Chapter 2 (commencing with Section 29800) of Division 9 of Title 4 of Part 6.

(3) Dismissal of an accusatory pleading underlying a conviction pursuant to this section does not permit a person prohibited from holding public office as a result of that conviction to hold public office.

(4) Dismissal of an accusation or information pursuant to this section does not release the defendant from the terms and conditions of an unexpired criminal protective order that has been issued by the court pursuant to paragraph (1) of subdivision (i) of Section 136.2, subdivision (j) of Section 273.5, subdivision (l) of Section 368, or subdivision (k) of Section 646.9. These protective orders shall remain in full effect until expiration or until any further order by the court modifying or terminating the order, despite the dismissal of the underlying accusation or information.

(d) This section applies to a conviction specified in subdivision (a) or (b) that occurred before, as well as those occurring after, the effective date of this section, except that this section does not apply to the following:

(1) A misdemeanor violation of subdivision (c) of Section 288.

(2) A misdemeanor falling within the provisions of Section 42002.1 of the Vehicle Code.

(3) An infraction falling within the provisions of Section 42001 of the Vehicle Code.

(e)

(1) A petition for relief under this section shall not be denied due to an unfulfilled order of restitution or restitution fine.

(2) An unfulfilled order of restitution or a restitution fine shall not be grounds for finding that a defendant did not fully comply with and perform the sentence of the court or a finding that a defendant has not lived an honest and upright life and has not conformed to and obeyed the laws of the land.

(3) When the court considers a petition for relief under this section, in its discretion and in the interest of justice, an unpaid order of restitution or restitution fine shall not be grounds for denial of the petition for relief.

(f) A petition for dismissal of an infraction pursuant to this section shall be by written declaration, except upon a showing of compelling need. Dismissal of an infraction shall not be granted under this section unless the prosecuting attorney has been given at least 15 days' notice of the petition for dismissal. It shall be presumed that the prosecuting attorney has received notice if proof of service is filed with the court.

(g) Any determination of amount made by a court under this section shall be valid only if either (1) made under procedures adopted by the Judicial Council or (2) approved by the Judicial Council.

Amended by Stats 2022 ch 734 (SB 1106),s 4, eff. 1/1/2023.
Added by Stats 2021 ch 257 (AB 177),s 28.5, eff. 9/23/2021.
Amended by Stats 2021 ch 209 (AB 1281),s 2, eff. 1/1/2022.
Amended by Stats 2021 ch 257 (AB 177),s 27, eff. 9/23/2021.
Amended by Stats 2013 ch 76 (AB 383),s 153.5, eff. 1/1/2014.
Amended by Stats 2011 ch 304 (SB 428),s 10, eff. 1/1/2012.
Amended by Stats 2011 ch 285 (AB 1402),s 18.5, eff. 1/1/2012, op. 1/1/2012.
Amended by Stats 2011 ch 284 (AB 1384),s 1, eff. 1/1/2012.
Amended by Stats 2010 ch 99 (AB 2582),s 1, eff. 1/1/2011.
Amended by Stats 2010 ch 178 (SB 1115),s 77, eff. 1/1/2011, op. 1/1/2012.
Amended by Stats 2005 ch 22 (SB 1108),s 150, eff. 1/1/2006

Amended by Stats 2001 ch 824 (AB 1700) s 36, eff. 1/1/2002.

Section 1203.4b - Special consideration for defendants who participated in California Conservation Camp Program or county incarcerated individual hand crew

(a)

(1) If a defendant successfully participated in the California Conservation Camp program as an incarcerated individual hand crew member, as determined by the Secretary of the Department of Corrections and Rehabilitation, or successfully participated as a member of a county incarcerated individual hand crew, as determined by the appropriate county authority, or successfully participated at an institutional firehouse, as determined by the Secretary of the Department of Corrections and Rehabilitation, and has been released from custody, the defendant is eligible for relief pursuant to this section, except that incarcerated individuals who have been convicted of any of the following crimes are automatically ineligible for relief pursuant to this section:

(A) Murder.

(B) Kidnapping.

(C) Rape as defined in paragraph (2) or (6) of subdivision (a) of Section 261 or paragraph (1) or (4) of subdivision (a) of Section 262.

(D) Lewd acts on a child under 14 years of age, as defined in Section 288.

(E) Any felony punishable by death or imprisonment in the state prison for life.

(F) Any sex offense requiring registration pursuant to Section 290.

(G) Escape from a secure perimeter within the previous 10 years.

(H) Arson.

(2) Any denial of relief pursuant to this section shall be without prejudice.

(3) For purposes of this subdivision, successful participation in a conservation camp program or a program at an institutional firehouse and successful participation as a member of a county incarcerated individual hand crew, as determined by the appropriate county authority, means the incarcerated individual adequately performed their duties without any conduct that warranted removal from the program.

(b)

(1) The defendant may file a petition for relief with the court in the county where the defendant was sentenced. The court shall provide a copy of the petition to the secretary, or, in the case of a county incarcerated individual hand crew member, the appropriate county authority.

(2) If the secretary or appropriate county authority certifies to the court that the defendant successfully participated in the incarcerated individual conservation camp program, or institutional firehouse, or successfully participated as a member of a county incarcerated individual hand crew, as determined by the appropriate county authority, as specified in subdivision (a), and has been released from custody, the court, in its discretion and in the interests of justice, may issue an order pursuant to subdivision (c).

(3) To be eligible for relief pursuant to this section, the defendant is not required to complete the term of their probation, parole, or supervised release. Notwithstanding any other law, the court, in providing relief pursuant to this section, shall order early termination of probation, parole, or supervised release if the court determines that the defendant has not violated any terms or conditions of probation, parole, or supervised release prior to, and during the pendency of, the petition for relief pursuant to this section.

(4) All convictions for which the defendant is serving a sentence at the time the defendant successfully participates in a program as specified in subdivision (a) are subject to relief pursuant to this section, except that a defendant convicted of any offense listed in subparagraphs (A) to (H), inclusive, of paragraph (1) of subdivision (a) is ineligible for relief pursuant to this section.

(5)

(A) A defendant who is granted an order pursuant to this section shall not be required to disclose the conviction on an application for licensure by any state or local agency.

(B) This paragraph does not apply to an application for licensure by the Commission on Teacher Credentialing, a position as a peace officer, public office, or for contracting with the California State Lottery Commission.

(c)

(1) If the requirements of this section are met, the court, in its discretion and in the interest of justice, may permit the defendant to withdraw the plea of guilty or plea of nolo contendere and enter a plea of not guilty, or, if the defendant has been convicted after a plea of not guilty, the court shall set aside the verdict of guilty, and, in either case, the court shall thereupon dismiss the accusations or information against the defendant and the defendant shall thereafter be released from all penalties and disabilities resulting from the offense of which the defendant has been convicted, except as provided in Section 13555 of the Vehicle Code.

(2) The relief available pursuant to this section shall not be granted if the defendant is currently charged with the commission of any other offense.

(3) The defendant may make the application and change of plea in person or by attorney.

(d) Relief granted pursuant to this section is subject to the following conditions:

(1) In any subsequent prosecution of the defendant for any other offense, the prior conviction may be pleaded and proved and shall have the same effect as if the accusation or information had not been dismissed.

(2) The order shall state, and the defendant shall be informed, that the order does not relieve the defendant of the obligation to disclose the conviction in response to any direct question contained in any questionnaire or application for licensure by the Commission on Teacher Credentialing, a peace officer, public office, or for contracting with the California State Lottery Commission.

(3) Dismissal of an accusation or information pursuant to this section does not permit a person to own, possess, or have in the person's custody or control any firearm or prevent their conviction under Chapter 2 (commencing with Section 29800) of Division 9 of Title 4 of Part 6.

(4) Dismissal of an accusation or information underlying a conviction pursuant to this section does not permit a person prohibited from holding public office as a result of that conviction to hold public office.

(5) Dismissal of an accusation or information pursuant to this section does not release the defendant from the terms and conditions of any unexpired criminal protective order that has been issued by the court pursuant to paragraph (1) of subdivision (i) of Section 136.2, subdivision (j) of Section 273.5, subdivision (l) of Section 368, or subdivision (k) of Section 646.9. These protective orders shall remain in full effect until expiration or until any further order by the court modifying or terminating the order, despite the dismissal of the underlying accusation or information.

(e)

(1) Relief shall not be granted under this section unless the prosecuting attorney has been given 15 days' notice of the petition for relief.

(2) It shall be presumed that the prosecuting attorney has received notice if proof of service is filed with the court.

(f) If, after receiving notice pursuant to subdivision (e), the prosecuting attorney fails to appear and object to a petition for dismissal, the prosecuting attorney may not move to set aside or otherwise appeal the grant of that petition.

Amended by Stats 2023 ch 311 (SB 883),s 8, eff. 1/1/2024.
Amended by Stats 2023 ch 47 (AB 134),s 7, eff. 7/10/2023.
Amended by Stats 2022 ch 734 (SB 1106),s 5, eff. 1/1/2023.
Amended by Stats 2022 ch 771 (AB 160),s 16, eff. 9/29/2022.
Amended by Stats 2022 ch 197 (SB 1493),s 22, eff. 1/1/2023. Not implemented per s 40.
Amended by Stats 2021 ch 434 (SB 827),s 9, eff. 1/1/2022.
Amended by Stats 2021 ch 209 (AB 1281),s 3, eff. 1/1/2022.
Added by Stats 2020 ch 60 (AB 2147),s 2, eff. 1/1/2021.

Section 1203.41 - Relief and conditions

(a) If a defendant is convicted of a felony, the court, in its discretion and in the interest of justice, may order the following relief, subject to the conditions of subdivision (b):

(1) The court may permit the defendant to withdraw their plea of guilty or plea of nolo contendere and enter a plea of not guilty, or, if the defendant has been convicted after a plea of not guilty, the court shall set aside the verdict of guilty, and, in either case, the court shall dismiss the accusations or information against the defendant and the defendant shall be released from all penalties and disabilities resulting from the offense of which they have been convicted, except as provided in Section 13555 of the Vehicle Code.

(2) The relief available under this section may be granted only after the lapse of one year following the defendant's completion of the sentence, if the sentence was imposed pursuant to subparagraph (B) of paragraph (5) of subdivision (h) of Section 1170, or after the lapse of two years following the defendant's completion of the sentence, if the sentence was imposed pursuant to subparagraph (A) of paragraph (5) of subdivision (h) of Section 1170 or if the defendant was sentenced to the state prison.

(3) The relief available under this section may be granted only if the defendant is not on parole or under supervision pursuant to subparagraph (B) of paragraph (5) of subdivision (h) of Section 1170, and is not serving a sentence for, on probation for, or charged with the commission of, an offense.

(4) The defendant shall be informed, either orally or in writing, of the provisions of this section and of their right, if any, to petition for a certificate of rehabilitation and pardon at the time of sentencing.

(5) The defendant may make the application and change of plea in person or by attorney, or by a probation officer authorized in writing.

(6) If the defendant seeks relief under this section for a felony that resulted in a sentence to the state prison, the relief available under this section may only be granted if that felony did not result in a requirement to register as a sex offender pursuant to Chapter 5.5 (commencing with Section 290) of Title 9 of Part 1.

(b) Relief granted pursuant to subdivision (a) is subject to all of the following conditions:

(1) In any subsequent prosecution of the defendant for any other offense, the prior conviction may be pleaded and proved and shall have the same effect as if the accusation or information had not been dismissed.

(2) The order shall state, and the defendant shall be informed, that the order does not relieve them of the obligation to disclose the conviction in response to a direct question contained in a questionnaire or application for public office, for licensure by a state or local agency or by a federally recognized tribe, for enrollment as a provider of in-home supportive services and waiver personal care services pursuant to Article 7 (commencing with Section 12300) of Chapter 3 of Part 3 of Division 9 of the Welfare and Institutions Code or pursuant to Section 14132.95, 14132.952, 14132.956, or 14132.97 of the Welfare and Institutions Code, or for contracting with the California State Lottery Commission.

(3) Dismissal of an accusation or information pursuant to this section does not permit a person to own, possess, or have in their custody or control a firearm or prevent their conviction under Chapter 2 (commencing with Section 29800) of Division 9 of Title 4 of Part 6.

(4) Dismissal of an accusation or information underlying a conviction pursuant to this section does not permit a person prohibited from holding public office as a result of that conviction to hold public office.

(c) This section applies to any conviction specified in subdivision (a) that occurred before, on, or after January 1, 2021.

(d) When the court considers a petition for relief under this section, in its discretion and in the interest of justice, an unpaid order of restitution or restitution fine shall not be grounds for denial of the petition for relief.

(e)

(1) Relief shall not be granted under this section unless the prosecuting attorney has been given 15 days' notice of the petition for relief. The probation officer shall notify the prosecuting attorney when a petition is filed, pursuant to this section.

(2) It shall be presumed that the prosecuting attorney has received notice if proof of service is filed with the court.

(f) If, after receiving notice pursuant to subdivision (e), the prosecuting attorney fails to appear and object to a petition for dismissal, the prosecuting attorney shall not move to set aside or otherwise appeal the grant of that petition.

(g) Relief granted pursuant to this section does not release the defendant from the terms and conditions of any unexpired criminal protective orders that have been issued by the court pursuant to paragraph (1) of subdivision (i) of Section 136.2, subdivision (j) of

Section 273.5, subdivision (l) of Section 368, or subdivision (k) of Section 646.9. These protective orders shall remain in full effect until expiration or until any further order by the court modifying or terminating the order, despite the dismissal of the underlying accusation or information.

(h) Relief granted pursuant to this section does not affect the authority to receive, or take adverse action based on, criminal history information, including the authority to receive certified court records received or evaluated pursuant to Section 1522, 1568.09, 1569.17, or 1596.871 of the Health and Safety Code, or pursuant to any statutory or regulatory provisions that incorporate the criteria of those sections. Relief granted pursuant to this section does not make eligible a person who is otherwise ineligible under state or federal law or regulation to provide, or receive payment for providing, in-home supportive services and waiver personal care services pursuant to Article 7 (commencing with Section 12300) of Chapter 3 of Part 3 of Division 9 of the Welfare and Institutions Code, or pursuant to Section 14132.95, 14132.952, 14132.956, or 14132.97 of the Welfare and Institutions Code.

Amended by Stats 2023 ch 47 (AB 134),s 8, eff. 7/10/2023.
Amended by Stats 2022 ch 842 (SB 1260),s 1.5, eff. 1/1/2023.
Amended by Stats 2022 ch 814 (SB 731),s 5, eff. 1/1/2023.
Amended by Stats 2022 ch 734 (SB 1106),s 6, eff. 1/1/2023.
Added by Stats 2013 ch 787 (AB 651),s 1, eff. 1/1/2014.

Section 1203.42 - Relief for defendants sentenced prior to 2011 Realignment legislation

(a) If a defendant was sentenced prior to the implementation of the 2011 Realignment Legislation for a crime for which the defendant would otherwise have been eligible for sentencing pursuant to subdivision (h) of Section 1170, the court, in its discretion and in the interest of justice, may order the following relief, subject to the conditions of subdivision (b):

(1) The court may permit the defendant to withdraw their plea of guilty or plea of nolo contendere and enter a plea of not guilty, or, if the defendant has been convicted after a plea of not guilty, the court shall set aside the verdict of guilty, and, in either case, the court shall thereupon dismiss the accusations or information against the defendant and the defendant shall be released from all penalties and disabilities resulting from the offense of which they have been convicted, except as provided in Section 13555 of the Vehicle Code.

(2) The relief available under this section may be granted only after the lapse of two years following the defendant's completion of the sentence.

(3) The relief available under this section may be granted only if the defendant is not under supervised release, and is not serving a sentence for, on probation for, or charged with the commission of, an offense.

(4) The defendant may make the application and change of plea in person or by attorney, or by a probation officer authorized in writing.

(b) Relief granted pursuant to subdivision (a) is subject to the following conditions:

(1) In a subsequent prosecution of the defendant for any other offense, the prior conviction may be pleaded and proved and shall have the same effect as if the accusation or information had not been dismissed.

(2) The order shall state, and the defendant shall be informed, that the order does not relieve the defendant of the obligation to disclose the conviction in response to a direct question contained in a questionnaire or application for public office, for licensure by a state or local agency, or for contracting with the California State Lottery Commission.

(3) Dismissal of an accusation or information pursuant to this section does not permit a person to own, possess, or have in their custody or control a firearm or prevent a conviction under Chapter 2 (commencing with Section 29800) of Division 9 of Title 4 of Part 6.

(4) Dismissal of an accusation or information underlying a conviction pursuant to this section does not permit a person prohibited from holding public office as a result of that conviction to hold public office.

(c) When the court considers a petition for relief under this section, in its discretion and in the interest of justice, an unpaid order of restitution or restitution fine shall not be grounds for denial of the petition for relief.

(d)

(1) Relief shall not be granted under this section unless the prosecuting attorney has been given 15 days' notice of the petition for relief. The probation officer shall notify the prosecuting attorney when a petition is filed, pursuant to this section.

(2) It shall be presumed that the prosecuting attorney has received notice if proof of service is filed with the court.

(e) If, after receiving notice pursuant to subdivision (d), the prosecuting attorney fails to appear and object to a petition for dismissal, the prosecuting attorney may not move to set aside or otherwise appeal the grant of that petition.

Amended by Stats 2023 ch 47 (AB 134),s 9, eff. 7/10/2023.
Amended by Stats 2022 ch 734 (SB 1106),s 7, eff. 1/1/2023.
Added by Stats 2017 ch 207 (AB 1115),s 1, eff. 1/1/2018.

Section 1203.425 - [Effective Until 7/1/2024] Monthly review of criminal justice databases; automatic conviction record relief

(a)

(1)

(A) Commencing July 1, 2022, and subject to an appropriation in the annual Budget Act, on a monthly basis, the Department of Justice shall review the records in the statewide criminal justice databases, and based on information in the state summary criminal history repository and the Supervised Release File, shall identify persons with convictions that meet the criteria set forth in subparagraph (B) and are eligible for automatic conviction record relief.

(B) A person is eligible for automatic conviction relief pursuant to this section if they meet all of the following conditions:

(i) The person is not required to register pursuant to the Sex Offender Registration Act.

(ii) The person does not have an active record for local, state, or federal supervision in the Supervised Release File.

(iii) Based upon the information available in the department's record, including disposition dates and sentencing terms, it does not appear that the person is currently serving a sentence for an offense and there is no indication of pending criminal charges.

(iv) Except as otherwise provided in subclause (III) of clause (v), there is no indication that the conviction resulted in a sentence of incarceration in the state prison.

(v) The conviction occurred on or after January 1, 1973, and meets either of the following criteria:

(I) The defendant was sentenced to probation and, based upon the disposition date and the term of probation specified in the department's records, appears to have completed their term of probation without revocation.

(II) The defendant was convicted of an infraction or misdemeanor, was not granted probation, and, based upon the disposition date and the term specified in the department's records, the defendant appears to have completed their sentence, and at least one calendar year has elapsed since the date of judgment.

(2)

(A) Except as specified in subdivision (b), the department shall grant relief, including dismissal of a conviction, to a person identified pursuant to paragraph (1) without requiring a petition or motion by a party for that relief if the relevant information is present in the department's electronic records.

(B) The state summary criminal history information shall include, directly next to or below the entry or entries regarding the person's criminal record, a note stating "relief granted," listing the date that the department granted relief and this section. This note shall be included in all statewide criminal databases with a record of the conviction.

(C) Except as otherwise provided in paragraph (4) and in Section 13555 of the Vehicle Code, a person granted conviction relief pursuant to this section shall be released from all penalties and disabilities resulting from the offense of which the person has been convicted.

(3)

(A) Commencing July 1, 2022, and subject to an appropriation in the annual Budget Act, on a monthly basis, the department shall electronically submit a notice to the superior court having jurisdiction over the criminal case, informing the court of all cases for which a complaint was filed in that jurisdiction and for which relief was granted pursuant to this section. Commencing on January 1, 2023, for any record retained by the court pursuant to Section 68152 of the Government Code, except as provided in paragraph (4), the court shall not disclose information concerning a conviction granted relief pursuant to this section or Section 1203.4, 1203.4a, 1203.41, or 1203.42, to any person or entity, in any format, except to the person whose conviction was granted relief or a criminal justice agency, as defined in Section 851.92.

(B) If probation is transferred pursuant to Section 1203.9, the department shall electronically submit a notice as provided in subparagraph (A) to both the transferring court and any subsequent receiving court. The electronic notice shall be in a mutually agreed upon format.

(C) If a receiving court reduces a felony to a misdemeanor pursuant to subdivision (b) of Section 17, or dismisses a conviction pursuant to law, including, but not limited to, Section 1203.4, 1203.4a, 1203.41, 1203.42, 1203.43, or 1203.49, it shall furnish a disposition report to the department with the original case number and CII number from the transferring court. The department shall electronically submit a notice to the superior court that sentenced the defendant. If probation is transferred multiple times, the department shall electronically submit a notice to all other involved courts. The electronic notice shall be in a mutually agreed upon format.

(D) If a court receives notification from the department pursuant to subparagraph (B), the court shall update its records to reflect the reduction or dismissal. If a court receives notification that a case was dismissed pursuant to this section or Section 1203.4, 1203.4a, 1203.41, or 1203.42, the court shall update its records to reflect the dismissal and shall not disclose information concerning a conviction granted relief to any person or entity, in any format, except to the person whose conviction was granted relief or a criminal justice agency, as defined in Section 851.92.

(4) Relief granted pursuant to this section is subject to the following conditions:

(A) Relief granted pursuant to this section does not relieve a person of the obligation to disclose a criminal conviction in response to a direct question contained in a questionnaire or application for employment as a peace officer, as defined in Section 830.

(B) Relief granted pursuant to this section does not relieve a person of the obligation to disclose the conviction in response to a direct question contained in a questionnaire or application for public office, for enrollment as a provider of in-home supportive services and waiver personal care services pursuant to Article 7 (commencing with Section 12300) of Chapter 3 of Part 3 of Division 9 of the Welfare and Institutions Code or pursuant to Section 14132.95, 14132.952, 14132.956, or 14132.97 of the Welfare and Institutions Code, or for contracting with the California State Lottery Commission.

(C) Relief granted pursuant to this section has no effect on the ability of a criminal justice agency, as defined in Section 851.92, to access and use records that are granted relief to the same extent that would have been permitted for a criminal justice agency had relief not been granted.

(D) Relief granted pursuant to this section does not limit the jurisdiction of the court over a subsequently filed motion to amend the record, petition or motion for postconviction relief, or collateral attack on a conviction for which relief has been granted pursuant to this section.

(E) Relief granted pursuant to this section does not affect a person's authorization to own, possess, or have in the person's custody or control a firearm, or the person's susceptibility to conviction under Chapter 2 (commencing with Section 29800) of Division 9 of Title 4 of Part 6, if the criminal conviction would otherwise affect this authorization or susceptibility.

(F) Relief granted pursuant to this section does not affect a prohibition from holding public office that would otherwise apply under law as a result of the criminal conviction.

(G) Relief granted pursuant to this section does not release a person from the terms and conditions of any unexpired criminal protective order that has been issued by the court pursuant to paragraph (1) of subdivision (i) of Section 136.2, subdivision (j) of Section 273.5, subdivision (l) of Section 368, or subdivision (k) of Section 646.9. These protective orders shall remain in full effect until expiration or until any further order by the court modifying or terminating the order, despite the dismissal of the underlying conviction.

(H) Relief granted pursuant to this section does not affect the authority to receive, or take adverse action based on, criminal history information, including the authority to receive certified court records received or evaluated pursuant to Section 1522, 1568.09, 1569.17, or 1596.871 of the Health and Safety Code, or pursuant to any statutory or regulatory provisions that incorporate the criteria of those sections.

(I) Relief granted pursuant to this section does not make eligible a person who is otherwise ineligible under state or federal law or regulation to provide, or receive payment for providing, in-home supportive services and waiver personal care services pursuant to Article 7 (commencing with Section 12300) of Chapter 3 of Part 3 of Division 9 of the Welfare and Institutions Code, or pursuant to Section 14132.95, 14132.952, 14132.956, or 14132.97 of the Welfare and Institutions Code.

(J) In a subsequent prosecution of the defendant for any other offense, the prior conviction may be pleaded and proved and shall have the same effect as if the relief had not been granted.

(K)

(i) Relief granted pursuant to this section does not affect the authority to receive, or take adverse action based on, criminal history information, including the authority to receive certified court records received or evaluated pursuant to Article 1 (commencing with Section 44000) of Chapter 1, Article 3 (commencing with Section 44240) and Article 8 (commencing with Section 44330) of Chapter 2, Article 1 (commencing with Section 44420) of Chapter 3, Article 3 (commencing with Section 44930) of Chapter 4, and Article 1 (commencing with Section 45100) and Article 6 (commencing with Section 45240) of Chapter 5, of Part 25 of Division 3 of Title 2 of the Education Code, or pursuant to any statutory or regulatory provisions that relate to, incorporate, expand upon, or interpret the authority of those provisions.

(ii) Notwithstanding clause (i) or any other law, information relating to a conviction for a controlled substance offense listed in Section 11350 or 11377, or former Section 11500 or 11500.5, of the Health and Safety Code that is more than five years old, for which relief is granted pursuant to this section, shall not be disclosed.

(5) This section shall not limit petitions, motions, or orders for relief in a criminal case, as required or authorized by any other law, including, but not limited to, Sections 1203.4 and 1204.4a.

(6) Commencing July 1, 2022, and subject to an appropriation in the annual Budget Act, the department shall annually publish statistics for each county regarding the total number of convictions granted relief pursuant to this section and the total number of convictions prohibited from automatic relief pursuant to subdivision (b), on the OpenJustice Web portal, as defined in Section 13010.

(b)

(1) The prosecuting attorney or probation department may, no later than 90 calendar days before the date of a person's eligibility for relief pursuant to this section, file a petition to prohibit the department from granting automatic relief pursuant to this section, based on a showing that granting that relief would pose a substantial threat to the public safety. If probation was transferred pursuant to Section 1203.9, the prosecuting attorney or probation department in either the receiving county or the transferring county shall file the petition in the county of current jurisdiction.

(2) The court shall give notice to the defendant and conduct a hearing on the petition within 45 days after the petition is filed.

(3) At a hearing on the petition pursuant to this subdivision, the defendant, the probation department, the prosecuting attorney, and the arresting agency, through the prosecuting attorney, may present evidence to the court. Notwithstanding Sections 1538.5 and 1539, the hearing may be heard and determined upon declarations, affidavits, police investigative reports, copies of state summary criminal history information and local summary criminal history information, or any other evidence submitted by the parties that is material, reliable, and relevant.

(4) The prosecutor or probation department has the initial burden of proof to show that granting conviction relief would pose a substantial threat to the public safety. In determining whether granting relief would pose a substantial threat to the public safety, the court may consider any relevant factors including, but not limited to, either of the following:

(A) Declarations or evidence regarding the offense for which a grant of relief is being contested.

(B) The defendant's record of arrests and convictions.

(5) If the court finds that the prosecutor or probation department has satisfied the burden of proof, the burden shifts to the defendant to show that the hardship of not obtaining relief outweighs the threat to the public safety of providing relief. In determining whether the defendant's hardship outweighs the threat to the public safety, the court may consider any relevant factors including, but not limited to, either of the following:

(A) The hardship to the defendant that has been caused by the conviction and that would be caused if relief is not granted.

(B) Declarations or evidence regarding the defendant's good character.

(6) If the court grants a petition pursuant to this subdivision, the court shall furnish a disposition report to the Department of Justice pursuant to Section 13151, stating that relief pursuant to this section was denied, and the department shall not grant relief pursuant to this section. If probation was transferred pursuant to Section 1203.9, the department shall electronically submit a notice to the transferring court, and, if probation was transferred multiple times, to all other involved courts.

(7) A person denied relief pursuant to this section may continue to be eligible for relief pursuant to Section 1203.4 or 1203.4a. If the court subsequently grants relief pursuant to one of those sections, the court shall furnish a disposition report to the Department of Justice pursuant to Section 13151, stating that relief was granted pursuant to the applicable section, and the department shall grant relief pursuant to that section. If probation was transferred pursuant to Section 1203.9, the department shall electronically submit a notice that relief was granted pursuant to the applicable section to the transferring court and, if probation was transferred multiple times, to all other involved courts.

(c) At the time of sentencing, the court shall advise a defendant, either orally or in writing, of the provisions of this section and of the defendant's right, if any, to petition for a certificate of rehabilitation and pardon.

(d) This section shall become inoperative on July 1, 2024, and, as of January 1, 2025, is repealed.

Amended by Stats 2023 ch 47 (AB 134),s 10, eff. 7/10/2023.
Amended by Stats 2022 ch 842 (SB 1260),s 2, eff. 1/1/2023.
Amended by Stats 2022 ch 814 (SB 731),s 6, eff. 1/1/2023.
Amended by Stats 2022 ch 58 (AB 200),s 13, eff. 6/30/2022.
Amended by Stats 2021 ch 209 (AB 1281),s 4.3, eff. 1/1/2022.
Amended by Stats 2021 ch 202 (AB 898),s 1, eff. 1/1/2022.
Amended by Stats 2021 ch 80 (AB 145),s 4, eff. 7/16/2021.

Amended by Stats 2020 ch 29 (SB 118),s 16, eff. 8/6/2020.
Added by Stats 2019 ch 578 (AB 1076),s 8, eff. 1/1/2020.
This section is set out more than once due to postponed, multiple, or conflicting amendments.
Section 1203.425 - [Operative 7/1/2024] Monthly review of criminal justice databases; automatic conviction record relief
(a)

    (1)

        (A) Commencing July 1, 2024, and subject to an appropriation in the annual Budget Act, on a monthly basis, the Department of Justice shall review the records in the statewide criminal justice databases, and based on information in the state summary criminal history repository and the Supervised Release File, shall identify persons with convictions that meet the criteria set forth in subparagraph (B) and are eligible for automatic conviction record relief.

        (B) A person is eligible for automatic conviction relief pursuant to this section if they meet all of the following conditions:

            (i) The person is not required to register pursuant to the Sex Offender Registration Act.

            (ii) The person does not have an active record for local, state, or federal supervision in the Supervised Release File.

            (iii) Based upon the information available in the department's record, including disposition dates and sentencing terms, it does not appear that the person is currently serving a sentence for an offense and there is no indication of pending criminal charges.

            (iv) The conviction meets either of the following criteria:

                (I) The conviction occurred on or after January 1, 1973, and meets either of the following criteria:

                    (ia) The defendant was sentenced to probation and, based upon the disposition date and the term of probation specified in the department's records, appears to have completed their term of probation without revocation.

                    (ib) The defendant was convicted of an infraction or misdemeanor other than one eligible under sub-subclause (ia), and, based upon the disposition date and the term specified in the department's records, the defendant appears to have completed their sentence, and at least one calendar year has elapsed since the date of judgment.

                (II) The conviction occurred on or after January 1, 2005, the defendant was convicted of a felony other than one for which the defendant completed probation without revocation, and based upon the disposition date and the sentence specified in the department's records, appears to have completed all terms of incarceration, probation, mandatory supervision, postrelease community supervision, and parole, and a period of four years has elapsed since the date on which the defendant completed probation or supervision for that conviction and during which the defendant was not convicted of a new felony offense. This subclause does not apply to a conviction of a serious felony defined in subdivision (c) of Section 1192.7, a violent felony as defined in Section 667.5, or a felony offense requiring registration pursuant to Chapter 5.5 (commencing with Section 290) of Title 9 of Part 1.

    (2)

        (A) Except as specified in subdivision (b), the department shall grant relief, including dismissal of a conviction, to a person identified pursuant to paragraph (1) without requiring a petition or motion by a party for that relief if the relevant information is present in the department's electronic records.

        (B) The state summary criminal history information shall include, directly next to or below the entry or entries regarding the person's criminal record, a note stating "relief granted," listing the date that the department granted relief and this section. This note shall be included in all statewide criminal databases with a record of the conviction.

        (C) Except as otherwise provided in paragraph (4) and in Section 13555 of the Vehicle Code, a person granted conviction relief pursuant to this section shall be released from all penalties and disabilities resulting from the offense of which the person has been convicted.

    (3)

        (A) Commencing July 1, 2022, and subject to an appropriation in the annual Budget Act, on a monthly basis, the department shall electronically submit a notice to the superior court having jurisdiction over the criminal case, informing the court of all cases for which a complaint was filed in that jurisdiction and for which relief was granted pursuant to this section. Commencing on January 1, 2023, for any record retained by the court pursuant to Section 68152 of the Government Code, except as provided in paragraph (4), the court shall not disclose information concerning a conviction granted relief pursuant to this section or Section 1203.4, 1203.4a, 1203.41, or 1203.42, to any person or entity, in any format, except to the person whose conviction was granted relief or a criminal justice agency, as defined in Section 851.92.

        (B) If probation is transferred pursuant to Section 1203.9, the department shall electronically submit a notice as provided in subparagraph (A) to both the transferring court and any subsequent receiving court. The electronic notice shall be in a mutually agreed upon format.

        (C) If a receiving court reduces a felony to a misdemeanor pursuant to subdivision (b) of Section 17, or dismisses a conviction pursuant to law, including, but not limited to, Section 1203.4, 1203.4a, 1203.41, 1203.42, 1203.43, or 1203.49, it shall furnish a disposition report to the department with the original case number and CII number from the transferring court. The department shall electronically submit a notice to the superior court that sentenced the defendant. If probation is transferred multiple times, the department shall electronically submit a notice to all other involved courts. The electronic notice shall be in a mutually agreed upon format.

        (D) If a court receives notification from the department pursuant to subparagraph (B), the court shall update its records to reflect the reduction or dismissal. If a court receives notification that a case was dismissed pursuant to this section or Section 1203.4, 1203.4a, 1203.41, or 1203.42, the court shall update its records to reflect the dismissal and shall not disclose information concerning a conviction granted relief to any person or entity, in any format, except to the person whose conviction was granted relief or a criminal justice agency, as defined in Section 851.92.

    (4) Relief granted pursuant to this section is subject to the following conditions:

        (A) Relief granted pursuant to this section does not relieve a person of the obligation to disclose a criminal conviction in response to a direct question contained in a questionnaire or application for employment as a peace officer, as defined in Section 830.

(B) Relief granted pursuant to this section does not relieve a person of the obligation to disclose the conviction in response to a direct question contained in a questionnaire or application for public office, for enrollment as a provider of in-home supportive services and waiver personal care services pursuant to Article 7 (commencing with Section 12300) of Chapter 3 of Part 3 of Division 9 of the Welfare and Institutions Code or pursuant to Section 14132.95, 14132.952, 14132.956, or 14132.97 of the Welfare and Institutions Code, or for contracting with the California State Lottery Commission.

(C) Relief granted pursuant to this section has no effect on the ability of a criminal justice agency, as defined in Section 851.92, to access and use records that are granted relief to the same extent that would have been permitted for a criminal justice agency had relief not been granted.

(D) Relief granted pursuant to this section does not limit the jurisdiction of the court over a subsequently filed motion to amend the record, petition or motion for postconviction relief, or collateral attack on a conviction for which relief has been granted pursuant to this section.

(E) Relief granted pursuant to this section does not affect a person's authorization to own, possess, or have in the person's custody or control a firearm, or the person's susceptibility to conviction under Chapter 2 (commencing with Section 29800) of Division 9 of Title 4 of Part 6, if the criminal conviction would otherwise affect this authorization or susceptibility.

(F) Relief granted pursuant to this section does not affect a prohibition from holding public office that would otherwise apply under law as a result of the criminal conviction.

(G) Relief granted pursuant to this section does not release a person from the terms and conditions of any unexpired criminal protective order that has been issued by the court pursuant to paragraph (1) of subdivision (i) of Section 136.2, subdivision (j) of Section 273.5, subdivision (l) of Section 368, or subdivision (k) of Section 646.9. These protective orders shall remain in full effect until expiration or until any further order by the court modifying or terminating the order, despite the dismissal of the underlying conviction.

(H) Relief granted pursuant to this section does not affect the authority to receive, or take adverse action based on, criminal history information, including the authority to receive certified court records received or evaluated pursuant to Section 1522, 1568.09, 1569.17, or 1596.871 of the Health and Safety Code, or pursuant to any statutory or regulatory provisions that incorporate the criteria of those sections.

(I) Relief granted pursuant to this section does not make eligible a person who is otherwise ineligible under state or federal law or regulation to provide, or receive payment for providing, in-home supportive services and waiver personal care services pursuant to Article 7 (commencing with Section 12300) of Chapter 3 of Part 3 of Division 9 of the Welfare and Institutions Code, or pursuant to Section 14132.95, 14132.952, 14132.956, or 14132.97 of the Welfare and Institutions Code.

(J) In a subsequent prosecution of the defendant for any other offense, the prior conviction may be pleaded and proved and shall have the same effect as if the relief had not been granted.

(K)

(i) Relief granted pursuant to this section does not affect the authority to receive, or take adverse action based on, criminal history information, including the authority to receive certified court records received or evaluated pursuant to Article 1 (commencing with Section 44000) of Chapter 1, Article 3 (commencing with Section 44240) and Article 8 (commencing with Section 44330) of Chapter 2, Article 1 (commencing with Section 44420) of Chapter 3, Article 3 (commencing with Section 44930) of Chapter 4, Article 1 (commencing with Section 45100) and Article 6 (commencing with Section 45240) of Chapter 5, of Part 25 of Division 3 of Title 2 of the Education Code, or pursuant to any statutory or regulatory provisions that relate to, incorporate, expand upon, or interpret the authority of those provisions.

(ii) Notwithstanding clause (i) or any other law, information for a conviction for a controlled substance offense listed in Section 11350 or 11377, or former Section 11500 or 11500.5, of the Health and Safety Code that is more than five years old, for which relief is granted pursuant to this section, shall not be disclosed.

(L) Relief granted pursuant to this section does not release the defendant from the terms and conditions of any unexpired criminal protective orders that have been issued by the court pursuant to paragraph (1) of subdivision (i) of Section 136.2, subdivision (j) of Section 273.5, subdivision (l) of Section 368, or subdivision (k) of Section 646.9. These protective orders shall remain in full effect until expiration or until any further order by the court modifying or terminating the order, despite the dismissal of the underlying accusation or information.

(5) This section does not limit petitions, motions, or orders for relief in a criminal case, as required or authorized by any other law, including, but not limited to, Sections 1016.5, 1203.4, 1203.4a, 1203.4b, 1203.41, 1203.42, 1203.49, and 1473.7. This section does not limit petitions for a certificate of rehabilitation or pardon pursuant to Chapter 3.5 (commencing with Section 4852.01) of Title 6 of Part 3.

(6) Commencing July 1, 2022, and subject to an appropriation in the annual Budget Act, the department shall annually publish statistics for each county regarding the total number of convictions granted relief pursuant to this section and the total number of convictions prohibited from automatic relief pursuant to subdivision (b), on the OpenJustice Web portal, as defined in Section 13010.

(7) Upon request from the subject of the record, the department shall provide confirmation that relief was granted pursuant to this section.

(b)

(1) The prosecuting attorney or probation department may, no later than 90 calendar days before the date of a person's eligibility for relief pursuant to this section, file a petition to prohibit the department from granting automatic relief pursuant to this section, based on a showing that granting that relief would pose a substantial threat to the public safety. If probation was transferred pursuant to Section 1203.9, the prosecuting attorney or probation department in either the receiving county or the transferring county shall file the petition in the county of current jurisdiction.

(2) The court shall give notice to the defendant and conduct a hearing on the petition within 45 days after the petition is filed.

(3) At a hearing on the petition pursuant to this subdivision, the defendant, the probation department, the prosecuting attorney, and the arresting agency, through the prosecuting attorney, may present evidence to the court. Notwithstanding Sections 1538.5 and 1539, the hearing may be heard and determined upon declarations, affidavits, police investigative reports, copies of state summary criminal history information and local summary criminal history information, or any other evidence submitted by the parties that is material, reliable, and relevant.

(4) The prosecutor or probation department has the initial burden of proof to show that granting conviction relief would pose a substantial threat to the public safety. In determining whether granting relief would pose a substantial threat to the public safety, the court may consider any relevant factors, including, but not limited to, either of the following:

(A) Declarations or evidence regarding the offense for which a grant of relief is being contested.

(B) The defendant's record of arrests and convictions.

(5) If the court finds that the prosecutor or probation department has satisfied the burden of proof, the burden shifts to the defendant to show that the hardship of not obtaining relief outweighs the threat to the public safety of providing relief. In determining whether the defendant's hardship outweighs the threat to the public safety, the court may consider any relevant factors, including, but not limited to, either of the following:

(A) The hardship to the defendant that has been caused by the conviction and that would be caused if relief is not granted.

(B) Declarations or evidence regarding the defendant's good character.

(6) If the court grants a petition pursuant to this subdivision, the court shall furnish a disposition report to the Department of Justice pursuant to Section 13151, stating that relief pursuant to this section was denied, and the department shall not grant relief pursuant to this section. If probation was transferred pursuant to Section 1203.9, the department shall electronically submit a notice to the transferring court, and, if probation was transferred multiple times, to all other involved courts.

(7) A person denied relief pursuant to this section may continue to be eligible for relief pursuant to law, including, but not limited to, Section 1203.4, 1203.4a, 1203.4b, or 1203.41. If the court subsequently grants relief pursuant to one of those sections, the court shall furnish a disposition report to the Department of Justice pursuant to Section 13151, stating that relief was granted pursuant to the applicable section, and the department shall grant relief pursuant to that section. If probation was transferred pursuant to Section 1203.9, the department shall electronically submit a notice that relief was granted pursuant to the applicable section to the transferring court and, if probation was transferred multiple times, to all other involved courts.

(c) At the time of sentencing, the court shall advise a defendant, either orally or in writing, of the provisions of this section and of the defendant's right, if any, to petition for a certificate of rehabilitation and pardon.

(d) This section shall become operative on July 1, 2024.

Amended by Stats 2023 ch 444 (AB 567),s 1, eff. 1/1/2024.
Amended by Stats 2023 ch 131 (AB 1754),s 159, eff. 1/1/2024.
Amended by Stats 2023 ch 47 (AB 134),s 11, eff. 7/10/2023.
Amended by Stats 2022 ch 842 (SB 1260),s 3, eff. 1/1/2023.
Added by Stats 2022 ch 814 (SB 731),s 7, eff. 1/1/2023.

Section 1203.426 - [Repealed]
Repealed by Stats 2023 ch 47 (AB 134),s 12, eff. 7/10/2023.
Added by Stats 2022 ch 494 (AB 1803),s 1, eff. 1/1/2023.

Section 1203.43 - Withdrawal of certain pleas of guilty or nolo contendere
(a)

(1) The Legislature finds and declares that the statement in Section 1000.4, that "successful completion of a deferred entry of judgment program shall not, without the defendant's consent, be used in any way that could result in the denial of any employment, benefit, license, or certificate" constitutes misinformation about the actual consequences of making a plea in the case of some defendants, including all noncitizen defendants, because the disposition of the case may cause adverse consequences, including adverse immigration consequences.

(2) Accordingly, the Legislature finds and declares that based on this misinformation and the potential harm, the defendant's prior plea is invalid.

(b) For the above-specified reason, in any case in which a defendant was granted deferred entry of judgment on or after January 1, 1997, has performed satisfactorily during the period in which deferred entry of judgment was granted, and for whom the criminal charge or charges were dismissed pursuant to Section 1000.3, the court shall, upon request of the defendant, permit the defendant to withdraw the plea of guilty or nolo contendere and enter a plea of not guilty, and the court shall dismiss the complaint or information against the defendant. If court records showing the case resolution are no longer available, the defendant's declaration, under penalty of perjury, that the charges were dismissed after he or she completed the requirements for deferred entry of judgment, shall be presumed to be true if the defendant has submitted a copy of his or her state summary criminal history information maintained by the Department of Justice that either shows that the defendant successfully completed the deferred entry of judgment program or that the record is incomplete in that it does not show a final disposition. For purposes of this section, a final disposition means that the state summary criminal history information shows either a dismissal after completion of the program or a sentence after termination of the program.

Added by Stats 2015 ch 646 (AB 1352),s 1, eff. 1/1/2016.

Section 1203.44 - [Effective Until 7/1/2029] Secured Residential Treatment Pilot Program
(a) The Counties of Sacramento and Yolo may offer a voluntary secured residential treatment pilot program, known as "Hope California," consistent with this section for individuals suffering from substance use disorders (SUDs) who have been convicted of drug-motivated felony crimes that qualify pursuant to the criteria and conditions described in subdivisions (b) and (c). If offered, the pilot programs shall align with the resolutions adopted by the counties in recognition of the goal of ensuring that people with behavioral health conditions receive treatment out of custody wherever possible. The counties may offer the pilot program to eligible individuals if the program meets all of the following conditions:

(1) The program facility is licensed by the State Department of Health Care Services as an alcoholism or drug abuse recovery or treatment facility pursuant to Chapter 7.5 (commencing with Section 11834.01) of Part 2 of Division 10.5 of the Health and Safety Code.

(2)

(A) The program facility is a clinical setting managed and staffed by the county's health and human services agency (HHSA) with oversight provided by the county's probation department.

(B) The program facility shall not be a jail, prison, or other correctional setting.

(C) The program facility shall be secured but shall not include a lockdown setting.

(3) The individual, upon a judge pronouncing a sentence to be served in a county jail or state prison, shall choose and consent to participate in the voluntary program in lieu of incarceration.

(4) The program is limited to one facility site per county.

(5) The State Department of Health Care Services monitors the program facility to ensure the health, safety, and well-being of program participants.

(6) The State Department of Health Care Services has authority to access the program facility to investigate complaints by program participants and to ensure the facility complies with applicable statutes and regulations.

(7) The program facility ensures that participants have visitation rights, including through the use of a telephone.

(8) The county develops and staffs the program in partnership with relevant community-based organizations and drug treatment service providers to provide support services, including, but not limited to, employment skill assessments, money management, technology education, tutoring, career planning, developing resumes and cover letters, and searching and applying for employment.

(9) HHSA ensures that a risk, needs, and biopsychosocial assessment, utilizing the Multidimensional Assessment of the American Society of Addiction Medicine (ASAM), as part of the ASAM Criteria, be performed for each individual identified as a candidate for the program.

(10) The participant's treatment, in terms of length and intensity, within the program is based on the findings of the risk, needs, and biopsychosocial assessment and the recommendations of treatment providers that may include an addiction medicine physician.

(11) The program adopts the Treatment Criteria of ASAM. The program may take into consideration evolving best practices in the SUD treatment community.

(12) The program has a comprehensive written curriculum that informs the operations of the program and outlines the treatment and intervention modalities.

(13) The program provides an individualized, medically assisted treatment plan for each resident, including, but not limited to, medically assisted treatment options and counseling based on the recommendations of a substance use disorder specialist, which may include a medical doctor or doctor of osteopathy specializing in addiction medicine.

(14) A judge determines the length of the treatment program after being informed by, and based on, the risk, needs, and biopsychosocial assessment and recommendations of treatment providers. After leaving the secured residential treatment facility, the participant continues outpatient treatment for a period of time and may also be referred to a "step-down" residential treatment facility, subject to the time limit described in paragraph (2) of subdivision (c).

(15) A judge shall also determine that the program will be carried out in lieu of a jail or prison sentence after making a finding that the defendant's decision to choose the alternative treatment program is knowing, intelligent, and voluntary.

(16) The program provides, for each participant successfully leaving the program, a comprehensive continuum of care plan that includes recommendations for outpatient care, counseling, housing recommendations, and other vital components of successful recovery.

(17) To the extent permitted under federal and state law, treatment provided to a participant during the program is reimbursable under the Medi-Cal program, if the participant is a Medi-Cal beneficiary and the treatment is a covered benefit under the Medi-Cal program. If treatment services provided to a participant during the program are not reimbursable under the Medi-Cal program or through the participant's personal health care coverage, funds allocated to the state from the 2021 Multistate Opioid Settlement Agreement, subject to an appropriation by the Legislature, may be used to reimburse those treatment services to the extent consistent with the terms of the Settlement Agreement and the Final Judgment (People v. McKinsey & Co. (Alameda County Superior Court, No. RG21087649, Feb. 4, 2021)).

(18)

(A) An outcomes assessment of the secured residential treatment pilot program is completed by an independent evaluator and submitted to the Assembly Committee on Health, the Assembly Committee on Public Safety, the Senate Committee on Health, the Senate Committee on Public Safety, and the Legislature by October 1, 2028.

(B) The outcomes assessment shall include pilot program data, including overall data and data by county, and shall include, but not be limited to, all of the following:

(i) A summary of the pertinent data collected under paragraphs (19) and (20) over the course of the pilot program.

(ii) The clinical efficacy of the secured residential treatment pilot program based on the data collected under paragraphs (19) and (20).

(iii) The effects of the secured residential treatment pilot program on participant recidivism and sustainable recovery.

(iv) A recommendation for the continuation and expansion of the secured residential treatment pilot project model beyond the pilot program.

(C) The outcomes assessment shall not be performed or managed by the State Department of Health Care Services but may be performed by a postsecondary institution.

(D) The independent evaluator may be provided with criminal offender record information, if necessary for the completion of the outcomes assessment, as provided in Section 13202.

(19) The county collects and monitors all of the following data for participants in the program:

(A) The participant's demographic information, including age, gender, race, ethnicity, marital status, familial status, and employment status.

(B) The participant's criminal history.

(C) The participant's risk level, as determined by the risk, needs, and biopsychosocial assessment.

(D) The treatment provided to the participant during the program, and if the participant completed that treatment.

(E) The participant's outcome at the time of program completion, six months after completion, and one year after completion, including subsequent arrests and convictions.

(20) The county reports all of the following information annually to the State Department of Health Care Services and, in compliance with Section 9795 of the Government Code, to the Legislature, excluding any personally identifiable information of participants:

(A) The risk, needs, and biopsychosocial assessment tool used for the program.

(B) The curriculum used by each program.

(C) The number of participants with a program length other than one year and the alternative program lengths used.

(D) Individual data on the number of participants participating in the program.

(E) Individual data for the items described in paragraph (19).

(F) A one- and three-year evaluation of the number of subsequent arrests and convictions of the participants.

(b)

(1) Eligible drug-motivated crimes shall include any felony crime other than the following:

(A) Sex crimes listed in subdivision (c) of Section 290.

(B) A "serious felony" as defined in subdivision (c) of Section 1192.7 or in Section 1192.8.

(C) A "violent felony" as defined in subdivision (c) of Section 667.5.

(D) "Domestic violence" as defined in the Domestic Violence Prevention Act (Division 10 (commencing with Section 6200) of the Family Code).

(E) Driving under the influence in violation of Section 191.5 of this code or Section 23152, 23153, 23550, or 23550.5 of the Vehicle Code.

(2) Notwithstanding paragraph (1), a "nonviolent drug possession offense" specified in subdivision (a) of Section 1210 may not be diverted pursuant to this program.

(c)

(1) At the time of sentencing or pronouncement of judgment in which sentencing is imposed, the judge shall offer the defendant voluntary participation in the pilot program, as an alternative to a jail or prison sentence that the judge would otherwise impose, consistent with the other provisions of this section and if all of the following conditions are met:

(A) The defendant's crime was caused in whole or in part by the defendant's SUD.

(B) The defendant's crime meets the criteria described in subdivision (b).

(C) The judge makes their determination based on the recommendations of the treatment providers who conducted the assessment, on a finding by HHSA that the defendant's participation in the program would be appropriate, and on the report described in subdivision (d).

(2) The amount of time in the secured residential treatment facility shall be determined by the recommendations of the treatment providers who conducted the assessment. The amount of time, combined with any outpatient treatment or "step-down" residential treatment pursuant to the program, shall not exceed the term of imprisonment to which the defendant would otherwise be sentenced, not including any additional term of imprisonment for enhancements, for the drug-motivated crime. The court shall not place the defendant on probation for the underlying offense. The defendant shall be eligible to receive credits pursuant to Section 4019.

(3) During the period that an individual is participating in the pilot program, the individual shall be on supervision with the probation department.

(d) To assist the court in making the determination as to whether to offer the defendant placement in the secured residential treatment program pursuant to subdivision (c), a report shall be prepared with input from any of the interested parties, including the district attorney, the attorney for the participant, the probation department, HHSA, and any contracted drug treatment program provider.

(e) If, at any time during the individual's participation in the program, it is determined by the treatment providers or program administrators that continued participation in the program would not be in the best interests of the individual, other participants, or the program itself, the treatment providers or program administrators may recommend to the court that the individual's participation be terminated and that the individual be transferred out of the secured residential treatment program.

(f) If the court, based on the recommendations of the treatment providers or program administrators, determines that the participant should be transferred out of the secured residential treatment phase of the program prior to the end of the original order, the court shall make that subsequent order, and the participant shall complete the remainder of the original sentence imposed prior to their consent to enter the program.

(g) If, at any time during the individual's participation in the program, the individual determines that they no longer wish to participate in the program, the individual may make a request to the court for termination of their participation and be transferred out of the secured residential treatment program to complete the remainder of their originally imposed sentence after accounting for any credits to which the individual is entitled pursuant to Section 4019.

(h) If the treatment providers make a recommendation to the court that the participant should be released prior to the end of the original order based on the treatment providers' assessment that the participant no longer needs to be in the secured residential treatment program, the court shall make that subsequent order, and paragraph (16) of subdivision (a) shall apply.

(i) If the participant successfully completes the court-ordered drug treatment pursuant to this program, the conviction shall be set aside, and the court shall dismiss the accusation or information against the participant. The court shall also have discretion to set aside the conviction and to dismiss the accusation or information of any previous drug possession or drug use crimes on the participant's record, including those offenses listed in Sections 11350, 11364, 11377, and 11550 of the Health and Safety Code. A participant's successful completion of treatment shall be defined and determined by the treatment providers and not by the court, district attorney's office, or probation department and does not require the participant to complete the duration of the treatment originally ordered by the court.

(j) The court shall ensure that the rights of any victim pursuant to Section 28 of Article I of the California Constitution (Marsy's Law) are honored before setting aside the conviction and dismissing the accusation or information.

(k) This section shall remain in effect only until July 1, 2029, and as of that date is repealed unless a later enacted statute that is enacted before July 1, 2029, deletes or extends that date.

Added by Stats 2023 ch 685 (AB 1360),s 2, eff. 1/1/2024.

Section 1203.45 - Petition for sealing of records by person under age of 18 years at time of commission of misdemeanor

(a) When a person was under 18 years of age at the time of commission of a misdemeanor and is eligible for, or has previously received, the relief provided by Section 1203.4 or 1203.4a, that person, in a proceeding under Section 1203.4 or 1203.4a, or a separate proceeding, may petition the court for an order sealing the record of conviction and other official records in the case, including records of arrests resulting in the criminal proceeding and records relating to other offenses charged in the accusatory pleading, whether the defendant was acquitted or charges were dismissed. If the court finds that the person was under 18 years of age at the time of the commission of the misdemeanor, and is eligible for relief under Section 1203.4 or 1203.4a or has previously received that relief, it may issue its order granting the relief prayed for. Thereafter the conviction, arrest, or other proceeding shall be deemed not to have occurred, and the petitioner may answer accordingly any question relating to their occurrence.

(b) This section applies to convictions that occurred before, as well as those that occur after, the effective date of this section.

(c) This section shall not apply to offenses for which registration is required under Section 290, to violations of Division 10 (commencing with Section 11000) of the Health and Safety Code, or to misdemeanor violations of the Vehicle Code relating to operation of a vehicle or of a local ordinance relating to operation, standing, stopping, or parking of a motor vehicle.

(d) This section does not apply to a person convicted of more than one offense, whether the second or additional convictions occurred in the same action in which the conviction as to which relief is sought occurred or in another action, except in the following cases:

(1) One of the offenses includes the other or others.

(2) The other conviction or convictions were for the following:

(A) Misdemeanor violations of Chapters 1 (commencing with Section 21000) to 9 (commencing with Section 22500), inclusive, Chapter 12 (commencing with Section 23100), or Chapter 13 (commencing with Section 23250) of Division 11 of the Vehicle Code, other than Section 23103, 23104, 23105, 23152, 23153, or 23220.

(B) Violation of a local ordinance relating to the operation, stopping, standing, or parking of a motor vehicle.

(3) The other conviction or convictions consisted of any combination of paragraphs (1) and (2).

(e) This section shall apply in a case in which a person was under 21 years of age at the time of the commission of an offense as to which this section is made applicable if that offense was committed prior to March 7, 1973.

(f)

(1) A petition for relief under this section shall not be denied due to an unfulfilled order of restitution or restitution fine.

(2) An unfulfilled order of restitution or a restitution fine shall not be grounds for finding that a defendant did not fulfil the conditions of probation for the entire period of probation.

(3) When the court considers a petition for relief under this section, in its discretion and in the interest of justice, an unpaid order of restitution or restitution fine shall not be grounds for denial of the petition for relief.

(g) In an action or proceeding based upon defamation, a court, upon a showing of good cause, may order the records sealed under this section to be opened and admitted into evidence. The records shall be confidential and shall be available for inspection only by the court, jury, parties, counsel for the parties, and any other person who is authorized by the court to inspect them. Upon the judgment in the action or proceeding becoming final, the court shall order the records sealed.

Amended by Stats 2023 ch 47 (AB 134),s 13, eff. 7/10/2023.
Amended by Stats 2022 ch 734 (SB 1106),s 8, eff. 1/1/2023.
Amended by Stats 2015 ch 388 (SB 504),s 1, eff. 1/1/2016.
Amended by Stats 2009 ch 606 (SB 676),s 8, eff. 1/1/2010.
Amended by Stats 2007 ch 682 (AB 430),s 4, eff. 1/1/2008.
Amended by Stats 2005 ch 705 (SB 67),s 6, eff. 10/7/2005.

Section 1203.47 - Petition for sealing of records by person described in Welfare and Institutions Code Section 602

(a) A person who was found to be a person described in Section 602 of the Welfare and Institutions Code by reason of the commission of an offense described in subdivision (b) of Section 647 or in former Section 653.22 may, upon reaching 18 years of age, petition the court to have their record sealed, as provided in Section 781 of the Welfare and Institutions Code, except that, as pertaining to any records regarding the commission of an offense described in subdivision (b) of Section 647 or in former Section 653.22, it shall not be a requirement in granting the petition for the person to show that they have not been convicted of a felony or of any misdemeanor involving moral turpitude, or that rehabilitation has been attained to the satisfaction of the court. Upon granting the petition, all records relating to the violation or violations of subdivision (b) of Section 647 or of former Section 653.22, or both, shall be sealed pursuant to Section 781 of the Welfare and Institutions Code.

(b) The relief provided by this section does not apply to a person adjudicated pursuant to subdivision (b) of Section 647 who paid money or any other valuable thing, or attempted to pay money or any other valuable thing, to any person for the purpose of prostitution as defined in subdivision (b) of Section 647.

(c) This section applies to adjudications that occurred before, as well as those that occur after, the effective date of this section.

(d) A petition granted pursuant to this section does not authorize the sealing of any part of a person's record that is unrelated to a violation of subdivision (b) of Section 647.

Amended by Stats 2022 ch 86 (SB 357),s 7, eff. 1/1/2023.
Amended by Stats 2013 ch 59 (SB 514),s 4, eff. 1/1/2014.
Added by Stats 2012 ch 197 (AB 2040),s 1, eff. 1/1/2013.

Section 1203.49 - Conviction for solicitation or prostitution; relief for victims of human trafficking

If a defendant has been convicted of solicitation or prostitution, as described in subdivision (b) of Section 647, and if the defendant has completed any term of probation for that conviction, the defendant may petition the court for relief under this section. If the defendant can establish by clear and convincing evidence that the conviction was the result of his or her status as a victim of human trafficking, the court may issue an order that does all of the following:

(a) Sets forth a finding that the petitioner was a victim of human trafficking when he or she committed the crime.

(b) Orders any of the relief described in Section 1203.4.

(c) Notifies the Department of Justice that the petitioner was a victim of human trafficking when he or she committed the crime and the relief that has been ordered.

Added by Stats 2014 ch 708 (AB 1585),s 4, eff. 1/1/2015.

Section 1203.5 - Ex officio probation officers

The chief probation officers, assistant probation officers, and deputy probation officers appointed in accordance with Chapter 16 (commencing with Section 27770) of Part 3 of Division 2 of Title 3 of the Government Code shall be ex officio adult chief probation officers, assistant adult probation officers, and deputy adult probation officers except in any county or city and county whose charter provides for the separate office of adult probation officer. When the separate office of adult probation officer has been established he or she shall perform all the duties of probation officers except for matters under the jurisdiction of the juvenile court.

Added by Stats 2017 ch 17 (AB 103),s 28, eff. 6/27/2017.

Repealed by Stats 2017 ch 17 (AB 103),s 27, eff. 6/27/2017.

Section 1203.6 - [Repealed]

Repealed by Stats 2017 ch 17 (AB 103),s 29, eff. 6/27/2017.

Amended by Stats 2002 ch 784 (SB 1316), s 548, eff. 1/1/2003.

Section 1203.7 - Inquiry into person over 16 years of age by probation officer; written report

(a) Either at the time of the arrest for a crime of any person over 16 years of age, or at the time of the plea or verdict of guilty, the probation officer of the county of the jurisdiction of the crime shall, when so directed by the court, inquire into the antecedents, character, history, family environment and offense of that person. The probation officer shall report that information to the court and file a written report in the records of the court. The report shall contain his or her recommendation for or against the release of the person on probation.

(b) If that person is released on probation and committed to the care of the probation officer, the officer shall keep a complete and accurate record of the history of the case in court and of the name of the probation officer, and his or her acts in connection with the case. This information shall include the age, sex, nativity, residence, education, habits of temperance, marital status, and the conduct, employment, occupation, parents' occupation, and the condition of the person committed to his or her care during the term of probation, and the result of probation. This record shall constitute a part of the records of the court and shall at all times be open to the inspection of the court or any person appointed by the court for that purpose, as well as of all magistrates and the chief of police or other head of the police, unless otherwise ordered by the court.

(c) Five years after termination of probation in any case subject to this section, the probation officer may destroy any records and papers in his or her possession relating to the case.

(d) The probation officer shall furnish to each person released on probation and committed to his or her care, a written statement of the terms and conditions of probation, and shall report to the court or judge appointing him or her, any violation or breach of the terms and conditions imposed by the court on the person placed in his or her care.

Amended by Stats 2003 ch 296 (SB 66), s 25.1, eff. 1/1/2004.

Added by Stats 2001 ch 473 (SB 485) s 9, eff. 1/1/2002.

Section 1203.71 - Performance of duties by probation officer and deputy probation officers; powers of peace officer

Any of the duties of the probation officer may be performed by a deputy probation officer and shall be performed by him or her whenever detailed to perform those by the probation officer; and it shall be the duty of the probation officer to see that the deputy probation officer performs his or her duties.

The probation officer and each deputy probation officer shall have, as to the person so committed to the care of the probation officer or deputy probation officer, the powers of a peace officer.

The probation officers and deputy probation officers shall serve as such probation officers in all courts having original jurisdiction of criminal actions in this state.

Added by Stats 2001 ch 473 (SB 485) s 10, eff. 1/1/2002.

Section 1203.72 - Availability of probation report prior to pronouncement of judgment

Except as provided in subparagraph (D) of paragraph (2) of subdivision (b) of Section 1203, no court shall pronounce judgment upon any defendant, as to whom the court has requested a probation report pursuant to Section 1203.7, unless a copy of the probation report has been made available to the court, the prosecuting attorney, and the defendant or his or her attorney, at least two days or, upon the request of the defendant, five days prior to the time fixed by the court for consideration of the report with respect to pronouncement of judgment. The report shall be filed with the clerk of the court as a record in the case at the time the court considers the report.

If the defendant is not represented by an attorney, the court, upon ordering the probation report, shall also order the probation officer who prepares the report to discuss its contents with the defendant.

Amended by Stats 2002 ch 787 (SB 1798), s 22, eff. 1/1/2003.

Added by Stats 2001 ch 473 (SB 485) s 11, eff. 1/1/2002.

Section 1203.73 - Incidental expenses of probation officers

The probation officers and deputy probation officers in all counties of the state shall be allowed those necessary incidental expenses incurred in the performance of their duties as required by any law of this state, as may be authorized by a judge of the superior court; and the same shall be a charge upon the county in which the court appointing them has jurisdiction and shall be paid out of the county treasury upon a warrant issued therefor by the county auditor upon the order of the court; provided, however, that in counties in which the probation officer is appointed by the board of supervisors, the expenses shall be authorized by the probation officer and claims therefor shall be audited, allowed and paid in the same manner as other county claims.

Amended by Stats 2002 ch 787 (SB 1798), s 23, eff. 1/1/2003.

Added by Stats 2001 ch 473 (SB 485) s 12, eff. 1/1/2002.

Section 1203.74 - Notification of insufficient staff and financial resources

Upon a determination that, in his or her opinion, staff and financial resources available to him or her are insufficient to meet his or her statutory or court ordered responsibilities, the probation officer shall immediately notify the presiding judge of the superior court and the board of supervisors of the county, or city and county, in writing. The notification shall explain which responsibilities cannot be met and what resources are necessary in order that statutory or court ordered responsibilities can be properly discharged.
Added by Stats 2001 ch 473 (SB 485) s 13, eff. 1/1/2002.

Section 1203.8 - Multiagency plan to prepare and enhance nonviolent felony offenders' successful reentry into community

(a) A county may develop a multiagency plan to prepare and enhance nonviolent felony offenders' successful reentry into the community. The plan shall be developed by, and have the concurrence of, the presiding judge, the chief probation officer, the district attorney, the local custodial agency, and the public defender, or their designees, and shall be submitted to the board of supervisors for its approval. The plan shall provide that when a report prepared pursuant to Section 1203.10 recommends a state prison commitment, the report shall also include, but not be limited to, the offender's treatment, literacy, and vocational needs. Any sentence imposed pursuant to this section shall include a recommendation for completion while in state prison, all relevant programs to address those needs identified in the assessment.

(b) The Department of Corrections and Rehabilitation is authorized to enter into an agreement with up to three counties to implement subdivision (a) and to provide funding for the purpose of the probation department carrying out the assessment. The Department of Corrections and Rehabilitation, to the extent feasible, shall provide to the offender all programs pursuant to the court's recommendation.
Added by Stats 2005 ch 603 (SB 618),s 2, eff. 1/1/2006.

Section 1203.9 - Transfer of case when person released on probation or mandatory supervision

(a)

(1)Except as provided in paragraph (3), whenever a person is released on probation or mandatory supervision, the court, upon noticed motion, shall transfer the case to the superior court in any other county in which the person resides permanently with the stated intention to remain for the duration of probation or mandatory supervision, unless the transferring court determines that the transfer would be inappropriate and states its reasons on the record.

(2)Upon notice of the motion for transfer, the court of the proposed receiving county may provide comments for the record regarding the proposed transfer, following procedures set forth in rules of court developed by the Judicial Council for this purpose, pursuant to subdivision (f). The court and the probation department shall give the matter of investigating those transfers precedence over all actions or proceedings therein, except actions or proceedings to which special precedence is given by law, to the end that all those transfers shall be completed expeditiously.

(3)If victim restitution was ordered as a condition of probation or mandatory supervision, the transferring court shall determine the amount of restitution before the transfer unless the court finds that the determination cannot be made within a reasonable time from when the motion for transfer is made. If a case is transferred without a determination of the amount of restitution, the transferring court shall complete the determination as soon as practicable. In all other aspects, except as provided in subdivisions (d) and (e), the court of the receiving county shall have full jurisdiction over the matter upon transfer as provided in subdivision (b).

(4)The receiving court shall send a receipt of records to the transferring court including the new case number, if any. The receipt of records shall be in a mutually agreed upon format.

(5)Pursuant to Section 13151, the transferring court shall report to the Department of Justice that probation or mandatory supervision was transferred, once the receiving court accepts the transfer. A probation or mandatory supervision transfer report shall identify the receiving court and the new case number, if any.

(b)The court of the receiving county shall accept the entire jurisdiction over the case effective the date that the transferring court orders the transfer.

(c)The order of transfer shall contain an order committing the probationer or supervised person to the care and custody of the probation officer of the receiving county. A copy of the orders and any probation reports shall be transmitted to the court and probation officer of the receiving county within two weeks of the finding that the person does permanently reside in or has permanently moved to that county, and the receiving court shall have entire jurisdiction over the case, except as provided in subdivisions (d) and (e), with the like power to again request transfer of the case whenever it seems proper.

(d)

(1)Notwithstanding subdivision (b) and except as provided in subdivision (e), if the transferring court has ordered the defendant to pay fines, forfeitures, penalties, assessments, or restitution, the transfer order shall require that those and any other amounts ordered by the transferring court that are still unpaid at the time of transfer be paid by the defendant to the collection program for the transferring court for proper distribution and accounting once collected.

(2)The receiving court and receiving county probation department shall not impose additional local fees and costs.

(e)

(1)Upon approval of a transferring court, a receiving court may elect to collect all of the court-ordered payments from a defendant attributable to the case under which the defendant is being supervised, provided, however, that the collection program for the receiving court transmits the revenue collected to the collection program for the transferring court for deposit, accounting, and distribution. A collection program for the receiving court shall not charge administrative fees for collections performed for the collection program for the transferring court.

(2)A collection program for a receiving court collecting funds for a collection program for a transferring court pursuant to paragraph (1) shall not report revenue owed or collected on behalf of the collection program for the transferring court as part of those collections required to be reported annually by the court to the Judicial Council.

(f)The Judicial Council shall promulgate rules of court for procedures by which the proposed receiving county shall receive notice of the motion for transfer and by which responsive comments may be transmitted to the court of the transferring county. The Judicial Council shall adopt rules providing factors for the court's consideration when determining the appropriateness of a transfer, including, but not limited to, the following:

(1)Permanency of residence of the person released on probation or mandatory supervision.

(2)Local programs available for the person released on probation or mandatory supervision.

(3)Restitution orders and victim issues.

(g)The Judicial Council shall consider adoption of rules of court as it deems appropriate to implement the collection, accounting, and disbursement requirements of subdivisions (d) and (e).

(h)This section shall become operative on January 1, 2022.

Amended by Stats 2022 ch 197 (SB 1493),s 23, eff. 1/1/2023.

Added by Stats 2021 ch 257 (AB 177),s 30.5, eff. 9/23/2021.

Amended by Stats 2020 ch 92 (AB 1869),s 53, eff. 9/18/2020.

Amended by Stats 2015 ch 251 (AB 673),s 1, eff. 1/1/2016.

Amended by Stats 2014 ch 111 (AB 2645),s 1, eff. 1/1/2015.

Amended by Stats 2013 ch 13 (AB 492),s 1, eff. 1/1/2014.

Amended by Stats 2012 ch 43 (SB 1023),s 32, eff. 6/27/2012.

Amended by Stats 2009 ch 588 (SB 431),s 1, eff. 1/1/2010.

Added by Stats 2004 ch 30 (AB 1306) s 1, eff. 4/12/2004.

Section 1203.10 - Report on person over 18 years of age

(a) At the time of the plea or verdict of guilty of any person over 18 years of age, a probation officer of the county of the jurisdiction of the criminal shall, when so directed by the court, inquire into the antecedents, character, history, family environment, and offense of such person, and must report the same to the court and file his or her report in writing in the records of such court. When directed, his or her report shall contain a recommendation for or against the release for the person on probation. If any such person shall be released on probation and committed to the supervision of a probation officer, such officer shall keep a complete and accurate record in suitable books of the history of the case and supervision, including the names of probation officers assigned to the case, and their actions in connection with the case; also the age, sex, nativity, residence, education, habit of temperance, whether married or single, and the conduct, employment and occupation, and parents' occupation, if relevant, and condition of such person during the term of the probation and the result of the probation. The record of the probation officer is a part of the records of the court, and shall at all times be open to the inspection of the court or of any person appointed by, or allowed access by order of, the court for that purpose, as well as of all magistrates, and the chief of police, or other heads of the police, and other probation agencies, unless otherwise ordered by the court.

(b) Five years after termination of probation in any case subject to this section, the probation officer may destroy any records and papers in his or her possession relating to such case.

Amended by Stats 2016 ch 59 (SB 1474),s 4, eff. 1/1/2017.

Section 1203.11 - Service of process

A probation or parole officer or parole agent of the Department of Corrections may serve any process regarding the issuance of a temporary restraining order or other protective order against a person committed to the care of the probation or parole officer or parole agent when the person appears for an appointment with the probation or parole officer or parole agent at their office.

Added by Stats. 1991, Ch. 866, Sec. 5.

Section 1203.12 - Written statement of terms of probation

The probation officer shall furnish to each person who has been released on probation, and committed to his care, a written statement of the terms and conditions of his probation unless such a statement has been furnished by the court, and shall report to the court, or judge, releasing such person on probation, any violation or breach of the terms and conditions imposed by such court on the person placed in his care.

Amended by Stats. 1968, Ch. 1222.

Section 1203.13 - Committees to prevent crime

The probation officer of any county may establish, or assist in the establishment of, any public council or committee having as its object the prevention of crime, and may cooperate with or participate in the work of any such councils or committees for the purpose of preventing or decreasing crime, including the improving of recreational, health, and other conditions in the community.

Added by Stats. 1947, Ch. 876.

Section 1203.14 - Prevention of adult delinquency

Notwithstanding any other provision of law, probation departments may engage in activities designed to prevent adult delinquency. These activities include rendering direct and indirect services to persons in the community. Probation departments shall not be limited to providing services only to those persons on probation being supervised under Section 1203.10, but may provide services to any adults in the community.

Added by Stats. 1973, Ch. 512.

Section 1203a - Authority of courts regarding probation for misdemeanors

(a) In all counties and cities and counties, the courts therein, having jurisdiction to impose punishment in misdemeanor cases, may refer cases, demand reports, and to do and require anything necessary to carry out the purposes of Section 1203, insofar as that section applies to misdemeanors. The court may suspend the imposition or execution of the sentence and make and enforce the terms of probation for a period not to exceed one year.

(b) The one-year probation limit in subdivision (a) shall not apply to any offense that includes specific probation lengths within its provisions.

Amended by Stats 2020 ch 328 (AB 1950),s 1, eff. 1/1/2021.

Section 1203b - Suspension of imposition or execution of sentence

All courts shall have power to suspend the imposition or execution of a sentence and grant a conditional sentence in misdemeanor and infraction cases without referring such cases to the probation officer. Unless otherwise ordered by the court, persons granted a conditional sentence in the community shall report only to the court and the probation officer shall not be responsible in any way for supervising or accounting for such persons.

Amended by Stats. 1982, Ch. 247, Sec. 2. Effective June 9, 1982.

Section 1203c - Report to Department

(a)

(1) Notwithstanding any other law, whenever a person is committed to an institution under the jurisdiction of the Department of Corrections and Rehabilitation, whether probation has been applied for or not, or granted and revoked, it shall be the duty of the probation officer of the county from which the person is committed to send to the Department of Corrections and Rehabilitation a report of the circumstances surrounding the offense and the prior record and history of the defendant, as may be required by the Secretary of the Department of Corrections and Rehabilitation.

(2) If the person is being committed to the jurisdiction of the department for a conviction of an offense that requires him or her to register as a sex offender pursuant to Section 290, the probation officer shall include in the report the results of the State-Authorized Risk Assessment Tool for Sex Offenders (SARATSO) administered pursuant to Sections 290.04 to 290.06, inclusive, if applicable.

(b) These reports shall accompany the commitment papers. The reports shall be prepared in the form prescribed by the administrator following consultation with the Board of State and Community Corrections, except that if the defendant is ineligible for probation, a report of the circumstances surrounding the offense and the prior record and history of the defendant, prepared by the probation officer on request of the court and filed with the court before sentence, shall be deemed to meet the requirements of paragraph (1) of subdivision (a).

(c) In order to allow the probation officer an opportunity to interview, for the purpose of preparation of these reports, the defendant shall be held in the county jail for 48 hours, excluding Saturdays, Sundays, and holidays, subsequent to imposition of sentence and prior to delivery to the custody of the Secretary of the Department of Corrections and Rehabilitation, unless probation officer has indicated the need for a different period of time.

(d) Whenever a person is committed to an institution under the jurisdiction of the Department of Corrections and Rehabilitation or a county jail pursuant to subdivision (h) of Section 1170, or is placed on postrelease community supervision or mandatory supervision, and the court has ordered the person to pay restitution to a victim, the following shall apply:

(1) If the victim consents, the probation officer of the county from which the person is committed may send the victim's contact information and a copy of the restitution order to the department or to the county agency designated by the board of supervisors to collect and distribute restitution for the sole purpose of distributing the restitution collected on behalf of the victim.

(2) Notwithstanding paragraph (1), the district attorney of the county from which the person is committed may send the victim's contact information and a copy of the restitution order to the department or to the county agency designated by the board of supervisors to collect and distribute restitution for the sole purpose of distributing the restitution collected on behalf of the victim if the district attorney finds it is in the best interest of the victim to send that information. If the victim affirmatively objects, the district attorney shall not send the victim's contact information. The district attorney shall not be required to inform the victim of the right to object.

(3) The victim's contact information shall remain confidential and shall not be made part of the court file or combined with any public document.

Amended by Stats 2014 ch 517 (SB 1197),s 1, eff. 1/1/2015.
Amended by Stats 2012 ch 124 (AB 2251),s 1, eff. 1/1/2013.
Amended by Stats 2009 ch 49 (SB 432),s 1, eff. 1/1/2010.
Amended by Stats 2006 ch 337 (SB 1128),s 39, eff. 9/20/2006.

Section 1203d - Probation report

No court shall pronounce judgment upon any defendant, as to whom the court has requested a probation report pursuant to Section 1203.10, unless a copy of the probation report has been made available to the court, the prosecuting attorney, and the defendant or his or her attorney, at least two days or, upon the request of the defendant, five days prior to the time fixed by the court for consideration of the report with respect to pronouncement of judgment. The report shall be filed with the clerk of the court as a record in the case at the time the court considers the report.

If the defendant is not represented by an attorney, the court, upon ordering the probation report, shall also order the probation officer who prepares the report to discuss its contents with the defendant. Any waiver of the preparation of the report or the consideration of the report by the court shall be as provided in subdivision (b) of Section 1203, with respect to cases to which that subdivision applies. The sentence recommendations of the report shall also be made available to the victim of the crime, or the victim's next of kin if the victim has died, through the district attorney's office. The victim or the victim's next of kin shall be informed of the availability of this information through the notice provided pursuant to Section 1191.1.

Amended by Stats. 1996, Ch. 123, Sec. 2. Effective January 1, 1997.

Section 1203e - Facts of Offense Sheets

(a) Commencing June 1, 2010, the probation department shall compile a Facts of Offense Sheet for every person convicted of an offense that requires him or her to register as a sex offender pursuant to Section 290 who is referred to the department pursuant to Section 1203. The Facts of Offense Sheet shall contain the following information concerning the offender: name; CII number; criminal history, including all arrests and convictions for any registerable sex offenses or any violent offense; circumstances of the offense for which registration is required, including, but not limited to, weapons used and victim pattern; and results of the State-Authorized Risk Assessment Tool for Sex Offenders (SARATSO), as set forth in Section 290.04, if required. The Facts of Offense Sheet shall be included in the probation officer's report.

(b) The defendant may move the court to correct the Facts of Offense Sheet. Any corrections to that sheet shall be made consistent with procedures set forth in Section 1204.

(c) The probation officer shall send a copy of the Facts of Offense Sheet to the Department of Justice within 30 days of the person's sex offense conviction, and it shall be made part of the registered sex offender's file maintained by the Department of Justice. The Facts of Offense Sheet shall thereafter be made available to law enforcement by the Department of Justice, which shall post it with the offender's record on the Department of Justice Internet Web site maintained pursuant to Section 290.46, and shall be accessible only to law enforcement.

(d) If the registered sex offender is sentenced to a period of incarceration, at either the state prison or a county jail, the Facts of Offense Sheet shall be sent by the Department of Corrections and Rehabilitation or the county sheriff to the registering law enforcement agency in the jurisdiction where the registered sex offender will be paroled or will live on release, within three days of the person's release. If the registered sex offender is committed to the State Department of State Hospitals, the Facts of Offense Sheet shall be sent by the State Department of State Hospitals to the registering law enforcement agency in the jurisdiction where the person will live on release, within three days of release.

Amended by Stats 2016 ch 59 (SB 1474),s 5, eff. 1/1/2017.
Amended by Stats 2012 ch 24 (AB 1470),s 24, eff. 6/27/2012.
Amended by Stats 2010 ch 709 (SB 1062),s 13, eff. 1/1/2011.
Added by Stats 2006 ch 337 (SB 1128),s 40, eff. 9/20/2006.

Section 1203f - High risk offenders

Every probation department shall ensure that all probationers under active supervision who are deemed to pose a high risk to the public of committing sex crimes, as determined by the State-Authorized Risk Assessment Tool for Sex Offenders, as set forth in Sections 290.04 to 290.06, inclusive, are placed on intensive and specialized probation supervision and are required to report frequently to designated probation officers. The probation department may place any other probationer convicted of an offense that requires him or her to register as a sex offender who is on active supervision to be placed on intensive and specialized supervision and require him or her to report frequently to designated probation officers.

Added by Stats 2006 ch 337 (SB 1128),s 41, eff. 9/20/2006.

Section 1203h - Crimes where minor is victim; psychological investigation

If the court initiates an investigation pursuant to subdivision (a) or (d) of Section 1203 and the convicted person was convicted of violating any section of this code in which a minor is a victim of an act of abuse or neglect, then the investigation may include a psychological evaluation to determine the extent of counseling necessary for successful rehabilitation and which may be mandated by the court during the term of probation. Such evaluation may be performed by psychiatrists, psychologists, or licensed clinical social workers. The results of the examination shall be included in the probation officer's report to the court.

Amended by Stats. 1982, Ch. 282, Sec. 1.

Section 1204 - Testimony of witnesses

The circumstances shall be presented by the testimony of witnesses examined in open court, except that when a witness is so sick or infirm as to be unable to attend, his deposition may be taken by a magistrate of the county, out of court, upon such notice to the adverse party as the court may direct. No affidavit or testimony, or representation of any kind, verbal or written, can be offered to or received by the court, or a judge thereof, in aggravation or mitigation of the punishment, except as provided in this and the preceding section. This section shall not be construed to prohibit the filing of a written report by a defendant or defendant's counsel on behalf of a defendant if such a report presents a study of his background and personality and suggests a rehabilitation program. If such a report is submitted, the prosecution or probation officer shall be permitted to reply to or to evaluate the program.

Amended by Stats. 1971, Ch. 1080.

Section 1204.1 - Probation regarding environmental crimes

(a) The Legislature finds and declares that environmental crimes are public welfare offenses resulting from violations of statutes designed to safeguard against threats or injury to the health and safety of the public and California's environment and precious natural resources.

(b) Notwithstanding Section 1203.1 or 1203a, if an entity is granted probation upon conviction of an environmental crime, the term of probation shall not exceed five years, which may include a period of summary probation as appropriate. For purposes of this section, environmental crimes means violations of any crimes in the following sections:

    (1) Division 9 (commencing with Section 12000) and Section 5650 of the Fish and Game Code.

    (2) Section 12996 of the Food and Agricultural Code.

    (3) Sections 132 and 133 of the Harbors and Navigation Code.

    (4) Part 14 (commencing with Section 117600) of Division 104 of the Health and Safety Code.

    (5) Article 3 (commencing with Section 42400) of Chapter 4 of Part 4 of Division 26 of the Health and Safety Code.

    (6) Chapters 6.5 (commencing with Section 25100), Chapter 6.67 (commencing with Section 25270), Chapter 6.7 (commencing with Section 25280), and Chapter 6.95 (commencing with Section 25500) of Division 20 of the Health and Safety Code.

    (7) Chapter 7.4 (commencing with Section 8670.1) of Division 1 of Title 2 of the Government Code.

    (8) Sections 374.2, 374.3, 374.5, 374.7, 374.8, 597, 653o, 653p, and 653q of the Penal Code.

    (9) Section 32001 and subdivision (b) of Section 34506 of the Vehicle Code.

    (10) Section 13387 of the Water Code.

(c) For purposes of subdivision (b), an entity means a trust, firm, partnership, joint stock company, joint venture, association, limited liability company, corporation, or other legal entity with more than 10 employees.

Added by Stats 2023 ch 264 (AB 508),s 1, eff. 1/1/2024.

Section 1204.5 - Considerations before plea

(a) In any criminal action, after the filing of any complaint or other accusatory pleading and before a plea, finding, or verdict of guilty, no judge shall read or consider any written report of any law enforcement officer or witness to any offense, any information reflecting the arrest or conviction record of a defendant, or any affidavit or representation of any kind, verbal or written, without the defendant's consent given in open court, except as provided in the rules of evidence applicable at the trial, or as provided in affidavits in connection with the issuance of a warrant or the hearing of any law and motion matter, or in any application for an order fixing or changing bail, or a petition for a writ.

(b) This section does not preclude a judge, who is not the preliminary hearing or trial judge in the case, from considering any information about the defendant for the purpose of that judge adopting a pre-trial sentencing position or approving or disapproving a guilty plea entered pursuant to Section 1192.5, if all of the following occur:

(1) The defendant is represented by counsel, unless he or she expressly waives the right to counsel.

(2) Any information provided to the judge for either of those purposes is also provided to the district attorney and to the defense counsel at least five days prior to any hearing or conference held for the purpose of considering a proposed guilty plea or proposed sentence.

(3) At any hearing or conference held for either of those purposes, defense counsel or the district attorney is allowed to provide information, either on or off the record, to supplement or rebut the information provided pursuant to paragraph (2).

Amended by Stats. 1995, Ch. 86, Sec. 1. Effective January 1, 1996.

Section 1205 - Judgment that defendant pay fine

(a) A judgment that the defendant pay a fine, with or without other punishment, may also direct that the defendant be imprisoned until the fine is satisfied and may further direct that the imprisonment begin at and continue after the expiration of any imprisonment imposed as a part of the punishment or of any other imprisonment to which the defendant may have been sentenced. The judgment shall specify the term of imprisonment for nonpayment of the fine, which shall not be more than one day for each one hundred twenty-five dollars ($125) of the base fine, nor exceed the term for which the defendant may be sentenced to imprisonment for the offense of which the defendant has been convicted. A defendant held in custody for nonpayment of a fine shall be entitled to credit on the fine for each day the defendant is held in custody, at the rate specified in the judgment. When the defendant has been convicted of a misdemeanor, a judgment that the defendant pay a fine may also direct that the defendant pay the fine within a limited time or in installments on specified dates, and that in default of payment as stipulated be imprisoned in the discretion of the court either until the defaulted installment is satisfied or until the fine is satisfied in full; but unless the direction is given in the judgment, the fine shall be payable. If an amount of the base fine is not satisfied by jail credits, or by community service, the penalties and assessments imposed on the base fine shall be reduced by the percentage of the base fine that was satisfied.

(b) Except as otherwise provided in case of fines imposed, as a condition of probation, the defendant shall pay the fine to the clerk of the court, or to the judge if there is no clerk, unless the defendant is taken into custody for nonpayment of the fine, in which event payments made while the defendant is in custody shall be made to the officer who holds the defendant in custody, and all amounts paid shall be paid over by the officer to the court that rendered the judgment. The clerk shall report to the court every default in payment of a fine or any part of that fine, or if there is no clerk, the court shall take notice of the default. If time has been given for payment of a fine or it has been made payable in installments, the court shall, upon any default in payment, immediately order the arrest of the defendant and order the defendant to show cause why they should not be imprisoned until the fine or installment is satisfied in full. If the fine or installment is payable forthwith and it is not paid, the court shall, without further proceedings, immediately commit the defendant to the custody of the proper officer to be held in custody until the fine or installment is satisfied in full.

(c) This section applies to any violation of any of the codes or statutes of this state punishable by a fine or by a fine and imprisonment.

(d) Nothing in this section shall be construed to prohibit the clerk of the court, or the judge if there is no clerk, from turning these accounts over to another county department or a collecting agency for processing and collection.

(e) This section shall not apply to restitution fines and restitution orders.

(f) This section shall become operative on January 1, 2022.

Added by Stats 2021 ch 257 (AB 177),s 32, eff. 9/23/2021.

Section 1205.3 - Specification of community service

In any case in which a defendant is convicted of an offense and granted probation, and the court orders the defendant either to pay a fine or to perform specified community service work as a condition of probation, the court shall specify that if community service work is performed, it shall be performed in place of the payment of all fines and restitution fines on a proportional basis, and the court shall specify in its order the amount of the fine and restitution fine and the number of hours of community service work that shall be performed as an alternative to payment of the fine.

Amended by Stats. 1996, Ch. 1077, Sec. 23. Effective January 1, 1997.

Section 1207 - Entry of judgment

When judgment upon a conviction is rendered, the clerk must enter the judgment in the minutes, stating briefly the offense for which the conviction was had, and the fact of a prior conviction, if any. A copy of the judgment of conviction shall be filed with the papers in the case.

Amended by Stats 2007 ch 263 (AB 310),s 28, eff. 1/1/2008.

Section 1208 - Designation of facility for confinement of prisoners classified for the work furlough program

(a)

(1) The provisions of this section, insofar as they relate to employment, shall be operative in any county in which the board of supervisors by ordinance finds, on the basis of employment conditions, the state of the county jail facilities, and other pertinent circumstances, that the operation of this section, insofar as it relates to employment, in that county is feasible. The provisions of this section, insofar as they relate to job training, shall be operative in any county in which the board of supervisors by ordinance finds, on the basis of job training conditions, the state of the county jail facilities, and other pertinent circumstances, that the operation of this section, insofar as it relates to job training, in that county is feasible. The provisions of this section, insofar as they relate to education, shall be operative in any county in which the board of supervisors by ordinance finds, on the basis of education conditions, the state of the county jail facilities, and other pertinent circumstances, that the operation of this section, insofar as it relates to education, in that county is feasible. In any ordinance the board shall prescribe whether the sheriff, the probation officer, the director of the county department of corrections, or the superintendent of a county industrial farm or industrial road camp in the county shall perform the functions of the work furlough administrator. The board may, in that ordinance, provide for the performance of any or all functions of the work furlough administrator by any one or more of those persons, acting separately or jointly as to any of the functions; and may, by a subsequent ordinance, revise the provisions within the authorization of this section. The board of supervisors may also terminate the

operation of this section, either with respect to employment, job training, or education in the county, if the board finds by ordinance that because of changed circumstances, the operation of this section, either with respect to employment, job training, or education in that county, is no longer feasible.

(2) Notwithstanding any other law, the board of supervisors may by ordinance designate a facility for confinement of prisoners classified for the work furlough program and designate the work furlough administrator as the custodian of the facility. The work furlough administrator may operate the work furlough facility or, with the approval of the board of supervisors, administer the work furlough facility pursuant to written contracts with appropriate public or private agencies or private entities. No agency or private entity may operate a work furlough program or facility without a written contract with the work furlough administrator, and no agency or private entity entering into a written contract may itself employ any person who is in the work furlough program. The sheriff or director of the county department of corrections, as the case may be, is authorized to transfer custody of prisoners to the work furlough administrator to be confined in a facility for the period during which they are in the work furlough program.

(3) All privately operated local work furlough facilities and programs shall be under the jurisdiction of, and subject to the terms of a written contract entered into with, the work furlough administrator. Each contract shall include, but not be limited to, a provision whereby the private agency or entity agrees to operate in compliance with all appropriate state and local building, zoning, health, safety, and fire statutes, ordinances, and regulations and the minimum jail standards for Type IV facilities as established by regulations adopted by the Board of State and Community Corrections. The private agency or entity shall select and train its personnel in accordance with selection and training requirements adopted by the Board of State and Community Corrections as set forth in Subchapter 1 (commencing with Section 100) of Chapter 1 of Division 1 of Title 15 of the California Code of Regulations. Failure to comply with the appropriate health, safety, and fire laws or minimum jail standards adopted by the board may be cause for termination of the contract. Upon discovery of a failure to comply with these requirements, the work furlough administrator shall notify the privately operated program director that the contract may be canceled if the specified deficiencies are not corrected within 60 days.

(4) All private work furlough facilities and programs shall be inspected biennially by the Board of State and Community Corrections unless the work furlough administrator requests an earlier inspection pursuant to Section 6031.1. Each private agency or entity shall pay a fee to the Board of State and Community Corrections commensurate with the cost of those inspections and a fee commensurate with the cost of the initial review of the facility.

(b) When a person is convicted and sentenced to the county jail, or is imprisoned in the county jail for nonpayment of a fine, for contempt, or as a condition of probation for any criminal offense, the work furlough administrator may, if the administrator concludes that the person is a fit subject to continue in the person's regular employment, direct that the person be permitted to continue in that employment, if that is compatible with the requirements of subdivision (c), or may authorize the person to secure employment for themselves, unless the court at the time of sentencing or committing has ordered that the person not be granted work furloughs. The work furlough administrator may, if the administrator concludes that the person is a fit subject to continue in the person's job training program, direct that the person be permitted to continue in that job training program, if that is compatible with the requirements of subdivision (c), or may authorize the person to secure local job training for themselves, unless the court at the time of sentencing has ordered that person not be granted work furloughs. The work furlough administrator may, if the administrator concludes that the person is a fit subject to continue in the person's regular educational program, direct that the person be permitted to continue in that educational program, if that is compatible with the requirements of subdivision (c), or may authorize the person to secure education for themselves, unless the court at the time of sentencing has ordered that person not be granted work furloughs.

(c) If the work furlough administrator so directs that the prisoner be permitted to continue in the prisoner's regular employment, job training, or educational program, the administrator shall arrange for a continuation of that employment or for that job training or education, so far as possible without interruption. If the prisoner does not have regular employment or a regular job training or educational program, and the administrator has authorized the prisoner to secure employment, job training, or education for themselves, the prisoner may do so, and the administrator may assist the prisoner in doing so. Any employment, job training, or education so secured shall be suitable for the prisoner. The employment, and the job training or educational program if it includes earnings by the prisoner, shall be at a wage at least as high as the prevailing wage for similar work in the area where the work is performed and in accordance with the prevailing working conditions in that area. In no event may any employment, job training, or educational program involving earnings by the prisoner be permitted where there is a labor dispute in the establishment in which the prisoner is, or is to be, employed, trained, or educated.

(d)

(1) Whenever the prisoner is not employed or being trained or educated and between the hours or periods of employment, training, or education, the prisoner shall be confined in the facility designated by the board of supervisors for work furlough confinement unless the work furlough administrator directs otherwise. If the prisoner is injured during a period of employment, job training, or education, the work furlough administrator shall have the authority to release the prisoner from the facility for continued medical treatment by private physicians or at medical facilities at the expense of the employer, workers' compensation insurer, or the prisoner. The release shall not be construed as assumption of liability by the county or work furlough administrator for medical treatment obtained.

(2) The work furlough administrator may release any prisoner classified for the work furlough program for a period not to exceed 72 hours for medical, dental, or psychiatric care, or for family emergencies or pressing business which would result in severe hardship if the release were not granted, or to attend those activities as the administrator deems may effectively promote the prisoner's successful return to the community, including, but not limited to, an attempt to secure housing, employment, entry into educational programs, or participation in community programs.

(e) The earnings of the prisoner may be collected by the work furlough administrator, and it shall be the duty of the prisoner's employer to transmit the wages to the administrator at the latter's request. Earnings levied upon pursuant to writ of execution or in other lawful manner shall not be transmitted to the administrator. If the administrator has requested transmittal of earnings prior to levy, that request shall have priority. In a case in which the functions of the administrator are performed by a sheriff, and the sheriff receives a writ of execution for the earnings of a prisoner subject to this section but has not yet requested transmittal of the prisoner's earnings pursuant to this section, the sheriff shall first levy on the earnings pursuant to the writ. When an employer or educator transmits earnings to the administrator pursuant to this subdivision, the sheriff shall have no liability to the prisoner for those earnings. From the earnings the administrator shall pay the prisoner's board and personal expenses, both inside and outside the jail, and shall deduct so much of the costs of administration of this section as is allocable to the prisoner or if the prisoner is unable to pay that sum, a lesser sum as is reasonable, and, in an amount determined by the administrator, shall pay the support of the prisoner's dependents, if any. If sufficient funds are available after making the foregoing payments, the administrator may, with the consent of the prisoner, pay, in whole or in part, the preexisting debts of the prisoner. Any balance shall be retained until the prisoner's discharge. Upon discharge the balance shall be paid to the prisoner.

(f) The prisoner shall be eligible for time credits pursuant to Sections 4018 and 4019.

(g) If the prisoner violates the conditions laid down for the prisoner's conduct, custody, job training, education, or employment, the work furlough administrator may order the balance of the prisoner's sentence to be spent in actual confinement.

(h) Willful failure of the prisoner to return to the place of confinement not later than the expiration of any period during which the prisoner is authorized to be away from the place of confinement pursuant to this section is punishable as provided in Section 4532.

(i) The court may recommend or refer a person to the work furlough administrator for consideration for placement in the work furlough program or a particular work furlough facility. The recommendation or referral of the court shall be given great weight in the determination of acceptance or denial for placement in the work furlough program or a particular work furlough facility.

(j) As used in this section, the following definitions apply:

(1) "Education" includes vocational and educational training and counseling, and psychological, drug abuse, alcoholic, and other rehabilitative counseling.

(2) "Educator" includes a person or institution providing that training or counseling.

(3) "Employment" includes care of children, including the daytime care of children of the prisoner.

(4) "Job training" may include, but shall not be limited to, job training assistance.

(k) This section shall be known and may be cited as the "Cobey Work Furlough Law."

(l) This section shall become operative July 1, 2021.

Added by Stats 2020 ch 92 (AB 1869),s 56, eff. 9/18/2020.

Section 1208.2 - Fees for work furlough program, electronic home detention program, or county parole program

(a)

(1)This section shall apply to individuals authorized to participate in a work furlough program pursuant to Section 1208, or to individuals authorized to participate in an electronic home detention program pursuant to Section 1203.016 or 1203.018, or to individuals authorized to participate in a county parole program pursuant to Article 3.5 (commencing with Section 3074) of Chapter 8 of Title 1 of Part 3.

(2)As used in this section, as appropriate, "administrator" means the sheriff, probation officer, director of the county department of corrections, or county parole administrator.

(b)

(1)A board of supervisors that implements programs identified in paragraph (1) of subdivision (a) shall not impose a program administrative fee.

(2) Privately operated electronic home detention programs pursuant to Section 1203.016 or 1203.018 or work furlough programs pursuant to Section 1208 shall not impose program administrative fees or application fees.

(c) In all circumstances where a county board of supervisors has approved a program administrator, as described in Section 1203.016, 1203.018, or 1208, to enter into a contract with a private agency or entity to provide specified program services, the program administrator shall ensure that the provisions of this section are contained within any contractual agreement for this purpose. All privately operated home detention programs shall comply with all appropriate, applicable ordinances and regulations specified in subdivision (a) of Section 1208.

Amended by Stats 2022 ch 57 (AB 199),s 17, eff. 6/30/2022.

Added by Stats 2020 ch 92 (AB 1869),s 58, eff. 9/18/2020.

Section 1208.3 - Verification by administrator

The administrator is not prohibited from verifying any of the following:

(a) That the prisoner is receiving wages at a rate of pay not less than the prevailing minimum wage requirement as provided for in subdivision (c) of Section 1208.

(b) That the prisoner is working a specified minimum number of required hours.

(c)

(1) That the prisoner is covered under an appropriate or suitable workers' compensation insurance plan as may otherwise be required by law.

(2) The purpose of the verification shall be solely to ensure that the prisoner's employment rights are being protected, that the prisoner is not being taken advantage of, that the job is suitable for the prisoner, and that the prisoner is making every reasonable effort to make a productive contribution to the community.

(d) This section shall become operative on July 1, 2021.

Added by Stats 2020 ch 92 (AB 1869),s 60, eff. 9/18/2020.

Section 1208.5 - Transfer of person in work furlough program from one county to another

The boards of supervisors of two or more counties having work furlough programs may enter into agreements whereby a person sentenced to, or imprisoned in, the jail of one county, but regularly residing in another county or regularly employed in another county, may be transferred by the sheriff of the county in which he or she is confined to the jail of the county in which he or she resides or is employed, in order that he or she may be enabled to continue in his or her regular employment or education in the other county through the county's work furlough program. This agreement may make provision for the support of transferred persons by the county from which they are transferred. The board of supervisors of any county may, by ordinance, delegate the authority to enter into these agreements to the work furlough administrator.

This section shall become operative on January 1, 1999.

Amended (as added by Stats. 1991, Ch. 437, Sec. 8) by Stats. 1994, Ch. 770, Sec. 5. Effective January 1, 1995. Section operative January 1, 1999, by its own provisions.

Section 1209 - Ability to pay costs of administration of sentence served on weekends or other nonemployment days

Upon conviction of any criminal offense for which the court orders the confinement of a person in the county jail, or other suitable place of confinement, either as the final sentence or as a condition of any grant of probation, and allows the person so sentenced to continue in his or her regular employment by serving the sentence on weekends or similar periods during the week other than their regular workdays and by virtue of this schedule of serving the sentence the prisoner is ineligible for work furlough under Section 1208, the county may collect from the defendant according to the defendant's ability to pay so much of the costs of administration of this section as are allocable to such defendant. The amount of this fee shall not exceed the actual costs of such confinement and may be collected prior to completion of each weekly or monthly period of confinement until the entire sentence has been served, and the funds shall be deposited in the county treasury pursuant to county ordinance.

The court, upon allowing sentences to be served on weekends or other nonemployment days, shall conduct a hearing to determine if the defendant has the ability to pay all or a part of the costs of administration without resulting in unnecessary economic hardship to the defendant and his or her dependents. At the hearing, the defendant shall be entitled to have, but shall not be limited to, the opportunity to be heard in person, to present witnesses and other documentary evidence, and to confront and cross-examine adverse witnesses, and to disclosure of the evidence against the defendant, and a written statement of the findings of the court. If the court determines that the defendant has the ability to pay all or part of the costs of administration without resulting in unnecessary economic hardship to the defendant and his or her dependents, the court shall advise the defendant of the provisions of this section and order him or her to pay all or part of the fee as required by the sheriff, probation officer, or Director of the County Department of Corrections, whichever the case may be. In making a determination of whether a defendant has the ability to pay, the court shall take into account the amount of any fine imposed upon the defendant and any amount the defendant has been ordered to pay in restitution.

As used in this section, the term "ability to pay" means the overall capability of the defendant to reimburse the costs, or a portion of the costs, and shall include, but shall not be limited to, the following:

(a) The defendant's present financial position.

(b) The defendant's reasonably discernible future financial position. In no event shall the court consider a period of more than six months from the date of the hearing for purposes of determining reasonably discernible future financial position.

(c) Likelihood that the defendant shall be able to obtain employment within the six-month period from the date of the hearing.

(d) Any other factor or factors which may bear upon the defendant's financial capability to reimburse the county for the costs. Execution may be issued on the order in the same manner as a judgment in a civil action.

The order to pay all or part shall not be enforced by contempt. At any time during the pendency of the judgment, a defendant against whom a judgment has been rendered may petition the rendering court to modify or vacate its previous judgment on the grounds of a change of circumstances with regard to the defendant's ability to pay the judgment. The court shall advise the defendant of this right at the time of making the judgment.

Amended by Stats. 1983, Ch. 779, Sec. 1.

Section 1209.5 - Community service in lieu of fine imposed on person convicted of infraction

(a) Notwithstanding any other law, the court shall permit a person convicted of an infraction, upon a showing that payment of the total fine would pose a hardship on the defendant or the defendant's family, to elect to perform community service in lieu of the total fine that would otherwise be imposed.

(b) For purposes of this section, the term "total fine" means the total bail, including the base fine and all assessments, penalties, and additional moneys to be paid by the defendant.

(c)

(1) For purposes of this section, the hourly rate applicable to community service performed pursuant to this section shall be double the minimum wage set for the applicable calendar year, based on the schedule for an employer who employs 25 or fewer employees, as established in paragraph (2) of subdivision (b) of Section 1182.12 of the Labor Code.

(2) Notwithstanding paragraph (1), a court may by local rule increase the amount that is credited for each hour of community service performed pursuant to this section, to exceed the hourly rate described in paragraph (1).

(d)

(1) If the court determines that a person who has been convicted of an infraction has shown that payment of the total fine would pose a hardship pursuant to subdivision (a) and the person has elected to perform community service in lieu of paying the total fine, the person may elect to perform that community service in the county in which the infraction violation occurred, the county of the person's residence, or any other county to which the person has substantial ties, including, but not limited to, employment, family, or education ties.

(2) Regardless of the county in which the person elects to perform community service pursuant to paragraph (1), the court shall retain jurisdiction until the community service has been verified as complete.

(e)

(1) If the court determines that a person who has been convicted of an infraction has shown that payment of the total fine would pose a hardship pursuant to subdivision (a) and the person has elected to perform community service in lieu of paying the total fine pursuant to subdivision (d), the court may, in its discretion, permit a person to participate in an educational program to satisfy community service hours.

(2) As used in this subdivision, an educational program includes, but is not limited to, high school or General Education Development classes, college courses, adult literacy or English as a second language programs, and vocational education programs.

Amended by Stats 2021 ch 598 (SB 71),s 1, eff. 1/1/2022.

Amended by Stats 2019 ch 138 (SB 164),s 1, eff. 1/1/2020.

Amended by Stats 2018 ch 280 (AB 2532),s 1, eff. 1/1/2019.

Section 1210 - Definitions

As used in Sections 1210.1 and 3063.1 of this code, and Division 10.8 (commencing with Section 11999.4) of the Health and Safety Code, the following definitions apply:

(a) The term "nonviolent drug possession offense" means the unlawful personal use, possession for personal use, or transportation for personal use of any controlled substance identified in Section 11054, 11055, 11056, 11057, or 11058 of the Health and Safety Code, or the offense of being under the influence of a controlled substance in violation of Section 11550 of the Health and Safety Code. The term "nonviolent drug possession offense" does not include the possession for sale, production, or manufacturing of any controlled substance and does not include violations of Section 4573.6 or 4573.8.

(b) The term "drug treatment program" or "drug treatment" means a state licensed or certified community drug treatment program, which may include one or more of the following: drug education, outpatient services, narcotic replacement therapy, residential treatment, detoxification services, and aftercare services. The term "drug treatment program" or "drug treatment" includes a drug treatment program operated under the direction of the Veterans Health Administration of the Department of Veterans Affairs or a program specified in Section 8001. That type of program shall be eligible to provide drug treatment services without regard to the licensing or certification provisions required by this subdivision. The term "drug treatment program" or "drug treatment" does not include drug treatment programs offered in a prison or jail facility.

(c) The term "successful completion of treatment" means that a defendant who has had drug treatment imposed as a condition of probation has completed the prescribed course of drug treatment as recommended by the treatment provider and ordered by the court. Completion of treatment shall not require cessation of narcotic replacement therapy.

(d) The term "misdemeanor not related to the use of drugs" means a misdemeanor that does not involve (1) the simple possession or use of drugs or drug paraphernalia, being present where drugs are used, or failure to register as a drug offender, or (2) any activity similar to those listed in (1).

Amended by Stats 2023 ch 481 (SB 46),s 2, eff. 1/1/2024.
Amended by Stats 2006 ch 63 (SB 1137),s 6, eff. 7/12/2006.
Amended by Stats 2003 ch 155 (SB 762), s 1, eff. 1/1/2004.
Amended by Stats 2001 ch 721 (SB 223), s 2, eff. 10/11/2001.
36 (2000).

Section 1210.1 - Probation for person convicted of nonviolent drug possession offense

(a) Notwithstanding any other provision of law, and except as provided in subdivision (b), any person convicted of a nonviolent drug possession offense shall receive probation. As a condition of probation the court shall require participation in and completion of an appropriate drug treatment program. The court shall impose appropriate drug testing as a condition of probation. The court may also impose, as a condition of probation, participation in vocational training, family counseling, literacy training and/or community service. A court may not impose incarceration as an additional condition of probation. Aside from the limitations imposed in this subdivision, the trial court is not otherwise limited in the type of probation conditions it may impose. Probation shall be imposed by suspending the imposition of sentence. No person shall be denied the opportunity to benefit from the provisions of the Substance Abuse and Crime Prevention Act of 2000 based solely upon evidence of a co-occurring psychiatric or developmental disorder. To the greatest extent possible, any person who is convicted of, and placed on probation pursuant to this section for a nonviolent drug possession offense shall be monitored by the court through the use of a dedicated court calendar and the incorporation of a collaborative court model of oversight that includes close collaboration with treatment providers and probation, drug testing commensurate with treatment needs, and supervision of progress through review hearings. In addition to any fine assessed under other provisions of law, the trial judge may require any person convicted of a nonviolent drug possession offense who is reasonably able to do so to contribute to the cost of his or her own placement in a drug treatment program.

(b) Subdivision (a) shall not apply to any of the following:

(1) Any defendant who previously has been convicted of one or more violent or serious felonies as defined in subdivision (c) of Section 667.5 or subdivision (c) of Section 1192.7, respectively, unless the nonviolent drug possession offense occurred after a period of five years in which the defendant remained free of both prison custody and the commission of an offense that results in a felony conviction other than a nonviolent drug possession offense, or a misdemeanor conviction involving physical injury or the threat of physical injury to another person.

(2) Any defendant who, in addition to one or more nonviolent drug possession offenses, has been convicted in the same proceeding of a misdemeanor not related to the use of drugs or any felony.

(3) Any defendant who, while armed with a deadly weapon, with the intent to use the same as a deadly weapon, unlawfully possesses or is under the influence of any controlled substance identified in Section 11054, 11055, 11056, 11057, or 11058 of the Health and Safety Code.

(4) Any defendant who refuses drug treatment as a condition of probation.

(5) Any defendant who has two separate convictions for nonviolent drug possession offenses, has participated in two separate courses of drug treatment pursuant to subdivision (a), and is found by the court, by clear and convincing evidence, to be unamenable to any and all forms of available drug treatment, as defined in subdivision (b) of Section 1210. Notwithstanding any other provision of law, the trial court shall sentence that defendant to 30 days in jail.

(c)

(1) Any defendant who has previously been convicted of at least three non-drug-related felonies for which the defendant has served three separate prison terms within the meaning of subdivision (b) of Section 667.5 shall be presumed eligible for treatment under subdivision (a). The court may exclude the defendant from treatment under subdivision (a) where the court, pursuant to the motion of the prosecutor or its own motion, finds that the defendant poses a present danger to the safety of others and would not benefit from a drug treatment program. The court shall, on the record, state its findings, the reasons for those findings.

(2) Any defendant who has previously been convicted of a misdemeanor or felony at least five times within the prior 30 months shall be presumed to be eligible for treatment under subdivision (a). The court may exclude the defendant from treatment under subdivision (a) if the court, pursuant to the motion of the prosecutor, or on its own motion, finds that the defendant poses a present danger to the safety of others or would not benefit from a drug treatment program. The court shall, on the record, state its findings and the reasons for those findings.

(d) Within seven days of an order imposing probation under subdivision (a), the probation department shall notify the drug treatment provider designated to provide drug treatment under subdivision (a). Within 30 days of receiving that notice, the treatment provider shall prepare a treatment plan and forward it to the probation department for distribution to the court and counsel. The treatment provider shall provide to the probation department standardized treatment progress reports, with minimum data elements as determined by the department, including all drug testing results. At a minimum, the reports shall be provided to the court every 90 days, or more frequently, as the court directs.

(1) If at any point during the course of drug treatment the treatment provider notifies the probation department and the court that the defendant is unamenable to the drug treatment being provided, but may be amenable to other drug treatments or related programs, the probation department may move the court to modify the terms of probation, or on its own motion, the court may modify the terms of probation after a hearing to ensure that the defendant receives the alternative drug treatment or program.

(2) If at any point during the course of drug treatment the treatment provider notifies the probation department and the court that the defendant is unamenable to the drug treatment provided and all other forms of drug treatment programs pursuant to subdivision (b) of Section 1210, the probation department may move to revoke probation. At the revocation hearing, if it is proved that the defendant is unamenable to all drug treatment programs pursuant to subdivision (b) of Section 1210, the court may revoke probation.

(3) Drug treatment services provided by subdivision (a) as a required condition of probation may not exceed 12 months, unless the court makes a finding supported by the record, that the continuation of treatment services beyond 12 months is necessary for drug treatment to be successful. If that finding is made, the court may order up to two six-month extensions of treatment services. The provision of treatment services under the Substance Abuse and Crime Prevention Act of 2000 shall not exceed 24 months.

(e)

(1) At any time after completion of drug treatment and the terms of probation, the court shall conduct a hearing, and if the court finds that the defendant successfully completed drug treatment, and substantially complied with the conditions of probation, including refraining from the use of drugs after the completion of treatment, the conviction on which the probation was based shall be set aside and the court shall dismiss the indictment, complaint, or information against the defendant. In addition, except as provided in paragraphs (2) and (3), both the arrest and the conviction shall be deemed never to have occurred. The defendant may additionally petition the court for a dismissal of charges at any time after completion of the prescribed course of drug treatment. Except as provided in paragraph (2) or (3), the defendant shall thereafter be released from all penalties and disabilities resulting from the offense of which he or she has been convicted.

(2) Dismissal of an indictment, complaint, or information pursuant to paragraph (1) does not permit a person to own, possess, or have in his or her custody or control any firearm capable of being concealed upon the person or prevent his or her conviction under Chapter 2 (commencing with Section 29800) of Division 9 of Title 4 of Part 6.

(3) Except as provided below, after an indictment, complaint, or information is dismissed pursuant to paragraph (1), the defendant may indicate in response to any question concerning his or her prior criminal record that he or she was not arrested or convicted for the offense. Except as provided below, a record pertaining to an arrest or conviction resulting in successful completion of a drug treatment program under this section may not, without the defendant's consent, be used in any way that could result in the denial of any employment, benefit, license, or certificate. Regardless of his or her successful completion of drug treatment, the arrest and conviction on which the probation was based may be recorded by the Department of Justice and disclosed in response to any peace officer application request or any law enforcement inquiry. Dismissal of an information, complaint, or indictment under this section does not relieve a defendant of the obligation to disclose the arrest and conviction in response to any direct question contained in any questionnaire or application for public office, for a position as a peace officer as defined in Section 830, for licensure by any state or local agency, for contracting with the California State Lottery, or for purposes of serving on a jury.

(f)

(1) If probation is revoked pursuant to the provisions of this subdivision, the defendant may be incarcerated pursuant to otherwise applicable law without regard to the provisions of this section. The court may modify or revoke probation if the alleged violation is proved.

(2) If a defendant receives probation under subdivision (a), and violates that probation either by committing an offense that is not a nonviolent drug possession offense, or by violating a non-drug-related condition of probation, and the state moves to revoke probation, the court may remand the defendant for a period not exceeding 30 days during which time the court may receive input from treatment, probation, the state, and the defendant, and the court may conduct further hearings as it deems appropriate to determine whether or not probation should be reinstated under this section. If the court reinstates the defendant on probation, the court may modify the treatment plan and any other terms of probation, and continue the defendant in a treatment program under the Substance Abuse and Crime Prevention Act of 2000. If the court reinstates the defendant on probation, the court may, after receiving input from the treatment provider and probation, if available, intensify or alter the treatment plan under subdivision (a), and impose sanctions, including jail sanctions not exceeding 30 days, a tool to enhance treatment compliance.

(3)

(A) If a defendant receives probation under subdivision (a), and violates that probation either by committing a nonviolent drug possession offense, or a misdemeanor for simple possession or use of drugs or drug paraphernalia, being present where drugs are used, or failure to register as a drug offender, or any activity similar to those listed in subdivision (d) of Section 1210, or by violating a drug-related condition of probation, and the state moves to revoke probation, the court shall conduct a hearing to determine whether probation shall be revoked. The trial court shall revoke probation if the alleged probation violation is proved and the state proves by a preponderance of the evidence that the defendant poses a danger to the safety of others. If the court does not revoke probation, it may intensify or alter the drug treatment plan and in addition, if the violation does not involve the recent use of drugs as a circumstance of the violation, including, but not limited to, violations relating to failure to appear at treatment or court, noncompliance with treatment, and failure to report for drug testing, the court may impose sanctions including jail sanctions that may not exceed 48 hours of continuous custody as a tool to enhance treatment compliance and impose other changes in the terms and conditions of probation. The court shall consider, among other factors, the seriousness of the violation, previous treatment compliance, employment, education, vocational training, medical conditions, medical treatment, including narcotics replacement treatment, and including the opinion of the defendant's licensed and treating physician if immediately available and presented at the hearing, child support obligations, and family responsibilities. The court shall consider additional conditions of probation, which may include, but are not limited to, community service and supervised work programs. If one of the circumstances of the violation involves recent drug use, as well as other circumstances of violation, and the circumstance of recent drug use is demonstrated to the court by satisfactory evidence and a finding made on the record, the court may, after receiving input from treatment and probation, if available, direct the defendant to enter a licensed detoxification or residential treatment facility, and if there is no bed immediately available in that type of facility, the court may order that the defendant be confined in a county jail for detoxification purposes only, if the jail offers detoxification services, for a period not to exceed 10 days. The detoxification services must provide narcotic replacement therapy for those defendants presently actually receiving narcotic replacement therapy.

(B) If a defendant receives probation under subdivision (a), and for the second time violates that probation either by committing a nonviolent drug possession offense, or a misdemeanor for simple possession or use of drugs or drug paraphernalia, being present where drugs are used, or failure to register as a drug offender, or any activity similar to those listed in subdivision (d) of Section 1210, or by violating a drug-related condition of probation, and the state moves to revoke probation, the court shall conduct a hearing to determine whether probation shall be revoked. The trial court shall revoke probation if the alleged probation violation is proved and the state proves by a preponderance of the evidence either that the defendant poses a danger to the safety of others or is unamenable to drug treatment. In determining whether a defendant is unamenable to drug treatment, the court may consider, to the extent relevant, whether the defendant (i) has committed a serious violation of rules at the drug treatment program, (ii) has repeatedly committed violations of program rules that inhibit the defendant's ability to function in the program, or (iii) has continually refused to participate in the program or asked to be removed from the program. If the court does not revoke probation, it may intensify or alter the drug treatment plan, and may, in addition, if the violation does not involve the recent use of drugs as a circumstance of the violation, including, but not limited to, violations relating to failure to appear at treatment or court, noncompliance with treatment, and failure to report for drug testing, impose sanctions including jail sanctions that may not exceed 120 hours of continuous custody as a tool to enhance treatment compliance and impose other changes in the terms and conditions of probation. The court shall consider, among other factors, the seriousness of the violation, previous treatment compliance, employment, education, vocational training, medical conditions, medical treatment, including narcotics replacement treatment, and including the opinion of the defendant's licensed and treating physician if immediately available and presented at the hearing, child support obligations, and family responsibilities. The court shall consider additional conditions of probation, which may include, but are not limited to, community service and supervised work programs. If one of the circumstances of the violation involves recent drug use, as well as other circumstances of violation, and the circumstance of recent drug use is demonstrated to the court by satisfactory evidence and a finding made on the record, the court may, after receiving input from treatment and probation, if available, direct the defendant to enter a licensed detoxification or residential treatment facility, and if there is no bed immediately available in the facility, the court may order that the defendant be confined in a county jail for detoxification purposes only, if the jail offers detoxification services, for a period not to exceed 10 days. Detoxification services must provide narcotic replacement therapy for those defendants presently actually receiving narcotic replacement therapy.

(C) If a defendant receives probation under subdivision (a), and for the third or subsequent time violates that probation either by committing a nonviolent drug possession offense, or by violating a drug-related condition of probation, and the state moves for a third or subsequent time to revoke probation, the court shall conduct a hearing to determine whether probation shall be revoked. If the alleged probation violation is proved, the defendant is not eligible for continued probation under subdivision (a) unless the court determines that the defendant is not a danger to the community and would benefit from further treatment under subdivision (a). The court may then either intensify or alter the treatment plan under subdivision (a) or transfer the defendant to a highly structured drug court. If the court continues the defendant in treatment under subdivision (a), or drug court, the court may impose appropriate sanctions including jail sanctions as the court deems appropriate.

(D) If a defendant on probation at the effective date of this act for a nonviolent drug possession offense violates that probation either by committing a nonviolent drug possession offense, or a misdemeanor for simple possession or use of drugs or drug paraphernalia, being present where drugs are used, or failure to register as a drug offender, or any activity similar to those listed in subdivision (d) of Section 1210, or by violating a drug-related condition of probation, and the state moves to revoke probation, the court shall conduct a hearing to determine whether probation shall be revoked. The trial court shall revoke probation if the alleged probation violation is proved and the state proves by a preponderance of the evidence that the defendant poses a danger to the safety of others. If the court does not revoke probation, it may modify or alter the treatment plan, and in addition, if the violation does not involve the recent use of drugs as a circumstance of the violation, including, but not limited to, violations relating to failure to appear at treatment or court, noncompliance with treatment, and failure to report for drug testing, the court may impose sanctions including jail sanctions that may not exceed 48 hours of continuous custody as a tool to enhance treatment compliance and impose other changes in the terms and conditions of probation. The court shall consider, among other factors, the seriousness of the violation, previous treatment compliance, employment, education, vocational training, medical conditions, medical treatment, including narcotics replacement treatment, and including the opinion of the defendant's licensed and treating physician if immediately available and presented at the hearing, child support obligations, and family responsibilities. The court shall consider additional conditions of probation, which may include, but are not limited to, community service and supervised work programs. If one of the circumstances of the violation involves recent drug use, as well as other circumstances of violation, and the circumstance of recent drug use is demonstrated to the court by satisfactory evidence and a finding made on the record, the court may, after receiving input from treatment and probation, if available, direct the defendant to enter a licensed detoxification or residential treatment facility, and if there is no bed immediately available in that type of facility, the court may order that the defendant be confined in a county jail for detoxification purposes only, if the jail offers detoxification services, for a period not to exceed 10 days. The detoxification services must provide narcotic replacement therapy for those defendants presently actually receiving narcotic replacement therapy.

(E) If a defendant on probation at the effective date of this act for a nonviolent drug possession offense violates that probation a second time either by committing a nonviolent drug possession offense, or a misdemeanor for simple possession or use of drugs or drug paraphernalia, being present where drugs are used, or failure to register as a drug offender, or any activity similar to those listed in subdivision (d) of Section 1210, or by violating a drug-related condition of probation, and the state moves for a second time to revoke probation, the court shall conduct a hearing to determine whether probation shall be revoked. The trial court shall revoke probation if the alleged probation violation is proved and the state proves by a preponderance of the evidence either that the defendant poses a danger to the safety of others or that the defendant is unamenable to drug treatment. If the court does not revoke probation, it may modify or alter the treatment plan, and in addition, if the violation does not involve the recent use of drugs as a circumstance of the violation, including, but not limited to, violations relating to failure to appear at treatment or court, noncompliance with treatment, and failure to report for drug testing, the court may impose sanctions including jail sanctions that may not exceed 120 hours of continuous custody as a tool to enhance treatment compliance and impose other changes in the terms and conditions of probation. The court shall consider, among other factors, the seriousness of the violation, previous treatment compliance, employment, education, vocational training, medical conditions, medical treatment including narcotics replacement treatment, and including the opinion of the defendant's licensed and treating physician if immediately available and presented at the hearing, child support obligations, and family responsibilities. The court shall consider additional conditions of probation, which may include, but are not limited to, community service and supervised work programs. If one of the circumstances of the violation involves recent drug use, as well as other circumstances of violation, and the circumstance of recent drug use is demonstrated to the court by satisfactory evidence and a finding made on the record, the court may, after receiving input from treatment and probation, if available, direct the defendant to enter a licensed detoxification or residential treatment facility, and if there is no bed immediately available in that type of facility, the court may order that the defendant be confined in a county jail for detoxification purposes only, if the jail offers detoxification services, for a period not to exceed 10 days. The detoxification services must provide narcotic replacement therapy for those defendants presently actually receiving narcotic replacement therapy.

(F) If a defendant on probation at the effective date of this act for a nonviolent drug offense violates that probation a third or subsequent time either by committing a nonviolent drug possession offense, or by violating a drug-related condition of probation, and the state moves for a third or subsequent time to revoke probation, the court shall conduct a hearing to determine whether probation shall be revoked. If the alleged probation violation is proved, the defendant is not eligible for continued probation under subdivision (a), unless the court determines that the defendant is not a danger to the community and would benefit from further treatment under subdivision (a). The court may then either intensify or alter the treatment plan under subdivision (a) or transfer the defendant to a highly structured drug court. If the court continues the defendant in treatment under subdivision (a), or drug court, the court may impose appropriate sanctions including jail sanctions.

(g) The term "drug-related condition of probation" shall include a probationer's specific drug treatment regimen, employment, vocational training, educational programs, psychological counseling, and family counseling.

Amended by Stats 2010 ch 178 (SB 1115),s 78, eff. 1/1/2011, op. 1/1/2012.

Amended by Stats 2006 ch 63 (SB 1137),s 7, eff. 7/12/2006.

Amended by Stats 2001 ch 721 (SB 223), s 3, eff. 10/11/2001.

36 (2000).

Section 1210.2 - [Effective until 1/1/2026] Grant program for demonstration projects to reduce the recidivism of high-risk misdemeanor probationers

(a)

(1) Upon appropriation by the Legislature, the Board of State and Community Corrections shall award funding for a grant program to four or more county superior courts or county probation departments to create demonstration projects to reduce the recidivism of high-risk misdemeanor probationers.

(2) The demonstration projects shall use risk assessments at sentencing when a misdemeanor conviction results in a term of probation to identify high-risk misdemeanants and to place these misdemeanants on formal probation that combines supervision with individually tailored programs, graduated sanctions, or incentives that address behavioral or treatment needs to achieve rehabilitation and successful completion of probation. The formal probation program may include incentives such as shortening probation terms as probationers complete the individually tailored program or probation requirements.

(3) The demonstration projects shall evaluate the probation completion and recidivism rates for project participants and may compare them to control groups to evaluate program efficacy. The board shall determine criteria for awarding the grants on a competitive basis that shall take into consideration the ability of a county to conduct a formal misdemeanor probation project for high-risk misdemeanor probationers, including components that align with evidence-based practices in reducing recidivism, including, but not limited to, risk and needs assessment, programming to help with drug or alcohol abuse, mental illness, or housing, and the support of the superior court if the application is from a county probation department.

(b) The board shall develop reporting requirements for each county receiving a grant to report the results of the demonstration project. The reports may include, but are not limited to, the use of risk assessment, the formal probation program components, the number of individuals who were placed on formal probation, the number of individuals who were placed on informal probation, and the number of individuals in each group who were subsequently convicted of a new offense.

(c)

(1) The board shall prepare a report that compiles the information it receives from each county receiving a grant, as described in subdivision (b). The report shall be completed and distributed to the Legislature and county criminal justice officials two years after an appropriation by the Legislature for this section.

(2) A report to be submitted pursuant to paragraph (1) shall be submitted in compliance with Section 9795 of the Government Code.

(d) This section shall remain in effect until January 1, 2026, and as of that date is repealed.

Added by Stats 2022 ch 856 (AB 2294),s 6, eff. 9/30/2022.

Section 1210.5 - Drug testing

In a case where a person has been ordered to undergo drug treatment as a condition of probation, any court ordered drug testing shall be used as a treatment tool. In evaluating a probationer's treatment program, results of any drug testing shall be given no greater weight than any other aspects of the probationer's individual treatment program.

Added by Stats 2001 ch 721 (SB 223), s 4, eff. 10/11/2001.

Section 1210.6 - Unfulfilled order of restitution or restitution fine

(a) When the court considers a petition for relief under this chapter, in its discretion and in the interests of justice, an unfulfilled order of restitution or restitution fine shall not be grounds to deny relief under this chapter to a person whose probation was conditioned on making victim restitution, if the person otherwise qualifies for relief pursuant to this chapter.

(b) An unfulfilled order of restitution or restitution fine shall not be grounds for finding that a defendant did not fulfill the conditions of probation for the entire period of probation.

(c) An unfulfilled order of restitution or restitution fine shall not be grounds for finding that a defendant did not fully comply with, and perform the sentence of, the court or finding that a defendant has not lived an honest and upright life and has not conformed to and obeyed the laws of the land.

Added by Stats 2022 ch 734 (SB 1106),s 9, eff. 1/1/2023.

Amended by Stats 2019 ch 25 (SB 94),s 38, eff. 6/27/2019.

Added by Stats 2018 ch 803 (AB 1065),s 8, eff. 1/1/2019.

Chapter 1.4 - ELECTRONIC MONITORING

Section 1210.7 - Continuous electronic monitoring

(a) Notwithstanding any other provisions of law, a county probation department may utilize continuous electronic monitoring to electronically monitor the whereabouts of persons on probation, as provided by this chapter.

(b) Any use of continuous electronic monitoring pursuant to this chapter shall have as its primary objective the enhancement of public safety through the reduction in the number of people being victimized by crimes committed by persons on probation.

(c) It is the intent of the Legislature in enacting this chapter to specifically encourage a county probation department acting pursuant to this chapter to utilize a system of continuous electronic monitoring that conforms with the requirements of this chapter.

(d) For purposes of this chapter, "continuous electronic monitoring" may include the use of worldwide radio navigation system technology, known as the Global Positioning System, or GPS. The Legislature finds that because of its capability for continuous surveillance, continuous electronic monitoring has been used in other parts of the country to monitor persons on formal probation who are identified as requiring a high level of supervision.

(e) The Legislature finds that continuous electronic monitoring has proven to be an effective risk management tool for supervising high-risk persons on probation who are likely to reoffend where prevention and knowledge of their whereabouts is a high priority for maintaining public safety.

Added by Stats 2005 ch 484 (SB 619),s 1, eff. 10/4/2005.

Section 1210.8 - Continuous electronic monitoring device

A county probation department may utilize a continuous electronic monitoring device pursuant to this section that has all of the following attributes:

(a) A device designed to be worn by a human being.

(b) A device that emits a signal as a person is moving or is stationary. The signal shall be capable of being received and tracked across large urban or rural areas, statewide, and being received from within structures, vehicles, and other objects to the degree technically feasible in light of the associated costs, design, and other considerations as are determined relevant by the county probation department.

(c) A device that functions 24 hours a day.

(d) A device that is resistant or impervious to unintentional or willful damage.

Added by Stats 2005 ch 484 (SB 619),s 1, eff. 10/4/2005.

Section 1210.9 - Capacity of continuous electronic monitoring system

(a) A continuous electronic monitoring system may have the capacity to immediately notify a county probation department of violations, actual or suspected, of the terms of probation that have been identified by the monitoring system if the requirement is deemed necessary by the county probation officer with respect to an individual person.

(b) The information described in subdivision (a), including geographic location and tampering, may be used as evidence to prove a violation of the terms of probation.

Added by Stats 2005 ch 484 (SB 619),s 1, eff. 10/4/2005.

Section 1210.10 - Standards to enhance public safety

A county probation department shall establish the following standards as are necessary to enhance public safety:

(a) Standards for the minimum time interval between transmissions of information about the location of the person under supervision. The standards shall be established after an evaluation of, at a minimum, all of the following:

    (1) The resources of the county probation department.

    (2) The criminal history of the person under supervision.

    (3) The safety of the victim of the persons under supervision.

(b) Standards for the accuracy of the information identifying the location of the person under supervision. The standards shall be established after consideration of, at a minimum, all of the following:

    (1) The need to identify the location of a person proximate to the location of a crime, including a violation of probation.

    (2) Resources of the probation department.

    (3) The need to avoid false indications of proximity to crimes.

Added by Stats 2005 ch 484 (SB 619),s 1, eff. 10/4/2005.

Section 1210.11 - Prohibitions against unauthorized access to, and use of, information

(a) A county probation department operating a system of continuous electronic monitoring pursuant to this section shall establish prohibitions against unauthorized access to, and use of, information by private or public entities as may be deemed appropriate. Unauthorized access to, and use of, electronic signals includes signals transmitted in any fashion by equipment utilized for continuous electronic monitoring.

(b) Devices used pursuant to this section shall not be used to eavesdrop or record any conversation, except a conversation between the participant and the person supervising the participant that is to be used solely for the purposes of voice identification.

Added by Stats 2005 ch 484 (SB 619),s 1, eff. 10/4/2005.

Section 1210.12 - Discretion of county chief probation officer; guidelines

(a) A county chief probation officer shall have the sole discretion, consistent with the terms and conditions of probation, to decide which persons shall be supervised using continuous electronic monitoring administered by the county probation department. No individual shall be required to participate in continuous electronic monitoring authorized by this chapter for any period of time longer than the term of probation.

(b) The county chief probation officer shall establish written guidelines that identify those persons on probation subject to continuous electronic monitoring authorized by this chapter. These guidelines shall include the need for enhancing monitoring in comparison to other persons not subject to the enhanced monitoring and the public safety needs that will be served by the enhanced monitoring.

Added by Stats 2005 ch 484 (SB 619),s 1, eff. 10/4/2005.

Section 1210.13 - Revocation of continuous monitoring

A county chief probation officer may revoke, in his or her discretion, the continuous monitoring of any individual.

Added by Stats 2005 ch 484 (SB 619),s 1, eff. 10/4/2005.

Section 1210.14 - Reasonable cause to take into custody without a warrant

Whenever a probation officer supervising an individual has reasonable cause to believe that the individual is not complying with the rules or conditions set forth for the use of continuous electronic monitoring as a supervision tool, the probation officer supervising the individual may, without a warrant of arrest, take the individual into custody for a violation of probation.

Added by Stats 2005 ch 484 (SB 619),s 1, eff. 10/4/2005.

Section 1210.15 - [Repealed]

Amended by Stats 2020 ch 92 (AB 1869),s 61, eff. 9/18/2020.

Added by Stats 2005 ch 484 (SB 619),s 1, eff. 10/4/2005.

Section 1210.16 - Legislative intent

It is the intent of the Legislature that continuous electronic monitoring established pursuant to this chapter maintain the highest public confidence, credibility, and public safety. In the furtherance of these standards, the following shall apply:

(a) The chief probation officer may administer continuous electronic monitoring pursuant to written contracts and appropriate public or private agencies or entities to provide specified supervision services. No public or private agency or entity may operate a continuous electronic monitoring system as authorized by this section in any county without a written contract with the county's probation department. No public or private agency or entity entering into a contract may itself employ any person who is a participant in continuous electronic monitoring surveillance.

(b) The county board of supervisors, the chief probation officer, and designees of the chief probation officer shall comply with Section 1090 of the Government Code in the consideration, making, and execution of contracts pursuant to this section.

Added by Stats 2005 ch 484 (SB 619),s 1, eff. 10/4/2005.

Chapter 1.5 - CERTIFICATION OF DRUG DIVERSION PROGRAMS

Section 1211 - Minimum requirements for drug diversion programs

(a) In order to ensure the quality of drug diversion programs provided pursuant to this chapter and Chapter 2.5 (commencing with Section 1000) of Title 6, and to expand the availability of these programs, the county drug program administrator in each county, in consultation with representatives of the court and the county probation department, shall establish minimum requirements, criteria, and fees for the successful completion of drug diversion programs, which shall be approved by the county board of supervisors no later than January 1, 1995. These minimum requirements shall include, but not be limited to, all of the following:

(1) An initial assessment of each divertee, which may include all of the following:

(A) Social, cultural, linguistic, economic, and family background.

(B) Education.

(C) Vocational achievements.

(D) Criminal history.

(E) Medical history.

(F) Drug history and previous treatment.

(2) A minimum of 20 hours of either effective education or counseling or any combination of both for each divertee. The education and counseling program shall include education about how the use of controlled substances affects the body and brain, factors that contribute to physical dependence, how to recognize and respond to the signs of drug overdose, and the dangers of using controlled substances unless under appropriate medical supervision. This education shall be culturally and linguistically appropriate and may include, but is not limited to, informing program participants about the physical and mental health risks associated with substance use disorders, the grave health risk to those who are exposed to controlled substances and the extreme danger to human life when controlled substances are manufactured and distributed.

(3) An exit conference which shall reflect the divertee's progress during their participation in the program.

(4) Fee exemptions for persons who cannot afford to pay.

(b) The county drug program administrator shall implement a certification procedure for drug diversion programs.

(c) The county drug program administrator shall recommend for approval by the county board of supervisors programs pursuant to this chapter. No program, regardless of how it is funded, may be approved unless it meets the standards established by the administrator, which shall include, but not be limited to, all of the following:

(1) Guidelines and criteria for education and treatment services, including standards of services that may include lectures, classes, group discussions, and individual counseling. However, any class or group discussion other than lectures shall not exceed 15 persons at any one meeting.

(2) Established and approved supervision, either on a regular or irregular basis, of the person for the purpose of evaluating the person's progress.

(3) A schedule of fees to be charged for services rendered to each person under a county drug program plan in accordance with the following provisions:

(A) Fees shall be used only for the purposes set forth in this chapter.

(B) Fees for the treatment or rehabilitation of each participant receiving services under a certified drug diversion program shall not exceed the actual cost thereof, as determined by the county drug program administrator according to standard accounting practices.

(C) Actual costs shall include both of the following:

(i) All costs incurred by the providers of diversion programs.

(ii) All expenses incurred by the county for administration, certification, or management of the drug diversion program in compliance with this chapter.

(d) The county shall require, as a condition of certification, that the drug diversion program pay to the county drug program administrator all expenses incurred by the county for administration, certification, or management of the drug diversion program in compliance with this chapter. No fee shall be required by any county other than that county where the program is located.

Amended by Stats 2023 ch 481 (SB 46),s 3, eff. 1/1/2024.

Amended by Stats. 1993, Ch. 850, Sec. 4. Effective January 1, 1994.

Chapter 2 - THE EXECUTION

Section 1213 - Furnishing of information to officer

(a) When a probationary order or a judgment, other than of death, has been pronounced, a copy of the entry of that portion of the probationary order ordering the defendant confined in a city or county jail as a condition of probation, or a copy of the entry of the judgment, or, if the judgment is for imprisonment in the state prison or imprisonment pursuant to subdivision (h) of Section 1170, either a copy of the minute order or an abstract of the judgment as provided in Section 1213.5, certified by the clerk of the court, and a Criminal Investigation and Identification (CII) number shall be forthwith furnished to the officer whose duty it is to execute the probationary order or judgment, and no other warrant or authority is necessary to justify or require its execution.

(b) If a copy of the minute order is used as the commitment document, the first page or pages shall be identical in form and content to that prescribed by the Judicial Council for an abstract of judgment, and other matters as appropriate may be added thereafter.

Amended by Stats 2011 ch 39 (AB 117),s 68, eff. 6/30/2011.

Amended by Stats 2011 ch 15 (AB 109),s 457, eff. 4/4/2011, but operative no earlier than October 1, 2011, and only upon creation of a community corrections grant program to assist in implementing this act and upon an appropriation to fund the grant program.

Amended by Stats 2007 ch 263 (AB 310),s 29, eff. 1/1/2008.

Section 1213.5 - Abstract of judgment

The abstract of judgment provided for in Section 1213 shall be prescribed by the Judicial Council.

Amended by Stats. 1986, Ch. 248, Sec. 164.

Section 1214 - Enforcement of judgment for fine, including restitution fine

(a) If the judgment is for a fine, including a restitution fine ordered pursuant to Section 1202.4, 1202.44, or 1202.45, or Section 1203.04 as operative on or before August 2, 1995, or Section 13967 of the Government Code, as operative on or before September 28, 1994, with or without imprisonment, or a diversion restitution fee ordered pursuant to Section 1001.90, the judgment may be enforced in the manner provided for the enforcement of money judgments generally. Any portion of a restitution fine or restitution fee that remains unsatisfied after a defendant is no longer on probation, parole, postrelease community supervision pursuant to Section 3451, or mandatory supervision pursuant to subparagraph (B) of paragraph (5) of subdivision (h) of Section 1170, after a term in custody pursuant to subparagraph (A) of paragraph (5) of subdivision (h) of Section 1170, or after completing diversion is enforceable by the California Victim Compensation Board pursuant to this section. Notwithstanding any other provision of law prohibiting disclosure, the state, as defined in Section 900.6 of the Government Code, a local public entity, as defined in Section 900.4 of the Government Code, or any other entity, may provide the California Victim Compensation Board any and all information to assist in the collection of unpaid portions of a restitution fine for terminated probation or parole cases, or of a restitution fee for completed diversion cases. For purposes of the preceding sentence, "state, as defined in Section 900.6 of the Government Code," and "any other entity" shall not include the Franchise Tax Board. A local collection program may continue to collect restitution fines and restitution orders once a defendant is no longer on probation, postrelease community supervision, or mandatory supervision or after a term in custody pursuant to subparagraph (A) of paragraph (5) of subdivision (h) of Section 1170.

(b) In any case in which a defendant is ordered to pay restitution, the order to pay restitution (1) is deemed a money judgment if the defendant was informed of his or her right to have a judicial determination of the amount and was provided with a hearing, waived a hearing, or stipulated to the amount of the restitution ordered, and (2) shall be fully enforceable by a victim as if the restitution order were a civil judgment, and enforceable in the same manner as is provided for the enforcement of any other money judgment. Upon the victim's request, the court shall provide the victim in whose favor the order of restitution is entered with a certified copy of that order and a copy of the defendant's disclosure pursuant to paragraph (5) of subdivision (f) of Section 1202.4, affidavit or information pursuant to paragraph (6) of subdivision (f) of Section 1202.4, or report pursuant to paragraph (8) of subdivision (f) of Section 1202.4. The court also shall provide this information to the district attorney upon request in connection with an investigation or prosecution involving perjury or the veracity of the information contained within the defendant's financial disclosure. In addition, upon request, the court shall provide the California Victim Compensation Board with a certified copy of any order imposing a restitution fine or order and a copy of the defendant's disclosure pursuant to paragraph (5) of subdivision (f) of Section 1202.4, affidavit or information pursuant to paragraph (6) of subdivision (f) of Section 1202.4, or report pursuant to paragraph (8) of subdivision (f) of Section 1202.4. A victim shall have access to all resources available under the law to enforce the restitution order, including, but not limited to, access to the defendant's financial records, use of wage garnishment and lien procedures, information regarding the defendant's assets, and the ability to apply for restitution from any fund established for the purpose of compensating victims in civil cases. Any portion of a restitution order that remains unsatisfied after a defendant is no longer on probation, parole, postrelease community supervision under Section 3451, or mandatory supervision imposed pursuant to subparagraph (B) of paragraph (5) of subdivision (h) of Section 1170 or after a term in custody pursuant to subparagraph (A) of paragraph (5) of subdivision (h) of Section 1170 is enforceable by the victim pursuant to this section. Victims and the California Victim Compensation Board shall inform the court whenever an order to pay restitution is satisfied. A local collection program may continue to enforce victim restitution orders once a defendant is no longer on probation, postrelease community supervision, or mandatory supervision or after completion of a term in custody pursuant to subparagraph (A) of paragraph (5) of subdivision (h) of Section 1170.

(c) A defendant who owes a restitution fine, a restitution order, or any portion thereof, and who is released from the custody of a county jail facility after a term in custody pursuant to subparagraph (A) of paragraph (5) of subdivision (h) of Section 1170 shall have a continuing obligation to pay the restitution fine or restitution order in full.

(d) Except as provided in subdivision (d), and notwithstanding the amount in controversy limitation of Section 85 of the Code of Civil Procedure, a restitution order or restitution fine that was imposed pursuant to Section 1202.4 in any of the following cases may be enforced in the same manner as a money judgment in a limited civil case:

(1) In a misdemeanor case.

(2) In a case involving violation of a city or town ordinance.

(3) In a noncapital criminal case where the court has received a plea of guilty or nolo contendere.

(e) Chapter 3 (commencing with Section 683.010) of Division 1 of Title 9 of Part 2 of the Code of Civil Procedure shall not apply to any of the following:

(1) A judgment for court-ordered fines, forfeitures, penalties, fees, or assessments.

(2) A restitution fine or restitution order imposed pursuant to Section 1202.4, 1202.44, or 1202.45, or Section 1203.04, as operative on or before August 2, 1995, or Section 13967 of the Government Code, as operative on or before September 28, 1994.

(3) A diversion restitution fee ordered pursuant to Section 1001.90.

Amended by Stats 2016 ch 31 (SB 836),s 242, eff. 6/27/2016.
Amended by Stats 2014 ch 513 (SB 419),s 1.5, eff. 1/1/2015.
Amended by Stats 2012 ch 762 (SB 1210),s 2, eff. 1/1/2013.
Amended by Stats 2010 ch 720 (SB 857),s 29, eff. 10/19/2010.
Amended by Stats 2004 ch 223 (SB 631), s 5, eff. 8/16/2004.
Amended by Stats 2002 ch 784 (SB 1316), s 549, eff. 1/1/2003.
Amended by Stats 2000 ch 545 (AB 2371) s 2, eff. 1/1/2001.

Section 1214.1 - Civil assessment

(a)On or after July 1, 2022, in addition to any other penalty in infraction, misdemeanor, or felony cases, the court may impose a civil assessment of up to one hundred dollars ($100) against a defendant who fails, after notice and without good cause, to appear in court for a proceeding authorized by law or who fails to pay all or any portion of a fine ordered by the court or to pay an installment of bail as agreed to under Section 40510.5 of the Vehicle Code. This assessment shall be deposited with the county treasurer as provided in Section 1463.001, and transmitted to the State Treasurer for deposit into the General Fund.

(b)

(1)The assessment imposed pursuant to subdivision (a) shall not become effective until at least 20 calendar days after the court mails a warning notice to the defendant by first-class mail to the address shown on the notice to appear or to the defendant's last known address. If the defendant appears within the time specified in the notice and shows good cause for the failure to appear or for the failure to pay a fine or installment of bail, the court shall vacate the assessment.

(2)Payment of bail, fines, penalties, fees, or a civil assessment shall not be required in order for the court to vacate the assessment at the time of appearance pursuant to paragraph (1). Payment of a civil assessment shall not be required to schedule a court hearing on a pending underlying charge.

(c)If a civil assessment is imposed pursuant to subdivision (a), no bench warrant or warrant of arrest shall be issued with respect to the failure to appear at the proceeding for which the assessment is imposed or the failure to pay the fine or installment of bail. An outstanding, unserved bench warrant or warrant of arrest for a failure to appear or for a failure to pay a fine or installment of bail shall be recalled prior to the subsequent imposition of a civil assessment.

(d)The assessment imposed pursuant to subdivision (a) shall be subject to the due process requirements governing defense and collection of civil money judgments generally.

(e)Each court and county shall maintain the collection program that was in effect on July 1, 2005, unless otherwise agreed to by the court and county. If a court and a county do not agree on a plan for the collection of civil assessments imposed pursuant to this section, or any other collections under Section 1463.010, after the implementation of Sections 68085.6 and 68085.7 of the Government Code, the court or the county may request arbitration by a third party mutually agreed upon by the Administrative Director of the Courts and the California State Association of Counties.

Amended by Stats 2022 ch 57 (AB 199),s 18, eff. 6/30/2022.
Amended by Stats 2015 ch 385 (SB 405),s 1, eff. 9/30/2015.
Amended by Stats 2007 ch 738 (AB 1248),s 41, eff. 1/1/2008.
Amended by Stats 2005 ch 706 (AB 1742),s 36, eff. 1/1/2006
Amended by Stats 2005 ch 705 (SB 67),s 7, eff. 10/7/2005.
Amended by Stats 2005 ch 74 (AB 139),s 59, eff. 7/19/2005.

Section 1214.2 - Enforcement of payment of fine as condition of probation

(a) Except as provided in subdivision (c), if a defendant is ordered to pay a fine as a condition of probation, the order to pay a fine may be enforced during the term of probation in the same manner as is provided for the enforcement of money judgments.

(b) Except as provided in subdivision (c), an order to pay a fine as a condition of probation may also be enforced as follows:

(1) With respect to a willful failure to pay during the term of probation, in the same manner as a violation of the terms and conditions of probation.

(2) If any balance remains unpaid at the end of the term of probation, in the same manner as a judgment in a civil action.

(c) If an order to pay a fine as a condition of probation is stayed, a writ of execution shall not issue until the stay is lifted.

Added by Stats. 1987, Ch. 454, Sec. 1. Effective September 9, 1987.

Section 1215 - Judgment for imprisonment, or fine and imprisonment until it be paid

If the judgment is for imprisonment, or a fine and imprisonment until it be paid, the defendant must forthwith be committed to the custody of the proper officer and by him or her detained until the judgment is complied with. Where, however, the court has suspended sentence, or where, after imposing sentence, the court has suspended the execution thereof and placed the defendant on probation, as provided in Section 1203, the defendant, if over the age of 16 years, shall be placed under the care and supervision of the probation officer of the court committing him or her, until the expiration of the period of probation and the compliance with the terms and conditions of the sentence, or of the suspension thereof. Where, however, the probation has been terminated as provided in Section 1203, and the suspension of the sentence, or of the execution revoked, and the judgment pronounced, the defendant shall be committed to the custody of the proper officer and be detained until the judgment be complied with.

Amended by Stats. 1987, Ch. 828, Sec. 80.

Section 1216 - Judgment for imprisonment in state prison

If the judgment is for imprisonment in the state prison, the sheriff of the county shall, upon receipt of a certified abstract or minute order thereof, take and deliver the defendant to the warden of the state prison. The sheriff also shall deliver to the warden the certified abstract of the judgment or minute order, a Criminal Investigation and Identification (CII) number, a Confidential Medical/Mental Health Information Transfer Form indicating that the defendant is medically capable of being transported, and take from the warden a receipt for the defendant.

Amended by Stats. 1998, Ch. 767, Sec. 1. Effective January 1, 1999.

Section 1217 - Judgment of death

When judgment of death is rendered, a commitment signed by the judge, and attested by the clerk under the seal of the court must be drawn and delivered to the sheriff. It must state the conviction and judgment, and must direct the sheriff to deliver the defendant, within 10 days from the time of judgment, to the warden of the State prison of this State designated by the State Board of Prison Directors for the execution of the death penalty, to be held pending the decision upon his appeal.

Amended by Stats. 1943, Ch. 107.

Section 1218 - Transmission to governor after judgment of death

The judge of the court at which a judgment of death is had, must, immediately after the judgment, transmit to the Governor, by mail or otherwise, a statement of the conviction and judgment, and a complete transcript of all the testimony given at the trial including any arguments made by respective counsel and a copy of the clerk's transcript.

Amended by Stats. 1961, Ch. 1648.

Section 1219 - Opinion required by governor

The Governor may thereupon require the opinion of the Justices of the Supreme Court and of the Attorney General, or any of them, upon the statement so furnished.

Enacted 1872.

Section 1227 - Execution of judgment of death

(a) If for any reason other than the pendency of an appeal pursuant to subdivision (b) of Section 1239 of this code a judgment of death has not been executed, and it remains in force, the court in which the conviction was had shall, on application of the district attorney, or may upon its own motion, make and cause to be entered an order specifying a period of 10 days during which the judgment shall be executed. The 10-day period shall begin no less than 30 days after the order is entered and shall end no more than 60 days after the order is entered. Immediately after the order is entered, a certified copy of the order, attested by the clerk, under the seal of the court, shall, for the purpose of execution, be transmitted by registered mail to the warden of the state prison having the custody of the defendant; provided, that if the defendant be at large, a warrant for his apprehension may be issued, and upon being apprehended, he shall be brought before the court, whereupon the court shall make an order directing the warden of the state prison to whom the sheriff is instructed to deliver the defendant to execute the judgment within a period of 10 days, which shall not begin less than 30 days nor end more than 60 days from the time of making such order.

(b) From an order fixing the time for and directing the execution of such judgment as herein provided, there shall be no appeal.

Amended by Proposition 66, approved by the voters at the November 8, 2016 election, effective immediately upon enactment.

Section 1227.5 - Execution of judgment of death on day after period of stay or reprieve

Notwithstanding Section 1227, where a judgment of death has not been executed by reason of a stay or reprieve granted by the Governor, the execution shall be carried out on the day immediately after the period of the stay or reprieve without further judicial proceedings.

Added by Stats. 1961, Ch. 1648.

Chapter 3 - CALIFORNIA COMMUNITY CORRECTIONS PERFORMANCE INCENTIVES

Section 1228 - Legislative findings and declarations

The Legislature finds and declares all of the following:

(a) In 2007, nearly 270,000 felony offenders were subject to probation supervision in California's communities.

(b) In 2007, out of 46,987 new admissions to state prison, nearly 20,000 were felony offenders who were committed to state prison after failing probation supervision.

(c) Probation is a judicially imposed suspension of sentence that attempts to supervise, treat, and rehabilitate offenders while they remain in the community under the supervision of the probation department. Probation is a linchpin of the criminal justice system, closely aligned with the courts, and plays a central role in promoting public safety in California's communities.

(d) Providing sustainable funding for improved, evidence-based probation supervision practices and capacities will improve public safety outcomes among adult felons who are on probation. Improving felony probation performance, measured by a reduction in felony probationers who are sent to prison because they were revoked on probation or convicted of another crime while on probation, will reduce the number of new admissions to state prison, saving taxpayer dollars and allowing a portion of those state savings to be redirected to probation for investing in community corrections programs.

Added by Stats 2009 ch 608 (SB 678),s 2, eff. 1/1/2010.
Repealed by Stats 2010 ch 709 (SB 1062),s 14, eff. 1/1/2011.
Repealed by Stats 2010 ch 328 (SB 1330),s 167, eff. 1/1/2011.
Added by Stats 2009 ch 28 (SB X3-18),s 36, eff. 1/1/2010.

Section 1229 - Definitions

As used in this chapter, the following definitions apply:

(a) "Community corrections" means the placement of persons convicted of a felony offense under probation supervision, mandatory supervision, or postrelease community supervision for a specified period.

(b) "Chief probation officer" or "CPO" means the chief probation officer for the county or city and county in which an adult offender is subject to probation for the conviction of a felony offense.

(c) "Community corrections program" means a program established pursuant to this act consisting of a system of services for felony offenders under local supervision dedicated to all of the following goals:

(1) Enhancing public safety through the management and reduction of offender risk while under local supervision and upon reentry from jail or prison into the community.

(2) Providing a range of supervision tools, sanctions, and services applied to felony offenders subject to local supervision based on a risk and needs assessment for the purpose of reducing criminal conduct and promoting behavioral change that results in reducing recidivism and promoting the successful reintegration of offenders into the community.

(3) Maximizing offender restitution, reconciliation, and restorative services to victims of crime.

(4) Holding offenders accountable for their criminal behaviors and for successful compliance with applicable court orders and conditions of supervision.

(5) Improving public safety outcomes for persons subject to local supervision for a felony offense, as measured by their successful completion of the period of local supervision and the commensurate reduction in the rate of offenders sent to prison as a result of a revocation of supervision or conviction of a new crime.

(d) "Evidence-based practices" refers to supervision policies, procedures, programs, and practices demonstrated by scientific research to reduce recidivism among individuals under local supervision.

(e) "Local supervision" means the supervision of an adult felony offender on probation, mandatory supervision, or postrelease community supervision.

Amended by Stats 2013 ch 31 (SB 75),s 10, eff. 6/27/2013.
Amended by Stats 2010 ch 328 (SB 1330),s 168, eff. 1/1/2011.
Added by Stats 2009 ch 608 (SB 678),s 2, eff. 1/1/2010.
Repealed by Stats 2010 ch 709 (SB 1062),s 14, eff. 1/1/2011.
Repealed by Stats 2010 ch 328 (SB 1330),s 167, eff. 1/1/2011.
Added by Stats 2009 ch 28 (SB X3-18),s 36, eff. 1/1/2010.

Section 1230 - Community Corrections Performance Incentives Fund

(a) Each county is hereby authorized to establish in each county treasury a Community Corrections Performance Incentives Fund (CCPIF), to receive all amounts allocated to that county for purposes of implementing this chapter.

(b) Notwithstanding any other law, in any fiscal year for which a county receives moneys to be expended for the implementation of this chapter, the moneys, including any interest, shall be made available to the CPO of that county, within 30 days of the deposit of those moneys into the fund, for the implementation of the community corrections program authorized by this chapter.

(1) The community corrections program shall be developed and implemented by probation and advised by a local Community Corrections Partnership.

(2) The local Community Corrections Partnership shall be chaired by the CPO and comprised of the following membership:

(A) The presiding judge of the superior court, or his or her designee.

(B) A county supervisor or the chief administrative officer for the county or a designee of the board of supervisors.

(C) The district attorney.

(D) The public defender.

(E) The sheriff.

(F) A chief of police.

(G) The head of the county department of social services.

(H) The head of the county department of mental health.

(I) The head of the county department of employment.

(J) The head of the county alcohol and substance abuse programs.

(K) The head of the county office of education.

(L) A representative from a community-based organization with experience in successfully providing rehabilitative services to persons who have been convicted of a criminal offense.

(M) An individual who represents the interests of victims.

(3) Funds allocated to probation pursuant to this act shall be used to provide supervision and rehabilitative services for adult felony offenders subject to local supervision, and shall be spent on evidence-based community corrections practices and programs, as defined in subdivision (d) of Section 1229, which may include, but are not limited to, the following:

    (A) Implementing and expanding evidence-based risk and needs assessments.

    (B) Implementing and expanding intermediate sanctions that include, but are not limited to, electronic monitoring, mandatory community service, home detention, day reporting, restorative justice programs, work furlough programs, and incarceration in county jail for up to 90 days.

    (C) Providing more intensive local supervision.

    (D) Expanding the availability of evidence-based rehabilitation programs including, but not limited to, drug and alcohol treatment, mental health treatment, anger management, cognitive behavior programs, and job training and employment services.

    (E) Evaluating the effectiveness of rehabilitation and supervision programs and ensuring program fidelity.

(4) Notwithstanding any other law, the CPO shall have discretion to spend funds on any of the above practices and programs consistent with this act but, at a minimum, shall devote at least 5 percent of all funding received to evaluate the effectiveness of those programs and practices implemented with the funds provided pursuant to this chapter. A CPO may petition the Judicial Council to have this restriction waived, and the Judicial Council shall have the authority to grant such a petition, if the CPO can demonstrate that the department is already devoting sufficient funds to the evaluation of these programs and practices.

(5) Each probation department receiving funds under this chapter shall maintain a complete and accurate accounting of all funds received pursuant to this chapter.

Amended by Stats 2015 ch 26 (SB 85),s 14, eff. 6/24/2015.
Amended by Stats 2013 ch 76 (AB 383),s 154, eff. 1/1/2014.
Amended by Stats 2013 ch 31 (SB 75),s 11, eff. 6/27/2013.
Amended by Stats 2011 ch 136 (AB 116),s 33, eff. 7/27/2011.
Amended by Stats 2011 ch 39 (AB 117),s 32, eff. 6/30/2011, 7/27/2011.
Amended by Stats 2010 ch 328 (SB 1330),s 169, eff. 1/1/2011.
Added by Stats 2009 ch 608 (SB 678),s 2, eff. 1/1/2010.
Repealed by Stats 2010 ch 709 (SB 1062),s 14, eff. 1/1/2011.
Repealed by Stats 2010 ch 328 (SB 1330),s 167, eff. 1/1/2011.
Added by Stats 2009 ch 28 (SB X3-18),s 36, eff. 1/1/2010.

Section 1230.1 - Local plan for implementation of public safety realignment

(a) Each county local Community Corrections Partnership established pursuant to subdivision (b) of Section 1230 shall recommend a local plan to the county board of supervisors for the implementation of the 2011 public safety realignment.

(b) The plan shall be voted on by an executive committee of each county's Community Corrections Partnership consisting of the chief probation officer of the county as chair, a chief of police, the sheriff, the District Attorney, the Public Defender, the presiding judge of the superior court, or his or her designee, and one department representative listed in either subparagraph (G), (H), or (J) of paragraph (2) of subdivision (b) of Section 1230, as designated by the county board of supervisors for purposes related to the development and presentation of the plan.

(c) The plan shall be deemed accepted by the county board of supervisors unless the board rejects the plan by a vote of four-fifths of the board, in which case the plan goes back to the Community Corrections Partnership for further consideration.

(d) Consistent with local needs and resources, the plan may include recommendations to maximize the effective investment of criminal justice resources in evidence-based correctional sanctions and programs, including, but not limited to, day reporting centers, drug courts, residential multiservice centers, mental health treatment programs, electronic and GPS monitoring programs, victim restitution programs, counseling programs, community service programs, educational programs, and work training programs.

Amended by Stats 2011 ch 136 (AB 116),s 33, eff. 7/27/2011.
Amended by Stats 2011 ch 39 (AB 117),s 68, eff. 6/30/2011.
Amended by Stats 2011 ch 39 (AB 117),s 33, eff. 6/30/2011, Amended by Stats 2011 ch 36 (SB 92),s 23, eff. 6/30/2011, 7/27/2011 .
  7/27/2011.
Added by Stats 2011 ch 15 (AB 109),s 458, eff. 4/4/2011, but operative no earlier than October 1, 2011, and only upon creation of a community corrections grant program to assist in implementing this act and upon an appropriation to fund the grant program.

Section 1231 - Outcome-based measures

(a) Community corrections programs funded pursuant to this chapter shall identify and track specific outcome-based measures consistent with the goals of this act.

(b) The Judicial Council, in consultation with the Chief Probation Officers of California, shall specify and define minimum required outcome-based measures, which shall include, but not be limited to, all of the following:

    (1) The percentage of persons subject to local supervision who are being supervised in accordance with evidence-based practices.

    (2) The percentage of state moneys expended for programs that are evidence based, and a descriptive list of all programs that are evidence based.

    (3) Specification of supervision policies, procedures, programs, and practices that were eliminated.

    (4) The percentage of persons subject to local supervision who successfully complete the period of supervision.

(c) Each CPO receiving funding pursuant to Sections 1233 to 1233.6, inclusive, shall provide an annual written report to the Judicial Council, evaluating the effectiveness of the community corrections program, including, but not limited to, the data described in subdivision (b).

(d) The Judicial Council, shall, in consultation with the CPO of each county and the Department of Corrections and Rehabilitation, provide a quarterly statistical report to the Department of Finance including, but not limited to, the following statistical information for each county:

(1) The number of felony filings.

(2) The number of felony convictions.

(3) The number of felony convictions in which the defendant was sentenced to the state prison.

(4) The number of felony convictions in which the defendant was granted probation.

(5) The adult felon probation population.

(6) The number of adult felony probationers who had their probation terminated and revoked and were sent to state prison for that revocation.

(7) The number of adult felony probationers sent to state prison for a conviction of a new felony offense, including when probation was revoked or terminated.

(8) The number of adult felony probationers who had their probation revoked and were sent to county jail for that revocation.

(9) The number of adult felony probationers sent to county jail for a conviction of a new felony offense, including when probation was revoked or terminated.

(10) The number of felons placed on postrelease community supervision, commencing January 1, 2012.

(11) The number of felons placed on mandatory supervision, commencing January 1, 2012.

(12) The mandatory supervision population, commencing January 1, 2012.

(13) The postrelease community supervision population, commencing January 1, 2012.

(14) The number of felons on postrelease community supervision sentenced to state prison for a conviction of a new felony offense, commencing January 1, 2012.

(15) The number of felons on mandatory supervision sentenced to state prison for a conviction of a new felony offense, commencing January 1, 2012.

(16) The number of felons who had their postrelease community supervision revoked and were sent to county jail for that revocation, commencing January 1, 2012. This number shall not include felons on postrelease community supervision who are subject to flash incarceration pursuant to Section 3453.

(17) The number of felons on postrelease community supervision sentenced to county jail for a conviction of a new felony offense, including when postrelease community supervision was revoked or terminated, commencing January 1, 2012.

(18) The number of felons who had their mandatory supervision revoked and were sentenced to county jail for that revocation, commencing January 1, 2012.

(19) The number of felons on mandatory supervision sentenced to county jail for a conviction of a new felony offense, including when mandatory supervision was revoked or terminated, commencing January 1, 2012.

Amended by Stats 2015 ch 26 (SB 85),s 15, eff. 6/24/2015.

Amended by Stats 2013 ch 360 (SB 100),s 5, eff. 9/26/2013.

Amended by Stats 2013 ch 31 (SB 75),s 12, eff. 6/27/2013.

Amended by Stats 2012 ch 41 (SB 1021),s 63, eff. 6/27/2012.

Amended by Stats 2010 ch 328 (SB 1330),s 170, eff. 1/1/2011.

Added by Stats 2009 ch 608 (SB 678),s 2, eff. 1/1/2010.

Repealed by Stats 2010 ch 709 (SB 1062),s 14, eff. 1/1/2011.

Repealed by Stats 2010 ch 328 (SB 1330),s 167, eff. 1/1/2011.

Added by Stats 2009 ch 28 (SB X3-18),s 36, eff. 1/1/2010.

Section 1232 - Report on implementation of act

Commencing no later than 18 months following the initial receipt of funding pursuant to this chapter and annually thereafter, the Judicial Council, in consultation with the Department of Corrections and Rehabilitation, the Department of Finance, and the Chief Probation Officers of California, shall submit to the Governor and the Legislature a comprehensive report on the implementation of this chapter. The report shall include, but not be limited to, all of the following information:

(a) The effectiveness of the community corrections program based on the reports of performance-based outcome measures required in Section 1231.

(b) The percentage of offenders subject to local supervision whose supervision was revoked and who were sent to prison for the year on which the report is being made.

(c) The percentage of offenders subject to local supervision who were convicted of crimes during their term of supervision for the year on which the report is being made.

(d) The impact of the moneys appropriated pursuant to this chapter to enhance public safety by reducing the percentage and number of offenders subject to local supervision whose supervision was revoked for the year being reported on for violations or new convictions, and to reduce the number of offenders subject to local supervision who are sentenced to prison for a new conviction for the year on which the report is being made.

(e) Any recommendations regarding resource allocations or additional collaboration with other state, regional, federal, or local entities for improvements to this chapter.

Amended by Stats 2015 ch 26 (SB 85),s 16, eff. 6/24/2015.

Amended by Stats 2013 ch 31 (SB 75),s 13, eff. 6/27/2013.

Added by Stats 2009 ch 608 (SB 678),s 2, eff. 1/1/2010.

Repealed by Stats 2010 ch 709 (SB 1062),s 14, eff. 1/1/2011.

Repealed by Stats 2010 ch 328 (SB 1330),s 167, eff. 1/1/2011.

Added by Stats 2009 ch 28 (SB X3-18),s 36, eff. 1/1/2010.

Section 1233 - [Repealed]

Repealed by Stats 2015 ch 26 (SB 85),s 17, eff. 6/24/2015.

Amended by Stats 2013 ch 31 (SB 75),s 14, eff. 6/27/2013.

Amended by Stats 2011 ch 36 (SB 92),s 24, eff. 6/30/2011.

Added by Stats 2009 ch 608 (SB 678),s 2, eff. 1/1/2010.
Repealed by Stats 2010 ch 709 (SB 1062),s 14, eff. 1/1/2011.
Repealed by Stats 2010 ch 328 (SB 1330),s 167, eff. 1/1/2011.
Added by Stats 2009 ch 28 (SB X3-18),s 36, eff. 1/1/2010.

Section 1233.1 - Required calculations for calendar year

After the conclusion of each calendar year, the Director of Finance, in consultation with the Department of Corrections and Rehabilitation, the Joint Legislative Budget Committee, the Chief Probation Officers of California, and the Judicial Council, shall calculate the following for that calendar year:

(a) The cost to the state to incarcerate in a contract facility and supervise on parole an offender who fails local supervision and is sent to prison.

(b) The statewide probation failure rate shall be calculated as the total number of adult felony probationers statewide sent to state prison as a percentage of the average statewide adult felony probation population for that year.

(c) The probation failure rate for each county shall be calculated as the total number of adult felony probationers sent to state prison from that county, as a percentage of the county's average adult felony probation population for that year.

(d) An estimate of the number of adult felony probationers each county successfully prevented from being incarcerated in state prison. For each county, this estimate shall be calculated based on the reduction in the county's probation failure rate as calculated annually pursuant to subdivision (c) for that year and the county's probation failure rate from the previous year.

(e) In calculating probation failure to prison rates for the state and individual counties, the number of adult felony probationers sent to state prison shall include those adult felony probationers sent to state prison for a revocation of probation, as well as adult felony probationers sent to state prison for a conviction of a new felony offense. The calculation shall also include adult felony probationers who are sent to state prison for a conviction of a new crime and who simultaneously have their probation terms terminated.

(f) The statewide mandatory supervision failure to prison rate. The statewide mandatory supervision failure to prison rate shall be calculated as the total number of offenders supervised under mandatory supervision pursuant to subparagraph (B) of paragraph (5) of subdivision (h) of Section 1170, statewide, sent to prison in the previous calendar year as a percentage of the average statewide mandatory supervision population for that year.

(g) A mandatory supervision failure to prison rate for each county. Each county's mandatory supervision failure to prison rate shall be calculated as the number of offenders supervised under mandatory supervision pursuant to subparagraph (B) of paragraph (5) of subdivision (h) of Section 1170 sent to prison from that county in the previous calendar year as a percentage of the county's average mandatory supervision population for that year.

(h) An estimate of the number of felons on mandatory supervision each county successfully prevented from being incarcerated in state prison. For each county, this estimate shall be calculated based on the reduction in the county's mandatory supervision failure to prison rate as calculated annually pursuant to subdivision (g) for that year and the county's mandatory supervision failure to prison rate from the previous year.

(i) The statewide postrelease community supervision failure to prison rate. The statewide postrelease community supervision failure to prison rate shall be calculated as the total number of offenders supervised under postrelease community supervision pursuant to Title 2.05 (commencing with Section 3450) of Part 3, statewide, sent to prison in the previous calendar year as a percentage of the average statewide postrelease community supervision population for that year.

(j) A postrelease community supervision failure to prison rate for each county. Each county's postrelease community supervision failure to prison rate shall be calculated as the number of offenders supervised under postrelease community supervision pursuant to Title 2.05 (commencing with Section 3450) of Part 3 sent to prison from that county in the previous calendar year as a percentage of the county's average postrelease community supervision population for that year.

(k) An estimate of the number of felons on postrelease community supervision each county successfully prevented from being incarcerated in state prison. For each county, this estimate shall be calculated based on the reduction in the county's postrelease community supervision failure to prison rate as calculated annually pursuant to subdivision (i) for that year and the county's postrelease community supervision failure to prison rate from the previous year.

(l) The statewide return to prison rate. The statewide return to prison rate shall be calculated as the total number of offenders supervised by probation departments as felony probationers, or subject to mandatory supervision pursuant to subdivision (h) of Section 1170, or subject to postrelease community supervision, who were sent to prison, as a percentage of the average statewide adult felony probation, mandatory supervision, and postrelease community supervision population.

(m) The county return to prison rate. The combined individual county return to prison rate shall be calculated as the total number of offenders supervised by a county probation department as felony probationers, or subject to mandatory supervision pursuant to subdivision (h) of Section 1170, or subject to postrelease community supervision, who were sent to prison, as a percentage of the average adult felony probation, mandatory supervision, and postrelease community supervision population for that county.

Amended by Stats 2015 ch 26 (SB 85),s 18, eff. 6/24/2015.
Added by Stats 2013 ch 310 (SB 105),s 7, eff. 9/12/2013.

Section 1233.15 - [Repealed]

Repealed by Stats 2015 ch 26 (SB 85),s 19, eff. 6/24/2015.
Amended by Stats 2014 ch 26 (AB 1468),s 22, eff. 6/20/2014.
Amended by Stats 2013 ch 31 (SB 75),s 16, eff. 6/27/2013.
Added by Stats 2011 ch 12 (AB X1-17),s 14, eff. 9/20/2011, op. 10/1/2011.

Section 1233.2 - [Repealed]

Repealed by Stats 2015 ch 26 (SB 85),s 20, eff. 6/24/2015.
Amended by Stats 2013 ch 31 (SB 75),s 17, eff. 6/27/2013.
Added by Stats 2009 ch 608 (SB 678),s 2, eff. 1/1/2010.
Repealed by Stats 2010 ch 709 (SB 1062),s 14, eff. 1/1/2011.

Repealed by Stats 2010 ch 328 (SB 1330),s 167, eff. 1/1/2011.
Added by Stats 2009 ch 28 (SB X3-18),s 36, eff. 1/1/2010.

Section 1233.3 - Probation failure reduction incentive payment

Annually, the Director of Finance, in consultation with the Department of Corrections and Rehabilitation, the Joint Legislative Budget Committee, the Chief Probation Officers of California, and the Judicial Council, shall calculate a statewide performance incentive payment for each eligible county for the most recently completed calendar year, as follows:

(a) For a county identified as having a return to prison rate less than 1.5 percent, the incentive payment shall be equal to 100 percent of the highest year of funding that a county received for the California Community Incentive Grant Program from the 2011-12 fiscal year to the 2014-15 fiscal year, inclusive.

(b) For a county identified as having a return to prison rate of 1.5 percent or greater, but not exceeding 3.2 percent, the incentive payment shall be equal to 70 percent of the highest year of funding that a county received for the California Community Incentive Grant Program from the 2011-12 fiscal year to the 2014-15 fiscal year, inclusive.

(c) For a county identified as having a return to prison rate of more than 3.2 percent, not exceeding 5.5 percent, the incentive payment shall be equal to 60 percent of the highest year of funding that a county received for the California Community Incentive Grant Program from the 2011-12 fiscal year to the 2014-15 fiscal year, inclusive.

(d) For a county identified as having a return to prison rate of more than 5.5 percent, not exceeding 6.1 percent, the incentive payment shall be equal to 50 percent of the highest year of funding that a county received for the California Community Incentive Grant Program from the 2011-12 fiscal year to the 2014-15 fiscal year, inclusive.

(e) For a county identified as having a return to prison rate of more than 6.1 percent, not exceeding 7.9 percent, the incentive payment shall be equal to 40 percent of the highest year of funding that a county received for the California Community Incentive Grant Program from the 2011-12 fiscal year to the 2014-15 fiscal year, inclusive.

(f) A county that fails to provide information specified in Section 1231 to the Administrative Office of the Courts is not eligible for a statewide performance incentive payment.

(g) This section shall not be used to calculate incentive payments for the 2021-22 fiscal year.

Amended by Stats 2021 ch 80 (AB 145),s 5, eff. 7/16/2021.
Amended by Stats 2015 ch 26 (SB 85),s 21, eff. 6/24/2015.
Added by Stats 2013 ch 310 (SB 105),s 9, eff. 9/12/2013.

Section 1233.4 - County performance incentive payments

The Director of Finance, in consultation with the Department of Corrections and Rehabilitation, the Joint Legislative Budget Committee, the Chief Probation Officers of California, and the Judicial Council, shall, for the most recently completed calendar year, annually calculate a county performance incentive payment for each eligible county. A county shall be eligible for compensation for each of the following:

(a) The estimated number of felons on probation that were successfully prevented from being incarcerated in the state prison as calculated in subdivision (d) of Section 1233.1, multiplied by 35 percent of the state's costs to incarcerate a prison felony offender in a contract facility, as defined in subdivision (a) of Section 1233.1.

(b) The estimated number of felons on mandatory supervision that were successfully prevented from being incarcerated in the state prison as calculated in subdivision (h) of Section 1233.1, multiplied by 35 percent of the state's costs to incarcerate a prison felony offender in a contract facility, as defined in subdivision (a) of Section 1233.1.

(c) The estimated number of felons on postrelease community supervision that were successfully prevented from being incarcerated in the state prison as calculated in subdivision (k) of Section 1233.1, multiplied by 35 percent of the state's costs to incarcerate a prison felony offender in a contract facility, as defined in subdivision (a) of Section 1233.1.

(d) This section shall not be used to calculate incentive payments for the 2021-22 fiscal year.

Amended by Stats 2021 ch 80 (AB 145),s 6, eff. 7/16/2021.
Added by Stats 2015 ch 26 (SB 85),s 23, eff. 6/24/2015.
Repealed by Stats 2015 ch 26 (SB 85),s 22, eff. 6/24/2015.
Added by Stats 2013 ch 310 (SB 105),s 11, eff. 9/12/2013.

Section 1233.5 - Use of best available data

If data of sufficient quality and of the types required for the implementation of this chapter are not available to the Director of Finance, the Director of Finance, in consultation with the Department of Corrections and Rehabilitation, the Joint Legislative Budget Committee, and Judicial Council, shall use the best available data to estimate the statewide performance incentive payments and county performance incentive payments utilizing a methodology that is as consistent with that described in this chapter as is reasonably possible.

Amended by Stats 2015 ch 26 (SB 85),s 24, eff. 6/24/2015.
Added by Stats 2009 ch 608 (SB 678),s 2, eff. 1/1/2010.
Repealed by Stats 2010 ch 709 (SB 1062),s 14, eff. 1/1/2011.
Repealed by Stats 2010 ch 328 (SB 1330),s 167, eff. 1/1/2011.
Added by Stats 2009 ch 28 (SB X3-18),s 36, eff. 1/1/2010.

Section 1233.6 - Payment of incentive payments and grants

(a) A statewide performance incentive payment calculated pursuant to Section 1233.3 and a county performance incentive payment calculated pursuant to Section 1233.4 for any calendar year shall be provided to a county in the following fiscal year. The total annual payment to a county shall be divided into four equal quarterly payments.

(b) The Department of Finance shall include an estimate of the total statewide performance incentive payments and county performance incentive payments to be provided to counties in the coming fiscal year as part of the Governor's proposed budget released no later than January 10 of each year. This estimate shall be adjusted by the Department of Finance, as necessary, to reflect the actual calculations of probation failure reduction incentive payments and high performance grants completed by the Director of Finance, in consultation with the Department of Corrections and Rehabilitation, the Joint Legislative Budget Committee, the Chief Probation Officers of California, and the Judicial Council. This adjustment shall occur as part of standard budget revision processes completed by the Department of Finance in April and May of each year.

(c) There is hereby established, in the State Treasury, the State Community Corrections Performance Incentives Fund, which is continuously appropriated. Moneys appropriated for purposes of statewide performance incentive payments and county performance incentive payments authorized in Sections 1230 to 1233.6, inclusive, shall be transferred into this fund from the General Fund. Any moneys transferred into this fund from the General Fund shall be administered by the Judicial Council and the share calculated for each county probation department shall be transferred to its Community Corrections Performance Incentives Fund authorized in Section 1230.

(d) For each fiscal year, the Director of Finance shall determine the total amount of the State Community Corrections Performance Incentives Fund and the amount to be allocated to each county, pursuant to this section and Sections 1230 to 1233.5, inclusive, and shall report those amounts to the Controller. The Controller shall make an allocation from the State Community Corrections Performance Incentives Fund authorized in subdivision (c) to each county in accordance with the amounts provided.

(e) Notwithstanding Section 13340 of the Government Code, commencing July 1, 2014, and each fiscal year thereafter, the amount of one million dollars ($1,000,000) is hereby continuously appropriated from the State Community Corrections Performance Incentives Fund to the Judicial Council for the costs of implementing and administering this program, pursuant to subdivision (c), and the 2011 realignment legislation addressing public safety.

(f) This section does not apply to incentive payments made during the 2021-22 fiscal year.

Amended by Stats 2021 ch 80 (AB 145),s 7, eff. 7/16/2021.
Amended by Stats 2015 ch 26 (SB 85),s 25, eff. 6/24/2015.
Amended by Stats 2014 ch 26 (AB 1468),s 23, eff. 6/20/2014.
Amended by Stats 2013 ch 31 (SB 75),s 20, eff. 6/27/2013.
Amended by Stats 2012 ch 41 (SB 1021),s 65, eff. 6/27/2012.
Amended by Stats 2011 ch 36 (SB 92),s 26, eff. 6/30/2011.
Added by Stats 2009 ch 608 (SB 678),s 2, eff. 1/1/2010.
Repealed by Stats 2010 ch 709 (SB 1062),s 14, eff. 1/1/2011.
Repealed by Stats 2010 ch 328 (SB 1330),s 167, eff. 1/1/2011.
Added by Stats 2009 ch 28 (SB X3-18),s 36, eff. 1/1/2010.

Section 1233.61 - Distribution of remaining money

(a) The Department of Finance shall increase to no more than two hundred thousand dollars ($200,000) the award amount for any county whose statewide performance incentive payment and county performance incentive payment, as calculated pursuant to Sections 1233.3 and 1233.4, totals less than two hundred thousand dollars ($200,000).

(b) The Department of Finance shall adjust the award amount up to two hundred thousand dollars ($200,000) per county, to those counties that did not receive a statewide performance incentive payment and county performance incentive payment, as calculated pursuant to Sections 1233.3 and 1233.4.

(c) Any county receiving funding through subdivision (b) shall submit a report to the Judicial Council and the Chief Probation Officers of California describing how it plans on using the funds to enhance its ability to be successful under this chapter. Commencing January 1, 2014, a county that fails to submit this report by March 1 annually shall not receive funding pursuant to subdivision (b) in the subsequent fiscal year.

(d) A county that fails to provide the information specified in Section 1231 to the Judicial Council shall not be eligible for payment pursuant to this section.

(e) This section shall not be used to calculate incentive payments for the 2021-22 fiscal year.

Amended by Stats 2021 ch 80 (AB 145),s 8, eff. 7/16/2021.
Amended by Stats 2015 ch 26 (SB 85),s 26, eff. 6/24/2015.
Amended by Stats 2014 ch 26 (AB 1468),s 24, eff. 6/20/2014.
Amended by Stats 2013 ch 31 (SB 75),s 21, eff. 6/27/2013.
Amended by Stats 2012 ch 41 (SB 1021),s 66, eff. 6/27/2012.
Added by Stats 2011 ch 36 (SB 92),s 27, eff. 6/30/2011.

Section 1233.7 - Use of money appropriated

The moneys appropriated pursuant to this chapter shall be used to supplement, not supplant, any other state or county appropriation for a CPO or a probation department.

Amended by Stats 2010 ch 328 (SB 1330),s 172, eff. 1/1/2011.
Added by Stats 2009 ch 608 (SB 678),s 2, eff. 1/1/2010.
Repealed by Stats 2010 ch 709 (SB 1062),s 14, eff. 1/1/2011.
Repealed by Stats 2010 ch 328 (SB 1330),s 167, eff. 1/1/2011.
Added by Stats 2009 ch 28 (SB X3-18),s 36, eff. 1/1/2010.

Section 1233.8 - [Repealed]

Repealed by Stats 2013 ch 31 (SB 75),s 22, eff. 6/27/2013.
Added by Stats 2009 ch 608 (SB 678),s 2, eff. 1/1/2010.
Repealed by Stats 2010 ch 709 (SB 1062),s 14, eff. 1/1/2011.
Repealed by Stats 2010 ch 328 (SB 1330),s 167, eff. 1/1/2011.
Added by Stats 2009 ch 28 (SB X3-18),s 36, eff. 1/1/2010.

Section 1233.9 - Recidivism Reduction Fund

(a) There is hereby created in the State Treasury the Recidivism Reduction Fund for moneys to be available upon appropriation by the Legislature, for activities designed to reduce the state's prison population, including, but not limited to, reducing recidivism. Funds available in the Recidivism Reduction Fund may be transferred to the State Community Corrections Performance Incentives Fund.

(b) Any funds in the Recidivism Reduction Fund not encumbered by June 30, 2016, shall revert to the General Fund upon order of the Department of Finance.

(c) The Recidivism Reduction Fund shall be abolished once all funds encumbered in the Recidivism Reduction Fund are liquidated.

Amended by Stats 2015 ch 26 (SB 85),s 27, eff. 6/24/2015.

Added by Stats 2013 ch 310 (SB 105),s 12, eff. 9/12/2013.

Section 1233.10 - Competitive grant program to fund community recidivism and crime reduction services

(a) Upon agreement to accept funding from the Recidivism Reduction Fund, created in Section 1233.9, a county board of supervisors, in collaboration with the county's Community Corrections Partnership, shall develop, administer, and collect and submit data to the Board of State and Community Corrections regarding a competitive grant program intended to fund community recidivism and crime reduction services, including, but not limited to, delinquency prevention, homelessness prevention, and reentry services.

(1) Commencing with the 2014-15 fiscal year, the funding shall be allocated to counties by the State Controller's Office from Item 5227-101-3259 of Section 2.00 of the Budget Act of 2014 according to the following schedule:

County	Amount
Alameda	$ 250,000
Alpine	$ 10,000
Amador	$ 10,000
Butte	$ 50,000
Calaveras	$ 10,000
Colusa	$ 10,000
Contra Costa	$ 250,000
Del Norte	$ 10,000
El Dorado	$ 50,000
Fresno	$ 250,000
Glenn	$ 10,000
Humboldt	$ 50,000
Imperial	$ 50,000
Inyo	$ 10,000
Kern	$ 250,000
Kings	$ 50,000
Lake	$ 25,000
Lassen	$ 10,000
Los Angeles	$1,600,000
Madera	$ 50,000
Marin	$ 50,000
Mariposa	$ 10,000
Mendocino	$ 25,000
Merced	$ 50,000
Modoc	$ 10,000
Mono	$ 10,000
Monterey	$ 100,000
Napa	$ 50,000
Nevada	$ 25,000
Orange	$ 500,000
Placer	$ 50,000
Plumas	$ 10,000
Riverside	$ 500,000
Sacramento	$ 250,000
San Benito	$ 25,000
San Bernardino	$ 500,000
San Diego	$ 500,000
San Francisco	$ 250,000
San Joaquin	$ 250,000
San Luis Obispo	$ 50,000
San Mateo	$ 250,000
Santa Barbara	$ 100,000
Santa Clara	$ 500,000
Santa Cruz	$ 50,000
Shasta	$ 50,000
Sierra	$ 10,000
Siskiyou	$ 10,000
Solano	$ 100,000
Sonoma	$ 100,000
Stanislaus	$ 100,000
Sutter	$ 25,000
Tehama	$ 25,000

Trinity	$ 10,000
Tulare	$ 100,000
Tuolumne	$ 25,000
Ventura	$ 250,000
Yolo	$ 50,000
Yuba	$ 25,000

(2) Commencing with the 2015-16 fiscal year, the funding shall be allocated to counties by the State Controller's Office from Item 5227-101-3259 of Section 2.00 of the Budget Act of 2015 according to the following schedule:

Alameda	$ 125,000
Alpine	$ 5,000
Amador	$ 5,000
Butte	$ 25,000
Calaveras	$ 5,000
Colusa	$ 5,000
Contra Costa	$ 125,000
Del Norte	$ 5,000
El Dorado	$ 25,000
Fresno	$ 125,000
Glenn	$ 5,000
Humboldt	$ 25,000
Imperial	$ 25,000
Inyo	$ 5,000
Kern	$ 125,000
Kings	$ 25,000
Lake	$ 12,500
Lassen	$ 5,000
Los Angeles	$ 800,000
Madera	$ 25,000
Marin	$ 25,000
Mariposa	$ 5,000
Mendocino	$ 12,500
Merced	$ 25,000
Modoc	$ 5,000
Mono	$ 5,000
Monterey	$ 50,000
Napa	$ 25,000
Nevada	$ 12,500
Orange	$ 250,000
Placer	$ 25,000
Plumas	$ 5,000
Riverside	$ 250,000
Sacramento	$ 125,000
San Benito	$ 12,500
San Bernardino	$ 250,000
San Diego	$ 250,000
San Francisco	$ 125,000
San Joaquin	$ 125,000
San Luis Obispo	$ 25,000
San Mateo	$ 125,000
Santa Barbara	$ 50,000
Santa Clara	$ 250,000
Santa Cruz	$ 25,000
Shasta	$ 25,000
Sierra	$ 5,000
Siskiyou	$ 5,000
Solano	$ 50,000
Sonoma	$ 50,000
Stanislaus	$ 50,000
Sutter	$ 12,500
Tehama	$ 12,500
Trinity	$ 5,000
Tulare	$ 50,000
Tuolumne	$ 12,500

Ventura	$ 125,000
Yolo	$ 25,000
Yuba	$ 12,500

(b) For purposes of this section, "community recidivism and crime reduction service provider" means a nongovernmental entity or a consortium or coalition of nongovernmental entities, that provides community recidivism and crime reduction services, as described in paragraph (2) of subdivision (c), to persons who have been released from the state prison, a county jail, a juvenile detention facility, who are under the supervision of a parole or probation department, or any other person at risk of becoming involved in criminal activities.

(c)

(1) A community recidivism and crime reduction service provider shall have a demonstrated history of providing services, as described in paragraph (2), to the target population during the five years immediately prior to the application for a grant awarded pursuant to this section.

(2) A community recidivism and crime reduction service provider shall provide services that are designed to enable persons to whom the services are provided to refrain from engaging in crime, reconnect with their family members, and contribute to their communities. Community recidivism and crime reduction services may include all of the following:

(A) Self-help groups.

(B) Individual or group assistance with basic life skills.

(C) Mentoring programs.

(D) Academic and educational services, including, but not limited to, services to enable the recipient to earn his or her high school diploma.

(E) Job training skills and employment.

(F) Truancy prevention programs.

(G) Literacy programs.

(H) Any other service that advances community recidivism and crime reduction efforts, as identified by the county board of supervisors and the Community Corrections Partnership.

(I) Individual or group assistance with referrals for any of the following:

(i) Mental and physical health assessments.

(ii) Counseling services.

(iii) Education and vocational programs.

(iv) Employment opportunities.

(v) Alcohol and drug treatment.

(vi) Health, wellness, fitness, and nutrition programs and services.

(vii) Personal finance and consumer skills programs and services.

(viii) Other personal growth and development programs to reduce recidivism.

(ix) Housing assistance.

(d) Pursuant to this section and upon agreement to accept funding from the Recidivism Reduction Fund, the board of supervisors, in collaboration with the county's Community Corrections Partnership, shall grant funds allocated to the county, as described in subdivision (a), to community recidivism and crime reduction service providers based on the needs of their community.

(e)

(1) The amount awarded to each community recidivism and crime reduction service provider by a county shall be based on the population of the county, as projected by the Department of Finance, and shall not exceed the following for each Budget Act allocation:

(A) One hundred thousand dollars ($100,000) in a county with a population of over 4,000,000 people.

(B) Fifty thousand dollars ($50,000) in a county with a population of 700,000 or more people but less than 4,000,000 people.

(C) Twenty-five thousand dollars ($25,000) in a county with a population of 400,000 or more people but less than 700,000 people.

(D) Ten thousand dollars ($10,000) in a county with a population of less than 400,000 people.

(2) The total amount of grants awarded to a single community recidivism and crime reduction service provider by all counties pursuant to this section shall not exceed one hundred thousand dollars ($100,000) per Budget Act allocation.

(f) The board of supervisors, in collaboration with the county's Community Corrections Partnership, shall establish minimum requirements, funding criteria, and procedures for the counties to award grants consistent with the criteria established in this section.

(g) A community recidivism and crime reduction service provider that receives a grant under this section shall report to the county board of supervisors or the Community Corrections Partnership on the number of individuals served and the types of services provided, consistent with paragraph (2) of subdivision (c). The board of supervisors or the Community Corrections Partnership shall report to the Board of State and Community Corrections any information received under this subdivision from grant recipients.

(h) Of the total amount granted to a county, up to 5 percent may be withheld by the board of supervisors or the Community Corrections Partnership for the payment of administrative costs.

(i) Any funds allocated to a county under this section shall be available for expenditure for a period of four years and any unexpended funds shall revert to the state General Fund at the end of the four-year period.

Amended by Stats 2015 ch 323 (SB 102),s 7, eff. 9/22/2015.

Amended by Stats 2015 ch 26 (SB 85),s 28, eff. 6/24/2015.

Added by Stats 2014 ch 26 (AB 1468),s 21, eff. 6/20/2014.

Section 1233.11 - State Community Corrections Performance Incentives Fund

(a) Notwithstanding Sections 1233.3 and Section 1233.4, for the 2021-22 fiscal year, the amount of one hundred twenty-two million, eight hundred twenty-nine thousand, three hundred ninety-seven dollars ($122,829,397) is hereby appropriated from the General Fund to the State Community Corrections Performance Incentives Fund, established pursuant to Section 1233.6, for the community corrections program. Funds shall be allocated by the Controller to counties according to the requirements of the program and pursuant to the following schedule:

County	Amount
Alameda	$ 2,760,919
Alpine	$ 200,000
Amador	$ 233,777
Butte	$ 416,404
Calaveras	$ 512,027
Colusa	$ 267,749
Contra Costa	$ 6,643,176
Del Norte	$ 200,000
El Dorado	$ 348,495
Fresno	$ 3,156,754
Glenn	$ 223,171
Humboldt	$ 1,055,456
Imperial	$ 203,247
Inyo	$ 222,098
Kern	$ 1,519,187
Kings	$ 1,105,869
Lake	$ 465,073
Lassen	$ 253,037
Los Angeles	$ 37,413,530
Madera	$ 1,237,543
Marin	$ 988,095
Mariposa	$ 200,000
Mendocino	$ 592,510
Merced	$ 1,032,961
Modoc	$ 202,975
Mono	$ 257,466
Monterey	$ 300,463
Napa	$ 329,767
Nevada	$ 669,278
Orange	$ 4,973,540
Placer	$ 545,848
Plumas	$ 442,681
Riverside	$ 6,954,331
Sacramento	$ 12,329,233
San Benito	$ 282,215
San Bernardino	$ 8,357,087
San Diego	$ 2,930,998
San Francisco	$ 3,060,552
San Joaquin	$ 2,227,270
San Luis Obispo	$ 1,322,460
San Mateo	$ 1,175,827
Santa Barbara	$ 1,416,944
Santa Clara	$ 1,747,784
Santa Cruz	$ 1,746,643
Shasta	$ 512,037
Sierra	$ 215,489
Siskiyou	$ 284,355
Solano	$ 807,241
Sonoma	$ 1,067,821
Stanislaus	$ 1,286,879
Sutter	$ 738,100
Tehama	$ 458,088
Trinity	$ 200,000
Tulare	$ 1,864,437
Tuolumne	$ 382,373
Ventura	$ 783,267
Yolo	$ 1,504,870
Yuba	$ 200,000

(b) The total annual payment to each county, as scheduled in subdivision (a), shall be divided into four equal quarterly payments.
(c) A county that fails to provide the information required in Section 1231 to the Judicial Council shall not be eligible for payment pursuant to this section.

(d) This section shall remain in effect only until July 1, 2022, and as of that date is repealed.

Added by Stats 2021 ch 80 (AB 145),s 9, eff. 7/16/2021.

Section 1233.12 - [Effective until 1/1/2025] Appropriations to the State Community Corrections Performance Incentives Fund

(a) Notwithstanding Sections 1233.3 and 1233.4, in each of the 2022-23 and 2023-24 fiscal years, the amount of one hundred twenty-two million eight hundred twenty-nine thousand three hundred ninety-seven dollars ($122,829,397) is hereby appropriated from the General Fund to the State Community Corrections Performance Incentives Fund, established pursuant to Section 1233.6, for the community corrections program. Funds shall be allocated by the Controller to counties according to the requirements of the program and pursuant to the following schedule:

County	Amount
Alameda	$ 2,760,919
Alpine	$ 200,000
Amador	$ 233,777
Butte	$ 416,404
Calaveras	$ 512,027
Colusa	$ 267,749
Contra Costa	$ 6,643,176
Del Norte	$ 200,000
El Dorado	$ 348,495
Fresno	$ 3,156,754
Glenn	$ 223,171
Humboldt	$ 1,055,456
Imperial	$ 203,247
Inyo	$ 222,098
Kern	$ 1,519,187
Kings	$ 1,105,869
Lake	$465,073
Lassen	$ 253,037
Los Angeles	$ 37,413,530
Madera	$ 1,237,543
Marin	$ 988,095
Mariposa	$ 200,000
Mendocino	$ 592,510
Merced	$ 1,032,961
Modoc	$ 202,975
Mono	$ 257,466
Monterey	$ 300,463
Napa	$ 329,767
Nevada	$ 669,278
Orange	$ 4,973,540
Placer	$ 545,848
Plumas	$ 442,681
Riverside	$ 6,954,331
Sacramento	$ 12,329,233
San Benito	$ 282,215
San Bernardino	$ 8,357,087
San Diego	$ 2,930,998
San Francisco	$ 3,060,552
San Joaquin	$ 2,227,270
San Luis Obispo	$ 1,322,460
San Mateo	$ 1,175,827
Santa Barbara	$ 1,416,944
Santa Clara	$ 1,747,784
Santa Cruz	$ 1,746,643
Shasta	$ 512,037
Sierra	$ 215,489
Siskiyou	$ 284,355
Solano	$ 807,241
Sonoma	$ 1,067,821
Stanislaus	$ 1,286,879
Sutter	$ 738,100
Tehama	$ 458,088
Trinity	$ 200,000
Tulare	$ 1,864,437
Tuolumne	$ 382,373
Ventura	$ 783,267
Yolo	$ 1,504,870

(b)The total annual payment to each county, as scheduled in subdivision (a), shall be divided into four equal quarterly payments.
(c)A county that fails to provide the information required in Section 1231 to the Judicial Council shall not be eligible for payment pursuant to this section.
(d)This section shall remain in effect only until January 1, 2025, and as of that date is repealed.
Added by Stats 2022 ch 58 (AB 200),s 14, eff. 6/30/2022.

Chapter 4 - SUPERVISED POPULATION WORKFORCE TRAINING GRANT PROGRAM

Section 1234 et seq - [Repealed]
Amended by Stats 2017 ch 96 (SB 106),s 13, eff. 7/21/2017.
Amended by Stats 2016 ch 100 (AB 2061),s 2, eff. 1/1/2017.
Added by Stats 2014 ch 383 (AB 2060),s 2, eff. 1/1/2015.

Title 9 - APPEALS IN FELONY CASES

Chapter 1 - APPEALS, WHEN ALLOWED AND HOW TAKEN, AND THE EFFECT THEREOF

Section 1235 - Appeal on questions of law
(a) Either party to a felony case may appeal on questions of law alone, as prescribed in this title and in rules adopted by the Judicial Council. The provisions of this title apply only to such appeals.
(b) An appeal from the judgment or appealable order in a felony case is to the court of appeal for the district in which the court from which the appeal is taken is located.
Amended by Stats. 1998, Ch. 931, Sec. 397. Effective September 28, 1998.

Section 1236 - Appellant; respondent
The party appealing is known as the appellant, and the adverse party as the respondent, but the title of the action is not changed in consequence of the appeal.
Enacted 1872.

Section 1237 - Appeal taken by defendant
An appeal may be taken by the defendant from both of the following:
(a) Except as provided in Sections 1237.1, 1237.2, and 1237.5, from a final judgment of conviction. A sentence, an order granting probation, or the commitment of a defendant for insanity, the indeterminate commitment of a defendant as a mentally disordered sex offender, or the commitment of a defendant for controlled substance addiction shall be deemed to be a final judgment within the meaning of this section. Upon appeal from a final judgment the court may review any order denying a motion for a new trial.
(b) From any order made after judgment, affecting the substantial rights of the party.
Amended by Stats 2015 ch 194 (AB 249),s 1, eff. 1/1/2016.

Section 1237.1 - Appeal by defendant on ground of error in calculation of presentence custody credits
No appeal shall be taken by the defendant from a judgment of conviction on the ground of an error in the calculation of presentence custody credits, unless the defendant first presents the claim in the trial court at the time of sentencing, or if the error is not discovered until after sentencing, the defendant first makes a motion for correction of the record in the trial court, which may be made informally in writing. The trial court retains jurisdiction after a notice of appeal has been filed to correct any error in the calculation of presentence custody credits upon the defendant's request for correction.
Amended by Stats 2015 ch 194 (AB 249),s 2, eff. 1/1/2016.

Section 1237.2 - Appeal on grounds of error in imposition or calculation of fines, penalty, fees, etc.
An appeal may not be taken by the defendant from a judgment of conviction on the ground of an error in the imposition or calculation of fines, penalty assessments, surcharges, fees, or costs unless the defendant first presents the claim in the trial court at the time of sentencing, or if the error is not discovered until after sentencing, the defendant first makes a motion for correction in the trial court, which may be made informally in writing. The trial court retains jurisdiction after a notice of appeal has been filed to correct any error in the imposition or calculation of fines, penalty assessments, surcharges, fees, or costs upon the defendant's request for correction. This section only applies in cases where the erroneous imposition or calculation of fines, penalty assessments, surcharges, fees, or costs are the sole issue on appeal.
Added by Stats 2015 ch 194 (AB 249),s 3, eff. 1/1/2016.

Section 1237.5 - Appeal by defendant from judgment of conviction upon plea of guilty or nolo contendere or revocation of probation following admission of violation
No appeal shall be taken by the defendant from a judgment of conviction upon a plea of guilty or nolo contendere, or a revocation of probation following an admission of violation, except where both of the following are met:
(a) The defendant has filed with the trial court a written statement, executed under oath or penalty of perjury showing reasonable constitutional, jurisdictional, or other grounds going to the legality of the proceedings.
(b) The trial court has executed and filed a certificate of probable cause for such appeal with the clerk of the court.
Amended by Stats 2002 ch 784 (SB 1316), s 550, eff. 1/1/2003.

Section 1238 - Appeal by people
(a) An appeal may be taken by the people from any of the following:
    (1) An order setting aside all or any portion of the indictment, information, or complaint.
    (2) An order sustaining a demurrer to all or any portion of the indictment, accusation, or information.
    (3) An order granting a new trial.
    (4) An order arresting judgment.
    (5) An order made after judgment, affecting the substantial rights of the people.

(6) An order modifying the verdict or finding by reducing the degree of the offense or the punishment imposed or modifying the offense to a lesser offense.

(7) An order dismissing a case prior to trial made upon motion of the court pursuant to Section 1385 whenever such order is based upon an order granting the defendant's motion to return or suppress property or evidence made at a special hearing as provided in this code.

(8) An order or judgment dismissing or otherwise terminating all or any portion of the action including such an order or judgment after a verdict or finding of guilty or an order or judgment entered before the defendant has been placed in jeopardy or where the defendant has waived jeopardy.

(9) An order denying the motion of the people to reinstate the complaint or a portion thereof pursuant to Section 871.5.

(10) The imposition of an unlawful sentence, whether or not the court suspends the execution of the sentence, except that portion of a sentence imposing a prison term which is based upon a court's choice that a term of imprisonment (A) be the upper, middle, or lower term, unless the term selected is not set forth in an applicable statute, or (B) be consecutive or concurrent to another term of imprisonment, unless an applicable statute requires that the term be consecutive. As used in this paragraph, "unlawful sentence" means the imposition of a sentence not authorized by law or the imposition of a sentence based upon an unlawful order of the court which strikes or otherwise modifies the effect of an enhancement or prior conviction.

(11) An order recusing the district attorney pursuant to Section 1424.

(b) If, pursuant to paragraph (8) of subdivision (a), the people prosecute an appeal to decision, or any review of such decision, it shall be binding upon them and they shall be prohibited from refiling the case which was appealed.

(c) When an appeal is taken pursuant to paragraph (7) of subdivision (a), the court may review the order granting the defendant's motion to return or suppress property or evidence made at a special hearing as provided in this code.

(d) Nothing contained in this section shall be construed to authorize an appeal from an order granting probation. Instead, the people may seek appellate review of any grant of probation, whether or not the court imposes sentence, by means of a petition for a writ of mandate or prohibition which is filed within 60 days after probation is granted. The review of any grant of probation shall include review of any order underlying the grant of probation.

Amended by Stats. 1999, Ch. 344, Sec. 25. Effective September 7, 1999.

Section 1238.5 - Reinstatement of time for defendant to seek review

Upon appeal by the prosecution pursuant to Section 1238, where the notice of appeal is filed after the expiration of the time available to defendant to seek review of an otherwise reviewable order or ruling and the appeal by the prosecution relates to a matter decided during the time available to the defendant to seek review of the otherwise reviewable order or ruling, the time for defendant to seek such review is reinstated to run from the date the notice of appeal was filed with proof of service upon defendant or his counsel.

The Judicial Council shall provide by rule for the consolidation of such petition for review with the prosecution appeal.

Added by Stats. 1975, Ch. 1195.

Section 1239 - Appeal in manner provided in rules; automatic appeal of judgment of death

(a) Where an appeal lies on behalf of the defendant or the people, it may be taken by the defendant or his or her counsel, or by counsel for the people, in the manner provided in rules adopted by the Judicial Council.

(b) When upon any plea a judgment of death is rendered, an appeal is automatically taken by the defendant without any action by him or her or his or her counsel. The defendant's trial counsel, whether retained by the defendant or court appointed, shall continue to represent the defendant until completing the additional duties set forth in paragraph (1) of subdivision (e) of Section 1240.1.

Amended (as added by Stats. 1982, Ch. 917, Sec. 4) by Stats. 1988, Ch. 551, Sec. 1.

Section 1239.1 - Duty of the Supreme Court in capital cases

(a) It is the duty of the Supreme Court in a capital case to expedite the review of the case. The court shall appoint counsel for an indigent appellant as soon as possible. The court shall only grant extensions of time for briefing for compelling or extraordinary reasons.

(b) When necessary to remove a substantial backlog in appointment of counsel for capital cases, the Supreme Court shall require attorneys who are qualified for appointment to the most serious non-capital appeals and who meet the qualifications for capital appeals to accept appointment in capital cases as a condition for remaining on the court's appointment list. A "substantial backlog" exists for this purpose when the time from entry of judgment in the trial court to appointment of counsel for appeal exceeds 6 months over a period of 12 consecutive months.

Added by Proposition 66, approved by the voters at the November 8, 2016 election, effective immediately upon enactment.

Section 1240 - Appointment of state public defender

(a) When in a proceeding falling within the provisions of Section 15421 of the Government Code a person is not represented by a public defender acting pursuant to Section 27706 of the Government Code or other counsel and he is unable to afford the services of counsel, the court shall appoint the State Public Defender to represent the person except as follows:

(1) The court shall appoint counsel other than the State Public Defender when the State Public Defender has refused to represent the person because of conflict of interest or other reason.

(2) The court may, in its discretion, appoint either the State Public Defender or the attorney who represented the person at his trial when the person requests the latter to represent him on appeal and the attorney consents to the appointment. In unusual cases, where good cause exists, the court may appoint any other attorney.

(3) A court may appoint a county public defender, private attorney, or nonprofit corporation with which the State Public Defender has contracted to furnish defense services pursuant to Government Code Section 15402.

(4) When a judgment of death has been rendered the Supreme Court may, in its discretion, appoint counsel other than the State Public Defender or the attorney who represented the person at trial.

(b) If counsel other than the State Public Defender is appointed pursuant to this section, he may exercise the same authority as the State Public Defender pursuant to Chapter 2 (commencing with Section 15420) of Part 7 of Division 3 of Title 2 of the Government Code.

Added by Stats. 1975, Ch. 1125.

Section 1240.1 - Duty to provide counsel and advice as to whether arguably meritorious grounds for reversion or modification exist

(a) In any noncapital criminal, juvenile court, or civil commitment case wherein the defendant would be entitled to the appointment of counsel on appeal if indigent, it shall be the duty of the attorney who represented the person at trial to provide counsel and advice as to whether arguably meritorious grounds exist for reversal or modification of the judgment on appeal. The attorney shall admonish the defendant that he or she is not able to provide advice concerning his or her own competency, and that the State Public Defender or other counsel should be consulted for advice as to whether an issue regarding the competency of counsel should be raised on appeal. The trial court may require trial counsel to certify that he or she has counseled the defendant as to whether arguably meritorious grounds for appeal exist at the time a notice of appeal is filed. Nothing in this section shall be construed to prevent any person having a right to appeal from doing so.

(b) It shall be the duty of every attorney representing an indigent defendant in any criminal, juvenile court, or civil commitment case to execute and file on his or her client's behalf a timely notice of appeal when the attorney is of the opinion that arguably meritorious grounds exist for a reversal or modification of the judgment or orders to be appealed from, and where, in the attorney's judgment, it is in the defendant's interest to pursue any relief that may be available to him or her on appeal; or when directed to do so by a defendant having a right to appeal. With the notice of appeal the attorney shall file a brief statement of the points to be raised on appeal and a designation of any document, paper, pleading, or transcript of oral proceedings necessary to properly present those points on appeal when the document, paper, pleading, or transcript of oral proceedings would not be included in the normal record on appeal according to the applicable provisions of the California Rules of Court. The executing of the notice of appeal by the defendant's attorney shall not constitute an undertaking to represent the defendant on appeal unless the undertaking is expressly stated in the notice of appeal.

If the defendant was represented by appointed counsel on the trial level, or if it appears that the defendant will request the appointment of counsel on appeal by reason of indigency, the trial attorney shall also assist the defendant in preparing and submitting a motion for the appointment of counsel and any supporting declaration or affidavit as to the defendant's financial condition. These documents shall be filed with the trial court at the time of filing a notice of appeal, and shall be transmitted by the clerk of the trial court to the clerk of the appellate court within three judicial days of their receipt. The appellate court shall act upon that motion without unnecessary delay. An attorney's failure to file a motion for the appointment of counsel with the notice of appeal shall not foreclose the defendant from filing a motion at any time it becomes known to him or her that the attorney has failed to do so, or at any time he or she shall become indigent if he or she was not previously indigent.

(c) The State Public Defender shall, at the request of any attorney representing a prospective indigent appellant or at the request of the prospective indigent appellant himself or herself, provide counsel and advice to the prospective indigent appellant or attorney as to whether arguably meritorious grounds exist on which the judgment or order to be appealed from would be reversed or modified on appeal.

(d) The failure of a trial attorney to perform any duty prescribed in this section, assign any particular point or error in the notice of appeal, or designate any particular thing for inclusion in the record on appeal shall not foreclose any defendant from filing a notice of appeal on his or her own behalf or from raising any point or argument on appeal; nor shall it foreclose the defendant or his or her counsel on appeal from requesting the augmentation or correction of the record on appeal in the reviewing court.

(e)

(1) In order to expedite certification of the entire record on appeal in all capital cases, the defendant's trial counsel, whether retained by the defendant or court-appointed, and the prosecutor shall continue to represent the respective parties. Each counsel's obligations extend to taking all steps necessary to facilitate the preparation and timely certification of the record of all trial court proceedings.

(2) The duties imposed on trial counsel in paragraph (1) shall not foreclose the defendant's appellate counsel from requesting additions or corrections to the record on appeal in either the trial court or the California Supreme Court in a manner provided by rules of court adopted by the Judicial Council.

Amended by Stats 2003 ch 62 (SB 600), s 232, eff. 1/1/2004.
Amended by Stats 2002 ch 784 (SB 1316), s 551, eff. 1/1/2003.
Amended by Stats 2000 ch 287 (SB 1955) s 17, eff. 1/1/2001.

Section 1241 - Compensation of appointed counsel

In any case in which counsel other than a public defender has been appointed by the Supreme Court or by a court of appeal to represent a party to any appeal or proceeding, such counsel shall receive a reasonable sum for compensation and necessary expenses, the amount of which shall be determined by the court and paid from any funds appropriated to the Judicial Council for that purpose. Claim for the payment of such compensation and expenses shall be made on a form prescribed by the Judicial Council and presented by counsel to the clerk of the appointing court. After the court has made its order fixing the amount to be paid the clerk shall transmit a copy of the order to the State Controller who shall draw his warrant in payment thereof and transmit it to the payee.

Amended by Stats. 1975, Ch. 1125.

Section 1242 - Effect of appeal by people on judgment in favor of defendant

An appeal taken by the people in no case stays or affects the operation of a judgment in favor of the defendant, until judgment is reversed.

Enacted 1872.

Section 1243 - Stay of execution of judgment

An appeal to the Supreme Court or to a court of appeal from a judgment of conviction stays the execution of the judgment in all cases where a sentence of death has been imposed, but does not stay the execution of the judgment or order granting probation in any other case unless the trial or appellate court shall so order. The granting or refusal of such an order shall rest in the discretion of the court, except that a court shall not stay any duty to register as a sex offender pursuant to Section 290. If the order is made, the clerk of the court shall issue a certificate stating that the order has been made.

Amended by Stats. 1998, Ch. 960, Sec. 3. Effective January 1, 1999.

Section 1244 - Duties of sheriff if certificate issues

If the certificate provided for in the preceding section is filed, the Sheriff must, if the defendant be in his custody, upon being served with a copy thereof, keep the defendant in his custody without executing the judgment, and detain him to abide the judgment on appeal.

Enacted 1872.

Section 1245 - Suspension of execution of judgment

If before the granting of the certificate, the execution of the judgment has commenced, the further execution thereof is suspended, and upon service of a copy of such certificate the defendant must be restored, by the officer in whose custody he is, to his original custody.

Amended by Stats. 1905, Ch. 538.

Section 1246 - Record of appeal

The record on appeal shall be made up and filed in such time and manner as shall be prescribed in rules adopted by the Judicial Council.

Amended by Stats. 1945, Ch. 40.

Chapter 1a - JUDICIAL COUNCIL RULES

Section 1247k - Power to prescribe rules

The Judicial Council shall have the power to prescribe by rules for the practice and procedure on appeal, and for the time and manner in which the records on such appeals shall be made up and filed, in all criminal cases in all courts of this state.

The rules shall take effect on July 1, 1943, and thereafter all laws in conflict therewith shall be of no further force or effect.

Amended by Stats 2004 ch 193 (SB 111), s 143, eff. 1/1/2005.

Chapter 2 - DISMISSING AN APPEAL FOR IRREGULARITY

Section 1248 - Dismissal of irregular appeal

If the appeal is irregular in any substantial particular, but not otherwise, the appellate court may order it to be dismissed.

Amended by Stats. 1945, Ch. 40.

Chapter 3 - ARGUMENT OF THE APPEAL

Section 1252 - Continuances; consideration and passing upon rulings of trial court

On an appeal in a criminal case, no continuance shall be granted upon stipulation of counsel, and no continuance shall be granted for any longer period than the ends of justice shall require. On an appeal by a defendant, the appellate court shall, in addition to the issues raised by the defendant, consider and pass upon all rulings of the trial court adverse to the State which it may be requested to pass upon by the Attorney General.

Amended by Stats. 1945, Ch. 40.

Section 1253 - Failure to appear

The judgment may be affirmed if the appellant fail to appear, but can be reversed only after argument, though the respondent fail to appear.

Enacted 1872.

Section 1254 - Counsel

Upon the argument of the appeal, if the offense is punishable with death, two counsel must be heard on each side, if they require it. In any other case the Court may, in its discretion, restrict the argument to one counsel on each side.

Enacted 1872.

Section 1255 - Appearance of defendant

The defendant need not personally appear in the appellate Court.

Enacted 1872.

Section 1256 - Cooperation of district attorney

It shall be the duty of the district attorney to cooperate with and assist the attorney general in presenting all criminal matters on appeal.

Added by Stats. 1927, Ch. 620.

Chapter 4 - JUDGMENT UPON APPEAL

Section 1258 - Judgment

After hearing the appeal, the Court must give judgment without regard to technical errors or defects, or to exceptions, which do not affect the substantial rights of the parties.

Enacted 1872.

Section 1259 - Review of question of law or instruction

Upon an appeal taken by the defendant, the appellate court may, without exception having been taken in the trial court, review any question of law involved in any ruling, order, instruction, or thing whatsoever said or done at the trial or prior to or after judgment, which thing was said or done after objection made in and considered by the lower court, and which affected the substantial rights of the defendant. The appellate court may also review any instruction given, refused or modified, even though no objection was made thereto in the lower court, if the substantial rights of the defendant were affected thereby.

Amended by Stats. 1939, Ch. 1016.

Section 1260 - Reversal, affirmance, or modification of judgment or order

The court may reverse, affirm, or modify a judgment or order appealed from, or reduce the degree of the offense or attempted offense or the punishment imposed, and may set aside, affirm, or modify any or all of the proceedings subsequent to, or dependent upon, such judgment or order, and may, if proper, order a new trial and may, if proper, remand the cause to the trial court for such further proceedings as may be just under the circumstances.

Amended by Stats. 1978, Ch. 1166.

Section 1261 - New trial

When a new trial is ordered it must be directed to be had in the Court of the county from which the appeal was taken.

Enacted 1872.

Section 1262 - Reversal

If a judgment against the defendant is reversed, such reversal shall be deemed an order for a new trial, unless the appellate court shall otherwise direct. If the appellate court directs a final disposition of the action in the defendant's favor, the court must, if he is in custody, direct him to be discharged therefrom; or if on bail that his bail may be exonerated; or if money or other property was deposited instead of bail, that it be refunded to the defendant or to the person or persons found by the court to have deposited said money or other property on behalf of said defendant. If a judgment against the defendant is reversed and the case is dismissed, or if the appellate court directs a final disposition of the action in defendant's favor, and defendant has theretofore paid a fine in the case, such act shall also be deemed an order of the court that the fine, including any penalty assessment thereon, be returned to defendant.

Amended by Stats. 1963, Ch. 1609.

Section 1263 - Affirmance

If a judgment against the defendant is affirmed, the original judgment must be enforced.

Enacted 1872.

Section 1265 - Jurisdiction

(a) After the certificate of the judgment has been remitted to the court below, the appellate court has no further jurisdiction of the appeal or of the proceedings thereon, and all orders necessary to carry the judgment into effect shall be made by the court to which the certificate is remitted. However, if a judgment has been affirmed on appeal no motion shall be made or proceeding in the nature of a petition for a writ of error coram nobis shall be brought to procure the vacation of that judgment, except in the court which affirmed the judgment on appeal. When a judgment is affirmed by a court of appeal and a hearing is not granted by the Supreme Court, the application for the writ shall be made to the court of appeal.

(b) Where it is necessary to obtain personal jurisdiction of the defendant in order to carry the judgment into effect, upon a satisfactory showing that other means such as contact by mail, phone, or notification by means of the defendant's counsel have failed to secure the defendant's appearance, the court to which the certificate has been remitted may issue a bench warrant.

Amended by Stats. 1992, Ch. 128, Sec. 1. Effective July 7, 1992.

Title 10 - MISCELLANEOUS PROCEEDINGS

Chapter 1 - BAIL

Article 1 - IN WHAT CASES THE DEFENDANT MAY BE ADMITTED TO BAIL

Section 1268 - Admission to bail

Admission to bail is the order of a competent Court or magistrate that the defendant be discharged from actual custody upon bail.

Enacted 1872.

Section 1269 - Taking of bail

The taking of bail consists in the acceptance, by a competent court or magistrate, of the undertaking of sufficient bail for the appearance of the defendant, according to the terms of the undertaking, or that the bail will pay to the people of this state a specified sum. Upon filing, the clerk shall enter in the register of actions the date and amounts of such bond and the name or names of the surety or sureties thereon. In the event of the loss or destruction of such bond, such entries so made shall be prima facie evidence of the due execution of such bond as required by law.

Whenever any bail bond has been deposited in any criminal action or proceeding in a municipal or superior court or in any proceeding in habeas corpus in a superior court, and it is made to appear to the satisfaction of the court by affidavit or by testimony in open court that more than three years have elapsed since the exoneration or release of said bail, the court must direct that such bond be destroyed.

Amended by Stats. 1998, Ch. 931, Sec. 398. Effective September 28, 1998.

Section 1269a - Defendant charged in warrant of arrest with public offense

Except as otherwise provided by law, no defendant charged in a warrant of arrest with any public offense shall be discharged from custody upon bail except upon a written order of a competent court or magistrate admitting the defendant to bail in the amount specified in the indorsement referred to in Section 815a, and where an undertaking is furnished, upon a written order of such court or magistrate approving the undertaking. All such orders must be signed by such court or magistrate and delivered to the officer having custody of the defendant before the defendant is released. Any officer releasing any defendant upon bail otherwise than as herein provided shall be guilty of a misdemeanor.

Amended by Stats. 1941, Ch. 366.

Section 1269b - Acceptance of bail; bail schedule

(a)The officer in charge of a jail in which an arrested person is held in custody, an officer of a sheriff's department or police department of a city who is in charge of a jail or is employed at a fixed police or sheriff's facility and is acting under an agreement with the agency that keeps the jail in which an arrested person is held in custody, an employee of a sheriff's department or police department of a city who is assigned by the department to collect bail, the clerk of the superior court of the county in which the offense was alleged to have been committed, and the clerk of the superior court in which the case against the defendant is pending may approve and accept bail in the amount fixed by the warrant of arrest, schedule of bail, or order admitting to bail in cash or surety bond executed by a certified, admitted surety insurer as provided in the Insurance Code, to issue and sign an order for the release of the arrested person, and to set a time and place for the appearance of the arrested person before the appropriate court and give notice thereof.

(b)If a defendant has appeared before a judge of the court on the charge contained in the complaint, indictment, or information, the bail shall be in the amount fixed by the judge at the time of the appearance. If that appearance has not been made, the bail shall be in the amount fixed in the warrant of arrest or, if no warrant of arrest has been issued, the amount of bail shall be pursuant to the uniform countywide schedule of bail for the county in which the defendant is required to appear, previously fixed and approved as provided in subdivisions (c) and (d).

(c)It is the duty of the superior court judges in each county to prepare, adopt, and annually revise a uniform countywide schedule of bail for all bailable felony offenses and for all misdemeanor and infraction offenses except Vehicle Code infractions. The penalty schedule for infraction violations of the Vehicle Code shall be established by the Judicial Council in accordance with Section 40310 of the Vehicle Code.

(d)A court may, by local rule, prescribe the procedure by which the uniform countywide schedule of bail is prepared, adopted, and annually revised by the judges. If a court does not adopt a local rule, the uniform countywide schedule of bail shall be prepared, adopted, and annually revised by a majority of the judges.

(e)In adopting a uniform countywide schedule of bail for all bailable felony offenses the judges shall consider the seriousness of the offense charged. In considering the seriousness of the offense charged the judges shall assign an additional amount of required bail for each aggravating or enhancing factor chargeable in the complaint, including, but not limited to, additional bail for charges alleging facts that would bring a person within any of the following sections: Section 667.5, 667.51, 667.6, 667.8, 667.85, 667.9, 667.10, 12022, 12022.1, 12022.2, 12022.3, 12022.4, 12022.5, 12022.53, 12022.6, 12022.7, 12022.8, or 12022.9 of this code, or Section 11356.5, 11370.2, or 11370.4 of the Health and Safety Code. In considering offenses in which a violation of Chapter 6 (commencing with Section 11350) of Division 10 of the Health and Safety Code is alleged, the judge shall assign an additional amount of required bail for offenses involving large quantities of controlled substances.

(f)

(1)The countywide bail schedule shall contain a list of the offenses and the amounts of bail applicable for each as the judges determine to be appropriate. If the schedule does not list all offenses specifically, it shall contain a general clause for designated amounts of bail as the judges of the county determine to be appropriate for all the offenses not specifically listed in the schedule. A copy of the countywide bail schedule shall be sent to the officer in charge of the county jail, to the officer in charge of each city jail within the county, to each superior court judge and commissioner in the county, and to the Judicial Council.

(2)The countywide bail schedule shall set zero dollars ($0) bail for an individual who has been arrested in connection with a proceeding in another state regarding an individual performing, supporting, or aiding in the performance of an abortion in this state, or an individual obtaining an abortion in this state, if the abortion is lawful under the laws of this state.

(g)Upon posting bail, the defendant or arrested person shall be discharged from custody as to the offense on which the bail is posted. All money and surety bonds so deposited with an officer authorized to receive bail shall be transmitted immediately to the judge or clerk of the court by which the order was made or warrant issued or bail schedule fixed. If, in the case of felonies, an indictment is filed, the judge or clerk of the court shall transmit all of the money and surety bonds to the clerk of the court.

(h)If a defendant or arrested person so released fails to appear at the time and in the court so ordered upon their release from custody, Sections 1305 and 1306 apply.

Amended by Stats 2022 ch 627 (AB 1242),s 6, eff. 9/27/2022.

Amended by Stats 2003 ch 149 (SB 79), s 76, eff. 1/1/2004.

Amended by Stats 2001 ch 176 (SB 210) s 42, eff. 1/1/2002.

Previously Amended July 12, 1999 (Bill Number: SB 966) (Chapter 83).

Section 1269c - Defendant arrested without warrant for bailable felony offense or misdemeanor offense of violating domestic violence restraining order; higher bail

If a defendant is arrested without a warrant for a bailable felony offense or for the misdemeanor offense of violating a domestic violence restraining order, and a peace officer has reasonable cause to believe that the amount of bail set forth in the schedule of bail for that offense is insufficient to ensure the defendant's appearance or to ensure the protection of a victim, or family member of a victim, of domestic violence, the peace officer shall prepare a declaration under penalty of perjury setting forth the facts and circumstances in support of his or her belief and file it with a magistrate, as defined in Section 808, or his or her commissioner, in the county in which the offense is alleged to have been committed or having personal jurisdiction over the defendant, requesting an order setting a higher bail. Except where the defendant is charged with an offense listed in subdivision (a) of Section 1270.1, the defendant, either personally or through his or her attorney, friend, or family member, also may make application to the magistrate for release on bail lower than that provided in the schedule of bail or on his or her own recognizance. The magistrate or commissioner to whom the application is made is authorized to set bail in an amount that he or she deems sufficient to ensure the defendant's appearance or to ensure the protection of a victim, or family member of a victim, of domestic violence, and to set bail on the terms and conditions that he or she, in his or her discretion, deems appropriate, or he or she may authorize the defendant's release on his or her own recognizance. If, after the application is made, no order changing the amount of bail is issued within eight hours after booking, the defendant shall be entitled to be released on posting the amount of bail set forth in the applicable bail schedule.

Amended by Stats 2010 ch 176 (SB 1049),s 1, eff. 1/1/2011.

Section 1270 - Recognizance release

(a) Any person who has been arrested for, or charged with, an offense other than a capital offense may be released on his or her own recognizance by a court or magistrate who could release a defendant from custody upon the defendant giving bail, including a defendant arrested upon an out-of-county warrant. A defendant who is in custody and is arraigned on a complaint alleging an offense which is a misdemeanor, and a defendant who appears before a court or magistrate upon an out-of-county warrant arising out of a case involving only misdemeanors, shall be entitled to an own recognizance release unless the court makes a finding on the record, in accordance with Section 1275, that an own recognizance release will compromise public safety or will not reasonably assure the appearance of the defendant as required. Public safety shall be the primary consideration. If the court makes one of those findings, the court shall then set bail and specify the conditions, if any, whereunder the defendant shall be released.

(b) Article 9 (commencing with Section 1318) shall apply to any person who is released pursuant to this section.

Amended by Stats. 1995, Ch. 51, Sec. 1. Effective January 1, 1996.

Section 1270.1 - Hearing

(a)Except as provided in subdivision (e), before a person who is arrested for any of the following crimes may be released on bail in an amount that is either more or less than the amount contained in the schedule of bail for the offense, or may be released on the person's own recognizance, a hearing shall be held in open court before the magistrate or judge:

(1) A serious felony, as defined in subdivision (c) of Section 1192.7, or a violent felony, as defined in subdivision (c) of Section 667.5, but not including a violation of subdivision (a) of Section 460 (residential burglary).

(2) A violation of Section 136.1 where punishment is imposed pursuant to subdivision (c) of Section 136.1, Section 273.5 or 422 if the offense is punished as a felony, or Section 646.9, or former Section 262.

(3) A violation of paragraph (1) of subdivision (e) of Section 243.

(4) A violation of Section 273.6 if the detained person made threats to kill or harm, has engaged in violence against, or has gone to the residence or workplace of, the protected party.

(b) The prosecuting attorney and defense attorney shall be given a two-court-day written notice and an opportunity to be heard on the matter. If the detained person does not have counsel, the court shall appoint counsel for purposes of this section only. The hearing required by this section shall be held within the time period prescribed in Section 825.

(c) At the hearing, the court shall consider evidence of past court appearances of the detained person, the maximum potential sentence that could be imposed, and the danger that may be posed to other persons if the detained person is released. In making the determination whether to release the detained person on their own recognizance, the court shall consider the potential danger to other persons, including threats that have been made by the detained person and any past acts of violence. The court shall also consider any evidence offered by the detained person regarding the detained person's ties to the community and ability to post bond.

(d) If the judge or magistrate sets the bail in an amount that is either more or less than the amount contained in the schedule of bail for the offense, the judge or magistrate shall state the reasons for that decision and shall address the issue of threats made against the victim or witness, if they were made, in the record. This statement shall be included in the record.

(e) Notwithstanding subdivision (a), a judge or magistrate, pursuant to Section 1269c, may, with respect to a bailable felony offense or a misdemeanor offense of violating a domestic violence order, increase bail to an amount exceeding that set forth in the bail schedule without a hearing, provided an oral or written declaration of facts justifying the increase is presented under penalty of perjury by a sworn peace officer.

Amended by Stats 2022 ch 197 (SB 1493),s 24, eff. 1/1/2023.

Amended by Stats 2021 ch 626 (AB 1171),s 52, eff. 1/1/2022.

Amended by Stats 2010 ch 176 (SB 1049),s 2, eff. 1/1/2011.

Amended by Stats 2003 ch 30 (AB 1488), s 1, eff. 1/1/2004.

Amended October 10, 1999 (Bill Number: AB 1284) (Chapter 703).

Section 1270.2 - Review of order fixing amount of bail

When a person is detained in custody on a criminal charge prior to conviction for want of bail, that person is entitled to an automatic review of the order fixing the amount of the bail by the judge or magistrate having jurisdiction of the offense. That review shall be held not later than five days from the time of the original order fixing the amount of bail on the original accusatory pleading. The defendant may waive this review.

Added by Stats. 1986, Ch. 658, Sec. 1.

Section 1270.5 - Defendant charged with offense punishable by death

A defendant charged with an offense punishable with death cannot be admitted to bail, when the proof of his or her guilt is evident or the presumption thereof great. The finding of an indictment does not add to the strength of the proof or the presumptions to be drawn therefrom.

Added by renumbering Section 1270 (as enacted in 1872) by Stats. 1986, Ch. 248, Sec. 165.

Section 1271 - Admission to bail before conviction

If the charge is for any other offense, he may be admitted to bail before conviction, as a matter of right.

Enacted 1872.

Section 1272 - Bail after conviction of offense not punishable with death or life without the possibility of parole

After conviction of an offense not punishable with death or life without the possibility of parole, a defendant who has made application for probation or who has appealed may be admitted to bail:

(a) As a matter of right, before judgment is pronounced pending application for probation in cases of misdemeanors, or when the appeal is from a judgment imposing a fine only.

(b) As a matter of right, before judgment is pronounced pending application for probation in cases of misdemeanors, or when the appeal is from a judgment imposing imprisonment in cases of misdemeanors.

(c) As a matter of discretion in all other cases, except that a person convicted of an offense subject to this subdivision, who makes a motion for release on bail subsequent to a sentencing hearing, shall provide notice of the hearing on the bail motion to the prosecuting attorney at least five court days prior to the hearing.

Amended by Stats 2023 ch 545 (AB 791),s 2, eff. 1/1/2024.

Amended by Stats. 1984, Ch. 1202, Sec. 2. Effective September 17, 1984.

Section 1272.1 - Release on bail pending appeal as matter of discretion

Release on bail pending appeal under subdivision (3) of Section 1272 shall be ordered by the court if the defendant demonstrates all the following:

(a) By clear and convincing evidence, the defendant is not likely to flee. Under this subdivision the court shall consider the following criteria:

(1) The ties of the defendant to the community, including his or her employment, the duration of his or her residence, the defendant's family attachments and his or her property holdings.

(2) The defendant's record of appearance at past court hearings or of flight to avoid prosecution.

(3) The severity of the sentence the defendant faces.

(b) By clear and convincing evidence, the defendant does not pose a danger to the safety of any other person or to the community. Under this subdivision the court shall consider, among other factors, whether the crime for which the defendant was convicted is a violent felony, as defined in subdivision (c) of Section 667.5.

(c) The appeal is not for the purpose of delay and, based upon the record in the case, raises a substantial legal question which, if decided in favor of the defendant, is likely to result in reversal. For purposes of this subdivision, a "substantial legal question" means a close question, one of more substance than would be necessary to a finding that it was not frivolous. In assessing whether a substantial legal question has been raised on appeal by the defendant, the court shall not be required to determine whether it committed error.
In making its decision on whether to grant defendants' motions for bail under subdivision (3) of Section 1272, the court shall include a brief statement of reasons in support of an order granting or denying a motion for bail on appeal. The statement need only include the basis for the order with sufficient specificity to permit meaningful review.
Amended by Stats. 1989, Ch. 150, Sec. 1.

Section 1273 - Admission to bail before conviction

If the offense is bailable, the defendant may be admitted to bail before conviction:
First-For his appearance before the magistrate, on the examination of the charge, before being held to answer.
Second-To appear at the Court to which the magistrate is required to return the depositions and statement, upon the defendant being held to answer after examination.
Third-After indictment, either before the bench warrant is issued for his arrest, or upon any order of the Court committing him, or enlarging the amount of bail, or upon his being surrendered by his bail to answer the indictment in the Court in which it is found, or to which it may be transferred for trial.
And after conviction, and upon an appeal:
First-If the appeal is from a judgment imposing a fine only, on the undertaking of bail that he will pay the same, or such part of it as the appellate Court may direct, if the judgment is affirmed or modified, or the appeal is dismissed.
Second-If judgment of imprisonment has been given, that he will surrender himself in execution of the judgment, upon its being affirmed or modified, or upon the appeal being dismissed, or that in case the judgment be reversed, and that the cause be remanded for a new trial, that he will appear in the Court to which said cause may be remanded, and submit himself to the orders and process thereof.
Amended by Code Amendments 1875-76, Ch. 80.

Section 1274 - Admission to bail as matter of discretion

When the admission to bail is a matter of discretion, the Court or officer to whom the application is made must require reasonable notice thereof to be given to the District Attorney of the county.
Enacted 1872.

Section 1275 - Factors to consider in setting, reducing, or denying bail

(a)
    (1) In setting, reducing, or denying bail, a judge or magistrate shall take into consideration the protection of the public, the seriousness of the offense charged, the previous criminal record of the defendant, and the probability of his or her appearing at trial or at a hearing of the case. The public safety shall be the primary consideration. In setting bail, a judge or magistrate may consider factors such as the information included in a report prepared in accordance with Section 1318.1.
    (2) In considering the seriousness of the offense charged, a judge or magistrate shall include consideration of the alleged injury to the victim, and alleged threats to the victim or a witness to the crime charged, the alleged use of a firearm or other deadly weapon in the commission of the crime charged, and the alleged use or possession of controlled substances by the defendant.
(b) In considering offenses wherein a violation of Chapter 6 (commencing with Section 11350) of Division 10 of the Health and Safety Code is alleged, a judge or magistrate shall consider the following:
    (1) the alleged amounts of controlled substances involved in the commission of the offense, and
    (2) whether the defendant is currently released on bail for an alleged violation of Chapter 6 (commencing with Section 11350) of Division 10 of the Health and Safety Code.
(c) Before a court reduces bail to below the amount established by the bail schedule approved for the county, in accordance with subdivisions (b) and (c) of Section 1269b, for a person charged with a serious felony, as defined in subdivision (c) of Section 1192.7, or a violent felony, as defined in subdivision (c) of Section 667.5, the court shall make a finding of unusual circumstances and shall set forth those facts on the record. For purposes of this subdivision, "unusual circumstances" does not include the fact that the defendant has made all prior court appearances or has not committed any new offenses.
Amended by Stats 2014 ch 71 (SB 1304),s 128, eff. 1/1/2015.
Amended by Stats 2013 ch 17 (AB 805),s 1, eff. 1/1/2014.

Section 1275.1 - Acceptance of bail; hold on release of defendant

(a) Bail, pursuant to this chapter, shall not be accepted unless a judge or magistrate finds that no portion of the consideration, pledge, security, deposit, or indemnification paid, given, made, or promised for its execution was feloniously obtained.
(b) A hold on the release of a defendant from custody shall only be ordered by a magistrate or judge if any of the following occurs:
    (1) A peace officer, as defined in Section 830, files a declaration executed under penalty of perjury setting forth probable cause to believe that the source of any consideration, pledge, security, deposit, or indemnification paid, given, made, or promised for its execution was feloniously obtained.
    (2) A prosecutor files a declaration executed under penalty of perjury setting forth probable cause to believe that the source of any consideration, pledge, security, deposit, or indemnification paid, given, made, or promised for its execution was feloniously obtained. A prosecutor shall have absolute civil immunity for executing a declaration pursuant to this paragraph.
    (3) The magistrate or judge has probable cause to believe that the source of any consideration, pledge, security, deposit, or indemnification paid, given, made, or promised for its execution was feloniously obtained.
(c) Once a magistrate or judge has determined that probable cause exists, as provided in subdivision (b), a defendant bears the burden by a preponderance of the evidence to show that no part of any consideration, pledge, security, deposit, or indemnification paid, given, made, or promised for its execution was obtained by felonious means. Once a defendant has met such burden, the magistrate or judge shall release the hold previously ordered and the defendant shall be released under the authorized amount of bail.

(d) The defendant and his or her attorney shall be provided with a copy of the declaration of probable cause filed under subdivision (b) no later than the date set forth in Section 825.

(e) Nothing in this section shall prohibit a defendant from obtaining a loan of money so long as the loan will be funded and repaid with funds not feloniously obtained.

(f) At the request of any person providing any portion of the consideration, pledge, security, deposit, or indemnification paid, given, made, or promised for its execution, the magistrate or judge, at an evidentiary hearing to determine the source of the funds, may close it to the general public to protect the person's right to privacy in his or her financial affairs.

(g) If the declaration, having been filed with a magistrate or judge, is not acted on within 24 hours, the defendant shall be released from custody upon posting of the amount of bail set.

(h) Nothing in this code shall deny the right of the defendant, either personally or through his or her attorney, bail agent licensed by the Department of Insurance, admitted surety insurer licensed by the Department of Insurance, friend, or member of his or her family from making an application to the magistrate or judge for the release of the defendant on bail.

(i) The bail of any defendant found to have willfully misled the court regarding the source of bail may be increased as a result of the willful misrepresentation. The misrepresentation may be a factor considered in any subsequent bail hearing.

(j) If a defendant has met the burden under subdivision (c), and a defendant will be released from custody upon the issuance of a bail bond issued pursuant to authority of Section 1269 or 1269b by any admitted surety insurer or any bail agent, approved by the Insurance Commissioner, the magistrate or judge shall vacate the holding order imposed under subdivision (b) upon the condition that the consideration for the bail bond is approved by the court.

(k) As used in this section, "feloniously obtained" means any consideration, pledge, security, deposit, or indemnification paid, given, made, or promised for its execution which is possessed, received, or obtained through an unlawful act, transaction, or occurrence constituting a felony.

Added by Stats. 1998, Ch. 726, Sec. 2. Effective January 1, 1999.

Section 1276 - Bail bond or undertaking on bail

(a) A bail bond or undertaking of bail of an admitted surety insurer shall be accepted or approved by a court or magistrate without further acknowledgment if executed by a licensed bail agent of the insurer under penalty of perjury and issued in the name of the insurer by a person authorized to do so by an unrevoked power of attorney on file in the office of the clerk of the county in which the court or magistrate is located.

(b) One person may both execute and issue the bail bond or undertaking of bail if qualified as provided in this section.

Added by Stats. 1982, Ch. 517, Sec. 316.

Section 1276.1 - Bail premiums

(a) On and after January 1, 2022, no insurer, bail agent, or other bail licensee shall enter into a contract, agreement, or undertaking of bail that requires the payment of more than one premium for the duration of the agreement, and the duration of the agreement shall be until bail is exonerated. On and after January 1, 2022, no insurer, bail agent, or other bail licensee, shall charge, collect, or receive a renewal premium in connection with a contract, agreement, or undertaking of bail.

(b) On and after July 1, 2022, no insurer or insurance licensee shall enter into a contract, agreement, or undertaking to post an immigration bond that requires the payment of more than one premium for the duration of the agreement, and the duration of the agreement shall be until the bond is exonerated. An insurer or insurance licensee shall not charge, collect, or receive a renewal premium in connection with a contract, agreement, or undertaking to post an immigration bond entered into on and after July 1, 2022.

(c) The violation of this section by an insurer, insurance licensee, bail agent, or other bail licensee shall make the violator liable to the person affected by the violation for all damages that person may sustain by reason of the violation plus statutory damages in the sum of three thousand dollars ($3,000). Any person affected by a violation of this section shall be entitled, if they prevail, to recover court costs and reasonable attorney's fees as determined by the court in any action brought to enforce this section.

Added by Stats 2021 ch 444 (AB 1347),s 1, eff. 1/1/2022.

Section 1276.5 - Disclosure to property owner

(a) At the time of an initial application to a bail bond licensee for a bail bond which is to be secured by a lien against real property, the bail bond licensee shall provide the property owner with a written disclosure statement in the following form:"DISCLOSURE OF LIEN AGAINST REAL PROPERTY DO NOT SIGN THIS DOCUMENT UNTIL YOU READ AND UNDERSTAND IT! THIS BAIL BOND WILL BE SECURED BY REAL PROPERTY YOU OWN OR IN WHICH YOU HAVE AN INTEREST. THE FAILURE TO PAY THE BAIL BOND PREMIUMS WHEN DUE OR THE FAILURE OF THE DEFENDANT TO COMPLY WITH THE CONDITIONS OF BAIL COULD RESULT IN THE LOSS OF YOUR PROPERTY!"

(b) The disclosure required in subdivision (a) shall be made in 14-point bold type by either of the following means:

    (1) A separate and specific document attached to or accompanying the application.

    (2) A clear and conspicuous statement on the face of the application.

(c) The property owner shall be given a completed copy of the disclosure statement and of the note and deed of trust or other instrument creating the lien against real property prior to the execution of any instrument creating a lien against real property. The failure to fully comply with subdivision (a) or (b), or this subdivision, shall render the deed of trust or other instrument creating the lien against real property voidable.

(d) Within 30 days after notice is given by any individual, agency, or entity to the surety or bail bond licensee of the expiration of the time for appeal of the order exonerating the bail bond, or within 30 days after the payment in full of all moneys owed on the bail bond obligation secured by any lien against real property, whichever is later in time, the bail bond licensee shall deliver to the property owner a fully executed and notarized reconveyance of title, a certificate of discharge, or a full release of any lien against real property to secure performance of the conditions of the bail bond. If a timely notice of appeal of the order exonerating the bail bond is filed with the court, that 30-day period shall begin on the date the determination of the appellate court affirming the order exonerating the bail bond becomes final. Upon the reconveyance, the licensee shall deliver to the property owner the original note and deed of trust, security agreement, or other instrument which secures the bail bond obligation. If the licensee fails to comply with this subdivision, the property owner may petition the superior court to issue an order directing the clerk of the superior court to execute a full reconveyance of title, a certificate of discharge, or a full release of any lien against real property created to secure performance of the conditions of the bail bond. The petition shall be verified and shall allege facts showing that the licensee has failed to comply with this subdivision.

(e) The violation of this section shall make the violator liable to the person affected by the violation for all damages which that person may sustain by reason of the violation plus statutory damages in the sum of three hundred dollars ($300). The property owner shall be entitled, if he or she prevails, to recover court costs and reasonable attorney's fees as determined by the court in any action brought to enforce this section.

Added by Stats. 1991, Ch. 838, Sec. 1.

Article 2 - BAIL UPON BEING HELD TO ANSWER BEFORE INDICTMENT

Section 1277 - Admission to bail

When the defendant has been held to answer upon an examination for a public offense, the admission to bail may be by the magistrate by whom he is so held, or by any magistrate who has power to issue the writ of habeas corpus.

Enacted 1872.

Section 1278 - Undertaking of bail

(a) Bail is put in by a written undertaking, executed by two sufficient sureties (with or without the defendant, in the discretion of the magistrate), and acknowledged before the court or magistrate, in substantially the following form: An order having been made on the ____ day of ____, 20__, by ____, a judge of the ____ Court of ____ County, that ____ be held to answer upon a charge of (stating briefly the nature of the offense), upon which he or she has been admitted to bail in the sum of ____ dollars ($____); we, ____ and ____, of ____ (stating their place of residence and occupation), hereby undertake that the above-named ____ will appear and answer any charge in any accusatory pleading based upon the acts supporting the charge above mentioned, in whatever court it may be prosecuted, and will at all times hold himself or herself amenable to the orders and process of the court, and if convicted, will appear for pronouncement of judgment or grant of probation, or if he or she fails to perform either of these conditions, that we will pay to the people of the State of California the sum of ____ dollars ($____) (inserting the sum in which the defendant is admitted to bail). If the forfeiture of this bond be ordered by the court, judgment may be summarily made and entered forthwith against the said (naming the sureties), and the defendant if he or she be a party to the bond, for the amount of their respective undertakings herein, as provided by Sections 1305 and 1306.

(b) Every undertaking of bail shall contain the bail agent license number of the owner of the bail agency issuing the undertaking along with the name, address, and phone number of the agency, regardless of whether the owner is an individual, partnership, or corporation. The bail agency name on the undertaking shall be a business name approved by the Insurance Commissioner for use by the bail agency owner, and be so reflected in the public records of the commissioner. The license number of the bail agent appearing on the undertaking shall be in the same type size as the name, address, and phone number of the agency.

Amended by Stats 2004 ch 104 (SB 761), s 1, eff. 1/1/2005.

Section 1279 - Qualifications of bail

The qualifications of bail are as follows:

1. Each of them must be a resident, householder, or freeholder within the state; but the court or magistrate may refuse to accept any person as bail who is not a resident of the county where bail is offered;

2. They must each be worth the amount specified in the undertaking, exclusive of property exempt from execution, except that if any of the sureties is not worth the amount specified in the undertaking, exclusive of property exempt from execution, but owns any equity in real property, a hearing must be held before the magistrate to determine the value of such equity. Witnesses may be called and examined at such hearing and if the magistrate is satisfied that the value of the equity is equal to twice the amount of the bond such surety is justified. In any case, the court or magistrate, on taking bail, may allow more than two sureties to justify severally in amounts less than that expressed in the undertaking, if the whole justification be equivalent to that of sufficient bail.

Amended by Stats. 1931, Ch. 1172.

Section 1280 - Affidavit

The bail must in all cases justify by affidavit taken before the magistrate, that they each possess the qualifications provided in the preceding section. The magistrate may further examine the bail upon oath concerning their sufficiency, in such manner as he may deem proper.

Enacted 1872.

Section 1280a - Content of affidavit

All affidavits for the justification of bail shall set forth the amount of the bail undertaking, a notice that the affidavit shall constitute a lien upon the real property described in the affidavit immediately upon the recordation of the affidavit with the county recorder pursuant to Section 1280b, and the legal description and assessor's parcel numbers of the real estate owned by the bail, which is scheduled as showing that they each possess the qualifications provided in the preceding sections, the affidavit shall also show all encumbrances upon the real estate known to affiants and shall show the number of bonds, if any, on which each bail has qualified, within one year before the date of the affidavit, together with the amount of each such bond, the date on which, the county in which, and the name of the principal for whom each bond was executed.

The affidavit shall also state the amount of each bail's liability on bonds executed in previous years and not exonerated at the date of the execution of the affidavit and be signed and acknowledged by the owner of the real property.

Amended by Stats. 1987, Ch. 828, Sec. 82.

Section 1280b - Filing of affidavits

It shall be the duty of the judge or magistrate to file with the clerk of the court, within 24 hours after presentation to him or her, all affidavits for the justification of bail, by delivering or mailing them to the clerk of the court. Certified copies of the affidavits for justification of bail involving equity in real property may upon the written order of the judge or magistrate be recorded with the county recorder.

Amended by Stats. 1988, Ch. 676, Sec. 1.

Section 1280.1 - Attachment lien

(a) From the time of recording an affidavit for the justification of bail, the affidavit shall constitute an attachment lien governed by Sections 488.500, 488.510 and 489.310 of the Code of Civil Procedure in the amount of the bail undertaking, until exonerated, released, or otherwise discharged. Any release of the undertaking shall be effected by an order of the court, filed with the clerk of the court, with a certified copy of the order recorded in the office of the county recorder.

(b) If the bail is forfeited and summary judgment is entered, pursuant to Sections 1305 and 1306, the lien shall have the force and effect of a judgment lien, by recordation of an abstract of judgment, which, may be enforced and satisfied pursuant to Section 1306 as well as through the applicable execution process set forth in Title 9 (commencing with Section 680.010) of Part 2 of the Code of Civil Procedure.

Amended by Stats 2001 ch 854 (SB 205) s 45, eff. 1/1/2002.

Section 1281 - Discharge order

Upon the allowance of bail and the execution and approval of the undertaking, the magistrate must, if the defendant is in custody, make and sign an order for his discharge, upon the delivery of which to the proper officer the defendant must be discharged.

Amended by Stats. 1927, Ch. 733.

Section 1281a - Release order

A judge of the superior court within the county, wherein a cause is pending against any person charged with a felony, may justify and approve bail in the said cause, and may execute an order for the release of the defendant which shall authorize the discharge of the defendant by any officer having said defendant in custody.

Amended by Stats 2002 ch 784 (SB 1316), s 552, eff. 1/1/2003.

Article 3 - BAIL UPON AN INDICTMENT BEFORE CONVICTION

Section 1284 - Offense not punishable with death; appearance before magistrate

When the offense charged is not punishable with death, the officer serving the bench warrant must, if required, take the defendant before a magistrate in the county in which it is issued, or in which he is arrested, for the purpose of giving bail. If the defendant appears before such magistrate without the bench warrant having been served upon him, the magistrate shall deliver him into the custody of the sheriff for the purpose of immediate booking and the recording of identification data, whereupon the sheriff shall deliver the defendant back before the magistrate for the purpose of giving bail.

Amended by Stats. 1961, Ch. 2198.

Section 1285 - Offense punishable by death; delivery into custody

If the offense charged is punishable by death, the officer arresting the defendant must deliver him into custody, according to the command of the bench warrant.

Amended by Code Amendments 1880, Ch. 47.

Section 1286 - Holding by sheriff

When the defendant is so delivered into custody he must be held by the Sheriff, unless admitted to bail on examination upon a writ of habeas corpus.

Enacted 1872.

Section 1287 - Undertaking of bail

(a) The bail shall be put in by a written undertaking, executed by two sufficient sureties (with or without the defendant, in the discretion of the court or magistrate), and acknowledged before the court or magistrate, in substantially the following form: An indictment having been found on the ____ day of ____, 20__, in the Superior Court of the County of ____, charging ____ with the crime of ____ (designating it generally) and he or she having been admitted to bail in the sum of ____ dollars ($____), we, ____ and ____, of ____ (stating their place of residence and occupation), hereby undertake that the above-named ____ will appear and answer any charge in any accusatory pleading based upon the acts supporting the indictment above mentioned, in whatever court it may be prosecuted, and will at all times render himself or herself amenable to the orders and process of the court, and, if convicted, will appear for pronouncement of judgment or grant of probation; or, if he or she fails to perform either of these conditions, that we will pay to the people of the State of California the sum of ____ dollars ($____) (inserting the sum in which the defendant is admitted to bail). If the forfeiture of this bond be ordered by the court, judgment may be summarily made and entered forthwith against the said (naming the sureties, and the defendant if he or she be a party to the bond), for the amount of their respective undertakings herein, as provided by Sections 1305 and 1306.

(b) Every undertaking of bail shall contain the bail agent license number of the owner of the bail agency issuing the undertaking along with the name, address, and phone number of the agency, regardless of whether the owner is an individual, partnership, or corporation. The bail agency name on the undertaking shall be a business name approved by the Insurance Commissioner for use by the bail agency owner, and be so reflected in the public records of the commissioner. The license number of the bail agent appearing on the undertaking shall be in the same type size as the name, address, and phone number of the agency.

Amended by Stats 2004 ch 104 (SB 761), s 2, eff. 1/1/2005.

Section 1288 - Applicability of statutory provisions

The provisions contained in sections 1279, 1280, 1280a and 1281, in relation to bail before indictment, apply to bail after indictment.

Amended by Stats. 1927, Ch. 736.

Section 1289 - Change in amount of bail

After a defendant has been admitted to bail upon an indictment or information, the Court in which the charge is pending may, upon good cause shown, either increase or reduce the amount of bail. If the amount be increased, the Court may order the defendant to be committed to actual custody, unless he give bail in such increased amount. If application be made by the defendant for a reduction of the amount, notice of the application must be served upon the District Attorney.

Amended by Code Amendments 1880, Ch. 47.

Article 4 - BAIL ON APPEAL

Section 1291 - Admission to bail

In the cases in which defendant may be admitted to bail upon an appeal, the order admitting him to bail may be made by any Magistrate having the power to issue a writ of habeas corpus, or by the Magistrate before whom the trial was had.
Amended by Code Amendments 1877-78, Ch. 89.

Section 1292 - Qualifications of bail

The bail must possess the qualifications, and must be put in, in all respects, as provided in Article II of this Chapter, except that the undertaking must be conditioned as prescribed in Section 1273, for undertakings of bail on appeal.
Enacted 1872.

Article 5 - DEPOSIT INSTEAD OF BAIL

Section 1295 - Deposit of money

(a) The defendant, or any other person, at any time after an order admitting defendant to bail or after the arrest and booking of a defendant for having committed a misdemeanor, instead of giving bail may deposit, with the clerk of the court in which the defendant is held to answer or notified to appear for arraignment, the sum mentioned in the order or, if no order, in the schedule of bail previously fixed by the judges of the court, and, upon delivering to the officer in whose custody defendant is a certificate of the deposit, the defendant must be discharged from custody.

(b) Where more than one deposit is made with respect to any charge in any accusatory pleading based upon the acts supporting the original charge as a result of which an earlier deposit was made, the defendant shall receive credit in the amount of any earlier deposit.

(c) The clerk of the court shall not accept a general assistance check for this deposit or any part thereof.
Amended by Stats. 1997, Ch. 17, Sec. 104. Effective January 1, 1998.

Section 1296 - Deposit after bail given

If the defendant has given bail, he may, at any time before the forfeiture of the undertaking, in like manner deposit the sum mentioned in the recognizance, and upon the deposit being made the bail is exonerated.
Enacted 1872.

Section 1297 - Receipt

When money has been deposited, a receipt shall be issued in the name of the depositor. If the money remains on deposit at the time of a judgment for the payment of a fine, the clerk shall, under the direction of the court, if the defendant be the depositor, apply the money in satisfaction thereof, and after satisfying restitution to the victim or the Restitution Fund, fines, and costs, shall refund the surplus, if any, to the defendant. If the person to whom the receipt for the deposit was issued was not the defendant, the deposit after judgment shall be returned to that person within 10 days after the person claims it by submitting the receipt, and, if a claim is not made within 10 days of the exoneration of bail, the clerk shall immediately notify the depositor of the exoneration of bail.
Amended by Stats. 1995, Ch. 313, Sec. 11. Effective August 3, 1995.

Section 1298 - Deposit of bonds

In lieu of a deposit of money, the defendant or any other person may deposit bonds of the United States or of the State of California of the face value of the cash deposit required, and these bonds shall be treated in the same manner as a deposit of money or the defendant or any other person may give as security any equity in real property which he or she owns, provided that no charge is made to the defendant or any other person for the giving as security of any equity in real property. A hearing, at which witnesses may be called or examined, shall be held before the magistrate to determine the value of the equity and if the magistrate finds that the value of the equity is equal to twice the amount of the cash deposit required he or she shall allow the bail. The clerk shall, under order of the court, when occasion arises therefor, sell the bonds or the equity and apply the proceeds of the sale in the manner that a deposit of cash may be required to be applied.
Amended by Stats 2008 ch 699 (SB 1241),s 14, eff. 1/1/2009.

Article 5.5 - BAIL FUGITIVE RECOVERY PERSONS ACT

Section 1299 - Short title

This article shall be known as the Bail Fugitive Recovery Persons Act.
Added by Stats 2012 ch 747 (AB 2029),s 1, eff. 1/1/2013.

Section 1299.01 - Definitions

(a) For purposes of this article, the following terms shall have the following meanings:

(1) "Bail fugitive" means a defendant in a pending criminal case who has been released from custody under a financially secured appearance, cash, or other bond and has had that bond declared forfeited, or a defendant in a pending criminal case who has violated a bond condition whereby apprehension and reincarceration are permitted.

(2) "Bail" means a bail agent, bail permittee, or bail solicitor licensed by the Department of Insurance pursuant to Section 1802, 1802.5, or 1803 of the Insurance Code.

(3) "Depositor of bail" means a person who or entity that has deposited money or bonds to secure the release of a person charged with a crime or offense.

(4) "Bail fugitive recovery agent" means a person licensed pursuant to Section 1802.3 of the Insurance Code who is provided written authorization pursuant to Section 1300 or 1301 by the bail or depositor of bail, and is contracted to investigate, surveil, locate, and arrest a bail fugitive for surrender to the appropriate court, jail, or police department, and any person who is employed to assist a bail or depositor of bail to investigate, surveil, locate, and arrest a bail fugitive for surrender to the appropriate court, jail, or police department.

(b) This section shall become operative on July 1, 2023.
Added by Stats 2022 ch 768 (AB 2043),s 19, eff. 1/1/2023.
Amended by Stats 2022 ch 768 (AB 2043),s 18, eff. 1/1/2023.
Added by Stats 2012 ch 747 (AB 2029),s 1, eff. 1/1/2013.

Section 1299.02 - Right to apprehend, detain, or arrest bail fugitive

(a) No person, other than a certified law enforcement officer, shall be authorized to apprehend, detain, or arrest a bail fugitive unless that person meets one of the following conditions:

(1) Is a bail as defined in paragraph (2) of subdivision (a) of Section 1299.01 who is also a bail fugitive recovery agent as defined in paragraph (4) of subdivision (a) of Section 1299.01.

(2) Is a bail fugitive recovery agent as defined in paragraph (4) of subdivision (a) of Section 1299.01.

(3) Is a licensed private investigator as provided in Chapter 11.3 (commencing with Section 7512) of Division 3 of the Business and Professions Code who is also a bail fugitive recovery agent as defined in paragraph (4) of subdivision (a) of Section 1299.01.

(b) This article shall not prohibit an arrest pursuant to Sections 837, 838, and 839, provided that no consideration is paid or allowed, directly or indirectly, to any person effecting an arrest pursuant to Sections 837, 838, and 839.

(c) Individuals who hold a bail license, bail fugitive recovery license, bail enforcer license, bail runner license, or private investigator license issued by another state shall not apprehend, detain, or arrest bail fugitives in California, unless that individual obtains a bail fugitive recovery agent license issued in this state and complies with California law.

(d) A person authorized, pursuant to subdivision (a), to apprehend, detain, or arrest a bail fugitive shall not apprehend, detain, or arrest a bail fugitive admitted to bail in another state whose alleged offense or conviction was for the violation of the laws of another state that authorize a criminal penalty to an individual performing, receiving, supporting, or aiding in the performance or receipt of sexual or reproductive health care, including, but not limited to, an abortion, contraception, or gender-affirming care if the sexual or reproductive health care is lawful under the laws of this state, regardless of the recipient's location. A person who violates this subdivision is guilty of an infraction punishable by a fine of five thousand dollars ($5,000), is ineligible for a license issued pursuant to Chapter 11.3 (commencing with Section 7512) of Division 3 of the Business and Professions Code or Section 1800 of the Insurance Code, and shall forfeit any license already obtained pursuant to those laws. A person who is taken into custody by a bail agent in violation of this subdivision may institute and prosecute a civil action for injunctive, monetary, or other appropriate relief against the bail fugitive recovery agent within three years after the cause of action accrues.

(e) This section shall become operative on July 1, 2023.

Amended by Stats 2023 ch 260 (SB 345),s 16, eff. 1/1/2024.

Amended by Stats 2022 ch 768 (AB 2043),s 20, eff. 1/1/2023.

Added by Stats 2012 ch 747 (AB 2029),s 1, eff. 1/1/2013.

Section 1299.04 - Compliance with Sections 1800 to 1823 of the Insurance Code

(a) A bail fugitive recovery agent, bail agent, bail permittee, or bail solicitor who contracts their services to another bail agent or surety as a bail fugitive recovery agent for the purposes specified in paragraph (4) of subdivision (a) of Section 1299.01, and any bail agent, bail permittee, or bail solicitor who obtains licensing after January 1, 2000, and who engages in the arrest of a defendant pursuant to Section 1301 shall comply with Sections 1800 to 1823, inclusive, of the Insurance Code, and any regulations promulgated by the Insurance Commissioner.

(b) This section shall become operative on July 1, 2023.

Added by Stats 2022 ch 768 (AB 2043),s 23, eff. 1/1/2023.

Section 1299.05 - Compliance with laws applicable to apprehension

In performing a bail fugitive apprehension, an individual authorized by Section 1299.02 to apprehend a bail fugitive shall comply with all laws applicable to that apprehension.

Added by Stats 2012 ch 747 (AB 2029),s 1, eff. 1/1/2013.

Section 1299.06 - Documentation of authority to apprehend

Before apprehending a bail fugitive, an individual authorized by Section 1299.02 to apprehend a bail fugitive shall have in his or her possession proper documentation of authority to apprehend issued by the bail or depositor of bail as prescribed in Sections 1300 and 1301. The authority to apprehend document shall include all of the following information: the name of the individual authorized by Section 1299.02 to apprehend a bail fugitive and any fictitious name, if applicable; the address of the principal office of the individual authorized by Section 1299.02 to apprehend a bail fugitive; and the name and principal business address of the bail agency, surety company, or other party contracting with the individual authorized by Section 1299.02 to apprehend a bail fugitive.

Added by Stats 2012 ch 747 (AB 2029),s 1, eff. 1/1/2013.

EFFECTIVE 1/1/2000. Added September 16, 1999 (Bill Number: AB 243) (Chapter 426).

Section 1299.07 - Prohibited representations

(a) An individual authorized by Section 1299.02 to apprehend a bail fugitive shall not represent himself or herself in any manner as being a sworn law enforcement officer.

(b) An individual authorized by Section 1299.02 to apprehend a bail fugitive shall not wear any uniform that represents himself or herself as belonging to any part or department of a federal, state, or local government. Any uniform shall not display the words United States, Bureau, Task Force, Federal, or other substantially similar words that a reasonable person may mistake for a government agency.

(c) An individual authorized by Section 1299.02 to apprehend a bail fugitive shall not wear or otherwise use a badge that represents himself or herself as belonging to any part or department of the federal, state, or local government.

(d) An individual authorized by Section 1299.02 to apprehend a bail fugitive shall not use a fictitious name that represents himself or herself as belonging to any federal, state, or local government.

(e) An individual authorized by Section 1299.02 to apprehend a bail fugitive may wear a jacket, shirt, or vest with the words "BAIL BOND RECOVERY AGENT," "BAIL ENFORCEMENT," or "BAIL ENFORCEMENT AGENT" displayed in letters at least two inches high across the front or back of the jacket, shirt, or vest and in a contrasting color to that of the jacket, shirt, or vest.

Added by Stats 2012 ch 747 (AB 2029),s 1, eff. 1/1/2013.

Section 1299.08 - Notification of local police department or sheriff's department

(a) Except under exigent circumstances, an individual authorized by Section 1299.02 to apprehend a bail fugitive shall, prior to and no more than six hours before attempting to apprehend the bail fugitive, notify the local police department or sheriff's department of the intent to apprehend a bail fugitive in that jurisdiction by doing all of the following:

(1) Indicating the name of an individual authorized by Section 1299.02 to apprehend a bail fugitive entering the jurisdiction.

(2) Stating the approximate time an individual authorized by Section 1299.02 to apprehend a bail fugitive will be entering the jurisdiction and the approximate length of the stay.

(3) Stating the name and approximate location of the bail fugitive.

(b) If an exigent circumstance does arise and prior notification is not given as provided in subdivision (a), an individual authorized by Section 1299.02 to apprehend a bail fugitive shall notify the local police department or sheriff's department immediately after the apprehension, and upon request of the local jurisdiction, shall submit a detailed explanation of those exigent circumstances within three working days after the apprehension is made.

(c) This section shall not preclude an individual authorized by Section 1299.02 to apprehend a bail fugitive from making or attempting to make a lawful arrest of a bail fugitive on bond pursuant to Section 1300 or 1301. The fact that a bench warrant is not located or entered into a warrant depository or system shall not affect a lawful arrest of the bail fugitive.

(d) For the purposes of this section, notice may be provided to a local law enforcement agency by telephone prior to the arrest or, after the arrest has taken place, if exigent circumstances exist. In that case the name or operator number of the employee receiving the notice information shall be obtained and retained by the bail, depositor of bail, or bail fugitive recovery person.

Added by Stats 2012 ch 747 (AB 2029),s 1, eff. 1/1/2013.

Section 1299.09 - Forcible entry of premises

An individual, authorized by Section 1299.02 to apprehend a bail fugitive shall not forcibly enter a premises except as provided for in Section 844.

Added by Stats 2012 ch 747 (AB 2029),s 1, eff. 1/1/2013.

Section 1299.10 - Carrying or firearm or other weapon

An individual authorized by Section 1299.02 to apprehend a bail fugitive shall not carry a firearm or other weapon unless in compliance with the laws of the state.

Added by Stats 2012 ch 747 (AB 2029),s 1, eff. 1/1/2013.

Section 1299.11 - Violations

Any person who violates this act, or who conspires with another person to violate this act, or who hires an individual to apprehend a bail fugitive, knowing that the individual is not authorized by Section 1299.02 to apprehend a bail fugitive, is guilty of a misdemeanor punishable by a fine of five thousand dollars ($5,000) or by imprisonment in a county jail not to exceed one year, or by both that imprisonment and fine.

Added by Stats 2012 ch 747 (AB 2029),s 1, eff. 1/1/2013.

Section 1299.12 - No exemption from licensure as private investigator

Nothing in this article is intended to exempt from licensure persons otherwise required to be licensed as private investigators pursuant to Chapter 11.3 (commencing with Section 7512) of Division 3 of the Business and Professions Code.

Added by Stats 2012 ch 747 (AB 2029),s 1, eff. 1/1/2013.

Article 6 - EXONERATION

Section 1300 - Surrender of defendant

(a) At any time before the forfeiture of their undertaking, or deposit by a third person, the bail or the depositor may surrender the defendant in their exoneration, or he may surrender himself, to the officer to whose custody he was committed at the time of giving bail, in the following manner:

(1) A certified copy of the undertaking of the bail, a certified copy of the certificate of deposit where a deposit is made, or an affidavit given by the bail licensee or surety company listing all that specific information that would be included on a certified copy of an undertaking of bail, must be delivered to the officer who must detain the defendant in his custody thereon as upon a commitment, and by a certificate in writing acknowledge the surrender.

(2) The bail or depositor, upon surrendering the defendant, shall make reasonable effort to give notice to the defendant's last attorney of record, if any, of such surrender.

(3) The officer to whom the defendant is surrendered shall, within 48 hours of the surrender, bring the defendant before the court in which the defendant is next to appear on the case for which he has been surrendered. The court shall advise the defendant of his right to move the court for an order permitting the withdrawal of any previous waiver of time and shall advise him of the authority of the court, as provided in subdivision (b), to order return of the premium paid by the defendant or other person, or any part of it.

(4) Upon the undertaking, or certificate of deposit, and the certificate of the officer, the court in which the action or appeal is pending may, upon notice of five days to the district attorney of the county, with a copy of the undertaking, or certificate of deposit, and the certificate of the officer, order that the bail or deposit be exonerated. However, if the defendant is released on his own recognizance or on another bond before the issuance of such an order, the court shall order that the bail or deposit be exonerated without prejudice to the court's authority under subdivision (b). On filing the order and papers used on the application, they are exonerated accordingly.

(b) Notwithstanding subdivision (a), if the court determines that good cause does not exist for the surrender of a defendant who has not failed to appear or has not violated any order of the court, it may, in its discretion, order the bail or the depositor to return to the defendant or other person who has paid the premium or any part of it, all of the money so paid or any part of it.

Amended by Stats. 1998, Ch. 223, Sec. 1. Effective January 1, 1999.

Section 1301 - Arrest of defendant

For the purpose of surrendering the defendant, the bail or any person who has deposited money or bonds to secure the release of the defendant, at any time before such bail or other person is finally discharged, and at any place within the state, may himself arrest defendant, or by written authority indorsed on a certified copy of the undertaking or a certified copy of the certificate of deposit, may empower any person of suitable age to do so.

Any bail or other person who so arrests a defendant in this state shall, without unnecessary delay, and, in any event, within 48 hours of the arrest, deliver the defendant to the court or magistrate before whom the defendant is required to appear or to the custody of the sheriff or police for confinement in the appropriate jail in the county or city in which defendant is required to appear. Any bail or other person who arrests a defendant outside this state shall, without unnecessary delay after the time defendant is brought into this state, and, in any event, within 48 hours after defendant is brought into this state, deliver the defendant to the custody of the court or magistrate before whom the defendant is required to appear or to the custody of the sheriff or police for confinement in the appropriate jail in the county or city in which defendant is required to appear.

Any bail or other person who willfully fails to deliver a defendant to the court, magistrate, sheriff, or police as required by this section is guilty of a misdemeanor.

The provisions of this section relating to the time of delivery of a defendant are for his benefit and, with the consent of the bail, may be waived by him. To be valid, such waiver shall be in writing, signed by the defendant, and delivered to such bail or other person within 48 hours after the defendant's arrest or entry into this state, as the case may be. The defendant, at any time and in the same manner, may revoke said waiver. Whereupon, he shall be delivered as provided herein without unnecessary delay and, in any event within 48 hours from the time of such revocation.

If any 48-hour period specified in this section terminates on a Saturday, Sunday, or holiday, delivery of a defendant by a bail or other person to the court or magistrate or to the custody of the sheriff or police may, without violating this section, take place before noon on the next day following which is not a Saturday, Sunday, or holiday.

Amended by Stats. 1965, Ch. 1859.

Section 1302 - Return of deposit

If money has been deposited instead of bail, and the defendant, at any time before the forfeiture thereof, surrenders himself or herself to the officer to whom the commitment was directed, in the manner provided in Sections 1300 and 1301, the court shall order a return of the deposit to the defendant or to the person or persons found by the court to have deposited said money on behalf of the defendant, upon the production of the certificate of the officer showing the surrender, and upon a notice of five days to the district attorney, with a copy of the certificate.

Amended by Stats. 1987, Ch. 828, Sec. 84.

Section 1303 - Dismissal of action

If an action or proceeding against a defendant who has been admitted to bail is dismissed, the bail shall not be exonerated until a period of 15 days has elapsed since the entry of the order of dismissal. If, within such period, the defendant is arrested and charged with a public offense arising out of the same act or omission upon which the action or proceeding was based, the bail shall be applied to the public offense. If an undertaking of bail is on file, the clerk of the court shall promptly mail notice to the surety on the bond and the bail agent who posted the bond whenever the bail is applied to a public offense pursuant to this section.

Added by Stats. 1971, Ch. 1790.

Section 1304 - Exoneration after release on own recognizance

Any bail, or moneys or bonds deposited in lieu of bail, or any equity in real property as security in lieu of bail, or any agreement whereby the defendant is released on his or her own recognizance shall be exonerated two years from the effective date of the initial bond, provided that the court is informed in writing at least 60 days prior to 2 years after the initial bond of the fact that the bond is to be exonerated, or unless the court determines otherwise and informs the party executing the bail of the reasons that the bail is not exonerated.

Added by Stats. 1984, Ch. 284, Sec. 1.

Article 7 - FORFEITURE OF THE UNDERTAKING OF BAIL OR OF THE DEPOSIT OF MONEY

Section 1305 - Forfeiture

(a)

(1) A court shall in open court declare forfeited the undertaking of bail or the money or property deposited as bail if, without sufficient excuse, a defendant fails to appear for any of the following:

(A) Arraignment.

(B) Trial.

(C) Judgment.

(D) Any other occasion prior to the pronouncement of judgment if the defendant's presence in court is lawfully required.

(E) To surrender himself or herself in execution of the judgment after appeal.

(2)

(A) Notwithstanding paragraph (1), except as provided in subparagraph (B), the court shall not have jurisdiction to declare a forfeiture and the bail shall be released of all obligations under the bond if the case is dismissed or if no complaint is filed within 15 days from the date of arraignment.

(B) The court's jurisdiction to declare a forfeiture and authority to release bail may be extended for not more than 90 days from the arraignment date originally set by the jailer pursuant to subdivision (a) of Section 1269b if either of the following occur:

(i) The prosecutor requests in writing or in open court that the arraignment be continued to allow the prosecutor time to file the complaint.

(ii) The defendant requests the extension in writing or in open court.

(b)

(1) If the amount of the bond or money or property deposited exceeds four hundred dollars ($400), the clerk of the court shall, within 30 days of the forfeiture, mail notice of the forfeiture to the surety or the depositor of money posted instead of bail. At the same time, the court shall mail a copy of the forfeiture notice to the bail agent whose name appears on the bond. The clerk shall also execute a certificate of mailing of the forfeiture notice and shall place the certificate in the court's file. If the notice of forfeiture is required to be mailed pursuant to this section, the 180-day period provided for in this section shall be extended by a period of five days to allow for the mailing.

(2) If the surety is an authorized corporate surety, and if the bond plainly displays the mailing address of the corporate surety and the bail agent, then notice of the forfeiture shall be mailed to the surety at that address and to the bail agent, and mailing alone to the surety or the bail agent shall not constitute compliance with this section.

(3) The surety or depositor shall be released of all obligations under the bond if any of the following conditions apply:

 (A) The clerk fails to mail the notice of forfeiture in accordance with this section within 30 days after the entry of the forfeiture.

 (B) The clerk fails to mail the notice of forfeiture to the surety at the address printed on the bond.

 (C) The clerk fails to mail a copy of the notice of forfeiture to the bail agent at the address shown on the bond.

(c)

 (1) If the defendant appears either voluntarily or in custody after surrender or arrest in court within 180 days of the date of forfeiture or within 180 days of the date of mailing of the notice if the notice is required under subdivision (b), the court shall, on its own motion at the time the defendant first appears in court on the case in which the forfeiture was entered, direct the order of forfeiture to be vacated and the bond exonerated. If the court fails to so act on its own motion, then the surety's or depositor's obligations under the bond shall be immediately vacated and the bond exonerated. An order vacating the forfeiture and exonerating the bond may be made on terms that are just and do not exceed the terms imposed in similar situations with respect to other forms of pretrial release.

 (2) If, within the county where the case is located, the defendant is surrendered to custody by the bail or is arrested in the underlying case within the 180-day period, and is subsequently released from custody prior to an appearance in court, the court shall, on its own motion, direct the order of forfeiture to be vacated and the bond exonerated. If the court fails to so act on its own motion, then the surety's or depositor's obligations under the bond shall be immediately vacated and the bond exonerated. An order vacating the forfeiture and exonerating the bond may be made on terms that are just and do not exceed the terms imposed in similar situations with respect to other forms of pretrial release.

 (3) If, outside the county where the case is located, the defendant is surrendered to custody by the bail or is arrested in the underlying case within the 180-day period, the court shall vacate the forfeiture and exonerate the bail.

 (4) In lieu of exonerating the bond, the court may order the bail reinstated and the defendant released on the same bond if both of the following conditions are met:

  (A) The bail is given prior notice of the reinstatement.

  (B) The bail has not surrendered the defendant.

(d) In the case of a permanent disability, the court shall direct the order of forfeiture to be vacated and the bail or money or property deposited as bail exonerated if, within 180 days of the date of forfeiture or within 180 days of the date of mailing of the notice, if notice is required under subdivision (b), it is made apparent to the satisfaction of the court that both of the following conditions are met:

 (1) The defendant is deceased or otherwise permanently unable to appear in the court due to illness, insanity, or detention by military or civil authorities.

 (2) The absence of the defendant is without the connivance of the bail.

(e)

 (1) In the case of a temporary disability, the court shall order the tolling of the 180-day period provided in this section during the period of temporary disability, provided that it appears to the satisfaction of the court that the following conditions are met:

  (A) The defendant is temporarily disabled by reason of illness, insanity, or detention by military or civil authorities.

  (B) Based upon the temporary disability, the defendant is unable to appear in court during the remainder of the 180-day period.

  (C) The absence of the defendant is without the connivance of the bail.

 (2) The period of the tolling shall be extended for a reasonable period of time, at the discretion of the court, after the cessation of the disability to allow for the return of the defendant to the jurisdiction of the court.

(f) In all cases where a defendant is in custody beyond the jurisdiction of the court that ordered the bail forfeited, and the prosecuting agency elects not to seek extradition after being informed of the location of the defendant, the court shall vacate the forfeiture and exonerate the bond on terms that are just and do not exceed the terms imposed in similar situations with respect to other forms of pretrial release.

(g) In all cases of forfeiture where a defendant is not in custody and is beyond the jurisdiction of the state, is temporarily detained, by the bail agent, in the presence of a local law enforcement officer of the jurisdiction in which the defendant is located, and is positively identified by that law enforcement officer as the wanted defendant in an affidavit signed under penalty of perjury, and the prosecuting agency elects not to seek extradition after being informed of the location of the defendant, the court shall vacate the forfeiture and exonerate the bond on terms that are just and do not exceed the terms imposed in similar situations with respect to other forms of pretrial release.

(h) In cases arising under subdivision (g), if the bail agent and the prosecuting agency agree that additional time is needed to return the defendant to the jurisdiction of the court, and the prosecuting agency agrees to the tolling of the 180-day period, the court may, on the basis of the agreement, toll the 180-day period within which to vacate the forfeiture. The court may order tolling for up to the length of time agreed upon by the parties.

(i) As used in this section, "arrest" includes a hold placed on the defendant in the underlying case while he or she is in custody on other charges.

(j) A motion filed in a timely manner within the 180-day period may be heard within 30 days of the expiration of the 180-day period. The court may extend the 30-day period upon a showing of good cause. The motion may be made by the surety insurer, the bail agent, the surety, or the depositor of money or property, any of whom may appear in person or through an attorney.

(k) In addition to any other notice required by law, the moving party shall give the prosecuting agency a written notice at least 10 court days before a hearing held pursuant to subdivision (f), (g), or (j), as a condition precedent to granting the motion.

Amended by Stats 2016 ch 79 (AB 2655),s 1, eff. 1/1/2017.

Amended by Stats 2012 ch 129 (SB 989),s 1, eff. 1/1/2013.

EFFECTIVE 1/1/2000. Amended September 29, 1999 (Bill Number: AB 476) (Chapter 570).

Section 1305.1 - Excuse for failure to appear

If the defendant fails to appear for arraignment, trial, judgment, or upon any other occasion when his or her appearance is lawfully required, but the court has reason to believe that sufficient excuse may exist for the failure to appear, the court may continue the case for a period it deems reasonable to enable the defendant to appear without ordering a forfeiture of bail or issuing a bench warrant. If, after the court has made the order, the defendant, without sufficient excuse, fails to appear on or before the continuance date set by the court, the bail shall be forfeited and a warrant for the defendant's arrest may be ordered issued.

Repealed and added by Stats. 1993, Ch. 524, Sec. 4. Effective January 1, 1994.

Section 1305.2 - Assessment

If an assessment is made a condition of the order to set aside the forfeiture of an undertaking, deposit, or bail under Section 1305, the clerk of the court shall within 30 days mail notice thereof to the surety or depositor at the address of its principal office, mail a copy to the bail agent whose name appears on the bond, and shall execute a certificate of mailing and place it in the court's file in the case. The time limit for payment shall in no event be less than 30 days after the date of mailing of the notice.

If the assessment has not been paid by the date specified, the court shall determine if a certificate of mailing has been executed, and if none has, the court shall cause a notice to be mailed to the surety, depositor, or bail agent whose name appears on the bond, and the surety, depositor, or bail agent whose name appears on the bond shall be allowed an additional 30 days to pay the assessment.

Amended by Stats. 1995, Ch. 56, Sec. 2. Effective January 1, 1996.

Section 1305.3 - Recovery of costs

The district attorney, county counsel, or applicable prosecuting agency, as the case may be, shall recover, out of the forfeited bail money, the costs and attorney's fees incurred in successfully opposing a motion to vacate the forfeiture and in collecting on the summary judgment prior to the division of the forfeited bail money between the cities and counties in accordance with Section 1463.001.

Amended by Stats 2016 ch 378 (AB 1854),s 1, eff. 1/1/2017.

Section 1305.4 - Extension of 180-day period

Notwithstanding Section 1305, the surety insurer, the bail agent, the surety, or the depositor may file a motion, based upon good cause, for an order extending the 180-day period provided in that section. The motion shall include a declaration or affidavit that states the reasons showing good cause to extend that period. The court, upon a hearing and a showing of good cause, may order the period extended to a time not exceeding 180 days from its order. A motion may be filed and calendared as provided in subdivision (j) of Section 1305. In addition to any other notice required by law, the moving party shall give the prosecuting agency a written notice at least 10 court days before a hearing held pursuant to this section as a condition precedent to granting the motion.

Amended by Stats 2013 ch 59 (SB 514),s 6, eff. 1/1/2014.

Amended by Stats 2012 ch 129 (SB 989),s 2, eff. 1/1/2013.

EFFECTIVE 1/1/2000. Amended September 29, 1999 (Bill Number: AB 476) (Chapter 570).

Section 1305.5 - Rules applicable to appeal from order on motion to vacate bail forfeiture

Notwithstanding Sections 85, 580, 904.1, and 904.2 of the Code of Civil Procedure, the following rules apply to an appeal from an order of the superior court on a motion to vacate a bail forfeiture declared under Section 1305:

(a) If the amount in controversy exceeds thirty-five thousand dollars ($35,000), the appeal is to the court of appeal and shall be treated as an unlimited civil case.

(b) Except as provided in subdivision (c), if the amount in controversy does not exceed thirty-five thousand dollars ($35,000), the appeal is to the appellate division of the superior court and shall be treated as a limited civil case.

(c) If the bail forfeiture was in a felony case, or in a case in which both a felony and a misdemeanor were charged, and the forfeiture occurred at or after the sentencing hearing or after the indictment or the legal commitment by a magistrate, the appeal is to the court of appeal and shall be treated as an unlimited civil case.

Amended by Stats 2023 ch 861 (SB 71),s 14, eff. 1/1/2024.

Added by Stats 2012 ch 470 (AB 1529),s 49, eff. 1/1/2013.

Section 1305.6 - Vacation of forfeiture and exoneration of bail

(a) If a person appears in court after the end of the 180-day period specified in Section 1305, the court may, in its discretion, vacate the forfeiture and exonerate the bond if both of the following conditions are met:

(1) The person was arrested on the same case within the county where the case is located, within the 180-day period.

(2) The person has been in continuous custody from the time of his or her arrest until the court appearance on that case.

(b) Upon a showing of good cause, a motion brought pursuant to paragraph (3) of subdivision (c) of Section 1305 may be filed within 20 days from the mailing of the notice of entry of judgment under Section 1306.

(c) In addition to any other notice required by law, the moving party shall give the applicable prosecuting agency written notice of the motion to vacate the forfeiture and exonerate the bond under this section at least 10 court days before the hearing.

Added by Stats 2012 ch 812 (AB 1824),s 1, eff. 1/1/2013.

Section 1306 - Summary judgment against bondsman

(a) When any bond is forfeited and the period of time specified in Section 1305 has elapsed without the forfeiture having been set aside, the court which has declared the forfeiture shall enter a summary judgment against each bondsman named in the bond in the amount for which the bondsman is bound. The judgment shall be the amount of the bond plus costs, and notwithstanding any other law, no penalty assessments shall be levied or added to the judgment.

(b) If a court grants relief from bail forfeiture, it shall impose a monetary payment as a condition of relief to compensate the people for the costs of returning a defendant to custody pursuant to Section 1305, except for cases where the court determines that in the best interest of justice no costs should be imposed. The amount imposed shall reflect the actual costs of returning the defendant to custody. Failure to act within the required time to make the payment imposed pursuant to this subdivision shall not be the basis for a summary judgment against any or all of the underlying amount of the bail. A summary judgment entered for failure to make the payment imposed under this subdivision is subject to the provisions of Section 1308, and shall apply only to the amount of the costs owing at the time the summary judgment is entered, plus administrative costs and interest.

(c) If, because of the failure of any court to promptly perform the duties enjoined upon it pursuant to this section, summary judgment is not entered within 90 days after the date upon which it may first be entered, the right to do so expires and the bail is exonerated.

(d) A dismissal of the complaint, indictment, or information after the default of the defendant shall not release or affect the obligation of the bail bond or undertaking.

(e) The district attorney or county counsel shall:

(1) Demand immediate payment of the judgment within 30 days after the summary judgment becomes final.

(2) If the judgment remains unpaid for a period of 20 days after demand has been made, shall forthwith enforce the judgment in the manner provided for enforcement of money judgments generally. If the judgment is appealed by the surety or bondsman, the undertaking required to be given in these cases shall be provided by a surety other than the one filing the appeal. The undertaking shall comply with the enforcement requirements of Section 917.1 of the Code of Civil Procedure. Notwithstanding Sections 85, 580, 904.1, and 904.2 of the Code of Civil Procedure, jurisdiction of the appeal, and treatment of the appeal as a limited civil case or an unlimited civil case, is governed by Section 1305.5.

(f) The right to enforce a summary judgment entered against a bondsman pursuant to this section shall expire two years after the entry of the judgment.

Amended by Stats 2012 ch 470 (AB 1529),s 50, eff. 1/1/2013.

Section 1306.1 - Payment of bail deposits pursuant to Vehicle Code provisions

The provisions of Sections 1305 and 1306 shall not affect the payment of bail deposits into the city or county treasury, as the case may be, pursuant to Section 40512 of the Vehicle Code in those cases arising under Section 40500 of the Vehicle Code.

Added by Stats. 1965, Ch. 1926.

Section 1307 - Payment of money deposited to county treasurer

If, by reason of the neglect of the defendant to appear, money deposited instead of bail is forfeited, and the forfeiture is not discharged or remitted, the clerk with whom it is deposited must, at the end of 180 days, unless the court has before that time discharged the forfeiture, pay over the money deposited to the county treasurer.

Amended by Stats. 1965, Ch. 1926.

Section 1308 - Acceptance of person or corporations as surety on bail

(a) No court or magistrate shall accept any person or corporation as surety on bail if any summary judgment against that person or corporation entered pursuant to Section 1306 remains unpaid after the expiration of 30 days after service of the notice of the entry of the summary judgment, provided that, if during the 30 days an action or proceeding available at law is initiated to determine the validity of the order of forfeiture or summary judgment rendered on it, this section shall be rendered inoperative until that action or proceeding has finally been determined, provided that, if an appeal is taken, an appeal bond is posted in compliance with Section 917.1 of the Code of Civil Procedure.

(b) The clerk of the court in which the judgment is rendered shall serve notice of the entry of judgment upon the judgment debtor within five days after the date of the entry of the summary judgment.

EFFECTIVE 1/1/2000. Amended September 29, 1999 (Bill Number: AB 476) (Chapter 570).

Article 8 - RECOMMITMENT OF THE DEFENDANT, AFTER HAVING GIVEN BAIL OR DEPOSITED MONEY INSTEAD OF BAIL

Section 1310 - Arrest of defendant and commitment

The court to which the committing magistrate returns the depositions, or in which an indictment, information, or appeal is pending, or to which a judgment on appeal is remitted to be carried into effect, may, by an order entered upon its minutes, direct the arrest of the defendant and his or her commitment to the officer to whose custody he or she was committed at the time of giving bail, and his or her detention until legally discharged, in the following cases:

(a) When, by reason of his or her failure to appear, he or she has incurred a forfeiture of his or her bail, or of money deposited instead thereof.

(b) When it satisfactorily appears to the court that his or her bail, or either of them, are dead or insufficient, or have removed from the state.

(c) Upon an indictment being found or information filed in the cases provided in Section 985.

Amended by Stats. 1987, Ch. 828, Sec. 85.

Section 1311 - Recommitment order

The order for the recommitment of the defendant must recite generally the facts upon which it is founded, and direct that the defendant be arrested by any sheriff, marshal, or policeman in this state, and committed to the officer in whose custody he or she was at the time he or she was admitted to bail, to be detained until legally discharged.

Amended by Stats. 1996, Ch. 872, Sec. 120. Effective January 1, 1997.

Section 1312 - Arrest of defendant

The defendant may be arrested pursuant to the order, upon a certified copy thereof, in any county, in the same manner as upon a warrant of arrest, except that when arrested in another county the order need not be indorsed by a magistrate of that county.

Enacted 1872.

Section 1313 - Failure of defendant to appear for judgment upon conviction

If the order recites, as the ground upon which it is made, the failure of the defendant to appear for judgment upon conviction, the defendant must be committed according to the requirement of the order.

Enacted 1872.

Section 1314 - Fixing amount of bail

If the order be made for any other cause, and the offense is bailable, the Court may fix the amount of bail, and may cause a direction to be inserted in the order that the defendant be admitted to bail in the sum fixed, which must be specified in the order.

Enacted 1872.

Section 1315 - Taking of bail

When the defendant is admitted to bail, the bail may be taken by any magistrate in the county, having authority in a similar case to admit to bail, upon the holding of the defendant to answer before an indictment, or by any other magistrate designated by the Court. Enacted 1872.

Section 1316 - Undertaking of bail

When bail is taken upon the recommitment of the defendant, the undertaking must be in substantially the following form:

An order having been made on the ____ day of ____, A.D. eighteen ____, by the Court (naming it), that A. B. be admitted to bail in the sum of ____ dollars, in an action pending in that Court against him in behalf of the people of the State of California, upon an (information, presentment, indictment, or appeal, as the case may be), we, C. D. and E. F., of (stating their places of residence and occupation), hereby undertake that the above named A. B. will appear in that or any other Court in which his appearance may be lawfully required upon that (information, presentment, indictment, or appeal, as the case may be), and will at all times render himself amenable to its orders and process, and appear for judgment and surrender himself in execution thereof; or if he fails to perform either of these conditions, that we will pay to the people of the State of California the sum of ____ dollars (insert the sum in which the defendant is admitted to bail).

Enacted 1872.

Section 1317 - Qualifications of bail

The bail must possess the qualifications, and must be put in, in all respects, in the manner prescribed in Article II of this Chapter. Enacted 1872.

Article 9 - PROCEDURE RELATING TO RELEASE ON OWN RECOGNIZANCE

Section 1318 - Release agreement

(a) The defendant shall not be released from custody under an own recognizance until the defendant files with the clerk of the court or other person authorized to accept bail a signed release agreement which includes:

(1) The defendant's promise to appear at all times and places, as ordered by the court or magistrate and as ordered by any court in which, or any magistrate before whom the charge is subsequently pending.

(2) The defendant's promise to obey all reasonable conditions imposed by the court or magistrate.

(3) The defendant's promise not to depart this state without leave of the court.

(4) Agreement by the defendant to waive extradition if the defendant fails to appear as required and is apprehended outside of the State of California.

(5) The acknowledgment of the defendant that he or she has been informed of the consequences and penalties applicable to violation of the conditions of release.

Amended (as amended by Stats. 1985, Ch. 1432) by Stats. 1988, Ch. 403, Sec. 4.

Section 1318.1 - Investigative staff; investigative report

(a) A court, with the concurrence of the board of supervisors, may employ an investigative staff for the purpose of recommending whether a defendant should be released on his or her own recognizance.

(b) Whenever a court has employed an investigative staff pursuant to subdivision (a), an investigative report shall be prepared in all cases involving a violent felony, as described in subdivision (c) of Section 667.5, or a felony in violation of subdivision (a) of Section 23153 of the Vehicle Code, recommending whether the defendant should be released on his or her own recognizance. The report shall include all of the following:

(1) Written verification of any outstanding warrants against the defendant.

(2) Written verification of any prior incidents where the defendant has failed to make a court appearance.

(3) Written verification of the criminal record of the defendant.

(4) Written verification of the residence of the defendant during the past year. After the report is certified pursuant to this subdivision, it shall be submitted to the court for review, prior to a hearing held pursuant to Section 1319.

(c) The salaries of the staff are a proper charge against the county.

Amended by Stats. 1992, Ch. 1009, Sec. 2. Effective January 1, 1993.

Section 1319 - Violent felony

(a) No person arrested for a violent felony, as described in subdivision (c) of Section 667.5, may be released on his or her own recognizance until a hearing is held in open court before the magistrate or judge, and until the prosecuting attorney is given notice and a reasonable opportunity to be heard on the matter. In all cases, these provisions shall be implemented in a manner consistent with the defendant's right to be taken before a magistrate or judge without unreasonable delay pursuant to Section 825.

(b) A defendant charged with a violent felony, as described in subdivision (c) of Section 667.5, shall not be released on his or her own recognizance where it appears, by clear and convincing evidence, that he or she previously has been charged with a felony offense and has willfully and without excuse from the court failed to appear in court as required while that charge was pending. In all other cases, in making the determination as to whether or not to grant release under this section, the court shall consider all of the following:

(1) The existence of any outstanding felony warrants on the defendant.

(2) Any other information presented in the report prepared pursuant to Section 1318.1. The fact that the court has not received the report required by Section 1318.1, at the time of the hearing to decide whether to release the defendant on his or her own recognizance, shall not preclude that release.

(3) Any other information presented by the prosecuting attorney.

(c) The judge or magistrate who, pursuant to this section, grants or denies release on a person's own recognizance, within the time period prescribed in Section 825, shall state the reasons for that decision in the record. This statement shall be included in the court's minutes. The report prepared by the investigative staff pursuant to subdivision (b) of Section 1318.1 shall be placed in the court file for that particular matter.

Amended by Stats. 1992, Ch. 1009, Sec. 3. Effective January 1, 1993.

Section 1319.5 - Arrest for new offense

(a) A person described in subdivision (b) who is arrested for a new offense shall not be released on his or her own recognizance until a hearing is held in open court before the magistrate or judge.

(b) Subdivision (a) shall apply to the following:

(1) Any person who is currently on felony probation or felony parole.

(2) Any person who has failed to appear in court as ordered, resulting in a warrant being issued, three or more times over the three years preceding the current arrest, except for infractions arising from violations of the Vehicle Code, and who is arrested for any of the following offenses:

(A) Any violation of the California Street Terrorism Enforcement and Prevention Act (Chapter 11 (commencing with Section 186.20) of Title 7 of Part 1).

(B) Any violation of Chapter 9 (commencing with Section 240) of Title 8 of Part 1 (assault and battery).

(C) A violation of Section 459 (residential burglary).

(D) Any offense in which the defendant is alleged to have been armed with or to have personally used a firearm.

(E) Any offense involving domestic violence.

(F) Any offense in which the defendant is alleged to have caused great bodily injury to another person.

(G) Any other felony offense not described in subparagraphs (A) through (F), inclusive, unless the person is released pursuant to a court-operated pretrial release program or a pretrial release program with approval by the court, in which case subdivision (a) shall not apply.

(c) This section does not change the requirement under Section 1270.1 to hold a hearing in open court before the magistrate or judge in cases in which the person has been arrested for an offense specified in that section.

(d) This section does not alter or diminish the rights conferred under Section 28 of Article I of the California Constitution (Marsy's Law).
Amended by Stats 2017 ch 554 (AB 789),s 1, eff. 1/1/2018.

Article 10 - VIOLATIONS

Section 1320 - Failure to appear

(a) Every person who is charged with or convicted of the commission of a misdemeanor who is released from custody on his or her own recognizance and who in order to evade the process of the court willfully fails to appear as required, is guilty of a misdemeanor. It shall be presumed that a defendant who willfully fails to appear within 14 days of the date assigned for his or her appearance intended to evade the process of the court.

(b) Every person who is charged with or convicted of the commission of a felony who is released from custody on his or her own recognizance and who in order to evade the process of the court willfully fails to appear as required, is guilty of a felony, and upon conviction shall be punished by a fine not exceeding five thousand dollars ($5,000) or by imprisonment pursuant to subdivision (h) of Section 1170, or in the county jail for not more than one year, or by both that fine and imprisonment. It shall be presumed that a defendant who willfully fails to appear within 14 days of the date assigned for his or her appearance intended to evade the process of the court.
Amended by Stats 2011 ch 39 (AB 117),s 68, eff. 6/30/2011.
Amended by Stats 2011 ch 15 (AB 109),s 459, eff. 4/4/2011, but operative no earlier than October 1, 2011, and only upon creation of a community corrections grant program to assist in implementing this act and upon an appropriation to fund the grant program.

Section 1320.5 - Failure to appear by person charged with or convicted of felony

Every person who is charged with or convicted of the commission of a felony, who is released from custody on bail, and who in order to evade the process of the court willfully fails to appear as required, is guilty of a felony. Upon a conviction under this section, the person shall be punished by a fine not exceeding ten thousand dollars ($10,000) or by imprisonment pursuant to subdivision (h) of Section 1170, or in the county jail for not more than one year, or by both the fine and imprisonment. Willful failure to appear within 14 days of the date assigned for appearance may be found to have been for the purpose of evading the process of the court.
Amended by Stats 2011 ch 39 (AB 117),s 68, eff. 6/30/2011.
Amended by Stats 2011 ch 15 (AB 109),s 460, eff. 4/4/2011, but operative no earlier than October 1, 2011, and only upon creation of a community corrections grant program to assist in implementing this act and upon an appropriation to fund the grant program.

Chapter 1.7 - PRETRIAL RISK ASSESSMENT TOOL VALIDATION

Section 1320.35 - Validation of pretrial risk assessment tools

(a) It is the intent of the Legislature in enacting this section to understand and reduce biases based on gender, income level, race, or ethnicity in pretrial release decisionmaking.

(b) For the purposes of this section, the following terms have the following meanings:

(1) "Pretrial risk assessment tool" means an instrument used to determine the risks associated with individuals in the pretrial context.

(2) "Pretrial services agency" means a local public agency that elects to perform pretrial risk assessments on individuals and provides the assessment information to a court.

(3) "Release conditions framework" means the guidelines used by the pretrial services agency and the court to categorize varying degrees of risk for purposes of recommending whether to release or detain a person, whether to impose pretrial release conditions on a person, and guidance regarding those conditions.

(4) "Validate" means using scientifically accepted methods to measure both of the following:

(A) The accuracy and reliability of the risk assessment tool in assessing (i) the risk that an assessed person will fail to appear in court as required and (ii) the risk to public safety due to the commission of a new criminal offense if the person is released before the adjudication of the current criminal offense for which they have been charged.

(B) Any disparate effect or bias in the risk assessment tool based on gender, race, or ethnicity.

(c)

(1) Any pretrial risk assessment tool used by a pretrial services agency shall be validated by July 1, 2021, and on a regular basis thereafter, but no less frequently than once every three years. A pretrial services agency may coordinate with the Judicial Council to validate a pretrial risk assessment tool.

(2) A pretrial risk assessment tool shall be validated using the most recent data collected by the pretrial services agency within its jurisdiction, or, if that data is unavailable, using the most recent data collected by a pretrial services agency in a similar jurisdiction within California.

(d)

(1) In order to increase transparency, a pretrial services agency shall, with regard to a pretrial risk assessment tool that it utilizes, make the following information publicly available:

(A) Line items, scoring, and weighting, as well as details on how each line item is scored, for each pretrial risk assessment tool that the agency uses.

(B) Validation studies for each pretrial risk assessment tool that the agency uses.

(2) A pretrial services agency shall, when selecting which pretrial risk assessment tool to utilize, ensure that the agency would be able to comply with paragraph (1) if that tool was selected.

(e) The Judicial Council shall maintain a list of pretrial services agencies that have satisfied the validation requirement described in subdivision (c) and complied with the transparency requirements described in subdivision (d).

(f) Beginning on or before June 30, 2021, and on or before June 30 of each year thereafter, the Judicial Council shall publish on its internet website a report with data related to outcomes and potential biases in pretrial release. The report shall, at a minimum, include:

(1) The following information on each county pretrial release program:

(A) The name of the pretrial risk assessment tool that is used to inform release decisions by the court.

(B) The release conditions framework used in the county.

(C) Whether a pretrial services agency is conducting interviews as part of the risk assessment.

(2) The following information by superior court in large and medium courts and otherwise aggregated by superior court size:

(A) Rates of release granted prearraignment and rates of release granted pretrial, aggregated by gender, race or ethnicity, ZIP Code of residency and offense type.

(B) The percent of released individuals who make their required court appearances, aggregated by offense type and whether they were released on bail or pursuant to a risk assessment. For those released pursuant to a risk assessment, this information shall be aggregated by risk level.

(C) The percent of released individuals who are not charged with a new offense during the pretrial stage, aggregated by offense type and whether they were released on bail or pursuant to a risk assessment. For those released pursuant to a risk assessment, this information shall be aggregated by risk level.

(D) The number of assessed individuals by age, ZIP Code of residency, gender, and race or ethnicity.

(E) The number of assessed individuals by risk level, ZIP Code of residency, booking charge level, and release decision.

(F) The number and percentage of assessed individuals who receive pretrial supervision by level of supervision.

(G) The number and percentage of assessed individuals, by supervision level, who fail to appear in court as required, are arrested for a new offense during the pretrial period, or have pretrial release revoked.

(3) The following information on each risk assessment tool:

(A) The percent of released individuals who attend all of their required court appearances and are not charged with a new offense during the pretrial stage, aggregated by risk level.

(B) Risk levels aggregated by race or ethnicity, gender, offense type, ZIP Code of residency, and release or detention decision.

(C) The predictive accuracy of the tool by gender, race or ethnicity, and offense type.

(D) The proportion of cases in which the release or detention recommendation derived from the risk assessment is different than the release or detention decision imposed by the judicial officer.

(4) If feasible, the Judicial Council shall provide information on any disparate effect in the tools based on income level.

(g)

(1) Pretrial services agencies and courts shall provide the Judicial Council the requisite data, as determined by the Judicial Council, to meet the requirements of this section.

(2) The Department of Justice shall work with the Judicial Council to provide the data necessary to fulfill the requirements of this section.

(3) The Judicial Council shall not share any individual-level data with any outside entity unless it has entered into a contract for research purposes with the entity and privacy protections are established to anonymize the data.

(h) The requirements of subdivisions (f) and (g) shall apply to pretrial services agencies that perform risk assessments pursuant to a contractual agreement with the courts, including all of the following:

(1) Agencies funded pursuant to the Budget Act of 2019 as pretrial pilot projects.

(2) Agencies otherwise funded by the state to perform risk assessments.

(3) Other agencies that perform risk assessments as long as sufficient funding is provided to the Judicial Council, the superior courts, and pretrial services agencies to ensure their ability to meet the data reporting requirements and standards set by the Judicial Council.

(i)

(1) By January 1, 2023, the Judicial Council shall provide a report to the courts and the Legislature containing recommendations to mitigate bias and disparate effect in pretrial decisionmaking.

(2) A report to be submitted pursuant to this subdivision shall be submitted in compliance with Section 9795 of the Government Code.

Amended by Stats 2020 ch 36 (AB 3364),s 42, eff. 1/1/2021.

Added by Stats 2019 ch 589 (SB 36),s 2, eff. 1/1/2020.

Chapter 2 - WHO MAY BE WITNESSES IN CRIMINAL ACTIONS

Section 1321 - Applicable rules

The rules for determining the competency of witnesses in civil actions are applicable also to criminal actions and proceedings, except as otherwise provided in this Code.

Enacted 1872.

Section 1324 - Refusal to answer question or produce evidence in felony proceeding

In any felony proceeding or in any investigation or proceeding before a grand jury for any felony offense if a person refuses to answer a question or produce evidence of any other kind on the ground that he or she may be incriminated thereby, and if the district attorney of the county or any other prosecuting agency in writing requests the court, in and for that county, to order that person to answer the question or produce the evidence, a judge shall set a time for hearing and order the person to appear before the court and show cause, if any, why the question should not be answered or the evidence produced, and the court shall order the question answered or the evidence produced unless it finds that to do so would be clearly contrary to the public interest, or could subject the witness to a criminal prosecution in another jurisdiction, and that person shall comply with the order. After complying, and if, but for this section, he or she would have been privileged to withhold the answer given or the evidence produced by him or her, no testimony or other information compelled under the order or any information directly or indirectly derived from the testimony or other information may be used against the witness in any criminal case. But he or she may nevertheless be prosecuted or subjected to penalty or forfeiture for any perjury, false swearing or contempt committed in answering, or failing to answer, or in producing, or failing to produce, evidence in accordance with the order. Nothing in this section shall prohibit the district attorney or any other prosecuting agency from requesting an order granting use immunity or transactional immunity to a witness compelled to give testimony or produce evidence.

Amended by Stats. 1996, Ch. 302, Sec. 1. Effective January 1, 1997.

Section 1324.1 - Refusal to answer question or produce evidence in misdemeanor proceeding

In any misdemeanor proceeding in any court, if a person refuses to answer a question or produce evidence of any other kind on the ground that he may be incriminated thereby, the person may agree in writing with the district attorney of the county, or the prosecuting attorney of a city, as the case may be, to testify voluntarily pursuant to this section. Upon written request of such district attorney, or prosecuting attorney, the court having jursidiction of the proceeding shall approve such written agreement, unless the court finds that to do so would be clearly contrary to the public interest. If, after court approval of such agreement, and if, but for this section, the person would have been privileged to withhold the answer given or the evidence produced by him, that person shall not be prosecuted or subjected to penalty or forfeiture for or on account of any fact or act concerning which, in accordance with such agreement, he answered or produced evidence, but he may, nevertheless, be prosecuted or subjected to penalty or forfeiture for any perjury, false swearing or contempt committed in answering or in producing evidence in accordance with such agreement. If such person fails to give any answer or to produce any evidence in accordance with such agreement, that person shall be prosecuted or subjected to penalty or forfeiture in the same manner and to the same extent as he would be prosecuted or subjected to penalty or forfeiture but for this section.

Added by Stats. 1968, Ch. 528.

Section 1324.2 - Immunity from drug and alcohol charges in sexual assault cases

(a) Testimony of a victim or witness in a felony prosecution for a violation or attempted violation of Section 220, 243.4, 261, 261.5, 286, 287, 288, or 289, that states that the victim or witness, at or around the time of the violation or attempted violation, unlawfully possessed or used a controlled substance or alcohol is inadmissible in a separate prosecution of that victim or witness to prove illegal possession or use of that controlled substance or alcohol.

(b) Evidence that the testifying witness unlawfully possessed or used a controlled substance or alcohol is not excluded in the felony prosecution of a violation or attempted violation of Section 220, 243.4, 261, 261.5, 286, 287, 288, or 289.

(c) Evidence that a witness received use immunity for testimony pursuant to subdivision (a) is not excluded in the felony prosecution of a violation or attempted violation of Section 220, 243.4, 261, 261.5, 286, 287, 288, or 289.

Added by Stats 2020 ch 241 (AB 1927),s 1, eff. 1/1/2021.

Chapter 3 - COMPELLING THE ATTENDANCE OF WITNESSES

Section 1326 - Subpoena

(a) The process by which the attendance of a witness before a court or magistrate is required is a subpoena. It may be signed and issued by any of the following:

(1) A magistrate before whom a complaint is laid or their clerk, the district attorney or their investigator, or the public defender or their investigator, for witnesses in the state.

(2) The district attorney, their investigator, or, upon request of the grand jury, any judge of the superior court, for witnesses in the state, in support of an indictment or information, to appear before the court in which it is to be tried.

(3) The district attorney or their investigator, the public defender or their investigator, or the clerk of the court in which a criminal action is to be tried. The clerk shall, at any time, upon application of the defendant, and without charge, issue as many blank subpoenas, subscribed by them, for witnesses in the state, as the defendant may require.

(4) The attorney of record for the defendant.

(b) A subpoena issued in a criminal action that commands the custodian of records or other qualified witness of a business to produce books, papers, documents, or records shall direct that those items be delivered by the custodian or qualified witness in the manner specified in subdivision (b) of Section 1560 of the Evidence Code. Subdivision (e) of Section 1560 of the Evidence Code shall not apply to criminal cases.

(c)

(1) Notwithstanding subdivision (b), a provider of health care, health care service plan, or contractor shall not release medical information related to a person or entity allowing a child to receive gender-affirming health care or gender-affirming mental health care in response to any foreign subpoena that is based on a violation of another state's laws authorizing a criminal action against a person or entity that allows a child to receive gender-affirming health care or gender-affirming mental health care.

(2) For the purpose of this subdivision, "gender-affirming health care" and "gender-affirming mental health care" shall have the same meaning as provided in Section 16010.2 of the Welfare and Institutions Code.

(d) In a criminal action, no party, or attorney or representative of a party, may issue a subpoena commanding the custodian of records or other qualified witness of a business to provide books, papers, documents, or records, or copies thereof, relating to a person or entity other than the subpoenaed person or entity in any manner other than that specified in subdivision (b) of Section 1560 of the Evidence Code. When a defendant has issued a subpoena to a person or entity that is not a party for the production of books, papers, documents, or records, or copies thereof, the court may order an in camera hearing to determine whether or not the defense is entitled to receive the documents. The court may not order the documents disclosed to the prosecution except as required by Section 1054.3.

(e) This section shall not be construed to prohibit obtaining books, papers, documents, or records with the consent of the person to whom the books, papers, documents, or records relate.

Amended by Stats 2022 ch 810 (SB 107),s 10, eff. 1/1/2023.

Amended by Stats 2007 ch 263 (AB 310),s 30, eff. 1/1/2008.

Amended by Stats 2004 ch 162 (AB 1249), s 2, eff. 1/1/2005.

Section 1326.1 - Order for production of utility records

(a) An order for the production of utility records in whatever form and however stored shall be issued by a judge only upon a written ex parte application by a peace officer showing specific and articulable facts that there are reasonable grounds to believe that the records or information sought are relevant and material to an ongoing investigation of a felony violation of Section 186.10 or of any felony subject to the enhancement set forth in Section 186.11. The ex parte application shall specify with particularity the records to be produced, which shall be only those of the individual or individuals who are the subject of the criminal investigation. The ex parte application and any subsequent judicial order shall be open to the public as a judicial record unless ordered sealed by the court, for a period of 60 days. The sealing of these records may be extended for 60-day periods upon a showing to the court that it is necessary for the continuance of the investigation. Sixty-day extensions may continue for up to one year or until termination of the investigation of the individual or individuals, whichever is sooner. The records ordered to be produced shall be returned to the peace officer applicant or his or her designee within a reasonable time period after service of the order upon the holder of the utility records.

(b) As used in subdivision (a), "utility records" include, but are not limited to, subscriber information, telephone or pager number information, toll call records, call detail records, automated message accounting records, billing statements, payment records, and applications for service in the custody of companies engaged in the business of providing telephone, pager, electric, gas, propane, water, or other like services. "Utility records" do not include the installation of, or the data collected from the installation of pen registers or trap-tracers, nor the contents of a wire or electronic communication.

(c) Nothing in this section shall preclude the holder of the utility records from notifying a customer of the receipt of the order for production of records unless a court orders the holder of the utility records to withhold notification to the customer upon a finding that this notice would impede the investigation. Where a court has made an order to withhold notification to the customer under this subdivision, the peace officer or law enforcement agency who obtained the utility records shall notify the customer by delivering a copy of the ex parte order to the customer within 10 days of the termination of the investigation.

(d) No holder of utility records, or any officer, employee, or agent thereof, shall be liable to any person for (A) disclosing information in response to an order pursuant to this section, or (B) complying with an order under this section not to disclose to the customer, the order or the dissemination of information pursuant to the order.

(e) Nothing in this section shall preclude the holder of the utility records from voluntarily disclosing information or providing records to law enforcement upon request.

(f) Utility records released pursuant to this section shall be used only for the purpose of criminal investigations and prosecutions.

Added by Stats. 1998, Ch. 757, Sec. 5. Effective January 1, 1999.

Section 1326.2 - Order for production of escrow or title records

(a) An order for the production of escrow or title records in whatever form and however stored shall be issued by a judge only upon a written ex parte application by a peace officer showing specific and articulable facts that there are reasonable grounds to believe that the records or information sought are relevant and material to an ongoing investigation of a felony violation of Section 186.10 or of any felony subject to the enhancement set forth in Section 186.11. The ex parte application shall specify with particularity the records to be produced, which shall be only those of the individual or individuals who are the subject of the criminal investigation. The ex parte application and any subsequent judicial order shall be open to the public as a judicial record unless ordered sealed by the court, for a period of 60 days. The sealing of these records may be extended for 60-day periods upon a showing to the court that it is necessary for the continuance of the investigation. Sixty-day extensions may continue for up to one year or until termination of the investigation of the individual or individuals, whichever is sooner. The records ordered to be produced shall be returned to the peace officer applicant or his or her designee within a reasonable time period after service of the order upon the holder of the escrow or title records.

(b) As used in subdivision (a), "holder of escrow or title records" means a title insurer that engages in the "business of title insurance," as defined by Section 12340.3 of the Insurance Code, an underwritten title company, or an escrow company.

(c) Nothing in this section shall preclude the holder of the escrow or title records from notifying a customer of the receipt of the order for production of records unless a court orders the holder of the escrow or title records to withhold notification to the customer upon a finding that this notice would impede the investigation. Where a court has made an order to withhold notification to the customer under this subdivision, the peace officer or law enforcement agency who obtained the escrow or title records shall notify the customer by delivering a copy of the ex parte order to the customer within 10 days of the termination of the investigation.

(d) No holder of escrow or title records, or any officer, employee, or agent thereof, shall be liable to any person for (A) disclosing information in response to an order pursuant to this section, or (B) complying with an order under this section not to disclose to the customer, the order or the dissemination of information pursuant to the order.

(e) Nothing in this section shall preclude the holder of the escrow or title records from voluntarily disclosing information or providing records to law enforcement upon request.

Added by Stats. 1998, Ch. 757, Sec. 6. Effective January 1, 1999.

Section 1327 - Form of subpoena

A subpoena authorized by Section 1326 shall be substantially in the following form:

The people of the State of California to A. B.:

You are commanded to appear before C. D., a judge of the _____ Court of _____ County, at (naming the place), on (stating the day and hour), as a witness in a criminal action prosecuted by the people of the State of California against E. F.

Given under my hand this _____ day of _____, A.D. 19_____. G. H., Judge of the _____ Court (or "J. K., District Attorney," or "J. K., District Attorney Investigator," or "D. E., Public Defender," or "D. E., Public Defender Investigator," or "F. G., Defense Counsel," or "By order of the court, L. M., Clerk," or as the case may be).

If books, papers, or documents are required, a direction to the following effect must be contained in the subpoena: "And you are required, also, to bring with you the following" (describing intelligibly the books, papers, or documents required).

Amended by Stats. 1998, Ch. 931, Sec. 403. Effective September 28, 1998.

Section 1328 - Service of subpoena

(a) A subpoena may be served by any person, except that the defendant may not serve a subpoena in the criminal action to which he or she is a party, but a peace officer shall serve in his or her county any subpoena delivered to him or her for service, either on the part of the people or of the defendant, and shall, without delay, make a written return of the service, subscribed by him or her, stating the time and place of service. The service is made by delivering a copy of the subpoena to the witness personally.

(b)

    (1) If service is to be made on a minor, service shall be made on the minor's parent, guardian, conservator, or similar fiduciary, or if one of them cannot be located with reasonable diligence, then service shall be made on any person having the care or control of the minor or with whom the minor resides or by whom the minor is employed, unless the parent, guardian, conservator, or fiduciary or other specified person is the defendant, and on the minor if the minor is 12 years of age or older. The person served shall have the obligation of producing the minor at the time and place designated in the subpoena. A willful failure to produce the minor is punishable as a contempt pursuant to Section 1218 of the Code of Civil Procedure. The person served shall be allowed the fees and expenses that are provided for subpoenaed witnesses.

    (2) If the minor is alleged to come within the description of Section 300, 601, or 602 of the Welfare and Institutions Code, and the minor is not residing with a parent or guardian, regardless of the age of the minor, service shall also be made upon the designated agent for service of process at the county child welfare department or the probation department under whose jurisdiction the child has been placed.

    (3) The court having jurisdiction of the case shall have the power to appoint a guardian ad litem to receive service of a subpoena of the child and shall have the power to produce the child ordered to court under this section.

(c) If any peace officer designated in Section 830 is required as a witness before any court or magistrate in any action or proceeding in connection with a matter regarding an event or transaction which he or she has perceived or investigated in the course of his or her duties, a criminal subpoena issued pursuant to this chapter requiring his or her attendance may be served either by delivering a copy to the peace officer personally or by delivering two copies to his or her immediate superior or agent designated by his or her immediate superior to receive the service or, in those counties where the local agencies have consented with the district attorney's office, marshal's office, or sheriff's office, where appropriate, to participate, by sending a copy by electronic means, including electronic mail, computer modem, facsimile, or other electronic means, to him or her personally, or to his or her immediate superior or agent designated by the immediate superior to receive the service. If the service is made by electronic means, the peace officer named in the subpoena, or his or her immediate superior or agency designated by his or her immediate superior shall acknowledge receipt of the subpoena by telephone or electronic means to the sender of origin. If service is made upon the immediate superior or agent designated by the immediate superior, the immediate superior or the agent shall deliver a copy of the subpoena to the peace officer as soon as possible and in no event later than a time which will enable the peace officer to comply with the subpoena.

(d) If the immediate superior or his or her designated agent upon whom service is attempted to be made knows he or she will be unable to deliver a copy of the subpoena to the peace officer within a time which will allow the peace officer to comply with the subpoena, the immediate superior or agent may refuse to accept service of process and is excused from any duty, liability, or penalty arising in connection with the service, upon notifying the server of that fact.

(e) If the immediate superior or his or her agent is tendered service of a subpoena less than five working days prior to the date of hearing, and he or she is not reasonably certain he or she can complete the service, he or she may refuse acceptance.

(f) If the immediate superior or agent upon whom service has been made, subsequently determines that he or she will be unable to deliver a copy of the subpoena to the peace officer within a time which will allow the peace officer to comply with the subpoena, the immediate superior or agent shall notify the server or his or her office or agent not less than 48 hours prior to the hearing date indicated on the subpoena, and is thereby excused from any duty, liability, or penalty arising because of his or her failure to deliver a copy of the subpoena to the peace officer. The server, so notified, is therewith responsible for preparing the written return of service and for notifying the originator of the subpoena if required.

(g) Notwithstanding subdivision (c), in the case of peace officers employed by the California Highway Patrol, if service is made upon the immediate superior or upon an agent designated by the immediate superior of the peace officer, the immediate superior or the agent shall deliver a copy of the subpoena to the peace officer on the officer's first workday following acceptance of service of process. In this case, failure of the immediate superior or the designated agent to deliver the subpoena shall not constitute a defect in service.

Amended by Stats 2016 ch 59 (SB 1474),s 6, eff. 1/1/2017.

Amended by Stats 2002 ch 1008 (AB 3028), s 26, eff. 1/1/2003.

Previously Amended October 10, 1999 (Bill Number: SB 218) (Chapter 662).

Section 1328.5 - Residence of peace officer

Whenever any peace officer is a witness before any court or magistrate in any criminal action or proceeding in connection with a matter regarding an event or transaction which he has perceived or investigated in the course of his duties, where his testimony would become a matter of public record, and where he is required to state the place of his residence, he need not state the place of his residence, but in lieu thereof, he may state his business address.

Added by Stats. 1971, Ch. 636.

Section 1328.6 - Residence of criminalist, questioned document examiner, latent print analyst, etc.

Whenever any criminalist, questioned document examiner, latent print analyst, polygraph examiner employed by the Department of Justice, a police department, a sheriff's office, or a district attorney's office, an intelligence specialist or other technical specialist employed by the Department of Justice, a custodial officer employed in a local detention facility, or an employee of the county welfare department or the department which administers the county public social services program, is a witness before any court or magistrate in any criminal action or proceeding in connection with a matter regarding an event or transaction which he or she has perceived or investigated in the course of his or her official duties, where his or her testimony would become a matter of public record, and where he or she is required to state the place of his or her residence, he or she need not state the place of his or her residence, but in lieu thereof, he or she may state his or her business address, unless the court finds, after an in camera hearing, that the probative value of the witness's residential address outweighs the creation of substantial danger to the witness.

Nothing in this section shall abridge or limit a defendant's right to discover or investigate this information. This section is not intended to apply to confidential informants.

Amended by Stats. 1984, Ch. 535, Sec. 1.

Section 1328a - [Repealed]

Repealed by Stats 2019 ch 851 (SB 471),s 1, eff. 1/1/2020.

Section 1328b - [Repealed]

Repealed by Stats 2019 ch 851 (SB 471),s 2, eff. 1/1/2020.

Section 1328c - [Repealed]

Repealed by Stats 2019 ch 851 (SB 471),s 3, eff. 1/1/2020.

Section 1328d - Delivery of subpoena; methods

(a) Notwithstanding Section 1328, except as specified in subdivision (c) of Section 1328, a subpoena may be delivered by mail, messenger, electronic mail, or facsimile transmission. Service shall be effected when the witness acknowledges receipt of the subpoena to the sender, by telephone, by mail, over the internet by email or by completion of the sender's online form, or in person, and identifies themselves by reference to their date of birth and driver's license number or Department of Motor Vehicles identification card number. The sender shall make a written notation of the identifying information obtained during any acknowledgment by telephone or in person. The sender shall retain a copy of any acknowledgment received over the internet until the court date for which the subpoena was issued or until any further date as specified by the court. A subpoena issued and acknowledged pursuant to this section shall have the same force and effect as a subpoena personally served. Failure to comply with a subpoena issued and acknowledged pursuant to this section may be punished as a contempt and the punishment may so state; provided, that a warrant of arrest or a body attachment may not be issued based upon a failure to appear after being subpoenaed pursuant to this section.

(b) A party requesting a continuance, based upon the failure of a witness to appear in court at the time and place required for their appearance or testimony pursuant to a subpoena, shall prove to the court that the party has complied with this section. That continuance shall only be granted for a period of time that would allow personal service of the subpoena and in no event longer than that allowed by law, including the requirements of Sections 861 and 1382.

Amended by Stats 2019 ch 851 (SB 471),s 4, eff. 1/1/2020.

Amended by Stats 2010 ch 709 (SB 1062),s 16, eff. 1/1/2011.

Section 1329 - Witness fees

(a) When a person attends before a magistrate, grand jury, or court, as a witness in a criminal case, whether upon a subpoena or in pursuance of an undertaking, or voluntarily, the court, at its discretion, if the attendance of the witness be upon a trial may by an order upon its minutes, or in any criminal proceeding, by a written order, direct the county auditor to draw his warrant upon the county treasurer in favor of such witness for witness' fees at the rate of twelve dollars ($12) for each day's actual attendance and for a reasonable sum to be specified in the order for the necessary expenses of such witness. The court, in its discretion, may make an allowance under this section, or under any appropriate section in Chapter 1 (commencing with Section 68070), Title 8, of the Government Code, other than Section 68093. The allowances are county charges.

(b) The court, in its discretion, may authorize payment to such a witness, if he is employed and if his salary is not paid by his employer during the time he is absent from his employment because of being such a witness, of a sum equal to his gross salary for such time, but such sum shall not exceed eighteen dollars ($18) per day. The sum is a county charge. A person compensated under the provisions of this subdivision may not receive the payment of witness' fees as provided for in subdivision (a).

Amended by Stats. 1981, Ch. 184, Sec. 5.

Section 1329.1 - Notice of entitlement to fees and mileage

Any witness who is subpoenaed in any criminal action or proceeding shall be given written notice on the subpoena that the witness may be entitled to receive fees and mileage. Such notice shall indicate generally the manner in which a request or claim for fees and mileage should be made.

Added by Stats. 1979, Ch. 67.

Section 1330 - Distance of 150 miles from place of residence to place of trial

No person is obliged to attend as a witness before a court or magistrate out of the county where the witness resides, or is served with the subpoena, unless the distance be less than 150 miles from his or her place of residence to the place of trial, or unless the judge of the court in which the offense is triable, or a justice of the Supreme Court, or a judge of a superior court, or, in the case of a minor concerning whom a petition has been filed pursuant to Article 16 (commencing with Section 650) of Chapter 2 of Part 1 of Division 2 of the Welfare and Institutions Code, by the judge of the juvenile court hearing the petition, upon an affidavit of the district attorney or prosecutor, or of the defendant, or his or her counsel, or in the case involving a minor in whose behalf a petition has been filed in the juvenile court, of the probation officer approving the filing of the petition or of any party to the action, or his or her counsel, stating that he or she believes the evidence of the witness is material, and his or her attendance at the examination, trial, or hearing is material and necessary, shall endorse on the subpoena an order for the attendance of the witness.

When a subpoena duces tecum is duly issued according to any other provision of law and is served upon a custodian of records or other qualified witness as provided in Article 4 (commencing with Section 1560) of Chapter 2 of Division 11 of the Evidence Code, and his or her personal attendance is not required by the terms of the subpoena, the limitations of this section shall not apply.
Amended by Stats. 1987, Ch. 828, Sec. 86.

Section 1331 - Disobedience to subpoena or refusal to be sworn or to testify as witness

Disobedience to a subpoena, or a refusal to be sworn or to testify as a witness, may be punished by the Court or magistrate as a contempt. A witness disobeying a subpoena issued on the part of the defendant, unless he show good cause for his nonattendance, is liable to the defendant in the sum of one hundred dollars, which may be recovered in a civil action.
Enacted 1872.

Section 1331.5 - Agreement to appear at another time

Any person who is subpoenaed to appear at a session of court, or at the trial of an issue therein, may, in lieu of appearance at the time specified in the subpoena, agree with the party at whose request the subpoena was issued, to appear at another time or upon such notice as may be agreed upon. Any failure to appear pursuant to such agreement may be punished as a contempt, and a subpoena shall so state. The facts establishing such agreement and the failure to appear may be shown by the affidavit of any person having personal knowledge of the facts and the court may grant such continuance as may be appropriate.
Added by Stats. 1972, Ch. 393.

Section 1332 - Undertaking to appear by witness

(a) Notwithstanding the provisions of Sections 878 to 883, inclusive, when the court is satisfied, by proof on oath, that there is good cause to believe that any material witness for the prosecution or defense, whether the witness is an adult or a minor, will not appear and testify unless security is required, at any proceeding in connection with any criminal prosecution or in connection with a wardship petition pursuant to Section 602 of the Welfare and Institutions Code, the court may order the witness to enter into a written undertaking to the effect that he or she will appear and testify at the time and place ordered by the court or that he or she will forfeit an amount the court deems proper.

(b) If the witness required to enter into an undertaking to appear and testify, either with or without sureties, refuses compliance with the order for that purpose, the court may commit the witness, if an adult, to the custody of the sheriff, and if a minor, to the custody of the probation officer or other appropriate agency, until the witness complies or is legally discharged.

(c) When a person is committed pursuant to this section, he or she is entitled to an automatic review of the order requiring a written undertaking and the order committing the person, by a judge or magistrate having jurisdiction over the offense other than the one who issued the order. This review shall be held not later than two days from the time of the original order of commitment.

(d) If it is determined that the witness must remain in custody, the witness is entitled to a review of that order after 10 days.

(e) When a witness has entered into an undertaking to appear, upon his or her failure to do so the undertaking is forfeited in the same manner as undertakings of bail.
Amended by Stats. 1987, Ch. 828, Sec. 87.

Chapter 3a - ATTENDANCE OF WITNESSES OUTSIDE THE STATE

Section 1334 - Short title

This chapter may be cited as the Uniform Act to Secure the Attendance of Witnesses from without the State in Criminal Cases.
Added by Stats. 1937, Ch. 262.

Section 1334.1 - Definitions

As used in this chapter:

(a) "Witness" includes any person whose testimony is desired in any proceeding or investigation by a grand jury or in any criminal action, prosecution, or proceeding.

(b) "State" means any State or Territory of the United States and the District of Columbia.

(c) "Grand jury investigation" means any grand jury investigation which has commenced or is about to commence.

(d) "Per diem" means a sum of money the purpose of which is to provide for personal expenses, including, but not limited to, food and lodging.
Amended by Stats. 1987, Ch. 322, Sec. 1.

Section 1334.2 - Persons within state; certificate; hearing

(a) Except as provided in subdivision (f), if a judge of a court of record in any state, which by its laws provides for commanding persons within that state to attend and testify in this state, issues a certificate under the seal of the court that there is a criminal prosecution pending in the court, or that there is a grand jury investigation, that a person within this state is a material witness in that prosecution or grand jury investigation, and that their presence will be required for a specified number of days, then, upon presentation of the certificate to a judge of a court of record in the county in which the person is, a time and place for a hearing shall be fixed by the judge and the judge shall make an order directing the witness to appear at the hearing.

(b) If, at the hearing, the judge determines that the witness is material and necessary, that it will not cause undue hardship to the witness to be compelled to attend and testify in the prosecution or grand jury investigation in the other state, and that the laws of the state in which the prosecution is pending or in which there is a grand jury investigation will give to the witness protection from arrest and service of civil and criminal process and will furnish in advance to the witness the sum of ten cents ($0.10) for each mile necessarily traveled if the witness elects surface travel or the minimum round trip scheduled airline fare plus twenty cents ($0.20) a mile for necessary surface travel at either end of the flight if the witness elects air travel, and, except as provided in subdivision (b) of Section 1334.3, a per diem of twenty dollars ($20) for each day that they are required to travel and attend as a witness and that the judge of the court in which the witness is ordered to appear will order the payment of witness fees authorized by law for each day the witness is required to attend the court plus reimbursement for any additional expenses of the witness which the judge of the court in which the witness is ordered to appear shall find reasonable and necessary, the judge shall issue a subpoena, with a copy of the certificate attached, directing the witness to attend and testify in the court where the prosecution is pending, or where the grand jury investigation is, at a time and place specified in the subpoena. In any of these hearings the certificate shall be prima facie evidence of all the facts stated therein.

(c) If the certificate recommends that the witness be taken into immediate custody and delivered to an officer of the requesting state to assure the witness' attendance therein, the judge may, in lieu of notification of the hearing, direct that the witness be forthwith brought before the judge for the hearing.

(d) If the judge at the hearing is satisfied of the desirability of the custody and delivery, for which determination the certificate shall be prima facie proof of this desirability, the judge may, in lieu of issuing a subpoena, order that the witness be forthwith taken into custody and delivered to an officer of the requesting state.

(e) If the witness, who is subpoenaed as provided in this section, after being paid or tendered by some properly authorized person the sum or fare, and per diem set forth in this section, fails without good cause to attend and testify as directed in the subpoena, the witness shall be punished in the manner provided for the punishment of any witness who disobeys a subpoena issued from a court of record in this state.

(f) A judge shall not issue an order directing a witness to appear pursuant to this section if the criminal prosecution is based on the laws of another state that authorize a criminal penalty to an individual performing, receiving, supporting, or aiding in the performance or receipt of sexual or reproductive health care, including, but not limited to, an abortion, contraception, or gender-affirming care if the sexual or reproductive health care is lawful under the laws of this state.

Amended by Stats 2023 ch 260 (SB 345),s 17, eff. 1/1/2024.

Amended by Stats. 1988, Ch. 160, Sec. 133.

Section 1334.3 - Persons outside state; certificate

(a) If a person in any state, which by its laws has made provision for commanding persons within its borders to attend and testify in criminal prosecutions or grand jury investigations in this state, is a material witness in a prosecution pending in a court of record in this state, or in a grand jury investigation, a judge of such court may issue a certificate under the seal of the court stating these facts and specifying the number of days the witness will be required. This certificate shall be presented to a judge of a court of record in the county of such other state in which the witness is found. If the certificate recommends that the witness be taken into immediate custody and delivered to an officer of this state to assure his or her attendance in this state, the judge may direct that the witness be forthwith brought before him or her. If the judge is satisfied of the desirability of the custody and delivery, for which determination the certificate shall be prima facie proof, he or she may order that the witness be forthwith taken into custody and delivered to an officer of this state. This order shall be sufficient authority to the officer to take the witness into custody and hold him or her unless and until he or she may be released by bail, recognizance, or order of the judge issuing the certificate.

If the witness is subpoenaed to attend and testify in this state, he or she shall be tendered the sum of ten cents ($0.10) for each mile necessarily traveled if the witness elects surface travel or the minimum round trip scheduled airlines fare plus twenty cents ($0.20) a mile for necessary surface travel at either end of the flight if the witness elects air travel, and except as provided in subdivision (b), a per diem of twenty dollars ($20) for each day that he or she is required to travel and attend as a witness. The judge of the court in which the witness is ordered to appear shall order the payment of witness fees authorized by law for each day the witness is required to attend the court plus reimbursement for any additional expenses of the witness which the judge of the court shall find reasonable and necessary. A witness who has appeared in accordance with the provisions of the subpoena shall not be required to remain within this state a longer period of time than the period mentioned in the certificate, unless otherwise ordered by the court. If the witness fails without good cause to attend and testify as directed in the subpoena, he or she shall be punished in the manner provided for the punishment of any witness who disobeys a subpoena issued from a court of record in this state.

(b) If the witness subpoenaed to attend and testify in this state is at the time he or she is required to appear and testify an inmate of a state prison, county jail, or other penal facility, the witness shall, while attending in this state as a witness, be furnished food and lodging in the jail or other appropriate penal facility in the county in which the witness is attending court, and food and lodging of that penal facility shall be rendered in lieu of the per diem specified in subdivision (a).

Amended by Stats. 1987, Ch. 322, Sec. 3.

Section 1334.4 - Person coming into state not subject to arrest or service of process

If a person comes into this State in obedience to a subpoena directing him to attend and testify in this State, he shall not, while in this State pursuant to the subpoena or order, be subject to arrest or the service of process, civil or criminal, in connection with matters which arose before his entrance into this State under the subpoena.

Added by Stats. 1937, Ch. 262.

Section 1334.5 - Person passing through not subject to arrest or service of arrest

If a person passes through this State while going to another State in obedience to a subpoena or order to attend and testify in that State or while returning therefrom, he shall not while so passing through this State be subject to arrest or the service of process, civil or criminal, in connection with matters which arose before his entrance into this State under the subpoena or order.

Added by Stats. 1937, Ch. 262.

Section 1334.6 - Construction of chapter

This chapter shall be so interpreted and construed as to effectuate its general purpose to make uniform the law of the States which enact similar legislation.

Added by Stats. 1937, Ch. 262.

Chapter 4 - EXAMINATION OF WITNESSES CONDITIONALLY

Section 1335 - Conditional examination of witnesses by defendant charged with public offense or serious felony or in case of domestic violence

(a) If a defendant has been charged with a public offense triable in a court, he or she in all cases, and the people in cases other than those for which the punishment may be death, may, if the defendant has been fully informed of his or her right to counsel as provided by law, have witnesses examined conditionally in his or her or their behalf, as prescribed in this chapter.

(b) If a defendant has been charged with a serious felony or in a case of domestic violence, the people or the defendant may, if the defendant has been fully informed of his or her right to counsel as provided by law, have a witness examined conditionally as prescribed in this chapter, if there is evidence that the life of the witness is in jeopardy.

(c)

(1) If a defendant has been charged with human trafficking, pursuant to Section 236.1, and there is evidence that the victim or material witness has been or is being dissuaded by the defendant or a person acting on behalf of the defendant, by intimidation or physical threat, from cooperating with the prosecutor or testifying at trial, the people or the defendant may, if the defendant has been fully informed of his or her right to counsel as provided by law, have a witness examined conditionally as prescribed in this chapter.

(2) If a defendant has been charged with human trafficking, pursuant to Section 236.1, and the court finds that there is a reasonable basis to believe that the material witness will not attend the trial because he or she is under the direct control of the defendant or another person involved in human trafficking and, by virtue of this relationship, the defendant or other person seeks to prevent the witness or victim from testifying, and if the defendant has been fully informed of his or her right to counsel as provided by law, the court may have a witness examined conditionally as prescribed in this chapter.

(d) If a defendant has been charged with a case of domestic violence and there is evidence that a victim or material witness has been or is being dissuaded by the defendant or a person acting on behalf of the defendant, by intimidation or a physical threat, from cooperating with the prosecutor or testifying at trial, the people or the defendant may, if the defendant has been fully informed of his or her right to counsel as provided by law, have a witness examined conditionally as prescribed in this chapter.

(e) For the purposes of this section, the following definitions shall apply:

(1) "Domestic violence" means a public offense arising from acts of domestic violence as defined in Section 13700.

(2) "Serious felony" means a felony listed in subdivision (c) of Section 1192.7 or a violation of Section 11351, 11352, 11378, or 11379 of the Health and Safety Code.

Amended by Stats 2014 ch 709 (AB 1610),s 1, eff. 1/1/2015.

Amended by Stats 2009 ch 567 (SB 197),s 1, eff. 1/1/2010.

Amended by Stats 2005 ch 305 (AB 620),s 1, eff. 1/1/2006

Section 1336 - Conditional examination of material witness

(a) When a material witness for the defendant, or for the people, is about to leave the state, or is so sick or infirm as to afford reasonable grounds for apprehension that he or she will be unable to attend the trial, or is a person 65 years of age or older, or a dependent adult, the defendant or the people may apply for an order that the witness be examined conditionally.

(b) When there is evidence that the life of a witness is in jeopardy, the defendant or the people may apply for an order that the witness be examined conditionally.

(c) As used in this section, "dependent adult" means a person, regardless of whether the person lives independently, who is between the ages of 18 and 65, who has physical or mental limitations which restrict his or her ability to carry out normal activities or to protect his or her rights, including, but not limited to, persons who have physical or developmental disabilities or whose physical or mental abilities have diminished because of age. "Dependent adult" includes any person between the ages of 18 and 65, who is admitted as an inpatient to a 24-hour facility, as defined in Sections 1250, 1250.2, and 1250.3 of the Health and Safety Code.

Amended by Stats 2018 ch 70 (AB 1934),s 4, eff. 1/1/2019.

Amended by Stats 2005 ch 305 (AB 620),s 2, eff. 1/1/2006

Amended by Stats 2000 ch 186 (AB 1891) s 1, eff. 1/1/2001.

Section 1337 - Application

The application shall be made upon affidavit stating all of the following:

(a) The nature of the offense charged.

(b) The state of the proceedings in the action.

(c) The name and residence of the witness, and that his or her testimony is material to the defense or the prosecution of the action.

(d) That any of the following are true:

(1) The witness is about to leave the state, or is so sick or infirm as to afford reasonable grounds for apprehending that he or she will not be able to attend the trial, or is a person 65 years of age or older, or a dependent adult, or that the life of the witness is in jeopardy.

(2) That the witness is a victim or a material witness in a human trafficking case who has been or is being intimidated or threatened, as described in paragraph (1) of subdivision (c) of Section 1335, from cooperating with the prosecutor or testifying at trial.

(3) That the witness is a victim or material witness in a domestic violence case who has been or is being intimidated or threatened, as described in subdivision (d) of Section 1335 from cooperating with the prosecutor or testifying at trial.

Amended by Stats 2014 ch 709 (AB 1610),s 2, eff. 1/1/2015.

Amended by Stats 2009 ch 567 (SB 197),s 2, eff. 1/1/2010.

Amended by Stats 2005 ch 305 (AB 620),s 3, eff. 1/1/2006

Amended by Stats 2004 ch 405 (SB 1796), s 13, eff. 1/1/2005.

Section 1338 - Making of application

The application may be made to the court or a judge thereof, and must be made upon three days' notice to the opposite party.

Amended by Stats. 1905, Ch. 540.

Section 1339 - Order for conditional examination of witness

If the court or judge is satisfied that the examination of the witness is necessary, an order must be made that the witness be examined conditionally, at a specified time and place, and before a magistrate designated therein.

Amended by Stats. 1905, Ch. 540.

Section 1340 - Presence of defendant; infirm or sick witness

(a) The defendant has the right to be present in person and with counsel at the examination, and if the defendant is in custody, the officer in whose custody he or she is, must be informed of the time and place of the examination, and must take the defendant thereto, and keep him or her in the presence and hearing of the witness during the examination.

(b) If the court determines that the witness to be examined is so sick or infirm as to be unable to participate in the examination in person, the court may allow the examination to be conducted by a contemporaneous, two-way video conference system, in which the parties and the witness can see and hear each other via electronic communication.

(c) Nothing in this section is intended to require the court to acquire two-way video conference equipment for these purposes.

Amended by Stats 2008 ch 14 (AB 1158),s 1, eff. 1/1/2009.

Section 1341 - Required showing for examination to take place

If, at the designated time and place, it is shown to the satisfaction of the magistrate that the stated ground for conditional examination is not true or that the application was made to avoid the examination of the witness at the trial, the examination cannot take place.

Amended by Stats 2009 ch 567 (SB 197),s 3, eff. 1/1/2010.

Amended by Stats 2005 ch 305 (AB 620),s 4, eff. 1/1/2006

Amended by Stats 2004 ch 405 (SB 1796), s 14, eff. 1/1/2005.

Section 1342 - Attendance of witness

The attendance of the witness may be enforced by a subpoena, issued by the magistrate before whom the examination is to be taken.

Enacted 1872.

Section 1343 - Testimony of witness

The testimony given by the witness shall be reduced to writing and authenticated in the same manner as the testimony of a witness taken in support of an information. Additionally, the testimony may be video-recorded.

Amended by Stats. 1997, Ch. 19, Sec. 1. Effective January 1, 1998.

Section 1344 - Deposition

The deposition taken must, by the magistrate, be sealed up and transmitted to the Clerk of the Court in which the action is pending or may come for trial.

Enacted 1872.

Section 1345 - Reading deposition into evidence or showing of video-recording

The deposition, or a certified copy of it, may be read in evidence, or if the examination was video-recorded, that video-recording may be shown by either party at the trial if the court finds that the witness is unavailable as a witness within the meaning of Section 240 of the Evidence Code. The same objections may be taken to a question or answer contained in the deposition or video-recording as if the witness had been examined orally in court.

Amended by Stats. 1997, Ch. 19, Sec. 2. Effective January 1, 1998.

Chapter 4.5 - EXAMINATION OF VICTIMS OF SEXUAL CRIMES

Section 1346 - Order for victim's testimony at preliminary hearing to be recorded on videotape if victim under 15 years of age or developmentally disabled as result of intellectual disability

(a) When a defendant has been charged with a violation of Section 220, 243.4, 261, 261.5, 264.1, 269, 273a, 273d, 285, 286, 287, 288, 288.5, 288.7, 289, or 647.6, or former Section 288a, and the victim either is a person 15 years of age or younger or is developmentally disabled as a result of an intellectual disability, as specified in subdivision (a) of Section 4512 of the Welfare and Institutions Code, the people may apply for an order that the victim's testimony at the preliminary hearing, in addition to being stenographically recorded, be video recorded and the video recording preserved.

(b) The application for the order shall be in writing and made three days prior to the preliminary hearing.

(c) Upon timely receipt of the application, the magistrate shall order that the testimony of the victim given at the preliminary hearing be taken and preserved as a video recording, in addition to being stenographically recorded. The video recording shall be transmitted to the clerk of the court in which the action is pending.

(d) If at the time of trial the court finds that further testimony would cause the victim emotional trauma so that the victim is medically unavailable or unavailable within the meaning of Section 240 of the Evidence Code, the court may admit the video recording of the victim's testimony at the preliminary hearing as former testimony under Section 1291 of the Evidence Code.

(e) A video recording that is taken pursuant to this section is subject to a protective order of the court for the purpose of protecting the privacy of the victim. This subdivision does not affect the provisions of subdivision (b) of Section 868.7.

(f) A video recording made pursuant to this section shall be made available to the prosecuting attorney, the defendant, and his or her attorney for viewing during ordinary business hours. A video recording that is made available pursuant to this section is subject to a protective order of the court for the purpose of protecting the privacy of the victim.

(g) The video recording shall be destroyed after five years have elapsed from the date of entry of judgment, except that if an appeal is filed, the video recording shall not be destroyed until a final judgment on appeal has been rendered.

Amended by Stats 2018 ch 423 (SB 1494),s 97, eff. 1/1/2019.

Amended by Stats 2017 ch 320 (AB 993),s 1, eff. 1/1/2018.

Amended by Stats 2014 ch 160 (AB 1900),s 1, eff. 1/1/2015.

Amended by Stats 2012 ch 457 (SB 1381),s 40, eff. 1/1/2013.

Amended by Stats 2012 ch 448 (AB 2370),s 40, eff. 1/1/2013.

Section 1346.1 - Order for victim's testimony at preliminary hearing to recorded on videotape if defendant charged with violation of Section 261 or Section 273.5(a)

(a) When a defendant has been charged with a violation of Section 261, if the victim is the spouse of the defendant, former Section 262, or subdivision (a) of Section 273.5, the people may apply for an order that the victim's testimony at the preliminary hearing, in addition to being stenographically recorded, be video recorded and the video recording preserved.

(b) The application for the order shall be in writing and made three days prior to the preliminary hearing.

(c)Upon timely receipt of the application, the magistrate shall order that the testimony of the victim given at the preliminary hearing be taken and preserved as a video recording, in addition to being stenographically recorded. The video recording shall be transmitted to the clerk of the court in which the action is pending.

(d)If the victim's prior testimony given at the preliminary hearing is admissible pursuant to the Evidence Code, then the video recording of that testimony may be introduced as evidence at trial.

Amended by Stats 2022 ch 197 (SB 1493),s 25, eff. 1/1/2023.

Amended by Stats 2021 ch 626 (AB 1171),s 53, eff. 1/1/2022.

Amended by Stats 2014 ch 160 (AB 1900),s 2, eff. 1/1/2015.

Section 1347 - Alternative court procedures involving a child witness

(a) It is the intent of the Legislature in enacting this section to provide the court with discretion to employ alternative court procedures to protect the rights of a child witness, the rights of the defendant, and the integrity of the judicial process. In exercising its discretion, the court necessarily will be required to balance the rights of the defendant or defendants against the need to protect a child witness and to preserve the integrity of the court's truthfinding function. This discretion is intended to be used selectively when the facts and circumstances in an individual case present compelling evidence of the need to use these alternative procedures.

(b) Notwithstanding any other law, the court in a criminal proceeding, upon written notice by the prosecutor made at least three days prior to the date of the preliminary hearing or trial date on which the testimony of the minor is scheduled, or during the course of the proceeding on the court's own motion, may order that the testimony of a minor 13 years of age or younger at the time of the motion be taken by contemporaneous examination and cross-examination in another place and out of the presence of the judge, jury, defendant or defendants, and attorneys, and communicated to the courtroom by means of closed-circuit television, if the court makes all of the following findings:

(1) The minor's testimony will involve a recitation of the facts of any of the following:

(A) An alleged sexual offense committed on or with the minor.

(B) An alleged violent felony, as defined in subdivision (c) of Section 667.5.

(C) An alleged felony offense specified in Section 273a or 273d of which the minor is a victim.

(2) The impact on the minor of one or more of the factors enumerated in subparagraphs (A) to (E), inclusive, is shown by clear and convincing evidence to be so substantial as to make the minor unavailable as a witness unless closed-circuit testimony is used.

(A) Testimony by the minor in the presence of the defendant would result in the child suffering serious emotional distress so that the child would be unavailable as a witness.

(B) The defendant used a deadly weapon in the commission of the offense.

(C) The defendant threatened serious bodily injury to the child or the child's family, threatened incarceration or deportation of the child or a member of the child's family, threatened removal of the child from the child's family, or threatened the dissolution of the child's family in order to prevent or dissuade the minor from attending or giving testimony at any trial or court proceeding, or to prevent the minor from reporting the alleged sexual offense, or from assisting in criminal prosecution.

(D) The defendant inflicted great bodily injury upon the child in the commission of the offense.

(E) The defendant or his or her counsel behaved during the hearing or trial in a way that caused the minor to be unable to continue his or her testimony. In making the determination required by this section, the court shall consider the age of the minor, the relationship between the minor and the defendant or defendants, any handicap or disability of the minor, and the nature of the acts charged. The minor's refusal to testify shall not alone constitute sufficient evidence that the special procedure described in this section is necessary to obtain the minor's testimony.

(3) The equipment available for use of closed-circuit television would accurately communicate the image and demeanor of the minor to the judge, jury, defendant or defendants, and attorneys.

(c) If the court orders the use of closed-circuit television, two-way closed-circuit television shall be used, except that if the impact on the minor of one or more of the factors enumerated in subparagraphs (A) to (E), inclusive, of paragraph (2) of subdivision (b), is shown by clear and convincing evidence to be so substantial as to make the minor unavailable as a witness even if two-way closed-circuit television is used, one-way closed-circuit television may be used. The prosecution shall give the defendant or defendants at least 30 days' written notice of the prosecution's intent to seek the use of one-way closed-circuit television, unless the prosecution shows good cause to the court why this 30-day notice requirement should not apply.

(d)

(1) The hearing on a motion brought pursuant to this section shall be conducted out of the presence of the jury.

(2) Notwithstanding Section 804 of the Evidence Code or any other law, the court, in determining the merits of the motion, shall not compel the minor to testify at the hearing, nor shall the court deny the motion on the ground that the minor has not testified.

(3) In determining whether the impact on an individual child of one or more of the five factors enumerated in paragraph (2) of subdivision (b) is so substantial that the minor is unavailable as a witness unless two-way or one-way closed-circuit television is used, the court may question the minor in chambers, or at some other comfortable place other than the courtroom, on the record for a reasonable period of time with the support person, the prosecutor, and defense counsel present. The defendant or defendants shall not be present. The court shall conduct the questioning of the minor and shall not permit the prosecutor or defense counsel to examine the minor. The prosecutor and defense counsel shall be permitted to submit proposed questions to the court prior to the session in chambers. Defense counsel shall be afforded a reasonable opportunity to consult with the defendant or defendants prior to the conclusion of the session in chambers.

(e) When the court orders the testimony of a minor to be taken in another place outside of the courtroom, the court shall do all of the following:

(1) Make a brief statement on the record, outside of the presence of the jury, of the reasons in support of its order. While the statement need not include traditional findings of fact, the reasons shall be set forth with sufficient specificity to permit meaningful review and to demonstrate that discretion was exercised in a careful, reasonable, and equitable manner.

(2) Instruct the members of the jury that they are to draw no inferences from the use of closed-circuit television as a means of facilitating the testimony of the minor.

(3) Instruct respective counsel, outside of the presence of the jury, that they are to make no comment during the course of the trial on the use of closed-circuit television procedures.

(4) Instruct the support witness, outside of the presence of the jury, that he or she is not to coach, cue, or in any way influence or attempt to influence the testimony of the minor.

(5) Order that a complete record of the examination of the minor, including the images and voices of all persons who in any way participate in the examination, be made and preserved as a video recording in addition to being stenographically recorded. The video recording shall be transmitted to the clerk of the court in which the action is pending and shall be made available for viewing to the prosecuting attorney, the defendant or defendants, and his or her attorney during ordinary business hours. The video recording shall be destroyed after five years have elapsed from the date of entry of judgment. If an appeal is filed, the video recording shall not be destroyed until a final judgment on appeal has been ordered. A video recording that is taken pursuant to this section is subject to a protective order of the court for the purpose of protecting the privacy of the witness. This subdivision does not affect the provisions of subdivision (b) of Section 868.7.

(f) When the court orders the testimony of a minor to be taken in another place outside the courtroom, only the minor, a support person designated pursuant to Section 868.5, a nonuniformed bailiff, any technicians necessary to operate the closed-circuit equipment, and, after consultation with the prosecution and the defense, a representative appointed by the court, shall be physically present for the testimony. A video recording device shall record the image of the minor and his or her testimony, and a separate video recording device shall record the image of the support person.

(g) When the court orders the testimony of a minor to be taken in another place outside the courtroom, the minor shall be brought into the judge's chambers prior to the taking of his or her testimony to meet for a reasonable period of time with the judge, the prosecutor, and defense counsel. A support person for the minor shall also be present. This meeting shall be for the purpose of explaining the court process to the child and to allow the attorneys an opportunity to establish rapport with the child to facilitate later questioning by closed-circuit television. No participant shall discuss the defendant or defendants or any of the facts of the case with the minor during this meeting.

(h) When the court orders the testimony of a minor to be taken in another place outside the courtroom, nothing in this section prohibits the court from ordering the minor to be brought into the courtroom for a limited purpose, including the identification of the defendant or defendants as the court deems necessary.

(i) The examination shall be under oath, and the defendant or defendants shall be able to see and hear the minor witness, and if two-way closed-circuit television is used, the defendant's image shall be transmitted live to the witness.

(j) Nothing in this section affects the disqualification of witnesses pursuant to Section 701 of the Evidence Code.

(k) The cost of examination by contemporaneous closed-circuit television ordered pursuant to this section shall be borne by the court out of its existing budget.

(l) Nothing in this section shall be construed to prohibit a defendant from being represented by counsel during any closed-circuit testimony.

Amended by Stats 2015 ch 155 (SB 176),s 1, eff. 1/1/2016.
Amended by Stats 2014 ch 160 (AB 1900),s 3, eff. 1/1/2015.
Amended by Stats 2005 ch 480 (SB 138),s 1, eff. 1/1/2006.
Amended by Stats 2000 ch 207 (SB 1715) s 2, eff. 1/1/2001.

Section 1347.1 - Testimony regarding human trafficking

(a) In any criminal proceeding in which a defendant is charged with a violation of Section 236.1, upon written notice by the prosecutor made at least three days prior to the date of the preliminary hearing or trial date on which the testimony of the minor is scheduled, or during the course of the proceeding on the court's own motion, may order that the testimony of a minor 15 years of age or younger at the time of the motion be taken by contemporaneous examination and cross-examination in another place and out of the presence of the judge, jury, defendant or defendants, and attorneys, and communicated to the courtroom by means of closed-circuit television, if the court makes all of the following findings:

(1) The minor's testimony will involve a recitation of the facts of an alleged offense of human trafficking, as defined in Section 236.1.

(2)

(A) The impact on the minor of one or more of the factors enumerated in clauses (i) to (v), inclusive, is shown by clear and convincing evidence to be so substantial as to make the minor unavailable as a witness unless closed-circuit testimony is used.

(i) Testimony by the minor in the presence of the defendant would result in the minor suffering serious emotional distress so that the minor would be unavailable as a witness.

(ii) The defendant used a deadly weapon in the commission of the offense.

(iii) The defendant threatened serious bodily injury to the minor or the minor's family, threatened incarceration or deportation of the minor or a member of the minor's family, threatened removal of the minor from the minor's family, or threatened the dissolution of the minor's family in order to prevent or dissuade the minor from attending or giving testimony at any trial or court proceeding, or to prevent the minor from reporting the alleged offense, or from assisting in criminal prosecution.

(iv) The defendant inflicted great bodily injury upon the minor in the commission of the offense.

(v) The defendant or his or her counsel behaved during the hearing or trial in a way that caused the minor to be unable to continue his or her testimony.

(B) In making the determination required by this paragraph, the court shall consider the age of the minor, the relationship between the minor and the defendant or defendants, any handicap or disability of the minor, and the nature of the acts charged. The minor's refusal to testify shall not alone constitute sufficient evidence that the special procedure described in this section is necessary to obtain the minor's testimony.

(3) The equipment available for use of closed-circuit television would accurately communicate the image and demeanor of the minor to the judge, jury, defendant or defendants, and attorneys.

(b) If the court orders the use of closed-circuit television, two-way closed-circuit television shall be used, except that if the impact on the minor of one or more of the factors enumerated in clauses (i) to (v), inclusive, of subparagraph (A) of paragraph (2) of subdivision (a), is shown by clear and convincing evidence to be so substantial as to make the minor unavailable as a witness even if two-way closed-circuit television is used, one-way closed-circuit television may be used. The prosecution shall give the defendant or defendants at least 30 days' written notice of the prosecution's intent to seek the use of one-way closed-circuit television, unless the prosecution shows good cause to the court why this 30-day notice requirement should not apply.

(c)

(1) The hearing on a motion brought pursuant to this section shall be conducted out of the presence of the jury.

(2) Notwithstanding Section 804 of the Evidence Code or any other law, the court, in determining the merits of the motion, shall not compel the minor to testify at the hearing, nor shall the court deny the motion on the ground that the minor has not testified.

(3) In determining whether the impact on an individual minor of one or more of the five factors enumerated in clauses (i) to (v), inclusive, of subparagraph (A) of paragraph (2) of subdivision (a) is so substantial that the minor is unavailable as a witness unless two-way or one-way closed-circuit television is used, the court may question the minor in chambers, or at some other comfortable place other than the courtroom, on the record for a reasonable period of time with the support person, the prosecutor, and defense counsel present. The defendant or defendants shall not be present. The court shall conduct the questioning of the minor and shall not permit the prosecutor or defense counsel to examine the minor. The prosecutor and defense counsel shall be permitted to submit proposed questions to the court prior to the session in chambers. Defense counsel shall be afforded a reasonable opportunity to consult with the defendant or defendants prior to the conclusion of the session in chambers.

(d) When the court orders the testimony of a minor to be taken in another place outside of the courtroom, the court shall do all of the following:

(1) Make a brief statement on the record, outside of the presence of the jury, of the reasons in support of its order. While the statement need not include traditional findings of fact, the reasons shall be set forth with sufficient specificity to permit meaningful review and to demonstrate that discretion was exercised in a careful, reasonable, and equitable manner.

(2) Instruct the members of the jury that they are to draw no inferences from the use of closed-circuit television as a means of facilitating the testimony of the minor.

(3) Instruct respective counsel, outside of the presence of the jury, that they are to make no comment during the course of the trial on the use of closed-circuit television procedures.

(4) Instruct the support witness, outside of the presence of the jury, that he or she is not to coach, cue, or in any way influence or attempt to influence the testimony of the minor.

(5) Order that a complete record of the examination of the minor, including the images and voices of all persons who in any way participate in the examination, be made and preserved as a video recording in addition to being stenographically recorded. The video recording shall be transmitted to the clerk of the court in which the action is pending and shall be made available for viewing to the prosecuting attorney, the defendant or defendants, and his or her attorney during ordinary business hours. The video recording shall be destroyed after five years have elapsed from the date of entry of judgment. If an appeal is filed, the video recording shall not be destroyed until a final judgment on appeal has been ordered. A video recording that is taken pursuant to this section is subject to a protective order of the court for the purpose of protecting the privacy of the witness. This subdivision does not affect the provisions of subdivision (b) of Section 868.7.

(e) When the court orders the testimony of a minor to be taken in another place outside the courtroom, only the minor, a support person designated pursuant to Section 868.5, a nonuniformed bailiff, any technicians necessary to operate the closed-circuit equipment, and, after consultation with the prosecution and the defense, a representative appointed by the court, shall be physically present for the testimony. A video recording device shall record the image of the minor and his or her testimony, and a separate video recording device shall record the image of the support person.

(f) When the court orders the testimony of a minor to be taken in another place outside the courtroom, the minor shall be brought into the judge's chambers prior to the taking of his or her testimony to meet for a reasonable period of time with the judge, the prosecutor, and defense counsel. A support person for the minor shall also be present. This meeting shall be for the purpose of explaining the court process to the minor and to allow the attorneys an opportunity to establish rapport with the minor to facilitate later questioning by closed-circuit television. A participant shall not discuss the defendant or defendants or any of the facts of the case with the minor during this meeting.

(g) When the court orders the testimony of a minor to be taken in another place outside the courtroom, this section does not prohibit the court from ordering the minor to be brought into the courtroom for a limited purpose, including the identification of the defendant or defendants as the court deems necessary.

(h) The examination shall be under oath, and the defendant or defendants shall be able to see and hear the minor witness, and if two-way closed-circuit television is used, the defendant's image shall be transmitted live to the witness.

(i) This section does not affect the disqualification of witnesses pursuant to Section 701 of the Evidence Code.

(j) The cost of examination by contemporaneous closed-circuit television ordered pursuant to this section shall be borne by the court out of its existing budget.

(k) This section shall not be construed to prohibit a defendant from being represented by counsel during any closed-circuit testimony.

Amended by Stats 2017 ch 269 (SB 811),s 9, eff. 1/1/2018.

Amended by Stats 2017 ch 561 (AB 1516),s 190, eff. 1/1/2018.

Added by Stats 2016 ch 635 (AB 1276),s 1, eff. 1/1/2017.

Section 1347.5 - Alternative court procedures involving adults and children with disabilities

(a) It is the intent of the Legislature, in enacting this section, to provide the court with discretion to modify court procedures, as a reasonable accommodation, to ensure that adults and children with disabilities who have been victims of an alleged sexual or otherwise specified offense are able to participate effectively in criminal proceedings. In exercising its discretion, the court shall balance the rights of the defendant against the right of the victim who has a disability to full access and participation in the proceedings, while preserving the integrity of the court's truthfinding function.

(1) For purposes of this section, the term "disability" is defined in paragraphs (1) and (2) of subdivision (c) of Section 11135 of the Government Code.

(2) The right of the victim is not to confront the perpetrator, but derives under both Section 504 of the Rehabilitation Act of 1973 (29 U.S.C. Sec. 794) and the Americans with Disabilities Act of 1990 (42 U.S.C. Sec. 12101 et seq.) as a right to participate in or benefit from the same services or services that are equal or as effective as those enjoyed by persons without disabilities.

(b) Notwithstanding any other law, in any criminal proceeding in which the defendant is charged with a violation of Section 220, 243.4, 261, 261.5, 264.1, 273a, 273d, 285, 286, 287, 288, 288.5, or 289, or former Section 288a, subdivision (1) of Section 314, Section 368, 647.6, or with any attempt to commit a crime listed in this subdivision, committed with or upon a person with a disability, the court in its discretion may make accommodations to support the person with a disability, including, but not limited to, any of the following:

(1) Allow the person with a disability reasonable periods of relief from examination and cross-examination during which he or she may retire from the courtroom. The judge may also allow other witnesses in the proceeding to be examined when the person with a disability retires from the courtroom.

(2) Allow the person with a disability to utilize a support person pursuant to Section 868.5 or a regional center representative providing services to a developmentally disabled individual pursuant to Article 1 (commencing with Section 4620) or Article 2 (commencing with Section 4640) of Chapter 5 of Division 4.5 of the Welfare and Institutions Code. In addition to, or instead of, allowing the person with a disability to utilize a support person or regional center representative pursuant to this paragraph, the court may allow the person with a disability to utilize a person necessary to facilitate the communication or physical needs of the person with a disability.

(3) Notwithstanding Section 68110 of the Government Code, the judge may remove his or her robe if the judge believes that this formal attire prevents full participation of the person with a disability because it is intimidating to him or her.

(4) The judge, parties, witnesses, support persons, and court personnel may be relocated within the courtroom to facilitate a more comfortable and personal environment for the person with a disability as well as accommodating any specific requirements for communication by that person.

(c) The prosecutor may apply for an order that the testimony of the person with a disability at the preliminary hearing, in addition to being stenographically recorded, be video recorded and the video recording preserved.

(1) The application for the order shall be in writing and made three days prior to the preliminary hearing.

(2) Upon timely receipt of the application, the judge shall order that the testimony of the person with a disability given at the preliminary hearing be taken and preserved as a video recording, in addition to being stenographically recorded. The video recording shall be transmitted to the clerk of the court in which the action is pending.

(3) If at the time of trial the court finds that further testimony would cause the person with a disability emotional trauma so that he or she is medically unavailable or otherwise unavailable within the meaning of Section 240 of the Evidence Code, the court may admit the video recording of his or her testimony at the preliminary hearing as former testimony under Section 1291 of the Evidence Code.

(4) A video recording that is taken pursuant to this subdivision is subject to a protective order of the court for the purpose of protecting the privacy of the person with a disability. This subdivision does not affect the provisions of subdivision (b) of Section 868.7.

(d) Notwithstanding any other law, the court in any criminal proceeding, upon written notice of the prosecutor made at least three days prior to the date of the preliminary hearing or trial date on which the testimony of the person with a disability is scheduled, or during the course of the proceeding on the court's own motion, may order that the testimony of the person with a disability be taken by contemporaneous examination and cross-examination in another place and out of the presence of the judge, jury, and defendant, and communicated to the courtroom by means of two-way closed-circuit television, if the court makes all of the following findings:

(1) The person with a disability will be called on to testify concerning facts of an alleged sexual offense, or other crime as specified in subdivision (b), committed on or with that person.

(2) The impact on the person with a disability of one or more of the factors enumerated in subparagraphs (A) to (D), inclusive, is shown by clear and convincing evidence to be so substantial as to make the person with a disability unavailable as a witness unless closed-circuit television is used. The refusal of the person with a disability to testify shall not alone constitute sufficient evidence that the special procedure described in this subdivision is necessary in order to accommodate the disability. The court may take into consideration the relationship between the person with a disability and the defendant or defendants.

(A) Threats of serious bodily injury to be inflicted on the person with a disability or a family member, of incarceration, institutionalization, or deportation of the person with a disability or a family member, or of removal of the person with a disability from his or her residence by withholding needed services when the threats come from a service provider, in order to prevent or dissuade the person with a disability from attending or giving testimony at any trial or court proceeding or to prevent that person from reporting the alleged offense or from assisting in criminal prosecution.

(B) Use of a firearm or any other deadly weapon during the commission of the crime.

(C) Infliction of great bodily injury upon the person with a disability during the commission of the crime.

(D) Conduct on the part of the defendant or defense counsel during the hearing or trial that causes the person with a disability to be unable to continue his or her testimony.

(e)

(1) The hearing on the motion brought pursuant to this subdivision shall be conducted out of the presence of the jury.

(2) Notwithstanding Section 804 of the Evidence Code or any other law, the court, in determining the merits of the motion, shall not compel the person with a disability to testify at the hearing, nor shall the court deny the motion on the ground that the person with a disability has not testified.

(3) In determining whether the impact on an individual person with a disability of one or more of the factors enumerated under paragraph (2) of subdivision (d) is so substantial that the person is unavailable as a witness unless the closed-circuit television

procedure is employed, the court may question the person with a disability in chambers, or at some other comfortable place other than the courtroom, on the record for a reasonable period of time with the support person described under paragraph (2) of subdivision (b), the prosecutor, and defense counsel present. At this time the court shall explain the process to the person with a disability. The defendant or defendants shall not be present; however, the defendant or defendants shall have the opportunity to contemporaneously observe the proceedings by closed-circuit television. Defense counsel shall be afforded a reasonable opportunity to consult with the defendant or defendants prior to the conclusion of the session in chambers.

(f) When the court orders the testimony of a victim who is a person with a disability to be taken in another place outside of the courtroom, the court shall do all of the following:

(1) Make a brief statement on the record, outside of the presence of the jury, of the reasons in support of its order. While the statement need not include traditional findings of fact, the reasons shall be set forth with sufficient specificity to permit meaningful review and to demonstrate that discretion was exercised in a careful, reasonable, and equitable manner.

(2) Instruct the members of the jury that they are to draw no inferences from the use of closed-circuit television as a means of ensuring the full participation of the victim who is a person with a disability by accommodating that individual's disability.

(3) Instruct respective counsel, outside of the presence of the jury, that they are to make no comment during the course of the trial on the use of closed-circuit television procedures.

(4) Instruct the support person, if the person is part of the court's accommodation of the disability, outside of the presence of the jury, that he or she is not to coach, cue, or in any way influence or attempt to influence the testimony of the person with a disability.

(5) Order that a complete record of the examination of the person with a disability, including the images and voices of all persons who in any way participate in the examination, be made and preserved as a video recording in addition to being stenographically recorded. The video recording shall be transmitted to the clerk of the court in which the action is pending and shall be made available for viewing to the prosecuting attorney, the defendant, and his or her attorney, during ordinary business hours. The video recording shall be destroyed after five years have elapsed from the date of entry of judgment. If an appeal is filed, the video recording shall not be destroyed until a final judgment on appeal has been ordered. A video recording that is taken pursuant to this section is subject to a protective order of the court for the purpose of protecting the privacy of the person with a disability. This subdivision does not affect the provisions of subdivision (b) of Section 868.7.

(g) When the court orders the testimony of a victim who is a person with a disability to be taken in another place outside the courtroom, nothing in this section shall prohibit the court from ordering the victim to appear in the courtroom for a limited purpose, including the identification of the defendant or defendants as the court deems necessary.

(h) The examination shall be under oath, and the defendant shall be able to see and hear the person with a disability. If two-way closed-circuit television is used, the defendant's image shall be transmitted live to the person with a disability.

(i) Nothing in this section shall affect the disqualification of witnesses pursuant to Section 701 of the Evidence Code.

(j) The cost of examination by contemporaneous closed-circuit television ordered pursuant to this section shall be borne by the court out of its existing budget.

(k) This section shall not be construed to obviate the need to provide other accommodations necessary to ensure accessibility of courtrooms to persons with disabilities nor prescribe a lesser standard of accessibility or usability for persons with disabilities than that provided by Title II of the Americans with Disabilities Act of 1990 (42 U.S.C. Sec. 12101 et seq.) and federal regulations adopted pursuant to that act.

(l) The Judicial Council shall report to the Legislature, no later than two years after the enactment of this subdivision, on the frequency of the use and effectiveness of admitting the videotape of testimony by means of closed-circuit television.

Amended by Stats 2018 ch 423 (SB 1494),s 98, eff. 1/1/2019.

Amended by Stats 2014 ch 160 (AB 1900),s 4, eff. 1/1/2015.

Amended by Stats 2004 ch 823 (AB 20), s 16, eff. 1/1/2005.

Section 1348.5 - [Repealed]

Repealed by Stats 2001 ch 115 (SB 153), s 26, eff. 1/1/2002.

Chapter 5 - EXAMINATION OF WITNESSES ON COMMISSION

Section 1349 - Examination of material witness residing out of state

When an issue of fact is joined upon an indictment or information, the defendant may have any material witness, residing out of the state, examined in his behalf, as prescribed in this chapter, and not otherwise.

Amended by Stats. 1980, Ch. 676, Sec. 253.

Section 1350 - Order that witness be examined on commission

When a material witness for the defendant resides out of the State, the defendant may apply for an order that the witness be examined on a commission.

Enacted 1872.

Section 1351 - Commission

A commission is a process issued under the seal of the Court and the signature of the Clerk, directed to some person designated as Commissioner, authorizing him to examine the witness upon oath on interrogatories annexed thereto, to take and certify the deposition of the witness, and to return it according to the directions given with the commission.

Enacted 1872.

Section 1352 - Application upon affidavit

The application must be made upon affidavit, stating:

1. The nature of the offense charged;

2. The state of the proceedings in the action, and that an issue of fact has been joined therein;

3. The name of the witness, and that his testimony is material to the defense of the action;

4. That the witness resides out of the State.

Enacted 1872.

Section 1353 - Making of application
The application may be made to the Court, or a Judge thereof, and must be upon three days' notice to the District Attorney.
Amended by Code Amendments 1880, Ch. 25.

Section 1354 - Order
If the Court to whom the application is made is satisfied of the truth of the facts stated, and that the examination of the witness is necessary to the attainment of justice, an order must be made that a commission be issued to take his testimony; and the Court may insert in the order a direction that the trial be stayed for a specified time, reasonably sufficient for the execution and return of the commission.
Amended by Code Amendments 1880, Ch. 47.

Section 1355 - Service of interrogatories and cross-interrogatories
When the commission is ordered, the defendant must serve upon the District Attorney, without delay, a copy of the interrogatories to be annexed thereto, with two days' notice of the time at which they will be presented to the Court or Judge. The District Attorney may in like manner serve upon the defendant or his counsel cross-interrogatories, to be annexed to the commission, with the like notice. In the interrogatories either party may insert any questions pertinent to the issue. When the interrogatories and cross-interrogatories are presented to the Court or Judge, according to the notice given, the Court or Judge must modify the questions so as to conform them to the rules of evidence, and must indorse upon them his allowance and annex them to the commission.
Enacted 1872.

Section 1356 - Return of commission
Unless the parties otherwise consent, by an indorsement upon the commission, the Court or Judge must indorse thereon a direction as to the manner in which it must be returned, and may, in his discretion, direct that it be returned by mail or otherwise, addressed to the Clerk of the Court in which the action is pending, designating his name and the place where his office is kept.
Enacted 1872.

Section 1357 - Execution of commission
The commissioner, unless otherwise specially directed, may execute the commission in the following order:
(a) He or she shall publicly administer an oath to the witness that his or her answers given to the interrogatories shall be the truth, the whole truth, and nothing but the truth.
(b) He or she shall cause the examination of the witness to be reduced to writing and subscribed by the witness.
(c) He or she shall write the answers of the witness as near as possible in the language in which he or she gives them, and read to the witness each answer as it is taken down, and correct or add to it until it conforms to what he or she declares is the truth.
(d) If the witness declines to answer a question, that fact, with the reason assigned by him or her for declining, shall be stated.
(e) If any papers or documents are produced before him or her and proved by the witness, they, or copies of them, shall be annexed to the deposition subscribed by the witness and certified by the commissioner.
(f) The commissioner shall subscribe his or her name to each sheet of the deposition, and annex the deposition, with the papers and documents proved by the witness, or copies thereof, to the commission, and shall close it up under seal, and address it as directed by the indorsement thereon.
(g) If there is a direction on the commission to return it by mail, the commissioner shall immediately deposit it in the nearest post office. If any other direction is made by the written consent of the parties, or by the court or judge, on the commission, as to its return, the commissioner shall comply with the direction. A copy of this section shall be annexed to the commission.
Amended by Stats. 1989, Ch. 1360, Sec. 115.

Section 1358 - Duties of agent
If the commission and return be delivered by the Commissioner to an agent, he must deliver the same to the Clerk to whom it is directed, or to the Judge of the Court in which the action is pending, by whom it may be received and opened, upon the agent making affidavit that he received it from the hands of the Commissioner, and that it has not been opened or altered since he received it.
Amended by Code Amendments 1880, Ch. 47.

Section 1359 - Agent unable to deliver commission and return
If the agent is dead, or from sickness or other casualty unable personally to deliver the commission and return, as prescribed in the last section, it may be received by the Clerk or Judge from any other person, upon his making an affidavit that he received it from the agent; that the agent is dead, or from sickness or other casualty unable to deliver it; that it has not been opened or altered since the person making the affidavit received it; and that he believes it has not been opened or altered since it came from the hands of the Commissioner.
Enacted 1872.

Section 1360 - Filing
The clerk or judge receiving and opening the commission and return shall immediately file it, with the affidavit mentioned in Sections 1358 and 1359, in the office of the clerk of the court in which the indictment is pending. If the commission and return is transmitted by mail, the clerk to whom it is addressed shall receive it from the post office, and open and file it in his or her office, where it must remain, unless otherwise directed by the court or judge.
Amended by Stats. 1987, Ch. 828, Sec. 89.

Section 1361 - Inspection by parties
The commission and return must at all times be open to the inspection of the parties, who must be furnished by the Clerk with copies of the same or of any part thereof, on payment of his fees.
Enacted 1872.

Section 1362 - Reading of deposition into evidence
The depositions taken under the commission may be read in evidence by either party on the trial if the court finds that the witness is unavailable as a witness within the meaning of Section 240 of the Evidence Code. The same objections may be taken to a question in the interrogatories or to an answer in the deposition as if the witness had been examined orally in court.

Chapter 6 - INQUIRY INTO THE COMPETENCE OF THE DEFENDANT BEFORE TRIAL OR AFTER CONVICTION

Section 1367 - Mental incompetence of defendant

(a) A person shall not be tried or adjudged to punishment or have their probation, mandatory supervision, postrelease community supervision, or parole revoked while that person is mentally incompetent. A defendant is mentally incompetent for purposes of this chapter if, as a result of a mental health disorder or developmental disability, the defendant is unable to understand the nature of the criminal proceedings or to assist counsel in the conduct of a defense in a rational manner.

(b) Section 1370 applies to a person who is charged with a felony or alleged to have violated the terms of probation for a felony or mandatory supervision and is incompetent as a result of a mental health disorder. Section 1370.01 applies to a person who is charged with a misdemeanor or misdemeanors only, or a violation of formal or informal probation for a misdemeanor, and the judge finds reason to believe that the defendant has a mental health disorder, and may, as a result of the mental health disorder, be incompetent to stand trial. Section 1370.1 applies to a person who is incompetent as a result of a developmental disability and applies to a person who is incompetent as a result of a mental health disorder, but also has a developmental disability. Section 1370.02 applies to a person alleged to have violated the terms of the person's postrelease community supervision or parole.

Amended by Stats 2019 ch 9 (AB 46),s 4, eff. 1/1/2020.

Amended by Stats 2014 ch 759 (SB 1412),s 1, eff. 1/1/2015.

Section 1367.1 - [Repealed]

Repealed by Stats 2014 ch 759 (SB 1412),s 2, eff. 1/1/2015.

Section 1368 - Doubt about mental competence of defendant during pendency of action

(a) If, during the pendency of an action and prior to judgment, or during revocation proceedings for a violation of probation, mandatory supervision, postrelease community supervision, or parole, a doubt arises in the mind of the judge as to the mental competence of the defendant, he or she shall state that doubt in the record and inquire of the attorney for the defendant whether, in the opinion of the attorney, the defendant is mentally competent. If the defendant is not represented by counsel, the court shall appoint counsel. At the request of the defendant or his or her counsel or upon its own motion, the court shall recess the proceedings for as long as may be reasonably necessary to permit counsel to confer with the defendant and to form an opinion as to the mental competence of the defendant at that point in time.

(b) If counsel informs the court that he or she believes the defendant is or may be mentally incompetent, the court shall order that the question of the defendant's mental competence is to be determined in a hearing which is held pursuant to Sections 1368.1 and 1369. If counsel informs the court that he or she believes the defendant is mentally competent, the court may nevertheless order a hearing. Any hearing shall be held in the superior court.

(c) Except as provided in Section 1368.1, when an order for a hearing into the present mental competence of the defendant has been issued, all proceedings in the criminal prosecution shall be suspended until the question of the present mental competence of the defendant has been determined. If a jury has been impaneled and sworn to try the defendant, the jury shall be discharged only if it appears to the court that undue hardship to the jurors would result if the jury is retained on call.

If the defendant is declared mentally incompetent, the jury shall be discharged.

Amended by Stats 2014 ch 759 (SB 1412),s 3, eff. 1/1/2015.

Section 1368.1 - Preliminary examination; demurrer or dismissal of complaint

(a)

(1) If the action is on a complaint charging a felony, proceedings to determine mental competence shall be held prior to the filing of an information unless the counsel for the defendant requests a preliminary examination under Section 859b. At the preliminary examination, counsel for the defendant may either demur, move to dismiss the complaint on the ground that there is not reasonable cause to believe that a felony has been committed and that the defendant is guilty thereof, or make a motion under Section 1538.5. A proceeding to determine mental competence or a request for a preliminary examination pursuant to this paragraph does not preclude a request for a determination of probable cause pursuant to paragraph (2).

(2) If the action is on a complaint charging a felony involving death, great bodily harm, or a serious threat to the physical well-being of another person, the prosecuting attorney may, at any time before or after a defendant is determined incompetent to stand trial, request a determination of probable cause to believe the defendant committed the offense or offenses alleged in the complaint, solely for the purpose of establishing that the defendant is gravely disabled pursuant to subparagraph (B) of paragraph (1) of subdivision (h) of Section 5008 of the Welfare and Institutions Code, pursuant to procedures approved by the court. In making this determination, the court shall consider using procedures consistent with the manner in which a preliminary examination is conducted. A finding of probable cause shall only be made upon the presentation of evidence sufficient to satisfy the standard set forth in subdivision (a) of Section 872. The defendant shall be entitled to a preliminary hearing after the restoration of his or her competence. A request for a determination of probable cause pursuant to this paragraph does not preclude a proceeding to determine mental competence or a request for a preliminary examination pursuant to paragraph (1).

(b) If the action is on a complaint charging a misdemeanor, counsel for the defendant may either demur, move to dismiss the complaint on the ground that there is not reasonable cause to believe that a public offense has been committed and that the defendant is guilty thereof, or make a motion under Section 1538.5.

(c) If the proceeding involves an alleged violation of probation, mandatory supervision, postrelease community supervision, or parole, counsel for the defendant may move to reinstate supervision on the ground that there is not probable cause to believe that the defendant violated the terms of his or her supervision.

(d) In ruling upon any demurrer or motion described in subdivision (a), (b), or (c), the court may hear any matter which is capable of fair determination without the personal participation of the defendant.

(e) A demurrer or motion described in subdivision (a), (b), or (c) shall be made in the court having jurisdiction over the complaint. The defendant shall not be certified until the demurrer or motion has been decided.

Amended by Stats 2017 ch 246 (SB 684),s 1, eff. 1/1/2018.

Amended by Stats 2014 ch 759 (SB 1412),s 4, eff. 1/1/2015.

Section 1369 - Trial by court or jury of question of mental competence

Except as stated in subdivision (g), a trial by court or jury of the question of mental competence shall proceed in the following order:

(a)

(1)The court shall appoint a psychiatrist or licensed psychologist, and any other expert the court may deem appropriate, to examine the defendant. If the defendant or the defendant's counsel informs the court that the defendant is not seeking a finding of mental incompetence, the court shall appoint two psychiatrists, licensed psychologists, or a combination thereof. One of the psychiatrists or licensed psychologists may be named by the defense and one may be named by the prosecution.

(2)

(A) The examining licensed psychologists or psychiatrists shall evaluate the nature of the defendant's mental disorder, if any, the defendant's ability or inability to understand the nature of the criminal proceedings or the defendant's ability to assist counsel in the conduct of a defense in a rational manner as a result of a mental disorder, and whether treatment with antipsychotic medication, as defined in subdivision (l) of Section 5008 of the Welfare and Institutions Code, is appropriate for the defendant. The evaluation of whether treatment with antipsychotic medication is appropriate shall be done in accordance with subparagraphs (B) and (C). The examining licensed psychologists or psychiatrists shall also opine whether the defendant lacks the capacity to make decisions regarding antipsychotic medication, as outlined in subclauses (I) and (II) of clause (i) of subparagraph (B) of paragraph (2) of subdivision (a) of Section 1370.

(B)If a licensed psychologist examines the defendant and opines that treatment with antipsychotic medication may be appropriate, their opinion shall be based on whether the defendant has a mental disorder that is typically known to benefit from that treatment. A licensed psychologist's opinion shall not exceed the scope of their license. That opinion about the potential benefit of antipsychotic medication is not a prescription for that medication.

(C)If a psychiatrist examines the defendant and opines that treatment with antipsychotic medication is appropriate, the psychiatrist shall inform the court of their opinion as to the likely or potential side effects of the medication, the expected efficacy of the medication, and possible alternative treatments, as outlined in subclause (III) of clause (i) of subparagraph (B) of paragraph (2) of subdivision (a) of Section 1370.

(3)If it is suspected the defendant has a developmental disability, the court shall appoint the director of the regional center established under Division 4.5 (commencing with Section 4500) of the Welfare and Institutions Code, or the director's designee, to examine the defendant to determine whether the defendant has a developmental disability. The regional center director or their designee shall determine whether the defendant has a developmental disability, as defined in Section 4512 of the Welfare and Institutions Code, and is therefore eligible for regional center services and supports. The regional center director or their designee shall provide the court with a written report informing the court of this determination.

(4)The regional center director shall recommend to the court a suitable residential facility or state hospital. Prior to issuing an order pursuant to this section, the court shall consider the recommendation of the regional center director. While the person is confined pursuant to order of the court under this section, they shall be provided with necessary care and treatment.

(b)

(1)The counsel for the defendant shall offer evidence in support of the allegation of mental incompetence.

(2)If the defense declines to offer any evidence in support of the allegation of mental incompetence, the prosecution may do so.

(c)The prosecution shall present its case regarding the issue of the defendant's present mental competence.

(d)Each party may offer rebutting testimony, unless the court, for good reason in furtherance of justice, also permits other evidence in support of the original contention.

(e)When the evidence is concluded, unless the case is submitted without final argument, the prosecution shall make its final argument and the defense shall conclude with its final argument to the court or jury.

(f)In a jury trial, the court shall charge the jury, instructing them on all matters of law necessary for the rendering of a verdict. It shall be presumed that the defendant is mentally competent unless it is proved by a preponderance of the evidence that the defendant is mentally incompetent. The verdict of the jury shall be unanimous.

(g)Only a court trial is required to determine competency in a proceeding for a violation of probation, mandatory supervision, postrelease community supervision, or parole.

(h)

(1)The State Department of State Hospitals, on or before July 1, 2017, shall adopt guidelines for education and training standards for a psychiatrist or licensed psychologist to be considered for appointment by the court pursuant to this section. To develop these guidelines, the State Department of State Hospitals shall convene a workgroup comprised of the Judicial Council and groups or individuals representing judges, defense counsel, district attorneys, counties, advocates for people with developmental and mental disabilities, state psychologists and psychiatrists, professional associations and accrediting bodies for psychologists and psychiatrists, and other interested stakeholders.

(2)When making an appointment pursuant to this section, the court shall appoint an expert who meets the guidelines established in accordance with this subdivision or an expert with equivalent experience and skills. If there is no reasonably available expert who meets the guidelines or who has equivalent experience and skills, the court may appoint an expert who does not meet the guidelines.

Amended by Stats 2022 ch 47 (SB 184),s 41, eff. 6/30/2022.

Amended by Stats 2018 ch 1008 (SB 1187),s 1, eff. 1/1/2019.

Amended by Stats 2016 ch 405 (AB 1962),s 1, eff. 1/1/2017.

Amended by Stats 2014 ch 759 (SB 1412),s 5, eff. 1/1/2015.

Amended by Stats 2007 ch 556 (SB 568),s 2, eff. 1/1/2008.

Amended by Stats 2004 ch 486 (SB 1794),s 1, eff. 1/1/2005.

Section 1369.1 - [Repealed]

Repealed by Stats 2022 ch 47 (SB 184),s 42, eff. 6/30/2022.
Amended by Stats 2015 ch 26 (SB 85),s 29, eff. 6/24/2015.
Amended by Stats 2014 ch 759 (SB 1412),s 6, eff. 1/1/2015.
Amended by Stats 2012 ch 24 (AB 1470),s 25, eff. 6/27/2012.
Amended by Stats 2009 ch 140 (AB 1164),s 148, eff. 1/1/2010.
Amended by Stats 2009 ch 35 (SB 174),s 12, eff. 1/1/2010.
Amended by Stats 2008 ch 179 (SB 1498),s 181, eff. 1/1/2009.
Added by Stats 2007 ch 556 (SB 568),s 3, eff. 1/1/2008.

Section 1369.5 - Confidentiality of documents

(a) A document submitted to a court pursuant to this chapter, including, but not limited to, Sections 1369, 1370, 1370.01, 1370.1, and 1372, is presumptively confidential, except as otherwise provided by law.

(b) A document described in subdivision (a) shall be retained in the confidential portion of the court's file. Counsel for the defendant and the prosecution shall maintain the documents as confidential.

(c)

(1) The defendant, counsel for the defendant, and the prosecution may inspect, copy, or utilize the documents, and any information contained in the documents, without an order from the court for purposes related to the defense, prosecution, treatment, and safety of the defendant, and for the safety of the public.

(2) A motion, application, or petition to access the documents shall be decided in accordance with subdivision (h) of Rule 2.551 of the California Rules of Court.

Added by Stats 2019 ch 251 (SB 557),s 1, eff. 1/1/2020.

Section 1370 - Effect of finding of mental competence or mental incompetence

(a)

(1)

(A) If the defendant is found mentally competent, the criminal process shall resume, the trial on the offense charged or hearing on the alleged violation shall proceed, and judgment may be pronounced.

(B) If the defendant is found mentally incompetent, the trial, the hearing on the alleged violation, or the judgment shall be suspended until the person becomes mentally competent.

(i) The court shall order that the mentally incompetent defendant be delivered by the sheriff to a State Department of State Hospitals facility, as defined in Section 4100 of the Welfare and Institutions Code, as directed by the State Department of State Hospitals, or to any other available public or private treatment facility, including a community-based residential treatment system approved by the community program director, or their designee, that will promote the defendant's speedy restoration to mental competence, or placed on outpatient status as specified in Section 1600.

(ii) However, if the action against the defendant who has been found mentally incompetent is on a complaint charging a felony offense specified in Section 290, the prosecutor shall determine whether the defendant previously has been found mentally incompetent to stand trial pursuant to this chapter on a charge of a Section 290 offense, or whether the defendant is currently the subject of a pending Section 1368 proceeding arising out of a charge of a Section 290 offense. If either determination is made, the prosecutor shall notify the court and defendant in writing. After this notification, and opportunity for hearing, the court shall order that the defendant be delivered by the sheriff to a State Department of State Hospitals facility, as directed by the State Department of State Hospitals, or other secure treatment facility for the care and treatment of persons with a mental health disorder, unless the court makes specific findings on the record that an alternative placement would provide more appropriate treatment for the defendant and would not pose a danger to the health and safety of others.

(iii) If the action against the defendant who has been found mentally incompetent is on a complaint charging a felony offense specified in Section 290 and the defendant has been denied bail pursuant to subdivision (b) of Section 12 of Article I of the California Constitution because the court has found, based upon clear and convincing evidence, a substantial likelihood that the person's release would result in great bodily harm to others, the court shall order that the defendant be delivered by the sheriff to a State Department of State Hospitals facility, as directed by the State Department of State Hospitals, unless the court makes specific findings on the record that an alternative placement would provide more appropriate treatment for the defendant and would not pose a danger to the health and safety of others.

(iv)

(I) If, at any time after the court finds that the defendant is mentally incompetent and before the defendant is transported to a facility pursuant to this section, the court is provided with any information that the defendant may benefit from diversion pursuant to Chapter 2.8A (commencing with Section 1001.35) of Title 6, the court may make a finding that the defendant is an appropriate candidate for diversion.

(II) Notwithstanding subclause (I), if a defendant is found mentally incompetent and is transferred to a facility described in Section 4361.6 of the Welfare and Institutions Code, the court may, at any time upon receiving any information that the defendant may benefit from diversion pursuant to Chapter 2.8A (commencing with Section 1001.35) of Title 6, make a finding that the defendant is an appropriate candidate for diversion.

(v) If a defendant is found by the court to be an appropriate candidate for diversion pursuant to clause (iv), the defendant's eligibility shall be determined pursuant to Section 1001.36. A defendant granted diversion may participate for the lesser of the period specified in paragraph (1) of subdivision (c) or the applicable period described in subparagraph (C) of paragraph (1) of subdivision (f) of Section 1001.36. If, during that period, the court determines that criminal proceedings should be reinstated pursuant to subdivision (g) of Section 1001.36, the court shall, pursuant to Section 1369, appoint a psychiatrist, licensed psychologist, or any other expert the court may deem appropriate, to determine the defendant's competence to stand trial.

(vi) Upon the dismissal of charges at the conclusion of the period of diversion, pursuant to subdivision (h) of Section 1001.36, a defendant shall no longer be deemed incompetent to stand trial pursuant to this section.

(vii) The clerk of the court shall notify the Department of Justice, in writing, of a finding of mental incompetence with respect to a defendant who is subject to clause (ii) or (iii) for inclusion in the defendant's state summary criminal history information.

(C) Upon the filing of a certificate of restoration to competence, the court shall order that the defendant be returned to court in accordance with Section 1372. The court shall transmit a copy of its order to the community program director or a designee.

(D) A defendant charged with a violent felony may not be delivered to a State Department of State Hospitals facility or treatment facility pursuant to this subdivision unless the State Department of State Hospitals facility or treatment facility has a secured perimeter or a locked and controlled treatment facility, and the judge determines that the public safety will be protected.

(E) For purposes of this paragraph, "violent felony" means an offense specified in subdivision (c) of Section 667.5.

(F) A defendant charged with a violent felony may be placed on outpatient status, as specified in Section 1600, only if the court finds that the placement will not pose a danger to the health or safety of others. If the court places a defendant charged with a violent felony on outpatient status, as specified in Section 1600, the court shall serve copies of the placement order on defense counsel, the sheriff in the county where the defendant will be placed, and the district attorney for the county in which the violent felony charges are pending against the defendant.

(G) If, at any time after the court has declared a defendant incompetent to stand trial pursuant to this section, counsel for the defendant or a jail medical or mental health staff provider provides the court with substantial evidence that the defendant's psychiatric symptoms have changed to such a degree as to create a doubt in the mind of the judge as to the defendant's current mental incompetence, the court may appoint a psychiatrist or a licensed psychologist to opine as to whether the defendant has regained competence. If, in the opinion of that expert, the defendant has regained competence, the court shall proceed as if a certificate of restoration of competence has been returned pursuant to paragraph (1) of subdivision (a) of Section 1372.

(H)

(i) The State Department of State Hospitals may, pursuant to Section 4335.2 of the Welfare and Institutions Code, conduct an evaluation of the defendant in county custody to determine any of the following:

(I) The defendant has regained competence.

(II) There is no substantial likelihood that the defendant will regain competence in the foreseeable future.

(III) The defendant should be referred to the county for further evaluation for potential participation in a county diversion program, if one exists, or to another outpatient treatment program.

(ii) If, in the opinion of the department's expert, the defendant has regained competence, the court shall proceed as if a certificate of restoration of competence has been returned pursuant to paragraph (1) of subdivision (a) of Section 1372.

(iii) If, in the opinion of the department's expert, there is no substantial likelihood that the defendant will regain mental competence in the foreseeable future, the committing court shall proceed pursuant to paragraph (2) of subdivision (c) no later than 10 days following receipt of the report.

(2) Prior to making the order directing that the defendant be committed to the State Department of State Hospitals or other treatment facility or placed on outpatient status, the court shall proceed as follows:

(A)

(i) The court shall order the community program director or a designee to evaluate the defendant and to submit to the court within 15 judicial days of the order a written recommendation as to whether the defendant should be required to undergo outpatient treatment, or be committed to the State Department of State Hospitals or to any other treatment facility. A person shall not be admitted to a State Department of State Hospitals facility or other treatment facility or placed on outpatient status under this section without having been evaluated by the community program director or a designee. The community program director or designee shall evaluate the appropriate placement for the defendant between a State Department of State Hospitals facility or the community-based residential treatment system based upon guidelines provided by the State Department of State Hospitals.

(ii) Commencing on July 1, 2023, a defendant shall first be considered for placement in an outpatient treatment program, a community treatment program, or a diversion program, if any such program is available, unless a court, based upon the recommendation of the community program director or their designee, finds that either the clinical needs of the defendant or the risk to community safety, warrant placement in a State Department of State Hospitals facility.

(B) The court shall hear and determine whether the defendant lacks capacity to make decisions regarding the administration of antipsychotic medication. The court shall consider opinions in the reports prepared pursuant to subdivision (a) of Section 1369, as applicable to the issue of whether the defendant lacks capacity to make decisions regarding the administration of antipsychotic medication, and shall proceed as follows:

(i) The court shall hear and determine whether any of the following is true:

(I) Based upon the opinion of the psychiatrist or licensed psychologist offered to the court pursuant to subparagraph (A) of paragraph (2) of subdivision (a) of Section 1369, the defendant lacks capacity to make decisions regarding antipsychotic medication, the defendant's mental disorder requires medical treatment with antipsychotic medication, and, if the defendant's mental disorder is not treated with antipsychotic medication, it is probable that serious harm to the physical or mental health of the defendant will result. Probability of serious harm to the physical or mental health of the defendant requires evidence that the defendant is presently suffering adverse effects to their physical or mental health, or the defendant has previously suffered these effects as a result of a mental disorder and their condition is substantially deteriorating. The fact that a defendant has a diagnosis of a mental disorder does not alone establish probability of serious harm to the physical or mental health of the defendant.

(II) Based upon the opinion of the psychiatrist or licensed psychologist offered to the court pursuant to subparagraph (A) of paragraph (2) of subdivision (a) of Section 1369, the defendant is a danger to others, in that the defendant has inflicted, attempted to inflict, or made a serious threat of inflicting substantial physical harm on another while in custody, or the defendant had inflicted, attempted to inflict, or made a serious threat of inflicting substantial physical harm on another that resulted in the defendant being taken into custody, and the defendant presents, as a result of mental disorder or mental defect, a demonstrated danger of inflicting substantial physical harm on others. Demonstrated danger may be based on an assessment of the defendant's present mental condition, including a consideration of past behavior of the defendant within six years prior to the time the defendant last attempted to inflict, inflicted, or threatened to inflict substantial physical harm on another, and other relevant evidence.

(III) The people have charged the defendant with a serious crime against the person or property, and based upon the opinion of the psychiatrist offered to the court pursuant to subparagraph (C) of paragraph (2) of subdivision (a) of Section 1369, the involuntary administration of antipsychotic medication is substantially likely to render the defendant competent to stand trial, the medication is unlikely to have side effects that interfere with the defendant's ability to understand the nature of the criminal proceedings or to assist counsel in the conduct of a defense in a reasonable manner, less intrusive treatments are unlikely to have substantially the same results, and antipsychotic medication is medically necessary and appropriate in light of their medical condition.

(ii)

(I) If the court finds the conditions described in subclause (I) or (II) of clause (i) to be true, and if pursuant to the opinion offered to the court pursuant to paragraph (2) of subdivision (a) of Section 1369, a psychiatrist has opined that treatment with antipsychotic medications is appropriate for the defendant, the court shall issue an order authorizing the administration of antipsychotic medication as needed, including on an involuntary basis, to be administered under the direction and supervision of a licensed psychiatrist.

(II) If the court finds the conditions described in subclause (I) or (II) of clause (i) to be true, and if pursuant to the opinion offered to the court pursuant to paragraph (2) of subdivision (a) of Section 1369, a licensed psychologist has opined that treatment with antipsychotic medication may be appropriate for the defendant, the court shall issue an order authorizing treatment by a licensed psychiatrist on an involuntary basis. That treatment may include the administration of antipsychotic medication as needed, to be administered under the direction and supervision of a licensed psychiatrist.

(III) If the court finds the conditions described in subclause (III) of clause (i) to be true, and if pursuant to the opinion offered to the court pursuant to paragraph (2) of subdivision (a) of Section 1369, a psychiatrist has opined that it is appropriate to treat the defendant with antipsychotic medication, the court shall issue an order authorizing the administration of antipsychotic medication as needed, including on an involuntary basis, to be administered under the direction and supervision of a licensed psychiatrist.

(iii) An order authorizing involuntary administration of antipsychotic medication to the defendant when and as prescribed by the defendant's treating psychiatrist at any facility housing the defendant for purposes of this chapter, including a county jail, shall remain in effect when the defendant returns to county custody pursuant to subparagraph (A) of paragraph (1) of subdivision (b) or paragraph (1) of subdivision (c), or pursuant to subparagraph (C) of paragraph (3) of subdivision (a) of Section 1372, but shall be valid for no more than one year, pursuant to subparagraph (A) of paragraph (7). The court shall not order involuntary administration of psychotropic medication under subclause (III) of clause (i) unless the court has first found that the defendant does not meet the criteria for involuntary administration of psychotropic medication under subclause (I) of clause (i) and does not meet the criteria under subclause (II) of clause (i).

(iv) In all cases, the treating hospital, county jail, facility, or program may administer medically appropriate antipsychotic medication prescribed by a psychiatrist in an emergency as described in subdivision (m) of Section 5008 of the Welfare and Institutions Code.

(v) If the court has determined that the defendant has the capacity to make decisions regarding antipsychotic medication, and if the defendant, with advice of their counsel, consents, the court order of commitment shall include confirmation that antipsychotic medication may be given to the defendant as prescribed by a treating psychiatrist pursuant to the defendant's consent. The commitment order shall also indicate that, if the defendant withdraws consent for antipsychotic medication, after the treating psychiatrist complies with the provisions of subparagraph (C), the defendant shall be returned to court for a hearing in accordance with subparagraphs (C) and (D) regarding whether antipsychotic medication shall be administered involuntarily.

(vi) If the court has determined that the defendant has the capacity to make decisions regarding antipsychotic medication and if the defendant, with advice from their counsel, does not consent, the court order for commitment shall indicate that, after the treating psychiatrist complies with the provisions of subparagraph (C), the defendant shall be returned to court for a hearing in accordance with subparagraphs (C) and (D) regarding whether antipsychotic medication shall be administered involuntarily.

(vii) A report made pursuant to paragraph (1) of subdivision (b) shall include a description of antipsychotic medication administered to the defendant and its effects and side effects, including effects on the defendant's appearance or behavior that would affect the defendant's ability to understand the nature of the criminal proceedings or to assist counsel in the conduct of a defense in a reasonable manner. During the time the defendant is confined in a State Department of State Hospitals facility or other treatment facility or placed on outpatient status, either the defendant or the people may request that the court review any order made pursuant to this subdivision. The defendant, to the same extent enjoyed by other patients in the State Department of State Hospitals facility or other treatment facility, shall have the right to contact the patients' rights advocate regarding the defendant's rights under this section.

(C) If the defendant consented to antipsychotic medication as described in clause (iv) of subparagraph (B), but subsequently withdraws their consent, or, if involuntary antipsychotic medication was not ordered pursuant to clause (v) of subparagraph (B), and the treating psychiatrist determines that antipsychotic medication has become medically necessary and appropriate, the treating psychiatrist shall make efforts to obtain informed consent from the defendant for antipsychotic medication. If informed consent is not obtained from the defendant, and the treating psychiatrist is of the opinion that the defendant lacks capacity to make decisions regarding antipsychotic medication based on the conditions described in subclause (I) or (II) of clause (i) of subparagraph (B), the treating psychiatrist shall certify whether the lack of capacity and any applicable conditions described above exist. That certification shall contain an assessment of the current mental status of the defendant and the opinion of the treating psychiatrist that involuntary antipsychotic medication has become medically necessary and appropriate.

(D)

(i) If the treating psychiatrist certifies that antipsychotic medication has become medically necessary and appropriate pursuant to subparagraph (C), antipsychotic medication may be administered to the defendant for not more than 21 days, provided, however, that, within 72 hours of the certification, the defendant is provided a medication review hearing before an administrative law judge to be conducted at the facility where the defendant is receiving treatment. The treating psychiatrist shall present the case for the certification for involuntary treatment and the defendant shall be represented by an attorney or a patients' rights advocate. The attorney or patients' rights advocate shall be appointed to meet with the defendant no later than one day prior to the medication review hearing to review the defendant's rights at the medication review hearing, discuss the process, answer questions or concerns regarding involuntary medication or the hearing, assist the defendant in preparing for the hearing and advocating for the defendant's interests at the hearing, review the panel's final determination following the hearing, advise the defendant of their right to judicial review of the panel's decision, and provide the defendant with referral information for legal advice on the subject. The defendant shall also have the following rights with respect to the medication review hearing:

(I) To be given timely access to the defendant's records.

(II) To be present at the hearing, unless the defendant waives that right.

(III) To present evidence at the hearing.

(IV) To question persons presenting evidence supporting involuntary medication.

(V) To make reasonable requests for attendance of witnesses on the defendant's behalf.

(VI) To a hearing conducted in an impartial and informal manner.

(ii) If the administrative law judge determines that the defendant either meets the criteria specified in subclause (I) of clause (i) of subparagraph (B), or meets the criteria specified in subclause (II) of clause (i) of subparagraph (B), antipsychotic medication may continue to be administered to the defendant for the 21-day certification period. Concurrently with the treating psychiatrist's certification, the treating psychiatrist shall file a copy of the certification and a petition with the court for issuance of an order to administer antipsychotic medication beyond the 21-day certification period. For purposes of this subparagraph, the treating psychiatrist shall not be required to pay or deposit any fee for the filing of the petition or other document or paper related to the petition.

(iii) If the administrative law judge disagrees with the certification, medication may not be administered involuntarily until the court determines that antipsychotic medication should be administered pursuant to this section.

(iv) The court shall provide notice to the prosecuting attorney and to the attorney representing the defendant, and shall hold a hearing, no later than 18 days from the date of the certification, to determine whether antipsychotic medication should be ordered beyond the certification period.

(v) If, as a result of the hearing, the court determines that antipsychotic medication should be administered beyond the certification period, the court shall issue an order authorizing the administration of that medication.

(vi) The court shall render its decision on the petition and issue its order no later than three calendar days after the hearing and, in any event, no later than the expiration of the 21-day certification period.

(vii) If the administrative law judge upholds the certification pursuant to clause (ii), the court may, for a period not to exceed 14 days, extend the certification and continue the hearing pursuant to stipulation between the parties or upon a finding of good cause. In determining good cause, the court may review the petition filed with the court, the administrative law judge's order, and any additional testimony needed by the court to determine if it is appropriate to continue medication beyond the 21-day certification and for a period of up to 14 days.

(viii) The district attorney, county counsel, or representative of a facility where a defendant found incompetent to stand trial is committed may petition the court for an order to administer involuntary medication pursuant to the criteria set forth in subclauses (II) and (III) of clause (i) of subparagraph (B). The order is reviewable as provided in paragraph (7).

(3) When the court orders that the defendant be committed to a State Department of State Hospitals facility or other public or private treatment facility, the court shall provide copies of the following documents prior to the admission of the defendant to the State Department of State Hospitals or other treatment facility where the defendant is to be committed:

(A) The commitment order, which shall include a specification of the charges, an assessment of whether involuntary treatment with antipsychotic medications is warranted, and any orders by the court, pursuant to subparagraph (B) of paragraph (2), authorizing involuntary treatment with antipsychotic medications.

(B) A computation or statement setting forth the maximum term of commitment in accordance with subdivision (c).

(C)

(i) A computation or statement setting forth the amount of credit for time served, if any, to be deducted from the maximum term of commitment.

(ii) If a certificate of restoration of competency was filed with the court pursuant to Section 1372 and the court subsequently rejected the certification, a copy of the court order or minute order rejecting the certification shall be provided. The court order shall include a new computation or statement setting forth the amount of credit for time served, if any, to be deducted from the defendant's maximum term of commitment based on the court's rejection of the certification.

(D) State summary criminal history information.

(E) Jail classification records for the defendant's current incarceration.

(F) Arrest reports prepared by the police department or other law enforcement agency.

(G) Court-ordered psychiatric examination or evaluation reports.

(H) The community program director's placement recommendation report.

(I) Records of a finding of mental incompetence pursuant to this chapter arising out of a complaint charging a felony offense specified in Section 290 or a pending Section 1368 proceeding arising out of a charge of a Section 290 offense.

(J) Medical records, including jail mental health records.

(4) When the defendant is committed to a treatment facility pursuant to clause (i) of subparagraph (B) of paragraph (1) or the court makes the findings specified in clause (ii) or (iii) of subparagraph (B) of paragraph (1) to assign the defendant to a treatment facility other than a State Department of State Hospitals facility or other secure treatment facility, the court shall order that notice be given to the appropriate law enforcement agency or agencies having local jurisdiction at the placement facility of a finding of mental incompetence pursuant to this chapter arising out of a charge of a Section 290 offense.

(5) When directing that the defendant be confined in a State Department of State Hospitals facility pursuant to this subdivision, the court shall commit the defendant to the State Department of State Hospitals.

(6)

(A) If the defendant is committed or transferred to the State Department of State Hospitals pursuant to this section, the court may, upon receiving the written recommendation of the medical director of the State Department of State Hospitals facility and the community program director that the defendant be transferred to a public or private treatment facility approved by the community program director, order the defendant transferred to that facility. If the defendant is committed or transferred to a public or private treatment facility approved by the community program director, the court may, upon receiving the written recommendation of the community program director, transfer the defendant to the State Department of State Hospitals or to another public or private treatment facility approved by the community program director. In the event of dismissal of the criminal charges before the defendant recovers competence, the person shall be subject to the applicable provisions of the Lanterman-Petris-Short Act (Part 1 (commencing with Section 5000) of Division 5 of the Welfare and Institutions Code). If either the defendant or the prosecutor chooses to contest either kind of order of transfer, a petition may be filed in the court for a hearing, which shall be held if the court determines that sufficient grounds exist. At the hearing, the prosecuting attorney or the defendant may present evidence bearing on the order of transfer. The court shall use the same standards as are used in conducting probation revocation hearings pursuant to Section 1203.2. Prior to making an order for transfer under this section, the court shall notify the defendant, the attorney of record for the defendant, the prosecuting attorney, and the community program director or a designee.

(B) If the defendant is initially committed to a State Department of State Hospitals facility or secure treatment facility pursuant to clause (ii) or (iii) of subparagraph (B) of paragraph (1) and is subsequently transferred to any other facility, copies of the documents specified in paragraph (3) shall be electronically transferred or taken with the defendant to each subsequent facility to which the defendant is transferred. The transferring facility shall also notify the appropriate law enforcement agency or agencies having local jurisdiction at the site of the new facility that the defendant is a person subject to clause (ii) or (iii) of subparagraph (B) of paragraph (1).

(7)

(A) An order by the court authorizing involuntary medication of the defendant shall be valid for no more than one year. The court shall review the order at the time of the review of the initial report and the six-month progress reports pursuant to paragraph (1) of subdivision (b) to determine if the grounds for the authorization remain. In the review, the court shall consider the reports of the treating psychiatrist or psychiatrists and the defendant's patients' rights advocate or attorney. The court may require testimony from the treating psychiatrist and the patients' rights advocate or attorney, if necessary. The court may continue the order authorizing involuntary medication for up to another six months, or vacate the order, or make any other appropriate order.

(B) Within 60 days before the expiration of the one-year involuntary medication order, the district attorney, county counsel, or representative of any facility where a defendant found incompetent to stand trial is committed may petition the committing court for a renewal, subject to the same conditions and requirements as in subparagraph (A). The petition shall include the basis for involuntary medication set forth in clause (i) of subparagraph (B) of paragraph (2). Notice of the petition shall be provided to the defendant, the defendant's attorney, and the district attorney. The court shall hear and determine whether the defendant continues to meet the criteria set forth in clause (i) of subparagraph (B) of paragraph (2). The hearing on a petition to renew an order for involuntary medication shall be conducted prior to the expiration of the current order.

(8) For purposes of subparagraph (D) of paragraph (2) and paragraph (7), if the treating psychiatrist determines that there is a need, based on preserving their rapport with the defendant or preventing harm, the treating psychiatrist may request that the facility medical director designate another psychiatrist to act in the place of the treating psychiatrist. If the medical director of the facility designates another psychiatrist to act pursuant to this paragraph, the treating psychiatrist shall brief the acting psychiatrist of the relevant facts of the case and the acting psychiatrist shall examine the defendant prior to the hearing.

(b)

(1) Within 90 days after a commitment made pursuant to subdivision (a), the medical director of the State Department of State Hospitals facility or other treatment facility to which the defendant is confined shall make a written report to the court and the community program director for the county or region of commitment, or a designee, concerning the defendant's progress toward recovery of mental competence and whether the administration of antipsychotic medication remains necessary. If the defendant is in county custody, the county jail shall provide access to the defendant for purposes of the State Department of State Hospitals conducting an evaluation of the defendant pursuant to Section 4335.2 of the Welfare and Institutions Code. Based upon this evaluation, the State Department of State Hospitals may make a written report to the court within 90 days of a commitment made pursuant to subdivision (a) concerning the defendant's progress toward recovery of mental incompetence and whether the administration of antipsychotic medication is necessary. If the defendant remains in county custody after the initial 90-day report, the State Department of State Hospitals may conduct an evaluation of the defendant pursuant to Section 4335.2 of the Welfare and Institutions Code and make a written report to the court concerning the defendant's progress toward recovery of mental incompetence and whether the administration of antipsychotic medication is necessary.

If the defendant is on outpatient status, the outpatient treatment staff shall make a written report to the community program director concerning the defendant's progress toward recovery of mental competence. Within 90 days of placement on outpatient status, the community program director shall report to the court on this matter. If the defendant has not recovered mental competence, but the report discloses a substantial likelihood that the defendant will regain mental competence in the foreseeable future, the defendant shall remain in the State Department of State Hospitals facility or other treatment facility or on outpatient status. Thereafter, at six-month intervals or until the defendant becomes mentally competent, if the defendant is confined in a treatment facility, the medical director of the State Department of State Hospitals facility or person in charge of the facility shall report, in writing, to the court and the community program director or a designee regarding the defendant's progress toward recovery of mental competence and whether the administration of antipsychotic medication remains necessary. If the defendant is on outpatient status, after the initial 90-day report, the outpatient treatment staff shall report to the community program director on the defendant's progress toward recovery, and the community program director shall report to the court on this matter at six-month intervals. A copy of these reports shall be provided to the prosecutor and defense counsel by the court.

(A) If the report indicates that there is no substantial likelihood that the defendant will regain mental competence in the foreseeable future, custody of the defendant shall be transferred without delay to the committing county and shall remain with the county until further order of the court. The defendant shall be returned to the court for proceedings pursuant to paragraph (2) of subdivision (c) no later than 10 days following receipt of the report. The court shall not order the defendant returned to the custody of the State Department of State Hospitals under the same commitment. The court shall transmit a copy of its order to the community program director or a designee.

(B) If the report indicates that there is no substantial likelihood that the defendant will regain mental competence in the foreseeable future, the medical director of the State Department of State Hospitals facility or other treatment facility to which the defendant is confined shall do both of the following:

(i) Promptly notify and provide a copy of the report to the defense counsel and the district attorney.

(ii) Provide a separate notification, in compliance with applicable privacy laws, to the committing county's sheriff that immediate transportation will be needed for the defendant pursuant to subparagraph (A).

(C) If a county does not take custody of a defendant committed to the State Department of State Hospitals within 10 calendar days following notification made pursuant to clause (ii) of subparagraph (B), the county shall be charged the daily rate for a state hospital bed, as established by the State Department of State Hospitals.

(2) The reports made pursuant to paragraph (1) concerning the defendant's progress toward regaining competency shall also consider the issue of involuntary medication. Each report shall include, but not be limited to, all of the following:

(A) Whether or not the defendant has the capacity to make decisions concerning antipsychotic medication.

(B) If the defendant lacks capacity to make decisions concerning antipsychotic medication, whether the defendant risks serious harm to their physical or mental health if not treated with antipsychotic medication.

(C) Whether or not the defendant presents a danger to others if the defendant is not treated with antipsychotic medication.

(D) Whether the defendant has a mental disorder for which medications are the only effective treatment.

(E) Whether there are any side effects from the medication currently being experienced by the defendant that would interfere with the defendant's ability to collaborate with counsel.

(F) Whether there are any effective alternatives to medication.

(G) How quickly the medication is likely to bring the defendant to competency.

(H) Whether the treatment plan includes methods other than medication to restore the defendant to competency.

(I) A statement, if applicable, that no medication is likely to restore the defendant to competency.

(3) After reviewing the reports, the court shall determine if grounds for the involuntary administration of antipsychotic medication exist, whether or not an order was issued at the time of commitment, and shall do one of the following:

(A) If the original grounds for involuntary medication still exist, any order authorizing the treating facility to involuntarily administer antipsychotic medication to the defendant shall remain in effect.

(B) If the original grounds for involuntary medication no longer exist, and there is no other basis for involuntary administration of antipsychotic medication, any order for the involuntary administration of antipsychotic medication shall be vacated.

(C) If the original grounds for involuntary medication no longer exist, and the report states that there is another basis for involuntary administration of antipsychotic medication, the court shall determine whether to vacate the order or issue a new order for the involuntary administration of antipsychotic medication. The court shall consider the opinions in reports submitted pursuant to paragraph (1) of subdivision (b), including any opinions rendered pursuant to Section 4335.2 of the Welfare and Institutions Code. The court may, upon a showing of good cause, set a hearing within 21 days to determine whether the order for the involuntary administration of antipsychotic medication shall be vacated or whether a new order for the involuntary administration of antipsychotic medication shall be issued. The hearing shall proceed as set forth in subparagraph (B) of paragraph (2) of subdivision (a). The court shall require witness testimony to occur remotely, including clinical testimony pursuant to subdivision (d) of Section 4335.2 of the Welfare and Institutions Code. In-person witness testimony shall only be allowed upon a court's finding of good cause.

(D) If the report states a basis for involuntary administration of antipsychotic medication and the court did not issue such order at the time of commitment, the court shall determine whether to issue an order for the involuntary administration of antipsychotic medication. The court shall consider the opinions in reports submitted pursuant to paragraph (1) of subdivision (b), including any opinions rendered pursuant to Section 4335.2 of the Welfare and Institutions Code. The court may, upon a finding of good cause, set a hearing within 21 days to determine whether an order for the involuntary administration of antipsychotic medication shall be issued. The hearing shall proceed as set forth in subparagraph (B) of paragraph (2) of subdivision (a). The court shall require witness testimony to occur remotely, including clinical testimony pursuant to subdivision (d) of Section 4335.2 of the Welfare and Institutions Code. In-person witness testimony shall only be allowed upon a court's finding of good cause.

(4) If it is determined by the court that treatment for the defendant's mental impairment is not being conducted, the defendant shall be returned to the committing court, and, if the defendant is not in county custody, returned to the custody of the county. The court shall transmit a copy of its order to the community program director or a designee.

(5) At each review by the court specified in this subdivision, the court shall determine if the security level of housing and treatment is appropriate and may make an order in accordance with its determination. If the court determines that the defendant shall continue to be treated in the State Department of State Hospitals facility or on an outpatient basis, the court shall determine issues concerning administration of antipsychotic medication, as set forth in subparagraph (B) of paragraph (2) of subdivision (a).

(c)

(1) At the end of two years from the date of commitment or a period of commitment equal to the maximum term of imprisonment provided by law for the most serious offense charged in the information, indictment, or complaint, or the maximum term of imprisonment provided by law for a violation of probation or mandatory supervision, whichever is shorter, but no later than 90 days prior to the expiration of the defendant's term of commitment, a defendant who has not recovered mental competence shall be returned

to the committing court, and custody of the defendant shall be transferred without delay to the committing county and shall remain with the county until further order of the court. The court shall not order the defendant returned to the custody of the State Department of State Hospitals under the same commitment. The court shall notify the community program director or a designee of the return and of any resulting court orders.

(2)

(A) The medical director of the State Department of State Hospitals facility or other treatment facility to which the defendant is confined shall provide notification, in compliance with applicable privacy laws, to the committing county's sheriff that immediate transportation will be needed for the defendant pursuant to paragraph (1).

(B) If a county does not take custody of a defendant committed to the State Department of State Hospitals within 10 calendar days following notification pursuant to subparagraph (A), the county shall be charged the daily rate for a state hospital bed, as established by the State Department of State Hospitals.

(3) Whenever a defendant is returned to the court pursuant to paragraph (1) or (4) of subdivision (b) or paragraph (1) of this subdivision and it appears to the court that the defendant is gravely disabled, as defined in subparagraph (A) or (B) of paragraph (1) of subdivision (h) of Section 5008 of the Welfare and Institutions Code, the court shall order the conservatorship investigator of the county of commitment of the defendant to initiate conservatorship proceedings for the defendant pursuant to Chapter 3 (commencing with Section 5350) of Part 1 of Division 5 of the Welfare and Institutions Code. Hearings required in the conservatorship proceedings shall be held in the superior court in the county that ordered the commitment. The court shall transmit a copy of the order directing initiation of conservatorship proceedings to the community program director or a designee, the sheriff and the district attorney of the county in which criminal charges are pending, and the defendant's counsel of record. The court shall notify the community program director or a designee, the sheriff and district attorney of the county in which criminal charges are pending, and the defendant's counsel of record of the outcome of the conservatorship proceedings.

(4) If a change in placement is proposed for a defendant who is committed pursuant to subparagraph (A) or (B) of paragraph (1) of subdivision (h) of Section 5008 of the Welfare and Institutions Code, the court shall provide notice and an opportunity to be heard with respect to the proposed placement of the defendant to the sheriff and the district attorney of the county in which the criminal charges or revocation proceedings are pending.

(5) If the defendant is confined in a treatment facility, a copy of any report to the committing court regarding the defendant's progress toward recovery of mental competence shall be provided by the committing court to the prosecutor and to the defense counsel.

(d) With the exception of proceedings alleging a violation of mandatory supervision, the criminal action remains subject to dismissal pursuant to Section 1385. If the criminal action is dismissed, the court shall transmit a copy of the order of dismissal to the community program director or a designee. In a proceeding alleging a violation of mandatory supervision, if the person is not placed under a conservatorship as described in paragraph (3) of subdivision (c), or if a conservatorship is terminated, the court shall reinstate mandatory supervision and may modify the terms and conditions of supervision to include appropriate mental health treatment or refer the matter to a local mental health court, reentry court, or other collaborative justice court available for improving the mental health of the defendant.

(e) If the criminal action against the defendant is dismissed, the defendant shall be released from commitment ordered under this section, but without prejudice to the initiation of proceedings that may be appropriate under the Lanterman-Petris-Short Act (Part 1 (commencing with Section 5000) of Division 5 of the Welfare and Institutions Code).

(f) As used in this chapter, "community program director" means the person, agency, or entity designated by the State Department of State Hospitals pursuant to Section 1605 of this code and Section 4360 of the Welfare and Institutions Code.

(g) For the purpose of this section, "secure treatment facility" does not include, except for State Department of State Hospitals facilities, state developmental centers, and correctional treatment facilities, any facility licensed pursuant to Chapter 2 (commencing with Section 1250) of, Chapter 3 (commencing with Section 1500) of, or Chapter 3.2 (commencing with Section 1569) of, Division 2 of the Health and Safety Code, or any community board and care facility.

(h) This section does not preclude a defendant from filing a petition for habeas corpus to challenge the continuing validity of an order authorizing a treatment facility or outpatient program to involuntarily administer antipsychotic medication to a person being treated as incompetent to stand trial.

Amended by Stats 2023 ch 311 (SB 883),s 9, eff. 1/1/2024(not implemented per sec. 30).
Amended by Stats 2023 ch 42 (AB 118),s 57, eff. 7/10/2023.
Amended by Stats 2022 ch 735 (SB 1223),s 2, eff. 1/1/2023.
Amended by Stats 2022 ch 738 (AB 204),s 11, eff. 9/29/2022.
Amended by Stats 2022 ch 197 (SB 1493),s 26, eff. 1/1/2023. Not implemented per s 40.
Amended by Stats 2022 ch 47 (SB 184),s 43, eff. 6/30/2022.
Amended by Stats 2021 ch 143 (AB 133),s 343, eff. 7/27/2021.
Amended by Stats 2018 ch 1008 (SB 1187),s 2, eff. 1/1/2019.
Amended by Stats 2018 ch 34 (AB 1810),s 25, eff. 6/27/2018.
Amended by Stats 2017 ch 246 (SB 684),s 2, eff. 1/1/2018.
Amended by Stats 2017 ch 17 (AB 103),s 30, eff. 6/27/2017.
Amended by Stats 2015 ch 260 (SB 453),s 1, eff. 1/1/2016.
Amended by Stats 2015 ch 26 (SB 85),s 30, eff. 6/24/2015.
Amended by Stats 2014 ch 759 (SB 1412),s 7.3, eff. 1/1/2015.
Amended by Stats 2014 ch 742 (AB 2625),s 1, eff. 1/1/2015.
Amended by Stats 2014 ch 733 (AB 2186),s 1, eff. 1/1/2015.
Amended by Stats 2014 ch 26 (AB 1468),s 25, eff. 6/20/2014.
Amended by Stats 2012 ch 162 (SB 1171),s 128, eff. 1/1/2013.

Added by Stats 2012 ch 24 (AB 1470),s 27, eff. 6/27/2012.
Added by Stats 2011 ch 654 (AB 366),s 2, eff. 1/1/2012.

Section 1370.01 - Resumption of criminal process or order directing confinement in treatment facility or placement on outpatient status

(a) If the defendant is found mentally competent, the criminal process shall resume, and the trial on the offense charged or hearing on the alleged violation shall proceed.

(b) If the defendant is found mentally incompetent, the trial, judgment, or hearing on the alleged violation shall be suspended and the court may do either of the following:

(1)

(A) Conduct a hearing, pursuant to Chapter 2.8A (commencing with Section 1001.35) of Title 6, and, if the court deems the defendant eligible, grant diversion pursuant to Section 1001.36 for a period not to exceed one year from the date the individual is accepted into diversion or the maximum term of imprisonment provided by law for the most serious offense charged in the misdemeanor complaint, whichever is shorter.

(B) If the court opts to conduct a hearing pursuant to this paragraph, the hearing shall be held no later than 30 days after the finding of incompetence. If the hearing is delayed beyond 30 days, the court shall order the defendant to be released on their own recognizance pending the hearing.

(C) If the defendant performs satisfactorily on diversion pursuant to this section, at the end of the period of diversion, the court shall dismiss the criminal charges that were the subject of the criminal proceedings at the time of the initial diversion.

(D) If the court finds the defendant ineligible for diversion based on the circumstances set forth in subdivision (b), (c), (d), or (g) of Section 1001.36, the court may, after notice to the defendant, defense counsel, and the prosecution, hold a hearing to determine whether to do any of the following:

(i) Order modification of the treatment plan in accordance with a recommendation from the treatment provider.

(ii) Refer the defendant to assisted outpatient treatment pursuant to Section 5346 of the Welfare and Institutions Code. A referral to assisted outpatient treatment may only occur in a county where services are available pursuant to Section 5348 of the Welfare and Institutions Code, and the agency agrees to accept responsibility for treatment of the defendant. A hearing to determine eligibility for assisted outpatient treatment shall be held within 45 days after the date of the referral. If the hearing is delayed beyond 45 days, the court shall order the defendant, if confined in county jail, to be released on their own recognizance pending that hearing. If the defendant is accepted into assisted outpatient treatment, the charges shall be dismissed pursuant to Section 1385.

(iii) Refer the defendant to the county conservatorship investigator in the county of commitment for possible conservatorship proceedings for the defendant pursuant to Chapter 3 (commencing with Section 5350) of Part 1 of Division 5 of the Welfare and Institutions Code. A defendant shall only be referred to the conservatorship investigator if, based on the opinion of a qualified mental health expert, the defendant appears to be gravely disabled, as defined in subparagraph (A) of paragraph (1) of subdivision (h) of Section 5008 of the Welfare and Institution Code. Any hearings required in the conservatorship proceedings shall be held in the superior court in the county of commitment. The court shall transmit a copy of the order directing initiation of conservatorship proceedings to the county mental health director or the director's designee and shall notify the county mental health director or their designee of the outcome of the proceedings. Before establishing a conservatorship, the public guardian shall investigate all available alternatives to conservatorship pursuant to Section 5354 of the Welfare and Institutions Code. If a petition is not filed within 60 days of the referral, the court shall order the defendant, if confined in county jail, to be released on their own recognizance pending conservatorship proceedings. If the outcome of the conservatorship proceedings results in the establishment of conservatorship, the charges shall be dismissed pursuant to Section 1385.

(iv) Refer the defendant to the CARE program pursuant to Section 5978 of the Welfare and Institutions Code. A hearing to determine eligibility for CARE shall be held within 14 court days after the date on which the petition for the referral is filed. If the hearing is delayed beyond 14 court days, the court shall order the defendant, if confined in county jail, to be released on their own recognizance pending that hearing. If the defendant is accepted into CARE, the charges shall be dismissed pursuant to Section 1385.

(2) Dismiss the charges pursuant to Section 1385. If the criminal action is dismissed, the court shall transmit a copy of the order of dismissal to the county behavioral health director or the director's designee.

(c) If the defendant is found mentally incompetent and is on a grant of probation for a misdemeanor offense, the court shall dismiss the pending revocation matter and may return the defendant to supervision. If the revocation matter is dismissed pursuant to this subdivision, the court may modify the terms and conditions of supervision to include appropriate mental health treatment.

(d) It is the intent of the Legislature that a defendant subject to the terms of this section receive mental health treatment in a treatment facility and not a jail. A term of four days will be deemed to have been served for every two days spent in actual custody against the maximum term of diversion. A defendant not in actual custody shall otherwise receive day for day credit against the term of diversion from the date the defendant is accepted into diversion. "Actual custody" has the same meaning as in Section 4019.

(e) This section shall apply only as provided in subdivision (b) of Section 1367.

Amended by Stats 2023 ch 283 (SB 35),s 1, eff. 1/1/2024.
Amended by Stats 2022 ch 735 (SB 1223),s 3.5, eff. 1/1/2023.
Amended by Stats 2022 ch 319 (SB 1338),s 4, eff. 1/1/2023.
Added by Stats 2021 ch 599 (SB 317),s 2, eff. 1/1/2022.
Repealed by Stats 2021 ch 599 (SB 317),s 1, eff. 1/1/2022.
Amended by Stats 2021 ch 143 (AB 133),s 344, eff. 7/27/2021.
Amended by Stats 2018 ch 34 (AB 1810),s 26, eff. 6/27/2018.
Amended by Stats 2014 ch 759 (SB 1412),s 8, eff. 1/1/2015.
Amended by Stats 2012 ch 440 (AB 1488),s 35, eff. 9/22/2012.
Amended by Stats 2004 ch 486 (SB 1794),s 3, eff. 1/1/2005.

Section 1370.015 - Eligibility for compassionate release

A person committed to the care of the State Department of State Hospitals because he or she is incompetent to stand trial or to be adjudged to punishment is eligible for compassionate release pursuant to Section 4146 of the Welfare and Institutions Code. In any case in which the criteria for compassionate release apply, the State Department of State Hospitals shall follow the procedures and standards in Section 4146 of the Welfare and Institutions Code to determine if the department should recommend to the court that the person's commitment for treatment and the underlying criminal charges be suspended for compassionate release.

Added by Stats 2016 ch 715 (SB 955),s 2, eff. 1/1/2017.

Section 1370.02 - Finding of competence or incompetence; effect on revocation proceedings

(a) If the defendant is found mentally competent during a postrelease community supervision or parole revocation hearing, the revocation proceedings shall resume. The formal hearing on the revocation shall occur within a reasonable time after resumption of the proceedings, but in no event may the defendant be detained in custody for over 180 days from the date of arrest.

(b) If the defendant is found mentally incompetent, the court shall dismiss the pending revocation matter and return the defendant to supervision. If the revocation matter is dismissed pursuant to this subdivision, the court may, using the least restrictive option to meet the mental health needs of the defendant, also do any of the following:

(1) Modify the terms and conditions of supervision to include appropriate mental health treatment.

(2) Refer the matter to any local mental health court, reentry court, or other collaborative justice court available for improving the mental health of the defendant.

(3) Refer the matter to the public guardian of the county of commitment to initiate conservatorship proceedings pursuant to Sections 5352 and 5352.5 of the Welfare and Institutions Code. The public guardian shall investigate all available alternatives to conservatorship pursuant to Section 5354 of the Welfare and Institutions Code. The court shall order the matter to the public guardian pursuant to this paragraph only if there are no other reasonable alternatives to the establishment of a conservatorship to meet the mental health needs of the defendant.

(c)

(1) Notwithstanding any other law, if a person subject to parole pursuant to Section 3000.1 or paragraph (4) of subdivision (b) of Section 3000 is found mentally incompetent, the court shall order the parolee to undergo treatment pursuant to Section 1370 for restoring the person to competency, except that if the parolee is not restored to competency within the maximum period of confinement and the court dismisses the revocation, the court shall return the parolee to parole supervision.

(2) If the parolee is returned to parole supervision, the court may, using the least restrictive option to meet the mental health needs of the parolee, do any of the following:

(A) Modify the terms and conditions of parole to include appropriate mental health treatment.

(B) Refer the matter to any local mental health court, reentry court, or other collaborative justice court available for improving the mental health of the parolee.

(C) Refer the matter to the public guardian of the county of commitment to initiate conservatorship proceedings pursuant to Sections 5352 and 5352.5 of the Welfare and Institutions Code. The public guardian shall investigate all available alternatives to conservatorship pursuant to Section 5354 of the Welfare and Institutions Code. The court shall order the matter to the public guardian pursuant to this subparagraph only if there are no other reasonable alternatives to the establishment of a conservatorship to meet the mental health needs of the parolee.

(d) If a conservatorship is established for a defendant or parolee pursuant to subdivision (b) or (c), the county or the Department of Corrections and Rehabilitation shall not compassionately release the defendant or parolee or otherwise cause the termination of his or her supervision or parole based on the establishment of that conservatorship.

Added by Stats 2014 ch 759 (SB 1412),s 9, eff. 1/1/2015.

Section 1370.1 - Resumption of criminal process or order directing confinement in treatment facility or placement on outpatient status

(a)

(1)

(A) If the defendant is found mentally competent, the criminal process shall resume, the trial on the offense charged or hearing on the alleged violation shall proceed, and judgment may be pronounced.

(B) If the defendant is found mentally incompetent and has been determined by a regional center to have a developmental disability, the trial or judgment shall be suspended until the defendant becomes mentally competent.

(i) Except as provided in clause (ii) or (iii), the court shall consider a recommendation for placement. The recommendation shall be made to the court by the director of a regional center or the director's designee. In the meantime, the court shall order that the mentally incompetent defendant be delivered by the sheriff or other person designated by the court to a state hospital, developmental center, or any other available residential facility approved by the director of a regional center established under Division 4.5 (commencing with Section 4500) of the Welfare and Institutions Code as will promote the defendant's speedy attainment of mental competence, or be placed on outpatient status pursuant to the provisions of Section 1370.4 and Title 15 (commencing with Section 1600).

(ii) When the action against a defendant who has been found mentally incompetent is on a complaint charging a felony offense specified in Section 290, the prosecutor shall determine whether the defendant previously has been found mentally incompetent to stand trial pursuant to this chapter on a charge of a Section 290 offense, or whether the defendant is currently the subject of a pending Section 1368 proceeding arising out of a charge of an offense specified in Section 290. If either determination is made, the prosecutor shall so notify the court and defendant in writing. After this notification, and opportunity for hearing, the court shall order that the defendant be delivered by the sheriff to a state hospital or other secure treatment facility for the care and treatment of persons with developmental disabilities unless the court makes specific findings on the record that an alternative placement would provide more appropriate treatment for the defendant and would not pose a danger to the health and safety of others.

(iii) If the action against the defendant who has been found mentally incompetent is on a complaint charging a felony offense specified in Section 290 and the defendant has been denied bail pursuant to subdivision (b) of Section 12 of Article I of the

740

California Constitution because the court has found, based upon clear and convincing evidence, a substantial likelihood that the person's release would result in great bodily harm to others, the court shall order that the defendant be delivered by the sheriff to a state hospital for the care and treatment of persons with developmental disabilities unless the court makes specific findings on the record that an alternative placement would provide more appropriate treatment for the defendant and would not pose a danger to the health and safety of others.

(iv) The clerk of the court shall notify the Department of Justice, in writing, of a finding of mental incompetence with respect to a defendant who is subject to clause (ii) or (iii) for inclusion in his or her state summary criminal history information.

(C) Upon becoming competent, the court shall order that the defendant be returned to the committing court pursuant to the procedures set forth in paragraph (2) of subdivision (a) of Section 1372 or by another person designated by the court. The court shall further determine conditions under which the person may be absent from the placement for medical treatment, social visits, and other similar activities. Required levels of supervision and security for these activities shall be specified.

(D) The court shall transmit a copy of its order to the regional center director or the director's designee and to the Director of Developmental Services.

(E) A defendant charged with a violent felony may not be placed in a facility or delivered to a state hospital, developmental center, or residential facility pursuant to this subdivision unless the facility, state hospital, developmental center, or residential facility has a secured perimeter or a locked and controlled treatment facility, and the judge determines that the public safety will be protected.

(F) For purposes of this paragraph, "violent felony" means an offense specified in subdivision (c) of Section 667.5.

(G) A defendant charged with a violent felony may be placed on outpatient status, as specified in Section 1370.4 or 1600, only if the court finds that the placement will not pose a danger to the health or safety of others.

(H) As used in this section, "developmental disability" has the same meaning as in Section 4512 of the Welfare and Institutions Code.

(2) Prior to making the order directing that the defendant be confined in a state hospital, developmental center, or other residential facility, or be placed on outpatient status, the court shall order the regional center director or the director's designee to evaluate the defendant and to submit to the court, within 15 judicial days of the order, a written recommendation as to whether the defendant should be committed to a state hospital, a developmental center, or to any other available residential facility approved by the regional center director. A person shall not be admitted to a state hospital, developmental center, or other residential facility or accepted for outpatient status under Section 1370.4 without having been evaluated by the regional center director or the director's designee.

(3) If the court orders that the defendant be confined in a state hospital or other secure treatment facility pursuant to clause (ii) or (iii) of subparagraph (B) of paragraph (1), the court shall provide copies of the following documents, which shall be taken with the defendant to the state hospital or other secure treatment facility where the defendant is to be confined:

(A) State summary criminal history information.

(B) Any arrest reports prepared by the police department or other law enforcement agency.

(C) Records of a finding of mental incompetence pursuant to this chapter arising out of a complaint charging a felony offense specified in Section 290 or a pending Section 1368 proceeding arising out of a charge of an offense specified in Section 290.

(4) When the defendant is committed to a residential facility pursuant to clause (i) of subparagraph (B) of paragraph (1) or the court makes the findings specified in clause (ii) or (iii) of subparagraph (B) of paragraph (1) to assign the defendant to a facility other than a state hospital or other secure treatment facility, the court shall order that notice be given to the appropriate law enforcement agency or agencies having local jurisdiction at the site of the placement facility of a finding of mental incompetence pursuant to this chapter arising out of a charge of an offense specified in Section 290.

(5)

(A) If the defendant is committed or transferred to a state hospital or developmental center pursuant to this section, the court may, upon receiving the written recommendation of the executive director of the state hospital or developmental center and the regional center director that the defendant be transferred to a residential facility approved by the regional center director, order the defendant transferred to that facility. If the defendant is committed or transferred to a residential facility approved by the regional center director, the court may, upon receiving the written recommendation of the regional center director, transfer the defendant to a state hospital, a developmental center, or to another residential facility approved by the regional center director. In the event of dismissal of the criminal action or revocation proceedings before the defendant recovers competence, the person shall be subject to the applicable provisions of the Lanterman-Petris-Short Act (Part 1 (commencing with Section 5000) of Division 5 of the Welfare and Institutions Code) or to commitment or detention pursuant to a petition filed pursuant to Section 6502 of the Welfare and Institutions Code.

The defendant or prosecuting attorney may contest either kind of order of transfer by filing a petition with the court for a hearing, which shall be held if the court determines that sufficient grounds exist. At the hearing, the prosecuting attorney or the defendant may present evidence bearing on the order of transfer. The court shall use the same standards as used in conducting probation revocation hearings pursuant to Section 1203.2.

Prior to making an order for transfer under this section, the court shall notify the defendant, the attorney of record for the defendant, the prosecuting attorney, and the regional center director or designee.

(B) If the defendant is committed to a state hospital or secure treatment facility pursuant to clause (ii) or (iii) of subparagraph (B) of paragraph (1) and is subsequently transferred to another facility, copies of the documents specified in paragraph (3) shall be taken with the defendant to the new facility. The transferring facility shall also notify the appropriate law enforcement agency or agencies having local jurisdiction at the site of the new facility that the defendant is a person subject to clause (ii) or (iii) of subparagraph (B) of paragraph (1).

(b)

(1) Within 90 days of admission of a person committed pursuant to subdivision (a), the executive director or the director's designee of the state hospital, developmental center, or other facility to which the defendant is committed, shall make a written report to the committing court and the regional center director or a designee concerning the defendant's progress toward becoming mentally competent. If the defendant is placed on outpatient status, this report shall be made to the committing court by the regional center

director or the director's designee. If the defendant has not become mentally competent, but the report discloses a substantial likelihood the defendant will become mentally competent within the next 90 days, the court may order that the defendant remain in the state hospital, developmental center, or other facility or on outpatient status for that period of time. Within 150 days of an admission made pursuant to subdivision (a), or if the defendant becomes mentally competent, the executive director or the director's designee of the state hospital, developmental center, or other facility to which the defendant is committed shall report to the court and the regional center director or the director's designee regarding the defendant's progress toward becoming mentally competent. If the defendant is placed on outpatient status, the regional center director or the director's designee shall make that report to the committing court. The court shall provide copies of all reports under this section to the prosecutor and defense counsel. If the report indicates that there is no substantial likelihood that the defendant has become mentally competent, the committing court shall order the defendant to be returned to the court for proceedings pursuant to paragraph (2) of subdivision (c). The court shall transmit a copy of its order to the regional center director or the director's designee and to the executive director of the developmental center.

(2) If it is determined by the court that treatment for the defendant's mental impairment is not being conducted, the defendant shall be returned to the committing court. A copy of this order shall be sent to the regional center director or the director's designee and to the executive director of the developmental center.

(3) At each review by the court specified in this subdivision, the court shall determine if the security level of housing and treatment is appropriate and may make an order in accordance with its determination.

(c)

(1)

(A) At the end of two years from the date of commitment or a period of commitment equal to the maximum term of imprisonment provided by law for the most serious offense charged in the information, indictment, or misdemeanor complaint, or the maximum term of imprisonment provided by law for a violation of probation or mandatory supervision, whichever is shorter, a defendant who has not become mentally competent shall be returned to the committing court.

(B) The court shall notify the regional center director or the director's designee and the executive director of the developmental center of that return and of any resulting court orders.

(2)

(A) Except as provided in subparagraph (B), in the event of dismissal of the criminal charges before the defendant becomes mentally competent, the defendant shall be subject to the applicable provisions of the Lanterman-Petris-Short Act (Part 1 (commencing with Section 5000) of Division 5 of the Welfare and Institutions Code), or to commitment and detention pursuant to a petition filed pursuant to Section 6502 of the Welfare and Institutions Code. If it is found that the person is not subject to commitment or detention pursuant to the applicable provision of the Lanterman-Petris-Short Act (Part 1 (commencing with Section 5000) of Division 5 of the Welfare and Institutions Code) or to commitment or detention pursuant to a petition filed pursuant to Section 6502 of the Welfare and Institutions Code, the individual shall not be subject to further confinement pursuant to this article and the criminal action remains subject to dismissal pursuant to Section 1385. The court shall notify the regional center director and the executive director of the developmental center of any dismissal.

(B) In revocation proceedings alleging a violation of mandatory supervision in which the defendant remains incompetent upon return to court under subparagraph (A), the defendant shall be subject to the applicable provisions of the Lanterman-Petris-Short Act (Part 1 (commencing with Section 5000) of Division 5 of the Welfare and Institutions Code), or to commitment and detention pursuant to a petition filed pursuant to Section 6502 of the Welfare and Institutions Code. If it is found that the person is not subject to commitment or detention pursuant to the applicable provision of the Lanterman-Petris-Short Act (Part 1 (commencing with Section 5000) of Division 5 of the Welfare and Institutions Code) or to commitment or detention pursuant to a petition filed pursuant to Section 6502 of the Welfare and Institutions Code, the court shall reinstate mandatory supervision and modify the terms and conditions of supervision to include appropriate mental health treatment or refer the matter to a local mental health court, reentry court, or other collaborative justice court available for improving the mental health of the defendant. Actions alleging a violation of mandatory supervision are not subject to dismissal under Section 1385.

(d) Except as provided in subparagraph (B) of paragraph (2) of subdivision (c), the criminal action remains subject to dismissal pursuant to Section 1385. If at any time prior to the maximum period of time allowed for proceedings under this article, the regional center director concludes that the behavior of the defendant related to the defendant's criminal offense has been eliminated during time spent in court-ordered programs, the court may, upon recommendation of the regional center director, dismiss the criminal charges. The court shall transmit a copy of any order of dismissal to the regional center director and to the executive director of the developmental center.

(e) For the purpose of this section, "secure treatment facility" does not include, except for state mental hospitals, state developmental centers, and correctional treatment facilities, a facility licensed pursuant to Chapter 2 (commencing with Section 1250) of, Chapter 3 (commencing with Section 1500) of, or Chapter 3.2 (commencing with Section 1569) of, Division 2 of the Health and Safety Code, or a community board and care facility.

Amended by Stats 2018 ch 1008 (SB 1187),s 3, eff. 1/1/2019.
Amended by Stats 2014 ch 759 (SB 1412),s 10, eff. 1/1/2015.
Amended by Stats 2013 ch 76 (AB 383),s 156, eff. 1/1/2014.
Amended by Stats 2012 ch 457 (SB 1381),s 41, eff. 1/1/2013.
Amended by Stats 2012 ch 448 (AB 2370),s 41, eff. 1/1/2013.

Section 1370.2 - Dismissal of misdemeanor charge

If a person is adjudged mentally incompetent pursuant to the provisions of this chapter, the superior court may dismiss any misdemeanor charge pending against the mentally incompetent person. Ten days notice shall be given to the district attorney of any motion to dismiss pursuant to this section. The court shall transmit a copy of any order dismissing a misdemeanor charge pursuant to this section to the community program director, the county mental health director, or the regional center director and the Director of Developmental Services, as appropriate.

Amended by Stats. 1992, Ch. 722, Sec. 14. Effective September 15, 1992.

Section 1370.3 - Placement on outpatient status

A person committed to a state hospital or other treatment facility under the provisions of this chapter may be placed on outpatient status from such commitment as provided in Title 15 (commencing with Section 1600) of Part 2.

Repealed and added by Stats. 1980, Ch. 547, Sec. 12.

Section 1370.4 - Order to undergo outpatient treatment

If, in the evaluation ordered by the court under Section 1370.1, the regional center director, or a designee, is of the opinion that the defendant is not a danger to the health and safety of others while on outpatient treatment and will benefit from such treatment, and has obtained the agreement of the person in charge of a residential facility and of the defendant that the defendant will receive and submit to outpatient treatment and that the person in charge of the facility will designate a person to be the outpatient supervisor of the defendant, the court may order the defendant to undergo outpatient treatment. All of the provisions of Title 15 (commencing with Section 1600) of Part 2 shall apply where a defendant is placed on outpatient status under this section, except that the regional center director shall be substituted for the community program director, the Director of Developmental Services for the Director of State Hospitals, and a residential facility for a treatment facility for the purposes of this section.

Amended by Stats 2012 ch 440 (AB 1488),s 36, eff. 9/22/2012.

Section 1370.5 - Escape

(a) A person committed to a state hospital or other public or private mental health facility pursuant to the provisions of Section 1370, 1370.01, 1370.02, or 1370.1, who escapes from or who escapes while being conveyed to or from a state hospital or facility, is punishable by imprisonment in a county jail not to exceed one year or in the state prison for a determinate term of one year and one day. The term of imprisonment imposed pursuant to this section shall be served consecutively to any other sentence or commitment.

(b) The medical director or person in charge of a state hospital or other public or private mental health facility to which a person has been committed pursuant to the provisions of Section 1370, 1370.01, 1370.02, or 1370.1 shall promptly notify the chief of police of the city in which the hospital or facility is located, or the sheriff of the county if the hospital or facility is located in an unincorporated area, of the escape of the person, and shall request the assistance of the chief of police or sheriff in apprehending the person, and shall within 48 hours of the escape of the person orally notify the court that made the commitment, the prosecutor in the case, and the Department of Justice of the escape.

Amended by Stats 2014 ch 759 (SB 1412),s 11, eff. 1/1/2015.

Section 1370.6 - Restoration of competency treatment

(a)If a mentally incompetent defendant is admitted to a county jail treatment facility pursuant to Section 1370, the department shall provide restoration of competency treatment at the county jail treatment facility and shall provide payment to the county jail treatment facility for the reasonable costs of the bed during the restoration of competency treatment as well as for the reasonable costs of any necessary medical treatment not provided within the county jail treatment facility, unless otherwise agreed to by the department and the facility.

(1)If the county jail treatment facility is able to provide restoration of competency services, upon approval by the department and subject to funding appropriated in the annual Budget Act, the county jail treatment facility may provide those services and the State Department of State Hospitals may provide payment to the county jail treatment facility for the reasonable costs of the bed during the restoration of competency treatment as well as the reasonable costs of providing restoration of competency services and for any necessary medical treatment not provided within the county jail treatment facility, unless otherwise agreed to by the department and the facility.

(2)Transportation to a county jail treatment facility for admission and from the facility upon the filing of a certificate of restoration of competency, or for transfer of a person to another county jail treatment facility or to a state hospital, shall be provided by the committing county unless otherwise agreed to by the department and the facility.

(3)In the event the State Department of State Hospitals and a county jail treatment facility are determined to be comparatively at fault for any claim, action, loss, or damage which results from their respective obligations under such a contract, each shall indemnify the other to the extent of its comparative fault.

(b)If the community-based residential system is selected by the court pursuant to Section 1370, the State Department of State Hospitals shall provide reimbursement to the community-based residential treatment system for the cost of restoration of competency treatment as negotiated with the State Department of State Hospitals.

(c)The State Department of State Hospitals may provide payment to either a county jail treatment facility or a community-based residential treatment system directly through invoice, or through a contract, at the discretion of the department in accordance with the terms and conditions of the contract or agreement.

Amended by Stats 2022 ch 47 (SB 184),s 44, eff. 6/30/2022.

Amended by Stats 2017 ch 17 (AB 103),s 31, eff. 6/27/2017.

Added by Stats 2015 ch 26 (SB 85),s 31, eff. 6/24/2015.

Section 1371 - Exoneration of bail

The commitment of the defendant, as described in Section 1370, 1370.1, 1370.01, or 1370.02, exonerates his or her bail, or entitles a person, authorized to receive the property of the defendant, to a return of any money he or she may have deposited instead of bail, or gives, to the person or persons found by the court to have deposited any money instead of bail on behalf of the defendant, a right to the return of that money.

Amended by Stats 2014 ch 759 (SB 1412),s 12, eff. 1/1/2015.

Section 1372 - Restoration of mental competency

(a)

(1)If the medical director of a state hospital, a person designated by the State Department of State Hospitals at an entity contracted by the department to provide services to a defendant prior to placement in a treatment program or other facility to which the defendant is committed, or the community program director, county mental health director, or regional center director providing outpatient services, determines that the defendant has regained mental competence, the director or designee shall immediately certify that fact to the court by filing a certificate of restoration with the court by certified mail, return receipt requested, or by confidential electronic transmission. This shall include any certificate of restoration filed by the State Department of State Hospitals based on an evaluation conducted pursuant to Section 4335.2 of the Welfare and Institutions Code. For purposes of this section, the date of filing shall be the date on the return receipt.

(2)The court's order committing an individual to a State Department of State Hospitals facility or other treatment facility pursuant to Section 1370 shall include direction that the sheriff shall redeliver the patient to the court without any further order from the court upon receiving from the state hospital or treatment facility a copy of the certificate of restoration.

(3)The defendant shall be returned to the committing court in the following manner, except that a defendant in county custody that the State Department of State Hospitals has evaluated pursuant to Section 4335.2 of the Welfare and Institutions Code and filed a certificate of restoration with the court shall remain in county custody:

(A)A patient who remains confined in a state hospital or other treatment facility shall be redelivered to the sheriff of the county from which the patient was committed. The sheriff shall immediately return the person from the state hospital or other treatment facility to the court for further proceedings.

(B)The patient who is on outpatient status shall be returned by the sheriff to court through arrangements made by the outpatient treatment supervisor.

(C)In all cases, the patient shall be returned to the committing court no later than 10 days following the filing of a certificate of restoration. The state shall only pay for 10 hospital days for patients following the filing of a certificate of restoration of competency. The State Department of State Hospitals shall report to the fiscal and appropriate policy committees of the Legislature on an annual basis in February, on the number of days that exceed the 10-day limit prescribed in this subparagraph. This report shall include, but not be limited to, a data sheet that itemizes by county the number of days that exceed this 10-day limit during the preceding year.

(b)If the defendant becomes mentally competent after a conservatorship has been established pursuant to the applicable provisions of the Lanterman-Petris-Short Act, Part 1 (commencing with Section 5000) of Division 5 of the Welfare and Institutions Code, and Section 1370, the conservator shall certify that fact to the sheriff and district attorney of the county in which the defendant's case is pending, defendant's attorney of record, and the committing court.

(c)

(1) When a defendant is returned to court with a certification that competence has been regained, including a certification of restoration provided pursuant to Section 4335.2 of the Welfare and Institutions Code, the court shall notify either the community program director, the county mental health director, the State Department of State Hospitals, or the regional center director and the Director of Developmental Services, as appropriate, of the date of any hearing on the defendant's competence and whether or not the defendant was found by the court to have recovered competence.

(2)If the court rejects a certificate of restoration, the court shall base its rejection on a written report of an evaluation, conducted by a licensed psychologist or psychiatrist, that the defendant is not competent. The evaluation shall be conducted after the certificate of restoration is filed with the committing court and in compliance with Section 1369. A copy of the written report shall be provided to the department pursuant to paragraph (3) of subdivision (a) of Section 1370. The court shall also provide a copy of the court order or minute order rejecting the certification of restoration to the department, pursuant to clause (ii) of subparagraph (C) of paragraph (3) of subdivision (a) of Section 1370, including any minute orders continuing the hearing for the court's determination.

(d)If the committing court approves the certificate of restoration to competence as to a person in custody, the court shall notify the State Department of State Hospitals by providing the State Department of State Hospitals with a copy of the court order or minute order approving the certificate of restoration to competence. The court shall hold a hearing to determine whether the person is entitled to be admitted to bail or released on own recognizance status pending conclusion of the proceedings. If the superior court approves the certificate of restoration to competence regarding a person on outpatient status, unless it appears that the person has refused to come to court, that person shall remain released either on own recognizance status, or, in the case of a developmentally disabled person, either on the defendant's promise or on the promise of a responsible adult to secure the person's appearance in court for further proceedings. If the person has refused to come to court, the court shall set bail and may place the person in custody until bail is posted.

(e)A defendant subject to either subdivision (a) or (b) who is not admitted to bail or released under subdivision (d) may, at the discretion of the court, upon recommendation of the director of the facility where the defendant is receiving treatment, be returned to the hospital or facility of their original commitment or other appropriate secure facility approved by the community program director, the county mental health director, or the regional center director. The recommendation submitted to the court shall be based on the opinion that the person will need continued treatment in a hospital or treatment facility in order to maintain competence to stand trial or that placing the person in a jail environment would create a substantial risk that the person would again become incompetent to stand trial before criminal proceedings could be resumed.

(f)Notwithstanding subdivision (e), if a defendant is returned by the court to a hospital or other facility for the purpose of maintaining competency to stand trial and that defendant is already under civil commitment to that hospital or facility from another county pursuant to the Lanterman-Petris-Short Act (Part 1 (commencing with Section 5000) of Division 5 of the Welfare and Institutions Code) or as a developmentally disabled person committed pursuant to Article 2 (commencing with Section 6500) of Chapter 2 of Part 2 of Division 6 of the Welfare and Institutions Code, the costs of housing and treating the defendant in that facility following return pursuant to subdivision (e) shall be the responsibility of the original county of civil commitment.

Amended by Stats 2022 ch 47 (SB 184),s 45, eff. 6/30/2022.
Amended by Stats 2021 ch 143 (AB 133),s 345, eff. 7/27/2021.
Amended by Stats 2018 ch 34 (AB 1810),s 27, eff. 6/27/2018.
Amended by Stats 2017 ch 17 (AB 103),s 32, eff. 6/27/2017.
Amended by Stats 2012 ch 24 (AB 1470),s 28, eff. 6/27/2012.
Amended by Stats 2004 ch 405 (SB 1796), s 15, eff. 1/1/2005.
Amended by Stats 2004 ch 183 (AB 3082), s 271, eff. 1/1/2005.
Amended by Stats 2003 ch 356 (AB 941), s 1, eff. 1/1/2004.

Section 1373 - Expenses

The expense of sending the defendant to the state hospital or other facility, and of bringing him or her back, are chargeable to the county in which the indictment was found, information was filed, or revocation proceeding was held; but the county may recover the expense from the estate of the defendant, if he or she has any, or from a relative, bound to provide for and maintain him or her.
Amended by Stats 2014 ch 759 (SB 1412),s 13, eff. 1/1/2015.

Section 1373.5 - Interest

In every case where a claim is presented to the county for money due under the provisions of section 1373 of this code, interest shall be allowed from the date of rejection, if rejected and recovery is finally had thereon.
Added by Stats. 1939, Ch. 441.

Section 1374 - Recovery of competence by defendant on outpatient status

When a defendant who has been found incompetent is on outpatient status under Title 15 (commencing with Section 1600) of Part 2 and the outpatient treatment staff is of the opinion that the defendant has recovered competence, the supervisor shall communicate such opinion to the community program director. If the community program director concurs, that opinion shall be certified by such director to the committing court. The court shall calendar the case for further proceeding pursuant to Section 1372.
Amended by Stats. 1985, Ch. 1232, Sec. 9. Effective September 30, 1985.

Section 1375 - Processing and payment of claims

Claims by the state for all amounts due from any county by reason of the provisions of Section 1373 of this code shall be processed and paid by the county pursuant to the provisions of Chapter 4 (commencing with Section 29700) of Division 3 of Title 3 of the Government Code.
Amended by Stats. 1965, Ch. 263.

Section 1375.5 - Credit for time spent in treatment facility or county jail

(a) Time spent by a person in a treatment facility or county jail as a result of proceedings under this chapter shall be credited against the sentence, if any, imposed in the underlying criminal case or revocation matter giving rise to the competency proceedings.

(b) As used in this section, "time spent in a treatment facility" includes days a person is treated as an outpatient pursuant to Title 15 (commencing with Section 1600) of Part 2.

(c) A person subject to this chapter shall receive credits pursuant to Section 4019 for all time during which he or she is confined in a county jail and for which he or she is otherwise eligible.
Amended by Stats 2018 ch 1008 (SB 1187),s 4, eff. 1/1/2019.
Amended by Stats 2014 ch 759 (SB 1412),s 14, eff. 1/1/2015.

Section 1376 - Hearing to determine intellectual disability in case in which prosecution seeks death penalty

(a) As used in this section, the following definitions shall apply:

(1) "Intellectual disability" means the condition of significantly subaverage general intellectual functioning existing concurrently with deficits in adaptive behavior and manifested before the end of the developmental period, as defined by clinical standards.

(2) "Prima facie showing of intellectual disability" means that the defendant's allegation of intellectual disability is based on the type of evidence typically relied on by a qualified expert in diagnosing intellectual disability, as defined in current clinical standards, or when a qualified expert provides a declaration diagnosing the defendant as intellectually disabled.

(b)

(1) When the prosecution seeks the death penalty, the defendant may, at a reasonable time prior to the commencement of trial, apply for an order directing that a hearing to determine intellectual disability be conducted. Upon a prima facie showing that the defendant is a person with an intellectual disability, the court shall order a hearing to determine whether the defendant is a person with an intellectual disability. At the request of the defendant, the court shall conduct the hearing without a jury prior to the commencement of the trial. The defendant's request for a court hearing prior to trial shall constitute a waiver of a jury hearing on the issue of intellectual disability. If the defendant does not request a court hearing, the court shall order a jury hearing to determine if the defendant is a person with an intellectual disability. The jury hearing on intellectual disability shall occur at the conclusion of the phase of the trial in which the jury has found the defendant guilty with a finding that one or more of the special circumstances enumerated in Section 190.2 are true. Except as provided in paragraph (3), the same jury shall make a finding that the defendant is a person with an intellectual disability or that the defendant does not have an intellectual disability.

(2) For the purposes of the procedures set forth in this section, the court or jury shall decide only the question of the defendant's intellectual disability. The defendant shall present evidence in support of the claim that they are a person with an intellectual disability. The prosecution shall present its case regarding the issue of whether the defendant is a person with an intellectual disability. Each party may offer rebuttal evidence. The court, for good cause in furtherance of justice, may permit either party to reopen its case to present evidence in support of or opposition to the claim of intellectual disability. Nothing in this section shall prohibit the court from making orders reasonably necessary to ensure the production of evidence sufficient to determine whether or not the defendant is a person with an intellectual disability, including, but not limited to, the appointment of, and examination of the defendant by, qualified experts. A statement made by the defendant during an examination ordered by the court shall not be admissible in the trial on the defendant's guilt.

(3) At the close of evidence, the prosecution shall make its final argument, and the defendant shall conclude with their final argument. The burden of proof shall be on the defense to prove by a preponderance of the evidence that the defendant is a person with an intellectual disability. The jury shall return a verdict that either the defendant is a person with an intellectual disability or the defendant does not have an intellectual disability. The verdict of the jury shall be unanimous. When the jury is unable to reach a unanimous verdict that the defendant is a person with an intellectual disability, and does not reach a unanimous verdict that the defendant does not have an intellectual disability, the court shall dismiss the jury and order a new jury impaneled to try the issue of intellectual disability. The issue of guilt shall not be tried by the new jury.

(c) When the hearing is conducted before the court prior to the commencement of the trial, the following shall apply:

(1) If the court finds that the defendant is a person with an intellectual disability, the court shall preclude the death penalty and the criminal trial thereafter shall proceed as in any other case in which a sentence of death is not sought by the prosecution. If the defendant is found guilty of murder in the first degree, with a finding that one or more of the special circumstances enumerated in Section 190.2 are true, the court shall sentence the defendant to confinement in the state prison for life without the possibility of parole. The jury shall not be informed of the prior proceedings or the findings concerning the defendant's claim of intellectual disability.

(2) If the court finds that the defendant does not have an intellectual disability, the trial court shall proceed as in any other case in which a sentence of death is sought by the prosecution. The jury shall not be informed of the prior proceedings or the findings concerning the defendant's claim of intellectual disability.

(d) When the hearing is conducted before the jury after the defendant is found guilty with a finding that one or more of the special circumstances enumerated in Section 190.2 are true, the following shall apply:

(1) If the jury finds that the defendant is a person with an intellectual disability, the court shall preclude the death penalty and shall sentence the defendant to confinement in the state prison for life without the possibility of parole.

(2) If the jury finds that the defendant does not have an intellectual disability, the trial shall proceed as in any other case in which a sentence of death is sought by the prosecution.

(e) When the defendant has not requested a court hearing as provided in subdivision (b), and has entered a plea of not guilty by reason of insanity under Sections 190.4 and 1026, the hearing on intellectual disability shall occur at the conclusion of the sanity trial if the defendant is found sane.

(f) A person in custody pursuant to a judgment of death may apply for an order directing that a hearing to determine intellectual disability be conducted as part of a petition for a writ of habeas corpus. When the claim of intellectual disability is raised in a petition for habeas corpus and a petitioner makes a prima facie showing of intellectual disability, the reviewing court shall issue an order to show cause if the petitioner has met the prima facie standard. The petitioner bears the burden of proving by a preponderance of the evidence that the petitioner is a person with an intellectual disability. The state may present its case regarding the issue of whether the petitioner is a person with an intellectual disability. Each party may offer rebuttal evidence. During an evidentiary hearing under this subdivision, an expert may testify about the contents of out-of-court statements, including documentary evidence and statements from witnesses when those types of statements are accepted by the medical community as relevant to a diagnosis of intellectual disability if the expert relied upon these statements as the basis for their opinion.

(g) The results of a test measuring intellectual functioning shall not be changed or adjusted based on race, ethnicity, national origin, or socioeconomic status.

Amended by Stats 2020 ch 331 (AB 2512),s 2, eff. 1/1/2021.
Amended by Stats 2012 ch 457 (SB 1381),s 42, eff. 1/1/2013.
Amended by Stats 2012 ch 448 (AB 2370),s 42, eff. 1/1/2013.
Added by Stats 2003 ch 700 (SB 3), s 1, eff. 1/1/2004.

Chapter 7 - COMPROMISING CERTAIN PUBLIC OFFENSES BY LEAVE OF THE COURT

Section 1377 - Compromise misdemeanor offense

When the person injured by an act constituting a misdemeanor has a remedy by a civil action, the offense may be compromised, as provided in Section 1378, except when it is committed as follows:

(a) By or upon an officer of justice, while in the execution of the duties of his or her office.

(b) Riotously.

(c) With an intent to commit a felony.

(d) In violation of any court order as described in Section 273.6 or 273.65.

(e) By or upon any family or household member, or upon any person when the violation involves any person described in Section 6211 of the Family Code or subdivision (b) of Section 13700 of this code.

(f) Upon an elder, in violation of Section 368 of this code or Section 15656 of the Welfare and Institutions Code.

(g) Upon a child, as described in Section 647.6 or 11165.6.

Amended by Stats. 1997, Ch. 243, Sec. 1. Effective January 1, 1998.

Section 1378 - Order staying proceedings and discharging defendant

If the person injured appears before the court in which the action is pending at any time before trial, and acknowledges that he has received satisfaction for the injury, the court may, in its discretion, on payment of the costs incurred, order all proceedings to be stayed upon the prosecution, and the defendant to be discharged therefrom; but in such case the reasons for the order must be set forth therein, and entered on the minutes. The order is a bar to another prosecution for the same offense.

Amended by Stats. 1957, Ch. 102.

Section 1379 - Compromise of public offense prohibited

No public offense can be compromised, nor can any proceeding or prosecution for the punishment thereof upon a compromise be stayed, except as provided in this Chapter.

Enacted 1872.

Section 1380 - [Repealed]

Added by Stats 2008 ch 208 (AB 1767),s 1, eff. 1/1/2009.

Chapter 8 - DISMISSAL OF THE ACTION FOR WANT OF PROSECUTION OR OTHERWISE

Section 1381 - Action within 90 days required

Whenever a defendant has been convicted, in any court of this state, of the commission of a felony or misdemeanor and has been sentenced to and has entered upon a term of imprisonment in a state prison or has been sentenced to and has entered upon a term of imprisonment in a county jail for a period of more than 90 days or has been committed to and placed in a county jail for more than 90 days as a condition of probation or has been committed to and placed in an institution subject to the jurisdiction of the Department of the Youth Authority or whenever any person has been committed to the custody of the Director of Corrections pursuant to Chapter 1 (commencing with Section 3000) of Division 3 of the Welfare and Institutions Code and has entered upon his or her term of commitment, and at the time of the entry upon the term of imprisonment or commitment there is pending, in any court of this state, any other indictment, information, complaint, or any criminal proceeding wherein the defendant remains to be sentenced, the district attorney of the county in which the matters are pending shall bring the defendant to trial or for sentencing within 90 days after the person shall have delivered to said district attorney written notice of the place of his or her imprisonment or commitment and his or her desire to be brought to trial or for sentencing unless a continuance beyond the 90 days is requested or consented to by the person, in open court, and the request or consent entered upon the minutes of the court in which event the 90-day period shall commence to run anew from the date to which the consent or request continued the trial or sentencing. In the event that the defendant is not brought to trial or for sentencing within the 90 days the court in which the charge or sentencing is pending shall, on motion or suggestion of the district attorney, or of the defendant or person confined in the county jail or committed to the custody of the Director of Corrections or his or her counsel, or of the Department of Corrections, or of the Department of the Youth Authority, or on its own motion, dismiss the action. If a charge is filed against a person during the time the person is serving a sentence in any state prison or county jail of this state or while detained by the Director of Corrections pursuant to Chapter 1 (commencing with Section 3000) of Division 3 of the Welfare and Institutions Code or while detained in any institution subject to the jurisdiction of the Department of the Youth Authority it is hereby made mandatory upon the district attorney of the county in which the charge is filed to bring it to trial within 90 days after the person shall have delivered to said district attorney written notice of the place of his or her imprisonment or commitment and his or her desire to be brought to trial upon the charge, unless a continuance is requested or consented to by the person, in open court, and the request or consent entered upon the minutes of the court, in which event the 90-day period shall commence to run anew from the date to which the request or consent continued the trial. In the event the action is not brought to trial within the 90 days the court in which the action is pending shall, on motion or suggestion of the district attorney, or of the defendant or person committed to the custody of the Director of Corrections or to a county jail or his or her counsel, or of the Department of Corrections, or of the Department of the Youth Authority, or on its own motion, dismiss the charge. The sheriff, custodian, or jailer shall endorse upon the written notice of the defendant's desire to be brought to trial or for sentencing the cause of commitment, the date of commitment, and the date of release. Amended by Stats. 1987, Ch. 828, Sec. 91.

Section 1381.5 - Bringing of trial or for sentencing within 90 days from request or consent

Whenever a defendant has been convicted of a crime and has entered upon a term of imprisonment therefor in a federal correctional institution located in this state, and at the time of entry upon such term of imprisonment or at any time during such term of imprisonment there is pending in any court of this state any criminal indictment, information, complaint, or any criminal proceeding wherein the defendant remains to be sentenced the district attorney of the county in which such matters are pending, upon receiving from such defendant a request that he be brought to trial or for sentencing, shall promptly inquire of the warden or other head of the federal correctional institution in which such defendant is confined whether and when such defendant can be released for trial or for sentencing. If an assent from authorized federal authorities for release of the defendant for trial or sentencing is received by the district attorney he shall bring him to trial or sentencing within 90 days after receipt of such assent, unless the federal authorities specify a date of release after 90 days, in which event the district attorney shall bring the prisoner to trial or sentencing at such specified time, or unless the defendant requests, in open court, and receives, or, in open court, consents to, a continuance, in which event he may be brought to trial or sentencing within 90 days from such request or consent.

If a defendant is not brought to trial or for sentencing as provided by this section, the court in which the action is pending shall, on motion or suggestion of the district attorney, or representative of the United States, or the defendant or his counsel, dismiss the action. Amended by Stats. 1983, Ch. 793, Sec. 1.1.

Section 1382 - Dismissal of action

(a) The court, unless good cause to the contrary is shown, shall order the action to be dismissed in the following cases:

(1) When a person has been held to answer for a public offense and an information is not filed against that person within 15 days.

(2) In a felony case, when a defendant is not brought to trial within 60 days of the defendant's arraignment on an indictment or information, or reinstatement of criminal proceedings pursuant to Chapter 6 (commencing with Section 1367) of Title 10 of Part 2, or, in case the cause is to be tried again following a mistrial, an order granting a new trial from which an appeal is not taken, or an appeal from the superior court, within 60 days after the mistrial has been declared, after entry of the order granting the new trial, or after the filing of the remittitur in the trial court, or after the issuance of a writ or order which, in effect, grants a new trial, within 60 days after notice of the writ or order is filed in the trial court and served upon the prosecuting attorney, or within 90 days after notice of the writ or order is filed in the trial court and served upon the prosecuting attorney in any case where the district attorney chooses to resubmit the case for a preliminary examination after an appeal or the issuance of a writ reversing a judgment of conviction upon a plea of guilty prior to a preliminary hearing. However, an action shall not be dismissed under this paragraph if either of the following circumstances exists:

(A) The defendant enters a general waiver of the 60-day trial requirement. A general waiver of the 60-day trial requirement entitles the superior court to set or continue a trial date without the sanction of dismissal should the case fail to proceed on the date set for trial. If the defendant, after proper notice to all parties, later withdraws, in open court, his or her waiver in the superior court, the defendant shall be brought to trial within 60 days of the date of that withdrawal. Upon the withdrawal of a general time waiver in open court, a trial date shall be set and all parties shall be properly notified of that date. If a general time waiver is not expressly entered, subparagraph (B) shall apply.

(B) The defendant requests or consents to the setting of a trial date beyond the 60-day period. In the absence of an express general time waiver from the defendant, or upon the withdrawal of a general time waiver, the court shall set a trial date. Whenever a case is set for trial beyond the 60-day period by request or consent, expressed or implied, of the defendant without a general waiver, the defendant shall be brought to trial on the date set for trial or within 10 days thereafter. Whenever a case is set for trial after a defendant enters either a general waiver as to the 60-day trial requirement or requests or consents, expressed or implied, to the setting of a trial date beyond the 60-day period pursuant to this paragraph, the court may not grant a motion of the defendant to vacate the date set for trial and to set an earlier trial date unless all parties are properly noticed and the court finds good cause for granting that motion.

(3) Regardless of when the complaint is filed, when a defendant in a misdemeanor or infraction case is not brought to trial within 30 days after he or she is arraigned or enters his or her plea, whichever occurs later, if the defendant is in custody at the time of arraignment or plea, whichever occurs later, or in all other cases, within 45 days after the defendant's arraignment or entry of the plea, whichever occurs later, or in case the cause is to be tried again following a mistrial, an order granting a new trial from which no appeal is taken, or an appeal from a judgment in a misdemeanor or infraction case, within 30 days after the mistrial has been declared, after entry of the order granting the new trial, or after the remittitur is filed in the trial court, or within 30 days after the date of the reinstatement of criminal proceedings pursuant to Chapter 6 (commencing with Section 1367). However, an action shall not be dismissed under this subdivision if any of the following circumstances exists:

(A) The defendant enters a general waiver of the 30-day or 45-day trial requirement. A general waiver of the 30-day or 45-day trial requirement entitles the court to set or continue a trial date without the sanction of dismissal should the case fail to proceed on the date set for trial. If the defendant, after proper notice to all parties, later withdraws, in open court, his or her waiver in the superior court, the defendant shall be brought to trial within 30 days of the date of that withdrawal. Upon the withdrawal of a general time waiver in open court, a trial date shall be set and all parties shall be properly notified of that date. If a general time waiver is not expressly entered, subparagraph (B) shall apply.

(B) The defendant requests or consents to the setting of a trial date beyond the 30-day or 45-day period. In the absence of an express general time waiver from the defendant, or upon the withdrawal of a general time waiver the court shall set a trial date. Whenever a case is set for trial beyond the 30-day or 45-day period by request or consent, expressed or implied, of the defendant without a general waiver, the defendant shall be brought to trial on the date set for trial or within 10 days thereafter.

(C) The defendant in a misdemeanor case has been ordered to appear on a case set for hearing prior to trial, but the defendant fails to appear on that date and a bench warrant is issued, or the case is not tried on the date set for trial because of the defendant's neglect or failure to appear, in which case the defendant shall be deemed to have been arraigned within the meaning of this subdivision on the date of his or her subsequent arraignment on a bench warrant or his or her submission to the court.

(b) Whenever a defendant has been ordered to appear in superior court on a felony case set for trial or set for a hearing prior to trial after being held to answer, if the defendant fails to appear on that date and a bench warrant is issued, the defendant shall be brought to trial within 60 days after the defendant next appears in the superior court unless a trial date previously had been set which is beyond that 60-day period.

(c) If the defendant is not represented by counsel, the defendant shall not be deemed under this section to have consented to the date for the defendant's trial unless the court has explained to the defendant his or her rights under this section and the effect of his or her consent.

Amended by Stats 2009 ch 424 (AB 250),s 1, eff. 1/1/2010.
Amended by Stats 2005 ch 36 (SB 330),s 1, eff. 1/1/2006

Section 1383 - Continuance of action

If the defendant is not charged or tried, as provided in Section 1382, and sufficient reason therefor is shown, the court may order the action to be continued from time to time, and in the meantime may discharge the defendant from custody on his or her own undertaking of bail for his or her appearance to answer the charge at the time to which the action is continued.

Amended by Stats. 1987, Ch. 828, Sec. 92.

Section 1384 - Discharge after dismissal; exoneration of bail

If the judge or magistrate directs the action to be dismissed, the defendant must, if in custody, be discharged therefrom; or if admitted to bail, his bail is exonerated, or money deposited instead of bail must be refunded to him or to the person or persons found by the court to have deposited said money on behalf of said defendant.

Amended by Stats. 1980, Ch. 938, Sec. 6.

Section 1385 - Dismissal of enhancements

(a) The judge or magistrate may, either on motion of the court or upon the application of the prosecuting attorney, and in furtherance of justice, order an action to be dismissed. The reasons for the dismissal shall be stated orally on the record. The court shall also set forth the reasons in an order entered upon the minutes if requested by either party or in any case in which the proceedings are not being recorded electronically or reported by a court reporter. A dismissal shall not be made for any cause that would be ground of demurrer to the accusatory pleading.

(b)

(1) If the court has the authority pursuant to subdivision (a) to strike or dismiss an enhancement, the court may instead strike the additional punishment for that enhancement in the furtherance of justice in compliance with subdivision (a).

(2) This subdivision does not authorize the court to strike the additional punishment for any enhancement that cannot be stricken or dismissed pursuant to subdivision (a).

(c)

(1) Notwithstanding any other law, the court shall dismiss an enhancement if it is in the furtherance of justice to do so, except if dismissal of that enhancement is prohibited by any initiative statute.

(2) In exercising its discretion under this subdivision, the court shall consider and afford great weight to evidence offered by the defendant to prove that any of the mitigating circumstances in subparagraphs (A) to (I) are present. Proof of the presence of one or more of these circumstances weighs greatly in favor of dismissing the enhancement, unless the court finds that dismissal of the enhancement would endanger public safety. "Endanger public safety" means there is a likelihood that the dismissal of the enhancement would result in physical injury or other serious danger to others.

(A) Application of the enhancement would result in a discriminatory racial impact as described in paragraph (4) of subdivision (a) of Section 745.

(B) Multiple enhancements are alleged in a single case. In this instance, all enhancements beyond a single enhancement shall be dismissed.

(C) The application of an enhancement could result in a sentence of over 20 years. In this instance, the enhancement shall be dismissed.

(D) The current offense is connected to mental illness.

(E) The current offense is connected to prior victimization or childhood trauma.

(F) The current offense is not a violent felony as defined in subdivision (c) of Section 667.5.

(G) The defendant was a juvenile when they committed the current offense or any prior offenses, including criminal convictions and juvenile adjudications, that trigger the enhancement or enhancements applied in the current case.

(H) The enhancement is based on a prior conviction that is over five years old.

(I) Though a firearm was used in the current offense, it was inoperable or unloaded.

(3) While the court may exercise its discretion at sentencing, this subdivision does not prevent a court from exercising its discretion before, during, or after trial or entry of plea.

(4) The circumstances listed in paragraph (2) are not exclusive and the court maintains authority to dismiss or strike an enhancement in accordance with subdivision (a).

(5) For the purposes of subparagraph (D) of paragraph (2), a mental illness is a mental disorder as identified in the most recent edition of the Diagnostic and Statistical Manual of Mental Disorders, including, but not limited to, bipolar disorder, schizophrenia, schizoaffective disorder, or post-traumatic stress disorder but excluding antisocial personality disorder, borderline personality disorder, and pedophilia. A court may conclude that a defendant's mental illness was connected to the offense if, after reviewing any relevant and credible evidence, including, but not limited to, police reports, preliminary hearing transcripts, witness statements, statements by the defendant's mental health treatment provider, medical records, records or reports by qualified medical experts, or evidence that the defendant displayed symptoms consistent with the relevant mental disorder at or near the time of the offense, the court concludes that the defendant's mental illness substantially contributed to the defendant's involvement in the commission of the offense.

(6) For the purposes of this subdivision, the following terms have the following meanings:

(A) "Childhood trauma" means that as a minor the person experienced physical, emotional, or sexual abuse, physical or emotional neglect. A court may conclude that a defendant's childhood trauma was connected to the offense if, after reviewing any relevant and credible evidence, including, but not limited to, police reports, preliminary hearing transcripts, witness statements, medical records, or records or reports by qualified medical experts, the court concludes that the defendant's childhood trauma substantially contributed to the defendant's involvement in the commission of the offense.

(B) "Prior victimization" means the person was a victim of intimate partner violence, sexual violence, or human trafficking, or the person has experienced psychological or physical trauma, including, but not limited to, abuse, neglect, exploitation, or sexual violence. A court may conclude that a defendant's prior victimization was connected to the offense if, after reviewing any relevant and credible evidence, including, but not limited to, police reports, preliminary hearing transcripts, witness statements, medical records, or records or reports by qualified medical experts, the court concludes that the defendant's prior victimization substantially contributed to the defendant's involvement in the commission of the offense.

(7) This subdivision shall apply to all sentencings occurring after January 1, 2022.

Amended by Stats 2023 ch 131 (AB 1754),s 160, eff. 1/1/2024.
Amended by Stats 2022 ch 58 (AB 200),s 15, eff. 6/30/2022.
Amended by Stats 2021 ch 721 (SB 81),s 1, eff. 1/1/2022.
Amended by Stats 2018 ch 1013 (SB 1393),s 2, eff. 1/1/2019.
Amended by Stats 2014 ch 137 (SB 1222),s 1, eff. 1/1/2015.
Amended by Stats 2000 ch 689 (AB 1808) s 3, eff. 1/1/2001.

Section 1385.1 - Prohibited dismissal of special circumstance

Notwithstanding Section 1385 or any other provision of law, a judge shall not strike or dismiss any special circumstance which is admitted by a plea of guilty or nolo contendere or is found by a jury or court as provided in Sections 190.1 to 190.5, inclusive.
Added June 5, 1990, by initiative Proposition 115, Sec. 26.

Section 1386 - Abolishment of entry of nolle prosequi

The entry of a nolle prosequi is abolished, and neither the Attorney General nor the district attorney can discontinue or abandon a prosecution for a public offense, except as provided in Section 1385.
Amended by Stats. 1987, Ch. 828, Sec. 93.

Section 1387 - Bar to prosecution

(a) An order terminating an action pursuant to this chapter, or Section 859b, 861, 871, or 995, is a bar to any other prosecution for the same offense if it is a felony or if it is a misdemeanor charged together with a felony and the action has been previously terminated pursuant to this chapter, or Section 859b, 861, 871, or 995, or if it is a misdemeanor not charged together with a felony, except in those felony cases, or those cases where a misdemeanor is charged with a felony, where subsequent to the dismissal of the felony or misdemeanor the judge or magistrate finds any of the following:

(1) That substantial new evidence has been discovered by the prosecution that would not have been known through the exercise of due diligence at, or prior to, the time of termination of the action.

(2) That the termination of the action was the result of the direct intimidation of a material witness, as shown by a preponderance of the evidence.

(3) That the termination of the action was the result of the failure to appear by the complaining witness, who had been personally subpoenaed in a prosecution arising under subdivision (e) of Section 243, or Section 273.5, 273.6, or 261, where the complaining witness is the spouse of the defendant, or former Section 262. This paragraph shall apply only within six months of the original dismissal of the action, and may be invoked only once in each action. This section does not preclude a defendant from being eligible for diversion.

(4) That the termination of the action was the result of the complaining witness being found in contempt of court as described in subdivision (b) of Section 1219 of the Code of Civil Procedure. This paragraph shall apply only within six months of the original dismissal of the action, and may be invoked only once in each action.

(b) Notwithstanding subdivision (a), an order terminating an action pursuant to this chapter is not a bar to another prosecution for the same offense if it is a misdemeanor charging an offense based on an act of domestic violence, as defined in subdivisions (a) and (b) of Section 13700, and the termination of the action was the result of the failure to appear by the complaining witness, who had been personally subpoenaed. This subdivision shall apply only within six months of the original dismissal of the action, and may be invoked only once in each action. This subdivision does not preclude a defendant from being eligible for diversion.

(c) An order terminating an action is not a bar to prosecution if a complaint is dismissed before the commencement of a preliminary hearing in favor of an indictment filed pursuant to Section 944 and the indictment is based upon the same subject matter as charged in the dismissed complaint, information, or indictment. However, if the previous termination was pursuant to Section 859b, 861, 871, or 995, the subsequent order terminating an action is not a bar to prosecution if:

    (1) Good cause is shown why the preliminary examination was not held within 60 days from the date of arraignment or plea.

    (2) The motion pursuant to Section 995 was granted because of any of the following reasons:

        (A) Present insanity of the defendant.

        (B) A lack of counsel after the defendant elected to self-represent rather than being represented by appointed counsel.

        (C) Ineffective assistance of counsel.

        (D) Conflict of interest of defense counsel.

        (E) Violation of time deadlines based upon unavailability of defense counsel.

        (F) Defendant's motion to withdraw a waiver of the preliminary examination.

    (3) The motion pursuant to Section 995 was granted after dismissal by the magistrate of the action pursuant to Section 871 and was recharged pursuant to Section 739.

Amended by Stats 2022 ch 197 (SB 1493),s 27, eff. 1/1/2023.

Amended by Stats 2021 ch 626 (AB 1171),s 54, eff. 1/1/2022.

Amended by Stats 2012 ch 510 (AB 2051),s 2, eff. 1/1/2013.

Section 1387.1 - Refiling charges where prior dismissals due solely to excusable neglect

(a) Where an offense is a violent felony, as defined in Section 667.5 and the prosecution has had two prior dismissals, as defined in Section 1387, the people shall be permitted one additional opportunity to refile charges where either of the prior dismissals under Section 1387 were due solely to excusable neglect. In no case shall the additional refiling of charges provided under this section be permitted where the conduct of the prosecution amounted to bad faith.

(b) As used in this section, "excusable neglect" includes, but is not limited to, error on the part of the court, prosecution, law enforcement agency, or witnesses.

Added by Stats. 1987, Ch. 1211, Sec. 47.5.

Section 1387.2 - Proceeding on existing accusatory pleading

Upon the express consent of both the people and the defendant, in lieu of issuing an order terminating an action the court may proceed on the existing accusatory pleading. For the purposes of Section 1387, the action shall be deemed as having been previously terminated. The defendant shall be rearraigned on the accusatory pleading and a new time period pursuant to Section 859b or 1382 shall commence.

Added by Stats. 1992, Ch. 278, Sec. 2. Effective January 1, 1993.

Section 1388 - Filing another accusatory pleading after order for dismissal of felony action

(a) In any case where an order for the dismissal of a felony action is made, as provided in this chapter, and where the defendant had been released on his own recognizance for that action, if the prosecutor files another accusatory pleading against the same defendant for the same offense, unless the defendant is present in court at the time of refiling, the district attorney shall send a letter to the defendant at his last known place of residence, and shall send a copy to the attorney of record, stating that the case has been refiled, and setting forth the date, time and place for rearrangement.

(b) If the defendant fails to appear for arraignment as stated, or at such time, date, and place as has been subsequently agreed to by defendant's counsel and the district attorney, then the court shall issue and have delivered for execution a warrant for his arrest within 20 days after his failure to appear.

(c) If the defendant was released on his own recognizance on the original charge, he shall, if he appears as provided in subdivisions (a) and (b), be released on his own recognizance on the refiled charge unless it is shown that changed conditions require a different disposition, in which case bail shall be set at the discretion of the judge.

Added by Stats. 1976, Ch. 1024.

Chapter 8.5 - AGREEMENT ON DETAINERS

Section 1389 - Agreement on detainers

The agreement on detainers is hereby enacted into law and entered into by this State with all other jurisdictions legally joining therein in the form substantially as follows:

  The Agreement on Detainers

The contracting states solemnly agree that:

Article I The party states find that charges outstanding against a prisoner, detainers based on untried indictments, informations or complaints, and difficulties in securing speedy trial of persons already incarcerated in other jurisdictions, produce uncertainties which obstruct programs of prisoner treatment and rehabilitation. Accordingly, it is the policy of the party states and the purpose of this agreement to encourage the expeditious and orderly disposition of such charges and determination of the proper status of any and all detainers based on untried indictments, informations or complaints. The party states also find that proceedings with reference to such charges and detainers, when emanating from another jurisdiction, cannot properly be had in the absence of cooperative procedures. It is the further purpose of this agreement to provide such cooperative procedures.

Article II As used in this agreement:

(a) "State" shall mean a state of the United States; the United States of America; a territory or possession of the United States; the District of Columbia; the Commonwealth of Puerto Rico.

(b) "Sending state" shall mean a state in which a prisoner is incarcerated at the time that he initiates a request for final disposition pursuant to Article III hereof or at the time that a request for custody or availability is initiated pursuant to Article IV hereof.

(c) "Receiving state" shall mean the state in which trial is to be had on an indictment, information or complaint pursuant to Article III or Article IV hereof.

Article III

(a) Whenever a person has entered upon a term of imprisonment in a penal or correctional institution of a party state, and whenever during the continuance of the term of imprisonment there is pending in any other party state any untried indictment, information or complaint on the basis of which a detainer has been lodged against the prisoner, he shall be brought to trial within one hundred eighty days after he shall have caused to be delivered to the prosecuting officer and the appropriate court of the prosecuting officer's jurisdiction written notice of the place of his imprisonment and his request for a final disposition to be made of the indictment, information or complaint: provided that for good cause shown in open court, the prisoner or his counsel being present, the court having jurisdiction of the matter may grant any necessary or reasonable continuance. The request of the prisoner shall be accompanied by a certificate of the appropriate official having custody of the prisoner, stating the term of commitment under which the prisoner is being held, the time already served, the time remaining to be served on the sentence, the amount of good time earned, the time of parole eligibility of the prisoner, and any decisions of the state parole agency relating to the prisoner.

(b) The written notice and request for final disposition referred to in paragraph (a) hereof shall be given or sent by the prisoner to the warden, commissioner of corrections or other official having custody of him, who shall promptly forward it together with the certificate to the appropriate prosecuting official and court by registered or certified mail, return receipt requested.

(c) The warden, commissioner of corrections or other official having custody of the prisoner shall promptly inform him of the source and contents of any detainer lodged against him and shall also inform him of his right to make a request for final disposition of the indictment, information or complaint on which the detainer is based.

(d) Any request for final disposition made by a prisoner pursuant to paragraph (a) hereof shall operate as a request for final disposition of all untried indictments, informations or complaints on the basis of which detainers have been lodged against the prisoner from the state to whose prosecuting official the request for final disposition is specifically directed. The warden, commissioner of corrections or other official having custody of the prisoner shall forthwith notify all appropriate prosecuting officers and courts in the several jurisdictions within the state to which the prisoner's request for final disposition is being sent of the proceeding being initiated by the prisoner. Any notification sent pursuant to this paragraph shall be accompanied by copies of the prisoner's written notice, request, and the certificate. If trial is not had on any indictment, information or complaint contemplated hereby prior to the return of the prisoner to the original place of imprisonment, such indictment, information or complaint shall not be of any further force or effect, and the court shall enter an order dismissing the same with prejudice.

(e) Any request for final disposition made by a prisoner pursuant to paragraph (a) hereof shall also be deemed to be a waiver of extradition with respect to any charge or proceeding contemplated thereby or included therein by reason of paragraph (d) hereof, and a waiver of extradition to the receiving state to serve any sentence there imposed upon him, after completion of his term of imprisonment in the sending state. The request for final disposition shall also constitute a consent by the prisoner to the production of his body in any court where his presence may be required in order to effectuate the purposes of this agreement and a further consent voluntarily to be returned to the original place of imprisonment in accordance with the provisions of this agreement. Nothing in this paragraph shall prevent the imposition of a concurrent sentence if otherwise permitted by law.

(f) Escape from custody by the prisoner subsequent to his execution of the request for final disposition referred to in paragraph (a) hereof shall void the request.

Article IV

(a) The appropriate officer of the jurisdiction in which an untried indictment, information or complaint is pending shall be entitled to have a prisoner against whom he has lodged a detainer and who is serving a term of imprisonment in any party state made available in accordance with Article V (a) hereof upon presentation of a written request for temporary custody or availability to the appropriate authorities of the state in which the prisoner is incarcerated: provided that the court having jurisdiction of such indictment, information or complaint shall have duly approved, recorded and transmitted the request: and provided further that there shall be a period of thirty days after receipt by the appropriate authorities before the request be honored, within which period the governor of the sending state may disapprove the request for temporary custody or availability, either upon his own motion or upon motion of the prisoner.

(b) Upon receipt of the officer's written request as provided in paragraph (a) hereof, the appropriate authorities having the prisoner in custody shall furnish the officer with a certificate stating the term of commitment under which the prisoner is being held, the time already served, the time remaining to be served on the sentence, the amount of good time earned, the time of parole eligibility of the prisoner, and any decisions of the state parole agency relating to the prisoner. Said authorities simultaneously shall furnish all other officers and appropriate courts in the receiving state who have lodged detainers against the prisoner with similar certificates and with notices informing them of the request for custody or availability and of the reasons therefor.

(c) In respect of any proceeding made possible by this Article, trial shall be commenced within one hundred twenty days of the arrival of the prisoner in the receiving state, but for good cause shown in open court, the prisoner or his counsel being present, the court having jurisdiction of the matter may grant any necessary or reasonable continuance.

(d) Nothing contained in this Article shall be construed to deprive any prisoner of any right which he may have to contest the legality of his delivery as provided in paragraph (a) hereof, but such delivery may not be opposed or denied on the ground that the executive authority of the sending state has not affirmatively consented to or ordered such delivery.

(e) If trial is not had on any indictment, information or complaint contemplated hereby prior to the prisoner's being returned to the original place of imprisonment pursuant to Article V (e) hereof, such indictment, information or complaint shall not be of any further force or effect, and the court shall enter an order dismissing the same with prejudice.

Article V

(a) In response to a request made under Article III or Article IV hereof, the appropriate authority in a sending state shall offer to deliver temporary custody of such prisoner to the appropriate authority in the state where such indictment, information or complaint is pending against such person in order that speedy and efficient prosecution may be had. If the request for final disposition is made by the prisoner, the offer of temporary custody shall accompany the written notice provided for in Article III of this agreement. In the case of a federal prisoner, the appropriate authority in the receiving state shall be entitled to temporary custody as provided by this agreement or to the prisoner's presence in federal custody at the place for trial, whichever custodial arrangement may be approved by the custodian.

(b) The officer or other representative of a state accepting an offer of temporary custody shall present the following upon demand:

(1) Proper identification and evidence of his authority to act for the state into whose temporary custody the prisoner is to be given.

(2) A duly certified copy of the indictment, information or complaint on the basis of which the detainer has been lodged and on the basis of which the request for temporary custody of the prisoner has been made.

(c) If the appropriate authority shall refuse or fail to accept temporary custody of said person, or in the event that an action on the indictment, information or complaint on the basis of which the detainer has been lodged is not brought to trial within the period provided in Article III or Article IV hereof, the appropriate court of the jurisdiction where the indictment, information or complaint has been pending shall enter an order dismissing the same with prejudice, and any detainer based thereon shall cease to be of any force or effect.

(d) The temporary custody referred to in this agreement shall be only for the purpose of permitting prosecution on the charge or charges contained in one or more untried indictments, informations or complaints which form the basis of the detainer or detainers or for prosecution on any other charge or charges arising out of the same transaction. Except for his attendance at court and while being transported to or from any place at which his presence may be required, the prisoner shall be held in a suitable jail or other facility regularly used for persons awaiting prosecution.

(e) At the earliest practicable time consonant with the purposes of this agreement, the prisoner shall be returned to the sending state.

(f) During the continuance of temporary custody or while the prisoner is otherwise being made available for trial as required by this agreement, time being served on the sentence shall continue to run but good time shall be earned by the prisoner only if, and to the extent that, the law and practice of the jurisdiction which imposed the sentence may allow.

(g) For all purposes other than that for which temporary custody as provided in this agreement is exercised, the prisoner shall be deemed to remain in the custody of and subject to the jurisdiction of the sending state and any escape from temporary custody may be dealt with in the same manner as an escape from the original place of imprisonment or in any other manner permitted by law.

(h) From the time that a party state receives custody of a prisoner pursuant to this agreement until such prisoner is returned to the territory and custody of the sending state, the state in which the one or more untried indictments, informations or complaints are pending or in which trial is being had shall be responsible for the prisoner and shall also pay all costs of transporting, caring for, keeping and returning the prisoner. The provisions of this paragraph shall govern unless the states concerned shall have entered into a supplementary agreement providing for a different allocation of costs and responsibilities as between or among themselves. Nothing herein contained shall be construed to alter or affect any internal relationship among the departments, agencies and officers of and in the government of a party state, or between a party state and its subdivisions, as to the payment of costs, or responsibilities therefor.

Article VI

(a) In determining the duration and expiration dates of the time periods provided in Articles III and IV of this agreement, the running of said time periods shall be tolled whenever and for as long as the prisoner is unable to stand trial, as determined by the court having jurisdiction of the matter.

(b) No provision of this agreement, and no remedy made available by this agreement, shall apply to any person who is adjudged to be mentally ill.

Article VII Each state party to this agreement shall designate an officer who, acting jointly with like officers of other party states, shall promulgate rules and regulations to carry out more effectively the terms and provisions of this agreement, and who shall provide, within and without the state, information necessary to the effective operation of this agreement.

Article VIII This agreement shall enter into full force and effect as to a party state when such state has enacted the same into law. A state party to this agreement may withdraw herefrom by enacting a statute repealing the same. However, the withdrawal of any state shall not affect the status of any proceedings already initiated by inmates or by state officers at the time such withdrawal takes effect, nor shall it affect their rights in respect thereof.

Article IX This agreement shall be liberally construed so as to effectuate its purposes. The provisions of this agreement shall be severable and if any phrase, clause, sentence or provision of this agreement is declared to be contrary to the constitution of any party state or of the United States or the applicability thereof to any government, agency, person or circumstance is held invalid, the validity of the remainder of this agreement and the applicability thereof to any government, agency, person or circumstance shall not be affected thereby. If this agreement shall be held contrary to the constitution of any state party hereto, the agreement shall remain in full force and effect as to the remaining states and in full force and effect as to the state affected as to all severable matters.

Added by Stats. 1963, Ch. 2115.

Section 1389.1 - "Appropriate court" defined

The phrase "appropriate court" as used in the agreement on detainers shall, with reference to the courts of this State, means the court in which the indictment, information, or complaint is filed.

Added by Stats. 1963, Ch. 2115.

Section 1389.2 - Enforcement of agreement on detainer

All courts, departments, agencies, officers, and employees of this State and its political subdivisions are hereby directed to enforce the agreement on detainer and to co-operate with one another and with other states in enforcing the agreement and effectuating its purpose.
Added by Stats. 1963, Ch. 2115.

Section 1389.4 - Escape
Every person who has been imprisoned in a prison or institution in this State and who escapes while in the custody of an officer of this or another state in another state pursuant to the agreement on detainers is deemed to have violated Section 4530 and is punishable as provided therein.
Added by Stats. 1963, Ch. 2115.

Section 1389.5 - Giving over inmate
It shall be lawful and mandatory upon the warden or other official in charge of a penal or correctional institution in this State to give over the person of any inmate thereof whenever so required by the operation of the agreement on detainer. Such official shall inform such inmate of his rights provided in paragraph (a) of Article IV of the Agreement on Detainers in Section 1389 of this code.
Added by Stats. 1963, Ch. 2115.

Section 1389.6 - Administration of agreement
The Administrator, Interstate Probation and Parole Compacts, shall administer this agreement.
Added by Stats. 1963, Ch. 2115.

Section 1389.7 - Cooperative agreements to carry out term-fixing and parole functions
When, pursuant to the agreement on detainers or other provision of law, a person in actual confinement under sentence of another jurisdiction is brought before a California court and sentenced by the judge to serve a California sentence concurrently with the sentence of the other jurisdiction or has been transferred to another jurisdiction for concurrent service of previously imposed sentences, the Board of Prison Terms, and the panels and members thereof, may meet in such other jurisdiction, or enter into cooperative arrangements with corresponding agencies in the other jurisdiction, as necessary to carry out the term-fixing and parole functions.
Amended by Stats. 1979, Ch. 255.

Section 1389.8 - Responsibility of agent of receiving state
It shall be the responsibility of the agent of the receiving state to return the prisoner to the sending state upon completion of the proceedings.
Added by Stats. 1971, Ch. 1185.

Chapter 9 - PROCEEDINGS AGAINST CORPORATIONS

Section 1390 - Issuance of summons
Upon the filing of an accusatory pleading against a corporation, the court shall issue a summons, signed by the judge with his name of office, requiring the corporation to appear before him, at a specified time and place, to answer the charge, the time to be not less than 10 days after the issuing of the summons.
Amended by Stats. 1971, Ch. 1591.

Section 1391 - Form of summons
The summons shall be substantially in the following form:
County of (as the case may be).
The people of the State of California to the (naming the corporation):
You are hereby summoned to appear before me at (naming the place), on (specifying the day and hour), to answer an accusatory pleading, for (designating the offense generally).
Dated this ____ day of ____, 19__.
G. H., Judge, (name of the court).
Amended by Stats. 1971, Ch. 1591.

Section 1392 - Service of summons
The summons must be served at least five days before the day of appearance fixed therein, by delivering a copy thereof and showing the original to the president or other head of the corporation, or to the secretary, cashier, managing agent, or an agent of the corporation designated for service of civil process.
Amended by Stats. 1973, Ch. 248.

Section 1393 - Proceeding with charges
At the appointed time in the summons, the magistrate shall proceed with the charge in the same manner as in other cases.
Amended by Stats. 1971, Ch. 1591.

Section 1396 - Appearance
If an accusatory pleading is filed, the corporation may appear by counsel to answer the same, except that in the case of misdemeanors arising from operation of motor vehicles, or of infractions arising from operation of motor vehicles, a corporation may appear by its president, vice president, secretary or managing agent for the purpose of entering a plea of guilty. If it does not thus appear, a plea of not guilty shall be entered, and the same proceedings had thereon as in other cases.
Amended by Stats. 1973, Ch. 718.

Section 1397 - Collection of fine
When a fine is imposed upon a corporation on conviction, it may be collected by virtue of the order imposing it in the manner provided for enforcement of money judgments generally.
Amended by Stats. 1982, Ch. 497, Sec. 140. Operative July 1, 1983, by Sec. 185 of Ch. 497.

Chapter 10 - ENTITLING AFFIDAVITS

Section 1401 - Title of affidavit

It is not necessary to entitle an affidavit or deposition in the action, whether taken before or after indictment or information, or upon an appeal; but if made without a title, or with an erroneous title, it is as valid and effectual for every purpose as if it were duly entitled, if it intelligibly refer to the proceeding, indictment, information, or appeal in which it is made.

Amended by Code Amendments 1880, Ch. 47.

Chapter 11 - ERRORS AND MISTAKES IN PLEADINGS AND OTHER PROCEEDINGS

Section 1404 - Invalidity

Neither a departure from the form or mode prescribed by this Code in respect to any pleading or proceeding, nor an error or mistake therein, renders it invalid, unless it has actually prejudiced the defendant, or tended to his prejudice, in respect to a substantial right.

Enacted 1872.

Section 1405 - Motion for performance of forensic DNA testing

(a) A person who was convicted of a felony and is currently serving a term of imprisonment may make a written motion, pursuant to subdivision (d), before the trial court that entered the judgment of conviction in his or her case, for performance of forensic deoxyribonucleic acid (DNA) testing.

(b)

(1) An indigent convicted person may request appointment of counsel in order to prepare a motion pursuant to subdivision (d) by sending a written request to the court. The request shall include the person's statement that he or she was not the perpetrator of the crime and shall explain how the DNA testing is relevant to his or her assertion of innocence. The request also shall include the person's statement as to whether he or she previously has had counsel appointed under this section.

(2) If any of the information required in paragraph (1) is missing from the request, the court shall return the request to the convicted person and advise him or her that the matter cannot be considered without the missing information.

(3)

(A) Upon a finding that the person is indigent, he or she has included the information required in paragraph (1), and counsel has not previously been appointed pursuant to this subdivision, the court shall appoint counsel to investigate and, if appropriate, to file a motion for DNA testing under this section and to represent the person solely for the purpose of obtaining DNA testing under this section.

(B) Upon a finding that the person is indigent, and counsel previously has been appointed pursuant to this subdivision, the court may, in its discretion, appoint counsel to investigate and, if appropriate, to file a motion for DNA testing under this section and to represent the person solely for the purpose of obtaining DNA testing under this section.

(4) This section does not provide for a right to the appointment of counsel in a postconviction collateral proceeding, or to set a precedent for any such right, in any context other than the representation being provided an indigent convicted person for the limited purpose of filing and litigating a motion for DNA testing pursuant to this section.

(c) Upon request of the convicted person or convicted person's counsel, the court may order the prosecutor to make all reasonable efforts to obtain, and police agencies and law enforcement laboratories to make all reasonable efforts to provide, the following documents that are in their possession or control, if the documents exist:

(1) Copies of DNA lab reports, with underlying notes, prepared in connection with the laboratory testing of biological evidence from the case, including presumptive tests for the presence of biological material, serological tests, and analyses of trace evidence.

(2) Copies of evidence logs, chain of custody logs and reports, including, but not limited to, documentation of current location of biological evidence, and evidence destruction logs and reports.

(3) If the evidence has been lost or destroyed, a custodian of record shall submit a report to the prosecutor and the convicted person or convicted person's counsel that sets forth the efforts that were made in an attempt to locate the evidence. If the last known or documented location of the evidence prior to its loss or destruction was in an area controlled by a law enforcement agency, the report shall include the results of a physical search of this area. If there is a record of confirmation of destruction of the evidence, the report shall include a copy of the record of confirmation of destruction in lieu of the results of a physical search of the area.

(d)

(1) The motion for DNA testing shall be verified by the convicted person under penalty of perjury and shall include all of the following:

(A) A statement that he or she is innocent and not the perpetrator of the crime.

(B) Explain why the identity of the perpetrator was, or should have been, a significant issue in the case.

(C) Make every reasonable attempt to identify both the evidence that should be tested and the specific type of DNA testing sought.

(D) Explain, in light of all the evidence, how the requested DNA testing would raise a reasonable probability that the convicted person's verdict or sentence would be more favorable if the results of DNA testing had been available at the time of conviction.

(E) Reveal the results of any DNA or other biological testing that was conducted previously by either the prosecution or defense, if known.

(F) State whether any motion for testing under this section previously has been filed and the results of that motion, if known.

(2) Notice of the motion shall be served on the Attorney General, the district attorney in the county of conviction, and, if known, the governmental agency or laboratory holding the evidence sought to be tested. Responses, if any, shall be filed within 90 days of the date on which the Attorney General and the district attorney are served with the motion, unless a continuance is granted for good cause.

(e) If the court finds evidence was subjected to DNA or other forensic testing previously by either the prosecution or defense, it shall order the party at whose request the testing was conducted to provide all parties and the court with access to the laboratory reports, underlying data, and laboratory notes prepared in connection with the DNA or other biological evidence testing.

(f) If the court determines that the convicted person has met all of the requirements of subparagraphs (A) to (F), inclusive, of paragraph (1) of subdivision (d), the court may, as it deems necessary, order a hearing on the motion. The judge who conducted the trial, or accepted the convicted person's plea of guilty or nolo contendere, shall conduct the hearing unless the presiding judge determines that judge is unavailable. Upon request of either party, the court may order, in the interest of justice, that the convicted person be present at the hearing of the motion. Either party, upon request, may request an additional 60 days to brief issues raised in subdivision (g).

(g) The court shall grant the motion for DNA testing if it determines all of the following have been established:

(1) The evidence to be tested is available and in a condition that would permit the DNA testing requested in the motion.

(2) The evidence to be tested has been subject to a chain of custody sufficient to establish it has not been substituted, tampered with, replaced, or altered in any material aspect.

(3) The identity of the perpetrator of the crime was, or should have been, a significant issue in the case.

(4) The convicted person has made a prima facie showing that the evidence sought to be tested is material to the issue of the convicted person's identity as the perpetrator of, or accomplice to, the crime, special circumstance, or enhancement allegation that resulted in the conviction or sentence. The convicted person is only required to demonstrate that the DNA testing he or she seeks would be relevant to, rather than dispositive of, the issue of identity. The convicted person is not required to show a favorable result would conclusively establish his or her innocence.

(5) The requested DNA testing results would raise a reasonable probability that, in light of all the evidence, the convicted person's verdict or sentence would have been more favorable if the results of DNA testing had been available at the time of conviction. The court in its discretion may consider any evidence whether or not it was introduced at trial. In determining whether the convicted person is entitled to develop potentially exculpatory evidence, the court shall not decide whether, assuming a DNA test result favorable to the convicted person, he or she is entitled to some form of ultimate relief.

(6) The evidence sought to be tested meets either of the following conditions:

(A) The evidence was not tested previously.

(B) The evidence was tested previously, but the requested DNA test would provide results that are reasonably more discriminating and probative of the identity of the perpetrator or accomplice or have a reasonable probability of contradicting prior test results.

(7) The testing requested employs a method generally accepted within the relevant scientific community.

(8) The motion is not made solely for the purpose of delay.

(h)

(1) If the court grants the motion for DNA testing, the court order shall identify the specific evidence to be tested and the DNA technology to be used.

(2) The testing shall be conducted by a laboratory that meets the FBI Director's Quality Assurance Standards and that is mutually agreed upon by the district attorney in a noncapital case, or the Attorney General in a capital case, and the person filing the motion. If the parties cannot agree, the court shall designate a laboratory that meets the FBI Director's Quality Assurance Standards. Laboratories accredited by the following entities have been determined to satisfy this requirement: the American Association for Laboratory Accreditation (A2LA), the American Society of Crime Laboratory Directors/Laboratory Accreditation Board (ASCLD/LAB), and Forensic Quality Services (ANSI-ASQ National Accreditation Board FQS).

(3) If the accredited laboratory selected by the parties or designated by the court to conduct DNA testing is not a National DNA Index System (NDIS) participating laboratory that takes or retains ownership of the DNA data for entry into the Combined DNA Index System (CODIS), the laboratory selected to perform DNA testing shall not initiate analysis for a specific case until documented approval has been obtained from an appropriate NDIS participating laboratory's technical leader of acceptance of ownership of the DNA data from the selected laboratory that may be entered into or searched in CODIS.

(i) In accordance with the court's order pursuant to subdivision (h), the laboratory may communicate with either party, upon request, during the testing process. The result of any testing ordered under this section shall be fully disclosed to the person filing the motion, the district attorney, and the Attorney General. If requested by any party, the court shall order production of the underlying laboratory data and notes.

(j)

(1) The cost of DNA testing ordered under this section shall be borne by the state or the applicant, as the court may order in the interests of justice, if it is shown that the applicant is not indigent and possesses the ability to pay. However, the cost of any additional testing to be conducted by the district attorney or Attorney General shall not be borne by the convicted person.

(2) In order to pay the state's share of any testing costs, the laboratory designated in subdivision (h) shall present its bill for services to the superior court for approval and payment. It is the intent of the Legislature to appropriate funds for this purpose in the 2000-01 Budget Act.

(k) An order granting or denying a motion for DNA testing under this section shall not be appealable, and shall be subject to review only through petition for writ of mandate or prohibition filed by the person seeking DNA testing, the district attorney, or the Attorney General. The petition shall be filed within 20 days after the court's order granting or denying the motion for DNA testing. In a noncapital case, the petition for writ of mandate or prohibition shall be filed in the court of appeal. In a capital case, the petition shall be filed in the California Supreme Court. The court of appeal or California Supreme Court shall expedite its review of a petition for writ of mandate or prohibition filed under this subdivision.

(l) DNA testing ordered by the court pursuant to this section shall be done as soon as practicable. However, if the court finds that a miscarriage of justice will otherwise occur and that it is necessary in the interests of justice to give priority to the DNA testing, a DNA laboratory shall be required to give priority to the DNA testing ordered pursuant to this section over the laboratory's other pending casework.

(m) DNA profile information from biological samples taken from a convicted person pursuant to a motion for postconviction DNA testing is exempt from any law requiring disclosure of information to the public.

(n) Notwithstanding any other provision of law, the right to file a motion for postconviction DNA testing provided by this section is absolute and shall not be waived. This prohibition applies to, but is not limited to, a waiver that is given as part of an agreement resulting in a plea of guilty or nolo contendere.

(o) The provisions of this section are severable. If any provision of this section or its application is held invalid, that invalidity shall not affect other provisions or applications that can be given effect without the invalid provision or application.

Amended by Stats 2014 ch 554 (SB 980),s 1, eff. 1/1/2015.

Amended by Stats 2004 ch 405 (SB 1796), s 16, eff. 1/1/2005.

Added by Stats 2000 ch 821 (SB 1342) s 1, eff. 1/1/2001.

Amended by Stats 2001 ch 943 (SB 83) s 1, eff. 1/1/2002.

Section 1405.1 - Uploading DNA profile of unknown contributor; conditions

(a) When the court grants a motion for DNA testing pursuant to Section 1405 and a DNA profile of an unknown contributor is generated, the court may conduct a hearing to determine if the DNA profile should be uploaded into the State Index System, and if appropriate, the National DNA Index System. The court may issue an order directing the upload of the DNA profile into the State Index System, and if appropriate, the National DNA Index System, only if all of the following conditions are met:

(1) The source of the DNA profile is attributable to the putative perpetrator of the crime.

(2) The profile meets all requirements, whether technical or otherwise, for permanent inclusion into the State Index System, and if appropriate, the National DNA Index System, as determined by the Department of Justice, the Federal Bureau of Investigation, federal law, and California law.

(3) The convicted person or convicted person's counsel provides written notice to the California Combined DNA Index System (CODIS) State Administrator at the Department of Justice, the Attorney General, and the district attorney 30 court days prior to the hearing to determine if the DNA profile should be uploaded into the State Index System, and if appropriate, the National DNA Index System.

(b) A court shall not order an upload of a DNA profile into the State Index System or the National DNA Index System that violates any CODIS or state rule, policy, or regulation.

Added by Stats 2014 ch 554 (SB 980),s 2, eff. 1/1/2015.

Chapter 12 - DISPOSAL OF PROPERTY STOLEN OR EMBEZZLED

Section 1407 - stolen or embezzled property in custody of peace officer

When property, alleged to have been stolen or embezzled, comes into the custody of a peace officer, he shall hold it subject to the provisions of this chapter relating to the disposal thereof.

Amended by Stats. 1975, Ch. 774.

Section 1408 - Order of delivery

On the application of the owner and on satisfactory proof of his ownership of the property, after reasonable notice and opportunity to be heard has been given to the person from whom custody of the property was taken and any other person as required by the magistrate, the magistrate before whom the complaint is laid, or who examines the charge against the person accused of stealing or embezzling it, shall order it to be delivered, without prejudice to the state, to the owner, on his paying the necessary expenses incurred in its preservation, to be certified by the magistrate. The order entitles the owner to demand and receive the property.

Amended by Stats. 1971, Ch. 799.

Section 1409 - Stolen or embezzled property in custody of magistrate

If property stolen or embezzled comes into the custody of the magistrate, it shall be delivered, without prejudice to the state, to the owner upon his application to the court and on satisfactory proof of his title, after reasonable notice and opportunity to be heard has been given to the person from whom custody of the property was taken and any other person as required by the magistrate, and on his paying the necessary expenses incurred in its preservation, to be certified by the magistrate.

Amended by Stats. 1971, Ch. 799.

Section 1410 - Order of restoration to owner

If the property stolen or embezzled has not been delivered to the owner, the court before which a trial is had for stealing or embezzling it, upon the application of the owner to the court and on proof of his title, after reasonable notice and opportunity to be heard has been given to the person from whom custody of the property was taken and any other person as required by the court, may order it to be restored to the owner without prejudice to the state.

Amended by Stats. 1971, Ch. 799.

Section 1411 - Notification of owner of property

(a) If the ownership of the property stolen or embezzled and the address of the owner, and the address of the owner of a security interest therein, can be reasonably ascertained, the peace officer who took custody of the property shall notify the owner, and a person having a security interest therein, by letter of the location of the property and the method by which the owner may obtain it. This notice shall be given upon the conviction of a person for an offense involving the theft, embezzlement, or possession of the property, or if a conviction was not obtained, upon the making of a decision by the district attorney not to file the case or upon the termination of the proceedings in the case. Except as provided in Section 217 of the Welfare and Institutions Code, if the property stolen or embezzled is not claimed by the owner before the expiration of three months after the giving of this notice, or, in any case in which such a notice is not given, before the expiration of six months from the conviction of a person for an offense involving the theft, embezzlement, or possession of the property, or if a conviction was not obtained, then from the time the property came into the possession of the peace officer or the case involving the person from whom it was obtained is disposed of, whichever is later, the magistrate or other officer having it in custody may, on the payment of the necessary expenses incurred in its preservation, deliver it to the county treasurer or other proper county officer, by whom it shall be sold and the proceeds paid into the county treasury. However, notwithstanding any other law, if the person from whom custody of the property was taken is a secondhand dealer or licensed pawnbroker and reasonable but unsuccessful efforts have been made to notify the owner of the property and the property is no longer needed for the criminal proceeding, the property shall be returned to the secondhand dealer or pawnbroker who had custody of the property and be treated as regularly acquired property. If the property is transferred to the county purchasing agent it may be sold in the manner provided by Article 7 (commencing with Section 25500) of Chapter 5 of Part 2 of Division 2 of Title 3 of the Government Code for the sale of surplus personal property. If the county officer determines that any of the property transferred to him or her for sale is needed for a public use, the property may be retained by the county and need not be sold. The magistrate or other officer having the property in custody may, however, provide for the sale of the property in the manner provided for the sale of unclaimed property which has been held for at least three months pursuant to Section 2080.4 of the Civil Code.

(b) This section shall not govern the disposition of property placed on hold pursuant to Section 21647 of the Business and Professions Code, notwithstanding the current custodial status of the property, unless the licensed pawnbroker or secondhand dealer, after receipt of the written advisement required by subdivision (h) of Section 21647 of the Business and Professions Code, willfully refuses to consent to a statutory hold as provided by Section 21647 of the Business and Professions Code or a search warrant for the business of the licensed pawnbroker or secondhand dealer has resulted in the seizure of the property subject to this section.

Amended by Stats 2013 ch 318 (SB 762),s 3, eff. 1/1/2014.

Section 1412 - Receipts for money or other property taken from defendant

When money or other property is taken from a defendant, arrested upon a charge of a public offense, the officer taking it must at the time give duplicate receipts therefor, specifying particularly the amount of money or the kind of property taken; one of which receipts he must deliver to the defendant and the other of which he must forthwith file with the Clerk of the Court to which the depositions and statement are to be sent. When such property is taken by a police officer of any incorporated city or town, he must deliver one of the receipts to the defendant, and one, with the property, at once to the Clerk or other person in charge of the police office in such city or town.

Enacted 1872.

Section 1413 - Duties of clerk of property section for police department

(a) The clerk or person having charge of the property section for any police department in any incorporated city or town, or for any sheriff's department in any county, shall enter in a suitable book a description of every article of property alleged to be stolen or embezzled, and brought into the office or taken from the person of a prisoner, and shall attach a number to each article, and make a corresponding entry thereof. He may engrave or imbed an identification number in property described in Section 537e for the purposes thereof.

(b) The clerk or person in charge of the property section may, upon satisfactory proof of the ownership of property held pursuant to Section 1407, and upon presentation of proper personal identification, deliver it to the owner. Such delivery shall be without prejudice to the state or to the person from whom custody of the property was taken or to any other person who may have a claim against the property. Prior to such delivery such clerk or person in charge of the property section shall make and retain a complete photographic record of such property. The person to whom property is delivered shall sign, under penalty of perjury, a declaration of ownership, which shall be retained by the clerk or person in charge of the property section. This subdivision shall not apply to any property subject to forfeiture under any provision of law. This subdivision shall not apply unless the clerk or person in charge of the property section has served upon the person from whom custody of the property was taken a notice of a claim of ownership and a copy of the satisfactory proof of ownership tendered and has allowed such person reasonable opportunity to be heard as to why the property should not be delivered to the person claiming ownership. If the person upon whom a notice of claim and proof of ownership has been served does not respond asserting a claim to the property within 15 days from the date of receipt of the service, the property may be disposed of in a manner not inconsistent with the provisions of this section.

(c) The magistrate before whom the complaint is laid, or who examines the charge against the person accused of stealing or embezzling the property, or the court before which a trial is had for stealing or embezzling it, shall upon application by the person from whom custody of the property was taken, review the determination of the clerk or person in charge of the property section, and may order the property taken into the custody of the court upon a finding that the person to whom the property was delivered is not entitled thereto. Such court shall make its determination in the same manner as a determination is made when the matter is before the court pursuant to Sections 1408 to 1410, inclusive.

(d) The clerk or person in charge of the property section is not liable in damages for any official action performed hereunder in good faith.

Amended by Stats. 1981, Ch. 714, Sec. 332.

Chapter 13 - DISPOSITION OF EVIDENCE IN CRIMINAL CASES

Section 1417 - Retention of exhibits

All exhibits which have been introduced or filed in any criminal action or proceeding shall be retained by the clerk of the court who shall establish a procedure to account for the exhibits properly, subject to Sections 1417.2 and 1417.3 until final determination of the action or proceedings and the exhibits shall thereafter be distributed or disposed of as provided in this chapter.

Amended by Stats. 1990, Ch. 382, Sec. 3.

Section 1417.1 - Destruction of exhibit prior to final determination prohibited

No order shall be made for the destruction of an exhibit prior to the final determination of the action or proceeding. For the purposes of this chapter, the date when a criminal action or proceeding becomes final is as follows:

(a) When no notice of appeal is filed, 30 days after the last day for filing that notice.

(b) When a notice of appeal is filed, 30 days after the date the clerk of the court receives the remittitur affirming the judgment.

(c) When an order for a rehearing, a new trial, or other proceeding is granted and the ordered proceedings have not been commenced within one year thereafter, one year after the date of that order.

(d)

(1) In cases where the death penalty is imposed, 30 days after the date of execution of sentence.

(2) In cases where the death penalty is imposed and the defendant dies while awaiting execution, one year after the date of the defendant's death.

Amended by Stats 2012 ch 283 (SB 1489),s 2, eff. 1/1/2013.

Section 1417.2 - Delivery of exhibit to party prior to final determination

Notwithstanding Section 1417.5, the court may, on application of the party entitled thereto or an agent designated in writing by the owner, order an exhibit delivered to that party at any time prior to the final determination of the action or proceeding, upon stipulation of the parties or upon notice and motion if both of the following requirements are met:

(a) No prejudice will be suffered by either party.

(b) A full and complete photographic record is made of the exhibits so released. The party to whom the exhibit is being returned shall provide the photographic record. This section shall not apply to any material, the release of which is prohibited by Section 1417.6.
Added by Stats. 1985, Ch. 875, Sec. 3.

Section 1417.3 - Exhibits posing security, storage, or safety problem; toxic exhibits

(a) At any time prior to the final determination of the action or proceeding, exhibits offered by the state or defendant shall be returned to the party offering them by order of the court when an exhibit poses a security, storage, or safety problem, as recommended by the clerk of the court. If an exhibit by its nature is severable the court shall order the clerk to retain a portion of the exhibit not exceeding three pounds by weight or one cubic foot by volume and shall order the return of the balance of the exhibit to the district attorney. The clerk, upon court order, shall substitute a full and complete photographic record of any exhibit or part of any exhibit returned to the state under this section. The party to whom the exhibit is being returned shall provide the photographic record.

(b) Exhibits toxic by their nature that pose a health hazard to humans shall be introduced to the court in the form of a photographic record and a written chemical analysis certified by competent authority. Where the court finds that good cause exists to depart from this procedure, toxic exhibits may be brought into the courtroom and introduced. However, following introduction of the exhibit, the person or persons previously in possession of the exhibit shall take responsibility for it and the court shall not be required to store the exhibit.
Amended by Stats. 1990, Ch. 382, Sec. 4.

Section 1417.5 - Disposal of exhibits by clerk of court

Except as provided in Section 1417.6, 60 days after the final determination of a criminal action or proceeding, the clerk of the court shall dispose of all exhibits introduced or filed in the case and remaining in the clerk's possession, as follows:

(a) If the name and address of the person from whom the exhibit was taken is contained in the court record, the clerk shall notify the person that he or she may make application to the court for release of the exhibits within 15 days of receipt of the notification.

(b) The court shall order the release of exhibits free of charge, without prejudice to the state, upon application, to the following:

(1) First, the person from whom the exhibits were taken into custody, provided that the person was in lawful possession of the exhibits.

(2) Second, a person establishing title to, or a right to possession of, the exhibits.

(c) If the party entitled to an exhibit fails to apply for the return of the exhibit prior to the date for disposition under this section, the following procedures shall apply:

(1) Exhibits of stolen or embezzled property other than money shall be disposed of pursuant to court order as provided in Section 1417.6.

(2) Exhibits of property other than property which is stolen or embezzled or property which consists of money or currency shall, except as otherwise provided in this paragraph and in paragraph (3), be transferred to the appropriate county agency for sale to the public in the same manner provided by Article 7 (commencing with Section 25500) of Chapter 5 of Part 2 of Division 2 of Title 3 of the Government Code for the sale of surplus personal property. If the county determines that any property is needed for a public use, the property may be retained by the county and need not be sold.

(3) Exhibits of property, other than money, currency, or stolen or embezzled property, that are determined by the court to have no value at public sale shall be destroyed or otherwise disposed of pursuant to court order.

(4) Exhibits of money or currency shall be disposed of pursuant to Section 1420.
Amended by Stats. 1997, Ch. 133, Sec. 1. Effective January 1, 1998.

Section 1417.6 - Dangerous or deadly weapons, narcotic or poisonous drugs, explosives, or other property possession of which is prohibited by law

(a) The provisions of Section 1417.5 shall not apply to any dangerous or deadly weapons, narcotic or poisonous drugs, explosives, or any property of any kind or character whatsoever the possession of which is prohibited by law and that was used by a defendant in the commission of the crime of which the defendant was convicted, or with which the defendant was armed or that the defendant had upon his or her person at the time of the defendant's arrest. Any of this property introduced or filed as an exhibit shall be, by order of the trial court, destroyed or otherwise disposed of under the conditions provided in the order no sooner than 60 days following the final determination of the criminal action or proceeding.

(b)

(1) Every person who knowingly has in his or her possession any tool or device that is seized and of a type used in the commission of a violation of Section 10801, 10802, or 10803 of the Vehicle Code, shall be subject to having the tool or device intended for the above purpose deemed a nuisance as provided in paragraph (2).

(2) An evidentiary hearing shall be held only upon conviction of the defendant for a violation of Section 10801, 10802, or 10803 of the Vehicle Code and after 15 days' notice is given to the defendant of the state's intent to declare as a nuisance any property that is described in paragraph (1). All relevant evidence shall be admissible at the hearing and the state shall prove by a preponderance of the evidence that the property seized is of a type used in facilitating the commission of the crime of which the defendant was convicted.

(3) If a person purports to be the lawful owner of any tool or device the state seeks to be declared a nuisance, the person shall show proof by a preponderance of the evidence at the hearing pursuant to paragraph (2), that he or she owns the tool or device, and the illegal use of the tool or device was without his or her knowledge or consent.

(4) Following a determination that the property shall be declared a nuisance, the property shall be disposed of as provided in paragraph (2) or (3) of subdivision (c) of Section 1417.5.
Amended by Stats 2010 ch 709 (SB 1062),s 17, eff. 1/1/2011.

Section 1417.7 - Notification prior to disposition of exhibit

Not less than 15 days before any proposed disposition of an exhibit pursuant to Section 1417.3, 1417.5, or 1417.6, the court shall notify the district attorney or other prosecuting attorney, the attorney of record for each party, and each party who is not represented by counsel of the proposed disposition. Before the disposition, any party, at his or her own expense, may cause to be prepared a photographic or digital record of all or part of the exhibit by a person who is not a party or attorney of a party. The clerk of the court shall observe the taking of the photographic or digital record and, upon receipt of a declaration of the person making the photographic or digital record that the duplicate delivered to the clerk is a true, unaltered, and unretouched duplicate of the photographic or digital record taken in the presence of the clerk, the clerk shall certify the photographic or digital record as such without charge and retain it unaltered for a period of 60 days following the final determination of the criminal action or proceeding. For purposes of this section, a "photographic record" of the exhibit means a photographic image of the exhibit or its equivalent stored in any form. For purposes of this section, a "duplicate" means a counterpart produced by a mechanical, photographic, chemical, electronic, or other equivalent process or technique that accurately reproduces the original. A certified photographic or digital record of exhibits shall not be deemed inadmissible pursuant to Section 1521 or 1522 of the Evidence Code.

Amended by Stats 2017 ch 566 (SB 238),s 3, eff. 10/7/2017.

Section 1417.8 - Photograph of minor found to be harmful matter

(a) Notwithstanding any other provision of this chapter, the court shall direct that any photograph of any minor that has been found by the court to be harmful matter, as defined in Section 313, and introduced or filed as an exhibit in any criminal proceeding specified in subdivision (b) be handled as follows:

(1) Prior to the final determination of the action or proceeding, the photograph shall be available only to the parties or to a person named in a court order to receive the photograph.

(2) After the final determination of the action or proceeding, the photograph shall be preserved with the permanent record maintained by the clerk of the court. The photograph may be disposed of or destroyed after preservation through any appropriate photographic or electronic medium. If the photograph is disposed of, it shall be rendered unidentifiable before the disposal. No person shall have access to the photograph unless that person has been named in a court order to receive the photograph. Any copy, negative, reprint, or other duplication of the photograph in the possession of the state, a state agency, the defendant, or an agent of the defendant, shall be delivered to the clerk of the court for disposal whether or not the defendant was convicted of the offense.

(b) The procedure provided by subdivision (a) shall apply to actions listed under subdivision (c) of Section 290, and to acts under the following provisions:

(1) Section 261.5.

(2) Section 272.

(3) Chapter 7.5 (commencing with Section 311) of Title 9 of Part 1.

(4) Chapter 7.6 (commencing with Section 313) of Title 9 of Part 1.

(c) For the purposes of this section, "photograph" means any photographic image contained in a digital format or on any chemical, mechanical, magnetic, or electronic medium.

Amended by Stats 2007 ch 579 (SB 172),s 43, eff. 10/13/2007.

Amended by Stats 2001 ch 473 (SB 485), s 14, eff. 1/1/2002.

Section 1417.9 - Retention of biological material

(a) Notwithstanding any other law and subject to subdivisions (b) and (c), the appropriate governmental entity shall retain any object or material that contains or includes biological material that is secured in connection with a criminal case for the period of time that any person remains incarcerated in connection with that case. The governmental entity shall have the discretion to determine how the evidence is retained pursuant to this section, provided that the evidence is retained in a condition suitable for deoxyribonucleic acid (DNA) testing.

(b) A governmental entity may dispose of any object or material that contains or includes biological material before the expiration of the period of time described in subdivision (a) if all of the conditions set forth below are met:

(1) The governmental entity notifies all of the following persons of the provisions of this section and of the intention of the governmental entity to dispose of the material:

(A) Any person, who as a result of a felony conviction in the case is currently serving a term of imprisonment and who remains incarcerated in connection with the case. This notification shall be sent to the current location where the person is incarcerated.

(B) Any counsel of record.

(C) The public defender in the county of conviction.

(D) The district attorney in the county of conviction.

(E) The Attorney General.

(2) The notifying entity does not receive, within 180 days of sending the notification, any of the following:

(A) A motion filed pursuant to Section 1405. However, upon filing of that motion, the governmental entity shall retain the material only until the time that the court's denial of the motion is final.

(B) A request under penalty of perjury that the material not be destroyed or disposed of because the declarant will file a motion for DNA testing pursuant to Section 1405 within one year, unless a request for an extension is requested by the convicted person and agreed to by the governmental entity in possession of the evidence.

(C) A declaration of innocence filed with the court under penalty of perjury. However, the court shall permit the destruction of the evidence upon a showing that the declaration is false or there is no issue of identity that would be affected by additional testing. The convicted person may be cross-examined on the declaration at any hearing conducted under this section or on an application by or on behalf of the convicted person filed pursuant to Section 1405.

(3) No other law requires that biological evidence be preserved or retained.

(c) Notwithstanding any other law, the right to receive notice pursuant to this section is absolute and shall not be waived. This prohibition applies to, but is not limited to, a waiver that is given as part of an agreement resulting in a plea of guilty or nolo contendere.

Amended by Stats 2018 ch 972 (AB 2988),s 1, eff. 1/1/2019.

Amended by Stats 2014 ch 554 (SB 980),s 3, eff. 1/1/2015.

Amended by Stats 2002 ch 1105 (SB 1391), s 2, eff. 1/1/2003.

Amended by Stats 2001 ch 943 (SB 83), s 2, eff. 1/1/2002.

Added by Stats 2000 ch 821 (SB 1342) s 2, eff. 1/1/2001.

Chapter 14 - DISPOSITION OF UNCLAIMED MONEY HELD BY DISTRICT ATTORNEY OR COURT CLERK

Section 1420 - Deposit with county treasurer; notice

All money received by a district attorney or clerk of the court in any criminal action or proceeding, the owner or owners of which are unknown, and which remains unclaimed in the possession of the district attorney or clerk of the court after final judgment in the criminal action or proceeding, shall be deposited with the county treasurer. Upon the expiration of two years after the deposit, the county treasurer shall cause a notice pursuant to Section 1421 to be published in the county once a week for two successive weeks in a newspaper of general circulation published in the county.

Amended by Stats. 1985, Ch. 875, Sec. 5.

Section 1421 - Content of notice

The notice shall state the amount of money, the criminal action or proceeding in which the money was received by the district attorney or clerk of the court, the fund in which it is held and that it is proposed that the money will become the property of the county on a designated date not less than 45 days nor more than 60 days after the first publication of the notice.

Amended by Stats. 1985, Ch. 875, Sec. 6.

Section 1422 - Verified complaint

Unless some person files a verified complaint seeking to recover all, or a designated part, of the money in a court of competent jurisdiction within the county in which the notice is published, and serves a copy of the complaint and the summons issued thereon upon the county treasurer before the date designated in the notice, upon that date the money becomes the property of the county and shall be transferred by the treasurer to the general fund.

Added by Stats. 1959, Ch. 2016.

Chapter 15 - DISQUALIFICATION OF PROSECUTING ATTORNEYS

Section 1424 - Motion to disqualify district attorney or city attorney

(a)

(1) Notice of a motion to disqualify a district attorney from performing an authorized duty shall be served on the district attorney and the Attorney General at least 10 court days before the motion is heard. The notice of motion shall contain a statement of the facts setting forth the grounds for the claimed disqualification and the legal authorities relied upon by the moving party and shall be supported by affidavits of witnesses who are competent to testify to the facts set forth in the affidavit. The district attorney or the Attorney General, or both, may file affidavits in opposition to the motion and may appear at the hearing on the motion and may file with the court hearing the motion a written opinion on the disqualification issue. The judge shall review the affidavits and determine whether or not an evidentiary hearing is necessary. The motion may not be granted unless the evidence shows that a conflict of interest exists that would render it unlikely that the defendant would receive a fair trial. An order recusing the district attorney from any proceeding may be reviewed by extraordinary writ or may be appealed by the district attorney or the Attorney General. The order recusing the district attorney shall be stayed pending any review authorized by this section. If the motion is brought at or before the preliminary hearing, it may not be renewed in the trial court on the basis of facts that were raised or could have been raised at the time of the original motion.

(2) An appeal from an order of recusal or from a case involving a charge punishable as a felony shall be made pursuant to Chapter 1 (commencing with Section 1235) of Title 9, regardless of the court in which the order is made. An appeal from an order of recusal in a misdemeanor case shall be made pursuant to Chapter 2 (commencing with Section 1466) of Title 11, regardless of the court in which the order is made.

(b)

(1) Notice of a motion to disqualify a city attorney or city prosecutor from performing an authorized duty involving a criminal matter shall be served on the city attorney or city prosecutor and the district attorney at least 10 court days before the motion is heard. The notice of motion shall set forth a statement of the facts relevant to the claimed disqualification and the legal authorities relied on by the moving party. The district attorney may appear at the hearing on the motion and may file with the court hearing the motion a written opinion on the disqualification issue. The motion may not be granted unless the evidence shows that a conflict of interest exists that would render it unlikely that the defendant would receive a fair trial.

(2) An order recusing the city attorney or city prosecutor from a proceeding may be appealed by the city attorney or city prosecutor or the district attorney. The order recusing the city attorney or city prosecutor shall be stayed pending an appeal authorized by this section. An appeal from an order of disqualification in a misdemeanor case shall be made pursuant to Chapter 2 (commencing with Section 1466) of Title 11.

(c) Motions to disqualify the city attorney or city prosecutor and the district attorney shall be separately made.

Amended by Stats 2017 ch 299 (AB 1418),s 2, eff. 1/1/2018.

EFFECTIVE 1/1/2000. Amended September 7, 1999 (Bill Number: AB 154) (Chapter 363).

Section 1424.5 - Withholding of evidence by prosecuting attorney; violation; hearing; penalty

(a)

(1) Upon receiving information that a prosecuting attorney may have deliberately and intentionally withheld relevant, material exculpatory evidence or information in violation of law, a court may make a finding, supported by clear and convincing evidence, that a violation occurred. If the court finds such a violation, the court shall inform the State Bar of California of that violation if the prosecuting

attorney acted in bad faith and the impact of the withholding contributed to a guilty verdict, guilty or nolo contendere plea, or, if identified before conclusion of trial, seriously limited the ability of a defendant to present a defense.

(2) A court may hold a hearing to consider whether a violation occurred pursuant to paragraph (1).

(b)

(1) If a court finds, pursuant to subdivision (a), that a violation occurred in bad faith, the court may disqualify an individual prosecuting attorney from a case.

(2) Upon a determination by a court to disqualify an individual prosecuting attorney pursuant to paragraph (1), the defendant or his or her counsel may file and serve a notice of a motion pursuant to Section 1424 to disqualify the prosecuting attorney's office if there is sufficient evidence that other employees of the prosecuting attorney's office knowingly and in bad faith participated in or sanctioned the intentional withholding of the relevant, material exculpatory evidence or information and that withholding is part of a pattern and practice of violations.

(c) This section does not limit the authority or discretion of, or any requirement placed upon, the court or other individuals to make reports to the State Bar of California regarding the same conduct, or otherwise limit other available legal authority, requirements, remedies, or actions.

Amended by Stats 2016 ch 59 (SB 1474),s 7, eff. 1/1/2017.
Added by Stats 2015 ch 467 (AB 1328),s 2, eff. 1/1/2016.

Title 11 - PROCEEDINGS IN MISDEMEANOR AND INFRACTION CASES AND APPEALS FROM SUCH CASES

Chapter 1 - PROCEEDINGS IN MISDEMEANOR AND INFRACTION CASES

Section 1427 - Warrant of arrest

(a) When a complaint is presented to a judge in a misdemeanor or infraction case appearing to be triable in the judge's court, the judge must, if satisfied therefrom that the offense complained of has been committed and that there is reasonable ground to believe that the defendant has committed it, issue a warrant, for the arrest of the defendant.

(b) Such warrant of arrest and proceedings upon it shall be in conformity to the provisions of this code regarding warrants of arrest, and it may be in the following form: County of ____

The people of the State of California, to any peace officer in this state:

Complaint upon oath having been this day made before me that the offense of ____ (designating it generally) has been committed and accusing ____ (name of defendant) thereof you are therefore commanded forthwith to arrest the above-named defendant and bring the defendant forthwith before the ____ Court of ____ (stating full title of court) at ____ (naming place).

Witness my hand and the seal of said court this ____ day of ____, 19__.

____ (Signed). ____ ____ Judge of said court ____

If it appears that the offense complained of has been committed by a corporation, no warrant of arrest shall issue, but the judge must issue a summons substantially in the form prescribed in Section 1391. Such summons must be served at the time and in the manner designated in Section 1392 except that if the offense complained of is a violation of the Vehicle Code or a local ordinance adopted pursuant to the Vehicle Code, such summons may be served by deposit by the clerk of the court in the United States mail of an envelope enclosing the summons, which envelope shall be addressed to a person authorized to accept service of legal process on behalf of the defendant, and which envelope shall be mailed by registered mail or certified mail with a return receipt requested. Promptly upon such mailing, the clerk of the court shall execute a certificate of such mailing and place it in the file of the court for that case. At the time stated in the summons the corporation may appear by counsel and answer the complaint, except that in the case of misdemeanors arising from operation of motor vehicles, or of infractions arising from operation of motor vehicles, a corporation may appear by its president, vice president, secretary or managing agent for the purpose of entering a plea of guilty. If it does not appear, a plea of not guilty shall be entered, and the same proceedings had therein as in other cases.

Amended by Stats. 1998, Ch. 931, Sec. 409. Effective September 28, 1998.

Section 1428 - Docket; register of actions

In misdemeanor and infraction cases, the clerk of the superior court may keep a docket, instead of minutes pursuant to Section 69844 of the Government Code and a register of actions pursuant to Section 69845 or 69845.5 of the Government Code. In the docket, the clerk shall enter the title of each criminal action or proceeding and under each title all the orders and proceedings in such action or proceeding. Wherever by any other section of this code made applicable to such court an entry of any judgment, order or other proceeding in the minutes or register of actions is required, an entry thereof in the docket shall be made and shall be deemed a sufficient entry in the minutes or register of actions for all purposes.

Amended by Stats 2002 ch 784 (SB 1316), s 553, eff. 1/1/2003.

Section 1428.5 - Remote proceedings

(a) Notwithstanding any other law, courts may conduct proceedings, including arraignments and trials, remotely for all infractions.

(1) Courts shall obtain the defendant's consent to conduct proceedings remotely.

(2) The court may require the physical presence of any witness or party in court for a particular proceeding.

(3) This subdivision does not apply to misdemeanor or felony proceedings.

(b) Remote proceedings include use of technology for remote appearances.

(c) The Judicial Council may adopt rules of court to implement this section.

Added by Stats 2021 ch 79 (AB 143),s 35, eff. 7/16/2021.

Section 1429 - Plea of defendant

In a misdemeanor case the plea of the defendant may be made by the defendant or by the defendant's counsel. If such defendant pleads guilty, the court may, before entering such plea or pronouncing judgment, examine witnesses to ascertain the gravity of the offense committed; and if it appears to the court that a higher offense has been committed than the offense charged in the complaint, the court may order the defendant to be committed or admitted to bail, to answer any indictment which may be found against the defendant by the grand jury, or any complaint which may be filed charging the defendant with such higher offense.

Amended by Stats. 1998, Ch. 931, Sec. 411. Effective September 28, 1998.

Section 1429.5 - [Repealed]

Repealed by Stats 2002 ch 784 (SB 1316), s 554, eff. 1/1/2003.

Section 1445 - Plea of guilty or conviction

When the defendant pleads guilty, or is convicted, either by the court, or by a jury, the court shall render judgment thereon of fine or imprisonment, or both, as the case may be.

Amended by Stats. 1989, Ch. 1360, Sec. 117.

Section 1447 - Acquittal

When the defendant is acquitted in a misdemeanor or infraction case, if the court certifies in the minutes that the prosecution was malicious and without probable cause, the court may order the complainant to pay the costs of the action, or to give an undertaking to pay the costs within 30 days after the trial.

Amended by Stats. 1998, Ch. 931, Sec. 413. Effective September 28, 1998.

Section 1448 - Judgment for costs

If the complainant does not pay the costs, or give an undertaking therefor, the court may enter judgment against the complainant for the amount of the costs, which may be enforced in the manner provided for enforcement of money judgments generally.

Amended by Stats. 1983, Ch. 18, Sec. 25. Effective April 21, 1983.

Section 1449 - Time for pronouncing judgment

In a misdemeanor or infraction case, after a plea, finding, or verdict of guilty, or after a finding or verdict against the defendant on a plea of former conviction or acquittal, or once in jeopardy, the court shall appoint a time for pronouncing judgment which shall be not less than six hours, nor more than five days, after the verdict or plea of guilty, unless the defendant waives the postponement. The court may extend the time for not more than 10 days for the purpose of hearing or determining any motion for a new trial, or in arrest of judgment. The court also may extend the time for not more than 20 judicial days if probation is considered. Upon request of the defendant or the probation officer, that time may be further extended for not more than 90 additional days. In case of postponement, the court may hold the defendant to bail to appear for judgment. If, in the opinion of the court there is a reasonable ground for believing a defendant insane, the court may extend the time of pronouncing judgment and may commit the defendant to custody until the question of insanity has been heard and determined.

If the defendant is a veteran who was discharged from service for mental disability, upon his or her request, his or her case shall be referred to the probation officer, who shall secure a military medical history of the defendant and present it to the court together with a recommendation for or against probation.

Amended by Stats. 1998, Ch. 931, Sec. 414. Effective September 28, 1998.

Section 1457 - Payment of fine

Upon payment of the fine, the officer must discharge the defendant, if he is not detained for any other legal cause, and pay over the fine to the court which rendered the judgment.

Amended by Stats. 1949, Ch. 1517. Note: The condition in Sec. 5 of Ch. 1517 was satisfied by adoption of Prop. 3 on Nov. 7, 1950.

Section 1458 - Bail

The provisions of this code relative to bail are applicable to bail in misdemeanor or infraction cases. The defendant, at any time after arrest and before conviction, may be admitted to bail. The undertaking of bail in such a case shall be in substantially the following form:

A complaint having been filed on the ____ day of ____, 19__, in the ____ Court of ____ County of ____ (stating title and location of court) charging ____ (naming defendant) as defendant with the crime of ____ (designating it generally) and the defendant having been admitted to bail in the sum of ____ dollars ($____) (stating amount);

We, ____ and ____, of ____ (stating their places of residence and occupation), hereby undertake that the above-named defendant will appear and answer any charge in any accusatory pleading based upon the acts supporting the complaint above mentioned and all duly authorized amendments thereof, in whatever court it may be prosecuted, and will at all times hold himself or herself amenable to the orders and process of the court, and, if convicted, will appear for pronouncement of judgment or grant of probation or if the defendant fails to perform either of these conditions, that we will pay to the people of the State of California the sum of ____ dollars ($____) (inserting the sum in which the defendant is admitted to bail). If the forfeiture of this bond is ordered by the court, judgment may be summarily made and entered forthwith against the said ____ (naming the sureties and the defendant if the defendant is a party to the bond) for the amount of their respective undertakings herein, as provided by Sections 1305 and 1306 of the California Penal Code.

Amended by Stats. 1998, Ch. 931, Sec. 415. Effective September 28, 1998.

Section 1459 - Undertakings of bail filed by admitted surety insurers

Undertakings of bail filed by admitted surety insurers shall meet all other requirements of law and the obligation of the insurer shall be in the following form except to the extent a different form is otherwise provided by statute:

____ (stating the title and the location of the court).

Defendant ____ (stating the name of the defendant) having been admitted to bail in the sum of ____ dollars ($____) (stating the amount of bail fixed) and ordered to appear in the above-entitled court on ____, 19__ (stating the date for appearance in court), on ____ (stating only the word "misdemeanor" or the word "felony") charge/s;

Now, the ____ (stating the name of admitted surety insurer and state of incorporation) hereby undertakes that the above-named defendant will appear in the above-named court on the date above set forth to answer any charge in any accusatory pleading based upon the acts supporting the complaint filed against him/her and all duly authorized amendments thereof, in whatever court it may be prosecuted, and will at all times hold him/herself amenable to the orders and process of the court and, if convicted, will appear for pronouncement of judgment or grant of probation or if he/she fails to perform either of these conditions, that the ____ (stating the name of admitted surety insurer and state of incorporation) will pay to the people of the State of California the sum of ____ dollars ($____) (stating the amount of the undertaking of the admitted surety insurer).

If the forfeiture of this bond be ordered by the court, judgment may be summarily made and entered forthwith against the said ____ (stating the name of admitted surety insurer and state of incorporation) for the amount of its undertaking herein, as provided by Sections 1305 and 1306 of the California Penal Code.

(Stating the name of admitted surety insurer and state of incorporation),
(Signature)
By Attorney-in-fact (Corporate seal)
(Jurat of notary public or other officer authorized to administer oaths.)

Amended by Stats. 1998, Ch. 931, Sec. 416. Effective September 28, 1998.

Section 1462 - [Repealed]

Repealed by Stats 2002 ch 784 (SB 1316), s 554.1, eff. 1/1/2003.

Section 1462.2 - Proper court for trial

Except as otherwise provided in the Vehicle Code, the proper court for the trial of criminal cases amounting to misdemeanor shall be the superior court of the county within which the offense charged was committed.

If an action or proceeding is commenced in a court other than the court herein designated as the proper court for the trial, the action may, notwithstanding, be tried in the court where commenced, unless the defendant, at the time of pleading, requests an order transferring the action or proceeding to the proper court. If after that request it appears that the action or proceeding was not commenced in the proper court, the court shall order the action or proceeding transferred to the proper court. The judge shall, at the time of arraignment, inform the defendant of the right to be tried in the county where the offense was committed.

Amended by Stats 2003 ch 449 (AB 1712), s 35, eff. 1/1/2004.

Section 1462.25 - Defendant charged with violations of Vehicle Code section 14601 in different courts

(a) A defendant formally charged with a violation of Vehicle Code Section 14601 in one court ("the first court"), against whom a formal charge of a violation of Vehicle Code Section 14601 is pending in one or more other courts, may state in writing his or her agreement to plead guilty or nolo contendere to some or all of the charges pending in the other courts, to waive trial or hearing in the other courts, and to consent to disposition of the case in the first court. The defendant's agreement is ineffective unless the district attorney for the other county approves in writing. Upon receipt of the defendant's agreement and the district attorney's approval, the clerk of court in the other court shall transfer the pending matter to the first court, and transmit the papers or certified copies. The prosecution of each transferred matter shall proceed in the first court as part of the case pending against the defendant there, but shall be limited to proceedings upon the defendant's plea of guilty or nolo contendere, and sentencing or probation. If the defendant pleads not guilty, the clerk shall retransfer the transferred case to the court of origin, and the prosecution shall be resumed in that court. The defendant's statement that the defendant agreed to plead guilty or nolo contendere shall not be used against the defendant.

(b) The procedure specified in subdivision (a) may be used only if the defendant is represented by counsel in the other courts, or the defendant has expressly waived his or her right to counsel in the other courts.

(c) A defendant may request appointment of counsel in the other courts by a written request. Upon receiving the defendant's written request, the other court shall appoint counsel to represent the defendant if he or she otherwise qualifies for appointed counsel.

(d) The appearance of the defendant in proceedings transferred pursuant to subdivision (a) shall not commence the running of time limits under Section 859b, 860, 861, or 1382.

Added by Stats. 1994, Ch. 389, Sec. 20. Effective September 1, 1994.

Section 1462.5 - Proration of installment or partial payment of fine, penalty, forfeiture, or fee

Each installment or partial payment of a fine, penalty, forfeiture, or fee shall be prorated among the state and local shares according to the trial court revenue distribution guidelines established by the Controller pursuant to Section 71380 of the Government Code. In cases subject to Section 1463.18 of the Penal Code, proration shall not occur until the minimum amounts have been transferred to the Restitution Fund as provided in that section.

Amended by Stats 2016 ch 703 (AB 2881),s 18, eff. 1/1/2017.

Section 1463 - Distribution of fines and forfeitures; definitions

All fines and forfeitures imposed and collected for crimes shall be distributed in accordance with Section 1463.001.

The following definitions shall apply to terms used in this chapter:

(a)"Arrest" means any law enforcement action, including issuance of a notice to appear or notice of violation, which results in a criminal charge.

(b)"City" includes any city, city and county, district, including any enterprise special district, community service district, or community service area engaged in police protection activities as reported to the Controller for inclusion in the 1989-90 edition of the Financial Transactions Report Concerning Special Districts under the heading of Police Protection and Public Safety, authority, or other local agency (other than a county) which employs persons authorized to make arrests or to issue notices to appear or notices of violation which may be filed in court.

(c)"City arrest" means an arrest by an employee of a city, or by a California Highway Patrol officer within the limits of a city.

(d)"County" means the county in which the arrest took place.

(e)"County arrest" means an arrest by a California Highway Patrol officer outside the limits of a city, or any arrest by a county officer or by any other state officer.

(f)"Court" means the superior court or a juvenile forum established under Section 257 of the Welfare and Institutions Code, in which the case arising from the arrest is filed.

(g)"Division of moneys" means an allocation of base fine proceeds between agencies as required by statute, including, but not limited to, Sections 1463.003, 1463.9, 1463.23, and 1463.26 of this code, Sections 13001, 13002, and 13003 of the Fish and Game Code, and Section 11502 of the Health and Safety Code.

(h)"Offense" means any infraction, misdemeanor, or felony, and any act by a juvenile leading to an order to pay a financial sanction by reason of the act being defined as an infraction, misdemeanor, or felony, whether defined in this or any other code, except any parking offense as defined in subdivision (i).

(i)"Parking offense" means any offense charged pursuant to Article 3 (commencing with Section 40200) of Chapter 1 of Division 17 of the Vehicle Code, including registration and equipment offenses included on a notice of parking violation.

(j)"Penalty allocation" means the deposit of a specified part of moneys to offset designated processing costs, as provided by Section 1463.16 of this code and by Section 68090.8 of the Government Code.

(k)"Total parking penalty" means the total sum to be collected for a parking offense, whether as fine, forfeiture of bail, or payment of penalty to the Department of Motor Vehicles (DMV). It may include the following components:

    (1) The base parking penalty as established pursuant to Section 40203.5 of the Vehicle Code.

    (2) The DMV fees added upon the placement of a hold pursuant to Section 40220 of the Vehicle Code.

    (3) The surcharges required by Section 76000 of the Government Code.

    (4) The notice penalty added to the base parking penalty when a notice of delinquent parking violations is given.

(l)"Total fine or forfeiture" means the total sum to be collected upon a conviction, or the total amount of bail forfeited or deposited as cash bail subject to forfeiture. It may include, but is not limited to, the following components as specified for the particular offense:

    (1) The "base fine" upon which the state penalty and additional county penalty is calculated.

    (2) The "county penalty" required by Section 76000 of the Government Code.

    (3) The "DNA penalty" required by Sections 76104.6 and 76104.7 of the Government Code.

    (4) The "emergency medical services penalty" authorized by Section 76000.5 of the Government Code.

    (5) The "service charge" permitted by Section 853.7 of the Penal Code.

    (6) The "special penalty" dedicated for blood alcohol analysis, alcohol program services, traumatic brain injury research, and similar purposes.

    (7) The "state penalty" required by Section 1464.

Amended by Stats 2022 ch 57 (AB 199),s 19, eff. 6/30/2022.

Amended by Stats 2007 ch 302 (SB 425),s 16, eff. 1/1/2008.

Amended by Stats 2003 ch 62 (SB 600), s 233, eff. 1/1/2004.

Amended by Stats 2002 ch 784 (SB 1316), s 555, eff. 1/1/2003.

Amended by Stats 2000 ch 135 (AB 2539) s 136, eff. 1/1/2001.

Section 1463.001 - Deposit with county treasurer; distribution

Except as otherwise provided in this section, all fines and forfeitures imposed and collected for crimes other than parking offenses resulting from a filing in a court, including civil assessments imposed under Section 1214.1, shall as soon as practicable after receipt thereof, be deposited with the county treasurer, and each month the total fines and forfeitures which have accumulated within the past month shall be distributed, as follows:

(a) The state penalties, county penalties, special penalties, service charges, penalty allocations, and civil assessments imposed under Section 1214.1, shall be transferred to the proper funds as required by law.

(b) The base fines shall be distributed, as follows:

    (1) Any base fines which are subject to specific distribution under any other section shall be distributed to the specified funds of the state or local agency.

    (2) Base fines resulting from county arrest not included in paragraph (1), shall be transferred into the proper funds of the county.

    (3) Base fines resulting from city arrests not included in paragraph (1), an amount equal to the applicable county percentages set forth in Section 1463.002, as modified by Section 1463.28, shall be transferred into the proper funds of the county. Until July 1, 1998, the remainder of base fines resulting from city arrests shall be divided between each city and county, with 50 percent deposited to the county's general fund, and 50 percent deposited to the treasury of the appropriate city, and thereafter the remainder of base fines resulting from city arrests shall be deposited to the treasury of the appropriate city.

    (4) In a county that had an agreement as of March 22, 1977, that provides for city fines and forfeitures to accrue to the county in exchange for sales tax receipts, base fines resulting from city arrests not included in paragraph (1) shall be deposited into the proper funds of the county.

(c) Each county shall keep a record of its deposits to its treasury and its transmittal to each city treasury pursuant to this section.

(d) The distribution specified in subdivision (b) applies to all funds subject thereto distributed on or after July 1, 1992, regardless of whether the court has elected to allocate and distribute funds pursuant to Section 1464.8.

(e) Any amounts remitted to the county from amounts collected by the Franchise Tax Board upon referral by a county pursuant to Article 6 (commencing with Section 19280) of Chapter 5 of Part 10.2 of Division 2 of the Revenue and Taxation Code shall be allocated pursuant to this section.

Amended by Stats 2022 ch 771 (AB 160),s 17, eff. 9/29/2022.

Amended by Stats 2022 ch 57 (AB 199),s 20, eff. 6/30/2022.

Amended by Stats. 1998, Ch. 146, Sec. 14.5. Effective July 13, 1998.

Section 1463.002 - Base fine amounts from city arrests

The base fine amounts from city arrests shall be subject to distribution according to the following schedule:

County and city	Percentage
Alameda	
Alameda	18

Ventura

Fillmore	16
Ojai	16
Oxnard	16
Port Hueneme	16
Santa Paula	16
Ventura	16
County percentage	16

Yolo

Davis	22
Winters	19
Woodland	20
County percentage	20

Yuba

Marysville	15
Wheatland	38
County percentage	15

With respect to any city arrest from a city which is not set forth in the above schedule, the county percentage shall apply. A county and city therein may, by mutual agreement, adjust these percentages. Where a county and a city have, prior to June 1, 1991, entered into an agreement to adjust the percentage specified in this section, or where a county and a city have entered into an agreement governing the distribution of revenue from parking penalties, those agreements shall remain in full force and effect until changed by mutual agreement.
Added by Stats. 1991, Ch. 189, Sec. 20. Effective July 29, 1991.

Section 1463.004 - Percentage calculations to establish components of total fines or forfeitures

(a) If a sentencing judge specifies only the total fine or forfeiture, or if an automated case-processing system requires it, percentage calculations may be employed to establish the components of total fines or forfeitures, provided that the aggregate monthly distributions resulting from the calculations are the same as would be produced by strict observance of the statutory distributions.
(b) If a fund would receive less than one hundred dollars ($100) in monthly distributions of total fines and forfeitures by a particular court for at least 11 months of each year, the court may omit that fund from the system for calculating distributions, and shall instead apply the distribution provided for by Section 1463.001.
Added by Stats. 1991, Ch. 189, Sec. 22. Effective July 29, 1991.

Section 1463.005 - Deposit of bases fines not resulting from arrests not subject to allocation

Notwithstanding Section 1463.001, in a county subject to Section 77202.5 of the Government Code, of base fines resulting from arrests not subject to allocation under paragraph (1) of subdivision (b) of Section 1463.001, by a California Highway Patrol Officer on state highways constructed as freeways within the city whereon city police officers enforced the provisions of the Vehicle Code on April 1, 1965, 25 percent shall be deposited in the treasury of the appropriate city, 75 percent shall be deposited in the proper funds of the county.
Amended by Stats. 1997, Ch. 850, Sec. 51. Effective January 1, 1998.

Section 1463.006 - Payment by warrant of county auditor

Any money deposited with the court or with the clerk thereof which, by order of the court or for any other reason, should be returned, in whole or in part, to any person, or which is by law payable to the state or to any other public agency, shall be paid to that person or to the state or to the other public agency by warrant of the county auditor, which shall be drawn upon the requisition of the clerk of the court.
All money deposited as bail which has not been claimed within one year after the final disposition of the case in which the money was deposited, or within one year after an order made by the court for the return or delivery of the money to any person, shall be apportioned between the city and the county and paid or transferred in the manner provided by statute for the apportionment and payment of fines and forfeitures. This paragraph controls over any conflicting provisions of law.
Added by Stats. 1991, Ch. 189, Sec. 23. Effective July 29, 1991.

Section 1463.007 - Comprehensive collection program

(a) Notwithstanding any other law, a county or court that operates a comprehensive collection program may deduct the costs of operating that program, excluding capital expenditures, from any revenues collected under that program. The costs shall be deducted before any distribution of revenues to other governmental entities required by any other law. A county or court operating a comprehensive collection program may establish a minimum base fee, fine, forfeiture, penalty, or assessment amount for inclusion in the program.
(b) Once debt becomes delinquent, it continues to be delinquent and may be subject to collection by a comprehensive collection program. Debt is delinquent and subject to collection by a comprehensive collection program if any of the following conditions is met:
    (1) A defendant does not post bail or appear on or before the date on which the defendant promised to appear, or any lawful continuance of that date, if that defendant was eligible to post and forfeit bail.
    (2) A defendant does not pay the amount imposed by the court on or before the date ordered by the court, or any lawful continuance of that date.
    (3) A defendant has failed to make an installment payment on the date specified by the court.
(c) For the purposes of this section, a "comprehensive collection program" is a separate and distinct revenue collection activity that meets each of the following criteria:
    (1) The program identifies and collects amounts arising from delinquent court-ordered debt, whether or not a warrant has been issued against the alleged violator.

771

(2) The program complies with the requirements of subdivision (b) of Section 1463.010.

(3) The program engages in each of the following activities:

(A) Attempts telephone contact with delinquent debtors for whom the program has a telephone number to inform them of their delinquent status and payment options.

(B) Notifies delinquent debtors for whom the program has an address in writing of their outstanding obligation within 95 days of delinquency.

(C) Generates internal monthly reports to track collections data, such as age of debt and delinquent amounts outstanding.

(D) Uses Department of Motor Vehicles information to locate delinquent debtors.

(E) Accepts payment of delinquent debt by credit card.

(4) The program engages in at least five of the following activities:

(A) Sends delinquent debt to the Franchise Tax Board's Court-Ordered Debt Collections Program.

(B) Sends delinquent debt to the Franchise Tax Board's Interagency Intercept Collections Program.

(C) Initiates driver's license suspension or hold actions when appropriate for a failure to appear in court.

(D) Contracts with one or more private debt collectors to collect delinquent debt.

(E) Sends monthly bills or account statements to all delinquent debtors.

(F) Contracts with local, regional, state, or national skip tracing or locator resources or services to locate delinquent debtors.

(G) Coordinates with the probation department to locate debtors who may be on formal or informal probation.

(H) Uses Employment Development Department employment and wage information to collect delinquent debt.

(I) Establishes wage and bank account garnishments where appropriate.

(J) Places liens on real property owned by delinquent debtors when appropriate.

(K) Uses an automated dialer or automatic call distribution system to manage telephone calls.

(d) A comprehensive collection program shall also administer nondelinquent installment payment plans ordered pursuant to Section 68645.2 of the Government Code, and may recover up to and including thirty-five dollars ($35) per nondelinquent installment plan.

Amended by Stats 2021 ch 79 (AB 143),s 36, eff. 7/16/2021.

Amended by Stats 2017 ch 17 (AB 103),s 33, eff. 6/27/2017.

Added by Stats 2010 ch 720 (SB 857),s 31, eff. 10/19/2010.

Section 1463.009 - Allocation of bail forfeitures

Notwithstanding Section 1463, all bail forfeitures that are collected from any source in a case in which a defendant is charged and convicted of a violation of Section 261, 264.1, 286, 287, 288, 288.5, or 289, or former Section 288a, or of a violent felony as defined in subdivision (c) of Section 667.5 or a serious felony as defined in subdivision (c) of Section 1192.7, and that are required to be deposited with the county treasurer shall be allocated according to the following priority:

(a) The county shall be reimbursed for reasonable administrative costs for the collection of the forfeited property, the maintenance and preservation of the property, and the distribution of the property pursuant to this section.

(b) Out of the remainder of the forfeited bail money, a total of up to 50 percent shall be distributed in the amount necessary to satisfy any civil court judgment in favor of a victim as a result of the offense or a restitution order due to a criminal conviction to a victim who was under 18 years of age at the time of the commission of the offense if the defendant is convicted under Section 261, 264.1, 286, 287, 288, 288.5, or 289, or former Section 288a, and to a victim of any age if the defendant has been convicted of a violent felony as defined in subdivision (c) of Section 667.5 or a serious felony as defined in subdivision (c) of Section 1192.7.

(c) The balance of the amount collected shall be deposited pursuant to Section 1463.

Amended by Stats 2018 ch 423 (SB 1494),s 99, eff. 1/1/2019.

Section 1463.010 - Uniform imposition and enforcement of court-ordered debts

The uniform imposition and enforcement of court-ordered debts are recognized as an important element of California's judicial system. Prompt, efficient, and effective imposition and collection of court-ordered fees, fines, forfeitures, penalties, restitution, and assessments ensure the appropriate respect for court orders. The California State Association of Counties and the Judicial Council are jointly committed to identifying, improving, and seeking to expand access to mechanisms and tools that will enhance efforts to collect court-ordered debt. To provide for this prompt, efficient, and effective collection:

(a) The Judicial Council shall adopt guidelines for a comprehensive program concerning the collection of moneys owed for fees, fines, forfeitures, penalties, and assessments imposed by court order. As part of its guidelines, the Judicial Council may establish standard agreements for entities to provide collection services. As part of its guidelines, the Judicial Council shall include provisions that promote competition by and between entities in providing collection services to courts and counties. The Judicial Council may delegate to the Administrative Director of the Courts the implementation of the aspects of this program to be carried out at the state level.

(b) The courts and counties shall maintain the collection program that was in place on January 1, 1996, unless otherwise agreed to in writing by the court and county. The program may wholly or partially be staffed and operated within the court itself, may be wholly or partially staffed and operated by the county, or may be wholly or partially contracted with a third party. In carrying out this collection program, each superior court and county shall develop a cooperative plan to implement the Judicial Council guidelines. In the event that a court and a county are unwilling or unable to enter into a cooperative plan pursuant to this section, prior to the arbitration procedures required by subdivision (e) of Section 1214.1, the court or the county may request the continuation of negotiations with mediation assistance as mutually agreed upon and provided by the Administrative Director of the Courts and the California State Association of Counties.

(c) The Judicial Council shall develop performance measures and benchmarks to review the effectiveness of the cooperative superior court and county collection programs operating pursuant to this section. Each superior court and county shall jointly report to the Judicial Council, as provided by the Judicial Council, information requested in a reporting template on or before September 1, 2009, and annually thereafter. The Judicial Council shall report annually, on or before December 31, to the Legislature, the Joint Legislative Budget Committee, and the Department of Finance all of the information required to be collected and reported pursuant to subdivision (a) of Section 68514 of the Government Code.

(d) The Judicial Council may, when the efficiency and effectiveness of the collection process may be improved, facilitate a joint collection program between superior courts, between counties, or between superior courts and counties.

(e) The Judicial Council may establish, by court rule, a program providing for the suspension and nonrenewal of a business and professional license if the holder of the license has unpaid fees, fines, forfeitures, penalties, and assessments imposed upon them under a court order. The Judicial Council may provide that some or all of the superior courts or counties participate in the program. Any program established by the Judicial Council shall ensure that the licensee receives adequate and appropriate notice of the proposed suspension or nonrenewal of the licensee's license and has an opportunity to contest the suspension or nonrenewal. The opportunity to contest may not require a court hearing.

(f) Notwithstanding any other provision of law, the Judicial Council, after consultation with the Franchise Tax Board with respect to collections under Section 19280 of the Revenue and Taxation Code, may provide for an amnesty program involving the collection of outstanding fees, fines, forfeitures, penalties, and assessments, applicable either statewide or within one or more counties. The amnesty program shall provide that some or all of the interest or collections costs imposed on outstanding fees, fines, forfeitures, penalties, and assessments may be waived if the remaining amounts due are paid within the amnesty period.

Amended by Stats 2019 ch 637 (AB 1818),s 10, eff. 1/1/2020.
Amended by Stats 2008 ch 311 (SB 1407),s 28, eff. 1/1/2009.
Amended by Stats 2007 ch 132 (AB 367),s 3, eff. 1/1/2008.
Amended by Stats 2004 ch 183 (AB 3082), s 272, eff. 1/1/2005.
Amended by Stats 2003 ch 275 (SB 940), s 3, eff. 1/1/2004.

Section 1463.011 - Garnishment of wages or levy of bank accounts of homeless person under 25 years of age prohibited

(a) Notwithstanding any other provision of law, if a court, during the course of its routine process to collect fees, fines, forfeitures, or other penalties imposed by a court due to a citation issued for the violation of a state or local law, obtains information indicating that a person under 25 years of age, who has been issued a citation for truancy, loitering, curfew violations, or illegal lodging that is outstanding or unpaid, is homeless or has no permanent address, the court shall not garnish the wages or levy against bank accounts of that person until that person is 25 years of age or older, as that age is recorded by that person's credit report or other document already in the possession of, or previously provided to, the court.

(b) For purposes of this section a person is considered to be "homeless" or as having "no permanent address" if that person does not have a fixed, regular, adequate nighttime residence, or has a primary nighttime residence that is one of the following:

    (1) A supervised publicly or privately operated shelter designed to provide temporary living accommodations, including, but not limited to, welfare hotels, congregate shelters, and transitional housing for the mentally ill.

    (2) An institution that provides a temporary residence for individuals intended to be institutionalized.

    (3) A public or private place not designed for, or ordinarily used as, a regular sleeping accommodation for human beings.

(c) Nothing in this section shall be construed to prevent a court from engaging in any other lawful debt collection activities.

(d) Nothing in this section shall be construed to require a court to perform any further investigation or financial screening into any matter beyond the scope of its regular duties.

(e) Nothing in this section shall be construed to prevent the Judicial Council from altering any best practices or recommendations for collection programs pursuant to Section 1463.010.

(f) Nothing in this section shall be construed to prevent a court from garnishing a person's wages or levying against a person's bank accounts if the court, subsequent to its initial determination that the person was a homeless youth exempt from wage garnishment or levy under this section, obtains evidence that the individual is no longer homeless.

Added by Stats 2011 ch 466 (AB 1111),s 2, eff. 1/1/2012.

Section 1463.012 - Prohibited debt collection activities

(a) Notwithstanding any other law, if a court, during the course of its routine process to collect fees, fines, forfeitures, or other penalties imposed by a court due to a citation issued for the violation of a state or local law, obtains information indicating that a person who has been issued a citation for loitering, curfew violations, or illegal lodging that is outstanding or unpaid served in the military within the last eight years and is homeless or has no permanent address, the court shall not garnish the wages or levy against bank accounts of that person for five years from the date that the court obtained that information.

(b) For purposes of this section, a person is considered to be "homeless" or as having "no permanent address" if that person does not have a fixed, regular, adequate nighttime residence, or has a primary nighttime residence that is one of the following:

    (1) A supervised publicly or privately operated shelter designed to provide temporary living accommodations, including, but not limited to, welfare hotels, congregate shelters, and transitional housing for the mentally ill.

    (2) An institution that provides a temporary residence for individuals intended to be institutionalized.

    (3) A public or private place not designed for, or ordinarily used as, a regular sleeping accommodation for human beings.

(c) Nothing in this section shall be construed to prevent a court from engaging in any other lawful debt collection activities.

(d) Nothing in this section shall be construed to require a court to perform any further investigation or financial screening into any matter beyond the scope of its regular duties.

(e) Nothing in this section shall be construed to prevent the Judicial Council from altering any best practices or recommendations for collection programs pursuant to Section 1463.010.

(f) Nothing in this section shall be construed to prevent a court from garnishing a person's wages or levying against a person's bank accounts if the court, subsequent to its initial determination that the person was a homeless veteran exempt from wage garnishment or levy under this section, obtains evidence that the individual is no longer homeless, or that the court had, on a previous occasion, suspended garnishment of that person's wages or levying against that person's bank accounts pursuant to subdivision (a).

Added by Stats 2013 ch 234 (AB 508),s 2, eff. 1/1/2014.

Section 1463.02 - Task force to evaluate criminal and traffic-related court-ordered debts

(a) On or before June 30, 2011, the Judicial Council shall establish a task force to evaluate criminal and traffic-related court-ordered debts imposed against adult and juvenile offenders. The task force shall be comprised of the following members:

(1) Two members appointed by the California State Association of Counties.

(2) Two members appointed by the League of California Cities.

(3) Two court executives, two judges, and two Administrative Office of the Courts employees appointed by the Judicial Council.

(4) One member appointed by the Controller.

(5) One member appointed by the Franchise Tax Board.

(6) One member appointed by the California Victim Compensation Board.

(7) One member appointed by the Department of Corrections and Rehabilitation.

(8) One member appointed by the Department of Finance.

(9) One member appointed by each house of the Legislature.

(10) A county public defender and a city attorney appointed by the Speaker of the Assembly.

(11) A defense attorney in private practice and a district attorney appointed by the Senate Committee on Rules.

(b) The Judicial Council shall designate a chairperson for the task force. The task force shall, among other duties, do all of the following:

(1) Identify all criminal and traffic-related court-ordered fees, fines, forfeitures, penalties, and assessments imposed under law.

(2) Identify the distribution of revenue derived from those debts and the expenditures made by those entities that benefit from the revenues.

(3) Consult with state and local entities that would be affected by a simplification and consolidation of criminal and traffic-related court-ordered debts.

(4) Evaluate and make recommendations to the Judicial Council and the Legislature for consolidating and simplifying the imposition of criminal and traffic-related court-ordered debts and the distribution of the revenue derived from those debts with the goal of improving the process for those entities that benefit from the revenues, and recommendations, if any, for adjustment to the court-ordered debts.

(c) The task force also shall document recent annual revenues from the various penalty assessments and surcharges and, to the extent feasible, evaluate the extent to which the amount of each penalty assessment and surcharge impacts total annual revenues, imposition of criminal sentences, and the actual amounts assessed.

(d) The task force also shall evaluate and make recommendations to the Judicial Council and the Legislature on or before June 30, 2011, regarding the priority in which court-ordered debts should be satisfied and the use of comprehensive collection programs authorized pursuant to Section 1463.007, including associated cost-recovery practices.

Amended by Stats 2016 ch 31 (SB 836),s 243, eff. 6/27/2016.

Amended by Stats 2010 ch 720 (SB 857),s 32, eff. 10/19/2010.

Added by Stats 2007 ch 132 (AB 367),s 4, eff. 1/1/2008.

Section 1463.04 - Transfer to Winter Recreation Fund and county general fund to pay for California SNO-PARK Permit Program

Notwithstanding Section 1463, out of the moneys deposited with the county treasurer pursuant to Section 1463, there shall be transferred once a month into the State Treasury to the credit of the Winter Recreation Fund an amount equal to 50 percent of all fines and forfeitures collected during the preceding month upon conviction or upon the forfeiture of bail from any person of any violation of Section 5091.15 of the Public Resources Code, and an amount equal to the remaining 50 percent shall be transferred to the county general fund and deposited in a special account which shall be used exclusively to pay for the cost of furthering the purposes of the California SNO-PARK Permit Program, including, but not limited to, the snow removal, maintenance, and development of designated parking areas.

Added by Stats. 1991, Ch. 189, Sec. 25. Effective July 29, 1991.

Section 1463.07 - [Repealed]

Repealed by Stats 2021 ch 257 (AB 177),s 34, eff. 9/23/2021.

Added by Stats. 1997, Ch. 850, Sec. 56. Effective January 1, 1998.

Section 1463.1 - Deposit in bank account of all moneys deposited as bail

Notwithstanding any other provisions of law except Section 77009 of the Government Code, any trial court may elect, with prior approval of the Administrative Director of the Courts, to deposit in a bank account pursuant to Section 53679 of the Government Code, all moneys deposited as bail with the court, or with the clerk thereof.

All moneys received and disbursed through the bank account shall be properly and uniformly accounted for under any procedures the Controller may deem necessary. The Judicial Council may regulate the bank accounts, provided that its regulations are not inconsistent with those of the Controller.

Amended by Stats 2001 ch 812 (AB 223), s 25, eff. 1/1/2002.

Section 1463.5 - Distribution of funds and assessments upon basis of probability sampling

The distribution of funds required pursuant to Section 1463, and the distribution of assessments imposed and collected under Section 1464 and Section 42006 of the Vehicle Code, may be determined and made upon the basis of probability sampling. The sampling shall be procedural in nature and shall not substantively modify the distributions required pursuant to Sections 1463 and 1464 and Section 42006 of the Vehicle Code. The procedure for the sampling shall be prescribed by the county auditor and the procedure and its implementation shall be approved by the board of supervisors and a majority of the cities within a county. The reasonableness of the distribution shall be verified during the audit performed pursuant to Section 71383 of the Government Code.

Amended by Stats. 1989, Ch. 897, Sec. 40.

Section 1463.7 - Use of funds transferred to Regents of University of California

Funds transferred to the Regents of the University of California pursuant to Section 1462.3 may not be utilized to purchase land or to construct any parking facility. These funds shall be utilized for the development, enhancement, and operation of alternate methods of transportation of students and employees of the University of California and for the mitigation of the impact of off-campus student and employee parking in university communities.

Added by Stats. 1991, Ch. 189, Sec. 26. Effective July 29, 1991.

Section 1463.9 - Separation of percentage of fines and forfeitures for specified violations

Notwithstanding the provisions of Section 1463, 50 percent of all fines and forfeitures collected upon conviction, or upon forfeiture of bail, for violations of Section 13002 of the Health and Safety Code, Sections 23111 and 23112, and subdivision (a) of Section 23113 of the Vehicle Code, and Section 374.3 of this code shall be kept separate and apart from any other fines and forfeitures. These fines and forfeitures shall, as soon as practicable after their receipt, be deposited with the county treasurer of the county in which the court is situated and shall be distributed as prescribed in Section 1463, except that the money distributed to any county or city shall be expended only for litter cleanup activities within that city or county.

Added by Stats. 1991, Ch. 189, Sec. 27. Effective July 29, 1991.

Section 1463.10 - Allocation of fines and forfeitures collected for conviction of Health and Safety Code Section 11366.7

Notwithstanding Section 1463, fines and forfeitures which are collected for a conviction of a violation of Section 11366.7 of the Health and Safety Code and which are required to be deposited with the county treasurer pursuant to Section 1463 shall be allocated as follows:

(a) To reimburse any local agency for the reasonable costs of the removal and disposal, or storage, of any chemical or drug, or any laboratory apparatus or device, sold by a person convicted under Section 11366.7 of the Health and Safety Code.

(b) The balance of the amount collected, if any, shall be deposited by the county treasurer pursuant to Section 1463.

Added by Stats. 1994, Ch. 979, Sec. 4. Effective January 1, 1995.

Section 1463.11 - Allocation of money collected for specified violations of Vehicle Code

Notwithstanding Sections 1463 and 1464 of this code and Section 76000 of the Government Code, moneys that are collected for a violation of subdivision (a) or (c) of Section 21453 of, subdivision (c) of Section 21454 of, or subdivision (a) of Section 21457 of, the Vehicle Code, and which are required to be deposited with the county treasurer pursuant to Section 1463 of this code shall be allocated as follows:

(a) The first 30 percent of the amount collected shall be allocated to the general fund of the city or county in which the offense occurred.

(b) The balance of the amount collected shall be deposited by the county treasurer under Sections 1463 and 1464.

Added by Stats. 1997, Ch. 852, Sec. 2. Effective January 1, 1998.

Section 1463.12 - Allocation of moneys collection for specified violations of Vehicle Code involving railroad grade crossings

Notwithstanding Sections 1463 and 1464 of this code and Section 76000 of the Government Code, moneys that are collected for a violation of subdivision (c) of Section 21752 or Section 22450 of the Vehicle Code, involving railroad grade crossings, or Section 22451, 22452, or subdivision (c) of Section 22526 of the Vehicle Code, and that are required to be deposited with the county treasurer pursuant to Section 1463 of this code shall be allocated as follows:

(a) If the offense occurred in an area where a transit district or transportation commission or authority established under Division 12 (commencing with Section 130000) of the Public Utilities Code provides rail transportation, the first 30 percent of the amount collected shall be allocated to the general fund of that transit district or transportation commission or authority to be used only for public safety and public education purposes relating to railroad grade crossings.

(b) If there is no transit district or transportation commission or authority providing rail transportation in the area where the offense occurred, the first 30 percent of the amount collected shall be allocated to the general fund of the county in which the offense occurred, to be used only for public safety and public education purposes relating to railroad grade crossings.

(c) The balance of the amount collected shall be deposited by the county treasurer under Section 1463.

(d) A transit district, transportation commission or authority, or a county that is allocated funds pursuant to subdivision (a) or (b) shall provide public safety and public education relating to railroad grade crossings only to the extent that those purposes are funded by the allocations provided pursuant to subdivision (a) or (b).

Amended by Stats 2005 ch 716 (AB 1067),s 4, eff. 1/1/2006

EFFECTIVE 1/1/2000. Added October 10, 1999 (Bill Number: AB 923) (Chapter 841).

Section 1463.13 - Alcohol and drug problem assessment program

(a) Each county may develop, implement, operate, and administer an alcohol and drug problem assessment program for persons convicted of a crime in which the court finds that alcohol or substance abuse was substantially involved in the commission of the crime. This program may be operated in coordination with the program developed under Article 6 (commencing with Section 23645) of Chapter 4 of Division 11.5 of the Vehicle Code.

(1) A portion of any program established pursuant to this section shall include a face-to-face interview with each program participant.

(2) No person convicted of driving under the influence of alcohol or a controlled substance or a related offense shall participate in any program established pursuant to this section.

(b) An alcohol and drug problem assessment report shall be made on each person who participates in the program. The report may be used to determine the appropriate sentence for the person. The report shall be submitted to the court within 14 days of the completion of the assessment.

(c) In any county in which the county operates an alcohol and drug problem assessment program under this section, a court may order any person convicted of a crime that involved the use of drugs or alcohol, including any person who is found to have been under the influence of drugs or alcohol during the commission of the crime, to participate in the assessment program.

(d) Notwithstanding any other provision of law, in addition to any other fine or penalty assessment, there shall be levied an assessment of not more than one hundred fifty dollars ($150) upon every fine, penalty, or forfeiture imposed and collected by the courts for a public offense wherein the court orders the offender to participate in a county alcohol and drug problem assessment program. The assessment shall only be levied in a county upon the adoption of a resolution by the board of supervisors of the county making that county subject to this section.

(e) The court shall determine if the defendant has the ability to pay the assessment. If the court determines that the defendant has the ability to pay the assessment then the court may set the amount to be reimbursed and order the defendant to pay that sum to the county in the manner which the court determines is reasonable and compatible with the defendant's financial ability. In making a determination of whether a defendant has the ability to pay, the court shall take into account the amount of any fine imposed upon the defendant and any amount the defendant has been ordered to pay in victim restitution.

(f) Notwithstanding Section 1463 or 1464 of the Penal Code or any other provision of law, all moneys collected pursuant to this section shall be deposited in a special account in the county treasury and shall be used exclusively to pay for the costs of developing, implementing, operating, maintaining, and evaluating alcohol and drug problem assessment and monitoring programs.

(g) On January 15 of each year, the treasurer of each county that administers an alcohol and drug problem assessment and monitoring program shall determine those moneys in the special account which were not expended during the preceding fiscal year, and shall transfer those moneys to the general fund of the county.

Added by Stats 2000 ch 165 (SB 1386) s 1, eff. 1/1/2001.

Section 1463.14 - Deposit to special account used to pay for analysis of blood, breath, or urine for alcohol content or presence of drugs

(a) Notwithstanding the provisions of Section 1463, of the moneys deposited with the county treasurer pursuant to Section 1463, fifty dollars ($50) of each fine collected for each conviction of a violation of Section 23103, 23104, 23105, 23152, or 23153 of the Vehicle Code shall be deposited in a special account that shall be used exclusively to pay for the cost of performing for the county, or a city or special district within the county, analysis of blood, breath or urine for alcohol content or for the presence of drugs, or for services related to that testing. The sum shall not exceed the reasonable cost of providing the services for which the sum is intended. On November 1 of each year, the treasurer of each county shall determine those moneys in the special account that were not expended during the preceding fiscal year, and shall transfer those moneys into the general fund of the county. The board of supervisors may, by resolution, assign the treasurer's duty to determine the amount of money that was not expended to the auditor or another county officer. The county may retain an amount of that money equal to its administrative cost incurred pursuant to this section, and shall distribute the remainder pursuant to Section 1463. If the account becomes exhausted, the public entity ordering a test performed pursuant to this subdivision shall bear the costs of the test.

(b) The board of supervisors of a county may, by resolution, authorize an additional penalty upon each defendant convicted of a violation of Section 23152 or 23153 of the Vehicle Code, of an amount equal to the cost of testing for alcohol content, less the fifty dollars ($50) deposited as provided in subdivision (a). The additional penalty authorized by this subdivision shall be imposed only in those instances where the defendant has the ability to pay, but in no case shall the defendant be ordered to pay a penalty in excess of fifty dollars ($50). The penalty authorized shall be deposited directly with the county, or city or special district within the county, that performed the test, in the special account described in subdivision (a), and shall not be the basis for an additional assessment pursuant to Section 1464, or Chapter 12 (commencing with Section 76010) of Title 8 of the Government Code. For purposes of this subdivision, "ability to pay" means the overall capability of the defendant to pay the additional penalty authorized by this subdivision, taking into consideration all of the following:

(1) Present financial obligations, including family support obligations, and fines, penalties, and other obligations to the court.

(2) Reasonably discernible future financial position over the next 12 months.

(3) Any other factor or factors that may bear upon the defendant's financial ability to pay the additional penalty.

(c) The Department of Justice shall promulgate rules and regulations to implement the provisions of this section.

Amended by Stats 2007 ch 682 (AB 430),s 5, eff. 1/1/2008.

Amended by Stats 2005 ch 158 (SB 966),s 27, eff. 1/1/2006

Section 1463.15 - Deposit to special account to pay for vehicle inspection and sobriety checkpoint program

Notwithstanding Section 1463, if a county board of supervisors establishes a combined vehicle inspection and sobriety checkpoint program under Section 2814.1 of the Vehicle Code, thirty-five dollars ($35) of the money deposited with the county treasurer under Section 1463.001 and collected from each fine and forfeiture imposed under subdivision (b) of Section 42001.2 of the Vehicle Code shall be deposited in a special account to be used exclusively to pay the cost incurred by the county for establishing and conducting the combined vehicle inspection and sobriety checkpoint program. The money allocated to pay the cost incurred by the county for establishing and conducting the combined checkpoint program pursuant to this section may only be deposited in the special account after a fine imposed pursuant to subdivision (b) of Section 42001.2, and any penalty assessment thereon, has been collected.

Added by Stats 2003 ch 482 (SB 708), s 2, eff. 1/1/2004.

Section 1463.16 - Deposit to special account for alcohol programs and services for general population

(a) Notwithstanding Section 1203.1 or 1463, fifty dollars ($50) of each fine collected for each conviction of a violation of Section 23103, 23104, 23105, 23152, or 23153 of the Vehicle Code shall be deposited with the county treasurer in a special account for exclusive allocation by the county for the county's alcoholism program, with approval of the board of supervisors, for alcohol programs and services for the general population. These funds shall be allocated through the local planning process and expenditures reported to the State Department of Health Care Services pursuant to subdivision (c) of Section 11798.2 and subdivision (a) of Section 11818.5 of the Health and Safety Code. Programs shall be certified by the State Department of Health Care Services or have made application for certification to be eligible for funding under this section. The county shall implement the intent and procedures of subdivision (b) of Section 11812 of the Health and Safety Code while distributing funds under this section.

(b) In a county of the 1st, 2nd, 3rd, 15th, 19th, 20th, or 24th class, notwithstanding Section 1463, of the moneys deposited with the county treasurer pursuant to Section 1463, fifty dollars ($50) for each conviction of a violation of Section 23103, 23104, 23105, 23152, or 23153 of the Vehicle Code shall be deposited in a special account for exclusive allocation by the administrator of the county's alcoholism program, with approval of the board of supervisors, for alcohol programs and services for the general population. These funds shall be allocated through the local planning process and expenditures reported to the State Department of Health Care Services pursuant to subdivision (c) of Section 11798.2 and subdivision (a) of Section 11818.5 of the Health and Safety Code. For those services for which standards have been developed and certification is available, programs shall be certified by the State Department of Health Care Services or shall apply for certification to be eligible for funding under this section. The county alcohol administrator shall implement the intent and procedures of subdivision (b) of Section 11812 of the Health and Safety Code while distributing funds under this section.

(c) The Board of Supervisors of Contra Costa County may, by resolution, authorize the imposition of a fifty dollar ($50) assessment by the court upon each defendant convicted of a violation of Section 23152 or 23153 of the Vehicle Code for deposit in the account from which the fifty dollar ($50) distribution specified in subdivision (a) is deducted.

(d) It is the specific intent of the Legislature that funds expended under this part shall be used for ongoing alcoholism program services as well as for contracts with private nonprofit organizations to upgrade facilities to meet state certification and state licensing standards and federal nondiscrimination regulations relating to accessibility for handicapped persons.

(e) Counties may retain up to 5 percent of the funds collected to offset administrative costs of collection and disbursement.

Amended by Stats 2013 ch 22 (AB 75),s 78, eff. 6/27/2013, op. 7/1/2013.

Amended by Stats 2007 ch 682 (AB 430),s 6, eff. 1/1/2008.

Section 1463.17 - Deposit to special account to pay for performing analysis of blood, breath, or urine for alcohol content or presence of drugs

(a) In a county of the 19th class, notwithstanding any other provision of this chapter, of the moneys deposited with the county treasurer pursuant to Section 1463, fifty dollars ($50) for each conviction of a violation of Section 23103, 23104, 23105, 23152, or 23153 of the Vehicle Code shall be deposited in a special account to be used exclusively to pay the cost incurred by the county or a city or special district within the county, with approval of the board of supervisors, for performing analysis of blood, breath, or urine for alcohol content or for the presence of drugs, or for services related to the testing.

(b) The application of this section shall not reduce the county's remittance to the state specified in paragraph (2) of subdivision (b) of Section 77201, paragraph (2) of subdivision (b) of Section 77201.1, and paragraph (2) of subdivision (a) of Section 77201.3 of the Government Code.

Amended by Stats 2007 ch 682 (AB 430),s 7.5, eff. 1/1/2008.

Amended by Stats 2007 ch 383 (AB 227),s 5, eff. 1/1/2008.

Section 1463.18 - Allocation of moneys collection for conviction of violation of Vehicle Code Section 23152 or 23153

(a) Notwithstanding the provisions of Section 1463, moneys which are collected for a conviction of a violation of Section 23152 or 23153 of the Vehicle Code and which are required to be deposited with the county treasurer pursuant to Section 1463 shall be allocated as follows:

(1) The first twenty dollars ($20) of any amount collected for a conviction shall be transferred to the Restitution Fund. This amount shall be aggregated by the county treasurer and transferred to the State Treasury once per month for deposit in the Restitution Fund.

(2) The balance of the amount collected, if any, shall be deposited by the county treasurer pursuant to Section 1463.

(b) The amount transferred to the Restitution Fund pursuant to this section shall be in addition to any amount of any additional fine or assessment imposed pursuant to Sections 1202.4 and 1203.04, as operative on or before August 3, 1995, or Section 13967, as operative on or before September 28, 1994, of the Government Code. The amount deposited to the Restitution Fund pursuant to this section shall be used for the purpose of indemnification of victims pursuant to Section 13965 of the Government Code, with priority given to victims of alcohol-related traffic offenses.

Amended by Stats. 1996, Ch. 1077, Sec. 26. Effective January 1, 1997.

Section 1463.20 - Deposit of $50 of parking penalty in special account for altering public facilities to make them accessible to persons with disabilities

Notwithstanding any other law, fifty dollars ($50) of every parking penalty received by a local entity pursuant to Section 42001.5 of the Vehicle Code may be deposited by the treasurer of the local entity in a special account to be used by the local entity for the sole purposes of altering existing public facilities to make them accessible to persons with disabilities in compliance with the Americans with Disabilities Act of 1990 (42 U.S.C. Sec. 12101, et seq.), and federal regulations adopted pursuant to that act, and covering the actual administrative cost of setting aside fifty dollars ($50) of every parking penalty received pursuant to Section 42001.5 of the Vehicle Code for that purpose.

Added by Stats. 1993, Ch. 137, Sec. 1. Effective January 1, 1994.

Section 1463.21 - [Repealed]

Added by Stats 2002 ch 590 (AB 1886), s 2, eff. 1/1/2003.

See Stats 2002 ch 590 (AB 1886), s 5.

Section 1463.22 - Deposit of moneys deposited with county treasurer in special accounts

(a) Notwithstanding Section 1463, of the moneys deposited with the county treasurer pursuant to Section 1463, seventeen dollars and fifty cents ($17.50) for each conviction of a violation of Section 16028 of the Vehicle Code shall be deposited by the county treasurer in a special account and allocated to defray costs of municipal and superior courts incurred in administering Sections 16028, 16030, and 16031 of the Vehicle Code. Any moneys in the special account in excess of the amount required to defray those costs shall be redeposited and distributed by the county treasurer pursuant to Section 1463.

(b) Notwithstanding Section 1463, of the moneys deposited with the county treasurer pursuant to Section 1463, three dollars ($3) for each conviction for a violation of Section 16028 of the Vehicle Code shall be initially deposited by the county treasurer in a special account, and shall be transmitted once per month to the Controller for deposit in the Motor Vehicle Account in the State Transportation Fund. These moneys shall be available, when appropriated, to defray the administrative costs incurred by the Department of Motor Vehicles pursuant to Sections 16031, 16032, 16034, and 16035 of the Vehicle Code. It is the intent of this subdivision to provide sufficient revenues to pay for all of the department's costs in administering those sections of the Vehicle Code.

(c) Notwithstanding Section 1463, of the moneys deposited with the county treasurer pursuant to Section 1463, ten dollars ($10) upon the conviction of, or upon the forfeiture of bail from, any person arrested or notified for a violation of Section 16028 of the Vehicle Code shall be deposited by the county treasurer in a special account and shall be transmitted monthly to the Controller for deposit in the General Fund.

Amended by Stats. 1998, Ch. 931, Sec. 422. Effective September 28, 1998.

Section 1463.23 - [Repealed]

Repealed by Stats 2017 ch 537 (SB 239),s 18, eff. 1/1/2018.

Amended by Stats 2010 ch 328 (SB 1330),s 173, eff. 1/1/2011.

Section 1463.25 - Deposit in special county alcohol abuse and prevention fund

Notwithstanding Section 1203.1 or 1463, and in addition to any allocation under Section 1463.16, the moneys from alcohol abuse education and prevention penalty assessments collected pursuant to Section 23196 of the Vehicle Code shall be initially deposited by the county treasurer in a special county alcohol abuse and prevention fund for exclusive allocation by the county alcohol program administrator, subject to the approval of the board of supervisors, for the county's alcohol abuse education and prevention program pursuant to Section 11802 of the Health and Safety Code.

A county shall not use more than 5 percent of the funds deposited in the special account for administrative costs.

Added by Stats. 1991, Ch. 189, Sec. 33. Effective July 29, 1991.

Section 1463.26 - Transfer to city traffic fund

Notwithstanding Section 1463, out of moneys deposited with the county treasurer pursuant to Section 1463, there shall be transferred, once a month, to the traffic fund of the city, an amount equal to one-third of all fines and forfeitures collected during the preceding month upon the conviction of, or upon the forfeiture of bail by, any person charged with a violation of Section 21655.5 or 21655.8 of the Vehicle Code within that city, and an amount equal to one-third of those fines and forfeitures shall be transferred into the general fund of the county, and an amount equal to one-third of those fines and forfeitures shall be transferred to the agency whose approval is required for high-occupancy vehicle lanes on state highways pursuant to Section 21655.6 of the Vehicle Code. If the arrest for a violation of either Section 21655.5 or 21655.8 of the Vehicle Code was not within a city, then 50 percent of the fines and forfeitures shall be transferred to the general fund of the county and 50 percent shall be transferred to the agency having authority to approve high-occupancy vehicle lanes pursuant to Section 21655.6 of the Vehicle Code. Money received by the agency having the authority to approve high-occupancy vehicle lanes pursuant to Section 21655.6 of the Vehicle Code shall be used by that agency for the purposes of improving traffic flow and traffic operations upon the state highway system within the jurisdiction of that agency. In counties where there exists a county transportation commission created pursuant to Division 12 (commencing with Section 130000) of the Public Utilities Code, that commission is the agency for purposes of this section.

Added by Stats. 1991, Ch. 189, Sec. 34. Effective July 29, 1991.

Section 1463.27 - Fee to fund domestic violence prevention programs

(a) Notwithstanding any other provision of law, in addition to any other fine or penalty assessment, the board of supervisors of a county may, by resolution, authorize a fee of not more than two hundred fifty dollars ($250) upon every fine, penalty, or forfeiture imposed and collected by the courts for a crime of domestic violence specified in paragraph (1) of subdivision (e) of Section 243 and in Section 273.5. Notwithstanding Section 1463 or 1464, money collected pursuant to this section shall be used to fund domestic violence prevention programs that focus on assisting immigrants, refugees, or persons who live in a rural community. Counties with existing domestic violence prevention programs that assist those persons may direct funds to those programs.

(b) The court shall determine if the defendant has the ability to pay the fee imposed under this section. In making that determination, the court shall take into account the total amount of fines and restitution that the defendant is subject to, and may waive payment of this additional fee.

(c) The court shall deposit the moneys collected pursuant to this section in a fund designated by the board of supervisors, to be used as specified in subdivision (a).

Added by Stats 2008 ch 241 (AB 2405),s 2, eff. 1/1/2009.

Section 1463.28 - Resolution directing fines and forfeitures to be deposited in county general fund

(a) Notwithstanding any other provision of law, for each option county, as defined by Section 77004 of the Government Code, which has adopted the resolution specified in subdivision (b), that portion of fines and forfeitures, whether collected by the courts or by other processing agencies, which are attributable to an increase in the bail amounts adopted subsequent to the resolution pursuant to subdivision (c) of Section 1269b which would otherwise be divided between the county and cities within the county shall be deposited into the county general fund up to the annual limit listed in subdivision (b) for that county. Fine and forfeiture increments which exceed the specified annual limit shall be divided between the county and the cities within the county as otherwise provided by law. The scheduled bail amounts in such a county may exceed the bail amounts established by the Judicial Council pursuant to subdivision (c) of Section 1269b.

(b) The counties which may adopt a resolution directing that future increments in fines and forfeitures as specified in subdivision (a) be deposited in the county general fund and the annual limit applicable to those counties is as follows:

County	Annual Limit
Alpine	$ 300,000
Amador	200,000
Butte	900,000
Calaveras	300,000
Contra Costa	100,000
Del Norte	200,000
Fresno	700,000
Humboldt	200,000
Kings	300,000
Lake	400,000
Lassen	200,000
Los Angeles	15,000,000
Madera	600,000
Mariposa	200,000
Mendocino	600,000

Modoc	200,000
Mono	200,000
Plumas	200,000
San Benito	300,000
San Diego	5,200,000
San Joaquin	1,000,000
Santa Clara	3,200,000
Sierra	300,000
Stanislaus	1,900,000
Sutter	800,000
Trinity	200,000
Tulare	2,000,000
Tuolumne	400,000
Yolo	700,000
Yuba	900,000

(c) Except as provided in Sections 40200.3 and 40200.4 of the Vehicle Code, this section does not apply to the collection of parking penalties.
Amended by Stats 2003 ch 149 (SB 79), s 76.5, eff. 1/1/2004.

Section 1464 - State penalty for criminal offenses involving violation of Vehicle Code or local ordinance

(a)

(1) Subject to Chapter 12 (commencing with Section 76000) of Title 8 of the Government Code, and except as otherwise provided in this section, there shall be levied a state penalty in the amount of ten dollars ($10) for every ten dollars ($10), or part of ten dollars ($10), upon every fine, penalty, or forfeiture imposed and collected by the courts for all criminal offenses, including all offenses, except parking offenses as defined in subdivision (i) of Section 1463, involving a violation of a section of the Vehicle Code or any local ordinance adopted pursuant to the Vehicle Code.

(2) Any bail schedule adopted pursuant to Section 1269b or bail schedule adopted by the Judicial Council pursuant to Section 40310 of the Vehicle Code may include the necessary amount to pay the penalties established by this section and Chapter 12 (commencing with Section 76000) of Title 8 of the Government Code, and the surcharge authorized by Section 1465.7, for all matters where a personal appearance is not mandatory and the bail is posted primarily to guarantee payment of the fine.

(3) The penalty imposed by this section does not apply to the following:

(A) Any restitution fine.

(B) Any penalty authorized by Chapter 12 (commencing with Section 76000) of Title 8 of the Government Code.

(C) Any parking offense subject to Article 3 (commencing with Section 40200) of Chapter 1 of Division 17 of the Vehicle Code.

(D) The state surcharge authorized by Section 1465.7.

(b) Where multiple offenses are involved, the state penalty shall be based upon the total fine or bail for each case. When a fine is suspended, in whole or in part, the state penalty shall be reduced in proportion to the suspension.

(c) When any deposited bail is made for an offense to which this section applies, and for which a court appearance is not mandatory, the person making the deposit shall also deposit a sufficient amount to include the state penalty prescribed by this section for forfeited bail. If bail is returned, the state penalty paid thereon pursuant to this section shall also be returned.

(d) In any case where a person convicted of any offense, to which this section applies, is in prison until the fine is satisfied, the judge may waive all or any part of the state penalty, the payment of which would work a hardship on the person convicted or his or her immediate family.

(e) After a determination by the court of the amount due, the clerk of the court shall collect the penalty and transmit it to the county treasury. The portion thereof attributable to Chapter 12 (commencing with Section 76000) of Title 8 of the Government Code shall be deposited in the appropriate county fund and 70 percent of the balance shall then be transmitted to the State Treasury, to be deposited in the State Penalty Fund, which is hereby created, and 30 percent to remain on deposit in the county general fund. The transmission to the State Treasury shall be carried out in the same manner as fines collected for the state by a county.

(f) Notwithstanding any other law, the Director of Finance shall provide a schedule to the Controller for all transfers of funds made available by the Budget Act from the State Penalty Fund in the current fiscal year.

(g) Upon the order of the Department of Finance, sufficient funds may be transferred by the Controller from the General Fund for cashflow needs of the State Penalty Fund. A cashflow loan made pursuant to this provision shall be short term and does not constitute a General Fund expenditure. A cashflow loan and the repayment of a cashflow loan does not affect the General Fund reserve.
Amended by Stats 2017 ch 17 (AB 103),s 34, eff. 6/27/2017.
Amended by Stats 2007 ch 302 (SB 425),s 17, eff. 1/1/2008.
Amended by Stats 2000 ch 248 (AB 1053) s 1, eff. 8/25/2000.

Section 1464.05 - "Assessment" defined
Wherever the word "assessment" appears in any reference to Section 1464 in any law or regulation with regard to a fine, penalty, or bail forfeiture, it shall be deemed to refer to the penalty, state penalty, or additional penalty required by Section 1464.
Added by Stats. 1990, Ch. 1293, Sec. 3.

Section 1464.2 - [Repealed]
Repealed by Stats 2017 ch 17 (AB 103),s 35, eff. 6/27/2017.
Added 10/10/1999 (Bill Number: AB 975) (Chapter 610).

Section 1464.8 - Allocation and distribution based upon law in effect during accounting period when payment made

Notwithstanding any other provision of law, when an allocation and distribution of any fine, forfeiture, penalty, fee, or assessment collected in any criminal case is made, including, but not limited to, moneys collected pursuant to this chapter, Section 13003 of the Fish and Game Code, Chapter 12 (commencing with Section 76000) of Title 8 of the Government Code, and Sections 11372.5 and 11502 of the Health and Safety Code, the allocation and distribution of any payment may be based upon the law in effect during the accounting period when the payment is made.

Amended by Stats. 1991, Ch. 189, Sec. 37. Effective July 29, 1991.

Section 1465.5 - Imposition of assessment by county upon adoption of resolution

An assessment of two dollars ($2) for every ten dollars ($10) or fraction thereof, for every fine, forfeiture, or parking penalty imposed and collected pursuant to Section 42001.13 of the Vehicle Code for violation of Section 22507.8 of the Vehicle Code, may be imposed by each county upon the adoption of a resolution by the board of supervisors. An assessment imposed by this section shall be collected and disbursed as provided in Section 9545 of the Welfare and Institutions Code.

Amended by Stats 2003 ch 555 (AB 327), s 2, eff. 1/1/2004.

Section 1465.6 - Additional assessment

(a) In addition to an assessment levied pursuant to Section 1465.5 of this code, or any other law, an additional assessment equal to 10 percent of the fine imposed under Section 42001.5, 42001.13, or 42002 of the Vehicle Code shall be imposed by each county for a criminal violation of the following:

(1) Subdivisions (b), (c), and (d) of Section 4461 of the Vehicle Code.
(2) Subdivision (c) of Section 4463 of the Vehicle Code.
(3) Section 22507.8 of the Vehicle Code.
(4) Section 22522 of the Vehicle Code.

(b) An assessment imposed pursuant to this section shall be deposited with the city or county where the violation occurred.

Amended by Stats 2009 ch 415 (AB 144),s 1, eff. 1/1/2010.

Amended by Stats 2003 ch 555 (AB 327), s 3, eff. 1/1/2004.

Section 1465.7 - State surcharge

(a) A state surcharge of 20 percent shall be levied on the base fine used to calculate the state penalty assessment as specified in subdivision (a) of Section 1464.

(b) This surcharge shall be in addition to the state penalty assessed pursuant to Section 1464 of the Penal Code and may not be included in the base fine used to calculate the state penalty assessment as specified in subdivision (a) of Section 1464.

(c) After a determination by the court of the amount due, the clerk of the court shall cause the amount of the state surcharge collected to be transmitted to the General Fund.

(d) Notwithstanding Chapter 12 (commencing with Section 76000) of Title 8 of the Government Code and subdivision (b) of Section 68090.8 of the Government Code, the full amount of the surcharge shall be transmitted to the State Treasury to be deposited in the General Fund. Of the amount collected from the total amount of the fines, penalties, and surcharges imposed, the amount of the surcharge established by this section shall be transmitted to the State Treasury to be deposited in the General Fund.

(e) When any deposited bail is made for an offense to which this section applies, and for which a court appearance is not mandatory, the person making the deposit shall also deposit a sufficient amount to include the surcharge prescribed by this section.

(f) When amounts owed by an offender as a result of a conviction are paid in installment payments, payments shall be credited pursuant to Section 1203.1d. The amount of the surcharge established by this section shall be transmitted to the State Treasury prior to the county retaining or disbursing the remaining amount of the fines, penalties, and forfeitures imposed.

(g) Notwithstanding Sections 40512.6 and 42007 of the Vehicle Code, the term "total bail" as used in subdivision (a) of Section 42007 of the Vehicle Code does not include the surcharge set forth in this section. The surcharge set forth in this section shall be levied on what would have been the base fine had the provisions of Section 42007 not been invoked and the proceeds from the imposition of the surcharge shall be treated as otherwise set forth in this section.

Amended by Stats 2007 ch 176 (SB 82),s 63, eff. 8/24/2007.

Amended by Stats 2003 ch 365 (AB 1710), s 4, eff. 1/1/2004.

Added by Stats 2002 ch 1124 (AB 3000), s 46, eff. 9/30/2002.

Section 1465.8 - Assessment to assist in funding court operations

(a)

(1) To assist in funding court operations, an assessment of forty dollars ($40) shall be imposed on every conviction for a criminal offense, including a traffic offense, except parking offenses as defined in subdivision (i) of Section 1463, involving a violation of a section of the Vehicle Code or any local ordinance adopted pursuant to the Vehicle Code.

(2) For the purposes of this section, "conviction" includes the dismissal of a traffic violation on the condition that the defendant attend a court-ordered traffic violator school, as authorized by Sections 41501 and 42005 of the Vehicle Code. This court operations assessment shall be deposited in accordance with subdivision (d), and may not be included with the fee calculated and distributed pursuant to Section 42007 of the Vehicle Code.

(b) This assessment shall be in addition to the state penalty assessed pursuant to Section 1464 and may not be included in the base fine to calculate the state penalty assessment as specified in subdivision (a) of Section 1464. The penalties authorized by Chapter 12 (commencing with Section 76000) of Title 8 of the Government Code, and the state surcharge authorized by Section 1465.7, do not apply to this assessment.

(c) When bail is deposited for an offense to which this section applies, and for which a court appearance is not necessary, the person making the deposit shall also deposit a sufficient amount to include the assessment prescribed by this section.

(d) Notwithstanding any other law, the assessments collected pursuant to subdivision (a) shall all be deposited in a special account in the county treasury and transmitted therefrom monthly to the Controller for deposit in the Trial Court Trust Fund. The assessments collected pursuant to this section shall not be subject to subdivision (e) of Section 1203.1d, but shall be disbursed under subdivision (b) of Section 1203.1d.

(e) The Judicial Council shall provide for the administration of this section.

Amended by Stats 2012 ch 41 (SB 1021),s 67, eff. 6/27/2012.

Amended by Stats 2011 ch 40 (AB 118),s 6, eff. 6/30/2011.

Amended by Stats 2011 ch 10 (SB 78),s 8, eff. 3/24/2011.

Amended by Stats 2011 ch 10 (SB 78),s 10, eff. 3/24/2011.

Amended by Stats 2010 ch 720 (SB 857),s 34, eff. 10/19/2010.

Amended by Stats 2010 ch 720 (SB 857),s 33, eff. 10/19/2010.

Amended by Stats 2009 ch 342 (SB 75),s 5, eff. 1/1/2010.

Amended by Stats 2009 ch 22 (SB X4-13),s 29, eff. 7/28/2009.

Amended by Stats 2007 ch 302 (SB 425),s 18, eff. 1/1/2008.

Amended by Stats 2003 ch 159 (AB 1759), eff. 8/2/2003.

Section 1465.9 - Costs uncollectable after 7/2/2021

(a) The balance of any court-imposed costs pursuant to Section 987.4, subdivision (a) of Section 987.5, Sections 987.8, 1203, 1203.1e, 1203.016, 1203.018, 1203.1b, 1208.2, 1210.15, 1463.07, 3010.8, 4024.2, and 6266, as those sections read on June 30, 2021, shall be unenforceable and uncollectible and any portion of a judgment imposing those costs shall be vacated.

(b) On and after January 1, 2022, the balance of any court-imposed costs pursuant to Section 1001.15, 1001.16, 1001.90, 1202.4, 1203.1, 1203.1ab, 1203.1c, 1203.1m, 1203.4a, 1203.9, 1205, 1214.5, 2085.5, 2085.6, or 2085.7, as those sections read on December 31, 2021, shall be unenforceable and uncollectible and any portion of a judgment imposing those costs shall be vacated.

(c) On and after July 1, 2022, the balance of any court-imposed civil assessments pursuant to Section 1214.1 imposed prior to that date shall be unenforceable and uncollectible and any portion of a judgment imposing those assessments shall be vacated.

Amended by Stats 2023 ch 131 (AB 1754),s 161, eff. 1/1/2024.

Amended by Stats 2022 ch 57 (AB 199),s 21, eff. 6/30/2022.

Amended by Stats 2021 ch 257 (AB 177),s 35, eff. 9/23/2021.

Added by Stats 2020 ch 92 (AB 1869),s 62, eff. 9/18/2020.

Chapter 2 - APPEALS IN MISDEMEANOR AND INFRACTION CASES

Section 1466 - Appeal

An appeal may be taken from a judgment or order, in an infraction or misdemeanor case, to the appellate division of the superior court of the county in which the court from which the appeal is taken is located, in the following cases:

(a) By the people:

(1) From an order recusing the district attorney or city attorney pursuant to Section 1424.

(2) From an order or judgment dismissing or otherwise terminating all or any portion of the action, including such an order or judgment, entered after a verdict or finding of guilty or a verdict or judgment entered before the defendant has been placed in jeopardy or where the defendant has waived jeopardy.

(3) From sustaining a demurrer to any portion of the complaint or pleading.

(4) From an order granting a new trial.

(5) From an order arresting judgment.

(6) From any order made after judgment affecting the substantial rights of the people.

(7) From the imposition of an unlawful sentence, whether or not the court suspends the execution of sentence. As used in this paragraph, "unlawful sentence" means the imposition of a sentence not authorized by law or the imposition of a sentence based upon an unlawful order of the court that strikes or otherwise modifies the effect of an enhancement or prior conviction. A defendant shall have the right to counsel in the people's appeal of an unlawful sentence under the same circumstances that he or she would have a right to counsel under subdivision (a) of Section 1238.

(8) Nothing in this section shall be construed to authorize an appeal from an order granting probation. Instead, the people may seek appellate review of any grant of probation, whether or not the court imposes sentence, by means of a petition for a writ of mandate or prohibition that is filed within 60 days after probation is granted. The review of any grant of probation shall include review of any order underlying the grant of probation.

(b) By the defendant:

(1) From a final judgment of conviction. A sentence, an order granting probation, a conviction in a case in which before final judgment the defendant is committed for insanity or is given an indeterminate commitment as a mentally disordered sex offender, or the conviction of a defendant committed for controlled substance addiction shall be deemed to be a final judgment within the meaning of this section. Upon appeal from a final judgment or an order granting probation the court may review any order denying a motion for a new trial.

(2) From any order made after judgment affecting his or her substantial rights.

Amended by Stats 2011 ch 304 (SB 428),s 11, eff. 1/1/2012.

Section 1467 - Stay of execution of judgment

An appeal from a judgment of conviction does not stay the execution of the judgment in any case unless the trial or a reviewing court shall so order. The granting or refusal of such an order shall rest in the discretion of the court, except that a court shall not stay any duty to register as a sex offender pursuant to Section 290.

Amended by Stats. 1998, Ch. 960, Sec. 6. Effective January 1, 1999.

Section 1468 - Decisions; records on appeals

Appeals to the appellate divisions of superior courts shall be taken, heard and determined, the decisions thereon shall be remitted to the courts from which the appeals are taken, and the records on such appeals shall be made up and filed in such time and manner as shall be prescribed in rules adopted by the Judicial Council.

Amended by Stats. 1998, Ch. 931, Sec. 425. Effective September 28, 1998.

Section 1469 - Review of question of law or instruction

Upon appeal by the people the reviewing court may review any question of law involved in any ruling affecting the judgment or order appealed from, without exception having been taken in the trial court. Upon an appeal by a defendant the court may, without exception having been taken in the trial court, review any question of law involved in any ruling, order, instruction, or thing whatsoever said or done at the trial or prior to or after judgment, which thing was said or done after objection made in and considered by the trial court and which affected the substantial rights of the defendant. The court may also review any instruction given, refused or modified, even though no objection was made thereto in the trial court if the substantial rights of the defendant were affected thereby. The reviewing court may reverse, affirm or modify the judgment or order appealed from, and may set aside, affirm or modify any or all of the proceedings subsequent to, or dependent upon, such judgment or order, and may, if proper, order a new trial. If a new trial is ordered upon appeal, it must be had in the court from which the appeal is taken.
Amended by Stats. 1977, Ch. 1257.

Chapter 3 - TRANSFER OF MISDEMEANOR AND INFRACTION APPEALS

Section 1471 - Transfer to court of appeal
A court of appeal may order any case on appeal to a superior court in its district transferred to it for hearing and decision as provided by rules of the Judicial Council when the superior court certifies, or the court of appeal determines, that such transfer appears necessary to secure uniformity of decision or to settle important questions of law.

A court to which any such case is transferred shall have similar power to review any matter and make orders and judgments as the appellate division of the superior court by statute would have in such case, except as otherwise expressly provided.
Amended by Stats. 1998, Ch. 931, Sec. 427. Effective September 28, 1998.

Title 12 - OF SPECIAL PROCEEDINGS OF A CRIMINAL NATURE

Chapter 1 - OF THE WRIT OF HABEAS CORPUS

Section 1473 - Writ of habeas corpus to inquire into cause of imprisonment or restraint
(a) A person unlawfully imprisoned or restrained of their liberty, under any pretense, may prosecute a writ of habeas corpus to inquire into the cause of the imprisonment or restraint.
(b)
(1) A writ of habeas corpus may be prosecuted for, but not limited to, the following reasons:
(A) False evidence that is material on the issue of guilt or punishment was introduced against a person at a hearing or trial relating to the person's incarceration.
(B) False physical evidence, believed by a person to be factual, probative, or material on the issue of guilt, which was known by the person at the time of entering a plea of guilty, which was a material factor directly related to the plea of guilty by the person.
(C)
(i) New evidence exists that is presented without substantial delay, is admissible, and is sufficiently material and credible that it more likely than not would have changed the outcome of the case.
(ii) For purposes of this section, "new evidence" means evidence that has not previously been presented and heard at trial and has been discovered after trial.
(D) A significant dispute has emerged or further developed in the petitioner's favor regarding expert medical, scientific, or forensic testimony that was introduced at trial or a hearing and that expert testimony more likely than not affected the outcome of the case.
(i) For purposes of this section, the expert medical, scientific, or forensic testimony includes the expert's conclusion or the scientific, forensic, or medical facts upon which their opinion is based.
(ii) For purposes of this section, the significant dispute may be as to the reliability or validity of the diagnosis, technique, methods, theories, research, or studies upon which a medical, scientific, or forensic expert based their testimony.
(iii) Under this section, a significant dispute can be established by credible expert testimony or declaration, or by peer reviewed literature showing that experts in the relevant medical, scientific, or forensic community, substantial in number or expertise, have concluded that developments have occurred that undermine the reliability or validity of the diagnosis, technique, methods, theories, research, or studies upon which a medical, scientific, or forensic expert based their testimony.
(iv) In assessing whether a dispute is significant, the court shall give great weight to evidence that a consensus has developed in the relevant medical, scientific, or forensic community undermining the reliability or validity of the diagnosis, technique, methods, theories, research, or studies upon which a medical, scientific, or forensic expert based their testimony or that there is a lack of consensus as to the reliability or validity of the diagnosis, technique, methods, theories, research, or studies upon which a medical, scientific, or forensic expert based their testimony.
(v) The significant dispute must have emerged or further developed within the relevant medical, scientific, or forensic community, which includes the scientific community and all fields of scientific knowledge on which those fields or disciplines rely and shall not be limited to practitioners or proponents of a particular scientific or technical field or discipline.
(vi) If the petitioner makes a prima facie showing that they are entitled to relief, the court shall issue an order to show cause why relief shall not be granted. To obtain relief, all the elements of this subparagraph must be established by a preponderance of the evidence.
(2) For purposes of this subdivision, "false evidence" includes opinions of experts that have either been repudiated by the expert who originally provided the opinion at a hearing or trial or that have been undermined by the state of scientific knowledge or later scientific research or technological advances.
(3) Any allegation that the prosecution knew or should have known of the false nature of the evidence is immaterial to the prosecution of a writ of habeas corpus brought under subparagraph (A) or (B) of paragraph (1).
(4) This subdivision does not create additional liabilities, beyond those already recognized, for an expert who repudiates the original opinion provided at a hearing or trial or whose opinion has been undermined by scientific research, technological advancements, or

because of a reasonable dispute within the expert's relevant scientific community as to the validity of the methods, theories, research, or studies upon which the expert based their opinion.

(c) This section does not change the existing procedures for habeas relief.

(d) This section does not limit the grounds for which a writ of habeas corpus may be prosecuted or preclude the use of any other remedies.

(e) Notwithstanding any other law, a writ of habeas corpus may also be prosecuted after judgment has been entered based on evidence that a criminal conviction or sentence was sought, obtained, or imposed in violation of subdivision (a) of Section 745, if that section applies based on the date of judgment as provided in subdivision (k) of Section 745. A petition raising a claim of this nature for the first time, or on the basis of new discovery provided by the state or other new evidence that could not have been previously known by the petitioner with due diligence, shall not be deemed a successive or abusive petition. If the petitioner has a habeas corpus petition pending in state court, but it has not yet been decided, the petitioner may amend the existing petition with a claim that the petitioner's conviction or sentence was sought, obtained, or imposed in violation of subdivision (a) of Section 745. The petition shall state if the petitioner requests appointment of counsel and the court shall appoint counsel if the petitioner cannot afford counsel and either the petition alleges facts that would establish a violation of subdivision (a) of Section 745 or the State Public Defender requests counsel be appointed. Newly appointed counsel may amend a petition filed before their appointment. The court shall review a petition raising a claim pursuant to Section 745 and shall determine if the petitioner has made a prima facie showing of entitlement to relief. If the petitioner makes a prima facie showing that the petitioner is entitled to relief, the court shall issue an order to show cause why relief shall not be granted and hold an evidentiary hearing, unless the state declines to show cause. The defendant may appear remotely, and the court may conduct the hearing through the use of remote technology, unless counsel indicates that the defendant's presence in court is needed. If the court determines that the petitioner has not established a prima facie showing of entitlement to relief, the court shall state the factual and legal basis for its conclusion on the record or issue a written order detailing the factual and legal basis for its conclusion.

(f) If the court holds an evidentiary hearing and the petitioner is incarcerated in state prison, the petitioner may choose not to appear for the hearing with a signed or oral waiver on record, or they may appear remotely through the use of remote technology, unless counsel indicates that the defendant's presence in court is needed.

(g) For purposes of this section, if the district attorney in the county of conviction or the Attorney General concedes or stipulates to a factual or legal basis for habeas relief, there shall be a presumption in favor of granting relief. This presumption may be overcome only if the record before the court contradicts the concession or stipulation or it would lead to the court issuing an order contrary to law.

(h)

(1) If after the court grants postconviction relief under this section and the prosecuting agency elects to retry the petitioner, the petitioner's postconviction counsel may be appointed as counsel or cocounsel to represent the petitioner on the retrial if both of the following requirements are met:

(A) The petitioner and postconviction counsel both agree for postconviction counsel to be appointed.

(B) Postconviction counsel is qualified to handle trials.

(2) Counsel shall be paid under the applicable pay scale for appointed counsel. Otherwise, the court shall appoint other appropriate counsel.

Amended by Stats 2023 ch 381 (SB 97),s 1, eff. 1/1/2024.
Amended by Stats 2022 ch 982 (SB 467),s 1.5, eff. 1/1/2023.
Amended by Stats 2022 ch 739 (AB 256),s 3, eff. 1/1/2023.
Amended by Stats 2020 ch 317 (AB 2542),s 4, eff. 1/1/2021.
Amended by Stats 2016 ch 785 (SB 1134),s 1, eff. 1/1/2017.
Amended by Stats 2014 ch 623 (SB 1058),s 1, eff. 1/1/2015.
See Stats 2022 ch 739 (AB 256), s 1.

Section 1473.1 - Standards for appointment of private counsel

The Judicial Council shall promulgate standards for appointment of private counsel in superior court for claims filed pursuant to subdivision (f) of Section 1473 of the Penal Code by individuals who are not sentenced to death. These standards shall include a minimum requirement of 10 hours of training in the California Racial Justice Act of 2020. The training required by this section shall meet the requirements for Minimum Continuing Legal Education credit approved by the State Bar of California. Appointment standards for counsel where an individual has been sentenced to death shall be consistent with existing standards set forth in the California Rules of Court.

Added by Stats 2023 ch 34 (SB 133),s 20, eff. 6/30/2023.

Section 1473.5 - Writ of habeas corpus based on expert testimony relating to intimate partner battering

(a) A writ of habeas corpus also may be prosecuted on the basis that competent and substantial expert testimony relating to intimate partner battering and its effects, within the meaning of Section 1107 of the Evidence Code, was not presented to the trier of fact at the trial court proceedings and is of such substance that, had the competent and substantial expert testimony been presented, there is a reasonable probability, sufficient to undermine confidence in the judgment of conviction or sentence, that the result of the proceedings would have been different. Sections 1260 to 1262, inclusive, apply to the prosecution of a writ of habeas corpus pursuant to this section. As used in this section, "trial court proceedings" means those court proceedings that occur from the time the accusatory pleading is filed until and including judgment and sentence.

(b) This section is limited to violent felonies as specified in subdivision (c) of Section 667.5 that were committed before August 29, 1996, and that resulted in judgments of conviction or sentence after a plea or trial as to which expert testimony admissible pursuant to Section 1107 of the Evidence Code may be probative on the issue of culpability.

(c) A showing that expert testimony relating to intimate partner battering and its effects was presented to the trier of fact is not a bar to granting a petition under this section if that expert testimony was not competent or substantial. The burden of proof is on the petitioner to establish a sufficient showing that competent and substantial expert testimony, of a nature which would be competent using prevailing understanding of intimate partner battering and its effects, was not presented to the trier of fact, and had that evidence been presented, there is a reasonable probability that the result of the proceedings would have been different.

(d) If a petitioner for habeas corpus under this section has previously filed a petition for writ of habeas corpus, it is grounds for denial of the new petition if a court determined on the merits in the prior petition that the omission of expert testimony relating to battered women's syndrome or intimate partner battering and its effects at trial was not prejudicial and did not entitle the petitioner to the writ of habeas corpus.

(e) For purposes of this section, the changes that become effective on January 1, 2005, are not intended to expand the uses or applicability of expert testimony on battering and its effects that were in effect immediately prior to that date in criminal cases.

Amended by Stats 2012 ch 803 (AB 593),s 1, eff. 1/1/2013.
Amended by Stats 2008 ch 146 (AB 2306),s 1, eff. 1/1/2009.
Amended by Stats 2004 ch 609 (SB 1385), s 2, eff. 1/1/2005.
Amended by Stats 2003 ch 136 (SB 784), s 1, eff. 1/1/2004.
Repealed by Stats 2003 ch 136 (SB 784), s 1, eff. 1/1/2010.
Added by Stats 2001 ch 858 (SB 799), s 1, eff. 1/1/2002.

Section 1473.6 - Motion to vacate judgment

(a) Any person no longer unlawfully imprisoned or restrained may prosecute a motion to vacate a judgment for any of the following reasons:

(1) Newly discovered evidence of fraud by a government official that completely undermines the prosecution's case, is conclusive, and points unerringly to his or her innocence.

(2) Newly discovered evidence that a government official testified falsely at the trial that resulted in the conviction and that the testimony of the government official was substantially probative on the issue of guilt or punishment.

(3) Newly discovered evidence of misconduct by a government official committed in the underlying case that resulted in fabrication of evidence that was substantially material and probative on the issue of guilt or punishment. Evidence of misconduct in other cases is not sufficient to warrant relief under this paragraph.

(b) For purposes of this section, "newly discovered evidence" is evidence that could not have been discovered with reasonable diligence prior to judgment.

(c) The procedure for bringing and adjudicating a motion under this section, including the burden of producing evidence and the burden of proof, shall be the same as for prosecuting a writ of habeas corpus.

(d) A motion pursuant to this section must be filed within one year of the later of the following:

(1) The date the moving party discovered, or could have discovered with the exercise of due diligence, additional evidence of the misconduct or fraud by a government official beyond the moving party's personal knowledge.

(2) The effective date of this section.

Added by Stats 2002 ch 1105 (SB 1391), s 3, eff. 1/1/2003.

Section 1473.7 - Motion to vacate a conviction or sentence by person no longer in custody

(a) A person who is no longer in criminal custody may file a motion to vacate a conviction or sentence for any of the following reasons:

(1) The conviction or sentence is legally invalid due to prejudicial error damaging the moving party's ability to meaningfully understand, defend against, or knowingly accept the actual or potential adverse immigration consequences of a conviction or sentence. A finding of legal invalidity may, but need not, include a finding of ineffective assistance of counsel.

(2) Newly discovered evidence of actual innocence exists that requires vacation of the conviction or sentence as a matter of law or in the interests of justice.

(3) A conviction or sentence was sought, obtained, or imposed on the basis of race, ethnicity, or national origin in violation of subdivision (a) of Section 745.

(b)

(1) Except as provided in paragraph (2), a motion pursuant to paragraph (1) of subdivision (a) shall be deemed timely filed at any time in which the individual filing the motion is no longer in criminal custody.

(2) A motion pursuant to paragraph (1) of subdivision (a) may be deemed untimely filed if it was not filed with reasonable diligence after the later of the following:

(A) The moving party receives a notice to appear in immigration court or other notice from immigration authorities that asserts the conviction or sentence as a basis for removal or the denial of an application for an immigration benefit, lawful status, or naturalization.

(B) Notice that a final removal order has been issued against the moving party, based on the existence of the conviction or sentence that the moving party seeks to vacate.

(c) A motion pursuant to paragraph (2) or (3) of subdivision (a) shall be filed without undue delay from the date the moving party discovered, or could have discovered with the exercise of due diligence, the evidence that provides a basis for relief under this section or Section 745.

(d) All motions shall be entitled to a hearing. Upon the request of the moving party, the court may hold the hearing without the personal presence of the moving party provided that it finds good cause as to why the moving party cannot be present. If the prosecution has no objection to the motion, the court may grant the motion to vacate the conviction or sentence without a hearing.

(e) When ruling on the motion:

(1) The court shall grant the motion to vacate the conviction or sentence if the moving party establishes, by a preponderance of the evidence, the existence of any of the grounds for relief specified in subdivision (a). For a motion made pursuant to paragraph (1) of subdivision (a), the moving party shall also establish that the conviction or sentence being challenged is currently causing or has the potential to cause removal or the denial of an application for an immigration benefit, lawful status, or naturalization.

(2) There is a presumption of legal invalidity for the purposes of paragraph (1) of subdivision (a) if the moving party pleaded guilty or nolo contendere pursuant to a statute that provided that, upon completion of specific requirements, the arrest and conviction shall be

deemed never to have occurred, where the moving party complied with these requirements, and where the disposition under the statute has been, or potentially could be, used as a basis for adverse immigration consequences.

(3) If the court grants the motion to vacate a conviction or sentence obtained through a plea of guilty or nolo contendere, the court shall allow the moving party to withdraw the plea.

(4) When ruling on a motion under paragraph (1) of subdivision (a), the only finding that the court is required to make is whether the conviction is legally invalid due to prejudicial error damaging the moving party's ability to meaningfully understand, defend against, or knowingly accept the actual or potential adverse immigration consequences of a conviction or sentence. When ruling on a motion under paragraph (2) of subdivision (a), the court shall specify the basis for its conclusion.

(f) An order granting or denying the motion is appealable under subdivision (b) of Section 1237 as an order after judgment affecting the substantial rights of a party.

(g) A court may only issue a specific finding of ineffective assistance of counsel as a result of a motion brought under paragraph (1) of subdivision (a) if the attorney found to be ineffective was given timely advance notice of the motion hearing by the moving party or the prosecutor, pursuant to Section 416.90 of the Code of Civil Procedure.

Amended by Stats 2021 ch 420 (AB 1259),s 1, eff. 1/1/2022.
Amended by Stats 2020 ch 317 (AB 2542),s 5, eff. 1/1/2021.
Amended by Stats 2018 ch 825 (AB 2867),s 2, eff. 1/1/2019.
Added by Stats 2016 ch 739 (AB 813),s 1, eff. 1/1/2017.

Section 1474 - Petition

Application for the writ is made by petition, signed either by the party for whose relief it is intended, or by some person in his behalf, and must specify:

1. That the person in whose behalf the writ is applied for is imprisoned or restrained of his liberty, the officer or person by whom he is so confined or restrained, and the place where, naming all the parties, if they are known, or describing them, if they are not known;

2. If the imprisonment is alleged to be illegal, the petition must also state in what the alleged illegality consists;

3. The petition must be verified by the oath or affirmation of the party making the application.

Enacted 1872.

Section 1475 - Grant of writ of habeas corpus

The writ of habeas corpus may be granted in the manner provided by law. If the writ has been granted by any court or a judge thereof and after the hearing thereof the prisoner has been remanded, he or she shall not be discharged from custody by the same or any other court of like general jurisdiction, or by a judge of the same or any other court of like general jurisdiction, unless upon some ground not existing in fact at the issuing of the prior writ. Should the prisoner desire to urge some point of law not raised in the petition for or at the hearing upon the return of the prior writ, then, in case the prior writ had been returned or returnable before a superior court or a judge thereof, no writ can be issued upon a second or other application except by the appropriate court of appeal or some judge thereof, or by the Supreme Court or some judge thereof, and in the event the writ must not be made returnable before any superior court or any judge thereof. In the event, however, that the prior writ was returned or made returnable before a court of appeal or any judge thereof, no writ can be issued upon a second or other application except by the Supreme Court or some judge thereof, and the writ must be made returnable before said Supreme Court or some judge thereof.

Every application for a writ of habeas corpus must be verified, and shall state whether any prior application or applications have been made for a writ in regard to the same detention or restraint complained of in the application, and if any prior application or applications have been made the later application must contain a brief statement of all proceedings had therein, or in any of them, to and including the final order or orders made therein, or in any of them, on appeal or otherwise.

Whenever the person applying for a writ of habeas corpus is held in custody or restraint by any officer of any court of this state or any political subdivision thereof, or by any peace officer of this state, or any political subdivision thereof, a copy of the application for the writ must in all cases be served upon the district attorney of the county wherein the person is held in custody or restraint at least 24 hours before the time at which said writ is made returnable and no application for the writ can be heard without proof of service in cases where the service is required.

If the person is in custody for violation of an ordinance of a city which has a city attorney, a copy of the application for the writ must also be served on the city attorney of the city whose ordinance is the basis for the charge at least 24 hours before the time at which the writ is made returnable, provided that failure to serve the city attorney shall not deprive the court of jurisdiction to hear the application. If a writ challenging a denial of parole or the applicant's suitability for parole is then made returnable, a copy of the application for the writ and the related order to show cause shall in all cases be served by the superior court upon the office of the Attorney General and the district attorney of the county in which the underlying judgment was rendered at least three business days before the time at which the writ is made returnable and no application for the writ can be heard without proof of such service.

Amended by Stats 2006 ch 274 (AB 2272),s 1, eff. 1/1/2007.

Section 1476 - Endorsement

Any court or judge authorized to grant the writ, to whom a petition therefor is presented, must endorse upon the petition the hour and date of its presentation and the hour and date of the granting or denial of the writ, and must, if it appear that the writ ought to issue, grant the same without delay; and if the person by or upon whose behalf the application for the writ is made be detained upon a criminal charge, may admit him to bail, if the offense is bailable, pending the determination of the proceeding.

Amended by Stats. 1949, Ch. 1021.

Section 1477 - Direction of writ

The writ must be directed to the person having custody of or restraining the person on whose behalf the application is made, and must command him to have the body of such person before the Court or Judge before whom the writ is returnable, at a time and place therein specified.

Enacted 1872.

Section 1478 - Delivery for service

If the writ is directed to the sheriff or other ministerial officer of the court out of which it issues, it must be delivered by the clerk to such officer without delay, as other writs are delivered for service. If it is directed to any other person, it must be delivered to the sheriff or a marshal, and be by him served upon such person by delivering the copy to him without delay, and make his return on the original to the court of issuance. If the person to whom the writ is directed cannot be found, or refuses admittance to the officer or person serving or delivering such writ, it may be served or delivered by leaving it at the residence of the person to whom it is directed, or by affixing it to some conspicuous place on the outside either of his dwelling house or of the place where the party is confined or under restraint. Amended by Stats. 1968, Ch. 479.

Section 1479 - Attachment

If the person to whom the writ is directed refuses, after service, to obey the same, the Court or Judge, upon affidavit, must issue an attachment against such person, directed to the Sheriff or Coroner, commanding him forthwith to apprehend such person and bring him immediately before such Court or Judge; and upon being so brought, he must be committed to the jail of the county until he makes due return to such writ, or is otherwise legally discharged.
Enacted 1872.

Section 1480 - Return

The person upon whom the writ is served must state in his return, plainly and unequivocally:

1. Whether he has or has not the party in his custody, or under his power or restraint;

2. If he has the party in his custody or power, or under his restraint, he must state the authority and cause of such imprisonment or restraint;

3. If the party is detained by virtue of any writ, warrant, or other written authority, a copy thereof must be annexed to the return, and the original produced and exhibited to the Court or Judge on the hearing of such return;

4. If the person upon whom the writ is served had the party in his power or custody, or under his restraint, at any time prior or subsequent to the date of the writ of habeas corpus, but has transferred such custody or restraint to another, the return must state particularly to whom, at what time and place, for what cause, and by what authority such transfer took place;

5. The return must be signed by the person making the same, and, except when such person is a sworn public officer, and makes such return in his official capacity, it must be verified by his oath.
Enacted 1872.

Section 1481 - Production of party

The person to whom the writ is directed, if it is served, must bring the body of the party in his custody or under his restraint, according to the command of the writ, except in the cases specified in the next section.
Enacted 1872.

Section 1482 - Sickness or infirmity of person directed to be produced

When, from sickness or infirmity of the person directed to be produced, he cannot, without danger, be brought before the Court or Judge, the person in whose custody or power he is may state that fact in his return to the writ, verifying the same by affidavit. If the Court or Judge is satisfied of the truth of such return, and the return to the writ is otherwise sufficient, the Court or Judge may proceed to decide on such return, and to dispose of the matter as if such party had been produced on the writ, or the hearing thereof may be adjourned until such party can be produced.
Enacted 1872.

Section 1483 - Hearing and examination of return

The Court or Judge before whom the writ is returned must, immediately after the return, proceed to hear and examine the return, and such other matters as may be properly submitted to their hearing and consideration.
Enacted 1872.

Section 1484 - Hearing of proof

The party brought before the Court or Judge, on the return of the writ, may deny or controvert any of the material facts or matters set forth in the return, or except to the sufficiency thereof, or allege any fact to show either that his imprisonment or detention is unlawful, or that he is entitled to his discharge. The Court or Judge must thereupon proceed in a summary way to hear such proof as may be produced against such imprisonment or detention, or in favor of the same, and to dispose of such party as the justice of the case may require, and have full power and authority to require and compel the attendance of witnesses, by process of subpoena and attachment, and to do and perform all other acts and things necessary to a full and fair hearing and determination of the case.
Enacted 1872.

Section 1485 - Discharge

If no legal cause is shown for such imprisonment or restraint, or for the continuation thereof, such Court or Judge must discharge such party from the custody or restraint under which he is held.
Enacted 1872.

Section 1485.5 - Writ of habeas corpus or motion to vacate a judgment; facts binding on attorney general and board

(a) If the district attorney or Attorney General stipulates to or does not contest the factual allegations underlying one or more of the grounds for granting a writ of habeas corpus or a motion to vacate a judgment, the facts underlying the basis for the court's ruling or order shall be binding on the Attorney General, the factfinder, and the California Victim Compensation Board.

(b) The district attorney shall provide notice to the Attorney General no fewer than seven days before entering into a stipulation of facts that will be the basis for the granting of a writ of habeas corpus or a motion to vacate a judgment. A response from the Attorney General is not required to proceed with the stipulation.

(c) In a contested or uncontested proceeding, the express factual findings made by the court, including credibility determinations, during proceedings on a petition for habeas corpus, a motion to vacate judgment pursuant to Section 1473.6, or an application for a certificate of factual innocence, shall be binding on the Attorney General, the factfinder, and the California Victim Compensation Board.

(d) For the purposes of this section, "express factual findings" are findings established as the basis for the court's rulings or orders.

(e) For purposes of this section, "court" is defined as a state or federal court.

Amended by Stats 2023 ch 702 (SB 78),s 2, eff. 1/1/2024.
Amended by Stats 2021 ch 490 (SB 446),s 1, eff. 1/1/2022.
Amended by Stats 2016 ch 785 (SB 1134),s 2, eff. 1/1/2017.
Amended by Stats 2016 ch 31 (SB 836),s 244, eff. 6/27/2016.
Amended by Stats 2014 ch 28 (SB 854),s 73, eff. 6/20/2014.
Added by Stats 2013 ch 800 (SB 618),s 2, eff. 1/1/2014.

Section 1485.55 - Contested proceedings; finding of innocence; findings binding on board

(a) In a contested or uncontested proceeding, if the court has granted a writ of habeas corpus or when the court vacates a judgment pursuant to Section 1473.6 and if the court has found that the person is factually innocent, under any standard for factual innocence applicable in those proceedings, that finding shall be binding on the California Victim Compensation Board for a claim presented to the board, and upon application by the person, the board shall, without a hearing, approve payment to the claimant, pursuant to Section 4904, if sufficient funds are available, upon appropriation by the Legislature.

(b) In a contested or uncontested proceeding, if the court has granted a writ of habeas corpus or vacated a judgment pursuant to Section 1473.6 or paragraph (2) of subdivision (a) of Section 1473.7, the person may move for a finding of factual innocence by a preponderance of the evidence that the crime with which they were charged was either not committed at all or, if committed, was not committed by the petitioner.

(c) If the court makes a finding that the petitioner has proven their factual innocence by a preponderance of the evidence pursuant to subdivision (b), upon application by the person, the board shall, without a hearing, approve payment to the claimant, pursuant to Section 4904, if sufficient funds are available, upon appropriation by the Legislature.

(d)

(1) In a contested or uncontested proceeding, if the court has granted a writ of habeas corpus pursuant to common law, the California Constitution, the United States Constitution, or paragraphs (1) to (4), inclusive, of subdivision (b) of Section 1473, or vacated a judgment pursuant to Section 1473.6 or paragraph (2) of subdivision (a) of Section 1473.7, and the charges were subsequently dismissed, or the person was acquitted of the charges on a retrial, the petitioner may move the court for a finding that they are entitled to approval of a claim for compensation pursuant to Chapter 5 (commencing with Section 4900) of Title 6 of Part 3. The court shall grant the motion unless the district attorney objects in writing within 15 days from when the person files the motion and can establish by clear and convincing evidence that the person committed the acts constituting the offense and is therefore not entitled to compensation. The district attorney shall bear the burden of proving by clear and convincing evidence that the person committed the acts constituting the offense. The district attorney may request a single 30-day extension of time upon a showing of good cause. An extension of time beyond this period may be given if agreed upon by stipulation between both parties.

(2) If the district attorney does not object, or if the district attorney fails to establish by clear and convincing evidence that the person committed the acts constituting the offense as described in paragraph (1), the court shall grant the motion and the board shall, upon application by the person, without a hearing, approve payment to the claimant, pursuant to Section 4904, if sufficient funds are available, upon appropriation by the Legislature.

(3) If the motion is granted pursuant to a stipulation of the district attorney, and upon application by the person, the board shall, without a hearing, approve payment to the claimant, pursuant to Section 4904, if sufficient funds are available, upon appropriation by the Legislature.

(e) A conviction reversed and dismissed is no longer valid, thus the district attorney may not rely on the fact that the state still maintains that the claimant is guilty of the crime for which they were wrongfully convicted, that the state defended the conviction against the petitioner through court litigation, or that there was a conviction to establish that the petitioner is not entitled to compensation. The district attorney may also not rely solely on the trial record to establish that the petitioner is not entitled to compensation.

(f) A presumption does not exist in any other proceeding for failure to make a motion or obtain a favorable ruling pursuant to subdivisions (a) and (b). No res judicata or collateral estoppel finding in any other proceeding shall be made for failure to make a motion or obtain a favorable ruling pursuant to subdivision (a) or (b) of this section.

(g) If a federal court, after granting a writ of habeas corpus, pursuant to a nonstatutory motion or request, finds a petitioner factually innocent by no less than a preponderance of the evidence that the crime with which they were charged was either not committed at all or, if committed, was not committed by the petitioner, upon application of the person, the board shall, without a hearing, approve payment to the claimant, pursuant to Section 4904, if sufficient funds are available, upon appropriation by the Legislature.

(h) For the purposes of this section, unless otherwise stated, "court" is defined as a state or federal court.

Amended by Stats 2023 ch 702 (SB 78),s 3, eff. 1/1/2024.
Amended by Stats 2021 ch 490 (SB 446),s 2, eff. 1/1/2022.
Amended by Stats 2021 ch 434 (SB 827),s 10, eff. 1/1/2022.
Amended by Stats 2019 ch 473 (SB 269),s 1, eff. 1/1/2020.
Amended by Stats 2016 ch 785 (SB 1134),s 3, eff. 1/1/2017.
Amended by Stats 2016 ch 31 (SB 836),s 245, eff. 6/27/2016.
Added by Stats 2013 ch 800 (SB 618),s 3, eff. 1/1/2014.

Section 1486 - Remand

The Court or Judge, if the time during which such party may be legally detained in custody has not expired, must remand such party, if it appears that he is detained in custody:

1. By virtue of process issued by any Court or Judge of the United States, in a case where such Court or Judge has exclusive jurisdiction; or,

2. By virtue of the final judgment or decree of any competent Court of criminal jurisdiction, or of any process issued upon such judgment or decree.

Enacted 1872.

Section 1487 - Discharge subject to restrictions

If it appears on the return of the writ that the prisoner is in custody by virtue of process from any Court of this State, or Judge or officer thereof, such prisoner may be discharged in any of the following cases, subject to the restrictions of the last section:

1. When the jurisdiction of such Court or officer has been exceeded;

2. When the imprisonment was at first lawful, yet by some act, omission, or event which has taken place afterwards, the party has become entitled to a discharge;

3. When the process is defective in some matter of substance required by law, rendering such process void;

4. When the process, though proper in form, has been issued in a case not allowed by law;

5. When the person having the custody of the prisoner is not the person allowed by law to detain him;

6. Where the process is not authorized by any order, judgment, or decree of any Court, nor by any provision of law;

7. Where a party has been committed on a criminal charge without reasonable or probable cause.

Enacted 1872.

Section 1488 - No discharge on ground of mere defect of form in warrant of confinement

If any person is committed to prison, or is in custody of any officer on any criminal charge, by virtue of any warrant of commitment of a magistrate, such person must not be discharged on the ground of any mere defect of form in the warrant of commitment.

Amended by Stats. 1951, Ch. 1608.

Section 1489 - Subpoena to testify if party is guilty or ought not be discharged but charge is defective

If it appears to the Court or Judge, by affidavit or otherwise, or upon the inspection of the process or warrant of commitment, and such other papers in the proceedings as may be shown to the Court or Judge, that the party is guilty of a criminal offense, or ought not to be discharged, such Court or Judge, although the charge is defective or unsubstantially set forth in such process or warrant of commitment, must cause the complainant or other necessary witnesses to be subpoenaed to attend at such time as ordered, to testify before the Court or Judge; and upon the examination he may discharge such prisoner, let him to bail, if the offense be bailable, or recommit him to custody, as may be just and legal.

Enacted 1872.

Section 1490 - Writ of habeas corpus for purpose of giving bail

When a person is imprisoned or detained in custody on any criminal charge, for want of bail, such person is entitled to a writ of habeas corpus for the purpose of giving bail, upon averring that fact in his petition, without alleging that he is illegally confined.

Enacted 1872.

Section 1491 - Bail

Any judge before whom a person who has been committed upon a criminal charge may be brought on a writ of habeas corpus, if the same is bailable, may take an undertaking of bail from such person as in other cases, and file the same in the proper court. Whenever a writ of habeas corpus is returned to a court for hearing and the petitioner is charged with an offense other than a crime of violence or committed with a deadly weapon or involving the forcible taking or destruction of the property of another, but the prisoner does not stand convicted of any offense, the amount of the bail must be set immediately if no bail has theretofore been fixed.

Amended by Stats. 1933, Ch. 595.

Section 1492 - Remand to custody

If a party brought before the Court or Judge on the return of the writ is not entitled to his discharge, and is not bailed, where such bail is allowable, the Court or Judge must remand him to custody or place him under the restraint from which he was taken, if the person under whose custody or restraint he was is legally entitled thereto.

Enacted 1872.

Section 1493 - Commitment to restraint or custody of person entitled thereto

In cases where any party is held under illegal restraint or custody, or any other person is entitled to the restraint or custody of such party, the Judge or Court may order such party to be committed to the restraint or custody of such person as is by law entitled thereto.

Enacted 1872.

Section 1494 - Commitment to custody of sheriff or county

Until judgment is given on the return, the Court or Judge before whom any party may be brought on such writ may commit him to the custody of the Sheriff of the county, or place him in such care or under such custody as his age or circumstances may require.

Enacted 1872.

Section 1495 - Writ of habeas corpus may not be disobeyed for defect of form

No writ of habeas corpus can be disobeyed for defect of form, if it sufficiently appear therefrom in whose custody or under whose restraint the party imprisoned or restrained is, the officer or person detaining him, and the Court or Judge before whom he is to be brought.

Enacted 1872.

Section 1496 - Imprisonment after discharge upon habeas corpus

No person who has been discharged by the order of the Court or Judge upon habeas corpus can be again imprisoned, restrained, or kept in custody for the same cause, except in the following cases:

1. If he has been discharged from custody on a criminal charge, and is afterwards committed for the same offense, by legal order or process;

2. If, after a discharge for defect of proof, or for any defect of the process, warrant, or commitment in a criminal case, the prisoner is again arrested on sufficient proof and committed by legal process for the same offense.

Enacted 1872.

Section 1497 - Warrant commanding peace officer to bring person before court or judge

When it appears to any court, or judge, authorized by law to issue the writ of habeas corpus, that any one is illegally held in custody, confinement, or restraint, and that there is reason to believe that the person will be carried out of the jurisdiction of the court or judge before whom the application is made, or will suffer some irreparable injury before compliance with the writ of habeas corpus can be enforced, the court or judge may cause a warrant to be issued, reciting the facts, and directed to any peace officer, commanding the peace officer to take the person held in custody, confinement, or restraint, and immediately bring him or her before the court or judge, to be dealt with according to law.

Amended by Stats. 1983, Ch. 990, Sec. 8.

Section 1498 - Command for apprehension of person charged with illegal detention and restraint

The Court or Judge may also insert in such warrant a command for the apprehension of the person charged with such illegal detention and restraint.

Enacted 1872.

Section 1499 - Execution of warrant

The officer to whom such warrant is delivered must execute it by bringing the person therein named before the Court or Judge who directed the issuing of such warrant.

Enacted 1872.

Section 1500 - Return

The person alleged to have such party under illegal confinement or restraint may make return to such warrant as in case of a writ of habeas corpus, and the same may be denied, and like allegations, proofs, and trial may thereupon be had as upon a return to a writ of habeas corpus.

Enacted 1872.

Section 1501 - Discharge if held under illegal restraint or custody; restoration to care or custody of person entitled thereto

If such party is held under illegal restraint or custody, he must be discharged; and if not, he must be restored to the care or custody of the person entitled thereto.

Enacted 1872.

Section 1502 - Issuance and service

Any writ or process authorized by this Chapter may be issued and served on any day or at any time.

Enacted 1872.

Section 1503 - Issuance by clerk of court; seal; service and return

All writs, warrants, process, and subpoenas authorized by the provisions of this Chapter must be issued by the Clerk of the Court, and, except subpoenas, must be sealed with the seal of such Court, and served and returned forthwith, unless the Court or Judge shall specify a particular time for any such return.

Enacted 1872.

Section 1504 - Returnable before judge

All such writs and process, when made returnable before a Judge, must be returned before him at the county seat, and there heard and determined.

Amended by Code Amendments 1880, Ch. 6.

Section 1505 - Refusal forfeiture

If the officer or person to whom a writ of habeas corpus is directed, refuses obedience to the command thereof, he shall forfeit and pay to the person aggrieved a sum not exceeding ten thousand dollars ($10,000), to be recovered by action in any court of competent jurisdiction.

Amended by Stats. 1983, Ch. 1092, Sec. 322.5. Effective September 27, 1983. Operative January 1, 1984, by Sec. 427 of Ch. 1092.

Section 1506 - Appeal by people from final order discharging defendant

An appeal may be taken to the court of appeal by the people from a final order of a superior court made upon the return of a writ of habeas corpus discharging a defendant or otherwise granting all or any part of the relief sought, in all criminal cases, excepting criminal cases where judgment of death has been rendered, and in such cases to the Supreme Court; and in all criminal cases where an application for a writ of habeas corpus has been heard and determined in a court of appeal, either the defendant or the people may apply for a hearing in the Supreme Court. Such appeal shall be taken and such application for hearing in the Supreme Court shall be made in accordance with rules to be laid down by the Judicial Council. If the people appeal from an order granting the discharge or release of the defendant, or petition for hearing in either the court of appeal or the Supreme Court, the defendant shall be admitted to bail or released on his own recognizance or any other conditions which the court deems just and reasonable, subject to the same limitations, terms, and conditions which are applicable to, or may be imposed upon, a defendant who is awaiting trial. If the order grants relief other than a discharge or release from custody, the trial court or the court in which the appeal or petition for hearing is pending may, upon application by the people, in its discretion, and upon such conditions as it deems just stay the execution of the order pending final determination of the matter.

Amended by Stats. 1975, Ch. 1080.

Section 1507 - Appeal when application made by person other than defendant

Where an application for a writ of habeas corpus has been made by or on behalf of any person other than a defendant in a criminal case, an appeal may be taken to the court of appeal from a final order of a superior court granting all or any part of the relief sought; and where such application has been heard and determined in a court of appeal, either on an application filed in that court or on appeal from a superior court, and all or any part of the relief sought has been granted, an application may be made for a hearing in the Supreme Court. Such appeal shall be taken and such application for hearing in the Supreme Court shall be made in accordance with rules to be laid down by the Judicial Council. The court which made the order granting relief or the court in which the appeal or petition for hearing is pending may, in its discretion, and upon such conditions as it deems just stay the execution of the order pending final determination of the matter.

Amended by Stats. 1967, Ch. 17.

Section 1508 - Returnable before issuing judge or court

(a) A writ of habeas corpus issued by the Supreme Court or a judge thereof may be made returnable before the issuing judge or his court, before any court of appeal or judge thereof, or before any superior court or judge thereof.

(b) A writ of habeas corpus issued by a court of appeal or a judge thereof may be made returnable before the issuing judge or his court or before any superior court or judge thereof located in that appellate district.

(c) A writ of habeas corpus issued by a superior court or a judge thereof may be made returnable before the issuing judge or his court.

Added by Stats. 1969, Ch. 38.

Section 1509 - Collateral attack on judgment of death

(a) This section applies to any petition for writ of habeas corpus filed by a person in custody pursuant to a judgment of death. A writ of habeas corpus pursuant to this section is the exclusive procedure for collateral attack on a judgment of death. A petition filed in any court other than the court which imposed the sentence should be promptly transferred to that court unless good cause is shown for the petition to be heard by another court. A petition filed in or transferred to the court which imposed the sentence shall be assigned to the original trial judge unless that judge is unavailable or there is other good cause to assign the case to a different judge.

(b) After the entry of a judgment of death in the trial court, that court shall offer counsel to the prisoner as provided in Section 68662 of the Government Code.

(c) Except as provided in subdivisions (d) and (g), the initial petition must be filed within one year of the order entered under Section 68662 of the Government Code.

(d) An initial petition which is untimely under subdivision (c) or a successive petition whenever filed shall be dismissed unless the court finds, by the preponderance of all available evidence, whether or not admissible at trial, that the defendant is actually innocent of the crime of which he or she was convicted or is ineligible for the sentence. A stay of execution shall not be granted for the purpose of considering a successive or untimely petition unless the court finds that the petitioner has a substantial claim of actual innocence or ineligibility. "Ineligible for the sentence of death" means that circumstances exist placing that sentence outside the range of the sentencer's discretion. Claims of ineligibility include a claim that none of the special circumstances in subdivision (a) of Section 190.2 is true, a claim that the defendant was under the age of 18 at the time of the crime, or a claim that the defendant has an intellectual disability, as defined in Section 1376. A claim relating to the sentencing decision under Section 190.3 is not a claim of actual innocence or ineligibility for the purpose of this section.

(e) A petitioner claiming innocence or ineligibility under subdivision (d) shall disclose all material information relating to guilt or eligibility in the possession of the petitioner or present or former counsel for petitioner. If the petitioner willfully fails to make the disclosure required by this subdivision and authorize disclosure by counsel, the petition may be dismissed.

(f) Proceedings under this section shall be conducted as expeditiously as possible, consistent with a fair adjudication. The superior court shall resolve the initial petition within one year of filing unless the court finds that a delay is necessary to resolve a substantial claim of actual innocence, but in no instance shall the court take longer than two years to resolve the petition. On decision of an initial petition, the court shall issue a statement of decision explaining the factual and legal basis for its decision.

(g) If a habeas corpus petition is pending on the effective date of this section, the court may transfer the petition to the court which imposed the sentence. In a case where a judgment of death was imposed prior to the effective date of this section, but no habeas corpus petition has been filed prior to the effective date of this section, a petition that would otherwise be barred by subdivision (c) may be filed within one year of the effective date of this section or within the time allowed under prior law, whichever is earlier.

Added by Proposition 66, approved by the voters at the November 8, 2016 election, effective immediately upon enactment.

Section 1509.1 - Appeal of decision regarding habeas corpus on judgement of death

(a) Either party may appeal the decision of a superior court on an initial petition under Section 1509 to the court of appeal. An appeal shall be taken by filing a notice of appeal in the superior court within 30 days of the court's decision granting or denying the habeas petition. A successive petition shall not be used as a means of reviewing a denial of habeas relief.

(b) The issues considered on an appeal under subdivision (a) shall be limited to the claims raised in the superior court, except that the court of appeal may also consider a claim of ineffective assistance of trial counsel if the failure of habeas counsel to present that claim to the superior court constituted ineffective assistance. The court of appeal may, if additional findings of fact are required, make a limited remand to the superior court to consider the claim.

(c) The people may appeal the decision of the superior court granting relief on a successive petition. The petitioner may appeal the decision of the superior court denying relief on a successive petition only if the superior court or the court of appeal grants a certificate of appealability. A certificate of appealability may issue under this subdivision only if the petitioner has shown both a substantial claim for relief, which shall be indicated in the certificate, and a substantial claim that the requirements of subdivision (d) of Section 1509 have been met. An appeal under this subdivision shall be taken by filing a notice of appeal in the superior court within 30 days of the court's decision. The superior court shall grant or deny a certificate of appealability concurrently with a decision denying relief on the petition. The court of appeal shall grant or deny a request for a certificate of appealability within 10 days of an application for a certificate. The jurisdiction of the court of appeal is limited to the claims identified in the certificate and any additional claims added by the court of appeal within 60 days of the notice of appeal. An appeal under this subdivision shall have priority over all other matters and be decided as expeditiously as possible.

Added by Proposition 66, approved by the voters at the November 8, 2016 election, effective immediately upon enactment.

Chapter 2 - PRETRIAL REVIEW

Section 1510 - Review of denial of motion made pursuant to Section 995 or 1538.5

The denial of a motion made pursuant to Section 995 or 1538.5 may be reviewed prior to trial only if the motion was made by the defendant in the trial court not later than 45 days following defendant's arraignment on the complaint if a misdemeanor, or 60 days following defendant's arraignment on the information or indictment if a felony, unless within these time limits the defendant was unaware of the issue or had no opportunity to raise the issue.

Added by Stats. 1971, Ch. 944.

Section 1511 - Immediate appellate review of ruling setting trail or granting continuance

If in a felony case the superior court sets the trial beyond the period of time specified in Section 1049.5, in violation of Section 1049.5, or continues the hearing of any matter without good cause, and good cause is required by law for such a continuance, either party may file a petition for writ of mandate or prohibition in the court of appeal seeking immediate appellate review of the ruling setting the trial or granting the continuance. Such a petition shall have precedence over all other cases in the court to which the petition is assigned, including, but not limited to, cases that originated in the juvenile court. If the court of appeal grants a peremptory writ, it shall issue the writ and a remittitur three court days after its decision becomes final as to that court if such action is necessary to prevent mootness or to prevent frustration of the relief granted, notwithstanding the right of the parties to file a petition for review in the Supreme Court. When the court of appeal issues the writ and remittitur as provided herein, the writ shall command the superior court to proceed with the criminal case without further delay, other than that reasonably necessary for the parties to obtain the attendance of their witnesses. The Supreme Court may stay or recall the issuance of the writ and remittitur. The Supreme Court's failure to stay or recall the issuance of the writ and remittitur shall not deprive the respondent or the real party in interest of its right to file a petition for review in the Supreme Court.

Former Ca. Pen. Code, § 1511, as added by Chapter 560 of the Statutes of 1989, was renumbered as § 1512 by Stats 2001 ch 854 (SB 205), s 46, eff. 1/1/2002.

Added June 5, 1990, by initiative Proposition 115, Sec. 28.

Section 1512 - Review of order granting defendant's motion for severance or discovery

(a) In addition to petitions for a writ of mandate, prohibition, or review which the people are authorized to file pursuant to any other statute or pursuant to any court decision, the people may also seek review of an order granting a defendant's motion for severance or discovery by a petition for a writ of mandate or prohibition.

(b) In construing the legislative intent of subdivision (a), no inference shall be drawn from the amendment to Assembly Bill 1052 of the 1989-90 Regular Session of the Legislature which deleted reference to the case of People v. Superior Court, 69 Cal. 2d 491.

Renumbered from 1511 and amended by Stats 2001 ch 854 (SB 205), s 46, eff. 1/1/2002.

Chapter 3 - OF SEARCH WARRANTS

Section 1523 - Search warrant

A search warrant is an order in writing, in the name of the people, signed by a magistrate, directed to a peace officer, commanding him or her to search for a person or persons, a thing or things, or personal property, and, in the case of a thing or things or personal property, bring the same before the magistrate.

Amended by Stats. 1996, Ch. 1078, Sec. 1.5. Effective January 1, 1997.

Section 1524 - Grounds for search warrant

(a) A search warrant may be issued upon any of the following grounds:

(1) When the property was stolen or embezzled.

(2) When the property or things were used as the means of committing a felony.

(3) When the property or things are in the possession of any person with the intent to use them as a means of committing a public offense, or in the possession of another to whom that person may have delivered them for the purpose of concealing them or preventing them from being discovered.

(4) When the property or things to be seized consist of an item or constitute evidence that tends to show a felony has been committed, or tends to show that a particular person has committed a felony.

(5) When the property or things to be seized consist of evidence that tends to show that sexual exploitation of a child, in violation of Section 311.3, or possession of matter depicting sexual conduct of a person under 18 years of age, in violation of Section 311.11, has occurred or is occurring.

(6) When there is a warrant to arrest a person.

(7) When a provider of electronic communication service or remote computing service has records or evidence, as specified in Section 1524.3, showing that property was stolen or embezzled constituting a misdemeanor, or that property or things are in the possession of any person with the intent to use them as a means of committing a misdemeanor public offense, or in the possession of another to whom that person may have delivered them for the purpose of concealing them or preventing their discovery.

(8) When the property or things to be seized include an item or evidence that tends to show a violation of Section 3700.5 of the Labor Code, or tends to show that a particular person has violated Section 3700.5 of the Labor Code.

(9) When the property or things to be seized include a firearm or other deadly weapon at the scene of, or at the premises occupied or under the control of the person arrested in connection with, a domestic violence incident involving a threat to human life or a physical assault as provided in Section 18250. This section does not affect warrantless seizures otherwise authorized by Section 18250.

(10) When the property or things to be seized include a firearm or other deadly weapon that is owned by, or in the possession of, or in the custody or control of, a person described in subdivision (a) of Section 8102 of the Welfare and Institutions Code.

(11) When the property or things to be seized include a firearm that is owned by, or in the possession of, or in the custody or control of, a person who is subject to the prohibitions regarding firearms pursuant to Section 6389 of the Family Code, if a prohibited firearm is possessed, owned, in the custody of, or controlled by a person against whom a protective order has been issued pursuant to Section 6218 of the Family Code, the person has been lawfully served with that order, and the person has failed to relinquish the firearm as required by law.

(12) When the information to be received from the use of a tracking device constitutes evidence that tends to show that either a felony, a misdemeanor violation of the Fish and Game Code, or a misdemeanor violation of the Public Resources Code has been committed or is being committed, tends to show that a particular person has committed a felony, a misdemeanor violation of the Fish and Game Code, or a misdemeanor violation of the Public Resources Code, or is committing a felony, a misdemeanor violation of the Fish and Game Code, or a misdemeanor violation of the Public Resources Code, or will assist in locating an individual who has committed or is committing a felony, a misdemeanor violation of the Fish and Game Code, or a misdemeanor violation of the Public Resources Code. A tracking device search warrant issued pursuant to this paragraph shall be executed in a manner meeting the requirements specified in subdivision (b) of Section 1534.

(13) When a sample of the blood of a person constitutes evidence that tends to show a violation of Section 23140, 23152, or 23153 of the Vehicle Code and the person from whom the sample is being sought has refused an officer's request to submit to, or has failed to complete, a blood test as required by Section 23612 of the Vehicle Code, and the sample will be drawn from the person in a

reasonable, medically approved manner. This paragraph is not intended to abrogate a court's mandate to determine the propriety of the issuance of a search warrant on a case-by-case basis.

(14)Beginning January 1, 2016, the property or things to be seized are firearms or ammunition or both that are owned by, in the possession of, or in the custody or control of a person who is the subject of a gun violence restraining order that has been issued pursuant to Division 3.2 (commencing with Section 18100) of Title 2 of Part 6, if a prohibited firearm or ammunition or both is possessed, owned, in the custody of, or controlled by a person against whom a gun violence restraining order has been issued, the person has been lawfully served with that order, and the person has failed to relinquish the firearm as required by law.

(15)Beginning January 1, 2018, the property or things to be seized include a firearm that is owned by, or in the possession of, or in the custody or control of, a person who is subject to the prohibitions regarding firearms pursuant to Section 29800 or 29805, and the court has made a finding pursuant to subdivision (c) of Section 29810 that the person has failed to relinquish the firearm as required by law.

(16)When the property or things to be seized are controlled substances or a device, contrivance, instrument, or paraphernalia used for unlawfully using or administering a controlled substance pursuant to the authority described in Section 11472 of the Health and Safety Code.

(17)

(A)When all of the following apply:

(i)A sample of the blood of a person constitutes evidence that tends to show a violation of subdivision (b), (c), (d), (e), or (f) of Section 655 of the Harbors and Navigation Code.

(ii)The person from whom the sample is being sought has refused an officer's request to submit to, or has failed to complete, a blood test as required by Section 655.1 of the Harbors and Navigation Code.

(iii)The sample will be drawn from the person in a reasonable, medically approved manner.

(B)This paragraph is not intended to abrogate a court's mandate to determine the propriety of the issuance of a search warrant on a case-by-case basis.

(18)When the property or things to be seized consists of evidence that tends to show that a violation of paragraph (1), (2), or (3) of subdivision (j) of Section 647 has occurred or is occurring.

(19)

(A)When the property or things to be seized are data, from a recording device installed by the manufacturer of a motor vehicle, that constitutes evidence that tends to show the commission of a felony or misdemeanor offense involving a motor vehicle, resulting in death or serious bodily injury to any person. The data accessed by a warrant pursuant to this paragraph shall not exceed the scope of the data that is directly related to the offense for which the warrant is issued.

(B)For the purposes of this paragraph, "recording device" has the same meaning as defined in subdivision (b) of Section 9951 of the Vehicle Code. The scope of the data accessible by a warrant issued pursuant to this paragraph shall be limited to the information described in subdivision (b) of Section 9951 of the Vehicle Code.

(C)For the purposes of this paragraph, "serious bodily injury" has the same meaning as defined in paragraph (4) of subdivision (f) of Section 243 of the Penal Code.

(20)When the property or things to be seized consists of evidence that tends to show that a violation of Section 647.9 has occurred or is occurring. Evidence to be seized pursuant to this paragraph shall be limited to evidence of a violation of Section 647.9 and shall not include evidence of a violation of a departmental rule or guideline that is not a public offense under California law.

(b)The property, things, person, or persons described in subdivision (a) may be taken on the warrant from any place, or from any person in whose possession the property or things may be.

(c)Notwithstanding subdivision (a) or (b), a search warrant shall not be issued for any documentary evidence in the possession or under the control of any person who is a lawyer as defined in Section 950 of the Evidence Code, a physician as defined in Section 990 of the Evidence Code, a psychotherapist as defined in Section 1010 of the Evidence Code, or a member of the clergy as defined in Section 1030 of the Evidence Code, and who is not reasonably suspected of engaging or having engaged in criminal activity related to the documentary evidence for which a warrant is requested unless the following procedure has been complied with:

(1)At the time of the issuance of the warrant, the court shall appoint a special master in accordance with subdivision (d) to accompany the person who will serve the warrant. Upon service of the warrant, the special master shall inform the party served of the specific items being sought and that the party shall have the opportunity to provide the items requested. If the party, in the judgment of the special master, fails to provide the items requested, the special master shall conduct a search for the items in the areas indicated in the search warrant.

(2)

(A)If the party who has been served states that an item or items should not be disclosed, they shall be sealed by the special master and taken to court for a hearing.

(B)At the hearing, the party searched shall be entitled to raise any issues that may be raised pursuant to Section 1538.5 as well as a claim that the item or items are privileged, as provided by law. The hearing shall be held in the superior court. The court shall provide sufficient time for the parties to obtain counsel and make motions or present evidence. The hearing shall be held within three days of the service of the warrant unless the court makes a finding that the expedited hearing is impracticable. In that case, the matter shall be heard at the earliest possible time.

(C)If an item or items are taken to court for a hearing, any limitations of time prescribed in Chapter 2 (commencing with Section 799) of Title 3 of Part 2 shall be tolled from the time of the seizure until the final conclusion of the hearing, including any associated writ or appellate proceedings.

(3)The warrant shall, whenever practicable, be served during normal business hours. In addition, the warrant shall be served upon a party who appears to have possession or control of the items sought. If, after reasonable efforts, the party serving the warrant is unable to locate the person, the special master shall seal and return to the court, for determination by the court, any item that appears to be privileged as provided by law.

(d)

(1)As used in this section, a "special master" is an attorney who is a member in good standing of the California State Bar and who has been selected from a list of qualified attorneys that is maintained by the State Bar particularly for the purposes of conducting the searches described in this section. These attorneys shall serve without compensation. A special master shall be considered a public employee, and the governmental entity that caused the search warrant to be issued shall be considered the employer of the special master and the applicable public entity, for purposes of Division 3.6 (commencing with Section 810) of Title 1 of the Government Code, relating to claims and actions against public entities and public employees. In selecting the special master, the court shall make every reasonable effort to ensure that the person selected has no relationship with any of the parties involved in the pending matter. Information obtained by the special master shall be confidential and may not be divulged except in direct response to inquiry by the court.

(2)In any case in which the magistrate determines that, after reasonable efforts have been made to obtain a special master, a special master is not available and would not be available within a reasonable period of time, the magistrate may direct the party seeking the order to conduct the search in the manner described in this section in lieu of the special master.

(e) Any search conducted pursuant to this section by a special master may be conducted in a manner that permits the party serving the warrant or that party's designee to accompany the special master as the special master conducts the search. However, that party or that party's designee may not participate in the search nor shall they examine any of the items being searched by the special master except upon agreement of the party upon whom the warrant has been served.

(f) As used in this section, "documentary evidence" includes, but is not limited to, writings, documents, blueprints, drawings, photographs, computer printouts, microfilms, x-rays, files, diagrams, ledgers, books, tapes, audio and video recordings, films, and papers of any type or description.

(g) No warrant shall issue for any item or items described in Section 1070 of the Evidence Code.

(h) No warrant shall issue for any item or items that pertain to an investigation into a prohibited violation, as defined in Section 629.51.

(i) Notwithstanding any other law, no claim of attorney work product as described in Chapter 4 (commencing with Section 2018.010) of Title 4 of Part 4 of the Code of Civil Procedure shall be sustained where there is probable cause to believe that the lawyer is engaging or has engaged in criminal activity related to the documentary evidence for which a warrant is requested unless it is established at the hearing with respect to the documentary evidence seized under the warrant that the services of the lawyer were not sought or obtained to enable or aid anyone to commit or plan to commit a crime or a fraud.

(j) Nothing in this section is intended to limit an attorney's ability to request an in-camera hearing pursuant to the holding of the Supreme Court of California in People v. Superior Court (Laff) (2001) 25 Cal.4th 703.

(k) In addition to any other circumstance permitting a magistrate to issue a warrant for a person or property in another county, when the property or things to be seized consist of any item or constitute evidence that tends to show a violation of Section 530.5, the magistrate may issue a warrant to search a person or property located in another county if the person whose identifying information was taken or used resides in the same county as the issuing court.

(l) This section shall not be construed to create a cause of action against any foreign or California corporation, its officers, employees, agents, or other specified persons for providing location information.

Amended by Stats 2022 ch 627 (AB 1242),s 7, eff. 9/27/2022.
Amended by Stats 2020 ch 219 (AB 2655),s 2, eff. 1/1/2021.
Amended by Stats 2019 ch 196 (AB 1638),s 1, eff. 1/1/2020.
Amended by Stats 2017 ch 342 (AB 539),s 1, eff. 1/1/2018.
Amended by Proposition 63, approved by the voters at the 11/8/2016 election.
Amended by Stats 2015 ch 124 (AB 1104),s 1.5, eff. 1/1/2016.
Amended by Stats 2015 ch 118 (AB 539),s 1, eff. 1/1/2016.
Amended by Stats 2014 ch 872 (AB 1014),s 1, eff. 1/1/2015.
Amended by Stats 2013 ch 317 (SB 717),s 1, eff. 9/20/2013.
Amended by Stats 2012 ch 818 (AB 2055),s 1, eff. 1/1/2013.
Amended by Stats 2010 ch 178 (SB 1115),s 79, eff. 1/1/2011, op. 1/1/2012.
Amended by Stats 2009 ch 473 (AB 789),s 1.5, eff. 1/1/2010.
Amended by Stats 2009 ch 450 (AB 532),s 1, eff. 1/1/2010.
Amended by Stats 2006 ch 538 (SB 1852),s 507, eff. 1/1/2007.
Amended by Stats 2005 ch 294 (AB 333),s 24, eff. 1/1/2006.
Amended by Stats 2004 ch 2 (SB X4-2), s 8, eff. 1/1/2005.
Amended by Stats 2004 ch 182 (AB 3081), s 51, eff. 1/1/2005.
Amended by Stats 2003 ch 137 (AB 1773), s 1, eff. 1/1/2004.
Added by Stats 2002 ch 1059 (AB 2055), s 3.2, eff. 9/29/2002, op. 1/1/2003.

Section 1524.1 - HIV testing

(a) The primary purpose of the testing and disclosure provided in this section is to benefit the victim of a crime by informing the victim whether the defendant is infected with HIV. It is also the intent of the Legislature in enacting this section to protect the health of both victims of crime and those accused of committing a crime. This section does not authorize mandatory testing or disclosure of test results for the purpose of a charging decision by a prosecutor, and, except as specified in subdivisions (g) and (i), this section does not authorize breach of the confidentiality provisions contained in Chapter 7 (commencing with Section 120975) of Part 4 of Division 105 of the Health and Safety Code.

(b)

(1) Notwithstanding the provisions of Chapter 7 (commencing with Section 120975) of Part 4 of Division 105 of the Health and Safety Code, when a defendant has been charged by complaint, information, or indictment with a crime, or a minor is the subject of a petition filed in juvenile court alleging the commission of a crime, the court, at the request of the victim, may issue a search warrant for

the purpose of testing the accused's blood or oral mucosal transudate saliva with an HIV test, as defined in Section 120775 of the Health and Safety Code only under the following circumstances: when the court finds, upon the conclusion of the hearing described in paragraph (3), or when a preliminary hearing is not required to be held, that there is probable cause to believe that the accused committed the offense, and that there is probable cause to believe that blood, semen, or any other bodily fluid identified by the State Department of Public Health in appropriate regulations as capable of transmitting the human immunodeficiency virus has been transferred from the accused to the victim.

(2) Notwithstanding Chapter 7 (commencing with Section 120975) of Part 4 of Division 105 of the Health and Safety Code, when a defendant has been charged by complaint, information, or indictment with a crime under Section 220, 261, 261.5, 264.1, 266c, 269, 286, 287, 288, 288.5, 289, or 289.5, or former Section 262 or 288a, or with an attempt to commit any of the offenses, and is the subject of a police report alleging the commission of a separate, uncharged offense that could be charged under Section 220, 261, 261.5, 264.1, 266c, 269, 286, 287, 288, 288.5, 289, or 289.5, or former Section 262 or 288a, or of an attempt to commit any of the offenses, or a minor is the subject of a petition filed in juvenile court alleging the commission of a crime under Section 220, 261, 261.5, 264.1, 266c, 269, 286, 287, 288, 288.5, 289, or 289.5, or former Section 262 or 288a, or of an attempt to commit any of the offenses, and is the subject of a police report alleging the commission of a separate, uncharged offense that could be charged under Section 220, 261, 261.5, 264.1, 266c, 269, 286, 287, 288, 288.5, 289, or 289.5, or former Section 262 or 288a, or of an attempt to commit any of the offenses, the court, at the request of the victim of the uncharged offense, may issue a search warrant for the purpose of testing the accused's blood or oral mucosal transudate saliva with an HIV test, as defined in Section 120775 of the Health and Safety Code only under the following circumstances: when the court finds that there is probable cause to believe that the accused committed the uncharged offense, and that there is probable cause to believe that blood, semen, or any other bodily fluid identified by the State Department of Public Health in appropriate regulations as capable of transmitting the human immunodeficiency virus has been transferred from the accused to the victim. As used in this paragraph, "Section 289.5" refers to the statute enacted by Chapter 293 of the Statutes of 1991, penetration by an unknown object.

(3)

(A) Prior to the issuance of a search warrant pursuant to paragraph (1), the court, where applicable and at the conclusion of the preliminary examination if the defendant is ordered to answer pursuant to Section 872, shall conduct a hearing at which both the victim and the defendant have the right to be present. During the hearing, only affidavits, counter affidavits, and medical reports regarding the facts that support or rebut the issuance of a search warrant under paragraph (1) shall be admissible.

(B) Prior to the issuance of a search warrant pursuant to paragraph (2), the court, where applicable, shall conduct a hearing at which both the victim and the defendant are present. During the hearing, only affidavits, counter affidavits, and medical reports regarding the facts that support or rebut the issuance of a search warrant under paragraph (2) shall be admissible.

(4) A request for a probable cause hearing made by a victim under paragraph (2) shall be made before sentencing in the superior court, or before disposition on a petition in a juvenile court, of the criminal charge or charges filed against the defendant.

(c)

(1) When the person has been charged by complaint, information, or indictment with a crime, or is the subject of a petition filed in a juvenile court alleging the commission of a crime, the prosecutor shall advise the victim of the right to make this request. To assist the victim of the crime to determine whether the victim should make this request, the prosecutor shall refer the victim to the local health officer for prerequest counseling to help that person understand the extent to which the particular circumstances of the crime may or may not have put the victim at risk of transmission of HIV from the accused, to ensure that the victim understands both the benefits and limitations of the current tests for HIV, to help the victim decide whether the victim wants to request that the accused be tested, and to help the victim decide whether the victim wants to be tested.

(2) The Department of Justice, in cooperation with the California District Attorneys Association, shall prepare a form to be used in providing victims with the notice required by paragraph (1).

(d) If the victim decides to request HIV testing of the accused, the victim shall request the issuance of a search warrant, as described in subdivision (b). Neither the failure of a prosecutor to refer or advise the victim as provided in this subdivision, nor the failure or refusal by the victim to seek or obtain counseling, shall be considered by the court in ruling on the victim's request.

(e) The local health officer shall make provision for administering all HIV tests ordered pursuant to subdivision (b).

(f) Any blood or oral mucosal transudate saliva tested pursuant to subdivision (b) shall be subjected to appropriate confirmatory tests to ensure accuracy of the first test results, and under no circumstances shall test results be transmitted to the victim or the accused unless any initially reactive test result has been confirmed by appropriate confirmatory tests for positive reactors.

(g) The local health officer shall have the responsibility for disclosing test results to the victim who requested the test and to the accused who was tested. However, positive test results shall not be disclosed to the victim or to the accused without also providing or offering professional counseling appropriate to the circumstances.

(h) The local health officer and victim shall comply with all laws and policies relating to medical confidentiality subject to the disclosure authorized by subdivisions (g) and (i). An individual who files a false report of sexual assault in order to obtain test result information pursuant to this section shall, in addition to any other liability under law, be guilty of a misdemeanor punishable as provided in subdivision (c) of Section 120980 of the Health and Safety Code. An individual as described in the preceding sentence who discloses test result information obtained pursuant to this section shall also be guilty of an additional misdemeanor punishable as provided for in subdivision (c) of Section 120980 of the Health and Safety Code for each separate disclosure of that information.

(i) A victim who receives information from the health officer pursuant to subdivision (g) may disclose the test results as the victim deems necessary to protect their health and safety or the health and safety of the victim's family or sexual partner.

(j) A person transmitting test results or disclosing information pursuant to this section shall be immune from civil liability for any actions taken in compliance with this section.

(k) The results of any blood or oral mucosal transudate saliva tested pursuant to subdivision (b) shall not be used in any criminal proceeding as evidence of either guilt or innocence.

Amended by Stats 2021 ch 626 (AB 1171),s 55, eff. 1/1/2022.

Amended by Stats 2018 ch 423 (SB 1494),s 100, eff. 1/1/2019.
Amended by Stats 2003 ch 62 (SB 600), s 234, eff. 1/1/2004.
Amended by Stats 2002 ch 784 (SB 1316), s 556, eff. 1/1/2003.
Amended by Stats 2002 ch 787 (SB 1798), s 24, eff. 1/1/2003.
Amended by Stats 2002 ch 831 (AB 2794), s 2, eff. 1/1/2003.

Section 1524.2 - Search warrant for records in possession of foreign corporation that provides electronic communication services or remote computing services

(a)As used in this section, the following terms have the following meanings:

(1)The terms "electronic communication services" and "remote computing services" shall be construed in accordance with the Electronic Communications Privacy Act of 1986 in Chapter 121 (commencing with Section 2701) of Part I of Title 18 of the United States Code. This section does not apply to corporations that do not provide those services to the general public.

(2)An "adverse result" occurs when notification of the existence of a search warrant results in:

(A)Danger to the life or physical safety of an individual.

(B)A flight from prosecution.

(C)The destruction of or tampering with evidence.

(D)The intimidation of potential witnesses.

(E)Serious jeopardy to an investigation or undue delay of a trial.

(3)"Applicant" refers to the peace officer to whom a search warrant is issued pursuant to subdivision (a) of Section 1528.

(4)"California corporation" refers to any corporation or other entity that is subject to Section 102 of the Corporations Code, excluding foreign corporations.

(5)"Foreign corporation" refers to any corporation that is qualified to do business in this state pursuant to Section 2105 of the Corporations Code.

(6)"Properly served" means that a search warrant has been delivered by hand, or in a manner reasonably allowing for proof of delivery if delivered by United States mail, overnight delivery service, or facsimile to a person or entity listed in Section 2110 of the Corporations Code, or any other means specified by the recipient of the search warrant, including email or submission via an internet web portal that the recipient has designated for the purpose of service of process.

(b)The following provisions apply to any search warrant issued pursuant to this chapter allowing a search for records that are in the actual or constructive possession of a foreign corporation that provides electronic communication services or remote computing services to the general public, where those records would reveal the identity of the customers using those services, data stored by, or on behalf of, the customer, the customer's usage of those services, the recipient or destination of communications sent to or from those customers, or the content of those communications.

(1)When properly served with a search warrant issued by the California court, a foreign corporation subject to this section shall provide to the applicant, all records sought pursuant to that warrant within five business days of receipt, including those records maintained or located outside this state.

(2)If the applicant makes a showing and the magistrate finds that failure to produce records within less than five business days would cause an adverse result, the warrant may require production of records within less than five business days. A court may reasonably extend the time required for production of the records upon finding that the foreign corporation has shown good cause for that extension and that an extension of time would not cause an adverse result.

(3)A foreign corporation seeking to quash the warrant must seek relief from the court that issued the warrant within the time required for production of records pursuant to this section. The issuing court shall hear and decide that motion no later than five court days after the motion is filed.

(4)The foreign corporation shall verify the authenticity of records that it produces by providing an affidavit that complies with the requirements set forth in Section 1561 of the Evidence Code. Those records shall be admissible in evidence as set forth in Section 1562 of the Evidence Code.

(c)

(1)A California corporation that provides electronic communication services or remote computing services to the general public, when served with a warrant issued by another state to produce records that would reveal the identity of the customers using those services, data stored by, or on behalf of, the customer, the customer's usage of those services, the recipient or destination of communications sent to or from those customers, or the content of those communications, shall produce those records as if that warrant had been issued by a California court, but shall not produce records when the corporation knows or should know that the warrant relates to an investigation into, or enforcement of, a prohibited violation, as defined in Section 629.51.

(2)A California corporation shall not comply with subdivision (c) unless the warrant includes, or is accompanied by, an attestation that the evidence sought is not related to an investigation into, or enforcement of, a prohibited violation, as defined in Section 629.51.

(3)A California corporation served with a warrant described in paragraph (1) is entitled to rely on the representations made in an attestation described in paragraph (2) in determining whether the warrant relates to an investigation into, or enforcement of, a prohibited violation, as defined in Section 629.51.

(d)A cause of action shall not lie against any foreign or California corporation subject to this section, its officers, employees, agents, or other specified persons for providing records, information, facilities, or assistance in accordance with the terms of a warrant issued pursuant to this chapter.

Amended by Stats 2022 ch 627 (AB 1242),s 8, eff. 9/27/2022.
Amended by Stats 2016 ch 86 (SB 1171),s 231, eff. 1/1/2017.
Amended by Stats 2015 ch 57 (AB 844),s 3, eff. 1/1/2016.
EFFECTIVE 1/1/2000. Added October 10, 1999 (Bill Number: SB 662) (Chapter 896).

Section 1524.3 - Subscriber records or information

(a) A provider of electronic communication service or remote computing service, as used in Chapter 121 (commencing with Section 2701) of Title 18 of the United States Code, shall disclose to a governmental prosecuting or investigating agency the name, address, local and long distance telephone toll billing records, telephone number or other subscriber number or identity, and length of service of a subscriber to or customer of that service, the types of services the subscriber or customer utilized, and the contents of communication originated by or addressed to the service provider when the governmental entity is granted a search warrant pursuant to paragraph (7) of subdivision (a) of Section 1524.

(b) The search warrant shall be limited to only that information necessary to achieve the objective of the warrant, including by specifying the target individuals or accounts, the applications or services, the types of information, and the time periods covered, as appropriate.

(c) Information obtained through the execution of a search warrant pursuant to this section that is unrelated to the objective of the warrant shall be sealed and not be subject to further review without an order from the court.

(d)

(1) A governmental entity receiving subscriber records or information under this section shall provide notice to a subscriber or customer upon receipt of the requested records. The notification may be delayed by the court, in increments of 90 days, upon a showing that there is reason to believe that notification of the existence of the search warrant may have an adverse result.

(2) An "adverse result" for purposes of paragraph (1) means any of the following:

(A) Endangering the life or physical safety of an individual.

(B) Flight from prosecution.

(C) Tampering or destruction of evidence.

(D) Intimidation of a potential witness.

(E) Otherwise seriously jeopardizing an investigation or unduly delaying a trial.

(e) Upon the expiration of the period of delay for the notification, the governmental entity shall, by regular mail or email, provide a copy of the process or request and a notice, to the subscriber or customer. The notice shall accomplish all of the following:

(1) State the nature of the law enforcement inquiry with reasonable specificity.

(2) Inform the subscriber or customer that information maintained for the subscriber or customer by the service provider named in the process or request was supplied to or requested by the governmental entity, and the date upon which the information was supplied, and the request was made.

(3) Inform the subscriber or customer that notification to the subscriber or customer was delayed, and which court issued the order pursuant to which the notification was delayed.

(4) Provide a copy of the written inventory of the property that was taken that was provided to the court pursuant to Section 1537.

(f) A court issuing a search warrant pursuant to paragraph (7) of subdivision (a) of Section 1524, on a motion made promptly by the service provider, may quash or modify the warrant if the information or records requested are unusually voluminous in nature or compliance with the warrant otherwise would cause an undue burden on the provider.

(g) A provider of wire or electronic communication services or a remote computing service, upon the request of a peace officer, shall take all necessary steps to preserve records and other evidence in its possession pending the issuance of a search warrant or a request in writing and an affidavit declaring an intent to file a warrant to the provider. Records shall be retained for a period of 90 days, which shall be extended for an additional 90-day period upon a renewed request by the peace officer.

(h) No cause of action shall be brought against any provider, its officers, employees, or agents for providing information, facilities, or assistance in good faith compliance with a search warrant.

Amended by Stats 2015 ch 643 (AB 1310),s 2, eff. 1/1/2016.

Added by Stats 2002 ch 864 (SB 1980), s 2, eff. 1/1/2003.

Section 1524.4 - Law enforcement contact process

(a) This section applies to a service provider that is subject to the Electronic Communications Privacy Act (Chapter 3.6 (commencing with Section 1546)) and that operates in California. This section does not apply to a service provider that does not offer services to the general public.

(b)

(1) Every service provider described in subdivision (a) shall maintain a law enforcement contact process that meets the criteria set forth in paragraph (2).

(2) Every service provider described in subdivision (a) shall ensure, at a minimum, that its law enforcement contact process meets all of the following criteria:

(A) Provides a specific contact mechanism for law enforcement personnel.

(B) Provides continual availability of the law enforcement contact process.

(C) Provides a method to provide status updates to a requesting law enforcement agency on a request for assistance.

(3) Every service provider described in subdivision (a) shall, by July 1, 2017, file a statement with the Attorney General describing the law enforcement contact process maintained pursuant to paragraph (1). If a service provider makes a material change to its law enforcement contact process, the service provider shall, as soon as practicable, file a statement with the Attorney General describing its new law enforcement contact process.

(c) The Attorney General shall consolidate the statements received pursuant to this section into one discrete record and regularly make that record available to local law enforcement agencies.

(d) The exclusive remedy for a violation of this section shall be an action brought by the Attorney General for injunctive relief. Nothing in this section shall limit remedies available for a violation of any other state or federal law.

(e) A statement filed or distributed pursuant to this section is confidential and shall not be disclosed pursuant to any state law, including, but not limited to, the California Public Records Act (Division 10 (commencing with Section 7920.000) of Title 1 of the Government Code).

Amended by Stats 2021 ch 615 (AB 474),s 342, eff. 1/1/2022, op. 1/1/2023.

Added by Stats 2016 ch 514 (AB 1993),s 2, eff. 1/1/2017.

Section 1525 - Probable cause supported by affidavit

A search warrant cannot be issued but upon probable cause, supported by affidavit, naming or describing the person to be searched or searched for, and particularly describing the property, thing, or things and the place to be searched.

The application shall specify when applicable, that the place to be searched is in the possession or under the control of an attorney, physician, psychotherapist or clergyman.

Amended by Stats. 1996, Ch. 1078, Sec. 3. Effective January 1, 1997.

Section 1526 - Examination of person seeking warrant and witnesses

(a) Before issuing the search warrant, the magistrate may examine on oath the person seeking the warrant and any witnesses the person may produce, and shall take his or her affidavit or their affidavits in writing, and cause the affidavit or affidavits to be subscribed by the party or parties making them. If the affiant transmits the proposed search warrant and all affidavits and supporting documents to the magistrate using facsimile transmission equipment, email, or computer server, the conditions in subdivision (c) apply.

(b) In lieu of the written affidavit required in subdivision (a), the magistrate may take an oral statement under oath if the oath is made under penalty of perjury and recorded and transcribed. The transcribed statement shall be deemed to be an affidavit for the purposes of this chapter. The recording of the sworn oral statement and the transcribed statement shall be certified by the magistrate receiving it and shall be filed with the clerk of the court. In the alternative, the sworn oral statement shall be recorded by a certified court reporter and the transcript of the statement shall be certified by the reporter, after which the magistrate receiving it shall certify the transcript which shall be filed with the clerk of the court.

(c)

(1) The affiant shall sign under penalty of perjury his or her affidavit in support of probable cause for issuance of a search warrant. The affiant's signature may be in the form of a digital signature or electronic signature if email or computer server is used for transmission to the magistrate.

(2) The magistrate shall verify that all the pages sent have been received, that all the pages are legible, and that the declarant's signature, digital signature, or electronic signature is genuine.

(3) If the magistrate decides to issue the search warrant, he or she shall do both of the following:

(A) Sign the warrant. The magistrate's signature may be in the form of a digital signature or electronic signature if email or computer server is used for transmission by the magistrate.

(B) Note on the warrant the date and time of the issuance of the warrant.

(4) The magistrate shall transmit via facsimile transmission equipment, email, or computer server the signed search warrant to the affiant. The search warrant signed by the magistrate and received by the affiant shall be deemed to be the original warrant. The original warrant and any affidavits or attachments in support thereof shall be returned as provided in Section 1534.

Amended by Stats 2018 ch 176 (AB 2710),s 2, eff. 1/1/2019.

Amended by Stats 2016 ch 86 (SB 1171),s 232, eff. 1/1/2017.

Amended by Stats 2015 ch 193 (AB 39),s 1, eff. 1/1/2016.

Amended by Stats 2010 ch 98 (AB 2505),s 1, eff. 1/1/2011.

Section 1527 - Content of affidavit

The affidavit or affidavits must set forth the facts tending to establish the grounds of the application, or probable cause for believing that they exist.

Amended by Stats. 1957, Ch. 1883.

Section 1528 - Issuance of search warrant; duplicate original warrant

(a) If the magistrate is thereupon satisfied of the existence of the grounds of the application, or that there is probable cause to believe their existence, he or she must issue a search warrant, signed by him or her with his or her name of office, to a peace officer in his or her county, commanding him or her forthwith to search the person or place named for the property or things or person or persons specified, and to retain the property or things in his or her custody subject to order of the court as provided by Section 1536.

(b) The magistrate may orally authorize a peace officer to sign the magistrate's name on a duplicate original warrant. A duplicate original warrant shall be deemed to be a search warrant for the purposes of this chapter, and it shall be returned to the magistrate as provided for in Section 1537. The magistrate shall enter on the face of the original warrant the exact time of the issuance of the warrant and shall sign and file the original warrant and the duplicate original warrant with the clerk of the court as provided for in Section 1541.

Amended by Stats. 1996, Ch. 1078, Sec. 4. Effective January 1, 1997.

Section 1529 - Form of warrant

The warrant shall be in substantially the following form:

County of ____.

The people of the State of California to any peace officer in the County of ____:

Proof, by affidavit, having been this day made before me by (naming every person whose affidavit has been taken), that (stating the grounds of the application, according to Section 1524, or, if the affidavit be not positive, that there is probable cause for believing that ____ stating the ground of the application in the same manner), you are therefore commanded, in the daytime (or at any time of the day or night, as the case may be, according to Section 1533), to make search on the person of C. D. (or in the house situated ____, describing it, or any other place to be searched, with reasonable particularity, as the case may be) for the following property, thing, things, or person: (describing the property, thing, things, or person with reasonable particularity); and, in the case of a thing or things or personal property, if you find the same or any part thereof, to bring the thing or things or personal property forthwith before me (or this court) at (stating the place).

Given under my hand, and dated this ____ day of ____, A.D. (year).

E. F., Judge of the (applicable) Court.

Amended by Stats 2005 ch 181 (AB 182),s 1, eff. 1/1/2006

Section 1530 - Service of warrant

A search warrant may in all cases be served by any of the officers mentioned in its directions, but by no other person, except in aid of the officer on his requiring it, he being present and acting in its execution.
Enacted 1872.

Section 1531 - Breaking open house to execute warrant
The officer may break open any outer or inner door or window of a house, or any part of a house, or anything therein, to execute the warrant, if, after notice of his authority and purpose, he is refused admittance.
Enacted 1872.

Section 1532 - Breaking open door or window of house to liberate person
He may break open any outer or inner door or window of a house, for the purpose of liberating a person who, having entered to aid him in the execution of the warrant, is detained therein, or when necessary for his own liberation.
Enacted 1872.

Section 1533 - Time of service of warrant
Upon a showing of good cause, the magistrate may, in his or her discretion, insert a direction in a search warrant that it may be served at any time of the day or night. In the absence of such a direction, the warrant shall be served only between the hours of 7 a.m. and 10 p.m.

When establishing "good cause" under this section, the magistrate shall consider the safety of the peace officers serving the warrant and the safety of the public as a valid basis for nighttime endorsements.
Amended by Stats. 1986, Ch. 257, Sec. 1.

Section 1534 - Execution and return of warrant
(a) A search warrant shall be executed and returned within 10 days after date of issuance. A warrant executed within the 10-day period shall be deemed to have been timely executed and no further showing of timeliness need be made. After the expiration of 10 days, the warrant, unless executed, is void. The documents and records of the court relating to the warrant need not be open to the public until the execution and return of the warrant or the expiration of the 10-day period after issuance. Thereafter, if the warrant has been executed, the documents and records shall be open to the public as a judicial record.

(b)

(1) A tracking device search warrant issued pursuant to paragraph (12) of subdivision (a) of Section 1524 shall identify the person or property to be tracked and shall specify a reasonable length of time, not to exceed 30 days from the date the warrant is issued, that the device may be used. The court may, for good cause, grant one or more extensions for the time that the device may be used, with each extension lasting for a reasonable length of time, not to exceed 30 days. The search warrant shall command the officer to execute the warrant by installing a tracking device or serving a warrant on a third-party possessor of the tracking data. The officer shall perform any installation authorized by the warrant during the daytime unless the magistrate, for good cause, expressly authorizes installation at another time. Execution of the warrant shall be completed no later than 10 days immediately after the date of issuance. A warrant executed within this 10-day period shall be deemed to have been timely executed and no further showing of timeliness need be made. After the expiration of 10 days, the warrant shall be void, unless it has been executed.

(2) An officer executing a tracking device search warrant shall not be required to knock and announce their presence before executing the warrant.

(3) No later than 10 calendar days after the use of the tracking device has ended, the officer executing the warrant shall file a return to the warrant.

(4)

(A) No later than 10 calendar days after the use of the tracking device has ended, the officer who executed the tracking device warrant shall notify the person who was tracked or whose property was tracked pursuant to subdivision (a) of Section 1546.2.

(B) Notice under this paragraph may be delayed pursuant to subdivision (b) of Section 1546.2.

(5) An officer installing a device authorized by a tracking device search warrant may install and use the device only within California.

(6)

(A) As used in this section, "tracking device" means any electronic or mechanical device, or software, that permits the tracking of the movement of a person or object.

(B) Nothing in this section shall be construed to authorize the use of any device or software for the purpose of tracking the movement of a person or object.

(7) As used in this section, "daytime" means the hours between 6 a.m. and 10 p.m. according to local time.

(c) If a duplicate original search warrant has been executed, the peace officer who executed the warrant shall enter the exact time of its execution on its face.

(d) A search warrant may be made returnable before the issuing magistrate or their court.
Amended by Stats 2020 ch 63 (AB 904),s 1, eff. 1/1/2021.
Amended by Stats 2016 ch 541 (SB 1121),s 1, eff. 1/1/2017.
Amended by Stats 2012 ch 818 (AB 2055),s 2, eff. 1/1/2013.

Section 1535 - Receipt for property taken
When the officer takes property under the warrant, he must give a receipt for the property taken (specifying it in detail) to the person from whom it was taken by him, or in whose possession it was found; or, in the absence of any person, he must leave it in the place where he found the property.
Enacted 1872.

Section 1536 - Retention of property taken
All property or things taken on a warrant must be retained by the officer in his custody, subject to the order of the court to which he is required to return the proceedings before him, or of any other court in which the offense in respect to which the property or things taken is triable.
Amended by Stats. 1957, Ch. 1885.

Section 1536.5 - Seizure of business records

(a) If a government agency seizes business records from an entity pursuant to a search warrant, the entity from which the records were seized may file a demand on that government agency to produce copies of the business records that have been seized. The demand for production of copies of business records shall be supported by a declaration, made under penalty of perjury, that denial of access to the records in question will either unduly interfere with the entity's ability to conduct its regular course of business or obstruct the entity from fulfilling an affirmative obligation that it has under the law. Unless the government agency objects pursuant to subdivision (d), this declaration shall suffice if it makes a prima facie case that specific business activities or specific legal obligations faced by the entity would be impaired or impeded by the ongoing loss of records.

(b)

(1) Except as provided in paragraph (2), when a government agency seizes business records from an entity and is subsequently served with a demand for copies of those business records pursuant to subdivision (a), the government agency in possession of those records shall make copies of those records available to the entity within 10 court days of the service of the demand to produce copies of the records.

(2) In the alternative, the agency in possession of the original records, may in its discretion, make the original records reasonably available to the entity within 10 court days following the service of the demand to produce records, and allow the entity reasonable time to copy the records.

(3) No agency shall be required to make records available at times other than normal business hours.

(4) If data is recorded in a tangible medium, copies of the data may be provided in that same medium, or any other medium of which the entity may make reasonable use. If the data is stored electronically, electromagnetically, or photo-optically, the entity may obtain either a copy made by the same process in which the data is stored, or in the alternative, by any other tangible medium through which the entity may make reasonable use of the data.

(5) A government agency granting the entity access to the original records for the purpose of making copies of the records, may take reasonable steps to ensure the integrity and chain of custody of the business records.

(6) If the seized records are too voluminous to be reviewed or be copied in the time period required by subdivision (a), the government agency that seized the records may file a written motion with the court for additional time to review the records or make the copies. This motion shall be made within 10 court days of the service of the demand for the records. An extension of time under this paragraph shall not be granted unless the agency establishes that reviewing or producing copies of the records within the 10 court day time period, would create a hardship on the agency. If the court grants the motion, it shall make an order designating a timeframe for the review and the duplication and return of the business records, deferring to the entity the priority of the records to be reviewed, duplicated, and returned first.

(c) If a court finds that a declaration made by an entity as provided in subdivision (a) is adequate to establish the specified prima facie case, a government agency may refuse to produce copies of the business records or to grant access to the original records only under one or both of the following circumstances:

(1) The court determines by the preponderance of the evidence standard that denial of access to the business records or copies of the business records will not unduly interfere with the entity's ability to conduct its regular course of business or obstruct the entity from fulfilling an affirmative obligation that it has under the law.

(2) The court determines by the preponderance of the evidence standard that possession of the business records by the entity will pose a significant risk of ongoing criminal activity, or that the business records are contraband, evidence of criminal conduct by the entity from which the records were seized, or depict a person under the age of 18 years personally engaging in or simulating sexual conduct, as defined in subdivision (d) of Section 311.4.

(d) A government agency that desires not to produce copies of, or grant access to, seized business records shall file a motion with the court requesting an order denying the entity copies of and access to the records. A motion under this paragraph shall be in writing, and filed and served upon the entity prior to the expiration of 10 court days following the service of the demand to produce records specified in subdivision (a), within any extension of that time period granted under paragraph (6) of subdivision (b), or as soon as reasonably possible after discovery of the risk of harm.

(e) A hearing on a motion under subdivision (d) shall be held within two court days of the filing of the motion, except upon agreement of the parties.

(f)

(1) Upon filing a motion under subdivision (d) opposing a demand for copies of records, the government agency may file a request in writing, served upon the demanding entity, that any showings of why the material should not be copied and released occur in an ex parte, in camera hearing. If the government agency alleges in its request for an in camera hearing that the demanding entity is, or is likely to become, a target of the investigation resulting in the seizure of records, the court shall hold this hearing outside of the presence of the demanding entity, and any representatives or counsel of the demanding entity. If the government agency does not allege in its request for an in camera hearing that the demanding entity is, or is likely to become, a target of the investigation resulting in the seizure of records, the court shall hold the hearing in camera only upon a particular factual showing by the government agency in its pleadings that a hearing in open court would impede or interrupt an ongoing criminal investigation.

(2) At the in camera hearing, any evidence that the government agency may offer that the release of the material would pose a significant risk of ongoing criminal activity, impede or interrupt an ongoing criminal investigation, or both, shall be offered under oath. A reporter shall be present at the in camera hearing to transcribe the entirety of the proceedings.

(3) Any transcription of the proceedings at the in camera hearing, as well as any physical evidence presented at the hearing, shall be ordered sealed by the court, and only a court may have access to its contents, unless a court determines that the failure to disclose the contents of the hearing would deprive the defendant or the people of a fair trial.

(4) Following the conclusion of the in camera hearing, the court shall make its ruling in open court, after notice to the demanding entity.

(g) The reasonable and necessary costs of producing copies of business records under this section shall be borne by the entity requesting copies of the records. Either party may request the court to resolve any dispute regarding these costs.

(h) Any motion under this section shall be filed in the court that issued the search warrant.

(i) For purposes of this section, the following terms are defined as follows:

(1) "Seize" means obtaining actual possession of any property alleged by the entity to contain business records.

(2) "Business" means an entity, sole proprietorship, partnership, or corporation operating legally in the State of California, that sells, leases, distributes, creates, or otherwise offers products or services to customers.

(3) "Business records" means computer data, data compilations, accounts, books, reports, contracts, correspondence, inventories, lists, personnel files, payrolls, vendor and client lists, documents, or papers of the person or business normally used in the regular course of business, or any other material item of business recordkeeping that may become technologically feasible in the future.

Added by Stats 2004 ch 372 (AB 1894), s 1, eff. 1/1/2005.

Section 1537 - Return of warrant; inventory of property taken

The officer must forthwith return the warrant to the magistrate, and deliver to him a written inventory of the property taken, made publicly or in the presence of the person from whose possession it was taken, and of the applicant for the warrant, if they are present, verified by the affidavit of the officer at the foot of the inventory, and taken before the magistrate at the time, to the following effect: "I, R. S., the officer by whom this warrant was executed, do swear that the above inventory contains a true and detailed account of all the property taken by me on the warrant."

Enacted 1872.

Section 1538 - Delivery of copy of inventory

The magistrate must thereupon, if required, deliver a copy of the inventory to the person from whose possession the property was taken, and to the applicant for the warrant.

Enacted 1872.

Section 1538.5 - Motion for return of property or to suppress evidence

(a)

(1) A defendant may move for the return of property or to suppress as evidence any tangible or intangible thing obtained as a result of a search or seizure on either of the following grounds:

(A) The search or seizure without a warrant was unreasonable.

(B) The search or seizure with a warrant was unreasonable because any of the following apply:

(i) The warrant is insufficient on its face.

(ii) The property or evidence obtained is not that described in the warrant.

(iii) There was not probable cause for the issuance of the warrant.

(iv) The method of execution of the warrant violated federal or state constitutional standards.

(v) There was any other violation of federal or state constitutional standards.

(2) A motion pursuant to paragraph (1) shall be made in writing and accompanied by a memorandum of points and authorities and proof of service. The memorandum shall list the specific items of property or evidence sought to be returned or suppressed and shall set forth the factual basis and the legal authorities that demonstrate why the motion should be granted.

(b) When consistent with the procedures set forth in this section and subject to the provisions of Sections 170 to 170.6, inclusive, of the Code of Civil Procedure, the motion should first be heard by the magistrate who issued the search warrant if there is a warrant.

(c)

(1) Whenever a search or seizure motion is made in the superior court as provided in this section, the judge or magistrate shall receive evidence on any issue of fact necessary to determine the motion.

(2) While a witness is under examination during a hearing pursuant to a search or seizure motion, the judge or magistrate shall, upon motion of either party, do any of the following:

(A) Exclude all potential and actual witnesses who have not been examined.

(B) Order the witnesses not to converse with each other until they are all examined.

(C) Order, where feasible, that the witnesses be kept separated from each other until they are all examined.

(D) Hold a hearing, on the record, to determine if the person sought to be excluded is, in fact, a person excludable under this section.

(3) Either party may challenge the exclusion of any person under paragraph (2).

(4) Paragraph (2) does not apply to the investigating officer or the investigator for the defendant, nor does it apply to officers having custody of persons brought before the court.

(d) If a search or seizure motion is granted pursuant to the proceedings authorized by this section, the property or evidence shall not be admissible against the movant at any trial or other hearing unless further proceedings authorized by this section, Section 871.5, 1238, or 1466 are utilized by the people.

(e) If a search or seizure motion is granted at a trial, the property shall be returned upon order of the court unless it is otherwise subject to lawful detention. If the motion is granted at a special hearing, the property shall be returned upon order of the court only if, after the conclusion of any further proceedings authorized by this section, Section 1238 or 1466, the property is not subject to lawful detention or if the time for initiating the proceedings has expired, whichever occurs last. If the motion is granted at a preliminary hearing, the property shall be returned upon order of the court after 10 days unless the property is otherwise subject to lawful detention or unless, within that time, further proceedings authorized by this section, Section 871.5 or 1238 are utilized; if they are utilized, the property shall be returned only if, after the conclusion of the proceedings, the property is no longer subject to lawful detention.

(f)

(1) If the property or evidence relates to a felony offense initiated by a complaint, the motion shall be made only upon filing of an information, except that the defendant may make the motion at the preliminary hearing, but the motion shall be restricted to evidence sought to be introduced by the people at the preliminary hearing.

(2) The motion may be made at the preliminary examination only if, at least five court days before the date set for the preliminary examination, the defendant has filed and personally served on the people a written motion accompanied by a memorandum of points and authorities as required by paragraph (2) of subdivision (a). At the preliminary examination, the magistrate may grant the defendant a continuance for the purpose of filing the motion and serving the motion upon the people, at least five court days before resumption of the examination, upon a showing that the defendant or his or her attorney of record was not aware of the evidence or was not aware of the grounds for suppression before the preliminary examination.

(3) Any written response by the people to the motion described in paragraph (2) shall be filed with the court and personally served on the defendant or his or her attorney of record at least two court days prior to the hearing at which the motion is to be made.

(g) If the property or evidence relates to a misdemeanor complaint, the motion shall be made before trial and heard prior to trial at a special hearing relating to the validity of the search or seizure. If the property or evidence relates to a misdemeanor filed together with a felony, the procedure provided for a felony in this section and Sections 1238 and 1539 shall be applicable.

(h) If, prior to the trial of a felony or misdemeanor, opportunity for this motion did not exist or the defendant was not aware of the grounds for the motion, the defendant shall have the right to make this motion during the course of trial.

(i) If the property or evidence obtained relates to a felony offense initiated by complaint and the defendant was held to answer at the preliminary hearing, or if the property or evidence relates to a felony offense initiated by indictment, the defendant shall have the right to renew or make the motion at a special hearing relating to the validity of the search or seizure which shall be heard prior to trial and at least 10 court days after notice to the people, unless the people are willing to waive a portion of this time. Any written response by the people to the motion shall be filed with the court and personally served on the defendant or his or her attorney of record at least two court days prior to the hearing, unless the defendant is willing to waive a portion of this time. If the offense was initiated by indictment or if the offense was initiated by complaint and no motion was made at the preliminary hearing, the defendant shall have the right to fully litigate the validity of a search or seizure on the basis of the evidence presented at a special hearing. If the motion was made at the preliminary hearing, unless otherwise agreed to by all parties, evidence presented at the special hearing shall be limited to the transcript of the preliminary hearing and to evidence that could not reasonably have been presented at the preliminary hearing, except that the people may recall witnesses who testified at the preliminary hearing. If the people object to the presentation of evidence at the special hearing on the grounds that the evidence could reasonably have been presented at the preliminary hearing, the defendant shall be entitled to an in camera hearing to determine that issue. The court shall base its ruling on all evidence presented at the special hearing and on the transcript of the preliminary hearing, and the findings of the magistrate shall be binding on the court as to evidence or property not affected by evidence presented at the special hearing. After the special hearing is held, any review thereafter desired by the defendant prior to trial shall be by means of an extraordinary writ of mandate or prohibition filed within 30 days after the denial of his or her motion at the special hearing.

(j) If the property or evidence relates to a felony offense initiated by complaint and the defendant's motion for the return of the property or suppression of the evidence at the preliminary hearing is granted, and if the defendant is not held to answer at the preliminary hearing, the people may file a new complaint or seek an indictment after the preliminary hearing, and the ruling at the prior hearing shall not be binding in any subsequent proceeding, except as limited by subdivision (p). In the alternative, the people may move to reinstate the complaint, or those parts of the complaint for which the defendant was not held to answer, pursuant to Section 871.5. If the property or evidence relates to a felony offense initiated by complaint and the defendant's motion for the return or suppression of the property or evidence at the preliminary hearing is granted, and if the defendant is held to answer at the preliminary hearing, the ruling at the preliminary hearing shall be binding upon the people unless, upon notice to the defendant and the court in which the preliminary hearing was held and upon the filing of an information, the people, within 15 days after the preliminary hearing, request a special hearing, in which case the validity of the search or seizure shall be relitigated de novo on the basis of the evidence presented at the special hearing, and the defendant shall be entitled, as a matter of right, to a continuance of the special hearing for a period of time up to 30 days. The people may not request relitigation of the motion at a special hearing if the defendant's motion has been granted twice. If the defendant's motion is granted at a special hearing, the people, if they have additional evidence relating to the motion and not presented at the special hearing, shall have the right to show good cause at the trial why the evidence was not presented at the special hearing and why the prior ruling at the special hearing should not be binding, or the people may seek appellate review as provided in subdivision (o), unless the court, prior to the time the review is sought, has dismissed the case pursuant to Section 1385. If the case has been dismissed pursuant to Section 1385, either on the court's own motion or the motion of the people after the special hearing, the people may file a new complaint or seek an indictment after the special hearing, and the ruling at the special hearing shall not be binding in any subsequent proceeding, except as limited by subdivision (p). If the property or evidence seized relates solely to a misdemeanor complaint, and the defendant made a motion for the return of property or the suppression of evidence in the superior court prior to trial, both the people and defendant shall have the right to appeal any decision of that court relating to that motion to the appellate division, in accordance with the California Rules of Court provisions governing appeals to the appellate division in criminal cases. If the people prosecute review by appeal or writ to decision, or any review thereof, in a felony or misdemeanor case, it shall be binding upon them.

(k) If the defendant's motion to return property or suppress evidence is granted and the case is dismissed pursuant to Section 1385, or the people appeal in a misdemeanor case pursuant to subdivision (j), the defendant shall be released pursuant to Section 1318 if he or she is in custody and not returned to custody unless the proceedings are resumed in the trial court and he or she is lawfully ordered by the court to be returned to custody. If the defendant's motion to return property or suppress evidence is granted and the people file a petition for writ of mandate or prohibition pursuant to subdivision (o) or a notice of intention to file a petition, the defendant shall be released pursuant to Section 1318, unless (1) he or she is charged with a capital offense in a case where the proof is evident and the presumption great, or (2) he or she is charged with a noncapital offense defined in Chapter 1 (commencing with Section 187) of Title 8 of Part 1, and the court orders that the defendant be discharged from actual custody upon bail.

(l) If the defendant's motion to return property or suppress evidence is granted, the trial of a criminal case shall be stayed to a specified date pending the termination in the appellate courts of this state of the proceedings provided for in this section, Section 871.5, 1238, or 1466 and, except upon stipulation of the parties, pending the time for the initiation of these proceedings. Upon the termination of these proceedings, the defendant shall be brought to trial as provided by Section 1382, and, subject to the provisions of Section 1382, whenever the people have sought and been denied appellate review pursuant to subdivision (o), the defendant shall be entitled to have the action dismissed if he or she is not brought to trial within 30 days of the date of the order that is the last denial of the petition. Nothing contained in this subdivision shall prohibit a court, at the same time as it rules upon the search and seizure motion, from dismissing a case pursuant to Section 1385 when the dismissal is upon the court's own motion and is based upon an order at the special hearing granting the defendant's motion to return property or suppress evidence. In a misdemeanor case, the defendant shall be entitled to a continuance of up to 30 days if he or she intends to file a motion to return property or suppress evidence and needs this time to prepare for the special hearing on the motion. In case of an appeal by the defendant in a misdemeanor case from the denial of the motion, he or she shall be entitled to bail as a matter of right, and, in the discretion of the trial or appellate court, may be released on his or her own recognizance pursuant to Section 1318. In the case of an appeal by the defendant in a misdemeanor case from the denial of the motion, the trial court may, in its discretion, order or deny a stay of further proceedings pending disposition of the appeal.

(m) The proceedings provided for in this section, and Sections 871.5, 995, 1238, and 1466 shall constitute the sole and exclusive remedies prior to conviction to test the unreasonableness of a search or seizure where the person making the motion for the return of property or the suppression of evidence is a defendant in a criminal case and the property or thing has been offered or will be offered as evidence against him or her. A defendant may seek further review of the validity of a search or seizure on appeal from a conviction in a criminal case notwithstanding the fact that the judgment of conviction is predicated upon a plea of guilty. Review on appeal may be obtained by the defendant provided that at some stage of the proceedings prior to conviction he or she has moved for the return of property or the suppression of the evidence.

(n) This section establishes only the procedure for suppression of evidence and return of property, and does not establish or alter any substantive ground for suppression of evidence or return of property. Nothing contained in this section shall prohibit a person from making a motion, otherwise permitted by law, to return property, brought on the ground that the property obtained is protected by the free speech and press provisions of the United States and California Constitutions. Nothing in this section shall be construed as altering (1) the law of standing to raise the issue of an unreasonable search or seizure; (2) the law relating to the status of the person conducting the search or seizure; (3) the law relating to the burden of proof regarding the search or seizure; (4) the law relating to the reasonableness of a search or seizure regardless of any warrant that may have been utilized; or (5) the procedure and law relating to a motion made pursuant to Section 871.5 or 995, or the procedures that may be initiated after the granting or denial of a motion.

(o) Within 30 days after a defendant's motion is granted at a special hearing in a felony case, the people may file a petition for writ of mandate or prohibition in the court of appeal, seeking appellate review of the ruling regarding the search or seizure motion. If the trial of a criminal case is set for a date that is less than 30 days from the granting of a defendant's motion at a special hearing in a felony case, the people, if they have not filed a petition and wish to preserve their right to file a petition, shall file in the superior court on or before the trial date or within 10 days after the special hearing, whichever occurs last, a notice of intention to file a petition and shall serve a copy of the notice upon the defendant.

(p) If a defendant's motion to return property or suppress evidence in a felony matter has been granted twice, the people may not file a new complaint or seek an indictment in order to relitigate the motion or relitigate the matter de novo at a special hearing as otherwise provided by subdivision (j), unless the people discover additional evidence relating to the motion that was not reasonably discoverable at the time of the second suppression hearing. Relitigation of the motion shall be heard by the same judge who granted the motion at the first hearing if the judge is available.

(q) The amendments to this section enacted in the 1997 portion of the 1997-98 Regular Session of the Legislature shall apply to all criminal proceedings conducted on or after January 1, 1998.

Amended by Stats 2007 ch 302 (SB 425),s 19, eff. 1/1/2008.

Amended by Stats 2002 ch 401 (AB 1590), s 1, eff. 1/1/2003.

Amended by Stats 2002 ch 784 (SB 1316), s 557, eff. 1/1/2003.

Amended by Stats 2001 ch 231 (AB 1304), s 1, eff. 1/1/2002.

Section 1539 - Special hearing

(a) If a special hearing is held in a felony case pursuant to Section 1538.5, or if the grounds on which the warrant was issued are controverted and a motion to return property is made (i) by a defendant on grounds not covered by Section 1538.5, (ii) by a defendant whose property has not been offered or will not be offered as evidence against the defendant, or (iii) by a person who is not a defendant in a criminal action at the time the hearing is held, the judge or magistrate shall proceed to take testimony in relation thereto, and the testimony of each witness shall be reduced to writing and authenticated by a shorthand reporter in the manner prescribed in Section 869.

(b) The reporter shall forthwith transcribe the reporter's shorthand notes pursuant to this section if any party to a special hearing in a felony case files a written request for its preparation with the clerk of the court in which the hearing was held. The reporter shall forthwith file in the superior court an original and as many copies thereof as there are defendants (other than a fictitious defendant) or persons aggrieved. The reporter is entitled to compensation in accordance with the provisions of Section 869. In every case in which a transcript is filed as provided in this section, the clerk of the court shall deliver the original of the transcript so filed to the district attorney immediately upon receipt thereof and shall deliver a copy of the transcript to each defendant (other than a fictitious defendant) upon demand without cost to the defendant.

(c) Upon a motion by a defendant pursuant to this chapter, the defendant is entitled to discover any previous application for a search warrant in the case which was refused by a magistrate for lack of probable cause.

Amended by Stats 2002 ch 71 (SB 1371), s 7, eff. 1/1/2003.

Section 1540 - Restoration of property

If it appears that the property taken is not the same as that described in the warrant, or that there is no probable cause for believing the existence of the grounds on which the warrant was issued, the magistrate must cause it to be restored to the person from whom it was taken.

Enacted 1872.

Section 1541 - Power to inquire into offense

The magistrate must annex the affidavit, or affidavits, the search warrant and return, and the inventory, and if he has not power to inquire into the offense in respect to which the warrant was issued, he must at once file such warrant and return and such affidavit, or affidavits, and inventory with the clerk of the court having power to so inquire.
Amended by Stats. 1957, Ch. 1881.

Section 1542 - Search of person charged with felony

When a person charged with a felony is supposed by the magistrate before whom he is brought to have on his person a dangerous weapon, or anything which may be used as evidence of the commission of the offense, the magistrate may direct him to be searched in his presence, and the weapon or other thing to be retained, subject to his order, or to the order of the Court in which the defendant may be tried.
Enacted 1872.

Section 1542.5 - Execution of warrant

Notwithstanding any other law, with regards to a search warrant issued upon the grounds specified in paragraph (14) of subdivision (a) of Section 1524, the following shall apply:

(a) The law enforcement officer executing the warrant shall take custody of any firearm or ammunition that is in the restrained person's custody or control or possession or that is owned by the restrained person, which is discovered pursuant to a consensual or other lawful search.

(b)

(1) If the location to be searched during the execution of the warrant is jointly occupied by the restrained person and one or more other persons and a law enforcement officer executing the warrant finds a firearm or ammunition in the restrained person's custody or control or possession, but that is owned by a person other than the restrained person, the firearm or ammunition shall not be seized if both of the following conditions are satisfied:

(A) The firearm or ammunition is removed from the restrained person's custody or control or possession and stored in a manner that the restrained person does not have access to or control of the firearm or ammunition.

(B) There is no evidence of unlawful possession of the firearm or ammunition by the owner of the firearm or ammunition.

(2) If the location to be searched during the execution of the warrant is jointly occupied by the restrained person and one or more other persons and a locked gun safe is located that is owned by a person other than the restrained person, the contents of the gun safe shall not be searched except in the owner's presence, and with his or her consent or with a valid search warrant for the gun safe.

(c) This section shall become operative on January 1, 2016.
Added by Stats 2014 ch 872 (AB 1014),s 2, eff. 1/1/2015.

Chapter 3.5 - DISCLOSURE OF MEDICAL RECORDS TO LAW ENFORCEMENT AGENCIES

Section 1543 - Disclosure

(a) Records of the identity, diagnosis, prognosis, or treatment of any patient maintained by a health care facility which are not privileged records required to be secured by the special master procedure in Section 1524, or records required by law to be confidential, shall only be disclosed to law enforcement agencies pursuant to this section:

(1) In accordance with the prior written consent of the patient; or

(2) If authorized by an appropriate order of a court of competent jurisdiction in the county where the records are located, granted after application showing good cause therefor. In assessing good cause, the court:

(A) Shall weigh the public interest and the need for disclosure against the injury to the patient, to the physician-patient relationship, and to the treatment services;

(B) Shall determine that there is a reasonable likelihood that the records in question will disclose material information or evidence of substantial value in connection with the investigation or prosecution; or

(3) By a search warrant obtained pursuant to Section 1524.

(b) The prohibitions of this section continue to apply to records concerning any individual who has been a patient, irrespective of whether or when he or she ceases to be a patient.

(c) Except where an extraordinary order under Section 1544 is granted or a search warrant is obtained pursuant to Section 1524, any health care facility whose records are sought under this chapter shall be notified of the application and afforded an opportunity to appear and be heard thereon.

(d) Both disclosure and dissemination of any information from the records shall be limited under the terms of the order to assure that no information will be unnecessarily disclosed and that dissemination will be no wider than necessary. This chapter shall not apply to investigations of fraud in the provision or receipt of Medi-Cal benefits, investigations of insurance fraud performed by the Department of Insurance or the California Highway Patrol, investigations of workers' compensation insurance fraud performed by the Department of Corrections and conducted by peace officers specified in paragraph (2) of subdivision (d) of Section 830.2, and investigations and research regarding occupational health and safety performed by or under agreement with the Department of Industrial Relations. Access to medical records in these investigations shall be governed by all laws in effect at the time access is sought.

(e) Nothing in this chapter shall prohibit disclosure by a medical facility or medical provider of information contained in medical records where disclosure to specific agencies is mandated by statutes or regulations.

(f) This chapter shall not be construed to authorize disclosure of privileged records to law enforcement agencies by the procedure set forth in this chapter, where the privileged records are required to be secured by the special master procedure set forth in subdivision (c) of Section 1524 or required by law to be confidential.
Amended by Stats 2005 ch 490 (SB 1344),s 2, eff. 1/1/2005.

Section 1544 - Extraordinary order delaying notice of application to health care facility

A law enforcement agency applying for disclosure of patient records under Section 1543 may petition the court for an extraordinary order delaying the notice of the application to the health care facility required by subdivision (f) of Section 1543 for a period of 30 days, upon a showing of good cause to believe that notice would seriously impede the investigation.

Added by Stats. 1980, Ch. 1080, Sec. 1.

Section 1545 - Definitions

For the purposes of this chapter:

(a) "Health care facility" means any clinic, health dispensary, or health facility, licensed pursuant to Division 2 (commencing with Section 1200) of the Health and Safety Code, or any mental hospital, drug abuse clinic, or detoxification center.

(b) "Law enforcement agency" means the Attorney General of the State of California, every district attorney, and every agency of the State of California expressly authorized by statute to investigate or prosecute law violators.

Added by Stats. 1980, Ch. 1080, Sec. 1.

Chapter 3.6 - ELECTRONIC COMMUNICATIONS PRIVACY ACT

Section 1546 - Definitions

For purposes of this chapter, the following definitions apply:

(a) An "adverse result" means any of the following:

    (1) Danger to the life or physical safety of an individual.

    (2) Flight from prosecution.

    (3) Destruction of or tampering with evidence.

    (4) Intimidation of potential witnesses.

    (5) Serious jeopardy to an investigation or undue delay of a trial.

(b) "Authorized possessor" means the possessor of an electronic device when that person is the owner of the device or has been authorized to possess the device by the owner of the device.

(c) "Electronic communication" means the transfer of signs, signals, writings, images, sounds, data, or intelligence of any nature in whole or in part by a wire, radio, electromagnetic, photoelectric, or photo-optical system.

(d) "Electronic communication information" means any information about an electronic communication or the use of an electronic communication service, including, but not limited to, the contents, sender, recipients, format, or location of the sender or recipients at any point during the communication, the time or date the communication was created, sent, or received, or any information pertaining to any individual or device participating in the communication, including, but not limited to, an IP address. "Electronic communication information" does not include subscriber information as defined in this chapter.

(e) "Electronic communication service" means a service that provides to its subscribers or users the ability to send or receive electronic communications, including any service that acts as an intermediary in the transmission of electronic communications, or stores electronic communication information.

(f) "Electronic device" means a device that stores, generates, or transmits information in electronic form. An electronic device does not include the magnetic strip on a driver's license or an identification card issued by this state or a driver's license or equivalent identification card issued by another state.

(g) "Electronic device information" means any information stored on or generated through the operation of an electronic device, including the current and prior locations of the device.

(h) "Electronic information" means electronic communication information or electronic device information.

(i) "Government entity" means a department or agency of the state or a political subdivision thereof, or an individual acting for or on behalf of the state or a political subdivision thereof.

(j) "Service provider" means a person or entity offering an electronic communication service.

(k) "Specific consent" means consent provided directly to the government entity seeking information, including, but not limited to, when the government entity is the addressee or intended recipient or a member of the intended audience of an electronic communication. Specific consent does not require that the originator of the communication have actual knowledge that an addressee, intended recipient, or member of the specific audience is a government entity.

(l) "Subscriber information" means the name, street address, telephone number, email address, or similar contact information provided by the subscriber to the service provider to establish or maintain an account or communication channel, a subscriber or account number or identifier, the length of service, and the types of services used by a user of or subscriber to a service provider.

Amended by Stats 2016 ch 541 (SB 1121),s 2, eff. 1/1/2017.

Amended by Stats 2016 ch 86 (SB 1171),s 233, eff. 1/1/2017.

Added by Stats 2015 ch 651 (SB 178),s 1, eff. 1/1/2016.

Section 1546.1 - Government access to electronic information

(a) Except as provided in this section, a government entity shall not do any of the following:

    (1) Compel the production of or access to electronic communication information from a service provider.

    (2) Compel the production of or access to electronic device information from any person or entity other than the authorized possessor of the device.

    (3) Access electronic device information by means of physical interaction or electronic communication with the electronic device. This section does not prohibit the intended recipient of an electronic communication from voluntarily disclosing electronic communication information concerning that communication to a government entity.

(b) A government entity may compel the production of or access to electronic communication information from a service provider, or compel the production of or access to electronic device information from any person or entity other than the authorized possessor of the device only under the following circumstances:

    (1) Pursuant to a warrant issued pursuant to Chapter 3 (commencing with Section 1523) and subject to subdivision (d).

    (2) Pursuant to a wiretap order issued pursuant to Chapter 1.4 (commencing with Section 629.50) of Title 15 of Part 1.

    (3) Pursuant to an order for electronic reader records issued pursuant to Section 1798.90 of the Civil Code.

    (4) Pursuant to a subpoena issued pursuant to existing state law, provided that the information is not sought for the purpose of investigating or prosecuting a criminal offense, and compelling the production of or access to the information via the subpoena is not

otherwise prohibited by state or federal law. Nothing in this paragraph shall be construed to expand any authority under state law to compel the production of or access to electronic information.

(5) Pursuant to an order for a pen register or trap and trace device, or both, issued pursuant to Chapter 1.5 (commencing with Section 630) of Title 15 of Part 1.

(c) A government entity may access electronic device information by means of physical interaction or electronic communication with the device only as follows:

(1) Pursuant to a warrant issued pursuant to Chapter 3 (commencing with Section 1523) and subject to subdivision (d).

(2) Pursuant to a wiretap order issued pursuant to Chapter 1.4 (commencing with Section 629.50) of Title 15 of Part 1.

(3) Pursuant to a tracking device search warrant issued pursuant to paragraph (12) of subdivision (a) of Section 1524 and subdivision (b) of Section 1534.

(4) With the specific consent of the authorized possessor of the device.

(5) With the specific consent of the owner of the device, only when the device has been reported as lost or stolen.

(6) If the government entity, in good faith, believes that an emergency involving danger of death or serious physical injury to any person requires access to the electronic device information.

(7) If the government entity, in good faith, believes the device to be lost, stolen, or abandoned, provided that the government entity shall only access electronic device information in order to attempt to identify, verify, or contact the owner or authorized possessor of the device.

(8) Except where prohibited by state or federal law, if the device is seized from an inmate's possession or found in an area of a correctional facility or a secure area of a local detention facility where inmates have access, the device is not in the possession of an individual, and the device is not known or believed to be the possession of an authorized visitor. This paragraph shall not be construed to supersede or override Section 4576.

(9) Except where prohibited by state or federal law, if the device is seized from an authorized possessor of the device who is serving a term of parole under the supervision of the Department of Corrections and Rehabilitation or a term of postrelease community supervision under the supervision of county probation.

(10) Except where prohibited by state or federal law, if the device is seized from an authorized possessor of the device who is subject to an electronic device search as a clear and unambiguous condition of probation, mandatory supervision, or pretrial release.

(11) If the government entity accesses information concerning the location or the telephone number of the electronic device in order to respond to an emergency 911 call from that device.

(12) Pursuant to an order for a pen register or trap and trace device, or both, issued pursuant to Chapter 1.5 (commencing with Section 630) of Title 15 of Part 1.

(d) Any warrant for electronic information shall comply with the following:

(1) The warrant shall describe with particularity the information to be seized by specifying, as appropriate and reasonable, the time periods covered, the target individuals or accounts, the applications or services covered, and the types of information sought, provided, however, that in the case of a warrant described in paragraph (1) of subdivision (c), the court may determine that it is not appropriate to specify time periods because of the specific circumstances of the investigation, including, but not limited to, the nature of the device to be searched.

(2) The warrant shall require that any information obtained through the execution of the warrant that is unrelated to the objective of the warrant shall be sealed and shall not be subject to further review, use, or disclosure except pursuant to a court order or to comply with discovery as required by Sections 1054.1 and 1054.7. A court shall issue such an order upon a finding that there is probable cause to believe that the information is relevant to an active investigation, or review, use, or disclosure is required by state or federal law.

(3) The warrant shall comply with all other provisions of California and federal law, including any provisions prohibiting, limiting, or imposing additional requirements on the use of search warrants. If directed to a service provider, the warrant shall be accompanied by an order requiring the service provider to verify the authenticity of electronic information that it produces by providing an affidavit that complies with the requirements set forth in Section 1561 of the Evidence Code. Admission of that information into evidence shall be subject to Section 1562 of the Evidence Code.

(e) When issuing any warrant or order for electronic information, or upon the petition from the target or recipient of the warrant or order, a court may, at its discretion, do either or both of the following:

(1) Appoint a special master, as described in subdivision (d) of Section 1524, charged with ensuring that only information necessary to achieve the objective of the warrant or order is produced or accessed.

(2) Require that any information obtained through the execution of the warrant or order that is unrelated to the objective of the warrant be destroyed as soon as feasible after the termination of the current investigation and any related investigations or proceedings.

(f) A service provider may voluntarily disclose electronic communication information or subscriber information when that disclosure is not otherwise prohibited by state or federal law.

(g) If a government entity receives electronic communication information voluntarily provided pursuant to subdivision (f), it shall destroy that information within 90 days unless one or more of the following circumstances apply:

(1) The government entity has or obtains the specific consent of the sender or recipient of the electronic communications about which information was disclosed.

(2) The government entity obtains a court order authorizing the retention of the information. A court shall issue a retention order upon a finding that the conditions justifying the initial voluntary disclosure persist, in which case the court shall authorize the retention of the information only for so long as those conditions persist, or there is probable cause to believe that the information constitutes evidence that a crime has been committed.

(3) The government entity reasonably believes that the information relates to child pornography and the information is retained as part of a multiagency database used in the investigation of child pornography and related crimes.

(4) The service provider or subscriber is, or discloses the information to, a federal, state, or local prison, jail, or juvenile detention facility, and all participants to the electronic communication were informed, prior to the communication, that the service provider may disclose the information to the government entity.

(h) If a government entity obtains electronic information pursuant to an emergency involving danger of death or serious physical injury to a person, that requires access to the electronic information without delay, the government entity shall, within three court days after obtaining the electronic information, file with the appropriate court an application for a warrant or order authorizing obtaining the electronic information or a motion seeking approval of the emergency disclosures that shall set forth the facts giving rise to the emergency, and if applicable, a request supported by a sworn affidavit for an order delaying notification under paragraph (1) of subdivision (b) of Section 1546.2. The court shall promptly rule on the application or motion and shall order the immediate destruction of all information obtained, and immediate notification pursuant to subdivision (a) of Section 1546.2 if that notice has not already been given, upon a finding that the facts did not give rise to an emergency or upon rejecting the warrant or order application on any other ground. This subdivision does not apply if the government entity obtains information concerning the location or the telephone number of the electronic device in order to respond to an emergency 911 call from that device.

(i) This section does not limit the authority of a government entity to use an administrative, grand jury, trial, or civil discovery subpoena to do any of the following:

(1) Require an originator, addressee, or intended recipient of an electronic communication to disclose any electronic communication information associated with that communication.

(2) Require an entity that provides electronic communications services to its officers, directors, employees, or agents for the purpose of carrying out their duties, to disclose electronic communication information associated with an electronic communication to or from an officer, director, employee, or agent of the entity.

(3) Require a service provider to provide subscriber information.

(j) This section does not limit the authority of the Public Utilities Commission or the State Energy Resources Conservation and Development Commission to obtain energy or water supply and consumption information pursuant to the powers granted to them under the Public Utilities Code or the Public Resources Code and other applicable state laws.

(k) This chapter shall not be construed to alter the authority of a government entity that owns an electronic device to compel an employee who is authorized to possess the device to return the device to the government entity's possession.

Amended by Stats 2016 ch 541 (SB 1121),s 3.5, eff. 1/1/2017.
Amended by Stats 2016 ch 511 (AB 1924),s 4, eff. 9/23/2016.
Amended by Stats 2016 ch 341 (SB 840),s 4, eff. 9/13/2016.
Amended by Stats 2016 ch 86 (SB 1171),s 234, eff. 1/1/2017.
Added by Stats 2015 ch 651 (SB 178),s 1, eff. 1/1/2016.

Section 1546.2 - Notice

(a)

(1) Except as otherwise provided in this section, any government entity that executes a warrant, or obtains electronic information in an emergency pursuant to Section 1546.1, shall serve upon, or deliver to by registered or first-class mail, electronic mail, or other means reasonably calculated to be effective, the identified targets of the warrant or emergency access, a notice that informs the recipient that information about the recipient has been compelled or obtained, and states with reasonable specificity the nature of the government investigation under which the information is sought. The notice shall include a copy of the warrant or a written statement setting forth facts giving rise to the emergency. The notice shall be provided contemporaneously with the execution of a warrant, or, in the case of an emergency, within three court days after obtaining the electronic information.

(2) Notwithstanding paragraph (1), notice is not required if the government entity accesses information concerning the location or the telephone number of an electronic device in order to respond to an emergency 911 call from that device.

(b)

(1) When a warrant is sought or electronic information is obtained in an emergency under Section 1546.1, the government entity may submit a request supported by a sworn affidavit for an order delaying notification and prohibiting any party providing information from notifying any other party that information has been sought. The court shall issue the order if the court determines that there is reason to believe that notification may have an adverse result, but only for the period of time that the court finds there is reason to believe that the notification may have that adverse result, and not to exceed 90 days.

(2) The court may grant extensions of the delay of up to 90 days each on the same grounds as provided in paragraph (1).

(3) Upon expiration of the period of delay of the notification, the government entity shall serve upon, or deliver to by registered or first-class mail, electronic mail, or other means reasonably calculated to be effective as specified by the court issuing the order authorizing delayed notification, the identified targets of the warrant or emergency access, a document that includes the information described in subdivision (a), a copy of all electronic information obtained or a summary of that information, including, at a minimum, the number and types of records disclosed, the date and time when the earliest and latest records were created, and a statement of the grounds for the court's determination to grant a delay in notifying the individual.

(c) If there is no identified target of a warrant or emergency access at the time of its issuance, the government entity shall submit to the Department of Justice within three days of the execution of the warrant or issuance of the request all of the information required in subdivision (a). If an order delaying notice is obtained pursuant to subdivision (b), the government entity shall submit to the department upon the expiration of the period of delay of the notification all of the information required in paragraph (3) of subdivision (b). The department shall publish all those reports on its Internet Web site within 90 days of receipt. The department may redact names or other personal identifying information from the reports.

(d) Except as otherwise provided in this section, nothing in this chapter shall prohibit or limit a service provider or any other party from disclosing information about any request or demand for electronic information.

Amended by Stats 2017 ch 269 (SB 811),s 10, eff. 1/1/2018.
Amended by Stats 2016 ch 541 (SB 1121),s 4, eff. 1/1/2017.

Amended by Stats 2016 ch 86 (SB 1171),s 235, eff. 1/1/2017.
Added by Stats 2015 ch 651 (SB 178),s 1, eff. 1/1/2016.

Section 1546.4 - Motion to suppress

(a) Any person in a trial, hearing, or proceeding may move to suppress any electronic information obtained or retained in violation of the Fourth Amendment to the United States Constitution or of this chapter. The motion shall be made, determined, and be subject to review in accordance with the procedures set forth in subdivisions (b) to (q), inclusive, of Section 1538.5.

(b) The Attorney General may commence a civil action to compel any government entity to comply with the provisions of this chapter.

(c) An individual whose information is targeted by a warrant, order, or other legal process that is inconsistent with this chapter, or the California Constitution or the United States Constitution, or a service provider or any other recipient of the warrant, order, or other legal process may petition the issuing court to void or modify the warrant, order, or process, or to order the destruction of any information obtained in violation of this chapter, or the California Constitution, or the United States Constitution.

(d) A California or foreign corporation, and its officers, employees, and agents, are not subject to any cause of action for providing records, information, facilities, or assistance in accordance with the terms of a warrant, court order, statutory authorization, emergency certification, or wiretap order issued pursuant to this chapter.

Added by Stats 2015 ch 651 (SB 178),s 1, eff. 1/1/2016.

Section 1546.5 - Participation in discovery prohibited for another state or a political subdivision for an investigation or enforcement of a prohibited violation as defined in Section 629.51

(a)A California corporation or a corporation whose principal executive offices are located in California that provides electronic communications services shall not, in California, provide records, information, facilities, or assistance in accordance with the terms of a warrant, court order, subpoena, wiretap order, pen register trap and trace order, or other legal process issued by, or pursuant to, the procedures of another state or a political subdivision thereof that relates to an investigation into or enforcement of a prohibited violation, as defined in Section 629.51.

(b)The Attorney General may commence a civil action to compel any California corporation or a corporation whose principal executive offices are located in California that provides electronic communications services to comply with the provisions of this section.

(c)A California corporation or a corporation whose principal executive offices are located in California, and its officers, employees, and agents, are not subject to any cause of action for providing records, information, facilities, or assistance in accordance with the terms of a warrant, court order, subpoena, wiretap order, pen register trap and trace order, or other legal process issued by, or pursuant to, the procedures of another state or a political subdivision thereof, except where the corporation knew or should have known that the warrant, court order, subpoena, wiretap order, pen register trap and trace order, or other legal process relates to an investigation into or enforcement of a prohibited violation, as defined in Section 629.51.

Added by Stats 2022 ch 627 (AB 1242),s 9, eff. 9/27/2022.

Chapter 4 - PROCEEDINGS AGAINST FUGITIVES FROM JUSTICE

Section 1547 - Reward for information leading to arrest and conviction

(a) The Governor may offer a reward of not more than fifty thousand dollars ($50,000), payable out of the General Fund, for information leading to the arrest and conviction of any of the following:

(1) Any convict who has escaped from a state prison, prison camp, prison farm, or the custody of any prison officer or employee or as provided in Section 3059 or 4530.

(2) Any person who has committed, or is charged with the commission of, an offense punishable by death.

(3)

(A) Any person engaged in the robbery or hijacking of, or any attempt to rob or hijack, any person upon or in charge of, in whole or in part, any public conveyance engaged at the time in carrying passengers within this state.

(B) As used in this paragraph, "hijacking" means an unauthorized person causing, or attempting to cause, by violence or threat of violence, a public conveyance to go to an unauthorized destination.

(4) Any person who attempts to murder either in the first or second degree, assaults with a deadly weapon, or inflicts serious bodily harm upon a peace officer or firefighter who is acting in the line of duty.

(5) Any person who has committed a crime involving the burning or bombing of public or private property, including any public hospital housed in a privately owned facility.

(6) Any person who has committed a crime involving the burning or bombing of any private hospital. A reward may be offered by the Governor in conjunction with that crime only if a reward in conjunction with the same crime is offered by the hospital, or any other public or private donor on its behalf. The amount of the reward offered by the Governor shall not exceed the aggregate amount offered privately, or fifty thousand dollars ($50,000), whichever is less. Nothing in this paragraph shall preclude a private hospital, or any public or private donor on its behalf, from offering a reward in an amount exceeding fifty thousand dollars ($50,000). If a person providing information for a reward under this paragraph so requests, his or her name and address shall remain confidential. This confidentiality, however, shall not preclude or obstruct the investigations of law enforcement authorities.

(7) Any person who commits a violation of Section 11413.

(8) Any person who commits a violation of Section 207.

(9) Any person who has committed a crime involving the burning or bombing of any bookstore or public or private library not subject to Section 11413. A reward may be offered by the Governor in conjunction with that crime only if a reward in conjunction with the same crime is offered by the bookstore or library, or any other public or private donor on its behalf. The amount of the reward offered by the Governor shall not exceed the aggregate amount offered privately, or fifty thousand dollars ($50,000), whichever is less. Nothing in this paragraph shall preclude a bookstore or public or private library, or any public or private donor on its behalf, from offering a reward in an amount exceeding fifty thousand dollars ($50,000). If a person providing information for a reward under this paragraph so requests, his or her name and address shall remain confidential. This confidentiality, however, shall not preclude or obstruct the investigations of law enforcement authorities.

(10) Any person who commits a violation of Section 454 or 463.

(11) Any person who willfully and maliciously sets fire to, or who attempts to willfully and maliciously set fire to, any property that is included within a hazardous fire area designated by the State Board of Forestry and Fire Protection pursuant to Section 4252 of the Public Resources Code or by the Director of Forestry and Fire Protection pursuant to Section 4253 of the Public Resources Code, if the fire, or attempt to set a fire, results in death or great bodily injury to anyone, including fire protection personnel, or if the fire causes substantial structural damage.

(12) Any person who has committed, or is charged with the commission of, a felony that is punishable under Section 422.75 and that resulted in serious bodily injury or in property damage of more than ten thousand dollars ($10,000).

(13) Any person who commits an act that violates Section 11411, if the Governor determines that the act is one in a series of similar or related acts committed in violation of that section by the same person or group.

(b) The Governor may offer a reward of not more than one hundred thousand dollars ($100,000) for information leading to the arrest and conviction of any person who kills a peace officer or firefighter who is acting in the line of duty.

(c) The Governor may offer a reward of not more than one hundred thousand dollars ($100,000), payable out of the General Fund, for information leading to the arrest and conviction of any person who commits arson upon a place of worship.

(d) The reward shall be paid to the person giving the information, promptly upon the conviction of the person so arrested, after a recommendation from the United States Attorney, or the California Attorney General, or the district attorney and the chief law enforcement officer, or his or her designate, in the jurisdiction where the crime occurred. Rewards shall only be paid to the person if the information is given voluntarily, at the person's own initiative. Rewards shall not be paid as part of any plea bargain.

(e) The reward may also be paid to the person giving the information if both of the following are met:

(1) The arrest or conviction of the person for an offense described in subdivision (a), (b), or (c) is rendered impossible by an intervening event, including, but not limited to, the death of the person during a pursuit by law enforcement, or while in custody.

(2) The appropriate law enforcement officials, after reviewing the evidence related to the crime or crimes, determine that the person is the individual responsible for the crime or crimes for which the reward was offered, and that the information would have reasonably led to the arrest and conviction of that person.

(f) If more than one claimant is eligible for any reward issued pursuant to this section, the Governor may apportion the reward money in a manner the Governor deems appropriate.

Amended by Stats 2002 ch 529 (AB 2339), s 1, eff. 1/1/2003.

Section 1548 - Definitions

As used in this chapter:

(a) "Governor" means any person performing the functions of Governor by authority of the law of this State.

(b) "Executive authority" means the Governor or any person performing the functions of Governor in a State other than this State.

(c) "State," referring to a State other than the State of California, means any other State or Territory, organized or unorganized, of the United States of America.

(d) "Laws of the United States" means:

(1) those laws of the United States passed by Congress pursuant to authority given to Congress by the Constitution of the United States where the laws of the United States are controlling, and

(2) those laws of the United States not controlling the several States of the United States but which are not in conflict with the provisions of this chapter.

Repealed and added by Stats. 1937, Ch. 554.

Section 1548.1 - Duty of governor

Subject to the provisions of this chapter, the Constitution of the United States, and the laws of the United States, it is the duty of the Governor of this State to have arrested and delivered up to the executive authority of any other State any person charged in that State with treason, felony, or other crime, who has fled from justice and is found in this State.

Added by Stats. 1937, Ch. 554.

Section 1548.2 - Recognition of demand for extradition

No demand for the extradition of a person charged with crime in another State shall be recognized by the Governor unless it is in writing alleging that the accused was present in the demanding State at the time of the commission of the alleged crime, and that thereafter he fled from that State. Such demand shall be accompanied by a copy of an indictment found or by information or by a copy of an affidavit made before a magistrate in the demanding State together with a copy of any warrant which was issued thereon; or such demand shall be accompanied by a copy of a judgment of conviction or of a sentence imposed in execution thereof, together with a statement by the executive authority of the demanding State that the person claimed has escaped from confinement or has violated the terms of his bail, probation or parole. The indictment, information, or affidavit made before the magistrate must substantially charge the person demanded with having committed a crime under the law of that State; and the copy of indictment, information, affidavit, judgment of conviction or sentence must be certified as authentic by the executive authority making the demand.

Added by Stats. 1937, Ch. 554.

Section 1548.3 - Investigation when demand made

When a demand is made upon the Governor of this State by the executive authority of another State for the surrender of a person so charged with crime, the Governor may call upon the Attorney General or any district attorney in this State to investigate or assist in investigating the demand, and to report to him the situation and circumstances of the person so demanded, and whether he ought to be surrendered according to the provision of this chapter.

Added by Stats. 1937, Ch. 554.

Section 1549 - Agreement for extradition of person before conclusion of proceedings or term of sentence in other state

When it is desired to have returned to this state a person charged in this state with a crime, and the person is imprisoned or is held under criminal proceedings then pending against him or her in another state, the Governor of this state may agree with the executive authority of the other state for the extradition of the person before the conclusion of the proceedings or his or her term of sentence in the other state, upon the condition that the person be returned to the other state at the expense of this state as soon as the prosecution in this state is terminated.

The Governor of this state may also surrender on demand of the executive authority of any other state any person in this state who is charged in the manner provided in Section 1548.2 with having violated the laws of the demanding state even though such person left the demanding state involuntarily.

Amended by Stats. 1987, Ch. 828, Sec. 101.

Section 1549.1 - Surrender of person

The Governor of this state may also surrender, on demand of the executive authority of any other state, any person in this state charged in the other state in the manner provided in Section 1548.2 with committing an act in this state, or in a third state, intentionally resulting in a crime in the state whose executive authority is making the demand. The provisions of this chapter, not otherwise inconsistent, shall apply to those cases, even though the accused was not in the demanding state at the time of the commission of the crime, and has not fled therefrom. Neither the demand, the oath, nor any proceedings under this chapter pursuant to this section need state or show that the accused has fled from justice from, or at the time of the commission of the crime was in, the demanding or other state.

Amended by Stats. 1987, Ch. 828, Sec. 102.

Section 1549.15 - Definitions

For purposes of this section, the following terms have the following meanings:

(a) "Gender-affirming health care" and "gender-affirming mental health care" have the same meaning as in paragraph (3) of subdivision (b) of Section 16010.2 of the Welfare and Institutions Code.

(b)

(1) "Legally protected health care activity" means any of the following:

(A) The exercise and enjoyment, or attempted exercise and enjoyment, by a person of rights to reproductive health care services, gender-affirming health care services, or gender-affirming mental health care services secured by the Constitution or laws of California or the provision by a health care service plan contract or a policy, or a certificate of health insurance, that provides for such services.

(B) An act or omission undertaken to aid or encourage, or attempt to aid or encourage, a person in the exercise and enjoyment or attempted exercise and enjoyment of rights to reproductive health care services, gender-affirming health care services, or gender-affirming mental health care services secured by the Constitution or laws of California.

(C) The provision of reproductive health care services, gender-affirming health care services, or gender-affirming mental health care services by a person duly licensed under the laws of California or the coverage of, and reimbursement for, those services or care by a health care service plan or a health insurer, if the service or care is lawful under the laws of California, regardless of the patient's location.

(2) "Legally protected health care activity" does not include any activity that would be deemed unprofessional conduct or that would violate antidiscrimination laws of California.

(c) "Reproductive health care services" means and includes all services, care, or products of a medical, surgical, psychiatric, therapeutic, diagnostic, mental health, behavioral health, preventative, rehabilitative, supportive, consultative, referral, prescribing, or dispensing nature relating to the human reproductive system provided in accordance with the constitution and laws of this state, whether provided in person or by means of telehealth services which includes, but is not limited to, all services, care, and products relating to pregnancy, the termination of a pregnancy, assisted reproduction, or contraception.

Added by Stats 2023 ch 260 (SB 345),s 18, eff. 1/1/2024.

Section 1549.2 - Warrant for arrest

If a demand conforms to the provisions of this chapter, the Governor or agent authorized in writing by the Governor whose authorization has been filed with the Secretary of State shall sign a warrant of arrest, which shall be sealed with the State Seal, and shall be directed to any peace officer or other person whom he may entrust with the execution thereof. The warrant must substantially recite the facts necessary to the validity of its issuance. The provisions of Section 850 shall be applicable to such warrant, except that it shall not be necessary to include a warrant number, address, or description of the subject, provided that a complaint under Section 1551 is then pending against the subject.

Amended by Stats. 1983, Ch. 793, Sec. 1.2.

Section 1549.3 - Authority of peace officer

Such warrant shall authorize the peace officer or other person to whom it is directed:

(a) To arrest the accused at any time and any place where he may be found within the State;

(b) To command the aid of all peace officers or other persons in the execution of the warrant; and

(c) To deliver the accused, subject to the provisions of this chapter, to the duly authorized agent of the demanding State.

Added by Stats. 1937, Ch. 554.

Section 1550 - [Repealed]

Repealed by Stats 2019 ch 204 (SB 192),s 2, eff. 1/1/2020.

Section 1550.1 - Magistrate

No person arrested upon such warrant shall be delivered over to the agent of the executive authority demanding him unless he is first taken forthwith before a magistrate, who shall inform him of the demand made for his surrender, and of the crime with which he is charged, and that he has the right to demand and procure counsel. If the accused or his counsel desires to test the legality of the arrest, the magistrate shall remand the accused to custody, and fix a reasonable time to be allowed him within which to apply for a writ of habeas corpus. If the writ is denied, and probable cause appears for an application for a writ of habeas corpus to another court, or justice or judge thereof, the order denying the writ shall remand the accused to custody, and fix a reasonable time within which the accused may again apply for a writ of habeas corpus. When an application is made for a writ of habeas corpus as contemplated by this section, a copy of the application shall be served as provided in Section 1475, upon the district attorney of the county in which the

accused is in custody, and upon the agent of the demanding state. A warrant issued in accordance with the provisions of Section 1549.2 shall be presumed to be valid, and unless a court finds that the person in custody is not the same person named in the warrant, or that the person is not a fugitive from justice, or otherwise subject to extradition under Section 1549.1, or that there is no criminal charge or criminal proceeding pending against the person in the demanding state, or that the documents are not on their face in order, the person named in the warrant shall be held in custody at all times, and shall not be eligible for release on bail.
Amended by Stats. 1983, Ch. 793, Sec. 2.

Section 1550.2 - Wilful disobedience in delivery of person in custody under governor's warrant

Any officer or other person entrusted with a Governor's warrant who delivers to the agent of the demanding State a person in his custody under such Governor's warrant, in wilful disobedience to the preceding section, is guilty of a misdemeanor and, on conviction thereof, shall be fined not more than $1,000 or be imprisoned not more than six months, or both.
Added by Stats. 1937, Ch. 554.

Section 1550.3 - Confinement of prisoner

The officer or persons executing the Governor's warrant of arrest, or the agent of the demanding State to whom the prisoner has been delivered may confine the prisoner in the jail of any county or city through which he may pass. The keeper of such jail must receive and safely keep the prisoner until the officer or person having charge of him is ready to proceed on his route. Such officer or person shall be charged with the expense of keeping the prisoner.

The officer or agent of a demanding State to whom a prisoner has been delivered following extradition proceedings in another State, or to whom a prisoner has been delivered after waiving extradition in such other State, and who is passing through this State with such a prisoner for the purpose of immediately returning such prisoner to the demanding State may confine the prisoner in the jail of any county or city through which he may pass. The keeper of such jail must receive and safely keep the prisoner until the officer or agent having charge of him is ready to proceed on his route. Such officer or agent shall be charged with the expense of keeping the prisoner. Such officer or agent shall produce and show to the keeper of such jail satisfactory written evidence of the fact that he is actually transporting such prisoner to the demanding State after a requisition by the executive authority thereof. Such prisoner shall not be entitled to demand a new requisition while in this State.
Added by Stats. 1937, Ch. 554.

Section 1551 - Warrant demanding apprehension of escaped person

(a)Whenever any person within this State is charged by a verified complaint before any magistrate of this State with the commission of any crime in any other State, or, with having been convicted of a crime in that State and having escaped from confinement, or having violated the terms of their bail, probation or parole or whenever complaint is made before any magistrate in this State setting forth on the affidavit of any credible person in another State that a crime has been committed in such other State and that the accused has been charged in such State with the commission of the crime, or that the accused has been convicted of a crime in that State and has escaped from bail, probation or parole and is believed to be in this State; then the magistrate shall issue a warrant directed to any peace officer commanding the officer to apprehend the person named therein, wherever the individual may be found in this State, and to bring them before the same or any other magistrate who is available in or convenient of access to the place where the arrest is made. A certified copy of the sworn charge or complaint and affidavit upon which the warrant is issued shall be attached to the warrant.

(b)Within 24 hours of the filing of any verified complaint pursuant to this section, the filing agency shall transmit electronically to the Attorney General a complete copy of the verified complaint, the out-of-state indictment, information, complaint, or judgment, out-of-state warrant, and the affidavit upon which the out-of-state warrant was issued.
Amended by Stats 2022 ch 627 (AB 1242),s 10, eff. 9/27/2022.
Repealed and added by Stats. 1937, Ch. 554.

Section 1551.05 - Extradition of person on outpatient status

(a) Any person on outpatient status pursuant to Title 15 (commencing with Section 1600) of Part 2 or pursuant to subdivision (d) of Section 2972 who leaves this state without complying with Section 1611, or who fails to return to this state on the date specified by the committing court, shall be subject to extradition in accordance with this section.

(b) If the return to this state is required by a person who is subject to extradition pursuant to subdivision (a), the Director of State Hospitals shall present to the Governor a written application for requisition for the return of that person. In the requisition application there shall be stated the name of the person, the type of judicial commitment the person is under, the nature of the underlying criminal act which was the basis for the judicial commitment, the circumstances of the noncompliance with Section 1611, and the state in which the person is believed to be, including the specific location of the person, if known.

(c) The application shall be verified, shall be executed in duplicate, and shall be accompanied by two certified copies of the court order of judicial commitment and of the court order authorizing outpatient status. The director may also attach any affidavits or other documents in duplicate as are deemed proper to be submitted with the application. One copy of the application, with the action of the Governor indicated by endorsement thereon, and one copy of the court orders shall be filed in the office of the Secretary of State. The other copies of all papers shall be forwarded with the Governor's requisition.

(d) Upon receipt of an application under this section, the Governor or agent authorized in writing by the Governor whose authorization has been filed with the Secretary of State, may sign a requisition for the return of the person.
Amended by Stats 2012 ch 440 (AB 1488),s 37, eff. 9/22/2012.

Section 1551.1 - Arrest without warrant

The arrest of a person may also be lawfully made by any peace officer, without a warrant, upon reasonable information that the accused stands charged in the courts of any other state with a crime punishable by death or imprisonment for a term exceeding one year, or that the person has been convicted of a crime punishable in the state of conviction by imprisonment for a term exceeding one year and thereafter escaped from confinement or violated the terms of his or her bail, probation or parole. When so arrested the accused shall be taken before a magistrate with all practicable speed and complaint shall be made against him or her under oath setting forth the ground for the arrest as in Section 1551.
Amended by Stats. 1987, Ch. 828, Sec. 104.

Section 1551.2 - Initial appearance; hearing

At the initial appearance of a person arrested under Section 1551 or 1551.1, he shall be informed of the reason for his arrest and of his right to demand and procure counsel. If the person denies that he is the same person charged with or convicted of a crime in the other state, a hearing shall be held within 10 days to determine whether there is probable cause to believe that he is the same person and whether he is charged with or convicted of a crime in the other state. At the hearing, the magistrate shall accept a certified copy of an indictment found, an information, a verified complaint, a judgment or sentence, or other judicial proceedings against that person in the state in which the crime is charged or the conviction occurred, and such copy shall constitute conclusive proof of its contents. Witnesses from the other state shall not be required to be present at the hearing.

Amended by Stats. 1983, Ch. 793, Sec. 4.

Section 1551.3 - Notice of arrest

Immediately upon the arrest of the person charged, the magistrate must give notice thereof to the district attorney. The district attorney must immediately thereafter give notice to the executive authority of the State, or to the prosecuting attorney or presiding judge of the court of the city or county within the State having jurisdiction of the offense, to the end that a demand may be made for the arrest and surrender of the person charged.

Added by Stats. 1937, Ch. 554.

Section 1552 - Commitment to county jail

If at the hearing before the magistrate, it appears that the accused is the person charged with having committed the crime alleged, the magistrate must, by a warrant reciting the accusation, commit him to the county jail for such a time, not exceeding thirty days and specified in the warrant, as will enable the arrest of the accused to be made under a warrant of the Governor on a requisition of the executive authority of the State having jurisdiction of the offense, unless the accused give bail as provided in section 1552.1, or until he shall be legally discharged.

Repealed and added by Stats. 1937, Ch. 554.

Section 1552.1 - Admission to bail by bond or undertaking

Unless the offense with which the prisoner is charged, is shown to be an offense punishable by death or life imprisonment under the laws of the state in which it was committed, or it is shown that the prisoner is alleged to have escaped or violated the terms of his parole following conviction of a crime punishable in the state of conviction by imprisonment for a term exceeding one year, the magistrate may admit the person arrested to bail by bond or undertaking, with sufficient sureties, and in such sum as he deems proper, conditioned upon the appearance of such person before him at a time specified in such bond or undertaking, and for his surrender upon the warrant of the Governor of this state. Nothing in this section or in Section 1553 shall be deemed to prevent the immediate service of a Governor's warrant issued under Section 1549.2.

Amended by Stats. 1983, Ch. 793, Sec. 5.

Section 1552.2 - Discharge or recommitment

If the accused is not arrested under warrant of the Governor by the expiration of the time specified in the warrant, bond, or undertaking, a magistrate may discharge him or may recommit him for a further period of 60 days. In the latter event a justice of the Supreme Court or court of appeal or a judge of the superior court may again take bail for his appearance and surrender, as provided in Section 1552.1 but within a period not to exceed 60 days after the date of such new bond or undertaking.

Amended by Stats. 1967, Ch. 17.

Section 1553 - Forfeiture of bond and order for immediate arrest without warrant

If the prisoner is admitted to bail, and fails to appear and surrender himself according to the conditions of his bond, the magistrate, by proper order, shall declare the bond forfeited and order his immediate arrest without warrant if he be within this State. Recovery may be had on such bond in the name of the people of the State as in the case of other bonds or undertakings given by a defendant in criminal proceedings.

Repealed and added by Stats. 1937, Ch. 554.

Section 1553.1 - Surrender on demand of executive authority of another state

(a) If a criminal prosecution has been instituted against a person charged under Section 1551 under the laws of this state and is still pending, the Governor, with the consent of the Attorney General, may surrender the person on demand of the executive authority of another state or hold him or her until he or she has been tried and discharged or convicted and served his or her sentence in this state.

(b) If a criminal prosecution has been instituted under the laws of this state against a person charged under Section 1551, the restrictions on the length of commitment contained in Sections 1552 and 1552.2 shall not be applicable during the period that the criminal prosecution is pending in this state.

Amended by Stats. 1983, Ch. 793, Sec. 6.

Section 1553.2 - Guilt or innocence of accused

The guilt or innocence of the accused as to the crime with which he is charged may not be inquired into by the Governor or in any proceeding after the demand for extradition accompanied by a charge of crime in legal form as above provided has been presented to the Governor, except as such inquiry may be involved in identifying the person held as the person charged with the crime.

Added by Stats. 1937, Ch. 554.

Section 1554 - Recall of arrest warrant; issuance of another warrant

The Governor may recall his warrant of arrest or may issue another warrant whenever he deems it proper.

Repealed and added by Stats. 1937, Ch. 554.

Section 1554.1 - Warrant commanding agent to receive person and to convey person to proper officer

Whenever the Governor of this State shall demand the return of a person charged with crime in this State or with escaping from confinement or violating the terms of his bail, probation or parole in this State, from the executive authority of any other State or of any foreign government or the chief justice or an associate justice of the Supreme Court of the District of Columbia authorized to receive such demand, he shall issue a warrant under the seal of this State to an agent, commanding him to receive the person so demanded and to convey him to the proper officer in the county in this State in which the offense was committed.

Added by Stats. 1937, Ch. 554.

Section 1554.2 - Application for return of person charged with crime

(a) When the return to this state of a person charged with crime in this state is required, the district attorney shall present to the Governor his written application for a requisition for the return of the person charged. In such application there shall be stated the name of the person so charged, the crime charged against him, the approximate time, place and circumstances of its commission, and the state in which he is believed to be, including the location of the accused therein at the time the application is made. Such application shall certify that, in the opinion of the district attorney, the ends of justice require the arrest and return of the accused to this state for trial and that the proceeding is not instituted to enforce a private claim.

(b) When the return to this state is required of a person who has been convicted of a crime in this state and who has escaped from confinement or has violated the terms of his bail, probation or parole the district attorney of the county in which the offense was committed, the Board of Prison Terms, the Director of Corrections, the California Institution for Women, the Youth Authority, or the sheriff of the county from which escape from confinement was made, shall present to the Governor a written application for a requisition for the return of such person. In such application there shall be stated the name of the person, the crime of which he was convicted, the circumstances of his escape or of the violation of the terms of his bail, probation or parole, and the state in which he is believed to be, including the location of such person therein at the time application is made.

(c) The application shall be verified, shall be executed in duplicate, and shall be accompanied by two certified copies of the indictment, the information, or the verified complaint made to the magistrate stating the offense with which the accused is charged, or the judgment of conviction or the sentence. The officer or board requesting the requisition may also attach such affidavits and other documents in duplicate as are deemed proper to be submitted with such application. One copy of the application, with the action of the Governor indicated by endorsement thereon, and one of the certified copies of the indictment, verified complaint, information, or judgment of conviction or sentence shall be filed in the office of the Secretary of State. The other copies of all papers shall be forwarded with the Governor's requisition.

(d) Upon receipt of an application under this section, the Governor or agent authorized in writing by the Governor whose authorization has been filed with the Secretary of State, may sign a requisition for the return of the person charged and any other document incidental to that requisition or to the return of the person charged.

Amended by Stats. 1983, Ch. 793, Sec. 7.

Section 1554.3 - Commitment to county jail with prescribed bail

After a person has been brought back to this state by extradition proceedings, the person shall be committed to a county jail with bail set in the amount of one hundred thousand dollars ($100,000) in addition to the amount of bail appearing on the warrant. A 48-hour noticed bail hearing, excluding weekends and holidays, is required to deviate from this prescribed bail amount. Nothing in this section is intended to preclude the application of subdivision (e) of Section 1270.1 to enhance the bail amount for the felony charge appearing on the warrant.

Added by Stats 2011 ch 67 (SB 291),s 1, eff. 1/1/2012.

Section 1555 - Service of process in civil actions arising out of same facts as criminal proceedings

A person brought into this State on, or after waiver of extradition based on a criminal charge shall not be subject to service of process in civil actions arising out of the same facts as the criminal proceedings for which he is returned, until he has been convicted in the criminal proceeding, or, if acquitted, until he has had reasonable opportunity to return to the State from which he was extradited.

Repealed and added by Stats. 1937, Ch. 554.

Section 1555.1 - Waiver of issuance and service of governor's warrant

Any person arrested in this state charged with having committed any crime in another state or alleged to have escaped from confinement, or broken the terms of his or her bail, probation or parole may waive the issuance and service of the Governor's warrant provided for in this chapter and all other procedure incidental to extradition proceedings, by subscribing in the presence of a magistrate within this state a writing which states that he or she consents to return to the demanding state; provided, however, that before such waiver shall be subscribed by such person, the magistrate shall inform him or her of his or her rights to require the issuance and service of a warrant of extradition as provided in this chapter.

If such waiver is executed, it shall forthwith be forwarded to the office of the Governor of this state, and filed therein. The magistrate shall remand the person to custody without bail, unless otherwise stipulated by the district attorney with the concurrence of the other state, and shall direct the officer having such person in custody to deliver such person forthwith to the duly authorized agent of the demanding state, and shall deliver to such agent a copy of such waiver.

Nothing in this section shall be deemed to limit the rights of the accused person to return voluntarily and without formality to the demanding state, provided that state consents, nor shall this procedure of waiver be deemed to be an exclusive procedure or to limit the powers, rights or duties of the officers of the demanding state or of this state.

Amended by Stats. 1983, Ch. 793, Sec. 8.

Section 1555.2 - Hearing if arrested person refuses to sign waiver of extradition

(a) If the arrested person refuses to sign a waiver of extradition under Section 1555.1, a hearing shall be held, upon application of the district attorney, to determine whether the person is alleged to have violated the terms of his release within the past five years on bail or own recognizance while charged with a crime punishable in the charging state by imprisonment for a term exceeding one year, or on probation or parole following conviction of a crime punishable in the state of conviction by imprisonment for a term exceeding one year, and whether, as a condition of that release, the person was required to waive extradition.

(b) At the hearing, the district attorney shall present a certified copy of the order from the other state conditionally releasing the person, including the condition that he was required to waive extradition together with a certified copy of the order from the other state directing the return of the person for violating the terms of his conditional release. The magistrate shall accept these certified copies as conclusive proof of their contents and shall presume the validity of the extradition waiver condition.

(c) If the magistrate finds that there is probable cause to believe that the arrested person is the same person named in the conditional release order and the order commanding his return, the magistrate shall forthwith issue an order remanding the person to custody without bail and directing the delivery of the person to duly accredited agents of the other state.

(d) Notwithstanding the provisions of subdivision (c), the district attorney may stipulate, with the concurrence of the other state, that the arrested person may be released on bail or own recognizance pending the arrival of duly accredited agents from the other state.

(e) If the arrested person or his counsel desires to test the legality of the order issued under subdivision (c), the magistrate shall fix a reasonable time to be allowed him within which to apply for a writ of habeas corpus. If the writ is denied and probable cause appears for an application for a writ of habeas corpus to another court, or justice or judge thereof, the order denying the writ shall fix a reasonable time within which the accused may again apply for a writ of habeas corpus. Unless otherwise stipulated pursuant to subdivision (d), the arrested person shall remain in custody without bail.

Added by Stats. 1983, Ch. 793, Sec. 10.

Section 1555.3 - No waiver by state
Nothing in this chapter shall be deemed to constitute a waiver by this state of its right, power or privilege to try any demanded person for crime committed within this state, or of its right, power or privilege to regain custody of such person by extradition proceedings or otherwise for the purpose of trial, sentence or punishment for any crime committed within this state; nor shall any proceedings had under this chapter which result in, or fail to result in, extradition be deemed a waiver by this state of any of its rights, privileges or jurisdiction in any manner whatsoever.

Added by renumbering Section 1555.2 by Stats. 1983, Ch. 793, Sec. 9.

Section 1556 - Trial for crimes
After a person has been brought back to this State by extradition proceedings, he may be tried in this State for other crimes which he may be charged with having committed in this State as well as for the crime or crimes specified in the requisition for his extradition.

Repealed and added by Stats. 1937, Ch. 554.

Section 1556.1 - Construction of provisions of chapter
The provisions of this chapter shall be so interpreted and construed as to effectuate its general purposes to make uniform the law of those states which enact legislation based upon the Uniform Criminal Extradition Act.

Added by Stats. 1937, Ch. 554.

Section 1556.2 - Short title
This chapter may be cited as the Uniform Criminal Extradition Act.

Added by Stats. 1937, Ch. 554.

Section 1557 - Payment of accounts of person employed to bring back fugitive
(a) This section shall apply when this state or a city, county, or city and county employs a person to travel to a foreign jurisdiction outside this state for the express purpose of returning a fugitive from justice to this state when the Governor of this state, in the exercise of the authority conferred by Section 2 of Article IV of the United States Constitution, or by the laws of this state, has demanded the surrender of the fugitive from the executive authority of any state of the United States, or of any foreign government.

(b) Upon the approval of the Governor, the Controller shall audit and pay out of the State Treasury as provided in subdivision (c) or (d) the accounts of the person employed to bring back the fugitive, including any money paid by that person for all of the following:

(1) Money paid to the authorities of a sister state for statutory fees in connection with the detention and surrender of the fugitive.

(2) Money paid to the authorities of the sister state for the subsistence of the fugitive while detained by the sister state without payment of which the authorities of the sister state refuse to surrender the fugitive.

(3) Where it is necessary to present witnesses or evidence in the sister state, without which the sister state would not surrender the fugitive, the cost of producing the witnesses or evidence in the sister state.

(4) Where the appearance of witnesses has been authorized in advance by the Governor, who may authorize the appearance in unusual cases where the interests of justice would be served, the cost of producing witnesses to appear in the sister state on behalf of the fugitive in opposition to his or her extradition.

(c) No amount shall be paid out of the State Treasury to a city, county, or city and county except as follows:

(1) When a warrant has been issued by any magistrate after the filing of a complaint or the finding of an indictment and its presentation to the court and filing by the clerk, and the person named therein as defendant is a fugitive from justice who has been found and arrested in any state of the United States or in any foreign government, the county auditor shall draw his or her warrant and the county treasurer shall pay to the person designated to return the fugitive, the amount of expenses estimated by the district attorney to be incurred in the return of the fugitive.

(2) If the person designated to return the fugitive is a city officer, the city officer authorized to draw warrants on the city treasury shall draw his or her warrant and the city treasurer shall pay to that person the amount of expenses estimated by the district attorney to be incurred in the return of the fugitive.

(3) The person designated to return the fugitive shall make no disbursements from any funds advanced without a receipt being obtained therefor showing the amount, the purpose for which the sum is expended, the place, the date, and to whom paid.

(4) A receipt obtained pursuant to paragraph (3) shall be filed by the person designated to return the fugitive with the county auditor or appropriate city officer or the Controller, as the case may be, together with an affidavit by the person that the expenditures represented by the receipts were necessarily made in the performance of duty, and when the advance has been made by the county or city treasurer to the person designated to return the fugitive, and has thereafter been audited by the Controller, the payment thereof shall be made by the State Treasurer to the county or city treasury that has advanced the funds.

(5) If the expenses of the person employed to bring back the fugitive are less than the amount advanced on the recommendation of the district attorney, the person employed to bring back the fugitive shall return to the county or city treasurer, as appropriate, the difference in amount between the aggregate amount of receipts so filed by him or her, and the amount advanced to the person upon the recommendation of the district attorney.

(6) When no advance has been made to the person designated to return the fugitive, the sums expended by him or her, when audited by the Controller, shall be paid by the State Treasurer to the person so designated.

(7) Any payments made out of the State Treasury pursuant to this section shall be made from appropriations for the fiscal year in which those payments are made.

(d) A city, county, or other jurisdiction shall not file, and the state shall not reimburse, a claim pursuant to this section that is presented to the Department of Corrections and Rehabilitation or to any other agency or department of the state more than six months after the close of the month in which the costs were incurred. Notwithstanding any other law, a person transporting a fugitive as authorized by the Governor pursuant to this section shall be reimbursed according to the rates in paragraphs (1) to (5), inclusive. Rates and rules for reimbursement of travel claims not specified in paragraphs (1) to (5), inclusive, shall be consistent with the rules of the Department of General Services.

(1) Reimbursement for breakfast is up to four dollars ($4).

(2) Reimbursement for lunch is up to seven dollars and twenty-five cents ($7.25).

(3) Reimbursement for dinner is up to twelve dollars ($12).

(4) Reimbursement for incidental expenses is up to three dollars and seventy-five cents ($3.75).

(5) Reimbursement for a meal for a prisoner, patient, ward, or fugitive is up to the amounts specified in paragraphs (1) to (3), inclusive.

Amended by Stats 2017 ch 17 (AB 103),s 36, eff. 6/27/2017.

Amended by Stats 2016 ch 31 (SB 836),s 246, eff. 6/27/2016.

Amended by Stats 2007 ch 175 (SB 81),s 6, eff. 8/24/2007.

Amended by Stats 2006 ch 538 (SB 1852),s 508, eff. 1/1/2007.

Section 1558 - Compensation as provided by statute

No compensation, fee, profit, or reward of any kind can be paid to or received by a public officer of this state, a corporation or firm, or other person, for a service rendered in procuring from the Governor the demand mentioned in Section 1557, or the surrender of the fugitive, or for conveying him or her to this state, or detaining him or her therein, except as provided for in that section. Every person who violates any of the provisions of this section is guilty of a misdemeanor.

Amended by Stats. 1990, Ch. 222, Sec. 1.

Chapter 5 - MISCELLANEOUS PROVISIONS RESPECTING SPECIAL PROCEEDINGS OF A CRIMINAL NATURE

Section 1562 - Complainant; defendant

The party prosecuting a special proceeding of a criminal nature is designated in this Code as the complainant, and the adverse party as the defendant.

Enacted 1872.

Section 1563 - Entitling affidavits

The provisions of Section 1401, in respect to entitling affidavits, are applicable to such proceedings.

Enacted 1872.

Section 1564 - Subpoenas

The Courts and magistrates before whom such proceedings are prosecuted may issue subpoenas for witnesses, and punish their disobedience in the same manner as in a criminal action.

Enacted 1872.

Title 13 - PROCEEDINGS FOR BRINGING PERSONS IMPRISONED IN THE STATE PRISON, OR THE JAIL OF ANOTHER COUNTY, BEFORE A COURT

Section 1567 - Order for production of imprisoned person

When it is necessary to have a person imprisoned in the state prison brought before any court, or a person imprisoned in a county jail brought before a court sitting in another county, an order for that purpose may be made by the court and executed by the sheriff of the county where it is made. The order shall be signed by the judge or magistrate and sealed with the seal of the court, if any. The order shall be to the following effect:

County of ____ (as the case may be).

The people of the State of California to the warden of ____ (or sheriff of ____, as the case may be):

An order having been made this day by me, that A. B. be produced in this court as witness in the case of ____, you are commanded to deliver him or her into the custody of ____.

Dated this ____ day of ____, 19__.

Amended by Stats. 1981, Ch. 714, Sec. 334.

Title 15 - OUTPATIENT STATUS FOR MENTALLY DISORDERED AND DEVELOPMENTALLY DISABLED OFFENDERS

Section 1600 - Placement on outpatient status

Any person committed to a state hospital or other treatment facility under the provisions of Section 1026, or Chapter 6 (commencing with Section 1367) of Title 10 of this code, or Section 6316 or 6321 of the Welfare and Institutions Code may be placed on outpatient status from that commitment subject to the procedures and provisions of this title, except that a developmentally disabled person may be placed on outpatient status from that commitment under the provisions of this title as modified by Section 1370.4. Any person committed as a sexually violent predator under the provisions of Article 4 (commencing with Section 6600) of Chapter 2 of Part 2 of Division 6 of the Welfare and Institutions Code may be placed on outpatient status from that commitment in accordance with the procedures described in Title 15 (commencing with Section 1600) of Part 2 of the Penal Code.

Amended by Stats. 1996, Ch. 462, Sec. 1. Effective September 13, 1996.

Section 1600.5 - Time spent on outpatient status not counted as actual custody

For a person committed as a mentally disordered sex offender under former Section 6316 or 6316.2 of the Welfare and Institutions Code, or committed pursuant to Section 1026 or 1026.5, or committed pursuant to Section 2972, who is placed on outpatient status under the provisions of this title, time spent on outpatient status, except when placed in a locked facility at the direction of the outpatient supervisor, shall not count as actual custody and shall not be credited toward the person's maximum term of commitment or toward the person's term of extended commitment. Nothing in this section shall be construed to extend the maximum period of parole of a mentally disordered offender.

Amended by Stats 2000 ch 324 (AB 1881) s 1, eff. 1/1/2001.

Section 1601 - Confinement in state hospital or treatment facility required prior to availability of outpatient status

(a) When a person charged with and found incompetent on a charge of, convicted of, or found not guilty by reason of insanity of murder, mayhem, aggravated mayhem, a violation of Section 207, 209, or 209.5 in which the victim suffers intentionally inflicted great bodily injury, robbery or carjacking with a deadly or dangerous weapon or in which the victim suffers great bodily injury, a violation of subdivision (a) or (b) of Section 451, a violation of paragraph (2), (3), or (6) of subdivision (a) of Section 261, a violation of paragraph (1) or (4) of subdivision (a) of former Section 262, a violation of Section 459 in the first degree, a violation of Section 220 in which the victim suffers great bodily injury, a violation of Section 288, a violation of Section 18715, 18725, 18740, 18745, 18750, or 18755, or any felony involving death, great bodily injury, or an act which poses a serious threat of bodily harm to another person, outpatient status under this title shall not be available until that person has actually been confined in a state hospital or other treatment facility for 180 days or more after having been committed under the provisions of law specified in Section 1600, unless the court finds a suitable placement, including, but not limited to, an outpatient placement program, that would provide the person with more appropriate mental health treatment and the court finds that the placement would not pose a danger to the health or safety of others, including, but not limited to, the safety of the victim and the victim's family.

(b) When a person charged with, and found incompetent on a charge of, or convicted of, any misdemeanor or any felony other than those described in subdivision (a), or found not guilty of any misdemeanor by reason of insanity, outpatient status under this title may be granted by the court prior to actual confinement in a state hospital or other treatment facility under the provisions of law specified in Section 1600.

Amended by Stats 2021 ch 626 (AB 1171),s 56, eff. 1/1/2022.

Amended by Stats 2014 ch 734 (AB 2190),s 1, eff. 1/1/2015.

Amended by Stats 2012 ch 24 (AB 1470),s 29, eff. 6/27/2012.

Amended by Stats 2010 ch 178 (SB 1115),s 80, eff. 1/1/2011, op. 1/1/2012.

Section 1602 - Satisfaction of conditions prior to placement on outpatient status for person charged or convicted of misdemeanor and certain felonies

(a)Before any person subject to the provisions of subdivision (b) of Section 1601 may be placed on outpatient status, the court shall consider all of the following criteria:

(1)In the case of a person who is an inpatient, whether the director of the state hospital or other treatment facility to which the person has been committed advises the court that the defendant will not be a danger to the health and safety of others while on outpatient status, and will benefit from such outpatient status.

(2)In all cases, whether the community program director or a designee, or pursuant to Section 4360.5 of the Welfare and Institutions Code, the independent evaluation panel, advises the court that the defendant will not be a danger to the health and safety of others while on outpatient status, will benefit from such status, and identifies an appropriate program of supervision and treatment.

(b)Prior to determining whether to place the person on outpatient status, the court shall provide actual notice to the prosecutor and defense counsel, and to the victim, and shall hold a hearing at which the court may specifically order outpatient status for the person.

(c)The community program director or a designee, or the independent evaluation panel, shall prepare and submit the evaluation and the treatment plan specified in paragraph (2) of subdivision (a) to the court within 15 calendar days after notification by the court to do so, except that in the case of a person who is an inpatient, the evaluation and treatment plan shall be submitted within 30 calendar days after notification by the court to do so.

(d)Any evaluations and recommendations pursuant to paragraphs (1) and (2) of subdivision (a) shall include review and consideration of complete, available information regarding the circumstances of the criminal offense and the person's prior criminal history.

Amended by Stats 2022 ch 47 (SB 184),s 46, eff. 6/30/2022.

Amended by Stats 2014 ch 734 (AB 2190),s 2, eff. 1/1/2015.

Section 1603 - Satisfaction of conditions prior to placement on outpatient status person charged with or convicted of certain felonies

(a)Before any person subject to subdivision (a) of Section 1601 may be placed on outpatient status the court shall consider all of the following criteria:

(1)Whether the director of the state hospital or other treatment facility to which the person has been committed advises the committing court and the prosecutor that the defendant would no longer be a danger to the health and safety of others, including themselves, while under supervision and treatment in the community, and will benefit from that status.

(2)Whether the community program director or a designee, or pursuant to Section 4360.5 of the Welfare and Institutions Code, the independent evaluation panel, advises the court that the defendant will benefit from that status, and identifies an appropriate program of supervision and treatment.

(b)

(1)Prior to release of a person under subdivision (a), the prosecutor shall provide notice of the hearing date and pending release to the victim or next of kin of the victim of the offense for which the person was committed where a request for the notice has been filed with the court, and after a hearing in court, the court shall specifically approve the recommendation and plan for outpatient status pursuant to Section 1604. The burden shall be on the victim or next of kin to the victim to keep the court apprised of the party's current mailing address.

(2)In any case in which the victim or next of kin to the victim has filed a request for notice with the director of the state hospital or other treatment facility, they shall be notified by the director at the inception of any program in which the committed person would be allowed any type of day release unattended by the staff of the facility.

(c)The community program director, their designee, or the independent evaluation panel, shall prepare and submit the evaluation and the treatment plan specified in paragraph (2) of subdivision (a) to the court within 30 calendar days after notification by the court to do so.

(d)Any evaluations and recommendations pursuant to paragraphs (1) and (2) of subdivision (a) shall include review and consideration of complete, available information regarding the circumstances of the criminal offense and the person's prior criminal history.

Amended by Stats 2022 ch 47 (SB 184),s 47, eff. 6/30/2022.

Amended by Stats 2014 ch 734 (AB 2190),s 3, eff. 1/1/2015.

Amended by Stats 2004 ch 628 (AB 1504), s 1, eff. 1/1/2005.

Section 1604 - Recommendation that person may be eligible for outpatient status; recommended plan for outpatient supervision and treatment; hearing

(a)Upon receipt by the committing court of the recommendation of the director of the state hospital or other treatment facility to which the person has been committed that the person may be eligible for outpatient status as set forth in subdivision (a)(1) of Section 1602 or 1603, the court shall immediately forward such recommendation to the independent evaluation panel described in Section 4360.5 of the Welfare and Institutions Code, prosecutor, and defense counsel. Notwithstanding any law, the court shall provide copies of the arrest reports and the state summary criminal history information to the panel. The panel shall share the recommendation and copies of the arrest reports and the state summary criminal history information with the community program director or designee.

(b)Within 30 calendar days the community program director, designee, or panel, shall submit to the court and, when appropriate, to the director of the state hospital or other treatment facility, a recommendation regarding the defendant's eligibility for outpatient status, as set forth in subdivision (a)(2) of Section 1602 or 1603 and the recommended plan for outpatient supervision and treatment. The plan shall set forth specific terms and conditions to be followed during outpatient status. The court shall provide copies of this report to the prosecutor and the defense counsel.

(c)The court shall calendar the matter for hearing within 15 judicial days of the receipt of the report described in subdivision (b) and shall give notice of the hearing date to the prosecutor, defense counsel, the panel, and, when appropriate, to the director of the state hospital or other facility. In any hearing conducted pursuant to this section, the court shall consider the circumstances and nature of the criminal offense leading to commitment and shall consider the person's prior criminal history.

(d)The court shall, after a hearing in court, either approve or disapprove the recommendation for outpatient status. If the approval of the court is given, the defendant shall be placed on outpatient status subject to the terms and conditions specified in the supervision and treatment plan. If the outpatient treatment occurs in a county other than the county of commitment, the court shall transmit a copy of the case record to the superior court in the county where outpatient treatment occurs, so that the record will be available if revocation proceedings are initiated pursuant to Section 1608 or 1609.

Amended by Stats 2022 ch 47 (SB 184),s 48, eff. 6/30/2022.

Amended by Stats. 1985, Ch. 1232, Sec. 14. Effective September 30, 1985.

Section 1605 - State Department of State Hospitals responsible for supervision of persons placed on outpatient status

(a) In accordance with Section 1615 of this code and Section 5709.8 of the Welfare and Institutions Code, the State Department of State Hospitals shall be responsible for the supervision of persons placed on outpatient status under this title. The State Department of State Hospitals shall designate, for each county or region comprised of two or more counties, a community program director who shall be responsible for administering the community treatment programs for persons committed from that county or region under the provisions specified in Section 1600.

(b) The State Department of State Hospitals shall notify in writing the superior court, the district attorney, the county public defender or public defense agency, and the county mental health director of each county as to the person designated to be the community program director for that county, and timely written notice shall be given whenever a new community program director is to be designated.

(c) The community program director shall be the outpatient treatment supervisor of persons placed on outpatient status under this title. The community program director may delegate the outpatient treatment supervision responsibility to a designee.

(d) The outpatient treatment supervisor shall, at 90-day intervals following the beginning of outpatient treatment, submit to the court, the prosecutor and defense counsel, and to the community program director, where appropriate, a report setting forth the status and progress of the defendant.

Amended by Stats 2012 ch 24 (AB 1470),s 30, eff. 6/27/2012.

Section 1606 - Period of outpatient status; hearing

Outpatient status shall be for a period not to exceed one year. At the end of the period of outpatient status approved by the court, the court shall, after actual notice to the prosecutor, the defense counsel, and the community program director, and after a hearing in court, either discharge the person from commitment under appropriate provisions of the law, order the person confined to a treatment facility, or renew its approval of outpatient status. Prior to such hearing, the community program director shall furnish a report and recommendation to the medical director of the state hospital, where appropriate, and to the court, which the court shall make available to the prosecutor and defense counsel. The person shall remain on outpatient status until the court renders its decision unless hospitalized under other provision of the law. The hearing pursuant to the provisions of this section shall be held no later than 30 days after the end of the one-year period of outpatient status unless good cause exists. The court shall transmit a copy of its order to the community program director or a designee.

Amended by Stats. 1985, Ch. 1232, Sec. 16. Effective September 30, 1985.

Section 1607 - Opinion of outpatient supervisor that person has regained competence

If the outpatient supervisor is of the opinion that the person has regained competence to stand trial, or is no longer insane, is no longer a mentally disordered offender, or is no longer a mentally disordered sex offender, the community program director shall submit his or her opinion to the medical director of the state hospital, where appropriate, and to the court which shall calendar the case for further proceedings under the provisions of Section 1372, 1026.2, or 2972 of this code or Section 6325 of the Welfare and Institutions Code. Amended by Stats 2000 ch 324 (AB 1881) s 2, eff. 1/1/2001.

Section 1608 - Request for revocation of outpatient status

If at any time during the outpatient period, the outpatient treatment supervisor is of the opinion that the person requires extended inpatient treatment or refuses to accept further outpatient treatment and supervision, the community program director shall notify the superior court in either the county which approved outpatient status or in the county where outpatient treatment is being provided of such opinion by means of a written request for revocation of outpatient status. The community program director shall furnish a copy of this request to the defense counsel and to the prosecutor in both counties if the request is made in the county of treatment rather than the county of commitment.

Within 15 judicial days, the court where the request was filed shall hold a hearing and shall either approve or disapprove the request for revocation of outpatient status. If the court approves the request for revocation, the court shall order that the person be confined in a state hospital or other treatment facility approved by the community program director. The court shall transmit a copy of its order to the community program director or a designee. Where the county of treatment and the county of commitment differ and revocation occurs in the county of treatment, the court shall enter the name of the committing county and its case number on the order of revocation and shall send a copy of the order to the committing court and the prosecutor and defense counsel in the county of commitment. Amended by Stats. 1985, Ch. 1232, Sec. 18. Effective September 30, 1985.

Section 1609 - Prosecutor's petition for hearing

If at any time during the outpatient period or placement with a local mental health program pursuant to subdivision (b) of Section 1026.2 the prosecutor is of the opinion that the person is a danger to the health and safety of others while on that status, the prosecutor may petition the court for a hearing to determine whether the person shall be continued on that status. Upon receipt of the petition, the court shall calendar the case for further proceedings within 15 judicial days and the clerk shall notify the person, the community program director, and the attorney of record for the person of the hearing date. Upon failure of the person to appear as noticed, if a proper affidavit of service and advisement has been filed with the court, the court may issue a body attachment for such person. If, after a hearing in court conducted using the same standards used in conducting probation revocation hearings pursuant to Section 1203.2, the judge determines that the person is a danger to the health and safety of others, the court shall order that the person be confined in a state hospital or other treatment facility which has been approved by the community program director. Amended by Stats. 1985, Ch. 1232, Sec. 19. Effective September 30, 1985.

Section 1610 - Confinement pending court's decision on revocation

(a) Upon the filing of a request for revocation under Section 1608 or 1609 and pending the court's decision on revocation, the person subject to revocation may be confined in a facility designated by the community program director when it is the opinion of that director that the person will now be a danger to self or to another while on outpatient status and that to delay confinement until the revocation hearing would pose an imminent risk of harm to the person or to another. The facility so designated shall continue the patient's program of treatment, shall provide adequate security so as to ensure both the safety of the person and the safety of others in the facility, and shall, to the extent possible, minimize interference with the person's program of treatment. Upon the request of the community program director or a designee, a peace officer shall take, or cause to be taken, the person into custody and transport the person to a facility designated by the community program director for confinement under this section. Within one judicial day after the person is confined in a jail under this section, the community program director shall apply in writing to the court for authorization to confine the person pending the hearing under Section 1608 or Section 1609 or subdivision (c). The application shall be in the form of a declaration, and shall specify the behavior or other reason justifying the confinement of the person in a jail. Upon receipt of the application for confinement, the court shall consider and rule upon it, and if the court authorizes detention in a jail, the court shall actually serve copies of all orders and all documents filed by the community program director upon the prosecuting and defense counsel. The community program director shall notify the court in writing of the confinement of the person and of the factual basis for the opinion that the immediate confinement in a jail was necessary. The court shall supply a copy of these documents to the prosecutor and defense counsel.

(b) The facility designated by the community program director may be a state hospital, a local treatment facility, a county jail, or any other appropriate facility, so long as the facility can continue the person's program of treatment, provide adequate security, and minimize interference with the person's program of treatment. If the facility designated by the community program director is a county jail, the patient shall be separated from the general population of the jail. In the case of a sexually violent predator, as defined in Section 6600 of the Welfare and Institutions Code, who is held pending civil process under the sexually violent predator laws, the person may be housed as provided by Section 4002. The designated facility need not be approved for 72-hour treatment and evaluation pursuant to the provisions of the Lanterman-Petris-Short Act (Part 1 (commencing with Section 5000) of Division 5 of the Welfare and Institutions Code); however, a county jail may not be designated unless the services specified above are provided, and accommodations are provided which ensure both the safety of the person and the safety of the general population of the jail. Within three judicial days of the patient's confinement in a jail, the community program director shall report to the court regarding what type of treatment the patient is receiving in the facility. If there is evidence that the treatment program is not being complied with, or accommodations have not been provided which ensure both the safety of the committed person and the safety of the general population of the jail, the court shall order the person transferred to an appropriate facility, including an appropriate state hospital. Nothing in this subdivision shall be construed as authorizing jail facilities to operate as health facilities, as defined in Section 1250 of the Health and Safety Code, without complying with applicable requirements of law.

(c) A person confined under this section shall have the right to judicial review of his or her confinement in a jail under this section in a manner similar to that which is prescribed in Article 5 (commencing with Section 5275) of Chapter 2 of Part 1 of Division 5 of the Welfare and Institutions Code and to an explanation of rights in the manner prescribed in Section 5325 of the Welfare and Institutions

Code. Nothing in this section shall prevent hospitalization pursuant to the provisions of Section 5150, 5250, 5350, or 5353 of the Welfare and Institutions Code.

(d) A person whose confinement in a treatment facility under Section 1608 or 1609 is approved by the court shall not be released again to outpatient status unless court approval is obtained under Section 1602 or 1603.

Amended by Stats 2001 ch 248 (AB 659), s 1, eff. 1/1/2002.

Section 1611 - Approval to leave state

(a) No person who is on outpatient status pursuant to this title or Section 2972 shall leave this state without first obtaining prior written approval to do so from the committing court. The prior written approval of the court for the person to leave this state shall specify when the person may leave, when the person is required to return, and may specify other conditions or limitations at the discretion of the court. The written approval for the person to leave this state may be in a form and format chosen by the committing court. In no event shall the court give written approval for the person to leave this state without providing notice to the prosecutor, the defense counsel, and the community program director. The court may conduct a hearing on the question of whether the person should be allowed to leave this state and what conditions or limitations, if any, should be imposed.

(b) Any person who violates subdivision (a) is guilty of a misdemeanor.

Added by Stats. 1988, Ch. 74, Sec. 2.

Section 1612 - Release only as provided by statute

Any person committed to a state hospital or other treatment facility under the provisions of Section 1026, or Chapter 6 (commencing with Section 1367) of Title 10 of this code, or former Section 6316 or 6321 of the Welfare and Institutions Code shall not be released therefrom except as expressly provided in this title or Section 1026.2.

Amended by Stats. 1984, Ch. 1488, Sec. 13.

Section 1614 - Outpatient status under this title

Persons ordered to undergo outpatient treatment under former Sections 1026.1 and 1374 of the Penal Code and subdivision (a) of Section 6325.1 of the Welfare and Institutions Code shall, on January 1, 1981, be considered as being on outpatient status under this title and this title shall apply to such persons.

Added by Stats. 1980, Ch. 547, Sec. 17.

Section 1615 - State Department of State Hospitals responsible for community treatment and supervision of judicially committed patients

Pursuant to Section 5709.8 of the Welfare and Institutions Code, the State Department of State Hospitals shall be responsible for the community treatment and supervision of judicially committed patients. These services shall be available on a county or regional basis. The department may provide these services directly or through contract with private providers or counties. The program or programs through which these services are provided shall be known as the Forensic Conditional Release Program.

The department shall contact all county mental health programs by January 1, 1986, to determine their interest in providing an appropriate level of supervision and treatment of judicially committed patients at reasonable cost. County mental health agencies may agree or refuse to operate such a program.

The State Department of State Hospitals shall ensure consistent data gathering and program standards for use statewide by the Forensic Conditional Release Program.

Amended by Stats 2012 ch 24 (AB 1470),s 31, eff. 6/27/2012.

Section 1616 - Study by research agency

The state shall contract with a research agency which shall determine the prevalence of severe mental disorder among the state prison inmates and parolees, including persons admitted to prison, the resident population, and those discharged to parole. An evaluation of the array of services shall be performed, including the correctional, state hospital, and local inpatient programs; residential-level care and partial day care within the institutions as well as in the community; and the individual and group treatment which may be provided within the correctional setting and in the community upon release. The review shall include the interrelationship between the security and clinical staff, as well as the architectural design which aids meeting the treatment needs of these mentally ill offenders while maintaining a secure setting. Administration of these programs within the institutions and in the community shall be reviewed by the contracting agency. The ability of treatment programs to prevent reoffenses by inmates with severe mental disorders shall also be addressed. The process for evaluating inmates and parolees to determine their need for treatment and the ability to differentiate those who will benefit from treatment and those who will not shall be reviewed.

The State Department of State Hospitals, the Department of Corrections and Rehabilitation, and the Department of Justice shall cooperate with the research agency conducting this study.

The research agency conducting this study shall consult with the State Department of State Hospitals, the Department of Corrections and Rehabilitation, the Department of Justice, and the Forensic Mental Health Association of California in the design of the study.

Amended by Stats 2012 ch 24 (AB 1470),s 32, eff. 6/27/2012.

Section 1617 - Evaluation of Forensic Conditional Release Program

The State Department of State Hospitals shall research the demographic profiles and other related information pertaining to persons receiving supervision and treatment in the Forensic Conditional Release Program. An evaluation of the program shall determine its effectiveness in successfully reintegrating these persons into society after release from state institutions. This evaluation of program effectiveness shall include, but not be limited to, a determination of the rates of reoffense while these persons are served by the program and after their discharge. This evaluation shall also address the effectiveness of the various treatment components of the program and their intensity.

The State Department of State Hospitals may contract with an independent research agency to perform this research and evaluation project. Any independent research agency conducting this research shall consult with the Forensic Mental Health Association concerning the development of the research and evaluation design.

Amended by Stats 2012 ch 24 (AB 1470),s 33, eff. 6/27/2012.

Section 1618 - No liability for criminal acts committed by persons on parole or judicial commitment status who receive supervision or treatment

The administrators and the supervision and treatment staff of the Forensic Conditional Release Program shall not be held criminally or civilly liable for any criminal acts committed by the persons on parole or judicial commitment status who receive supervision or treatment. This waiver of liability shall apply to employees of the State Department of State Hospitals, the Board of Parole Hearings, and the agencies or persons under contract to those agencies, who provide screening, clinical evaluation, supervision, or treatment to mentally ill parolees or persons under judicial commitment or considered for placement under a hold by the Board of Parole Hearings. Amended by Stats 2012 ch 24 (AB 1470),s 34, eff. 6/27/2012.

Section 1619 - Automation of criminal histories

The Department of Justice shall automate the criminal histories of all persons treated in the Forensic Conditional Release Program, as well as all persons committed as not guilty by reason of insanity pursuant to Section 1026, incompetent to stand trial pursuant to Section 1370 or 1370.2, any person currently under commitment as a mentally disordered sex offender, and persons treated pursuant to Section 1364 or 2684 or Article 4 (commencing with Section 2960) of Chapter 7 of Title 1 of Part 3. Amended by Stats. 1988, Ch. 37, Sec. 4.

Section 1620 - Access to criminal histories

The Department of Justice shall provide mental health agencies providing treatment to patients pursuant to Sections 1600 to 1610, inclusive, or pursuant to Article 4 (commencing with Section 2960) of Chapter 7 of Title 1 of Part 3, with access to criminal histories of those mentally ill offenders who are receiving treatment and supervision. Treatment and supervision staff who have access to these criminal histories shall maintain the confidentiality of the information and shall sign a statement to be developed by the Department of Justice which informs them of this obligation. Amended by Stats. 1987, Ch. 687, Sec. 6.

Made in the USA
Las Vegas, NV
20 May 2024

VOLUME 1

MASTERPIECES of
RUSSIAN STAGE DESIGN
1880-1930

(in Two Volumes)

John E. Bowlt, Nina and Nikita D. Lobanov-Rostovsky, and Olga Shaumyan

Russian Stage Design 1880-1930 (in two volumes)

VOLUME I

MASTERPIECES of RUSSIAN STAGE DESIGN

ISBN: 978 1 85149 688 4

Book design concept: Nikita D. Lobanov-Rostovsky
Catalogue Raisonné: Copyright © by John E. Bowlt, Nikita Lobanov-Rostovsky, and Nina Lobanov-Rostovsky
Photographs: Nikita D. Lobanov-Rostovsky
Colour separation and photocomposition: Antique Collectors' Club Ltd.

British Library Cataloguing-in-Publication Data:
A catalogue record for this book is available from the British Library

Published by Antique Collectors' Club, England
Printed in China for The Antique Collectors' Club Ltd.,
Woodbridge, Suffolk IP12 4SD

Endpapers. Mstislav Dobujinsky: *Curtain Design with Quarter-moons for the Chauve-Souris*, 1924 (No. 429 in Volume II).

Frontispiece. 1. Alexandre Benois: Design for a Program Cover, 1952 (No. 121 in Volume II)

Title page. Natalia Goncharova: Portrait of Leonide Massine, 1916 (No. 561)

Serge Tchehonine, *Three Theatrical Masks*, 1911 (No. 1019)

2. Nina Aizenberg: Costume Design for a Pioneer, 1926 (No. 2)

CONTENTS

RUSSIAN STAGE DESIGN 1880-1930

3. Mikhail Andreenko:
Costume Design for a
Boyar's Daughter,
Tsar Fedor Ioannovich,
1922 (No. 19)

ADDENDA

4. Mikhail Andreenko:
Costume Design for a
Young Man,
Tsar Fedor Ioannovich,
1922 (No. 20)

Foreword

Russian Stage Design 1880-1930 based on the collection of Nina and Nikita D. Lobanov-Rostovsky (hereafter: *Russian Stage Design*) guides the reader through the complex labyrinth of the movements, styles, productions, and projects that attracted many of Russia's early 20th century artists to the stage. It lists well over one thousand items by 176 artists, including Léon Bakst, Alexandre Benois, Alexandra Exter, Natalia Goncharova, Mikhail Larionov, Kazimir Malevich, Liubov Popova, Vladimir Tatlin, and other prime movers of the Modernist era. Volume I, *Masterpieces of Russian Stage Design*, includes color illustrations of selected designs plus an introduction, interview, indices to artists, theater companies, and primary productions, glossary of terms, and a comprehensive bibliography for the visual and performing arts in Russia. Volume II, *An Encyclopedia of Russian Stage Design*, contains the catalogue raisonné of the Lobanov-Rostovsky collection.

The scope of the collection extends the conventional idea of the history of Russian stage design because it focuses attention on many scenic phenomena outside Sergei Diaghilev's celebrated Ballets Russes. True, the Diaghilev era is well represented by contributions to famous and less famous productions, but the diversity of the collection makes us question the assumed dominance of Diaghilev's artists in modern Russian stage design and reassesses those designers and producers who worked concurrently in Russia / Soviet Union. Indeed, it becomes clear from the collection that, if Diaghilev's artists created a revolution in theatrical art before World War I, a second revolution was achieved by artists such as Liubov Popova and Alexander Rodchenko working in Moscow, not in Paris, during the early 1920s.

The collection, begun in 1960, can scarcely be replicated. The reason for this is not simply a commercial one, even though the market price for a work by Bakst, Marc Chagall or Malevich, is now extremely high. Rather, it is a question of accessibility. Even if unlimited funds were available, a similar collection could not be assembled today because most Western and Russian sources have been exhausted (the remainder of Serge Lifar's collection, one of the last major Western sources of ballet material in private hands, was auctioned in Geneva on March 13, 2012). Moreover, if, during the 1960s it was possible to export items by artists such as Malevich and Rodchenko from the Soviet Union, that privilege has long been revoked. It is, therefore, extremely difficult to acquire primary, high-quality designs today for, say, Diaghilev's Ballets Russes, either financially or physically, even though the international demand for such material is greater than ever.

In February, 2008, 810 items from the Lobanov-Rostovsky collection were acquired by the Konstantin Foundation (Fond Konstantinovskii) for the Konstantin Palace outside St. Petersburg, and another fifty subsequently,[1] and the works were transferred to a branch of the Glinka Museum of Theatrical and Musical Art in St. Petersburg where they can be viewed today.[2] The remaining works are in private collections and this is indicated in the entries in Volume II.

---

1. For information on the Konstantin Palace see T. Alekseeva, ed.: *Konstantinovskii dvortsovo-parkovyi ansambl. Khronika, materialy, issledovaniia. Sbornik statei,* SP: Gangut, 2010. For information on the transaction see, for example, J. Varoli: "Art Repatriated. The Lobanov-Rostovsky Collection" in *Russian Life,* SP, 2009, March-April, pp. 55-60. See N186 for a sampling of the items from the Lobanov-Rostovsky collection now under the auspices of the Konstantin Foundation. (A capital letter plus number, e.g. N186, refers to the Bibliography at the end of this volume.)
2. In September-October, 2008, the GMTMA (see List of Abbreviations) organized an exhibition of 400 works from the collection and in April, 2010, announced the formation of a dedicated space for the collection within a branch of the Museum in St. Petersburg. See E. Gerusova: "'Konstantinovskii' gastroliruet v Teatralnom muzee" in *Kommersant,* M, 2010, 15 April, No. 66.

5. Boris Anisfeld: Costume Design for a Member of the Peasant Chorus, *Sadko,* ca. 1911 (No. 27)

Acknowledgements

Preparing *Russian Stage Design* has been an exciting and rewarding, if complex, procedure. The fruit of long and exacting research, this catalogue raisonné has involved the cooperation of many people in many countries. Unfortunately, space does not permit us to name all those individuals who, with their various talents, contributed to the realization of this book, but special thanks go to the following artists, performers, and their relatives, many of whom, alas, are now deceased: Mikhail Andreenko, Lisa Aronson, Elena Balieva, Nicola Benois, René and Valeria Clémenti-Bilinsky, Dmitri Bouchène, Marochka Chatfield-Taylor, Alexandra Danilova, Vsevolod Dobujinsky, George Dunkel, Tamara Geva, Cyrille Grigoriev, André Houdiakoff, Marianna Jedrinsky, Alexandra Tomilina-Larionova, Serge Lifar, Simon Lissim, Leonid Remisoff, Varvara Rodchenko, Ekaterina and Alexandre Serebriakoff, Alexander Shlepianov, Jeanne Palmer-Soudeikine, Anna Tcherkessoff, Irène Zack, and Rusudama Zaitseva-Shervashidze.

Much of the research for the catalog was undertaken in the Soviet Union / Russian Federation, thanks, in part, to research awards from the Alfred and Elaine Borchard Foundation, the Fulbright-Hayes Program, and the International Research and Exchanges Board, and we would like to express our gratitude to the staff of the following institutions: Bakhrushin State Central Theater Museum, Moscow; Glinka Museum, Moscow; Glinka Museum of Theatrical and Musical Art, St. Petersburg; Russian National Library, Moscow; Russian State Archive of Literature and Art, Moscow; State Russian Museum, St. Petersburg; and State Tretiakov Gallery, Moscow. Extensive use was also made of museums and libraries in the West, especially the Biblioteca Nazionale, Rome; Biblioteca Teatrale "Bucardo," Rome; British Library, London; Institute of Modern Russian Culture, Los Angeles; Research Institute of the Getty Center for the History of Art and the Humanities, Los Angeles; Library of Congress, Washington, D.C.; McNay Art Museum, San Antonio; Metropolitan Museum, New York; Museum of Modern Art, New York; New York Public Library; Theatre Museum, London; and the libraries and archives of Sotheby's, London, and Christie's, London.

During our research for *Russian Stage Design*, we consulted with many colleagues over questions of provenance, dating, bibliography, etc., and we would like to acknowledge our appreciation to the following in particular: Oleg Antonov, Natalia Avtonomova, Sergei Balan, Alfred H. Barr, Jr., Michaela Bohmig, Boris Brodsky, Richard Buckle, Mary Chamot, Myroslava Ciszkewycz, Robert Craft, André de Saint-Rat, Irina Duksina, Elizabeth Durst, Igor Dychenko, Irina Dzutseva, Irina Evstigneeva, Elena Fedosova, Ildar Galeev, Yurii Gogolitsyn, Dmitrii Gorbachev, Elena Grushvitskaia, Evgeniia Iliukhina, Susan Kechekian, Mikhail Kiselev, Tatiana Klim, Dora Kogan, Mark Konecny, Georgii Kovalenko, Vera Krasovskaia, Alla Lukanova, Valentine and Jean-Claude Marcadé, John McKendry, Irina Menchova, Oleg Minin, Nicoletta Misler, Alexander Parnis, Militsa Pozharskaia, Irina Pruzhan, Alexander Rabinovich, Konstantin Rudnitsky, Alla and Yurii Rusakov, Andrei and Dmitrii Sarabianov, Alexander Schouvaloff, Dmtirii Severiukhin, Alexandra Shatskikh, Vladimir Shleev, Yuliia Solonovich, Bella Solovieva, Anatolii Strigalev, Elizaveta Surits, Flora Syrkina, Elena Terkel, Liudmila Tikhvinskaia, Andrei Tolstoi, Leonid Trauberg, Keith Tribble, Nancy Van Norman Baer, Alexandre Vassilieff, Raisa Vlasova, Tatiana Volodina, Viacheslav Zavalishin, and Ilia Zilbershtein.

6. Boris Anisfeld: Costume Design for an Arab Female Dancer, *Islamey*, ca. 1912 (No. 28)

Note to the Reader

Russian Stage Design makes no claim to be a complete history of modern Russian stage design. Rather, its main objectives are to register and describe the Lobanov-Rostovsky collection and, therefore, to furnish bio-bibliographical information on the Russian artists who contributed set and costume designs to theatrical productions during ca. 1880-ca. 1930. These chronological perimeters are, of course, not stable, but the renaissance of the Russian literary, visual, and theatrical arts identifiable with the late 19th and early 20th centuries attracted innovative artists who undertook a veritable revolution in the conventions of stage design. In turn, they left an indelible imprint on the development of the performing arts in Russia, Europe and the USA.

This scenic transformation was effected by many talented artists, the vast majority of whom are represented in the Lobanov-Rostovsky collection, a unique depository that serves as the constant point of reference for this book. Some of the artists represented in the collection such as Bakst and Benois enjoy international repute; others such as Mikhail Andreenko and Ilia Shlepianov are less familiar, but are still of immediate importance to the evolution of modern stage design. Consequently, every attempt has been made to provide comprehensive bio-bibliographical information on those artists who deserve to be better known to the Western public, whereas, for obvious reasons, the more celebrated figures receive less commentary. In many cases, the footnotes contain additional bio-bibliographical references, and the systematized Bibliography at the end of Volume I also provides essential information.

Dates referring to events in Russia before January, 1918, are in the Old Style. Consequently, if they are in the 19th century, then they are twelve days behind the Western calendar, whereas if they are between 1900 and 1918 they are thirteen days behind.

The city of St. Petersburg was renamed Petrograd in 1914, Leningrad in 1924, and then St. Petersburg again in 1991. However, both the names Petrograd and Petersburg continued to be used in common parlance and in publications until 1924. As a general rule, however, Petrograd has been retained here as the official name of St. Petersburg for the period 1914-1924.

Before the Soviet occupation in 1940, Tallinn was called Reval, Tartu Dorpat, and Helsinki Helsingfors.

Titles of books, catalogs, journals, and newspapers are italicized; titles of articles, exhibitions, and manuscripts are in quotation marks, but names of societies and institutions are not. Depending on the context, therefore, the name World of Art, which is associated variously with a journal, a society, and a series of exhibitions, may or may not appear in italics or quotation marks.

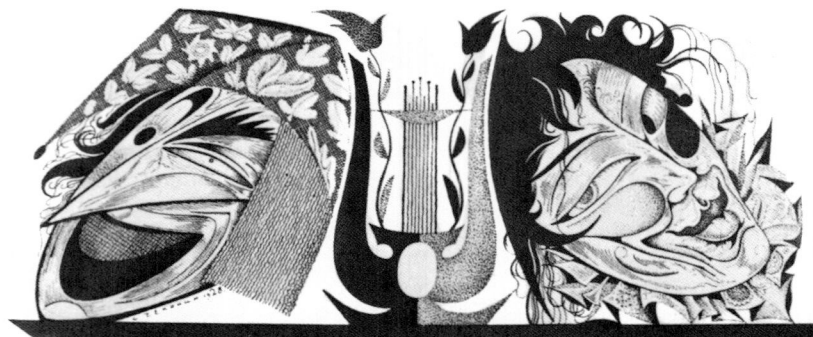

Serge Tchehonine, *Two Masks and Lyre*, 1928 (No. 1047)

7. Boris Anisfeld: Costume Design for Cleopatra's Slave worn by Michel Fokine,
An Egyptian Night, 1913. (No. 30)

Note on Transliteration

Many of the Russian artists, dancers, producers, and critics mentioned in this book spent their lives traveling from country to country. Often their names received diverse, often unconventional, transliterations from the original Russian into the language of their adopted home. Because of these discrepancies and because of the frequent variants in the spelling of Russian names in Western languages, the following transliteration system has been followed:

For those artists, dancers, producers, etc. who emigrated from Russia, took up permanent residence in the West, and established a consistent spelling of their names, this has been retained in the main text. In many cases, the spelling may contradict standard American or British transliteration systems, but this approach has been followed in deference to the individuals themselves. Examples are: Alexandre Benois (not Aleksandr Benua), Dimitri Bouchène (not Dmitrii Bushen), André Houdiakoff (not Andrei Khudiakov), Vladimir Jedrinsky (not Vladimir Zhedrinsky), Jean Pougny (not Ivan Puni), and Nicholas Roerich (not Nikolai Rerikh). In the main text, "Aleksandr", "Aleksandra", and "Aleksei" have been rendered as "Alexander", "Alexandra", and "Alexei" respectively.

For most of those artists and their colleagues who did not emigrate or who emigrated temporarily and returned to the Soviet Union, such as Ivan Bilibin and Vasilii Shukhaev, the names are transliterated in accordance with a modified system of the Library of Congress, although the Russian soft and hard signs have either been omitted or rendered by an "i" (e.g., Grigoriev). This system is also used throughout the footnotes and the bibliographical data where references involve Russian language sources.

Alexandre Benois: Portrait of Prince Alexandre Shervashidze, 1906 (No. 120)

8. Yurii Annenkov:
Costume Design for the
Baba-Yaga (Witch),
The First Distiller, 1919
(No. 43)

Note on Iconographic References

The Lobanov-Rostovsky Collection has been represented at exhibitions worldwide and many works have been reproduced in printed and electronic media. Such sources are usually indicated by a bibliographical code within the curatorial data for each item (e.g. B115, plate 1), together with comparative material. Exceptions are lithographs, silkscreens (pochoirs), and other works reproduced in multiple editions, unless a given item is exceptionally rare (e.g. No. 1116), and also Alexandre Benois's enormous cycle of variants and versions for his several interpretations of *Petrouchka*, which would warrant a separate compilation and analysis. A few of the items are double-sided (e.g. No. 1152) and wherever the verso is of particular importance, this has been given a sequential number (e.g. No. 1153). The iconographic references are not exhaustive and are intended only as a guide to the visual accessibility of the collection within the public domain.

Alexandre Benois: Portrait of Igor Stravinsky Playing the Piano Score of *Petrouchka* in the Hall of the Teatro Costanza, Rome, 1911 (No. 150)

9. Yurii Annenkov: Panorama "Festive Decoration for Uritsky Square",
The Storming of the Winter Palace, 1920 (No. 44)

List of Abbreviations

The following abbreviations have been used in both volumes (see Glossary for further explanation of terms):

AKhRR	Association of Artists of Revolutionary Russia
BTM	Bakhrushin State Central Theater Museum, Moscow
CSIAI	Central Stroganov Industrial Art Institute, Moscow
Comintern	Communist International
ed. khr.	*edinitsa khraneniia* (unit of preservation). This refers to the item number within a particular file in Russian archives
f.	*fond* (fund). This refers to the file number in Russian archives
GAKhN	See RAKhN
GAU	Chief Archive Administration, Soviet of Ministers of the USSR, Moscow
Ginkhuk	State Institute of Artistic Culture
GITIS	State Institute of Theater Art (now the Russian Academy of Theater Arts), Moscow
GMTMA	Glinka Museum of Theatrical and Musical Art, St. Petersburg
IAA	Imperial Academy of Arts, St. Petersburg
Inkhuk	Institute of Artistic Culture, Moscow
IZO	Subsection of NKP (Commissariat of Enlightenment) responsible for the visual arts
K	Kiev
l.	*list* (sheet). This refers to the sheet number in Russian archives
L	Leningrad
LEF	Left Front of the Arts
M	Moscow
MIPSA	Moscow Institute of Painting, Sculpture, and Architecture (Russian acronym MUZhVZ)
NIRE	Not In Russian Edition (i.e., not listed in B179)
NKP	People's Commissariat for Enlightenment
Obmokhu	Society of Young Artists
OMKh	Society of Moscow Artists
op.	(opus). This is the general heading used for a particular section within a Russian archive *fond*.
OST	Society of Studio Artists
P	Petrograd
Pegoskhum	Petrograd State Free Art Studios
RAKhN	Russian Academy of Artistic Sciences
RGA	Russian State Archive, Moscow
RGALI	Russian State Archive of Literature and Art, Moscow
RM	State Russian Museum, St. Petersburg
RSFSR	Russian Soviet Federative Socialist Republic
SCITD	Stieglitz Central Institute of Technical Drawing, St. Petersburg
SP	St. Petersburg
SSEA	School of the Society for the Encouragement of the Arts, St. Petersburg
Svomas	Free Studios
TG	State Tretiakov Gallery, Moscow
Unovis	Affirmers of New Art
Vkhutein	Higher State Art-Technical Institute
Vkhutemas	Higher State Art-Technical Studios
VNIITE	All-Union Scientific Research Institute of Technical Esthetics
Vsekokhudozhnik	All-Russian Cooperative Association "Artist"
Zhivskulptarkh	Collective for "Painting-Sculpture-Architecture" Synthesis

10. Léon Bakst: Costume Design for Cleopatra Worn by Ida Rubinstein, *Cléopatre*, 1909 (No. 75)

Glossary of Terms and Acronyms

0.10: Short title of the "Last Futurist Exhibition of Paintings, 0.10" held in Petrograd in 1915-16 with contributions by Kliun, Popova, Pougny, Rozanova, Tatlin et al. This was also the first public showing of Malevich's Suprematism.

5 x 5 = 25: Exhibition in Moscow in 1921 at which Exter, Popova, Rodchenko, Stepanova, and A. Vesnin contributed five works each. Generally regarded as a major development in the history of Constructivism.

Academy of Arts: See **Imperial Academy of Arts**

AKhRR: Assotsiatsiia khudozhnikov revoliutsionnoi Rossii (Association of Artists of Revolutionary Russia). Founded in 1922 by A. Grigoriev, Katsman and other artists who supported the style of Heroic Realism. Functioned primarily as an exhibition society based in Moscow. In 1928 changed its name to AKhR (Assotsiatsiia khudozhnikov revoliutsii – Association of Artists of the Revolution). Disbanded in 1932.

Apollo: Title of an art and literary journal (*Apollon*) published by S. Makovsky in St. Petersburg 1909-17 (last issues appeared in 1918). *Apollo* published articles and exhibition reviews dealing with the new art and also organized exhibitions in its editorial offices.

Askranov: Assotsiatsiia krainikh novatorov (Association of Extreme Innovators). Founded in Moscow in 1919 by Drevin, Gan, Rodchenko, and Stepanova.

Blue Rose (Golubaia roza)**:** Group of Moscow and Saratov Symbolist artists consisting of P. Kuznetsov, Sapunov, Sudeikin et al. Held one exhibition in Moscow in 1907.

Café Pittoresque: A bohemian café and cabaret founded in Moscow in 1917. Functioned for only a few months. Interior design by Yakulov, assisted by Rodchenko, Udaltsova et al.

Central Stroganov Industrial Art Institute: (also known as the Central Stroganov Institute of Technical Drawing), Moscow. After 1917 it merged with the Moscow Institute of Painting, Sculpture, and Architecture to form Svomas (q.v.).

Comintern: Communist International. Unification of Communist Parties worldwide through debate and convocation. Tatlin designed his Tower for the III International in Moscow in 1919.

Contemporary Trends (Sovremennye techeniia)**:** Exhibition organized by Kulbin in St. Petersburg in 1908. D. Burliuk, Lentulov et al. took part.

Donkey's Tail (Oslinyi khvost)**:** Group organized by Larionov in 1911. Held one exhibition in Moscow in 1912 with contributions by Goncharova, Larionov, Malevich, Shevchenko et al.

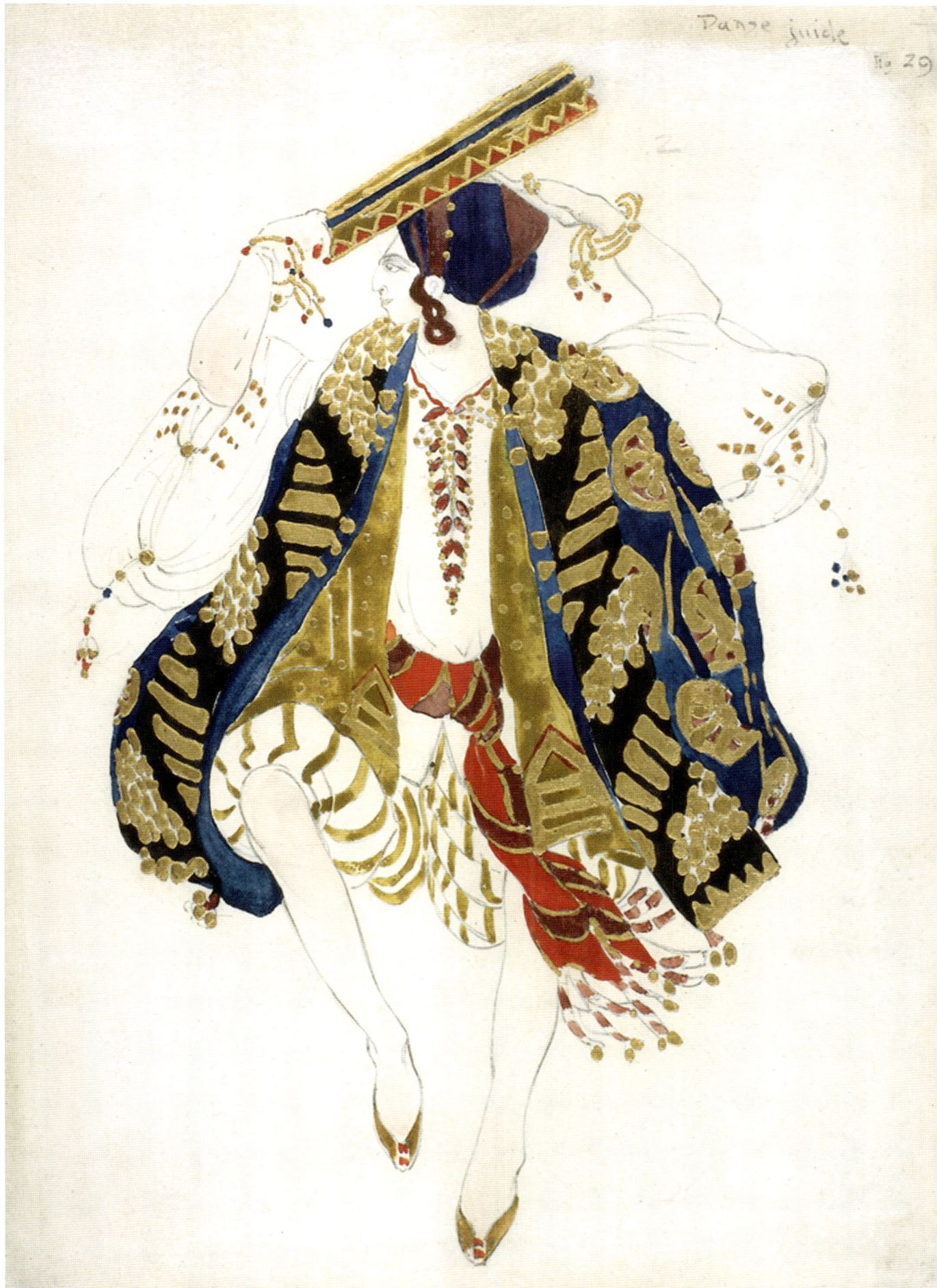

11. Léon Bakst: Costume Design for a Male Dancer Holding a Tambourine
in the "Danse Juive," *Cléopatre*, 1910 (No. 77)

Erste Russische Kunstausstellung: The first major Soviet art exhibition abroad, held at the Galerie Van Diemen, Berlin, in 1922, before traveling on to Amsterdam in modified form. Although the avant-garde was well represented, this commercial exhibition was a survey of many trends.

Exhibition of Paintings by Petrograd Artists of All Directions: Broad survey of new trends organized in Petrograd in 1923. Among the many contributors were Chashnik, Filonov, Mansurov, and Tatlin.

Exposition Internationale des Arts Décoratifs et Industriels: International exhibition of industrial design and applied art in Paris in 1925. Many of the Soviet Suprematists and Constructivists such as Chashnik, Popova, Rodchenko, Stepanova, and A. Vesnin contributed to the Soviet Pavilion designed by Melnikov.

GAKhN: See **RAKhN**

Ginkhuk: Gosudarstvennyi institut khudozhestvennnoi kultury (State Institute of Artistic Culture). The Petrograd / Leningrad counterpart to Inkhuk (q.v.). which developed from the Petrograd affiliation of the Museums of Painterly Culture (q.v.) in 1923 (ratified 1924). The Museums / Ginkhuk contained five basic departments: 1) Department of Form and Theory headed by Malevich; 2) Department of Material Culture headed by Tatlin (1922-25); 3) Department of Organic Culture headed by Matiushin; 4) Department of Experimentation headed by Pavel Mansurov; 5) Department of General Ideology headed by Filonov and then Punin.

Golden Fleece (Zolotoe runo): Title of an art and literary journal published by N. Riabushinsky in Moscow 1906-09 (last issues actually appeared in 1910). The *Golden Fleece* also organized three exhibitions that did much to propagate the cause of Goncharova and Larionov, i.e. "Salon of the *Golden Fleece*" (Moscow, 1908; contributions by Russian and W. European artists); "Golden Fleece" (Moscow, 1909; contributions by Russian and W. European artists); "Golden Fleece" (Moscow, 1909-10; contributions by Russian artists only).

Imperial Academy of Fine Arts: Founded in 1757 in St. Petersburg; first president was Catherine the Great. In 1918 the Academy was replaced by Svomas (q.v.) and then reinstated in 1921. In the 1920s it was also referred to as Vkhutemas (q.v.).

Inkhuk: Institut khudozhestvennoi kultury (Institute of Artistic Culture). Founded as a research institute in Moscow in 1920. Many of the avant-garde were associated with it and Kandinsky was its first president. Inkhuk had affiliations in Petrograd, Vitebsk, and other cities. Active through 1924.

Izdebsky Salons: Izdebsky organized two important exhibitions or salons of the new Russian art, i.e. the "International Exhibition of Paintings, Sculpture, Engravings, and Drawings" (Odessa, St. Petersburg, and other cities, 1909-10; contributions by Russian and W. European artists), "Salon 2" (Odessa 1910, opened 1911; contributions by Russian artists only).

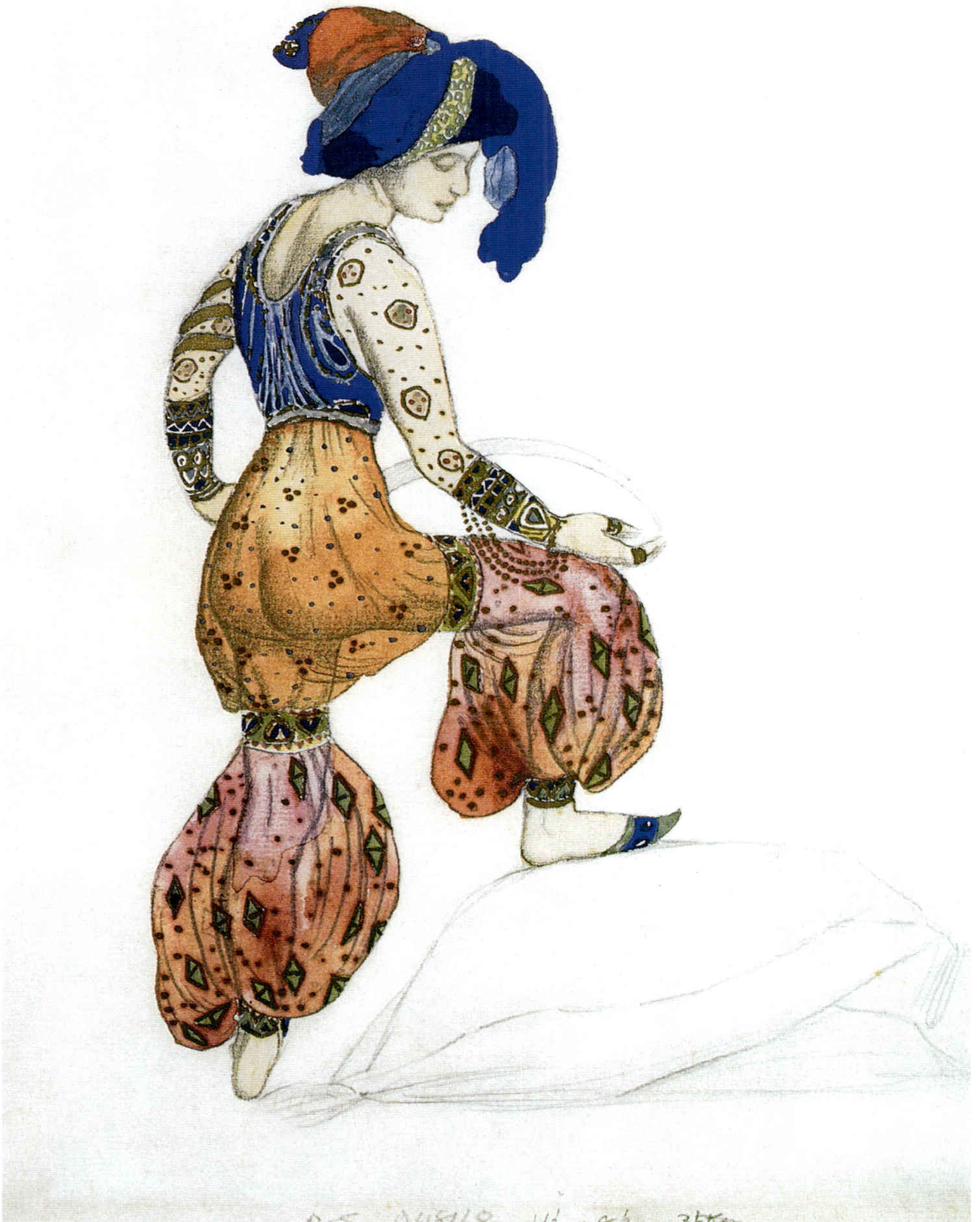

12. Léon Bakst: Costume Design for the Blue Sultana, *Schéhérazade*, 1910 (No. 81)

IZO: Izobrazitelnye iskusstva (the Visual Arts). The Visual Arts Section of NKP (q.v.) founded in 1918 under Shterenberg. IZO was responsible for art exhibitions, official commissions, art institutes, art education, etc. At first, many of the avant-garde were involved in its activities.

Jack of Diamonds (Bubnovyi valet): Group organized by Larionov in Moscow in 1910 and supported at first by many radical artists, including Goncharova and Malevich. After the first exhibition in Moscow in 1910-11, the group split into two factions, one led by Larionov giving rise to the Donkey's Tail (q.v.), the other by Falk, Konchalovsky, Lentulov, Mashkov et al. The Jack of Diamonds organized regular exhibitions in Moscow and St. Petersburg between 1910 and 1917, some of them international in scope.

Lef: Levyi front iskusstv (Left Front of the Arts). A Moscow group of radical writers and artists including Maiakovsky, Rodchenko, and S. Tretiakov. Published a journal of the same name in 1923-25 and then *Novyi lef* (New Lef) in 1927-28. The group was an enthusiastic proponent of Constructivism and new media such as photography and cinematography.

Link (Zveno): Exhibition organized by D. Burliuk, Bogomazov, Exter and other artists in Kiev in 1908. Accompanied by a manifesto, this was one of the first avant-garde exhibitions of Russian and Ukrainian art.

Lubok: A cheap, handcolored print or broadsheet often depicting allegorical and satirical scenes from Russian life. The bright colors and crude outlines of the lubok attracted many 20th century Russian artists.

Morozov Gallery: The Moscow collection of Impressionist and Post-Impressionist paintings belonging to the businessman Ivan Morozov. In 1918 the collection was nationalized.

Moscow Institute of Painting, Sculpture and Architecture: The main Moscow art school at which many of Russia's 19th and 20th century artists studied, including most of the avant-garde. After 1917 it merged with the Central Stroganov Industrial Art Institute to form Svomas (q.v.).

Moscow Painters: See **OMKh**

Moscow Salon: A society that held regular exhibitions in Moscow between 1910 and 1918, at which some of the avant-garde, including Goncharova, Konchalovsky, and Stepanova were represented.

Museums of Painterly Culture: In 1919 a network of Museums of Painterly (also called Artistic or Plastic) Culture was established for Moscow, Petrograd and other cities. Altman, Kandinsky, Rodchenko and other avant-garde artists were involved in the organization of this network, the purpose of which was to collect works by modern Russian artists. The most important Museum was the Moscow one that functioned 1919-24.

Narkompros: See **NKP**

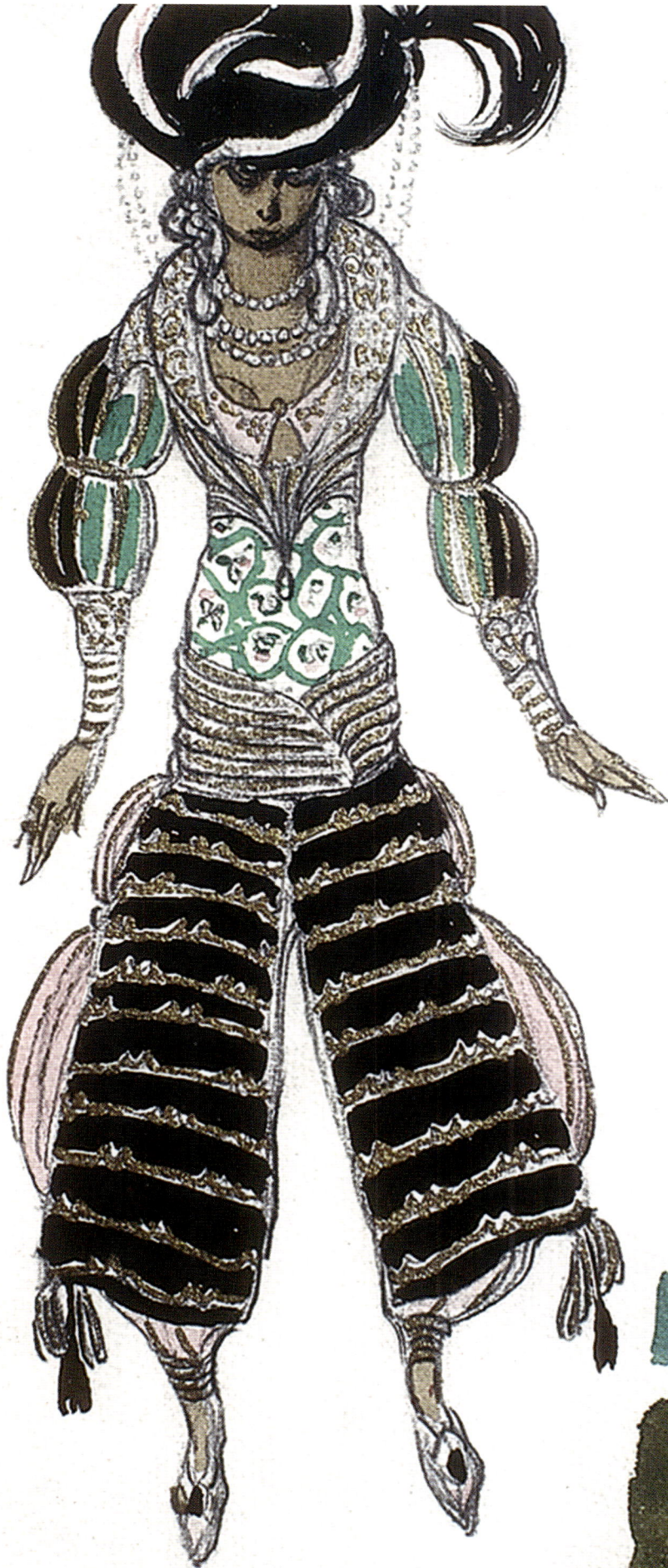

Pour 5 costumes changer la roux pur le vert clair
et alors le Turban sera ce vert foncé

13. Léon Bakst: Costume Design for a Slave, *Schéhérazade*, 1910 (No. 84)

27

New Society of Artists: A society that held regular exhibitions in St. Petersburg between 1904 and 1915, at which some of the avant-garde, including Exter, Kandinsky, Konchalovsky, and Mashkov were represented.

NKP: Narodnyi komissariat prosveshcheniia (People's Commissariat for Enlightenment). Established under Lunacharsky just after the Revolution, this radical ministry of culture opened various subsections responsible for the arts, including IZO (visual arts, q.v.). LITO (literature), MUZO (music), and TEO (theater).

No. 4: Group organized by Larionov in 1914. Held one exhibition in Moscow with contributions by Exter, Goncharova, Larionov, Shevchenko et al.

Obmokhu: Obshchestvo molodykh khudozhnikov (Society of Young Artists). A society that held four exhibitions in Moscow between 1919 and 1923 with contributions by Medunetsky, Rodchenko, the Stenberg brothers et al. Obmokhu was a primary exponent of Constructivism.

October: A Moscow group, founded in 1928, that supported the principles of Constructivist applied and industrial art. Among the members were Eisenstein, Klutsis, Telingater, Rodchenko, and A. Vesnin. One of the last avant-garde groups, it was disbanded in 1932.

OMKh: Obshchestvo moskovskikh khudozhnikov (Society of Moscow Artists). A society based on the Moscow Painters group of 1925, which was based, in turn, on the Jack of Diamonds. Held two exhibitions in 1928 and 1929, at which Drevin, Falk, Lentulov, Rozhdestvensky, Udaltsova et al. were represented.

OST: Obshchestvo khudozhnikov-stankovistov (Society of Studio Artists). A group of young painters and sculptors that often used Expressionist and Surrealist styles to illustrate the new reality of industry, sports, etc. It held exhibitions between 1925 and 1928, at which Deineka, Pimenov, Tyshler, Shterenberg et al. were represented.

Pegoskhum: Petrogradskie gosudarstvennye khudozhestvennye masterskie (Petrograd State Art Studios). See Svomas (q.v.).

Plan of Monumental Propaganda: In 1918 Lenin composed his Plan of Monumental Propaganda whereby many Tsarist monuments, reliefs, and street-names were to be removed from the cities and replaced by revolutionary ones. The Plan, which attracted numerous artists, was implemented only in part.

Proletkult: Proletarskaia kultura (Proletarian Culture). This movement, established formally in February, 1917, maintained that only the proletariat could create a proletarian art and that much of Russia's cultural heritage could be ignored. Supported by a number of the avant-garde artists, including Rozanova, Proletkult operated studios in urban centers and its emphasis on industry allied it with the emergent Constructivist groups. It was annexed to NKP (q.v.) in 1922.

14. After Léon Bakst: Set Design for the Last Scene: The Return of the Sultan Shariar, *Schéhérazade*, 1910 (No. 82).

Pushkin Museum of Fine Arts: The principal Moscow collection of Western art, ancient and modern. Founded in 1912, it was called the Alexander III Museum of Fine Arts until 1917.

RAKhN: Rossiiskaia Akademiia khudozhestvennykh nauk (Russian Academy of Artistic Sciences). Founded in Moscow in 1921 under P. Kogan, RAKhN, also known as GAKhN (Gosudarstvennaia Akademiia khudozhestvennykh nauk -- State Academy of Artistic Sciences), was a research institution that attracted a number of important artists and critics, including Bakushinsky, Kandinsky, Shmit and Shpet. It functioned until 1931.

RSFSR: Rossiiskaia Sovetskaia Federativnaia Sotsialisticheskaia Respublika (Russian Soviet Federative Socialist Republic).

Russian Museum: The principal St. Petersburg collection of Russian art. Founded in St. Petersburg in 1898, it was called the Alexander III Russian Museum until 1917.

Shchukin Gallery: The Moscow collection of Impressionist and Post-Impressionist paintings belonging to the businessman Sergei Shchukin. In 1918 the collection was nationalized.

Society of Studio Artists: See **OST**

State Exhibitions: IZO NKP (q.v.) organized 21 state exhibitions in Moscow in 1919-21, of which the following were particularly important: the tenth "Non-Objective Creativity and Suprematism" (1919), the twelfth "Color-Dynamos and Tectonic Primitivism" (1919), the sixteenth (one man show of Malevich, 1919), and the nineteenth (1920).

Stieglitz Central Institute of Technical Drawing: The main institute in St. Petersburg for studying technical drawing and industrial design. After 1917 it merged with the Imperial Academy of Arts (q.v.) to form Pegoskhum (q.v.)

Store (Magazin): Title of exhibition organized by Tatlin in Moscow in 1916 with contributions by Bruni, Exter, Malevich, Pestel, Stepanova, Udaltsova, Vassilieff et al.

Stroganov Institute: See Central Stroganov Industrial Art Institute

Supremus: A Moscow group of artists consisting of Kliun, Malevich, Popova, Tatlin, Udaltsova et al. formed in 1916 to propagate the new art, particularly Suprematism, through lectures, discussions and a journal (projected, but not realized). Ceased activities in 1917.

Svomas: Svobodnye gosudarstvennye khudozhestvennye masterskie (Free State Art Studios). In 1918 the Moscow Institute of Painting, Sculpture and Architecture (q.v.) and the Central Stroganov Industrial Art Institute (q.v.) were integrated to form Svomas, and the St. Petersburg Academy of Arts and the Stieglitz Central Institute of Technical Drawing (q.v.) were abolished to be replaced by the Petrograd State Art Studios (Pegoskhum -- late Svomas). In 1920, however, Svomas, Moscow, was

15. Léon Bakst: Costume Design for a Bacchante, *Narcisse*, 1911 (No. 85)

renamed Vkhutemas (q.v.) and the Academy of Arts was reinstated in Petrograd; in 1926 Vkhutemas became Vkhutein (q.v.). Similar changes were implemented in other cities. Many avant-garde artists, including Kliun, Malevich, Popova, Rodchenko, and Tatlin, contributed to the radical pedagogical and administrative developments that accompanied these name changes.

Target (Mishen): Group organized by Larionov in 1913. Held one exhibition in Moscow in 1913 with contributions by Chagall, Goncharova, Larionov, Malevich, Shevchenko et al.

Tramway V: Short title of "Tramway V, the First Futurist Exhibition of Paintings" held in Petrograd in 1915 with contributions by Kliun, Malevich, Popova, Rozanova, Tatlin et al.

Tretiakov Gallery: The principal Moscow collection of Russian art. Founded in 1892 on the basis of the collection of Pavel Tretiakov, a Moscow businessman.

Triangle: Exhibition organized by Kulbin in St. Petersburg in 1910 and supported by some of the avant-garde artists, including the Burliuks.

Union of Russian Artists: A society that held regular exhibitions in Moscow / St. Petersburg between 1903 and 1924 with contributions by predominantly moderate artists such as I. Ostroukhov, Vinogradov, and Yuon.

Union of Youth (Soiuz molodezhi): Group of artists, critics, and esthetes initiated by Markov, Rozanova, Shkolnik et al. in St. Petersburg in 1910. Published an art journal under the same name 1912-13 and sponsored a series of exhibitions, 1910-1914, to which many of the avant-garde contributed, including D. Burliuk, Filonov, Larionov, and Pougny.

Unovis: Utverditeli novogo iskusstva (Affirmers of the New Art). A group of Suprematist artists founded by Malevich in Vitebsk at the end of 1919 and including Chashnik, Kogan, Lissitzky, and Suetin. Unovis had affiliations in Smolensk, Samara, and other cities, and held exhibitions in Vitebsk and Moscow.

Victory over the Sun (Pobeda nad solntsem): The Cubo-Futurist opera produced in St. Petersburg in 1913 with libretto by Kruchenykh and Khlebnikov, music by Matiushin and designs by Malevich.

Vkhutein: Vysshii gosudarstvennyi khudozhestvenno-tekhnicheskii institut (Higher State Art-Technical Institute). Vkhutein replaced Vkhutemas (q.v.) in 1926 and was replaced by the Moscow Institute of Visual Arts in 1930.

Vkhutemas: Vysshie gosudarstvennye khudozhestvenno-tekhnicheskie masterskie (Higher State Art-Technical Studios). Vkhutemas replaced Svomas (q.v.) in 1920 and was replaced by Vkhutein (q.v.) in 1926. Although the Moscow Vkhutemas is the most famous, the name was also applied to other art schools such as the reinstated Academy of Arts in Petrograd/Leningrad.

16. Léon Bakst: Costume Design for a Boeotian, *Narcisse*, 1911 (No. 86)

VNIITE: Vsesoiuznyi nauchno-issledovatelskii institut tekhnicheskoi estetiki (All-Union Scientific Research Institute of Technical Esthetics). Founded in Moscow in the early 1960s, VNIITE brought together theorists, philosophers, and designers concerned especially with 20th century industrial design and with its debt to the Russian avant-garde.

Vsekokhudozhnik: Vserossiiskoe kooperativnoe tovarishchestvo "Khudozhnik" (All-Russian Cooperative Association "Artist"). Founded in Moscow in 1934 as an artists' trade union with exhibition and publishing facilities. Discontinued with the practical establishment of the Union of Artists of the USSR in 1939.

Wanderers (Peredvizhniki): Short title of the Association of Wandering Exhibitions founded in 1870. Held regular exhibitions in St. Petersburg, Moscow, and other cities between 1871 and 1923 with contributions by Levitan, Repin, Surikov, and other Realist artists.

World of Art: Group of St. Petersburg artists, critics, and esthetes founded by Benois, Diaghilev et al. in the late 1890s. Published an art journal under the same name (*Mir iskusstva*) in 1898-1904 and sponsored a series of exhibitions in 1899-1906 so as to propagate contemporary art. Revived as an exhibition society in 1910 (through 1924).

Wreath: Exhibition organized in St. Petersburg in 1908 with contributions by the Burliuks, Exter, Lentulov et al.

Wreath-Stephanos: Exhibition organized in Moscow in 1907-08 with contributions by the Burliuks, Larionov, Lentulov, Yakulov et al.; also opened in St. Petersburg and other cities with a similar contingent.

Year 1915: Short title of "Exhibition. The Year 1915" organized by Kandaurov in Moscow in 1915 with contributions by Kamensky, Larionov, Lentulov, Malevich, Rozanova et al.

Zhivskulptarkh: Kollektiv zhiviopisno-skulpturno-arkhitekturnogo sinteza (Collective of Painting-Sculpture-Architecture Synthesis). Group founded in Moscow in 1919 consisting of Korolev, Krinsky, Ladovsky, Rodchenko, Shevchenko et al.

Sonia Delaunay: *Fabric Design No. 1*, ca. 1918 (No. 407)

17. Léon Bakst: Poster Advertising a *Dance Recital* by Caryathis (Elise Jouhandeau), ca. 1916 (No. 93)

18. Léon Bakst: Costume Design for One of the Bayadères Carrying a Peacock, *Le Dieu Bleu*, 1911 (No. 91)

19. Léon Bakst: Costume Design for the Péri, *La Péri*, 1911 (No. 90)

Conversation between Nina and Nikita Lobanov-Rostovsky and John E. Bowlt, London, 25 September, 2010

John: First of all, I want to thank Nina and Nikita for taking the time to be here today to talk to us. I have a few questions to ask Nina and Nikita with regard to the collection, with which they have lived for over fifty years — they more than I of course, but I have also been very close to the collection since 1970. Naturally, we have developed a very close working relationship and inasmuch as we have continued to work with the collection, publications, and exhibitions and so on, it seems logical and justifiable to talk about these things. So I have put together — compiled — a number of questions which I would like both Nina and Nikita to address, if they don't mind.

My very first question concerns, I suppose, the basic reason why Nina and Nikita collected, or to use American language, what has driven them to collect. What is the drive which makes them collect, to continue to collect, and what really stimulated them to collect all these years? Of course, there could be many answers to that basic question: financial investment, connoisseurship, a general wish to expose Russian art to the rest of the world. So, Nina, I wonder if you have an answer to that question: Where did the inspiration come from?

Nina: What really turned me on was I met a delightful young man in 1959 who seemed to talk about little else than Diaghilev and the Ballets Russes and the Diaghilev exhibition, which he had seen in 1954 in London and which had transformed his life. Fortunately, I was very fond of ballet and opera, too, and, therefore, listened attentively and became very interested in what he was telling me. Of course, eventually, I myself got hooked — to use the parlance — by the subject and became a helpmate. On my own I've really only gone against Nikita's wishes twice, when I acquired the designs for the *Tricorne,* which we can see on the walls around us and which are omitted from the catalogue raisonné because they are not Russian. Then some Exter costumes, because I wished to fill out the holdings we already had for *Aelita* (Ill. 66) — I saw those wonderful costumes at an auction in Paris and decided to buy them (Ills. 67-68). Most of the other things have been joint decisions. Later on, when we talk about costumes and what made us want to buy one thing and not the other, I will explain why I insisted on buying these particular pieces. But basically, it was love of two sorts: first of a human being and then falling in love with these wonderful pictures that he was showing me.

John: That's a very graceful answer. Thank you, Nina. So I guess, Nikita, we turn to you because you seem to have been fascinated by this subject even before you met Nina. So what was driving you before Nina?

Nikita: The impact of the Diaghilev exhibition, which I saw in London in 1954, left a very strong impression on me, possibly because I had just arrived from Bulgaria, where I had never been to a museum to see pictures hanging on the wall. What I saw attracted me so much that there and then I decided that one day I must have the same thing. It is one of the great satisfactions in life when such early ambitions ultimately come to fruition — it doesn't happen very often. Now, was it one-upmanship? For sure not, because at that time one could take little pride in owning such art, as, by and large, nobody was interested in it. We were living in America, where such art was available, but where there were very few buyers — in New York, for example, there were only three people who were buying it. A monetary investment? Not really,

20. Léon Bakst: Hunting Costume Design for the Duchess, *The Sleeping Princess*,
ca. 1921 (No. 99)

because back then it could not have been considered so. The amounts were so insignificant that, for people who had a normal salary, a $2 purchase of a costume by Goncharova was hardly considered an investment. To put it in perspective, a pen and ink drawing by Rembrandt in those days used to cost $1,200 dollars and such drawings were still available on the market. So, were we to have sought investments and were we to have had any money, I would have suggested that we collect 17th century works by Rembrandt and those of his contemporaries. As you may know, the *Financial Times* study of the values of paintings over two hundred years showed that Rembrandt is the one artist whose paintings have never experienced a price drop and consistently moved with inflation without major jumps up and down in value. Sensual attraction? For sure! You can't escape that in the designs of Léon Bakst. With the utmost elegance, they depict the sensuality germane to costume designs of the time. Were we tempted to show to Western audiences something new? Yes. Our first exhibition in New York was in 1966, six years after we had started collecting, followed by a larger exhibition at the Metropolitan Museum of Art in 1967. It then went on tour.

John: Thank you. Nina, do you wish to comment?

Nina: Yes, Mrs. Annemarie Pope of the International Exhibitions Foundation wrote to us asking whether she could tour our collection. We thought: how wonderful this person is for having noticed our collection. However, the real reason was that Mrs. Pope had been trying for years to have a connection with the Metropolitan Museum and tour some of their holdings. She had never managed to do this, so our exhibition presented her at last with an opportunity. Mrs. Pope toured the show and in later years, other parts of our collection to fifty American museums.

John: In some sense your commentary addresses the second question that I was going to ask you — a very general one about whether you both felt that your amazing efforts in collecting Russian art over so many years has been a rewarding experience. Did it satisfy some private, inner need or were you more concerned with the public at large? Nina, are you satisfied that the collection has appealed both to you and to a more universal public?

Nina: Of course it's a joy to live with these wonderful, colorful, dynamic pictures; and as I tend to live at home, see relatives and friends at home, I like having my books and pictures around me. But as for showing to the public, I'm not quite sure what to make of that. What I do know is that it has been wonderful to see the reaction or recognition from people who were established in the field of art. In 1970 we moved to 49 East 96th Street, where the Barrs were living. Alfred Barr came to see our paintings. I think that Nikita really felt gratified when Mr. Barr said, "You must go on. This is marvelous. I remember seeing such things in 1927 and 1928 in the USSR. This is important, an unexplored field of art." Barr was the first person to put Russian art in the mainstream, showing how, as a tributary, it flows into the main river of art. And then of course there wasn't only Mr. Barr. Bit by bit we met other people. Even before, in 1965 in Paris, at Anna Tcherkesoff's apartment, we met Professor Zilbershtein, a giant in Russian art history, who treated us as equals. He greeted Nikita and, after learning that we had been collecting and had many works by Benois, Zilbershtein, who greatly admired Benois, asked, "When did you buy your first Benois?" Nikita replied, "Well, actually it was Nina who bought our first Benois." After that Zilbershtein always treated me as a granddaughter. In 1970 we first went to the USSR on the invitation of the Central State Archive

21. Léon Bakst: Costume Design for Prince Charming at Court, *The Sleeping Princess*, ca. 1921 (No. 100)

of Literature and Art following the Metropolitan Museum exhibition. It took three years for the trip to be worked out. In Moscow we met other collectors like George Costakis and Yakov Rubinshtein, then Abram Chudnovsky and Solomon Shuster in Leningrad, David Sigalov and Gleb Ivakin in Kiev. They, of course, flew in a higher orbit, but it was a fellowship, as though we belonged to the same club. And they greatly respected Nikita because they were amazed at his passion for theatrical art. As every single Russian artist has done some theatrical design, they had to admit that yes, here was a valid field of collecting. I think that those relationships were very enriching and satisfying; and then, John, in 1970 you also walked into our lives and broadened our scope.

John: Nikita, do you want to add to that, has collecting been rewarding for you?

Nikita: Yes. In hindsight it has been extraordinarily rewarding. Look at it in context. Here are two young people with very limited resources. We lived on one salary and collected on the other. In practice, my salary at the bank was $86 a week after taxes. Nina's salary perhaps was a little bit less. Anyway, there we are after ten years of collecting with that type of budget — and the Metropolitan Museum of Art, one of the foremost art institutions of the world, is showing our collection. Now, you must admit this is almost a miracle. It is a phenomenal ego trip to be able to see the confirmation of the right choices that you have been betting on. And again, let us put it in context: that art was unknown and it was obliterated in its country of origin. In the Soviet Union you could not talk about, write about, or show it. So, with a minimal amount of knowledge, simply if we liked what we saw, we bought it. And the ultimate accolade — that the country which produced those artists, i.e. its government — bought our collection and at the price at which Sotheby's had valued it. So that again proved that what we had been collecting was relevant and worthwhile. Esthetically it has been a success, as the collection was shown in more than fifty museums in the United States, plus museums in Japan, Europe, and Canada, as well as twice in Russia. And then, Russia buys it. I feel that the privations that Nina and I imposed on ourselves in order to buy pictures for our collection, plus the great amount of time and effort in gathering Russian stage design, were all worth it. So, it has been a supremely rewarding experience, John.

John: It is wonderful to hear that. Of course we will return to this question of the collection in its Russian home, perhaps in a minute. But, Nina, did you want to add a qualification?

Nina: I think I would like to add something essential about the show at the Metropolitan Museum. I would like to pay tribute to the late John J. McKendry, an extremely gifted and original curator. We met McKendry through James Rorimer's niece Edie Dushkin, who was working at the *Reader's Digest* with me. Edie asked whether she could bring McKendry to see our watercolors. McKendry was curator in the Prints and Drawings Department of the Metropolitan Museum of Art. When he came to see our designs, he immediately said, "Oh, but this is wonderful! Have they been exhibited?" Nikita replied, "No." McKendry then said, "Well, I would like, if possible, for us to have an exhibition at the Metropolitan Museum." And he went ahead and made it happen. This man, who was in charge of prints in this vast institution, looked at this group of theatrical watercolor designs and saw something in them, something that made him want to exhibit them. Therefore, I would want to make sure that John McKendry's name is in this conversation, because it was his eye and enthusiasm that made the exhibition possible, thereby confirming Nikita's original vision.

22. Léon Bakst: Costume Design for a Female Dancer Holding the Train of Her Dress,
Artémis Troublée, 1922 (No. 102)

John: I'd like to move on to a perhaps more glamorous question regarding the high point or zenith of your, how can I say, acquisition program. You have both been collecting for many years now and have witnessed many ups and downs in the market and in the whole process of acquiring these works. I am sure that both of you have fond memories of high points — of certain intersections, meetings, episodes that you remember with great fervor and that, you feel, perhaps influenced the direction of your collection or have remained, let's say, the centerpieces in the necklace of the collection. So, Nina, I would like to begin with you: Do you have some very poignant memory that you feel is of particular interest to you, one which you would like to perpetuate vis-à-vis the collection?

Nina: I think that one of the most exciting moments for me was when Nikita returned from Milan, having managed to purchase most of the working sketches for the costumes and stage designs for *Petrouchka* that, for some reason, the Scala Museum was letting go. The Joffrey ballet in New York bought the actual costumes and décors, while we got the blueprints, so to speak. This was exciting because *Petrouchka* is my favorite ballet and I like Alexandre Benois's work so much. Both Nikita and I enjoyed the chase. But besides the connoisseurial challenge of identifying unsigned drawings piled unsorted at a dealer's store, or picking out a misattributed watercolor in an international sale, there were other instances of real serendipity. It happened to me when I decided to acquire the folio of Picasso's silkscreens for *Tricorne* you see on the walls around you. Incredible though it seems, it ultimately cost me nothing, due to a cataloguing mistake, but that is another story. Now, what is very interesting — and I've noticed this over time — is that, basically, what we collected were seemingly the blueprints for costumes and for set designs. Yet, many of these items are not really blueprints. Many of Bakst's things are very pretty pictures that he made for exhibitions or duplicates of famous costumes made at the request of wealthy collectors. Whereas Benois — his costume sketches and Picasso's are blueprints. They are for the costumier, sometimes with instructions written on them, explaining materials to be used and embroidery. These are not pretty designs for sale, these are working sketches. And there is a great difference in the collection between the blueprints that are working sketches and others that are attractive designs and, usually, one doesn't differentiate between them. But this is something I've become aware of and it's what has made me like the Benois pieces so much because they were real working sketches.

John: Thank you, Nina, and thank you for that happy memory. Nikita, did you want to add something? Probably you also remember a high point?

Nikita: As to the zenith in our collecting career I could relate one such event that made our hearts palpitate. In the summer of 1966 we stopped for a lemonade in a café in Athens in Stadio Street called "Petrograd". We chose it from a number of other cafés in the street because of its Russian name. Whilst we waited for the waiter to bring us lemonade, I looked at the walls and I could hardly believe my eyes — for what was on the walls were costume designs that to me looked like Tchelitchew. They were unsigned. And ultimately it proved to be so. We got to know the owner, Mr. Niki Yakovlev. In his office above the café was a huge collection of Russian costume designs. That's where we bought one Tchelitchew and missed the three Kandinskys which he had. My heart also palpitated (to add to Nina's story), when on one of my periodic visits to Nicola Benois at his office at the Scala, he proudly told me that they were staging *Petrouchka* with new designs. So I said, "How come? You staged it

23. Vladimir Baranoff-Rossiné, Stage Design on the Theme of the Birth of Venus (No. 108)

some 15-20 years ago. You must still have all the costume designs, all the sketches." He replied, "Well, we have a budget for a new production. Why not?" Then I asked him, "What are you going to do then with the old décor designs and the costumes?" "Well, we usually chuck them out." Just before I left for Italy, Robert Joffrey told us that he was having difficulties in staging *Petrouchka* in New York because Massine had only about seventeen of Benois's sketches. But, as you know, there are over one hundred costume designs in that ballet, a prologue curtain plus three décors. So I asked Benois, if he would sell the whole production which Milan was going to throw away for $5,000. He said, "Done." I was able to make that offer because I knew that Joffrey's budget was $20,000! So, this is how Joffrey got the *vestimenta* plus décor, while we got the sketches. That was a wonderful coincidence and Joffrey sent Nina a bouquet of a hundred white roses to say thank you.

Nina: In all programs ever since, whenever the Joffrey company stages *Petrouchka,* they mention Nikita in the credits. Anyway, back to Nikita seeing the Tchelitchews on the wall of the Petrograd – I'm thinking of another episode, when you, Nikita, were wandering down the streets of Paris on the Left Bank and were staring at some old programs in a secondhand bookstore...

Nikita: Hard to believe. That was 1966. A shabbily dressed man approached me, asking, "Are you interested in what you're seeing?" Among the programs in the bookstore was the one for the 1907 Diaghilev production of *Khovanshchina* (Ills. 78-80) in Paris and of *Boris Godunov* in 1908. I said, "Yes, I am," and the man told me, "Follow me." We walked around to a warehouse — and there we saw huge designs. What do I mean by huge? Two meters by a meter and a half. Fedorovsky's designs for *Khovanshchina*. The price he asked was minimal, but the problem was how to move them. So I phoned my uncle who came with his car and we put them on the roof. That was a fabulous find. What the Russians call a *nakhodka*!

Nina: Actually, some of Fedorovsky's costumes are at the Centre National du Costume de Scène in Moulins, the actual costumes used at the Théâtre des Champs-Elysées. I'm seeing them next week when I travel to France. Fedorovsky was one of those who went back to Russia before the First World War and he took most of his sketches with him. So, there are very few Fedorovskys abroad.

Nikita: Still, on the other hand, some people simply were only too happy to give away the designs they had. For example, we visited Bilinsky's daughter in France, tracking her down after her six changes of address. She was very surprised to see that somebody would be so interested in her father's art. We were there with Viscount Georges-Martin du Nord and I felt that legally, if we did not pay even a minimal amount, there could be problems for us. So I begged her to accept $10 per design, which she did reluctantly (Ill. 8). She was only too happy that somebody else might assume responsibility for the welfare of the pictures. It just shows you what the situation was in the 1950s and the 1960s in the field of Russian costume and stage design. Remember that in the Soviet Union there was only one collector of this type of art, Dr. Levitin in Leningrad.

John: Was it a collection of exclusively theater design?

Nikita: Yes, he had over 3,000 designs, mostly of the 1950s and 1960s.

24. Alexandre Benois: Design for the Catalog of *The Diaghilev Exhibition*, 1954 (No. 159)

Nikita: In those days we had a very small flat in New York. Keeping all these big designs was difficult. I therefore gave three large Fedorovskys to the Wadsworth Atheneum in Hartford, Connecticut.

Nina: John knew us at 49 East 96th Street. Before that we had a flat only twice the size of this room.

Nikita: So, actually, our Exters were hanging on the stairs and on the landing.

John: These were happy moments, but I suppose that we should also address negative moments. We start with you, Nina. Were there any anticlimaxes, desperate moments, profound disappointments or mistakes during your years of acquisition? Does something bother you still?

Nina: Yes, I talked Nikita out of acquiring a Bakst that he liked, because of its fantastic colors and I hated it because of its angularity, and that's the great Firebird figure. It's not a working sketch. It's one of these pictures made, I think, for sale and exhibition at Brentano's or whatever. But it belonged to Mrs. Havemeyer and she was selling it and it would have meant emptying out our small savings account. But that wasn't the reason I said no. I just disliked it. It was ugly, I thought. Then Nikita said, "Well, it is angular, but the design is wonderful, it's so Russian." Well, you know, we have equal votes and I said no, I really couldn't live with that. So he didn't buy it and, of course, it is considered one of the very great Bakst costumes. That was definitely a mistake on my part.

John: The one at the Museum of Modern Art?

Nina: Yes. Anyway I know I was wrong and Nikita was right. I will always regret that we were so incredibly ignorant. George Riabov, a fellow collector, was *kulturnyi*; he knew about art, had studied it, and had a BA in art. We knew the names of the major Russian artists, but we did not know their works. It was impulse buying, a lot of it. I will always regret that we didn't understand enough about Exter at the time. We could have bought the whole Exter *atelier*. And even more so that Nikita arranged for Chauvelin and Nakov to buy from Lissim all the Exters. Well, you know, we could have had some major Exters on our walls. But we have theatrical ones, which are top quality. Had we had a bit more art historical knowledge and better paid jobs, we might have tried to borrow money from relatives, well-off friends or even borrow from a bank against our salaries, like a mortgage, but we didn't dare.

Nikita: We were embarrassed to ask someone for a loan for pictures. For instance, when we saw those designs in Athens in the café Petrograd, we were staying with one of the foremost wealthy Greek families in Athens. But we couldn't make ourselves ask them for a loan, so, as I have just mentioned, on that visit we bought only one design by Tchelitchew (Ill. 217) — which was chosen for the cover of the catalog of the Metropolitan Museum exhibition. To buy it, we used the last $100 traveler's check we had with us. So, subsequently, I had to buy some of the Tchelitchews from Georges-Martin du Nord that he had bought from Yakovlev. There have been many lost opportunities. We could have bought all the *atelier* of Exter rather than just selected pieces. Similarly, we could have bought three-fourths of Bakst's studio from his nephew and nieces. Their attitude to their uncle's work at the time

25. Alexandre Benois: Costume Designs for One of the Ladies and Gentlemen in
Waiting at the Court of Armide, *Le Pavillon d'Armide*, 1907 (No. 129)

was lukewarm. Kliachko (Bakst's nephew) had inherited works which he kept on the balcony under a tarpaulin! The nieces kept their lots in their flats and I could probably have bought hundreds of designs, but we did not have the money. The same thing with Mrs. Tomilina in 1958 — $2 a Goncharova design, which was to do her a favor because one walked over Goncharova designs in the flat full of junk (Ills. 92-96).

John: Ah, because she didn't like Goncharova.

Nikita: $2 at the time equaled Fr1,000, but I assure you we didn't have that kind of money. So, we have had many opportunities that were missed. I feel that our collection of Russian theatrical art would have been even greater, had we had the means we have today. Well, perhaps that made us more careful. We spent a lot of time studying, seeking information. You know yourself that in the 1950s and 1960s you had to buy all the old programs to learn who had been performing when and what. These were the leads that we started from. Today, I envy collectors. They just go to the internet and have whatever they want. For us there was nobody to ask.

John: I know. I remember that myself. We might come back to the question of resources of knowledge later — leading on from the question I have just asked regarding the high points and the low points, I'd like to turn to Nina again and ask whether you feel there are major gaps, omissions, in the collection or whether, basically, as a reflection of Russian stage design everything is covered.

Nina: I believe that as a reflection of Russian stage design, basically the major artists who worked on the Russian stage — we have them. Except perhaps Polenov. We don't have a Polenov as it's very difficult to buy one, and until recently we didn't have a Kandinsky, but I don't feel that there are important lacunae in our collection.

John: What about you, Nikita? Do you agree that there is nothing serious which is missing?

Nikita: Correct. We have almost two hundred painters in our collection and the reason why we don't have a Polenov is that in fifty years of collecting there's never been a largish Polenov of quality for sale. Yes, frequently there have been small ones, A5 in size, but I never thought they were representative enough in order to have them in the collection. Hence I was very pleased to hear one of the employees of the Theater Museum in St. Petersburg, Elena Grushvitskaia, when they were checking our collection prior to the Russian government buying it, say, "But this is a museum within a museum that you have here and not a collection."

John: I'm glad to hear that, as far as you're concerned, the collection is comprehensive and has no serious omissions. Which is very important if we think of it as a teaching collection, as a didactic instrument. Now, I do have another question that is personal in a sense, I guess. Sometimes I'm rather romantic in my attitude towards the collection. Perhaps for Nikita it's less evident what I have in mind. But for both of you, I'm wondering whether you could think of any — how can I say — magic moments, secrets, incomprehensible designs, costumes that you felt to be absurd in the sense that they could never been constructed on stage? Or whether you can think of any surprises, for example,

26. Alexandre Benois: Stage Design for Armide's Garden, Scene II, *Le Pavillon d'Armide*, 1909 (No. 139)

a certain artist who was famous as a studio painter and here you find him suddenly as a stage designer. So, I was wondering, Nina, whether you have any surprises of that kind as you were collecting all these years, surprises that prompted you to exclaim, "Ah, this is very strange!"

Nina: Yes. I certainly had surprises, or at least I was intrigued and mystified when we acquired costume designs for Larionov's *Chout* because I couldn't understand how people could dance in them. I couldn't understand the whole point of these costumes. Then later I read Serge Grigoriev, the *régisseur*, who reminisced that all the dancers complained about dancing in them, and, indeed, *Chout* was not a success. Years later, when I saw the wonderful collection of *Chout* costumes at the Victoria and Albert Museum repository at Olympia, Sarah Woodcock, who was then in charge of the costumes, explained that nearly always (there are exceptions like *The Rite of Spring* and other ballets) — nearly always the costumes one sees that people have collected, are the costumes of the unsuccessful ballets. Because they weren't used a lot and, therefore, survived. *Chout* (Ills. 128-130), I think, was danced five times, perhaps? So they weren't subjected to the stresses and strains of dancing, ripping them off to quickly put on the next costume for the next scene. They weren't sweated into, so the cloth hasn't suffered. And, therefore, in the exhibition today at the Victoria and Albert Museum, if one were to judge merely by quantity and quality of the *Chout* costumes, you might think: Oh, this is a very successful ballet, not realizing that it was because it was unsuccessful that the costumes are still so beautiful. So this was for me an enigma. I never quite understood until I met Sarah Woodcock and heard her talk, as she does brilliantly on the subject, and with breadth and depth of knowledge, about the relationship between the blueprints and the costumes, and why, for some of these wonderful blueprints there are no costumes. Now I know.

John: Yes, one of those paradoxes. Another question that interests me and which I would like to ask of both of you, is how you confront a work of art that becomes available. Let's say that it's a design for a costume or a set design or a prop. What really induces you at that particular moment to acquire that piece or not to acquire it. In other words, are you guided by a sudden flash of inspiration? Are you guided by a divine power, by scientific knowledge, by a friend whispering over your shoulder or, perhaps, by a financial issue? Nina, how would you answer that question? What really makes you acquire that particular work at that particular moment?

Nina: I like it or I don't like it — and that's it. Yes, recently there've been lots of monographs and studies, one learns so much more, but the eye can be cluttered by what the mind knows. True, we did the major part of our collecting before so much information was available. One could read two or three books and, as Nikita said, there were the programs. We studied these and looked at them again and again, always asking ourselves whether we still liked the piece. But basically, what attracted me was the color and the design, a gut reaction. Not all art historians, I am sure, have this capacity.

Nikita: I'll give you a good example of what Nina said. In about 1963 we went with George Riabov to Petr Pavlovich Tretyakov in his New York gallery, where he had a number of theatrical works for sale. Two designs had the same price: $100. One was a prologue curtain for *Petrouchka* (Ill. 28). The other was a small version of the stunning Bakst stage design

La Pavillon
d'Armide

(Version de
Paris)
1909.

Le Marquis
en
Roi
Hidrao

Alexandre
Benois

27. Alexandre Benois: Costume Design for the Marquis de Fierbois Dressed as King
Hydrao in the Land of Dreams, *Le Pavillon d'Armide*, 1909 (No. 142)

for *The Blue God,* which you must have seen yesterday at the exhibition at the Victoria and Albert. with those snakes coming down from the cliffs. We both decided on the Benois, and George Riabov was delighted to buy the Bakst. So this confirms to you that we were really buying with the heart, because marketwise the Bakst even then must have been three times more valuable than the Benois, particularly a piece for *Petrouchka,* which he designed fourteen times. Forty-five years later the Benois has just kept up with inflation, whereas the Bakst design would fetch at least a hundred times more at auction.

John: One spoke to you and the other did not.

Nina: No, I think there we let our minds close our eye, because for the eye the Bakst one was more beautiful. But this was a prologue curtain for *Petrouchka, Petrouchka* — ooh!

Nikita: This approach prevailed for the first ten years. Subsequently we had your guidance, when you mentioned that with the critical mass we had already acquired, we had a substantial collection — which was reaching a significance beyond a collection for personal enjoyment. You suggested that we start broadening it and going into the so-called Russian avant-garde. At the time, esthetically, it was not something that I was particularly drawn to. But we started buying then and rounding up and expanding our collection numerically. Because initially, we were focused on the twenty-one Russian artists amongst the forty designers that had worked with Diaghilev, as we intended to have every Russian designer that had worked with Diaghilev with some of his or her representative pieces.

John: I think, we have all been aware of the fact that certainly in the 1960s and 1970s information about these artists and these productions was very scant indeed and that it could take days, if not weeks, to find the death date of an artist, for example. It was a difficult process of acquiring knowledge, producing biographies for artists and talking about productions, simply because you had to go through libraries and archives, and so on and so forth. Now, as we know, it's very different today, because we have the internet, we have regular auctions of Russian art, where in many cases Russian stage designs appear, we have more scholars, both in Russia especially and in the West, who are working in this field, and there are many more books now as sources of possible information. So, I'm wondering whether this has changed your attitude towards the field of Russian stage design, and I address this question first to Nina. In a sense, perhaps the subject was more romantic, more mysterious, more attractive, simply because it was forbidden fruit. But today it's all become so instantaneous. Does that detract from your relationship to the collection? Or on the contrary, the accessibility of information, the information boom, makes it perhaps closer to you, more immediate? Would you like to comment on that?

Nina: It hasn't changed my attitude in any way, because all the publications about stage design (and some of the best ones are by you, John), basically, at one point or another refer to our collection: they take illustrations from it, comment on it. So, I feel as if we were the seminal thing, this is publication data. We were there in the pioneering days. There were theater sales for many years at Sotheby's, but they stopped about five or six years ago. Having reached their peak in 1995, Russian stage designs have gone down and now the new Russians or, excuse me, the Russians who are buying today, like large

28. Alexandre Benois: Design for the Backdrop for the Fair, Scenes 1 and 4, *Petrouchka*, 1947 (No. 162)

29. Alexandre Benois: Design for the Backdrop for Petrouchka's Room, Scene 2, *Petrouchka*, 1948 (No. 163)

30. Alexandre Benois: Design for the Backdrop for the Moor's Room, *Petrouchka*, 1956 (No. 165)

31. Alexandre Benois: Curtain Design with Night Scene with Fantastic Creatures in the Sky and with the Admiralty Tower in the Background, *Petrouchka*, 1957 (No. 166)

32. Alexandre Benois: Stage detail: Petrouchka Kissing the Ballerina, *Petrouchka*, 1945 (No. 171)

59

oil paintings to hang in their offices so people can see them and so on. I'm generalizing, of course. There are people who buy works of art on paper, but very few and, therefore, many stage designs today are worth less than they were half a dozen years ago. Benois has not moved with inflation. Bakst is one of those who has, but even he has come way down in price. On the whole it's not a field that the new market is interested in. So it hasn't really changed my attitude one way or another. I feel exactly as I did a dozen years ago before things slowed down.

John: Do you tend to agree, Nikita, that all this has not influenced your personal attitude?

Nikita: Correct. Not at all. All the new information that is available today simply reinforces our original concentration and is an affirmation of our taste. The fact that publications today continuously refer to, and illustrate, what we have collected over time indirectly confirms this. The question of price doesn't even come into it. Whether or not some pieces cost us so much money doesn't make it more or less esthetically attractive.

John: It's very refreshing to hear that. I'd like to ask the penultimate question, which is a loaded one, a difficult and complicated question in the sense that the collection is now in Russia and was acquired by the Russian government and, ostensibly, for public consumption in Russia. I know this was a long and burdensome decision, but the decision was taken and the collection moved from West to East. I think that some of us had hoped that the collection would remain in the West for Western consumption inasmuch so many people in the West do not know about Russian stage design, Russian art. Therefore, wouldn't it have been wonderful to have given the Western audience access to such an extraordinary and brilliant collection? But never mind. It is in Russia. Nina, I'd like to ask you in all frankness a very difficult question: What is your attitude to the fact that this collection is now permanently in Russia and returned to the country of its birth? Are you pleased or not?

Nina: I was unhappy with the sale because of where the 810 items were going — the Konstantin Palace outside St. Petersburg, where they have no conception of how to treat a work of art on paper. They have no light, or temperature, or humidity control. I was happier when we managed to get the buyer to agree to store it at the Theater Museum in St. Petersburg until 2013, giving the Konstantin Foundation time to build an equipped art center. You refer to the "collection". The collection had 1093 pieces of which thirty-one *Sadko* designs by Alexandre Benois plus five others were sold off or lost over the years. Only four-fifths were sold to Russia. The 212 pieces that I own remained here at Oakwood Court. I was not willing to let my beloved Petrouchkas dry up and fade away in the Konstantin Palace. Should the purchaser of the collection see fit one day to loan it to the Museum in perpetuity, then I would agree to these 212 pictures going there. Furthermore, it is not quite correct to say that it went back to its country of origin for at least one-third of the pieces sold were created abroad by Russian émigré artists. Sorry to reply negatively to this question. Nikita feels differently and that is why, ultimately, I agreed to sell my part of what we owned jointly. Well, perhaps they have gone home in the sense that no one quite looks at Russian art the way the Russians do. I remember people at the Pushkin Museum of Fine Arts in Moscow and the Manège in Leningrad coming with their children on their shoulders, showing them this picture and that, and welcoming it to Russia. But at that time the collection was not in the hands where it is now.

33. Alexandre Benois: Costume Design for Petrouchka, *Petrouchka* (No. 180)

34. Alexandre Benois: Costume Design for the Ballerina, *Petrouchka*, 1947 (No. 181)

35. Alexandre Benois: Costume Design for the Moor, *Petrouchka*, 1945 (No. 184)

John: Nikita, would you like to comment on this? Are you happy that the collection is in the hands of Mother Russia now?

Nikita: Yes, I am. Now, to address your main question: As you know, the Library of Congress had contemplated acquiring the collection. But it so happened that we received an offer in writing from Russia rather than from Washington, D.C., and hence we replied to Russia affirmatively. I am delighted that the collection was bought in Russia. Similarly to Nina, I'm saddened that it is kept in conditions different to those outlined in the sale contract. I hope that eventually the Konstantin Foundation will realize that they are not geared to be the custodians of this collection, because at least it is housed in the Theater Museum until they build their center, which is supposed to be somewhat like Lincoln Center with exhibition halls, performances, libraries, and so forth. I think that it will be legally impossible for the Konstantin Foundation to give the collection in perpetuity to the Theater Museum, while retaining its ownership. In other words, the Konstantin Foundation may lend it to the Theater Museum whilst retaining it on its balance sheets. That would be a very good solution because the Theater Museum in St. Petersburg has stated publicly that our collection complements theirs. They have a vast collection, but they don't have so many pieces of the Diaghilev and émigré artists represented in our collection. The dedicated space at the Theater Museum in St. Petersburg offers a good resting place for our collection. Nevertheless, there are significant snags. The Theater Museum is not equipped with air-conditioning and presents a great hazard to works on paper, because temperature fluctuations there can be more than 45° Centigrade, from +40°C in the summer to -5°C in the winter. Whether they in time (2012-13) receive funds in order to have air-conditioning installed and keep the collection in better circumstances, I do not know. I will continue to bring up this topic with the Foundation. We will see what will happen. But on balance, I am very happy with this outcome.

Nina: Well, what I'm worried about all the time is that the collection might suddenly be dispersed. They may fail to build the center, they may decide not to go on lending it to the Theater Museum. Nothing to stop them.

John: Well, we're down to the ultimate question on my shopping list, which is a rather facetious question, but it may touch on things that are dear to the hearts of Nina and Nikita. The question is this: If for some curious reason you were both exiled to the utmost island of the Outer Hebrides in the cold North Sea and forever, but the court that exiled you allowed you to take one item from your collection, then I would be very interested to know what that choice would be. So, Nina, what would you take with you?

Nina: One design would have to be *The Coq d'Or* stage design by Goncharova (Ill. 87), which usually hangs on that wall because it encapsulates all the joy and the joyousness of Diaghilev stage production, and the Russian colors, and everything that a certain group of Russian artists were known for. And then I would of course like to have one *Petrouchka* (Ill. 28) stage set just to remind me of Benois and St. Petersburg — the fairground of the time of Nicholas I, all that other kind of Russianness.

John: Nikita, what would be your choice on your island?

Petrouchka

Covent Garden 1913

N°7
(Liste Inzenhof 11)

Second Organ Grinder

Второй Шарманщик

↓ clochettes

cuivre

drap
en
loques

très
usé

Alexandre Benois
1911 - 1916

Perelin Reconstruct
1914

36. Alexandre Benois: Costume Design for the Second Barrel Organ Grinder, *Petrouchka* (No. 189)

65

37. Alexandre Benois: Costume Design for One of the Blue Mandarins, *Le Rossignol*, 1914 (No. 281)

38. Alexandre Benois: Costume Design for the Third Japanese Envoy, *Le Rossignol*, 1914 (No. 283)

Nikita: My choice would be to have a stage design for *Chout* by Larionov, in which the Chout is selling his whip to the gullible peasants (Ill. 128). For me it's joyful, colorful and it synthesizes most of those qualities that I like in Russian stage design. But for me also it is very important that you were kind enough to propose an outer island in the Hebrides, as opposed to somewhere within Russia like Vorkuta or Solovki, to be exposed to the terrible conditions there and to be sucked bloodless by mosquitoes.

John: Do you feel that you have left a legacy of universal value with your collection?

Nikita: There are certain facts that are worthwhile mentioning. What is the merit of our having created our collection? One, it is a massive physical accumulation. But that physical accumulation was prompted by the fact that we realized very early, in late 1950s, that what we were collecting and what was available on the market had a relevance within Western art and, more specifically, within Russian art. Many other people could have done the same thing, many other people had much more knowledge and funds, and possibilities to travel to acquire such things, but did not do it. We did — and I think this is probably our foremost merit, i.e. that we attained this goal long before anyone else did.

John: I think that one asset lies in the fact that, in producing this extraordinary collection, you have demonstrated to the world that Russian art is not out on the limb somewhere in some remote province, but is very much part of the European mainstream. I think that's graphically represented by the collection itself. It must have been appealing to Western viewers and American ones in particular. Otherwise the International Exhibition Foundation over those twenty years would not have shown it in fifty museums throughout the United States. In retrospect I'm very puzzled: How come that there were no others collecting exclusively Russian theatrical art? Maybe there were many other opportunities in other fields?

Nikita: For example, in France, René Guerra could have done it. He had the funds. He became a phenomenal accumulator of pictures, and much more importantly, literary archives. He created a large and diversified repository of Russian history. In New York, George Riabov had the same opportunities that we did. He specialized in easel painting, probably because he had already an artistic background. He studied art history at university. I was a geologist: I had no connection to art whatsoever; and had I had, I probably would have followed Riabov's example. I would have collected Borovikovsky, Levitsky, and Tropinin, and bought all the marvelous pictures in the Ansonia Hotel from Mrs. Kamyshnikova. But no, we went for something different. After we were married, we could also have been buying easel art such as Sverchkov's *Troika,* the first oil that I bought from Mr. Tyutchev. But the ballet designs were a consensus with Nina and me. Collecting the Realist art of the *peredvizhniki* would be a dead bore for Nina because their equivalent in France, the Barbizon School, is similar in spirit and style, but much better.

Nina: Could there be something about the fact that we were both very fond of ballet and opera? We used to go a lot to the New York City Ballet, the Balanchine company. We loved his ballets but we always regretted the fact that there were very basic costumes and no décor, because a visual feast is a pleasant thing. Balanchine was such an extraordinary choreographer that his ballets never degenerated into just gymnastics, whereas a lot of these modern plotless ballets with no costumes or backdrop end up looking a bit like gymnastics.

John: Fascinating. I'm glad that both of you are naming the various personages who were part of the trajectory of your acquisitions, people like Mr. Vladimir Hessen and Mrs. Pope. Actually, I wanted to ask you since I also met Mrs. Pope very briefly: How did she relate to the collection? Did she come to your apartment and say suddenly, "Aah! We must do an exhibition!"

Nina: We did mention when answering your earlier question that Mrs. Pope got in touch with us when an exhibition was in the process of being organized for the Metropolitan Museum and then asked if she could stage the exhibition, pay the expenses, and, in exchange, show it afterwards in some museums in the USA. Mrs. Pope had studied at the Kunsthistorisches Institut at the University of Vienna, which turned out many art historians. I think she considered our collection second-class art, but she realized somehow that it was sexy, that people came and always all the catalogs were sold. She said that she never made a loss on touring our collection. She had organized the International Exhibitions Foundation in Washington, D.C. This was in the days when American curators rarely crossed the Atlantic. She had her contacts in New York, and in Europe. She was married to Mr. John Pope, director of the Freer Gallery. Mrs. Pope traveled to Europe every year and always stayed at the best hotels and ate at the best restaurants. That is tax-deductible in the US, if you have a profitable foundation, which she did. When we moved to England, she was no longer touring our collection, but she used to touch base with us and invite us to dinner at the grill of the Connaught Hotel near the American Embassy and pick our brains about interesting exhibitions we had seen during our travels. She was a remarkably resourceful person and a force in the American museum world of her time.

Nikita: Very significant. While she may have considered our art to be low-grade, she always made money exhibiting our collection. This is why she came again, and again, and again.

John: Well, Nina and Nikita, surely, our conversation has come full circle. This afternoon we have touched upon many topics and issues pertaining to the history of Russian stage design, but my single and parting observation would be to add that your collection is also a visual feast – and one which, for half a century, has brought moments of satisfaction to so many people in so many countries.

Sonia Delaunay: *Fabric Design No. 2*, ca. 1918 (No. 408)

40. Alexandre Benois: Set Design for Act II, *La Dame aux Camélias*, 1923 (No. 289)

RUSSIAN STAGE DESIGN 1880-1930

Preamble

The majority of the artists represented in the Lobanov-Rostovsky collection achieved international recognition as stage designers and most of the works discussed here were, precisely, set and costume projects for ballets, operas, dramas, the circus, movies, cabarets, and other kinds of theatrical spectacle. But what is stage design and to what exactly does it relate — to the physical stage, the actor, the audience, or all these elements together? Is it the mere illustrating of a plot that makes the action on stage more appealing, more convincing? Should sets and costumes decorate and entertain in their own right? Such questions are difficult to answer because the sheer diversity of theatrical forms precludes a single, comprehensive response. Perhaps, in any case, stage design as a whole is, inevitably, a fragmentary and "inconsequential" discipline inasmuch as a set or costume design that comes down to us is already divorced from its living context. As Yurii Annenkov observed in one of his deliberations on the theater:

> Essentially, each theatrical production is like a butterfly. It comes to life one evening and within three or four hours vanishes forever. No murals, no sketches or cinematographic films can provide an accurate recording of the production.[3]

Consequently, we tend to examine a stage design for its visual appeal rather than for its degree of functionality in the sequence of the spectacle — which, in many cases, cannot be remembered or reconstructed. Looking at Léon Bakst's sensuous costumes for *Cléopâtre* (Ills. 10, 11; Nos. 75-79) or *Schéhérazade* (Ills. 12, 13; Nos. 81-84), Boris Bilinsky's sparkling backdrop for *Ruslan and Liudmila* (Ill. 47; No. 377) or Mikhail Larionov's vibrant group of dancers for *Le Soleil de Nuit* [Midnight Sun] (Ill. 122; No. 703), we suspend our disbelief and almost disregard the question as to how they would have functioned on stage, in three-dimensional space. But, albeit approximately, we can at least try to identify a given stage design with one of the two fundamental approaches to the subject — with the painted décor deriving from the decorative fresco or with the plastic décor deriving from architecture.[4] Whether we interpret a set or costume as plane or volume, and however we define its task (as a principal mover of the action, as an auxiliary illustration, or as an independent esthetic object) the Russian contribution is extraordinary, and the Lobanov-Rostovsky collection is ample testimony to this.

The collection covers over fifty years of stage design with a concentration on the period 1905-25, when the constellation of radical personalities and ideas known as the avant-garde changed the face of Russian culture. Indeed, the activities of the artists included in these two volumes encompass the entire history of modern Russian art from Neo-Nationalism and Symbolism through Cubo-Futurism and Suprematism to Constructivism and Socialist Realism: Bakst, Alexandre Benois, Alexandra Exter, Pavel Filonov, Natalia Goncharova, Konstantin Korovin, Larionov, Kazimir Malevich, Liubov Popova, Alexander Rodchenko, and Vladimir Tatlin formulated bold new perceptions of art and design. Their theories revolutionized conventional attitudes toward painting,

---

3 Yu. Annenkov. Untitled, undated manuscript in RGALI, f. 2618, op. 1, ed. khr. 15, l. 147.
4 G6, pp. 9-10.

41. Alexandre Benois Costume Design for the Ethiopian, *Le Médecin malgré lui*, 1923 (No. 283)

sculpture, architecture, and the applied arts, and contributed to the international prestige of the Russian stage just before and after the Revolution of October, 1917. The Imperial Ballet, Savva Mamontov's Private Opera, Nikita Baliev's Chauve-Souris cabaret, Vera Komissarzhevskaia's Theater, Sergei Diaghilev's Ballets Russes, Alexander Tairov's Chamber Theater, Vsevolod Meierkhold's Theater of the RSFSR No.1 — these enterprises are unthinkable without the cooperation of such artists.

Some of them worked both in Russia and in the West. For example, a total of twenty-two Russian-born artists worked for Diaghilev and the Ballets Russes, often relying on Western methods and technology to realize their ideas. Yet, at heart, they remained Russian; they depicted Russian motifs, alluded frequently to Russian art forms, and even their color combinations and figural stylizations were often derived immediately from domestic traditions. In addition, many Russian designers turned repeatedly to their rich legacy of myth and ritual in the land of the midnight sun. Like Ivan Tsarevich in the fairy-tale, they invoked the magic favors of the Firebird (*L'Oiseau de Feu*, Ill. 100; Nos. 370, 391, 533, 569, 739, 1156), receiving the Firebird's consolation and inspiration. It was this "Russianness," especially the riot of colors and vibrant forms, that astounded and captivated the audiences at the Saisons Russes in Paris, London, and New York. The imprint was permanent, prompting the theater historian Léon Moussinac to declare summarily in 1931 that "Les réalisations théâtrales des russes ont eu une énorme influence en Europe et en Amérique."[5]

The purpose of this introductory essay is to provide a broad assessment of the scenic renaissance that the Russians achieved during the Modernist period (late 19th through early 20th centuries). The text is divided into four major chronological sections of particular periods during the development of the modern Russian theater (the 19th century cultural legacy, the *fin de siècle*, the avant-garde experiments of ca. 1908-1920, and the post-Revolutionary period), and is intended to serve as a general background to the extensive data provided in the catalogue raisonné of Volume II.

---

5 G14, p. 21.

Sonia Delaunay: *Fabric Design No. 3*, ca. 1918 (No. 409)

42. Nicola Benois: Costume Design for the General, *Amour et Hiérarchie.* ca. 1924 (No. 345)

1. BETWEEN EAST AND WEST

Imperial Predilections

On a state visit to the city of Kharkov in the 1830s, Tsar Nicholas I made an official inspection of the university building. Halting in front of its august facade, he suddenly remarked, "Your university has too many windows facing West." "Your Imperial Majesty," was the hurried rejoinder, "these are false windows."[6]

This episode, whether apocryphal or not, points to two salient features of Russian cultural and social ritual: the ambivalent attitude towards the West and the urge to disguise or redesign the world of actual appearances. Russia's constant oscillation between East and West, Slavophilism and Westernism, patriarchal tradition and contemporary technology, has been, since at least the time of Ivan the Terrible (reigned 1547-84), an identifying characteristic of Russian culture and a vital source for its national character.

The resulting dualism left its imprint on many of Russia's artistic achievements, not least, the applied arts — landscape architecture, propaganda art, book illustration, and, of course, stage design. Even the thoroughly "Russian" Kremlin in Moscow was designed in part by Italian architects (e.g. the Palace of the Facets), and perhaps the very incongruity of the heavy Baroque and Neo-Classical edifices rising from the marshes of St. Petersburg with Greek and Roman statues transplanted from the Mediterranean sunshine to the fastnesses of Russia's winter epitomizes this fundamental dichotomy. Yet it is precisely the assimilation, reprocessing, and application of these imported ideas to the indigenous patrimony that makes Russian culture so intriguing. The result is sometimes a brilliant hybrid, an effervescent cocktail that at once attracts and repels, charms and corrodes. Diaghilev's Ballets Russes (1909-29) is a primary example of this esthetic integration, since, to a considerable extent, the enterprise acted as a showcase of "Russianness" for Western consumption.

How can we explain this dual tradition, this mixture of the sophisticated and the "barbaric"? With the enforced and accelerated Westernization of Russia under Peter the Great (reigned 1682-1725) and Catherine the Great (reigned 1762-96), Russia suddenly assimilated cultural, technological, and commercial concepts that, in Western Europe, had already been evolving for centuries. It is worth remembering that before their ascension to the throne, Russia could boast no equivalent to Louis XIV and his brilliant court, no professional theater, and certainly no real understanding of stage design. In the early 17th century in Western Europe, Inigo Jones was designing for Ben Jonson, the Emperor Leopold was filling his Austrian court with Baroque spectacles, and Giacomo Torelli da Fano was pleasing the Sun King with his perspectival stagings; whereas Russia at that time had no navy, no advanced school of studio painting or sculpture, no professional drama, opera or ballet theater, and very little stone architecture. A century later, however, she had all these things.

However, far from erasing all signs of popular culture, Westernization tended to create two parallel cultures, divided and differentiated: one, so to speak, above ground; the other, underground. These categories rarely interwove, at least not until the Silver Age (ca. 1895-1914). Even Peter the Great, the arch apologist of Western

---

civilization, retained immediate links with his native Russian culture — for example, he established an intricate Order of Buffoons (the so-called *Orden shutov*), which indulged in hearty excesses while parodying official ceremonies and rituals. In this manner, Russian folk art also struggled to compete with the Western import until at least the middle of the 19th century — as in the cases of the *lubok* (a cheap handcolored print) and the peasant toy, which contained many a sly reference, explicit and implicit, to unwanted reformation and modernization.

One way to approach the study of this dual tradition within the context of the Russian arts is to identify the various points at which Western ideas were borrowed and absorbed. With whom did the first professional Russian artists spend their apprenticeship? Which foreign professors taught at the Imperial Academy of Arts (established in St. Petersburg in 1757) during its early years? Which Russian students were allowed to go abroad? Whom did they respect at their various points of sojourn in Paris and Rome? These questions have been discussed and answered in various publications, but in order to better understand the initial impetus to the making of theatrical decoration in Russia, it is worth detailing specific connections to 18th-century Russian architectural, landscape, interior, and stage design.

To begin with, we must take note of the forceful presence of Italians — such as Giuseppe Valeriani, who actually taught "perspectival" painting at the Academy of Sciences in St. Petersburg under the Empress Elizabeth Petrovna (reigned 1741-62). Giacomo Quarenghi worked as an architect and stage designer for Catherine, building, among other things, her Hermitage Theater. Alessandro and Carlo Galli of the Bibiena dynasty also worked in Russia, as did the Venetian Pietro Gonzaga, an enthusiast of Carlo Bibiena's work, whom Prince Nikolai Yusupov invited to become chief artist for the Imperial Theaters in 1792. In other words, as the St. Petersburg historian and connoisseur Ivan Bozherianov affirmed much later, Russia's best — and perhaps only — stage designers before the 19th century were Italian.[7] Naturally, their canons were later diluted and neglected, although, even in the 20th century, the Italian Baroque influence can still be discerned. There are, for example, references to the Bibienas as well as to Valeriani and Gonzaga in the sumptuous works of Andrea Beloborodoff (No. 118), Alexandre Serebriakoff (Ills. 185-87; Nos. 897-902), and also Alexandre Benois (Ill. 26; Nos. 136-39). Sometimes even Bakst brings to mind the classical conventions of Longhi and Guardi, as in his designs for *The Good-Humored Ladies*, *Sleeping Beauty* (No. 94), and *The Sleeping Princess* (Ills. 20, 21; Nos. 96-101).[8]

Eclecticism and the Russian Stage

In the mid-19th century the *bella prospettiva* cultivated by Valeriani and then Gonzaga in particular was replaced by a more luxurious form of spectacle — by a love of visual flamboyance — that linked the Russian Imperial stage of the 1860s onwards to Victorian England's Alhambra and Empire Theaters. The designers of these late Romantic extravanganzas such as Mikhail Bocharov, Anatolii Geltser, Andrei Roller (not to be confused with the more famous Alfred Roller active in Austria and Germany), and Matvei

---

7 I. Bozherianov: "Nechto o dekoratsiiakh, kostiumakh i dekoratorakh" in G2, pp. X-XIV.
8 According to Cyril Beaumont. See G19, p. 10.

44. Alexander Bilibin: Design for the Proscenium Curtain for Act I, *Boris Godunov*, 1941 (No. 363)

Shishkov created "flights, magic transformations, fires, destructions, etc."[9] that changed every ballet, opera or play, whether Alexander Pushkin's *Ruslan and Liudmila* or Johann von Schiller's *Jungfrau von Orleans*, into a celebration of the picturesque. Essentially, this is the concept that Shishkov taught at the Academy of Arts, where, beginning in 1876, he gave classes in decorative painting and stage design. Among his followers were Pavel Dmitriev (Nos. 418-21), Pavel Grigoriev (No. 575), and Petr Lambin (No. 691), who maintained the artisan tradition of stage-painting, contributing much to the technical mastery of the Imperial theaters.

These grandiose productions resulted in a marked tendency towards eclecticism and the unscrupulous mixing of styles resulted in the most curious combinations — dancers in tights, for example, with mustaches à la Wilhelm dancing the ballet *Pharaoh's Daughter.*[10] The young dancer and choreographer, Michel Fokine, was especially disturbed by this laxity:

> ...in their attempts to add variety to the performance, they [authors] neglected integrity of style, forgetting completely the character of the ballet... on the bottom of the Nile, in ancient Egypt, the Neva River danced in the costume of a Moscow boyar... mazurkas and csardases were used in almost all ballets.[11]

Cyril Beaumont described the visual effect of the Russian Imperial ballet at the end of the 19th century in similar terms:

> The costumes presented a strange contrast in that those of the supers were often historically correct according to the period of the ballet, while the dancers, from *corps de ballet* to *danseuse étoile*, wore the ballet-skirt, pink tights and satin shoes of tradition. Period and nationality were suggested by decorative motifs applied to the ballet-skirt. Another curious convention was the dancer's *coiffure*, which followed the fashion of the moment, whatever the character represented, and was often decorated with a diamond crescent or tiara.[12]

A striking characteristic of the Russian designers of the Silver Age (from the late 1890s to just after the October Revolution), whether in the Ballets Russes, Tairov's Chamber Theater or Meierkhold's Theater of the RSFSR No. 1, was their avoidance of these defects. The artists Bakst, Exter, Popova, and Georgii Yakulov, for example, displayed a remarkable integrity and consistency of style, whatever the national or historical demand. Furthermore, they were willing to investigate and analyze the "ethnographic" significance of a given theme: Bakst's serious study of the cultures of Ancient Hellas (Ill. 15, 16; Nos. 57, 58; 85, 86) and Siam (Ill. 18; No. 91); Benois's vast knowledge of 17th- and 18th-century France (Ills. 25-27; Nos. 123-58); Pavel Kuznetsov's interest in Indian culture in connection with his work on *Sakuntala* (No. 690); Goncharova's and Larionov's assembling and documenting of Russian folk art (Ills. 87, 100-01, 122-23, 127-34; Nos. 534-37, 569-70, 703-04, 711-13, 716-21) — these activities are symptomatic of the modern Russian designer's readiness to provide interpretations that, while imaginative, retain historical credibility.

---

9 G25, p. 24.
10 F19, pp. 200-03.
11 F19 (English edition), p. 109.
12 G19, p. 7.

45. Ivan Bilibin: Costume Design for a Boyar, *Boris Godunov*, 1908 (No. 366)

The "purification" of the Russian theater from the excesses of the later 19th century can best be discussed and explained through reference to two specific influences, one foreign, the other domestic. In a long article on stage design written in 1913, Fedor Komissarzhevsky, then artistic director of the Imperial theaters, asserted that there were essentially two kinds of decorative art at the disposal of the contemporary designer — the "psychological" and the "spectacular."[13] Rejecting the latter, Komissarzhevsky wrote that:

> With all these thousands of meters of canvas for productions, with these props and apparatuses... we have reached the stage where the décor storage areas of our theaters are much bigger than the theaters themselves. We must lighten the theater.[14]

The design system that was to replace "these thousands of meters of canvas" was the more economical "psychological" one which "does not disperse the viewer's attention all over the stage, but concentrates it on the actor or the action"[15] — and it was the Moscow Art Theater (MKhAT), founded in 1898 under Konstantin Stanislavsky's supervision (see Nos. 741, 1032), that helped to move the art of the stage towards a deeper and more psychological conception. While the first MKhAT productions still owed something to the recent Realist tradition, the very fact that Anton Chekhov's "psychological dramas" were first produced there with designs by Viktor Simov (No. 951) testifies to the refreshing and experimental approach of this theater. Of course, it was precisely this psychological approach that lay at the basis of both Adolphe Appia's and Edward Gordon Craig's theories of stage design, whose ideas were promoted in Russia by the critics Mikhail Babenchikov and Sergei Volkonsky (one-time director of the Imperial theaters), the historian Evgenii Znosko-Borovsky, and — in a practical way — by Tairov at his Chamber Theater.[16] Appia's and Craig's new concepts found an enthusiastic audience in St. Petersburg and Moscow, and they helped to cleanse Russian stage design of the more cumbersome elements of the 19th-century heritage. Craig's co-production with Konstantin Stanislavsky and Leopold Sulerzhitsky of *Hamlet* at the Moscow Art Theater in 1911 was one result of this international cooperation — even though by then his Symbolist principles were *passé*.

The Russians were well aware of Western European innovations through publications and frequent travels to Berlin, Munich, and Paris. Meierkhold, for example, encouraged his artists to produce psychological designs based on Appia's sparse, emotive forms, as his 1907 production of Leonid Andreev's *Life of a Man* at Komissarzhevskaia's Theater, with designs by Viktor Kolenda, indicates. The pioneering exhibition "Stage Design in the USSR 1917-X-1927," organized by Erik Gollerbakh in Leningrad in 1927, also emphasized this European connection, placing particular emphasis on the significance of Max Reinhardt for the Russians:

13 F. Komissarzhevsky: "'Dekoratsiia' v sovremennom teatre" in *Maski*, M, 1913-14, No. 6, p. 10.
14 Ibid., p. 12.
15 Ibid., p. 11.
16 For commentary on Appia and Craig and the Russian theater see M. Babenchikov: "Ot Appia i Krega k budushchemu teatra" in *Novaia studiia*, SP, 1912, 9 November, No. 10, pp. 10-12; E. Znosko-Borovsky: "Tvorchestvo aktera i Gordon Kreg," ibid., pp. 14-15; and 17 November, No. 11, pp. 7-10; also see S. Volkonsky: "Adolf Appia" in *Apollon*, SP, 1912, No. 6, pp. 25-31; and his *Khudozhestvennye otkliki*, SP: Apollon, 1912; L. Senelick: *Gordon Craig's Moscow Hamlet: a Reconstruction*, Westport, Connecticut: Greenwood Press, 1982.

„Царъ Салтанъ."
Стражникъ.

И. Б.
1929
J. Bilibine

46. Ivan Bilibin: Costume Design for the Guard, *The Tale of Tsar Saltan*, 1929 (No. 368)

The work of the Munich Art Theater [of Reinhardt] with its "stage in relief" and its light effects arranged as a single style of painting revealed new methods of resolving the architectonic problems of the theater.[17]

Not all Russians regarded the German (and Austrian) influence as beneficial, however, and some, including Meierkhold, even maintained that its "bad taste" had ruined the Russian theater.[18]

The Tradition of Russian Folk Culture

When all is said and done, we do not praise the modern Russian stage for its reliance on Italian, German or English models, although there are, of course, many instances of borrowing and reprocessing— Exter's 1916 sets for *Thamira Khytharedes* (Ills. 61-63; Nos. 460-62) are directly inspired by Appia, and no doubt Craig would have been happy with the restoration décors used by the St. Petersburg Antique Theater (Nos. 693, 694). Yet the decorative resolutions by Benois and Sudeikin for *Petrouchka* (Ills. 28-36, 194-201; Nos. 159-280, 987-1004), by Vera Ermolaeva, El Lissitzky, and Malevich for *Victory over the Sun* (Ills. 138-46, 147-55; Nos. 458, 752-64, 770-84), by Tatlin for *The Emperor Maximilian and his Disobedient Son Adolf* (Ill. 203; No. 1014) and *A Life for the Tsar* (Ill. 204; Nos. 1015, 1016), by Popova for *The Magnanimous Cuckold* (Nos. 974, 975), by Varvara Stepanova for *The Death of Tarelkin* (Ill. 192; Nos. 974-80), by Alexander Rodchenko for *The Bed Bug* (Nos. 867-74), etc. cannot be accommodated within this tradition. Instead, they depend upon more domestic stimuli, especially the fairground and the *balagan* (fairground booth), and, in general, on the rediscovery of Russian folk art in the late 19th and early 20th centuries.

As early as the 1830s, the Academy of Arts in St. Petersburg commissioned the artist Fedor Solntsev to study and sketch antiquities and monuments in the Russian countryside. The ensuing decades also witnessed a proportionate increase in expeditions, debates, and publications devoted to Russian art and architecture. These culminated in the establishment of prestigious journals such as *Russkaia starina* [Russian Antiquity] in St. Petersburg (1870-1900) and the creation of de luxe editions such as Ivan Snegirev and Solntsev's *Pamiatniki moskovskoi drevnosti* [Monuments of Moscow Antiquity] (1842-45) and Vladimir Stasov's *Slavianskii i vostochnyi ornament* [Slav and Eastern Ornament] in 1887. In addition to this scholarly interest in traditional Russian art, there were attempts in the early 19th century to incorporate local motifs into music and *belles lettres*, as in the case of Mikhail Glinka's songs and Pushkin's fairy-tales. In fact, the latter became a major source of inspiration to many artists of the late 19th and early 20th centuries, as the numerous jubilee editions of 1899 celebrating the centenary of Pushkin's birth — illustrated by Ivan Bilibin, Sergei Maliutin, Viktor Vasnetsov, etc. — confirm. The design for *Vasilisa the Beautiful* (No. 364) and the interpretations of *L'Oiseau de Feu* (Ills. 100, 101; Nos. 370, 381, 533, 569, 570, 739, 1156), *Ruslan and Liudmila* (Ills. 47, 190, 211; Nos. 377-79, 959, 1053-56), and *Le Coq d'Or* (Ills. 87, 228; Nos. 299-303, 534-40, 896, 1093, 1094) also acknowledge the rediscovery of indigenous traditions. In turn, this lexicon became an identifying characteristic of émigré culture

17 E. Gollerbakh: "Teatr kak zrelishche" in I3, p. 20.
18 F. Komissarzhevsky: "Nemtsy i russkii teatr" in *Maski*, 1912-13, No. 7-8, p. 10. The whole article is on pp. 1-11. For a contextual commentary see C146.

47. Boris Bilinsky: Stage Design for Prince Svetozar's Feast for Liudmila's Wedding, *Ruslan and Liudmila*, 1930 (No. 377)

in the 1920s onwards: from the *Firebird* magazine (*Zhar-ptitsa*, Paris-Berlin, 1921-1926) to the Russian Tea Room in New York City, from the sets and costumes for Baliev's Chauve-Souris in France and the USA to Goncharova's pochoirs for the Paris edition of the *Conte du Tsar Saltan* (1921).[19]

Many modern Russian artists, including those of the avant-garde, looked to their heritage for artistic inspiration. They were able to create a vigorous and exotic product that Western audiences perceived immediately as "Russian" or "oriental," even though it contained many European references, Diaghilev's production of *Schéhérazade* (1910) being a case in point (Ills. 12-14; Nos. 81-84). Perhaps the marriage of East and West was consummated during the Diaghilev epoch, but the betrothal occurred much earlier. In the specific context of the Russian theater and stage design, there had already been a number of earlier attempts to bridge the gap between high and low, between the studio and the street. That is why the presence of the *balagan* (fairground booth) is so important and no discussion of modern Russian stage design is complete without ample reference to this theatrical form. In his memoirs, Benois described his childhood impressions of the *balagany* in St. Petersburg:

> These *balagany* served as the main attraction of that promenading that, "since time immemorial," or more exactly since the 18th century, had been the most important popular pastime in Russia, especially in the two capitals. This promenading corresponded to what are called *foires,* or fairs, in Western Europe. In many respects our entertainments were copies of what had been elaborated in the West, but still, whatever came from abroad was imbued with a specifically "Russian spirit." The merriment in these promenades was of a more tempestuous, more elemental character. Apart from that, it was possible to see much of a distinctive local flavor, something ultra-amusing and picturesque. And there were more drunks around here than any place in Europe, and they were noisier, more tempestuous, and also terrifying. The general drunkenness of the simple folk who by the evening remained as the real proprietors of the squares that were allotted to these amusements, gave them some kind of downright demonically dashing character — communicated so wonderfully in Scene IV of Stravinsky's *Petrouchka*.[20]

The panoramas and dioramas for the Field of Mars in St. Petersburg designed by Pavel Dmitriev (Nos. 418-21) relate directly to the world of the *balagan* that so nurtured Benois's and Stravinsky's artistic imagination, and the Lobanov-Rostovsky collection contains many other works inspired by the same tradition. These include Andreenko's costume designs for Riccardo Drigo's *Millions d'Arlequin* (Nos. 17, 18) as well as Tatlin's for *The Emperor Maximilian and His Disobedient Son Adolf* (Ill. 203), Stepanova's for *The Death of Tarelkin* (Ill. 192), and Vladimir Kozlinsky's depiction of a street theater in which the touter is about to close (or open) the makeshift drop curtain (No. 682).

The *balagan* was a vital part of popular Russian culture in the 18th and 19th centuries, a culture that encompassed bazaars and buffoons, minstrels and hawkers, quacks and Punch and Judy shows. By the late 19th century much of that culture was fast disappearing or, rather, was undergoing an urban metamorphosis relying more on the circus, the traveling prestidigitator, and the flea market. Productions such as *Victory over the Sun*, *The First Distiller* (Ill. 8; Nos. 42, 43), and *The Death of Tarelkin* were often regarded by contemporary critics as extensions of the *balagan*,

---

19 N. Gontcharova: *Le Conte du Tsar Saltan*, Paris: Sirène, 1921.
20 F54, Vol. 1, pp. 289, 298. For further commentary on the *balagany* see E60.

48. Boris Bilinsky: Costume Design for a Boyar, *La Princesse Cygne*, ca. 1932 (No. 381)

constituting a finale, so to speak, to the traditional *balagany* of Benois's youth. Presenting folk dramas, especially Punch and Judy shows, to a willing audience, the *balagany* depended for their effect on rude actions, colorful language, and simple cues, making the spectacle not so much a "theater of movement in general, but a theater of verbal dynamics," as Viktor Shklovsky wrote in 1920.[21] The *balagan*, therefore, contained theatrical possibilities — a mobile stage, a wide variety of acts, audience participation — that the Modernists investigated and adapted. Their rediscovery of the *balagan* and other manifestations of popular culture does, indeed, help to explain certain key developments in the recent history of the Russian theater and theatrical design.

Yet, by the late 19th century, the *balagan* had blended with an emerging entertainment industry that enabled an eager public to enjoy not only a folk drama, but also a colored diorama of some great battle (No. 419), acrobatics, lantern slides of exotic countries, peep shows, etc. The fairgrounds in St. Petersburg, Moscow, Nizhnii Novgorod, Kishinev, and other cities constituted the theater and the various booths, its acts, with the crowds of onlookers promenading from one show to the next. Of course, the crowd moved separately from the action, but its position was contradictory to the conventional notion of the static audience held at a predetermined and constant distance from the stage.

The "Style Russe"

It is in this context that the *style russe* with its various interpretations and applications just before and after 1900 assumes such importance. True, this tendency was part of the international reassessment of the handicrafts of the time, especially by William Morris and the Arts and Crafts movement in England, of which the Russians were well aware. However, the Russian contribution to this reawakening took on a somewhat different form and left an indelible imprint on modern stage design, more so than did the concurrent revivals in England and Germany. Largely responsible for this particular orientation within Russian art and design were two maecenases — the railroad magnate Savva Mamontov and Princess Mariia Tenisheva — who used their financial and creative resources not only to refurbish the traditions of popular Russian culture, but also to establish private experimental theaters. To some extent, their theatrical endeavors might be regarded as anticipations of Diaghilev's Ballets Russes of 1909 onwards and of the Moscow and St. Petersburg cabarets of 1908.

After the exclusive Imperial monopoly on the Russian stage was lifted in 1882, a number of important private companies were established, among them Fedor Korsh's Theater in 1882 and Mamontov's opera company in 1885. In managing the so-called Krotkov Private Opera Troupe in Moscow, Mamontov implemented his desire to integrate the arts and, more egocentrically, to build a monument that would help him overcome the identity crisis that he had suffered as a young man:

> I am not a writer yet or a philosopher or a public figure. After me nothing
> will remain that might remind people that there once lived Savva Ivanovich
> Mamontov and that this is how he lived.[22]

---

21 V. Shklovsky: "Narodnaia komediia i '1-yi vinokur'" in *Zhizn iskusstva*, P, 1920, 17-18-19 April, No. 425-426-427, p. 1.
22 Savva Mamontov: [Autobiography], 1869 in RGALI, f. 799, op. 2, ed. khr. 2, l. 2 (verso).

49. Tatiana Bruni: Costume Design for Kozelkov's Girlfriend in Act II, *Bolt*, 1931 (No. 393)

Костюму.
1 костю.м

Приятельница Ленки

349.

50. Tatiana Bruni: Costume Design for Lenka Gulba's Girlfriend, *Bolt*, 1931 (No. 394)

51. Tatiana Bruni: Costume Design for a Komsomol Girl on a Rope Ladder (Act III, Scene 2), *Bolt*, 1931 (No. 395)

When Mamontov founded his opera company, he was drawing on the theatrical and scenic experience that he had gained since the early 1870s when the Abramtsevo circle of artists, writers, and actors had first begun to stage plays and charades, some of them written by Mamontov himself. These were in the tradition of Victorian family entertainment, except that the "family" included many gifted artists who contributed directly to the success of these *tableaux vivants*, Isaak Levitan, Ilia Ostroukhov (No. 803), Vasilii Polenov, Viktor Vasnetsov (Ill. 232; No. 1115), and Mikhail Vrubel (Nos. 1152-55) among them. For example, Vasnetsov designed the production of Alexander Ostrovsky's play *Snegurochka* in the winter of 1882-83 (cf. Ills. 115, 181-83; Nos. 651-59) and Polenov made the decorations for Mamontov's own play *The Crimson Rose* in January, 1883.[23] Moreover, the circle often used genuine peasant costumes in their plays as, for example, in the case of *Snegurochka*, something that lent a special vitality and immediacy to the productions; and, certainly, the emphasis on a repertoire of Russian myth and fairy-tale served as an important precedent to the promotion of Russian music and opera in Europe and America by Diaghilev, Marie Kousnezoff, and other impresarios during the 1910s and 1920s. For example, *The Maid of Pskov (Pskovitianka), Snegurochka,* and *The Tale of Tsar Saltan* interpreted by Nicholas Roerich (Ills. 178-83; Nos. 880, 881, 883-90), *Sadko* interpreted by Boris Anisfeld, A. Benois, Korovin, and Alexandra Shchekatikhina-Pototskaia (Ills. 5, 113; Nos. 26, 27, 113, 308-38, 642, 915), *The Golden Cockerel,* or *Le Coq d'Or,* interpreted by Natalia Goncharova (Ill. 87; Nos. 534-40), and *Tale of the Invisible City of Kitezh and the Maid Fevronia* interpreted by Bilibin and Alexei and Konstantin Korovin (Ills. 110-12; Nos. 369, 630-41, 643). The Abramtsevo circle worked with the spirit of true amateurs, and their productions carried none of the dry routine that accompanied those of the Imperial theaters. Stanislavsky, who frequented Abramtsevo and Mamontov's Moscow house, recalled these intimate and lively spectacles:

> [Mamontov] was in charge of all these activities and at the same time wrote plays, joked with the young people, dictated business letters and telegrams connected with his complicated railroad affairs.[24]

During the first series of the operas produced by the Krotkov Troupe at Abramtsevo and Moscow between 1885 and 1887 (e.g. *Rusalka* and *Snegurochka* with décors by Vasnetsov, *Aida* designed by Polenov, and *Carmen* designed by Ostroukhov),[25] the public responded with only mild enthusiasm and there was much criticism of the musical organization and the acting. In spite of the appearance of such impressive singers as Ivan Ershov and Nadezhda Salina, the Krotkov Troupe closed temporarily in 1887, although Mamontov contracted the Italian tenors Angelo Masini and Francesco Tamagno to sing in Moscow in 1890 and 1895 respectively. In 1896 the company reopened, inaugurating its second and more successful phase including, for example, the appearance of Nadezhda

---

23 Details of the spectacles produced by the Mamontov circle can be found in the large folio entitled *Khronika nashego khudozhestvennogo kruzhka*, M:Mamontov, 1894. For further information on Mamontov and Abramtsevo see M. Jacobs: *The Good and Simple Life*, Oxford: Phaidon, 1985, pp. 111-8; and B184.
24 F2 (1936 edition), pp. 123, 124.
25 For a detailed list of operas produced by the Krotkov Private Opera Troupe in Moscow and Kharkov in 1885-87 see RGALI, f. 799, op. 1, ed. khr. 292, ll. 1-84, and V. Rossikhina: *Opernyi teatr Mamontova*, M: Muzyka, 1985; and B184.

52. Marc Chagall: Costume Designs for Aleko and Zemfira, *Aleko*, ca. 1942 (No. 404)

53. Sonia Delaunay: Costume Design for Cleopatra, *Cleopatra*, ca. 1918 (No. 413)

54. Sonia Delaunay: Costume Design in Simultanist Style for Amneris, *Aida*, 1920 (No. 414)

Zabela (Vrubel's wife; see No. 1153) in *Hansel and Gretel* designed by Vrubel, and of Fedor Chaliapin in Modest Mussorgsky's *Khovanshchina* designed by Konstantin Korovin and Sergei Maliutin (cf. Ills. 78-80; Nos. 500-02). The fact that Mamontov invited young professional studio artists to come and work for him such as Korovin, Levitan, Polenov, Ilia Repin, Vasnetsov, and Vrubel, imparted a vision and energy to the company and to the general concept of stage design. Just like his German contemporary, the Duke of Saxe-Meiningen, Mamontov encouraged his designers to respect historical accuracy, to avoid the extravagant, and to allow the actor maximum freedom of movement. Within these conditions, Korovin and Polenov, in particular, helped to create a "revolt in stage design."[26] Benois, who was present at the St. Petersburg debut of the Mamontov troupe in 1898, wrote:

> Mamontov's enterprise was, in fact, very far from being a "folly"... we all were able to see for ourselves how original and interesting Korovin's treatment of scenic painting was. I did not like everything — the planning was rather poor at times, and there was a certain roughness of technique — but... on the whole, Korovin's décors amazed us by their daring approach to the problem and, above all, by their high artistic value — the very quality that was so often missing in the elaborate productions of the Imperial stage.[27]

The activities of Princess Tenisheva, Mamontov's rival, were also pertinent to the development of the *style russe* and the new ideas of Russian design. After all, it was at her estate, Talashkino, near Smolensk, and through her some-time curator there, Nicholas Roerich, that Igor Stravinsky found some of his primary material for *Le Sacre du Printemps* (No. 662). Sharing Mamontov's aspirations, although at a later date (Talashkino did not function as an art colony until the late 1890s), Tenisheva felt her vocation to be the revival and propagation of Russian peasant art. To this end, she invited many artists and writers to visit her estate, among them Golovin (Nos. 530-33), Korovin (Ills. 113-18; Nos. 642-78), Maliutin, Roerich (Ills. 177-83; Nos. 880-90), Dmitrii Stelletsky (cf. Ill. 190; No. 959), Vrubel (Nos. 1152-55), and Sergei Makovsky. She also established workshops for training young peasants in traditional crafts and opened a theater that gave particular attention to the dramatization of fairy-tales. Due to the civic disturbances in 1905-06, Tenisheva loosened her ties with Talashkino and concentrated her subsequent artistic activities in Paris, even though she did return in 1908 and two years later commissioned Roerich to decorate the exterior and interior of the church. While Roerich was working there, Stravinsky also visited — gathering much new material for his new ballet *Le Sacre du Printemps* (No. 882), which Diaghilev produced in Paris with Roerich's designs.

Roerich had the following to say about the artistic environment of Talashkino:

> In Talashkino the broad home-like spirit is unexpectedly combined with the freedom of art; a country house with ornate chambers; a hand-written chronicle with the latest utterances of the Occident. Much is conflicting. But in this conflict is a special pulse which reflects our many-sided life... On the sacred hearth, away from the contamination of the city, the people

---

26 Anon.: "Na khudozhestvennykh vystavkakh" in *Kulisy*, M, 1917, January, No. 1, p. 11.
27 F7, p. 197.

55. Sonia Delaunay: Three Costume Studies, left to right: Costume Design for a Lady, 1923; Simultanist Dress, Rhythm without End, 1919; Costume, 1919 (No. 416)

create again newly conceived objects... We are reminded of the covenants of our forefathers... The degrees of higher and lower become more pliable.[28]

The surviving photographs of the exterior and interior of the buildings at Talashkino indicate that Tenisheva, Roerich, and their colleagues such as Maliutin, Shchekatikhina-Pototskaia, and Vrubel, tried to realize this stylistic synthesis by designing the furniture, wall decorations, and utensils according to a common denominator. The workshops for embroidery and woodcarving that Tenisheva subsidized seemed also to operate according to the same uniform principle, i.e. they reproduced folk art that was interpreted and "modernized"[29] by a professional artist, whether Roerich, Maliutin or Tenisheva herself.

Folk tradition, stylistic totality, ornament, and artistic integration were important components of the Abramtsevo and Talashkino theaters. True, Tenisheva did not have a private opera and her theater was of modest dimensions (seating only 200), but she ensured that the dramatic repertoire consisted of Russian titles based on legends and fables and that they were acted by peasants — one example being the opera *The Tale of the Dead Tsarevna and the Seven Bogatyrs*. Tenisheva also founded a balalaika orchestra, inviting Vrubel and other artists to decorate the sounding boards of the instruments.

Not surprisingly, both Tenisheva and Mamontov introduced personal concepts of peasant culture into their enterprises, linking these with the conventions of professional, high theater, and thereby creating the kind of amalgam that was later developed by Diaghilev in productions such as the *Polovtsian Dances* (Ill. 177; No. 880), *Le Sacre du Printemps* (No. 882), *Le Coq d'Or* (Ill. 87; Nos. 534-40), *Soleil de Nuit* (Ills. 122-23; Nos. 703-04), and *Contes Russes* (Ill. 127; Nos. 711-13). The panels, costumes, and sets that they commissioned may have incorporated siren birds and ears of wheat, but they were painted by studio artists conversant with the ideas of Art Nouveau (e.g., No. 1156); the themes they selected may have involved village maidens, monsters, and witches, but the key prop was no longer the imagination of the sympathetic crowd of villagers or humble townsfolk, but a mechanical complex that changed scenes, dropped curtains, and modified lighting. Above all, the audiences of Mamontov's opera and Tenisheva's theater included literati, students, critics, and professional artists who, through this conspiracy of methods, were encouraged to view the presentation not as a rowdy entertainment, but rather as an esthetic experience. Abramtsevo and Talashkino "beautified" peasant culture, making it palatable to the urbane consumer. To some extent, they also anesthetized it — just as did Nikolai Drizen and Nikolai Evreinov and their artists such as Evgenii Lanceray with Medieval dramaturgy at their Antique Theater in St. Petersburg in 1907-12 (Nos. 693, 694), or as did Diaghilev with his Ballets Russes.

---

28 N. Roerich: *Realm of Light*, New York: Roerich Museum Press, 1931, pp. 299-301. On Talashkino see M. Tenisheva: *Vpechatleniia moei zhizni*, Paris: Russkoe Istoriko-genealogicheskoe obshchestvo vo Frantsii, 1933; L. Zhuravleva: *Kniaginia Mariia Tenisheva*, Smolensk: Poligramma, 1994; A. Shkurko et al.: *Kniagina Mariia Tenisheva v zerkale Serebrianogo veka*. Catalog of exhibition at the State Historical Museum, Moscow, 2008; and K273. For general discussion of the folk art revival in Russia see B202.
29. C. de Danilowicz: "Art Décoratif Russe Ancien. Collection de la Princesse Marie Tenicheff" in *L'Art Décoratif*, Paris, 1907, December, p. 145.

56. Mstislav Dobujinsky: Costume Designs for Two Cossacks Flirting with Two Girls,
Platov's Cossacks in Paris, 1926 (No. 430)

57. Mstislav Dobujinsky: Costume Design for the Chinese Doll, *Coppélia*, 1956 (No. 449)

58. Mstislav Dobujinsky: Costume Design for the Astrologer Doll, *Coppélia*, 1956 (No. 451)

II. THE SILVER AGE

The World of Art: towards Artistic Synthesism

It is important to remember that many artists who spent their "apprenticeship" years with Mamontov or Tenisheva achieved their true reputations as designers while working for the Ballets Russes and other famous companies both in Russia and in the West. Furthermore, most of them — Golovin, Korovin, Roerich — were closely associated with the group of artists, writers, esthetes, and musicians known as the World of Art (*Mir iskusstva*), which, to a considerable extent, acted as a laboratory for the cultivation and creation of the Ballets Russes itself.

The World of Art group was founded by Diaghilev and his friends (Bakst, Benois, Konstantin Somov, et al.) in St. Petersburg in the late 1890s. It did much to develop and legitimize the design experiments of Mamontov and Tenisheva through publications, especially the journal *Mir iskusstva* [World of Art] (1898-1904), and through two cycles of exhibitions (1899-1906; 1910-24). The World of Art relied heavily on subsidies provided by its two patrons — so much so that Bakst even declared that:

> the most powerful enemies of the new journal are Mamontov and the Princess. Mamontov because he dreams that the journal be an aide to craftsmen... We were looking for a title for the journal, e.g. *Aurora, Forward, The New Art*... and as a joke I suggested calling it *The Russian Artisan's Handbook* and I'm afraid that this is what would suit Mamontov and the Princess best of all![30]

While not applying the name Secession to their group, the World of Art opposed the canons of both Realism and academic art and evinced a primary interest in the Western Secessionist style and Symbolist art in general, running articles and reproductions relating to Aubrey Beardsley, Arnold Böcklin, Thomas T. Heine, Gustav Klimt, Charles Rennie Mackintosh, Josef Maria Olbrich, Franz Stuck, et al. Many of them spent shorter or longer periods studying in Munich and participated in exhibitions at the centers of *Jugendstil* — Munich, Berlin, Prague, Vienna, and Warsaw. In turn, the World of Art artists, especially Bakst, Benois, Ivan Bilibin, Lanceray, Roerich, and Somov, elaborated, refined, and disseminated the new esthetic ideas by applying them to many disciplines, especially book and stage design.

The World of Art was fascinated by the cultures of Greece and Italy as well as by grandiose cultural symbols such as the Versailles of Louis XIV. Diaghilev, in particular, did much to restore public interest in Russia's 17th and 18th centuries, organizing a vast, unprecedented exhibition of Russian historic portraits in 1905 (No. 692). In any case, this retrospective tendency, the aspiration towards artistic synthesism, new concepts of design, and the emphasis on individual creative expression — can also be identified with the Ballets Russes, especially during the first phase (1909-14). In fact, as Serge Lifar affirmed later,[31] the Ballets Russes should be regarded as the

---

30 Letter from Léon Bakst to Alexandre Benois dated 25 March, 1898, in RGALI, f. 938, op. 1, ed. khr. 46, inserted as Note 3 to l. 83. For detailed information on the World of Art see B18, B24, B123, B186, and B238.
31 See D8, especially Part III.

59. Boris Erdman: Costume Design for a Circus Horse-Rider, ca. 1921 (No. 457)

direct extension of the esthetic principles advocated by the St. Petersburg group. It is important, therefore, to examine the ways in which Bakst, Benois, Diaghilev, Somov, and their colleagues approached the notion of theater in the early days, and to pinpoint possible connections between their perceptions and the Ballets Russes. True, the World of Art members were not especially interested in the ballet as such during the period 1898-1906 and the discipline was hardly discussed on the pages of the *World of Art*. However, as Benois maintained, their "mania for the theater"[32] prompted them to visit all manner of productions in St. Petersburg and abroad, even though, by and large, they seemed to prefer opera over drama and the ballet. Benois was so attracted to the theater that in 1905 he predicted that his professional future might well lie in that direction:

> Over the past five or six years I've been living in some kind of kaleidoscope... I'm dreaming of having just one enduring cause in the future. And insofar as I know myself, I would do best of all in the theater.[33]

The general attitude of the World of Art artists and writers towards the function of theater in its widest sense was closely connected to the esthetic demands that they made of all artistic activity: they felt that art should reflect the creator's personality, that it should be independent of "usefulness,"[34] and that it should disclose the "real reality" beyond the world of tawdry appearances. That is why the World of Art members, such as the poet Valerii Briusov, did not sympathize with Stanislavsky's Realist methods at the Moscow Art Theater (also established in 1898, the same year as the *World of Art* magazine), referring to them as an "unnecessary truth."[35]

As far as dramatic repertoire was concerned, the World of Art was catholic in its taste, welcoming the classics (Euripides's *Hippolytus* [Nos. 57, 58] and Sophocles's *Oedipus at Colona*), Shakespeare's (*Julius Caesar*), and the plays of Maurice Maeterlinck — even running a translation of one of Maeterlinck's essays on contemporary drama in the journal.[36] In opera, however, Benois and Diaghilev, at least, had very definite opinions: paying homage to a vogue of their time, they praised Wagner and the operatic drama, published appreciations of *Tristan und Isolde*, *Die Walkyrie*, and *Die Götterdämmerung*,[37] and also included a translation of Nietzsche's statements on Wagner at Bayreuth.[38] "I'm fed up with Beethoven," wrote Benois in 1896, "What is he in comparison with Bach!! Or Wagner!!!"[39] As for the ballet, neither Diaghilev, nor Benois manifested a particular interest in it, perhaps because during those early years it was difficult to predict the renaissance that the Russian ballet would soon experience. Their attitude towards the Imperial ballet was, to say the least, restrained,

32 F15, Vol. 2, p. 26.
33 Letter from Alexandre Benois to Walter Nouvel dated 20 October, 1905, l. 197 in RGALI, f. 938, op. 1, ed. khr. 46.
34 Sergei Volkonsky, an associate of the World of Art, wrote: "works of art... are foreign to the element of usefulness" in his article "Iskusstvo" in *Mir iskusstva*, SP, 1899, No. 3-4, p. 82.
35 V. Briusov: "Nenuzhnaia pravda," ibid., 1902, Vol. 7, Khudozhestvennaia khronika, No. 4, pp. 67-74.
36 M. Maeterlinck: "Sovremennaia drama," ibid., 1901, Vol. 4, pp. 272-32. Also see his "Povsednevnyi tragizm," ibid., 1899, Vol. 2, Khudozhestvennaia khronika, pp. 71-74.
37 See D[iaghilev]: "K postanovke 'Tristana i Izoldy'," ibid., 1899, Vol. 1, Khudozhestvennaia khronika, pp. 135-37; A. Benois: "Postanovka Valkirii," ibid., 1900, Vol. 4, Literaturnyi otdel, pp. 241-43; S. Diaghilev: "Gibel bogov." ibid., 1903, No. 4, pp. 35-38.
38 F. Nitsshe [Nietzsche]: "R. Vagner v Bairete," ibid., 1900, Vol. 3, Literaturnaia khronika, pp. 59-63, 99-102.
39 Letter from Alexandre Benois to Walter Nouvel dated late November, 1896, in RGALI, f. 938, op. 1, ed. khr. 46, l. 45

60. Erté: Costume Design with Chinese Dragons, *Aladin*, Folies Bergère, Paris, 1929 (No. 459)

something that Diaghilev made clear in a review of 1902, entitled "In the Theater. 1. The Ballets of Delibes", in which he described performances at the Mariinsky Theater:

> Here we saw how the eternal Petipa stormed around so clumsily, how the corps de ballet idly went through its tedious "pas"... [40]

The critic and philosopher Vasilii Rozanov, in his appreciation of the Siamese ballet, which visited St. Petersburg in 1900, even implied that the Western classical ballet as a whole was moribund, since "our heads may be ablaze, but our body hardly lives."[41]

Essentially, the World of Art members saw little of merit in the productions of the state-controlled ballet. In fact, Diaghilev's abrupt disengagement from the Mariinsky Theater after the abortive *Sylvia* episode in 1901[42] and his general intolerance of the cumbersome state bureaucracy impelled him rapidly towards the establishment of his own troupe in 1909. Nevertheless, it would be wrong to assume that all was unwell in the Imperial theaters in the late 19th and early 20th centuries. After all, most of Diaghilev's key dancers received their training within the Imperial ballet system and a number of Diaghilev's experimental ballets actually had their premieres (albeit in tamer versions) on the Imperial stage. For example, *Egyptian Night* (also called *Egyptian Nights*), which became *Cléopâtre* in 1909 in Paris (Ills. 7, 10, 11, 53; Nos. 30, 75-79, 407-13), was first produced by Michel Fokine at the Mariinsky in 1908, as was *Le Pavillon d'Armide* in 1907 (Ills. 25-27; Nos. 121-51). Furthermore, Enrico Cecchetti, who coached many of Diaghilev's dancers, was balletmaster for the Mariinsky and ballet teacher for the Theater Institute in St. Petersburg from 1892-1902. Of course, it would have been impossible for the Imperial ballet to have staged the avant-garde productions that Diaghilev realized in Paris, such as *Schéhérazade* in 1910 and *Jeux* in 1913. However, as far as dancing and choreographic technique were concerned, Diaghilev and his colleagues actually maintained and enhanced, rather than destroyed, the Imperial tradition.

In the specific context of stage design, the World of Art made scant reference to particular principles or even productions. In fact, commentary was limited to a few appraisals of spectacles undertaken by members of the group — Bakst, Benois, Golovin. Evidently, at this juncture, the World of Art artists had little understanding of the revolution that was already occurring in Western European design, thanks especially to Appia, and their remarks, sporadic and subjective, were not especially enlightening. Dmitrii Filosofov, the literary factotum of the group, liked Bakst's sets and costumes for the 1902 production of *Hippolytus* :

> Bakst's idea of depicting the goddesses in the hieratic, frozen poses of primitive art and of making them larger than human scale is very successful.[43]

Diaghilev felt that Benois and Korovin's resolution of *Die Götterdämmerung* of 1903 "did not have much to do with Wagner"[44] (an assumption that Benois

---

40 S. Diaghilev: "V teatre. 1. Balety Deliba" in *Mir iskusstva*, 1902, Vol. 8, Khudozhestvennaia khronika, p. 32.
41 V. Rozanov: "Balet ruk" in his *Sredi khudozhnikov,* P, 1914, p. 41.
42 For details see D8, pp. 112, 114, 116, 130; D12, pp. 140, 145.
43 D. Filosofov: "Teatralnye zametki. I. Pervoe predstavlenie 'Ippolita'" in *Mir iskusstva*, 1902, Vol. 8, Khudozhestvennaia khronika, p. 30.
44 S. Diaghilev: "Gibel bogov," ibid., 1903, No. 4, Khronika, p. 35.

61. Alexandra Exter: Costume Design for a Bacchante with Hands Outstretched,
Thamira Khytharedes, 1916 (No. 460)

62. Alexandra Exter: Costume Design for a Female Dancer with Part of the Tunic Held out in Front, *Thamira Khytharedes*, 1916 (No. 461)

63. Alexandra Exter: Costume Design for Dancing Bacchante with Bare Bosom,
Thamira Khytharedes, 1916 (No. 462)

protested).[45] Benois, in turn, argued that Golovin's designs for *The Magic Mirror* of 1903 were too "chintzy."[46]

These tenuous remarks notwithstanding, stage design became probably the most exciting and enduring area of activity for the World of Art artists. As far as Diaghilev's Ballets Russes was concerned, it was the stage designs that astounded, angered or perplexed the Edwardian public as least as much as Nijinsky's leap or Stravinsky's brave discordance. Yet ironically — in view of the success — not one of Diaghilev's Russian designers was actually trained as a designer or decorator, and all came to the stage by way of studio painting. Moreover, most of the artists were graduates not of the Academy of Arts, but of less prestigious, private schools such as those of Princess Tenisheva in St. Petersburg and Elizaveta Zvantseva (at first in Moscow and then, after 1905, in St. Petersburg). Some, above all Benois, were simply brilliant amateurs. As Filosofov once remarked, "The World of Art... was a cult of dilettantism in the good and true sense of the word."[47]

Far from hindering Diaghilev's designers, the absence of a strict, academic mentality provided them with a necessary flexibility, enabling Bakst, for example, to move easily from 19th century St. Petersburg in *La Fée des Poupées* (Nos. 59-71) to London's Bloomsbury in *Jeux*, from Greece in *Hippolytus* to 17th-century France in *The Sleeping Princess*. Perhaps their initial study as easel painters also stood them in good stead: all of them were fond of nature painting and of the outdoors; they delighted in the malleability of pencil drawing and watercolor; and, paying homage to a current European fashion, they could also regard the sketch and the study as independent works, self-contained and intrinsically valid. Benois knew from firsthand experience that a Brittany field and a Norwegian fjörd demanded very different perceptions and renderings of light, just as Bakst realized that an Ancient Egyptian costume should not be confused with a Persian one. Of course, Benois, Bakst, and their colleagues maintained recognizable styles and, especially in their middle periods, they did repeat points of view, color combinations, and thematic motifs. However, their initial "open" training as artists contributed much to their stylistic vitality, to their automatic suspension of disbelief each time they were confronted with a new design commission.

Furthermore, the stage presented the artists of the *fin de siècle* with the possibility of exploring a large decorative space, i.e. a pictorial area that, traditionally, the fresco and the wallpainting had also provided.[48] Since there were few opportunities to decorate public spaces at that time (a situation that changed dramatically after the October Revolution with the inauguration of agit-art and monumental propaganda), artists such as Bakst, Benois, Roerich, Nikolai Sapunov, Sergei Sudeikin, and Vrubel welcomed the theater as an environment for the wider display of pictorial ideas. This circumstance also helps explain the popularity of the panneau for St. Petersburg and Moscow villas at the turn of the century (No. 1156). By and large, this approach benefited the stage, although, as Raymond Cogniat pointed out in the context of the Ballets Russes:

> Serge de Diaghilew impose ce qui, par excès, deviendra parfois une erreur: le peintre au théâtre. Plus tard on découvrira cette erreur: la toile de chevalet démesurément agrandie à l'échelle de la scène.[49]

---

45 Benois protested in his article "Ruslan i Liudmila," ibid., 1904, No. 11-12, p. 234.
46 A. Benois: "Volshebnoe zerkaltse," ibid., 1904, No. 1, Khronika, pp. 1-6.
47 Quoted in A. Grishchenko and N. Lavrsky: *A. Shevchenko*, M: IZO NKP, 1919, p. 5.
48 G6, p. 10.
49 G12, p. 12.

64. Alexandra Exter: Curtain Design for the Chamber Theater, Moscow, 1920 (No. 463)

The Designers of the Ballets Russes

There can be no question that, within the history of the modern stage, a primary influence on theatrical design, on choreography, on dance repertoire, indeed, on the very evolution of ballet itself, derived from the seasons of the Ballets Russes that Diaghilev opened in Paris in 1909. Ever since Richard Buckle's pioneering exhibition in Edinburgh and London in 1954 (Ills. 1, 24; Nos. 121, 159),[50] there has been an ever increasing public awareness and appreciation of the Diaghilev era — its dancers, its artists, its intrigues and scandals. Visual and documentary materials abound, and much has been written about Diaghilev as impresario, the great dancers such as Tamara Karsavina and Nijinsky, the patrons such as Gabriel Astruc, Lady Juliet Duff, and Misia Sert,[51] as well as the designers. The Lobanov-Rostovsky collection illustrates the evolution of the Ballets Russes from its pre-First World War decorative phase through its later, more international, and more "modern" one. Apart from designs for the famous productions already mentioned above, the collection also contains a number of related pieces for less familiar productions such as *Boris Godunov* in 1908 and 1913 with contributions by Dmitrii Stelletsky (No. 955) and Konstantin Yuon (Nos. 1172-74), *Les Orientales* with designs by Bakst and Korovin (No. 649), *Pskovitianka* with designs by Roerich (No. 881), *Judith* with designs by Valentin Serov (Nos. 910, 911), and *Mavra* with designs by Léopold Survage (Nos. 1012, 1013). There is little sense in repeating the familiar chronology here, but concentration on four of the principal designers — Bakst, Benois, Goncharova, and Larionov — helps us to appreciate the originality and diversity of the sets and costumes produced for the Ballets Russes between 1909 and 1929.

Alexandre Benois and Léon Bakst

As the supporters of two different, often conflicting, approaches to stage design, Benois and Bakst deserve particular attention. Both artists played major roles in the opening seasons of the Ballets Russes — Benois with *Le Pavillon d'Armide* and Bakst with *Cléopâtre* — and both contributed directly to the "transports of admiration"[52] that the company elicited among their Paris audiences. While like Bakst, Benois, though less imaginatively, was able to move from century to century, from France (*Le Pavillon d'Armide*) to Russia (*Petrouchka* [Ills. 28-36; Nos. 159-280]) to China (*Le Rossignol* [Ills. 37, 38; Nos. 281-84]), he was always consistent in his historical evocation of a given epoch and, correspondingly, was outraged when a designer, such as Golovin (No. 530), preferred "irrelevant" luxury of ornament to an ethnographically correct reconstruction. On the other hand, Benois's sense of history was so acute that he knew exactly when and how to enliven a certain costume or set with the spirit of its time. Consequently, with his encyclopedic knowledge of 17th and 18th century France and his personal passion for Versailles, Benois was an ideal interpreter of the ballet *Le Pavillon d'Armide* staged by Fokine in 1907 and then taken to Paris in modified form by Diaghilev in 1909.

With the exception of a few designs for an unrealized production of his own ballet *The Prodigal Son* (spring, 1907), *Le Pavillon* was Benois's first professional theatrical engagement since 1903 (when he designed the Mariinsky production of *Die*

---

50 See I7. Also see the following exhibition catalogs: I15, I42, and I51.
51 See, in particular, D18, D26, D32, F4, F7, F10, F15, F28, F54 and F63.
52 G6, p. 55.

65. Alexandra Exter: Costume Design for a Barber, Hand on Hip, *La Cueva de Salamanca*, 1924 (No. 464)

Götterdämmerung), and it was one of his most successful. As Fokine recalled:

> Alexandre Nikolaevich seemed to be — immediately and exclusively — a theatrical artist. All his colors, his lines related directly and obviously to the particular juncture on stage. The costumes, the sets, the lighting — everything was aimed at expressing the content of the piece.[53]

Benois's interpretation of *Le Pavillon* was a striking one, expressing the "fantasy of Berain allied to a delicate colour sense of Bocquet."[54] He demonstrated clearly how well he understood the historical era — especially in his celebrated décors for Scenes I, II and III (Ill. 26; Nos. 123, 136, 137, 139) and his numerous costumes as for Armide's Favorite Slave, the Vicomte, and various ladies and gentlemen in waiting (Ill. 25; Nos. 124, 141, 144).

Although Benois was sometimes guilty of pedantic compilation of historical detail, this failing was not especially evident in *Le Pavillon* or in any early productions such as *Le Festin* (1909, costumes only), *Giselle* (1910; Nos. 152-58), *Petrouchka*, and *Le Rossignol*. For example, Benois's designs for *Giselle* were so well received at its Paris premiere that the original Benois version was reconstructed many times thereafter. Benois's lyrical evocation of Giselle, his fantastic castle, and romantic cemetery of the Wilis became images enjoyed by many audiences — in spite of Diaghilev's initial reluctance to produce this particular ballet. Still, both Diaghilev and Benois knew quite well that the French also expected a measure of "barbarism" from the Russians, and, of course, Diaghilev satisfied this desire with his productions of *Petrouchka* and *Le Sacre du Printemps*, presenting the "pagan" music of Stravinsky to the Paris audiences. *Petrouchka* was especially close to Benois's heart since he associated it with fond childhood memories of a time when the bazaars, fairs, and *balagany* were still part of St. Petersburg folk life. The dancer Nathalie Trouhanova, who was not an enthusiast of Diaghilev's company (Ill. 17; Nos. 89; 767), admitted grudgingly that *Petrouchka* did, indeed, evoke the sense of play, although for her it was the "cretin" Nijinsky who stole the show.[55]

In the introduction to his *Reminiscences of the Russian Ballet,* Benois stated:

> It is with particular pleasure that I have accepted the suggestion that I should write my reminiscences of the ballet; yet I am not, strictly speaking, a devotee of the ballet, or even a *balletomane*.[56]

Justifiably, Benois felt that he had, nonetheless, contributed much to the global success of the Russian ballet, but it is important to realize that at heart he remained an illustrator and studio painter and gave his first attention to the "picture." Bakst, however, understood that the set and costume designer, the dancer, the actor, the singer, etc., were of equal importance within the spectacle, and he perceived the stage in three dimensions, not as a mere extension of the easel — something that is immediately apparent from his achievements such as *Cléopâtre*, *Schéhérazade*, and *Le Dieu Bleu* (Ill. 18; No. 91). True, Bakst did not believe in audience participation

---

53 F19 (English edition), p. 188.
54 G19, p. 9.
55 N. Trukhanova: *Ogni rampy. Vospominaniia*, Part 3. RGALI, f. 1403, op. 1, ed. khr. 932, l. 74. For contextual commentary on the genesis and role of Petrouchka in Russian culture see C95 and C127.
56 F7, page v.

66. Alexandra Exter: Costume Design for Aelita, Queen of the Martians, *Aelita*, 1924 (No. 465)

67. Alexandra Exter: Costume Design for a Female, *Aelita*, 1924 (No. 468)

68. Alexandra Exter: Costume Design for a Martian, *Aelita*, 1924 (No. 469)

and he distinguished emphatically between the proscenium and the auditorium, but his concentration on elements such as diagonal axis, occult symmetry, and rhythmicality of the body broke the pictorial, i.e. painterly, convention of 19th-century stage design, and, therefore, built a solid bridge between performer and public.

Bakst's approach to stage design was an exciting one because, while joining "l'outrancière d'un barbare au raffinement sensuel d'un décadent,"[57] he also made every effort to coordinate the decoration and the human figure. Like the Constructivist designers of the 1920s, especially Exter, Popova, and Stepanova, Bakst regarded the body as a kinetic force that was to be exposed and amplified in its movements, not enveloped and disguised. Instead of the constrained, static unit that the body tended to represent on the academic stage (a tradition that Benois never finally rejected), Bakst tried to make the body itself as expressive as possible. He also supplemented the physical motions of the body either by attaching appendages such as veils, feathers, and jewelry (e.g., Ills. 10, 12, 15-17, 19; Nos. 75, 81, 85, 86, 89, 90, 93) or by creating intricate abstract patterns of dress (e.g., Nos. 77, 80, 88, 102, 103) — so as to extend and emphasize the body's movement through space. While Bakst liberated the body from its traditional fixed role on stage, he did not expose it merely for erotic appeal and he did not sympathize with the trend towards nudity on stage that Evreinov and other St. Petersburg theater people were promoting in the 1910s. However much Bakst loved the human anatomy, he perceived its beauty as lying in the tension between the seen and the unseen, something that he achieved so masterfully in his costume design for the Blue Sultana in Schéhérazade (Ill. 12; No. 81) and in the costume design for the Péri in the ballet of the same name of 1911 (Ill. 17; Nos. 89, 90). True, sometimes Bakst could digress from his measure of good taste, especially when erotic fantasy clouded esthetic vision — as in the luxurious poster for Caryathis (Ill. 19; No. 93).

Bakst's gravitation towards exotic ballets — Cléopâtre, Schéhérazade, La Péri, Narcisse, Le Dieu Bleu — coincided, too, with the fashion for the Orient that affected Moscow and St. Petersburg almost as much as it did Paris and London. Diaghilev's production of Judith in 1909 with designs by Bakst and Valentin Serov (Ill. 188; Nos. 910, 911), Fokine's production of Islamey in 1912 with designs by Boris Anisfeld (Ill. 6; No. 28), Tairov's production of Sakuntala in 1914 with designs by Kuznetsov (No. 690), and Mikhail Mordkin's preparation of Nur and Anitra with designs by Anatolii Petritsky in 1923 (Ills. 160, 161; Nos. 812, 813) were also gestures to this vogue. Bakst, however, should not be identified exclusively with this trend, even though he was fascinated by the sex and violence of the East, for he also possessed a shy, "Magdalenian" character[58] that sometimes dictated restrained and sober artistic forms. A case in point is Jeux, produced by Diaghilev in Paris in 1913.

With music by Debussy, choreography by Nijinsky, and designs by Bakst, Jeux tells the story of a flirtation during a game of tennis "placed in the year 1925."[59] Against a romantic set of stylized trees, electric lanterns, and a rambling villa in London's Bloomsbury, Bakst dressed his tennis players in simple, economical, utilitarian costumes that anticipated the Constructivist costume and set designs of the 1920s by Nina Aizenberg (Ill. 2; Nos. 1-2), Tatiana Bruni (Ills. 49-51; Nos. 393-95),

---

57 G6, p. 56.
58 Letter from Alexandre Benois to Walter Nouvel dated 3 November, 1897, in RGALI, f. 938, op. 1, ed. khr. 46, l. 66.
59 Unsigned article entitled "Gowns of the Sexes" in The Daily Mirror, London, 1913, 3 April.

69. Alexandra Exter: Costume Design for a Woman with a Fan, *La Dama Duende*, ca. 1924 (No. 470)

70. Alexandra Exter: Costume Design for a Man with a Ruff, *La Dama Duende*, 1924 (No. 471)

71. Alexandra Exter: Costume Design for a Woman with a Farthingale, *La Dama Duende*, 1924 (No. 472)

Popova (Ill. 171; No. 847), and Stepanova (Ill. 192; 977-80). Indeed, it is not very distant from the monochrome functional sportswear of Bakst to the *sportodezhda* (sports clothes) of Stepanova, Aizenerg's uniforms, or even Popova's blue denims for the workers in *The Magnanimous Cuckold* (1922) and Rodchenko's coverall of 1923. Furthermore, Bakst's knee-length skirt for the female tennis player represented an audacious development in fashion, at once enhancing her sexuality and, at the same time, symbolizing woman's freedom from the strictures of her 19th-century social round. In this respect, Bakst was actually continuing his search for a new *haute couture* that he had begun in 1912, and the dynamism of sports obviously attracted him no less than the dynamism of the dance. Perhaps he even wondered whether one day sports might replace ballet.

As far as the visual effect of *Jeux* is concerned, there is one element in particular that connects this piece to the productions of the avant-garde in the 1910s and 1920s — and that is the restrained use of color and the consistent application of contrast between white and dark colors. The critic A. E. Johnson even referred to the cinematographic quality of *Jeux*.[60] Anticipating the exercises in black and white of Sergei Eisenstein and Dziga Vertov, Bakst and Nijinsky dismissed color from the dance composition (except for the male player's red necktie), providing a visual compensation via sharp formal juxtapositions rather than the decorative exuberance of the early Ballets Russes productions. Nijinsky's reliance on geometric movements in his choreography (Debussy even accused him of being subject to the power of Emile Jaques-Dalcroze, "one of the greatest enemies of music")[61] brings to mind parallel developments in the visual arts such as Tatlin's uncolored reliefs of 1914 onwards, Malevich's *Black Square* of 1915, Rodchenko's black on black paintings of ca. 1918 and his photographs of 1923 onwards, even Naum Gabo's translucent constructions for *La Chatte* of 1927 (No. 512). Bakst and Nijinsky's involuntary connections with the Russian avant-garde become even clearer when we recall that in *Jeux* Nijinsky wanted to have an airplane fall on to the stage — just as the Cubo-Futurists had in their transrational opera *Victory over the Sun* of the same year (Ills. 147-55; Nos. 752-64), for which, incidentally, Malevich also designed a sportsman's costume.[62]

Natalia Goncharova and Mikhail Larionov: "What imagination!" [63]

The innovative force of *Jeux* puts into question the conventional division of the chronology of the Ballets Russes into the pre-War "decorative" phase and the post-War "modern" phase. True, Diaghilev did concentrate on revolutionary (some even said proletarian) ballets in the 1920s, such as *La Chatte* and *Le Pas d'Acier* (Nos. 1165-67), but the position of *Jeux* within the early engagements indicates that the pictorial, narrative ballet (e.g. *Schéhérazade*) was not the exclusive focus of the Ballets Russes even at that time.

The question of the Ballets Russes and the avant-garde is a complex one and many relevant designs in the Lobanov-Rostovsky collection carry the imprint of Neo-Primitivism, Cubism, Futurism, Constructivism, and Surrealism. There is, however,

60 A. E. Johnson: *The Russian Ballet*, New York: Houghton Mifflin, 1913, pp. 195, 196.
61 Letter from Claude Debussy to Robert Godet dated 9 June, 1913. Quoted in D18, p. 290.
62 See G2, item No. 1146.
63 S. Volkonsky: *Otkliki teatra*, P: Sirius, N.D., p. 57.

72. Alexandra Exter: Stage Design for a Revue, ca. 1925 (No. 474)

73. Alexandra Exter: Stage Design for a Spanish Pantomime, ca. 1926 (No. 476).

74. Alexandra Exter: Stage Design and Lighting Study for Scene 3, *Don Juan*, ca. 1926 (No. 477)

75. Alexandra Exter: Stage Design for an Operetta with Action on Five Platforms (No. 488)

76. Alexandra Exter: Stage Design for a Revue with Action in Center and on Both Sides of Stage (No. 492)

one curious aspect that is worth emphasizing, namely that the true experiments and innovations in sets and costumes were made by Russian rather than by Western artists. Of course, Giacomo Balla, Georges Braque, Max Ernst, Henri Matisse, Pablo Picasso, Giorgio de Chirico, and other Western painters also contributed to the development of the Ballets Russes, but, ultimately, the styles that they applied (e.g. Cubism and Surrealism) tended to be two-dimensional, pictorial systems appropriate to the intimate space of the studio, but not always operative within the public space of the theater. Primary exceptions are Picasso's creations for *Parade* (1917) and Balla's for *Feu d'Artifice* (1917), but Braque's resolutions for *Zéphyr et Flore* (1925) or de Chirico's for *Le Bal* (1929), while visually appealing, hardly relate to the dynamic, architectonic demands of the ballet in action.

In our search for those designers who made a determined effort to construct rather than to paint the sets and costumes for the Ballets Russes, we must give first attention to the work of Goncharova and Larionov, even though some of their key commissions for Diaghilev (e.g. *Liturgie* [Ills. 88-97; Nos. 541-58] and *Histoires Naturelles* [Ill. 125; Nos. 707-09]) were not implemented. Skeptical of the sometimes false finesse of their St. Petersburg colleagues, both artists, representing the new Moscow culture, were of a younger generation than Bakst and Benois. Goncharova and Larionov, when they joined Diaghilev's company in 1914, were already acknowledged leaders of the Russian avant-garde and brought to their new vocation a wide array of pictorial ideas deriving from their own explorations of Neo-Primitivism, Cubo-Futurism, and Rayism.

Of particular significance for Goncharova and Larionov were "primitive" art forms such as children's drawing, graffiti, the *lubok*, naive painting, toys, icons, etc, and in the bright colors, emphatic lines, intense stylization, and general optimism of Russian peasant art they found a vigor and integrity that seemed to be lacking in their contemporary bourgeois culture. Goncharova, Larionov, and their immediate colleagues such as Malevich, Alexander Shevchenko, and Tatlin regarded the traditional arts and crafts as a decisive element in the renovation of Russian art and design, even arguing in 1913 that Russia was part of the East and that the East was the real birthplace of all modern art. "Painted wooden dolls sold at [Russian] fairs", proclaimed Goncharova, "are... Cubist works".[64]

Drawing on their knowledge and appreciation of indigenous art forms, Goncharova and Larionov transformed the Russian stage into an effervescent buffoonery. With their reds, oranges, and yellows, distorted perspectives, and love of play, they imbued the theater with an ebullience and vitality that reminded spectators — once again — of the *balagany*, the fairground, and the circus. Both artists restored the energy of farce to the modern stage, often accomplishing this through the introduction of illogical, absurd or "capricious" elements. Larionov's designs for *Le Soleil de Nuit* of 1915, *Histoires Naturelles* of 1916, *Contes Russes* of 1917 (Ill. 127; No. 711), *Chout* of 1921 (Ills. 129, 130; Nos. 716-20), and *Le Renard* of 1922 (Ills. 131-34; Nos. 721-24), or Goncharova's for *Le Coq d'Or* of 1914, *Liturgie* of 1915, and *España* of 1916 (Ill. 98; No. 559) rely for their effect on this tension between narrative sequence and what the Russian Cubo-Futurists referred to as

---

64 N. Goncharova: "Cubism" (1912). English translation in B12, p. 78. Also see other Neo-Primitivist statements by Goncharova and Alexander Shevchenko, e.g. her preface to the catalog of her exhibition in Moscow in 1913 (English translation in B12, pp. 55-60) and Shevchenko's Neo-Primitivist manifesto of the same year (ibid., pp. 44-54).

77. Robert Falk: Set Design, *The Travels of Benjamin III*, 1927 (No. 499)

78. Fedor Fedorovsky: Two Costume Designs for Prince Khovansky, *Khovanshchina*, 1912 (No. 500)

79. Fedor Fedorovsky: Costume Designs for Persian Slave Dancers in Act 2, *Khovanshchina*, 1912 (No. 501)

"shift" or "displacement."[65] Larionov's several versions for the single set for *Le Renard* express the very essence of this story about a cockerel, a fox, a cat, and a ram, who dance, sing, and mime on an improvised platform outside a Russian hut in winter. It was quite in keeping with this mood that in the 1929 revival of *Le Renard* Lifar employed circus acrobats to mime the roles of the dancers, thus creating a double action and returning the ballet to the status of "burlesque activity."[66] Larionov's conception was simple, unadorned, and functional, providing the bare necessities for the plot and extending the mood of Stravinsky's candid, humorous music. Larionov was not averse to low taste, fooling around, eclecticism, and plagiarization, and he combined these qualities in a vivid, clever manner that seemed very distant from the staid elegance of *Le Pavillon d'Armide* and *Giselle*.

Goncharova also joined forces with Stravinsky in her sets and costumes for *Les Noces* of 1923 (Nos. 568) and *L'Oiseau de Feu* of 1926 (Ill. 101; Nos. 569, 570). In her backdrop for the latter, she broke the expected sequence of the churches by piling them on top of each other, using them, therefore, not as the architectural description of a certain city, but as a geometric pattern — a method that integrates with the staccato, angular composition of Stravinsky's music. Goncharova's calculated rendering for *L'Oiseau de Feu* was rather different from Bakst and Golovin's scintillating designs for Diaghilev's original production of 1910 (No. 533) and also from her own Neo-Primitivist interpretation of *Le Coq d'Or*, which, to use her own words, "creates, psychologically and visually, an overall theatrical unity."[67] The Lobanov-Rostovsky collection is fortunate to possess one of the several versions for the first scene of *Le Coq d'Or*, which, rather like Larionov's set for *Le Soleil de Nuit*, indicates the artist's orientation towards the *lubok*, the painted tray, the store signboard, and the carved woodwork of the *izba* (Russian hut). When the curtain rose on *Le Coq d'Or* on 21 May, 1914, Paris audiences applauded its raucous, "Eastern" colors, even if the moderate Benois was rather taken aback, "Least of all did I like the protrusion of her scenery, which seemed to impede the action."[68] No doubt, Benois preferred the restrained, stylized designs that his World of Art colleague Bilibin, made for Sergei Zimin's production of *Le Coq d'Or* in Moscow in 1909 — "looking like a book illustration." (No. 370).[69]

In its more stylized, more elegant version, Goncharova's and Larionov's Neo-Primitivism had a large following among Russian artists in the 1910s and early 1920s. Posters, theater bills, book illustrations with scenes of fairy-tales or with depictions of toys and dolls became very popular as "collectibles," evoking a growing nostalgia for the Russia of yesteryear. Even though the Goncharova and Larionov designs for the Diaghilev Ballets Russes are distinctive and unmistakably of their hand, the return to Russia's past and the evocation of her Orthodox and mercantile rituals is identifiable with the most diverse artists of this time — from Re-mi (Ill. 175; No. 858) to Stelletsky (Ill. 190; No. 959), from Fedor Fedorovsky (Ills. 78-80; Nos. 500-02) to Konstantin Yuon (Nos. 1172-75).

---

65 "Shift" or "displacement" translates the Russian word *sdvig*, a concept often invoked by the Russian Cubo-Futurists. In its most basic sense "shift" meant the transference of an object from its normal context into a strange or illogical one, e.g. Kazimir Malevich's application of a wooden spoon to his picture *Englishman in Moscow* of 1913. The poet Alexei Kruchenykh even wrote a tract on the use and function of "shift" in Russian poetry; see his *Sdvilogiia russkogo stikha*, M: MAF, 1923.
66 "Burlesque activity" translates the first two words of the text of the cover of Alexandre Benois's souvenir program for *Petrouchka* (Paris, 1911).
67 Quoted in G28, p. 86.
68 A. Benois: "Vospominaniia o balete" in *Russkie zapiski*, Paris, 1939, No. 18, p. 101.
69 F30, p. 12.

80. Fedor Fedorovsky: Costume Designs for the Boyar Shaklovityi and the Scribe,
Khovanshchina, 1913 (No. 502)

Streamlining the Ballets Russes

Perhaps it was this retrospective repletion that encouraged Diaghilev, always open to new solutions, to move away from his emphasis on Russian folklore towards the "industrial ballets" of the 1920s. It is a tribute to Diaghilev's unfailing curiosity about the new in art and to his instant recognition of authentic innovation that his most experimental, "modern" productions were staged at the end of his life — *La Chatte* (1927; Nos. 512, 823), *Le Pas d'Acier* (1927; Nos. 1165-67), and *Ode* (1928; Nos. 1095-97). These ballets integrated new concepts of music, choreography, and visual dynamics, and actually have more in common with developments in ballet today than they do with the heyday of Bakst and Benois.

La Chatte, choreographed by George Balanchine, premiered in Monte Carlo in April, 1927, and then in Paris the following month. Telling the story of a young man in love with a cat who becomes a woman only to change back into a cat, *La Chatte* deals with the central theme of metamorphosis and instability. In order to emphasize these qualities, the designers Gabo and his brother Antoine Pevsner applied their abstract principles of Constructivism: by building transparent and refractive surfaces from mica, celluloid, black oilcloth, etc., they created a plastic, variable décor and costumes that reflected and magnified the movements of the dancers. The shapes distributed about the stage were deprived of figurative value (except for Pevsner's towering statue of Venus) and the circular stage itself revolved, ever changing the physical appearance of its own appurtenances.

La Chatte was one of several "industrial" spectacles inside and outside Russia that relied for their scenic effect on modern, hi-tech materials and streamlined actions. Meierkhold's Constructivist presentations in the 1920s, such as *The Magnanimous Cuckold* and *Death of Tarelkin*, the movie *Aelita* (Ills. 66-68; Nos. 465-69), Bronislava Nijinska's *Le Train Bleu* of 1924 (designed by Henri Laurens; cf. Nos. 728-29), and, of course, Leonide Massine's *Le Pas d'Acier,* were other expressions of this esthetic. The latter, in particular, symbolized Diaghilev's wish to modernize ballet by bringing it close to contemporary themes and topical issues. Produced in Paris in June, 1927, with music by Sergei Prokofiev and sets and costumes by Yakulov, *Le Pas d'Acier* portrayed the new Socialist Russia with her glorification of the factory and the machine, to which end Yakulov introduced mechanical, moving parts, including real hammers. Not surprisingly, Diaghilev was criticized for this "Communist" tendency, as he had been in May, 1917, when he had allowed a red banner to be waved in the final scene of *L'Oiseau de Feu*,[70] although neither Diaghilev, Yakulov, nor Massine seemed especially interested in the political interpretations of *Le Pas d'Acier*. Massine enthused:

> The wheels and pistons on the rostrums moved in time to the hammering movements of the young factory workers, and by strengthening the tableau with a large ensemble group in front of the rostrums, so evolving a multi-level composition which welded together the scenic and the bodily movements, I was able to create a climax of overwhelming power.[71]

The success of the Ballets Russes, and not least of its experiments in design, depended fundamentally on the inspiration of Diaghilev, and with his passing in 1929

---

70 Reported in untitled, anonymous note in *Kulisy*, M, 1917, 14 May, No. 20, p. 15.
71 F28, p. 172.

81. Petr Galadzhev: Poster Design for a Street Cinema on Wheels for Lev Kuleshov's Film *Death Ray*, Moscow, 1925 (No. 516)

82. Petr Galadzhev: Poster Design for the Film *Circle*, 1927 (No. 517)

83. Pier Galadzhev: Petr Galadzhev: Poster Design for the film *The Knot*, Moscow, 1927 (No. 519)

the company disbanded. Its artists, dancers, and choreographers diversified their interests, a fission that stimulated the formation of smaller troupes in Europe and the USA or the enhancement of ones already in existence. The Nijinska Ballets and Théâtre de la Danse Nijinska, Marie Kousnezoff's Opéra Privé de Paris (Ills. 110-12, 115; Nos. 630-41, 651-59), Vera Nemtchinova's Ballets Russes (Nos. 1057-63, 1180, 1181), and the Ida Rubinstein Company (Nos. 305-07) were among the enterprises that benefited from this distribution of talents. The principal heir to the Diaghilev legacy, Colonel W. de Basil's Ballet Russe (1931-52), never really attained the synthetic level of the Diaghilev enterprise, even though it boasted many famous names and was well organized. Ultimately, it merely crystallized prior discoveries and, scenically, never produced the equals of *Schéhérazade, Contes Russes* or *La Chatte.*

Intimate Theater in St. Petersburg and Moscow

One of the paradoxes associated with the Ballets Russes is that the company never performed in Russia. On several occasions Diaghilev expressed the desire to take certain of his productions to St. Petersburg, but each time his plans were thwarted.[72] Naturally, many Russian artists and intellectuals saw the Diaghilev productions on their various trips to the European capitals, but the full impact of the Ballets Russes was never felt in Moscow or St. Petersburg. However, prior or parallel to the establishment of the Ballets Russes, a number of sophisticated theatrical enterprises opened at home — not on the grandiose scale of the Diaghilev operation, but, certainly, of strong artistic value. Some of these were Symbolist "little theaters" where young artists such as Anisfeld, Mikhail Bobyshev, Vladimir Denisov, Nikolai Kalmakov, Sapunov, and Sudeikin interpreted a repertoire of Decadent plays by Leonid Andreev, Alexander Blok (Ills. 135, 159; Nos. 738, 800), Maurice Maeterlinck (Nos. 31, 746), Gerhart Hauptmann, Stanislaw Przybyszewski, Oscar Wilde, and other writers of the *fin de siècle*. Of primary importance in this context was the theater that the actress Vera Komissarzhevskaia (sister of Fedor Komissarzhevsky) founded in St. Petersburg in 1906. Evreinov, one of her greatest admirers, even asserted that she did more for the public propagation of the new art than all the exhibitions and journals did together, simply because every evening she forced her public to confront the new art for two or three hours at a stretch.[73]

During the 1906-07 season, Komissarzhevskaia commissioned a number of experimental productions, which were staged by Meierkhold, including Hauptmann's *Hedda Gabler* (designed by Vasilii Milioti and Sapunov), Maeterlinck's *Soeur Béatrice* (designed by Sudeikin), and Blok's *Balaganchik* [Fairground Booth] (designed by Sapunov). Meierkhold joined Komissarzhevskaia after his brief collaboration with Stanislavsky and his so-called Theater-Studio attached to the Moscow Art Theater. Even though Stanislavsky shared his colleague's enthusiasm for the Symbolist dramas of Andreev, Henrik Ibsen, and Maeterlinck, and, for example, encouraged Meierkhold to prepare Maeterlinck's *La Mort de Tintagiles* (designed by Sapunov and

---

72 According to Sergei Grigoriev (D11, p. 59) Diaghilev wished to present a season of the Ballets Russes in St. Petersburg in 1911, but the theater that he had reserved — the People's House — burned down. According to a note in *Novaia studiia*, 1912, No. 3, p. 24, Diaghilev "has decided to put on in St. Petersburg Igor Stravinsky's *L'Oiseau de Feu* and *Petrouchka* and then Claude Debussy's *Dieu Bleu* and *Faune."*

73 N. Evreinov: "Khudozhniki v teatre V.F. Komissarzhevskoi" in *Alkonost*, SP, 1911, p. 127.

84. Iraklii Gamrekeli: Stage Design for Act I (Version), *Mystery-Bouffe*, 1924 (No. 520)

85. Iraklii Gamrekeli: Stage Design for Act II, *Mystery-Bouffe*, 1924 (No. 523)

86. Iraklii Gamrekeli: Stage Design for Act III, *Mystery-Bouffe*, 1924 (No. 524)

Sudeikin) and Hauptmann's *Schluck und Jau* (designed by Nikolai Ulianov) at the Theater-Studio, the two men were essentially of different artistic psychologies.

Stanislavsky's basic orientation was towards the Realist presentation, as he demonstrated in his productions of Anton Chekhov's plays and in his famous 1909 production of Ivan Turgenev's *A Month in the Country* designed by Mstislav Dobujinsky at the Moscow Art Theater (cf. No. 453). For Stanislavsky the actor remained the dominant and dynamic force, while the décor served only to supplement the speech and gestures, a perception that, essentially, contravened the new principles espoused by Appia and Meierkhold. Of course, Stanislavsky was not altogether foreign to the new radical trends and he manifested an interest even in the theatrical experiments of the avant-garde, but, ultimately, he regarded stage design as description and commentary, as a static rather than a dynamic element — something evident from the remark he made to Dobujinsky when they were working on *A Month in the Country*. "The décor should grow out of the floor."[74] True, the Theater-Studio that Stanislavsky founded in 1905 and the four subsequent Moscow Art Theater Studios[75] were intended as experimental laboratories for acting and design, but, always in the shadow of their august flagship, they were not the keen practitioners of avant-garde ideas — as is manifest from the 1914 production of *A Cricket on the Hearth* with designs by Mikhail Libakov (No. 741) or from Matrunin's and Simov's various interpretations (Nos. 788, 951).

Meierkhold — and Komissarzhevskaia — wished to redress this imbalance and, certainly, their choice of plays and artists demonstrated their preference for the radical and the unorthodox. The production of *Soeur Béatrice*, for example, elicited harsh criticism both for its "conditional" acting and for its "abstract" sets and costumes, leading Walter Nouvel to dismiss it as a "sad and hopeless" production.[76] Sapunov's decorative arrangement for *Hedda Gabler* was also provocative: the action took place not within the usual three walls, but against a backdrop of a single panneau located close to the front of the stage and leaving only a narrow area of the stage for the actors. Komissarzhevsky described the effect as follows:

> It was romantic. A blue northern harmony. The colors did not whirl about, they were not restless. Everything was tranquil. Everything was like a phantom. The stage seemed to be enveloped in a bluish-green, silver smoke. The back curtain was blue.[77]

Komissarzhevskaia, Meierkhold, and Sapunov further undermined the principles of Stanislavsky's Realism in their most famous collective endeavor, the production of *Balaganchik* [Fairground Booth], also in 1906. Blok's play, dedicated to Meierkhold, was both an immediate outgrowth of the Symbolist esthetic, relying on fabulous visions of the "other world," and also a satire on Symbolism as a philosophical worldview. Judging from the décor, Sapunov fully understood the dual significance of the play with its motifs of depersonalization, spiritual insolvency, and inescapability. The artist created a stage within a stage, the outer one hung with blue canvases, the inner one denuded to reveal the ropes, footlights, boards, prompter's box, etc. — as if to affirm

---

74 F45, p. 352.
75 For information on Stanislavsky and the Moscow Art Theater Studios see C31, Vol. 1, pp. 384-90; Vol. 2, pp. 160-96; C42 (both volumes).
76 Letter from Walter Nouvel to Sergei Diaghilev dated 22 November, 1906. Inserted as note 5 to a letter from Benois to Nouvel dated 14 (1) December, 1906, in RGALI, f. 938, op. 1, ed. khr. 46, ll. 224-26.
77 F. Komissarzhevsky: "Sapunov-dekorator" in *Apollon*, 1914, No. 4, p. 16.

87. Natalia Goncharova: Stage Design for Act I, *Le Coq d'Or*, ca. 1914 (No. 534)

that the ulterior reality that the Symbolists aspired to disclose was just as mundane as the everyday world of appearances. The theme of the philosophical impasse — the fear that "there" was the same as "here" — that Blok expressed in his play was further communicated through Sapunov's emphasis on the elements of prosaic bourgeois reality, such as the florid wallpaper, the pseudo-Rococo table, and other images of domesticity, realia that we also recognize in the stage designs for *Uncle Vanya* (Ill. 184; No. 893). Incidentally, Meierkhold and Sapunov's interpretation anticipated an artistic device that was a central ingredient in Evreinov's philosophy of the theater, i.e. the exposure and accentuation of the theater's conditionality.

The productions of *Soeur Béatrice*, *Hedda Gabler*, and *Balaganchik* focused attention on the Symbolist and Decadent drama and reinforced an artistic tendency in the Russian theater that endured until at least the Revolution, as is indicated by Vladimir Baranoff-Rossiné's exuberant interpretation of the birth of Venus of 1917 (Ill. 23; No. 108). In spite of her apparent naïveté, Komissarzhevskaia was one of the most liberated producers in St. Petersburg and, until her death in 1910, was involved in several scandalous episodes. After all, her theater was responsible for the notorious production of *Salomé* in 1908 (with designs by Kalmakov), which was banned by the Holy Synod, but which seems to have initiated a renewed interest in eroticism and nudity in the theater in general (Ills. 105, 106; Nos. 594-98)[78] and to have reinforced the balletic and operatic interepretations of *Salomé*, in particular, witness to which is Diaghilev's staging of *La Tragédie de Salomé* with designs by Sergei Sudeikin in 1913 (Ill. 193; No. 983). In stage design, she encouraged an ornamental "Bakstian" style easily identifiable with the early work of Anisfeld (Ill. 6; No. 28), Bobyshev, Denisov, and Kalmakov, and clearly supported the kind of décor that "demanded that the audience be only an eye, an enormous eye with absolute sensitivity."[79] On the one hand, it was this emphasis on what Sudeikin called "painterliness" and "color orchestration"[80] that attracted Tairov, prompting him to invite painters such as Kuznetsov (No. 690), Aristarkh Lentulov, and Sudeikin to design his productions at the Chamber Theater. On the other hand, one suspects that it was Komissarzhevskaia's preference for heightened decorativism and morbid themes that compelled her to break with Meierkhold in 1907. He then went on to pursue his very different interests — in eurhythmics, the Japanese theater, and the circus, even if, apparently, he did return to *Salomé* in 1920 (Ill. 157; No. 798).

Komissarzhevskaia's esthetic of a refined Decadence was preached and practised at an entire array of elite establishments in St. Petersburg from the Stray Dog cabaret to Yuliia Sazonova's Marionette Theater (No. 599). Incidentally, Levkii Zheverzheev, the foremost St. Petersburg collector of stage designs, whose collection became the basis of the Leningrad Theater Museum, seems obviously to have favored this spicy, highly decorative kind of theatrical activity (No. 929).[81] Meierkhold, on the other hand, was suspicious of it, as he demonstrated in his magazine *Liubov k trem apelsinam* [Love for Three Oranges] during 1914-16,[82] and his famous productions

---

78 See N. Evreinov, ed.: *Nagota na stsene*, SP: Butkovskaia, 1910. This collection of articles contains the "Manifesto on Nudity" by Ivan Miasoedov.
79 A. Efros: "Zhivopis teatra" in *Apollon*, 1914, No. 10, p. 28.
80 Statement by Sergei Sudeikin. Quoted in G39, p. 171.
81 See the listing of his collection in G2.
82 A number of articles in Meierkhold's *Liubov k trem apelsinam* stressed the formal and constructive aspect of stage design. See, for example, S. Vermel: "Moment formy v iskusstve," 1914, No. 1, pp. 15-17; V. Meierkhold: "Benua-rezhisser," 1915, No. 1-3, pp. 95-126.

88. Natalia Goncharova: Costume Design for a Cherub, *Liturgie*, 1915 (No. 544)

89. Natalia Goncharova: Costume Design for St. Andrew, *Liturgie*, 1915 (No. 545)

90. Natalia Goncharova: Costume Design for St. Mark, *Liturgie*, 1915 (No. 546)

91. Natalia Goncharova: Costume Design for One of the Magi (the Abyssinian King?), *Liturgie*, 1915 (No. 548)

92. Natalia Goncharova: Costume Design for St. John, *Liturgie*, 1915 (No. 549)

93. Natalia Goncharova: Costume Design for St. Peter, *Liturgie*, 1915 (No. 551)

94. Natalia Goncharova: Costume Design for the Six-Winged Seraph, *Liturgie*, 1915 (No. 552)

95. Natalia Goncharova: Costume Design for an Apostle, *Liturgie*, 1915 (No. 555)

96. Natalia Goncharova: Costume Design for St. Matthew, *Liturgie*, 1915 (No. 556).

of the early 1920s are anything but Symbolist. In any case, the Komissarzhevskaia Theater provided a firm basis for the establishment of a recognizable school of St. Petersburg-Leningrad stage design that reached its fruition in the 1920s, when a number of talented young artists came to the fore. Artists such as Nikolai Akimov (Nos. 13-14), Valentina Khodasevich, who worked almost extensively for the Theater of People's Comedy (Nos. 601-04), Moisei Levin (No. 740), Semeon Mandel (No. 787), and Elizaveta Yakunina (No. 1171) dominated the exhibition "Stage Design in the USSR 1917-X-1927" held in Leningrad in 1927.

The Cabaret Theater

In 1912 Evreinov staged a play called *In the Side-scenes of the Soul* at the St. Petersburg cabaret called the Crooked Mirror. The distinguishing feature of this short piece, designed by Bobyshev, was that the dramatic events took place inside the human body. Here you could actually see the mounting excitement through the inflating lungs and beating of the heart. This was intimate theater in the true sense of the word and it symbolized a primary aspiration of Russian experimental theater of the 1910s — to move inwards psychologically and physically. Such performances were, of course, close to the theatrical searches of the avant-garde and also represented an essential characteristic of the cabaret, a theatrical form that prospered and multiplied in St. Petersburg, Moscow, Odessa, Kiev, and Tiflis/Tbilisi in the 1910s and early 1920s and then in the émigré communities of Berlin, Paris, and New York.

Some of the Russian (as well as Ukrainian and Georgian) cabarets such as the Crooked Mirror (founded in St. Petersburg in 1908), the Bat/Chauve-Souris (founded in Moscow in 1908), the Stray Dog (founded in St. Petersburg in 1911), the Comedians' Halt (founded in Petrograd in 1916), Khimerioni (founded in Tiflis in 1917), and Crooked Jimmy (founded in Kiev in 1919) received wide recognition for their literary and artistic achievements. Others such as the Café Pittoresque (Moscow, 1918; Ill. 135; No. 738), the Peacock's Tail (Moscow 1922-23), the Little Berry (Petrograd, 1923), the Cricket on the Hearth (Leningrad, 1925; No. 1100), and the Stable of Pegasus (Moscow, 1919; Ill. 239; No. 1158) were too ephemeral to make a major contribution to the evolution of stage design. In the German and Austrian tradition, the cabaret was often used to criticize and censure social and political mores. The Simplicissimus in Munich and the Fledermaus in Vienna, for example, were arenas for incisive political discourse. It should be noted, however, that their Russian counterparts did not, as a rule, support or condemn any particular ideological system. Satire and parody were applied, but in esthetic or "domestic" contexts (the love triangle, the boudoir, the mother-in-law), rather than for the coverage of a political event, at least until the opening of the Blue Blouse "agit-cabarets" in 1923 (Ill. 2; Nos. 1-12).

The format of the Russian cabaret — a confined stage housed in a small restaurant or café providing amusement through variety sequences — owed much to Western models (Nikita Baliev's Bat, for example, carried an obvious reference to the Fledermaus). However, the Russian cabaret was also indebted to local traditions and perhaps one reason why this theatrical form flourished so well on Russian soil is because of its links with the conventions of the indigenous folk theater — the *balagan*, the *skomorokhi* (traveling buffoons), the *narodnoe gulianie*

97. Natalia Goncharova: Costume Design for One of the Magi, *Liturgie*, 1915 (No. 557)

(popular promenading). The Russian cabaret incorporated various elements from the folk theater — quick repartee, rapid sequence of numbers, clowning, the *pliaska* (Russian dance) and so on. There were many other expressions of this "vulgarity" in Modernist Russian theater, including the 1911 and 1912 productions of *The Emperor Maximilian and His Disobedient Son Adolf* with designs by Tatlin and the 1913 extravaganza *Victory over the Sun* with designs by Malevich. These loud, ingenuous productions were, to a large extent, also examples of vaudeville, which entertained not so much by their plotlines as by their riot of colors, crazy costumes, burlesque antics, noise — and by what Vasilii Kandinsky (No. 600), in an appreciation of the circus, called a "completely unconscious approach to the meaning of movement."[83]

There were, however, several elements that distinguished dramatic productions such as *The Emperor Maximilian* and *Victory over the Sun* from the cabarets. At the Stray Dog, the Bat, and Jascha Juschny's Blue Bird (Berlin, 1920s), for example, the audience was baited and abated by the interpolations of the impresario — who continued the tradition of the *zazyvala* (barker or touter) of the *balagan*. For example, the writer Teffi (pseudonym of Nadezhda Buchinskaia), who composed many of the numbers for the Bat, recalled that:

> Everything... was the invention of one man — N.F. Baliev. He asserted his individuality so directly and totally that assistants would only hinder him... He is a real sorcerer.[84]

Within the specific context of the cabaret, the communication between the *zazyvala* (whom we would now call the impresario) and the audience was of vital significance, although successful contact also presupposed a particular kind of public — a public that had the time, means, and inclination to attend the cabaret evenings, that possessed a degree of sophistication, and that was willing to listen to, and interact with, the impresario. By 1908, at the height of her Capitalist boom, Russia had such an audience, a fact demonstrated by the mushrooming of intimate societies and clubs in the metropolitan areas such as the Society of Free Esthetics in Moscow. Socialite salons also flourished, offering entertainment and sometimes enlightenment.

During the decade before 1917 there were many little theaters, nightclubs, and restaurants in St. Petersburg and Moscow that called themselves cabarets. The functions and artistic levels at these institutions varied considerably. Some relied for their effect on "singers, nude dancers, choirs, circus numbers, and gypsy choruses";[85] others focused on a particular group, such as the Moscow Cubo-Futurists; and their collected names constitute a kaleidoscope of the most exotic epithets — Bi-Ba-Bo, the Green Lampshade, the Pink Lantern, the Stable of Pegasus, Petrouchka, and the like. In general, however, the Russian (and European) cabarets confronted artists with a set of circumstances that forced them to rethink the question of design. The close proximity of the audience to the actors, the miniature stage, the ever-changing repertoire, and the need to switch sets and costumes rapidly (something that Aizenberg fulfilled with her universal costumes — see No. 1),

83 V. Kandinsky: *Programma Instituta khudozhestvennoi kultury* (1920). Translation in K. Lindsay and P. Vergo: *Kandinsky. Complete Writings on Art*, Boston: Hall, 1982, Vol. 1, p. 467.
84 RGALI, f. 1174, op. 1, ed. khr. 10, l. 79.
85 E. Gershuni: *Rasskazyvaiu ob estrade*, L: Iskusstvo, 1968, p. 16.

98. Natalia Goncharova: Costume Design for a Spanish Dancer, *España*, ca. 1916. (No. 559)

the extension of the decorative scheme to the walls and even on to the ceiling (as in the case of the Café Pittoresque) — such conditions caused the critic André Boll to observe in 1926 that this kind of theater was the "ultime refuge où le décorateur puisse exercer sa fantasie et son imagination."[86]

The Bat (Chauve-Souris)

On 29 February, 1908 (a leap year), Nikita Baliev, an actor with the Moscow Art Theater, and a few colleagues opened a tiny theater, the Bat, in Moscow. The idea of establishing such a cabaret derived from the famous *kapustniki,* or "cabbage parties" (from the Russian word *kapusta* meaning "cabbage"), organized by the supporters of MKhAT to celebrate Shrovetide and the end of winter. At first, the Bat, housed in a cellar (decorated by Sapunov) of the Pertsov House near Red Square, served as a night spot for actors to unwind after performances, to parody the seriousness of Stanislavsky's method (Stanislavsky himself frequented the cellar), to discuss new roles, etc.:

> The footlights were abolished... Often the seating area itself became the scenic area... At The Bat the numbers were often played amidst the tables.[87]

In 1910 Baliev moved his enterprise to another cellar on Miliutinskii Lane and redesigned the space to resemble a European cabaret, with a small stage at one end of the room and small tables seating eighty people in the remaining space. Baliev now began to organize regular revues, even though, strictly speaking, the cabaret was still open only to Moscow Art Theater employees — however, non-members were allowed in if they could produce a petition signed by twelve Moscow Art Theater actors. In 1915 Baliev made his final move in Moscow to spacious premises decorated by Sudeikin on the Bolshoi Gnezdnikovskii Lane. By then the Bat was a focal point of Moscow night life and remained so until its closure in 1919.

Baliev invited prominent writers and producers to work for him, including Andreev, Andrei Bely, Briusov, Sergei Gorodetsky, and Alexei Tolstoi, and Vasilii Luzhsky, Meierkhold, and Ivan Moskvin, although his favorite script writers were Tatiana Shchepkina-Kupernik and Boris Sadovskoi. In the early days many important artists performed at the Bat, including Fedor Chaliapin, Leonid Sobinov, and Stanislavsky, and in 1916-18 the director of performances was Kasian Goleizovsky, the great Constructivist balletmaster of the 1920s; the musical director both in Russia and in emigration was Alexander Arkhangelsky. The kind of dramatic repertoire that Baliev commissioned was the short skit, often the parody of a famous classic such as Gogol's *Inspector General,* and he was also fond of "animating" themes, an antique porcelain group, for example, or a *lubok.* Baliev liked hyperbole, numbers that alternated rapidly between the comic and the tragic, and a steady interchange with the audience. Once, for example, he asked everyone to sing "Akh, akh, ekh, im!" — to impersonate someone sneezing.[88]

---

86 G6, p. 69.
87 As reported by Liudmila Tikhvinskaia in her doctoral thesis entitled *Russkii dorevoliutsionnyi teatr miniatiur,* submitted to the Lunacharsky Institute of Theatrical Art, Moscow, in 1976. This information on p. 54. Also see her monograph E52, pp. 19-36, 340-77; and A54, pp. 52-53, 308-10. A Bat cabaret also operated in St. Petersburg in 1913-17, although this had nothing to do with Baliev's enterprise. See E56, pp. 136-37.
88 Ibid., p. 82.

99. Natalia Goncharova: Costume Design for the Shah Shahriar, *Le Mariage d'Aurore*, or
Le Mariage de la Belle au Bois Dormant, ca. 1922 (No. 567)

As far as stage design was concerned, the tiny stage precluded lavish productions or majestic experiments of the type that Tairov and his artists were undertaking at the Chamber Theater. Rather, stage design for Baliev and his artists, who included Re-mi (Ill. 175; Nos. 656-62) and Sudeikin (No. 985), consisted of either a literal representation of characters and periods (Baliev was fond of the 18th century) or the application of special technical effects. For example, cinematography and a theater of shadows were used in a number called *Life's Metamorphoses,* and Baliev once installed red lamps under the tables that went on and off in time with the music. Young artists and producers found this environment attractive, for it provided the "opportunity to experiment... and a great number of purely technical assignments that, in turn, stimulated a number of, so to speak, laboratory tests."[89]

According to his autobiography, at the beginning of 1919 Baliev took part of his company to Kiev, hoping to recapture a middle-class public fast disappearing.[90] However, Baliev's brief sojourn there was of little consolation, so he returned to Moscow in the winter of 1919 to reinstate the Bat in the old premises "without heating, among burst pipes, flooded, with boards piled high in the foyer."[91] In spite of these adversities, Baliev decided to celebrate the twelfth birthday of the Bat in as grand a style as possible and presented a traditional extravaganza of fast revues:

> Remnants of old Moscow and actors from all the theaters were at the jubilee. The Bolsheviks were also there... Went on until three a.m. Big party at home the next day. Illegal use of electricity. Five days later arrested.[92]

Shortly thereafter, Baliev was freed, and he immediately left Moscow, arriving in Paris by way of Tiflis and Constantinople, early in 1920.[93] With his indefatigable energy, Baliev soon regrouped the far-flung members of his troupe and reformed them into the Chauve-Souris at the Théâtre Femina, Paris, later that year. Until January, 1922, when Morris Gest brought the Baliev company to the USA, the Chauve-Souris toured France, Germany, and England, scoring immediate success: between 1920 and 1924 Baliev put on 273 performances in Paris, 175 in London, and many more in the USA. After 1922 the Roof Theater of the old Century Theater in New York became the more or less permanent home of the Bat, and Baliev continued to welcome enthusiastic wealthy audiences there until his death in 1936. With his passing, the Bat closed, although it enjoyed a brief, but uninspired revival in 1943 under the directorship of Leon Greanim.

Rather like Diaghilev with his productions of *Petrouchka*, *L'Oiseau de Feu,* and *Le Sacre du Printemps,* Baliev propagated a mythology of Russia. He reinforced the public's desired interpretation of Russia as a colorful, exuberant nation consisting of samovars, bears, merchants and peasants in high leather boots, lovely country maidens, sleighs hastening across the snow, carousing hussars, etc. Baliev commissioned talented artists

---

89 Yurii Ozarovsky cited in Dovle (pseudonym):: "Sezon v 'Letuchei myshi'" in *Rannee utro*, M, 1913, 2 October, p. 5.
90 N. Baliev: "Avtobiografiia" (undated). Published as "Sny o Rossii" in C121 (2004), pp. 214-38. Tikhvinksaia, op. cit., p. 146, gives the beginning of 1918 as the time of Baliev's move from Moscow to Kiev.
91 Baliev, op. cit., p. 2.
92 Ibid.
93 Part of the Bat company stayed in Moscow and continued to perform at the old premises on the Bolshoi Gneednikovskii Lane until 1923.

100. Natalia Goncharova: Costume Design for One of the Monsters, *The Firebird*, ca. 1926 (No. 569)

to render these images, including Nicola Benois (Ill. 42; Nos. 345-46), Lado Gudiashvili (No. 578), Vasilii Shukhaev (Nos. 948-49), Stelletsky (Ill. 190; No. 959), and Serge Tchehonine (Ills. 209-212; Nos. 1047-56), as well as Re-mi (Ill. 175; Nos. 857-62) and Sudeikin (Nos. 985-86). Even before the Revolution, the Bat identified itself with this sentimental evocation, and its numbers made frequent reference to a bygone Russia — such as *The Coachman's Yard*, *Village Women*, *The Hawker*, and *The Wooden Soldiers*. Baliev included gentle satires sometimes of a slightly erotic nature under titles such as *Love in the Ranks* [known in Paris as *Amour et Hiérarchie* [Ill. 42; Nos. 345-46]), *Platov's Cossacks in Paris* (Ill. 56; No. 430), *What the Prompter Sees from His Box*, *An Entrepreneur under the Sofa*, *A Virgin's Mirror*, and so on.

Baliev also stressed the appeal of Old Russia during his American years, playing to the taste of his émigré audience and of his clientele from Newport and the Hamptons, who refused to regard Russia as anything but Imperial pomp and circumstance or a mercantile bacchanalia. They wanted to see the expansive Russian soul and Baliev gave it to them: "If Russia laughs, the sky resounds with her laughter; if she weeps, her tears pass through countries like a tempest."[94] The result was a noticeable influence of this "counterfeit Russian provincialism"[95] on many aspects of American life in the 1920s. The critic Oliver Sayler wrote in 1927:

> Arriving unheralded, [The Bat] became at once the "thing to see"... Its music permeated our orchestras. *The Wooden Soldiers* traveled across the continent as fast as trains could carry people whistling it. Jazz received a staggering blow and never since has it been so raucous. The unabashed colors and designs of the costumes of the Chauve-Souris started a vogue that revolutionized our raiment.[96]

The Blue Bird (Der Blaue Vogel)

Baliev and the Bat inspired many imitations, both at home and abroad, although most of them were ephemeral. However, at least one, the Blue Bird (Der Blaue Vogel) deserves some attention since it attracted several important designers, including Pavel Tchelitchew, more often remembered for his contribution to the Ballets Russes (Ill. 229; Nos. 1095-97) and his Surrealist painting (cf. Ill. 230; No. 1098). Founded by the actor Jascha Juschny (Yasha Yuzhnyi) on Golzstrasse in Berlin in 1920,[97] the Blue Bird attracted a number of experimental artists and actors, achieving some degree of international prestige (touring the USA, for example, in 1931-32). Ksenia Boguslavskaia decorated the interior walls, while she, André Houdiakoff (Khudiakov) (No. 580), Elena Liessner-Blomberg (cf. Ill. 136; No. 743), Georges Pogedaieff, Jean Pougny (cf. Ill. 173; No. 850), Tchelitchew, and others painted the sets and costumes "almost for free, in return for breakfast."[98] In particular, the young Tchelitchew (Ills. 224-25; Nos. 1084-85) scored an immediate success with his luminous colors and spiralic forms, evident in the six productions that he designed for the Blue Bird, including *Der König rief seinen Tambour* and

---

94 *Chauve-Souris*. Program of the 1924-25 season, Paris, p. 1.
95 V. Shklovsky: *Zoo or Letters Not about Love*. Translated by Richard Sheldon, Ithaca: Cornell University Press, 1971, p. 89.
96 *The Bat*. Program of the 1927-28 New York season, unpaginated.
97 For information on the Blue Bird see A54, pp. 696-97; E19, H31, and H37.
98 E12.

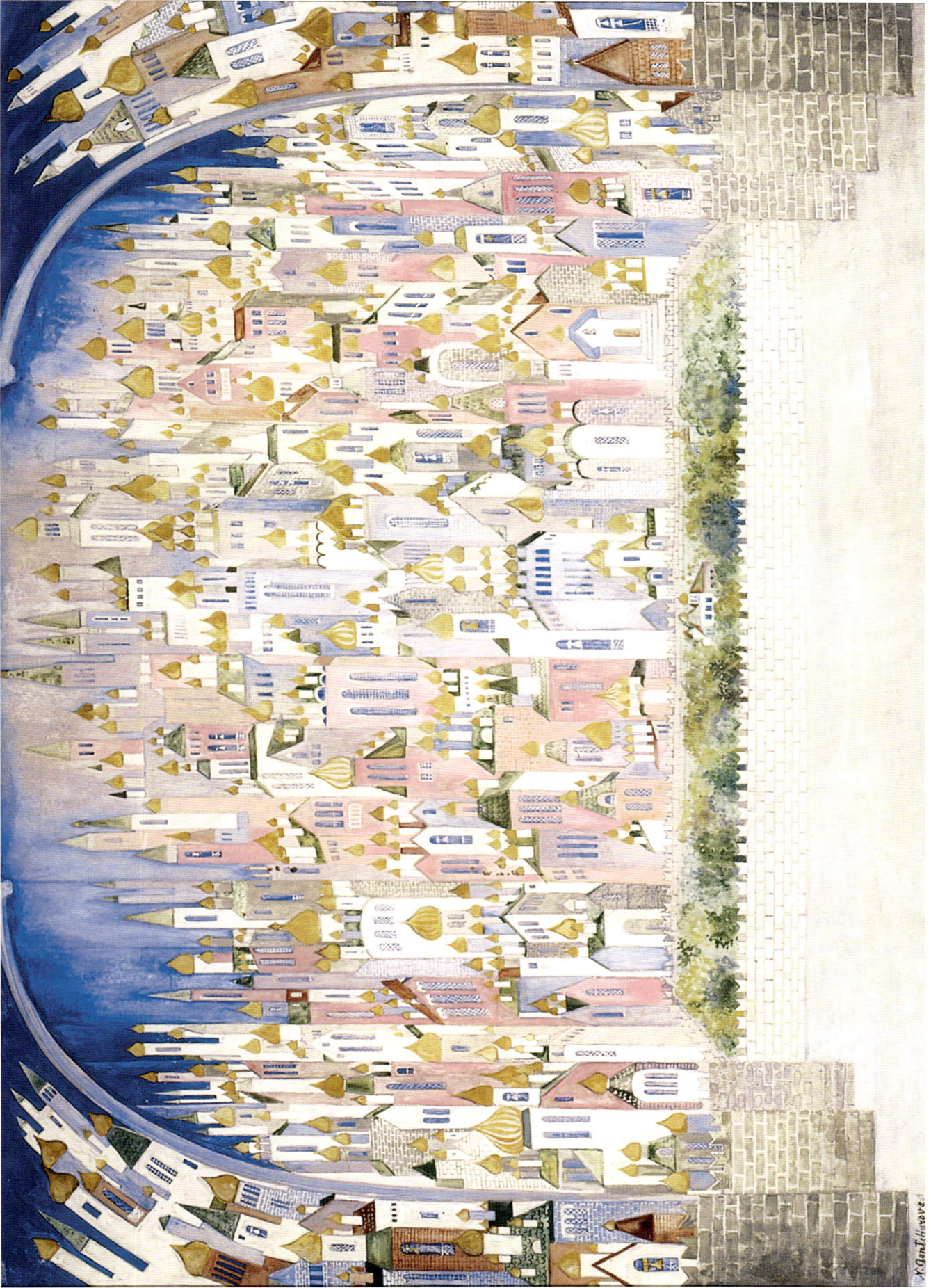

101. Natalia Goncharova: Backcloth Design for the Finale, *The Firebird*, ca. 1926 (No. 570)

Die Dreie Trommler, and for other concurrent theatrical engagements (Ills. 214-28; Nos. 1067-94).

During the 1920s, the Blue Bird, like other émigré cabarets in Berlin, such as the Carousel, Vanka-Vstanka, and the Romantisches Theater (Nos. 1178-79), provided a source of income for many jobless entertainers and painters as well as an emotional placebo for many displaced countrymen:

> Tired of politics and everyday life, the Russian visits his cabaret to search for a complete escape from the reality of life, searches for a cheerful self-oblivion in music, color, and play.[99]

The cabarets also attracted Germans, but, as one Russian reviewer noted, they "merely guffaw at those moments when we feel like crying."[100]

The Stray Dog

The Bat and the Blue Bird maintained a high professional standard, but they were not radical theaters either dramatically or visually and, in spite of their gifted personnel, they tended to attract an audience without especially high aspirations. The St. Petersburg cabarets, however, especially the Stray Dog and the Comedians' Halt (Ill. 102; No. 572), attracted prominent intellectuals from all disciplines and tended to commission lectures and recitations and to lead debates and polemics on "hot issues" rather than rely only on musical sketches and *tableaux vivants*. They were at once more international and more provocative, even though they, too, were indebted to the new middle classes for financial support.

The Stray Dog, for example, compered by Nikolai Petrov and Boris Pronin, hosted many important cultural events during its brief active life (1911-15), and it encouraged discussions on a wide range of issues, some as esoteric as:

> ... the Tarot, Theosophy, Alexandrian Christianity, the French magic revival, Russian Orthodoxy, neo-Platonism, Jacob Boehme, the monks of Athos.[101]

The Stray Dog did not espouse the cause of the avant-garde as represented by Malevich and Tatlin, but it was at the head of Russian intellectual life, and included Andreev, Evreinov, Karsavina, Mikhail Kuzmin, Lanceray, Alexei Radakov, Savelii Sorin, and Teffi among its corresponding members.[102]

The Stray Dog organized a wide variety of artistic and literary engagements, inviting, for example, Sergei Gorodetsky to speak on "Symbolism and Acmeism," Sergei Auslender to speak on "Theatrical Dilettantism," Marinetti to recite his poetry (introduced by Nikolai Kulbin; cf. No. 684), and young musicians to perform their works. Sudeikin, as artist-in-residence, often marked these events by designing special programs, panneaux, and even fancy dress costumes. The poet

---

99 *Der Blaue Vogel.* Undated Program of 1923 (?) Berlin season, p. 24.
100 Baian: "Russkoe iskusstvo za granitsei" in *Teatr i zhizn*, Berlin, 1922, No. 10, p. 14.
101 J. Moore: *Gurdjieff and Mansfield*, London: Routledge and Kegan Paul, 1980, pp. 54-55.
102 The documents in f. 212 at BTM contain much data on the programs and associates of the Stray Dog. Also see A54, pp. 85-86; E32; E56, pp. 48-51; E57; and A. Gribanov: "Iskusstvo, 'Sobaka' i 'farmatsevty'" in *Russkaia mysl*, Paris, 1987, 29 May, p. 12.

102. Boris Grigoriev: Four Dancers on a Stage, St. Petersburg, 1913 (No. 572)

Benedikt Livshits left the following description of the ambiance and programs of the Stray Dog:

> On so-called "extraordinary" Saturdays and Wednesdays, guests were told to put paper hats on their heads. They were handed these at the entrance to the cellar. Illustrious lawyers or members of the State Duma, famous the length and breadth of Russia, were taken unawares and, uncomplainingly, submitted to this requirement.
>
> At Twelfth-night and Shrove-tide masquerades actors, sometimes whole companies, would turn up in theatrical costume...
>
> The programs were the most diverse — from Kulbin's lecture "On the New Worldview" or Piast's "On the Theater of the Word and the Theater of Movement" to the "Musical Mondays," Karsavina's dancing or a banquet in honor of the Moscow Art Theater.
>
> In some cases the program dragged on for several days. It swelled into a "Caucasian Week" with lectures on travels in the Fergana Valley and the Zaravshan Mountains, with an exhibition of Persian miniatures, majolica, and fabrics, evenings of Oriental music and dances, or into a "Marinetti Week" or a "Week of Paul Fort, King of French Poets", etc. However, the main point of the program was not the scheduled part, but the unscheduled one — the unforeseen performances which would usually enthrall us the whole night through.[103]

As Livshits implies, until its closure in 1915, the Stray Dog entertained a wide and varied clientele, although its activities presupposed a literary and artistic awareness, and many key representatives of Russian (and European) Modernism were to be seen there. The rapid interchange of numbers, rehearsed or impromptu, the close alliance between spectacle and spectator, the marriage of "life" (the guests eating and drinking) and "art" (the performance) accommodated the Stray Dog easily within the genre of cabaret — and connected it directly to another intellectual cabaret of the time, i.e. Moscow's Café Pittoresque.

Café Pittoresque

In July, 1917, the Moscow entrepreneur, Nikolai Filippov, owner of the chain of Filippov cafés and patisseries in Moscow, acquired a disused iron foundry at No. 5 on Kuznetsky Most. Filippov wished to turn the foundry into an elegant, exotic, and fast-moving café, and, to this end, he invited Yakulov to propose a decorative scheme for the interior. Yakulov was confronted with a narrow, high space that culminated in a huge glass, hangar-like roof, which he proceeded to disguise with a series of "fairground-like"[104] colored areas composed according to his Simultanist system; he also painted the walls and stage cupola with motifs from Blok's play *The Unknown Lady* (cf. Ill. 35; No. 738).[105] The result, therefore, was a scenographic extension into the immediate environment of the audience, so that stage design now became "interior design" just as it did in the Chamber Theater decorated by Exter (Ill. 64; No. 463) and the First Soviet Theater in Orenburg "suprematized" by Ivan Kudriashev

---

103 F48, p. 215.
104 Yakulov said of his decorations for the Café Pittoresque that they were "fairground-like" (GAU [Chief Archive Administration, Moscow], f. 2306, op. 24, ed. khr. 54, l.1).
105 For more details on this see GAU, f. 2306, op. 24, ed. khr. 54, ll. 1-43.

103. Boris Grigoriev: Four Masked Actors, 1920 (No. 573)

(No. 633). Yakulov ensured that particular attention was paid to the fixtures, and he invited several avant-garde artists to assist him, including Lev Bruni, Sofia Dymshits-Tolstaia, Rodchenko, Boris Shaposhnikov, Tatlin, and Nadezhda Udaltsova. When the so-called Café Pittoresque opened for business on 30 January, 1918, visitors saw the following interior:

> There were all sorts of fantastic configurations made out of cardboard, plywood and fabric; lyres, wedges, circles, funnels, spiral constructions. Sometimes light bulbs were inside these solids. All this was interfused with light, everything revolved, vibrated — it seemed that the whole decoration was moving... All these things were hanging from the ceilings, from the corners, and from the walls.[106]

The bold transformation of the Pittoresque did not really extend to the dramatic repertoire produced on its tiny stage. True, the audience was the most heterogenous (from Blok to Vladimir Maiakovsky, from Anna Akhmatova to Meierkhold), but the Pittoresque operated more as a rendezvous for disoriented bohemians rather than as an experimental theater — just like the other intellectual venues of the time, such as the Poets' Café and the Stable of Pegasus. True, Meierkhold staged *The Unknown Lady* there in March, 1918, with designs by Lentulov; and Yakulov tried to involve Maiakovsky, the composer Arthur-Vincent Lourié (No. 1168-69), Annenkov, Kuznetsov et al. in various productions. But it seems that by September, 1918, the Café had degenerated into a "café chantant," and its premises — including its potted palms — were requisitioned by TEO NKP (Theater Section of the People's Commissariat for Enlightenment).[107] On the other hand, according to a detailed statement by Vasilii Kamensky dated 2 October, 1918, the Café could still have become an avant-garde center for the arts: among Kamensky's proposals for future programs were excerpts from his own and Maiakovsky's plays, verses by proletarian poets, ballet and rhythmical gymnastics, spontaneous questions from the floor and answers from the stage, the Café's own newspaper, etc.[108] True, the Café reopened at the beginning of 1919 as a "Club-Studio" under the title Red Rooster, and, like the Café Pittoresque, continued to attract Yakulov and his Imaginist friends, Sergei Esenin and Anatolii Marienhof (cf. Nos. 967-68), but it seems to have done little more than put on occasional concerts of music and served afternoon tea.[109]

The Blue Blouse
Intimate theater survived well into the 1920s in the Soviet Union, especially as a result of the implementation of the New Economic Policy (NEP) in 1921 that allowed a partial return to the free enterprise system and, therefore, the reestablishment of private restaurants, theaters, publishing-houses, etc. Advertisements for all kinds of "Hermitages," "Aquariums," "Grands Palais," and other cabarets and music-halls abounded in Soviet theatrical magazines of the early 1920s and as late as 1928 the Moscow telephone book still listed four theaters of a "lighter genre." For some political observers, including Anatolii Lunacharsky, Commissar for Enlightenment,

---

106 As recalled by the artist Nikolai Lakov. Quoted in B7, p. 101.
107 According to GAU, f. 2396, op. 24, ed, khr. 54, ll. 26-30.
108 List of proposals by Vasilii Kamensky for the Café Pittoresque dated 2 October, 1918, in GAU, Moscow, f. 2306, op. 24, ed. khr. 54, ll. 12-14.
109 Ibid. ll. 39, 40.

104. Karl von Hoerschelmann: Poster Design for a Conjuror, 1923? (No. 579)

the presence of so many night-spots was an unsavory development, a "corruptive theater. . one of the poisons of the bourgeois world,"[110] acceptable perhaps in post-World War I Berlin, but not on the front line of world Communism.

To some extent, the antidote to this poison was found in the cabaret itself. A flexible and accessible medium, it was simply adapted to political ends, and the result was the system of theaters known as the Blue Blouse (Ill. 2; Nos. 1-12). These Soviet versions of the variety theater presented contemporary revues, were highly politicized, and catered to a mass audience. For obvious reasons, the Blue Blouse could not depend for its effect on subtle allusions to Symbolist literature, to 18th-century aristocratic culture, or to middle-class values, as the Bat and the Stray Dog had done. The Blue Blouse was born of the Revolution, extended the genre of the agit-theater, and used the emblems of the Revolutionary cause (Red Army uniforms, factory songs, ideological slogans) to communicate the message. True, the Blue Blouse was influenced by the Constructivists with their propagation of "labor acrobatics and gymnastics" (see No. 1193),[111] but it was incapable of autoparody and lacked the basic component of the pre-Revolutionary cabarets, i.e. the forceful presence of the impresario.

The Blue Blouse attracted a number of talented young actors and designers, including Aizenberg and Boris Erdman (Ill. 59; No. 457), it was extremely popular, and even toured abroad. However, with the imposition of Socialist Realism in Soviet culture in the early 1930s and with the sharp attacks on "bourgeois" forms of art, the Blue Blouse, along with other latterday versions of vaudeville and the cabaret, was disbanded. In spite of enthusiastic attempts to maintain the Russian cabaret as a living expression in the Soviet Union, its further successes occurred only in emigration, thanks largely to the activities of Baliev and the Bat.

---

110 A. Lunacharsky: "Revoliutsiia i iskusstvo" (1920). Translation in B12, p. 195.
111 Ippolit Sokolov was the apologist of these principles. See, for example, his booklet *Sistema trudovoi gimnastiki*, M: TsIT, 1922.

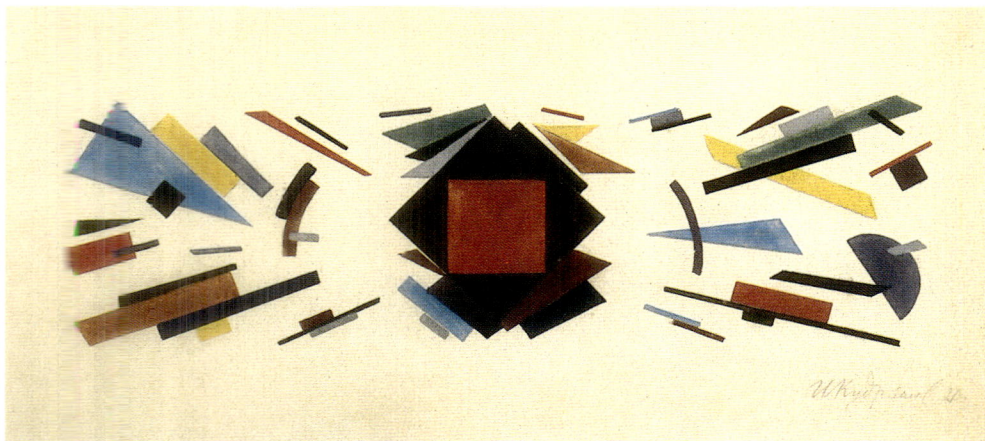

Ivan Kudriashev: Design for the Interior of the First Soviet Theater in Orenburg, 1920 (No. 683)

105. Nikolai Kalmakov: Costume Design for Salomé, *Salomé*, 1908 (No. 594)

III. THE AVANT-GARDE

A Brazen Can-Can in the Temple of Art [112]

Many of the artists represented in the Lobanov-Rostovsky collection belonged to what has come to be known as the Russian avant-garde: David Burliuk, Alexandra Exter, Pavel Filonov, Natalia Goncharova, Vasilii Kandinsky, Ivan Kliun, Mikhail Larionov, Aristarkh Lentulov, El Lissitzky, Kazimir Malevich, Liubov Popova, Jean Pougny, Alexander Rodchenko, Olga Rozanova, Varvara Stepanova, Vladimir Tatlin, and Georgi Yakulov are closely associated with this complex of personalities and ideas that transformed the course of Russian art in the 1910s and 1920s. The avant-garde stood for many different, often conflicting ideas: Filonov with his system of Analytical Art, Goncharova and Larionov with their Neo-Primitivism and Rayism, Kliun, Lissitzky, and Malevich with their Suprematism, Exter, Popova, Rodchenko, the Stenberg brothers, and Alexander Vesnin with their Constructivism. Although these artists were rarely interconnected by constant bonds of friendship or by the common support of a uniform style, they all believed passionately in the new art and felt that Russia was destined to play a primary role in the development of contemporary culture. Some of them, especially Filonov, Lissitzky, and Malevich, considered their art to be eschatological, maintaining that "Cubism and Futurism were revolutionary movements in art, anticipating the revolution in the economic and political life of 1917."[113] Consequently, they argued that the old world had to be destroyed and a new civilization projected and designed. The opera *Victory over the Sun* can be read as a metaphor for this belief.

The deliberate elevation of "vulgar" art forms to a higher position within the hierarchy of the arts was a service that many Russian artists, poets, and directors rendered in the early years of this century. They aspired to remove false auras from traditional styles, to "throw Pushkin, Dostoevsky, Tolstoi, et al., overboard from the Ship of Modernity," as the Cubo-Futurists declared in their 1912 manifesto[114] to challenge Raphael with the signboard, to replace Verdi with Vampuka.[115] The artists of the avant-garde also found that one way in which "sacred" art could be "desanctified" was to remove the traditional gap between the artifact and the spectator and to welcome and explore all styles, past and present, Western and Eastern (see No. 701). The intimate space of the cabaret, the improvisations of the circus, the impromptu gestures of the fairground — such elements served to extend the proscenium into the auditorium and, for this reason, attracted artists eager to take art from the studio into the street. No doubt, this attitude encouraged Pougny to design and wear "abstract" costumes for the Cubist street procession organized by the Sturm Gallery in Berlin in February, 1921

---

112 See Note 125.
113 K. Malevich: *O novykh sistemakh v iskusstve* (1919). Translation in B12, p. xxxiii.
114 From the Futurist manifesto *Poshchechina obshchestvennomu vkusu* (1912). Translated as "A Slap in the Face of Public Taste" in V. Markov: *Russian Futurism*, Berkeley, California: University of California Press, 1968, pp. 45-46.
115 *Vampuka, the African Bride,* a "model opera in two acts" composed by Vladimir Erenburg with a libretto by M. N. Volkonsky, was produced at the Crooked Mirror, St. Petersburg, in 1909. It was a parody of the classical opera and poked fun at the scenic stereotype, especially of Grand Opera. Consequently, in common parlance, *Vampuka* became a synonym for hackneyed routine and vulgar taste.

106. Nikolai Kalmakov: Costume Design for a 'Cellist, *Salomé*, 1908 (No. 595)

(Ill. 173; No. 850), and Aizenberg, Natan Altman (No. 15), Annenkov (Ills. 8-9; Nos. 42-44), Tatiana Bruni (Ills. 49-51; Nos. 393-96), Popova, and other champions of the avant-garde to involve themselves in agit-theater and mass actions just after the Revolution.

Much of the output — pictorial and verbal — of the avant-garde can, in fact, be accommodated within this context of market-place magic. It is a context that is often evoked casually and superficially, but the relation between the conventions of the *balagan* and the circus to the artistic behavior of, say, David Burliuk, Goncharova, Larionov, and Malevich runs deep and deserves particular attention. There are images and motifs in their paintings and designs that can be explained or, at least, illuminated by reference to popular amusements; and even though there can never be a single, primary reason for the formulation of a particular artistic style, the causes and effects of Rayism (Larionov), *zaum*, or transrationalism (Malevich), and Constructivism (Popova, Rodchenko, Stepanova, Yakulov) can certainly be connected to the canons of mass entertainment.

The social and cultural milieu that formed the essential worldview of Larionov, Malevich, and Tatlin was very different from that of Bakst, Benois, and Somov. They were often born into humble families that had no pretentions to cultural grandeur and they often left secondary school in their early teens. In other words, Larionov and his colleagues were not exposed to the intellectual régime of the World of Art artists and it is misleading to connect them too readily with the sophisticated ideas of Symbolist philosophy on the one hand and higher mathematics on the other. Here were spontaneous, impetuous artists who operated more by instinctive response than by sober calculation, and the kind of cultural endeavor that distracted them was not the spiritualist séance or the ordering of the chemical elements, but the life of the street. Certainly, in the case of the World of Art, the more studious artists such as Benois were also interested in the primitive, but for them this was a scholarly exercise to be adjusted upwards to high art, whereas the avant-garde favored the contrary approach, maintaining that high art should be demoted. Many of their actions were aimed at doing just that — rude pictorial subjects, explicit eroticism, mystifications, scandalous names and titles (e.g. Larionov's "Jack of Diamonds," "Donkey's Tail," and "Target" exhibitions, see Nos. 737, 700, and 701, respectively), and body painting. In a primary sense, therefore, the avant-garde simply applied and expanded the traditions of the clown, the charlatan, and the conjuror.

The circus and other forms of "magic" enjoyed remarkable popularity in Russia at the end of the 19th century: the circus troupe of Ciniselli, the clowns Anatolii Durov, Ivan Kozlov, and Vitalii Lazarenko, and the magician Leoni (pseudonym of Vladimir Larionov; not a relative of Mikhail) were household names,[116] and, clearly, Karl von Hoerschelmann was drawing on such precedents for his poster design of a conjuror (Il. 104; No. 579). As the *skomorokhi* and *balagany* receded into history (Benois records that the last *balagany* closed in St. Petersburg in ca. 1900),[117] new forms of mass entertainment developed, including the professional circus (often staffed by Italians, Turks, and gypsies) and, beginning in 1896, the movie industry. Catering to an eager public, these recreations concocted and proffered "illusions"

---

116 On the circus in Russia during the late 19th and early 20th centuries see Anatolii Durov's memoirs (first published in Voronezh in 1914), i.e. E29. Also see E5 and E72.
117 F7, p. 325.

107. Viktor Kiselev: Costume Design for Beelzebub, *Mystery-Bouffe,* ca. 1921 (No. 615)

(the Russian word for "conjuror" is *illiuzionist* and the early cinemas in Russia were called "*illiuziony*"), illusions that became ever more complex and spellbinding as technological possibilities advanced. In fact, we must remember that the making of these factories of dreams just before and after 1900 paralleled the development of other, more pragmatic wizardries, i.e. the telephone, the phonograph, the telegraph, and various other mechanical and electrical apparatuses that could also create miracles. Conjurors and clowns — and also the artists of the avant-garde — referred increasingly to such machines in order to enhance their creative gestures.

Levitations, beheadings, sawing ladies in half, face painting, dressing up, ventriloquy, divinations by fakirs, X-ray photography, electric motors, movies, mobile theatrical lighting — these are just some of the tricks that can be associated with the great Russian circuses and also with the avant-garde, and a number of intriguing parallels can be traced. The 1913 production of *Victory over the Sun*, for example, relied substantially on a sophisticated illumination system;[113] Larionov's *Peacock* (Ill. 125; No. 708) was supposed to be operated by a curious vocal mechanism; whole theatrical productions such as *The First Distiller* (Il. 8; Nos. 42-43), *Mystery-Bouffe* (Ills. 84-86, 107-08; Nos. 520-24, 608-18, 194), and *The Bed Bug* (Nos. 821, 867-74) — were clearly modeled on the circus; and some artists such as Vladimir Bekhteev (Nos. 109-17) and Boris Erdman (Il. 59; No. 457) even designed costumes for the circus itself. The weird clothes and painted faces of clowns are referenced in the costumes and face painting of David Burliuk, Goncharova, Larionov, Mikhail Le-Dantiu, and Ilia Zdanevich (No. 1184). The great Russian clown Durov used to enter the circus ring on a pig, shocking and amusing his public — just as Larionov did with the pig that trots in and out of his Neo-Primitivist paintings; moreover, Durov would dress up his pig and other animals in the most outrageous costumes, much as Larionov did with the insects and animals for *Histoires Naturelles* (Ill. 125; Nos. 707-09) and *Le Renard* (Ils. 131-34; Nos. 721-24).

The conjuring trick, the art of ventriloquy (transmuted by the Cubo-Futurists into their concept of *sdvig*, or shift, and into their appliqués of words or materials on the painted surface as in Petritsky's costumes for *Nur and Anitra* of 1923; Ills. 160-61; Nos. 812-13), and the powers of the magician contributed much to the theatricality of the avant-garde artists. However, unlike the clown and the conjuror, they did not make a strong division between "art" and "life," and the exhibitions, rude paintings, rowdy behavior and raucous manifestoes aimed to "shock the bourgeoisie" — were all components of a total spectacle. That is why Goncharova, Larionov, I. Zdanevich et al. propagated the idea of face painting in public places, including art exhibitions, as they declared in their 1913 article "Why We Paint Ourselves":

> We have joined art to life. After the long isolation of artists, we have
> loudly summoned life, and life has invaded art. It is time for art to invade
> life. The painting of our faces is the beginning of the invasion. That is
> why our hearts are beating so hard.[119]

---

113 See Benedikt Livshits's description of the lighting system at *Victory over the Sun* in F48, p. 164.
119 M. Larionov and I. Zdanevich: "Pochemu my raskrashivaemsia" (1913). Translation in B12, p. 81.

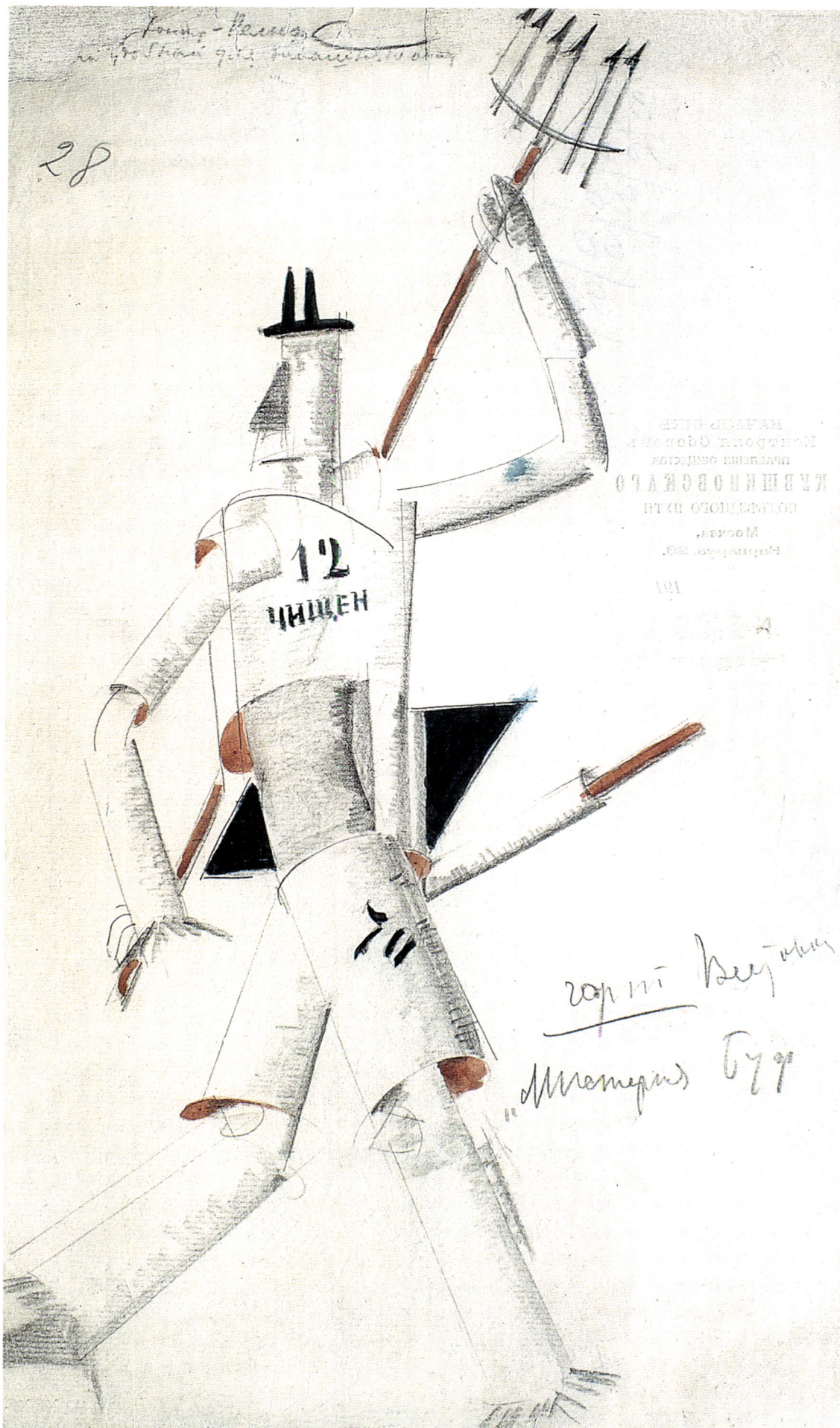

108. Viktor Kiselev: Costume Design for the Devil Herald, *Mystery-Bouffe*, ca. 1921 (No. 616)

Exhibitionism: from the Jack of Diamonds to the Pink Lantern

The avant-garde artists used many opportunities to disseminate their art in the public arena — street promenades, provincial tours, cabarets, and the professional stage, as in the case of Goncharova's and Larionov's involvement in the Ballets Russes. They also regarded the art exhibition as a means of theatrical expression, often dressing and acting at their venues to attract attention and enter into polemics with the public. A clear example of the exhibition as exhibitionism was the "Jack of Diamonds" of 1910-11, one of the first major confrontations between the avant-garde (Goncharova, Kandinsky, Larionov, Malevich et al.) and the bourgeoisie. Later on, its founder-members, particularly Larionov and Lentulov, claimed various explanations for the title, but whoever coined the term, it was eminently successful as a publicity stunt. When the poster advertising the show was hung up on 10 December, 1910, people thought it referred to a gambling casino, a lunatic asylum, a house of ill-repute, even a theater, but few imagined that this was an art exhibition. The title had many associations — with the *valet de carreau* (a rascal who appears in Molière's plays), with a pornographic novel by Pierre Alexis de Ponson du Terrail, with the patterns of aces of diamonds on prisoners' uniforms of the time, and, of course, with the card tricks of both conjurors and gamblers.[120] Such associations aroused much righteous indignation and the Governor of Moscow even forbade the opening of the exhibition (although it opened on time regardless).

It is in the context of exhibitionism — of public spectacle — that the projects of the avant-garde acquired their full significance, for with them the artists hoped to carry the stage into the street and, literally, to rebuild the "old house of the theater."[121] Moreover, although the artists of the avant-garde pretended to spurn and malign their public, obviously they were interested in the response of the community at large to their paintings, decorations, and manifestoes, which is why the theater was a vital means of expression for them. After all, practically all the radical Russian artists of the 1910s and 1920s were directly involved in theatrical productions, often as set and costume designers.

A case in point is the short-lived Pink Lantern cabaret that opened in Moscow in October, 1913. Projected as a Futurist theater by Goncharova, Larionov, Ilia Zdarevich, and the poets Konstantin Bolshakov and Maiakovsky, the Pink Lantern was to have had a Futurist dramatic repertoire and the scenic resolution to have been Rayist and *zaum* (transrational) with:

> . . the stage mobile and moving to different parts of the auditorium. The décors are also mobile and follow the actor... the music and lighting play an important role since they correspond to the free movements of the dance.
> In many plays the language is beyond the limits of the language of ideas, being a free and invented onomatopoeia.[122]

The Pink Lantern closed after only one performance, but even so Larionov and the "followers of Futurist novelties"[123] managed to paint the faces of members of the

---

120 For a discussion of the name Jack of Diamonds, see G. Pospelov: "O 'valetakh' bubnovykh i valetakh chervonnykh" in *Panorama iskusstv 77*, M, 1978, pp. 127-42.
121 G12, p. 9.
122 Anon: "Okolo khudozhestvennogo mira. Grimasy v iskusstve. K proektu futuristicheskogo teatra Moskve" in *Teatr v karikaturakh,* M, 1913, 8 September, No. 1, p. 14.
123 One of the practitioners of Larionov's face painting was the Moscow socialite Antonina Privalova described in *Teatr v karikaturakh* as the "first follower of Futurist novelties" (ibid., 1913, 21 September, No. 3, p. 14.)

109. Gustav Klutsis: Design for Decoration of the Moscow Kremlin Celebrating the IV Congress of the Communist International and the Fifth Anniversary of the Revolution, 1922 (No. 622)

audience even though, according to some observers, the result was not especially "Futurist."[124] The point is that the public responded in the same way as it did to the painted faces of clowns, rebutting or accepting the outlandish invitation to have a pig painted on the cheek or forehead, and certainly not taking the "illusions" seriously. One correspondent described such an evening:

> The Futurists abused the "crowd" with all the words at their disposal, and the audience tormented these "clowns of art" mercilessly... as a result the artist Goncharova slapped a certain barrister...
> A disgraceful, brazen and talentless can-can reigns dissolutely in the temples of art, and grimacing and wriggling on its altars are these shaggy young guys in their orange shirts and painted physiognomies.[125]

Of course, Larionov and his comrades were aware of the Italian Futurists' theatrical innovations, especially as described by Marinetti, even though in 1912-14 Larionov had little respect for his rival — "he's a renegade, a traitor, and we'll throw rotten eggs at him."[126] Marinetti's ideas on the "polydimensional Futurist spatio-stage" and "electro-dynamic architecture... plastic, luminous elements moving at the center of the theatre pit"[127] were translated and discussed widely in the Russian press.[128] and Larionov integrated them with his own Rayist system. We remember, for example, his vigorous costume design for a *Lady with Fans* of 1915-16 (Ill. 126; No. 710) created probably for Catherine Devillier (Devilliers), who rehearsed in *Histoires Naturelles* and *España* (Ill. 98; No. 559) in Lausanne in 1915. Although Larionov's *Lady with Fans* derives in part from his Rayist experiments, it also brings to mind the contemporary work of the Italians, especially of Fortunato Depero. After all, although he did not work for the Ballets Russes until 1916, Depero was much concerned with the theme of dance, drawing and painting works such as *Ballerina* (1916) and *Futurista — Movimento d'Uccello* (1916). The former work is especially close to Larionov's *Lady with Fans*, and, highly indignant, Depero himself noted the apparent borrowing.[129]

Victory over the Sun

Just as Goncharova and Larionov were acting up in Moscow and then in Paris, Malevich and Tatlin were also investigating the possibilities of theater as a medium of creative expression. If Larionov was impetuous and "dissolute," then Malevich and Tatlin were perhaps more calculating — in modern parlance, "they had their act together." Ultimately, their experiments in stage design in 1911-13 were of greater import to the formation of a genuinely new design esthetic — one that would be

124 P. K.: "Rozovyi fonar," ibid., 1913, 13 October, No. 6, p. 15.
125 Anon.: "Opiat futuristy (vmesto peredovoi)" in *Akter*, M, 1913, No. 4, pp. 1-2.
126 N. Serpinskaia: "Memuary intelligentki dvukh epokh" in RGALI, f. 1604, op. 1, ed. khr. 1248, l. 78/34.
127 F. Marinetti: "La scenografia futurista" in *La Biennale*, Venice, 1928, June, pp. 14-15. Sources dealing with Italian Futurist theater can be found in the relevant sections of I61 and I62.
128 See, for example, B. Shaposhnikov: "Futurizm i teatr" in *Maski*, 1912-13, No. 7-8, pp. 29-38 (with translations from Marinetti's statements). For indications of Russian translations of relevant Italian manifestoes see M. Drudi Gambillo and T. Fiori: *Archivi del futurismo*, Roma: De Luca, 1958, Vol. 1, pp. 495-53.
129 An undated prospectus by Depero for the *Chant du Rossignol* (*Il Canto dell'Usignuolo*) on display at the Civico Museo Depero, Rovereto, Italy, carries clear indications that Depero was highly incensed by Larionov's apparent plagiarism.

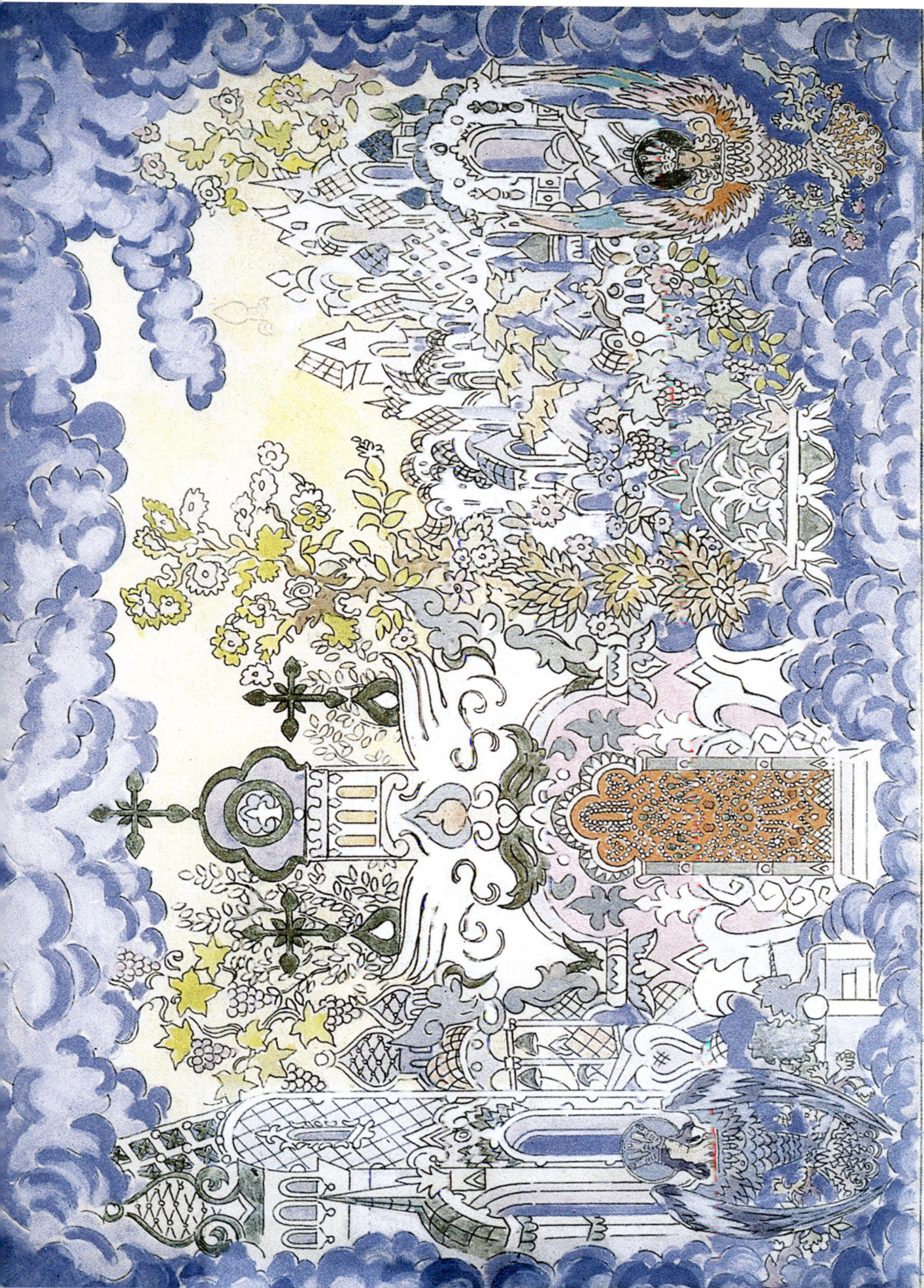

LÉGENDE DE LA VILLE INVISIBLE DE KITEGE . ACTE IV TABLEAU II

AlEXiS Korovine

110. Alexei Korovin: Stage Design for Paradise (the City of Greater Kitezh),
The Tale of the Invisible City of Kitezh and the Maid Fevronia, ca. 1929 (No. 630)

171. Alexei Korovin: Costume Design for Bediai, the Tatar Chief, *The Tale of the Invisible City of Kitezh and the Maid Fevronia*, ca. 1929 (No. 636)

112. Alexei Korovin: Costume Design for Burundai, a Tatar Chieftain, *The Tale of the Invisible City of Kitezh and the Maid Fevronia*, ca. 1929 (No. 637)

developed by the Constructivists — than Larionov's histrionic, but still pictorial, decorations. Malevich and Tatlin were very different artists and their early involvement in the theater, i.e. *The Emperor Maximilian and His Disobedient Son Adolf* of 1911-12 with designs by Tatlin and *Victory over the Sun* of 1913 with designs by Malevich demonstrated their distinctive approaches. Essentially, the simple narrative of *The Emperor*, edited by the Cubo-Futurist poet Kamensky (cf. Ill. 237-38 Nos. 1144-47), and the partly *zaum* libretto written by Alexei Kruchenykh (see No. 634) for *Victory over the Sun*, had little in common; however, both pieces advanced or at least pointed towards the notion of *Bühnenarchitektur*, of a three-dimensional, kinetic, interactive totality.

Tatlin designed his costumes for *The Emperor* (No. 1014) before his momentous discovery of Picasso's reliefs in Paris in 1914,[130] but even so, he already expressed a spatial, volumetrical sensation in this spectacle, while relying substantially on the attributes of the *balagan*. By the time he came to work on his second major commission, *A Life for the Tsar (Ivan Susanin)* (Ill. 203; Nos. 1015-16) in the winter of 1913, Tatlin's definition of stage design was a more dynamic, more architectural one. His emphasis on a spiralic structure, as in the costumes for the peasant girl, provides his composition with an emphatic vertical impulse and continuum — something less apparent in a Benois or Dobujinsky of the same period. Tatlin's attempt to "put the eye under the control of touch"[131] was especially evident in his sets for both *The Emperor* and *A Life for the Tsar*. The "Gothic" architecture for the former and the pyramidal construction of the forest for the latter pointed towards certain Constructivist designs of the 1920s, e.g. towards Tatlin's own resolution of Velmir Khlebnikov's *Zangezi* in 1923 and Isaak Rabinovich's sets foregrounding Exter's costumes for *Aelita* in 1924 (Ills. 66-68; Nos. 465-69). Moreover, as the critic Auslender noted, there seemed to be a sincere effort to integrate actor and audience in *The Emperor*: footlights were absent and actors passed freely from stage to audience, a procedure reminiscent of the cabaret routine.[132]

The productions of *The Emperor* in St. Petersburg and Moscow alluded to design possibilities without fully exploring them. A greater force was needed to bring about a "complete fracture of concepts and words... antiquated décor, and... musical harmony";[133] and just such a force was provided by the opera *Victory over the Sun* staged in St. Petersburg in December, 1913, one of the two "First Futurist Spectacles in the World" as we see from Rozanova's poster (No. 891). This Cubo-Futurist *balagan* with prologue by Khlebnikov and libretto by Kruchenykh, music by Mikhail Matiushin, and designs by Malevich narrated how a band of Futurist strongmen set out to conquer the sun. The text drew substantially on *zaum* (although the end result was fairly comprehensible), the music was chromatic and dissonant, and the designs were caricatural, exaggerating the salient characteristics of this or that character (e.g. Ill. 53; No. 779). Malevich's costume designs are drawn mostly in profile and they seem to derive more from children's cut-out and stick figures than from sophisticated

130 See A. Strigalev: "Vladimir Tatlin" in *Arkhitektura SSSR*, M, 1985, November-December, No. 6, pp. 86-93.

131 This was Tatlin's slogan in 1913. In 1920 he replaced it by "Via the exposure of material towards the new object." Both slogans appear on the last page (unnumbered) of N. Punin: *Tatlin (Protiv kubizma)*, P: IZO NKP, 1921.

132 S. Auslender: "Vecher Soiuza molodezhi" in *Russkaia khudozhestvennaia letopis*, SP, 1911, No. 4, p. 10.

133 M. Matiushin in *Futuristy. Pervyi zhurnal russkikh futuristov*, M, 1914, No. 1-2, p. 157.

113. Konstantin Korovin: Stage Design for a Square in Novgorod, *Sadko*, 1912 (No. 642)

interpretations of Cubism and Futurism. It is hard to determine whether the costumes were successful as volumetrical arrangements on stage, although, like Larionov's costumes for other extravaganzas such as *Chout*, they appealed, no doubt, more by their improbable shapes and bright colors than by their easy integration with the scenic space. Visually, Malevich's costumes are striking and resemble an illustrated compendium of buffoons and clowns, but it is hard to imagine them functioning as material, physical personages.

On the other hand, Malevich's sets and props for *Victory over the Sun* (Ills. 147-48; Nos. 770-72) seem more successful as effective architectural agents on stage — including the famous décor for Act(ion) I, Scene 5, which presented a square within a square divided into two unrelieved areas of black and white. These visual components, both abstract and descriptive, provided the background against which various geometrical forms, often created by mobile lighting, were distributed about the stage. The poet Livshits, who saw the production, recalled:

> Painterly stereometry was created within the confines of the scenic box for the first time, and a strict system of volumes was established, one that reduced the element of chance which the movements of the human figures might have introduced to a minimum. These figures were cut up by the blades of the lights and were deprived alternately of hands, legs, head, etc., because, for Malevich, they were merely geometric bodies subject not only to disintegration into their component parts, but also to total dissolution in painterly space.
>
> Abstract form was the only reality, a form that completely absorbed the entire Luciferan futility of the world.[134]

Victory over the Sun broke with many artistic, theatrical, and philosophical conventions, although in some ways it posed more questions than it answered. It continued the tradition of the fairground and yet carried a clear, apocalyptic message; it reminded the audience of the old mummers and buffoons and yet it paid homage to the new industrial age (the airplane crashing onto the stage); it gave the audience familiar figures (e.g. Nero at Ill. 150; No. 774) and also "men of the future" (Ill. 154; No. 782). Perhaps the very fluidity and diversity of the opera were the qualities that impelled other avant-garde artists to design later interpretations, not least Vera Ermolaeva in 1920 and Lissitzky in 1923.

One regrets that Lissitzky's ten marionettic figures for *Die plastische Gestaltung der elektromechanischen Schau "Sieg über die Sonne"* were not used in an actual production (Ills. 138-46; Nos. 770-94). Costumes such as the *Old Man,* or *Old Fogy,* (Ill. 144; No. 762) and the *Anxious One* (Ill. 140; No. 757) are entirely theatrical beings, as absurd — and as credible — as Benois's designs for *Petrouchka*. The importance of Lissitzky's costumes lies precisely in their destruction of a central axis and in their reliance on the principles of disharmony, asymmetry, and arhythmicality. Instead of one focus, the Lissitzky figure has many; instead of one particular entrance and exit for the spectator, the figure is open on all sides; instead of terrestrial dependence and gravity, the figure almost floats in space. Lissitzky's frustration of our conditioned responses to space destroys our equilibrium, makes us "circle like a planet" round the figure,[135] and in this sense, Lissitzky's marionettes for *Victory over the Sun* are

134 F48, p. 164.
135 El Lissitzky: "Suprematism in World Reconstruction" (1920). Translation in S. Lissitzky-Küppers: *El Lissitzky. Life, Letters, Texts*, London: Thames and Hudson, 1968, p. 328.

114. Konstantin Korovin: Costume Design fo Tsarevich Gvidon, *The Tale of Tsar Saltan*, 1912 (No. 650)

subtle extensions of his theory of the Proun (=Project for the Affirmation of the New):

> PROUN is the creative building of form (deriving from mastery of space)
> via the economic construction of the material being used. The aim of the
> PROUN is to be a phased movement along the path of concrete creativity
> and not a foundation, a clarification or a popularization of life.[136]

The disturbance of the traditional axis in the work of art — the *sdvig,* or displacement, so fundamental to the development of the Russian avant-garde — occurred in all the arts just before World War I. Conventional progressions were changing. One no longer "read" the painting as in the 19th century, one was now asked to appreciate it simply as a combination of colors, forms, and textures. The poem no longer described a sentimental episode or a moral issue, but lived as a self-sufficient experiment in sound and rhythm. Music abandoned social and religious subservience and returned to its abstract principle. Correspondingly, Russian stage designers of the avant-garde also began to seek the essence of theatrical space, action, and gesture — and once again, it was a little theater, Tairov's Chamber Theater, that assisted them in this assignment.

The Dynamic Use of Immobile Form: the Art of Alexandra Exter [137]

If 19th-century stage design had tended towards an overabundance of historical and social data, the early Modernist stage, of which the Ballets Russes was an organic part, tended to be at once less pedantic and more plastic. However, both approaches still emphasized the illustrative and narrative function of the theatrical decoration and despite the remarkable talents of Fedor Chaliapin (No. 354), Mariia Ermolova, Nijinsky, Pavlova (Nos. 118, 909, 947), Alexander Yuzhin, etc., the performer tended to act and move "externally," in accordance with the plotline. In other words, movement on the professional stage played an auxiliary role — dictated, controlled, refined, and infinitely reproducible. With the advent of Tairov and his Chamber Theater, however, primary attention passed to the "actor's inner technique"[138] and to the liberated movement as the central force of theater. It was within the perimeter of Tairov's company, established in Moscow in 1914, that the professional theater in Russia became a kinetic, rather than a purely literary or descriptive experience. Suffice it to recall the names of the principal actors, e.g. Alisa Koonen and Nikolai Tsereteli (Ill. 191, Nos. 969-70), and artists, e.g. Exter, the Stenberg brothers, Vesnin, and Yakulov, to realize the importance of the Chamber Theater as a forum for the propagation of new and vital ideas in acting and stage design.

It was a fortunate combination of circumstances that Exter, one of Russia's foremost stage designers, should have returned from Paris to reside in Russia also in 1914, and that she should have accepted Tairov's invitation to come and work at the Chamber Theater. As Tairov himself wrote later:

> [Exter was] an artist with an extraordinary sensitivity, one who was very
> responsive to my stage projects and who, from the very first, manifested
> a wonderful sense of the active element of the theater.[139]

---

136 El Lissitzky: "Tezisy k Prounu (ot zhivopisi k arkhitekture)" (1920) in M. Barkhin et al., eds.: *Mastera arkhitektury ob arkhitekture,* M: Iskusstvo, 1975, Vol. 2, p. 134.
137 Ya. Tugendkhold: "Pismo iz Moskvy" in *Apollon,* 1918, No. 1, p. 72.
138 C35, p. 602.
139 Ibid., p. 163.

Snegourotchka   Le Carnaval

115. Konstantin Korovin: Costume Design for the Carnival, *The Snow Maiden*, ca. 1928 (No. 656)

113 Konstantin Korovin: Costume Design for Prince Igor with a Shield, *Prince Igor*, 1928 (No. 661)

Prince Igor   *Le Khan Kontchak*

Korovine Paris 1928.

117. Konstantin Korovin: Costume Design for Khan Konchak, *Prince Igor*, 1928 (No. 664)

Along with Popova, Exter was among the few members of the Russian avant-garde who was able to transcend the confines of the pictorial surface and to organize forms in their interaction with space. Her acute awareness of this interaction became apparent in her first collaborations with Tairov on the productions of *Thamira Khytharedes* in 1916 (Ills. 61-63; Nos. 460-62) and *Salomé* in 1917, and then in her later endeavors such as *Romeo and Juliet* in 1921 and *Death of Tarelkin* also in 1921 (not produced). Paying homage to Appia, Exter applied his programmatic principle of arranging a counterpoint of particular architectural shapes on stage in order to elicit particular emotional responses as, for example, in the pointed triangles of the cypresses and the gradual incline of the steps in *Thamira Khytharedes*. Exter's concentration on the rhythmic organization of space, on the "rhythmic frame of the action",[140] was the common denominator of her stylistic approach to the theater, whether Cubist as in *Thamira Kytharedes* or Constructivist as in the Paris projects of the mid-1920s (Ills. 74-76; Nos. 477-97), whether for a dramatic costume or for a marionette.

While Exter emerged as a pioneer in the new design, she was always "above isms,"[141] interpreted their codes freely, and in the case of Constructivism, did not support the taut economy and sparsity favored by, say, Rodchenko and the Stenberg brothers. She was not the most austere and laconic of artists and, for example, in her fashion designs of 1923, she favored a richness of pattern and a mélange of styles that combined Suprematist geometry, Egyptian motifs, and fur appendages. Similarly, in the designs that she made to replace Alexander Vesnin's for *Romeo and Juliet* (Ill. 234; No. 1133), Exter indulged in a luxury and splendor that even for Tairov were "too visual," and in their decorative excess and Bakstian brilliance seemed more suited to a pantomime or circus — and the production was a failure. Some critics even referred to the 1921 *Romeo and Juliet* as the "most bitter page"[142] in the history of the Chamber Theater and although Tairov never lost his admiration for Exter, as we see from his preface to her album *Alexandra Exter: Décors de Théâtre* (Ills. 75-76; Nos. 483-97), they did not collaborate in the theater again. It is understandable, therefore, why Tairov welcomed the architect Alexander Vesnin into the Chamber Theater in order to design the 1920 production of Paul Claudel's *L'Annonce faite à Marie* (Ill. 235; No. 1136). A Neo-Classicist in his architectural training, Vesnin possessed the rigor and sense of measure that Exter did not, qualities that helped him create his elegant resolution for *Phèdre* in 1922 (No. 1139) and build his construction for *The Man Who Was Thursday* in 1923. Obviously, Tairov was attracted by the same calculated reserve in the art of the Stenberg brothers (Ill. 181; Nos. 960-73) whom he also invited to design a number of plays at the Chamber Theater, including *The Storm* and *St. Joan* in 1924.

Exter might have favored a luxury of forms not always practical in the post-Revolutionary theater, but she never lost sight of the medium with which she was dealing. After her interlude with Tairov, she worked on a variety of projects such as her collection of marionettes (which she designed together with Nechama Szmuszkowicz in 1926), her interior décor for the Berlin apartment of the dancer Elza

---

140 C11, p. 68.
141 Untitled, unsigned text on the invitation ticket to the exhibition "Alexandra Exter (1882-1949)" held at BTM, May, 1987, unpaginated.
142 G17, p. XXXII.

118. Konstantin Korovin: Costume Design for a Persian Slave Girl Holding Flowers, *Prince Igor*, ca. 1928 (No. 670)

Kruger in 1927, and her set of pochoirs published in 1930 (Ills. 75, 76; Nos. 483-97). Yet surely, her most impressive designs of the 1920s pertain to her work for Yakov Protazanov's production of the movie *Aelita* in 1924. Aided by Nadezhda Lamanova and Vera Mukhina, with whom she also worked at the Chamber Theater (Ills. 158, 159; Nos. 798-800), Exter designed the costumes, while her pupil Rabinovich, aided by Sergei Kozlovsky, designed the sets.

The costumes for *Aelita* are remarkable. Alexei Tolstoi's fantastic novel of a journey by a Soviet engineer to Mars, on which the motion picture was based, created a highly imaginative, fantastic scenario, while most of the characters, e.g. the Queen of the Martians (Ill. 66; No. 465), had no parallels in theatrical literature. On paper, Exter's costumes may look unwieldy and even rather absurd, but in the movie they function perfectly. The medium of film provided Exter with a high degree of momentum: just as she intended her marionettes to operate as a kinetic totality (they were also for a movie), so she relied on the cinematic method to "move" the characters, providing the spectator with constantly changing points of view. Accustomed to the comparative intimacy of the Chamber Theater, Exter was confronted with the question of trying to overcome the barrier between spectacle and spectator and for her a motion picture such as *Aelita* supplied one clear answer: through the illusion of film the designer could draw the audience, virtually, into the action of the fabrication. With its double love story, visionary descriptions of life on Mars, and unadorned commentary on everyday Soviet life, *Aelita* combined dream and reality, "happily ever after" and "now," just as Mary Pickford and Douglas Fairbanks did. Actually, it is worth remembering the primary box-office draw in Moscow in the early 1920s was not the Eisenstein or Vertov experiment, but the make-believe movie (often a Hollywood import) and the thriller – for which Petr Galadzhev made his arresting posters (Ills. 81-83; Nos. 516-19).

In turn, the cinema supplied Exter with an additive or artificial space, and the bizarre patterns on the costumes, the asymmetries, and mechanical attributes were appropriate to the constantly changing space in which they functioned. Exter ensured the success of her costumes by the care and deliberation with which she constructed them. They are different from the exuberance of her pieces for *Thamira Khytharedes* (cf. Nos. 460-62) and perhaps have more in common with the simplicity and severity of Vesnin's costumes for *Phèdre* (Nos. 1140-41). Knowing that in the medium of black and white film, color in her designs would be superfluous, Exter resorted to other systems of formal definition — to dependence on sharp contrasts between the material textures of metal, metal foil, glass, cloth. Such "industrial" materials, of course, were part of the Futurists' and Constructivists' cult of the machine — manifest also in *La Chatte* (Nos. 512, 823) and *Le Pas d'Acier* (Nos. 1154-67), but for Exter they served a purpose beyond that of "novelty" — they defined form in the absence of color and with their transparency or reflectivity, integrated perfectly with the surrounding space.

Exter's constructed costumes harmonized well with the sets designed by her student Rabinovich. His general conception of the stage was essentially an architectural rather than a decorative one, as he demonstrated in perhaps his most successful resolution — for the *Love for Three Oranges* in 1927 (Ill. 174; No. 866), and even in the most florid period of Soviet art (1930s-50s) he remained loyal to this conviction. In his designs for *Aelita*, Rabinovich emphasized verticals, both as

119. Boris Kustodiev: Poster Advertising *The Flea*, 1925 (No. 685)

unrelieved "metal" (plaster and wood) columns ascending in elliptical forms and as semi-transparent curtains of cord or metal. The austerity of these surfaces was tempered by the actual progression of the movie and by the extensive application of beams of light amplified through mirrors incorporated into various parts of the floor, walls, etc. Exter herself made considerable use of panels of light in her projects for various spectacles in the mid-1920s (e.g., Ill. 74; Nos. 477-80).

Centrifuge: the Avant-Garde in the Ukraine, Georgia, and Armenia [143]

The fact that Rabinovich worked with Exter on *Aelita* is not fortuitous. Exter, along with Malevich, was one of the very few members of the Russian avant-garde to have created a "school." In Kiev, especially between 1916 and 1919, Exter was in close contact with many young Ukrainian artists, including Andreenko (Ills. 3-4; Nos. 18-24), Boris Aronson (No. 54), Alexander Bogomazov (Nos. 388-90), Alexander Khvostenko-Khvostov (Nos. 605-07), Simon Lissim (Nos. 744-50), Vadim Meller (Ill. 156; Nos. 791-96), Petritsky (Ills. 160-62; Nos. 812-18), Rabinovich, Nisson Shifrin, Tchelitchew (Ills. 214-30; Nos. 1066-98), and Alexander Tyshler (Nos. 1102-07), and some took lessons from her. Many were Jewish and, born in remote parts of the Ukraine, aspired from the very beginning to leave their local environments and enter a more cosmopolitan cultural community. All the major Jewish contributors to modern Russian art — Bakst, Chagall (Ill. 52; Nos. 403-04), Iosif Chaikov, Sonia Delaunay (Ills. 53-55; Nos. 407-16), Robert Falk (Ill. 77; No. 499), Lissitzky, David Shterenberg, Iosif Shkolnik (Nos. 928-29), Tyshler (Nos. 1102-07) — moved from their native towns and villages to Kiev, Moscow or St. Petersburg / Petrograd / Leningrad, or to Paris and New York, where they achieved their prestige precisely as Soviet or European or American artists, i.e. not as the bearers of local Jewish traditions.

No doubt, this state of affairs explains in part the success of Exter's school in Kiev in 1917-19 and also of Malevich's pedagogical experiments in Vitebsk in 1919-22. The majority of their students were local Jews who esteemed their mentors not only because of charisma, but also because of bold esthetic systems that transcended ethnic folklore. Indeed, just after the Revolution, Exter's Kiev studio became a point of pilgrimage for many displaced intellectuals (again, many of them Jewish), and as the historian Flora Syrkina has observed, alongside Exter's own residence, it was also a *pied-à-terre* for writers such as Ilya Ehrenburg, Livshits, Osip Mandelshtam, Shklovsky, and Natan Vengrov.[144]

During those turbulent years, Kiev was an extraordinary center of cultural activity. Cabaret life thrived with the hot numbers at the cabarets Bi-Ba-Bo (see No. 814) and Khlam [Junk]. Art magazines and literary reviews mushroomed, reflecting the most diverse tendencies — from the weekly *Teatr* [Theater] (1920) (see No. 793) to the almanac *Germes* [Hermes] (1919).[145] Exter presided in the Art Section of the Ministry for Great Russian Affairs, while her friend Elza Kriuger performed Evenings of Dances

---

143 The reference here is not only to the geographical dissemination of the ideas of the Russian avant-garde, but also, more specifically, to the Moscow group and publishing-house Tsentrifuga (Centrifuge) active in 1913-20, whose publications included Ivan Aksenov's study of Picasso in 1917, *Pikasso i okrestnosti*, with illustrations by Exter.

144 F. Syrkina: *Aleksandr Grigorievich Tyshler*, M: Sovetskii khudozhnik, 1966, p. 11.

145 Of particular importance is the "annual of art and humanistic knowledge" *Germes* (K, 1919; one issue only). This publication carried a cover design by Exter and several reproductions of her works. Other contributors included Ilya Ehrenburg, Nikolai Evreinov, Viacheslav Ivanov, Benedikt Livshits, Vladimir Makkaveisky, and Grigorii Petnikov.

120. Boris Kustodiev: Stage Design for Act 2, Scene 1: Tula, *The Flea*, 1925 (No. 687)

et the Art Theater. An exhibition of Chinese and Japanese engravings opened at the Society of Art Workers just as Alexander Deich announced the end of proletarian art.[146] Here was an atmosphere that could only inspire young artists to forget the misery of the *mestechko* (local Jewish colony), where the "streets are cleaned only sporadically ,[147] and to experiment at all costs. Logically, therefore, Aronson, Rabinovich, Shifrin, Tyshler, and others proceeded to follow Exter's Cubist teaching and their artistic achievements in studio painting, street decoration, and stage design e.g. Rabinovich's decorations for *Salomé* and Shifrin's for *The Green Island* in 1919) display a strong debt to this — and, incidentally, a complete rejection of the Jewish milieu. Only when these artists reached Moscow did they sometimes recall their Jewish roots, involving themselves in productions at the Habimah and the Jewish Chamber and State Theaters, a development now well documented and researched.[148]

In greater or lesser degree, these artists supported Exter's lyrical adaptation of Cubism. For example, there is a striking similarity between the early costumes of Meller (Ill. 156; Nos. 791, 792, 794), Petritsky (Ills. 160-61; Nos. 812-13) and even Tchelichew (e.g. Ill. 219; No. 1077). Petritsky's costumes of the mid-1920s and Tchelitchev's of 1919-21 rely on a sculptural, often spiralic structure that brings to mind Exter's costumes for Tairov's productions. At the same time, Petritsky, at least, referred to his ethnic context, whether in his choice of commission or in his actual introduction of folkloric elements (Ills. 160-61; Nos. 812-13). However, he was also concerned with formal combinations and syncopations in sets and costumes, and applied subtle collages of materials — gold paper on cotton prints, geometric motifs on floric backgrounds, etc. (Ill. 162; No. 815). Perhaps in this curious dissonance we can detect the very spirit of the Ukrainian avant-garde, at once professional and primitive, constructive and ornamental. As the critic Vasyl Khmury wrote in 1929, Petritsky gave "decorative functions to constructive deformation,"[149] a sentiment that seems particularly valid of his work for the productions at the Berezil and Franko Theaters in Kharkov in the 1920s (see No. 818).

The vitality of the Ukrainian contingent within the renaissance of stage design underlines an important aspect of the "Russian" avant-garde: many of the modern artists and designers, generally categorized as Russian in the West, were, strictly speaking, not of Russian origin, and their inspiration owed much to national traditions outside the geographical confines of Russia, i.e. Ukrainian, Georgian, Armenian, Lithuanian Latvian, Polish, Jewish, etc. Ultimately, Moscow and St. Petersburg, if not Paris and New York, remained the real centers of artistic activity and the arbiters of taste, but local connections and commitments, especially in the Ukrainian context, cannot be ignored. True, the cultural links between Kiev and Moscow were close thanks to the common traditions of language, literature, and religion — and we should not be surprised to find Tatlin teaching at the Kiev Art Institute in the mid-1920s or Petritsky designing productions for the Bolshoi Theater in the 1950s — but there were many "Russian" artists who had no Slavic blood at all and who came to the modern movement bearing a very different set of cultural criteria. Among them were Lado Guclashvili, Martiros Sarian, and Georgii Yakulov.

146 A. Deich: ' Krakh proletarskogo iskusstva" in *Teatralnaia zhizn*, K, 1918, No. 18, pp. 8-10.
147 L. Rokhlin: *Mestechko Krasnopolie Mogilevskoi gubernii*, SP: Sever, 1909. p. 11.
148 See, for example, C40, C154, and M. Kohansky: *The Hebrew Theatre*, Jerusalem: Israel Universities Press, 1969.
149 V. Khmury: *Anatol Petritskii. Teatralni stroi*. Kharkov: State Publishing-House, 1929, p. 15.

121. Lev Lapin: Costume Design for a Russian Peasant Woman Dancing, 1929 (No. 696)

Gudiashvili (Nos. 576-78), for example, arrived at his individual style not only after a first-hand examination of the latest Russian and Western ideas, but also through the study of his national traditions — the Georgian fresco, the Georgian miniature, and Georgian church architecture. Many of the formal devices peculiar to Gudiashvili's paintings and designs can, indeed, be traced back to ancient Georgian wall-painting, examples of which he saw during his archaeological expeditions. Gudiashvili's exaggerated curvation and elongation of figures might well derive from this source, although, certainly, his familiarity with the work of André Derain and Amedeo Modigliani should not be disregarded. Gudiashvili was also active as a decorator and wall painter for many cafés and residences in Tiflis (Tbilisi) and Paris, and he achieved some success as a stage designer for the Chauve-Souris in Paris (No. 578) and then for the Georgian theater in the late 1920s onwards. Among the Tfis interiors that he designed in 1918-19 was the cabaret called Khimerioni, a bohemian meeting place frequented by the poets of the Blue Horns group. David Kakabadze- Kirill Zdanevich (Nos. 1186-87), Sudeikin (Nos. 981-1010), and Sigizmund Valishevsky (No. 1183) were also part of this café culture and it seems probable that Gudiashvili arrived at his concept of feminine beauty at this time, partly under the influence of Sudeikin's sensual "Arabian" nudes. The Expressionist style of Boris Grigoriev, who collaborated with Sudeikin on the decorative scheme for the Comedians' Halt cabaret in Petrograd, also comes to mind here (Ills. 102-03; Nos. 572-73).

After spending five years in Paris, Gudiashvili returned to Tbilisi, beckoned by the generous promises of fame and abundance in Soviet Georgia, and his initial period there was auspicious — a one-man show in Tbilisi in 1926, a commission to design Konstantin Mardzhanov's production of *Lamara* and to decorate the interior of the Hotel Oriant in downtown Tbilisi, and a professorship at the new Tbilisi Academy of Arts. Undoubtedly, the principal reason for Gudiashvili's immediate success at home was that his art had never been distant from his native Georgia, nor had it assimilated the extreme methods of Cubism, Futurism or Suprematism. As the painter and historian Georgii Lukomsky wrote in Paris in 1921:

> How valuable it is that [Gudiashvili], unlike most, is not losing his characteristic flavor, is not falling under the influence of Paris, is not being infected by this terrible "mass" hypnosis, by these "angles" which are becoming so banal and tedious.[150]

Like Gudiashvili, Sarian and Yakulov also resisted the "angular infection," and they did so, in part, because of their attachment to the "non-constructive" art of the East.[151] When, in 1922, Yakulov called for the need of an "Oriental Renaissance,"[152] he was, in fact, expressing a life-long desire, for as early as 1905, he was painting according to what he regarded as the canons of Oriental art. This came about not only because of his Armenian background, but also because he studied Oriental languages at the Lazarev Institute of Eastern Languages in Moscow in the 1890s

150 G. Lukomsky. Quoted in L. Zlatkevich: *Lado Gudiashvili*, Tbilisi: Ganatleba, 1971, p. 29.
151 The Lithuanian critic and painter Vladimir Markov (Voldemārs Matvejs), a member of the Union of Youth and a close associate of Malevich, Rozanova, and other avant-garde artists, characterized the art of the West as "constructive" and the art of the East as "non-constructive." See his essay "The Principles of the New Art" (1912). Translation in B12, pp. 25-38.
152 G. Yakoulov: "La définition de soi" in *Notes et Documents,* Paris: Société des amis de Georges Yakoulov, 1967, No. 1, p. 16.

122. Mikhail Larionov: Stage Design with Group of Dancers and Mask on Floor, *Le Soleil de Nuit*, 1915 (No. 703)

when Sudeikin was also there) and made a series of optical and meteorological observations *in situ* when he was serving in Manchuria in 1904-05. Yakulov was also friendly with Sarian (No. 896), his fellow countryman, especially in Moscow in the 1900s, and their early works are rather similar in color and ornamental impetus. Although Yakulov and Sarian, the "Russian Matisse," came to support different styles, they retained many "oriental" links. Yakulov, for example, designed the cover for Marietta Shaginian's book of verse called *Orientalia* in 1912 (published in 1913) and Sarian did the same for the fourth edition in 1918.

Whether his source of artistic inspiration was Armenian, Parisian or Far Eastern, Yakulov brought to the theater a sense of play and a fluency that contrasted sharply with more classical approaches. Tairov must have been overjoyed when he saw Yakulov's scenic ideas in practice in the three productions at the Chamber Theater — *Princess Brambilla* (1920; in which Yakulov himself performed), *Giroflé-Girofla* (1922), and *Signor Formica* (1922; Nos. 1159-60). Yakulov transformed the theater into a circus, relying on chance, coincidence, and intuition, resulting either in total failure (as was the case with *Signor Formica*) or in remarkable success (as was the case with *Giroflé-Girofla*). These were the qualities — spontaneity, illogicality, accident — that Yakulov identified with Armenian and Eastern art and that he felt were lacking in the "archaic art of Europe."[153] Of course, Yakulov combined many ideas from many countries, including the Simultanism of Sonia and Robert Delaunay (I.B. 53-55; Nos. 407-16), but his familiarity with Asiatic art, his specific study of elements such as spiral and vertical perspective, his rejection of the straight line, and his belief that the Chinese actually possessed a different optical perception contributed to the peculiar sense of aeriality in his paintings and designs.

---

153 G. Yakulov, B. Livshits and A. Lurie: *My i Zapad,* SP, 1914. See Nos. 1168 and 1169.

Dmitrii Bouchène: Curtain Design, *L'Oiseau de Feu*, ca. 1969 (No. 391)

123. Mikhail Larionov: Costume Design for a Young Peasant Girl, *Le Soleil de Nuit*, 1915 (No. 704)

124. Mikhail Larionov: Stage Mask. Portrait of Leonide Massine, 1916 (No. 706)

125. Mikhail Larionov: Costume Design for a Peacock, *Histoires Naturelles*, ca 1917 (No. 708)

IV. THE THEATER OF REVOLUTION

Deprivation and Dispersal

The October Revolution and Civil War in Russia (1917-22) were a time of economic chaos, material deprivation, and cultural disorientation. While we might savor the political optimism and enjoy the surprising wealth of visual material of those years, it is easy to forget just how dislocated Russian society was. Already ravaged by the misfortunes of World War I and now torn by mass emigration and Civil War, the Russian population experienced extreme hardships and deprivations at all levels. It was a case of bare survival, not least for the artists, and a principal reason why so many leftists and rightists, responded to the call for politicized art forms (Lenin's Plan of Monumental Propaganda, agit-art, mass actions) was perhaps more a material than an ideological one. In spite of the valiant efforts by Anatolii Lunacharsky to provide special rations for art workers, they were in dire straits — and victimized by a rapidly expanding bureaucracy, as the following note, circulated in the Theater Section (TEO) of the Commissariat, indicates:

> Forwarded herewith: 145 coupons for the Section workers to receive cabbage, 10 lbs per head at a price of 4 rubles per lb. The Executive Committee asks that these coupons be distributed among the Section workers after the recipient's first and last name have been entered both on the coupon and on the counterfoil...[154]

Consequently, such straitened circumstances, fear of Bolshevik reprisal, and experience of the licentious behavior of ignorant plenipotentiaries in 1917-18 resolved many artists and writers to leave Russia. This was particularly true of those who had been a part of the Moscow and St. Petersburg cultural bohemia, who had hobnobbed with patrons, dandies, and merchants' wives at nightspots such as the Stray Dog and the Comedians' Halt, who had achieved fame — if not for their art, then for their tangos and foxtrots, and who had passed nights of pleasure at weekend dachas. These artists included Annenkov (Nos. 40-41), Grigoriev (Ill. 102; No. 572), Mak (Nos. 766-77), and Sudeikin (Ill. 193; Nos. 981-1010), whose emigration was also motivated by the sudden disappearance of that very class — the bourgeoisie — that had guaranteed the artist patronage and well-being.

One result of the diaspora was that groups of Russian artists converged in the most unlikely places as they traveled towards Western Europe and the Americas. One such bohemian center was Tiflis (Tbilisi), capital of the still independent Georgia, which maintained the "café culture" of St. Petersburg and Moscow. Gudiashvili and the Zdanevich brothers were still resident in Tiflis in 1919 and they were joined by Evreinov, Alexandre Shervashidze (Nos. 924-27), Shukhaev (Nos. 947-50), Sudeikin, and other intellectuals moving south. Their combined forces inspired the production of plays, designs for café interiors, lectures, and exhibitions. By the end of 1919, however, this remarkable state of affairs terminated, since it was clear that Georgia, in economic and political turmoil, would soon capitulate to the Bolsheviks. For the numerous Russian, Ukrainian, Armenian, and Georgian artists in Tiflis in 1919-20,

---

154 RGA, Moscow, f. 837, op. 2, ed. khr. 727, l. 50. The undated letter is addressed to a certain Erasov associated with the Theater Section of the People's Commissariat for Enlightenment.

126. Mikhail Larionov: Costume Design for a Lady with Fans, ca. 1915 (No. 710)

Berlin and Paris beckoned as securer havens, and the mass exodus from Tiflis began in the fall of 1919.

In their emigration westward, Russian artists designed productions in many cities. Tchelitchew worked for a ballet company in Istanbul before moving to Berlin (Ill. 2-4; Nos. 1066-98), Andreenko passed through Bucharest and Prague (Ills. 3-4; Nos. 13-24), Jedrinsky was active in Belgrade (Nos. 589-93), and Bilibin (Ills. 45-46; Nos. 364-71) and Shchekatikhina-Pototskaia (Nos. 915-23) even worked in Egypt before going on to Paris. Still, for many Russian artists just after the Revolution, Berlin was the primary destination,[155] where the most diverse personalities, ideas, and events could be encountered in the early 1920s, an exodus of Russian intellectuals and business people that culminated in the presence of over a quarter of a million Russian refugees in Berlin by 1923. One consequence of this emigration was a brilliant mosaic of Russian artistic, literary, and theatrical enterprises, fragile and short-lived, but vital to the development of the "other" Russian culture. Altman, Alexander Arnshtam (Nos. 50-53), Boguslavskaia, Chagall, Gabo, Grigoriev, Kandinsky (Nl. 600), Lissitzky, Pevsner (Nos. 822-23), Pogedaieff (Ill. 163; Nos. 824-27), Pougny (Ills. 850-53), Tchelitchew, Zack (Nos. 1176-81) — not to mention their numerous literary colleagues, such as Andrei Bely, Ilya Ehrenburg, Shklovsky, and Alexei Tolstoi — all lived and worked in Berlin in the early 1920s. They contributed to a cosmopolitan mix of the most diverse personalities, ideas, and events: the elegant, though anachronistic *Zhar-ptitsa* [Firebird] magazine, Korovin's exhibition at the Galerie Carl Nicolai in 1923, and Der Blaue Vogel cabaret on the one hand; and the Constructivist review *Veshch/Gegenstand/Objet*, Pougny's one-man show at Der Sturm in 1921 (Ill. 173; No. 850), and Tairov's Chamber Theater on tour in 1923 (No. 72) on the other. As Chagall said of those days:

> After the war, Berlin had become a kind of caravansary where everyone traveling between Moscow and the West came together... In the apartments round the Bayerische Platz there were as many samovars and theosophical and Tolstoyan countesses as there had been in Moscow... In my whole life I've never seen so many wonderful rabbis or so many Constructivists as in Berlin in 1922.[156]

This spectacular and dramatic context returns us to the peculiar artistic position of artists such as Houdiakoff (No. 580), Pogedaieff, Pougny, and Tchelitchew, in the early emigration. For them Berlin represented not only the first auspicious halting place on their outward journey, where they could recapture something of the cultural complexity to which they had been used in St. Petersburg, Moscow, and Kiev, but also a crossroads in their artistic careers. For many reasons, logical and casual, the Berlin confrontation displaced esthetic axes and often harbingered or witnessed a sudden reversal of pictorial styles (e.g. Pogedaieff's move towards Orientalism; Pougny's towards Post-Impressionism, and Tchelitchew's towards Surrealism), hardly predictable during their Russian or Ukrainian periods. Of course, these new stylistic preferences were part of a universal "return to order" that affected many masters of the avant-garde in the 1920s — from Picasso and Severini to Ivan Kliun (No. 621) and Malevich. However, for practical, material reasons, the Berlin experience also forced Russian artists to investigate new genres and new media,

155 For information on Russians in Berlin see H25, H28, H29, H31, H36, H43, and H72.
156 E. Roditi: "Entretien avec Marc Chagall" in *Preuves,* Paris, 1958, February, p. 27.

127. Mikhail Larionov: Design for Backdrop for the Haunted Forest, the Home of the Witch (Baba-Yaga), *Contes Russes*, 1916 (No. 711)

128. Mikhail Larionov: Stage Design for Scene I, *Chout*, ca 1921 (No. 716)

129. Mikhail Larionov: Stage Design for Scene V: The Bedroom, *Chout*, 1915 (No. 717)

especially stage design, book illustration, and *haute couture.* To make ends meet, for example, Boguslavskaia created embroidery and dress designs for magazines and fulfilled textile commissions for the Baruch fashion and accessories firm, while Pougny turned to creative writing, publishing his story "The Flying Dutchman" in the children's miscellany *Tsveten* [Pollen] in 1922. Pougny also made three black-and-white illustrations for this story about the fat merchant Peter, his passion for cocoa, and his servant Hans. It is a comic mix of food, lethargy, cantankerous servant, magic weightless, and levitation that brings to mind Gogol's *Nose,* Goncharov's *Oblomov,* and Chagall's topsy-turvy people. Yet the story is perhaps also an allegory about Pougny's uneasy suspension in a foreign city, a disorientation reflected in the author's closing lines: "I am telling you this story, because I have absolutely no friends."

After Berlin, Paris and then New York became the major points for the emigration, and Russian artists, especially the younger generation, contributed to many productions. The artistic level of the Russian opera and ballet companies, cabarets, publishing-houses, fashion ateliers, movie companies, and restaurants where the émigré artists worked was of course, extremely uneven. However, the decorative style that dominated the Russian stage in emigration was precisely decorative, and its representatives continued to paint "palaces with staircases that no one used, archways beneath which no one passed, doors that did not open."[157] Konstantin Korovin and his son Alexei (Ills. 110-12; Nos. 630-41) were typical of this movement and to an audience meditating on the irrevocable charms of Old Russia, their tinsel Christmas card effect had particular appeal. Bakst, who exerted a considerable influence on the young generation of émigré designers, especially Boris Bilinsky (Ills. 47-48; Nos. 372-87), Erté (Ill. 60; No. 459), and Lissim, had always managed to preserve a scenic harmony, i.e. to induce a constant interchange of all components. Bilinsky, Erté, Eugene Dunkel (No. 454), the Korovins, and Pogedaieff tended to disrupt this harmony, but the "oriental Constructivism"[158] of their Art Deco style still created dazzling scenic effects, even if they did not always illustrate the respective ballet or drama in an appropriate manner.

Mass Action: from Surface to Space

The kind of art generated by the October Revolution — the mass action, the flying banners, the plaster of Paris and cement statues — actually disguised a dearth of solid, durable artistic creations during the first years of the new Republic; and the history of the theater and the visual arts then is as much the history of what was not produced as of what was. It was a time of elaborate theory and meager practice, of visionary projects for a utopian future, of models and prototypes that could never be manufactured — and also of theatrical spectacles that were prepared but never realized such as Boris Sushkevich's *Death of Tarelkin* with designs by Exter, Valerii Bebutov's *Rienzi* with designs by Yakulov (No. 1160), and Vakhtangov's *Inspector General* with designs by Rabinovich.[159] Moreover, not all were keen to offer their services to the Revolution and, as Platon Kerzhentsev observed in his book on the

157 BKE, pp. 90-91.
158 BKE, p. 131.
159 Samuil Margolin even wrote a book on the subject of unrealized productions for the Lakshin publishing-house, Moscow, in 1922, under the title *Neosushchestvlennyi teatr.* See *Teatr i muzyka*, M, 1922, 28 November, No. 9, p. 116.

130. Mikhail Larionov: Costume Design for the Merchant, *Chout*, 1921 (No. 720)

early Soviet theater in 1922, many artists had to be asked importunately to "join in."[160] Even though Lenin's Plan of Monumental Propaganda of April, 1918, onwards (whereby statues to the heroes of Socialism were to be erected in the streets and squares) and the program of agit-art (redesigning and redecorating buildings with posters, banners, and hoardings celebrating the Revolution, as is manifest for example, in Vladimir Kozlinsky's images (Nos. 681-82), attracted many avant-garde artists, everyday reality did not seem to change much, as Kerzhentsev also observed:

> You go into a Soviet restaurant, or any institution, a railroad station, a club or a new theater. Do you see the hand of an artist? Everywhere is filth, disorder, and a lack of even the most primitive cultivation of beauty. For the most part they're just pigsties, repulsive sewers. Why aren't the artists indignant? Why don't they hang their paintings, their posters, their panneaux here? Why don't they paint the walls of these rooms?[161]

It is difficult to disperse the accumulated mythology surrounding the Revolution, especially as far as the visual arts are concerned, and to assess the real predicament of the artist, the producer, and the designer. However, perhaps at least one misconception should be questioned, i.e. the notion of October, 1917, as representing a clear dividing-line between the old culture and the new in Russia. The more we examine the process of Russian culture during the Modernist period, especially in the context of stage design, the more we find that the apparent innovations of the early 1920s (e.g. Constructivism) derived immediately from artistic concepts elaborated well before the Revolution. Of course, the social and political ramifications of the Bolshevik coup could not fail to affect the thematic orientation of the theater, and in the late 1920s there was an increasing pressure on producers and designers, as on all artists, to create an art form that was narrative, illustrative, and accessible. However, the historic experimental productions, such as Meierkhold's *Magnanimous Cuckold* and *The Death of Tarelkin* at his Theater of the RSFSR No. 1 in 1922, could not have been implemented without the laboratory stage of theatrical and scenic development in the late 19th century onwards. Perhaps there is a paradox in the fact that it was precisely the intimate, bourgeois theaters of Mamontov, Komissarzhevskaia, Baliev, Tairov, and Evreinov that prepared the ground for the "democratic" theater of the Constructivists in the early 1920s — which, in point of fact, was elitist, unpopular, and very distant from the realities of contemporary Soviet life.

One immediate problem was that there was no extensive repertoire of revolutionary or "modern," socially didactic plays, ballets, and operas, at least during the first decade after October, 1917. Most theaters continued to orient themselves towards the old middle-class favorites such as *Le Corsaire* designed by Petritsky (Ill. 162; No. 315), *A Midsummer Night's Dream* designed by Vasilii Komardenkov (No. 625), and *The Mikado* designed by Meller (No. 796). In this respect, Tairov's emphasis on the classics, e.g. *Phèdre* (Nos. 789, 969-72, 1137-42), is typical of the post-Revolutionary period. Spectacles with a relevant ideological content were few and far between, and even when 19th-century Russian plays, relevant to burning social issues were produced — such as Igor Terentiev's rendering of Nikolai Gogol's *Inspector General* designed by Pavel Filonov's students in 1927 (Nos. 506-09) — the

---

160 P. Kerschenzew: *Das schöpferische Theater*, Hamburg: Carl Hoym Nachf, 1922, p. 149.
161 Ibid. p. 150.

131. Mikhail Larionov: Stage Design, *Le Renard*, ca. 1922 (No. 721)

133. Mikhail Larionov: Costume Design for the Fox Disguised as a Nun, *Le Renard*, ca. 1922 (No. 723)

aristic in erpretation was often so far-fetched that the tendentious meaning was lost from view. That is why Meierkhold was so pleased when Maiakovsky brought him *Mystery-Scuffe* in 1918 — which, in turn, attracted several different designers for productions, including Malevich, Viktor Kiselev (Ills. 107-08; Nos. 608-18), and Iraklii Gamrekeli (Ills. 84-86; Nos. 520-24). *The End of Krivorylsk* designed by Akimov (No. 13) Isaac Babel's *Sunset* designed by Ilia Shlepianov (No. 931), and Kamensky's *Szenka-Fazin* designed by Konstantin Vialov (Ills. 237-38; Nos. 1144-47) were other plays that connected immediately to the socio-economic transformations of the time, but they were the exception, rather than the rule.

Even the so-called mass action — the reenactment of Revolutionary events such as *The Storming of the Winter Palace* in 1920 (Ill. 9; No. 44) — derived in part from more ancient theatrical forms such as the Orthodox procession. The French theater critic Léon Moussinac also regarded these spectacles as extensions of the Medieval mystery play such as the *Mystery of the Incarnation and the Nativity* given in Rouen in 1474, [162] and Shklovsky even referred to one of the mass actions, the *Hymn to Liberated Labor* presented in Petrograd in May, 1920, as a "May Day mysterium."[163] In any case there were clear historical precedents such as the public fêtes organized in France in the 1790s and designed by David, De Machy, Naudet et al. The debt of the mass action to tradition did not, however, prevent some artists and critics from regarding it as a genre created expressly for the Revolution, and Alexei Gan (Nos. 525-29), one of the more enthusiastic theorists of Constructivism, even saw it as the generator of Constructivism. For him, the mass action was the "organization and cementation of the life of the working society,"[164] the "action not of a civic society, but of a human one — wherein material production will fuse with intellectual production."[165]

The proposals to reproduce the historic events of 1917 as in *The Storming of the Winter Palace*, or to celebrate the Communist International as in *Towards the World Commune* (1920, designed by Altman) or Tatlin's *Monument to the III International* (Ill. 137 No. 751) were ambitious ventures. Both mass actions expressed the concept of total theater and, with a cast of thousands and an audience of tens of thousands could have implemented the demand of the Symbolists that

> the theater must stop being "theater" in the sense of spectacle — *zu schaffen, nicht zu schauen.* The crowd of spectators must fuse into a choral body, like the mystical community of ancient "orgies" and "mysteries."[166]

In the case of *The Storming of the Winter Palace*, décor in the traditional sense consisted of very little — wooden platforms in front of the Winter Palace in Petrograd and a diorama of agit-hoardings on the buildings themselves — and the real spirit of the production was to have been expressed precisely by "mass action." Ultimately, the spectacle merely regenerated or rather distorted historical facts and called for little imagination or interpretation on the part of cast or audience. As one of the

162 G14, p. 12.
163 V. Shklovsky: "O gromkom golose" in *Zhizn iskusstva*, P, 1920, 8-9 May, No. 446-47, p. 2.
164 Unsigned article (by Alexei Gan?): "Konstruktivisty" in *Ermitazh*, M, 1922, No. 13, p. 3.
165 A. Gan: "Borba za massovoe deistvo" in C3, p. 73.
166 V. Ivanov: "Novaia organicheskaia epokha i teatr budushchego" in *Po zvezdam*, SP: Ory, 1909, p. 205.

134. Mikhail Larionov: Costume Design for the Rooster *Le Renard* ca. 1922 (No. 724)

producers of *Towards the World Commune* indicated, the mass action proved to be a tedious experience:

> The spectacle begins... We have flags, telephones, electric bells in our hands. Actors come out on to the steps of the Stock Exchange. I press the bell and, obediently, they all sit down. I make a pause... ring again, and they take off their hats. I ring once more, and they open their books... There were four hundred Red Army soldiers who had been rounded up from goodness knows where... They moved, wandered about, sang, ran... just as all soldiers do on parade when they're fed up with the whole business. It was obvious that they were not touched or excited by the idea of the scenario or by the project itself.[167]

As this description would indicate, the mass action was both uninspiring and unwieldy. Demanding such enormous human and material resources, it was an impractical venture in the harsh conditions of War Communism, and the number of mass actions produced was very small. The genre was, however, transmuted into the propaganda parades, gymnastic displays, and carnivals of the 1920s onwards, which, with their elaborate floats, clear political messages, and festive mood, were reminiscent of the old church procession and the *narodnoe gulianie*. Gustav Klutsis's decorations for the Moscow Kremlin of 1922 (Ill. 109; No. 622) and Solomon Telingater's detail for a motorcade ten years later (Ill. 231; No. 1101) belong to this belated extension of traditional folk ritual.

Whatever the faults of the mass action, it did achieve one very important objective: it transferred the stage from the intimacy of the theater-house to the public square, a development that — consciously or unconsciously — producers and artists had entertained since the Neo-Nationalist revival some forty years before. The theater, like the *balagan* and the circus, was about to become public and itinerant. Meierkhold's desire that the theater become part of everyday life, accessible to the worker, the peasant, and the intellectual at any time and place, now seemed a distinct possibility. After all, this conception lay at the basis of some of the Constructivist productions of the early 1920s, such as Meierkhold's production of *Earth on End* with designs by Popova in 1923 (see No. 848).

The Constructivists: "Urbanistic, Formalistic, Jazzbandistic"

Constructivism affected not only the "decorative" aspect of the theater, often transforming the stage into a truly three-dimensional experience, but also the dramatic text, the music (or other) accompaniment, and the actors themselves. Meierkhold's system of bio-mechanics, with its debt to the eurhythmic principles of Jacques-Dalcroze, to the work-study programs of Frederick Taylor, and to the devices of the Japanese theater, was a principal element in the Constructivist concept of the performer: "maximum effect through minimum means" and "function determines form" were the basic assumptions on which Meierkhold constructed his system and which he taught to students such as Shlepianov (Nos. 930-46) and Elizaveta Yakunina (No. 1170) at his State Higher Theater Studios in 1922 onwards.[168]

---

37. Quoted in C5, pp. 428-29

38 Nikolai Aseev, tongue-in-cheek, proposed that the letters GVYTM (Gosudarstvennye vysshie teatralnye masterskie [State Higher Theater Studios]) could also be rendered as Genialnaia vycumka tovarishcha Meierkholda (the brilliant invention of comrade Meierkhold). See N. Aseev: "Pisma iz Moskvy. Budushchii teatralnyi sezon" in *Teatr, literatura, muzyka, balet, grafika, zhivopis, kino*, Kharkov, 1922, 16 September, No. 2, p. 12.

135. Aristarkh Lentulov: Stage Design for Scene I, *The Unknown Lady*, 1918 (No. 738)

In 1920 Meierkhold was given the premises of the former Zon Theater in Moscow where he :

> ... stripped bare his stage after throwing the old decorations into a shed...
> and unashamedly denuding the brick walls of the building. Meierkhold
> destroyed the illusory theater.[169]

Meierkhold opened his Theater of the RSFSR No. 1 with a production of Emile Verhaeren's *Les Aubes* with designs by Vladimir Dmitriev in November, 1920. The play was politically relevant inasmuch as it was a treatment of a Capitalist war that turned into a revolution of the international proletariat. The audience, however, found certain methods, such as the presence of a Greek chorus in the orchestra pit, the interruption of the narrative by episodes of a purely agitational nature, and the abstract cylinders, spheres, cones, and discs scattered on stage, to be perplexing and illogical. Clearly, both Meierkhold and Dmitriev wished to renounce the use of illustrative décor, but, in effect, the conglomeration of volumes produced merely another kind of superficial decoration. Fortunately, Dmitriev did better in his subsequent designs, e.g. for *The Love for Three Oranges* of 1926 (Nos. 422-23), but what Meierkhold needed immediately was a designer who, above all, would be able to use material in three dimensions in close conjunction with the essential component of movement on stage. It was in the art of Rodchenko, Stepanova, and, above all, Popova that Meierkhold found the necessary support for his "art of conscious theater."[170]

Popova was first involved in stage design in 1920 when she was commissioned to design costumes for the children's play *The Tale of the Country Priest and His Dunderhead Servant* (Ills. 164-67; Nos. 840-43). In 1921 she designed sets and costumes for Lunacharsky's play *The Chancellor and the Locksmith* (Ill. 171; No. 847), and also prepared sets and costumes for an unrealized production of *Romeo and Juliet* at the Chamber Theater (Ills. 168-69; Nos. 845-46). The same year she worked with Vesnin and Meierkhold on a project for an open-air mass spectacle intended to celebrate the theme of *Struggle and Victory* for the Third Congress of the International. With a cast of 200 cavalry, 2,300 infantry, 16 artillery batteries, tanks, motorcycles, and five airplanes carrying projectors, the spectacle was clearly impracticable, but it gave Popova valuable experience for her less ambitious scheme for *Earth on End* two years later.

The turning-point in Popova's career, and in the evolution of Constructivist theater, came in September, 1921, with the opening of the exhibition "5 x 5 = 25," to which five artists — Exter, Popova, Rodchenko, Stepanova, and Vesnin — contributed five abstract works each. One of the visitors was Meierkhold, who, seeing the works of Popova and her colleagues, concluded that they could be used as the basis for stage designs and "would allow him to fulfill his long cherished dream of an extra-theatrical spectacle."[171] The result was that Meierkhold invited Popova to compile a program for a course in material, three-dimensional stage design at his State Higher Theater Studios, and it was here that Popova developed the basic ideas for her extraordinary construction for *The Magnanimous Cuckold*, which was staged by Meierkhold on 25 April, 1922 (Nos. 974-75).

---

169 G16, p. 16.
170 This is the title of Marjorie Hoover's monograph on Meierkhold (C46).
171 I. Aksenov: "Prostranstvennyi konstruktivizm na stsene" in *Teatralnyi Oktiabr*, L-M, 1926, No. 1, p. 31.

E.Л. 1921 II   москва

136. Elena Liessner-Blomberg: Costume Design for a Man with Stick and Hat, 1921 (No. 743)

Meierhold took Fernand Crommelynck's farce about a miller duped by his adulterous wife and used it merely as an experiment in pure acting and pure form, "taking the circus, not literature as his departure-point."[172] Although Popova is generally credited with the whole visual design of this spectacle, it should be remembered that she started with suggestions by other artists already working in the Studios, including Sergei Eisenstein, and with a model developed by Vladimir Liutse. Still, the definitive conception belonged to Popova. Yurii Elagin recalled his impression of the production:

> On the evening of the first presentation Muscovites... saw on the stage completely denuded of curtain, backdrop, portals, and footlights — a wooden installation of the strangest shape, a construction. It was assembled to look like a peculiar windmill and was a combination of platforms, ladders, gangways, revolving doors, and revolving wheels. The installation itself did not depict anything. It served merely as a support, a device for the actors' performance and resembled something in the order of an intricate combination of trampolines, trapezes, and gymnastic installations.[173]

Inevitably, Popova's construction elicited censure as well as praise. Ippolit Sokolov, for example, wrote:

> ... t is difficult to imagine anything more vulgar, coarser, and more tasteless than the revolving red and black wheels of Popova's construction for *The Cuckold* enhancing the emotions of jealousy or lust.[174]

He then went on to argue that the real turning-point in the history of the Constructivist theater was Yakulov's *Giroflé-Girofla* — the "embodiment of the economy of use in the expressive means of human and physical material."[175] On the other hand, Yakulov was accused by other critics of plagiarizing directly from Popova in his major works for the Chamber Theater.[176]

Whatever the responses to *The Magnanimous Cuckold*, neither Popova, nor Meierhold regarded it as a standard prototype, although it certainly influenced other theatrical resolutions of the 1920s, including Stepanova's designs for *The Death of Tarelkin* (Ill. 192; No. 977-80) and Vesnin's *The Man Who Was Thursday* (1923). Popova's next and last theatrical endeavor, her design for Meierkhold's production of Sergei Tretiakov's *Earth on End* of 1923, relied on a totally representational setting and employed a real automobile, a real tractor, real telephones, etc. As one critic said: "The abstraction of *The Magnanimous Cuckold* turned into the documentation of *Earth on End*." Rodchenko also incorporated real objects into the theater for his rendering of Meierkhold's production of Maiakovsky's *The Bed Bug* in 1929 (Nos. 867-74).

As far as the designs for *The Death of Tarelkin* are concerned, Stepanova may, consciously or unconsciously, have paraphrased Popova's basic principle of the

> ... organization of the material elements of the spectacle as an apparatus, a kind of installation or contrivance for the given action.[178]

---

172 "Kronika" in *Ermitazh*, 1922, No. 1, p. 8.
173 Iu. Elagin: *Temnyi genii*, New York: Chekhov, 1955, pp. 248-49.
174 I. Sokolov: "Teatralnyi konstruktivizm (Kamernyi teatr)" in *Teatr i muzyka*, 1922, 19 December, No. 12, p. 288.
175 Ibid.
176 About-Fanfreliush [=V. Shershenevich]: "Kamernyi" in *Zrelishcha*, M, 1922, 10-16 October, No. 7, p. 19.
177 E. Rakitina: "Liubov Popova. Iskusstvo i manifesty" in G44, Vol. 1, 1975, p. 164.
178 From a lecture on *The Magnanimous Cuckold*, which Popova gave at Inkhuk, Moscow, on 27 April, 1922. Quoted in G44, Vol. 1, pp. 153-54.

137. El Lissitzky: Vladimir Tatlin at Work on the Monument to the III International ca. 1922 (No. 751)

Even so, her use of a series of wooden constructions of abstract form produced an unprecedented, variable scenario: as the actors moved about the stage, their formal, physical definitions changed constantly because the laths and slats of the constructions served as a kind of Op-Art mechanism. From the costumes for *The Death of Tarelkin*, it is clear that Stepanova was particularly concerned with the "proletarian esthetic" — with simplicity of form and maximum of efficiency. As in her *sportodezhda* (sports clothes) of 1923, Stepanova regarded emotion, illusion, and ornament as alien to production art, endeavoring

> ... [to eradicate] the ingrown view of the ideal artistic drawing as the
> imitation and copying of nature; to grapple with organic design and orient
> it towards the geometrization of forms; to propagate the productional
> tasks of Constructivism.[179]

Stepanova maintained that each profession — factory worker, doctor, actor, sportsman, etc. — demanded its own costume, which should be constructed according to the norms of expediency and convenience dictated by that profession. The most exciting instance of Stepanova's experiments in this area was, indeed, her designs for sports clothes (not unlike some of the stage costumes in *The Death of Tarelkin*) incorporating lightness of form (for mobility), economy of material (to maintain body temperature), and clear colors (for identification). They were not mass produced, but *The Death of Tarelkin* provided her with the opportunity to test her uniforms within a three-dimensional, living environment. Stepanova's husband, Rodchenko, was also active as a clothes and textile designer in the early 1920s. He produced his own *prozodezhda* (industrial clothing) in the form of a worker's coverall and a uniform for the martial arts (Ill. 176; No. 866-68), testing his ideas in the laboratory of the theater, as with Nikolai Gorchakov's production of *One Sixth of the World* (Nos. 875-79).

There is a clear connection here between Stepanova's, Rodchenko's, and also Popova's experimental costumes and the doctrine of Taylorism, industrial gymnastics, and ergatocratic gesture being researched concurrently at the Institute of Rhythm in Moscow. Reprocessing the eurhythmic ideas of Jaques-Dalcroze, the Soviet theorists of rational movement, among them Ippolit Sokolov (No. 1193), affirmed that:

> The new physical culture is the departure point for the new productional art.
> The *artistic design of the labor processes (the physical culture of labor) is a
> production art...* Labor gymnastics are a *psycho-physiological gymnastics.*[180]

Clearly, Popova, Stepanova, and their colleagues were adjusting their costumes to this demand for physical efficiency, agreeing that:

> Well-balanced, rhythmical lines exert an influence on the masses, make
> them more rational, more organized, and strengthen their aspiration
> towards self-discipline.[181]

Their streamlined designs might have functioned well in the theater and, theoretically, in the workplace, too. The problem was that this economy of gesture

---

179 V. Stepanova quoted in T. Strizhenova: *Iz istorii sovetskogo kostiuma.* M: Sovetskii khudozhnik, 1972, p. 97.
180 Sokolov, *Sistema trudovoi gimnastiki*, op. cit., p. 5.
181 L. Zalevsky: *Iskusstvo i proletariat*, M: Vserossiiskii tsentralnyi ispolnitelnyi komitet sovetov R.S.K. i Krasnykh deputatov, 1918, p. 47.

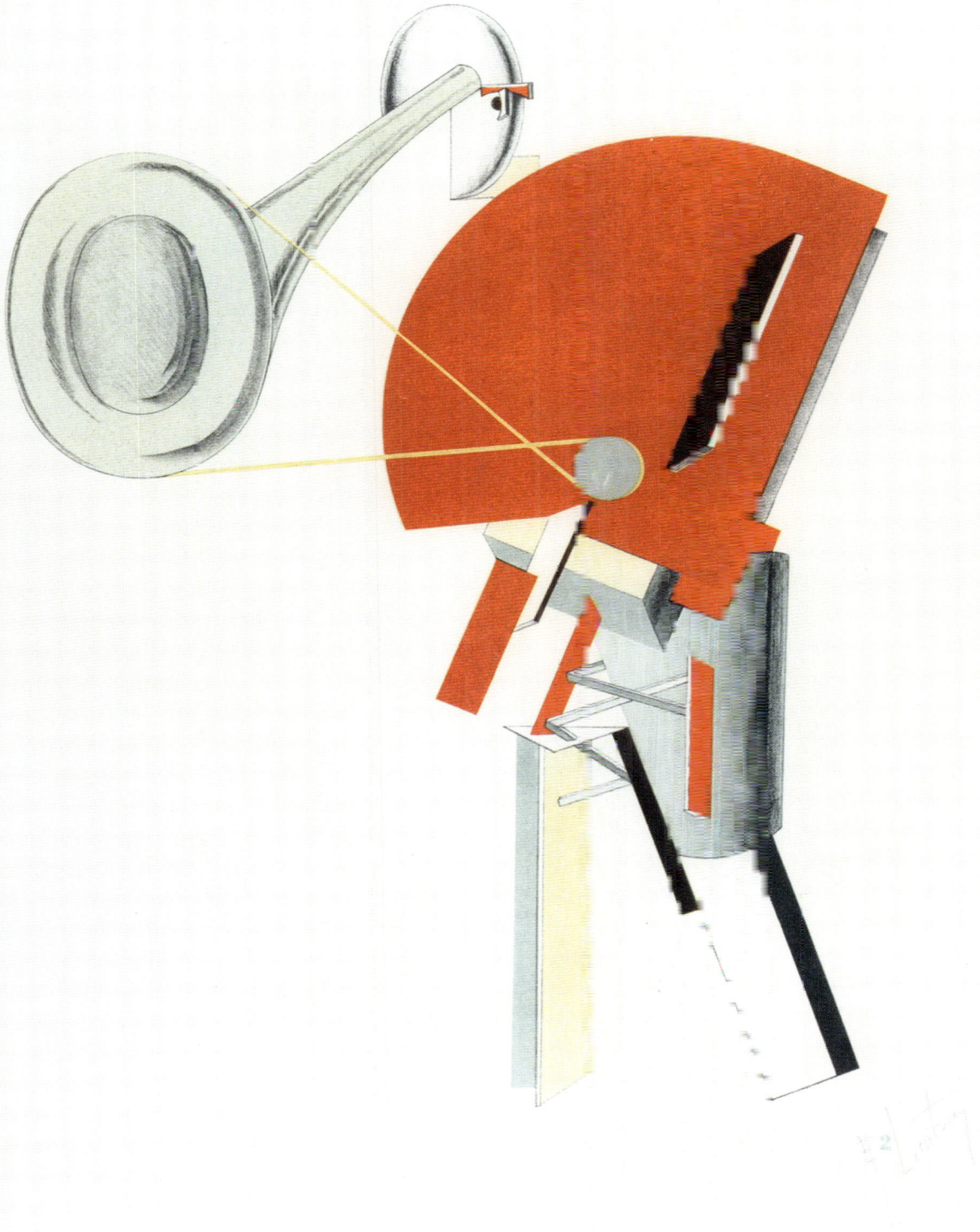

138. El Lissitzky: Design for the Announcer (Ansager, Figure 2), *Victory over the Sun*, 1923 (No. 755)

139. El Lissitzky: Design for the Sentinel (Posten, Figure 3), *Victory over the Sun*, 1923 (No. 756)

140. El Lissitzky: Design for the Anxious One (Ängstliche, Figure 4), *Victory over the Sun*, 1923 (No. 757)

141. El Lissitzky: Design for the Globetrotter in Time (Globetrotter in der Zeit, Figure 5), *Victory over the Sun*, 1923 (No. 759)

142. El Lissitzky: Design for the Sportsmen (Sportsmänne_ Fig_e 6),
Victory over the Sun, 1923 (No. 760)

143. El Lissitzky: Design for the Troublemaker (Zankstifter, Figure 7),
Victory over the Sun, 1923 (No. 761)

144. El Lissitzky: Design for the Old Man: Head Two Steps Back (Alter: Kopf 2 Schritt Hinten, Figure 8), *Victory over the Sun*, 1923 (No. 732)

145. El Lissitzky: Design for the Gravediggers (Totengräber, Figure 9), *Victory over the Sun*, 1923 (No. 763)

146. El Lissitzky: Design for The New Man (Neuer, Figure 10), *Victory over the Sun*, 1923 (No. 764)

and material presupposed a willingness on the part of the masses to understand these principles, i.e. an active psychological involvement. However, simple working people, confronted with "light, air, hygiene, convenience, cleanliness, economy," wondered where the art was,[182] and they certainly did not identify themselves with *prozodezhda, sportodezhda,* or any other kind of newfangled clothing.

There is a certain logic in the fact that many of the avant-garde artists, especially the Constructivists, worked with such enthusiasm for the theater and the cinema. The stage or screen acted as their laboratory — confined, concentrated, controlled — for research into the creation of prototypes for the land of the future. The critic and sculptor Boris Ternovets wrote in his catalog essay for the Soviet pavilion at the "Exposition des Arts Décoratifs" in Paris in 1925:

> Mais la nouvelle culture s'affirme peut-être plus combative, plus intrépide, plus impitoyable à l'égard des formes périmées que partout ailleurs, dans notre Section théâtrale. Ici le problème n'est pas seulement posé: il reçoit sa solution.[183]

But the "solution" was meaningful only in the theater. Once taken out into everyday life, this "modern culture" perished, for there was neither the popular demand, nor the technological wherewithal to produce it. As the critic Boris Brodsky observed in the context of Rodchenko's furniture designs for *The Bed Bug* in 1929: "The sofa-bed was displayed not in a store but on the stage, as a gibe at everyday life."[184]

Popova's *Magnanimous Cuckold*, Stepanova's *Death of Tarelkin*, Rodchenko's *Bed Bug* — here were scenic resolutions that made form follow function and expressed a modern, industrial era. These spectacles seemed to confirm the Constructivists' claim that their art, with its emphasis on factory culture, engineering, and mass entertainment, such as the circus, was in step with the working class, and that Constructivism, therefore, was the genuine artistic counterpart to the socio-political revolution of 1917. The argument is reasonable, but ultimately invalid, simply because, as the Gabo-Pevsner *La Chatte* demonstrated (Nos. 512, 823), the same machine esthetic was also operative in the Capitalist West, e.g. in Monte Carlo and Paris, where the audiences were not especially proletarian. This discrepancy can be noted on many levels of early Soviet design and it became a point of especially heated debate in the wake of the "Exposition des Arts Décoratifs," where it was noted that designers from bourgeois countries, for example, Marie Vassilieff (Ill. 233; No. 1116) and Sonia Delaunay (Ill. 55; No. 416), were creating projects and patterns for their rich clienteles very similar to those of the Soviet Constructivists. Perhaps, as the critic Yakov Tugendkhold concluded, Constructivism, therefore, was not especially revolutionary.[185] Conversely, the Russian Constructivists themselves were not always true to their mechanical credo, sometimes offering a more lyrical and visceral decoration instead of their severe, geometrical resolutions, a case in point being Popova's costume for a soldier with billowing scarf that she designed for a production of *Tarquinius, the High Priest* ca. 1923 (Ill. 172; No. 849).

---

182 A. Mikhailov: *IZO iskusstvo rekonstruktivnogo perioda*, M-L: Ogiz-Izogiz, 1932, p. 205.
183 B. T. (=Boris Ternovets): "En guise d'introduction" in catalog of the "Exposition des Arts Décoratifs." 1925, i.e. *Exposition de 1925. Section URSS. Catalogue*, Paris, 1925, p. 19.
184 E. Brodsky: "The Psychology of Urban Design in the 1920s and 1930s" in *Journal of Decorative and Propaganda Arts,* Miami, 1987, No. 5, p. 82.
185 Ya. Tugendkhold: *Khudozhestvennaia kultura Zapada*, M-L: GIZ, 1928, p. 130.

зелеными
до
похороны

2ᵉ Картина Зеленая и ~~черная~~
1ᵃ Действо

N.162г

IV.

⁶/₁₃₁

147. Kazimir Malevich: Design for the Backcloth for Action I, Scene 2, *Victory over the Sun*, 1913 (1973) (No. 770)

One can still maintain, however, that the Revolution, fired by the industrial proletariat, did make artists more aware of the machine-made object, of industrial production and of utilitarian design. Obviously, the Revolution also confronted them with the tastes of the new spectator, but it should not be forgotten that most of the avant-garde artists who became Constructivist designers after 1917 had already been active in applied geometric art before that date contributing designs for utilitarian objects to a number of pre-Revolutionary exhibitions.[186] In the immediate context of stage design, mention should be made once again of the "industrial" precedents of *Jeux* and *Victory over the Sun,* which, with their airplanes and other "modern" paraphernalia, pointed forwards to Popova's inclusion of real automobiles and tractors on stage in *Earth on End* in 1923. Could we perhaps interpret this esthetic consistency as a desire on the part of avant-garde artists to extend élite and private ideas from before the Revolution into the public forum after the Revolution? Did the new artists such as Malevich, Popova, and Rodchenko turn to the theater because they wished to move from the studio to the street?

In spite of the Constructivists' eloquent statements on the architecture of the stage and on the micro-environment, most of their scenic resolutions still carried a pictorial or illustrative element. Their set and costume designs, with few exceptions, relied on a receptive, static audience placed at a certain distance from the stage; and the traditional space between the viewer and the painting hanging on the wall was repeated in the space between the proscenium and the public. The set was examined frontally just like a painting in a museum, it related to the wings just as the solid oil related to its gilt frame, it relied on a false perspective, it was a visual unit defined and confined. Each play, ballet or opera dictated a single, one-time, individual resolution, just as the painted landscape, still life or abstract composition did. In other words, the Constructivist artists tended to use the stage as a "blow-up" of their earlier studio paintings and sculptures, perhaps even as an impressive piece of publicity. They geometrized objects and figures, reduced the actors to formal elements, and borrowed ideas from the low arts, but in the same sophisticated and intellectual manner in which they had appropriated images and devices from the *lubok* or store signboard into their professional studio paintings. Tatlin's conception of *Zangezi* in 1923 as a gigantic relief or Rodchenko's of *One Sixth of the World* in 1931 as a mobile, revolving construction (No. 875) are clear illustrations of this transference of essential ideas from one discipline to another.

The artists of the avant-garde who, by and large, evolved primarily as studio artists and whose practical training in design was minimal, found the theater to be an attractive and even comfortable medium. For them it was a closed laboratory and a haven for experiment protected from the brutal reality outside. The inevitable conclusion, then, is that, to a considerable extent, the avant-garde of the 1920s thought more about itself than about the masses, for they continued their refined, cerebral experiments initiated well before the Revolution, "cluttered the scenic space with abstract objects deprived of any figurative sense,"[187] dreamed of floating cities when people were living in slums, and transformed the theater into an esoteric

---

186 See, for example, the "Exhibition of Contemporary Decorative Art" (1915), the "Exhibition of Industrial Art" (1915-1916) (both at the Lemercier Gallery, Moscow), and the "Second Exhibition of Contemporary Decorative Art" (1917) (at the Mikhailova Salon, Moscow). Among the contributors were Exter, Malevich, Popova, Pougny, Rozanova, Nadezhda Udaltsova, and Yakulov.
187 G38, pp. 254, 255.

233

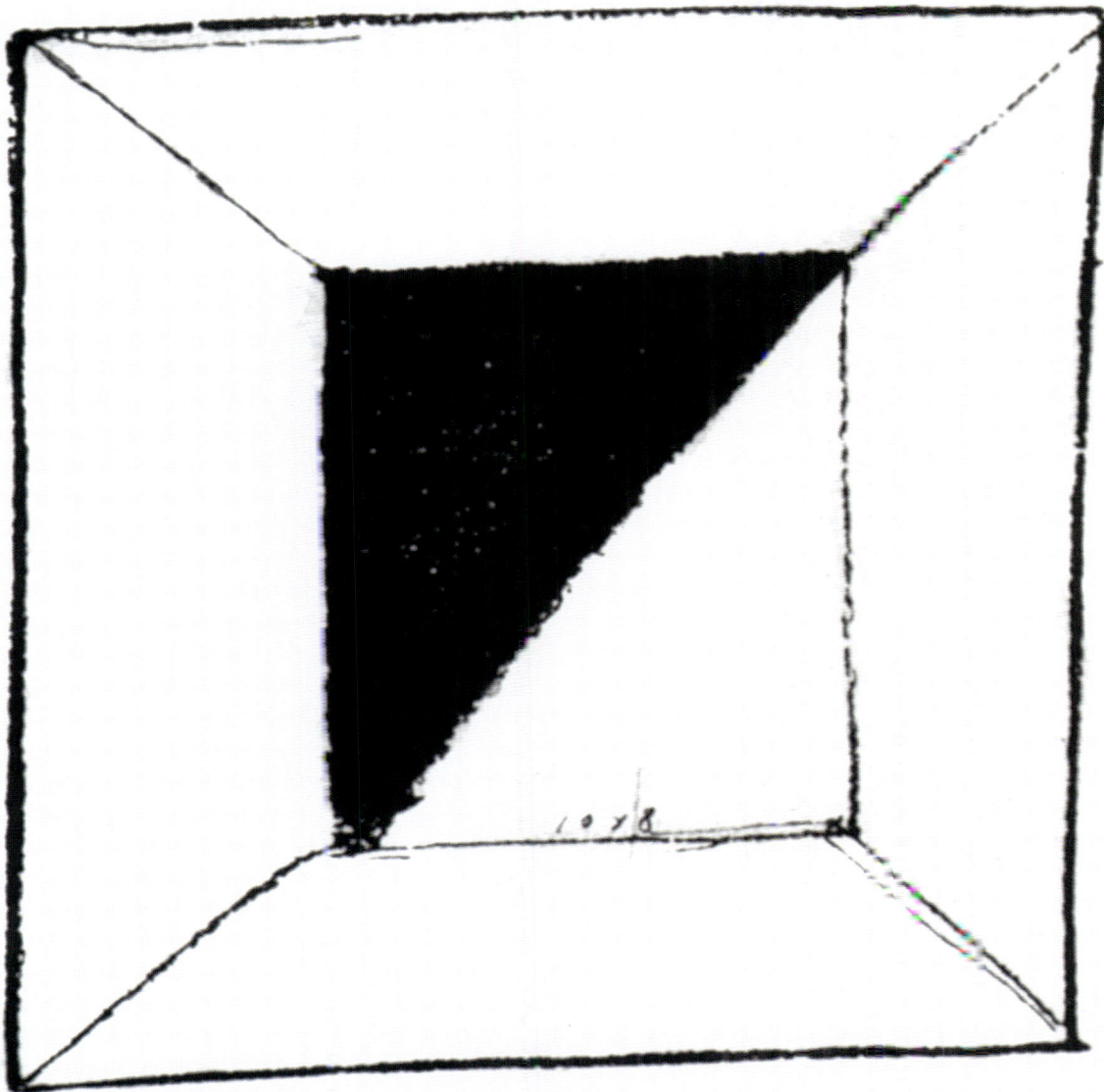

148. Kazimir Malevich: Design for the Backcloth, Action II, Scene 5, *Victory over the Sun*, 1913 / 1973 (No. 771)

debate when much of the population could neither read, nor write. Boris Arvatov was justified in his appeal of 1922:

> Abandon the stage and the productions. Enter life so as to relearn and learn. Assimilate not esthetic methods, but the methods of constructing society and life in general. Be engineers, be the assemblers of everyday life.
> The working class does not want illusions, it wants concrete forms scientifically organized. It does not need an imitation of life, it needs the construction of life.[188]

True, the avant-garde had created, as Isaiah Berlin noted, "a culture of unusual vitality and achievement, an extraordinary upwards curve in European civilisation" — but "plainly, all this was too good to last."[189]

Socialist Realism and Beyond

The formal severity and intellectual complexity of the Constructivist designs were alien to the average theater-goer in the Soviet Union. By and large, the new public was operating with a 19th-century concept of spectacle and what people wanted was the melodrama, the epic movie, the distracting entertainment with an accessible plotline and recognizable sets and costumes. A direct result of this pressure from below was that by the late 1920s Soviet stage design was returning rapidly from space to surface, forcing the "replacement of construction by decoration."[190] There are many examples of Constructivist compromise, some of them very beautiful. Who is to say that Gamrekeli's lively designs for *Mystery-Bouffe*, Meller's for *The Mikado*, Petritsky's for *The Flea* (No. 818), Vialov's for *Stenka Razin*, Lev Lapin's rendering of a Russian peasant dancing (Ill. 121; No. 696) or even Tchehonine's projects (e.g. Ills. 206-08; Nos. 1038-46) are any less successful as stage or costume designs than Popova's or Rodchenko's? Malleable in composition, they are imaginative, colorful, alive, and often funny, qualities not always identifiable with the main line Constructivist productions at Tairov's and Meierkhold's theaters in the early 1920s.

The late 1920s are an extremely complex period in the history of Soviet culture and many circumstances must be borne in mind in any assessment of this kind. Soviet art and design moved towards a more narrative, more illustrative esthetic — and eventually towards Socialist Realism — because of a variety of conditions, not just because the masses or the state bureaucracy wanted it that way. The petty jealousies among the avant-garde artists always threatened their collective power (illusory or real); key representatives of the new artistic ideas such as Chagall, Gabo, Goncharova, Kandinsky, and Larionov went on to develop their ideas in emigration; and of particular importance here, the more classical, more conservative artistic styles that had never really disappeared during the Modernist period, now began to play an ever stronger role. Artists such as Alexandre and Nicola Benois, Ivan Biilibin (Ills. 45-46; Nos. 364-71), Dobujinsky (Ills. 56-58; Nos. 452-53), Alexandre Jacovleff (Nos. 584-88), Kuzma Petrov-Vodkin (Nos. 819-21), and Shukhaev (Nos. 947-50) lived and worked outside the confines of the avant-garde and, consciously or

188 B. Arvatov: "Ot rezhissury teatra k montazhu byta" in *Ermitazh*, 1922, No. 11, p. 3.
189 I. Berlin: *Personal Impressions,* London: Hogarth, 1980, p. 148.
190 A. Fevralsky: "Detskaia bolezn pravizny i konstruktivizm" in *Zrelishcha*, 1923, No. 34, p. 6.

Будетлянскій силачъ

4-2...

149. Kazimir Malevich: Costume Design for a Futurist Strongman, *Victory over the Sun*, 1913 / 1973 (No. 773)

50. Kazimir Malevich: Costume Design for Nero, *Victory over the Sun*, 1913 / 1973 (No. 774)

151. Kazimir Malevich: Costume Design for a Mugger, *Victory over the Sun*, 1913 / 1973 (No. 775)

костюм трусливых

152 Kazimir Malevich: Costume Design for a Coward, *Victory over the Sun*, 1913 / 1973 (No. 776)

153. Kazimir Malevich Costume Design for a Fat Man, *Victory over the Sun*, 1913 / 1973 (No. 779)

154 Kazimir Malevich: Costume Design for a New Man, *Victory over the Sun*, 1913 / 1973 (No. 782)

155. Kazimir Malevich: Costume Design for the Enemy, *Victory over the Sun*, 1913 / 1973 (No. 784)

unconsciously, fought against its extremism. Jacovleff and Shukhaev, for example, never betrayed their allegiance to the canons of the Italian Renaissance, while a younger generation of émigré artists such as Dimitri Bouchène (No. 391), Alexander Bilibin (Ill. 44; Nos. 362-63), Georges Pogedaieff (Ill. 163; Nos. 824-27), and Alexandre Serebyakoff (Ills. 185-87; Nos. 897-902) continued to uphold the principles of the World of Art. Petrov-Vodkin also contributed to this retention of traditional values by taking the Russian icon as a source of inspiration. He reinterpreted sacred images, as in his paraphrase of St. George and the Dragon in his *Bathing of the Red Horse* (1912), perceiving space "iconically" — something that might also explain the curved, planetary surface of his set for *The Brothers Karamazov* of 1927 (No. 819). Even Filonov, a stellar member of the avant-garde, firmly upheld the accomplishments of 19th-century Realism and the Imperial Academy of Arts, regarding Ivan Aivazovsky, Ilia Repin, and Konstantin Savitsky as accomplished predecessors worthy of emulation. True, neither Petrov-Vodkin, nor Filonov was especially sympathetic to the principles of Socialist Realism, but their appreciation of the "verdict of ages," their unswerving belief in the validity of figurative art, and their recognition of a hallowed tradition as a major esthetic criterion brought them into line with the leading practitioners of Socialist Realism in the 1930s.

Obviously, all these conditions affected the subsequent development of the Soviet theater, including stage design. Yet, in spite of a few innovative projects realized by talented artists such as Vladimir Dmitriev and Petr Viliams, the "Great Experiment"[191] was — by the late 1930s — lost from view. As Shlepianov wrote in 1938: "Moscow theaters... are now like a row of interlocking retorts in which the water level is the same."[192] However, after Stalin's death in 1953, ballets, operas, and plays, once dismissed as "decadent" or "formalist," were reintroduced into the theatrical repertoire and a new generation of artists came forward, including Eduard Kochergin, Valer Levental, and Enar Stenberg. They refurbished the luminous traditions of the Silver Age so that, once again, Russian stage design recaptured the spirit of bold reform and lasting iridescence.

---

191 This is the title of the first edition of Camilla Gray's pioneering study of the Russian avant-garde (E2).
192 E. Graeva, ed.: *Ilia Shlepianov,* M: Iskusstvo, 1969, p. 22.

Alexandre Benois: Curtain Design with Night Scene with Fantastic Creatures in the Sky, *Petrouchka*, ca. 1957 (No. 166)

156. Vadim Meller: Ccstume design for Bronislava Nijinska. *Мерi̇̈хс́ ̇ ́а/z,* 1919 (No. 792)

STYLES AND MOVEMENTS IN EARLY
20TH-CENTURY WESTERN ART

1. Art Nouveau (1895-ca. 1920)

This phrase was coined by Samuel Bing in 1895 at the opening of his Salon de l'Art Nouveau in Paris. The style relevant especially to architecture and interior decoration, is characterized by asymmetry of line, sinuous, fluid forms, bright colors, and the extensive use of decorative motifs derived from nature, especially plant life and the female form. Among the best-known exponents are Gallé, Lalique, and Daum in France, and Tiffany in the United States. Beardsley in England may be considered the progenitor of Art Nouveau with his drawings for the first issue of *The Studio* (1893), a periodical which helped to disseminate the style. In Germany the movement was called *Jugendstil*, and in Russia it is known as the *style moderne*.

Example: Yakimchenko, No. 1156.

2. Cubism (1907-20)

A technique and style of representing three-dimensional reality on a calculated, reintegrated two-dimensional surface. Streets, people, and houses are reduced to geometric outlines, e.g. cubes, and are then depicted simultaneously from more than one viewpoint. In addition, the artist fragments the objects into geometric, faceted forms, reassembling them into a loosely overlapping structure with intersecting spaces. Initiated by Georges Braque and Pablo Picasso.

Examples: Larionov, Ill. 124 (No. 706); Pougny, Ill. 173 (No. 850).

3. Simultanism (1912 onwards)

A style based on the use of constrasting luminous colors that bounce off and balance one another across whirls of circular forms. Concentric rings overlap and interlock, and are stabilized and interrupted by horizontal and vertical axes. The result is a play between rectangularity and circularity, color and form. Initiated by Robert and Sonia Delaunay.

Examples: S. Delaunay, Ills. 53-54, Nos. 407-16.

4. Surrealism (1920s-30s)

Pictorial or verbal imagery created according to irrational dictates of the subconscious mind and vision. Promoted by Salvador Dalí.

Examples: Berman, No. 361; Tchelitchew, Ill. 230 (No. 1098).

5. Art Deco (1925 onwards)

The term is an abbreviation for "Art Décoratif" and was inspired by the "Exposition Internationale des Arts Décoratifs et Industriels Modernes" held in Paris in 1925. The simple, geometric forms typical of Art Deco had their origins at the turn of the century, when, in Europe and America, artists and artisans reacted against the excesses of late 19th-century taste. The Wiener Werkstätte craftsmen in Vienna, Frank Lloyd Wright in Chicago, Mackintosh in Glasgow, and Lalique in France were all pioneers of this movement. Representative objects are angular rather than curved, opalescent instead of iridescent, and contain large areas of pure color as well as flat surfaces. The style was strongly influenced by fashion houses and ballet designers.

Examples: Bilinsky, Ill. 47, Nos. 376, 377; Dunkel, No. 454; Lissim, No. 746;
Pogedaieff, Ill. 163, Nos. 825-27.

157. Grigorii Miller: Costume Design for King Herod, *Salome*, ca. 1920 (No. 798)

STYLES AND MOVEMENTS IN EARLY 20TH-CENTURY RUSSIAN ART

1. Neo-Nationalism or the Neo-Russian Style (1880s-early 1900s)

Reacting against the strictures of the international academic style, Russian artists turned to native arts and crafts for inspiration, often deriving subject matter from Russian history and fairy-tales. Using a narrative and representational style, the artists sought to repeat the bright and stylized qualities of indigenous arts such as icons and wood carvings. A parallel to this style existed in the Arts and Crafts Movement in England.

> Theoretician: The movement was not accompanied by any significant published manifesto.
>
> Principal representatives: I. Bilibin, Kustodiev, Nesterov, Polenova, Riabushkin, V. Vasnetsov, Yakunchikova, and their colleagues at Abramtsevo and Talashkino.
>
> Examples: Riabushkin, No. 865; Vasnetsov, Ill. 232, No. 1115.

2. Symbolism (late 1890s-ca. 1910)

Concerned with the evocation of mood and subjective vision rather than with the depiction of concrete reality. Tended to use the intrinsic elements of painting (color, line, texture) for highly emotional, psychological expression. Symbolism was supported by two important art groups in Russia — by the World of Art in St. Petersburg (ca. 1898-1906) and the Blue Rose in Moscow (ca. 1904-1908).

> Theoretician: Diaghilev (leader of the World of Art): various articles in the magazines *Mir iskusstva* (SP, 1898-1904), and *Zolotoe runo* (M, 1906-1909 [=1910]).
>
> Principal representatives: Bakst, Borisov-Musatov, Čiurlionis, Kalmakov, Kuznetsov, Sapunov, Somov, Sudeikin, Vrubel.
>
> Examples: Kalmakov, Ill. 106, No. 595; Vrubel, No. 1152; Yakimchenko, No. 1156.

3. Neo-Primitivism (ca. 1907-14)

This style is defined by intentional use of naive, primitive forms and subjects in painting, with the emphasis on primary colors not necessarily germane to nature, i.e. trees could be red and people blue. In the Russian variant, Neo-Primitivism borrows from the simple forms of folk art (e.g. the *lubok* [broadsheet], the primitive icon, store signs, toys) and applies methods such as the distortion or rejection of academic perspective and proportion, the laconic emphasis on highly expressive and humorous elements, the attention to trivial and provincial themes. The principal reason why artists chose such methods and forms was to oppose both the earlier styles of Naturalism and Realism and to renounce the refined subjects of Symbolism together with the eclecticism of the *style moderne*. Russian Neo-Primitivism has affinities with French Fauvism and German Expressionism.

> Theoretician: A. Shevchenko: *Neoprimitivizm, ego teoriia, ego vozmozhnosti, ego dostzheniia* (M, 1913).
>
> Principal representatives: Burliuks, Chagall, Goncharova, Larionov, Malevich, Shevchenko, Sudeikin, Tatlin.
>
> Examples: Goncharova, Ill. 87, No. 534; Larionov, Ills. 122, 128, 129, Nos. 702, 703, 716, 717.

4. Rayism (also known as Rayonism, 1912-14)

Allegedly, one of the first variants of non-figurative art (out of perhaps three or four). Rayism is based on an attempt to identify artistic form with the movement of light rays emanating from objects and to express the linear dynamism of the pictorial plane. The object is not presented in its apparent visual form, but is composed of parallel, convergent, and interpenetrating rays. These in turn derive from the radiations of the objects as seen by the painter. According to Larionov, a Rayism painting is also intended to convey the sensation of the fourth dimension.

> Theoretician: M. Larionov *Luchizm* (M, 1913).
> Principal representatives: Goncharova, Larionov, Le-Dantiu, Romanovich, Shevchenko.
> Examples: Larionov, Nos. 705, 713.

5. Cubo-Futurism (1912-16)

The combination of Cubism with the basic Futurist principle, i.e. the visual representation of motion in time. (In their essential forms, French Cubism and Italian Futurism were not practised widely in Russian art.) In other words, this principle advocates the combination in one picture of several stages of movement or of sequential views of objects. Both provide the pictorial composition with a dynamic form.

> Theoreticians: D. Burliuk, Rozanova: various articles. See the miscellanies
> *Poshchechina obshchestvennomu vkusu* (M, 1912); *Sadok sudei No. 2* (M, 1913).
> Principal representatives: Burliuks, Malevich, Popova, Pougny, Rozanova,
> Tatlin, Udaltsova.
> Examples: Bogomazov, No. 389; Meller, No. 795; Pougny, Ill. 173, (No. 850);
> Yakulov, Ill. 239, No. 1158.

6. Suprematism (1915-early 1920s)

One of the primary categories of non-figurative painting. The painter uses simple geometric forms, covering the pictorial surface with minimal geometric units — the square, the circle, the cross, the triangle — painted in contrasting colors. These elements are presented, as it were, "in infinity," and in free interrelationships, independent of the laws of gravity.

> Theoretician: K. Malevich: *Ot kubizma i futurizma k suprematizmu* (P, 1915).
> Principal representatives: Chashnik, Chervinka, Kliun, Kudriashev, Lissitzky,
> Malevich, Pougny, Rozanova, Suetin.
> Examples: Chervinka, Nos. 405-06; Kudriashev, No. 683; Lissitzky, Ill. 144, (No. 762).

7. Constructivism (1921 onwards)

The development of studio painting into an artistic and mechanical approach in which function determines form. There is a tendency to show the structural elements of form and the composition of materials. Consequently, Constructivism finds its most concrete expression in architecture and industrial design. In the field of stage design its manifestation is evident in multifaceted constructions occupying the entire stage. These are often enhanced by the application of mechanically moved components.

> Theoretician: A. Gan: *Konstruktivizm* (Tver, 1922).
> Principal representatives: Gabo, Klutsis, Lissitzky, Medunetsky, Popova,
> Rodchenko, G. and V. Stenberg, Stepanova, Tatlin, Telingater, A. Vesnin, Yakulov.
> Examples: Exter, Ills. 72, 73, Nos. 474, 476, 478; Rodchenko, No. 875; Vialov, Ills.
> 235-238, (Nos. 1143, 1145, 1147).

159. Vera Mukhina: Costume Design for Bertrand, the Knight of Misfortune,
The Rose and the Cross, ca. 1916 (No. 800

STYLES AND MOVEMENTS IN RUSSIAN ART AS REPRESENTED IN THE LOBANOV-ROSTOVSKY COLLECTION

Antecedents to the Russian Avant-Garde

1.	Neo-Nationalism (1880s-1900s)		No. in Vol II (Ill. in Vol. I)
	Bilibin, Ivan	Boyar, *Boris Godunov*	366 (Ill. 45)
	Kustodiev	*Flea* stage set	687 (Ill. 120)
	Ryabushkin	*At the Wedding*	865
	Vasnetsov, Victor	*Russian Maiden*	1115 (Ill. 232)
	Yekimchenko	*Firebird Panneau*	1156
2.	Symbolism (late 1890s - ca.1910)		
	Kalmakov	*Salomé*	594
	Sapunov	Costume, *Princess Turandot*	895
	Sudeikin	*Salomé*	983
	Vrubel	*Lady with Cothurni*	1152

The Avant-Garde

3.	Neo-Primitivism (ca. 1907-14)		
	Goncharova	*Coq d'Or* stage design	534 (Ill. 87)
	Larionov	*Chout* sets and costume	716-18 (Ills. 128-29)
		Soleil de Nuit set and costume	703-04 (Ills. 122-23)
	Malevich	*Victory over the Sun* costumes	779-80 (Ill. 153)
	Tatlin	*Emperor Maximilian* costume	1014 (Ill. 203)
4.	Rayism (1912-14)		
	Larionov	*Dancer*	705
		Haunted Forest, *Contes Russes*	711 (Ill. 127)
5.	Cubo-Futurism (1912-16)		
	Bogomazov	*Female dancer*	389
	Malevich	*Victory over the Sun* stage designs	770, 772 (Ill. 147)
	Meller	*Carnival* costume design	795
	Udaltsova	Stage design	1109
	Yakulov	Stable of Pegasus interior design	1158 (Ill. 239)
6.	Suprematism (1915-20s)		
	Chashnik	Textile designs	405-406
	Ermolaeva	*Victory over the Sun* stage design	458
	Kudriashev	Orenburg Theater interior design	683
	Lissitzky	Old man, *Victory over the Sun*	762 (Ill. 144)
	Suetin	Textile design	1011
	Tchernovine	Stage designs	1020, 1025
7.	Constructivism (1921 onwards)		
	Gabo	Costume for woman, *La Chatte*	512
	Exter	Stage designs	474, 476, 478 (Ills. 72-73)
		Costumes, *Aelita*	465-69 (Ills. 66-68)
	Klutsis	Decoration for Kremlin	622
	Meerzsky	Headgear, *Phèdre*	789
	Popova	*The Chancellor & the Locksmith* Set	847 (Ill. 171)
	Pougny	Costume for a street procession	850 (Ill. 173)
	Rodchenko	Set, *One Sixth of the World*	875
	Stenbergs	Headgear, *Phèdre* 969-71 (Ill. 191)	
	Stepanova	Costume for Raspliuev, *Death of Tarelkin*	979
	Vesnin, A.	Stage Design, *Phèdre*	1139
	Vialov	Stage Designs, *Stenka Razin*	1145, 1147 (Ills. 237-38)

160. Anatolii Petritsky: Costume Design for Nur, *Nur and Anitra*, 1923 (No. 812)

161. Anatolii Petritsky: Costume Design for the Musician, *Nur and Anitra*, 1923 (No. 813)

162. Anatolii Petritsky: Costume Design for Medora, *Le Corsaire*, 1925 (No. 815)

RUSSIAN ART GROUPS

World of Art (*Mir iskusstva*) (1898-1924)

Group of graphic and decorative artists, poets, and musicians who accepted "art for art's sake." By and large, they were distant to contemporary socio-political reality, a fact sometimes reflected in their highly stylized, retrospective depictions of historical themes executed with technical finesse.

Original Members	Pictorial Example	No. in Vol II
Bakst	Wise Man, *Hippolytus*, 1902	57
Benois, A.	Suzanne de S., *Pavillon d'Armide*, 1907	125
Bilibin, I.	Boyar, *Boris Godunov*, 1908	366 (Ill. 45)
Dobujinsky	Portrait of Benois, 1908	424
Lanceray	Stage Detail, *El Purgatorio de San Patricio*, 1911	693
Roerich	Five Costumes, *Le Sacre du Printemps*, 1913	882
Somov	Drop Curtain for Free Theater, Moscow, 1913	953

Union of Russian Artists (*Soiuz russkikh khudozhnikov*) (1903-22)

Name of an exhibition group in Moscow that promoted a Naturalist style of painting, focusing primarily on interiors, church architecture, landscapes, and portraits.

Original Members	Pictorial Example	No. in Vol II
Golovin	Carmen's Hairstyle, 1908	532
Korovin, K.	Square in Novgorod, *Sadko*, 1912	642
Maliavin	Portraits	785-86
Ostroukhov	Street Scene	803
Serov	Holophernes's Camp, *Judith*, 1908	910 (Ill. 188)
Vrubel	Union of Russian Artists Exhibition Poster, 1904	1155
Yuon	Costumes, *Boris Godunov*, 1913	1172-74

Blue Rose (*Golubaia roza*) (ca. 1904-1908)

Name of an exhibition held in Moscow in 1907. Adopted as a group name for Symbolist painters, among them: Kuznetsov, Sapunov, and Sudeikin. Their aim was to break with Naturalism and to distort form in order to incite subjective, psychological experiences, replacing analytical observation with individualistic interpretation. United in their emphasis on the "flowing," melodic quality of the canvas, they consciously used symbols, especially the female figure. Their basic form was the curve or the circle, while their basic colors were blue, gray, and green.

Original Members	Pictorial Example	No. in Vol II
Kuznetsov	Costume, *Sakuntala*, 1914	690
Milioti	Costume, *Princesse de Carizme*, 1925	797
Sapunov	Costume, *Princess Turandot*, ca. 1912	895
Sarian	Costume, *Golden Cockerel*, 1931	896
Sudeikin	Costume, *La Tragédie de Salomé*, 1913	982 (Ill. 193)

163. Georges Pogedaieff: Costume for a Male Dancer, ca 19⬛ (No. 827)

Jack (Knave) of Diamonds *(Bubnovyi valet)* (1910-18)

Group of Moscow painters who adopted ideas from Post-Impressionism. They used brilliant colors with intense surface patterning and radical simplification of form. Their painting was not photographic, but was instead an exercise in color, line, and texture, with a deliberate simplification and vulgarization of form. Indebted to Cézanne and, to some extent, Cubism, they painted mainly still-lifes and portraits.

Original Members	Pictorial Example	No. in Vol II
Goncharova	Man from the people, *Liturgie*, 1915	542
Larionov	Portrait of a soldier, 1914	702
Lentulov	Stage design, *Unknown Lady*, 1918	738 (Ill. 135)
Tatlin	Peasant girl, *A Life for the Tsar*, 1913	1015 (Ill. 204)

Union of Youth *(Soiuz molodezhi)* (1910-1915)

Group of avant-garde artists based in St. Petersburg that followed various artistic styles beginning with Neo-Primitivism, followed by Neo-Symbolism and Expressionism, and ending with analytical painting.

Original Members	Pictorial Example	No. in Vol II
Annenkov	Portrait of Evreinov, ca. 1915	45
Goncharova	Stage design, *Coq d'Or*, 1914	534 (Ill. 87)
Kubin	Portrait of Kruchenykh, 1913	684
Larionov	*Dancer in Movement*, 1915	705
Malevich	Backcloth, *Victory over the Sun*, 1913	770 (Ill. 147)
Rozanova	Poster, *Futurist Theater*, 1913	891
Shkolnik	Stage design, 1910s	928
Tatlin	Pipe player, *Emperor Maximilian*, 1911	1014 (Ill. 203)

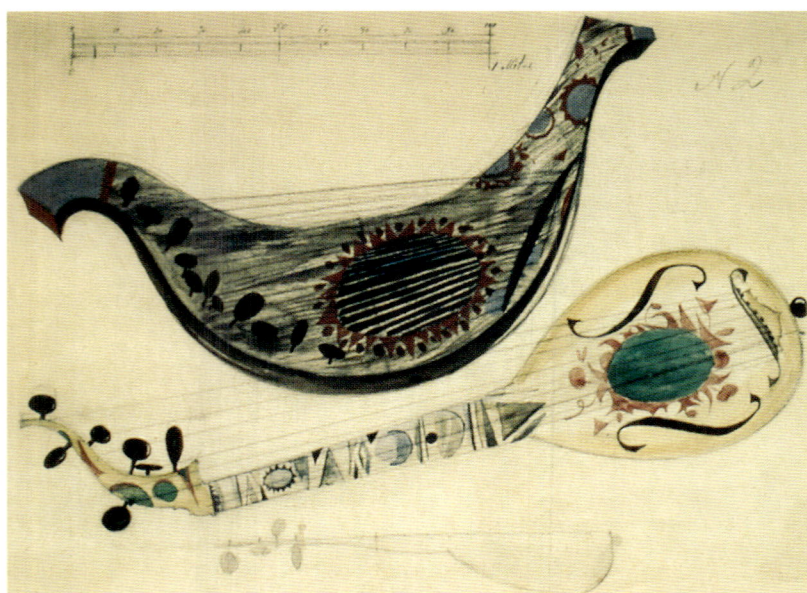

Serge Tchehonine: Stage Detail for Gusli and Mandolin, *The Blind Street Musician*, ca. 1929 (No. 1049)

164. Liubov Popova: Costume Design for the Dunderhead Servant with Hat, *The Tale of the Country Priest and His Dunderhead Servant*, ca. 1920 (No. 340)

165. Liubov Popova: A Second Costume Design for the Dunderhead Servant without Hat, *The Tale of the Country Priest and His Dunderhead Servant*, ca. 1920 (No. 841)

166. Liubov Popova: Costume Design for the Priest's Daughter, *The Tale of the Country Priest and His Dunderhead Servant*, ca. 1921 (No. 8–2)

GUIDE TO BALLETS, BALLS, MOVIES, OPERAS, OPERETTAS, PANTOMIMES, PLAYS, AND REVUES

167. Liubov Popova Costume Design for the Devil, *The Tale of the Country Priest and His Dunderhead Servant*, ca. 1920 (No. 843)

Name of Spectacle / Cultural Event: No. in Vol. II (Ill. in Vol. I)

168. Liubov Popova: Costume Design for a Lady in a Blue Cape, *Romeo and Juliet*, ca. 1920 (No. 844)

Name of Spectacle / Cultural Event: No. in Vol. II (III. in Vol. I)

169. Liubov Popova: Costume Design for a Man in Green, with Feather in Cap,
Romeo and Juliet, ca. 1920 (No. 345)

170. Liubov Popova: Costume Design for a Woman, *Romeo and Julie, 920* (No. 846)

171. Liubov Popova: Set Design for the Chancellor's Study, *The Chancellor and the Locksmith*, ca. 1921 (No. 847)

BALLETS AND OPERAS PRODUCED
OR PROJECTED BY SERGEI DIAGHILEV

1908	*Boris Godunov* (opera) (Golovin et al.)
1909	*Le Pavillon d'Armide* (A. Benois)
	Prince Igor (Roerich)
	Le Festin (K. Korovin)
	Les Sylphides (A. Benois)
	Cléopâtre (Bakst)
	Ivan the Terrible (Golovin)
	Ruslan and Liudmila (K. Korovin)
1910	*Carnaval* (Bakst)
	Schéhérazade (Bakst)
	Giselle (A. Benois)
	L'Oiseau de Feu (Golovin)
	Les Orientales (K. Korovin)
1911	*Le Spectre de la Rose* (Bakst)
	Narcisse (Bakst)
	Sadko (Anisfeld)
	La Péri (Bakst)
	Petrouchka (A. Benois)
	Swan Lake (Golovin and K. Korovin)
1912	*Le Dieu Bleu* (Bakst)
	Thamar (Bakst)
	L'Après-midi d'un Faune (Bakst)
	Daphnis et Chloé (Bakst)
1913	*May Night* (Fedorovsky)
	Boris Godunov (opera) (Fedorovsky)
	Khovanshchina (opera) (Fedorovsky)
	Jeux (Bakst)
	Le Sacre du Printemps (Roerich)
	La Tragédie de Salomé (Sudeikin)
1914	*Papillons* (Dobujinsky)
	La Légende de Joseph (J.-M. Sert)
	Le Coq d'Or (Goncharova)
	Le Rossignol (A. Benois)
	Midas (Dobujinsky)
1915	*Liturgie* (Goncharova) (not produced)
	Soleil de Nuit (Larionov)
1916	*Till-Eulenspiegel* (Jones)
	Las Meninas (Sert)
	Kikimora (Larionov)
	Histoires Naturelles (Larionov) (not produced)
	España (Goncharova) (not produced)
	Foire Espagnole (Goncharova) (not produced)
	Triana (Goncharova) (not produced)

172. Liubov Popova: Costume Design for a Soldier with Billowing Scarf *Tarquinius, the High Priest*, ca. 1923 (No. 849)

Ballets and Operas Produced or Projected by Diaghilev (continued)

1917   *Contes Russes* (Larionov)
Feu d'Artifice (Balla)
Les Femmes de Bonne Humeur (Bakst)
Parade (Picasso)

1919   *La Boutique Fantasque* (Derain)
Le Tricorne (Picasso)

1920   *Le Chant du Rossignol* (Matisse)
Pulcinella (Picasso)
Les Astuces Féminines (Sert)

1921   *Chout (Le Bouffon)* (Larionov)
Il Cuadro Flamenco (Picasso)
La Belle au Bois Dormant (Bakst)

1922   *Le Mariage d'Aurore* (A. Benois, Golovin, Bakst)
Renard (Larionov)
Mavra (opera) (Survage)

1923   *Les Noces* (Goncharova)

1924   *Les Tentations de la Bergère ou l'Amour Vainqueur* (Gris)
Les Biches (Laurencin)
Cimarosiana (excerpt from *Les Astuces Féminines*, 1920)
Les Facheux (Braque)
La Nuit sur le Mont Chauve (Goncharova)
Le Train Bleu (Laurens and Picasso)
Le Médécin malgré lui (A. Benois)
Philémon et Baucis (A. Benois)

1925   *Zéphyr et Flore* (Braque)
Les Matelots (Pruna)
Barabau (Utrillo)

1926   *Roméo et Juliette* (Miró and Ernst)
La Pastorale (Pruna)
Jack-in-the-Box (Derain)
Le Triomphe de Neptune (Shervashidze)

1927   *La Chatte* (Gabo and Pevsner)
Mercure (Picasso)
Le Pas d'Acier (Yakulov)
Oedipus-Rex (Oratorio) (Cocteau)

1928   *Ode* (Tchelitchew)
Apollon-Musagète (Bauchant)
Les Dieux Mendiants (Gris)

1929   *Le Bal* (de Chirico)
Le Fils Prodigue (Rouault)

173. Jean Pougny: Costume Design for a Lady with the Figure 8, *Street Procession*, February, 1921 (No. 850)

ARTISTS BORN IN THE RUSSIAN EMPIRE WHO WORKED ON PRODUCTIONS REALIZED BY SERGEI DIAGHILEV

Sergei Pavlovich Diaghilev (1872-1929) is now remembered primarily as the founder of the Ballets Russes, the spectacular company of accomplished dancers, musicians, and designers that toured the Western world between 1909 and 1929. Often divided by historians into pre- and post-War phases, the Ballets Russes at first offered an artistic homage to "barbaric" Russia and the Orient with the celebrated productions of *Cléopâtre* and *Schéhérazade,* but ended as a confirmation of the new Classicism as in ballets such as *Zéphyr et Flore* and *Le Fils Prodigue.* Although Diaghilev never issued a manifesto of intent or declaration of principles, at least in the context of the dance, his clear mission was to refurbish the traditions of the Imperial ballet and to encourage radical innovation in movement, sound, and image. To this end, he invited Bakst, Benois, Braque, Fokine, Dolin, Goncharova, Karsavina, Larionov, Lifar, Massine, Nijinsky, Picasso, Prokofiev, Stravinsky, and many other innovators to work for his enterprise, guiding and molding them with a ruthless discipline and quality control that allowed for neither protest, nor deviation. He welcomed new artistic resolutions such as Primitivism (Goncharova in *Le Coq d'Or* or Larionov in *Le Soleil de Minuit*), Cubism (Picasso in *Parade*), Constructivism (Gabo and Pevsner in *La Chatte* and Yakulov in *Le Pas d'Acier*), and even Surrealism (Ernst and Miro in *Roméo et Juliette*). If experimental dance, discordant music, and bold color distinguished many of Diaghilev's productions, such as *Le Sacre du Printemps, L'Oiseau de Feu,* and *Le Train Bleu,* he never betrayed his commitment to good taste, technical precision, and esthetic synthesis. In this respect, Diaghilev's Ballets Russes proved to be perhaps the most remarkable expression of the *Gesammtkunstwerk* of which Richard Wagner (one of Diaghilev's cultural heroes) had spoken so earnestly in the 19th century

It is always difficult to place an impresario within an artistic hierarchy. Of course, we all know that the great works of dance, music and design associated with the Ballets Russes would never have existed without Diaghilev; but what exactly did he do, beyond bringing all the other artists — the "real" artists — together in the right way at the right time? He ed. He was a collector, a patron, an organiser, a participant in all sorts of ways. He floated ideas and made seemingly impossible projects actually happen. Somehow he succeeded in staying at a sufficient distance to allow his artists freedom to express themselves, while at the same time immersing himself in their creative process.

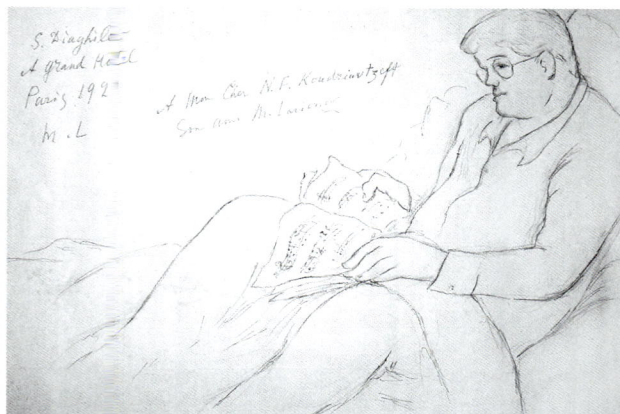

Mikhail Larionov:
Sergei Diaghilev
in Bed at the
Grand Hotel,
Paris, 1929
(No. 732)

174. Isaak Rabinovich: Costume Design for the Glutton, *Love for Three Oranges*, 1927 (No. 855)

	Artist	No. in Vol. II	Production
1.	Anisfeld	26-27	*Sadko,* 2 costume designs
2.	Bakst	75-79	*Cléopâtre,* 5 costume designs
		81, 83-84, 82	*Schéhérezade,* 3 costume and 1 stage design
		85-86	*Narcisse,* 2 costume designs
		89	*La Péri,* 1 costume design
		91	*Le Dieu Bleu,* 1 costume design
		96-101	*Sleeping Princess,* 6 costume designs
3	Benois, A.	123, 136-139	*Le Pavillon d'Armide,* 5 stage designs
		124-35, 140-51	and 22 costumes
		153-58, 152	*Giselle,* 6 costume designs and 1 stage design
		162-69, 170-79	*Petrouchka,* 8 stage designs, 10 stage details,
		180-280	and 101 costume designs
		281-84	*Le Rossignol,* 4 costume designs
		280	*Le Médecin malgré lui,* 1 stage design
		291-94	and 4 costume designs
4.	Bilibin, I.	366	*Boris Godunov,* 1 costume design
		370	*Firebird,* 1 costume design
5.	Delaunay	407-10	*Cléopâtre,* 3 cloth designs,
		411-12, 413	2 stage details, and 1 costume design
6.	Dobujinsky	425-427	*Midas,* 3 postcards of costume designs
7.	Fedorovsky	500-02	*Khovanschina,* 3 costume designs
8.	Gabo	512	*La Chatte,* 1 costume design
9.	Golovin	533	*L'Oiseau de Feu,* 1 costume design
10.	Goncharova	536-37, 534-35	*Coq d'Or,* 2 costume designs and 2 stage designs
		542-58	*Liturgie,* 17 costume designs
		559	*España,* 1 costume design
		567	*Aurora's Wedding,* 1 costume design
		568	*Les Noces,* 1 costume design
		569, 570	*L'Oiseau de Feu,* 1 costume and 1 stage design
11.	Korovin, K.	649	*Les Orientales,* 1 stage design
12.	Larionov	703, 704	*Soleil de Nuit,* 1 décor and 1 costume design
		707-10	*Histoires Naturelles,* 4 costume designs
		713, 711-12	*Contes Russes,* 1 décor, 2 stage details
		718-20, 716-17	*Chout,* 3 costume designs and 2 stage designs
		721, 722-24	*Le Renard,* 1 stage design and 3 costume designs
13.	Pevsner	823	*La Chatte,* 1 stage detail
14.	Roerich	881	*Maid of Pskov,* 1 stage design
		882	*Sacre du Printemps,* 1 costume design
15.	Serov	910, 911	*Judith,* 1 stage design and 1 costume design
16.	Stelletsky	955	*Boris Godunov,* 1 costume design
17.	Sudeikin	982	*Salomé,* 1 costume design
18.	Survage	1012-13	*Mavra,* 2 costume designs
19.	Tchelitchew	1097	*Ode,* 1 group of figures
20.	Yakulov	1165-66	*Le Pas d'Acier,* 2 stage designs
		1167	and 1 costume design
21.	Yuon	1172-74	*Boris Godunov,* 3 costume designs

175. Nicholas Remisoff: Stage Design, *The Miracle of the Holy Virgin*, ca. 1921 (No. 858)

PLAYS PRODUCED OR PROJECTED BY
VSEVOLOD MEIERKHOLD AND ALEXANDER TAIROV

Vsevolod Meierkhold

Unafraid of change or paradox, Vsevolod Emilievich Meierkhold (1874-1940) followed his private theatrical instinct without compromise or scruple, an artistic absolutism that could only clash with external dictates, whether esthetic or political. Meierkhold's theatrical experiments were distinguished by this intransigence, something that explains the brevity and discomfort of his collaborations with fellow directors and actors. On the other hand, his spasmodic contact with Stanislavsky, Komissarzhevskaia, and Evreinov left a formative impression on his approach to the stage and, ultimately, on the credo of his Theater of the RSFSR No. 1, which he founded in 1920 and which functioned as the Meierkhold Theater from 1923 until 1938. Meierkhold's system was a brilliant integration of many ideas, including the Realism of the Moscow Art Theater, Komissarzhevskaia's Symbolism, Evreinov's quirkiness, and the respective systems of Jaques-Dalcroze, Craig, Taylorism, and even the circus. However, Meierkhold is celebrated above all for his avant-garde renderings of the early 1920s, especially those dependent upon the new principles of Constructivism: productions such as *The Magnanimous Cuckold* (designs by Popova, 1922), *The Death of Tarelkin* (designs by Stepanova, 1923), and *The Bed Bug* (designs by Rodchenko, 1929) were unique in their radical reform of the dramatic, visual, and musical components of the stage. Much indebted to his elaboration of bio-mechanics, according to which actors used economical and controlled gesture for maximum effect within an unadorned and often kinetic scenography, Meierkhold's main productions were powerful, unrelenting expressions

Designer unknown: Poster advertising events at the Moscow Art Masters Club in connection with Vsevolod Meierkhold's 35th anniversary as actor and director, 1934 (no. 873).

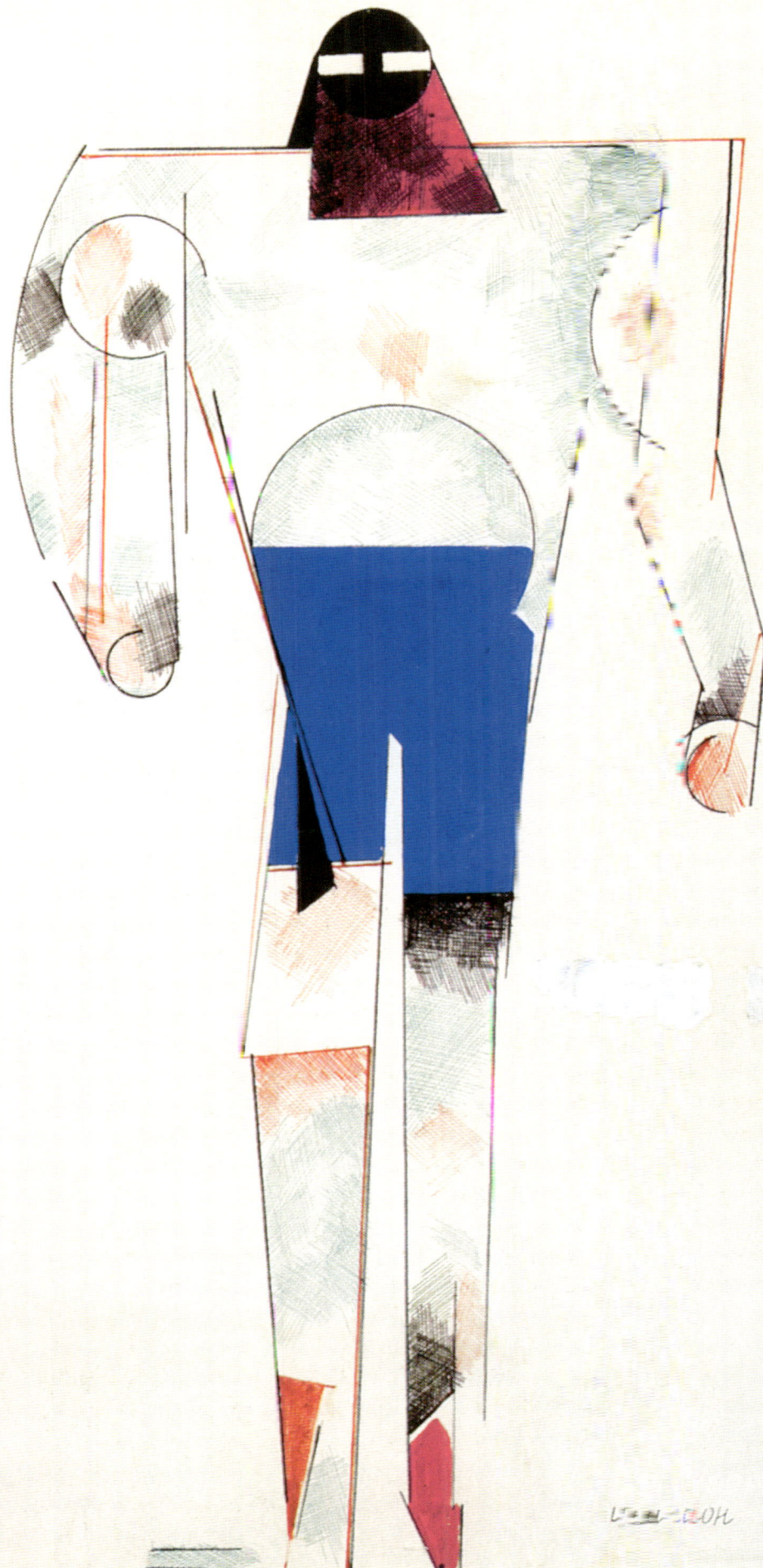

176. Alexander Rodchenko: Costume Design for the Black Mask Champion (Holland), 1918 (No. 866)

of the revolutionary era of industrial automation, mechanical efficiency, and proletarian uniformity — and in this sense seemed appropriate to the demands of the new regime. However, the alliance was illusory, for Meierkhold refused to adjust to the didactic exhortations of Socialist Realism and, after the enforced closure of his Theater in 1938, was arrested and executed.

Designer	Productions	No. in Vol. II
Annenkov	*First Distiller* by L. Tolstoi Hermitage Theater, Petrograd, 1919	42, 43
Bakst	*Pisanella* by Gabriele d'Annunzio Théâtre du Châtelet, Paris, 1913	92
Galadzhev	*Lake Liul* by Faiko Theater of Revolution, Moscow, 1923	513
Kiselev	*Mystery-Bouffe* by Maiakovsky Theater of the RSFSR No. 1, Moscow, 1921	608-17
Lentulov	*Unknown Lady* by Blok Café Pittoresque, Moscow, 1918	738
Rodchenko	*Bed Bug* by Maiakovsky Theater of the RSFSR No. 1, Moscow, 1929	867-68
Stepanova	*Death of Tarelkin* by Sukhovo-Kobylin Theater of the RSFSR No. 1, Moscow, 1922	977-80

Projects

Miller	*Salomé* by Wilde Theater of the RSFSR No. 1, Moscow, 1920	798

Alexander Tairov

Alexander Yakovlevich Tairov (1885-1950) founded the Chamber Theater in Moscow in 1914 and remained its director until it was closed by official decree in 1950. Although the Chamber Theater was eclectic in its repertoire, acting techniques, and stage designs, Tairov's primary emphasis was on the ancient and modern classics, with plays by Annensky, Molière, Ostrovsky, Racine, Shakespeare, Shaw, and Verhaeren taking pride of place. Like Diaghilev, Tairov gave particular attention to the technique of scenic performance (gesture, deportment, gait) and, while open to the ideas of Appia, Craig, and Reinhardt, also respected the dramatic traditions of the 19th century. Consequently, the Chamber Theater was recognized for its lead actresses and actors such as Koonen and Tsereteli, and for its rhetorical declamation and hieratic movement (as in *Phèdre*). But if Tairov's playwrights were restrained rather than boisterous, his designers were certainly unorthodox, introducing brave new geometries and color combinations in their sets and costumes. Among Tairov's collaborators were Exter (as in *Salomé*), Vesnin (as in *Phèdre*), the Stenberg brothers (as in *The Lawyer from Babylon*), and Yakulov (as in *Giroflé-Girofla*), who, if not quite as radical as Popova and Rodchenko (Meierkhold's leading designers), still brought an energy and panache to the staid conventions of the traditional stage. If Tairov

177. Nicholas Roerich: Costume Design for Ovlur, *Polovtsian Dances*, 1909 (No. 880)

was not the most iconoclastic of Russian directors, he was certainly the most professional. He was able to integrate disparate styles into a harmonious totality, often leading to the peculiar "Baroque Cubism" with which his scenography is commonly identified. Subject to increasing criticism for "formalism" and "bourgeois tendencies" in the 1930s and 1940s, the Chamber Theater was renamed the Pushkin Moscow Dramatic Theater shortly before Tairov's death.

Designer	Productions	No. in Vol II
Kuznetsov	*Sakuntala* by Kalidasa, 1914	690
Sudeikin	*Le Carnaval de la Vie* by Saint-Georges de Bouhélier (?), 1915	983
Exter	*Thamira Khytharedes,* 1916	460-62
Vesnin	*L'Annonce Faite à Marie* by Claudel, 1920	1134-36
Medunetsky	*Phèdre* by Racine, 1922	789
Stenberg, G.	same	969-70
Stenberg, V.	same	971
Vesnin	same	1137-39
Yakulov	*Signor Formica* by V. Sokolov based on E.T.A Hoffmann, 1922	1159
Komardenkov	same	625-26
Stenberg G.+ V.	*The Lawyer from Babylon* by Mariengof, produced by Sokolov, 1924	967-68

Projects

Mukhina	*La Cena delle Beffe* by Benelli, 1916	798-99
	The Rose and the Cross by Blok, 1916	800
Popova	*Romeo and Juliet* by Shakespeare, 1920	844-46
Vesnin	*Romeo and Juliet* by Shakespeare, 1921	1133

Georgii Stenberg: Portrait of Alexander Tairov behind Bars, 1922 (No. 962)

178. Nicholas Roerich: Costume Design for a Warrior, *The Tale of Tsar Saltan*, 1919 (No. 883)

179. Nicholas Roerich: Costume Design for a Standard Bearer, *The Tale of Tsar Saltan*, ca. 1919 (No. 884)

180. Nicholas Roerich: Costume Design for a Boyar's Wife, *The Tale of Tsar Saltan* ca. 1919 (No. 885)

RUSSIAN-BORN ARTISTS ACTIVE AS SET AND COSTUME DESIGNERS OUTSIDE RUSSIA (1909-62)

Diaghilev's Ballets Russes, Paris

1909-29	Opera	Anisfeld, Bakst, A. Benois, I. Bilibin, Delaunay, Dobujinsky,
1911-14	Ballet	Fedorovsky, Gabo, Golovin, Goncharova, K. Korovin,
1920-29	Opera + Ballet	Larionov, Pevsner, Roerich, Serov, Sudeikin, Shervashidze,
		Stelletsky, Survage, Tchelitchew, Yakulov, Yuon

Anna Pavolova Company, worldwide

1914-31	Ballet	Anisfeld, Bakst, A. Benois, I. Bilibin, Dobujinsky,
		K. Korovin, Sudeikin, Zack

Ida Rubinstein Company, Paris

1928-34	Ballet	Bakst, A. Benois

Opéra Privé de Paris

1929-30	Opera	A. Benois, A. Korovin, I. Bilibin

Vera Nemtchinova's Ballets Russes de Paris, Paris

1930	Ballet	Tchehonine, Zack

Opéra Russe à Paris, Paris

1931	Opera	Bilinsky, K. Korovin, Shchekatikhina-Pototskaia

Diaghilev Successor Companies:
René Blum + Colonel de Basil (Ballet Russe de Monte Carlo), Monte Carlo

1932-35	Ballet	Annenkov, Bilinsky, Bouchène, Dobujinsky

Ballets Russes du Colonel de Basil, New York

1935-47	Ballet	A. Benois, Zack

René Blum + de Basil (Ballet Russe de René Blum), Monte Carlo

1936	Ballet	Goncharova, Tchelitchew, Zack

Marcel Sablon (Nouveau Ballet de Monte Carlo), Monte Carlo

1942-44	Ballet	A. Benois, Zack

Ballet Russe de Monte Carlo, New York

1938-62	Ballet	Dunkel, Goncharova, Jedrinsky

Baliev's Chauve-Souris, Berlin-Paris, New York
(1,214 performances in the U.S., 383 in Paris, 378 in the U.K. – 1,975 in all)

1920-27	Cabaret	A. Benois, N. Benois, Dobujinsky, Gudiashvili, Pogedaieff,
		Remisoff, Sarian, Shukhaev, Stelletsky, Sudeikin

Jascha Juschny's Blue Bird, Berlin (3,850 performances)

1921-31	Cabaret	Houdiakoff, Jedrinsky, Liessner-Blomberg, Pogedaieff,
		Pougny, Tchelitchew

Folies Bergère, Paris

1869-present	Revues	Erté (R. de Tirtoff)

181. Nicholas Roerich: Costume Design for a Village Maiden, *The Snow Maiden*, 1920 (No. 887)

ARMENIAN, GEORGIAN, JEWISH, LATVIAN AND UKRAINIAN ARTISTS

Artist	Works	No. in Vol. II
Armenian		
1. Sarian	1 costume design	896
2. Yakulov	7 costume designs + 3 stage designs + 1 portrait	1157-67
Georgian		
1. Gamrekeli	5 stage designs	520-24
2. Guciashvil	1 stage design + 2 costume designs	576-78
3. Shervashidze	3 costume designs + 1 stage design	924-927
4. Shukhaev	1 costume design + 1 stage design + 2 portraits	947-50
5. Valishevsky	1 portrait	1183
6. Zdanevich. I.	2 posters	1184-85
7. Zdanevich. K.	2 stage designs	1186-87
Jewish		
1. Aizenberg	2 costume designs + 10 posters	1-2, 3-12
2. Altman	1 portrait	14
3. Anisfeld	1 portrait	25
	13 costume designs	26-35, 37-39
	1 stage detail	36
4. Aronson	1 costume design	54
5. Bakst	27 costume designs	57-58, 75-81, 83-86, 88-92, 94, 96-103
	4 stage designs	82, 104-06
	3 posters	74, 87, 93
	12 postcards + 1 wrapper	59-71
	3 portraits	56, 95, 107
6. Baranoff-Rossiné	1 stage design	108
7. Chagall	2 costume designs	373-74
8. Delaunay	4 fabric designs	407-10
	2 stage details	411-12
	4 costume designs	413-16
9. Falk	1 set design	499
10. Foregger	1 costume design	511
11. Gabo	1 costume design	512
12. Levin	1 costume design	740
13. Lissitzky	1 photomontage	751
	12 lithographs + 1 cardboard wrapper	752-64
14. Mandel	1 costume design	787
15. Pasternak	3 portraits	804-06
16. Pevsner	1 stage detail	823
17. Rabinovich	1 self-portrait	854
	1 costume design	855
18. Shkolnik	1 set design	928
	1 poster	929

182. Nicholas Roerich: Costume Design for a Maiden, *The Snow Maiden*, 1921 (No. 888)

Artist	Works	No. in Vol. II
19. Tellngater	1 propaganda truck	1101
20. Tyshler	3 costume designs	1104-06
	2 stage designs	977-978
21. Zack	2 self-portraits	1176-77
	1 stage set	1178
	3 costume designs	1179-81
Latvian		
1. Klutsis	1 street decoration + reverse	622-23
2. Liberts	1 stage design	742
Ukrainian		
1. Asimov	2 costume designs	13-14
2. Andreenko	1 self-portrait	16
	6 costume designs	17-22
	2 stage designs	23-24
3. Bilinsky	1 self-portrait	372
	1 stage design	377
	12 costume designs	373-76, 378-87
4. Bogomazov	1 self-portrait + 2 costume designs	388-90
5. Burluk D.	3 portraits	398-400
6. Burluk V.	1 portrait	397
7. Chervinka	2 textile designs	405-06
8. Exter	8 stage designs	463, 474-480
	16 costume designs	460-62, 464-73, 481-82, 498
	15 silk screens	483-97
9. Galadznev	1 stage design	513
	6 movie posters	514-19
10. Khvostenko-Khvostov	1 stage design + 1 costume design	606-608
11. Lattry	1 costume design	735
12. Lssim	2 stage designs	747, 750
	3 costume designs	746, 748-49
13. Malevich	1 self-portrait	768
	1 study for Architekton	769
	15 silkscreens for *Victory over the Sun*	770-84
14. Meler	5 costume designs	791-792, 794-96
	1 magazine cover	793
15. Petritsky	6 costume designs	812-17
	1 stage design	818
16. Shlepianov	1 self-portrait	930
	1 costume design	931

183. Nicholas Roerich: Costumes for Snegurochka and Tsar Berendei, *The Snow Maiden*, 1921 (No. 889)

WOMEN ARTISTS
IN THE LOBANOV-ROSTOVSKY COLLECTION

Artist	Design	No. in Vol. II
1. Aizenberg	Set of 3 variable shirts	1
	Pioneer costume	2
2. Benois, Nadia	1 costume	343
3. Bruni	3 costumes	393-95
	Set design for a procession	396
4. Delaunay	4 fabric designs	407-10
	4 simultanist costumes	413-16
	2 stage details	411, 412
5 Ermilova-Platova	Portrait	1108
6 Ermolaeva	Victory Over the Sun décor	458
7 Exter	39 décors + costumes	460-98
8 Goncharova	38 décors + costumes	534-71
9 Khodasevich	2 costumes + 1 poster	601-03
10. Korbut	1 poster	12
11. Liessner-Blomberg	1 costume	743
12. Melnikova	1 female profile	1146
13. Mukhina	3 costumes	798-800
14. Pestel	2 portraits	807, 808
	2 costumes	810, 811
15. Poret	Panel Poor People	510
16. Popova	1 self-portrait	839
	8 costumes + 1 set + 1 poster	840-49
17. Serebriakova	7 portraits	903-08
18. Shchekatikhina-Pototskaia	1 self-portrait	905
	1 set + 7 costumes	916-23
19. Stepanova	3 posters + 4 costumes	974-80
20. Udaltsova	1 set + 1 costume	1109-10
21. Vassilieff	Poster	1116

DESIGNS FOR PRODUCTION OR
INDUSTRIAL CLOTHING (*PROZODEZHDA*)
IN THE LOBANOV-ROSTOVSKY COLLECTION

Prozodezhda, an abbreviation for *proizvodstvennaia odezhda* (lit. "production clothing"), was clothing designed in simple, undecorated patterns, manufactured with mechanical precision and industrial efficiency. This concept of clothing was advocated by the Constructivists in 1922-24.

Artist	Design	No. in Vol. II
1. Aizenberg	set of 3 vests + costume design	1-2
2. Bruni	3 costume designs	393-95
3. Kiselev	7 costume designs	608-14
4. Lebedev	1 costume design	736
5. Rodchenko	2 costume designs	867-68
6. Stenberg, G. and V.	2 costume artigsns	967-68
7. Stepanova	4 costume designs	977-80

184. Nikolai Sapunov: Set for Act II, The Dining-Room in the Serebriakov House, *Uncle Vania. Scenes from Country Life*, 1908 (No. 893)

185. Alexandre Serebriakoff: *The Ballroom Frescoed by G.B. Tiepolo, the Arrival of the Giants,*
Ball at the Palazzo Labia, Venice, 1951 (No. 897)

186. Alexandre Serebriakoff: The Arrival of the Couturier Jacques Fath (Dressed as the Sun King), His Wife Geneviève, and Other Guests, *Ball at the Palazzo Labia, Venice* (No. 898)

TYPOGRAPHICAL DESIGNS
IN THE LOBANOV-ROSTOVSKY COLLECTION

Artist	Design	No. in Vol. II
1. Annenkov	Cover design for a book with a portrait of Evreinov	45
2. Arnshtam	Cover for Evreinov's *Teatr kak takovoi*	52
3. Bakst	Poster for Red Cross Society	74
	Poster for *Le Martyre de Saint Sebastien*	87
	Lithograph for *La Péri*	90
	Poster for Caryathis	93
	Wrapper and postcards for *La Fée des Poupées*	59-71
4. Beloborodoff	Poster: Anna Pavolva in *Les Sylphides*	118
5. Benois, A.	2 designs for program and catalog covers (Diaghilev)	121, 159
	Program cover (Baliev)	295
6. Bilibin, I.	2 postcard designs	365-66
	Program cover (de Basil)	371
7. Chekhlarov	Poster for Mystery-Bouffe	1194
8. Doboujinsky, M.	3 postcards for *Midas*	425-27
9. Fi'onov School	Poster for *The Inspector General*	506
10. Galadzhev	1 theater + 6 movie posters	513-519
11. Gan	4 Posters (Maiakovsky)	525-28
12. Goncharova	Liturgie portfolio label	541
	Cover for *14 Portraits de Théâtre*	560
	3 publicity items for Artists' Balls, Paris	564-66
13. Hoerschelmann	Poster with a magician	579
14. Khocasevich	Poster for *Volpone*	603
15. Korbut	Poster for the Blue Blouse	12
16. Kozlinsky	2 St. Petersburg linocuts	681-82
17. Kustodiev	Poster for "The Russian Exhibition"	685
	Poster for *The Flea*	686
18. Lanceray	Poster for "The Exhibition of Historic Portraits"	692
19. Larionov	4 publicity items for Artists' Balls, Paris	725-28
20. Lissitzky	Wrapper and title page for *Victory over the Sun*	752-53
21. Mak (P. Ivanov) et al.	Poster for *Teatr v karrikaturakh*	767
22. Meller	Cover for magazine *Teatr*	793
23. Remisoff	Program/Poster for The Bat	856
24. Rodchenko	Posters for *The Bed Bug* (2-sided)	871-72
25. Rozanova	Poster for Futurist Theater	891
26. Serov	Poster for the first Russian Season at the Théâtre du Châtelet	909
27. Shkolnik	Poster for Zheverzheev Collection Exhibition	929
28. Shlepianov	11 posters for Meierkhold Productions	932-38, 941-44
29. Stelletsky	Poster for a Benefit for Russian artists	956
30. Stenberg, V. + G.	Poster for performance by the Moscow Chamber Theater at the Théâtre des Champs-Elysées	972
	Poster for *Desire under the Elms*	973
31. Suceikin	Poster for *The Chief Thing*	1008
	Poster for *The Patriot*	1009

187. Alexandre Serebriakoff: The Entrance of Arturo Lopez as the Emperor of China together with His Suite, *Ball at the Palazzo Labia*, Venice, 1951 (No. 899)

188. Valentin Serov: Stage Design for the Orgy in Holophernes's Camp, *Judith*, 1908 (No. 910)

GUIDE TO PORTRAITS IN THE LOBANOV-ROSTOVSKY COLLECTION

Part I: Portraits By Artist

Artist	Sitter	No. in Vol. II
Natan Altman	Martiros Sarian	15
Mikhail Andreenko	self	16
Boris Anisfeld	self	25
Yuri Annenkov	self	40
	Natan Altman	46
	Nikolai Evreinov	45
	Mikhail Larionov	49
Anonymous	Léon Bakst	55
	Sergei Diaghilev	540
	Natalia Goncharova	540
	Kazimir Malevich	768
Alexander Arnshtam	self	50
	Nikita Baliev	51
	Nikolai Evreinov	52
	Ivan Moskvin	53
Leon Bakst	Vladimir Argutinsky-Dolgorukov	107
	Ivan Bunin	95
	Konstantin Somov	56
Vladimir Bekhteev	self	109
Andrea Beloborodoff	Anna Pavlova	108
Alexandre Benois	Vladimir Argutinsky-Dolgorukov	304
	Nikolai Cherepnin	122
	Mstislav Dobujinsky	119
	Sergei Esenin	286
	Jean Giraudoux	304
	Maurice Ravel	285
	Alexandre Shervashidze	120
	Vasilii Shukhaev	298
	Igor Stravinsky	160
	Viktor Valter	122
Nicola Benois	Fedor Chaliapin	354
	Nikita Lobanov-Rostovsky	358-60
	self	344
Boris Bilinsky	self	372
Alexander Bogomazov	self	388
David Burliuk	Nikolai Burliuk	398
	Vladimir Maiakovsky	399
	Nicholas Roerich	400
Vladimir Burliuk	David Burliuk	397
Civis (Sergei Tsivinsky)	Simon Lissim	745

189. Valentin Serov: *The Rape of Europa*, 1910 (No. 914)

Artist	Sitter	No. in Vol. II
Nikolai Denisovsky	Osip Brik	417
	Vladimir Maiakovsky	417
Mstislav Dobujinsjky	Alexandre Benois	424
	Nicholas Zverev	432
	Vera Nemtchinova	433
Efrosinia Ermilova-Platova	Nadezhda Udaltsova	1108
Natalia Goncharova	Sergei Diaghilev	562
	Leonide Massine	561
Alexandre Jacovleff	self	584
	Sergei Sudeikin	588
Vladimir Jedrinsky	self	589
Vasilii Kniazev	Konstantin Stanislavsky	767b
	Vladimir Nemirovich-Danchenko	767b
Vasilii Komardenkov	Charlie Chaplin	624
	Vladimir Sokolov	626
	Igor Ilinsky	627
Konstantin Korovin	Fedor Chaliapin	678
Nikolai Kulbin	Alexei Kruchenykh	684
Mikhail Larionov	Catherine Devilliers	710
	Georgii Yakulov	730
	Igor Stravinsky	734
	Leonide Massine	706
	Natalia Goncharova	697-98
	Serge Lifar	731
	Sergei Diaghilev	731-33
	Vladimir Tatlin	699
Mikhail Le–Dantiu (?)	Ilia Zdanevich	1183
El Lissitzky	Vladimir Tatlin	751
Mak (Pavel Ivanov)	self	765
	Alexander Yuzhin-Sumbatov	767g
	Konstantin Varlamov	766
	Valentina Piontkovskaia	767
Filipp Maliavin	self	785
	Anatolii Lunacharsky	786
	Vladimir Lenin	786
	Lev Trotsky	786
Konstantin Mikhailov (Ten)	Alexander Bakhrushin	767c
	Konstantin Mardzhanov	767g
	Natalia Trukhanova (Trouhanova)	767d
	Sergei Zimin	767e
Dmitrii Moor	Alexander Khvostenko-Khvostov	605
Ignatii Nivinsky	Alexandra Exter	802
Leonid Pasternak	self	804
	Fedor Chaliapin	806
	Lev Tolstoi	805
Vera Pestel	self	807
Georges Pogedaieff	self	824
Liubov Popova	self	839

190. Dmitrii Stelletsky: Stage Design, *Rite Matrimonial Russe*, 1926 (No. 959)

Artist	Sitter	No. in Vol. II
Isaak Rabinovich	self	854
Nicholas Remisoff	self	856
	Arkadii Stoianovsky	859
	George Birse	859
	Mikhail Vavitch	859
	Nikita Baliev	859
	Zotoff	859
Zina de Serebriakova	self	903-04
	Alexandre Benois	908
	Alexandra Danilova	905
	Alexandre Serebriakoff	907, 1196
	Georges Tcherkessoff	906
Valentin Serov	Anna Pavlova	909
	Fedor Chaliapin	911, 912
	Ida Rubinstein (?)	914
Alexandra Shchekatikhina-Pototskaia	self	915
Ilia Shlepianov	self	930
Vasilii Shukhaev	Anna Pavlova	947
	Nikita Baliev	948
Georgii Stenberg	Alexander Tairov	962
Sergei Sudeikin	self	981
	Alexei Ermolov	985
	Mikhail Gorchakov	985
	Grand Duke Nikolai Pavlovich (Tsar Nicholas I)	985
	Vasilii Orlov-Denisov	985
	Vera Sudeikina	982
Alexei Taskin	Nikolai Legat	72
	Sergei Legat	73
Pavel Tchelitchew	self	1066
	Serge Lifar	1095-96
Georges Tcherkessoff	self	1099
Sigizmund Valishevsky (?)	Ilia Zdanevich	1183
Georgii Vereisky	Alexandre Benois	1122, 1131
	Osip Braz	1123
	Alexander Golovin	1130
	Mstislav Dobujinsky	1124
	Boris Kustodiev	1119
	Dmitrii Mitrokhin	1125
	Petr Neradovsky	1117
	Anna Ostroumova-Lebedeva	1118
	Sergei Prokofiev	1132
	Zinaida Serebriakova	1126
	Konstantin Somov	1127, 1129
	Stepan Yaremich	1128
Georgii Yakulov	self	1157
Léon Zack	self	1176-77
Fedor Zakharov	Konstantin Somov	1182

191. Georgii Stenberg: Drawing of the Headgear for Fhèdre, Phèdre, 1923 (No. 969)

Part II: Portraits by Sitter

Sitter	Artist	No. in Vol. II
Altman, Natan	Annenkov, Yurii	46
Andreenko, Mikhail	Self	16
Aristfek, Boris	Self	25
Annenkov, Yurii	Self	40
Argutinsky-Dolgorukov, Vladimir	Bakst, Léon	107
	Benois, Alexandre	304
Arnshtam, Alexander	Self	50
Bakhrushin, Alexander	Mikhailov, Konstantin (Ten)	767c
Bakst, Léon	Anonymous	55
Baliev, Nikita	Arnshtam, Alexander	51
	Re-mi (Remisoff, Nicholas)	859
	Shukhaev, Vasilii	948
Beknteev, Vladimir	Self	109
Benois, Alexandre	Dobujinsky, Mstislav	424
	Serebriakova, Zinaida	908
	Vereisky, Georgii	1122, 1131
Benois, Nicola	Self	344
Blinsky, Boris	Self	372
Birse, George	Re-mi (Remisoff, Nicholas)	859
Bogomazov, Alexander	Self	388
Braz, Osip	Vereisky, Georgii	1123
Brik, Osip	Denisovsky, Nikolai	417
Bunin, Ivan	Bakst, Léon	95
Burliuk, David	Burliuk, Vladimir	397
Burliuk, Nikolai	Burliuk, David	398
Chaliapin, Fedor	Benois, Nicola	354
	Korovin, Konstantin	678
	Pasternak, Leonid	806
	Serov, Valentin	911-12
Chaplin, Charlie	Komardenkov, Vasilii	624
Cherepnin, Nikolai (Tcherepnine)	Benois, Alexandre	122
Danilova, Alexandra	Serebriakova, Zinaida	905
Devilliers, Catherine	Larionov, Mikhail	710
Diaghilev, Sergei	Anonymous	540
	Goncharova, Natalia	562
	Larionov, Mikhail	731-33
Dobujinsky, Mstislav	Benois, Alexandre	119
	Vereisky, Georgii	1124
Ermolov, Alexei	Sudeikin, Sergei	985
Esenin, Sergei	Benois, Alexandre	286
Evreinov, Nikolai	Annenkov, Yurii	45
	Arnshtam, Alexander	52
Exter, Alexandra	Nivinsky, Ignatii	802
Giraucoux, Jean	Benois, Alexandre	304
Golovin, Alexander	Vereisky, Georgii	1130
Goncharova, Natalia	Anonymous	540
	Larionov, Mikhail	697-98
Gorchakov, Mikhail	Sudeikin, Sergei	985

ТАРЕЛКИН

192. Varvara Steparova: Costume Design for Tarelkin, *The Death of Tarelkin* 1922 (No. 977)

Sitter	Artist	No. in Vol. II
Grand Duke Nikolai Pavlovich (Tsar Nicholas I)	Sudeikin, Sergei	985
Ilinsky, Igor	Komardenkov, Vasilii	627
Jacovleff, Alexandre	Self	584
Jedrinsky, Vladimir	Self	589
Khvostenko-Khvostov, Alexander	Moor, Dimitrii (Orlov, D.S.)	605
Kruchenykh, Alexei	Kulbin, Nikolai	684
Kustodiev, Boris	Vereisky, Georgii	1119
Larionov, Mikhail	Annenkov, Yurii	49
Legat, Nikolai	Taskin, Alexei	72
Legat, Serge	Taskin, Alexei	73
Lenin (Ulianov, Vladimir)	Maliavin, Filipp	786
Lifar, Sergei	Larionov, Mikhail	731
	Tchelitchew, Pavel	1095-96
Lissim, Simon	Civis (Tsivinsky, Sergei)	745
Lobanov-Rostovsky, Nikita	Benois, Nicola	358-60
Lunacharsky, Anatolii	Maliavin, Filipp	786
Maiakovsky, Vladimir	Burliuk, David	399
	Denisovsky, Nikolai	417
Mak (Ivanov, Pavel)	Self	765
Malevich, Kazimir	Anonymous	768
Maliavin, Filipp	Self	785
Mardzhanov, Konstantin	Mikhailov, Konstantin (Ten)	767g
Massine, Leonide	Goncharova, Natalia	561
	Larionov, Mikhail	706
Mitrokhin, Dmitrii	Vereisky, Georgii	1125
Moskvin, Ivan	Arnshtam, Alexander	53
Nemirovich-Danchenko, Vladimir	Kniazev, Vasilii (Joe)	767b
Nemtchinova, Vera	Dobujinsky, Mstislav	433
Neradovsky, Petr	Vereisky, Georgii	1117
Orlov-Denisov, Vasilii	Sudeikin, Sergei	985
Ostroumova-Lebedeva, Anna	Vereisky, Georgii	1118
Pasternak, Leonid	Self	804
Pavlova, Anna	Beloborodoff, Andrea	108
	Serov, Valentin	909
	Shukhaev, Vasilii	947
Pestel, Vera	Self	807
Pionkovskaia, Valentina	Mak (Ivanov, Pavel)	767f
Pogedaieff, Georges	Self	824
Popova, Liubov	Self	839
Prokofiev, Sergei	Vereisky, Georgii	1132
Rabinovich, Isaak	Self	854
Ravel, Maurice	Benois, Alexandre	285
Re-mi (Remisoff, Nicholas)	Self	856
Roerich, Nicholas	Burliuk, David	400
Rubinstein, Ida	Serov, Valentin	914
Sarian, Martiros	Altman, Natan	15
Serebriakoff, Alexandre	Serebriakova, Zinaida	907, 1196
Serebriakova, Zinaida	Self	903-04
	Vereisky, Georgii	1126

193. Sergei Sudeikin: Costume Design for Salomé Danced by Tamara Karsavina, *La Tragédie de Salomé*, 1913 (No. 983)

Vladimir Kozlinsky:
Man Drawing Curtain,
from the linocut album
on contemporary St.
Petersburg, ca. 1919
(No. 682)

194. Sergei Sudeikin: Costume Design for the Bear Tamer, *Fetrouchka*, 1925 (No. 992)

BIBLIOGRAPHY

The Bibliography is intended as a guide to further reading on the history of Russian art and stage design of the period ca. 1890-1930. It is not exhaustive, although particular attention has been paid to books and catalogs published over the last decades. References are to major published sources and take no account of the many archival sources in private and public hands in the countries of the former Soviet Union and the West. Bibliographical details for particular artists are listed in the appropriate catalog entries of Volume. II.

As a general rule, 2011 has been set as the final date for bibliographical entries. The Bibliography is divided into twenty-one sections (A-W). Listings within each section are in chronological sequence.

A. Reference Manuals Relevant to the Scenic Arts in Russia
B. General Works on Twentieth-Century Russian Art
C. The Modern Stage in Russia
D. The Russian Ballet
E. Music-Hall, the Cabaret, the Circus, the Puppet Theater, and the Early Movie Industry in Russia
F. Memoirs, Collections of Letters, Diaries, etc., Relating to Modern Russian Stage Design
G. Modern Russian Costume and Set Design
H. Russian Art and the Theater in the Early Emigration
I. Catalogs of Exhibitions Relating to Stage Designs by Modern Russian Artists
J. Auction Catalogs Relating to Stage Designs by Modern Russian Artists
K. Catalogs of Exhibitions Relating to Modern Russian Art
L. Auction Catalogs Relating to Modern Russian Art
M. Publications by Nikita D. Lobanov-Rostovsky Relating to Modern Russian Art
N. Commentaries on the Lobanov-Rostovsky Collection, Including Reviews of Exhibitions in the US
O. Reviews of the Exhibitions of the Lobanov-Rostovsky Collection at the Pushkin Art Museum, Moscow, and the Manege, Leningrad in 1988-89 (I68)
P. Articles and Reviews Relating to the Exhibition of the Lobanov-Rostovsky Collection in Germany in 1991-92, i.e. "Die Russische Avantgarde und die Bühne 1890-1930" at the Schleswig-Holsteinisches Landesmuseum, Schloss Gottorf, Schleswig, and other institutions (I77)
Q. Reviews of the Russian Catalogue Raisonné of the Lobanov-Rostovsky collection, *Khudozhniki russkogo teatra*, compiled by John E. Bowlt and published by Iskusstvo, Moscow, 1994 (B179)
R. Articles and Reviews Relating to the Exhibition "Modernist Movements in Russian Art and Their Reflection on the Stage. Selections from the Nina and Nikita Lobanov-Rostovsky Collection" at the Museum of Private Collections, Moscow, November, 1994 – January, 1995 (I87)
S. Articles and Reviews Relating to the Exhibition "Russian Stage Designs 1910-1930 (from the Lobanov-Rostovsky Collection) and Marc Chagall and the Jewish Theater" at Megaron, Athens, 24 February – 25 May, 1997 (I92)

T. Articles and Reviews Relating to the Exhibition "L'avant-garde russe et la scène, 1910 - 1930. La collection Lobanov-Rostovsky" at the Musée d'Ixelles, Brussels, 11 March – 30 May, 1998 (I96)
U. Articles and Reviews in English and Russian Relating to the Exhibition "Russian Avant-Garde and the Stage, 1900 - 1930: The Collection of Nina and Nikita D. Lobanov-Rostovsky" at the Yokohama Museum of Art, Yokohama, Japan, 3 October – 6 December, 1998 (I97)
V. Articles and Reviews Relating to the Exhibition "Vozvrashchenie v Rossiiu" [Return to Russia], at the Museum of Theater and Musical Art, St. Petersburg, 25 September – 26 October 2008.
W. Articles and Reviews Relating to the Exhibition "Vozvrashchenie v Rossiiu" [Return to Russia], at the Radishchev Art Museum, Saratov, 3 December 2010 – 30 January 2011.

A. Reference Manuals Relevant to the Scenic Arts in Russia

Note: The standard, global reference works on artists such as E.-C. Bénézit, ed.: *Dictionnaire critique et documentaire des peintres, sculpteurs, dessinaterus et graveurs,* Paris: Gründ, 1976 (first edition 1911-23) and U. Thieme and F. Becker, eds.: *Künstlerlexikon,* Leipzig: Seemann, 1907-50 (37 vols.) are not included here.

1. W. Gamble: *The Development of Scenic Art and Stage Machinery; A List of References in the New York Public Library,* New York: New York Public Library, 1920.
2. *Teatralnaia Moskva,* M, 1924 onwards. (An annual guide to Who's Who in Moscow theater. Of particular value are the annuals for 1927-28 and 1935).
3. S. d'Amico, ed.: *Enciclopedia dello Spettacolo,* Rome: Le Maschere, 1955-65 (eleven volumes, including *Aggiornamento.*).
4. F. Gadan and R. Maillard, eds.: *A Dictionary of Modern Ballet,* London: Methuen, 1959.
5. Various editors: *Tsentralnyi Gosudarstvennyi arkhiv literatury i iskusstva SSSR. Putevoditel,* M: Glavnoe arkhivnoe upravlenie / Rossiiskaia politicheskaia entsiklopediia, 1959-2011 (ten volumes)
6. N. Glagoleva et al., comps.: *Sovetskie khudozhestvennye filmy,* M: Iskusstvo, 1961 (three volumes).
7. S. Mokulsky et al., eds.: *Teatralnaia entsiklopediia,* M: Sovetskaia entsiklopediia, 1961-66 (five volumes).
8. Kh. Abdusamatov et al., eds.: *Kratkaia literaturnaia entsiklopediia,* M: Sovetskaia entsiklopediia, 1962-78 (nine volumes).
9. E. Butorina, ed.: *Vystavki sovetskogo izobrazitelnogo iskusstva. Spravochnik,* M: Sovetskii khudozhnik, 1965-76 (five volumes); and supplementary volume *Personalnye i gruppovye vystavki sovetskikh khudozhikov 1917-1947,* 1989.
10. B. Shteinpress and I. Yampolsky: *Entsiklopedicheskii muzykalnyi slovar,* M: Sovetskaia entsiklopediia, 1966.
11. S. Yutkevich et al., eds.: *Kinoslovar,* M: Sovetskaia entsiklopediia, 1966-70 (two volumes).
12. G. Berngart, comp.: *Slovar oper 1736-1959,* M: Muzyka, 1967.
13. A. Alekseev et al., eds.: *Russkaia khudozhestvennaia kultura kontsa* XIX – *nachala* XX *veka,* M: Nauka, 1968-80 (four volumes).

195. Sergei Sudeikin: Costume Design for the Wet Nurse, *Petrouchka*, 1925 (No. 995)

14. O. Voltsenburg et a ., eds.: *Khudozhniki narodov SSSR. Biobibliograficheskii slovar v shesti tomakh*, M: Iskusstvo, 1970-84; SP: Gumanitarnoe agentstvo, 1995 (five of six volumes have appeared).

15. G. Sternin: *Khudozhestvennaia zhizn Rossii na rubezhe XIX-XX vekov*. M: Iskusstvo, 1970. German translation: G. Sternin: *Das Kunstleben Russlands an der Jahrhundertwende*, Dresden: VEB Kunst, 1976.

16. G. Berngar and I. Yampolsky: *Kto pisal o muzyke*, M: Sovetskii kompozitor, 1971-79 (three volumes).

17. New York Public Library: *Dictionary Catalog of the Dance Collection*, Boston: Hall, 1974. Supplementary volumes appear under the title *Bibliographical Guide to Dance*, 1975 onward.

18. A. Shneer and R. Slavsky: *Tsirk. Malaia entsiklopediia*, M: Sovetskaia entsiklopediia, 1979.

19. G. Sternin: *Khudozhestvennaia zhizn Rossii nachala XX veka*. M: Iskusstvo, 1976. German translation: G. Sternin: *Das Kunstleben Russlands zu Beginn des zwanzigsten Jahrhunderts*. Dresden: VEB Kunst, 1980.

20. Yu. Grigorovich, ed.: *Balet. Entsiklopediia*, M: Sovetskaia entsiklopediia, 1981.

21. F. Derra de Moroda: *The Dance Library. A Catalogue,* Munich: Wölfle, 1982.

22. *225 let Akademii khudozhestv SSSR*. Catalog of the exhibition at the Academy of Arts of the USSR, Leningrad, M: Izobrazitelnoe iskusstvo, 1983 (two volumes covering the periods 1757-1917 and 1917-82).

23. S. Neef: *Handbuch der russischen und sowjetischen Oper*, Berlin: Henschelverlag, 1985.

24. O. Schneider: *Tanzlexikon*, Vienna: Hollinek; Mainz: Schott, 1985.

25. Various authors: *Pipers Enzyklopädie des Musiktheaters*. Laaber: Laaber-Verlag, 1986 (eight volumes).

26. G. Sternin: *Khudozhestvennaia zhizn Rossii 1900-1910-kh godov,* M: Iskusstvo, 1988.

27. A. Ho and D. Feofanov: *Biographical Dictionary of Russian/Soviet Composers*, New York: Greenwood Press, 1989.

28. A. Prokhorov et al.: *Russkie pisateli 1800-1917. Biograficheskii slovar,* M: Sovetskaia entsiklopediia, Vol. 1, 1989; Vol. 2, 1992; Vol. 3, 1994; Vol. 4; 1999.

29. Yu. Abyzov: *Russkoe pechatnoe slovo v Latvii: 1917-1944,* Stanford: Stanford Slavic Studies, 1990-91 (four volumes).

30. R. Bartmann: *Picture Postcard Encyclopedia of Russia,* Erlangen: publisher not indicated, 1992.

31. A. Kudritsky, ed.: *Mistsi Ukraini*, K: Ukrainska entsiklopediia, 1992.

32. D. Severiukhin and O. Leikind: *Zolotoi vek khudozhestvennykh obiedinenii v Rossii i SSSR (1820-1932). Spravochnik,* SP: Chernyshev, 1992.

33. G. Vanechkova, ed.: *V. Bulgakov* (author)*: Slovar russkikh zarubezhnykh pisatelei,* New York: Ross, 1993

34. J. Milner: *A Dictionary of Russian and Soviet Artists,* Woodbridge, England: Antique Collectors' Club, 1993.

35. O. Ostroi: *Istoriia iskusstvovedcheskoi bibliografii v Rossii 1917-1991,* SP: Russkaia natsionalnaia biblioteka, 1994.

36. W. Brumfield: *An Architectural Survey of St. Petersburg, 1840-1916: Building Inventory,* Washington, D.C.: Kennan Institute for Advanced Russian Studies, 1994.

37. N. Bogomolov: *Materialy k bibliografii russkikh literaturno-khudozhestvennykh almanakhov i sbornikov 1900-1917,* M: Lanterna-Vita, 1994, Vol. 1.

38. Anon.: *Izobrazitelnoe iskusstvo. Rossiia XX vek,* M: SEI, 1995.

39. V. Afanasiev et al., eds.: *Mistetstvo Ukraini,* K: Ukrainska entsiklopediia, 1995.

40. V. Vishnevsky: *Dokumentalnye filmy dorevoliutsionnoi Rossii 1907-1916,* M: Muzei kino, 1996.

41. V. Soloviev: *Russkie khudozhniki XVIII-XX vv.,* Dnepropetrovsk: Porogi, 1996.

42. V. Shelokhaev, ed.: *Russkoe zarubezhie. Zolotaia kniga emigratsii. Pervaia tret XX veka,* M: Rosspen, 1997.

43. A. Kantor, ed.: *Terminlogicheskii slovar, "Apollon". Izobrazitelnoe i dekorativnoe iskusstvo, arkhitekura,* M: Ellis Lak, 1997.

44. V. Kozlov, P. Grimsted, and L. Repulo, eds.: *Arkhivy Rossii. Moskva i Sankt-Peterburg,* M: Arkheologicheskii tsentr, 1997.

45. E. Belova et al., eds.: *Russkaia baletnaia entsiklopediia,* M: Soglasie, 1997.

46. A. Kiselev et al., eds.: *Tsentralnyi moskovskii arkhiv dokumentov na spetsialnykh nositeliakh, Kinofotofonoarkhiv,* M: Mosgorarkhiv, 1997.

47. I. Kondakova, comp.: *Otkrytyi arkhiv,* M: Bumprint, 1997.

48. F. Lévèque and S. Plantureux: *Dictionnaire des illustrateurs de livres d'enfants russes,* Paris: Agence Culturelle de Paris, 1997.

49. M. Bown: *A Dictionary of 20th Century Russian and Soviet Painters,* London: Izoram, 1998.

50. A. Kats et al.: *Tsentralnye arkhivy Moskvy. Fondy lichnogo proiskhozhdeniia,* M: Mosgorarkhiv, 1998.

51. A. Melik-Pashaev, ed.: *Sovremennyi slovar-spravochnik po iskusstvu,* M: Olimp-AST, 1999.

52. T. Pavlova, ed.: *Fondy russkogo zagranichnogo istoricheskogo arkhiva v Prage. Mezharkhivnyi putevoditel,* M: Rosspen, 1999.

53. V. Chuvakov, ed.: *Nezabytye mogily. Rossiiskoe zarubezhie: nekrologi 1917-1997 v shesti tomakh,* M: Rossiiskaia gosudarstvennaia biblioteka, 1999-2007 (six volumes in eight books).

54. E. Uvarova, ed.: *Estrada Rossii. XX vek. Leksikon,* M: Rosspen, 2000.

55. V. Vlasov, ed.: *Bolshoi entsiklopedicheskii slovar izobrazitelnogo iskusstva,* SP: LITA, 2000.

56. V. Vlasov, ed.: *Novyi entsiklopedicheskii slovar izobrazitelnogo iskusstva,* M: Azbuka-klassika, 2005 onwards (ten volumes).

57. M. Sandler et al.: *Russian and Ukrainan Avant-Garde and Constructivist Books and Serials in the New York Public Library,* New York: NYPL, 2000.

58. V. Ivanova et al., comps.: *Velikii Kinemo: Katalog sokhranivshikhsia igrovykh fil'mov Rossii (1908-1919),* M: NLO, 2002.

59. A. Markunas: *Spravochnik po russkomu iskusstvu,* Poznan: Wydawnictwo naukowe uniwersytetu, 2002.

60. O. Ostroi and I. Saksonova: *Izobrazitelnoe i prikladnoe iskusstvo: russkie spravochnye izdaniia,* SP: Bulanin, 2002.

61. I. Preobrazhenskaia, ed.: *Putevoditel po rukopisnym fondam Gosudarstvennogo tsentralnogo teatralnogo muzeia im. A.A. Bakhrushina,* M: Bakhrushin Museum, 2002.

62. C. Wilhelmi: *Künstlergruppen im östlichen und südlichen Europa seit 1900,* Stuttgart: Hauswedell, 2002.

63. V. Gorbatsky: *Kinooperatory ot A do Ya. Spravochnik-katalog,* M: Materik, 2005.

64. D. Severiukhin: *"Vystavochnaia proza" Peterburga: Iz istorii khudozhestvennogo rynka,* SP: Novikov, 2003.

65. N. Bogomolov: *Materialy k bibliografii russkikh literaturno-khudozhestvennykh almanakhov i sbornikov 1900-1937,* M: Vita, 2004.

66. E. Fomin, ed.: *Letopis rossiiskogo kino, 1863-1929,* M: Materik, 2004.

196. Sergei Sudeikin: Costume Design for the Rooster, *Fetouche*, ca. 1925 (No. 997)

67. O. Leikind and D. Severiukhin: *Novyi khudozhestvennyi Peterburg,* SP: Novikov, 2004.

68. M. Shrub: *Literaturnye obiedineniia Moskvy i Peterburga 1890-1917,* M: NLO, 2004.

69. E. Uvarova et al., comps.: *Estrada Rossii. XX vek. Entsiklopediia,* M: Olma-Press, 2005.

70. I. Chubarov, comp.: *Slovar khudozhestvennykh terminov. GAKhN, 1923-1929,* M: Logo-Altera, 2005.

71. A. Morozov: *Konstruktivizm: Annotirovannyi bibliograficheskii ukazatel,* M: Kontakt-Kultura, 2005.

72. E. Tomkina: *Anglo-russkii i russko-angliiskii slovar iskusstv,* M: Flinta/Nauka, 2005.

73. V. Vlasov and N. Lunina: *Avangardizm. Modernizm. Postmodernizm. Terminologicheskii slovar,* M: Azbuka-klassika, 2005.

74. A. Bannikov, S. Sapozhnikov et al.: *Sobirateli i khraniteli prekrasnogo. Entsiklopedicheskii slovar rossiiskikh kollektsionerov,* M: Tsentrpoligraf, 2007.

75. A. Azarov: *Anglo-russkii enstiklopedicheskii slovar iskusstv i khudozhestvennykh remesel,* M: Flinta/Nauka, 2007 (two volumes).

76. E. Konovalov: *Novyi polnyi biograficheskii slovar russkikh khudozhnikov,* M: Eksmo, 2008.

77. V. Kulakov and V. Pappe: *2500 khoreograficheskikh premier XX veka 1900-1945. Entsiklopedicheskii slovar,* M: Deka-VS, 2008.

78. A. Astakhov: *1000 russkikh khudozhnikov,* M: Belyi gorod, 2009.

79. E. Gordon, comp.: *Russkie khudozhniki ot A do Ya,* M: Slovo, 2009.

80. Yu. Poliakov and O. Budnitsky: *Periodicheskaia pechat rossiiskoi emigratsii. 1900-2000,* M: Institut rossiiskoi istorii, 2009.

81. E. Rasshivalova, ed.: *Bolshaia Rossiiskaia entsiklopediia muzeev,* M: Ripol Klassik, 2009.

82. A. Bartoshevich and E. Khaichenko, comps.: *Zarubezhnyi teatr v rossiiskoi kritike (1954-2001): Biliograficheskii ukazatel,* M: RATI-GITIS, 2010.

83. S. Voznesensky: *Pervye sto let istorii Ekspeditsii zagotovleniia gosudarstvennykh bumag, 1818-1918,* SP: Nestor-Istoriia, 2009.

84. Yu. Vulfson: *Katalog otkrytykh pisem v polzu Obshchiny Sv. Evgenii,* M: Bonfi, Vol. 1, 2009, Vols. 2-4, 2010.

85. O. Beliakova et al.: *Putevoditel po kinofotodokumentam Rossiiskogo gosudarstvennogo arkhiva kinofotodokumentov (RGAKFD),* M: Rosspen, 2010.

86. A. Dybo, ed.: *Teatralnye terminy i poniatiia: Materialy k slovariu* SP: Rossiiskii institut istorii iskusstv, 2010.

87. V. Kuchmii: *Staryi novyi Gollivud. Entsiklopediia kino 1903-2010,* M: Chelovek, 2010 (two volumes).

88. T. Kuznetsova: *Khronika Bolshogo baleta,* M: Ripol Klassik, 2011.

B. General Works on Twentieth-Century Russian Art

1. I. Grabar et al., eds.: *Istoriia russkogo iskusstva,* M: Nauka, 1953-69, especially Volumes 10 (Books 1 and 2) and 11 (sixteen volumes in all).

2. C. Gray: *The Great Experiment. Russian Art 1863-1922,* London: Thames and Hudson, 1962. Reissued as *The Russian Experiment in Art: 1863-1922,* London: Thames and Hudson, 1970. Revised edition, London: Thames and Hudson, 1986.

3. A. Leonov. ed.: *Russkoe dekorativnoe iskusstvo,* M: Iskusstvo, 1965, Volume 3 (three volumes in all).

4. T. Andersen: *Moderne russisk kunst 1910-1930,* Copenhagen: Borgen, 1967.

5. A. Sidorov: *Russkaia grafika nachala XX veka,* M: Iskusstvo, 1969.

6. J. Billington, ed.: *The Horizon Book of the Arts of Russia,* New York: American Heritage, 1970.

7. A. Galushkina et al., eds.: *Agitatsionno-massovoe iskusstvo pervykh let Oktiabria,* M: Iskusstvo, 1971.

8. V. Marcadé: *Le Renouveau de l'art pictural russe,* Lausanne: L'Age d'Homme, 1971.

9. L. Zinger et al., eds.: *Istoriia iskusstva narodov SSSR,* M: Izobrazitelnoe iskusstvo, 1971, Volume 7 (nine volumes).

10. S. Bojko: *New Graphic Design in Revolutionary Russia,* New York: Praeger, 1972.

11. V. Petrov: *"Mir iskusstva,"* M: Izobrazitelnoe iskusstvo, 1975.

12. J. Bowlt, ed.: *Russian Art of the Avant-Garde. Theory and Criticism 1902-1934,* New York: Viking, 1976; second edition: London: Thames and Hudson, 1988; Japanese translation: Tokyo: Shoten, 1988.

13. J. Bowlt: *Russian Art 1875-1975. A Collection of Essays,* New York: MSS, 1976.

14. J. Bowlt, ed.: *Soviet Constructivism.* Special issue of *Soviet Union,* Pittsburgh, 1976, Volume 3, Part 2.

15. N. Khardzhiev: *K istorii russkogo avangarda,* Stockholm: Almqvist and Wiksell, 1976.

16. V. Shleev: *Revoliutsiia 1905-07 godov i izobrazitelnoe iskusstvo,* M: Izobrazitelnoe iskusstvo, 1977-89 (four volumes). Vol. 1 (1977) on St. Petersburg; Vol. 2 (1978) on Moscow and the Russian provinces; Vol. 3 (1981) on the Ukraine and Moldavia; Vol. 4 (1989) on Latvia and Estonia.

17. G. Harrison: *Ex Libris 6. Constructivism and Futurism: Russian and Other,* New York: TJ Art, 1977.

18. Kennedy: *The "Mir iskusstva" Group and Russian Art, 1898-1912,* New York: Garland, 1977.

19. M. Kolpakchi, ed.: *Skulptura i risunski skulptorov kontsa XIX–nachala XX veka,* M: Sovetskii khudozhnik, 1977.

20. N. Lapshina: *"Mir iskusstva",* M: Iskusstvo, 1977.

21. S. Compton: *The World Backwards. Russian Futurist Books 1912-16,* London: The British Library, 1978.

22. P. Dragone et al., eds.: *Arte e rivoluzione. Documenti delle avanguardie tedesche e sovietiche 1918-1932,* Milan: Unicopli, 1978.

23. L. Shadowa: *Suche und Experiment. Russische und sowjetische Kunst 1910 bis 1930,* Dresden: VEB Kunst, 1978.

24. J. Bowlt: *The Silver Age. Russian Art of the Early Twentieth Century and the "World of Art" Group,* Newtonville: ORP, 1979.

25. H. Gassner and E. Gillen: *Zwischen Revolutionskunst und Sozialistischen Realismus. Dokumente und Kommentare. Kunstdebatten in der Sowjetunion von 1917 bis 1934,* Cologne: DuMont, 1979.

26. M. Guerman: *Art of the October Revolution,* New York: Abrams, 1979. Editions also in Russian, German, and French.

27. J. Milner: *Russian Revolutionary Art,* London: Oresko, 1979.

28. N. Nilsson, ed.: *Art, Society, Revolution. Russia 1917-1921,* Stockholm: Almqvist and Wiksell, 1979.

29. R. Williams: *Russian Art and American Money,* Cambridge, Mass.: Harvard University Press, 1980.

30. R. Auty and D. Obolensky, eds.: *Companion to Russian Studies, Vol. 3. An Introduction to Russian Art and Architecture,* Cambridge: Cambridge University Press, 1980.

197. Sergei Sudeikin: Costume Design for a Gypsy Man, *Petouchka* 1925 (No. 998)

31. J. Bowlt, ed.: *Soviet Art of the 1920s*. Special issue of *Soviet Union*, Tempe, Arizona 1980, Vol. 7, Parts 1-2.

32. S. Massie: *Land of the Firebird. The Beauty of Old Russia*, New York: Simon and Schuster, 1980.

33. M. Milotvorskaia, ed.: *Istoriia russkogo iskusstva*, M: Iskusstvo, 1981, Volume 2, Book 2 (two volumes).

34. A. Rudenstine, S. F Starr, and G. Costakis, eds.: *Russian Avant-Garde Art: The George Costakis Collection*, New York: Abrams, 1981.

35. H. McCooey and M. Binyan: "Russian Art: The Shock of the Old" in *The Sunday Times Magazine*, London, 11 October, 1981, pp. 68-75.

36. A. Fedotova: *Znivopis pervoi piatiletki*, L: Khudozhnik RSFSR, 1981.

37. A. Flaker and D. Ugrešič, eds.: *Književnost Avangarda Revolucija*, Zagreb: University of Zagreb, 1981.

38. R. Grübel: *Russischer Konstruktivismus*, Wiesbaden: Harrassowitz, 1981.

39. A. Nakov: *Abstrait Concret. Art Non-Objectif Russe et Polonais*, Paris: Editions de Minuit, 1981.

40. M. Alpatow: *Über Westeuropäische und Russische Kunst*, Dresden: VEB Kunst, 1982.

41. M. Davydova et al., eds.: *Iskusstvo Sovetskogo Soiuza*, L: Aurora, 1982.

42. L. Denisova and N. Bespalov, eds.: *Russkaia sovetskaia khudozhestvennaia kritka (1917-1941)*, M: Izobrazitelnoe iskusstvo, 1982.

43. A. Ermakov and I. Sats, eds.: *A. V. Lunacharsky ob iskusstve*, M: Iskusstvo, 1982 (two volumes).

44. N. Jernakoff, ed.: *On Russian Art*. Special issue of *Transactions of the Association of Russian-American Scholars in USA / Zapiski Russkoi akademicheskoi gruppy v SShA*, New York, 1982, Vol. 15.

45. V. Kemenov: *The USSR Academy of Arts*, L: Aurora, 1982.

46. N. Khardzhiev and V. Trenin: *La Culture Poètique de Maïakovski*. Lausanne: L'Age d'Homme, 1982 (French translation of the 1976 Soviet edition).

47. L. Magarotto et al., eds.: *L'Avanguardia a Tiflis*, Venice: Università degli Studi, 1982.

48. V. Pushkarev: *Akvareli i risunki v Gosudarstvennom Russkom muzee. XVIII—nachalo XX veka*, M: Izobrazitelnoe iskusstvo, 1982.

49. N. Rozanova: *Moskovskaia knizhnaia ksilografiia 1920-30-ykh godov*, M: Kniga, 1982

50. E. Goheen, ed.: *Constructivism and the Geometric Tradition*. Special issue of *The Nelson-Atkins Museum of Art Bulletin*, Kansas City, 1982, October.

51. T. Omuka, ed.: *Russian Art 1900-1930*. Special issue of *Art Vivant*, Tokyo, 1982, Nr. 7-8.

52. C. Bauermeister and N. Hertling, ed.: *Sieg über die Sonne. Aspekte russischer Kunst zu Beginn des 20. Jahrhunderts*, W. Berlin: Frolich and Kaufmann, 1983.

53. S. Chan-Magomedow: *Pioniere der sowjetischen Architektur*, Dresden: VEB Kunst, 1983. English translation: S. Khan-Magomedov: *Pioneers of Soviet Architecture*, New York: Rizzoli, 1987. Russian version *Arkhitektura sovetskogo avangarda*, M: Stroiizdat, 1996 and 2001 (two volumes).

54. C. Cooke, ed.: *Russian Avant-Garde. Art and Architecture*. Special issue of *Architectural Design*, London, 1983, Vol. 53.

55. A. Gofman et al., eds.: Special issue of *Tekhnicheskaia estetika* (VNIITE), M, 1983, No. 41, devoted to issues of design in the 1920s.

56. S. Gollerbakh: *Zametki khudozhnika*, London: Overseas Publications Exchange, 1983.

57. B. Kean: *All the Empty Palaces*, London: Barrie and Jenkins, 1983.

58. V. Lapshin: *Khudozhestvennaia zhizn Moskvy i Petrograda v 1917 godu*, M: Sovetskii khudozhnik, 1983.

59. C. Lodder: *Russian Constructivism*, New Haven: Yale University Press, 1983.

60. J. Milner: *Vladimir Tatlin and the Russian Avant-Garde*, New Haven: Yale University Press, 1983.

61. A. Tellini, ed.: Il'ja Erenburg. *Eppur si muove! Per una internazionale costruttivista*, Rome: Officina Edizioni, 1983.

62. V. Tolstoi: *U istokov sovetskogo monumentalnogo iskusstva 1917-1923*, M: Izobrazitelnoe iskusstvo, 1983.

63. J. Willett: *L'Avanguardia Europea. Anni venti a Mosca e a Weimar*, Rome: Editori Riuniti, 1983 (a translated version of *The New Sobriety: Art and Politics in the Weimar Period 1917-33*, London: Thames and Hudson, 1978).

64. B. Zelinsky: *Russische Avantgarde, 1907-1921, Vom Primitivismus zum Konstruktivismus*, Bonn: Grundmann, 1983.

65. J. Bowlt et al.: *Mir iskusstva*, Rome: E/O, 1984.

66. G. Janecek: *The Look of Russian Literature. Avant-Garde Experiments 1900-1930*, Princeton: Princeton University Visual Press, 1984.

67. N. Misler: *Pavel Florenskij: La prospettiva rovesciata e altri scritti*, Rome: La Casa del Libro, 1984.

68. N. Misler and J. Bowlt: *Pavel Filonov. A Hero and His Fate*, Austin: Silvergirl, 1984.

69. A. Nakov: *L'Avant-Garde Russe*, Paris: Hazan, 1984.

70. V. Vasilenko et al., eds.: *Sovetskoe dekorativnoe iskusstvo 1917-1945*, M: Iskusstvo, 1984.

71. C. Leclanche-Boule: *Typographies et Photomontages Constructivistes en URSS*, Paris: Papyrus, 1984.

72. V. Tolstoi, ed.: *1917-1932. Agitatsionno-massovoe iskusstvo. Oformlenie prazdnenstv*. M: Iskusstvo, 1984 (2 volumes).

73. J. Kowtun: *Die Wiedergeburt der kunstlerischer Druckgraphik*, Dresden: VEB Kunst, 1984.

74. A. Flaker and D. Ugrešič: *Pojmovnik ruske avangarde*, Zagreb: Grafički zavod Hrvatske, 1984.

75. A. Flaker: *Ruska avangarda*, Zagreb: Globus, 1984.

76. T. Andersen, ed.: *Louisiana Revy*, Humlebaek, 1985, September. Entire issue devoted to the Russian avant-garde 1910-1930, Museum Ludwig, Cologne.

77. M. Mudrak: *The New Generation and Artistic Modernism in the Ukraine*, Ann Arbor: UMI, 1986.

78. A. Erjavec et al., eds.: *Slowenische Historische Avantgarde / Slovene Historical Avant-Garde*, Ljubljana: Aesthetics Society, 1986.

79. A. Erjavec, ed.: *Soobstoj avantgard / Coexistence among the Avant-Gardes*, Ljubljana: Drustvo za estetiko, 1986 (two volumes).

80. S. Gohr: *Museum Ludwig. Illustrated Catalog*, New York: Prestel / Neues, 1986.

81. J. Stapanian: *Mayakovsky's Cubo-Futurist Vision*, Houston: Rice, 1986.

82. *Rassegna sovietica*, Rome, 1986, No. 2, March-April. Part of the issue is devoted to the Russian avant-garde with essays on Khlebnikov, Rodchenko, Kandinsky, Florensky, Yakulov et al.

83. A. Turowski: *Existe-t-il un art de l'Europe de l'est?*, Paris: Les Editeurs de la Villette, 1986.

84. D. Elliott: *New Worlds. Russian Art and Society 1900-1937*, London: Thames and Hudson, 1986.

198. Sergei Sudeikin: Costume Design for a Gypsy Woman, *Petrouchka*, ca. 1925 (No. 999)

85. V. Kostin: *Sredi khudozhnikov*, M: Sovetskii khudozhnik, 1986.
86. M. Anikst, ed. *Soviet Graphic Design of the Twenties*, New York: Abbeville, 1987.
87. A. Bird: *A History of Russian Painting*, Oxford: Phaidon, 1987.
88. J. Bowlt, ed.: *Journal of Decorative and Propaganda Arts*, Miami, 1987, No. 5. Special issue devoted to Russian design 1880-1980.
89. E. Kovtun et al.: *Sovetskoe iskusstvo 20-30-kh godov*, L: Iskusstvo, 1988.
90. M. German: *Soviet Art 1920s-1930s: Russian Museum, Leningrad*, New York: Abrams, 1988.
91. E. Borisova and G. Sternin: *Russian Art Nouveau*, New York: Rizzoli, 1988.
92. S. Fauchereau et al.: *Moscow 1900-1930*, New York: Rizzoli, 1988.
93. A. Flaker: *Nomadi ljepote*, Zagreb: Grafički zavod Hrvatske, 1988.
94. J. Bowlt, ed.: *Journal of Decorative and Propaganda Arts*, Miami, 1989, No. 11. Special issue devoted to Russian design 1880-1980, Part II.
95. K. Kuzminsky et al.: *Zabytyi avangard*, Vienna: Kohlweis, 1989.
96. J.-C. Marcadé: *Le Futurisme Russe*, Paris: Dessain et Tolra, 1989.
97. N. Beliaeva et al., eds.: *Sergei Diagilev i khudozhestvennaia kultura XIX-XX vv.*, Perm: Permskoe knizhnoe izdatelstvo, 1989.
98. *Constructivisme*. Special issue of *Ligeia*, Paris, 1989, No. 5-6.
99. N. Misler: *Avanguardie russe*, Roma: Giunti, 1989.
100. A. Brambatti et al.: *Grafica Art Nouveau nelle riviste russe*, Florence: Cantini, 1989.
101. P. Railing: *From Science to Systems of Art. On Russian Abstract Art and Language 1910-1920*, Forest Row, England: Artists Bookworks, 1989.
102. V. Manine: *L'Art Russe 1900-1935. Tendances et Mouvements*, Paris: Sers, 1989.
103. E. Kovtun et al: *Avangard, ostanovlennyi na begu*, L: Aurora, 1989.
104. E. Kovtun: *Russkaia futuristicheskaia kniga*, M: Kniga, 1989.
105. V. Tolstoi et al.: *Art décoratif soviétique 1917-1937*, Paris: Editions du Regard 1989.
106. A. Flaker, ed.: *Glossarium der russischen Avantgarde*, Graz: Droschl, 1989.
107. N. Misler and L. Tonini, eds.: *Tradizione artigianale e rivoluzione industriale in Russia tra '800 e '900*. Special issue of *Ricerche di Storia dell'arte*, Rome, 1989, No. 39.
108. D. Sarabianov: *Russian Art. From Neo-Classicism to the Avant-Garde*, London: Thames and Hudson, 1990.
109. M. Yablonskaya: *Women Artists of Russia's New Age 1900-1935*, London: Thames and Hudson, 1990.
110. V. Tolstoy, I. Bibikova, C. Cooke: *Street Art of the Revolution*, London: Thames and Hudson, 1990.
111. L. Cerwinske: *Russian Imperial Style*, London: Barrie and Jenkins, 1990.
112. O. Kuprin et al: *V chetyre chasa popoludni*, L: LenArt, 1990.
113. I. Smolnikov: *Masterskaia solntsa*, L: Detskaia literatura, 1990.
114. M. Anikst and E. Cherrevich: *Russian Graphic Design 1880-1917*, New York: Abbeville, 1990.
115. J. Bowlt: *Khudozhniki russkogo teatra 1880-1930. Sobranie Nikity i Niny Lobanovykh-Rostovskikh*, M: Iskusstvo, 1990.
116. V. Ruban: *Zabytye imena*, K: Naukova dumka, 1990.

117. G. Conio, ed.: *L'Avant-garde russe et la synthèse des arts*, Lausanne: L'Age d'homme, 1990.
118. L. Lang: *Konstruktivismus und Buchkunst*, Leipzig: Edition Leipzig, 1990.
119. A. Turowski: *Wielka utopia awangardy*, Warsaw: Państwowe Wydawnictwo Naukowe, 1990.
120. E. Borisova and G. Sternin: *Russkii modern*, M: Sovetskii khudozhnik, 1991.
121. S. Chan-Magomedov: *Vkhutemas-Vkhutein*, Paris: Sers, 1991.
122. E. Kirichenko: *The Russian Style*, London: Laurence King, 1991.
123. V. Petrov and A. Kamensky: *The World of Art Movement*, L: Aurora, 1991.
124. J. Kovtun: *Russische Avantgarde*, Munich: Neimanis, 1991. French edition: E. Kovtoune: *Avant-Garde Russe Années 1920-1930*, Bournemoth: Parkstone,1996 (B206).
125. J. van der Eug and W. Weststeijn, eds.: *Avant Garde. USSR*. Special issue of the journal *Avant Garde*, Amsterdam, 1991, No, 5-6.
126. E. Clowes et al., eds.: *Between Tsar and People*. Princeton: Princeton University Press, 1991.
127. W. Brumfield: *The Origins of Modernism in Russian Architecture*, Berkeley: University of California Press, 1991.
128. E. Kirichenko and M. Anikst: *Russian Design and the Fine Arts 1750-1917*, New York: Abrams, 1991.
129. V. Marcadé: *L'Art d'Ukraine*, Lausanne: L'Age d'Homme, 1991.
130. L. Magarotto et al.: *Zaumnyi futurizm i dadaizm v russkoi kulture*, Bern: Lang, 1991.
131. V. Quilici: *Il Costruttivismo*, Rome: Laterza, 1991.
132. A. Povelikhina and E. Kovtun: *Russian Painted Shop Signs and Avant-Garde Artists*, L: Aurora, 1991.
133. M. Allenov et al.: *L'Art Russe*, Paris: Citadel, 1991.
134. E. Kuznecov: *L'Illustrazione del libro per bambini e l'avanguardia russa*, Florence: Cantini, 1991.
135. B. Taylor: *Art and Literature under the Bolsheviks*, London: Pluto, 1991.
136. J. Fraser and T. Shima: *Musée Imaginaire 1. 1920-1930*, Tokyo: Libro-port, 1991.
137. D. Lichačev: *Le Radici dell'arte russa*, Milan: Fabbri, 1992.
138. A. Sarabianov and N. Gurianova: *Neizvestnyi avangard*, M: Sovetskii khudozhnik, 1992.
139. N. Lobanov-Rostovsky et al.: *Rossia 1850-1910*, Athens: Aprilioz, 1992.
140. M. C. Bown and B. Taylor: *Art of the Soviets: Painting, Sculpture and Architecture in a One-Party State, 1917-1922*, Manchester: Manchester University Press, 1992.
141. G. Roman and V. Marquardt, eds.: *The Avant-Garde Frontier. Russia Meets the West, 1910-1930*, Gainesville, Florida: University of Florida Press, 1992.
142. C. Marsh and W. Roslyn, eds.: *Russian and Yugoslav Culture in the Age of Modernism*, Nottingham: Astra, 1992.
143. B. Brodskij: *Tesori vietati*, Florence: Ponte alle Grazie, 1992.
144. J. Howard: *The Union of Youth*, Manchester: Manchester University Press, 1992.
145. N. Dumova: *Moskovskie metsenaty*, M: Molodaia gvardiia, 1992.
146. S. Compton: *Russian Avant-Garde Books 1917-1934*, Cambridge, Mass.: MIT Press, 1992.
147. C. Burrus: *Les Collectioneurs Russes*, Paris: Chêne, 1992 (English edition: Art Collectors of Russia: the private treasures revealed. New York: Rizzoli, 1994).

199. Sergei Sudeikin: Costume Design for The Moor, *Petroushka* ca. 1925 (No. 1000)

148. V. Turchin: *Po labirintam avangarda,* M: MGU, 1993.
149. V. Cherepov et al.: *Avangardnye napravleniia v sovetskom izobrazitelnom iskusstve,* Ekaterinburg: Ural University, 1993.
150. R. Vroon and J. Malmstad: *Kultura russkogo modernizma,* Los Angeles: UCLA Slavic Studies, 1993, Vol. 1.
151. V. Arwas, ed.: *The Great Russian Utopia,* London: Art and Design, 1993.
152. M. C. Bown and B. Taylor, eds.: *Art of the Soviets,* Manchester: Manchester University Press, 1993.
153. V. Abashev, comp.: *Vremia Diaghileva. Universalii Serebrianogo veka,* Perm: Arabesk, 1993.
154. J. Bowlt and N. Misler: *The Thyssen-Bornemisza Collection: Twentieth Century Russian and East European Painting,* London: Wilson, 1993.
155. J. Bowlt and B. Hernad: *Aus vollem Halse. Russische Buchillustration und Typographie 1900-1930,* Munich: Prestel, 1993.
156. N. Thun: *Majakowski: Maler und Dichter,* Tübingen: Francke, 1993.
157. S. Fitzpatrick: *The Cultural Front: Power and Culture in Revolutionary Russia,* Ithaca: Cornell University Press, 1993.
158. W. Brumfield: *History of Russian Architecture,* Cambridge: Cambridge University Press, 1993.
159. A. Kantsedikas (series editor): *Shedevry evreiskogo iskusstva,* M: Image, 1993 (five volumes on the painting, architecture, and applied arts of the Jewish people).
160. R. Messina: *Majakovskij Artista 1893-1993,* Rieti, Italy: Biblioteca Paroniana, 1993.
161. J. Norman, ed.: *New Perspectives on Russian and Soviet Artistic Culture.* New York: St. Martin's Press, 1993.
162. E. Moch-Bickert: *Kolombina desiatykh godov,* Paris-SP: Grzhebin, 1993.
163. N. Borisovkaia, ed.: *Proizvedeniia russkikh i zapadnoevropeiskikh masterov XVI–nachala XX veka iz sobraniia I.S. Zilbershteina,* M: GMII/Rodina, 1993.
164. S. Khan-Magomedov: *Zhivskulptarkh,* M: Arkhitektura, 1993 (two volumes).
165. D. Sarabianov: *Istoriia russkogo iskusstva kontsa XIX–nachala veka,* M Moskovskii universitet, 1993.
166. D. Sarabianov et al.: *Iskusstvo avangarda. Materialy mezhdunarodnoi konferentsii 10-11 dekabria 1992 g.,* Ufa: Vostok, 1993.
167. E. Kowtun: *Sangesi. Die russische Avantgarde. Chlebnikow und seine Maler,* Zurich: Stemmle, 1993.
168. L. Boersma: *0.10. The Last Futurist Exhibition of Painting,* Rotterdam: Zero Ten Publshers, 1994.
169. G. Zaitsev: *Iskusstvo XX veka. Vzgliad na razvitie,* Ekaterinburg: Ural University, 1994.
170. N. Gurianova: *Rozanova, Filonov, Tatlin, Goncharova, Larionov, Malevich, Kulbin,* M: Avant-Garde; and Paris: La Hune, 1994.
171. S. Khan-Magomedov: *Inkhuk i rannii konstruktivizm,* M: Arkhitektura, 1994.
172. I. Ilina: *Istoriia iskusstv. Otechestvennoe iskusstvo,* M: Vysshaia shkola. 1994.
173. P. Roberts: *George Costakis: A Russian Life in Art,* New York: Braziller, 1994.
174. V. Ivanov et al., eds.: *Russkii avangard v krugu evropeiskoi kultury,* M: Radiks, 1994.
175. I. Danilova, ed.: *Dialog kultur,* M: GMII im. A.S. Pushkina 1994, No. 25.

176. P. Cate et al.: *The George Riabov Collection of Russian Art,* New Brunswick: Jane Voorhees Zimmerli Art Museum, 1994.
177. P. Hellyer, ed.: *A Catalogue of Russian Avant-Garde Books 1912-1934,* London: The British Library, 1994.
178. E. Sidorina: *Skvoz ves dvadtsatyi vek,* M: Russkii mir, 1994.
179. Dzh. Boult (J. Bowlt and N.D. Lobanov-Rostovsky): *Khudozhniki russkogo teatra. Katalog–rezone,* M: Iskusstvo, 1994. This is the Russian version of the catalogue raisonné of the Lobanov-Rostovsky collection of Russian stage designs.
180. N. Udaltsova: *Zhizn russkoi kubistki,* M: RA, 1994.
181. R. Anderson and P. Debreczeny: *Russian Narrative and Visual Art. Varieties of Seeing,* Gainesville: University of Florida Press, 1994.
182. A. Rusakova: *Simvolizm v russkoi zhivopisi 19–nachala 20 vv.,* M: Iskusstvo, 1995.
183. *Experiment,* Los Angeles (1995-2011). On the classical Russian avant-garde (No. 1), artistic movements in Russia in the 1910s and 1920s (No. 2), the Russian Academy of Artistic Sciences (No. 3), the Apocalypse (No. 4), the Khardzhiev archive (No. 5), Organica (No. 6), Art Nouveau (No. 7), Vasilii Kandinsky (Nos. 8, 9), Performing Arts and the Avant-Garde (No. 10), Pavel Filonov (No. 11), Cabaret (No. 12), the diaries of Vera Sudeikina (No. 13), the 19th century Russian Realists (No. 14), Omsk Modernism (No. 15), Vladimir Sterligov and Tatiana Glebova (No. 16), and the Ballets Russes (No. 17).
184. V. Rakitin and A. Sarabianov, eds.: *Aleksei Kruchenykh. Nash vykhod,* M: RA, 1995. English translation: *Alexei Kruchenykh. Our Arrival,* M: RA, 1995.
185. A. Morozov: *Konets utopii. Iz istorii iskusstva v SSSR 1930-kh godov,* M: Galart, 1995.
186. G. Kazanov: *Sankt-Peterburg: Obrazy prostranstva,* M: Indrik, 1995.
187. A. Yakimovich: *Magicheskaia vselennaia,* M: Galart, 1995.
188. I. Danilova, ed.: *Chastnoe kollektsionirovanie v Rossii. Materialy nauchnoi konferentsii "Vipperovskie chteniia, 1994",* M: GMII im. A.S. Pushkina, 1995.
189. Yu. Linnik: *Russkii kosmizm i russkii avangard,* Petrozavodsk: Sviatoi Ostrov, 1995.
190. J.-C. Marcadé : *L'Avant-garde russe,* Paris: Flammarion, 1995.
191. A. Aronov: *Zolotoi vek russkogo metsenatstva,* M: Moskovskii gosudarstvennyi universitet kultury, 1995.
192. A. Kafetsi, ed.: *Russian Avant-Garde 1910-1930. The George Costakis Collection: Theory and Criticism,* Athens: National Gallery and Alexandros Soutzos Museum, 1995.
193. E. Lazarev: *Tre secoli di pittura russa,* Milan: Fabbri, 1995.
194. V. Strada, ed.: *I russi e l'Italia,* Milan: Scheiwiller, 1995.
195. V. Shcherbakivsky: *Ukrainske mistetstvo,* K: Libid, 1995 (in Ukrainian).
196. B. Wismer: *Karo Dame,* Baden: Müller, 1995.
197. V. Mirimanov: *Russkii avangard i esteticheskaia revoliutsiia XX veka,* M: RGGU, 1995.
198. S. Khan-Magomedov: *Pionery sovetskogo dizaina,* M: Galart, 1995.
199. E. Sidorina: *Russkii konstruktivizm: Istoki, idei, praktika,* M: Galart, 1995.
200. J. Bowlt and O. Matich, eds.: *Laboratory of Dreams: The Russian Avant-Garde,* Stanford: Stanford University Press, 1996.
201. C. Cooke: *Russian Avant-Garde,* London: Academy, 1996.
202. W. Salmond: *Arts and Crafts in Late Imperial Russia,* Cambridge: Cambridge University Press, 1996.

200. Sergei Sudeikin: Costume Design for the Tea Vendor, *Petrouchka*, c. 1925 (No. 1002)

203. A. Krusanov: *Russkii avangard, 1907-1932,* SP: Novoe literaturnoe obozrenie, 1996. New edition: *Russkii avangard*, M: NLO, 2003-10 (three volumes).

204. Anon.: *Soviet Art, Origins and Development,* Washington, D.C.: Russian Information and Business Center, 1996.

205. V. Lebedeva, comp.: *Vek nyneshnii i vek minuvshii,* M: Gosudarstvennyi Institut iskusstvoznaniia, 1996.

206. E. Kovtoune: *L'Avant-Garde Russe dans les Années 1920-1930,* Bournemouth: Parkstone, and SP: Aurora, 1996. (Translation of B124).

207. T. Kniazevskaia, comp.: *Russkoe podvizhnichestvo,* M: Nauka, 1996.

208. L. Rapatskaia: *Iskusstvo "Serebrianogo veka",* M: Prosveshchenie, 1996.

209. E. Allenova et al.: *Russkie khudozhniki ot A do Ya,* M: Slovo, 1996.

210. E. Vinogradova and G. Kovalenko, eds.: *Ot konstruktivizma do siurrealizma: Sbornik statei,* M: Nauka, 1996.

211. A. Parton, *Mikhail Larionov and the Russian Avant-Garde*, Princeton, NJ: Princeton University Press, 1996 (1st ed. 1993).

212. D. Gorbachev *Ukrainskiy avangard*, K: Mistetstvo, 1996.

213. J.-L. Cohen, D. Woodruff, L. Grubišič: *Russian Modernism*, Oxford: Windsor Books, 1997.

214. V. Margolin: *The Struggle for Utopia. Rodchenko, Lissitzky, Moholy-Nagy,* Chicago: University of Chicago Press, 1997.

215. Yu. Molok: *Staraia detskaia knizhka. 1900-1930-e gody. Iz sobraniia professora Marka Ratsa,* M: AiB, 1997.

216. E. Landini: *Artisti delle avanguardie russe.* Milan: Mondadori, 1997.

217. V. Rakitin and A. Sarabianov, eds.: *Nikolai Khardzhiev. Stati ob avangarde.* M: RA, 1997.

218. O. Ilnytzkyj: *Ukrainian Futurism, 1914-1930.* Cambridge, Mass.: Harvard University Press, 1997.

219. A.B. Nakov: *Bespredmetnyi mir.* M: Iskusstvo, 1997.

220. V. Petrov: *Russian Art Nouveau. The Diaghilev Group of Russian Artists.* Bournemouth: Parkstone, 1997.

221. V. Butromeev *Iskusstvo Rossii,* M: Sovremennik, 1997.

222. M. Chegodaeva: *Iskusstvo, kotoroe bylo,* M: GMII im. A.S. Pushkina, 1997.

223. J. Chirac et al.: *Les Survivants des Sables Rouges. Art Russe du Musée de Noukous, Ouzbekistan 1920-1940,* Malherbe-Caen, France: Conseil Régional Basse-Normande, 1998.

224. S. Foster and G. Janecek, eds.: *The Eastern Dada Orbit: Russia, Georgia, Ukraine, Central Europe and Japan,* New York: Hall, 1998.

225. J. Hercher and P. Urban, comps.: *Erstens, zweitens, Dichtungen russischer Maler / Zeichnungen russischer Dichter,* Hamburg: Material-Verlag, 1998 (two volumes).

226. V. Poliakov: *Knigi russkogo kubofuturizma,* M: Gileia, 1998.

227. D. Sarabianov: *Russkaa zhivopis. Probuzhdenie pamiati,* M: Iskusstvoznanie, 1998.

228. *Ligeia,* Paris, 1998, Nos. 21-24. Collective issue devoted to Cubo-Futurism.

229. N. Rzhevsky, ed.: *Modern Russian Culture,* Cambridge: Cambridge Unviersity Press 1998.

230. G. Kovalenko, ed.: *Avangard 1910-kh-1920-kh gg.,* M: GII, 1998.

231. E. Gollerbakh, ed.: *Erik Gollerbakh. Vstrechi i vpechatleniia,* SP: Inapress, 1998.

232. I. Ilin, ed.: *Iskusstvo i religiia,* M: Gitis, 1998.

233. A. Ivanov and A. Petrova, eds.: *Azbuka Mira iskusstva,* M: Nahe nasledie, 1998.

234. V. Shestakov: *Iskusstvo i mir v "Mire iskusstva",* M: Slavianskii dialog, 1998.

235. L. Beliakova-Kazanskaia: *Ekho Serebrianogo veka,* SP: Kanon, 1998.

236. R. Davis et al.: *Russian and Ukrainian Avant-Garde and Constructivist Books and Serials in the New York Public Library,* New York: Ross, 1998.

237. E. Kashuba: *Pervye avangardnye vystavki v Kieve 1908-1910 gg.,* K: Triumf, 1998.

238. E. Petrova et al.: *Mir iskusstva,* SP: Palace, 1998.

239. A. Turowski, ed.: *Między sztuką a komuną. Teksty avangardy rosyjskiej 1910-1932,* Cracow: Universitas, 1998.

240. G. Anisimov: *Mira vostorg bespredelnyi. Rasskazy o khudozhnikakh,* M: Lira, 1999.

241. A. Aronov: *Mirovaia khudozhestvennaia kultura. Rossiia XX veka,* M: Profizdat, 1999.

242. B. Gribanov: *Kartiny i zhizn: Zapiski kollektsionera,* M: Prava cheloveka, 1999.

243. G. Kovalenko, ed.: *Avangard 1910-kh—1920-kh godov. Vzaimodeistvie iskusstv,* M: GII, 1999.

244. P. Leek: *Russian Painting from the XVIII until the XX Century,* Bournemouth: Parkstone, 1999.

245. V. Manin: *Iskusstvo v rezervatsii. Khudozhestvennaia zhizn Rossii 1917-1941 gg.,* M: Editorial URSS, 1999.

246. V. Petrov-Stromsky: *Tysiacha let russkogo iskusstva,* M: Terra, 1999.

247. G. Pospelov: *Russkoe iskusstvo nachala XX veka. Sudba i oblik Rossii,* M: Nauka, 1999.

248. I. Sakhno: *Avangard zhivopisi,* M: Dialog-MGU, 1999.

249. A. Strigalev et al.: *Dialog istorii iskusstva,* SP: GII, 1999.

250. V. Terekhina and A. Zimenkov: *Russkii futurizm. Teoriia. Praktika. Kritika. Vospoinaniia,* M: Nasledie, 1999.

251. A. Trofimov: *Ot Imperatorskogo muzeia k bloshinomu rynku,* M: Nashe nasledie, 1999.

252. A. Tsukor et al., eds.: *Iskusstvo na rubezhe vekov,* Rostov-on-Don: Rostovskaia gosudarstvennaia konservatoriia, 1999.

253. M. Allenov: *Russkoe iskusstvo XVIII—nachala XX veka,* M: Trilistnik, 2000.

254. P. Beletsky et al.: *Ukrainske mistetstvo ta arkhitektura kintsia XIX—pochatku XX st.,* K: Naukova dumka, 2000.

255. E. Bobrinskaia: *Futurizm i kubofuturizm,* M: Galart, 2000.

256. Yu. Daniel, ed.: *Yu.A. Rusakov. Izbrannye iskusstvovedcheskie trudy,* SP: Aleteiia, 2000.

257. S. Daniel: *Ot ikony do avangarda,* SP: Azbuka, 2000.

258. I. Danilova, ed.: *Rossiia-Germaniia. Kulturnye sviazi, iskusstvo, literatura v pervoi polovine XX v.,* M: GMII, 2000.

259. E. Degot: *Russkoe iskusstvo XX veka,* M: Trilistnik 2000 (new edition 2009).

260. I. Gofman: *Golubaia roza,* M: Pinakoteka, 2000.

261. I. Gofman: *Golubaia roza,* M: Elizium, 2000.

262. F. Ingold: *Der grosse Bruch. Russland im Epochenjahr 1913,* Munich: Beck, 2000.

263. F. Ingold: *Kunstleben und Lebenskunst. Russlands kulturelle Szene im Umbruch,* Zug: Stiftung der Freunde Kunsthaus, 2000.

264. E. Itkina, ed.: *Stranitsy khudozhestvennogo naslediia Rossii XVI-XX vekov,* M: GII, 2000.

265. C. Kelly and S. Lowell, eds.: *Russian Literature, Modernism and the Visual Arts,* Cambridge: Cambridge University Press, 2000.

266. V. Kostin and T. Rein: *Khudozhestvennaia sudba i velikii perelom,* M: Palmir, 2000.

201. Sergei Sudekin: Costume Design for the Chimney Sweep, *Petrouchka*, ca. 1925 (No. 1003)

267. G. Kovalenko, ed.: *Russkii avangard 1910-1930-kh godov v evropeiskom kontekste,* M: Nauka, 2000.

268. W. Kruglow: *Symbolismus in Russland,* Bad Breisig: Palace Editions, 2000.

269. V. Kruglov and V. Leniashin: *Russkii impressionizm,* SP: Palace Editions, 2000.

270. A. Lavrentiev: *Laboratoriia konstruktivizma,* M: Grant, 2000.

271. D. Likhachev: *Russkaia khudozhestvennaia kultura,* M: Iskusstvo. 2000.

272. M. Meilakh, ed.: *Poeziia i zhivopis. Sbornik trudov pamiati N.I. Khardzhieva,* M: Yazyki russkoi kultury, 2000.

273. T. Nikolskaia: *Fantasticheskii gorod. Russkaia khudozhestvennaia zhizn v Tbilisi (1917-1921),* M: Piataia strana, 2000.

274. E. Paston et al.: *Stil zhizni, stil iskusstva,* M: TG, 2000.

275. E. Petrova et al.: *Russkii futurizm,* SP: Palace Editions, 2000.

276. O. Petrova: *Simvolizm v russkom izobrazitelnom iskusstve,* SP: Sankt-peterburgskii gumanitarnyi universitet profsoiuzov, 2000.

277. N. Stepanian: *Iskusstvo Rossii XX veka,* M: EKSMO, 2000.

278. V. Tretiakov: *Otkrytye pisma Serebrianogo veka,* SP: Slaviia, 2000.

279. M. Zalambani: *L'arte della produzione,* Ravenna: Longo, 2000.

280. L. Azizian: *Dialog iskusstv Serebrianogo veka,* M: Progress-Traditsiia, 2001.

281. G. Kovalenko, ed.: *Amazonki avangarda,* M: Nauka, 2001.

282. O. Kuznetsova: *Russkii modernizm. Sbornik statei,* SP: Aleteiia, 2001.

283. E. Petrova et al. *Russkii avangard: problemy reprezentatsii i interpretatsii,* SP: Palace Editions, 2001.

284. D. Sarabianov: *Istoriia russkogo iskusstva kontsa XIX–nachala XX veka.* M: Galart, 2001.

285. D. Sarabianov: *Modern. Istoriia stilia,* M: Galart, 2001.

286. J. Bowlt and M. Konecny, eds.: *A Legacy Regained: Nikolai Khardzhiev and the Russian Avant-Garde,* St. Petersburg: Palace Editions, 2002.

287. I. Karasik, comp.: *The Russian Avant-Garde: Personality and School,* SP: Palace Editions, 2002.

288. G. Kovalenko, ed.: *Simvolizm v avangarde,* M: Nauka, 2002.

289. G. Kovalenko, ed.: *Russkii kubo-futurizm,* M: Nauka, 2002.

290. T. Nikolskaia: *Avangard i okrestnosti,* SP: Limbakh, 2002.

291. A. Raev: *Russische Künstlerinnen der Moderne (1870-1930),* Munich: Fink, 2002.

292. I. Shteiner: *Avangard i postroenie novogo cheloveka,* M: NLO, 2002.

293. N. Avtonomova et al., eds.: *Russkii avangard 1910-1920-ykh godov i problema ekspressionizma,* M: Nauka, 2003.

294. E. Bobrinskaia: *Russkii avangard: Istoki i metamorfozy,* M: Gileia, 2003.

295. S. Khan-Magomedov: *Konstruktivizm. Kontseptsiia formoobrazovaniia,* M: Stroizdat, 2003.

296. G. Kovalenko, ed.: *Russkii avangard 1910-kh-1920-kh godov. Problema kollazha,* M: Nauka, 2003.

297. K. Vashik (C. Waschik) and I. Baburina: *Realnost utopii. Iskusstvo russkogo plakata XX veka,* M: Progress-Traditsiia, 2003.

298. E. Petrova et al.: *Origins of the Russian Avant-Garde,* SP: Palace Editions, 2003.

299. M. Valiaeva: *Morfologiia russkoi bespredmetnosti,* M: RA, 2003.

300. D. Krvavich et al., eds.: *Ukrainske mistetstvo,* Lvov: Svit, 2003-05 (three volumes; in Ukrainian).

301. M. Adamchik: *500 shedevrov russkogo iskusstva,* Minsk: Kharvest, 2004.

302. D. Anfam et al. *My People Is the World,* M: Museum of Avant Garde Masters, 2004.

303. T. Goriaeva et al.: *Russkii avangard iz sobraniia Rossiiskogo Gosudarstvennogo arkhiva literatury i iskusstva,* M: RGALI, 2004.

304. A. Nakov: *Aux avant-gardes de l'art moderne,* Paris: Découvertes–Gallimard Arts. 2004.

305. N. Pavlova et al., eds.: *Modern, modernizm, modernizatsiia,* M: RGGU, 2004.

306. E. Petrova et al.: *100 neznakomykh kartin iz fondov Russkogo muzeia,* SP: Palace Editions, 2004.

307. O. Roitenberg: *Neuzheli kto-to vspomnil, chto my byli,* M: Galart, 2004.

308. S. Baiman, ed.: *Russkaia khudozhestvennaia kultura. Kontury dukhovnogo opyta,* SP: Aleteiia, 2004.

309. N. Avtonomova et al., eds.: *Voldemar Matvei i "Soiuz molodezhi",* M: Nauka, 2005.

310. V. Dudakov and M. Kashuro: *Russkoe iskusstvo. Chastnoe sobranie,* SP: Zolotoi vek, and M: Artprior, 2005.

311. D. Gorbachov, ed.: *Ukrainski avangardisti yak teoretiki i publitsisti,* Kiev: Triumf, 2005.

312. M. Gough: *The Artist as Producer. Russian Constructivism in Revolution,* Berkeley: University of California Press, 2007.

313. V. Terekhina: *Russkii ekspressionizm. Teoriia. Praktika. Kritika,* M: IMLI RAN, 2005.

314. I. Salnikova: *My byli… Iz istorii gosudarstvennogo i chastnogo sobiratelstva,* SP: Blits, 2005.

315. W. Bayer: *Gerettete Kultur. Private Kunstsammler in der Sowjetunion (1917-1991),* Vienna: Turia und Kant, 2006.

316. R. Blakesley and S. Reid, eds.: *Russian Art and the West,* Dekalb: Northern Illinois Press, 2006.

317. E. Bobrinskaia: *Russkii avangard: Granitsy iskusstva,* M: NLO, 2006.

318. J. Howard: *East European Art,* Oxford: Oxford University Press, 2006.

319. E. Petinova: *Ot akademizma k modernu,* SP: Iskusstvo-SPb, 2006.

320. T. Rein, comp.: *Khudozhnik, sudba i velikii perelom: VKhUTEMAS-VKhUTEIN-Poligrafinstitut–MIII,* M: Palmir. 2006.

321. Yu. Stepanov et al., eds.: *Semiotika i avangard: Antologiia,* M: Kultura / Akademicheskii proekt, 2006.

322. I. Golitsyna: *Istoriia russkoi zhivopisi: Rubezh XIX i XX vekov,* M: Belyi gorod, 2007.

323. J. Kowtun: *Russische Avantgarde,* Ho-Chi Minh City: Baseline, 2007.

324. N. Maiorova and G. Skokov: *Istoriia russkoi zhivopisi. V 12 tomakh. Tom 12. Vtoraia polovina XX veka,* M: Belyi gorod, 2007.

325. V. Manin: *Russkaia zhivopis XX veka,* SP: Aurora, 2007 (three volumes).

326. A. Raev and I. Wünsche, eds.: *Kursschwankungen. Russische Kunst im Wertesystem der europäischen Moderne,* Berlin: Lukas, 2007.

327. G. Sternin: *Dva veka: Ocherki russkoi khudozhestvennoi kultury,* M: Galart, 2007.

328. P. Fokin and S. Kniazeva, eds.: *Serebrianyi vek. Portretnaia galereia kulturnykh geroev rubezha XIX-XX vekov,* SP: Amfora, 2007-08 (three volumes).

329. G. Kovalenko, ed.: *Russkoe iskusstvo XX vek,* M: Nauka, 2007-09 (three volumes).

330. N. Adaskina, ed.: *I.A. Aksenov. Iz tvorcheskogo naslediia,* M: RA, 2008 (two volumes).

331. M. Allenov, ed.: *Istoriia russkogo iskusstva. Iskusstvo XVIII-nachala XX veka:* M: Belyi gorod, 2008.

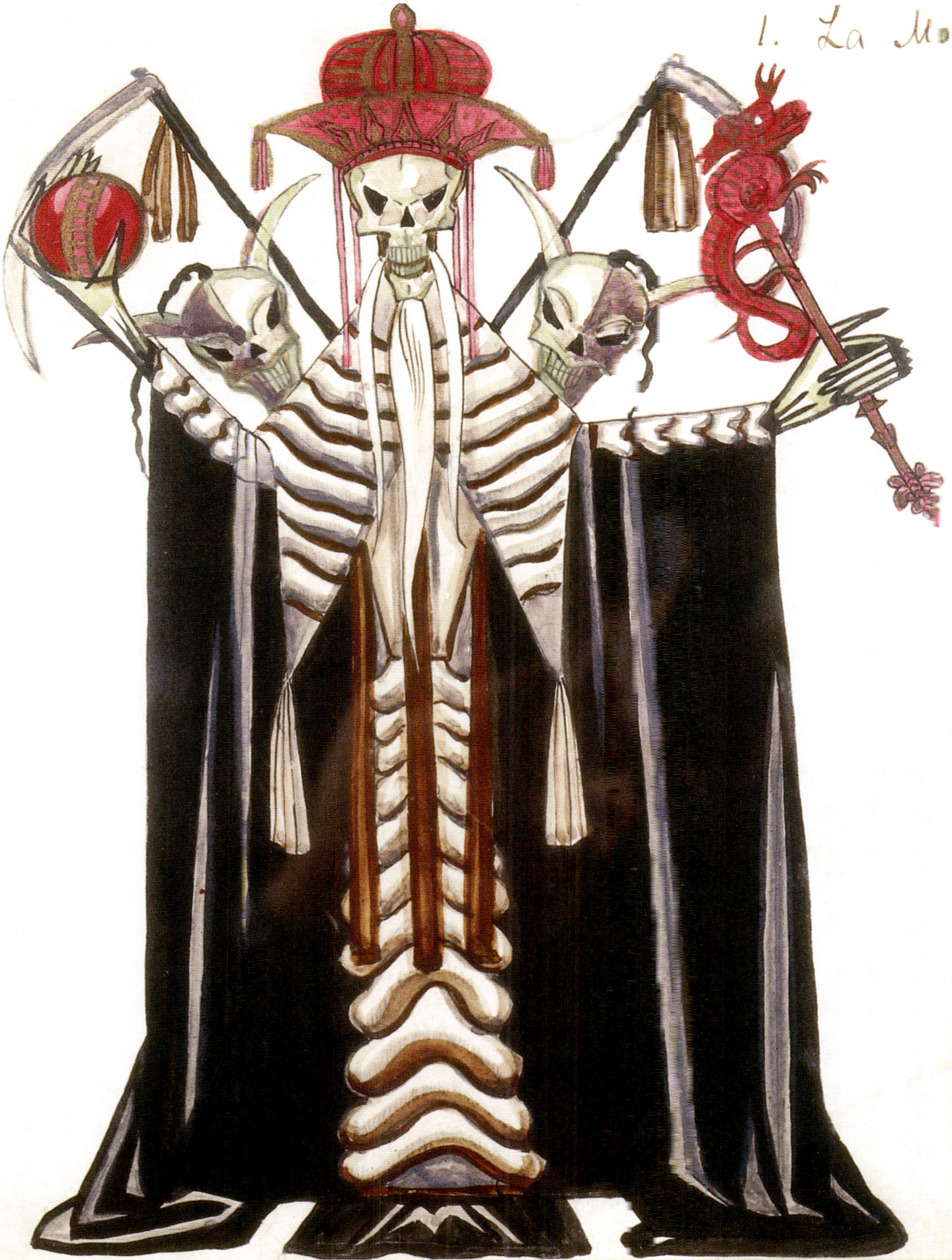

202. Sergei Sudeikin: Costume Design for Death, *Le Rossignol*, ca 1926 (No. 1005)

332. J. Bowlt: *Moscow and St. Petersburg 1900-1920. Art, Life and Culture of the Russian Silver Age,* New York: Vendome, 2008.

333. E. Chernevich: *Graficheskii dizain v Rossii, 1900-1920,* M: Slovo, 2008.

334. P. Fokin and S. Kniazeva: *Serebrianyi vek,* M: Amfora, 2008.

335. E. Murina: *Rannii avangard. Ekspressionizm. Fovizm. Neoprimitivizm,* M: Galart, 2008.

336. G. Pospelov: *Bubnovyi valet,* M: Pinakoteka, 2008.

337. E. Sabashnikova, ed.: *Russkaia zhivopis i grafika kontsa XIX–nachala XX veka,* M: Slovo, 2008.

338. D. Severiukhin: *Staryi khudozhestvennyi Peterburg. Rynok i samoorganizatsiia khudozhnikov ot nachala XVIII veka do 1932 goda,* SP: Mir, 2008.

339. A. Spira: *The Avant-Garde Icon. Russian Avant-Garde Art and the Icon Painting Tradition,* London: Lund Humphries, 2008.

340. I. Svetlov, ed.: *Simvolizm i modern – fenomeny evropeiskoi kultury,* M: Kompaniia Sputnik, 2008.

341. V. Volodarsky et al.: *Russian Painting and Graphic Art of the Late 19th And Early 20th Century,* M: Slovo, 2008.

342. I. Vorobiev: *Russkii avangard. Manifesty, deklaratsii, programmnye stati (1908-1917),* SP: Kompozitor, 2008.

343. O. Yushkova: *Stantsiia bez ostanovki. Russkii avangard 1910-1920-e gody,* M: Galart, 2008.

344. N. Zlydneva: *Izobrazhenie i slovo v ritorike russkoi kultury XX veka,* M: Indrik, 2008.

345. N. Firtich et al.: *Ot Gogolia k "Pobede nad solntsem": Traektoriia russkogo avangarda.* Special issue of *Zapiski russkoi akademicheskoi gruppy v SShA,* New York, 2009, Vol. 35.

346. K. Ichin, comp.: *Avangard i ideologiia: Russkie primery,* Belgrade: Belgrade University, 2009.

347. D. Likhachev: *Russkoe iskusstvo: Ot drevnosti do avangarda,* SP: Iskusstvo-SPb, 2009.

348. G. Sternin: *Ot Repina do Vrubelia,* M: Galart, 2009.

349. V. Terekhina et al., comps.: *Russkii futurizm. Stikhi, stati, vospominaniia,* SP: Poligraf, 2009.

350. L. Tonini, ed.: *Il collezionismo in Russia da Pietro I all'Unione Sovietica,* Formia: Artistic Publishing Company, 2009.

351. *Apollon No. 2* "Ot i do: Traektorii peterburgskogo avangarda", SP: Apollon, 2010.

352. K. Baudin and E. Knorpp, eds.: *Der Kubofuturismus und der Aufbruch der Moderne in Russland. Russische Avantgarde im Museum Ludwig,* Cologne: Wienaud, 2010.

353. Yu. Girin, ed.: *Avangard v kulture XX veka: 1900-1930 gg. Teoriia, istoriia, poetika,* M: MLI RAN, 2010 (two volumes).

354. V. Krichevsky and K. Blagodatskikh: *Modern v pechati,* M: Tipoligon-AB, 2010.

355. E. Kuznetsov: *Grafinia pokidaet bal,* M: Artist. Rezhisser. Teatr, 2010.

356. I. Makaryk and V. Tkacz, eds.: *Modernism in Kyiv, Jubilant Experimentation,* Toronto: University of Toronto Press, 2010.

357. V. Nedoshivin: *Progulki po Serebrianomu veku,* SP: ACT, 2010.

358. G. Romanov: *Mir iskusstva, 1898-1927,* M: Global-viu, 2010.

359. V. Tolstoi, ed.: *Khudozhestvennaia zhizn Sovetskoi Rossii, 1917-1932,* M: Galart, 2010.

360. G. Dadamian: *Atlantida sovetskogo iskusstva 1917-1932,* M: GITIS, 2010.

361. E. Turchinskaia: *Avangard na Dalnem Vostoke. "Zelenaia koshka". Burliuk i drugie,* M: Aleteiia, 2011.

362. T. Harte: *Fast Forward. The Aesthetics and Ideology of Speed in Russian Avant-Garde Culture, 1910-1930,* Madison: University of Wisconsin Press, 2011.

363. V. Chaikovskaia: *K istorii russkogo iskusstva: evreiskaia nota,* M: Tri kvadrata, 2011.

364. A. Uspensky: *Mezhdu avangardom i sotsrealizmom,* M: Iskusstvo-XXI vek, 2011.

365. N. Gurianova: *The Aesthetics of Anarchy. Art and Ideology in the Early Russian Avant-Garde,* Berkeley: University of California Press, 2012.

C. The Modern Stage in Russia

1. A. Bakshy: *The Path of the Modern Russian Stage and Other Essays,* London: Palmer and Heywood, 1916.

2. O. Sayler: *The Russian Theater under the Revolution,* Boston: Little, Brown, 1920.

3. I. Aksenov et al.: *O teatre,* Tver: Tverskoe izdatelstvo, 1922.

4. H. Carter: *The New Theatre and Cinema in Soviet Russia,* New York: Chapman and Dodd, 1924.

5. E. Znosko-Borovsky: *Russkii teatr nachala XX veka,* Prague: Plamia, 1925.

6. A. Redko: *Teatr i evoliutsiia teatralnykh form,* L: Sabashnikov, 1926.

7. J. Gregor and R. Fülöp-Miller: *Das Russische Theater,* Vienna: Amalthea, 1927. English translation: *The Russian Theatre,* London: Harrap, 1930; American edition: New York: Blom, 1968; Spanish translation: *El teatro ruso,* Barcelona: Gili, 1931.

8. H. Carter: *The New Spirit in the Russian Theatre, 1917-1928,* London: Brentano's, 1929.

9. V. Vsevolodsky (Gerngross): *Istoriia russkogo teatra,* L-M: Teakino-pechat, 1929 (two volumes).

10. V. Rafalovich, ed.: *Istoriia sovetskogo teatra,* L: Gosizdat, 1933.

11. K. Derzhavin: *Kniga o Kamernom teatre,* L: Khudozhestvennaia literatura, 1934.

12. L. Okhitovich, ed.: *Kamernyi teatr. Stati, zametki, vospominaniia,* M: Khudozhestvennaia literatura, 1934.

13. T. Komisarjevsky: *The Theatre,* London: Lane, 1935.

14. *Theatre Arts Monthly,* New York, September 1936. Issue devoted to the Soviet theater.

15. Ya. Boiarsky, ed.: *Moskovskii khudozhestvennyi teatr v illiustratsiiakh i dokumentakh 1898-1938,* M: MKhAT, 1938.

16. N. Evreinov: *Le Théâtre en Russie Soviétique,* Paris: Editions techniques et artistiques, 1946.

17. N. Evreinov: *Histoire du Théâtre Russe,* Paris: Chêne, 1947.

18. V. Nemirovich-Danchenko: *Teatralnoe nasledie,* M: Iskusstvo, 1952-54 (two volumes).

19. N. Zograf et al., eds.: *Ocherki istorii russkogo sovetskogo dramaticheskogo teatra,* M: Akademiia nauk, 1954 (two volumes).

20. K. Stanislavsky: *Sobranie sochinenii v 8-mi tomakh,* M: Iskusstvo, 1954-61 (eight volumes).

21. N. Evreinov: *Istoriia russkogo teatra,* New York: Chekhov, 1955.

22. N. Gorchakov: *Istoriia sovetskogo teatra,* New York: Chekhov, 1956.

23. M. Rylsky, ed.: *Ukrainskyi dramatychnyi teatr,* K: Naukova dumka, 1959-67 (two volumes).

24. E. Grosheva, ed.: *Fedor Ivanovich Shaliapin,* M: Iskusstvo, 1976-79 (three volumes; a two-volume edition appeared in 1960).

25. E. Lo Gatto: *Storia del teatro russo,* Florence: Sansoni, 1963.

26. A. Raskina: *Shaliapin i russkie khudozhniki,* L-M: Iskusstvo, 1963.

Дудильщик

203. Vladimir Tatlin: Costume Design for a Pipe Player, *The Emperor Maximilian and His Disobedient Son Adolf*, ca. 1911 (No. 1014)

27. A. Ripellino: *Maiakovski et le théâtre russe d'avant-garde,* Paris: L'Arche, 1965.

28. N. Akimov: *Ne tolko o teatre,* L-M: Iskusstvo, 1966.

29. A. Afanasiev et al., eds.: *Istoriia sovetskogo dramaticheskogo teatra,* M: Nauka, 1966-71 (six volumes).

30. M. Valentei et al., eds.: *Vstrechi s Meierkholdom,* M: VTO, 1967.

31. A. Yufit et al., eds.: *Sovetskii teatr. Dokumenty i materialy 1917-1967,* L: Iskusstvo, 1968-84 (four volumes): Vol. 1, *Russkii sovetskii teatr 1917-1921,* 1968; Vol. 2, *Teatr narodov SSSR 1917-1921,* 1972; Vol. 3, *Russkii sovetskii teatr 1921-1926,* 1975; Vol. 4, *Russkii sovetskii teatr 1926-1932,* 1982.

32. A. Fevralsky et al., eds.: *V. E. Meierkhold. Stati, pisma, rechi, besedy,* M: Iskusstvo, 1968 (two volumes).

33. K. Rudnitsky: *Rezhisser Meierkhold,* M: Nauka, 1969 (see C72).

34. E. Braun, trans. and ed.: *Meyerhold on Theatre,* New York: Hill and Wang, 1969.

35. P. Markov, ed.: *A. Ya. Tairov. Zapiski rezhissera. Stati, besedy, rechi, pisma,* M: VTO, 1970. Includes the Russian text of the 1923 Potsdam edition of *Das Entfesselte Theater* (see C44).

36. E. Krag et al., eds.: *Russisk teater,* Oslo: Aschehung, 1971.

37. A. de Salzmann: *Notes from the Theatre,* Far West Press (city not indicated), 1972.

38. L. Hoffmann and D. Wardetzky, eds.: *Meyerhold, Tairow, Wachtangow: Theateroktober,* Leipzig: Reclam, 1972.

39. B. Picon-Vallin (trans.): *Vsevolod Meyerhold. Ecrits sur le Théâtre,* Lausanne: L'Age d'Homme, 1973-92 (four volumes).

40. B. Picon-Vallin: *Le Théâtre juif soviétique pendant les années vingt,* Lausanne: L'Age d'Homme, 1973.

41. C. Proffer and E. Proffer, eds.: Special issue of *Russian Literature Triquarterly,* Ann Arbor, 1973 devoted to Russian theater.

42. M. Stroeva: *Rezhisserskie iskanniia Stanislavskogo 1898-1917,* M: Nauka, 1973; *Rezhisserskie iskaniia Stanislavskogo 1917-1938;* M: Nauka, 1977.

43. B. Zakhava: *Evgueni Vakhtangov et son école,* M: Progress, 1973.

44. C. Amiard-Chevrel, ed.: *Alexandre Tairov. Le Théâtre libéré,* Lausanne: l'Age d'Homme, 1974. (Cf. C36).

45. V. Dubrovsky: *Moskovskii akademicheskii teatr im. Vl. Maiakovskogo 1922-72.* M: Iskusstvo, 1974.

46. M. Hoover: *Meyerhold. The Art of Conscious Theater,* Amherst: University of Massachusetts, 1974.

47. V. Korzhunova and M. Sitkovetskaia: *Bibliograficheskii ukazatel knig, statei, perevodov, besed, dokladov, vyskazyvanii, pisem V.E. Meierkholda,* M: Iskusstvo, 1974.

48. Z. Udaltsova, ed. *P.A. Markov o teatre,* M: Iskusstvo, 1974-77 (four volumes).

49. A. Fevralsky: *Zapiski rovesnika veka,* M: Sovetskoe iskusstvo, 1976.

50. V. Korzhunova and M. Sitkovetskaia, comps.: *V.E. Meierkhold. Perepiska,* M: Iskusstvo, 1976.

51. D. Zolotnitsky: *Zori teatralnogo Oktiabria,* L: Iskusstvo, 1976.

52. S. Apostolov, ed.: *Stati o tvorchestve N.D. Mordvinova,* M: VTO, 1976.

53. B. Alpers: *Teatralnye ocherk,* M: Iskusstvo, 1977 (two volumes).

54. V. Borovsky: *Moskovskaia opera S.I. Zimina,* M: Iskusstvo, 1977.

55. H. Marshall: *The Pictorial History of the Russian Theater,* New York: Crown, 1977.

56. A. Yufit: *Revoliutsiia i teatr,* L: Iskusstvo, 1977.

57. C. Amey et al.: *Le Théâtre d'agit-prop de 1917 à 1932,* Lausanne: L'Age d'Homme, 1977-78 (four volumes).

58. I. Abalkin, ed.: *Maly teatr 1824-1917,* M: VTO, 1978 (Vol. 1); *Maly teatr 1917-74,* M: VTO, 1984 (Vol. 2).

59. P. Diezel: *Exiltheater in der Sowjetunion 1932-1937,* W. Berlin: Henhschverlag, 1978.

60. E. Groteva, ed.: *Bolshoi teatr Soiuza SSR,* M: Muzyka, 1978.

61. S. Tsimbal, ed.: *Akimov. Teatralnoe nasledie,* L: Iskusstvo, 1978 (two volumes).

62. L. Vendrovskaia et al., eds.: *Tvorcheskoe nasledie V.E. Meierkholda,* M: VTO, 1978.

63. N. Zaitsev et al., eds.: *Problemy teorii i praktiki russkoi sovetskoi rezhissury 1917-1925,* L: Leningradskii Institut teatra, muzyki i kinematografii, 1978.

64. N. Zaitsev et al., eds.: *Problemy teorii i praktiki russkoi sovetskoi rezhissury 1925-1932,* L: Leningradskii institut teatra, muzyki i kinematografii, 1978.

65. D. Zolotnitsky: *Budni i prazdniki teatralnogo Oktiabria,* L: Iskusstvo, 1978.

66. C. Amiard-Chevrel: *Le Théâtre Artistique de Moscou 1889-1917,* Paris: CNRS. 1979.

67. I. Danilova, ed.: *Teatralnoe prostranstvo. Materialy nauchnoi konferentsii,* M: Sovetskii khudozhnik, 1979.

68. I. Petrovskaia: *Teatr i zritel v provintsialnoi Rossii. Vtoraia polovina XIX veka.* L: Iskusstvo, 1979.

69. D. Bablet, ed.: *Les Voies de la Création Théâtrale. Mises en scène années 20 et 30,* Paris: Centre National de la recherche scientifique. Various volumes, 1979 onwards.

70. L. Kleberg: *Teatern som Handling. Sovjetisk avantgard-estetik 1917-27,* Stockholm: Kontrakurs, 1980.

71. C. Mailand-Hausen: *Mejerchol'ds Theaterästhetik in den 1920er Jahren,* Copenhagen: Rosenkilde and Bagger, 1980.

72. K. Rudnitsky: *Meyerhold The Director,* Ann Arbor: Ardis, 1981 (English version of C33).

73. G. Abensour, comp.: *Nicolas Evreinov. L'Apôtre russe de la théâtralité,* Paris : Institut des Etudes Slaves, 1981.

74. E. Proffer, ed.: *Evreinov. Fotobiografiia,* Ann Arbor: Ardis, 1981.

75. K. Rudnitsky, ed.: *Mikhoels. Stati, besedy, rechi. Stati i vospominaniia o Mikhoelse,* M: Iskusstvo, 1981.

76. C. Solivetti: *Konstantin Miklasevskij. La Commedia dell'Arte,* Venice: Marsilio, 1981.

77. L. Senelick: *Gordon Craig's Moscow "Hamlet,"* Westport: Greenwood, 1982.

78. D. Zolotnitsky: *Akademicheskie teatry na putiakh Oktiabria,* L: Iskusstvo, 1982.

79. T. Krutiaeva, comp.: *Teatr opery i baleta imeni S.M. Kirova,* L: Muzyka, 1983.

80. L. Kleberg and N.A. Nilsson, eds.: *Theater and Literature in Russia 1900-1930,* Stockholm: Almqvist and Wiksell, 1984.

81. A. Anisimov: *Teatry Moskvy,* M: Moskovskii rabochii, 1984.

82. Yu. Dmitriev: *Akademicheskii malyi teatr 1917-1941,* M: Iskusstvo, 1984.

83. O. Ivanov and K. Krivitsky: *Vakhtangov i vakhtangovtsy,* M: Moskovskii rabochii, 1984.

84. S. Golub: *Evreinov. The Theatre of Paradox and Transformation,* Ann Arbor: UMI Press, 1985.

85. N. Kuziankina et al, eds.: *Les Kurbas. Stati i vospominaniia o L. Kurbase. Literaturnoe nasledie,* M: Iskusstvo, 1987.

86. E. Zotova and T. Lukina, comps.: *N.P. Okhlopkov. Stati. Vospominaniia,* M: VTO, 1986.

87. A. Schouvaloff: *The Theatre Museum,* London: Scala, 1987.

204. Vladimir Tatlin: Costume Design for a Peasant Girl, *A Life for the Tsar*, 1913 (No. 1015)

88. N. Godzina and I. Shchedrovitskaia: *Po stranitsam teatralnykh rukopisei,* M: Bakhrushin Museum, 1988.

89. K. Rudnitsky: *Russian and Soviet Theater 1905-1932,* New York: Abrams, 1988.

90. O. Poliakova and F. Fainshtein: *Resheniia stsenicheskogo prostranstva. Spektakli Gosudarstvennogo Akademicheskogo tsentralnogo teatra kukol.* M: Soiuz teatralnykh deiatelei, 1988.

91. K. Rudnitsky: *Russkoe rezhisserskoe iskusstvo 1898-1907,* M: Nauka, 1989.

92. S. Carnicke: *The Theatrical Instinct. Nikolai Evreinov and the Russian Theatre of the Twentieth Century,* New York: Lang, 1989.

93. M. Dolinsky, ed.: *Sergei Yutkevich. Sobranie sochinenii v trekh tomakh,* M: Iskusstvo, 1990 (three volumes).

94. I. Rom-Lebedev: *Ot tsyganskogo khora k teatru "Romen,"* M: Iskusstvo, 1990.

95. C. Kelly: *Petrushka,* Cambridge: Cambridge Univiersity Press, 1990.

96. N. Worrall: *Modernism to Realism on the Soviet Stage,* Cambridge: Cambridge University Press, 1991.

97. Anon.: *Teatralnye musei SSSR. Spravochnik,* M: Bakhrushin Museum, 1991.

98. V. Petrova, comp.: *Materialy k istorii teatralnoi kultury Rossii XVII-XX vv.,* SP: Rossiiskaia natsionalnaia biblioteka,1992 (issue No. 3 dedicated to individuals, Vol. 1, A-K; Vol. 2, L-Ya).

99. M. Valentei et al.: *Meierkholdovskii sbornik,* M: Meierkhold Creative Center, 1992 (two volumes).

100. S. Bushueva (intro.): *Russkoe akterskoe iskusstvo XX veka,* SP: RIII, 1992.

101. D. Clayton: *Pierrot in Petrograd,* Montreal: McGill–Queen's University Press, 1993.

102. N. Chechel: *Ukrainske teatralne vidrozheniia,* K: Chechel, 1993 (in Ukrainian).

103. *Teatr,* M, 1993, No. 5. Whole issue devoted to Russian Symbolist theater.

104. V. Zarubin: *Bolshoi teatr. Pervye postanovki oper na russkoi stsene: 1825-1993,* M: Ellis Luck, 1994.

105. C. Amiard-Chevrel: *Les symbolistes russes et le théâtre,* Lausanne: L'Age d'Homme, 1994.

106. S. Golub: *The Recurrence of Fate. Theatre and Memory in Twentieth Century Russia,* Iowa City: University of Iowa, 1994.

107. I. Petrovskaia and V. Somina, eds.: *Teatralnyi Peterburg. Nachalo XVIII veka–Oktiabr 1917 goda,* SP: RIII, 1994.

108. R. Leach: *Vsevolod Meyerhold,* Cambridge: Cambridge University Press, 1994.

109. E. Fradkina: *Zal Dvorianskogo Sobraniia,* SP: Kompozitor, 1994.

110. H. Robinson: *The Last Impresario. The Life, Times and Legacy of Sol Hurok,* New York: Penguin, 1994.

111. E. Poliakova: *Zerkalo stseny. Evoliutsiia stsenicheskogo obraza v russkom teatre XVIII-XIX vv.,* M: Nauka, 1994.

112. G. Titova: *Tvorcheskii teatr i teatralnyi konstruktivizm,* SP: Sankt-Peterburgskaia Gosudarstvennaia Akademiia teatralnogo iskusstva, 1995.

113. N. Rabiniants: *Kamernyi teatr,* SP: Akademiia teatralnogo iskusstva, 1996.

114. I. Sergeeva et al.: *Teatr im. Evgeniia Vakhtangova,* M: Russkaia kniga, 1996.

115. A. Konechnyi: *Byt i zrelishchnaia kultura Sankt-Peterburga-Petograda XVIII–nachalo XX veka, Materialy i bibliografii,* SP: Rossiisskii Institut istorii iskusstv, 1997.

116. A. Bartoshevich et al., eds.: *Dialog kultur: Problema vzaimodeistviia russkogo i mirovogo teatra XX veka,* SP: Bulanin, 1997.

117. O. Radishcheva: *Nemirovich-Danchenko / Stanislavsky. Istoriia teatralnykh otnoshenii 1897-1908,* M: Artist, Rezhisser. Teatr, 1997.

118. T. Smirnova: *Natsionalnye teatry Petograda-Leningrada 1917-1941,* SP: Nestor, 1997.

119. T. Zabozlaeva: *Russkie imperatory i Alexandrinskii teatr — vzgliad iz-za kulis,* SP: Borei, 1997.

120. N. Pesochinsky et al., comps.: *Meierkhold v russkoi teatralnoi kritike 1892-1918,* M: Artist. Rezhisser. Teatra, 1997.

121. *Mnemozina,* M, 1997-2009 (four issues).

122. E. Deich, ed.: *Nikolai Evreinov. V shkole ostroumiia,* M: Iskusstvo, 1998.

123. V. Koliazin: *Tairov, Meierkhold i Germaniia / Piskator, Brekht i Rossiia,* M: Gitis, 1998.

124. *Theater,* New Haven, 1998. Special number dedicated to Vsevolod Meierkhold.

125. V. Varunets, ed.: *I.F. Stravinsky. Perepiska s russkimi korrespondentami,* M: Kompozitor, 1998 (Vol. 1); 2000 (Vol. 2).

126. I. Vakar, ed.: *Teatr i russkaia kultura na rubezhe XIX-XX vekov,* M: Bakhrushin Museum, 1998.

127. A. Wachtel, ed.: *Petrushka. Sources and Contexts,* Evanston: North Western University Press, 1998.

128. V. Kozintseva and Ya. Butovsky: *Perepiska G.M. Kozintseva,* M: Artist. Rezhisser. Teatr, 1998.

129. S. Carnicke: *Stanislavsky in Focus,* Amsterdam: Harwood Academic Publishers, 1998.

130. O. Feldman, ed.: *N.M. Tarabukin o V.E. Meierkholde,* M: OGI, 1998.

131. B. Golubovsky: *Bolshie malenkie teatry,* M: Sabashnikovy, 1998.

132. B. Zingerman et al.: *V.E. Meierkhold. Nasledie,* M: OGI, 1998 (Vol. 1); 2000 (Vol. 2).

133. M. Geizer: *Mikhoels. Zhizn i smert,* M: Geizer, 1998.

134. A. Smeliansky et al., eds.: *Moskovskii Khudozhestvennyi teatr. Sto let,* M: Moscow Art Theater, 1998 (two volumes). English translation C158.

135. M. Svetaeva, ed.: *V.A. Teliakovsky. Dnevnik direktora Imperatorskikh teatrov 1898-1901,* M: Artist, Rezhisser. Teatr, 1998.

136. A. Bretanitskaia: *Petr Suvchinsky i ego vremia,* M: Kompozitor, 1999.

137. O. Feldman, ed.: *Meierkholdovskii sbornik,* M: OGI, 1998-2000 (two volumes).

138. Yu. Gamalei: *"Mariinka" i moia zhizn,* SP: Papirus, 1999.

139. D. Korolev: *Ocherki iz istorii izdaniia i rasprostraneniia teatralnoi knigi v Rossii XIX–nachala XX vekov,* SP: Russian National Library, 1999.

140. A. Kolganova, comp.: *Solomon Mikhoels,* M: RGBI, 1999.

141. O. Krasilnikova: *Istoriia ukrainskogo teatru XX storichchia,* K: Libid, 1999.

142. T. Kotovich: *Igra s koordinatami smyslov,* Vitebsk-Minsk: Belorussian State Dramatic Academic Theater, 1999.

143. S. Serova: *Teatralnaia kultura Serebrianogo veka v Rossii i khudozhestvennaia traditsiia Vostoka,* M: Institut vostokovedeniia, 1999.

144. D. Zolotnitsky: *Sergei Radlov. Rezhissura. Sudba,* SP: RIII, 1999.

145. J. Buckler: *The Literary Lorgnette. Attending Opera in Imperial Russia,* Stanford: Stanford University Press, 2000.

146. S. Carnicke: *Stanislavsky in Focus,* Amsterdam: Harwood Academic Publishers, 2000.

147. G. Dadamian: *Teatr v kulturnoi zhizni Rossii (1914-1917),* M: Dar-Ekspo, 2000.

148. Yu. Dmitriev: *Teatralnaia Moskva (1920-e gody),* M: GII, 2000.

205. Serge Tchehonine: Costume with Celestial Motifs for a Clown, 1922 (No. 1029)

149. V. Ivanov: *Russkie sezony teatra "Gabima"*, M: Artist. Rezhisser. Teatr, 2000.
150. G. Kovalenko: *Russkii avangard 1910-kh-1920-kh godov i teatr*, SP: Bulanin, 2000.
151. G. Serova: *Teatralnaia kultura Serebrjanogo veka*, M: Institut Vostokovedeniia, 2000.
152. *Teatr/Theater* (No. 1 only), Idylwild, CA, 2000.
153. J. Veidlinger: *The Moscow State Yiddish Theater*, Bloomington: Indiana University Press, 2000.
154. A. Vislova: *"Serebrianyi vek" kak teatr: Fenomen teatralnosti v iskusstve rubezha XIX-XX vv.*, M: Gosudartvennyi institut kulturologii, 2000
155. V. Borovsky: *A Triptych from the Russian Theatre*, London: Hurst, 2001.
156. A. Kolganova, ed.: *Sudba evreiskogo teatra v Rossii. XX vek*, M: Russian State Art Library, 2001.
157. R. Messina: *Giselle*, Rieti: Comune di Rieti, 2001.
158. A. Smeliansky et al., eds.: *Moscow Art Theatre. One Hundred Years*, M: MKhAT, 2001. Translation of C134.
159. O. Calvarese, ed.: *La Febbre del Teatro. Pagine sconosciute dell'avanguardia russa*. Special issue of *Culture Teatrali*, Bologna, 2002, No. 6.
160. A. Dekhtereva and E. Kostina, eds.: *Za zanavesom veka. Issledovaniia i publikatsii po iskusstvu russkoi stsenografii XX veka*, M: Russkoe slovo, 2004.
161. D. Utsky: *Meierhold. Roman s sovetskoi vlastiu*, M: Agraf, 2000.
162. N. Pivovarova et al.: *Russikii teatr*, M: Interros, 2004 (two volumes).
163. D. Varygin et al.: *Ermitazhnyi teatr*, SP: Slaviia, 2005.
164. V. Maksimova: *Teatra radostnye teni*, SP: Bulanin, 2006.
165. V. Dmitrievsky: *Teatr i zritel: Otechestvennyi teatr v sisteme otnoshenii stseny i publiki: Ot istokov do nachala XX veka*, SP: Bulanin, 2007.
166. A. Egidio: *Aleksandr Tairov e il Kamernyj teatr di Mosca, 1907-1922*, Roma: Bulzoni, 2007.
167. G. Emelianova-Zubovskaia: *Zhizel*, SP: Peterburg XX vek, 2007.
168. B. Harshav: *The Moscow Yiddish Theater*, New Haven: Yale University Press, 2007.
169. V. Ivanov: *Goset: Politika i iskusstvo 1919-1928*, M: GITIS, 2007.
170. V. Maksimova, ed.: *PRO SCENIUM: Voprosy teatra*, M: KomKniga, 2007.
171. V. Pronina, comp.: *Chastnaia opera v Rossii*, M: Pokoleniia, 2007.
172. I. Solovieva: *Khudozhestvennyi teatr: Zhizn i prikliucheniia idei*, M: MKhAT, 2007.
173. N. Vagapova: *Russkaia teatralnaia emigratsiia v Tsentralnoi Evrope i na Balkanakh: Ocherki*, M: Aleteiia, 2007.
174. O. Radishcheva and V. Shingareva, eds.: *Moskovskii khudozhestvennyi teatr v russkoi teatralnoi kritike 1897-1943*, M: Artist. Rezhisser. Teatr, Vol. 1, 2007; Vols. 2-3, 2010 (three volumes).
175. N. Avtonomova et al., eds.: *Avangard i teatr 1910-1920-kh godov. Sbornik*, M: Nauka, 2008.
176. A. Elkana: *Aleksandr-Alisa-Kamernyi teatr*, M: KRUK-Prestizh, 2009.
177. T. Kuzovleva, comp.: *Sankt-Peterburgskaia gosudarstvennaia Akademiia teatralnogo iskusstva. Stranitsy istorii 1779-2009*, SP: St. Petersburg State Academy of Theatrical Art, 2009.
178. M. Rolf: *Sovetskie massovye prazdniki*, M:ROSSPEN, 2009.
179. E. Streltsova: *Chastnyi teatr v Rossii ot istokov do nachala XX veka*, M: GITIS, 2009.
180. N. Afonin et al.: *Vysshee teatralnoe uchilishche (institut) imeni M.S. Shchepkina. Dva veka istorii v illiustratsiiakh*, M: Tonchu, 2010.
181. V. Dmitrievsky: *Formirovanie otnoshenii stseny i zala v otechestvennom teatre v 1917-1930 gg.*, M: RATI-GITIS, 2010.
182. I. Solovieva and A. Smeliansky, eds.: *MKhAT Vtoroi. Opyt vosstanovleniia biografii*, M: Moskovskii Khudozhestvennyi teatr, 2010.
183. S. Sboeva: *Tairov: Evropa i Amerika*, M: Artist. Rezhisser. Teatr, 2010.
184. O. Haldey: *Mamontov's Private Opera*, Bloomington: Indiana University Press, 2010.
185. P. Volkova, ed.: *Evgenii Vakhtangov: Na puti k Turandot*, M: Zebra, 2010.
186. L. Bogov and A. Smeliansky: *Nash Chekhov. Proizvedeniia A.P. Chekhova na stsene Moskovskogo khudozhestvennogo teatra (1980-2010 gody)*, M: Moscow Art Theater, 2010.
187. V. Ivanov, ed.: *Evgenii Vakhtangov. Dokumenty i svidetelstva*, M: Indrik, 2011 (two volumes).
188. Yu. Orlov: *Moskovskii khudozhestvennyi teatr, 1898-1917*, M: Tvorchestvo, 2011.
189. M. Tereshina, ed.: *Istoriia russkogo teatra*, M: EKSMO-Press, 2011.
190. E. Binevich: *Karikaturisty idut v teatr*, SP: Petropolis, 2011.
191. A. Bobyleva: *Zapadnoevropeiskii i russkii teatr XIX-XX vekov*, M: GITIS, 2011.
192. Z. Udaltsova: *MKhAT Vtoroi. Svidetelstva i dokumenty 1926-1936*, M: MKhAT, 2011.
193. A. Kolganova, comp.: *Istoriia teatra v arkhivnykh i knizhnykh sobraniiakh*, M: Tri kvadrata, 2011.

D. The Russian Ballet

Note: Only a small selection of titles is provided here. For detailed bibliographical information on twentieth-century Russian ballet, the reader may wish to consult the bibliographical sections of D14, D19 and D26 in particular.

1. W. Propert: *The Russian Ballet in Western Europe 1909-1920*, London: Lane, 1921.
2. *La Revue Musicale*, Paris, 1930, 1 December. Special issue devoted to the Ballets Russes de Serge de Diaghilev.
3. W. Propert: *The Russian Ballet 1921-1929*, London: Lane, 1931.
4. C. Beaumont: *The Monte Carlo Ballet*, London: Beaumont, 1934.
5. C. Beaumont: *Michael Fokine and His Ballets*, London: Beaumont, 1935 (reprinted New York: Dance Horizons, 1981).
6. P. Lieven: *The Birth of Ballets Russes*, London: Allen and Unwin, 1936 (reprinted 1956).
7. C. Beaumont: *The Diaghilev Ballet in London*, London: Maclehose, 1940 (reprinted in an expanded edition as *Bookseller at the Ballet. Memoirs 1891-1929*, London: Beaumont, 1975).
8. S. Lifar: *Serge Diaghilev, His Life, His Work, His Legend*. London: Putnam, 1940. English version of the Russian edition (*Diagilev i s Diagilevym*, Paris: Dom knigi, 1939) republished as *Diagilev*, SP: Kompozitor, 1993.
9. J. Gregor: *Kulturgeschichte des Balletts*, Vienna: Gallus, 1944.
10. B. Kleiber: *Russisk Ballett*, Oslo: Nasjonalforlaget, 1946.
11. S. Grigoriev: *The Diaghilev Ballet 1909-1929*, London: Constable, 1953 (reprinted New York: Dance Horizons, n.d.).
12. A. Haskell and W. Nouvel: *Diaghileff. His Artistic and Private Life*, London: Gollancz, 1955.

206. Serge Tchehonine: Costume Design for a Clown with Protuding Belly, 1926 (No. 1038)

13. R. Buckle: *In Search of Diaghilev*, New York: Nelson, 1956.
14. V. Krasovskaia: *Russkii baletnyi teatr vtoroi poloviny XIX veka*, L-M: Iskusstvo, 1963.
15. N. Roslavleva: *Era of the Russian Ballet*, London: Gollancz, 1966.
16. A. Haskell: *Ballet Russe*, London: Weidenfeld and Nicolson, 1968.
17. B. Kochno: *Diaghilev and the Ballets Russes*, New York: Harper and Row, 1970.
18. R. Buckle: *Nijinsky*, London: Weidenfeld and Nicolson, 1971.
19. V. Krasovskaia: *Russkii baletnyi teatr nachala XX veka*. Vol. 1. *Khoreografy*, L: Iskusstvo, 1971; Vol. 2. *Tantsovshchiki*, L: Iskusstvo, 1972.
20. J. Percival: *The World of Diaghilev*, London: Studio Vista, 1971.
21. A. Haskell: *Balletomane at Large*, London: Heinemann, 1972.
22. F. Lopukhov: *Khoreograficheskie otkrovennosti*, M: Iskusstvo, 1972.
23. C. Spencer: *The World of Serge Diaghilev*, London: Elek, 1974.
24. N. MacDonald: *Diaghilev*, London: Weidenfeld and Nicolson, 1979.
25. V. Krasovskaia: *Sovetskii baletnyi teatr*, M: Iskusstvo, 1976.
26. R. Buckle: *Diaghilev*, London: Weidenfeld and Nicolson, 1979.
27. V. Krasovskaya: *Nijinsky*, New York: Schirmer, 1979.
28. E. Surits: *Khoreograficheskoe iskusstvo dvadtsatykh godov*, M: Iskusstvo, 1979. English translation D44.
29. J. Andersen: *The One and Only: The Ballet Russe de Monte Carlo*, New York: Dance Horizons, 1981.
30. J. and R. Lazzarini: *Pavlova — Repertoire of a Legend*, New York: Schirmer, 1981.
31. K. Walker: *De Basil's Ballets Russes*, London: Hutchinson, 1982.
32. R. Buckle: *In the Wake of Diaghilev*, New York: Holt, Rinehart and Winston, 1983.
33. O. Rozanova: *Elena Liukom*, L: Iskusstvo, 1983.
34. N. Chernova et al.: *Kasian Goleizovsky. Zhizn i tvorchestvo*, M: VTO, 1984.
35. U. Steiner: *Tanz und Karikatur*, Cologne: Steiner, 1984.
36. P. Migel: *Great Ballet Stars in Historic Photographs*. New York: Dover, 1985.
37. G. Shmakov: *Great Russian Dancers*, New York: Knopf, 1985.
38. S. Volkov: *Balanchine's Tchaikovsky*, New York: Simon and Schuster, 1985.
39. M. de Cossart: *Ida Rubinstein (1885-1960). A Theatrical Life*, Liverpool: Liverpool University Press, 1987.
40. R. Buckle: *George Balanchine Ballet Master*, New York: Random House, 1988.
41. M. Pozharskaia: *Russkie sezony v Parizhe*, M: Iskusstvo 1988. English translation: *The Art of the Ballets Russes*, London: Aurum, 1990.
42. L. Garafola: *Diaghilev's Ballets Russes*, New York: Oxford University Press, 1989.
43. R. Shead: *Ballets Russes*, Secaucus, NJ: Wellfleet, 1989.
44. E. Souritz: *Soviet Choreographers in the 1920s*, Durham, NC: Duke University Press, 1990. English translation of D28.
45. R.J. Wiley: *A Century of Russian Ballet*, Oxford: Clarendon Press, 1990.
46. V. García-Márquez: *The Ballets Russes. Colonel de Basil's Ballets Russes de Monte Carlo 1932-1952*, New York: Knopf, 1990.
47. N. Baburina and M. Avvakumov: *Russkii sovetskii balet v plakate*, M: Panorama, 1991.
48. N. Tikhonova: *Ballets Russes. Devushka v sinem*, M: Art, 1992.
49. A. Volynsky: *Kniga likovanii*, M: Artist. Rezhisser. Teatr, 1992

(reprint of the 1925 edition with introduction by V. Gaevsky; second reprint: *Kniga likovani. Azbuka klassicheskogo tantsa*, M: Planeta muzyki, 2008).
50. T. Kasatkina, comp.: *Aisadora: Gastroli v Rossii*, M: Artist. Rezhisser. Teatr, 1992.
51. M. Kahane et al.: *Les Ballets Russes à l'Opéra*, Paris: Bibliothèque Nationale, 1992.
52. M. Plissetskaia: *Moi, Maia Plissetskaia*, Paris: Gallimard, 1994.
53. S. Snezhko and V. Shleev, comps.: Sergei Lifar. *Stradnye gody s Diagilevym. Vospominaniia*, K: Muza, 1994.
54. A. Dunkan [Duncan]: *Moia ispoved*, Minsk: Universitetskoe, 1994.
55. D. Cherkassky: *Zapiski baletomana*, M: Artist. Rezhisser. Teatr, 1994.
56. I. Nestiev: *Diaghilev i muzykalnyi teatr XX veka*, M: Muzyka, 1994.
57. V. García-Márquez: *Massine*, New York: Knopf, 1995.
58. C. Dumais-Lvowski, trans.: *Nijinski-Cahiers. Version Non Expurgée*, Le Méjan: Actes Sud, 1995.
59. O. Petrov: *Russkaia baletnaia kritika vtoroi poloviny XIX veka: Peterburg*, Ekaterinburg: Sfera, 1995.
60. O. Levenkov, comp.: *Permskii ezhegodnik. Khoreografiia*, Perm: Arabesk, 1995; 1996.
61. C. Jeschke, ed.: *Spiegelungen. Ballets Russes / Kunst / Reception*, Leipzig: Institut für Theaterwissenschaft, 1997.
62. E. Surits (intro.): *Leonid Miasin. Moia zhizn v balete*, M: Artist. Rezhisser.Teatr, 1997.
63. C. Jeschke et al.: *Spielungen. Die Ballets Russes und die Künste*, Leipzig: Institut für Theaterwissenschaft, 1997.
64. S. Carandini and E. Vaccarini: *La Generazione Danzante: L'arte del movimento in Europa del primo Novecento*, Rome: Di Giacomo, 1997.
65. Yu. Gromov: *Tanets i ego rol v vospitanii plasticheskoi kultury aktera*, SP: Sankt-Peterburgskii gumanitarnyi universitet profsoiuzov, 1997.
66. N. Alovert: *Balet Mariinskogo teatra. Vchera, segodnia, XXI vek...*, SP: GPU, 1997.
67. J. Drummond, ed.: *Speaking of Diaghilev*, London: Faber and Faber, 1997.
68. E. Diagileva: *Semeinaia zapis o Diagilevykh*, SP/Perm: Bulanin, 1998.
69. M. Plissetskaja et al: *Russisches Ballett. Kunst und Choreographie*, Bournemouth: Parkstone, 1998.
70. R. Messina, ed.: *Ritratto di Nižinskij da Fauno*, Rieti, Italy: Biblioteca Paroniana, 1998.
71. V. Kiselev: *A Bouquet for Tamara Karsavina*, M: Kompozitor, 1998.
72. N. Baer and L. Garafola, eds.: *The Ballets Russes and Its World*, New Haven: Yale University Press, 1999.
73. V. Krasovskaia: *Pavlova, Nizhinsky, Vaginova*, M: Agraf, 1999.
74. A. Alekseeva: *Dvigatsia i dumat*, M: Prest, 2000.
75. V. Gaevsky: *Dom Petipa*, M: Artist. Rezhisser. Teatr, 2000.
76. E. Surits and E. Belova, eds.: *Baletmeister A.A. Gorsky*, SP: Bulanin, 2000.
77. V. Teider: *Kasian Goleizovsky. "Iosif Prekrasnyi"*, M: Nauka, 2001.
78. O. Amirgamzaeva and Yu. Usova: *Samye znamenitye mastera baleta Rossii*, M: Veche, 2002.
79. S. Jordan, trans.: *Fedor Lopukhov. Writings on Ballet and Music*, Seattle: University of Washington Press, 2002.
80. V. Fédorovski: *L'Histoire secrète des Ballets russes*, Paris: Rocher, 2002. Russian version D82.

207. Serge Tchehonine: Costume Design for a Clown Wearing a Woman's Shoe, 1927 (No. 1041)

81. A. Degen and I. Stupnikov: *Peterburgskii balet, 1903-2003. Spravochnik,* M. 2003.

82. V. Fedorovsky: *Sergej Djagilev ili zakulisnaia istoriia russkogo baleta,* SP: Eksmo-Press, 2003. Russian translation of D80.

83. A. Ignatenko, comp.: *Marius Petipa. Memuary baletmeistera,* SP: Soiuz khudozhnikov, 2003.

84. E. Kurilenko: *Problema khudozhestvennogo sinteza v baletnom spektakle,* M: GII, 2003.

85. A. Laskin: *Dolgoe puteshestvie s Diagilevym,* Ekaterinburg: U-Faktoriia, 2007.

86. G. Murygin: *S.P. Diagilev,* Novosibirsk: Nauka, 2003.

87. E. Surits: *Artist baleta Mikhail Mikhailovich Mordkin,* M: Editorial URSS, 2003.

88. E. Zharnitsky, ed.: Natalia Ignatieva-Trukhanova: *Na stsene i za kulisami: vospominaniia,* M: Zakharov, 2003.

89. G. Dobrovolskaia: *Mikhail Fokin. Russkii period,* SP: Giperion, 2004.

90. S. Press: *Prokofiev's Ballets for Diaghilev,* Ashgate: Aldershot and Burlington, 2006.

91. Yu. Smirnov, comp.: *Baletmeister Yurii Grigorovich: Stati. Issledovaniia. Razmyshleniia,* M: Foliant, 2006.

92. E. Tomina-Petrova: *Zhemchuzhina russkogo baleta - Olga Spesivtseva,* M: Logos. 2006.

93. O. Brezgin, comp.: *Persona Diagileva v khudozhestvennoi kulture Rossii, Zapadnoi Evropy i Ameriki,* Perm: Perm State Art Gallery, 2007.

94. I. Kuznetsov and A. Lapidus, comps.: *Sergei Pavlovich Diagilev 1872-1929. Materialy k bibliografii,* SP: SPbGUKI, 2007.

95. S. Dubkova: *Elistatel'nyi mir baleta,* M: Belyi gorod, 2007.

96. O. Levenkov et al.: *S.P. Diagilev i sovremennaia kultura,* Perm, 2007 onwards.

97. V. Gaevsky: *Khoreograficheskie portrety,* M: Artist. Rezhisser. Teatr, 2008.

98. L. Iovleva, ed.: Special issue of *Tretiakovskaia galereia,* M, 2009, No. 3.

99. M. Meilakh: *Evterpa, ty? Khudozhestvennye zametki. Besedy s artistami russkoi emigratsii,* M: NLO, 2008 (Vol. 1: Ballet).

100. S. Nuridzhanova: *K istorii Geptakhora. Ot Aisedory Dunkan k Muzykalnomu dvizheniiu,* SP: DNK, 2008.

101. S. Rabinowitz, ed.: *Ballet's Magic Kingdom. Selected Writings on Dance in Russia, 1911-1925, by Akim Volynsky,* New Haven: Yale University Press, 2008.

102. V. Gurkov: *Bludnyi syn Sergei Diagilev,* M: Tsentr sovremennogo iskusstva, 2009.

103. L. Iovleva, ed.: *Tretiakovskaia galereia/Tretiakov Gallery,* 2009, No. 3. Whole issue devoted to the Ballets Russes, dance and stage design.

104. S. Kaufman: *Bolshoi balet. Vzgliad iznutri,* M, 2009.

105. S. Khudekov: *Illustrirovannaia istoriia tantsa,* M: EKSMO-Press, 2009 (new printing).

106. S. Khudekov: *Vseobshchaia istoriia tantsa,* M: EKSMO-Press, 2009 (new printing).

107. V. Krasovskaia: *Zapadnoevropeiskii baletnyi teatr,* SP: Lan, 2009.

108. I. Krotevich: *Ekho russkikh sezonov,* SP: Hermitage, 2009.

109. A. Pleshcheev: *Nash balet,* SP: Lan, 2009.

110. G. Pospelov and E. Surits: *Istoriia "Russkogo baleta", realnaia i fantasticheskaia, v risunkakh, memuarakh i fotografiiakh Mikhaila Larionova,* M: Interros, 2009.

111. S. Scheijen: *Sergej Diagilev,* Amsterdam: Prometheus; London: Profile, 2009.

112. Yu. Abdokov: *Muzykalnaia poetika khoreografii,* M: RATI-GITIS, 2009.

113. A. Aldzheranov: *Anna Pavlova,* M: Tsentrpoligraf, 2009.

114. J. Homans: *Apollo's Angels. A History of Ballet,* New York: Random House, 2010.

115. A. Lavrov et al., comps.: *Ot slova k telu. Sbornik statei k 60-letiiu Yuriia Tsiviana,* M: NLO, 2010.

116. N. Misler: *Vnachale bylo telo,* M: Iskusstvo XXI vek, 2010.

117. S. Naborshchikova: *Videt muzyku, slyshat tanets: Stravinskii i Balanchin: K probleme muzykalno-khoreograficheskogo sinteza,* M: Moscow Conservatoire, 2010.

118. Yu. Tsivian: *Na podstupakh k karpalistike. Dvizhenie i zhest v literature, iskusstve i kino,* M: NLO, 2010.

119. V. Vanslov: *V mire baleta,* M: Vanslov, 2010.

120. O. Zakharova: *Russkii bal XVIII-nachala XX veka,* M: Tsentropoligraf, 2010.

121. N. Chernyshev-Melnik: *Sergei Diagilev. Operedivshii vremia,* M: Molodaia gvardiia. 2010.

122. L. Garafola and J. Bowlt, eds.: *Sergei Diaghilev and the Ballets Russes: A Tribute to the First Hundred Years.* Special issue of *Experiment,* Los Angeles and Leiden, 2011.

123. O. Kovalik: *Povsednevnaia zhizn balerin russkogo imperatorskogo teatra,* M: Molodaia gvardiia, 2011.

124. V. Pasiutinskaia: *Puteshestvie v mir tantsa,* SP: Aleteiia, 2011.

125. I. Sirotkina: *Svobodnoe dvizhenie i plasticheskii tanets v Rossii,* M: NLO, 2011.

126. V. Kotykhov: *Vospominaniia o tantse,* M: Kanon-Plius, 2012.

E. Music-Hall, the Cabaret, the Circus, the Puppet Theater, and the Early Movie Industry in Russia

For a comprehensive listing of relevant actors, artists, and producers see A54.

1. N. Efros: *Teatr "Letuchaia mysh" N.F. Balieva,* M: Solntse Rossii, 1918.

2. B. Zemenkov: *Oformlenie sovetskikh karnavalov i demonstratsii,* M: AKhRR 1930.

3. N. Efimova: *Adventures of a Russian Puppet Theatre,* Birmingham, Michigan: Puppetry Imprints, 1935.

4. J. Leyda: *Kino,* London: Allen and Unwin, 1960.

5. Yu. Dmitriev: *Sovetskii tsirk. Ocherki istorii 1917-1941,* M: Iskusstvo, 1963.

6. N. Smirnova: *Sovetskii teatr kukol,* M: Akademiia nauk, 1963.

7. G. Khaichenko: *Russkii narodyi teatr kontsa XIX–nachala XX veka,* L: Nauka, 1975.

8. L. Kuleshov and A. Khokhlova: *50 let v kino,* M: Iskusstvo, 1975.

9. D. Moldavsky: *S Maiakovskim v teatre i kino. Kniga o Sergee Yutkeviche,* M: VTO, 1975.

10. G. Rapisarda: *Cinema e avanguardia in Unione Sovietica,* Rome: Officina Edizioni, 1975.

11. A Birkos: *Soviet Cinema. Directors and Films,* Hamden: Archon, 1976.

12. M. Khazinov: "Teatr 'Siniaia ptitsa' v Berline v 1921 g." in *Russkaia mysl,* Paris, 1976, 11 March.

13. V. Kukaretin: *Nasledniki "Sinei bluzy,"* M: Molodaia gvardiia, 1976.

14. M. Mestechkin: *V teatre i v tsirke,* M: Iskusstvo, 1976.

15. E. Uvarova, ed.: *Russkaia sovetskaia estrada,* Vol. 1: 1917-29, M: Iskusstvo, 1976; Vol. 2: *Russkaia sovetskaia estrada:* 1930-45, M: Iskusstvo, 1977.

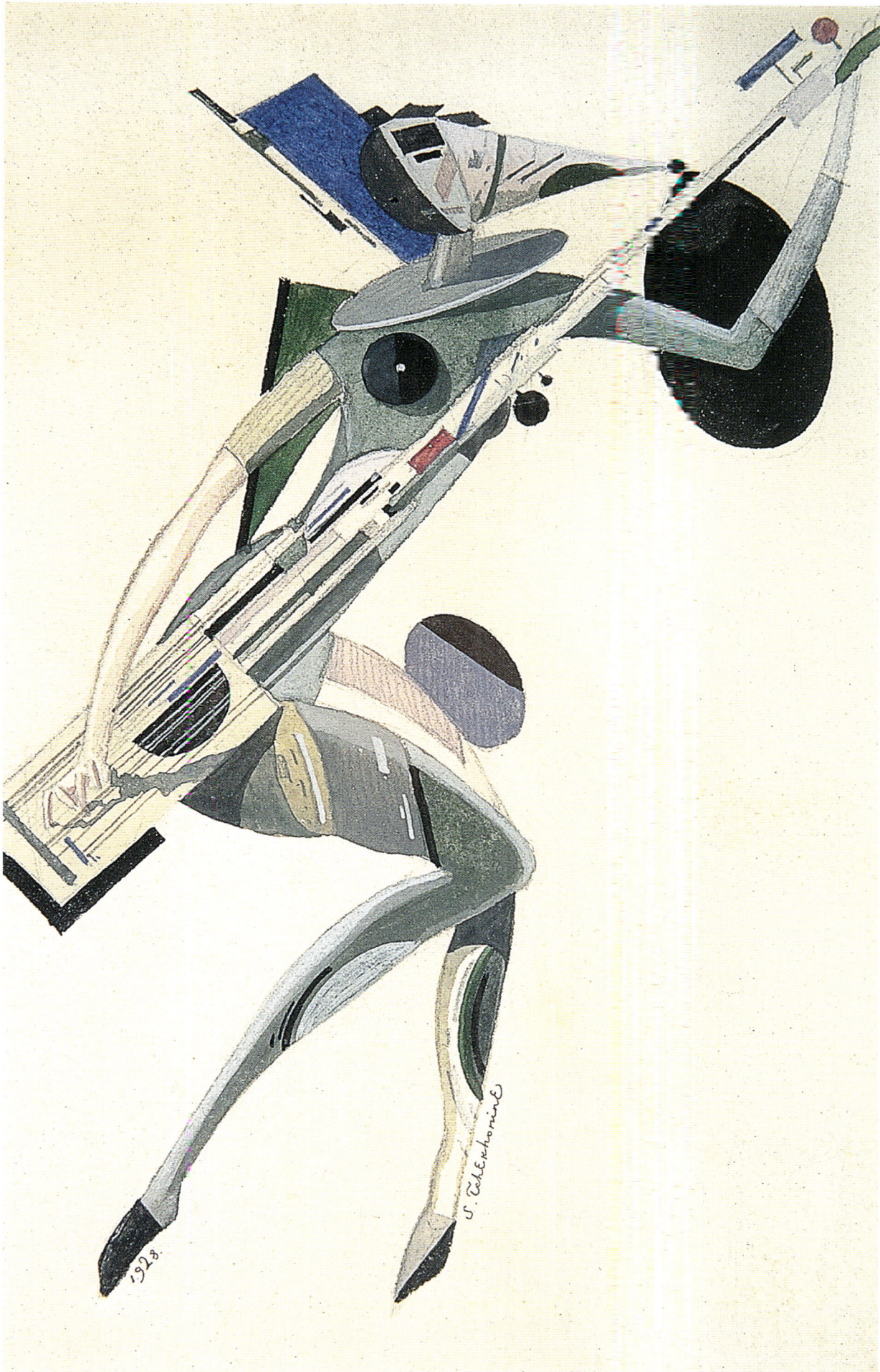

208. Serge Tchehonine: Costume Design for a Guitar Player, 1928 (No. 1043)

16. N. Zorkaia: *Na rubezhe stoletii. U istokov massovogo iskusstva v Rossii 1900-1910 godov*, M: Nauka, 1976.

17. K. Kazansky: *Cabaret Russe*, Paris: Orban, 1978.

18. I. Ivanov-Vano, ed.: *Khudozhniki sovetskogo multfilma*, M: Sovetskii khudozhnik, 1978.

19. G. Wolf, J. Renner, and W. Schmidt: *Elena Liessner-Blomberg oder die Geschichte vom Blauen Vogel*, Berlin: Der Morgen, 1978.

20. R. Taylor: *The Politics of the Soviet Cinema 1917-1929*, Cambridge: Cambridge University, 1979.

21. I. Safrazbekian: *Nikita Baliev and His Theatre "The Bat,"* Erevan: The Armenian Theatrical Society, 1980 (in Armenian).

22. V. Kisunko, ed.: *A. V. Lunacharsky o muzyke i muzykalnom teatre*, M: Muzyka, 1981.

23. S. Obraztsov: *Moia professiia*, M: Iskusstvo, 1981.

24. G. Kozintsev: *Sobranie sochinenii v 5 tt.*, L: Iskusstvo, 1982-84 (five volumes).

25. J. Leyda and Z. Voynow: *Eisenstein at Work*, New York: Pantheon, 1982.

26. S. Obraztsova: *Estafeta iskusstv*, M: Iskusstvo, 1983.

27. E. Uvarova: *Estradnyi teatr: miniatiury, obozreniia, miuzik-kholly (1917-1945)*, M: Iskusstvo, 1983.

28. J. Bowlt: "When Life Was a Cabaret" in *Art News*, New York, 1984, December, pp. 122-27.

29. A. Durov: *V zhizni i na arene*, M: Iskusstvo, 1984.

30. A. Michelson, ed.: *Kino-Eye. The Writings of Dziga Vertov*, Berkeley: University of California, 1984.

31. A. Nekrylova: *Russkie narodnye gorodskie prazdniki, uveseleniia i zrelishcha. Konets XVIII–nachalo XX veka*, L: Iskusstvo, 1984.

32. A. Parnis and R. Timenchik: "Programmy 'Brodiachei sobaki'" in I. Andronnikov et al. eds.: *Pamiatniki kultury. Novye otkrytiia. Ezhegodnik 1983*, L: Nauka, 1985, pp. 160-257.

33. P. Carden, ed.: *Canadian-American Slavic Studies*, Irvine, CA., 1985, Vol. 19, No. 4. Special issue devoted to performance, cabaret, etc. in Russia.

34. N. Sheremetievskaia: *Tanets na estrade*, M: Iskusstvo, 1985.

35. L. Senelick: "Nikita Baliev's Le Théâtre de la Chauve-Souris: An Avant-Garde Theater" in *Dance Research Journal*, Edinburgh, 1986-87, Winter, Vol. 13, No. 2 (Russian Folklore Abroad), p. 17-29.

36. H. Segel: *Turn of the Century Cabaret*, New York: Columbia University, 1987.

37. A. Konechnyi et al. "Artisticheskoe kabare 'Prival komediantov'" in I. Andronnikov et al., eds.: *Pamiatniki kultury. Novye otkrytiia 1988*, M: Nauka, 1989, pp. 96-154.

38. P. Usai et al, eds.: *Silent Witnesses. Russian Films 1908-1919 / Testimoni silenziosi. Film Russi 1908-1919*, London: British Film Institute; and Rome: Edizione Biblioteca dell'Immagine, 1989 (in English and Italian).

39. T. Lapina: *Govorit artistka estrady*, L: Redaktor, 1991.

40. R. Stites: *Russian Popular Culture*, Cambridge: Cambridge University Press, 1992.

41. D. Youngblood: *Movies for the Masses*, Cambridge: Cambridge University Press, 1992.

42. S. Abarbarchuk: "Gde sobiralas bogema" in *Novoe russkoe slovo*, New York, 1992, 30 October and 13 November.

43. B. Savchenko: *Kumiry zabytoi estrady*, M: Znanie, 1992.

44. L. Senelick, ed.: *Cabaret Performance*, Baltimore: Johns Hopkins University Press, 1989 and 1993 (two volumes).

45. A. Raikin: *Vospominaniia*, SP: Kult-inform-press, 1993.

46. Yu. Tsivian: *Early Cinema in Russia and Its Cultural Reception*, London: Routledge, 1991.

47. N. Noussinova, ed.: *Leonid Trauberg et l'Excentrisme*, Crisnée (Belgium): Yellow Now, 1993.

48. N. Plevitskaia: *Dezhkin karagod*, SP: Logos, 1994.

49. Yu. Nikulin: *Pochti seriozno*, M: Terra, 1994.

50. N. Zorkaia: *Folklor. Lubok. Ekran*, M: Iskusstvo, 1995.

51. B. Ziukov: *Vera Kholodnaia*, M: Iskusstvo, 1995.

52. L. Tikhvinskaia: *Kabare i teatry miniatiur v Rossii. 1908-1917*, M: Kultura, 1995.

53. S. Pack: *Film Posters of the Russian Avant-Garde*, Cologne: Taschen 1995.

54. M. Litavrina: *Amerikanskie sady Ally Nazimovoi*, M: RIO, 1995.

55. B. Savchenko: *Estrada retro*, M: Iskusstvo, 1996.

56. Yu. Alianskii: *Uveselitelnye zavedeniia starogo Peterburga*, SP: PF, 1996.

57. S. Shults: *Brodiachaia sobaka*, SP: Almaz, 1997.

58. E. Aronzon, comp.: *Valentin Parnakh. Zhirafovidnyi istukan*, M: Piataia strana, 2000.

59. K. Kazansky: *Cabaret Russe*, Paris: Chapitre, 2000.

60. A. Konechnyi, comp.: *Peterburgskie balagany*, SP: Giperion, 2000.

61. K. Tribble, ed.: *Marionette Theater of the Symbolist Era*, Lewiston, NY: Mellen, 2002.

62. N. Nusinova: *Kogda my v Rossiiu vernemsia. Russkoe kinematograficheskoe zarubezhie, 1918-1939*, M: Eisenstein Center, 2003.

63. B. Poiurovsky, ed.: *Mastera estrady*, M: Ast-Press Kniga, 2003.

64. E. Uvarova: *Kak razvlekalis v rossiisikh stolitsakh*, M: Aleteiia, 2003.

65. G. Skorokhodov: *Tainy grammofona*, M: Eksmo: Algoritm, 2004.

66. I. Grashchenkova: *Kino Serebrianogo veka*, M: Grashchenkova, 2005.

67. L. Tikhvinskaia: *Povsednevnaia zhizn teatralnoi bogemy Serebrianogo veka*, M: Molodaia gvardiia, 2005.

68. S. Ginzburg: *Kinematografiia dorevoliutsionnoi Rossii*, M: Agraf, 2007.

69. D. Zolotnitsky: *Fars… i chto tam eshche?. Teatr farsa v Rossii 1893-1917*, SP: Netor-Istoriia, 2006.

70. D. Dragilev: *Labirinty russkogo tango*, SP: Aleteiia, 2008.

71. S. Makarov: *Ot starinnykh razvlechenii k zrelishchnym iskusstvam*, M: Librokom, 2010.

72. S. Makarov: *Teatralizatsiia tsirka*, M: Librokom, 2010.

73. A. Deriabin, ed.: *Letopis Rossiiskogo kino 1946-1965: Nauchnaia monografiia*, M: Kanon, 2010.

F. Memoirs, Collections of Letters, Diaries, etc., relating to Modern Russian Stage Design

1. N. Drizen: *Sorok let teatra. Vospominaniia 1875-1915*, P: Prometei, 1915.

2. K. Stanislavsky: *Moia zhizn v iskusstve*, M: GAKhN, 1926, and subsequent editions.

3. K. Valts: *65 let v teatre*, L: Akademiia, 1928.

4. T. Karsavina: *Theatre Street*, London: Heinemann, 1930, and later printings.

5. A. Ostroumova-Lebedeva: *Avtobiograficheskie zapiski*, L: Izdatelstvo Oblastnogo Soiuza sovetskikh khudozhnikov, 1935 (Vol. 1); *Avtobiograficheskie zapiski*, L-M: Iskusstvo, 1945 (Vol. 2).

6. N. Legat: *Ballet Russe. Memoirs of Nicolas Legat*, London: Methuen, 1939.

7. A. Benois: *Reminiscences of the Russian Ballet*, London: Putnam, 1941.

209. Serge Tchehonine: Costume Design for an Old Gusli Player, *The Blind Street Musician*, ca. 1929 (No. 1048)

8. S. Hurok: *Impresario*, New York: Random House, 1946.

9. A. Aleksandrovich: *Zapiski pevtsa*, New York: Chekhov, 1955.

10. A. Benua: *Zhizn khudozhnika*, New York: Chekhov, 1955 (two volumes) (see F15 and F54).

11. S. Hurok: *The World of Ballet*, London: Hale, 1955.

12. S. Makovsky: *Portrety sovremennikov*, New York: Chekhov, 1955.

13. L. Leonidov: *Rampa i zhizn*, Paris: Russkoe teatralnoe izdatelstvo za granitsei, 1955.

14. S. Shcherbatov: *Khudozhnik v ushedshei Rossii*, New York: Chekhov, 1955.

15. A. Benois: *Memoirs*, London: Chatto and Windus, 1960-64 (two volumes) (see F10 and F54).

16. A. Movshenzon: *Aleksandr Yakovlevich Golovin*, L-M: Iskusstvo, 1960.

17. L. Sokolova: *Dancing for Diaghilev*, New York: MacMillan, 1961.

18. S. Makovsky: *Na Parnase serebrianogo veka*, Munich: TsOPE, 1962.

19. M. Fokin: *Protiv techeniia*, L-M: Iskusstvo, 1962 (2nd edition, 1981). This is the Russian version of M. Fokine's *Memoirs of a Ballet Master*, London: Constable, 1961.

20. I. Stravinsky: *An Autobiography*, New York: Norton, 1962.

21. N. Moleva: *Konstantin Korovin. Zhizn i tvorchestvo*, M: Akademiia khudozhestv, 1963.

22. E. Sakharova: *Vasilii Dmitrievich Polenov, Elena Dmitrievna Polenova. Khronika semii khudozhnikov*, M: Iskusstvo, 1964.

23. S. Lifar: *Ma Vie*, Paris: Julliard, 1965.

24. M. Chagall: *My Life*, London: Owen, 1965 (and other editions).

25. Yu. Annenkov: *Dnevnik moikh vstrech*, New York: Inter-Language Literary Associates, 1966 (two volumes).

26. M. Etkind, comp.: *Boris Mikhailovich Kustodiev*, L: Khudozhnik RSFSR, 1967.

27. A. Ivanovsky: *Vospominaniia kinorezhissera*, M: Iskusstvo, 1967.

28. L. Massine: *My Life in Ballet*, London: MacMillan, 1968.

29. I. Zilbershtein and A. Savinov, comps.: *Aleksandr Benua razmyshliaet*, M: Sovetskii khudozhnik, 1968.

30. S. Golynets, comp. *Ivan Yakovlevich Bilibin*, L: Khudozhnik RSFSR, 1970.

31. S. Lifar: *Ma Vie. From Kiev to Kiev*, New York: World Publishing, 1970.

32. I. Stravinsky: *Dialogi. Vospominaniia. Razmyshleniia. Kommentarii*, L: Sovetskii kompozitor, 1971.

33. I. Zilbershtein and V. Samkov, comps.: *Konstantin Korovin vspominaet*, M: Izobrazitelnoe iskusstvo, 1971 (second edition, 1990).

34. I. Zilbershtein and V. Samkov, comps.: *Valentin Serov v vospominaniiakh, dnevnikakh i perepiske sovremennikov*, L: Khudozhnik RSFSR, 1971 (two volumes).

35. V. Milashevsky: *Vchera, pozavchera*, L: Khudozhnik RSFSR, 1972.

36. A. Alekseev: *Sereznoe i smeshnoe*, M: Iskusstvo, 1972.

37. L. Diachkova, comp.: *I.F. Stravinsky. Stati i materialy*, M: Sovetskii kompozitor, 1973.

38. V. Komardenkov: *Dni minuvshie*, M: Sovetskii khudozhnik, 1973.

39. T. Kazhdan et al., comps.: *Igor Grabar. Pisma 1891-1917*, M: Nauka, 1974; *Igor Grabar. Pisma 1917-1941*, M: Nauka, 1977; *Igor Grabar. Pisma. 1941-1960*, M: Nauka, 1983.

40. V. Veregina: *Vospominaniia*, L: Iskusstvo, 1974.

41. R. Yurenev, comp.: *Eizenshtein v vospominaniiakh sovremennikov*, M: Iskusstvo, 1974.

42. Erté: *Things I Remember*, New York: New York Times Book Company, 1975.

43. A. Koonen: *Stranitsy zhizni*, M: Iskusstvo, 1975 (second edition 1985).

44. L. Pasternak: *Zapisi raznykh let*, M: Sovetskii khudozhnik, 1975. English translation by J. Bradshaw with an introduction by J. Pasternak, *The Memoirs of Leonid Pasternak*, London: Quartet, 1982.

45. M. Dobuzhinsky: *Vospominaniia*, New York: Put zhizni, 1976.

46. G. Kryzhitsky: *Dorogi teatralnye*, M: VTO, 1976.

47. E. Kuzmina: *O tom, chto pomniu*, M: Iskusstvo, 1976-79.(two volumes).

48. J. Bowlt, trans.: *B. Livshits: "The One and a Half-Eyed Archer"*, Newtonville: ORP, 1977. Second edition: SP: Palace Editions, 2004. This is the English translation of the Russian edition, *Polutoroglazyi strelets* (L, 1933; new Russian editions: L: Sovetskii pisatel, 1989; M: Khudozhestvennaia literatura, 1991). French translation by J.-C. Marcadé: *L'archer à un œil et demi*, Lausanne: L'Age d'Homme, 1971; Italian translation from the French: *L'Arciere da un Occhio e Mezzo*, Florence: Hopefulmonster, 1989.

49. G. Wakhevitch: *L'Envers des décors*, Paris: Laffont, 1977.

50. A. Faiko: *Zapisi starogo teatralshchika*, M: Iskusstvo, 1978.

51. Yu. Podkopaeva et al., comp.: *Konstantin Andreevich Somov*, M: Iskusstvo, 1979.

52. O. Sergievsky: *Memoirs of a Dancer*, New York: Dance Horizons, 1979.

53. V. Vilenkin: *V. I. Nemirovich-Danchenko. Izbrannye pisma*, M: Iskusstvo, 1979 (two volumes).

54. N. Aleksandrova, ed.: *Alexandr Benua. Moi vospominaniia*, M: Iskusstvo, 1979 (two volumes) (see F10 and F15).

55. N. Sats: *Novelly moei zhizni*, M: Iskusstvo, 1979 (two volumes).

56. S. Delaunay: *Nous irons jusqu'au soleil*, Paris: Laffont, 1980.

57. N. Reznikova: *Ognennaia pamiat*, Berkeley: Berkeley Slavic Specialties, 1980.

58. B. Nijinska: *Early Memoirs*, New York: Holt, Rinehart and Winston, 1981.

59. Z. Gippius: *Peterburgskie dnevniki (1914-1919)*, New York: Orpheus, 1982.

60. V. Khodasevich: *Belyi koridor. Vospominaniia*, New York: Silver Age, 1982.

61. N. Kuzmin: *Davno i nedavno*, M: Sovetskii khudozhnik, 1982.

62. E. Shvarts: *Memuary*, Paris: La Presse Libre, 1982.

63. I. Zilbershtein and V. Samkov, comps.: *Sergei Diagilev. Literaturnoe nasledie. Perepiska. Vospominaniia sovremennikov*, M: Izobrazitelnoe iskusstvo, 1982 (two volumes).

64. B. Zakhava: *Vospominaniia. Spektakli i roli*, M: VTO, 1982.

65. N. Berezov: *Zhizn i balet*, London: Beriozoff, 1983.

66. P. Markov: *Kniga vospominanii*, M: Iskusstvo, 1983.

67. I. Ilinsky: *Sam o sebe*, M: Iskusstvo, 1984.

68. N. Chernova, ed.: *Kasian Goleizovsky. Zhizn i tvorchestvo*, M: VTO, 1984.

69. I. Zilbershtein and V. Samkov, eds.: *Valentin Serov v perepiske, dokumentakh i interviu*, L: Khudozhnik RSFSR, 1985.

70. R. Craft, ed.: *Dearest Bubushkin. Selected Letters and Diaries of Vera and Igor Stravinsky*, London: Thames and Hudson, 1985.

71. A. Danilova: *Choura. The Memoirs of Alexandra Danilova*, New York: Knopf, 1986.

72. G. Chugunov, ed.: *M.V. Dobuzhinsky: Vospominaniia*, M: Nauka, 1987.

210. Serge Tchehcnine: Costume Design for a Blind Barrel Organ Player, *The Blind Street Musician*, ca. 1929 (No. 1050)

73. I. Annenkov: *La révolution derrière la porte*, Paris: Lieu Commun, 1987.

74. A. Deich: *Po stupeniam vremeni*, K: Mistetstvo, 1988.

75. M. Tenisheva: *Vpechatleniia moei zhizni*, L: Iskusstvo, 1991 (reprint of the Paris edition of 1929).

76. G. Kostaki: *Moi avangard*, M: Modus graffiti, 1993.

77. Yu. Bakhrushin: *Vospominaniia*, M: Khudozhestvennaia literatura, 1994.

78. N. Zubkova, ed.: *D D. Burliuk. Fragmenty iz vospominanii futurista*, SP: Pushkirsdi fond, 1994.

79. S. Gollerbakh: *Moi dom*, Paris: Albatros, 1994.

80. V. Kurdov: *Pamiatnye dni i gody*, SP: Arsis, 1994.

81. I. Danilova, ed.: *M. Alpatov: Vospominaniia*, M: Iskusstvo, 1994.

82. I. Kozhevnikova, comp.: *Uroki postizheniia. Khudozhnik Varvara Bubnova. Vospominaniia, stati, pisma*, M: Istina i zhizn, 1994.

83. G. Kozintsev: *"Chernoe, likhoe vremia....."*, M: Artist. Rezhisser. Teatr, 1994.

84. O. Tsinger: *Gde v gostiakh, a gde doma*, Paris: Albatros and Moscow: Moskovskaia palitra, 1994.

85. J. Bowlt, ed.: *The Salon Album of Vera Sudeikin-Stravinsky*, Princeton: Princeton University Press, 1995.

86. N. Tamrazov: *Galereia*, M: Kh.G.S., 1995.

87. A. Beniaminov: *Artist bez grima. Vospominaniia*, Tenafly, New Jersey: Hermitage, 1995.

88. V. Nikitina: *Dom of nami na zakat, Vospominaniia*, M: Semeinyi arkhiv, 1996.

89. J. Rubenstein, trans.: *Tangled Loyalties. The Life and Times of Ilya Ehrenburg*. New York: Basic Books, 1996.

90. V. Marquardt, ed.: *Survivor from a Dead Age. The Memoirs of Louis Lozowick*, Washington, D.C.: Smithsonian, 1997.

91. E. Chukovskaia, ed.: *Chukokkala*, M: Premiera, 1999.

92. G. fon Mekk: *Kak ya ikh pomniu*, M: Sytin, 1999.

93. A. Shchegolev: *Vospominaniia. Dokumenty*, Omsk: Omskii dom pechati, 1999.

94. L. Utesov: *Spasibo, serdtse!*, M: Vagrius, 1999.

95. E. Kovtun, intro.: *Pavel Filonov. Dnevniki*, SP: Azbuka, 2000.

96. P. Gnedich: *Kniga zhizni. Vospominaniia 1855-1918*, M: Agraf, 2000.

97. G. Chugunov, ed.: *M.V. Dobuzhinsky. Pisma*, SP: Bulanin, 2001.

98. T. Khvostenko: *Vechera na Maslovke bliz Dinamo. Zabytye imena*, M: Olimpiia Press, 2003.

99. T. Khvostenko: *Vechera na Maslovke bliz Dinamo. Za fasadom proletarskogo iskusstva*, M: Olimpiia Press, 2003.

100. N. Lobanov-Rostovsky: *"Vospominaniia (Zapiski kollektsionera)"* in *Pamiatniki kultury. Novye otkrytiia*, M: Nauka, 2003, pp. 64-280.

101. I. Vydrin and V. Tretiakov, comps.: *Stepan Petrovich Yaremich*, SP: Sam iskusstv, 2005 (two volumes).

102. A. Chegodaev: *Moia zhizn i liudi, kotorykh ya znal: Vospominaniia*, M: Zakharov, 2006.

103. D. Likhachev: *Vospominaniia*, M: Logos, 2006.

104. A. Kats, ed.: *Serafima Rudneva: Vospominaniia schastlivogo cheloveka*, M, 2007.

105. V. Vanslov: *Pod seniu muz. Vospominaniia i etiudy*, M: Pamiatniki istoricheskoi mysli, 2007.

106. R. Polchaninov: *Molodezh russkogo zarubezhia: Vospominaniia, 1941-1951*, Munich: Posev, 2009.

107. N. Lobanov-Rostovsky: *Epokha-Sudba-Kollektsiia*, M: Russkii put, 2010 (290 color and 330 b/w ills.).

108. A. Panina and T. Pereslegina, eds.: *M.V. Sabashnikov: Zapiski. Pisma*, M: Sabashnikov, 2011.

G. Modern Russian Costume and Set Design

1. F. Komissarzhevsky: "Kostium" in *Entsiklopediia stsenicheskogo samoobrazovaniia*, SP: Teatr i iskusstvo, 1911 (Vol. 4).

2. L. Zheverzheev (intro.): *Opis vystavlennykh v polzu lazareta shkoly narodnogo iskusstva ee Velichestva Gosudaryni Imperatritsy Aleksandry Fedorovny pamiatnikov Russkogo teatra iz sobraniia L.I. Zheverzheeva*, P: Schmidt, 1915.

3. *Collection des plus beaux numéros de Comoedia Illustré et des Programmes consacrés aux Ballets et Galas Russes depuis le début à Paris 1909-1921*, Paris: Brunoff, 1922.

4. O. Fischel: *Das Moderne Buhnenbilt*, Berlin: Wasmuth, 1923.

5. J. Harker: *Studio and Stage*, London: Nisbet, 1924.

6. A. Boll: *Du Décor de théâtre. Ses tendances modernes*, Paris: Chiron, 1926.

7. A. Yanov: *Teatralnaia dekoratsiia*, L: Blago, 1926.

8. E. Gollerbakh, ed.: *Teatralno-dekoratsionnoe iskusstvo v SSSR 1917-1927*. L: Komitet vystavki teatralno-dekoratsionnogo iskusstva, 1927.

9. J. Laver and G. Sheringham: *Design in the Theatre*, London: Studio, 1927.

10. W. Fuerst and S. Hume: *Twentieth-Century Stage Decoration*, New York: Knopf, 1929 (two volumes). Reprinted by Dover, New York, 1967.

11. J. Rouché: *L'Art théâtral moderne*, Paris: Blond et Gay, 1929.

12. R. Cogniat: *Décors du théâtre*, Paris: Chroniques du jour, 1930.

13. M. Georges-Michel, W. George and N. Gontcharova: *Les Ballets Russes de Serge de Diaghilew. Décors et costumes*, Paris: Vorms, 1930.

14. L. Moussinac: *Tendances nouvelles du théâtre*. Paris: Lévy, 1931. English translation: *The New Movement in the Theater*, New York: Blom, 1967.

15. F. Komissarzhevskii and L. Simonson: *Settings and Costumes of the Modern Stage*, New York: Studio, 1933.

16. S. Margolin: *Khudozhniki teatra za 15 let*, M: Ogiz, 1933.

17. A. Efros: *Kamernyi teatr i ego khudozhniki 1914-1934*, M: VTO, 1934.

18. N. Izvekov: *Stsena. Arkhitektura stseny*, M: Khudozhestvennaia literatura, 1935.

19. C. Beaumont: *Design for the Ballet*, New York: Studio, 1937.

20. C. Beaumont: *Five Centuries of Ballet Design*, London: Studio, 1939.

21. G. Amberg: *Art in Modern Ballet*, New York: Pantheon, 1946.

22. C. Beaumont: *Ballet Design: Past and Present*, New York: Studio, 1946.

23. R. Buckle: *Modern Ballet Design*, London: Black, 1955.

24. N. Gontcharova, M. Larionov, and P. Vorms: *Les Ballets russes. Serge de Diaghilew et la décoration théâtrale*, Paris: Vorms, 1955.

25. F. Syrkina: *Russkoe teatralno-dekoratsionnoe iskusstvo vtoroi poloviny XIX veka*, M: Iskusstvo, 1956.

26. D. Kliuchnikov and L. Snezhnitsky: *Teatralnye drapirovki*, M: VTO, 1957.

27. D. Bablet: *La Mise en scène contemporaine. Vol. 1 (1887-1914)*, Brussels: La Renaissance du livre, 1968.

28. H. Rischbieter: *Art and the Stage in the 20th Century*, New York: New York Graphic, 1968.

29. N. Sokolova, ed.: *Khudozhniki teatra*, M: Sovetskii khudozhnik, 1969.

30. L. Haskell: "Russian Paintings and Drawings in the Ashmolean Museum Oxford," *Oxford Slavonic Papers*, Oxford (new series), 1969, Vol. 2, pp. 1-38. Published in book form by the Ashmolean Museum, Oxford, in 1970; second and revised edition in 1989.

211. Serge Tchehonine: Costume Design for Ruslan, *Ruslan and Liudmila*, ca. 1929 (No. 1054)

31. M. Pozharskaia: *Russkoe teatralno-dekoratsionnoe iskusstvo kontsa XIX–nachala XX veka*, M: Iskusstvo, 1970.

32. M. Larionov: *Diaghilev et les Ballets Russes*, Paris: Bibliothèque des arts, 1970.

33. A. Shifrina and N. Yesulovich: *Muzei imeni Bakhrushina*, M: Sovetskii khudozhnik, 1972.

34. T. Strizhenova: *Iz istorii sovetskogo kostiuma*, M: Sovetskii khudozhnik, 1972. English translation: *From the History of Soviet Costume*. Liverpool: Liverpool Polytechnic, n.d.

35. L. Golova: *O khudozhnikakh teatra*, L: Khudozhnik RSFSR, 1972.

36. L. Haskell: "Russian Drawings in the Victoria and Albert Museum" in *Oxford Slavonic Papers* (New Series), Oxford, 1972, Vol. 5, pp. 1-51.

37. T. Silantieva: *Khudozhniki sovetskogo kino*, M: Sovetskii khudozhnik, 1972.

38. F. Syrkina, comp.: *Khudozhniki teatra o svoem tvorchestve*, M: Sovetskii khudozhnik, 1973.

39. M. Davydova: *Ocherki istorii russkogo teatralno-dekoratsionnogo iskusstva XVIII–nachala XX v.*, M: Nauka, 1974.

40. D. Bablet: *Esthétique générale du décor de théâtre de 1870 à 1914*, Paris: Centre Nacional de la Recherche Scientifique, 1975.

41. F. Mancini: *L'Evoluzione dello spazio scenice. Dal naturalismo al teatro epico*, Bari: Dedalo Libri, 1975.

42. D. Oenslager: *Stage Design. Four Centuries of Scenic Invention*. New York: Viking 1975.

43. V. Kuznetsova: *Kostium na ekrane*, L: Iskusstvo, 1975.

44. E. Rakitina, comp.: *Khudozhnik. Stsena. Ekran*, M: Sovetskii khudozhnik, 1975 and 1978 (two volumes).

45. A. Shifrina: *Viliam Shekspir v tvorchestve sovetskikh khudozhnikov teatra*, M: Sovetskii khudozhnik, 1975.

46. V. Kozlinsky and E. Freze: *Khudozhnik i teatr*, M: Sovetskii khudozhnik, 1975

47. V. Berezkin: *Khudozhniki Bolshogo teatra*, M: Sovetskii khudozhnik, 1976

48. D. Brownell: *The Nutcracker Ballet from the Designs by Alexandre Benois*. San Francisco: Bellerophon, 1977. See also his *Sleeping Beauty Ballet. Léon Bakst's Designs for the Music of Tchaikovsky*, San Francisco: Bellerophon, 1977.

49. D. Bablet: *Revolutions in Stage Design of the XXth Century*, Paris and New York: Ameil, 1977.

50. A. Vasiliev et al., eds.: *Sovetskie khudozhniki teatra i kino*, M: Sovetskii khudozhnik, 1977 and subsequent issues.

51. M. Clarke and C. Crisp: *Design for Ballet*, New York: Hawthorne books, 1978.

52. D. Keller, ed.: *Maler im Banne des Balletts*. Special issue of *Du*, No 405, Nov. 1974, Zürich.

53. F. Syrkina and E. Kostina: *Russkoe teatralno-dekoratsionnoe iskusstvo*. M: Iskusstvo, 1978.

54. V. Berezkin: *V.V. Dmitriev*, L: Khudozhnik RSFSR, 1981.

55. J. Bowlt, ed.: *Twentieth Century Russian Stage Design*. Special issue of *Russian History*, Tempe, 1981, Vol. 8, parts 1-2.

56. R. Strong et al.: *Designing for the Dance*, London: Elron, 1981.

57. I. Verikivska: *Stanovlennia ukrainskoi radianskoi stsenografii*, K: Naukova dumka, 1981.

58. P. Williams: *Masterpieces of Ballet Design*, London: Phaidon, 1981.

59. A. Schouvaloff and V. Borovsky: *Stravinsky on Stage*, London: Stainer and Bell 1982

60. E. Pankratova: *Russkoe teatralno-dekoratsionnoe iskusstvo kontsa XIX–nachala XX veka*, L: Leningradskii gosudarstvennyi institut teatra, muzyki i kinematografii, 1983.

61. I. Zilbershtein: "Poisk prodolzhaetsia" in *Ogonek*, M, 1983, 14 May, pp. 8, 25.

62. Yu. Nekhoroshev: *Khudozhnik V.A. Simov*, M: Sovetskii khudozhnik, 1984.

63. R. Vlasova: *Russkoe teatralno-dekoratsionnoe iskusstvo nachala XX veka*, L: Khudozhnik RSFSR, 1984.

64. V. Vanslov, ed.: *O khudozhnikakh teatra, kino i televideniia*, L: Khudozhnik RSFSR, 1984.

65. R. Hansen: *Scenic and Costume Design for the Ballets Russes*, Ann Arbor: UMI, 1985.

66. *Treasures of the Bakhrushin Museum*, M: Vneshtorg, 1986 (an unauthored brochure of reproductions of works in the Bakhrushin Museum, Moscow).

67. V. Berezkin: *Khudozhnik v teatre Chekhova*, M: Izobrazitelnoe iskusstvo, 1987.

68. A. Schouvaloff: *The Thyssen-Bornemisza Foundation. Set and Costume Designs for Ballet and Theatre*, London: Sotheby's 1987.

69. M. Bogomolova: *Dekoratsionnye materialy–khudozhniki teatra*, M: Soiuz teatralnykh deiatelei, 1988.

70. M. Kolesnikov: "Shedevry Zolotogo veka russkoi stsenografii" in *Sovetskii balet*. M, 1988, No. 5, pp. 63-68.

71. A. Vasiliev et al., eds.: *Khudozhnik i stsena*, M: Sovetskii khudozhnik, 1988.

72. N. Metelitsa, ed.: *Balet Peterburga, Petrograda, Leningrada*, L: GMTMA, 1989.

73. A. Vasiliev et al., eds.: *Khudozhnik i zrelishche*, M: Sovetskii khudozhnik, 1990.

74. V. Berezkin: *Sovetskaia stsenogafiia 1917-1941*, M: Nauka, 1990.

75. L. Chaim: *Khudozhnik. Teatr. Revoliutsiia*, Saratov: Saratov State University, 1990.

76. D. Afanasiev and N. Gromov: *Khudozhnik stseny: Problemy obucheniia professii. Sbornik nauchnykh trudov*, SP: Institute of Theater, Music and Cinematography, 1992.

77. A. Kozlov: *Ogni lagernoi rampy. Iz istorii Magadanskogo teatra 30-50-kh godov*, M: Raritet, 1992.

78. N. Tarabukin: *Ocherki po istorii kostiuma*, M: GITIS, 1994.

79. Dzh. Boult (Bowlt): "Khudozhniki des Ballets Russes" in *Nashe nasledie*, M, 1995, No. 33, pp. 129-34.

80. T. Bentley: *Costumes by Karinska*, New York: Abrams, 1995.

81. V. Berezkin: *Istoriia stsenografii mirovogo teatra*, M: Gosudarstvennyi Institut iskusstvoznaniia, 1995; second edition, M: URSS, 1997.

82. A. Mikhailova: *Meierkhold i khudozhniki*, M: Galart, 1995.

83. R. Kirsanova: *Kostium v russkoi khudozhestvennoi kulture 18–pervoi poloviny 20 vv.*, M: Bolshaia Rossiiskaia entsiklopediia, 1995.

84. R. Kirsanova: *Stsenicheskii kostium i teatralnaia publika v Rossii XIX veka*, Kaliningrad: Yantarnyi skaz; and M: Artist. Rezhisser. Teatr, 1997.

85. E. Pankratova: *Russkaia zhivopis i teatr*, SP: SPbGTU, 1997.

86. A. Schouvaloff: *The Art of Ballets Russes. The Serge Lifar Collection of Theater Designs, Costumes and Paintings at the Wadsworth Atheneum, Hartford, Connecticut*, New Haven: Yale University Press, 1997.

87. E. Strutinskaia: *Iskaniia khudozhnikov teatra. Peterburg-Petrograd-Leningrad, 1910-1920 gg.*, M: GII, 1998.

88. N. Makerova: *Istoriia otechestvennogo teatralno-dekoratsionnogo iskusstva*, M: RGGU, 1999.

89. M. Davydova: *Khudozhnik v teatre nachala XX veka*, M: Nauka, 1999.

212. Serge Tchehonine: Costume Design for a Male Dancer Wearing a Turban. ca. 1929 (No. 1055)

90. L. Efimova: *Kostium v Rossii XV–nachala XX veka,* M: Art-Rodnik, 2000.

91. E. Kostina: *Khudozhniki stseny russkogo teatra XX veka*, M: Russkoe slovo, 2002

92. J. Blake et al.: *An Eye for the Stage. The Tobin Collection of Theatre Arts at the McNay Art Museum,* San Antonio, TX: McNay Museum, 2003.

93. L. Oves: *Khudozhniki stseny,* SP: LIK, 2003.

94. V. Berezkin: *Teatr khudozhnika: Istoki i nachala,* M: URSS, 2006.

95. V. Berezkin: *Teatr khudozhnika: Mastera,* M: URSS, 2006.

96. I. Duksina and T. Kim: *Obrazy russkogo teatra v kollektsii Valentina Solianikova.* M: SSV, 2006.

97. V. Berezkin: *Teatr khudozhnika: Rossiia. Germaniia,* M: Agraf, 2007.

98. V. Vanslov: *Volshebnik teatralnoi stseny,* M: Teatral, 2008.

99. A. Purvis, P. Rand and A. Winestein, eds.: *The Ballets Russes and the Art of Design,* New York: Monacelli, 2009 (French translation: *Les Ballets Russes, Arts et Design,* Paris: Hazan, 2009).

100. C. Rouane: *The Empire's New Clothes: A History of the Russian Fashion Industry,* New Haven: Yale Univerrsity Press, 2009.

101. S. Batrakova: *Teatr-Mir i Mir-Teatr. Tvorcheskii metod khudozhnika XX veka,* M: Pamiatniki istoricheskoi mysli, 2010.

102. V. Berezkin: *Iskusstvo stsenografii mirovogo teatra: Teatr khudozhnika. Ot istokov do serediny XX veka*, M: LKI, 2011 (Vol. 1).

103. O. Naumova et al.: *Dvizhenie, forma, tanets,* SP: Palace Editions, 2011.

H. Russian Art and the Theater in the Early Emigration

1. *Teatr i zhizn / Theater und Leben,* Berlin, 1921-22. Russian émigré journal.

2. *Teatr / Das Theater / Le Théâtre,* Berlin, 1921-23. Russian émigré journal.

3. *Zhar-ptitsa / Jar-ptitza,* Berlin-Paris, 1921-26. Russian émigré journal; summaries variously in French, German, and English.

4. *Illliustrirovannaia Rossiia,* Paris, 1924-39. Russian émigré journal.

5. *Perezvony,* Riga, 1925-28. Russian émigré journal.

6. D. Burliuk: *Russkie khudozhniki v Amerike,* New York: Burliuk, 1928.

7. *Le Théâtre et la vie / Teatr i zhizn,* Paris, 1929-32. Russian émigré journal.

8. *Mir i iskusstvo / Le Monde et l'Art,* Paris, 1930-31. Russian émigré journal.

9. *Chisla.* Paris, 1930-34. Russian émigré journal.

10. L. Lvov (Lwoff): *Russkie khudozhniki v Parizhe / L'Art Russe à Paris,* Paris: La Russie et le Monde Slave, 1931.

11. N. Martinoff, ed.: *Almanac. Russian Artists in America,* New York: Martianoff, 1932.

12. V. Bulgakov and A. Yupatov, comps.: *Russkoe iskusstvo za rubezhom,* Prague-Riga, 1938.

13. N. Evreinov: *Pamiatnik mimoletnomu,* Paris: Navarre, 1953.

14. S. Bertenson: *Vokrug iskusstva,* Hollywood: Bertenson, 1957.

15. I. Okuntsov: *Russkaia emigratsiia v Severnoi i Yuzhnoi Amerike,* Buenos Aires: Sembrador, 1967.

16. K. Arensky: *Pisma v Khollivud,* Monterey: Arensburger, 1968.

17. L. Foster: *Bibliografiia russkoi zarubezhnoi literatury 1918-1968,* Boston: Hall, 1970.

18. M. Beyssac: *La Vie Culturelle de l'Emigration Russe en France. Chronique (1920-1930),* Paris: PUF, 1971.

19. R. Williams: *Culture in Exile*, Ithaca, N.Y.: Cornell University Press, 1972.

20. P. Kovalevsky. *Zarubezhnaia Rossiia,* Paris: Librairie des Cinq Continents, 1971-73 (two volumes).

21. *Russian Literature and Culture in the West: 1922-1972.* Special issue of *Triquarterly,* Evanston, Ill., 1973, No. 28.

22. G. Ozeretskovsky: *Russkii blistatelnyi Parizh do voiny,* Paris: Beresniak, 1973.

23. G. Ozeretskovsky: *Voina i posle voiny,* Paris: Impressions Internationales, 1975.

24. R. Gul: *Ya unes Rossiiu,* New York: Bridge, 1981.

25. L. Fleishman et al.: *Russkii Berlin 1921-1923,* Paris: YMCA, 1983.

26. I. Odoevtseva: *Na beregakh Seny,* Paris: La Presse Libre, 1983.

27. V. Yanovsky: *Polia Eliseiskie,* New York: Silver Age, 1983.

28. F. Mierau, ed.: *Russen in Berlin. Literatur, Malerei, Theater, Film 1918-1933,* Leipzig: Reclam, 1987.

29. T. Beyer, G. Kratz, X. Werner: *Russische Autoren und Verlage in Berlin nach der Ersten Weltkrieg,* Berlin: Spitz, 1987.

30. R. de Ponfilly: *Guide des Russes en France,* Paris: Horay, 1990.

31. M. Böhmig: *Das Russische Theater in Berlin 1919-1931,* Munich: Sagner, 1991.

32. M. Parkhomovsky, ed.: *Evrei v kulture russkogo zarubezhia,* Jerusalem: Parkhomovsky, 1992-2009 (nineteen volumes).

33. L. Senelick, ed.: *Wandering Stars: Russian Emigré Theatre, 1905-1940,* Iowa City: Iowa University Press, 1993.

34. D. Severiukhin and O. Leikind: *Khudozhniki russkoi emigratsii (1917-1941),* SP: Chernyshev, 1994; second edition with K. Makhrov: *Khudozhniki russkogo zarubezhia*, SP: Notabene, 1999. References in the text are to the second edition.

35. L. Mnukhin, ed.: *Russkoe zarubezhie 1920-1940. Frantsiia. Khronika,* Paris: YMCA / M: EKSMO, 1995. Cf. H44.

36. K. Schlögel ed.: *Russische Emigration in Deutschland 1918-bis 1941,* Berlin: Akademie, 1995.

37. L. Schirmer: "Das russische-deutsche Theater 'Der blaue Vogel'" in *Museums Journal,* Berlin, 1995, July, pp. 30-33.

38. F. Albera: *Albatros: des Russes à Paris 1919-1929,* Paris: Cinémathèque française. 1995.

39. L. Fleishman et al.: *Russkaia pechat v Rige. Iz istorii gazety "Segodnia" 1930-kh godov,* Oakland: Berkeley Slavic Specialities, 1997 (four volumes).

40. S. Chervonnaia: *Litovskaia khudozhestvennaia emigratsiia 1945-85 gg.,* M: NII Teorii i istorii izobrazitelnykh iskusstv, 1998.

41. E. Taskina: *Russkii Kharbin,* M: MGU, 1998; second edition, 2005.

42. A. Korliakov: *L'émigration russe en photos. France, 1917-1947,* Paris: YMCA, 1999.

43. K. Schlögel: *Chronik des russischen Lebens in Deutschland 1918-1941,* Berlin: Akademie, 1999.

44. L. Mnukhin, ed.: *Russkoe zarubezhie. Khronika nauchnoi, kulturnoi i obshchestvennoi zhizni 1940-1975. Frantsiia,* Paris: YMCA / M: Russkii put, 2000 (Vol. 1). Cf. H35.

45. A. Vassiliev: *Beauty in Exile,* New York: Abrams, 2000.

213. Serge Tchehonine: Costume Designs for a Male and a Female Dancer. 1930 (No. 1063)

46. E. Menegaldo: *Russkie v Parizhe. 1919-1939*, M: Kstati, 2001.
47. M. Litavrina: *Russkii teatralnyi Parizh*, SP: Aleteiia, 2003.
48. V. Cherniaev et al., eds.: *Zarubezhnaia Rossiia 1917-1945*, SP: Liki Rossii, 2004.
49. E. Aleksandrov: *Russkie v Severnoi Amerike*, San Francisco: Congress of Russian Americans, 2005.
50. Di Mino, V.: *Gde moi dom?*, Caracas: Novaia rech, 2005.
51. A. Tolstoi: *Khudozhniki russkoi emigratsii*, M: Iskusstvo XXI vek, 2005.
52. M. Talalai, ed.: *Russkie v Italii: Kulturnoe nasledie emigratsii*, M: Russkii put, 2006
53. V. Kosik: *"Chto mne do Vas, mostovye Belgrada?" Russkaia diaspora v Belgrade*, M: Institut slavianovedeniia, 2007.
54. H. Robinson: *Russians in Hollywood*, Boston: Northwestern University Press, 2007.
55. V. Ershov: *Rossiiskaia khudozhestvennaia emigratsiia vo Frantsii v 1920-1930-e gg.*, M: Maks Press, 2008.
56. O. Leikind et al., eds.: *Izobrazitelnoe iskusstvo, arkhitektura i iskusstvovedenie russkogo zarubezhia*, SP: Bulanin, 2008.
57. K. Makhrov, ed.: *Russkaia koloniia v Tunise. Sbornik*, 1920-2000, M: Russkii put, 2008.
58. S. Nechaev: *Russkaia Nitstsa*, M: Veche, 2008.
59. B. Nosik and V. Zherlitsyn: *Russkie khudozhniki v emigratsii*, SP: APT, 2008.
60. G. Vzdornov et al., eds.: *Khudozhestvennaia kultura russkogo zarubezhia 1917-1939. Sbornik statei*, M: Indrik, 2008.
61. N. Komandorova: *Russkii Stambul*, M: Veche, 2009.
62. S. Romanov: *Russkii London*, M: ACT-Astrel, 2009.
63. R. Gerra: *"Kogda my v Rossiiu vernemsia…"*, SP: Rostok, 2010.
64. G. Goriachkin: *Russkaia Aleksandriia. Sudby emigratsii v Egipte*, M: Russkii put, 2010.
65. A. Khisamutdinov: *Russkaia Yaponiia*, M: Veche, 2010.
66. V. Kosik: *Russkie kraski na balkanskoi palitre*, M: Institut slavianovedeniia RAN, 2010.
67. L. Kozlov and R. Gagkuev: *Russkoe zarubezhe. Velikie sootechestvenniki*, M: Drofa, 2010.
68. L. Mnukhin et al.: *Rossiiskoe zarubezhie vo Frantsii 1919-2000. Biograficheskii slovar*, M: Nauka, 2010 (three volumes).
69. S. Nechaev: *Russkie v Latinskoi Amerike*, M: Veche, 2010.
70. N. Nepomniashchy: *Russkaia Indiia*, M: Veche, 2010.
71. B. Nosik: *S Lazurnogo berega na Kolymu (Russkie khudozhniki-neoakademiki doma i v emigratsii)*, SP: KOSTA, 2010.
72. A. Popova: *Russkii Berlin*, M: Veche, 2010.
73. V. Schastnyi: *Khudozhniki Parizhskoi shkoly iz Belarusi: Esse, biografii, putevodite. Literaturno-khudozhestvennoe izdanie*, Minsk: Chetyre chetverti, 2010.
74. V. Susak: *Ukrainian Artists in Paris 1900-1939*, Lviv: Lviv Art Gallery, 2010.
75. A. Vaisberg and R. Gerra: *Sem dnei v marte, Besedy ob emigratsii*, SP: Russkaia kultura, 2010.
76. A. Vasiliev: *Russkii Gollivud*, M: Slovo, 2010.
77. A. Kravtsov: *Russkaia Avstraliia*, M: Veche, 2011.
78. M. Shishkin: *Russkaia Shveitsariia. Literaturno-istoricheskii putevoditel*, M: AST-Astrel, 2011.
79. L. Babka et al.: *Russkii zagranichnyi istoricheskii arkhiv v Prage – dokumentatsiia*, Prague: Národní knihovna České republiky, 2011.
80. O. Peresypkin: *Russkaia Palestina*, M: Vostok-Zapad, 2011.
81. O. Korostelev and M. Shruba, eds.: *"Sovremennye zapiski". Parizh, 1920-1940. Iz arkhiva redaktsii*, M: NLO, 2011 (Vol. I) and 2012 (Vol. II).

82. O. Korostelev and M. Shruba, eds.: *Vokrug redaktsionnogo arkhiva "Sovremennykh zapisok". Parizh, 1920-1940*, M: NLO, 2012.

Note: The titles given above constitute only a small section from a large, but still unclassified bibliography on Russian art and the theater in emigration. An essential guide to Russian stage design in Berlin, Paris, and New York is provided by the various programs and brochures issued by companies such as Jascha Jushny's Der Blaue Vogel / The Blue Bird, Nikita Baliev's Chauve-Souris / The Bat, and Marie Kousnezoff's Opéra Privé de Paris. The reader should also consult the programs for the Diaghilev and de Basil Ballets Russes companies for the 1920s and 1930s.

I. Catalogs of Exhibitions Relating to Stage Designs by Modern Russian Artists

1. *Teatralno-dekoratsionnoe iskusstvo za 5 let*, M: Museum of Decorative Painting, 1924 (catalog published in Kazan, 1924).
2. *Internationale Ausstellung neuer Theatertechnik*, Vienna: Konzerthaus, 1924.
3. *Vystavka teatralno-dekoratsionnogo iskusstva 1917-X-1927*, L: Academy of Arts, 1927.
4. *Memorial Exhibition of the Russian Ballet*, London: Claridge Gallery, 1930.
5. *Khudozhniki sovetskogo teatra za XVII let (1917-1934)*, M: State Historical Museum, 1935. Exhibition also went to Leningrad.
6. *Ballets Russes de Diaghilev*, Paris: Musée des Arts Décoratifs, 1939.
7. *The Diaghilev Exhibition*, Edinburgh: Edinburgh Festival; London: Forbes House, 1954.
8. *Fifty Years of Ballet Design*. Indianapolis: John Herron Art Museum; and other institutions, 1959-60.
9. *Stravinsky and the Dance*, New York: New York Public Library, 1962.
10. *Stravinsky and the Theatre*, New York: New York Public Library, 1962.
11. *The Serge Lifar Collection of Ballet Set and Costume Designs*, Hartford: Wadsworth Atheneum, 1965 (published on the occasion of the opening of the Harkness House for Ballet Arts, New York).
12. *Stage and Costume Designs by Russian Painters from the Collections of Mr. and Mrs. Nikita D. Lobanov-Rostovsky and Mr. George Riabov*, New York: Harkness House for Ballet Arts, 1966.
13. *Diaghilev. An Exhibition of Ballet Designs*, Plymouth and other cities: Arts Council of Great Britain, 1967-68.
14. *Russian Stage and Costume Designs: A Loan Exhibition from the Lobanov-Rostovsky, Oenslager and Riabov Collections*, circulated by the International Exhibitions Foundation, Washington, D.C., 1967-69. (See N2-20).
15. *Les Ballets Russes de Serge Diaghilev 1909-1929*, Strasbourg: Conseil de l'Europe, 1969.
16. *Explosion: Color: Paris: 1909. Russian Theatre Designs Drawn from the collection of Robert L.B. Tobin*, San Antonio, Texas: McNay Art Institute, 1969.
17. *The Boris Kochno collection: Designs for Diaghilev*, New York: New York Public Library, 1971.
18. *Hommage à Diaghilew. Collections Boris Kochno et Serge Lifar*, Paris: Musée Galliera, 1972.

214. Pavel Tchelitchew: Costume Design for the Geisha, *The Geisha* 1919 (No. 1067)

19. *Ricordi di Serge de Diaghilev,* Milan: Museo Teatrale alla Scala, 1972.

20. *Diaghilev and Russian Stage Designers. A Loan Exhibition of Stage and Costume Designs from the Collection of Mr. and Mrs. N. Lobanov-Rostovsky,* circulated by the International Exhibitions Foundation, Washington, D.C., 1972-74. (See N21-44).

21. *Stravinsky-Diaghilev,* New York: Cordier and Ekstrom Gallery, 1973.

22. *Diaghilev / Cunningham,* New York: Hofstra University, 1974.

23. *Theatre. An Exhibition of Twentieth Century Theatrical Designs and Drawings,* London: Annely Juda Fine Art, and other cities, 1974-75.

24. *Omaggio ai disegnatori di Diaghilev,* Venice: Palazzo Grassi, 1975.

25. *The Diaghilev Ballets Russes 1909-1929,* Chicago: University of Chicago, 1975.

26. *Majakovskij, Mejerchol'd, Stanislavskij,* Milan: Castello Sforzesco, Sala della balla, 1975.

27. *Vsevolod Mejerchold. Yubileinaia vystavka k stoletiiu so dnia rozhdeniia,* M: Bakhrushin Museum, 1976.

28. *American Ballet Theatre. Thirty-Six Years of Scenic and Costume Design 1940-1976,* circulated by the International Exhibitions Foundation, Washington, D.C., 1976.

29. *The Golden Age of Ballet Design,* Palm Beach, Florida: The Society of the Four Arts, 1976.

30. *Khudozhniki Bolshogo teatra za 200 let,* M: Museum of the Bolshoi Theater, 1976.

31. *The George Verdak Collection. Eras of the Dance,* Huntsville: Museum of Art, and elsewhere, 1976-77.

32. *Stage Designs and the Russian Avant-Garde (1911-1929). A Loan Exhibition of Stage and Costume Designs from the Collection of Mr. and Mrs. Nikita Lobanov-Rostovsky,* circulated by the International Exhibitions Foundation. Washington, D.C., 1976-78. (See N45-64).

33. *Mastera Sovetskoi stsenografii / Mistři sovětské scénografie,* M and Prague, 1977.

34. *Diaghilev i balletti russi e il loro tempo,* Rome: Libreria e Galleria Pan, 1977.

35. *Diaghilev's Ballets Russes 1909-1929,* Cambridge, Mass.: Harvard University, 1977.

36. *La Galaxie Diaghilev 1909-1929,* Le Mans: Musée du Mans, 1977.

37. *Russkoe teatralno-dekoratsionnoe iskusstvo iz sobranii I.V. Khachurina i Ya. E. Rubinshteina,* Tallin: State Art Museum of Estonia, 1978. (An earlier version of this exhibition took place in Yaroslavl in 1974, and a later version, *Khudozhnik i teatr. Zhivopis iz sobraniia Ya. E. Rubinshteina,* opened in Moscow and Arkhangelsk in 1982).

38. *Designs for the New York Stage,* New York: Pace University, 1978.

39. *Diaghilev: Costumes and Designs for the Ballets Russes,* New York: Metropolitan Museum of Art, 1978.

40. *Russian Painters and the Stage 1884-1965. A Loan Exhibition of Stage and Costume Designs from the Collection of Mr. and Mrs. Nikita Lobanov-Rostovsky,* Austin, Texas: University of Texas, 1978-79.

41. *Dance Image. A Tribute to Serge Diaghilev,* Jackson, Mississippi: Mississippi Museum of Art, 1979 (see N65-70).

42. *Diaghilev: Les Ballets Russes,* Paris: Bibliothèque Nationale, 1979.

43. *The Diaghilev Ballet in England,* Norwich: Sainsbury Centre for Visual Arts, 1979.

44. *Russian Theater and Costume Designs,* San Francisco: The Fine Arts Museums, 1980.

45. *Igor Stravinsky. La carrière européenne,* Paris: Musée d'Art Moderne de la Ville de Paris and other institutions, 1980-1982.

46. *The Diaghilev Heritage. Selections from the Collection of Robert L.B. Tobin,* Houston: Museum of Fine Arts, 1981.

47. *Costumes for the Ballet: Diaghilev to Balanchine,* Fort Worth: Kimbell Museum, 1981.

48. *Russian Stage Designs: Tradition and Modernism. An Exhibition Selected from the Collection of Mr. and Mrs. Nikita D. Lobanov-Rostovsky,* Austin: Archer M. Huntington Art Gallery, University of Texas, 1981 (see N71-77).

49. *Mir iskusstva — il Mondo dell'arte,* Naples: Museo Pignatelli and other institutions, 1982.

50. *Art and Dance,* Boston: Institute of Contemporary Art and other institutions, 1982.

51. *Russian Stage Design. Scenic Innovation 1900-1930 from the Collection of Mr. and Mrs. Nikita D. Lobanov-Rostovsky,* Jackson: Mississippi Museum of Art and other institutions, 1982-1984 (see N78-107).

52. *Il balletto russo dalle origini ai nostri giorni,* Naples: Sala Gemito, 1983.

53. *Khudozhniki teatra 1917-1983 gg.,* L: The Kirov State Academic Theater of Opera and Ballet and other instititutions, 1983.

54. *Strawinsky. Sein Nachlass. Sein Bild,* Basel: Kunstmuseum, 1984.

55. *Russkaia stsenografiia 1900-1930 iz kollektsii N.D. Lobanovykh-Rostovskikh,* M: Spaso House, 1984.

56. *L'Avventura del Sipario,* Prato: Teatro Metastasio, 1984.

57. *The Book of the Dance in the 20th Century,* Oakland, California: Mills College, 1984.

58. *Artists Design for Dance,* Bristol: Arnolfini, 1984-85.

59. *XIII Theatrical Sketches from Igor S. Dychenko's Collection,* M: Spaso House, 1985.

60. *Avant-Garde Alchemy. Russian Stage Design 1900-1930,* Allentown: Muhlenberg College, 1986.

61. *Die Maler und das Theater im 20. Jahrhundert,* Frankfurt: Kunsthalle, 1986.

62. *Raumkonzepte. Konstruktivistische Tendenzen in Bühnen- und Bildkunst 1910-1930,* Cologne: Universität zu Köln; Frankfurt: Städtische Galerie, 1986.

63. *The Operatic Muse,* Santa Fe: Museum of Fine Arts; and San Antonio: Marion Koogler McNay Art Museum, 1986.

64. *Serge Lifar. Une vie pour la danse,* Lausanne: Musée Historique de l'Ancien-Evêché, 1986.

65. *Bronislava Nijinska. A Dancer's Legacy,* New York: Cooper-Hewitt Museum; San Francisco: Palace of the Legion of Honor, 1986-87.

66. *Thespis Adorned,* San Antonio: Marion Koogler McNay Museum, 1987.

67. *The Art of Enchantment. Diaghilev's Ballets Russes 1909-1929,* San Francisco: Fine Arts Museums, 1988.

68. *Russkoe teatralno-dekoratsionnoe iskusstvo 1880-1930,* M: GMII im. A.S. Pushkina; and L: Manège Exhibition Hall, 1988.

69. *Russische Avant-Garde. Theater 1914-1934,* Amsterdam: Theatermuseum, 1989.

70. *100 Years of Russian Ballet 1830-1930,* New York: Edward Nakhamkin Fine Arts, 1989.

71. *Russian Constructivist Theatre Design,* Louisville: J.B. Speed Art Museum, 1989.

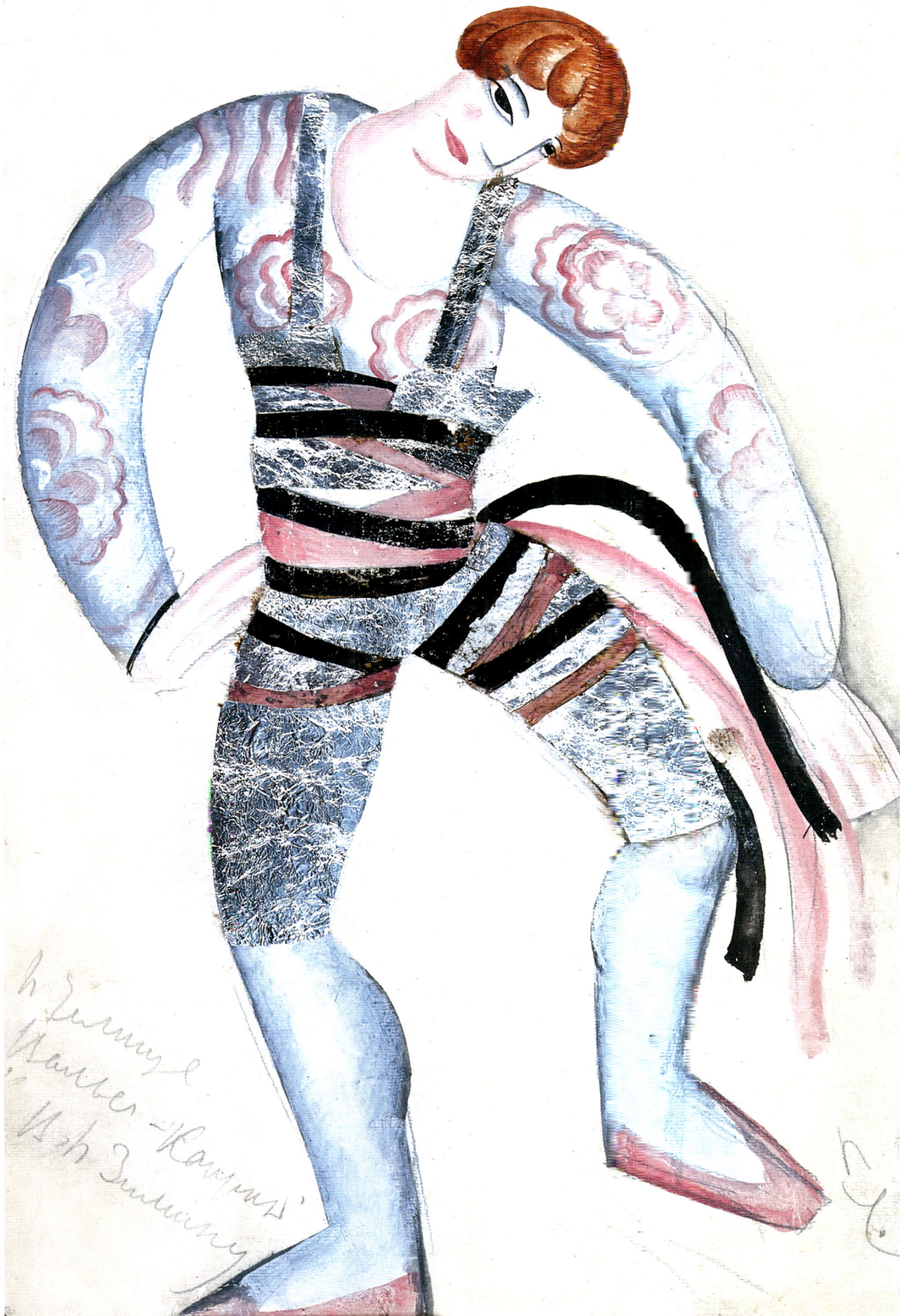

215. Pavel Tchelitchew: Costume Design for a Male Dancer in the Ballet Sketch *Caprice*, 1920 (No. 1071)

72. *Von Eisenstein bis Tarkowsky*, Munich: Lenbachhaus, 1990.

73. *Russia 1900-1930. L'Arte della Scena*, Venice: Ca' Pesaro, 1990.

74. *Arte e Moda negli Anni Venti.* Milan: Padiglione d'Arte Contemporanea, and other institutions, 1990.

75. *Russian Theatrical Artists 1900's-1930's*, London: The Harrington Gallery, 1990.

76. *Kostbarkeiten aus der Sammlung des Theatermuseums A.A. Bachruschin in Moskau*, Kassel, 1990.

77. *Die Russische Avantgarde und die Bühne 1890-1930*, Schleswig: Schleswig-Holsteinisches Landesmuseum Schloss Gottorf, and other institutions 1991-1992.

78. *I. Sakharoff. Un mito della danza*, Argenta: Convento dei Cappuccini, 1991.

79. *L'Art du Ballet en Russie 1738-1940*, Paris: Opéra de Paris Garnier, 1991.

80. *Khudozhniki Gosudarstvennogo evreiskogo teatra*, M: Bakhrushin Museum, 1991.

81. *Theatre in Revolution. Russian Avant-Garde Stage Design 1913-1935*, San Francisco: California Palace of the Legion of Honor, and other institutions, 1991-92.

82. *The Decorative Tradition in Russian Stage Design*, San Antonio: Marion Koogler McNay Art Museum, 1992-93.

83. *I balletti in bozzetto*, Brera: Galleria Anna Perez, 1993.

84. *Russische Theaterkunst 1910-1936*, Vienna: österreichisches Theatermuseum, 1993.

85. *An Exhibition of Designs for the Ballet*, London: Julian Barran, 1994

86. *Entfesselt. Die russische Bühne 1900-1930*, Munich: Bayerische Akademie der Schönen Künste, 1994.

87. *Modernist Movements in Russian Art and Their Reflection on the Stage. Selections from the Nina and Nikita Lobanov-Rostovsky Collection*, M: Museum of Private Collections,1994-1995.

88. *Studio Albatros. L'école russe de Montreuil*, Montreuil: Musée de l'Histoire Vivante, 1995.

89. *Diaghilev, Creator of the Ballets Russes. Art, Music, Dance*, London: Barbican Art Centre, 1996.

90. *Overdadets konst / The Art of Extravagance*, Stockholm: Dansmuseet, 1996.

91. *In Search of Diaghilev*, SP: State Academy of Culture, 1997.

92. *Russian Stage Designs 1910-1930 (from the Lobanov-Rostovsky Collection) and Marc Chagall and the Jewish Theater*, Athens: Megaron, 1997

93. *Teatralno-dekcratsionnoe iskusstvo russkikh khudozhnikov iz sobraniia Yuriia Vasilievicha Riabova*, SP: RM, 1997.

94. *The Russian Imperial Theater*, Petersburg Museum, Otaru, Japan: 1997.

95. *Plastyka teatralna*, Torun: Muzeum Okręgowe, 1997.

96. *L'avant-garde russe et la scène, 1910-1930. La collection Lobanov-Rostovsky*. Brussels: Musée d'Ixelles, 1998.

97. *Russian Avant-Garde and the Stage, 1900-1930: The Collection of Nina and Nikita D. Lobanov-Rostovsky*, Yokohama: Yokohama Museum of Art, 1998.

98. *Diaghilev's Ballets Russes 1909-1929. Art, Dance, Music*, Tokyo: Sezon Museum of Art and Shiga: Museum of Modern Art, 1998.

99. *Polifonia. Da Malevic a Tat'jana Bruni 1910-1930*, Milan: Padiglione d'Arte Contemporanea, 1998.

100. *Théâtre et Ballet Russe 1910-1930*, Milan-Munich: Galerie Michael Hasenclever, 1998-99.

101. *Out of Russia. A Gift of Scene Designs from Robert L.B. Tobin*, San Antonio, Texas: Marion Koogler McNay Art Museum, 1999.

102. *Kostümentwürfe der Russischen Avangarde*, Apolda: Kunsthaus, 1999.

103. *From Russia with Love. Costumes of the Ballets Russes 1909-1933*, Canberra: National Gallery of Australia, 1999.

104. *In principio era il corpo. L'Arte del movimento a Mosca negli anni '20*, Rome: Acquario Romano, 1999.

105. *Kostümentwürfe der Russischen Avantgarde*, Apolda: Kunsthaus, 1999.

106. *Automi, marionette e ballerine nel teatro d'avanguardia*, MART (Museo di Arte Moderna e Contemporanea di Trento e Rovereto), Rovereto, 2000.

107. *Chelovek plasticheskii. Russkoe iskusstvo dvizheniia, Moskva, 1910-20-ye gg.*, M: Bakhrushin Museum, 2000.

108. *El teatro de los pintores en la Europa de las vanguardias*, Madrid: Museo Naional Centro de Arte Reina Sofia, 2000.

109. *Vaslav Nijinsky, Legend and Modernist*, Stockholm: Dansmuseet, 2000.

110. *Diagilev i ego epokha*, SP: Russian Museum, 2001.

111. *Nijinsky 1889-1950*, Paris: Musée d'Orsay, 2000-01.

112. *The Bestiary of the Russian Cabaret: Flying Mice and Blue Birds, Black Cats and Stray Dogs. Designs and Documents from the Institute of Modern Russian Culture and Other Collections*, Los Angeles: Doheny Library, University of Southern California, 2002.

113. *A World of Stage Design for Theater, Opera and Dance (from the George Riabov Collection of Russian Art)*, New Brunswick, NJ: Jane Voorhees Zimmerli Art Museum, 2004.

114. *Muses and Masks. Theater and Music in Antiquity*, SP: State Hermitage.

115. *Working for Diaghilev*, Groningen, Netherlands: Groninger Museum, 2004-05.

116. *Pamiatniki russkogo teatralnogo avangarda*, M: Elizium, 2006.

117. *La Danza delle Avanguardie. Dipinti, scene e costume: da Degas a Picasso, da Matisse a Keith Haring*, Rovereto: MART (Museo di Arte Moderna e Contemporanea di Trento e Rovereto), 2006-07.

118. *Artists of the Theater and Cinema. Paintings and Photographs from the Russian State Archive of Literature and Art (RGALI)*, M: RGALI, 2006.

119. *A Theatrical Mosaic. Russian and Soviet Stage Design of the First Half of the 20th Century*, M: Gallery na Leninke, 2007.

120. *A World of Stage: Russian Designs for Theater, Opera and Dance*, Kyoto: National Museum of Modern Art, and other cities, 2007.

121. *Danser vers la Gloire. L'Age d'Or des Ballets Russes*, Paris: at Sotheby's Galerie Charpentier, 2008.

122. *Chagall and the Artists of the Russian Jewish Theater*, New York: Jewish Museum, 2008-09.

123. *Diaghilev. Nachalo*, SP: Russian Museum, 2009.

124. *Khudozhnik v zerkale stseny. Pervaia polovina XX veka. Teatralnaia kollektsiia V. Solianikova*, M: Museum of Private Collections, 2009.

125. *Die Ballets Russes, 1909-1929: Schwäne und Feuervögel*, Munich: Deutsche Theatermuseum, 2009.

126. *Treasures of Diaghilev's Ballets Russes. Olga and Ivor Mazure Collection*, M: Museum of Decorative, Applied and Popular Art, 2009.

216. Pavel Tchelitchew: Costume Design for a Dancing Bacchante (in profile) ca. 1920 (No. 1072)

127. *Etonne-moi: Sergei Diaghilev et Les Ballets Russes / A Feast of Wonders. Serge Diaghilev and the Ballets Russes*, Monaco: Nouveau Musée de Monte Carlo, and M: Tretiakov Gallery, 2009-10

128. *Opéras Russes à l'Aube des Ballets Russes 1901-1913. Costumes et Documents*, Moulins: Centre National du Costume du Scène, 2009-10.

129. *Ballets Russes. The Art of Costume*, Canberra: National Gallery of Australia, 2010-11.

130. *Diaghilev and the Golden Age of the Ballets Russes 1909-1929*, London: Victoria and Albert Museum, 2010-11.

131. *Kunst und Bühne. Film, Music, Tanz, Theater, Varieté, Zirkus*, Zurich: Galerie Orlando, 2010-11.

J. Auction Catalogs Relating to Stage Designs by Modern Russian Artists

1. *Diaghilev Ballet Material,* London: Sotheby's, 13 June, 1967.

2. *Costumes and Curtains from Diaghilev and de Basil Ballets,* London: Sotheby's, 17 July, 1968.

3. *Diaghilev Ballet Material,* London: Sotheby's, 18 July, 1968.

4. *Diaghilev and Reinhardt Ballet Material,* London: Sotheby's, 9-10 July, 1969.

5. *S. Diaghilev, B. Kniaseff and M. Reinhardt Ballet and Theatre Material,* London: Sotheby's, 15-16 December, 1969.

6. *Costumes and Curtains from Diaghilev and de Basil Ballets,* London: Sotheby's, 19 December, 1969.

7. *Designs for Costumes and Décors: Ballet, Opera, Theater,* New York: Parke Bernet, 6 May, 1970.

8. *Ballet, Theatre and Opera Décor and Costume Designs; Portraits and Posters,* London: Sotheby's, 3 June, 1971.

9. *20th Century Paintings, etc. from the Collection of Leonide Massine,* London: Sotheby's, 7 July, 1971.

10. *Costume and Décor Designs,* London: Sotheby's (Belgravia Galleries), 17 November, 1971.

11. *Costumes and Curtains from the Diaghilev and de Basil Ballets,* London: Sotheby's, 3 March, 1973.

12. *Décor and Costume Designs, Portraits, Manuscripts and Posters,* London: Sotheby's, 21 June, 1973.

13. *Costume and Décor Designs for Ballet, Theatre and Opera,* London: Sotheby's, 30 May, 1974.

14. *Collection Serge Lifar; Les Ballets Russes,* Paris: Ader Picart Tajan, 20 June, 1974.

15. *Ballet and Theatre Material,* London: Sotheby's, 5 June, 1975.

16. *Ballet, Opéra, Théâtre, Music-Hall. Projets de Costumes et de Décors,* Monte Carlo: Sotheby's, Parke Bernet, 26 June, 1976.

17. *Impressionists, etc., and Ballet and Theatre Material,* London: Sotheby's, 20 October, 1976.

18. *Ballet and Theater Material,* London: Sotheby's, 25 May, 1977.

19. *Dance, Theatre, Opera,* New York: Sotheby, Parke Bernet, 15 December, 1977.

20. *Ballet and Theatre Material,* London: Sotheby's, 17 May, 1978.

21. *Dance, Theater, Opera,* New York: Sotheby, Parke Bernet, 24 November, 1978.

22. *Ballet and Theatre Material,* London: Sotheby's, 6 June, 1979.

23. *Dance, Theater, Opera, Cabaret,* New York: Sotheby, Parke Bernet, 6 December, 1979.

24. *Ballet and Theatre Material,* London: Sotheby's, 13 March, 1980.

25. *Good American and European Paintings, and Ballet, Theater and Opera Material,* New York: Sotheby, Parke Bernet, 22 May, 1980.

26. *Royal Opera House, Covent Garden. Royal Gala Auction,* London: Sotheby, Parke Bernet, 1 October, 1980.

27. *Theatre, Ballet and Music-Hall Material,* London: Sotheby's, 23 October, 1980.

28. *Costumes from the Monte Carlo Opera House,* London: Sotheby's, 16 November, 1980.

29. *Dance, Theater, Opera, Music Hall,* New York: Sotheby, Parke Bernet, 18 December, 1980.

30. *Ballet Designs,* London: Sotheby's, 4 June, 1981.

31. *Dance, Theater, Opera, Music-Hall,* New York: Sotheby, Parke Bernet, 12 June, 1981.

32. *Ballet, Theatre and Music-Hall Material,.* London: Sotheby's, 29 October, 1981.

33. *Dance, Theater, Opera, Music-Hall and Film. Décor and Costume Designs, Books, Posters and Photographs,* New York: Sotheby, Parke Bernet, 15 December, 1981.

34. *Ballet and Theatre Material and Related Reference Books.* London: Sotheby's, 4 March 1982.

35. *Ballet and Theatre Material,* London: Sotheby's, 28 October, 1982.

36. *Modern Paintings, Drawings and Sculpture. Dance, Theater and Opera,* New York: Sotheby, Parke Bernet, 10 December, 1982.

37. *Ballet and Theatre Material,* London: Sotheby's, 9 June, 1983.

38. *Modern Paintings, Drawings and Sculpture. Dance, Theater and Opera,* New York: Sotheby, Parke Bernet, 22 June, 1983.

39. *The Modern Movement (Ballet and Theatre Material),* London: Christie's, 29 June, 1983.

40. *Ballet, Theatre and Music Hall Material,* London: Sotheby's, 26 October, 1983.

41. *Modern Paintings, Drawings and Sculpture; Dance, Theater and Opera,* New York: Sotheby, Parke Bernet, 15 and 16 December, 1983.

42. *The Modern Movement, Including Ballet and Theatre Material,* London: Christie's, 17 April, 1984.

43. *Ballet Material and Manuscripts from the Serge Lifar Collection.* London: Sotheby's, 9 May, 1984.

44. *Dance, Theater, Opera, Music Hall and Film,* New York: Sotheby, Parke Bernet, 21 November, 1984.

45. *Art Russe,* Paris: Nouveau Drouot, 12 March, 1985 (included a Russian theatrical section).

46. *Ballet and Theatre Material,* London: Sotheby's, 28 May, 1985.

47. *L'Art, le Music-Hall et le Théâtre,* Paris: Nouveau Drouot, 20 April, 1986.

48. *Dance, Theater, Opera and Music Hall,* New York: Sotheby's, 23 April, 1986.

49. *Ballet and Theatre Material,* London: Sotheby's, 22 October, 1987.

50. *Ballets Russes, Theatre, Atelier Maliavine,* Paris: Nouveau Drouot, 4 November, 1987.

51. *Collection Boris Kochno,* Monaco: Sotheby's, 11-12 October, 1991.

52. *The Ruth Page Collection,* New York: Sotheby's, 7 November, 1991.

53. *The Diaghilev and Ballets Russes Costumes from Castle Howard,* London: Sotheby's, 14 December, 1995.

217. Pavel Tchelitchew: Costume Design for a Male Dancer with a Leopard Motif on Trousers, ca. 1920 (No. 1075)

54. *Music in Art,* London: Phillips, 4 November, 1997.
55. *Dance, Theater and Opera,* New York: Sotheby's, 9 December, 1998.
56. *Music in Art,* London: Phillips, 29 November, 1999.
57. *Music in Art,* London: Phillips, 21 November, 2000.

Since 2000 the major auction houses have included Russian stage design materials in general sales of Russian art, a major exception being L223.

K. Catalogs of Exhibitions Relating to Modern Russian Art

1. *Exposition Russe d'Art Ancien et Moderne,* Paris: Chez Devambez, 1921.
2. *Le Monde Artiste,* Paris: Galerie Dancy, 1921.
3. *Die Erste russische Kunstausstellung,* Berlin: Galerie Van Diemen, 1922.
4. *Exhibition of Russian Painting and Sculpture,* Brooklyn: Brooklyn Museum, 1923.
5. *Russian Art Exhibition,* New York: Grand Central Palace, 1924.
6. *L'Exposition Internationale des Arts Décoratifs et Industriels Modernes* (Section russe: Art décoratif et industriel de l'URSS), Paris, 1925.
7. *Le Monde Artiste,* Paris: Galerie Bernheim-Jeune, 1927.
8. *Art Russe,* Brussels: Palais des Beaux-Arts, 1928.
9. *Exposition d'Art Russe,* Paris: Galerie La Renaissance, 1932.
10. *Exhibition of Russian Art,* London: Belgrave Square, 1935.
11. *Russian Painting 1700-1917,* London: Society for Cultural Relations with the USSR, 1948.
12. *Two Decades of Experiment in Russian Art (1902-1922),* London: Grosvenor Gallery, 1962.
13. *Il Contributo Russo alle Avanguardie Plastiche,* Milan: Galleria del Levante, 1964.
14. *Vystavka kartin, risunkov i akvarelei russkikh khudozhnikov iz sobraniia Ya. E. Rubinshteina,* Tallin: State Art Museum of Estonia, 1966.
15. *Agitatsionno-massovoe iskusstvo pervykh let Oktiabrskoi revoliutsii,* M: TG, 1967.
16. *Avantgarde Osteuropa 1910-1930,* W. Berlin: Akademie der Künste, 1967.
17. *Russische Künstler aus dem 20. Jahrhundert,* Cologne: Galerie Gmurzynska, 1968.
18. *L'Art d'Avant-Garde Russe, 1905-1925,* Paris: Musée d'Art Moderne, 1968.
19. *Aspects de L'Avant-Garde Russe, 1905-1925,* Paris: Galerie Jean Chauvelin, 1969.
20. *The Non-Objective World 1914-1924,* London: Annely Juda Fine Art, and other cities, 1971.
21. *The Non-Objective World 1924-1939,* London: Annely Juda Fine Arts, and other cities, 1971.
22. *Osteuropäische Avantgarde,* Cologne: Galerie Gmurzynska, 1970-71.
23. *Russian Art of the Revolution,* Ithaca, N.Y.: Andrew Dickson White Museum of Art; Brooklyn: Brooklyn Museum, 1971.
24. *Russian Art of the Avant-Garde 1908-1922,* New York: Leonard Hutton Galleries, 1971.
25. *Art in Revolution. Soviet Art and Design Since 1917,* London:

Hayward Gallery, and other cities, 1971-1972. Opened as *Kunst in der Revolution* in Frankfurt, W. Germany, and other cities, 1972-73.
26. *Konstruktivismus. Entwicklungen und Tendenzen seit 1913,* Cologne: Galerie Gmurzynska, 1972.
27. *Progressive Russische Kunst,* Cologne: Galerie Gmurzynska, 1973.
28. *Vision Russe,* Geneva: Galerie Motte, 1973.
29. *Tatlin's Dream. Russian Suprematist and Constructivist Art 1910-23,* London: Fischer Fine Art, 1974.
30. *Der Beitrag Russlands zur der Geschichter der Avantgarde der zehner und zwanziger Jahre,* Nuremberg: Galerie R. Johanna Ricard, 1974.
31. *Von der Fläche zum Raum / From Surface to Space. Russland / Russia 1916-24,* Cologne: Galerie Gmurzynska, 1974.
32. *2 Stenberg 2. The "Laboratory" Period (1919-1921) of Russian Constructivism,* Paris: Galerie Jean Chauvelin, 1975.
33. *Die 20er Jahre in Osteuropea / The 1920s in Eastern Europe,* Cologne: Galerie Gmurzynska, 1975.
34. *Echoes of Russia,* Washington, Conn.: Washington Art Gallery, 1975.
35. *Dibujos y acuarelas de la vanguardia rusa,* Caracas: Sala de esposiciones, 1975.
36. *Portret v russkoi zhivopisi kontsa XIX–nachala XX veka,* L: RM, 1975.
37. *Russian Avant Garde,* New York: Carus Gallery, 1975.
38. *Maïakovski 20 Ans de Travail,* Paris: Centre Georges Pompidou, 1975-1976. The exhibition then opened at the Neue Gesellschaft für bildende Kunst, W. Berlin, in 1978 under the title "Majakovskij: 20 Jahre Arbeit"; and then at the Museum of Modern Art, Oxford, England, in 1982, under the title "Vladimir Mayakovsky: Twenty Years of Work."
39. *Russian Pioneers at the Origins of Non-Objective Art,* London: Annely Juda Fine Art, 1976.
40. *Russian Suprematist and Constructivist Art 1910-1930,* London: Fischer Fine Art, 1976.
41. *Russische Malerei 1890-1917,* Frankfurt: Städelsches Kunstinstitut, 1976-77.
42. *Die Kunstismen in Russland / The Isms of Art in Russia,* Cologne: Galerie Gmurzynska, 1977.
43. *Russian And Soviet Painting,* New York: Metropolitan Museum of Art, 1977.
44. *Sammlung Costakis,* Düsseldorf: Kunstmuseum, 1977.
45. *The Suprematist Straight Line: Malevich, Suetin, Chashnik, Lissitzky,* London: Annely Juda Fine Art, 1977.
46. *Revolution: Russian Avant-Garde 1912-1930,* New York: Museum of Modern Art, 1978.
47. *Russische Avantgarde 1910-1930,* Cologne: Galerie Bargera, 1978.
48. *Vystavka novykh postuplenii, XVIII – nachala XX veka,* L: Russian Museum, 1978-1979; a) *Zhivopis*; b) *Risunok i akvarel*; c) *Graviura i litografii.*
49. *Russian Graphic Art XVIII-XX cc.,* Newcastle: University of Newcastle, 1978-79.
50. (a) *Paris-Moscou 1900-1930,* Paris: Centre Pompidou, 1979; (b) *Moskva-Parizh 1900-1930,* M: GMII im. A.S. Pushkina, 1981.
51. *The Russian Revolution of Art,* New York: Rosa Esman Gallery, 1979.
52. *Künstlerinnen der russischen Avantgarde / Women-Artists of the Russian Avant-Garde 1910-30,* Cologne: Galerie Gmurzynska, 1979-1980.

218. Pavel Tchelitchew: Costume Design for a Male Turkish Dancer Wearing a Turban, 1920 (No. 1076)

53. *L'altra metà dell'avanguardia 1910-1940,* Milan: Comune di Milano, 1980. French version: *L'autre moitié de l'avant garde 1910-1940,* Paris: Des Femmes, 1982.

54. *The Avant-Garde in Russia 1910-1930, New Perspectives,* Los Angeles: Los Angeles County Museum; Washington, D.C.: Hirshhorn Museum and Sculpture Garden, 1980-81.

55. *Invention and Tradition. Selected Works from the Julia A. Whitney Foundation and the Thomas P. Whitney Collection of Modernist Russian Art,* Charlottesville, VA: University of Virginia, and other cities 1980-81.

56. *Plakat pervogo desiatiletiia Oktiabria i proizvedeniia teatralnykh khudozhnikov iz sobraniia Ya.E. Rubinshteina,* M: Yablochkina Centra House of the Actor, 1981.

57. *Herwarth Walden and Der Sturm,* New York: La Boetie, 1981.

58. *Russian Painting and Graphics: 1812-1945. A Selection from the Collections of Mr. and Mrs. A.L. de Saint-Rat and the Walter Havighurst Special Collections,* Oxford, Ohio: Miami University, 1981.

59. *Von der Malerei zum Design / From Painting to Design,* Cologne: Galerie Gmurzynska, 1981.

60. *Art of the Avant-Garde in Russia: Selections from the George Costakis Collection,* New York: Guggenheim Museum, and other cities, 1981-83.

61. *Art and Revolution,* Tokyo: Seibu Museum of Art, 1982.

62. *Plastyka Radziecka. Sztuka okresu października 1917-1930,* Warsaw: Zacheta. 1982.

63. *Russkaia grafika XVIII-XX vekov (iz sobraniia O. V. Kachurina i Ya. E. Rubinshteina,* L: Leningrad Soviet Executive committee, 1982; M: GMII m. A.S. Pushkina, 1982.

64. *Architettura nel paese dei Soviet 1917-1933,* Rome: Palazzo delle Esposizioni, 1982-83.

65. *L'Avant-Garde au Féminin. Moscou, Saint-Petersbourg, Paris (1907-1930),* Paris: Artcurial, 1983.

66. *Umetnost Oktobarske epohe,* Belgrade: Museum of Contemporary Art; Zagreb: Gallery of Contemporary Art, 1983.

67. *100 oeuvres du Musée Trétiakov de Moscou,* Geneva: Petit Palais, 1983.

68. *The First Russian Show,* London: Annely Juda Fine Art, 1983.

69. *Russisk maleri fra slutten av det 19. og begynnelsen av det 20 århundre,* Oslo: Munch-Museet, 1983.

70. *The Russian Avant-Garde and American Abstract Artists,* Coral Gables: Lowe Art Museum, 1983.

71. *Dada-Constructivism,* London: Annely Juda Fine Art, 1984.

72. *Russian Avant-Garde Art from the Schreiber Collection,* New Rochelle, NY: Castle Gallery, 1984.

73. *Meisterwerke russischer Malerei,* Cologne: Josef-Haubrich-Kunsthalle, 1984.

74. *Russische Kunst des 20 Jahrhunderts. Sammlung Semjonow,* Esslingen am Neckar: Galerie der Stadt, 1984.

75. *Sieben Moskauer Künstler / Seven Moscow Artists 1910-1930,* Cologne: Galerie Gmurzynska, 1984.

76. *Art into Production,* Oxford: Museum of Modern Art, 1984-85.

77. *Russische und Sowjetische Kunst. Tradition-Gegenwart,* Düsseldorf: Städtische Kunsthalle, and other institutions, 1984-85.

78. *Art for the Masses. Russian Revolutionary Art from the Merrill C. Berman Collection,* Williamstown, MA: Williams College Museum of Art; Middletown, CT: Wesleyan University: Davison Art Center, 1985.

79. *Vanguardia Rusa 1910-1930. Museo y colección Ludwig,* Madrid: Fundación Juan March, 1985.

80. *Russkoe izobrazitelnoe iskusstvo nachala XX veka. Iz chastnykh sobranii Leningrada,* L: Manège, 1985.

81. *Vom Klang der Bilder,* Stuttgart: Staatsgalerie, 1985.

82. *Masterpieces of the Avantgarde,* London: Annely Juda Fine Art / Juda Rowan Gallery, 1985.

83. *Contrasts of Form. Geometric Abstract Art 1910-1980,* New York: Museum of Modern Art, 1985.

84. *Of Absence and Presence,* New York: Kent Fine Art, 1986.

85. *Futurismo i futurismi,* Venice: Palazzo Grassi, 1986.

86. *Pioniere der abstrakten Kunst aus der Sammlung Thyssen-Bornemisza,* Cologne: Galerie Gmurzynska, 1986.

87. *Russia. The Land, The People,* Washington: Renwick Gallery, and other institutions, October, 1986-87.

88. *Avant-Garde Russe 1910-1930,* Paris: Galerie Georges Lavrov, 1987.

89. *Meister des XX Jahrhunderts,* Cologne: Galerie Gmuryznska, 1987.

90. *Iskusstvo i revoliutsiia II / Art and Revolution II,* Tokyo: Seibu Museum, 1987.

91. *Müvészet és Forradalom / Art and Revolution,* Budapest: Palace of Exhibitions; then opened under the title *Kunst und Revolution / Art and Revolution,* Vienna: Österreichische Museum für angewandte Kunst, 1987-1988.

92. *Novoe iskusstvo, Novyi byt, 1917-1927,* M: Collectors' Club, 1987.

93. *Muutoksen aika förändringens tid / Time of Change, 1905-1930,* Helsinki: Art Hall, 1988.

94. *Moderne – Postmoderne,* Geneva: Cabinet des estampes, 1988.

95. *1000-letie russkoi khudozhestvennoi kultury / 1000 Jahre russische Kunst,* M: TG, and Hamburg: Schloss Gottorf, 1988.

96. *Vystavka khudozhestvennykh proizvedenii XVI-XX vekov iz sobraniia G. Basmadzhiana,* M: TG, and L: Hermitage, 1988.

97. *Russian and Soviet Painting 1900-1930.* Washington, D.C.: Hirshhorn Museum and Sculpture Garden, 1988.

98. *Revolutionäre Kunst aus sowjetischen Museen 1910-1930,* Lugano: Fondazione Thyssen-Bornemisza, 1988.

99. *A New Spirit,* New York: Barry Friedman, 1988.

100. *Avant-Garde Revolution Avant-Garde. Russian Art from the Michail Grobman Collection,* Tel Aviv: Tel Aviv Museum of Art, 1988.

101. *Michail Grobman. Künstler und Sammler,* Bochum: Museum Bochum, 1988.

102. *Shedevry zhivopisi XX veka iz sobraniia Tissen-Bornemisa,* L: RM, 1988.

103. *Dada and Constructivism,* Tokyo: Seibu Museum and elsewhere, 1988-89.

104. *Konstruktivismus – Suprematismus,* Zürich: Galerie Stolz, 1988-89.

105. *Osteuropäische Avantgarde,* Bochum: Museum Bochum, 1988-89.

106. *The Russian and Soviet Avant-Garde. Works from the Collection of George Costakis,* Montreal: Montreal Museum of Fine Arts, 1989.

107. *Avanguardia Russa dalle collezioni private sovietiche. Origini e percorso 1904-1934,* Milan: Palazzo Reale, 1989.

108. *Avantgarde. Neuostotaidetta 1920-1930,* Helsinki: Galerie Art, 1989.

109. *100 Years of Russian Art 1889-1989 from Private Collections in the USSR,* London: Barbican Gallery, and Oxford: Museum of Modern Art, 1989.

110. *Arte Russa e Sovietica 1870-1930,* Turin: Lingotto, 1989.

219. Pavel Tchelitchew: Costume Design for a Female Dancer Wearing a Bead Necklace, 1920 (No. 1077)

111. *Avantgarde 1910-1930. Russian-Soviet Art,* Turku: Art Museum, 1989

112. *Von der Revolution zur Perestroika. Sowjetische Kunst aus der Sammlung Ludwig,* Lucerne: Kunstmuseum, 1989.

113. *Russische Kunst 1900-1930,* Munich: Galerie Pabst, 1989.

114. *Vor den Toren der unbekannten Zukunft. Russische Avantgarde der 10er und 20er Jahre. Werke aus Schweizer Privatbesitz,* Zürich: Stiftung für konstruktive und konkrete Kunst, 1989.

115. *Kunst der 20er und 30er Jahre,* Iserlohn: Stadmuseum, 1989.

116. *Artistes Russes de l'Ecole de Paris,* Paris: Musée d'Art Moderne, 1989.

117. *Kunst und Propaganda. Sowjetische Plakate bis 1953,* Zürich: Museum für Gestaltung, and other institutions, 1989-90.

118. *The Russian Avant-Garde 1920-1935,* Los Angeles: Turner Dailey Gallery, 1990.

119. *Russland 1910-193. Buchkunst und Literatur der Avantgarde,* Cologne: Venator und Hanstein, 1990.

120. *Grafica Russa 1917-1930,* Florence: Palazzo Strozzi, 1990.

121. *Tradition and Revolution in Russian Art,* Manchester: City Art Gallery and other insitutions, 1990.

122. *Russian Avant-Garde,* London: Cooling Gallery, 1990.

123. *The Russian Experiment,* New Rochelle, NY: College of New Rochelle, 1990.

124. *Russische und Sowjetische Zeichnungen und Aquarelle von 1900 bis 1930 aus dem Puschkin-Museum, Moskau,* Mannheim: Städtische Kunsthalle, 1990.

125. *Moscow Treasures and Traditions,* Washington, D.C.: Smithsonian Traveling Exhibition Service, 1990.

126. *Art Treasures from the Russian Tsar Court,* Aarhus: Aarhus Art Museum, 1990.

127. *Russishche Avantgarde 1910-1930,* Duisburg: Wilhelm-Lehmbruck Museum, 1990.

128. *Art into Life,* Seattle: Henry Art Gallery, 1990.

129. *Color. Form. Texture: The Russian Avant-Garde, 1910-1920,* Los Angeles: Institute of Modern Russian Culture 1990.

130. *Simvolizm v Russii 1890-1930 iz chastnykh kollektsii,* M: Soviet Culture Foundation, 1990.

131. *Ukrajinska Avangarda 1910-1930,* Zagreb: Muzej suvremene umjetnosti, 1990.

132. *50 Años de Arte sovietico,* Barcelona: Centre Cultural Metropolità, 1990.

133. *La Tipografia Russa 1890-1930,* Città di Castello, Palazzo Vitelli a Sant'Egidio, 1990.

134. *Majakovskij e l'avanguardia russa del primo '900,* Senigalia: Rocca Roveresca, 1990.

135. *La epoca heroica. Obra grafica de las vanguardias rusa y hungara 1912-1925,* Valencia: IVAM Centre Julio Gonzalez, 1990.

136. *Viisi Vuosisataa Ukrainan Taidetta / Five Centuries of Ukrainian Art,* Tampere, Finland: Tampere Art Museum, 1990.

137. *Artisti Russi 1900-1930,* Rome: Palazzo delle Esposizioni, 1990-1991.

138. *Moskovskie khudozhniki. 20-30-e gody,* M: Union of Artists of the RSFSR, 1991.

139. *Twilight of the Tsars,* London: Hayward Gallery, 1991.

140. *Avantgarde I 1900-1923. Russisch-sowjetische Architektur,* Tübingen: Kunsthalle, 1991.

141. *Proizvedeniia russkikh khudozhnikov iz muzeev i chastnykh kollektsii Italii,* L: RM, 1991.

142. *Avanguardie Russe,* Milan: Fonte d'Abisso d'Arte, 1991.

143. *Russian Constructivism and Suprematism, 1914- 1930,* London: Annely Juda Fine Art, 1991.

144. *Russian Avant-Garde Art — 1910-1930 from the Gilbert Collection,* Akron, OH: Akron Art Museum, 1991.

145. *Sovetskoe iskusstvo 1920-1930-kh godov iz sobraniia Gosudarstvennogo muzeia iskusstv Karakalpakskoi ASSR,* L: RM, 1991.

146. *Matjuschin und die Leningrader Avantgarde,* Karlsruhe: Zentrum für Kunst und Medientechnologie, 1991.

147. *Vanguardismo Ruso 1900-1935 de Collecciones Privadas,* Valencia: Museo de la Ciudad, 1991.

148. *Suprematisti Russi degli Anni 20,* Milan: Galleria Marconi, 1991.

149. *Russie-URSS 1914-1991, Changements de regards,* Paris: Musée d'Histoire Contemporaine, 1991.

150. *Spirit of Ukraine. 500 Years of Painting,* Winnipeg: Winnipeg Art Gallery, 1991.

151. *Taide Tulevaisuutta Luomassa 1920-1930,* Helsinki: Taideteollisuusmuseo, 1991.

152. *Abstraktion und Konstruktion,* Berlin: Stolz, 1992.

153. *Il Simbolismo russo,* Venice: Fondazione Georgio Cini, 1992.

154. *Die Grosse Utopie. Die russische Avantgarde 1915-1932,* Frankfurt: Kunsthalle; *De Grote Utopie. Russische Avantgarde 1915-1932,* Amsterdam: Stedelijk Museum; *The Great Utopia. The Russian and Soviet Avant-Garde 1915-1932,* New York: Solomon R. Guggenheim Museum, 1992-1993; *Velikaia utopiia 1915-1932,* M: TG; and SP: RM, 1993.

155. *Avanguardie Russe,* Rome: Galleria Fontanella Borghese, 1992.

156. *Avant-Garde and Russian Art 1900-1930,* Sapporo: Maruiimai, 1992.

157. *Die Welt der Lilja Brik,* Berlin: Galerie Natan Fedorowskij, 1992.

158 *Arte Nascosta. Itinerario attraverso la pittura russa del primo '900,* Milan: Galleria Capitani; and Cuneo: Galleria d'Arte Il Prisma, 1992-95 (three volumes).

159. *L'avant-garde russe, 1905-1925. Chefs-d'oeuvre des musées de Russie,* Nantes: Musée des Beaux-Arts, 1993.

160. *I collezionisti,* Vol. 1: *Arte russa e sovietica nelle raccolte italiane,* Modena: Galleria Civica, 1993.

161. *Avant Garde and Ukraine,* Munich: Villa Stuck, 1993.

162. *Regard sur l'avant-garde russe:* 1910-25, Yonne Tanlay: Centre d'Art Contemporain, 1993.

163. *Russische Avantgarde und Volkskunst,* Baden-Baden: Staatliche Kunsthalle, 1993.

164. *Partners,* London: Annely Juda Fine Art, 1993.

165. *Una mirada sobre la vanguardia rusa (1910-1930),* Zaragoza: Centro de Exposiciones y Congresos, 1993.

166. *Pays-Paysage. Livres d'artistes russes et soviètiques 1910-1933,* Uzerche, France: Bibliothèque Nationale, 1993.

167. *Russian Painting of the Avant-Garde 1906-1924,* Edinburgh: Scottish National Gallery, 1993.

168. *Avantgarde 1900-1930,* Helsinki: Atheneum, 1993-94.

169. *L'Art en Ukraine,* Toulouse: Musée des Augustins, 1993-94.

170. *From Malevich to Kabakov: The Russian Avant-Garde in the 20th Century,* Cologne: Josef-Haubrich-Kunsthalle, 1993-94.

171. *Russische Avant-garde 1900-1930,* Antwerp: Hessenhuis, 1993-94.

172. *L'Avant-Garde Russe,* Paris: Galerie Gloria Cohen, 1994.

173. *Kreuzwege. Russische Avantgarde im 20. Jahrhundert / Trials and Tribulations. Russian Avant-Garde in the 20th Century,* Berlin: Galerie Stolz, 1994.

220. Pavel Tchelitchew: Costume Design for a Female Dancer with a Tambourine, ca. 1920 (No. 1079)

174. *The Avant-Garde Heritage,* Storrs, Connecticut: William Benton Museum of Art, 1994.

175. *Affiches russes et soviètiques 1905-1953,* Paris: Galerie Basmadjian, 1994.

176. *Tradition and the Vanguard. Jewish Culture in the Russian Revolutionary Era,* San Diego: Founders Gallery, University of San Diego,1994.

177. *Avanguardia e ritorno. Arte russa 1900-1940,* Milan: Fonte d'Abisso Arte, 1994.

178. *All Change. Russian Avant-Garde Books 1912-1934,* London: King's Library, 1994.

179. *Veseliashchii Peterburg,* SP: RM, 1994.

180. *La Vanguardia Rusa 1905-1925,* Barcelona: Centro Atlantico de Arte Moderno, 1994.

181. *Der Zarenschatz der Romanov,* Speyer: Museum der Pfalz, 1994.

182. *Europa, Europa. Das Jahrhundert der Avantgarde in Mittel- und Osteuropa,* Bonn: Kunsthalle, 1994.

183. *Biliofil'skaia kniga v Rossii pervoi treti XX veka,* SP: Anna Akhmatova Museum, 1994.

184. *Ori e Ore. Arte sacra e profana al tempo degli Zar,* Milan: Galleria Ottavo Piano, 1994-1995.

185. *Five Centuries of Russian Art,* St. Petersburg, Florida: Museum of Fine Arts, 1995.

186. *Treasures of the Czars: from the Moscow Kremlin Museums,* St. Petersburg, Florida: Florida International Museum, 1995.

187. *Russische Avant-garde 1900-1930 (40 paintings and 30 works on paper from the collection of the late Abram Chudnovsky),* The Hague: Het Palais, 1995.

188. *Staatliches Russisches Museum, St. Petersburg,* Bonn: Kunsthalle, 1995.

189. *They Bore Russia with Them,* M: TG, 1995; *L'Exil de la peinture russe en France 1920-1970,* Nice: Musée d'Art Moderne et d'Art Contemporain, 1995 (selections from René Guerra's collection of Russian émigré artists).

190. *Paul Mansouroff et l'avant-garde russe à Pétrograd / Les Arts Appliqués à Pétrograd,* Nice: Musée d'Art Moderne et d'Art Contemporain, 1995. Traveled to the Petersburg Museum, Otaru, Japan, in 1996.

191. *Aspects of Futurism,* Cologne: Galerie Gmurzynska, 1995.

192. *Suprematism and Constructivism in Russia,* New York: Howard Schickler Gallery, 1995.

193. *Zeichen und Wunder: Niko Pirosmani (1862-1918) und die Kunst der Gegenwart,* Zürich: Kunsthalle, 1995.

194. *Die Russen in Berlin / The Russians in Berlin / Russkii Berlin,* Berlin: Galerie Stolz, 1995.

195. *Il tempo delle illusioni. Arte russa degli anni Venti.* Genoa: Palazzo Ducale, 1995.

196. *Opere da una collezione di arte russa moderna e contemporanea* (Dalla collezione di Alberto Sandretti), Sesto San Giovanni (Milan): Villa Zorn, 1995.

197. *Okkultismus und Avantgarde. Von Munch bis Mondrian 1900-1915,* Frankfurt: Schirn Kunsthalle, 1995.

198. *Paul Gauguin e l'avanguardia russa,* Ferrara: Palazzo dei Diamanti, 1995.

199. *Kandinskij, Malevich e le avanguardie russe 1905-1925,* Turin: Palazzo Bricherasio, 1995-96. Traveled to the Art Gallery of New South Wales, Sydney, under the title *Kandinsky and the Russian Avant-Garde* in 1996.

200. *Moskau-Berlin,* Berlin: Berlinische Galerie, 1995-1996; and then *Berlin-Moscow,* M: GMII im. A.S. Pushkina, 1996.

201. *Russian Jewish Artists in a Century of Change, 1890-1988,* New York: Jewish Museum, and other cities,1995-96.

202. *The Women Artists of the Russian Avant-garde,* Cologne: Galerie Gmurzynska, 1995-96.

203. *Glaube, Hoffnung-Anpassung. Sowjetische Bilder 1928-1945,* Essen: Museum Folkwang, 1995-96.

204. *Russian Avant-Garde 1910-1930. The G. Costakis Collection,* Athens: National Gallery and Alexandros Soutzos Museum; and other cities, 1995-96.

205. *Arte Russa 1900-1935,* Milan: Galleria Capitani, 1996.

206. *Building the Collective. Soviet Graphic Design 1917-1937. Selections from the Merrill C. Berman Collection,* New York: Schermerhorn Hall, Columbia University, New York, 1996.

207. *Les Russes en France,* Paris: Musée Carnavalet, 1996.

208. *Utopia, Ilusiòn y Adaptaciòn: Arte Sovietica 1928-1945,* Valencia: IVAM Centre Julio Gonzalez, 1996.

209. *Simvolizm v Rossii,* SP: RM, 1996.

210. *Posviashchenie Shostakovichu,* M: GMII im. A.S. Pushkina, 1996-97.

211. *Krasnyi tsvet v russkom iskusstve,* SP: RM, 1997.

212. *Russian Constructivist Roots: Present Concerns,* College Park, Maryland: University of Maryland, 1997.

213. *Staraia detskaia kniga 1900-30-ye gody iz sobraniia professora Marka Ratsa,* M: Literary Museum, 1997.

214. *Masterskaia konstruktivizma,* M: TG, 1998.

215. *Art from Russia's Turning-Point. Isaak Brodsky and His Collection,* Billings, Montana: Yellowstone Art Museum, 1998.

216. *Russkii avangard. Muzei v muzee,* SP: Russian Museum, 1998.

217. *Pol Sezan [Paul Cézanne] i russkii avangard nachala XX veka,* M: GMII im. A.S. Pushkina, 1998.

218. *Vystavka khudzhnikov kruga "Bubnovogo valeta" 1910-1930 iz kollektsii Andreia Eremina,* M: Art-Salon, 1998.

219. *Stanovlenie russkogo zhivopisnogo simvolizma,* Saratov: Radishchev Museum of Art, 1998.

220. *A Taste for Splendor. Russian Imperial and European Treasures from The Hillwood Museum,* Washington, D.C.: Art Services International, 1998.

221. *Chagall, Kandinsky, Malewitsch und die russische Avantgarde,* Hamburg: Kunsthalle; and Zürich: Kunsthaus, 1998-99.

222. *100 dessins et aquarelles russes de 1790 à 1920,* Paris: Galerie de la Scala, 1999.

223. *Defining Russian Graphic Arts: From Diaghilev to Stalin, 1898-1934,* New Brunswick, New Jersey: Zimmerli Museum, 1999.

224. *New Art for a New Era. Malevich's Vision of the Russian Avant-Garde.,* London: Barbican Center, 1999.

225. *Pioneros del arte moderno. Arte ruso y sovietcio 1900-1930,* Bogota: Banca de la Republica,1999.

226. *"Mir iskusstva" i vozrozhdenie originalnoi graviury v Rossii,* M: TG, 1999.

227. *Igra i strast.* SP: RM,1999. A smaller version traveled to the Moscow Center of the Arts in 2001.

228. *Treasures of Russia from Peterhof, Palaces of the Tsars,* Las Vegas: Rio All-Suite Casino Resort, 1999.

229. *Treasures of the Last Russian Emperor,* Los Angeles: Queen Mary, 1999.

230. *Souvenirs Moscovites 1860-1930,* Paris: Musée Galliera, 1999.

231. *Risunki masterov "Bubnovogo valeta",* M: Elizium, 1999.

232. *Kandinsky, Chagall, Malevich e lo spiritualismo russo,* Verona: Palazzo Forti, 1999-2000.

221. Pavel Tchelitchew: Costume Design for a Female Dancer with Chair, ca. 1920 (No. 1080)

233. *Organica. The Non-Objective World of Nature and the Russian Avant-Garde of the 20th Century*, Cologne: Galerie Gmurzynska, 1999-2000.

234. *Le Fauvisme ou l'Epreuve du feu*, Paris: Musée d'Art Moderne de la Ville de Paris, 1999-2000.

235. *El simbolismo ruso / Le symbolisme russe*, Madrid and Barcelona: Fundacíon "la Caixa"; Bordeaux: Musée des Beaux-Arts, 1999-2000.

236. *Amazonen der Avantgarde / Amazons of the Avant-Garde*, Berlin: Deutsche Guggenheim; Royal Academy, London; Peggy Guggenheim Museum, Venice; Guggenheim Museum, Bilbao; and Solomon R. Guggenheim Museum, New York, 1999-2000.

237. *Painting Revolution. Kandinsky, Malevich and the Russian Avant-Garde*, Phoenix, AZ: Phoenix Art Museum, and other cities. 1999-2001.

238. *Parizhskoe kafe*, M: Moscow Center of the Arts, 2000.

239. *Tri ognia. Baku v izobraziltelnom iskusstve 19-20 vekov*. M: Moscow Center of the Arts, 2000.

240. *XX vek. My – v oblozhke*, M: GMII im. A.S. Pushkina, 2000.

241. *The Collection of George Costakis*, Thessaloniki: State Museum of Contemporary Art, 2000-01.

242. *Russi 1900-1920. Larionov, Goncharova, Kandinsky e gli altri. Le radici dell'avanguardia*, Brescia: Palazzo Martinengo, 2000-01.

243. *Kollektsiia peterburgskikh sobiratelei bratiev Rzhevskikh*. SP: RM, 2001.

244. *Mit voller Kraft. Russische Avant-garde 1910-1934*, Hamburg: Museum für Kunst und Gewerbe, 2001.

245. *Paris-Moscow. Crosscurrents*, London: Grosvenor Gallery, 2001.

246. *Jack of Diamonds*, Moscow: Elizium, 2001-02.

247. *Women Artists in the Art of Russia*, M: TG, 2001-02.

248. *Modernism in the Russian Far East, 1918-1928*, Tokyo: Machida City Museum of Graphic Arts; and other cities, 2002.

249. *The Russian Avant-Garde Book 1910-1934*, New York: Museum of Modern Art, 2002.

250. *Art and Utopia*, Thessaloniki: State Museum of Contemporary Art, 2003.

251. *The New Barbarians: the Russian Avant-Garde and Its Primitive Sources*, Baltimore: Walters Art Gallery; and San Francisco: Legion of Honor Museum, 2003.

252. *Russkii Parizh, 1910-1960*, SP: RM and other venues, 2003.

253. *La Russie et les avant-gardes*, Saint-Paul de Vence: Fondation Maeght, 2003.

254. *Jack of Diamonds*, SP: RM, 2004.

255. *The Russian Avant-Garde from the Collection of the Russian State Archive of Literature and Art*, M: TG, 2004.

256. *Le Valet de Carreau*, Monte Carlo: Grimaldi Forum, 2004.

257. *The World of Art* circulated in the US by the International Arts and Education Foundation, Bethesda, 2004.

258. *Licht und Farbe der Russischen Avantgarde. Die Sammlung Kostakis in Staatlichen Museen für zeitgenössiche Kunst*, Berlin: Martin-Gropius-Bau; and Vienna: Museum Moderner Kunst Stiftung Ludwig, 2004-05.

259. *Arkhumas (The Kazan Avant-Garde)*, M: Art-Divage, 2005.

260. *Exhibition in Memory of Solomon Shuster*, M: Our Artists Gallery, 2005.

261. *For the Voice. The Book of the Russian Avant-Garde 1910-1934 / The Book of the Artist 1970-2004*, SP: Anna Akhmatova Museum, 2005.

262. *St. Petersburg, 1900*, Perth: Art Gallery of Western Australia, 2005.

263. *Avant-garde in Rusland, 1900-1935*, Brussels: Paleis voor Schone Kunsten; and SP: RM, 2005-06.

264. *Russia!*, New York: Solomon R. Guggenheim Museum; and Bilbao: Solomon R. Guggenheim Museum, 2005- 06.

265. *Ukrainskii modernism / Ukrainian Modernism*, Kiev: National Art Museum of the Ukraine, 2005; circulated in the US by the International Arts and Education Foundation, Bethesda, 2005-06.

266. *From Symbolism to the Avant-Garde: Graphics and Sculpture of the First Thirty years of the 20th Century from the Collection of Mariia and Sergei Krivosheev*, M: Museum of Private Collections, 2006.

267. *Vanguardias rusas*, Madrid: Museo Thyssen, and Fundación Caja Madrid, Madrid, 2006.

268. *Von Kandinsky bis Tatlin. Konstruktivismus in Europa*, Schwerin: Staatlisches Museum, 2006.

269. *A Slap in the Face! Futurists in Russia*, London: Estorick Collection of Modern Italian Art; and Newcastle-upon-Tyne: Hatton Gallery, 2007.

270. *From Russia: French and Russian Master Paintings 1870-1925 from Moscow and St. Petersburg*, Düsseldorf: Museum Kunst Palast; and London: Royal Academy of Arts, 2007-08.

271. *Five Seasons of the Russian Avant-Garde*, Athens: State Museum of Cycladic Art, 2008.

272. *Futurism – A Radical Revolution, Italy and Russia*, M: GMII im. A.S. Pushkina, 2008.

273. *Kniaginia M.K.Tenisheva v zerkale Serebrianogo veka*, M: State Historical Museum, 2008.

274. *Lost Vanguard Found*, Thessaloniki: State Museum of Contemporary Art, 2008.

275. *Russische Avantgarde. Wurzeln der Sammlung Otten*, Hohenems, Austria: Otten Kunstraum, 2008.

276. *Sobranie kniagini M.K. Tenishevoi*, SP: RM, 2008.

277. *Futurism*, London: Tate Modern, 2009.

278. *Vers des Nouveaux Rivages – Oeuvres de la collection Georges Costakis*, Paris: Musée Maillol, 2009.

279. *Tanz der Farben. Nijinskys Auge und die Abstraktion*, Hamburg: Kunsthhalle, 2009.

280. *The Great Experiment: Russian Art. Homage to Camilla Gray*, London: Annely Juda Fine Art, 2009.

281. *OST. Grafika Obshchestva stankovistov, 1925-1932*, M: Elizium Gallery, 2009.

282. *The Spring-time of the Russian Avant-Garde*, Saitama, Japan: Museum of Modern Art, 2009.

283. *Dreams of Russia: Russian Avant-Garde, 1917-1937*, Satama, Japan: Museum of Modern Art; Russia and other venues, 2009-10.

284. *Parizhachii. Les Russes de Paris*, M: Our Artists Gallery, 2010.

285. *Russie! Memoria, misificazione, immaginario*, Venice: Ca' Foscari Esposizioni, 2010.

286. *El Cosmos de la vanguardia rusa. Arte y exploración espacial 1900-1930*, Santander: Fundacion Marcelino Botin; and Thessoloniki: State Museum of Contemporary Art, 2010-11.

287. *Klub kollektsionerov izobrazitelnogo iskusstva Moskvy. Premiera kollektsii 2010*, M: Club of the Collectors of Visual Art, 2010-11.

288. *Pioniere der deutschen und russischen Avangarde*, Zurich: Galerie Orlando, 2010-11.

289. *Venok Savitskomu. Zhivopis, risunok, fotografii, dokumenty*, M: Galeev Gallery, 2011.

290. *Russian Drawings and Watercolors*, London: Ivan Samarine / Jean-Luc Baroni, 2011.

222. Pavel Tchelitchew: Costume Design for a Fishmonger (c. 1920 No. 1081)

291. *Bespredmetnost kak novyi realizm / Nonfigurativeness as New Realism*, SP: RM; and Samara: Victoria Gallery, 2011.
292. *Avanguardia russa. Esperienze di un mondo nuovo*, Vicenza: Palazzo Leoni Montanari, 2011-12.
293. *Kollektsiia Mikhaila i Sergeia Botkinykh*, SP: RM, 2011-12.

L. Auction Catalogs Relating to Modern Russian Art

Note: This section does not list the sales devoted only to Russian *objets d'art*, icons, silver and gold or contemporary and non-conformist art held regularly at the main auction houses in the USA and Europe

1. *Twentieth Century Russian Paintings, Drawings and Watercolors 1900-1925,* London: Sotheby's, 1 July, 1970.
2. *Twentieth Century Russian Paintings, Drawings and Watercolors 1900-1930,* London: Sotheby's, 12 April, 1972.
3. *Twentieth Century Russian Paintings, Drawings and Watercolors 1900-1930,* London: Sotheby's, 29 March, 1973.
4. *Twentieth Century Russian and East European Paintings, Drawings and Sculpture 1900-1930,* London: Sotheby's, 4 July, 1974.
5. *Russian and European Avant-Garde Art, 1905-1930,* New York: Sotheby, Parke Bernet, 3 November, 1978.
6. *Russian and European Avant-Garde Art and Literature, 1905-1930,* New York: Sotheby, Parke Bernet, 6-7 November, 1979.
7. *Russian Paintings, Drawings, Watercolours and Sculpture,* London: Sotheby's, 14 May, 1980.
8. *Russian Paintings, Drawings, Watercolours and Sculpture,* London: Sotheby's, 5 March, 1981.
9. *Russian Paintings, Drawings, and Watercolors,* London: Sotheby's, 3 March, 1982.
10. *Art Russe,* Paris: Nouveau Drouot, 15 and 16 February, 1982.
11. *Art Russe,* Paris: Nouveau Drouot, 17 and 18 May, 1982.
12. *Nineteenth and Twentieth Century European Paintings, Drawings, Watercolours and Sculpture and Russian Paintings, Drawings and Watercolors,* London: Sotheby's, 28 February, 1983.
13. *Russian Pictures, Icons and Russian Works of Art,* London: Sotheby's, 15 February, 1984.
14. *Icons, Russian Pictures, Works of Art and Fabergé,* London: Sotheby's, 20 February, 1985.
15. *Art Russe,* Paris: Nouveau Drouot, 12 and 13 March, 1985.
16. *Art Russe,* Paris: Hôtel des Ventes de l'Isle-Adam, 17 March, 1985.
17. *Art Russe,* Paris: Nouveau Drouot, 24 May, 1985.
18. *Art Russe,* Paris: Hôtel des Ventes de l'Isle-Adam, 20 October, 1985.
19. *Russian Pictures, Works of Art and Fabergé,* London: Sotheby's, 13 February, 1986.
20. *Icons, Russian Pictures and Works of Art,* London: Christie's, 6 March, 1986.
21. *Livres et Tableaux Russes des Années 1910-1930,* Paris: Binoche et Godeau, 23 April, 1986.
22. *Important Modern and Contemporary Prints,* London: Christie's, 25 June, 1986.
23. *Art Russe,* Paris: Nouveau Drouot, 15 December, 1986.
24. *Russian Twentieth Century and Avant-Garde Art* London: Sotheby's, 2 April, 1987.

25. *Icons, Russian Pictures and Works of Art,* London: Sotheby's, 1 May, 1987.
26. *Icons, Russian Pictures and Works of Art,* London: Christie's, 21 October, 1987.
27. *Alexandre Sementchenkoff Collection,* London: Christie's, 22 October, 1987.
28. *Icons, Russian Pictures and Works of Art.* London: Christie's, 21 April, 1988.
29. *Art Russe,* Paris: Verrières-le-Buisson, 15 May, 1988.
30. *Impressionist and Modern Art, Twentieth Century Russian and Avant-Garde Art,* London: Sotheby's, 18 May, 1988.
31. *Russian Avant-Garde and Contemporary Art,* M: Sotheby's, 7 July, 1988.
32. *Artwork of the Soviet Union,* New York: Guernsey's, 22 and 23 October, 1988.
33. *Icons, Russian Pictures and Works of Art,* London: Sotheby's 14 November, 1988.
34. *Collection of Russian and German Works of Art,* Phelps, New York: Davis Auction House, 26 February, 1989.
35. *Russian Twentieth Century and Avant-Garde Art,* London: Sotheby's, 6 April, 1989.
36. *Art Russe Impérial et Post-Révolutionnaire,* Paris: Drouot Montaigne, 23 April, 1989.
37. *Icons, Russian Pictures and Works of Art,* London: Sotheby's, 7 April, 1989.
38. *Imperial and Post-Revolutionary Russian Art,* London: Christie's, 5 October, 1989.
39. *Avant-Garde du XXe Siècle,* Paris: Hôtel Drouot, 20 October, 1989.
40. *Collection Léon Aronson dit Dominique (1893-1984),* Paris: Drouot, 15 November, 1989.
41. *Russian 20th Century and Avant-Garde Art,* London: Phillips, 27 November, 1989.
42. *Russian Pictures, Works of Art, and Icons,* London: Sotheby's, 6 December, 1989.
43. *Russian Art,* London: Phillips, 2 April, 1990.
44. *Russian Avant-Garde. Pictures from the Collection formed by George Costakis,* London: Sotheby's, 4 April, 1990.
45. *A Selection of Russian Avant-Garde Works Formerly the Property of Kurt Benedikt,* London: Christie's, 5 April, 1990.
46. *Important Russian Works of Art,* New York: Christie's, 19 April, 1990.
47. *Icons, Russian Pictures and Works of Art,* London: Christie's, 27 April, 1990.
48. *Tableaux Russes,* Paris: Drouot, 14 May, 1990.
49. *Art Russe,* Paris: Drouot, 16 May, 1990.
50. *Russian Twentieth Century and Avant-Garde Art,* London: Sotheby's, 23 May, 1990.
51. *Moderne Literatur und Kunst,* Cologne: Venator und Hanstein, 20 September, 1990.
52. *Imperial and Post-Revolutionary Russian Art,* London: Christie's, 10 October, 1990.
53. *Russian Works of Art,* New York: Christie's, 31 October, 1990.
54. *Russian Art,* London: Phillips, 26 November, 1990.
55. *Icons, Russian Pictures and Works of Art,* London: Christie's, 27 November, 1990.
56. *Icons, Russian Pictures and Works of Art,* London: Sotheby's, 30 November, 1990.
57. *Art russe XXe siècle,* Paris: Drouot-Richelieu, 10 February, 1991.

223. Pavel Tchelitchew: Costume Design for a Spanish Dancer, *Danse Espagnole*, 1921 (No. 1084)

58. *Les Avant-Gardes Russes XXe Siècle, Rares Affiches, Oeuvres sur Papier,* Paris: Drouot-Richelieu, 22 May, 1991.

59. *Russian Art,* London: Phillips, 23 April, 1991.

60. *Icons, Russian Pictures, Avant-Garde Books and Works of Art,* London: Christie's, 24 April, 1991.

61. *Icons, Russian Pictures and Works of Art,* London: Sotheby's, 24 November. 1991.

62. *Icons, Imperial and Post-Revolutionary Russian Art,* London: Christie's, 27 November, 1991.

63. *Nineteenth and Twentieth Century Scandinavian, Russian and Continental Pictures and Water-Colours,* London: Christie's, 22 May, 1992.

64. *Icons, Russian Pictures and Works of Art,* London: Sotheby's, 16 June, 1992.

65. *Icons, Russian Pictures and Works of Art,* London: Sotheby's, 24 November, 1992.

66. *Icons, Russian Pictures and Works of Art,* London: Sotheby's 17 June, 1993.

67. *Icons, Russian Pictures and Works of Art,* London: Sotheby's, 15 June, 1993.

68. *Icons, Russian Pictures and Works of Art,* London: Sotheby's, 15 December, 1993.

69. *USSR in Construction. Posters, Designs, and Drawings,* New York: Sotheby's, 10 March, 1994.

70. *The Russian Library of an American Collector,* New York: Christie's, 8 June, 1994.

71. *Icons, Russian Pictures and Works of Art,* London: Sotheby's, 16 June, 1994.

72. *A Collection of Russian Works of Art,* London: Phillips,15 November, 1994.

73. *Soviet Realist and Impressionist Paintings,* London: Phillips, 15 November, 1994.

74. *Russian Pictures and Works of Art,* London: Sotheby's, 15 December, 1994.

75. *Fabergé, Russian Works of Art and Objects of Vertu,* New York: Sotheby's, 6 June, 1995.

76. *Icons, Russian Pictures and Works of Art,* London: Christie's, 14 June, 1995.

77. *Icons, Russian Pictures and Works of Art,* London: Sotheby's, 15 June, 1995.

78. *Fabergé, Russian Works of Art and Objects of Vertu,* New York: Sotheby's, 6 December, 1995.

79. *Imperial and Post-Revolutionary Russian Art and Icons,* London: Christie's, 13 December, 1995.

80. *The Russian Sale,* London, Sotheby's, 14-15 December, 1995.

81. *The Russian Tea Room,* New York: William Doyle Galleries, 16 January, 1996.

82. *Russian Works of Art, Paintings and Fabergé,* New York: Christie's, 18 April, 1996.

83. *Fabergé, Russian Works of Art and Objects of Vertu,* New York: Sotheby's, 12 June, 1996.

84. *The Russian Sale,* London: Sotheby's, 17 July, 1996.

85. *Imperial and Post-Revolutionary Russian Art and Icons,* London: Christie's, 18 July, 1996.

86. *Fabergé, Russian Works of Art and Obejcts of Vertu,* New York: Sotheby's, 11 December, 1996.

87. *Imperial and Post-Revolutionary Russian Art and Icons,* London: Christie's, 18 December, 1996.

88. *The Russian Sale,* London: Sotheby's, 19 December, 1996.

89. *The Russian Sale,* London: Sotheby's, 11 and 12 June, 1997.

90. *Imperial and Post-Revolutionary Russian Art and Icons,* London: Christie's, 12 June, 1997.

91. *Imperial and Post-Revolutionary Russian Art and Icons,* London: Christie's, 20 November, 1997.

92. *The Provatoroff Collection of Russian Works of Art, Icons and Pictures,* London, Christie's, 20 November, 1997.

93. *The Russian Sale, Including the Nicholas Lynn Collection of Soviet Revolutionary Porcelain,* London: Sotheby's, 19 February, 1998.

94. *Imperial and Post-Revolutionary Russian Art and Icons,* London: Christie's, 15 July, 1998.

95. *The Russian Sale,* London: Sotheby's, 7-8 October, 1998.

96. *Icons, Russian Pictures and Works of Art,* London: Sotheby's, 8 October, 1998.

97. *20th Century Art,* London: Christie's, 7 December, 1998 (carried a section on Russian theatrical art).

98. *Imperial and Post-Revolutionary Russian Art and Icons,* London: Christie's, 17 December, 1998.

99. *Russische Kunst,* Vienna: Palais Dorotheum, 22 February, 1999.

100. *The Russian Sale,* London: Sotheby's, 29 April, 1999.

101. *Russian Art and Icons,* London: Christie's, 14 July, 1999.

102. *Russische Kunst,* Vienna: Palais Dorotheum, 16 November, 1999.

103. *Russische Kunst,* Vienna: Palais Dorotheum, 17 November, 1999.

104. *The Russian Sale,* London: Sotheby's, 18 November, 1999.

105. *Russian Works of Art and Objects of Vertu,* New York: Sotheby's, 15 December, 1999.

106. *Russian Art and Icons.* London: Christie's, 17 December, 1999.

107. *Russische Kunst,* Vienna: Dorotheum, 26 April, 2000.

108. *The Russian Sale,* London: Sotheby's, 10 May, 2000.

109. *Kazimir Malevich: Suprematist Composition*, New York: Phillips, 11 May, 2000.

110. *Russian Paintings and Works of Art,* London: Christie's, 7 July, 2000.

111. *Russische Kunst,* Vienna: Dorotheum, 15 November, 2000.

112. *The Russian Sale,* London: Sotheby's, 23 November, 2000.

113. *Russian Paintings and Works of Art,* London: Christie's, 15 December, 2000.

114. *Russische Kunst,* Vienna: Dorotheum, 16 May, 2001.

115. *The Russian Sale,* London: Sotheby's, 31 May, 2001.

116. *The Russian Sale,* London: Sotheby's, 20 November, 2001.

117. *Russian Paintings and Works of Art,* London: Christie's, 21 November, 2001.

118. *Russian Paintings and Works of Art,* London: Christie's, 21 November, 2001.

119. *Russische Kunst,* Vienna: Dorotheum, 30 April, 2002.

120. *Russian Pictures,* London: Sotheby's 22 May, 2002.

121. *Russian Pictures,* London: Sotheby's, 20 November, 2002.

122. *Russian Paintings and Works of Art,* London: Christie's, 26 November, 2002.

123. *Russian Pictures,* London: Sotheby's, 21 May, 2003.

124. *Russian Pictures,* London: Sotheby's, 19 November, 2003.

125. *Russian Art,* New York: Sotheby's, 23 April, 2004.

126. *The Russian Sale,* London: Sotheby's, 26 May, 2004.

127. *Russian Pictures, Russian Works of Art,* London: Christie's, 30 November, 2004.

128. *Russian Art Auction,* London: MacDougall's, 30 November, 2004.

224. Pavel Tchelitchew: Costume Design for a Spanish Guitar Player, *Danse Espagnole*, 1921 (No. 1085)

129. *Russian Pictures, Works of Art and Icons,* London: Sotheby's, 2 December, 2004.

130. *Russian Sale,* Stockholm: Stockholms Auktionsverk, 16 December, 2004.

131. *Russian Art Auction,* London: MacDougall's, 18 May, 2005.

132. *Russian Pictures,* Works of Art and Icons, London: Sotheby's, 20 May, 2005.

133. *The Russian Sale,* London: Bonhams, 28 November, 2005.

134. *Russian Pictures,* London: Christie's, 30 November, 2005.

135. *The Russian Auction,* Stockholm: Stockholms Auktionsverk, 9 December, 2005.

136. *Property from the Collection of Ambassador Charles R. Crane, New* York: Christie's, 24 April, 2006.

137. *Russian Paintings and Works of Art,* New York: Christie's, 24 April, 2006.

138. *Russian Art,* New York: Sotheby's, 26 April, 2006.

139. *Russian Art,* New York: Sotheby's, 28 April, 2006.

140. *Russian Art Auction,* London: MacDougall's, 30 May, 2006.

141. *The Russian Sale,* London: Sotheby's, 31 May, 2006.

142. *Russian Pictures, Works of Art and Icons,* London: Sotheby's, 1 June, 2006.

143. *The Russian Sale,* London: Bonhams, 13 June, 2006.

144. *The Russian Sale,* London: Bonhams, 27 November, 2006.

145. *The Russian Sale,* London: Sotheby's, 28 November, 2006.

146. *Important Russian Pictures,* London: Christie's, 29 November, 2006.

147. *The Russian Sale. Pictures,* London: Sotheby's, 28 November, 2006.

148. *Russian Pictures, Works of Art and Icons,* London: Sotheby's, 30 November, 2006.

149. *The Russian Auction,* Stockholm: Stockholms Auktionsverk, 15 March, 2007.

150. *Russian Art,* New York: Sotheby's, 16 April, 2007.

151. *Russian Art,* New York: Sotheby's, 17 April, 2007.

152. *Russian Paintings and Works of Art,* New York: Christie's, 18 April, 2007.

153. *Sonderteil. Russische Kunst des 20. Jahrhunderts,* Stuttgart: Nagel, 26 April, 2007.

154. *The Russian Sale,* London: Bonhams, 31 May, 2007.

155. *Russian Art,* London: Sotheby's, 12 June, 2007.

156. *Russian Art,* London: Christie's, 13 June, 2007.

157. *Russian Pictures, Works of Art and Icons,* London: Sotheby's, 14 June, 2007.

158. *Russian XIX and XX Century Art Auction,* London: MacDougall's, 15 June, 2007.

159. *The Rostropovich-Vishnevskaya Collection,* London: Sotheby's, 18-19 September, 2007.

160. *The Russian Auction,* Stockholm: Stockholms Auktionsverk, 4-5 October, 2007.

161. *Russian Art Evening,* London: Sotheby's, 26 November, 2007.

162. *The Russian Sale,* London: Bonhams, 26 November, 2007.

163. *Important Russian Works from the Schreiber Collection,* London: Sotheby's, 26-27 November, 2007.

164. *Russian Art,* London: Sotheby's, 27 November, 2007.

165. *Important Russian Pictures,* London: Christie's, 28 November, 2007.

166. *The Somov Collection,* London: Christiie's, 28 November, 2007.

167. *Russian Icons and Pictures including Works by Nonconformist Artists,* London: Christiie's, 29 November, 2007.

168. *Russian XIX and XX Century Art Auction,* London: MacDougall's, 29-30 November, 2007.

169. *The Russian Auction,* Stockholm: Stockholms Auktionsverk, 13-14 March, 2008.

170. *Russian Art,* New York: Sotheby's, 15 April, 2008.

171. *Russian Art,* London: Sotheby's, 16 April, 2008.

172. *Russian Art,* New York: Christie's, 18 April, 2008.

173. *Russian Art Evening,* London: Sotheby's, 9 June, 2008.

174. *The Russian Sale,* London: Bonhams, 9 June, 2008.

175. *Russian Art,* London: Christie's, 11 June, 2008.

176. *Art Russe,* Paris: Tajan, 27 June, 2008.

177. *The Russian Auction,* Stockholm: Stockholms Auktionsverk, 2-3 October, 2008.

178. *Important Russian Art,* London: Sotheby's, 3-5 November, 2008.

179. *The Russian Sale,* London: Bonhams, 24 November, 2008.

180. *Russian Works of Art,* London: Christie's, 24 November, 2008.

181. *Russian Art Evening,* London: Sotheby's, 24 November, 2008.

182. *Russian Art Paintings,* London: Sotheby's, 25 November, 2008.

183. *Russian Pictures including Post-War and Contemporary Art,* London: Christie's, 26 November, 2008.

184. *Russian Pictures, Icons and Works of Art,* London: Christie's, 27 November, 2008.

185. *The Russian Auction,* Stockholm: Stockholms Auktionsverk, 12 March, 2009.

186. *Russian Art,* New York: Sotheby's, 22 April, 2009.

187. *Russian Art,* New York: Christie's, 24 April, 2009.

188. *Russian Art Evening,* London: Sotheby's, 3 June, 2009.

189. *The Russian Sale,* London: Bonhams, 8 June, 2009.

190. *Russian Art,* London: Christie's, 9 June, 2009.

191. *Russian Art Paintings,* London: Sotheby's, 10 June, 2009.

192. *Russian Art,* London: Christie's, 11 June, 2009.

193. *Galerie Popoff,* Part I, London: Christie's, 12 October, 2009.

194. *Galerie Popoff,* Part II, London: Christie's, 13 October, 2009.

195. *Russian Art,* New York: Sotheby's, 2 November, 2009.

196. *Russian Art Evening,* London: Sotheby's, 30 November, 2009.

197. *The Russian Sale,* London: Bonhams, 30 November, 2009.

198. *Russian Art,* London: Christie's, 1 December, 2009.

199. *Russian Art Painting,* London: Sotheby's, 1 December, 2009.

200. *Russian Art,* London: Christie's, 3 December, 2009.

201. *Russian XIX and XX Century Art Auction,* London: MacDougall's, 3 December, 2009.

202. *Russian Art,* New York: Sotheby's, 21-22 April, 2010.

203. *Russian Art,* New York: Christie's, 23 April, 2010.

204. *Important Russian Art,* London: Sotheby's, 7 June, 2010.

205. *The Russian Sale,* London: Bonhams, 7 June, 2010.

206. *Russian Art,* London: Christie's, 8 June, 2010.

207. *Russian Art,* London: Sotheby's, 9 June, 2010.

208. *Russian Art,* London: Christie's, 10 June, 2010.

209. *Russian Classic and Contemporary Art,* London: MacDougall's, 11 June, 2010.

210. *Russian Works on Paper,* London: MacDougall's, 11 June, 2010.

211. *Important Russian Art,* New York: Sotheby's, 4 November, 2010.

212. *Russian Art,* London: Christie's, 29 November, 2010.

213. *Russian Art,* London: Sotheby's, 30 November, 2010.

214. *The Russian Sale,* London: Bonhams, 1 December, 2010.

215. *Russian Art,* New York: Sotheby's, 12 April, 2011.

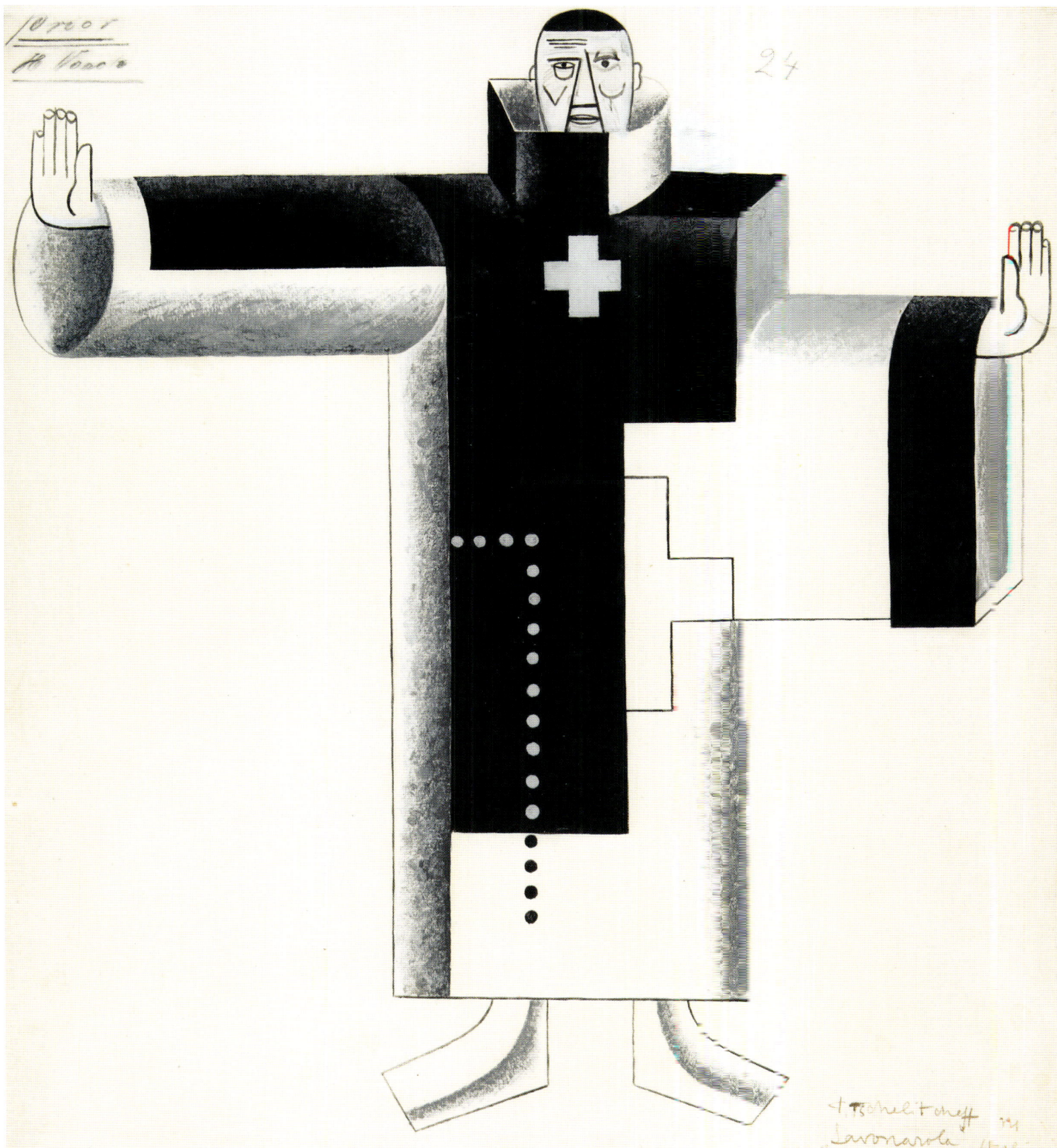

225. Pavel Tchelitchew: Costume Design for Girlolamo Savonarola, *Savonarola*, Berlin, 1921 (No. 1087)

216. *Russian Art,* London: Christie's, 13 April, 2011.
217. *Russian Classic Art,* London: MacDougall's, 8 June, 2011.
218. *Russian Works on Paper,* London: MacDougall's, 9 June, 2011.
219. *Russian Icons and Works of Art,* London: MacDougall's, 9 June, 2011.
220. *Important Russian Art,* New York: Sotheby's, 1 November, 2011.
221. *Important Russian Art,* London: Sotheby's, 28 November, 2011.
222. *Russian Art,* London: Christie's, 28 November, 2011.
223. *Russian Art,* London: Sotheby's, 29 and 30 November, 2011.
224. *Russian Art Auctions,* London: MacDougall's, 30 November-1 December, 2011.
225. *Art Russe,* Paris: CAZO, 11 December, 2011.
226. *Collection Serge Lifar,* Geneva: Hôtel des Ventes, 13 March, 2012.
227. *Important Russian Art,* London: MacDougall's, 27 May, 2012.
228. *Russian Art,* New York: Christie's, 28 May, 2012.
229. *Russian Art,* Part I, London: MacDougall's, 30 May, 2012.
230. *Russian Art,* Part II, London: MacDougall's, 30 May, 2012.

M. Publications by Nikita D. Lobanov-Rostovsky Relating to Modern Russian Art

1. N.L. (Lobanov): "Vosproizvedenie russkikh postanovok i kostiumov" in *Russkaia mysl,* Paris, 1967, 21 September.
2. "Russian Painters and the Stage" in *Transactions of the Association of Russian-American Scholars in USA / Zapiski Russkoi Akademicheskoi gruppy v SShA,* New York, 1968, Vol. 2, pp. 131-210; 1969, Vol. 3, pp. 207-09; 1972, Vol. 6, pp. 89-93.
3. "Nakhodka na bloshinom rynke — Kartiny Nikolaia Kalmakova" in *Novoe russkoe slovo,* New York, 1969, 17 August, p. 4.
4. "Pavel Fedorovich Chelishchev" in *Novoe russkoe slovo,* New York, 1972, 21 April.
5. "The Pictures of Nikolai Kalmakov" in A. Flegon: *Eroticism in Russian Art,* London: Flegon, 1976, pp. 306-07.
6. "Kratkoe opredelenie piati levykh techenii v russkoi zhivopisi" in *Russkaia mysl,* Paris, 1979, 28 June, p. 7.
7. "My Collection of Costume and Stage Designs by Russian-Born Artists" in G55, 1981, pp. 265-71 (19 ills.).
8. with J. Bowlt (interviewer): "Russkaia teatralnaia zhivopis. Interviu s N.D. Lobanovym-Rostovskim" in *Russkaia mysl,* Paris, 1982, 25 March, pp. 13-14.
9. "Sem voprosov Igoriu Dychenko" in *Novoe russkoe slovo,* New York, 1984, 11 March, p. 4 (3 ills.).
10. "Russians Who Painted the Stage" in *Art and Design,* London, 1986, April, pp. 53-55 (5 color ills.).
11. "Modernist Russian Art and the Stage" in *Art and Design,* London, 1986, June, pp. 18-19 (3 color ills.).
12. "Vospriiatie russkoi zhivopisi na Zapade" in *Russkaia mysl,* Paris, 1986, 22 August, p. 11 (4 color ills.).
13. "Russkii teatralnyi dizain" in *Russkaia mysl,* Paris, 1987, 10 April, p. 12 (1 ill.).
14. "Teatralnyi dizain prishel iz Rossii" in *Novoe russkoe slovo,* New York, 15 April, 1987, p. 3.
15. "Po sledam khudozhnitsy (A. Exter)" in *Ogonek,* M, 1988, January, No, 4, p. 9 and centerfold (10 color ills.).
16. "Cutting through the Bureaucratic Tangle in Soviet Culture?" in *Apollo,* London, 1988, February, pp. 123-24 (1 ill.).
17. "Russkie auktsiony v Londone" in *Ezhemesiachnik Otdela emigrantov iz Rossii pri Jewish Community Center,* San Diego, 1990, June, pp. 13-14.
18. "Spomeni za ruskite khudozhnitsi v chuzhbina" in *Orfei,* Sofia, 1991, No. 2, December, pp. 64-67 (3 color and 1 b/w ills.).
19. "Tseny na iskusstvo russkogo avangarda" in *Menedzher,* M, 1991, No. 4, February, p. 4.
20. "Useshtane za uprichastnost" in *Orfei,* Sofia, 1992, No. 2, pp. 16-21 (5 ills.).
21. "Theatre Artists from Russia. Notes of a Collector" in H32, Vol. 1, pp. 390-420.
22. "Spomeni za ruski khudozhnitsi emigranti" in *Literaturen vestnik,* Sofia, 1993, 26 April – 2 May, pp. 1 and 7 (2 ills.).
23. "Vyrvannye iz zabveniia" in *Kultura,* M, 1993, No. 28, 17 July, pp. 10-11 (part 1); No. 29, 27 July, pp. 10-11 (part 2); No. 30, 31 July, pp. 10-11.
24. "Reception of Russian Art at Auctions is Lukewarm" in *The Moscow Tribune,* M, 1993, 4 August, p. 4.
25. "Sergei Lifar i ego kollektsiia teatralnoi zhivopisi" in *Russkaia mysl,* Paris, 1993, 3 November, p. 17. Reprinted in D53, pp. 321-26; and *Kollektsioner,* M, 1995, No. 3, pp. 4-5.
26. "Sudba ego kollektsii (Sergei Lifar)" in *Kultura,* M, 1993, 18 December, p. 11 (2 ills.).
27. "For Russian Art Collectors, 1993 Was a Good Year" in *The Moscow Tribune,* M, 1993, 31 December, p. 8.
28. "Bankiry liubiat Vasnetsova" in *Chelovek i kariera,* M, 1993, No. 3, p. 15 (1 ill.).
29. "Birth of a Unique Museum" in *The Moscow Tribune,* M, 1994, 11 January, p. 8.
30. "Tak kuda zhe otpravilsia russkii boiarin?" in *Kultura,* M, 1994, 5 February, No. 4, p. 10 (part 1); and 12 February, No. 5, pp. 10-11 (part 2) (2 ills.).
31. "Lish nekotorye bankiry predpochitaiut avangard" in *Chelovek i kariera,* M, 1994, No. 1, p. 15 (1 ill.).
32. "Iskusstvo izmeriaetsia tonnami, kogda ono vyvozitsia iz Rossii" in *Chelovek i kariera,* M, 1994, No. 3, p. 15.
33. "Russkii plakat pokupaiut v Niu-Yorke" in *Chelovek i kariera,* M, 1994, No. 4, p. 15 (1 ill.).
34. "The Ultimate in Art Research is Bound to Please" in *The Moscow Tribune,* M, 1994, 11 March, p. 7.
35. "Kto bolee Maiakovskogo tsenen?" in *Vechernii klub,* M, 1994, 15 March, p. 7 (1 ill.).
36. "Russkii i vostochnoevropeiskii avangard iz znamenitoi kollektsii" in *Russkaia mysl,* Paris, 1994, 25-31 March, p. 13 (1 ill.).
37. "Annenkova kupili po telefonu" in *Chelovek i kariera,* M, 1994, No. 12, p. 15 (1 ill.).
38. "Russkii plakat, 1917-1940" in *Russkaia mysl,* Paris, 1994, 6 April, p. 15 (1 ill.).
39. "Ne imeia ni grosha, ya poklialsia sobrat kollektsiiu i sdelal eto" in *Vechernii klub,* M, 1994, 7 April (1 ill.).
40. "Anatolii Nikolaevich Demidov, Kniaz San-Donato" in *Russkaia mysl,* Paris, 1994, 7 April, p. 16.
41. "Eksponaty kollektsii Demidovykh rasprodany poodinochke" in *Vechernii klub,* M, 1994, 14 April.
42. "Un labirinto oscuro in cui è facile smarrirsi" in *Il giornale dell'arte,* Rome, 1994, April, No. 121.
43. "Muzei lichnykh kollektsii" in *Kvartirier,* M, 1994, May, No. 6-7, p. 15 (2 ills.).
44. "Collecting Russian art: a Hazardous Adventure" in *The Art Newspaper,* London, 1994, June, No. 39.
45. "Russian Works Sell Well at Sotheby's" in *The Moscow Tribune,* M, 1994, 29 June (1 ill.).

226. Pavel Tchelitchew. Costume Design for a Gentleman at Court and His Moorish Boy Servant, *Savonarola*, ca. 1921 (No. 1089)

46. "Russkoe iskusstvo v Londone" in *Kultura,* M, 1994, 9 July, p. 10 (2 ills.).

47. "Temnye labirinty russkogo avangarda" in *Segodnia,* M, 1994, July, p. 9 (2 ills.).

48. with N. Shcheglova: "Kak stat kollektsionerom bez grosha v karmane" in *Chelovek i kariera,* M, 1994, No. 4, p. 14 (2 ills.).

49. "Tragediia — ne vyvoz Malevicha, a poteria arkhiva" in *Chelovek i kariera,* M, 1994, No. 8.

50. "Russian Art at Sotheby's" in *The Art Newspaper,* London, 1994, No. 40, July-September, p. 33.

51. "Fantasticheskaia realnost" in *Kultura,* M, 1994, 5 August, p. 10 (1 ill.).

52. "Pleiboi siurrealizma, papa sotsarta..." in *Mir iskusstva,* M, 1994, 20 August, p. 7 (prepared by N. Danilevich) (1 ill.).

53. "Vospominaniia o russkikh khudozhnikakh za rubezhom" in *Transactions of the Association of Russian-American Scholars in USA / Zapiski Russkoi Akademicheskoi gruppy v SShA,* New York, 1994, Vol. XXVI, pp. 64-95 (20 ills.).

54. "Russkoe iskusstvo za granitsei" in *Kultura,* M, 1994, 17 September, p. 10 (3 ills.).

55. with John E. Bowlt (interviewer): "Sled ot poleta babochki" in *Kultura,* M, 1994, 8 October, p. 4 (3 ills.).

56. "Russkie khudozhniki pokorili mir" in *Kultura,* M, 1994, 15 October, p. 4 (3 ills.).

57. with John E. Bowlt (interviewer): "Sobiratel fantazii" in *Rodina,* M, 1994, No. 11, pp. 90-96 (9 color and 3 b/w ills.).

58. Anon.: "Lifetime of Russian Art Goes for a Song" in *The Moscow News,* M, 1994, 8 December, p. 9 (1 ill.).

59. with Elena Skvortsova (interviewer): "Russkie kollektsii vystavliaiutsia i prodaiutsia" in *Obshchaia gazeta,* M, 1994, 9-15 December, p. 11 (3 ills.).

60. "Auktsiony. Nasledie Dory i Richarda na 'Fillipse'" in *Kultura,* M, 1994, 10 December, p. 2.

61. "Frantsuzskie interiery Aleksandra Serebriakova" in *Chelovek i kariera,* M, 1994, No. 14, p. 13 (2 ills.).

62. with Peter Batkin, Aleksandr Solodkov, John Stuart, Aleksei Tisenkhauzen: "Kupit v Londone, privezti v Moskvu!" in *Kultura,* M, 1995, 28 January, pp. 9-10 (3 ills.).

63. "Vmesto epitafii. A. Serebriakov, maestro interiera" in *Kultura,* M, 1995, 28 January, p. 10.

64. with Vladimir Enisherlov (interviewer): "Etu 'diversiiu' ya gotovil vsiu zhizn" in *Illiustrirovannaia Rossiia,* M, 1995, January, pp. 59-63 (14 color ills.).

65. with Alexander Poliakov (interviewer): "Russkii kniaz v kontse XX veka" in *Kollektsioner,* M, 1995, No. 1, pp. 8-11 (3 ills.).

66. with Elena Skvortsova (interviewer): "Strast aristokrata" in *Obshchaia gazeta,* M, 1995, 16-22 February, p. 16 (5 ills.).

67. "Khudozhniki-emigranty" in *Delovaia zhizn,* M, 1995, February, p. 18 (3 ills.).

68. with John E. Bowlt (interviewer): "Ya vzial by kostium Kleopatry" in *Mir muzeia,* M, 1995, No. 4, pp. 60-64 (3 ills.).

69. "Palitra emigratsii" in *Obshchaia gazeta,* M, 1995, 20 June – 5 July, p. 16 (10 ills.).

70. "Kollekstionery" in *Art Prestige,* M, 1995, July-August, p. 56 (1 ill.).

71. with John E. Bowlt (interviewer): "Ya vzial by kostium Kleopatry" in *Vsemirnoe slovo,* SP, 1995, No. 8, pp. 60-63, 90 (5 ills.).

72. with Igor Kokhanovsky (interviewer): "Potomok Riurikovichei v segodniashnei Rossii" in *Inostranets,* M, 1995, 20 September, pp. 30-31 (1 ill.).

73. "Karl Briullov i kniaz San Donato" in *Kultura,* M, 1995, 4 November.

74. "Russkaia kollektsiia prineset 'Sotheby's' okolo 7 millionov dollarov" in *Delovoi mir,* M, 1995, 8 November, p. 22. The same page carries the unsigned article "Bakst i Sudeikin u Juliana Barrana" (3 ills.).

75. "Avangard—minnoe pole antikvarnogo rynka" in *Delovoi mir,* M, 1995, 8 November, p. 23. The same page carries the unsigned article "'Bestsennoe' iskusstvo na evropeiskikh rynkakh" (2 ills.).

76. "Vozvrashchenie Karla Briullova" in *Obshchaia gazeta,* M, 1995, 23-29 November, p. 11.

77. "'Sotbis' vnov delaet stavku na russkii avangard" in *Chelovbek i kariera,* M, 1995, No. 15, p. 14 (6 ills.).

78. "Million nemetskikh marok za odnu russkuiu 'konstruktsiiu'" in *Chelovek i kariera,* M, 1995, No. 16, p. 15 (1 ill.).

79. "Bespretsedentnyi russii auktsion" in *Kultura,* M, 1995, 2 December, p. 10.

80. (with Sergei Drozhin): "Berlin exhibition hailed" in *The Moscow News,* M, 1995, 7 December, p. 8 (2 ills.).

81. "'Novye russkie' — novaia klientura 'Sotbis'" in *Obshchaia gazeta,* M, 1995, 7-13 December, p. 11.

82. "Proekt goda: uspekh ili fiasko?" in *Obshchaia gazeta,* M, 1996, 11-17 January, p. 11 (1 ill.).

83. "Vstrechi na marshrute 'Moskva-Berlin'" in *Kultura,* M, 1996, 27 January, p. 11 (3 ills.).

84. "Eltsin ukhazhva edin mlad pretendent za ruski tsar" in *24 chasa,* Sofia, 31 January, 1996, p. 21 (1 ill.).

85. "Kollektsionirovanie russkikh kostiumov i dekoratsii" in *Muzykalnaia akademiia,* M, 1996, No. 1, pp. 223-25 (introduced by Vadim Kiselev) (4 ills.).

86. "Moskva-Berlin 1900-1950" in *Art-Prestige,* M, 1996, No. 2, p. 36 (5 color ills.).

87. with Sergei Nikolaevich and Edvard Gurevich (interviewers): "Russkii inostranets Nikita Lobanov-Rostovsky" in *Domovoi,* M, 1996, February, pp. 30-36 (2 color ills.).

88. "Bespretsedentnyi russkii auktsion v 'Sotbis'" in *Magnifikat,* M, 1996, April (2 color ills.).

89. "Russkii avangard iz sobraniia Georgiia Kostaki" in *Art and Prestige,* M, 1996, No. 4, p. 32 (2 ills.).

90. "Kollektsii, kotoroi net analogov" in *Delovoi mir,* M, 1996, 22 May, p. 22.

91. with Nadezhda Danilevich (interviewer): "Predotvrashchenie ushcherba" in *Delovoi mir,* M, 1996, May, p. 22 (2 ills.).

92. "Sobranie russkogo avangarda" in *Evropeiskii vestnik,* London, 1996, June, p. 14 (1 ill.).

93. "Russian Avant-Garde Lives on in Costakis Collection" in *The Moscow News,* M, 1996, 19 July, p. 15 (1 ill.).

94. with DV (interviewer): "Problemy strakhovaniia proizvedenii isusstva v Rossii" in *Evropeiskii vestnik,* London, 1996, July, p. 13.

95. with Nadezhda Danilevich (interviewer): "Massovaia emigratsiia khudozhnikov vyzvana poterei rynka v Rossii" in *Delovoi mir,* M, 1996, 9-15 August, p. 9 (1 ill.).

96. with Jeanne Vronskaya (interviewer): "Bum na rynke iskusstv v Rossii zatikh...iz-za krizisa v bankakh" in *Evropeiskii vestnik,* London, 1996, August, pp. 11-12 (1 ill.).

97. with Jeanne Vronskaya (interviewer): "Kem by vy khoteli byt? Lorentso Medichi" in *Evropeiskii vestnik,* London, 1996, August, pp. 11-12.

98. with Olga Speranskaia (interviewer): "Gori, gori, moia zvezda" in *London Courier,* London, 1996, No. 39, August, p. 12; No. 40, 16 (1 ill.).

99. "Valuation for Russian Artworks" in *European Herald,* London, 1996, September, p. 11.

227. Pavel Tchelitchew: Costume Design for Cornazano, a Knight, *Savonarola* 1921 (No. 1091)

100. with Valerii Dudakov (interviewer): "Art-rynok. Zakonomernoe i anomalnoe" in *Art-Prestige,* M, 1997, No. 1-2, pp. 134-36 (1 color ill.).

101. with Natalia Aleksandrova (interviewer): "Roskosh — eto kogda" in *Stil zhizni,* M, 1997, January-February, No. 1-2, p. 3 (4 color ills.).

102. with Nadezhda Danilevich (interviewer): "Ya khotel by byt Lorentso Medichi" in *Dengi,* M, 1997, No. 6, February, pp. 55-59 (8 color ills.).

103. with Elena Druzhinina (interviewer): "Kniaz Nikita Dmitrievich Lobanov-Rostovsky. Istoriia odnogo uspekha" in *Intellektualnyi kapital,* SP, 1997, No. 4, April, p. 9 (1 ill.).

104. "Moe sobranie russkoi teatralnoi zhivopisi" in *Art-Prestige,* M, 1997, No. 5-6, pp. 122-25. (2 color ill.).

105. with Svetlana Balashova (interviewer): "'Kem by Vy khoteli byt?' — 'Lorentso Medichi'" in *Intellektualnyi kapital,* SP, 1997, June-July, No. 6, p. 10 (2 ills.).

106. "Moe sobran e russkoi teatralnoi zhivopisi" in *Russkaia mysl,* Paris, 1997, 18-24 September, No. 4189, p. 16 (4 ills.).

107. with Vladimir Skosyrev (interviewer): "Priobretet li Moskva kollektsiiu Lobanova-Rostovskogo?" in *Izvestiia,* M, 1997, 16 October, p. 5 (2 ills.).

108. with E.B. (unidentified interviewer): "Rossiiskii muzeinyi rynok samyi bezopasnyi v mire" in *Intellektualnyi kapital,* SP, 1997, October, No. 9, p. 8.

109. N. Lobanov-Rostovsky: "Moe sobranie russkoi teatralnoi zhivopisi" in *Novoe russkoe slovo,* New York, 1997, 3 November, p. 18 (7 color ills.).

110. "Moskovskomu pravitelstvu potrebovalos 27 let" in *Evropeiskii vestnik,* London, 1997, 15 November, No. 16, p. 14.

111. "Almaznaia monopoliia: vzgliad izvnutri" in *Ekspert,* M, 1998, 26 January, No. 3, pp. 34-35 (1 ill.).

112. "Almaznaia monopoliia: vzgliad izvnutri" in *Yuvelirnyi mir,* M, 1998, No. 1, pp. 12-14 (1 ill.).

113. "Russian Diamonds — Conflicting Interests under Scrutiny" in *European Herald.* London, 1998, No. 18, pp. 5, 6 (1 ill.).

114. "Moe sobranie russkoi teatralnoi zhivopisi" in *Intellektualnyi kapital,* SP, 1998, January, No. 1, p. 9; and No. 2, p. 9 (2 ills.).

115. with Vladimir Teslenko (interviewer): "Ne slishkom dorogaia kollektsiia" in *Ekspert,* M, 1998, 6 April, pp. 100-01 (2 color and 1 b/w ills.).

116. with Liusiena Krumova (interviewer): "2000 kartini ne izlizat ot doma mi" in *Standart,* Sofia, 1998, 8 May, p. 22 (1 ill.).

117. with Nada Nesheva (interviewer): "Neudobno e da bdesh tsar" in *Trud,* Sofia, 1998, 10 May, p. 5 (2 color ills.).

118. with Valia Stoianova (interviewer): Streliana ptitsa sum" in *Novinar,* Sofia, 1998, 10 May, p. 9 (2 ills.).

119. (interviewer anonymous): "Portreti ot lagera 'Belene' kuta dirigent Veselin Baichev" in *Noshten trud,* Sofia, 1998, 11-12 May, p. 4 (2 ills.).

120. with Elena Druzhinina (interviewer): "...Eta kollektsiia ne uidet po chastiam" in *Novosti Peterburga,* SP, 1998, 14 May, p. 21 (1 ill.).

121. with Magdalena Gigova (interviewer): "V sasht kazvat 'Da go napravim', a u vas 'Niama dna stane'" in *Noshten trud,* Sofia, 1998, 27 May (1 ill.).

122. with Lev Mints (interviewer): "De Birs i Rossiia" in *Intellektualnyi kapital,* SP, 1998, May, pp. 4-5 (3 ills.).

123. "O russkikh khudozhnikakh za rubezhom" in *Krug chteniia,* M, 1998, No. 6, pp. 7-119 (33 color and 13 b/w ills.).

124. with Vladimir Gadzhev (interviewer): "Klanta Openkhaimer" in *Banker,* Sofia, 1998, 15 June, pp. 28-31 (4 ills.).

125. "Bakst, Benua i drugie" in *Business International,* Linz, summer, 1998, pp. 42-47 (16 ills.).

126. with Julian Barran, Annely Juda, André B. Nakov, and Olga Speranskaia (interviewer): "Avangard na rynke" in *Novoe russkoe slovo,* New York, 1998, 4 (p. 44), 7 (p. 15), 9 (p. 17) and 11 (p. 35) September (9 ills.).

127. with Valia Stoianova (interviewer): "Avantiuristi zavzekha vlastta na 7 noemvri" in *Novinar,* Sofia, 1998, 7 November, p. 7 (1 ill.).

128. with unnamed interviewer: "'Bylgarskiat tsar' se okaza germanski" in *Banker,* Sofia, 1998, 7 December, p. 30 (1 ill.).

129. with Julian Barran, Annely Juda, André B. Nakov, Dmitrii Sarabianov, and Olga Speranskaia (interviewer): "Russkii avangard. Za kulilsami torgov" in *Nashe nasledie,* M, 1998, No. 4, December, pp. 123-35 (16 color ills.).

130. with unnamed interviewer: "Almazy tozhe 'zamerzaiut'" in *Yuvelirnoe obozrenie,* M, 1998, December, p. 5 (1 ill.).

131. with Julian Barran, Annely Juda, André B. Nakov, and Olga Speranskaia (interviewer): "Avant-Garde. Za kulisami torgov" in *Business Lunch Magazine,* Linz, 1998-99, Vol. 2, No. 3-4, pp. 62-72 (7 color ills.).

132. with Nadezhda Danilevich (interviewer): "Privilegiia malchishki, proshedshego cherez ad i ne ispugavshegosia" in *Rossiia segodnia,* M, 1999, 20 January, p. 5 (1 ill.).

133. with I. Kokhanovskaia (interviewer): "Budushchee chelovechestva — v kartinakh proshlogo" in *Russkaia gazeta,* Riga, 1999, 29 January, p. 29 (1 ill.).

134. with Valia Stoianova (interviewer): "V Bylgariia ima khora, koito mogat da platiat 100 khil. dolara za platno na Vereshchagin" in *Novinar,* Sofia, 1999, 31 March, p. 9 (1 ill.).

135. with Nicola Benois, John E. Bowlt, and Elena Druzhinina (editor): "Iz mira realnosti — v Mir iskusstva i obratno" in *Intellektualnyi kapital,* SP, 1999, March, No. 1, p. 11.

136. with Ivan Kogin (interviewer): "Nikita Lobanov: Sudba" in *Intellektualnyi kapital,* SP, 1999, April, No. 2, pp. 6-7 (5 ills.).

137. with Nicola Benois and John E. Bowlt: "Odnazhdy v Parizhe" in *Business Lunch Magazine,* Linz, 1999, Vol. 4, No. 1, pp. 66-71, 92.

138. with Yurii Osipov (interviewer): "'Uchityvaite sootnoshenie tseny i kachestva'" in *Bakhus,* M, 1999, May-June, p. 16 (1 color ill.).

139. with Vladimir Teslenko (interviewer): "Nikita Lobanov-Rostvosky: 'ne sobiraite to, chto chitaetsia modnym'" in *Kommersant,* M, 1999, 10 July p. 7 (2 ills.).

140. "Kapitalisticheskite 'Mobifoni'" in *Banker,* Sofia, 1999, 27 July, No. 30., p. 30 (1 ill.).

141. "Russkaia levaia zhivopis na auktsione Christie's" in *European Herald,* London, 1999, 13 August, pp. 4,5 (3 ills.).

142. "Russkaia levaia zhivopis. Obzor auktsiona Kristis — leto 1999 goda" in *Londonskii kurier,* London, 1999, 13 August-3 September, No. 106, p. 26.

143. "Russkii avangard" in *Intellektualnyi kapital,* SP, 1999, September, No. 3, pp. 6-7 (6 ills.); November, No. 4, p. 9 (3 ills.); January, 2000, No. 1, p. 9.

144. with unnamed interviewer: "Potomok Riurikovichei kniaz Nikita Lobanov-Rostovsky" in *Intellektualnyi kapital,* SP, 1999, November, No. 4, pp. 8-9.

145. with Sergei Ivio (interviewer): "U nas raznye vzgliady na biznes" in *Londonskii kurier,* London, 1999, 19 November – 3 December, No. 112, p. 14 (2 ills.).

228. Pavel Tchelitchew: Costume Design for Three Turks, *Le Coq d'Or*. 1923 (No. 1093)

146. with Liliia Vlakhiiska (interviewer): "Kniaz Nikita Lobanov-Rostovsky" in *Klub M*, Sofia, 1999, December, No. 12, pp. 70-72 (2 color ills.).

147. "Zhivopis russkogo avangarda. Obzor auktsiona Kristis. Dekabr 1999 goda" in *Londonskii kurier*, London, 2000, 14 January, p. 14.

148. with L. Krumova: "Kollektsionirane ne e investitsiia" in *Standart*, Sofia, 2000, 24 January, p. 20.

149. "Obzor dekabrskikh auktsionov Kristis" in *Russkaia mysl*, Paris, 2000, 27 January, p. 16.

150. "Zhivopis russkogo avangarda" in *Novoe russkoe slovo*, New York, 2000, 31 January, p. 15.

151. "Tarelka Malevicha stoit ochen dorogo — Obzor zimnego russkogo auktsiona doma Kristis v Londone" in *Intellektualnyi kapital*, SP, 2000, March, No. 2, p. 11.

152. "17 millionov za Malevicha" in *Londonskii kurier*, London, 2000, 2 June, p. 6. Also in *Russkaia mysl*, Paris, 2000, 8-14 June, p. 18.

153. "Russkii avangard na poslednikh auktsionnykh torgakh" in *Russkaia mysl*, Paris, 2000, 8-14 June, p. 18. Also in *Evropeiskii vestnik*, London, 2000, 7 July, p. 11.

154. "Moi vstrechi s Isaiei Berlinym in *Evropeiskii vestnik*, London, 2000, 7 July, p. 8.

155. "Russkoe iskusstvo na auktsione Kristis" in *Londonskii kurier*, London, 2000, 15 July, p. 23.

156. "Triumpf Kazimira Malevicha" in *Intellektualnyi kapital*, SP, 2000, July, No. 4 (24), p. 11.

157. "Russkie dni na auktsione Kristis" in *Chisla*, Marigny, France, 2000, September, No. 3, p. 6.

158. "Serge Lifar's Collections" in *Chisla*, Marigny, France, 2000, October, No. 4, pp. 14-15 (2 ills.).

159. with Olga Speranskaia: "Russian Avant-Garde" (Speranskaia talks to N.D. Lobanov-Rostovsky, A. Juda, J. Barran, A. Nakov and Prof. D. Sarabianov) in *Chisla*, Marigny, France, 2000, 23 November, No. 5, pp. 8-17 (2 ills.).

160. with Speranskaia: "Za kulisami auktsiona": in *Drevo*, monthly supplement to *Rossiiskie vesti*, M, 2000, 27 December, No. 8 (12), pp. x-xi (4 b/w ills.; Russian version of 159).

161. "Kak ulybaetsia iskusstvo": in *Drevo*, monthly supplement to *Rossiiskie vesti*, M, 2000, 27 December, No. 8 (12), pp. vi-vii.

162. "Tseny na russkoe iskusstvo rastut" in *Russkaia mysl*, Paris, 2000, 30 November, No. 4343, p. 16. Also in *Londonskii kurier*, London, 2000, 1 December, No. 135, p. 16; in *Novoe russkoe slovo*, New York, 2000, 5 December, p. 10; and in *Intellektualnyi kapital*, SP, 2000, December, No. 8 (28), p. 7.

163. "Russkii avangard ili poddelka?" in *Londonskii kurier*, London, 2000, 15 December, No. 136, p. 10.

164. with N.A. Benois and John Bowlt: "Razgovor s N.A. Benua" in *Novyi zhurnal*, New York, 2000, December, No. 221, pp. 151-174.

165. "Tseny na russkoe iskusstvo rastut" in *Chisla*, Marigny, France, 2000, 23 January, No. 6, pp. 18-20.

166. "Byloe i dumy kniazia kollektsionera" in *Drevo, monthly supplement to Rossiiskie vesti*, M, 2001, 14 June, pp. 16-17 (3 b/w ills.).

167. with Nadezhda Danilevich: "Blagorodnoe sobranie (Kollektsionirovanie — eto ne biznes, a beskonechnye zhertvy)" in *Mir i dom*, M, 2001, September, No. 9 (81), p. 202-209 (14 ills.).

168. "Vot eto da! 626 000 dollarov za kartinu Z. Serebriakovoi" in *Londonskii kurier*, London, 2001, 1-13 December, pp. 14-15. Also as "Russkie auktsiony v Londone" in *Russkaia mysl*, Paris, 2001, 29 November – 5 December, p. 11 (1 ill.).

169. "Nikita Dm. Lobanov-Rostovskii, kollektsioner" in *Novyi zhurnal*, New York, 2001, December.

170. "K sozdaniiu v Rossii Natsionalnoi portretnoi galerei (NPG)" in *Dvorianskii vestnik*, 2001, No. 9-10 (88-89), pp. 1-2.

171. "Zhivopis na Ukraine: vzgliad russkogo londontsa" in *Literaturnyi Krym*, Simferopol, 2002, July, No. 27-28 (30-31), p. 8.

172. with V. Leonidov: "V stranu nevozmozhno vvezti nichego tsennogo" in *Kultura*, 2002, 8-14 August, No. 31-32, p. 7 (3 b/w ills). Also in *Novoe russkoe slovo*, New York, 2002, 14 August.

173. "Chomu nemae suchasnogo ukrainskogo mistetstva v ukrainskikh muzeiakh" in *Visokii zamok*, Lvov, 2002, 1 October, p. 7 (in Ukrainian).

174. Natsionalna portretna galereia mae buti in *Obrazotvorche mistetstvo*, Kiev, 2001, No. 4, pp. 18-19 (in Ukrainian).

175. "Vospominaniia o khudozhnikakh za rubezhom" in *Kulturnoe nasledie rossiiskogo gosudarstva*, issue III, SP: IPK Vesti, 2002, pp. 234-260.

176. "Russkii antikvarnyi rynok na rubezhe XX-XXI vekov" in *Nashe nasledie*, 2002, No. 62, pp. 77-92.

177. with K. Meleshko: "Agent avangarda" in *Argumenty i fakty v Ukraine*, Kiev, 2003, June, No. 26, p. 16.

178. with Georgina Adam: "Roubles galore" (an auction review) in *The Art Newspaper*, London, 2003, July-August, p. 42.

179. with Alevtina Riabinina: "Kolekcjas veidošana vienmēr ir laime / Collecting is always delight" in *Studija*, Riga, 2003, August-September, pp. 50-52 / 6-7 (2 ills.; in Latvian / English).

180. "Saruna pie pusdienām / A conversation over lunch in the restaurant of the Intercontinental Hotel in Paris (conversation with Benois)" in *Studija*, Riga, 2003, August-October, pp. 53-55 / 7-9, (2 ills., in Latvian/English). Russian version: "Odnazhdy v Parizhe. Razgovor s N.A. Benua 15 noiabria 1981g." in *Antikvarnye vedomosti*, M, 2004, 20 January, No. 3-4, pp. 4-6 (26 ills.).

181. "Pamiati Dzhona Stiuarta (nekrolog)" in *Londonskii kurier*, London, 2003, 3 October, No. 197, p. 33 (5 ills.). Also in *Russkaia mysl*, Paris, 2003, 13-19 November, No. 42 (4479) p. 9; and as "Dom, kotoryi pokinul Dzhon" in *Nashe nasledie*, M, 2003, December, No. 67, pp. 176-177.

182. "Iskusstvo dolzhno udivliat (obzor auktsiona Sotbis)" in *Russkaia mysl*, Paris, 2003, 27 November – 3 December, No. 44 (4481), p. 8. Also in *Nezavisimaia gazeta*, M, 2003, 27 November, p. 2; in *Londonskii kurier*, London, 2003, 5 December, No. 201, p. 17; and in *Telegraf*, Riga, 2003, 1 December, p. 21 (5 ills).

183. with G. Vasilieva: "'Obnazhennaia' dlia Abramovicha?" in *Argumenty i fakty*, Moscow, 2003, 27 November, No. 48 (1205), p. 28.

184. with Alevtina Riabinina: "Prognoz popal v tochku" in *Telegraf*, Riga, 2003, 1 December, No. 231 (519), p. 201 (2 ills.).

185. with Dmitrii Butkevich: "U Kristis byl povtor, Sotbis v minore" in *Nezavisimaia gazeta*, Moscow, 2003, 5 December, p. 23.

186. "O teatre" in *Novyi zhurnal*, New York, 2003, December, No. 233, pp. 129-137.

187. "V Rossii nuzhna natsionalnaia portretnaia galereia" in *Nezavisimaia gazeta*, M, 2004, 1 April, p. 6.

188. "Samoe vazhnoe — sdelat pervyi shag (muzei russkogo zarubezhia)" in *Antikvarnye vedomosti*, No. 9, Moscow, 2004, 5 April, pp. 1 and 3 (2 ills.).

189. with M. Petruk: "Ukrainskim avangardom zaimetsia russkaia aristokratiia" in *Segodnia*, K, 2004, 3 August, p. 9 (1 ill.).

190. "Portret Salomei Andronikovoi raboty Aleksandra Yakovleva" in *Russkaia gazeta*, Sofia, 2005, 4-10 April, No. 12 (83), p. 10.

229. Pavel Tchelitchew: Portrait of Serge Lifar in *Ode*, ca. 1935 (No. 1096)

191. "Khraniteli russkogo zarubezhia / Guardians of Russian culture" in *antiq.info*, 2005, July-August, No. 30/31, pp. 132-137 (1 b/w and 8 color ills.).

192. "Kollektsioner" in *Novyi zhurnal*, New York, 2005, December, vol. 241, pp. 303-311.

193. with V.P. Enisherlov of *Nashe nasledie*: "Russkoe iskusstvo — 2005 god" in *Londonskii kurier*, London, 2006, 3-16 March, No. 250, pp. 13 (1 ill.). Also in *Russkaia gazeta*, Sofia, 2006, 6-12 March, No. 8 (130), p. 10.

194. "Natsionalnaia portretnaia galereia Ukrainy. Nakhodki i atributsii" in *Ukrainskii vymir*, Nizhin, 2006, issue 5, p. 129. (In Ukrainian.)

195. with V.P. Enesherlov: "Pokupaite vse, krome falshivok" in *Nashe nasledie*, 2006, June, No. 78, pp. 114-123 (9 color ills.).

196. "Andergraund: Anatolii Brusilovskii" in *Nash dom – Amerika*, New York, 2006, 10 November, No. 120 (426), pp. 54-55 (2 b/w ills.).

197. with Galina Chermenskaia: "Slivki sbili v kuchu" in *Novaia gazeta*, M, 2006, 13 November.

198. with N. Sazonov: "'Russkii bum' v kontekste novorusskoi kultury" in *Novyi zhurnal*, New York, 2006, December, vol. 243, pp. 285-291.

199. "Falshivye proizvedeniia iskusstva" in *Reklama*, Chicago, 2007, 8-14 March, No. 9 (620), pp. 124-125 (2 ills.). Also in *Nash dom – America*, New York, 2007, 22 July, p. 30; and in *Kievskoe slovo*, Kiev, 2007, May, No. 14, p. 13 (1 ill.).

200. "Ne obmanesh — ne prodash" in *Novoe russkoe slovo*, 2007, 21-22 April (1 ill.).

201. "Fakes forever!" in *Moskovskie novosti*, M, 2007, 11-17 May, No. 18 (1385), p. 45. Also as: "Podlinnik ili poddelka?" in *Vernisazh*, M, 2007, p. 20; and as "Falshivye proizvedeniia iskusstva" in *Ukrainskii vymir*, Nizhin, 2007, issue 6, pp. 141-143.

202. "Ukraina – SShA: tvorcheskii most" in *Yarmarok*, Sumy, 2007, 5 June, No. 27 (339), p. 1 (1 b/w ill.).

203. with Olga Smetanskaia: "Dazhe Putinu nedavno podarili falshivogo Shagala" in *Fakty*, K, 2008, 9 June, p. 6.

204. with Dmitrii Butkevich: "Iskusstvo nastoiashchee i poddelnoe" in *Moskovskie novosti*, 2007, 29 June – 5 July, No. 25 (1392), p. 48 (2 color ills.).

205. with Alevtina Riabinina: "Kollektsionirovanie — eto pochti detektiv" in *VIP Lounge*, Riga, 2007, September-October, No. 4 (10), pp. 105-110 (8 color ills.).

206. "Natsionalnaia portretnaia galereia" in *Russkoe slovo*, Prague, 2007, November, No. 5, p. 19, 1 color ill.).

207. "Vospominaniia kollektsionera" in *Svoi*, M, 2007, No. 8-9, . 98-107 (12 color ills.).

208. with Elena Plotnik: "Spasennye ot zabveniia" in *Graal Collection*, K, 2008, February, No. 2, pp. 137-146 (13 color ills.).

209. with Nadezhda Sikorskaia: "Borshch, de Kiriko i geneticheskaia liubov k Rossii" in *Nasha gazeta*, Geneva, Switzerland, 2008, 12 March (1 color ill.).

210. "Metsenatstvo" in *Informatsionnyi biulleten MSRS*, 2008, March, p. 77 (2 color ills.).

211. with E. Verlin: "Kollektsiia Lobanovykh-Rostovskikh budet vystavlena v Teatralnom muzee v Sankt-Peterburge" in *Russkii mir.ru*, Moscow, 2008, 18 June. Also in *Nash dom – Amerika*, New York, 2008, 26 June, pp. 4-5 (4 color ills.).

212. with Nadezhda Danilevich: "Vozvrashchenie bludnogo Baksta" in *Izvestiia*, M, 2008, 20 June, No. 110, pp. 1 and 14 (4 color ill.).

213. with Elena Druzhinina: "Ob uchasti kollektsii Lobanovykh-Rostovskikh" in *Sankt-Peterburg*, SP, 2008, 29 August.

214. with Natalia Kostitsyna: "Vystavka 'Vozvrashchenie v Rossiiu. Kollektsiia Lobanovykh-Rostovskikh'" on radio show "Razvorot na Peterburg", Radio "Ekho Moskvy", 2008, 24 September.

215. "Rynok iskusstva" in *Londonskii kurier*, 2009, 6-19 March, No. 315, p. 15. Also in *Art-gorod*, SP, 2009, March, No. 11 (21), pp. 86-87 (4 color ills.).

216. "Iskusstvo vo vremia krizisa" in *Russkaia mysl*, Paris-London, 2009, 13-19 March, No. 10 (4737), p. 8.

217. with Galina Chermenskaia: "Dana komanda 'Anfas'" in *Novaia gazeta*, M, 2010, 19 February, No. 18 (1576), p. 13 (1 ill.).

218. with Aleksandr Kovtunenko: "V Rossii sozdadut Natsionalnuiu portretnuiu galereiu", on TV channel "Mir", M, 2010, 28 March.

219. with Natalia Markova: "Litso natsii i profil" in Rossiiskii istoricheskii muzei (RIM), 2010, March-April, No. 1 (18), pp. 4-5 (2 color and 7 b/w ills.).

220. "Initsiativa MSRS" in *Informatsionnyi biulleten MSRS*, 2010, July, pp. 46-47 (6 color ills.).

Note that F107 (N. Lobanov: *Epokha Sudba Kollektsiia*, M: Russkii put, 2010), contains a full bibliography of Nikita Lobanov-Rostovsky's publications until 2010.

N. Commentaries on the Lobanov-Rostovsky Collection, including Reviews of Exhibitions in the US

Note: Wherever a publication in Sections N-W carries illustrations of works in the Lobanov-Rostovsky collection, this is indicated in parentheses following the entry. Unless stated otherwise, the reproductions are in black and white.

Stage and Costume Designs by Russian Painters from the Collections of Mr. and Mrs. Nikita D. Lobanov-Rostovsky and Mr. George Riabov, New York: Harkness House for Ballet Arts, 1966 (I12):

1. N. N. "Vystavka v Kharkness Khauz" in *Novoe russkoe slovo*, New York, 1966, 24 February, p. 3.

Russian Stage and Costume Designs: A Loan Exhibition from the Lobanov-Rostovsky, Oenslager and Riabov Collections. Circulated by the International Exhibitions Foundation, Washington, D.C., 1967-69 (I14):

2. Yu. Annenkov: "Znachenie russkhikh khudozhnikov v iskusstve stsenicheskogo oformleniia" in *Novoe russkoe slovo*, New York, 1967, 28 May, pp. 4 and 6.

3. V. Z-n [=V. Zavalishin]: "Russkie khudozhniki stseny v Muzee Metropoliten" in *Novoe russkoe slovo*, New York, 1967, 22 June.

4. V. Gessen: "Vystavka russkogo iskusstva v Niu-Yorke" in *Russkaia mysl*, Paris, 1967, 3 August.

5. P. Wilson: "Stage and Costume Designs" in *Christian Science Monitor*, Boston, 1967, 25 August, p. 8 (2 ills.).

6. Anon.: "Russian Costumes on Display" in *Daily Utah Chronicle*, Salt Lake City, 1968, 12 January (1 ill.).

7. G. Dibble: "Utah Museum Shows Russian Designs" in *N.A.*, Salt Lake City, 1968, January, pp. W9, W10.

8. N. N.: "Theater Art" in *Minneapolis Sunday Tribune*, Minneapolis, 1968, 30 June (2 ills.).

9. N. N. "Stage Designs Exhibited" in *St. Paul Sunday Pioneer Press*, St. Paul, 1968, 30 June.

10. N. N.: "Russian Exhibits to be Shown at Walter Art Center through July 31" in *North St. Paul Review*, St. Paul, July 8-15.

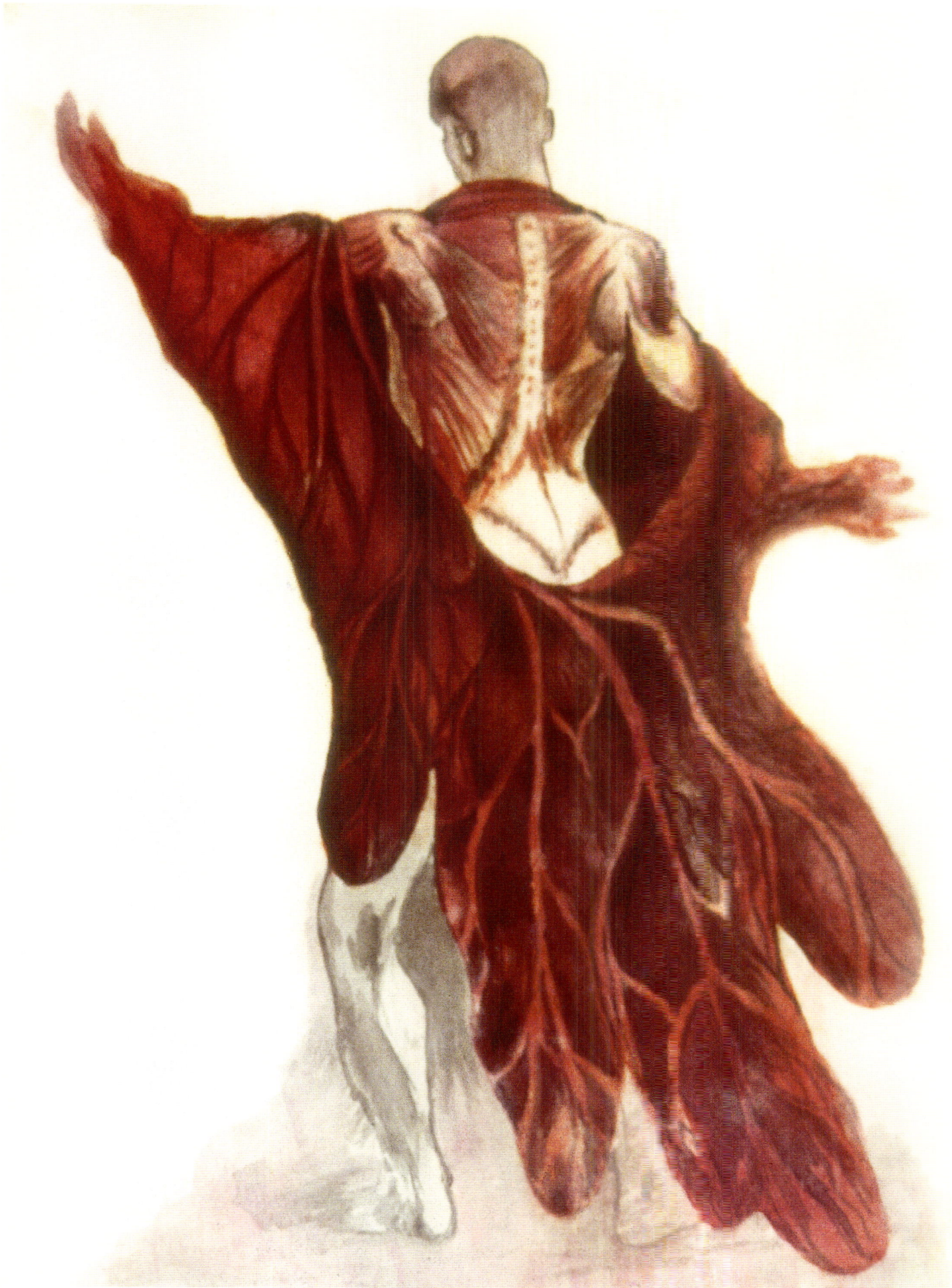

230. Pavel Tchelitchew: Costume Design for a Scarlet Demon, *Orpheus and Eurigce*, 1936 (No. 1098)

11. P. Whitaker: "Encounter" in *Columbia Record*, Columbia, SC, 1968, 28 September, pp. 1C and 2C.

12. Anon.: "Russian Watercolor Exhibit Opens" in *Star and the Columbia Record*, Columbia, SC, 1968, 29 September, p. 6-B (1 ill.).

13. Anon.: Russian Stage Design" in *Columbia Museum of Art News*, Columbia, SC 1968, October, Vol. 19, No. 7, unpaginated.

14. Anon.: "Exhibition of Designs" in *Providence Sunday Journal*, Rhode Island, 1968, 10 November, p. W-19.

15. Anon.: "Russian Stage and Costume Designs" in *Ringling Museum Newsletter*, Sarasota, 1969, March, Vol. 2, No. 3, unpaginated (1 ill.).

16. C. Burnett: "Russian Exhibit" in *Sarasota Herald Tribune*, Sarasota, FL, 1969, 6 May.

17. K. Belousov: "Pisma v redaktsiiu. 'Smena est'" in *Novoe russkoe slovo*, New York, 1969, 12 May.

18. V. Z-n [=Zavalishin]: "Russkoe iskusstvo v galeree Rait, Khepburn, Vebster" in *Novoe russkoe slovo*, New York, 1969, 22 October.

19. Anon.: "Russian Theatrical Design" in *Virginia Museum Members' Bulletin*, Richmond, VA, 1970, February, Vol. 30, No. 6, unpaginated (2 ills.).

20. V. Z-n [=Zavalishin]: "Vystavka sovetskogo dekorativnogo iskusstva" in *Novoe russkoe slovo*, New York, 1970, 12 March.

Diaghilev and Russian Stage Designers. *A Loan Exhibition of Stage and Costume Designs from the Collection of Mr. and Mrs. N. Lobanov-Rostovsky.* Circulated by the International Exhibitions Foundation, Washington, D.C., 1972-74 (l20):

21. Anon. "Russian Stage and Costume Design" in *Apollo*, London, 1970, September (1 ill.).

22. P. Ekstrom: "Russkie khudozhniki i balet" in *Novoe russkoe slovo*, New York, 1972, 30 January.

23. H. Kissel: "Designs for Diaghilev" in *Women's Wear Daily*, New York, 1972, 25 February, p. 9 (1 ill.).

24. A. Kisselgoff: "Astor Display Draws on Diaghilev and Designers" in *The New York Times*, New York, 1972, 25 February (1 ill.).

25. Anon.: "Russian Art on Exhibit" in *Sunday News*, New York, 1972, 27 February.

26. Anon.: "Diaghilev Era" in *Manhattan East*, New York, 1972, 29 February (1 ill.).

27. D. Boult (J. Bowlt): "Diaghilev i russkie teatralnye khudozhniki" in *Novoe russkoe slovo*, New York, 1972, 5 March, p. 2.

28. R. Shepard: "Design" in *The New York Times*, New York, 1972, 14 March.

29. V. G. [=Vladimir Gessen]: "Russkoe iskusstvo v Niu-Yorke" in *Russkaia mysl*, Paris, 1972, 16 March.

30. Anon.: "Diaghilev and Russian Designers" in *Antiques Magazine*, New York, 1972, May.

31. A. Brown: "Outstanding Exhibits on Display at Museum" in *The State*, Columbia, SC, 1972, 13 and 15 October, pp. 3-E (1 ill.).

32. J. Butterfield: "Diaghilev and Russian Stage Designers" in *Fort Worth Star Telegram*, Fort Worth, 1972, 10 December.

33. J. Kutner: "Diaghilev and Russian Stage Designers" in *Dallas Morning News*, Dallas, 1972, 31 December.

34. Anon.: "Russian Ballet Captured in Print" in *Detroit Free Press*, Detroit, 1973, 24 February (4 ills.).

35. Anon.: "Costume Design for Ballet" in *Sunday Call-Chronicle*, Allentown, Pa., 1973, 11 March, p. F7 (1 ill.)

36. D. Tarzan: "Russian Stage Design" in *Seattle Times*, Seattle, 1973, 17 June (1 ill.).

37. Anon.: "Designs from the Era of Diaghilev" in *Seattle Post-Intelligencer*, Seattle, 1973, 24 June (1 color ill.).

38. M. Hawthorn: "The Russians Are Here at the Frye" in *Post-Intelligence Book World*, Seattle, 1973, 24 June.

39. Anon. "Russian Design" in *The Seattle Times*, Seattle, 1973, 27 June, p. E12 (1 ill.).

40. Anon.: "High Jinks" in *Apollo*, London, 1973, July (1 ill.).

41. Anon.: "Diaghilev and Russian Stage Designers" in *West Texas Museum Association Quarterly*, Lubbock, 1973, July-September, p. 9 (1 ill.).

42. Anon.: "Art, Ballet Linked" in *Lubbock Avalanche Journal*, Lubbock, TX, 1973, 26 August.

43. Anon.: "Diaghilev and Russian Stage Design" in *Virginia Museum Bulletin*, Richmond, 1973, October, Vol. 34, No. 2, pp. 4, 5. (3 ills.).

44. F. Brock: "Diaghilev at Allen" in *Oberlin Review*, Oberlin, OH, 1974, 1 October, p. 6 (two ills.).

Stage Designs and the Russian Avant-Garde (1911-1929). *A Loan Exhibition of Stage and Costume Designs from the Collection of Mr. and Mrs. Nikita Lobanov-Rostovsky.* Circulated by the International Exhibitions Foundation, Washington, D.C., 1976-78 (l32):

45. Anon.: "Russian Stage and Costume Designs" in *Antiques Magazine*, New York 1976, September, pp. 444 and 460 (1 ill.).

46. Yu. Zorin: "Otbleski burnogo vremeni" in *Novoe russkoe slovo*, New York, 1976, 24 October, p. 5.

47. V. Z-n [=V. Zavalishin]: "Vystavka russkikh avangardistov" in *Novoe russkoe slovo*, New York 1976, 13 October.

48. A. Kisselgoff: "Art of Russian Stage Design Is Shown" in *The New York Times*, New York, 1976, 12 November (1 ill.).

49. Anon.: "Stage Designs of the Russian Avant-Garde" in *Print Collectors Newsletter*, New York, 1977, January-February, p. 184.

50. Anon. "Russian Avant-Garde" in *Theater Crafts*, New York, 1977, January-February (1 ill.).

51. Anon.: "Russian Stage and Costume Design" in *Antiques Magazine*, New York, 1977, March, p. 460.

52. Anon.: "Designs for Ballet" in *San Francisco Examiner and Chronicle*, San Francisco, 1977, 2 October, p. 42 (2 ills.).

53. Anon.: "The Golden Age of Costume Design" in *Oakland Tribune*, Oakland, 1977, 9 October, pp. 1E, 7 (3 ills.).

54. Anon.: "Russian Art Exhibit Opens" in *Greensboro Daily News*, Greensboro, 1978, 5 February, p. C12 (1 ill.).

55. B. Greenberg: "Russian Exhibit: A Touch of Magic" in *The Herald*, Durham, N.C., 1978, 22 February.

56. Anon.: "Russian Avant-Garde Design Featured at Ackland" in *North Carolina Leader*, Raleigh, 1978, 23 February.

57. Anon.: "Russian Avant-Garde Design Display at 'Y'" in *The Herald*, Provo, UT, 1978, 23 July, p. 31 (1 ill.).

58. Anon.: "Russian Art Show in HFAC" in *Daily Universe*, Provo, UT, 1978, 21 August.

59. Anon.: "Avant-Garde Design on Display at HFAC" in *Daily Universe*, Provo, UT, 1978, 31 August.

60. Anon.: "USSR Art Featured in HFAC" in *Daily Universe*, Provo, UT, 1978, 31 August.

61. Anon.: "Stage Designs of the Russian Avant-Garde" in *Los Angeles Times*, Los Angeles, 1978, 10 September, p. 86.

62. Anon.: "Rare Russian Art on Display in Galleries" in *Union*, California State University, Long Beach, 1978, 11 September, Vol. 3, No. 4 (1 ill.).

63. Anon.: "Art on Campus" in *Daily Forty-Niner*, Long Beach, 1976, 12 September, p. 3.

231. Solomon Telingater: Design for a Propaganda Truck for the Red Army, 1932 (No. 1101)

64. T. Rutten: "Russia's Avant-Garde" in *Los Angeles Times,* Los Angeles, 1978, 2 October, p. 8 (1 ill.).
65. D. Hitchcock: "Russian Art" in *University Daily,* Lawrence, KS, 1979, 2 February, p. 8 (1 ill.).
66. L. Bretz: "Stage Art" in *Lawrence Journal-World,* Lawrence, KS, 1979, 18 February (1 ill.).

Dance Image: A Tribute to Serge Diaghilev. Jackson, Mississippi: Mississippi Museum of Art, 18-29 June, 1979 (I41):

67. M. Hill: "Sergei Diaghilev and the Ballets Russes" in *Museum Journal,* Jackson, MS, Vol. 2, No. 10, June, 1979, p. 27.
68. J. Dunning: "Dolin, Elder Statesman of Ballet, Recalls Diaghilev" in *The New York Times,* New York, 30 June, 1979, p. 10.
69. J. Bowlt: "Dance Image: A Tribute to Sergei Diaghilev: in *The Clarion-Ledger. Jackson Daily News,* Jackson, MS, 1979, 21 June.
70. Anon.: "Recalling World of Diaghilev" in *The New York Times,* New York, 1980, 18 January.
71. A. Temko: "Russian Theater Designs" in *San Francisco Chronicle and Examiner,* San Francisco, 1980, 27 January, p. 39 (2 ills.).
72. Anon.: *Malevich The Non-Objective World. From the Collection of N. Lobanov-Rostovsky.* Booklet for exhibition at the Mississippi Museum of Art, Jackson, 4 May – 15 June, 1980.

Russian Stage Designs: Tradition and Modernism.
An Exhibition Selected from the Collection of Mr. and Mrs. Nikita D. Lobanov-Rostovsky at the Archer M. Huntington Art Gallery, University of Texas, Austin, 1981, 3 September – 3 November (I48):

73. H. Tackett: "Russian Designs for Stage Come to Art Museum" in *On Campus,* Austin, 1980, vol. 8, No. 4, p. 1 (1 ill.).
74. Anon.: "Five Year Loan of the Lobanov-Rostovsky Collection" in *UT Calendar,* Austin, 1980, 7 December, p. 106.
75. Anon.: "UT Art Museum is loaned extensive collection of Russian theater designs" in *Discovery,* Austin, 1981, Spring, p. 31.
76. Anon.: "Scenery Costume Design by Russian Artists on Exhibit" in *On Campus,* Austin, 1981, 7-13 September, p. 23 (2 ills.).
77. P. McAlpin: "Rothgeb Explains Progression of Russian Art" in *On Campus,* Austin, 1981, 7-13 September, p. 4.
78. M. Sandoval: "Exhibit Shows Change in Russian Stage Design" in *On Campus,* Austin, 1981, 7-13 September, p. 5 (1 ill.).
79. V. Z-n: [= Zavalishin] "Kollektsiia Lobanova-Rostovskogo" in *Novoe russkoe slovo,* New York, 1982, 16 April, p. 4.

Russian Stage Design. Scenic Invention 1900-1930. From the Collection of Mr. and Mrs. Nikita D. Lobanov-Rostovsky. Circulated by the Mississippi Museum of Art, Jackson, Mississippi, June, 1982-July, 1984. (I51):

80. Anon.: "Russian Exhibit Opens June 18" in *Nexus,* Jackson, MS, 1982, Vol. 1, No. 20, 11 June-9 July, p. 1 (1 color ill.).
81. Anon.: "Exhibits, Displays. Happenings" in *The Clarion-Ledger. Jackson Daily News,* Jackson, MS, 1982, 13 June, p. 3E (1 ill.).
82. Anon.: "A Summer Festival" in *The Clarion-Ledger. Jackson Daily News,* Jackson, MS, 1982, 20 June, p. 21.
83. B. Nichols: "Staging a Landmark Exhibit" in *The Clarion-Ledger. Jackson Daily News,* Jackson, MS, 1982, 20 June, Section E, front page (4 ills.).
84. J. Williams: "Russian Immigrant's Collection Comes to MMA" in *The Clarion-Ledger. Jackson Daily News,* Jackson, MS, 1982, 23 June (2 ills.).

85. [V. Zavalishin]: "Prazdnik russkogo iskusstva" in *Russkaia mysl,* Paris, 1982, 1 July, p. 13.
86. V. Zavalishin: "Prazdnik russkogo iskusstva" in *Novoe russkoe slovo,* New York, 1982, 2 July, p. 9.
87. Anon.: "Russian Stage Designs" in *Antiques,* New York, 1982, July, pp. 56-60 (1 ill.)
88. O. Carlisle: "'Scenic Innovation' Comes to Jackson" in *Nexus,* Jackson, MS, 1982, August, p. 9 (2 ills.).
89. J. Reiff: "Russian Stage Design" in *Nexus,* Jackson, MS, 1982, August, p. 8 (1 ill.).
90. Anon.: "Russian Stage Design: Scenic innovation, 1900-1930" in *Dance Magazine,* New York, 1982, August (1 ill.).
91. D. Sutton: "The Vitality of Russian Stage Design" in *Apollo,* London, 1982, September, pp. 136-39 (10 ills.).
92. V. Zavalishin: "S chego nachinaetsia teatr" in *Novaia gazeta,* New York, 1982, 13-19 November, p. 15-17 (10 ills.).
93. C. Crisp: [Book review of I51] in *Dance Gazette,* London, 1983, March, No. 182.
94. I. Zilbershtein: "Rasskaz o russkikh teatralnykh khudozhnikakh nachala 20 veka, pokorivshikh mir svoim iskusstvom. Poisk prodolzhaetsia" in *Ogonek,* M, 1983, 14 May, No. 20, pp. 8, 25 (5 ills., 4 in color).
95. B. Trethewy: "Galleries Offer Summer Full of Art" in *The Chandler Arizonian,* Phoenix, AZ, 1983, 29 June.
96. B. Trethewy: "Russian Set Designs Shown in Phoenix" in *Mesa Tribune,* Mesa, AZ, 1983, 29 June.
97. Anon.: "Russian Stage Design" in *The Phoenix Gazette,* Phoenix, AZ, 1983, 30 June, p. F2 (1 ill.).
98. I. Dzutseva: "Gruzinskie temy v russkoi teatralnoi zhivopisi" in *Vechernii Tiflis,* Tbilisi, 1983, 2 July, p. 3 (4 ills.).
99. Anon.: "Galleries Display Versatility" in *The Arizona Republic,* Phoenix, 1983, 6 July, pp. 5-6 (1 ill.).
100. P. Leonard: "Museum Hosts Russian Design Era" in *Summer State Press,* Phoenix, AZ, 1983, 14 July, p. 10 (1 ill.).
101. J. Young: "Russian Art Is Worth Attention" in *Daily Progress,* Scottsdale, AZ, 1983, 22 July, p. 16 (3 ills.).
102. D. Balazs: "Museum To Show Russian Stage Art" in *Art News,* New York, 1983, July, p 15.
103. M. Barrack: "Russian Stage Sets, Costumes Entertain Museum Goers" in *Arizona Business Gazette,* Phoenix, 1983, 8 August, Section A, p. 8 (3 ills.).
104. M. Barrack: "Russian Art Recalls Diaghilev Style" in *Arizona Living Magazine,* Phoenix, 1983, August, p. 42 (2 ills.).105
105. V. Zavalishin: "Ob odnoi kollektsii" in *Novaia gazeta,* New York, 1983, 2-8 October, p. 26.
106. K. Andreev: "Iz teatralnogo plena" in *Novoe russkoe slovo,* New York, 1984, 1 April, p. 5 (2 ills.).
107. A. Chorley: "Russian Avant-Garde Stage Designs in the Lobanov-Rostovsky Collection" in *The Antique Dealer and Collectors' Guide,* London, 1984, March, pp. 78-80 (9 ills.).
108. V. Zavalishin: "Russkoe iskusstvo i voprosy sovremennoi stsenografii" in *Russkaia zhizn,* San Francisco, 1984, 12 September, p. 6; 13 September, p. 6.
109. A. Shukalo: "Russian Design Show Splashes Imagination throughout Gallery" in *Austin American Statesman,* Austin, TX, 1984, 10 July, pp. 6-7.

Various Other Articles

110. V. Chirikba: "V kataloge — imia Chachba-Shervashidze" in *Sovetskaia Abkhaziia,* Sukhumi, 1985, 6 February.

232. Viktor Vasnetsov: Russian Maiden in Medieval Dress, 1880s (No. 1115)

111. R. Cohen: "Russian Stage Design" in *Drawing,* New York, 1985, March-April, p. 136 (1 ill.).

112. R. Pacher-Theinburg: "Das russische Buhnenbild und die Sammlung Lobanov-Rostovsky" in *Artis,* Bern/Stuttgart, 1986, March, pp. 54-59 (eight color ills.).

113. I. Zilbershtein: "Shedevry teatralnoi zhivopisi" in *Ogonek,* M, 1986, 16-23 August, No. 33, (7 ills., 6 color).

114. I. Zilbershtein: "Delo zhizni" in *Ogonek,* M, 1986, No. 36, pp. 8, 9; No. 37, pp. 22-24.

115. D. Boult (J. Bowlt: "O kollektsii kn. N. D. Lobanova-Rostovskogo" in *Russkaia mysl,* Paris, 1986, 17 October, p. 14 (2 ills.).

116. S. D[edulin]: "'Ogonek' o kollektsii kn. Lobanova-Rostovskogo" in *Russkaia mysl,* Paris, 1986, 17 October, p. 10.

117. G. Eremian: "Suvremenna pamet za minaloto" in *Zemledelsko zname,* Sofia, 1987, 29 April.

118. N. Shcheglova: "Lobanov iz roda kollektsionerov" in *Golos rodiny,* M, 25 May 1987, p. 14 (3 ills.).

119. V. Zavalishin: "Kollektsiia kniazia Lobanova-Rostovskogo" in *Novoe russkoe slovo,* New York, 18 September, 1987, p. 5.

120. T. Trucco: "Nikita Lobanov-Rostovsky. Glasnost for Schéhérazade" in *Art News,* New York, 1988, February, pp. 93-94 (4 color ills.)

121. V. Kassis: "Sotni mil po Anglii" in *Golos rodiny,* M, 1988, July, p. 14.

122. R. Fizdale and A. Gold: "Costume and Stage Designs of the Lobanov-Rostovsky Collection" in *Architectural Digest,* London, 1988, September, pp. 106, 110-12 (5 color ills.)

123. Anon.: "Russkoe teatralno-dekoratsionnoe iskusstvo. Vystavka kollektsii N. D. Lobanova-Rostovkogo v S.Sh.A." in *Amerika,* Washington, D.C., 1988, No. 382.

124. Anon.: "Contact with Experts Flourishes" in *Soviet Weekly,* M, 1989, 15 April.

125. L. Shchukina: "Korolevskii podarok" in *Leningradskaia pravda,* L, 1989, 12 December, p. 4.

126. V. Zavalishin: "Prazdnik tsvetomuzyki" in *Novyi zhurnal,* New York, 1989, No. 74, pp. 302-10.

127. M. Meilakh: "Vliiaem li na zarubezhie" in *Vechernii Leningrad,* L, 1990, 26 March, p. 3.

128. V. Kassis and N. Shcheglova: "Kollektsioner i prosvetitel" in *Golos Rodiny,* M, 1990, March, No. 13, pp. 14-15 (6 ills.); and April, No. 14, pp. 14-15 (8 ills.). Reprinted in V. Kassis and N. Shcheglova: *Svet volshebnogo fonaria,* M, Moskovskaia pravda, 1991, pp. 21-27.

129. M. Meilakh: "Nedelia russkikh auktsionov v Londone" in *Russkaia mysl,* Paris, 1990, 20 April, p. 11 (3 ills.).

130. S. Balashova: "Russkii dom v angliiskoi stolitse" in *Sovetskaia kultura,* M, 1990, 28 April, p. 14 (4 ills.).

131. N. Aleksandrova and V. Udin: "Kropotkinskaia 21" in *Golos Rodiny,* M, 1990, May, No. 22, p. 14 (4 ills.).

132. E. Druzhinina: "Kultura nedelima" in *Sovetskii soiuz,* M, 1990, No. 6, p. 52.

133. B. Nikolov: "Kniaz Lobanov-Rostovsky" in *Demokratiia,* M, 1990, 20 June, p. 3 (1 ill.).

134. V. Kassis and N. Shcheglova: "Liudi, knigi, arkhivy" in *Golos Rodiny,* M, 1990, June, No. 24, p. 14 (4 ills.).

135. L. Lozinsky and N. Shcheglova: "S soznaniem chesti i dolga" in *Golos Rodiny,* M, 1990, July, No. 26, p. 4 (1 ill.).

136. E. Druzhinina: "Avtoritet natsii sozdaet kulturu" in *Gudok,* M, 1990, 8 August.

137. E. Druzhinina: "Obidno kniaziu za Rossiiu" in *Trud,* L, 1990, 3 August.

138. S. Balashova: "Kniaz Nikita Lobanov i negovia Klondaik" in *Memori,* Sofia, 1990, September, pp. 42-45 (7 ills., 2 in color).

139. S. Balashova: "Voskhozhdenie. Kniaz Lobanov-Rostovsky" in *Mir zvezd,* M, 1990, No. 1, October, pp. 11-13 (7 ills.).

140. G. Romanov: "Proslavliaia masterov teatralnogo iskusstva" in *RAU,* M, 1991, No. 0 [sic], pp. 46-47. In Russian and in English. (6 color ills.).

141. L. Rovnianskaia: "'Russkii amerikanets'" in *Moskovskii zhurnal,* M, 1991, No. 2, pp. 59-61 (2 ills.).

142. N. Shcheglova: "Kollektsiia na bumage" in *Golos Rodiny,* M, 1991, No. 3, January, p. 14 (3 ills.)

143. I. Beziazychnaia: "Glaz i serdtse Nikity Lobanova-Rostovskogo" in *Miloserdie,* M, 1991, February, No. 7, p. 11 and 13 (2 ills.).

144. N. Aleksandrova: "Khudozhniki russkogo teatra" in *Izvestiia,* M, 1991, 16 March, No. 65, p. 6.

145. S. Balashova: "Kollektsiia priiatnaia glazu..." in *Sovetskaia kultura,* M, 1991, 20 April, p. 14 (3 ills.).

146. E. Druzhinina: "Kniaz Lobanov-Rostovsky: Za Otchiznu obidno" in *Russkoe zarubezhie,* M, 1991, 23 April, p. 4 (2 ills.).

147. A. Sazonov: "Revoliutsionnaia keramika" in *Tvorchestvo,* M, 1991, No 5, inside back cover.

148. N. Shcheglova: "The Theatre of Marc Chagall, Mikhail Vrubel and Others" in *Moscow News,* M, 1991, No. 5, p. 11 (4 ills., 3 in color).

149. E. Baskakov: "Nuzhen muzei rossiisskogo zarubezhia" in *Golos Rodiny,* M, 1991, No. 28, p. 3.

150. N. Shcheglova: "'Tsarskaia kollektsiia kniazia" in *Vecherniaia Moskva,* M, 1991, 8 July, p. 4 (2 ills.).

151. Anon.: "London-Permi" in *Golos Rodiny,* M, 1992, No. 30. p. 12 (3 ills.).

152. S. Adrianova: "Gde vy, nasledniki?" in *Orlovskaia pravda,* Orel, 1992, 26 August, No. 157, p. 2.

153. V. Vlasov: "Zemli rodnoi minuvshaia sudba" in *Dosug,* M, 1992, 24 September, p. 7.

154. V. Gadzhev: "Kniaz Lobanov-Rostovsky tyrsi svoia bashta" in *Pari,* Sofia, 1992, 7 December, p. 18 (3 ill.).

155. R. Todorov: "Kniazyt s chuvalenia gashterizon" in *Vrabets,* Sofia, 1992, 10 December, p. 4 (1 ill.).

156. J. Bowlt: "Costume and Stage Design Masterpieces" in *Russian Heritage,* M, 1993, No. 2, pp. 74-81 (13 color ills.).

157. L. Univerg: "Sekretnaia kollektsiia russkogo kniazia" in *Den sedmoi — novosti nedeli,* Jerusalem, 1993, 14 August, pp. 24-25 (3 ills.).

158. Anon. "Diviatsia britantsy" in *Kultura,* M, 1993, 11 December, p. 10 (1 ill.).

159. N. Aleksandrova and A. Loginova: *Iz kollektsii N.D. Lobanova-Rostovskogo i S.I. Pankova,* M: Museum of Private Collections, 1993.

160. S. Sergeev: "Vechnoe dvizhenie iskusstva" in *Nedelia,* M, 1994, No. 4, p. 11 (3 ills.).

161. L. Gamova: "Ne imeia ni grosha, ya poklialsia sobrat kollektsiiu i sdelal eto" in *Vechernii klub,* M, 1994, 7 April (1 ill.).

162. J. Murray: "Portrait of an Obsessive Collector" in *The Moscow Tribune,* M, 1994, 13 September, p. 8.

163. N. Lobanov-Rostovsky: "Russkoe iskusstvo epokhi 'shagaem s pesnei'" in *Moskovskie novosti,* M, 1994, 8 December, p. 9.

164. T. Kolesnik: "Chto ishchet kniaz v kraiu dalekom?" in *Khobbi,* M, 1994, November.

165. V. Kiselev: "Odna, no plamennaia strast" in *Balet,* M, 1995, November-December, pp. 37-38 (3 ills.).

166. I. Kokhanovsky: "Potomok Riurikovichei o znachenii iskusstva v istorii tsivilizatsii" in *Elita,* 1995, December, pp. 78-81.

233. Marie Vassilieff: Poster Advertising the Deuxième Bal des Artistes, 1924 (No. 1116)

167. R. Bakl (R. Buckle): "Kollektsiia Lobanova-Rostovskogo" in *Muzykalnaia akademiia,* M, 1996, No. 1, pp. 226-29 (2 ills.).

168. S. Filcheva: "Zashto Natsionalnata galeriia osudi Vasil Stoilov" in *Kontinent,* Sofia, 1996, 10-11 February (1 ill.).

169. G. Ruleva: "Trudno vryshtane kum rodinata" in *Bulgarski zhurnalist,* Sofia, 1996, No. 2, p. 20 (1 ill.)

170. J. Vronskaya: "Kollektsionery... kollektsii..." in *London Courier,* London, 1996, No. 31, March, p. 15.

171. N. Danilevich: "Kniaz-izgnannik stal metsenatom" in *Delovoi mir,* M, 1996, 12 July, p. 12 (3 ills.).

172. E. Skvortsova: "Sredstvo ot falshivok — na etot raz silnodeistvuiushchee" in *Obshchaia gazeta,* M, 1996, 5-11 September, p. 7.

173. V. Skosyrev: "Nevolnik russkogo avangarda" in *Izvestiia,* M, 1996, 6 September, p. 6 (2 ills.).

174. N. Danilevich: "Moskva reshila kupit krupneishee sobranie diagilevskikh khudozhnikov" in *Art-biznes,* M, 1997, 15-18 August, p. 8 (1 ill.).

175. V. Gadzhev: "Kogato Niu York e khremav, London kikha" in *Banker,* Sofia, 1997, 8-14 September, p. 30 (1 ill).

176. N. Danilevich: "Moskva reshila kupit krupneishee sobranie diagilevskikh khudozhnikov" in *Novoe russkoe slovo,* New York, 1997, 3 November, p. 18 (4 color ills.).

177. V. Gadzhev: "'Salon na bulgarskoto izkustvo' v 'Internet'" in *Banker,* Sofia, 1997, 3-9 November, No. 44, p. 30 (1 ill.).

178. V. Gadzhev: "Kniaz Nikita Lobanov-Rostovski podir senkite na minaloto" in *Literaturen,* Sofia, 1997, 11 November, p. 14 (3 ills.).

179. Z. Tsereteli: [interview] in *Kommersant,* M, 1998, 21 February, No. 30, p. 10.

180. E. Skvortsova: "Neprosto naiti 'chestnye' dengi" in *Obshchaia gazeta,* M, 1998, 9 April, No, 14, p. 10 (1 ill.).

181. V. Gadzhev, ed.: "Svetoven kolektsioner zamislia portretna galeriia v stolitsata" in *Natsionalen vsekidnevnik,* Sofia, 1998, 5 May, No. 115, p. 17 (3 ills.).

182. N. Danilevich: "Vozvrashchenie legendy" in *Evropatsentr,* Berlin, 1998, 28 August – 10 September, p. 8 (1 ill.).

183. Yu. Osipov: "Kniaz. Shtrikhi k portretu N.D. Lobanova-Rostovskogo" in *Litsa,* M, 1998, August, pp. 48-50 (6 color ills.).

184. Yu. Osipov: "Uchityvaite sootnoshenie tsen i kachestva" in *Bakhus,* M, 1999, May-June, pp. 16-17 (1 color ill.).

185. D. Arnaudova: "Sudbata na kniaz Nikita Lobanov i unikalnata mu kolektsia" in *Maritsa biznes,* Plovdiv, 1999, 21 August, No. 196, p. 6 (1 ill.)

186. V. Myznikov: "Kniaz Nikita Dmitrievich Lobanov-Rostovsky" in *Bereg,* SP, 1999, April, p. 18.

187. N. Lapidus: "Sluzhenie otechestvu" in *Tserkov i mir,* Riga, 1999, No. 6, p. 5 (1 ill.).

188. Anon.: *Russkoe teatralno-dekoratsionnoe iskusstvo 1880-1930-ykh godov,* SP: Internatonal Konstantinovsky Foundation, 2011.

189. V. Dudakov: "Nikita Dmitrievich Lobanov-Rostovsky" in *Antikvariat,* M, 2012, January-February, pp. 30-33 (24 color ills.).

O. Reviews of the Exhibitions of the Lobanov-Rostovsky Collection in Moscow and Leningrad in 1988-89 (168)

Moscow Venue

"Russian Stage Design 1880-1930 from the Collection of Nikita and Nina Lobanov-Rostovsky." The exhibition opened at the Pushkin Museum of Fine Arts, Moscow, on 26 February, 1988.

1. A. Krivopalov: "'Vdokhnovlennye Melpomenoi'. Operezhaia sobytiia" in *Nedelia,* M, 1987, No. 47, p. 13.

2. Anon.: "Mastera stsenografii" in *Vecherniaia Moskva,* M, 1988, 26 February.

3. N. Alexandrova: "Iz znamenitogo sobraniia" in *Sovetskaia kultura,* M, 1988, 27 February (three illustrations), p. 6.

4. N. Spiridonova: "Dogadka Lobanova" in *Stroitelnaia gazeta,* M, 1988, 27 February.

5. L. Nekrasova: "Siniaia sultansha" in *Moskovskaia pravda,* M, 1988, 27 February, p. 4.

6. O. Sugrobova: "Russkoe iskusstvo iz Anglii" in *Pravda,* M, 1988, 1 March (1 ill.).

7. Anon.: "Kartinka s vystavki" in *Literaturnaia gazeta,* M, 1988, 2 March (1 ill.).

8. I. Lagunina: "Vtoroe litso teatra" in *Novoe vremia,* M, 1988, 4 March (3 ills.).

9. I. Smirnova: "Colours of the Past Stage" in *Moscow News,* M, 1988, 6 March, No. 10. Also published in Russian as "Kraski bylykh podmostkov" in *Moskovskie novosti,* M, 1988, 6 March.

10. Xan Smiley: "Art's Secret Millionaires" in *The Daily Telegraph,* London, 1988, 7 March.

11. T. Khoroshilova: "I znoi nariada Kleopatry" in *Komsomolskaia pravda,* M, 1988, 13 March, p. 4 (1 ill.).

12. N. Shcheglova: "Vernisazh na Volkhonke" in *Golos rodiny,* M, 1988, 9 March (4 ills.), p. 15.

13. N. Shcheglova: "Nikita Lobanov-Rostovsky iz roda kollektsionerov" in N. Shcheglova: *Sokhranit dlia potomkov,* M: Sovetskaia Rossiia, 1988, pp. 109-35 (11 ills.).

14. B. B. [B. Bernshtein]: "Russkaia stsenografiia poseshchaet Moskvu" in *Russkaia mysl,* Paris, 1988, 25 March, p. 11 (3 ills.).

15. S. Dedulin: "O kataloge vystavki iz sobraniia N.D. Lobanova-Rostovskogo" in *Russkaia mysl,* Paris, 1988, 25 March, p. 11.

16. G. Belkova (interview): "Shedevry stsenografii" in *Nashe nasledie,* London, 1988, No. 3, pp. 10-20 (13 color and 2 b/w ills.).

17. V. Nekrasov: "The Lobanov-Rostovsky Collectors" in *Soviet Woman,* M, 1989, March (7 ills.).

18. Anon.: "Spektr" in *Lik,* 1988, Sofia, 1 April (1 ill.).

19. D. Kogan: "Zhivopis teatra" in *Izvestiia,* M, 1988, 5 April, p. 3.

20. K. Kaurinkovski: "Ihmelapsia siperiasta" in *Turun sanomat,* Turku, 1988, 29 April (2 ills.).

21. V. Chirikba: "Razmyshlenie posle stolichnoi vystavki" in *Sovetskaia Abkhaziia,* Sukhumi, 1988, 30 April.

22. N. Traikova: "Sykrovishtata na Volkhonka 12" in *Zemledelsko zname,* Sofia, 1988, 18 May.

23. B. B. [B. Bernshtein]: "Teatralnyi eskiz kak proizvedenie iskusstva" in *Russkaia mysl,* Paris, 1988, 24 June, p. 11 (1 ill.).

24. "Russkoe teatralno-dekoratsionnoe iskusstvo" in *Amerika,* Washington, D.C., 1988, September.

25. M. Kolesnikov: "Shedevry zolotogo veka russkoi stsenografii" in *Sovetskii balet,* M, 1988, September-October, No. 5, pp. 62-64 (6 color and 3 b/w ills.).

26. I. Dzutseva: "Vystavka, kotoraia ne proidet bessledno" in *Sabchota halovneba,* Tbilisi, 1988, No. 11 (7 b/w ills.).

27. E. Poliakova: "Pamiat teatra — buduschee teatra" in *Teatr,* M, 1988, No. 11 November (17 color ills.).

28. V. Kiselev: "Stsenograficheskaia simfoniia" in *Sovetskaia muzyka,* M, 1988, No. 12, December (2 color and 3 b/w ills.).

29. M. Pozharskaia: "Sokrovishcha, spasennye ot zabveniia" in *Tvorchestvo,* M, 1988, December, No. 12 (5 color and 4 b/w ills.).

234. Alexander Vesnin: Costume Design for Romeo, *Romeo and Juliet*, 1922 (No. 1133)

Leningrad Venue

"Russian Stage Design 1830-1930 from the Collection of Nikita and Nina Lobanov-Rostovsky." The exhibition opened at the Manège Exhibition Hall, Leningrad, on 5 April, 1988.

30. J. Bowlt and J. Barran: *Review of the Exhibition "Stage and Costume Designs by Russian Painters (1900-1930)" from the Collection of Mr. and Mrs. Nikita D. Lobanov-Rostovsky*, L: Cultural Foundation of the USSR, 1988.
31. Julian Barran: "Volshebnyi mir teatra" in *Vechernii Leningrad*, L, 1988, 4 April, p. 3.
32. M. Vladimirova: "Shchastliv, chto moe sobranie uvidiat leningradtsy" in *Leningradskaia pravda*, L, 1988, 6 April.
33. Anon.: "I raspakhnetsia zanaves!" in *Televidenie-radio*, L, 1988, No. 19, 9-15 May, p. 5.
34. B. Bernstein: "Vene stsenograafia külastab Moskvat" in *Teatr-muzyka-kino*, Tallin, 1988, Nos. 2, 5, 7 (12 color and 13 b/w ills.).

P. Articles and Reviews Relating to the Exhibition of the Lobanov-Rostovsky Collection in Germany in 1991-92, "Die Russische Avantgarde und die Bühne 1890-1930"

At the Schleswig-Holsteinisches Landesmuseum, Schloss Gottorf, Schleswig, 10 March – 16 June, 1991; the Landesmuseum, Wiesbaden, 4 August – 17 November, 1991; the Saarland Museum, Saarbrücken, 1 December, 1991 – 11 January, 1992; and the Kunsthalle, Tübingen, 18 January – 15 March, 1992

1. Anon.: "Påny russisk kunst" in *Flensborg Avis*, Flensburg, 1991, 9 February.
2. Anon.: "Russische Avantgarde auf Schloss Gottorf" in *Welt am Sonntag*, Schleswig, 1991, No. 9, 3 March, p. 91.
3. H. Glossner: "Fortschritt in Russland" in *Deutsches Allgemeineines Sonntagsblatt*, Schleswig, 1991, 8 March.
4. T. Schulze: "'Mit Sorgfalt und Methodik'" in *Flensborg Avis*, Flensburg, 1991, 8 March, No. 57, p. 10 (1 ill.)
5. R. Gaska: "Was russische Avantgarde dem Theater schenkte" in *Kieler Nachrichten*, Kiel, 1991, 9 March, No. 58, p. 23 (2 ills., 1 in color).
6. A. Carstens: "Russlands einstige Kunst-Avantgarde und das Theater" in *Lübecker Nachrichten*, Lübeck, 1991, 9 March (2 ills.).
7. K. Hoyer: "Da wird der 'Reitstall' zur Ikone" in *Schleswig-Holsteinische Landeszeitung*, Schleswig, 1991, 9 March, No. 58.
8. Anon.: "'Ballets Russes' om Bildern in Schleswig" in *Schleswiger Nachrichten*, Schleswig, 1991, 9 March (1 ill.).
9. W. Jahn: "Dokumente bewegter Zeit" in *Hamburger Morgenpost*, Hamburg, 1991, 9 March (1 ill.).
10. B. Dohm: "Russiske scenebilleder på Gottorp Slot" in *Flensborg Avis*, Flensburg, 1991, 9 March, pp. 1, 7 (1 color and 3 b/w ills.).
11. R. Drommert: "Fürstliche Schätze" in *Die Zeit*, 1991, 22 March, No. 13, p. 76.
12. E. Entz and V. Zerssen: "Theaterideen grosser Maler" in *Land und Leute*, 1991, 23 March, pp. 28-29.
13. A. Glanz: "Die Revolution entlässt ihr Theater" in *Hersfelder Zeitung*, Hersfeld, 1991, 26 April (1 ill.).
14. U. Faust-Lichtenberger: "Das Genre der Russischen Avantgarde" in *Schleswig-Holstein*, Schleswig, 1991, No, 4, pp. 28-29.
15. Anon.: "Theaterkunst der Russen-Moderne" in *Der Spiegel*, Berlin, 1991, April, No. 12, p. 258 (2 ills.).

16. Anon.: "Kubismus. Futurismus. Volkskunst" in *Pan*, Munich, 1991, 31 May, No. 6, pp. 54-55 (8 color ills.).
17. M. Tschechne: "Von der Ikone zur Revolution" in *Art*, Frankfurt, 1991, May, No. 5, p. 126 (3 color ills.).
18. P. Winter: "Zwischen Folklore und Suprematismus" in *Frankfurter Allgemeine Zeitung*, Frankfurt, 1991, 5 June (1 ill.).
19. Anon.: "Russische Avantgarde und die Bühne" in *Rhein-Main-Presse*, Wiesbaden, 1991, 1 August (1 ill.).
20. Anon.: "Russische Theater-Avantgarde in Wiesbaden" in *Höchstädter Kreisblatt*, Wiesbaden, 1991, 9 August.
21. Anon.: "Anekdoten rund um die Sammlung" in *Rhein-Main-Presse*, Wiesbaden, 17 August (1 ill.).
22. Anon.: "Die Versammlung der Künste auf der Bühne" in *Giessener Anzeiger*, 1991, Wiesbaden, 17 August.
23. VF: "Als Sammler teetrinkend die Schätze im Keller aufspüren...." in *Wiesbadener Kurier*, Wiesbaden, 1991, 17-18 August (1 ill.).
24. Anon.: "Russische Avantgarde" in *Wiesbadener Kurier*, Wiesbaden, 1991, 18 August.
25. Anon.: "Anknüpfung an enge kulturelle Beziehung" in *Rhein-Main-Presse*, Wiesbaden, 1991, 18 August.
26. K. Crüwell: "Der futuristische Kraftmensch und das Kostüm für eine Pfarrerstochter" in *Frankfurter Allgemeine Zeitung*, Frankfurt, 1991, 18 August (3 ills.).
27. K. Crüwell: "Uberraschung in Athen" in *Frankfurter Allgemeine Zeitung*, Frankfurt, 1991, 19 August (1 ill.).
28. Anon.: "Russische Avantgarde" in *Wiesbadener Kurier*, Wiesbaden, 1991, 19 August.
29. A. Krämer: "Vorhang auf im Museum" in *Darmstädter Echo*, Darmstadt, 1991, 20 August (1 ill.).
30. B. Melten: "Reiche Früchte einer Wechselwirkung" in *Rhein-Main-Presse*, Wiesbaden, 1991, 21 August (2 ills.).
31. B. Rechberg: "Theatergeschichte im Spiegel einer Sammlung" in *Allgemeine*, Wiesbaden, 1991, 21 August (2 ills.).
32. DL: "Russische Avangardekunst im Museum" in *Wiesbadener Wochenblatt*, Wiesbaden, 1991, 22 August.
33. R. Tauer: "Kunst für eine neue Zeit" in *Morgen*, Wiesbaden, 1991, 23 August (1 ill.).
34. C. Huther: "Die Maler auf der Bühne" in *Main-Echo*, Aschaffenburg, 1991, 23 August.
35. D. Trauth-Marx: "Die Sonne vom Himmel herabgerissen" in *Die Rheinplatz*, Ludwigshaffen, 1991, 24 August (3 ills.).
36. V. Flick: "Die Tradition der Ikonen tanzt unter einem Hauch von Apokalypse" in *Wiesbadener Kurier*, Wiesbaden, 1991, 24 August (2 ills.).
37. B. Scharpen: "Die Maske des Autofahrers ist nicht die Maske der Waschfrau" in *Frankfurter Neue Presse*, Frankfurt, 1991, 3 September (1 ill.).
38. D. Baer-Bogenschütz: "Kreative Künstler-Kostüme" in *Neue Rhein-Ruhr Zeitung*, Essen, 1991, 4 September (2 ills.).
39. E. Buck: "Rückblick auf Avantgarde" in *Offenbach Post*, Offenbach, 1991, 4 September (2 ills.).
40. Anon.: "Wiesbaden: Russisches Avantgarde" in *Rhein Zeitung*, Koblenz, 1991, 10 September.
41. I.M.: "Bühnenzauber der russischen Avantgarde" in *Sexualmedizin*, Wiesbaden, 1991, September (2 ills.).
42. S. Broos: "Kunst für die Bühne" in *Prinz*, Hamburg, 1991, September (1 ill.)
43. Anon.: "Die russische Avantgarde und die Bühne 1890-1930" in *Rhein Main aktuell*, Frankfurt, 1991, October (1 ill.).
44. Anon.: "Die russische Avantgarde und die Bühne 1890-1930" in *Wiesbaden International*, Wiesbaden, 1991, October (1 ill.).

235. Alexander Vesnin: Costume Design for Jacques, *L'Annonce Faite à Marie*, 1921 (No. 1136)

45. Anon.: "Die russische Avantgarde und die Bühne" in *Kunstmarkt*, Würzburg, 1991, No. 10, p. 4 (7 ills.).
46. ADL: "Russische Avantgarde in Saarbrücken ausgestellt" in *Die Rheinplatz*, Saarbrücken, 1991, 2 December.
47. Anon.: "Chagalls Kostümentwürfe" in *Saarbrücker Zeitung*, Saarbrücken,1991, 4 December (1 ill.).
48. U. Giessler: "Kühne Szenen-Konstruktionen statt Dekor" in *Saarbrücker Zeitung*, Saarbrücken, 1991, 5 December, No. 281, p. 13.
49. Anon.: "Saarbrücken: Arbeiten russischer Künstler" in *Rhein Zeitung*, Koblenz 1991, 6 December (1 ill.).
50. P. Olszowska: "Kaufhaus des Ostens" in *Die Tageszeitung*, Berlin, 1991, 10 December, p. 15 (1 ill.).
51. Anon.: "Kurz gemeldet" in *Schweinfurter Volkszeitung*, Schweinfurt, 1991, 18 December.
52. Anon.: "Theater-Arbeiten russischer Künstler in Saarbrücken" in *Hanauer Anzeiger*, Hanau, 1991, 23 December.
53. Anon.: "Die russische Avantgarde und die Bühne 1890-1930" in *Mannheimer Morgen*, Mannheim, 1991, 28 December, p. 32 (1 ill.).
54. Anon.: "Die russische Avantgarde und die Bühne 1890-1930" in *Saarländisches Kulturjournal*, Saarbrücken, 1992, January, p. 15 (1 ill.).
55. H. Dietsch: "Moderne Galerie des Saarland-Museums" in *Saarheimat*, Saarbrücken, 1992, No. 1-2, pp. 30-31 (5 ills.).
56. Anon.: "Bilder gegen den Status quo" in *Schwäbisches Tagblatt*, 1992, 13 March (6 ills.).
57. H. Koegler: "Explosion der Farben und Formen" in *Stuttgarter Zeitung*, Stuttgart, 1992. No. 63 (4 ills.).
58. H. Hornbogen. "Und das Dekor wird dynamisch. Die Russische Avantgarde und die Bühne 1890 bis 1930 in der Kunsthalle Tübingen" in *Schwäbisches Tageblatt*, Tübingen, 1992, 16 March.
59. Anon.: "Die Russen in Tübingen" in *Süddeutsche Zeitung*, Munich, 1992, 24 March (1 ill.).
60. E. D.: "Russia on stage" in *The Art Newspaper*, London, 1992, March, No. 16.
61. BEA: "Russische Bühnenkunst" in *Süddeutsche Zeitung*, Munich, 1992, 7 April (1 ill.).
62. G. Gampert: "Der neue Bühnen-Mensch" in *Die Zeit*, Hamburg, 1992, 24 April, No. 18 (1 ill.).
63. V. Pakhomov: "Ne toko o vystavke. Beseda s kollektsionerom Nikitoi Lobanovym-Lobanovskim" in *Russkaia mysl*, Paris, 1992, 15 May, p. 16 (two ills.).

Q. Reviews of *Khudozhniki russkogo teatra*

The Russian catalogue raisonné of the Lobanov-Rostovsky collection, compiled by John E. Bowlt and published by Iskusstvo, Moscow, in 1994 (B179)

1. N. Danilevich: "Restavratsiia istorii iskusstva" in *Kultura*, M, 1994, 24 September, p. 4 (1 ill.).
2. N. Danilevich: "Khudozhniki na stsene" in *Kultura*, M, 1994, 29 October, p. 11 (1 ill.).
3. L. Levchev: "Kto Vy, kniaz Lobanov-Rostovsky?" in *Kultura*, M, 1994, 29 October, p. 11 (1 ill.).
4. Anon.: "Nikita and Nina Lobanov-Rostovsky's Collection" in *The Art Newspaper*, London, 1994, October, p. 26.
5. N. Danilevich: "Katalog kollektsii Lobanovykh-Rotovskikh" in *Kultura*, M, 1994, 5 November.
6. Yu. Molok: "Sledy ischeznuvshei teatralnoi Atlantidy obnaruzheny v Londone" in *Izvestiia*, M, 1994, 9 November, p. 5.

7. N. Lobanov-Rostovsky: "Pismo vdogonku. Bolshoe Vam spasibo" in *Kultura*, M, 1994, 12 November, p. 2.
8. E. Dzhamaeva: "Rossii nuzhen monarkh kalibra angliiskoi korolevy" in *Vek, Gazeta delovykh krugov*, M, 1994, 25 November-1 December, p. 11.
9. O. Vasilieva: "Moia kollektsiia — dostoianie russkoi kultury" in *Delovoi mir*, M, 1994, 28 November – 4 December, p. 23 (1 ill.).
10. A. Tolstoi: "Khudozhniki Serebrianogo veka" in *Literaturnaia Rossiia*, M, 1994, 23 December, p. 15 (1 ill.).
11. Yu. Molok: "Korotkii vek teatra: Kniga o teatre" in *Oko*, Paris, 1994, No. 9, pp. 132-34.
12. F. Ingold: "Immer neue Entdeckungen" in *Neue Züriche Zeitung*, Zürich, 1995, 24 May, p. 81 (1 ill.).
13. M. Meilakh: "Khudozhniki russkogo teatra" in *Russkaia mysl*, Paris, 1995, 1-7 June, p. 13 (3 ills.).
14. A. Shatskikh: "John E. Bowlt, N.D. Lobanov-Rostovsky: Khudozhniki russkogo teatra 1880-1890" in *Voprosy iskusstvoznaniia*, M, 1995, No. 1-2, pp. 578-80.
15. T. Omuka: "The Avant-Garde and the Collector: with Special Reference to the New Russian Catalog Raisonné of the Nikita D. Lobanov-Rostovsky Collection" in *Slavic Studies*, Hokkaido, 1996, No. 43, pp. 229-37.
16. M. Böhmig: "Sobranie Nikity i Niny Lobanovykh-Rostovskikh" in *Russica Romana*, Roma, 1996, Vol. 1, pp. 377-79.

R. Articles and Reviews Relating to the Exhibition "Modernist Movements in Russian Art and Their Reflection on the Stage. Selections from the Nina and Nikita Lobanov-Rostovsky Collection"

At the Museum of Private Collections, Moscow, November, 1994 – January, 1995 (I87)

1. N. Danilevich: "Kartinki s vystavki. Khobbi kniazia Lobanova-Rostovskogo" in *Ekran i stsena*, M, 1994, 13-20 October, pp. 1, 16 (6 ills.).
2. D. Boult (J. Bowlt): "Podobnykh kollektsii poprostu ne sushchestvuet" in *Chelovek i kariera*, M, 1994, No. 17, p. 11 (3 ills.).
3. N. Semenova: "Lobanovy-Rostovskie khoteli by nadeiatsia, chto ikh kollektsiia ostanetsia v Rossii" in *Kommersant*, M, 1994, 3 November, p. 13 (1 ill.).
4. S. Drozhin: "Legendary Theatre Graphics Collection on Show" in *The Moscow Tribune*, M, 1994, November 4, p. 6 (1 ill.).
5. Anon.: "Chastnye kollektsii iz SShA — na Volkhonke" in *Moskovskii komsomolets*, M, 1994, 5 November.
6. Anon.: "What's To be Done? Theater Memorabilia" in *The Moscow Times*, M, 1994, 5 November, p. 20.
7. R. Gray and S. Coudenhove: "Theater That Danced to a New Beat Called Art" in *The Moscow Times*, M, 1994, 15 November, p. 7 (1 ill.).
8. E. Skvortsova: "Vse nachalos s Petrushki" in *Obshchaia gazeta*, M, 1994, 17 November, p. 11.
9. A. Sarabianov: "'Russkie sezony' v Moskve" in *Kultura*, M, 1994, 20-27 November, p. 18 (1 ill.).
10. N. Selivanova: "Angely Malevicha" in *Utro Rossii*, M, 1994, 24-30 November, p. 9 (1 ill.).
11. O. Torchinsky: "Kniazheskaia kollektsiia na Volkhonke" in *Moskovskaia pravda*, M, 1994, 25 November (4 ills.).
12. A. Sarabianov: "Early 20th Century Theater Design Returns to Russia" in *Moscow News*, M, 1994, 25 November – 1 December, p. 11 (1 ill.).

236. Konstantin Vialov: Costume Design for an Abbot Wearing Glasses,
The Camorra of Seville, ca. 1923 (No. 113)

237. Konstantin Vialov: Stage Design for Razin's Boat with Mast in the Center, *Stenka Razin*, ca. 1924 (No. 1145)

САРЫНЬ НА КИЧКУ

худ. К.ВЯЛОВ

238. Konstantin Vialov. Stage Design for the Upper Deck of Razin's Boat, *Sten'ka Razin*, ca. 1924 (No. 1147)

13. Anon.: "Orthodox Violation" in *Moscow Tribune,* M, 1994, 2 December, p. 11.

14. Anon.: "Museum of Private Collections. Theatre Collection" in *Moscow Revue,* M, 1994, 4-20 December.

15. N. Semenova: "Khudozhniki russkogo teatra" in *Ogonek,* M, 1994, December, unpeginated (11 color ills.).

16. N. Alexandrova: "340 shedevrov dlia spektaklia zhizni" in *Chelovek i kariera,* M, 1994, No. 23, p. 12 (3 ills.).

17. S. Khachaturov: "Karnaval krasok" in *Nakanune,* M, 1995, January, p. 31 (1 ill.)

18. V. Kiselev: "Kniazheskaia kollektsiia" in *Sezon,* M, 1995, January, pp. 20-23 (3 color ills.).

19. O. Saragareva: "Muzyka dlia svoikh i dlia bogatykh" in *Stolitsa,* M, 1995, January (1 color ill.).

20. N. Danilevich: "Assotsiatsiia 'Chetyre iskusstva'" in *Sobesednik,* M, 1995, January, p. 13 (1 ill.).

S. Articles and Reviews Relating to the Exhibition "Russian Stage Designs 1910-1930 (from the Lobanov-Rostovsky Collection) and Marc Chagall and the Jewish Theater"

At Megaron, Athens, 24 February-25 May, 1997 (I92)

City and year of publication are Athens, 1997, unless stated otherwise

1. Anon.: "E retoriki taeni sto Megaro" in *Auriani,* 15 February.
2. Anon.: "E rosiki protoporia sto theatro" in *Augi,* 15 February.
3. Anon.: "Erga rosiki protoporias" in *Nautemporik,* 15 February.
4. Anon.: "E rosiki protoporeia" in *Logos,* 16 February.
5. Anon.: "Eikastikes notes sto Megaro" in *Niki,* 18 February.
6. Anon.: "Oi toiho graphies too Marc Chagall gia to kratino. Ebraiko theatro tis Moshas sto Megaro Moosikis" in *Eletheia Ora,* 19 February.
7. Anon.: "Dia heiros Chegall" in *Nautemporiki,* 20 February.
8. Anon.: "Marc Chagall kai rosiki skenographia" in *Isotimia,* 22 February.
9. Anon.: "O Chagall kai ti alloi, rosiki protoporia sto theatro" in *Radioteleorasi,* 22 February.
10. Anon.: "Oramata kai elpides zois me to hrostira too Chagall" in *Kathimerinii* 22 February.
11. Anon.: "E rosiki protoporia zographiki sto theatro" in *Nautemporiki,* 22 February.
12. Anon.: "O Marc Chagall... paroosiaze" in *Niki,* 22 February.
13. Anon.: "Rosiki protoporia sto theatro" in *Pizospatis,* 22 February.
14. Anon.: "Otan e rosiki protoporia zographizei gia to theatro" in *Nea,* 22 February.
15. Anon.: "Rosiki protoporia" in *Eleutheros,* 22 February.
16. Anon.: "E rosiki protoporia sto Megaro" in *Apogaeoomatini,* 22 February.
17. Anon.: "Epoche Chegal" in *Adesmeutostinos,* 22 February.
18. Anon: "Ena 'theatro oneiron' sto megaro moosikis" in *Ethnos,* 22 February.
19. A. Stauraki: "Ekthesi sto Megaro Moosikis gia ti zographiki sto theatro" in *Eleutheria Larsis,* 23 February.
20. Anon.: "Erga Chagall sto Megaro Moosikis" in *Auriani,* 23 February.
21. Anon.: "To aristoorgima too Chagall" in *Exormis,* 23 February.
22. Anon.: "E tekni tis apoaotis" in *Bima,* 23 February, p. 42.
23. Anon.: [Untitled] in *Expres,* 23 February.
24. Anon.: "Eleutherias—Lobanow-Rostowskij" in *Nees Epohes,* 23 February, p. 43.
25. K. Vidos: "E tekhne tes apolutes eleutherias" in *Nees Epokhas,* 1997, 23 February, p. 42.
26. Anon. "Exthesis zographikis too Marc Chagall sto megaro" in *Exoosia,* 24 February.
27. Anon.: "Rosiki zographikis too Marc Chagall sto Megaro" in *Eleutherotoopia,* 24 February.
28. Anon.: "Art-draseis. Rosiki protoporia 1910-1930" in *Expres,* 25 February.
29. M. Pana: "E rosiki protoporia sto theatro" in *To onoma,* 25 February.
30. Anon.:"Eikastiki Pandaisia" in *Nea,* 26 February.
31. Anon.: "E rosiki protoporia pano sti skini" in *Nea,* 27 February.
32. Anon.: "Aeikastiki pandaisia sto theatro" in *Exousia,* 28 February.
33. M. Kaltaki: "E rosiki protoporia stin athina" in *Ependutis,* 1 March, p. E4.
34. Anon.: "Ekrixeis hromaton" in *Exipno Hrima,* 1 March.
35. Anon.: "E rosiki protoporia sto theatro" in *Isotimia,* 1 March.
36. B. Psorraki: "Tragoodo san pooli aelaegae o Chagall" in *Apogeoomatini,* 2 March.
37. K. Vidos: "Perusing through Marc Chagall and the Russian avant-garde scene" in *Athens News,* 2 March.
38. Anon.: "Megali rosiki ekthesi sto Megaro Moosikis" in *Gnomi Patron,* 3 March.
39. Anon.: [Untitled] in *Teeletheatis,* 8 March, p. 32.
40. B. Sarakazianou: "Erotas epi skinis" in *Anti,* March 14, pp..52-53.
41. L. Petmezas: "O Marc Chagall kai e rosiki protoporia sto Megaro Moosikis Athenon" in *Eleuthery Ora,* 16 March.
42. Anon.: "Ena aexairetikis simasia—eiastiko gegonos" in *Einai,* 18 March.
43. Anon.: "E rosiki protoporia sto Megaro Musikes" in *Eleutherias Larsis,* 19 March.
44. Anon.: "Sunizetai sto Megaro Moosikis Athenon e megali ekthesi me titlo: 'Rosiki protoporia too theatroo 1910-1918'" in *Gnomi Pathron,* 21 March.
45. Anon.: "E rosiki protoporia sto megaro musikesî" in *Eleutherias Larsis,* 19 March.
46. Anon.: "E rosiki protoporia sto Megaro Mousikis" in *Eleuthery Ora,* 28 March.
47. Anon.: "Kai an einai...." in *Account,* 3 April.
48. Anon.: "Erga Chagall sto Megaro" in *Aurian,* 14 April.
49. Anon.: "Zographiki sto theatro" in *Logos,,* 14 April.
50. Anon.: "Megaro Moosikis" in *Niki,* 14 April.
51. N. Danilevich: "Afiny prinimaiut russkoe iskusstvo" in *Delovoi mir,* M, 1997, 18-21 April, 1997.
52. Anon.: "Rosiki protoporia" in *Eleutherotoopia,* 29 April.
53. Anon.: "E rosiki protoporia sto Megaro" in *Einai,* 29 April.
54. Anon.: "O Marc Chagall... paroosiazei" in *Niki,* 30 April.
55. Anon.: "Aistiki apolausi kai mathimata istorias" in *Crash,* April.
56. Anon.:"Biolistis sti stegi kai alla erga" in *Madame Figaro,* April.
57. Anon.: "E peripeteia tou Mark Chagall" in *Marie Claire.* April, p. 246.
58. Anon.: "E rosiki protoporia sto Megaro Moosikis" in *Thlerama,* April.

239. Georgii Yakulov: Design for the Interior of the Stable of Pegasus Café, 1919 (No. 1158)

405

59. Anon.: "To Megaro proscaley tous mathitis" in *Thessalia Bolou,* April.

60. Anon.: "Megaro Moosikis" in *Monopoli,* April-May.

61. Anon.: "To agnos-o prosope..." in *Bima,* 6 May, p. 8.

62. Anon.: "E aekthesi ergon M. Chagall sto Megaro — Anoixiti prosklisi stoos Marrth tis olis tes elladas" in *Thessalias Bolou,* May 10.

63. Anon.: "Rosiki prctoporia" in *Radiothleorasi,* May 10, p. 86.

64. Anon.: "Me to blemma strammeno stin kardia tis outopias" in *Tempo Newsweek,* May 17.

65. B. Basilopooloo: "O Chagall kai e rosiki protoporia" in *Ependutis,* 17-18 May.

66. Anon.: "E rosiki pro oporia sto theatro 1920-1930" in *Palco,* May.

67. Anon.: "O Marc Chagall kai e rosiki skini" in *Elle,* May.

68. Anon.: "M. Chagall. Rosiki protoporia 1910-1930. Zographiki sto theatro. Makates, phocographies, afises" in *Optikon,* May-June.

69. N. Hatziantonioo: "Chagall epi toihoo" in *Diphono,* June, p. 112.

T. Articles and Reviews Relating to the Exhibition "L'avant-garde russe et la scène, 1910-1930. La collection Lobanov-Rostovsky"

At the Musée d'Ixelles Brussels, 11 March-30 May, 1998 (I96).

City of publication is Brussels unless stated otherwise

1. Anon.: [Announcement] in *Le Soir,* 1998, 11 March (1 ill.)

2. Anon.: "L'Avant-Garde Russe et la Scène" in *La Libre Belgique,* 1998, 13 March.

3. D. Gilleeman: "L'avant-garde russe dans son éblouissant costume" in *Arts-Plastiques,* 1998, 18 March, p. 37 (1 color ill.).

4. B. Popelier: "Schitte ende modellen" in *Tijd-Cultur,* 1998, 18 March (2 ills.).

5. Anon.: "Bal costumé russe" in *La Libre Belgique,* 1998, 20 March (1 ill.).

6 R.P. Turine: "Exceptionelle collection d'art russe au Musée d'Ixelles" in *La Libre Culture,* 1998, 20 March, p. 12 (4 color ills.).

7. P.-O. Rollin: "Les costumes de l'avant-garde russe" in *Le Matin,* 1998, 26 March, p. 28 (1 ill.).

8. N. Degand: "Aelita, reine des Martiens" in *Le Journal du Médecin,* 1998, 27 March, p. 36 (2 ills.).

9. J. Dustin: "Une Avant-Garde Occultée" in *Art et Culture,* 1998, March, p. 31 (2 ills.).

10. G.G.: "La Collection Lobanov au Musée d'Ixelles" in *AAA,* March, 1998 (1 ill.).

11. Anon.: "Musée d'Ixelles" in *Si on sortait,* 1998, March.

12. Anon.: "L'avant-garde russe et la scène 1910-1930" in *Park Mail Pocket,* 1998, 1 April (1 ill.).

13. P. Verduyckt: "Kleur is alles" in *Artsenkrant,* 1998, 3 April (1 ill.).

14. G. Gilsoul: "La Russie des théâtres" in *Le Vif – L'Express,* 1998, 3 April (1 ill.)

15. J. De Geest: "Dans van de Russische avant-garde" in *De Standaard,* 1998, 4-5 April.

16. M. Vershvovsky: "Potomok Riurikovichei pokoriaet belgiitsev" in *Russkaia Germaniia,* Berlin, 1998, 6-12 April, No. 94, p. 2.

17. Anon.: "Russische Avant-Garde en Theater 1900-1930" in *Klasse,* 1998, 7 April (1 ill.).

18. Anon.: "L'avant-garde russe et la scène 1910-1930" in *Télémoustique,* 1998, 8 April (1 ill.).

19. Anon.: [Announcement] in *Laatste Nieuws,* 1998, 15 April.

20. P. Verduyckt: "Russische avant-garde en theater 1910-1930" in *Knack,* 15 April (1 ill.).

21. Anon.: "Exposiciones: La vanguardia rusa y la escena 1910-1930" in *El Sol de Bélgica,* 1998, 22 April, p. 34 (1 ill.).

22. M. Holthof: "Russisch" in *Weekend Knack,* 29 April.

23. Anon.: "Art Scénique Russe" in *Femme d'Aujourdhui / Libelle,* 1998, 30 April (1 ill.).

24. M. Vershvovsky: "Vystavka russkogo iskusstva v Briussele" in *Nasha gazeta,* Hanover, 1998, April, No. 4, p. 11 (2 ills.).

25. M. Vershvovsky: "Kniaz Nikita Dmitrievich Lobanov-Rostovsky" in *Nasha gazeta,* Hanover, 1998, April, No. 4, p. 11.

26. Anon.: [Announcement] in *Ons Brussel,* 1998, April, p. 27 (1 ill.).

27. J. Florizoone: "Notenkraker" in *Kunst en Cultuur,* 1998, April, p. 40 (1 ill.).

28. E.V.: "De Russische avant-garde en het theater" in *Kunst en Cultuur,* 1998, April, p. 52 (1 ill.).

29. Anon.: "L'avant-garde russe à Bruxelles" in *Ideart,* 1998, April-May, p. 25 (1 ill.).

30. M. Holthof: "Doublé réussi à Ixelles" in *Art-Expo,* 1998, April-June (1 ill.).

31. Anon.: "Les coulisses de l'avant-garde russe" in *L'Evénement,* 1998, 5 May (1 ill.).

32. A. Hustache: "Costumes d'éclats" in *Le Généraliste,* 1998, 6 May (1 ill.).

33. V. Liévine: 'Une pièce pas comme les autres...' in *Le Semaine médicale,* 1998, 7 May.

34. V. Liévine: "Een ongewoon stuk..." in *Het Medisch Weekblad,* 1998, 7 May.

35. Anon.: "Exposition: L'avant-garde russe et la scène" in *La Libre Belgique,* 1998, 12 May.

36. Anon.: "Expos: L'avant-garde russe et la scène" in *Paris Match* (encart belge), 1998, 14 May (2 ills.).

37. E. Druzhinina: "Petrushka v Briussele" in *Intellektualnyi kapital,* SP, 1998, May, p. 2 (1 ill.).

38. Anon.: "Die russische Avantgarde und die Bühne (1910-1930)" in *Thalyscope,* 1998. May.

39. Anon.: "L'avant-garde russe et la scène 1910-1930" in *Nouvel Age,* 1998, May (1 ill.).

40. Anon.: "Bruxelles: Le théâtre russe" in *L'Eventail,* May (1 ill.).

41. M. Meilakh: "Vystavka iz sobraniia Nikity i Niny Lobanovykh-Rostovskikh" in *Russkaia mysl,* Paris, 1998, 6-12 August.

42. S. de Bodt: "Kostuums gebaseerd op onwrikbare schema's" in *Zaterdag,* 1998, 4 April (2 ills.).

U. Articles and Reviews Relating to the Exhibition "Russian Avant-Garde and the Stage, 1900-1930: The Collection of Nina and Nikita D. Lobanov-Rostovsky"

At the Yokohama Museum of Art, Yokohama, Japan, 3 October – 6 December, 1998 (I97)

1. Anon.: "Coming This Month" in *Asahi Evening News Weekend,* Yokohama, 1998, 1 October, p. 11 (1 ill.).

2. Anon.: "Today" in *Kanagawa Shinbun,* Yokohama, 1998, 3 October, p. 18.

3. E. Boriatinskaia: "Ukrainskii avangard v Yaponii" in *Zerkalo nedeli,* K, 1998, 12 December, p. 16 (1 ill.).

4. M. Meilakh: "Vystavki iz sobraniia Nikity i Niny Lobanovykh-Rostovskikh" in *Londonskii kurier,* London, 1999, 5-18 February, p. 21.

240. Georgii Yakulov: Costume Design for the Earl of Gloucester (?) *King Lear*, ca. 1925 (No. 1163)

V. Articles and Reviews Relating to the Exhibition "Vozvrashchenie v Rossiiu (Return to Russia): Stage Designs, 1900-30 from the Lobanov-Rostovsky Collection," St. Petersburg

At the Museum of Theater and Musical Art, St. Petersburg, 25 September – 26 October 2008.

1. S. Khodnev: "Sdelka antikvariat", *Kommersant*, M, 2008, 9 June, No. 98 (2 ills.).

2. E. Verlin: "Kollektsiia Lobanovykh-Rostovskikh budet vystavlena v Teatralnom muzee Peterburga" in *Russkii Mir.ru*, M, 2008, 16 June, 3 pp. Reprinted in *Nash dom – Rossiia*, New York, 2008, 27 June, pp. 4-5 (4 color ills.).

3. N. Danilevich: "Vozvrashchenie bludnogo Baksta" in *Izvestiia*, M, 2008, 20 June, p. 14 (4 color ills.).

4. A. Tolstova: "Kollektsiia Lobanovykh-Rostovskikh upokoitsia v Peterburge" in *Kommersant*, M, 2008, 23 June, No. 105.

5. Anon.: "Returning to Russia, the Lobanov-Rostovsky Collection / Vozvrashchenie v Rossiiu, Kollektsiia Lobanovykh-Rostovskikh (in English and Russian) in *St. Petersburg Travel Pages* quarterly, 2008, autumn, No. 3, pp. 6-9 (7 color ills.).

6. Anon.: "Exhibition of Theater Art" in *Heritage*, 2008, autumn, No. 3 (2 color ills.).

7. I. Titova: "Performing Art" in *St. Petersburg Times*, 2008, September, p. 9 (3 color ills.).

8. A. Matveea: "Rodina prikupila iskusstva" [Motherland bought art]" in *Kommersant Weekend*, 2008, 19 September, No. 169, p. 39 (2 ills.)

9. A. Matveeva: "Odnoi nogoi v Rossii" in *Kommersant*, 2008, 26 September, p. 22 (1 color ill.).

10. Anon.: "Kollektsiiu Lobanovykh-Rostovskikh mozhno uvidet za 150 rublei" in *Komsomolskaia pravda*, SP, 2008, 26 September.

11. Anon.: "Teatralnoe iskusstvo nachala veka" in *Novosti Peterburga*, 2008, 29 September, p. 2 (1 ill.).

12. Anon.: "Vystavka vozvrashchaetsia v Rossiiu" in *Interfax*, 2008, 29 September.

13. T. Bulbenko: "Vozvrashchenie v Rossiiu" in *Kultura*, M, 2008, 2 October, No. 40.

14. Anon.: "'Konstantinovskii' gastroliruet v Teatralnom muzee. Kollektsiiu Lobanovykh-Rostovskikh pokazhut v fondovom khranilishche" in *Kommersant-SPb*, SP, 2010, 15 April, No. 66 (4366).

W. Articles and Reviews Relating to the Exhibition "Vozvrashchenie v Rossiiu (Return to Russia): Stage Designs, 1900-30 from the Lobanov-Rostovsky Collection," Saratov

At the Radishchev Art Museum, Saratov, 3 December 2010 – 30 January 2011.

1. Anon.: "Zhiteli goroda uvidiat 'Vozvrashchenie v Rossiiu'" in *Izvestiia*, Saratov, 2010, 1 December.

2. Anon.: "V Saratov pribyla unikalnaia khudozhestvennaia kollektsiia" in *Chetvertaia vlast* (internet-gazeta), Saratov, 2010, 3 December (1 color ill.).

3. Anon.: "Vozvrashchenie na Rodinu", *Nasha versiia*, Saratov, 2010, 6 December (6 color ills.).

4. L. Sokolova: "'Russkie sezony' v Radishchevskom" in *Bogatei*, Saratov, 2010, 9 December, No. 42 (556).

5. E. Talpeu: "Kniazheskii dar" in *Saratovskii Vzgliad*, Saratov, 2010, 9-15 December, No. 5 (303), p. 18 (1 ill.).

6. Anon.: "Vystavka teatralno-dekorativnogo iskusstva iz kollektsii Lobanovykh-Rostovskikh v Saratove" in *ARTinvestment.ru*, 2011, 2 January.

7. Anon.: "'Vozvrashchenie v Rossiiu' prodolzhaetsia" in *Izvestiia*, Saratov, 2011, 14 January.

Mikhail Larionov: *Sergei Diaghilev Watching Serge Lifar and Other Dancers at Rehearsal*, 1927 (No.731)

241. Pavel Filonov school (Andrey Sashin?): Costume for a Warden, ПЕРЕД, *General*, 1927 (No.508)

LIST OF ILLUSTRATIONS

412

TAILPIECE ILLUSTRATIONS

242. Alexandre Benois: Portrait of Mstislav Dobujinsky, Lake Lugano, Switzerland, 1908 (No. 119)

Alexander Yakimchenko: Design for a Panneau for the Dining Room in Vera Firsanova's House, Moscow, 1909 (No. 1156)